THIS classic reference work, the best one-volume music dictionary available, has been brought completely up to date in this new edition. Combining authoritative scholarship and lucid, lively prose, the Fourth Edition of *The Harvard Dictionary of Music* is the essential guide for musicians, students, and everyone who appreciates music.

The Harvard Dictionary of Music has long been admired for its wide range as well as its reliability. This treasure trove includes entries on all the styles and forms in Western music; comprehensive articles on the music of Africa, Asia, Latin America, and the Near East; descriptions of instruments enriched by historical background; and articles that reflect today's beat, including popular music, jazz, and rock.

Throughout this Fourth Edition, existing articles have been fine-tuned and new entries added so that the dictionary fully reflects current music scholarship and recent developments in musical culture. Encyclopedia-length articles by notable experts alternate with short entries for quick reference, including definitions and identifications of works and instruments. More than 220 drawings and 250 musical examples enhance the text. This is an invaluable book that no music lover can afford to be without.

THE HARVARD DICTIONARY OF MUSIC

Edited by DON MICHAEL RANDEL

THE HARVARD DICTIONARY OF MUSIC

Fourth Edition

The Belknap Press of Harvard University Press
Cambridge, Massachusetts, and London, England 2003

Instrument drawings by Carmela Ciampa and Laszlo Meszoly.
Musical examples by A-R Editions, Inc.

Library of Congress Cataloging-in-Publication Data
The Harvard dictionary of music / edited by Don Michael Randel.—4th ed.
p. cm.
"Fourth edition proceeds rather directly from New Harvard dictionary of music"—Pref.
Includes bibliographical references.
ISBN 0-674-01163-5 (alk. paper)
1. Music—Dictionaries. I. Randel, Don Michael.
ML100.H37 2003 780′.3—dc22 2003058262

Preface to the Fourth Edition

Whereas *The New Harvard Dictionary of Music* relied very little on the first two editions of *The Harvard Dictionary of Music,* this fourth edition does proceed rather directly from its predecessor. Numerous changes, including outright additions and deletions, have been incorporated, however. These reflect new developments in musical scholarship, especially the expanding range of subjects now being studied by scholars, as well as the fact that the world and its political boundaries have changed substantially since the last edition. Revised bibliographies point to recent literature but do not cite larger standard reference works.

I am very grateful to all of the contributors listed in the following pages—both those who contributed first to the previous edition and those whose work appears for the first time in the present edition. Members of the Editorial Board have been very helpful in suggesting revisions and in recruiting new contributors.

In the course of the preparation of this edition, the locus of activity changed from Cornell University to the University of Chicago. Thus, I must now thank assistants at both institutions. At the University of Chicago and new to this project are Peter Martens, Ryan Minor, and Pelarin Bacos. Those at Cornell University are listed in the Preface to the previous edition. The libraries of both institutions have of course provided essential support.

As always, the staff at Harvard University Press has been extraordinarily professional and helpful. I am especially grateful to Margaretta Fulton for her work on dictionary projects going back now over twenty-five years. Her labors on this edition have been more essential than ever.

Don Michael Randel
Chicago, Illinois

Preface to *The New Harvard Dictionary of Music*

The present dictionary carries on the tradition of the first and second editions of the *Harvard Dictionary of Music,* edited by Willi Apel. The greatly expanded scope of current musical scholarship and changes in the character of musical life in recent decades, however, have made it necessary to conceive the dictionary afresh. As a result, *The New Harvard Dictionary of Music* includes only a handful of articles based on the earlier dictionaries. The coverage of non-Western and popular music and of musical instruments of all cultures has been much enlarged. Within the tradition of Western art music, which remains its central concern, the dictionary reflects recent scholarship on all periods and the growing proportion of scholarship and criticism devoted to more recent music. On all of these topics, it aims, like its predecessors, to serve as a convenient reference work for laymen, students, performers, composers, scholars, and teachers.

The bibliographies that accompany many of the articles will serve as guides to further reading. These bibliographies do not in general cite other standard reference works, however. Both general and specialized reference works are listed in the article Dictionaries and encyclopedias.

In addition to the editorial board and the contributors who are listed on the following pages, numerous people helped to make this book possible. Principal among these were assistants in Ithaca, New York, who did research, verified bibliographies and other information, keyboarded material by contributors, and drafted or wrote many of the unsigned articles. These assistants (with the special areas, if any, in which they worked) included Matthew Brown (theory), Jennifer Brown (bibliography), William Cowdery, Charlotte Greenspan (opera, individual countries), Bettie Jean Harden, Christopher C. Hill (a broad range of medieval and other topics), Paul Horsley (individual countries), Barry Kernfeld (jazz and popular music), Mark S. Laporta (theory), Wayne Schneider (individual works), Robert Seletsky (performance practice), John Spitzer (instruments used in non-Western and popular music), Shirlene Ward, and Patrick T. Will (popular music). Shirlene Ward was the chief assistant during the first years of the project, and Bettie Jean Harden was the chief assistant thereafter, playing a major role in the final typing, editing, bibliographical verification and updating, and proofreading. Dennis Libby, of South Paris, Maine, provided expert editorial assistance at several stages. Among those who gave valuable help on the use of computers were Tom Hughes, Dean Jacobs, and Ray Tim Teitelbaum. The project was housed in the Department of Music at Cornell University and could not have been carried out without the facilities and collection of the Cornell Music Library and the generous assistance of its staff, headed by Lenore Coral.

With the exception of the organ diagrams, which were drawn by Marcia Tucker, and the diagram of the modern piano action, for which thanks are due Steinway, the instrument drawings are by Carmela Ciampa and Laszlo Meszoly. Other line art was supplied by Deborah Schneck. Notation for *Concert for Piano and Orchestra* by John Cage, ©1960 by Henmar Press Inc., is reproduced by permission of the publisher. Notation from *in memoriam . . . CRAZY HORSE (symphony)* by Robert Ashley is reproduced by permission of the composer.

Don Michael Randel
Ithaca, New York

Contributors

A.B. André Barbera, St. John's College, Annapolis (Greece I, related articles)

A.J.N. Arthur J. Ness, Daemen College (Canzona, Fantasia, Intabulation, Prelude, Ricercar, Tablature, Toccata, related articles)

A.K.R. Anne K. Rasmussen, College of William and Mary (Islamic music, Quranic chant)

A.P. Ardal Powell, Folkers and Powell, Makers of Historical Flutes (Flute, Fife)

A.R.R. Albert R. Rice, Fiske Musical Instrument Museum (Basset horn, *Chalumeau,* Clarinet, Winds, Woodwinds, related articles)

A.Z. Albin Zak, University of Michigan (Country, Rock, Rock and roll, Rockabilly, related articles)

B.G. Bruce Gustafson, Franklin and Marshall College (Organ Mass, Suite, articles on related dances)

B.H.H. Bruce Haynes, Montreal, Canada (Oboe)

B.J.H. Bettie Jean Harden, University of North Texas (*Musica ficta,* Solmization)

B.K. Barry Kernfeld, *The New Grove Dictionary of Jazz* (Jazz articles)

B.N. Bruno Nettl, University of Illinois (American Indian music, Ethnomusicology, Folk music, Improvisation, Near and Middle East, related articles)

B.O. Barbara Owen, Newburyport, Massachusetts (Organ IV, rev. related articles)

B.R.L. Barbara Rose Lange, University of Houston (Gypsy music)

C.C. Charles Capwell, University of Illinois (South Asia, related articles)

C.C.H. Christopher C. Hill, Cornell University *(Ars nova)*

C.G. Charlotte Greenspan, Ithaca, New York (Opera, related articles)

C.Hy. Camille Hardy, Department of Dance, New York University (Ballet and theatrical dance)

C.J.R. Carl J. Rahkonen, Indiana University of Pennsylvania (Baltic countries)

C.K. Carol Krumhansl, Department of Psychology, Cornell University (Absolute pitch)

C.R.	Christopher Rouse, Eastman School of Music (Orchestra, Orchestration)
C.T.G.	Chris T. Goertzen, University of Southern Mississippi (Fiddling)
D.A.B.	Donna A. Buchanan, University of Illinois (Russian folk and popular music, Bulgaria)
D.A.S.	Douglas Alton Smith, The Martindale Press (Lute)
D.B.	David Brackett, State University of New York at Binghamton (Song, American popular)
D.C.	Dale Cockrell, Vanderbilt University (Minstrel 2)
D.E.C.	Dimitri E. Conomos, Oxford, England (Byzantine chant, Russian and Slavonic chant, Syrian chant, related articles)
D.E.S.	Daniel E. Sheehy, Smithsonian Institution (articles on Latin America)
D.F.	David Fuller, State University of New York at Buffalo (Automatic instrument, Ornamentation, related articles)
D.S.	David Stigberg, University of Illinois (articles on Latin America)
E.A.	Elizabeth Aubrey, University of Iowa (Troubadour, Trouvère, related articles)
E.A.B.	Edmund A. Bowles, Falls Church, Virginia (Cymbals, Drum, Timpani)
E.C.	Eric Charry, Wesleyan University (Africa)
E.D.M.	Ernest D. May, University of Massachusetts, Amherst (Fugue, Organ chorale)
E.G.	Edward Gollin
E.K.W.	Eugene K. Wolf, University of Pennsylvania (Binary and ternary form, Classical, Concerto, Development, Divertimento, Mannheim school, Overture, Partita, Rococo, Rondo, Scherzo, Serenade, Sinfonia, Sonata form, String quartet, Symphony, Trio, related articles)
E.M.G.	Edwin M. Good, Eugene, Oregon (Piano)
E.M.R.	Edwin M. Ripin (Clavichord)
E.S.	Elaine Sisman, Columbia University (Chaconne, Ground, Ostinato, Passacaglia, Strophic variations, Variation)
E.W.M.	Elizabeth W. Marvin, Eastman School of Music (rev. Absolute pitch)
F.H.	Frank Hubbard (Harpsichord)
G.A.T.	Gary A. Tomlinson, University of Pennsylvania (Academy, Baroque, Camerata, Monody)
H.E.S.	Harold E. Samuel (Bibliography, Conservatory, Copyright and performance right, Dictionaries and encyclopedias, Editions, Libraries, National anthems, Periodicals, Printing, Publishing, Societies, Sources, Thematic catalog, related articles)

H.F. Henry Fogel, President, Chicago Symphony Orchestra (Radio and television broadcasting, Recording III)

H.P. Harrison Powley, Brigham Young University (rev. Percussion instruments)

H.S. Howard Schott, Brookline, Massachusetts (*Arpicordo, Cembal d'amour,* Chekker, Keyboard, Spinet, Virginal, related articles)

H.Sm. Howard Smither, University of North Carolina (rev. Cantata, Oratorio)

H.S.P. Harold S. Powers, Princeton University (Melody, Rhythm)

I.K.F.W. Isabel K. F. Wong, University of Illinois (East Asia, related articles)

J.A.O. Jessie Ann Owens, Brandeis University (Motet)

J.Be. Jamshed Bharucha, Department of Psychology, Cornell University (Absolute pitch)

J.B. John Beckwith, University of Toronto (Canada)

J.H. James Haar, University of North Carolina (*Frottola,* Madrigal, related articles)

J.H.A. Jon H. Appleton, Dartmouth College (Electro-acoustic music)

J.J.J. James J. John, Department of History, Cornell University (Paleography, Textual criticism)

J.K. Janet Knapp (*Clausula, Conductus, Copula,* Discant, Hocket, *Magnus liber organi,* Rhythmic modes, Notre Dame, Organum)

J.Ko. John Koster, America's Shrine to Music Museum (Keyboard instruments)

J.P. James Porter, Stirling, United Kingdom (Ballad)

J.S. John Spitzer, University of Michigan (Authenticity)

J.T.F. John T. Fesperman (Organ I–III, related articles)

J.Y. Jeremy Yudkin, Boston University *(Ars antiqua, ars vetus)*

K.McM. Kathleen McMorrow, University of Toronto (Canada)

K.S. Kenneth Slowik, University of Maryland (rev. Violin and related articles)

L.C. Lenore Coral, Music Librarian, Cornell University (rev. Bibliography, Conservatory, related articles)

L.D.B. Lester D. Brothers, University of North Texas (rev. *Musica ficta,* Solmization)

L.E.F. Laurel E. Fay, Staten Island, New York (Russia I)

L.H.M. Lawrence H. Moe, University of California, Berkeley (Passamezzo, *Romanesca,* articles on music and dance of the Renaissance)

L.K.S. Louise K. Stein, University of Michigan *(Tonadilla, Zarzuela)*

L.L.C. Lola L. Cuddy, Queen's University, Ontario (Music cognition)

L.T.	Laurel Trainor, McMaster University (Musical ability, development of)
M.A.S.	Mary Ann Smart, University of California, Berkeley (Gender and music)
M.B.	Matthew Brown, Eastman School of Music (Consonance and dissonance, Rhetoric, Theory)
M.Dev.	Mark DeVoto, Tufts University (Analysis, Atonality, Counterpoint, Harmonic analysis, Harmonic rhythm, Harmony, Modulation, Schenker analysis, Species counterpoint, Tonality)
M.D.S.	Mark Davis Scatterday, Eastman School of Music (Wind ensemble)
M.E.F.	Margot E. Fassler, Yale University (Liturgical drama)
M.H.	Martin Hatch, Cornell University (Southeast Asia, related articles)
M.H.A.	Matthew Harp Allen, Wheaton College (Guitar in popular and folk music)
M.J.T.	Mark Jude Tramo, Harvard Medical School (The Brain and music)
M.K.	Mark Katz, Peabody Conservatory (Compact disc, Recording I–II, Turntablism)
M.McL.	Mervyn McLean, University of Auckland (Oceania and Australia)
M.S.	Michael Seyfrit, Washington, D.C. (Wind instruments, Woodwinds, related articles)
O.J.	Owen Jander (Cantata, Oratorio)
P.A.	Putnam Aldrich (*Appuy,* Double appoggiatura, Grace, Grace note)
P.K.D.	Peter K. Danner, Palo Alto, California (Guitar)
P.E.	Paul Evans (Sequence, Trope, Troubadour, Trouvère, related articles)
P.J.	Peter Jeffery, Princeton University (Ambrosian chant, Beneventan chant, Coptic chant, Ethiopic chant, Gallican chant)
P.K.	Peter Kivy, Department of Philosophy, Douglass College, Rutgers University (Aesthetics)
P.M.	Panayotis Mavromatis, Eastman School of Music (Set theory)
P.T.	Pamela Thompson, Chief Librarian, Royal College of Music (Czech Republic, Slovakia)
P.T.W.	Patrick T. Will, Cornell University (Radio and television broadcasting, Reception, Sociology of music)
P.V.B.	Philip V. Bohlman, University of Chicago (Jewish music, Klezmer)
R.A.B.	Rebecca A. Baltzer, University of Texas (rev. *Clausula, Conductus,* Hocket, related articles)
R.A.H.	Robert A. Hall, Jr., Department of Modern Languages and Linguistics, Cornell University (Prosody)

R.A.L. Robin A. Leaver, Westminster Choir College (rev. Anglican chant, Church music, related articles)

R.B. Rob Bowman, York University (Hip Hop, Music video, Rap, Reggae)

R.C. Richard Crawford, University of Michigan (Album, Bay Psalm Book, Musical [comedy], United States, related articles)

R.E.E. Robert E. Eliason, Lyme Center, New Hampshire (Brass instruments, related articles)

R.E.W. Robert E. Witmer, York University (African American music)

R.F.F. Richard F. French (Anglican chant, Anglican church music, Chorale, Church music, Hymn, Lutheran church music, Psalter, Service, related articles)

R.H. Rufus Hallmark, Queens College, City University of New York (*Ballade* 2, Lied, *Mélodie,* Song, Song cycle)

R.H.S. Robert H. Silsbee, Department of Physics, Cornell University (Acoustics)

R.J.C. Richard J. Colwell, Emeritus, University of Illinois (Symphonic band, Education in the U.S.)

R.L. Robert Lundberg, Portland, Oregon (Archlute, Bandora, Cittern, Theorbo, *Vihuela,* related instruments)

R.M. Ryan Minor, University of Chicago (Hermeneutics, Modernism, Nationalism, Voice)

R.P.L. Ralph P. Locke, Eastman School of Music (Absolute music, Program music, Program symphony, Symphonic poem)

R.P.M. Robert P. Morgan, Yale University (Aleatory music, Expressionism, Impressionism, Mixed media, Music theater, Neoclassical, Serial music, Twelve-tone music, Twentieth century)

R.S. Richard Sherr, Smith College (Mass, Paraphrase, Parody Mass, Requiem)

S.B. Stephen Bonta, Hamilton College (Sonata, *Sonata da camera, Sonata da chiesa,* Trio sonata)

S.C.D.V. Sue Carole De Vale, University of California, Los Angeles (Harp)

S.Z. Steven Zohn, Temple University (Performance articles)

T.A.J. Travis A. Jackson, University of Michigan (Jazz, related articles)

T.L. Theodore Levin, Dartmouth College, Silk Road Project (Central Asia)

V.P. Vincent Pollina, Department of Romance Languages, Tufts University (*Chanson de toile,* Tenso)

W.L.M. William L. Monical, Staten Island, New York (Violin, related articles)

W.P.M. William P. Malm, University of Michigan (Instrument)

Z.B. Zdravko Blažeković *RILM* (Balkan countries)

Abbreviations

Abbreviations employed in this dictionary are listed below in the following groups: General Bibliography, *Festschriften* and Congress Reports, Languages, and General. The shortened forms of publishers' names generally follow the model of *Books in Print.*

General Bibliography

AfMf	*Archiv für Musikforschung* (Leipzig, 1936–43)
AfMw	*Archiv für Musikwissenschaft* (Leipzig, 1918–27, 1952–)
AM	*Acta musicologica* (Basel, 1928–)
AMI	*L'arte musicale in Italia,* ed. Luigi Torchi (Milan, Rome: Ricordi, 1897–1908; R: Milan: Ricordi, 1970)
AMP	*Antiquitates musicae in Polonia* (Warsaw: Warsaw U Pr, 1963–76)
AmZ	*Allgemeine musikalische Zeitung* (Leipzig, 1798–1848, 1863–68)
AMz	*Allgemeine Musikzeitung* (Leipzig, 1874–1943)
AnM	*Anuario musical* (Barcelona, 1946–)
AnMca	*Analecta musicologica* (Cologne, 1963–)
AnnM	*Annales musicologiques* (Neuilly-sur-Seine, 1953–77)
AntMon	*Antiphonale monasticum pro diurnis horis* (Tournai: Desclée, 1934)
AntRom	*Antiphonale Sacrosanctae Romanae Ecclesiae pro diurnis horis* (Rome: Typis Polyglottis Vaticanis, 1912; later eds. include Paris: Desclée, 1924)
AsM	*Asian Music* (New York, 1968–)
BAMS	*Bulletin of the American Musicological Society* (New York, 1936–48)
BamZ	*Berliner allgemeine musikalische Zeitung* (Berlin, 1824–30)
BaJb	*Bach-Jahrbuch* (Leipzig, 1904–)
BBM	*Collezione di trattati e musiche edite in fac-simile* (Milan: Bolletino bibliografico musicale, 1930–ca. 1936)
BeJb	*Beethoven-Jahrbuch* (Bonn, 1953–)
BJEdP	*British Journal of Educational Psychology* (Birmingham, Eng., 1931–)
BJP	*British Journal of Psychology* (London, 1904–)
BMB	*Bibliotheca musica bononiensis* (Bologna: Forni, 1967–)

BMBSI	*Bulletin of the Musical Box Society, International* (Morgantown, Ind., 1957–)
BrownI	Howard M. Brown, *Instrumental Music Printed before 1600* (Cambridge, Mass.: Harvard U Pr, 1965)
BWQ	*Brass and Woodwind Quarterly* (Durham, N.H., 1966–69)
BzMw	*Beiträge zur Musikwissenschaft* (Berlin, 1959–)
CCT	*Translations,* general ed. Albert Seay (Colorado Springs: Colo Coll Mus, 1967–)
CEKM	*Corpus of Early Keyboard Music* (n.p.: AIM, 1963–)
CEMF	*Corpus of Early Music in Facsimile* (Brussels: Éditions culture et civilization, 1970–)
CLLA	Klaus Gamber, *Codices liturgici latini antiquiores* (Freiburg, Switzerland: Universitätsverlag, 1963; 2nd ed., 1968)
CM	*Current Musicology* (New York, 1965–)
CMI	*I classici musicali italiani* (Milan: I classici musicali italiani, 1941–43, 1956)
CMM	*Corpus mensurabilis musicae* (n.p.: AIM, 1948–)
CMS	*College Music Symposium* (Madison, Wis., 1961–)
CPL	*Clavis patrum latinorum,* 3rd ed., ed. Emil Gaar. Corpus Christianorum Series Latina (Brepols: Turnhout & Steenbrugge, 1995)
CS	*Scriptorum de musica medii aevi,* ed. Edmond de Coussemaker (Paris, 1864–76; R: Hildesheim: Olms, 1963)
CSM	*Corpus scriptorum de musica* (Rome: AIM, 1950–)
Cw	*Das Chorwerk* (Wolfenbüttel: Kallmeyer, 1929)
DDT	*Denkmäler deutscher Tonkunst* (Leipzig: Breitkopf & Härtel, 1892–1931; R: Wiesbaden: Breitkopf & Härtel; Graz: Akadem Druck- & V-a, 1957–61)
DJbMw	*Deutsches Jahrbuch der Musikwissenschaft* (Leipzig, 1956–)
DM	*Documenta musicologica* (Kassel: Bärenreiter, 1951–)
DMA	*Dictionary of the Middle Ages* (New York: Scribner, 1982–)
DTB	*Denkmäler der Tonkunst in Bayern,* Denkmäler deutscher Tonkunst, 2. Folge (Brunswick: H Litolff [etc.], 1900–38; rev. ed., Wiesbaden: Breitkopf & Härtel, 1962)
DTÖ	*Denkmäler der Tonkunst in Österreich* (Vienna: Österreichischer Bundesverlag, 1894–1959; Graz: Akadem Druck- & V-a, 1960–; R: Graz: Akadem Druck- & V-a, 1959)
EDM	*Das Erbe deutscher Musik,* 1. Reihe (Kassel: Nagel; Wiesbaden: Breitkopf & Härtel; Leipzig: Kistner & Siegel, 1935–; R: Kiel: Das Erbe deutscher Musik, 1953–)
EitnerQ	Robert Eitner, *Biographisch-bibliographisches Quellen-Lexikon* (Leipzig: Breitkopf & Härtel, 1900; 2nd ed., Graz: Akadem Druck- & V-a, 1959)
EitnerS	Robert Eitner, *Bibliographie der Musik-Sammelwerke des XVI. und XVII. Jahrhunderts* (Berlin, 1877; R: Hildesheim: Olms, 1977)
EKM	*Early Keyboard Music* (London: Stainer & Bell, 1955–)

ELS	*The English Lute Songs* (Menston, Eng.: Scolar Pr, 1968–)
EM	*Early Music* (London, 1973–)
EMH	*Early Music History*
EMS	*The English Madrigal School,* ed. Edmond H. Fellowes (London: Stainer & Bell, 1913–24; rev. ed. 1956–)
ESLS	*The English School of Lutenist-Songwriters,* ed. Edmond H. Fellowes, Ser. 1–2 (London: Winthrop Rogers; New York: G Schirmer, 1920–32; rev. ed., London: Stainer & Bell, 1959–)
Ethno	*Ethnomusicology* (Middletown, Conn., 1953–)
FAM	*Fontes artis musicae* (Kassel, 1954–)
Fellerer	Karl Gustav Fellerer, *Geschichte der katholischen Kirchenmusik* (Kassel: Bärenreiter, 1972–1976)
FétisB	François-Joseph Fétis, *Biographie universelle des musiciens* (Brussels, 1837–44 and later eds.)
FP	*Feedback Papers* (Cologne, 1971–83)
GMB	*Geschichte der Musik in Beispielen,* ed. Arnold Schering (Leipzig: Breitkopf & Härtel, 1931)
Grove 1–5	*Grove's Dictionary of Music and Musicians* (London, New York: Macmillan, 1879–89; 2nd ed., 1904–20; 3rd ed., 1927–28; 4th ed., 1940; 5th ed., 1954)
Grove 6	*The New Grove Dictionary of Music and Musicians* (London: Macmillan, 1980; 2nd ed., 2001).
GrRom	*Graduale Sacrosanctae Romanae Ecclesiae de tempore et de sanctis* (Rome: Typis Vaticanis, 1908; later eds. include Paris: Desclée, 1924)
GS	*Scriptores ecclesiastici de musica sacra,* ed. Martin Gerbert (St. Blasien, 1784; R: Hildesheim: Olms, 1963)
GSJ	*The Galpin Society Journal* (Oxford, 1948–)
HAM	*Historical Anthology of Music,* ed. Willi Apel and Archibald Thompson Davison (Cambridge, Mass.: Harvard U Pr, 1946–50)
HJb	*Händel-Jahrbuch* (Leipzig, 1928–33, 1955–)
HM	*Hortus musicus* (Kassel: Bärenreiter, 1936–)
HMT	*Handwörterbuch der musikalischen Terminologie* (Wiesbaden: Steiner, 1971–)
HS	*Haydn Studien* (Munich, 1965–)
HYb	*Haydn Yearbook* (Bryn Mawr, Pa., 1962–)
IRASM	*International Review of the Aesthetics and Sociology of Music* (Zagreb, 1970–)
ITO	*In Theory Only* (Ann Arbor, 1975–)
JAF	*Journal of American Folklore* (Philadelphia, 1888–)
JAMIS	*Journal of the American Musical Instrument Society* (Shreveport, La., 1974–)
JAMS	*Journal of the American Musicological Society* (Richmond, 1948–)
JASA	*Journal of the Acoustical Society of America* (Menasha, Wis., 1929–)

JbfmV	*Jahrbuch für musikalische Volks- und Völkerkunde* (West Berlin, 1963, 1966–68, 1970, 1972–73; Cologne, 1977–)
JEdP	*Journal of Educational Psychology* (Baltimore, 1910–)
JIFMC	*Journal of the International Folk Music Council* (Cambridge, Eng., 1948–68)
JJS	*Journal of Jazz Studies* (New Brunswick, N.J., 1973–79)
JM	*Journal of Musicology* (St. Joseph, Mich., 1982–)
JMP	*Jahrbuch der Musikbibliothek Peters* (Leipzig, 1895–1941)
JMT	*Journal of Music Theory* (New Haven, 1957–)
JRME	*Journal of Research in Musical Education* (Chicago, 1953–)
KmJb	*Kirchenmusikalisches Jahrbuch* (Regensburg, 1886–1911, 1930–38, 1950–)
LBCM	*Contemporary Music in Europe,* ed. Paul Henry Lang and Nathan Broder (New York: G Schirmer, 1966)
LU	*Liber usualis* (Tournai and New York: Desclée, 1959, and other eds.)
MB	*Musica britannica* (London: Stainer & Bell, 1951–; 2nd ed., 1954–)
MD	*Musica disciplina* (Rome, 1948–)
Mf	*Die Musikforschung* (Kassel, 1948–)
MfMg	*Monatshefte für Musikgeschichte* (Leipzig, 1869–1905)
MGG	*Die Musik in Geschichte und Gegenwart* (Kassel: Bärenreiter, 1949–79)
MJb	*Mozart-Jahrbuch* (Salzburg, 1950–)
ML	*Music and Letters* (London, 1920–)
MM	*Modern Music* (New York, 1924–46)
MMB	*Monumenta musicae byzantinae* (Copenhagen: Levin & Munksgaard, 1935–)
MME	*Monumentos de la música española* (Barcelona: CSIC, 1941–)
MMFTR	*Monuments de la musique française au temps de la renaissance,* ed. Henry Expert (Paris: Editions M Senart, 1924–29, 1958–; R: New York: Broude Bros, 1952)
MMMA	*Monumenta monodica medii aevii* (Kassel: Bärenreiter, 1956–)
MMML	*Monuments of Music and Music Literature in Facsimile* (New York: Broude Bros, 1965–)
MMR	*Masters and Monuments of the Renaissance* (New York: Broude Bros, 1980–)
MMRF	*Les maîtres musiciens de la renaissance française,* ed. Henry Expert (Paris: Leduc, 1894–1908; R: New York: Broude Bros, 1952)
MQ	*The Musical Quarterly* (New York, 1915–)
MR	*The Music Review* (Cambridge, Eng., 1940–)
MRM	*Monuments of Renaissance Music* (Chicago: U of Chicago Pr, 1964–)
MSD	*Musicological Studies and Documents* (Rome: AIM, 1951–)
MT	*The Musical Times* (London, 1844–)

MTT	*Music Theorists in Translation* (Brooklyn: Institute of Mediaeval Music, 1959–)
Mw	*Das Musikwerk* (Cologne: Arno Volk, 1958–76), also issued in English as *Anthology of Music*
NA	*Note d'archivio per la storia musicale* (Rome, 1924–27, 1930–43; Nuova serie, 1983–)
NeuO	Frederick Neumann, *Ornamentation in Baroque and Post-Baroque Music* (Princeton: Princeton U Pr, 1978)
NOHM	*The New Oxford History of Music* (London: Oxford U Pr, 1954–)
Notes	*Notes of the Music Library Association* (Ann Arbor, 1943–)
NRMI	*Nuova rivista musicale italiana* (Turin, 1967–)
NZfM	*Neue Zeitschrift für Musik* (Leipzig, 1834–43, 1950–74, 1979–)
PAMS	*Papers of the American Musicological Society* (Richmond, 1936–38, 1940–41)
PB	*Psychological Bulletin* (Washington, 1904–)
PL	*Patrologiae cursus completus,* Series latina, ed. Jacques-Paul Migne (Paris, 1844–64; supps. 1958–74)
PM	*Paléographie musicale* (Solesmes: Imprimerie St. Pierre [Tournai: Société Saint-Jean l'Évangéliste], 1889–1958; R: Bern: H Lang, 1969–). Monumentale (Tournai: Société Saint-Jean l'Évangéliste, Desclée, 1900–24; R: Bern: H Lang, 1968–70)
PMA	*Proceedings of the Musical Association* (London, 1874–1944), continued as *PRMA*
PNM	*Perspectives of New Music* (Princeton, 1962–)
PO	*Patrologia orientalis* (Paris: Didot, 1904–)
POM	*Psychology of Music* (Manchester, Eng., 1973–)
PP	*Perception and Psychophysics* (Goleta, Calif., 1966–)
PR	*Psychological Review* (Washington, D.C., 1894–)
PRMA	*Proceedings of the Royal Musical Association* (London, 1944–), continuation of *PMA*
PsM	*Psychological Monographs* (Evanston, Ill., 1895–1966)
RBM	*Revue belge de musicologie* (Brussels, 1946–)
RdM	*Revue de musicologie* (Paris, 1917–39, 1945–)
ReM	*La revue musicale* (Paris, 1920–40, 1946–)
RFsC	*Fourscore Classics of Music Literature,* ed. Gustave Reese (New York: Liberal Arts Pr, 1957)
RILM	*Répertoire international de littérature musicale* (Flushing, N.Y., 1967–)
RiHM	Hugo Riemann, *Handbuch der Musikgeschichte* (Leipzig: Breitkopf & Härtel, 1904–13; 8th ed., Berlin: M Hesse, 1922)
RIM	*Rivista italiana di musicologia* (Florence, 1966–)
RISM	*Répertoire international des sources musicales* (Munich: Henle, 1960–)
RMARC	*Royal Musical Association Research Chronicle* (London, 1961–)

RMFC	*Recherches sur la musique française classique* (Paris, 1960–)
RMI	*Rivista musicale italiana* (Milan, 1894–1932, 1936–43, 1946–55)
RRMBE	*Recent Researches in the Music of the Baroque Era* (Madison, Wis.: A-R Edit, 1964–)
RRMCE	*Recent Researches in the Music of the Classical Era* (Madison, Wis.: A-R Edit, 1975–)
RRMR	*Recent Researches in the Music of the Renaissance* (Madison, Wis.: A-R Edit, 1964–)
SartoriB	Claudio Sartori, *Bibliografia della musica strumentale stampata in Italia fino al 1700* (Florence: Olschki, 1952)
SIMG	*Sammelbände der Internationalen Musik-Gesellschaft* (Leipzig, 1899–1914)
SM	*Studia musicologica academiae scientiarum hungaricae* (Budapest, 1961–)
SR	*Source Readings in Music History,* comp. Oliver Strunk (New York: Norton, 1950; rev. ed., ed. Leo Treitler, 1998)
STMf	*Svensk tidskrift för musikforskning* (Stockholm, 1919–)
SzMw	*Studien zur Musikwissenschaft* (Vienna, 1913–34, 1955–)
TCM	*Tudor Church Music* (London: Oxford U Pr, 1922–29; appendix, 1948; R: New York: Broude Bros, 1963)
TVNM	*Tijdschrift van de Vereniging voor Nederlandse muziekgeschiedenis* (Amsterdam, 1882–)
VogelB	Emil Vogel, *Bibliothek der gedruckten weltlichen Vocalmusik Italiens aus den Jahren 1500–1700* (Berlin, 1892; R: Hildesheim: Olms, 1962)
VfMw	*Vierteljahrsschrift für Musikwissenschaft* (Leipzig, 1885–94)
WE	*The Wellesley Edition* (Wellesley, Mass.: Wellesley College, 1950–)
YIFMC	*Yearbook of the International Folk Music Council* (Urbana, 1969–80); *Yearbook for Traditional Music* (1981–)
YTS	*Music Theory Translation Series* (New Haven: Yale U Pr, 1963–)
ZfMw	*Zeitschrift für Musikwissenschaft* (Leipzig, 1918–35)
ZIMG	*Zeitschrift der Internationalen Musik-Gesellschaft* (Leipzig, 1899–1914)
ZPP	*Zeitschrift für Psychologie und Physiologie der Sinnesorgane* (Leipzig, 1890–)

Festschriften and Congress Reports

Albrecht, 1980 *Studies in Musicology in Honor of Otto E. Albrecht,* ed. John Walter Hill (Kassel: Bärenreiter, 1980)

Anderson, 1984 *Gordon Athol Anderson (1929–1981): In Memoriam von seinen Studenten, Freunden und Kollegen,* 2 vols., Musicological Studies 39 (Henryville, Pa.: Institute of Mediaeval Music, 1984)

Apel, 1968 *Essays in Musicology: A Birthday Offering for Willi Apel,* ed. Hans Tischler (Bloomington: School of Music, Indiana Univ., 1968)

Basel, 1924 *Bericht über den musikwissenschaftlichen Kongress in Basel: Veranstaltet anlässlich der Feier des 25-jährigen Bestehens der Ortgruppe Basel der Neue Schweizerischen Musikgesellschaft,* ed. Wilhelm Merian (Leipzig: Breitkopf & Härtel, 1925; R: Wiesbaden: M Sändig, 1969)

Beethoven, 1970 *Beethoven-Studien: Festgabe der österreichischen Akademie der Wissenschaften zum 200. Geburtstag von Ludwig van Beethoven,* ed. Erich Schenk (Vienna: Böhlau, 1970)

Berkeley, 1977 *International Musicological Society: Report of the Twelfth Congress, Berkeley 1977,* ed. Daniel Heartz and Bonnie Wade (Kassel: Bärenreiter, 1981)

Besseler, 1961 *Festschrift Heinrich Besseler zum sechzigsten Geburtstag,* ed. Eberhardt Klemm (Leipzig: Deutscher Verlag für Musik, 1961)

Blume, 1963 *Festschrift Friedrich Blume zum 70. Geburstag,* ed. Anna Amalie Abert and Wilhelm Pfannkuch (Kassel: Bärenreiter, 1963)

Bonn, 1970 *Bericht über den internationalen musikwissenschaftlichen Kongress Bonn 1970,* ed. Carl Dahlhaus, Hans Joachim Marx, Magda Marx-Weber, and Günther Massenkeil (Kassel: Bärenreiter, 1972)

Brno, 1967 *Studia instrumentorum musicae popularis I: Bericht über die 2. Internationale Arbeitstagung der Study Group on Folk Musical Instruments des International Folk Music Council in Brno 1967,* ed. Erich Stockmann (Stockholm: Musikhistoriska museet, 1969)

Brook, 1985 *Music in the Classic Period: Essays in Honor of Barry S. Brook,* ed. Allan W. Atlas, Festschrift series no. 5 (New York: Pendragon, 1985)

Certaldo, 1959 *L'ars nova italiana del trecento: Primo convegno internazionale,* ed. Bianca Becherini (Certaldo: Centro di studi sull'ars nova italiana del trecento, 1962)

Certaldo, 1969 *L'ars nova italiana del trecento: Secondo convegno internazionale,* ed. F. Alberto Gallo (Certaldo: Centro di studi sull'ars nova italiana del trecento, 1970)

CNRS, 1953 *Musique et poésie au XVIe siècle, Paris, 30 juin–4 juillet 1953,* Colloques internationaux du Centre national de la recherche scientifique (Paris: CNRS, 1954; R: 1973)

CNRS Abbaye de Royaumont, 1955 *Les fêtes de la Renaissance I: Journées internationales d'études,* Royaumont, July 8–13, 1955, ed. Jean Jacquot (Paris: CNRS, 1956; 2nd ed., 1973)

CNRS Tours, 1972 *Les fêtes de la Renaissance III: Quinzième colloque international d'études humanistes,* Tours, July 10–22, 1972, ed. Jean Jacquot and Élie Konigson (Paris: CNRS, 1975)

Copenhagen, 1972 *International Musicological Society: Report of the Eleventh Congress Copenhagen 1972,* 2 vols. (Copenhagen: Hansen, 1974)

Davison, 1957 *Essays on Music in Honor of Archibald Thompson Davison, by His Associates* (Cambridge, Mass.: Harvard Univ., Dept. of Music, 1957)

Dorfmüller, 1984 *Ars iocundissima: Festschrift für Kurt Dorfmüller zum 60. Geburtstag,* ed. Horst Leuchtmann and Robert Münster (Tutzing: Schneider, 1984)

Dufay, 1974 *Papers Read at the Dufay Quincentenary Conference, Brooklyn College, December 6–7, 1974,* ed. Allan W. Atlas (New York: Dept. of Music, School of Performing Arts, Brooklyn College of the City Univ. of New York, 1976)

Emsheimer, 1974 *Studia instrumentorum musicae popularis III: Festschrift to Ernst Emsheimer on the Occasion of His 70th Birthday, January 15th 1974,* ed. Gustaf Hilleström (Stockholm: Musikhistoriska museet, 1974)

Fellerer, 1962 *Festschrift Karl Gustav Fellerer zum sechzigsten Geburtstag,* ed. Heinrich Hüschen (Regensburg: G Bosse, 1962)

Freidus, 1929 *Studies in Jewish Bibliography and Related Subjects, in Memory of Abraham Solomon Freidus (1867–1923)* (New York: Alexander Kohut Memorial Foundation, 1929)

Fusignano, 1968 *Studi Corelliani: Atti del primo congresso internazionale (Fusignano, 5–8 settembre 1968),* ed. Adriano Cavicchi, Oscar Mischiati, and Pierluigi Petrobelli (Florence: Olschki, 1972)

Geiringer, 1970 *Studies in Eighteenth-Century Music: A Tribute to Karl Geiringer on His Seventieth Birthday,* ed. H. C. Robbins Landon, in collaboration with Roger E. Chapman (New York: Oxford U Pr, 1970)

Grout, 1968 *New Looks at Italian Opera: Essays in Honor of Donald J. Grout,* ed. William W. Austin (Ithaca, N.Y.: Cornell U Pr, 1968)

Gudewill, 1978 *Beiträge zur Musikgeschichte Nordeuropas: Kurt Gudewill zum 65. Geburtstag,* ed. Uwe Haensel (Wolfenbüttel: Möseler, 1978)

Handschin, 1962 *In memoriam Jacques Handschin,* ed. Higini Anglès et al. (Argentorati: Heitz, 1962)

Haydn, 1975 *Haydn Studies: Proceedings of the International Haydn Conference,* ed. Jens Peter Larsen, Howard Serwer, and James Webster (New York: Norton, 1981)

Helmuth Osthoff, 1969 *Helmuth Osthoff zu seinem siebzigsten Geburtstag,* ed. Wilhelm Stauder, Ursula Aarburg, and Peter Cahn (Tutzing: Schneider, 1969)

Hughes, 1995 *Essays on Medieval Music in Honor of David G. Hughes,* ed. Graeme M. Boone (Cambridge, Mass.: Harvard Univ., Dept. of Music, 1995)

Indiana Univ., 1965 *Music in the Americas,* ed. George List and Juan Orrego-Salas, Inter-American Music Monograph Series 1 (Bloomington, Ind.: Indiana Univ. Research Center in Anthropology, Folklore, and Linguistics, 1967)

Isham Library, 1957 *Instrumental Music,* ed. David H. Hughes (Cambridge, Mass., Harvard U Pr, 1959)

Isham Library, 1961 *Chanson and Madrigal, 1480–1530: Studies in Comparison and Contrast,* ed. James Haar (Cambridge, Mass.: Harvard U Pr, 1964)

Isham Library, 1979 *The String Quartets of Haydn, Mozart, and Beethoven: Studies of the Autograph Manuscripts,* ed. Christoph Wolff (Cambridge, Mass.: Dept. of Music, Harvard Univ., 1980)

Jeppesen, 1962 *Natalicia musicologica Knud Jeppesen septuagenario collegis oblata,* ed. Bjørn Hjelmborg and Søren Sørensen (Hafniae: Hansen, 1962)

Johnson, 1990 *Essays in Musicology: A Tribute to Alvin Johnson,* ed. Lewis Lockwood and Edward Roesner (American Musicological Society, 1990)

Josquin, 1971 *Josquin des Prez: Proceedings of the International Josquin Festival-Conference Held at The Juilliard School at Lincoln Center in New York City, 21–25 June 1971,* ed. Edward E. Lowinsky in collaboration with Bonnie J. Blackburn (New York: Oxford U Pr, 1976)

Kassel, 1962 *Gesellschaft für Musikforschung: Bericht über den internationalen musikwissenschaftlichen Kongress Kassel 1962,* ed. Georg Reichert and Martin Just (Kassel: Bärenreiter, 1963)

Kaufmann, 1981 *Music East and West: Essays in Honor of Walter Kaufmann,* ed. Thomas Noblitt (New York: Pendragon, 1981)

King, 1980 *Music and Bibliography: Essays in Honour of Alec Hyatt King,* ed. Oliver Neighbour (New York: Saur, C Bingley, 1980)

La Laurencie, 1933 *Mélanges de musicologie offerts à m. Lionel de la Laurencie* (Paris: Droz, 1933)

Lenaerts, 1969 *Renaissance-musiek 1400–1600: Donum natalicium Rene Bernard Lenaerts,* ed. Jozef Robijns, Musicologica lovaniensia 1 (Louvain: Katholieke Universiteit, Seminarie voor Muziekwetenschap, 1969)

Ljubljana, 1967 *Report of the Tenth Congress of the International Musicological Society, Ljubljana 1967,* ed. Dragotin Cvetko (Kassel: Bärenreiter, 1970)

Lockwood, 1997 *Music in Renaissance Cities and Courts: Studies in Honor of Lewis Lockwood,* ed. Jessie Ann Owens and Anthony M. Cummings (Warren, Mich.: Harmonie Park Press, 1997)

Lüneburg, 1950 *Kongress-Bericht: Gesellschaft für Musikforschung Lüneburg 1950,* ed. Hans Albrecht, Helmut Osthoff, and Walter Wiora (Kassel: Bärenreiter, n.d.)

Merritt, 1972 *Words and Music: The Scholar's View,* ed. Laurence Berman (Cambridge, Mass.: Harvard Univ., Dept. of Music, 1972)

Neumann, 1975 *Bach-Studien: Eine Sammlung von Aufsätzen (Werner Neumann zum 65. Geburtstag),* ed. Rudolf Eller and Hans-Joachim Schulze, Bach-Studien 5 (Leipzig: Breitkopf & Härtel, 1975)

New York, 1961 *International Musicological Society: Report of the Eighth Congress, New York 1961* (Kassel: Bärenreiter, 1961)

Palermo, 1954 *Atti del Congresso internationale di musiche popolari mediteranee e del Convegno dei bibliotecari musicali* (Palermo: Tip. F.lli De Magistris & C successori V Bellotti & F, 1959)

Paris, 1953 = *CNRS,* 1953

Plamenac, 1969 *Essays in Musicology: In Honor of Dragan Plamenac on His 70th Birthday,* ed. Gustave Reese and Robert J. Snow (Pittsburgh: U of Pittsburgh Pr, 1969)

Queens College, 1964 *Queens College, Flushing, N.Y., Department of Music: Twenty-Fifth Anniversary Festschrift, 1937–1962,* ed. Albert Mell (Flushing, N.Y., 1964)

Reese, 1966 *Aspects of Medieval and Renaissance Music: A Birthday Offering to Gustave Reese,* ed. Jan LaRue (New York: Norton, 1966; R: New York: Pendragon, 1978)

Riemann, 1909 *Riemann-Festschrift: Gesammelte Studien. Hugo Riemann zum sechzigsten Geburtstag* (Leipzig: M Hesse, 1909)

Rome, 1950 *Atti del [I] congresso internationale di musica sacra,* Rome, May 25–30, 1950, ed. Higini Anglès (Tournai: Desclée, 1952)

Sachs, 1965 *The Commonwealth of Music: In Honor of Curt Sachs,* ed. Gustave Reese and Rose Brandel (New York: Free Press of Glencoe, 1965)

Schmidt-Görg, 1957 *Festschrift Joseph Schmidt-Görg zum 60. Geburtstag,* ed. Dagmar Weise (Bonn: Beethovenhaus, 1957)

Schering, 1937 *Festschrift Arnold Schering zum sechzigstem Geburtstag,* ed. Helmut Osthoff, Walter Serauky, Adam Adrio, Max Schneider, and Gotthold Frotscher (Berlin: A Glass, 1937)

Schneider, 1955 *Festschrift Max Schneider zum achtzigsten Geburtstage,* ed. Walter Vetter (Leipzig: Deutscher Verlag für Musik, 1955)

Schrade, 1973 *Gattungen der Musik in Einzeldarstellung: Gedenkschrift Leo Schrade,* ed. Wulf Arlt, Ernst Lichtenhahn, Hans Oesch, and Max Haas (Bern: Francke, 1973)

Smits van Waesberghe, 1963 *Organicae voces: Festschrift Joseph Smits van Waesberghe, anlässlich seines 60. Geburtstages 18. April 1961* (Amsterdam: Instituut voor Meddeleeuwse Muziekwetenschap, 1963)

Strunk, 1968 *Studies in Music History: Essays for Oliver Strunk,* ed. Harold Powers (Princeton: Princeton U Pr, 1968)

Utrecht, 1952 *Kongressbericht der Internationalen Gesellschaft für Musikwissenschaft, 5. Kongress, Utrecht, 1952* (Amsterdam: G Alsbach, 1953)

Van den Borren, 1964 *Liber amicorum Charles van den Borren* (Antwerp: Lloyd Anversois, 1964)

Vetter, 1969 *Musa—Mens—Musici: Im Gedenken an Walther Vetter,* ed. Institut für Musikwissenschaft der Humboldt-Universität zu Berlin (Leipzig: Deutscher Verlag für Musik, 1969)

Vienna, 1954 *Zweiter internationaler Kongress für katholische Kirchenmusik: Zu Ehren des Heiligen Papstes Pius X: Bericht,* Vienna, October 4–10, 1954 (Vienna: Exekutivkomitee des II. Internationalen Kongresses für katholische Kirchenmusik, 1955)

von Fischer, 1973 *Studien zur Tradition in der Musik: Kurt von Fischer zum 60. Geburtstag,* ed. Hans Heinrich Eggebrecht and Max Lutolf (Munich: Katzbichler, 1973)

Wachsmann, 1977 *Essays for a Humanist: An Offering to Klaus Wachsmann,* ed. Charles Seeger and Bonnie Wade (New York: Town House, 1977)

Warsaw, 1960 *The Book of the First International Musicological Congress Devoted to the Works of Frederick Chopin,* ed. Zofia Lissa (Warsaw: Polish Scientific Publishers, 1963)

Wégimont, 1954 *Les colloques de Wégimont, 1 (1954): Ethnomusicologie I,* ed. P. Collaer (Brussels: Elsevier, 1956)

Wégimont, 1955 *Les colloques de Wégimont, 2 (1955): L'ars nova,* Bibliothèque de la faculté de philosophie et lettres de l'Université de Liège 149 (Paris: Société d'édition "Les belles lettres," 1959)

Wégimont, 1956 *Les colloques de Wégimont, 3 (1956): Ethnomusicologie II,* Bibliothèque de la faculté de philosophie et lettres de l'Université de Liège 157 (Paris: Société d'édition "Les belles lettres," 1960)

Wégimont, 1957 *Les colloques de Wégimont, 4 (1957): Le "baroque" musical,* Bibliothèque de la faculté de philosophie et lettres de l'Université de Liège 171 (Paris: Société d'édition "Les belles lettres," 1963)

Wégimont, 1958–60 *Les colloques de Wégimont, 5 (1958–60): Ethnomusicologie III,* Bibliothèque de la faculté de philosophie et lettres de l'Université de Liège 172 (Paris: Société d'édition "Les belles lettres," 1964)

Wellesz, 1966 *Essays Presented to Egon Wellesz,* ed. Jack Westrup (London: Oxford U Pr, 1966)

Wiora, 1967 *Festschrift für Walter Wiora zum 30. Dezember 1966,* ed. Ludwig Finscher and Christoph-Hellmut Mahling (Kassel: Bärenreiter, 1967)

Wiora, 1979 *Über Symphonien (Festschrift Walter Wiora zum 70. Geburtstag),* ed. Christoph-Hellmut Mahling (Tutzing: Schneider, 1979)

Languages

Ar.	Arabic	Kor.	Korean
AS	Anglo-Saxon	Lat.	Latin
Brit.	British usage	ME	Middle English
Bulg.	Bulgarian	MHG	Middle High German
Cat.	Catalan	Nor.	Norwegian
Chin.	Chinese	Occ.	Occitan
Cz.	Czechoslovakian	OE	Old English
Dan.	Danish	OFr.	Old French
Du.	Dutch	OHG	Old High German
Eng.	English	ON	Old Norse
Finn.	Finnish	Per.	Persian
Fr.	French	Pol.	Polish
Gael.	Gaelic	Port.	Portuguese
Ger.	German	Prov.	Provençal
Gr.	Greek	Rom.	Romanian
Heb.	Hebrew	Russ.	Russian
Hin.	Hindi	Serb.-Cro.	Serbo-Croatian
Hung.	Hungarian	Skt.	Sanskrit
Icel.	Icelandic	Sp.	Spanish
IE	Indo-European	Swed.	Swedish
It.	Italian	Tel.	Telugu
Jap.	Japanese	Turk.	Turkish
Jav.	Javanese		

General

An asterisk (*) before a term indicates a separate article on that subject.

Middle C is designated c′, the C's below that c, C, C_1, etc. The C's above middle C are designated c″, c‴, etc. See Pitch names.

abbr.	abbreviated, abbreviation
anon.	anonymous
app.	appendix
art.	article
b.	born
bapt.	baptized
B.C.E.	before the common era
bibl.	bibliography
bk.	book
ca.	circa
C.E.	of the common era
cent.	century
chap.	chapter
col.	column
comp.	compiled by, compiler
d.	died
dim.	diminutive
ed.	edition, edited by, editor
ex.	example (plural exx.)
f.	and following (plural ff.)
facs.	facsimile
fasc.	fascicle
fem.	feminine
fig.	figure
fl.	flourished
fol.	folio
fr.	from
ill.	illustration
incl.	inclusive, including
l.	line (plural ll.)
lit.	literally
M:	microform edition
maj.	major
masc.	masculine
min.	minor
movt.	movement
MS, MSS	*manuscriptorum(-a),* manuscript(s)
n.	note (plural nn.)
no.	number
N.S.	New Style
op.	opus
orch.	orchestra
O.S.	Old Style
p.	page (plural pp.)
par.	paragraph
perf.	performance, performed
pl.	plural
prod.	produced
Ps.	Psalm (for the numbering of the Psalms, see Psalter)
pt.	part
publ.	published by
R:	reprint
r	recto
rev.	revised, revised by
sec.	section
supp.	supplement
trans.	translation, translated by, translator
vol.	volume
v	verso
Univ.	University

THE HARVARD DICTIONARY OF MUSIC

A

A. (1) See Pitch names, Letter notation, Hexachord, Pitch. (2) An abbreviation for *alto or *altus.* (3) *A* [It.], *à* [Fr.]. To, at, with, for; *a 2* [etc.] *voci,* for two [etc.] voices. Phrases beginning with this word should be sought under the word immediately following, e.g., *Battuta, Beneplacito, Cappella, Deux, Due, Peine entendu, Piacere, Tempo.*

Ab [Ger.]. Off, as for a mute or an organ stop.

Abandonné [Fr.], **abbandonatamente, con abbandono** [It.]. With abandon, unrestrained.

Abbassare [It.]. To lower, e.g., the pitch of a string.

Abbellimento [It.]. Ornament.

Abbreviations. For abbreviated or shorthand forms of musical notation, see Notation. Abbreviations of words, including performance directions, should be sought at the appropriate place in the alphabet.

Abdämpfen [Ger.]. To damp, to mute.

Abduction from the Seraglio. See *Entführung aus dem Serail, Die.*

Abegg Variations. Schumann's variations for piano op. 1 (1829–30), dedicated to his friend Meta Abegg, whose name is represented in the first five notes of the theme: a′, b♭′, e″, g″, g″.

Abendmusik [Ger.]. An evening concert in a church; specifically the performances at the Marienkirche in Lübeck, north Germany, begun in the 17th century and lasting until 1810. Paid for by local businessmen, the concerts came to prominence under Dietrich Buxtehude (organist at Lübeck from 1668 until 1707), who established them on five Sundays preceding Christmas. At first they included organ music and a variety of vocal music. Buxtehude and his successors, however, composed five-part oratorios to be performed over the course of the five Sundays.

Bibl.: Wilhelm Stahl, "Die Lübecker Abendmusiken im 17. und 18. Jahrhunderts," *Verein für lübeckische Geschichte und Altertumskunde* 29/1 (1937): 1–64. Georg Karstädt, *Die "extraordinairen" Abendmusiken Dietrich Buxtehudes* (Lübeck: M Schmidt-Römhild, 1962).

Abgesang [Ger.]. See Bar form.

Abgestossen [Ger.]. *Staccato.

Abnehmend [Ger.]. **Diminuendo.*

Absetzen [Ger.]. (1) To separate; to articulate. (2) To intabulate, i.e., to transcribe in *tablature.

Absolute music [fr. Ger. *absolute Musik, absolute Tonkunst*]. Instrumental music that is "free of" [Lat. *absolutus*] any explicit or implied connection with, or reference to, extramusical reality. The term, little-used today, long served as a polemical weapon in a debate, now largely resolved, about the validity of *program music; in this debate, the category of absolute music (sometimes also called "abstract music") was often defined as the antithesis of program music.

The term absolute music was used repeatedly by Wagner to condemn any music that was in his view deprived of the necessary solid basis in poetry or drama. He included in this category not only much instrumental music, but also the sections of *bel canto* operas in which tunefulness and vocal display often take precedence over dramatic truth. Subsequent writers have restricted the term to instrumental music. Eduard Hanslick praised absolute music (in this sense) as the only "pure" music and attacked the programmatic symphonic poems of Liszt and the operas of Wagner as attempts to subjugate music or to assign it tasks for which it is manifestly unfit.

The debate between the proponents of absolute and program music has continued for over a century, overlapping, but only in part, with a debate over the extent to which music is a form of *expression. In the 20th century, the proponents of absolute music have generally had the upper hand; the influence of the doctrine can be seen in many works of musical *aesthetics, in Schenkerian and other approaches to musical analysis, and not least in the relatively objective, intellectual, or formalistic character of much recent music. Nonetheless, the dichotomy between absolute and program music is essentially misleading, for it obscures the complex intertwining of extramusical associations and "purely" musical substance that can be found even in pieces that bear no verbal clues whatever.

Bibl.: Eduard Hanslick, *On the Musically Beautiful: A Contribution towards the Revision of the Aesthetics of Music,* 8th ed. (1891), trans. and ed. Geoffrey Payzant (Indianapolis: Hackett, 1986). Carl Dahlhaus, *The Idea of Absolute Music,* trans. Roger Lustig (Chicago: U of Chicago Pr, 1989). Leo Treitler, "Mozart and the Idea of Absolute Music," in his *Music and the Historical Imagination* (Cambridge, Mass.: Harvard U Pr, 1989), pp. 176–215. Lydia Goehr, *The Imaginary Museum of Musical Works: An Essay in the Philosophy of Music* (Oxford: Clarendon, 1992), pp. 211–218. Scott Burnham, "How Music Matters: Poetic Content Revisited," in *Rethinking Music,* ed. Nicholas Cook and Mark Everist (Oxford: Oxford U Pr, 1999), pp. 193–216. Daniel K. L. Chua, *Absolute Music and the Construction of Meaning* (Cambridge: Cambridge U Pr, 1999). R.P.L.

Absolute pitch. The ability to name a pitch (in reference to the musical scale, generally by letter name) or to produce a pitch designated by name without recourse to any external source or standard. The term perfect pitch is misleading because varying degrees of ability are observed. Most trained musicians have excellent *relative pitch; only some have absolute pitch, which has more limited practical value.

At the high end of the absolute pitch ability range, errors are rare and tend to differ from the correct response by a semitone, an octave, or an octave plus or minus a semitone. This suggests that there are two independent stages: locating the octave (pitch height) and determining the pitch name regardless of octave (pitch class, or chroma). Ability differences are attributed primarily to accuracy of pitch class. Octave errors may partially reflect the frequent use in these tests of complex tones, often piano tones, but errors are also found with pure tones (sine waves). Pure tones are generally more difficult to name, indicating that characteristics of musical instruments (overtones, inharmonic partials, timbre variations with pitch) may be used in identifying pitches. Recent research has found that pitches associated with white keys on the piano are identified by absolute pitch possessors faster and with greater accuracy than those associated with black keys.

Theories of absolute pitch assume that individuals with this ability possess an internal standard pitch in long-term memory. The ability appears to be most easily acquired in childhood. Some theories maintain that the ability is largely innate, but a few cases of apparently successful training have been reported. There is no general agreement as to whether absolute pitch is continuously distributed in the population or if there are distinct subgroups, although recent studies have found a higher incidence of absolute pitch among musicians than in the general population and a higher incidence among Asian music students than non-Asian music students. It is unclear whether this effect is due to genetics or to cultural differences in training. Underlying neurological mechanisms have not been identified.

Bibl.: Karl Stumpf, *Tonpsychologie* (Leipzig: S Hirzel, 1883–90). J. von Kries, "Über das absolut Gehör," *ZPP* 3 (1891–92): 257–79. Max Meyer, "Is the Memory of Absolute Pitch Capable of Development by Training?" *PR* 6 (1899): 514–16. Géza Révész, *Zur Grundlegung der Tonpsychologie* (Leipzig: Veit, 1913). Carl Emil Seashore, *The Psychology of Musical Talent* (Boston: Silver Burdett, 1919). Laurence A. Petran, "An Experimental Study of Pitch Recognition," *PsM* 42/6 (1932): 1–124. A. Bachem, "Various Types of Absolute Pitch," *JASA* 9 (1937–38): 146–51. D. Morgan Neu, "A Critical Review of the Literature on 'Absolute Pitch,'" *PB* 44 (1947): 249–66. A. Bachem, "Absolute Pitch," *JASA* 27 (1955): 1180–85. Paul T. Brady, "Fixed-Scale Mechanism of Absolute Pitch," *JASA* 48 (1970): 883–87. Jane A. Siegel and William Siegel, "Absolute Identification of Notes and Intervals by Musicians," *PP* 21 (1977): 143–52. Gregory R. Lockhead and Robert Byrd, "Practically Perfect Pitch," *JASA* 70 (1981): 387–89. W. Dixon Ward and Edward M. Burns, "Absolute Pitch," in *The Psychology of Music,* ed. Diana Deutsch (New York: Acad Pr, 1982), pp. 431–51. Ken'ichi Miyazaki, "Absolute Pitch Identification: Effects of Timbre and Pitch Region," *Music Perception* 7 (1989): 1–14. Ken'ichi Miyazaki, "The Speed of Musical Pitch Identification by Absolute-Pitch Possessors," *Music Perception* 8 (1990): 177–88. Annie H. Takeuchi and Stewart H. Hulse, "Absolute Pitch," *PB* 113 (1993): 345–61. Peter Gregersen et al., "Absolute Pitch: Prevalence, Ethnic Variation, and Estimation of the Genetic Component," *American Journal of Human Genetics* 65 (1999): 911–13. Elizabeth W. Marvin and Alexander R. Brinkman, "The Effect of Key Color and Timbre on Absolute Pitch Recognition in Musical Contexts," *Music Perception* 18 (2000): 111–37. C.K., J.B., rev. E.W.M.

Abstossen [Ger.]. (1) To detach; to play *staccato. (2) In organ playing, to take off a stop.

Abstract music. *Absolute music.

Abstrich [Ger.]. Down-bow. See Bowing (1).

Abwechseln [Ger.]. To alternate, as when a single player alternates in playing two instruments.

Abzug [Ger.]. (1) *Scordatura tuning, especially on the lute; by extension, in the writings of Praetorius, additional open bass strings. (2) The softening of an *appoggiatura as it tapers into its resolution; or, according to Löhlein, a **Schneller.* D.F.

Academic Festival Overture [Ger. *Akademische Festouvertüre*]. An orchestral composition by Brahms, op. 80 (1880), dedicated to the University of Breslau in recognition of the honorary doctorate awarded him in 1879. It makes free use of several German student songs, notably "Gaudeamus igitur."

Academy. A scholarly or artistic society. The term first referred to a grove in Athens sacred to the mythological hero Academus, where Plato established a school as early as 385 B.C.E. It gained new currency with the revival of Platonic and Neoplatonic thought in the Renaissance. Marsilio Ficino (1433–99), the central figure in this revival, created around 1470 a loosely structured "Platonic Academy" in Florence, whose members included the most illustrious poets and men of letters of that city. Many of these men were also accomplished musicians, including Ficino himself, Lorenzo de' Medici ("The Magnificent"), and Baccio Ugolini; and music, whose moral and curative effects played a large part in Ficino's thought, figured importantly in the meetings of the Academy.

By the mid-16th century more than 200 academies had sprung up in Italian towns in imitation of Ficino's group, most of them now formally organized with written statutes and statements of their scholarly goals. In literary and philosophical academies such as the Accademia fiorentina and Accademia della crusca of Florence (established, respectively, in 1540 and 1582), music was a frequent topic of discussion and source of entertainment. And alongside these groups there arose academies in which musical composition and performance were the primary or even sole aims, such as the Accademia filarmonica of Verona (established 1543) and the Accademia degli elevati of Florence (established 1607). Finally, numerous informal groups of learned aristocrats gathered at private palaces in the 16th and 17th centuries. Many of these *camerate* or *ridotti,* such as those meeting in late 16th-century Florence at the palaces of Giovanni de' Bardi and Jacopo Corsi, featured musical discussion and experimentation.

France too participated in the Renaissance rebirth of academies, in conscious emulation of Italian developments. The first French academy officially instituted by royal decree gave pride of place to music: the Académie de poésie et de musique, established in 1570 by the poet Jean-Antoine de Baïf and the musician Joachim Thibault de Courville. The Académie aimed to rediscover the legendary effects of ancient music through a new style of quantitative poetry and music—*vers mesuré et *musique mesurée à l'antique.*

The French academic tradition languished during the period of religious wars, but was rejuvenated, now with the express aim of authoritarian cultural uniformity, by Cardinal Richelieu in the mid-17th century. After the institution in 1635 of the Académie française, whose purview was purely linguistic, numerous other similar groups followed, devoted to such subjects as painting and sculpture, dance, and the sciences. In 1669 the Académie Royale de Musique was founded, with letters patent granted to the poet Pierre Perrin and composer Robert Cambert (the patent passing to Jean-Baptiste Lully in 1672). It was not a learned society for musical experimentation and discussion like Baïf's, but rather an opera company with royal sponsorship. This survives as the Paris Opéra, the official title of which through most of its history has included the term *académie.* Such use of the term grew more prevalent throughout the 18th century, until by 1800 almost any concert with aristocratic support might be termed an academy. Musical academies since that time have assumed various forms, from schools of music, to groups promoting musical performance, to learned associations devoted to studies of music theory and history.

Bibl.: Michele Maylender, *Storia delle accademie d'Italia,* 5 vols. (Bologna: L Cappelli, 1926–30). Giuseppe Turrini, *L'Accademia filarmonica di Verona dalla fondazione (Maggio 1543) al 1600* (Verona: Tip Veronese, 1941). Frances A. Yates, *The French Academies of the Sixteenth Century* (London: Warburg Institute, 1947). Claude V. Palisca, "The Alterati of Florence, Pioneers in the Theory of Dramatic Music," *Grout,* 1968, pp. 9–38. Edmond Strainchamps, "New Light on the Accademia degli Elevati of Florence," *MQ* 62 (1976): 507–35. David S. Chambers and François Quiviger, eds., *Italian Academies of the Sixteenth Century* (London: Warburg Institute, 1995). G.A.T.

A cappella [It.]. See *Cappella.*

Accelerando, accelerato [It., abbr. *accel.*]. Becoming faster; faster.

Accent. (1) Emphasis on one pitch or chord. An accent is dynamic if the pitch or chord is louder than its surroundings, tonic if it is higher in pitch, and agogic if it is of longer duration. In measured music [see Meter], the first beat of each measure is the strong beat and thus carries a metrical accent. The creation of regularly recurring metrical accents depends on the manipulation of groups of pitches or chords (e.g., according to the principles of tonality) and not solely on the placement of dynamic, tonic, or agogic accents. Thus, the strong beat in a measure need not be louder, higher, or longer than the remaining weak beats in order to retain its quality of strength with respect to its surroundings. When the regular recurrence of metrical accents is contradicted by means of loudness, pitch, or duration, *syncopation results. In vocal music, the coordination of musical accent with the various sonorous characteristics (including accent) of a text is termed *declamation. For the role of tonic accent in Gregorian chant, see Cursive and tonic, Gregorian chant V.

A dynamic accent on a single pitch or chord may be specified with the symbols > and ^, the second calling for greater loudness and sharper attack than the first. See also *Sforzando, sforzato;* Dynamic marks; Notation.

(2) [Fr., Ger.; It. *accento*] From the late 16th through the 18th century, any of various ornaments such as the *springer, *appoggiatura, **Schneller* (according to Printz), and small groups of notes (see *NeuO,* pp. 577–78 for a list). The most common French meaning was springer (an *échappée*), and *accent* was J. S. Bach's term for an appoggiatura. Diruta (1593) used *accento* for the springer.

(3) [Fr.] In the 17th and 18th centuries, a type of **Nachschlag* in which the upper neighbor is added to the very end of the main note. The following note most often lies below the main note or is a return to the pitch of the main note. It is also called an *aspiration* and sometimes a *plainte.* See Ornamentation.

(4) For the signs associated with Greek prosodic accents and with cantillation of Semitic texts, see Ecphonetic notation. (2) D.F.

Accentuation. The placement of *accents. For the musical treatment of text accent, see also Declamation.

Accentus, concentus [Lat.]. Two broad classifications of liturgical chant, *accentus* referring to recitation tones of various types, and *concentus* referring to more elaborate melodies such as antiphons, responsories, and hymns. Andreas Ornithoparchus (*Musicae activae micrologus,* 1517) is among the first to make this distinction. It is not found in the works of medieval writers.

Accessist [Ger.]. See *Akzessist.*

Acciaccatura [It., perhaps from *acciaccare,* to crush]. An ornament of 17th- and 18th-century keyboard playing, particularly in the Italian style of accompanying recitatives, consisting of a nonharmonic tone that is sounded simultaneously with a harmonic tone or tones but that is neither prepared nor resolved; sometimes referred to as a *Zusammenschlag* and by extension as a simultaneous appoggiatura. Francesco Gasparini (1708) and Francesco Geminiani (1749) seem to distinguish between striking and immediately releasing the semitone below the main note, termed *mordente* by Gasparini and *tatto* by Geminiani, and striking and sustaining a whole tone below one or more main notes, termed *acciaccatura.* Non-Italian writers of the 18th century and modern writers after them have often used the term *acciaccatura* for both the semitone and the whole-tone dissonance and have prescribed the very nearly immediate release of both. Although the 18th-century Italian practice was improvisatory and not indicated by any sign, the term *acciaccatura* has sometimes been applied to extremely dissonant chords occurring in keyboard compositions by Domenico Scarlatti and others. This has led, probably inappropriately and because of the confusion surrounding the term, to the suggestion that the dissonant pitches in such chords are not to be sustained for the full duration of the chord.

C. P. E. Bach and Friedrich W. Marpurg give the term *acciaccatura* as the equivalent of the *arpégé figuré* or figurate *arpeggio, i.e., an arpeggio into which are introduced one or more nonharmonic tones that are not sustained. Some modern writers have termed such a tone a passing *acciaccatura.* Both Bach and Marpurg, however, treat the simultaneously sounded but immediately released dissonance as a type of *mordent. In 1762, Marpurg terms this ornament a *Zusammenschlag* and equates it with the Italian term *acciaccatura* and, probably incorrectly, with the French **pincé étouffé.* See Ornamentation.

Accidental. In musical notation, any of the symbols used to raise or lower a pitch by one or two semitones or to cancel a previous sign or part of a *key signature. The five symbols used for this purpose are given in the table with their names in English, French, German, Italian, and Spanish. A sharp raises and a flat lowers a pitch by one semitone. A double sharp raises and a double flat lowers a pitch by two semitones. A natural cancels any preceding sign, including an element of the prevailing key signature. The combinations ♮♯ and ♮♭ are sometimes used to cancel one element of the double sharp and double flat, respectively, and ♮♮ is sometimes used to cancel the double sharp or double flat altogether. The simple forms ♯, ♭, and ♮ suffice for these purposes, however. An accidental is placed on a line or space of the staff immediately to the left of the note to which it applies. According to modern notational practice, an accidental remains in force for all notes occurring on the same line or space in the remainder of the measure in which it appears. This practice is not well established until the 19th century.

	♯	♭	𝄪
Eng.	sharp	flat	double sharp
Fr.	dièse	bémol	double dièse
Ger.	Kreuz	Be	Doppelkreuz
It.	diesis	bemolle	doppio diesis
Sp.	sostenido	bemol	doble sostenido

	𝄫	♮
Eng.	double flat	natural
Fr.	double bémol	bécarre
Ger.	Doppel-Be	Auflösungszeichen, Quadrat
It.	doppio bemolle	bequadro
Sp.	doble bemol	becuadro

In tonal music, certain conventions govern the choice between enharmonically equivalent sharps and flats, e.g., between F-sharp and G-flat. In general, if the note to be altered is followed immediately by a higher pitch it is altered by means of a sharp; if followed by a lower pitch, a flat is used. Alterations to the pure minor *scale result from "raising" the sixth and seventh scale degrees, with the result that a natural note is used to substitute for a prevailing flat and a sharped note to substitute for a prevailing natural. In some atonal music, in order to avoid ambiguity, accidentals are applied to every note and thus apply only to the note immediately following.

The sharp, flat, and natural derive from the two forms of the letter b employed to represent B-natural and B-flat in the medieval *Gamut. For B-natural, a square-shaped b, called *b quadratum* (square b) or *b durum* (hard b), was used. For B-flat a rounded b, called *b rotundum* (round b) or *b molle* (soft b), was used. This terminology is reflected in the terminology still in use for flats and naturals in German and the Romance languages as well as in the German *Dur* for major and *Moll* for minor. Since, according to the principles of *solmization and the use of the *hexachord, B-flat was to be sung with the syllable *fa* and B-natural with the syllable *mi,* the round b or ♭ meant principally that a note before which it appeared should be sung as *fa.* This did not necessarily entail lowering the pitch by a semitone, for when ♭ appeared before an F there was no need to alter the pitch in order to use the syllable *fa* appropriately. Only with the extension of the system to include all chromatic pitches did the ♭ come to mean universally that the pitch in question should be lowered by a semitone. Similar considerations governed the use of the square b, except that here several different forms developed: ⅃, ♮, ♯, and ⨳. Until the latter part of the 15th century, these signs, especially the last three, were used without distinction to specify the syllable *mi* and thus were in some cases (as on F) the equivalent of the modern sharp and in some cases (as on E) the equivalent of the modern natural. Only beginning in the later 15th century is there theoretical support for the notion that all notes could be sharp, flat, or natural, a notion essential to the modern understanding of accidentals. The first of these four forms sometimes resembled an h in German practice of the 15th and 16th centuries, and as a result, German pitch nomenclature still refers to B-flat as B and to B-natural as H. The last of these forms was the preferred form in the 16th century and remained in use as the equivalent of the modern sharp into the 18th century. For the use of unnotated accidentals in some early music, see *Musica ficta.*

Acclamation. An elaborate musical salutation addressed to the Byzantine emperor, his family, the Patriarch, and other dignitaries of church or state. Known also as *Euphymia* ("song of praise") and *Polychronion,* it wished the personage "many years." Musical documents preserving acclamations date only from the 14th century, but according to written tradition (*De ceremoniis,* ii, 19) the practice is much older. Acclamations may have been used as models for the Carolingian *Laudes regiae* of the late 8th century. Apparently the performance was antiphonal, with two groups of singers: *kraktai* at secular ceremonies (sometimes accompanied by instruments) and *psaltai* on religious occasions. Each group was led by a *praipositos* or precentor, respectively. D.E.C.

Accolade [Fr.]. *Brace.

Accompagnato [It.]. Accompanied. See Recitative.

Accompanied (keyboard) sonata. A sonata for harpsichord or piano with one or more accompanying melodic instruments such as violin or flute, the keyboard part being written out in full rather than realized from a thoroughbass part. A product of the middle third of the 18th century with both French and German antecedents, it was a widely cultivated and very prominent form through the 1770s, and its influence was felt into the 19th century in the standard repertory of solo sonatas, trios, and the like. It was not an outgrowth of the sonata with thoroughbass accompaniment, but rather coexisted with it for several decades, some composers writing both types. By the 1770s, the accompanying instrumental parts were often distinctly subordinate (sometimes even marked as not obligatory) to the keyboard part, and this treatment of instruments was employed for types of music other than the sonata. Although the chamber music with keyboard by the masters of the Classical period often exhibits something approaching equality among participants and gives prominence to the nonkeyboard instruments, much of it shows very clear links to the tradition of the accompanied keyboard sonata. See also Sonata II.

Bibl.: David Fuller, "Accompanied Keyboard Music," *MQ* 60 (1974): 222–45. William S. Newman, *The Sonata in the Classic Era* (Chapel Hill: U of NC Pr, 1963; 3rd ed., New York: Norton, 1983).

Accompaniment. The musical background for a principal part or parts. This term is used in two somewhat different ways, one referring to manner of performance, the other to texture. The first is appropriate when the performers of a musical work are divided into two components of contrasting and complementary function: a principal part in which musical interest and the listener's attention are mainly centered, and the accompaniment, subordinate to it, whose main purpose is in some sense supportive. The principal part may be one or more solo performers, vocal or instrumental, or a group of performers, such as a chorus. The accompaniment is usually instrumental, either a single instrument (usually one capable of chords), an ensemble, or an orchestra. The relation between accompaniment and principal part can vary from a completely and unobtrusively subordinate role for the accompaniment, like that of guitar chords strummed with a song or that of the church organist in congregational singing, to what is usually called *obbligato accompaniment, found in more complex music, where the accompaniment is an essential part of the texture. Obbligato parts can remain in a subordinate relation to the principal part, as in much Baroque music, or can interact with it to varying degrees, as in much music from the Classical period onward. It is in such music that accompaniment makes its greatest artistic demands on performers.

This is the usual and original meaning of accompaniment. By extension the term has also been applied to musical textures, as in the phrase "melody and accompaniment," when one or more primary melodic parts are supported by other material subordinate in musical interest, often of a primarily harmonic rather than melodic character, commonly chords or chordal figuration, e.g., the *Alberti bass and similar formulas. Melody and accompaniment may be performed on a single instrument or by different performers in an ensemble. In many cases these two uses of the term are both applicable at the same time.

Instruments and voices were frequently used together in the Middle Ages and Renaissance, as documentary evidence shows, but the reconstruction of accompanimental practice is difficult because the written music lacks precise indications of when instruments were used, and which ones. Very likely this lack reflects a degree of flexibility on both points. The monophonic songs of the troubadours and trouvères were probably often accompanied in some way, but modern attempts to reproduce this practice are highly speculative. (The organ accompaniment of Gregorian chant often heard in Catholic churches in later centuries was not based on historical considerations but on a distaste for monophony.) Polyphonic chansons of the 14th and 15th centuries frequently have lines that appear to be more instrumental than vocal, but scholars are not in complete agreement on their implications. In the equal-voice polyphony of the 16th century, instruments were sometimes used to replace or reinforce some of the singers [see Performance practice].

Accompaniment takes on a new and more essential role in the Baroque, because of the development of new kinds of texture in which vocal and instrumental parts of different functions and styles are clearly distinguished and because of the stronger differentiation of harmony and melody that arises with the tonal system. In Baroque music, accompaniment is often present on more than one level at once. The *thoroughbass pervades the background of most music for more than one performer, while obbligato accompaniment is often present in the foreground of many late Baroque vocal works and concertos. In much Baroque vocal music, the accompaniment has also a symbolic function, forming a tissue of musical elements representative of aspects of the text, in keeping with the principles of musical *rhetoric and the doctrine of *affections.

In the Classical period, the relation between principal part and accompaniment tends to become more varied and dynamically interactive. Mozart represents a peak of achievement in this regard, especially in his operas (where his accompaniments to the voices often convey a sense of gesture and movement very important to the dramatic effect) and concertos (where the dialectic of soloist and accompanying orchestra involves almost every possible relation between the two). In chamber music, the breakdown of the distinction between principal part and accompaniment becomes clear in, for example, Haydn's String Quartets op. 33 and later works. See also Accompanied keyboard sonata.

In the Romantic period, the growth of the orchestra, an increasing complexity of harmony and its growing importance as an element of expression, and the Romantic aesthetic position that music had more expressive potential by itself than with words (a reversal of earlier opinion) all tended to shift more importance to the accompaniment, especially in vocal music. These trends were more evident in German music than elsewhere, as in the climactic moments of Wagner's operas, where the orchestra sometimes challenges the primacy of the voice, or as in the contribution of the piano part to the musical design and expressive effect of many lieder [see Lied]. This continues a general difference between German and other national styles of accompaniment already apparent in the 18th century and persisting into the 20th. Schoenberg and associated composers sometimes explicitly distinguish between a leading part (**Hauptstimme*) and subordinate parts, though Boulez and others have sought to abolish the distinction.

Until the decline of the thoroughbass, improvisation played a prominent role in accompaniment. Since that time, it has been restricted within art music to a few domains, notably organ accompaniment of congregational singing, where improvisation is sometimes quite elaborate. In folk and popular music, accompaniment is often improvised, though ensembles may rely on written *arrangements for the purpose. There is a centuries-long tradition of providing composed accompaniments for folk songs that includes not only works by composers such as Haydn and Ives, but also what are now regarded as the misguided efforts of some 19th- and 20th-century collectors. In some non-Western musics, *heterophony is a prominent feature of accompaniment. See also Additional accompaniment.

Bibl.: Gerald Moore, *Singer and Accompanist* (London: Methuen, 1953). Kurt Adler, *The Art of Accompanying and Coaching* (Minneapolis: U of Minn Pr, 1965; corr. ed., New York: Da Capo, 1971). Gerhard Krapf, *Organ Improvisation: A Practical Approach to Chorale Elaborations for the Service* (Minneapolis: Augsburg, 1967). Philip Cranmer, *The Technique of Accompaniment* (London: Dobson, 1970).

Accoppiare [It.]. In organ playing, to couple.

Accord [Fr.]. (1) Chord; *accord parfait,* triad. (2) The set of pitches to which an instrument such as the lute is tuned. Various tunings have been used for a single instrument. See also *Accords nouveaux,* Scordatura.

Accordare [It.]. To tune.

Accordatura [It.]. The set of pitches to which an instrument, especially a stringed instrument, is tuned; in stringed instruments, often the usual as opposed to some less common set. See also Scordatura.

Accorder [Fr.]. To tune.

Accordion. A bellows-operated, hand-held wind instrument sounded by free reeds. It consists in effect of two reed organs, each with its own keyboard, joined by a rectangular bellows. The organ in the player's right hand is the higher pitched, and in the prevalent design, its reeds are sounded by means of a piano keyboard. The left-hand organ, designed for accompani-

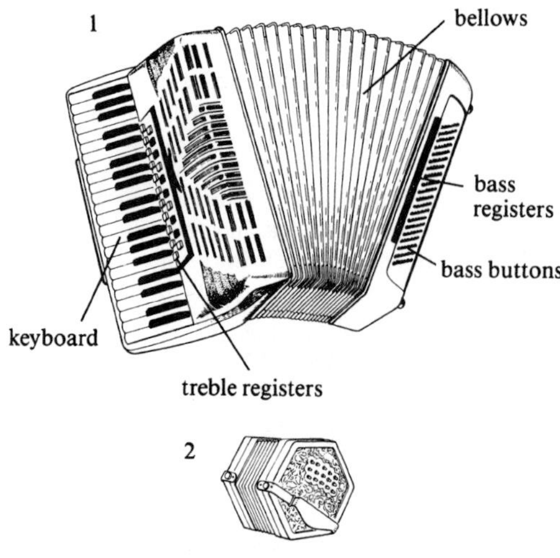

1. Accordion. 2. Concertina.

ment, is played on rows of buttons, some sounding single bass notes, others producing major, minor, diminished, and seventh chords. In standard double-action models, the steel reeds are arranged in pairs, one reed sounded by pressure (pushing), the other by suction (pulling). Supplementary sets of reeds in the right-hand organ are activated by register switches above the keyboard and provide a variety of tone colors.

Related instruments like the *concertina and *mouth organ were developed in the early 19th century, inspired by the Chinese *sheng. The first instrument of this type to incorporate bellows and a button keyboard was patented as the Handäoline in 1821 by Friedrich Buschmann of Berlin. The first instrument with the name accordion was patented in 1829 by Cyrillus Demian in Vienna and included a button keyboard and chords for accompaniment. The piano keyboard and steel reeds were introduced in the 1850s.

Accordo [It.]. Chord.

Accords nouveaux [Fr., new tunings]. The various 17th-century tunings for the lute and related instruments. To facilitate playing in diverse keys, at least 25 tunings appear in manuscript and printed sources of lute music, particularly in the French repertory of the Gaultier circle. These tunings, which stabilized into the standard "D-minor" tuning around 1640, stress intervals of thirds rather than the fourths used in the Renaissance tuning (**vieil ton*). Among the most common are the following (for others, see Radke, 1963): G c f′ a c′ f′ *(ton de la harpe par b dur);* G c f a♭ c′ f′ ("harpe way, flat"; *ton de la harpe par b mol*); A d g b d′ f♯′ ("tuning Gaultier"); A d g b♭ d′ f′ ("flat French"); B♭ d f a d′ f′ *(accord Mercure);* B♭ d f b♭ d′ f′ ("trumpet tuning"); A d f♯ a d′ f♯′ ("English tuning"; *Accord dur*); and A d f a d′ f′ ("D-minor"; *ton enrhumé*).

Bibl.: Hans Radke, "Beiträge zur Erforschung der Lautentabulaturen des 16.–18. Jahrhunderts," *Mf* 16 (1963): 34–51. A.J.N.

Accoupler [Fr.]. In organ playing, to couple.

Accusé [Fr.]. Marked, emphasized.

Achtel, Achtelnote; Achtelpause [Ger.]. Eighth note; eighth rest. See Note.

Achtfuss [Ger.]. Eight-foot stop.

Acid rock. A genre of American *rock music often meant to evoke or to accompany an experience on psychedelic drugs such as LSD (termed acid). Performances were sometimes combined with light shows to enhance this effect. Most songs combined blues-derived song forms with heavy amplification and distortion. The genre emerged in San Francisco in the late 1960s; its originators include Jimi Hendrix, the Jefferson Airplane, and the Grateful Dead. The term lost currency in the early 1970s.

Bibl.: Ralph J. Gleason, *The Jefferson Airplane and the San Francisco Sound* (New York: Ballantine, 1969). P.T.W.

Acis and Galatea. Handel's two-act dramatic work, variously described as a *masque, *pastorale, or *serenata, to a libretto by John Gay with additions by Pope and Dryden, composed and first performed in 1718 at Cannons, the estate of the future Duke of Chandos. It was revived in London in 1732 with additions from his cantata *Aci, Galatea e Polifemo,* completed in Naples in 1708. The work makes significant use of the chorus and was evidently intended to be staged (elaborately so in the London performances), but without action.

Acoustic. (1) Not electric, especially with reference to the guitar or double bass (acoustic guitar, acoustic bass). (2) The acoustical character of a space.

Acoustic bass. An effect comparable in pitch to that of a 32-foot stop on an organ, obtained by playing a 16-foot stop with a stop pitched a fifth above. Also termed resultant bass or harmonic bass, the effect is produced by the acoustical phenomenon of *combination or resultant tones. See also Acoustic (1).

Acoustics. The science of the production, propagation, and perception of sound. Sound will be taken here in the physical sense and will refer to mechanical vibrations or pressure oscillations of various sorts. The production of musical sound entails mechanical vibrations such as those of stretched strings (violin or piano), wooden or metal plates (violin body, piano soundboard, or cymbal), stretched membranes (head of a drum or tambourine), wooden or metal bars (marimba or celesta), and the oscillatory motion of air columns (the vocal tract, trumpet, clarinet, or organ). The propagation of sound involves pressure oscillations and associated vibrational motion of a medium, usually air but sometimes a liquid or solid material, that carries the vibrational energy, or sound, from source to listener. The perception of sound requires the transmission of sound energy, again as mechanical vibrations, by the eardrum via the small bones of the middle ear to the fluid of the inner ear and finally to the hair cells of the inner ear where the information contained in the details of the vibrational motion is encoded into patterns of nerve impulses. The brain interprets these impulses, with extremely subtle discrimination, as the psychological sound of which we are consciously aware [see Psychology of music].

It is convenient to represent the physical sound as a graph that records the variation with time of the vibration, perhaps the displacement from its resting position of a particular point on a violin string or the air pressure at a particular position within a trumpet. Fig. 1a represents such an oscillatory motion for a string vibrating in a particularly simple way; the associated sound is called a pure tone, and its graph is a sine wave. The frequency, f, of this pure tone is the number of full oscillations that occur each second. For example, since there are 4 full oscillations occurring in the duration .0091 second of the graph, the frequency is (4 cycles/.0091 second) = 440 cycles per second (cps or Hertz, abbrev. Hz). The approximate range of frequencies to which the human ear is sensitive, 20 to 20,000 cps, defines the frequencies of interest in musical acoustics. As is discussed more fully below, the frequency of a pure tone determines its *pitch, higher frequencies corresponding to higher pitches. The frequency 440 cps corresponds to the "concert A" produced when the tines of the tuning fork vibrate back and forth 440 times each second. Doubling frequency raises the pitch by one octave. The maximum displacement or pressure of the vibration, as recorded on the vertical axis of the graph, is the amplitude of the vibration, which is related to the amount of energy in the vibrating system and available to be transmitted to the surrounding medium. The amount of energy reaching any point in the surrounding medium is the intensity of the sound at that point. An increase in the intensity of a sound is heard as an increase in loudness. The relationship between intensity and perceived loudness is rather more complex than that between frequency and pitch.

I. *The representation of complex sounds and its relation to pitch.* Almost all musical sounds have a much more complex graph than Fig. 1a. Figs. 1b and 1d represent two examples of more complicated forms. An important mathematical theorem (Fourier's theorem) states that any such graph may be represented as the superposition or sum of sine waves, such as 1a, 1c, and 1d, with different frequencies and amplitudes. For example, 1b is obtained by adding together 1a and 1c. The vertical displacement B at the time 0.0047 second is the sum of the displacements A and C at that same time. Similarly, the displacement D, in the complex waveform 1d, is the sum of A and E. Quite generally, any complex musical tone may be represented as the sum of a number of pure tones of different frequencies and different amplitudes. If one strikes a metallic lampshade or pan lid and listens carefully, one can hear at least a couple of the distinct frequencies that make up the full complex tone. These different components, which together make up the sound produced by the flute, violin, or cymbal, are called partials, and their individual frequencies are called partial frequencies. For many practical purposes, the complete specification of a continuously sounding musical tone, and to a fair approximation decaying tones as well, requires only the enumeration of the frequencies and amplitudes (strengths) of the different partials. The partial frequencies are typically listed in order, the lowest first, as a series of numbers $f_1, f_2, f_3, \ldots$. The sound represented by graph 1b has partial frequencies $f_1 = 440$ and $f_2 = 880$ cps; 1d reflects partials with frequencies $f_1 = 440$ and $f_2 = 1{,}000$ cps.

For many musical sounds, specifically those that are continuously produced by a single source such as the bowed violin, trumpet, oboe, or voice, a special relationship exists among the partial frequencies: they are all equal to an integer times a single frequency, called the fundamental. The partial frequencies $f_1, f_2, f_3, \ldots$ of the A played by the oboist will be 440, 880, 1320, 1760, . . . cps, or $1f_1, 2f_1, 3f_1, 4f_1, \ldots$, where $f_1 = 440$ cps. A convenient statement of the relationship, assuming none of the partial frequencies in the simple sequence happens to be missing, is that the frequency of the nth partial is n times the frequency of the fundamental. A set of frequencies related to one another in this way is called a harmonic set. Continuously produced musical tones are characterized by a harmonic set of partial frequencies.

The pitch of such a musical tone is well defined (identifiable without difficulty by a musician) and is related to the frequency of the fundamental of the harmonic set making up that tone. Although the frequencies making up the complex oboe tone when it is playing a "concert A" are 440, 880, 1320, . . . cps, the pitch is unambiguously concert A or 440 cps. Equally important in the composition of the tone nevertheless are the 880 cps partial (pitch an octave higher), the 1320 cps partial (pitch an octave and a fifth higher), etc. The tone is heard as a single entity, not as a chord corresponding to the various individual partials. So important is the psychological identification of the pitch of a tone with the fundamental of the harmonic set of partials making up that tone that the pitch remains identified with the fundamental even if the partial at the fundamental happens to be completely absent from the tone.

Musical sounds that are percussively produced, such as the tones of the bell, piano, cymbal, guitar, marimba, pizzicato violin, and drum, will have partial frequencies that are not harmonic sets. In some instances, for example the middle range of the piano or the guitar, the partial frequencies so nearly approximate a harmonic set that they may be considered harmonic, and the remarks of the preceding paragraphs are relevant; in particular, the pitch of such sounds is well defined. At the other extreme are the tones of the cymbal, gong, and many drums, in which there is a rich set of partials with no simple relationship among the partial frequencies and for which there is no defined pitch. Intermediate are some of the instruments of the percussion section, e.g., marimba, timpani, and some bells, which are constructed so that several of the lowest partial frequencies are harmonically related. The harmonically related partials establish a well-defined pitch, while additional partials, which are not harmonically related to the pitch, contribute importantly to the tone quality of the instrument. There are also examples such as the bass strings on small pianos, from which one hopes to hear a defined pitch but for which the partial frequencies are so far from harmonic that no meaningful pitch is established.

Figs. 1b and 1d illustrate the contrast between the wave forms characteristic of continuously produced

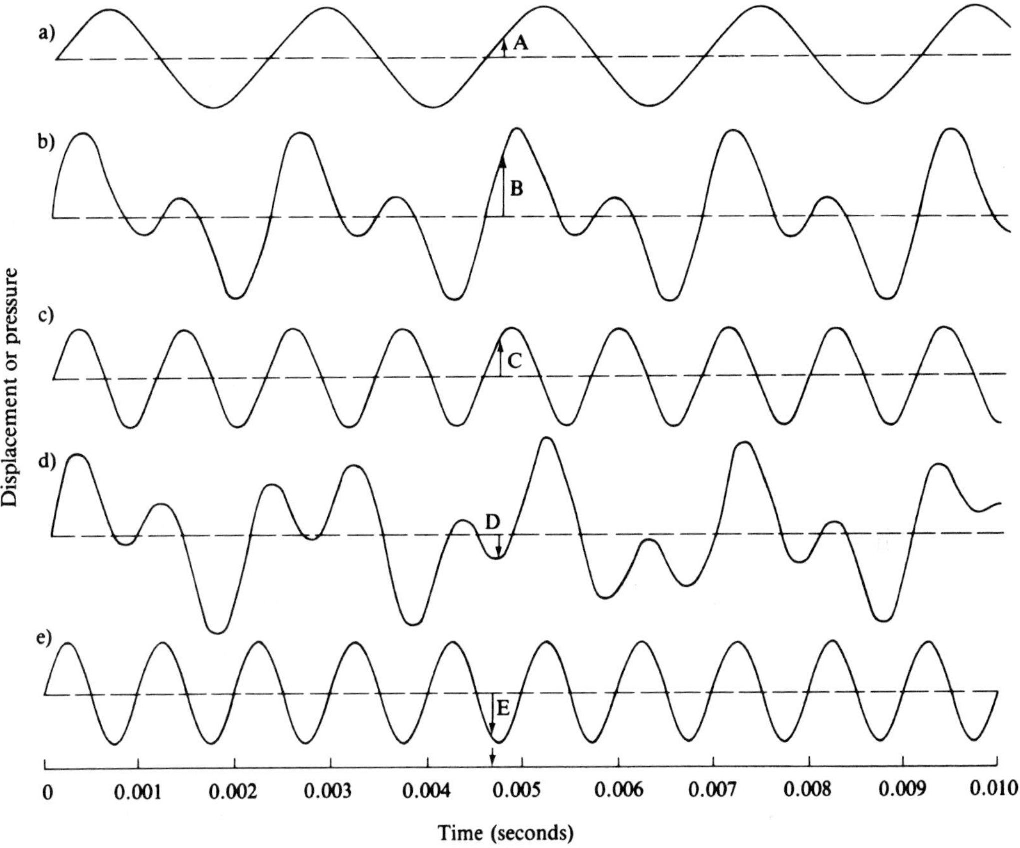

Fig. 1. a) pure sine wave at 440 cps; b) superposition of 1a and 1c; c) pure sine wave at 880 cps; d) superposition of 1a and 1e; e) pure sine wave at 1000 cps.

sound and those of percussively produced sound. The continuously produced sound, Fig. 1b, is the sum of two pure tones, or partials, of frequency 440 and 880 cps (Fig. 1a plus Fig. 1c), which are the first two members of a harmonic set; the wave form shows a clear pattern that repeats at the fundamental frequency of the partials that combine to make the full tone. The percussively produced sound of Fig. 1d is the sum of two partials (Figs. 1a and 1e) with frequencies 440 and 1,000 cps, frequencies not harmonically related to one another. The wave form now does not show a repeating pattern, a consequence of the anharmonic relation between the two partials.

II. *Sound production.* The first essential in the sound production by a musical instrument is the vibration of some part of the instrument. The simplest mechanisms to excite such motion are those used in the percussion instruments, plucking or hammering, for which the excitation is of short duration. The subsequent motion of the vibrating part is usually quite complex, but may be represented as the superposition or sum of many simple motions all taking place concurrently. Figs. 2a, b, and c represent some of the simple kinds of motion, or normal modes of motion, possible for a stretched string. The solid and dotted lines are meant to represent the extremes of the motion. Any point on the string oscillates back and forth between the extremes in a fashion similar to the graph of Fig. 1a. Each normal mode of motion, i.e., each pattern of Fig. 2, has associated with it a characteristic frequency. For the "ideal" stretched string, these frequencies happen to form a harmonic set. For modes other than the first, such a string vibrates in segments of equal length termed loops; the stationary points between loops are termed nodes. A drumhead, a straight wooden bar, or a cymbal also has a series of normal modes of vibration, or "ways in which it can vibrate," but in these examples the frequencies of the normal modes are not harmonically related. When an instrument is percussively excited, many normal modes of the instrument are set into vibration, and the partial frequencies of the tone produced by the instrument are just the frequencies characteristic of the normal modes of motion of the instrument.

The excitation of vibrations in instruments such as the winds and the bowed strings is a continuous rather

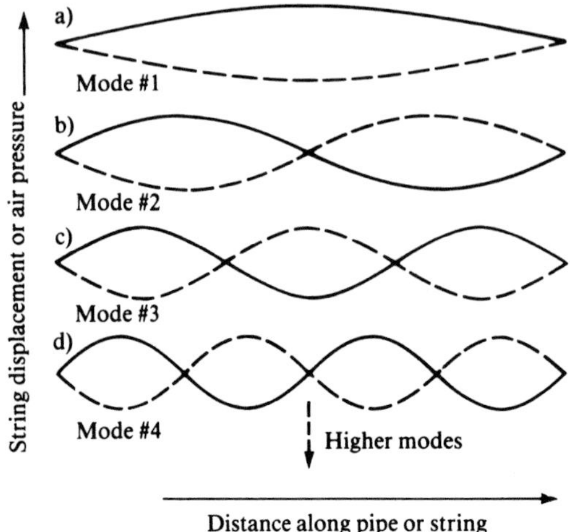

Fig. 2. Displacement patterns for the first four normal modes of the stretched string.

than an instantaneous process and is more complicated to describe. Essential is some device to convert continuous motion, such as airflow from the lungs or the movement of a bow, into the oscillatory motion of an air column or a string. As noted already, the partial frequencies of the sound produced by such an instrument will be a harmonic set of frequencies, and although the partials are often approximately equal to the normal mode frequencies of the instrument, that relationship is less direct than in the case of the percussively produced sound.

Understanding the determining factors in the pitch produced by an instrument requires a knowledge of the natural or normal-mode frequencies of the pitch-determining element, often a stretched string or an air column. As noted above, the natural modes of vibration of an ideal stretched string, represented schematically in Fig. 2, have frequencies that are a harmonic set, $f_n = nf_1$, with a fundamental frequency given by the following equation:

$$f_1 = \sqrt{(\text{tension})/(\text{mass per unit length})} / 2(\text{length})$$

This equation is used intuitively by all string players, who tune their instruments by increasing the tension in the strings to raise the frequency f_1 and hence the pitch. The strings intended to sound at higher pitch are thinner and hence have smaller mass per unit length. The effective length of a string is shortened, and the pitch raised, by stopping the string against the fingerboard. The equation gives quantitative expression to these principles.

In a wind instrument, the vibration is an oscillatory motion of the air along the instrument pipe. For the lowest mode of oscillation in the flute, for example, the air flows alternately from both ends toward the middle of the instrument and back toward the ends. At the middle, the air is not moving, but the pressure rises as the air flows in from both ends, then falls as the air flows away. There are large pressure oscillations at the center of the instrument. Fig. 2a may in fact be interpreted schematically as representing the pressure variation along the flute, the solid line corresponding to the time when the pressure at the center is maximum, the dotted line to a half cycle later when some of the air has moved out of the ends, leaving decreased pressure at the center. Similarly, Figs. 2b and c may be interpreted as the pressure variations for the second and third modes of oscillation of the air column of the flute. It is the natural frequencies of these modes that define the pitches in the higher registers of the flute. Again, as in the case of the string, a formula something like the one above is appropriate to describe the dependence of the fundamental-mode frequency upon the physical parameters of the instrument; and again the higher mode frequencies are (approximately) members of the harmonic set based upon the fundamental, although for certain instruments only the odd-numbered harmonics are present. The proportionality of the fundamental frequency to the inverse of the effective length of the instrument is again essential to the idea of controlling the sounding pitch by varying, in one way or another, the effective length of the air column.

For most percussion instruments, stretched membranes, metal plates or bars, bells, etc., the formulas giving the natural frequencies are more complicated than those for strings or air columns. These formulas show, however, that stiff objects of small mass and small size produce sounds of high pitch; objects that are heavy, large, and flexible have low fundamental frequencies. The complicated formulas also show that the natural frequencies do not typically form a harmonic set, though some instruments are specifically constructed and tuned so that a few of the frequencies are harmonically related; and to the extent that the frequency set is strongly anharmonic, the pitch is ill defined.

A second essential feature of musical instruments is a mechanism to transfer the energy of the vibrations within the instrument to the surrounding air. This occurs naturally with an instrument such as a drum, in which the vibrations are set up in the drumhead, which provides a large moving area that is relatively efficient in forcing vibrational motion into the surrounding air. By contrast, a vibrating string, rigidly fixed at each end, is extremely inefficient in transferring the energy to the surrounding air. The purpose of the bridge and soundboard of the piano, or of the bridge and thin wooden body of the violin or guitar, is to provide the needed transfer. The bridge of the violin transfers the vibrational energy to the belly and via the sound post to the back; the motion of these front and back plates transfers the sound to the surrounding air. The efficiency of energy transfer and its variation with the frequency of vibration depend critically upon the thickness and shape of the walls of the stringed instrument or the construction of the piano or harpsichord soundboard. These parts of the instrument are important in determining such properties of the instrument as tone quality, ease of playing, and carrying power.

III. *Tone quality.* The timbre or tone quality of an instrument is determined by many properties of the sound. Probably the most important properties—certainly the ones the scientist can most easily measure, characterize, and discuss—are the number, frequencies, and amplitudes of the various partials. One important characteristic of timbre is the number of partials that make up the tone. The tone of the flute, for example, has very few partials, while that of the violin has many.

The harmonicity of the partials of the piano tone contrasts dramatically with the anharmonicity of the sound of the chime or gong. The importance of the harmonicity of the set of partial frequencies is easily heard in an experiment with a guitar string or piano string (with the pedal holding the damper up). Compare the tone quality of the plucked (or hammered) bare string with the sound heard when a paper clip is clipped (not hung) onto the string. The variations in timbre are principally the consequence of the large deviations from harmonicity when the string is made "nonideal" by adding the weight of the paper clip.

The characteristic sound of some instruments results from the relative intensities of the partials. The clarinet, played in the low register, has strong odd-numbered partials and weak even ones. In the electronic synthesis of instrumental sounds, the first step in imitating a clarinet is to assure this alternation in the relative amplitudes of successive partials.

A special quality may also be provided by one or several relatively narrow ranges of frequency in which the coupling from the instrument to the surrounding air is stronger than at other frequencies. These ranges in frequency are referred to as formants. In the human voice, the several formant frequencies are varied by adjusting the shape of the vocal tract, and in speaking, the distinction among the various vowel sounds is made by appropriate subconscious adjustment or tuning of the various formant frequencies. In the singing voice these same adjustments are heard not only as differences among vowel sounds but also as changes in vocal timbre or tone quality.

Nevertheless, the specification of frequencies and relative amplitudes, though easy to measure, is by no means the only clue used by the ear and brain in identifying instrumental sounds. Just as, in a spoken language, the consonants that begin and end syllables are crucial in conveying the meaning of the syllable, so in the musical context the way in which tones start and end in different instruments is characteristic of, and important in the identification of, those instruments. If a tape recording of a piano piece is played backward, the sound is most likely to be identified as a strange-sounding organ, not as a piano. The way in which a tone starts and reaches a steady state is its attack. The way in which a tone ends or dies away is its decay. The combination of characteristics defining the attack, steady state, and decay of a tone taken together constitute its envelope. The envelope, attack, and decay controls on an electronic synthesizer regulate these essential transient characteristics of the synthesized tones.

IV. *Architectural acoustics.* The mechanisms and characteristics of tone production are not, of course, the sole determinants of the quality of sound heard by the auditor. One must consider as well how the sound is transferred from source to listener and how it is modified in that process. The two most important and relevant physical phenomena are the reflection of sound and the finite speed of propagation of sound. The phenomenon of reflection implies that in the concert hall the sound is heard both as it comes directly, by line of sight so to speak, from the performer and in addition as it propagates to a side wall or ceiling and is reflected to the listener from those surfaces. There are many paths, a direct one and ones involving one, two, or more reflections from walls and ceilings, by which any feature of the musical performance reaches the ear. Because of the finite speed of sound, about 350 meters per second, and because the various paths by which the sound reaches the ear involve different distances, each feature of the music in fact reaches the ear many times in close succession. This multiplicity has a number of consequences.

If the reflected sound is too long delayed with respect to the direct sound, as can be the case in a very large auditorium or sports arena, the reflected sound will be heard as a distinct echo, and the effect will be most objectionable. More usually, the reflected sound is not heard in this obtrusive fashion, but rather fuses, psychologically at least, with the directly received sound and is heard as richer, fuller sound. A "live" room is one in which the reflected sound is very apparent, though not as a series of discrete echoes, and contributes in a major way to the total sound heard. A "dead" room is one in which most of the sound reaching the surfaces of the room is absorbed, perhaps by carpeting, drapes, or sound-absorbing ceiling tiles, and the reflected sound is only a minor contributor, compared with the direct sound, to the perceived sound.

Both audiences and performers consider a substantial contribution of reflected sound, or reverberation, desirable in a concert hall. The reverberation increases the loudness of the sound heard by the listener and, perhaps more important, it creates a certain degree of overlap of one note in a melodic line with the next. Excessive reverberation, however, even when it is not heard as distinct echoes, is undesirable. Extensive overlap of successive sounds resulting from a too live room, though perhaps pleasing to the amateur singer in the shower, can destroy the intelligibility of both speech and music.

Controlling the amount of reverberation is only one concern, perhaps the most important and probably the easiest to quantify, in the acoustic design of a concert hall. Other considerations include freedom from extraneous noise, even distribution of sound throughout the hall, good balance between high and low frequencies, and a sense of acoustic intimacy.

V. *Beats and intervals.* An acoustical effect particularly relevant in music is the phenomenon of beats. Suppose that in a complex sound reaching the ear, two of the partials, perhaps from two different instruments, are comparable in loudness and very nearly equal in frequency, say within a few cycles per second of one another. Over time, the two partials alternately reinforce and tend to cancel each other [see Fig. 3]. The subjective impression is of a single partial varying in amplitude at a "beat frequency" equal to the difference in frequencies of the two original partials. If the source of one of the two partials is tuned to reduce the beat frequency to zero, the frequencies of the two partials become identical, a convenient method for tuning unisons. In general, beats will occur for two complex tones of different pitch whenever the frequency of one or more of the partials in one tone matches very nearly the frequency of partials in the second.

It is interesting to examine the relation between the pitches of two complex tones for which a partial from one matches in frequency, or nearly matches, one from the other. These matching partials will beat with one another if the tones are slightly mistuned. Suppose the fundamental of one tone is f_1, with the associated set of partials $f_1, 2f_1, 3f_1, \ldots nf_1$, and the harmonic set composing the other tone is $f_2, 2f_2, 3f_2, \ldots mf_2$. Beats will occur whenever a partial from one set nearly matches a partial from the other set, or when $nf_1 \approx mf_2$, where n and m are integers. The beats disappear when the approximate relation (denoted by $\approx$) becomes exact, that is, when $nf_1 = mf_2$.

There is thus a special relationship between pitch pairs whose corresponding fundamental frequencies are in the ratio of integers: small variations in the pitch of one tone or the other will change or eliminate the beats between some of the higher partials of each. The effect will be strong and obvious if the integers are small, say 1, 2, 3, and 4, becoming less obvious for larger m and n and becoming finally weak and unlikely to be evident for integers in the ratio larger than 7 or 8. The musical intervals with these special beatless relationships are the intervals of *just intonation; the just intervals of octave, fifth, fourth, major third, minor third, etc., correspond to ratios between the fundamentals of the harmonic sets of the two tones of 2/1, 3/2, 4/3, 5/4, 6/5, etc. In contrast, the frequency ratios of intervals in the system of equal *temperament only approximately satisfy these relationships, and these intervals will have beating upper partials. The frequency of this beating is used by piano tuners to adjust the tuning to the "imperfect" intervals characteristic of equal temperament.

VI. *Resonance.* The phenomenon of resonance plays an important role in a number of musical contexts. Resonance refers to the large oscillatory response of a system to a weak driving force whose frequency matches precisely one of the natural frequencies of the driven system. A swing can be set into a large amplitude of motion by a number of successive small pushes if the pushes are given at a frequency

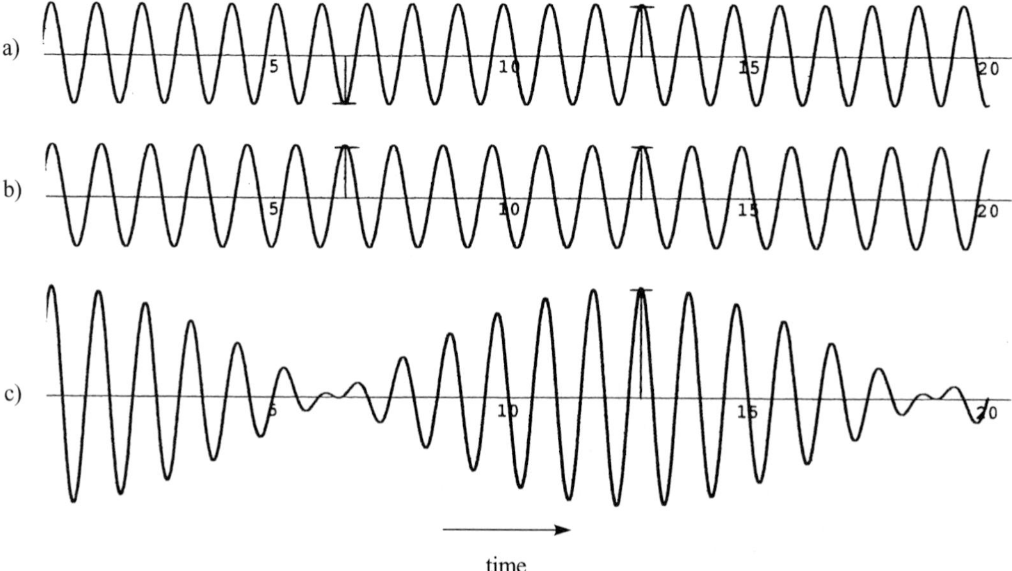

Fig. 3. Beats produced by the superposition of two sine waves of nearly the same frequency.

that matches the swing's natural, or freely swinging, frequency.

A soprano can make her voice "carry" better by shaping her vocal tract so that one or several of its resonances, or formants, have the same frequency as that of some partials of the note being sung; this more effectively transfers to the surrounding room the acoustic energy generated by the vocal cords. The lowest tones on a violin would be nearly inaudible were it not for several resonances of the front and back plates of the instrument and of the air chamber within the box that promote the efficient coupling of energy from the strings to the surrounding air. The judicious tuning of the frequencies of these resonances is an essential part of the art of violin making. The excitation of sympathetic strings in the viola d'amore and the change in quality of the sound of a piano when the damper pedal is depressed are the results of resonance. A wind instrument is the more easily played the more nearly the resonant frequencies of the higher normal modes match the frequencies of the harmonic set corresponding to the desired pitch.

Bibl.: Hermann L. F. von Helmholtz, *Die Lehre von der Tonempfindung* (Brunswick, 1863; 4th ed., 1877); trans. Eng. Alexander Ellis, *On the Sensations of Tone* (London, 1875; 2nd ed., 1885; R: New York: Dover, 1954). *Journal of the Acoustical Society of America* (New York: American Institute of Physics, 1929–). Alexander Wood, *The Physics of Music* (London: Methuen, 1944; 7th ed., New York: Wiley, 1975). Lothar Cremer, *Die wissenschaftlichen Grundlagen der Raumakustik,* 3 vols. (Stuttgart: Hirzel, 1948–61; rev. ed., Helmut Müller, 1978). *Acustica* (Stuttgart: Hirzel, 1951–). Leo L. Beranek, *Music, Acoustics, and Architecture* (New York: Wiley, 1962). Siegmund Levarie and Ernst Levy, *Tone: A Study in Musical Acoustics* (Kent, Ohio: Kent St U Pr, 1968; 2nd ed., 1980). John Backus, *The Acoustical Foundations of Music* (New York: Norton, 1969; 2nd ed., 1977). Cornelis J. Nederveen, *Acoustical Aspects of Woodwind Instruments* (Amsterdam: Frits Knuf, 1969). Juan G. Roederer, *Introduction to the Physics and Psychophysics of Music* (New York: Springer, 1973; rev. ed., 1995). Arthur H. Benade, *Fundamentals of Musical Acoustics* (London: Oxford U Pr, 1976). Earle L. Kent, ed., *Musical Acoustics: Piano and Wind Instruments, BPA* 9 (1977). *Music, Room and Acoustics* (Stockholm: Royal Swedish Academy of Music, 1977). Thomas D. Northwood, ed., *Architectural Acoustics, BPA* 10 (1977). Frederick Vinton Hunt, *Origins in Acoustics: The Science of Sound from Antiquity to the Age of Newton* (New Haven: Yale U Pr, 1978). Donald E. Hall, *Musical Acoustics: An Introduction* (Belmont, Calif.: Wadsworth, 1980; rev. ed., 2002). John R. Pierce, *The Science of Musical Sound* (New York: Scientific American Library, 1983; rev. ed., 1992). Michael J. Moravcsik, *Musical Sound: An Introduction to the Physics of Music* (New York: Paragon, 1987). Murray Campbell and Clive Greated, *The Musician's Guide to Acoustics* (New York: Schirmer, 1988). Johan Sundberg, *The Science of Musical Sounds* (San Diego: Acad Pr, 1991). A. Hirschberg, J. Kergomard, G. Weinreich, eds., *Mechanics of Musical Instruments* (New York: Springer, 1995). James Beament, *The Violin Explained: Components, Mechanism, and Sound* (New York: Oxford U Pr, 1997). Malcolm J. Crocker, ed., *Encyclopedia of Acoustics* (New York: Wiley, 1997). Carleen Maley Hutchins and Virginia Benade, eds., *Research Papers in Violin Acoustics, 1975–1993: With an Introductory Essay, 350 Years of Violin Research* (Woodbury, N.Y.: American Institute of Physics, 1997). Neville H. Fletcher and Thomas D. Rossing, *The Physics of Musical Instruments* (New York: Springer, 1998). Thomas D. Rossing, *Science of Percussion Instruments* (Singapore; River Edge, N.J.: World Scientific, 2000). R.H.S.

Action. (1) In keyboard instruments, the mechanism that causes a string or pipe to sound when a key is depressed [see Piano, Organ, Harpsichord, Clavichord]. (2) In the *harp, the mechanism that alters the pitch of strings when a pedal is depressed.

Act tune. A composition played between acts of an opera or play. See also *Entr'acte.*

Actus musicus [Lat.]. In German Protestant music of the late 17th and early 18th centuries, a dramatic vocal work on a Biblical subject. Like the less elaborate *historia,* it is an antecedent of the German Protestant *oratorio.

Actus tragicus. Bach's Cantata no. 106, *Gottes Zeit ist die allerbeste Zeit* (God's Time Is Best), perhaps composed in Mühlhausen in 1707 and performed at the funeral of his mother's uncle.

Adagietto [It., diminutive of *adagio*]. (1) A tempo slightly faster than **adagio.* (2) A movement in a slow tempo, but shorter or less somber in character than the typical **adagio.*

Adagio [It.]. (1) A slow tempo, often said to be slower than *andante* but not as slow as *largo.* Some writers of the 18th and 19th centuries, however, regarded the term as designating the slowest of all tempos, though the term itself could be modified to call for still slower tempos, e.g., *adagissimo.* In the 18th century, the term sometimes implied the need for ornamentation. See also Tempo marks. (2) A composition with a slow tempo (perhaps, but not necessarily, specified by the term *adagio* itself), especially the slow movement of a sonata, symphony, or similar multimovement work.

Adagissimo [It.]. Extremely slow. See also *Adagio* (1).

Added sixth. A sixth added above the root of a triad, or the chord thus produced; thus, f–a–c′–d′. The traditional theory of chord *inversion derived from Rameau requires such a structure to be viewed as the first inversion of a *seventh chord (the root in this example being d, making the chord a ii^7 in the context of C major and implying a resolution to the dominant). But Rameau himself observed that the chord can also function as an embellished triad (usually, as in this example in C major, the subdominant) and thus resolve in different ways. Such chords are often used in jazz and popular music as embellished triads and are specified by the letter indicating the root of the triad followed by the arabic numeral 6 (e.g., F6), as distinct from what is termed the minor seventh chord (specified, in the example above, Dm7).

Additional accompaniment. The reworking of the accompaniments of older vocal works to fit them to later concepts of sonority and orchestration. The practice began with the continued performance of works by Handel in the changed musical conditions of the late 18th century. Mozart rescored, sometimes radically altering, *Messiah, Alexander's Feast, Acis and Galatea,* and the *Ode for St. Cecilia's Day.* His *Messiah* became the basis for several 19th-century versions. With the revival of Bach's music, similar treatment was applied to it, most notably by Robert Franz, whose reworkings of the *St. Matthew Passion,* Magnificat, and several cantatas were considered models of good taste. He filled out accompanying textures that were too thin by later standards, adjusted scoring to balance choruses much larger than intended, and rescored to compensate for changes in makeup of the orchestra and the disappearance of Baroque instruments. Mendelssohn also indulged in the practice, but is said to have later regretted it. Similar tendencies were also manifested in other genres, such as the reinforcing of the orchestration of Mozart's operas or Grieg's composition of a second piano part to accompany some of Mozart's sonatas.

The stronger historical awareness of the 20th century worked against the practice, although the continued existence of large choral societies has been an obstacle to its complete disappearance, particularly with Handel oratorios. More recently it has reappeared in the newly resurrected genre of 17th-century Venetian opera, the thinness of whose accompaniment has similarly been thought by some to require such treatment in order to appeal to modern audiences. See also Performance practice.

Addolorato [It.]. Pained, afflicted.

Adelaide. A song by Beethoven, op. 46 (1794–95), to a poem by Friedrich von Matthisson.

Adélaïde Concerto. A Concerto in D major for violin and orchestra attributed to Mozart, K. Anhang 294a. The work exists in a simple two-stave sketch, supposedly written in 1766, and dedicated to the French Princess Adélaïde. Although a letter exists in which Mozart dedicates such a work to the Princess, it is almost certainly not this concerto. The sketch was completed and published by Marius Casadesus in 1933.

Adeste fideles [Lat.]. A hymn often sung in the English translation beginning "O come, all ye faithful" by Frederick Oakeley (1802–80). The Latin text and the well-known tune have been dated ca. 1740 and attributed to John Francis Wade (d. 1786). It was published in 1751 and used thereafter in the Portuguese Embassy Chapel in London, whence the title "Portuguese Hymn" by which it is also known.

Adieux, Les [Fr.]. Beethoven's Piano Sonata no. 26 in E♭ *major op. 81a (1809–10), titled Das Lebewohl, Abwesenheit und Wiedersehn* and subtitled *Les adieux, l'absence, et le retour* (The Farewell, Absence, and Return). It was inspired by the departure from Vienna of Beethoven's patron the Archduke Rudolph, to whom the work is dedicated.

Ad libitum [Lat.]. At the pleasure of the performer. The phrase may indicate that a part for voice or an instrument may be omitted (in contrast to **obbligato*); that the performer is to improvise either ornaments or altogether new material such as a *cadenza; or that the tempo may be varied.

Adriana Lecouvreur. Opera in four acts by Francesco Cilea (libretto by Arturo Colautti after Eugène Scribe and Ernest Legouvé), produced in Milan in 1902. Setting: Paris, 1730, the year of the death of the celebrated French actress of this name.

A due [It.]. See *Due.*

Aeolian, aeolian mode. See Mode.

Aeolian harp. A zither whose strings are set in motion by the wind. A variable number of strings of varying thickness but equal length are stretched over a sound box (usually rectangular and as much as a meter or more in length) and tuned to the same fundamental pitch. The wind generates different harmonics in each string, producing a chord whose texture changes as the wind rises and falls. Instruments of this type were known in antiquity. It was popular in late 18th- and early 19th-century Europe and was a frequent subject of Romantic literature. See also Anémocorde.

Bibl.: Stephen Bonner, ed., *Aeolian Harp,* 3 vols. (Cambridge: Bois de Boulogne, 1968–70).

Aeoline. (1) A free-reed keyboard instrument invented by Bernhard Eschenbach ca. 1810. An antecedent of the *harmonium, it incorporated knee-operated bellows and permitted variations in loudness. (2) A soft string-tone organ stop.

Aeolodicon. Any of several free-reed keyboard instruments developed from the *aeoline.

Aeolo melodicon. A reed organ patented in Warsaw in 1824 with tubes attached to the reeds and permitting variations in loudness.

Aeolopantalon. An instrument combining the *aeolo melodicon and the piano, patented in Warsaw in 1824, and on which Chopin performed in 1825.

Aequal [Lat.], **Aequalstimmen** [Ger.]. See *Equale;* Equal voices.

Aerophon. See Aerophor.

Aerophone. An instrument in which a column of air is the primary vibrating system. In most cases the player sets the air in motion by blowing. There are three main categories of aerophone: *flutes, in which the turbulence produced by blowing across a sharp edge sets the air column in motion; lip-vibrated aerophones (primarily *brass instruments), in which the air is set in motion by the vibration of the player's lips; *reedpipes (most *woodwinds), in which air is set in motion by a vibrating *reed. In addition there are free aerophones, in which the vibrating air is not confined to a column (e.g., the *accordion, *bull-roarer, *mouth organ, *harmonium) or in which the column serves merely as a *resonator (e.g., the *sheng). See also Instrument.

Aerophor. A device permitting the player of a wind instrument to sustain a tone indefinitely. A foot-operated bellows pumps air to the player's mouth through a tube, thus maintaining air pressure to the instrument while allowing breathing through the nose. Invented ca. 1912 by Bernhard Samuel, it was prescribed by Richard Strauss (incorrectly as an "aerophon") in his *Alpensinfonie.*

Aesthetics. First coined as a technical term in 1735 by Alexander Baumgarten, now denoting almost exclusively the constellation of philosophical problems raised in our thinking about the fine arts. Hence, music aesthetics is taken here to comprise those issues of a philosophical character surrounding the art of music since antiquity, excluding, insofar as such distinctions can be uncontroversially made, issues that belong more properly to music theory, musicology, the psychology of music, and normative compositional doctrine.

By far the most pervasive question of music aesthetics, if historical longevity and sheer quantity are any measures, is the question of whether music possesses a "content" beyond its purely musical "syntax" and structure: whether, that is, it denotes, conveys, or is even describable in terms of anything but what Kant felicitously called "the beautiful play of sensations." But in recent years another question has surfaced, of a logical or ontological kind, as to the exact nature of the musical work itself. These two questions, if not the alpha and omega of music aesthetics, are at least the major part of its alphabet.

I. *Musical content.* Theories of musical content can best be divided into the emotive and the nonemotive, emotive theories being the most numerous by far in modern times, and with us since Plato and Aristotle. In general, all such theories state that music is describable in emotive terms. They diverge sharply as to the construction to be put on such descriptions.

Historically, and perhaps currently as well, if "the man on the street," rather than the philosopher, is consulted, the most ubiquitous form that the emotive content theory takes is the "arousal" variety. On this view, to say that "the music is sad" is to say that, one way or another, the music arouses sadness in the listener: that is to say, literally makes the listener sad. Both Plato and Aristotle speak of music as "imitating" or "representing" the characters and passionate tones of men, but seem to suggest that the end for which this imitation or representation exists is the arousal of such passions in the listener, for good (Aristotle) and often for ill (Plato). And in the 17th and 18th centuries, the arousal theory gains almost absolute dominance, to the extent that Descartes actually *defines* music in terms of emotive arousal, thus: "Its medium is sound. Its end is to please and to move the various affections in us."

An important historical appendage to the arousal theory, deserving separate mention, is the "speech" theory of musical emotion, which amounts to the claim that "sad" music arouses sadness in the listener, by a kind of "sympathy," because of its resemblance to the passionate tones of human speech when the speaker is under the influence of that particular emotion. The theory flourished among the theorists and composers of the Florentine Camerata and functioned not only as a philosophical account of musical emotion, but as a basis for a compositional practice as well. It survived well into the 18th century.

With the rise of the Romantic movement—although not owing to that historical event alone—another emotive theory took form. The "self-expression" theory, as many have called it, concentrates on the composer rather than the listener and avers that sad music is, first and foremost, the "expression" of the composer's emotion, and this, somehow, perhaps by arousal, gives us an insight into or lets us share the emotion of the composer, which, it is supposed, if the composer is a great artist, must be a very special and great emotion, beyond the ordinary run of such things. Perhaps the leading proponent of this view in our own century was J. W. N. Sullivan, scientist and biographer of Beethoven, for whom the theory served the purpose of explaining the greatness of Beethoven's music in terms of the greatness of his "soul" (as opposed, in Sullivan's view, to the mean-spiritedness of Wagner's). But it has outlived its specific purpose and become an example of its kind in the writings of philosophers of music.

By far the most interesting and fruitful direction that emotive theories have taken since the 18th century has been *away* both from arousal and self-expression. Schopenhauer characterized music as a "direct copy" of the will and the emotions, meaning not the individual human psyche but the "metaphysical" will, which he saw as the basis of reality. Earlier, the 18th-century composer, critic, and musical theorist Johann Mattheson presented a theory of musical expression (the final flowering of the Baroque *Affektenlehre* [see Affections, Doctrine of]) that, at least on a charitable interpretation, can be taken for an attempt to see music not as an emotive stimulus but rather as a kind of musical "icon" or "copy" of specific human emotional states, *recognized* by the listener *in* the music, not experienced or felt. This notion, that emotions are apprehended in music rather than stimulated by it, has taken two distinct forms in recent years. The "semantic" approach, adumbrated by Carroll Pratt and made famous by Susanne Langer, made out the apprehension of the emotive in music to be the apprehension of music as an emotive *symbol.* More recently, in contrast, Peter Kivy and others have seen emotions as expressive *properties* of music, much in the way that the sadness is seen as a property of the Saint Bernard's face, or of a weeping willow, without it being thought that the dog or the tree is "expressing" sadness or the viewer "feeling" it.

Closely related to music's emotive "content" is the question of its power to emotionally move the listener. If music is sad, for example, in virtue of arousing sadness, as the old arousal theory has it, then it is ipso facto emotionally moving. But if the arousal theory of musical content is given up, does that mean music does not move us emotionally at all? It is generally agreed that rejecting the old arousal theory of musical expression does not commit one to the view that our reaction to music lacks emotive involvement. However, what that emotive involvement consists in is a matter of vigorous and unresolved debate.

Until recently, few writers in modern times have seen in music a content of much significance beyond the emotive. There has, of course, since antiquity been the belief in some divine mystery uniting music, mathematics, and the *harmonia mundi,* the last manifestation of which is Leibniz's oft-quoted (and much inflated) remark that the beauty of music arises "in the counting, which we do not perceive but which the soul nevertheless continues to carry out." Many 18th-century thinkers recognized musical imitations of sounds and even "tone painting" as part of the art. Most, however, shared the view of James Harris that it is "*at best* . . . but an imperfect thing." And even 19th-century champions of "program music" and the "tone poem" were inclined to see them as Beethoven had seen the *Pastorale,* "not a painting, but an expression of those sentiments evoked in men by their enjoyment of the country," thus conflating musical representation with musical expression and falling back into some form of the emotive content theory.

But particularly among philosophically inclined musicologists, and some philosophers as well, there has arisen a renewed interest in the possibility of giving at least some works in the *absolute music repertoire a "narrative" content, sometimes understood in terms of what Anthony Newcomb has called "plot archetypes." The project is to try to give such works interpretations that are interesting enough to be aesthetically significant, while avoiding the kind of detailed "storytelling" that ceases to be interpretation and lapses into personal fantasy. What success such theorists have had is still a matter of dispute.

Numerous, however, are those who do not want to allow music any content at all. The name most often associated with such musical "purism" is that of the 19th-century German critic Eduard Hanslick, who likened music to arabesque and the evanescent colors and shapes of the kaleidoscope. But perhaps more worthy of philosophical notice is the theory of Edmund Gurney, a generation later, worked out in far more detail than Hanslick's influential though unsystematic sketch.

II. *The musical work.* Substantial work in recent years has concerned the question of what kind of "ontological" object the musical work might be. The question is generated by the observation that there is at least a prima facie obviousness about what kind of object a painting or statue is: it is a material object, of such-and-such a physical description, in such-and-such a place. But *where,* it might be wondered, is the *Eroica* Symphony? And if we cannot give any intelligible answer to this question (and it is hard to see how we can), it would then appear that the *Eroica* cannot be a *material* object at all, at least of the ordinary kind, located, fetched, carried, and measured.

In response, metaphysicians in the grand manner, like Collingwood, wished to say that music exists, ultimately, as an "object" in the imagination, although Collingwood did not think any of the *other* arts, as a matter of fact, differed from music in this respect. Others, eschewing such metaphysical imponderables as "imaginary objects," have tried to construe music as merely a more complex and diffuse physical manifestation, identifying the *Eroica* (say) with the class of all its physical realizations in sound-vibrations, thus making it, if not a physical "object," at least a class of perturbations of a purely physical medium. And Nelson Goodman, with an admirable rigor seldom seen in the field, has given a careful logical analysis of the musical score, concluding that "a score . . . defines a work," and the work is the class of all "compliants" with it.

However, difficulties with the Goodmanian analysis of the musical work have led to an upsurge of interest in traditional but hard-edged Platonic metaphysics and the attempt to construe the musical work as a nonphysical Platonic universal and performances as instances of the universal or, in the terminology of C. S. Peirce, tokens of the type. Pioneering this work was Nicholas Wolterstorff. More recently, two versions of musical Platonism have emerged: a "moderate" version, advocated by Jerrold Levinson, which has it that musical works are "created types," and a more "extreme" form, in which they are eternal, "discovered" types and composers are those who discover and, as Jerrold Katz puts it, "first-token" them.

III. *The musical experience.* Finally, a philosophical task has emerged in recent years of trying to say something about what might be called the "purely musical experience." The musical theorist Leonard Meyer was, in some ways, the inspiration to philosophers to pursue this work. It has now become one of the most active areas as well as *the* most difficult area for the philosopher of music to handle. But it seems fair to say that, in spite of the predominance over the centuries of interest in the question of music and the emotions, this question lies at the heart of musical aesthetics, and if the purely musical experience is not understood, it seems doubtful that anything else will be (or is) understood either.

Bibl.: Plato, *Republic.* Aristotle, *Politics.* René Descartes, *Compendium musicae* (Amsterdam, 1656; ed. and trans. Walter Robert, *MSD* 8, 1961; facs., *MMML* ser. 2, 87, 1968). Gottfried Wilhelm von Leibniz, "The Principles of Nature and Grace" (1714), *Philosophical Papers and Letters,* ed. and trans. Leroy Loemker (Chicago: U of Chicago Pr, 1956). Alexander Baumgarten, *Meditationes philosophicae de nonnullis ad poema pertinentibus* (Halle, 1735). Johann Mattheson, *Der vollkommene Capellmeister* (Hamburg, 1739; facs., *DM* ser. 1, 5, 1954). James Harris, *Discourse on Music, Painting, and Poetry* (London, 1744). Immanuel Kant, *Kritik der Urteilskraft* (Berlin, 1790). Arthur Schopenhauer, *Die Welt als Wille und Vorstellung* (Leipzig, 1819). Eduard Hanslick, *Vom Musikalisch-Schönen* (Leipzig, 1854); trans. Gustav Cohen, *The Beautiful in Music* (London, 1891; R: New York: Da Capo, 1974; ed. Morris Weitz, New York: Liberal Arts Pr, 1957). Edmund Gurney, *The Power of Sound* (London, 1880; R: New York: Basic Bks, 1966). John William Navin Sullivan, *Beethoven: His Spiritual Development* (New York: A A Knopf, 1927). Carroll Pratt, *The Meaning of Music* (New York: McGraw-Hill, 1932). Robin George Collingwood, *The Principles of Art* (Oxford: Clarendon Pr, 1938). Susanne Langer, *Philosophy in a New Key* (Cambridge, Mass.: Harvard U Pr, 1942; 3rd ed., 1957). Leonard B. Meyer, *Emotion and Meaning in Music* (Chicago: U of Chicago Pr, 1956). Carl Dahlhaus, *Musikästhetik* (Cologne: H Gerig, 1967); trans. Eng. William W. Austin, *Esthetics of Music* (Cambridge: Cambridge U Pr, 1982). Nelson Goodman, *Languages of Art* (Indianapolis: Bobbs-Merrill, 1968). Peter Kivy, *The Corded Shell: Reflections on Musical Expression* (Princeton: Princeton U Pr, 1980). Nicholas Wolterstorff, *Works and Worlds of Art* (Oxford: Clarendon Pr, 1980). Jerrold Levinson, *Music, Art, and Metaphysics: Essays in Philosophical Aesthetics* (Ithaca: Cornell U Pr, 1990). Peter Kivy, *Music Alone: Philosophical Reflections on the Purely Musical Experience* (Ithaca: Cornell U Pr, 1990). Peter Kivy, *The Fine Art of Repetition: Essays in the Philosophy of Music* (Cambridge: Cambridge U Pr, 1993). Jerrold Levinson, *Music in the Moment* (Ithaca: Cornell U Pr, 1997). Roger Scruton, *The Aesthetics of Music* (Oxford: Clarendon, 1997). Jerrold J. Katz, *Realistic Rationalism* (Cambridge, Mass.: MIT Pr, 2000). P.K.

Aevia. An abbreviation for *alleluia consisting of its vowels (*v* representing *u*), sometimes used in manuscripts of liturgical chant. See also *Euouae.*

Affabile [It.]. Affable, pleasing.

Affannato, affanoso [It.]. Breathless, anxious, excited.

Affections (affects), doctrine of [Ger. *Affektenlehre*]. The belief, widely held in the 17th and early 18th centuries, that the principal aim of music is to arouse the passions or affections (love, hate, joy, anger, fear, etc., conceived as rationalized, discrete, and relatively static states). By the later 17th century, the view also included the notion that a composition (or at least a single movement or major section of a larger work) should have a unity of affection. The general notion that music should move or arouse the affections is taken up by writers on music in the later 16th century (including Gioseffo Zarlino, 1558), evidently by analogy with the aims of *rhetoric as described by classical writers and their followers. Major attention is devoted to the subject by writers from the mid-17th to the mid-18th century, among them René Descartes (1618), Marin Mersenne (1636), Athanasius Kircher (1650), Wolfgang Caspar Printz (1696), Andreas Werckmeister (1686, 1702), Johann David Heinichen (1711), Johann Mattheson (1713, 1739), Johann Joachim Quantz (1752), and Friedrich Wilhelm Marpurg (1763).

Although these writers often described the affective character of intervals, scales, types of pieces, and the like, they did not share a precisely formulated "doctrine of affections" relying on the use of stereotyped musical figures, as was implied by the German scholars (Kretschmar, Goldschmidt, Schering) who gave currency to the term *Affektenlehre* (Buelow, 1980). The enumeration and description of musical *figures beginning in the 17th century was a separate aspect of the general effort to conceive music in the terms provided by rhetoric. For bibl. see Rhetoric.

Affektenlehre [Ger.]. See Affections, doctrine of.

Affetto [It., pl. *affetti*]. An affection or passion such as, in the view of 16th-, 17th-, and 18th-century writers, could be aroused or moved by music. See Affections, doctrine of.

Affettuoso [It.]. Affectionate, tender.

Affinales [Lat.]. In medieval theory, the pitches a, b, and c′, which could serve as the finals of transpositions of the *modes with finals on d, e, and f, respectively. There was no *affinalis* corresponding to the final g.

Affrettando [It.]. Hurrying.

Afghanistan. See Near and Middle East.

Africa. Second-largest continent (one-fifth of the earth's land surface), encompassing more than 50 nations and a population of approximately 800 million. Within most sub-Saharan nations several local languages predominate, and many more are spoken in smaller pockets, yielding for the continent about 1,000 distinct languages, often used to identify ethnic groupings. This great linguistic diversity is also reflected musically, most notably in the hundreds or thousands of distinct musical instruments.

North Africa is often discussed apart because of its cultural affinity to West Asian Arab and Mediterranean cultures. However, human movement in all directions through the Sahara (forced and otherwise) and the vast spread of Islam from the north into the Sahara and farther south as well as along the eastern coast indicate that the Sahara may profitably be viewed as a bridge rather than a barrier. Saharan peoples have a long shared history with their neighbors to the north and south, resulting in multidirectional cultural flows that have shaped all concerned.

Unlike vast parts of Asia where great musical traditions canonized for centuries in theoretical and historical writings span large territories, Africa is home to hundreds of local music cultures. Some of these are fairly compact, uniting small groups of people numbering in the thousands; others are more expansive, encompassing several modern nations and tens of millions of people (Mande, Swahili). Diversity marks the continent, although certain widespread aesthetic preferences may also be discerned.

Although scholars have moved away from earlier notions of the continent as made up of bounded static traditions forming a mosaic or jigsaw puzzle, Africans do use music to distinctly mark or unite themselves in various ways, in effect setting themselves apart from their neighbors. This does not preclude them from claiming several kinds of group identities. An affinity for embracing outside ideas and shaping them for local usage (e.g., in religion, technology, music, instruments) is a defining aspect of African notions of tradition. Allowing that musical traditions in Africa can expand, contract, die out, and accommodate new ideas, the notion of a distinct tradition associated with certain groups of people located in some geographic place—no matter that various parties may contest the borders of that tradition—can be an effective vantage point from which to examine how music helps define various kinds of identity, such as generation, lineage, class, nationality, gender, and ethnicity (a difficult concept to pin down, but still occasionally useful).

I. *Climate zones.* Other than narrow bands of temperate zones at the extreme north and south, four main types of vegetation zones define the continent: desert, sahel (the transitional area at the southern Sahara border), savanna, and forest. The main deserts are the Sahara in the north (home to camel-herding nomads) and the Kalahari in the south (home to small bands of hunter-gatherers). Forests line most of the West African coastline from Guinea into Central Africa, where they cover much of the inland center of the continent, home to forest peoples known as pygmies. The sahel stretches the breadth of the continent just south of the Sahara, from Senegal through Sudan. The savanna, south of the sahel, also spans the continent and is home to some of the great empires. Major rivers facilitating trade and linking peoples include the Niger (west), Congo (central), Zambezi (southeast), and Nile (northeast).

Climate zones affect music making in the materials available for the construction of instruments and in the lifestyles and social organizations that shape the way music is used. Several nations encompassing desert, sahel, and savanna environments have desert peoples playing string instruments in the north and savanna peoples playing xylophones in the south, where there is a ready supply of wood (Mali, Chad). Gourds, abundant in the savanna, are used in all kinds of instruments there (e.g., drums, resonators on string instruments). Portable string instruments, made of materials that can be found almost anywhere, are widespread. Hunter-gatherers and pastoral nomads are unlikely to carry bulky musical instruments or to play in large ensembles. Sedentary agricultural societies in the savanna are more likely to spawn large civilizations, including professional classes of musicians. The Central African rain forests, which are inhospitable to large settlements, are home to vocal-based music cultures in smaller, nonhierarchical societies that encourage more or less equal participation among all present.

II. *Language, cultural areas, and religion.* Language maps of Africa recognize four large families: Afroasiatic (Somali, Hausa, Berber) in the north and the Sahara; Nilo-Saharan (Nuer, Teda, Songhai) in pockets in and around the Sahara; Khoisan (Khoikhoi, San) in and around the Kalahari Desert; and the most populous, Niger-Kordofanian (formerly Niger-Congo), covering most of the sub-Saharan region, including Atlantic (Wolof, Fulbe), Mande (Bamana, Maninka), Kwa (Ewe, Akan, Yoruba), and Bantu (the most widespread family). Perhaps the most significant internal migration was that of Bantu-speaking peoples, beginning about 3,500 years ago. From their homeland around the present Nigeria-Cameroon border they migrated east toward Lake Victoria and also south through the Central African forests. Some continued southward (Xhosa and Zulu are the southernmost languages). Swahili (a mixture of Arabic and Bantu languages) is unique as an indigenous language that serves as the lingua franca in several nations (Tanzania, Kenya, and other parts of the eastern, or Swahili, coast).

Melville Herskovits's notion of broad cultural areas in Africa solidified into music culture areas via his student Alan Merriam and others after him who continued to view Africa as consisting of a number of broad cultural regions (between eight and a dozen). Along the same lines, and with much more detailed documentation to work with, Kubik divided West Africa into nine cultural zones and the nation of Tanzania into eight style areas.

Identifying certain cultural areas, from local to supraregional, helps bring to the forefront certain musical features, but it may also obscure others. Neighboring groups in one region might have less in common musically than each group might have with more distant peoples. For example, distribution maps of harps, plucked lutes, and xylophones in West Africa show links among peoples spread out over thousands of kilometers. Some instruments may reflect affinities of occupation, such as blacksmithing, hunting, or praise singing, rather than affinities of language or ethnicity.

The impact of Islam and Christianity further undermine notions of regional cultural areas. Indigenous religions, which revere ancestral spirits or more abstract spiritual forces, have been overlain but not transplanted by Islam and Christianity, which have shaped, and been shaped by, local musical traditions. The impact of Islam includes the introduction of new musical instruments, sound materials (vocal styles, melodic materials), classes of musicians, and genres of music, and the alteration or suppression of some genres, such as the drumming with wooden masks associated with power societies.

Christianity entered via European seafaring travelers along the western, central, and southern coastlines. As a result, many West African countries have a Muslim north and Christian south. Missionary education, including hymn singing, has introduced new genres and instruments and influenced local singing styles, to the extent that in South Africa it merged with Zulu choral singing and developed into a tradition that reflects elements of both worlds.

III. *Colonial histories and modern nations.* The indigenous language map is overlain with another map of languages coming from outside the continent. Because of Muslim invasions from the Arabian peninsula, Arabic is the lingua franca in the north. Classical Arabic, the language of the Qur'ān, is known among devout Muslims in the African Islamic world. Throughout most of the rest of the continent English and French are predominant official languages, reflecting the intense period of colonization of the 1890s to early 1960s. (European presence south of the Sahara dates from the mid-15th century.) Portuguese colonization was much more limited and lasted into the 1970s, ending with bitterly contested wars. Germany, Belgium, and Italy were the other European powers with significant involvement in colonization. The primary languages of scholarship in African music reflect this colonial past: English and French, with a significant amount in German.

Colonial histories are significant for music histories for several reasons. In the colonial era, travel, communication, and European-style education were greatly facilitated among colonies. The French colonized much of North and West Africa and parts of Central Africa; the British had a significant presence in West, East, and most of southern Africa. There was much communication between anglophone Nigeria and Ghana in the development of their modern popular musics, as there was between francophone Guinea, Mali, and Ivory Coast. Cuban music had a particularly strong impact throughout francophone Africa.

British music schools offered correspondence courses and examinations in Britain's colonies, eventually leading to the establishment of music departments at the college level in Ghana, Nigeria, Uganda, and Kenya. Appreciation for European art music was thereby fostered, and several generations of African composers have been actively engaged with combining European and African musical techniques.

The gaining of political independence between 1957 and 1963 in most of Africa led to the development of national styles of music. Capital cities attracted talented artists from across the country, and disparate musical genres bounded within one country began to mix in new ways. National dance groups and orchestras were formed to promote national identities that downplayed ethnic divisions.

IV. *Regional overviews.* With such a vast area to comprehend, it has been convenient to divide the continent geographically.

1. North Africa. Because of the early and intense Islamization process, begun within decades of the death of Muhammad (632 C.E.), Arab culture dominates the region. Egypt, with its own unique history of ancient dynasties, civilizations, and music culture dating back 5,000 years, may be distinguished from the rest of North Africa, known as the Maghreb (Arabic for *west*). An Arab-Andalusian urban music tradition, stemming from 9th-century C.E. Baghdad and transplanted to southern Spain, was brought to the Maghreb by Muslim and Jewish refugees from Spain in the 10th to 15th centuries.

Egyptian popular vocal idioms, exemplified by Umm Kulthum, the most beloved singer in the whole Arab world, and schools of *Quranic chant have been particularly influential. Algeria has in the past few decades spawned a popular vocal music with electronic instruments called Rai. Sub-Saharan culture was carried to the Maghreb several centuries ago by slaves, known as Gnawa, who acted as spiritual healers and played large lutes (called gimbri), drums, and metal castanets. Berber groups, including the desert-dwelling Moor and Tuareg, are known for their poetry and harp and lute playing. Saharan women play musical instruments, uncommon in the rest of Africa.

2. East Africa. The kingdoms of Buganda, Rwanda, and Burundi in the vicinity of Lake Victoria were important centers attracting virtuoso harp soloists and ensembles of drums, flutes, horns, or xylophones. Ethiopia is unique, owing to the early introduction of Christianity there (4th century) and a chanted liturgy that has been notated since at least the 16th century, probably the oldest indigenous musical notation system in Africa. Along the Swahili coast, Taarab, a genre of poetry sung to the accompaniment of ensembles reflecting their late-19th-century Egyptian origin, mixed with electric guitars, basses, and accordions, is widely popular and is performed at concerts and weddings.

3. West Africa. Drumming traditions abound in West Africa, as do active lineages of praise singers and court musicians associated with the great empires of ancient Ghana, Mali (Mande), Songhai, and the Hausa states. Prolific research into southern Ghanaian drum ensembles has been especially influential in theories of African rhythm, but the bell patterns that regulate Akan (Asante, Fante) and Ewe drum ensembles may not be as representative of African drumming as previously thought. The hourglass-shaped squeeze drum traditions, like the Senegalese Wolof *tama,* Ghanaian Dagbamba *luna,* and Nigerian Yoruba *dundun*

do not use bells. Many societies have classes of nobles, who do not usually play music, and artisans, including griots, known by local terms such as *jali* or *jeli* (Mandinka, Maninka), who are oral historians, singers, and instrumentalists. An elaborate system of court musicians exists among the Hausa, with varying degrees of status being according to players of different instruments, such as long trumpets, drums, lutes, and fiddles. Cattle-herding Fulbe (Fula, Fulani) peoples in the sahel and savanna are probably the most widely dispersed (from Senegal to Cameroon), and they carried their lute traditions with them and also spread Islam in a series of 18th- and 19th-century holy wars of conversion.

Ghana is home to a popular guitar-based music called highlife. Yoruba drumming and praise singing are the basis of popular styles that arose in the 20th century, most notably juju and fuji. Fela Kuti, one of Africa's most outspoken and prolific recording artists in the 1970s and 1980s, single-handedly created the Nigerian style known as Afrobeat. Since the 1980s Mali and Senegal have produced internationally known singers, such as Salif Keita, Youssou Ndour, and Oumou Sangare.

4. Central Africa. Central Africa is perhaps best known for the complex polyphonic singing of pygmies and the very popular guitar-based dance music known as Congolese rumba or soukous. Bantu interaction with forest peoples, known by their local names BaBenzele, BaMbuti, and BaAaka, among others, resulted in the pygmies' losing their own language and borrowing musical instruments such as drums and string instruments. Bantu peoples in turn apparently borrowed pygmy-style polyphony and interlocking techniques (as in the large horn and flute ensembles of the Banda of the Central African Republic). Bantu groups such as the Kongo, Cokwe, and Kuba employ xylophones, metal bells, and drum ensembles with masking traditions.

In the 1940s and 1950s a guitar-based music developed in Kinshasa (formerly Léopoldville) and Brazzaville, capitals of the former Belgian Congo and French Congo, respectively, based on local interpretations of Cuban popular music. Products of a local private recording industry, bands such as OK Jazz and African Fiesta gained great popularity. OK Jazz leader Franco Luambo became one of the most prolific and beloved electric guitarists in Africa in the 1960s and 1970s.

5. Southern Africa. Mbiras (Zimbabwe), homophonic choral singing (Republic of South Africa), and orchestras of xylophones of different sizes (Mozambique) are hallmarks of southern Africa. Musical bows are very common, being staple instruments of the oldest inhabitants of the south, the Khoikhoi pastoralists and the San hunter-gatherers, called Hottentots and Bushmen, respectively, by Europeans. Khoisan clicks, borrowed by Nguni speakers (Xhosa and Zulu) are featured in the famous "Click Song" of South African Miriam Makeba, perhaps Africa's most beloved singer. Zulu are known for their choral singing, in which indigenous traditions mixed with influences from late-19th-century visiting African American minstrel troupes and Christian missionary choral practices, producing a popular male a capella style known as *mbube* ("The Lion") or *isicathamiya.* Ladysmith Black Mambazo is the most well known group in that tradition. Mozambique is home to xylophone orchestras attached to Chopi chiefs. Drumming traditions are relatively absent in this part of the continent. The island of Madagascar is home to diverse string traditions (tube zithers, lutes) that bear some influence from Indonesia.

V. *Uses and social roles of music.* Music in Africa is intimately linked with the four major life-cycle events (naming just after birth, initiation into adulthood, marriage, and death); the agricultural calendar; spiritual, religious, and healing ceremonies; work activities; and the creation and reification of personal, group, national, and transnational identities.

Initiation into adulthood, which can entail male circumcision or female excision, is typically accompanied by drumming, singing, and dancing. Children are sent off to and welcomed from the bush with grand celebrations, and in the actual initiation camps they may learn songs and dances that teach them about the responsibilities of adulthood. Among the Venda of South Africa girls play drums for initiation dances, rare elsewhere. Marriage is probably the most elaborate affair throughout Africa, and music is an integral part of the celebration, which can last many days. In Muslim societies funerals do not usually involve music; in non-Muslim societies music can be a major part of funeral ceremonies, as with drumming in southern Ghana. For each of these life-cycle events, music unique to the particular occasion may be performed.

Masking traditions (wooden face masks or outfits that can cover the body from head to toe) involving drumming and dancing are widespread in sub-Saharan Africa among agriculturally based Niger-Congo–speaking peoples. Agricultural fertility may be sought in ceremonies involving drums and masked dancers, fields are prepared accompanied by singing or drumming, and the harvest is often celebrated with song and dance. Power societies, often secret with closed membership (such as the male Poro and female Sande associations of the western Guinea coast), use drumming and dancing with mask emblems to solidify their status as sources of spiritual power. Daily work and household activities are often supported with music. Women throughout Africa pound grain with mortar and pestles, and they often perform interlocking patterns with occasional claps or vocal sounds as two or three women work together.

Music is also an integral part of possession or trance ceremonies, which take place throughout the continent. Professional musicians retain the expertise needed to properly induce possession, which is the state in which direct communication with ancestors, local spirits, or gods takes place. Typically the ceremonies are used for physical or psychic healing. Diverse examples are found among Shona of Zimbabwe, who use the *mbira;* Hausa of Nigeria, who use the *garaya* (lute) and *goge* (fiddle) in their *bori* cult; Tumbuka of Malawi and Akan of Ghana, who use drums; and Gnawa of Morocco.

Individual identities can be shaped by performances of praise singers and court musicians, as among Maninka of Mali or Dagbamba of northern Ghana. Certain instruments are reserved for royalty and can reinforce the status of the patron, as among Hausa of Nigeria. The reification of some kind of group identity is perhaps the most widespread purpose of music in Africa. Instruments and repertories belong to certain groups of people, distinguishing them from their neighbors. In the process of nation building during the postcolonial era (after 1960 for most African nations), music has been one of the primary means of creating a national identity. Whether through independent artists who synthesize the influences they have absorbed since childhood, or through governments that form national performance ensembles, African nations have clear and well-understood musical traditions that uniquely define their identities. With increased media circulation in the 20th century and migration to northern-hemisphere cities in the second half of the 20th century, transnational music communities have also developed, with African musicians permanently relocating to the major cities of Europe and North America and assuming a significant cultural presence in their new host countries.

Music makers can range from highly trained specialists whose family lineages have been responsible for guarding musical traditions for centuries to virtually any member of the community participating in group events by singing or hand clapping.

VI. *Musical instruments.* Like languages and dialects, the number and variety of musical instruments in Africa is staggering. Kubik's investigation of internal migrations and the historical implications of the seemingly endless variations in form of African instruments summarizes current research. Various instrument types and forms tend to cluster within certain regions, reflecting the availability of local resources and also stylistic preferences. The contexts in which instruments play often mark them for special social status, although such status is locally defined and can vary according to place. Drums may be high-status symbols of royalty in one culture and low-status instruments requiring no special care in another.

1. Drums. The greatest diversity of musical instruments occurs among drums, with hundreds, if not thousands, of them distributed across most of the continent, especially in West Africa, probably home to the greatest variety of drums in the world. Most ethnic groups use one or more drums, each named and uniquely identified by some morphological feature. Using the method of attaching the skin head to the body and the shape of the body as distinctive features, clear cultural areas emerge. For example, hourglass-shape squeeze drums, many of which are able to imitate rising and falling intonations of local languages and thereby communicate speech, are found primarily in the West African sahel and savanna. Farther south in Kwa-speaking regions (Ewe, Akan, Fon) drums with heads attached with a unique kind of cord-and-peg tension mechanism resemble those used in the Americas in religious contexts for the worship of African deities. In the past decade the jembe, indigenous to Mande peoples in western Africa, has become the most popular African drum outside the continent.

2. Strings. String instruments are more or less evenly distributed across the whole continent. Musical bows, the most primitive technologically, are used all over; in the South they may have originated with San peoples. Zithers, such as the *mvet* in Cameroon that has a wooden trough resonator, or the *valiha* in Madagascar, with a wooden tube resonator, are primarily used in central and southeastern Africa. Lyres are primarily used in East Africa among Nilo-Saharan, Afroasiatic, and some Bantu language speakers, perhaps disseminated from ancient Egypt. Several morphological varieties of harps, each with its own relatively compact distribution, are used north of the equator (Gabon), and are perhaps remnants of ancient Saharan culture. Fiddles are primarily used in West Africa and farther north, and plucked lutes are widely disseminated. Lutes and harps in West Africa (including the twenty-one-string harp *kora*) are particularly suited to accompany the epic recitations of griots and hunter's musicians. The guitar, introduced from Europe at varying times in different parts of the continent, is played virtually everywhere and has been the primary instrument used to modernize local musics and integrate them into more popular idioms aimed at international audiences.

3. Xylophones, wooden slit drums, lamellophones. Wooden percussion instruments are widespread south of the Sahara. Distinctions can be made between free-key xylophones (single slats of wood sitting freely across a player's legs or on the ground), frame xylophones (slats of wood set on top of a frame and held in place by pegs or rope tied around them), and slit drums (a single slab or cylinder of hollowed-out wood, which may also have carved slits for different pitches). Slit drums are usually found in forested areas where wood is plentiful. Xylophones are more often found in the savanna regions. Slit drums played with wooden sticks can be heard over long distances and have been used for speechlike communication. Lamellophones (with plucked metal or reed rods) are found throughout the sub-Sahara, although they probably originated in the southeast, where the greatest concentration occurs. *Mbira* (Zimbabwe), *kalimba,* and *likembe* (Central Africa) are some of the local names used.

4. Winds. Wind instruments, such as wooden flutes

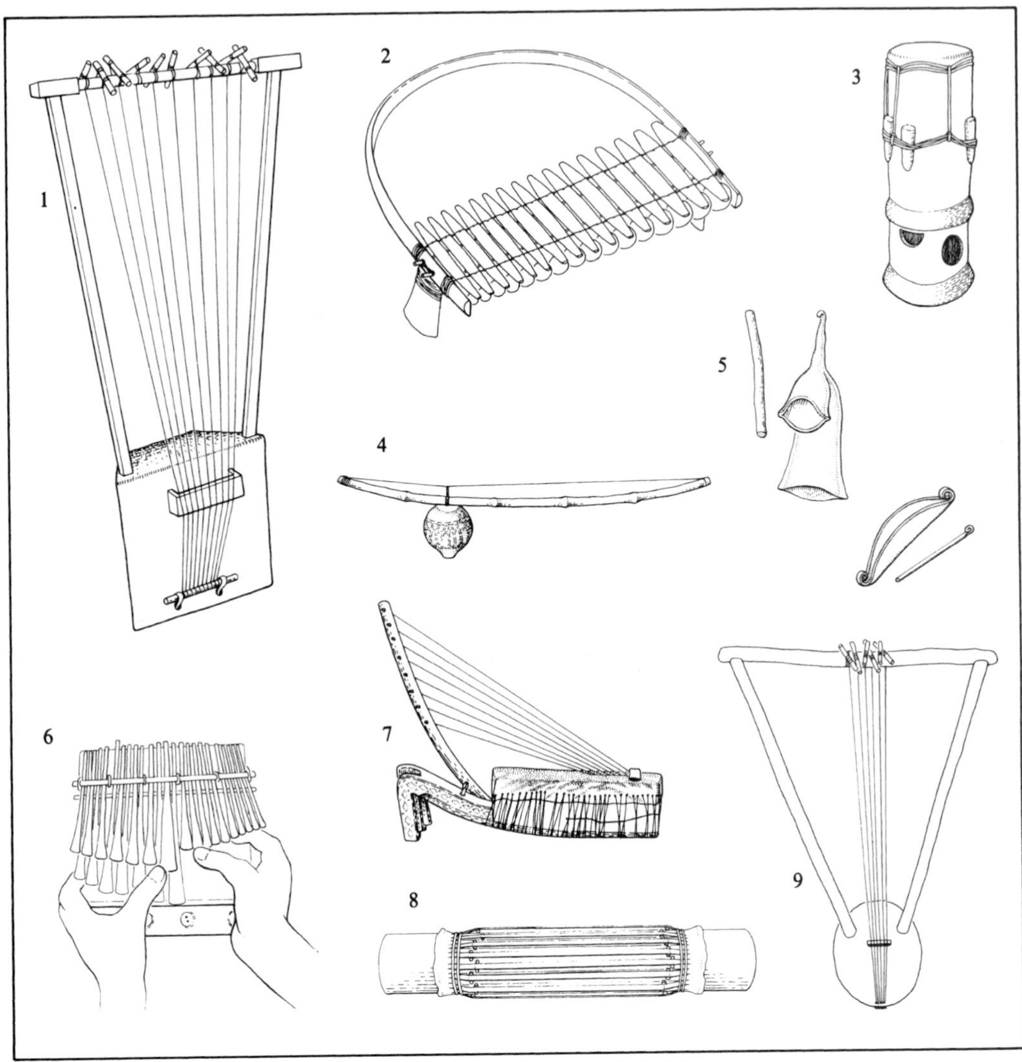

African instruments: 1. Bagana. 2. Xylophone. 3. Drum. 4. Musical bow. 5. Bells. 6. Mbira. 7. Harp. 8. Valiha. 9. Krar.

and horns, are less common than other instruments. Often horns (which can play only one or two notes) are played in ensembles, with each instrument playing short simple phrases that interlock with a dozen or more other horns, forming a complex texture. Fulbe flute players in western Africa sing into their instrument while they play melodies that may be in free meter.

VII. *Musical aesthetics.* Even with the great diversity of musical expression across the continent, much music exhibits features that mark it as uniquely African. Scholars have debated the exact nature of these features and how to define them, and any generalization about the continent is rightfully bound to draw criticism of oversimplification. Nevertheless, it would be difficult to ignore the following traits.

1. Filling in the sound spectrum. There is a remarkable preference for devices that add rattling, jingling, or buzzing sounds to musical instruments. On xylophones, the gourd resonators under the slats have holes over which are stretched membranes (made of thin paper or plastic) that buzz like kazoos. On *mbiras,* shells or bottle caps attached to the wooden soundboard rattle when a rod is plucked. On lutes and harps, metal plaques with rings around them are attached to the bridge or end of the neck so they jingle when a string is plucked. *Dagbamba* (Ghana) bass drums have a leather cord stretched across the skin that

buzzes like a snare. Drummers and xylophone players often wear metal jingles on their wrists that sound when they move their arms. In recording studios these devices are often taken off, perhaps in deference to non-African or modern sensibilities.

2. Cyclic form. Pieces are based on rhythmic, melodic, or harmonic cycles that can continue as long as the performers wish; they are open-ended and require improvisational skills. While musicians do not talk about technical aspects of the music, such as beats and their combinations or divisions, scholars have theorized some of the basic concepts using the terms *pulse, beat,* and *cycle.* One cycle of a piece is made up of a fixed number of beats (usually multiples of 2 or 3, such as 4, 6, 8, 9, 12, or 16), which in turn consist of a fixed number of pulses (usually 2, 3, or 4). African musicians are not concerned with defining the beginning of a cycle, and in performance they may start in any number of places within a cycle, although certain beats may be favored.

Example 1 shows two *mbira* parts for a well-known piece, *Nhemamusasa.* Each part, the *kushaura* (leader) and *kutsinhira* (follower), is based on a 48-pulse cycle and is played against a ternary (3-pulse) beat marked off by a rattle *(hosho),* shown at the bottom. The transcription reveals polyrhythm in the *kushaura,* wherein the lowest registral level groups beats into 4 pulses each, yielding 12 beats per cycle (the middle and upper levels group beats into 4 or 2 pulses). The *kutsinhira* part groups beats into 3 pulses each (aligning them with the *hosho*), yielding 16 beats per cycle. The harmonies (indicated by roman numerals) change every 12 pulses (4 ternary beats), yielding four harmonic areas, somewhat similar to a chord progression with four chords. This principle of a cycle consisting of groups of beats defining harmonic areas is widespread, whether on *mbiras,* xylophones, string instruments, or voices.

3. Dialogue, conversation, call and response. Equally pervasive is a preference for musical dialogue, conversation, or response. This can be achieved by a solo performer, as in the dialogic relation between the various levels in the *kushaura* part [ill.] or the well-known pygmy recording of Arom, in which a solo performer responds to her own singing with a whistle on the offbeat. Responding is also a hallmark of group performance. A leader (vocalist or instrumentalist) might receive regular responses from a single person or from a group of vocalists or instrumentalists interjecting between phrases or playing regular patterns. Several kinds of conversations might take place simultaneously, as among different drums in an ensemble, the vocal polyphony of forest peoples, or interlocking horn orchestras.

4. Polyrhythm and offbeat phrasing. Related to the idea of a dialogue are the technical distinctions of polyrhythm (two or more different rhythms played simultaneously) and offbeat phrasing (accentuation of the spaces in between beats). Sometimes called cross-rhythm, polyrhythm typically involves three beats played in the space of two or four (or vice versa). Polyrhythm is exploited in Africa perhaps more so than in any other part of the world, although not uniformly around the continent or even within any one region. Offbeat phrasing is much more ubiquitous.

5. Tuning, scale, and melody. No single tuning standard exists for even relatively small cultural regions. Specific tunings may vary from musician to musician in a region, suggesting that tunings may be a matter of personal style. A willingness to accept and even embrace a variety of ways to render an abstract scale into a concrete tuning, or to have two or more different tuning systems in a single ensemble, can be perplexing for non-Africans. While instruments are tuned with a high degree of precision when appropriate (e.g., a xylophone orchestra), instruments from different towns may exhibit differences.

Scales range from pentatonic to heptatonic, with no credible indication of any kind of evolutionary movement from one to another. Seven equal tones in an octave are frequently used for xylophones. Rarely will more than seven tones be used in a single piece of music (or repertory); altering one or two tones of a scale is more common, especially among peoples exposed to Islam (hence Quranic chant and the Arab tonal system that conveys it). Observers have noted that vocal melodies often descend in a terrace-like manner.

VIII. *Sound recordings.* A series of discographies (see Bibl.) provide a good overview of recordings in Africa over the past century. Two streams can be distinguished: ethnographic and commercial, although by the late 20th century they began to merge.

The ethnographic stream dates to the first three decades of the 20th century, when German and British anthropologists began making sporadic field recordings in their colonial territories. In the 1930s and 1940s American and French anthropologists (such as Laura Boulton and Gilbert Rouget) expanded the field. The most prolific producer of recordings and the first to make a systematic survey was Hugh Tracey of southern Rhodesian (Zimbabwe). In 1954 Tracey established the South Africa–based International Library of African Music, and by the early 1970s he had recorded and released some 210 LPs from central, eastern, and southern Africa in the library's Sound of Africa series.

Ethnographic recordings feature local musics that show little outward sign of European or American influence. Usually recorded by anthropologists or ethnomusicologists, copious notes are standard, ranging from several pages to the exquisitely documented booklets issued by the Berlin Museum (edited by Artur Simon) and the Musée Royal de l'Afrique Centrale in Tervueren, Belgium (edited by Jos Gansemans). Important labels include those from France (OCORA, Vogue, Inedit), the United States (Folk-

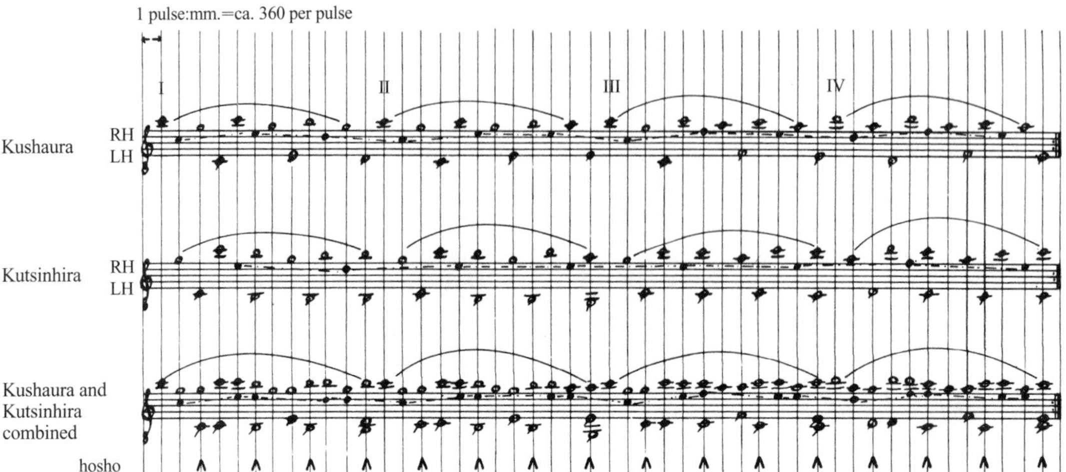

Ex. 1. From Paul F. Berliner, *The Soul of Mbira: Music and Traditions of the Shona People of Zimbabwe.* Reproduced courtesy University of Chicago Press.

ways), and Germany (Barenreiter Musicaphon, Berlin Museum). Folkways was particularly prolific; the label issued more than 110 LPs from thirty African countries between the early 1950s and early 1980s.

Beginning in the late 1920s commercial recording companies began to record Africans in Europe and at home in mobile studios. By the 1940s private labels were recording and issuing local guitar-based popular music in the Belgian Congo, which by the 1960s would have an enormous impact on the rest of the continent in the form of Congolese rumba. After the colonial period, European labels accelerated their interest and LPs became more abundant. The World Music boom, which coincided with the rise of CD technology in the mid-1980s, fueled intense independent-label interest and established African music as a viable commercial market with no signs of subsiding.

IX. *History and scholarship.* Several bibliographies (see Bibl.) provide a good overview of scholarly writing from the past century. Early Arabic (from the 9th century) and European (from the 15th century) travelers' accounts, often tangentially describing music, have been an important source in writing music histories, as have oral traditions actively collected over the past century. Material culture from the past—including items such as the 16th-century Benin copper plaques depicting musicians, instruments from ancient Egypt, and archeological evidence of new technologies (e.g., iron smelting, agriculture)—support speculation about artisanal or subsistence activities related to uses of music.

The first major work on music in Africa was based on the musical instrument collection at the Museum für Völkerkunde Berlin, which continues to spawn monographs on instrument types. Scholarly interest in African music accelerated after von Hornbostel's (1928) "African Negro Music," in the inaugural issue of the journal *Africa.* Monographs were slow in coming over the next several decades. The establishment of the South Africa–based journal *African Music* in 1954 gave a major boost to African music research, with a flurry of detailed articles on very specific traditions. Ghanaian J. H. Kwabena Nketia, one of the first black African scholars of African music, is one of the most prolific writers and has been a major presence since the 1950s. Many others, primarily from Ghana and Nigeria, have followed in his footsteps.

Current trends in scholarship demonstrate a new historical and ethnographic consciousness. Since the late 1970s scholarship has increased exponentially, with perhaps half a dozen books now being published annually in English. Highly focused analyses continue, now bringing new analytical tools to the table, including native fluency in language. Single book-length surveys of the continent have not been taken up in force, perhaps in recognition of the enormity of the task. African composers working out of European-based choral and instrumental art music traditions are gaining recognition, as are the varied roles that women play in making music. Finally, modern or popular musics have enjoyed a surge of scholarly attention. While these musics often reflect national identities, it is clear that increased globalization has not eradicated more local kinds of identity, which are still viable and vital.

Bibl.: *Bibliographies.* Douglas H. Varley, *African Native Music: An Annotated Bibliography* (London: Royal Empire Society, 1936; R: Folkestone: Dawsons of Pall Mall, 1970). Alan Merriam, "An Annotated Bibliography of African and African-Derived Music since 1936," *Africa* 21, no. 4 (1951): 319–29. Darius L. Thieme, *African Music: A Briefly Annotated Bibliography* (Washington, D.C.: Library of Congress,

1964). L. J. P. Gaskin, *A Select Bibliography of Music in Africa* (London: International African Institute, 1965). John Gray, *African Music: A Bibliographical Guide to the Traditional, Popular, Art, and Liturgical Musics of Sub-Saharan Africa* (Westport, Conn.: Greenwood, 1991). Carol Lems-Dworkin, *African Music: A Pan-African Annotated Bibliography* (London: Hans Zell, 1991).

Discographies. Alan Merriam, *African Music on LP: An Annotated Discography* (Evanston: Northwestern U Pr, 1970). Hugh Tracey, *Catalogue, The Sound of Africa Series: 210 Long Playing Records of Music and Songs from Central, Eastern and Southern Africa,* 2 vols. (Roodepoort, South Africa: International Library of African Music, 1973). Ruth M. Stone and Frank J. Gillis, *African Music and Oral Data: A Catalog of Field Recordings, 1902–1975* (Bloomington: Ind U Pr, 1976). Chantal Nourrit and Bill Pruitt, *Musique traditionelle de l'Afrique noire: Discographie,* 17 country vols. (Paris: Centre de documentation africaine, Radio France International, 1978–85). Ronnie Graham, *The Da Capo Guide to Contemporary African Music* (New York: Da Capo, 1988). Ronnie Graham, *The World of African Music: Stern's Guide to Contemporary African Music, Volume 2* (London: Pluto Pr; Chicago: Research Associates, 1992). Simon Broughton, Mark Ellingham, and Richard Trillo, eds., *World Music: The Rough Guide,* vol. 1: *Africa, Europe and the Middle East,* new ed. (London: Rough Guides, 1999).

Other references. Bernhard Ankermann, "Die Afrikanische Musikinstrumente," *Ethnologisches Notizblatt* 3, no. 1 (1901). Erich M. von Hornbostel, "African Negro Music," *Africa* 1 (1928): 30–62. Percival K. Kirby, *The Musical Instruments of the Native Races of South Africa* (London: Oxford U Pr, 1934; 2nd ed. Johannesburg: Witwatersrand U Pr, 1965). Hugh Tracey, *Chopi Musicians: Their Music, Poetry, and Instruments* (London: Oxford U Pr, 1948; R: 1970). J. H. Kwabena Nketia, *Funeral Dirges of the Akan People* (Legon: U of Ghana, 1955; R: Westport, Conn.: Greenwood, 1974). A. M. Jones, *Studies in African Music,* 2 vols. (London: Oxford U Pr, 1959). *Musikgeschichte in Bildern:* 1 (8), *Nord-Afrika* (P. Collaer and J. Elsner, 1983); 1 (9), *Zentralafrika* (J. Gansemans and B. Schmidt-Wrenger, 1986); 1 (10) *Ostafrika* (G. Kubik, 1982); 1 (11), *Westafrika* (G. Kubik, 1989); 2 (1), *Ägypten* (H. Hickmann, 1961) (Leipzig: VEB Deutscher Verlag für Musik Leipzig). Klaus Wachsmann, "Human Migration and African Harps," *JIFMC* 16 (1964): 84–88. Simha Arom with Geneviève Taurelle, eds., *UNESCO Collection, An Anthology of African Music,* vol. 3: *The Music of the Ba-Benzélé Pygmies* (LP) (Bärenreiter Musicaphon, BM 30L2303, 1965; reissued on Rounder, CD5107, 1998). Lois A. Anderson, "The African Xylophone," *African Arts* 1 (1967): 46–49, 66, 68–69. H. T. Norris, *Shinqiitii Folk Literature and Song* (Oxford: Oxford U Pr, 1968). John Blacking, *Venda Children's Songs: A Study in Ethnomusicological Analysis* (Johannesburg: Witwatersrand U Pr, 1967; R: Chicago: U of Chicago Pr, 1995). David Rycroft, *Zulu, Swazi and Xhosa Instrumental and Vocal Music* (LP) (Tervueren, Belgium: Musée Royal de l'Afrique Centrale, 1969). Francis Bebey, *Musique de l'Afrique* (Paris: Horizons de France, 1969); trans. as *African Music: A People's Art* (Brooklyn: Lawrence Hill, 1975). David W. Ames and Anthony V. King, *Glossary of Hausa Music and Its Social Contexts* (Evanston: Northwestern U Pr, 1971). Klaus P. Wachsmann, ed., *Essays on Music and History in Africa* (Evanston: Northwestern U Pr, 1971). Hugo Zemp, *Musique Dan: La musique dans la pensée et la vie sociale d'une société africaine* (Paris: Mouton, 1971). J. H. Kwabena Nketia, *The Music of Africa* (New York: Norton, 1974). Georges Lapassade, "Les Gnaoua d'Essaouira," *L'Homme et la société* 39/40 (1976): 191–215. Thomas A. Sebeok and Donna Jean Umiker-Sebeok, eds., *Speech Surrogates: Drum and Whistle Systems* (The Hague: Mouton, 1976). Paul Berliner, *The Soul of Mbira: Music and Traditions of the Shona People of Zimbabwe* (Berkeley: U of Cal Pr, 1978; R: Chicago: U of Chicago Pr, 1993). Philip Schuyler, "A Repertory of Ideas: The Music of the Rwais, Berber Professional Musicians from Southwestern Morocco," Ph.D. diss., U of Wash, 1979. Jacqueline Cogdell DjeDje, *Distribution of the One-String Fiddle in West Africa* (Los Angeles: Program in Ethnomusicology, Dept. of Music, UCLA, 1980). Gerhard Kubik, *Angola: Mukanda Na Makisi* (LP) (Berlin: Museum für Völkerkunde, Museum Collection MC 11, 1981). David Locke, "Principles of Offbeat Timing and Cross-Rhythm in Southern Eve Dance Music," *Ethno* 26 (1982): 217–46. Alan Merriam, *African Music in Perspective* (New York: Garland, 1982). Fremont E. Besmer, *Horses, Musicians, and Gods: The Hausa Cult of Possession-Trance* (Zaria, Nigeria: Ahmadu Bello U Pr, 1983). Larry Godsey, "The Use of Variation in Birifor Funeral Music," *Selected Reports in Ethnomusicology* 5 (1984): 67–80. Ulrich Wegner, *Afrikanische Saiteninstrumente* (Berlin: Staatliche Museen Preussischer, 1984). David Coplan, *In Township Tonight! South Africa's Big City Music and Theatre* (London: Longman, 1985). Gilbert Rouget, *Music and Trance: A Theory of the Relations between Music and Possession* (Chicago: U of Chicago Pr, 1985). Jacqueline Cogdell DjeDje, ed., and William G. Carter, assoc. ed., *African Musicology: Current Trends,* vol. 1 (Los Angeles: African Studies Center, UCLA, 1989). Akin Euba, *Yoruba Drumming: The Dùndún Tradition* (Bayreuth: E. Breitinger/Bayreuth U Pr, 1990). Christopher Waterman, *Jùjú: A Social History and Ethnography of an African Popular Music* (Chicago: U of Chicago Pr, 1990). Patrick R. McNaughton, "Is There History in Horizontal Masks? A Preliminary Response to the Dilemma of Form," *African Arts* 24 (1991): 40–53, 88–90. John Collins, *West African Pop Roots* (Philadelphia: Temple U Pr, 1992). Roderic Knight, *Music of the Mande* (video) (Original Music, 1992; dist. by the author). Kay Kaufman Shelemay and Peter Jeffery, eds., *Ethiopian Christian Liturgical Chant: An Anthology,* 3 vols. (Madison, Wis.: A-R Eds, 1993–97). Esther A. Dagan, ed., *Drums: The Heartbeat of Africa* (Montreal: Galerie Amrad African Art Publications, 1993). Kofi Agawu, *African Rhythm: A Northern Ewe Perspective* (Cambridge: Cambridge U Pr, 1995). Peter Cooke, "Music in a Uganda Court," *EM* 24 (1996): 439–52. Ruth Davis, "Arab-Andalusian Music in Tunisia," *EM* 24 (1996): 423–37. Veit Erlmann, *Nightsong: Performance, Power, and Practice in South Africa* (Chicago: U of Chicago Pr, 1996). Steven Friedson, *Dancing Prophets: Musical Experience in Tumbuka Healing* (Chicago: U of Chicago Pr, 1996). Carol Lems-Dworkin, *Videos of African and African-Related Performance: An Annotated Bibliography* (Evanston: C. Lems-Dworkin, 1996). Virginia Danielson, *The Voice of Egypt: Umm Kulthuum, Arabic Song, and Egyptian Society in the Twentieth Century* (Chicago: U of Chicago Pr, 1997). Andreas Meyer, *Afrikanische Trommeln: West- und Zentralafrika* (Berlin: Museum für Völkerkunde, 1997). Michelle Kisliuk, *Seize the Dance! BaAka Musical Life and the Ethnography of Performance* (New York: Oxford U Pr, 1998). Judith Perani and Fred T. Smith, *The Visual Arts of Africa: Gender, Power, and Life Cycle Rituals* (Upper Saddle River, N.J.: Prentice Hall, 1998). Ruth Stone, ed., *Garland Encyclopedia of World Music,* vol. 1: *Africa* (New York: Garland, 1998). Hugh Tracey and Andrew Tracey, "Historical Recordings by Hugh Tracey" (CD series) (Grahamstown: International Library of African Music/Utrecht: Sharp Wood Productions, SWP 07–, 1998–). Lucy Durán, "Stars and Songbirds: Mande Female Singers in Urban Music, Mali, 1980–99" (Ph.D. diss., U of London, 1999). Scott Kiehl, *Akom: The Art of Possession* (CD) (Seattle: Village Pulse, VPU 1009, 1999). Marc Schade-Poulsen, *Men and Popular Music in Algeria: The Social Significance of Raï* (Austin: U of Tex Pr, 1999). Eric Charry, *Mande Music: Traditional and Modern Music of the Maninka and Mandinka of Western Africa* (Chicago: U of Chicago Pr, 2000). Eric Charry, "Music and Islam in Sub-Saharan Africa," in Nehemia Levtzion and Randall Pouwels, eds., *The History of Islam in Africa* (Athens: Ohio U Pr, 2000), pp. 545–73. Gary Stewart, *Rumba on the River: A History of the Popular Music of the Two Congos* (London: Verso, 2000). Thomas Turino, *Nationalists, Cosmopolitans, and Popular Music in Zimbabwe* (Chicago: U of Chicago Pr, 2000). Michael E. Veal, *Fela: The Life and Times of an African Musical Icon* (Philadelphia: Temple U Pr, 2000). Gerhard Kubik, "Africa," in *Grove 6,* 2nd ed. (London: Macmillan, 2001), pp. 190–210. Thomas Van Buren, "The Music of Manden in New York City: A Study of Applied Ethnomusicology in a Western African Immigrant Community" (Ph.D. diss., U of Md College Park, 2001). Kelly Askew, *Performing the Nation: Swahili Music and Cultural Politics in Tanzania* (Chicago: U of Chicago Pr, 2002). E.C.

Africaine, L' [Fr., The African Woman]. Opera in five acts by Meyerbeer (libretto by Eugène Scribe; final revisions to libretto following Scribe's death in 1861 and to music following Meyerbeer's death in 1864 by François-Joseph Fétis), produced in Paris in 1865. Setting: Lisbon and Madagascar at the end of the 15th century.

African American music. In the context of the music history and musical life of the U.S., those musical genres and styles created and practiced predominantly by members of the resident population with African roots. In some quarters of the musical, academic, and African American communities this definition is expanded to include any music, including concert music in the Euro-American tradition, conceived by African Americans and any music expressing the African American experience. Earlier designations for this vast body of materials have included African-American music (distinguished from the current designation only by the presence of a hyphen), black music, Afro-American music, Negro music. (The latter three terms have been used to designate not only U.S. musical practices, it should be noted.) All of these terms can be problematic in their overt association of race and ethnicity with a broad and diverse range of specific musical practices, and in their corresponding potential to deflect attention from other commonalities and distinctions of perhaps equal or greater significance in certain circumstances.

I. *Genres and history.* Documentary evidence has revealed the existence of a rich African American folk culture during the days of slavery, particularly in the plantation regions of the deep South. Aspects of this culture are still in evidence. Principal musical genres included: (1) *field hollers and *work songs, i.e., song types associated with particular occupations or kinds of labor (rowing songs, etc.); (2) social and recreational music, e.g., *ballads, children's songs, game songs, fife and drum ensembles, and instrumental dance music (e.g., *breakdowns); (3) religious music of converts to Christianity (e.g., *spirituals, *ring shouts).

In and around New Orleans, a cosmopolitan but essentially Latin-Catholic cultural base nurtured an African American culture more similar to that found in parts of Latin America and the West Indies than in the rest of North America, where an Anglo-Protestant cultural base predominated [see Latin America].

African Americans created distinctive musical cultures in North America by retaining certain features of African music and musical culture while simultaneously adapting to new circumstances. The circumstances of slavery, especially the policy of dispersal, made the preservation of tribally specific African musical practices virtually impossible. What was retained of African music in North America during slavery was mainly a general conceptual approach to music making—a set of overall African aesthetic preferences—which of necessity made use of available materials. Some instruments, such as drums and banjos, were constructed with little variation from their African prototypes, while European instruments and genres were adapted to African performance ideals. As African Americans became acquainted with Euro-American music and performance practices, some became expert practitioners. By the mid-19th century, as slavery neared its end in the U.S., aspects of African and European musical practices and ideals were being juxtaposed and blended by persons of all manner of ethnocultural roots, leading ultimately to new and distinctively U.S. vernacular musics and music cultures straddling and fusing European and African elements in a variety of configurations.

From the mid-19th century and continuing into the present, successive African American musical practices have had an impact far beyond their initial ethnic and regional confines. The first widespread manifestation of Anglo-American (and European) interest in the music of African Americans is to be found in blackface *minstrelsy. While the Euro-American professional minstrels' characterizations of African American music and culture are open to debate, blackface minstrelsy initiated and exemplifies a long-standing pattern in the history of American music and mass entertainment: the fascination of Euro-Americans with African American expressive culture and the ongoing appropriation and often callous exploitation of it by Euro-American professional entertainers and entrepreneurs.

During the latter third of the 19th century and well into the 20th century, the spiritual, albeit in a Europeanized guise, had a considerable impact on concert life in North America and, to some extent, Europe. In the first two decades of the 20th century, *ragtime, largely the creation of African American musicians, was a major international phenomenon, and its rhythmic organization changed popular music irrevocably. The influence of the various kinds of *jazz that have emerged since World War I has been even greater and more varied. During the 1920s, a number of African American musical practices became staples of the popular music industry [see Race record], e.g., *blues (and its instrumental cousins *barrelhouse and *boogie-woogie) and *gospel music. This trend has continued to the present, but some of the marketing terms and other designations for African American popular music have changed periodically, as have some stylistic features [see Rhythm and blues, Soul, Funk, Disco, Motown, Rap].

Sometimes also included in the category of African American music is the *zydeco music of Louisiana and the *reggae, *calypso, and *steel drum music of the African Caribbean population now resident in the U.S. Overview monographs and articles on U.S. African American music (see Literature, below) have as yet had little or nothing to say on these genres, preferring to focus on the founding African American population.

As training, educational, and performance opportunities for African American composers of concert music were limited until the mid-20th century at least, concert music constitutes a relatively small proportion of African American music as a whole. African American composers since the mid-20th century have produced works that embrace all of the stylistic developments of contemporary concert music, including serialism, minimalism, and music employing chance procedures. Such works frequently (but not necessarily) include stylistic features that can be linked to an African aesthetic.

II. *Musical values and behaviors.* Much of what is distinctive about African American music is attributable to the preservation and transmission from one generation to the next of sub-Saharan African musical values and behaviors [see Africa] in the New World. Some sub-Saharan African musical values and behaviors persisting in African American music, from a Western analytic perspective at least, are (1) a performance style that combines individual inventiveness, energy, and expressivity with maximal community participation and social interaction; (2) a predilection for cellular organization consisting of numerous repetitions of a short musical unit, sometimes varied improvisationally, and in which the performers use *call-and-response patterns; (3) an emphasis on rhythmic features including *cross-rhythm, *polyrhythm, asymmetric rhythms (e.g., 3 + 3 + 2 figures), strict time keeping, prominence of percussion (including handclapping and a percussive approach to melodic materials); (4) imaginative exploitation of the timbral potential of voices and instruments (e.g., buzzy or blurry tone, shouty or raspy vocal delivery). Individually, none of these traits is exclusive to sub-Saharan Africa, but the particular combination of features listed has been prominent in that region for centuries, so far as is known, and it is this bundle of characteristics that seems to have been most clearly retained in the New World.

African American musical styles and genres have developed as admixtures of various African musics and the musics of Native Americans, Europeans, and European-Americans that African Americans encountered in the New World environment, such as *psalmody, hymn singing, and Euro-American *popular, martial, and social dance music. The essence of African American music is its hybrid nature: African, European, and New World or newly created elements have combined and recombined in numerous ways over many years to create a rich and varied musical tradition.

Bibl.: *Research tools. Bibliographic Guide to Black Studies* (Boston: G K Hall, 1975–97). John Szwed and Roger Abrahams, *Afro-American Folk Culture,* pt. 1: *North America* (Philadelphia: Institute for the Study of Human Issues, 1978). Dominique-René de Lerma, *Bibliography of Black Music* (Westport, Conn.: Greenwood, 1981). Eileen Southern, *Biographical Dictionary of Afro-American and African Musicians* (Westport, Conn.: Greenwood, 1982). Samuel A. Floyd, Jr., ed., *International Dictionary of Black Composers,* 2 vols. (Chicago: Fitzroy Dearborn, 1999). Kwame Anthony Appiah and Henry Louis Gates, Jr., eds., *Africana: The Encyclopedia of the African and African American Experience* (New York: Basic Books, 1999). Ellen Koskoff, ed., *The Garland Encyclopedia of World Music,* vol. 3: *The United States and Canada* (New York: Garland, 2001).

Periodicals. American Music (1983–), *The Black Perspective in Music* (1973–90), *Black Music Research Journal* (1980–), *Popular Music* (1981–).

Literature. Richard Waterman, "African Influences in the Music of the Americas," in Sol Tax, ed., *Acculturation in the Americas* (Chicago: U of Chicago Pr, 1952), pp. 207–18. Harold Courlander, *Negro Folk Music, U.S.A.* (New York: Columbia U Pr, 1963). LeRoi Jones (Amiri Baraka), *Blues People: Negro Music in White America* (New York: Basic Books, 1971). John Storm Roberts, *Black Music of Two Worlds* (New York: Praeger, 1972; 2nd ed., Schirmer, 1998). Eileen Southern, *The Music of Black Americans: A History* (New York: Norton, 1971, 1983; 3rd ed., 1997). Eileen Southern, ed., *Readings in Black American Music* (New York: Norton, 1971; 2nd ed., 1983). Hildred Roach, *Black American Music: Past and Present* (Boston: Crescendo Pub Co, 1973; 2nd ed., Krieger Pub Co, 1992). Dena Epstein, *Sinful Tunes and Spirituals: Black Folk Music to the Civil War* (Urbana: U of Ill Pr, 1977). David Evans, "African Elements in Twentieth-Century United States Black Folk Music," (Berkeley: U of Cal Pr, 1977), pp. 54–66. Lawrence Levine, *Black Culture and Black Consciousness* (New York: Oxford U Pr, 1977). Tilford Brooks, *America's Black Musical Heritage* (Englewood Cliffs, N.J.: Prentice Hall, 1984). Philip Tagg, "Open Letter about 'Black Music,' 'Afro-American Music' and 'European Music,'" *Popular Music* 8, no. 3 (1989): 285–98. Portia K. Maultsby, "Africanisms in African-American Music," in Joseph E. Holloway, ed., *Africanisms in American Culture* (Bloomington: Ind U Pr,

1990), pp. 185–210. Michael T. Coolen, "Senegambian Influences on Afro-American Musical Culture," *Black Music Research Journal* 11, no. 1 (1991): 1–18. Gerhard Kubik, "Transplantation of African Musical Cultures into the New World: Research Topics and Objectives in the Study of African-American Music," in Wolfgang Binder, ed., *Slavery in the New World* (Würzburg: Königshausen und Neumann, 1993), pp. 421–52. Samuel A. Floyd, Jr., *The Power of Black Music: Interpreting Its History from Africa to the United States* (New York: Oxford U Pr, 1995). Christopher Small, *Music of the Common Tongue: Survival and Celebration in African American Music* (Hanover, N.H.: U Pr of New England/Wesleyan U Pr, 1998). Jacqueline Cogdell Djedje, "African American Music to 1900," in David Nicholls, ed., *The Cambridge History of American Music* (Cambridge: Cambridge U Pr, 1998), pp. 103–34. R.E.W.

Afro-Cuban jazz. See Latin jazz.

Afro-Cuban music. See Cuba.

Afterbeat. A beat falling after a metrically stronger beat, especially the second and fourth quarter notes in a measure of 4/4 and, by extension, the second and fourth eighth notes in a measure of 2/4.

After-dance. The second of a pair of dances, in a fast tempo, danced with skips, hops, and leaps that contrast with the slow, elegant steps of the preceding dance [see also *Nachtanz*]. As a rule, the melodic or the harmonic materials or both of the first dance are used in the second, but in a different meter. The earliest extant examples are in a 14th-century manuscript (*GB-Lbm* Add. 29987) where two monophonic dances, "Lamento di Tristano" (*HAM,* no. 59a; *GMB,* no. 28^1) and "La Manfredina" (*GMB,* no. 28^2) are followed by dances called "La *Rotta." In each, the melodic material of the first dance is used in a varied form for the second, but contrary to later practices, the first dance of each set is in triple meter and the second in duple. In the 15th century, the most common pairings were the *bassadanza* with the **saltarello* in Italy, the **basse danse* with the **pas de Brabant* in France, and the *bassadanza* with the **alta* in Spain. In the second dance, the tenor *cantus firmus* was played twice as fast as for the *basse danse.* Since the instrumental parts around the tenor were improvised, it is not possible to ascertain whether the same added musical material was used in both dances. In the 16th and 17th centuries, it was the **pavana* and *saltarello,* the **pass'e mezo* and *saltarello,* the *pavana* and **gagliarda,* and the *pass'e mezo* and *gagliarda* that were most commonly paired. Other combinations also occur in Italian tablatures, however. In France, the **recoupe* and **tourdion* appeared as after-dances to the *basse danse.* L.H.M.

Afternoon of a Faun. See *Prelude to "The Afternoon of a Faun."*

Agende [Ger.]. In the German Protestant (Evangelical) Church, the formularies for divine service; synonymous with *Kirchenordnung, Kirchenamt.* The term *Agende* was used from the 4th century C.E. to designate liturgical acts and subsequently the liturgical books containing directions for the execution of such acts. The *Rituale romanum* of 1614, as revised, is the Roman Catholic counterpart. Neither an *Agende* in any form nor the *Rituale romanum* has ever been universally applied or adopted. R.F.F.

Agevole [It.]. Easy, unconstrained.

Aggradevole [It.]. Pleasing.

Agiato, agiatamente [It.]. Sedate, with ease.

Agile, agilmente [It.]. Agile, with agility.

Agitato [It.]. Agitated.

Agnus Dei [Lat., Lamb of God]. The fifth item of the *Ordinary of the Roman *Mass, the received form consisting of three acclamations, each beginning "Agnus Dei" and derived from John 1:29. It was apparently added to the Mass late in the 7th century as a chant associated with the breaking of the communion bread. Numerous melodies were composed for the Agnus Dei during the Middle Ages, and their form (including at first even the number of acclamations) was quite varied. Like the *Kyrie, it is found in medieval sources with texts that have usually been thought to be additions to or elaborations of the received official text, though the priority of the latter is a matter of some debate [see Trope, Prosula]. The Agnus Dei has been widely used, though not prescribed, in the Anglican service of Holy Communion. For the complete text with translation, see Mass.

Bibl.: Martin Schildbach, "Das einstimmige Agnus Dei und seine handschriftliche Überlieferung vom 10. bis zum 16. Jahrhundert" (diss., Univ. of Erlangen, 1967). Charles M. Atkinson, "The Earliest Agnus Dei Melody and Its Tropes," *JAMS* 30 (1977): 1–19.

Agogic. (1) An agogic *accent is one created by duration rather than by loudness or metrical position. (2) In the plural form, *agogics,* those aspects of performance related to duration, and by extension tempo, in the way that *dynamics* are related to loudness; thus, the use of *rubato or other departures from strictly notated durations. Hugo Riemann coined the German term *Agogik* by analogy with *Dynamik* in 1884.

Agon [Gr., contest]. A ballet by Stravinsky (choreography by George Balanchine) composed in 1953–54 and 1956–57, and first produced in New York in 1957.

Agréments [Fr.]. Ornaments introduced in French music of the 17th century and soon widely used throughout Europe. They were generally indicated by stenographic signs or notes in small type. See Ornamentation.

Aguinaldo [Sp.]. A traditional religious song, most characteristically associated with the Christmas season, found in Iberia and in several countries of Latin America. It is a particularly important folk genre in

Puerto Rico, with sacred as well as secular texts and sharing many musical traits with the Puerto Rican *seis. D.S.

Ähnlich [Ger.]. Similar, like.

Aida. Opera in four acts by Verdi (libretto by Antonio Ghislanzoni from the French prose version by Camille du Locle of a scenario by Auguste Mariette Bey), produced in Cairo in 1871. Setting: Memphis and Thebes during the time of the pharaohs.

Air. A tune, whether vocal or instrumental. In the 16th century in France and England [see Ayre], the term applied essentially to vocal melodies, but its meaning was soon loosened. In operas and cantatas, simpler and more dancelike airs are distinguished from *recitatives, but in French Baroque style they are more declamatory than Italian *arias. Instrumental operatic excerpts are *airs à jouer* (as against *airs à chanter*), including dances *(airs de mouvement).* Seventeenth-century French serious songs (**airs de cour*) are a separate category from light ones (*airs à boire,* drinking songs). In Baroque suites, the practice of transcribing operatic airs resulted in the use of the title for newly composed tuneful movements that did not fit any dance category. B.G.

Air de cour [Fr., court air]. A type of French secular vocal music prominent in the last quarter of the 16th century and the first half of the 17th. The first published collection was printed by Le Roy and Ballard in 1571 and contains works for solo voice with lute accompaniment by Adrian Le Roy, who remarks in his preface that such pieces were formerly known as *voix de ville* [see *Vaudeville*]. Some of Le Roy's pieces are in fact arrangements of works for four voices by Nicolas de la Grotte published in 1570. Pieces for four or five voices predominate in the later 16th century and exist alongside the accompanied solos that predominate in the 17th. They are generally syllabic, homophonic, and without fixed meter, resembling in this respect **musique mesurée.* The texts are usually strophic, the first collections containing poems by Ronsard, Desportes, Baïf, and others. Later collections include translations of Italian poets such as Tasso and Guarini. Composers of 17th-century collections include Pierre Guédron (ca. 1570–ca. 1620), Antoine Boësset (1586–1643), Etienne Moulinié (ca. 1600–after 1669), and Jean de Cambefort (ca. 1605–61). Such works were also published in England, sometimes in translation.

Bibl.: D. P. Walker, "The Influence of *Musique mesurée* . . . on the *Airs de cour*," *MD* 2 (1948): 141–63. Kenneth Levy, "Vaudeville, vers mesurés, et airs de cour," in *Musique et poésie au XVIe siècle* (Paris: CNRS, 1953), pp. 185–201. Don Lee Royster, "Pierre Guédron and the *Air de cour*" (Ph.D. diss., Yale Univ., 1972).

Aires, los [Sp.]. See *Escondido.*

Air on the G String. Popular name for the second movement of Bach's Orchestral Suite no. 3 in D major BWV 1068, composed ca. 1729–31. In 1871, August Wilhelmj published an arrangement of the air for violin and piano, transposing it to C major in such a way that the tune could be played solely on the violin's lowest string, the G string.

Ais [Ger.]. A-sharp. See Pitch names.

Aisé [Fr.]. With ease.

Aisis [Ger.]. A-double-sharp. See Pitch names.

Ajouter [Fr.]. To add, e.g., an organ stop.

Akathistos [Gr.]. A celebrated, anonymous Byzantine **kontakion* in praise of Mary, possibly dating from the 6th century (and believed by some scholars to be the work of St. Romanos the Melode), that is chanted in Eastern churches in the Morning Office of the fifth Saturday of Lent. It consists of 2 *prooimia* and 24 *oikoi* [see Byzantine Chant], each *oikos* beginning with one of the 24 letters of the Greek alphabet. To each of the odd-numbered *oikoi* is appended a number of salutations for the Virgin. Music for the entire poem exists in manuscript; the earliest available settings date from the 13th century and are written in a highly melismatic style for soloist. It is very probable that the original chant was simple and syllabic. D.E.C.

Akkord [Ger.]. Chord.

Akolouthia [Gr.]. A late Byzantine anthology of settings both simple and florid for hymns, psalms, and other chants used in the *Divine Liturgy and the Office. St. Joannes Koukouzeles (active ca. 1300) is believed to have first edited this volume, which also bore the name *Papadikē.* In addition to compositions by Palaeologan composers, the earlier *Akolouthiai* also preserve vestiges of Constantinopolitan repertories from the 12th and 13th centuries, and a handful, both early and late, contain musical treatises. At present there exist 20 *Akolouthiai* from the 14th century, nearly three times that number from the 15th, and a great profusion after the fall of the empire. Chants in *kalophonic* style occupy the bulk of these collections. This style is chiefly recognizable by its use of the meaningless *teretismata* [see *Anenajki*] and its demanding virtuosity. D.E.C.

Akzessist, Accessist [Ger.]. In the 18th century, a younger member of a princely musical establishment who performed for little or no salary until a permanent position became available. Because payment lists do not usually include the unpaid *Akzessisten,* such lists may not reflect the true size of a princely *Kapelle.* E.K.W.

Al [It.]. To the, at the; e.g., *al *fine, al *segno.* See also *All', alla.*

À la, à l' [Fr.]. To the, at the; in the manner of, e.g., *à l'espagnol,* in the Spanish manner.

Alabado, alabanza [Sp.]. A religious song of praise originating in Spain and brought to the New World by Spanish missionaries. Often with modal melodies and other features reminiscent of earlier styles, *alabados* and *alabanzas* are found today in the folk traditions of several Latin American countries and among Hispanic communities in the U.S. D.S.

Alalá. A type of folk song from the Spanish province of Galicia, examples of which use syllables such as *la-la* and *ai-le-lo-la,* especially as refrains.

A la mi re, Alamire. See Hexachord.

Ālāp, ālāpa(na) [Hin., Skt., Tel.]. An unmetered and unpulsed, improvised prelude or vocalise in Indian music. Broadly speaking, it may include types of pulsed music, but drum accompaniment and meter are now rarely used. An abbreviated *ālāp (āocār ālāp)* normally precedes lighter forms of Hindustani instrumental music and performances of **khyāl* in which *ālāp* types of improvisation figure prominently. C.C.

Alba [Occ., dawn], **aube** [Fr.]. In the troubadour and trouvère repertories, a song portraying the parting of two lovers, who, after a secret, often illicit, nocturnal tryst, are awakened at sunrise and lament the too sudden arrival of day. A night watchman—at times the lovers' friend and ally—often plays a significant role. According to Bec, there are, at most, 18 such pieces in Old Occitan, 5 in Old French. Melodies survive for two southern examples (Giraut de Bornelh's well-known "Reis glorios" and Cadenet's "S'anc fui belha") as well as for one from the north (the anonymous "Gaite de la tor"). The genre may be of popular origin, and examples are found in Latin and German as well as Occitan and French. The few melodies that survive suggest a musical style not appreciably different from that of the courtly **canso.* The *Tagelied* (or *Wächterlied*) is the medieval German counterpart.

Bibl.: R. J. Taylor, "The Melodies of Mediaeval Romance and German Dawn Songs," in Arthur T. Hatto, ed., *Eos: An Enquiry into the Theme of Lovers' Meetings and Partings at Dawn in Poetry* (The Hague: Mouton, 1965), pp. 825–26. Peter Dronke, *The Medieval Lyric,* 2nd ed. (Cambridge: Cambridge U Pr, 1977), chap. 5. Pierre Bec, *La Lyrique française au moyen-âge,* 2 vols. (Paris: A & J Picard, 1977–78), 1:90–106, 2:24–30. Martín de Riquer, ed., *Las albas provezales* (Barcelona, 1944). Elizabeth W. Poe, "The Three Modalities of the Old Provençal Dawn Song," *Romance Philology* 37 (1984): 259–72. Elizabeth Aubrey, *The Music of the Troubadours* (Bloomington: Ind U Pr, 1996), pp. 102–105. Samuel N. Rosenberg, Margaret Switten, and Gérard Le Vot, eds., *Songs of the Troubadours and Trouvères* (New York: Garland, 1998), pp. 190–94. P.E., V.P., rev. E.A.

Albania. Art music began to be cultivated in Albania largely after World War II and received substantial state support from the communist government. Although the country was musically as well as politically isolated for several decades following the war, performing groups for opera, dance, and choral and instrumental music were established in Tiranë and elsewhere, as were institutions for advanced musical training. Notable Albanian art music composers of this generation include Tish Daija (b. 1926), Nikolla Zoraqi (1929–91), Tonin Harapi (1928–91), Feim Ibrahimi (1935–92), and Kristo Kono (1907–91), who wrote Albania's first indigenous operatic works.

The fall of communism in 1990–91 had a dramatic effect on the country's musical life. A great many of Albania's professional musicians left the country during this short time, causing ensembles and music schools to close or reduce their activities substantially. Composition and support of serious music continued, however, under the leadership of Daija, and the 1990s saw several new festivals founded as well as private and international arts partnerships forged. The next generation of Albanian composers, including Sokol Shupo (b. 1954), Thoma Gaqi (b. 1948), Shpëtim Kushta (b. 1949), Aleksandër Peçi (b. 1951), and Vasil Tole (b. 1963), has been quick to explore previously restricted styles and genres.

The folk music of Albania shows effects of early Greek, Roman, and especially Turkish occupation. Even today, urban popular music manifests the "oriental" influence of the Turks, who dominated the land from 1470 to 1912; nomadic rural peoples largely escaped this assimilation by withdrawing into isolated mountain villages. The musical dialects of the northern Gegs and the southern Tosks differ significantly. Vocal music of the former is dominated by monophonic epics, principally the heroic *këngë trimash* and *këngë kreshnikësh,* sung in recitative style and accompanied by a *çifteli* (two-string lute) or *lahutë* (one-string fiddle). The southern Tosks emphasize part-singing of two principal types: one employing two solo voices and choral drone, another entirely choral. The songs of both regions consist generally of regular strophes or of loosely arranged phrase pairs. Also important are lullabies and laments, usually sung by women, and the northern *maje krahe,* semimelodic mountain cries.

The chief instrumental music of Albania is that of shepherds, who play melodies relating to daily duties on wind instruments such as the *fyell* and *kavall* (end-blown flutes), the *zumare* (double clarinet), the *gajdë* (bagpipe), and the *cyla-diare* (double flute). Semiprofessional urban instrumental ensembles employ the *saze* (10-string lute), the *dajrë* (tambourine), and factory-made violins and clarinets. Field work for research on Albanian music lags behind that of neighboring countries, though recently groups such as the Institute of Folklore at the University of Tiranë have made significant advances. Albanian music began to be studied at the Institute of Folklore during the 1970s and 1980s, and since the opening of Albania's borders, the country's rich musical past has attracted increasing international attention.

Bibl.: Pyrrhus J. Ruches, *Albanian Historical Folksongs 1716–1943* (Chicago: Argonaut, 1967). Spiro Shituni, "The Relationship of Poetry and Music in the Albanian Folk

Songs," in *Probleme der Volksmusikforschung* (Bern: Lang, 1990): 232–40. June Emerson, *The Music of Albania* (Ampleforth, U.K.: Emerson, 1994). Fatmir Hysi, "Muzika Shqiptare ne nje kuader Mesdhetar [The Albanian Music in a Mediterranean Scope]," in *Mediterranean Music Conference/ Conferenza Musicale Mediterranea* (Mediterraneo Musica [MEMUS], 1995), pp. 51–65. Sokol Shupo, *Folklori muzikor shqiptar* (Tiranë: Botimet Enciklopedike, 1997). Bruno Reuer, "Musik in Albanien vor und nach der Wende 1991," in *Musik im Umbruch: Kulturelle Identitat und gesellschaftlicher Wandel in Sudosteuropa/New Countries, Old Sounds? Cultural Identity and Social Change in Southeastern Europe* (Munich: Sudostdeutsches Kulturwerk, 1999), pp. 123–33.

Albert Herring. Comic opera in three acts by Benjamin Britten (libretto by Eric Crozier, adapted from the short story "Le rosier de Madame Husson" by Guy de Maupassant), produced in Glyndebourne in 1947. Setting: a small market town in East Suffolk, 1900.

Alberti bass. An accompaniment figure, found frequently in the left hand of 18th-century keyboard music, in which the pitches of three-pitch chords are played successively in the order lowest, highest, middle, highest, as in the accompanying example by Mozart (Sonata in C major K. 545). The figure takes its

name from the composer Domenico Alberti (ca. 1710–40), who employed it frequently. The term is sometimes inappropriately extended to refer to any arpeggiated accompaniment figure in the left hand.

Albisiphone [It. *albisiphon, albisifono*]. A metal *Boehm-system flute of large bore invented in 1910 by Abelardo Albisi of Milan. The head section has a loop of tubing allowing the instrument to be held vertically. The name is usually applied to the bass instrument (the *baritono,* with lowest pitch B), but other sizes were made as well. M.S.

Alborada [Sp., dawn]. (1) Music performed at dawn, especially on a festive occasion or to honor an individual, as on a bride's wedding day. Other terms used in various regions of Spain include *alba, albae,* and *alborá.* (2) A type of Spanish folk music accompanied by the *dulzaina* (a double-reed instrument) and *tamboril* (drum). Some examples employ 6/8 meter in a way that is perhaps echoed in Ravel's composition for piano *Alborada del gracioso* (The Fool's Dawn Song, 1905) from *Miroirs.*

Album. The commercial unit for distributing recorded works longer than the approximately 6-minute maximum established by the two-sided, 10-inch, 78-rpm recording. The term also applies to the package in which more than two song-length performances ("singles") are sold.

In the 78-rpm era, very few recorded performances of popular music (including jazz numbers) exceeded 3 minutes. Because many classical compositions were longer, a 12-inch format was developed with them in mind. By the 1920s, sonatas, symphonies, and operas were being recorded in full, and the packages in which they appeared—typically several 12-inch recordings in a bound "book" of record sleeves—came to be called albums.

The record album's first purpose, then, was to reproduce larger works without having to shorten them drastically. Its second was established by the 1930s: to gather and reissue collections of records available only singly or no longer in circulation. By the early 1940s, jazz fans could buy multirecord sets featuring Louis Armstrong, Bix Beiderbecke, Earl Hines, Bessie Smith, and other artists in performances recorded during the 1920s and 1930s. Together with albums by particular artists, companies brought out anthologies focused on different styles (blues, boogie-woogie), locales (New Orleans, Kansas City), and instruments *(Hot Trombones, Tenor Saxophobia).*

The album's third purpose, to make a unified artistic statement, was promoted by the advent of the 33⅓-rpm long-playing (*LP) record, introduced in 1948 and containing up to 25 minutes per side. In jazz, unity could be established by events such as famous concerts: *The Duke Ellington Carnegie Hall Concerts: January 1943,* Charlie Parker and Dizzy Gillespie's *The Greatest Jazz Concert Ever* at Toronto's Massey Hall (1953), Keith Jarrett's *The Köln Concert* (1975). Or a landmark recording session might produce an album whose identity is thereafter preserved: the selection of tunes on Miles Davis's *Kind of Blue* (1959), for example, or John Coltrane's *A Love Supreme* (1965), a single album-length piece. In the popular mainstream, Frank Sinatra and his arrangers used the LP to record such "concept albums" as *Frank Sinatra Sings Only the Lonely* (1958), whose ten songs—composed over three decades by different songwriters—share a melancholy mood.

Many popular and jazz LPs from the 1950s into the 1980s were simply compilations of varied song-length selections, new or reissued. Yet the way record-jacket space could be filled—with pictures on the cover and explanatory words ("liner notes") on the back—encouraged the making of concept albums. (Folkways Records, which included liner notes with every issue, brought traditional music into the world of the album with such recordings as *Mountain Music Bluegrass Style* [1959].) In the late 1960s, rock bands such as the Moody Blues, the Who, and the Beatles created song albums based around a single theme, perhaps most famously the latter's *Sergeant Pepper's Lonely Hearts Club Band,* issued with full-color images of group members dressed in the mythical band's uniforms, and including the lyrics of every song. Another familiar rock and pop approach was the compilation of favorite numbers, as in *Elvis' Golden Records* (1958) or Ray Charles's *The Best of Atlantic,* anthologized from the years 1951–61.

In the 1980s, the arrival of digitized sound and the compact disc relegated the LP album to the past. The new unit, called the *CD, could hold more than 70 minutes of music, so even the longest works could be recorded in small, space-saving packages. In the classical sphere, the standard repertory was rerecorded and the reach of recordings extended by an archival impulse. More albums containing the whole of some repertory appeared: the complete piano music of Dvořák, for example, or, on a grander scale, the complete music of Mozart. In popular music and jazz, reissues abounded, with a vast proportion of the earlier recorded repertory made newly available, often in packages built around star performers or even composers (e.g., a two-disc set, *Gershwin Plays Gershwin*). Many older albums were reissued, and new ones were assembled from old parts. The "boxed set"—several CDs of a particular artist or group, such as the complete Miles Davis–Gil Evans collaborations of the 1950s, with a lengthy essay and precise discographical data—became a familiar album format of the 1990s. So did such annotated anthologies as *The Smithsonian Collection of Classic Country Music* (1990), offering gems from more than half a century of record making. Moreover, borrowing from the popular sphere, some classical musicians made concept albums of their own. For example, the Kronos Quartet's *Black Angels* (1990) brings together fresh recordings of works linked by subject matter (images related to war), in the belief that their mutual resonances have a collective impact beyond that of any one piece on the album. R.C.

Albumblatt [Ger., album leaf]. A fanciful title in the 19th century for short pieces, usually for piano, of a type once inscribed in autograph albums. The name does not imply any particular character or musical form.

Alceste. Opera in three acts by Gluck (Italian libretto by Raniero de Calzabigi after Euripides) produced in Vienna in 1767. A revised French version (translated by François Louis Gaud le Bland du Roullet) was produced in Paris in 1776. Gluck's dedication to the first edition (1769) sets out his views on the reform of opera (trans. in *SR,* pp. 673–75). Setting: Thessaly in ancient times.

Aleatory music. Music in which deliberate use is made of chance or indeterminacy; the term chance music is preferred by many composers. The indeterminate aspect may affect the act of composition, the performance, or both. In the first instance, some random process, such as throwing dice (the original meaning of aleatory being "according to the throw of a die"), is used to fix certain compositional decisions: e.g., the choice of pitches or rhythmic values. In the second, the performer (or performers) makes certain compositional decisions in a given realization of a piece: e.g., the number of segments played or the order in which they are played or the specific pitches or durations used.

Although aleatory music, especially in its more extreme forms, is principally a phenomenon of the later 20th century, precedents are found throughout Western musical history. Medieval theorists, for example, occasionally recommend the permutation of a given succession of pitches as a mechanical aid to melodic invention; and musical dice games, in which choices are made among a number of available possibilities with the aid of dice, were popular in the 18th century. In the early 20th century, Charles Ives at times allowed the performer certain alternatives (for example, the number of times a measure is to be played, or even whether or not an entire section will be played), and such tendencies were later developed further by Henry Cowell, especially in his String Quartet no. 3 of 1935, known as the *Mosaic* Quartet, which consists of a number of separate segments that have to be "assembled" by the players. The terms open form and mobile form have since been applied to works of this type. It should also be noted that the use of chance played a significant role in the work of Marcel Duchamp, as well as other artists and writers associated with the Dada movement.

The major figure in the evolution of modern aleatory music is John Cage, whose *Music of Changes,* a piano piece composed in 1951, was the first composition to be largely determined by random procedures. For this work, Cage tossed coins and used the results to choose configurations from the *I Ching,* a Chinese book of oracles, which in turn led to the selection of pitches, durations, dynamics, etc. Cage, along with Morton Feldman and Earle Brown (with whom he was in close association during the early 1950s), had an important influence on a number of younger composers and artists working in America, including those involved with the Fluxus movement in New York (Nam June Paik), the ONCE group in Ann Arbor (Robert Ashley, Gordon Mumma, Roger Reynolds), and the San Francisco Tape Center (Pauline Oliveros, Morton Subotnick), all active during the 1960s.

Cage visited Europe several times during the 1950s, and his ideas also had a significant impact on a number of younger European composers of the time, including Pierre Boulez and Karlheinz Stockhausen. But whereas Cage's own approach to indeterminacy has always been essentially unsystematic, even mystical, in character, the Europeans tended to a more theoretical conception of aleatory music with a more limited range of choices. In Stockhausen's *Zyklus* for one percussionist, for example, all pitches and timbres are strictly specified; choice is allowed only in the temporal placement of individual events (and even these must be placed within certain carefully prescribed boundaries) and in the determination of a starting point and the "direction" (i.e., whether backward or forward) in which the piece will be played.

The degree of leeway left to a performer may vary widely in aleatory music and is closely tied to the notational system used. Certain scores by Brown, Robert Moran, and Anestis Logothetis, for example, are purely graphic, containing no traditional notation at all. The performer is thus allowed to interpret the "score" more or less freely, with little if any specific instruction. Other works, such as LaMonte Young's "instructive" scores and Stockhausen's *Aus den sieben Tagen,* are completely verbal. More commonly, however, one finds a mixture of traditional and graphic notation, with some elements specified while others are left to the performer's choice (e.g., Brown's *Available Forms*). The incorporation of indeterminate processes in computer music applications, dating back to the "stochastic" works of Iannis Xenakis, has contributed to its continued importance in more recent music. See also Notation.

Bibl.: Pierre Boulez, "Alea," *Nouvelle revue française,* no. 59 (1957); trans. in *PNM* 3 (1964/65): 42–53. John Cage, "Indeterminacy," in his *Silence* (Middletown, Conn.: Wesleyan U Pr, 1961), pp. 35–40. Roger Reynolds, "Indeterminacy: Some Considerations," *PNM* 4 (1965/66): 136–40. Leonard G. Ratner, "*Ars combinatoria:* Chance and Choice in 18th-Century Music," *Geiringer,* 1970, pp. 343–63. Michael Nyman, *Experimental Music: Cage and Beyond* (London: Cassell and Collier Macmillan, 1974). Terence J. O'Grady, "Aesthetic Value in Indeterminate Music," *MQ* 67 (1981): 366–81. James Pritchett, *The Music of John Cage* (New York: Cambridge U Pr, 1993). R.P.M.

Alexander Nevsky. Music by Prokofiev for a film directed in 1938 by Sergei Eisenstein. In 1939, Prokofiev reworked it as a cantata for mezzo soprano, chorus, and orchestra with text by himself and Vladimir Lugorsky.

Al fine [It.]. See *Fine.*

Algorithmic composition. The use of a predefined procedure or set of rules (an algorithm), often automated by computer, to produce a musical work. Such works need not be intended for reproduction by electro-acoustic means. Although examples can be found throughout the history of Western music, widespread use of the technique and of the term emerged in the second half of the 20th century. Early examples from this period occur in the works of Lejaren Hiller and Iannis Xenakis. The technique has followed closely advances in computing and artificial intelligence.

Bibl.: Curtis Roads, ed., *The Music Machine: Selected Readings from the Computer Music Journal* (Cambridge, Mass.: MIT Pr, 1989). Bruce L. Jacob, "Algorithmic Composition as a Model of Creativity," *Organised Sound* 1, no. 3 (1996).

Aliquotstimmen [Ger.]. Organ stops sounding intervals above the unison other than the octave (i.e., twelfth, 2⅔′; seventeenth, 1⅗′; etc.).

Aliquot string. A *sympathetic string. The terms aliquot stringing and aliquot scaling are applied to pianos (such as those by the firm of Blüthner) that employ such strings or that arrange the strings of the upper register in such a way that the portion of each string between the bridge and the hitch pin will act as a sympathetic string.

All', alla [It.]. To the, at the; in the manner of. See, e.g., *Ongarese, Ottava, Unisono, Turca, Zingarese.*

Alla breve [It., at the breve]. The *meter indicated with the sign ¢, in which each measure is conceived as consisting of two half notes, each given one beat, rather than the four quarter notes indicated with the sign c. It is thus the equivalent of 2/2 as compared with 4/4. It is sometimes referred to as cut time. In modern practice this implies relatively rapid tempo, as in military marches, which often employ this meter. But its use with respect to tempo varied considerably from the 17th through the 19th century, so it cannot always be regarded as indicating rapid tempo. Historically *alla breve* derives from the system of *proportions, in use in the Middle Ages and Renaissance, in which it indicated that the *tactus* or metrical pulse was to be "at the breve" rather than "at the semibreve" [see Mensural notation]. Thus it represented in theory, as it still does, a diminution of the duration of any note value by one-half, given a fixed tempo or rate of beats, and was known as *tempus imperfectum diminutum* or *proportio dupla.* It could also be represented in that system by the fraction 2/1. When occurring in all voices simultaneously, however, it could represent a faster *tactus,* but not necessarily in the ratio 2:1.

Allant [Fr.]. (1) Going, stirring; continuing. (2) **An-dante.*

Allargando [It.]. Broadening, becoming slower, sometimes with an accompanying **crescendo.*

Alle [Ger.]. All, *tutti.

Allegramente [It.]. **Allegro.*

Allegretto [It.]. (1) Slightly less fast than **allegro,* often implying lighter texture or character as well. See Performance marks. (2) A short piece with the tempo mark *allegro* or *allegretto.*

Allegro [It., merry, lively]. (1) Fast. Although the term has been used since the 17th century to indicate a fast or moderately fast tempo and is the single most widely used term for such a tempo since the 18th century, it continued to be used into the 18th century as an indication of character or mood without respect to tempo. See Performance marks. (2) A movement in a fast or moderately fast tempo, especially the first movement, in *sonata form (whence sonata-allegro), of a sonata, symphony, or similar work.

Allein [Ger.]. Alone.

Alleluia [Lat., fr. Heb. **hallelujah,* praise ye the

Lord]. (1) An expression of praise to God occurring in Psalms 110–18 (111–13, 115–17) and in the Book of Revelation (19:1, 3, 4, 6), in the latter case as the cry "of a great multitude" in heaven. As a general expression of rejoicing both inside and outside the liturgy it is attested by St. Augustine (d. 430) and others, and as such it plays a prominent part in the liturgy of the Christian church. In *Gregorian chant, it is found in different types of chants especially for the Easter season, which celebrates the resurrection. It is absent from seasons of somber character such as Lent.

(2) In Gregorian chant, the item of the *Proper of the *Mass sung before the reading of the Gospel except in the period from Septuagesima Sunday through Lent to Holy Saturday, when the *tract is sung instead, and in three of the four groups of Ember Days [see Liturgy]. From Saturday after Easter to Friday after Pentecost two alleluias are sung, one substituting for the gradual. Its texts consist of the word alleluia followed by a verse often drawn from the Psalms. Its melodies are *melismatic, and a characteristic feature is the melisma, called the *jubilus,* with which the setting of the word alleluia itself concludes. This melisma often recurs at the end of the verse and may include internal repetitions in various forms. Alleluia and verse may be similar in other respects as well. The first part of the alleluia itself is sung by soloists, after which the choir repeats the first part and continues with the *jubilus.* The soloists then sing the verse except for the conclusion, which is sung by the choir, and repeat the alleluia, the concluding *jubilus* again being sung by the choir. The alleluia is thus usually regarded as an example of responsorial *psalmody. Some are preserved in early sources with two or three verses. It is unlikely that these are remnants of complete Psalms. Pope Gregory the Great (pope from 590 to 604) is often credited with distributing the singing of alleluia through parts of the year other than the Easter season. But there is no evidence for the origins of the specific form with one or more verses that is preserved in liturgical documents beginning in the 8th or 9th century. The alleluia repertory grew steadily in the following centuries, and even in the earliest part of the repertory, some melodies are shared by more than one text.

Bibl.: Karl-Heinz Schlager, *Thematischer Katalog der ältesten Alleluia-Melodien aus Handschriften des 10. und 11. Jahrhunderts* (Munich: W Ricke, 1965). Id., ed., *Alleluia-Melodien I: bis 1100, MMMA* 7 (Kassel: Bärenreiter, 1968). James W. McKinnon, "Preface to the Study of the Alleluia," EMH, 15 (1996): 213–49.

Allemande [Fr., German; It. *alemana, allemanda;* Eng. allemand, almain, alman]. (1) A Renaissance and Baroque dance that was cultivated as an independent instrumental piece ca. 1580–1750. It became the first of the four core movements of the solo *suite. In its mature Baroque form (ca. 1660–1750), its characteristics had more to do with idiomatic instrumental writing than with dance rhythms. In solo harpsichord, lute, and viol music, it ordinarily has quadruple meter and binary form, beginning with one or more upbeats and proceeding to cadences on downbeats in phrases of irregular lengths. Its texture is permeated with imitation and **style brisé* figures that obscure a sense of clear-cut melodic phrases; its mood is serious and its tempo moderately slow [see Ex. 1]. Fast allemandes exist as well, but are more common in instrumental ensemble music, in which the texture is often less imitative [see Ex. 2].

The allemande originated in the early or mid-16th

1. D'Anglebert, Allemande (1689). 2. Corelli, Allemanda, Trio Sonata op. 2 no. 3 (1685).

century as a "German dance" *(Teutschertanz, bal tedesco).* It was a fast dance in duple meter often followed by a triple-meter *Nachtanz.* It continued to be danced throughout the 17th and 18th centuries, but was already stylized by the Elizabethan virginalists (e.g., in the *Fitzwilliam Virginal Book*), who often wrote successive strains of music that exploited scalar figuration and motivic interchange. French lutenists (Denis Gaultier) and harpsichordists (Chambonnières) developed the richer texture described above, and these usually slower allemandes were the principal models for German harpsichordists (Froberger, Bach). Allemandes for chamber ensembles tended to retain the homophonic texture of choreographed music (H. L. Hassler, Scheidt, Pachelbel), but were more imitative in Italy and especially England (William Lawes). They varied widely in tempo from *largo* to *presto* (Corelli). In the late 18th century, when composers occasionally wrote allemandes, they returned even in keyboard music to the fast duple meter with homophonic texture of the dance as it was performed then in Switzerland and Germany, although Mozart wrote one in the Baroque style (K. 385i).

(2) A dance in triple meter originating in the mid-18th century. It involved the giving of both hands to the partner, from which evolved the American square-dance call. The name was applied loosely to a number of waltzlike dances through the 19th century as an equivalent of "German Dance."

Bibl.: Ernst Mohr, *Die Allemande* (Leipzig: Kommissionsverlag von gebr. Hug, 1932). Richard Hudson, *The Allemande, the Balletto, and the Tanz* (Cambridge: Cambridge U Pr, 1986). B.G.

Allentando, allentamente [It.]. Slowing down.

Alliteration. The use of two or more words in close succession that begin with (or include) the same sound, usually a consonant. It is an important feature of the oldest poetry in all of the Germanic languages (in which context it is known as *Stabreim*) and was taken up by Wagner in imitation of this tradition in his *Der Ring des Nibelungen.*

Allmählich [Ger.]. Gradually.

Allo. [It.]. Abbr. for **allegro.*

All' ottava [It.]. See *Ottava.*

All' unisono [It.]. See Unison.

Almain, alman. In early English sources, the *allemande.

Alma Redemptoris Mater [Lat., Nourishing Mother of the Redeemer]. One of the four *antiphons for the Blessed Virgin Mary. Formerly attributed to Hermannus Contractus (d. 1054), it is sung in modern practice at Compline through Advent to the Purification (February 2). The more ornate of the two melodies preserved in modern chant books was set polyphonically numerous times beginning in the 13th century (in the Montpellier, Bamberg, and Las Huelgas MSS), especially in the 15th and 16th centuries (by Dufay, Dunstable, Obrecht, Ockeghem, Josquin, Palestrina, Victoria), and provided material for some polyphonic Masses of the Renaissance as well (by Power, Mouton, Victoria).

Almérie [Fr.]. A type of lute invented by Jean Lemaire (d. ca. 1650), the name being an anagram of his own name.

Alpensinfonie, Eine [Ger., An Alpine Symphony]. A symphonic poem by Richard Strauss, op. 64 (1911–15), describing a day in the Alps. The work is in 22 short, continuously connected sections and requires an orchestra of over 150 players.

Alphorn. A long wooden trumpet of the Alps made in various forms, usually straight with a small upturned bell, but also S-shaped. It ranges in length from 1.5 to 4 m. and is characteristically a shepherd's instrument, used for signaling over long distances. It is known by various names elsewhere in Europe. See ill. under Brass instruments; see also Lur (2), *Trutruka.*

Alpine Symphony, An. See *Alpensinfonie, Eine.*

Al segno [It.]. See *Segno.*

Also sprach Zarathustra [Ger., Thus Spake Zarathustra]. A symphonic poem by Richard Strauss, op. 30 (1896), based on Friedrich Nietzsche's prose work of the same title.

Alt. (1) [Ger.] *Alto, as a designation both for voices and (in compounds such as *Altklarinette, Altsaxophon*) instruments. (2) [fr. It. *in alto*] In the phrase *in alt,* the range of pitches lying one octave above the treble staff, from g″ to f‴. The pitches of the next higher octave are said to be *in altissimo.*

Alta [It., Sp.]. (1) A 15th-century dance that, according to the Italian dance master Antonio Cornazano (*Libro dell'arte del danzare,* ca. 1455), was the Spanish equivalent of the **saltarello* or the *passo brabante* [Fr. **pas de Brabant*]. An *alta* could be danced to any of the *bassedanze* (**basse danse*) tunes. The extant music of the 15th-century *bassedanze* consists only of long-note tenors, but an *Alta* by Francesco de la Torre (ca. 1500) written for three instruments on the tenor "Il Re de Spagna" [see *Spagna*] provides an excellent example of the kind of music that might have been improvised on a *bassadanza* tune in the earlier period (*HAM,* no. 102a). (2) In the 15th century, an ensemble of loud instruments, usually two or three *shawms and a *sackbut (see Johannes Tinctoris, *De inventione et usu musicae,* ca. 1487). The ensemble might also include trumpets and drums. See also *Haut.* L.H.M.

Altenberg Lieder [Ger., Altenberg Songs]. Five songs for voice and orchestra by Berg, op. 4 (1912). The full title is *Fünf Orchesterlieder nach Ansichts-*

kartentexten von Peter Altenberg (Five Orchestral Songs on Picture-Postcard Texts by Peter Altenberg).

Alteration. (1) The raising or lowering of a pitch by means of an *accidental, also termed chromatic alteration. (2) See Mensural notation.

Altered chord. In tonal harmony, a chord in which one or more pitches has been altered by an accidental and thus does not belong to the scale of the operative key, e.g., the Neapolitan and augmented *sixth chords. See Harmonic analysis.

Alternatim [Lat., alternately]. The practice of two or more contrasting forces taking turns in performing music for a liturgical text, each taking only one verse or short section at a time. The contrast might be of soloists *(cantores)* versus choir *(schola),* polyphony versus monophonic plainchant, organ *versets versus vocal plainchant, or more complicated juxtapositions of any of these elements. The practice can be traced back to antiphonal psalmody in the early Christian church and later included the alternation of Notre Dame organum with plainchant. By the 15th century, alternatim practice was widespread for a great variety of liturgical categories, including the Ordinary of the Mass. One element of the alternation remained monophonic plainchant, but the contrasting verses might be sung in **fauxbourdon* or newly composed polyphony (Dufay). In the later Renaissance, vocal polyphony for use in alternatim performance was quite significant (Palestrina, Morales, Taverner), but was more common for the Magnificat, sequences, and hymns than for the Mass Ordinary. As early as the 14th century, the organ supplied polyphony, in which case the odd-numbered verses of text were omitted altogether. This role for the organ grew steadily in importance in the late Renaissance [see Organ Mass]. Until the middle of the 17th century, organ versets were based on the chants they replaced, thus invoking if not presenting the appropriate words. During the next hundred years this large organ literature made little reference to a *cantus firmus,* reaching its artistic zenith and liturgical nadir in France (François Couperin). The church eventually stipulated that the omitted words be spoken by the choir, but the practice of improvising alternatim organ music survived even the reforms of the 1903 *motu proprio;* it can still be heard occasionally in Paris. B.G.

Alternativo [It.], **alternativement** [Fr.]. Eighteenth-century indications to play two movements as a pair in alternation, that is, to repeat the first one after playing the second. The terms are attached to either member of a pair of dances such as minuets, bourrées, passepieds, etc. The second is often labeled trio because of its reduced texture and is generally in the opposite mode or in a related key. In modern tradition, documented rarely in the 18th century, the internal repetitions of the first dance are often omitted during its second playing. *Alternativo* was used by Schumann to designate the middle sections of intermezzos in his op. 4. B.G.

Altgeige [Ger.]. (1) *Viola alta. (2) Viola (now rarely).

Althorn [Ger.]. See Alto horn.

Altissimo [It.]. See *Alt* (2).

Altistin [Ger.]. A contralto singer.

Alto [It.]. (1) A low female voice, also called a contralto. For its approximate range see Voice. (2) A high male voice, sung with *falsetto, often called a countertenor. (3) The second highest part (thus lying below the soprano and above the tenor) in the normal four-part vocal texture. (4) [It., Fr.] Viola. (5) In families of instruments such as the flute, clarinet, and saxophone, the second, third, or even fourth highest member, depending upon whether there are members higher than the soprano (e.g., sopranino, piccolo). See also Clef.

Alto horn [Ger. *Althorn;* Fr. *saxhorn tenor;* Eng. also tenor horn; It. *flicorno contralto;* Sp. *bugle contralto*]. A valved brass instrument in E♭, a fifth lower than the modern cornet or trumpet. It has about 2.1 m. (7 ft.) of tube length, usually folded in an upright tuba form with the bell straight up or turned partly forward. Small circular models called mellophones, large circular ones called cavalry horns, as well as trumpet, oval, and over-shoulder shapes are also encountered. All of these instruments came into being as members of various families of brass instruments invented during the 1830s and 1840s. Alto horns found extensive use in European and American brass bands during the last half of the 19th century. In concert bands of the turn of the century, however, their solo and obbligato roles were largely lost to the French horn and euphonium. They continue to be used in English brass bands as well as in some military and school bands. Their written range is that of the cornet (f♯ to c‴), and they sound a major sixth lower than written. Their tone is mellow and undistinguished, blending well with similar instruments. Their proportions are based on those of the *bugle-*flugelhorn family. See ills. under Brass instruments. R.E.E.

Alto moderne [Fr.]. **Viole-ténor.*

Alto Rhapsody. See *Rhapsodie (Fragment aus Goethe's Harzreise im Winter).*

Altra volta [It.]. *Encore.

Altus [Lat.]. *Alto (3). See also Contratenor.

Alzato, alzati [It.]. Raised, removed (e.g., a mute or mutes).

Amabile [It.]. Amiable, lovable.

Amahl and the Night Visitors. Opera in one act by Gian Carlo Menotti (setting his own libretto), composed for and produced on television in New York in 1951; first produced on the stage at Indiana University in 1952. Setting: near Bethlehem at the time of the birth of Jesus.

Amaro, amarevole [It.]. Bitter, bitterly.

Ambitus [Lat.]. The range of pitches employed in a melody or voice. It is an important determinant of mode in the usual description of the system of church modes employed in liturgical chant and in some repertories of early polyphony. For the ambitus of individual modes, see Mode.

Amboss [Ger.]. *Anvil.

Ambrosian chant. Latin liturgical chant tradition of Milan, preserved in about 300 northern Italian manuscripts, mostly of the 12th century and later (*CLLA* 501–95). Though named for the great Milanese bishop St. Ambrose (ca. 340–97, bishop from 374), most of the repertory developed after his time. Ambrose did, however, write a few strophic hymns in iambic meter (*CPL* 163) that became models for the medieval "Ambrosian" hymn, and it was during Ambrose's reign that a new kind of congregational psalmody was introduced at Milan.

Because of its reputed link to St. Ambrose, the rite of Milan was better able to resist the repeated efforts at Romanization that overwhelmed the other local Western chant traditions; thus it preserved many interesting archaic features. The Ambrosian office preserves some of the structures of the 4th-century Greek rite of Jerusalem: the morning Office includes three canticles, Gospel readings, and a procession to the Cross, while Vespers begins with a *lucernarium,* or lamplighting. Besides the antiphons of the psalmody, there are more substantial antiphons *in choro* and *ad crucem,* processional *psallendae,* and responsorial *lucernaria.* The responsories *cum pueris,* sung by the boys' choir, are embellished with lengthy *melodiae,* the repeated-phrase structure of which recalls the Gregorian *sequences. A 9th-century Carolingian reform brought in some Gregorian antiphons, and the singing of Psalms 109 [110]–147 at Vespers, as in the Gregorian and Benedictine Offices. Psalms 1–108 [109] were sung in the morning, but distributed over a two-week period instead of one week as at Rome. This may reflect a time when the monastic practice of singing all 150 psalms in one week had not yet become the Western norm.

Some Mass chants are textually and musically related to pieces in the *Gregorian and *Old Roman traditions, but there are also important differences. The eight church modes were never adopted at Milan. The Ambrosian *ingressa* and *transitorium* lack the psalm verses of the corresponding Gregorian introit and communion. The offertories are often responsorial, like the Gregorian offertories. The *psalmellus* is generally more melismatic than the Gregorian gradual, as is the small repertory of alleluias, which have a longer *jubilus* at the repeat than at the beginning. The Ambrosian *cantus* is often shorter and simpler than the Gregorian tract. The antiphons *post evangelium* (and *ante* for high feasts) have no Roman equivalent but may be related to the chants sung in the Jerusalem Mass while the clergy washed their hands. Indeed many Ambrosian chants are related to texts sung in the Greek rites. A variable *confractorium* is sung instead of Agnus Dei. The Ambrosian Mass Ordinary consists only of Gloria, Credo, and Sanctus, though like many Psalms in the Office, the Gloria ends in a triple Kyrie. Litanies replace the Gloria in Lent. There are few melodies for the Ordinary chants; in the 15th century, the polyphonic *motetti missales* were often sung in their place.

Reformed after the Council of Trent by St. Carlo Borromeo (b. 1538, archbishop of Milan 1566–84), the Ambrosian chant was revived in the 20th century under bishops Achille Ratti (later Pope Pius XI) and Ildefonso Schuster, with the melodies edited by Dom Gregorio Sunyol. The liturgical books were completely revised and translated into Italian during the 1970s after Vatican Council II.

Bibl.: *PM* 5–6. Marco Magistretti, ed., *Beroldus, sive Ecclesiae Ambrosianae Mediolanensis Kalendarium et Ordines, saec. XII* (Milan: 1894). Marco Magistretti, *Monumenta veteris liturgiae ambrosianae,* 3 vols. (Milan: U Hoepli, 1897–1905). *Breviarium Ambrosianum S. Carolo Archiepiscopo editus,* 2 vols. in 4 (Milan: Cogliati, 1902). Achille Ratti and Marco Magistretti, eds., *Missale Ambrosianum duplex (Proprium de Tempore) Editt. Puteobonellianae et Typicae (1751–1902) cum critico commentario continuo ex manuscriptis schedis Ant. M. Ceriani,* Monumenta Sacra et Profana 4 (Milan: R. Ghirlanda, 1913). W. C. Bishop, *The Mozarabic and Ambrosian Rites* (London: A R Mowbray, 1924). *Antiphonale Missarum juxta ritum Sanctae Ecclesiae Mediolanensis* [ed. Gregorio M. Sunyol] (Rome: Desclée, 1935). *Liber Vesperalis juxta rium Sanctae Ecclesiae Mediolanensis* [ed. Gregorio M. Sunyol] (Rome: Desclée, 1939). Gregorio Suñol, "La Restaurazione ambrosiana," *Ambrosius* 14 (1938): 145–50, 174–77, 196–200, 296–304; 15 (1939): 113–16; 16 (1940): 12–16, 108–12. Michel Hugo et al., *Fonti e paleografia del canto ambrosiano* (Milan, 1956). Rembert Weakland, "The Performance of Ambrosian Chant in the Twelfth Century," *Reese,* 1966, pp. 856–66. Thomas Noblitt, "The Ambrosian Motetti Missales Repertory," *MD* 22 (1968): 77–103. Gabriele Winkler, "Das Offizium am Ende des 4. Jahrhunderts und das heutige chaldäische Offizium," *Ostkirchliche Studien* 19 (1970): 289–311. Josef Schmitz, *Gottesdienst im altchristlichen Mailand* (Cologne: P Hanstein, 1975). E. T. Moneta Caglio, "Manoscritti di canto ambrosiano rinvenuti nell'ultimo ventennio," *Ambrosius* 52 (1976): 27–36. Terence Bailey, "Ambrosian Choral Psalmody: The Formulae," *Rivista internazionale di musica sacra* 1 (1980): 300–328. Terence Bailey, *The Ambrosian Alleluias* (Englefield Green, Surrey: Plainsong and Mediaeval Music Soc, 1983). Chrysogonus Waddell, ed., *The Twelfth-Century Cistercian Hymnal,* 2 vols., Cistercian Liturgy Series 1–2 (Trappist, Ky.: Gethsemani Abbey, 1984). Terence Bailey, *The Ambrosian Cantus,* Musicological Studies 47 (Ottawa:

Institute of Mediaeval Music, 1987). Terence Bailey and Paul Merkley, *The Antiphons of the Ambrosian Office,* Musicological Studies 50/1 (Ottawa: Institute of Mediaeval Music, 1989). Bailey and Merkley, *The Melodic Tradition of the Ambrosian Office-Antiphons.* Musicological Studies 50/2 (Ottawa: Institute of Mediaeval Music, 1990). Angelo Paredi, *Storia del rito ambrosiano* (Milan: Edizioni O. R., 1990). Jacques Fontaine et al., eds., *Ambroise de Milan: Hymnes: Texte établi, traduit et annoté* (Paris: Cerf, 1992). Ansgar Franz, *Tageslauf und Heilsgeschichte: Untersuchungen zum literarischen Text und liturgischen Kontext der Tagzeitenhymnen des Ambrosius von Mailand* (St. Ottilien, 1994). Terence Bailey, *Antiphon and Psalm in the Ambrosian Office,* Musicological Studies 50/3 (Ottawa: Institute of Mediaeval Music, 1994). Terence Bailey, "The Development and Chronology of the Ambrosian Sanctorale: The Evidence of the Antiphon Texts," *The Divine Office in the Latin Middle Ages: Methodology and Source Studies, Regional Developments, Hagiography,* ed. Margot E. Fassler, Rebecca A. Baltzer (Oxford: Oxford U Pr, 2000), pp. 257–77. Rembert Weakland, "The Office Antiphons of Ambrosian Chant," Ph.D. diss., Columbia U, 2000. P.J.

Ambrosian hymns. The hymns of the Gregorian and Ambrosian chant repertories attributed to St. Ambrose (ca. 340–97). Although a great many hymns were formerly attributed to him, only six can be so ascribed with any confidence: four ("Aeterne rerum conditor," "Deus Creator omnium," "Jam surgit hora tertia," and "Veni Redemptor gentium") on the basis of statements by St. Augustine and two ("Illuxit orbi" and "Bis ternas horas") on the basis of statements by Cassiodorus. It is not certain that any of the surviving melodies is by Ambrose. See also Hymn, *Te Deum.*

Âme [Fr., soul]. *Sound post.

Amen [Heb., so be it]. An expression used variously by Christians, Jews, and Muslims as an affirmative response to prayers, readings, hymns, or other texts. In the Roman rite and the liturgical music associated with it, Amen occurs at the end of the lesser *doxology and at the end of the Gloria and Credo of the Mass. In polyphonic settings of the Gloria and Credo, it is often set as a separate section, and from the 17th century onward, settings of it are often in fugal style. It is treated similarly in nonliturgical music (e.g., the Amen chorus in Handel's *Messiah*). In Protestant traditions, it is often sung to a plagal *cadence following hymns.

Amen cadence. A plagal *cadence, frequently sung to the word Amen at the conclusion of Protestant hymns.

Amener [Fr., from *branle à mener*]. A Baroque dance movement in moderate triple time with phrases of six measures (3 + 3 or 4 + 2). Like a sarabande, it tends to have accented dotted notes on the second beat. In the first half of the 17th century, it was a type of *branle, similar in style to early versions of the *minuet. It is occasionally found in instrumental suites (J. C. F. Fischer, Poglietti). By ca. 1700 it could refer to any sort of branle, and later composers (Telemann) used the title occasionally in this looser manner. B.G.

American Federation of Musicians. The largest union of professional musicians, formed in 1896 and chartered by the American Federation of Labor; in 1900 it expanded its representation to include Canada as well as the U.S. James Petrillo, president from 1940 to 1968, became a widely known and pivotal figure in the union's development.

American Guild of Organists. See Societies, musical.

American Indian music. Also termed Native American music and, in Canada, First Nations music. The traditional, and traditionally based, music of culturally separate societies of aboriginal peoples of North, Central, and South America. Most of it is distinct from the European- and African-derived music in which these peoples also participate, but it does include musical forms and social contexts combining traditional and Western elements. [For the mixed styles of Central and South America, see *Latin America.] Although it comprises hundreds of cultures and discrete musical systems of varying degrees of complexity, American Indian music is essentially unified, sharing important characteristics: it is almost exclusively monophonic, predominantly vocal with percussion accompaniment, and although entirely an oral tradition, it consists of composed songs that are transmitted intact, with little if any improvisation. A very large proportion is religious or ritual expression, and much of it accompanies dancing. A good deal of it is sung to meaningless though set vocables. A small number of formal and scalar principles dominate. Music plays a very important role in the religious, social, recreational, and even political life of these cultures. While North and South American Indian musics exhibit similarities, each continent has its distinctive characteristics.

I. *Music in Indian culture.* Tribes that have similar cultures also tend to have similar musical styles. For example, the buffalo-hunting Plains Indians of North America and the sedentary Pueblo Indians of the southwestern U.S. account for two musical style areas. The Andean highlands constitute another such area. Musical style does not correlate as well with areas determined by language relationships. Peoples with complex cultures, such as the Hopi or Zuñi, normally have more complex music than the much simpler and smaller tribes of central California or the Amazon valley.

Music played a variety of roles in Indian societies before contact with Europe. In addition to forming part of many religious services and of quasi-religious events such as ritual gambling games and social ceremonies, music was an accompaniment of social dances, healing, events in the year and life cycle, preparation for and conclusion of war, recounting of history, and informal social gatherings. In many cultures, music symbolized and personalized supernatural power, which was transmitted from spirits to humans through the teaching of songs. Although most Indians had relatively simple material culture and economic organization, each tribe had a large number and variety of ceremonies, public and private, that required specific music, and tribal repertories went into thousands of songs.

Music was usually judged by the degree to which it fulfilled religious and other functions and effectively helped to provide food, water, and health, rather than by specifically musical criteria. Music played an important role in origin myths, underscoring its important role in society. The Havasupai of the Grand Canyon believed that spirits who preceded humanity on earth sang rather than spoke to each other. The Amuesha of Peru believed that learning to sing brought order and human culture out of chaos. In Montana Blackfoot mythology, music was given by the culture hero to be used as an aid in times of trouble.

While some peoples recognized strictly human composition of songs, there was a widespread belief that music comes to humans from the supernatural in dreams and visions, and in some tribes these visions, central events in spiritual life, were legitimized by the singing of new songs. The Pima of Arizona thought that songs existed unheard in the cosmos and had to be "unraveled" by humans who dreamed them. Most Indian tribes did not have systematic methods for teaching music, but accurate rendition was required by some cultures, such as the Navaho, in whose ceremonies an error required the repetition of hourlong sections, and the Kwakiutl of British Columbia, who punished mistakes. Ordinarily, there were no professional musicians; the musical specialists were those who had special ceremonial and religious roles—medicine men, shamans, and priests.

Most Indian poetry is sung. Language may be altered in singing, syllables and words repeated, meaningless syllables inserted. While rhyme and meter are normally absent, linguistic features such as accent, syllable length, and (in *tone languages) pitch are observed in musical setting. Except for imitation of animal cries, musical representation of nonmusical ideas or objects was not found; but the fact that different functions such as gambling, dancing, and narration provided the basis for musical distinction is a related phenomenon.

Little music, though some, was performed strictly for passive listening. Performers were judged by their religious powers, but also by the extent of their repertories and in some cases by their ability to sing high (in the Plains) or low (in the Pueblos), to drum accurately, and to lead a singing group. In some cultures, such as the Pima of Arizona, social deviants occupied special roles in musical life. In most North American cultures, men appear to have played a greater musical role than women, largely on account of their prominence in ceremonies; but women were in some cases the carriers of tradition who knew and taught much of the repertory. While formal music theory was generally absent, many tribes had at least a modest set of terms to indicate genres of songs, sections within a song, and types of performance practice.

II. *Musical styles.* A number of distinct styles can be briefly characterized. The simplest Indian music consists of one or two phrases with an inventory of two, three, or four pitches repeated many times, usually with variations. In a number of tribes, such as the Yana in northern California, peoples of the Amazon valley, and the Ona of Tierra del Fuego, this simple style accounts for the entire repertory. Despite strict limits, such repertories provide variety by introducing many kinds of formal relationships between the phrases making up a song and by creating interesting melodic variations. Where it does not dominate the repertory, this style often exists beside a more complex style and is used for a special group of genres: love songs, children's songs, songs for children's and adults' games, and those sung as part of telling tales. As this style was widespread, associated with archaic uses of music, and prominent in isolated areas, it may reflect an archaic stage in the development of Indian music. This suggestion is supported by the fact that the style is shared by very simple tribal peoples outside the Americas such as the Vedda of Sri Lanka and tribes of eastern Siberia.

The most widely known Indian style, that of the Plains, consists of a variety of pentatonic modes along with four-tone and six-tone scales, sharply descending melodic contours, a tense, harsh-sounding singing style with pulsations on the longer tones and some falsetto, and complex rhythmic structure. Forms are commonly strophic and consist of an initial repeated phrase followed by a longer section, also repeated, which ends with a variation of that phrase an octave lower. Drum accompaniment is systematically slightly off the beat. The music of the southwestern U.S. has several styles. The Navaho is characterized by triadic melodies, a variety of forms in many of which high phrases alternate with repetitions of a low tonic, and a less harsh nasal manner of singing. The Pueblo Indians have a greater variety of scales, many of them diatonic, a tendency to sing low in the vocal range, and complex forms that require six to eight minutes without strophic repetition. The Yuman tribes of southern Arizona irregularly alternate a low section comprising several isorhythmic phrases with a higher one they refer to as the "rise." They sing in a relaxed style with little pulsation and use anhemitonic pentatonic scales and simple duple and triple meters.

The peoples of the Great Basin of Nevada and Utah have many songs with a characteristic form in which each of two or three phrases of varying length is sung twice, the entire song using a range of a fifth or sixth. The Indians of the North Pacific Coast have a great variety of styles that include relatively complex rhythms in the percussion accompaniment, the use of minor seconds, and a distinctive singing style of considerable intensity and tension but without the great harshness and heavy pulsation of the Plains. This style is also found among the Eskimo, whose music is characterized by rhythmic complexity, restricted scales, and many songs in a nonmetric recitative style, along with a great variety of uses of the voice including the widely known "throat games." The peoples originally living in the eastern U.S. have music similar to that of the Plains peoples, but with greater regularity of phrase and more consistent use of pentatonic scales, less falsetto, and the widespread use of antiphonal and responsorial forms.

While Indian peoples of the U.S. and Canada remained relatively isolated from whites and thus retained their distinctive styles, the larger populations of *Latin America were more thoroughly absorbed into Hispanic culture, and their musics combine Western and traditional elements. Those cultures retaining tribal styles are the simpler ones, including the peoples of northern Mexico, the interior lowlands of Ecuador, Peru, and adjoining parts of Brazil, and southern Argentina and Chile. The music of northern Mexico is related to Yuman, Pueblo, and Navaho styles. In northern South America, typical features include triadic melodies, prominence of female singers, greater use of instrumental music, some polyphony based on hocket technique, and varieties of ceremonial speech intermediate between language and music. In the Gran Chaco of northern Brazil, some of the music is similar to that of the North American Plains. The Araucanians of the tip of South America also use restricted triadic scales with short forms ceaselessly varied. In general, instrumental music plays a greater role in South than in North America, and there is more participation by women.

III. *Instruments.* Idiophones of various sorts predominate, principally rattles, notched sticks, and hollow log drums (**teponaztli* in Mexico). While their musical functions are limited, there is enormous variety in construction and decoration of these instruments, attesting to their ceremonial and religious importance. A single tribal group may use many types of rattles, including (in the case of the Arapaho, for example) seeds or stones enclosed in sewn rawhide, in gourds, and in containers made of turtle shell; strings of deer hooves; and groups of metal bells. Drums of many sizes and with one and two skins, normally beaten with sticks, accompanied public ceremonies and singing throughout North America and large parts of South America. Buffalo skins suspended from sticks and beaten by groups of singers were found in the North American Plains.

The only aboriginal stringed instrument is the musical bow, found in the southwestern U.S. and parts of Central and South America. Approximating a small hunting bow, it is usually held in the mouth to enable the player to manipulate the overtones and provide a triadic melody against a fundamental drone. The influence of Western stringed instruments on the musical bow resulted in combinations such as the "Apache fiddle," a bowed instrument with one horsehair string on a tubular body, and the Ecuadorian shaman's fiddle, shaped roughly like a violin but with two or three strings.

Aerophones include the *bull-roarer, widely used for initiation rites and to assemble people, and many types of flutes. These are mostly vertical fipple flutes, sometimes with external duct, and with a variety of finger-hole arrangements (four and five holes being most common). In western South America, panpipes are widespread, and in the Amazonian jungle their component pipes may be up to 1.5 m (5 ft.) long. In most cases, flutes have no separate repertory but perform the melodies of songs. Other instruments, mainly with quasi-musical ceremonial uses, include reed pipes, bone whistles, and reeds made of leaves. The areas in which instruments are most developed include the North Pacific Coast, southern Mexico, and the Andean highlands and interior lowlands of South America.

IV. *Modern developments.* Much of the musical culture of Native American people in North America results, directly or indirectly, from the events of American Indian history in the 19th and 20th centuries. Of greatest significance are the physical and cultural devastation visited on Indian people by white incursions and settlements in the 19th century, the removal of tribes to reservations and the resulting breakdown—and sometimes reconstitution—of tribal cultures, various experiments for assuring physical and cultural survival in the early 20th century, the rebuilding of Native American cultures on both tribal and intertribal bases beginning about 1950, and various attempts to establish bases of political power in the later 20th century. All of these events had significant results in musical life, and, conversely, musical activity has played important roles in the various reactions and initiatives of Indian societies in their relationship to the dominant culture. Among the indirect results is the increased diversity of tribal repertories through modern intertribal religious movements such as the *Ghost Dance style, introduced from the Great Basin to Plains tribes ca. 1880; the *Peyote style, from stylistic elements of several areas beginning late in the 19th century; and a pan-Indian style, largely based on traits of Plains music, which spread throughout reservations and urban Indian settlements in the U.S. and Canada in the 20th century. The most visible change after 1950 is the development of the powwow as the most prominent venue for traditional music and dance. Powwows are social celebrations of family, tribal, or intertribal cultural identity that feature various types of dances—the solo "War" or "Grass" or "Intertribal" dance, round dances, and line dances; traditional and fancy (virtuosic) dancing; and dancing contests—to the accompaniment of singing groups of six to eight singers, known as Drums, singing in traditional Plains style. Small powwows may be gatherings of an extended family with friends, and be accompanied by one Drum; large tribal and intertribal powwows have large audiences of Native Americans and tourists, and have as many as 25 Drums alternating in singing one song at a time. Powwows began among southern Plains cultures but have become the hallmark of Native American gatherings throughout North America. Their role is to foster cultural integrity, but as most of them are attended by spectators, they are consciously used for cultural bridge-building and education. Various Native American Christian churches have translated standard American hymns into traditional languages and also set Christian texts to tunes in traditional styles. Although the reaction to European incursions has resulted in certain unique musical developments, there is no doubt that a major result was the impoverishment of and standardization of repertories, as in the adoption of concerts and similar musical occasions, and the disappearance of ceremonies. Secular parts of the repertories have survived better than the sacred. Combinations with Western music are of enormous importance in Latin America but, in part because of the incompatibility of styles, less common in North America.

Among the developments after ca. 1970, the following are important: (1) a distinct Native American record industry has been established, including several large and a number of small independent recording labels producing LPs, audiotapes, and CDs largely for the Native American market, providing an intertribal repertory of traditional and modernized music; (2) a body of Native American popular music was gradually established that includes music in mainstream American popular styles, with texts that speak to Native American political and social issues, performed largely by Native American musicians, and sometimes with traditional musical style elements and even traditional but harmonized tunes; among the prominent Native popular musicians, the singer Buffy Saint-Marie, the jazz and rock musician Jim Pepper, and the female trio Ulali should be mentioned; (3) the role of women in Native American music has been greatly expanded; (4) after decades of neglect following the "Indianist" movement among white American composers in the period around 1900, Indian music and musicians have begun to play a role in the mainstream performing arts world, as in the work of Native American composer Louis Ballard, in the choreography of the American Indian Dance Theater, and in the use of Indian motifs in the so-called New Age music movement. Schools for young members of many tribes, such as the Institute for American Indian Arts in Santa Fe, have developed choruses singing harmonized Indian songs from many styles. As North American Indian daily life becomes more Westernized, there is an increasing role for music and dance as the principal symbols of American Indian ethnic identity.

V. *Research.* American Indian music played a dominant role in the development of ethnomusicology, in part because of its physical accessibility. It remains the best-known area of tribal musics of the world and provides some of the paradigms of ethnomusicological method. Studies by Baker and Stumpf are among the first landmarks of the field, and many of the leading scholars, e.g., Hornbostel, George Herzog, Helen H. Roberts, David P. McAllester, and Alan P. Merriam, contributed to this research. The largest body of work is by Frances Densmore, who wrote over 20 monographs with thousands of transcriptions on many North American tribes. Herzog developed techniques for comprehensive analytical explication of repertories, McAllester explored the study of musical and cultural values, and Merriam provided a model for the presentation of comprehensive musical ethnography. Important developments after 1980 include studies of the repertories of individual Shoshone women by Judith Vander; attempts to construct a culture's system of ideas about music by Nettl; contributions by Native American scholars, including Charlotte Heth and Tara Browner; and studies dealing in various ways with the representation of Native American music, in scholarship by Beverley Diamond and Victoria Levine.

Bibl.: Theodore Baker, *Über die Musik der nordamerikanischen Wilden* (Leipzig, 1882). Carl Stumpf, "Lieder der Bellakula Indianer," *VfMw* 2 (1886): 405–26. Alice C. Fletcher, *The Hako: A Pawnee Ceremony* (Washington, D.C., 1904). Frances Densmore, *Chippewa Music,* 2 vols. (Washington, D.C.: Government Printing Office, 1910–13). Id., *Teton Sioux Music* (Washington, D.C.: Government Printing Office, 1918). Raoul and Marguerite d'Harcourt, *La musique des Incas et ses survivances* (Paris: P Geuthner, 1926). George Herzog, "The Yuman Musical Style," *Journal of American Folklore* 41 (1928): 183–231. Id., "Plains Ghost Dance and Great Basin Music," *American Anthropologist* 37 (1935): 403–19. Karl Gustav Izikowitz, *Musical and Other Sound Instruments of the South American Indians* (Göteborg: Elander Boktrykeri Aktiebolag, 1934; R: East Ardsley, U.K.: S R Pubs, 1970). George Herzog, "Special Song Types in North American Indian Music," *Zeitschrift für vergleichende Musikwissenschaft* 3 (1935): 23–34. Id., "A Comparison of Pueblo and Pima Musical Styles," *Journal of American Folklore* 49 (1936): 286–417. Helen H. Roberts, *Musical Areas in Aboriginal North America* (New Haven: Yale U Pr, 1936). David P. McAllester, *Peyote Music,* Viking Fund Publications in Anthropology (New York, 1949). Zygmunt Estreicher, "Die Musik der Eskimos," *Anthropos* 45 (1950): 659–720. Willard Rhodes, "North American Indian Music: A Bibliographical Survey of Anthropological Theory," *Notes* 10 (1952): 33–45. David P. McAllester, *Enemy Way Music* (Cambridge, Mass.: Peabody Museum, 1954). Bruno Nettl, *North American Indian Musical Styles,* American Folk-lore Society, Memoirs 45 (Philadelphia, 1954). Charles Haywood, *A Bibliography of North American Folklore and Folk Song,* 2nd ed., vol. 2 (New York: Dover, 1961). Gilbert Chase, *A Guide to the Music of Latin America,* 2nd ed. (Washington, D.C.: Pan American Union, 1962). Bruno Nettl, "The Songs of Ishi," *MQ* 51 (1965): 460–77. Charlotte J. Frisbie, *Kinaalda: A Study of the Navajo Girl's Puberty Ceremony*

(Middletown, Conn.: Wesleyan U Pr, 1967). Alan P. Merriam, *Ethnomusicology of the Flathead Indians* (Chicago: Aldine, 1967). Gertrude P. Kurath and Antonio Garcia, *Music and Dance of the Tewa Pueblos* (Santa Fe: Museum of New Mexico Pr, 1970). Carol E. Robertson–de Carbo, "Tayil as Category and Communication among the Argentine Mapuche," *YIFMC* 8 (1976): 35–52. John Bierhorst, *A Cry from the Earth* (New York: Four Winds Pr, 1979). Anthony Seeger, "What Can We Learn When They Sing? Vocal Genres of the Suya Indians of Central Brazil," *Ethno* 23 (1979): 373–94. Charlotte J. Frisbie, *Southwestern Indian Ritual Drama* (Albuquerque, 1980). Marcia Herndon, *Native American Music* (Darby, Pa.: Norwood Edns, 1982). Anthony Seeger, *Why Suya Sing: A Musical Anthropology of an Amazonian People* (Cambridge: Cambridge U Pr, 1988). Judith Vander, *Songprints: The Musical Experience of Five Shoshone Women* (Urbana: U of Ill Pr, 1988). Bruno Nettl, *Blackfoot Musical Thought: Comparative Perspectives* (Kent, Ohio: Kent St U Pr, 1989). William K. Powers, *War Dance: Plains Indian Musical Performance* (Tucson: U of Ariz Pr, 1990). Richard Keeling, *Cry for Luck: Sacred Song and Speech among the Yurok, Hupa, and Karok Indians of Northwestern California* (Berkeley: U of Cal Pr, 1992). Thomas Turino, *Moving Away from Silence: Music of the Peruvian Altiplano and the Experience of Urban Migration* (Chicago: U of Chicago Pr, 1993). Tara Browner, *Heartbeat of the People: Music and Dance of the Northern Pow-wow* (Urbana: U of Ill Pr, 2002). Victoria Lindsay Levine, *Writing American Indian Music* (Madison, Wis.: A-R Eds, 2002).

B.N.

American in Paris, An. A symphonic poem by George Gershwin, composed in 1928, describing a sightseer's day in Paris. The work makes use of automobile horns, bluesy tunes, and the rhythms of the Charleston.

American Musicological Society. See Societies, musical.

American organ. A *harmonium operated by suction rather than by compression.

Amfiparnaso, L'. See Madrigal comedy.

Am Frosch [Ger.]. At the *frog; hence, an instruction to bow the violin or other stringed instrument with that portion of the bow nearest the hand.

Am Griffbrett [Ger.]. At the *fingerboard; hence, an instruction to bow the violin or other stringed instrument near or above the fingerboard. See Bowing (12).

Amor brujo, El [Sp., Love the Sorcerer]. A ballet by Manuel de Falla, composed in 1914–15 and produced in Madrid in 1915 (choreography by Pastora Imperio), on a gypsy subject, and including numerous folk-inspired dances, the best known of which is the "Ritual Fire Dance." The work includes several songs originally intended to be sung by the ballerina, but now most often sung from the orchestra pit by a singer.

Amore, con; amorevole; amoroso [It.]. With love, lovingly. Instruments with names including the phrase *d'amore* are usually thought to have an especially mellow tone; in the case of stringed instruments this is usually attributable to the presence of *sympathetic strings in addition to the strings actually played upon.

Amorschall [Ger.]. A French horn having two side holes with keys and some kind of cover or insert for its bell, invented by a Bohemian horn player named Kölbel, ca. 1766. It was one of the first attempts to complete the scale of the horn, and Kölbel, employed in St. Petersburg, attracted considerable attention performing on it. R.E.E.

Amour des trois oranges, L'. See *Love for Three Oranges.*

Amplitude. See Acoustics.

Am Steg [Ger.]. At the *bridge; hence, an instruction to bow the violin or other stringed instrument near or on the bridge. See Bowing (11).

Anacrusis [fr. Gr.]. One or more notes preceding the first metrically strong beat of a phrase; upbeat, pickup.

Analysis. The study of musical structure applied to actual works or performances. In ethnomusicology, analysis includes the study of the relation among musical structure, performance, and culture. The analysis of Western art music deals substantively with questions of technique and is therefore considered a branch of music *theory, but it is distinct in that it addresses music already composed or performed; analysis has no bearing on music-as-it-might-be or on the properties of the raw materials of music. Much analysis aims to demonstrate the organic unity of a work or works. Many practitioners see it as having no bearing on larger aesthetic issues, such as expressiveness, or on questions of the value of individual works. With respect to these and many other topics, the relationship between analysis and *criticism of music is not well defined.

The analysis of any repertory of music necessarily rests on some view (whether or not expressed) about which features of the repertory are significant as well as on the aims of the analyst. It may rest on a widely shared theory of a repertory and simply describe the work in terms of that theory, or it may be advanced as evidence for the correctness of a theory. Its aim may be to elucidate the individual work in strictly technical terms without direct reference to other works, or it may seek to situate the work in a larger theoretical, biographical, historical, or cultural context. In Western art music, the aim of analysis is sometimes to guide the performer's interpretation. At issue with respect to every repertory is the extent to which analysis can or should be carried out in terms that do not form an explicit part of the musical and cultural traditions of the repertory itself. This issue is forcefully present in *ethnomusicology, where, for example, the study of non-Western musics in analytical terms derived from Western art music poses serious risks of distortion. Similarly, the study of the history of Western art music requires choosing an analytical vocabulary appropriate to the period and repertory in question, though the vocabulary need not be restricted to that of contemporaneous theorists.

The analysis of Western tonal music may deal comprehensively with all of the structural aspects of a work, including identification of its larger outlines or *form, variability within types of form, specific gestures, special devices, and relationship to a text. The analysis of form may subsume motivic analysis [see Motive] and *harmonic analysis, which considers aspects of *tonality, *modulation, function (determined in turn by root analysis, or, less accurately, "roman-numeral analysis"), and *harmonic rhythm. The analysis of melody, rhythm, and instrumentation may be applicable to larger questions of structure. *Schenker analysis is a technique that stresses the linear motions of tonal works.

The analysis of works from before the period of tonality is often carried out in terms of concepts such as *mode that form a part of contemporaneous theory, though considerable study (and some controversy) surrounds the relationship of this music to the emergence of the tonal system. The aim of such analysis is often historical. Some styles of art music of the 20th century, notably *twelve-tone and *serial music, have developed along with a related body of theory that provides terms for analysis. This theory has inspired the development of techniques for the analysis (principally of pitch relations) of other atonal music as well. In contrast, *aleatory music, by undermining the fixity of the individual work, radically calls into question analysis as traditionally conceived.

All of the techniques of analysis may be subsumed under *style analysis, which usually has aims reaching beyond the individual work. It may concern itself with a composer's growth and evolution; with the similarities and differences between the works of a single composer or between those of one composer and those of another; with the trends and idiosyncrasies of musical eras and national heritages; with the humanistic aspect of music and the relationship between music and other arts and human activities. Some analysis has used the techniques of information theory, linguistics, semiotics, and computer science [see bibl. below]. See also Criticism, Theory.

Bibl.: Donald Francis Tovey, *Essays in Musical Analysis,* 7 vols. (London: Oxford U Pr, 1935–44). Rudolph Réti, *The Thematic Process in Music* (New York: Macmillan, 1951; new ed., London: Faber, 1961). Walter Piston, *Orchestration* (New York: Norton, 1955). Leo Treitler, "Music Analysis in a Historical Context," *CMS* 6 (1966): 75–88. Jan LaRue, *Guidelines for Style Analysis* (New York: Norton, 1970). Harry B. Lincoln, ed., *The Computer and Music* (Ithaca: Cornell U Pr, 1970). Leonard B. Meyer, *Explaining Music* (Berkeley and Los Angeles: U of Cal Pr, 1973). Jean-Jacques Nattiez, *Fondements d'une sémiologie de la musique* (Paris: Union génerale d'éditions, 1975). Eugene Narmour, *Beyond Schenkerism: The Need for Alternatives in Music Analysis* (Chicago: U of Chicago Pr, 1977). Walter Piston and Mark DeVoto, *Harmony,* 4th ed. (New York: Norton, 1978). Douglass M. Green, *Form in Tonal Music,* 2nd ed. (New York: Holt, Rinehart and Winston, 1979). Ian D. Bent, "Analysis," *Grove 6.* Joseph Kerman, "How We Got into Analysis, and How to Get Out," *Critical Inquiry,* vol. 7, no. 2 (Winter, 1980): 311–31. George Perle, *Serial Composition and Atonality,* 5th ed. (Berkeley and Los Angeles: U of Cal Pr, 1981). Allen Forte and Steven Gilbert, *Introduction to Schenkerian Analysis* (New York: Norton, 1982). Jean-Jacques Nattiez, "Varèse's 'Density 21.5': A Study in Semiological Analysis," trans. Anna Barry, *Music Analysis* 1 (1982): 244–340. Fred Lerdahl and Ray Jackendoff, *A Generative Theory of Tonal Music* (Cambridge, Mass.: MIT Pr, 1983). See also Theory, Schenker analysis. M.DEV.

Anapest, anapaest. See Prosody.

Anche [Fr.]. *Reed. The plural, *anches,* denotes the reed stops of the organ.

Ancia [It.]. *Reed.

Ancora [It.]. (1) Again, often as a request to repeat a performance. (2) Still, more; *ancora più forte,* still louder.

Ancus [Lat.]. See Neume.

Andacht, mit; andächtig [Ger.]. With devotion, devoutly.

Andamento [It.]. (1) A fugue subject of some length, often consisting of more than one phrase, as distinct from the **attaco* and **soggetto.* (2) *Sequence (2). (3) An episode in a *fugue.

Andante [It., walking]. (1) Moderately slow, and since the late 18th century, usually regarded as a tempo lying between **adagio* and **allegro.* The term was first used as a performance instruction independent of tempo, particularly with reference to bass lines with a steadily moving or "walking" character in even note-values. Its position between tempos that are thought of as clearly slow and clearly fast leads to some ambiguity when the term is combined with others, as in the phrases *molto andante, più andante,* and *meno andante.* Although the first two are probably most often intended to call for a tempo slower and the last to call for a tempo faster than *andante,* the reverse may be true in some cases, as in Brahms's Sonata for Violin and Piano no. 1 in G major op. 78, second movement, in which the opening, marked *adagio,* is followed by a passage marked *più andante,* meaning faster, or Beethoven's Piano Sonata op. 109, variation 4 of the last movement, which is marked "Un poco meno andante ciò è un più adagio come il tema," meaning "a little less fast, that is, somewhat slower than the theme," the theme itself being marked *andante.* A similar ambiguity exists with respect to **andantino.* See Performance marks. (2) A movement in moderately slow tempo, perhaps not as slow as an *adagio* and in any case less somber in character.

Andante con moto [It.]. See *Moto.*

Andantino [It.]. In present usage, usually slightly less slow than **andante.* The term is ambiguous, however, in part because of the ambiguity associated with *andante.* In the late 18th century, *andantino* seems to have called for a tempo slower than *andante.* Beethoven wrote to his publisher in Edinburgh, George Thomson, that the term could be used for a tempo either faster or slower than *andante.* See Performance marks.

An die ferne Geliebte [Ger., To the Distant Beloved]. A cycle of six songs by Beethoven, op. 98 (1815–16), on poems by Alois Jeitteles.

Andrea Chénier. Opera in four acts by Umberto Giordano (libretto by Luigi Illica), produced in Milan in 1896. Setting: Paris before, during, and after the French Revolution.

Anémocorde [Fr.]. A mechanical *aeolian harp invented by Johann Jacob Schnell in Paris in 1789. Wind was supplied by bellows and channeled past tuned strings by a mechanism activated by a keyboard. See also Sostenente piano.

Anenajki [Russ.]. In ornate **Znamenny* chant, the interpolation of the meaningless syllables *a, ne, na.* Adjunct to this practice are the *khomonie,* distortions in the text produced by applying vowel sounds (*e* and *o*) to letters normally silent. Both procedures stem from Byzantine kalophonic chant, which contains *teretismata,* the intercalated syllables *te, re, re.* D.E.C.

Anfang [Ger.]. Beginning; *vom Anfang,* from the beginning, and thus the equivalent of **da capo.*

Angelica [It.; Fr. *angélique;* Eng. angel lute]. An archlute of the 17th and 18th centuries with 16 or 17 single gut strings tuned diatonically, D to e′. Played like a harp, it was popular with amateurs because of the full, clear, sustained tone of the open plucked strings. R.L.

Angenehm [Ger.]. Pleasant.

Angklung [Jav.]. An Indonesian instrument made of tuned lengths of bamboo. In East Java, 12 to 14 tubes are set on a frame and struck with mallets. In West Java and in Bali, 2 or 3 tubes tuned in octaves are fastened loosely to a frame and shaken by hand like a *rattle.

Anglaise, anglois [Fr.]. A fast, late Baroque dance movement in a harpsichord or orchestral suite (Bach, Telemann). The term was used loosely to refer to any of the English dance types whose popularity spread from the court of Louis XIV across Europe [see *Contredanse,* Country Dance, Hornpipe, *Écossaise*]. Anglaises usually have folkish simplicity and are strongly accented. They continued to be written until the end of the 18th century. B.G.

Angle harp. A *harp in which the neck forms an angle (usually acute) with the sound box and which lacks a pillar, thus having only two sides. Angle harps are now common only in Africa, having been replaced elsewhere by *frame harps. See also Arched harp.

Anglican chant. Harmonized formulas for singing Psalms and canticles in the daily Offices of the Anglican Church [see also Anglican church music]. Origins are found in the medieval tradition of improvised chant harmonizations, known in England as **farburden* and in continental Europe as **fauxburden.* Before the Restoration (mid-17th century), simple harmonizations of Gregorian *psalm tones with the chant in the tenor were used (examples in Thomas Morley's *A Plaine and Easie Introduction,* 1597). After the Restoration, the connection between Anglican chant and the Gregorian psalm tones became gradually less direct. The melody was moved to the top voice, but the bipartite form of the Gregorian tones was retained. Eventually Anglican chant came to be a small binary form, each part opening with an expandable, unmeasured reciting chord (to accommodate the varying number of syllables per verse in the prose texts) and closing with a measured cadential pattern. The harmonization of the first psalm tone shown in the example (called Christ Church Tune by Edward Lowe in a publication of 1661) is used for the opening of the *Venite* (Psalm 95) in the first volume of William Boyce's *Cathedral Music* (3 vols., 1760–73).

Where suitable, the halves of the formula can be divided in performance between the halves of the choir (**decani* and *cantoris*). In a single chant, one statement of the formula encompasses one verse of text; in a double chant, one statement encompasses two verses; in a triple chant, one statement encompasses three verses; in a quadruple chant, four.

From the Restoration through the 18th century, musical performances of Anglican chant were largely confined to cathedrals and collegiate churches. The choirs of these institutions could be taught to adapt Psalm verses to the formulas by rote without written notation, and they eagerly accepted the many new chants being composed. Thus, the Anglican tradition of chanting never died out. Neither did metrical and rhymed texts (e.g., by Sternhold and Hopkins or, later, Tate and Brady), and the associated tunes ever threatened to overwhelm the older custom.

In the latter part of the 18th century some Evangelicals, notably Jonathan Gray in York, began promoting Anglican chant for congregational singing of the Psalms. But it was the Oxford (or Tractarian) Movement of the 19th century that was largely responsible for establishing the parochial practice. All churches were encouraged to adopt the practice, which had hitherto been associated with rather elaborately equipped ecclesiastical establishments. Experience revealed that if such chanting was to be successful, some orderly manner of indicating in print the correlations between text and music was needed. To meet that need, systems of pointing were established (the first published being in Robert Janes, *The Psalter or*

1
O Come let
us sing un-
to the Lord
Let us heartily
rejoice in the
strength of
our sal- va-
tion

Anglican chant.

Psalms of David, 1837); some were more arcane than others, but all tended toward simplification to encourage congregational use, and all were dependent on a standard binary musical form. One of the most widely used collections in 19th-century England was William Mercer's *Church Psalter and Hymn Book,* first issued in 1854. In the mid-20th century the most widely used was Sydney H. Nicholson's *Parish Psalter With Chants* (1928; rev. 1967). Since the publication in 1980 of *The Alternative Service Book,* with its (then) new liturgical psalter, a variety of Anglican chant books have been in use.

In America, Lowell Mason was an early advocate of such congregational chanting, usually identified with the Episcopal church. Trinity Church, on Wall Street in New York City, introduced its own *Psalter* in 1870, much reprinted and revised, and widely used in Episcopal churches. Late 19th- and 20th-century Episcopal hymnals generally included Anglican chant, and a specific *Anglican Chant Psalter,* edited by Alec Wyton, was issued in 1987.

Bibl.: Nicholas Temperley, *Jonathan Gray and Church Music in York, 1770–1840* (York: St Anthony's Pr, 1977). Nicholas Temperley, *The Music of the English Parish Church* (New York: Cambridge U Pr, 1979). Ruth Mack Wilson, *Anglican Chant and Chanting in England, Scotland, and America, 1660 to 1820* (New York: Oxford U Pr, 1996). Ruth Mack Wilson, "Harmonized Chant," in *The Hymnal 1982 Companion,* ed. Raymond Glover, vol. 1 (New York: Church Hymnal Corp, 1990), pp. 215–237. Ian Spink, *Restoration Cathedral Music, 1660–1714* (New York: Oxford U Pr, 1995). R.F.F., rev. R.A.L.

Anglican church music. The music of the Church of England *(Anglicana Ecclesia)* is inseparably bound to its peculiar history. Its repertory and style affirm the church's nature as a confluence of medieval, Reformation, and humanistic ideals.

Three principles have guided Anglican church music: that it adopt the English vernacular, that it have verbal clarity, and that it utilize texts prescribed by the Book of Common (i.e., public) Prayer (1549, 1552, 1559, and 1662). Musically, the most important texts have been those of the Psalter and the four canticles "Te Deum" and "Benedictus" (for Morning Prayer) and "Magnificat" and "Nunc dimittis" (for Evening Prayer). Musical settings of these (or alternate) canticles, Psalm 95 *(Venite),* and portions of the Communion service (e.g., Byrd's *Great Service,* Gibbons's *Short Service,* Greene's *Service in C,* Stainer's three Communion services, Vaughan Williams's *Morning, Communion, and Evening Services*) constitute a basic repertory of Anglican church music. Virtually all notable English composers—as well as less gifted ones—of every generation have made contributions to Anglican church music.

Increments to this basic repertory (*anthems, settings of metrical Psalms, canticles, and hymns and other texts) were added at different times for different reasons. The Elizabethan Injunctions of 1559, by permitting the singing of "an Hymn, or such like song, to the praise of Almighty God," encouraged composers to embellish the basic liturgy with musical settings of other texts; the history of the English anthem thus becomes an indispensable adjunct to liturgical history and also exhibits changing musical tastes and styles (unaccompanied, verse and full, Handelian, Victorian, cathedral, parochial).

Elaborate musical settings of the basic and embellished repertory presupposed the correspondingly elaborate and expert musical forces of cathedrals, collegiate churches, and the Chapel Royal (particularly before and immediately after the Commonwealth), whose choirs, supplanting congregations, performed the services, anthems, and chanting of Psalms. In the mid-19th century, however, the Oxford Movement encouraged universal imitation of the relatively elaborate cathedral style (memorialized in Barnard's *First Book of Selected Church Musick,* 1641, and Boyce's *Cathedral Music,* 1760–73). The congregations of parish churches, on the other hand, had cultivated a distinctive musical repertory utilizing metrical translations of the Psalter (Sternhold and Hopkins, 1562; Tate and Brady, 1696), not always with admirable musical results (Burney, de Quincey); later they enlisted the support of charity children's choirs for the Psalms and anthems and, in the 18th century, modest orchestras, which were replaced in the early 19th century by the barrel organ and harmonium. By the end of the 19th century, parish music had generally become an imitation (often pale) of the cathedral style.

The comprehensive authorized use of congregational hymnody in the Anglican Church was long delayed, in part because of theological opposition to texts other than Psalms and despite many attempts to introduce new texts (e.g., Wither, 1623) or texts with a non-Psalmodic point of view (Watts, 1707; John and Charles Wesley). The case of *Holy and Ward* v. *Cotterill* in 1820 had decisive consequences, striking down restrictions on the free choice of texts for congregational singing. This decision led to a flood of composition, setting, and publication (Heber, 1827; Neale, 1851; Kemble, 1853), reaching a climax in *Hymns Ancient and Modern* (1861), which celebrated the Victorian hymn and became virtually the authorized hymnal of the Anglican Church. No subsequent collection has been as successful.

In common with other denominations, music in Anglican churches since the 1960s has become fragmented by the different popular styles engendered by folk music, charismatic choruses, and, more recently, by contemporary Christian music. The older tradition, however, continues in cathedrals and collegiate chapels—such as Christ Church, Oxford, and King's College, Cambridge—where newly composed music is heard alongside music from earlier generations.

Bibl.: John Jebb, *The Choral Service of the United Church of England and Ireland* (London: Parker, 1843). Christopher Dearnley, "English Church Music, 1650–1750," in *Royal Chapel, Cathedral, and Parish Church* (New York: Oxford U Pr, 1970). Bernarr Rainbow, *The Choral Revival in the Anglican Church (1839–1872)* (New York: Oxford U Pr, 1970). Kenneth R. Long, *The Music of the English Church* (New York: St Martin's, 1972). Friedrich Blume, et al., *Protestant Church Music: A History* (New York: Norton, 1974). Peter Le Huray, *Music and the Reformation in England, 1549–1660,* corrected ed. (New York: Cambridge U Pr, 1978). Nicholas Temperley, *The Music of the English Parish Church* (New York: Cambridge U Pr, 1979). Kenneth Walter Cameron, *Early Anglican Church Music in America . . . 1763–1830* (Hartford: Transcendental Books, 1983). Ian Spink, *Restoration Cathedral Music, 1660–1714* (New York: Oxford U Pr, 1995). Dale Adelmann, *The Contribution of Cambridge Ecclesiologists to the Revival of Anglican Choral Worship 1839–62* (Aldershot: Ashgate, 1997). R.F.F., rev. R.A.L.

Angosciosamente [It.]. With anguish.

Ängstlich [Ger.]. Anxiously.

Anhalten, anhaltend [Ger.]. To hold or continue (e.g., sounding, as when a tone is not damped); continuing.

Anhemitonic. Lacking semitones; e.g., the whole-tone scale or the pentatonic scale c d e g a.

Anima [It., soul]. *Sound post.

Animando, animandosi, animato [It.]. Animating, becoming animated, animated; usually with the implication of (increasingly) rapid tempo.

Animé [Fr.]. Animated; thus, in a moderately fast tempo.

Animo, animoso [It.]. Spirit, spirited.

Anmutig [Ger.]. Graceful.

Années de pèlerinage [Fr., Years of Pilgrimage]. Three volumes of piano music by Liszt, composed during the years 1835–77. The first (published in 1855) is titled *Suisse,* the second (1858) *Italie,* and the third (1883) is untitled. Each contains pieces with descriptive titles. Many of the pieces in the first volume were composed in 1835–36, published in 1840 as *Album d'un voyageur,* and later revised.

Anreissen [Ger.]. In string playing, to pluck forcefully.

Ansatz [Ger.]. (1) In the playing of wind instruments, *embouchure. (2) The adjustment of the organs contributing to vocal production. (3) *Attack.

Anschlag [Ger.]. (1) In piano playing, touch. (2) An ornament mainly associated with German music of the mid-18th century and consisting most commonly of two notes, the first a step below the main note and the second a step above. These notes precede the main note and take their value from it; they are executed more lightly than the main note, however, unlike an

*appoggiatura. C. P. E. Bach and Marpurg illustrated *Anschläge* beginning at intervals larger than a second below the main note. Tartini (before 1756) showed the *Anschlag (appoggiatura composta in altro modo)* with the first note longer than the second; Marpurg gave a dotted variety. For bibl., see Ornamentation.

(2) D.F.

Anschwellend [Ger.]. Becoming louder.

Answer. In a fugue, a statement of the subject immediately following its statement in the prevailing key. Answers usually result from imitation of the subject at an interval other than the unison or octave, most often the perfect fifth above or the perfect fourth below, and the term is sometimes reserved for only such cases. Depending on the nature of their similarity to the original subject, answers may be either tonal or real [see Tonal and real].

Antar. Rimsky-Korsakov's Second Symphony op. 9, composed in 1868 and revised in 1875 and 1897 as a symphonic suite. It is based on the legend of Antar, an

Arabian hero of the 6th century, as recounted by Osip Senkovsky.

Antara [Quechua]. Andean *panpipes of cane or clay.

Antecedent, consequent. Two musical phrases, the second of which is a concluding response to or resolution of the first. The two phrases often have the same or similar rhythms, but have complementary pitch contours and/or tonal implications, e.g., a rising contour in the first and a falling contour in the second, or a conclusion on the dominant in the first and a conclusion on the tonic in the second. In the accompanying example from the first movement of Mozart's Symphony no. 40 in G minor K. 550, this relationship obtains at two levels simultaneously. Phrases c and d form one antecedent-consequent pair, as do phrases e and f. At the same time, the two pairs, understood as phrases A and B, respectively, are also related to one another as antecedent and consequent.

Ante-Communion. That part of the Anglican service of Holy Communion concluding with the "prayer for the whole state of Christ's Church." It does not include Communion itself and is thus analogous to the Roman Mass of the Catechumens.

Anthem [fr. *antiphon]. A choral composition with a sacred or moralizing text in English, performed in a liturgical or ceremonial context. In the worship of Protestant churches, it is the analogue of the *motet in the Roman Catholic Church.

There have been three great periods of anthem composition in English history. The first of these, 1549–1644, opened with an affirmation of Renaissance and Reformation principles (Christopher Tye, 1500–73; Thomas Tallis, 1505–85; William Mundy, 1529–91), the style being represented by the anthems and "prayers" in the four partbooks of John Day's anthology, begun in 1560 as *Certaine notes* but not issued until 1565 under the title *Mornyng and evenyng prayer . . . in foure partes.* It continued with the evolution of the verse anthem, in which sections or "verses" for one or more soloists with instrumental accompaniment alternate with sections for full chorus, and the full anthem, which is entirely choral (William Byrd, 1542–1623; Thomas Morley, 1557–1622). Finally, this period responded to the religious and political turmoil of the early Stuart years with textural contrast and declamatory interjection and the compositional shapes implied by such changes in elocution (Thomas Tomkins, 1572–1656; Thomas Weelkes, 1575–1623; Orlando Gibbons, 1583–1676; Adrian Batten, 1591–1637). The work of this whole period is summed up in the 124 compositions contained in John Barnard's *First Book of Selected Church Musick* (1641).

The second period opened with the brilliant anthems of the Restoration and the Chapel Royal in the reign of Charles II (1660–85), celebrating the return of monarchy and the Anglican Communion (Book of Common Prayer, 1662), the vigor of the monarch's French connections during his exile (Paris, and Lully, under Louis XIV), and the importation of continental Baroque musical styles (solo and choral voices, instruments and instrumental passages, continuo). The music of Matthew Locke (1630–77), Pelham Humfrey (1647–74), and John Blow (1649–1708) led to the dominant figure of Purcell, rivaled only by Handel (e.g., *Chandos Anthems*), whose long shadow obscured the native composers Maurice Greene (1695–1755), who projected the collection *Cathedral Music,* and William Boyce (1711–79), who completed it (3 vols., 1760–73). Boyce expanded the pre-Commonwealth repertory with a strong representation of music from the Restoration period. Whereas Barnard's collection (1641) had been published in partbooks, that of Boyce was in score; the very style of publication provides a clue to changes in musical conception and performance practice.

The third period, stimulated by the Oxford Movement and the tireless inventiveness of Samuel Sebastian Wesley (1810–76), brought the republication of Purcell's sacred music (1828–32), the revival of chant and folk song, the full flowering of the Victorian anthem with the music (and musicology) of Sir John Stainer (1840–91) and Sir Charles Stanford (1852–1924), and the beginnings of the republication of the Elizabethan repertory (e.g., *Tudor Church Music,* 10 vols., 1922–29), all presuming the proliferation of cathedral style and practices into the parish churches.

Antecedent, consequent.

The effects of this proliferation still prevail, and the needs of parish churches continue to be met by English composers of the first rank.

William Billings (1746–1800), Lowell Mason (1792–1872), Horatio Parker (1863–1919), and Charles Ives (1875–1954) are only the most visible of the legions of composers who have supplied anthems for American denominations. In the 20th century, however, relatively few of the best-known American composers have contributed to the genre. Thus, though the anthem in America is a by-product of the English tradition, it is only in England that one finds a single liturgy reinterpreted by successive generations of its best composers and ornamented with their anthems, the entire tradition being sustained and available for current use. However, the production of small-scale, three- to four-minute anthems by scores of American composers continue to fill the catalogs of many U.S. publishers, and are sung by choirs of many different denominations. See also Anglican church music.

Bibl.: Robert Stevenson, *Protestant Church Music in America* (New York: Norton, 1966). Leonard Ellinwood, *The History of American Church Music,* rev. ed. (New York: Da Capo, 1970). Ralph T. Daniel, *The Anthem in New England before 1800* (Evanston: Northwestern U Pr, 1966; R: New York: Da Capo, 1979). Elwyn A. Wienandt and Robert H. Young, *The Anthem in England and America* (New York: Free Pr, 1970). Nicholas Temperley, *The Music of the English Parish Church* (New York: Cambridge U Pr, 1979). Ian Spink, *Restoration Cathedral Music, 1660–1714* (New York: Oxford U Pr, 1995). R.F.F., rev. R.A.L.

Anthems, national. See National anthems.

Anticipation. See Counterpoint, *Nachschlag.*

Antienne [Fr.]. *Antiphon.

Antimasque. See Masque.

Antiphon. A type of liturgical chant common to the *Gregorian and other Western chant repertories and associated principally with antiphonal psalmody. It is generally a relatively short melody in a simple, syllabic style that serves as a refrain in the singing of the verses of a Psalm or canticle. For the relationship of antiphon to accompanying verses and the methods of performing these, see Psalmody, Latin, and Psalm tone.

The antiphons sung with the Psalms of the Office, of which several thousand survive, are the most numerous type. These are also the simplest melodies. A large part of this repertory resulted from the adaptation to new texts of a relatively small number of prototypical melodies, as some of the earliest manuscripts make clear in indicating that one text is to be sung to the melody of some other. Gevaert (1895) identified 47 such melodies or *thèmes,* basing his categories on the *tonary of Regino of Prüm; other scholars (Frere, Hucke, Apel) have analyzed the repertory along these or related lines. Some melodies in the repertory seem to have resulted from the combining of common melodic elements, a process associated with oral transmission and often termed *centonization (as in the analyses of Ferretti).

The *introit, *communion, and *offertory of the Mass are also sometimes termed antiphons *(antiphona ad introitum, a. ad communionem, a. ad offertorium).* The first two of these clearly represent antiphonal psalmody in the Mass, even though the accompanying verses sung to a psalm tone were greatly reduced in the introit and eliminated altogether in the communion. It is much less certain that the offertory was ever an example of antiphonal psalmody as it is usually understood, since even the earliest sources preserve very much more elaborate melodies for both antiphon and verses.

Two types of antiphon are not associated with psalmody at all. The processional antiphons, first preserved in graduals and later in separate books and sung at processions on such occasions as the feast of the Purification (Candlemas) on 2 February, the Greater Litanies on 25 April, and Palm Sunday, sometimes include verses after the fashion of responsories. Some of this repertory derives from *Gallican chant. Of the Marian antiphons (antiphons for the Blessed Virgin Mary), the most important are the four sung at the end of Compline, one for each season of the year: *"Alma Redemptoris Mater," *"Ave Regina caelorum," *"Regina caeli laetare," and *"Salve Regina." These date from the 11th century and after, are rather more elaborate than the antiphons of the Psalms and canticles, and have been set polyphonically by numerous composers, especially in the 15th and 16th centuries.

The Latin term *antiphona* was borrowed directly from Greek, where it meant the octave. In the first century C.E., *antiphonia* was used in the East to describe the singing of two choirs in alternation, one of men and one of women (presumably singing an octave apart), and subsequently it referred simply to psalmody consisting of the alternation of two choirs. By the 4th century, when the term was first used in the West and when St. Ambrose (d. 397) introduced antiphonal singing there, *antiphona* referred, as it has in general since, to a melody that accompanied the antiphonal singing of a Psalm.

Bibl.: François-Auguste Gevaert, *La mélopée antique dans le chant de l'Église latine* (Ghent, 1895–96; R: Osnabrück: Zeller, 1967). Walter Howard Frere, ed., *Antiphonale sarisburiense* (London: Plainsong and Mediaeval Music Soc, 1901–25; R: Farnborough: Gregg, 1966). Helmut Hucke, "Die Entwicklung des christlichen Kultgesangs zum Gregorianischen Gesang," *Römische Quartalschrift* 48 (1953): 147–94. Id., "Zur Formenlehre der Offiziumsantiphonen," *KmJb* 37 (1953): 7–33. Jacques Hourlier, "Notes sur l'antiphonie," *Schrade,* 1973, pp. 116–43. See also Gregorian chant, Psalmody. D.M.R.

Antiphonal singing. Singing in which two choirs alternate. In liturgical chant it is present in one of the three basic forms of *psalmody. The term is also applied to any *polychoral music.

Antiphoner, antiphonal, antiphonary [Lat. *antiphonale, antiphonarium, antiphonarius*]. The *liturgical book of the Western Christian rites containing the chants for the Office and thus antiphons as well as responsories and other types of chant. The comparable book for the Mass is the *gradual. Some of the earliest uses of the Latin terms, however, beginning in the 8th century and thus before the development of musical notation, refer to books containing the texts of antiphonal chants [see Psalmody] for both Mass and Office and in some cases to books containing the texts of chants for the Mass alone (as in the phrase *antiphonale missarum,* "antiphoner of the Mass").

Antiphonia [Gr.]. In Greek theory, the octave.

Antiphony. The use of two (or more) spatially separated performers or ensembles that alternate or oppose one another in a musical work or performance. Music employing choirs in this way is said to be *polychoral.

Antony and Cleopatra. Opera in three acts by Samuel Barber (libretto by Franco Zeffirelli after Shakespeare), produced in New York in 1966; a revised version (libretto revised by Gian Carlo Menotti) was produced at the Juilliard American Opera Center in 1975. Setting: Alexandria and Rome in the first century B.C.E.

Anvil [Fr. *enclume;* Ger. *Amboss;* It. *incudine;* Sp. *yunque*]. A percussion instrument, often intended to represent the sound of the metal-working tool, consisting of a small metal bar struck with a hard wooden or metal mallet. It may or may not be of definite pitch. Sometimes the blacksmith's anvil itself is used. Works calling for one or more anvils include the "Anvil Chorus" in Verdi's *Il trovatore,* Wagner's *Das Rheingold,* and Varèse's *Ionisation.*

Anwachsend [Ger.]. Growing, swelling.

À peine entendu [Fr.]. See *Peine entendu, à.*

Aperto [It., open]. (1) In horn playing, with the bell open, i.e., not stopped *(chiuso)* [see Horn, Stopped tones]. (2) In 14th-century music, the first of two endings for a section of a piece; thus, equivalent to the French **ouvert.*

A piacere [It.]. See *Piacere, a.*

Apollo. See *Apollon Musagète.*

Apollo Club. Any of a number of choral societies, at first usually all male, founded in the late 19th century in American cities, including Boston (1871), Chicago (1872), Brooklyn (1878), Cincinnati (1882), and St. Louis (1893).

Apollonicon. A large organ built by Flight and Robson of London between 1812 and 1817 that attempted to imitate the sound of an orchestra and that could be played either manually by five players or automatically by means of three pinned barrels, each 2.4 m (8 ft.) long. See also Automatic instruments.

Apollon Musagète [Fr., Apollo, Leader of the Muses]. A ballet, scored for string orchestra, by Stravinsky. It was produced in Washington, D.C., in 1928 (with choreography by Adolph Bolm) and in Paris later the same year (with choreography by George Balanchine). Stravinsky revised the work in 1947 and published it two years later; at some later time it was renamed simply *Apollo.*

Apostropha [Gr.]. See Neume.

Apothéose [Fr.]. Apotheosis, sometimes used as a title for works glorifying a deceased composer, e.g., François Couperin's *L'Apothéose de Corelli.*

Apotome [Gr.]. See Pythagorean scale.

Appalachian dulcimer. A plucked *zither of European derivation found chiefly in the Appalachian mountains. The narrow sound box is 70 to 100 cm (ca. 3 ft.) long and gently bulging, often in the shape of a figure 8. Three or four metal strings, often tuned c′ g′ g′, run the length of the instrument over a fingerboard with 13 or 14 frets. It is held horizontally in the player's lap and strummed with a quill or the thumb of the right hand. The string nearest the player (g′) is the melody string and is stopped either with a finger or with a wooden bar, called a noter, held in the left hand. The remaining strings are drones. It is used today principally to accompany folk singing. See ill. under Zither; see also *Hummel, Langleik, Scheitholt.*

Appalachian Spring. A ballet, scored for 13 instruments, by Copland (choreography by Martha Graham, who chose the title of the work from a Hart Crane poem and to whom the piece is dedicated), produced in Washington, D.C., in 1944. Its setting is a pioneer wedding at a Pennsylvania farmhouse. Much of the music is incorporated in a suite for full orchestra of the same name completed in 1945. The work includes variations on the Shaker hymn "Simple Gifts."

Appassionata; Sonata appassionata [It., impassioned]. Beethoven's Piano Sonata no. 23 in F minor op. 57 (1804–5). The title was first added to the work in 1838 by the publisher of an arrangement of it for piano four-hands.

Appassionato [It.]. Impassioned.

Appena [It.]. Scarcely.

Applied dominant. The *dominant of a pitch other than the tonic. See also Tonicization.

Appoggiando [It., leaning]. With succeeding notes stressed and closely connected.

Appoggiatura [It.]. (1) A dissonant pitch occurring in a strong metrical position and resolving by ascending or descending step to a consonance in a relatively weaker metrical position. See Counterpoint II, 4.

(2) An ornamental note falling on the beat, that is, one that replaces the main note at the moment of its attack, then resolves to the pitch of that note [Ex. 1]. The meaning of the word itself, "a leaning," suggests that

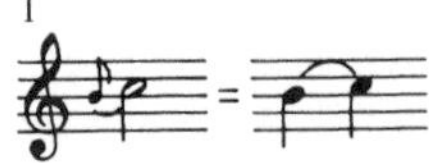

the ornament should be accented relative to its resolution; the term is often used for unaccented, single-note ornaments that anticipate the beat, however. Tartini (before 1756) described the *appoggiatura breve di passaggio* (short passing appoggiatura) in terms that are confusing and partly contradictory but clearly include anticipation of the beat and, even if on the beat, unaccented performance. As defined and discussed here, therefore, the term is not the exact equivalent of the German *Vorschlag,* the French *port de voix,* or of Tartini's *appoggiatura,* all of which may designate prebeat and/or unaccented, single-note ornaments. For these see *Port de voix* and Ornamentation.

The chief difficulties presented by the appoggiatura are: first, the two principal signs for it, a small note or a hook preceding the main note, can also stand for ornaments that precede the beat (*Nachschlag,* "grace note," *coulé*); second, the length, which is seldom specified by the notation, may vary from a small fraction of the main note to its whole value, and this length is sometimes governed by localized conventions, sometimes not; third, in recitative, where 18th- and 19th-century sources agree that appoggiaturas are obligatory in certain circumstances, they are rarely indicated by any sign, and the rules for their use are variable and sometimes conflicting; and fourth, there is vigorous disagreement in modern scholarship on all these matters. This article partially avoids these disputes by restricting the application of the term to on-beat graces.

Feminine phrase endings in recitative are a special case. When these consist of two notes on the same pitch, the first may be entirely replaced by a different note (usually a second or a fourth higher) [Ex. 2, in which Ex. 2c extends the practice to repeated notes in mid-phrase]. Whether such notes, which are never indicated by sign but are often written out in full, are ornaments in the usual meaning of the term is arguable; usage, however, has confirmed the term appoggiatura for the convention, probably in analogy to similar melismatic configurations of masculine endings [Exx. 2c and 3].

Except in the case of feminine endings in recitative, appoggiaturas are slurred to their note of resolution; many authorities also prescribe dynamic emphasis or shaping of the ornamental note. Appoggiaturas very often resolve on other ornaments, especially trills (for descending appoggiaturas) and mordents (for ascending ones). In such cases, the appoggiatura is

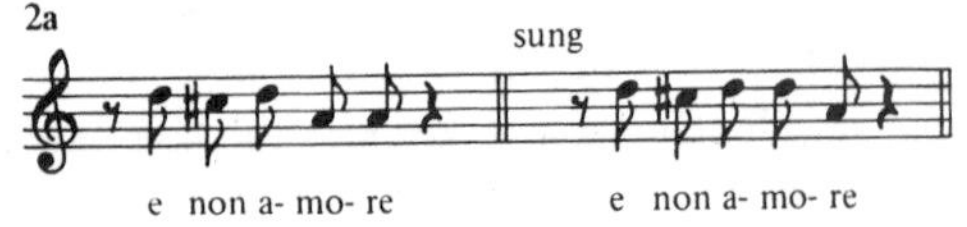

2a. Agricola, *Anleitung zur Singkunst,* p. 154.
2b, 2c, 3. Telemann, *Harmonischer Gottesdienst* (1725), after Spitta (trans. Eng.), II, 311, 312.
4. Leopold Mozart, *Versuch einer gründliche Violinschule* (trans. Eng.), p. 173.

generally accounted a part (often the "preparation") of the following ornament and is classified with it. Appoggiaturas may resolve via some intermediate ornament *(Zwischenschlag),* sometimes to correct the voice leading. Leopold Mozart gives several examples [Ex. 4].

The ornamental appoggiatura first appeared as one of a large number of possible embellishments to an existing melody in Giovanni B. Bovicelli's *Regole, passaggi di musica* (1594). Some of these were taken up in Praetorius's *Syntagma musicum* (1614–19) and thence into later German treatises [Ex. 5]. There were no conventional signs for the ornament in vocal or ensemble music, its introduction being left up to the performer. It is encountered in connection with lute music as early as 1615 in Nicolas Vallet's *Secretum musarum* and in 1636 in Mersenne's *Harmonie universelle.* Here it was indicated by signs, as also in a mid-17th-century German keyboard manuscript, *US-NH* Hintze (see *NeuO*). Something like it was also described by various Italian and German writers from Bovicelli on under the term *intonatio* or *intonazione.* This was a way of attacking the first note of a song from one or more degrees below and sliding up to the written pitch. Otherwise, the appoggiatura, if named at all, was included under the generic term *accent* or one of its variants—a term applied loosely to many short ornaments in the 17th century. It was in French music for lute and keyboard in the last third of the 17th century that the appoggiatura and the signs for it—either a small note or a hook preceding the main note—began to take their place in a code of graces, the most influential figure being D'Anglebert (1689), who used the terms *chûte* and *port de voix.* Neither in his nor in any other French usage, however, was any term established that applied exclusively to the appoggiatura as understood here [Ex. 6]. In England, the falling appoggiatura was termed backfall (Simpson, 1659, and others), while the rising one had several names: rise, half-fall (Mace, 1676), and, most commonly, forefall (Purcell and others). These terms appear not to have been used for graces anticipating the beat. The signs were strokes slanting in the desired direction and placed before or above the note [see table under Ornamentation].

In the 18th century, the appoggiatura began to assume a dominant role among the single-note ornaments, and at the same time to be indicated more and more commonly by a small note to the exclusion of the older signs. (In spite of a few attempts to make the values of the small notes reflect the actual length, they usually bore no relation to their duration in practice.) In 1723, Tosi wrote of former times, probably the late 17th century, when Italian singers knew where to place their appoggiaturas (which he regarded as essential to the art), and lamented the growing habit of marking them in the music; his English translator noted in 1743 that "in all the modern Italian compositions the Appoggiatura's are mark'd, supposing the

5

6

7

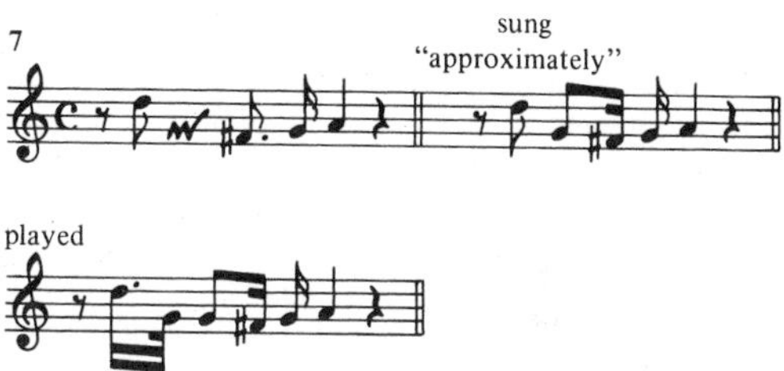

8a

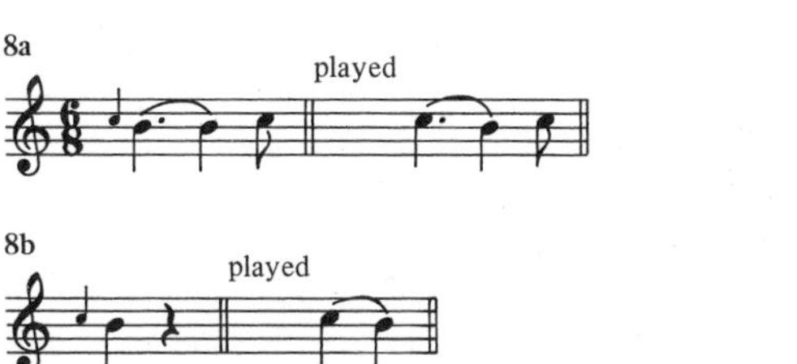

5. Bovicelli, *Diversi modi di diminuire,* from *Regole, passaggi* (1594), p. 17. 6. D'Anglebert, *Pièces de clavecin* (1689). 7. Heinichen, *Der Generalbass in der Composition* (1728), after *NeuO,* p. 179.

singers to be ignorant where to place them." In Germany, the term *Accent,* still used by J. S. Bach, gave way to *Vorschlag* (e.g., Heinichen, 1728, who distinguished the instrumental from the vocal appoggiatura by prefixing the former with a short anticipation, as in Ex. 7). With the rise of the *galant* style and the appearance of the great treatises of the 1750s [see Ornamentation], the appoggiatura assumed an importance unequaled before or since. It was treated most exhaustively by C. P. E. Bach, who insisted upon it as a replacement for *Nachschläge* and other prebeat graces, and who implied that the extremes of both shortness and length required by the taste of his time were relatively new, thus presumably not characteristic of his father's formative years.

C. P. E. Bach distinguished between variable or long appoggiaturas and invariable short ones. His rules for the variable ones were accepted generally—though with due regard for exceptions occasioned by different contexts—well into the 19th century: variable appoggiaturas occupied half the value of notes divisible in two equal parts and two-thirds the value of triple ones. They might also occupy the whole value of the first of two tied notes or of a note followed by a rest, the rest being replaced by the resolution of the appoggiatura [Ex. 8]. Neither Bach nor anyone else applied these rules rigidly, as they could lead to musical absurdities, but they were a point of departure. Bach's invariable appoggiatura was supposed to be so short that it took hardly any value from the main note; it could be lengthened in gentle pieces, however, to soften its snap. And since in practice the sign for it was the same as for the long one and the contexts appropriate to the two types overlapped, the distinction between it and the variable appoggiatura was far from rigorous. In the end, the rules for the length of appoggiaturas given by Bach and the other theorists provide the modern performer with sure answers in a minority of real musical situations, but the performer is saved by two circumstances: the wealth of examples in the many treatises, if studied and absorbed, can give an excellent sense of what would be in or out of style; and composers are very apt to write out appoggiaturas in contexts resembling those in which they use signs, thus suggesting the probable interpretation to be placed on the signs. This salutary situation helps to resolve the other problems raised by appoggiaturas: when to insert unmarked ones, what notes to use, what accidentals, etc.

In the 19th century, the short appoggiatura was increasingly replaced by the short grace note before the beat, while the long one was incorporated into the essential (fully notated) melody, becoming a salient characteristic of the styles of Wagner, Brahms, and Mahler. This evolution was gradual, however, and Chopin insisted on the execution of single grace notes simultaneously with the bass, citing as his model the *bel canto* of Italian opera singers (Eigeldinger, 1979, pp. 91–92, 165–66, 192).

See also Double appoggiatura; for bibl. see Ornamentation. (2) D.F.

Apprenti sorcier, L' [Fr., The Sorcerer's Apprentice]. A symphonic poem by Paul Dukas composed in 1897 and based on Goethe's ballad "Der Zauberlehrling."

Appuy [Fr.]. An 18th-century term for a note having the quality of an appoggiatura. It usually refers to the appoggiatura that constitutes the first note of the *tremblement* or *cadence* [see Trill]. P.A.

Appuyé [Fr.]. Accented.

Après-midi d'un faune, L'. See *Prelude to "The Afternoon of a Faun."*

Aquitanian neume, notation. See Neume.

Arabella. Opera ("lyrical comedy") in three acts by Richard Strauss (libretto by Hugo von Hofmannsthal after his short novel *Lucidor*), produced in Dresden in 1933. Setting: Vienna, 1860.

Arabesque [Fr.], **Arabeske** [Ger.]. An ornament characteristic of Arabic art and architecture; hence, similarly decorative or florid musical material or a composition employing such material. As a title, the term is used by Schumann (op. 18), Debussy, and others.

Arab music. See Islamic music; Near and Middle East; Quranic chant.

Aragonesa [Sp.], **aragonaise** [Fr.]. From Aragón [see *Jota*].

Arará [Sp.]. A Cuban cult drum. See Rada drum.

Arcata [It.]. Bow stroke; *a. in giù,* down-bow; *a. in su,* up-bow.

Arcato [It.]. Bowed.

Archduke Trio. Popular name for Beethoven's Piano Trio in B♭ major op. 97 (1810–11), dedicated to his patron the Archduke Rudolph.

Arched harp. A *harp with a curved neck, usually forming a continuous line with the sound box. The arched harp thus resembles a musical bow with several strings instead of one. Such instruments are depicted in the third millennium B.C.E. in Mesopotamia and Egypt. They are important today in Burma and sub-Saharan Africa. See *Saùng-gauk.*

Archet [Fr.], **archetto** [It.]. The bow of a stringed instrument.

Archi [It.]. Bows; hence, an instruction to resume bowing after a passage marked *pizzicato.

Architectural acoustics. See Acoustics IV.

Archlute [Fr. *archiluth;* Ger. *Erzlaute;* It. *arciliuto, liuto attiorbato;* Sp. *archilaúd*]. A small six- or seven-course lute to which an extended pegbox has been added to hold six or seven unfretted bass courses. Used in Italy for solo and continuo in the 17th and 18th centuries, it retained the Renaissance tuning with added basses, F_1 G_1 A_1 B_1 C D E F G c f a d′ g′. Alessandro Piccinini (1623) claimed its invention. R.L.

Arcicembalo, arciorgano [It.]. Keyboard instruments (a harpsichord and an organ, respectively) with divided keys that permit the playing of intervals smaller than a semitone and/or the playing of pure as against tempered [see Temperament] intervals in a variety of keys. Such instruments were described by Nicola Vicentino in his *L'antica musica ridotta a la moderna prattica* (1555) and *Descrizione dell' arciorgano* (1561). His instruments were intended to make possible the performance of the diatonic, chromatic, and enharmonic genera of ancient Greek theory. The later, somewhat simpler instruments to which the terms have been applied were intended primarily to provide alternatives to tempered tuning.

Arco [It.]. The bow of a stringed instrument; hence, also an instruction (sometimes in the phrase *col arco,* with the bow) to resume bowing after a passage marked *pizzicato.

Arditamente, ardito [It.]. Boldly.

A re, are. See Hexachord.

Areito. A ceremonial dance among the pre-Conquest inhabitants of Hispaniola, according to the Spanish chronicler Gonzalo Fernández de Oviedo (1478–1557). The term appears frequently in other early descriptions of indigenous musical life elsewhere in the Greater Antilles, in Mexico, and in Central America.
D.S.

Argentina. Of all South American countries, Argentina has one of the richest art music traditions and perhaps the most active contemporary musical life.

I. *Contemporary institutions.* Buenos Aires boasts of several professional orchestras, including the Orquesta sinfónica nacional, the Orquesta filarmónica de Buenos Aires, the Ensemble musical de Buenos Aires, and the Camerata Bariloche. Many provincial cities also have professional orchestras. The Teatro Colón in Buenos Aires, inaugurated in 1908, is one of the largest opera houses in the world. It has its own orchestra and mounts a season with standard repertory and international stars. There are occasional productions of opera in other Argentine cities.

Public support for art music in Argentina is extensive. The Teatro Colón is subsidized by the municipal government of Buenos Aires, and most major orchestras receive some form of government financing. The Fondo nacional de las artes, created in 1958, lends money and provides subsidies to musical organizations. It also organizes concerts, gives prizes to composers and performers, publishes music and books about music, and issues recordings. The Radio nacional and the Radio municipal in Buenos Aires not only broadcast music but sponsor concerts and recordings. Many private organizations contribute to Argentine musical life, among them the Asociación Amigos de música, which runs an orchestra and sponsors the Buenos Aires Bach Festival, the Mozarteum argentino, modeled on the Salzburg Mozarteum, and the Asociación wagneriano. Several societies foster and promote contemporary Argentine art music.

Several conservatories offer professional music education in Argentina. Among them are the Conservatorio de música de Buenos Aires (Conservatorio Williams), the Conservatorio nacional de música Carlos López Buchardo, and the Conservatorio municipal de música (Manuel de Falla). The Teatro Colón operates an Instituto de arte, which concentrates on music for the theater and ballet. The Universidad Católica Argentina offers a doctorate in music. Despite the resources of Argentine music education, many contemporary Argentine musicians—performers, conductors, and composers—have gone abroad for training, and many have remained abroad.

II. *History.* In the 17th and the first half of the 18th century, art music in Argentina was cultivated mainly by the church, especially by the Jesuits. With the growth and commercial prosperity of Buenos Aires in the late 18th century, the theater became a vital force in Argentine musical life. By the end of the 19th century, Buenos Aires had a large number of theaters, and most provincial capitals had one or more, offering Italian and French operas and Spanish **zarzuelas,* plus concerts by touring virtuosi. Italian music and musicians were very influential in Argentina during the 19th and the early 20th century, in part because of the large number of Italian immigrants. But operas and salon music were composed by Argentinians as well, including Francisco Hargreaves (1847–1900) and Juan Gutiérrez (1840–1906). Nationalism became an important force in Argentine music in the late 19th century. Composers such as Alberto Williams (1862–1952), Julián Aguirre (1868–1924), Arturo Berutti (1862–1938), and Felipe Boero (1884–1952) wrote music that drew from Argentine traditions, literature, and folk music, particularly the songs and dances of the gauchos. This nationalist trend continued well into the 20th century, but in the 1930s several Argentine composers began to espouse a cosmopolitan and modernist style, influenced by *twelve-tone techniques and *serialism. The most noted exponents of this trend were Juan Carlos Paz (1901–72) and Alberto Ginastera (1916–83). By the 1960s, avant-garde music was thriving in Argentina. From 1963 to 1970 the Centro interamericano de altos estudios musicales, financed by the Rockefeller Foundation, brought internationally famous composers to work and teach in Buenos Aires and also established an electronic music studio. Among the new Argentine composers active during this period were Roberto Garcia Morillo (b. 1911), Roberto Caamaño (b. 1923), Antonio Tauriello (b. 1931), Alcides Lanza (b. 1929), Francisco Kröpfl (b. 1928), Gerardo Gandini (b. 1936), and Armando Krieger (b. 1940). Younger Argentine composers who made considerable reputations and established residence abroad include Mario Davidovsky (b. 1934) and Mauricio Kagel (b. 1931).

III. *Folk and popular music.* The indigenous population of Argentina is relatively small in comparison with that of other Latin American countries. Nevertheless, some tribes and groups preserve aspects of their traditional musics along with features borrowed from European culture. The folk music of the European-descended and mixed population flows from Spanish, African, and Andean sources. Characteristic song types are the **vidala, vidalita, *estilo, *triste, cifra,* and **milonga,* the last two traditionally sung by *payadores* (minstrels). Among traditional dances are the **zamba, *gato, malambo, *milonga,* and **chacarera.* The **tango,* which is a song type as well as a dance, developed in Buenos Aires in the late 19th century and is often considered the national music of Argentina. *Cuarteto* dance music of Córdoba attracted massive audiences in the late 20th century. See also Latin America.

Bibl.: Carlos Vega, *Panorama de la música popular argentina* (Buenos Aires: Editorial Losada, 1944). Isabel Aretz, *El folklore musical argentino* (Buenos Aires: Ricordi americana, 1952). Francisco Curt Lange, *La música eclesiástica en Córdoba durante la dominación hispánica* (Córdoba: Impr de la Universidad, 1956). Horacio A. Ferrer, *El tango: Su historia y evolución* (Buenos Aires: A Peña Lillo, 1960). Vincente Gesualdo, *Historia de la música en la Argentina* (Buenos Aires: Editorial Beta, 1961). *Folklore musical y música folklórica argentina* [6 records with booklets] (Buenos Aires: Fondo nacional de las artes República Argentina, 1966). Roberto Caamaño, *La historia del Teatro Colón* (Buenos Aires: Editorial Cinetea, 1969). Rodolfo Arizaga, *Enciclopedia de la música argentina* (Buenos Aires: Fondo nacional de las artes, 1971). Julie M. Taylor, "Tango: Theme of Class and Nation," *Ethno* 20 (1976): 273–91.

Arghūl [Ar.]. A Middle Eastern *double clarinet made of cane. The shorter pipe has six finger holes; the longer is a drone. See also *Zummārah;* see ill. under Near and Middle East.

Aria [It.]. A self-contained composition for solo voice, usually with instrumental accompaniment and occurring within the context of a larger form such as opera, oratorio, or cantata.

The term first appeared at the end of the 14th century signifying a manner or style of singing or playing. This meaning continued into the 15th and 16th centuries (when the word was joined to certain place names, as in *aria veneziana* or *aria napoletana*), but the term came increasingly to mean tune or lyrical piece. Aria could also refer to a melodic scheme or pattern used for singing texts of similar poetic structure, such as the sonnet, *terza rima,* or *ottava rima,* and was sometimes used to designate strophic pieces for three or four voices in homophonic texture—pieces that might otherwise be called **canzonetta* or **villanella.* The term was further attached to instrumental pieces, either accompaniments of songs or independent works such as the **romanesca* and **ruggiero.*

In the 17th century, the aria existed as a portion of a larger work, such as an opera, or as an independent piece sometimes published in a collection like Giulio Caccini's *Le nuove musiche* (first collection 1601/2, second collection 1614). The forms favored were strophic or strophic-bass [see Strophic variations]. In many cases the strophes were separated by a *ritornello played either by strings or by the basso continuo. An example of a strophic-bass aria is the prologue sung by Musica in Monteverdi's *Orfeo.* Although arias at this time differed from recitative in their formal organization, they could be similar to recitative in melodic style. By the second third of the 17th century, triple meter became a characteristic feature of arias. About that time, ostinato arias—arias over a *ground bass—also came into use, particularly for laments.

In the later 17th century, the da capo aria became increasingly important. Composers found this form not merely useful but vital for close to a century. Its crystallization in the first decades of the 18th century was due in part to a standardization concomitant with rapid production (composers such as Hasse, Handel, Porpora, Leo, and Vinci each having written perhaps over 1,000 da capo arias) and in part to the perfect balance it achieved, judged by the aesthetic standards of the time, of drama, poetry, and music. The text for a da capo aria, as seen in the librettos of Zeno and Metastasio, was typically a poem in two strophes, each strophe normally containing three to six lines. Whatever the rhythmic and metric scheme of the strophes as a whole, the final line of the strophe normally ended with an accented syllable, and the final lines of the two strophes formed a rhyme. The first strophe of the poem provided the text for the first section of the da capo aria. By the 1720s and 1730s, a typical scheme for the first part had emerged: an instrumental ritornello; a full statement of the first strophe with a harmonic movement from tonic to dominant; a further ritornello in the dominant; a second full statement of the first strophe either beginning in the tonic or moving quickly back to it; a final statement of the ritornello in the tonic. The second strophe provided the text for the middle section of the da capo aria. This section usually provided harmonic contrast by avoiding the tonic, often using the relative key. The middle section might be more lightly scored than the outer sections and generally presented the full strophe only once, although internal text might be repeated. Then came the return of the first strophe and its music, a repetition that the singer was usually expected to vary with improvised ornamentation. But the form of the da capo aria was predictable only on the largest level: ABA. Matters such as the relation of the melodic material of the ritornello to that of the voice, the orchestration of the ritornello, the balance of the tonic- and dominant-controlled sections within the first part, and the degree of contrast between the first and second sections were all variable.

The da capo aria came under increasing criticism from Gluck and others by the final third of the 18th century, for both musical and dramatic reasons. In some instances, it became merely a virtuoso singer's plaything—not only undramatic but antidramatic. The impossibility of dramatic progress in a form that returned to the words with which it began was also criticized. In the second half of the 18th century, a number of alternative forms for the aria emerged. One possibility was an abridgment of the da capo—the dal segno aria, in which the return was not to the beginning of the aria but to a point marked by a sign after the ritornello, often the beginning of the second full statement of the first strophe. Arias were also constructed along the lines of instrumental movements, in binary, sonata, or rondo forms. New procedures emerged, such as the intrusion of a chorus or another soloist. Nevertheless, the form of the da capo aria was still to be found, though fully written out, in the early *opere serie* of Mozart. Comic opera in particular showed a notable variety of formal procedures during the 18th century. One particularly striking innovation was the "double" aria, in which two tempos (usually slow–fast) outlined two contrasting emotions.

In 19th-century Italian opera, at least from Rossini onward, this double aria became the norm and was typically expanded into an entire scene. First came the *scena,* an orchestrally accompanied recitative setting of unrhymed lines of variable length; then the first lyrical section, sometimes called *cantabile* and usually slow; then the *tempo di mezzo,* effecting a change of mood, usually by the arrival or interjection of secondary characters or the chorus; and finally the *cabaletta,* usually faster and more energetic than the *cantabile,* nearly always repeated literally with choral interjections. Each of these last three sections was set to rhymed, metrically stable verse, though typically the line length and syllabic stress changed from section to section. This double aria remained the standard form for Bellini, Donizetti, and early Verdi, and was even extended to duets and larger ensembles, usually with an added confrontational movement (the *tempo d'attacco*) between the *scena* and *cantabile.* After *La traviata* (1853), however, Verdi became increasingly wary of the *cabaletta,* often preferring to end his scenes with a *coup de théâtre* at the *tempo di mezzo* stage.

In French grand opera, as represented by the works of Meyerbeer, the aria plays a less significant role. For example, in *Les Huguenots,* with seven significant roles for soloists, only four characters receive full-fledged arias. Some of the grandest, most imposing of Meyerbeer's arias are cast in a modified version of the Italian form; others make use of ternary, strophic, or refrain forms. The variety of terms used for arialike pieces in German romantic opera before Wagner is a reflection of the variety of formal procedures used. The terms *arie, arietta, solo, Lied, romanza, rondo, cavatina* are present in the works of Spohr, Schubert, Weber, and Marschner. Procedures run the gamut from simple strophic songs to complex multitempoed works. In the course of Wagner's life work, the aria, understood as a lyric, self-sufficient piece, gradually became less and less important, a reform whose impact was felt well beyond the bounds of German opera.

The aria has had a restricted role in 20th-century opera. One role is in situations in which the character is actually singing, as in the tenor's aria in Richard Strauss's *Der Rosenkavalier* or Marie's lullaby in Berg's *Wozzeck.* Some 20th-century operas, sometimes dubbed neoclassical, use arias in a frankly retrospective manner, for example Stravinsky's *The Rake's Progress* or Hindemith's *Cardillac.*

Bibl.: Nigel Fortune, "Italian Secular Monody from 1600 to 1635: An Introductory Survey," *MQ* 39 (1953): 171–95. Harold Powers, "Il Serse trasformato," *MQ* 47 (1961): 481–92, 48 (1962): 73–92. Michael Robinson, "The Aria in Opera Seria, 1725–1780," *PRMA* 88 (1961–62): 31–43. Sieghart Döhring, "Die Arienformen in Mozarts Opern," *MJb* (1968–70): 66–76. Warren Kirkendale, *L'aria di Fiorenza, id est Il ballo del gran duca* (Florence: Olschki, 1972). Friedrich Lippmann, *Vincenzo Bellini und die italienische Opera seria seiner Zeit, AnMca* 16 (1976). Julian Budden, *The Operas of Verdi,* 3 vols. (New York: Oxford U Pr, 1978–81). Charles Rosen, *Sonata Forms* (New York: Norton, 1980). Nino Pirrotta and Elena Povoledo, *Music and Theatre from Poliziano to Monteverdi,* trans. Karen Eales (Cambridge: Cambridge U Pr, 1981). Mary Hunter, "Text, Music, and Drama in Haydn's Italian Opera Arias: Four Case Studies," *JM* 7 (1989): 29–57. James Webster, "The Analysis of Mozart's Arias," *Mozart Studies,* ed. Cliff Eisen (New York: Oxford U Pr, 1991), pp. 101–99. C.G.

Aria del Gazzella [It.]. See *Bel fiore.*

Ariadne auf Naxos. Opera in one act and a prologue by Richard Strauss (libretto by Hugo von Hofmannsthal). In its original form, produced in Stuttgart in 1912, the opera was in one act only and was performed together with a condensed version of Molière's *Le bourgeois gentilhomme* (translation by Hofmannsthal, incidental music by Strauss). In 1916, it was produced in Vienna as an independent work with the addition of a prologue establishing a dramatic situation similar to that in Molière's play, whereby an *opera seria* is interwoven with the antics of a *commedia dell'arte* troupe. Setting: Vienna in the 18th century and Naxos, ancient Greece.

Arietta [It.]. A small aria or a song, less elaborate than an aria, sometimes sung by a secondary character in an opera. The term was in use by the middle of the 17th century.

Ariette [Fr.]. (1) In French opera of the first half of the 18th century, a virtuoso aria, written in imitation of the Italian style. It might contain runs, trills, or long sustained notes in the vocal part, and was frequently in da capo form. (2) In French comic opera of the second half of the 18th century, simply a song. The **comédie mêlée d'ariettes* is thus a spoken play with added songs.

Arioso [It.]. A lyrical manner of setting a text, usually a recitative text, in an opera, cantata, or oratorio. The term was in use in Italy by the 1630s. An *arioso* may grow directly out of recitative and be distinguished from it by text repetition, more florid or expressive melodic line, melodic sequence, or a more regular harmonic rhythm. For such a passage, *recitativo arioso* may be a more accurate designation. *Arioso* may also indicate a small aria that, although songlike and tonally self-contained, does not have the formal shape of a regular aria (e.g., strophic or *da capo,* depending on the period). Handel's operas and oratorios contain numerous examples of such pieces, "Ombra mai fù" from *Serse* being one of the best known. The term may also be applied to instrumental movements in *arioso* style, as in Beethoven's Piano Sonata op. 110.

Arithmetic and harmonic mean. The arithmetic mean between two numbers exceeds one number by the same amount that it falls short of the other. Thus, a is the arithmetic mean between x and y if, assuming $x > y$, $x - a = a - y$. The harmonic mean between two numbers exceeds one number by a part of that number and falls short of the other number by the same part of the other. Thus, h is the harmonic mean between x and y if, assuming $x > y$, $(h - y) \div y = (x - h) \div x$. Ancient Pythagoreans recognized the musical application of these means, noting that the arithmetic mean and harmonic mean of the octave produced the fourth and fifth. Usually they represented the octave by 12:6, which in most cases represents a ratio of string lengths, and thus noted that the arithmetic mean 9 produced the fourth 12:9 and the fifth 9:6. The harmonic mean 8 produced the fifth 12:8 and the fourth 8:6 [see Pythagorean hammers]. In antiquity, the arithmetic and harmonic means were always discussed along with the geometric mean *(g)*. Assuming $x > y$, $x \div g = g \div y$. Aristides Quintilianus made the observation that if arithmetic means (a and b) are inserted between members of a continuous geometric proportion *(x:g:y),* then harmonic means are produced (*De musica,* iii.5). In other words, if a is the arithmetic mean between x and g, and b the arithmetic mean between g and y, then g is the harmonic mean between a and b. Algebraically, $(x + \sqrt{xy})\,(y + \sqrt{xy}) \,/\, (x + y + 2\sqrt{xy}) = \sqrt{xy}$.

Walter Odington argued that the Pythagorean ditone (81:64) was dissonant and in no way formed a mean of the fifth (96:64) (*Summa de speculatione musice,* i.9 and ii.10). Zarlino, in his numerological justification for the use of imperfect consonances in counterpoint, observed that the pure major (5:4) and minor (6:5) thirds can be got by harmonic and arithmetic means of the fifth (*Le istitutioni harmoniche,* iii.31). If C = 30 and G = 20, then the harmonic mean is 24 or E. The arithmetic mean is 25 or E♭. A.B.

Arlésienne, L' [Fr., The Woman of Arles]. Incidental music by Bizet, composed in 1872, to Alphonse Daudet's play of the same name. Bizet arranged an orchestral suite from this work in 1872. A second suite was arranged posthumously by Ernest Guiraud in 1879.

Armed Man. See *Homme armé, L'.*

Armenian chant. The ecclesiastical monody of the Armenian Apostolic Church. From the inauguration of its autonomy in 552, the Armenian Church developed a liturgical, literary, and artistic tradition independent from the rest of Christendom. One firm musical connection, however, is the employment of an **oktoēchos* and of *ecphonetic and neumatic notations for lections and hymns. According to Lazarus of Parb (5th century), Armenians at first used alphabetical letters to fix the music of their chants. A much later source, however, declares that the music was transmitted orally up to the 12th century.

The Armenian Divine Office comprises 1,166 *shakaran* (hymns), which are arranged in an *oktoēachos (dzayn)* and collected in a book known as the *Sharaknots.* Its present form constitutes the reworking of the Catholicos Nerses IV Klayetsi (1112–73), "the Gracious," who enlarged the volume and introduced popular elements. The most ancient hymn texts had been in prose and many were translations from Greek, but during the renaissance in Lesser Armenia (Cilicia) under the Rubenid dynasty (ca. 1080), a new literary and musical life began. Hymns in verse were written, and musical notation was developed.

Armenian manuscripts of the 9th century contain an indigenous ecphonetic notation used for the cantillation of readings from the Old and New Testaments. Like the Byzantine lectionary notation, the Armenian also developed from prosodic accents. Three groups of signs have been discerned: (1) those indicating pitch; (2) those indicating rhythm; and (3) those denoting special formulas at the beginning and end of lessons. A contemporaneous melodic notation called *khaz* notation survives. Its invention is dubiously attributed to the Abbot Khachatur of Taron (1100–1184), whose celebrated *tagh* (an Armenian hymnodic form) is still sung at the beginning of the *Divine Liturgy. As with the Palaeobyzantine systems and the unheighted Latin neumes, the *khaz* system is not a diastematic notation; it merely identifies the rising and falling direction of the melody. It also outlines conventional formulas and indicates rhythm and expression. In addition to approximately 25 neumes, it comprises 12 consonants. The lack of any medieval Armenian musical treatise precludes absolute knowledge or interpretation of the *khaz* system.

Armenian chants exist in both simple and florid styles, the latter predominating in the later Middle Ages. By the 16th century, *khaz* notation was incapable of describing new progressive musical developments. Finally, in 1813, the system was reformed, and although certain of the old *khaz* neumes were retained, they were given new meanings.

Bibl.: Léonce Dayan, *Les hymnes de l'église arménienne* (Venice: Congrégation mékhitariste à St Lazare, 1954). Heinrich Husmann, "Die Gesänge der armenischen Liturgie," in *Geschichte der katholischen Kirchenmusik,* ed. Karl Gustav Fellerer, 1 (Kassel: Bärenreiter, 1972): 99–108. Bernard Outtier, "Recherches sur la genèse de l'octoéchos arménien," *Études grégoriennes* 14 (1973): 127–211. V. Nersessian, ed., *Essays on Armenian Music* (London, 1978). V. Nersessian, *The Armenian Neume System of Notation* (London, 1999).

D.E.C.

Armonica. *Glass harmonica.

Armonica a bocca [It.]. *Mouth organ.

Armure [Fr.]. *Key signature.

Arpa [It., Sp.]. Harp.

Arpanetta [It.; Ger. *Spitzharfe*]. A double *zither popular in Italy and Germany in the 16th, 17th, and 18th centuries. It has strings on both sides of its trapezoidal sound box: steel strings on one side for the melody and brass strings on the other for accompaniment. The player sets the instrument upright with the steel strings on the right and plucks it like a harp with the fingers of both hands.

Arpège [Fr.]. *Arpeggio; in earlier writing also *arpègement, arpégé*. See also *Acciaccatura*.

Arpeggiando, arpeggiato [It.]. See Bowing (9).

Arpeggiate, arpeggiation. To sound the pitches of a chord successively, as in an *arpeggio, rather than simultaneously; the sounding of a chord in this way. See also Schenker analysis.

Arpeggio [It., fr. *arpa,* harp; Fr. *arpège;* Sp. *arpegio*]. A chord whose pitches are sounded successively, usually from lowest to highest, rather than simultaneously. In current notational practice, it may be indicated by any of the methods shown in Ex. 1, all of which should be interpreted to mean performance from lowest to highest pitch unless the contrary is specifically indicated by additional signs or the reversal of the order of the smaller notes. A distinction between simultaneous arpeggios in the two hands in keyboard music and a single arpeggio in which the

1

2a 2b

two hands play successively is often indicated by the distinction between separate wavy lines for the two hands [Ex. 2a] and a single wavy line spanning the chords of the two hands [Ex. 2b]. Although some modern authorities insist that arpeggios should always begin on the beat, the treatises on *ornamentation of the 17th and 18th centuries do not explicitly state any such rule, and musical context often suggests the contrary, as when the topmost pitch has melodic and rhythmic functions that would be contradicted by its displacement from the beat [Ex. 3] (see *NeuO*).

Writers of the 17th and 18th centuries use a variety of signs to indicate the ascending arpeggio *(arpègement en montant)* [Ex. 4] and the descending arpeggio *(arpègement descendant)* [Ex. 5]. The earliest of these seems to be the diagonal stroke used by French lutenists of the early 17th century. Although the angle of the stroke sometimes indicates whether the arpeggio rises or falls, later writers (e.g., Marpurg, 1749) do not always maintain this distinction, the rising arpeggio being indicated by a stroke below the chord, the falling arpeggio by a stroke sloping in either direction above it.

3

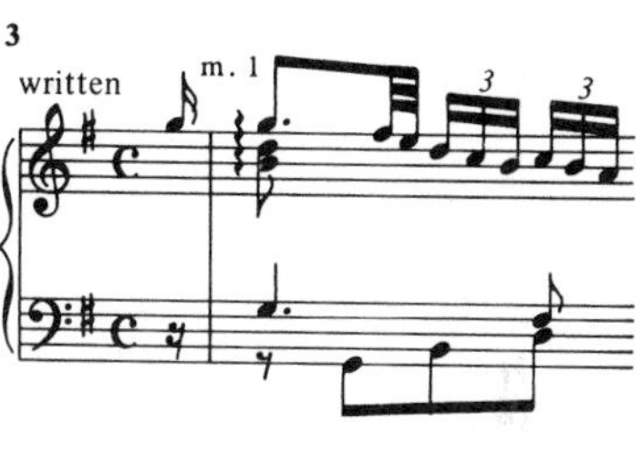

3. Bach, Allemande, Partita no. 5 BWV 829 (after *NeuO*).

The figurate or figured arpeggio (*arpégé* or *arpègement figuré*) is one in which nonharmonic tones are introduced into the arpeggio and not sustained [Ex. 6; see also *Acciaccatura*]. These added tones may be indicated in various ways, e.g., with a diagonal stroke

4 5

6

between or a vertical curved line connecting the two chordal tones between which a nonharmonic tone is to be added.

Although the arpeggio is particularly associated

with plucked instruments, such as the harp, lute, and guitar, and stringed keyboard instruments, it is common also in music for bowed instruments, such as the members of the violin and viol families, where, however, it is often a technical necessity deriving from the limited ability of such instruments to sustain three or more pitches simultaneously [see Bowing]. For bibl. see Ornamentation.

Arpeggione. (1) A bowed guitar invented by J. G. Staufer in 1824. It is the size of a cello, its bridge and fingerboard are curved, its neck is fretted, and its six strings are tuned like those of the guitar, E A d g b e′. (2) A sonata in A minor by Schubert, D. 821 (1824), for arpeggione and piano, now often played on the cello.

Arpichordum. On Flemish *muselar* (i.e., center-plucking) *virginals of the Renaissance, and reportedly on later German *harpsichords, a mechanism consisting of a sliding wooden batten with metal hooks that could be pressed against the strings at one end, causing them to buzz when plucked. The buzzing tone was sometimes compared to the sound of organ reeds *(Schnarrwerk)* or of the Renaissance harp with brays. In virginals, the *arpichordum* effect was almost always limited to the lowest 25–30 notes. References occur in Sebastian Virdung, *Musica getutscht* (Basel, 1511); Michael Praetorius, *Syntagma musicum,* vol. 2, *De organographia* (Wolfenbüttel, 1619), ch. 43; Jakob Adlung, *Anleitung zu der musikalischen Gelahrtheit* (Erfurt, 1758), par. 246, n. *r;* and Peter Nathanael Sprengel, *Handwerk und Künste in Tabelen,* 11 (Berlin, 1773): 265. H.S.

Arpicordo [It.]. In 16th- and early 17th-century Italy, one of the names used for virginals, because the layout of their bridges and strings is like a harp (It. *arpa*). Publications whose titles include the term are *Intabolatura nova di varie sorte de balli da sonare per arpichordi, clauicembali, spinette, et manachordi* (1551) and Giovanni Picchi's *Intavolatura di balli d'arpicordo* (1620). H.S., rev. J.Ko.

Arraché [Fr., torn]. Forceful pizzicato.

Arrangement [Ger. *Bearbeitung*]. (1) The adaptation of a composition for a medium different from that for which it was originally composed, usually with the intention of preserving the essentials of the musical substance; also the result of such a process of adaptation. The practice is widespread at least as early as the 14th through the 16th century, when numerous vocal works (both sacred and secular) were arranged for keyboard instruments and the lute [see Intabulation]. Bach provides the most celebrated examples from the Baroque era in his arrangements of works by Vivaldi. Mozart in turn arranged some fugues by Bach for string trio and quartet.

Numerous works from the 18th and 19th centuries were arranged for piano, often, in the case of operas, orchestral works, and some chamber music, to aid the study and dissemination of the works. Some such arrangements, however, notably those of Liszt, were clearly intended to have artistic merit in their own right as well as to serve as vehicles for the display of virtuosity by performers. Earlier in the 20th century, there was a considerable vogue for arranging works (including keyboard works) by Bach for the modern symphony orchestra. This has largely been displaced by the increasing concern for authentic *performance practice. There are also numerous examples from the 18th century to the present of composers arranging their own works for a new medium of performance. The motives for this may be as much commercial as artistic.

The terms transcribe and transcription are sometimes used interchangeably with arrange and arrangement. Often, however, the former imply greater fidelity to the original. Transcription also means the translation of works from earlier forms of musical notation into the notation now in use. See also Additional accompaniment, Orchestration.

(2) In popular music and jazz, a specific version, including orchestration if for an ensemble, of a tune and its harmonies. In such repertories, it is usually assumed that the composer's role has been to specify the melody and to name the accompanying harmonies in a rather straightforward way, leaving the arranger complete freedom with respect to performance medium and orchestration, and considerable latitude with respect to rhythmic and harmonic detail. An arrangement is in general something written down or at least preserved essentially unchanged from performance to performance rather than improvised. This model, in which a tune may circulate widely in a number of quite different arrangements, is somewhat less characteristic of recent jazz and rock than of popular music and jazz up until about 1960. The role of the arranger is crucial in the music of the *big bands and in a significant proportion of music for films, television, and musicals. Among the more notable arrangers are Robert Russell Bennett, Quincy Jones, and Nelson Riddle. See also Head arrangement.

Bibl.: Evlyn Howard-Jones, "Arrangements and Transcriptions," *ML* 16 (1935): 305–11. Russell Garcia, *The Professional Arranger-Composer* (New York: Criterion Music Corp, 1954). Robert Russell Bennett, *Instrumentally Speaking* (Melville, N.Y.: Belwin-Mills, 1975). Walter Koller, *Aus der Werkstatt der Wiener Klassiker: Bearbeitungen Haydns, Mozarts und Beethovens* (Tutzing: Schneider, 1975). Marlin Skiles, *Music Scoring for TV and Motion Pictures* (Blue Ridge Summit, Pa.: Tab Bks, 1976).

Ars antiqua, arts vetus [Lat., ancient art, old art]. The style, genres, and notational devices of late 12th- and 13th-century (mostly French) polyphonic music, as contrasted with those of the *ars nova* of the 14th century. The self-conscious terms were highlighted in the early 14th century by Johannes de Muris, Philippe de Vitry, and Jacques de Liège, who were vaunting either the superiority or the decadence of the practices of their own time. In his *Notitia artis musicae* [*Ars novae musicae*] (1321) Johannes de Muris introduced the idea of an equipollence of binary to ternary mensurations, systematizing the set of rules governing all four levels of temporal measurement. The author lauds the work of those he terms *moderni musici.* The *Ars nova* (1322–23) of Philippe de Vitry appears in four manuscript sources, of which two contain a condensed first section, and one a reference to the same, that is entitled *Ars vetus.* Vitry confirmed the validity of duple ("imperfect") mensurations and proposed signs to indicate the four different combinations of duple and triple at the breve and semibreve levels. He also established the minim as an integral element of musical theory and performance. Jacques de Liège completed his magnum opus, the *Speculum musicae,* sometime between 1324 and 1325. In it he attacks the innovations of Johannes de Muris and other *moderni* and urges a return to the practice of the *antiqui,* among whom he cites Lambertus and Franco of Cologne. This conservative view was not limited to notation, however. Jacques complains about modern musical practice: words are lost, the measure is confused, genres such as organum and conductus are abandoned.

This seesaw between innovation and reaction in musical thought is not confined to the 14th century; it is manifested in similar and recurring controversies from Greek antiquity to the present day. In the case of the Middle Ages, the terminology of this antithesis between an ancient and a modern art or teaching is borrowed from Scholastic philosophy. Until the 12th century only the early works *(ars vetus)* of Aristotle had been known to the West; by the early 13th century almost the entirety of the remainder of his works *(ars nova)* had become available in Latin. J.Y.

Arsis and thesis [fr. Gr., raising, lowering]. (1) Originally, the raising and lowering of the foot in ancient Greek dance. By extension with respect to Greek verse, thesis referred to the long syllable of the poetic foot and arsis to the remainder of the foot. (2) Among Roman writers, who associated the rise and fall with the voice, and for many writers since then, the reverse of (1), i.e., arsis referring to the long syllable of the foot and thesis to the remainder; with respect to accentual verse, the accented and unaccented parts of the foot, respectively. (3) In musical usage, the metrically unaccented and accented parts of a measure, respectively [see Accent, Meter]; hence, often the equivalent of upbeat and downbeat, respectively. For writers of the 16th and 17th century (e.g., Zarlino and Morley), *per arsin et thesin* meant by inversion, usually with respect to canons. In the 18th century, however, Marpurg used the phrase to refer to a fugue in which the answer reverses the pattern of metrically strong and weak beats found in the subject.

Ars nova [Lat., new technique, new craft]. (1) A stylistic era of European (especially French and Italian) art music whose beginning may be conveniently marked by the manuscript *F-Pn* 146 (dated 1316) [see *Fauvel, Roman de*], and whose end is variously placed ca. 1330 (Schrade, 1955), ca. 1370 (Günther, 1963), ca. 1440 (Pirrotta, 1973), or sometime between the latter two dates. See also *Ars subtilior.*

The notion of a new art has been used at several junctures of music's history. Its association with the 14th century in particular is due to the prestige of Philippe de Vitry's treatise *Ars nova,* to Edmond de Coussemaker's 19th-century titles for 14th-century treatises, and, especially, to Hugo Riemann, who used the notational term to name an era in his widely influential *Handbuch der Musikgeschichte* (Leipzig: Breitkopf & Härtel, 1904–23). In the 14th century itself, "new" could denote at least three different styles. The new schools censured by Pope John XXII in his *Docta sanctorum patrum* (1324–25) are as much those of the 13th century as they are of the *ars nova* (witness John's particular dislike of *hocket, a genre that Jacques de Liège associates with the *antiqui*). The anonymous *De musica antiquae et nova* contrasts early 14th-century notation with previous practice. And the *Tractatus magistri Phillopoti Andree artis nove* (copied 1391; ed. *CS* 3 as *Tractatus de diversis figuris* attributed to Philipus de Caserta) discusses notational refinements associated with the last quarter of the century. In Italy, 14th-century music was seen more as a continuation of than a departure from the music of the 13th century. In light of this, many authors believe that the era is more justly known by its literary designation, *trecento.* Yet Italian scholars themselves continue to use the term *ars nova italiana.* See also *Ars antiqua,* Middle Ages.

(2) Two related but autonomous 14th-century repertories, centered in France and northern Italy, that are characterized by new conventions of notation and a new emphasis on polyphonic song (in France principally the **ballade,* **virelai,* and **rondeau;* in Italy the *madrigal, **caccia,* and **ballata*). The French repertory further gives prominence to polyphonic settings of Mass movements and *isorhythmic principles of construction, chiefly in motets.

In France the new techniques are first described in six contemporary treatises: Anonymous O[xford] P[aris], *Tractatus de musica* (ca. 1316–20); Jehan des Murs, *Notitia artis musicae* (1321); id., *Compendium musicae practicae* (1322); Philippe de Vitry, *Ars nova* (1322–23); Jacques de Liège, *Speculum musicae,* bk. 7 (1324–25; describes but does not advocate); Jehan des Murs, *Musica speculativa,* second version (1325) [for editions, see Theory]. These are antedated by several transitional works such as Anonymous VI (*CS* 1) and Anonymous II (*CS* 3, ca. 1300–10), which together illustrate the variety of notational practices competing for general adoption in early 14th-century Paris.

The methodology and vocabulary of scholastic argumentation permeate the central texts of the *ars* *nova.* Intellectually, the new craft attempts further to rationalize the theory of durations and to place it on an equal footing with the theory of consonances inherited from antiquity. To do this, an inherited typology of additive rhythmic patterns (or modes) is placed within the broader context of a theory of proportionately related metric levels. This accords equal status to binary and ternary divisions of the *brevis* and, especially, the *semibrevis,* and results in a system of four *prolations or meters equivalent to the modern 9/8, 6/8, 3/4, and 2/4 [see Mensural notation]. Two further and somewhat inconsistent features of *ars nova* notation are: first, the extension of earlier contextual rules to a broader class of note groups; and second, the limiting of contextual rules through the proliferation of new note shapes as unique and noncontextual signs for different durations and the broadened use of the *punctum* or dot to free older note shapes from contextual associations.

In Italy, the early *trecento* is marked by the fusion of indigenous 13th-century theory (e.g., Amerus, *Practica artis musice,* 1271) with notational practices of the French **ars antiqua.* The earliest sources are Guidonis Frater, *Ars musice mensurate* (1310–15); Marchetto da Padova, *Lucidarium musicae planae* (1316–17); id., *Pomerium musicae mensurabilis* (1317–18). Since 13th-century Italian theory already accounts for duple rhythm, the first and third of these treatises do not present this aspect of notation as revolutionary. In their use of the *punctum perfectionis,* these works expound a north Italian variant of the late 13th-century French notational practices associated with Petrus de Cruce. Accordingly, rhythmic patterns remain conceptually prior to meter. On the other hand, Marchetto adopts the new and noncontextual *semibrevis minima* from his French contemporaries.

Bibl.: Nino Pirrotta, "Marchettus da Padua and the Italian Ars Nova," *MD* 9 (1955): 57–71. Id., "Cronologia e denominazione dell' Ars Nova italiana," *Wégimont,* 1955, pp. 93–104. Leo Schrade, "The Chronology of the Ars Nova in France," *Wégimont,* 1955, pp. 37–59. Rudolf Bockholdt, "Semibrevis minima und Prolatio temporis: Zur Entstehung der Mensuraltheorie der Ars nova," *Mf* 16 (1963): 3–21. Ursula Günther, "Das Ende der *ars nova,*" *Mf* 16 (1963): 105–20. Marie Louise Martinez-Göllner, *Die Musik des frühen Trecento* (Tutzing: Schneider, 1963). Viola L. Hagopian, *Italian Ars nova Music: A Bibliographic Guide to Modern Editions and Related Literature* (Berkeley and Los Angeles: U of Cal Pr, 1964; 2nd ed., 1973). Francis J. Smith, "Ars Nova—a Re-Definition?," *MD* 18 (1964): 19–35, 19 (1965): 83–97. Nino Pirrotta, "Novelty and Renewal in Italy: 1300–1600," *von Fischer,* 1973, pp. 49–63. Daniel Leech-Wilkinson, "Ars Antiqua–Ars Nova–Ars Subtilior," *Antiquity and the Middle Ages,* ed. J. McKinnon (London, 1990), pp. 218–40. C.C.H.

Ars subtilior [Lat., more subtle art]. The intricate style of late 14th-century music by composers after Machaut such as Anthonello de Caserta, Egidius (the name of several musicians), Grimace, Matteo da Perugia, Philipoctus de Caserta, Jacob Senleches, Solage, and Trebor, about most of whom little is known. The term was introduced by Ursula Günther for a repertory whose notation (termed mannered by Willi Apel, whence also "manneristic style") combines features of French and Italian notation and can be extremely complex. The compositions, usually in one of the French **formes fixes,* often exhibit textures that are very complicated rhythmically. The repertory seems to have been centered in southern France and northern Spain.

Bibl.: Willi Apel, *The Notation of Polyphonic Music 900–1600* (Cambridge, Mass.: Mediaeval Acad, 1942, and later eds.). Id., *French Secular Compositions of the Fourteenth Century, CMM* 53, 3 vols. (1970, edition with commentary). Ursula Günther, "Das Ende der *Ars Nova,*" *Mf* 16 (1963): 105–20. Nigel Wilkins, "The Post-Machaut Generation of Poet-Musicians," *Nottingham Mediaeval Studies* 12 (1968): 40–84. Wulf Arlt, "Der Traktatus figurarum—Ein Beitrag zur Musiklehre des 'ars subtilior,'" *Schweizer Beiträge zur Musikwissenschaft* 1 (1972): 35–53.

Articulation. (1) In performance, the characteristics of attack and decay of single tones or groups of tones and the means by which these characteristics are produced. Thus, for example, *staccato and *legato are types of articulation. In the playing of stringed instruments, this is largely a function of *bowing; in wind instruments, of *tonguing. Groups of tones may be articulated (i.e., "phrased") so as to be perceived as constituting phrases [see Phrase, Phrasing]. Notational symbols for articulation first occur around 1600, are not uncommon in compositions from ca. 1620 to 1750, and occur with increasing attention to detail in works thereafter. See also Performance practice.

(2) In the analysis of musical form, a boundary or point of demarcation between formal segments, e.g., that produced by a cadence or rest. As a compositional process, articulation is comparable to punctuation in language.

Art of Fugue, The [Ger. *Die Kunst der Fuge*]. A didactic keyboard work by Bach, BWV 1080 (ca. 1745–50), first published in 1751, though the publication was partly overseen by Bach before his death in 1750. This printed edition contains 14 fugues, called *contrapuncti* (numbers 12 and 13 being completely invertible and thus in two versions each), 4 canons, 2 mirror fugues arranged for two keyboards, and an incomplete quadruple fugue, all based on the same theme [see Ex.]. The work exploits a wide variety of contrapuntal devices—inversion, stretto, augmentation, diminution, canon, double fugue, triple fugue, and quadruple fugue. A concluding chorale prelude,

"Wenn wir in höchsten Nöten sein" BWV 668, was added to the work by its editors to "compensate" for missing and incomplete material. The printed edition, however, represents a reordering of Bach's extant autograph score and adds several movements. Consequently, extended controversies have arisen as to the proper order of the *contrapuncti* and canons, the intended medium for performance (Bach having had the work engraved in open score without specifying the medium), the added chorale, and the role of the last fugue.

Bibl.: Donald Francis Tovey, *A Companion to "The Art of Fugue" (Die Kunst der Fuge) of J. S. Bach* (London: Oxford U Pr, H Milford, 1931). Christoph Wolff et al., "Bach's 'Art of Fugue': An Examination of the Sources," *CM* 19 (1975): 47–77. Walter Kolneder, *Die Kunst der Fugue: Mythen des 20. Jahrhunderts* (Wilhelmshaven: Heinrichshofen, 1977). Christoph Wolff, "Zur Chronologie und Kompositionsgeschichte von Bachs Kunst der Fuge," *BzMw* 25 (1983): 130–42; trans. in *Bach: Essays on His Life and Music* (Cambridge, Mass.: Harvard U Pr, 1991). Erich Bergel, *Bachs letzte Fuge: Die "Kunst der Fuge"* (Bonn: Brockhaus, 1985). Hans Heinrich Eggebrecht, *J. S. Bach's The Art of Fugue: The Work and Its Interpretation,* trans. Jeffrey L. Prater (Ames: Iowa St U Pr, 1993).

Art Rock. A subgenre of *rock music characterized by the use of larger forms and more complex harmonies than is common to most popular music. Some ensembles working in this genre have appropriated material from the orchestral repertory (such as Mussorgsky's *Pictures at an Exhibition,* arranged by Emerson, Lake, and Palmer), while others utilize more general formal principles of art music (e.g., *sonata form in "Close to the Edge" by the group Yes). Art Rock is synonymous with the term Progressive Rock, coined in the late 1970s. P.T.W.

Art song. A song intended for the concert repertory, as distinct from a folk or popular song. An art song traditionally is a setting of a text of high literary quality and, unlike most folk and popular songs, includes an accompaniment that is specified by the composer rather than improvised or arranged by or for the performer. See also Song.

As, ases [Ger.]. A-flat, A-double-flat. See Pitch names.

ASCAP. Abbr. for American Society of Composers, Authors, and Publishers. See Copyright and performance right.

Asia. See East Asia, South Asia, Southeast Asia, Near and Middle East.

Aspiration [Fr.]. (1) The French *accent* [see Appoggiatura]. (2) A one-finger vibrato *(plainte)* on the viola da gamba. (3) The substitution of silence for the last part of a note-value, indicated by a vertical stroke over the note.

Assai [It.]. Much, very much, e.g., *allegro assai,* very fast. Some 18th-century writers, however, use the term to mean *rather* and thus in a way similar to the French *assez.*

Assez [Fr.]. Sufficiently, rather, e.g., *assez vite,* rather fast.

Assyria. See Mesopotamia.

Atabal [Sp.]. (1) *Timpani. (2) A cylindrical drum; in Spain a large bass drum, in Central America and the West Indies a smaller drum sometimes played in sets of three. (3) In Cuba, a *slit drum. (4) In the Dominican Republic, a single-headed frame drum, also called a *palo.* See *Baile de palos.*

Atabaque [Port.]. A single-headed, barrel-shaped drum used in Afro-Brazilian cults and generally played in sets of three.

Atem [Ger.]. Breath; *atempause,* breathing pause, usually indicated in musical notation with an apostrophe and often a guide to phrasing as much as an indication of where wind players or singers should take a breath.

A tempo [It.]. In *tempo; hence, an instruction to return to the original tempo after some deviation from it.

Atonality. Literally, the absence of tonality, the absence of key; the opposite of *tonality. Atonal music is marked by a weakening or suppression of the defining conditions of tonality. At first used to describe characteristics of certain pioneering works by Schoenberg, Webern, and Berg, atonality meant the elimination of the necessity for a central tonic triad and for diatonic harmonies functionally relating to it; it also meant the consideration of the twelve pitch-classes of the chromatic scale in such a way that these would be employed on a freely and equally associated basis rather than with any overriding reference to a diatonic scale.

Historically, atonality appeared gradually in Western art music. Even in the early 18th century, examples are common of tonality destabilized by successive modulation or temporarily suspended by chromatic operations such as sequences of diminished seventh chords. Bach's *Chromatic Fantasy* is a familiar instance. Both of these tendencies were carried to extremes by Wagner, Liszt, and others in the mid-19th century. Debussy, a few decades later, by systematically eliminating classical harmonic formulas and by introducing a whole new vocabulary of chord types, developed a very individual idiom that displaced many of the classically familiar features of tonality. Yet both Wagner and Debussy presupposed the primacy of triadic harmony and diatonic scales.

In the characteristic early atonal works of Schoenberg (e.g., Three Piano Pieces op. 11; Five Orchestra Pieces op. 16; *Erwartung* op. 17; and most of the last movement of the String Quartet no. 2 op. 10, a borderline case; all of these works dating from 1908–9) and in Webern's works from op. 3 on, the harmony is marked by a constant chromaticism, dense chordal structures of many intervallic types, and a virtually total suppression of classical consonant sonorities. The search for a structural justification for atonality, comparable to that developed over the centuries for tonal music, led initially to works exhibiting a wide variety of autonomous and synthetic forms (e.g., Berg's *Wozzeck,* 1917–22; Schoenberg's *Pierrot lunaire* op. 21, 1912) and ultimately to Schoenberg's invention, about 1921–23, of the *twelve-tone serial technique (dodecaphony). Since about 1960, atonality, with or without dodecaphony, has characterized the works of many of the leading composers of art music in Europe and America, though since the mid-1970s, the prominence of atonality has steadily receded.

Some composers, notably Berg (e.g., in his Violin Concerto, 1935), have sought to combine a complex structural chromaticism (even using twelve-tone technique) with elements specifically suggesting tonality. The term paratonality has been suggested for this hybrid phenomenon. See also Harmony VII.

Bibl.: Allen Forte, *The Structure of Atonal Music* (New Haven: Yale U Pr, 1973). Arnold Schoenberg, *Style and Idea,* ed. Leonard Stein (London: Faber, 1975). John Rahn, *Basic Atonal Theory* (New York: Longman, 1980). George Perle, *Serial Composition and Atonality,* 6th ed. (Berkeley: U of Cal Pr, 1991). M.DEV.

Attacca, attacca subito [It.]. Attack, attack immediately; hence, when placed at the end of one movement, an instruction to begin the next movement immediately without the customary pause.

Attacco [It., attack]. A short motive that is treated imitatively, either as the subject for a fugue or within a work using imitation. It is to be distinguished from the **andamento* and **soggetto.*

Attack. The characteristics of the beginning of a sound, either as described technically by the science of *acoustics or more loosely as a function of *articulation in performance; also the degree of precision with which members of an ensemble coordinate the beginnings of pitches.

Aubade [Fr.]. Originally, music played in the morning for a specific person or persons, as opposed to the *serenade, which is intended for the evening. In the 17th and 18th centuries, such music was often played for members of the royalty or civil authorities. More recently, composers (e.g., Bizet, Rimsky-Korsakov, Poulenc) have sometimes used the term as a title for instrumental works. See also *Alba, Alborada.*

Aube [Fr.]. **Alba.*

Au chevalet [Fr.]. At the bridge; hence, an instruction to bow the violin or other stringed instrument near or on the bridge. See Bowing (11).

Auctoralis [Lat.]. Authentic as opposed to plagal. See Mode.

Audition. (1) A hearing given to a performer, often for the purpose of determining the performer's level of ability and therefore admissibility to a particular school, class, or ensemble; to perform for such a purpose; to listen to or preside over such a performance. (2) The sense of hearing.

Aufforderung zum Tanz [Ger., Invitation to the Dance]. A composition for piano by Carl Maria von Weber, J. 260 (1819), consisting of an introduction (the "invitation"), a waltz, and an epilogue. It was arranged for orchestra by Berlioz and by Felix Weingartner.

Aufführungspraxis [Ger.]. *Performance practice.

Aufgeregt [Ger.]. Excited.

Auflösung [Ger.]. (1) Resolution, as of a dissonance. (2) Cancellation of an accidental or element of a key signature; *Auflösungszeichen,* the natural sign.

Aufstrich [Ger.]. Up-bow.

Auftakt [Ger.]. Upbeat.

Auftritt [Ger.]. Entrance; scene, as of a dramatic work.

Aufzug [Ger]. (1) An act of an opera, play, etc. (2) In ceremonial trumpet music of the 18th and 19th centuries, a processional fanfare, sometimes followed by a **Tusch.*

Augenmusik [Ger.]. *Eye music.

Augmentation and diminution. The statement of a theme in uniformly longer or shorter note-values, respectively, than those originally associated with it. Thus, if the ratio between old and new values is 2 to 1, in augmentation what was originally a quarter note becomes a half note, etc., whereas in diminution what was originally a quarter note becomes an eighth note. Other ratios may apply as well. These devices are particularly characteristic of music based on imitation, such as the *fugue, *canon (including especially the augmentation canon), *ricercar, and early *fantasia. In fugues, augmentation of the subject is most likely to occur near the end (e.g., in Bach's *Well-Tempered Clavier* vol. 1 no. 8; for an example of diminution see vol. 2 no. 9). Complex examples such as are found in Bach's *The Art of Fugue,* nos. 6 and 7, may include simultaneous use of augmentation and diminution at various ratios. The fugue in the final movement of Beethoven's Piano Sonata op. 110 includes a passage (beginning in m. 16 of the section that begins with the subject in inversion) in which the subject is presented in augmentation together with a countersubject, derived from the subject, presented in diminution.

Music of the Middle Ages and Renaissance based on a **cantus firmus* (including **clausulae* of the Notre Dame repertory) also sometimes makes use of these devices, as do some *isorhythmic works, and they are important in the ricercars and fantasias of composers such as Andrea Gabrieli, Sweelinck, and Frescobaldi. Apart from works based primarily on the technique of imitation, works or sections of works with contrapuntal texture, such as the development sections of some movements in sonata form, may employ augmentation and diminution, though not always in the strictest form.

In the 15th and 16th centuries, the system of *proportions employed in musical notation embodied augmentation and diminution; in much the same way in modern notation the meter ¢ implies a diminution or halving of the duration of the values of **C**, a half note of the former taking the place of a quarter note of the latter as the basic unit of metrical pulse. In this sense, however, the terms do not refer necessarily to the restatement in augmented or diminished form of musical material already heard. See also Diminutions.

Augmented. See Intervals, Sixth chords, Triads.

Aulos [Gr., also *kalamos;* Lat. *tibia*]. The most important wind instrument of ancient Greece. The aulos of classical times (600–300 B.C.E.) was a slender pipe made of cane, wood, bone, or ivory with three to five finger holes plus a thumb hole and a reed affixed to the top. Auloi were always played in pairs. The player put both reeds in the mouth and held the pipes apart in a *V* shape, with the left hand fingering one pipe and the right hand the other [see ill. under Greece]. They ranged from 30 to over 60 cm (2 ft.) in length. Later auloi often had more finger holes, the unfingered holes being filled with wax or shut off by sliding metal rings. There is much debate over whether the aulos had a single or double *reed. It has been suggested that the left-hand pipe was pitched lower than the right-hand pipe or that it served as a drone. Aulos players are often depicted wearing a halter *(phorbeia)* fitted around the head and passing across the cheeks, but the purpose of this device is not known.

The aulos was used in many social contexts. It accompanied both solo and choral singing and was played as a solo instrument at public festivals and private banquets. By the 5th century B.C.E., many aulos players were professionals. Women are described and depicted playing auloi only for private entertainments.

Aulos players are represented in statues dating from as early as the 3rd millennium B.C.E., and the aulos is mentioned in the *Iliad.* Many accounts assert, however, that it was imported to Greece from Asia Minor (Phrygia) around the 7th century B.C.E., and most descriptions and depictions of the aulos in Greek life date from the 7th century B.C.E. and later. The aulos was exported in Hellenistic times to Egypt and to Etruria and Rome, where it was called *tibia* and served many of the same purposes as in Greece. Paired reedpipes survived in Europe into the Middle Ages.

The words *aulos* and *tibia* were often used in a generic sense by Greek and Latin writers to denote any blown pipe, whether a reedpipe or a flute.

Bibl.: Heinz Becker, *Zur Entwicklungsgeschichte der antiken und mittelalterlichen Rohrblattinstrumente* (Hamburg: H Sikorski, 1966). Annie Bélis, "Studying and Dating Ancient Greek *Auloi* and *Tibiae,*" in *The Archaeology of Early Music Cultures,* ed. Ellen Hickmann and David W. Hughes (Bonn: Verlag für systematische Musikwissenschaft, 1988).

Aurresku, aurésku [Basque]. A Basque dance consisting of several sections (including a **zortziko*) that takes its name from the leader of a line of dancers. It is accompanied by the *txistu* and *tamboril,* the Basque equivalent of the *pipe and tabor.

Ausdruck, mit; Ausdrucksvoll [Ger.]. With expression.

Aushalten [Ger.]. To sustain.

Aus Italien [Ger., From Italy]. A symphonic fantasy, op. 16, composed in 1886 by Richard Strauss and inspired by his trip to Italy in that year.

Auslösung [Ger.]. The escapement of the *piano.

Äusserst [Ger.]. Extremely.

Australia. Musical life in Australia is decentralized. Each of the six states and two territories has at least one conservatory or school of music and university or college with a music department; all but the Northern Territory also have one or more orchestras and opera companies.

Australia's first European settlement was a British penal colony at Sydney, established in the late 18th century. Notable activity in art music began after the arrival of large numbers of free settlers in the 1830s and was accelerated by mass migrations that started in the 1850s. In the latter half of the 19th century, numerous choral and instrumental performing organizations, including opera companies, were founded. From before 1850 until about 1913, opera held a prominent position in musical life. The first university chair in music, conservatory, and professional orchestra were established before the turn of the century. With the start of World War I, musical activity dropped off markedly; its revival was assisted substantially when in 1932 the ABC (Australian Broadcasting Commission) set up studio ensembles in the capital cities of several states. Soon these were enlarged and more were formed.

After World War II, public concern for music grew, and the radio orchestras were established as permanent municipal symphonies. In the 1960s, 20th-century music began to arouse more widespread interest. A change in governmental policy in the early 1970s increased funding for the arts substantially, which enhanced musical activities nationwide and especially encouraged the composition and performance of new music. The three main musical organizations today are the ABC, Musica Viva Australia, and the Australian Chamber Orchestra, who with the government are major supporters of many performing, compositional, and educational programs. In addition, there are dozens of amateur and professional performing organizations, including orchestras, opera companies, choruses, and chamber ensembles, plus nearly a hundred educational institutions that offer instruction in music. The Sydney Opera House (1973) has attracted considerable international attention, and the Australian Music Centre (1973) functions as a primary source of information on Australian compositional activity, commissioning new works and publishing books on Australian music.

Prominent Australian composers of the 20th century, some of whom have spent major parts of their careers abroad, include Percy Grainger (1882–1961), Roy Agnew (1893–1944), Margaret Sutherland (1897–1984), John Antill (1904–86), Peggy Glanville-Hicks (1912–90), Dorian Le Gallienne (1915–63), Peter Sculthorpe (b. 1929), Malcolm Williamson (b. 1931), and Richard Meale (b. 1932). Younger Australian composers of note are Gillian Whitehead (b. 1941), Ross Edwards (b. 1943), Roger Smalley (b. 1943 in England), Alison Bauld (b. 1944), Anne Boyd (b. 1946), Brian Howard (b. 1951), Brenton Broadstock (b. 1952), Carl Vine (b. 1954), Graham John Koehne (b. 1956), Julian Jing-Jun Yu (b. 1957 in China), Andrew Ford (b. 1957 in England), Michael Smetanin (b. 1958), Nigel Westlake (b. 1958), Andrew Schultz (b. 1960), Gordon Kerry (b. 1961), and Elliott Gyger (b. 1968).

For ethnic musics, see Oceania and Australia.

Bibl.: James Murdoch, *A Handbook of Australian Music* (Melbourne: Sun Bks, 1983). Brenton Broadstock, ed., *Sound Ideas: Australian Composers Born since 1950* (The Rocks, NSW: Australia Music Centre, 1995). Bill Coackley, *Music and Drama in Western Australia,* 2 vols. Armadale, WA: Coackley, 1995. Brenton Broadstock, *Aflame with Music: 100 Years of Music at the University of Melbourne* (Parkville, Vic.: Centre for Studies in Australian Music, University of Melbourne, 1996. Nicole Saintilan, Andrew Schultz, and Paul Stanhope, *Biographical Directory of Australian Composers* (The Rocks, NSW: Australia Music Centre, 1996). Warren Bebbington, ed., *The Oxford Companion to Australian Music* (Melbourne: Oxford U Pr, 1997). Caitlin Rowley, *Australia: Exploring the Musical Landscape* (Grosvenor Place, NSW: Australia Music Centre, 1998). Tony Bennett and David Carter, *Culture in Australia: Policies, Publics, and Programs* (Cambridge: Cambridge U Pr, 2001). Diane Collins, *Sounds from the Stables: The Story of Sydney's Conservatorium* (Crows Nest, NSW: Allen & Unwin, 2001).

Austria. The musical center of Austria is Vienna, the capital of the present Republic of Austria and for centuries the seat of the Hapsburg monarchy. A number of other cities in Austria are also very active musically.

I. *Art music.* 1. Opera. There are three opera companies in Vienna: the Vienna State Opera, the Volksoper, and the Vienna Chamber Opera. In Salzburg, opera is performed during the summer and during the Easter festival in three opera theaters—the Grosses Festspielhaus, the Kleines Festspielhaus, and the Felsenreitschule. Opera is also associated with a summer festival in Bregenz and with an autumn festival in Graz. Seasons of opera also take place in Innsbruck, Linz, and Klagenfurt.

2. Performing groups. Perhaps the most renowned Austrian performing group is the Vienna Philharmonic Orchestra, which is identical with the Vienna State Opera Orchestra. Vienna boasts other important orchestras including the Vienna Symphony Orchestra and the Lower Austrian Tonkünstler Orchestra. Salzburg has three orchestras—the Mozarteum Orchestra, the Camerata Academica, and the Symphony Orchestra of the province of Salzburg. Several other provincial capitals, e.g., Linz, Innsbruck, and Graz, have symphony orchestras. Another performing group of international fame is the Vienna Boys Choir. In the past few decades Vienna has become a center for performances of early music; the most notable group specializing in early music is the Concentus musicus directed by Nikolaus Harnoncourt.

3. Festivals. The Salzburg festival, which takes place in July and August, features concerts, ballets, and contemporary music as well as opera. Another festival in Salzburg at Easter offers the music of Wagner. The festival in Vienna in May and June and that in Bregenz from June to August have performances of opera, ballet, and concerts. The festival in Graz, called the Styrian Autumn, takes place in October and November.

4. Education. The principal institution for the training of musicians in Austria is the Hochschule (formerly Akademie) für Musik und darstellende Kunst in Vienna, descended from the Konservatorium der Gesellschaft der Musikfreunde. Vienna also has a city-run conservatory that offers professional training for both performers and teachers of music. Of great fame and prestige is the Mozarteum in Salzburg, which also offers an internationally attended series of summer school courses. There are state conservatories in several other provincial capitals—Linz, Klagenfurt, Innsbruck, and Graz. Musicology is taught at the universities in Vienna, Salzburg, Graz, and Innsbruck.

5. Publishing. Vienna was the home of a number of music publishing houses in the 18th and 19th centuries, among them Artaria, Haslinger, and Diabelli, but all of these ceased to function before the end of the 19th century. The most important music publisher in Austria today is Universal Edition, significant both for editions of 20th-century music and for Urtext editions of earlier music.

6. Broadcasting. Radio broadcasting in Austria is guided by the Österreichischer Rundfunk (ÖRF), which supports symphony orchestras in Vienna and Bregenz and a professional chorus in Vienna. The ÖRF is also an important sponsor of contemporary music.

7. History. In the Middle Ages, sacred music was cultivated in many monasteries in Austria, particularly those of the Benedictine and Cistercian orders, such as Kremsmünster, Göttweig, Heiligenkreuz, St. Lambrecht, St. Florian, and Klosterneuburg. Secular song was cultivated by the *Minnesinger, including Walther von der Vogelweide, and polyphonic secular song by Oswald von Wolkenstein. The Renaissance vogue

for humanist *odes was initiated in Austria by Conrad Celtis, professor of poetry at the University of Ingolstadt. The Hapsburg emperors were important patrons of music and some, such as Ferdinand II, Leopold I, and Joseph I, were estimable composers in their own right. Netherlandish domination of the court chapel in the Renaissance was succeeded by Italian domination in the Baroque. Important contributions to the development of instrumental music were made by Froberger (works for keyboard) and Biber (works for violin).

The most important genres of instrumental music in the Classical era—*symphony, *string quartet, *concerto, and keyboard *sonata—were developed and brought to full fruition by composers born in various parts of the Hapsburg realm and drawn to Vienna for significant portions of their careers, especially Haydn, Mozart, Beethoven, and Schubert. At the same time, Vienna was a leading center in the production of opera in both German and Italian. In the middle of the 19th century, the musical form most often associated with Vienna was the *waltz, but by the last quarter of the century, Vienna once again became the home of some of the most prominent composers and writers on music, such as Brahms, Bruckner, Mahler, Wolf, and the critic Eduard Hanslick.

*Twelve-tone music was developed in Austria by Schoenberg, Berg, and Webern, sometimes referred to collectively as the second Viennese school. Among more recent composers, Gottfried von Einem (1918–96) is primarily known for his operas and ballets, but he has also composed orchestral and instrumental works. Friedrich Cerha (b. 1926), professor of composition at the Viennese Hochschule, was an important avant-garde composer in the generation immediately following the second Viennese school, and with Kurt Schwertsik (b. 1935) founded the Vienna Ensemble for New Music, better known as Die Reihe. Other noteworthy figures of this period include Paul Angerer (b. 1927), Theodor Berger (1905–92), Robert Schollum (1913–87), Karl Schiske (1916–69), and Alfred Uhl (1909–92). Foreign-born composers György Ligeti (b. 1923), Roman Haubenstock-Ramati (1919–94), and Anestis Logothetis (1921–94) eventually settled in Vienna and furthered the city's reputation as an international center for the musical avant-garde during the 1950s and 1960s. Ligeti was a proponent of *Klangflächenkomposition,* favoring timbre and texture in his works over melody, harmony, and rhythm, while the latter two composers are known especially for their graphic notations.

During this same period, many young Austrian composers traveled to Darmstadt to take part in the International Summer Course for New Music (founded 1946). Several of these composers (Schwertsik, Gösta Neuwirth [b. 1937], Erich Urbanner [b. 1936], Otto M. Zykan [b. 1935], Günther Kohowez [b. 1940], Iván Eröd [b. 1936]), together with Heinz Karl Gruber (b. 1943) and Herbert Willi (b. 1956), are notable members of Austria's next generation. Other recent additions to new music in Austria are the ensemble Klangforum Wien (1985), and the festival Wien Modern (1988).

II. *Folk music.* Much Austrian folk music has characteristics that can be traced to the *yodel or the **Ländler,* broadly defined. Much of it, both vocal and instrumental, is performed in semi-improvised polyphony, often in three, sometimes in more or fewer parts; the melody is normally in a middle voice. The most common instruments, usually employed in trios or quartets, are fiddle, accordion (diatonic), harp, dulcimer (chromatic and diatonic), string bass, and various winds (particularly clarinet and flugelhorn).

Despite general similarities, various regions do have distinctive traditions. For example, vocal music is predominant in Carinthia and Burgenland, instrumental music in Vorarlberg. Most instrumental ensembles are made up of either all winds or all strings, often with an accordion acting as a harmony instrument. The harp is peculiar to the Tyrol, where it is the favorite instrument and carries the harmony in ensembles. In a portion of Upper Austria, the usual dance band is made up of two violins and winds, rather than the more common two violins, accordion, and string bass. Distinctive folk music has also developed around Salzburg and, particularly, Vienna. The Croatian minority in Burgenland has an independent musical tradition, which, although quite active, has had little effect on the folk music of the rest of the country.

Bibl.: Siegried Lang, *Lexikon österreichischer U-Musik-Komponisten in 20. Jahrhundert* (Vienna: Arbeitskreis U-Musik, 1986). Rudolf Flotzinger, *Geschichte der Musik in Österreich: Zum Lesen und Nachschlagen* (Graz: Styria, 1988). Otto Kolleritsch, ed., *Die Wiener Schule und das Hakenkreuz: Das Schicksal der Moderne im gesellschaftspolitischen Kontext des 20. Jahrhunderts* (Vienna: Universal Edition, 1990). Rudolf Flotzinger and Gernot Gruber, eds., *Musikgeschichte Österreichs,* 3 vols. (Graz: Styria & Böhlau, 1977–95). David Wyn Jones, ed., *Music in Eighteenth-Century Austria* (Cambridge: Cambridge U Pr, 1996). Peter Wehle, "Zur Auffuhrungspraxis alter Musik an Osterreichs Hohen Schulen," in Bekenntnis zur osterreichischen Musik in *Lehre und Forschung: Eine Festschrift fur Eberhard Wurzl zum achtzigsten Geburtstag am 1. November 1995* (Vienna: Vom Pasqualatihaus, 1996), pp. 341–46. Hartmut Krones, "175 Jahre Auffuhrungspraxis Alter Musik in Wien," in *Alte Musik und Musikpadagogik* (Vienna: Böhlau, 1997), pp. 15–21. Harald Goertz, *Music in Austria, from Its Early Beginnings to the Present Day: An overview* (Vienna: Federal Press Service, 2000).

Auszug [Ger.]. Extract, excerpt; *Klavierauszug,* a reduction for piano of a work for larger forces such as an opera.

Authentic. (1) Of a musical text, unequivocally linked with the composer to whom the work is attributed. See Authenticity. (2) In the study of folklore and folk music, belonging to a living, continuous folk tradition (often orally transmitted), as opposed to the corruption, imitation, or revival of a tradition. (3) In *performance practice, instruments or styles of playing that are historically appropriate to the music being performed. This usage of the term has been criticized as value-laden. (4) See Cadence. (5) See Mode.

Authenticity. The nature and validity of the link between a composer and a work that bears his or her name. When a piece of music is transmitted in a manuscript or printed source, the name of a composer is very often transmitted with that work, either written in the source or by some other means. Three questions may be asked about the link between the music in the source and the named composer. First, is the piece authentic or spurious? Second, is this an authentic version, or has the music been altered or arranged by another hand? Third, is this the authentic text, or has the text been edited by someone else or corrupted in transmission? An *autograph may help to answer all three questions. If no autograph is available, the musicologist subjects the available sources to critical examination, trying to establish whether any of them can be traced back to the named composer, and which versions or which readings must be closest to the hypothetical autograph. When source criticism fails at these tasks, the musicologist resorts to style criticism, comparing the work in question with other works by the named composer to evaluate the probability of authorship and to establish the most plausible readings [see Textual criticism]. Often an unequivocal answer is not possible, particularly regarding the authenticity of versions or of text readings. It is widely assumed that authentic is better than inauthentic—that the text written by the composer is better than an edited or corrupted text, that the composer's version is better than an arrangement, that a work securely attributed to a composer is better than a spurious work. This may be true in a large number of cases, but there is no reason that it must be true, and to make authenticity an absolute critical principle can be dangerous.

Since the *performance practice movement of the 20th century, the concept of authenticity has also been used to characterize the link between a modern performance of a work and its composer. The assertion that a performance is "authentic" is a claim that the link between the modern performance and the composer is strong: the composer would have performed the work on this instrument; the composer intended the work to be performed at this tempo; the composer would have expected the ornaments to be realized in this way, etc. Claims about the authenticity of a performance, unlike claims about the authenticity of attributions, versions, or texts, cannot be verified by critical methods. At base they amount to assertions of value and taste.

In *ethnomusicology, the concept of authenticity is sometimes applied to a musical tradition or practice that belongs uniquely to one culture or that preserves old and distinctive features in unaltered form. Again, the implication is that authentic is better than inauthentic. The search for authentic musical traditions has inspired much research and documentation on non-Western musics, but it runs the risk of ignoring mixed or syncretic traditions that may be socially important and musically valuable.

Bibl.: *Isham Library,* 1959, *passim.* Jan LaRue, "Major and Minor Mysteries of Identification in the 18th-Century Symphony," *JAMS* 13 (1960): 181–96. Georg Feder, "Die Bedeutung der Assoziation und des Wertvergleiches für das Urteil in Echtheitsfragen," in *Copenhagen,* 1972, pp. 365–77. Allan Atlas, "Conflicting Attributions in Italian Sources of the Franco-Netherlandish Chanson, c. 1460–c. 1505: A Progress Report on a New Hypothesis," in Iain Fenlon, ed., *Music in Medieval and Early Modern Europe* (Cambridge, 1981), pp. 249–94. Hanspeter Bennwitz et al., eds., *Opera incerta: Echtheitsfragen als Problem musikwissenschaftlicher Gesamtausgaben,* Kolloquium Mainz 1988 (Stuttgart, 1991). Richard Taruskin, *Text and Act: Essays on Music and Performance* (New York, 1995). John Spitzer, "Style and the Attribution of Musical Works," in Fotis Jannidis et al., eds., *Rückkehr des Autors* (Tübingen, 1999), pp. 495–510. J.S.

Auto [Sp.]. A Spanish dramatic work in one act with a prologue, often on a sacred or allegorical subject. By the middle of the 16th century, *autos* were performed especially on the feast of Corpus Christi and dealt in one way or another with the miracle of transubstantiation in the sacrament of communion, whence the term *auto sacramental.* They were written in verse and made use of music in varying degrees. *Autos* were written by Juan del Encina (fl. 1500) and Gil Vicente (1492–1557), and the *auto sacramental* reached its peak in the works of Lope de Vega (1562–1635), Tirso de Molina (1584?–1648), and, especially, Calderón de la Barca (1600–81). Such plays were taken by missionaries in the 16th century to the Spanish and Portuguese colonies of Latin America, where there are accounts of *autos* performed with music.

Autograph. A manuscript of a musical work written in its composer's hand, as opposed to music in the hand of a copyist or printed music; also holograph. The term usually refers to the score of an entire piece or movement, although a composer's corrections in a copy or print may be "autograph" in an adjectival sense. There are very few autographs of musical works from as early as the 16th century. From the 18th century on, autographs survive in considerable quantity and have played an important role in 20th-century efforts to produce reliable editions.

Autographs are valued for several reasons apart from their often considerable monetary worth. An autograph provides convincing evidence of a work's *authenticity, and in many cases it can help determine the date of composition. Since it represents what the composer actually wrote, uncorrupted by editorial license or errors of transmission, an autograph is particularly useful for establishing a good text of a work. Changes or revisions in an autograph offer insight into the compositional process. And an autograph may also transmit information about how the composer wanted the work performed.

The value of autographs is not absolute or unequivocal in all respects, however. Composers sometimes improve their works in the course of rehearsals or in the process of editing. An autograph may be a copy in one composer's hand of a work by another composer. And composers, like copyists, may simply make mistakes in copying their works from earlier drafts or sketches.

Bibl.: Emanuel Winternitz, *Musical Autographs from Monteverdi to Hindemith* (Princeton: Princeton U Pr, 1955; R: New York: Dover, 1965). Alfred Dürr, "Zur Chronologie der Leipziger Vokalwerke Johann Sebastian Bachs," *BaJb* 44 (1957): 5–162. Georg von Dadelsen, "Die 'Fassung letzter Hand' in der Musik," *AM* 33 (1961): 1–14. Walter Gerstenberg and Martin Hürlimann, eds., *Composers' Autographs,* trans. Ernest Roth (Madison, N.J.: Fairleigh Dickinson U Pr, 1968). John Cage, *Notations* (New York: Something Else Pr, 1969). Lewis Lockwood, "On Beethoven's Sketches and Autographs: Some Problems of Definition and Interpretation," *AM* 42 (1970): 32–47. Alan Tyson, *Mozart: Studies of the Autograph Scores* (Cambridge, Mass.: Harvard U Pr, 1987). Jessie Ann Owens, *Composers at Work: The Craft of Musical Composition, 1450–1600* (New York: Oxford U Pr, 1997).

Autoharp. A *zither on which chords are produced with the aid of dampers mounted on a set of bars above the strings. The dampers are mounted on each bar in such a way as to allow only the strings for a designated chord to sound when that bar is depressed. The player plucks or strums the strings with the right hand while depressing the bars with the left. Invented in Germany in the late 19th century, it was patented in the U.S. in 1881 by C. F. Zimmermann, who produced and sold hundreds of thousands before the turn of the century. It became established in folk music in the 1920s and gained popular currency through the commercially recorded music of the Carter Family. It was for a time also used in schools as a pedagogical instrument. See ill. under Zither.

Automatic instrument. An instrument that plays itself without the agency of a living performer; also automatophone. Instruments are also called automatic if the sounding of the notes is caused by a self-actuating mechanism, even if the motive power is supplied by someone who turns a crank or treads on pedals and who also may have control over such aspects of the music as tempo, dynamics, or registration. Some instruments can be played either manually or automatically. The most common are player pianos and player organs, which have a normal keyboard as well as a built-in mechanism that can operate it. Another type of automatic device is the accessory mechanism applied to a normal instrument; for example, the Pianola and *Vorsitzer,* which stand in front of a piano keyboard and play upon it automatically.

In principle, any instrument can be played automatically, given the technology, and from the early 19th century, attempts have been made to simulate whole orchestras, using organ pipes and automatic percussion instruments. For such a machine (Maelzel's Panharmonicon) Beethoven wrote his *Wellington's Victory* (1813). During the first two decades of the 20th century, several types of automatic violin were developed, usually combined with a piano but sometimes with other violins or a cello. Of these, the Violano-Virtuoso (Mills Novelty Co., U.S.) and the Violina (Ludwig Hupfeld, Germany) reached production figures in the thousands. Automatic zithers, banjos, harps, and accordions were also made.

All automatic instruments before the advent of electronic memories were governed by the relative motion of the data-bearing element and the sound-producing portions. This motion could be produced by human power, either acting directly (cranking) or indirectly (supplying wind for a pneumatic machine, as in a player piano). In fully automatic instruments, water pressure, weights, springs, steam, or electricity furnished the power. Until the late 19th century, the data-bearing element was most commonly a cylinder studded with pegs or pins corresponding to the notes of the music. As the cylinder revolved, the pegs or pins acted upon the sound-producing part of the instrument. Large wheels or flat moving panels sometimes served the same function. In more recent times, revolving discs of metal or cardboard, either pierced or bearing teeth bent out from their surfaces, partially replaced cylinders. Along with paper rolls, cards, or folded "books," these had the advantages of cheapness and easy interchangeability, and they greatly enlarged the potential repertory of the instruments to which they were applied. Rolls and "books" offered the additional advantages of easy duplication and longer playing times. Recently, magnetic tape has been used to record electrical impulses taken from the action of an organ or piano while it is being played. The tape can then be played back immediately, causing the organ or piano to repeat what has been played upon it for critical evaluation by the player. Electronic memories can be used in the same way.

In the simplest automatic instruments, pins on the cylinder or projections from the disc engage the teeth of a metal comb, sometimes through the intermediary of a star wheel, causing them to vibrate and make a sound. No mechanism is needed beyond that required to rotate the cylinder. This is the principle of the music box, and it goes back to the 18th century. Other types require some intermediate link between the data-bearing element and the sounding parts. It is here that the greatest variety obtains. Sometimes, as in carillons, spinets, harp clocks, or barrel pianos, the motion of the cylinder acts directly through a mechanical linkage to strike or pluck. In wind instruments—pipe or reed organs, accordions, etc.—valves must be opened to admit or exhaust wind. In the simplest kind, holes in a paper roll pass over openings to become valves themselves. Most, however, employ a mechanical or pneumatic action. More commonly, the paper passes over a tracker bar with openings like those in the mouthpiece of a harmonica connected to the pneumatic action. As a hole in the paper passes over one of these openings, wind is admitted to or exhausted from the action, playing the required note. Sometimes the paper passes over spring-loaded fingers that pop through the holes. Wind is supplied by bellows connected to whatever provides the motive power. The American Trumpetto of the 1870s was winded by being blown into. In the 16th and 17th centuries, large outdoor organs were winded by aerated water under pressure. Bubbles rose from the water in a large chamber that acted as the wind reservoir, the exhaust water then falling further to turn a wheel geared to the pinned cylinder (Caus, Kircher, Jeans).

There are two quite separate arts in the making of automatic instruments. One is the art of the technician and musical instrument maker. The other is that of the artisan who "enters the data," that is, places pins in the barrel, lays out the paper roll, or punches the disc. It is possible to record on the moving band of a paper roll by means of pencils attached to the action of a keyboard instrument. Such mechanisms were invented in 1752 by Johann Friederich Unger (1716–81) and ca. 1780 by John Joseph Merlin (1735–1803). They enable the performance of a particular artist to be recorded in great detail for punching or transference to a cylinder. Not until the early 20th century, however, was a reproducing piano developed that was able—by means of extra perforations in the paper roll—not only to render the exact rhythms of a particular performance but also to approximate the dynamics (touch) and pedaling (Ampico, Duo-Art, Welte-Mignon, etc.).

The vast majority of automatic performances were creations not of musicians playing in "real time," however, but of artisans working from scores and charts, according to traditional methods. When Joseph Engramelle introduced a new method of notating music, designed to enable pinners of cylinders to reproduce the minute details of articulation and rhythmic nuance that characterized the best keyboard playing (*La tonotechnie,* 1775), he became one of the first writers to show a concern for the artistic possibilities of automatic instruments and an appreciation of their historical value for future generations.

The history of automatic instruments may extend, via Byzantine and Arab civilization, back to antiquity. In more recent times, it is closely bound up with the history of clockwork and automata (mechanical birds, moving figures, etc.). There has always been an element of magic associated with automatic phenomena, and this magic has colored historical research on the subject, endowing much of it with the quality of pure fancy. The best and most detailed research concerns the 19th and 20th centuries, but it is not to be found in the writings of musicologists. Rather one must consult the books and periodicals of collectors and enthusiasts.

Among the earliest surviving automatophones are little carillons in late medieval and early Renaissance astronomical clocks. With the development of large cylinder mechanisms, tower carillons could be played automatically and their tunes changed by rearranging the pegs on the cylinders, which were pierced over their whole surface. Other early types of automatophones were barrel organs associated with Alpine **Hornwerke.* These were signaling devices placed in towers and consisting of a large number of organ pipes tuned like one note of a vast mixture stop and all sounding at once (*Salzburger Stier,* 1502). Water organs on the principle described above were combined with other automata and erected in Italian gardens of the mid-16th century (Tivoli, Villa d'Este). They were said to play madrigals, perhaps in intabulations like Peter Philips's of Alessandro Striggio Sr.'s "Chi fara fed' al ciel," whose pinning is described and illustrated by Caus (1615).

The art of making barrel organs and spinets was well established by the end of the 16th century, and barrel spinets by the Bidermann family of Augsburg from the early 17th century survive in playing condition. Quantities of high quality automatic instruments of all types were made in the late 18th and early 19th centuries. In Vienna, especially, major pieces by the best composers were pinned on barrel organs of great technical refinement. In England, barrel organs were widely used in country churches to accompany singing. Flute clocks contained miniature barrel organs that played tunes on the hour. The construction and pinning of barrel organs is dealt with exhaustively by Dom Bédos de Celles (1778).

By the beginning of the 20th century, the production of automatic instruments reached well into the millions, and though greatly reduced after about 1930 owing to the competition of the phonograph, production continues today. The Musical Box Society International (U.S.A.) had over 2,500 members in 1980. Automatic instruments constitute a vast and almost entirely untapped reservoir of musical documentation.

Bibl.: Salomon de Caus, *Les raisons des forces mouvantes* (Frankfurt am Main, 1615: R: Amsterdam: Frits Knupf, 1973). Athanasius Kircher, *Musurgia universalis* (Rome, 1650). Marie Dominique Joseph Engramelle, *La tonotechnie ou l'art de noter les cylindres* (Paris, 1775). Dom François Bédos de Celles, *L'art du facteur d'orgues,* vol. 4 (Paris, 1778; facs., *DM* ser. 1, 26, 1966). Henry Farmer, *The Organ of the Ancients from Eastern Sources (Hebrew, Syriac and Arabic)* (London: W Reeves, 1931). Albert Protz, *Mechanische Musikinstrumente* (Kassel: Bärenreiter, 1941). *BMBSI* (quarterly, 1955–). Alexander Buchner, *Mechanical Musical Instruments* (London: Batchworth Pr, 1959). Susi Jeans, "Water Organs," in *Music Libraries and Instruments,* Hinrichsen's Eleventh Music Book, ed. Unity Sherrington and Guy Oldham (London: Hinrichsen, 1961), pp. 189–96. Lyndesay G. Langwill and Noel Boston, *Church and Chamber Barrel-Organs: Their Origin, Makers, Music, and Location,* 2nd ed. (Edinburgh: L G Langwill, 1970). Q. David Bowers, *Encyclopedia of Automatic Musical Instruments* (Vestal, N.Y.: Vestal Pr, 1972). Arthur W. J. G. Ord-Hume, *Clockwork Music* (New York: Crown Pubs, 1973). Id., *The Mechanics of Mechanical Music: The Arrangement of Music for Automatic Instruments* (London: Ord-Hume, 1973). David R. Fuller, *Mechanical Musical Instruments as a Source for the Study of Notes Inégales* (Cleveland Heights, Ohio:

Music Box Society International, 1979). Id., "Analyzing the Performance of a Barrel Organ," *The Organ Yearbook* 11 (1980): 104–15. George Frideric Handel, *Two Ornamented Organ Concertos as Played by an Early Barrel Organ,* ed. David R. Fuller (Hackensack, N.J.: Jerona, 1980). Arthur W. J. G. Ord-Hume, *Musical Box: A History and Collector's Guide* (London: Allen & Unwin, 1980). *EM* 11, no. 2 (April 1983) [special issue]. J. J. L. Haspels, *Automatic Instruments: Their Mechanics and Their Musics, 1580–1820* (Koedijk: Nirota, 1987). Herbert J. Jüttemann, *Mechanische Musikinstrumente* (Frankfurt: E. Bochinsky, 1987). D.F.

Automelon [Gr.]. See *Idiomelon.*

Auxiliary tone. Neighbor note [see Counterpoint].

Ave Maria [Lat., Hail, Mary]. (1) A prayer of the Roman Catholic Church (text and melody in *LU,* p. 1861). Its text begins with parts of two verses of Scripture (Luke 1:28, 42) and concludes with a petition added in the 15th century. The melody associated with the first part of the text as an antiphon for the Annunciation (*LU,* pp. 1416–17) dates from the 10th century. There are numerous polyphonic settings of the text from the Renaissance (by Fogliano, Ockeghem, Josquin, Mouton, Willaert, de Orto, Victoria), some based on the melody, and there are Renaissance Masses based on this material as well (by La Rue, Morales, Peñalosa). (2) A song by Schubert, D. 839 (1825), based on verses from Sir Walter Scott's *Lady of the Lake.* (3) A song by Gounod (1859) in which Bach's prelude in C major from *The Well-Tempered Clavier* vol. 1 provides the harmonic background for a new melody.

Ave maris stella [Lat., Hail, Star of the Sea]. A hymn of the Roman Catholic Church sung to several different melodies (*LU,* pp. 1259–63). Its melodies (most often the first given in *LU*) were frequently used during the Renaissance as the basis for polyphonic settings of the text (by Dufay, Martini, Porta), Masses (by Josquin, Morales, Animuccia, Victoria), and keyboard works (by Cabezón, Girolamo Cavazzoni, Du Caurroy, Titelouze).

Ave Regina caelorum [Lat., Hail, Queen of Heaven]. One of the four *antiphons for the Blessed Virgin Mary, sung in modern practice at Compline from the Purification (February 2) until Wednesday in Holy Week (*LU,* pp. 274–75). During the Renaissance it was often set polyphonically (by Dufay, the setting mentioned in his will being a special case in point; Palestrina, Victoria) and used as the basis for polyphonic Masses (by Dufay, Weerbecke, Arcadelt, Victoria, Palestrina).

Ayre. (1) The English lute-accompanied song of the late 16th and early 17th centuries. Such pieces were often published with an optional bass viol part or with three additional vocal parts printed in such a way that they could be read from a single copy by singers seated around a table. They range in style from serious songs with contrapuntal texture to lighter, homophonic, strophic songs. The first published collection was John Dowland's *First Booke of Songes or Ayres* of 1597. Other composers who contributed to the genre include Campion, Cavendish, Danyel, Jones, Pilkington, and Rosseter. Among the antecedents of the genre are the English *consort song, for solo voice accompanied by four viols, and the French **air de cour.* (2) In the 17th century, a movement in a suite [see Air]. (3) [also aire, air] In 17th-century English writers, mode or key; also the general character of a work.

Bibl.: See Editions V, 32. Peter Warlock, *The English Ayre* (London: Oxford U Pr, 1926; R: Westport, Conn.: Greenwood, 1970). Warlock and Philip Wilson, eds., *English Ayres, Elizabethan and Jacobean,* 6 vols. (London: Oxford U Pr, 1927–31; R: 1964). *English Lute Songs, 1597–1632: A Collection of Facsimile Reprints* (Menston, U.K.: Scolar Pr, 1967–71). Ian Spink, *The English Song: Dowland to Purcell* (New York: Scribner, 1974). Franklin B. Zimmerman, "*Air,* A Catchword for New Concepts in Seventeenth-Century English Music Theory," *Albrecht,* 1980, pp. 142–57. Winifred Maynard, *Elizabethan Lyric Poetry and Its Music* (Oxford: Oxford U Pr, 1986. Ulrich Sommerrock, *Das englische Lautenlied (1597–1622)* (Regensburg: S Roderer, 1990).

B

B. (1) See Pitch names, Letter notation, Hexachord, Pitch. (2) In German nomenclature for pitch, B-flat. (3) An abbreviation for *bass, or *bassus.*

Babylonia. See Mesopotamia.

Bacchetta [It.]. (1) *Baton. (2) The stick of the *bow of a stringed instrument. (3) Drumstick; *b. di legno,* wooden; *b. di spugna,* sponge-headed.

B-A-C-H. The letters of J. S. Bach's surname. If read in the context of German nomenclature for pitch (in which B denotes B-flat and H denotes B-natural), these letters represent the succession of pitches B♭ A C B♮, which has been used in works (especially as a fugue subject) by various composers, including Bach himself (*The *Art of Fugue*), Albrechtsberger, Schumann, Liszt, Reger, Piston, Casella, and Busoni. See also Cryptography.

Bach-Gesellschaft. See Societies.

Bachiana [Port.]. A title employed by Heitor Villa-Lobos (1887–1959) for compositions in which he applied Bach's contrapuntal techniques to Brazilian folk music. He wrote nine such works (for solo piano, full orchestra, voice, chorus, and chamber ensembles), each a suite bearing two titles: one evoking the Baroque and the other referring to a Brazilian popular form.

Backbeat. In *rock and some other genres in *popular music and *jazz, a sharp attack on beats two and four of a 4/4 measure, often sounded continuously on the snare drum.

Back check. See Piano.

Backfall, forefall. In 17th-century England, two types of *appoggiatura, the former approaching the main note from above, the latter from below, notated and played as in the accompanying example. When the backfall is combined with a shake (trill), it occupies

half the value of the written note unless the note is dotted, in which case it takes two-thirds. Dieupart (1701–2) translates *port de voix* as "fore fall up" and *cheute (chûte)* as "back fall"; the interpretations are in even eighths.

Bibl.: Henry Purcell, *A Choice Collection of Lessons for the Harpsichord or Spinnet* (London, 1699). Charles Dieupart, *Six suittes de clavessin* (Amsterdam, 1701–2), ed. Paul Brunold (Paris: L'oiseau-lyre, 1934), rev. Kenneth Gilbert (Monaco: L'oiseau-lyre, 1979). Howard Ferguson, *Keyboard Interpretation* (New York: Oxford U Pr, 1975), pp. 148–52.
D.F.

Background. See Schenker analysis.

Badinage, badine, badinerie [Fr., banter]. A playful or coy movement. It was both a descriptive title and a category in 18th-century suites (Bach, Telemann, Claude-Bénigne Balbastre). The term implies lightness but no specific rhythmic characteristics. B.G.

Bagana, beganna [Amharic]. An Ethiopian *lyre with a large, rectangular frame, a rectangular sound box, and up to ten gut strings, plucked with the fingers of both hands. Considered an aristocratic instrument, it is played almost exclusively by men, usually to accompany sacred songs. See ill. under Africa; see also Kithara, *Krar.*

Bagatelle [Fr., trifle]. A short, unpretentious piece, often for piano and often presented in sets with contrasting tempos and moods. Marin Marais used the title in 1692 *(Pièces en trio),* and it appeared occasionally throughout the late 18th century. Beethoven's three sets for piano (opp. 33, 119, and 126) became models for many later composers. Most (e.g., Sibelius, op. 97) added descriptive titles [see Character piece]. Anton Webern wrote *Six Bagatelles* for string quartet in 1913. B.G.

Bağlama [Turk.]. A long-necked lute of Turkey. See *Saz.*

Bagpipe. Any of a family of wind instruments in which one or more *reedpipes are attached to a windbag, usually made of animal skin. The player holds the windbag under the arm and squeezes it with the elbow to provide a steady stream of air to the pipes. The windbag is filled by means of either a mouth pipe or a set of bellows operated by the player's free elbow. One or two of the pipes, called *chanters, have finger holes and play a melody. The other pipes, called *drones, have no finger holes and sound a single pitch.

The bagpipe is, or has been, a popular instrument in Europe, North Africa, the Middle East, Central Asia, and India, taking on various forms in different regions. Broadly speaking, Eastern European and Asian bagpipes have single-reed, cylindrical-bore chanters, while Western European bagpipes have double-reed, conical-bore chanters. Most North African and Middle Eastern bagpipes have no drone pipes, and their chanter consists of two pipes side by side like a *dou-

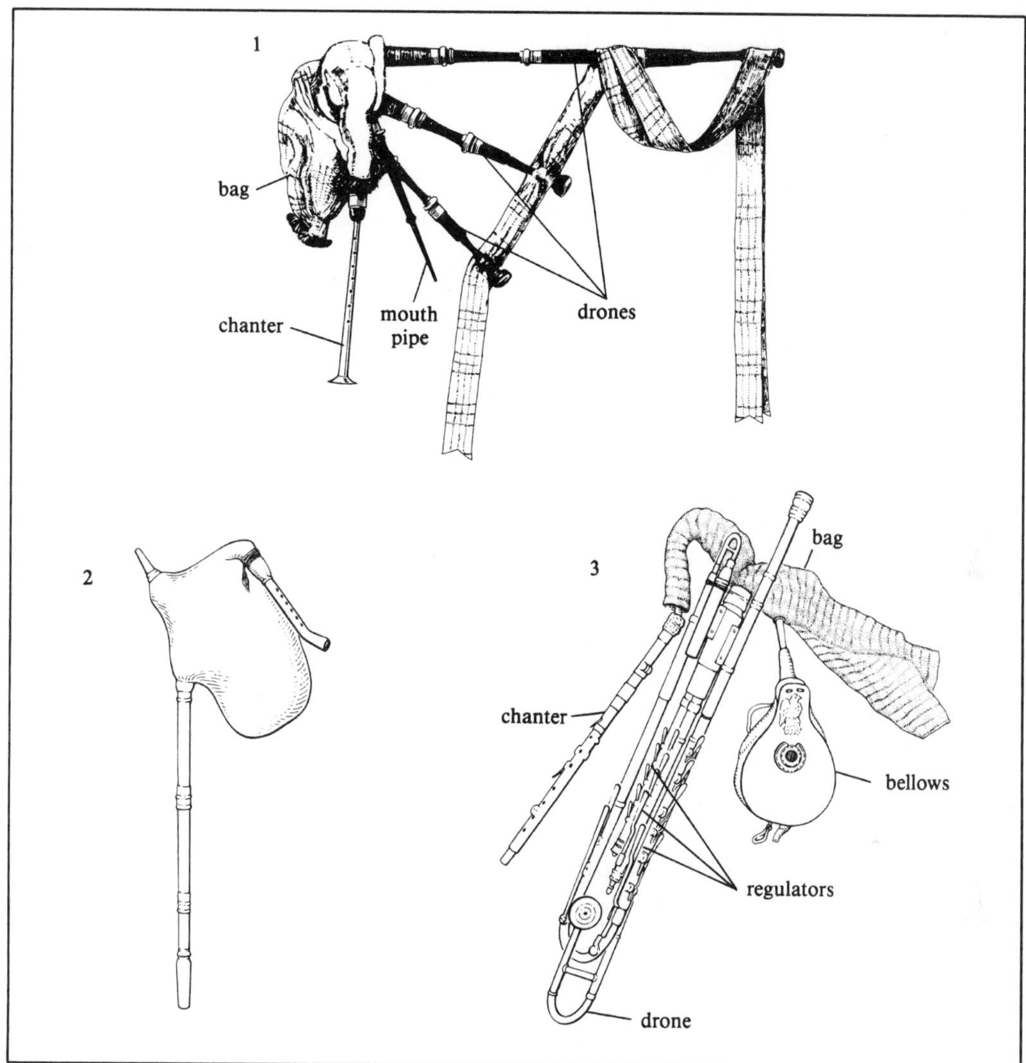

1. Highland bagpipe. 2. Bulgarian gaida. 3. Union pipe.

ble clarinet. The French *cornemuse,* Spanish **gaita,* Irish *union pipe, and Scottish *highland pipes all combine a double-reed, conical-bore chanter with one or more single-reed, cylindrical-bore drones.

Mouth-blown reedpipes have been known since the third millennium B.C.E., and it is possible that an animal-skin bag was combined with such a pipe in India or the Middle East as early as 1000 B.C.E. The first secure record of the bagpipe is of the Roman Emperor Nero performing on such an instrument *(tibia utricularis)* in the 1st century C.E. After Roman times there is no record of the bagpipe in Europe until the 9th century. By the 12th century, there is extensive literary and pictorial documentation of the bagpipe in many areas of Europe.

Throughout its geographic range, the bagpipe is typically a folk, outdoor, and pastoral instrument. In the 17th century, the **musette* enjoyed a brief vogue at the French court. In modern Europe, piping traditions are still strong in Scotland, Ireland, and the Balkans, especially Bulgaria. See also *Biniou, Gaita,* Highland bagpipe, Union pipe, *Zampogna.*

Bibl.: Anthony Baines, *Bagpipes* (Oxford: Oxford U Pr, 1960). Theodor H. Podnos, *Bagpipes and Tunings* (Detroit: Info Coord, 1974).

Baguala. A traditional song genre of northwestern Argentina and neighboring Paraguay and Bolivia, most typically sung by groups of men, women, and children, often with drum accompaniment, during the celebration of Carnival. Reflecting indigenous tonal systems of the region, *baguala* melodies are characteristically tritonic, with pitches corresponding to the major triad. The use of falsetto and vocal ornaments known as *kenko (kenkito)* is also common. D.S.

Baguette [Fr.]. (1) *Baton. (2) The stick of the *bow of a stringed instrument. (3) Drumstick; *b. de bois,* wooden; *b. d'éponge,* sponge-headed.

Baião [Port.]. A traditional dance genre of northeastern Brazil, associated in performance with the textually virtuosic and improvisatory song types known as **desafio* and **embolada;* also an urban dance popularized in Brazil in the 1940s. D.S.

Bailecito [Sp.]. A couple dance of Bolivia and northern Argentina. Its melodies, often in parallel thirds, are sung to *seguidilla* verses or played by **quenas,* violin, harp, or accordion; guitar, **charango,* **caja,* and **bombo* are typical accompanying instruments. In lively tempo, its rhythmic patterns combine elements of both simple triple and compound duple meters. It also incorporates a characteristically Andean pentatonicism and bimodality. D.S.

Baile de palos [Sp.]. Ritual dance music of the Dominican Republic. Strongly African in character, it is typically performed by vocal soloist and chorus with an ensemble of *guayos* (metal scrapers) and single-headed membranophones, known as *palos* or *atabales,* of three different sizes: *palo mayor* or *grande, palo mediano* or *adulón,* and *alcahuete.* D.S.

Baile pastoril [Port., pl. *bailes pastoris*]. A Brazilian play with songs and dances, of Iberian origin, performed during the Christmas season and dramatizing the shepherds' visit to the manger in Bethlehem. D.S.

Baisser [Fr.]. To lower, e.g., the tuning of a string.

Bajón [Sp.]. An early form of the bassoon, made in several sizes (the smaller examples termed *bajoncillos*) and sometimes played together in ensembles. It was much used in Spanish sacred music beginning in the 17th century.

Bajoncillo [Sp., dim. of *bajón*]. (1) A small **bajón.* (2) An organ reed stop of trumpet scale, often mounted horizontally in the facade.

Bajo sexto [Sp.]. A large 12-string guitar of northern Mexico, typically played in ensemble with an accordion. See also *Música norteña.*

Balalaika [Russ.]. A *long-necked lute of Russia with three strings, a fretted neck, and a flat-backed triangular body. It has been popular in accompaniment for song and dance since the 18th century, when it replaced its antecedent the **dömbra.* Since the 19th century it has been built in six different sizes that are played together in balalaika orchestras. See ill. under Guitar.

Balancement [Fr.]. In singing, a rather slow vibrato of loudness, not pitch; sometimes used synonymously with **Bebung.*

Balg [Ger.]. Bellows (of an organ).

Bali. See Southeast Asia IX, 4.

Ballabile [It.]. In 19th-century opera, a piece suitable for dancing. Such pieces may be purely instrumental or performed with chorus. Examples are found in Meyerbeer *(Robert le diable, Les Huguenots)* and Verdi *(Ernani, Macbeth, Aida).*

Ballad [Lat. *ballare,* to dance]. A popular song, usually with narrative content and in strophic form. The term refers to a variety of historical subgenres: the medieval French art song; the orally transmitted type originating in the later Middle Ages; the popular street song of the 16th to 18th centuries; the sentimental drawing-room song of the 19th century; and a song in a slow tempo dating from the 1920s. *Ballade* in the 14th century originally designated the French art lyric with its fixed form, or referred to the dance song more often known as the *carole.* By the late 16th century the Anglicized term *ballad* became loosely associated with popular song or lyric verse. It continued in this sense into the 18th century, when it was first associated with narrative song, and into the 19th century, when in the usage of specialists it was increasingly applied to orally transmitted, traditional narrative songs. This type, the oral-traditional ballad, first developed in France and the Low Countries after 1400, the connection with dance being partly through the French *carole,* which involved a solo singer and unison choral refrain. Through minstrelsy and trade the form found its way into Scandinavia, central and eastern Europe, the northern Mediterranean, and to Britain and Ireland, whence variants were carried to the New World with the first European settlers in the 17th century. Ballads, or balladlike forms influenced by epic song, are still found throughout the European subcontinent. Some ballad plots of a generalized type are distributed in multiple variant forms across many regions: "Lady Isabel and the Elf-Knight" (Child 4), for instance, which probably originated in the Low Countries, is well known under localized names in Scandinavia, Central and Eastern Europe, the Mediterranean, and North America.

Compared with sung epics, oral-traditional ballads are not expansive but compress action into a limited number of stanzas (sometimes with refrains), at the same time handling the story objectively. The general tone of the older ballads is impersonal: in performance the story is allowed to develop without subjective intrusion or comment, although this does not preclude the singer's emotional involvement in the drama. The subject matter of the texts is varied and includes: usually domestic dramas involving a triangular relationship (e.g., "Edward," "Little Musgrave and Lady Barnard"), feuds and historic battles ("Chevy Chase," "Harlaw"), supernatural events ("The Wife of Usher's

Well," "Tam Lin"), outlaws and criminals ("Captain Kidd," "Jesse James"), disasters ("Sir Patrick Spens," "The Titanic"), murders ("Lamkin," "Pearl Bryan"), and a variety of occupations. Because of their oral nature, individual ballads exist in multiple and fluid variants of both text and tune. The most common meter is "ballad meter," a four-line strophe with alternating lines of eight and six syllables (8, 6, 8, 6) with four and three stresses, respectively. Ballad tunes, with their memorable shape, regular two-bar structure and four phrases to the strophe, often influence the versification. The tunes are not distinct from other folksong melodies, and each regional tradition has developed a pool of melodies apt for both ballads and other strophic types.

The broadside ballads of Europe (and later, North America), were popular from the mid-16th to the 20th century. They embodied an urban revival through printers who adapted older versions and cobbled newer ballads on topical themes. These cheap broadsheets ("broadsides") were sold in the streets, in bookstalls, and at fairs; the songs were learned by city dwellers, thus attracting the interest of 17th-century literary men in London such as Samuel Pepys. The ballad text was often printed on one side of a folio page with the instruction, "to the tune of," but in the 18th century broadsides began to include tunes. Ballads also enjoyed popularity in the theater, as ballad operas such as John Gay's *The Beggar's Opera* (1728) borrowed currently fashionable tunes. Collectors with a literary or antiquarian bent increasingly published ballads from traditional sources, but versions were sometimes doctored or even invented. At the same time, city ballad hawkers in Europe and North America developed parallel forms, such as the German *Bänkellieder* ("mountebank songs") on topics of interest to the working classes, such as crimes or disasters; such songs were performed from a stage in a public place where the singer could sell his ballad sheets. The modern period also saw the rise of subtypes such as the "come-all-ye" with its moralistic tone and, in the American South, the "blues ballad" with its slight narrative line and blues-influenced melody.

Impressive compilations of ballad texts appeared in the 19th century, such as the multivolume editions of Danish ballads by Svend Grundtvig, and of English and Scottish ballads by Francis James Child; these were eventually followed by greater attention to the tunes. Translations of English and Scottish ballads, meanwhile, as well as German ballads, appeared in arrangements by composers such as Loewe, Schubert, Schumann, and Brahms. Ballad collecting in Europe and North America flourished again just before World War I and again after World War II, in the fieldwork of figures such as Cecil Sharp in England and John A. Lomax in the United States. The folksong revival of the mid-20th century made the oral traditions of Europe and North America available through recording technology and thus contributed to a fresh interest in the ballad form: newer ballads have been composed since World War II, often on political or satirical themes. Study of the oral-traditional ballad has widened to include the living traditions of southern Europe and such types as the Judeo-Hispanic *romance* or Mexican *corrido.*

In the modern period the term ballad has had applications other than to the oral-traditional type. During Victorian times it referred to a wide variety of popular, often middle-class forms that were sung in the drawing room or parlor, most of them rarely confined to oral tradition. Within British and American popular music of the late 19th and early 20th centuries, the term was generally used to refer to a song with sentimental text in slow or moderate tempo and usually in a form consisting of two or more 16-bar strophes, each followed by an 8-bar (or multiple thereof) refrain, the whole sometimes designated as "a ballad and refrain" or "a song and chorus." Again, in British and American popular music from the 1920s the term refers to a song in slow tempo. Many such songs consist of an introductory "verse" of 16 or 32 bars followed by a chorus or refrain of 32 bars made up of four 8-bar phrases arranged AABA. Phrase B in such a scheme is called the bridge or release; the verse is often omitted in performance, and some songs lack it altogether.

Bibl.: Svend Grundtvig et al., *Danmarks gamle folkeviser* (Copenhagen: Akademisk forlag, 1843–1976), vol. 9 (1976) [tunes]. Francis James Child, *The English and Scottish Popular Ballads* (Boston: Houghton Mifflin, 1882–98). George Doncieux, *Le Romancéro populaire de la France* (Paris: E. Bouillon, 1904). G. H. Gerould, *The Ballad of Tradition* (Oxford: Clarendon, 1932). John Meier et al., *Deutsche Volkslieder mit ihren Melodien* (Berlin: de Gruyter, 1935–), vol. 9 (1992). Joseph W. Hendren, *A Study of Ballad Rhythm, with Special Reference to Ballad Music* (Princeton: Princeton U Pr, 1936). W. J. Entwistle, *European Balladry* (Oxford: Clarendon, 1939). Vicente T. Mendoza, *El corrido mexicano* (Mexico City: Fondo de Cultura Económica, 1954). Jan Schinhan, *The Music of the Ballads,* The Frank C. Brown Collection of North Carolina Folklore, 4 (Durham: Duke U Pr, 1957). D. K. Wilgus, *Anglo-American Folksong Scholarship since 1898* (New Brunswick: Rutgers U Pr, 1959). Bertrand H. Bronson, *The Traditional Tunes of the Child Ballads* (Princeton: Princeton U Pr, 1959–72). Claude M. Simpson, *The British Broadside Ballad and Its Music* (New Brunswick: Rutgers U Pr, 1966). Bertrand H. Bronson, *The Ballad as Song* (Berkeley: U of Cal Pr, 1969). I. J. Katz, *Judeo-Spanish Traditional Ballads from Jerusalem: An Ethnomusicological Study* (Brooklyn: Institute of Medieval Music, 1972–75). R. Leydi, *I canti popolari italiani* (Milan: Montadori, 1973). Peter Kennedy, *Folksongs of Britain and Ireland* (New York: Schirmer, 1975). Rita Benmayor, *Romances judeo-españoles de Oriente* (Madrid: Seminario Menéndez Pidal, 1979). Lajos Vargyas, *Hungarian Ballads and the European Ballad Tradition* (Budapest: Akadémiai Kiadó, 1983). Hugh Shields, *Narrative Singing in Ireland* (Dublin: Irish U Pr, 1993). J.P.

Ballade. (1) [Fr.] One of the three **formes fixes* prominent in the poetry and music of France in the 14th and 15th centuries. In the variety usually set to music, the poem has three seven- or eight-line stanzas, all with the same metrical and rhyme scheme; most often the stanzas also share a *refrain, consisting of one or (occasionally) two lines. The poetic form of the stanza may be ababcdE or ababcdeF (capital letters denoting a textual and musical refrain) or any of a number of other patterns. Two or more of the lines after the second b often rhyme with each other; one or more may rhyme with a or b, as in the very common ababbcC. The whole of the poem sometimes concludes with an **envoi.*

The music of a *ballade* stanza is in two sections (X and Y), the first setting the initial couplet ab and repeated for the next couplet, the second setting the remainder. The musical form can be described as XXY. When the latter portion of a stanza is made up of an even number of lines, Y may be used twice, each statement providing music for half of the relevant section, the musical form then being XXYY. Any repeated music may have first and second endings. Subsequent stanzas have the same music as the first.

The word *ballade* probably originated with the Occitan verb *balar,* "to dance," indicating a connection with dance forms like the *rondet de *carole.* In French the word *balade* is found in the early 13th century, but it does not seem to refer to any particular poetic or musical structure. The 20 "balades" of Jehannot de Lescurel (early 14th century) found in the Fauvel MS assume the more distinctive musical and poetic features of the standardized form of the 14th century.

Guillaume de Machaut (ca. 1300–1377) composed settings of 42 *ballades,* most of them courtly love songs. He usually employed one-line refrains and set *ballades* polyphonically. In these compositions, most often one part carries the text and is evidently meant to be sung, while the other parts (up to three) might have been performed instrumentally or sung on a neutral syllable. The final portions of the second statement of X and of the complete piece (perhaps including all or a substantial part of the refrain) are often alike or quite similar (a feature often termed musical *rhyme).

Composers of the later 14th century retained the framework that Machaut employed, but often incorporated into their *ballades* considerable contrapuntal and rhythmic intricacy [see *Ars subtilior*]. In the early 15th century, the *ballade* receded in importance in music, although as poetry, the form continued to be cultivated. In their relatively few *ballades,* Burgundian composers wrote comparatively simple music and, more significantly, often attached instrumental introductions. See also Chanson, Bar form, *Ballata,* Trouvère, Troubadour; for bibl. see *Formes fixes.*

(2) [Ger.] A narrative poem or song in German, or an instrumental work associated with a narrative poem. Related to the folk *ballad, the German *Ballade* flourished as a literary and musical genre in the last quarter of the 18th and first half of the 19th century. Its subjects, usually drawn from popular (often medieval) history and legend, are largely serious, even tragic (though sometimes light or even comic), frequently with supernatural elements. The tale is told suspensefully but impersonally, often employing dialogue. In imitation of its folk model, the *Ballade* is cast in strophic form; quatrains with three- and four-stress lines and simple rhyme (sometimes with refrains) are common. As a musical work, the *Ballade* is most often a solo song with piano accompaniment. Settings may be *strophic (like traditional folk ballads) or modified strophic, or they may be *through-composed. The stylistic development generally parallels that of the *lied.

The origin and vogue of the German *Ballade* can be related to the view, advanced in the 1760s by Johann Gottfried Herder (1744–1803), that poetry, especially folk poetry and song, is the most characteristic and profound utterance of a people. Gottfried August Bürger (1747–94) created the literary *Ballade* with his poem "Lenore" (1773). Other poets followed Herder's and Bürger's examples of adapting or writing *Balladen* in folklike style, chief among them Goethe, Schiller, Uhland, Fontane, Freiligrath, Heine, Rückert, Chamisso, and Platen.

Precursors of the musical *Ballade* are found in the "Fabeln" and "Erzählungen" of Johann Ernst Bach (1683–1739) and Valentin Herbing (1735–66). Other composers, such as Johann Friedrich Reichardt (1752–1814) and Carl Friedrich Zelter (1758–1832) of the second *"Berlin school," numbered *Balladen* among their songs, but the most important *Ballade* composer of the 18th century was Johann Rudolf Zumsteeg (1760–1802), whose *Kleine Balladen und Lieder* (7 vols., 1798–1805) feature long, rambling, through-composed settings.

Schubert developed a more economical and integrated style in his famous setting of Goethe's "Erlkönig" (1815), but this is an exceptional work even within his own output. Carl Loewe (1796–1869) set the same poem (op. 1, 1818), and he became the most productive (17 vols.) and most celebrated *Ballade* composer of the 19th century. Examples by other composers include Schumann's "Die beiden Grenadiere" (poem by Heine), "Der Soldat" (Andersen), "Die Löwenbraut" (Chamisso); Liszt's "Die Vätergruft" (Uhland); Brahms's "Das Lied vom Herrn von Falkenstein" (Uhland); Wolf's "Der Feuerreiter" (Mörike). *Balladen* occasionally appear as set pieces in operas; e.g., Senta's *Ballade* in Wagner's *Der fliegende Holländer.* In some instances, composers employed *melodrama for their *Ballade* settings; e.g., Schumann's "Ballade der Haidenknabe" (Hebbel), Liszt's "Lenore" (Bürger), Richard Strauss's "Enoch Arden" (Tennyson).

Toward the middle of the 19th century a new genre appeared, the choral *Ballade,* which used mixed choirs and often vocal soloists with orchestral (or other instrumental) accompaniment; e.g., Schumann's "Des Sängers Fluch" (Uhland), Cornelius's "Die Vätergruft" (Uhland), Reger's "Die Nonnen" (Boelitz). The *Ballade* is related to the *romance, commonly a strophic, narrative song in a more lyrical style; e.g., Pedrillo's "Im Mohrenland" in Mozart's *Die Entführung aus dem Serail.*

Some purely instrumental compositions are entitled *Ballade,* with sometimes explicit, sometimes inferable relation to the literary genre. Chief among them are piano works, the best known being Chopin's four *Ballades* (thought by some to be based on poems by Adam Mickiewicz), but also including the *Balladen* of Liszt and Brahms (whose first *Ballade* is headed "after the Scottish ballad 'Edward'"). These pieces display a variety of forms. The points of reference to the literary genre are most likely to be narrative style; the suggestion of a refrain; and archaism (as in Chopin's *Ballade* no. 2 and Brahms's *Ballade* in G minor).

Bibl.: Philipp Spitta, "Die Ballade," *Musikgeschichtliche Aufsätze* (Berlin: Gebrüder Paetel, 1894), pp. 405–61. Adolf König, *Die Ballade in der Musik* (Langensalza: H Beyer, 1904). Hans Joachim Moser, *Die Ballade* (Wolfenbüttel: Möseler, 1959). Id., "Die Ballade und Karl Loewe," *Das deutsche Lied seit Mozart* (Berlin: Atlantis, 1937; rev ed., Tutzing: Schneider, 1968), pp. 105–13. Wolfgang J. Kayser, *Geschichte der deutschen Ballade* (Berlin: Junker und Dünnhaupt, 1936). Sydney Northcote, *The Ballade in Music* (London: Oxford U Pr, 1942). Hans Joachim Moser, *Das deutsche Sololied und die Ballade, Mw* 14 (Cologne: A Volk, 1957; trans. Eng., 1958). David Charles Ossenkop, "The Earliest Settings of German Ballads for Voice and Clavier" (Ph.D. diss., Columbia Univ., 1968). H. Laufhütte, *Die deutsche Kunstballade: Grundlegung einer Gattungsgeschichte* (Heidelberg, 1979). Walther Dürr, *Das deutsche Sololied im 19. Jahrhundert: Untersuchungne zu Aprache und Musik* (Wilhelmshaven, 1984). (2) R.H.

Ballade style. The style of the polyphonic *ballade* [see *Ballade* (1)] of the 14th century, as found, e.g., in the works of Guillaume de Machaut (ca. 1300–1377). Such pieces typically employ three-part texture (cantus, tenor, and contratenor) with the text carried only in the uppermost part, which is also the most animated part of the three. Other forms, both sacred (*Mass, *motet) and secular (**formes fixes*), were composed in the same style, which has also been termed *cantilena style and treble-dominated style.

Ballad meter. See Ballad.

Ballad of Baby Doe. Opera in two acts by Douglas Moore (libretto by John Latouche), first produced in Central City, Colorado, in 1956. Setting: Colorado and Washington, D.C., 1880–99.

Ballad opera. A musico-dramatic genre popular in England, Ireland, and the American colonies in the 18th century in which spoken dialogue alternates with songs consisting of new words fit to traditional or familiar tunes. The musical collaborator in the creation of a ballad opera was primarily a compiler and adapter rather than a composer. He was eclectic with regard to sources, making use of collections of dance tunes; English, Irish, Scottish, or French folk tunes; instrumental or vocal music by composers such as Purcell, Handel, Corelli, and Geminiani; as well as the broadside *ballads that gave the genre its name. The texts are often satirical, taking as their targets aspects of English political, social, or economic life; the conventions of Italian opera, very popular in London at that time, are also a favorite target. The tunes often show dance origins; jigs are especially preferred, but hornpipes and minuets also appear. Frequently, the melody is doubled by strings and accompanied by continuo instruments.

The first and most famous ballad opera was *The *Beggar's Opera* (1728), text by John Gay, music arranged by Johann Christoph Pepusch. Ballad opera flourished for about a decade, after which the earlier works continued to be played, but none of the new works written was successful. The term ballad opera is also applied, somewhat imprecisely, to English operas with spoken dialogue composed in the second half of the 18th century, such as Thomas Arne's *Thomas and Sally* (1760) or Charles Dibdin's *The Padlock* (1768). These works differ from the earliest ballad operas in that they contain a large percentage of newly composed music. The ballad opera was probably influenced by the French *comédie en *vaudeville,* which it resembles and examples of which John Gay knew. The ballad opera, in its turn, influenced the development of north German **Singspiel,* with Charles Coffey's *The Devil to Pay* (1731) and *The Merry Cobbler* (1735) playing a direct and significant role. Kurt Weill's *Die *Dreigroschen Oper* (1921) is a modern reworking of *The Beggar's Opera.*

Bibl.: William Barclay Squire, "An Index of Tunes in the Ballad Operas," *The Musical Antiquary* 2 (1910/11): 1–17. Oscar G. Sonneck, *Early Opera in America* (New York: G Schirmer, 1915). Frank Kidson, *The Beggar's Opera: Its Predecessors and Successors* (Cambridge: Cambridge U Pr, 1922; R: New York, Johnson Repr, 1969). William Schultz, *Gay's Beggar's Opera: Its Content, History, and Influence* (New Haven: Yale U Pr, 1923; R: New York: Russell & Russell, 1967). Arthur Berger, "The Beggar's Opera, the Burlesque, and Italian Opera," *ML* 17 (1936): 93–105. Edmond Gagey, *Ballad Opera* (New York: Columbia U Pr, 1937; R: Bronx: B Blom, 1965). Walter Rubsamen, "The Ballad Burlesques and Extravaganzas," *MQ* 36 (1950): 551–61. Harold Gene Moss, "Popular Music and the Ballad Opera," *JAMS* 26 (1973): 365–82. Roger Fiske, *English Theatre Music in the Eighteenth Century* (London: Oxford U Pr, 1973). Walter Rubsamen, ed., *The Ballad Opera: A Collection of 171 Original Texts of Musical Plays Printed in Photo-facsimile in 28 Volumes* (New York: Garland, 1974). Robert D. Hume, *Henry Fielding and the London Theatre, 1728–1737* (Oxford: Oxford U Pr, 1988). See also Ballad. C.G.

Ballata [It., fr. *ballare,* to dance]. A principal Italian musical and poetic form of the mid-13th to 15th centuries. The *ballata* was intensely cultivated as art music, usually polyphonic, in the 14th century [see *Ars nova* (2)].

Initially the *ballata* was a popular form. Texts without music survive from the second half of the 13th century. Literary references, describing the *ballata* as a dance-song, survive from the very early 14th century. From the mid-14th century, the *ballata* was also cultivated as art song; surviving examples reveal no connection with the dance.

The *ballata* of the 14th century is formally similar to the contemporaneous French **virelai* (not **ballade*). The poetic form of a single stanza with refrain can be outlined AbbaA (capital letters indicating the refrain), and the musical form XYYXX. Each letter may stand for one or several lines. The refrain (A) is called the *ripresa,* the other sections *piedi* (b) and *volta* (a). Most *ballate* have three stanzas; it is not clear whether the refrain should always be repeated between them. Many *ballate,* however, have only one stanza.

The *ballata* of the 14th century is almost always polyphonic. It became the most prominent of Italian song types soon after attaining its position as an art form. In contrast, settings of the formally similar *virelai* are usually monophonic, except for examples composed very late in the 14th century; also, the *virelai* was the least used of the **formes fixes.* Although the musical style of early *ballate* resembles that of the Italian *madrigal, the style of later *ballate* approximates that of French polyphonic songs of the period.

The *ballata* was cultivated by such composers as Niccolò da Perugia, Andreas de Florentia, Bartolino da Padova, Johannes Ciconia, and Francesco Landini. Some of the latest examples were written by Guillaume Dufay and Arnold de Lantins. See also *Barzeletta, Lauda.*

Bibl.: W. Thomas Marrocco, "The Ballata: A Metaphoric Form," *AM* 31 (1959): 32–37. Nino Pirrotta, "On Text Forms from Ciconia to Dufay," *Reese,* 1966, pp. 673–82. Beate Regina Suchla, *Studien zur Provenienz der Trecento-Ballata* (Kassel: Bärenreiter-Antiquariat, 1976). See also *Ars nova.*

Ballet and theatrical dance. The following is a survey of Western theatrical dance. See also Ballet in opera.

Although theatrical dance was important in the civilizations of ancient Greece and Rome, relatively little concrete choreographic detail survives from before the 15th century, and the specific relationship between descriptions of dance and the surviving musical repertory remains ambiguous. The earliest dance of which some distinct impression can be gained is the **carole.* Among instrumental dance pieces surviving in actual examples and in accounts of theorists (especially Johannes de Grocheo) are the **estampie, *ductia,* and **saltarello.*

A wealth of detail is available from the 15th century onward. As authorities in deportment, music, and dance, Italian dancing masters of the 15th and 16th centuries were extremely influential. Domenico da Piacenza (ca. 1390–ca. 1470), Guglielmo Ebreo da Pesaro (b. ca. 1425), Antonio Cornazano (ca. 1430–84), Fabritio Caroso (ca. 1530–after 1605), and Cesare de' Negri (ca. 1535–after 1604) not only trained courtiers to dance but also wrote manuals that recorded steps and music, the most famous of which is *Orchésographie* (1588) by Jehan Tabourot [Thoinot Arbeau] (1520–95). Many of the dances described in these primers are familiar as musical forms. See Afterdance, *Alta, Ballo, Basse danse, Bel fiore, Branle, Calata, Canarie, Cascarda, Chiarenzana, Cinque passi, Favorita, Folia, Forlana, Gagliarda, Hoftanz, Haye, Montirandé, Moresca, Nachtanz, Padovana, Pas de Brabant, Pass'e mezo, Pavana, Pavaniglia, Piva, Quaternaria, Recoupe, Rotta, Saltarello, Sciolta, Spagna, Spagnoletta, Spingardo, Tourdion, Volta.*

Theatrical dancing was merely one aspect of the Renaissance festivals. Royal entries, tournaments, equestrian ballets, and indoor *divertissements* were executed to commemorate births, marriages, or the visits of monarchs and their families. The *divertissements* were elaborate spectacles with lavish scenery and costumes. They combined poetry, music, and *balli* or *balletti* (staged ballroom dances) in a complex allegorical framework. Directed by the dancing masters, these events fall into three major categories: the Italian **intermedio,* the French **ballet de cour,* and the English *masque. The details of these extravaganzas, documented in costly volumes that were distributed to participants and guests, were known and emulated throughout Europe.

With the wedding of Catherine de' Medici and Henri Valois in 1533, Italian supremacy in festival artistry was transferred to France. To support her political strategy and to eliminate the violence associated with jousting, Catherine produced five complex fêtes between 1564 and 1581 that transformed *ballet de cour* into an identifiable form. The fête of Fontainebleau (1564), the festival of Bayonne (1565), the *Paradis d'Amour* (1572), and the *Ballet Polonais* (1573) increasingly refined her use of the arts in support of the state. *Ballet comique de la Reine* (1581), commissioned by Catherine, unified music, poetry, and dance with a single dramatic plot. Staged by Balthasar de Beaujoyeulx, this work contained two monodic solos. The score, composed by Lambert de Beaulieu and Jacques Salmon, featured **musique mesurée* and was strongly supported by the Académie de poésie et de musique, established in 1570 by Jean-Antoine de Baïf and Joachim Thibault de Courville. The performance technique for Beaujoyeulx's ballet, which was danced by noble amateurs, was based on a lexicon of steps, a turnout of the feet, and a firm vertical torso, all of which remain characteristics of classical dance.

Economic depression as well as the political turmoil that ended the Valois line brought about a concurrent decline for the *ballet de cour.* Simpler, less expensive variations appeared. The *ballet mascarade* (1600–10), the *ballet mélodramatique* (1610–21), and the *ballet à entrées* (1620–50) departed from the mythological theme and consecutive plot of *Ballet comique de la Reine.*

As a result of the guidance and financial backing of

Louis XIV, ballet flourished again during the Baroque period. A fine dancer himself, the king performed from 1651, when he made his debut in *Cassandre,* until 1670, when his vanity and corpulence kept him off the stage. More important was his founding of the Académie royale de danse in 1661. Under the direction of Pierre Beauchamp, 13 ballet masters set the standards for training that prevailed at the subsequent institution, the Académie royale de musique et de danse, which opened in 1672. A fine teacher and virtuosic soloist, Beauchamp codified the five positions of the feet with accompanying *port de bras.* Along with his colleagues, he defined the academic terminology of the *danse d'école.*

Beauchamp collaborated on productions with two other favorites of the king, the playwright Molière (Jean-Baptiste Poquelin) and the composer Jean-Baptiste Lully (1632–87), who had been officially in charge of royal dance music since 1653. Their first of many joint efforts, *Le mariage forcé* (1664), introduced the *comédie-ballet,* an amusing amalgam of stage play and dancing. With the librettist Philippe Quinault, Lully brought about a number of reforms in French opera. He imposed quicker tempos for the ballets in his operas and composed prolifically for Versailles's favorite dance forms: canarie, chaconne, minuet, passepied, courante, and contredanse. The Baroque dancing style emphasized a stiff torso. Small steps were ornamented for the men with *cabrioles, entrechats,* and *tours en l'air.* Louis Pécour and Pierre Rameau were among the Académie's other highly regarded masters. In 1700, Raoul-Auger Feuillet published Beauchamp's system of notation, thus spreading French terminology and method all over Europe. For examples of dance music of the 17th and 18th centuries see Allemande, Amener, Anglaise, Bourrée, Canarie, Contredanse, Courante, Gavotte, Gigue, Hornpipe, Loure, Minuet, Sarabande, Passepied, Rigaudon, Tambourin, Traquenard. See also Suite.

By 1660 dancing on the orchestra level of the theater was abolished, and all action receded onto a raked stage behind a proscenium arch. Casts for the ballets were male courtiers. But in 1681 in *Le triomphe de l'amour,* Mlle. de LaFontaine (1665–1738) and three other women set the precedent for female professional dancers. Paris was the leading center for dance, and audiences began to single out performers such as Jean Balon, Marie Thérèse Subligny (1666–1736), and Françoise Prévost (1680–1741) for special adulation. By the end of the 17th century, the *opéra-ballet* and André Campra's (1660–1744) first ballet of **entrées, L'Europe galante* (1697), were in vogue.

A series of substantial reforms and an intense aesthetic dualism characterize theatrical dancing in the 18th century. The central issue in the artistic dispute was whether to place an emphasis on expressiveness or on virtuosity. The struggle between those who preferred organic forms over artifice also appeared in musical circles. The "Lullists" continued to uphold the ideals of Lully, which placed an equal value on music, plot, and dancing. The "Ramists," who sided with Jean-Philippe Rameau (1683–1764), gave greater freedom to exoticism and *divertissements.* On the stage, the rivalry of the two leading ballerinas was based on the same debate. Marie Sallé (1707–56) threw off her *panniers* and donned Greek draperies for the role of Galatea in *Pygmalion,* which demonstrated her sensitive pantomime. Marie-Anne Cupis de Camargo (1710–70) shortened her skirts to show off her brilliant *entrechat quatre. Danse haute* was praised by those who admired exhibitionism and verticality but was decried by *basse danse* enthusiasts.

The elimination of the verbal text from ballet and the maturation of *ballet d'action* were two of the century's major developments. Experiments in France by the Duchesse du Maine in 1708 and in England by John Weaver in 1717 proved that dance, mime, and music could convey a narrative without recourse to poetry, prose, or song. The insistence on a single plot along with the simultaneous unification of dance, decor, and music with the elements of action, character, and locale were characteristics of the new form, *ballet d'action.* Franz Hilverding van Wewen, Gaspero Angiolini, and Vincenzo Galeotti gained acceptance for *ballet d'action* in Vienna, Stuttgart, St. Petersburg, and Copenhagen. Jean-Georges Noverre (1727–1810) articulated his innovative reforms in his invaluable *Lettres sur la danse et sur les ballets* (1760). Enlightening manuals on dance were published by John Weaver, Pierre Rameau, John Essex, Abbé Jean-Baptiste Dubos, and others. Several interesting musical collaborations also occurred. Noverre did a series of epic ballets with Gluck, and he choreographed *Les petits riens* by Mozart.

While Paris retained its dominance, vigorous dance activity also took place in the capital cities of Russia, Denmark, England, and Austria. Dance masters, *danseurs,* and *danseuses* moved easily among the royal opera houses. Some of the dancers celebrated in more than one country were La Barbarina, Charles Le Picq (1749–1806), and Charles Louis Didelot (1767–1836). The principal international star was Gaetano Vestris (1729–1808). Along with his brother, Angiolo (1730–1809), he established the first of the skillful Italian ballet families who captivated spectators for more than 200 years. His son, Auguste (1760–1842), was the leading male dancer of the late 18th and early 19th centuries. Vestris's wife, Anna Heinel (1753–1808), was the first woman to perform the *pirouette à la seconde.*

Costume reforms altered the ballet *mise en scène* dramatically. Contemporary fashions were replaced by attempts at historical accuracy in terms of the period and locale of the production. Following the example of Gaetano Vestris, dancers appeared on stage without masks.

Although transitional choreographers such as Jean Dauberval (1742–1806) and Salvatore Viganò (1769–

1821) added strength to ballet's independence as an art form, French Romanticism revolutionized technique. Trained by her father, Filippo, Marie Taglioni (1804–84) astonished Paris in 1827 by dancing on the tips of her toes with an ease that seemed supernatural. Her delicate pointe work was perfectly suited to the sylphs, wilis, undines, and fairies that began to fill the stage of the Paris Opéra. From 1832 until 1850, French Romantic ballet blossomed with choreography by Filippo Taglioni (1778–1871), Jules Perrot (1810–92), Arthur Saint-Léon (ca. 1815–70), and Jean Coralli (1779–1854). **Giselle,* with choreography by Coralli and Perrot to a score by Adolphe Adam (1803–56), was first produced in 1841 and remains one of the masterpieces of the international repertory. Other works of the period include *La *sylphide, *Coppélia,* and **Sylvia.* Ballerinas like Marie Taglioni, Fanny Elssler (1810–84), Fanny Cerrito (1817–1909), Carlotta Grisi (1819–99), and Lucile Grahn (1819–1907) brought theatrical dance to an increasingly large audience.

At mid-century, French ascendance was ceded to Copenhagen, where August Bournonville (1805–79) stocked the repertory of the Royal Danish Ballet with dozens of fine Romantic works, many of which are still performed today. As ballet elsewhere became an all-female spectacle, the grand climax of the period took place in Russia. Marius Petipa (1819–1910) arrived to dance in St. Petersburg in 1847. When he retired as ballet master in 1903, he had created dances for more than 100 productions, highlighted by definitive versions of **Don Quixote* (1869), *La *bayadère* (1877), *The *Sleeping Beauty* (1890), *The *Nutcracker* (1892 with Lev Ivanov), **Cinderella* (1893), **Swan Lake* (1895 with Ivanov), and *Raymonda* (1898). He invented the structure of the classical *pas de deux* and brought staging for the *corps de ballet* to a level that has seldom been equaled. He imported the second generation of Italian ballerinas trained by the remarkable Carlo Blasis (1795–1878), but he did not allow the Maryinsky Theatre to become dependent on their attractions. In collaborations with Léon Minkus (1826–1917) and Tchaikovsky, Petipa set a pattern that singularly influenced the 20th century: the teaming of a gifted choreographer with an equally talented composer.

The marvels of Russian ballet were not known in Europe until Sergei Diaghilev (1872–1929) formed his Ballets russes in 1909. Dedicated to the concept of total unity of production, Diaghilev hired some of the world's finest artists to mount works for his company. Léon Bakst, Pablo Picasso, and Maurice Utrillo were among his designers. Scores were commissioned from Stravinsky (*L'*oiseau de feu, *Petrushka, Le *sacre du printemps*), Debussy (**Jeux*), Falla (*El *sombrero de tres picos*), Milhaud (*Le train bleu,* 1924), Satie (*Parade,* 1917), Ravel (**Daphnis et Chloé*), and others. Vaclav Nijinsky, Tamara Karsavina, Alexandra Danilova, Anton Dolin, Serge Lifar, and for one season, Anna Pavlova were members of his ensemble. A revolution was accomplished by Diaghilev's principal choreographers: Michel Fokine (1880–1942), Léonide Massine (1896–1979), and George Balanchine (1904–84). Abstract ballet—classical dancing with no narrative—was introduced. Because of Diaghilev, ballet came to be regarded as a serious art and as a leading force in modern aesthetics. With his death in 1929, his troupe disbanded. Former dancers and staff scattered and founded what became internationally prestigious companies—the Ballet russe de Monte Carlo, Britain's Royal Ballet, and the New York City Ballet.

In 1925 Balanchine was given his first choreographic assignment for Diaghilev: he was to revise the dances in Stravinsky's *Le chant du rossignol* [see *Nightingale, The*]. Three years later the two men collaborated on the first project in a lifelong partnership that enriched the repertories of both music and dance. The 1928 production of **Apollon Musagète* (called *Apollo* since 1947) was a rediscovery of the classical language for Balanchine. It was also the birth of neoclassical dancing, the most significant extension of ballet technique in the 20th century. Trained in St. Petersburg's Imperial School as a dancer and musician, Balanchine was able to translate Stravinsky's new meters and rhythms into equally novel visual and spatial dynamics that fused sight with sound.

At the invitation of Lincoln Kirstein, Balanchine came to the U.S. and founded a conservatory. The School of American Ballet opened in 1934 and began to cultivate the tall, swift dancers necessary to his intricate choreographic designs. In 1948 the performance unit of the SAB changed its name from Ballet Society to New York City Ballet. With his dancers, Balanchine defined the American balletic style. To traditional classicism he added a flexible torso, turned-in positions for the feet, instantaneous changes of direction, asymmetry, and a startling rapidity of movement. To maintain this style he built a school, company, and repertory. The scope of his work is prodigious. The 425 documented choreographies have already been danced by more than 200 different ensembles.

The dispersal of Russian artists after the Bolshevik Revolution took rigorous technical standards to many parts of the world. As a result, ballet companies emerged in China, Japan, Canada, Latin America, and across the U.S. England produced a celebrated group of choreographers, including Frederick Ashton, Antony Tudor, and John Cranko. Although Soviet attitudes limited the range of the contemporary repertory in the U.S.S.R., the Russian system of training produced stars of international magnitude, such as Rudolf Nureyev, Natalia Makarova, and Mikhail Baryshnikov (all three of whom emigrated in search of wider opportunity).

One of the subtler influences on classicism in the 20th century was the development of modern dance. A revolt against the spectacle, formality, scale, and inflexibility of Western European ballet in the late 19th century brought about the search for a form of dance based on a vocabulary of natural human motions. On the stages of commercial theaters in America, three soloists created personal styles that established the iconoclastic nature of modern dance. Each artist generated an individual technique to express movement design concepts. Loie Fuller used extensive draperies and colored light projections to enhance her notions of organic imagery. The theatrical, exotic presentations of Ruth St. Denis were inspired by the ethnic dances of the Orient. Isadora Duncan turned to ancient Greece for the bold, heroic spirit that motivated her choreography. Similar experiments in Europe were carried out by Rudolf von Laban, Mary Wigman, and later, Kurt Jooss and Hanya Holm.

In 1915 St. Denis and her husband, Ted Shawn, opened Denishawn, the school in Los Angeles where Doris Humphrey, Martha Graham, and Charles Weidman studied. Resident music director Louis Horst influenced all three of these artists in their selection of scores and in their investigations of preclassic dances. Graham and Humphrey left Denishawn in the 1920s to form their own companies. Through her choreography, articles, and classes, Humphrey elevated the craft of dance composition. Her ideas also generated much of the repertory for the José Limón Dance Company. Collaborations with Horst, Aaron Copland, William Schuman, and Samuel Barber contributed to the distinctively American viewpoint of the Graham oeuvre. From the great number of Graham's former dancers, Paul Taylor, Robert Cohan, and Merce Cunningham founded important troupes of their own.

Cunningham's fascination with pure movement—stripped of any contextual framework—fomented the next rebellion. In close alliance with composer John Cage, Cunningham created a body of dance works that exist simultaneously with, but independently of, their musical scores. The only relationship between music and dance is that they occur in the same moment. Through improvisation and aleatoric methods, Cunningham expanded the limits of the creative process. His choreographic patterns are often decentralized, shifting value and focus to many different points on the stage. Cunningham's dictum, "Any movement can be a dance movement," launched the next generation of modernists.

A concert at New York's Judson Memorial Church on July 6, 1962, inaugurated the era of postmodern dancing. With a violence characteristic of the decade, young artists repudiated the formulas and aesthetic principles of their predecessors, decrying them as romantic, outdated, and too expressive. In efforts to rescale dance from ideal to human proportions, untrained performers were frequently placed in task-oriented composites that could take place anywhere from rooftops to parking lots. Work clothes became costumes. Sound, noise, even silence were used as accompaniment. Repetition and reductivist techniques heightened the perception of minimalist material. David Gordon, Deborah Hay, Trisha Brown, Lucinda Childs, Yvonne Rainer, Meredith Monk, Laura Dean, and Kei Takei were participants in a choreographic field in which visual artists and musicians also made dances.

"New" or "next wave" dances succeeded postmodernism by the late 1970s. Led by the technical innovations of Twyla Tharp, artistic directors began to sustain their works by incorporating athleticism, virtuosity, and handsomely designed costumes and properties. Performances moved back into more formal spaces where dances could be framed by a proscenium arch or sculpted by professional lighting effects. Theatricality served as a means of attracting larger audiences. Notable productions of this type have been produced by Mark Morris and the experimentalist Tricia Brown. European theaters and festivals continue to sponsor numerous tours by avant-garde and classical American troupes. As to nontraditional choreography on the Continent, works by Pina Bausch, Maguy Marin, Anna Teresa de Keersmaker, and Mats Ek are best known internationally.

The genre of *musical comedy has provided an important link between *popular music and concert dance. Along with Graham, Humphrey, Holm, and Balanchine, Agnes De Mille, Jack Cole, Jerome Robbins, Michael Bennett, and many others have created new parameters and styles of American dance in the musical theater. Susan Stroman redefined the collaborative role of director/choreographer with such productions as the dance play *Contact* (1999), *The Music Man* (2000 revival), *The Producers* (2001), and *Thou Shalt Not* (2001). She is the only person to win Broadway's coveted Antoinette Perry Award, or Tony, for best director/choreographer in two consecutive years.

Bibl.: John Martin, *The Modern Dance* (New York: Barnes, 1933; R: 1965). Lincoln Kirstein, *Dance: A Short History of Classical Theatrical Dancing* (New York: Putnam, 1935; R: Brooklyn: Dance Horizons, 1969; Princeton, N.J.: Princeton Bk Co, 1987). Curt Sachs, *World History of the Dance,* trans. Bessie Schönberg (New York: Norton, 1937; 1st ed. in Ger., 1933). Margaret M. McGowan, *L'art du ballet de cour en France, 1581–1643* (Paris: CNRS, 1963). Leo Kirsley and Janet Sinclair, *A Dictionary of Ballet Terms,* 3rd ed. (London: A & C Black, 1973). Natalia René [Natal'ia Roslavleva], *Era of the Russian Ballet* (London: Gollancz, 1966). Anatole Chujoy and P. W. Manchester, comp. and ed., *The Dance Encyclopedia,* rev., enl. ed. (New York: Simon & Schuster, 1967). George Balanchine, *Balanchine's New Complete Stories of the Great Ballets,* ed. Francis Mason (Garden City, N.Y.: Doubleday, 1968 rev. enl. ed., 1977). Lincoln Kirstein, *Movement and Metaphor* (New York: Praeger, 1970; R: *Four Centuries of Ballet,* New York: Dover, 1984). New York Public Library, *Dictionary Catalog of the Dance Collection: A List of Authors, Titles, and Subjects of Multimedia Materials in the Dance Collection of the Performing Arts Research Center of the New York Public Library,* 10 vols. (Boston: G K Hall, 1974; rev. ed. 26 vols., 2000). G. B. L. Wilson, *A Dictionary of Ballet,* 3rd ed. (London: A&C Black, 1974). Marian Hannah Winter, *The Pre-Romantic Ballet*

(Brooklyn: Dance Horizons, 1975). Selma Jeanne Cohen, ed., *Dance as a Theatre Art: Source Readings in Dance History from 1581 to the Present* (New York: Harper & Row, 1976). Don McDonagh, *The Complete Guide to Modern Dance* (Garden City, N.Y.: Doubleday, 1976). Sally Banes, *Terpsichore in Sneakers: Post-Modern Dance* (Boston: Houghton Mifflin, 1980). Ivor Guest, *The Romantic Ballet in Paris,* 2nd rev. ed. (London: Dance Bks, 1980). Wendy Hilton, *Dance of Court and Theater: The French Noble Style, 1690–1725,* ed. Caroline Gaynor (Princeton, N.J.: Princeton Bk Co, 1981). Horst Koegler, *The Concise Oxford Dictionary of Ballet,* 3rd ed. (London: Oxford U Pr, 1987). George Balanchine, *Choreography by George Balanchine: A Catalogue of Works,* comp. Leslie George Kate, Nancy Lassalle, and Harvey Simmonds (New York: Eakins Pr Found, 1983). Paul Taylor, *Private Domain, An Autobiography* (New York: Knopf, 1987). Lynn Garafola, *Diaghilev's Ballets Russes* (New York: Oxford U Pr, 1990). Twyla Tharp, *Push Comes to Shove, An Autobiography* (New York: Linda Grey Bantam Books, 1992). Joan Acocella, *Mark Morris* (New York: Farrar, Straus & Giroux, 1993). Sasha Anawalt, *Joffrey Ballet: Robert Joffrey and the Making of an American Dance Company* (New York: Scribner, 1996). Ivor Guest, *The Ballet of the Enlightenment: Establishment of the Ballet d'Action in France 1770–1793* (London: Dance Books, 1996). Knud Arne Jürgensen, *The Bournonville Tradition: The First Fifty Years, 1829–1879,* 2 vols. (London: Dance Books, 1997). Jennifer Dunning, *Alvin Ailey: A Life in Dance* (New York: Da Capo, 1998). Selma Jeanne Cohen, founding ed., *International Encyclopedia of Dance,* 6 vols. (New York: Oxford U Pr, 1998). Jack Anderson, *Art without Boundaries: The World of Modern Dance* (Ames: U of Iowa Pr, 1999). Suki Schorer, with Russell Lee, *Suki Schorer on Balanchine Technique* (New York: Knopf, 1999). David Vaughan, *Merce Cunningham: Fifty Years, Chronicle and Commentary* (New York: Aperture Foundation, 1999). Marian Smith, *Ballet and Opera in the Age of Giselle* (Princeton: Princeton U Pr, 2000). Jane C. Desmond, ed., *Dancing Desires: Choreographing Sexualities on and off the Stage* (Madison: U of Wis Pr, 2001). C.HY.

Ballet de cour [Fr., court ballet]. The chief French courtly amateur entertainment of the 16th and 17th centuries, succeeding the 15th-century *entremet* and influenced by the Italian **intermedio, mascherata,* and *trionfo.* Produced in a decorated hall, the ballet consisted of up to five mythological or allegorical *entrées* (sets of dances and choruses) with corresponding *vers* (verses printed and distributed to participants), each introduced by a spoken or sung *récit.* The whole commenced with an *ouverture* and concluded with a *grand ballet* in which at least once a year the king himself danced. Each ballet owed its composition to a team of at least one vocal composer, instrumental composer, poet, choreographer, and machinist, coordinated by a master of revels and produced by a royal or courtly patron.

Under the late Valois kings, Queen Catherine de' Medici imported fellow Florentine ballet-master Baltazarini de Belgioioso (Beaujoyeulx), who unified the spectacle by dramatic continuity and made its diction conform to the humanistic philosophy of the Pléiade and Baïf's Académie de poésie et de musique. His ballet for the Magnificences of 1581, *Balet comique de la Royne,* on the overthrow of Circe, epitomized a resultant complex genre that foreshadowed operatic developments of later eras.

Dramatic unification waned under the early Bourbon kings; politically topical themes gained in importance. In 1641, Cardinal Richelieu produced the *Ballet de la prospérité des armes de France,* importing Florentine machinist Giacomo Torelli, who mounted the spectacle for the first time on stage. Cardinal Mazarin continued this practice under Louis XIV, casting the young monarch in major roles—among them the Sun in *Ballet de la nuit* (1653), whence the sobriquet "Roi soleil." The *ballet de cour* reached its apogee in the 1650s with the poet Isaac de Benserade and the young Florentine musician Giambattista Lulli (Lully). From the 1660s, the autocratic and influential Lully transformed the ballet, first with Molière into the professional *comédie-ballet,* finally with Quinault into the operatic *tragédie-lyrique.*

Bibl.: James R. Anthony, *French Baroque Music* (New York: Norton, 1974). Robert M. Isherwood, *Music in the Service of the King* (Ithaca, N.Y.: Cornell U Pr, 1973). Marie-Françoise Christout, *Le ballet de cour au XVIIè siècle* (Geneva: Minkoff, 1987). David J. Buch, *Dance Music from the Ballets de Cour 1575–1651* (Stuyvesant, N.Y.: Pendragon, 1993).

Ballet in opera. The roots of opera are in spectacles that involve singing, mime, and dance, such as the **intermedio, *pastorale, *ballet de cour,* and *masque [see also Ballet]. And the earliest Italian operas—Peri's and Caccini's **Euridice* (both 1600), Monteverdi's **Orfeo* (1607), Marco da Gagliano's **Dafne* (1608)—conclude with scenes of celebration that call for group singing and dancing. (Peri's score instructs "Ballo à 5. Tutto il Coro insieme cantano, e Ballano"; Monteverdi's ends with a **moresca.*) Dance remained an important part of court operas, which placed a high value on lavish display and spectacle. Cesti's *Il pomo d'oro* (Vienna, 1667) has ballets in each act and a triple ballet at the conclusion. Commercial opera in Italy, on the other hand, gradually dispensed with both chorus and ballet.

In 17th-century France, ballet was a more firmly established genre than opera. One may speak of opera grafted onto ballet rather than ballet inserted into opera. Jean-Baptiste Lully, who laid the foundation and set the model for French opera for the next several generations, was a dancer and choreographer as well as a composer. Operas by him and his successors normally contained dances in each act—dances that were integrated into the action or dances that caused a break in the action, that is, **divertissements.* In the **opéra-ballet,* a genre that flourished after Lully's death, the *divertissement* function of the dances outweighed considerations of dramatic continuity. Popular ballroom dances such as the courante, minuet, passepied, gigue, and bourrée were pressed into service for ballets; extended choral dances, chaconnes and passacaglias, were preferred for the ends of acts. The music for the dance in Rameau's operas and *opéras-ballet* was expanded and more richly orchestrated; at the same time dance was more fully integrated into the action. The librettist for several of Rameau's works, Louis de Cahusac, was the author of an influential treatise on the dance, *La danse ancienne et moderne* (Paris, 1754).

Ballet developed as an independent art in 18th-century Italy, but there was little place for ballet in the Italian operas of the time—serious or comic. The occasional exceptions were likely to be a response to a particular situation, such as the presence of an important dancer or dance troupe at a certain time. For example, Handel's *Il pastor fido* (second version, 1734), *Ariodante* (1735), and *Alcina* (1735) have a considerable amount of ballet music, which was not typical of Handel's operas in general but a response to the presence of Marie Sallé in London during the 1734 season. The second half of the 18th century saw reform movements in the ballet (promoted by Franz Hilverding, Gasparo Angiolini, and Jean-Georges Noverre) as well as in Italian opera (promoted by Gluck, Jommelli, and Traetta). Indeed these reformers sometimes collaborated—Noverre and Jommelli in Stuttgart, Gluck and Angiolini in Vienna, Gluck and Noverre in Paris. In the reform operas of Jommelli, Traetta, and Gluck, ballet and chorus, well integrated into the action, once more played an important role.

Despite the many political, social, and cultural changes that took place in France in the 19th century, ballet remained an important feature of opera, particularly of grand opera. Ballets were valued for the contributions they made to the spectacular or atmospheric facets of the opera. On occasion the ballet was integrated into the plot, as in the sensational dance of the spectral nuns in Meyerbeer's *Robert le diable* (1831). The close connection of ballet and opera in 19th-century France is suggested by the careers of Adolphe Adam and Léo Delibes, who composed both successful operas and successful ballets, and that of Eugène Scribe, who wrote ballet scenarios as well as opera librettos. Of the operas adapted to the French style by the addition of ballet scenes, Wagner's *Tannhäuser* (1845; revised for Paris in 1861) is perhaps the most notorious example; Verdi added ballets for the Paris performances of *I lombardi* (rewritten and renamed *Jérusalem,* 1847), *Macbeth* (1847; Paris, 1865), *Il trovatore* (1853; Paris, 1857), and *Otello* (1887; Paris, 1894).

Ballet did not usually play an important role in the operas composed by Rossini, Bellini, and Donizetti for Italian premieres. In many Italian theaters, independent ballets were presented between the acts of operas instead. Nevertheless, the atmosphere of the dance, in the background, permeates the opening scenes of *Rigoletto* (1851) and *La traviata* (1853) and contributes to the irony of the last scene of *Un ballo in maschera* (1859), all written for Italian theaters. With the exception of Weber's *Der Freischütz* (1821), ballet did not make an important contribution to German opera in the 19th century, in part because ballet itself was not significantly developed or cultivated in Germany at that time except in certain court theaters such as Stuttgart.

Ballet played a significant role in 19th-century Russian opera. Glinka's *A Life for the Tsar* (1836) and *Ruslan and Lyudmila* (1842), Borodin's *Prince Igor* (1869–87), and Musorgsky's *Boris Godunov* (1868–74) all have important dance scenes, as do most of the operas by Tchaikovsky and Rimsky-Korsakov. Tchaikovsky, like Adam and Delibes, whom he much admired, was active as a composer of operas and of ballets. Ballets in Russian operas were sometimes choreographed by major figures. For example, Lev Ivanov, who choreographed *The Nutcracker* (1892) and rechoreographed some scenes of *Swan Lake* (1877), also choreographed the Polovtsian Dances in *Prince Igor.*

Dance (though generally not classical ballet) still had a certain place in operas of the 20th century. Often that place is to express emotional excess, as in Strauss's *Elektra* (1909), in which Elektra dances herself into a frenzied collapse; in Schoenberg's *Moses und Aron* (1930–32), the scene of the orgy around the golden calf; in Berg's *Wozzeck* (1925), when Marie's infidelity is brought home to Wozzeck as he sees her dancing with the drum major in a tavern. Other 20th-century operas use dance in a more traditional manner, often to evoke the atmosphere of the period in which the work is set. Britten's *Gloriana* (1953) evokes Elizabethan England in its use of a volta, galliard, pavanne, and morris dance; in Prokofiev's *War and Peace* (1941–43, rev. 1946–52), the ball scenes are likewise important for suggesting the atmosphere of Russia before the Napoleonic wars. In Tippett's *A Midsummer Marriage* (1946–52), the dance is both a central symbol and a means for manifesting the action. C.G.

Ballett. See *Balletto* (2).

Balletto [It.]. (1) A 15th-century choreographed Italian dance using pantomimic gesture; the term was also used for composed dances, for dance groups, and for dance in general in the 16th and 17th centuries. See *Ballo.*

(2) A vocal piece in homophonic, dance-rhythm style, with strophic texts punctuated by nonsense refrains such as "fa-la-la." The earliest known collection, Giovanni Gastoldi's *Balletti a cinque voci con li suoi versi per cantare, sonare e ballare* (1591), is arranged so as to indicate an evening's entertainment of costumed dance and song. Adriano Banchieri, Orazio Vecchi, Sigismondo d'India, and others continued writing *balletti* in the early 17th century. The *balletto* was taken up in Germany (by Hans Leo Hassler, 1601) and especially in England, where Thomas Morley (*Balletts to Five Voyces,* 1595) imitated Gastoldi

with great success, producing a sophisticated genre that under Thomas Weelkes (*Balletts and Madrigals to Five Voyces,* 1598) drew close to the madrigal in freedom of rhythm and contrapuntal style.

(3) An instrumental dance, mainly for lute in the late 16th century, and for guitar, keyboard, and chamber ensemble (especially strings and continuo) throughout the 17th century. In Italy the term was often used for a foreign dance, especially one of German origin (hence its close relationship with the *allemande; in Italian usage the two terms are nearly indistinguishable). Bipartite in structure, simple and tuneful in texture, varied in tempo and meter (usually duple), the *balletto* was often used as an introductory dance in a suite. It was a popular dance in Germany through much of the 17th century. J.H.

Ballo [It., sometimes also *bal, balletto,* dance, ball]. (1) In the late Middle Ages, any social dancing. (2) In the 15th century, a lively dance that contrasted with the slower-moving *bassadanza* [see *Basse danse*]. (3) In the 15th and 16th centuries, a professionally choreographed dance performed socially or as an entertainment [see Dance; *Balletto*]. (4) In the titles of 16th-century collections of instrumental music, any of various specific dances (e.g., **pavana, *gagliarda*). (5) Around 1600, a stage work in which dance is of central importance (e.g., Monteverdi's *Il ballo delle ingrate,* 1608) or a dance forming a part of a larger stage work.

Ballo in maschera, Un [It., A Masked Ball]. Opera in three acts by Verdi (libretto by Antonio Somma, based on Eugène Scribe's libretto for Auber's opera *Gustave III, ou Le bal masqué* of 1833), first produced in Rome in 1859. It was originally to be set in Stockholm at the end of the 18th century. In order to appease government censors, who objected to the staged portrayal of a successful assassination of a king, the setting was transferred to Boston and its surroundings at the end of the 17th century. Modern productions may use Boston, Stockholm, Naples, or other cities; the epoch is also variable.

Baltic countries. Estonia, Latvia, and Lithuania were established as independent nations from 1918 to 1940, and were reestablished in the early 1990s. Throughout most of their history they were under foreign domination; thus they absorbed many cultural influences from their neighbors. In spite of these influences, each country developed its own unique folk and art music.

The oldest folk music of this relatively remote agrarian area was connected directly to year-cycle events of the agricultural calendar and to life-cycle events, such as weddings and funerals. In general, women sang and men played instrumental music. Latvian and Lithuanian are among the oldest Indo-European languages; Estonian is a Uralic language, related to Finnish and Hungarian. The oldest vocal texts in Latvia and Lithuania were called *dainas,* and in Estonia *runos.* A wide variety of folksong genres prevail in the region.

The most important folk instrument is the so-called Baltic psaltery, in Estonia the *kannel,* in Latvia the *kokle,* and Lithuania the *kanklės.* This is a small, trapezoidal zither with five to ten strings, closely related to the Finnish *kantele.* Each nation considers its type of Baltic psaltery as its national instrument. Bagpipes were also played in the region, as well as a variety of herdsman's aerophones. Since the late 1960s, a strong folk music revival has emerged in each of the Baltic countries. The Baltica International Folklore Festival has contributed significantly to the revival movement since 1988. All three countries have established large archival research collections of their folk music.

Art music in the region grew initially out of church music. Estonia and Latvia are predominantly Lutheran, while Lithuania is Catholic. Many composers of the region studied in St. Petersburg. Perhaps the most significant influence has been nationalism, prompting the use of native folk music as a basis for composition. Although all genres of art music flourish, vocal genres predominate. Since the 19th century, each Baltic nation has had a strong tradition of choral singing that has manifested itself in large song festivals. In recent years these song festivals served as a kind of resistance against foreign domination. The reestablishment of independence in the 1990s has been called the "Singing Revolution."

Bibl.: *The Garland Encyclopedia of World Music,* vol. 8: *Europe* (New York: Garland, 2000), s.v.v. "Estonia," "Latvia," "Lithuania." *Grove 6,* 2nd ed. (London: Macmillan, 2001), s.v.v. "Estonia," "Latvia," "Lithuania." Guntis Šmidchens, "A Baltic Music: The Folklore Movement in Lithuania, Latvia, and Estonia, 1968–1991" (Ph.D. diss., Indiana Univ., 1996). C.R.

Bamberg, Codex. Bamberg, Staatliche Bibliothek, Lit. 115 [Ba]. 80 leaves. France, 13th century. This manuscript consists of *conductus, clausulae,* 100 motets, and a treatise by Amerus, *Practica artis musice.* Modern editions: Pierre Aubry, *Cent motets du XIIIe siècle,* 3 vols. (Paris: Rouart & Lerolle, 1908); Gordon Anderson, *CMM* 75 (1977).

Bibl.: Gordon Anderson in *MD* 32 (1978): 19–67.

Bambuco [Sp.]. An important traditional dance of the Andean region of Colombia. It is characteristically performed by one or, more commonly, two singers with an ensemble of guitar, **bandola* or *requinto* (a small eight-string guitar), and **tiple,* accompanying couples that dance with advance-retreat figures symbolizing courtship. Rhythmically complex and lively, it typically displays melodies that alternate patterns in compound duple and simple triple meters, combined in disjunct relationship with accompaniments in a syncopated, simple triple meter. A stylistically distinct but probably related dance of the same name is found among black populations in the Pacific lowlands of Colombia and Ecuador. D.S.

Band [Fr. *bande;* Ger. *Kapelle;* It., Sp. *banda*]. (1) Any instrumental ensemble larger than a chamber ensemble, including, especially in British usage, the orchestra. Early ensembles bearing the name include the 17th-century **Vingt-quatre violons du roi (La grande bande)* and the 24 fiddlers of Charles II (The King's Private Band). (2) An ensemble of wind instruments, sometimes also with percussion. See Brass band, Military music, Symphonic band. (3) Any ensemble other than one of the traditional combinations of Western art music, sometimes identified by the type of instrument(s) included or by the repertory performed, e.g., accordion band, jazz band, dance band, *big band, *string band, *jug band, *bluegrass band, *rock band. (4) [It.] The brass and percussion sections of the orchestra.

Bandola [Sp.]. A plucked stringed instrument similar to the **bandurria* and used in Colombia. It has six courses of strings tuned in fourths.

Bandoneon. A square, entirely button-operated *accordion invented in the 1840s by Heinrich Band, after whom it is named. It is used in Argentine popular music, especially the *tango, notably in the compositions and performances of Astor Piazzolla. David Tudor and Gordon Mumma have played and composed music for it, sometimes modifying the sound electronically.

Bandora [Fr. *bandore, pandore, pandura;* Ger. *Pandora, Bandoer;* It., Sp. *pandora*]. A wire-strung plucked instrument with a festooned outline invented by John Rose of London in 1562. A bass instrument with six courses, tuned C D G c e a, it was used to accompany the first printed English solo songs (in the publisher William Barley's *A New Booke of Tabliture for the Bandora,* London, 1596) and was one of the continuo instruments in a mixed consort. The limited solo repertory (including pieces in Barley's collection) sometimes requires a seventh course tuned to G_1. See also Orpharion; ill. under Lute.

Bibl.: Donald Gill, "Orpharion and Bandora," *GSJ* 13 (1960): 14–25. R.L.

Bandura, bandoura [Ukrainian]. (1) A Ukrainian *zither, combining features of the *psaltery and the *lute. It has a circular body with a flat back and a short, unfretted neck placed far to one side. Its 30 or more strings are tuned chromatically. It is held upright in the player's lap and played with a plectrum. (2) A Ukrainian *archlute.

Bandurria [Sp.]. A small Spanish plectrum instrument found also in Latin America [see ill. under Guitar]. Juan Bermudo (1555) derives it from the guitar, but its deep sides and cittern-shaped body suggest that it is a hybrid. The modern instrument has six courses of metal strings tuned in fourths. It often plays the treble part in small ensembles, producing sustained tones by means of a tremolo with the plectrum. A similar Latin American instrument is the **bandola.* R.L.

Banjo. A plucked stringed instrument with a long, fretted neck and a circular body in the form of a shallow, one-headed drum. The five-string banjo has four strings (often metal) running the length of the neck plus a shorter fifth string placed next to the lowest string and fastened to a peg at the fifth fret [see ill. under Guitar]. The most common tunings are g′ c g b d′ and g′ d g b d′. Tenor banjos and plectrum banjos have four strings. The former is tuned c g d′ a′, the latter d g b e′. Four-string banjos are strummed with a plectrum. Five-string banjos may be plucked with the thumb and forefinger, the thumb and first three fingers, or the thumb and first two fingers, often using finger picks. The fifth string serves primarily as a drone.

The earliest banjos were brought by slaves from Africa to the U.S. and Caribbean islands. The instrument was given its modern form with five strings and flat, circular body in the first half of the 19th century by white minstrel-show performers like J. W. Sweeney and Dan Emmett. By the 1880s, inlaid frets were common. In the early 20th century, fretted four-string banjos surpassed five-string models in popularity, particularly as rhythm instruments in jazz and dance bands. In this period, numerous hybrids were produced as well, e.g., a four-string banjo-ukulele, and banjo clubs were formed, some of them in conjunction with the *glee clubs of colleges and universities. The five-string tradition was preserved in the southern mountains by players such as Pete Steele and was revived after World War II by performers like Pete Seeger and especially Earl Scruggs, who, with his virtuoso three-finger style, made the banjo an important instrument in *bluegrass music.

Bibl.: Hans Nathan, *Dan Emmett and the Rise of Early Negro Minstrelsy* (Norman: U of Okla Pr, 1962). Pete Seeger, *How to Play the Five-String Banjo,* 3rd ed. (Beacon, N.Y., 1962). Dena J. Epstein, "The Folk Banjo: A Documentary History," *Ethno* 19 (1975): 347–71. Robert B. Winans, "The Folk, the Stage, and the Five-String Banjo in the Nineteenth Century," *Journal of American Folklore* 89 (1976): 407–37. Robert Lloyd Webb, *Ring the Banjar! The Banjo in America from Folklore to Factory* (Cambridge, Mass.: MIT Museum, 1984).

Bar. (1) *Measure. (2) *Bar line. (3) *Bar form.

Barber of Seville, The. See *Barbiere di Siviglia, Il.*

Barbershop singing. A style of popular singing for four unaccompanied male voices, arranged from highest to lowest as tenor, lead, baritone, and bass. The melody is almost always sung by the lead and harmonized in characteristically "close" part writing in which triads and seventh chords predominate, with frequent chromatic passing tones [Ex.]. Performers attempt to cause individual chords to "ring" by singing acoustically pure rather than tempered intervals [see Temperament]. The style was developed in the late 19th century and is still cultivated in much the same

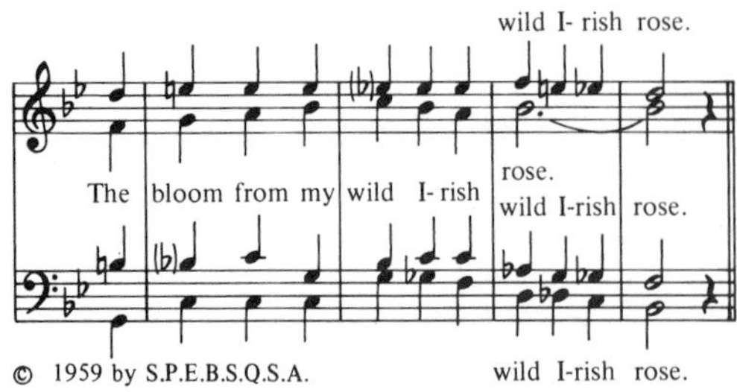
wild I- rish rose.
The bloom from my wild I- rish
rose.
wild I-rish rose.
© 1959 by S.P.E.B.S.Q.S.A.
wild I-rish rose.

form by the 40,000 members of the Society for the Preservation and Encouragement of Barbershop Quartet Singing in America.

Bibl.: Deac (C. T.) Martin, *Deac Martin's Book of Musical Americana* (Englewood Cliffs, N.J.: Prentice-Hall, 1970).

Barbiere di Siviglia, Il [It., The Barber of Seville]. (1) Opera in two acts by Rossini, produced in Rome in 1816. The libretto by Cesare Sterbini, based on Beaumarchais's *Le barbier de Seville* and on the libretto for Paisiello's opera [see (2) below], was originally titled *Almaviva, ossia L'inutile precauzione,* possibly to avoid direct comparison with Paisiello's opera. Setting: 18th-century Seville. (2) Opera in four parts by Giovanni Paisiello with a libretto by Giuseppe Petrosellini (after Beaumarchais), produced in St. Petersburg in 1782. Setting: 18th-century Seville.

Barbiton, barbitos [Gr.]. A type of ancient Greek *lyre. Several scholars identify it as the large lyre with gracefully curving arms often depicted in Greek art.

Barcarole [Fr. *barcarolle;* It. *barcarola*]. A song of the Venetian gondoliers, or a vocal or instrumental composition modeled on such a song. In the latter, a rhythmically repetitive accompaniment, usually in moderate 6/8 or 12/8 meter, evokes the motion of a boat in the waves. Various 18th- and 19th-century operas contain vocal barcaroles (e.g., Paisiello's *Il Re Theodoro,* Weber's *Oberon,* Rossini's *Otello,* Verdi's *I due Foscari,* and Offenbach's *Les contes d'Hoffmann*). Well-known examples for piano include three (each titled "Venezianisches Gondellied") from Mendelssohn's *Songs without Words* (op. 19 no. 6; op. 30 no. 6; op. 62 no. 5); Chopin's *Barcarolle* op. 60; *13 Barcarolles* by Fauré; Schoenberg's "Heimfahrt" from *Pierrot lunaire* (op. 21 no. 20); and Bartók's "Barcarolla" from *Out of Doors* (op. 81 no. 2).

Bard. A poet-musician of the Celts, especially of Wales, Ireland, and Scotland. Greek and Roman writers mention the bards as early as the 2nd century B.C.E., and in the 1st century B.C.E., Diodorus Siculus reports that they used an instrument similar to the lyre. They were later associated with the *harp and, especially, the *crwth. In the 10th century, their position in Welsh society was fixed in the laws of King Howel the Good. They held high rank in noble households, where they played and sang verse of various kinds, including elegies, eulogies, and sagas. They also gathered for an annual competition, known from the 18th century as an *eisteddfod, at which their elaborate procedures and regulations were discussed. In the 12th and 13th centuries, their numbers increased, but with the conquest of Wales by Edward I in 1284, their position began to decline, and in the 15th and 16th centuries they were subjected to some political persecution. By this time, too, the bard could be either a poet or a musician—not necessarily both. The tradition of household musicians, especially harpists, continued in Wales in some measure into the 19th century. The tradition of bardic poetry in classical Gaelic continued in Ireland until the end of the 17th century and in Scotland until the middle of the 18th.

The music of the Welsh bards has been the subject of some controversy, especially as regards the antiquity of examples preserved in a 17th-century manuscript belonging to Robert ap Huw (*GB-Lbm* 14905, also called the Penllyn manuscript; facs., Cardiff: University of Wales, 1936). The notation employed is a modified form of late 16th-century German organ tablature, and the music for harp that it transmits, instead of deriving from the 6th century or before (as Arnold Dolmetsch claimed), probably does not antedate the 15th century.

Bibl.: Arnold Dolmetsch, *Translations from the Penllyn Manuscript of Ancient Harp Music* (Glynteg Llangefni: Early Welsh Music Society, 1937). Peter Crossley-Holland, "Secular Homophonic Music in Wales in the Middle Ages," *ML* 23 (1942): 135–62. Thurston Dart, "Robert ap Huw's Manuscript of Welsh Harp Music (c. 1613)," *GSJ* 21 (1968): 52–65. James Travis, *Miscellanea musica celtica* (Brooklyn: Institute of Mediaeval Music, 1968), pp. 1–46. Joseph P. Clancy, comp. and trans., *The Earliest Welsh Poetry* (London: Macmillan, 1970).

Bar form [Ger. *Barform*]. In musicology, the formal design AAB, common to music and poetry of many times and places, but particularly associated with German strophic song (both secular and liturgical) from the late 12th century onward.

Among the German *Meistersinger (from whom the term bar is borrowed), the strophe of a new song was typically written to one of the preexisting *Töne* (authoritative tunes with associated verse forms). Doctor Mügling's Long *Ton* (given in Puschman, 1571) follows the scheme: a_{12} a_{12} b_{10} (first *Stoll*) c_{12} c_{12} b_{10} (second *Stoll*) d_8 e_{11} d_8 e_{11} / f_8 g_{11} f_8 g_{11} / h_8 i_6 j_8 k_4 l_8 i_6 *(Abgesang).* The organization into two *Stollen* (making up one *Aufgesang*) and an *Abgesang* is typical of most Meistersinger *Töne;* it defines the bar form, both in terminology and formal scope. (In primary sources, *Stoll* is the singular; in recent literature, *Stollen* is both singular and plural.) The Meistersinger, however, employed the term *Bar* for the whole song and not for the individual strophe or *Ton.*

The form AAB also describes the sequence of strophe, antistrophe, and epode found in the Greek *ode as cultivated by Pindar and later imitated by Horace. Medieval songs with an AAB arrangement include many 12th- and 13th-century Provençal **canzos* and

French *chansons* (sources for the bar form of the Minnesinger and Meistersinger), as well as 14th- and 15th-century French **ballades* [see also Troubadour, Trouvère, *Formes fixes*].

Modern musicological interest in the bar form was stimulated during the later 19th century by Wagner's opera *Die *Meistersinger.* Mey (1901, pp. 340–68, especially 357, 363ff.) and Lorenz (1924–34 and 1930) established the extension of bar form to broader formal scales in *Die Meistersinger*'s text and music, respectively. Interest in the bar form was further heightened by the pivotal role assigned by Spitta (1873–80) to the use of Lutheran chorales (virtually all in bar form) in what he took to be the most mature of Bach's cantatas. At the same time, Brahms discovered that the bar form of the chorale "Jesu, meine Freude" generates larger formal structures in Bach's motet of the same name.

The 16th-century Meistersinger themselves seem to have used the term to denote rule-governed verse in contrast to rule-governed melody: "Then with much haste I studied a great deal about the *Bar* and the *Töne*" (Hans Sachs). "[In this book] there are 221 of these *Bars* set to 121 master *Töne*" (Bartel Weber, 1549; cited in Wagenseil, 1697, p. 501). Yet Puschman, a student of Sachs, never once uses the term *Bar* in his *Gründtlicher Bericht,* the first publication to give the rules governing the Meistersinger's song contests. In Wagenseil (1697), on the other hand, attention is given to the origin and etymology of the term. Discussions of etymology in Plate (1887) and Petzsch (1971) conclude that *Bar* is related to a fencing term designating a skillful thrust. It was Wagner who (misreading Wagenseil) transferred the notion of the *Bar* from the highest (and additive) formal level of *Meistergesang* to the level of the tripartite structure of the strophe (or *Ton*).

Bibl.: Adam Zacharias Puschman, *Gründtlicher Bericht des deudschen Meistergesangs* (Görlitz, 1571); facs., ed. Richard Jonas (Halle: Niemeyer, 1888). Johann Christoph Wagenseil, *De sacri rom. imperii libera civitate noribergensi commentatio,* appendix *Buch von der Meister-Singer Holdseligen Kunst* (Altdorf, 1697; facs. of appendix, Göppingen: A Kümmerle, 1975). Philipp Spitta, *Johann Sebastian Bach,* 2 vols. (Leipzig: Breitkopf & Härtel, 1873–80). Otto Plate, "Die Kunstausdrücke der Meistersinger," *Salzburger Studien: Zeitschrift für Geschichte, Sprache und Litteratur des Elsasses* 3 (1887): 147–237. Curt Mey, *Der Meistergesang in Geschichte und Kunst* (Karlsruhe, 1892); 2nd expanded ed. (Leipzig: H Seemann, 1901). Alfred Lorenz, *Das Geheimnis der Form bei Richard Wagner,* 4 vols. (Berlin: Hesse, 1924–34). Id., "Das Relativitätsprinzip in den musikalischen Formen," *Adler,* 1930, pp. 179–86. Kurt Gudewill, "Zur Frage der Formstrukturen deutscher Liedtenores," *Mf* 1 (1948): 112–21. Christoph Petzsch, "Parat-(Barant-) Weise, Bar und Barform: Eine terminologische Studie," *AfMw* 28 (1971): 33–43.

Bariolage [Fr.]. In the playing of bowed stringed instruments such as the violin, an effect produced by playing in rapid alternation on two strings, one open and the other stopped, with a resulting contrast in tone color. The pitches played on the two strings may be the same (producing a kind of *tremolo) or different, and the bowing may be slurred or separate. The type of bowing required is termed **ondeggiando* or *ondulé.*

Baritone [Fr. *baryton;* Ger. *Bariton;* It. *baritono;* Sp. *barítono*]. (1) The male *voice lying below the tenor and above the bass. (2) In families of instruments such as the saxophone, the member pitched below the tenor and above the bass. (3) The baritone horn. See Euphonium.

Baritone clef. See Clef.

Bar line [Fr. *barre de mesure;* Ger. *Taktstrich;* It. *stranghetta;* Sp. *barra de compás*]. A line drawn vertically through one or more staves to mark off a *measure [see also Meter]. In the modern sense, it is not a regular feature of musical notation until the 17th century. Prior to that time, it is found most frequently in *tablatures for keyboard and fretted instruments (particularly the Spanish **vihuela*) and in keyboard music produced in *score (the earliest being Faenza, Biblioteca comunale, 117, from ca. 1400). Here, however, it may serve primarily to aid in the alignment of the parts and not as a guide to the metrical organization of the music. In some cases, where account of an initial *upbeat is not taken, the placement of the bar line may contradict the regular recurrence of metrical strong beats in the music. In other cases, because it merely marks the duple division of one note value, it may obscure a meter that is prevailingly triple. Both phenomena are found in the accompanying example (where the meter implied by the music is shown below the staff) from the "Pavana muy llana" in Diego Pisador's *Libro de musica de vihuela* of 1552. They occur in some 17th-century music as well.

The bar line is in general absent from vocal or ensemble music that is presented in *partbooks and becomes a regular feature of notation only with increasing use of the score in the late 16th century. This fact is reflected in a variety of ways in *editions of early music, most editors having accommodated to some degree the modern reader's reliance on the bar line as an aid to reading. Some have employed bar lines in precisely the way in which they are used in more recent music and have further employed ties for note values that, according to modern conventions, must be divided. Some have employed a line [Ger. *Mensurstrich*] drawn between the staves rather than through them, thus avoiding the need for ties. Others have used dotted lines, apostrophes, or small wedges to mark recurring metrical units. All agree, however, that the performer should be aware of the absence of bar lines in the original notation and avoid the undue sense of regular stress that the bar line sometimes elicits. See also Notation.

Baroque. The period of Western music history extending from the end of the 16th century to ca. 1750; also the musical styles of that period.

I. *History and usage of the term.* Two contrasting derivations of the word were posited already in the 18th century: (1) from the Portuguese *barroco,* describing an irregularly shaped pearl; and (2) from the Italian *baroco*, a logical term referring to an extraordinary type of syllogism. The first derivation is now generally accepted. Both etymologies suggest the bizarre, unnatural, and strained as connotations of the term; it was used in the 18th and 19th centuries (and still is occasionally in the 20th) with pejorative intent. The rehabilitation of the term and its modern usage to signify a stylistic period in the arts began in 1888 with the publication of the art historian Heinrich Wölfflin's *Renaissance und Barock.* Later, in his *Principles of Art History* (1915; trans. 1932), Wölfflin distinguished Renaissance and Baroque style in the plastic arts through five neat stylistic antitheses (linear vs. painterly representation, closed vs. open form, etc.).

Sachs (1919) matched specific musical techniques to Wölfflin's stylistic criteria, but other writers (e.g., Haas, 1928) soon challenged Sachs's overly precise analogies between the plastic arts and music. They turned instead to the enumeration of purely musical stylistic features that might be termed Baroque by virtue of (1) their contemporaneity to developments in the plastic arts and literature already so labeled and (2) a general spiritual and artistic unity of the post-Renaissance period. Most of the subsequent literature on the subject stands in this tradition. Bukofzer (1947) remains a standard survey of musical styles within the period 1600–1750, though many of the general contrasts he draws between Renaissance and Baroque styles (p. 16) need qualification in light especially of recent scholarship on the Renaissance. He does not attempt to illuminate general cultural impulses behind Baroque music.

Palisca (1981), instead, singles out a static, rationalistic view of human affections and a conviction that music should arouse these affections as two decisive cultural features reflected in all Baroque music. The first is indeed an important component of Baroque musical thought. But the second demonstrates the difficulty of investing broader cultural significance in a term that refers first to a congeries of stylistic features, since the urge to emotional expression may be traced at least to the end of the 15th century and beyond that to classical antiquity. It arises as a corollary to the preoccupation of Italian Renaissance humanists with rhetorical persuasion, and it therefore provides no clear point of demarcation between the Renaissance and Baroque periods. Similar difficulties, and a distorted picture of the Renaissance as a period of placid rationalism, undermine the effort of Wolf (1957) to discern a *mannerist period between the Renaissance and the Baroque. The term Baroque is best employed to connote the stylistic features of music from a period whose borders, by now, have been set largely by scholarly convention.

II. *Baroque style.* Baroque music typically shows a homophonic texture in which the uppermost part carries the melody over a bass line with strong harmonic implications. The resulting soprano-bass polarity leads from around 1600 to the employment of the *thoroughbass (*basso continuo* or figured bass), an instrumental bass line with the inner parts improvised chordally above it. The division of labor implied in this melody–bass line dichotomy manifests itself also in the *stile *concertato* (concerted style), in which performing forces diverse in function and timbre are united, and later in the *concerto, with its functional contrast of soloist(s) and **ripieno.* Throughout the period, stylistic diversity is enhanced by a pervasive feature of Baroque musical thought (one clearly anticipated in the late Renaissance): the self-conscious discrimination of separate styles for separate musical functions. Baroque theorists often recognized three such styles, destined for church, chamber, and theater, though these distinctions embraced important subdivisions (e.g., concerted church music vs. that in the Palestrinian *stile antico* or "old style"; see Palestrina style) and were often blurred in practice (e.g., in the *oratorio; that is, theatrical church music).

The Baroque period is usually divided into three subperiods. The early Baroque (ca. 1590–1640) is a period of experimentation characterized by the new hegemony of monodic styles (which had persisted, if not predominated, throughout the Renaissance; see Monody) in such genres as solo *madrigal and *aria, *opera (uniting aria and dramatic monody or *recitative), sacred vocal concerto, and the nascent solo and trio *sonatas. The expressive chromaticism and dissonance of the polyphonic madrigal are transferred to a monodic context. But the pitch hierarchies of modern tonality begin to emerge from the freer tonal practices of the polyphonic madrigalists (which had been based on the harmonic elaboration of hexachordal degrees). This process is aided by the new importance, in the monodic texture, of bass-line structures with clear tonal implications, especially repeating bass lines [see Ground bass] and *strophic variation forms taken over from 16th-century dances and poetic reciting formulas.

The middle Baroque, from around 1640 to 1690, is a period of consolidation. Dissonance is more strictly controlled than in the early Baroque. The expressive recitative of earlier years declines in importance, while the lyrical, *bel canto* aria, in new, regularized forms (one of them the da capo form, ABA), takes on greater expressive weight. Operatic features appear in other vocal genres: the *cantata, built from a simple alternation of aria and recitative, displaces earlier lyrical monody, and the oratorio and (in Protestant countries) church cantata transform the sacred concerto. Solo and especially trio sonatas are standardized in movement order and style.

In the late Baroque, from ca. 1690 to the mid-18th century, the tonal regularity attained gradually through the preceding century generates large formal patterns: the grand da capo aria, and *ritornello form in the concerto. The *stile antico,* maintained for religious and instrumental music throughout the 17th century, culminates in the tonally ordered fugal style of Bach and others. The moderate, triple-time motion typical of the *bel canto* style gives way to insistent, motoristic rhythms that emphasize motives designed to project a single, static affection—here the rationalist conception of the passions discussed by Palisca reveals itself clearly in music. Indeed, in some cases too clearly: in the 1720s the rigidity of its application joined with new philosophical currents to inspire simpler, more tuneful, less rigorous musical idioms. These new idioms, especially prominent in comic opera and *intermezzi,* adumbrate the Classical style.

Bibl.: Curt Sachs, "Barockmusik," *JMP* 26 (1919): 7–15. Robert Haas, *Die Musik des Barocks* (Wildpark-Potsdam: Akademische V-g, 1928). Manfred F. Bukofzer, *Music in the Baroque Era: From Monteverdi to Bach* (New York: Norton, 1947). Suzanne Clercx, *Le baroque et la musique: Essai d'esthétique musicale* (Brussels: Librairie encyclopédique, 1948). Robert Erich Wolf, "Renaissance, Mannerism, Baroque: Three Styles, Three Periods," *Wégimont,* 1957, pp. 35–80. Lorenzo Bianconi, *Music in the Seventeenth Century,* trans. David Bryant (New York: Cambridge U Pr, 1987). Claude Palisca, "'Baroque' as a Music-Critical Term," *French Musical Thought, 1600–1800,* ed. Georgia Cowart (Ann Arbor: UMI Res Pr, 1989), pp. 7–21. Paolo Gozza, *La musica nella rivoluzione scientifica del seicento* (Bologna: Società editrice il Mulino, 1989). Claude V. Palisca, *Baroque Music,* 3rd ed. (Englewood Cliffs, N.J.: Prentice Hall, 1991). Ellen Rosand, *Opera in Seventeenth-Century Venice: The Creation of a Genre* (Berkeley: U of Cal Pr, 1991). Julie Ann Sadie, ed., *Companion to Baroque Music* (New York: Schirmer, 1991). Tim Carter, *Music in Late Renaissance and Early Baroque Italy* (Portland, Ore.: Amadeus, 1992). John H. Baron, *Baroque Music: A Research and Information Guide* (New York: Garland, 1993). Suzanne G. Cusick, "Gendering Modern Music: Thoughts on the Monteverdi-Artusi Controversy," *JAMS* 46, no. 1 (1993): 1–25. Nicholas Anderson, *Baroque Music: From Monteverdi to Handel* (London: Thames & Hudson, 1994). Margaret Murata, ed., Leo Treitler, gen. ed., *Source Readings in Music History,* vol. 4: *The Baroque Era* (New York: Norton, 1998). G.A.T.

Barré, grand-barré [Fr.; Sp. *ceja, cejilla*]. In guitar and lute playing, the stopping of all strings with the forefinger at some specified fret; sometimes termed in English capotasto, which, however, also refers to a device [see Capotasto (1)]. In the *petit-barré* [Sp. *media ceja;* Eng. half-capotasto], the forefinger stops only the highest-pitched three, four, or five strings.

Barre de mesure [Fr.]. *Bar line.

Barrel. (1) In some *automatic instruments, including the most common variety of music box, a cylinder studded with pins or pegs that engage the sound-producing mechanism (often a metal comb) when the cylinder is made to rotate. (2) The short section of the clarinet that connects the mouthpiece to the first section or joint with finger holes. Barrels of differing length are sometimes used to adjust pitch.

Barrelhouse. In early jazz, raucous piano playing; also a style of piano playing, related to *boogie-woogie, and associated with the noisy, informal atmosphere of barrooms (barrelhouses).

Barrel organ [Fr. *orgue à cilindre, o. à manivelle, o. de Barbarie;* Ger. *Drehorgel, Leierkasten;* It. *organetto;* Sp. *organillo*]. A small organ in which a *barrel with pins or staples is made to rotate by a hand crank (which also operates a bellows), the pins or staples engaging a mechanism that causes individual pipes to sound [see also Automatic instruments]. A barrel might have eight or ten tunes encoded on it side by side, each tune requiring one complete revolution; larger instruments may accommodate three or more barrels, thus reducing the frequency with which the barrels need to be changed. Such instruments were developed in the 18th century and were widely used in English parish churches into the 19th. Smaller instruments that could be supported by a strap over the shoulder were also developed in the 18th century and survived into the 20th, along with instruments on wheels, as the street organs (sometimes also termed hand organs) of itinerant "organ grinders." See also Barrel piano.

Bibl.: Noel Boston and Lyndesay G. Langwill, *Church and Chamber Barrel-Organs* (Edinburgh: Langwill, 1967). Arthur W. J. G. Ord-Hume, *Barrel Organ: The Story of the Mechanical Organ and Its Repair* (New York: A S Barnes, 1978).

Barrel piano. An upright piano operated by a *barrel-and-pin mechanism and used especially by itinerant street musicians; sometimes also called a hand organ or street organ. See also Barrel organ.

Bartered Bride, The [Cz. *Prodaná nevěsta;* Ger. *Die verkaufte Braut*]. Opera in three acts by Smetana (libretto by Karel Sabina), produced in Prague in 1866 in a version with spoken dialogue and two acts, revised three times, and produced in the definitive version in three acts with recitatives instead of spoken dialogue in 1870. Setting: a village in Bohemia in the middle of the 19th century.

Baryton [Ger.; It. *viola di bordone*]. An 18th-century bowed stringed instrument similar to the bass viol, with six bowed strings and seven fingerboard frets, but with a festooned body outline and a very broad neck hollowed in the rear to accommodate as many as twenty sympathetic strings [see ill. under Viol]. The baryton enjoyed its greatest popularity in Austria and southern Germany and has been often likened to a bass form of the *viola d'amore. The bowed strings are commonly tuned like those of the bass viol, D G c e a′ d′, with sympathetics in diatonic or chromatic progression. While fingering the six fretted bowed strings, the left hand is also required to pluck with the thumb the exposed sympathetics behind the neck, creating an accompaniment or "lutelike" effect. Although the sound is transparent and pleasingly resonant, the complexity of its technique has limited the instrument's popularity. Today it is seldom played. The first known collection of works for baryton is *IX. Partien auf die Viola Paradon* by Johann Georg Krause II, which dates from the early 18th century. There are about 170 chamber works requiring baryton, including some 126 trios for baryton, viola, and violoncello composed by Joseph Haydn for his patron Prince Nikolaus Esterházy, who loved and played the baryton. Other works include 24 divertimenti by Luigi Tomasini (1741–1808) and a variety of compositions by Joseph Weigl (1766–1846).

Bibl.: Georg Kinsky, *Musikhistorischen Museums von Wilhelm Heyer in Köln, Katalog von Georg Kinsky* (Cologne: Breitkopf & Härtel, 1912), pp. 496–504. W.L.M.

Barzelletta [It.]. The most often used verse form in the 16th-century **frottola*. Like the *ballata,* it consists of a *ripresa* (refrain) followed by *piedi* or *mutazioni* and a *volta* leading back to the *ripresa.* A typical rhyme scheme is abba *(ripresa)* cdcd *(piedi)* d(ee)a *(volta).* In meter (usually a jingly eight-syllable trochaic) and lightness of subject matter, it differs from the *ballata.* A common musical form (one stanza) is AB *(ripresa)* AA *(piedi)* (A)B *(volta).* J.H.

Bas [Fr.]. See *Haut.*

Basis [Gr.]. In some humanist-inspired writings of the 16th century, the *bass part of a polyphonic composition or of a passage or chord.

Bass [Fr. *basse;* Ger. *Bass;* It. *basso;* Sp. *bajo*]. (1) The lowest-sounding male voice [see Voice]. (2) The *double bass. (3) In families of instruments such as the clarinet or trombone, the lowest sounding member. (4) The BB♭ *tuba. (5) From the 15th century (when it emerged as the **contratenor bassus*), the lowest part in a polyphonic composition; by extension, the lowest pitch of any single chord and the succession of such lowest pitches even if produced by different voices or instruments in turn. In music composed in the language of triadic *tonality, the bass part (or line, if not confined to a single instrument or voice) is usually regarded as having a primary structural role in determining *harmony; and *harmonic analysis takes it as fundamental, though the bass is subject to the principles of *counterpoint as much as is any other part. The role of the bass part becomes particularly important around 1600 with the advent of the *thoroughbass (or *basso continuo*). See also Clef; Ground bass; Bass horn.

Bassa [It.]. Low; *ottava bassa* (abbr. *8va bassa*), an octave lower than notated; *con ottava bassa,* an instruction to double the notated pitches with those an octave lower.

Bassadanza [It.]. **Basse danse.*

Bass-bar [Fr. *barre;* Ger. *Bassbalken;* It. *catena;* Sp. *cadena, barra*]. In the violin and other bowed stringed instruments, a long vertical strip of even-grained spruce glued under tension to the inside of the table beneath the bass foot of the bridge. It strengthens the table and aids the distribution and amplification of string vibrations, especially those of the lower register. Average dimensions for the violin are: length, 25 cm.; width, .6 cm.; height, 1.1 cm. beneath the bridge, tapering toward the ends. Prior to the adoption of these more or less standard dimensions in the mid-19th century, bass-bar sizes varied greatly; 17th- and 18th-century bass-bars were usually smaller and slimmer. W.L.M.

Bass-course. On some plucked stringed instruments, a low-pitched *course or string that is not over the fingerboard and thus cannot be stopped.

Bass drum. See Drum I, 3.

Basse [Fr.]. *Bass; *b. à pistons,* *euphonium; *b. chiffrée,* *figured bass; *b. continue,* *thoroughbass; *b. contrainte,* *ground bass; *b.-contre,* an especially deep bass voice or the lowest member of the *viol family; *b. de Flandre,* *bladder and string; *b. d'harmonie,* *ophicleide; *b. fondamentale,* *fundamental bass; *b.-taille,* in the 18th century, the baritone voice. For *b. chantante, profonde,* see Voice.

Basse danse [Fr.; It. *bassadanza*]. A family of related dances including the *basse danse* proper *(bassadanza),* the **quaternaria,* the **pas de Brabant* (**saltarello*), and the **piva,* widely cultivated in the courts of Europe in the 15th century and, because of early literary sources, thought to be of French origin. The earliest manuals describing *bassedanze* are ten treatises in manuscript: one by the master teacher Domenico da Piacenza, *De arte saltandi e choreas ducendii* (ca. 1420); one by his student Antonio Cornazano, *Libro dell'arte del danzare* (1455); and eight copies of the work of his student Guglielmo Ebreo da Pesaro (one under his Christian name, Giovanni Ambrosio), *De pratica seu arte tripudii vulgare opusculum* (1455–1510). Only three of them contain music: Cornazano's (*I-Rvat* 203), Guglielmo's (*F-Pn* it. 973, dated 1463), and Giovanni Ambrosio's (*F-Pn* 476). The main sources of the Burgundian repertory are the elegant Brussels *basse danse* manuscript (*B-Br* 9085, written with gold and silver on black paper), an anonymous manual copied in the late 15th century that includes steps and music from an era several decades earlier, and the single surviving copy of Michel de Toulouse's printed *L'art et instruction de bien dancer* (ca. 1496).

The *basse danse* itself was a sedate dance performed by couples. It was danced with slow, gliding steps that contrasted with the livelier movements of the *pas de Brabant* or the *saltarello.* The Burgundian manuals list only five basic steps, abbreviated as follows: R *(Révérence),* b *(branle),* ss *(simples),* d *(double),* and r *(reprise).* They were combined into sequences to form measures, and it took several measures to make a complete dance. In the Italian manuals, greater freedom was allowed in the variety and sequence of steps and in the number of participants. Indeed, the Italian manuals suggest that measures from the *bassadanza,* the *quaternaria,* the *saltarello,* and the *piva* could be interpolated in any of the dances of the family. The music of the *basse danse* consists of a series of long-note tenors that served as *cantus firmi.* One step was danced to each note, and, as with the sequence of steps, it took several notes to make up a measure. For the rest of the music, the dance band, usually consisting of two or three *shawms and a *sackbut, improvised livelier parts around the tenor [for the ensemble and reference to a notated example, see *Alta;* see also the example in Bukofzer, 1950]. Only three tenor melodies, the most famous of which is the **Spagna,* are included in Cornazano's manual, but more than 50 are preserved in the collections of the Brussels manuscript and in the print by Toulouse. Many of these tenors find their origin in French chansons.

The theoreticians are not entirely lucid when explaining the mensuration of the dances. In the *basse danse,* four steps of a measure were danced to six beats of the music, i.e., a meter of 6/1 divided into 3 plus 3 (which could be interpreted in reduction as a meter of 3/2 × 2). For the *pas de Brabant* or *saltarello,* the mensuration was diminished by half, i.e., 6/1 became 6/2 (a mensuration that could be interpreted as 6/8 meter). The explanations for the *quaternaria* and the *piva* are even more ambiguous. The tempo for the *quaternaria,* between that of the *basse danse* (6/1) and the *saltarello* (3/1 = 6/2), was given the relationship of 4/1 and was translated into some form of duple or quadruple meter. (The *quaternaria* was not used in France at all, and Cornazano says it was danced more in Germany than in Italy.) For the *piva,* the mensuration of the *saltarello* was diminished by half to become 6/4 plus 6/4, a meter which by using the same reduction would be 12/16, but which in early 16th-century examples is usually transcribed as 12/8. The dance masters suggest that the *piva* was a peasant dance, too low and vulgar to be danced at court.

In 16th-century Italy, the *bassadanza* was superseded by the **pavana.* In France, it continued well into the 16th century as a simpler dance with a more stereotyped order of steps, and it used as source materials discant tunes rather than long-note tenors. Most of the *basses danses* in Pierre Attaingnant's collections (*Dixhuit basses dances,* 1530, and *Neuf basses dances,* 1530) are in traditional triple meter, but a few are in duple. Sometimes a *basse danse* is followed by a **tourdion* and sometimes by a **recoupe* and a *tourdion* to form an embryonic suite. In Germany, the 16th-century counterpart is the **Hoftanz* with its accompanying **Nachtanz.*

Bibl.: *Trattato dell'arte del ballo di Guglielmo Ebreo, Scelta di curiosità letterarie,* vol. 131 (Bologna: Presso Gaetano Romagnoli, 1873). Ernest Closson, ed., *Le manuscrit dit des basses danses de la Bibliothèque de Bourgogne* (Brussels: Société des bibliophiles et iconophiles de Belgique, 1912). Otto Kinkeldey, "A Jewish Dancing Master of the Renaissance (Guglielmo Ebreo)," *Freidus,* 1929, pp. 329–72; publ. separately (Brooklyn: Dance Horizons, 1966). Victor Scholderer, ed., *L'art et instruction de bien dancer (Michel Toulouze, Paris),* facs. (London: Royal College of Physicians of London, 1936). Manfred Bukofzer, "A Polyphonic Basse Dance of the Renaissance," *Studies in Medieval and Renaissance Music* (New York: Norton, 1950), pp. 190–216. Otto Gombosi, "The Cantus Firmus Dances," *Compositione di Meser Vincenzo Capirola* (Neuilly-sur-Seine: Société de musique d'autrefois, 1955), pp. xxxvi–lxiii. Ingrid Brainard, "Die Choreographie der Hoftänze in Burgund, Frankreich und Italien" (diss., Univ. of Göttingen, 1956). Otto Kinkeldey, "Dance Tunes of the Fifteenth Century" "*Isham Library,* 1957, pp. 3–30 and 89–152. Daniel Heartz, "The Basse Dance: Its Evolution circa 1450 to 1550," *AnnM* 6 (1958–63): 287–340. Eileen Southern, "Some Keyboard Basse Dances of the Fifteenth Century," *AM* 35 (1963): 114–24. Daniel Heartz, "Basses Dances," *Preludes, Chansons, and Dances for Lute Published by Pierre Attaingnant, Paris (1529–1530)* (Neuilly-sur-Seine: Société de musique d'autrefois, 1964), pp. xxxi–xxxviii. James L. Jackman, ed., *Fifteenth Century Basses Dances, WE,* no. 6 (Wellesley, Mass.: Wellesley College, 1964). Daniel Heartz, "A 15th-century Ballo: *Rôti Boulli Joyeux,*" *Reese,* 1966, pp. 359–75. Id., "Hoftanz and Basse Dance," *JAMS* 19 (1966): 13–36. Eileen Southern, "Basse-dance Music in Some German Manuscripts of the 15th Century," *Reese,* 1966, pp. 738–55. Frederick Crane, *Materials for the Study of the Fifteenth Century Basse Danse* (Brooklyn: Institute of Mediaeval Music, 1968). Raymond Meylan, *L'énigme de la musique des basses danses du quinzième siècle* (Bern: P Haupt, 1968). W. Thomas Marrocco, *Inventory of 15th Century Bassedanze, Balli & Balletti* (New York: Cord, 1981). L.H.M.

Basset horn [Fr. *cor de basset;* Ger. *Bassetthorn;* It. *Corno di bassetto, clarinetto d'amore*]. A form of *clarinet pitched in F, a fourth lower than the normal B♭ clarinet. Its key mechanism always includes basset keys operated by the right thumb and/or left little finger that extend the written range down to c. The instrument has a bore that is narrow in proportion to its length, about the same diameter as a normal B♭ clarinet. Modern instruments are made in the shape of a bass clarinet with a Boehm or Oehler system of keys, and sometimes include the larger bore of an alto clarinet.

Anton and Michael Mayrhofer of Passau probably invented the basset horn. This attribution is based primarily on three surviving basset horns made about 1770 that include a stamp reading "ANT et MICH MAYRHOFER/INVEN & ELABOR/PASAVII." The curved or sickle-shaped oboe da caccia served as a model for the earliest instruments, which had four or five keys, a curved wooden tube covered with leather, and a bore consisting of three parallel internal bore channels housed in a wooden box [Ger. *Kasten* or *buch*] connected to a flared metal bell. Because of the arrangement of keys, these basset horns are equivalent in technical capability to the baroque three-key clarinet. These earliest basset horns are anonymous instruments made in Austria about 1760. Later basset horns with six, seven, and eight keys correspond to classical clarinets with four, five, and six keys. During the 1780s, the Viennese maker Theodor Lotz created the angled basset horn with two straight sections connected by a short elbow joint, a D key, and keys mounted on metal saddles [see ill. under Reed]. The earliest instruments were pitched in G and F with circular-shaped brass bells; later instruments have oval-shaped brass bells and were sometimes made in E, E♭, and D. John Mahon and Johann Backofen included instructions concerning the basset horn in their clarinet tutors (ca. 1803). During the early 19th century, makers constructed basset horns without boxes, straight finger hole sections, and fully chromatic basset keys. The basset horn repertory is quite large. Composers for the instrument in chamber music and opera include J. C. Bach (who wrote for instruments in D that he called clarinetto d'amore), Mozart, Danzi, Mendelssohn, Cherubini, Donizetti, Massenet, and Richard Strauss. Concertos were written by Carl Stamitz (in G), Druschetsky, and Rolla.

Bibl.: Josef Samm, *Das Bassetthorn, seine Erfindung und Weiterbildung* (Mainz: B Schott's Söhne, 1971). Albert R. Rice, "The Clarinette d'Amour and Basset Horn," *GSJ* 39 (1986): 97–111. John P. Newhill, *The Basset-Horn and Its Music* (Sale, Cheshire: J. P. Newhill, 1986). Colin Lawson, "The Basset Clarinet Revived," *EM* 15, no. 4 (Nov. 1987): 487–501. Nicholas Shackleton, "The Earliest Basset Horns," *GSJ* 40 (1987): 2–23. Jürgen Eppelsheim, "Bassetthorn-Studien," *Studia Organologica: Festschrift für John Henry van der Meer zu seinem fünfundsechzigsten Geburtstag,* ed. F. Hellwig (Tutzing: H. Schneider, 1987), pp. 69–125. Phillip T. Young, *4900 Historical Woodwind Instruments: An Inventory of 200 Makers in International Collections* (London: Tony Bingham, 1993). T. Eric Hoeprich, "A Trio of Basset Horns by Theodor Lotz," *GSJ* 50 (1997): 228–36. A.R.R.

Bassett, bassetgen, bassettl [Ger.], **bassetto** [It.]. (1) In the 18th century, the *violoncello. (2) In the Baroque era, a part exercising the function of the bass part, but sounding in a higher register than normal.

Bass horn. (1) An English variety of the *serpent, made of two sections of conical brass tubing joined to form a tall, narrow V. The larger section is topped with an expanded opening or bell, the other with a long, looped mouth pipe. It has six finger holes, three or four keys, approximately 2.45 m. (8 ft.) of tube length, and is in the key of C. Its range and playing technique are the same as those of the serpent. The bass horn was invented in the 1790s by Louis Alexandre Frichot (1760–1825), a French serpent player then performing in England. (2) In modern high school band usage, a *tuba or *sousaphone. R.E.E.

Bassist. (1) In jazz and popular music, a player of the *double bass or *electric bass. (2) [Ger.] A bass singer.

Basso [It.]. *Bass; *col basso,* with the bass.

Basso buffo [It.]. See Voice.

Basso cantante [It.]. See Voice.

Basso continuo [It.]. *Thoroughbass.

Basson [Fr.]. *Bassoon; *b. quinte,* *tenoroon; *b. russe,* *Russian bassoon.

Bassoon [Fr. *basson;* Ger. *Fagott;* It. *fagotto;* Sp. *fagot*]. A conical-bore, double-reed woodwind instrument that has its bore folded in the center in order to reduce its exterior dimensions. To further aid in making the finger holes reachable, several of them are drilled at an extreme angle into the bore. The bassoon has been made in a variety of sizes, but the only instruments that have survived in current use are the normal bassoon (range B♭$_1$ to e″, written at pitch) and the *contrabassoon (range A_2 or B♭$_2$ to g, usually written an octave higher). From the Baroque period to the present, bassoons have been built in four sections, usually called the wing (or tenor), the boot (or butt), the long (or bass), and the bell. The reed is connected to the wing by an S-shaped tube called a *bocal. Modern bassoons may be divided into two types, the French and the German, which differ in design and in fingering. The German instrument is usually made of maple, the French instrument of rosewood. The German instrument dominates most of Europe and the U.S., while the French instrument remains solidly entrenched in France, with a few adherents in French Canada as well. See ill. under Reed.

Ranges.

The bassoon is descended from the various folded-bore instruments of the Renaissance, such as the *curtal and the **sordone.* It is impossible to trace the development of the true bassoon to a specific place of origin. Upon its introduction into England in the late 17th century, however, it was referred to as the "French basson." The Baroque version of the instrument had four (earlier, three) keys: for B♭, D, F, and G♯. By the end of the 18th century, the instrument had acquired additional keys for E♭ and F♯. More keys were subsequently added to improve certain trills and for the purpose of reaching more easily the notes at the extreme upper end of the range.

Carl Almenräder redesigned the instrument in the 1820s. He entered into partnership with Johann Adam

Heckel in 1831, and by 1843, the year of Almenräder's death, the German form of the bassoon, as made by Heckel, was substantially established. Almenräder's principal contributions were perhaps no more logical than the features found on previous instruments; but their aim, at least, was the easier execution of trills and easier slurring of difficult intervals, especially in remote keys. The Heckel firm has continued to make changes and improvements in the instrument.

The French bassoon has proceeded along slightly different lines and retains more of the earlier *cross fingerings than the German instrument. Its principal developers were Eugène Jancourt (1815–1901; performer, composer, and teacher at the Paris Conservatoire) and the firms of Guillaume and his son Frédéric Triébert and Jean Nicolas Savery (known as Savery *jeune*). In 1855, the firm of Buffet-Crampon began building the instruments and continued the modifications that Jancourt requested. Bassoons incorporating Theobald Boehm's ideas [see Boehm system] and the design innovations of Adolphe Sax were never widely accepted.

Besides those in current use, there have been instruments pitched an octave higher (octave bassoon, *fagottino*), tenors pitched a fifth higher (often called *tenoroons; also *basson quinte*), and instruments a fourth or a fifth below the normal bassoon *(Quartfagott, Quintfagott)*. Subcontrabass instruments have also been constructed, but have never achieved much use.

Bibl.: Lindesay Langwill, *The Bassoon and Contrabassoon* (New York: Norton, 1965). Will Jansen, *The Bassoon: Its History, Construction, Makers, Players and Music* (Buren: Frits Knuf, 1978–84). Gunther Joppig, *The Oboe and the Bassoon,* trans. Alfred Clayton (Portland, Ore.: Amadeus, 1988). M.S.

Basso ostinato [It.]. See Ground, *Ostinato.*

Basso profondo [It.]. See Voice.

Basso ripieno [It.]. In a *concerto grosso, a bass part for the **ripieno* or tutti passages only.

Basso seguente [It.]. In the late 16th and early 17th centuries, a part composed of the lowest-sounding pitches of a composition and played on the organ or some other instrument in the fashion of a *thoroughbass (or *basso continuo*). It is thus not a truly independent part, as is a thoroughbass proper. It might include the theme of an imitative work introduced in a high register and repeated as successively lower voices enter. Such parts were added to works as early as Giovanni Croce's collection of motets for eight voices with instruments of 1594, and later *basso seguente* parts were sometimes added to previously published madrigals, as in the 1615 edition of Monteverdi's fourth book of madrigals (originally published in 1603). The term is used in the title of Adriano Banchieri's *Ecclesiastiche sinfonie, dette canzoni in aria francese, per sonare, et cantare, et sopra un basso seguente* op. 16 (1607).

Bassus [Lat., fr. **contratenor bassus*]. *Bass (5).

Bastien und Bastienne. **Singspiel* in one act (libretto by Friedrich Wilhelm Weiskern after Favart's parody of Rousseau's *Le devin du village*) composed by Mozart at the age of 12 and first performed, probably, at the home of Anton Mesmer in Vienna in 1768.

Batá [Sp.]. A set of three Afro-Cuban hourglass-shaped drums used in the Lucumí cult. The drums are graduated in size, and each has two heads, one much larger than the other. Played only by men, each is held horizontally in a player's lap and played with bare hands.

Bathyphone [Ger. *Bathyphon*]. A type of contrabass clarinet designed in 1839 by Wilhelm Wieprecht (1802–72). It was manufactured first by Eduard Skorra of Berlin and subsequently by Franz Karl Kruspe of Erfurt. The instrument was built in bassoon shape of either metal or wood, with a metal bell. It was pitched two octaves lower than the normal clarinet and was usually constructed in C. M.S.

Baton. (1) A thin, tapered stick, about 45 cm. (18 in.) in length and now often painted white, used in *conducting. (2) The stick, nearly a meter (3.25 ft.) or more in length, often ornamented with braid, used by the drum major in a military or other marching band.

Battaglia [It., battle]. A composition that depicts a battle, sometimes with quite naturalistic attempts to imitate the cries and noise of the battlefield. There are examples from as early as the late 14th century (Grimace's "Alarme, alarme") and from the 15th century ("Alla bataglia" for three voices, ca. 1470, in the Chansionnier Pixérécourt), but the earliest well-known example is Clement Janequin's chanson "La guerre," commemorating the Battle of Marignano (1515) and published in 1528. Monteverdi's *Madrigali guerrieri et amorosi* (1638) include vocal works of a similar type. The later history of the genre is typically instrumental and includes works by Byrd, Cabanilles, Banchieri, Kerll, Frescobaldi, Scheidt, Kuhnau, and Couperin. A rather large repertory of such pieces was composed in the second half of the 18th century and in the first half of the 19th. It includes František Kočžwara's *Battle of Prague,* for piano or harpsichord with optional violin, cello, and percussion (ca. 1788), James Hewitt's *Battle of Trenton,* for piano (1792), and Beethoven's **Wellingtons Sieg.*

Battement [Fr.]. (1) An acoustical *beat. (2) In Baroque music, a *mordent, or a two-finger gamba vibrato, or a trill beginning on the main note, or (in Georg Simon Löhlein and Leopold Mozart) a multiple mordent beginning on the lower auxiliary; also the separate oscillations of a trill or multiple mordent. See Ornamentation.

Batterie [Fr.]. (1) The percussion section of the orchestra. (2) In jazz, a drum set. (3) A formulaic drum pattern used as a military signal. (4) In the 18th century, an arpeggiated or broken chord repeated several times. (5) In guitar playing, strumming the strings rather than plucking.

Battery. (1) The percussion section of the orchestra. (2) *Batterie (4).

Battle of the Huns, The. See *Hunnenschlacht, Die.*

Battle of Victoria, The. See *Wellingtons Sieg.*

Battle pieces. See *Battaglia.*

Battre [Fr.]. To beat, with respect to both time in conducting and percussion instruments.

Battuta [It.]. Beat; measure; *a battuta,* return to a strict tempo after some deviation from it. Beethoven's direction "ritmo di tre [quattro] battute" in the scherzo of his Symphony no. 9 indicates that measures, each of which takes only a single beat, should be grouped in threes (or fours).

Batuque [Port.]. In Brazil, any of a variety of African-derived traditional dances and dance music, the music characteristically performed by ensembles consisting largely or entirely of percussion instruments. Like the Brazilian **samba,* it may originally have been an Afro-Brazilian circle dance of Angolese or Congolese derivation. D.S.

Bauernflöte, Bauernpfeiffe [Ger.]. An organ register of stopped pipes, found at 2′ or 1′ pitch in the Pedal.

Bauernkantate [Ger., Peasant Cantata]. A secular cantata by Bach, BWV 212, setting a text by Picander in Saxon dialect ("Mer hahn en neue Oberkeet"; We have a new magistrate) and performed in 1742 on the installation of a new magistrate in the rural town of Klein-Zschocher, Saxony. It makes use of several popular tunes.

Bayadère, La [Fr., The Indian Dancing Girl]. A ballet in three acts by Léon Minkus, first produced in St. Petersburg in 1877 with choreography by Marius Petipa.

Bay Psalm Book. *The Whole Booke of Psalms Faithfully Translated into English Metre,* the first book printed in North America (Cambridge, Mass., 1640). Twenty-six editions were published, the last in 1744. The first edition employed only six metrical patterns (chiefly common meter) for the entire Psalter, referring users to 48 tunes for singing them in congregations, smaller groups, or alone. The third edition (1651) provided Psalm translations that were more poetic and added passages of Scripture, under the new title *The Psalms, Hymns, and Spiritual Songs of the Old and New Testament faithfully translated into English meetre. For the use, edification, and comfort of the saints in publick and private, especially in New England.* It remained the model for later ones. The ninth edition (Boston, 1698) included settings in two voice parts for 13 tunes, the first music printed in North America. Editions from the twelfth (1705) through the twenty-third (1730) carried a dozen monophonic tunes or fewer. The appearance in 1737 (twenty-fourth edition) of 39 three-part tune settings suggests a rising performance standard sparked by the spread of singing schools. See also Psalter.

Bibl.: Irving Lowens, "The Bay Psalm Book in 17th-Century New England," *JAMS* 8 (1955): 22–29. Allen P. Britton, Irving Lowens, and Richard Crawford, *American Sacred Music Imprints 1698–1810: A Bibliography* (Worcester: American Antiquarian Society, 1990), pp. 107–15. R.C.

BB♭ bass [pronounced "double-B-flat"]. See Tuba.

B.c. Abbr. for *basso continuo.* See Thoroughbass.

Be [Ger.]. The flat sign, ♭ [see Accidental, Pitch names].

Beak(ed) flute [Fr. *flûte à bec;* Ger. *Schnabelflöte*]. A *duct flute with beak-shaped upper end; specifically the *recorder.

Bearbeitung [Ger.]. *Arrangement, *transcription; including any polyphonic setting of a liturgical chant or hymn *(Choralbearbeitung).*

Beat [Fr. *temps;* Ger. *Zählzeit, Schlag;* It. *battuta;* Sp. *tiempo*]. (1) A metrical pulse; also the marking of such a pulse by movements of the hand in *conducting. For the grouping of beats in recurring patterns of strong and weak beats, see Meter. For metrical pulse in early music, see *Tactus.* See also Accent (1), Downbeat, Upbeat, Afterbeat, Backbeat. (2) The English term for *mordent, indicated by a wavy line without a stroke through it and, by the 18th century, other signs [see

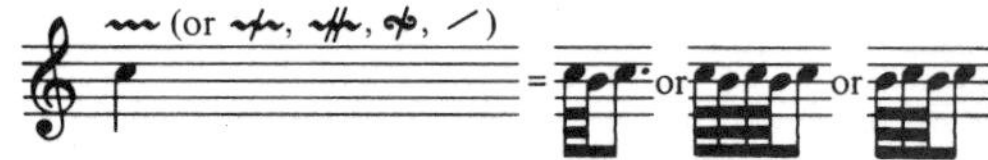

Ex.]. There is some evidence that by this time, owing to an apparent error in the ornament table in Purcell's *A Choice Collection* (1699), the beat had become merged with the "forefall and beat" [see Backfall, forefall], resulting in normal execution as a mordent beginning on the lower auxiliary. A "shaked beat" is a mordent with several repercussions. (3) See Beats.

Bibl. for (2): Howard Ferguson, *Keyboard Interpretation* (New York: Oxford U Pr, 1975), pp. 148–52. (2) D.F.

Béatitudes, Les [Fr., The Beatitudes]. An oratorio by César Franck for soloists, chorus, and orchestra, op. 53 (1869–79), a setting of texts adapted from the Beatitudes of the Sermon on the Mount (Matt. 5:3–12).

Beats. A slight, steady pulsation in intensity that results from the interference between two sound waves of slightly different frequencies. The frequency of the beats will be equal to the difference between the frequencies of the sound waves. Since the beats will disappear if the two frequencies are made identical, the phenomenon is useful in the tuning of musical instruments. Beats can occur between the fundamental of one pitch and a higher harmonic of another as well as between the two fundamentals. Hence, beats are also useful in tuning intervals other than the unison. If, for example, a string is tuned so as to be beatless with the third harmonic of another string whose fundamental is a fifth lower, the fifth will be an acoustically pure fifth rather than a tempered fifth. If the frequency of beats is above about 30 per second, they are not likely to be perceived. See also Acoustics, Temperament, Tuning, Interval. For an organ stop making use of beats, see *Céleste*.

Bebization. See Solmization.

Bebop, bop. A jazz style stressing melodic improvisation and extreme tempos that first gained public attention with recordings made in the mid-1940s. Typically, a small combo presents 12-bar *blues or 32-bar popular tunes in a theme-solos-theme format. In performance, musicians stress formulaic, jagged, fast-moving melodies and/or rhythms. Pianists combine silence with punctuations that reinterpret traditional harmonies through chordal extension, alteration, or substitution. Drummers add asymmetrical accents, while *swinging cymbal patterns and *walking bass lines mark the beat. A number of substyles, including *Latin, *cool, *West Coast, and *soul jazz, as well as *hard bop and *free bop, emerged thereafter and established bebop conventions as the lingua franca of jazz performance. For further detail, see Jazz. B.K., rev. T.A.J.

Bebung [Ger.; Fr. *balancement*]. (1) A *vibrato produced on the clavichord by varying the pressure with which a key is held and thus varying the tension of the string that has been struck [see Clavichord]. Notated as in Ex. 1, it is mentioned in the writings of Wolfgang Caspar Printz (1668), Johann Mattheson (1735), Friedrich Wilhelm Marpurg (1750, 1755, 1765), C. P. E. Bach (who specifies it for long, affective notes, 1753, 1762), and Daniel Gottlob Türk (who associates it with compositions of tragic character, 1789). The term is also used to refer to a vocal vibrato (Johann Friedrich Agricola), a violin vibrato (Georg Simon Löhlein), or any vibrato (Johann Samuel Petri). See Ornamentation.

(2) [Ger. *Mannheimer Bebung*] A melodic figure consisting of five notes beginning on the downbeat in the pattern of Ex. 2 and associated by Hugo Riemann (*DTB* 7/2, 1906, p. xvii) with the melodic style of the *Mannheim school.

Bec [Fr.]. The *mouthpiece of a clarinet or recorder; *flûte à bec,* recorder.

Bécarre [Fr.]. The natural sign, ♮ [see Accidental, Pitch names].

Becken [Ger.]. Cymbals.

Becuadro [Sp.]. The natural sign, ♮ [see Accidental, Pitch names].

Bedächtig [Ger.]. Deliberate, slow.

Bedeckt [Ger.]. With respect to the kettledrum, muffled.

Bedrohlich [Ger.]. Threatening.

Be fa, befa. See Hexachord.

Beggar's Opera, The. A *ballad opera with music arranged by Johann Christoph Pepusch (libretto by John Gay), produced in London in 1728. It presents a satirical view of 18th-century London (including the fashion for Italian opera, the subsequent course of which in England was strongly affected by the vogue for ballad opera that *The Beggar's Opera* initiated) through a cast of criminals and harlots. It has been revived and reworked several times in the 20th century (by Frederic Austin, Edward J. Dent, Benjamin Britten, Darius Milhaud). A work based on the libretto but with new music is Kurt Weill's *Die *Dreigroschenoper.*

Begleitung [Ger.]. Accompaniment.

Béguine [Fr.]. A social dance popular in Europe and America from the 1930s, with a rhythm similar to that of the **bolero*.

Behende [Ger.]. Agile, quick.

Beisser [Ger.]. In the 18th century, *mordent.

Beklemmt [Ger.]. Anxious, oppressed.

Bel. See Decibel.

Bel canto [It., beautiful singing]. A manner of singing that emphasizes beauty of sound, with an even tone throughout the full range of the voice; fine legato phrasing dependent on a mastery of breath control; agility in florid passages; and an apparent ease in attaining high notes. This manner is distinguishable from a more declamatory style in which a weightier vocal tone is projected with more dramatic force. The term is also used, by some musicologists (notably Bukofzer, 1947), to characterize the more lyric style of mid-17th-century composers of vocal music in Venice and Rome, in contrast to the more declamatory style of the earlier Florentine composers [see Opera].

The period from the middle of the 17th century to the beginning of the 19th is thought of as the golden age of *bel canto.* This period coincides with the flourishing of the *castrato* singer in Italian opera. During this time, beautiful singing meant not only good tone production and flexibility of voice but also the ability of the singer to incorporate tasteful and artistic ornaments (often prepared by others) that would both flatter the characteristic traits of his or her voice and enhance the expressivity of the piece. The term *bel canto* comes into active use only toward the middle of the 19th century—only when that manner of singing was under attack because of changes in musical style and when it was thought to be in decline or disappearing. The imprecision with which the term is used today is due, in part, to the fact that the singers who are now associated with *bel canto* sing the music for which the term is appropriate as only a portion of their total repertory.

Bibl.: Manfred Bukofzer, *Music in the Baroque Era* (New York: Norton, 1947). Philip A. Duey, *Bel Canto in Its Golden Age* (New York: King's Crown Pr, 1951). William Weaver, *The Golden Century of Italian Opera from Rossini to Puccini* (London: Thames & Hudson, 1980). Rodolfo Celletti, *Storia del belcanto* (Fiesole: Discanto, 1983).

Belebend, belebt [Ger.]. Lively, animated.

Bel fiore [It.]. (1) A **ballo* in the 15th-century Faenza Codex (*I-FZc* 117; Fa) that may be as old as the 14th century, and one in the 15th-century manual by Domenico da Piacenza *(De arte saltandi & choreas ducendi).*

(2) An Italian popular dance and dance song of the 16th century that, like many of the *arie per cantar,* was composed on a specific isometric harmonic pattern [see Ex.]. The music of the 16th-century *Bel fiore* bears no relation to that of the earlier compositions [see (1)]. This pattern crystallized early in the century, and many dances composed on it are found in English,

French, German, and Italian sources, some with the title *Bel fiore* and others merely with the title of a type of dance. Toward the end of the century, the pattern was expanded into two different dances and dance songs that remained popular well into the 17th century, the *Paganina* and the *Aria del Gazzella* (the latter appearing under other titles as well). Each has a middle section added to the original pattern.

Bibl.: Lawrence H. Moe, "Dance Music in Printed Italian Lute Tablatures from 1507 to 1611" (Ph.D. diss., Harvard Univ., 1956). L.H.M.

Belgium. Because of its geographic and linguistic situation, Belgium has close cultural relations with both France and the Netherlands. Belgium has existed as an independent political unit, separate from the Netherlands, only since 1830.

I. *Contemporary musical life and institutions.* Much musical activity is supported by local or national government. Opera is performed on a regular basis in Antwerp at the Vlaamse Operastichting, founded in 1893, in Brussels at the Théâtre Royal de la Monnaie (also the site of Maurice Béjart's Ballet du XXe siècle), and in Ghent, Liège, and Verviers. Notable performing organizations other than opera companies are the state-supported Belgian National Orchestra, based in Brussels, L'Orchestre Royal de Liège, and the several orchestras and choirs maintained by the Radiodiffusion-télévision belge, also centered in Brussels. The contribution of this broadcasting company to the promotion and diffusion of music in Belgium has been considerable. The CeBeDeM (Centre Belge de Documentation Musicale), started in 1951, publishes the works of contemporary composers and scholars and also subsidizes recordings and concerts.

Festivals take place throughout the year. The two largest are the Festival of Flanders and the Festival de Wallonie, comprising performances of opera and dance, concerts, and recitals in numerous cities during the spring, summer, and fall. Two festivals are devoted to contemporary music: the Ars Musica festival (founded 1988), and November Music (1992), an international festival with concerts in Ghent as well as Essen, Germany, and 's Hertogenbosch, the Netherlands.

The principal conservatories of music in Belgium are located at Antwerp, Brussels, Ghent, and Liège. Musicology is taught at the universities in Brussels, Ghent, Liège, and Louvain and liturgical music at the Lemmens Institute in Mechelen.

II. *History.* The region encompassing what is now Belgium was especially prominent in the domain of art music in the 15th and 16th centuries, producing a number of Europe's leading composers [see Renaissance]. In the 18th and 19th centuries, composers of Belgian birth and European-wide reputation included François Gossec (1734–1829), André Modeste Grétry (1741–1813), Henri Vieuxtemps (1820–81), and César Franck (1822–90). Among the most important Belgian musical scholars of the 19th century were François-Joseph Fétis (1784–1871) and François-Auguste Gevaert (1828–1908). The career of Peter Benoit (1834–1901) was dedicated to the development of a distinctly Flemish musical language; although he produced many interesting compositions, he had few significant followers. A tradition of violin virtuosos was most prominently represented by Eugène Ysaÿe (1858–1931). The most influential composers of the first part of the 20th century were Paul Gilson (1865–1942), Joseph Jongen (1873–1953), and Flor Alpaerts (1876–1954). The next generation included Jean Absil (1893–1974) and Marcel Poot (1901–88), both students of Gilson, and René Bernier (b. 1905). These composers actively promoted the ideals of contemporary music, with Gilson and Poot founding *La Revue musicale Belge* in 1925, and Absil founding another review, *Syrinx,* and a concert series, La Sirène, in 1934; the outbreak of hostilities in the late 1930s ended all of these ventures. Several students of Absil, Pierre Froidebise (1914–62), Marcel Quinet (1915–86), and Victor Legley (1915–94), rose to prominence in the postwar years, along with Raymond Chevreuille (1901–76) and David van de Woestijne (1915–79).

The best-known Belgian composer of the past 40 years, Henri Pousseur (b. 1929), continues the lineage of Belgian composers, having studied with Froidebise. Other notable composers of his generation are André Laporte (b. 1931), Philippe Boesmans (b. 1936), Frederik van Rossum (b. 1939), and Pierre Bartholomée (b. 1937), a founding member of the Brussels-based ensemble Musique Nouvelle. Electronic music has been an important part of Belgian composition since the founding of the Instituut voor Psychoacoustica en Electronische Muziek in Ghent (1962) by Louis de Meester (1904–87). Karel Goeyvaerts (1923–93) and Lucien Goethals (b. 1931) are also associated with this institute.

For folk music, see Netherlands.

Bibl.: Charles Leirens, *Belgian Music,* 5th ed. (New York: Belgian Government Information Center, 1963). Albert Van der Linden, "Belgium from 1914 to 1964," *MQ* 51 (1965): 92–96. Elaine Brody and Claire Brook, *The Music Guide to Belgium, Luxembourg, Holland, and Switzerland* (New York: Dodd, Mead, 1977). Colley Cibber Music, *French and Belgian Music* (Guildford: Colley Cibber Music, 1987). Willem Elders, *Composers of the Low Countries* (Oxford: Clarendon, 1991). Mark Delaere, Yves Knockaert, and Helge Sabbe, *Nieuwe muziek in Vlaanderen* (Bruges, 1998). Société philharmonique de Bruxelles, *In Praise of Music: 150 Years of Musical Life in Brussels* (Tielt: Lannoo, 1998). Hubert Boone and Wim Bosmans, *Volksinstrumenten in België* (Leuven: Peeters, 2000).

Bell. (1) Any of a variety of objects that, when struck, emit a ringing sound. There are three basic types of bell: open, cup-shaped bells, usually made of metal, that are struck at the rim; closed, spherical *pellet bells; and *tubular bells (orchestral chimes). Only the first type is discussed here.

Open bells may be hemispheric, quadrilateral, or beehive-shaped, but the characteristic bell of the Occident is tulip-shaped or "campaniform," with a well-defined shoulder and flaring sides. Quadrilateral bells (e.g., the *cowbell) are typically made of sheet metal, hammered and soldered. Other metal bells are cast, most often of bronze. The smallest bells, such as those hung on clothing or animal harnesses, may weigh only a few grams. The largest bell ever cast weighed approximately 200,000 kg. Church tower bells generally weigh from 4,000 to 10,000 kg., though a few approach 20,000 kg. (44,000 lb.).

Bells are struck either from the inside by a *clapper or from the outside by a hammer or a mechanical striking device. Chiming consists in swinging a bell so as to cause the clapper to strike it. Ringing consists in rotating a bell vertically through a full circle, causing the clapper to strike it more forcefully. Clocking consists in moving a bell's clapper so as to cause it to strike the stationary bell.

A bell produces a complicated, nonharmonic vibrational pattern [see Acoustics]. A bell can be tuned, however, so that its five lowest partials approximate a familiar chord. This is done for each partial by removing metal from a specific part of the bell after casting, causing the pitch of the partial in question to be lowered. The fundamental is the strongest pitch; the hum tone lies an octave below the fundamental, and the nominal an octave above; the tierce is a minor third and the quint a perfect fifth above the fundamental. In addition, there are many untuned higher partials and a momentary strike note lying near the fundamental. This pattern of vibrations characterizes only the large, tulip-shaped bells of the Occident. Cowbells, hemispheric bells, the bells of the Far East, and handbells have considerably different patterns.

Bells are ancient and widely distributed. Chinese bells can be dated back to before 1500 B.C.E., and the Chinese knew how to tune bells as early as the 5th century C.E. Multiclapper wooden bells and metal pellet bells from the 8th to 10th centuries have been excavated in South America. In the Far East, large, single bells and sets of tuned bells (bell *chimes) have been associated since ancient times with religion and temple worship. Both handbells and tower bells have been associated with Christian worship from about the 5th century. The craft of bell casting and tuning developed in Europe between the 12th and 14th centuries. Sets of large bells were installed in towers on top of or next to churches and were rung to mark the hours, to call people to worship, to signal emergencies, and to toll for the dead. Bell wheels and mechanisms for ringing bells automatically were introduced in the 14th century. The *carillon (a set of tuned bells operated by a keyboard mechanism) was developed during the 15th and 16th centuries in the Low Countries. In England, the practice of *change ringing arose during the same period. Bell manufacture was an empirical art until the late 19th century, when bell acoustics were investigated scientifically. See also Celesta, Cymbalum, Gong, Idiophone.

(2) [Fr. *pavillon;* Ger. *Schallbecher, Schallstück, Schalltrichter, Stürze;* It. *padiglione, campana;* Sp. *pabellón, campana*] The opening of a wind instrument at the end opposite the mouthpiece. The flaring bells of *brass instruments serve two acoustical purposes: they alter the vibrational modes of the air column, making them approximate more closely the harmonic series, and they reinforce certain partials, thus molding the tone color of the instrument [see Acoustics]. The bell of a woodwind affects primarily the tone color of only those pitches produced with most or all of the finger holes closed, since for other pitches much of the sound is radiated through the open finger holes.

Bibl.: (1) Josef Pfunder, "Über dem Schlagton der Glocken," *Acustica* 12 (1962): 153–57. Wendell Westcott, *Bells and Their Music* (New York: Putnam, 1970). C.-R. Schad and Hans Warlimont, "Akustische Untersuchungen zum Einfluss des Werkstoffes auf den Klang von Glocken," *Acustica* 29 (1973): 1–14. John Camp, *Bell Ringing: Chimes, Carillons, Handbells* (Newton Abbot: David & Charles, 1974). Percival Price, *Bells and Man* (London: Oxford U Pr, 1983).

Bell gamba. An organ register of tapered metal pipes of medium scale, surmounted by a conical bell.

Bell harp. A type of zither invented ca. 1700, perhaps by John Simcock of Bath, with 14 to 24 courses of 3 or 4 strings. It was held in both hands, plucked with the thumbs, and swung back and forth while being played. A form manufactured in the 19th century was known as fairy bells.

Bell lyra, bell lyre. A portable *glockenspiel in the shape of a lyre, used principally in marching bands.

Bell ringing. See Change ringing.

Bells. In the context of music for orchestra or band, either the *glockenspiel or the *tubular bells. See also Bell.

Belly [Ger. *Decke;* Fr. *table (d'harmonie);* It. *tavola armonica;* Sp. *tapa (tabla) de armonía*]. (1) On stringed instruments such as the violin or lute, the upper face of the body or sound box, over which the strings pass and which plays a major part in transmitting the vibrations of the strings to the surrounding atmosphere; also called the table. See ill. under Violin. (2) The soundboard of the *piano.

Be mi, bemi. See Hexachord.

Bémol [Fr.], **bemol** [Sp.], **bemolle** [It.]. The flat sign, ♭ [see Accidental, Pitch names].

Ben, bene [It.]. Well; as in *ben marcato,* well marked.

Benedicamus Domino [Lat., Let us bless the Lord]. A *versicle sung or recited at the end of the hours of the *Office of the Roman rite and in place of the **Ite missa est* at the conclusion of Masses in which the Gloria is omitted or which are followed by a procession. It is followed by the response "Deo gratias" (To God be praise). (For the tones employed in the Office, see *LU,* pp. 124–27, and *AntMon,* pp. 1242–49; for the Mass, see the cycles of Ordinary chants in *LU,* pp. 16–63.) Its melodies, preserved in the Middle Ages in processionals and graduals, often served as tenors of polyphonic compositions in the repertories of *St. Martial and *Notre Dame.

Benedicite [Lat., Bless ye (the Lord)]. The *Canticle of the Three Children in the Fiery Furnace (Vulgate, Daniel 3:57–88 and 56).

Benediction. (1) A blessing, especially one pronounced on the congregation at the conclusion of a service of worship. (2) In the Roman Catholic Church and some communities of the Anglican Communion, a service in which the congregation is blessed with the Host (see *LU,* pp. 93*–95*).

Benedictus Dominus Deus Israel [Lat., Blessed be the Lord God of Israel]. The *Canticle of Zachary on the birth of his son St. John the Baptist (Luke 1:68–79). In the monastic Office of the Roman Catholic Church it is sung at Lauds; in the Anglican Church at Morning Prayer.

Benedictus (qui venit) [Lat., Blessed is he who comes in the name of the Lord]. Matthew 21:9, the second part of the *Sanctus of the *Mass, usually set as a separate composition in polyphonic works.

Beneplacito, A [It.]. At the pleasure of the performer, especially as regards tempo.

Beneventan chant. The medieval Latin chant of southern Italy, centered in the archdiocese of Benevento and the monastery of Montecassino. The original local chant tradition was replaced by Gregorian chant at some time before 838, so that it is only known from fragmentary MSS and a few pieces that were copied into MSS of Gregorian chant (*CLLA* 430–83). The major exception is the *Exsultet* blessing of the Easter candle on Holy Saturday, preserved in some beautifully illuminated parchment scrolls (*CLLA* 485–99). In the Middle Ages the old local tradition was called "Ambrosian" chant to distinguish it from the Gregorian, though it was not the same as the *Ambrosian chant sung at Milan. Some preserved Beneventan chants are related to *Byzantine chants, notably the Good Friday antiphon *O quando in cruce.* After the introduction of Gregorian chant, some Gregorian melodies were adapted to new words for local use: *sequences and *prosulae continued to be composed locally.

Bibl.: *PM* ser. 1, 14–15, 20–21. Egon Wellesz, *Eastern Elements in Western Chant, MMB,* Subsidia 2 (Oxford: Byzantine Institute, 1947), pp. 68–110. Thomas Forrest Kelly, *The Beneventan Chant* (New York: Cambridge U Pr, 1989). Thomas Forrest Kelly, *The Exultet in Southern Italy* (New York: Oxford U Pr, 1996). Jean Mallet and André Thibaut, *Les Manuscrits en écriture bénéventaine de la Bibliothèque Capitulaire de Bénévent,* 3 vols. (Paris: CNRS, 1984–97; vols. 2–3 also Turnhout: Brepols, and Ottawa: Institute of Mediaeval Music). Alejandro Planchart and John Boe, *Beneventanum Troporum Corpus,* Recent Researches in the Music of the Middle Ages and Early Renaissance 16–27 (Madison, Wis.: A-R Eds, 1989–). Bonifacio Baroffio, "The Musical Repertories of the Liturgy of Southern Italy and Beneventan Sources," *Songs of the Dove and the Nightingale: Sacred and Secular Music c. 900–c. 1600,* ed. Greta Mary Hair and Robyn E. Smith, Musicology 17 (Basel: Gordon & Breach, 1995), pp. 1–32. Thomas Forrest Kelly, "New Evidence of the Old Beneventan Chant," *Plainsong and Medieval Music* 9 (2000): 81–93. P.J.

Benvenuto Cellini. Opera in two acts by Berlioz (libretto by Léon de Wailly and Auguste Barbier, after Cellini's autobiography), first produced in Paris in 1838. It was revised in three acts for performance in Weimar in 1852. Setting: Italy in the 16th century.

Bequadro [It.]. The natural sign, ♮ [see Accidental, Pitch names].

Berceuse [Fr.; Ger. *Wiegenlied*]. Lullaby. In instrumental works, especially for piano, 19th- and early 20th-century composers (including Chopin, Schumann, Brahms, Liszt, Grieg, Debussy, Ravel, Busoni, and Stravinsky) captured the steady rocking of the lullaby through an ostinato accompaniment in compound meter or triplets. Chopin's Berceuse op. 57 in particular provided a model for others.

Bergamasca [It.]. (1) A dance, dance song, or popular poem from the district of Bergamo in northern Italy. Early musical examples occur in Giacomo Gorzanis's *Il terzo libro de intabolatura di liuto* (1564, no. 12, "Saltarello dito il Bergamasco") and in Filippo Azzaiolo's *Il terzo libro delle villotte del fiore alla padoana con alcune napolitane e bergamaschi* (1569, nos. 3 and 7, "Bergamasca"). Gorzanis's title suggests that it is music for a Bergamascan dance; Azzaiolo's refers to the texts in Bergamascan dialect. The music is different in each case and is unrelated to the harmonic pattern described below (2). Many compositions from the 17th, 18th, and 19th centuries bear the title because of a real or fancied relationship to Bergamo. For Claude Debussy's work with this title, see *Suite bergamasque.*

(2) Late in the 16th century, any of a number of pieces composed on repetitions of a specific harmonic pattern [Ex.]: I–IV–V–I (e.g., Giulio Cesare Barbetta, *Intavolatura de liuto,* 1585, p. 14, "Moresca quarta detta la Bergamasca"; Giulio Abondante, *Il quinto libro de tabolatura da liuto,* 1587, p. 58, "Bergamasca"). In the 17th century, hundreds of compositions, largely for the guitar but also for the lute, for keyboard instruments, and for instrumental and vocal ensembles, were written on the pattern, and *bergamaschi* are found in collections in France, Germany, and England (sometimes under the title "Bergomask") as well as Italy. Early in the 17th century, a single discant began to be associated with the harmonic pattern and in some cases supplanted the pattern itself (cf. Giovanni Salvatore's "Canzone francese . . . Bergamasca," 1541, in *CEKM,* vol. 3, which is written only on the discant tune; and Frescobaldi's "Bergamasca"

in the *Fiori musicali,* 1635, which starts with the discant tune and incorporates the bass pattern before the set of variations is finished). Both the harmonic pattern and the discant tune became clichés in the 18th and 19th centuries—clichés that have survived in popular music to the present day. The German folk tune "Kraut und Rüben" used by Bach in the final quodlibet of his **Goldberg Variations* is the *bergamasca* discant, and the harmony for the first phrase of a well-known evangelical hymn, "The Old Rugged Cross" (1913), follows the *bergamasca* harmonic pattern.

The I–IV–V–I pattern has a long history predating its association with the title *bergamasca.* Adumbrated forms occur in late 15th- and early 16th-century sources such as the *Cancionero musical de palacio* and Italian manuscripts dating from the turn of the century. The earliest examples of variations on the pattern proper are found in Antonio Casteliono's *Intabolatura de leuto* ([1536], fol. 24v, "Le riprese" of the "Saltarelo chiamato el Mazolo") and Melchioro de Barberis's *Intavolatura di lauto,* 9 (1549; no. 17, "Vesentino," and no. 25, "Saltarello"). L.H.M.

Bergerette [Fr.]. (1) In the 15th century, a form related to the **formes fixes* that dominated French poetry and music of the period. The *bergerette* appeared early in the century, experienced a surge in popularity in the latter half, and then largely died out by about 1500. The form is often described today as a one-stanza **virelai* but was commonly defined by 15th- and early 16th-century writers in terms of the **rondeau.* Busnois composed a number of *bergerettes.* (2) [rare] In the 16th century, an instrumental dance in quick triple time. (3) In the 18th century, a French *air* with frequent pastoral references.

Bergomask. See *Bergamasca.*

Bergreihen [Ger., mountain dance]. Popular poems of the 16th and 17th centuries on sacred and secular subjects, primarily from a mountainous region of Saxony called the Erzgebirge. Two of the numerous publications of such poems include music: Erasmus Rotenbucher's *Bergkreihen* (1551) and Melchior Franck's *Musicalischer Bergkreyen* (1602). The instruction "in the manner of Bergreihen" occurs in collections of sacred music by Johann Walter (1551) and Kaspar Othmayr (1547?), but its meaning is not clear. In 18th-century sources, the term *Bergmannslied* is used in its place.

Berimbau [Port.]. A Brazilian *musical bow. *Berimbau* ensembles provide the main accompaniment for the **capoeira* dance of the state of Bahia.

Berlin school. A group of composers, also known as the North-German School, working in Berlin in the second half of the 18th century, principally at the court of Frederick the Great (reigned 1740–86). They included Johann Joachim Quantz (1697–1773), Johann Gottlieb Graun (1703–71), Carl Heinrich Graun (1704–59), Franz Benda (1709–86), C. P. E. Bach (1714–88), Christoph Nichelmann (1717–62), Friedrich Wilhelm Marpurg (1718–95), Johann Philipp Kirnberger (1721–83), and Johann Friedrich Agricola (1720–74).

As song composers, they sought a folklike quality in their works, first published in Christian Gottfried Krause's (1719–70) *Oden mit Melodien* (1753; works by C. P. E. Bach, Agricola, Benda, and others). C. P. E. Bach, a key figure in what is sometimes called the Berlin Lieder School, prepared toward the end of his life a collected edition of his songs *(Polyhymnia).* Although this large-scale project was never published (MS in the Sing-Akademie Collection, Berlin), his extensive revisions indicate that he continued to be involved with songs into the 1780s. A younger generation (called the Second Berlin Lieder School), which included Johann Abraham Peter Schulz (1747–1800), Johann Friedrich Reichardt (1752–1814), and Carl Friedrich Zelter (1758–1832), turned away from the folklike element to the poetry of Klopstock and Goethe. See Lied.

Bersag horn. A type of military *bugle adopted by the Bersaglieri corps of the Italian army in 1861. The soprano was similar to a three-valve *flugelhorn. The contralto, tenor, baritone, and bass had one valve lowering the pitch a fourth. Modern versions of this instrument often have two valves and are seen in drum and bugle corps. R.E.E.

Beruhigend, beruhigt [Ger.]. Calming, calm.

Bes [Ger.]. B-double-flat. See Pitch names.

Beschleunigend, beschleunigt [Ger.]. **Accelerando, accelerato.*

Besetzung [Ger.]. Setting, scoring, orchestration.

Bestimmt [Ger.]. Decisively.

Betont [Ger.]. Accented, stressed.

Betrothal in a Monastery. See *Duenna, The* (2).

Beweglich [Ger.]. Nimbly.

Bewegt [Ger.]. Agitated.

Bezifferter Bass [Ger.]. Figured bass, *thoroughbass.

B fa. See Hexachord.

Bharata-nāṭyam [Skt.]. A major solo dance tradition of South India performed by women. The standard recital contains pieces that range from abstract dance to mime; some mix the two. The dancer is accompanied by a vocalist, a wind instrument, a drum, and a dance master who recites rhythmic compositions. C.C.

Bibliography. A list of compositions or writings about music, organized alphabetically by author or title or by topic according to content, instrumentation, opus number, date of origin, etc.; also the science of describing books. A bibliography differs from a catalog in that the latter is normally limited to the contents of a particular collection or library. Separately published bibliographies fall naturally into two categories, bibliographies of music and of music literature.

History. Early bibliographies are important today as historical records, not as finding guides to the literature. Among the early sources are the catalogs of books and music exhibited at the book-trade fairs in Frankfurt and Leipzig in the 16th, 17th, and 18th centuries. The musical items have been excerpted and listed separately in Albert Göhler, *Verzeichnis der in den Frankfurter und Leipziger Messkatalogen der Jahre 1564 bis 1759 angezeigten Musikalien* (Leipzig: C F Kahnt, 1902; R: Hilversum: F A M Knuf, 1965). Sébastien de Brossard intended to compile a comprehensive list of writings on music but abandoned the project as too large to accomplish, though he does list 900 writings in an appendix to his *Dictionnaire de musique,* published in 1703 (facs., Amsterdam: Antiqua, 1964). The first independent bibliography of music literature is that of Jakob Adlung, *Anleitung zur musikalischen Gelahrtheit* (Erfurt, 1758; facs., Kassel: Bärenreiter, 1953). This was followed by Johann Nikolaus Forkel's *Allgemeine Litteratur der Musik* (Leipzig, 1792; facs., Hildesheim: Olms, 1962), listing about 3,000 items, and subsequently updated to 1826 by Peter Lichtenthal, *Dizionario e bibliografia della musica* (Milan, 1826); to 1838 by Carl Ferdinand Becker, *Systematisch-chronologische Darstellung der musikalischen Literatur* (Leipzig, 1836–39); to 1846 by Robert Eitner, *Bücherverzeichnis der Musik-Literatur . . . 1839–1846* (*Beilage* to *MfMg,* 1885); and to 1866 by Adolf Büchting, *Bibliotheca musica* (Nordhausen, 1867). From Forkel to Büchting the coverage emphasizes German publications. No comprehensive list has subsequently been published. Current publications have been listed in music periodicals, beginning with *VfMw* in 1885, *ZIMG* (1899–1914), *ZfMw* (1918–1933), and subsequently by several journals, but best accomplished by *Notes* (1943–) and *FAM* (1954–).

Bibliographies of music. Of great value to the researcher are bibliographies limited to early music, usually before 1800, and giving the locations of copies of items listed. The first such work and still today a landmark in music bibliography is Robert Eitner's *Biographisch-Bibliographisches Quellen-Lexikon* (Leipzig: Breitkopf & Härtel, 1900–1904; R: Graz, Akademische Druck- und Verlagsanstalt, 1959–60), which in ten volumes lists all known manuscript and published works of individual composers born before 1771. While Eitner's listing of manuscripts has not been superseded, the listing and location of published works were greatly expanded in *Einzeldrucke vor 1800,* series A of **RISM,* an international project to list all musical sources prior to 1800. Similarly useful are national projects such as *The British Union-Catalogue of Early Music Printed before the Year 1801* (London: Butterworths Scientific Publications, 1957), done in preparation for *RISM,* and *Katalog der Filmsammlung* of the Deutsches Musikgeschichtliches Archiv in Kassel, a project begun after World War II to film all early German music existing in German and foreign collections. Early music in Parisian libraries is listed in François Lesure, *Catalogue de la musique imprimée avant 1800 conservée dans les bibliothèques publiques de Paris* (Paris: Bibliothèque nationale, 1981). Volumes containing music by two or more composers and published in the 16th and 17th centuries are listed by Robert Eitner in his *Bibliographie der Musik-Sammelwerke* (Berlin, 1877; R: Hildesheim: Olms, 1977). This has been upgraded and expanded to include the 18th century in *Recueils imprimés XVIe–XVIIe siècles* and . . . *XVIIIe siècle* (Munich-Duisburg: Henle, 1960), in Series B of *RISM.*

Among the bibliographies limited to early music that are devoted to special topics are Emil Vogel, *Bibliothek der gedruckten weltlichen Vokalmusik italiens, aus den Jahren 1500 bis 1700* (Berlin, 1892; new ed. by François Lesure and Claudio Sartori, *Bibliografia della musica italiana vocale profana pubblicata dal 1500 al 1700,* Pomezia: Staderini-Minkoff Editori, 1976–77); Howard Mayer Brown, *Instrumental Music Printed before 1600* (Cambridge, Mass.: Harvard U Pr, 1965); Claudio Sartori, *Bibliografia della musica strumentale italiana stampata in Italia fino al 1700* (Florence: Olschki, 1952–68); Solange Corbin, *Répertoire de manuscrits médiévaux* (Paris: CNRS, 1965–74); *Census-Catalogue of Manuscript Sources of Polyphonic Music 1400–1550* (Neuhausen-Stuttgart: Hänssler, 1979–); and various volumes in *RISM.* American music before 1800 is listed by Oscar Sonneck, *Bibliography of Early Secular American Music* (Washington, D.C., 1905; rev. ed. William Treat Upton, Library of Congress, Music Division, 1945). The next 25 years are covered by Richard J. Wolfe, *Secular Music in America, 1801–1825* (New York: New York Public Library, 1964). National coverage of current publications includes the following: for Great Britain: *The British Catalogue of Music* (London: Council of the British National Bibliography, 1957–); for France: Bernard Pierreuse, *Catalogue général de l'édition musicale en France* (Paris: Éditions musicales transatlantiques, 1984); for Germany: *Hofmeisters Jahresverzeichnis* (Leipzig, 1852–), which is a continuation of Whistling (see below) and lists music and music literature published in German-speaking countries; the only comparable publication for the United States is the *Catalogue of Copyright Entries. Part 3, Musical Compositions* (Washington, D.C.: Government Printing Office, 1891–). A valuable source for American archival materials is *Resources of American Music History: A Directory of Source Materials from Colonial Times to World War II* (Urbana: U of Ill Pr, 1981).

Performers and music dealers have long desired a "Music in Print," comparable to the widely used *Books in Print.* Carl Friedrich Whistling compiled such a work early in the last century, *Handbuch der musikalischen Literatur* (Leipzig, 1817), which was supplemented by Hofmeister. Early in this century the brothers Bohumil and František Pazdírek compiled from publishers' catalogs their remarkable 34-volume *Universal-Handbuch der Musikliteratur* (Vienna: Pazdírek, 1904–10). Subsequent bibliographers, unable to match this feat, have turned to music-in-print compilations limited to a particular instrument or class of instruments, or to the individual catalogues of publishers now available online or the compilations made by major national music vendors on their websites.

Bibliographies of music literature. Writings about music published before 1800 are listed in *Écrits imprimés concernant la musique,* 2 vols. (Munich-Duisburg: Henle, 1971), in Series B of *RISM.* For later publications or for bibliographies on a very wide variety of particular topics, one must consult lists in monographs and encyclopedias or separately published special bibliographies. A good starting point is *Music Reference and Research Materials,* 5th ed. (New York: Schirmer, 1997). Doctoral dissertations in music can be found in Doctoral Dissertations in Musicology Online, *http://www.music.indiana.edu/ddm/.*

The science of describing books. The study of manuscripts and publications as physical objects—how they are made and how they are recorded in a bibliography—has until recently been largely neglected in music. Outside music the topic is well covered in Fredson T. Bowers, *Principles of Bibliographical Description* (Princeton: Princeton U Pr, 1949; R: New York: Russell & Russell, 1962), and Philip Gaskell, *A New Introduction to Bibliography* (Oxford: Clarendon Pr, 1972). The chief interest in music has been the various methods of establishing dates for undated works, a topic explored by Donald W. Krummel, *A Guide for Dating Early Published Music* (Hackensack, N.J.: Boonin, 1974). While music printed from movable type is normally dated, dates are lacking in the imprints of most of the engraved music published after 1700. Among the methods of establishing dates, all of which have limitations, are: (1) Plate numbers [see Publishers' numbers]: to facilitate storage, publishers assigned a number to the engraved plates of each edition. If the numbers were assigned chronologically, which unfortunately is not always the case, and if earlier and later numbers can be dated, the intervening numbers are assumed to fall within the outside dates. (2) City directories: throughout the 18th century and into the 19th, publishers traditionally included their address in the imprint. Fortunately, publishers moved rather frequently and street numbering also changed, so that by checking the address in contemporary postal or other city directory, an approximate date for an address can be determined. (3) Publishers' catalogues and newspaper announcements: a comparison of successive catalogues or advertisements might reveal a new publication and its possible date. Such a study is Cari Johansson, *French Music Publishers' Catalogues of the Second Half of the Eighteenth Century,* 2 vols. (Stockholm: 1955). (4) Paper: the paper a work is written or printed on can reveal the date of manufacture of that paper and thus establish a date before which the item could not have been produced. The main paper-dating technique is the study of *watermarks, particularly in handmade paper created before ca. 1850. (5) Copyright: the date of copyright or legal deposit as given on the printed item or as recorded in a central (usually national) office might approximate the date of publication.

Bibl.: Donald W. Krummel and Stanley Sadie, *Music Printing and Publishing* (New York: Norton, 1990). Donald W. Krummel, *The Literature of Music Bibliography: An Account of the Writings on the History of Music Printing and Publishing* (Berkeley: Fallen Leaf, 1992). H.E.S., rev. L.C.

Bicinium [Lat.]. A two-voice composition for voices, instruments, or keyboard without further accompaniment, especially one from the 15th through the early 17th century. The term was principally associated with a large repertory of didactic works cultivated in German-speaking regions, especially by Lutherans. The first major published collection from this repertory was Georg Rhau's *Bicinia gallica, latina, germanica* (Wittenberg, 1545; ed. Bruce Bellingham, Basel: Bärenreiter, 1980), which included pieces in a variety of textures (some being two-voice sections of larger works of Josquin and others) with sacred and secular texts in several languages (some of which were newly adapted **contrafacta*). Similar works continued to be published into the 17th century, often in association with pedagogical manuals.

The term has also been applied more recently to Italian and French repertories of two-voice works of the period, including secular vocal works and instrumental *ricercars. The first published collection of these works was Eustachio Romano's *Musica* (Rome, 1521; ed. *MRM* 6, 1975). Later publications include Jhan Gero's *Il primo libro de madrigali italiani et canzoni francese, 2vv* (Venice, 1541; ed. Lawrence Bernstein and James Haar, *MMR* 1, 1980); collections brought out by the publishers Gardane, Scotto, Attaingnant, and Le Roy & Ballard; Bernardino Lupacchino and Gioan Maria Tasso's frequently reprinted collection of textless pieces, *Il primo libro a due voci* (Venice, 1559); Orlande de Lassus's *Novae . . . ad duas voces cantiones* (Munich, 1577); and Vincenzo Galilei's *Contrapunti* (Florence, 1584). See also *Tricinium.*

Bibl.: Dietrich Kämper, "Das Lehr- und Instrumentalduo um 1500 in Italien," *Mf* 18 (1965): 242–53. Bruce Bellingham, "The Bicinium in the Lutheran Latin Schools during the Reformation Period" (Ph.D. diss., U of Toronto, 1971). Lawrence F. Bernstein, "French Duos in the First Half of the 16th Century," *Albrecht,* 1980, pp. 43–87.

Big band. A large jazz or popular music ensemble of the type that dominated American popular music of the period 1935–45. Typically, a rhythm section of piano, double bass, drums [see Drum set], and guitar accompanies as many as five saxophones (two altos, two tenors, and one baritone, some of which may occasionally be replaced by clarinet and/or flute), three or four trumpets, and three or four trombones. A female or male vocalist frequently performs with such a group. Such ensembles, now often called stage or repertory bands, have enjoyed a considerable revival in recent decades in high schools and colleges in the U.S. as well as in nightcubs and such cultural institutions as Lincoln Center and Carnegie Hall. See also Jazz, Popular music.

Billy Budd. Opera in four acts by Britten (libretto by E. M. Forster and Eric Crozier, adapted from the story by Herman Melville), produced in London in 1951. A two-act revision was completed by Britten in 1960. Setting: aboard H.M.S. Indomitable, 1797.

Billy the Kid. A ballet in one act by Copland (choreography by Eugene Loring, book by Lincoln Kirstein on the American West and the outlaw of the same name), first produced in Chicago in 1938. An orchestral suite derived from it has become part of the concert repertory.

Bimusicality. The full participation of an individual in two musical systems, e.g., Western and Japanese, somewhat in the manner of bilingualism. The concept was developed by Mantle Hood (ca. 1958) for the training of ethnomusicologists who may be required to present competence as performers of a non-Western instrument as part of their research. Non-Western musicians who perform both traditional and Western music may also be considered bimusical.

Bibl.: Mantle Hood, *The Ethnomusicologist* (New York: McGraw, 1971). B.N.

Bīn [Hin.]. A North Indian *stick zither. Four playing strings and three drone strings are stretched over a fretted fingerboard with a gourd resonator attached at either end. Tuning and playing techniques are similar to those of the South Indian **vīṇā*. See ill. under South Asia.

Binary and ternary form. Two fundamental musical forms, the first consisting of two parts, the second of three. These forms are found in a vast number of works from the tonal period. Despite the similarity of nomenclature, the binary and ternary principles represent two substantially different approaches to musical structure.

I. *Binary form.* A movement in binary form contains two parts, each usually repeated. The first generally modulates from the tonic to a related key, ordinarily the dominant if the tonic is major, the relative major (less often the dominant minor) if the tonic is minor. In short binary movements there is often no modulation, the first part merely ending with a half *cadence. The second part reverses this motion, progressing back to the tonic either directly or via one or more additional keys. Binary form is thus an archetypal example of *open* tonal structure at the large scale, in which motion away from the tonic in one part requires a complementary return to the tonic in a second.

Though certain examples of overt contrast between parts 1 and 2 of a binary form exist, the relationship of the two parts is normally close: the thematic material, like the harmony, may be said to be complementary rather than contrasting. Typically, the two parts parallel each other thematically, beginning and ending alike except for the difference in key. Even when new material is introduced after the double bar, it generally continues the style of the preceding part or serves as a brief transition to part 2 proper. Hence, the appropriate symbolization for most binary forms is AA′ (more precisely, AAA′A′), not AB.

The accompanying diagram (Fig. 1) presents the most important characteristics of a typical simple (i.e., nonrounded) binary structure in major (roman numerals symbolize keys, arrows indicate modulations, "Cl." = closing material).

Binary form in which part 2 is significantly longer than part 1 may be referred to as asymmetrical binary form, in contrast to the symmetrical type just described. In one scheme common in the late Baroque, part 2 is divided into two sections, each approximately equivalent in length to part 1. The first half of part 2 begins as usual in the dominant or relative major, but cadences in a related key (in major, usually a modal degree such as the submediant or mediant); the second half begins in or leads to the tonic, but without a decisive return to the principal theme (see, e.g., the gavotte and bourrée of Bach's French Suite no. 5, and compare the symmetrical loure that follows).

Binary form already appears with some frequency in dances of the 16th century, and it becomes increasingly common in dance movements of the early Baroque. These pieces are inconsistent in their tonal organization by comparison with later examples, often remaining in the same key throughout. The high point in the cultivation of simple binary form comes in the middle and late Baroque periods, which utilize it in most dance movements and in many other movement-types. Simple binary form (both symmetrical and asymmetrical) is still the most common form in dance movements of the early Classical period, and it survives in the later 18th and 19th centuries as a frequent choice for short character pieces and for themes of theme-and-variation movements (as in the finale to Beethoven's Piano Sonata op. 109).

For a thematically more differentiated binary type common in instrumental music of the early Classical period, designated as polythematic binary form or binary sonata form, see Sonata form II.

II. *Rounded binary form.* In the early 18th century, composers began frequently to introduce a coordinated return of the main theme and the tonic key within part 2 of binary forms, producing a rounded or recapitulating binary form that may be diagrammed as shown in Fig. 2.

The idea of a return to primary material at this point in the form probably originated in ternary forms such as the da capo *aria and especially in the ritornello form of the concerto, one version of which, tritornello form, closely resembles rounded binary form without repeat signs [see Concerto (2) I, 2–3, Overture (1)]. Many works emphasize the parallelism of part 1 and the second half of part 2 by turning to new (but still mostly noncontrasting) material after the double bar. This type of form is often erroneously described as ternary, a description that disregards not only the repetition structure, open tonal plan, and generally continuous style of these movements, but also the unanimous view of the theorists of the time.

Rounded binary form is common in late Baroque dance and sonata movements and is found in most minuets, scherzos, and trios of later Classical symphonies and other instrumental works. Equally important, it serves as the principal structural basis for the emerging *sonata form, part 1 becoming the (repeated) exposition, the first half of part 2 the development, and the second half of part 2 the recapitulation.

III. *Ternary form.* Movements in ternary form consist of three parts, the first and third identical or closely related, the second contrasting to a greater or lesser degree. The form may therefore be symbolized ABA. Both A parts end in the tonic key, usually after a central modulation to a related key or keys. The B part generally begins in a related key and cadences in the same or another related key before the reentry of the A part. Thus, in contrast to binary form, ternary form is *closed* in structure; the two A parts, and often the B part, are complete within themselves, not interdependent or complementary like the parts of a binary movement. It should be noted that the return of the A part in a ternary form is often indicated by placing a *da capo or *dal segno marking at the end of the B part rather than writing it out in full.

A typical ternary movement proceeds as shown in Fig. 3 (N = new key or keys).

The basic ternary principle of return after contrast occurs throughout Western music history, for example in Gregorian chant (the Kyrie–Christe–Kyrie succession of the Mass), Renaissance polyphony (numerous works based on the ternary melody **L'homme armé*, many chansons), and 17th-century opera (e.g., the final duet of Monteverdi's *L'incoronazione di Poppea,*

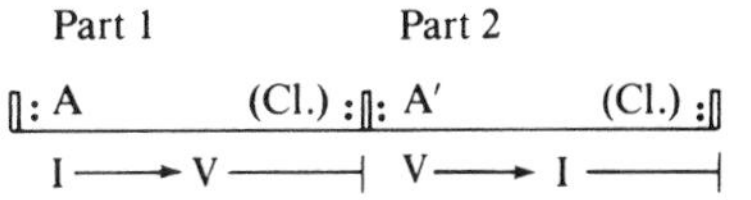

Part 1 Part 2
‖: A (Cl.) :‖: A′ (Cl.) :‖
I → V ⊣ V → I ⊣

Fig. 1.

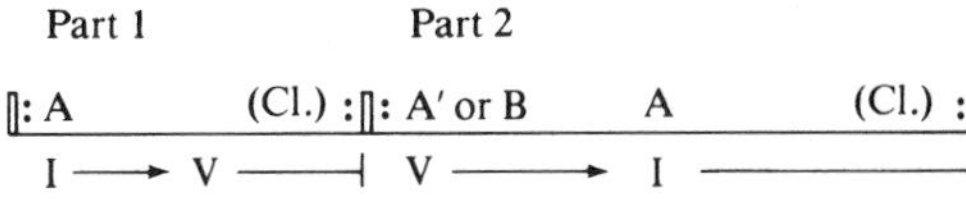

Part 1 Part 2
‖: A (Cl.) :‖: A′ or B A (Cl.) :‖
I → V ⊣ V → I ⊣

Fig. 2.

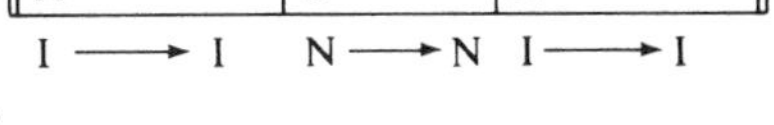

‖ A | B | A ‖
I → I N → N I → I

Fig. 3.

the authenticity of which is, however, questionable). It appears most prolifically and characteristically, in the da capo *aria of the late 17th and 18th centuries, the minuet (or scherzo)–trio–minuet alternation of the symphony and other instrumental genres, and the character piece of the Romantic period (e.g., Chopin's nocturnes and Brahms's intermezzos).

IV. *Mixed and related forms.* In addition to the types discussed above, there are several short forms that fall somewhere between the binary and ternary poles, containing elements of each. For instance, a fair number of minuets and trios of the 18th century that are otherwise binary in form (simple or rounded) do *not* modulate in part 1; that part ends with a tonic chord rather than in or on the dominant. (Such movements do, however, usually move to the dominant after the double bar, as in the trio of Mozart's Symphony no. 39 K. 543.) A similar case, but one leaning more toward ternary form, is provided by the countless melodies in AABA and related forms in which each A ends on the tonic, B on the dominant (e.g., folk songs such as "Au clair de la lune," the majority of American popular songs). Actually, AABA forms derive from stanzaic structure; they are perhaps best classified as distinct "quatrain" or "quaternary" forms (Bartha, 1975).

Bibl.: Edward J. Dent, "Binary and Ternary Forms," *ML* 17 (1936): 309–21. Ian Spink, *An Historical Approach to Musical Form* (London: Bell, 1967). Jan LaRue, *Guidelines for Style Analysis* (New York: Norton, 1970). Dénes Bartha, "Song Form and the Concept of 'Quatrain,'" *Haydn,* 1975, pp. 353–55. William E. Caplin, *Classical Form: A Theory of Formal Functions for the Instrumental Music of Haydn, Mozart, and Beethoven* (New York: Oxford U Pr, 1998).

E.K.W.

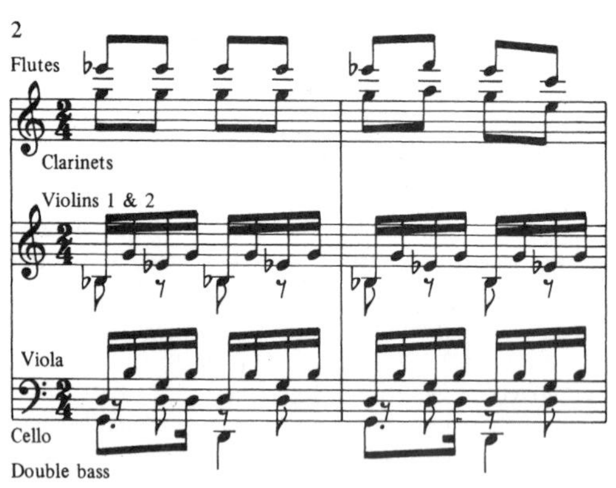

Bind. *Tie.

Biniou [Fr.]. A small, mouth-blown *bagpipe of Brittany, usually played in ensemble with the **bombarde.*

Bird, The. Popular name for Haydn's String Quartet no. 32 in C major Hob. III:39, published in 1782. The grace notes in the main subject of the first movement and the duet in dialogue between the violins in the trio of the scherzando suggest the chirping of birds.

Bis [Lat., twice]. (1) An instruction to repeat a passage. (2) [Fr., Ger.] Said by an audience as a request for an *encore.

Bisbigliando [It., whispering]. In harp playing, a rapid, back-and-forth motion of the fingers producing a soft tremolo.

Biscroma [It.]. Thirty-second note. See Note.

Bisdiapason [Lat.]. The interval of two octaves.

Bistropha [Lat.]. See Neume.

Bitonality, polytonality. The simultaneous use of two or more tonalities or keys. This may occur briefly or over an extended span. (When two tonal triads or other chords are combined, the result is said to be a bichord or polychord.) The device was widely used in the first half of the 20th century, Ex. 1 from Richard Strauss's *Salome* (1905) being a passage to which he later applied the term himself. It was employed by Ravel, Stravinsky, Prokofiev, and many others, but is particularly characteristic of the music of Darius Milhaud (1892–1974). Ex. 2 includes the relevant elements of a passage from his *Le boeuf sur le toit* (1919) and shows bitonality used in conjunction with a folk melody (in this case from Brazil), here played simultaneously in the keys of E♭ major (by flutes and violins) and G major (by clarinets, violas, cellos, and double basses). Other composers wishing to draw on folk materials used bitonality in this way as well, since it permits the presentation of tonal materials in complex sonorities. Some other composers and critics, however, have heartily disapproved of the device (Strauss himself said that it was not recommended for imitation), arguing either that the simultaneous presence of two tonalities is not perceived or that one tonality necessarily subordinates the others.

The history of bitonality as a programmatic device, often with humorous or satirical intent, includes Mozart's *Ein musikalischer Spass* (A Musical Joke K. 522, 1787) and Charles Ives's *Variations on America* for organ (1891?), in which the keys of F major and A♭ major are juxtaposed but distinguished by the dynamic markings *ppp* and *ff*.

Biwa [Jap.]. A Japanese lute, similar in form and playing technique to the Chinese *p'i-p'a.* See ill. under East Asia.

Bkl. [Ger.]. Abbr. for *Bassklarinette,* bass clarinet.

Black-Key Etude. Popular name for Chopin's Etude op. 10 no. 5 in G♭ major (1830), for piano, in which the right hand plays only on the black keys.

Black music. See Afro-American music.

Bladder and string. A stringed instrument consisting of a single gut string fastened at both ends to a curved stick, with an inflated animal bladder inserted between them that keeps the string taut and serves as a resonator. The string is usually scraped with a horsehair bow or a notched stick. The stick and bow are often hung with bells or jingles that sound when the instrument is struck against the ground. Instruments of this type include the *basse de Flandre, bumba,* and *Bumbass* and have been known widely in Europe since at least the 17th century.

Bladder pipe. A wind instrument consisting of a short blowpipe, an animal bladder, and a *chanter whose reed is enclosed in the bladder. The bladder acts as a reservoir to enable continuous playing. Bladder pipes have been played in Europe since at least the 13th century. See also Bagpipe.

Blanche [Fr.]. Half note. See Note.

Bläserquartett, -quintett, -trio [Ger.]. Wind quartet, quintet, trio.

Blasinstrument [Ger.]. Wind instrument.

Blasmusik [Ger.]. Music for wind instruments.

Blatt [Ger.]. (1) Sheet, as of music. (2) Reed *(Rohrblatt).*

Blech, Blechinstrumente [Ger.]. Brass instruments.

Blechmusik [Ger.]. Music for brass instruments.

Blind octaves. A technique of piano playing in which the two hands alternate playing octaves in such a way that the thumbs of the two hands combine to produce a scale, trill, arpeggio, etc., alternating notes of which are doubled at the octave above or below [see Ex.].

Block chords, harmony. (1) Chords played in such a way that all pitches are attacked simultaneously, especially on the keyboard, as in the simplest hymn settings. The resulting texture is described as *homophony. (2) *Parallel chords.

Blockflöte [Ger.]. (1) *Recorder. (2) An organ stop with open or tapered wide-scaled flue pipes, most often found at 2′ pitch.

Blockwerk, Werck [Ger.], **Blokwerk** [Du.]. The main division of the medieval organ, consisting of the fundamental, octave, and fifth-sounding ranks, all sounding at once, without individual stops for each rank.

Blown fifth. In the theory of Erich M. von Hornbostel (1877–1935), a fifth equal to 678 cents (as compared with the pure fifth of 702 cents or the tempered fifth of 700; see Interval) resulting from the *overblowing of a stopped bamboo pipe. From this he derived a circle of blown fifths and an associated pitch system that he found to be widely distributed geographically. The theory has been seriously questioned, however.

Bibl.: "Blasquinte," *MGG.*

Bluebeard's Castle [Hung. *A Kékszakállú Herceg Vára*]. Opera in one act by Bartók (libretto by Béla Balázs, after Maeterlinck), produced in Budapest in 1918. Setting: Bluebeard's castle.

Bluegrass music. A style of *country music brought to prominence in the mid-1940s, first on broadcasts of the Grand Ole Opry, by Bill Monroe and his Blue Grass Boys. The term refers to Monroe's native state, Kentucky (the Bluegrass State). The style is formed principally from the Anglo-American traditions of white musicians of rural Appalachia and was seen from the beginning as consciously preserving those traditions in the face of the increasing commercialization of what was termed hillbilly music generally.

Monroe himself, however, recognized the influence of black musicians. Bluegrass is typically performed by a "string band" consisting of a combination of nonelectric instruments such as violin, *mandolin, guitar, five-string banjo, and double bass, with some or all of the instrumentalists also singing. The style is technically demanding, with instrumental solos or breaks alternating with the singing in often spectacular, virtuosic displays. The vocal melody occupies a relatively high tessitura and is the second voice from the top when harmonized. Characteristic instrumental styles are those of Earl Scruggs on the *banjo, Lester Flatt on the guitar, and Monroe on the mandolin.

Bibl.: Robert Cantwell, *Bluegrass Breakdown: The Making of the Old Southern Sound* (Urbana: U of Ill Pr, 1984). Neil V. Rosenberg, *Bluegrass: A History* (Urbana: U of Ill Pr, 1985).

Blue note. In African American music, especially in *blues and *jazz, a pitch, frequently the third, seventh, or fifth scale degree, that is deliberately sharpened or flattened in performance. The degree of inflection may vary considerably.

Blues. (1) A troublesome emotion. Recognized long before blues as a musical genre, blues as emotion came hand-in-hand with the troubles of black Americans. *Blue notes, falsetto cries, hums, growls, moans, and shouts express these troubles vocally and are imitated on instruments.

(2) A body of 20th-century black American poetry; also a verse form in that poetry. Poems range from coherent, composed stories to discontinuous, improvised stanzas drawn from a common pool of formulas. Delivered in black American vernacular speech, lyrics comment upon day-to-day concerns, such as romantic relationships or financial difficulties, and—according to writers like Ralph Ellison and Albert Murray—provide listeners with ways of managing or reflecting on them. By far the dominant form is a rhymed couplet with the first line repeated, yielding the structure AAB. Line B, which often rhymes with A, usually resolves A with a humorous or ironic twist. In one alternative structure, each stanza ends with a refrain.

(3) A standard rhythmic-harmonic structure in which the 12-bar progression I–I–I–I–IV–IV–I–I–V–IV–I–I is tied to the AAB couplet in three 4-bar phrases. Although 8- and 16-bar patterns occur, the 12-bar blues predominates and is highly flexible. It may be rendered literally, as in *boogie-woogie, or radically altered, as in modern jazz improvisation. Secondary dominants and dominant substitutions are common in jazz styles, and the use of the lowered seventh degree in bar 4 (producing the dominant seventh of the IV of bar 5) is especially common.

(4) A title. Some "blues" make no reference to blues emotions and structures.

(5) A secular, 20th-century black American vocal or instrumental genre, and the source for a vital set of expressive resources, e.g., "blues feeling," in related genres. Unlike blues emotion, blues music is entertainment whose function is to dispel blue feelings. As a genre, blues "proper" falls into three general categories:

I. In country (or downhome) blues, a male singer plays an acoustic steel-stringed guitar. All singers use blues inflections [see above], but timbre, enunciation, contour, and range vary greatly, individuality being especially prized. Lyrics are highly flexible; many titles refer to one or two traditional verses rather than to a fixed text, and verses migrate from one melody to another. Accompaniments sometimes refer only obliquely, if at all, to what is now regarded as the normative 4/4 meter and 12-bar structure. In one approach, string bending and *bottleneck techniques produce nondiatonic pitches in melodies that parallel or answer the vocal line; these treble lines may alternate with a tonic drone, as melody alone suggests a blues progression. In another, finger-picked ostinatos outline blues harmonies; unpredictable placement in relation to the vocal line confounds the strong metrical implications of clichéd patterns.

Country blues originated ca. 1890–1905 in the Mississippi delta and east Texas. Concurrently in Southern logging camps, little-known pianists probably sang blues and developed the boogie-woogie bass formulas that found their way into all subsequent blues styles. Wide dissemination of downhome blues began only with Blind Lemon Jefferson's emergence as a recording star in 1926. The style flourished before and after the Depression; the most famous of scores of talented singer-guitarists were Charley Patton, Blind Blake, Blind Willie McTell, Son House, Blind Boy Fuller, Peetie Wheatstraw (a pianist on records), and Robert Johnson. Leadbelly, Bukka White, Big Bill Broonzy, Lightnin' Hopkins, and Mississippi John Hurt were among folk-bluesmen later discovered and supported by the white community.

II. In classic blues, a *ragtime or *stride pianist or a *New Orleans style jazz band accompanies a female singer. Designed for formal presentation on stage, a song pursues a coherent theme through stanzas divided into introductory verse and chorus; 12-bar AAB structures provide only one element of the multithematic repertory. Concentrating on lyrics and leaving florid melodic responses and extended solos to the instrumentalists, the singers play with blues inflections within a narrow vocal range. The style derives from country blues through performers (e.g., Ma Rainey, whose black minstrel band toured the South in the early 1900s) and composers (e.g., W. C. Handy, who began to publish and popularize "blues" in 1912). The decade-long classic blues craze started in 1920, when the astounding success of Mamie Smith's rendition of Perry Bradford's "Crazy Blues" revealed a market for *race records. Smith and her first competitors (Lucille Hegamin, Ethel Waters) had clear, trained voices, but Rainey, Ida Cox, Victoria Spivey, and the renowned Bessie Smith brought roughness and a concomitant directness to the style.

III. In post–World War II Chicago and urban blues,

which employ electronic amplification, a male singer leads an instrumental group. Composed lyrics frequently tell a story. In Chicago blues, a sound and style associated with Howlin' Wolf, Muddy Waters, Little Walter, and Sonny Boy Williamson (Rice Miller), harmonica, piano, and especially electric guitar improvisations rival *gospel-influenced, melismatic vocal lines. Usually adhering to 12-bar, AAB forms, drums and bass establish strong dance rhythms with ostinato patterns. In urban blues groups, saxophones or brass sustain chords and play accompanimental *riffs. Widely influential in the creation of the style were singer–electric guitarists T-Bone Walker and B. B. King.

A movement away from country blues had already begun in the late 1920s with recordings by the eclectic Lonnie Johnson and by the team of pianist Leroy Carr and guitarist Scrapper Blackwell. While retaining traditional aspects of vocal delivery and instrumental technique, Chicago blues performers from the Depression through World War II addressed ghetto life, regularized musical structures to facilitate group performance, and experimented with amplification; Big Bill Broonzy, John Lee "Sonny Boy" Williamson, Tampa Red, Big Maceo Merriweather, and others constantly avoided the archaic aspects of country blues. After the war, musicians from the Mississippi delta migrated to Chicago and Detroit and created the amplified sounds of the postwar era that were in many ways as archaic (John Lee Hooker, early Muddy Waters) as the country blues of the prewar era, while urban blues (B. B. King) drew closer to jazz. The 1960s saw an upsurge of interest in blues among white musicians and scholars, sometimes termed the blues revival.

The entire genre of blues proper, through its inflections and expressive practices, stands in complex relationship to *jazz (especially to Jimmy Rushing, Joe Turner, and fellow Kansas City "shouters"), *boogie-woogie (Pete Johnson, Meade Lux Lewis, Albert Ammons), *jug band music (Will Shade, Gus Cannon), *rhythm and blues (Dinah Washington, Chuck Berry), *rock (the Rolling Stones, Jimi Hendrix, Eric Clapton, and others, who borrowed Chicago blues tunes and gave back innovations in electronic playing), *soul (Ray Charles, Bobby Blue Bland), and white American folk music. It provides a series of expressive resources that allow performers to invoke the blues even in the absence of its characteristic lyrical concerns and harmonic formulas, thus leading some commentators to see it as the source uniting all African American musical styles and even providing inspiration for black literature.

Bibl.: *Blues Unlimited* (1963–). Samuel Charters, *The Poetry of the Blues* (New York: Oak Pubns, 1963). LeRoi Jones (Imamu Baraka), *Blues People* (New York: W Morrow, 1963). Ralph Ellison, *Shadow and Act* (New York: Random House, 1964). Charles Keil, *Urban Blues* (Chicago: U of Chicago Pr, 1966). Mike Leadbitter and Neil Slaven, *Blues Records January 1943 to December 1966* (London: Hanover Bks, 1968). John Godrich and Robert Dixon, comps., *Blues and Gospel Records 1902–1942* (London: Storyville Pbns, 1969). Paul Oliver, *The Story of the Blues* (Harmondsworth: Penguin, 1972). Albert Murray, *Stomping the Blues* (New York: McGraw-Hill, 1976). Jeff Todd Titon, *Early Downhome Blues* (Urbana: U of Ill Pr, 1977). Sheldon Harris, *Blues Who's Who* (New Rochelle, N.Y.: Arlington House, 1979). Robert Palmer, *Deep Blues* (New York: Penguin, 1981). David Evans, *Big Road Blues: Tradition and Creativity in the Folk Blues* (Berkeley and Los Angeles: U of Cal Pr, 1982). Paul Oliver, "Blues Research: Problems and Possibilities," *JM* (1983): 377–90. Houston A. Baker, Jr., *Blues, Ideology, and Afro-American Literature: A Vernacular Theory* (Chicago: U of Chicago Pr, 1984). Paul Oliver, *Blues off the Record* (Tunbridge Wells: Baton Pr, 1984). William Tallmadge, "Blue Notes and Blue Tonality," *Black Perspective in Music* 12 (1984): 155–165. Daphne Duval Harrison, *Black Pearls: Blues Queens of the 1920s* (New Brunswick: Rutgers U Pr, 1988). Lawrence Cohn, ed., *Nothing But the Blues: The Music and the Musicians* (New York: Abbeville Pr, 1993). Hans Weisthaunet, "Is There Such a Thing as the 'Blue Note'?" *Popular Music* 20 (2001): 99–116. B.K., rev. T.A.J.

Blumen [Ger.]. Coloratura passages in the music of the *Meistersinger.

B mi. See Hexachord.

BMI. Abbr. for Broadcast Music, Inc. See Copyright and performance right.

B-minor Mass. A Latin Mass by Bach, BWV 232, for soloists, chorus, and orchestra, assembled in the years 1747–49. The principal parts of the Ordinary are subdivided into many sections treated as choruses, arias, duets, etc. Some of these are reworkings of material from earlier cantatas, among them the *Crucifixus* (from BWV 12, *Weinen, Klagen, Sorgen, Sagen*). The Sanctus was first performed in 1724. The Kyrie and the Gloria were sent by Bach to the Catholic Elector of Saxony in 1733 as part of a request to be appointed court composer, a request granted only in 1736.

BMV. Abbr. for *Beatae Mariae Virginis,* of the Blessed Virgin Mary; used to designate feasts as well as the four Marian *antiphons.

Bobization. See Solmization.

Bocal. (1) The curved metal tube to which the reed of the bassoon, English horn, or similar instrument is attached; sometimes also called the crook. (2) [Fr.] Mouthpiece.

Bocca chiusa [It.]. **Bouche fermée.*

Bocca ridente [It., laughing mouth]. In singing, a smiling position of the lips.

Bocedization. See Solmization.

Bockstriller [Ger.]. *Goat's trill.

Boehm system. A system of fingering for woodwind instruments developed starting in the 1830s by Theobald Boehm (1794–1881) of Munich. There are two parts to Boehm's developments: the rational placement of tone holes and the mechanized key system developed to cover them. The former was an attempt to place the holes at their most acoustically advantageous positions and to provide a separate hole for each chromatic pitch so that all notes on the instrument would be of the same tone quality. The key mechanism was designed to provide full venting (in which all holes below the first open hole are open), and to bring distant holes under easy control by the fingers. Boehm himself applied his system primarily to the flute; others, influenced by his thinking, applied it successfully to the clarinet, oboe, bassoon, and other instruments. Although Boehm's ideas have influenced woodwind construction and the fingering of all modern instruments, only the Boehm flute and clarinet have retained all of the essential features of the system. True Boehm fingering systems may usually be distinguished by the mechanism for the right (lower) hand. The seven-, six-, five-, and four-fingered notes produce the first four pitches of a major scale. The addition of finger five or six to the three-fingered note produces the raised fourth degree of the scale.

Bibl.: Theobald Boehm, *Die Flöte und das Flötenspiel* (Munich: Joseph Aibl, 1871; R: Frankfurt: Zimmermann, 1980), trans. Dayton C. Miller, *The Flute and Flute-Playing in Acoustical, Technical and Artistic Aspects,* 2nd ed., rev. (Cleveland: Case School of Applied Science, 1922; R: New York: Dover, 1964). Id., *An Essay on the Construction of Flutes,* trans. W. S. Broadwood (London: Rudall, Carte, 1882). Christopher Welch, *History of the Boehm Flute,* 3rd ed. (New York: G Schirmer, 1896). Henry Clay Wysham, *The Evolution of the Boehm Flute* (Elkhart, Ind.: Charles G Conn, 1898). Karl Ventzke, *Die Boehmflöte: Werdegang eines Musikinstrumentes* (Frankfurt am Main: Musikinstrument, 1966). M.S.

Boethian notation. See Letter notation.

Bogen [Ger.]. (1) The bow of a bowed stringed instrument; *Bogenführung,* bowing; *Bogenstrich,* bow stroke; *Bogenflügel, Bogenklavier,* *bowed keyboard instrument [see also Sostenente piano]. (2) [also *Haltebogen*] *Tie.

Bogenform [Ger.]. Bow or arch form, i.e., a musical *form that is roughly symmetrical; thus, ABA, ABCBA, etc.

Bohème, La. Opera in four acts by Puccini (libretto by Giuseppe Giacosa and Luigi Illica, after Henri Murger's novel *Scènes de la vie de Bohème*), produced in Turin in 1896. Setting: the Latin Quarter in Paris, 1830.

Bohemia. See Czech Republic.

Böhm system. See Boehm system.

Bois [Fr., wood]. (1) Woodwind instruments. (2) *Avec le bois,* an instruction to bow or strike the strings of a violin or similar instrument with the wood or stick of the bow.

Boîte [Fr.]. (1) *Swell box. (2) *Boîte à musique,* music box [see Automatic instruments].

Bolero [Sp.]. (1) A Spanish dance in moderate triple meter traditionally said to have been invented by the dancer Sebastián Cerezo of Cádiz around 1780. It is most often danced by a couple with castanets, includes a variety of intricate steps, and is in three parts, each of which concludes with the characteristic gesture (termed *bien parado*) formed with one arm arched over the head and the other crossed in front of the chest. Typical rhythms are those of Ex. 1. Art music evoking this dance includes Beethoven's "Bolero a solo" WoO 158a no. 19 and "Bolero a due" WoO 158a no. 20; numbers in operas by Weber *(Preciosa),* Auber *(La muette de Portici),* and Berlioz *(Benvenuto Cellini);* Chopin's *Boléro* op. 19 for piano (1833); and Ravel's *Boléro* for orchestra, composed as a ballet in one act (choreography by Bronislava Nijinska), produced by Ida Rubinstein in Paris in 1928.

(2) A Cuban song and dance-music form, of 19th-century origin, and an important element in the repertories of Afro-Cuban urban dance ensembles as well as among other Cuban popular musicians to the present. It is also well established in most of the rest of Latin America, often independent of the popularity of other Cuban forms. The bolero is in slow to moderate duple meter, with the characteristic bass and accompanying percussion figures of Ex. 2. It sets sentimental

texts, most typically in binary structures with two contrasting periods of 16 measures each, but also frequently in the 32-measure AABA form of North American popular song. Its role in Latin American urban popular music is closely analogous to that of the North American ballad. (2) D.S.

Bologna school. A group of composers active in Bologna, Italy, in the second half of the 17th century and associated with one or both of the city's two principal musical institutions: the church of San Petronio and the Accademia filarmonica [see Academy]. San Petronio had maintained a significant performing establishment since at least the 16th century, but the prominence of instrumental music increased significantly during the years 1657–71 when Maurizio Cazzati (ca. 1620–77) was chapel master. In this period and the years following, an ensemble of strings was supported, and this was regularly augmented by other performers from the region. Especially characteristic of instrumental music at San Petronio were works for trumpet and strings, the first of which were sonatas by Cazzati himself. Later works for this combination, including some of the earliest examples of the Baroque concerto grosso style [see Concerto I], were by Domenico Gabrielli (1651–90, also a virtuoso cellist and composer of demanding works for cello), Giacomo Antonio Perti (1661–1756), Giuseppe Aldrovandini (1672–1707), and Giuseppe Torelli (1658–1709). Other composers active in Bologna in this period or associated with musical styles developed there include Giovanni Battista Vitali (1632–92, influential in the development of the solo and trio sonatas), Giovanni Paolo Colonna (1637–95, who succeeded Cazzati at San Petronio in 1674), Pietro Degli Antoni (1648–1720), Giovanni Battista Bassani (ca. 1657–1716), Tomaso Antonio Vitali (1663–1745), and Giovanni Bononcini (1670–1747). Arcangelo Corelli (1653–1713) is also sometimes associated with the Bologna school, having gone to Bologna in 1666 and having become a member of the Accademia filarmonica in 1670. He was active in Rome, however, from perhaps as early as 1671. The fortunes of the musical establishment at San Petronio itself declined considerably after 1696.

Although the term Bologna school is most often associated with important developments in instrumental styles, particularly in the sonata and concerto, many of the composers in question were equally active in the composition of concerted sacred and secular vocal music.

Bibl.: Francesco Vatielli, *Arte e vita musicale a Bologna* (Bologna: N Zanichelli, 1927; R: Bologna: Forni, 1969). Henry G. Mishkin, "The Solo Violin Sonata of the Bologna School," *MQ* 29 (1943): 92–112. Sanford E. Watts, "The Stylistic Features of the Bolognese Concerto" (Ph.D. diss., Indiana Univ., 1964). Anne Schnoebelen, "The Concerted Mass at San Petronio in Bologna, ca. 1660–1730" (Ph.D. diss., Univ. of Illinois, 1966). Id., "Performance Practices at San Petronio in the Baroque," *AM* 41 (1969): 37–55. Id., "Cazzati vs. Bologna: 1657–1671," *MQ* 57 (1971): 26–39. Oscar Mischiati, "Aspetti dei rapporti tra Corelli e la scuola bolognese," *Fusignano,* 1968, pp. 23–31.

Bomba [Sp.]. Traditional dance music of Puerto Rico's coastal lowlands, with many African-derived traits. *Bailes de bomba* (*bomba* dances), of which there are many named varieties (*belén, candungué, cuembé, yubá,* etc.) are characterized by call-and-response singing between leader and chorus, with complex percussion accompaniment. A typical instrumental ensemble consists of two membranophones (*bombas,* a large *burlador* and a smaller *requinto*); two *palillos* (sticks) played on a drum-side or other wooden surface; and a single *maraca.* In Yucatán, Mexico, a short, often improvised poetic stanza recited during a break in the performance of the dance called *jarana.* D.S.

Bombard [Ger., also *Bomhardt, Bombhardt, Pomhart, Pommer;* Fr. *bombarde;* It. *bombarda*]. (1) The tenor or bass member of the *shawm family of woodwinds, named after a type of artillery. It dates from the 14th century and seems to be of French origin. A folk *bombarde* is still played in Brittany. (2) On the organ, a brilliant reed stop with full-length, flared resonators, at 16′ or 8′ pitch. See also *Bombardon.*

Bombardon. (1) In Germany in the 1820s, an early *ophicleide. (2) In the 1830s, a German military valved *tuba. (3) A full-toned organ reed stop occurring in the pedal at 16′ and 32′ pitch and found on 19th-century instruments built by Walcker.

Bombo. (1) [Sp.] A bass drum of Latin America with two heads, usually played with two sticks. It is especially popular in Hispanic-derived music of the Andean region from Colombia to Chile and in Argentina. (2) [It.] In the 17th century, a figure of repeated notes. (3) [It.] In the 17th and 18th centuries, a string *tremolo.

Bomhardt [Ger.]. **Bombard.*

Bonang [Jav.]. A Javanese *gong set employed in a *gamelan* ensemble. Ten to fourteen kettle-shaped, knobbed gongs are set open-side down in two rows on taut cords in a wooden frame. The player strikes the kettles with two padded sticks. The set is tuned to either **slendro* or **pelog* scales, each pitch represented by a pair of gongs an octave apart. See Southeast Asia IX, 5 and ill.

Bones. European and American *clappers originally made of animal ribs and later of hardwood. The player holds a pair in one hand and clicks them together. They figured prominently in 19th-century *minstrel shows, in which one of the two "end men" was called Bones (from his use of bones) and the other Tambo (from his use of the tambourine).

Bongos, bongo drums. A permanently attached pair of small, single-headed, cylindrical or conical drums of Afro-Cuban origin. One drum of slightly larger diameter is tuned about a fifth below the smaller, and the pair is held between the knees and struck with both hands. They are widely used in the urban popular music of Latin America. See ill. under Percussion instruments.

Boogie. A *blues-derived form of *rock dance music characterized by approximated triplet rhythms and minor-mode blues progressions played at a fast tempo. The term is derived from *boogie-woogie. Numerous rock bands, particularly in the 1950s and 1960s, have used the form. Its musical antecedents can be found in the music of black performers such as John Lee Hooker.

Boogie-woogie. A piano blues style featuring percussive ostinato accompaniments such as that of the accompanying example. The steadily repeated bass patterns, one or two bars long, delineate the 12-bar blues progression, sometimes with IV in measure 2 or 10 [see Blues (3)]. Melodies range from series of repeated figures reinforcing the explicit beat (including

tremolos, *riffs, rapid triplets) to polyrhythmic improvisations. The style first flourished in the late 1930s and early 1940s with the rediscovery of 1920s pioneers like Meade "Lux" Lewis and Albert Ammons, though the style is older than the 1920s. The bass lines have survived in blues, rhythm and blues, and rock.

Bibl.: Max Harrison, "Boogie-Woogie," in *Jazz,* ed. Nat Hentoff and Albert J. McCarthy (New York: Rinehart, 1959), pp. 105–35. Eric Kriss, *Barrelhouse and Boogie Piano* (New York: Oak Pubns, 1974). Eli H. Newberger, "Archetypes and Antecedents of Blues and Boogie Woogie Style," *JJS* 4 (1976): 84–109. B.K.

Book of Common Prayer. The basic Anglican liturgical book. See Liturgical books II.

Bop. *Bebop.

Bordone [It.], **Bordun** [Ger.]. (1) Drone. (2) Drone bass strings that do not pass over the fingerboard on plucked stringed instruments such as the theorbo. (3) *Bourdon (3).

Bore. The cross section of the column of air contained in the tube of a *wind or *brass instrument. If the bore is of uniform size over most of the length of the tube, it is said to be cylindrical; if it increases in size over a significant part of the length of the tube, it is said to be conical.

Bore, borea, boree. *Bourrée.

Boris Godunov. Opera by Musorgsky (libretto by Musorgsky after a play by Pushkin and Karamzin's *History of the Russian State*). The first version consisted of seven scenes and was composed in 1868–69 but not produced until 1928 in Leningrad. The second version, which has a prologue and four acts, was composed in 1871–72, revised in 1873, and produced in St. Petersburg in 1874. In 1896, Rimsky-Korsakov thoroughly revised the work, reorchestrating it and making both major omissions and additions. This version was produced in Russia a number of times in the years following. Rimsky-Korsakov prepared yet another version in 1906–8; this version was produced in Paris in 1908, the work's first production outside of Russia. Setting: Russia and Poland, 1598–1605.

Borre, borree, borry. *Bourrée.

Borstwerk [Du.]. A keyboard division of Dutch organs, usually based on a 2′ or 4′ *Prestant. See also *Brustwerk.*

Bosnia and Herzegovina. I. *Current musical life and related institutions.* The population consists of Bosnian Muslims (44%), Orthodox Christian Serbs (31%), and Roman Catholic Croats (17%). In irregular orchestral and theater performances before World War I, mainly amateur and military musicians participated. The first symphonic concert in Sarajevo, the country's capital, was organized in 1881, and the first opera production in 1882. The Sarajevska filharmonija was founded in 1923, and the permanent opera and ballet ensembles in 1946. Radio-Television Sarajevo has maintained its symphony orchestra since 1962. The first music school was opened in 1908 by the Czech pianist and composer Franjo Matějovský (1871–1938), and university-level music education was established in 1955 at the Sarajevo Academy of Music. Research on Bosnian traditional music was grounded at the Institut za proučavanje folklora (1947–57) under the leadership of Cvjetko Rihtman (1902–89). The Udruženje kompozitora Bosne i Hercegovine was founded in 1949 and the Muzikološko društvo Bosne i Hercegovine in 1997. Scholarship on national music appears in the journal *Muzika* (started in 1997).

II. *History of art music.* The Ottoman occupation of Bosnia (1463) and Herzegovina (1482) disconnected the development of art music, and although no music from pre-Ottoman times survives, archival sources point toward an exchange of musicians between the Bosnian court and Adriatic towns, particularly Dubrovnik. Among Bosnian refugees settling in Dalmatia and Venice soon after the Ottoman occupation was Petrucci's editor and composer of lute ricercari, Franciscus Bossinensis (fl. 1509–11). Throughout the Ottoman period the Franciscan order maintained its presence among the Roman Catholic population, producing several composers and theorists: Matheus Bartl (Mato Banjalučanin) wrote *Regulae cantus plani pro incipientibus* (MS in *BA-KS,* 1687); Mass settings were composed in the 18th century by Marijan Aljinić, Augustin Soljanin, and Vice Vicić (1734–96), and later by Stjepan Marjanović (d. 1848). The first organ was installed in 1801 in the Franciscan church in Fojnica.

Austrian administration of Bosnia (1878–1918) brought a period of resilient musical life in which choral ensembles, military bands, and their conductors (Franz Lehár, Sr., Julius Fučik, Josip Chládek) played central roles. The first significant composers were Matějovský and his student Beluš Jungić (1892–1968) in Sarajevo, and Aleksa Šantić in Mostar (1868–1924). After World War II appeared a generation of native composers whose musical identity was shaped by Bosnian folk music (Cvjetko Rihtman; Milan Prebanda, 1907–79; Vlado Milošević, 1901–91), neoclassicism (Nada Ludvig-Pečar, b. 1929), and avant-garde trends (Avdo Smailović, 1917–84; Vojin Komadina, 1933–97; Josip Magdić, b. 1937).

From the mid-1960s Sarajevo gained a reputation as a center of pop and rock music, the most famous rock bands being Indexi (founded 1962) and Bijelo Dugme (1973), led by Goran Bregović (b. 1950). Their hits usually combined rock sound and Bosnian folk music.

III. *Traditional music.* The rural music tradition is dominated by vocal forms, many related to annual (St. Lazarus and flax combers', reapers', haymakers' songs) and life-cycle rituals (lullabies, wedding songs, laments). Isolated by rugged terrain, music of the rural population was less exposed to Ottoman influences and remained closer to neighboring Croatian and Serbian musical practice. Most vocal forms are polyphonic (two-voice), performed by small, mainly single-sex groups. In chords, dominant is the major second, which is perceived as a consonant interval. The tone row of melodies, rarely exceeding a range of fourth or fifth, consists of narrow intervals, different from the Western tempered system. In the mountainous regions of Herzegovina, *ganga* singing is characteristic, with melismatic melodic movements based on narrow, nontempered tonal relations dominated by the major second. The name of the genre comes from its performance style: one voice sings melody and lyrics while the accompanying voice *produces a drone, with words imitating the sound of the **gusle* (*gn-gn* or *gan-gan*).

The central vocal form of the urban population is the *sevdalinka* (known as *turčija* until the 1880s), a love song performed solo with the *saz* or, since the late 19th century, accordion accompaniment. Its balladic text is in eight- or ten-syllable verses, and the melody has a wide tonal range, with a distinct augmented second inserted between half-tones.

Instruments used until the 20th century were adopted from the East, most popular being long-necked lutes *(tambura, šargija, saz)* and the double-reed *zurna.* Among the cattle-breeding population, single *(jednojke)* and double *(dvojnice)* pipes are common. The *gusle,* used for accompaniment of narrative and epic songs, normally has one string (two in northwestern Bosnia).

Among the Bosnian Muslims exist several orders of Sufi dervishes (the Kadiri, Naqšabandi, Mavlevi), whose songs, known by the Slavicized Turkish term of Arabic provenance *ilahija,* represent a tradition halfway between folk and art music. Stylistically close to rural musical practice, they are sung solo or in a group, with no instruments save occasional drum accompaniment: *bimbim halka (bendīr), kudum* (kettledrum), and *zil* (cymbal). The text eulogizes God, the Prophet, or prominent members of Sufi brotherhoods. Among the poets of *ilahije* in Serbian, Croatian, Turkish, and Arabic languages are Abdurrahman Sirri (1785–1846/47), Muhamed Mejli (d. 1853), Omer Humo (1808–80), and Mehmed-beg Kapetanović Ljubušak (1839–1902), and recently Selim Sami and Sheik Fejzulah Hadžibajrić (d. 1990). In the 1990s the *ilahija* was transformed to a new form of neotraditional Muslim religious music, often performed in concerts.

Sephardic Jewish music had a distinctive tradition from the 16th to the mid-20th century. It was exclusively urban and influenced by the local Muslim idiom. Religious singing was performed by men, in Hebrew, while secular songs were sung by women, in Ladino language (locally called Djideo).

Bibl.: Zija Kučukalić, *Likovi savremenih bosansko-hercegovačkih kompozitora* [Contemporary Composers in Bosnia and Herzegovina] (Sarajevo: Udruženje kompozitora BiH, 1961). Cvjetko Rihtman, "Orientalische Elemente in der traditionellen Musik Bosniens und der Herzegowina," *Grazer und Münchener Balkanologische Studien* 2 (1967): 97–105. Zija Kučukalić, *The Development of Musical Culture in Bosnia-Hercegovina* (Sarajevo: Udruženje kompozitora BiH, 1967). Ankica Petrović, "Paradoxes of Music in Bosnia and Herzegovina," *AsM* 20, no. 1 (1988): 128–47. Tünde Polomik, "Quellen zur Erforschung der Tätigkeiten und Rollen von Militärorchestern in Bosnien und Herzegowina zur Zeit der österreichisch-ungarischen Verwaltung (1878–1918)," *SM* 32, nos. 1–4 (1990): 383–408. Ankica Petrović, "Les Techniques du chant villageois dans les Alpes Dubaruqyes (Yugoslavie)," *Cahiers de musique traditionnelle* 4 (1991): 103–15. Ankica Petrović, "Perceptions of Ganga," *The World of Music* 14, no. 2 (1995): 241–56. Tünde Polomik, "Sketches from the Musical Cultural Life of the Sephardic Jews in Sarajevo at the Time of Austro-Hungarian Administration 1878–1918," *Muzika* 1, no. 4 (1997): 55–60.

Discography. Bosnia: Echoes from an Endangered World, produced by Ankica Petrović and Ted Levin, Smithsonian/Folkways, 1993. Z.B.

Bossa nova [Port.]. A movement in Brazilian popular music, and in particular, a new style of *samba, pioneered by Antonio Carlos Jobim, João Gilberto, and others in the late 1950s. Characteristics of the bossa nova samba, some of which reflect the influence of *cool jazz styles of the period, include increased harmonic and melodic complexity, a detached, unemotional singing style, the acoustic guitar as principal accompanying instrument, and a departure from the older samba's emphasis on percussion. Although bossa nova accompaniments retain some of the rhythmic features of the older samba (e.g., duple meter, with constant sixteenth-note activity and on-the-beat bass emphasis), distinctive patterns [see Ex.] performed by guitar or percussion give the bossa nova a quite different character. D.S.

Boston dip waltz, Boston waltz. Dances to popular songs in 3/4 meter. Americans introduced the former in the 1870s, the latter in 1913. The terms have been used rather casually with resulting confusion in their relation to the hesitation waltz (further confused with the Viennese hesitation waltz). In general, the Boston dip featured a dip on the first beat of one-bar patterns; the Boston and hesitation waltzes featured three steps syncopated through two-bar patterns, a hemiola rhythm that Paul Hindemith used in the "Boston" of his *Suite 1922* for piano. B.K.

Bottleneck. A *blues guitar technique. Holding a bottleneck or metal tube on either the ring or the little finger of the fretting hand and tuning to an open (usually major) chord, the player produces a vibrato by shaking the device above a fret, or a wail by running it along the steel strings. The effect is sometimes produced with the dull edge of a knife blade. B.K.

Bouché [Fr.]. In horn playing, *stopped tones.

Bouche fermée [Fr. closed mouth; It. *bocca chiusa;* Ger. *Brummstimme*]. Singing with the mouth closed, i.e., humming. The effect is called for in the last act of Verdi's *Rigoletto* and in a considerable number of 20th-century choral works.

Bouffons [Fr.]. Costumed dancers of the 15th and 16th centuries who danced the **moresca* or **matasin.*

Bouffons, Querelle (guerre) des [Fr., Quarrel (War) of the Buffoons]. A dispute, carried on principally in an exchange of several dozen published letters and pamphlets in Paris in the years 1752–54, over the relative merits of French and Italian music. It was occasioned by the appearance in Paris in 1752 of a troupe of Italians who performed Pergolesi's *La serva padrona* and other examples of **opera buffa* and who became known as the Bouffons, though the question had earlier been posed by Jean-Jacques Rousseau and Friedrich Melchior Grimm, both of whom took the Italian side. The Italian partisans, including D'Alembert and Diderot, claimed that Italian music was more in accord with natural principles and that it was superior to French music in its melody (owing in part to the softness of the Italian language), its harmony (French harmonies being too full), its expressive power, and its dramatic force as displayed in Italian operas (see Rousseau's *Lettre sur la musique française,* 1753, translated in part in *SR,* pp. 636–54). Defenders of French music included Rameau, whose works, along with those of Destouches and Mondonville, played an important part in the defense.

Bibl.: Louisette Richebourg, *Contribution à l'histoire de la "Querelle des Bouffons"* (Paris: Librairie Nizet et Bastard, 1937). Noël Boyer, *La Guerre des Bouffons et la musique française* (Paris: Les Éditions de la Nouvelle France, 1945). Alfred Richard Oliver, *The Encyclopedists as Critics of Music* (New York: Columbia U Pr, 1947). Arnold M. Whittall, "La Querelle des Bouffons" (Ph.D. diss., Univ. of Cambridge, 1964). Denise Launay, ed., *La Querelle des Bouffons* (Geneva: Minkoff, 1973) [facs. of pamphlets publ. 1752–54].

Boulevard Solitude. Opera in seven scenes by Hans Werner Henze (libretto by Grete Weil, based on the Manon Lescaut story), produced in Hanover in 1952. Setting: Paris, 1950.

Bourdon [Fr.]. (1) *Drone; a string or pipe that produces a drone. See also *Burdo.* (2) An organ stop of capped flue pipes, made of wood or metal, of medium scale, and dark in tone quality. (3) In a theory put forward by Heinrich Besseler to explain the origins in the first half of the 15th century of the term **fauxbourdon,* a low instrumental contratenor part that functioned as a bass. He identified such parts in the works of Ciconia, Dufay, and others. There is no documentary evidence attesting the use of the term in this way, however.

Bourrée [Fr.]. A lively, fluent Baroque dance movement in duple meter and binary form. It usually has four-measure phrases in ¢ (or 2), a quarter-note upbeat, dactylic figures in quarters and eighths, and syncopations in quarters and halves (especially in the second or fourth measures of phrases). Like a *rigaudon, it is moderately quick, faster than a *gavotte. It was danced frequently at the court of Louis XIV and in Lully's operas, and it was an independent instrumental

Nicolas-Antoine Lebègue, Bourrée (1687).

form throughout the Baroque era (Michael Praetorius, Johann Caspar Ferdinand Fischer, Johann Krieger, Georg Muffat, Bach), keeping the simple rhythms, phrasing, and homophonic texture of music to be danced. Bourrées are often arranged in pairs to be played **alternativement* and may be among the movements following the sarabande in solo *suites. The folk dance, in duple or triple meter, is still cultivated, especially in the Auvergne region of France. B.G.

Bout. (1) A curve in the side of a stringed instrument such as the violin, including the outward curves at the upper and lower parts of the body and the inward curves forming the waist [see ill. under Violin]. (2) [Fr.] The point of the bow.

Boutade [Fr.]. According to Johann Mattheson (1717) and Jean-Jacques Rousseau (1767), a dance or ballet of improvisatory character; also an instrumental piece of similar character, such as might otherwise be called a *caprice* or *fantaisie.*

Bouzouki [Gr.]. A *long-necked lute of modern Greece. Developed in the early 20th century from the Turkish **saz,* it has a fretted neck, a pear-shaped body, and metal strings in courses of two. Older models have three courses; the melody is plucked on the upper two strings while the lower serves as a drone. Newer examples have four courses tuned like the upper strings of a guitar, and all strings are fingered. It is often electronically amplified. In Greece it is the leading instrument in some forms of urban popular music. The four-string *bouzouki* has been imported to Ireland, where it provides chordal and rhythmic background in instrumental ensembles.

Bow [Fr. *archet;* Ger. *Bogen;* It. *arco, archetto;* Sp. *arco*]. A device for setting in motion the strings of some types of stringed instruments. It consists of a stick that is shaped (often simply curved) to permit a string or fibers such as horsehair to be attached at both ends and held away from the stick itself. When the bow string or hair is drawn across a string of an instrument, the instrument's string is made to sound by being repeatedly displaced slightly and released by the friction between the two. Bowed stringed instruments are widely distributed and include members of the Western *violin and *viol families and the **ching-hu,* **erh-hu,* **gusle,* **kamānjah,* **lira,* **rabāb,* and **sārangī.* See also Musical bow.

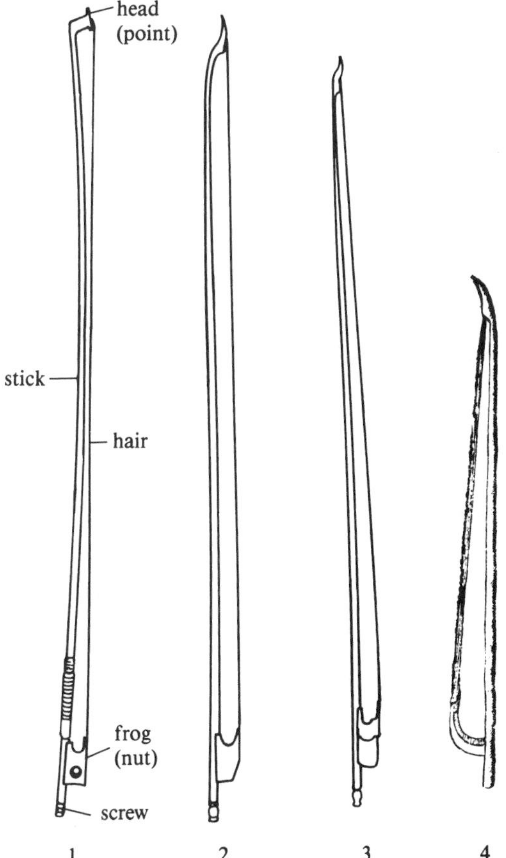

Bows: 1. Tourte, ca. 1800. 2. Thomas Smith, 1760–70. 3. Anonymous, 1694. 4. Marin Mersenne, *Harmonie universelle,* 1636–37.

The violin bow was given its present form in about 1785 by François Tourte (1747–1835). The stick curves slightly inward toward a ribbon of horsehair or, occasionally, similar synthetic material that is held away from the stick at one end by the head and at the other by the frog. The tension of the hair is adjusted by means of a screw mechanism that moves the frog along the stick. The stick, the best examples of which are made of Pernambuco wood, is octagonal in cross section at the frog and usually round and tapering slightly above the frog. The frog is of ebony, ivory, or tortoise shell, sometimes inlaid with mother-of-pearl. At the head, the hair passes through an ivory or metal plate; at the frog, it passes through a metal ferrule that spreads it evenly. According to Tourte's specifications, the stick is about 75 cm. (29.5 in.) long and the hair about 65 cm., with the center of gravity 19 cm. above the frog. Viola and cello bows are 74 and 73 or 72 cm. long, respectively. For the double bass, the French style of bow (held with the palm down) is about 71 cm. long, the German or Simandl bow (with a higher frog and held with the palm up; see Bowing) about 77 cm. long.

The earliest bows, illustrated beginning in about the 10th century, were convex like the hunting bow, the stick curving away from the hair. The gradual straightening of the stick in the 16th and 17th centuries made necessary the creation of a horn-shaped frog and, subsequently, a distinct head to hold the hair away from the stick. Movable frogs for adjusting the tension of the hair by means of a screw mechanism were first introduced around 1700. In the decades preceding, this purpose was sometimes served by a metal catch on the frog that could be engaged in one or another of a set of teeth (dentated or *crémallère* bow). By about 1700, the stick was straight or only very slightly curved outward and had increased in length to between 60 and 70 cm. or more. Eighteenth-century bows before Tourte were in general lighter and more flexible than the modern bow, with the center of gravity closer to the player's hand. These features contributed to a lighter style of articulation in the playing of that period than has since prevailed. As bows became increasingly concave after 1750, a more pronounced head was required.

Bibl.: Joseph Roda, *Bows for Musical Instruments of the Violin Family* (Chicago: William Lewis & Son, 1959). William Charles Retford, *Bows and Bow Makers* (London: The Strad, 1964). See also bibls. under Bowing, Violin.

Bowed harp. Otto Andersson's term for bowed *lyres of northern Europe. See also Crwth.

Bowed keyboard instrument. A stringed keyboard instrument in which the strings are bowed mechanically rather than being struck or plucked. See Sostenente piano.

Bow harp. See Arched harp.

Bowing. The technique of using the *bow on stringed instruments such as the violin. Instruments of the violin family are bowed overhand, i.e., with the palm downward, the bow being held on the stick just above the frog between the thumb (which is kept slightly bent) and the middle fingers. On the violin and viola, the hand is angled so that the index finger rests on the stick between the first and second joints, and the tip of the little finger just touches the stick. The angling of the hand allows the index finger to apply the necessary pressure to the bow. On the cello, the hand is held more squarely, the little finger extending slightly over the stick. The bow is generally tilted slightly away from the player and is drawn perpendicular to the string. Finger pressure, wrist motion, and arm weight contribute to the consistency of tone production in bowing. The most important bowing techniques are briefly described below.

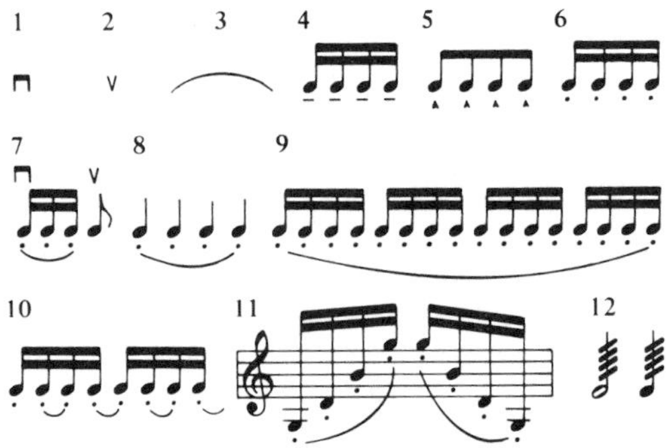

(1) *Legato* [It.]. Legato bowing consists of two basic strokes: down-bow [Fr. *tiré;* Ger. *Abstrich, Herabstrich, Herstrich, Herunterstrich, Niederstrich;* It. *arcata in giù;* Sp. *arco abajo*] and up-bow [Fr. *poussé;* Ger. *Aufstrich, Heraufstrich, Hinstrich;* It. *arcata in su;* Sp. *arco arriba*]. During the down-bow, indicated by the sign in Ex. 1, the hand moves away from the violin; during the up-bow [Ex. 2], the hand moves toward the violin. Care must be taken to equalize the naturally stronger down-stroke and the weaker up-stroke in order to produce an evenly sustained tone. Arm weight and movement control the volume of the strokes, while small motions of the wrist and fingers are used to achieve virtually unnoticeable changes in bow direction. The slur [Ex. 3] indicates the number of notes to be taken in a single stroke.

(2) *Détaché* [Fr.]. The basic stroke in which notes are taken one per bow. While the notes may be played in a detached manner, with slight articulations or separations between them, *détaché* bow-strokes are usually intended to produce a seamless flow of up- and down-bows. Lines appearing above or below the notes [Ex. 4] indicate a broad, vigorous stroke.

(3) *Martelé* [Fr., hammered; It. *martellato*]. An effect obtained by releasing each stroke forcefully and suddenly. It can be played in any section of the bow and is indicated by an arrowhead [Ex. 5].

(4) *Sautillé* [Fr., bounced; It. *saltando;* Ger. *Springbogen;* Sp. *saltillo*]. A short stroke played at rapid tempos in the middle of the bow so that the bow bounces slightly off the string. It is indicated by dots [Ex. 6]. The same indication is used for the *spiccato* [It., detached], in which the bow is dropped on the string and lifted again after each note.

(5) *Ricochet* [Fr., also *jeté*]. The upper third of the bow is "thrown" on the string so that it bounces a series of rapid notes on the down-bow [Ex. 7]. Usually from two to six notes are taken in one stroke, but up to ten or eleven can be played.

(6) *Louré* [Fr.], *portato* [It.]. A stroke in which each of several notes is separated slightly within a slur [Ex. 8], i.e., without a change in the direction of the bow. It is used for passages of a *cantabile* character.

(7) *Staccato* [It.]. A solo effect theoretically consisting of a number of *martelé* notes taken in the same stroke. It can be executed either up- or down-bow, but the latter is more difficult. When the bow is allowed to spring slightly from the string, it is known as *staccato volante* (flying staccato) [Ex. 9]. See also Staccato.

(8) *Viotti-stroke.* A variant of the staccato, attributed to Giovanni Battista Viotti (1755–1824). It consists of two detached and strongly marked notes, the first of which is unaccented and given very little bow, while the second comes on the accented part of the beat and takes much more bow. Its use is practically limited to the works of Viotti, Rodolphe Kreutzer (1766–1831), and Pierre Rode (1774–1830) [Ex. 10].

(9) *Arpeggio, arpeggiando* [It.]. A bouncing stroke played on broken chords in such a way that successive bounces fall on different strings [Ex. 11].

(10) *Tremolo* [It.]. An effect much used in orchestral music and produced by playing extremely short, rapid up- and down-strokes on one note [Ex. 12]. See Tremolo.

(11) *Sul ponticello* [It.; Fr. *au chevalet;* Ger. *am Steg;* Sp. *sobre el puentecillo*]. A nasal, brittle effect produced by bowing very close to the instrument's bridge.

(12) *Sul tasto, sulla tastiera* [It.; Fr. *sur la touche;* Ger. *am Griffbrett*]. A flutelike effect (hence also called *flautando*) produced by bowing over the end of the fingerboard.

(13) *Col legno* [It.]. Striking the string with the stick rather than the hair.

(14) *Ondulé* [Fr.; It. *ondeggiando*]. A stroke in which the bow alternates between two adjacent strings, either in the same bow-stroke or within a slur. **Bariolage* is a form of *ondulé* in which the same pitch is thus alternated, generally using one stopped and one open string. See Tremolo.

Earlier styles of bowing differed considerably from present-day methods. Violin treatises of the 19th century stress the use of a higher wrist and a lower arm; the arm was used less to control the stroke. The lighter, more flexible bows of the 17th and 18th centuries, with their natural clarity of articulation, made a non-legato the customary stroke; on rapid notes, the effect is similar to the modern *sautillé*. Composers before ca. 1750 used the terms *staccato, détaché,* and *spiccato* somewhat interchangeably when they desired the further separation of bow-strokes, occasionally indicating these with dots and strokes over and under the notes. The *sforzando* effect of the modern *martelé* stroke was not easily produced by earlier bows, nor was it called for by composers. While the evenly sustained bow-stroke was a part of the string player's training, 17th- and 18th-century writings stress the greater importance of mastering such expressive dynamic shadings as the *crescendo-diminuendo* (**messa di voce*), codified as "bow divisions" by Leopold Mozart. Prior to the 19th century, the term *tremolo* was used in the sense given above, but in other ways as well [see Tremolo]. The Italian bow grip was not too unlike the modern grip, but the hand was usually held several inches above the frog; the style of bowing involved less pressure and arm movement. The 17th-century French violin bow grip, used to emphasize the metric accents in dance music, placed the thumb on the playing hair; strong beats were played with a down-bow.

Viols are bowed underhand, i.e., with the palm upward. The bow is supported by the thumb and the forefinger; the middle fingers press against the inner side of the bow hair and control much of the articulation, particularly in French Baroque viol music. Contrary to violin bowing, the up-bow is the stronger stroke in viol playing.

The double bass, a hybrid of the viol and violin families of instruments, may be played with either of two styles of bow. The French or Bottesini bow is held in a manner similar to the bows for other instruments of the violin family; the German or Simandl bow, with its high frog producing a considerable distance between stick and hair, is held with the fingers parallel to the stick and the palm upward. The two middle fingers wrap around the frog, the index finger is placed just under the stick, the little finger below the frog, and the thumb on top of and pressing the stick.

Most non-Western fiddles are bowed with the palm upward.

Bibl.: Christopher Simpson, *The Division-Violist* (London, 1659); 2nd ed., *The Division-Viol* (London, 1665; facs., London: J Curwen, 1955). Francesco Geminiani, *The Art of Playing on the Violin* (London, 1751; facs., London: Oxford U Pr, 1951). Leopold Mozart, *Versuch einer gründlichen Violinschule* (Augsburg, 1756); trans. Editha Knocker, *A Treatise on the Fundamental Principles of Violin Playing* (London: Oxford U Pr, 1948; 2nd ed., 1951). Louis Spohr, *Violinschule* (Vienna, 1831); trans. and ed. U. C. Hill, *Spohr's Grand Violin School* (Boston: Ditson, 1852). Pierre Baillot, *L'art du violon: Nouvelle méthode* (Paris, 1834); *The Art of the Violin,* ed. and trans. Louise Goldberg (Evanston: Northwestern U Pr, 1991). Carl Flesch, *Die Kunst des Violinspiels,* 2 vols. (Berlin: Ries & Erler, 1923–28); trans. Frederick H. Martens, *The Art of Violin Playing* (New York: C Fischer, 1924–30). David D. Boyden, *The History of Violin Playing from its Origins to 1761* (London: Oxford U Pr, 1965). John Hsu, *A Handbook of French Baroque Viol Technique* (New York: Broude Bros, 1981). Robin Stowell, *Violin Technique and Performance Practice in the Late Eighteenth and Early Nineteenth Centuries* (Cambridge: Cambridge U Pr, 1985).

Braccio [It.]. Arm; **viola da braccio,* a bowed stringed instrument held on the arm rather than on or between the knees [cf. *Viola da gamba*]. The German term *Bratsche* for the viola is a corruption of this term.

Brace [Fr. *accolade*]. The bracket connecting two or more staves to form a *score; also the staves so connected, for which the term system is sometimes used.

Braille musical notation. A system of musical notation for the blind, based on the Braille system, and first proposed by Louis Braille (1809–52) himself. The system employs six dots arranged in two columns of three each, any combination of which may be raised so as to form a pattern that can be felt by the reader. The letter names of notes are indicated by varying combinations of the four uppermost dots [see Ex., where enlarged dots represent those that are raised on the page]. The lowest two dots indicate the rhythmic value: an eighth note if neither is raised, a

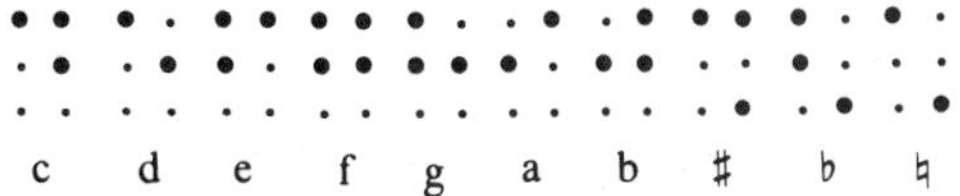

quarter note if the one on the right is raised, a half note if the one on the left, and a whole note if both. The same combinations of the lowest two dots are also used to indicate values equal to one-sixteenth of these. Additional patterns formed from the group of six dots are used to indicate the octave for one or more pitches following, accidentals, rests, time signatures, and the like.

Bibl.: H. V. Spanner, *Revised International Manual of Braille Music Notation 1956 Based on Decisions Reached at the International Conference on Braille Music, Paris, 1954,* 1: *Western Music* (Paris: World Council for the Welfare of the Blind, 1956; Amer. ed., Louisville: Amer Printing House for the Blind, 1961; R: 1982). Id., *Lessons in Braille Music* (Louisville: Amer Printing House for the Blind, 1961).

The brain and music. All aspects of intellectual and aesthetic life are generated by the human brain—a 1000-cubic-cm, 1.5-kg organ composed of billions of information processing units (nerve cells, or neurons) that make trillions of connections with one another. This massive neural network mediates conscious and subconscious experience through three basic information processing systems: (1) modality-specific systems (auditory, visual, tactile, motor, olfactory, gustatory, vestibular), which operate at the interface between the self and the external world; (2) multimodal systems, which integrate information across modalities (e.g., auditory-motor integration when we dance); and (3) supramodal systems, which can transcend sensory and motor processing at the interface between the self and the external world to generate ideas, desires, emotions, memories, foresight, and our will to act and think. Supramodal systems also exert "top-down" influences on the "bottom-up" processing of sensory stimuli by the modality-specific system and the multimodal system.

Brain functions can be understood in terms of three fundamental disciplines of neuroscience: neuroanatomy, neurophysiology, and neurochemistry. Neuroanatomy is concerned with the size, shape, and organization of the brain and its cellular elements. Neurophysiology is concerned with electrical, magnetic, and metabolic aspects of brain function. Neurochemistry is concerned with the effects of chemicals (neurotransmitters and hormones) on brain function. Amusia or dysmusia refers to a disorder of music perception, performance, or cognition.

I. *Neuroanatomy.* The central nervous system (CNS) consists of the brain and the spinal cord. First-order subdivisions of the brain are: (1) the cerebral hemispheres, including the cerebral cortex, a 3-mm-thick peel of gray matter (neuron-containing, grayish-looking tissue) that forms the surface of each hemisphere; the underlying mass of hemispheric white matter, which houses myelinated axons—insulated cables that conduct electricity and interconnect brain cells near and far throughout the CNS; and the basal ganglia, gray-matter structures lying deep within each hemisphere that also play an important role in motor, cognitive, and emotional aspects of behavior; (2) the brainstem, which is juxtaposed between the cerebral hemispheres and spinal cord; and (3) the cerebellum, which is attached to the brainstem and connected with many neurons at all levels of the CNS. The peripheral nervous system (PNS) consists mostly of nerves, the "arms and legs" of neurons (bundled axons), that reach out from the cell body to send information from peripheral sensory organs to the CNS (e.g., spiral ganglion cell axons that connect hair cells in the cochlea of the inner ear to the cochlear nucleus in the brainstem) and from the CNS to muscles (e.g., from the anterior horn cells in the spinal cord to the muscles of the hand).

Most neuroscientific studies of music processing have focused on the functional role of the cerebral cortex because its neurons are known to play a critical role in conscious experience, cognition, perception, and motor functions; many of its gross anatomical subdivisions are readily identifiable on brain scans; and damage caused by neurological diseases and surgical treatment often leads to relative, specific mental effects without overwhelming disability or death (unlike brainstem damage). The cortex in the left and right hemispheres is folded into four major subdivisions: the frontal, temporal, parietal, and occipital lobes [see ill.]. The folds of gray and white matter within each lobe are called *gyri;* the spaces between them, *sulci.* More than 20 gyri populate each hemisphere. The size and shape of the hemispheres and regions of interest within them can be analyzed using magnetic resonance imaging (MRI). There is neuroanatomical evidence that size and shape of regions within the cerebral cortex and corpus callosum (the mass of 200 million axons interconnecting the two hemispheres) can be influenced by musical experience.

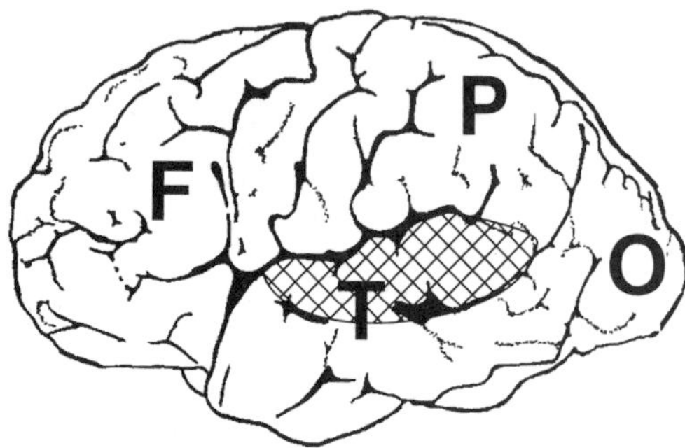

F = frontal lobe; T = temporal; P = parietal; O = occipital. Hatched area of the brain is the auditory cortex.

The sound waves we consciously perceive as music cease to exist in the form of acoustical energy once they penetrate the inner ear. Music takes shape through the concerted activity of neuron ensembles at multiple stations within the (modality-specific) auditory PNS and CNS: organ of Corti in the cochlea (PNS) to spiral ganglion and auditory nerve (PNS) to cochlear nucleus (brainstem) to superior olivary complex (brainstem) to nuclei of the lateral lemniscus (brainstem) to inferior colliculus (brainstem) to auditory thalamus (brainstem) to auditory cortex (cerebral hemispheres). Thus the auditory cortex [hatched area in ill.] is the "highest" station within the auditory CNS—the one farthest up from the ear that receives and transmits the most highly processed auditory information. The auditory cortex is housed inside the transverse gyrus of Heschl and the superior temporal gyrus in the left and right temporal lobes. In right-handed individuals who have little or no experience playing or reading music, the transverse gyrus and superior temporal gyrus of the right cerebral hemisphere typically play a critical role in pitch perception; the transverse gyrus and superior temporal gyrus of the left hemisphere are essential to the recognition of words that are spoken or sung. Axons from neurons in the superior temporal gyrus send acoustic information about music to other parts of the temporal lobe and to the frontal and parietal lobes for processing by multimodal and supramodal systems. These regions are critical for apprehending, feeling, learning, remembering, creating, and moving to music.

II. *Neurophysiology.* Neurons throughout the auditory CNS and PNS represent sound using a neural code that is based on the electrical pattern of their activity. When music is played, these neurons fire a series of brief sparks, or spikes, at rates varying between a few spikes per second to hundreds of spikes per second. In the brain, the sound of music is represented in patterns of spikes—a kind of Morse code, loosely speaking—produced by tens of millions of auditory neurons. Candidate neural codes include place codes, rate codes, and time codes. Place codes use the anatomical location of neural activity to encode information about a stimulus. For example, a pure tone of a give frequency (e.g., 440 Hz) will evoke activity in only a small proportion of neurons at each level of the auditory nervous system; since the frequency of a pure tone strongly determines its pitch, the place of neural activity may thus carry information about pitch. Rate codes use the rate of neural firing (spikes per second) to encode information about sound. For example, A4 played fortissimo may cause a neuron to fire more than A4 played pianissimo; the firing rate may thus carry information about loudness. Time codes use the timing of spikes to encode information about sound. There are several types of time codes; one that uses information about the time between spikes (interspike interval) appears to be important for the coding of pitch and harmony by the auditory nerve. Neurophysiologists interested in cracking the neural code for pitch, harmony, timbre, and other aspects of music processing study the electrical activity of individual neurons and small clusters of neurons occurring every few thousandths of a second using microelectrodes (single-unit physiology). Changes in electrical and magnetic field potentials generated by large populations of neurons every few tenths of a second can be studied using detectors outside the head and electrodes placed on the scalp, on the brain, or in the brain (evoked potentials [EPs], event-related potentials [ERPs], magnetoencephalography [MEG], electroencephalography [EEG]). Changes in blood flow, oxygen metabolism, and glucose metabolism that reflect activity in large populations of neurons (millions) over long time intervals (seconds to minutes) can be studied using *functional imaging* techniques (positron emission tomography [PET], functional magnetic resonance imagining [fMRI], single photon emission tomography [SPECT], nuclear magnetic resonance [NMR] spectroscopy).

III. *Neurochemistry.* The brain and body make more than three dozen chemicals that directly or indirectly influence whether or not a given neuron will fire a spike, how many spikes it will fire, and when. There are two broad classes of neuroactive chemicals: neurotransmitters, which are splashed by one neuron onto another at close range; and hormones, which reach neurons from distant sites through the blood. Neurotransmitters and hormones influence the excitability of neurons throughout the brain in anatomically and physiologically specific ways. In the cerebral cortex, two types of neurons (pyramidal cells and stellate cells) use two neurotransmitters: glutamate, which excites neurons, and gamma-aminobutyric acid (GABA), which inhibits neurons. Substances produced elsewhere in the brain (e.g., noradrenaline, serotonin, beta-endorphin) or body (e.g., thyroid hormone, cortisol) also influence neuronal activity in the cortex. Listening to music and participating in musical activities have been associated with changes in the concentrations of certain neurotransmitters and hormones (and their breakdown products) in the blood and urine. Some of these systemic chemical changes appear to correlate with behavioral effects in normal individuals and in neurological and psychiatric patients. M.J.T.

Brande [Old Ger.]. *Branle.

Brandenburg Concertos. Six concertos (BWV 1046–51) composed by Bach beginning perhaps as early as 1708 and dedicated to Christian Ludwig, Margrave of Brandenburg, on 24 March 1721. They are notable for the variety both of their instrumental forces and of the formal procedures employed in individual movements. Nos. 2, 4, and 5 are most closely related to the concerto grosso [see Concerto (2) I, 1], though the treatment of the violin in no. 4 and of the harpsichord in no. 5 links these works to the solo concerto as well.

Branle [Fr.; It. *brando;* Eng. brawl, brall, brangill]. In the 15th century, one of the steps of the **basse danse,* indicated in dance notation by the letter *b.* In the 16th century, the *branle* was a popular French group dance. A characteristic motion was a side step as the group, holding hands, moved in a large, perhaps circular pattern. As the century progressed, a large number of local varieties developed. Thoinot Arbeau (*Orchésographie,* 1588) enumerates 23. The *branle double* and the *branle simple* were sedate dances in duple meter, the former with phrases of four and the latter with phrases of three measures. The *branle gay* was lively and in a triple meter. A more complicated type was the Burgundian *branle,* which was yet livelier and had mixed meters and an irregular number of measures per phrase. An early example of a *branle* in Italy is a *double* in Melchiore de Barberis's lute tablature *Intabolatura di lauto libro nono* (1549, fol. c3). Other examples are in Antonio Terzi's *Il secondo libro de intavolatura di liuto* (1599, pp. 67 and 68) and in Cesare Negri's dance manual, *Le gratie d'amore* (1602; facs., Bologna: Forni, 1969, and New York: Broude Bros, 1969, pp. 129–30, 154–55, 167–68, and 294–96).

Bibl.: Daniel Heartz, ed., *Preludes, Chansons, and Dances for Lute Published by Pierre Attaingnant, Paris (1529–1530)* (Neuilly-sur-Seine: Société de musique d'autrefois, 1964), pp. xxxix–xlviii. L.H.M.

Brass band. An ensemble composed entirely of brass instruments; especially one consisting of 24 or 25 players including 1 E♭ soprano cornet; 1 *repiano, 4 or 5 solo, 2 second, and 1 or 2 third B♭ cornets; 1 B♭ flugelhorn; 3 E♭ tenor horns (solo, first, and second); 2 B♭ baritones (first and second); 2 B♭ euphoniums; 2 B♭ tenor trombones (first and second); 1 B♭ bass trombone; 2 E♭ basses; and 2 BB♭ basses. Percussion instruments are sometimes added. The American brass band instrumentation is slightly different and less standardized than the English, using the higher E♭ bugles or cornets as the main melodic voice instead of B♭ cornets. Bands of this type usually have 2–4 first and second E♭ bugles or cornets, 2–4 first and second B♭ bugles or cornets, 2–4 first and second alto horns, 1–2 tenor horns, 1 euphonium, 1 B♭ bass, 2–4 E♭ basses, and 2–3 percussion instruments.

Such bands came to prominence in the 1830s not only as military bands, especially for cavalry or militia units, but also as community bands and groups of amateurs. Instrumentation varied through the 19th century and often included various types of *saxhorn and keyed instruments such as the *keyed bugle and *ophicleide. In Great Britain, where the tradition of such bands has remained strong, they have often been established as part of recreational and educational programs offered by industry, religious groups, and schools. The Salvation Army has played an especially prominent role in this tradition. Festivals and contests for ensembles with the instrumentation described above continue to be held. In the U.S., such bands were popular through the 1870s but began to decline thereafter in favor of ensembles that mixed brass and reed instruments, as did the bands of Patrick Gilmore and John Philip Sousa. In the last quarter of the 20th century they were revived to some extent, especially in connection with Civil War reenactment activities. See also Symphonic band.

Bibl.: Harold C. Hind, *The Brass Band* (London: Hawkes, 1934; rev. ed., 1952). John F. Russell and John H. Elliot, *The Brass Band Movement* (London: Dent, 1936). Denis Wright, *Scoring for Brass Band* (Colne, Lancs.: J Duckworth, 1935; 4th ed., London: Baker, 1967). Id., *The Brass Band Conductor* (Colne, Lancs.: J Duckworth, 1948). Arthur R. Taylor, *Labour and Love: An Oral History of the Brass Band Movement* (London: Elm Tree Bks, 1983). Margaret Hindle Hazen and Robert M. Hazen, *The Music Men: An Illustrated History of Brass Bands in America, 1800–1920,* (Washington, D.C.: Smithsonian, 1987). Jon T. Borowicz, "The Mid-Nineteenth Century Brass Band: A Rebirth," *Historic Brass Journal* 2 (1990): 123. Trevor Herbert, ed., *The British Brass Band: A Musical and Social History* (Oxford: Oxford U Pr, 2000).

Brass instruments. A family of tubular wind instruments or aerophones most often made of brass and sounded by the buzzing of the player's lips. Each consists of a more or less expanding length of tube with a mouthpiece at one end and a rapidly enlarging or flared opening called a bell at the other end. Common members of this family are the *trumpet, *cornet, *horn, *trombone, *euphonium, and *tuba of European and American bands and orchestras.

I. *Types.* Brass instruments used for musical purposes can be divided into three main types. (1) Short instruments such as the *cornett, *serpent, and *ophicleide are designed to play from the lowest octave of the *harmonic series. These are now all obsolete. (2) Medium-length instruments have ranges that usually begin with the second octave of the series. The trombone as well as most present-day valved brasses belong to this category. (3) Long instruments begin their most useful range in the third octave of the harmonic series. These include the present-day French horn and the Baroque and Classical trumpets.

The medium-length instruments can be further divided according to the profile of their tubes. At least two types can be identified, although these are not clearly defined except in the soprano and tenor ranges: narrow-bore instruments such as the trumpet and trombone, and wide-bore instruments like the flugelhorn and euphonium.

The sound of brass instruments is forceful. It ranges from bright and piercing in more cylindrical, smaller-bore instruments like the trumpet and trombone to dark and mellow in the more conical, large-bore instruments such as the flugelhorn and euphonium.

Not all brass instruments are made of brass. Other materials commonly used are German silver, silver, and copper. Since the middle of the 19th century, brass has also been electroplated with nickel, silver, and gold. Unusual instruments in this family have been made of ceramics, glass, tortoise shell, and solid gold. Recently sousaphones have also been made of fiberglass. Earlier instruments were fashioned from conch shells, animal horns, and hollow wood or cane as well as from tubes made of spirally wound wood strips or hollowed-out, glue-joined wood halves, sometimes covered with leather (*alphorn, cornett, serpent). Most of the metals used tarnish rapidly, but are kept shiny today by a coating of lacquer.

Simple brasses such as military *bugles will sound only a limited number of tones spaced approximately according to the *harmonic series. There are, for instance, only four pitches available in the first two octaves and four more in the next octave. The player controls the tone to be sounded by the compression of the lips and the force with which the instrument is blown.

In order to produce additional tones, most brasses are fitted with *valves or a *slide, either of which can lengthen the instrument and provide an additional series of tones with fundamentals on each of several successive half-steps lower. Earlier brasses changed their sounding length by hand stopping, by adding sections of tubing called crooks (natural horn, trumpet), or by opening side holes similar to those on flutes or saxophones (cornett, serpent, keyed trumpet, *keyed bugle, ophicleide).

II. *History.* The use of natural objects as lip-vibrated aerophones is common to most early civilizations. Bronze, brass, copper, or silver instruments awaited only the necessary skills in metal working. At least by

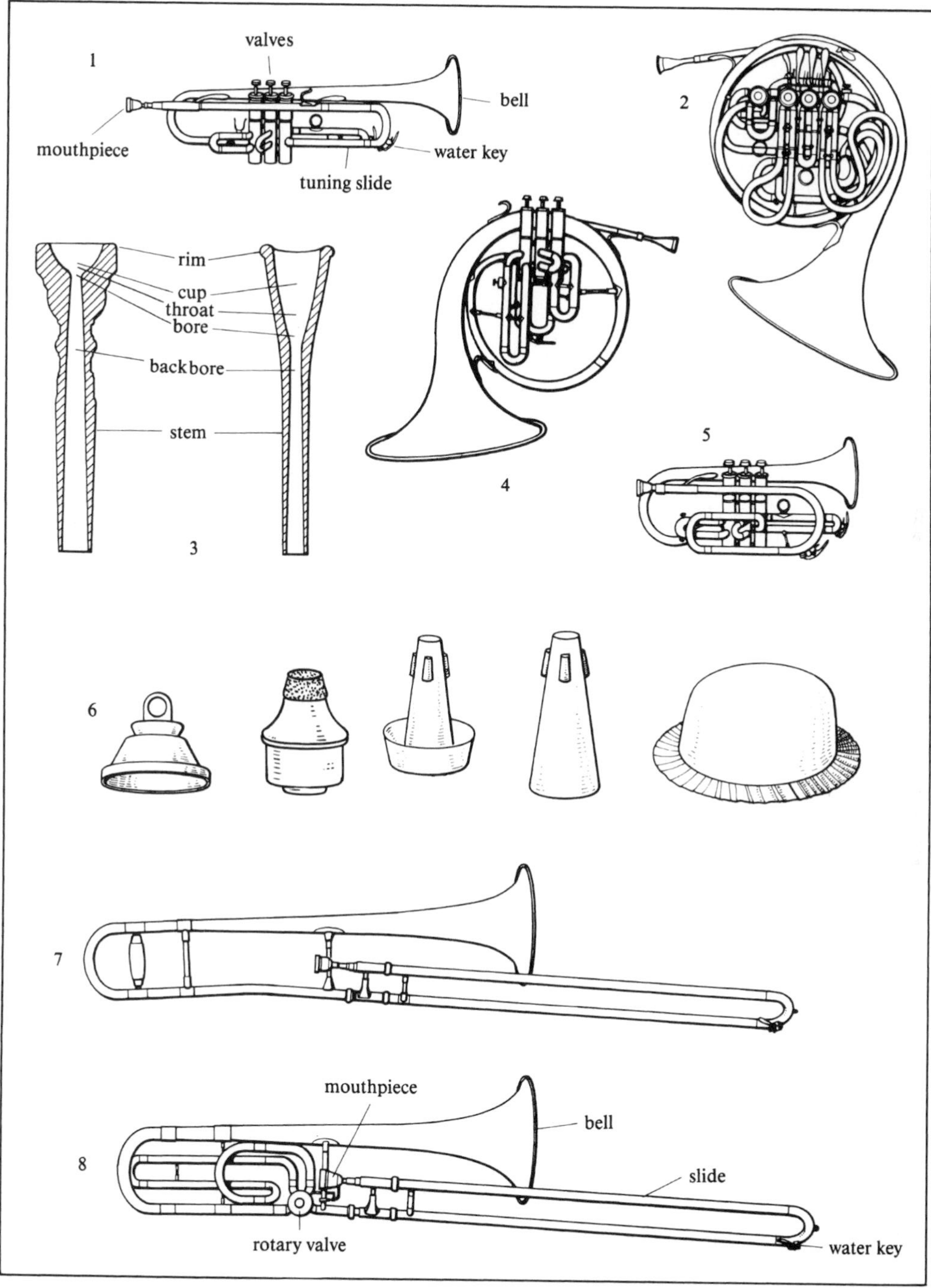

Brass instruments: 1. Trumpet in B♭. 2. French horn. 3. Mouthpieces (not to scale): left, trumpet; right, French horn. 4. Mellophone. 5. Cornet in B♭. 6. Mutes for trumpet (not to scale): plunger, Harmon or wow-wow, cup, straight, hat. 7. Tenor trombone. 8. Bass trombone.

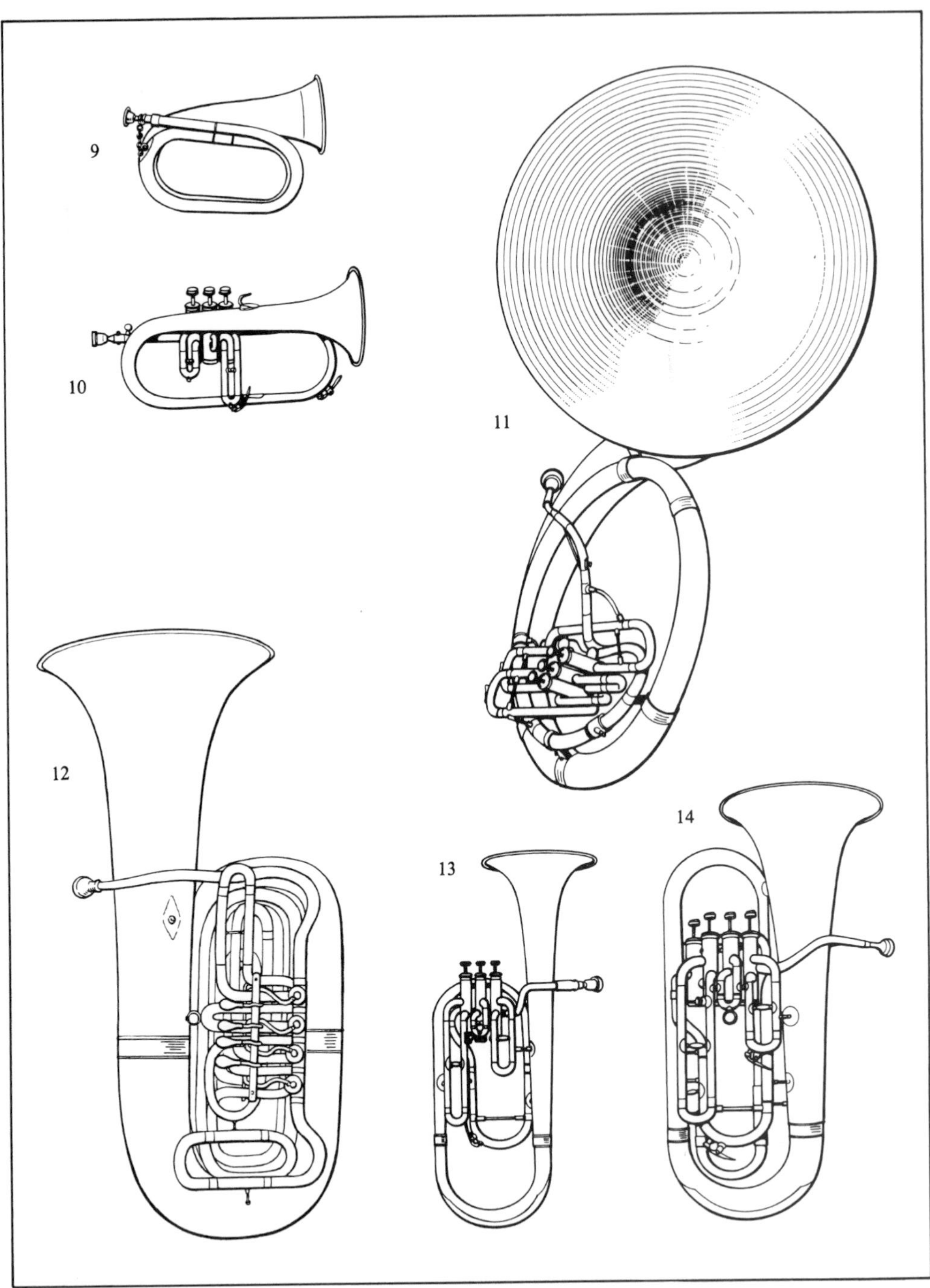

Brass instruments: 9. Bugle. 10. Flugelhorn. 11. Sousaphone. 12. Tuba. 13. Alto horn. 14. Euphonium.

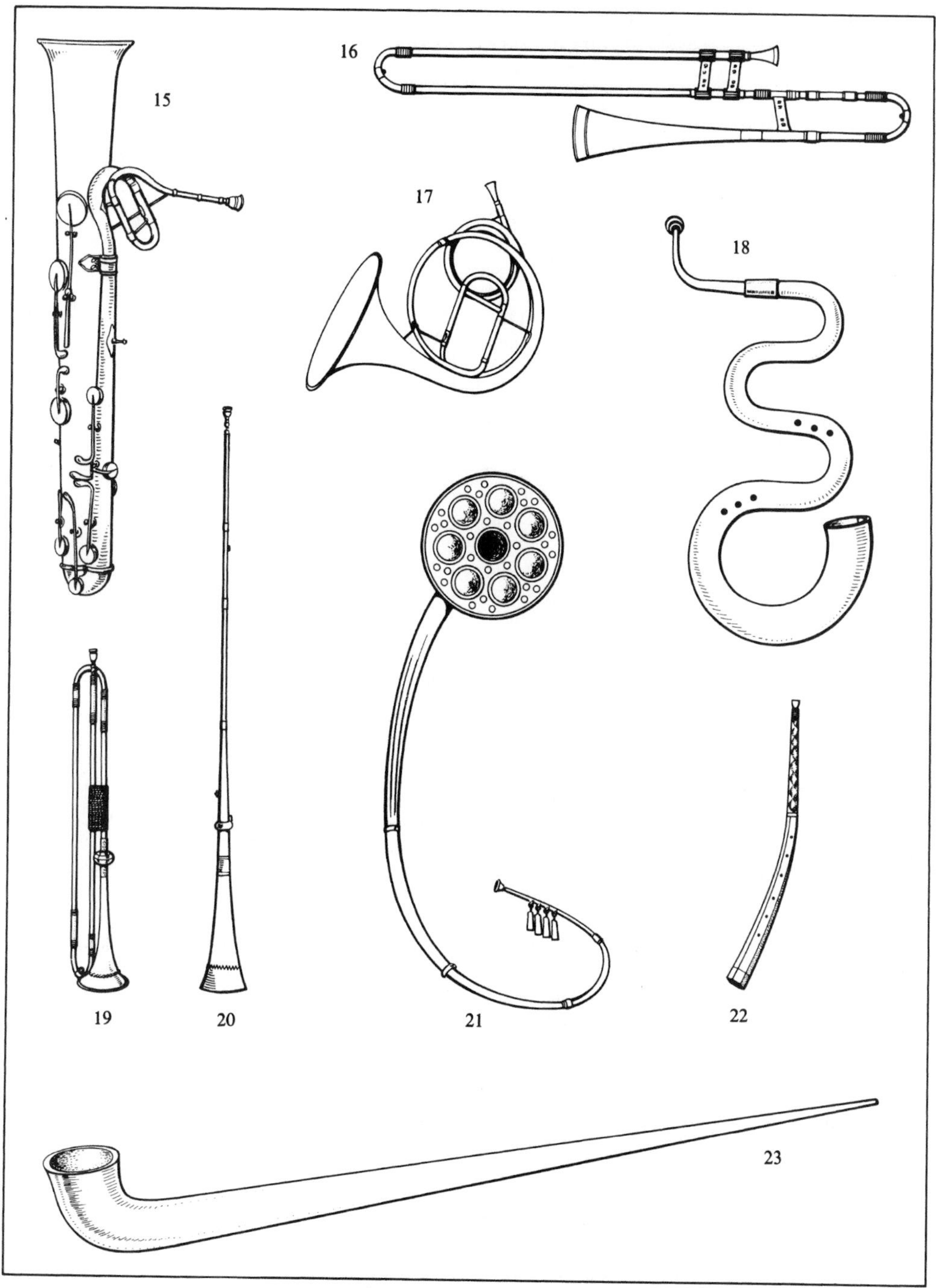

Brass instruments: 15. Ophicleide. 16. Sackbut. 17. Natural horn. 18. Serpent. 19. Natural trumpet. 20. Buisine. 21. Lur. 22. Cornetto. 23. Alphorn (shown half size in relation to others).

1500 B.C.E. in Egypt, metal signaling trumpets were in use. By about 1000 B.C.E., Scandinavian metal workers were producing the tenor-sized **lur.* The Romans used a number of signal and ceremonial brasses for military as well as civilian occasions. The **buccina, *lituus, *cornu,* and **tuba* appear in the literature and art of the first few centuries B.C.E. and C.E.

Evidence of the use of brasses for more musical purposes in Europe begins to appear in the late 14th and early 15th centuries. This evidence centers on the longer trumpet of two sizes then in use in Europe, both the natural version of this instrument and one equipped with a single slide at the mouth pipe. At the same time the cornett or *Zink,* a wooden instrument covered with leather and provided with finger holes, began to appear. By the end of the 16th century it formed, with trombones, the nucleus of the Venetian ensembles for which Andrea and Giovanni Gabrieli composed.

By the second half of the 15th century, the trombone with U-shaped slide had appeared. During that same period the famous Nuremberg brass-making dynasties were founded. From at least 1500 on, the sound of the *post horn was familiar in Europe. And late in the 16th century, the serpent joined the choir in French churches. The next brass instrument, the French horn, evolved from the hunting horn in the late 17th century. Its final musical taming took place in the following century.

Late in the 18th century, keys covering side holes were tried on horns and trumpets. It was not until the early 19th century, however, that keys found some success when applied to the wide-bore bugle and its offspring, the ophicleide. Other side-hole brasses were made during the same period in attempts to improve the serpent. Among them were the bass horn and several so-called *Russian bassoons.

Valves were invented about 1815 and precipitated the invention of brasses of many kinds. By 1850, valve instruments from BB♭ tubas to E♭ sopranos were available, and the saxhorns made by Adolphe Sax had set the pattern for modern band instruments.

Older instruments were rapidly made obsolete by the new instruments with valves. Only the slide trombone survived basically intact. Late in the 18th century, the natural trumpet in D had been shortened to F so that it could be crooked for orchestral use to keys from F down to C or B♭. This instrument was then made with valves in place of crooks and continued in this guise through much of the 19th century. It was replaced late in the century by shorter cornet-like valved trumpets in D, C, or B♭, instruments not directly related to the earlier long trumpets. The post horn with valves retained some of its earlier character and was an important part of the development of the cornet. The French horn also retained its essential character as valves were added, although eventually a double instrument in F/B♭ was required to cover the wide range of tonalities formerly provided by additions of several crooks.

New instruments that were a direct result of the invention of the valve include the modern trumpet, *alto horn, baritone, euphonium, and tuba.

Bibl.: Adam Carse, *Musical Wind Instruments* (London: Macmillan, 1939). Anthony Baines, *European and American Musical Instruments* (New York: Viking, 1966). Horace Fitzpatrick, *The Horn and Horn Playing and the Austro-Bohemian Tradition from 1680–1830* (London: Oxford U Pr, 1970). Anthony Baines, *Brass Instruments* (London: Faber, 1976). Bernhard Brüchle and Kurt Janetzky, *A Pictorial History of the Horn* (Tutzing: Schneider, 1976). Philip Bate, *The Trumpet and Trombone: An Outline of Their History, Development and Construction,* 2nd ed. (New York: Norton, 1978). Clifford Bevan, *The Tuba Family* (New York: Scribner, 1978). Emilie Mende and Jean-Pierre Mathez, *Pictorial Family Tree of Brass Instruments in Europe* (Bulle, Switzerland: Editions BIM, 1978). Trevor Herbert and John Wallace, eds., *The Cambridge Companion to Brass Instruments* (Cambridge: Cambridge U Pr, 1997). Clifford Bevan, *The Tuba Family,* 2nd ed. (Winchester: Piccolo, 2000). R.E.E.

Bratsche [Ger., fr. It. **braccio*]. Viola.

Brautlied [Ger.]. Bridal song.

Bravura [It., skill, bravery]. Virtuosic display of skill by a performer; a composition requiring such display, as in the type of aria known in the 18th century as an *aria di bravura.*

Brawl. **Branle.*

Brazil. I. *Contemporary musical life and institutions.* Art music in Brazil is cultivated extensively in Rio de Janeiro and São Paulo. Regular opera seasons are presented in the municipal theaters of both cities. Both have several symphonic and chamber orchestras, including notably the Orquestra sinfônica brasileira of Rio de Janeiro and the Orquestra sinfônica municipal of São Paulo. Orchestras exist elsewhere in Porto Alegre, Recife, and Salvador. Choral societies abound, among them the choir of the Instituto israelita brasileiro and the Associação de canto coral of Rio de Janeiro, and the University choir and Coral Paulistano of São Paulo. Rio de Janeiro hosts a multitude of musical festivals and contests, including the Festival Villa-Lobos and international piano and singing competitions. Regular festivals take place also in São Paulo and Belo Horizonte.

Musical conservatories and academies in Rio de Janeiro include the Federal University School of Music, the Brazilian Conservatory of Music, and the Lorenzo Fernândez Academy of Music; in São Paulo the Dramatic and Musical Conservatory, the Paulist Academy of Music, the Musical Institute, and the University School of Communications and Arts; and in Salvador the Musical Institute of Bahia, the Musical School of Bahia, and the Free Seminaries of Music. The professional Academia brasileira de música, founded in Rio de Janeiro by Heitor Villa-Lobos, includes composers, performers, critics, and scholars among its members.

Dissemination of music is advanced by the publishing houses of Ricordi and Casa Vitali of São Paulo, Anchieta Foundation television of São Paulo, and the radio station of the Ministry of Education of Rio de Janeiro. The cultural ministries of both cities have established orchestras, choirs, and chamber ensembles. The national musicians' union has its headquarters in Rio de Janeiro.

II. *History.* Franciscans and Jesuits brought European music to Brazil in the 16th century, and in the 17th, the Jesuits established large plantations in Santa Cruz, near Rio de Janeiro, and organized musical instruction for their black slaves. The earliest art music to survive, however, dates from the second half of the 18th century, most of it liturgical music by the chapel masters at Bahia, Recife, Rio de Janeiro, and elsewhere. There was a particularly active musical life in the province of Minas Gerais. Composers of this period include Caetano de Mello Jesus, Luiz Álvarez Pinto, José Joaquim Emérico Lobo de Mesquita, Marcos Coelho Metto, Francisco Gomes da Rocha, Ignacio Parreira Neves, and Jerónimo José Ferreira. The leading composer of the late 18th and early 19th century was the mulatto José Maurício Nunes Garcia (1767–1830), chapel master of the cathedral in Rio de Janeiro from 1798 and chapel master of the royal chapel of João VI and the Portuguese court there from 1808. Over 200 of his works survive, including an opera, Masses, and much other sacred music.

The establishment of the Portuguese court helped to make Rio de Janeiro one of the most brilliant musical centers of South America in the first half of the 19th century. The Portuguese composer Marcos Antônio Portugal (1762–1830) arrived there in 1811 to become general director of music and helped to found the Teatro São João, which from 1813 until the end of the Empire (1889) produced grand opera on a large scale. Another prominent European was the Austrian Sigismund Neukomm, who was at the court from 1816 until 1821. The most important Brazilian composer of the period was Francisco Manuel da Silva (1795–1865), composer of the national anthem, much sacred music, and a few piano pieces and songs. He was a conductor and composer to the imperial court and, in 1847, founded the Imperial Conservatory of Music, which ultimately became the National School of Music of the University of Brazil. Da Silva's immediate successor was Henrique Alves de Mesquita (1830–1906), composer of operas and operettas with French, Portuguese, and Italian librettos. His contemporary Antônio Carlos Gomes (1836–96) became Latin America's foremost composer of operas modeled on Italian styles. He was trained in Italy, and several of his works, especially *Il Guarany* (1870), were acclaimed at La Scala in Milan. Other composers working in European styles included Leopoldo Américo Miguez (1850–1902; Wagnerian), Henrique Oswald (1852–1931; French), and Francisco Braga (1868–1945; late Romanticism).

The first composer to develop a national style was Alberto Nepomuceno (1864–1920; e.g., in *Série brasileira* for orchestra, 1892). Alexandre Lévy (1864–92) worked along similar lines.

Brazil's most important composer of the 20th century is Heitor Villa-Lobos (1887–1959), who composed over 1,000 works for every conceivable medium. His most distinguished successor is Camargo Guarnieri (b. 1907), whose generation also includes Radamés Gnatalli (b. 1906) and Luiz Cosme (b. 1908). A slightly younger generation of composers is headed by César Guerra Peixe (b. 1914), Claudio Santoro (b. 1919), and the German-born Hans Joachim Koellreutter (b. 1915). The best-known of still younger composers include Edino Krieger (b. 1928), Osvaldo Lacerda (b. 1927), and Marlos Nobre (b. 1939). Music of the avant-garde has been cultivated especially in São Paulo by members of a group called Música nova, including Damiano Cozzella (b. 1929), Rogério Duprat (b. 1932), and Gilberto Mendes (b. 1922).

III. *Folk and popular music.* There are three principal tributaries to Brazilian folk and popular music: the Iberian, principally Portuguese, brought to Brazil by its colonizers; the African, resulting from the centuries of slave trade; and the indigenous Indian. All three have intersected in various ways, though the indigenous Indian traditions are the least well studied and perhaps the least influential outside of their own sometimes isolated communities. In general, Indian music performance is often integrated with dance, is central to shamanistic rituals, and embraces a wide range of musical instruments. In the mixture that has resulted, many aspects of melody and harmony are Iberian or simply European in origin, as are various instruments of the guitar family such as the *viola* and the **cavaquinho.* Iberian or Iberian-derived genres include the **romance, *desafío,* and **embolada.* The **modinha* and **maxixe* are still more broadly European. The African contribution is especially prominent in dances such as the **batuque, *capoeira, *congada,* and **samba.* The urban popular *samba* and its offshoot the **bossa nova* became staples of popular music throughout Latin America and, in some measure, beyond. Musical performance is central to various Afro-Brazilian religious cults such as the **macumba* and *candomblé.* Instruments of African origin include various drums such as the **atabaque,* a *musical bow termed *berimbau,* and the **cabaça* or *piano de cuia.* The high-pitched *cuica* friction drum marks the samba sound and signifies Brazilian identity. The **reco-reco* and rattles of various types, which are widely used, are often difficult to identify with a single source. See also Latin America.

Bibl.: Renato Almeida, *História da música brasileira,* 2nd ed. (Rio de Janeiro: F Briguiet, 1942). Albert T. Luper, *The Music of Brazil* (Washington, D.C.: Pan American Union, 1943). Vasco Mariz, *Figuras da música brasileira contemporânea* (Pôrto, Portugal: Impr Portuguesa, 1948; 2nd ed., São Paulo: Universidade de Brasília, 1970). Luiz Heitor Corrêa de Azevedo, *150 anos de música no Brasil, 1800–1950* (Rio de Janeiro: J Olympio, 1956). Francisco Curt Lange, *A organização musical durante o período colonial brasileiro* (Coimbra, 1966). José Geraldo de Souza, *Características da música folclórica brasileira* (Rio de Janeiro:

Campanha de defesa do folclore brasileira, 1969). Gerard Béhague, *The Beginnings of Musical Nationalism in Brazil* (Detroit: Info Coord, 1971). Lúcio Rangel, *Bibliografia da música popular brasileira* (Rio de Janeiro: Livraria São José, 1976). Ary Vasconcelos, *Raízes da música popular brasileira (1500–1889)* (São Paulo: Livraria Martins Editora, 1977). David P. Appleby, *The Music of Brazil* (Austin: U of Tex Pr, 1983). Gerard Béhague, "Patterns of *Candomblé* Music Performance: An Afro-Brazilian Religious Setting," in *Performance Practice: Ethnomusicological Perspectives,* ed. Gerard Béhague (Westport, Conn.: Greenwood, 1984), pp. 222–54. Anthony Seeger, *Why the Suyá Sing: A Musical Anthropology of an Amazonian People* (Cambridge: Cambridge U Pr, 1987). See also Latin America.

Break. (1) In jazz, a brief, fast-moving, improvised solo, usually played without any accompaniment, that serves as an introduction to a more extended solo or that occurs between passages for the ensemble. It is typically performed in the final measure (or two, especially in the case of the *blues) of the preceding chorus, after the final arrival at the tonic. (2) In *bluegrass and related styles, an improvised instrumental solo occurring within the framework of an ensemble performance. (3) In singing, the point in the vocal range at which the shift from one register to another takes place.

Breakdown. In U.S. folk music of the rural South beginning about 1850, an animated instrumental (especially fiddle) tune in duple meter, often to accompany dancing; also the associated lively dance.

Breit [Ger.]. **Largo,* broad.

Breve, brevis [Lat., short]. At the time of the first systematization of *mensural notation in the 13th century, the prevailing short note-value, as distinct from the *longa* or long note-value; now the equivalent of two whole notes or semibreves. See also Note, *Alla breve.*

Breviary [Lat. *breviarium*]. See Liturgical books.

Bridge. (1) [Fr. *chevalet;* Ger. *Steg;* It. *ponticello;* Sp. *puente*] In bowed stringed instruments, a slender wedge-shaped wooden device, usually of unfigured maple, that holds the strings in place and transmits string vibration to the table for amplification by the body of the instrument [see ill. under Violin]. The bridge, with two feet, is held in place on the table between the sound holes by string pressure alone. The left (bass) foot covers the interior *bass-bar, while the right (treble) foot lies above and slightly forward of the interior *sound post. The height of the bridge ensures free bowing without striking the sides of the body, while the precisely curved upper edge allows the strings to be bowed independently of one another. The geometry of bridge design and the location and size of holes within the bridge have an important role in sound production. The modern violin-family bridge is a French adaptation of the 17th- and 18th-century Italian forms, which seem to have been more open in profile and perhaps a bit thicker.

(2) A transitional passage whose primary function is to connect two passages of greater weight or importance in the work as a whole. Such passages often embody a modulation, as between the keys of the first and second themes of a work in sonata form.

(3) In jazz and popular music, the 8-bar B section of a tune in 32-bar AABA form; also release or channel.

(1) W.L.M.

Brillante [It.]. Brilliant.

Brillenbass [Ger., fr. *Brille,* eyeglasses]. A pejorative term for accompaniment figures abbreviated as in the accompanying example:

Brindisi [It.]. In 19th-century Italian opera, a drinking song, most often set for a soloist with a choral response. Examples are found in Verdi's *Macbeth, La traviata,* and *Otello.*

Brio, con; brioso [It.]. With vivacity, spirited.

Brisé [Fr.]. Broken, as in the arpeggiation of chords or detached bowing. Louis-Joseph Francoeur, in the manuscript additions to his *Diapason général* (1772), shows a **Schneller* on the middle of three stepwise descending quarters, which he labels *pincé* [?*ou*] *brissé.*

D.F.

Britain. See England, Ireland, Scotland, Wales.

Broadcasting. See Radio and television broadcasting.

Broadside ballad. See Ballad (1).

Broderie [Fr.]. (1) Ornament; [pl. *broderies*] vocal ornaments. (2) Auxiliary tone, neighboring tone. See Counterpoint II, 2.

Broken chord. *Arpeggio; also any figure in which the pitches of a chord are stated successively rather than simultaneously, e.g., the *Alberti bass.

Broken consort. See Consort.

Broken octave. The lowest octave of a keyboard, with one or more accidentals omitted; rare after 1800. See Short octave.

Browning. Any of a number of 16th- and 17th-century English sets of variations for keyboard, lute, or instrumental ensemble, based on a melody associated with texts such as "The leaves be greene, the nuts be browne," "Browning Madame, browning Madame, so merrily we sing," and "Browninge my dere." Examples include keyboard works in the *Fitzwilliam Virginal Book, a set of 20 variations for five parts by William Byrd, and 14 variations for solo lute by John Danyel (1606).

Brummen, Brummstimme [Ger.]. To hum; **bouche fermée.*

Brunette [Fr.]. A type of French song of the 17th and 18th centuries for one to three voices, with or without accompaniment, and with pastoral or amorous texts. The name perhaps derives from a well-known example, "Le beau berger Tirsis," with the refrain "Ah petite brunette, ah tu me fais mourir" [*GMB,* no. 217]. The firm of Ballard in Paris published three collections of *Brunetes ou petits airs tendres* (1703, 1704, 1711), and collections continued to appear into the second half of the 18th century. A few examples are incorporated in works for harpsichord by Chambonnières and D'Anglebert and in later comic operas.

Bibl.: Gustave Cammaert, "Les brunettes," *RBM* 11 (1957): 35–51.

Brush. A fan-shaped array of relatively flexible wires bound together in a retractable handle and used in pairs in playing principally the snare drum and cymbals in jazz and popular music, especially in pieces with slow tempo. Typically, one brush is rubbed in a circular motion on the head of the snare drum, and the other is used to strike either the drum or the cymbals [see ill. accompanying the drum set under Percussion instruments]. See also *Rute.*

Brustwerk, Brustpositiv [Ger.], **Borstwerk** [Du.]. A division of an organ, usually based on 2′ or 4′ pitch, located above the keyboards directly in front of the player.

Buccina [Lat.]. A Roman horn or trumpet. Its precise appearance is unknown, but it is described by Latin authors as curved. It was used primarily for military signaling and is not to be confused with the **cornu.* In medieval Latin, *buccina* denoted the straight trumpet [see Tuba (1)]. See also *Buisine.*

Buckwheat note. See Shape-note.

Buffet [Fr.]. Organ case.

Buffo [It.]. Comic; *opera buffa,* comic opera; *basso buffo,* a male singer of comic roles. A *buffo* role (e.g., Bartolo in Rossini's *Il barbiere di Siviglia*) may call for rapid-fire enunciation of texts. See Patter song.

Buffoons. See *Bouffons.*

Buff stop. See Harpsichord, Harp stop.

Bügelhorn [Ger.]. Bugle.

Bugle [Fr. *bugle, clairon;* Ger. *Flügelhorn, Signalhorn, Bügelhorn;* It. *cornetta segnale;* Sp. *bugle, corneta*]. (1) A very large-bore soprano brass instrument in *trumpet form [see ill. under Brass instruments]. It was used in the 18th century as a signaling instrument, first for hunting and later by military units. Early in the 19th century, the addition of keys [see Keyed bugle] and then *valves gave it a complete chromatic scale and a place as the solo voice of early *brass bands. Complete sets of valved bugles patterned after the *saxhorns of Adolphe Sax (1814–94) filled out the instrumentation of brass bands of the 1850s and 1860s. Usual sizes ranged from E♭ soprano to E♭ contrabass, alternating at E♭ and B♭ pitches. [See Flugelhorn.]

(2) A soprano brass signaling instrument without valves used by the military. The most common type in the United States is proportioned like a *trumpet or *cornet. It is pitched from B♭ to F (the same or lower than the B♭ trumpet), is 1.4 to 1.8 m. (4.5 to 6 ft.) in tube length, and usually only plays pitches two through six of the *harmonic series.

(3) An instrument with one or two valves made in various sizes for modern drum and bugle corps [see Bersag horn]. R.E.E.

Bühne [Ger.]. Stage. *Bühnenmusik,* *incidental music for a play; also music played on stage in an opera.

Buisine [OFr., also *busine, buysine, buzine,* etc.; related terms are **buccina* and **Posaune*]. From the 12th through the 16th centuries, a trumpet, especially a ceremonial and military signaling instrument. The term is first encountered in the *Chanson de Roland* (ca. 1100) and may have referred to both horns and trumpets. The earlier trumpets in question were slightly curved. In the 13th century, the term was applied to the straight instrument imported from the Middle East and used in association with *kettledrums. See ill. under Brass instruments.

Bulgaria. A parliamentary democracy in southeastern Europe encompassing 110,994 sq km. The population speaks Bulgarian, a South Slavic language. Orthodox Christianity is the official religion. Prominent minority groups include Pomaks (Slavic Bulgarian Muslims), Turks, and Roma.

I. *Traditional music before 1944.* Although women are considered the primary bearers of song traditions, both men and women sing, as soloists and in gender-specific groups, for entertainment and to accompany customs or work. Groups typically sing in unison or antiphonally. In the Shop and Pirin regions of western Bulgaria they also perform songs *(pesni)* in narrow-interval two- and three-voice part-singing styles *(mnogoglasie)* utilizing drone. The predominant vocal production is slightly nasal, full and reverberant, emanating from the open throat and chest. Women tend to sing in a low tessitura, and men in their upper range. Both instrumental and vocal melodies are richly embellished with glottal ornaments (vocal), timbral ornaments (instrumental), trills, portamenti, grace notes, mordents, turns, and other melismatic figures, which are often distinguished by indigenous terminology. Songs and instrumental tunes may be metered or unmetered; the latter are termed "slow songs" *(bavni pesni)* or "slow melodies" *(bavni melodii).* Many pulsed melodies are in simple or compound duple time (2/4, 6/8); others exhibit complex asymmetrical meters (5/8, 7/8, 9/8, 11/16, 13/16) related to those of other Balkan nations.

1. Vocal music. Prior to liberation from the Ottoman Empire in 1878, most Bulgarians lived in small vil-

lages and practiced agriculture and animal husbandry. Ritual life was tightly interwoven with pre-Christian life-cycle and agrarian calendrical customs, both of which that had been mapped onto Christian observances following conversion in the 860s. Songs greeted the solstices and equinoxes, the changing seasons, saint's days, and other Christian feasts. Muslim communities celebrated *sunet* (circumcision) and religious holidays such as Ramadan and Bairam with music making. Everywhere, weddings were accompanied extensively by song, including powerful bridal laments related in imagery and performance style to women's death laments. Secular genres include mythological songs, teasing and game songs, love songs, historical ballads, and work songs. Table songs *(pesni na trapeza)* provided entertainment at celebratory meals; these were usually mythological, historical, or love songs executed as elaborately embellished slow songs by a soloist, sometimes accompanied heterophonically by an instrumentalist. Metered lyric songs *(horovodni pesni),* initiated by a song leader and performed antiphonally with the rest of the group, accompanied dancing.

2. Instrumental music. Until the mid-20th century all instruments were handmade by master craftsmen. Sizes and tunings were nonstandardized, rendering collective performance difficult. Instrumental performance was largely a male pastime associated with herding or entertainment. Shepherds improvised dance tunes *(hora)* and expressive, florid *bavni melodii* (or *svirni*) to calm their flocks and while away the hours, played on *kaval* (wooden flute, blown obliquely), *gaida* (bagpipe), and in the central- and northwestern *duduk* (whistle flute) and *dvoyanka* (wooden double-block fipple flute). Community line and circle dances, held Sundays after church, at summer fairs, and at numerous social events, especially weddings, were once typically accompanied by a solo instrument, usually the *gaida.* In the southwest (Pirin-Macedonia), Rom musicians accompanied such dances with two *zurni* (shawms), one sounding a melody and the other a drone, and a *tupan* (large double-headed frame drum). By the late 1800s small, heterogeneous ensembles featuring *gaida, kaval, gudulka* (vertical three-stringed wooden fiddle), *tambura* (long-necked strummed lute typical of Pirin-Macedonia), or *tupan* became increasingly popular alternatives. Such groups improvised *hora* in repetitive phrases *(kolyana)* derived from songs or original material, in unison or heterophony. Additionally, professional Rom and foreign musicians playing violin, clarinet, accordion, and brass instruments performed at dances and weddings, and in taverns or restaurants.

II. *Art music and related institutions.* Facilitated by an escalating national consciousness, the 1800s witnessed an era of cultural growth characterized by the development of urban musical life. Numerous Czech- and Russian-led civic and school choirs, singing societies, and military and civic wind bands, whose repertories included folk song arrangements, medleys of traditional tunes, and classical compositions, established western European performance practice in Bulgarian townships. String, chamber, and symphony orchestras soon followed. By 1950 professional, state-funded symphony orchestras, concert choirs, and opera and theater companies were arising in most major cities. The National Music Conservatory in Sofia dates from 1921, and Plovdiv's National Music Academy, which trains professional folk musicians and dancers, from the 1970s. Three secondary music schools were established to provide additional early training. The Union of Bulgarian Composers, which greatly influenced compositional practices during the socialist era, was instituted in 1947.

The first generations of composers created programmatic and nationalistic works inspired by indigenous music and lore, a trend that remained common in the post-1944 climate of socialist realism. By the late 1960s composers were experimenting with heterometer, serialism, aleatorism, tone clusters, sound masses, and other modernistic techniques. Recent works are showcased at the annual midwinter New Bulgarian Music Festival. Since the political transition of 1989, interest in contemporary and especially electronic music has greatly intensified, resulting, since 1992, in an international Musica Nova Festival each June.

III. *Socialist traditional music.* Between 1944 and 1989 the socialist government supervised all musical activity through the Ministry of Culture, Unions, and Center for Artistic Amateur Activity. In 1951, emulating Soviet models, Philip Kutev established the first professional State Ensemble for Folk Songs and Dances in Sofia. Such ensembles, which comprised a women's folk choir, a predominantly male folk orchestra of newly-constructed and modified traditional instruments, and a dance troupe of both men and women, quickly became the primary venue for both professional and amateur traditional music performance. Their repertories featured staged, stylized arrangements *(obrabotki)* of village music and dance written by classically trained composers using Western European harmonies and techniques, often strung together in suites or dramatic presentations of traditional customs.

IV. *Popular culture and post-socialist musical life.* After 1989, funding for the hundreds of state-supported folk ensembles and music and dance collectives greatly diminished. Public interest turned to rock music *(rok muzika)* whose development had largely followed that of European and American bands since the 1960s, and new, hybridic forms of ethnopop *(etnopop)* combined local idioms with elements of European and American popular music and Middle Eastern and other Balkan styles. The latter include wedding music *(svatbarska muzika),* disco folk *(disko folk),* rock music colored by indigenous instruments or styles, rock music remakes of traditional songs,

Macedonian-influenced pop songs in Pirin, and Rom- and Turkish-influenced dance music *(chalga; pop-folk).*

Bibl.: Venelin Krustev, ed., *Entsiklopediya na bulgarskata muzikalna kultura* (Sofia: BAN, 1967). Venelin Krustev, *Bulgarian Music* (Sofia, 1978). Stoyan Dzhudzhev, *Bulgarska narodna muzika,* 2 vols. (Sofia: Muzika, 1975/1980). Donna A. Buchanan, "Bibliografiya na bulgarska traditsionna muzika v angloezichni izvori," *Bulgarsko muzikoznanie* 17, no. 3 (1993): 78–85. Timothy Rice, *"May It Fill Your Soul": Experiencing Bulgarian Music* (Chicago: U of Chicago Pr, 1994). Martha Forsyth, *Listen, Daughter, and Remember Well . . . : The Songs and Life of Linka Gekov Gergova* (Sofia: St. Kliment Ohridski U Pr, 1996). Timothy Rice, "Bulgaria," in *The Garland Encyclopedia of World Music,* vol. 8: *Europe,* ed. Timothy Rice et al. (New York: Garland, 2000), pp. 890–910. Donna A. Buchanan, "Bulgaria," in *Grove 6,* 2nd ed. Donna A. Buchanan, *Performing Democracy: Bulgarian Music and Musicians in Transition* (in press). D.A.B.

Bull-roarer. An instrument made by attaching a flat, narrow, elongated object to a string and whirling it overhead. As it circles the player, it rotates on its own axis, causing the air to vibrate and producing a roaring or screaming sound. Examples have been discovered in paleolithic excavations and are distributed worldwide. In primitive societies, it is often used in connection with initiation, funeral, curing, or fertility rites, its sound being equated with the voice of spirits or ancestors.

Bumbass [Ger.]. See Bladder and string.

Bund [Ger.]. *Fret; for *bundfrei,* see Clavichord.

Burden. (1) Refrain, especially that of the 15th-century *carol. (2) In 14th- and 15th-century England, the lowest part in a polyphonic complex, whence perhaps the term *faburden.

Burdo [Lat.]. From the late 13th century, *drone, including the sustained tenors of *organum and the pipes and strings producing invariable pitches on instruments. See also *Bourdon.*

Burgundian cadence. See Cadence.

Burgundian school. A group of composers of the 15th century with ties of varying kinds to the court of the Dukes of Burgundy, especially Philip the Good (1419–67) and Charles the Bold (1467–77), or born or active at some time in the duchy of Burgundy, which included eastern France and the Low Countries. Composers loosely grouped under this rubric, the usefulness of which may be doubted, have included Guillaume Dufay (1397 or 1398–1474), Gilles Binchois (ca. 1400–1460), Hayne van Ghizeghem (ca. 1445–between 1472 and 1497), Pierre Fontaine (d. ca. 1450), Nicolas Grenon (ca. 1380–1456), Robert Morton (ca. 1430–ca. 1476), and Antoine Busnois (ca. 1430–92). Particularly characteristic of the period were three-voice *chansons with French text in the uppermost part alone, especially settings of *rondeaux,* a form cultivated and circulated internationally. Most of these composers also composed Latin sacred music, however. See also Chanson, Middle Ages, Renaissance.

Bibl.: Jeanne Marix, *Histoire de la musique et des musiciens de la cour de Bourgogne sous le règne de Philippe le Bon (1420–1467)* (Paris: L'oiseau-lyre, 1937; R: Baden-Baden: Koerner, 1974). Craig Wright, *Music at the Court of Burgundy 1364–1419: A Documentary History,* Musicological Studies 28 (Henryville, Pa.: Institute of Mediaeval Music, 1979). Walter H. Kemp, *Burgundian Court Song in the Time of Binchois* (Oxford: Oxford U Pr, 1990).

Burla [It.]. (1) In 18th-century Italian opera, a colloquial term for a comic work. (2) In instrumental music, a humorous piece, for example the "Burla" in Schumann's *Albumblätter* op. 124.

Burlesca [It.]. A playful or comical piece. Examples of instrumental burlescas include the fifth movement of Bach's Partita in A minor, Richard Strauss's *Burleske* for piano and orchestra, and works by Hiller, Heller, Paderewski, Reger, and Bartók, among others.

Burlesque [Fr.]. (1) *Burlesca. (2) In England beginning in the late 17th century, a satirical parody of a stage work, often of an opera or *ballad opera. Examples include *The Opera of Operas, or Tom Thumb the Great* (1733, after Fielding's *The Tragedy of Tragedies*), with music for two versions by C. John Frederick Lampe and Thomas Arne, respectively, and a parody of Weber's *Der Freischütz.* The genre was most prominent in the 19th century and includes works by James Planché and W. S. Gilbert. (3) In America until about 1860, works similar to those of (2) above; after about 1860 and up to the present, a variety show likely to include comedians and other entertainers, but the principal ingredient of which is striptease.

Bibl.: Victor C. Clinton-Baddeley, *The Burlesque Tradition in the English Theatre after 1660* (London: Methuen, 1952). Roger Fiske, *English Theatre Music in the Eighteenth Century* (London: Oxford U Pr, 1973). George Rowell, *The Victorian Theatre, 1792–1914: A Survey,* 2nd ed. (Cambridge: Cambridge U Pr, 1978). Robert Klein Allen, *Horrible Prettiness: Burlesque and American Culture* (Chapel Hill: U of NC Pr, 1991).

Burletta. In England in the late 18th and early 19th centuries, an Italian comic opera such as Pergolesi's *La serva padrona* or an English imitation of such a work, the first example of the latter being Kane O'Hara's *Midas* (Belfast, 1760; music anonymously compiled). English examples were often satires of Italian *opera seria.* Later examples were often comic plays with five or six songs inserted and accompanied by the piano. See also Burlesque.

Burma. See Southeast Asia II.

Busine. See *Buisine.*

Buxheimer Orgelbuch [Ger., Buxheim Organ Book]. A manuscript (Munich, Bayerische Staatsbibliothek, Cim. 352b, formerly Mus. 3725) from ca. 1470 containing more than 250 compositions for organ, including preludes, liturgical works, **basses danses,* *intabulations of German and French songs, Conrad Paumann's **Fundamentum organisandi,* and two anonymous collections similar to Paumann's. It is notated in a form of German organ *tablature in which the uppermost line is written on a staff and everything below that in letters.

Bibl.: Facs., *DM* 2nd ser., 1 (1955). *EDM* 37–39, ed. Bertha A. Wallner. Eileen Southern, *The Buxheim Organ Book* (Brooklyn: Institute of Mediaeval Music, 1963). Hans Rudolf Zöbeley, *Die Musik des Buxheimer Orgelbuchs* (Tutzing: Schneider, 1964).

Buysine, buzanne, buzine. See *Buisine.*

Buzuq [Ar.]. A *long-necked lute of Syria, Lebanon, and northern Iraq. It has a fretted fingerboard and two or three courses of two or three strings, and it is played with a plectrum. Similar instruments are the Turkish **saz* and Greek **bouzouki.*

B.V.M. Abbr. for Blessed Virgin Mary [Lat. *B.M.V., Beatae Mariae Virginis*].

BWV. Abbr. for *Bach-Werke-Verzeichnis,* the short title of Wolfgang Schmieder's *Thematisch-systematisches Verzeichnis der musikalischen Werke von Johann Sebastian Bach: Bach-Werke-Verzeichnis* (Wiesbaden: Breitkopf & Härtel, 1990), a *thematic catalog of the works of J. S. Bach.

Byzantine chant. The medieval sacred music of the Christian churches following the Eastern Orthodox rite. This tradition, principally encompassing the Greek-speaking world [for others see Armenian chant, Syrian chant, Georgian chant, Russian and Slavonic chant], developed in Byzantium from the establishment of its capital, Constantinople, in 330 until its conquest in 1453. It is undeniably of composite origin, drawing on the artistic and technical productions of the classical age and on Jewish music, and inspired by the plainsong that evolved in the early Christian cities of Alexandria, Antioch, and Ephesus.

Byzantine chant manuscripts date from the 9th century, while lectionaries of Biblical readings with *ecphonetic notation begin about a century earlier. Our knowledge of the older period is derived from the church ordos, patristic writings, and medieval histories. In common with other dialects in the East and West, Byzantine music is purely vocal and exclusively monodic. Apart from the *acclamations, the texts are solely designed for the several Eastern liturgies and offices. The most ancient evidence suggests that hymns and Psalms were originally syllabic or near-syllabic in style, stemming, as they did, from pre-*oktoēch* [see *Ēchos*] congregational recitatives. Later, with the development of monasticism, at first in Palestine and then in Constantinople, and with the augmentation of rites and ceremonies in new and magnificent edifices (such as Hagia Sophia), trained choirs, each with its own leader (the *protopsaltes* for the right choir; the *lampadarios* for the left) and soloist (the *domestikos* or *kanonarch*), assumed full musical responsibilities. Consequently after ca. 850 there began a tendency to elaborate and to ornament, and this produced a radically new melismatic and ultimately *kalophonic* style [see *Anenajki*].

I. *Notation.* Fully diastematic Byzantine notation, which can be readily converted into the modern system, surfaces in the last quarter of the 12th century. Currently known as round or middle Byzantine notation, it differs decisively from earlier forms (paleobyzantine notation) in that it represents an explicit technique of writing, accounting even for minor details of performance. When reading the earlier, simple notation, the singer was expected to interpret or realize the stenography by applying certain established rules (generally unknown now but absolutely familiar to him) in order to provide an accurate and acceptable rendition of the music. The change to greater precision came about initially in response to an urgent need: to capture the vestiges of an old and dying melodic tradition then losing its supremacy in the face of more progressive and complex musical styles. But the actual process of substitution from the implicit to the explicit system is not easily explained, since mixed traditions characterize notational procedures used in the Byzantine world, each new manuscript revealing a variance, an inconsistency, or a deviation. Broadly speaking, scholars have discerned two principal paleobyzantine notations, of common origin yet distinct and contemporaneous in their development: Coislin and Chartres (the names are taken from two exemplars, MS Coislin and a fragment of MS Lavra Γ. 67, which was formerly at Chartres). Their origins are believed to lie in the ancient grammatical accents, and they are comparable to the Latin staffless neumes.

Specifically, Coislin is a notation that chiefly employs a limited number of rudimentary diastematic neumes (*oxeia, bareia, apostrophos, petastē,* and *klasma*) independently and in combination, with the addition of a small number of simple auxiliaries and incidental signs. Chartres notation, on the other hand, is mainly characterized by its use of elaborate signs that stand for melodic groups. Around 1050 these two primitive systems terminated their coexistence, the former superseding the latter and continuing its development until ca. 1106. Toward the end of the century it succumbed to the totally explicit round method. The new system embodied a uniformity that is inherent in any written tradition, but, more than this, it established a number of influential precedents both in manuscript transmission and in musical theory. It suppressed the instability of oral tradition, and it countered the inconsistencies of diverse musical practices. Melodies written in round notation developed an aura of sanctity and became models for subsequent generations of composers. One immediate result of this was the appearance of new music books for soloists (the *Psaltikon*), for choristers (the *Asmatikon*), and for both (the **Akolouthia*). But much more was involved in the substitution of notations than a mere evolution to greater clarity. Other changes were taking place in liturgical ordos and in performance practices, and the advent of the round system satisfied the demands placed on music by a new class of professional musicians (the *maistores*), who naturally favored an exact method of writing that could capture the nuances and elaborations of their highly specialized art. Marked developments in the liturgical tradition, which had reached a culminating stage by the end of the 12th century, gave the scribes an additional incentive to provide appropriate musical material in newly edited choirbooks.

Following an independent development and surviving until the 14th century in a relatively unchanged state is the notation that was devised to accommodate Biblical lessons: ecphonetic or lectionary notation. It comprises a small set of signs that occur as couples, one at the beginning and one at the end of every phrase in the text, presumably requiring the application of different kinds of cantillation formulas. Like the Coislin and Chartres systems, ecphonetic notation was of value for the singer, who used it only as a memory aid; but complete reconstruction of the melody line is impossible today.

Byzantine chant notation in its fully developed and unambiguous form represents a highly ingenious system of interrelationships among a handful of symbols that enabled scribes to convey a great variety of rhythmic, melodic, and dynamic nuances. Certain signs called *somata* (bodies) refer to single steps up or down; others called *pneumata* (spirits) denote leaps. Five of the former group also carry dynamic value, and when combined with the *pneumata,* they lose their step value but indicate the appropriate stress or nuance. For example, the *oxeia* (acute) / marks an ascending second with emphasis (usually denoted by >). When placed with the *hypsēlē* (high), the ascending fifth /ᶫ , the *oxeia* loses its intervallic value but has its dynamic quality applied to the new note. Standing apart from these is the *ison* (equal) ⌞, which asks for a repetition of the note sung before. Another group of signs refers to rhythmic duration (note lengthenings), and another (the *hypostases*) to ornaments. At the beginning of the chant, a special signature *(martyria)* indicates the mode and starting pitch. Therefore, in order to sing from a medieval Greek chant book, the trained cantor *(psaltēs)* would work his way through the piece by steps and leaps, applying the necessary nuances and durations as required by the neumes. To avoid confusion, scribes frequently drew the *somata* and *pneumata* in black or brown ink and the *hypostases* in red.

II. *Psalmody and hymnody.* Unlike the acclamations and lectionary recitatives, Byzantine psalmody and hymnody were systematically assigned to the eight ecclesiastical modes that, from about the 8th century, provided the compositional framework for Eastern and Western musical practices. Research has demonstrated that, for all practical purposes, the *oktoēchos,* as the system is called, was the same for Latins, Greeks, and Slavs in the Middle Ages [see *Ēchos*]. Each mode is characterized by the deployment of a restricted set of melodic formulas that is peculiar to the mode and that constitutes the substance of the hymn. Although these formulas may be arranged in many different combinations and variations, most of the phrases of any given chant are nevertheless reducible to one or another of this small number of melodic fragments.

Both psalmody and hymnody are represented by florid and syllabic settings in the manuscript tradition. Byzantine syllabic psalm tones display extremely archaic features such as the rigidly organized four-element cadence that is mechanically applied to the last four syllables of the verse, regardless of accent or quantity. The florid Psalm verses such as those for communion, which first appear in 12th- and 13th-century choirbooks, demonstrate a simple motivic uniformity that transcends modal ordering and undoubtedly reflects a pre-*oktoēch* congregational recitative.

A special position, however, was accorded to non-Biblical hymnody, within which the generic term *troparion* came to signify a monostrophic stanza, or one of a series of stanzas, in poetic prose of irregular length and accentuated patterns. The earliest *troparia* may have been interpolated after Psalm verses or Biblical canticles, while others acted as invitatory prefaces to liturgical chants. At first restricted to the Office, they are in later times found in all Byzantine services. Two venerable examples, still used, are the Vesperal "Phos hilaron" (O Gladsome Light) and "Ho Monogēnēs Huios" (Only Begotten Son) from the *Divine Liturgy. The development of larger forms began in the 5th century with the rise of the *kontakion* (scroll), a long and elaborate metrical sermon, reputedly of Syriac origin, which finds its acme in a work of St. Romanos the Melode (6th century). This dramatic homily, which usually paraphrases a Biblical narrative, comprises some 20 to 30 stanzas and was sung during the Morning Office in a simple and direct syllabic style. The earliest extant musical versions, however, are melismatic, belonging to the time (beginning in the 9th century) when the *kontakia* were reduced to the *prooimion* (introductory strophe) and the first *oikos* (stanza, lit. house).

In the second half of the 7th century, the *kontakion* was supplanted by a new type of hymn, the *kanōn* (rule), initiated by St. Andrew of Crete (ca. 660–ca. 740) and developed by Saints John of Damascus and Kosmas of Jerusalem (both 8th century). Essentially, the *kanōn* is a hymnodic complex comprising nine *ōdēs* that were originally attached to the nine Biblical canticles and related to these by means of corresponding poetic allusion or textual quotation. The nine canticles are: (1) and (2) the two songs of Moses (Exodus 15:1–19 and Deuteronomy 32:1–43); (3)–(7) the prayers of Hannah, Habbakuk, Isaiah, Jonah, and the

Three Children (I Kings [I Samuel] 2:1–10; Habbakuk 3:1–19; Isaiah 26:9–20; Jonah 2:3–10; Apoc. Daniel 3:26–56); (8) the song of the Three Children (Apoc. Daniel 3:57–88); (9) the Magnificat and Benedictus (Luke 1:46–55 and 68–79). Each ode consists of an initial model *troparion,* the **heirmos,* followed by three, four, or more *troparia* that are exact metrical reproductions of the *heirmos,* thereby allowing the same music to fit all *troparia* equally well. The nine *heirmoi,* however, are metrically dissimilar; consequently, an entire *kanōn* comprises nine independent melodies (eight, when *ōdē* 2 is omitted) that are united musically by the same mode and textually by references to the general theme of the liturgical occasion as well as sometimes by an acrostic. *Heirmoi* in syllabic style are gathered in the *Heirmologion,* a bulky volume that first appeared in the middle of the 10th century and may contain over a thousand model *troparia* arranged into an *oktoēchos.*

Another kind of hymn, important both for its number and for the variety of its liturgical uses, is the **sticheron.* Proper *stichera,* accompanying both the fixed Psalms at the beginning and end of Vespers and the psalmody of Lauds in the Morning Office, exist for all the feast days of the year, for the Sundays and weekdays of Lent, and for the recurrent cycle of eight weeks that begins with Easter and that employs the modes in order, one per week. Their melodies, preserved in the *Sticherarion,* are distinctly more elaborate and varied than those in the tradition of the *Heirmologion.* Nevertheless, all forms and styles of Byzantine chant, as exhibited in the early sources, are strongly formulaic in design. Only in the final period of the chant's development did new composers abandon this procedure in favor of the highly ornate *kalophonic* style. The most celebrated of these composers, and one entirely representative of the new school, was the *maistor* St. Joannes Koukouzeles (fl. ca. 1300), who organized the new chants into large anthologies [see *Akolouthia*]. This final phase of Byzantine musical activity provided the main thrust that was to survive throughout the Ottoman period and that continues to dominate the current tradition.

Bibl.: Henry J. W. Tillyard, *Handbook of the Middle Byzantine Notation, MMB,* subsidia 1 (Copenhagen: Levin & Munksgaard, 1935). Egon Wellesz, *Eastern Elements in Western Chant, MMB,* subsidia 2 (Boston: Byzantine Institute, 1947). Kenneth Levy, "The Byzantine Sanctus and Its Modal Tradition in East and West," *AnnM* 6 (1958–63): 7–67. Egon Wellesz, *A History of Byzantine Music and Hymnography* (Oxford: Clarendon Pr, 1949; 2nd ed., 1961; R: 1971). Kenneth Levy, "A Hymn for Thursday in Holy Week," *JAMS* 16 (1963): 127–75. Max Haas, *Byzantinische und slavische Notationen* (Cologne: A Volk, 1973). Miloš Velimirović, "Byzantine Chant," *NOHM* 2, no. 2 (1990): 26–68. Dimitri E. Conomos, *Byzantine Trisagia and Cheroubika of the Fourteenth and Fifteenth Centuries: A Study of Late Byzantine Liturgical Chant* (Thessalonika: Patriarchal Institute for Patristic Studies, 1974). Oliver Strunk, *Essays on Music in the Byzantine World* (New York: Norton, 1977). Dimitri E. Conomos, *The Late Byzantine and Slavonic Communion Cycle* (Washington, D.C.: Dumbarton Oaks Research Library, 1985).

D.E.C.

C

C. (1) See Pitch names, Letter notation, Hexachord, Pitch. (2) Abbr. for *con (col, colla),* with, as in **c.a.,* **c.b.,* **c.d.,* **c.o.,* **c.s.;* for *capo,* as in *D.C.* for **da capo;* in guitar music, for *ceja* or *cejilla* [see *Barré*]; for **cantus;* for *contralto. (3) In modern musical notation, a sign used to specify 4/4 meter. Though it is sometimes said to be an abbreviation for "common meter," it derives from the incomplete circle (C) used in *mensural notation to specify imperfect *tempus* with minor prolation.

C.a. [It.]. Abbr. for *col arco,* with the bow.

Cabaça [Port.]. An Afro-Brazilian *rattle consisting of a small gourd covered with a loose network of strung beads. It is held by a handle and shaken with a rotating motion. See ill. under Percussion instruments.

Cabaletta [It.]. In 19th-century Italian opera, the concluding portion of an aria or a duet with several sections. Cabalettas are usually in a rapid, audience-rousing tempo with regular phrase structure. The usual order in the operas of Rossini, Bellini, Donizetti, and their contemporaries (including Verdi through the 1850s) is orchestral introduction; vocal statement; orchestral or orchestral and choral interlude; literal repetition of vocal statement; coda in faster tempo.

Caça [Sp.]. **Chace.*

Caccia [It., hunt]. An Italian poetic and musical genre of the 14th and early 15th centuries. The texts usually deal with hunting scenes or with similar realistic subjects (e.g., a fire, cries of street vendors, market scenes), often in dialogue. Most of the 25 surviving musical works have two texted upper voices in canon and a textless (and hence presumably instrumental) tenor that does not participate in the canon. *Cacce* often conclude with a similarly constructed ritornello or refrain. *Madrigal texts set to music in this way are sometimes called canonic madrigals. Composers of *cacce* include Magister Piero, Giovanni da Cascia, Gherardello da Firenze, Jacopo da Bologna, and Francesco Landini. See also *Chace.*

Bibl.: Nino Pirrotta, "Per l'origine e la storia della 'caccia' e del 'madrigale' trecentesco," *RMI* 48 (1946): 305–23, 49 (1947): 121–42. W. Thomas Marrocco, ed., *Fourteenth-Century Italian Cacce,* rev. ed. (Cambridge, Mass.: Mediaeval Acad, 1961). Kosaku Toguchi, "Sulla struttura e l'esecuzione di alcune cacce italiane: Un cenno sulle origini delle cacce arsnovistiche," *Certaldo,* 1969, pp. 67–81. Virginia Newes, "Chace, Caccia, Fuga: The Convergence of French and Italian Traditions," *MD* 51 (1987): 27–57.See also *Ars nova.*

Cachua, kashua, quashwa. A courtship circle-dance of the Aymara Indians of Bolivia and Peru, one of several genres traditionally performed by large ensembles consisting variously of panpipes *(sicus),* notched and fipple flutes (*quenas, pincullos,* etc.), and drums *(bombo, tambor, caja).* In one characteristic practice, amorous verses are sung by groups of male and female vocalists in alternation, accompanied by an ensemble of *pincullos* playing in rhythmic unison and often in parallel fifths and octaves and by a continuous drum roll.

D.S.

Cachucha [Sp.]. A popular dance of Andalusia in triple meter, related to the **fandango.* Fanny Elssler included an example in the ballet *Le diable boiteux* (1836).

Cadence. (1) [Fr.] In the 17th and 18th centuries, *trill.

(2) [Fr. *cadence;* Ger. *Kadenz, Schluss;* It. *cadenza;* Sp. *cadencia*] A melodic or harmonic configuration that creates a sense of repose or resolution. Cadences thus most often mark the end of a phrase, period, or complete composition. The strength or finality of cadences varies considerably, however. In all cases, the effect of the cadence derives from the musical context and the conventions associated with it. The cadences of Western tonal music [see Tonality] are usually classified through the *harmonic analysis of their constituent elements and, to a lesser extent, according to the voice leading of the highest and lowest parts. The names that have been assigned to these cadences are for the most part an accumulation of historical accidents. Cadences are the principal means by which tonal music projects the sense of one pitch as a central or tonic pitch in a passage or work.

I. *Tonal music.* The strongest cadence in tonal music is the progression from the dominant harmony to the tonic harmony, V–I, and is termed an authentic cadence [Ex. 1]. Other terms for the authentic cadence are final cadence, full cadence, and full close [Fr. *cadence parfaite, c. authentique;* Ger. *Ganzschluss, authentische Kadenz, vollkommene K.;* It. *cadenza perfetta;* Sp. *cadencia perfecta*]. The force of this cadence derives in large measure from the presence in the dominant harmony of the supertonic and the leading tone [see Scale degrees], both of which have functioned historically as tending toward the tonic pitch. This cadence is a microcosm of the tonal system and is the most direct means of establishing a pitch as tonic. It is virtually obligatory as the final structural cadence of a tonal work. When a seventh is added to the dominant harmony, the result is a dominant seventh cadence, V^7–I [Ex. 2].

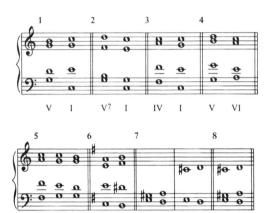

The progression IV–I is termed a plagal cadence [Ex. 3; Fr. *cadence plagale;* Ger. *plagale Kadenz, unvollkommene K., Kirchenschluss;* It. *cadenza plagale;* Sp. *cadencia plagal*]. Because it is sung to the word amen at the conclusion of Protestant hymns, it is also termed an amen cadence. As at the conclusion of hymns, it often follows immediately on an authentic cadence and is interpreted in this context as elaborating or prolonging the tonic harmony by means of neighboring-tone motions to the sixth and fourth scale degrees from the fifth and third, respectively.

A deceptive cadence (also termed interrupted) is one in which the dominant is followed by a harmony other than the tonic, most often VI [Ex. 4], but sometimes IV or some other harmony instead [Fr. *cadence interrompue, c. évitée;* Ger. *Trugschluss;* It. *cadenza evitata, c. d'inganno;* Sp. *cadencia evitada, c. interrumpida*]. In the great majority of deceptive cadences, the leading tone in V resolves normally to the tonic pitch, which is contained in the following chord (V–VI, V–IV, V–V^7/♭II, etc.), but is harmonized as the third or fifth of the chord rather than as the root. Such cadences can serve to establish or maintain clearly the identity of the tonic while avoiding full closure on the tonic harmony itself.

A half cadence (also termed a half close or an imperfect cadence) ends on the dominant [Ex. 5; Fr. *demi-cadence, cadence suspendue;* Ger. *Halbschluss;* It. *cadenza imperfetta, c. sospesa;* Sp. *semicadencia, cadencia suspendida*]. The dominant is most often preceded by the tonic. The dominant frequently follows a six-four chord with the same bass note, the so-called cadential tonic six-four. When the dominant is preceded by its own dominant [see Tonicization], a half cadence, in which the final harmony must be heard as the dominant, may be difficult to distinguish from a cadence that effects a modulation to the dominant, which is then heard as the local tonic. The half cadence is frequently encountered at the conclusion of the first part of shorter pieces in *binary form.

In the context of tonal music, a Phrygian cadence is one in which the root of the final chord is approached from a semitone above, most often in the form IV^6–V in minor [Ex. 6]. A Phrygian cadence is thus a type of half cadence, concluding as it does on the dominant. It is a characteristic gesture of Baroque music and often concludes a slow movement that is to be followed immediately by a faster one.

In terms of voice leading, authentic and plagal cadences are termed perfect if both harmonies are in root position and the tonic pitch is sounded in the uppermost voice; otherwise they are imperfect. If one or both harmonies is sounded in inversion rather than root position, a cadence may be termed medial or inverted rather than radical [fr. Lat. *radix,* root].

II. *History.* In Western monophonic music, the final [see Mode] or tonic pitch is very often approached by step from above. In Gregorian chant, for example, this is the most common type of cadence, followed in frequency by the approach from the third above. Motion from below the final proceeds most often from the step below, though it rarely occurs in the form of the semitone from E to F. In polyphonic music, the 13th century saw the emergence of those elements that make up the familiar cadences of tonal music. Principal among these is the approach to a perfect consonance (either perfect fifth or perfect octave) by stepwise contrary motion in two voices, one voice moving a whole tone, the other a semitone. Thus, for example, a major third expands to a perfect fifth and a major sixth to an octave [Ex. 7]. In three-voice music of the 14th century, these two may be combined in the most characteristic cadence of the period [Ex. 8]. Since in this example, both the fifth and the octave are approached by semitone from below, this cadence is sometimes termed the double leading-tone cadence. Because these semitone relationships occur naturally in the Lydian mode with final on F, it is also termed a Lydian cadence. If some other pitch is the final or cadential goal, accidentals are required, though they may not be explicitly notated in contemporaneous sources [see *Musica ficta*]. The same principles also apply in the Phrygian cadence, however, in which the lowest voice moves down a semitone and the upper two upward by a whole tone [Ex. 9]. This occurs naturally in the Phrygian mode with final on E and by means of accidentals on other pitches. When combined with motion in the uppermost part to the sixth scale degree above the cadential goal [Ex. 10], the double leading-tone cadence is sometimes termed a Landini cadence, after Francesco Landini (ca. 1325–97), in whose music it occurs frequently. Cadences of this general type, often including motion to the sixth in one form or another, remained prominent through the 15th century.

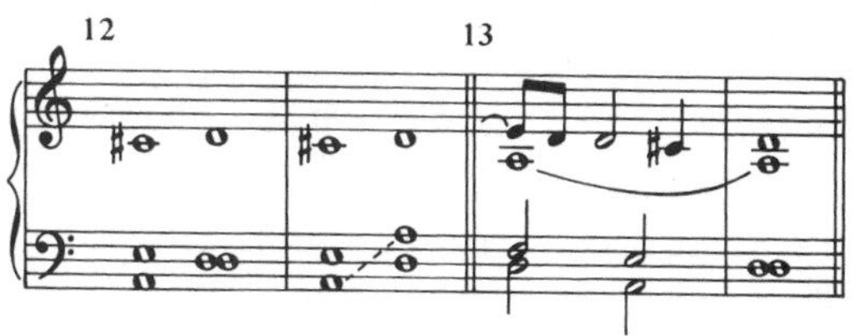

The form given in Ex. 11 is sometimes termed Burgundian because of its regular occurrence in the so-called Burgundian chanson of the middle and late 15th century. In this three-voice cadence, the stepwise descent to the cadential goal occurs in the tenor and the ascent to its octave in the uppermost part. If the penultimate simultaneity is to be wholly consonant, the third voice must sound either the third above the tenor or the fifth below. The latter, followed by a leap up a fourth to the cadential goal or up an octave to the fifth [Ex. 12], begins to occur regularly in music of the second half of the 15th century at about the same time that four-voice texture begins to be the norm in sacred music. In four-voice texture, harmonization of the sixth to octave progression with the fifth below the tenor is the only practical alternative if the fourth voice is to avoid parallel fifths or octaves or the awkward voice leading that would result from the doubling of one of the two leading tones or of the supertonic of the double leading-tone cadence. The harmonization with the fifth below the tenor in either three or four voices of course results in a cadence identical in structure to the V–I of tonal harmony, but through the end of the 16th century, theorists such as Gioseffo Zarlino continue to describe it as deriving from the combination of pairs of voices, one of which is the soprano and tenor pair moving from a major sixth to an octave. Only with the advent of the *thoroughbass in the 17th century and the development of harmonic theory by Rameau and others in the 18th does this cadence come to be understood as arising from the root motion V–I in the bass.

Although this basic cadential structure remains at the heart of Western polyphony from the late 15th century through all of tonal music up to the present, it has been elaborated and ornamented in a variety of ways. Until about 1500, the final sonority, at least at the conclusion of pieces or major sections of them, was made up only of perfect consonances, omitting the third. From the 16th century through much of the 18th, the third of the final sonority was always made major regardless of the prevailing mode [see Picardy third]. In the 16th century, this cadence is often introduced by means of a suspension [Ex. 13]. In the 17th and 18th, an anticipation is common [Ex. 14], the supertonic often being ornamented with a trill. The combination of suspension and anticipation in two voices produces a dissonant succession termed a Corelli clash [Ex. 15]. The *cadenza of the Classical concerto is an elaboration of the cadence I^6_4–V–I.

In music of the 19th century, quite dense harmonies often occur within the framework of a V–I progression as a result of more elaborate suspensions or rhythmic displacements. In Ex. 16 (Chopin, Prelude op. 28 no. 20), the E♭ that is attacked with the dominant seventh on G is in effect suspended from the submediant (A♭) of the first beat. In Ex. 17 (Brahms, Intermezzo op. 119 no. 1), a suspension results in a dominant ninth chord, which is itself suspended over its resolution in the bass, producing briefly a chord of seven different pitches.

Some works of the 20th century exploit traditional voice-leading procedures in the context of an expanded tonality or modality [Ex. 18, Hindemith, *Sonate für Klavier,* 1936]. In works that largely abandon tonality but that project a single or a few pitches as central, cadential gestures may rely on traditional rhythmic and melodic elements, such as a weak beat followed by a strong beat and descending stepwise motion, while avoiding the traditional harmonic elements, as in the first movement of Bartók's String Quartet no. 4 [Ex. 19]. Some *serial works that strive for a continuous unfolding of texture may avoid cadential gestures altogether, however, as may works in which *texture or sonority (broadly defined) are the principal compositional elements. In much jazz and popular music, traditional tonal functions are retained but with characteristic substitutions and additions, e.g., the substitution of a seventh, ninth, or more complex chord on the lowered supertonic for the dominant and the addition of a major seventh or ninth above the tonic in the final tonic harmony [Ex. 20].

Bibl.: Alfredo Casella, *L'evoluzione della musica a traverso la storia della cadenza perfetta* [parallel texts in It., Fr., Eng.] (London: J & W Chester, 1924; rev. 2nd ed., 1964). Robert W. Wienpahl, "The Evolutionary Significance of 15th-Century Cadential Formulae," *JMT* 4 (1960): 131–52. Don M. Randel, "Emerging Triadic Tonality in the Fifteenth Century," *MQ* 57 (1971): 73–86. Margaret Bent, "The Grammar of Early Music: Preconditions for Analysis," *Tonal Structures in Early Music,* ed. Cristle Collins Judd (New York: Garland, 1998), pp. 15–59. See also Counterpoint.

Cadent. In 17th-century England, a falling note of anticipation, indicated by a line slanting down toward the note to be anticipated (Christopher Simpson, 1659) [see *Nachschlag*].

Cadenza [It., cadence]. In music for soloist, especially a *concerto or other work with accompanying ensemble, an improvised or written-out ornamental passage performed by the soloist, usually over the penultimate or antepenultimate note or harmony of a prominent cadence. During a cadenza the accompaniment either pauses or sustains a pitch or a chord.

Although a cadenza may occur elsewhere, it most typically ornaments a prominent tonic cadence, such as one before a final *ritornello or *coda. If improvised, it may be indicated by a *fermata in all parts, as in the accompanying example from Mozart's Piano Concerto in B♭ major K. 595, first movement. Here the cadenza should commence with the righthand b♭′, continue at the pianist's discretion, and conclude with a trill and chord, as written, to signal the orchestra's reentry. This is typical of the principal cadenza in the Classical concerto in being an elaboration of the progression from the tonic second-inversion or six-four chord, on which the orchestra pauses, to the dominant, the conclusion of which is often marked by a trill by the soloist, to the tonic, with which the orchestra reenters to begin the coda. An *Eingang* is a passage of similar character but smaller dimensions that introduces a section of a work, such as the recurring material in rondo form. If improvised, it may be indicated by a fermata over a dominant seventh chord.

From early times, soloists have optionally embellished final cadences. Theorists of *discant in the 12th through the 14th century, including Franco of Cologne, Jehan des Murs, and Jacques de Liège, attest that a discanting voice might perform an unmeasured point of *organum over the penultimate cadential note of a *cantus.* Places for improvised melismas within a piece of discant or polyphony might bear a fermata over the appropriate note in each voice, as in the medieval *cantus coronatus* and certain works of Dufay.

Sixteenth-century theorists of polyphony discussed cadential embellishments, which the Italians Pietro Aaron (1523) and Sylvestro di Ganassi (1535) for the first time called cadenzas. Rather than being rhythmically free, they consisted of *divisions that implied a preservation, if slackening, of tempo. In 1585, Giovanni Bassano published a collection of written-out *cadentie* to be inserted in certain formulaic cadences, deriving from an instrumental style of the late Renaissance. In contrast, the cadenza in Monteverdi's embellished version of the aria "Possente spirto" from *Orfeo* (1607) reflects a vocal style of ornamentation devised by contemporary composers of *monody.

Virtuosic cadenzas gained importance in the Baroque era. Corelli notated cadenzas in the first *allegro* movements of his Violin Sonatas op. 5 nos. 1, 3, and 5; Torelli, Vivaldi, and J. S. Bach occasionally wrote them out in concertos. Italian opera singers placed cadenzas at any of the three vocal cadences in the

Cadenza.

standard three-part *aria, particularly the last. Some unaccompanied music contained written-out cadenzas, e.g., keyboard works of J. S. Bach, Domenico Scarlatti, and, later, Mozart and Beethoven. The standard cadential progression expanded from V–I to I^6_4–V–I (as in the example), thereby strengthening the cadenza's harmonic thrust. C. P. E. Bach and Johann Joachim Quantz discussed the improvisation of cadenzas at length in their treatises on performance.

As cadenzas became more elaborate, their thematic reference to the composition increased. This occurred in the later works of Mozart, who wrote optional cadenzas to many of his concertos for friends and students. Beethoven integrated obligatory cadenzas in his Piano Concerto no. 5. In the 19th century, obligatory cadenzas, often placed in unorthodox positions, became a common feature of vocal and instrumental music, notably in piano works of Chopin and Liszt and the later operas of Verdi. Beethoven, Brahms, and others wrote out cadenzas to earlier composers' concertos, often in anachronistic style. Performers today generally use cadenzas already composed for the standard repertory, though some create their own.

Bibl.: Paul Mies, *Die Krise der Konzertkadenz bei Beethoven* (Bonn: Bouvier, 1970). Id., *Das Konzert im 19. Jahrhundert: Studien zu Formen und Kadenzen* (Bonn: Bouvier, 1972). Charles W. Warren, "Punctus Organi and Cantus Coronatus in the Music of Dufay," *Dufay,* 1974, pp. 128–43. David Lasocki and Betty Bang Mather, *The Classical Woodwind Cadenza: A Workbook* (New York: McGinnis & Marx, 1978). Howard Mayer Brown, "Embellishing Eighteenth-Century Arias: On Cadenzas," in *Opera and Vivaldi,* ed. Michael Collins and Elise K. Kirk (Austin: U of Tex Pr, 1984), pp. 258–76. Joseph S. Swain, "Form and Function of the Classical Cadenza," *JM* 6 (1988): 27–59. Eduard Melkus, "On the Problem of Cadenzas in Mozart's Violin Concertos," in *Perspectives on Mozart Performance,* ed. R. Larry Todd and Peter Williams (Cambridge: Cambridge U Pr, 1991). Christoph Wolff, "Cadenzas and Styles of Improvisation in Mozart's Piano Concertos," in *Perspectives on Mozart Performance,* pp. 228–38. Philip Whitmore, *Upremeditated Art: The Cadenza in the Classical Keyboard Concerto* (Oxford: Clarendon, 1991). Eva Badura-Skoda, "On Improvised Embellishments and Cadenzas in Mozart's Piano Concertos," in *Mozart's Piano Concertos: Text, Context, Interpretation,* ed. Neal Zaslaw (Ann Arbor: U of Mich Pr, 1996), pp. 365–72.

Cadenzato [It.]. Rhythmical.

Cadereta [Sp.]. A keyboard division of the classic Spanish organ, often with a case behind the player *(exterior)* containing high-pitched stops and an additional chest in the main case *(interior)* for lower-pitched stops.

Caesura [Fr. *césure;* Ger. *Zäsur;* It., Sp. *cesura*]. (1) In modern prosody, a pause or interruption occurring within a line of poetry, usually coinciding with the end of a word and sometimes marked by punctuation. (2) The boundary between two musical phrases, sometimes, but by no means always, marked by a rest or by a breathing *pause (indicated with an apostrophe above the staff).

Caisse [Fr.]. Drum.

Caja [Sp.]. Any of a variety of two-headed drums of Spain and Latin America. They are most often played with sticks and are sometimes struck on the frame as well as the heads.

Cajun. See Zydeco.

Cakewalk. (1) A dance originating among plantation slaves in the 1840s as a strutting promenade mocking the owner's manners. It became a commercial entertainment in the 1890s and an international hit in social dancing in the period 1898–1903. (2) During the period in which the dance of the same name was popular, a multithematic instrumental march with syncopated melodic rhythms, the simplest of which became a trademark: ♪ ♩ ♪ in 2/4. Cakewalks formed a subgenre of *ragtime and American marching band repertories.

Bibl.: Brooke Baldwin, "The Cakewalk: A Study in Stereotype and Reality," *Journal of Social History* 15 (1981): 205–18. B.K.

Calamus [Lat.]. (1) In Classical Latin poetry, the **tibia* or the **syrinx.* (2) In the Middle Ages, a *shawm.

Calando [It.]. Decreasing in loudness and often also in tempo.

Calata [It.]. An Italian dance of the early 16th century known only by 13 examples in Joan Ambrosio Dalza's *Intabulatura de Lauto* (1508). Because the tablature does not include choreographies, the style of the dance cannot be defined. The meters suggest, however, that for the *calata* Dalza was following the patterns of the *bassadanza* [see *Basse danse*]. Two of the dances are in a 3/2 meter reminiscent of the *bassadanza* proper. Two are in an unequivocal 3/4 meter that might stem from the **quaternaria.* Seven are in a 6/8 meter (with interspersed hemiolas) typical of the **saltarello.* And two are in the 12/8 meter of a **piva.* L.H.M.

Calcant [Ger.]. See *Kalkant.*

Calenda, kalinda. See Calypso.

Calendric Song. A song associated with a particular time of year (harvest, planting, solstice, equinox) or the life cycle (birth, puberty, marriage). Calendric functions are among the most widespread and oldest in folk music. B.N.

Call and response. Sometimes overlapping alternation between two performers or groups of performers, especially between a solo singer and a group of singers. Diverse African-derived musics, including 20th-century popular styles in the U.S., the Caribbean, and Latin America, employ such exchanges between a lead singer's or instrumentalist's improvisations and a group's recurring responses. African American popular musics adapt it, for example, in interplays between a blues or rock singer and a guitar, two sections of a jazz ensemble, or a soul singer and an audience. Many scholars see this practice as evidence of conceptual links among the musics of the African diaspora.

B.K., rev. T.A.J.

Calliope [the Muse of epic poetry]. An instrument consisting of tuned steam whistles played from a keyboard or operated by a barrel-and-pin mechanism. A patent for such an instrument with this name was granted to Joshua C. Stoddard of Worcester, Mass., in 1855, and it soon thereafter became a feature of showboats, carnivals, and circuses, with which it is still associated. The extraordinary loudness of which it is capable is intended to attract spectators from considerable distances.

Callithump. *Charivari.

Calmando, calmato [It.]. Becoming calm, quiet.

Calm Sea and Prosperous Voyage. See *Meeresstille und glückliche Fahrt.*

Calore, con; caloroso [It.]. With warmth, passionately.

Calypso. A song style of Trinidad, also established in Jamaica and elsewhere in the Caribbean. Calypso is most distinctive in its texts, which are topical in subject matter—wry and witty commentaries on social conditions, events, and personalities. Calypso singer-composers are specialists esteemed for their verse-making ability, colorful figures with grandiose names (Lord Executor, Atilla the Hun, Mighty Sparrow), frequently enjoying national and sometimes international recognition. Calypso is intimately associated with Carnival; annually, new calypso texts are composed, often set to preexisting calypso melodies, and performed by calypsonians in temporary theaters or "tents" for several weeks prior to Lent as well as in the street parades of Carnival itself.

The principal antecedent of calypso is found in the *kalindas,* which were quarterstaff duels involving processions of fighters that were accompanied by bands of their supporters. The supporters carried African-derived percussion instruments and were led by singers *(chantuelles, shantwells)* skilled at making verses that praised their champions and insulted their opponents. *Kalindas* became a prominent part of Carnival celebrations after the emancipation of the slaves in Trinidad in 1834. Even though modern calypso performance by singers with small, conventional dance bands is common, the traditional percussion accompaniment of older calypsos and *kalindas* remains important and today is most characteristically performed by steel bands [see Steel drum], which were established in Trinidad in the 1940s.

D.S.

Cambia, cambiano, cambiare [It.]. Change, to change, as when a player is instructed to change instruments or tuning. See also Muta.

Cambiata, nota cambiata [It.; Fr. *note de rechange;* Ger. *Wechselnote;* Sp. *nota cambiada*]. See Counterpoint II, 7.

Cambodia. See Southeast Asia V.

Camera [It.]. Chamber, as in *chamber music *(musica da camera).* In the Baroque period (ca. 1600–1750), the term identifies music intended for performance outside the church *(*chiesa),* especially the **concerto da camera* and the **sonata da camera.*

Camerata [It.]. An informal gathering, usually for the purposes of literary, philosophical, or artistic discussion. Specifically, a group of noblemen and musicians who met in the salon of Giovanni de' Bardi in Florence from ca. 1573 to ca. 1582 to discuss poetry, music, and other subjects. The only known participants are the noblemen Bardi and Piero Strozzi, and the musicians Vincenzo Galilei and Giulio Caccini. The influence of the Camerata on the first operas (written in the 1590s) was of a general, indirect nature, and took the form of a desire to re-create the expressive power of ancient Greek music through a new manner of solo song and a belief that ancient Greek drama was sung throughout. These positions, advanced especially in Galilei's *Dialogo della musica antica, et della moderna* (1581), reflect the views of the philologist and antiquarian Girolamo Mei, the mentor of the Camerata.

Bibl.: Nino Pirrotta, "Temperaments and Tendencies in the Florentine Camerata," *MQ* 40 (1954): 169–89. Gary Tomlinson, "Rinuccini, Peri, Monteverdi, and the Humanist Heritage of Opera" (Ph.D. diss., Univ. of California, Berkeley, 1979), chap. 6. Claude V. Palisca, *The Florentine Camerata: Documentary Studies and Translations* (New Haven: Yale U Pr, 1989). Claude V. Palisca, *Studies in the History of Italian Music and Music Theory* (Oxford: Oxford U Pr, 1994).

G.A.T.

Camminando [It.]. Walking, moving along.

Campana [It., Lat., Sp.]. *Bell (1) (2).

Campane [It.]. *Tubular bells.

Campanelli [It.]. *Glockenspiel.

Campo aperto [Lat., open field]. *Neumes are said to be written *in campo aperto* if they are not written on a line or lines and are thus nondiastematic, i.e., imprecise with respect to pitch.

Can. [Lat.]. Abbr. for *cantoris.* See *Decani* and *cantoris.*

Canada. I. *General issues.* Canada's culture, like that of every Western Hemisphere country, coordinates aboriginal and colonial elements. Canada is one of only two countries bordering on the U.S., and the more prevalent of its two official languages is also the official language of the U.S. Its proximity to the U.S., added to Canada's vast size and small, sparsely distributed population, are often regarded as barriers to cultural distinctness. For example, recording, radio and television music, music publishing, and concert management are all areas dominated by U.S. agencies.

The term Canadian content arose in the wave of cultural nationalism just after WWII, denoting—in such bodies as the Canada Council for the Arts (founded 1957) and the Canadian Radio-Television Commission, or CRTC (founded 1967; renamed the Canadian Radio-Television and Telecommunications Commission 1976)—rules designed to assure a degree of homemade creative work in the music the agencies supported. The council's subsidies characteristically insisted on a certain measure of local repertoire or involvement by local artists, and the CRTC licensed only broadcasters who met minimum percentage levels under its definition of Canadian content.

II. *Contemporary musical life and institutions.* The postwar wave of nationalism established strong organizations in performance, education, research, and management. Among the country's 96 professional or semiprofessional orchestras in 2001–2002, 2 had annual budgets over $10 million, 2 over $7.5 million, another 4 over $5 million. Special mandates govern the classical-size National Arts Centre Orchestra, Ottawa, and the Tafelmusik Baroque Orchestra, Toronto; the former is supported by federal grants and the latter is widely known from its tours and recordings. From 1980 through 2001, almost all the major civic orchestras endured serious financial crises. The opera audience burgeoned in the 1990s and early 2000s, active companies being the Canadian Opera Company (Toronto), Vancouver Opera, Opéra de Montréal, Opéra de Québec, Manitoba Opera (Winnipeg), Edmonton Opera, and Pacific Opera Victoria. Thriving smaller groups include Opera Atelier and Tapestry Music Theatre (both in Toronto), the former devoted to Baroque and Classical pieces, the latter to new works by Canadian composers. Choral music, historically the main focus of Canadian social music making, continues to attract both participants and auditors in large numbers: variously sized professional and amateur ensembles are found in every city and town. The Association of Canadian Choral Conductors (begun 1980) had 600 members in 2002 and acts as liaison with the provincial choral federations. An emphasis on youth and children's choirs was notable in the last decades of the 20th century. The annual Canadian Broadcasting Corporation (CBC) radio competitions for eight categories of choirs afford the best amateur groups nationwide attention.

In 2000, the Canadian University Music Society (founded 1964) had a membership of approximately 40 university or college music departments. Conservatories include the long-established independent Royal Conservatory (Toronto), the provincially supported Conservatoire du Québec (Montreal, branches in six other centers), and smaller schools in London (Ontario), Calgary, Halifax, and elsewhere. The summer program of the Banff Centre plays a special role, offering symposia and master classes. The Canadian Music Centre (founded 1959; Toronto, regional offices in four other centers) provides scores, recordings, and research materials on works by Canadian composers, past and present. The largest holdings of papers of distinguished musicians are in the Music Division of the National Library of Canada (Ottawa). Member firms of the Canadian Record Industry Association (formed 1963 as the Canadian Record Manufacturers Association) produce 95 percent of sound recordings made and sold in Canada. In 1997–98, 15.2 percent of new releases were of Canadian content or by Canadian artists. National and international performing rights are administered by the Society of Composers, Authors, and Music Publishers of Canada (SOCAN).

III. *History, repertoire.* Any account of the musical repertoire initially must be almost entirely based on secondary sources. The earliest evidence from the myriad aboriginal communities are instruments in the archeological collections of museums in Victoria, Vancouver, Toronto, Ottawa, Montreal, and Quebec City, and descriptions in writings of explorers and travelers before 1800, some of which contain notation. Two musical numbers constituting the score of *Le Théâtre de Neptune,* a masque enacted by settlers and aboriginals at Port Royal in 1606, possibly the earliest composed art-music pieces, are lost. The 17th-century carol "Jesous Ahatonhia," a French popular melody with Huron text, exemplifies the use of music as a teaching tool by Christian missionaries of the period. A Quebec-born priest, Charles-Amador Martin, is the likely composer of a late-17th-century plainchant sequence, the first surviving original work. Manuscripts preserved from the 18th century cover a wider gamut: a theory manual compiled in 1718; motets of the same period, some perhaps locally composed; a collection of 398 compositions for organ solo (16 identified as by Nicolas Lebègue, the rest anonymous), discovered in 1978 and dubbed the *Livre d'orgue de Montréal;* a *Cahier de contre-danses* dated 1768; and other dance-music collections. Starting in 1771 the elaborate musical program of the Moravian mission at Nain, serving the Inuit of Labrador—including a large repertoire of traditional chorales as well as choruses by Mozart and Haydn—continued uninterrupted into the late 20th century.

Growing cities—Quebec City, Halifax—began in the late eighteenth century to cultivate European musical features such as home chamber music and public concerts. The German-born bandsman Frédéric-Henri Glackemeyer, at Quebec City, led a busy life as performer, teacher, composer, and dealer in instruments and sheet music, typical of many urban musicians well into the 19th century. Music publishing began in 1800 with the church-music volume *Le Graduel romain,* and the first decades of the 19th century produced Protestant tune books in several regions of the country, paralleling the contemporaneous U.S. compilations in format and often also in repertoire. Original published items by immigrant composers (Antoine Dessane from France, J. P. Clarke from Scotland) tended to be short choruses, piano solos (variations, dances), or songs. The early published legacy is well represented in the anthology series *The Canadian Musical Heritage.*

Grand-opera touring and local operatic performances took place regularly from 1841 on, but none of the early composers cultivated the form. There is, however, a steady history of original light operas, from *Colas et Colinette* (1790, words and music by Joseph Quesnel—the first stage work with music in North America) to *Le Fétiche* (Joseph Vézina, 1912). Another contributor in this genre was the outstanding composer of the period, Calixa Lavallée, who departed for the U.S. in 1880, ironically after writing his best-known song, now the country's national anthem, "O Canada." The favored large-scale musical form was not opera but cantata or oratorio, and the years 1880–1920 produced examples by Alexis Contant, Guillaume Couture, Charles A. E. Harriss, and others.

In many regions during the first half of the 20th century the professional leaders were organist-choirmasters, immigrants from Britain, and often prolific composers of choral music (Alfred Whitehead) or in larger genres as well (Healey Willan). The best-known figure, (Sir) Ernest MacMillan, though born in Canada, had a British formation and outlook; a gifted composer in his early career, he later concentrated on conducting. Early echoes of international modernism are discerned in the writings of the composer-critic Léo-Pol Morin and in the music of Rodolphe Mathieu, a disciple of Scriabin. But it was with the maturing of composers born in the years 1910–20 that the full impact of new music was felt. Violet Archer, Barbara Pentland, John Weinzweig, and Jean Papineau-Couture broke with their mentors not only in style but also in attitude, studying in North America rather than in Europe, and composing as professionals rather than as a sideline—though all became influential teachers.

The post-WWII period favored new directions, as Canada Council study grants and CBC commissions created a fresh climate for composers (Harry Somers, Pierre Mercure, Serge Garant, R. Murray Schafer, Gilles Tremblay) and brought their music to international notice. Newcomers from Europe—often war refugees—added to the richness of these times (Oskar Morawetz, Otto Joachim, István Anhalt, Talivaldis Kenins, Udo Kasemets). Results ranged from Somers's deliberate Canadianism (historical subjects, folk quotations) and the site-specific outdoor music-theater works of Schafer to Bruce Mather's delicate microtonalism. Studios for electro-acoustic music flourished in all major centers beginning around 1960. At this period also, recalling the worldwide success of the Canadian-born soprano Emma Albani at the turn of the century, several Canadian performers rose to sensational careers, notably the opera singers Jon Vickers and Teresa Stratas and the pianist Glenn Gould.

Public responsibility for culture and art slackened in the succeeding era; this is sometimes cited as a reason for the late-20th-century call for "accessibility." From the late 1960s on, work of younger composers—not all of it accessible in the desired sense—was fostered by the rise of local societies for new-music performance in the larger cities. Among the main talents are Chan Ka-Nin, Henry Kucharzyk, Alexina Louie, Denys Bouliane, Linda Bouchard, Linda C. Smith, Rodney Sharman, and James Rolfe.

IV. *Traditional and popular music.* Amerindian and Inuit musics in Canada continue to exhibit adaptations from the settler cultures—phrases of hymns and ballads in the 19th century, latterly the contours of rock and country; the reverse influence occurs far more rarely. Scholars observe since 1980 a marked resurgence of traditional ceremonial music. The collections of the Canadian Museum of Civilization (Hull, Quebec) and other institutions preserve tens of thousands of recordings and transcriptions not only of aboriginal music but also of aurally transmitted pieces from colonial and immigrant communities: the Anglo-Celtic repertoires of Atlantic Canada and Ontario; the vast francophone song repertoire of Quebec; Ukrainian, Czech, and Hungarian songs from the Prairies; and more lately music of Japanese-Canadians, Caribbean-Canadians, and others. In Atlantic and central Canada, as well as among the Métis of the Great Plains, a fiddling tradition thrives in recordings and annual competitions.

Montreal has produced a succession of outstanding jazz performers, from Willie Eckstein in the 1920s to Oscar Peterson in the later 20th century. Popular songwriting has shown steady vitality through recording and publishing since the mid-19th century, with many notable hits. The *Canadian Musical Heritage* volumes illustrate the frequent connection of these with topical events and values. The *chansonnier* movement of the 1950s and 1960s, with singer-composers such as Félix Leclerc, Gilles Vigneault, and Robert Charlebois, gave effective expression to the sentiments of francophone Canadians in a period of decisive political change. Among performer-writers of the later 20th century, Neil Young, k.d. lang, and Céline Dion dominated pop charts both at home and abroad.

Bibl.: Helmut Kallmann, *A History of Music in Canada, 1534–1914* (Toronto: U of Toronto Pr, 1960). *The Canadian Musical Heritage / Le Patrimoine musical canadien,* 25 vols. (Ottawa: Canadian Musical Heritage Society, 1983–99). Marie-Thérèse Lefebvre, *La Création musicale des femmes au Québec* (Montreal: Les Éditions du remue-ménage, 1991). Helmut Kallmann and Gilles Potvin, eds., *Encyclopedia of Music in Canada,* 2nd ed. (Toronto: U of Toronto Pr, 1992). Beverley Diamond and Robert Witmer, eds., *Canadian Music: Issues of Hegemony and Identity* (Toronto: Canadian Scholars' Pr, 1994). Carl Morey, *Music in Canada: A Research and Information Guide* (New York: Garland, 1997). Ellen Koskoff, ed., *Garland Encyclopedia of World Music,* vol. 3: *The United States and Canada* (New York: Garland, 2001). J.Be., K.McM.

Canarie [Fr.; Eng. canary; It., Sp. *canario*]. A very fast Baroque dance movement in duple-compound or triple meter, a fast and heavily accented French *gigue in style. It sometimes begins with an upbeat and has a dotted note on most strong beats, with regular four-measure phrases and little counterpoint. It was particularly popular in French stage and harpsichord music (Lully, Louis and François Couperin), as well as in German *suites for orchestra or harpsichord (Georg Muffat, J. C. F. Fischer, Telemann). The dance originated in the Canary Islands and was characterized by jumping and foot stamping. By the 16th century, it was known in Spain with more than one set of musical characteristics. As it spread to France and then across Europe, its music became standardized in style, but it retained connotations of the exotic and primitive that are sometimes reflected as syncopations. B.G.

Cancan [Fr.]. A French dance of the 19th century in a fast duple meter and derived from the *quadrille. It is most characteristically danced by a line of female dancers in full skirts and ruffled petticoats, with much kicking and thus exposure of the legs. The most celebrated example is in Offenbach's **Orphée aux enfers* (1874).

Cancel. A device for disconnecting all stops and couplers, found on electric-action organs.

Canción [Sp.]. (1) Song. (2) In the 15th and early 16th centuries, a type of **villancico.* (3) After about 1530, a type of Spanish poem, largely derived from Italian models (particularly the **canzone* stanza), in which 7- and 11-syllable lines alternate freely and which makes use of freely invented rhyme schemes; also a musical setting of such a poem.

Cancionero [Sp., fr. *canción,* song]. A collection of lyric poems, often poems intended for singing, and sometimes including music. In the history of music, the term is often specifically applied to collections of Spanish secular polyphony from the 15th through the early 17th centuries [see also *Romance* (1), *Villancico*].

Cancrizans [Lat., crabwise]. *Retrograde.

Candomblé. In the Bahian region of Brazil, any of various religious groups with beliefs derived from those of West Africa, sometimes including Christian elements. The term may also refer to the place of such a group's or cult's activities and to the specifically musical public ceremony that is also termed *xirê* and includes a series of songs and dances. Drums termed **atabaques* play a prominent role, including the summoning of the gods. Similar ceremonies in other parts of Brazil include the *macumba* of Guanabara.

Bibl.: Gerard Béhague, "Patterns of *Candomblé* Music Performance: An Afro-Brazilian Religious Setting," in Gerard Béhague, ed., *Performance Practice: Ethnomusicological Perspectives* (Westport, Conn.: Greenwood Pr, 1984), pp. 222–54.

Canntaireachd [Gael.]. The notation used for a *pibroch.

Canon [Lat.; fr. Gr. *kanōn,* rule, precept]. (1) The *monochord of ancient Greece, used for acoustical experiments, not for music making. (2) In medieval Europe, a *psaltery. See also *Qānūn.* (3) In the Roman Catholic Mass, the prayer consecrating the elements of communion, said immediately following the Sanctus. (4) A rule or instruction for realizing a composition. In the Middle Ages and Renaissance, such rules were sometimes stated in cryptic fashion and might entail a variety of ways of interpreting a composition's notation, only one of which is the strict form of imitation with which the term has since come to be almost exclusively associated [see (5) below].

(5) Imitation of a complete subject by one or more voices at fixed intervals of pitch and time. If each successive following voice *(comes)* follows the leading voice *(dux)* in every detail, the canon is strict; if, however, the *comes* modifies the *dux* by minor changes in accidentals, the canon is free. Originally, canon referred to the verbal motto or rule by which the *comes* could be derived from the *dux.* In such cases only the *dux* would be notated. Canons may be self-contained entities or may occur within larger pieces (canonic imitation). They may also be combined with independent lines (mixed or accompanied canons) or even with other canons (group or compound canons). In the simple two-part canon of Ex. 1, Bach wrote the *dux* on a single staff and marked the entry of the *comes* with a sign (*signum congruentiae* or *presa*).

I. *Types.* Canons are usually classified on the basis of the following elements.

1. The time between entries—*canon ad minimam* (at the half note), *ad semibrevem* (at the whole note), etc.

2. The interval between entries—*canon ad unisonum* (at the unison), *ad epidiapente* (at the fifth above). For example, Bach's *Goldberg Variations* (BWV 988) include nine canons at increasing intervals from a unison to a ninth, and the fifth of Bach's *Canonic Variations on Vom Himmel hoch* (BWV 769) contains four canons by inversion on the chorale theme at the sixth, third, second, and ninth [see Ex. 2].

3. Transformations of the subject, as follows: (a) Inversion (*canon per motu contrario, per arsin et thesin* [see also Arsis and thesis]), in which the *comes* imi-

tates the *dux* upside down [Ex. 2]. (b) Retrograde (*canon cancrizans, al rovescio,* crab canon), in which the *comes* gives the *dux* backward [Ex. 3]. (c) Retrograde inversion *(canon al contrario riverso),* in which the *comes* gives the *dux* upside down and backward. (d) Augmentation, in which the note-values of the *comes* are longer by a fixed ratio. (e) Diminution, in which the note-values of the *comes* are shorter [Ex. 4]. (f) A mensuration canon is one in which the *dux* is interpreted simultaneously in different mensurations or *proportions [see also Mensural notation], with the result that the temporal relationship between the voices may shift because of the different interpretation of individual note-values [see II below].

4. Ending. Finite canons have a definite ending that may either add notes to the *dux* to make up the time lag between the first and last entries or perhaps add a short coda; infinite canons (perpetual canon, circle canon, *round, **rota*) lead straight back to the beginning with an arbitrary ending shown by a fermata *(corona).* In the case of the modulating canon (spiral canon), the *dux* ends in a key different from the one in which it begins; a specific case is the *canon per tonos,* in which the *dux* ends in a key a whole tone higher than the key in which it begins, returning to the original key only after six statements, as in the example in Bach's *Musical Offering* (BWV 1079).

5. Number of canons. Canons combined with other canons (group or compound canons) are indicated by the number of canons (double canon has two, triple canon has three, etc.) and by the number of parts. A two-part double canon has four parts and is thus a canon "four-in-two" [Ex. 5].

Canons are also described in other ways. The term mirror canon normally refers to canons by inversion but may also denote canons by retrograde or retrograde inversion. Canons that are fully transcribed are said to be resolved canons whereas those that must be deciphered (i.e., in which only the *dux* is written out) are unresolved. Unresolved canons inscribed with cryptic instructions for resolution are called riddle or enigmatic canons [see II below]. If a canon is capable of more than one solution it is termed polymorphous. Accompaniments to mixed canons may be based on freely composed melodies (*Goldberg Variations,* canons 1–8), preexistent *cantus firmi (Musical Offering),* or a ground bass (14 canons BWV 1087).

II. *History.* Although the precise origins of the canon are unclear, it seems certain that canons existed long before the term was coined. Canonic imitation can be traced back at least to the 13th century and was possibly related to the principle of *voice exchange as found, for example, in motets and the three-part English **rondellus.* First described by Walter Odington (ca. 1300), the *rondellus* used voice exchange between all three parts or between the upper two over an ostinato tenor *(pes).* Although each individual part has the same melodic material as the others, the *rondellus* differs from the canon in two respects: first, the voices of the *rondellus* start together, whereas they are staggered in the canon; second, the order of melodic elements differs in each voice of the *rondellus,* whereas in the canon the order of events is always the same in all voices.

The earliest known canon is the 13th-century English round *"Sumer is icumen in," a four-part infinite canon sung over a two-voice *pes.* Voice exchange within the *pes* suggests links with the *rondellus.* Apart from "Sumer is icumen in," canons do not appear as complete pieces before the four **chaces* of the Ivrea codex (ca. 1360). Like its Italian counterpart the **caccia,* the French *chace* is a finite canon, normally in three parts. In the *chace,* all three parts are canonic; in the *caccia,* the lowest part is independent (making the *caccia* a mixed canon). The two-part refrain structure of the *caccia* is similar to that found in 14th-century canonic *madrigals such as Landini's "De' dimmi tu." The terms *chace, caccia, caça* [Sp.], and *catch all refer to the process of one voice chasing another before capture. This image was paralleled by the Latin equivalent *fuga* (flight), introduced by Jacques de Liège (ca. 1330). Chase also means hunt, and a number of pieces of this type evoke hunting scenes in both text and music. Several outstanding examples of 14th-century canon are found in the works of Machaut—the three-voice ballade "Sanz cuer" is a three-part canon with a different vernacular text for each voice, the three-voice rondeau "Ma fin est mon commencement, et mon commencement ma fin" is the earliest known example of a crab canon, and some of his **lais,* though notated monophonically, were intended to be realized as canons.

The 15th century saw not only the flowering of canonic art in both sacred and secular repertories, but also the first use of the term itself. In the *Terminorum musicae diffinitorium* (1475), Tinctoris defines canon as "a rule showing the purpose of a composer behind a certain obscurity." This definition illustrates the practice of notating only the *dux* and showing explicit or cryptic rules for resolution. The complex combinations of subject transformation including mensuration canon may be seen, for example, in the Agnus Dei of Dufay's *Missa L'homme armé,* which has the rule "cancer eat plenus et redeat medius" (tenor in full note-values backward, then forward in half note-values; *HAM,* no. 66). Other famous examples of mensuration canons from the period 1475–1550 include Ockeghem's *Missa prolationum* and the *L'homme armé* Masses of Josquin Desprez and Pierre de La Rue (*HAM,* nos. 89, 92). Such works were described at length by theorists including Sebald Heyden (1537) and Glarean (1547). Other writers, however, were less enthusiastic and highlighted changing attitudes toward canon—Adam of Fulda (1490) warned against excessive use of canon and Nicola Vicentino (1555) regarded canon as inferior to free imitation. Changes are also apparent in the writings of Zarlino (*Istitutione harmoniche,* 1558–73), who was the first

1. Canon. Bach, BWV 1075. 2. Canon by inversion. Bach, *Canonic Variations on Vom Himmel hoch* BWV 769, var. 5. 3. Retrograde canon. Bach, *Musical Offering* BWV 1079. 4. Canon by diminution. Bach, 14 canons BWV 1087. 5. Double canon at the octave. Bach, Chorale prelude *In dulci jubilo* BWV 608.

major theorist to distinguish between fugue and imitation. Zarlino equated *fuga legata* with strict canon at perfect intervals, whereas *imitatione legata* could refer to free canons at any interval. In the 1573 edition of the *Istitutione,* Zarlino reserved the term *consequenza* for canons notated on a single staff. Zarlino also added detailed instructions for improvising two-part canons on a plainsong in the 1573 edition. See also Imitation.

During the 17th century, canon was generally associated with the **prima prattica* and, following Zarlino's example, was widely used for teaching counterpoint. German keyboard composers were particularly attracted to canon, often using a chorale melody as the *dux* or as an independent *cantus firmus* (e.g., Schein's *Tabulatura nova,* 1624). Nevertheless, throughout the century, theorists attempted to clarify the meaning of canon and sharpen the distinctions between canon, fugue, and imitation. For Zarlino, canon still referred to the rule for solving the canon, and theorists such as Artusi, Cerone, and Zacconi carried on this tradition. Silverio Picerli (1630), however, took the decisive step and used canon to mean the piece itself. Later in the century, Giovanni Maria Bononcini went further by separating canons written on a single part *(canone chiuso)* and those notated in full *(canone aperto).* Two other trends may be seen in the 17th century: first, a vogue for polymorphous canons, e.g., Pier Francesco Valentini's *Canone . . . sopra le parole del Salve regina . . .* (1629), which had over 2,000 solutions; second, an expanding output of popular canons, especially rounds, e.g., Ravenscroft's collection *Pammelia* or the numerous catches by Purcell and others. Lighter canons remained prominent throughout the 18th and 19th centuries in examples by Caldara, Mozart, Beethoven, Brahms, and others.

At the same time, canon continued to serve as an essential pedagogical aid. The monumental achievements of Bach reflect this serious purpose. Except for some extended canons in chamber works (Sonata for Violin BWV 1015, Suite for Flute BWV 1067) and several isolated items, the core of Bach's canonic output comes from the last two decades of his life—the *Goldberg Variations* BWV 988, the 14 canons BWV 1087, the *Musical Offering* BWV 1079, the *Canonic Variations on Vom Himmel hoch* BWV 769, and the *Art of Fugue* BWV 1080. Several of Bach's contemporaries, including Johann Friedrich Fasch, Telemann, and Handel, also wrote canons. Music theory texts from the following decades confirm that the role of canon was primarily didactic (e.g., those by Marpurg, Kirnberger, Albrechtsberger, Kollmann).

Despite declining interest in canon as a major compositional technique at the end of the 18th century, strict imitative counterpoint had a significant impact on the music of Haydn, Mozart, and Beethoven. All three composers studied canon and incorporated it into their works. For example, both Haydn and Mozart wrote canonic minuets for large-scale pieces—Haydn, Symphonies 3, 23, 44, 47, and the String Quartet op. 76 no. 2; Mozart, String Quartet K. 171 and Serenade K. 388 (384a). Beethoven wrote extended canons in the middle sections of the "Vivace alla marcia" from the Piano Sonata op. 101 and the scherzo to the *Hammerklavier* Sonata op. 106. Canons also appear in the works of many 19th-century composers: Schubert, scherzo from the Piano Trio op. 100; Schumann, 3/8 movement from the Piano Trio op. 80, six canonic movements in op. 56; Franck, last movement of the Violin Sonata; Brahms, opp. 9, 21, 24, and 113. But the significance of canon in 19th-century music should not be overestimated. Canon remained the exception rather than the rule for most composers.

In the 20th century, however, particularly with the spread of serialism, canon once again proved a vital technique of composition. Schoenberg (trio from the minuet in the Piano Suite op. 25; *Pierrot Lunaire,* nos. 17, 18), Berg (Violin Concerto), Messiaen *(Cantéyodjaya),* Hindemith *(Ludus tonalis),* Stravinsky *(In memoriam Dylan Thomas),* Bartók (String Quartet no. 3, *Mikrokosmos*), and many others have contributed to the literature of the canon. Perhaps no 20th-century composer has relied on canon more heavily than Webern. Following his edition of Isaac's **Choralis constantinus,* Webern drew upon canon as early as op. 2, a short choral work in three sections, each section in double canon. Webern's last free atonal works also employ canon—the five canons op. 16 consist of two- and three-part canons while the last movement of op. 15 is a double canon in contrary motion. The heights of Webern's canonic achievement, however, are reached in the twelve-tone compositions opp. 21, 22, 24, and 31, which rival the works of the Netherlanders and J. S. Bach in their ingenious solutions to the problems of canonic writing.

Bibl.: Ebenezer Prout, *Double Counterpoint and Canon* (London, 1893; R: New York: Greenwood, 1969). Paul Mies, "Der Kanon in mehrsätzigen klassischen Werk," *ZfMw* 8 (1925–26): 10–23. Walter Piston, *Counterpoint* (New York: Norton, 1947). Fritz Jöde, ed., *Der Kanon* (Wolfenbüttel: Möseler, 1948–51). Alfred Mann, *The Study of Fugue* (New Brunswick: Rutgers U Pr, 1958), incl. trans. of part of Johann G. Albrechtsberger, *Gründliche Anweisung zur Komposition* (1790). Robert Falk, "*Rondellus,* Canon, and Related Types before 1300," *JAMS* 25 (1972): 38–57. Virginia Newes, "Fuga and Related Contrapuntal Procedures in European Polyphony ca. 1350–1420" (Ph.D. diss., Brandeis Univ., 1987). D. B. Collins, "Canon in Music Theory from c. 1550 to c. 1800" (Ph.D. diss., Stanford Univ., 1992).

Canonical hours. The services making up the *Office.

Canonic imitation. Strict *imitation, as in a *canon.

Canso, chanso [Occ., song; Fr. *chanson;* It. *canzo*]. In the *troubadour and *trouvère repertories, the principle vehicle for the expression of *fin'amor* [Occ., refined love]. At first, the term seems to have been used interchangeably with *vers* [fr. Lat. *versus*] in a general sense, but by the end of the 12th century it came to be applied more specifically to the love song. As with other strophic forms used by the troubadours and trouvères, the poem may end with a shortened stanza [Occ. *Tornada;* Fr. *envoy*] referring to the person to whom the song is addressed, the "messenger" who delivers the song, a patron, or another troubadour. Most *canso* melodies of the troubadours are essentially thorough-composed (e.g., Bernart de Ventadorn's famous "Can vei la lauzeta mover"), though often with one or two phrases repeated. Many troubadour *cansos* and most trouvère *chansons* are cast in a more regular musical scheme, most often AAB [see Bar form]. The term *grand chant courtois* is often used to refer to the highest form of Old French lyric, the love song.

Bibl.: Robert H. Perrin, "A Note on Troubadour Melodic Types," *JAMS* 9 (1956): 12–18. Roger Dragonetti, *La Technique poétique des trouvères dans la chanson courtoise* (Brugge: De Tempel, 1960; R: Geneva: Slatkine, 1979). Pierre Bec, *La Lyrique française au moyen-âge,* 2 vols. (Paris: A & J Picard, 1977–78). Elizabeth Aubrey, *The Music of the Troubadours* (Bloomington: Ind U Pr, 1996), pp. 86–95. Elizabeth Aubrey, "Genre as a Determinant of Melody in the Songs of the Troubadours and Trouvères," in *Medieval Lyric: Genres in Historical Context,* ed. William D. Paden (Urbana: U of Ill Pr, 2000), pp. 273–96. E.A.

Cantabile [It.]. Singable, songlike.

Cantando [It.]. Singing, **cantabile.*

Cantare super librum [Lat., to sing from the book; Fr. *chant sur le livre*]. In common usage, vocal improvisation on a preexisting melody (from "the book," which might be any book of music, most often but not always one of liturgical chant). The French phrase *chant sur le livre* definitely referred to improvisation in the 18th century and perhaps earlier; similar practices apparently existed in some places in Italy and Germany. According to Bent (1983), the Latin term (usually with the verb *cantare,* never with the noun *cantus*) first occurs in the works of Tinctoris (ca. 1435–1511) and implies, rather, the singing of carefully prepared counterpoints to a given melody, each part at minimum constructed with regard to the given melody alone, at best taking account of all other parts as well. Singing *super librum* involved successive mental composition of voices and was not a matter of spontaneous improvisation. See also Discant.

Bibl.: Abbé Jean Prim, "*Chant sur le livre* in French Churches in the 18th Century," *JAMS* 14 (1961): 37–49. Margaret Bent, "*Resfacta* and *Cantare super librum,*" *JAMS* 36 (1983): 371–91.

Cantata [It.]. A composite vocal genre of the Baroque era, consisting of a succession of *recitatives, *ariosos, and set-pieces (e.g., *arias, duets, and choruses). A cantata may be either secular or sacred in subject matter and function, and its treatment may be lyrical, allegorical, or dramatic (although almost never actually staged). Cantatas range from intimate, small-scale works for solo singer or singers and restricted accompanimental forces (sometimes called chamber cantatas) to large ones with chorus and orchestral accompaniment. Such large cantatas were often composed to celebrate or commemorate specific events. The cantata originated early in the 17th century in Italy, where the term was first used simply to indicate a piece to be sung (as opposed to **sonata,* to be played on instruments). The most frequently performed cantatas today are those of Bach; they are sacred works with German texts and were intended for performance during Lutheran church services. The typical Bach cantata employs several soloists and chorus and is accompanied by a small orchestra.

I. *The Italian cantata.* The 17th-century Italian cantata was a distinctly secular work intended for performance at private social gatherings; and it was composed, most often, for a solo voice accompanied by only *basso continuo* [see Thoroughbass]. The evolution of the Italian cantata can be roughly divided into three periods. In the first period, through about 1620, the repertory was usually published, a circumstance suggesting that this music was apt for both professional singers and competent amateurs. It includes simple strophic arias, *strophic variations, and monodic *madrigals [see also Monody]. For the subsequent evolution of the genre, monodic madrigals were of particular importance, for in them recitative was gradually transformed into rhythmically controlled arioso. The arioso material involves a dual statement of the culminating line of the text (a process taken over from the polyphonic motet and madrigal). The resulting AA′ at the end of such a monodic madrigal became the seed-ground of the later aria (see Jeppesen, *La flora,* 2:16–17). These germinal lyric elements then expanded into slightly more complex patterns such as ABB′ or ABB′A′; and as the overall form expanded, its several sections took on contrasting characters. Generically this early published repertory is known to historians as monody, although that term rarely appears in the prints. Its leading composers include Giulio Caccini (ca. 1550–1618), Sigismondo d'India (ca. 1580–1629), and Stefano Landi (ca. 1590–1639).

In the second period—the 1630s and 40s—this monodic repertory was printed with decreasing regularity, a circumstance indicating that amateur performers were leaving it to professionals—opera singers in particular, but also church musicians, who in Italy were often barred from singing in the theater. The principal locale for the cultivation of the cantata during this period was Rome, whose highly competitive social scene featured musical entertainments usually consisting of one or more cantatas. The music itself survives in thousands of manuscript collections (in which the term *cantata* never appears until late in the 17th century). For more imposing evening entertainments, cantatas on a larger scale were in order: *serenatas, which called for several singers along with a pair of obbligato violins or even a small orchestra.

The forms of cantatas during this period are, like

those of monody, characterized by amazing variety. The texts are more consciously constructed to produce narrative passages that motivate periodic contemplation, with corresponding musical divisions into recitative and aria. Arias grew in size, and in the latter half of the century a new form-dynamic reigned briefly, the aria in two strophes. This probably came into the cantata from opera, although the interacting influences of opera and cantata constitute a historical problem as yet insufficiently explored. Among the many interesting composers of this rich period are Luigi Rossi (1598–1653), Marco Marazzoli (ca. 1602–62), Giacomo Carissimi (1605–74), Antonio Cesti (1623–69), Alessandro Stradella (1644?–82), and Agostino Steffani (1654–1728).

The third period is characterized by the prevailing use of the da capo *aria. Although the da capo aria is anticipated in the 17th-century ternary forms, the most interesting precedents for the large-scale 18th-century manifestations of the da capo aria are certain aria pairs found, for example, in the serenatas of Alessandro Stradella (see his *Qual prodigio* in Supplement 3 of the Chrysander edition of Handel). A typical early 18th-century Italian cantata involves a sequence of two or three da capo arias, each of which is prepared by a recitative. The repetitiousness of this format is mitigated by a high degree of innovation, particularly an expressive new harmonic vocabulary and an exploration of key relationships unimagined in earlier generations.

As more orchestras came into existence (most of them associated with courts and with court theaters) in the 18th century, composers produced a large repertory of cantatas that, though still involving solo voices and lacking choruses, now had rather ample orchestral accompaniments. Such accompaniments provided an element of musical interest that helped the cantata to become voguish outside Italy, though such works were still composed to Italian texts and were usually sung by Italian singers.

The demand for Italian cantatas in the first half of the 18th century stimulated prodigious output by, among others, Alessandro Scarlatti (1660–1725), Giovanni Bononcini (1670–1747), Handel (1685–1759), Benedetto Marcello (1686–1739), Nicola Porpora (1686–1768), and Johann Adolf Hasse (1699–1783).

II. *The early cantata outside Italy.* During this same period, there appeared numerous composers in northern Europe (England and France as well as the German-speaking countries) who set texts in their own languages, producing cantatas that were inspired by the Italian models. That this repertory is not of greater size is largely due to different social habits and different regional traditions of musical entertainments. Among the French composers were André Campra (1660–1744), Michel Montéclair (1667–1737), Louis-Nicolas Clérambault (1676–1749), and Jean-Philippe Rameau (1683–1764). Among the English composers were John Pepusch (1667–1752), John Stanley (1713–86), and Thomas Arne (1710–88).

III. *The Lutheran cantata.* As the Lutheran motet developed in the 17th century, it became longer, often expanding into a work with many sections. Along with the chorus, it frequently employed solo singers (sometimes two of them in a spiritual dialogue) as well as instruments. This large repertory assumed many forms, often inspiring such genre names as *symphoniae sacrae* and *geistliche Konzerte.* An element of religious authority second only to the Bible itself was the Lutheran *chorale, the melodies of which were repeatedly incorporated into new compositions, most often as a **cantus firmus.* This extremely varied repertory came under the influence of the Italian cantata as it began to include passages of recitative and arias in da capo form. A particularly significant figure in this new development was Pastor Erdmann Neumeister (1671–1756), who during the first decades of the 18th century produced several cycles of cantata texts, mostly poetic paraphrases of scriptural passages appropriate for various feasts of the church year. Within the Lutheran service, these often quite lengthy sacred cantatas functioned as sermons in music, preceding the actual sermon itself.

The approximately 200 surviving cantatas of Bach (out of a substantially greater number that he is thought to have composed) embody much of this long tradition. A few, particularly among the early ones, are close to the sectional and fluid construction of the older Lutheran motet. Others incorporate, especially in recitatives and arias, the techniques of emotional and dramatic expression of contemporary Italian secular cantatas and operas. Most of Bach's cantatas employ a chorus, but a few are for solo singers only. Chorales are also employed in a variety of ways, many works concluding with a largely homophonic four-part setting of one strophe. See also Chorale cantata.

IV. *Later history.* During the latter half of the 18th century and continuing into the 19th and 20th centuries, the cantata evolved into a miniature *oratorio, usually secular and frequently involving classical or allegorical motifs. Such works, requiring the forces of an orchestra, a chorus, and soloists, were often produced on special commission to celebrate some important occasion. Many cantatas composed to meet the academic requirements of the French **Prix de Rome* (the most celebrated of which is Debussy's *L'enfant prodigue,* 1884) emphasize tradition. Lacking the social or religious framework that would stimulate constant production and encourage creative innovation, the cantata gradually ceased to be widely cultivated on the Continent. In England, however, the 19th and 20th centuries have seen a steadier cultivation of the cantata, including works by Parry, Sullivan, Stanford, Elgar, Vaughan Williams, and Britten.

The varied compositions to which the term cantata has been applied in the 20th century include works by Hindemith, Milhaud, Bartók (*Cantata profana,* 1930),

Prokofiev (*Alexander Nevsky,* 1939), Webern (op. 29, 1939, and op. 31, 1943), and Stravinsky (*Cantata on Old English Texts,* 1952). Two of Benjamin Britten's cantatas for special occasions are *Cantata academica* (1960) for the 500th anniversary of Basle University and *Cantata misericordium* (1963) for the centenary of the International Red Cross at Geneva.

Bibl.: *Anthologies.* Knud Jeppesen, *La flora, arie antiche italiane,* 3 vols. (Copenhagen: Hansen, 1949). Karl Gustav Fellerer, *Die Monodie, Mw* 31, trans. Eng. Robert Kolben (Cologne: A Volk, 1968). Richard Jakoby, *Die Kantate, Mw* 32, trans. Eng. Robert Kolben (Cologne: A Volk, 1968). Carol MacClintock, *The Solo Song, 1580–1730* (New York: Norton, 1973). Carolyn Gianturco, *The Italian Cantata in the Seventeenth Century,* 16 vols. (New York: Garland, 1985–87). David Tunley, *The Eighteenth-Century French Cantata in Facsimile,* 17 vols. (New York: Garland, 1990–91).

Literature. Eugen Schmitz, *Geschichte der weltlichen Solokantate* (Leipzig, 1914; 2nd ed. rev., Leipzig: Breitkopf & Härtel, 1955). William Gillies Whittaker, *The Cantatas of Johann Sebastian Bach, Sacred and Secular,* 2 vols. (London: Oxford U Pr, 1959; 2nd ed., 1964). David Burrows, "Antonio Cesti on Music," *MQ* 51 (1965): 518–29. Malcolm Boyd, "English Secular Cantatas in the 18th Century," *MR* 30 (1969): 85–97. Gloria Rose, "The Italian Cantata of the Baroque Period," *Schrade,* 1973, pp. 655–77. Friedrich Blume and Ludwig Finscher, *Protestant Church Music: A History* (New York: Norton, 1974). David Tunley, *The Eighteenth-Century French Cantata* (London: Dobson, 1974). Carolyn Gianturco, "*Cantate spirituali e morali,* with a Description of the Papal Sacred Cantata Tradition for Christmas 1676–1740," *ML* 73 (1992): 1–31. Friedhelm Krummacher, *Bachs Zyklus der Choralkantaten: Aufgaben und Lösungen* (Göttingen: Vandenhoeck & Ruprecht, 1995). Michael Märker, *Die protestantische Dialogkomposition in Deutschland zwishen Heinrich Schütz und Johann Sebastian Bach: eine stilkritische Studie* (Cologne: Studio, 1995). Ulrich Wüster, *Felix Mendelssohn Bartholdys Choralkantaten—Gestalt und Idee: Versuch einer historisch-dritischen Interpretation* (Frankfurt: Peter Lang, 1996). David Tunley, *The Eighteenth Century French Cantata* (Oxford: Clarendon, 1997).

O.J., rev. H.Sm.

Cantatorium [Lat.]. See Liturgical books I.

Cante flamenco, cante hondo, cante jondo [Sp.]. See Flamenco.

Canti carnascialeschi [It.]. Any of various kinds of Florentine carnival part songs sung by masquers on foot or by costumed performers on decorated carts, as part of the festivities at pre-Lenten Carnival, at Calendimaggio (1 May), and on the feast of San Giovanni (24 June). The surviving repertory comes chiefly from the first 20 years of the 16th century. The texts, mostly anonymous, celebrate (with many *double entendres*) Florentine arts and trades; there are also allegorical and moralizing themes. Most of the poems are in some kind of refrain form, and all have multiple stanzas; poetic meters range from the popular eight-syllable trochaic to the more refined seven- and eleven-syllable iambic. The surviving music (most of which is from the early 16th century) is homophonic, rhythmically crisp, and of appropriately choral, "outdoor" character. It is on the whole through-composed, refrains and stanzas having different music. About 70 pieces survive, in manuscript sources different from the north Italian *frottola* repertory.

Bibl.: Federico Ghisi, *I canti carnascialeschi* (Florence: Olschki, 1937). Joseph Gallucci, ed., *Florentine Festival Music, 1480–1520, RRMR* 40 (Madison, Wis.: A-R Edit, 1981). Piero Gargiulo, ed., *La musica a Firenze al tempo di Lorenzo il Magnifico* (Florence: Olschki, 1993). Patrick Macey, *Bonfire Songs: Savonarola's Musical Legacy* (Oxford: Oxford U Pr, 1998).

J.H.

Canticle [Lat. *canticum,* dim. *canticulum*]. A song or lyrical passage from a book of the Bible other than the Book of Psalms; sometimes also the *"Te Deum." Canticles play an ancient and important role in the liturgies of both the Eastern and Western Christian churches. In the Roman rite, three canticles from the New Testament, *"Benedictus Dominus Deus Israel," *"Magnificat," and *"Nunc dimittis," are sung daily at Lauds, Vespers, and Compline, respectively [see Office]. In the Anglican rite, the first of these is sung at Morning Prayer, and the last two at Evening Prayer. Lauds of the Roman rite includes in addition a different Old Testament canticle for each day of the week. These are sung with *antiphons in the same fashion as the four psalms with which they are associated at that hour [see Psalmody] and include the Canticle of the Three Children ("Benedicite," Vulgate, Daniel 3:57–88, 56; also used in some Masses of the Roman and other Latin rites during the Middle Ages), the Canticle of Isaiah ("Confitebor tibi, Domine," Isaiah 12:1–6), the Canticle of Hezekiah ("Ego dixi," Isaiah 38:10–20), the Canticle of Anna ("Exultavit cor meum," 1 Samuel 2:1–10), the Canticle of Habakkuk ("Domine audivi," Habakkuk 3:2–19), and the two Canticles of Moses ("Cantemus Domino," Exodus 15:1–19, and "Audite caeli," Deuteronomy 32:1–43). Canticles are also sung at Matins. See also Byzantine chant II.

Canticum [Lat.]. Song, *canticle.

Cantiga [Sp., Port.]. A medieval monophonic song of the Iberian peninsula. Although the term is generic and may refer to both sacred and secular poems (including, e.g., *cantigas de amigo,* love poems in feminine voice), it refers in the musicological literature principally to the *Cantigas de Santa María* of Alfonso el Sabio (Alfonso the Wise, 1221–84, King of Castile and León from 1252). This repertory of more than 400 songs has texts in Galician-Portuguese, cast in the form of the **zajal* (hence the family of the **villancico* and **virelai*), most of which narrate miracles of the Virgin Mary. Approximately 30 are simply in praise of the Virgin. The texts are preserved with melodies in three manuscripts of the 13th or 14th century (a fourth having blank musical staves) along with a rich collection of miniatures depicting performers with musical instruments. The miniatures provide invaluable material for the study of medieval instruments, but their relevance for the performance practice of this and other repertories has been debated, as have the extent of Islamic influence (said by Ribera to be great) in the repertory as a whole and the nature of the rhythm (said by Anglès to include modal, nonmodal but metrical, and free rhythms) of the melodies. The repertory was evidently collected under King Alfonso's supervision and may include some works by him.

Bibl.: Julián Ribera, *La música de las Cantigas* [includes one MS in facs.] (Madrid: Real academia española, 1922); trans. Eng., abridged, Eleanor Hague and Marion Leffingwell, *Music in Ancient Arabia and Spain* (London: H Milford, Oxford U Pr, 1929; R: New York: Da Capo, 1970). Higini Anglès, *La música de las cantigas,* 3 vols. in 4 [complete ed. with facs.] (Barcelona: Diputación provincial de Barcelona, Biblioteca central, 1943–64). Israel J. Katz, "The Study and Performance of the *Cantigas de Santa Maria:* A Glimpse at Recent Musicological Literature," *Bulletin of the Cantiqueiros de Santa Maria* 1 (1987): 51–60.

Cantilena [Lat.]. (1) In the Middle Ages, song, melody, including liturgical chant as well as secular song. (2) From the 13th through the 15th century, polyphonic song, especially the French *chanson; whence the use in musicological literature of the term cantilena style to describe music, whether sacred or secular, in which the texture of the three-voice chanson prevails, with the leading melody and text in the uppermost part and two, often textless (hence presumably instrumental) accompanying parts. The terms *ballade* style and treble-dominated style have also been used to describe this texture. (3) In England in the late 13th and in the 14th century, three-voice pieces with sacred texts in Latin, not usually based on a **cantus firmus,* and making extensive use of six-three chords (hence said to be in *sixth-chord style). Such pieces were copied in score, with the text under the lowest voice. (4) In the 19th century and since, a lyrical vocal melody or an instrumental melody of similar character.

Bibl.: Ernest H. Sanders, "Cantilena and Discant in 14th-Century England," *MD* 19 (1965): 7–52.

Cantillation. The speechlike chanting of a liturgical text. The term is used especially, though not exclusively, with respect to *Jewish music. For the notation used for such chanting, see Ecphonetic notation.

Cantino [It.; Fr. *chanterelle;* Ger. *Sangsaite*]. The highest-pitched string of a stringed instrument, especially the E string of the violin.

Cantio [Lat.]. Song, especially the monophonic song of the Middle Ages with Latin, sacred, nonliturgical, strophic text, often with a refrain. See also *Cantio sacra.*

Cantionale [Lat.; Ger. also *Kantionale*]. A collection from the late 16th or early 17th century of chorales or hymns intended for German Protestant liturgical use, especially one containing homophonic settings in four parts with the melody in the uppermost part. Settings of this type are said to be in cantional style. Examples of such collections include Lucas Osiander's *Funffzig geistliche Lieder und Psalmen* (1586) and J. H. Schein's *Cantional oder Gesangbuch Augspurgischer Confession* (1627).

Cantio sacra [Lat., pl. *cantiones sacrae*]. Sacred song; especially in the 16th and 17th centuries, the *motet.

Cantique [Fr.]. Canticle; hymn; any religious song with French text.

Canto [It.; Sp.]. (1) Song, melody; *c. piano* [It.], *c. llano* [Sp.], plainsong; *c. fermo, *cantus firmus; col c.,* an instruction for the accompanist to follow the lead of the singer of the melody. See also *Bel canto, Canti carnascialeschi, Canto de órgano.* (2) The soprano or highest part in vocal music. (3) The art of singing.

Canto de órgano [Sp.]. In Spain from the 14th through the 18th centuries, measured or *mensural music, especially vocal polyphony, as distinct from plainsong *(canto llano).*

Cantometrics. A system of ethnomusicological analysis developed by Alan Lomax. A piece or a repertory is described by indication of the degree to which each of 37 "parameters" is present. Special attention is given to organization of ensembles and to *singing style.

Bibl.: Alan Lomax, *Folk Song Style and Culture* (Washington, D.C.: Amer Assoc for the Advancement of Science, 1968). Id., *Cantometrics: An Approach to the Anthropology of Music* (Berkeley: U of Cal, Extension Media Center, 1976). B.N.

Cantor [Lat.; Heb. *chazzan*]. (1) In Jewish and Latin-Christian liturgical music, a solo singer. In Gregorian and related repertories, certain melodies or parts of them are sung by one or more such soloists as distinct from the chorus or *schola* [see Psalmody]. Writers of the Middle Ages often distinguish between a *cantor,* who is a singer and practical musician, and a *musicus,* who is a learned student of music theory, though the distinction is modified and qualified in a variety of ways. (2) In the Lutheran Church, the director of music of a church [see Kantor].

Bibl.: Erich Reimer, "Musicus und Cantor: Zur Sozialgeschichte eines musikalischen Lehrstücks," *AfMw* 35 (1978): 1–32.

Cantoris [Lat.]. See *Decani* and *cantoris.*

Cantus [Lat., song, tune, melody]. (1) Chant, liturgical plainsong; i.e., a single piece of chant, or a repertory of such pieces, such as *cantus gregorianus, ambrosianus, romanus,* etc.; in *Ambrosian chant, the equivalent of the Gregorian *tract. (2) In 9th- to 13th-century polyphony, a chant or a portion of a chant to which an added voice was improvised or composed. The term was equivalent to, and superseded by, *tenor. (3) In 14th-, 15th-, and especially 16th-century polyphony, the topmost part of a polyphonic work, regardless of vocal range, though usually synonymous with *superius* (soprano), *discantus* (discant), or *triplex* (treble). Typically, the part bore a designation (abbr. *C.*) in *partbook format but not in *choirbook format. (4) Any song or vocal work.

Cantus choralis [Lat., choral song]. **Cantus planus.*

Cantus coronatus [Lat., crowned song; Fr. *chanson couronnée*]. (1) A medieval song awarded a prize, or "crowned," in competitions such as those sponsored by the *puys* of 13th-century France. Theorist Johannes de Grocheio (ca. 1300), in his taxonomy of secular genres, says that the *cantus coronatus* was about "delightful and difficult material like friendship and charity" and was composed by nobles and performed in their courts to inspire them to courage and generosity. About 30 songs are designated "couronnée" in medieval manuscripts. (2) The term *cantus coronatus,* like *cantus fractus* and *contrapunctus diminutus,* also designated the improvisation of divisions to other chants, or their *fauxbourdons, as practiced in certain Kyries, Glorias, graduals, and alleluias. In the polyphony of Dufay's generation, the presence of a *fermata or *corona* over a note called for similar embellishment.

Bibl.: Hendrik vender Werf and Wolf Frobenius, "Cantus coronatus," *Handwörterbuch der musikalischen Terminologie,* ed. Hans Heinrich Eggebrecht (Wiesbaden: Steiner, 1971–). Hendrik van der Werf, *The Chansons of the Troubadours and Trouvères: A Study of the Melodies and Their Relation to the Poems* (Utrecht: A Oosthoek, 1972). Charles W. Warren, "Punctus Organi and Cantus Coronatus in the Music of Dufay," *Dufay,* 1974, pp. 128–43. Christopher Page, "Johannes de Grocheio on Secular Music: A Corrected Text and a New Translation," *Plainsong and Medieval Music* 2 (1993): 17–41. Elizabeth Aubrey, "Genre as a Determinant of Melody in the Songs of the Troubadours and the Trouvères," in *Medieval Lyric: Genres in Historical Context,* ed. William D. Paden (Urbana: U of Ill Pr, 2000), pp. 273–96.

E.A.

Cantus durus, mollis, naturalis [Lat., hard, soft, natural song]. In medieval theory, the three types of *hexachord.

Cantus figuralis, figuratus, indentatus, mensuratus [Lat., figural, figured, pricked, measured melody]. In medieval theory, music written in *mensural notation, as distinct from *cantus planus* or *plainsong.

Cantus firmus [Lat., pl. *cantus (canti) firmi;* It., *canto fermo*]. A preexistent melody used as the basis of a new polyphonic composition. A *cantus firmus* may be derived from sacred or secular music or may be freely invented; its pitch may be preserved intact or elaborated in the new composition; its rhythm or phrase structure may or may not be retained.

Preexistent melodies are present in the majority of early polyphonic compositions, including most of the polyphony of *St. Martial and of *Notre Dame and virtually all *motets of the 13th century. By convention, however, the term *cantus firmus* is usually used in reference to later music only, beginning with the 14th century. Composition on a *cantus firmus* dominated the music of the 14th and 15th centuries, particularly sacred vocal music. In the 16th century, the technique continued in use but was not dominant, having been supplanted in part by other methods of using preexistent material, such as *parody; nevertheless, it was still prominent in certain types of instrumental music, particularly keyboard music. Thereafter, *cantus firmi* were seldom used except in repertories closely tied to preexisting tunes (such as Lutheran music based on *chorales), in deliberately archaic styles (for instance, *Palestrina style in sacred music), and in counterpoint manuals as given melodies to which a student was to add voices.

In the 14th century, *cantus firmi* were most commonly used in *isorhythmic pieces, in which pitch (as *color*) but not rhythm or phrase structure of a preexistent melody was preserved in a comparatively slow-moving tenor. Its speed made the *cantus firmus* audibly distinct from the surrounding texture. Although after about 1450 isorhythm fell into disuse, the statement of a *cantus firmus* in long notes remained a common device throughout the 15th and 16th centuries.

Before the end of the 14th century, "migrant" *cantus firmi* began to be employed; that is, the borrowed melody was divided among the voices, occupying first one part, then another. Initially this technique was most used in England, but it later became common on the Continent. Paraphrased *cantus firmi,* in which a preexistent melody was elaborated rather than quoted strictly, had a similar history. Particularly in the 15th century, a paraphrased *cantus firmus* was often employed as the highest voice of a polyphonic complex in the setting of antiphons and hymns [see Paraphrase].

In the late 14th and early 15th centuries, single Mass movements were sometimes based on melodies not from the corresponding plainchant of the Mass. Subsequently, pairs of movements with the same *cantus firmus* began to be composed, and finally, complete polyphonic Mass settings using one *cantus firmus* throughout were composed. The latter is termed a cyclic *Mass, the first example of which was composed about 1440.

In the later 15th century, the field from which *cantus firmi* could be chosen broadened considerably. Earlier, most had come from plainchant. Now, secular or freely invented melodies or single parts, especially tenors, from polyphonic pieces were often used. By the end of the 15th century, a *cantus firmus* was not always distinguishable from other members of a polyphonic texture. Often all parts incorporated motives from the *cantus firmus;* that melody frequently migrated among the parts and was paraphrased; and in many cases its rhythm was similar to that of accompanying musical lines.

Perhaps the most important use of preexistent melodies after the 16th century was in Lutheran organ and vocal music, commonly based on chorale melodies [see Organ chorale]. The employment of given melodies for instruction in counterpoint, still common today, is probably most firmly linked to the name of Johann Joseph Fux (1660–1741) [see Species counterpoint].

Bibl.: Manfred F. Bukofzer, *Studies in Medieval and Renaissance Music* (New York: Norton, 1950). Edgar H. Sparks, *Cantus Firmus in Mass and Motet, 1420–1520* (Berkeley and Los Angeles: U of Cal Pr, 1963).

Cantus fractus [Lat., broken melody]. See *Cantus coronatus.*

Cantus planus [Lat.]. Since the 13th century, *plainsong, as distinct from measured music; in earlier writings, a song in a low register, as distinct from *cantus acutus.*

Cantus planus binatim [Lat., double plainchant]. In Italy from the 13th century through the end of the 15th, the practice of singing plainsong in improvised note-against-note, nonparallel counterpoint, by two voices of equal ambitus.

Bibl.: F. Alberto Gallo, "'Cantus planus binatim,' polifonia primitiva in fonti tardive . . . ," *Quadrivium* 7 (1966): 79–89.

Cantus prius factus [Lat., previously made song]. See *Cantus firmus.*

Canzo [It.]. See *Canso, chanso.*

Canzona [It., song; see also *Canzone*]. An instrumental composition of the 16th and 17th centuries having as its prototype the French *chanson [It. *canzona francese*]. Chansons published in Paris by Pierre Attaingnant between 1528 and 1550 enjoyed continued and widespread popularity, especially in Italy, where they were often cultivated in instrumental transcriptions, or *intabulations. With their animated chordal textures, casual imitation, simple harmonies, and rhythmic vitality, these chansons were ideally suited to instrumental transcription. Above all, their flexible, sectional repetitions (ABBA, AABC, ABA′CA, etc.) provided logic for an untexted, purely instrumental idiom and gradually stimulated original canzonas derived in style and form from the earlier vocal models. The ensemble canzona *(canzona da sonare)* eventually influenced and gave way to the *sonata, *concerto, and other multimovement genres of the Baroque, while the keyboard canzona, along with the *ricercar, laid a foundation for the *fugue.

The Italian vogue for transcriptions of chansons by composers such as Claudin de Sermisy, Clément Janequin, Pierre Certon, and Sandrin began in 1536 and continued sporadically, peaking in the lute prints of 1546–48 by Giulio Abondante, Francesco Canova da Milano, Domenico Bianchini, Melchiore de Barberiis, Giovanni Maria da Crema, Antonio Rotta, and their contemporaries. Lute transcriptions remained a staple throughout the century, although they seldom spawned original works, as did transcriptions in the keyboard and ensemble repertories.

Early keyboard prints by Marco Antonio Cavazzoni (Venice, 1523) and his son Girolamo (Venice, 1543) contain several pieces called *canzon:* an instrumental *parody of a chanson by Josquin and paraphrases of the popular melodies "Il est bel et bon" and "Faulte d'argent." But these works belong more to the 15th-century instrumental **carmen* and the emerging parody and paraphrase *fantasia and ricercar than to the independently conceived keyboard canzonas that followed only after 1570. Organists such as Andrea Gabrieli (Venice, 1571, 1605), Antonio Valente (Naples, 1576), Sperindio Bertoldo (Venice, 1591), and Claudio Merulo (Venice, 1588, 1592, 1608, and 1611) produced ornate intabulations of chansons by Janequin, Thomas Crecquillon, Orlande de Lassus, Clemens non Papa, and others. Andrea Gabrieli's are sometimes followed by *ricercari ariosi* that rework the thematic materials of the preceding chanson, and Merulo's output includes a large number of canzonas that are given descriptive and dedicatory titles (e.g., "La cortese," "La bovia," "La Leonora," "La Rolanda") and that do not have vocal antecedents but are instead transcribed from ensemble canzonas (one ed. in both versions in *Mw* 12). Nevertheless, such arrangements prepared the way for the independently conceived keyboard canzona that reached its culmination early in the 17th century in the works of Girolamo Frescobaldi.

Although sharing a single root and, in many instances, pieces in common, the ensemble canzona grew in directions quite separate from the keyboard one. Apart from works in the 15th-century *carmen* tradition, original ensemble canzonas antedate those for solo instruments by nearly two decades. The earliest include *La bella canzona da sonare* by Nicola Vicentino (Milan, 1572) and two pieces titled *Aria di canzon francese per sonar* by Marc'Antonio Ingegneri (Venice, 1579). Among reworkings of chansons by Adrian Willaert and Crequillon in Giacomo Vincenti's anthology (Venice, 1588) are two canzonas by Merulo and two by Gioseffo Guami, the latter's being called elsewhere *Fantasia in modo di canzon francese,* a term that Giovanni Gabrieli used in 1599. Merulo's student Florentio Maschera, a viol player and organist, composed the most successful canzonas of his day (Brescia, 1584; one in *HAM,* no. 175). They passed through at least nine editions, ca. 1570–1612, and were drawn upon for published transcriptions for cittern (Paolo Virchi, Venice, 1574), lute (Giovanni Antonio Terzi, Venice, 1593), and organ (the younger Bernhard Schmid, Strasbourg, 1607; Johann Woltz, Basel, 1617). Maschera's 21 canzonas are replete with lively rhythms, including the pervading terse chanson/canzona rhythmic tattoo, ♩ ♫ , sectional and interlocutory repetitions, and an idiomatic flexibility and charm that assured their continued popularity.

A retrospective anthology published by Alessandro

Ravierii (Venice, 1608; see Bartholomew, 1965) for four-, five-, and eight-part ensembles with organ *basso seguente* provides a summary cross section of some 36 canzonas by Merulo, Guami, Maschera, Constanzo Antegnati, Luzzasco Luzzaschi, Giovanni Battista Grillo, the young Frescobaldi, and (among others) the great Venetian master of the genre, Giovanni Gabrieli, who is represented by six early canzonas *a 4.* In some 40 canzonas, Giovanni Gabrieli (Venice, 1597, 1615) absorbed its legacy and realized its potential in works that exploit the color contrasts of the **cori spezzati* tradition at the Basilica of St. Mark. His canzonas and sonatas *a 4* to *a 22* for cornetts, violins, trombones, and organ continuo (although specific instruments are often not given in the prints) divide into sections, some very short, almost "quiltlike," that pit from two to five groups of instruments *(cori)* against one another in alternation, one group echoing another, or repeating or contrasting textures of sound in a spatially oriented style. Some groupings set a refrain *(tutti)* in chordal style against a duo of cornetts or violins playing virtuoso figuration with organ continuo, thus anticipating important features of the later Baroque concerto and, with the polarity of these "solo" parts, the *trio sonata. His canzonas were imitated by German composers, such as Hans Leo Hassler (Nuremberg, 1601), Johann Hermann Schein (Wittenberg, 1609; Leipzig, 1615), and especially Samuel Scheidt (Hamburg, 1621), whose canzonas include several based on popular melodies.

Tarquinio Merula (Venice, 1615, 1637), Maurizio Cazzati (Venice, 1642), and others wrote canzonas for two violins and continuo that trace the gradual fusion of the canzona and the trio sonata; one by Bernardo Pasquini (1637–1710) is in three distinct movements. Frescobaldi's (Venice, 1635) canzonas mark formal changes toward the **sonata da chiesa,* with expanded chordal adagios separating spirited fugal sections in a variety of meters and tempos, unified by thematic variation. By the second half of the 17th century, sonata had virtually ousted canzona as a name for the central tradition of ensemble music, though William Young (Innsbruck, 1653), Henry Purcell (London, 1697), and Antonio Luigi Baldacini (Rome, 1699) retained the term to indicate fast fugal movements in their *sonate da chiesa.* The canzona's influence in 17th-century opera *sinfonias—by Stefano Landi, Francesco Cavalli, and others—is also evident.

The earliest original keyboard canzonas include 13 by Vincenzo Pellegrini (Venice, 1599) and 5 by Giovanni Gabrieli, both of whom worked within the northern Italian milieu of the ensemble canzona. A southern school of Giovanni de Macque (Rome, 1586; Basel, 1617), Ascanio Mayone (Naples, 1609), and Giovanni Maria Trabaci (Naples, 1603, 1615; *HAM,* no. 191) provides a link with Frescobaldi. Neapolitan canzonas lace together one to three ingeniously combined and varied subjects (some use contrary motion) in contrasting sections with sudden changes of meter, tempo, and figuration, providing examples of both the "quilt" and variation canzona. Frescobaldi's (Rome, 1615, 1627, 1628, and Venice, 1635, 1645; *HAM,* no. 194) are essays concentrated in three to six sections of imitation connected with toccatalike flourishes or *adagio* interludes. They alternate duple and triple meter and are unified either by continuous thematic variation and running countersubjects or by a return to the opening section at the end. Except for a few examples by Merula, Giovanni Salvatore (Naples, 1641), Giovanni Battista Fasolo (Venice, 1645), and Bernardo Pasquini, the canzona declined in Italy after Frescobaldi, being sustained through the 17th century and into the 18th mainly by south German composers such as Johann Kaspar Kerll, Gottlieb Muffat, and Frescobaldi's student Johann Jacob Froberger. Froberger's canzonas feature a succession of fugal expositions in which a subject is recast in fresh rhythmic guises.

Toward the 17th century's end, differences began to widen between the canzona and the ricercar, capriccio, and fantasia, which all draw upon similar constructive principles. By the early 18th century, the fantasia and capriccio had become freely organized, nearly improvisational structures, whereas the ricercar and canzona had merged into the fugue. Nevertheless, the slower-moving *alla breve* meter and archaic contrapuntal devices of the ricercar distinguish it from the faster, lighter subjects and moods of the canzona. During the Mass, for example, organists played canzonas and capriccios before or during the Gradual and Ite missa est, while the severe ricercar (or a **toccata di durezze e ligature*) was reserved for the elevation. Michael Praetorius (Wolfenbüttel, 1612) equated the mood of the canzona with dance music, "ein lustig Canzon, Gailliard, oder dergleichen," and described it as a succession of *fuge,* a term that Bernhard Schmid used to label Italian canzonas in his 1607 edition. Thus, the two canzonas by Dietrich Buxtehude and the one by Bach (BWV 588) are retrospective in name as well as conception.

Bibl.: Knud Jeppesen, *Die italienische Orgelmusik am Anfang des Cinquecento,* 2nd ed. rev. and enl., 2 vols. (Copenhagen: Hansen, 1960). Leland Bartholomew, *Alessandro Rauerij's Collection of "Canzoni per sonare" (Venice, 1608)* (Fort Hays: Kansas St Col Pr, 1965). Dietrich Kämper, *Studien zur instrumentalen Ensemblemusik des 16. Jahrhunderts in Italien, AnMca* 10 (1970). Willi Apel, *The History of Keyboard Music,* trans. and rev. Hans Tischler (Bloomington: Ind U Pr, 1972). Eleanor Selfridge-Field, *Venetian Instrumental Music from Gabrieli to Vivaldi* (New York: Praeger, 1975). Id., "Canzona and Sonata: Some Differences in Social Identity," *IRASM* 9 (1978): 111–19. John G. Suess, "The Ensemble Sonatas of Maurizio Cazzati," *AnMca* 19 (1979): 146–85. Alexander Silbiger, "The Roman Frescobaldi Tradition, c. 1640–1670," *JAMS* 33 (1980): 42–87. For editions of many of the works discussed, see *CEKM.* Andrew Dell'Antonio, *Syntax, Form and Genre in Sonatas and Canzonas 1621–1635* (Lucca: Libreria musicale italiana, 1997). A.J.N.

Canzona francese [It.]. See Canzona.

Canzone [It., pl. *canzoni*]. (1) Song, in both art and popular music. (2) A poetic form defined by Dante and made popular by Petrarch, having five to seven stanzas of identical scheme and often ending with a shorter final stanza *(commiato).* Each stanza includes a *fronte* of several groups of lines with shared rhymes, and a longer *sirima* metrically distinct from the *fronte.* Iambic lines of seven and eleven syllables are freely mixed. Petrarch's *canzoni* are love lyrics; they were popular with 16th-century madrigalists, who set whole *canzoni* as cycles or, more often, chose individual stanzas. Many 16th-century poets imitated Petrarch's *canzoni,* and their poems also found favor among musicians; these often show free adaptations of the Petrarchan form. *Canzone* was used as a general term for serious madrigals; it was also employed for lighter forms, with words such as **villanesca* attached. The instrumental genre now known as the *canzona was often spelled *canzon* or *canzone* in the 16th century.

(3) Song. In the 18th and 19th centuries (sometimes spelled *canzona*), a songlike work for voice (e.g., "Voi che sapete" in Mozart's *Le nozze di Figaro*) or instruments (e.g., the slow movement of Tchaikovsky's Symphony no. 4).

Bibl.: Alfred Einstein, *The Italian Madrigal* (Princeton: Princeton U Pr, 1949). Don Harrán, "Verse Types in the Early Madrigal," *JAMS* 22 (1969): 27–53. (2) J.H.

Canzonet [Eng.], **canzonetta** [It.]. A light vocal piece popular in Italy from the 1560s, in England at the end of the 16th century, and in Germany in the early 17th century. The texts took various forms, from the *canzone* stanza to the refrain structure of the **villanella;* they were originally many-stanza strophic pieces. The collections of Giovanni Ferretti (1567) and Girolamo Conversi (1572) are among the first musical settings of this poetry; they are homophonic in style but of greater refinement than the *villanella.* Luca Marenzio and Claudio Monteverdi contributed to the genre, as did Orazio Vecchi, Adriano Banchieri, and others. Thomas Morley's canzonets are madrigals in all but name, though he assigns the genre to "the second degree of gravity" as compared with the madrigal and describes such pieces as "little short songs . . . which is, in composition of the music, a counterfeit of the madrigal"; German settings (e.g., by Hans Leo Hassler and Jacob Regnart) are closer to Italian models. Later the term came to mean, in England and Germany, a strophic solo song. J.H.

Caoine [Gael., pronounced *keen*]. In Ireland from the 8th to the 20th centuries, a lament sung at a funeral or wake. See also Coronach.

Capelle, Capellmeister [Ger.]. Older spellings of **Kapelle,* **Kapellmeister.*

Capitolo [It.]. A verse form used by the frottolists [see *Frottola*], consisting of three-line stanzas of eleven-syllable iambic meter in an interlocking rhyme scheme (aba bcb cdc; the last stanza sometimes had a fourth line). Despite its resemblance to Dante's *terza rima,* the frottolists' *capitolo* is in content a lightweight poem. *Capitoli* by 16th-century poets occasionally found their way into the madrigal literature. J.H.

Capo, capotasto [It.]. (1) A device for transposing on a fretted stringed instrument such as a guitar. It consists of a bar that can be affixed to the fingerboard by means of a spring mechanism or elastic, thereby stopping all strings at a desired fret and raising the pitch by a desired number of semitones without requiring a change in fingering by the player. (2) **Barré.* See also *Da capo.*

Capoeira [Port.]. Among the Afro-Bahians of Brazil, a ritual combat-dance for several male participants. The music of the *capoeira,* or *capoeira angola,* involves responsorial singing [see Call and response] accompanied by a distinctive ensemble of *berimbaus* (*musical bows), *caxixi* (basket rattles), and other percussion instruments. *Capoeira* popularity has spread throughout urban Brazil and abroad, and has attracted many practitioners in countries such as the U.S. D.S.

Cappella [It.]. *Chapel; *a cappella* (in the manner of a chapel), pertaining to choral music without instrumental accompaniment. Until the 19th century, the latter phrase was applied only to sacred choral music, especially that of the 16th century in the *Palestrina style. For the role of instruments in early vocal music, see Performance practice.

Capriccio [It., whim; Eng., Fr. *caprice*]. A humorous, fanciful, or bizarre composition, often characterized by an idiosyncratic departure from current stylistic norms. Throughout its history the capriccio has been closely allied with pieces called *fantasia, but more extreme in contrasts and more daring in deviating from conventions of harmony and counterpoint.

The earliest uses of the word in a general musical sense occur as the title for Jacquet de Berchem's madrigal cycle on Ariosto's *Orlando furioso* (Venice, 1561) and in Giovanni Croce's *Triaca musicale* ("musical cure for animal bites") (Venice, 1595), with its comic scenes from Venetian life. More frequently, capriccio identifies instrumental pieces such as the ensemble ones by Vincenzo Ruffo (Milan, 1564), Ottavio Bariolla (Milan, 1594), Paolo Fonghetto (Verona, 1598), and others. Many bear fanciful titles. Beginning with Giovanni Piero Manenti (Venice, 1586), the capriccio may also be a dance-song or movement in a suite, partita, or *sonata da camera,* as with Maurizio Cazzati (Bologna, 1669), Vivaldi (op. 2, Venice, 1709), and Bach (BWV 826, 1727).

One type of capriccio, a precursor of the fugue, draws upon the abstract contrapuntal learnedness of the contemporaneous fantasia and canzona [see Fantasia II]. Capriccios of this type have shorter sections that are often repeated, contrast textures and moods more strikingly, and use fugal subjects that are more sprightly; they may also have unexpected chromatic twists. These capriccios are prominent in works by Italian keyboard composers such as Giovanni de Macque (Rome, 1586), Ascanio Mayone (Naples, 1603, 1609), Giovanni Maria Trabaci (Naples, 1603), Tarquinio Merula (Venice, 1615), and Frescobaldi (Rome, 1615, 1624). Praetorius (*Syntagma musicum,* 1619) called such pieces hastily contrived fantasias.

Another type of Baroque capriccio is programmatic. Frescobaldi, Johann Kaspar Kerll, Johann Jacob Froberger, and Alessandro Poglietti, among other mid-17th-century composers, employ figural variation or ostinato and imitate the calls of the cuckoo and nightingale, recall the sounds of bells and war, or depict a pastoral scene. Bach's *Capriccio on the Departure of His Most Beloved Brother* (BWV 992, ca. 1704), with its fugal writing and sounds of the post horn, combines the two Baroque types.

The instruction *a capriccio* indicates a passage played in free tempo, e.g., a cadenza. Locatelli's 24 Capriccios (1733), originally cadenzas for violin concertos, are virtuoso technical etudes in all keys. They lead a tradition that includes similar sets for solo violin by Veracini (in op. 2, 1744), Rodolphe Kreutzer (*40 Études ou caprices,* 1796), Paganini (24 Caprices op. 1, ca. 1805), and Pierre Rode (*24 Caprices en forme d'études* op. 22, ca. 1815). Paganini's capriccios spawned similar sets of etude-capriccios in all keys for other instruments, such as those by Ernesto Cavallini for clarinet (opp. 1–5, ca. 1840–44), by Theobald Boehm for flute (op. 26, 1852), and by Alfredo Piatti for cello (op. 25, 1875), and were the subject of concert variations and transcriptions for piano by Chopin, Schumann, Liszt, Brahms, and Rachmaninoff.

A fanciful mood permeates the capriccios of Weber and Mendelssohn, with their scherzo style of fast, evenly moving, light staccato figuration; a similar agitation characterizes the capriccios in Brahms's op. 76 (1878) and op. 116 (1892). Notable 20th-century capriccios include Stravinsky's for piano and orchestra (1929, rev. 1949) and Penderecki's for oboe and strings (1965) and for cello alone (1968). For bibl., see Fantasia.

(2) Opera in one act by Richard Strauss (libretto by Clemens Krauss, with contributions by the composer and others), produced in Munich in 1942. The authors call the work "a conversation piece for music." Setting: near Paris, around 1775. (1) A.J.N.

Capriccio espagnol [Fr., Spanish Capriccio]. A symphonic suite in five sections, op. 34 (1887), by Rimsky-Korsakov employing some characteristic Spanish rhythms and melodic figures.

Capriccio italien [Fr., Italian Capriccio]. A symphonic poem by Tchaikovsky, op. 45 (1880), composed during a visit to Italy and employing Italian folk songs.

Capriccioso, capricciosamente, a capriccio [It.]. Capricious, capriciously, at the player's whim. See Capriccio.

Caprice [Fr.]. *Capriccio.

Caput. The concluding melisma, over the word *caput,* in the *Sarum antiphon "Venit ad Petrum." The melody was used as a **cantus firmus* in a Mass by Dufay (though the attribution to him has been questioned) and in closely related Masses by Obrecht and Ockeghem. The source of the melisma was first identified by Bukofzer (1950).

Bibl.: Manfred Bukofzer, "*Caput:* A Liturgico-musical Study," *Studies in Medieval and Renaissance Music* (New York: Norton, 1950), pp. 217–310. Alejandro Planchart, "Guillaume Dufay's Masses: Notes and Revisions," *MQ* 58 (1972): 1–23. Reinhard Strohm, "Quellenkritische Untersuchungen an der Missa 'Caput,'" *Datierung und Filiation von Musikhandschriften der Josquin-Zeit,* ed. Ursula Günther and Ludwig Finscher (Kassel: Bärenreiter, 1984).

Cara cosa [It.]. An Italian popular dance of the 16th century, sometimes called "La gamba." Its music is based upon one of the many harmonic patterns that led to the development of the isometric **folia.* Apparently it was considered primarily a bass pattern [see Ex., from Giulio Abondante's *Intabolatura sopra el lauto,* 1546] because several different discant melodies are set to it. The dance is adapted to the meters of a **pavana,* a *passamezzo, a **saltarello,* or a **gagliarda.*

Bibl.: Lawrence H. Moe, "Dance Music in Printed Italian Lute Tablatures from 1507 to 1611" (Ph.D. diss., Harvard Univ., 1956), pp. 232–34. L.H.M.

Caramba [Sp.]. A *musical bow of Central America. Other names for the same or closely related instruments of the region are *carimba, quijongo,* and *zambumbia.*

Card Game, The. See *Jeu de cartes.*

Cardillac. Opera in three acts by Hindemith (libretto by Ferdinand Lion after E. T. A. Hoffmann), produced in Dresden in 1926; produced with libretto revised by the composer in Zurich in 1952. Setting: Paris, 17th century.

Carezzando [It.]. Caressingly, soothingly.

Carillon. A set of large, tuned *bells, usually hung in a tower and played from a keyboard and pedalboard.

Cara cosa.

A carillon may contain anywhere from 25 to 40 bells, tuned chromatically and covering from two to four octaves. The bells, the largest weighing as much as 10,000 kg, do not move but are fixed to beams and struck by moving clappers. The keyboard consists of two rows of wooden batons arranged like a piano keyboard but played with the fists rather than the fingers. The batons are attached to the clappers by a system of wires, springs, and counterweights.

Carillons originated in the Low Countries during the 15th century. The first record of a keyboard being attached to a set of bells comes from Antwerp in 1480. In the mid-16th century, the Hemony brothers produced 40 to 50 carillons for churches and municipalities. Many of these are still extant and in use and are considered outstanding instruments. Interest in carillons declined in the 18th and 19th centuries, but revived in the late 19th and early 20th centuries, especially in the Low Countries, where a school for carilloneurs was founded in 1922 by Jef Denyn (1862–1941). The carillon became popular in the U.S. during the 1920s, both in churches and on university campuses. There are at present about 70 mechanical carillons in the Netherlands, about 70 in Belgium, about 30 in northern France, and about 100 in the U.S. Many carillons can be played by automatic mechanisms as well as from a keyboard. In the 1950s, electronic carillons were developed, most of them using tuned rods or *tubular bells greatly amplified.

Much carillon music is transcribed from works for other instruments. Among the most important examples of 17th- and 18th-century carillon music are works by Matthias van den Gheyn (1721–85). Composers of the 20th century who have contributed to the repertory include Jef Denyn, J. A. F. Wagenaar, Daniel Pinkham, and John Cage. See also Chimes, Cymbalum.

Bibl.: F. Percival Price, *The Carillon* (London: Oxford U Pr, 1933). Arthur L. Bigelow, *Carillon* (Princeton: Princeton U Pr, 1948). Id., *The Acoustically Balanced Carillon* (Princeton: Dept of Graphics, School of Engineering, Princeton U, 1961). Englebert W. van Heuven, *Acoustical Measurements on Church-bells and Carillons* ('s Gravenhage: Gebroeders Van Cleef, 1949).

Carimba [Sp.]. See *Caramba.*

Carioca [Port., someone from Rio de Janeiro]. **Samba.*

Carmen [Lat., pl. *carmina*]. (1) Song, poem. In the Middle Ages and Renaissance, the term is applied to a wide variety of kinds of music, including monophonic popular song and the French *chanson. (2) In Germany in the late 15th and early 16th centuries, compositions for instrumental ensemble, often in three voices. Such pieces are found in the Glogauer Liederbuch (ca. 1480) and among the works of Isaac, Senfl, and Hofhaimer. The term is also applied to pieces of similar character derived from vocal models. See also Canzona. (3) [Sp. proper name] Opera in four acts by Bizet (libretto by Henri Meilhac and Ludovic Halévy, after Mérimée), produced in Paris in 1875. Setting: Seville and environs, about 1820.

Carmina burana [Lat., songs of Beuren]. (1) A title given in the 19th century to a collection of over 200 Latin secular poems preserved in a manuscript of the 13th century at the monastery of Benediktbeuren (where, however, it probably did not originate) until 1803 and now in the Bayerische Staatsbibliothek in Munich (Codex Latinus 4660; facs. ed. Bernhard Bischoff, Brooklyn: Institute of Mediaeval Music, 1967). The great majority are love poems (often obscene) belonging to an international repertory reaching back to the 12th century and beyond and preserved also principally in French and English manuscripts. Some poems are provided with nondiastematic neumes, but can be transcribed with the help of concordances in the repertories of *Notre Dame and *St. Martial. The collection also includes about 48 poems in German. See also Goliards. (2) A scenic oratorio (1937) by Carl Orff for soloists, choruses, and orchestra, based on 24 Latin poems from the collection described under (1).

Carnatic. Of or pertaining to the classical music of South India; also Karnatic. See South Asia.

Carnaval: Scènes mignonnes sur quatre notes [Fr., Carnival: Dainty Scenes on Four Notes]. A work for piano by Schumann, op. 9 (1833–35), consisting of 21 short pieces bearing programmatic titles. The notes in question are derived from the name of a Bohemian town, Asch, the home of the young Schumann's sweetheart Ernestine von Fricken, by means of German *pitch names. The results are a four-note group —A, E♭ (from the *S* interpreted as *Es*), C, and B♮ (called *H* in German)—and a three-note group—A♭ (from *As*), C, and B♮. See also *Davidsbündlertänze.*

Carnaval des animaux, Le [Fr., The Carnival of the Animals]. A "Grand Zoological Fantasy" composed in 1886 by Saint-Saëns for chamber orchestra and two pianos. It consists of short descriptive pieces named for various animals.

Carnavalito [Sp.]. A collective dance of Bolivia and northern Argentina, associated with the pre-Lenten celebration of Carnival but performed on other occasions as well. It is also popular as a salon dance and is distinctive in its numerous intricate choreographic figures. The music of the *carnavalito* exhibits features in common with the **huayno* and other Andean dance genres. D.S.

Carnaval romain, Le [Fr., The Roman Carnival]. An overture ("ouverture caractéristique") by Berlioz, op. 9 (1844), based on themes from his opera *Benvenuto Cellini* (produced in Paris in 1838).

Carnival songs. **Canti carnascialeschi.*

Carol. In the Middle Ages, a song of English origin,

with text in English or Latin (or a mixture of the two) and dealing with any subject, but most often having to do with the Virgin Mary or some aspect of Christmas. The medieval carol began with a burden (refrain), which was followed by verses (stanzas) of uniform structure; the burden was repeated after each verse. Many such texts survive without music. Although the alternation between burden and verse seems originally to have corresponded to an alternation between chorus and soloist(s), this correspondence was steadily blurred in the course of the 15th century as forms, sometimes including a double burden, became more complex. In present-day usage, the term designates a strophic song, often traditional and usually (but not always) connected with the celebration of Christmas. Informally, similar songs not of English origin (such as the French **noël* or the German *Weihnachtslied*) are sometimes called carols. For Spanish songs associated with Christmas, see *Villancico.*

In the repertory of the Middle Ages and early Renaissance, several types of carol may be distinguished according to style or function. First, many such pieces were apparently associated with bodily movement, both dancing (cf. the French **carole*) and walking in procession. Second, there existed popular religious carols with monophonic music, similar to the French **noël* and the Italian **lauda.* Finally, the 15th and 16th centuries saw the composition of numerous polyphonic carols, which may themselves be divided into two general types: conductuslike pieces of the 15th century that were copied in score format in liturgical manuscripts and that seem to have served as processional pieces; and more elaborate polyphonic works of the late 15th and early 16th centuries by Cornysh, Davy, and others, copied in choirbook format (e.g., in the Fayrfax manuscript, *GB-Lbm* Add. 5465), composed in increasingly varied forms (e.g., with new music for successive verses), and setting texts that might be contemplative, courtly, or political.

At the time of the Reformation in England, works that were more motetlike began to be composed in place of the polyphonic carol; and in the 17th century, the monophonic carol was strongly disapproved by Puritan reformers. With the Restoration, however, came a resurgence of the popular carol, which had never gone entirely out of use; and the composition and publication of popular carols have continued uninterrupted ever since. The carol of art music never regained its former prominence.

Bibl.: Richard L. Greene, ed., *The Early English Carols* (Oxford: Clarendon Pr, 1935). Manfred F. Bukofzer, *Studies in Medieval and Renaissance Music* (New York: Norton, 1950), pp. 113–75. John Stevens, *Mediaeval Carols, MB* 4 (1952; rev. ed. 1958). Frank L. Harrison, *Music in Medieval Britain* (London: Routledge & Kegan Paul, 1958). Manfred Bukofzer, "Popular and Secular Music in England (to *c.* 1470)," *NOHM* 3 (1960): 107–33. John Stevens et al., "The English Carol" (Round Table), *Ljubljana,* 1967, pp. 284–309. Id., *Early Tudor Songs and Carols, MB* 36 (1975). William E. Studwell, *Christmas Carols: A Reference Guide* (New York: Garland, 1985). Hugh Keyte and Andrew Parrott, eds., *The New Oxford Book of Carols* (Oxford: Oxford U Pr, 1992).

Carole [Fr.]. A social dance of the 12th and 13th centuries, common in both courtly and popular society and danced to refrain songs *(cançon de carole)* sung by a soloist on the verses alternating with the full group (chorus) singing the refrain. The term derives from Gr. *choraules,* Lat. *corolla/carolla,* meaning a musician accompanying a dance. Numerous literary references suggest it was a circle-dance. The word *tresca, tresche, tresce* [Occ., It., Fr.] is sometimes used synonymously, but it may have been performed in a line rather than a circle. The presence of a refrain in extant examples and the occasional term *rondet de carole* after ca. 1250 suggest an association with the developing **rondeau* and other refrain types. About 20 monophonic examples survive, most of them notated in triple meter.

Bibl.: Margit Sahlin, *Étude sur la carole médiévale* (Uppsala: Almqvist & Wiksells, 1940). Pierre Bec, *La Lyrique française au moyen-âge,* 2 vols. (Paris: A & J Picard, 1977–78), 1: 220–28, 2: 150–64. Robert Mullaly, "Cançon de Carole," *Acta Musicologica* 58 (1986): 224–31. Christopher Page, *The Owl and the Nightingale: Musical Life and Ideas in France 1100–1300* (Berkeley: U of Cal Pr, 1989). Nico H. J. van den Boogaard, *Rondeaux et refrains du XIIe siècle au début du XIVe* (Paris: Klincksieck, 1969). E.A.

Carrée [Fr.]. A double whole note or breve. See Note.

Cascabeles [Sp.]. (1) Sleigh bells. (2) In Spanish organs, a set of small, untuned bells mounted on a rotating device propelled by a jet of air. See also *Cimbelstern.*

Cascarda [It.]. A court dance of the late 16th and early 17th centuries found only in Fabritio Caroso's dance books (*Il ballarino,* 1581, and later editions titled *Nobilità di dame,* 1600, 1605, and 1630). All editions include music and choreographies. The music of most *cascarde* is in a compound duple (6/8) meter and resembles the music of a **saltarello* and a **gagliarda.* However, three of them are in a compound quadruple (12/8) meter and resemble a **padovana* or a **piva.* The *cascarda* is a dance for couples, occasionally for three persons, and uses any of the typical step patterns of the late Renaissance. L.H.M.

Cassa [It.]. *Drum.

Cassation. An informal instrumental genre of the Classical period, usually intended for performance outdoors as a kind of street serenade. Cassations were most common in Austria and its dominions. The term probably derived from the colloquial German expression "gassatim gehen" (to walk about or perform in the streets). Heinrich Christoph Koch (*Musikalisches Lexikon,* 1802), although acknowledging that the usual meaning of cassation is "a work designed for performance in the evening, outdoors or in the streets," states that the term refers literally to a work intended to close a concert [fr. It. *cassare,* to release or dismiss]. The term was often used interchangeably in the 18th century with *serenade and *notturno.

Cassations are normally in multiple movements, one or more of which is a minuet, march, or other light movement-type. They may be scored for either solo ensemble or orchestra. The cassations of Mozart and Michael Haydn, reflecting a local Salzburg tradition, are all orchestral, though Leopold Mozart in a letter referred to one of his son's soloistic divertimentos, K. 287, as a cassation.

Bibl.: Reimund Hess, "Serenade, Cassation, Notturno und Divertimento bei Michael Haydn" (diss., Univ. of Mainz, 1963). James Webster, "Towards a History of Viennese Chamber Music in the Early Classical Period," *JAMS* 27 (1974): 212–47. Id., "The Scoring of Mozart's Chamber Music for Strings," *Brook,* 1985, pp. 259–96. E.K.W.

Casse-noisette. See *Nutcracker, The.*

Castanets [Fr. *castagnettes;* Ger. *Kastagnetten;* It. *castagnette, nacchere;* Sp. *castañuelas*]. A percussion instrument of indefinite pitch consisting of two shell-shaped pieces of wood, the hollowed sides of which are clapped together. They are widely used in Spanish music, especially to accompany dancing. When played by dancers, they are loosely joined by a string that is looped over the thumb, permitting the remaining fingers to strike them together against the palm of the hand. For orchestral use they are often mounted on either side of a piece of wood that is held by the player and shaken. See ill. under Percussion instruments.

Castrato [It.]. A male singer, castrated as a boy so as to preserve his soprano or alto range after his chest and lungs had become those of an adult; also *evirato.* Castration for this purpose was practiced in Italy in the 16th through 18th centuries and into the 19th century. *Castrati* were members of the Sistine Chapel choir from the later 16th century until 1903 and were prominent in opera throughout the 17th and 18th centuries. They were especially important in *opera seria,* where they sang the leading male roles and were international stars. Among the most celebrated 18th-century *castrati* were Senesino (Francesco Bernardi, d. ca. 1750), Caffarelli (Gaetano Majorano, 1710–83), and Farinelli (Carlo Broschi, 1705–82). The last famous *castrato* was Giovanni Battista Velluti (1780–1861).

Bibl.: Franz Haböck, *Die Kastraten und ihre Gesangskunst* (Stuttgart: Deutsche Verlagsanstalt, 1927). Angus Heriot, *The Castrati in Opera* (London: Seeker & Warburg, 1956; R: New York: Da Capo, 1974).

Catalectic. Of a line of poetry, lacking the final syllable of the prevailing meter or concluding with an imperfect foot.

Catalog number. A number assigned by a manufacturer to a sound recording. Synonymous with issue number, it appears on the label and on the printed matter accompanying the recording. See also Matrix number, Discography.

Catch. A kind of English *round for three unaccompanied male voices, usually with lighthearted words. It was popular from the late 16th century into the 19th. The significance of the name has not been agreed upon. A derivation from **caccia,* often assumed earlier because of the use of canon common to the two genres, is now generally discounted. The term is usually explained, on no real evidence, as relating to each entering singer's catching the round from the preceding one.

The first known use of the word to designate a musical composition occurs in a manuscript collection of rounds dated 1580. Thomas Ravenscroft's anthology *Pammelia: Musicks Miscellanie, or Mixed Varietie of Pleasant Roundelayes, and Delightful Catches* (1609) was the first publication to include such pieces. It was followed by many others over the next two centuries. The singing of catches was a popular male social pastime from the late 16th century onward. At its beginning it seems to have been especially popular among working men and artisans, but it was soon widespread among all classes. The 17th-century catch became a sophisticated and often intricate genre, developing the manner of treating the words that was to remain characteristic. This involved calculating the words so that the interplay among the parts produced new combinations, usually comic or (especially during the Restoration period) bawdy in effect. The bawdy Restoration catch, much frowned upon in later periods, especially the Victorian, has contributed to a revival of interest in the genre in recent times. Late 17th-century composers of catches included Michael Wise (ca. 1647–87), Henry Aldrich (1648–1710), John Blow (1649–1708), and Henry Purcell (1659–95).

In the 18th century, social clubs organized around the singing of catches and similar music, as well as smoking and drinking (they usually met in taverns), were numerous. The Noblemen and Gentlemen's Catch Club, founded in London in 1761 and still in existence, exemplifies the wide social milieu of the catch in its later stages. Prominent among the numerous 18th-century composers of catches were Philip Hayes (1738–97), Samuel Webbe (1740–1816), and John Callcott (1766–1821). The catch gradually lost vitality in the 19th century.

Bibl.: Jill Vlasto, "An Elizabethan Anthology of Rounds," *MQ* 40 (1954): 222–34. Paul Hillier, ed., *The Catch Book: 153 Catches Including the Complete Catches of Henry Purcell* (Oxford: Oxford U Pr, 1987).

Cathedral music. See Anglican church music.

Catholicon. In Glareanus's *Dodecachordon* (1547), a composition that can be sung in more than one of the church *modes, for example, Ockeghem's *Missa cuiusvis toni* (Mass in any mode), which is notated without clefs.

Cat's Fugue. Popular name for a keyboard sonata in G minor by Domenico Scarlatti (L. 499, K. 30), so called because the theme consists of wide and irregular skips in ascending motion, as if produced by a cat bounding across the keyboard.

Cauda [Lat., tail]. (1) In *mensural notation, an ascending or descending stem attached to any of various note shapes. (2) A textless passage such as often occurs at the ends of lines in **conductus.*

Cavaco [Port.]. A Portuguese, fretted, stringed instrument related to the guitar and the mandolin, with four or six strings. See also *Cavaquinho.*

Caval, kaval [fr. Turk. *qawul*]. An *end-blown flute of the Balkans and Turkey made of cane or softwood. In construction and playing technique it is similar to the **nāy.* It is characteristically a shepherd's instrument.

Cavalleria rusticana [It., Rustic Chivalry]. Opera in one act by Pietro Mascagni (libretto by Guido Menasci and Giovanni Targioni-Tozzetti, after Giovanni Verga's play), produced in Rome in 1890. Setting: a Sicilian village in the late 19th century. See *Verismo.*

Cavaquinho [Port., dim. of **cavaco*]. A small, four-stringed, guitarlike instrument of Portugal and Brazil; also called a *machete.* It was taken by Portuguese sailors to Hawaii, where it became known as the *ukulele.

Cavata [It.]. A short, epigrammatic arioso found at the end of a long recitative *(recitativo con cavata).* Popular in 17th-century chamber cantatas, the procedure is also found in Bach's cantatas, although he does not use the term as such.

Cavatina [It.; Fr. *cavatine;* Ger. *Kavatine*]. A type of *aria. In 19th-century Italian opera, the cavatina is the entrance aria of a principal singer. It is in all formal ways identical to pieces labeled aria in the scores of Rossini, Donizetti, Bellini, Verdi, and their contemporaries. In this repertory, the cavatina is distinguished only by its position in the opera, that is, in the first act. In 19th-century French and German opera, a *cavatine* or *Kavatine* is a short aria in a moderate or slower than moderate tempo. Weber includes a *Kavatine* for the heroine in the last act of *Der Freischütz, Euryanthe,* and *Oberon.* Examples are also found in Gounod's *Faust* and Bizet's *La jolie fille de Perth* and *Les pêcheurs de perles.*

In the second half of the 18th century, a cavatina is a short aria, simpler than the da capo aria. When the text consists of a single strophe, often this is repeated (as in "Porgi amor" from Mozart's *Le nozze di Figaro*); when of two strophes, the music for the first strophe is repeated, cadencing on the tonic instead of the dominant.

Bibl.: Wolfgang Osthoff, "Mozarts Cavatinen und ihre Tradition," *Helmuth Osthoff,* 1969, pp. 139–77. C.G.

C.b. [It.]. Abbr. for *col basso,* with the bass, or *contrabasso,* double bass.

CD. Abbr. for *compact disc.

C.d. [It.]. Abbr. for *colla destra,* with the right hand.

Cebell. *Cibell.

Cecilian movement. A movement within the Roman Catholic Church, especially in Germanic countries, to reform church music in the spirit of 19th-century Romantic historicism. Eighteenth-century leagues named for St. Cecilia, patron of music, that had promoted the old *a cappella* style in the face of an increasingly secularized Baroque idiom, evolved under the influence of such theological reformers as Bishop J. M. Sailer and Cardinal Newman into a widespread movement to cultivate Gregorian chant, vernacular hymnody, and composition in the style of Palestrina. In 1869, Franz Xaver Witt founded the Allgemeine Cäcilien-Verein, which published music deemed proper for worship and spawned similar societies in Europe and, notably, in the U.S. under John B. Singenberger.

Bibl.: Karl Gustav Fellerer, *Geschichte der katholischen Kirchenmusik* (Düsseldorf: Schwann, 1939); trans. Eng., Francis A. Brunner, *The History of Catholic Church Music* (Baltimore: Helicon, 1961).

Cedendo [It.]. Becoming slower.

Cédez [Fr.]. Yield, slow down.

Cefaut. See Hexachord.

Ceja, cejilla [Sp.]. **Barré.*

Celere, celermente [It.]. Quickly, swiftly.

Celesta [Eng., Ger., It., Sp.; Fr. *célesta*]. An instrument in the form of a small upright piano in which the action causes hammers to strike metal bars suspended over resonators. Dampers for the bars are controlled by a damper pedal. The celesta has a range of five octaves upward from c and is notated on staves in the fashion of piano music, sounding an octave higher than notated. It was patented by Auguste Mustel of Paris in 1886. Among the best-known works of the orchestral repertory making use of the celesta are the "Dance of the Sugar-Plum Fairy" from Tchaikovsky's *The *Nutcracker* and Bartók's *Music for Strings, Percussion, and Celesta* (1936). See ill. under Percussion instruments. See also Dulcitone.

Range.

Céleste [Fr.]. (1) An organ stop with two ranks of pipes, one tuned slightly sharp to create an undulating sound. The *Voix céleste* was important in 19th-century French organs. (2) *Moderator (pedal).

Cello. *Violoncello.

Cellone [It.]. A large violoncello, tuned a fourth lower than the normal cello (G_1 D A e), designed by Alfred Stelzner of Dresden about 1890 to provide a bass part in chamber music. It found little acceptance by either composers or performers.

Cembal d'amour. A type of *clavichord invented by Gottfried Silbermann about 1721. According to an engraving published in 1723 it had the shape of an irregular trapezoid and had a 51-note compass (C to d‴). Its strings were approximately twice normal length and were struck near the middle, so that both segments of each string sounded the same pitch. The central tangent that struck the string also raised it off a damping block, which replaced the usual clavichord damper listing. Despite having greater volume, sustaining power, and dynamic range than did the normal clavichord, the *cembal d'amour* did not become popular, according to Forkel.

Bibl.: Johann Forkel, *Musikalischer Almanach für Deutschland* (Leipzig, 1782), p. 19. Edmund S. J. van der Straeten, "The Cembal d'Amour," *MT* 65 (1924): 40–42.

H.S.

Cembalo [It., abbr. of *clavicembalo;* Ger.]. *Harpsichord. On the piano, a cembalo or harpsichord stop is a device intended to imitate the sound of the harpsichord.

Cencerro [Sp.]. *Cowbell.

Cenerentola, La [It., Cinderella]. Opera in two acts by Rossini (libretto by Jacopo Ferretti, after Charles Perrault's fairy tale *Cendrillon,* Charles-Guillaume Étienne's libretto *Cendrillon,* and Felice Romani's libretto *Agatina*). First produced in Rome in 1817. Setting: Salerno in the 18th century (although the specific time and place have no great bearing on the work).

Cent. On the logarithmic scale used in measuring the size of the *interval between two pitches, 1/100 of a semitone in equal *temperament. The octave in this scheme is equal to 1,200 cents, since each of the twelve equally tempered semitones is equal to 100 cents. This system of measurement was introduced by Herrmann Helmholtz in 1863 and adapted for practical use in musicological research by Alexander J. Ellis in 1885.

Centitone. A unit of measurement equal to 1/100 of a whole tone in equal *temperament and thus equal to two *cents.

Centonization [fr. Lat. *cento,* patchwork]. The creation of a work from preexisting elements. The term has been much used (first by Ferretti, 1934) in connection with liturgical chants that make use of melodic formulas shared with other chants, usually of the same liturgical type and in the same mode. Such a chant is said to be centonate. The Gregorian tract, gradual, and responsory have often been described in this way. Although the existence of such formulas is not in dispute, the term has been found problematic (Treitler 1975) on the grounds that it implies a creative process in which a historical composer is imagined to have performed a specific act of composition by this method. It is argued instead that the role of formulas in liturgical chant is the result of the processes of oral *transmission.

Bibl.: Paolo Ferretti, *Estetica gregoriana,* vol. 1 (Rome: Pontificio istituto di musica sacra, 1934; trans. Fr., Paris: Desclée, 1938). Leo Treitler, "'Centonate' Chant: *Übles Flickwerk* or *E pluribus unus?*" *JAMS* 28 (1975): 1–23.

Central America. See Latin America.

Central Asia. A region of steppe, desert, mountains, and riverine oases occupying the central portion of the Eurasian landmass from the Caspian Sea to the northwest of China and from the southern reaches of Siberia to Afghanistan and northern Pakistan. Culture in the region has historically reflected the interaction of two broad socioeconomic domains: sedentary societies that have supported mercantile trade and urban nobilities, and pastoralists organized into clan-based lineages rooted in the life of the steppe. Notwithstanding millennia of cultural exchange, however, nomads and sedentary dwellers have maintained distinctive musical identities.

The deep impact of Islam as a spiritual and cultural force among Central Asia's sedentary populations resonates strongly in sophisticated urban art song and instrumental music called *maqām,* a name shared with other classical or court music traditions in the core Muslim world. Local repertories of Central Asian *maqām* include *Shash maqām,* identified with the city of Bukhara, Khorezm *maqām,* nourished by noble patronage in the city of Khiva, and Ferghana-Tashkent *maqām,* historically linked to the patronage of the Qoqand khanate. A related but somewhat more distant complex of local *maqām* traditions exists among the Turkic-speaking Uyghurs, who inhabit the oasis cities of northwest China. In Central Asia, *maqām* refers both to a melodic type or mode and to a cyclic form or suite consisting of as many as 25–30 canonical pieces. Many of the names of the Central Asian *maqām*s are identical or cognate with those in other Islamic court music traditions, e.g., *rāst, buzruk, segāh, irāq;* however, their scales and modal features are often different.

In Central Asia, music has been a key element of festivity and celebration linked to life-cycle events such as birthdays, weddings, and circumcisions, and to calendar events such as the celebration of *nawruz,* the Persian New Year that marks the beginning of spring. Among sedentary populations, an abiding tradition of separate festivities for men and women is reflected in distinct genres, repertories, and performance practices for male and female entertainers.

Central Asian pastoralists have historically been on the margins of Islamic cultural influence, and nomadic music has retained its strong roots in archaic practices of animism and shamanism. Among pastoralists, the preeminent musical figure is the bard, a solo performer of oral poetry who typically accompanies himself or herself (women are well represented in the Central Asian bardic tradition) on a strummed lute with silk or gut strings. Nomadic cultures have also produced virtuosic instrumental repertories performed by soloists on strummed lutes, jew's harps, flutes, fiddles, and zithers. A distinguishing feature of these repertories is their narrative quality: pieces typically tell stories by using musical onomatopeia imitating the sounds of horses, birds, the wind, and other natural sound sources. Rhythm in nomadic music tends toward asymmetry and, with the exception of the shaman's drum, is never expressed on percussion. In sedentary cultures, by contrast, metrical drumming is a highly developed art.

Bibl.: Jean During, *Musiques d'Asie centrale: L'esprit d'une tradition* (Paris: Actes Sud, 1998). *Garland Encyclopedia of World Music,* vol. 6: *The Middle East* (New York: Garland, 2001). Theodore Levin, *The Hundred Thousand Fools of God: Musical Travels in Central Asia (and Queens, New York)* (Bloomington: Ind U Pr, 1996). T.L.

Cephalicus [Lat.]. See Neume.

Cercar la nota [It., to seek the note]. In singing, a slight anticipation of the following pitch before pronouncing the syllable assigned to it.

Ceremony of Carols. A setting of nine medieval *carols in Middle English for treble voices and harp by Benjamin Britten, op. 28 (1942). The carols are framed by a Latin plainsong processional and recessional.

Cervelas, cervelat [Fr.]. *Racket.

Ces, ceses [Ger.]. C-flat, C-double-flat. See Pitch names.

Cesolfa(ut). See Hexachord.

Cetera [It.]. *Cittern.

Ceterone [Fr. *cisteron;* Ger. *gross Zittern*]. A large *cittern of the 17th century with an extended pegbox similar to the *theorbo. Wire strung, it was used for *thoroughbass.

Cetra [It.]. (1) *Zither. (2) *English guitar.

C.f. Abbr. for **cantus firmus.*

C fa ut, Cfaut, Cefaut. See Hexachord.

Chacarera [Sp.]. An important traditional couple dance of Argentina. Sung with texts in octosyllabic quatrains *(coplas),* or performed by instruments alone, it exhibits Andean influence in its characteristically pentatonic melodies and oscillation between major and relative minor tonal centers. In other respects, it is similar in style to such related Argentine dances as the **gato.* D.S.

Chace [Fr., hunt]. (1) In the 14th century, *canon. The term is used by Guillaume de Machaut to designate canonic sections of his three-voiced *lai* "Je ne cesse de prier." (2) A type of French composition of the 14th century employing canon in the setting of a text that includes naturalistic sounds, in one case, as in some examples of the Italian **caccia,* those of the hunt. Only a few such pieces survive. The *chace* is usually a finite canon in three parts and lacks the untexted, noncanonic tenor of the *caccia.* The Ivrea MS (begun after 1365) includes four *chaces* (ed. Willi Apel, *French Secular Compositions of the Fourteenth Century, CMM* 53, vol. 3, nos. 290–93), of which one is a perpetual canon and another may be a two-voiced work. The term for similar works from Spain is *caça,* of which three examples survive in the 14th-century *Llibre vermell* (ed. Higini Anglés in *AnM* 10 [1955]: 45–78).

Chachachá, cha cha cha [Sp.]. A Cuban dance-music genre, developed by traditional urban ensembles known as **charangas* in the early 1950s. Like the Cuban **rumba* and **mambo* before it, the *chachachá* was to enjoy international popularity. It is in moderate tempo and characterized by accompanimental patterns shown in the example. D.S.

Chaconne. A continuous variation form of the Baroque, similar to the *passacaglia, based on the chord progression of a late 16th-century dance imported into Spain and Italy from Latin America. Usually in triple meter and major mode, the dance had a few stereotyped bass lines and a basic series of chords (I–V–IV–V) that acted as melodic or melodic-harmonic *ostinatos. Other chords were possible, especially vi and iii, just before IV.

The first written versions in Spanish guitar books of the early 17th century show a simple progression sometimes repeating often enough over the bass line to create a set of ostinato variations; this suggests an originally improvised practice. By 1627, the first chaconne variations for keyboard appeared (Frescobaldi, *Partite sopra ciaconna*) and joined the growing body of keyboard variations on dance basses and progressions (e.g., the **folia,* *passamezzo, **romanesca,* **ruggiero*). Whereas the guitar chaconnes were largely made up of chords, keyboard chaconnes tended to include more counterpoint and intricate figurations over the ostinato. (Many examples of 17th-century chaconnes can be found in Hudson, 1982.) Vocal pieces also used the chaconne bass and harmonic formula, but with greater freedom in modulating and in the treatment of the melodic line, whose phrases might be longer than the bass (e.g., Frescobaldi, *Ceccona a due tenori,* in Hudson, 1981). The French chaconne of the same period, rather more sedate than its southern counterpart, often was presented "en rondeau," the first section returning as a refrain after couplets that may modulate or alter refrain material (e.g., Chambonnières, *Chaconne,* in *HAM,* no. 212). This type of chaconne became common in the harpsichord and chamber suite and also was a great favorite in French opera from Lully to Gluck, especially as a finale with chorus.

By the late 17th century, instrumental chaconnes on both the variation and *rondeau* schemes were popular in England, Germany, and Austria, and they remained so until around 1750. The ostinato often developed into an eight-bar pattern, as in Purcell's *Chacony* (in minor), Handel's Chaconne in G with 62 Variations, and Gottlieb Muffat's *Ciaconna.* The last two have virtually identical chord progressions; the same progression makes up the first reprise of the Aria in Bach's *Goldberg Variations.* Some pieces have a series of variations in the opposite mode to act as a large contrasting section and impose a three-part design on the whole, as in Bach's Chaconne from the Sonata for solo violin in D minor.

Although 18th-century theorists attempted to distinguish between the chaconne and the *passacaglia, no consistent differences are readily apparent from the 18th century onward, except that the chaconne was more frequently in major. Some pieces called passacaglia were actually closer to the original progressions of the chaconne, such as the passacaglia from Wenzel Raimond Pirck's (Birck, Pürk) G-major Trio (two violins and bass; MS copy in *A–Wgm,* IX: 31817). Unlike the passacaglia, the chaconne had few adherents after the Baroque. The 20th century produced a few examples, however (e.g., Britten, Second String Quartet, 3rd movt.; Mario Davidovsky, *Chacona* for violin, cello, and piano, which uses an ostinato of durations).

Bibl.: Paul Mies, "Die Chaconne (Passacaille) bei Händel," *HJb* 2 (1929): 13–24. Arnold Machabey, "Les origines de la chaconne et de la passacaille," *RdM* 25 (1946): 1–21. Kurt von Fischer, "Chaconne und Passacaglia: Ein Versuch," *RBM* 12 (1958): 19–34. Thomas Walker, "Ciaccona and Passacaglia: Remarks on Their Origin and Early History," *JAMS* 21 (1968): 300–320. Richard Hudson, "Further Remarks on the Passacaglia and Ciaccona," *JAMS* 23 (1970): 302–14. Id., *Passacaglio and Ciaccona: From Guitar Music to Italian Keyboard Variations in the 17th Century* (Ann Arbor: UMI Res Pr, 1981). Id., *The Folia, the Saraband, the Passacaglia, and the Chaconne, MSD* 35 (1982). E.S.

Chahārmezrāb [Per., four plectrums]. An instrumental genre of Persian classical and popular music, composed or improvised, usually accompanied by drum, with rapid tempo, rhythmic ostinato, frequent use of drone, and virtuosic passages. B.N.

Chair organ. A secondary division of English organs, having its own case and wind-chest, located behind the organist's bench or chair. See also Positive organ.

Chaldean chant. See Syrian chant.

Chaleur [Fr.]. Warmth, passion.

Chalumeau [Ger. *chalimo, chalimou, Schalümo;* It. *scialumò*]. (1) A cylindrical, single-reed instrument, often with two keys, developed during the late 17th century. A keyless *chalumeau* appeared about 1680, sold in England under the name mock trumpet, and was illustrated as late as 1767 in the *Recueil de Planches* of the *Encyclopédie.* An improved version with two diametrically opposed keys is credited to the Nuremberg woodwind maker Johann Christoph Denner (1655–1707), who is also credited with the invention of the clarinet. Unlike the similar-looking Baroque *clarinet, the *chalumeau* plays only in its fundamental register, does not have a speaker key to assist in producing an overblown register, and does not include a flared bell. Most *chalumeaux* are similar in profile to the recorder.

The earliest evidence of the use of the *chalumeau* is a 1687 invoice list showing "Ein Chor Chalimo von 4. stücken" purchased in Nuremberg for the duke of Römhild-Sachsen. It is quite possible that J. C. Denner made these *chalumeaux.* During the 18th century, Denner's son Jacob (1681–1735) received orders for *chalumeaux* as recorded in archival documents from Nuremberg (1710) and Göttweig (ca. 1720). The earliest musical evidence for the use of the *chalumeau* is an anonymous collection inscribed "Hannover 1690" and entitled "XIIe Concert Charivari ou nopce de village a 4 Violin, 2 Chalumeau 3 Pollisons et un Tambour les Viollons en Vielle." In 1722, a two-key *chalumeau* was briefly described by Buonanni, and ten years later Majer reported the existence of four sizes of *chalumeaux:* soprano, alto or quart, tenor, and bass. Many composers wrote for the two-key *chalumeau* in operas, oratorios, cantatas, and instrumental works, including Georg Philipp Telemann, Johann Christoph Graupner, Johann Joseph Fux, Christoph Willibald Gluck, Handel, Johann Christoph Molter, and Franz Anton Hoffmeister in a concerto as late as the 1770s. Extant two-key instruments are a tenor by J. C. Denner (ca. 1700), two tenors by Klenig (ca. 1750–60), an alto by Liebau (ca. 1750–60), and a soprano by an anonymous maker (ca. 1750). W. Kress (ca. 1700) constructed a bass *chalumeau* in a bassoon shape with an extended lower range and five keys. Other extant examples are an anonymous alto d'amour (ca. 1750) with three keys and a soprano by Muller (ca. 1760) with seven keys. Other documented makers of *chalumeaux* include Jacob Denner, Philipp Borkens, Jeremias Schlegel, Debey, Jan Steenbergen, and Andrea Fornari. Joos Verschuere Reynvaan (1795) gave the last description of the *chalumeau* and provided a fingering chart for a one-key tenor instrument with an idioglott reed mouthpiece. By 1800, the instrument disappeared.

(2) A shepherd's pipe made of a wheat stalk with an idioglott reed.

(3) A chanter of a bagpipe.

(4) The lowest register of the clarinet named by Valentin Roeser in a treatise of 1764.

(5) A register of a pipe organ first made during the 1730s by Gottfried Silbermann.

Bibl.: Filippo Buonanni, *Gabinetto armonico pieno d'istromenti sonori* (Rome: G Placho, 1722). J. F. B. C. Majer, *Museum musicum* (Schwäbisch Hall: G M Majer, 1732; R: Kassel: Bärenreiter, 1954). Valentin Roeser, *Essai d'instruction à l'usage de ceux qui composent pour la clarinette et le cor* (Paris: Le Menu, 1764; R: Geneva: Minkoff, 1972). Heinz Becker, "Das Chalumeau im 18. Jahrhundert," in *Speculum Musicae Artis, Festgabe für Heinrich Husmann* (Munich: Katzbichler, 1970), pp. 23–46. Colin Lawson, *The* Chalumeau *in Eighteenth-Century Music* (Ann Arbor: UMI Res Pr, 1981). Albert R. Rice, *The Baroque Clarinet* (Oxford: Clarendon, 1992). A.R.R.

Chamade [Fr.]. (1) In France, a reed stop whose pipes are mounted horizontally in the facade of an organ, *en chamade*. Stops of this type are a prominent feature of many Spanish organs [see *Lengueteria de la fachada*]. (2) **Chiamata*.

Chamber music. In present usage, music written for and performed by a small ensemble, usually instrumental, with one performer on a part. The term has been defined or delimited differently in various periods, reflecting changing social and musical conditions. For the 19th century and much of the 20th, it meant instrumental music for small ensembles in the tradition deriving from the Viennese Classical masters, Haydn, Mozart, and Beethoven. Much of this music is in four-movement *sonata format and bears abstract titles reflecting the number of instruments employed (*trio, *quartet, *quintet, *sextet, *septet, *octet, *nonet). Chamber music has most often been written for strings in standard groupings, most prominently the *string quartet, but piano and strings, mixed winds and strings, winds alone, and other combinations are often employed. Music for a solo performer, with or without accompaniment, is often excluded from this definition, because interplay of parts is considered an essential element of it.

From the 16th to the late 18th century, the term was used differently, with all music classified in three large categories: chamber, church, and—after the rise of opera—theater. This classification was based primarily on the music's social function and only secondarily on differences of style, form, or performing forces. The **sonata da camera* (chamber sonata) and **sonata da chiesa* (church sonata), the two main types of trio sonata, therefore fell into different categories. Chamber music included whatever secular music might be performed in the musical establishment of a private household, whether vocal or instrumental, solo or ensemble, including music for orchestra.

Mid-18th-century orchestras often were not much larger than solo ensembles with only one player on each part, and it is sometimes not easy to distinguish, on the basis of style, music written for one or the other. Some was intended to be suitable for either type of ensemble. Later in the century, there was an increasing divergence between the two in size and the style of their music, as the transference of the orchestra's center of activity to the public concert hall created conditions for its rapid growth. Small solo ensembles remained popular, especially with the period's growing numbers of musical amateurs. Of the large quantities of music produced for this market, much tended to be easy to play and simple in style, texture, and expression. Partly out of this environment, but in contrast to it, Haydn developed, especially in his string quartets, a style based on a high degree of equality, independence, and interplay of the parts. This greatly increased the musical interest and expressive possibilities of the genre, which were further explored by Mozart and Beethoven. The work of these three composers led to the concept of chamber music as an intimate art of wide expressive range, one increasingly distinct from the symphonic style being formulated at the same time in orchestral music.

As the orchestra grew in size and coloristic possibilities in the 19th century, chamber music with its more restricted scope came to be seen in a somewhat reverential light as the most intellectual and the most profound and purest of the instrumental genres (especially after the late quartets of Beethoven). With the increasing complexity of compositional styles, demands on performers rose; chamber-music concerts by professionals became more frequent, amateur performances less so.

For much of the century, most significant chamber music was produced by composers of the German school (principally Schubert, Mendelssohn, Schumann, Brahms, and Dvořák) who carried on enough of the characteristics of the Viennese composers to constitute a tradition for the genre. Composers such as Liszt, Bruckner, or Richard Strauss, stylistically more radical and inclined to program music or expansiveness of expression, produced relatively little in this genre. Although chamber music of this period tended to the abstract, there were notable attempts at extramusical suggestion or programs by Smetana (**From My Life*), Schoenberg (**Verklärte Nacht*), and others. Late in the century, chamber music had a flowering in France, with Franck, Fauré, Debussy, and others, and to some extent elsewhere in northern Europe. In the U.S., where opportunities for orchestral performance were less abundant, many composers put sustained (and often their best) effort into chamber music (Arthur Foote, George Chadwick, Charles Ives, Amy Beach, Charles Loeffler).

The Classical tradition remained strong in chamber music in the 20th century, with the string quartet much cultivated by composers of otherwise very different stylistic tendencies, such as Bartók, Schoenberg, Carter, Bloch, Milhaud, Villa-Lobos, Shostakovich, and many others. At the same time, there was wide-ranging experimentation with unusual combinations of instruments, the participation of voices, electronic elements, new forms, and compositional methods that expanded the boundaries of the genre and made necessary a broader definition of it.

The 20th-century revival of much medieval, Renaissance, and Baroque music had similar results, since much of it fell within an expanded concept of chamber music in which interplay of the members of small solo ensembles and intimacy of effect were the main determining criteria rather than the presence of instrumental groupings or musical forms belonging to a specific tradition.

Bibl.: Donald Francis Tovey, *Essays in Musical Analysis: Chamber Music,* ed. Hubert J. Foss (London: Oxford U Pr, 1944). Walter Cobbett, ed., *Cobbett's Cyclopedic Survey of Chamber Music,* 2nd ed. rev. (London: Oxford U Pr, 1963). Donald N. Ferguson, *Image and Structure in Chamber Music* (Minneapolis: U of Minn Pr, 1964). Homer Ulrich, *Chamber Music: The Growth and Practice of an Intimate Art,* 2nd ed. (New York: Columbia U Pr, 1966). Roger Fiske, *Chamber Music* (London: BBC, 1969). James Webster, "Towards a History of Viennese Chamber Music in the Early Classical Period," *JAMS* 27 (1974): 212–47. Hubert Unverricht, *Kammermusik, Mw* 46, trans. Eng. A. C. Howie (Cologne: A Volk, 1975). Ella Marie Forsyth, *Building a Chamber Music Collection: A Descriptive Guide to Published Scores* (Metuchen, N.J.: Scarecrow, 1979). John H. Baron, *Chamber Music: A Research and Information Guide* (New York: Garland, 1987). John H. Baron, *Intimate Music: A History of the Idea of Chamber Music* (Stuyvesant, N.Y.: Pendragon, 1998).

Chamber opera. An opera of small dimensions, of an intimate character, using relatively small performing resources. The earliest operas were *de facto* chamber operas in that they were performed in the rooms of noble residences rather than in theaters. The term can be applied to many 18th-century operas as an indication that they call for few singers and an orchestra made up of strings plus a few supporting winds. It is more meaningfully used in describing 20th-century works that deliberately eschew the use of a large orchestra, although many of the 20th-century works called chamber operas, such as Strauss's *Ariadne auf Naxos* or Stravinsky's *The Rake's Progress,* demand larger performing forces than were normally used in 18th-century Italian opera. Britten's *The Turn of the Screw* (requiring six or seven soloists, single woodwinds, a string quartet plus bass, harp, percussion, piano, and celesta) is a model example of chamber opera.

Chamber orchestra. A small orchestra, often of around 20 or 25 players, as distinct from the modern symphony *orchestra. Since this was about the normal size for orchestras in the 18th century, such ensembles today often devote themselves to the performance of 18th-century music [see also Chamber music], though the late 19th century and the 20th also produced works specifically for ensembles of this type.

Chamber organ. An organ of modest size (usually four to seven stops), with a single keyboard, intended for use in domestic rooms or other small spaces.

Bibl.: Michael I. Wilson, *The Chamber Organ in Britain, 1600–1830* (Aldershot: Ashgate, 2001).

Chamber pitch. See Pitch.

Chamber sonata. See *Sonata da camera.*

Chamber symphony. A symphony intended for performance by a *chamber orchestra rather than by a modern symphony orchestra. The term is not normally applied to works from earlier periods in which the normal size of the orchestra was that of what is now often termed a chamber orchestra.

Chance music. See Aleatory music.

Chandos Anthems. Twelve anthems for soloists, chorus, and orchestra by Handel, composed in the years 1717–18 for James Brydges, later Duke of Chandos. Included are a **Te Deum* and a *Jubilate.*

Change ringing. The English practice of ringing tower *bells (or, more recently, handbells) in a methodical order, the changes in the ringing sequence prescribed by arithmetical permutations. For instance, a set, or "ring," of six bells, 1 2 3 4 5 6, may be played in the orders, or "changes," 2 1 4 3 6 5, or 2 4 1 6 3 5, etc. The "peal," or total number of permutations, for six bells is 720 (6!, i.e., 6 × 5 × 4 × 3 × 2 × 1; for twelve bells, 479,001,660), but in actual performance, usually a limited selection of changes is played in succession, the main principle being the course, or path, of a bell among the other bells, effected chiefly by the exchange of pairs of bells. A complete system of changes, called a "method," always begins and ends with "rounds," the ring rung in order from highest to lowest pitch. Methods, some of which are extremely complicated, are known by such traditional names as "Grandsire Triple," "Treble Bob," and "Plain Hunt."

Groups of swinging bells in English church towers date from the 10th century, but it was the invention of the bell wheel in the 14th century that gave ringers enough control over the timing of bell strokes to make change ringing possible. By the 17th century, intricate methods had evolved, and prestigious change ringing societies were formed to perform them. The first such organization, the Ancient Society of College Youths, was founded in 1637 and is still active. Methods are performed from memory, in even rhythm, one person per bell. Important early treatises on the subject include Fabian Stedman's *Tintinnalogia* (1688) and his *Campanologia* (1677).

Bibl.: Dorothy L. Sayers, *The Nine Tailors: Changes Rung on an Old Theme in Two Short Touches and Two Full Peals* (London: Gollancz, 1934). Wilfrid G. Wilson, *Change Ringing* (London: Faber, 1965). John Camp, *Bell Ringing* (Newton Abbot: David & Charles, 1974).

Changes. In jazz and popular music, a harmonic *progression; also the entire series of chords or harmonies making up a piece.

Changing note. Cambiata. See Counterpoint II, 7.

Channel. *Bridge (3).

Chanson [Fr.]. (1) Song. The term has been in use since the Middle Ages and has referred to a very wide range of both poetry and music cultivated by all classes of society, including the medieval epic (**chanson de geste*), the *troubadour and *trouvère repertories, secular polyphony and the related poetry of the 14th through 16th centuries [see (2) below], the **air de cour* of the late 16th and early 17th centuries, the **brunette* of the 17th and 18th centuries, the **vaudeville* originating in the 16th century and spawning a tradition lasting into the 19th, the art song of the 19th and 20th centuries (more often referred to as the **mélodie*), and folk and popular song of all periods up to the present.

(2) French secular polyphonic song of the 14th through 16th centuries; sometimes, more narrowly, a late 15th- or 16th-century setting of a text not in one of the **formes fixes.*

Chansons setting one or another of the *formes fixes* are first encountered at the end of the 13th century, 14 three-voice **rondeaux* by Adam de la Halle being the earliest such works to survive with an attribution. These are homophonic in style with the principal voice generally occupying the middle position. It is in the works of Guillaume de Machaut (ca. 1300–77), however, that the tradition that dominated chanson composition until near the end of the 15th century was established. His chansons, among which the **ballade* predominates, are most often for three voices, the uppermost voice being the leading melodic part and the only one provided with text, the lower two voices, termed tenor and contratenor, being less animated, close together in range (though the tenor is the lowest voice at structurally important points), and perhaps intended for instruments. His poems treat the themes of courtly love and are the finest lyrics of their age.

Although sources of the 14th and 15th centuries frequently make it difficult for the modern editor to align specific syllables with specific notes, many passages reveal a clear concern for such matters on the part of Machaut and his successors through the end of the 15th century, when the *formes fixes* ceased to be cultivated. Both syllabic and melismatic passages occur, and the contrast often bears on features of the texts, as does the variety of register, texture, and dissonance treatment [see Text and music].

Rhythmic complexity characterizes many of the chansons by the generation of composers immediately following Machaut. The notation of these works has been termed mannered [see Mensural notation], and their style has been described as the **ars subtilior.* This style seems to have been developed and cultivated principally in Avignon and the courts of southern France and northern Spain. The *ballade* continues to predominate in this repertory, but the variety of texts increases somewhat to include a broader range of themes, personal and historical allusions, and, in some *virelais,* imitations of birdcalls and other realistic sounds. Underlying the rhythmic complexity, with extended syncopations and conflicting meters, is a control of dissonance rather stricter than that of Machaut, despite the sometimes dissonant character of the surface detail. By about 1400, a simpler style seems to have emerged, and the *rondeau* begins to be favored. Both styles are found among the works of Matteo da Perugia (d. ca. 1418).

Of composers born around 1400, Guillaume Dufay (ca. 1400–1474) and Gilles Binchois (ca. 1400–1460) were preeminent in establishing the character of what has been termed the *Burgundian chanson. Like them, many chanson composers of the period were from northern France and the Low Countries. But Dufay spent part of his career in Italy, and for the remainder of the century, the French chanson was as widely disseminated in Italy as in French-speaking territories, as the numerous *chansonniers copied in Italy clearly attest. For Dufay and Binchois, the *rondeau* was the favored form. The themes of courtly love are prominent among their texts, but other poetic registers are explored as well, especially in works by Dufay. Three parts continue to make up the usual texture, only the uppermost part of which is regularly texted in the sources. Although the uppermost part and the tenor make satisfactory two-part counterpoint, the contratenor is often carefully integrated into the texture and cannot be regarded simply as an afterthought. The tenor and contratenor have usually been thought to be instrumental parts, though one or both are sometimes texted, and some scholars and performers now favor singing all three parts. This music is overwhelmingly consonant compared with that of the 14th century.

Later composers, who brought this tradition of chansons in the *formes fixes* largely to an end, include Johannes Ockeghem (ca. 1410–97), Antoine Busnois (ca. 1430–92), and Hayne van Ghizeghem (ca. 1445–between 1472 and 1497). Their works exhibit somewhat more complex polyphony with less clearly outlined phrase structure. In this period, the **bergerette* assumed a place in the repertory, without rivaling the *rondeau,* however.

Only at the end of the 15th century does a significant transformation of the chanson begin to take place, a transformation embodied in the works of Josquin Desprez (ca. 1440–1521) and his contemporaries such as Jacob Obrecht (ca. 1450–1505), Alexander Agricola (ca. 1446?–1506), Antoine de Févin (ca. 1470–1511 or 1512), Antoine Brumel (ca. 1460–ca. 1515), Heinrich Isaac (ca. 1450–1517), Loyset Compère (ca. 1445–1518), Pierre de La Rue (ca. 1460–1518), and Jean Mouton (ca. 1459–1522). Although the *formes fixes* continued to be set, these composers turned increasingly to texts of popular character, often in strophic form. Such texts were often set with their associated melodies either paraphrased or treated in canon (a favorite device of Josquin) in a complex of three, four, or more voices employing extensive imitation. This is the repertory of Petrucci's

**Odhecaton* and related publications and is preserved in contemporaneous manuscripts as well.

Remnants of this style—notably its continuously imitative polyphony in four or more voices—persist through the mid-16th century in the works of later northern composers published in Antwerp and elsewhere in the north. These composers include Jean Richafort (ca. 1480–ca. 1547), Clemens non Papa (ca. 1515–1555 or 1556), Thomas Crecquillon (d. 1557), Nicolas Gombert (ca. 1495–ca. 1560), and Adrian Willaert (ca. 1490–1562).

A somewhat different style, or group of styles, was cultivated by composers from Paris and surrounding territories and published in Paris by Pierre Attaingnant (ca. 1494–1551 or 1552). Prominent within this repertory is a largely homophonic style associated with the Parisian composer Claudin de Sermisy (ca. 1490–1562) and sometimes termed the Parisian chanson. Pieces in this style often set decasyllabic quatrains and employ simple repetition schemes derived from the rhyme scheme of the text (e.g., a text rhymed abba yielding a piece with the form ABCAA). The poetry of Clément Marot, with its mixture of courtly and popular registers, plays an important role. A characteristic opening rhythm, 𝅗𝅥 ♩♩ | 𝅗𝅥., derives from the syllabic treatment of the four syllables preceding the caesura of the ten-syllable poetic line. Precedents for this simpler style reach back through the *Odhecaton* into the 15th century and include works by Févin and his contemporaries in the early 16th. This style also suggests a relationship with Italian music, notably the **frottola,* and Italian musicians active in France.

Clément Janequin (ca. 1485–1558), the other most prolific chanson composer represented in the Attaingnant prints, often cultivates styles that are different from Claudin's style and that point to the variety of the works in this repertory. Janequin's chansons include settings of many humorous narrative poems as well as the so-called programmatic chansons depicting battles, birdcalls, and the like. The repertory includes works by composers active in Paris and by composers from the provinces, the latter often displaying quite divergent styles. Represented in these prints are Pierre Passereau (fl. 1509–47), Pierre Sandrin (ca. 1490–after 1561), Pierre Certon (d. 1572), and many others. Furthermore, although there are distinctions to be made between the repertories of Attaingnant and the northern printers, those distinctions are not as rigid nor are the repertories as isolated from one another as the terms Parisian and Netherlandish have sometimes been allowed to suggest. Overlapping both of these repertories in some measure are the chanson collections published in the 1530s and 40s by Jacques Moderne in Lyons.

The second half of the 16th century saw further interpenetration of regional and national styles as new printers in France and the Low Countries became active. The homophonic style centered in Paris in the first half of the century had its successors in the works of many composers, including one of the most prominent of the period published principally in Paris, Jacques Arcadelt (1505?–68). A radically simple, chordal style had emerged in Paris by mid-century, termed the *voix de ville* or **vaudeville,* and this became the **air de cour,* the principal type of French secular vocal music of the late 16th and early 17th centuries. It bore, too, on the efforts of the poet Jean Antoine de Baïf (1532–89) to recapture the character of the music of antiquity through quantitative poetry and music termed **musique mesurée.* The principal composer associated with this particular enterprise, and France's most distinguished chanson composer of the later 16th century, was Claude Le Jeune (ca. 1530–1600).

Perhaps the most widespread effect on the chanson of the second half of the century was that of the Italian madrigal, evident in the first instance in works of international composers such as Arcadelt and Orlande de Lassus (1532–94) who cultivated both genres. This effect was paralleled by interest in Italian poetry on the part of Pierre de Ronsard (1524–85) and associated poets of the Pléiade. The works in question employ polyphonic texture and some of the techniques of text illustration found in the madrigal. Among French composers in this tradition were Claude Goudimel (ca. 1520–72), Guillaume Costeley (ca. 1530–1606), Anthoine de Bertrand (between 1530 and 1540–between 1580 and 1582), and Nicolas de la Grotte (1530–ca. 1600). Costeley and Bertrand also participated in classically inspired uses of *chromaticism and *microtones in setting some French texts. Composers from the Low Countries, many of whom pursued careers elsewhere in Europe and whose works were widely published and disseminated, include, in addition to Lassus, Philippe de Monte (1521–1603), Jean de Castro (ca. 1540–ca. 1600), and the last great exponent of this tradition, Jan Pieterszoon Sweelinck (1562–1621). See also *Chanson spirituelle.*

Bibl.: *Musique et poésie au XVIe siècle, CNRS,* 1953. Howard M. Brown, "The *chanson rustique:* Popular Elements in the 15th- and 16th-Century Chanson," *JAMS* 12 (1959): 16–26. Id., "The Genesis of a Style: The Parisian Chanson, 1500–1550," *Isham,* 1961, pp. 1–36. Id., *Music in the French Secular Theater, 1400–1550* (Cambridge, Mass.: Harvard U Pr, 1963). Daniel Heartz, "*Les goûts réunis,* or The Worlds of the Madrigal and the Chanson Confronted," *Isham,* 1961, pp. 88–123. Hubert Daschner, *Die gedruckten mehrstimmigen Chansons von 1500–1600: Literarische Quellen und Bibliographie* (inaug.-diss., Bonn, 1962). Howard M. Brown, "The Transformation of the Chanson at the End of the Fifteenth Century," *Ljubljana,* 1967, pp. 78–94. Nigel Wilkins, "The Post-Machaut Generation of Poet-Musicians," *Nottingham Mediaeval Studies* 12 (1968): 40–84. Id., *One Hundred Ballades, Rondeaux, and Virelais from the Late Middle Ages* (Cambridge: Cambridge U Pr, 1969). Wolfgang Dömling, *Die mehrstimmigen Balladen, Rondeaux und Virelais von Guillaume de Machaut* (Tutzing: Schneider, 1970). Gilbert Reaney, *Guillaume de Machaut* (London: Oxford U Pr, 1971). Lawrence F. Bernstein, "The 'Parisian Chanson': Problems of Style and Terminology," *JAMS* 31

(1978): 193–240. Leeman L. Perkins and Howard Garey, *The Mellon Chansonnier,* 2 vols. (New Haven: Yale U Pr, 1979). Lawrence F. Bernstein, "Notes on the Origin of the Parisian Chanson," *JM* 1 (1982): 275–326. Don Michael Randel, "Dufay the Reader," *Studies in the History of Music* 1 (New York: Broude Bros, 1983): 38–78. D.M.R.

Chanson avec des refrains [Fr.]. A type of song in 12th- and 13th-century France with several stanzas, each of which ends with a different "refrain" of varying length, poetic structure, and melody. Some of these refrains are found elsewhere, including as a voice in a motet and as independent insertions in long narrative works such as *Renart le Nouvel.*

Bibl.: Friedrich Gennrich, "Die Refrains aus den 'Chansons avec des Refrains,'" *Gesellschaft für romanische Literatur* 47 (1927): 255–350. Nico H. J. van den Boogaard, *Rondeaux et refrains du XIIe siècle au début du XIVe* (Paris: Klincksieck, 1969). Eglal Doss-Quinby, *Les Refrains chez les trouvères du XIIe siècle au Début du XIVe* (New York: P Lang, 1984). Mark Everist, *French Motets in the Thirteenth Century: Music, Poetry and Genre* (Cambridge: Cambridge U Pr, 1994).

Chanson balladée [Fr.]. See *Virelai.*

Chanson de geste [Fr., fr. Lat. *gesta,* actions]. A type of medieval French epic poetry of 1,000 to more than 20,000 lines in length, recounting the deeds of historical or legendary heroes. About 100 examples survive, the most famous, and among the oldest preserved, being the *Chanson de Roland,* which relates the story of the battle of Roncesvals and the exploits of Charlemagne's knight Roland. The earliest stories are based on events from the 8th century, but the first written examples do not appear until the 11th century. Thus scholars still debate whether the genre's origins were oral or written, by an individual in a single creative act or by many contributors over time. Most *chansons de geste* are constructed of 10-syllable lines grouped into *laisses* (sections) of variable length, delineated in the earliest examples by assonance, but from the end of the 12th century usually by rhyme. The *chansons de geste* were probably sung, perhaps to some recitational melodic formula. Theorist Johannes de Grocheio (13th century) says that all verses in a *laisse* (which he calls "versicle") are sung to a repeated melody. None of the poems is preserved together with its music, but possible examples of such melodic formulas do exist in later sources. The 13th-century play *Le Jeu de Robin et Marion* by Adam de la Halle quotes a single line of melody from the *chanson de geste* known as *Audigier* (*NOHM* 2: 223). Another such fragment appears in the epic *Bataille d'Annezin* (Chailley, 1948).

Bibl.: Friedrich Gennrich, *Der musikalische Vortrag der altfranzösischen chansons de geste* (Halle: M Niemeyer, 1923). Jacques Chailley, "Etudes musicales sur la chanson de geste et ses origines," *RdM* 30 (1948): 1–27. Martín de Riquer, *Los cantares de gesta franceses* (Madrid: Gredos, 1952); trans. Fr., Irénée Cluzel, 2nd ed. (Paris: Nizet, n.d.). Jacques Chailley, "Autour de la chanson de geste," *AM* 27 (1955): 1–12. Jean Rychner, *La chanson de geste* (Geneva/Lille: Droz/Girard, 1955). Jan van der Veen, "Les aspects musicaux des chansons de geste," *Neophilologus* 41 (1957): 82–200. Jacques Chailley, "Du 'Tu autem' de 'Horn' à la musique des chansons de geste," *La Chanson de geste et le mythe carolingien: Mélanges René Louis* (Saint-Père-sous-Vézelay, 1982), pp. 21–32. Edward A. Heinemann, *L'Art métrique de la chanson de geste: Essai sur la musicalité du récit* (Geneva: Droz, 1993). E.A.

Chanson de toile [Fr., literally "song of the cloth"]. Also known from 13th-century sources as a *"chanson d'histoire,"* a French lyric poem that relates a tale of a woman's disappointed love, often with a tragic ending. In most cases, the woman's given name appears at the outset of the poem, preceded by the adjective *bele* (fair). In a brief exordium, the woman is frequently portrayed as sewing, weaving, or spinning, hence the name *chanson de toile.* Like most other genres practiced by the trouvères, it is a strophic form, but it is further distinguished by the use of a refrain. Only about 20 texts survive. Of these, 4 anonymous poems are preserved with melodies, as are 3 or 4 by the 13th-century trouvère Audefroi la Bastart; several songs are interpolated into larger narrative works, such as Jean Renart's *Guillaume de Dole.* Some of the melodies, like that of the anonymous *Bele Doete,* are more ornate than the simple narrative nature of the texts might suggest. The origins of the genre are unclear, but the prominence of the woman's voice suggests that at least some of the lyrics were composed by women.

Bibl.: Pierre Bec, *La lyrique française au moyen-âge,* 2 vols. (Paris: A & J Picard, 1977–78), 1:107–19, 2:30–46. Michel Zink and Gérard Le Vot, *Belle: Essai sur les chansons de toile* (Paris: H Champion, 1978). Samuel N. Rosenberg, Margaret Switten, and Gérard Le Vot, eds., *Songs of the Troubadours and Trouvères* (New York: Garland, 1998), pp. 184–89. P.E., V.P., rev. E.A.

Chanson mesurée [Fr.]. See *Musique mesurée.*

Chansonnier [Fr., fr. *chanson*]. A manuscript or printed collection of French lyric poetry or musical settings of such poetry. Although the term may be applied to sources for the whole range of repertories, both text and music, referred to as *chansons [see, e.g., Troubadour, Trouvère], it is especially applied in the musicological literature to manuscript anthologies containing predominantly polyphonic chansons of the 15th century such as Bologna, Civico museo bibliogricomusical MS 016. These are usually rather small (e.g., 22 × 16 cm), upright rather than oblong, in *choirbook format, and often elegantly prepared as presentation copies. Most contain at least a few pieces with text in a language other than French, especially Italian and Spanish. A list of sources can be found in NG2, v. 23. "Sources," MS. Bibliography IX. Renaissance polyphony, 8. Chansonniers, 906–908.

Bibl.: Frédéric Lachèvre, *Bibliographie des recueils collectifs de poésies du XVIe siècle* (Paris: E Champion, 1922). Gustave Reese and Theodore Karp, "Monophony in a Group of Renaissance Chansonniers," *JAMS* 5 (1952): 4–15. Bianca Becherini, *Catalogo dei manoscritti musicali della Biblioteca nazionale di Firenze* (Kassel: Bärenreiter, 1959). Knud Jeppesen, *La frottola,* vol. 2 (Copenhagen: Hansen, 1969). Brian Jeffery, *Chanson Verse of the Early Renaissance,* 2 vols. (London: Tecla Editions, 1971–76). Joshua Rifkin, "Scribal Concordances for Some Renaissance Manuscripts in Florentine Libraries," *JAMS* 26 (1973): 305–26. Howard Mayer Brown, ed., *A Florentine Chansonnier from the Time of Lorenzo the Magnificent,* Monuments of Renaissance Music, vol. 7 (Chicago: U of Chicago Pr, 1983). Howard Mayer Brown, "A 'New' Chansonnier of the Early Sixteenth Century in the University of Uppsala: A Preliminary Report," *MD* 37 (1983): 171–233. Lawrence Bernstein, "A Florentine Chansonnier of the Early Sixteenth Century: Florence, Biblioteca Nazionale Centrale, MS Magliabechi xix 117," *EMH* 6 (1986): 1–107. Duff James Kennedy, "Six Chansonniers Français: The Central Sources of the Franco-Burgundian Chanson (Ph.D. diss., UC Santa Barbara, 1987). Courtney Adams, "The Early Chanson Anthologies Published by Pierre Attaingnant (1528–1530)," *JM* 5, no. 4 (Fall 1987): 526–48. Dennis Slavin, "Genre, Final and Range: Unique Sorting Procedures in a Fifteenth-Century Chansonnier," *MD* 43 (1989): 115–39. Howard Mayer Brown, "Theory and Practice in the Sixteenth Century: Preliminary Notes on Attaingnant's Modally Ordered Chansonniers," in *Essays in Musicology* (Philadelphia: AMS, 1990), pp. 52–74. Madeleine Tyssens, ed., *Lyrique Romane medievale: La tradition des chansonniers* (Liège: U of Liège, 1991). David Fallows, *Songs and Musicians in the Fifteenth Century* (Aldershot: Variorum, 1996). David Fallows, *A Catalogue of Polyphonic Music 1415–1480* (Oxford: Oxford U Pr, 1999). See also Sources.

Chanson spirituelle [Fr.]. In the middle and late 16th century, a polyphonic *chanson with a religious or moralizing text in French. Such pieces often resulted merely from the substitution of a new text for the original one in a secular chanson, the music remaining unchanged. Numerous chansons by Lassus were given this treatment. Composers of original works include Didier Lupi Second (fl. mid-16th cent.), Hubert Waelrant (1516/17–95), and Claude Le Jeune (ca. 1530–1600). Much of the repertory is specifically Protestant in character, though the genre was cultivated by Catholics as well.

Bibl.: Kenneth J. Levy, "'Susanne un jour': The History of a 16th-Century Chanson," *AnnM* 1 (1953): 375–408. Marc Honegger, *Les chansons spirituelles de Didier Lupi et les débuts de la musique protestante en France* (Lille: Univ. of Lille, 1971).

Chant. (1) *Plainsong, e.g., *Gregorian chant, *Byzantine chant. See also Anglican chant. (2) To sing plainsong or in the style of plainsong; to sing a single pitch or a limited range of pitches repetitively. (3) [Fr.] Song, melody; the voice part as distinct from the accompaniment.

Chantant, chanté [Fr.]. Singing, in a singing style.

Chanter. A pipe with finger holes for playing melody on a *bagpipe; as distinct from a drone, which sounds only a single pitch.

Chanterelle [Fr.]. **Cantino.*

Chantey, chanty. *Shanty.

Chanzoneta, chançonetta [Sp.]. From the 15th century through the early 17th, a type of poem and vocal music similar to the **villancico,* often with a sacred text. Works referred to in this way appear in Luis Venegas de Henestrosa's *Libro de cifra nueva* (1557; *MME* 2) and Francisco Guerrero's *Canciones y villanescas espirituales* (1589; *MME* 16, 19).

Chapel [Lat. *cappella, capella,* dim. of *cappa,* cloak; Fr. *chapelle;* Ger. *Capelle, Kapelle;* It. *cappella;* Sp. *capilla*]. (1) A place of worship within or dependent upon a larger church, institution, or residence; often small or private, though sometimes large and quite elaborate. (2) The staff of a chapel, including clergy and musicians, if any; also the specifically musical establishment of any church or chapel. In the later Middle Ages and Renaissance, the personal chapels of royalty, the nobility, and ecclesiastical dignitaries (including the Pope) as well as the musical chapels of churches were the most important musical institutions, employing many of the leading composers and musicians of the period. Such institutions might include up to 20 or 30 singers (both men and boys), an organist, and, especially later, other instrumentalists. Members of courtly chapels often provided secular entertainment for the court as well. The musical director of such an institution was called the *chapel master. (3) In Germany beginning in the 17th century, the entire musical establishment of a court, including the opera. (4) In Germany by the 19th century, any orchestra. See also *Kapelle, Kapellmeister.*

Chapel master [Fr. *maître de chapelle;* Ger. *Kapellmeister;* It. *maestro di cappella;* Sp. *maestro de capilla*]. The leader of a musical *chapel. In France, Italy, and Spain, this remained the title of the leader of a sacred institution. For German usage, see *Kapelle, Kapellmeister.*

Characteristic note. *Leading tone, note.

Character notation. *Shape-note.

Character (characteristic) piece [Ger. *Charakterstück;* Fr. *pièce caractéristique*]. In the late 18th and 19th centuries, any of a wide variety of kinds of *program music; now principally a short, lyric piano piece. The individual piece usually evokes a particular mood or scene, suggested more often than not by a descriptive title. Early examples for piano include G. C. Füger's *Charakteristische Klavierstücke* (1783 or 1784) and Carl Friedrich Zelter's *La malade, pièce caractéristique* (1787). Johann Baptist Cramer contributed the *Études caractéristiques* op. 70 (1825) and Ignaz Moscheles the *Charakteristische Studien* op. 95 (1836) to the burgeoning pedagogical literature of the 19th century. The best-known *Charakterstücke* are Mendelssohn's op. 7 (1827) and Schumann's *Davidsbündlertänze* op. 6 (1837).

The term derives from widespread discussion of the nature of character and characterization in vocal as well as instrumental music in the German lexical and aesthetic literature from the mid-18th century through the 19th. The origin of the discussion in the visual arts is betrayed by some of the 19th-century German synonyms for *Charakterstück,* such as *Tongemälde* (sound painting), *Genrebild* (genre picture; Fr. *pièce de genre*), and *Stimmungsbild* (mood picture). At issue was music's capacity to imitate, describe, and express, with and without the assistance of words. The complexity of these issues invited broad definitions: through the 1870s, some writers still made little distinction between program music and character pieces, and they listed as examples of the latter not only dances (a characteristic dance being one in a free form or one with national characteristics) and marches, but also "battle symphonies," "hunting overtures," and all types of "sound paintings." "Sound paintings" referred to little instrumental pieces with descriptive titles, and it is to this repertory, especially to the vast number of late 18th- and 19th-century lyric piano pieces, that the term character piece is loosely applied today. Given this unrestrictive usage, several writers have included in the repertory the descriptively titled keyboard works of C. P. E. Bach and François Couperin; Kahl (1955) extends the term to cover certain medieval, Renaissance, and Baroque works as well.

The Romantic lyric piano pieces generally thought of as character pieces frequently appeared in sets or cycles bearing titles such as *Handstücke, Kinderszenen, Albumblätter, Bagatelles, Nocturnes, Impromptus, Intermezzi, Capriccios, Rhapsodies, Eclogues,* and *Novelletten.* Individual pieces often had fanciful titles. Virtually every 19th-century keyboard composer from Beethoven to Richard Strauss wrote such pieces. Forms varied from Schumann's musically unified sets of miniatures to Chopin's large independent works, but song forms (ABA) were most common for individual pieces.

Bibl.: Martha Vidor, "Zur Begriffsbestimmung des musikalischen Charakterstückes mit besonderer Berücksichtigung der Charakterstückes für Klavier" (diss., Univ. of Leipzig, 1924). Willi Kahl, *Das Charakterstück, Mw* 8 (Cologne: A Volk, 1955; trans. Eng., 1961). Elfriede Glusman, "The Early Nineteenth-Century Lyric Piano Piece" (Ph.D. diss., Columbia Univ., 1969).

Charanga [Sp.]. A Cuban dance ensemble, characteristically consisting of flute, two or three violins, piano, double bass, *timbales with *cencerro, and güiro. Traditionally a prominent exponent of the Cuban **danzón,* the *charanga* was also principally responsible for the development of the **chachachá* in the early 1950s.
D.S.

Charango [Sp.]. A small guitar of the Andes with five double courses of strings. The back of the soundbox is characteristically of armadillo shell.

Charivari [Fr.; Ger. *Katzenmusik;* It. *scampata;* in the U.S., shivaree]. Deliberately cacophonous music, often including the use of pots and pans; especially music of this type played outside the home of newlyweds or of an unpopular person.

Charleston. (1) A fast, American dance that flourished in the 1920s. Said to have originated among southern blacks, it became a commercial hit with James P. Johnson's song "Charleston," composed for the show *Runnin' Wild* (1923). Subsequent Charlestons borrowed the catchy rhythmic motive of Johnson's melody: ¢ ♩ 𝄾 ♪♩. (2) [archaic] *Hi-hat cymbals.

Chart. (1) Statistical reports, such as those published in *Billboard,* measuring record sales, divided among categories of popular music. (2) Arrangement (2).

Chasse, La [Fr., the hunt]. A title sometimes given to compositions imitating the sound of hunting horns or some other aspect of the hunt. See *Hunt Quartet, Hunt Symphony.*

Chasseur maudit, Le [Fr., The Accursed Huntsman]. A symphonic poem by César Franck, op. 44 (1882), based on the ballad "Der wilde Jäger" by Gottfried Bürger (1747–94).

Check, check head. Back check. See Piano.

Chef d'attaque [Fr.]. *Concertmaster; the leader of a section.

Chef d'orchestre [Fr.]. *Conductor.

Chegança [Port.]. A Brazilian dramatic dance *(bailado),* also known as *marujada* or *chegança de marujos.* In the *chegança,* the traditions of Portuguese maritime adventure and the Iberian conflicts between Christians and Moors are combined in portrayals involving the singing of narrative **romances* and praise songs *(loas),* elaborate costume, and choreography.
D.S.

Cheironomy. See Chironomy.

Chekker [Fr. *échiquier, eschaquier, eschiquier;* Ger. *Schachtbrett;* Lat. *scacarum;* Sp. *esaquier*]. A stringed keyboard instrument first mentioned in a document of 1360, several decades before the earliest known occurrences of the names clavichord and *clavicembalum* (harpsichord). The term remained in occasional use until the early 16th century, but none of the sources describes the instrument. The name, borrowed from the French for chessboard or for the counting board used like an abacus for calculating, suggests that it was square or rectangular and had components crossing at right angles. Although various interpretations have been proposed, the clavichord, which is rectangular and has key levers roughly at right angles with the strings, is generally regarded as best fitting the nomenclature and historical circumstances. Especially after the term clavichord entered general use, chekker, *échiquier,* etc., might occasionally have been used generically for any rectangular stringed-keyboard instrument.

Bibl.: Edwin M. Ripin, "Towards an Identification of the Chekker," *GSJ* 28 (1975): 11–25. Christopher Page, "The

Myth of the Chekker," *EM* 7 (1976): 482–89. Nicolas Meeùs, "The Chekker," *Organ Yearbook* 16 (1985): 5–25. J.Ko.

Chelys [Gr.]. The Greek *lyra, so called because its soundbox was often made from a turtle shell. From the Middle Ages through the 17th century, the term could refer to lutes, viols, and violins.

Cheng (zheng) [Chin.]. A Chinese zither with 10 to 17 silk strings, each with its own movable bridge. The modern version has 16 metal strings tuned to three pentatonic octaves. Its playing technique is similar to that of the Japanese **koto.* See also *Ch'in, Kayago;* see ill. under East Asia I.

Cherubic Hymn. The offertory chant of the Byzantine *Divine Liturgy. For ordinary celebrations the text begins "Oi ta cherubim," but during Lent and Holy Week other hymns are used: "Nyn ai dynameis" for the Presanctified Liturgy; "Tou deipnou sou" on Holy Thursday; and "Sigēsato pasa sarx" on Holy Saturday. The oldest melodies for the Ordinary and for the Proper of Holy Saturday are preserved in 13th-century choirbooks, whereas the remainder first appear in the 14th-century **Akolouthiai.*

In a translated form, "Oi ta cherubim" was introduced to the West for the *Missa graeca;* and again in Latin translation ("Qui cherubim mystice"), it later appears as a processional antiphon for the Dedication—in both instances without notation. A Latin version was also used as a verse to the Trinity offertory, "Benedictus sit," with surviving music in unheighted neumes. D.E.C.

Chest of viols. In England in the 16th and 17th centuries, a matched (in size, shape, wood, and color) set of viols, usually two trebles, two tenors, and two basses, kept in an appropriately partitioned chest. For a description, see Thomas Mace, *Musick's Monument* (London, 1676), p. 245. See also Consort.

Chest voice, chest register. See Voice.

Cheute [Fr.]. See *Chûte.*

Chevalet [Fr.]. The *bridge of a bowed stringed instrument; *au chevalet,* an instruction to bow at or near the bridge. See Bowing (11).

Chevé method. A method of teaching sight-singing widely used in France and elsewhere in the 19th century. It employs a system of musical notation in which diatonic scale degrees, beginning with the tonic in whatever key, are numbered 1 through 7. The notation has its origins in one proposed by Jean Jacques Rousseau in 1742. The method was most vigorously promoted by Emile Chevé (*Méthode élémentaire de musique vocale,* 1844), having been jointly developed by him, his wife, Nanine Paris, and her brother Aimé Paris, based on the work of Aimé's teacher Pierre Galin. The notation was adapted for teaching purposes to Javanese *gamelan* music as the *kepatihan* notation and is still in use in Indonesia.

Cheville [Fr.]. In stringed instruments, a tuning peg; in the piano, a tuning or wrest pin.

Cheviller [Fr.]. *Pegbox.

Chevrotement [Fr.]. *Goat's trill.

Chiamata [It., call]. In 17th-century Italy, a trumpet fanfare, especially one sounded in battle, but also associated with hunting. Music of this kind is sometimes found in operas of the first part of the century. See also *Chamade.*

Chiarenzana, chirintana, giurintana [It.]. An Italian court dance of the Renaissance. It was performed in Florence as early as 1459 at a festival in honor of Pope Pius II. Although the music is not preserved, a choreography ascribed to Domenico da Piacenza is found in treatises by Guglielmo Ebreo da Pesaro (ca. 1450). Marcantonio del Pifaro includes 14 examples of music (without choreographies) in his *Intabolatura de lauto* (1546). His *chiarenzane* are indistinguishable from the common **pavana* or *passamezzo of the day. An isolated example of the music with a complicated choreography is found in Fabritio Caroso's *Il ballarino* (1581), where the dance is cast in the 6/8 meter of a **saltarello* or a **gagliarda.* L.H.M.

Chiaro, chiaramente [It.]. Clear, clearly.

Chiave [It.]. (1) *Clef. (2) On woodwind instruments, a key.

Chiavette [It.]. In 16th-century vocal polyphony, a coordinated collection of clefs (G2 C2 C3 F3/C4; Ex. 1) that locates the staves of individual parts (or the ten-line staff used by composers and theorists) a third lower on the gamut than do the usual *chiavi naturali* [It., natural clefs] (C1 C3 C4 F4; Ex. 2). The earliest source known to describe this phenomenon in these terms is Paolucci (1765). Bellermann (1862, p. 35) notes a third common clef grouping (C2 C4 F3 F5; Ex. 3)—sometimes termed *chiavi trasportati* [It., transposed clefs] or "low *chiavette*"—that locates most staves a third higher on the gamut than do the *chiavi naturali.*

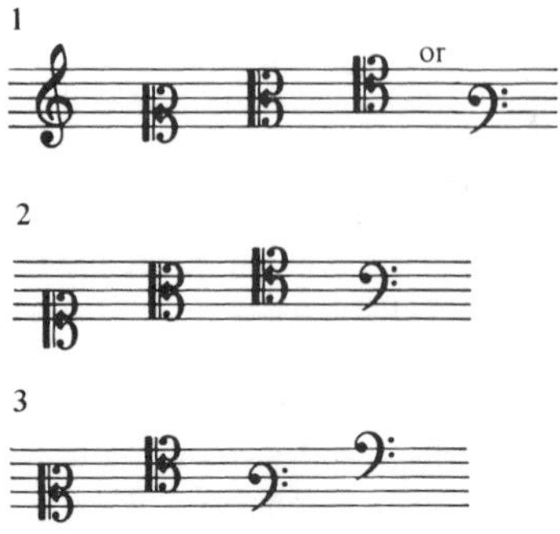

1. *Chiavette.* 2. *Chiavi naturali.* 3. *Chiavi trasportati.*

Transposition of staves on the gamut admits of two different interpretations. One claims that when clefs shift, pitch associations shift correspondingly, but vocal ranges remain the same. For example, given a normal superius range of c′–e″ and a shifted *chiavette* range of e′–g″, a c″ written in the normal clefs will sound a third lower than a c″ written with *chiavette.* This view is advanced by Kiesewetter (1827); a substantial body of evidence is marshaled in its support by Mendel (1948 and 1978). The alternative interpretation holds that when clefs shift, vocal ranges shift correspondingly, but pitch associations remain the same. Thus, in the example just given, a c″ written in either range will denote the same sounding pitch. Some evidence for this view is given by Ehrmann (1924) and Schering (1931).

Powers (1974 and 1981) observes that several central sources for 16th-century Italian polyphony use a systematic association of modes with clef groupings and system signature [see Mode]. In these sources, the *chiavette* grouping is in principle reserved for authentic (odd-numbered) modes, and the *chiavi naturali* for the plagal (even-numbered) modes. This suggests that in such sources, the first priority of the *chiavette* is to signal a feature of the modal system rather than to accommodate ranges. This use of *chiavette* seems to have been dominant. Smith (1982) gives a useful inventory of clef dispositions in late 16th-century sources.

Bibl.: Giuseppi Paolucci, *Arte pratica di contrappunto . . . Tomo primo* (Venice, 1765). Raphael Kiesewetter, "Über den Umfang der Singstimmen in den Werken der alten Meisters, in Absicht auf deren Ausführung in unserer Zeit," *AmZ* 29 (1827): 125–35, 145–56. Heinrich Bellermann, *Der Contrapunct* (Berlin, 1862). Richard Ehrmann, "Die Schlüsselkombinationen im 15. und 16. Jahrhundert," *SzMw* 11 (1924): 59–74. Arnold Schering, *Aufführungspraxis alter Musik* (Leipzig: Quelle & Meyer, 1931; R: Wiesbaden: M Sändig, 1969). Arthur Mendel, "Pitch in the 16th and Early 17th Centuries," *MQ* 34 (1948): 336–57. Siegfried Hermelink, *Dispositiones modorum* (Tutzing: Schneider, 1960). Id., "Ein neuer Beleg zum Ursprung der Chiavette," *Mf* 14 (1961): 44–46. Harold S. Powers, "The Modality of 'Vestiva i colli,'" *Mendel,* 1974, pp. 31–46. Arthur Mendel, "Pitch in Western Music Since 1500: A Reexamination," *AM* 50 (1978): 1–93. Harold S. Powers, "Mode," *Grove 6.* Id., "Tonal Types and Modal Categories in Renaissance Polyphony," *JAMS* 34 (1981): 428–70. Id., "Modal Representation in Polyphonic Offertories," *Early Music History* 2 (1982): 43–86. Anne Smith, "Über Modus und Transposition um 1600," *Basler Jahrbuch für historische Musikpraxis* 6 (1982): 9–43.

Chiavi naturali, trasportati [It.]. See *Chiavette.*

Chicago jazz. A modification of *New Orleans jazz made in the 1920s and 1930s by white musicians in the Midwest, on one hand, and by black musicians (some from New Orleans) on the South Side of Chicago, on the other. While some elements of the earlier style were retained, musicians in both instances increasingly emphasized solos, arrangements including accompanimental figures, a string bass playing on each beat in 4/4, and popular song forms. T.A.J.

Chiesa [It.]. Church. In the Baroque period (ca. 1600–1750), in which music was classified as belonging to the style of church, chamber (**camera*), or theater, the phrase *da chiesa* identifies music appropriate for use in church, especially the **concerto da chiesa* and the **sonata da chiesa.*

Chiff. The percussive attack sound of an organ pipe, preceding by a millisecond the fundamental pitch.

Chifonie [Fr., fr. Lat. *symphonia*]. In the Middle Ages, *hurdy-gurdy.

Childhood of Christ, The. See *Enfance du Christ, L'.*

Children's Corner. A suite of six piano pieces composed by Debussy in 1906–8 and dedicated to his daughter Claude-Emma, who is referred to in the dedication as "Chouchou." The original English titles of the pieces are "Doctor Gradus ad Parnassum" (a humorous allusion to Clementi's **Gradus ad Parnassum*), "Jimbo's Lullaby," "Serenade for the Doll," "The Snow Is Dancing," "The Little Shepherd," and "Golliwogg's Cake-Walk."

Chile. I. *Contemporary musical life and institutions.* Some of the most prominent institutions associated with art music in Chile are administered through the Faculty of Fine Arts at the University of Chile (Santiago), whose Musical Extension Institute controls the national symphony, ballet, and educational radio; it also oversees a university chorus, various chamber ensembles, the Chilean Music Festival, reestablished in 1998, and the publication of *Revista musical chilena.* The Institute of Music at the Catholic University of Santiago sustains chamber and early music ensembles as well as instructional programs and an electronic music studio. In addition, the Santiago Municipal Theater produces regular seasons of operas and concerts, for which purpose it maintains the Municipal Philharmonic Orchestra and Ballet. New music is supported notably at the Santiago School of Modern Music and at the Catholic University, which sponsors contemporary music festivals, and by Agrupación Musical Anacrusa (1984), a privately run association of primarily young composers and performers.

Several provincial universities support musical programs, especially that of Concepción, which has an orchestra, a radio station, and a noted chorus. Provincial orchestras include those of La Serena, Temuco, Valparaiso, and Viña del Mar. Conservatories exist in Concepción, Osorno, Temuco, and Viña del Mar.

II. *History.* Little has survived of music from Chile's colonial period; and through the 18th century, art music (principally sacred) was dominated by composers from Spain. The first native composers to achieve prominence became active in the period in which Chile won independence (1810–18) and the years following. These include Manuel Robles (1780–

1837), composer of the original national anthem; Isidora Zegers de Huneeus (1803–69), a composer of lighter works for piano and a founder of the Philharmonic Society in Santiago (1827) and active in the founding of the National Conservatory of Music there (1849); José Zapiola (1802–85), author of a book of musical reminiscences from the years 1810–40; Federico Guzmán (1837–85), a pianist and composer of over 200 works for piano, for voice, and for chamber ensembles. Émigré composers of the period include Guillermo Frick (1813–96) and Aquinas Ried (1810–69), composer of the first opera written in Chile (*La Telésfora,* 1846). The 1840s and 50s saw opera houses open in Valparaiso, Santiago, and elsewhere and began a steady succession of performances of zarzuelas and Italian operas. The most notable Chilean composer of operas by century's end was Eleodoro Ortíz de Zárate (1865–1953), whose *Juana la Loca* was performed in Milan in 1892 and *La florista de Lugano* in Santiago in 1896.

Enrique Soro (1884–1954), a composer in the Romantic tradition, was the most distinguished of the first generation of composers to come to prominence in the 20th century. Others in this generation were Pedro Humberto Allende Sarón (1885–1959), who made use of impressionist techniques and native rhythms, Próspero Bisquertt (1881–1959), Carlos Lavin (1883–1962), Carlos Isamitt (1887–1974), Acario Cotapos (1889–1969), and Alfonso Leng (1894–1974).

Only slightly younger was Domingo Santa Cruz Wilson (1899–1987), often simply "Santa Cruz," who gained a considerable reputation both at home and abroad. He was influential in the founding of the Bach Society (1917), the Fine Arts program at the University of Chile in Santiago (1930), and its Musical Extension Institute (1941). Composers who were born in the 20th century and have achieved recognition include Jorge Urrutia Blondel (1905–81), Alfonso Letelier Llona (1912–94), Juan Orrego-Salas (b. 1919), Eduardo Maturana (b. 1920), Claudio Spies (b. 1925), Gustavo Becerra-Schmidt (b. 1925), León Schidlowsky (b. 1931), José Vicente Asuar (b. 1933), Enrique Rivera (b. 1941), and Eduardo Cáceres (b. 1955). Orrego-Salas relocated to the United States in 1961 to found the Latin American Music Center at the Indiana School of Music.

III. *Folk music.* The relatively small indigenous populations have retained independent musical traditions, some of which may have pre-Columbian origins and some of which share features of the musics of neighboring peoples, e.g., Andean populations to the north. Otherwise, Chilean folk music is largely Hispanic in origin and character and has been little affected by the music of indigenous groups. Forms of Spanish origin include the **romance* and **villancico* and their derivatives such as the **tonada.* Artists performing left-leaning, folk-derived music, such as singer-guitarist Violeta Parra and the groups Quilpayún and Inti-Illimani, had major impact abroad in the era before and after the 1973 coup d'état. See also *Cuando, Cueca,* Latin America.

Bibl.: Eugenio Pereira Salas, *Los orígenes del arte musical en Chile* (Santiago: Imprenta universitaria, 1941). Vicente Salas Viu, *La creación musical en Chile* (Santa Cruz: Ediciones de la Universidad de Chile, 1952). Eugenio Pereira Salas, *Historia de la música en Chile, 1850–1900* (Santiago, 1957). Robert Stevenson, "Chilean Music in the Santa Cruz Epoch," *Inter-American Music Bulletin* 67 (1968): 1–18. Samuel Claro, *Panorama de la música contemporánea en Chile* (Santiago, 1969). Id. and Jorge Urrutia Blondel, *Historia de la música en Chile* (Santiago: Editorial Orbe, 1973). Luis Merino, "Instrumentos musicales, cultura mapuche, y el Cantiverio feliz del Mestre de Campo Francisco Nuñez de Pineda y Bascuñan, *Revista Musical Chilena* (1974) 28: 56–95. Numerous articles by Eugenio Pereira Salas, María Ester Grebe, and others on both folk and art music in *Revista musical chilena.* Roberto Escobar, *Creadores musicales chilenos* (Santiago: RiL Ediciones, 1995). Nick Caistor, *The Rainstick Pack: Explore the Mysteries and Traditions of Native Chilean Culture* (New York: Universe Publishing, 1997). Manuel Dannemann, *Enciclopedia del folclore de Chile* (Santiago: Editorial Universitaria, 1998). See also Latin America.

Chimes. (1) A set of tuned *idiophones (e.g., *gong chimes, stone chimes). (2) The *tubular bells of the orchestra and similar sets of struck tubes (e.g., doorbell chimes, wind chimes). (3) A set of stationary *bells or a small *carillon. Clock chimes, sounded by automatic mechanisms, have been popular in the West since the 15th century.

Chiming. See Bell (1).

Chimney flute [Ger. *Rohrflöte*]. An organ flue stop with half-length pipes, the caps or stoppers of which are pierced with a narrow tube or chimney. These pipes produce a brighter sound than other stopped registers and are usually made of metal, occasionally of wood.

Ch'in (qin) [Chin.]. A Chinese *zither made from a hollowed, slightly convex board approximately 120 cm (4 ft.) long, 20 cm wide, and 8 cm deep, over the length of which are stretched seven silk strings of varying thickness. The most common tuning pattern is C D F G A c d. It has neither frets nor bridges. Inlaid along one edge of the instrument are 13 small disks of ivory or mother-of-pearl marking points at which a string is to be fully stopped or touched lightly to produce harmonics. The pitches produced by stopping the C string at these points are D E♭ E F G A c e g c′ e′ g′ c″. Additional stopping positions are also used, however. The strings are plucked with the fingers in a variety of ways.

The instrument may have existed as early as the 15th century B.C.E. Archeological remains date from the 3rd century B.C.E. The earliest surviving work for it is thought to date from the 6th century and is preserved in tablature in a manuscript from the T'ang dynasty (618–906). Throughout its history, the *ch'in* has been prized as the instrument of the learned, and an extensive philosophical tradition attaches to it. See also East Asia I, including ill.

China. See East Asia I.

Chinese block [Fr. *bloc de bois, caisse chinoise;* Ger. *Holzblock, Holzblocktrommel;* It. *cassettina, blochetto;* Sp. *caja china*]. A percussion instrument consisting of a partially hollowed rectangular block of wood that is struck with wooden drumsticks or other beaters; also wood block. See ill. under Percussion instruments.

Chinese crescent, Chinese pavilion. *Turkish crescent.

Ch'ing (qing) [Chin.]. A Chinese sounding stone used in Confucian temple rituals. The *t'e ch'ing (te qing)* is a single thin piece of limestone or jade cut in an L-shape, hung from a frame, and struck with a wooden mallet. The *pien-ch'ing (bien qing)* is a set of such stones (usually 16) hung in two rows and carefully tuned. See ill. under East Asia I.

Ching-hu [Chin.]. A Chinese *spike fiddle similar in construction and playing technique to the **erh-hu,* though only about 45 cm tall; also called *hu-ch'in.* It is the principal melodic instrument in *Peking opera, where it plays along with the singer, ornamenting and elaborating the vocal line.

Chin rest [Fr. *mentionnière;* Ger. *Kinnhalter;* It. *mentoniera;* Sp. *mentonera, barbada*]. A holding device for the violin and other bowed stringed instruments played on the arm, allowing the player to grip the instrument firmly between chin and shoulder for ease of left-hand shifting without damping the sound by touching the table of the instrument with the chin. It is usually clamped at the bottom block area to the left of or directly above the tailpiece. The modern chin rest was developed in the first quarter of the 19th century, perhaps by Spohr, who illustrated it in his *Violinschule* of 1832. Prior to that time, musicians placed their chins usually above or to the right side of the tailpiece, or supported the instrument mainly on the shoulder.

W.L.M.

Chirimía [Sp.; Cat. *xirimía*]. (1) A *shawm of Spain and Latin America. The keyed *chirimía* is important in the **cobla* bands of Catalonia. In some Indian communities of Mexico, Guatemala, and Colombia, an ensemble of two *chirimías* and a drum plays for public processions. See also *Dulzaina, Tiple, Zūrnā.* (2) An organ reed stop of narrow scale, sometimes mounted horizontally in the facade.

Chironomy [fr. Gr. *cheir,* hand]. The use of movements of the hand to indicate approximate pitch or melodic contour to singers. The practice is evidently of great antiquity and is widely distributed (e.g., in ancient Egypt, Israel, and Greece, in Byzantine culture from about the 8th century, in India, and in Coptic and Jewish communities of the Near and Middle East to the present day), especially, it would seem, in cultures lacking musical notation. Chironomy is often used today in the teaching of schoolchildren, and it has been used as a supplement to musical notation in the teaching and conducting of Gregorian chant. According to one of several competing hypotheses, the notations developed in the traditions of *Jewish music, *Byzantine chant, and Western plainchant [see Neume] derive from the written tracing of hand gestures.

Bibl.: Egon Wellesz, *A History of Byzantine Music and Hymnography* (Oxford: Clarendon Pr, 1949; 2nd ed., 1961; R: 1971). Michel Huglo, "La chironomie médiévale," *RdM* 49 (1963): 155–71.

Chiroplast. A sliding frame attached to a piano keyboard for guiding and training the hands, patented in 1814 by Johann Bernhard Logier (1777–1846).

Chitarra [It.]. *Guitar.

Chitarra battente [It.]. A five-course (often with three strings per course), wire-strung, Italian folk guitar played with a plectrum and used for accompaniment. Developed in the 18th century, it resembles the 17th-century round-back guitar, with which it is often confused.

R.L.

Chitarrone [It.]. (1) In 16th-century Italy, a large bass *lute whose fingerboard strings were tuned like those of the descant lute, but with the first two courses tuned an octave lower than lute pitch, and with seven or eight contrabasses tuned diatonically: G_1 A_1 B_1 C D E F G A/A d/d g/g b/b e/e a/a. See ill. under Lute. (2) In the 17th century, the *theorbo. Michael Praetorius (*Syntagma musicum,* vol. 2, 1619) says that the long Roman theorbo is called *chitarrone.*

Bibl.: Douglas Alton Smith, "On the Origin of the Chitarrone," *JAMS* 32 (1979): 440–62.

Chiterna [It.]. *Gittern.

Chiuso [It., closed]. (1) In horn playing, stopped [see Horn, Stopped tones, *Aperto*]. (2) In 14th-century music, the second of two endings for a section of a piece [see also *Ouvert* and *clos*].

Choeur [Fr.]. (1) *Choir. (2) *Course.

Choir. (1) A group of singers, especially one dedicated to the performance of sacred music [see also Chorus]. (2) A group of instruments of similar type, sometimes forming part of a larger ensemble, e.g., brass choir, woodwind choir. (3) That part of a church in which the choir (1) is placed.

Choirbook. A manuscript of dimensions large enough and in a format designed to permit an entire choir (of 20 or more singers) to sing from it; any manuscript in such a format, regardless of size. Such manuscripts were especially characteristic of the late 15th and early 16th centuries and could be as large as 75 × 50 cm. Manuscripts (including much smaller ones) containing polyphony of the period were generally copied in choirbook format, in which all parts appear separately on a single opening. The norm in four-part polyphony was for the superius to be copied above the tenor on the left-hand page (verso) of the opening, with the alto above the bass on the right-hand page (recto). See also Partbook, Score.

Choir organ. (1) A secondary division of English and American organs with its wind-chest often located behind the Great organ; possibly a corruption of *Chair organ. (2) A small organ with a single keyboard, located in the choir of a church.

Choir pitch. See Pitch.

Chor [Ger.]. *Chorus, *choir.

Choral. (1) Of or pertaining to a choir or chorus. (2) [Ger.] *Plainchant. (3) [Ger.] *Chorale.

Choralbearbeitung [Ger.]. A composition based on sacred melody, whether a plainchant or a chorale. Examples thus include Notre Dame *organum, many *motets, *chorale cantatas, and *organ chorales (including chorale preludes).

Choral cantata. A *cantata employing a chorus, as distinct from one for soloist only. See also Chorale cantata.

Choralcelo. One of the earliest "electronic" (more properly, electromechanical) instruments, developed during the last decade of the 19th century by Melvin Severy and George B. Sinclair of Arlington, Massachusetts. Commercial production was begun in Boston in 1909 by the Choralcelo Co. under the direction of C. D. Farrington and A. Hoffman, who continued improving it. The sound was generated by a sophisticated system of tone-wheels that excited various wood and metal resonating bodies electrically, and it was entirely unamplified. A more successful and manageable instrument than its contemporary, the Telharmonium, approximately 100 Choralcelos were produced and sold before the company failed around 1920. Only a few remain today, none of them in playable condition.
B.O.

Chorale. The congregational song or hymn of the German Protestant (Evangelical) Church. The term derives from the German *Choral* (i.e., plainsong, in turn derived from the Latin *cantus choralis*) and first referred to the style of performance (as in plainsong, unison and unaccompanied, i.e., *choraliter* as opposed to *figuraliter*). Only later, in the 17th century, did the word denote the tune and subsequently the text and tune together. Luther's Latin terms *canticum vernaculum* and *psalmus vernaculus* clearly refer to the text, as do the German *Lied* and *Kirchenlied. Kirchengesang* and *Gemeindegesang* (church song and congregational song) are later terms, the latter being current, the former now denoting monodic chant forms.

Luther insisted upon the value of congregational singing in the vernacular as part of the liturgical action, and he recognized that texts for congregational song should be strophic in form, metrical in style, and vernacular in language. He provided the prototypes by adapting texts and tunes from a variety of sources and composing others. The texts of Luther's chorales are drawn from Psalms ("Ein' feste Burg," from Psalm 46), Gregorian seasonal hymns ("Nun komm' der Heiden Heiland," from "Veni Redemptor gentium," for Advent), antiphons ("Mitten wir im Leben sind," from "Media vita in morte sumus"), the Mass Ordinary ("Jesaia, dem Propheten," from the Sanctus), German sacred song ("Christ lag in Todesbanden," from "Christ ist erstanden"; see *Leise*), and paraliturgical Latin hymns ("Wir glauben all an einen Gott," from "Credo in unum Deum patrem omnipotentem"), with tunes adapted and readapted from these and secular sources or composed on similar models. A great many chorale melodies are in *bar form, with each strophe of text consisting of two lines for each *Stollen* and three for the *Abgesang,* and some show a relationship to the melodic procedures of the *Meistersinger.

In the liturgies devised by Luther (*Formula missae,* 1523, and *Deutsche Messe,* 1526), the use of chorales varied. In the *Formula missae,* Luther suggested that vernacular chorales be inserted into the purified Latin version; this led ultimately to a polyglot *Mass in which the congregational singing of chorales in the vernacular was found at least after the Epistle, after the Gospel, and after Communion. In the *Deutsche Messe,* on the other hand, Luther effected a complete vernacular transformation of the texts of the *Ordinary and *Proper, entailing the reordering of syllabic chant and the suggested substitution of vernacular metrical material for Ordinary and Proper. In both instances, specific *Agenden* [see *Agende*] varied greatly from place to place and reflected the blending of local tradition with reform. Nevertheless, the mixing of Latin and vernacular texts and the substitution or addition of metrical texts characterize the whole history of the Lutheran liturgy.

The earliest collection of texts and monophonic melodies was the so-called *Achtliederbuch* (Nuremberg, 1523–24, eight texts and four melodies); the earliest polyphonic collection was the *Geystliches Gesangk Buchleyn* of Johann Walter (1524, 32 texts, 35 melodies, 38 polyphonic settings in five partbooks). Various collections followed, including the two Erfurt *Enchiridia* (1524), and the succession of editions of the Wittenberg hymnal, published by Klug (1529–45). The last collection published in Luther's lifetime, Valentin Babst's *Geistliche Lieder* (1545), had 80 texts (with tunes) arranged in sections: those by Luther came first, followed by those of other contemporary authors (Speratus, Spengler, Adam von Fulda), and concluding with pre-Reformation German and Latin texts. Within the section of texts by Luther, the material was arranged for the convenience of liturgical or instructional use: *de tempore* lieder for the church year, catechism, Psalm paraphrases, litanies, and miscellaneous chorales. This selection and ordering was often imitated later.

During Luther's lifetime, the content of the chorales had been directed toward the public expression of confession, thanksgiving, and praise, and their melodies had been typically monophonic or, in polyphony, placed in the tenor part. Several factors combined, however, to alter radically the form and orientation of the chorales composed in the century and a half after Luther's death: the invasion of German-speaking territories by the melodies of the Genevan *Psalter (through the metrical translations of Ambrosius Lobwasser, 1573); the reform of German poetry (Martin Opitz, *Buch von der deutschen Poeterey,* 1624), moving away from quantitive measure to regularized meter, rhyme, and strophic form; the change in polyphonic setting from the 16th-century tenor *lied to the cantional style (Lucas Osiander, *Fünfftzig Geistische Lieder und Psalmen,* 1586; Johann Hermann Schein, *Cantional oder Gesangbuch*, 1627; see *Cantionale*), where the chorale melody rose to the top voice; the reorientation of texts away from God as object of adoration to God as object of meditative relief from personal anguish, frustration, and suffering (Johann Heerman, 1585–1647; Johann Rist, 1607–67; Paul Gerhardt, 1607–76; Johann Frank, 1618–77); the revitalized melodies of Johann Crüger (1598–1662), the first to be published (1640) with thoroughbass accompaniment suitable for home (keyboard) or church (organ) and subsequently given wide distribution as *Praxis pietatis melica* (1647) and as arrangements for voices, instruments, and thoroughbass under the title *Geistliche Kirchenmelodien* (1649); and finally the *Pia desideria* of the theologian Philip Spener (1635–1705), the manifesto of the Pietist movement that effected simpler forms for the chorale. The statistical climax was reached in Johann Balthasar König's *Harmonischer Lieder-Satz* of 1738, which contained 1,913 chorale melodies, with thoroughbass, including all the melodies from the Genevan Psalter. The artistic climax was reached in the music of Bach, who composed many four-part harmonizations (still often regarded as paradigms of tonal harmony) and employed chorale melodies in very diverse and often elaborate ways in works for voices and for organ [see Chorale cantata, Chorale concerto, Chorale fantasia, Chorale fugue, Chorale motet, Chorale variations, Organ chorale]. After Bach's death, innovation virtually ceased, though texts and melodies continued to play some role in works by Mendelssohn, Reger, Distler, Heinz Werner Zimmermann, and others. See also Hymn, Lutheran church music, Organ chorale.

Bibl.: Johannes Zahn, *Die Melodien der deutschen evangelischen Kirchenlieder* (Gütersloh, 1889–93; R: Hildesheim: Olms, 1963). John Julian, *Dictionary of Hymnology,* 2nd ed. (London, 1907; R: New York: Dover, 1957). Konrad Ameln, *Roots of German Hymnody of the Reformation Era* (St. Louis: Concordia, 1964). Johannes Riedel, *The Lutheran Chorale: Its Basic Traditions* (Minneapolis: Augsburg, 1967). Friedrich Blume, et al., *Protestant Church Music: A History* (New York: Norton, 1974). Konrad Ameln et al., eds., *Das deutsche Kirchenlied [I]: Verzeichnis der Drucke . . . bis 1800* [*RISM* B/VIII/1–2] (Kassel: Bärenreiter, 1975–80). Robin A. Leaver, *The Liturgy and Music: A Study of the Use of the Hymn in Two Liturgical Traditions,* Grove Liturgical Study 6 (Bramcote, Nottingham: Grove Books, 1976). Walter Blankenburg, "Johann Sebastian Bach und das evangelische Kirchenlied zu seiner Zeit," *Bachiana et alia Musicologica: Festschrift Alfred Dürr zum 65. Geburtstag,* ed. Wolfgang Rehm (Kassel: Bärenreiter, 1983), pp. 31–38. Joachim Stallmann et al., eds., *Das deutsche Kirchenlied III: Gesamtausgabe der Melodien aus gedruckten Quellen* (Kassel: Bärenreiter, 1993–). Robin A. Leaver, "The Chorale: Transcending Time and Culture," *Concordia Theological Quarterly* 56 (1993): 123–44. R.F.F., rev. R.A.L.

Chorale cantata [Ger. *Choralkantate*]. A cantata [see Cantata III] based on the words or on both words and melody of a German Protestant *chorale. Several types are found among the works of Bach: (i) Every movement is based on both words and melody of the chorale (*Christ lag in Todesbanden* BWV 4). (ii) The first and last strophes of the chorale text are retained, but some others are paraphrased poetically and set as arias and recitatives (*Ach Gott vom Himmel* BWV 2). (iii) The first and last strophes of the chorale text are retained, but some others are replaced by poetry that is set as arias and recitatives (*Wachet auf* BWV 140 and *Ein' feste Burg* BWV 80). The final strophe of all three types is characteristically a relatively simple four-part setting of the melody. Other movements that employ the melody, especially the first movement, may be elaborate choral settings that paraphrase it or treat it as a **cantus firmus* [see also Chorale motet]. Such works, type (i) above being the earliest, have their origins in the *chorale concerto of the 17th century and were composed through the middle of the 18th century by such composers, in addition to Bach, as Franz Tunder (1614–67), Johann Rosenmüller (ca. 1619–84), Sebastian Knüpfer (1633–76), Dietrich Buxtehude (ca. 1637–1707), Johann Schelle (1648–1701), Johann Philipp Krieger (1649–1725), Johann Pachelbel (1653–1706), and Johann Kuhnau (1660–1722).

Chorale concerto [Ger. *Choralkonzert*]. A setting for voices and instruments of a German Protestant *chorale, arising, like the **geistliches Konzert* of which it is a type, in the early 17th century under the influence of the Italian **concertato* style [see also Concerto (1)]. Such works could employ one or a few solo voices with *thoroughbass or *polychoral treatment of vocal and instrumental groups. Composers of such works include Michael Praetorius (ca. 1570–1621), Johann Hermann Schein (1586–1630), and Samuel Scheidt (1587–1654). See also Chorale cantata.

Chorale fantasia [Ger. *Choralfantasie*]. (1) A composition for organ in which a *chorale melody is treated freely. Successive phrases of the melody may be ornamented, broken into smaller motives, paraphrased, imitated, and the like. Such works are usually relatively long. The genre was developed and cultivated by north German organists from the middle 17th century through the middle 18th, including Heinrich Scheidemann (ca. 1595–1663), Franz Tunder (1614–67), Dietrich Buxtehude (ca. 1637–1707), Vincent Lübeck (1654–1740), Georg Böhm (1661–1733), and Bach. In the later part of his career, Bach applied the term fantasia to large-scale organ works in which the chorale melody is treated as a **cantus firmus* in the bass. See Organ chorale. (2) An elaborate choral movement based on a chorale melody, such as often occurs as the first movement of a Bach *chorale cantata.

Chorale fugue, chorale fughetta [Ger. *Choralfuge*]. A work for organ in which the first phrase of a *chorale is made the subject of a fugue. Such works were composed principally by middle-German composers of the later 17th and early 18th centuries, including J. S. Bach's great-uncle Heinrich Bach (1615–92), the latter's sons Johann Christoph Bach (1642–1703) and Johann Michael Bach (1648–94), Johann Pachelbel (1653–1706), and J. S. Bach himself. See also Organ chorale, Chorale motet.

Chorale motet [Ger. *Choralmotette*]. (1) A polyphonic vocal work in the style of a motet and based on a German Protestant *chorale melody. Examples from the early part of the 16th century usually treat the chorale melody as a **cantus firmus*. The term is most often applied, however, to settings from the later 16th century through the 18th in which successive phrases of the chorale are treated in imitation. Such works were often accompanied by instruments doubling the vocal parts. (2) A work for organ in the style of (1), also termed a chorale ricercar. See also Organ chorale.

Chorale partita. See Chorale variations.

Chorale prelude [Ger. *Choralvorspiel*]. A composition for organ based on a German Protestant *chorale melody and intended to serve as an introduction to the singing of the chorale. See Organ chorale.

Chorale ricercar. See Chorale motet.

Chorale variations. A composition for organ or harpsichord in which a German Protestant *chorale is made the basis of a set of variations. The genre was developed, under the influence of English keyboard variations, by Jan Pieterszoon Sweelinck (1562–1621), in whose works the chorale melody is presented in long notes, sometimes slightly ornamented, in a series of **cantus firmus* settings of varying texture and number of voices connected by transitional passages. Sweelinck's principal successors were Heinrich Scheidemann (ca. 1595–1663) and Samuel Scheidt (1587–1654), whose works omit transitional passages between settings. In the second half of the 17th century, compositions of this type give way to settings, often termed chorale *partitas, in which each variation retains the basic structural (including rhythmic) properties of the chorale in the fashion of what are now normally thought of as sets of *variations. In such settings, the melody may nevertheless be presented unadorned in one or another voice, as in works by Dietrich Buxtehude (ca. 1637–1707) and Johann Pachelbel (1653–1706). Bach's contributions include three early sets and the monumental *Canonic Variations on Vom Himmel hoch* BWV 769. See also Organ chorale.

Choralis constantinus. A three-volume collection of four-voice polyphonic settings of *Mass Propers for the liturgical year composed by Heinrich Isaac (ca. 1450–1517), completed and edited by his pupil Ludwig Senfl (ca. 1486–1542 or 1543), and published in Nuremberg in the years 1550–55 by Hieronymus Formschneider. The works in the second volume were commissioned in 1508 by the Cathedral of Constance, from which the collection takes its name. The remaining works were composed for the Hapsburg court chapel. Individual Masses normally include introit, alleluia or tract, sequence (especially for feasts of the saints), and communion. A very few include the gradual. The collection is indexed in *Grove 6,* s.v. "Isaac, Heinrich."

Choraliter [Lat.]. In the manner of *plainsong, as distinct from measured music.

Choral music. Music to be sung by a chorus or choir (i.e., with more than one singer for each part), with or without accompaniment. Choral singing was important in antiquity, but in the absence of any music, only general aspects of its character can be reconstructed. In the Middle Ages, choral music in Western Europe was confined primarily to *plainchant, since sacred polyphony and most secular music were intended for solo singers. The choral performance of sacred polyphony probably began early in the 15th century, though the size of choirs varied widely thereafter, and performances of sacred polyphony by ensembles with only one singer for each part undoubtedly continued to take place, perhaps as late as the 18th century [see Chorus]. Today, madrigals, chansons, and other kinds of early polyphony probably not intended for choral singing are frequently sung by small choruses.

The Renaissance has been seen in retrospect as a Golden Age of polyphonic choral music. Composers of this period perfected the medium itself, establishing the balanced distribution of voice parts over the full vocal range that has remained the norm. Their compositional methods were conceived in terms of this medium (though instruments were sometimes used in performance), and they extensively explored its many possibilities of sonority, texture, interrelationship of the parts, *polychoral writing, and manipulation of borrowed material. The unified setting of the *Mass Ordinary was established as a leading compositional genre (which it has since remained), joining the *motet, and the two underwent a rich and complex development.

Many of the basic aspects of choral writing formulated in the Renaissance were to remain standard thereafter, but the Baroque made new departures that were also to become traditional. Chief among these was the independent and increasingly idiomatic accompaniment of the chorus by instruments. Baroque emphasis on solo singing and contrast also influenced the formation of large works into sections or movements of differing setting, primarily choral, solo vocal, or instrumental. The chorus thus lost its formerly predominant position in sacred music, but broadened its scope as new genres in which it could participate—including for the first time secular ones—came into existence. Foremost among these were *oratorio and *opera. In the latter genre, the attention given the chorus is at times slight, as in Venetian and Neapolitan opera, but at others considerable, as in the works of Gluck.

Growing national differences and religious sectarianism also contributed to the creation of disparate bodies of music varying in their use of chorus. Italian composers, well into the 19th century, placed greater emphasis on solo singing, whereas the Germans maintained a stronger choral tradition, as in the *Passions, *cantatas, and motets of Bach and the oratorios and *anthems of Handel.

The Handel Commemoration concerts in England in the later 18th century, when many thousands of singers sang in performances of the oratorios, fostered the creation of municipal choral societies in the 19th century. This tendency was further advanced, first in Germany, then in England, following the success of Mendelssohn's revival of Bach's St. Matthew Passion in 1829. Regular performances of Handel's oratorios alternated with Mendelssohn's *Elijah* and *St. Paul,* as well as with the works of other composers such as Spohr and Gade, among others. Notable choral organizations founded in America during this period include the Handel and Haydn Society (Boston 1815) and the Bach Choir (Bethlehem, Pennsylvania, 1898). In Boston, Lowell Mason set up his Academy of Music, which was influential in promoting choral music in both church and school. Bethlehem (with Winston-Salem) was one of the two primary centers of the Moravian Church in America, a denomination that made significant use of choral music with instrumental accompaniment from the later 18th century.

The dramatic affective techniques of baroque expression gave it a certain theatricality that some considered less appropriate for sacred music than the Renaissance style, particularly the restrained Counter-Reformation style of Palestrina [see Palestrina style]. A stylistic split resulted, with composition in the so-called *stile antico* continuing to be cultivated along with the modern style into the 18th century.

The Classical masters reinterpreted the traditional procedures and genres of choral music in terms of Classical style, as Haydn did with the Handelian oratorio. Perhaps the most important innovation of the period was Beethoven's use of the chorus in his Choral Fantasy and Ninth Symphony. This innovation suggested a new concept of symphonic work with chorus that was pursued by many later composers in a variety of ways, from the use of a wordless chorus as adjunct to the orchestra (Debussy, Holst, Delius, Ravel) to the choral symphony (Berlioz, Mendelssohn, Liszt, Mahler, Scriabin, Vaughan Williams, Stravinsky, Berio).

The works of these classical masters did not affect the lives of people living in areas far away from European centers of music, but that does not mean they were without choral music. Emerging from the singing schools, created as part of the reform of psalmody in the early 18th century, a vigorous tradition of local choral singing developed in England and New England. Singing masters composed modest choral works, edited tune books, and taught in singing schools not only how these pieces should be sung but also the rudiments of music. The choral music of the singing schools was particularly strong in the U.S., spreading throughout most of the country and surviving (especially in the southern states) into the 20th century. William Billings, Lewis Edson, and Supply Belcher, among others, are characteristic of this American phenomenon that touched the lives of thousands.

In the 19th century, renewed debate over the proper style of sacred choral writing produced the *Cecilian movement, which reemphasized the Palestrina style as the proper model. This produced little music of lasting interest, although its ideal of restraint perhaps had an effect on the choral writing of Brahms, Bruckner, and even Fauré. By contrast, Berlioz and Verdi composed large-scale and elaborate works on the liturgical texts of the *Requiem and *Te Deum.

Amateur choral singing, which in the U.S. includes the choruses in virtually every secondary school, college, and university and most church choirs, has created an even greater market for varied choral music, which, however, is often conservative in style and of modest difficulty. Some composers have made radical innovations, at times through the influence of folk material (as in the percussive chanting invented by Stravinsky in *Les noces,* later adopted by Orff), or through avant-garde choral techniques, such as shouting, whispering, tone clusters, and glissandos, as in Krzysztof Penderecki's *St. Luke Passion.* See also Chorus.

Bibl.: Charles C. Perkins and John Sullivan Dwight, *History of the Handel and Haydn Society, Boston* (Boston: Mudge, 1889–93; R: New York: Da Capo, 1977). Raymond Walters, *The Bethlehem Bach Choir: A History and a Critical Compendium* (New York: Houghton Mifflin, 1923). Percy M. Young, *The Choral Tradition: An Historical and Analytical Survey from the Sixteenth Century to the Present Day* (New York: Norton, 1962). Robert Hines, ed., *The Composer's Point of View: Essays on Twentieth-Century Choral Music by Those Who Write It* (Norman: U of Okla Pr, 1963). Elwyn A. Wienandt, *Choral Music of the Church* (New York: Free Pr, 1965; R: New York: Da Capo, 1980). Nicholas Temperley,

The Music of the English Parish Church (New York: Cambridge U Pr, 1979). David P. DeVenney, *Nineteenth-Century American Choral Music* (Berkeley: Fallen Leaf, 1987). David P. DeVenney, *Early American Choral Music* (Berkeley: Fallen Leaf, 1988). David P. DeVenney, *American Choral Music since 1920* (Berkeley: Fallen Leaf, 1993). David P. DeVenney, *Source Readings in American Choral Music* (Missoula, Mont.: College Music Society, 1995).

Choralnotation [Ger.]. The notation of *plainsong; also notation of this type, especially that with square note-shapes, employed in the Middle Ages for other repertories, including secular monophonic music. See Neume.

Choralrhythmus [Ger.]. The rhythm of *plainsong. See Gregorian chant.

Choral Symphony. Popular name for Beethoven's Symphony no. 9 in D minor op. 125 (1822–24). The fourth and final movement, the introduction to which quotes themes from the preceding movements, is a setting for four soloists, chorus, and orchestra of Schiller's ode "To Joy" [Ger. "An die Freude"]. The first movement is an allegro, the second a scherzo with trio, and the third an adagio, all for orchestra alone.

Choralvorspiel [Ger.]. *Chorale prelude.

Chord [Fr. *accord;* Ger. *Akkord, Zusammenklang;* It. *accordo;* Sp. *acorde*]. Three or more pitches sounded simultaneously or functioning as if sounded simultaneously; two such pitches are normally referred to as an *interval. The most basic chords in the system of tonic-dominant or triadic *tonality are the major and minor *triads and their *inversions (the *sixth or six-three chord and the *six-four chord). Other chords that play an important though subordinate role are the *seventh chord (especially the dominant seventh), the augmented *sixth chord, the ninth chord, and the diminished triad, each of which is regarded in this context as dissonant [see Consonance, dissonance]. In the analysis of tonal music [see Harmonic analysis], all chords may be regarded as consisting of or deriving from two or more thirds (whether major or minor; see Interval) arranged one above another (e.g., G–B–D–F). When a chord is arranged in this most compact form containing only thirds, the lowest pitch is the root. A chord in which the root is the lowest pitch is said to be in root position regardless of the spacing of the pitches that lie above the root. The superposition of thirds may be extended to include ninth, eleventh, and thirteenth chords, each of which takes its name from the interval that separates the lowest and highest pitches when the chord is in the most compact form of root position. All such chords can be inverted, and, in some circumstances, one or more pitches other than the highest may be omitted.

In works of the 20th century not based on the tonal system, chords of numerous types are used, the concepts of consonance and dissonance being often irrelevant [see also Fourth chord, Tone cluster, Atonality, Twelve-tone music]. Discussions of such music often prefer the term simultaneity to chord, though the latter may appear in such compounds as trichord, tetrachord, pentachord, and *hexachord for collections of three, four, five, and six pitches, respectively, that may or may not be sounded simultaneously. Two pitches may be referred to as a dyad.

Chorda [Gr., Lat., string]. Pitch, note.

Chordal style. A style or texture consisting of *chords whose pitches are sounded simultaneously. Such texture is also described as homophonic or *homorhythmic. In strict chordal style, the number of pitches in each chord (and thus the number of parts making up the texture) remains constant (most often four, as in the Protestant chorale or hymn). In free chordal style, the number of pitches may vary.

Chordophone. Any instrument in which sound is produced by the vibration of a string. Chordophone strings are made of a variety of materials, including plant fiber, animal gut, steel, brass, silk, bamboo, and nylon [see also String]. They may be set in motion by plucking (as in the guitar), by striking (piano), or by bowing (violin). In some chordophones (such as the piano), strings are tuned to fixed pitches in advance and not normally altered during performance. In others (such as the violin), different pitches are produced in performance by altering the effective length or tension of a string. [For a discussion of the relationship of length, tension, and thickness of strings to their pitch, see Acoustics.] Many chordophones are provided with a *sound box or *resonator to amplify and prolong the sound. Chordophones are classified on the basis of their shape and construction into the following families: *harps, *lutes (including violins and guitars), *lyres, *musical bows, and *zithers (including pianos and harpsichords). See also Instrument.

Chorea [Lat.]. From the Middle Ages through the 17th century, a piece to be danced to, including specific types such as the *passamezzo.

Choreography. The planning or composing of movement in *dance, including ballet; the plan or composition that results for a specific work; also the basic pattern of movement in a social dance.

Chorister. A singer in a choir, especially a boy singer.

Chorlied [Ger.]. A choral song, especially one without accompaniment.

Chôro [Port.]. An ensemble of serenaders established in the later 19th century in Rio de Janeiro consisting of guitars, *cavaquinhos* (small, four-string guitars), flute and other winds, and percussion and dedicated to the polka and other dances of European derivation. In the early 20th century, it became prominently associated with such distinctive Brazilian popular dances as the **maxixe* and **samba.* The term *chôro* is also applied to various kinds of instrumental music that reflect the virtuosic, contrapuntal, and improvisatory character of the ensemble's typical performance and has been used in art music by Heitor Villa-Lobos, among others.

D.S.

Chororgel [Ger.; Du. *Koororgel*]. *Choir organ (2).

Chorton [Ger.]. See Pitch.

Chorus [fr. Gr. *choros;* Fr. *choeur;* Ger. *Chor;* It., Sp. *coro*]. (1) A body of singers who perform together, either in unison or in parts, usually with more than one on a part. A body of church singers is a choir, a term also sometimes used for a secular chorus. Other names for a secular chorus include glee club, choral society, and chorale. The most common kind of chorus at present, but not always in the past, is the mixed chorus of male and female voices, usually distributed soprano, alto, tenor, and bass, although other numbers of parts are not uncommon. Choruses of exclusively male, female, or boys' voices are also found. An *a *cappella* chorus sings without instrumental accompaniment.

The all-male Greek chorus of antiquity, a formative and essential element of the Greek drama, both sang and danced, and varied considerably in size at different times. For Western Europe, the chorus as a continuing tradition begins with Christianity. Whereas much of the singing in the very early Church seems to have been congregational, formal choral singing developed as the Church became institutionalized, a development resulting in highly trained choirs and virtuoso soloists with a variety of performance methods, including responsorial and antiphonal singing [see Psalmody].

In the Middle Ages and Renaissance, the use of the chorus was largely confined to church music. Formal secular choruses did not exist, secular vocal music being, with few exceptions, performed by soloists. Because of St. Paul's prohibition, church choirs included only male voices (except, of course, in convents). Further, the medieval choir was restricted to the performance of the monophonic music of the Church, *plainchant. Medieval polyphony was the domain of solo singers.

Choral performance of polyphonic sacred music seems to have begun early in the 15th century, though the singing of such music with only one singer on each part survived until as late as the 18th century. Some 15th-century music clearly calls for alternation between a group of soloists and a chorus. The 15th century saw a change from a usual three-part texture of tenor and contratenor equal in range supporting a higher discant to a norm of four parts with *contratenor bassus* (later shortened to bass) below the tenor, *contratenor altus* (later shortened to alto) above it, and discant as the highest part. This occupation of different vocal ranges by sections of the chorus was essential to the development of the equal-voice imitative style of Renaissance polyphony.

Before ca. 1525, the highest parts were usually sung by falsettists [see Falsetto], thus setting an upper pitch limit around d″. Thereafter, the use of boy sopranos allowed for parts of true soprano range, pulling up the alto as well and finally achieving the stratification of soprano, alto, tenor, and bass that has remained the norm. In the second half of the 16th century, perhaps because of the growing popularity of female sopranos in secular music, the soprano **castrato* came into vogue in Italian choirs, remaining so into the 19th century. Elsewhere boys and falsettists continued in use until the 19th century, when women began to replace them in Protestant choirs. In England the falsetto tradition never disappeared.

The principal innovation of Baroque choral practice was the development of concerted instrumental accompaniment. In the Renaissance, instrumentalists had not had independent parts [see Performance practice]. In the Baroque, too, secular music began to employ the chorus, particularly for dramatic or quasi-dramatic genres such as opera and oratorio. But even within sacred music, the importance of the chorus was limited by the new emphasis on solo singing, especially in Italianate music.

The size of choruses was generally small until the late 18th century, though it varied considerably from place to place depending on the resources available to pay their members. Church and court payment records provide considerable evidence, though they do not always make clear who sang what kinds of music and the extent to which persons not listed as musicians might also have sung polyphonic music. The papal chapel employed 18 singers in 1450, rising gradually thereafter to the limit of 32 set in 1625. The chapel of Philip the Good included 30 men and boys in 1467. The average for the 15th and 16th centuries probably fell in the range from 20 to 30. Lassus, on the other hand, had available 62 singers at the court chapel in Munich around 1570. In the course of the 17th and 18th centuries, some choruses included 30 to 40 and more: 36 at St. Mark's in Venice in the late 17th century, between 35 and 45 at the Chapel Royal in England in the same period, and up to 30 for Buxtehude's **Abendmusik* concerts in Lübeck. Yet in Protestant Germany, church choirs usually consisted of 1 singer per part (concertists), sometimes with 1 to 5 supplementary vocalists (ripienists) providing reinforcement in less elaborate movements. These were the forces available to Buxtehude, Bach in Leipzig, and Telemann in Frankfurt for cantatas and larger works. Choruses were sometimes combined for special occasions, and the late 18th century saw some performances, notably the Handel festivals in England, with singers numbering in the hundreds and up to 1,000. In the 19th century, amateur choral societies became popular in northern Europe and America, particularly all-male ones (**Liedertafel, *Liederkranz, *Orphéon*) and large mixed choruses of 200 to 300 voices, with even more at festivals. This increase in size led to distorted performances of earlier choral music conceived for smaller numbers [see Additional accompaniment].

Amateur choral singing remained popular in the 20th century. In the U.S., this included the activities of choruses in virtually every secondary school, college, and university, of church choirs, and of many community choruses, including *glee clubs. School choruses often included 100 or more members. But since the mid-20th century, a developing sense of historicity has encouraged the use of smaller choruses—still usually mixed—for pre-19th century music. The number of paid professional church choirs, and professional choruses of any other kind, is now extremely small. See also Choral music.

(2) A piece intended to be sung by a chorus, often a movement within a larger work.

(3) The *refrain, or *burden, of a strophic song, both text and music of which are repeated after each verse, or stanza, of changing text. This usage derives from the frequent performance of the verse by the soloist, with others joining in the refrain. See also Ballad (2) (3).

(4) In jazz, a single statement of the harmonic-melodic pattern (as of a 32-bar popular song in AABA form or the 12-bar *blues chord progression) whose varied repetition constitutes a performance of a piece. The first and last choruses will usually be the same or similar in presenting the least varied statement of the given melody and harmonies. Intervening choruses are usually improvisations based on the pattern. To "take a chorus" is to improvise in this way. This meaning derives from (3). See also Ballad (2) (3).

(5) In organ registration, the combined sound of unison- and fifth-sounding stops of the same tone family, i.e., 16′, 8′, 4′, 2⅔′, 2′, 1⅓′, 1′. See *Plein jeu.*

(6) [Lat.] In the Middle Ages, any of several instruments including the *bagpipe, *crwth, and *string drum.

Bibl.: Wilhelm Ehmann, *Das künstlerische Singen,* vol. 2, *Die Chorführung* (Kassel: Bärenreiter, 1949), trans. George D. Wiebe, *Choral Directing* (Minneapolis: Augsburg, 1968). Manfred Bukofzer, "The Beginnings of Choral Polyphony," *Studies in Medieval and Renaissance Music* (New York: Norton, 1950), pp. 176–89. Royal Stanton, *The Dynamic Choral Conductor* (Delaware Water Gap, Pa.: Shawnee Pr, 1971). Harold A. Decker and Julius Herford, eds., *Choral Conducting: A Symposium* (New York: Appleton-Century-Crofts, 1973). Percy M. Young, *The Choral Tradition: An Historical Survey from the Sixteenth Century to the Present Day,* 2nd ed. rev. (New York: Norton, 1981). Robert L. Garretson, *Choral Music: History, Style, and Performance Practice* (Englewood Cliffs, N.J.: Prentice Hall, 1993). Reinhard Kapp, "Wagners Dresdner Chorwerke und der Chor der Hofoper," *Berliner Beitrage zur Musikwissenschaft* 8 (1993): 5–21. Mary Cyr, "The Paris Opéra Chorus during the Time of Rameau," *ML* 76 (1995): 32–51. Mary Cyr, "The Dramatic Role of the Chorus in French Opera: Evidence for the Use of Gesture, 1670–1770," in *Opera and the Enlightenment,* ed. Thomas Bauman and Marita Petzoldt McClymonds (Cambridge: Cambridge U Pr, 1995), 105–18. John Morehen, ed., *English Choral Practice c. 1400–c. 1650: A Memorial Volume to Peter le Huray* (Cambridge: Cambridge U Pr, 1995). Lawrence Schenbeck, *Joseph Haydn and the Classical Choral Tradition* (Chapel Hill, N.C.: Hinshaw Music, 1996). Andrew Parrott, *The Essential Bach Choir* (Woodbridge: Boydell, 2000).

Christmas Concerto. Popular name for Corelli's Concerto Grosso in G minor op. 6 no. 8 (first printed in 1714), headed "Fatto per la notte di Natale" (made for Christmas night). The last movement is a *pastorale.

Christmas Oratorio. (1) [Ger. *Weihnachts-Oratorium;* Lat., *Oratorium tempore Nativitatis Christi*]. A work by Bach, BWV 248 (performed in 1734/35), consisting of six church cantatas intended to be performed on six successive days between Christmas Day and Epiphany. It includes a number of pieces used in earlier cantatas. (2) [Ger. *Historia, der freuden- und gnadenreichen Geburth Gottes und Marien Sohnes, Jesu Christi,* Story of the Joyful and Merciful Birth of the Son of God and Mary, Jesus Christ]. A work by Heinrich Schütz, SWV 435, published in 1664. See also Cantata, Oratorio.

Christ on the Mount of Olives. See *Christus am Ölberge.*

Christophe Colomb [Fr., Christopher Columbus]. Opera in two parts by Darius Milhaud (libretto by Paul Claudel) composed in 1928 and first produced in Berlin in 1930. Setting: Spain at the end of the 15th century. Milhaud also composed substantially unrelated incidental music for Claudel's play.

Christus. (1) An oratorio by Liszt with texts from the Bible and the Roman Catholic liturgy, composed in 1862–67 and first performed in Weimar in 1873. (2) An unfinished oratorio by Mendelssohn.

Christus am Ölberge [Ger., Christ on the Mount of Olives]. An oratorio by Beethoven, op. 85 (libretto by Franz Xaver Huber), first performed in Vienna in 1803, and revised in 1804.

Chroai [Gr.]. In ancient Greek theory, the shades or colors of genera obtained by tuning the movable notes of a *tetrachord [see Greece I, 3 (i)]. Assuming the fourth to equal 2½ tones exactly, Aristoxenus specified three chromatic and two diatonic chroai (as in the accompanying table, where the unit is equal to a whole tone). Other ancient theorists, especially Ptolemy, provided chroai different from those of Aristoxenus.

Chroai	Internal intervals in descending order
Tense diatonic	1 — 1 — ½
Soft diatonic	1¼ — ¾ — ½
Tonic chromatic	1½ — ½ — ½
Hemiolic chromatic	1¾ — ⅜ — ⅜
Soft chromatic	1⅚ — ⅓ — ⅓

Bibl.: C. André Barbera, "Arithmetic and Geometric Divisions of the Tetrachord," *JMT* 21 (1977): 294–323. A.B

Chromatic [Gr., colored]. (1) The *scale that includes all of the 12 pitches (and thus all of the 12 semitones) contained in an octave, as distinct from the *diatonic scale. (2) Harmony or melody that employs some if not all of the pitches of the chromatic scale in addition to those of the diatonic scale of some particular key, whether or not the harmony or melody in question can be understood within the context of any single key. See Chromaticism. (3) An instrument capable of playing a chromatic scale, e.g., *brass instruments with valves as distinct from natural instruments [but see also Harp]. (4) One of the three genera (the other two being *diatonic and *enharmonic) of the music of ancient *Greece. It employs a *tetrachord bounded by a perfect fourth and in which the lower two intervals are both semitones. (5) [It. *cromatico.*] In the 16th century, works notated with black notes. See *Note nere.*

Chromatic Fantasy and Fugue. A composition for harpsichord in D minor by Bach, BWV 903 (ca. 1720, rev. ca. 1730). The fantasy makes extensive use of chromatic harmonies, and the fugue is based on a chromatic subject.

Chromaticism. The use of at least some pitches of the *chromatic scale in addition to or instead of those of the *diatonic scale of some particular key. It can occur in limited degrees that do not detract from the sense of key or tonal center; thus it can function fully within the system of tonic-dominant *tonality. The term may also refer, however, to the procedures employed in music in which no single diatonic scale or key predominates and in which, therefore, chromaticism cannot be regarded as the elaboration of an underlying diatonic structure [see also Atonality; Twelve-tone music].

In tonal music, chromaticism may occur as a surface detail or on a deeper structural level. At the surface or foreground, it may result simply from the filling in of whole steps with half steps. Chromatic pitches introduced in this way can usually be understood as resulting from an extension of the principles of *counterpoint or voice leading that produce *nonharmonic tones in general: passing tones, neighboring tones, suspensions, and the like, each of which may thus have both diatonic and chromatic forms. Chromaticism may also be associated at this level with modal mixture, i.e., the introduction of pitches from the parallel major or minor of the prevailing key. At a somewhat deeper level of musical structure, chromatic tones may bring about the *tonicization of a pitch other than the prevailing tonic. In this context, they most often occur as either the leading tone or the fourth scale degree of some key other than the prevailing tonic. The resulting harmonies are usually described as applied or secondary dominants. At the deepest level of structure, chromaticism is associated with *modulation from the prevailing tonic to other keys, especially keys whose tonics do not occur as diatonic pitches in the original key.

In the analysis of chromatic voice leading, a distinction is made between chromatic inflection and chromatic substitution (Salzer and Schachter, 1969). Inflection results when a chromatic tone precedes or follows its diatonic counterpart. Substitution results when the chromatic tone replaces its diatonic counterpart.

To some extent, the different structural levels of chromaticism may be independent of one another. A composition may employ considerable chromatic voice leading, perhaps in a chromatic melody or in chromatic counterpoint and harmony supporting a largely diatonic melody, without modulating to any new key at all or at least not to any keys other than relatively closely related ones. The music of Mozart, for example, is sometimes rather more chromatic in this way than that of Haydn. Conversely, a composition may modulate rather quickly to several relatively remote keys, in each of which a relatively diatonic tonal language may prevail. The music of Schubert, where motion to third-related keys such as the mediant or flatted submediant may be prominent, is sometimes chromatic in this way.

The harmonies resulting from chromatic voice leading, whether or not for the sake of modulation to remote keys, are often described as altered chords. Among the most prominent of these are various types of *sixth chords, including the Neapolitan sixth, formed on the flatted supertonic, and the several augmented sixth chords. The diminished *seventh chord is inherently chromatic, since it cannot be constructed from the diatonic pitches of a single key (though it can occur on the raised leading tone in the harmonic minor scale). Because its four pitches are disposed symmetrically with respect to the octave, it functions equally well as the diminished seventh on the seventh scale degree in four different keys (and in other ways in other keys) and thus facilitates modulation. Also inherently chromatic, though much less prominent in tonal music, is the augmented *triad. See also Harmonic analysis.

From the mid-19th century onward, increasing amounts of music deploy the resources of chromaticism at all structural levels. The result sometimes undermines the procedures of tonality to such a degree that individual works are not easily described as belonging to a single key. Examples of such works include Chopin's Prelude op. 28 no. 2 and the prelude to Wagner's *Tristan und Isolde.* Wagner's opera is sometimes seen as marking a crisis in the tonal language, leading ultimately to its abandonment in the 20th century in the atonal works of Schoenberg and others (Kurth, 1920). Of at least equal historical importance, however, is the rather different chromaticism of Debussy, which is not satisfactorily explained as resulting from an organic process of unchecked and ultimately destructive growth of the chromaticism latent within tonality. The chromaticism of much 20th-century music can only be seen as a radical alternative to the procedures of tonal music. The resurgence of tonality in some art music of recent decades, however, reasserts the historical relationship between chromaticism and diatonicism. The sometimes considerable chromaticism of much jazz and popular music can also be understood as elaborating underlying diatonic structures.

Although chromaticism is a prominent feature of the music of ancient Greece, it has a restricted role in the music of the Middle Ages, even though all of the pitches in question were discussed by theorists and available on instruments by the 14th century. Until the 16th century, nondiatonic pitches except for B♭ were regarded as belonging to *musica ficta* as distinct from *musica recta* (the pitches of the *gamut, which included B♭'s). Although liturgical chant in the Middle Ages normally includes no accidentals other than B♭ (the status of which itself is in doubt in this repertory), polyphonic music of the period, especially from the 14th century onward, sometimes makes considerable use of chromatic tones and may include harmonies such as F♯–A–C♯. There has been considerable scholarly debate over the extent to which chromatic tones have been left unspecified in the sources of the period and over the principles to be employed in identifying unspecified chromatic tones [see *Musica ficta*].

In the 16th century, various theorists (particularly Nicola Vicentino, in his *L'antica musica ridotta alla moderna prattica* of 1555) sought to revive the musical system of classical antiquity and with it chromaticism. Some composers (including Vicentino himself and Anthoine de Bertrand, ca. 1535–ca. 1580) pursued similar goals. Edward Lowinsky (1946) has proposed the existence of a "secret chromatic art" in which were composed works that could be interpreted either diatonically or as embodying distant chromatic modulations. Independent of these programmatic efforts, the use of chromaticism increased steadily in the middle and later 16th century. A well-known early example of explicit chromaticism is Cipriano de Rore's "Calami sonum ferentes" (1555). A high point is reached in the Italian madrigals of Luca Marenzio (1553 or 1554–1613) and especially Carlo Gesualdo (ca. 1561–1613).

From the late 16th century through the 17th century and into the first half of the 18th, chromaticism is encountered especially in abstract keyboard works such as the *ricercar, *fantasia, and *fugue and in vocal works expressing grief (with which a descending chromatic bass line is closely associated). To the former category belong works of Bull, Sweelinck, Frescobaldi, and others, including Bach (*Chromatic Fantasy and Fugue,* ricercar from the *Musical Offering*). Examples of the latter include works by Purcell ("Thy hand, Belinda!" and Dido's lament from *Dido and Aeneas*) and by Bach ("Crucifixus" from the *B-minor Mass*).

The later 18th century sees wider-ranging chromaticism in fantasies of C. P. E. Bach, persistent chromatic voice leading in works of Mozart (String Quintet in G minor K. 516, first movt.), and striking juxtapositions of key in works of Haydn (String Quartet op. 76 no. 6 in E♭ major, second movt.; the "Representation of Chaos" from the *Creation*). In the early 19th century, Beethoven often makes the semitone an organizing structural element as well as a component of foreground voice leading (D♭–C in the first movement of the Piano Sonata in F minor op. 57, "Appassionata"; the surrounding of B♭ by B♮ and A in the introduction to the fugue of the last movement of the Piano Sonata in B♭ major op. 106, "Hammerklavier"; C♯–D in the first two movements of the String Quartet in C♯ minor op. 131). But whereas the chromaticism of Beethoven most often rests on a strongly developed polarity between tonic and dominant, that of his successors often abandons this fundamental relationship and with it one of the principal elements of tonality.

Bibl.: Ernst Kurth, *Romantische Harmonik und ihre Krise in Wagners 'Tristan'* (Bern and Leipzig: P Haupt, 1920; 3rd ed., Berlin: M Hesse, 1923; R: Hildesheim: Olms, 1968). Edward E. Lowinsky, *Secret Chromatic Art in the Netherlands Motet,* trans. Carl Buchman (New York: Columbia U Pr, 1946; R: New York: Russell & Russell, 1967). Id., "Adrian Willaert's Chromatic 'Duo' Re-examined," *TVNM* 18 (1956): 1–36. Felix Salzer, *Structural Hearing* (New York: C Boni, 1952). William J. Mitchell, "The Study of Chromaticism," *JMT* 6 (1962): 2–31. Roger Bullivant, "The Nature of Chromaticism," *MR* 29 (1963): 97–129, 279. Felix Salzer and Carl Schachter, *Counterpoint in Composition: The Study of Voice Leading* (New York: McGraw-Hill, 1969). James Haar, "False Relations and Chromaticism in Sixteenth-Century Music," *JAMS* 30 (1970): 391–94. Jim Samson, *Music in Transition* (London: Dent, 1977). Karol Berger, *Theories of Chromatic and Enharmonic Music in Late 16th-Century Italy* (Ann Arbor: UMI Res Pr, 1980). Howard Boatwright, *Chromaticism: Theory and Practice* (Fayetteville, N.Y.: Walnut Grove, 1994).

Chronos, chronos protos [Gr.]. In ancient Greek music, the temporal unit. Theoretically indivisible, it takes the time of a short syllable of text and is usually transcribed as an eighth note. Aristides Quintilianus makes the analogy between it and the monad, or the point in geometry (*De musica,* i.14). Longer temporal values in music were multiples of the *chronos protos.*

A.B.

Chrotta [Lat.]. See *Rote.*

Church mode. See Mode.

Church music. Music composed, adapted, or deemed suitable for church use, or for Christian worship, prayer, meditation, thanksgiving, or commemoration, public or private. Western church music has a distinctive character that differentiates it from other church musics and even from its own Judeo-Christian roots (Werner, 1959). Its nature, its materials, and the forms and forces it utilizes have been peculiarly shaped by theological, historical, and cultural factors over two millennia.

The church in the West has always regarded music as an important feature of ritual. *Plainchant and *psalmody have been associated with the Western church since its beginnings, both having clear pre-Christian roots; together they pose and to some extent define two fundamental issues of church music style:

(i) What is the proper manner of performance? and (ii) What are the range and depth of the sentiments it may seek to express?

The historical evolution of church music (Blume, 1965; Fellerer, 1972–76) has provoked as many difficulties as it has solved, but all of them deal with or rise out of what are perceived as fundamental categories of church music: an appropriate textual and melodic repertory and an appropriate compositional and performing style. The nature of that appropriateness and the authority to determine it are the primary issues that the historical evolution has sought to address (Hayburn, 1979).

Since the Book of *Psalms, generally viewed as exploring the totality of relationships between humanity and God, its pervasive use by the Christian church accounts in large measure for the catholicity of sentiment that characterizes Western church music. The prosody of the Psalms, where structure and meaning are virtually inseparable (Lowth, 1787), has also permeated church music, especially in its clear implications for recitation and performance growing out of parallelism of structure—implications found within all chanted music in the Western church.

Since about the beginning of the second millennium of Christian history, plainchant has been the locus of polyphonic invention in Western music, a practice perhaps adapted from folk usage but then, as *organum (Waite, 1954) and later as *motet, evolving as a musico-textual trope to the chant. The adaptation of polyphony to plainchant is significant on two counts: It is the ultimate origin of all polyphonic music, liturgical or otherwise, and it witnesses the initial (and continuing) use of chant as **cantus firmus* (Sparks, 1963).

Most church music is associated with text in some way: as bearer of it, symbol of it, or meditator upon it. Textually, the Holy Bible (Old and New Testaments) is the primary source, but before it can be used by church musicians, it must exist in specific and canonically satisfactory form—in a particular language and rhetorical style deemed suitable and authorized for ecclesiastical use. For the most part, the authoritative prose style has been the Latin Vulgate, mostly the work of St. Jerome (ca. 342–420), much of whose translation from Greek and Hebrew survives in the oldest extant Vulgate manuscripts from the early 8th century. For English-speaking peoples, the most widely used text has been the so-called Authorized or King James version (1611), based on many previous sources and translations, both Roman Catholic and Protestant. The sanctity of the Latin Biblical text derives as much from its age and long liturgical use as it does from prosodic and syntactical inflections that permit the most succinct, precise, and musically fecund expression. How to invest a vernacular language with just those qualities was the test facing all subsequent translators and one that the makers of the Book of Common Prayer and the Authorized Version passed brilliantly. The work facing Martin Luther (1483–1546) and John Calvin (1509–64), insofar as it relates to music, was different in nature but equal in difficulty: for Lutheran lieder, a German diction and imagery suitable for congregational expression (Babst, 1545); for Calvin and Clément Marot (d. 1544) in French and their co-workers (notably Sternhold) in English, the fitting of Psalm texts into meters and rhyme schemes in which sound should cooperate with sense.

In the 18th century, congregational hymnody gave rise to a new body of vernacular texts (Wesley, 1788) that succeeded the use of metrical Psalms and grew dramatically in quality and importance in the 19th and 20th centuries by virtue of reinterpretation of Biblical or quasi-Biblical imagery in terms of the secular, the personal, and the patriotic, often phrased in pseudo-Biblical imagery. Of all these experiments, the English Victorian hymn (Temperley, 1979) and the American *gospel song (Sankey, 1894) are by far the most significant.

Plainchant is the foundation of the melodic repertory of Western church music, and the major bodies of melodic repertory that join it in chronological succession—*chorale melody, metrical *psalter tune, and *hymn tune—have had, in order to survive and flourish, to find ways of adjusting their own styles to certain qualities of chant melody that account for its substantial importance. The most significant of these are predictable singability and unpredictable plasticity. Plainchant is predictably singable because its melodies have a limited range that for the most part barely exceeds an octave and thus makes them accessible to any voice, trained or untrained, and also because they are woven of melodic locutions that seem to make minimal technical demands (pitch, interval) on singers. Nevertheless, despite these comparative simplicities, the plasticity of plainchant—its surprising melodic turns folded around and into the most elastic phraseology—gives it an openness, a sense of eternal meditative incompleteness, that is unique and makes it adaptable to metrical or polyphonic settings (because it can bend and stretch itself without losing its identity).

The three late bodies of melodic repertory—chorale, Psalm tune, and hymn tune—being conceived for congregational use and adapted to strophic vernacular texts, must also satisfy other needs: They must come to an end, and seem to do so; they must tolerate strophic repetition without doing too much violence to change of strophic content; they must be melodically and metrically memorable. The chorale melody, really a late medieval construct, drawing advantageously on its poetic roots (*bar form and corresponding contemporary prosody), nevertheless achieves the most successful reinterpretation of chant in restrictive modern terms. It was the melodies that gave the Lutheran texts entrance into any language and that enabled the translated texts to rise above mere vernacular intelligibility to a universality of meaning and use that eluded the metrical Psalms, despite their musical popularity (Lobwasser, 1573). The tunes of the metrical psalter in their original Genevan version (Pidoux, 1962) are rhythmically much more avant-garde (Blankenburg, in Blume, 1965), making the most elaborately contrived use of rhythmic stencils in the most modern 16th-century manner. In startling contrast to the history of chorale melody composition, however, the composition of metrical Psalm tunes virtually ceases by the early 17th century, and this closing off of the repertory prevents its reaching and sustaining a universality of theological significance attained by chant and chorale. The modern hymn tune, beginning in the 18th century, continues to produce a huge repertory of memorable melodies often maligned for poverty of melodic invention but just as often attaining a widespread dissemination. The repertory of hymn melodies is the only one of the three modern types still in process of formation. A fourth melodic type, the *spiritual (Jackson, 1933, 1939), is now also a virtually closed repertory, but it more perfectly satisfies congregational needs than any of the other three. Its structure immediately evokes its performing style, which arises out of its social setting, and represents a kind of liturgical wholeness.

Church music has always been composed in relation to the circumstances of its performance, e.g., who is to do it and where (Temperley, 1979). The interior arrangement of many Western churches, often disposing performers in apparently awkward patterns, diffuses acoustical concentration and blurs acoustical clarity. Surmounting these difficulties sometimes is made impossible by impediments such as the sheer size of the buildings, acoustically hostile furnishings and materials, and architectural details—lofts or balconies—that tend to disperse the sound sources even further. The performers of church music may be one or many—priest or minister, clerk, choir, organ, instruments, congregation—and music may engage them separately or together, and from (and to and from) various points and elevations within and around the acoustical shell. But a church is not a concert hall, nor are the performers of church music necessarily concert artists. Thus, no matter how desirable, technical excellence in performing church music is not necessarily the first requirement, nor can one insist on other aspects of modern concert hall manners, e.g., attentiveness, or only one music at one time. Even text (let alone intelligible text) is dispensable: the textually mute organ, for instance, has had a connection with the Western church since the 8th century (Williams, 1980; Ochse, 1975), its literature is overwhelmingly liturgical or ecclesiastical in origin, intent, or association, and major performers on it have always had to learn to be skilled church musicians. But though organs cannot speak words, their music can salute, sing, ornament, elaborate, and combine melodies that convey words and thus come to symbolize those words and project their meanings, despite their absence. Almost every other instrument has had some relationship with church performance. None, however, has enjoyed the prestige—or license—granted to the organ.

The forms and styles of polyphonic church music constitute the substance of any historical account or discussion, but virtually none of these exists apart from some relation to the corpus of texts and melodies and their liturgical content and the peculiar performing circumstances of the church. In this respect, every church composition is obliged to take some position vis-à-vis tradition, which it is joining, continuing, rejecting, modifying, or amplifying. All the major compositional forms employing text (e.g., *Mass, *motet, *canticle, *hymn, *passion, *oratorio, *cantata) are intelligible as church music only in terms of their function, which entails relating them to a particular liturgy at a particular time and place. Mass, motet, and canticle are liturgical embellishments, often calling on traditional textual or melodic materials; the *anthem appears as an interpolation into an otherwise completed liturgy, tolerated but not essential; the musical passion also begins as liturgical interpolation, as does the church cantata. On the other hand, the oratorio's history is that of liturgical substitute rather than embellishment or interpolation, even though Biblical characters, imagery, or language may be used or suggested. The history of the hymn is sui generis. Since much music in most of these categories is difficult to perform, it presupposes expert musical forces of a quality usually found only in the grandest establishments of church or court and thus constitutes special music for notable ceremonial occasions. All of it, by style and technique, has kinship with other musics contemporaneous with it. Thus, one can speak of Medieval, Renaissance, Baroque, Classical, Romantic, and 20th-century church music styles (and their subdivisions) and expect some correlation with all the music composed in such periods—some evidence, in other words, of kinship (e.g., by domination, appropriation, submission, rejection) with current styles.

The surviving sacred music of the Middle Ages and early Renaissance is largely liturgical and is largely responsible for the origins and development of *cantus firmus* polyphony. All 16th-century music measures itself by its relation to the word and its intelligibility, adopting the technique of imitative polyphony and placing enormous and unbearable strains on the traditional *cantus firmus* techniques. The disintegration and reconstruction of polyphony in the Baroque period is evident in church music (Lewis, 1975) that borrows from its operatic and instrumental surroundings recitative, aria, and the concerted instrumental style and adds them to a redeveloped polyphonic texture with or without *cantus firmus*. Up to this point, ca. 1750, the best church music and the best music are generally synonymous. After 1750, the comparison breaks down, stylistic and imaginative innovation passing outside the church, which, finding itself swept up and carried along by what are now perceived as secular styles (symphonic and even revolutionary music), withdraws and seeks, not for the first time, to redirect itself into a less clamorous and more devout course by drawing on historical models (Palestrina and Bach) or interpreting archival materials (Mocquereau, 1908, 1927), all of whose influences are evident in 19th-century music. In the 20th century, church music toyed with the trivial as well as continued to seek out a "church" style, but by doing so it further alienated itself from the mainstream of musical development.

At the beginning of the 21st century, there is in North America a vast diversity of musical style, much of it of a popular nature—e.g., contemporary Christian. Nevertheless there are signs that the Latin mass, together with chant and polyphony, is returning to some Catholic churches, while other churches are equally rediscovering chant and exploring new music, much of it inspired by such composers as Tavener and Pärt, among others.

Western church music continues to struggle with fundamental difficulties whose defiance of final resolution may be the hallmark of the vitality of church and culture, or merely a sign of intractability. In secular terms, such difficulties may be considered as aesthetic, political, sociological, or even purely technical matters, but they have theological meaning as well. Can there be a true church music style? The evidence of history provides no answers, but it raises the question continuously, and certain patterns, though not prevailing, now and then emerge. The criterion of verbal intelligibility, for instance, affected all the music of the Reformation and Counter-Reformation, but it has to be seen as a burning contemporaneous theological issue that then sought to realize itself in musical terms (*Council of Trent). Almost its exact artistic opposite prevailed in the later 19th century, when the *a cappella* style, ideally implying no instruments and utilizing recognizable triadic harmony, set the standard by which church music could be identified, irrespective of verbal clarity or even verbal source. Instruments themselves, other than the organ, have come and gone over the years, their use often explained by local traditions and arrangements, their rejection resulting from theocratic displeasure that not even the organ escaped. But no judgments a priori about text, style, or musical forms—whether identifiable or exclusively ecclesiastical or integral to the larger culture—have ever provided satisfactory answers or produced by themselves a church music style of quality.

There are, however, two more fundamental issues that persist, one deriving from the nature of music itself, the other related to the nature of music as an invocation of the divine. In its relation to the church and the performing arts to which it may there be allied (poetry, movement, drama), music tends quickly to occupy a dominating position from which it orders and controls, and even comes to interpret, content; and if left to their own devices, its practitioners—those who compose or perform it—may tend to forget church music's raison d'être and take delight only in their own activity. As a result, church music has occasionally been criticized for not being so much reinforcement of the liturgy as interference with it. The various reasons all attach to a notion of excess: too opulent, too complex, too busy, too dissonant, too noisy, in the context of the music's use. Cultural experience conditions such judgments, of course, so that the content of the notion of excess changes with history, but the notion itself persists. Such negative criticism, wholly directed at what music should *not* be, leads by default to the more important issue: how church music acquires authenticity, i.e., inherent authority that compels attention not to itself but to its larger religious aims.

Bibl.: Robert Lowth, *Lectures on the Sacred Poetry of the Hebrews,* trans. G. Gregory (London, 1787; R: New York: Garland, 1971). Ira D. Sankey, *Gospel Hymns Nos. 1–6 Complete* (New York: Biglow & Main, 1894). André Mocquereau, *Le Nombre musical grégorien* (Tournai: Desclée, 1908–27; trans. Aileen Tone, Paris: Desclée, 1932–51). George Pullen Jackson, *Spiritual Folk-Songs of Early America* (New York: Augustin, 1939; R: New York: Dover, 1964). William G. Waite, *The Rhythm of Twelfth-Century Polyphony* (New Haven: Yale U Pr, 1954). Eric Werner, *The Sacred Bridge* (New York: Columbia U Pr, 1959–84). Pierre Pidoux, *Le Psautier huguenot* (Basel: Bärenreiter, 1962). Edgar Sparks, *Cantus Firmus in Mass and Motet, 1420–1520* (Berkeley: U of Cal Pr, 1963). Karl Gustav Fellerer, ed., *Geschichte der katholischen Kirchenmusik* (Kassel: Bärenreiter, 1972–76). Friedrich Blume et al., *Protestant Church Music: A History* (New York: Norton, 1974). Orpha C. Ochse, *History of the Organ in the United States* (Bloomington: Ind U Pr, 1975). Carl Schalk, *Key Words in Church Music* (St. Louis: Concordia, 1978). Robert F. Hayburn, *Papal Legislation on Sacred Music 95 A.D.. to 1977 A.D.* (Collegeville: Liturgical Pr, 1979). Peter Williams, *A New History of the Organ* (Bloomington: Ind U Pr, 1980). Richard C. Von Ende, *Church Music: An International Bibliography* (Metuchen: Scarecrow, 1980). J. A. Smith, "The Ancient Synagogue, the Early Church, and Singing," *Music and Letters* 65 (1984): 1–16. James W. McKinnon, "On the Question of Psalmody in the Ancient Synagogue," *EMH* 6 (1986): 159–91. James W. McKinnon, *Music in Early Christian Literature* (Cambridge: Cambridge U Pr, 1987). Margot E. Fassler and Peter Jeffery, "Christian Liturgical Music from the Bible to the Renaissance," in *Sacred Sound and Social Change: Liturgical Music in Jewish and Christian Experience,* ed. Lawrence A. Hoffman and Janet R. Walton (Notre Dame: U of Notre Dame Pr, 1992), pp. 84–123. Victor H. Matthews and Ivor H. Jones, "Music and Musical Instruments," *The Anchor Bible Dictionary,* ed. David Noel Freedman et al. (New York: Doubleday, 1992), 4: 930–939. David Hiley, *Western Plainchant: A Handbook* (Oxford: Clarendon, 1993). Edward Foley, *Foundations of Christian Music: The Music of Pre-Constantinian Christianity* (Collegeville: Liturgical Pr, 1996). E. Gardner Rust, *The Music and Dance of the World's Religions: A Comprehensive, Annotated Bibliography of Materials in the English Language* (Westport, Conn.: Greenwood, 1996). James W. McKinnon, *The Temple, the Church Fathers, and Early Western Chant* (Aldershot: Ashgate, 1998). Edward Foley,

ed., *Worship Music: A Concise Dictionary* (Collegeville: Liturgical Pr, 2000). James W. McKinnon, *The Advent Project: The Later-Seventh-Century Creation of the Roman Mass Proper* (Berkeley: U of Cal Pr, 2000). Craig A. Monson, "The Council of Trent Revisited," *JAMS* 55 (2002): 1–38.
R.F.F., rev. R.A.L.

Church sonata. *Sonata da chiesa.*

Chûte [Fr.]. In the 17th and 18th centuries, (1) a *cadent; (2) an *appoggiatura, falling or rising; (3) a figured *arpeggio with one or two inserted dissonances.

Ciaccona [It.]. *Chaconne.

Ciaramella [It.]. A south Italian *shawm, usually played in ensemble with the **zampogna.*

Cibell, cebell. An English harpsichord or ensemble piece ca. 1695–1710 in imitation of the *gavotte "Descente de Cybelle" in Jean-Baptiste Lully's opera *Atys* (1676), act 1 (LWV 53/58). Henry Purcell's version (an "old cibell") was itself imitated, creating a second generation of the genre that continued to the 1760s. B.G.

Címbala [Sp.]. In Spanish and Mexican organs, a mixture stop of higher pitch than the **lleno* or main mixture.

Cimbal d'amour. *Cembal d'amour.*

Cimbalom [fr. Gr. *kymbalon*]. Either of two types of Hungarian *dulcimer: a smaller instrument similar to the Middle Eastern **santur* or a larger instrument developed in the 1870s in Budapest by Joseph Schunda. The larger instrument has a large sound box and is set on legs. Metal strings arranged in courses of three or four and tuned chromatically run over individual bridges. A pedal mechanism operates dampers. This is a favorite instrument in Hungarian Gypsy orchestras and has also been used in orchestral works by Liszt, Kodály, Bartók, and Stravinsky. See ill. under Zither.

Cimbasso [It.]. (1) A term used in Italian scores for the contrabass of the brass section. Depending on the period and composer, it could mean *serpent, *bass horn, *Russian bassoon, *ophicleide, *bombardon, *tuba, or contrabass valve *trombone. (2) A slide bass trombone with two valves, designed by Hans Kunitz in 1959.

Bibl.: Renato Meucci, "The Cimbasso and Related Instruments in 19th-Century Italy," *GSJ* 49 (March 1996): 143.

Cimbel [Du.; Ger. *Zimbel*]. The highest-pitched *mixture in the classical Dutch or German organ, usually with 2/3′ as its lowest pitch at C (an octave higher than the **Scharff* or *Scherp*). A repeating *Cimbel* has the same pitches in each octave throughout its compass.

Cimbelstern [Du.; Ger. *Zimbelstern*]. A set of high-pitched, untuned bells made to sound by a rotating wheel or star-shaped frame; often found on classical northern European organs.

Cinderella. (1) **Cenerentola, La.* (2) Ballet in three acts by Prokofiev (book by Nicolai Volkov, choreography by Rostislav Zakharov), composed in 1940–44 and first produced in Moscow in 1945. Prokofiev's music (with some omissions) was also used in a production with book and choreography by Frederick Ashton in London in 1948. Prokofiev employed music from the ballet in three orchestral suites and other works.

Cinelli [It.]. *Cymbals.

Cinfonía [Sp.]. *Hurdy-gurdy.

Cinque passi [It.; Fr. *cinq pas;* Eng. cinque pace, sinkapas, sink-a-pace, sink a part, etc.]. Five basic steps of the Renaissance **saltarello* and **gagliarda,* consisting of a forward thrust of alternate legs (L R L R) on the first four beats of the measure (coincidently with each thrust the other foot executed a bounce), a leap on the fifth beat, and a resting stance (posture) on the sixth. The *cinque passi* sequence was not danced continuously; dancers improvised many variations on simple steps for an indefinite number of measures and reserved the *cinque passi* for strategic cadences.
L.H.M.

Cipher. The continuous sounding of an organ pipe caused by wind leakage or by a malfunction of the valve beneath a pipe.

Circle of fifths [Ger. *Quintenzirkel*]. The arrangement in a closed circle of all 12 pitch names in such a way that, when proceeding clockwise along the circle, any pair of adjacent pitch names represents the *interval of a perfect fifth [see fig.]. Thus, C to G is a perfect fifth, as are G to D, D to A, A to E, E to B, etc. Literal closure of the circle requires the substitution of an enharmonically equivalent pitch name at some point; otherwise, extending the series of fifths from C results in arrival at B♯ rather than C. Thus, B to F♯ is a perfect fifth; F♯ is enharmonically equivalent to G♭; G♭ to D♭ is a perfect fifth. Closure also requires the use of tempered tuning [see Temperament; Tuning; Intervals, calculation of]. Acoustically pure fifths (i.e., the fifths that occur in the harmonic series and that equal 702 *cents) are larger by 2 cents than equally tempered fifths (700 cents). Thus, a succession of 12 acoustically pure fifths produces a pitch 24 cents (about one quarter of a semitone) higher than the starting point. That is, if on a piano, C to G were tuned as an acoustically pure fifth and then D were tuned as a pure fifth above the G, A a pure fifth above the D, and so forth, the C that would be produced as a pure fifth above the preceding F on the circle would not be the same as the C with which the circle began. Some or all of the fifths must therefore be made smaller than pure fifths by amounts totaling 24 cents. Historically, all 12 fifths were not necessarily reduced at all or by the same amount, as they are in the system of equal temperament.

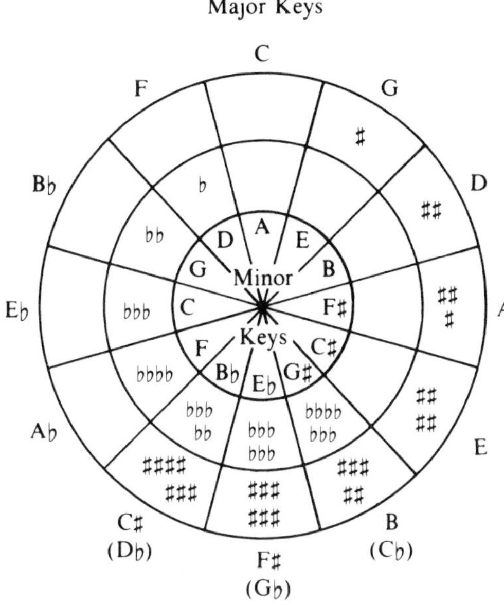

When each pitch name is taken to represent the tonic of a major *scale, the circle arranges keys in such a way that, beginning with C and proceeding clockwise, the number of sharps in each succeeding key increases by one; proceeding counterclockwise from C, the number of flats increases by one. The order in which sharps are added to a *key signature remains the same for all sharp keys, and this can be seen to be represented on the circle proceeding clockwise from F. Similarly, the pitches that must be flatted in the flat keys lie along the circle proceeding counterclockwise from B. The same relationships hold for minor keys, A minor (the relative minor of C major) being the minor key with no sharps and no flats in the key signature.

Because of the way in which sharps or flats are added to key signatures along the circle, the number of pitches in common between the starting key and each successive key outward in either direction decreases by one. Thus, the circle of fifths also illustrates the degree of relatedness of keys. The farther apart on the circle of fifths, the more distant in a musical sense are two keys from one another, since they will have fewer pitches in common.

The circle of fifths was first described and illustrated by Johann David Heinichen in his *Der General-Bass in der Composition* (Dresden, 1728).

Circular breathing. A technique employed in the playing of wind instruments, especially Western and non-Western woodwinds. The mouth is used to maintain a continuous stream of air through the instrument in such a way as to permit the player to draw breath through the nose.

Cis, cisis [Ger.]. C-sharp, C-double-sharp. See Pitch names.

Cister [Ger.], **cistre** [Fr.]. *Cittern.

Cithara [Lat.]. See Kithara.

Cither. *Cittern.

Cithrinchen [Ger.]. See Cittern.

Citole [Fr.; Eng. cythol, sitole, sytholle, etc.; Ger. *Zitole;* It. *cet(e)ra, cetula;* Sp. *cítola*]. A wire-strung, plucked-string instrument; the medieval form of the Renaissance *cittern. Its four-cornered, flattish body, neck or handhole, and pegbox are carved from one piece. Tinctoris (*De inventione et usu musicae,* ca. 1487) says that it is fitted with "certain wooden elevations, known as frets," and that the intervals between its four strings are a second, a fourth, and a second.

R.L.

Cittern [Fr. *cistre, sistre;* Ger. *Cister, Cither, Zither;* It. *cetula;* Sp. *cistro, cedra*]. A small, wire-strung, quill-plucked instrument of Renaissance Europe, second in popularity only to the lute. It was developed late in 15th-century Italy from the *cetra* (**citole*) to fill again the role of the ancient *kithara.

The body of the 16th-century cittern is usually pear-shaped, with a flat back and a top bearing an ornate rosette, often of Gothic design. Before 1570, the body and its neck were carved from one piece of wood. By 1600, a standardized form, built up from pieces, had emerged. See ill. under Guitar.

Giovanni Lanfranco (*Scintille di musica,* 1533) gives the basic Italian and English six-course tuning, e′ d′/d′ g′/g b c′ a, but requires diatonic fretting. So does Adrien Le Roy (*Breve et facile instruction,* 1565) with a tuning e′/e′ d′/d′ g′/g′/g a′/a′/a for a four-course instrument. Paolo Virchi (*Il primo libro . . . di citthara,* 1574) gives a six-course tuning for chromatic fretting, e′/e′ d′/d′ g/g b/b f/f d/d.

Cittern music ranges from intabulated dance tunes to elaborate polyphony. Much was published for solo cittern and cittern with solo voice. The instrument was especially valued for its role in the English mixed consort. It remained popular into the 18th century when it was supplanted by such regional derivatives as the *English guitar, Portuguese *guiterra,* Spanish **bandurria,* and German *Cithrinchen.*

Bibl.: Donald Gill, *Wire Strung Plucked Instruments* (Richmond: Lute Society, 1977). John M. Ward, *Sprightly and Cheerful Musick: Notes on the Cittern, Gittern, and Guitar in 16th- and 17th-Century England* (London: Lute Society, 1983).

R.L.

Cl. Abbr. for *clarinet.

Clair de lune [Fr., Moonlight]. The third movement of Debussy's **Suite bergamasque.*

Clairon [Fr.]. (1) *Bugle. (2) An organ reed stop with full-length, flared metal pipes, usually of 4′ pitch and always of brilliant sound.

Cláirseach [Gael.]. *Harp; especially the *Irish harp.

Clapper. (1) Any instrument consisting of two or

more similar objects that are struck together; hence, a concussion idiophone. The player may hold one object in each hand, like the *claves, or both in one hand, like the *bones. A clapper may also be formed by a split stick or two objects attached to a stick. Vessel clappers, in which two convex objects are struck, include *castanets and *cymbals. Clappers are distributed worldwide and are extremely ancient. (2) The tongue of a *bell.

Claquebois [Fr., obs.]. *Xylophone.

Clarin [Ger.]. **Clairon* (2).

Clarín [Sp.]. (1) *Clarino. (2) An organ reed stop of trumpet scale, usually mounted horizontally in the facade, and of brilliant tone quality.

Clarinet [Fr. *clarinette;* Ger. *Klarinette;* It. *clarinetto*]. (1) A family of single-reed woodwind instruments with a predominantly cylindrical bore. The modern instrument is generally made of grenadilla (African blackwood), less often of materials such as ebonite, plastic, and metal. See ill. under Reed.

The complete family usually comprises the following instruments: high A♭, E♭, B♭, A, basset horn in F, alto clarinet in E♭, bass clarinet in B♭, contra alto clarinet in E♭, and contra bass clarinet in B♭. All clarinets have approximately the same written range, e to c'''' in the treble staff; the lower-pitched instruments seldom use the higher octaves. Clarinets are notated as *transposing instruments. Some scores notate the bass instruments in the bass clef, one octave below the written range shown. Of the instruments listed, the clarinet in B♭ is the most common. Orchestral and chamber music parts often call for the clarinet in A. The player is expected either to double on the A clarinet or to transpose the part. During the 18th and early 19th centuries, clarinet parts were notated in tenor (for B♭ clarinet), soprano (for A clarinet), and alto (for D clarinet) clefs, especially in opera. Use of the treble clef was standardized for all transposing clarinets after 1850. Around 1800 clarinetists transposed parts having up to three flats and two sharps but in operas, clarinets in C and B♮ were required. Players were expected to have C and B♭ instruments with additional finger hole sections *(corps de rechange)* to change to B♮ and A clarinets. By about 1840, orchestral clarinetists preferred to play separate instruments in C, B♭, and A. Higher-pitched clarinets in E♭ and F were played in bands.

A distinctive feature of the clarinet is that it acts as a *stopped-pipe resonator—that is, it sounds an octave lower than one would expect [see Acoustics]. Thus, the flute and the B♭ clarinet are roughly the same length, but the clarinet's lowest sounding note is d, whereas the flute's is c′. Because a stopped pipe produces primarily the odd partials, the clarinetist must cope with the interval of a twelfth between its first two registers rather than the octave of most other woodwinds. This presents formidable difficulties for the de-

Ranges.

sign of a fingering system. The nine available fingers must govern 19 semitones rather than, for instance, the 11 of the flute.

The clarinet is closely related to the European **chalumeau.* The Nuremberg woodwind maker Johann Christoph Denner (1655–1707) is credited with improvements to the *chalumeau* and the invention of the clarinet, but the exact nature of his work is unknown. Denner's son Jacob Denner (1681–1735) is documented as the first to make clarinets in 1710 on a commission from the duke of Gronsfeld in Nuremberg. The Baroque clarinet has two or three keys and was used by Vivaldi, Telemann, Rathgeber, Handel, Molter, and Rameau in orchestral and chamber music and opera. By the 1770s, the classical clarinet with four to six keys (E/B, F♯/C♯, A♭/E♭, A, A/B trill, B♭/*speaker) had become standard. During the 18th century, the instrument was built in four sections: mouthpiece with a long socket, left-hand section, right-hand section, and stock-bell. Toward the end of the century, the mouthpiece was made with a separate barrel and the stock section was separated from the bell. A sixth key (A/B trill) was added about 1775 and a seventh key (C♯/G♯) by about 1790. Additional keys continued to be added to facilitate trills and the slurring of difficult intervals. In 1812, Ivan Müller devised a 13-key clarinet that was meant to be omnitonic, i.e., playable in all keys. A commission of the Conservatoire impériale de musique et de déclamation of Paris did not officially accept Müller's clarinet, fearing the loss of distinctive tone colors. After some changes to the original design and the addition of rollers devised by César Janssen in 1821, it emerged as the 13-key "simple-system" clarinet. In 1843, Louis-Auguste Buffet, in consultation with the clarinetist Hyacinthe Klosé (1808–80), applied Theobald Boehm's ideas to the clarinet [see *Boehm system]. The resulting *clarinette à anneaux mobiles* is known today as the Boehm system clarinet and is used far outside France. Adolphe Sax and other makers continued to experiment with key work. Today two principal key systems survive: the Boehm system, used throughout the French- and English-speaking worlds, and the Oehler system, used in German- and Russian-speaking countries. Clarinets of various types and pitch are also widely used in the folk music of Eastern Europe, India, and especially Turkey.

(2) An organ stop. See also Double clarinet.

Bibl.: Oskar Kroll, *Die Klarinette* (Kassel: Bärenreiter, 1965); trans. Hilda Morris, *The Clarinet* (New York: Taplinger, 1968). F. Geoffrey Rendall, *The Clarinet,* 3rd ed., rev. P. Bate (New York: Norton, 1971). Albert R. Rice, *The Baroque Clarinet* (Oxford: Clarendon, 1992). William Waterhouse, *The New Langwill Index: A Dictionary of Musical Wind-Instrument Makers and Inventors* (London: T Bingham, 1992). Colin Lawson, ed., *The Cambridge Companion to the Clarinet* (Cambridge: Cambridge U Pr, 1995). Nicholas Shackleton and Albert Rice, "César Janssen and the Transmission of Müller's 13-Keyed Clarinet in France," *GSJ* 52 (1999): 183–94. A.R.R.

Clarino [It.]. (1) The upper range of the Baroque *trumpet, from the eighth through the twentieth pitch of the *harmonic series or higher. (The lower range was called the *principale.*) (2) The style of trumpet playing that uses the natural trumpet in its highest register, where the diatonic scale is possible. (3) In the Middle Ages and Renaissance through the 18th century, a trumpet. R.E.E.

Clarin trumpet. A modern term for a natural trumpet on which the *clarino register or style of playing is exploited.

Clarion. (1) In the Middle Ages and Renaissance, a *trumpet. (2) An organ reed stop of brilliant quality, usually at 4′ pitch. See *Clairon* (2).

Clarone [It.]. (1) Bass *clarinet. (2) *Basset horn.

Clàrsach, clarsech, clarseth [Gael.]. **Cláirseach.*

Classical [fr. Lat. *classicus,* Roman citizen of the highest class; Fr. *classique*]. (1) In popular usage, art or "serious" music as opposed to popular music.

(2) In French writings about music, the period or style of Louis XIV (ruled 1643–1715), often extended to include the music of Jean-Philippe Rameau (1683–1764).

(3) The period or style that has its tentative beginnings in Italy in the early 18th century and extends through the early 19th century. In most periodizations of music history, the Classical period therefore succeeds the Baroque and precedes the Romantic, in both cases with sizable chronological overlaps.

In general usage, the terms classical and classic refer to *(a)* the Greco-Roman tradition and *(b)* such perceived characteristics of that tradition as poise, balance, proportion, simplicity, formal discipline and craftsmanship, and universal and objective (rather than idiosyncratic and subjective—i.e., "Romantic") expression. In addition, the terms classical and especially classic often refer to *(c)* a standard or model of excellence, one of enduring value. The last of these definitions, though important historiographically, has little relevance within a modern theory of periodization, for it is essentially evaluative. The first definition *(a)* corresponds to the meaning of neoclassical in the visual arts of the 18th century; in music the principal examples of this type of classicism occur in opera, for example Gluck's late or "reform" operas and, arguably, the Arcadianism of Metastasian **opera seria.* Hence, the primary meaning-complex of classical in music is that of *(b).* It must be stressed, however, that terms like classical constitute more a handy means of reference than an informative or even necessarily accurate description; a given work of, say, 1775 may be no more "classical" (poised, balanced, etc.) than one of 1675 is "baroque."

Charles Burney, in his *General History of Music* (1789), attributed the inception of what is here called the Classical style to the generation of composers that came to prominence in Naples starting about 1720, succeeding the older generation of Alessandro Scarlatti (1660–1725). In this view, the birth of the Classical style corresponds with the rise of Metastasian opera, with its classicizing tendencies. The most important of these composers, including Leonardo Vinci (ca. 1690 [1696?]–1730) and Leonardo Leo (1694–1744), had significant early experience in the burgeoning comic opera of the day, doubtless a major reason for the melodic and textural simplicity of their music. Burney considered Vinci revolutionary for "simplifying and polishing melody, and calling the attention of the audience chiefly to the voice-part, by disintangling [*sic*] it from fugue, complication, and laboured contrivance."

Though Burney oversimplified in various ways, most conspicuously by overemphasizing the role of Naples, he correctly identified the basic components of the new style as homophonic texture and simpler, more "natural" melody. (This style was labeled the **galant* style by theorists of the time.) To these characteristics we may add the development of hierarchical phrase and period structure (at first generally based on phrases of two bars, later of four), introduction of a greater degree of stylistic contrast within sections or movements, use of graded dynamics such as the *crescendo,* choice of more differentiated and contoured rhythmic values (as opposed to the more continuous beat-marking, unicellular rhythms of the late Baroque), simplification of the harmonic vocabulary, and slowing of the harmonic rhythm (the latter two points related to the growing preference for harmonic rather than linear bass lines). In the realm of expression, the new style tended to favor tender sentiment over strong passion, and Baroque unity of affect began to break down as composers cultivated a more variegated and nuanced spectrum of emotions.

Elements of the new style appear decisively in Italian instrumental music somewhat later than in opera, from ca. 1730 on [see Symphony, Overture, Sonata, Concerto]. Nevertheless, Classical tendencies such as slow harmonic rhythm and extensive use of literal phrase-repetition already appear in numerous instrumental works of the previous decades, for example Francesco Maria Veracini's first set of solo sonatas of 1716 and Vivaldi's later concertos. In addition to the characteristics already noted, orchestral music saw the development of various principles of *sonata form as well as a more idiomatic approach to orchestration. Music for soloists during the early part of this period tended to cultivate a highly ornamented melodic style based on constant subdivision of the beat and half-beat levels; figures involving triplet sixteenth notes, dotted sixteenths and thirty-seconds, and the like are ubiquitous. This tendency toward rhythmic intricacy reached its peak in the keyboard works of the north German **empfindsam* style.

The wide range of styles characteristic of the period from ca. 1720 to ca. 1765 has led some scholars to consider it a separate "pre-classical" period preceding what they regard as the "true" classicism of Haydn and Mozart. [For another frequent designation of this period, see Rococo.] Yet a principal trait of all early subperiods is diversity, as those composers dissatisfied with an earlier style and aesthetic strike out in many new directions at once. The period in question shows at least as much organic unity with later developments as do other early subperiods (e.g., the early Baroque), especially when one examines central genres like opera and symphony. Moreover, the term pre-classical deviates from the terminological usage accepted for every other period, relegating the music in question to antecedent status. For these reasons, many scholars now prefer to designate the period from ca. 1720 (later in other countries than Italy) through approximately the 1760s as simply the "early Classical period," in full realization of the oversimplification all such labels entail.

The period from approximately the 1760s until the end of the century brought a synthesis of the disparate idioms of the early phase into a more cosmopolitan "middle" style, one that was basically Italianate but that also increasingly introduced stylistic and formal complexity and expressive depth. The culmination of this approach is represented by the mature works of Haydn and Mozart.

The description late Classical is appropriate for those successors of Haydn and Mozart who generally avoided the new Romantic currents of the early 19th century. In the case of Beethoven, however, there has long been disagreement as to whether he is best regarded as a Classical or a Romantic composer. As should be obvious, he is to some extent both, and also neither. The most overtly Romantic aspects in Beethoven are biographical—his view of himself as an independent artist, his increasing tendency to turn away from the public, and the like. The use of extramusical "programs" in many of his works may also be considered a Romantic trait, though even here the content is generally universal and ideal rather than subjective or self-expressive, as it is in Berlioz or Schumann, for example. From the musical standpoint, much of Beethoven's style may be viewed as fundamentally an extension and expansion of the styles of Haydn and Mozart, as seen in his granitic formal control, unambiguous and forceful rhythm, continued use of structural rather than coloristic harmony, consistent devotion to thematic development as a principle, and interest in traditional contrapuntal techniques [see Sonata form, Symphony, Concerto]. Nevertheless, many of Beethoven's late works are too personal and idiosyncratic to relate directly to either a Classical or Romantic tradition. It may be noted that, in contrast to Beethoven, Schubert is now generally linked with early Romanticism.

Bibl.: Wilhelm Fischer, "Zur Entwicklungsgeschichte des Wiener klassischen Stils," *SzMw* 3 (1915): 24–84. Ernst Bücken, *Die Musik des Rokokos und der Klassik* (Potsdam: Akademische V-g Athenaion, 1927). *SR.* Helmut Hucke and Edward O. D. Downes, "The Neapolitan Tradition in Opera," *New York,* 1961, 1:253–84, 2:132–33. William S. Newman, *The Sonata in the Classic Era* (Chapel Hill: U of NC Pr, 1963; 3rd ed., New York: Norton, 1983). Reinhard G. Pauly, *Music in the Classic Period* (Englewood Cliffs, N.J.: Prentice-Hall, 1965; 2nd ed., 1973). Ludwig Finscher, "Zum Begriff der Klassik in der Musik," *DJbMw* 11 (1966): 9–34. Daniel Heartz et al., "Critical Years in European Musical History: 1740–1760," *Ljubljana,* 1967, pp. 159–93. Hugh Honour, *Neo-classicism* (Harmondsworth: Penguin, 1968). Friedrich Blume, *Classic and Romantic Music,* trans. M. D. Herter Norton (New York: Norton, 1970). Charles Rosen, *The Classical Style: Haydn, Mozart, Beethoven* (New York: Viking, 1971; 2nd ed., New York: Norton, 1997). *NOHM,* vol. 7, ed. Egon Wellesz and Frederick Sternfeld (London: Oxford U Pr, 1973). Warren Kirkendale, *Fugue and Fugato in Rococo and Classical Chamber Music,* 2nd ed., trans. Margaret Bent and Warren Kirkendale (Durham: Duke U Pr, 1979). Leonard G. Ratner, *Classic Music: Expression, Form, and Style* (New York: Schirmer Bks, 1980). Peter le Huray and James Day, *Music and Aesthetics in the Eighteenth and Early Nineteenth Centuries* (Cambridge: Cambridge U Pr, 1981). Eugene K. Wolf, *The Symphonies of Johann Stamitz: A Study in the Formation of the Classic Style* (Utrecht: Bohn, Scheltema & Holkema, 1981). Michael Broyles, "The Two Instrumental Styles of Classicism," *JAMS* 36 (1983): 210–42. Eric Weimer, *Opera seria and the Evolution of Classical Style, 1755–1772* (Ann Arbor: UMI Res Pr, 1984). Carl Dahlhaus, ed., *Die Musik des 18. Jahrhunderts,* vol. 5 of *Neues Handbuch der Musikwissenschaft* (Laaber: Laaber-Verlag, 1985). Howard Smither, *A History of the Oratorio,* vol. 3: *The Oratorio in the Classical Era* (Chapel Hill: U of NC Pr, 1987). Neal Zaslaw, ed., *The Classical Era: From the 1740s to the End of the 18th Century,* vol. 5 of *Man and Music / Music and Society,* ed. Stanley Sadie (Englewood Cliffs, N.J.: Prentice Hall, 1989). V. Kofi Agawu, *Playing with Signs: A Semiotic Interpretation of Classic Music* (Princeton: Princeton U Pr, 1991). James Webster, *Haydn's "Farewell" Symphony and the Idea of Classical Style* (Cambridge: Cambridge U Pr, 1991). Philip G. Downs, *Classical Music: The Era of Haydn, Mozart, and Beethoven* (New York: Norton, 1992). Daniel Heartz, *Haydn, Mozart and the Viennese School, 1740–1780* (New York: Norton, 1995). James Webster, "Between Enlightenment and Romanticism in Music History: 'First Viennese Modernism' and the Delayed Nineteenth Century," *19th-Century Music* 25 (2002): 108–26.

E.K.W.

Classical Symphony. Prokofiev's Symphony no. 1 in D major op. 25 (1916–17), composed in a style sometimes called *neoclassical. It is scored for a relatively small orchestra of strings with pairs of wind instruments reminiscent of the works of Haydn and Mozart.

Clausula [Lat., fr. *claudo, claudere,* to conclude]. (1) From the 11th to the 15th century, a cadence. The term is applied equally to monophony and polyphony, to plainchant, and to secular song. Sometimes used simply for the last note (or interval) of a piece, it may also refer more specifically to a cadence on the final of the mode (in the case of a song or dance, for example, often the *clos* or *chiuso* [see *Ouvert* and *clos*] ending) or to a cadential formula. The word *clausula* was largely replaced in the 16th century by *cadentia.*

(2) In the 12th and 13th centuries, a passage of (Parisian) liturgical polyphony, most often in *discant style. The tenor (the voice on which the piece is based) is typically a melismatic fragment from one of the responsorial chants of the Mass or the Office. A number of melismas, among them *Regnat, Dominus, In seculum,* [*Immo*]*latus,* and *Omnes,* are set with great frequency, in part, no doubt, because of their liturgical significance, but also, one is bound to assume, because of inherent musical qualities that make them particularly suitable for polyphonic treatment.

The principal sources for the *clausula* are the *Notre Dame manuscripts W1 and F, which together contain more than 900 pieces for two voices plus a handful for three and four. Many of these are embedded in larger organal settings of chants [see Organum]; many others are copied separately. Manuscript evidence suggests that the bulk of the latter are substitutes, that is, *clausulae* that could be inserted into existing organa (or conversely, had already been replaced by newer pieces).

In the earliest examples, the tenor proceeds in ternary longs [see Modes, rhythmic], each of which is matched in the second voice *(duplum)* by a binary long plus a breve or the equivalent of these [Ex. 1]. The uninterrupted succession of ternary longs persists throughout the period of *clausula* composition as the most popular form of tenor articulation, appearing

Clausulae. 1. MS W1, fol. 22. 2. MS F, fol. 149. 3. MS F, fol. 167.

eventually in conjunction with strictly modal *dupla* [Ex. 2]. Somewhat younger than the *clausulae* of the first type are those in which the tenor moves in duplex longs, the *duplum* in the so-called alternate third mode. The next chronological layer consists of *clausulae* in which both tenor and *duplum* are modally ordered. The tenor is characterized by short, fixed patterns, chiefly in the fifth mode, occasionally in the third [Ex. 3], whereas the *duplum,* in the same or a complementary mode, is more flexible in rhythm and in length of phrase. Multiple statements of the tenor are typical of this group of pieces. The latest of the *clausulae* have both tenors and *dupla* paired in first mode or in second mode, with a few *dupla* in sixth mode.

The *clausula* as such, which seems to have attracted little attention after ca. 1230, survived to the end of the century as the basis of the enormously popular *motet.

Bibl.: Rudolf Flotzinger, *Der Diskantussatz im Magnus Liber und seiner Nachfolge* (Vienna: Böhlau, 1969). Jürg Stenzl, *Die vierzig Clausulae der Handschrift Paris Bibliothèque Nationale Latin 15139 (Saint Victor-Clausulae),* Publikationen der Schweizerischen Musikforschenden Gesellschaft, ser. 2, vol. 22 (Bern: Paul Haupt, 1970). Norman E. Smith, "Some Exceptional Clausulae of the Florence Manuscript," *ML* 54 (1973): 405–14. Rebecca Baltzer, "Notation, Rhythm, and Style in the Two-Voice Notre Dame Clausula" (Ph.D. diss., Boston Univ., 1974). Norman E. Smith, "From Clausula to Motet: Material for Further Studies in the Origin and Early History of the Motet," *MD* 34 (1980): 29–65. Hendrik van der Werf, *Integrated Directory of Organa, Clausulae, and Motets of the Thirteenth Century* (Rochester, N.Y.: Author, 1989). Rebecca A. Baltzer, ed., *Le Magnus liber organi de Notre-Dame de Paris,* vol. 5: *Les Clausules à deux voix du manuscrit de Florence, Biblioteca Medicea-Laurenziana, pluteus 29.1, fasicule V,* ed. Edward H. Roesner, Musica Gallica (Monaco: Éditions de l'Oiseau-Lyre, 1995). Susan A. Kidwell, "The Selection of Clausula Sources for Thirteenth-Century Motets: Some Practical Considerations and Aesthetic Implications," *CM* 64 (2001): 73–103. See also *Magnus liber organi.* J.K.

Clavecin [Fr., occasionally *claveçin, clavessin*]. *Harpsichord.

Clavecín [Sp.]. *Harpsichord.

Clavecin d'amore. **Cembal d'amour.*

Claves [Sp.]. A Cuban *clapper consisting of a pair of solid, hardwood cylinders, each approximately 20 cm long; see ill. under Percussion instruments. One cylinder rests against the fingernails of a loosely formed fist (cupped to act as a resonator) and is struck with the other. They are widely used in the urban popular music of Latin America. The most characteristic rhythmic figure played on the *claves* is shown in the accompanying example.

Clavessin [Fr.]. *Harpsichord.

Clavicembalo [It.], **clavicémbalo** [Sp.]. *Harpsichord.

Clavichord [Fr. *clavicorde, manicorde;* Ger. *Clavichord, Klavichord, Clavier;* It. *clavicordo, manicordo, sordino;* Sp. *clavicordio, manicordio, monacordio*]. A stringed keyboard instrument in use from the 15th to 18th centuries and revived since the 1890s. It consists of a rectangular case with its keyboard projecting from or set into one of the long sides. The soundboard is to the right of the keyboard and the strings traverse the case from right to left. When a key is depressed, a brass blade or tangent at the far end strikes a pair of strings, remaining in contact until the key is released. To the left of the tangent, the strings are damped by a strip of cloth (or listing). But at the right, where they pass over a bridge that transmits their vibrations to the soundboard, the strings are sounded by the blow of the tangent [see ill.]. When the key is released, the listing silences the strings immediately. Since the tangent's striking point determines the strings' vibrating length, several different pitches can be produced on a single pair of strings by causing various tangents to strike at different points. But as one pair of strings can sound only one pitch at a time, keys whose tangents strike the same pair cannot be sounded simultaneously. Thus, from the earliest times makers took care that only notes forming dissonances with each other would be sounded on the same strings. Clavichords in which pairs of strings are struck by more than one tangent are called fretted [Ger. *gebunden*]; those in which each key has its own pair are termed unfretted or fret-free [Ger. *bundfrei*].

The sound of the clavichord is relatively small and soft, but it has a wide dynamic range: variations in the force with which the keys are depressed produce corresponding variations in loudness, much as on the piano. A special effect unavailable on any other keyboard instrument is the **Bebung,* a kind of vibrato produced by varying finger pressure on the key.

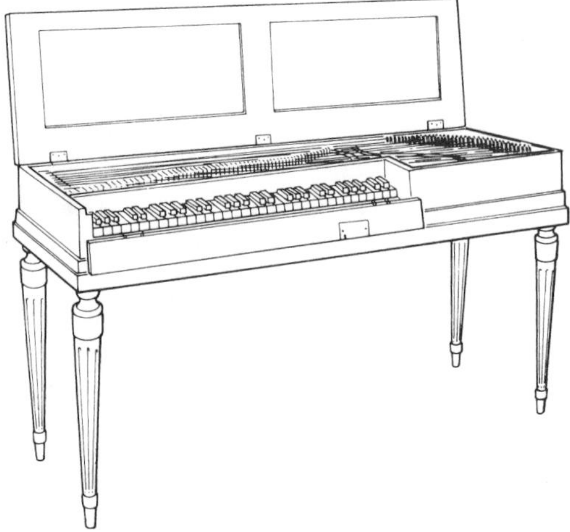

Clavichord.

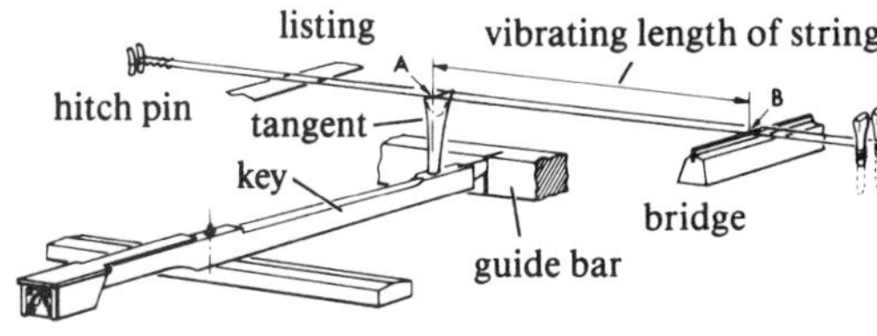

Clavichord mechanism.

The clavichord appears to have developed from the *monochord. The instrument was sometimes called *monochordum* in the 15th century; and until the third quarter of the century, its strings were of equal length and all tuned in unison. The earliest record of the name clavichord is in a Viennese will of 1397. Henri Arnaut de Zwolle's mid-15th-century manuscript shows a layout drawing of a three-octave instrument, and an intarsia of 1479–92 depicts a four-octave clavichord. A somewhat smaller compass (F to a″) seems to have been usual in the early 16th century. About 1540, C to c‴ became standard, but with a bass *short octave. This range was only rarely exceeded in the 17th century; but by the mid-18th century, clavichords with a compass of five octaves (F_1 to f‴) and even more were being made.

The earliest surviving clavichords are Italian and date from the mid-16th century. Interest in the instrument, however, seems to have died out in Italy by the end of the century; the vast majority of surviving 17th- and 18th-century examples are German. In contrast to Italian instruments, with their projecting keyboards and strings running parallel to the back of the case, the typical German clavichord has an inset keyboard and strings running obliquely from the right front to the left rear. Although clavichords in which some strings were struck by as many as four tangents continued to be built in the 17th century, larger instruments usually had only two tangents for each pair of strings. The only musical limitations of these fretted instruments lay, first, in their inflexible tuning in modified meantone temperament that excluded playing pieces in remote keys, and second, in the impossibility of playing certain combinations and, occasionally in a descending line, particular successions of notes where it was desired to sustain the higher tone while playing the lower one. Nevertheless, fretted clavichords continued to serve the needs of most musicians and were built by makers of the first rank well into the 1780s and beyond.

Unfretted clavichords, requiring about half again as many strings as the fretted type, and accordingly more difficult to tune and maintain, appeared in the last years of the 17th century. The exact date of introduction is difficult to establish. But Johann Speth in the preface to his *Ars magna consoni et dissoni* (1693) explicitly calls for a clavichord in which "each key has its own strings and not some [strings] touched by two, three, and even four keys." Large unfretted clavichords continued to be built in Germany and Scandinavia through the first decade of the 19th century, in most cases by makers who were also building pianos.

The precise role of the clavichord in the history of keyboard music is difficult to establish. Although the word *Clavier* appears frequently on the title pages of German publications, the term means keyboard instrument as well as clavichord, and such a collection as Bach's **Clavier-Übung* (4 pts., 1731–42) contains works explicitly designated for harpsichord and for organ. The clavichord, however, was the usual domestic instrument of the 16th, 17th, and 18th centuries in Germany, and its value as an instrument for teaching and practice had been emphasized since the 15th century. This popularity doubtless stemmed as much from musical considerations as from the more mundane ones of low cost and ease of maintenance and tuning. On the other hand, the clavichord seems to have been the preferred medium of performance only during the period of the **empfindsam* style in the second half of the 18th century, a period that produced the instrument's most ardent partisans, including C. P. E. Bach. His *Versuch über die wahre Art das Clavier zu spielen* (2 pts., 1753–62) is an eloquent appreciation of the clavichord as well as a thorough study of keyboard technique as he taught it. His F♯ minor fantasia "C. P. E. Bach's Empfindungen" and "Abschied von meinem Silbermannischen Claviere," with their abrupt contrasts, crescendos, diminuendos, and explicit *Bebung* indications, are among the most idiomatic clavichord pieces ever composed.

Bibl.: Michael Praetorius, *Syntagma musicum,* vol. 2, *De Organographia* (Wolfenbüttel, 1619; facs., *DM* ser. 1, 14, 1958). Carl Philip Emanuel Bach, *Versuch über die wahre Art das Clavier zu spielen,* 2 pts. (Berlin, 1753–62); trans. William J. Mitchell, *Essay on the True Art of Playing Keyboard Instruments* (New York: Norton, 1949). François Auguste Goehlinger, *Geschichte des Klavichords* (Basel: E Birkhäuser, 1910). Otto Kinkeldey, *Orgel und Klavier in der Musik des 16. Jahrhunderts* (Leipzig: Breitkopf & Härtel, 1910; R: Hildesheim: Olms, 1968). Hanns Neupert, *Das Klavichord,* 2nd ed. (Kassel: Bärenreiter, 1955), trans. Ann Feldberg, *The Clavichord* (Kassel: Bärenreiter, 1965). Cornelia Auerbach, *Die deutsche Clavichordkunst des 18. Jahrhunderts,* 3rd ed. (Kassel: Bärenreiter, 1959). Edwin M. Ripin, "The Early Clavichord," *MQ* 53 (1967): 518–38. Id., "A Reassessment of the Fretted Clavichord," *GSJ* 23 (1970): 40–48. Raymond Russell, *The Harpsichord and Clavichord: An Introductory Study,* 2nd ed. rev. Howard Schott (London: Faber, 1973). Donald H. Boalch, *Makers of the Harpsichord and Clavichord, 1440–1840,* 2nd ed. (Oxford: Clarendon Pr, 1974). Edmund A. Bowles, "A Checklist of 15th-Century Representations of Stringed Instruments," *Keyboard Instruments: Studies in Keyboard Organology, 1500–1800,* 2nd ed. rev. and enl., Edwin M. Ripin (New York: Dover, 1977), pp. 11–17, plates 1–31a. Bernard Brauchli, *The Clavichord* (Cambridge: Cambridge U Pr, 1998). E.M.R., rev. H.S., J.Ko.

Clavicor [Fr.; It. *clavicorno*]. An alto or tenor brass instrument in a tall, upright shape. It has a very narrow bore and three Stölzel *valves, one for the left hand and two for the right. Patented in 1837 by a Parisian named Danays, it was designed to replace the *ophicleide and was made in five sizes (alto in F and E♭;

tenor in D♭, C, and B♭) in Paris by the firm of Guichard. During the mid-19th century, clavicors were used in some French, English, and Italian bands. Later models had all three valves together in the usual right-hand position. R.E.E.

Clavicylinder. A keyboard instrument invented by Ernst Friedrich Chladni ca. 1800. Depressing a key pressed a tuned metal bar against a revolving glass cylinder, thus causing the bar to sound by friction. See also Sostenente piano.

Clavicytherium [Fr., also *clavecin vertical;* Ger. *Klaviziterium;* It. *claviciterio, cembalo verticale;* Sp. *claveciterio*]. An upright harpsichord and hence one in which the plane of the strings is vertical. The earliest surviving example is from the late 15th century. The term was first used and an illustration given by Sebastian Virdung, *Musica getutscht* (1511). Because such instruments required relatively little space, they were widely used in the 17th and 18th centuries.

Clavier [Eng., Fr., Ger.]. *Keyboard; in English, widely used to mean stringed keyboard instrument (harpsichord, clavichord, piano, etc.) in contradistinction to the organ; there is no instrument called in English clavier. This usage, which is perhaps best avoided, can be traced to J. N. Forkel (1749–1818; see *MGG* 7:1093), who wrote at a time when all three stringed keyboard instruments were used to some extent interchangeably, but were nevertheless distinguished from the organ. In the second half of the 18th century, *Clavier* was the normal German word for clavichord, though it was not rigorously confined to that meaning; in the 19th century, *Klavier* became the normal word for piano. Rousseau defined *clavier* as the system of pitches encompassed by the "great staff" of 12 lines, from F to b″, three octaves and a fourth (his top five lines had the G-clef on the first line, the "French violin clef"). D.F.

Clavier-Übung [Ger., Keyboard Study]. Bach's title for four publications of his keyboard music. *Clavier-Übung* I (published 1731) contains six partitas BWV 825–30; II (published 1735) the **Italian* Concerto BWV 971 and an *Ouvertüre nach französischer Art* (Overture in the French Manner) BWV 831; III (published 1739) nine chorale preludes for Mass and twelve for the catechism BWV 669–89 and four duets BWV 802–5 framed by the Prelude and Fugue (**St. Anne's Fugue*) in E♭ major BWV 552; IV (published 1741–42) the **Goldberg Variations.* Parts I, II, and IV are for harpsichord, whereas part III is for the organ. The term had earlier been used in the titles of Johann Kuhnau's *Neue* [New] *Clavier-Übung* (1689, 1692) and Johann Krieger's *Anmuthige* [Charming] *Clavier-Übung* (1698).

Clavilux. A *color organ introduced in 1925 by Thomas Wilfrid. It projected moving colors and shapes on a screen, but did not produce sounds. See also Color and music.

Claviorgan [Lat. *claviorganum;* Fr. *clavecin organisé;* Ger. *Orgelklavier;* It. *claviorgano;* Sp. *clavióorgano*]. A keyboard instrument combining a harpsichord or piano and an organ. Such instruments were described in the late 15th century, and examples survive from the 16th. They were built in the late 18th century by some of the best makers of stringed keyboard instruments, including Stein, Taskin, and Broadwood.

Clavis [Lat., key, as of a lock; pl. *claves*]. (1) *Clef. (2) Pitch, especially any of the pitches making up the *gamut.

Clef [fr. Lat. *clavis,* key; Fr.; Ger. *Schlüssel;* It. *chiave;* Sp. *clave*]. A sign placed at the beginning of a staff to indicate the position of some particular pitch and, by extension, the pitches represented by all of the staff's lines and spaces. There are three types of clefs now in general use: the G-clef, the C-clef (of which there are several shapes), and the F-clef [see Ex. 1]. The spiral of the lower part of the G-clef locates the position of g′ (the G above middle C) on some line, now almost exclusively on the second line from the bottom, in which case it is termed the treble or violin clef. The C-clef is now placed on either of two lines so as to locate the position of c′ (middle C): when placed on the third line it is termed the alto or viola clef; when placed on the fourth line it is the tenor clef. The F-clef locates f (the F below middle C) and is today employed almost exclusively on the fourth line, in which case it is termed the bass clef. The three clefs in their most common positions are illustrated in Ex. 2. The combination of clef and position is sometimes indicated by the letter of the clef followed by the number of the line; hence, the treble clef is G2, the alto clef C3, the bass clef F4.

The treble clef is now used for the violin, woodwinds, higher brasses, and the right hand in keyboard music. Some wind instruments so notated, however, may actually sound in higher or lower octaves [see also Transposing instruments]. The alto clef is employed principally for the viola, for which it is the normal clef. The tenor clef is occasionally used for the cello, bassoon, and trombone, the normal clef for all of which is the bass clef. The bass clef is employed, in addition, for lower brasses, the double bass, and the left hand in keyboard music. The G-clef on the second line is also regularly used for the tenor part in choral music and in this context is understood to represent transposition down one octave from the normal treble clef. This is sometimes made explicit, especially in editions of early music (where it may serve for parts other than the one actually called the tenor), in the ways shown in Ex. 3. Historically, all three clefs have been used in a variety of positions, as illustrated and identified in Ex. 4.

4a. French violin clef. b. Treble clef, violin clef. c. Soprano clef, descant clef. d. Mezzo-soprano clef. e. Alto clef. f. Tenor clef. g, h. Baritone clefs. i. Bass clef. j. Subbass clef.

Clefs were first used with regularity in the 12th century, F- and C-clefs being by far the most common. The modern form of the G-clef came into use in the 16th century. In the 17th and 18th centuries, G1 was more often used than G2, with the result that G1 is still sometimes termed the French violin clef. In the course of the 20th century, the use of the C-clef steadily declined except in the music of a few instruments, principally the viola and, to a lesser extent, the tenor trombone and bassoon. Thus, even in modern editions of earlier music that employed a variety of clefs, the treble, octave-treble, and bass clefs are now used almost exclusively. For the use in the Renaissance of certain standard combinations of clefs, see *Chiavette,* Mode. See also Notation.

Clemenza di Tito, La [It., The Clemency of Titus]. An *opera seria* in two acts by Mozart. The libretto, by Caterino Mazzolà, is an abridgment and adaptation of one by Pietro Metastasio. The simple recitatives were perhaps composed by Mozart's student Franz Xaver Süssmayr. The work was first produced in Prague in 1791 at the coronation of Emperor Leopold II as King of Bohemia. Setting: Rome, ca. 80 C.E.

Cleron [Fr.]. In the 17th century, **clairon.*

Climacus [Lat.]. See Neume.

Clivis [Lat.]. See Neume.

Cloche [Fr.]. *Bell; *cloches tubulaires,* *tubular bells.

Clocking. See Bell.

Clock Symphony. Popular name for Haydn's Symphony no. 101 in D major Hob. I:101 (1793–94; one of the **London* Symphonies), so called because of the ticking motif in the second movement (Andante).

Clockwork instruments. See Automatic instruments.

Clos [Fr.]. See *Ouvert* and *clos.*

Close. *Cadence.

Close harmony, position. In harmony in four voices, the placement of the three uppermost voices as close together as possible, i.e., without the omission of a chord tone between soprano and alto or alto and tenor. See also Spacing.

Closing theme. A theme occurring at the end of the exposition in *sonata form.

Cluster. See Tone cluster.

Clutsam keyboard. See Keyboard.

C.O. Abbr. for *Coll'*ottava.*

Cobla. (1) [Prov.] Stanza. (2) A Catalan ensemble consisting of *flaviol* and *tamboril* (*pipe and tabor), two treble and two tenor shawms, two trumpets, two flugelhorns, trombone, and double bass. It accompanies the dancing of the **sardana.*

Coda [It., tail]. In instrumental music following regular musical forms, a concluding section extraneous to the form as usually defined; any concluding passage that can be understood as occurring after the structural conclusion of a work and that serves as a formal closing gesture. Although codas may on occasion consist of only a few perfunctory chords, they may on other occasions assume considerable dimensions and cannot always be regarded as essentially superfluous.

In music before about 1750, the term is applied principally to the end of a canon, where voices cease canonic imitation, or to the end of a fugue following the last statement of the subject. Free polyphonic music might conclude with a coda composed over a pedal point, as might pieces based on *cantus firmi,* grounds, and variation sets. Binary dance forms, ternary aria forms, and ritornello forms rarely admitted of a coda, although French composers such as Couperin and Rameau often appended a *petite reprise* of the final bars of a piece; Bach followed this practice in the *Aria* of his Sixth Partita for harpsichord.

After 1750, the somewhat freer forms of sonata, rondo, scherzo, and the like often incorporated a coda. Composers before Beethoven generally employed codas to increase the sense of musical finality or symmetry, e.g., in the first movement of Haydn's Symphony no. 88 and the last movement of Mozart's *Jupiter* Symphony no. 41. Beethoven used codas most notably to delay or interrupt a final resolution, often with highly dramatic effect. In some cases, they may approach the weight and technical resources of a development. Many movements of Beethoven's symphonies, especially the first movements of nos. 3, 5, and 9, use codas to such ends; his Piano Sonata op. 2 no. 3 contains classic examples of codas (one of them so labeled) in each movement. Following Beethoven's lead, composers of the 19th century adopted the coda as a regular feature of sonata form. The term has also been applied to vocal music, following instrumental models. See also Codetta.

Codetta [It., little tail]. (1) In *sonata form, a brief coda concluding the exposition. (2) In an exposition of a *fugue, a modulatory passage connecting the end of a statement of the subject in the dominant with the beginning of the next statement in the tonic. (3) A brief coda concluding an inner section of a movement or piece as opposed to a coda at the end of the movement or piece as a whole.

Coffee Cantata. Popular name for Bach's secular cantata *Schweigt stille, plaudert nicht* [Ger., Be quiet, don't prattle] for soloists and orchestra BWV 211 (ca. 1734–35). The cantata relates the predicament of a burgher's daughter whose coffee habit her father wishes to break.

Cog rattle. An instrument consisting of a grooved cylinder attached to a handle and a wooden tongue, both set in a frame; also ratchet. The frame is whirled around the cylinder, causing the tongue to strike the cogs in rapid succession. See also *Matraca.*

Col, coll', colla, colle [It.]. With, with the. For phrases beginning with these words, see the word following, e.g., *arco, punta d'arco, destra, legno, ottava.*

Colachon [Fr.]. **Colascione.*

Colascione [It.; Fr. *colachon*]. A fretted, *long-necked lute of Eastern origin introduced first into 16th-century Italy and into France and Germany in the 17th century. Its two or three metal or sometimes gut strings were tuned (E) A d and played with a plectrum. It may have been used as a drone in popular and amateur ensembles, and, according to Johann Mattheson (1713), it was used as a continuo instrument in Germany. See ill. under Lute. R.L.

Colenda [Pol.], **colindă** [Rom.]. See *Kolęda.*

Coll', colla [It.]. See *Col.*

Collect [Lat. *oratio, collecta*]. A short prayer consisting of an invocation (e.g., "Almighty God, who hast . . ."), a petition ("Grant that . . ."), and a pleading of Christ's name or ascription of glory to God ("through the same our Lord Jesus Christ, who . . ."). In the Roman rite, it forms part of the Proper of the Mass and precedes the reading of the Epistle. On some occasions there may be two or three. It is either sung to a simple recitation tone (*LU,* pp. 98–102) or recited. Such prayers are well represented in the earliest *sacramentaries [see Gregorian chant]. The term derives from the collecting of the prayers of all present into a single prayer. In the Anglican rite, prayers of this type proper to the season or feast occur at Morning and Evening Prayer.

Collegium musicum [Lat., musical guild]. One of various types of musical societies arising in German and German-Swiss cities and towns during the Reformation and thriving into the mid-18th century. Generally while societies such as the *Kantorei* cultivated vocal music for church performance and the *convivium musicum* discussed musical philosophy over a banquet, the *collegium musicum* performed for pleasure both vocal and instrumental music, especially the latter as it rose in stature during the Baroque era. Though closed amateur societies in concept, *collegia* frequently included professionals to fill out the music and admitted auditors. Moreover, they often provided music for church, state, and academic occasions and gained the patronage of leading citizens. From the 1660s, their functions largely constituted the beginnings of public concert life in Germany.

Leipzig *collegia musica,* consisting mostly of university students, enjoyed a succession of particularly illustrious directors, including Johann Kuhnau (1688), Telemann (1702), and Bach (1729–37), who composed several concertos and *dramme per musica* for weekly performances at Zimmerman's coffeehouse and for "extraordinary" concerts. Telemann went on to promote professional concerts by Frankfurt and Hamburg *collegia* in the 1720s, thus fostering the emergence of public subscription concerts in Germany. With the Moravian emigration, American *collegia* sprang up beginning in 1744 in Pennsylvania, Maryland, Ohio, and the Carolinas.

In 1909, Hugo Riemann refounded the Leipzig *collegium* within the university, initiating a widespread modern trend in German and American universities to foster the performance of early music on original instruments or replicas. The term *collegium musicum* has thus come to be associated in large measure with university ensembles that perform early music, though from a historical perspective, the term need not imply any restriction in repertory.

Colophony. *Rosin.

Color [Lat.]. In the Middle Ages, embellishment of various kinds, including especially repetition, but also the use of **musica ficta.* In modern discussions of *isorhythm, the term refers specifically to a repeated series of pitches as distinct from a repeated series of rhythmic values (known as *talea*). See also Coloration, Coloratura.

Color and music. The senses of sight and hearing both distinguish a range of percepts associated with frequency spectra. Even before it was possible to confirm the intuition that extension is a property of color, many wished to believe that colors, like pitches, differ from each other according to geometrical proportions. In *De sensu et sensibilia,* Aristotle avers that the aesthetics of color groupings is governed by the same ratios that govern musical consonances. In more recent times, Kircher (1673) has argued that differences between colors as well as between sounds are caused by different rates and types of vibrations broadcast through the atmosphere to the body, then through the nervous system to the mind. Newton (1704) more rigorously demonstrates the quantitative physical relationship between light and sound.

Associations between pitch-class names and frequencies of the audible continuum have varied considerably during the recorded history of music. Nevertheless, there has persisted a class of listeners for whom specific vowels, pitches, timbres, chords and chord progressions, (more recently) keys, entire compositions, and even styles have specific color analogues (Vernon, 1930). This is explainable in large part by a cognitive anomaly known as synaesthesia, in which a given stimulus within the domain of one sense (in this case, sound waves) elicits percepts belonging to the domain of another sense (in this case, images). Galton (1883) was the first to study this phenomenon systematically. Vernon (1930) finds that 18 percent of her subjects visualize notes heard. Among 274 college students studied by Karwoski and Odbert (1938), 60 percent showed some synaesthetic sensitivity.

The first known attempt to project colors in association with specific pitches occurred when Father Louis Castel (1688–1757) built a *clavessin oculaire* (inspired partly by the magic lantern described in Kircher's *Ars magna lucis et umbrae,* Rome, 1646). Color projectors became more practical after the invention of the electric light in 1879. In popular music of the 1960s and after, it is common for live performances to include coordinated colored light shows, or even improvised light paintings (using overhead projectors and transparent media). In Classical music, the appearance of Wagner's *Parsifal* (1882), which attempts an amalgamation of art and religion, and of Helena P. Blavatsky's provocatively titled *The Secret Doctrine: The Synthesis of Science, Religion, and Philosophy* (London, 1888) suggested to some artists that the creative future lay in mounting total artworks as instruments of psychological or spiritual revolution. In exemplary works such as Scriabin's Fifth Symphony (*Prométhée,* 1908–10) and Schoenberg's opera *Die glückliche Hand* (1913), color is conceived as an integral and even structural element of the intended multimedia event. (For more on this intellectual movement, see Kandinsky, 1912; Gay, 1972.) After World War I, a different aesthetic atmosphere prevailed. Still the association of color and music continued in works such as Arthur Bliss's *A Colour Symphony* op. 24 (1921–22; rev. 1932). Other 20th-century contributions include Henry Brant's *Violin Concerto with Lights* (1961) and Viking Eggeling's *La notte fantastica* (1976) for prism and percussion. See also Mixed media.

Bibl.: Athanasius Kircher, *Phonurgia nova* (Kempten, 1673; facs., *MMML* ser. 2, 44, 1966). Isaac Newton, *Opticks* (London, 1704). Francis Galton, *Inquiries into Human Faculty and Its Development* (London: MacMillan, 1883). Wassily Kandinsky, *Über das Geistige in der Kunst, inbesonders in der Malerei* (Munich: R Piper, 1912); trans. M. T. H. Sadler, *The Art of Spiritual Harmony* (London: Constable, 1914). Alexander László, *Die Farblichtmusik* (Leipzig: Breitkopf & Härtel, 1925). Leonid Sabaneef, "The Relation between Sound and Colour," *ML* 10 (1929): 266–77. P. E. Vernon, "Synaesthesia in Music," *Psyche* 10/4 (Apr., 1930): 22–40. Adrian B. Klein, *Colour-Music: The Art of Light,* 3rd ed. enl. publ. as *Colored Light: An Art Medium* (London: Technical Pr, 1937). Theodore F. Karwoski and Henry S. Odbert, *Color Music,* American Psychological Association Psychological Monographs 50/2 (Columbus, Ohio: Psychological Review Co, 1938). Wilton Mason, "Father Castel and His Color Clavecin," *Journal of Aesthetics and Art Criticism* 17 (1958): 103–16. John F. Gay, "The Correlation of Sound and Color: Three Major Metaphysical Sources" (D.M.A. diss., Univ. of Missouri–Kansas City, 1972).

Coloration. (1) In *mensural notation, the use of colored notes (red or white in black notation, black in white notation). (2) Florid ornaments of a type written out in keyboard and lute music of the 15th and 16th centuries [see Colorists, Intabulation, Diminutions, Ornamentation]. (3) Any elaborate *ornamentation or figuration, whether written or improvised, of the type common in the 17th and 18th centuries and in some singing styles of the 19th. See Coloratura.

Coloratura [It.]. (1) Elaborate ornamentation or embellishment, including running passages and trills, whether written or improvised, and common in 18th- and 19th-century singing, e.g., that occurring in the arias for the Queen of the Night in Mozart's *Die Zauberflöte.* (2) A soprano with a high range who sings in the style of (1). (3) *Coloration (2).

Colorists [Ger. *Koloristen,* fr. med. Lat. *color,* embellishment]. A term applied derogatorily by August G. Ritter in his *Zur Geschichte des Orgelspiels* (Leipzig, 1884) to a group of north German organists of the late 16th century who transcribed polyphonic vocal works for keyboard, embellishing them heavily with formulaic ornamental figures in the style of Italian instrumental *divisions or *coloraturas. The colorists include Elias Nikolaus Ammerbach (ca. 1530–97), Bernhard Schmid Sr. (1535–92) and Jr. (1567–1625), and Jakob Paix (1556–after 1623). By analogy, the neutral term colored *(koloriert)* has been applied to later florid organ settings of German chorales, e.g., Bach's *Allein Gott in der Höh sei Ehr* BWV 662.

Color organ. An instrument for manipulating colors in a fashion analogous to that in which an organ manipulates sounds. The earliest instrument of this type, built in the first half of the 18th century, was Louis-Bertrand Castel's *clavecin oculaire,* in which depressing a key plucked a string and at the same time projected a color on a screen. The advent of electricity permitted the invention of much more sophisticated instruments. These included A. Wallace Rimington's Colour Organ (1895), Adrian Bernard Klein's Color

Projector (1921), Thomas Wilfrid's Clavilux (1925), Alexander László's Color Piano (1925), and George Lawrence Hall's Musichrome (1930s). Most such instruments produced colors without sound, but they were often used in connection with music. Wilfrid and others, however, sought to develop a new and independent visual art by analogy with music. Scriabin's *Prometheus: Poem of Fire* (1910) specifies the use of a keyboard instrument (It. *tastiera per luce*) for projecting colors. See also Color and music.

Colotomic structure. Musical structure of the type found in some music of *Southeast Asia in which gongs or similar instruments in hierarchical sets are sounded to mark the beginnings and endings of successive sections, each characterized by recurrent melodic and rhythmic patterns.

Colpo d'arco [It.]. Bow stroke.

Combattimento di Tancredi e Clorinda [It., The Duel between Tancred and Clorinda]. A dramatic scene composed by Monteverdi, first performed in 1624 and published in his eighth book of madrigals (1638). Partly acted and partly narrated, it is based on a passage from Torquato Tasso's *Gerusalemme liberata.* See *Concitato.*

Combination pedal. A mechanical device for bringing on or retiring a group of organ stops. As used by the 19th-century French builder Cavaillé-Coll, these were preset and not adjustable.

Combination piston. In electric-action organs, a device for changing combinations of stops, operated by small buttons (pistons) below the keyboards.

Combination tone [also resultant tone, obs.; Fr. *son combiné;* Ger. *Kombinationston;* It. *suono di combinazione;* Sp. *sonido de combinación*]. A tone produced by a nonlinear system (one that introduces distortion during transmission) when it is supplied with two tones having sufficient and similar intensities as well as a frequency difference that is itself an audible frequency. Examples of nonlinear systems include the resonating masses of musical instruments, certain electric circuits in receivers and transmitters, and—of particular importance—the cochlea of the inner ear, where perceived combination tones are produced. These include difference tones and summation tones.

Difference tones are the easiest to hear and include tones with the frequencies f_2-f_1 Hz (first order), $2f_1-f_2$ Hz (second order), and $3f_1-2f_2$ Hz (third order), where f_1 is the lower of the two input tones. For example, if a pitch of frequency 500 Hz is sounded with a pitch of frequency 400 Hz, a pitch of frequency 100 Hz will be heard even though it is not physically present outside the ear. Difference tones were discovered in normal conditions of music making. Early descriptions occur in Sorge (1745–47) and Tartini (1754, where the author, employing the term *terzo suono,* claims to have discovered them in 1714). The first-order difference tone is sometimes termed Tartini's tone.

Summation tones associated with the frequencies f_1+f_2 Hz and $2f_1+f_2$ Hz terms can be heard only in very favorable circumstances. They are harder to hear because lower frequency tones mask higher ones much more strongly than the reverse (see Plomp, 1965; Smoorenburg, 1972). Summation tones were discovered by Helmholz under laboratory conditions and were first discussed by him in 1856 (see Helmholz, 1863). See also Psychology of music.

Bibl.: Georg Andreas Sorge, *Vorgemach der musikalischen Composition* (Lobenstein, 1745–47). Giuseppe Tartini, *Trattato di musica secondo la vera scienza dell' armonia* (Padua, 1754; facs., *MMML* ser. 2, 8, 1966). Hermann von Helmholz, *Die Lehre von den Tonempfindungen als physiologische Grundlage für die Theorie der Musik* (Braunschweig, 1863); trans. of 4th (1877) ed. Alexander J. Ellis, *On the Sensations of Tone as a Physiological Basis for the Theory of Music* (London, 1875); R: of 2nd (1885) ed. (New York: Dover, 1954). R. Plomp, "Detectability Threshold for Combination Tones," *JASA* 37 (1965): 1110–23. Guido F. Smoorenburg, "Audibility Region of Combination Tones," *JASA* 52 (1972): 603–14. Id., "Combination Tones and Their Origin," *JASA* 52 (1972): 615–32. R. A. Rasch and R. Plomp, "The Perception of Musical Tones," *The Psychology of Music,* ed. Diana Deutsch (New York: Academic Pr, 1982): 1–24.

Combinatoriality. See Twelve-tone music.

Combo. In jazz and popular music, a small ensemble (i.e., "combination" of instruments or players).

Come [It.]. As, like; *c. prima,* to be performed as on the first playing; *c. sopra,* as above; *c. stà,* as it stands, as written.

Comédie-ballet [Fr.]. See Dance.

Comédie mêlée d'ariettes [Fr.]. A type of **opéra comique* appearing toward the middle of the 18th century. In it, spoken dialogue alternates with newly composed songs, duets, and, occasionally, larger ensembles. The plots, whether sentimental or fantastic, sometimes reflect the social philosophy of Rousseau and the Encyclopedists. Composers of such works in France included Philidor, Duni, Monsigny, and Grétry; the genre was also popular in Vienna, where Gluck contributed several examples.

Comes [Lat.]. See *Dux, comes.*

Comic opera. Opera with humorous or lighthearted subject matter. In this sense, comic opera stands in direct and simple analogy with spoken comedy and includes works in a wide range and variety of styles, e.g., Mozart's *Le nozze di Figaro,* Smetana's *The Bartered Bride,* Wagner's *Die Meistersinger,* and Britten's *Albert Herring.* The term is also applied, however, to opera with certain musical or structural characteristics, regardless of subject matter. The most important of these characteristics is the use of spoken dialogue in place of *recitative. French **opéra comique,* German

Singspiel, English *ballad opera, Spanish *tonadilla,* and *operetta in whatever language all employ spoken dialogue in alternation with musical numbers. (Italian *opera buffa,* on the other hand, uses recitative.) Comic operas frequently (but not invariably) are shorter, make use of music in a more popular style, and contain characters drawn from a wider social sphere than their more serious counterparts. Until the end of the 18th century, works called comic operas were usually comic both in sentiment and in structure, though Mozart's mature operas blend comic and serious elements. The 19th century, however, offers many examples of works that alternate music with spoken dialogue but are nevertheless serious or even tragic. Notable examples are Beethoven's *Fidelio* and Bizet's *Carmen* (in its original version). See Opera. C.G.

Comma, schisma. Minute differences that exist between two relatively large, nearly identical intervals that have been obtained by different methods. The Pythagorean comma is the interval by which the sum of six whole tones (each 9:8) exceeds the octave (2:1). Thus $(9:8)^6 - 2:1 = 531441:524288$, or 23.5 cents. This discrepancy was first observed in the Euclidean *Division of the Canon (Sectio canonis),* dating from perhaps as early as 300 B.C.E. Modern acoustical theory usually defines the Pythagorean comma as the interval by which twelve fifths (each 3:2) exceed seven octaves. The syntonic comma, named after Ptolemy's syntonic diatonic genus, is the interval by which the ditone exceeds the pure major third (5:4). Thus $(9:8)^2 - 5:4 = 81:80$, or 21.5 cents. Modern acoustical theory defines the syntonic comma as the interval by which four fifths exceed the sum of two octaves plus a major third.

Boethius (*De musica* 3.8) attributes to Philolaus, a Pythagorean of the 5th century B.C.E., a definition of schisma as one-half of a Pythagorean comma. Boethius notes further that the diaschisma equals one-half of the *diesis, and that the major semitone or apotome exceeds the diesis by a comma. Thus, Boethius concludes that the half tone exceeds the diesis by a schisma [see Pythagorean scale].

Some modern acousticians use diaschisma and schisma to refer to intervals different from those of Boethius. In this modern usage, the diaschisma is the interval by which three octaves exceed the sum of four fifths plus two major thirds, i.e., 19.6 cents; the schisma is the interval by which the sum of eight fifths plus a major third exceeds five octaves, i.e., 2.0 cents.

Bibl.: Boethius, *Fundamentals of Music,* trans. Calvin M. Bower (New Haven: Yale U Pr, 1989). A.B.

Commedia dell' arte [It., comedy by profession as distinct from amateur courtly theater]. A genre of improvised theater parodying Venetian and northern Italian society, arising in the early 16th century, and flourishing throughout Europe until the early 18th. Its stock characters included lecherous Pantalone, gullible Dottore Graziano, boastful Capitano or Scaramuccia, the ingenue Columbina, clown Pedrolino (Pierrot), and base comedians or *zanni* Arlecchino (Harlequin) and Pulcinella (Punch), each with stereotyped mask, costume, and accessories. Performances intermingled stock dramatic situations with improvised singing, dancing, and acrobatics. Operatic composers from Vecchi (*L'Amfiparnaso,* 1594) to Pergolesi and Mozart incorporated elements from the *commedia dell' arte* in their works, as did playwrights Shakespeare, Johnson, and Molière; more recent composers such as Schumann, Busoni, Debussy, Strauss, and Stravinsky have also drawn upon this tradition.

Commedia per musica, commedia in musica, commedia musicale [It.]. An *opera buffa* [see Opera] in two or three acts. The terms were used most frequently in Naples from the 1720s through the 1790s.

Commiato [It.]. See *Envoi.*

Common chord. Major *triad.

Common meter. In *prosody, a four-line strophe alternating lines of eight and six syllables. See also Ballad.

Common of the Mass. The Ordinary of the Mass. See Ordinary and Proper.

Common of the Saints [Lat. *commune sanctorum*]. See Liturgy.

Common Prayer, Book of. The basic Anglican liturgical text. See Liturgical books.

Common time. The *meter 4/4. For the use of **C** to designate this meter, see Mensural notation.

Commosso [It.]. Moved, excited.

Commune sanctorum [Lat.]. The Common of Saints. See Liturgy.

Communion [Lat. *communio*]. In *Gregorian chant, the final item of the *Proper of the *Mass, sung during communion. Since the 12th century, it has consisted of an *antiphon without verses, except in the *Requiem Mass. Communions range in style from short syllabic pieces to longer pieces with prominent melismas. Some are identical to *responsories of the Office. Their texts are most often drawn from either the Psalms or the Gospels. Earlier sources incorporate verses sung to the same *psalm tones employed for the verses of the *introit. The communion was thus originally an example of antiphonal *psalmody. The singing of Psalms during communion is mentioned in the 4th-century Apostolic Constitutions. *Ordo romanus I* [see Gregorian chant VI], deriving from Roman accounts of the first half of the 8th century, describes the singing of verses until all communicants have received the sacrament and a signal to begin the lesser *Doxology is given. This was also permitted in modern practice (*LU,* p. xvi) before the Second *Vatican Council and has since been formally prescribed.

Early accounts also mention the singing of **versus ad repetendum* with the communion.

Comodo, comodamente [It.]. With respect to tempo, comfortable, easy.

Compact disc (CD). A digital recording medium introduced in 1983. A thin, round plastic form typically 4¾ inches in diameter with a reflective aluminum coating on one side, the CD can store about 80 minutes of music in the form of binary code. Playback requires a laser-equipped CD player that converts the binary code into an analog signal from which sound can be produced. See also Recording.

Comparative musicology [Ger. *vergleichende Musikwissenschaft*]. See Ethnomusicology.

Comparsa [Sp.]. See Conga.

Compass. The complete range of pitches from lowest to highest of an instrument, voice, or part.

Comping [fr. accompany]. A style of jazz piano accompanying that tends to be discontinuous, concentrating more on rhythm and sound than on melody.

Complainte [Fr.]. See Lament.

Complement. (1) Of an *interval, the difference between that interval and the octave, i.e., its *inversion. (2) Of a hexachord in *twelve-tone music, the six remaining pitch classes not included in that hexachord. (3) Of any set of pitch classes, all of the remaining pitch classes.

Completorium [Lat.]. Compline. See Office.

Compline [Lat. *completorium*]. See Office.

Composition [fr. Lat. *componere,* to put together]. The activity of creating a musical work; the work thus created. The term is most often used in opposition to improvisation, implying an activity carried out prior to performance or a work whose features are specified in sufficient detail to retain its essential identity from one performance to another. This opposition, however, is not entirely clear-cut, and the status of the concepts varies widely with time and place. Non-Western cultures vary considerably in the extent to which the concepts implied by the term composition are applicable. For the relationship between premeditation and performance in some of these cultures, see Improvisation.

Art music in the Western tradition, especially as viewed in the wake of Romanticism, has been most closely bound up with the concept composition understood as the work (both activity and product) of some historical figure who is the composer. The extensive use of notation in this tradition reinforces such a concept to the point that the notation of a work is often regarded as coterminous with the work itself, independent of performance. Notation, however, has no meaning independent of a reader who realizes it in the terms that he or she brings to bear on it. In this respect, a composition must be understood as a function of the reader or listener. At a practical level, the relationship between composer and performer has changed steadily, performers in the 18th century, for example, being expected to contribute more fundamentally to the character of a work than was the norm in the mid-20th century [see Performance practice]. Then, too, notation may be used to fix music that has been created and transmitted by processes quite different from those of the Romantic figure of the composer [see Transmission].

Neither notation nor an identifiable composer suffices to define a composition, though these have been the principal preoccupations of students of Western music. Notation may simply record the materials (e.g., a mode or a melody type) from which performances are created, and a composer's name may be attached to some such materials even though those materials are never performed as such. Popular song offers a related phenomenon. Such a song is attributed to a composer and often disseminated in notation, which, however, is never reproduced literally in performance. The song's identity as a composition is thus preserved even under considerable transformations and cannot be uniquely defined by any single written version of it.

During the middle decades of the 20th century, the concept of composition as both activity and product underwent a radical change in some quarters within what must nevertheless be regarded as the tradition of art music. *Aleatory procedures of all kinds called into question the composer's status as the specifier of the work in advance and called into question the character of the work itself as something reproducible. A composition, furthermore, might comprise a variety of activities and effects in addition to or rather than sound. In contrast, composers of *serial music sought to integrate every feature of a musical work into a rational plan, and some composers of *electro-acoustic music merged the acts of composition and performance by creating works on tape for reproduction through loudspeakers.

As a result of the importance attached in the West to the figure of the composer, considerable study has been devoted to the compositional process—the means or at least the order of events by which a composer produces what is regarded as the finished work. This has entailed principally the study of *sketches. Another preoccupation of scholarship that derives from the status of the composer is the *authenticity of individual works.

Guido of Arezzo uses the term *componere* in the 11th century with reference to melodies, and in the 13th, Johannes de Grocheo describes polyphonic music as *musica composita* and refers to the composer as a *compositor.* The study of composition has traditionally entailed the study of music theory based on the styles or idioms current at the time. For a historical list of theory treatises, many of which were intended to provide instruction for composers, see Theory.

*Counterpoint has been an element of instruction in composition since the 13th century. Since the sharp decline of *tonality in art music in the 20th century, tonal counterpoint and harmony and imitation of the forms of tonal music have nevertheless remained aspects of much early training in composition, though their usefulness for this purpose has been disputed.

Through the 18th century, a composer was likely to be a performer as well, to have been trained as such, and to earn a living as such. Composition as a profession separate from that of the performer emerged largely in the 19th century. Composers of art music today are rarely able to support themselves entirely from composition, but more often support themselves from teaching than from performance. Composers of *popular music, on the other hand, may derive substantial sums from their compositions and, in recent decades, have often been celebrated performers.

Composition pedal, stop. A foot- or hand-operated button on the *organ permitting a preset selection of several stops to be drawn at once.

Compostela. See Santiago de Compostela, Repertory of.

Compound interval. An *interval that exceeds an octave.

Compound meter, time. A *meter that includes a triple subdivision within the beat, e.g., 6/8.

Compound stop. Any organ stop with two or more pipes per note, sounding the unison or octaves along with the fifth. *Sesquialtera and *Cornet stops also include the third. *Mixtures contain only octaves and fifths.

Comprimario [It.]. In opera, a singer of secondary roles.

Computers. See Electro-acoustic music for the use of computers in composition and performance. For other applications, see Recording, Theory, Analysis, Musicology, Ethnomusicology, Printing of music.

Con [It., Sp.]. With. For phrases beginning with this word, see the word following.

Concentus [Lat.]. See *Accentus, concentus.*

Concert. A public performance of music before an audience that has assembled for the purpose of listening to it. A performance by a soloist, with or without an accompanist, is usually called a *recital.

Until the 18th century, most secular music-making was private, confined to those households, usually royal or aristocratic, that could afford a musical establishment. The rise of public concerts was concomitant with that of a general public sufficiently knowledgeable and prosperous to support them, and so is first found primarily in cities with a well-developed middle class.

The origin of concerts is usually held to lie in the musical activities of *academies in Italy and **collegia musica* in Germany, beginning in the 16th and 17th centuries. Although both were private societies and so did not give public concerts in the modern sense, their musical performances were a move away from individual patronage to collective support. (Academy was long to be synonymous with concert.)

Concerts with paid admission began in London by 1664. In 1672–78, John Banister gave regular subscription concerts at his house. In the 18th century, numerous concert organizations were active in London, including that managed jointly by Johann Christian Bach and Carl Friedrich Abel (1765–81) and that of Johann Peter Salomon (1791–95). Beginning with the famous **Concert spirituel* (1725–90), 18th-century Paris also had several concert societies. Many of those in German cities grew out of *collegia musica.* The famous and still-continuing *Gewandhaus* concerts of Leipzig began in 1781. By the second half of the 18th century, many good-sized European cities had halls in which concerts were regularly given [see Concert hall]. Outdoor summer concerts in pleasure gardens had also become popular. The Mozart letters provide numerous glimpses into concert-giving in this period, as seen by the traveling virtuoso. Eighteenth-century concerts tended to be considerably longer and to consist of more varied fare (usually both vocal and instrumental, solo and ensemble) than modern ones. The high price of tickets to the most fashionable concerts in large cities put them beyond the means of the broader public.

In the 19th century, concerts assumed much of their present character. The Revolutionary and Napoleonic upheavals speeded the breakdown of princely and aristocratic patronage. Public concerts became more numerous and varied, concert halls larger. Many permanent orchestras emerged as concert-giving organizations (London Philharmonic Society, 1813; Berlin Philharmonic, 1826; Vienna Philharmonic, 1842; Philharmonic Society of New York, 1842; Boston Symphony, 1881). Programs tended to become more specialized (e.g., orchestra, chamber music, solo recital). The introduction of program notes was part of a tendency in some quarters to see the concert as an instrument of social improvement, manifested also in the "popular concert," which was developed by Louis Jullien and was intended to entertain and educate a wider public. To attract such a public, P. T. Barnum and others brought into music the rapidly refining techniques of modern publicity and advertising.

In the 20th century, the number of concert-giving organizations continued to increase, usually depending on financial support from government and business. At the same time, concert life became increasingly dominated by a relatively small number of international celebrities, with the result that persons attending the most prominent concerts in any large city in Europe or the U.S. and in many smaller cities as well were likely to hear the same artists being heard in every other city. Economic and public-relations factors, including the power of some recording companies and artists-management firms, continue to shape concert life to a considerable degree.

Also in the 20th century, concert presentations extended into popular idioms such as jazz, country, and rock. On February 12, 1924, Paul Whiteman's "Experiment in Modern Music" brought his popular jazz-inflected orchestra to Aeolian Hall in New York City. On January 16, 1938, Benny Goodman presented his band at Carnegie Hall. In 1943 Duke Ellington inaugurated a series of annual concerts at Carnegie Hall that continued through 1951. By the 1950s, jazz was featured regularly in concert settings, both large and small. Jazz festivals in Europe and in the United States showcased a number of performers and drew large audiences. At the same time, a chamber music–like atmosphere prevailed at concerts presented in venues on college campuses by groups such as the Modern Jazz Quartet and the Dave Brubeck Quartet. In the 1960s, avant-garde jazz musicians began playing concerts in alternative performance spaces such as Sam Rivers's Studio Rivbea in New York. In the 1990s, both Carnegie Hall and Lincoln Center sponsored their own resident jazz bands.

In country music, the successful launch in 1925 of the Grand Ole Opry (originally called the WSM Barn Dance) radio show on station WSM in Nashville led to a concert version presented in a series of venues including the Ryman Auditorium (1943–74). Since 1974, the Grand Ole Opry has been presented in its own theater, which is part of the Opryland amusement park outside Nashville. Similarly, rock and rhythm and blues have had their own dedicated concert venues in theaters such as the Fillmore Auditorium in San Francisco, Fillmore East in New York City, and the Apollo Theater in Harlem. The enormous appeal of rhythm and blues and early rock and roll and was immediately evident at one of the first concerts to feature such artists. Held at the Cleveland Arena on March 21, 1952, Alan Freed's Moondog Coronation Ball lasted for only one song before the concert was shut down due to an overcapacity crowd that flooded the 10,000-seat venue. In the 1960s rock concerts grew to even larger proportions with presentations at sports arenas and at outdoor festivals such as Monterey (1967) and Woodstock (1969), which drew hundreds of thousands of fans. Rock concerts also became increasingly extravagant spectacles, with elaborate staging, pyrotechnics, large-screen video, and massively amplified sound.

Bibl.: Michel Brenet [pseud.: Marie Bobillier], *Les concerts en France sous l'ancien régime* (Paris: Fischbacher, 1900; R: New York: Da Capo, 1970). Oscar Sonneck, *Early Concert Life in America: 1731–1800* (Leipzig: Breitkopf & Härtel, 1907; R: New York: Da Capo, 1978). Gerhard Pinthus, *Das Konzertleben in Deutschland: Ein Abriss seiner Entwicklung bis zum Beginn des 19. Jahrhunderts* (Strasbourg: Heitz, 1932). Stanley Sadie, "Concert Life in Eighteenth-Century England," *PRMA* 85 (1958–59): 17–30. José Subirá, "Conciertos espirituales españoles en el siglo XVIII," *Fellerer,* 1962, pp. 519–29. Percy Young, *The Concert Tradition: From the Middle Ages to the Twentieth Century* (London: Routledge & Kegan Paul, 1965). Jeffrey Cooper, *The Rise of Instrumental Music and Concert Series in Paris, 1828–1871* (Ann Arbor: UMI Res Pr, 1983). Eugene K. Wolf, "The 'Concert' in Munich under Elector Carl Theodor," in *Mozarts* Idomeneo *und die Musik in München zur Zeit Karl Theodors,* ed. Theodor Göllner and Stephan Hörner (Munich: Verlag der Bayerischen Akademie der Wissenschaften/C. H. Beck, 2001), pp. 223–36.

Concertant [Fr.], **concertante** [It.]. Beginning in the 18th century, adjectives applied to works for two or more performers (including orchestral works) in which one or more of the performers is called upon for soloistic display, e.g., Mozart's *Sinfonia concertante* K. 364 (320d) for violin, viola, and orchestra, and Weber's *Grand duo concertant* op. 48 for clarinet and piano. The form *concertante* has also been used as a noun to refer to pieces of this kind, particularly in the 18th century. See *Symphonie concertante,* Concerto, String quartet.

Concertato [It., concerted]. Of or pertaining to works of the early 17th century that combine and contrast vocal and instrumental forces, especially through the introduction of the *thoroughbass. The modern use of the term in this way was promoted by Manfred Bukofzer (*Music in the Baroque Era,* New York: Norton, 1947). The numerous sacred works of the period in this style were usually titled concerto [see Concerto (1)].

Concertgebouw [Du.]. Concert building, specifically the one constructed in Amsterdam in 1888 and from which The Netherlands' foremost orchestra takes its name.

Concert grand. The largest size of grand *piano, measuring approximately 2.75 m (9 ft.) in length.

Concert hall. A large room in which concerts are given. The beginnings of public indoor concerts are discernible in the 17th century, particularly in the music heard in taverns and coffee houses, London taverns that specialized in such performances being known as "Musick Houses." Concerts were also sometimes given in private houses with paid public admission. Taverns and coffee houses continued to be prominent in this respect in the 18th century, as exemplified by the places of performance of Bach's *collegium musicum* in Leipzig and some of Mozart's London concerts.

According to Burney, about 1680 a room designed primarily for music was built in London, but such rooms remained rare in the 18th century. As still happens today, concerts were often given in theaters and in halls not primarily or exclusively intended for them, although more or less suitable, e.g., Leipzig's Gewandhaus (Cloth Hall) (1781). Admission to concerts was often expensive, partly to ensure exclusivity. Information on the seating capacity of early concert halls is scanty. The size of the concert room at London's Carlisle House restricted the Bach-Abel concerts to 400 subscribers in the 1760s. These concerts later moved to the Hanover Square Rooms (1775), which had a capacity of almost 900; Salomon's concerts were also given there later. Paris's first real concert hall, that of the Conservatoire (1811), seated 1,055.

In the second half of the 19th century, many concert halls were built across northern Europe and North America. They tended to be larger than before, reflecting the increased size of performing bodies and the widening interest of the middle class. This made them less suitable for chamber music and solo recitals and sometimes led to the inclusion of smaller halls for these purposes along with larger ones, as in the second Gewandhaus (1884) and New York's Carnegie Hall (1891). The movement in this period to bring high culture to the masses helped stimulate the construction of very large halls, often temporary for special occasions, but sometimes permanent, e.g., London's Royal Albert Hall (1871, capacity 6,500).

A sizable number of concert halls were destroyed in World War II, especially in Germany and Great Britain, and this situation produced a new wave of building. Historic halls were reconstructed (e.g., Cologne's Gürzenich) and new halls were built, some of which incorporated new approaches to concert-hall design, such as Berlin's Philharmonie (1963). A prominent recent tendency has been to group halls and theaters used for various purposes together in performing-arts centers, such as London's South Bank (1951), Los Angeles's Music Center (1964), New York's Lincoln Center (1969), Sydney's Opera House complex (1973), and Philadelphia's Kimmel Center (2001). Other late-20th-century halls include Ireland's National Concert Hall (1981), the Glasgow Royal Concert Hall (1991), and Dallas's Morton H. Meyerson Symphony Center (1989). The proliferation of Western concert music in Asia has also led to the construction of concert halls and performing-arts centers, including Japan's Suntory Hall (1986) and China's National Chiang Kai Shek Cultural Center (1987).

See also Acoustics IV, Concert.

Bibl.: T. Busby, *Concert Room and Orchestra Anecdotes* (London: Clementi, 1825). H. Bagenal, "Musical Taste and Concert Hall Design," *PRMA* 78 (1951–2): 11–29. M. Forsyth, *Buildings for Music* (Cambridge, Mass.: MIT Pr, 1985). Y. Ando, *Concert Hall Acoustics* (New York: Springer-Verlag, 1985). Y. Ando, *Music and Concert Hall Acoustics* (London: Academic Pr, 1997).

Concertina. A free-reed [see Reed], bellows-operated instrument similar to the *accordion but hexagonal in shape and with a button keyboard for each hand. In 1844, Charles Wheatstone of London patented an instrument that was fully chromatic and on which each button produced the same pitch regardless of whether the bellows were pressed or drawn. Other (principally German) instruments that continued in use were diatonic and produced different pitches when pressed and drawn. The concertina became widely popular in Europe and in North and South America. It is employed in the popular music of some African countries as well. See ill. under Accordion; see also Bandoneon.

Concertino [It., dim. of *concerto*]. (1) The soloists in a concerto grosso [see Concerto (2) I]. (2) In the early and mid-18th century, a multimovement work for orchestra or chamber ensemble. Orchestral concertinos do not usually feature soloists, and they are generally lighter and less formal in style than early symphonies. See also String quartet I. (3) In the 19th and 20th centuries, a work in the style of a concerto, but freer in form and on a smaller scale, sometimes for one or a few instruments without orchestra and usually in a single movement. A common German title for works of this type is *Konzertstück.* Examples include Weber's Concertino in E♭ for clarinet and orchestra (1814), Schumann's Introduction and Allegro appassionato *(Concertstück)* for piano and orchestra (1849), Bruch's *Konzertstück* in F♯ minor for violin and orchestra, Stravinsky's Concertino for string quartet (1920), and Piston's Concertino for piano and chamber orchestra (1937). (4) [Sp.] *Concertmaster.

Concertmaster [Brit. leader; Fr. *chef d'attaque, de pupitre;* Ger. *Konzertmeister;* It. *primo violino;* Sp. *concertino*]. The principal first violinist of an orchestra and as such the person responsible for coordinating the bowing and attack of all strings and for playing solo violin passages. The concertmaster usually comes to the stage after the remainder of the orchestra is seated, oversees tuning, and takes his or her place on the conductor's immediate left. In smaller ensembles that perform without a conductor (as did orchestras of the 18th and early 19th centuries), such a person may fulfill all of the functions of musical leadership. See also Conducting, Orchestra.

Concerto [fr. It. *concertare,* to join together; pres. part. *concertante,* past part. *concertato;* related to Lat. *concertare,* to fight or contend]. (1) In the 16th through the early 18th centuries, a diverse ensemble of voices, instruments, or both, or a composition for such an ensemble. This usage derived from the original Italian meaning of *concertare* and its derivatives, "to join together" or "unite," a meaning present in English in such phrases as "to work in concert" and "concerted effort." The performers "joined together" in an early concerto are usually heterogeneous in some sense: soloists and chorus, two separate choruses, different instruments, or (most commonly of all) voice and instruments. In the course of the 17th century, the term concerto took on the additional Latin meaning of "fighting" or "contending," referring to the opposition between soloist(s) and orchestra of the modern concerto [see (2), below]. Which of the meanings of concerto and its derivatives was intended in a particular instance can often be determined only from the context.

In the 17th century, sacred works for voices and instruments were typically called concertos; secular works of similar character were more often entitled airs *(arie), musiche,* cantatas, and so forth [see Cantata]. Large-scale sacred concertos for chorus, soloists, and instruments were particularly common in Venice, appearing in collections by Andrea and Giovanni Gabrieli and Claudio Monteverdi from the late 16th century onward. More widely cultivated was the small sacred concerto for one to four solo voices, continuo, and (frequently) additional solo instruments. The earliest such settings, for example, Lodovico Viadana's *Cento concerti ecclesiastici* (1602), resemble adaptations of polyphonic style for the new medium of solo voice plus continuo. Before long, however, the influence of true monodic style came strongly to the fore in collections by Monteverdi (1610), Alessandro Grandi, and others. In Germany, the few-voiced sacred concerto appeared first in the chorale-based concertos of Johann Hermann Schein, Michael Praetorius, and Samuel Scheidt (1618 and thereafter), then in Heinrich Schütz's freely composed *Kleine geistliche Concerte* (Small Sacred Concertos) of 1636–39. J. S. Bach was thus reflecting a long-standing tradition when he used the title "concerto" for many of the works that we know as cantatas. See also Chorale cantata, Chorale concerto.

(2) From the latter part of the 17th century to the present, a multimovement (occasionally multisectional) work for soloist or soloists and orchestra.

I. *Baroque.* 1. Concerto grosso. The instrumental concerto of the middle and late Baroque comprised three basic types. The earliest of these was the concerto grosso, in which a small group of soloists is set against a larger orchestra. The smaller group, consisting most often of two solo violins and continuo, is known as the concertino (little ensemble). The larger group, generally a string orchestra plus continuo, is known variously as the concerto grosso (large ensemble), grosso, tutti, or—perhaps least confusingly—ripieno (from *concerto ripieno,* full ensemble, i.e., with doubled parts).

Several Baroque genres contributed to the creation of the concerto grosso. One was the multivoiced *canzona and *sonata, especially those polychoral works in which the groups of instruments contrast with one another (e.g., Giovanni Gabrieli's famous *Sonata pian e forte*). Another was the *trio sonata, which not only supplied the normal instrumentation of the concertino, but was also performed with doubled parts as the occasion demanded. In the latter case, division *ad libitum* into soloists and ripienists was an obvious stratagem, and this practice can be documented in Rome beginning in the 1660s. During the 1670s, numerous vocal works written by Alessandro Stradella for performance in Rome explicitly require concerto grosso instrumentation, both in their sinfonias and in accompaniments to arias. Stradella was also the composer of the earliest known independent concerto grosso (entitled "Sonata" in one source, "Sinfonia" in another, but with clearly specified concertino and ripieno groups; see *Concentus musicus* 5). In this work, the similarity of the material given to each group evidences a close relationship with the polychoral canzona and the trio sonata with *ad libitum* textural contrast.

It is against this background in Rome that Arcangelo Corelli produced his earliest concerti grossi, several of which were already in existence by ca. 1682 according to the composer Georg Muffat, who visited Rome at that time. It is probable that some of Corelli's famous Concerti grossi op. 6 (published posthumously in 1714) date from that period. Texturally, Corelli's concertos resemble others of the period in that the alternation of tutti and solo follows no set plan; the effect is generally that of a trio sonata in which additional contrast has been provided by entry of the ripieno at various points. Indeed, Corelli indicates on the title page that doubling of the ripieno parts is optional, and all the essential material is present in the concertino. Also rather conservative is the use of a flexible number and sequence of movements (five or more). Corelli nevertheless made frequent use of what has been called the concerto style (Bukofzer, 1947), an all-important Baroque style featuring idiomatic string figuration (often disposed in sequences), clearly directional harmony (often based on the circle of fifths), motoric rhythm, and relatively homophonic texture.

Corelli's model proved influential for many later composers, notably Pietro Locatelli in Holland (op. 1, 1721) and Francesco Geminiani and Handel (op. 6, 1739) in England. But beginning with Giuseppe Torelli and Antonio Vivaldi, the concerto grosso came more and more under the domination of the solo concerto in matters of form and instrumental treatment. While this tendency is most obvious in the so-called double concerto—less a concerto grosso than a concerto for two individual soloists—it may also be seen in concerti grossi such as Bach's **Brandenburg* Concertos (dedication dated 1721), often considered the greatest works in this genre. Here the influence of the solo concerto appears both in Bach's adoption of the formal procedures of Vivaldi [see below] and in the extraordinary virtuosity required of the concertino performers, who are given many extended solo passages (e.g., the famous harpsichord solo of the first movement of no. 5). Like Vivaldi, Bach wrote for an exceptionally wide range of instruments in these concertos. The result is a virtual compendium of late-Baroque concerto techniques, though Bach wholly transcends his models in the interrelated areas of intensive motivic development and the application of contrapuntal procedures to the concerto.

2. Ripieno concerto. A somewhat later type of concerto—here the term reverts to its earlier meaning of "work for an ensemble"—is the ripieno concerto, known in the Baroque as the *concerto ripieno* or *concerto a 4* (or *a 5* if the orchestra included two viola parts, a standard 17th-century scoring). These are

merely compositions for the ripieno alone (i.e., for string orchestra and continuo), with either no solo parts or manifestly subsidiary ones. Beginning with the six ripieno concertos of Giuseppe Torelli's op. 5 (1692), this genre enjoyed an efflorescence that extended until about 1740.

Most ripieno concertos fall into one of two distinct classes: a sonata type and a sinfonia type. The sonata type generally mirrors the form and style of the **sonata da chiesa* in its use of four-movement slow–fast–slow–fast cycles and predominantly fugal texture in the fast movements.

The more modern sinfonia type was firmly established in Torelli's second publication to include concertos, op. 6 (1698), and in Giulio Taglietti's *Concerti a quattro* op. 4 (1699), which turn to the three-movement (fast–slow–fast) pattern and more homophonic texture familiar to us from the solo concerto and opera sinfonia. The opening movements also parallel the solo concerto in utilizing a type of *ritornello form (without solo sections), in which the opening material recurs from one to several times in various keys, the last statement normally in the tonic. Slow movements range from full movements to brief transitions, while finales are most often binary in form and dancelike in style. The sinfonia type gradually merged with the early concert *symphony beginning in the 1720s, doubtless in part because the term concerto was by that time acquiring an indelible association with the notion of tutti-solo contrast.

3. Solo concerto. The last type of concerto to develop, and the one with the most far-reaching influence, was the concerto for a single soloist (most often violin during the Baroque) and orchestra. The earliest known solo concertos are nos. 6 and 12 of Torelli's op. 6 of 1698. These works employ both a three-movement cycle and clear (if diminutive) ritornello form, like that of the ripieno concerto except that sections for the soloist and continuo now separate the various orchestral ritornellos. Torelli, who was active at Bologna, was probably influenced in these concertos by the operatic aria and by the numerous sonatas and sinfonias for trumpet and strings produced in Bologna from the 1660s on [see Bologna school]; he himself composed over a dozen such works for trumpet, two dated in the early 1690s. Other early violin concertos are the four in Tomaso Albinoni's op. 2 (1700) and the six in Torelli's important op. 8 (1709; the other six works in this set are double concertos for two violins).

The most influential and prolific composer of concertos during the Baroque period was the Venetian Antonio Vivaldi (1678–1741). In addition to his nearly 60 extant ripieno concertos, Vivaldi composed approximately 425 concertos for one or more soloists, including about 350 solo concertos (two-thirds for solo violin) and 45 double concertos (over half for two violins). Vivaldi's concertos firmly established the three-movement cycle as the norm. In them the virtuosity of the solo sections increases markedly, especially in the later works, and concurrently the texture becomes more homophonic.

Ritornello form in Vivaldi, often described as procrustean, is actually rather flexible. It is true that in a large number of works, including the later published sets such as op. 8 (ca. 1725, containing *The Four Seasons*), Vivaldi utilized a fairly standardized scheme of four or five regularly recurring tutti sections or ritornellos (hereafter symbolized R_1, R_2, etc.). The first and last ritornellos are in the tonic, the second in the dominant or relative major, and the remainder in related keys, including the dominant minor in a minor-key work. Central (and often final) ritornellos are usually shorter than the opening one, merely stating material selected from it and frequently omitting the opening theme. The intervening solo sections (symbolized S_1, S_2, etc.), which may or may not incorporate material from the ritornello sections, normally have the function of carrying out the modulations from key to key, each new key being confirmed and stabilized by the eventual entry of the tutti.

In many other Vivaldi concertos, however—notably those from earlier sets such as op. 3 (1711)—the entire middle area from the beginning of S_2 to the final section is more varied, often simply alternating brief tutti and solo statements; ritornellos are irregular in length, placement, and choice of material. It should be stressed that it was primarily the latter, more fluid type of ritornello form that Bach became acquainted with by transcribing nine Vivaldi concertos for organ and clavier at Weimar ca. 1714–17; this fact provides one explanation for the relative freedom of form in the *Brandenburg* Concertos and the three Bach violin concertos, all from the Cöthen period, that survive in their original form (two for solo violin, one for two violins). Many virtuoso violinists of the late Baroque also adopted the Vivaldi model to a greater or lesser extent, the most important being Pietro Locatelli, Giuseppe Tartini (at least in his early period), and Jean-Marie Leclair.

Concertos for instruments other than violin began to appear early in the 18th century, including the cello concertos of Giuseppe Jacchini (op. 4, 1701) and Leonardo Leo, the oboe concertos of Handel and Albinoni, and the numerous concertos for flute, oboe, bassoon, cello, and other instruments by Vivaldi and Telemann. The earliest organ concertos can probably be credited to Handel (16 concertos, ca. 1735–51), the earliest harpsichord concertos to Bach (14 concertos for one to four harpsichords, ca. 1730–40). In the latter case, all but possibly one of the concertos are arrangements of preexistent works (including op. 3 no. 10 of Vivaldi), though Bach had already approached the idea of a harpsichord concerto before 1721 in the *Brandenburg* Concerto no. 5.

II. *Classical.* The Classical period brought the final ascendancy of the solo concerto over the group or multiple concerto; the only important manifestation of the latter type during this period was the **symphonie* *concertante,* a variety of concerto for two or more instruments fashionable after ca. 1770. Two different phenomena contributed to the popularity of the solo concerto: the continued rise of the virtuoso soloist and the growing demand for up-to-date works for performance by amateurs. The former trend appears most obviously in the large number of violin concertos written for use by their composers, including the Italians Pietro Nardini, Gaetano Pugnani, and later Giovanni Battista Viotti (from 1782 in Paris), the German Johann Gottlieb Graun (Berlin), the Bohemian Johann Stamitz (Mannheim) and his sons Carl and Anton, and the Frenchman Pierre Gaviniès.

Among numerous concertos by virtuosos on other instruments, one may cite the cello concertos of Luigi Boccherini, the 300 flute concertos of Johann Joachim Quantz, the oboe concertos of Johann Christian Fischer (active in London), and the horn concertos of the Bohemian Giovanni Punto (Johann Wenzel Stich). Quantz's concertos, written for performance by himself and his patron, Frederick the Great, illustrate the extraordinary vogue in the 18th century of the nobleman as amateur flutist; the literally thousands of such works epitomize Rococo grace and elegance.

The Classical period also witnessed the coming of age of the keyboard concerto. Until about 1770, the preferred instrument was generally the harpsichord, but thereafter the piano rapidly came to the fore. The most important composers of keyboard concertos before Mozart were Bach's sons, all highly gifted performers: Wilhelm Friedemann (Halle), Carl Philipp Emanuel (Berlin and Hamburg), and Johann Christian (Milan and London). Other early composers of keyboard concertos included Giovanni Benedetto Platti (op. 2, 1742) and Johan Joachim Agrell (10 concertos, 1751–61). Vienna provided an especially strong stimulus to the production of keyboard concertos, as seen early in the period in works by Matthias Georg Monn (d. 1750) and Georg Christoph Wagenseil, later in works by Joseph Anton Steffan (Štěpán), Leopold Hofmann, Johann Vanhal, Leopold Kozeluch, and of course Mozart. The last decades of the 18th century brought the rise of such traveling piano virtuosos as Jan Ladislav Dussek, Daniel Steibelt, and Johann Nepomuk Hummel, in whose oeuvre the concerto naturally figured prominently.

The concertos of this period show a broad transition from Baroque to Classical style, though often they are more conservative than contemporaneous symphonies, presumably owing in part to the greater weight of stylistic tradition associated with the concerto. Most are in three movements, though a significant minority adopt such lighter two-movement patterns as Allegro–Minuet and Allegro–Rondo. Dance and rondo finales are also frequent in three-movement concertos, while slow movements employ a variety of song, rondo, and variation forms.

Nearly all first movements during this period are in some variety of ritornello form, as are many finales. This form shows great fluidity until late in the Classical period. The number of ritornellos is most often four, and most sections tend to be longer and more variegated than in the Baroque. One particularly common plan illustrates the tendency of Classical ritornello form to assimilate principles of structure evident in *sonata form. This design is a modified version of the Vivaldi type with four ritornellos (R_1–R_4) and three solo sections (S_1–S_3). Here the final solo, S_3, begins and ends in the tonic and tends to parallel S_1 thematically. Thus, S_3 now resembles the recapitulation of a sonata-form movement. Moreover, S_1 had always been comparable to an exposition and S_2 to a development section, owing to their modulatory schemes (e.g., I–V for S_1, V–vi for S_2; real thematic development is uncommon in S_2 during the 18th century, however).

The 18th-century theorist Heinrich Christoph Koch, basing his analysis on works from the period under discussion, specifically equates the three solo sections of the form just described with the three principal divisions of sonata form; he considers the tutti sections subsidiary (*Versuch einer Anleitung zur Composition* 3, 1793). Koch's analysis is especially appropriate for that majority of Classical movements that deemphasize R_2 and R_4 by giving them material from the end of the preceding solo section rather than restating the main theme: in such cases R_2 and R_4 function partially as codettas, merely reinforcing the cadential areas of the solo sections that precede them, S_1 and S_3. Examples of the plan discussed by Koch, with S_3 serving as the recapitulation, appear from before mid-century until late in the Classical period (e.g., in the Mozart Clarinet Concerto, 1791).

The most variable element of 18th-century concerto form was the penultimate tutti, R_3 in a movement with four ritornellos. Many early Classical movements deemphasize this section, reducing it to a brief interpolation before the final solo. Other movements either omit it entirely, proceeding directly from S_2 to S_3 (the formal type described in Koch's *Musikalisches Lexikon* of 1802), or else assign it the function of a retransition (as in the Haydn Trumpet Concerto, 1796). But the most influential approach, found in concertos of J. C. Bach and Michael Haydn as early as the 1760s and in most of Mozart's piano concertos, was to accentuate the coordinated return of the main theme and the tonic key by assigning it to the orchestra rather than to the soloist, who then reenters at some convenient spot. The section as a whole thus combines the functions of R_3, S_3, and recapitulation [see fig.].

By approximately 1760, up-to-date composers had begun to introduce into R_1 and S_1 the kind of functional thematic contrast already common in expositions of sonata-form movements, including use of a secondary theme or themes. The relationship between the two sections themselves, however, remained flexible throughout the century. The opening tutti, R_1, may range from a brief introduction to a full-scale orches-

R_1/Orch. exp./Intro.	S_1/Solo exp.	R_2	S_2/Dev.	(Retr.)	R_3/S_3/Recap.	R_4 (Cad.)
I (i) ———	I (i) → V (III, v) ———		V (III, v)	⟿	I (i) ———	

Ritornello-sonata form of the late 18th and the early 19th century.

tral exposition, while S_1 may consist entirely of new material or basically parallel R_1 except that it ends in the dominant. (R_1 in Classical concertos often modulates to the dominant for the secondary theme, just as does S_1, but it nearly always returns to the tonic near the end; see, e.g., the first movement of Mozart's Piano Concerto K. 449.) When the sections are disparate, Mozart generally incorporates the principal material of both at some point within the recapitulation and final tutti, often in exceedingly clever fashion.

The accompanying figure presents an overview of concerto first-movement form of the late 18th and early 19th centuries, showing how it synthesizes the structural principles of both ritornello and sonata forms. (Roman numerals indicate keys, those in parentheses referring to minor-key movements; arrows indicate modulations.) The mutual adjustment of these dichotomous principles in what may be termed ritornello-sonata form stands as one of the signal achievements of the Classical period, and analysis or listening solely in terms of one or the other type may well result in a distorted impression of the work. For example, the entry of S_2 in a Mozart concerto never has the structural weight of the beginning of a sonata-form development section: it begins as a solo section, often rather inconspicuously, and only gradually takes on a more forceful developmental character. On the other hand, the next section, R_3/S_3, is obviously a recapitulation comparable to that of sonata form, in which the orchestra presents a dramatic dual return of the primary theme and the tonic, usually prepared by a retransition. It should be noted in regard to the accompanying figure that Mozart usually places a *cadenza within R_4, as indicated, whereas in earlier concertos it normally occurs in S_3 (or often not at all). In addition, Mozart frequently utilizes an *Eingang* (entry), a brief cadenzalike passage for the piano leading to the beginning of S_1 proper.

Mozart's 5 violin concertos are all Salzburg works dating from a single period in 1775. His 23 original piano concertos—17 from his Viennese period—represent the crowning achievement of the 18th-century concerto. Most of the works written for Vienna are of a type that he himself called "grand concertos"; these were intended for performance at his own subscription concerts, which were held in sizable halls. They thus call for an orchestra that is much larger and more diverse than that of the typical chamber concerto, especially in the expanded role assigned to the winds—an orchestra fully capable of sustaining a dramatic confrontation with the virtuosity and individuality of the soloist. In the same way, Mozart's approach in these concertos is often clearly symphonic, not only in the aforementioned application of formal principles associated with the symphony, but also in an almost Haydnesque interest in thematic derivation and unity in the later concertos. Finally, the range of styles and expression is incomparably greater than that of most other concertos of the period, extending from the comic-opera elements of K. 467 to the Italianate lyricism of K. 488, the tragic character of K. 466 and 491, and the Beethovenian heroism of K. 503. Haydn's concertos, with the exception of the Piano Concerto in D, the Cello Concerto in D (once attributed to Anton Kraft), and the Trumpet Concerto, are generally early and, for him, conventional.

III. *19th century.* Beethoven's five piano concertos (ca. 1793–1809, plus an early work of 1784) by and large accept the premises of Mozart's great series while at the same time extending the range of expression, the time scale, and the degree of virtuosity. Mozart would doubtless have been surprised at the secondary themes in the flat submediant in R_1 of nos. 1–2, less so at the much-criticized modulation to the relative major at the same point in no. 3, because he himself had followed the same procedure in the first movement of K. 466. Likewise, the influential use of piano in the opening bars of nos. 4–5 had been forecast in Mozart's Salzburg concerto K. 271. The dramatic second movement of no. 4, however, which has been likened to Orpheus subduing the Furies or the wild beasts, has no real counterpart in the Mozart concertos. These and other expansions in the role of the soloist benefited from the availability to Beethoven of a more powerful six-octave piano, in contrast to Mozart's five-octave instrument. Beethoven's Violin Concerto (1806), influenced by Viotti, transfers the achievements of the mature Classical piano concerto to a work for the violin, a step Mozart never had occasion to take.

A predominantly conservative tradition of the concerto after Beethoven can be traced from Mendelssohn's two piano concertos (1831–37) and his important Violin Concerto (1844) to concertos by Schumann (piano, cello, violin, 1841–53), Brahms (two for piano, one for violin, one for violin and cello, 1854–87), Grieg (piano, 1868), Max Bruch (three for violin, 1868–91), and Dvořák (piano, violin, cello, 1876–95). In France this tradition is represented primarily by Camille Saint-Saëns (ten concertos for piano, violin, and cello, 1858–1902), in Russia by Anton Rubinstein, Tchaikovsky (three piano concertos, one for violin, 1874–93), and Rachmaninoff (four piano concertos, 1890–1926).

Probably influenced by Weber's *Konzertstück* of 1821, and before that by Beethoven's use of the piano at the beginning of the last two piano concertos, Mendelssohn initiated a formal type for the first movement of concertos in which the opening ritornello and first solo section are merged into one unrepeated exposition; presentation of the themes is now freely shared by soloist and orchestra. Development, recapitulation, and coda follow as in the usual Romantic versions of sonata form, material again being assigned to tutti and solo at the discretion of the composer (though vestiges of ritornello procedure are often apparent). This structure may be considered a final stage in the previously described assimilation of sonata-form elements within the first-movement form of the concerto. A majority of the concertos listed in the previous paragraph follow this pattern. As might be expected, however, Brahms (and Dvořák in the Cello Concerto) returned to the model of Beethoven, specifically that of the first movements of the Piano Concertos nos. 4–5. Finales may utilize the new design, as well, though rondo and sonata-rondo schemes are more common. The Mendelssohn Violin Concerto contains another influential trait—the formal connection of all three movements without pause. Brahms's Piano Concerto no. 2 should also be mentioned as a rare example of a four-movement concerto, a passionate scherzo being inserted after the first movement.

A more overtly virtuosic trend appears in the concertos of such brilliant 19th-century performers as the violinists Pierre Rode, Louis Spohr, Nicolò Paganini, Henry Vieuxtemps, and Henryk Wieniawski, the cellist Bernhard Romberg, and the pianists Ignaz Moscheles, Chopin (two concertos, 1829–30), Henry Litolff, and Liszt (two concertos, original versions 1839–49). Movement structure in many of these works is patterned on the by-now conventional ritornello-sonata type perfected by Mozart and Beethoven. Liszt's two concertos, however, are anything but conventional: the first connects the five movements or sections both formally and thematically, whereas the second utilizes a still freer sectional structure. The first concerto in particular shows the influence of such continuous composite forms as those of Weber's *Konzertstück* and Schubert's *Wanderer Fantasy.* The extraordinary virtuosity of all these concertos was facilitated by—and, of course, helped to spur—technical developments in the instruments themselves [see Piano, Violin].

IV. *20th century.* Numerous works of the 20th century basically continued the 19th-century concept of the concerto (and often its forms and styles), including concertos by Sibelius (violin, 1903), Elgar (violin, cello), Carl Nielsen (violin, flute, clarinet), Prokofiev (five for piano, 1911–32; two for violin, 1916–17 and 1935), Poulenc (harpsichord, two pianos, organ, piano), William Walton (viola, violin, cello), Shostakovich (two each for piano, violin, and cello), and Joaquin Rodrigo (ten, including four for one–four guitars). The virtuoso tradition mirrored in these concertos also manifests itself, though in radically different guise, in the concertos of Bartók—himself a piano virtuoso, as was Prokofiev. Bartók's first two piano concertos (1926–31), notable for their arch forms, and his Violin Concerto (1937–38) rank among the outstanding concertos of the century.

The Viennese atonalists also produced several prominent concertos: Alban Berg's Chamber Concerto for piano, violin, and 13 winds (1923–25), not yet fully serial but incorporating many elements of Schoenberg's new system; Anton Webern's Concerto for nine instruments (1931–34), originally intended as a piano concerto; Berg's important Violin Concerto (1935); and Schoenberg's Violin Concerto (1935–36) and Piano Concerto (1942).

The *neoclassical movement of the period after World War I produced a long series of works that returned to pre-Romantic conceptions of the concerto. Stravinsky's Concerto for Piano and Winds (1923–24) is in his familiar neoclassical idiom, but his subsequent concertos are more specifically neo-Baroque in character. The Violin Concerto (1931), for example, is made up of a Toccata, two Arias, and a Capriccio, and the soloist is treated more as a member of the ensemble than as a virtuoso protagonist. Likewise, his *Dumbarton Oaks* Concerto (1937–38) is in effect a concerto grosso, its instrumental treatment modeled on that of the *Brandenburg* Concertos. Other group concertos of this type are the two concerti grossi of Ernst Krenek (1921–24), the two concerti grossi of Ernest Bloch (1924–52), and the *Capricorn* Concerto of Samuel Barber (1944). The solo concertos of Paul Hindemith (eight for various instruments, 1939–62) are more traditional than the foregoing works in their treatment of the relationship between soloist and orchestra. Though hardly neoclassical in the usual sense, Richard Strauss's Horn Concerto no. 2 (1942, following his first concerto by some 60 years) and Oboe Concerto (1945) also reach back to an earlier era, finding nostalgic inspiration in the wind concertos of Mozart.

A tendency related to neoclassical rejection of Romantic and traditional features is the use of jazz elements in many 20th-century concertos, for example Aaron Copland's Piano Concerto (1926), Ravel's Concerto for the Left Hand and Piano Concerto in G (1929–31), and Stravinsky's *Ebony* Concerto for clarinet and jazz band (1945). George Gershwin's *Rhapsody in Blue* (1924) and Concerto in F for piano (1925) provided obvious sources of inspiration for such works.

A special class of 20th-century concerto is the "concerto for orchestra." These works are not for the most part ripieno concertos in the Baroque sense [see (2) I, 2, above] but rather display pieces in which the orchestra itself is the virtuoso—from soloists to sections to choirs to tutti. Examples of this genre, best known through Bartók's popular work of 1943, include compositions by Hindemith (1925), Walter Piston (1933), Zoltán Kodály (1939–40), Michael Tippett (1962–

63), and Elliott Carter (1969). In the latter piece, Carter dramatically personifies or characterizes the various solo groupings, a technique he also exploits in his Double Concerto for harpsichord and piano (1961), his Piano Concerto (1964–65), and his Oboe and Violin Concertos (1986–87, 1990). Other noteworthy contemporary concertos include Ligeti's five concertos for various instruments (1966–93), Penderecki's six concertos (two each for violin and cello, one for viola, one for piano, 1967–2002), Berio's Concerto for Two Pianos (1972–73) and Piano Concerto (1988), Sofia Gubaidulina's concertos for bassoon, jazz band, piano, and violin (1975–80), Peter Maxwell Davies's concertos for violin, trumpet, piccolo, and piano (1985–97), and Oliver Knussen's Violin Concerto (2002).

Bibl.: Hans Engel, *Die Entwicklung des deutschen Klavierkonzertes von Mozart bis Liszt* (Leipzig: Breitkopf & Härtel, 1927). Arnold Schering, *Geschichte des Instrumentalkonzerts bis auf die Gegenwart,* 2nd ed. (Leipzig: Breitkopf & Härtel, 1927). Isabella Amster, *Das Virtuosenkonzert in der ersten Hälfte des 19. Jahrhunderts* (Wolfenbüttel: G Kallmeyer, 1931). Theofil Stengel, *Die Entwicklung des Klavierkonzerts von Liszt bis zur Gegenwart* (Berlin: P Funk, 1931). Adam Adrio, *Die Anfänge des geistlichen Konzerts* (Berlin: Junker & Dünnhaupt, 1935). Donald Francis Tovey, *Essays in Musical Analysis,* 6 vols. (London: Oxford U Pr, 1935–39; new ed. in 2 vols., 1981), vol. 3, *Concertos* (1936). Manfred F. Bukofzer, *Music in the Baroque Era* (New York: Norton, 1947). David D. Boyden, "When Is a Concerto Not a Concerto?" *MQ* 43 (1957): 220–32. Edwin J. Simon, "The Double Exposition in the Classic Concerto," *JAMS* 10 (1957): 111–18. Arthur Hutchings, *The Baroque Concerto* (London: Faber, 1961; 3rd ed., 1973). Walter Kolneder, *Antonio Vivaldi* (Wiesbaden: Breitkopf & Härtel, 1965); trans. Bill Hopkins (Berkeley and Los Angeles: U of Cal Pr, 1970). Owen Jander, "Concerto grosso Instrumentation in Rome in the 1660's and 1670's," *JAMS* 21 (1968): 168–80. Claude V. Palisca, *Baroque Music* (Englewood Cliffs, N.J.: Prentice-Hall, 1968; 3rd ed., 1991). Charles Rosen, *The Classical Style* (New York: Viking Pr, 1971; 2nd ed., New York: Norton, 1997). Hans Engel, *Das Instrumentalkonzert,* 2 vols. (Wiesbaden: Breitkopf & Härtel, 1971–74). Paul Mies, *Das Konzert im 19. Jahrhundert: Studien zu Formen und Kadenzen* (Bonn: Bouvier Verlag H Grundmann, 1972). Jane R. Stevens, "Theme, Harmony, and Texture in Classic-Romantic Descriptions of Concerto First-Movement Form," *JAMS* 27 (1974): 25–60. John A. Meyer, "The Solo Piano Concerto in the Twentieth Century," *Miscellanea musicologica (Adelaide Studies in Musicology)* 7 (1975): 193–95. Pippa Drummond, *The German Concerto: Five Eighteenth-Century Studies* (Oxford: Oxford U Pr, 1980). Leonard G. Ratner, *Classic Music: Expression, Form, and Style* (New York: Schirmer Bks, 1980). Chappell White, "First-Movement Form in the Violin Concerto from Vivaldi to Viotti," *Kaufmann,* 1981, pp. 183–97. Scott L. Balthazar, "Intellectual History and Concepts of the Concerto: Some Parallels from 1750 to 1850," *JAMS* 36 (1983): 39–72. Eugene K. Wolf, ed., "The Ripieno Concerto," in Barry S. Brook et al., eds., *The Symphony, 1720–1840* (New York: Garland, 1979–86), ser. A, vol. 1, *Antecedents of the Symphony* (1983). Jehoash Hirshberg, ed., *Ten Italian Violin Concertos from Fonds Blancheton, RRMCE* 19 (1984). Daniel E. Freeman, "The Earliest Italian Keyboard Concertos," *JM* 4 (1985–86): 121–45. Robert Layton, ed., *A Companion to the Concerto* (New York: Schirmer, 1989). Chappell White, *From Vivaldi to Viotti: A History of the Early Classical Violin Concerto* (Philadelphia: Gordon & Breach, 1992). Ingo Gronefeld, *Die Flötenkonzerte bis 1850: ein thematisches Verzeichnis,* 4 vols. (Tutzing: Hans Schneider, 1992–95). Konrad Küster, *Das Konzert: Form und Forum der Virtuosität* (Kassell: Bärenreiter, 1993). Michael T. Roeder, *A History of the Concerto* (Portland, Ore.: Amadeus, 1994). William E. Caplin, *Classical Form: A Theory of Formal Functions for the Instrumental Music of Haydn, Mozart, and Beethoven* (New York: Oxford U Pr, 1998). Stephan D. Lindeman, *Structural Novelty and Tradition in the Early Romantic Piano Concerto* (Stuyvesant, N.Y.: Pendragon, 1999). Joseph Kerman, *Concerto Conversations* (Cambridge, Mass.: Harvard U Pr, 1999). E.K.W.

Concerto Fantastique. Ralph Shapey's *Concerto Fantastique* (1991) was a joint commission from the Chicago Symphony Orchestra and the University of Chicago celebrating their respective centennials. The Pulitzer Prize music jury unanimously selected it for the 1992 Pulitzer Prize in music. Controversially, the Pulitzer board overruled the decision and awarded the prize to the second-place selection.

Concerto for Orchestra. See Concerto (2) IV.

Concerto grosso [It., large concerto]. A concerto for a small group of soloists (the concertino) and orchestra (the tutti or ripieno); also the tutti ensemble itself. See Concerto (2) I, 1.

Concerto ripieno [It.]. See Concerto (2) I, 2.

Concert pitch. The pitch at which the piano and other nontransposing instruments play. See Transposing instruments, Pitch.

Concert spirituel [Fr., sacred concert]. A series of concerts founded in Paris by Anne Danican Philidor (1681–1728) in 1725 and extending to 1790. Their purpose was to provide concerts on religious holidays when opera was not performed. Their repertory included instrumental as well as sacred vocal music. The series was revived in 1805.

Concitato [It., agitated]. A style *(stile concitato)* defined by Monteverdi (see *SR,* pp. 413–15) and employed in his **Combattimento di Tancredi e Clorinda* (1624) and *Madrigali guerrieri ed amorosi* (1638) to express anger and warfare. By analogy with classical Greek poetic meters, it was based on a division of the whole note into 16 sixteenth notes repeated on single pitches.

Concord, discord. *Consonance, dissonance.

Concord Sonata. Charles Ives's second piano sonata, composed in 1910–15. Its complete title is "Concord, Mass., 1840–1860," and its four movements are titled, respectively, "Emerson," "Hawthorne," "The Alcotts," and "Thoreau." The last movement includes an optional part for flute.

Concrete music [Fr. *musique concrète*]. See Electroacoustic music I.

Conducting [Fr. *direction;* Ger. *Dirigieren* (v.), *Taktschlag;* It. *direzione, concertazione;* Sp. *dirigir* (v.)]. Leading and coordinating a group of singers and/or instrumentalists in a musical performance or rehearsal. Conducting includes indicating the meter and tempo; signaling changes in tempo and dynamics; cueing entrances; adjusting timbral balances; identifying the source(s) of performance errors and helping to resolve these; demanding clear articulation and enunciation; and, generally, bearing responsibility for the coherent interpretation of musical works. A conductor may also serve in an administrative role (often with the title music director) and in this capacity reviews and revises the membership of the orchestra or chorus, selects repertory and guest artists, and participates in fundraising and public-relations events.

The conductor's skills seen by audiences are chiefly time-beating and expressive gesture, for which many conductors (especially of instrumental ensembles) use a baton. In the past, different patterns have been used to beat time in different meters. Patterns in current use for both choral and instrumental conducting are shown in the accompanying figure. For earlier patterns see Kienle (1885), Schwartz (1907), Chybiński (1908/9 and 1912), and Schünemann (1908/9 and 1913). Conductors usually follow a score in performance as well as rehearsal, but some often conduct from memory except when accompanying a soloist. Richard Wagner was the first to risk this (London, 1855), and Hans von Bülow (1830–94) popularized it. Some of the most essential skills of the modern conductor are displayed in rehearsals, which, because of their expense, are often kept to a minimum, especially in the U.S., and must therefore be used extremely efficiently.

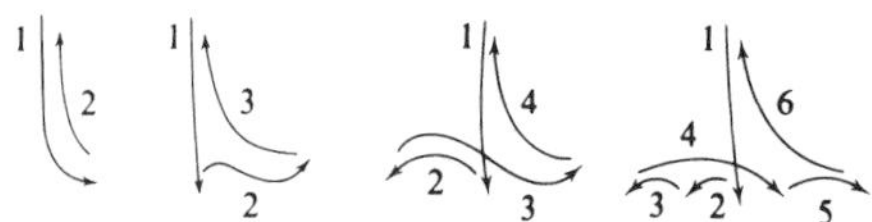

I. *Early history.* Evidence of conducting occurs on a Greek tablet dated 709 B.C.E.: "The Giver of Time beats with his stave up and down in equal movements so that all might keep together" (Murchard, 1825). Later, Marcus Fabius Quintilianus (*Institutio oratoria,* book 12, ca. 95 C.E.) writes that musical leaders "indicate intervals [of time] by stamping the feet, also [tapping] the toes." Pictorial evidence from as late as the 11th century shows that some instructors of liturgical chant reserved their right hands for *chironomy and grasped with their left hands a staff that was both a token of authority and an instrument of discipline (Kienle, 1885). Jerome of Moravia (before 1304) writes that "although all the singers [in a group] may be equally good, one of them is nevertheless appointed the conductor or director to whom the others most diligently pay attention" (*CS* 1:93).

After the 11th century, the widespread pedagogical use of the so-called *Guidonian hand, the development of notation, and the rise of musical literacy all helped to free conductors' hands for time-beating. Whether or not the beat should be kept visually or aurally became a practical matter connected with performing environment and ensemble size. Silent beat-keeping seems to have been preferred. Bartolomeo Ramos de Pareia (*Musica practica,* 1482) indicates that the choir director beats time with his foot, his hand, or his finger. Stephano Vanneo (*Recanetum de musica aurea,* 1533) says that one does not follow a percussive beat but rather a gesturing hand. Tomás de Santa María (*Arte de tañer fantasia,* 1565), on the other hand, emphasizes the use of the foot as a timekeeper. Two centuries later Rousseau (*Dictionnaire de musique,* 1768) still avers that intervals of time "are marked by equal motions of the hand or foot."

In 15th- and 16th-century choral polyphony, an important function of the conductor is the steady beating of the *tactus,* often with a roll of parchment or paper. At the beginning of the 17th century, changing notions of accent and meter as well as of the norms of musical rhetoric led many to abandon the steady and unvarying *tactus.* An argument between old and new practices of conducting came to a head in Rome in 1611. Agostino Pisa (*Battuta della musica,* 1611) argues for the old practice. The new school of thought is exemplified by Praetorius (*Syntagma musicum,* vol. 3, 1619): using a variety of gestures, the conductor signals the slowing down or speeding up of the *tactus* itself.

II. *Since 1600.* Baroque ensemble is founded on the structural interplay of two lines, the upper of which is subject to rules of melodic elaboration, the lower to rules of harmonic elaboration. It is characteristic of late-Baroque style that lower lines (but not necessarily upper) continuously articulate the beat (or some subdivision of it). Thus, the main instrument realizing the lower line (usually a keyboard instrument) is in solo groups the first among equals and in ensemble music the effective leader. C. P. E. Bach (*Versuch einer Anweisung die Flöte traversière zu spielen,* 1753) claims that "the tone of the keyboard, correctly placed [at the center of the instrumental ensemble], . . . can be heard by all" and that "performers located in front of or beside the keyboard will find the simultaneous motion of both hands an inescapable, visual portrayal of the beat."

Yet in 18th-century courts, the *maître de la musique* or *Kapellmeister* was often the concertmaster in performances. Writing of J. S. Bach, Johann Matthias Gesner (1738) makes clear that only the very greatest musicians were capable of playing continuo (the most complicated part in an ensemble) while at the same time guiding a typically underrehearsed group. A plate in Johann Jacob Walther's *Lexicon* (1732) shows a conductor leading an instrumental and vocal ensemble from a spot next to the organ continuo. Nevertheless, leadership from the keyboard continued to be a feature of some ensemble and opera performances throughout the 18th century. In Milan ca. 1770, the first three performances of an opera were customarily led by the composer from the *cembalo primo,* the remainder by the first violin. But in Turin ca. 1790, the opera was led by a *direttore dell'orchestra* who stood on a platform next to the leader of the first violins. Mozart sometimes conducted opera performances from the keyboard, as Haydn did his symphonies.

In Mannheim, beginning in 1745 or 1746, the composer, virtuoso, and concertmaster Johann Stamitz led the court orchestra in performances of unexcelled precision, using "nothing more than the nod of his head and the movement of his elbows," according to one observer, a result made possible by adequate rehearsal. Many of the Mannheim players imported their standards to the Parisian *Concert spirituel. In 19th-century Paris, that tradition was sustained by the Société des concerts du Conservatoire under the leadership (1828–49) of their concertmaster, François-Antoine Habeneck. Habeneck conducted from a first-violin part marked with added instrumental cues; until 1867, so did the leader of the Paris Opéra. But this should not be taken to mean that violin-bow conductors were any less attentive to the textural nuance than were contemporary baton conductors. It was Habeneck, for instance, who apparently began the practice (also recommended by Wagner, 1869, and others) of revising the scoring of Beethoven symphonies. As late as 1878, the cause of the violin-bow conductor was being pleaded in France by Deldevez.

The rise of the modern orchestral conductor can be attributed in part to increased attention to elements of timbre, texture, and dynamics in music. Beginning with the later works of Mozart and especially the works of Beethoven, the tendency in orchestral scores to fragment a single melodic line among two or more leading instruments (or an accompanimental figuration between different sections) demands levels of ensemble precision that were previously unknown.

The first well-known conductors were highly regarded composers: Weber, Spohr, Spontini, Mendelssohn, Berlioz, and Wagner. Carl Maria von Weber is sometimes credited with being the first (in 1817) to assume the role of the conductor in the modern sense. When in 1820 the visiting composer and violinist Louis Spohr took the leadership of the London Philharmonia into his own hands, it was the pianist's score that he appropriated. The keyboard player's billing was subsequently changed to Conductor (beginning 20 March 1820); yet it was only when Hippolyte Chélard led operas with a baton throughout the 1832/33 season that the Philharmonia installed its own podium conductor. And when in 1836 Mendelssohn assumed the direction of the Leipzig Gewandhaus Orchestra, its first violinist, Ferdinand David, complained volubly about the change from keyboard leadership to baton leadership. Berlioz's essay (1855) was the first to treat the conductor as a specialist in his own right. By 1880, conductors were accorded the same recognition as instrumental virtuosos.

Bibl.: Professor Murchard, "Discovery of Ancient Greek Tablets Relative to Music," *Harmonicon* 3 (1825): 56. Hector Berlioz, *Grand traité d'instrumentation et d'orchestration modernes . . . Nouvelle édition . . . suivie de l'art du chef d'orchestre* (Paris: Schonenberger, 1855); trans. Mary Cowden Clark, *A Treatise upon Modern Instrumentation and Orchestration [including] On the Whole Art of the Orchestral Conductor* (London: J A Novello, 1856). Richard Wagner, "Über das Dirigieren," *NZfM* 65 (1869): 405–8, 417–19, 425–27, 437–39, 445–47; 66 (1870): 4–8, 13–16, 25–27, 33–36; trans. Edward Dannreuther, *On Conducting,* 2nd ed. (London: W Reeves, 1897). E. M. E. Deldevez, *L'art du chef d'orchestre* (Paris: Firmin-Didot, 1878). P. Ambrosius Kienle, "Notizen über das Dirigiren mittelalterlicher Gesangschöre," *VfMw* 1 (1885): 158–69. Rudolf Schwartz, "Zur Geschichte des Taktschlagens," *JMP* 14 (1907): 59–70. Georg Schünemann, "Zur Frage des Taktschlagens und der Textbehandlung in der Mensuralmusik," *SIMG* 10 (1908–9): 73–114. Adolf Chybiński, "Zur Geschichte des Taktschlagens und des Kapellmeisteramtes in der Epoch der Mensuralmusik," *SIMG* 10 (1908–9): 385–95. Id., *Beitrage zur Geschichte des Taktschlagens* (Leipzig: Breitkopf & Härtel, 1912). Georg Schünemann, *Geschichte des Dirigierens* (Leipzig: Breitkopf & Härtel, 1913). Hermann Scherchen, *Handbook of Conducting,* trans. M. D. Calvocoressi (London: Oxford U Pr, H Milford, 1933). Archibald T. Davison, *Choral Conducting* (Cambridge, Mass.: Harvard U Pr, 1940). Imogen Holst, *Conducting a Choir: A Guide for Amateurs* (London: Oxford U Pr, 1973). Max Rudolf, *The Grammar of Conducting,* 2nd ed. (New York: Schirmer Bks, 1980; 3rd ed. 1993). Erich Leinsdorf, *The Composer's Advocate: A Radical Orthodoxy for Musicians* (New Haven: Yale U Pr, 1981). Donald Hunsberger and Roy Ernst, *The Art of Conducting* (New York: Knopf, 1983). Frederik Prausnitz, *Score and Podium: A Complete Guide to Conducting* (New York: Norton, 1983). Warren A. Bebbington, "The Orchestral Conducting Practice of Richard Wagner" (Ph.D. diss., CUNY, 1984). Hermann Dechant, *Dirigieren: Zur Theorie und Praxis der Musikinterpretation* (Vienna: Herder, 1985). Hans-Klaus Jungheinrich, *Der Musikdarsteller: Zur Kunst des Dirigenten* (Frankfurt: Fischer, 1986). D. Kern Holoman, "The Emergence of the Orchestral Conductor in Paris in the 1830s," in *Music in Paris in the Eighteen-Thirties* (Stuyvesant, N.Y.: Pendragon, 1987), pp. 374–430. Elliot W. Galkin, *A History of Orchestral Conducting: In Theory and Practice* (Stuyvesant, N.Y.: Pendragon, 1988). Jeannine Wagar, *Conductors in Conversation: Fifteen Contemporary Conductors Discuss Their Lives and Profession* (Boston: Hall, 1991); David Charlton, "A maitre d'orchestre . . . Conducts: New and Old Evidence on French Practice," *EM* 21 (1993): 340–53. Arthur Weisberg, *Performing Twentieth-Century Music: A Handbook for Conductors and Instrumentalists* (New Haven: Yale U Pr, 1993). Gunther Schuller, *The Compleat Conductor* (New York: Oxford U Pr, 1997).

Conductor. A person who, principally by means of gestures of the hands and arms, leads the performance of a musical ensemble. See Conducting.

Conductor's part. A condensed (as distinct from a full) *score, in which the entrances and principal parts of a composition are indicated, usually at actual pitch, on relatively few staves, for use by a conductor; also short score.

Conductus [pl. *conductus* or *conducti,* fr. Lat. *conducere,* to escort]. A medieval song for one or more voices with a serious, most often sacred, text in rhythmical Latin verse.

The term first appears in manuscripts of the mid-12th century (*E-Mn* 289, of Norman-Sicilian origin, and the so-called *Codex Calixtinus;* see Santiago de Compostela, repertory of), where it is written above a number of monophonic songs used as processional introductions to liturgical readings. Circumcision Offices compiled in the early 13th century for cities in the north of France identify as *conductus* songs that accompany a variety of liturgical and paraliturgical processions, and in the Beauvais Play of Daniel, the principal characters enter and retire to the accompaniment of similarly designated pieces.

The musical style of these songs is akin to that of one type of verse composition (**versus*) found in Aquitanian manuscripts dating from the end of the 11th century to the turn of the 13th. Textual declamation is simple, often strictly syllabic, and the melodies are highly repetitive. Other Aquitanian *versus* are enriched with long melismas; and eight of the freely composed songs, from a total of 100 or more, are for two voices. Sometimes the individual notes of the melody are sustained amid florid gestures in the added voice, and at other times the two parts move together in *discant.

There are no concordances between the Aquitanian repertory and that of Notre Dame of Paris (ca. 1150/60–ca. 1240), but the songs of the latter, although more numerous and generally larger-scaled, would seem to have their roots in the somewhat older, more southerly tradition.

Like the Aquitanian *versus,* the majority of Notre Dame *conductus* celebrate the great feasts of the church year; a goodly number, however, refer to contemporary events, and many decry the vices of simony and sloth, said to be rampant among clerics of every rank.

The nearly 200 multivoiced *conductus* from Paris are discant compositions. They differ from other types of Parisian polyphony in that the tenor or principal voice is almost always original rather than drawn from liturgical chant. The tenor is also usually similar in both melodic and rhythmic character to the other voice(s). Such pieces are notated in score with the tenor occupying the lowest position and underlaid with the text. Those for two and three voices are of two broad types, identified by the 13th-century English theorist Anonymous 4 as with and without melismas. Those without melismas are commonly, although by no means always, strophic, and the tenor is further subject to a certain amount of internal repetition, which may or may not extend to the added voice(s). The more elaborate pieces, nearly all of which are through-composed, vary in length and in the position of the melismas. They may be from ca. 35 to more than 300 measures long, and melismas occur regularly at the conclusion, often at the beginning or at interior verse endings, and at times in mid-verse. In contrast to the texted portions of these compositions, in which repetition plays a relatively small part, the melismas are full of repetition; some is literal, with or without *voice exchange, some is in the form of antecedent-consequent phrases differing only at the cadence, and some involves the use of two or three melodic-rhythmic cells, combined and recombined into larger structural units.

The *conductus* is included by 13th-century theorists among the categories governed by the rhythmic *modes, and the reading of the melismas, which are notated in ligature, is largely unproblematical. The breaking apart of the ligatures occasioned by the presence of text, on the other hand, results in some ambiguity. Many of the characteristically regular trochaic texts are declaimed in the first rhythmic mode, the long notes of which coincide with poetic stresses [Ex. 1]. The fifth-mode analogue of the foregoing declamatory rhythm is frequently encountered in melismatic compositions such as Perotin's *Salvatoris hodie.* Settings of irregular texts are more troublesome, inasmuch as consistent patterns congruent with those of the modes are wanting. Lines of six or eight syllables with iambic cadences may proceed in fifth-mode longs, with the substitution, at some point, of a duplex long for two ternary longs. The stresses are thus neu-

1

2

tralized, in effect, even as the integrity of the mode is maintained [Ex. 2]. Although there are some polyphonic *conductus* for which no satisfactory reading has been found, there is little reason to reject the testimony of the theorists as to the modal character of the repertory as a whole.

The situation is otherwise with the monophonic pieces, which are scarcely mentioned by the theorists. It is unclear whether this omission results from a preference for polyphony or indicates that the pieces were, in fact, not modal; but notational considerations suggest the greater probability of the latter.

By the middle of the 13th century, Parisian composers had lost interest in the *conductus*. A number of the older pieces lived on in manuscripts of the 14th century: the **Roman de Fauvel* (*F-Pn* 146); Las Huelgas (Burgos; *E-Hu*); and the **Carmina burana* (*D-Mbs Clm.* 4660). Continuing attention to the category in Germany and England in the 15th century produced little that was new and gradually died out.

Bibl.: Eduard Gröninger, *Repertoire-Untersuchungen zum mehrstimmigen Notre Dame–Conductus* (Regensburg: H Schiele, 1937). Jacques Handschin, "Zur Frage der Conductus-Rhythmik," *AM* 24 (1952): 1330. Heinrich Husmann, "Zur Grundlegung der musikalischen Rhythmik des mittellateinischen Liedes," *AfMw* 9 (1952): 3–26. Ruth Steiner, "Some Monophonic Songs of the Tenth Fascicle of the Manuscript Florence, Biblioteca Laurenziana, Pluteus 29.1" (Ph.D. diss., Catholic Univ. of America, 1963). Janet Knapp, ed., *Thirty-five Conductus for Two and Three Voices* (New Haven: Yale U Pr, 1965). Gordon Anderson, "Notre Dame and Related Conductus—A Catalogue Raisonné," *Miscellanea Musicologica—Adelaide Studies in Musicology* 6 (1972): 153–229; 7 (1975): 1–81. Id., "The Rhythm of *cum littera* Sections of Polyphonic Conductus in Mensural Sources," *JAMS* 26 (1973): 288–304. Id., ed., *Notre Dame and Related Conductus: Opera omnia* (Henryville, Pa.: Institute of Mediaeval Music, 1979–). Robert Falck, *The Notre Dame Conductus: A Study of the Repertory* (Henryville, Pa.: Institute of Mediaeval Music, 1981). Gordon A. Anderson, *Notre-Dame and Related Conductus,* vols. 1–6, 8–10 (Henryville, Pa.: Institute of Mediaeval Music, 1979–88); vol. 7 forthcoming. Ernest H. Sanders, "*Sine Littera* and *Cum Littera* in Medieval Polyphony," in *Music and Civilization: Essays in Honor of Paul Henry Lang,* ed. Edmond Strainchamps and Maria Rika Maniates, with Christopher Hatch (New York: Norton, 1984), pp. 215–31. Ernest H. Sanders, "Style and Technique in Datable Polyphonic Notre-Dame Conductus," *Gordon Athol Anderson In Memoriam,* 2 vols. (Henryville, Pa.: Institute of Mediaeval Music, 1984), 2: 505–30. Ernest H. Sanders, "Conductus and Modal Rhythm," *JAMS* 38 (1985): 439–69. Olga E. Malyshko, "The English Conductus Repertory: A Study of Style" (Ph.D. diss., New York Univ., 1989). Robert Falck, "Harmony in the Two-Part Notre Dame Conductus," in *Beyond the Moon: Festschrift Luther Dittmer,* ed. Bryan Gillingham and Paul Merkley (Ottawa: Institute of Mediaeval Music, 1990), pp. 75–99. Bryan Gillingham, "A New Entymology and Etiology for the Conductus," *MQ* 75 (1991): 59–73. Janet Knapp, "Which Came First, the Chicken or the Egg? Some Reflections on the Relationship between Conductus and Trope," in *Essays in Musicology: A Tribute to Alvin Johnson,* ed. Lewis Lockwood and Edward Roesner (Philadelphia: American Musicological Society, 1990), pp. 16–25. Thomas B. Payne, "Poetry, Politics, and Polyphony: Philip the Chancellor's Contribution to the Music of the Notre Dame School," 5 vols. (Ph.D. diss., Univ. of Chicago, 1991). Ernest H. Sanders, *"Rithmus,"* in *Essays on Medieval Music in Honor of David G. Hughes,* ed. Graeme M. Boone (Cambridge, Mass.: Harvard Univ. Dept. of Music, 1995), pp. 415–40. Christopher Page, *"Latin Poetry and Conductus Rhythm in Medieval France,"* RMA Monographs 8 (London: Royal Musical Association, 1997). Joseph Szövérffy, *Lateinische Conductus-Texte des Mittelalters (Medieval Latin Conductus Texts),* Musicological Studies 74 (Ottawa: Institute of Mediaeval Music, 2000). Hans Tischler, *Conductus and Contrafacta,* Musicological Studies 75 (Ottawa: Institute of Mediaeval Music, 2001). Thomas B. Payne, "Datable 'Notre Dame' Conductus: New Historical Observations on Style and Technique," *CM* 64 (2001): 104–51.

J.K.

Confinalis [Lat.]. The pitch lying a fifth above the final of a *mode. See also *Affinales.*

Conflicting signatures, partial signatures. In early music, "key" signatures with differing numbers of flats in the several voices of a polyphonic composition. As a rule, upper voices carry fewer flats than do lower voices. Common patterns include the following (top voice listed first; "-" indicates the absence of a flat): -♭; --♭, -♭♭, ♭♭♭♭♭; --♭♭. Such signatures occur as early as the 13th century and as late as the 16th century, but are most common in music of the 15th century.

Early theorists seldom mention them. Modern writers have variously explained them as expressions of a sort of bitonality (Apel, 1938) or bimodality (Hoppin, 1953, 1956), or practical reflections of cadence structures (Lowinsky, 1954). More recently, Margaret Bent has advanced the view that flat signatures indicate the transposition of the entire system of *musica recta* [see Hexachord, *Musica ficta*] and that a piece with conflicting signatures thus has voices lying in different *recta* realms.

Bibl.: Willi Apel, "The Partial Signatures in the Sources up to 1450," *AM* 10 (1938): 1–13, 11 (1939): 40–42. Richard H. Hoppin, "Partial Signatures and Musica Ficta in Some Early 15th-Century Sources," *JAMS* 6 (1953): 197–215. Edward E. Lowinsky, "Conflicting Views on Conflicting Signatures," *JAMS* 7 (1954): 181–204. Richard H. Hoppin, "Conflicting Signatures Reviewed," *JAMS* 9 (1956): 97–117. Margaret Bent, "Musica Recta and Musica Ficta," *MD* 26 (1972): 73–100.

B.J.H.

Confractorium [Lat.]. In the *Ambrosian, *Gallican, and *Mozarabic liturgies, the item of the Proper of the *Mass associated with the breaking of the communion bread and corresponding to the Gregorian *communion.

Conga [Sp.]. (1) An Afro-Cuban dance-music genre and an essential element in the performances of *comparsas*—groups of masqueraders that dance during the celebration of Carnival in Latin American countries. In the 1930s, it became popular as a ballroom dance in North America and Europe. The characteristic dance consists of three short steps and a forward leap, coordinated with the following continuously repeated rhythmic figure:

(2) A long, single-headed, Afro-Cuban drum played with bare hands. The head is generally larger than the open end, and the shell may bulge slightly below the head. See ill. under Percussion instruments. Some congas are tunable and may be used in a set containing drums of various sizes and pitches. Congas are essential in the urban popular music of Latin America and its derivatives. (1) D.S.

Congada [Port.]. A dramatic dance *(bailado)* widely known in Brazil. One of several *bailados* that dramatize the theme of conversion through portrayals drawn from the Iberian conflicts between Christians and Moors, the *congada* also incorporates characters and events deriving from Afro-Brazilian traditional lore. Many *bailados* found with the *congada* are performed in two major sections, with an opening procession (*cortejo,* cortege) followed by the dramatic action itself (*embaixada,* embassy), which is made up of a series of episodes *(jornadas).* In the *congada,* marches and songs, often in responsorial form, are performed with ensembles consisting of, e.g., *violas* (ten-string guitars), *rabeca* (fiddle), and various percussion instruments. D.S.

Congo [Sp., Port.]. **Congada.*

Congress report. A published collection of papers read at a congress or conference. Congresses are usually sponsored by *societies, some of which have published reports regularly. A few societies publish reports in their journals (e.g., *FAM, College Music Symposium*). Independent congresses normally deal with a special topic, such as Beethoven in the centennial year 1927 or Dufay in 1974, the 500th anniversary of his death. Congress reports are variously indexed in John Tyrrell and Rosemary Wise, *A Guide to International Congress Reports in Musicology 1900–1975* (New York: Garland, 1979). An earlier index, which includes titles of papers read at the congresses but not published in the reports, is Marie Briquet, *La musique dans les congrès internationaux (1835–1939)* (Paris: Société française de musicologie, 1961). Recent reports are indexed in *RILM.* H.E.S.

Conjunct, disjunct. Types of melodic *motion. Conjunct motion proceeds by step from one scale degree to the next (i.e., by the *interval of a second), and disjunct motion proceeds by leap (i.e., by intervals larger than a second). *Tetrachords in the music of ancient *Greece and the Middle Ages are conjunct if the last pitch of one is the first pitch of the other, and otherwise disjunct.

Conjuncta [Lat.]. See *Musica ficta.*

Conjunctura [Lat.]. In square *notation of the Middle Ages, a symbol derived from the neume called a *climacus* [see ill. under Neume] and consisting of a square note with a descending tail on the right followed by two or more diamond-shaped notes *(currentes)* descending scalewise.

Consecration of the House. See *Weihe des Hauses, Die.*

Consecutives. See Parallel fifths, octaves; Counterpoint.

Consequent. See Antecedent, consequent.

Conservatory [Fr. *conservatoire;* Ger. *Konservatorium* or *Hochschule für Musik;* It., Sp. *conservatorio*]. A school for the practical and theoretical training of musicians of all types and grades. Pupils can receive training in composition, individual instruments, voice, conducting, music education, and church music. Sight singing is normally an important part of a curriculum, and various courses in music history and theory and in nonmusical subjects are made available. Special classes and training are offered to children. Most conservatories are in cities that have an orchestra or opera house, whose members are employed to teach. In Europe, conservatories are supported and controlled by the government. They award diplomas or certificates; degree programs are offered only by universities, which give no training in applied music. In the U.S., conservatories are private and must compete with public and private universities, whose schools and departments of music combine professional and academic education; some university schools of music offer programs similar in every way to those of conservatories. U.S. conservatories award baccalaureate and master's degrees; a few award the Doctor of Musical Arts.

Conservatories originated in the 16th century in Italy, where the term (from the Latin *conservare,* to keep or preserve) designated an orphanage. The orphans received special training in music, for they could be employed in church choirs and later in opera. Thus music schools developed within the "conservatories." One such institution was the Conservatorio Santa Maria di Loreto, founded in 1537 in Naples. Numerous 17th- and 18th-century Italian composers were associated with conservatories, either as students or teachers, most notably Vivaldi, who was employed from 1703 on by the Pio Ospedale della Pietà, a Venetian orphanage for girls. Most Italian conservatories closed late in the 18th century, but the idea for music schools had spread to other countries. In France, the government, rather than the church, established the Conservatoire national de musique et de déclamation in Paris in 1795. Other nations followed this example of a state conservatory or a network of them. Among the early conservatories still in existence are the conservatory in Prague (1811), the Hochschule für Musik und darstellende Kunst in Vienna (1817), the Royal Academy of Music in London (1822), the Conservatoire Royal de Musique in Brussels (1832), and the Hochschule für Musik in Leipzig, which was founded by Mendelssohn in 1843 and attracted students from all over the world.

For information (names, addresses, dates of foundation, numbers of students and teachers, and names of directors), see the current edition of *The World of Learning.* For U.S. conservatories, see also the College Music Society's current *Directory of Music Faculties.*

Bibl.: Allen Sigel, "A Report on Six European Conservatories," *CMS* 8 (1968): 27–41. Karol Musiol, ed., "Bibliothèques des conservatoires, académies et écoles de musique," *FAM* 22 (1975): 97–154. Craig R. Short, ed., *Directory of Music Faculties in Colleges and Universities, U.S. and Canada* (Binghamton, N.Y.: College Mus Soc, 1972–[biennial]). *The World of Learning* (London: Allen & Unwin, 1947–[annual]). *International Directory of Music and Music Education Institutions,* comp. and ed. Graham A. R. Bell (Nedlands, W. Australia: Callaway International Centre for Music Education, 1996–). H.E.S.

Console. (1) In organs, the key desk, containing one or more manual keyboards, pedalboard, and the knobs controlling all of the stops. (2) A small upright *piano.

Consonance and dissonance. A means of classifying the interval between two simultaneous notes. Very generally, consonant intervals are regarded as primary and stable, whereas dissonant intervals are regarded as secondary and unstable. Theorists use this distinction to explain the sense of motion that occurs within pieces of music. When discussing consonance and dissonance they typically address three main issues: (1) deciding which intervals count as consonant and which as dissonant; (2) discriminating between the behavior of consonances and dissonances; and (3) establishing plausible criteria for distinguishing one type of interval from the other. Responses to these issues have changed significantly over time.

The words consonance and dissonance are, in fact, translations of the ancient Greek terms *symphonia and *diaphonia. Writing in the 5th century B.C.E., Pythagoras borrowed the Babylonian system of classifying intervals, in which the octave, fifth, octave-plus-fifth, fourth, and the double octave were regarded as consonant and all other intervals as dissonant. With a few refinements by Aristoxenus and Ptolemy, this system of classification was transmitted to the Middle Ages via Boethius's *De institutione musica* (ca. 500 C.E.). As musical styles changed, theorists were forced to modify this scheme. In the mid-13th century, John of Garland, Franco of Cologne, and others reclassified major and minor thirds as consonant, and in the mid-14th century their successors reclassified major and minor sixths as consonant and fourths as dissonant. By 1400, theorists generally classified consonances into two types: perfect consonances (unisons, octaves, fifths, and their compounds) and imperfect consonances (thirds, sixths, and their compounds). Seconds, fourths, sevenths, augmented/diminished intervals, and their compounds were classified as dissonant.

Although theorists were able to classify every interval as either consonant or dissonant in two-voice textures, they were unable to do so in textures with three or more voices. By insisting that polyphonic lines should primarily be consonant with the bass, they acknowledged that perfect and augmented fourths could sometimes be classified as consonant and sometimes as dissonant; in particular, they behave as consonances when they appear between upper voices and as dissonances when they appear above the bass. Seen in triadic terms, this meant that major and minor triads in root position and major, minor, and diminished triads in first inversion are consonant, whereas diminished triads in root position and major, minor, and diminished triads in second inversion are dissonant.

The development of functional tonality in the 17th and 18th centuries prompted further changes in the ways theorists classified intervals. Using the notion of triadic inversion, Rameau and others challenged contrapuntal theory by treating second-inversion triads not as dissonances but as essential harmonies. Debates also arose about whether diminished triads—e.g., viio in major keys and iio in minor keys—could be regarded as essential harmonies and hence whether they behave as consonances. This idea often intersected with Rameau's claim that seventh chords could serve as essential harmonies. Although Rameau's views reflected the growing freedom with which dominant seventh harmonies were treated in tonal contexts, they have not been universally accepted; Schenker and others have rejected the claim that tonal dissonances are ever generated harmonically, and they have also dismissed the notion that second-inversion chords can serve as essential harmonies. The question of whether to treat tonal dissonances as harmonic or contrapuntal phenomena continues to this day.

As the 19th century progressed, tonal practice developed considerably; not only did functional triads appear less and less frequently, but also other sonorities became more and more important to the texture. The *locus classicus* of such trends is the Prelude to Wagner's *Tristan und Isolde;* although this piece seems to establish the key of A minor, the single most prominent chord is the so-called Tristan Chord [see Ex. 1a]. Other examples of referential sonorities include the "Prometheus chord," from Scriabin's *Prometheus: The Poem of Fire* [Ex. 1b], and the "Petrushka chord," from Stravinsky's *Petrushka* [Ex. 1c]. The possibility of treating referential sonorities as essential harmonies prompted Schoenberg to reject any absolute distinction between consonance and dissonance and to call for "the emancipation of the dissonance" (*Harmonielehre,* 1911). Schoenberg's claim has been an important rallying cry for many 20th-century composers.

Just as theorists have changed the ways in which they have classified intervals as consonant or disso-

1

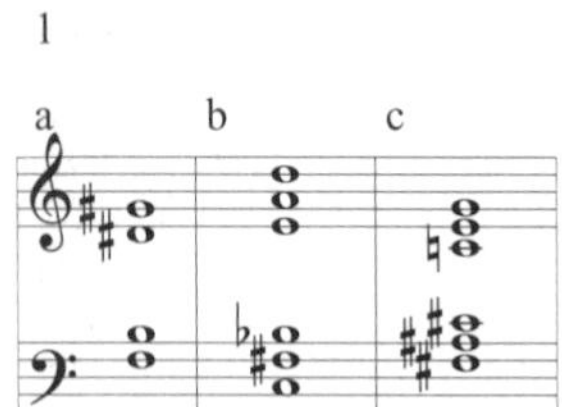

nant, so they have also modified their views about the ways in which consonant and dissonant intervals behave in musical contexts. During the Middle Ages, theorists generally believed that polyphonic textures were primarily consonant in nature and that imperfect consonances played a subordinate role to perfect consonances. They recognized that phrases begin and end on perfect consonances, and that the final perfect consonance is approached by step in contrary motion from the nearest imperfect consonance. They also claimed that, whereas perfect unisons, octaves, and fifths can never appear in parallel succession, imperfect consonances can form parallel strings.

Although 15th- and 16th-century theorists largely endorsed such views, they focused increasing attention on the behavior of dissonances. They found that dissonances arise from motion between consonances. Some dissonances, which Fux later referred to as nonessential dissonances, fill out the space between two consonant tones. For example, dissonant passing tones fill the space between two different consonances a third apart [see Ex. 2a], whereas dissonant neighbor tones fill the space between repetitions of the same consonant note [Ex. 2b]. Meanwhile, Fux's essential dissonances displace notes that are already an essential part of the musical fabric. For example, the 7–6 suspension in Ex. 2c arises from displacing the upper voice in a pair of parallel sixths in Ex. 2d. Since the dissonant note originally appears as a consonance, it is said to be prepared. It should be noted that dissonances seldom appear in direct succession; they tend to be surrounded by consonances. Besides passing tones, neighbor tones, and suspensions, other important dissonances of the period include the *nota cambiata* and the anticipation [see Counterpoint].

2

The shift toward functional tonality in the 17th century also brought with it significant changes in dissonance treatment. These changes prompted important theoretical debates, such as the famous exchange between Artusi and Monteverdi, as well as the recognition of two distinct compositional practices, *prima prattica* and *seconda prattica.* Of the many new types of dissonance, perhaps the most interesting are the appoggiatura and the changing note [see Counterpoint]. In tonal contexts, dissonances often appear in direct succession, though they again move between consonances. Having said this, Rameau's decision to classify seventh chords as essential harmonies suggests that, in tonal contexts, dissonances need not always be contrapuntal in origin; he proposed that they can be created simply by stacking thirds on top of triads. Although Schenker later dismissed this idea, even he accepted that, under special circumstances, dissonant sonorities can be composed out, a property that only consonances enjoy in his system.

The distinction between consonance and dissonance has changed considerably over time; different cultures and different periods treat different intervals as consonant and dissonant, and these intervals behave in various ways, depending on context. These observations are important because they also influence the various ways in which music theorists have sought to defend their classification of intervals. At least since classical antiquity, music theorists have found different ways to explain the differences between consonance and dissonance. Some have appealed to the acoustic properties of particular sounds. Pythagoras, for example, insisted that octaves, fifths, and fourths were consonant because they could be produced by dividing strings into simple arithmetic ratios: the octave (2:1), the fifth (3:2), the octave-plus-fifth (3:1), the fourth (4:3), and the double octave (4:1). Since the early 18th century, however, many theorists have turned their attention to the properties of the overtone series; Rameau, Schoenberg, and Schenker immediately spring to mind. Instead of providing acoustic explanations for consonance and dissonance, many theorists have appealed to how these sounds are perceived by listeners. Aristoxenus, for example, rejected Pythagoras's appeals to number and insisted that consonant intervals sound stable, whereas dissonant intervals sound unstable. As the discipline of music psychology has developed, theorists from Helmholtz to Meyer, Lerdahl, and Jackendoff have maintained that our theoretical concepts and analytical methods should reflect the ways in which human beings actually listen to and think about music. However, the fact that the distinction between consonance and dissonance has changed so much suggests that it will never be explained in any absolute acoustic terms.

M.B.

Consort [perhaps fr. Fr. *concert* and It. *concerto,* or fr. Lat. *consortio,* fellowship]. In 16th- and 17th-century England, an instrumental ensemble, usually of two to eight players, or a composition for such an ensemble. In the late 17th century, the term consort gave way to such foreign terms as concert, concerto, and sonata, as a preference for imported music and terminology took hold.

English consorts were principally of two types. One type combined instruments of only one family, such as viols, violins, recorders, shawms, or sackbuts; for example, a usual consort of six viols included two treble, two tenor, and two bass viols. The other type mixed families; a standard six-part mixed consort included recorder, treble viol, bass viol, lute, cittern, and bandora—for which Morley (1599) and Rossiter (1609) published sets of *lessons (i.e., pieces for performance). In the late 17th century, and even more in modern times, these two types have come to be called whole and broken consorts, respectively.

Broken consorts regularly provided music for plays, masques, banquets, and outdoor entertainments. English superiority in such music gained international recognition. Whole consort music was introduced in the late 1520s by an Italian ensemble at the court of Henry VIII. Quickly becoming popular, the genre flourished in the hands of Tye, Tallis, Parsons, White, and Byrd, perhaps providing a new outlet for choral composers after the church's abolition of vocal polyphony.

By the late 16th century, viol consort playing was a major form of domestic musical recreation and education, as many households possessed a *chest of viols. Music for such use, including fancies (fantasies), **In nomine*s, dance sets, grounds, variations on popular tunes, and, in the Stuart era, masque ayres, was written by Alfonso Ferrabosco the younger, Coprario, Gibbons, Jenkins, William Lawes, Purcell, and many others.

Consort songs were usually for treble solo or duet, with viol accompaniment. Perhaps first written for mid-16th-century "children's plays" performed by Chapel Royal choirboys, they remained popular for a century. A consort song with sacred text was called a consort anthem, often with organ substituted for viols. An expanded form, the verse *anthem, alternated full choir and solo voice or voices, accompanied throughout by viols or organ. Byrd and Gibbons developed these forms most notably. Published consort songs frequently bore the notice "apt for viols and voices," indicating a considerable freedom to substitute one for the other.

Bibl.: Thomas Mace, *Musick's Monument* (London, 1676; facs. Paris: CNRS, 1958; facs., *MMML* ser. 2, 17, 1966). John Wilson, ed., *Roger North on Music* (London: Novello, 1959). Phillip Brett, "The English Consort Song, 1570–1625," *PRMA* 88 (1961–62): 73–88. Ernest H. Meyer, "Concerted Instrumental Music," *NOHM* 4:550–601. Warwick Edwards, "The Performance of Ensemble Music in Elizabethan England," *PRMA* 97 (1970–71): 113–23. Craig Monson, *Voices and Viols in England, 1600–1650: The Sources and the Music* (Ann Arbor: UMI Res Pr, 1982).

Consul, The. Opera in three acts by Gian Carlo Menotti (libretto by the composer), produced in Philadelphia in 1950. Setting: a police state in the 20th century.

Contemporary music. See Twentieth century, Western art music of the.

Contes d'Hoffmann, Les [Fr., The Tales of Hoffmann]. An "opéra fantastique" in three acts with prologue and epilogue by Jacques Offenbach (libretto by Jules Barbier and Michel Carré, on three stories by E. T. A. Hoffmann), completed after the composer's death in 1880 by Ernest Guiraud, and first produced in Paris in 1881. Setting: Germany and Italy in the 19th century.

Continuo [It., abbr. for *basso continuo*]. *Thoroughbass.

Contra [Lat., It.]. (1) Against, counter to, as in compounds such as *contratenor (sometimes referred to simply as the contra), *contrapunctus* or *contrappunto* (*counterpoint), *contralto, and, in French, **haute-contre.* (2) With respect to pitch, lower octave. Thus, the contra-octave is the octave below the great octave [see Pitch names]. The names of instruments formed with this prefix are normally the lowest members of their families (though there are a few subcontrabass instruments).

Contrabass. (1) The lowest pitched member of some families of instruments, such as the *clarinet, often with a range extending down to around C_1 (three octaves below middle C). See also Contra. (2) *Double bass.

Contrabassoon. See Bassoon.

Contrabbasso [It.]. *Double bass.

Contradanza [It.]. **Contredanse.*

Contrafactum [Lat.]. A vocal work in which a new text has been substituted for the original one. The substitution of new texts in preexisting works was common through the 16th century, was restricted to fewer genres in the 17th and 18th centuries, and, in art music, largely disappeared in the 19th century.

From the Middle Ages, there are numerous examples of liturgical chant in which various texts have been set to what appears to be a single melody. In some categories, such as antiphons and alleluias, however, it is not always possible to identify the specific antecedent for any given example. The family resemblances in such cases may result from the mechanisms of *transmission from an oral to a written tradition. On the other hand, feasts introduced at a relatively late date [see Liturgy] often clearly adapt old melodies for new texts related to the feast. Specific connections are also somewhat easier to trace among hymns and sequences.

Other medieval repertories including *contrafacta* (sometimes identified as to antecedent) are those of the *troubadours, *trouvères, and *Minnesinger (including works on French models, on the basis of which some scholars have made conjectures about the rhythm of *Minnesang*), and the *motet. In the 16th century, the principal types of examples entail the adaptation of secular works to sacred texts and the adaptation of works from one religious tradition into another. Genres include the Italian **lauda*, the French **chanson spirituelle*, the German *chorale, and tunes for the *Psalter in various languages.

With respect to the 17th and 18th centuries, the term *parody is more often employed. The operas of Lully were sometimes provided with new text with humorous intent, and the use of new texts for old music was a common feature of **opéra comique* and *ballad opera [see also Timbre (2)]. Bach, among others, sometimes reused his own music for new texts (e.g., in the **B-minor Mass*).

Bibl.: Friedrich Gennrich, *Die Kontrafaktur im Liedschaffen des Mittelalters* (Langen, 1965). Walther Lipphardt, "Zur geistlichen Kontrafactur," *Wiora*, 1967, pp. 284–95. See also Parody.

Contrafagotto [It.]. Contrabassoon. See Bassoon.

Contralto [fr. Lat. **contratenor altus*]. (1) The lowest female voice, as distinct from the soprano and mezzo-soprano [see Voice], also called an alto. Through the 18th century, the term could refer to male altos (including **castrati*) as well as to females. (2) A large viola (67.5 cm in length), but with the range of the normal viola, designed by Jean-Baptiste Vuillaume in about 1855.

Contra-octave. The octave below the great octave and thus the third octave below middle C (C_1 to B_1). See Pitch names.

Contrappunto [It.]. *Counterpoint.

Contrapunctus [Lat.]. (1) *Counterpoint. (2) A contrapuntal composition, especially one employing *imitation.

Contrapuntal. (1) Of or pertaining to *counterpoint. (2) With respect to musical *texture, exhibiting counterpoint, i.e., a degree of independence among the lines or parts making up the texture; in this sense roughly synonymous with *polyphonic, as distinct from *homophonic.

Contrary motion. See Motion, Counterpoint.

Contratenor [Lat.]. In music of the 14th and 15th centuries, a part written "against" the tenor part. The contratenor part occupies approximately the same range as and frequently crosses the tenor; it forms the third part, in addition to the discant or *cantus* or *superius* (the highest-sounding part) and tenor parts, of the typical three-part texture. The contratenor part is often more disjunct than the tenor and may give the impression of being supplementary to the structural pair formed by discant and tenor. With the emergence of four-part texture in the later 15th century, the functions of the contratenor were divided between two parts: the *contratenor altus* or simply *altus* (whence the term *alto), lying between the *superius* and the tenor, and the *contratenor bassus* or simply *bassus* (whence the term *bass), lying below the tenor.

Contra-violin. A large-sized violin introduced in 1917 by Henry Newbold to play the second-violin parts in chamber music.

Contraviolon [Ger.]. A large *violone; also called *grosse Bassgeige, Bassviolon,* [Fr.] *grande basse de violon,* and [It.] *violone grosso.* It was comparable in function, and sometimes identical in tuning, to the *double bass.

Contrebasse [Fr.]. *Double bass; *c. à pistons,* *tuba.

Contrebasson [Fr.]. Contrabassoon. See Bassoon.

Contredanse [Fr.; Ger. *Kontertanz, Contratanz;* It. *contraddanza;* Sp. *contradanza*]. A fast dance movement in duple meter (usually simple, but sometimes compound), constructed of a series of repeated eight-measure strains that maintain the simple motivic and textural qualities of dance music. English *country dances enjoyed a great vogue at the court of Louis XIV, where the name and style were Gallicized before being disseminated across Europe. They were used in French operas from André Campra to Jean-Philippe Rameau, and borrowed elements from other duple dances (e.g., *gavotte, *rigaudon). They spawned the *quadrille and reached their height of bourgeois popularity in the late 18th century, not disappearing until the second third of the 19th century. Mozart wrote many for various ensembles, and Beethoven published a set of 12 in 1802 (WoO 14). B.G.

Convertible counterpoint. See Invertible counterpoint.

Cool jazz. A subdued adaptation of *Bebop. Players deemphasized the extremes of bebop in favor of medium volume, gentle tone colors, legato phrasing, dense harmonies, moderate tempos, and use of the middle registers of instruments. Emerging in the Miles Davis nonet's "Birth of the Cool" recordings (1949–50) and also associated in New York with teacher-pianist Lennie Tristano, the label became for some synonymous with *West Coast jazz in the 1950s.

B.K., rev. T.A.J.

Coon song. A racist song in "Negro" dialect. Songs of this type were present in 18th-century English comic operas. An integral part of American *minstrel music of the second half of the 19th century, coon songs flourished in the period 1883–1912 in the new, animated, verse-and-chorus style of *Tin Pan Alley. From the 1890s, they were identified with *ragtime because of ragtime arrangements of hit tunes, demeaning caricatures shared on sheet-music covers, and the inclusion in piano rags of derogatory verses.

B.K.

Coperto [It., pl. *coperti*]. Covered; in music for kettledrum, muted by the placing of a cloth on the head.

Copla [Sp.]. (1) Any of several Spanish verse types, including as many as 12 lines with varying rhyme schemes, in use from the 14th century. (2) A four-line octosyllabic strophe rhymed abcb, as found in the **romance;* poetry of similar construction used in popular song. (3) A part of the **villancico.*

Coppélia. A ballet in three acts with music by Léo Delibes, choreography by Arthur Saint-Léon, and book by Saint-Léon and Charles Nuitter after a story by E. T. A. Hoffmann, first produced in Paris in 1870. Later versions have included choreography by Lev Ivanov, Enrico Cecchetti, and Nicholas Sergeyev.

Coptic chant. The chant of the ancient Egyptian Christian liturgy, still used in the Coptic Orthodox church. It combines originally Greek traditions from Alexandria with Coptic-dialect material from the desert monasteries. The earliest sources, not well cataloged, include fragmentary texts written on papyrus, broken pottery, and pieces of wood. A few MSS contain rudimentary *ecphonetic notations, but the tradition was always essentially oral. Responsorial psalms are given in the lectionary (*PO* 24, 2–25, 2). Four biblical odes and the Marian *theotokia* form the nucleus of the *psalmodia,* the main chant book. A more developed form for the month of Khoiak (Advent) is full of Marian hymns. The later *difnar* contains hymns for the calendar of saints. The two "modes" *Adam* and *Watos* take their names from the Monday and Thursday *theotokia,* but there are other melody types as well. The chant is strongly rhythmic and is accompanied by triangles and small cymbals.

Bibl.: Hanna Malak, "Les Livres liturgiques de l'église copte," *Mélanges Eugène Tisserant* 3: *Orient chrétien* 2, Studi e Testi 233 (Vatican City: Biblioteca Apostolica Vaticana, 1964), pp. 1–35. Maria Cramer, *Koptische Hymnologie in deutscher Übersetzung: eine Auswahl aus saidischen und bohairischen Antiphonarien vom 9. Jahrhundert bis zur Gegenwart* (Wiesbaden: Harrassowitz, 1969). Oswald H. E. Khs-Burmester and Lothar Störk, *Koptische Handschriften,* 3 vols., Verzeichnis der orientalischen Handschriften in Deutschland 21 (Wiesbaden: F. Steiner, 1975–96). Robert McLachlan Wilson, *The Future of Coptic Studies* (Leiden: Brill, 1978), pp. 164–96, 227–45. Jørgen Raasted, "Musical Notation and Quasi Notation in Syro-Melkite Liturgical Manuscripts," *Cahiers de l'Institut du moyen-âge grec et latin de l'Université de Copenhague* 31 (1979): 11–37, 53–77. Ragheb Moftah et al., "Music," in *The Coptic Encyclopedia,* ed. Aziz S. Atiya (New York: Macmillan, 1991), 6: 1715–47. The International Association for Coptic Studies, *Acts of the Fifth International Congress of Coptic Studies, Washington, 12–15 August 1992* (Rome: Centro Italian Microfiches, 1993), vol. 1: *Reports on Recent Research,* ed. Tito Orlandi, pp. 9–49, 209–19; vol. 2, no. 2, *Papers from the Sections,* ed. David W. Johnson, pp. 355–67.

P.J.

Copula. (1) [Lat., also *copulatio*] A grammatical term first used by 12th-century writers on music to describe the joining of two voices in a cadential accord (see Eggebrecht and Zaminer, 1970). In the 13th century, Johannes de Garlandia used the word for a kind of polyphony between *organum and *discant, distinguished from the former by the modal [see Modes, rhythmic] organization of the second voice *(duplum).* Johannes's *copula* is further characterized by a plurality of similar phrases, restricted to small intervals and marked off by rests. Later authors, among them the St. Emmeram (Sowa) Anonymous and Franco of Cologne, understood the rhythm of the second voice to be irregular. According to the former, *copula* has the appearance of the first mode *(sub specie primi modi),* but it is more subtle than the discant. Franco identifies two kinds of *copula:* bound, i.e., written in ligature, and unbound. In both cases, the notes are sung more rapidly than is normal. The term *copula* is occasionally used in the 13th century to mean ligature.

(2) A stopped 8′ organ register, found from the late 17th century on in Austria and other European countries. The term is sometimes used in modern organ stop lists, often to denote a 4′ Koppelflöte. See also Coupler, *Koppel.*

Bibl.: (1) Hans H. Eggebrecht and Frieder Zaminer, *Ad organum faciendum* (Mainz: B Schott, 1970). Fritz Reckow, *Die Copula* (Wiesbaden: Steiner, 1972). Jeremy Yudkin, "The *Copula* according to Johannes de Garlandia," *MD* 34 (1980): 67–84. Id., "The Anonymous of St. Emmeram and Anonymous IV on the *Copula,*" *MQ* 70 (1984): 1–20.

(1) J.K.

Copyright and performance right. Laws providing protection to the authors of "original works of authorship" (Title 17, U.S. Code) began in England in 1710 and in the U.S. in 1790. The current U.S. copyright law, which replaced the Copyright Act of 1909, went into effect on 1 January 1978 and is referred to variously as Public Law 94-553, the Copyright Act of 1976, the Copyright Revision Act, or Title 17 of the U.S. Code. Under the new law, copyright is secured automatically when the work is created. For works published with the notice of copyright in the U.S., the law requires a deposit of two copies in the Copyright Office. Published and unpublished works can also be registered, but that is not a condition of copyright protection, though it is a prerequisite of the institution of an infringement suit. Registration can be made at any time during the copyright term by submitting the proper form and fee and depositing one copy of an unpublished work and two copies of a published work (which can also be registered at the time of the original deposit). Registration and renewal forms, the fee schedule, and general information can be obtained from the Register of Copyrights, Library of Congress, Washington, D.C. 20559. This office, which can be engaged to do a copyright search, has since 1891 published a *Catalog of Copyright Entries.*

The new law was amended in 2000 to extend the duration of copyright to 70 years after the author's death, which is the rule for most countries. For works created after 1 January 1978, the term is life plus 70 or, in the case of a joint work, 70 years after the last surviving author's death. This extension is also true for unpublished and unregistered works created before 1 January 1978; such works are guaranteed at least 45 years of protection, so that the copyright for work in this category will not expire before 31 December 2022; if the work was published before 1 January 1978, the term is extended another 25 years, to 2047. For works that were copyrighted before 1 January 1978, those in their first term of 28 years under the old law can be renewed for 67 years; those in their second term were automatically extended to 75 years from the date of the original copyright. Another feature of the new law is the recognition of the principle of "fair use" and factors for determining it (Section 107).

Three international conventions have resulted in copyright agreements between nations: the Bern Copyright Union (1886 and several revisions), the Universal Copyright Convention (1952, revised 1971), and the Buenos Aires Convention (1910).

Performance-right licensing agencies have been established in many countries to assist authors in collecting fees for the use of their copyrighted works. The two chief U.S. agencies are the American Society of Composers, Authors, and Publishers (ASCAP, 1914) and Broadcast Music, Inc. (BMI, 1940). A small, privately owned third agency is SESAC (formerly the Society of European Stage Authors and Composers, 1930). These agencies issue blanket licenses to corporate users of their authors' works, such as radio and television stations, nightclubs, and performing organizations; collect fees based on the amount of use; and distribute the proceeds among their members. A new source of income is provided by the Copyright Act of 1976, in that for the first time, jukeboxes are charged an annual fee of $8. This is collected by the Register of Copyrights and passed on to the performance-right agencies.

Bibl.: Lucia S. Schultz, "Performing-Right Societies in the United States," *Notes* 35 (1978–79): 511–36. William Lichtenwanger, "94-553 and All That: Ruminations on Copyright," *Notes* 35 (1978–79): 803–18, 36 (1979–80): 837–48. Mark E. Halloran, *Musician's Guide to Copyright,* rev. ed. (New York: Scribner, 1996). Sidney Shemel and M. William Krasilovsky, *This Business of Music,* 8th ed. (New York: Watson-Guptill, 2000). Music Library Association website: Copyright for Music Librarians *http://www.lib.jmu.edu/org/mla.* H.E.S., rev. L.C.

Coq d'or, Le [Fr.]. See *Golden Cockerel, The.*

Cor [Fr.]. *Horn; *c. anglais,* *English horn; *c. à pistons, c. d'harmonie,* valve horn; *c. de basset,* *basset horn; *c. de chasse,* hunting horn.

Coranto. See Courante.

Corda [It.], **corde** [Fr.]. *String; *snare; *corda vuota, corde à vide,* open string. See also *Una corda.*

Corelli clash. See Cadence.

Coriolan Overture. An orchestral work by Beethoven, op. 62 (1807), composed as an overture to a play by Heinrich Joseph von Collin on the same subject as Shakespeare's *Coriolanus.*

Cori spezzati [It., broken choirs]. See Polychoral.

Corista [It.]. (1) *Tuning fork. (2) *Concert pitch. (3) A singer in a chorus.

Cornamusa, cornemuse [It., Lat.]. A wind instrument mentioned but not described in 16th-century sources. It was probably a capped *shawm, perhaps identical with the **dolzaina.* (2) A *bagpipe of the Abruzzi mountains of Italy.

Cornemuse [Fr.]. *Bagpipe.

Cornet. (1) [formerly also cornopean; Fr. *cornet à pistons;* Ger. *Kornett;* It. *cornetta;* Sp. *corneta, cornetín*] A soprano brass instrument very similar to the modern trumpet but having a slightly more conical bore [see ill. under Brass instruments]. Its sound is somewhat more mellow than that of the trumpet (depending on the player). It is used in European and American military, community, and school bands. The cornet first appeared in France about 1830 when valves were applied to the *cornet simple* or *post horn. The instrument was built in C with *shanks and *crooks for most keys down to D. A deep conical *mouthpiece was used at first, as the instrument was originally intended for horn players. The lower crooks soon fell into disuse, however, and with a shallower mouthpiece the cornet became the leading voice and soloist for many kinds of bands. Its agility and flexibility were exploited in brilliant popular solos during the last half of the 19th century. In the 1920s, it was largely replaced by the trumpet in jazz and popular music. Its written range is from f♯ to c‴ or higher, sounding a whole tone lower on the common B♭ instrument. The soprano E♭ cornet has been widely used as a solo instrument and in *brass bands.

(2) [Fr.] The most important solo voice in French organs, consisting of five pitches (8′, 4′, 2⅔′, 2′, and 1⅗′), drawn either as one stop or as separate ranks. The *Cornet séparé* or *Cornet de récit* is played from its own keyboard, separate from the *Grand orgue.* It is also an important register in Dutch and English organs.

Bibl.: Richard I. Schwartz, *The Cornet Compendium: The History and Development of the Nineteenth-Century Cornet* (Author, 2000–2001; *Irisrick@aol.com*); also available in downloadable format at *http://www.angelfire.com/music2/thecornetcompendium.* Edward H. Tarr, "The Romantic Trumpet," *Historic Brass Society Journal* 5 (1993): 213.

(1) R.E.E.

Corneta [Sp.]. (1) *Cornet. (2) *Bugle. (3) *Cornett.

Cornett [Fr. *cornet à bouquin;* Ger. *Zink;* It. *cornetto;* Sp. *corneta*]. A wooden (or occasionally ivory) instrument of the brass family with a wide conical bore and side holes for a thumb and six fingers. It was used in church and chamber music, sometimes with very elaborate parts, from about 1550 to 1700. The English spelling of "cornet" was altered to "cornett" at the suggestion of Francis W. Galpin (1858–1945) to avoid confusion with the modern *cornet. Three sizes were made: small treble *(cornettino),* treble, and tenor *(cornone).* Of these the treble was by far the most important. The treble is about 60 cm (2 ft.) long with a range from a (which can be lipped down to g) to d‴. There are three types of treble cornett: curved, straight, and mute. The curved is the most common and is made of two hollowed-out wood halves glued together and covered with leather. The straight is made of one piece of wood bored and turned. The mute is made in the same way as the straight, but does not have a detachable mouthpiece. A turned cavity in the end of the instrument, deeper and more conical than the usual detachable mouthpiece, yields a muted or softened tone quality. See ill. under Brass instruments. R.E.E.

Cornetta [It.]. *Cornet.

Cornetto [It.]. *Cornett.

Cornett-ton [Ger.]. See Pitch (4).

Cornet voluntary. An organ composition, popular in England from the late 17th to the early 19th centuries, in which a florid solo line is given to the *Cornet stop.

Corno [It.]. (1) *Horn; *c. a macchina, a pistone, cromatico, ventile,* valve horn; *c. a mano,* natural horn; *c. da caccia,* hunting horn; *c. di bassetto,* *basset horn; *c. inglese,* *English horn; *c. storto,* *crumhorn. *Corno da tirarsi,* an instrument specified in some cantatas by Bach, perhaps a slide *trumpet. (2) [Sp.] Horn.

Cornone [It.]. A tenor *cornett, made in the shape of an S.

Cornopean. (1) An early form of the *cornet. (2) An organ stop of reed pipes at 8′ pitch with conical resonators.

Cornu [Lat.]. (1) A horn of ancient Rome. It was curved in the shape of a G and held vertically with the tubing passing around the player's shoulder and the bell pointing forward. Larger *cornua* had over three meters of tubing and a wooden crosspiece by which the instrument was held and that enabled it to rest on the player's shoulder. It is depicted often in Roman art, and two well-preserved specimens have been excavated in Pompeii. See ill. under Greece. (2) *Horn.

Coro [It., Sp.]. (1) Chorus. (2) *Course. See also *Cori spezzati.*

Corona [Lat., It.]. *Fermata. See also *Cantus coronatus.*

Coronach, corranach [Gael.]. In Scotland from the 16th century through the early 19th, a funeral lament sung over the corpse principally by women and including praise for the deceased and highly emotional wailing. It is thought to have been the equivalent of the Irish *caoine.* Very few melodies associated with the practice survive. Schubert's "Coronach" for women's chorus (D. 836; op. 52 no. 4) is a setting of such a text from Sir Walter Scott's *The Lady of the Lake.*

Coronation Anthems. (1) Four anthems for chorus and orchestra by Handel, composed for the coronation of George II in 1727: "Zadok the priest," "The King shall rejoice," "My heart is inditing," and "Let thy hand be strengthened." (2) An anthem for chorus and orchestra, "My heart is inditing," composed by Purcell for the coronation of James II in 1685.

Coronation Concerto. Mozart's Piano Concerto in D major K. 537 (1788), so called because he performed it (together with the Concerto in F major K. 459) at the coronation of the Emperor Leopold in Frankfurt in 1790.

Coronation Mass. Popular name for Mozart's Mass in C major K. 317 (1779), traditionally believed to have been composed for the annual crowning of the statue of the Virgin Mary at the shrine of Maria Plain near Salzburg, Austria.

Corps [Fr.]. (1) The resonating body of a stringed instrument. (2) *Corps de rechange,* a *tuning slide or *crook of a brass instrument.

Corrente [It.]. See Courante.

Corrido [Sp.]. A type of narrative ballad found in several countries of Latin America, derived from the Spanish **romance.* It is especially important in Mexico, where it treats heroic figures and episodes of legend and history as well as contemporary events; many widely known examples are associated with the Mexican revolution of 1910. Characteristically performed by a singer with self-accompaniment of guitar or harp, or by small vocal and instrumental ensemble, the Mexican *corrido* is strophic, made up typically of octosyllabic quatrains separated by instrumental interludes. *Corrido* texts contain many formulaic elements, particularly in introductory and concluding verses. D.S.

Cortège [Fr.]. A solemn procession; a composition appropriate to such a procession.

Corthol. *Curtal.

Così fan tutte, ossia La scuola degli amanti [It., All Women Act That Way, or The School of Lovers]. Comic opera in two acts by Mozart (libretto by Lorenzo da Ponte), produced in Vienna in 1790. Setting: Naples, 18th century.

Cotillon [Fr.], **cotillion.** (1) A social dance of the 18th and 19th centuries, related to the **contredanse* and *quadrille and often performed at the end of a ball, in which the numerously varied steps executed by a leading couple are imitated by others. Music for such a dance might include the waltz, polka, mazurka, and galop. (2) A formal occasion for social dancing, especially for young people.

Cottage piano. A small upright piano, especially the design made by Robert Wornum in 1813.

Coulé [Fr.]. (1) Slurred; often used as a noun for a pair of notes connected by a slur. In 18th-century France, it seems sometimes to have meant a pair of notes played unequally (long-short or short-long) according to the convention of **notes inégales;* as a direction heading a piece, it may occasionally have been a direction for inequality, and slurs written over pairs of notes of equal value may have had the same meaning. But it is likely that in the great majority of cases, both slurs and the term *coulé* meant simply connected or legato and had no rhythmic significance. When, however, there was a dot over the second of two slurred notes in the music of François Couperin and one or two other composers (e.g., Pierre-Claude Foucquet), reversed dotting (short-long) was intended. (2) In the French Baroque, a descending *appoggiatura. (3) A single-note ornament filling in a descending third *(coulé de tierce),* slurred to the second note but often taking its value from the first. (4) According to D'Anglebert, a rising or falling slide. See Ornamentation. D.F.

Coulisse [Fr.]. (1) The slide of a trombone or slide trumpet. (2) The *tuning slide of a brass instrument.

Council of Trent. A council of the Roman Catholic Church that was convened by Pope Paul III to meet in the city of Trento (now northern Italy) and that met intermittently from 1545 through 1563. Its work embodied the spirit of the Counter-Reformation and, among many other topics, dealt with the reform of liturgical music. It prohibited the use of *tropes and all but a few *sequences and considered prohibiting the use of all polyphony in the liturgy. The story that Palestrina's *Marcellus Mass saved polyphony from this prohibition is without foundation. More closely associated with the Council was the music of Jacobus de Kerle (1531 or 1532–91), whose *Preces speciales* for four voices (Venice, 1562) were dedicated to the Council's members. A principal aim of the reforms and of the music composed with them in view was the intelligibility of the liturgical texts.

Bibl.: Lewis Lockwood, "Vincenzo Ruffo and Musical Reform after the Council of Trent," *MQ* 43 (1957): 342–71. Edith Weber, *Le Concile de Trente et la musique: De la Réforme à la Contre-Réforme* (Paris: H Champion, 1982). James F. White, *Roman Catholic Worship: Trent to Today* (New York: Paulist Pr, 1995).

Counter. *Countertenor.

Counterexposition. In a *fugue, a second, complete exposition in the tonic and dominant.

Counterfugue. A *fugue in which the answer is an inversion of the subject, e.g., nos. 4, 5, and 6 of Bach's *The *Art of Fugue.* The technique dates from the 16th century and is sometimes described with the phrase *per arsin et thesin* [see Arsis and thesis (3)].

Countermelody. In a piece whose texture consists clearly of a melody with accompaniment, an accompanying part with distinct, though subordinate, melodic interest.

Counterpoint [Lat. *contrapunctus,* fr. *contra punctum,* against note; *contrepoint;* Ger. *Kontrapunkt;* It. *contrappunto;* Sp. *contrapunto*]. The combination of two or more melodic lines; the linear consideration of melodic lines sounding together; the technical principles governing such consideration.

I. *The nature of counterpoint.* The very elementary fragment of music in Ex. 1 has a notationally horizontal component, the moving upper part (x), and a vertical component, the interval of a third (y), which changes to a fourth (z). The notation expresses the temporal dimension: the A comes after the G in time (a melodic succession), and the fourth comes after the third (an intervallic succession). The G can be perceived as moving to the A, the ear being drawn to this moving part because it is the more active; and the E can be perceived as remaining stationary underneath the moving part. Alternatively, both of these parts can be perceived simultaneously; or the third can be perceived as changing to a fourth, the vertical intervals being measured by ear. In either case, the perception of these relationships simultaneously is the perception of counterpoint. The essence of contrapuntal perception is that horizontal motion of one part may be perceived and differentiated from the simultaneous horizontal motion of another, at the same time. Counterpoint, more than anything, has distinguished Western music from that of all other cultures for some nine centuries.

Although counterpoint is a property of *polyphony, its nature is indissolubly linked to the nature of melody. A melody must have coherence; its tones follow one another in a musically sensible way, and this is true for melodies combined contrapuntally no less than for those that are not. This is not to say that every melody used in counterpoint must be as distinctive as a theme or as memorable as a song, but it must be perceptible as a continuity, not just as a succession of isolated tones. So, too, do melodies relate to each other in counterpoint, with the result that a perceptual balance is struck between the individualities of the lines and their combination; the ear's attention will ideally be focused now on one line, now on the other, and simultaneously on both.

Counterpoint is a feature of all music in which combinations of two or more simultaneously sounding pitches are regularly employed. The term and its adjective form, contrapuntal, however, are often used to distinguish from one another musical *textures in which each of the several lines sounding together retains its character as a line and textures in which one line predominates and the remainder are clearly subservient, retaining little or no distinct character as lines. In this sense, a Bach fugue is considered more contrapuntal than a Schubert waltz, even though careful analysis might reveal that the two are equally well worked out in linear terms. Similarly, counterpoint, with its emphasis on the linear or horizontal aspect of music, is sometimes contrasted with *harmony, which concerns primarily the vertical aspect of music embodied in the nature of the simultaneously sounding combinations of pitches employed. Counterpoint and harmony are, nevertheless, fundamentally inseparable.

Contrapuntal motion is regulated by direction, by rhythmic differentiation, and by separation. Direction [see also Motion] refers to the way in which the parts may move with respect to each other: by contrary motion, that is, in opposite directions, one part moving up while the other moves down; and by similar motion, the parts moving in the same direction. Parallel motion is similar motion in which the parts keep the same interval between them as they move. Oblique motion, one voice moving while the other remains fixed, is illustrated by Ex. 1; it is the basis for rhythmic differentiation between parts, for the ear tends to follow the moving part in preference to the slower one. Separation refers to the intervals formed between simultaneous tones in the different parts. These intervals may be consonant or dissonant [see Consonance and dissonance]. Dissonant intervals in tonal counterpoint are those that are treated as requiring resolution to consonant intervals; resolution is characteristically achieved by the stepwise motion of one of the tones in the dissonant interval. "The essential quality of dissonance is its sense of movement and not, as is sometimes erroneously assumed, its degree of unpleasantness to the ear" (Piston, 1978, p. 7).

II. *Dissonance treatment in tonal counterpoint.* The principles usually taught under the heading of counterpoint (also called the principles of voice-leading) describe the types of motion permitted in individual lines with respect to one another and the types of dissonance and resolution permitted between two or more lines. One of the most important principles governing motion is the prohibition against motion in parallel fifths and octaves [see Parallel fifths, octaves]. The principal types of dissonance (sometimes called *nonharmonic tones or embellishing tones) occurring in tonal counterpoint are as follows:

1. Passing tone [Ex. 2], which connects two consonant pitches by stepwise motion and normally occurs in a metrically weak position. When it occurs in a metrical position stronger than that of its resolution [see Accent], it is called an accented passing tone.

2. Neighboring tone or auxiliary tone, a tone a step above (upper neighbor; Ex. 3) or a step below (lower neighbor; Ex. 4) a consonant tone. Upper and lower neighbors are sometimes combined to form double neighbors [Exx. 5 and 6], to which the term cambiata [see 7 below] is also sometimes applied [see also *échappée,* 6 below]. Single neighboring tones may be either strong or weak metrically.

3. Suspension [Ex. 7], normally a dissonant tone occurring in a strong metrical position, having been sustained (or "suspended" or "prepared") from an initial attack as a consonance and converted to a dissonance as a result of motion in another voice. It is most often resolved downward by step.

4. Appoggiatura [Ex. 8], a metrically strong dissonance, normally arrived at by leap and resolved by descending step. The term is also applied to accented dissonances similar to the suspension [Ex. 9], in which case it is said to be a prepared appoggiatura, and more loosely to any accented dissonance that is resolved by step in either direction. For the appoggiatura in the history of ornamentation, see Appoggiatura.

5. Anticipation [Ex. 10], a metrically weak dissonant tone that is immediately reharmonized as a consonance.

6. *Échappée* or escape tone [Ex. 11], a metrically weak dissonance approached by step and left by leap in the opposite direction. Such formations can also be understood as incomplete neighboring tones.

7. Cambiata (or *nota cambiata*), properly a five-note figure [Ex. 12], the second note of which is dissonant and the third of which is consonant. The term is also applied, however, to a similar figure moving in an upward direction [Ex. 13] and to several related

shorter figures [Exx. 14 and 15] as well as to the double neighboring tones described above [Exx. 5 and 6], to which the term changing notes is sometimes applied. All of these are common in music of the 15th and 16th centuries. The term cambiata has sometimes been further extended to include another figure [Ex. 16], the principal feature of which is that the motion to the dissonance is in the same direction (unlike the motion of the *échappée*) as the motion between the initial and final consonances.

Although all of the above formations serve primarily to introduce dissonance into an otherwise consonant succession, some of them, particularly the first three, may on occasion be entirely consonant. See also Species counterpoint.

III. *History.* Although the term counterpoint did not come into use until the 14th century, the principles that form the basis for counterpoint even into the period of tonality were formulated in 13th-century treatises on what was termed *discant. These principles include criteria for simultaneous, vertical combinations and for horizontal motion. The former consists in its essence of a list of intervals to be treated as consonant, the latter in a preference for contrary motion, especially when approaching a perfect consonance, and the banning of motion in parallel perfect intervals. Much of the history of counterpoint that follows, at least through the late 15th century, consists in redefinition, first in practice and then in theory, of the list of consonances, and the increasing strictness in practice of adherence to the prohibition against motion in parallel perfect intervals, which had been formulated by about 1300 [see Parallel fifths, octaves]. In the mid-13th century, the list of consonances included unison, octave, fifth, fourth, and major and minor thirds. By about the middle of the 14th century, however, this list included unison, octave, fifth (but not the fourth, which has since functioned as a consonance only when supported by a third or fifth below), major and minor thirds, and major and minor sixths (Crocker, 1962). This is the list that has remained in effect even in tonality. And it is from this list that the triad emerges, furthermore, for the major and minor triads and their inversions are the only three-pitch consonant sonorities that can be derived from it.

The prohibition against parallel perfect intervals begins to be very strictly observed only in about the middle of the 15th century (though some music in parallel imperfect consonances flourished; see *Fauxbourdon*). This coincides with an increasing preference for four-voice texture, which has formed a kind of norm ever since. Taken together with the list of consonances and the long-standing preference for contrary motion, especially when approaching perfect intervals, these two developments produce music with a greatly increased number of complete triads and with some of the most familiar harmonic progressions of tonality, notably the cadence since described as V–I or authentic (Randel, 1971).

Another distinguishing feature of the contrapuntal style that was formed in the late 15th century and that characterized much of the music of the Renaissance is *imitation, isolated instances of which are known earlier but which in the later 15th century was adopted by nearly every composer. Imitation is not a principle but an application of counterpoint, a means of projecting a theme or motive repeatedly but with intervallic and tonal variety. Strict imitation over a fairly long distance, at least a phrase, is called *canon; its appearance in music predates the widespread use of free imitation.

Renaissance counterpoint, with or without imitation, is characterized by smooth, chiefly stepwise melodic motion in all parts, from two to five or even more, with a maximum of rhythmic independence, and yet with essentially the same kind of freedom of motion in any one part. Dissonances are carefully controlled, appearing as passing tones between consonances, as suspensions or delayed motions, and (somewhat less frequently) in other ways. The concern for elegant shaping of the melodic line in all parts reaches a peak during this period, resulting in what is sometimes termed the *florid style. Some secular music of the Renaissance, on the other hand, shows a marked tendency toward *homophony, with a lessening of rhythmic differentiation between parts, although the rules of dissonance treatment still pertain; the genres of *chanson, *madrigal, **frottola,* and various instrumental forms and dance pieces illustrate these traits in various degrees.

Such stylistic differences did not weaken the essential uniformity of contrapuntal practice in the Renaissance, a fact that is reflected in the appearance during the period (and for some years after) of codifications of contrapuntal rules in an impressive variety of theoretical works by Johannes Tinctoris, Pietro Aaron, Heinrich Glarean, Gioseffo Zarlino, Thomas Morley, and others [see Theory, Palestrina style].

The increasing importance of homophonic styles in the late 16th century is linked to the emergence of a new musical dimension, functional *harmony, in which the vertical relationships formed by moving parts are not merely controlled coincidence but are the result of conscious attention to particular chords, with the perception of an actual foundation supporting the harmony from below. The Renaissance ideal of a balanced texture of several independent parts gave way to a texture in which top and bottom parts predominate over the interior parts in musical attention. The concept of melody and accompaniment, a category of musical texture which has remained vigorous ever since, achieved its first full realization in the *monody of the early Baroque, although the homophonic genres of the 16th century, which included accompanied solo song, certainly pointed in that direction. In the most characteristic invention of the early Baroque, *recitative, the contrapuntal essence is reduced to a freely ranging upper melody and a slowly moving harmonic support underneath it, a support that is itself no more than a bass line with symbols indicating chord pitches to be supplied above it [see Thoroughbass]; as in the comparable case of melismatic organum, the melodic identity of the supporting line is thus greatly diminished.

The harmonic dimension in the later Baroque became fused with a reinvigorated counterpoint that achieves its zenith in the works of Bach. The contrapuntal art of the late Baroque is marked by a melodic vitality that has never been surpassed; at the same time, this counterpoint is wrought upon a harmonic background that is itself organized by smooth linear means. Thus, in the counterpoint of the Baroque, two kinds of contrapuntal organization can be perceived: the successive note-to-note counterpoint of the individual melodies relating immediately to each other, and the at-a-distance counterpoint of the harmonic changes [see Schenker analysis].

The Baroque era is also identified by the appearance of specific compositional forms and procedures that are inherently dependent on a well-developed contrapuntal technique applied to a theme. The first of these procedures to appear was *variation technique, which achieved its fullest realization in the *chorale prelude and in *ostinato forms like the *passacaglia and *chaconne. In the *fugue, which stands at the pinnacle of formal invention in the Baroque, a single theme (or occasionally more than one) is developed repeatedly and imitatively in all parts, with all surrounding counterpoint being mobilized for its support [see also Ricercar].

The contrapuntal energy of the late Baroque was continued in the sacred music of the eras that followed, and masterly fugal technique is abundant in large-scale sacred works from Haydn and Mozart to Verdi and Brahms. But the characteristic genres of these years—symphony and sonata, song, character piece, and 19th-century opera—do not often rely on a rigorously contrapuntal texture, and the extended display of counterpoint is generally by way of a brilliant exception, particularly in a finale (Mozart's *Jupiter* Symphony K. 551; Beethoven's Piano Sonatas opp. 106 and 110 and String Quartet op. 133 *(Grosse Fuge)*; Verdi's *Falstaff*). Nevertheless, counterpoint is often a feature of the development sections of movements in sonata form. The 19th-century evolution of chromatic harmony was in large part a concomitant of contrapuntal procedures, and Wagner's treatment of the *leitmotif employs counterpoint to dramatic as well as specifically musical ends. As for late 19th-century diatonicism, the contrapuntal technique of Brahms's *Variations on a Theme by Haydn* op. 56a looks back to the styles of Bach's chorale preludes, and that of the first movement of Mahler's Fourth Symphony looks back to Haydn's symphonies.

In the 20th century, two extremes are represented by the attitude of Debussy, whose reaction against "classical" and "learned" compositional aesthetics included an antipathy to counterpoint in particular, and by that of Schoenberg, whose early virtuosity in the treatment of tonal counterpoint led him to evolve a chromatic language that eliminated tonality altogether [see Atonality]. Debussy's works are often marked by a stark homophony, with *parallel chords a commonplace (*Danse sacrée* for harp and strings); on the other hand, his orchestral works sometimes demonstrate a *heterophony in which myriad figurational and instrumental details are synthesized into a complex overall texture, a kind of "counterpoint of colors" *(La mer)*, which can be compared with the brush techniques of the impressionist painters [see Impressionism]. Schoenberg's atonal counterpoint occasionally superficially resembles Debussy's heterophony, but more characteristically it is worked out in complex motivic or imitative textures (Serenade; String Quartet no. 3), with a maximum of rhythmic differentiation and melodic angularity, sometimes in a dense polyphony without any motives or repetition at all (Orchestral Piece op. 16 no. 5). In between these two extremes can be found Stravinsky's primitivist textures, with contrapuntally opposed metrical groupings *(Petrushka)* and chordal layers *(The Rite of Spring)*, and his later *neoclassical styles (Octet; *Symphony of Psalms*), which adapted a whole era of 18th-century contrapuntal shapes, figurations, and forms to 20th-century harmony and dissonance treatment.

Spatial counterpoint, or counterpoint in three dimensions, is especially represented today by the compositional stereophony of electronic music [see Electro-acoustic music], a tendency that can be traced back to Bach's *St. Matthew Passion*, to the Venetian *cori spezzati* [see Polychoral], or even to antiphonal chant. In the electronic medium, the perception of spatiality can be controlled with a speed and accuracy not attainable by conventional performers. With multichannel equipment it is possible to create the impression of a multitude of different spatially moving musics at once.

See also Species counterpoint, Double counterpoint, Harmony.

Bibl.: A. Tillman Merritt, *Sixteenth-Century Polyphony: A Basis for the Study of Counterpoint* (Cambridge, Mass.: Harvard U Pr, 1939). Allen I. McHose, *The Contrapuntal Harmonic Technique of the 18th Century* (New York: F S Crofts, 1947). Walter Piston, *Counterpoint* (New York: Norton, 1947). Humphrey Searle, *Twentieth-Century Counterpoint* (London: Williams and Norgate, 1954). Leland Procter, *Tonal Counterpoint* (Dubuque, Iowa: W C Brown, 1957). Sergei Taneev, *Convertible Counterpoint in the Strict Style*, trans. G. Ackley Brower (Boston: B Humphries, 1962). Richard L. Crocker, "Discant, Counterpoint, Harmony," *JAMS* 15 (1962): 1–21. Carl Dahlhaus, *Untersuchungen über die Entstehung der harmonischen Tonalität* (Kassel: Bärenreiter, 1968). Felix Salzer and Carl Schachter, *Counterpoint in Composition* (New York: McGraw-Hill, 1969). Don M. Randel, "Emerging Triadic Tonality in the Fifteenth Century," *MQ* 57 (1971): 73–86. Ernst Apfel, *Grundlagen einer Geschichte der Satztechnik* (Saarbrücken: Apfel, 1974). John Rothgeb, "Strict Counterpoint and Tonal Theory," *JMT* 19 (1975): 260–84. The history of counterpoint is dealt with in a number of important articles in *The Music Forum* (New York: Columbia U Pr, 1967–). Harold Owen, *Modal and Tonal Counterpoint: From Josquin to Stravinsky* (New York:

Schirmer, 1992). See also Theory, Species counterpoint, Palestrina style, Canon, Discant. M.DEV.

Countersubject. In a *fugue, a subordinate subject that accompanies statements of the principal subject.

Countertenor. (1) *Contratenor. (2) A male alto who sings *falsetto.

Country. An American popular music idiom derived from traditional oral music brought by immigrants from the British Isles. Commercial recording companies began to tap rural Southern music in the early 1920s as part of a larger strategy to capitalize on the culture of various ethnic and minority groups. Victor recorded the fiddlers Henry Gilliland and Eck Robertson in 1922, Ralph Peer discovered Henry Whitter and "Fiddlin'" John Carson for Okeh the following year, and other companies rushed to build their own catalogs of what was first called old-time music. By the end of the decade, Uncle Dave Macon, Gid Tanner, Ernest "Pop" Stoneman, Riley Puckett, Vernon Dalhart, Clayton McMichen, and a host of other successful performers had been recorded, and the musicians who gave the most important definition to the new genre—the Carter family and Jimmie Rodgers—had begun their commercial careers. The label "hillbilly," a derogatory term for rural white Southerners, was now put on this music, taken from the name of a popular recording group from the vicinity of Galax, Virginia, the Hillbillies.

This music at first represented a cross section of the traditional repertory of the rural South. There were old narrative ballads brought to America from Britain and newer American ballads of the same sort, usually accompanied by banjo, fiddle, guitar, or some combination of these instruments. Many other songs had passed into oral tradition from the composed, popular-song literature of the 19th-century American parlor. There was also dance music—two-strain pieces played by one or more fiddles sometimes accompanied by banjo or guitar—as well as blues songs from the early 20th century. Some tunes retained elements of pentatonic or modal patterns, and the oldest style of accompaniment on the banjo or fiddle was nonharmonic, with heterophonic or ostinato figures. But the introduction of the guitar and other chord-playing instruments in the latter part of the 19th century, and the assimilation of pieces from the composed popular repertory at the same time, brought an increasing trend toward a tonal, triadic style.

By the middle of the 1930s, a mainstream style had crystallized, blending elements of traditional and more recent urban music. Roy Acuff was recognized as the first important practitioner of this consensus style in which vocal characteristics retain the nasal, "high-lonesome" sound of older music; instrumentation consists of one or two fiddles, a banjo, guitars (including a Hawaiian or steel instrument capable of producing a characteristic sliding sound [see Steel guitar]), and usually a bass; texts are often concerned with such harsh realities as death, alcoholism, desertion, crime, and thwarted love; both melody and accompaniment reflect a solid harmonic foundation.

The music soon spread beyond the South, thanks in large part to commercial radio. Stations such as WSB in Atlanta, WSM in Nashville, WBAP in Fort Worth, and WLS in Chicago played an important role in popularizing country music and its performers. Regional dialects emerged, all eventually encompassed under the term country, or country and western. In the 1920s, Carl Sprague and Jules Verne Allen performed and recorded songs reflecting the music and culture of the Southwest, and slightly later the image of the singing cowboy was brought to all parts of the country via films starring Gene Autry, Roy Rogers, and Tex Ritter. In the 1930s, an eclectic genre known as Western swing melded the rhythms, instruments, and improvised solos of swing-era jazz with traditional fiddle and guitar styles and vocal stylings influenced by urban pop; two of the most important early groups, the Texas Playboys and the Musical Brownies, were led by Bob Wills and Milton Brown, who had been bandmates in the Light Crust Doughboys. The Cajuns of rural Louisiana, led by performers such as Joe Falcon, Amédé Ardoin, and the Hackberry Ramblers, assimilated the instruments and general sound of country music into their own tradition, retaining the French language and the distinctive sound of the concertina. In the Southwest, particularly in Texas, a more urban sound emerged in the bars and roadhouses serving as social centers for the region. Ernest Tubb, Lefty Frizzell, and Hank Williams, Sr., were the most successful performers of this "honky-tonk" music, which typically featured amplified instruments and drums. Honky-tonk has retained a central influence in country music in terms of instrumentation, vocal style, and song topics. Later examples include the music of Buck Owens, Merle Haggard, and George Jones.

Since the mid-20th century, country music's appeal has grown continually. Several major recording companies, including Decca and RCA Victor, established studios in Nashville in the 1950s to take advantage of the city's concentration of successful singers, songwriters, and leading session musicians. The increasing popularity of the Grand Ole Opry, which had expanded from its beginnings in 1925 as a regional radio show on WSM to a nationwide broadcast of live concerts in the Ryman Auditorium, helped establish Nashville as the commercial center of country music. The Country Music Association, founded there in 1958, set out to improve, market, and publicize country music. At the same time, country audiences accepted a wider range of music. For example, early rock and roll performers such as Elvis Presley and Jerry Lee Lewis brought a new sound and a youthful energy to the country charts. And with the aid of record producers whose musical backgrounds and training spanned a wide stylistic range—Owen Bradley and Chet Atkins, for instance—country records took on some of the smooth trappings of mainstream pop, a style that became known as the Nashville sound. Performers such as Patsy Cline ("I Fall to Pieces") and Eddy Arnold ("Make the World Go Away") recorded songs that managed to retain the older country audience while also attracting new listeners. In the late 1960s and 1970s, the country/pop fusion continued with the so-called countrypolitan style that featured lush string arrangements and vocal choruses. Billy Sherrill became one of the most prominent countrypolitan producers, working with artists such as George Jones, Tammy Wynette, and Charlie Rich.

While some performers, such as Ricky Skaggs and Alison Krauss, have clung to a more traditional sound, country music in general has continued to incorporate elements of other popular music idioms, even among the so-called new traditionalists (Dwight Yoakum, Garth Brooks) who have reemphasized the honky-tonk ethos. Borrowing heavily from rock in the 1980s and 1990s, country records routinely appeared among the *Billboard* Hot 100. Country music's mainstream acceptance, which at this point is international in scale, and its willingness to conform stylistically to mainstream pop tastes are aptly illustrated by the success of Canadian singer and songwriter Shania Twain, whose songs are cowritten and whose records are produced by South African Robert John "Mutt" Lange, a producer of multiplatinum hits for rock groups such as AC/DC *(Back in Black),* Def Leppard *(Pyromania),* and the Cars *(Heartbeat City).* At the same time, artists working outside the Nashville mainstream in the "alternative country" vein have produced a range of hybrid styles that combine elements of traditional country with the sophisticated lyric sensibilities of songwriters such as Townes Van Zandt and Lyle Lovett and the musical influences of country-rock musicians such as Gram Parsons and Neil Young.

Bibl.: Bill C. Malone, *Country Music, U.S.A.* (Austin: U of Tex Pr, 1985). Jimmie N. Rogers, *The Country Music Message: Revisited* (Little Rock: U of Ark Pr, 1989). Paul Kingsbury, Laura Garrard, and Daniel Cooper, eds., *The Encyclopedia of Country Music: The Ultimate Guide to the Music* (New York: Oxford U Pr, 1998). David Goodman, *Modern Twang: An Alternative Country Music Guide and Directory* (Nashville: Dowling, 1999). Peter Guralnick, *Lost Highway: Journeys and Arrivals of American Musicians* (New York: Little, Brown, 1999). Charles K. Wolfe, *A Good-Natured Riot: The Birth of the Grand Ole Opry* (Nashville: Vanderbilt U Pr, 1999). Bill C. Malone, *Don't Get above Your Raisin': Country Music and the Southern Working Class* (Urbana: U of Ill Pr, 2002). A.Z.

Country dance. Any of numerous English dances of folk origin (shared, however, by all classes of society) known since the 16th century and usually danced by a line of women and a line of men facing one another. The music for such dances included folk tunes and usually consisted of a series of eight-measure phrases. Dances and tunes were collected in the numerous editions of John Playford's *The English Dancing Master* (2nd and later eds. titled *The Dancing Master*) published from 1651 through 1728 (R: London: B Schott, 1957). Such dances, including specific English examples, were taken up in France around 1700 as the **contredanse,* which in turn spread through Europe. Publications continued to appear through about 1830. In the 20th century, country dances were revived in both England and the U.S.

Bibl.: Cecil J. Sharp, *The Country Dance Book,* 6 vols. (London: Novello, 1909–18). Id., *Country Dance Tunes* (London: Novello, 1909–22). H. Thurston, "Bibliography of Country Dance Books," *Journal of the English Folk Dance and Song Society* 7 (1952).

Coup d'archet [Fr.]. Bow stroke.

Coup de langue [Fr.]. In the playing of wind instruments, a movement of the tongue so as to articulate a sound.

Coupler. A mechanical device in organs and harpsichords for connecting one keyboard to another at unison pitch, and in electric-action organs, often at octave and suboctave pitches as well.

Couplet [Fr.]. (1) Two successive lines of poetry forming a pair, often within a larger form. (2) In French poetry, any of the strophes in a poem that includes a refrain [for the related Spanish *copla,* see *Villancico*]. (3) In the late 17th and 18th centuries (e.g., in the music of François Couperin), the sections between recurrences of the main theme of a **rondeau;* also the similar sections of a *rondo. (4) In light opera of the 18th and 19th century and in derivative genres since, a humorous strophic song with refrain. (5) *Duplet.

Courante [Fr.; It. *corrente;* Eng. corant, coranto]. A Baroque dance movement in triple meter. It originated in the 16th century and became a regular member of the solo *suite, following the allemande, by ca. 1630. Two versions, ultimately considered French and Italian, coexisted; most composers used *courante* and *corrente* interchangeably as titles, however. The Italian type uses fast triple meter (3/4 or 3/8), often with triadic or scalar figuration in even eighth or sixteenth notes [see Ex. 1]. It generally has homophonic texture, but imitative openings are not uncommon. The mature French courante was described by contemporary theorists as solemn and grave, having the same pulse as a *sarabande. It is usually notated in 3/2, with a strong proclivity toward *hemiola figures that combine 6/4 and 3/2 accent patterns as well as related syncopated figures [see Ex. 2]. Somewhat contrapuntal texture or **style brisé* is the norm, and phrase structures are often ambiguous, as is the harmonic scheme. Both types are usually in binary form, although early examples may have three strains. Both begin with upbeats and end on the strong beat.

The dance was courtly and was known in the 16th century, becoming important in the 17th. In Italy, it

1. Arcangelo Corelli, Corrente from Trio Sonata op. 2 no. 10 (1685). 2. Louis Couperin, Courante (ca. 1660).

was a cheerful courtship dance. French choreography survives only from the 18th century, so that the early relationship of the courante to the corrente is unknown. The late French dance used a pattern of long-short steps. The courante was danced infrequently on the stage in France, but was one of the most important dances at court balls under Louis XIV, subsisting as late as 1725.

The courante/corrente was of central importance to solo and chamber suites. Music for both types is found in both France and Italy as early as the first third of the 17th century. Orchestral suites, which were derived directly from French stage music, rarely included the dance. There are early examples in keyboard music by Bernhard Schmid (1577) and in the Fitzwilliam Virginal Book (copied 1609–19). Girolamo Frescobaldi's correntes (1615–37) illustrate the two genres, with the simple type being in **C**3 (the equivalent of the later 3/4 or 3/8) and the rhythmically complex ("French") type being in 3 (the later 3/2 or 6/4). Michael Praetorius also used both types in *Terpsichore* (1612), which contains 163 examples and specifies a fast tempo. From the middle of the 17th century to the end of the Baroque era, the Italians showed a distinct preference for the straightforward (and fast) corrente in the **sonata da camera,* as well as in solo music (e.g., that by Michelangelo Rossi, Arcangelo Corelli, and Antonio Vivaldi). They also used hemiolas and syncopations in some correntes, nevertheless notating them in 3/4 and marking them allegro.

In France, the courante was first significant in lute music (by Robert Ballard and Ennemond Gaultier, among others). By the middle of the century, the complex type in 3 (i.e., 3/2) was used almost exclusively and was relatively slow. There are more courantes than any other dance type in French harpsichord music of the 17th century (e.g., that by Jacques Champion de Chambonnières, Louis Couperin, and Jean-Henri d'Anglebert), and a single suite may have two or three. English composers (e.g., Henry Purcell and John Blow) were influenced by the French variety, although the tempo was understood to be quick (see Thomas Mace, *Musick's Monument,* London, 1676, p. 129; facs., Paris: CNRS, 1958; facs., *MMML* ser. 2, 17, 1966). The Germans also drew from both traditions, often adopting the weightier courante as a result of the strong French influence on the solo suite (in works of Johann Jakob Froberger). They are typically barred in half measures compared to the French models (3/4 rather than 6/4 or 3/2) and seem to have assumed a quicker tempo (in works of Dietrich Buxtehude, for example).

In the first half of the 18th century, the distinction between corrente and courante was sometimes explicit. Bach specified "corrente" in the harpsichord partitas nos. 1, 3, 5, and 6; nos. 2 and 4 have "courantes" in style and title. (Most modern editors have not preserved Bach's distinction.) In his other suites, the titles give no clue to the type, but the choice of meter (3/4 or 3/8 for corrente and 3/2 for courante) does. François Couperin composed French courantes except when specifically invoking the Italian muse, as in the fourth *Concert royal.* The dance form died out completely at the end of the Baroque period.

Bibl.: Uwe Kraemer, "Die Courante in der deutschen Orchester- und Klaviermusik des 17. Jahrhunderts" (Ph.D.

diss., Hamburg, 1968). Wendy Hilton, *Dance of Court and Theater: The French Noble Style 1690–1725,* ed. Caroline Gaynor (Princeton: Princeton Bk Co, 1981). Meredith Little and Carol Marsh, *La Danse Noble: An Inventory of Dances and Sources* (Williamstown: Broude Trust, 1992). B.G.

Course [Fr. *choeur, rang;* Ger. *Chor, Saitenchor;* It. *coro;* Sp. *orden*]. A set of one, two, or three strings tuned and played as one; the term is usually used in reference to 16th-, 17th-, and 18th-century plucked instruments such as the lute, theorbo, archlute, guitar, bandora, and cittern. Multiple strings in a course are tuned in unison or in octaves. In either disposition they greatly enhance tone color [see Timbre]. This enrichment is caused by dissonance in the upper partials. Added benefits are a perception of greater volume, caused by unequal beating of the strings, as well as the augmentation of the weak tone of large bass strings, either of gut (as found on the lute and theorbo) or of wire (as on the bandora and cittern). R.L.

Courtaut, courtaud. A 17th-century double-reed woodwind instrument of cylindrical bore. It was constructed with two bore channels in a single block of wood and was usually played with a *wind cap. See also *Kortholt, Sordone.* M.S.

Covered fifths, octaves. See Parallel fifths, octaves.

Cover. In popular music since the 1960s, especially rock and sometimes jazz, a recording or performance that remakes an earlier, sometimes very successful, recording. The aim of such a recording, which may or may not directly acknowledge the original, is to reach a wider commercial market, often by adapting the original to the tastes of a new or somewhat different audience (e.g., a rock "cover" of a rhythm-and-blues recording).

Cowbell [Sp. *cencerro*]. A metal bell, usually with straight sides and a slightly expanding, nearly rectangular cross section. The type with clapper, associated with cattle, is sometimes specified in orchestral works. A type without clapper and played with a drumstick is widely used in Latin American popular music. See ill. under Percussion instruments.

Cow horn [Ger. *Stierhorn*]. A lip-vibrated wind instrument made from the horn of a cow, often used by herdsmen. The parts specified by Wagner for such instruments in the *Ring* and in *Die Meistersinger* are usually played on specially made straight brass instruments with perfectly conical bore.

Cps. Abbr. for cycles per second. See Hertz.

Crab canon. See Canon I, 3.

Crab motion. *Retrograde.

Cracovienne [Fr.]. **Krakowiak.*

Creation, The [Ger. *Die Schöpfung*]. An oratorio by Haydn for soloists, chorus, and orchestra, Hob. XXI:2 (1796–98). It is a setting of a poem compiled by an unknown Mr. Lidley (Lindley?) from Milton's *Paradise Lost,* the whole project having been suggested to Haydn by the concert manager Johann Peter Salomon during the composer's second stay in London (1794–95). Upon Haydn's return to Vienna, the text was translated into German by Baron Gottfried van Swieten as *Die Schöpfung.* The work was first performed in Vienna in 1798 and in this translation.

Creation Mass. Popular name for Haydn's Mass in B♭ major Hob. XXII:13 (1801), so called because a theme from his oratorio *The *Creation* appears in the "Qui tollis."

Creatures of Prometheus. See *Geschöpfe des Prometheus.*

Crécelle [Fr.]. *Cog rattle.

Credo [Lat., I believe; Eng. Creed]. The third item of the *Ordinary of the Roman Catholic *Mass, except on certain feasts when it is omitted. Its text is the Nicene *Creed, first used in association with the Eucharist in the East in the 5th century. In the 6th century it was prescribed for the Mozarabic Mass, and it was taken up in Gaul in the Carolingian period. It was not formally incorporated into the Roman Mass, however, until 1014 at the insistence of Emperor Henry II. Modern liturgical books include six melodies of varying antiquity, the earliest one being from the 11th century though perhaps derived from an earlier Greek model. In performance, the celebrant begins with the phrase "Credo in unum Deum," and the choir continues with the phrase "Patrem omnipotentem," with which most polyphonic settings therefore begin. For the complete text and translation, see Mass.

Creed [fr. Lat. *credo,* I believe; also Lat. *symbolum*]. A statement of religious belief, especially any of those adopted for use in the Christian liturgies. Three are of particular importance: (1) A text that is often called the "Nicene Creed" (after the Council of Nicaea of 325 C.E.) but is in fact the somewhat longer "Niceno-Constantinopolitan Creed," which is of uncertain date and origin. It is the *Credo of the Roman Mass and has been widely used in East and West in connection with both baptism and the Eucharist. (2) The "Apostles' Creed" (not, however, of apostolic origin), "Credo in Deum Patrem omnipotentem," used in the Western rites, including Roman and Anglican, in baptism and in the Office. (3) The "Athanasian Creed" (perhaps of Gallican origin), "Quicumque vult salvus esse" (Whosoever wants to be saved), used at the Office of Prime in the Roman rite and at Morning Prayer on some occasions in the Anglican rite.

Crembalum [Lat.]. *Jew's harp.

Cremona. An organ reed stop with cylindrical resonators, usually half-length, probably based on the French **Cromorne;* used in England from ca. 1680.

Crescendo, decrescendo [It., growing, decreasing;

abbr. *cresc., decresc., decr.*]. As *performance marks, increasing and decreasing loudness, respectively; sometimes indicated with the signs < and >. See also *Diminuendo*.

Crescendo pedal. In electric- or pneumatic-action organs, a device for bringing on each of the stops and couplers, from the softest to the loudest.

Crescent. *Turkish crescent.

Cretic meter. In the music of ancient *Greece, paeonic or quintuple meter.

Criticism. The elucidation and interpretation, based on the experience of an informed listener, of a work or performance. Its fundamental aim is the illumination of the individual work or performance as heard rather than the discovery of structural or other features common to many works. In this respect it sometimes stands in contrast to *analysis, though the two are not rigidly separable, and criticism inevitably makes use of some of the methods most often associated with analysis. Criticism focuses its energies on the work or performance as perceived and thus is likely to give greater weight to temporal factors and to the detailed musical surface than does much analysis. It is concerned with the underlying structural features of works to the extent that they bear directly on the listener's response. It does not necessarily aim to judge value. Here a distinction must be made between writing about the works in a widely accepted canon and writing about (often termed reviewing) recent performances and works whose status with respect to the canon, perhaps because of their novelty, is itself the subject of discussion. In criticism of the former type, the critic's evaluative judgment is likely to be expressed principally in the mere choice of subject. Criticism of the second type, especially as written for the mass media, often aims explicitly to report the critic's judgment of quality for readers or listeners who may wish to use it as a guide. Distinguished practitioners of both types share the same qualities: thorough technical training in music, broad experience of repertories and performances, gifted use of language, respect for the art of music, and respect for their readers.

I. *Criticism in musical scholarship.* Criticism for the serious if not professional student of music makes use of whatever technical and historical materials are necessary to provide the informed basis on which to give an account of a work as something heard. Its concern is, at least initially, the individual work and the individual listener. Indeed, it understands the work as existing only in relation to a listener who brings to bear on it the experienced perception that gives its features meaning. It is thus necessarily subjective and seeks to persuade the reader of its relevance to the reader's own experience rather than to reveal some inherent truth about the work. It derives its authority from its ability to persuade and to enrich the relationship between work and listener. In this respect, it differs from other discourse about music, however, only in the extent to which it places the listener in the foreground and knowingly operates on what may be contested terrain rather than on terrain sufficiently circumscribed or defined as to make the absence of contest resemble the discovery of objective truth. Even the most rigorous analysis derives its authority only from the extent to which its readers agree, at least tacitly, on the criteria for significance that it brings to bear on what it observes.

Criticism must persuade its reader that appropriate matters have been brought to bear on the work—that the work itself has been situated on an appropriate horizon of expectations. This requires the critic to have, in addition to a wide experience of other works, knowledge of the accuracy and completeness of the work's notated text, of the historical and cultural factors affecting the ways in which its composer might have composed and heard the work, and of the ways in which the *reception history of the work is likely to affect his or her own hearing of it.

Criticism of the individual work, with its presuppositions laid bare to the extent possible, may lead to enterprises on a larger scale. On a theoretical plane, this may be the study of the mechanisms by which musical works create meaning with and for a listener. It may also form a basis for the writing of history. All writing about the history of music necessarily relies on a critical position with respect to the works that it encompasses, whether this critical position is made explicit or not. The practice of criticism of individual works alone can ensure that this critical position grows from and responds to the works themselves rather than being forced upon them by received opinion or other factors external to them. Even the making of scientific editions of individual works requires critical judgment with respect to the significance of numerous details and the extent to which the written text is an adequate guide to its realization. This requires study of works as works of art and not simply as examples of notation or of some preconceived genre or style. It is in these respects that criticism can contribute to the discipline of *musicology even as traditionally conceived.

II. *Criticism in the mass media.* Criticism disseminated through the mass media must be produced and function within certain limits of time, space, editorial policy, and the musical sophistication of a large general audience. In part it must report the musical news, and in part it is often expected to serve as arbiter of taste and guide to musical consumption for its audience. Its responsibility for the character and quality of musical life can thus be considerable. Its emphasis is likely to be on describing and evaluating recent performances and newly composed works. Sustained interpretation of established works (or even new ones) is rarely possible except in a very few magazines with established traditions of this kind. The best criticism of this type gives a complete and accurate account of what was performed (perhaps including dates and other relevant facts about the works) and by whom, and it enables its reader to form a judgment that is in some measure independent of that expressed by the critic. This requires some attention to technical matters and a correspondingly appropriate vocabulary. It, too, aims more to persuade than to pontificate. Constant dangers in such criticism are that the value of novelty for the newsperson may affect the reasoned judgment of the critic and that the pressure of time and limitations of space may encourage hasty and facile judgments rather than carefully considered ones.

III. *History.* Critical accounts of individual works, as distinct from the mere mention of works that illustrate one theoretical construct or another, began to appear with some regularity in the 16th century in the context of a musical humanism that, under the influence of writers of classical antiquity, sought to privilege the effect of music on the listener. Heinrich Glarean's *Dodecachordon* of 1547 provides notable examples (see, e.g., the excerpts in *SR,* pp. 219–27). The same concern underlies much that was written about music in the years around 1600 in support of *monody and the changes in style now taken as marking the beginning of the *Baroque period, and in these writings, too, individual works are often cited and commented upon.

Controversy in both England and France over the merits of Italian opera in the early 18th century provided the context for much writing about music for a somewhat broader audience. In France, discussion of the relative merits of French and Italian music was carried on throughout the century, as in the *querelle des *bouffons.* In England, Joseph Addison's contributions to *The Spectator* in the years around 1710 mark the beginning of a tradition of critical writing about both literature and music for the informed but not necessarily professional reader. This tradition was soon imitated and began to flourish in Germany in periodicals such as Johann Mattheson's *Critica musica* (1722–25); Johann Scheibe's *Der critische Musikus* (1737–40); Friedrich Wilhelm Marpurg's *Der critische Musicus an der Spree* (1749–50), *Historisch-kritische Beyträge zur Aufnahme der Musik* (1754–62, 1778), and *Kritische Briefe über die Tonkunst* (1760–64); and Johann Adam Hiller's *Wöchentliche Nachrichten und Anmerkungen die Musik betreffend* (1766–70), perhaps the first specialized music periodical aimed at a general audience, and including among many things reviews of performances and new works.

Composers along with some literary figures assumed increasing prominence as critics in the 19th century, and much that characterized criticism even in the 20th century had its roots in the *Romanticism of this period, which took music as the paradigm for all of the arts. E. T. A. Hoffmann's essays in the *Allgemeine musikalische Zeitung* of Leipzig from 1809 to 1819 initiated this new era and were very influential in the reception of the works of Mozart, Haydn, and Beethoven. Berlioz was France's greatest composer-critic of the 19th century and Schumann, who founded the *Neue Zeitschrift für Musik* in 1834, was Germany's. Other composer-critics of the 19th century included Weber, Liszt, Wagner, and Hugo Wolf. In the meantime, music reviews became a regular feature of the daily press and of many nonmusic journals. Paris, the operatic capital of Europe throughout the first half of the century, had an especially active and diverse music press, contributors to which ranged from François-Joseph Fétis and Castil-Blaze to numerous anonymous hacks. Century's end saw a reaction to some features of Romantic criticism in the work of Vienna's most influential critic Eduard Hanslick, an ardent advocate of the music of Brahms as against that of Wagner and his followers. This was also the period of George Bernard Shaw's brilliant contributions to the press in London.

Debussy continued the tradition of the distinguished composer-critic in the early 20th century, but thereafter no composer of comparable stature wrote criticism for the popular press on a regular basis. The adoption by many composers of the complex technical language of *twelve-tone and *serial music, the further emergence of analysis as an attempt at the "objective" study of individual works, and the vogue in music scholarship for the "scientific" study of sources and the like combined with other factors to discourage the development of music criticism along the lines of the criticism that became central to the study and teaching of literature. Donald Francis Tovey is among the few writers in English in this mode from the first half of the century whose work continues to inspire both readers and writers. Joseph Kerman (a musicologist), Edward T. Cone (a composer), Leonard B. Meyer (a theorist), and Charles Rosen (a pianist) are among the leading exponents of scholarly criticism in English of recent decades. Distinguished critics for the popular press in English have included writers with diverse backgrounds, the best-known composer among them being Virgil Thomson. But newspapers in the major musical centers and magazines devoted to recordings and high-fidelity equipment have also included serious criticism for a general audience.

Bibl.: Charles Burney, "Essay on Musical Criticism," *A General History of Music,* bk. 3 (London, 1789; R: New York: Dover, 1957). Michel D. Calvocoressi, *The Principles and Methods of Musical Criticism* (London: Oxford U Pr, H Milford, 1923; 2nd ed., 1931). Theodore M. Greene, *The Arts and the Art of Criticism* (Princeton: Princeton U Pr, 1940; 2nd ed., 1947). Irving Kolodin, ed., *The Critical Composer: The Musical Writings of Berlioz, Wagner, Schumann, Tchaikovsky, and Others* (New York: Howell, Soskin, 1940; R: Port Washington, N.Y.: Kennikat Pr, 1969). Max Graf, *Composer and Critic: Two Hundred Years of Musical Criticism* (New York: Norton, 1946; R: 1971). Armand Machabey, *Traité de la critique musicale* (Paris: Richard-Masse, 1947). Norman Demuth, ed., *An Anthology of Musical Criticism from the Fifteenth to the Twentieth Century* (London: Eyre & Spottiswoode, 1947). Richard French, ed., *Music Criticism: A Symposium* (Cambridge, Mass.: Harvard U Pr, 1948). Virgil Thomson, *The Art of Judging Music* (New York: A A Knopf, 1948). "Music Critics and Criticism Today," *MT* 101 (1960): 220–25. George Bernard Shaw, *How to Become a Musical Critic,* ed. Dan H. Laurence (New York: Hill & Wang, 1961). Alan Walker, *An Anatomy of Musical Criticism* (London: Barrie & Rockliffe, 1966). Leon Plantinga, *Schumann as Critic* (New Haven: Yale U Pr, 1967; R: New York: Da Capo, 1976). Leonard B. Meyer, *Explaining Music* (Berkeley and Los Angeles: U of Cal Pr, 1973; R: Chicago: U of Chicago Pr, 1978). Joseph Kerman, "How We Got into Analysis and How to Get Out," *Critical Inquiry,* vol. 2, no. 2 (Winter, 1980): 311–31; as "The State of Academic Music Criticism," in *On Criticizing Music,* ed. Kingsley Price (Baltimore: Johns Hopkins U Pr, 1981). Edward T. Cone, "The Authority of Music Criticism," *JAMS* (1981): 1–18. Joseph Kerman, *Contemplating Music: Challenges to Musicology* (Cambridge, Mass.: Harvard U Pr, 1985). Mark N. Grant, *Maestros of the Pen: A History of Classical Music Criticism in America* (Boston: Northeastern U Pr, 1998). Lawrence Kramer, *Musical Meaning: Toward a Critical History* (Berkeley and Los Angeles: U of Calif Pr, 2002). D.M.R.

Croatia *(Hrvatska).* I. *Current musical life and related institutions.* The first music school in Zagreb was founded in 1788, followed by the school *Hrvatski glazbeni zavod* (1829) from which in 1921 grew the Academy of Music. Musicological research is carried out at the academy's *Zavod za sistematsku muzikologiju* (Institute of Systematic Musicology, 1967) and the *Odjel za povijest hrvatske glazbe* (Department for History of Croatian Music, 1980) affiliated with the *Hrvatska akademija znanosti i umjetnosti* (Croatian Academy of Sciences and Arts). Main periodicals are *Arti musicies* (1969) and *International Review for Aesthetics and Sociology of Music* (1970), both published by the *Hrvatsko muzikološko društvo* (Croatian Musicological Society, 1992). Research in folk music goes back to the 1860s, when Franjo Ksaver Kuhač (1834–1911) started collecting material for his collection *Južno-slovjenske narodne popievke* (South-Slav Folk Songs, Zagreb, 1878–81), and today is carried out at the *Institut za etnologiju i folkloristiku* (Institute for Ethnology and Folklore, 1948), which publishes *Narodna umjetnost* (1962).

Permanent opera companies are in Zagreb (1870), Osijek (1907), Split (1922/23), and Rijeka (1946), while the *Komedija* theater in Zagreb (1950) specializes in operetta and musicals. Main orchestras are the *Zagrebačka filharmonija* (1920), the symphony orchestra of the Croatian Radio (1957), and the chamber orchestra *Zagrebački solosti* (1953, known as *I solisti di Zagreb*). Music publishers are the *Društvo hrvatskih skladatelja* (Croatian Composers' Society, 1945) and the Music Information Center (1972). Festivals with an international reputation are the *Dubrovačke ljetne igre* (Dubrovnik, 1950), the *Splitsko ljeto* (Split, 1954), and the Zagreb Music Biennale (1961).

II. *History of art music.* Latin liturgical manuscripts with Gregorian chants were produced since the 11th century all over the Croatian territory, especially in Benedictine scriptoria of Osor, Zadar, Split, Dubrovnik, and Trogir. The Zagreb Diocese (founded in 1094) followed the Latin rites and inherited a large number of liturgical manuals (today at the *Metropolitanska knjižnica,* Zagreb) and customs from Hungary, while Dalmatia had contacts with Italian Beneventan scriptoria. The Zagreb cathedral developed its own ritual in the later part of the Middle Ages (sung until 1788). Being on the border between the Latin and Byzantine influences, the coastal areas and islands retained from the Middle Ages the Glagolitic liturgy in the Croatian variant of Church Slavonic language. Late Renaissance composers (Giulio Schiavetto, 1530/35–1590) were influenced by both the Venetian and Roman schools, while the Franco-Flemish polyphonic style reach as far to the southeast as Dubrovnik (Lambert Courtois, fl. 1542–83). This was also the time of the earliest transcriptions of Croatian folk songs (Petar Hektorović, 1558) and dances (Giulio Cesare Barbetta, 1569). The early-Baroque monody and Venetian style were instantly adopted along the Adriatic coast by Ivan Lukačić (?1587–1648), Tomaso Cecchino (ca. 1582–1644), and Marcantonio Romano (ca. 1552–1636). The Italian theater was promptly accepted. The first public theaters opened in Hvar (1612) and Dubrovnik (1682), and the 1617 translation of Rinuccini's *Euridice* by Paskoj Primović was probably the earliest translation of an Italian opera libretto into any other language. In the 17th and 18th centuries in the north a significant role was played by the Jesuits (who frequently organized elaborate theater performances in their residences), Paulists, and Franciscans, who were all prolific in outfitting folk songs with new, theologically approved texts suitable for pastoral work.

Classicism arrived promptly in noble households, many of which maintained instrumental ensembles, and in towns. Although sporadic, instrumental works in the early sonata form appeared in Dubrovnik as early as the 1750s (Luka Sorkočević, 1734–89), spreading to Split (Julije Bajamonti, 1744–1800) and Varaždin (Leopold Ebner, 1769–1830). Zagreb became the main music center in the early 19th century, particularly after the founding of the music society *Hrvatski glazbeni zavod* (1827). Early Romanticism coincided in the 1830s and 1840s with the movement for national revival, which inspired not only the first national operas by Vatroslav Lisinski (1819–54: *Ljubav i zloba,* 1846; *Porin,* 1851), but also Romantic lieder and instrumental miniatures. Through his teaching and conducting, musical life was strongly influenced by Ivan Zajc (1832–1914), himself a prolific composer. Under his directorship of the Zagreb Opera (1870–89), major works were staged soon after their European premieres. The generation of composers coming to the scene after World War I split into two streams, one inclining toward late Romanticism and modernism (Blagoje Bersa, 1873–1934; Josip Hatze, 1879–1959; Dora Pejačević, 1885–1923; Franjo Dugan, 1874–1948; Vjekoslav Rosenberg-Ružić, 1870–1954), and the other toward the style based on folklore (Antun Dobronić, 1878–1955; Fran Lhotka,

1883–1962; Krsto Odak, 1888–1965; Božidar Širola, 1889–1956; Krešimir Baranović, 1894–1976; Jakov Gotovac, 1895–1982; Josip Štolcer-Slavenski, 1896–1955; Ivo Parac, 1890–1954). This division persisted until the outburst of stylistic pluralism in the 1960s, greatly influenced by the Zagreb Music Biennale, in works of Boris Papandopulo (1906–91), Ivan Brkanović (1906–87), Milo Cipra (1906–85), Bruno Bjelinski (1909–92), Stjepan Šulek (1914–86), Natko Devčić (1914–97), Branimir Sakač (1918–79), Milko Kelemen (b. 1924), Ivo Malec (b. 1925), Stanko Horvat (b. 1930), Ruben Radica (b. 1931), Dubravko Detoni (b. 1937), Davorin Kempf (b. 1947), Silvio Foretić (b. 1940), Marko Ruždjak (b. 1946), and Franjo Parać (b. 1948).

III. *Traditional music.* Croatian traditional music reflects the overlap of Mediterranean, Central European (Pannonian and sub-Alpine), and Balkan musical styles. Polka, *tanac,* and *balun,* the most popular dances in Istria and the Kvarner Bay, are played on shawms, usually in pairs of *mala* (small) and *vela* (big) *sopila (sopela, roženica).* The *sopila* music has its parallel in a two-part singing style called *na tanko i debelo,* in which one singer performs a falsetto accompanied by the other in a lower register. In the Dinaric region (north Adriatic coast and islands with the mountainous hinterland of Dalmatia and the districts of Lika, Kordun, and Banovina) tunes are based on chromatic modes of narrow range, with intervals deviating from the system of equal half-tones. The *ojkanje* is a peculiar style of singing melisma with a sharp and prolonged shaking of the voice on the syllables "oj" or "hoj." Narrative songs are performed with the **gusle* accompaniment. In the dance repertoire, the *nijemo kolo* (silent kolo) is common, performed without accompaniment, to the rhythm of steps and the jingling sound of dancers' jewelry.

In Dalmatia, dances *(šotić, manfrina, kvadrilja, polka šaltina)* are accompanied by *mandolina* (pluck lute) ensembles. In the Dubrovnik area the *linđo (poskočnica)* is characteristic, accompanied by the *lirica (lijerica)* plucked lute. On the islands of Korčula and Lastovo the sword dances *moreška* and *moštra* are performed during carnival. The most prominent marker of the Dalmatian music identity is *klapa* singing. The term *klapa* refers to a group of five to ten men who sing in four- or sometimes three-part harmonies.

In northwestern Croatia (Hrvatsko Zagorje, Turopolje, Posavina, Bilogora, Žumberak, Gorski Kotar) tunes in major keys, couple dances (*drmeš* and *polka*), and instruments suitable for diatonic music prevail. Slavonia, Baranja, and Srijem (northeastern Croatia) are dominated by the *tambura* instruments (plucked lutes), played in ensembles composed of four sizes of instruments *(bisernica, brač, bugarija, berde)* or solo *(samica).* Dances are usually performed in closed circle *(kolo),* accompanied by singing or *tambura* ensembles. The *slavonsko kolo* and *šokačko kolo* are common today in Croatian traditional music and symbolize the identity of people of eastern Croatia. In Međimurje and Podravina (northern Croatia adjacent to Hungary) melodies are based on medieval modes and anhemitonic pentatonic scales. The most common instruments are the bourdon box zithers (*citura* in Podravina; *trontolje* in Međimurje), the dulcimer *(cimbal),* and the violin. Dominant since the late 19th century are couple dances imported from the north (*čardaš,* polka, *valcer,* and *zibnšrit*).

Bibl.: Koraljka Kos, *Musikinstrumente im mittelalterlichen Kroatien* (Zagreb: Muzička akademija, 1972). Josip Andreis, *Music in Croatia* (Zagreb: Muzička akademija, 1974, 1982). Miho Demović, *Musik und Musiker in der Republik Dubrovnik vom Anfang des 11. Jahrhunderts bis zur Mitte des 17. Jahrhunderts* (Regensburg: Bosse, 1981). Jerko Martinić, *Glagolitische Gesänge Mitteldalmatiens* (Regensburg: Bosse, 1981). Lovro Županović, *Centuries of Croatian Music* (Zagreb: Muzički informativni centar, 1984–89). Ivano Cavallini, *Musica, cultura e spettacolo in Istria tra '500 e '600* (Florence: Olschki, 1990). Ivano Cavallini, *I due volti di Nettuno: Studi su teatro e musica a Venezia e in Dalmazia dal Cinquecento al Settecento* (Lucca: LIM, 1994). Svanibor Pettan, ed., *Music, Politics, and War: Views from Croatia* (Zagreb: Institut za etnologiju i folkloristiku, 1998). Stanislav Tuksar, ed., *Mediaeval Music Cultures of the Adriatic Region* (Zagreb: Hrvatsko Muzikološko Društvo, 2000).

Discography: *Croatie: Musique d'aitrefois,* prod. by Grozdana Marošević, Ocora/Radio France, 1997. *Croatia,* prod. by Svanibor Pettan, Musiques traditionnelles d'aujourd'hui, Auvidis/UNESCO, 1998. Z.B.

Croche [Fr.]. Eighth *note.

Croiser les mains [Fr.]. An instruction to cross the hands in piano playing; also indicated with the forms *croisez, croisement.*

Croma [It.]. Eighth *note.

Cromatico [It.]. *Chromatic. For *madregali cromatici,* see *Note nere.*

Cromorne [Fr.]. (1) *Crumhorn. (2) A reed stop with half-length cylindrical resonators, especially important in the classic French organ.

Crook. (1) [Fr. *corps de rechange;* Ger. *Aufsatzbogen, Stimmbogen;* It. *ritorto;* Sp. *tonillo, cuerpo de recambio*] A curved segment of tubing that can be inserted into a brass instrument, especially a *natural horn or trumpet, in order to alter its fundamental pitch. See also Shank. (2) On the bassoon or English horn, the curved metal tube to which the reed is affixed.

Croon. To sing relatively softly and with inflections of pitch as in the style of such singers of sentimental popular songs as Rudy Vallee, Bing Crosby, Perry Como, and Frank Sinatra. The style was made possible by the advent of electronic amplification, which eliminated the need to project the voice as in the singing styles of Western art music. It was the dominant male singing style in popular music from the 1920s into the 1950s and has survived alongside other styles since.

Cross fingering. (1) On an instrument with finger holes, a fingering requiring a closed hole or holes below an open one. The *Boehm system was in part developed in order to obviate the need for many of the fingerings of this type that would otherwise be necessary in order to produce chromatic pitches. See also Fork fingering. (2) The use of a "cross" key to produce the semitones outside the basic scale of a wind instrument. The first key to which the name applied, the short F key of the flute, lay across the body of the instrument. Later any key that produced a note one semitone higher than the natural fingering below it was so termed. M.S.

Cross flute. The transverse *flute as distinct from the *recorder.

Crossover. A recording that is intended to appeal to the audience for one style of popular music or jazz or rock music but that becomes popular with another audience as well, usually audiences as defined by the *charts published by the music industry; also an artist who makes such a recording.

Cross-relation, false relation [Fr. *fausse relation;* Ger. *Querstand*]. The succession of a pitch in one voice by a chromatic alteration of that pitch (or its equivalent in another octave) in another voice. A simultaneous or vertical cross-relation is the simultaneous occurrence of two pitches related in this way. Such relations, especially between outer voices as in Ex. 1, are normally prohibited by the academic formulations of 18th- and 19th-century harmony and counterpoint on the grounds that such chromatic motion is most intelligible when it occurs within a single voice. Their appearance in music of this period, however, often mitigated by placement in inner voices or by accompanying passing tones [Ex. 2], is not infrequent.

Among the most frequent progressions giving rise to cross-relations are the following: the use of V^6 or V^6_5 in minor [Ex. 2]; the use in minor of the lowered seventh scale degree in a descending line in one voice (i.e., melodic minor) followed by the raised seventh degree (i.e., harmonic minor) in another [Ex. 3]; the *tonicization of the sixth scale degree [Ex. 4]; the use of a Neapolitan *sixth chord followed by the dominant [Ex. 5]. Modal mixture and other techniques associated with the increasing chromaticism of music in the late 19th and early 20th centuries (e.g., that of Mahler and Strauss) also regularly produced cross-relations.

Cross-relations occur in music of the Middle Ages and Renaissance as well, and the term is also applied to the creation of a tritone between two different voices in the music of this period. According to some interpretations of the notion of **musica ficta,* many of these cross-relations are to be eliminated by the addition of editorial accidentals. By no means all of them can be avoided, however, and the use of cross-relations is unambiguously attested in instrumental tablatures of the period. They are a feature of keyboard music on the Continent and in England into the 17th century [see also *Toccata di durezze e ligature*], and they are an important expressive device for some composers of the later madrigal, e.g., Gesualdo.

Cross-rhythm. A rhythm in which the regular pattern of accents of the prevailing meter is contradicted by a conflicting pattern and not merely by a momentary

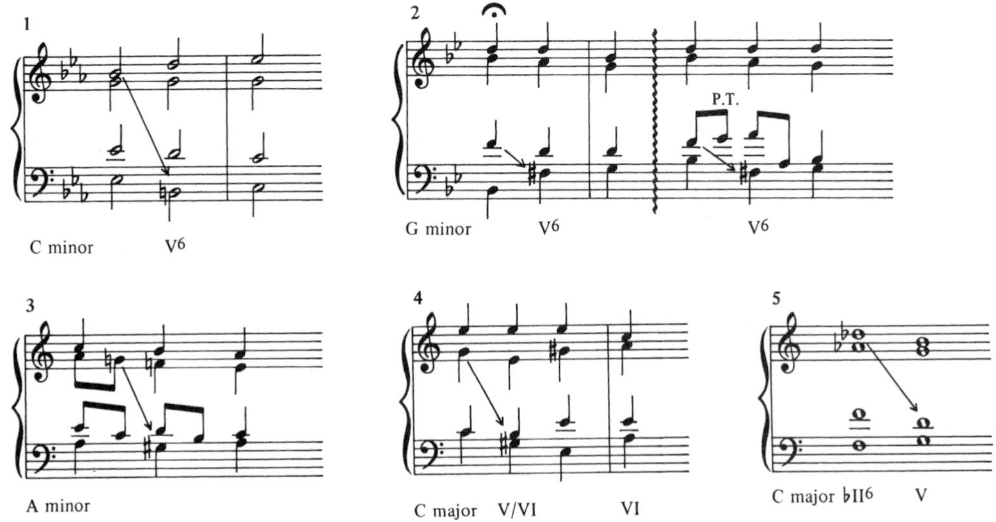

2. Bach, "Auf meinen lieben Gott." 3. Bach, "Helft mir Gotts Gute Preisen." 4. Bach, "Herr Jesu Christ, meins Lebens Licht."

displacement that leaves the prevailing meter fundamentally unchallenged. See also Syncopation, Polyrhythm.

Crot(t). See *Rote.*

Crotal. (1) **Crotalum.* (2) *Pellet bell.

Crotales [Fr., also *cymbales antiques,* antique cymbals]. Small, rather thick cymbals of definite pitch ranging in size from about 5 to 12.5 cm in diameter, now manufactured as a chromatic set mounted on a board. See ill. under Percussion instruments.

Crotalum [Lat., pl. *crotala;* Gr. *krotalon*]. *Clappers or *castanets of ancient Greece and Rome, made of wood, bone, bronze, etc. They were often used by dancers.

Crotchet. In British terminology, the quarter note [see Note, Notation]. The term derives from the representation in black notation beginning in the 14th century of the semiminim (the early equivalent of the quarter note) as a minim with a flag or crook (hence *crochata*) attached.

Crouth, Crowd. See Crwth, *Rote.*

Crucible, The. Opera in four acts by Robert Ward (libretto by B. Stambler after Arthur Miller's play), produced in New York in 1961. Setting: Salem, Mass., 1692.

Crucifixus [Lat., crucified]. The portion of the Credo of the *Mass dealing with the crucifixion, often set as a separate movement in large-scale polyphonic settings of the Mass text.

Cruit [Gael.]. A plucked stringed instrument of medieval Ireland. From the 12th to the 14th century, *cruit* denoted the *Irish harp, but the word may also have referred to plucked *lyres. See also *Rote, Tiómpán.*

Crumhorn [Fr. *cromorne, tournebout;* Ger. *Krummhorn;* It. *storto, piva torta;* Sp. *orlo*]. A *wind-cap, double-reed wind instrument of the 16th and 17th centuries. It has a narrow cylindrical bore and is shaped like the letter J. Several sizes of crumhorn are described by Praetorius (1619) and others. The fingering of the instrument is similar to that of the *recorder, though the lack of direct control of the reed prevents *overblowing. The larger sizes were provided with keys, usually protected with perforated metal covers. Unfingered tuning holes are present in the curve of the tube. See ill. under Reed. M.S.

Crwth, crowd [Welsh, pronounced "crooth"]. A bowed *lyre of Wales, now obsolete. It was rectangular in shape, the lower portion being a flat sound box, the upper part consisting of two arms and a yoke to which the strings were held by pegs. A fingerboard with three or four strings above it passed from the center of the yoke to the sound box. Two additional strings were sometimes added to one side. It is pictured in sources as early as the 11th century. Early models lacked a fingerboard and were most likely plucked. The bowed *crwth,* with a fingerboard and six strings, had come into use by the 14th century.

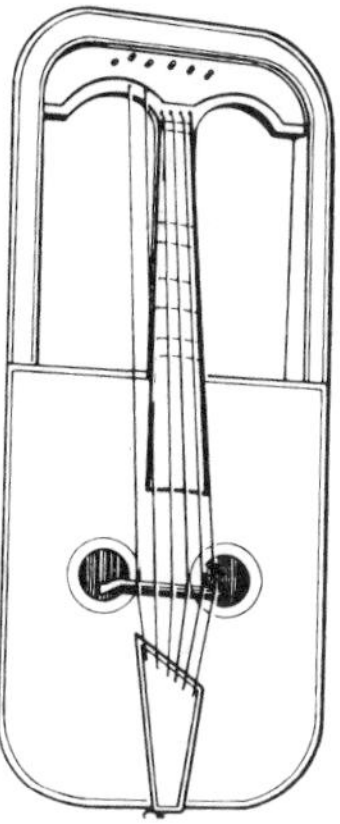

Crwth.

The *crwth* was known in England, Ireland, and on the Continent, but it was above all the instrument of the Welsh *bards. With the decline of the bardic tradition in the 16th century, the *crwth* became increasingly rare, and the last players died in the 19th century. Bowed lyres similar to the *crwth*—the Swedish **tal-harpa* and Finnish **jouhikantele*—are still played.

Bibl.: Otto Andersson, *The Bowed-Harp* (London: W Reeves, 1930; R: New York: AMS Pr, 1973).

Cryptography. In music, the use of music or musical notation to convey an extramusical idea or message. The simplest and most common method entails the use of the letter names of pitches to spell a word or abbreviation. *B-A-C-H is perhaps the single most widely known example; Schumann's **Carnaval* includes other well-known examples. A related technique employed beginning in the Renaissance makes use of *solmization syllables [see *Soggetto cavato*]. *Eye music constitutes another related technique. More elaborate schemes may produce equivalences for each of the letters of the alphabet by repeating the usual sequence of seven pitches (A–G) until the alphabet is exhausted (with the result that each of the seven pitches may represent as many as four letters) or by employing chromatic pitches and enharmonic equivalents. Composers who have made significant use of musical cryptography include Michael Haydn, Schumann, Brahms, Elgar, Ravel, Debussy, Honegger, Berg, Shostakovich, and Messiaen.

C.s. [It.]. Abbr. for *colla sinistra,* with the left hand.

Csárdás [Hung.]. A Hungarian dance first documented ca. 1835 and closely related to the fast *(friss)* part of the **verbunkos.* It is typically in fast duple meter (though a slow, *lassu,* form was also developed) and was a fashionable ballroom dance throughout the 19th century. Examples occur in the *Hungarian Rhapsodies* of Liszt.

C sol fa (ut), Csolfa(ut), Cesolfa(ut). See Hexachord.

Cuando [Sp.]. A traditional dance song of Chile and Argentina, originally cultivated in the salons and theaters of the early 19th century and rarely heard today. Closely related to the **minué montonero,* in triple meter, and with two sections in contrasting tempo, it derives its name from the refrain phrase "Cuando, cuando, ay cuando mi vida, cuando." D.S.

Cuatro [Sp.]. A small, four-stringed guitar of Latin America, especially Venezuela. Many examples have strings in courses of two. The Puerto Rican *cuatro* has five courses of two metal strings.

Cuba. The music of Cuba, popular music in particular, has deeply influenced musical life far beyond the country's national borders and out of proportion with its small size and 11 million inhabitants.

I. *History.* Cuba's aboriginal people, principally Arawak known as Taíno, swiftly died of disease and hardship in the wake of the Spanish conquest that began in 1492. Little is known of their music, though the *areito* celebration was a focus of music and dancing. Maracas and other idiophones fashioned from natural materials, and a conch shell trumpet, the *guamo,* were among their instruments. African people of many cultural backgrounds took their place as forced laborers, arriving in the 16th century to as late as the 1840s, and became a principal force in shaping Cuban musical life. European art music of Cuban origin was evident in church music of the 18th and 19th centuries, in the opera, *zarzuela,* and concert music of the 19th century, and in more nationalistic concert music in the 20th century. Compositions by Manuel Saumell (1817–70), such as *contradanzas* for piano, prefigured Cuban art music of later years. Nationalist composers Alejando García Caturla (1906–40) and Amadeo Roldán (1900–1939), were succeeded by the neoclassical Grupo de Renovación, headed by José Ardévol (1911–81), and its followers. Cuban folk music took many forms, derived principally from regional traditions. The **son, punto guajiro, canción,* **danzón,* and *rumba, roughly in this chronological order, emerged as major forms. African musical culture had great, though varying, impact on these forms, with perhaps the *punto guajiro* being the least affected and the rumba the most.

II. *Afro-Cuban music.* A large and diverse corpus of Cuban styles developed among or critically influenced by the island's black population and often strongly reflective of African musical traditions. These styles generally share: a predilection for percussion instruments, which are found in great variety in Cuba; vocal styles employing solo-chorus, call-and-response procedures; prevalence of both textual and musical improvisation; mixed vocal and instrumental ensemble performance; orientation to the dance; and an emphasis on rhythm, seen, e.g., in the pervasive use of syncopation, in rhythmically complex relationships between melody and accompanying parts, and in typically polyphonic accompaniments that combine layers of contrasting ostinato figures.

Among the most important Afro-Cuban musical traditions are the following: the ritual music of various religious groups (Lucumí, Abakuá, etc.) of African derivation; the **son,* a song and dance-music style of rural Cuba, most typically for small ensembles of voices, strings, and percussion; the several varieties of *rumba (*yambú, guaguancó,* and *columbia,* etc.), secular recreational music of liturgical origin involving dance, solo-choral singing, and percussion ensemble performance; and 20th-century urban popular music, including adaptations of the folk *son* and rumba, forms such as the *bolero and **danzón* that reflect 19th-century Cuban aristocratic traditions as well as African-derived influence, and numerous more recent genres, such as the *mambo and the **chachachá.* This popular music is performed by several kinds of ensembles, the most characteristic and long-lived being the *conjunto* developed in the 1930s, with vocalists, trumpets, and, variously, piano, guitar, *tres* (guitar with three double courses of strings), string bass, conga drums, *timbales,* and an array of handheld idiophones.

Afro-Cuban popular music has had a great impact in Europe, in North America, and above all in other Latin American countries.

Bibl.: Alejo Carpentier, *La música en Cuba* (Havana: Editorial Letras Cubanas, 1979). Fernando Ortiz, *La música afrocubana* (Madrid: Biblioteca Júcar, 1975). María Teresa Vélez, *Drumming for the Gods: The Life and Times of Felipe García Villamil, Santero, Palero, and Abakuá* (Philadelphia: Temple U Pr, 2000). (I) D.E.S. (II) D.S.

Cue. (1) In an individual part, an extract from some other, prominent part, usually printed in smaller notes, serving to alert the performer to an approaching entrance, especially after a long rest. (2) A gesture given by a conductor to signal the entrance of a player or section; to give such a gesture.

Cueca [Sp.]. The national dance of Chile, also found in Bolivia and Argentina, descended from the *zamacueca (zambacueca)* of colonial Peru. In rural Chile, it is sung with guitar, harp, and, most commonly today, accordion; this accompaniment is frequently supplemented with drumming on a wooden box or the side of the guitar. It is typically in the major mode, in rapid tempo, and with compound duple accompaniments to melodies combining patterns in 6/8, 3/4, and 2/4. D.S.

Cuíca [Port.]. A *friction drum of Brazil. It is widespread and popular, especially in dance music.

Cuivre [Fr.]. A player of a brass instrument; *les cuivres,* the brass instruments or section; *cuivré,* a harsh or brassy tone, especially on the horn.

Cumbia [Sp.]. An Afro-Hispanic dance-music genre

of Panama and the Atlantic coastal region of Colombia. It is performed by small ensembles with, e.g., accordion, drums, and other percussion instruments. Distinctive traits include moderate to rapid duple meter, short, syncopated melodic phrases, and sharp offbeat accompanimental accents, as in the accompanying examples.

In the 20th century, it became an important urban popular dance form in several Latin American countries.

Cunning Little Vixen, The [Cz. *Příhody Lišky Bystroušky*]. Opera in three acts by Leoš Janáček (libretto by the composer after Rudolf Těsnohlídek), produced in Brno in 1924. Setting: a mythical woodland.

Cup. See Mouthpiece and ill. under Brass instruments.

Cupo [It.]. Gloomy, somber.

Currentes [Lat.]. See *Conjunctura.*

Cursive and tonic. In *Gregorian and other Western liturgical chant, cadential melodic formulas that are, respectively, applied to a fixed number of the final syllables of the text without regard for accentuation or that are adjusted to the accentuation of the text by the addition or suppression of notes. The most prominent examples of the former are found in the tones for the great responsories; for the latter in the tones for the antiphonal psalmody of the Office [see Psalmody, Psalm tone]. The use of the term cursive for the invariable formulas derives from the theories of André Mocquereau (*PM,* vols. 3–4), elaborated further by Paolo Ferretti, that trace its origins to literary **cursus.*

Cursus [Lat.]. In classical Latin prose, any of several patterns (described by Cicero and Quintilian with the term *clausula*) of long and short syllables employed at the ends of clauses and sentences. In the late 12th century, the term *cursus* was applied to analogous patterns of accented and unaccented syllables *(cursus planus, c. velox, c. tardus).* In the view of André Mocquereau (disputed by, among others, Willi Apel, *Gregorian Chant,* 1958, pp. 297–301), the metrical *cursus* was the basis for certain invariable melodic cadential formulas in *Gregorian chant [see Cursive and tonic]. Paolo Ferretti (*Il cursus metrico e il ritmo delle melodie gregoriane,* 1913; *Estetica gregoriana,* 1934) developed further extended theories of the relationship between chant and literary *cursus.*

Curtain tune. **Entr'acte.*

Curtal. An English double-reed wind instrument of conical bore, used in the 16th and 17th centuries, equivalent to the German *Dulzian* or *chorist Fagott.* It was constructed of a single piece of wood containing two parallel bores connected at the bottom and had a small integral or separate bell at the top. The curtal was made in two sizes, the single (tenor) and the double (bass). The bass instrument is the precursor of the modern *bassoon. See ill. under Reed. M.S.

Custos [Lat.]. *Direct.

Cut time. The *meter indicated by the sign ¢, equivalent to 2/2.

Cutup. In an organ pipe, the distance between the upper and lower lips of the mouth [see ill. under Organ].

Cycle. (1) In *acoustics, one complete vibration of a vibrating system such as a string, the number of such vibrations per unit of time (usually described in cycles per second, or *Hertz) being the frequency of vibration and the principal determinant of pitch. (2) Any system of *tuning or *temperament in which the octave is divided into intervals of equal size. (3) See Song cycle. (4) The sequence or pattern of movements in a multimovement work such as a symphony or suite. (5) In discussions of polyphonic Masses of the 14th and 15th centuries, and to some extent of liturgical chant as well, settings of individual texts of the Mass (especially the Ordinary) that are intended to form a single work, whether or not unified musically. See also Cyclic form.

Cyclic form. Any musical form consisting of discrete movements in two or more of which the same or very similar thematic material is employed. The first large-scale works of this type were the cyclic Masses of the 15th century, in which a single **cantus firmus* is employed in all movements or in which all movements begin in the same way ("motto beginning") [see Mass]. The *parody Mass of the 16th century is also cyclic in this sense. Instrumental forms from the late 16th and early 17th centuries, such as the *canzona, *sonata, and *suite, often exhibit thematic recurrence among movements, but instrumental music of the 18th century does not in general employ cyclic forms (though some examples of suites, e.g., by Handel, carry forward the older tradition). The 19th century sees a steady increase in their use, however. Well-known early examples from this period include Schubert's **Wanderer-Fantasie* and Berlioz's **Symphonie fantastique.* In some works, whole movements recur, as in Schumann's **Davidsbündlertänze.* Other composers to make considerable use of the technique, sometimes in association with the *transformation of themes, are Schumann, Liszt, and Franck.

Cylinder. See Valve. See also Recording.

Cymbale [Fr.]. In the classical French organ, a mixture stop of three or more ranks, usually pitched with its lowest rank an octave higher than the **Fourniture,* with which it was intended to be used to complete the **Plein jeu.* Unlike the German **Cimbel,* the French

Cymbale breaks back in pitch as it ascends in the treble, often having 8′ as its lowest pitch at c‴.

Cymbalon [Hung.]. **Cimbalom.*

Cymbals [Fr. *cymbales;* Ger. *Becken;* It. *piatti;* Sp. *platillos*]. Broad-rimmed circular plates of indefinite pitch, slightly convex so that only the edges touch when two are struck together. In the center of each is a small hump, or boss, pierced by a hole, through which a holding strap is attached. Modern orchestral cymbals, made of copper and tin alloy with a touch of silver, are heavier and flatter than their predecessors and come in a variety of sizes, typically between 44 and 55 cm (17 and 22 in.) in diameter. Thickness and hence tone color vary as well. In orchestral music, they are most often held vertically and clashed together, the sound being damped if necessary against the chest. Cymbals can also be suspended and struck with some sort of beater or a pair of drum sticks; or one can be fastened to the top of a bass drum and hit with the other. For cymbals used in jazz and popular music, including hi-hat, ride, crash, and sizzle cymbals, see Drum set; for antique cymbals, see Crotales. See ill. under Percussion instruments.

Cymbals probably originated in Asia Minor as ritual instruments. They are mentioned frequently in the Bible (ca. 1100 B.C.E.), were used in the orgiastic rites connected with worship of the goddess Cybele (1200 B.C.E.), and appear in Babylonian and Assyrian sculpture (ca. 700 B.C.E.) and later on Greek and Roman monuments. They were widespread in the Far East, particularly in India and Tibet, and were included in a Turkestani orchestra established at the Imperial Court in Peking in 384 C.E. Gigantic instruments nearly 1 m in diameter were employed in Mongolian temples. The *gamelan* orchestras of Indonesia include smaller versions, and female dancers from many Oriental regions have used finger cymbals.

Cymbals came to Europe during the Middle Ages and were depicted, for example, in the **Cantigas de Santa María* (ca. 1270). Other medieval illuminated manuscripts often show angels or women playing cymbals, usually held horizontally in the Oriental manner.

Cymbals were probably first used in the modern orchestra by Nicolaus Strungk in his opera *Esther* (1680), but seem not to have been in general use until the craze for Turkish *Janissary music gripped Europe in the mid-18th century. Gluck used cymbals in *Iphigénie en Aulide* (1774) as did Mozart in *Die Entführung aus dem Serail* (1782), Haydn in his Symphony no. 100 (*Military,* 1793–94), and Beethoven in the *Ruins of Athens* (1812), *Wellington's Victory* or "Battle Symphony" (1813), and the Ninth Symphony (1822–24). Berlioz called for no fewer than ten cymbals in his *Requiem* (1837), and Wagner often wrote for them in the *Ring of the Nibelungen* (1848–76). The regular use of cymbals in the Romantic orchestra is typified by the works of Tchaikovsky and Rimsky-Korsakov. More recent composers, such as Mahler, Strauss, Schoenberg, Bartók, Stravinsky, Hindemith, and Walton, have called for a variety of effects, requiring cymbals of different sizes and tone colors and struck with a variety of devices, such as a wire brush, steel rod, coins, triangle beater, fingernails, or cello bow.

Bibl.: Carl Engel, *The Music of the Most Ancient Nations,* 2nd ed. (London, 1864; new ed., London: W Reeves, 1929). Joseph Baggers, "Les timbales, le tambour et les instruments à percussion," in *Encyclopédie de la musique et dictionnaire du Conservatoire,* pt. 2, vol. 3 (Paris: Delagrave, 1927). Hans Hickmann, "Die altägyptischen Becken," *Instrumentenbau Zeitschrift* 12 (1957–58): 2–6. Gerassimos Avgerinos, *Handbuch der Schlag- und Effektinstrumente* (Frankfurt am Main: Musikinstrument, 1967). Karl Peinkofer and Fritz Tannigel, *Handbuch des Schlagzeugs* (Mainz, 1969). Włodzimierz Kotoński, *Schlaginstrumente im moderne Orchester* (Mainz: B Schott, 1968). Reginald Smith Brindle, *Contemporary Percussion* (London: Oxford U Pr, 1970). James Blades, *Percussion Instruments and Their History,* rev. ed. (London: Faber, 1975). Jeremy Montagu, *Timpani and Percussion* (London/New York, 2002). E.A.B.

Cymbalum. (1) [Lat., pl. *cymbala*] In antiquity, *cymbala* were small cymbals. In the Middle Ages, they were a set of three to eight small, tuned bells, hung in a row and struck with a wooden rod or a small hammer. These were used in churches and monasteries to give intervals to singers and to accompany plainsong. (2) [Fr.] **Cimbalom.*

Bibl.: Joseph Smits van Waesberghe, *Cymbala: Bells in the Middle Ages* (Rome: AIM, 1951).

Cymbasso [Ital.]. **Cimbasso.*

Cymbelstern [Ger., Du.]. **Cimbelstern,* **Horologium.*

Cythara [Lat.]. *Kithara.

Cythringen [Ger.]. *Cittern.

Czakan [Hung.]. A walking stick whose upper portion is a *duct flute, usually detachable. It was popular in Austria and Hungary in the early 19th century. See also Walking-stick instrument.

Czardas [Hung.]. **Csárdás.*

Czech Republic. In 1993 the Czech and Slovak republics became autonomous states, no longer joined as Czechoslovakia, the independent country established in 1918 following centuries of Hapsburg rule. The Czech Republic includes the regions of Bohemia, Moravia, and part of Silesia, and Czech music has manifested their divergent traditions, in both art and folk music.

Czech art music had its beginnings around 863, when Christianity was established in the country; liturgical music was at first Byzantine, then Gregorian. Vocal polyphony reached its peak at the Prague court of Rudolf II (1576–1612). Native composers of this period included Jan Trojan Turnovský (ca. 1550–ca.

1595) and Kryštof Harant of Polžic (1564–1621). After the 1620 defeat of Czech Protestants, the music of the country showed the influence of the German and Italian Baroque, as is evident in the works of Heinrich Biber (1644–1794), Pavel Vejvanovský (ca. 1633–93), Jan Dismas Zelenka (1679–1745), František Tůma (1704–74), and František Xaver Brixi (1732–71). When patronage was withdrawn during the 18th century, many native composers went elsewhere: Johann Stamitz (1717–57) and Franz Xaver Richter (1709–89) to Mannheim, Georg Benda (1722–95) to Gotha, his brother Franz (1709–86) to Berlin, Josef Mysliveček (1737–81) to Naples and Munich, Jan Ladislav Dusík [Dussek] (1760–1812) and Antonín Rejcha [Reicha] to Paris, and a great many to Vienna, including Tůma, Florian Leopold Gassmann (1729–74), Leopold Koželuch (1747–1818), and Jan Václav Tomášek (1774–1850).

Principal Czech composers of the 19th century were Bedřich Smetana (1824–84), Antonín Dvořák (1841–1904), and Zdeněk Fibich (1850–1900). Active somewhat later and into the first half of the 20th century were Leoš Janáček (1854–1928), Josef Suk (1874–1935), Vítězslav Novák (1870–1949), Josef Foerster (1859–1951), Bohuslav Martinů (1890–1959), Ervin Schulhoff (1894–1942), and Viktor Ullmann (1898–1944). Alois Hába (1890–1959) and his followers produced significant atonal compositions.

After World War II and the establishment of a socialist state in 1948, many Czech composers wrote in a simplified style aimed at mass appeal and use. Others, including Zdeněk Lukáš (b. 1928), Václav Kučera (b. 1929), and Josef Berg (1927–71), maintained contact with international trends such as aleatoric and electronic music, laying the foundations for a number of experimental music groups in the 1960s and beyond. Since 1989 and the end of communism, there has been only slow recognition of a new generation of Czech composers, among them Ivana Loudová, Milan Slavický, and, preeminently, Petr Eben.

Musical life in today's Czech Republic, no longer state controlled and heavily subsidized, has nonetheless blossomed, with some large publishing and recording enterprises taken over by foreign companies and a multitude of new organizations and festivals. It remains dominated by opera at Prague's State, National, and Estates Theaters and the National Theatre in Brno, and by the Czech Philharmonic Orchestra. Festivals such as the Prague Spring Festival continue to attract musicians of international repute. Czech Radio began in 1923, providing the stimulus for radio orchestras in several cities, including Prague and Brno. Major archives in Prague and Brno, while somewhat depleted by the restitution of materials to their former owners, remain substantial. Central to the system of musical education and research are networks of local music schools and conservatories, the Academy of Musical Arts and Charles University in Prague, the Janáček Academy of Music and Dramatic Art in Brno, and the Czech Academy of Sciences.

Nearly all of the rich body of folk music from Bohemia and western Moravia is related to dance and has triadic melodies. Dances in triple meter include the pre-Christian *koleda, sousedská,* the *rejdovák* [see Redowa], and in duple the *obkročák* and its derivatives. By the 19th century, the *polka and waltz were entering the folk repertory. The most characteristic folk instrument is the *dudy* [see Bagpipe]. In contrast, the music of eastern Moravia makes substantial use of nondiatonic scales, rubato, and "pointed" rhythms. Typical dances from this area are the *sedlácka,* the *starosvětská,* the *verbunk,* and the *danaj.*

Bibl.: Paul Nettl, "The Czechs in 18th-Century Music," *ML* 21 (1940): 362–70. Jaroslav Pohanka, *Dějiny české hudby v příkladech* [A History of Czech Music in Examples] (Prague: Státní nakladatelství krásné literatury, hudby a umění, 1958). Karl Michael Komma, *Das böhmische Musikantentum* (Kassel: J P Hinnenthal, 1960). Jaroslav Markl and Vladimír Karbusický, "Bohemian Folk Music: Traditional and Contemporary Aspects," *JIFMC* 15 (1963): 25–29. Vladimír Stěpánek and Bohumil Karásek, *An Outline of Czech and Slovak Music* (Prague: Orbis, 1964). Čeněk Gardavský, ed., *Contemporary Czechoslovak Composers* (Prague: Panton, 1965). Jan Racek and Jiří Vysloužil, "Problems of Style in 20th-Century Czech Music," *MQ* 51 (1965): 191–204. *Dějiny české hudební kultury,* vol. 1: *1890–1945* (Prague: Academia, 1972). Jaroslav Šeda, "Česká hudba 1945–1980," *HV* 18 (1981): 195–237. *Hudba v českých dějinách: od středověku do nové doby* [Music in Czech History: From Medieval to Modern Times] (Prague, 1983). Joza Karas, *Music in Terezín* (Stuyvesant, N.Y., 1985). John Tyrrell, *Czech Opera* (Cambridge: Cambridge U Pr, 1988). Jaromír Havlík, *Česká symfonie 1945–1980* [The Czech Symphony 1945–1980] (Prague, 1989). Christopher Hogwood and Jan Smaczny, "The Bohemian Lands," in *Man and Music: The Classical Era,* ed. Niel Zaslaw (London, 1989), pp. 188–212. Jan Smaczny, "The Czech Symphony," in *A Guide to the Symphony,* ed. Robert Layton (Oxford: Oxford U Pr, 1993, 1995), pp. 221–61. Jiří Fukač and Jiří Vysloužil, *Slovník české hudební kultury* [Dictionary of Czech Musical Culture] (Prague: Editio Supraphon, 1997). P.T.

Czimbalom [Hung.]. **Cimbalom.*

D

D. (1) See Pitch names, Letter notation, Hexachord, Pitch. (2) In *harmonic analysis, *dominant. (3) In 16th-century sources, **discantus.* (4) Abbr. for Otto Erich Deutsch's (with Donald R. Wakeling) *Schubert: Thematic Catalogue of All His Works in Chronological Order* (New York: Norton, 1951; new Ger. ed. by the editors of the *Neue Schubert-Ausgabe* and Werner Aderhold, Kassel: Bärenreiter, 1978).

Da capo [It., abbr. *D.C.*]. From the beginning, and hence an indication that a piece is to be repeated from the beginning to the end, to a place marked *fine (da capo al fine),* or to a place marked with a specified sign (e.g., *da capo al segno,* or *al* 𝄋, or *al* 𝄌). On reaching the sign in the last case, the player is to skip ahead to the next occurrence of the same sign, often marking the beginning of a *coda. This may occur in conjunction with or as an alternative to the direction *da capo e poi la coda* (from the beginning, and then the coda). In the course of the repetition, other internal repetitions are normally omitted, as in the case of the minuet or scherzo with trio. This is sometimes made explicit with the direction *da capo senza repetizione.* The practice of omitting internal repetitions seems to have begun, however, only in the course of the 19th century (Rudolf, 1982). See also *Dal segno.*

Bibl.: Max Rudolf, "Inner Repeats in the *Da capo* of Classical Minuets and Scherzos," *Journal of the Conductors' Guild* 3 (1982): 145–50. Michael F. Robinson, "The Da Capo Aria as Symbol of Rationality," in *La musica come linguaggio universale: Genesi e storia de un'idea,* ed. Raffaele Pozzi (Florence: Olschki, 1990), pp. 51–63. Stephen A. Crist, "J. S. Bach and the Conventions of the Da Capo Aria, or, How Original Was Bach?" *Irish Musical Studies* 4 (1996): 71–85.

Da capo aria. See Aria.

Dactyl, dactylic. See Prosody.

Daff, duff [Ar.]. A Middle Eastern *frame drum. It may be round, square, or octagonal and may have one head or two. Some varieties have jingles and others have snares. In many regions it is primarily a women's instrument. See ill. under Near and Middle East.

Dafne. Opera in a prologue and six scenes by Jacopo Peri (libretto by Ottavio Rinuccini, after the classical story of Daphne and Apollo), first performed at the house of Jacopo Corsi, with whom Peri collaborated, in Florence at Carnival in 1598. This work, for which only some of the music survives, is the first opera. A revision of this libretto was set by Marco da Gagliano and produced in Mantua at Carnival in 1608. Giulio Caccini also claimed to have set this text. An adaptation by Martin Opitz of Rinuccini's libretto was set by Heinrich Schütz and performed in 1627. The music for this work, the first German opera, does not survive.

Dalcroze method. A system of musical education developed by Émile Jaques-Dalcroze (1865–1950), based on the idea of experiencing music and developing musical abilities through rhythmic movement. The system has three components: (1) eurhythmics, or the expression of musical concepts through body movements, (2) *solfège (with fixed *do*), and (3) improvisation at the piano.

Bibl.: Émile Jaques-Dalcroze, *Rhythm, Music, and Education,* trans. Harold F. Rubenstein (New York: Putnam, 1921; rev. ed., London: Dalcroze Society, 1967). Elsa Findlay, *Rhythm and Movement: Applications of Dalcroze Eurythmics* (Evanston, Ill.: Summy-Birchard, 1971).

Dal segno [It., abbr. *D.S.*]. From the sign, and hence an indication that a piece is to be repeated beginning at the place marked with the sign 𝄋. See also *Da capo.*

Dal segno aria. See Aria.

Ḍamaru [Hin., Bengali]. A small, double-headed hourglass drum of India. One or two cords or thongs, knotted at the ends, are tied to the middle of the shell. The instrument is twisted rapidly, causing the knots to strike the heads alternately. It is sacred to Siva and played by mendicants.

Dame blanche, La [Fr., The White Lady]. Opera in three acts by Adrien Boieldieu (libretto by Eugène Scribe after Sir Walter Scott's novels *Guy Mannering* and *The Monastery*), produced at the *Opéra comique* in Paris in 1825. Setting: 17th-century Scotland.

Damenization. See Solmization.

Damnation de Faust, La [Fr., The Damnation of Faust]. "Dramatic legend" in four parts by Berlioz (libretto by the composer with Almire Gandonnière after Gérard de Nerval's translation of Goethe's *Faust*). Described by Berlioz as a "concert opera," it was given a concert performance in 1846 and staged in Monte Carlo in 1893.

Damp. To cause the vibrations of a string or other vibrating system to stop.

Damper [Fr. *étouffoir;* Ger. *Dämpfer;* It. *sordina, smorzatore;* Sp. *apagador, sordina*]. In the action of a piano, a felt-covered device that prevents the string or strings associated with any one key from vibrating except when that key or the *damper pedal is depressed. In the harpsichord (which lacks a damper pedal), this function is served by a felt attached to each jack. See ills. under Harpsichord, Piano.

Damper pedal. On the piano, the rightmost pedal, which removes all of the *dampers from contact with the strings; also sustaining pedal, loud pedal. On early pianos this function was served by knee levers, sometimes divided to permit independent control of the dampers for the upper and lower halves of the keyboard.

Dämpfer [Ger.]. (1) *Damper. (2) *Mute.

Dance. See Ballet and theatrical dance, Ballet in opera, Suite, and entries for individual dances.

Dance band. A band that plays for social dancing; often synonymous with *big band.

Danse macabre [Fr.]. (1) The dance of death. (2) A symphonic poem by Saint-Saëns, op. 40 (1874), based on a poem of the same name (which he had earlier set as a song) by Henri Cazalis. Saint-Saëns's work depicts Death playing the violin and dancing in a graveyard at midnight. The music incorporates the *"Dies irae."

Dante Symphony [Ger. *Eine Symphonie zu Dantes Divina commedia*]. An orchestral work with choral ending by Liszt (1855–56), based on Dante's *Divina commedia.* It is in two movements, entitled "Inferno" and "Purgatorio," to which are added a choral Magnificat.

Danza tedesca [It.]. *_Ländler,_ *waltz.

Danzón [Sp.]. A Cuban instrumental dance-music genre, established by the later 19th century, prominent through the 1940s, and still retaining some popularity today. It is distinctive in its use of melodic and harmonic features reminiscent of the Cuban ballroom and salon traditions of the *contradanza* and *_habanera,_ while at the same time displaying some of the rhythmic complexity of more recent popular genres; in particular, the Afro-Cuban rhythmic patterns known as *cinquillo* and *tresillo* are employed extensively [see Ex.].

The *danzón* exhibits a kind of rondo structure, ABACAD. It typically consists of a short introduction (A) that functions as a refrain; two long sections (B and C) that contrast with each other in material and instrumentation; and a concluding rumba or *parte rumbeada* (D) of more vigorous character and often with improvisation over a repeated harmonic-rhythmic ground. D.S.

Daouli [Gr.]. See *Davul.*

Daphnis et Chloé [Fr.]. Ballet by Ravel (book, after the classical story by Longus, and choreography by Michel Fokine; décor by Léon Bakst), produced by Diaghilev's Ballets russes in Paris in 1912. Ravel arranged two concert suites from the ballet in 1911 and 1913, the second of which, like the ballet, includes a wordless chorus.

Darabukkah, darabuka, darbouka [Ar.]. A goblet-shaped drum of the Islamic world with a single head and made of clay, wood, or metal. It is held horizontally on the player's thigh and struck with the palms and fingers. The pitch may be varied by pressing the skin with one hand while striking with the other. See also *Dumbalak, Zarb;* see ill. under Near and Middle East.

Daseian notation. A system of musical notation used in *_Musica enchiriadis_ (ca. 900) and related treatises that employs modified versions of the Greek aspirate sign *(prosōdia daseia)* to indicate pitches. The four signs designating the tetrachord of *finales* (the finals of plainchant), d e f g, are inverted, reversed, and otherwise modified to provide the signs for the remaining pitches in the system [see fig.]. It is the earliest nonalphabetic Western European notation that is precise with respect to pitch.

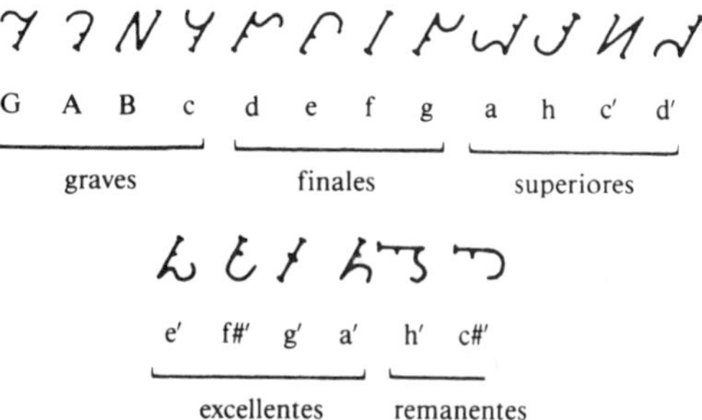

Dastgāh [Per., pattern or scheme]. The principal modal unit of Persian classical music, comprising a diatonic scale, a main cadential motif, a group of constituent melodies called *_gusheh,_ and ascribed musical character. There are seven main and five secondary *dastgahs* (also called *āvāz* or *mota'alleqāt*): *shūr,* the most important (with the related secondary *afshārī, dashti, abu-ātā,* and *bayāt-e tork*); *homāyoun* (with the secondary *bayāt-e isfahan*); *segāh* and *chahārgāh* (closely related); *māhour; navā;* and *rāst-panjgāh.* The first and characterizing part of a *dastgāh* is called *darāmad.* Major *gusheh*s may become independent *dastgāh*s.

Bibl.: Ella Zonis, *Classical Persian Music* (Cambridge, Mass.: Harvard U Pr, 1973). B.N.

Dauer, dauernd [Ger.]. Duration, lasting.

Daughter of the Regiment. See *Fille du régiment, La.*

Davidsbündlertänze [Ger., Dances of the David-Leaguers]. A cycle of 18 *character pieces by Schumann, op. 6 (1837). Schumann frequently wrote of an imaginary League of David that was to oppose the Philistines of his day. In the first edition, each piece is signed E. or F. (or both) for Eusebius and Florestan, who represented, respectively, Schumann's pensive, introverted and impulsive, extroverted sides. Both characters, along with a "March of the David-Leaguers against the Philistines," also appear in his **Carnaval.*

Davul [Turk.]. A cylindrical, double-headed bass drum of Turkey [see ill. under Near and Middle East]. It is slung from a strap over the right shoulder and beaten with a large stick held in the right hand and a light switch held in the left. It is inevitably paired with the **zurna* for dance, processional, and wedding music. The Greek *daouli,* the Indian *tāvil,* and the **tupan* of the Balkans are similar drums, also played with *shawms and for similar purposes.

DB. Abbr. for *decibel.

D.C. Abbr. for **Da capo.*

Deaconing. *Lining (out).

Dead interval. An interval formed between the last pitch of one phrase and the first pitch of the next and thus not strictly subject to the normal principles of melodic construction and voice leading.

Death and the Maiden. See *Tod und das Mädchen.*

Death and Transfiguration. See *Tod und Verklärung.*

Death in Venice. Opera in two acts by Britten (libretto by Myfanwy Piper after the story by Thomas Mann), produced at the Aldeburgh Festival in Suffolk in 1973. Setting: Munich, Venice, and the Lido, 1911.

Debole [It.]. Weak.

Decani and cantoris [Lat.]. In English churches, the two halves of the choir, one seated on the dean's side of the altar (the right side when facing it), the other on the cantor's side (the left). Some types of liturgical chant are sung in alternation between the two sides, and some polyphony exploits the division for *polychoral effects.

Decay. In *acoustics, the decline in intensity that results as the vibrations producing a sound are damped, whether artificially or by internal friction of the vibrating system.

Deceptive cadence. See Cadence.

Déchant [Fr.]. *Discant.

Decibel [abbr. dB]. A unit of measurement of the difference in intensity of two sounds (or the difference in power of two signals), expressed as 10 times the logarithm (to the base 10) of the ratio of the intensities of the two sounds (I_1 and I_0, measured, e.g., in watts per square meter): $10 \log_{10} (I_1/I_0)$. The difference between the threshold of hearing and the threshold of pain is approximately 120 decibels. One decibel is approximately the minimum difference in intensity that the ear can detect. In high-fidelity audio equipment, the ratio of signal to noise is also measured in decibels. One decibel equals one-tenth of a Bel, a unit named for Alexander Graham Bell. See also Acoustics.

Décidé [Fr.]. **Deciso.*

Deciso, decisamente [It.]. Decisive, resolutely.

Declamation. That aspect of the musical setting of a text that corresponds to the purely sonorous quality of the text itself. Since about the 16th century, good declamation has usually been said to require that musical *accent and textual accent coincide, both at the level of individual words and syllables and at the level of phrases and sentences. See also Text and music.

Decrescendo [It., abbr. *decr., decresc.*]. Becoming softer [see also *Diminuendo, Crescendo*].

Degree. See Scale degrees.

Dehors, en [Fr.]. Prominent, standing out.

Delasol(re), de la sol (re). See Hexachord.

Delicato [It.]. Delicate.

Délié [Fr.]. (1) Detached, not *legato. (2) Free.

Démancher [Fr.]. In string playing, to shift the left hand from one position to another.

Demi- [fr. Lat.]. Half. For demisemiquaver, *demi-pause, demi-soupir,* see Note; *demi-ton,* semitone; *demi-voix,* **mezza voce.*

Denkmäler [Ger.]. Monuments [see Editions].

Denmark. Musical activity in Denmark is decentralized and receives significant state support. Opera—old and new, native and foreign—is performed at the Royal Theater, the New Stage, and the Scala, all in Copenhagen, and at provincial theaters in Århus and Odense; concert life is further enriched by orchestras based in those cities and in Alborg, Randers, South Jutland, West Jutland, and Zealand. Denmark is a remarkably active center for contemporary music, with an unusually high density of composers per capita. The works of modern composers have been promoted internationally by the concerts and publications of Det Unge Tonkunstnerselskab (Society of Young Composers), formed in 1930, and in Denmark itself by that body, three regional societies for new music, and more than a dozen new music festivals. Advanced training in music and music history is available at conservatories in several cities and at Copenhagen University.

The S-shaped **lur* trumpets surviving from the Bronze Age are the earliest indication of musical activity in Denmark. The first known art music was Gregorian chant, imported with the advent of Christianity in the 10th and 11th centuries; during the 12th and 13th, clerics brought *Notre Dame polyphony from Paris. From 1250 to 1350 musicians at the Danish court cultivated the *folkevise* (folk ballad), whose origins probably lay in the imported French courtly **ballade.* The reorganization of the Danish church that followed the Reformation brought into use Lutheran collections such as Thomissøn's *Psalmebog* (1569) and Jespersøn's *Gradual* (1573). During the 16th and 17th centuries, Christian IV, Frederik III, and Christian V imported to their courts such internationally known musicians as Adrianus Coclico, John Dowland, and Heinrich Schütz.

Important early native composers include Mogens Pedersøn (ca. 1583–1623) and Hans Nielsen (ca. 1580–after 1626), both pupils of Giovanni Gabrieli in Venice. Dietrich Buxtehude (1637–1707) was possibly of Danish parentage and probably spent his early years in Danish territory. Both the **Singspiel,* cultivated by composers such as Johann Ernst Hartmann (1726–93) and Johann A. P. Schulz (1747–1800), and the **opéra comique,* introduced to the country in the latter part of the 18th century, were to have an influence on later Danish opera. The influence of the Viennese classicists can be seen in the instrumental music of Hartmann, Christoph Weise (1774–1842), and Friedrich Kuhlau (1786–1832). The Danish art song, particularly the *romance,* was cultivated by Weise, Niels Gade (1817–90), Peter Heise (1830–79), and Peter Lange-Müller (1850–1926). Composers who worked in a late Romantic style include Lange-Müller, Christian Horneman (1840–1906), Fini Henriques (1867–1940), and Rued Langgaard (1893–1952).

Nearly all 20th-century Danish composers felt the effect of the music of Carl Nielsen (1865–1931). Significant composers after Nielsen include Poul Schierbeck (1888–1949), Jørgen Bentzon (1897–1951), Knudåge Riisager (1897–1974), Ebbe Hamerik (1898–1951), Flemming Weis (1898–1981), and Finn Høffding (b. 1899). Prominent at the end of World War II were Herman David Koppel (1908–98), Svend Erik Tarp (1908–94), Vagn Holmboe (1909–96), Svend Schultz (1913–98), and Niels Viggo Bentzon (1919–2000). The next generation includes Poul Rovsing Olsen (1922–1982), Axel Borup-Jørgensen (b. 1924), Peder Holm (b. 1926), Jan Maegaard (b. 1926), Bernhard Lewkovitch (b. 1927), Tage Nielsen (b. 1929), Ib Nørholm (b. 1931), Pelle Gudmundsen-Holmgreen (b. 1932), Per Nørgård (b. 1932), Bent Lorentzen (b. 1935), Mogens Winkel Holm (b. 1936), and Ingolf Gabold (b. 1942).

The beginnings of Danish folk music are often said to be in medieval ballads, most of which tell of events of the first half of the 13th century. Among these are chivalric epics, magic songs, songs of giants, and romantic songs. From the 16th to the 18th century, the influence of German poetry and song brought about new song forms, heroic epics giving way to lyrical love songs. Important folk dances include the *polskdans* and the *tospring* ("two jump"). There was renewed interest in folk music during the second half of the 20th century, and much current activity occurs under the auspices of the amateur Folkemusikhusringen (Folk Music House Ring) and the professional Folkemusiksammenslutningen, or FMS (Folk Music Association), founded in 1980.

Bibl.: Vagn Kappel, *Contemporary Danish Composers against the Background of Danish Musical Life and History,* trans. O. A. Hansen (Copenhagen: Danske Selskab, 1950; 2nd ed. rev., 1967). Thorkild Knudsen and Nils Schiørring, *Folkevisen i Danmark* [Ballads in Denmark] (Copenhagen: Musikhøjskolens Forlag, 1960–65). Nils Schiørring, "Flerstemmighed i dansk middelalder" [Polyphony in Medieval Denmark], *Larsen,* 1972, pp. 11–25. Nils Schiørring, *Musikkens Historie i Danmark,* 3 vols. (Copenhagen: Politiken, 1977–78). Karl-Aage Rasmussen, *Noteworthy Danes: Portraits of Eleven Danish Composers* (Copenhagen: W. Hansen, 1991). Svend Nielsen, *Dansk Folkemusik: en indføring i den traditionelle musik i Danmark* (Copenhagen: Dansk folkemindesamling, 1993). Svend Ravnkilde, *Danish Music, 1800–1850: Golden Age* (Copenhagen: Danish Music Information Center, 1994). Gerhard Schepelern, *Operaens historie i Danmark 1634–1975* (Copenhagen: Munksgaard-Rosinante, 1995). Lansing D. McLoskey, *Twentieth-Century Danish Music: An Annotated Bibliography and Research Directory* (Westport, Conn.: Greenwood, 1998). Henrik Glahn, *Salmemelodien i Dansk tradition, 1569–1973* (Copenhagen: Anis, 2000).

Déploration [Fr.]. A poem, or the musical setting of such a poem, that is a *lament on someone's death. Well-known examples include Eustache Deschamps's double *ballade* "Armes, amours / O flour de flours," on the death of Machaut (d. 1377), set by F. Andrieu, and Jean Molinet's "Nymphes des bois," on the death of Ockeghem (d. 1497), set by Josquin.

De profundis [Lat.]. Psalm 129 (130). See Penitential Psalms.

Derb [Ger.]. Robust, rough.

Des, deses [Ger.]. D-flat, D-double-flat. See Pitch names.

Desafío [Sp., Port.]. A kind of singing contest or duel, generally between two improvising vocalists, known in Spain and Portugal and an important folk tradition in several countries of Latin America. D.S.

Descant [fr. Lat. *discantus*]. (1) *Discant. (2) A high-pitched (sometimes the highest) member of some families of instruments, e.g., the *recorder and *viol; the descant clef is the soprano *clef. (3) In hymn singing, a high ornamental part lying above the melody.

Descort [Occ.]. See *Lai.*

Deses [Ger.]. See *Des, deses.*

Desolre(ut), de sol re (ut). See Hexachord.

Dessus [Fr.]. *Treble, i.e., the normally highest part or member of a group of instruments. A still higher instrument is called a *pardessus,* e.g., the **pardessus de viole.*

Destra [It.]. The right hand *(mano destra).*

Détaché [Fr.]. See Bowing (2).

Deuterus [Gr.]. See Mode.

Deutlich [Ger.]. Clear, distinct.

Deutsch catalog. See D. (4), Thematic catalog.

Deutscher Tanz [Ger., German dance; pl. *Deutsche (Tänze)*]. In the late 18th and early 19th centuries, especially in South Germany and Austria, a dance for couples in a fast triple meter; not to be confused with the earlier *allemande, which was sometimes called a *Teutscher Tanz.* Numerous sets of such pieces for keyboard and for various combinations of instruments including orchestra were composed by Haydn, Mozart, Beethoven, and Schubert. The term was eventually superseded by *waltz.

Deutsches Requiem, Ein [Ger., A German Requiem]. A work for soprano, baritone, chorus, and orchestra by Brahms, op. 45 (1857–68). Its seven movements are settings of texts freely chosen from Martin Luther's translation of the Bible.

Deutschland über alles [Ger.]. See *Einigkeit und Recht und Freiheit.*

Deux [Fr.]. Two; *à deux, a *due.*

Deux journées, Les [Fr., The Two Days; also produced in English as The Water Carrier; Ger. *Der Wassertrager*]. Opera in three acts by Luigi Cherubini (libretto by Jean Nicolas Bouilly), produced in Paris in 1800. Setting: Paris and environs, 1617.

Development. (1) Structural alteration of musical material, as opposed to the exposition or statement of material. Development may affect any parameter of a theme; typical examples would include significant modification of pitch contour or rhythm, formal expansion or contraction, textural change, melodic fragmentation, and melodic or contrapuntal combination with other themes. Development may also usefully be distinguished from *variation, the former involving a true structural transformation, the latter merely an ornamental change such as a melodic elaboration or a shift in dynamics or orchestration.

Development occurs in all periods of Western art music. In early music it ranges from the formulaic melodic development of chant, through the *isorhythmic and isomelic techniques of the 14th century, to the **cantus firmus,* *paraphrase, and *parody techniques of the Renaissance. With the evolution of imitative counterpoint during the 15th century, it becomes a central principle of musical construction, extended in the Baroque fugue to encompass development of a single subject throughout an entire movement. Especially during the late Baroque, even nonfugal movements may make constant use of developmental manipulation of motives, as in Bach's *Brandenburg* Concertos.

Works of the Classical period tend to differentiate between areas devoted primarily to intensive development and those devoted to exposition [see (2) below], though development also occurs frequently in expositional areas and vice versa. A great deal of Romantic "development," including many examples of so-called *transformation of themes, is actually variation according to the distinction made above, since it merely restates a theme in different harmonic, timbral, dynamic, registral, and expressive contexts rather than altering its structure. The 20th century saw the formulation of an entire system based on development—serialism—as well as the continued employment of traditional techniques.

(2) The central section of a movement in sonata, sonata-rondo, or ritornello-sonata form [see Sonata form, Rondo (1) II, Concerto (2) II].

Bibl.: Heinrich Schenker, *Der freie Satz* (Vienna: Universal Ed, 1935); trans. Ernst Oster, *Free Composition* (New York: Longman, 1979). Jan LaRue, *Guidelines for Style Analysis* (New York: Norton, 1970; 2nd ed., Warren, Mich.: Harmonic Park Pr, 1992). E.K.W.

Devil and Daniel Webster, The. Opera in one act by Douglas Moore (libretto by the composer after Stephen Vincent Benét), produced in New York in 1939. Setting: New Hampshire in the 1840s.

Devil's Trill Sonata. A violin sonata in G minor by Tartini, probably composed no earlier than 1745 and first printed in 1798. It was said to have been inspired by a dream in which the devil appeared and, at the composer's request, played the violin. Among its many virtuosic effects, the work includes a long trill, for which it is named, in the last movement.

Devin du village, Le [Fr., The Village Soothsayer]. An *intermède* in one act by Jean-Jacques Rousseau (libretto by the composer), produced at Fontainebleau in 1752.

Devisenarie [Ger.]. See Motto.

Devoto [It.]. Devoutly.

Dholak [Hin.]. A two-headed, barrel-shaped drum of India, played with one hand and one stick.

Dhrupad [Hin.]. A type of Hindustani vocal or instrumental composition and its style of rendition, performed today by a few traditional specialists who are revered as the repositories of an old heritage. C.C.

Diabelli Variations [Ger. *33 Veränderungen über einen Walzer von Anton Diabelli,* 33 Variations on a Waltz by Anton Diabelli]. Beethoven's op. 120 (1819, 1822–23) for piano. The variations were composed in response to a request by the Viennese publisher Diabelli to 51 composers that each contribute one variation on his waltz tune to a set meant to represent contemporary musical composition in Austria. The entire collection was published under the title *Vaterländischer Kunstlerverein* (Society of Artists of the

Fatherland), in two volumes. The first contained the variations of Beethoven; the second, those of the other 50 composers (including Schubert, Moscheles, Kalkbrenner, and the 11-year-old Liszt).

Diabolus in musica [Lat., the devil in music]. In the late Middle Ages, the *tritone, the use of which was prohibited by various theorists. See *Mi-fa.*

Diacisma, diaschisma. According to Boethius, one-half of a *diesis [see Comma, schisma].

Dialogue [Fr.; Ger. *Dialog;* Lat. *dialogus;* It. *dialogo;* Sp. *diálogo*]. In the 16th to early 18th centuries, a setting of dialogue text between two or more characters in which opposing musical forces represent opposing roles.

In the early 16th-century four-part **frottola,* dialogue techniques often consisted of the alternation of pairs of sung parts, or the alternation of voices within the uppermost part of an otherwise instrumental piece. Later madrigalists such as Verdelot, Willaert, and Lassus set dialogues for five to eight sung parts by using opposing sonorities that contrasted both range and number of voices, a technique similar to that of **cori spezzati.* The dialogue style flourished in the dramatic **intermedio* and the sacred **lauda* and *madrigale spirituale* as well as in the madrigal proper.

After the advent of *monody, recitative dialogues became common both in the context of opera and as independent pieces, called *dialoghi fuor di scena.* Vecchi, Banchieri, and others published collections of the latter. Increasingly, such pieces incorporated arioso writing, for which reason the late 17th- and early 18th-century dialogues of Alessandro Scarlatti, Handel, and others generally bore the name *cantata. Parallel developments occurred in the French **air de cour* and the English *ayre.

The sacred recitative dialogue sprang from the secular and constituted an important antecedent of the mid-17th-century *oratorio. It became widespread in Germany, especially through the works of Schütz, Scheidt, and Schein; published collections of sacred dialogues by Andreas Hammerschmidt, Johann Rudolf Ahle, and Christoph Bernhard nurtured the development of the German cantata. Bach made frequent use of dialogue style in his cantatas and passions.

In a broader sense, dialogue may indicate any musical setting of a dialogue text, for example 10th-century liturgical dialogue tropes, certain 14th-century settings of *formes fixes,* and some 19th-century lieder. Some 17th-century French organ pieces are titled dialogues to describe the antiphonal use of two manuals.

Bibl.: Ian Spink, "English Seventeenth-Century Dialogues," *ML* 38 (1957): 155–63. Howard E. Smither, "The Latin Dramatic Dialogue and the Nascent Oratorio," *JAMS* 20 (1967): 403–33. Don Harrán, "Towards a Definition of Early Secular Dialogue," *ML* 51 (1970): 37–50. Johan Clarence Kliewer, "The German Sacred Dialogues of the Seventeenth Century" (Ph.D. diss., Univ. of Southern California, 1970). David Nutter, "The Italian Polyphonic Dialogue of the Sixteenth Century" (Ph.D. diss., Univ. of Nottingham, 1978). John Whenham, *Duet and Dialogue in the Age of Monteverdi* (Ann Arbor: UMI Res Pr, 1982). Frits Noske, *Saints and Sinners: The Latin Musical Dialogue in the Seventeenth Century* (Oxford: Oxford U Pr, 1992).

Dialogues des Carmélites [Fr., Dialogues of the Carmelites]. Opera in three acts by Francis Poulenc (libretto by Ernest Lavery after the play of Georges Bernanos), produced in Milan in 1957. Setting: France, 1789.

Diapason [fr. Gr.]. (1) In Greek and medieval theory, the octave [see Greece I, 3 (i); Interval]. (2) In English and American organs, the main open flue stop of the *Great manual, at 8′ or 16′ pitch, depending on the size of the organ [see Principal]. (3) The range of a voice or instrument. (4) [Fr., It.; Sp. *diapasón*] *Tuning fork. (5) [Fr.] *Diapason normal,* standard or concert *pitch.

Diapente [Gr.]. In ancient Greek and medieval theory, the interval of a fifth; *epidiapente,* the fifth above; *hypodiapente, subdiapente,* the fifth below.

Diaphone. A loud reed stop whose sound is generated by a beating valve rather than a reed tongue. It is found in theater organs.

Diaphonia [Gr.]. (1) In ancient Greek theory and in some medieval writings, dissonance, as opposed to **symphonia,* consonance. (2) In theoretical works of the Middle Ages, two-part polyphony, for which *discant [Lat. *discantus*] became the preferred term in the 13th century, though Jehan des Murs in the 14th century uses *diaphonia basilica* [fr. Gr. *basis,* base, foundation] for **organum duplum.*

Diaschisma. **Diacisma.*

Diastematic. Of or pertaining to notation that is precise with respect to pitch. See Neume.

Diatessaron [Gr.]. In ancient Greek and medieval theory, the interval of a fourth; *epidiatessaron,* the fourth above; *hypodiatessaron, subdiatessaron,* the fourth below.

Diatonic. (1) A *scale with seven different pitches (heptatonic) that are adjacent to one another on the *circle of fifths; thus, one in which each letter name represents only a single pitch and which is made up of whole tones and semitones arranged in the pattern embodied in the white keys of the piano *keyboard; hence, any major or pure minor scale and any church *mode, as distinct from the *chromatic scale, which employs only semitones. (2) Melody or harmony that employs primarily the pitches of a diatonic scale. (3) The genus of the music of ancient *Greece [see also Chromatic, Enharmonic] that employs a *tetrachord constructed from a whole tone, a semitone, and a whole tone. See also Pandiatonicism.

Dice music. See Aleatory music.

Dichterliebe [Ger., Poet's Love]. A *song cycle by Schumann, op. 48 (1840), consisting of settings of 16 poems by Heinrich Heine.

Dichtung [Ger.]. Poem; *symphonische Dichtung,* *symphonic poem.

Dictionaries and encyclopedias. Reference works in which subjects are arranged alphabetically. Encyclopedia suggests an exhaustive treatment of a subject, though a dictionary might have a more detailed list of articles. These works fall into four categories: terms only, biography only, terms and biography, and special topics, e.g., church music, popular music, instruments, or modern music. Dictionaries (used collectively here to include encyclopedias) are helpful as quick references, for basic information at the start of a research project, and as bibliographic guides. Although generally derivative, dictionaries often differ in their factual information as well as in their breadth of coverage, so that reference to various dictionaries is advisable. The lexicographer is expected to synthesize existing knowledge, not to undertake new research, though the latter has been stimulated during mammoth productions such as Eitner's *Quellen-Lexikon, MGG,* and *The New Grove,* the last two of which employed hundreds of contributors from around the world. The success of a dictionary is judged mainly on its factual detail, completeness of coverage, and clarity of presentation.

I. *History.* Although music was not neglected in numerous general lexicographic works of antiquity and the Middle Ages, the first independent dictionary of music is Johannes Tinctoris's *Terminorum musicae diffinitorium* (1495), which defines 299 terms. Music lexicography as a continuous branch of music literature did not begin until 200 years later, when Tomáš Baltazar Janovka and Sébastien de Brossard published their terminological dictionaries in 1701. The years between Tinctoris and Janovka/Brossard saw the advent of the new Italian style, with its host of terms that needed definitions as the style spread to other countries. This need was partly met by general encyclopedias and bilingual language dictionaries. But in Germany the need was met by alphabetical lists of terms appended to theoretical writings, beginning with Michael Praetorius in his *Syntagma musicum,* vol. 3 (1619; facs., Kassel: Bärenreiter, 1958–59), and continuing into the 18th century (see Coover, 1971). There was little or no need for biographical information, since until the 18th century, composers and performers were employed by the church and the court and their fame was largely local.

Janovka's dictionary covers 167 broad subjects, sometimes in lengthy essays. Brossard's *Dictionnaire,* compiled independently of Janovka, covers many more terms and, in the version first published in 1703, also has a list of 900 writers on music. The first general dictionary, containing both terms and biographies, is the *Musicalisches Lexicon* of Johann Gottfried Walther (1732), who thought of his work as an expansion of Brossard's, many of whose articles he used. The *Lexicon* defines about 3,000 terms; much of the biographical information stems from Walther's personal contacts with the musicians. The work is especially important for its information about the German Baroque. It was supplemented by Johann Mattheson's *Grundlage einer Ehren-Pforte* (1740), which contains biographies of 148 musicians, chiefly contemporary Germans, from whom Mattheson received the information directly. After Janovka, Brossard, and Walther, the pace of publication of dictionaries increased rapidly, reflecting the popularization of art during the Enlightenment. Many publications were condensations of other works and were directed at the amateur.

The three outstanding terminological dictionaries since Brossard are those of Jean-Jacques Rousseau, Heinrich Christoph Koch, and Willi Apel. Rousseau's *Dictionnaire* (1768) appeared in several editions and influenced many later lexicographers. He had written articles on music for the famous *Encyclopédie* of Diderot and D'Alembert (Paris, 1751–65), but his and especially Rameau's displeasure with the articles led him to compile a separate dictionary. The next important work is Koch's *Musikalisches Lexikon* (1802), which looks back on the Classical era as Walther's *Lexicon* looks back on the Baroque. Another original terminological dictionary was not compiled until 1944, when Apel published his *Harvard Dictionary of Music.* A helpful approach to terminological dictionaries is Hans Heinrich Eggebrecht's *Handwörterbuch* (1972–), which traces the meaning and usage of each term throughout its history; additional pages are issued as information becomes available or as earlier articles are revised.

The first major biographical work after Walther is Ernst Ludwig Gerber's *Historisch-biographisches Lexicon* (1790–92), published first in two volumes and then enlarged to four volumes in 1812–14. A larger, eight-volume work is the well-known *Biographie universelle* of François Joseph Fétis (1835–44). This was followed by Robert Eitner's remarkable *Biographisch-bibliographisches Quellen-Lexikon* (1900–1904), a ten-volume dictionary famous for its archival information about musicians born before 1771 and the locations of their publications and manuscripts. Series B of **RISM* has now superseded Eitner's lists of published works, but his dictionary continues to be a useful reference source for locations of manuscripts and identifications of lesser-known musicians. The most helpful work in English is *Baker's Biographical Dictionary* (1900), now in its eighth enlarged edition.

Multiple-volume general dictionaries, covering both terms and biographies, were a feature of the 19th century. First among them, and the first new general dictionary after Walther, was Gustav Schilling's *Encyclopädie* (1835–38) in six volumes, followed by

Eduard Bernsdorf's four volumes (1856–65), Hermann Mendel's eleven volumes (1870–79), and George Grove's four volumes (1879–89). Hugo Riemann's highly regarded *Musik-Lexikon* (1882), now in its twelfth edition, was the first to employ the scientific methods of musicology.

Two remarkable recent works, aiming to bring together in one alphabetical order all of the most important knowledge about music, are *Die Musik in Geschichte und Gegenwart,* edited by Friedrich Blume, which is now appearing in its second edition, edited by Ludwig Finscher. This edition is divided into Sachteil (terminology), 9 volumes and register (1994–1999), and Personenteil (biography), which will be complete in 17 volumes (1999–) (Kassel: Bärenreiter; Stuttgart: Metzler), and *The New Grove Dictionary of Music and Musicians,* now also in a revised edition of 29 volumes (London, 2001), edited by Stanley Sadie; *New Grove* is also available by subscription on the web. Some articles in these dictionaries are of monographic length and have been published separately. *MGG* is being issued in volumes, *Grove* all at once. Also notable is the *Garland Encyclopedia of World Music,* 10 vols. (New York: Garland, 1998–2002).

The high degree of specialization and the explosion of information over the past century have led to a vast literature of special dictionaries, useful to both the amateur and the professional. Major categories include terminological dictionaries, biographical dictionaries, and dictionaries of church music, jazz, musical instruments, new music, opera, and popular music.

Bibl.: Hans H. Eggebrecht, "Walthers musikalisches Lexicon in seinen terminologischen Partien," *AM* 29 (1957): 10–27. Friedrich Blume, "*Die Musik in Geschichte und Gegenwart:* A Postlude," *Notes* 24 (1967): 217–44 (German text in *MGG* 14 [1968]: xi–xxxiv). Hans H. Eggebrecht and Fritz Reckow, "Das Handwörterbuch der musikalischen Terminologie," *AfMw* 25 (1968): 241–77; 27 (1970): 214–22. James B. Coover, *Music Lexicography,* 3rd ed. (Carlisle, Pa.: Carlisle Bks, 1971). Vincent Duckles, "Some Observations on Music Lexicography," *CMS* 11 (1971): 115–22. Stanley Sadie, "The New Grove," *Notes* 32 (1975): 259–68. Paul Henry Lang, "*Die Musik in Geschichte und Gegenwart:* Epilogue," *Notes* 36 (1979): 271–80. Don Michael Randel, "Defining Music," *Notes* 43 (1987): 751–62. *Music Reference and Research Materials,* 5th ed. (New York: Schirmer, 1997). Stanley Sadie, "The *New Grove,* Second Edition," *Notes* 57 (2000): 11–20. H.E.S., rev. L.C.

Didjeridu. An Australian aboriginal trumpet made of wood or bamboo. The player maintains a low-pitched drone that is punctuated with bursts of higher partials. In addition, the player sings into the instrument while blowing, thus producing a great variety of pitches, timbres, and rhythms. It originated in northern Australia, where it accompanies singers and dancers [see also Oceania and Australia].

Dido and Aeneas. Opera in three acts by Purcell (libretto by Nahum Tate after Book 4 of Virgil's *Aeneid*), produced at Josias Priest's boarding school for young ladies in Chelsea, London, in 1689. Setting: Carthage, after the fall of Troy.

Dièse [Fr.]. The sharp sign [see Accidental, Pitch names]. In the 17th century, the term was also used to indicate the major mode.

Dies irae [Lat., Day of wrath]. A rhymed *sequence, the text of which is attributed to Thomas of Celano (d. ca. 1250). One of four sequences retained by the *Council of Trent, it was officially made part of the *Requiem Mass (see *LU,* p. 1810) in the 16th century, but had been incorporated into the Requiem in some localities from as early as the 14th century. Its origin may lie in a trope to the responsory "Libera me," of which the verse "Dies illa, dies irae" begins with a similar melody (*LU,* p. 1767). From the early 16th century, composers have often set it polyphonically, sometimes in strikingly dramatic ways. It has also been used in works such as Berlioz's **Symphonie fantastique,* Liszt's *Totentanz* and **Dante Symphony,* and Saint-Saëns's **Danse macabre.*

Diesis. (1) [It.] The sharp sign [see Accidental, Pitch names]. The term is used in this sense as early as the Renaissance. See also *Dièse.* (2) [Gr.] In Pythagorean writings, the minor semitone, i.e., the difference between a perfect fourth (4:3) and two whole tones (each 9:8). Thus $4{:}3 - (9{:}8)^2 = 256{:}243$, or 90.2 *cents. The diesis was later called *limma. (3) According to Aristoxenus, the diesis is an interval contained in a pyknon, smaller than a half tone, and characteristic of a *genus. He gives a quarter tone as an enharmonic diesis, one-third and three-eighth tones as chromatic dieses. (4) According to Marchetto (*Lucidarium* ii. b), the diesis is one-fifth tone, which makes a whole tone in conjunction with the chroma (four-fifths tone). There exist still other intervallic designations for the diesis. For instance, in more recent writings on acoustics, greater diesis signifies the difference between four minor thirds (each 6:5) and the octave. Thus $(6{:}5)^4 - 2{:}1 = 648{:}625$, or 62.6 cents. Lesser diesis signifies the difference between the octave and three major thirds (each 5:4). Thus $2{:}1 - (5{:}4)^3 = 128{:}125$, or 41.1 cents. A.B.

Diezeugmenon [Gr.]. See Greece I, 3 (i).

Diferencia [Sp.]. In Spanish instrumental music of the 16th century, *variation. Luis de Narváez's *diferencias* for **vihuela* (*Delphín de música,* 1538) are among the earliest surviving examples of variations. Such pieces are also found among the works of keyboard composers of the period, including Antonio de Cabezón. See also *Glosa,* Division.

Difference. **Differentia* [see Psalm tone].

Difference tone, differential tone. See Combination tone.

Differentia [Lat.]. Any of the various final cadences of the antiphonal *psalm tones.

Diluendo [It.]. Dying away.

Dimeter. See Prosody.

Diminished interval. See Interval.

Diminished seventh chord. See Seventh chord.

Diminished triad. See Triad.

Diminuendo [It., abbr. *dim., dimin.*]. Becoming softer, *decrescendo* [see *Crescendo, decrescendo*].

Diminution. See Augmentation and diminution; Diminutions.

Diminutions. Also *divisions, *coloratura, passages. The division of the notes of a melody into shorter ones for the purpose of ornamentation, either written out or improvised. The terms diminutions and divisions are also sometimes used for fast-moving counterpoint to a slower *cantus firmus;* in this case it is imaginary note-against-note counterpoint that is "diminished." (This usage may be found in *De diminutione contrapuncti,* first half of the 14th century, *CS* 3:62–68, in *Ars contrapuncti secundum Johannem de Muris;* and Christopher Simpson's *The Division-Violist,* 1659.) In the 17th century, the verb "break" meant to improvise diminutions. By extension, diminutions and divisions designate ornamental passages, especially at cadences, that do not strictly "divide" any existing rhythmic units.

The term diminution is used most characteristically for the arithmetical division of melody notes into steadily running passages and simple rhythmic figures. Four procedures are used. In the first, the figure that replaces a melody note begins and ends on that note; thus the progression from the end of one ornamental figure to the beginning of the next is the same as the original melody-progression, and one runs little risk of contravening the rules of counterpoint by introducing parallels or other solecisms [Ex. 1]. In the second procedure, the ornamental figure begins with the melody note but ends with a different one. Here the executant must know what the other parts are doing so that the progression from the last note of the decorative figure to the next melody note does not spoil the part-writing [Ex. 2]; Hermann Finck (*Practica musica,* 1556), however, tolerated parallels if they were brief. In the third procedure, the original melody note is heard not at the beginning of the figure that decorates it but later [Ex. 3]. In the fourth, one or more melody notes are avoided altogether [Ex. 4]. All of these procedures but the first require a knowledge of counterpoint on the part of the performer, and the last

Diminutions. 1. Ortiz (1553). 2. Bovicelli (1594). 3. Dalla Casa (1584). 4. Bach, Sarabande from English Suite no. 2. 5. Quantz, *Versuch* (1752). 6. Mozart, K. 608.

should really be called paraphrase rather than diminution. In practice, and especially in composed diminutions, the four procedures are freely combined.

Simple, arithmetical diminutions reached the peak of their popularity in all media during the hundred years from 1550 to 1650. Diminution was applied not only to solo music, where it was most at home, but to polyphony, both written and improvised. Giovanni Battista Doni complained of the "endless passages" in the singing of the papal choir. The German *colorists of the late Renaissance carried the art to tedious extremes. Theorists (e.g., Conforti, 1593) gave tables of passages with which to decorate all the intervals, ascending and descending. Cadential passages, usually ending in written-out trills, were also provided. In English virginal music, written diminutions were commonly supplemented by symbols for ornaments (single or double slashes through the stem or above or below stemless notes). In early Baroque song, diminutions were often used for illustrative or expressive purposes on words such as *fuoco* or *ardore* (Caccini); this use continued along with the purely decorative throughout the period and beyond. Successive strophes of *airs de cour* were embellished with increasingly elaborate diminutions; Mersenne gave sample diminutions for a five-part viol *fantaisie* by Claude Le Jeune. During the 18th century, diminution techniques (albeit with much-increased rhythmic variety and admixture of stereotyped graces) continued to figure prominently, especially in the playing and singing of adagios. Quantz (*Versuch,* 1752) gave no fewer than 457 examples of "extempore variations on simple intervals" in the Italian style—much as the Renaissance manuals had done, though in a very different style [Ex. 5]. Jean Baptiste Cartier's violin method of 1798 included 16 extravagantly embellished versions of an adagio. In the florid organ chorales, Bach made free use of diminution techniques.

In 1736, Montéclair still defined the term diminution according to its traditional meaning, but Rousseau's dictionary of 1768 called it a *vieux mot* and referred the reader to *Roulade* (a passage sung to one syllable). Throughout the 17th and 18th centuries, "passage" and its cognates in the various languages served as an informal term for diminutions. Simple diminutions continued to be used in variation sets well into the Classical period [Ex. 6]. The improvised solos of jazz often amount to complex divisions or diminutions.

*Species counterpoint also embodies the concept of successively more complex levels of elaboration or diminution, as does *Schenker analysis. Schenker conceived of the structure of certain tonal works as a series of hierarchical levels extending from the *Ursatz* or background structure to the surface foreground, the piece itself. Each level represents a diminution of the next level closer to the background. For Schenker, "all foreground is diminution" (*Free Composition,* p. 96).

Bibl.: Giovanni Luca Conforti, *Breve e facile maniera . . . a far passaggi* (Rome, 1593); facs., *MMML* ser. 2, 115 (1978). Jean-Jacques Rousseau, *Dictionnaire de musique* (Paris, 1768; facs., Hildesheim: Olms, 1969); trans. William Waring (London, 1770; 2nd ed., 1779; facs., New York: AMS Pr, 1975). Jean Baptiste Cartier, *L'art du violon* (Paris, 1798; 3rd ed., 1803); facs., *MMML* ser. 1, 14 (1973). Hans Engel, "Diminution," *MGG.* Ernest Ferand, *Die Improvisation in Beispielen, Mw* 12 (Cologne: A Volk, 1956; trans. Eng., 1961). Id., "Improvisation," *MGG.* Howard Brown, *Embellishing Sixteenth-Century Music* (London: Oxford U Pr, 1976). Richard Erig, ed., *Italienische Diminutionen: Die zwischen 1553 und 1638 mehrmals bearbeiteten Sätze* (Zürich: Amadeus, 1979). Robert Donington, "Diminution," *Grove 6.* See also Ornamentation. Michael Beiche, "Diminutio/Diminution," in *Handworterbuch der musikalischen Terminologie,* ed. Hans Heinrich Eggebrecht (Stuttgart: Steiner, 1989). Cleveland Johnson, "A Keyboard Diminution Manual in Bartfa Manuscript 27: Keyboard Figuration in the Time of Scheidt," in *Church, Stage, and Studio: Music and Its Contexts in Seventeenth-Century Germany,* ed. Paul Walker (Ann Arbor: UMI Res Pr, 1990), pp. 279–347. D.F.

Di molto [It.]. Very; e.g., *allegro di molto,* very fast.

Di nuovo [It.]. Again.

Diphona [Gr.]. **Bicinium.*

Direct [Lat. *custos;* Fr. *guidon;* Ger. *Kustos;* It. *guida;* Sp. *custos*]. A sign placed on the staff at the end of one line of music to indicate the first pitch of the next. Among its various forms, two of the most common are signs similar to a check mark and a mordent. It was first employed in the 11th century in notations that, although *diastematic, sometimes do not employ a clef or more than a single line. Its use continued into the 18th century.

Directaneus [Lat.]. Direct *psalmody.

Direct fifths, octaves. See Parallel fifths, octaves.

Dirge [fr. Lat. *dirige,* the first word in an antiphon from the Office for the Dead]. A mournful song or hymn, usually slow and often with a repetitive quality, to accompany burial or memorial rites.

Dirigent, dirigieren [Ger.]. Conductor, to conduct.

Dis, disis [Ger.]. D-sharp, D-double-sharp; as late as the early 19th century, *Dis* may also mean E-flat. See Pitch names.

Discant [also descant, deschant; fr. Lat. *discantus,* singing apart]. Medieval polyphony, improvised or notated, in which all voices move at essentially the same speed.

The earliest polyphony, whether improvised or notated, is note-against-note polyphony, which was variously referred to as diaphony [Gr. *diaphonia*], *organum, and, somewhat later, discant (from the Latin equivalent of diaphony). From the middle of the 13th century on, the word organum was reserved for the relatively new style of florid polyphony, in which a single note of the first voice is ornamented by groups of notes in the second, whereas discant was used to identify note-against-note writing. Discant may also refer to the added or newly composed voice of a polyphonic complex, to the highest part of such a complex, or to the highest register of certain instruments.

The oldest extant examples of Western polyphony are preserved in two closely related treatises from ca. 900: **Musica enchiriadis* and *Scolica enchiriadis.* The anonymous authors describe three kinds of diaphony based on the plainchant. The first of these is singing at the octave. The second is the duplication of the given melody *(vox principalis)* at the fifth below *(vox organalis).* The two-voice example can be expanded by doubling one or both of the voices at the octave above.

Extemporizing on the chant in the manner described continued long after the advent of notated polyphony. The author of *Discantus positio vulgaris* (ca. 1240), essaying a classification of the several kinds of polyphony cultivated in his time, uses the term discant-as-such *(discantus ipse)* for the simultaneous doubling of the plainchant at the fifth, the octave, and the twelfth.

An offshoot of this long-standing type of improvisation is the practice of "fifthing" [Lat. *quintare;* Fr. *quintoier*], described in a number of short, technical essays and referred to in vernacular literary sources of the 13th and 14th centuries. A fifth above the chant is the normal discanting interval, but phrases open and close with a progression, in contrary motion, from or to the octave. Not infrequently, a dissonance falls between the two perfect consonances.

The third kind of diaphony described in *Musica enchiriadis* and its companion is governed by the fourth. The strict parallelism of the voices and the exclusive use of a single controlling interval in the first and second types sometimes give way here to a mixture of oblique and parallel motion and thus to a variety of intervals ranging from the unison to the fourth [see Ex. 1 under Organum]. Although the greater complexity of this type comes about as a result of the need to avoid the tritone or augmented fourth, its effect is to widen the stylistic possibilities of both improvised and notated polyphony.

The musical monuments of the 11th and early 12th centuries from England (the Winchester Troper) and the north of France (the Chartres manuscripts) and the theoretical treatises of the same period contain only note-against-note polyphony. As long as this situation obtained, the terms diaphony (discant) and organum could be used interchangeably. For some writers the terms maintain traditionally different shades of meaning, diaphony emphasizing the distinctness or the sounding apart of the voices, organum alluding to the intervals employed; for others, such as John of Afflighem, the words are synonymous. Only when a second, contrasting style of polyphonic composition was developed were the terms themselves sharply differentiated.

It is not possible to say exactly when or where the florid style had its origins, but it dominates the work of Aquitanian composers [see St. Martial] active from the end of the 11th century to the early years of the 13th. The new manner of writing did not displace the more traditional one, however, and the repertory contains a sizable number of pieces—nearly all settings of Latin rhythmical poems or **versus*)—in note-against-note polyphony. These freely composed songs are characterized chiefly by the contrary motion of the voices and by the use not only of the perfect intervals other than the fourth, which is conspicuous by its absence, but of both species of third.

Although there are no concordances between the Aquitanian repertory and that of the partially contemporaneous Parisian school of *Notre Dame (ca. 1150–1240), the polyphony of the latter is again of two types. The distinction between these was first fully understood by the mid-13th-century theorist Johannes de Garlandia, who calls the florid composition organum, the note-against-note writing discant.

The Notre Dame repertory contains two large bodies of discant composition, one made up of **clausulae,* short passages included in or intended for inclusion in the great liturgical organa, the other of freely composed songs known as **conductus.* The history of the *clausula,* which appeared in ever-increasing numbers as the 12th century drew to a close, is inseparable from the history of modal rhythm, without doubt the most original of all Parisian contributions [see Modes, rhythmic].

For Johannes de Garlandia, there is an intimate connection between the rhythmic and the harmonic structure of the discant. Consonances, which he describes as perfect (unison, octave), middle (fifth, fourth), and imperfect (major third, minor third), must fall with the long values of the rhythmic mode; dissonances, some stronger than others, may coincide with the shorter values. In practice, Parisian discant is even more consonant than he suggests.

Discant composition as exemplified in the Notre Dame repertory virtually disappeared in France after the middle of the 13th century. It is true that the motet, which originated as a *trope of the *clausula,* came to dominate the repertory in the latter part of the century, but the increasing differentiation of the several voices eventually destroyed the rhythmic unity essential to the discant. Among the few 14th-century reminders of the older compositions are scattered settings of the long texts of the Ordinary of the Mass, namely, Gloria and Credo.

English polyphony of the 13th, 14th, and early 15th centuries shows an almost exclusive preference for the discant style. This is true of the two-voice compositions for Marian liturgies copied in the 11th fascicle of the manuscript W1 and the ritual fragments for two and three voices through which most of the polyphony of this period is known [see Worcester, repertory of]. The discant is nearly always based on a **cantus firmus,* which in the later 13th century typically appears as the lowest voice. Later, in three-voice pieces, the *cantus firmus* is found in the middle or even the highest voice.

English theorists, like those from the Continent, stress the importance of contrary motion in discant composition, but in practice, successions of paired thirds or of thirds and sixths occur with considerable frequency. They are especially noticeable in the discant that is governed in part or in its entirety by the technique of the ever-popular **rondellus*. The rules governing written discant in England in the 14th and 15th centuries also apply to improvisation [see Sight].

The term discant begins to drop out of the theoretical vocabulary in the 14th century and is finally replaced toward the end of the 15th by *counterpoint.

Bibl.: Richard L. Crocker, "Discant, Counterpoint, and Harmony," *JAMS* 15 (1962): 1–21. Rudolf Flotzinger, *Der Discantussatz im Magnus liber und seiner Nachfolge* (Vienna: Böhlau, 1969). Erich Reimer, ed., *Johannes de Garlandia: De mensurabili musica,* 2 vols. (Wiesbaden: Steiner, 1972). Sarah Fuller, "An Anonymous Treatise *Dictus de Sancto Martiale:* A New Source for Cistercian Music Theory," *MD* 31 (1977): 5–30. Id., "Discant and the Theory of Fifthing," *AM* 50 (1978): 241–75. Ernst Apfel, *Die Lehre vom Organum, Diskant, Kontrapunkt und von der Komposition bis um 1480* (Saarbrucken, 1987). Cecily Sweeny, "The *Regulae Organi Guidonis Abbatis* and 12th-Century Organum/Discant Treatises," *MD* 43 (1989): 7–32. Nicky Loseff, *The Best Concords: Polyphonic Music in Thirteenth-Century England* (New York: Garland, 1994). Andreas Traub, "Die mittelalterlichen Grundlagen der europäischen Musik," *Württembergisch Franken* (Jahrbuch 1994): 217–28.

J.K.

Discant Mass. A *Mass or Mass section of the 14th or 15th century in which the **cantus firmus,* usually paraphrased, is presented in the uppermost voice or discant rather than in the tenor.

Discantus [Lat.]. *Discant.

Discantus supra librum [Lat.]. See *Cantare super librum,* Discant.

Discantus visibilis [Lat.]. *Sight.

Disco. (1) [fr. Fr. *discothèque*] A nightclub at which there is dancing to recorded rather than live music. (2) A type of urban American dance music that achieved enormous popularity worldwide in the late 1970s. Disco is characterized less by its musical forms, which are extensions of basic *pop formulas, than by its recording "mix," which emphasizes percussion, particularly the *hi-hat, and a thumping bass beating a straight 4/4 pattern in quarter notes. Representative artists include Donna Summer, Chic, the Bee Gees, and Sister Sledge. The motion picture *Saturday Night Fever* (1977) depicts the social setting of the genre.

P.T.W.

Discography. (1) The description and cataloging of sound recordings in general. (2) A catalog of a specific category of sound recordings. Although the term is loosely used for simple lists of recordings, or for comparative reviews thereof, in its most comprehensive sense discography entails identification of the music contained on the recordings (composer/author, title, language, transposition, edition, arrangement, completeness, duration, as applicable), personnel (including producer and engineer) and instrumentation, date and place of recording, the physical characteristics of the recordings' published form(s)—medium and size, manufacturer, *catalog (or issue) number, *matrix number, playing speed, as applicable—and the extent of their availability, both geographic and temporal.

Discographies of vernacular music most frequently follow a format initially developed for jazz, with entries arrayed alphabetically by principal performer or group, and chronologically within each entry. Discographies of art music are likely to be arranged by composer and title, although those devoted to the work of individual performers are usually ordered either by date of recording or by title. Specialized works may include historical detail about recording sessions, contracts, and the like; include correspondence and other relevant documents; identify the work of individual solo performers; incorporate the discographic listings into a biographical narrative ("bio-discography"); compare and evaluate the recordings. A "label discography" lists the recordings made by a company under all its matrix or catalog numbers; it may be based on surviving company documents, or may have to be reconstructed from catalogs and actual recordings. In addition to commercially published recordings, discographies may deal with such materials as piano or organ rolls, ethnic field recordings, radio broadcast transcriptions, privately made tapes, etc.

Bibl.: Gordon Stevenson, "Discography: Scientific, Analytical, Historical, and Systematic," *Library Trends* 21 (1972): 101–35. Steve Smolian, "Standards for the Review of Discographic Works," *Association for Recorded Sound Collections—Journal* 7, no. 3 (1976): 47–55. Michael H. Gray and Gerald D. Gibson, *Classical Music, 1925–75,* Bibliography of Discographies, 1 (New York: Bowker, 1977). Brian Rust, *Brian Rust's Guide to Discography* (Westport, Conn.: Greenwood, 1980). Daniel Allen, *Jazz, 1935–80,* Bibliography of Discographies, 2 (New York: Bowker, 1981). Michael H. Gray, *Popular Music,* Bibliography of Discographies, 3 (New York: Bowker, 1983). Michael H. Gray, *Classical Music Discographies, 1976–1988: A Bibliography* (New York: Greenwood, 1989).

Discord. Dissonance. See Consonance, dissonance.

Disinvolto [It.]. Free, easy, jaunty.

Disis [Ger.]. See *Dis, disis.*

Disjunct. See Conjunct, disjunct.

Disposition. In organs, the manner in which stops are disposed among the manual and pedal keyboards.

Dissonance. See Consonance, dissonance.

Dissonant (Dissonance) Quartet. Popular name for

Mozart's String Quartet in C major K. 465 (1785), so called because of the prominent dissonances in the slow introduction to the first movement.

Dital harp. A harp with a lutelike soundbox and buttons for raising the pitch of individual strings by a semitone, invented by Edward Light in 1819. See also Harp lute.

Dithyramb [Gr. *dithyrambos*]. In ancient Greece, a song in honor of the god Dionysus. These were choral until the period between the 6th and 4th centuries B.C.E., when solos and accompaniment by the *aulos were introduced. Thereafter they declined in importance. Aristotle described tragedy as having developed from the dithyramb. As a title for works of the 19th and 20th centuries, the term suggests music of a passionate, Dionysian character.

Ditonus [Lat.]. In the Middle Ages, the interval of a major third, which consists of two whole tones.

Div. [It.]. Abbr. for **Divisi.*

Diva [It.]. See *Prima donna.*

Divertimento [It.]. In the second half of the 18th century, especially in Austria, any of a wide variety of secular instrumental works for chamber ensemble or soloist. In the period ca. 1750–80, the term was applied both to lighter entertainment music of an occasional nature [see Cassation, Notturno, Partita, Serenade] and to more serious genres such as the *string quartet and keyboard *sonata. For example, all of Haydn's string quartets through op. 20 (1772), and most of his keyboard sonatas through ca. 1770, were entitled divertimento by the composer. Hence, at least for the period ca. 1750–80 in Austria, the traditional association of the term divertimento with entertainment and especially occasional music, as well as with specific cycles such as the five-movement fast–minuet–slow–minuet–fast plan, cannot be justified. Nor does the evidence support the frequent identification of the ensemble divertimento of this period with ripieno performance (i.e., with doubled parts); most such works are for soloists.

In the course of the 1770s, Austrian composers gradually turned to the more specific, precise titles familiar today (sonata, trio, etc.) for those "serious" or formal works previously entitled divertimento (Webster, 1974, 1985). After ca. 1780, the term divertimento, when it appeared at all, generally designated works that were light or informal (e.g., Mozart's Divertimento/String Trio K. 563, in a six-movement cycle with two minuets). It is in the latter sense—though mostly assuming ripieno performance—that 20th-century composers utilized the term, as in Stravinsky's Divertimento from *The Fairy's Kiss* of 1934 and Bartók's Divertimento for Strings of 1939. See also *Divertissement.*

Bibl.: Eve R. Meyer, "The Viennese Divertimento," *MR* 29 (1968): 165–71. James Webster, "Towards a History of Viennese Chamber Music in the Early Classical Period," *JAMS* 27 (1974): 212–47. Id., "The Scoring of Mozart's Chamber Music for Strings," *Brook,* 1985, pp. 259–96. E.K.W.

Divertissement [Fr.]. (1) A musical potpourri, frequently in the form of pieces extracted from an opera. (2) A group of musical pieces (dances, vocal solos, or ensembles) inserted within the acts or between the acts of an opera, play, or ballet. *Divertissements* are sometimes related to the dramatic action, but more often are decorative digressions. The genre originated in France at the end of the 17th century. (3) A French Baroque *pièce d'occasion,* on a mythological or allegorical subject, produced to enhance a celebration. (4) *Divertimento.

Divided stop. In organs, the separation of a *stop into treble and bass halves in such a way that the two halves of the keyboard could use different registrations. In English and French organs, the separation was usually between b and c′; in Spanish instruments, usually between c′ and c♯′. See *Medio registro.*

Divine Liturgy. The Byzantine Mass. Three formularies are used: for ordinary celebrations, that of St. John Chrysostom; for special feasts, that of St. Basil; and for Lent, the Presanctified. See also Byzantine chant. D.E.C.

Divine Office. See Office.

Divisi [It., abbr. *div.*]. Divided; hence, an indication in ensemble music that a group of players normally playing the same part (e.g., the first violins of an orchestra) are to be divided so as to play different parts, sometimes notated on the same staff. See also *Due, a.*

Divisio [Lat.]. (1) *Divisio modi,* a short vertical dash used in modal notation of the 12th and 13th centuries to mark the end of an *ordo* [see Modes, rhythmic]. It is often transcribed in modern notation as a rest, though it implies no fixed duration. The symbols used in the later 13th century to indicate rests of fixed duration derive from this sign. (2) In Italian notation of the 14th century, any of the several metrical schemes that result from the subdivision of the *brevis.* See also Mensural notation.

Division. In 17th- and 18th-century England, a type of *variation, normally of a bass or *ground (whence "divisions on a ground"), performed by dividing the bass itself into running passages or other figuration in smaller note-values, by playing such figuration above the bass, or by a mixture of the two. As described by Christopher Simpson (*The Division-violist,* London, 1659), the technique is largely employed in *improvisation, though he refers to composed divisions for two or more instruments as well. Other treatises on the subject include John Playford's *The Division Violin* (London, 1684) and the anonymous *The Division Flute* (London, 1722). See also Diminutions.

Division viol [It. *viola bastarda*]. An English bass

*viol, smaller than the normal bass, but larger than the *lyra viol, used in playing *divisions.

Dixie. (1) Popular song by Daniel D. Emmett (1815–1904), written for Bryant's Minstrels traveling show and first published in 1860. (2) *Dixieland jazz.

Dixieland jazz. *New Orleans jazz and adaptations thereof; or that style only when played by white musicians, as in the Original Dixieland Jazz Band (see Jazz). Included among the adaptations are *Chicago jazz of the 1920s, the small combo music of white New York contemporaries (Red Nichols, Miff Mole, the Dorsey brothers, et al.), and since the 1940s, a somewhat integrated international revival. B.K.

DJ. Originally, one who announces and/or selects records for radio broadcast; a disc jockey. The term now also refers to those who play records at social events or nightclubs (mobile and club DJs) and those who create new compositions by mixing records in live performance (scratch DJs or turntablists). See also Turntablism.

D la sol (re), Dlasol(re), Delasol(re). See Hexachord.

Do, doh. See Pitch names, Solmization, Tonic sol-fa.

Dobro. A guitar with a large, circular, metal resonator under the bridge; also called resonator or resophonic guitar. It has been manufactured in the U.S. since the 1920s and is used in Hawaiian and in *country music.

Doctrine of affections. See Affections, doctrine of; Rhetoric.

Doctrine of figures. See Figures, doctrine of; Rhetoric.

Dodecachordon [fr. Gr., instrument of twelve strings]. A treatise by the Swiss humanist and theorist Heinrich Glarean (1488–1563) published in Basel in 1547 (facs., *MMML* ser. 2, 65, 1967; trans. Eng. Clement A. Miller, *MSD* 6, 1965). Its principal contribution is the systematic expansion of the system of eight *modes of medieval theory to twelve, which are discussed with respect to both monophonic and polyphonic music of the day. Glarean justified his names for the four new modes by appeal to classical authority.

Bibl.: Clement A. Miller, "The *Dodecachordon:* Its Origins and Influence on Renaissance Musical Thought," *MD* 15 (1961): 155–66.

Dodecaphonic. *Twelve-tone.

Doigté [Fr.]. *Fingering; *d. fourchu,* *cross fingering.

Dolcan. An organ stop of mild sound with open conical pipes.

Dolce [It.]. (1) Sweet; usually also soft; *dolcemente,* sweetly, softly; *dolcissimo,* extremely sweet, soft. (2) An organ stop of soft tone with narrow-scaled open flue pipes, found in late-19th-century American organs.

Dolcian, dolcino. *Dulzian* [see Curtal], *Dulcian.

Dolente [It.]. Sad.

Doloroso [It.]. Painful, sorrowful.

Dolzaina [It.]. A wind instrument of the 16th and 17th centuries, perhaps a *shawm and possibly very similar to the earlier **douçaine.* See also *Dulzaina.*

Dombak [Per.]. See *Dumbalak.*

Dömbra, domra [Russ.]. A *long-necked lute of Soviet Central Asia and an antecedent of the *balalaika. It has either two or three strings and may or may not have frets. See also *Dutār.*

Domchor [Ger.]. The choir of a German cathedral *(Dom).*

Domestic Symphony. See *Symphonia domestica.*

Dominant. (1) The fifth *scale degree of the major or minor scale. The *triad and the *seventh chord built on this degree as root are the dominant triad and dominant seventh, respectively. As part of a *cadence, both of these chords are most often resolved to the *tonic triad because of the presence in both of the leading tone and the supertonic. The relationship of dominant and tonic expressed in such a cadence, which is a function of both *counterpoint and *harmony, is the most powerful in *tonal music and is fundamental to the structure of tonal melodies and of both small- and large-scale forms [see Binary and ternary form, Sonata form]. When serving as the root of a chord, the fifth scale degree is identified in *harmonic analysis by the numeral V or the letter D (for dominant). Secondary dominants [see also Tonicization] are the dominants of degrees other than the tonic and are designated as follows: V of II (or simply V/II; e.g., in the key of C, the fifth above D, namely A), V of III (V/III), etc. (2) For the dominant of the modes, see Mode, Psalm tone.

Dominant seventh chord. See Seventh chord, Dominant.

Dominica [Lat.]. Sunday. See also *Feria.*

Domp(e). See Dump.

Don Carlos. Opera in five acts by Verdi (libretto in French by François Joseph Méry and Camille DuLocle, based on Schiller's play), produced in Paris in 1867. A revised version in four acts and in Italian was produced in Milan in 1884. Setting: Spain, mid-16th century.

Don Giovanni [It., Don Juan]. Opera *(*dramma giocoso)* in two acts by Mozart. The libretto, by Lorenzo da Ponte, has literary predecessors in Tirso de Molina's *El burlador de Sevilla,* Molière's *Le festin de pierre,* Goldoni's *Don Giovanni Tenorio ossia Il dis-*

soluto, and most directly Giovanni Bertati's libretto *Don Giovanni Tenorio, ossia Il convitato di pietra.* The opera was first produced in Prague in 1787 under the title *Il dissoluto punito, ossia Il Don Giovanni* (The Rake Punished or Don Giovanni). Mozart made a few changes in the work for the first performance in Vienna in 1788. Setting: Seville, 17th century.

Don Juan. Symphonic poem by Richard Strauss, op. 20 (1888–89), based on a verse play of the same name by Nicolaus Lenau.

Donnermaschine [Ger.]. *Thunder machine.

Don Pasquale. Opera in three acts by Donizetti (libretto by the composer and Giovanni Ruffini after Angelo Anelli's libretto *Ser Marc'Antonio*), produced in Paris in 1843. Setting: Rome in the early 19th century.

Don Quixote. (1) "Fantastic Variations on a Theme of Knightly Character" for orchestra by Richard Strauss, op. 35 (1896–97), based on the novel by Cervantes. Don Quixote and Sancho Panza are often represented musically by prominent solo cello and viola parts, respectively. (2) Ballet by Léon Minkus (book and choreography by Marius Petipa), produced in Moscow in 1869. A version with choreography revised by Alexander Gorsky was produced in Moscow in 1900. A revival of the latter, with some new music and dances, was produced in Moscow in 1940 and has remained in the repertory. (3) Opera [Fr. *Don Quichotte*] in five acts by Massenet (libretto by Henri Cain after Jacques Le Lorrain's play based on Cervantes's novel), produced in Monte Carlo in 1910. (4) Three songs [Fr. *Don Quichotte à Dulcinée*] by Ravel on poems by Paul Morand composed in 1932–33 for baritone and chamber orchestra (also in a version with piano) intended for use in a film.

Don Rodrigo. Opera in three acts by Alberto Ginastera (libretto by Alejandro Casona), produced in Buenos Aires in 1964. Setting: Spain in the 8th century.

Doo wop. A form of *rhythm and blues that flourished commercially in the late 1940s and 1950s. The ensemble most often featured a solo singer backed by a vocal trio or quartet and an instrumental unit. The name doo wop, which derives from the nonsense syllables commonly sung by the backing vocalists, was applied to the genre long after its popularity had passed. Representative groups included the Drifters, the Platters, and the Ravens. P.T.W.

Doppel [Ger.]. Double; *Doppel-Be,* double flat; *Doppelchörig,* for double chorus, with a course of two strings; *Doppelgriff,* double stop; *Doppelkreuz,* double sharp; *Doppelpedal,* double pedal, double action pedal (as in the harp); *Doppelpunkt,* double dot; *Doppelschlag,* turn; *Doppelstrich,* double bar; *Doppelzunge,* double tonguing; with reference to instruments such as the horn, duplex.

Doppelflöte. A wooden organ stop with double mouths, popular as a solo stop in the 19th century.

Doppelt so schnell [Ger.]. Twice as fast.

Doppio [It.]. Double; *d. bemolle,* double flat; *d. diesis,* double sharp; *d. movimento,* twice as fast; *d. pedale,* double pedal.

Dorian. See Mode, Greece I, 3 (ii). The Dorian sixth is the interval of a major sixth formed above the tonic in a minor key (e.g., D–B♮ in D minor), since in the conventional description of the church modes, the Dorian mode differs from the pure minor scale only in having a major sixth above the tonic.

Dorian Toccata and Fugue. Popular name for Bach's Toccata and Fugue in D minor for organ BWV 538 (composed during Bach's Weimar years, 1708–17), written without B♭ in the key signature and thus having the appearance of a composition in the *Dorian mode. B♭ is consistently specified as an accidental, however, in keeping with a common practice in the 17th and early 18th centuries of supplying in the key signatures of minor keys one less flat (namely the one affecting the sixth scale degree, which will often be canceled in any case) than is now the norm (e.g., one flat for G minor, two flats for C minor).

Dot [Fr. *point;* Ger. *Punkt;* It. *punto;* Sp. *puntillo*]. (1) In modern musical *notation, a sign placed after a note so as to increase its duration by one-half. For its antecedents, see Mensural notation, *Punctus.* See also Dotted notes. (2) A sign placed above or below a note to indicate *staccato. (3) In some keyboard music of the early 16th century, a sign placed above or below a note to indicate chromatic alteration. See also Tablature.

Dotted notes. Notes written with a dot of addition (other uses of the dot are discussed under Notation, Staccato, *Notes inégales,* Lombard rhythm). A dot written after a note increases its value by half. A second dot adds a quarter of the value and a third dot, an eighth [Ex. 1]. Double dotting is rare before the 19th century, but may be found as early as *Les pièces de Clavessin* (Paris, 1670) of Jacques Champion de Chambonnières [Ex. 2]. Triple dotting is very rare but occurs in the music of Robert Schumann. In music before 1800, dots were often written as in Ex. 2, that is, they were positioned where a note of equivalent value would come in the measure, even if a bar line separated them from the parent note. Such dots are easy to mistake for staccato dots pertaining to another part.

Although early theory and instruction books almost invariably define dotted notes as above, dots were in practice very frequently used to prolong the value of a note as long as necessary to fill in the time preceding the complementary short note or group [Ex. 3]. If the

Dotted notes. 2. Chambonnières, Courante, *Les pièces de clavessin,* bk. 1 (1670). 3. Rameau, "La Boucon," *Pièces de clavecin en concerts* (1741).

short notes were played slowly or quickly, according to the discretion of the executant, then the dotted note was curtailed or lengthened to compensate.

In French Baroque music, extra beams or flags on complementary notes or groups are sometimes encountered. The meaning of these is uncertain. To the eye, it seems as though an exaggeration of the dotted effect was intended, and the dot was to be prolonged until it was time to play the very short note or group. But John O'Donnell (1979) has suggested that at least in the *Livre pour musique d'orgue* (Paris, 1685) of Nicolas Gigault, the beaming followed a different system according to which the number of beams doubled as the values halved. Thus, one beam meant an eighth note, two a sixteenth, four a thirty-second, and eight a sixty-fourth. This left three beams for a triplet of sixteenths, five for a quintuplet, etc. The system does not always work in the music of François Couperin (1668–1733), one of the most prodigious users of beams [Ex. 4]. Guillaume-Gabriel Nivers, in his *Premier livre d'orgue* (Paris, 1665), used dotted eighths followed by undotted eighths to suggest a gentler inequality than the 3:1 ratio of long and short note values that occurs in true dotting.

From the 17th to the early 19th century, dotted figures were commonly used against triplets [Ex. 5a] instead of the notation in Ex. 5b. But they can also be found against metrical ternary groups, as in variation 26 of J. S. Bach's *Goldberg Variations* [Ex. 6]. Ordinarily, the short note of the dotted figure should coincide with the last note of the triplet, as clearly it must in Ex. 5. But J. F. Agricola reported that Bach taught his pupils to distinguish between the dotted figure and the triplet rhythm (*Allgemeine deutsche Bibliothek* 3 [1769]: 757), and Quantz agreed. Yet assimilation to triplets was recommended by C. P. E. Bach (*Versuch über die Wahre Art das Clavier zu spielen,* 1753, pt. 1, chap. 3, sec. 27). The question has been argued by Jacobi (1960) and Harich-Schneider (1959). It should be observed that in many pieces containing both triplets and dotted figures by Bach and others, the two rhythms are not mixed but kept separate; this is especially true of arias where the vocal divisions consist of triplet motion. There may also be instances where

4. François Couperin, "Les fauvétes plaintives," *Pièces de clavecin,* bk. 3 (1722). 5. Bach, Toccata in G minor BWV 915.

6. Bach, *Goldberg Variations,* var. 26. 7. Bach, "Wie zweifelhaftig ist mein Hoffen," Cantata 109.

triplet notation is to be resolved to duple rhythm (Collins, 1966).

In passages executed in **notes inégales,* dots whose value is the same as that of the unequal notes (i.e., where dots after notes double that value) should be lengthened in the same proportion as unequal notes on "strong" subdivisions of the beat, producing an overdotted effect (Morel de Lescer, in *Sçience de la musique vocale,* ca. 1760, is one of the clearest exponents of this commonsense rule). Dotting on the same metrical level as notes that would ordinarily be unequal (e.g., dotted eighth/sixteenth figures where eighths are unequal) may be a cautionary indication of *notes inégales* and thus should be rendered freely, perhaps in a ratio less sharp than the 3:1 of true dotting, or it may indicate a contrast with inequality, i.e., true dotting or overdotting. Theoretical opinion and the evidence of music are divided on this question, and the answer is certainly different in different contexts.

It often happens that dotted figures on different metrical levels will coincide [Ex. 7], and the question arises whether the figures in larger values should be overdotted so that the short notes (connected by dotted lines in Ex. 7) sound simultaneously. Modern opinion is sharply divided, and the performer must decide whether the diffuse and imprecise effect of observing the exact values better suits the music than the rhythmic energy produced by synchronism. In Ex. 7, the text "zweifelhaftig" (doubtful) is perhaps better served by the former approach. The same division of opinion exists in regard to overdotting in general. Agricola, glossing his translation of Pier Francesco Tosi's *Opinioni de'cantori antichi e moderni . . .* (Bologna, 1723; trans. as *Anleitung zur Singkunst,* Berlin, 1757), the most influential singing treatise of the 18th century, wrote, "Short notes after a dot, either sixteenths or thirty-seconds, or in ¢, eighths, whether in fast or slow tempo, whether there are one or several, are always played very short and at the very end of their value" (p. 133). This and similar, though less sweeping, statements by theorists of the 17th and 18th centuries have led modern writers, especially Thurston Dart (1954), to affirm overdotting as a principle for the performance of much music of the 17th and 18th centuries. His view was vigorously disputed by Frederick Neumann in a series of articles beginning in 1965 and just as vigorously defended by several other scholars. Moderate but differently argued positions on the question of French overtures have been taken by John O'Donnell (1979) and Graham Pont (1980).

Bibl.: Thurston Dart, *The Interpretation of Music* (London: Hutchinson, 1954; 4th ed., 1967). Eta Harich-Schneider, "Über die Angleichung nachschlagender Sechzehntel an Triolen," *Mf* 12 (1959): 35–59. Erwin R. Jacobi, "Über die Angleichung nachschlagender Sechzehntel an Triolen," *Mf* 13 (1960): 268–81. Frederick Neumann, "La note pointée et la soi-disant 'manière française,'" *RdM* 51 (1965): 66–92; trans., "The Dotted Note and the So-Called French Style," *EM* 5 (1977): 310–24. Michael Collins, "The Performance of Triplets in the Seventeenth and Eighteenth Centuries," *JAMS* 19 (1966): 281–328. Id., "A Reconsideration of French Overdotting," *ML* 50 (1969): 111–23. Frederick Neumann, "The Question of Rhythm in Two Versions of Bach's French Overture, BWV 831," *Mendel,* 1974, pp. 183–94. David Fuller, "Dotting, the 'French Style,' and Frederick Neumann's Counter-Reformation," *EM* 5 (1977): 517–43. Frederick Neumann, "Facts and Fiction about Overdotting," *MQ* 63 (1977): 155–85. Id., "Once More: The 'French Overture Style,'" *EM* (1979): 39–45. John O'Donnell, "The French Style and the Overtures of Bach," *EM* 7 (1979): 190–96, 336–45. Graham Pont, "French Overtures at the Keyboard: 'How Handel Rendered the Playing of Them,'" *Musicology* 6 (1980): 29–50. Frederick Neumann, "The Overdotting Syndrome: Anatomy of a Delusion," *MQ* (1981): 305–47. David Fuller, "The 'Dotted Style' in Bach, Handel, and Scarlatti," *Bach, Handel, Scarlatti: Tercentenary Essays,* ed. Peter Williams (Cambridge: Cambridge U Pr, 1985), pp. 99–117. William Malloch, "Bach and the French Ouverture," *MQ* 75 (1991): 174–97. Ivan Rosanoff and Alexei Panov, *Essays on Problems of Rhythm in Germany in the XVIIIth Century: Overdotting and the So-called Taktenlehre (A Research of Sources)* (Heilbronn: Musik-Edition Lucie Galland, 1996). Ido Abravaya, "A French Overture Revisited: Another Look at the Two Versions of BWV831," *EM* 25 (1997): 47–61. Matthew Dirst, "Bach's French Overtures and the Politics of Overdotting," *EM* 25 (1997): 35–44. D.F.

Double. (1) To perform or to specify the performance of the same note or notes by two parts, either at the same pitch level or in octaves. Two identical instruments may double one another, as well as two different instruments, an instrument and a voice, or even two lines of a keyboard composition. (2) To play two instruments in a single piece; to be capable of playing two different instruments; to sing two roles (or to sing one and understudy another) in an opera. (3) Instruments of low pitch, usually an octave below the normal pitch, e.g., *double bass, double bassoon; thus often a synonym for *contra. (4) Two instruments combined in one, e.g., *double clarinet, double *horn. A double *harpsichord has two manuals. For the double action harp, see Harp. (5) [Fr.] A melodic variation, particularly for **airs de cour* and then in French harpsichord pieces where there was usually consistent motion in note-values twice (or three times) as fast as the original movement. *Doubles* were usually presented after both strains of the original dance rather than being interpolated as in the English Virginal style (e.g., |: A :|: B :||: A′ :|: B′ :| rather than |: A :|: A′ :|: B :|: B′ :|). (5) B.G.

Doublé [Fr.]. In 17th- and 18th-century French harpsichord music, *turn.

Double action. See Harp.

Double appoggiatura. Any of the three ways in which two *appoggiaturas can be used: (1) two appoggiaturas performed simultaneously, at the interval of a third or a sixth; (2) two conjunct appoggiaturas approaching the main note from the interval of a third above or below it [see Slide]; (3) two disjunct appoggiaturas, one being placed below the main note, the other above it [see *Anschlag*]. P.A., rev. D.F.

Double ballade. In 14th-century French poetry and music, a poem consisting of two **ballades* or a musical work in which two *ballades* are set simultaneously, e.g., Guillaume de Machaut's "Ne quier vëoir / Quant Theseüs."

Double bar. Two parallel lines drawn vertically through a staff or the staves of a score to indicate the end of a composition or a section of it.

Double bass [Fr. *contrebasse;* Ger. *Kontrabass;* It. *contrabbasso;* Sp. *contrabajo*]. The lowest-pitched member of the family of bowed stringed instruments and a hybrid of the *viol and *violin families; also bass viol, contrabass, string bass, bass. Its four strings are tuned E_1 A_1 D G, notated one octave higher. Some instruments have a fifth string tuned C_1 (in jazz and popular music more often c), and in orchestras, the E string of the four-stringed instrument is often fitted with an extension that, by means of levers along the fingerboard, permits playing down to C_1. The highest pitch in orchestral works is rarely above a (notated a′). Tuning is by means of a mechanism incorporating worm gears. The overall length of instruments in current use ranges from 180 to 200 cm (71 to 79 in.), the length of the vibrating string being from 105 to 110 cm (41 to 43 in.). The sloping shoulders and flat back of most instruments testify to ancestry in the viol family, as does the tuning in fourths rather than fifths [see ill. under Violin]. Two types of bow are used: the French type, held with the palm downward, and the German type, held with the palm upward [see Bow, Bowing].

Shape, size, number of strings, and tuning varied considerably into the 20th century. The instrument's earliest ancestors were 16th-century members of the viol family, whence the term double-bass viol. The Italian term **violone* was and is applied to some of these ancestors. As late as the late 18th century, the most common instrument of this general type in use in Austria seems to have been one with five strings, tuned F_1 A_1 D F♯ A, and frets, though writers of the period also mention four- and three-stringed instruments without frets. Three-stringed instruments, tuned A_1 D G, G_1 D G, or G_1 D A, were well known in the 18th century and common throughout Europe in the 19th, persisting into the 20th. The modern tuning of the four-stringed instrument originated in the late 17th century but became standard only in the 19th as the four-stringed instrument itself began its rise to prominence. The first consistent extensions of the range down to C_1 also took place in the 19th century.

The double bass has been a regular member of the orchestra since the 18th century, and a considerable solo literature emerged beginning in the late 18th century in the works of composers active in Austria. Although it does not belong to any of the most usual combinations found in chamber music, it has been employed in chamber music by Mozart, Beethoven, Schubert, Spohr, Hummel, and Dvořák. It is sometimes included in the symphonic band. One of the first and most celebrated virtuosos on the double bass was Domenico Dragonetti (1763–1846). Later virtuosos include Giovanni Bottesini (1821–89), for whom the French style of bow is sometimes named, and Franz Simandl (1840–1912), whose name is sometimes given to the German style. Bottesini and Simandl were also composers and authors of influential methods.

Played pizzicato, the double bass has been an essential participant in *jazz and much popular music. In these contexts, it is often amplified and is increasingly replaced by instruments more closely related to the *electric guitar.

Bibl.: Alfred Planyavsky, *Geschichte des Kontrabasses* (Tutzing: Schneider, 1970). Murray Grodner, *Comprehensive Catalogue of Available Literature for the Double Bass,* 3rd ed. (Bloomington, Ind.: Lemur Musical Research, 1974). Paul Brun, *Histoire des contrebasses à cordes* (Paris: La flûte de Pan, 1982). Alfred Planyavsky, *Der Barockkontrabass Violone* (1985); trans. James Barket, *The Baroque Double Bass Violone* (Lanham, Md.: Scarecrow Pr, 1998). Paul Brun, *A New History of the Double Bass* (Villeneuve d'Ascq: P Brun, 2000).

Double-bass clarinet. Contrabass *clarinet.

Double C (D, etc.). See Pitch names.

Double cadence [Fr.]. See Turn.

Double chorus. Two choruses that perform in a single work, often in alternation. See Polychoral.

Double clarinet. A wind instrument consisting of two cane or wooden pipes, side by side, with a single reed at the top of each. In some, the finger holes of the two pipes are next to one another, each pair of holes being covered by one finger. Other examples have holes in one pipe only, the other pipe being a drone. In a few cases, the pipes are separate, each fingered with one hand. Usually both reeds are taken into the mouth, and *circular breathing is used to maintain an uninterrupted sound. Double clarinets are depicted in Egyptian art as early as 2700 B.C.E. Today they are distributed throughout the Middle East, in the Balkans, and in India. See also *Arghūl,* Bagpipe, *Launeddas, Zummārah.*

Double concerto. A *concerto for two solo instruments and orchestra.

Double counterpoint. *Invertible counterpoint in two parts.

Double croche [Fr.]. Sixteenth *note.

Double cursus. In some types of medieval music, the repetition (to new words with the same poetic form) of a section that may itself consist of repeated elements, as in some examples of the *sequence (e.g., AABBCC AABBCC); also the repetition of a melody in its entirety, as in the tenors of some **clausulae* and *motets.

Double dot, double dotting. A second dot adds a quarter of the value of the plain written note to its dotted value; e.g., a double-dotted quarter note equals seven sixteenth notes. Double dots are found in a manuscript written ca. 1660 and containing music by Louis Couperin, D'Anglebert, and Chambonnières (see Guy Oldham in *RMFC* 1 [1960]: 51–59) and in Chambonnières's engraved *Pièces de clavessin* (1670). They are rare, however, until the 19th century. See Dotted notes. D.F.

Double flat. See Accidental.

Double fugue. (1) A *fugue in which two subjects are first given full and independent treatment, each in its own turn, and then treated in contrapuntal combination with one another. Fugues that treat three and four subjects in a similar way are termed triple and quadruple fugues, respectively. Examples of double fugues in the works of Bach include the fugue in G♯ minor in the second book of *The Well-Tempered Clavier* and the fugue from the Toccata and Fugue in F major for organ BWV 540. Triple fugues include the fugue in F♯ minor from the second book of *The Well-Tempered Clavier* and the Fugue in E♭ major for organ BWV 552 ("St. Anne"). In addition, *The Art of Fugue* includes double (nos. 9 and 10) and triple (nos. 8 and 11) fugues as well as an unfinished quadruple fugue. (2) A fugue in which the subject is accompanied consistently and from the outset by a countersubject, thus giving the impression of a fugue based on two subjects simultaneously.

Double horn. See Horn, Duplex instruments.

Double leading tone. In a *cadence (especially in music of the 14th and 15th centuries), two leading tones, one of which rises by half step to the primary cadential pitch, the other rising by half step to the fourth below or its equivalent in another octave.

Double motet. A *motet in which two different texts are set simultaneously in different voices.

Double organ. Since the 17th century, an English organ with two keyboards, i.e., *Great and *Chair.

Double pedal. On the organ, the playing of two pitches or parts simultaneously in the pedal. The technique is encountered as early as the 15th century (in the tablature of Adam Ileborgh) and figures prominently in works of 17th- and 18th-century north German organists (e.g., Franz Tunder, Johann Adam Reincken, Vincent Lübeck) as well as in some works of Bach (e.g., the organ chorale on "Aus tiefer Not" BWV 686).

Double reed. See Reed.

Doubles cordes [Fr.]. *Double stop.

Double sharp. See Accidental.

Double stop. The execution of two (or more, in which case the terms triple or quadruple stop are sometimes employed) pitches simultaneously or in such a way as to create the effect of a simultaneity on a bowed, stringed instrument; also multiple stop. This is accomplished by means of stopping (i.e., fingering) strings with the left hand in such a way as to allow two or more pitches to sound simultaneously, even if the technique of *bowing [see also Bow], because of the curvature of the *bridge on such instruments, requires that they be bowed in succession. The technique is described and illustrated in Sylvestro di Ganassi's *Regola rubertina* (Venice, 1542–43; facs., *BMB* ser. 2, 18, 1970; ex. in *HAM,* no. 119). It is exploited considerably in works by Biagio Marini (ca. 1587–1663) and Heinrich Biber (1644–1704). Among numerous examples from works by 18th-century composers, those from the unaccompanied works for violin and for cello by Bach are the most celebrated. The technique is particularly prominent in virtuosic works of the 19th century, notably those of Paganini.

Double time. In jazz, the use of rhythmic values twice as fast as the prevailing values without, however, changing the tempo of the chord progressions, which in such a case is typically slow. Often introduced in the course of an improvised solo.

Double tonguing. See Tonguing.

Double touch. In electric-action theater organs of the early 20th century, a feature of keyboards that were equipped with two sets of contacts, one above the other, in such a way that by pressing with greater force, the player could cause both contacts to operate and thus produce accents by added sounds (usually percussion).

Double trill. In keyboard music, two trills on two different pitches, often a third apart, performed simultaneously with the same hand. Louis-Claude Daquin claimed that the triple trills (double in the right hand) in his harpsichord piece *Les trois cadences* (1735) had never before appeared in music. Characteristic examples occur in Beethoven's Piano Concerto no. 4 in G major op. 58. In violin music, the same effect is called for as early as the 17th century in works by Johann Schop.

Doublette [Fr.]. An organ stop of *Principal scale found at 2′ pitch on French organs.

Doubling. See Double.

Douçaine [Fr.]. A wind instrument of the 14th and 15th centuries, perhaps a *shawm and possibly similar to the later **dolzaina.*

Doucement [Fr.]. Gently, softly.

Douloureux [Fr.]. Painful, sorrowful.

Doux [Fr.]. Sweet, soft.

Downbeat. (1) The first and thus metrically strongest beat of a measure [see Meter], usually signaled in *conducting with a downward motion. (2) The first beat of a piece and thus also the conductor's signal to begin a piece.

Down-bow. See Bowing (1).

Down in the Valley. Folk opera in one act by Kurt Weill (libretto by Arnold Sundgaard), produced in Bloomington, Indiana, in 1948. Setting: the U.S. in the 1940s.

Doxology. An expression of praise to God. In the Roman Catholic *Mass the Greater Doxology is the *Gloria ("Gloria in excelsis Deo"). The Lesser Doxology is the text "Gloria Patri et Filio et Spiritui Sancto; sicut erat in principio, et nunc, et semper, et in saecula saeculorum. Amen." (Glory be to the Father and to the Son and to the Holy Ghost; as it was in the beginning, is now, and ever shall be, world without end. Amen.) The Lesser Doxology is sung following the Psalms of the Office (an association that dates from the 4th century) [see Psalmody], the verse of the introit, most canticles, and in a few other circumstances. Other doxologies are used in both Eastern and Western rites, including metrical texts following hymns. In Protestant churches, the term may refer to the metrical text "Praise God from whom all blessings flow," often sung to the *Old Hundredth tune.

Drag. A common stroke on the snare drum, the first two notes played with one hand, the concluding main note with the other:

Dragma [fr. Gr.?]. A note form introduced in the late 14th century consisting of a semibreve with upward and downward stems. Its meaning depends wholly on context [see Mensural notation].

Drame lyrique [Fr.], **dramma lirico** [It.]. From the middle of the 19th century, the term *drame lyrique* has been used, with no great precision, to refer to French operas that cannot be comfortably accommodated by the designations *opéra comique* or *grand opéra.* Massenet called his opera *Werther* a *drame lyrique,* as did Debussy his *Pelléas et Mélisande. Dramma lirico* is used as a subtitle occasionally by Verdi (*Nabucco, I Lombardi, Ernani, Otello,* among others) and Puccini *(Manon Lescaut, Turandot).*

Dramma giocoso [It.]. A comic opera with some serious elements. The term was introduced in the middle of the 18th century by Carlo Goldoni to describe his librettos in which serious characters, from an aristocratic social class, interacted with comic servants and peasants. The most famous example of *dramma giocoso* is Mozart's *Don Giovanni.*

Dramma lirico [It.]. See *Drame lyrique.*

Dramma per musica [It.]. A designation that commonly follows the title in 17th- and 18th-century librettos, usually meaning that the text has been written expressly to be set to music. It is sometimes used to refer to the text alone and sometimes to refer to the entire opera, but the former is more common. Bach used the term for secular cantatas in dialogue form that were designed for a modest stage performance (e.g., *Der *Streit zwischen Phöbus und Pan* and the **Coffee Cantata*).

Dramma sacro [It.]. (1) An *oratorio. (2) A sacred opera.

Drängend [Ger.]. Pressing on, quickening.

Draw stop. A knob mounted on a shaft of wood, connected to a *slider in the organ wind-chest, and employed to draw or retire a stop. In some electric-action organs, small tabs of ivory or plastic are used instead of the more traditional arrangement.

Dreher [Ger.]. A dance in 3/4 meter related to the **Ländler.*

Drehleier [Ger.]. *Hurdy-gurdy.

Drehorgel [Ger.]. *Barrel organ.

Dreigroschenoper, Die [Ger., The Threepenny Opera]. Opera in a prologue and eight scenes by Kurt Weill (libretto by Bertolt Brecht after *The *Beggar's Opera*), produced in Berlin in 1928. An English adaptation by Marc Blitzstein was first produced in 1952.

Dreiklang [Ger.]. *Triad.

Dreitaktig [Ger.]. Three-beat.

Drone. (1) Any instrument that plays only a constant pitch or pitches. See *Tamburā.* (2) On a *bagpipe, those pipes that have no finger holes and thus sound a single pitch. They may be pitched above or below the *chanter, which plays the melody. (3) A long, sustained tone in a piece of music, often intended to imitate the sound of (1), usually pitched below the melody. See also *Bourdon,* Pedal point.

Drum [Fr. *tambour;* Ger. *Trommel;* It. *tamburo;* Sp. *tambor*]. Any of the instruments known as *membranophones, with skin (or plastic) stretched over a frame or vessel of, usually, wood or metal; a few instruments also termed drums are *idiophones (e.g., the *slit drum). While most drums are struck with the hand(s) or a beater, in some cultures they are also shaken (*rattle drums), rubbed (*friction drums), or plucked (drums with a tensioned string attached [see String drum]). These instruments are found in a large variety of sizes and shapes ranging from bowls, cylinders, and barrels to cones, hourglasses, and simple frames. They have one or two heads that are either laced, nailed, or glued to the body, or in their modern form, held in place by a counterhoop and bolts. Drums are found throughout the world, from the most primitive African or South American tribal cultures to sophisticated cultures of China, India, and Muslim lands. In most musical cultures, drums are of indefinite pitch, though in *Africa, the *Near East, *Southeast Asia, and elsewhere, the contrast of two or more higher and lower indefinite pitches on one, two, or more drums is a central feature of drumming. European *timpani, however, must be tuned to definite pitches, as must drums used in the art music of *South Asia, such as the **tablā* and **mṛdaṅgam.* Drums play an important role in communication and ceremony as well as in high art. As ritual instruments, they have often been imbued with magical powers. For the use of drums in jazz and popular music, see Drum set.

I. *Drums of indefinite pitch in Western art music* [see ills. under Percussion instruments]. 1. Side drum, snare drum [Fr. *caisse claire, tambour militaire;* Ger. *kleine Trommel;* It. *tamburo militare;* Sp. *tambor, caja militar*]. A cylindrical shell made of wood or metal with two heads, the lower being furnished with snares—gut strings or wires running parallel to one another across the center of the head. When the upper or batter head is struck, the snares, if appropriately adjusted, vibrate against the lower or snare head. The two heads were tensioned in earlier times by ropes laced between them around the shell. Today threaded rods are employed, sometimes permitting separate adjustment of the tension on each head. Most modern instruments also have a lever for the quick release of the snares. The instrument used in the modern orchestra and in the *drum set of jazz and popular music is about 35 cm (14 in.) in diameter and about 13 cm (5 in.) deep. It is mounted on a stand horizontally or at a slight angle. The instrument used in marching is at least 30 cm (12 in.) in diameter and at least 38 cm (15 in.) deep. It is suspended at an angle at the player's left side (whence the term side drum) from a strap worn over the right shoulder. The snare drum is played with wooden sticks that taper to a slightly elongated knob at the tip. In jazz and popular music, the snare drum may also be played with wire brushes. For characteristic strokes employed on the side drum, see Drag, Flam, Paradiddle, Roll, Ruff.

The snare drum developed from the big tabor [see II below] and appeared toward the end of the Middle Ages as an important military instrument popularized by Swiss mercenary regiments. However, it was also found along with fifes, cornetts, trumpets, and kettledrums in ensembles for court and civic music-making, particularly out of doors. Its use in the orchestra was at first generally limited to works with a martial flavor, such as Handel's *Music for the Royal Fireworks* (1749), Haydn's *Military* Symphony, no. 100 (1793–94), and Beethoven's *Wellington's Victory* or "Battle

Symphony" (1813). Rossini gave the snare drum an important solo in the overture to his opera *La gazza ladra* (1817). Encouraged by Berlioz's pioneering use of percussion, the 19th-century orchestra made increasing use of this instrument. It is featured prominently in the music of Rimsky-Korsakov and Elgar, for example. In Nielsen's Symphony no. 5 (1921–22), the drummer is called upon to improvise in counterpoint to the orchestra, and in Ravel's *Boléro* (1928) the first snare drum provides a constant rhythmic underpinning. Both Stravinsky and Bartók carried on this tradition, the latter specifying contrasting tones by the hitting of the drum at different spots. Contemporary composers regularly call for instruments of various sizes, with and without snares. *Rim shots are employed by Milhaud in his *La création du monde* (1923), Copland in his Symphony no. 3 (1944–46), and Carter in his Variations for Orchestra (1954–55).

2. Tenor drum [Fr. *caisse roulante;* Ger. *Rührtrommel, Wirbeltrommel;* It. *cassa rullante;* Sp. *redoblante*]. A cylindrical drum, similar in diameter to the side drum, but rather deeper (25 to 30 cm or more). Its construction is like that of the snare drum except that it has no snares. It is played either with felt-headed or snare-drum sticks. Although the tenor drum has always been primarily a military or marching instrument, it was used in the orchestra by Berlioz in his *Requiem* (1837), Wagner in several of his operas, Strauss in *Ein Heldenleben* (1897–98), as well as by Elgar, Stravinsky, Milhaud, and Britten.

3. Bass drum [Fr. *grosse caisse;* Ger. *grosse Trommel;* It. *gran cassa;* Sp. *bombo*]. A large instrument, approximately 90 cm (almost 36 in.) in diameter and 40 cm (16 in.) deep, consisting of a cylindrical wooden shell with two heads tensioned as are those of the side drum. In the symphony orchestra, it is suspended from a swivel frame or placed on a stand and hit with a large, felt-headed stick. A roll can be performed with timpani sticks or a double-headed beater. The bass drum was rare in Europe until the vogue for Turkish *Janissary music in the 18th century, reflected in works such as Gluck's opera *Le cadi dupé* (1761), Mozart's *Die Entführung aus dem Serail* (1782), and Haydn's Symphony no. 100 (*Military,* 1793–94). Beethoven used the instrument effectively in his Ninth Symphony (1822–24), as did Berlioz in his *Symphonie fantastique* (1830) and *Damnation of Faust* (1845–46). Romantic composers often called for bass drum and cymbals simultaneously, the syncopated beats in Tchaikovsky's music being a typical example. Verdi asked for hard, loud blows in the *Dies Irae* section of his *Requiem* (1874) and provided a dramatic solo in the final scene of *Otello* (1887). Britten called for strokes with a snare-drum stick in *Peter Grimes* (1944–45).

II. *Early history and distribution.* The popularity of drums in ancient civilizations is confirmed by their widespread appearance in art. A man-sized bass drum is depicted on a Sumerian vase (ca. 3000 B.C.E.), and at least four types of drums in different sizes were used in Mesopotamia. Actual instruments from ancient Egypt (ca. 1800 B.C.E.) have been preserved. Drums are mentioned in one of the earliest Chinese poems (1135 B.C.E.), and a bass drum was supposedly installed in the Imperial Palace in Peking around the same time. In India, especially, drumming was raised to a highly sophisticated art with a variety of instruments played with different techniques. Hand drums, used chiefly by women, accompanied songs and dances in Arabia and Persia. The Greeks seem not to have employed drums to any great extent; only the tambourine is depicted regularly in their artifacts.

The most common form of drum during the European Middle Ages was the cylindrical tabor, a rope-tensioned, double-headed instrument of varying size with a snare on the struck (or batter) head. It was introduced to Europe during the Crusading era, and the earliest known pictorial evidence is a 12th-century English manuscript illumination showing a juggler disguised as a bear striking a small barrel drum suspended from his neck. The tabor was played with a single stick, and very often the performer blew a small pipe at the same time. This combination proved ideal for accompanying dance and is portrayed over and over again in artifacts of the period [see Pipe and tabor]. The tabor reappears from time to time in the modern orchestra as the *tambour* or *tambourin provençal.* Bizet employed it in *L'Arlésienne* Suite no. 2 (1872), Copland in *El Salón México* (1933–36), Milhaud in his *Suite française* (1944), and Sessions in his Symphony no. 3 (1957).

More significant was the introduction of the Arabian naker (**naqqārah*), a small *kettledrum used in pairs and ordinarily carried around the waist. Nakers were at first military instruments but soon joined the ensembles of so-called loud instruments found at all important feudal events.

See ill. under Percussion instruments. See also Bongo, *Caja,* Conga, *Daff, Darabukkah, Davul, Ḍholak, Dombalak,* Drum set, Frame drum, *Mṛdaṅgam, Naqqārah,* Slit drum, Steel drum, *Ṭabl, Tablā, Timbales,* Timpani, *Tombak,* Tom-tom, *Zarb.*

Bibl.: Jehan Tabourot [Thoinot Arbeau], *Orchésographie* (Lengres, 1588); trans. Mary Stewart Evans (New York: Kamin Dance Pubs, 1948; R:New York: Dover, 1967). Anonymous, *Kurze Anweisung das Trommel-Spielen* (Berlin, 1777). Samuel Potter, *The Art of Beating the Drum* (London: H Potter, 1817). Georg Fechner, *Die Pauken und Trommeln in ihren neueren und vorzüglicheren Konstruktionen* (Weimar: Voigt, 1862). Jacob Adam Kappey, *Military Music* (London: Boosey, 1894). Henry George Farmer, *Military Music and Its Story: The Rise and Development of Military Music* (London: W Reeves, 1912). Joseph Baggers, "Les timbales, le tambour et les instruments à percussion," in *Encyclopédie de la musique et dictionnaire du Conservatoire,* pt. 2, vol. 3 (Paris: Delagrave, 1927), pp. 1684–1707. Richard St. Barbe Baker, *Africa Drums,* rev. ed. (Oxford: G Ronald, 1951). Evert Elsenaar, *De geschiedenis der slaginstrumenten* (Hilversum: J J Lispet, 1951). Charles L. White, *Drums through the Ages*

(Los Angeles: Sterling Pr, 1960). Mervin W. Britton, *The International Percussion Reference Library Catalogue* (Tempe: Music Dept., Ariz State U, 1963–). Gerassimos Avgerinos, *Handbuch der Schlag- und Effektinstrumente* (Frankfurt am Main: Musikinstrument, 1967). Włodzimierz Kotoński, *Schlaginstrumente im modernen Orchester* (Mainz: B Schott, 1968). Karl Peinkofer and Fritz Tannigel, *Handbuch des Schlagzeugs* (Mainz, 1969). Reginald Smith Brindle, *Contemporary Percussion* (London: Oxford U Pr, 1970). F. Michael Combs, *Solo and Ensemble Literature for Percussion* (Knoxville, Tenn.: Percussive Arts Soc, 1972). James Blades, *Percussion Instruments and Their History,* rev. ed. (London: Faber, 1975). J. Blades and J. P. S. Mantagu, *Early Percussion Instruments from the Middle Ages to the Baroque* (London: Oxford U Pr, 1976). R. Vaughan, *The Drumset Owner's Manual: A Heavily Illustrated Guide to Selecting, Setting Up, and Maintaining All Components of the Acoustic Drumset* (Jefferson, N.C., 1993). H. Powley, "The Drum Tablature Tradition of American Military Music of the Early Nineteenth Century: Levi Lovering's *The Drummer's Assistant or The Art of Drumming Made Easy,*" 21 *JAMIS* (1995): 5–29. *Encyclopedia of Percussion,* ed. John Beck (New York: Garland, 1995). Renato Meucci, "I timpani e gli strumenti a percussione nell'ottocento italiano," *Studi Verdiana* 13 (1995): 183–254. Jeremy Montagu, *Timpani and Percussion* (London and New York, 2002). E.A.B., rev. H.P.

Drum kit. *Drum set.

Drum-Roll Symphony. Popular name for Haydn's Symphony no. 103 in E♭ major Hob. I:103 (1795, the 11th of the *Salomon Symphonies), so called because of the timpani roll in the opening measure of the introduction to the first movement.

Drum set. A collection of percussion instruments played by a single player; characteristic of jazz, rock, and other forms of American popular music. It typically includes the following drums: a pedal-operated bass *drum, a snare drum, and two or more *tom-toms. The normal complement of cymbals includes a hi-hat: a pair of cymbals mounted horizontally on a stand and clashed together by a pedal mechanism. In the most characteristic use of the hi-hat, the pedal is sharply depressed, producing a choked clash, on beats two and four in a measure of 4/4. This may be combined with the accompanying rhythm played with a snare-drum stick on the upper of the two cymbals, often with the pedal released on beats one and three to allow the cymbals to ring. The drum set also usually includes one or more single cymbals, each mounted at an angle on a stand. These may include a ride cymbal (used to play the rhythm shown in the accompanying example, often for prolonged periods), a crash cymbal, and a sizzle cymbal (a large cymbal with loose rivets inserted in a ring of holes near the edge).

To all of these may be added *bongos, *timbales, *cowbells, *wood blocks, etc. The seated drummer plays with sticks, hard or soft mallets, and wire brushes. See ill. under Percussion instruments.

Drum Stroke Symphony. See *Surprise* Symphony.

D.S. Abbr. for **Dal segno.*

Dsolre(ut), D sol re (ut), Desolre(ut). See Hexachord.

Dualism, dualistic theory. A theory that regards major and minor modes as being of equal weight and that rests in considerable measure on the observation that the minor triad is the inversion of the major triad. In this view, the major triad is generated upward from the root, the minor triad downward from the fifth. Elements of such a view are present in the writings of Zarlino and Rameau. It is elaborated in the work of Moritz Hauptmann and developed further by Arthur van Oettingen and Hugo Riemann.

Bibl.: Moritz Hauptmann, *Die Natur der Harmonik und der Metrik zur Theorie der Musik* (Leipzig, 1853; trans. Eng., 1888). Arthur van Oettingen, *Harmoniesystem in dualer Entwickelung* (Dorpat and Leipzig, 1866; 2nd ed. *Das duale Harmoniesystem,* Leipzig: Siegel, 1913). Hugo Riemann, *Das Problem des harmonischen Dualismus* (Leipzig: C F Kahnt, 1905), originally publ. in *NZfM* 72 (1905). Carl Dahlhaus, "War Zarlino Dualist?" *Mf* 10 (1957): 286–90. Dale Jorgenson, "A Résumé of Harmonic Dualism," *ML* 44 (1963): 31–42. Martin Vogel, "Arthur van Oettingen und das harmonische Dualismus," in *Beiträge zur Musiktheorie des 19. Jahrhunderts* (Regensburg: G Bosse, 1966). Daniel Harrison, *Harmonic Function in Chromatic Music: A Renewed Dualist Theory and an Account of Its Precedents* (Chicago: U of Chicago Pr, 1994).

Duct flute. A flute, also called a fipple flute or whistle flute, that is blown at one end through a mouthpiece that directs the air stream through a narrow passage across the sharp edge of a hole in the pipe. The upper end of the pipe is usually plugged by a block or fipple with only the duct left open. Most duct flutes have finger holes, but there are also single-pitch and plunger varieties. Examples are the *flageolet, *penny whistle, and *recorder.

Ductia [Lat.]. According to Johannes de Grocheio (*De musica,* ca. 1300), either of two types of piece, one vocal and the other instrumental. He describes the vocal type as a simple piece sung while dancing. The instrumental type is described as similar to the *stantipes* [see *Estampie*] but with a stronger beat, and having only three *puncta* (sections) of uniform length instead of six or seven of varying length. No firmly identified examples of a *ductia* survive.

Bibl.: Siegmund Levarie, "Communication," *JAMS* 27 (1974): 367–69. Hans J. Moser, "Stantipes und Ductia," *Zeitschrift für Musikwissenschaft* 2 (1944): 194–206. Christopher Page, "Johannes de Grocheio on Secular Music: A Corrected Text and a New Translation," *Plainsong and Medieval Music* 2 (1993): 17–41. Timothy J. McGee, *Medieval Instrumental Dances* (Bloomington: Ind U Pr, 1989).

Dudelsack [Ger.]. *Bagpipe.

Due [It.]. Two; *a due,* an indication in orchestral scores that a single part notated on a staff that normally carries parts for two different players (e.g., first and second flutes) is to be played by both players, or conversely, that two pitches or parts notated on a staff that normally carries only a single part (e.g., first violins) are to be played by different players or groups of players; also [Fr.] *à deux; a due corde,* on two strings [for the use of this phrase in piano music, see *Una corda*].

Duenna, The. (1) Comic opera in three acts by Thomas Linley the son in collaboration with his father (libretto by Richard B. Sheridan), produced in London in 1775. (2) Opera [Russ. *Obrucheniye v monastïre,* Betrothal in a Monastery] in four acts by Prokofiev (libretto by Prokofiev and Mira Mendelson after Sheridan), composed in 1940–41 and produced in Leningrad in 1946. Setting: Seville in the 18th century.

Duet [Fr. *duo;* Ger. *Duett, Duo;* It. *duetto;* Sp. *dúo, dueto*]. A composition for two performers, with or without accompaniment. The term is most frequently used in vocal music and for two performers on one piano [see Piano duet], while duets for two instruments are frequently called duos. The two parts of a duet are ideally thought of as equal in importance, but this is not always true, especially in keyboard music.

The vocal duet became part of opera almost at its inception and has since remained one of its most important elements, in a wide variety of forms and styles. The chamber duet for voices and continuo was much cultivated in the Baroque, notably by Handel, Agostino Steffani, Francesco Durante, and Giovanni Carlo Maria Clari.

The piano duet became popular with amateurs in the late 18th century and produced a large body of new music and arrangements in the 19th. Mozart and Schubert made important contributions. Unaccompanied duets for two violins and, less frequently, other combinations were popular in the same period, with notable examples by Haydn and Spohr. Usually in sonata format, they are often used in teaching. See also *Bicinium.*

Duff [Ar.]. **Daff.*

Dugazon. See *Soubrette.*

Duke Bluebeard's Castle. See *Bluebeard's Castle.*

Dulce melos [Lat.]. A dulcimer fitted with a keyboard and an action that causes the strings to be struck when keys are depressed. The instrument, of which there is no surviving example, is described in the treatise of Henri Arnaut de Zwolle (written ca. 1436–54) and appears to have features of some later pianos, though it is also related to the *clavichord and similar instruments. The assertion that the *chekker was a similar instrument remains unsubstantiated.

Dulcian [Ger. *Dulzian*]. An organ reed stop of modest-scaled, cylindrical resonators, usually half-length and covered at the top; not to be confused with *Dulciana.

Dulciana. An organ register of cylindrical, rather narrow-scaled pipes producing a mild principal tone. It was probably introduced by John Snetzler in England ca. 1750.

Dulcimer. A *zither sounded by striking rather than plucking. Instruments of the dulcimer family usually have trapezoidal sound boxes and metal strings, in courses of two to four, divided into unequal lengths by high bridges. The strings run parallel to the long side, which is closest to the player, the instrument being placed horizontally. Most commonly, dulcimers have two long bridges or two rows of bridges, the first course of strings passing over the right-hand bridge and through a hole in the left-hand bridge, the next over the left-hand bridge and through a hole in the right-hand bridge, and so on in alternation, thus producing two slightly inclined planes of strings that cross in the middle. The strings are struck with light wooden hammers of various types. See ill. under Zither.

The dulcimer seems to have originated in Persia around the 10th century C.E. By the 12th century, dulcimers were known in the Balkans and Spain, by the 15th century in most of Europe, and by the 18th century they had reached the Far East. In Europe they have remained folk instruments for the most part. Nevertheless, Hebenstreit's **pantaleon* in the 18th century and Schunda's **cimbalom* in the 19th century both enjoyed popularity on the concert stage. In the U.S., the instrument is sometimes termed a hammered dulcimer to distinguish it from the *Appalachian dulcimer. See also Psaltery, *Santur, Yang-ch'in.*

Dulcitone. A keyboard instrument similar to the *celesta, but which employs tuning forks rather than metal plates.

Dulzaina [Sp.]. A *shawm of Spain, made of wood or metal with seven finger holes. It is played in ensemble with a drum. See also *Chirimía, Dolzaina, Zūrnā.*

Dulzian [Ger.]. (1) *Curtal. (2) *Dulcian.

Dumbalak [Ar.; Per. *dombak*]. A goblet-shaped drum of the Middle East. See also *Darabukkah.*

Dumbarton Oaks. Popular name for a concerto for 15 instruments by Stravinsky, composed in 1937–38 in the style of a *concerto grosso. The name is that of the then residence of Mr. and Mrs. Robert Woods Bliss (who commissioned the work) in Washington, D.C.

Dumka [dim. of Ukrainian *duma,* pl. *dumky*]. Either of two types of folk music and poetry of Ukrainian origin taken up in Poland and Bohemia in the 19th century: a narrative type with features of the epic and the ballad, and a lament. Elements of the two were often combined. Examples include melismatic sections along with sudden alternation between slow-moving, melancholy sections and faster, livelier ones. A popular Polish example was Karol Kurpiński's "Dumka włoscian Jabłonny" (Dumka of the Jabłonna Peasants,

1821). Instrumental pieces of related character were composed by Liszt, Mussorgsky, Tchaikovsky, and above all Dvořák (*Dumka* for piano op. 35, 1876; **Furiant with Dumka* for piano op. 12, 1884; Piano Trio op. 90, "Dumky Trio," 1891).

Dump, domp. A type of piece for lute or keyboard of which about 20 examples survive from the late 16th and early 17th centuries. Most are continuous variations on *ground basses that alternate tonic and dominant harmonies (e.g., for one measure each, TTDD or DTDT or TTDT) or on one of the familiar patterns such as the **romanesca.* Like the dump mentioned in literary sources, these pieces are probably *laments. The earliest example is "My Lady Carey's Dompe" for keyboard (ca. 1525).

Bibl.: John Ward, "The 'Dolfull Domps,'" *JAMS* 4 (1951): 111–21.

Duo. (1) *Duet. (2) An ensemble of two players. See also Duo sonata.

Duole [Ger.], **duolet** [Fr.]. *Duplet.

Duo sonata. In the Baroque period, a *sonata *a 2,* i.e., for one melody instrument and continuo.

Dupla [Lat.]. (1) The ratio 2:1; hence, in early discussions of intervals, the octave; in the system of rhythmic *proportions, the diminution of durations by half. (2) Plural of **duplum.*

Duple meter, time. See Meter.

Duplet [Fr. *duolet;* Ger. *Duole;* It. *duina;* Sp. *dosillo*]. A group of two notes of equal duration to be played in the time normally taken up by three notes of the same type, e.g., two eighth notes (marked with the figure 2) in the time of three eighth notes in 6/8, 9/8, or 12/8.

Duplex instrument. A brass instrument that combines two instruments in one, the player switching between the two by means of a valve. The two most common examples are the double-belled *euphonium and the double *horn.

Duplex longa [Lat.]. In *mensural notation, the note value next larger than the *longa,* also called a *maxima.*

Duplum [Lat., pl. *dupla*]. In music of the *Notre Dame repertory (except for the *motet, where it was termed the *motetus*), the part immediately above the tenor; *organum duplum,* *organum in two parts. See also *Triplum, Quadruplum.*

Dur, moll [Ger., fr. Lat. *durus,* hard, *mollis,* soft]. Major, minor. The terms originally denoted the two forms of the letter b in the *hexachord system of the Middle Ages and Renaissance: "hard" or "square" b for B-natural, and "soft" or "round" b for B-flat [see also Accidental]. They seem to have been used with their present meanings for the first time in Andreas Werckmeister's *Die nothwendigsten Anmerckungen* (1698).

Bibl.: Carl Dahlhaus, "Die Termini Dur und Moll," *AfMw* 12 (1955): 280–96.

Duramente [It.]. Harshly.

Duration. The time that a sound or silence lasts. This can be measured in seconds or similar units, though for this purpose common musical notation employs *notes and rests of various shapes whose values are fixed with respect to one another. The absolute duration of individual notes and rests in the system is fixed either approximately, through the use of terms such as *allegro* (fast), or precisely, by the specification of the number of occurrences per minute of some particular value. See also Tempo, Performance marks, Metronome.

Durchbrochene Arbeit [Ger.]. A technique of composition, often encountered in works of the Classical period, in which melodic material is broken into fragments and distributed among two or more instruments or parts.

Durchdringend [Ger.]. Piercing, shrill.

Durchführung [Ger.]. (1) In a movement in *sonata form, the development. (2) In a *fugue, an exposition.

Durchkomponiert [Ger.]. *Through-composed.

Duret, duretto. (1) A *courante melody or courante-like dance mentioned in some early 17th-century English *masque texts (e.g., *Masque of Flowers,* 1614). According to Michael Praetorius (*Terpsichore,* 1612), the courante tune "La Durette" was named for its composer. The term was also known in England and may have been synonymous with the dance category. (2) A German corruption of **durezza.* B.G.

Durezza [It.]. (1) Harshness. (2) In 17th-century Italy, a dissonance, as in a **toccata di durezze e ligature.*

Dutār [Per.]. A *long-necked lute of Iran and Central Asia with two strings of silk or metal, a fretted neck, and a pear-shaped body. See also *Dömbra.*

Dux, comes [Lat.]. In compositions employing *imitation, such as the *canon and *fugue, the leading voice and the following or imitating voice, respectively.

Dyad. Two pitches, whether sounded simultaneously or successively. The term is used principally with reference to nontonal music.

Dynamic marks. Terms, abbreviations, and symbols used in musical notation to indicate degrees of loudness and transitions from one to another. See Performance marks.

Dynamics. (1) That aspect of music relating to degrees of loudness. (2) *Dynamic marks.

E

E. See Pitch names, Letter notation, Hexachord, Pitch.

Ear training. Training intended to improve musical perception, including the ability to recognize by ear alone and reproduce in musical notation melodies, intervals, harmonies, rhythms, and meters and the ability to sing at sight. Practice in the former is often termed dictation; in the latter, sight-singing. See also Solfège, Sight-reading, Sight-singing.

East Asia. There are five distinctive cultural areas in this geographical region: Chinese, Mongolian, Tibetan, Korean, and Japanese. In the Chinese cultural area, Tibet and Inner Mongolia are autonomous regions within the People's Republic of China. East Asian cultures have long interacted with one another through trade, diplomatic and cultural exchange, warfare, and religious pilgrimages. As a result, in the sphere of music, there has been much borrowing and exchange of musical instruments, styles, scales and modes, and ideas. In what follows, the official Chinese pinyin system is used in the transliteration of Chinese names and terms.

I. *Chinese cultural area.* 1. Introduction. The Chinese cultural area includes the People's Republic of China (PRC) on the East Asian continent, and Taiwan, the island situated off the southeastern coast of China, which China claims as a province. Although the Chinese people are relatively homogeneous, in the PRC and to a much lesser extent in Taiwan also, a variety of cultures exist that comprise diverse ethnic groups and languages. The flag of the PRC symbolizes the multinational nature of the country: on the upper left corner of a solid red background are one large star and four small ones. The large star represents the Han ethnic community, which has been dominant in the land for centuries and accounts for 94 percent of the population. The small stars represent Inner Mongolia, Manchuria, Xinjiang, and Xizang (Tibet), the homelands of the major non-Han groups absorbed by the Chinese state. Within the country as a whole there are more than 60 non-Han groups, called minority nationalities. The Han speak a number of related Sinitic languages that are known collectively as Chinese; the major form is *putonghua* (the General Tongue, or Mandarin, as it is known in the West), which is also the lingua franca. The languages of the minority nationalities are unintelligible both to other minority groups and to the Han Chinese, resulting in much bilingualism among individuals who deal with the Han.

2. History. (i) Prehistory to the founding of the Chinese state. The main development in prehistoric times was concentrated in northern China, where conditions favored primitive agriculture. The Xia dynasty (ca. 2205–1766? B.C.E.) was considered by the West to be a legendary state until 1978, when its existence was confirmed by archeological evidence. Our knowledge of music in the Xia dynasty and before is based on written records dating from around 400 B.C.E. that focus mainly on court ritual music, and also on archeological data, which include musical instruments such as end-blown bone flutes, clay whistles, ocarinas, rattles, and clapperless handbells.

The Shang dynasty (ca. 1766–ca. 1154 B.C.E.) was the first highly organized state from which we have records. It was also the first culture to use metal (bronze). An extensive collection of late Shang oracle bones made of ox bone or turtle shell with proto-Chinese inscriptions, discovered in the early 20th century, inform us of names of instruments and also of shamanistic rituals that used music and dance to connect in a highly personal way with ancestral, martial, and rain spirits. The musical instruments mentioned include *xing* (individual or sets of suspended stone chimes), *zhong* (individual or sets of suspended clapperless bronze bells), *xiao* (panpipes and end-blown flutes), *yu* and *sheng* (mouth organs), *qin* and *se* (7-stringed and 25-stringed zithers, respectively), and *gu* (drums of varying sizes). In recent years, ongoing archeological excavations at Shang sites in Henan province have unearthed several clay ocarinas and bone flutes as well as numerous bronze bells, either single ones or sets that are tuned mostly in thirds. Each of these range from one to two feet in diameter. There are also ornately decorated stone chimes.

The Shang was replaced by the Zhou dynasty (ca. 1122–771 B.C.E.), which controlled most of northern and northeastern China and administered the territory through a system of fiefs. After 771 B.C.E. the central authority of the Zhou declined. Gradually the larger feudal states absorbed the smaller, until by the 3rd century B.C.E. only a handful of powerful states remained. During its heyday the Zhou regime continued many ritual practices of the Shang but developed a more rationalistic and impersonal approach that found expression in elaborate and complex rituals; it also developed highly sophisticated concepts of music, education, religion, philosophy, and statecraft that served as models for later dynasties.

The age when the central authority of the Zhou was in decline, known as the Spring and Autumn (772–431 B.C.E.) and the Warring States (403–221 B.C.E.) periods, saw the flowering of many schools of philosophy. Philosophers and teachers such as Kong Fuzi (Confucius), Laozi, Zhuangzi, and others explored ethical values and investigated the meanings of music in the ethical system. The Confucian views on music were later incorporated into a work known as the *Classic of Music,* which served as the foundation of orthodox Chinese music ideology until the 20th century. The *Shujing* (Book of History) and the *Shijing* (Book of Poetry) are two extant important documents of this period that inform us of the musical life and the function and ideology of music in the time of Zhou. The latter, consisting of a collection of 305 song texts said to be compiled by Confucius, provides us with information on the musical practice and ideology of the ruling class and some glimpses of the everyday life of common people. It is important to note that the Chinese word for music *(yue)* always connotes a combination of music, dance, literature (words), and fine arts that involve not only the aural and visual sensations but the tactile as well. In various rituals, music functioned as an emblematic marker to differentiate strata in a hierarchical class system. In its heyday around 1058 B.C.E. the Zhou court established a music bureau to supervise and codify court ritual and secular music and dance. This music bureau became the prototype for court music bureaus established in subsequent ages.

Zhou's concept of music had an enduring influence on later Chinese thinking. Music was conceived of as a cosmological manifestation of the sound of nature, and was integrated into a binary universal order of opposites: yin (negative force) and yang (positive force), female and male, earth and heaven, etc. Out of this conception grew an idea that there was cosmologically "correct" music and "incorrect" music; the former, played by correct instrumentation correlating to the five elements of nature (metal, wood, water, fire, and earth), would bring equilibrium and harmony to man and nature. Instruments were thus classified into eight categories according to materials used and timbres produced: stone (chimes), metal (bronze bells), silk (zithers), bamboo (flutes), wood (percussion), clay (ocarinas), gourd (mouth organs), and skin (drums), and were collectively known as *bayin* (eight kinds of timbre).

Around or before the 7th century B.C.E. a system of pitch generation appeared that grew out of the ideal for cosmic harmony based on a ratio of 2:3, symbolizing heaven and earth, respectively. An ancient pentatonic scale was derived through a process of calculation based on a cycle-of-fifths theory. According to this, a given length of pitch pipe is regarded as the fundamental pitch, called *huangzhong* (yellow bell), from which the remaining pitches are generated through the cycle-of-fifths process. Later theoreticians used this system to generate an entire chromatic scale. The excavation in 1978 of the spectacular set of 64 suspended bronze bells on the tomb of Marquis Yi of the state of Zeng (722–331 B.C.E.) of the Warring States period greatly enhanced our knowledge of the late Zhou period. Chinese musicologists and archeologists determined that 19 of the bells were designated for tuning and the remaining 45 were designated as performance bells grouped into six sections; each of these 45 bells had two striking positions on the lower portion of the bell that produced two different pitches having intervals of either a major third, minor third, perfect fourth, or diminished fifth. Together the 64-bell set encompassed a range of five octaves.

(ii) The founding of the Chinese empire and the first flowering of Chinese civilization. Among the warring states in the late Zhou period, the Qin in the northwest was the most powerful. In 221 B.C.E. it overcame the last of its rivals and unified all of China under a single centralized empire. Relying on a harsh legalist ideology that stressed the supremacy of the state and harsh punishment for offenders, the short-lived Qin dynasty (221–206 B.C.E.) nonetheless accomplished much, not only militarily, and brought about the standardization of weights and measures. Writing was also standardized and unified. It is from the Qin that we have the first record of a zither with movable bridges, called the *zheng,* which was popular in northwest China.

The Qin was superseded by the great Han empire, which lasted 450 years (202 B.C.E.–220 C.E.). Under Han rule China enjoyed unprecedented prosperity and stability. The Han adopted a modified form of Confucianism, with elements of legalism, as its state ideology, and the Confucian *Classic of Music* and the classical Zhou conception of music served as the foundation for a repertory of court ritual music known as *yayue* (elegant music). Following the Zhou model, a Bureau of Music, known as Yuefu, was established at court to supervise and codify court ritual music and secular entertainments; in addition, Yuefu officials oversaw the collection and compilation of folk songs into anthologies. This gigantic undertaking served a political purpose: the government scrutinized the collective data closely to find out what the common people thought and sang about.

In the sphere of popular music, the musical narrative *xianghe ge* (narrative songs with rhythmic accompaniment) was prevalent in the Han time; its songs were partly derived from preexistent folk tunes and partly newly composed. In its later development *xianghe ge* included dance and instrumental accompaniment, and out of this grew the sophisticated multimovement *da qu* (grand suites) with alternating song, dance, and instrumental movements in varying speeds and moods. The *qin* (a seven-stringed zither) emerged as an important solo instrument during the Han, and several famous *qin* pieces created during this period exist today with the same names. Stability in the Han empire encouraged the growth of commerce and urban commercial centers, and in turn stimulated many urban popular entertainments that involved dance, music, and acrobatic skills. For example, on an engraved Han-period stele is a depiction of a *panwu* (drum dance) featuring a performer dancing on a series of small flat drums placed on the floor, with an accompanying female chorus and a sizable male and female instrumental ensemble playing instruments such as small flat drums, panpipes, ocarina, zither, horizontal flute, mouth organ, suspended two-headed barrel drum, bronze bells, and a stone chime set. Existing written and pictorial records from the Han depict the popular entertainment *bai xi* (hundred variety shows), made up of acrobatic shows, dances, and short dramatic skits with musical accompaniment. Some members of the educated leisure class developed the intellectual pursuit of relating music to cosmology, manifested in a system of pitch calculation correlated with special dates and seasons of the year for divination purposes. This eventually developed into a system of pitch calculation called *lulu,* which increased the 12 pitches per octave to 60 micropitches by generating new pitches through cycles of fifths.

Han economic growth in northern China stimulated foreign trade and military expansion. The great east-west caravan trade route, later dubbed the Silk Road, was opened up by the Han emissary Zhang Qin in the 3rd century B.C.E. This long route brought Chinese traders into contact with Persian, Syrian, and Greek traders, who transported goods to the Roman Empire through the help of Greek and Jewish merchants. The constant incursions in the Han's northern and northwestern frontiers by the Turkic nomads known as Xiongnu (the Huns) necessitated Han military expeditions across the Pamirs into Central Asia, and the formation of diplomatic, trade, and cultural alliances with other nomadic tribes along the Silk Road. These activities brought China into contact with the cultures of Tibet, Central Asia, and beyond. Imported foreign instruments that took root in China included a harp called *shukonghou;* a flute called the *di,* whose prototype probably came from Tibet; and most important of all, a pear-shaped lute from Persia that was the prototype for the Chinese plucked lute, the *pipa.* The Han empire eventually declined due to weakness in the central government and ultimately ended in 220 C.E. with a revolt. During this time of chaos, many thinking men turned to Taoism, *qin* playing, and poetry writing as means of self-cultivation.

(iii) Reunification and the Buddhist age. The revolt that overthrew the Han led to three centuries of disunion during which northern China was invaded by nomadic proto-Mongol people and by the Toba Turks, who set up states in northern China, took on the trappings of Chinese aristocratic families, and intermarried with the local Han people. The Toba Turks, who set up the northern Wei dynasty (386–535 C.E.), accepted Buddhist teaching, which had come to China from India in the 1st century C.E., bringing with it Indian Buddhist art, music, and musical modal practice. During these three centuries of disunity a process of assimilation of imported music and musical instruments took shape in northern China. Meanwhile, a large number of educated Han Chinese moved south to the Yangzi Valley, partly to seek refuge from foreigners and partly to live in a more temperate climate. Consequently, an Eastern Jin dynasty in the south was established, with Nanjing as its capital (317–420), where Han traditional culture was deliberately nurtured. Eventually Buddhism was also accepted in the south.

The 5th to 9th centuries were regarded as the great age of Buddhism, which eclipsed Confucianism, and Buddhist art and music flourished and exerted a profound and long-lasting effect on Chinese culture. In 581 northern and southern China were again reunited under the Sui empire (581–617), and China entered one of its most cosmopolitan periods before the 20th century. The ruling houses of both the Sui and the Tang were great patrons of Buddhism and Buddhist arts and music. During the Tang, the imported *pipa* became one of the most celebrated instruments in the empire, and Buddhist *bien wen,* narratives alternating songs and spoken passages, were performed by Buddhist monks in temples to tell stories about the life of Buddha and to teach compassion for all living things. The assimilation of imported music and musical instruments into remnants of Han music accelerated during this period, and new instrumental ensembles employing both Han and imported instruments were formed. This development was particularly evident in the huge repertory of court banquet music and dance known as *yenyue,* which included compositions derived from indigenous Han music as well as imported music and a mixed orchestra of Han and imported instruments. Murals depicting *yenyue* performances dating from the Sui and Tang periods can still be found in the Mogao Buddhist grottoes in the ancient city of Dunhuang in Western Gansu province.

(iv) The second flowering of Chinese civilization and the Mongol invasion. The highly centralized Tang state was challenged by powerful regional regimes, and from 907 to 960 China was split up into a series of five short-lived dynasties and small regimes, known as the Five Dynasties, which were later incorporated (except the northern territories occupied by foreign powers) into the Song empire in 979. Southern and central China under the Song enjoyed great internal prosperity, and Chinese civilization flourished. The intellectual leadership of the Song advocated Neo-Confucianism, a metaphysical reinterpretation of Confucianism emphasizing pragmatism and careful examination of political and social matters. This pragmatic attitude influenced writings on musical subjects. Buddhism was in decline, and Neo-Confucianism became the new orthodoxy.

Yayue (court ritual music), based on Song Neo-Confucian precepts, was once again in ascendancy and became the model for later dynasties. The *yayu* of the Song period employed an orchestra made up of idiophones (suspended bronze bells and stone chimes, and wooden percussion instruments), chordophones (the *qin* and *se* zithers), aerophones (transverse and end-blown flutes, panpipes, mouth organs, and ocarinas), and membranophones (suspended and barrel drums in different shapes and sizes), which were played by more than 200 instrumentalists. This orchestra was divided into two ensembles of unequal size. The smaller was chiefly made up of chordophones and aerophones played on the terrace of a pavilion, while the larger included all four categories of instruments arranged according to five directions (four points of the compass plus the center) and played in the large courtyard in front of the pavilion and below its terrace. (In Chinese traditional architecture, formal pavilions were built on a raised terrace facing a large courtyard.) The larger ensemble accompanied "civil" and "military" dances, each performed by 64 dancers (the number 64 has cosmological significance). *Yayue* ensembles also included a chorus that sang songs selected from a large repertory according to requirements of the occasion.

Theory on musical modes had been an intellectual preoccupation for a long time, and during the Song, theory on the modal system reached its fullest form, which defined a mode by a specific scale structure and the choice of a final. It was also during the Song that the indigenous seven-stringed zither, the *qin,* came to be regarded as the exclusive instrument for cultivated gentlemen, and an elaborate ideology for the *qin,* known as the *qin dao* (the way of the *qin*), also came into being. A large repertory of *qin* compositions notated in *jianze pu* (tablature in abbreviated characters) was developed. Rapid urbanization during the Song time ushered in large amusement quarters where highly specialized professional storytellers, actors, and other performers provided entertainment for a large and demanding audience. Enjoying a form of lyrical song called *ci,* whose lyrics were made up of two or more stanzas of unequal length, became the favorite pastime for the literati.

Meanwhile, from the 10th to the 12th century, northern China was divided into several states ruled by alien tribes from the northeast. In the early 12th century the Jurchen, a Tungusic people from Manchuria, conquered northern China and set up a new state of Gin, which in 1127 forced the Song to abandon their capital in central China and move south; this later period is designated as the Southern Song, during which a couple of rather crude theatrical traditions began to take shape, both in Southern Song and in the Jin. The former is called *nanxi* (southern drama), and the latter is known as Jin *yuanben* (dramatic scripts of the Jin). The rise of the Mongols in the early 13th century led to the conquest of Gin in 1234, and later to the conquest of the Southern Song in 1278. China under the Mongol Yuan dynasty (1260–1341) became a part of the Mongol empire, which stretched across Eurasia. It was during the Mongol period that the Jin *yuanben,* a plebeian form of musical theater ignored by the educated circles, came into maturity and achieved great artistic height as the *yuan zaju* (Yuan drama).

(v) Ming and Qing China. In 1368, with the establishment of the Ming dynasty, China was reunited under Chinese rule for the first time in more than four centuries. The Ming began as a great seafaring power, but after the mid-15th century the empire entered an inward-looking period, undergoing steady growth in trade, agriculture, and industry. Its population doubled from about 80 million to about 160 million. The Ming boasted of great achievements in education and philosophy, literature, art, and drama, reflecting the high cultural level of the elites. A mathematician called Zhu Zaiyu (1536–ca. 1610), who was a member of the royalty, succeeded in creating a tempered scale and published his results in *Lulu quanshu* (A Comprehensive Study of the Lulu, 1584–1606) and two other books, thus completing efforts to create a tempered scale since at least the Han period. In the mid-16th century, a highly literary and polished musical theater, known as *kunqu,* began to be developed jointly by literary men and professional singers and actors in the Kunshan-Souzhou area of the lower Yangzi. Its libretti were written in a dramatic form called *chuanqi* drama, which combined musical and literary elements from the southern drama of the Song period and the yuan drama. Patronized by the literary and wealthy elites, *kunqu* theater dominated the national stage from the late 16th century to the 18th century and is still performed today. Also during the Ming period, the art of *qin* playing achieved great heights, and scholarly writing on music theory, music, and drama, and the creation of *chuanqi* libretti for *kunqu,* became the favorite pastime of literary men.

In 1644 the Ming empire came to an end when it was conquered by the Manchus, descendants of the Jurchens who had formed the Jin state from 1127–1234, and the Qing dynasty was formed. The Manchus extended China's frontiers to incorporate Mongolia, Manchuria, Xinjiang, and Tibet. To retain power the Qing rulers adopted many Ming institutions and preserved the social and political order of imperial Confucianism, but they harshly discriminated against the Han populace. China prospered under the Qing, and under royal patronage scholarship flourished. However, from the 1840s on, Western powers began to force trading concessions from the Qing and to exert pressure on the Qing government. The Opium War (1830–42) exposed China's weakness in the face of modern Western military technology. In 1911 the Qing collapsed under external and internal pressures and vengeful Han nationalism.

Economic and political decline in the late Qing, particularly in the countryside, also affected the development of some musical genres. In the sphere of folk song, many lyrics reflected the harsh life of the common people in the increasingly impoverished countryside; one prevalent topic in folk songs in both northern and southern China after the Opium War was the necessity for peasants to plant opium as a cash crop, and the resulting widespread opium addiction. Musical narrative performances had deep roots in the countryside, but because of economic decline many rural performers migrated to cities seeking a better life. As they faced more exacting artistic demands from their city patrons, many narrative performers found it necessary to reform their genre by elevating the artistic content and tightening the structure of the narratives, and to improve their performing skills as well. Notable narrative genres such as the *Jing yun dagu* (Peking drum song) and the *tanci* (southern narrative) achieved a high artistic standard and flourished as a result. Various regional and local musical theaters became known during the late Qing. The internationally known musical theater *jingxi* (known as *jingju* today; both terms mean "Theater of the Capital [Beijing]," but in the West it is known by the somewhat misleading name Peking Opera) began to take shape in Beijing, the capital of Qing, during the late 18th century. Building on the foundation of the regional theaters of Anhui and Hubei, particularly their aria repertories and speech delivery styles—and later also cross-fertilized with Beijing's own local theater, the *gaochang,* and other imported theaters, such as the highly elegant *kunqu* from the south, and the lively *qinchang* theater originated in Shaanxi province, the territory of the former state of Qin, particularly its aria repertory known as *xipi* and its complex percussion elements—*jingju* became consolidated and mature in the mid-19th century, and by the early 20th century it dominated the national stage. The late Qing also saw the proliferation and development of various regional instrumental genres. Notable genres included the *si* (silk, or strings) and *zhu* (bamboo, or winds) ensembles of the lower Yangzi area, and the instrumental ensemble of Guangdong province in the south. Outstanding players of *qin* and *pipa* music also appeared during the late Qing, and a few aficionados of these instruments began to preserve, compile, and publish existing repertories into anthologies.

(vi) After 1911. The Nationalist Revolution of 1911 overthrew the Qing and transformed imperial China into a republic, but foreign expansion continued. The traditions of court ritual and entertainment music—the *yayue* and the *yenyue*—were discarded. The nationalist leaders and leading intellectuals looked toward the West for inspiration to modernize and industrialize China in order to catch up with the expanding Western powers; inhabitants of the highly populated coastal cities, notably Tianjin in the north, and Shanghai, Wuhan, Xiamen, and Guangzhou in the south, were exposed directly to Western influence through foreign trade and personal contact. Rapid social and institutional changes necessitated the establishment of a modern school system based on Western models, and the traditional civil service examination, based on knowledge of the Confucian classics, was discarded. Natural science and geography were included in the modern school curriculum; also included was classroom music, known as *xuetang gequ* (school song), which aimed to alleviate boredom in the classroom. As there was no precedent for school songs in China, a national debate concerning the musical content for the new *xuetang gequ* began in earnest. There was general consensus among modern education reformers, however, that school song ought to be used as a tool to inculcate the correct values for nation building; therefore, the body of existing music closely connected with theater, narrative, and other types of entertainment was not thought suitable for schoolchildren. Protestant hymnals and some Western school songs brought to China by Western missionaries and educators since the 19th century were readily available. So were Japanese school songs of the Meiji (1873–1904) and later periods that were themselves modeled on Western songs and were brought back by Chinese students who had studied in Japan. Many of the first generation of modern Chinese songwriters chose Western and Japanese songs as models for *xuetang gequ.* A few active songwriters at the turn of the 20th century had received their elementary musical training in Japan, and their songs, which are syllabic, diatonic, and often marchlike, had a distinctly Japanese flavor, albeit of Western inspiration. From such a humble beginning, the *xuetang gequ* evolved into a new genre of modern Chinese songs in the diatonic scale, no longer restricted to school; it later was transformed into the body of political songs known as Songs for the Masses of the People's Republic of China (1949–). Songs in the diatonic scale represented the largest output of modern Chinese music in the 20th century.

The modern curriculum of Westernized school songs totally excluded instruction in and acknowledgment of other existing forms of Chinese music, and as a result, generations of Chinese students were ignorant of and indifferent to China's former musical heritage, a situation that persists today. After World War I, some Chinese composers and educators received training in Europe and America and returned to China as enthusiastic advocates of Western music. The continued foreign expansion in China, plus China's own unstable political and economic situation, precipitated intellectual ferment and finally resulted in widespread student demonstrations May 4, 1919, which stimulated a profound national awakening and critical self-examination. With the slogan "New Culture," leading intellectuals and activists of the May Fourth movement advocated learning from Western knowledge and culture.

Under this impetus, in 1922, at National Peking University, the first extracurricular department of music was established, offering instruction in piano, violin, and harmony. It was headed by Xiao Youmei (1884–1940), a Japan- and then Leipzig-trained composer and educator. In 1927, Xiao Youmei left Beijing for Shanghai, where he established and headed the Shanghai Conservatory, the first modern conservatory in China. It was partially modeled after the Leipzig Conservatory of Music, Xiao's alma mater. The faculty of the conservatory included Western-trained musicians such as the Oberlin- and Yale-trained composer Huang Zi (Huang Tzu, 1904–1938), who used impressionist harmonic idioms to set Chinese words in his major choral works, and several expatriate Russian and European musicians. The curriculum included instruction in piano, violin, cello, organ, harmony, and Western music theory. Xiao, who was the author of many music textbooks and also the composer of many school songs and short piano pieces, believed that China must train a new generation of musicians, theorists, and educators in the scientific principles of Western music so that they could use their skills and knowledge to improve and reform Chinese music, which Xiao considered to be "unscientific." Because of its pioneering and influential status, and its location in Shanghai—the treaty port whence Western knowledge was transmitted to the rest of the nation—the Shanghai Conservatory profoundly influenced the attitude of the Chinese educated elites toward acceptance of Western art music and the adoption of harmony, tempered scales, and instrumental intonation, as well as Western concert behavior. It is important to note, however, that for the majority of the Chinese people living in smaller cities and rural areas, local music without a Western veneer was still their favorite, until the communist revolution.

Besides Xiao Youmei, other influential music figures of this period were Li Jinhui (1891–1967), Zhao Yuanren (Chao Yuen ren, or Y. R. Chao, 1892–1982), and Liu Tianhua (1895–1932). Li Jinhui was a pioneer who advocated writing songs specially for children, and was the creator of the first song-and-dance dramatic skits for schoolchildren; he later also created the commercial Shanghai Popular Song. Zhao Yuanren, a Cornell-trained linguist, was a composer by avocation. His piano composition "Heping Jinxing Qu" ("March of Peace") was the first for piano by a Chinese composer. Being a linguist, and therefore sensitive to the Chinese language, he also wrote several well-known songs based on Chinese folk style whose melodies reflect the linguistic tonal characteristics of the Chinese words. Liu Tianhua, a one-time colleague of Xiao Youmei in Beijing, took a drastically different track in developing modern Chinese music. He was a good player of the *erhu* and the *pipa* and frequently participated in the performance of traditional instrumental ensembles with professional musicians who were by and large shunned by the educated class, and he had a deep fondness and respect for traditional music. Nonetheless, under the influence of the New Culture movement of the May Fourth period, Liu felt compelled to reform Chinese instrumental music by borrowing Western elements. In his compositions for the *erhu* and the *pipa,* entitled "Liang Xiao" ("Beautiful Evening") and "Gewu yin" ("Introduction to Song and Dance"), respectively, he borrowed some Western concepts of musical structure and employed Western ideas of intonation.

In 1921, the Chinese Communist Party (CCP) was founded in Shanghai by an activist of the May Fourth movement. There began a competition between two political groups that would last for decades to come: the Nationalist Party (KMT), led by Chiang Kai-shek, and the CCP, led by Mao Zedong. In 1923 the impact of Marxism-Leninism on Chinese thought, and on arts and music, which were to be regarded as political tools, began to affect Chinese musical development. With the increase of Japanese aggression in China, Chinese song composers began to transform the school-song medium into anti-Japanese songs. In 1932, the Japanese government set up a puppet state in Manchuria in preparation for a full-scale invasion of China, which took place in 1937. Under military pressure by the Nationalists, members of the CCP escaped to Yan'an in northeastern China, where the party set up its wartime headquarters. The War of Resistance against Japan, as this war is called in China, fought by the Nationalists and the Communists, lasted until the Japanese surrender in 1945, and it stimulated an outpouring of war songs.

Composers who began their careers in the 1920s and 1930s included Ma Sicong (1912–87), a noted violinist and composer who was trained at the Paris Conservatory of Music. Ma composed several works for violin and cello, and was the first Chinese composer to write symphonies; he also attempted to employ harmony in folk materials. Another composer was the self-taught Nie Er (1912–35), who wrote numerous film songs and anti-Japanese songs; one of them, a film song called "March of the Volunteers," later became the national anthem of the PRC. Another composer active during this period was the French-trained Xian Xinghai (Hsien Hsing-hai, 1905–45). Xian returned to China in 1935 on the eve of the Japanese invasion, and he immediately threw himself into composing numerous anti-Japanese songs that he taught to thousands of participants in antiwar rallies in many cities. In 1938 Xian went to Yan'an to head the newly established music department of the Lushun Institute of Art, whose goals were to train a new generation of composers to serve the communist revolution. Xian composed several large-scale orchestral and choral works while at Yan'an. His most celebrated work is the *Huang He da hechang* (Yellow River Cantata). This work combines folk and Western musical elements for mixed male and female chorus and small vocal ensembles, which use singing and recitation accompanied by a small instrumental ensemble with piano and a few Chinese strings and percussion. The cantata later became the model for an internationally known piano concerto of the same name, the bombastic *Huang He Ganqin Xiezhou Qu* (Yellow River Piano Concerto). Both Nie and Xiang are lionized in China today.

Also during the 1930s, in Shanghai a new medium of acculturated Chinese popular songs sprang from the children's songs composed by Li Jinhui, who went on to write *qing ge* (love songs) for commercial purposes. Later, these songs were known as *liuxing gequ* (Shanghai popular song). Written primarily for commercial recordings and for social dancing, these acculturated songs in the diatonic scale borrowed elements from Tin Pan Alley ballads, film songs from American movies, and popular dance rhythms from Latin America, such as the tango and rumba.

Meanwhile, in communist-controlled Yan'an, the party leadership began to develop a coherent theoretical concept of using folk art for propaganda purposes. In 1942, Mao Zedong delivered his celebrated "Talk at the Yan'an Forum on Literature and Art," which mandated that literary and artistic production must have a political purpose and must be subjected to party control and direction; arts that reflected feudal and Western bourgeois values must be discarded. "The Talk," as it is called, has been the guideline for literature and arts ever since.

With the coming of peace in 1945 the Russian occupation of Manchuria and Inner Mongolia ensured communist dominance of these areas. After the outbreak of civil war with the Nationalists, the CCP armies rapidly overran the north, and in 1949 the PRC was established in mainland China, while the remaining members of the Nationalist government fled to Taiwan. Immediately after its establishment, the PRC set up a party organ known as the Association of All China Literature and Arts, to control and censor the arts and artists, under which a subcommittee, the Union of Chinese Musicians, had the responsibility to supervise musicians and set policies to coordinate musical output with China's political goals. During the 1950s the primary goals of the Chinese government were to consolidate power and to reconstruct the war-torn country according to ideals of Marxism-Leninism and Mao Zedong. Political songs for the masses were produced in large quantity to inform the Chinese people of these aims and to motivate them to participate in the reconstruction. The progenitor of these songs was the school song from the turn of the 20th century.

These songs with political messages represented the largest output of the 1950s and produced a new generation of composers whose songs are still sung today. Among these are the celebratory "Quan shijie renmin xin yi tiao" ("All the world's people are of the same mind") by the prolific female composer Qu Xixian (b. 1919), who was a graduate of the Shanghai Conservatory, and "Ge chang Erlaing shan" ("Song of the Erliang Mountain"), in Henan folk song style by Shi Lemeng (b. 1915). A composer and conductor who served in the People's Liberation Army, Shi was steeped in the traditions of Henan's folk music and theater, but he also studied composition at the Lushun Institute of Art in Yan'an under Xian Xinghai. Songs written by national minorities, particularly those by Tibetans and Uygurs, were also circulated.

Beginning in 1949, the Shanghai Conservatory came under direct state supervision, and new regional conservatories were also established, among them the prestigious Central Conservatory of Music in Beijing. The state also supported the establishment of many Western and Chinese orchestras and ensembles. A number of new acculturated genres, such as *geju* (opera), *hechang* (choral works), and *wuju* (dance drama) began to appear. Far-reaching reform of traditional musical theater, narrative, and instrumental music began to take place. All new and revised compositions had first to be inspected by the Union of Chinese Musicians to make sure that they were politically correct.

The ten years of the Cultural Revolution (1966–76) were a period of extreme xenophobia, partly triggered by the U.S. military involvement in Vietnam at the time, and partly due to power struggles at the highest levels of government. Culture, particularly in the form of musical theater, was used as a tool to eliminate political enemies under the guise of class struggle. During the Cultural Revolution, all existing institutions were dismantled and all schools and universities were closed. Educators, artists, composers, and others whose class backgrounds were considered polluted were sent to be reeducated through hard labor in the countryside. Only eight sanctioned "model musical works" were permitted to be performed; among them, five were labeled "Contemporary Revolutionary [Bei]jing Musical Drama" (*Red Lantern, Taking Tiger Mountain by Strategy, The Harbor, Shajia Coastal Village,* and *Ambush of the White Tiger Brigade*), and three were labeled "Contemporary Revolutionary Dance Drama" (*The Red Detachment of Women, White Haired Girl,* and *Shajia Coastal Village Revolutionary Symphony*). Musically, the five musical dramas were innovative in employing Western tempered scales for *jingju* arias and a mixed Chinese and Western orchestra to supply accompaniment and interludes. The dance dramas *Red Detachment of Women* and *White Haired Girl* also employed songs and dialogue, while the *Shajia Coastal Village Revolutionary Symphony* is neither a dance drama nor a symphony but a combination of nonstage *jingju* with arias in tempered scales alternating with orchestral interludes. After 1968, a few more "model works" were allowed to be performed, including, in 1970, the aforementioned *Yellow River Piano Concerto* by the Soviet-trained pianist Yin Chenzhong (b. 1941), since the piano—the bourgeois instrument par excellence—was now dubbed a "revolutionary instrument." In addition to these larger works, songs based on quotations of Mao Zedong, known as "quotation songs," were encouraged by Marshal Lin Biao, one of the members of the collective leadership in the Cultural Revolution during 1966–69. Lin's political purpose was to establish a cult of Mao that would bolster his own authority. In 1969 Mao's wife Jiang Qing, another authority in the collective leadership, emerged as the rival of Lin Biao and banned quotation songs for their "obscenity." From then on, only three songs were permitted to be sung: "East Is Red," "Sailing the Sea Relies on the Helmsman," and the army song "The Three Great Rules and Eight Attentions."

The Cultural Revolution officially ended in 1976.

As China emerged from those ruinous ten years, the Chinese government, under Deng Xiaoping's leadership, embarked on limited market reform and adopted an open-door policy to attract foreign investments and technology from the West and from Japan. Music conservatories, together with other educational institutions, were revived. Government support of the arts was also revived, and the Chinese musical stage became more diversified. Famous Western virtuosi, conductors, composers, and academics were invited to perform and lecture in China. A new generation of Chinese performers and composers also emerged, among them Tan Dun, Chen Yi, Zhou Long (all now living in the U.S.), and Qu Xiaosong. The open-door policy also ushered in popular music from the U.S., Japan, Taiwan, and Hong Kong, and many Chinese youths became fans of foreign popular music. To counteract this, the government sponsored China's own popular music, called *qing yinyue* (light music). As China became more prosperous during the late 1990s, a more confident Chinese government encouraged experimentation in the arts and took measures to ensure the survival of art forms that Chinese youths tended to neglect. In the late 1990s, the Chinese Ministry of Culture was successful in proposing that the United Nations proclaim *qin* music and the *jingju* and *kunqu* musical theaters as "masterpieces of the oral and intangible heritage of humanity" to help ensure their survival.

3. Instruments and their music. (i) Chordophones. Chinese chordophones have traditionally been classified as the "silk" instruments, as strings used to be made of silk thread (steel and nylon strings are commonly used today). There are four main types of chordophones: the zither *(qin),* the plucked lute *(pipa),* the bowed lute *(erhu),* and the struck lute *(yangqin).* The *qin* is a seven-stringed zither made of lacquered wood. It is highly revered for its antiquity and its association with sages and poets. The seven strings of varying thickness stretch over the entire length of the elongated soundbox. On the outer edge of the soundbox are 13 embedded studs called *hui* indicating positions for fingers. *Qin* playing involves various ways of plucking and pulling the strings with the player's right fingers, and pressing the strings at different positions with the fingers of the left hand to alter the pitch or to create ornaments. Practically all *qin* compositions have programmatic titles that serve to evoke a mood, atmosphere, or historical incident familiar to an educated Chinese listener. A typical *qin* composition contains several sections framed by meterless opening and ending sections.

The *pipa* is a four-stringed, pear-shaped, fretted, plucked lute with a bent neck. Its prototype was imported to China from Persia via the ancient Silk Road around the 4th century C.E., and it became extremely popular from the 7th century onward. All through its history, the *pipa,* an instrument associated with music for artistic entertainment rather than for ceremonies and rituals, has been played as a solo instrument, as a member of an instrumental ensemble, and to accompany musical narrative and drama. The *pipa* is placed upright on the player's crossed knees and played with the fingers. The strings are usually tuned to A-d-c-a, and the entire chromatic scale can be produced. The pipa player employs a large variety of playing techniques and an astonishing variety of sounds and moods can be produced.

The *erhu* is a two-stringed, bowed lute with a wooden, cylindrical soundbox covered with snake skin. The bow, of horsehair, is inserted between the two strings of the *erhu,* and the player alternately pushes the bow away and draws it inward to play on one or the other string. Of Central Asian origin, the *erhu* is used as a solo instrument, as a member of an instrumental ensemble, and as an accompanying instrument for musical narrative and musical theater. Liu Tianhua was responsible for transforming the *erhu* into an instrument for the modern concert stage. Between 1918 and 1932, Liu dedicated himself to improving the instrument and inventing new techniques borrowed from the Western violin. He wrote a dozen or so solo *erhu* compositions, and these have formed the foundation of the modern *erhu* solo repertory. A contemporary of Liu, the blind street musician Hua Xianjun (1893?–1950), known as Ah Bing the Blind, also contributed to the art, techniques, and repertory of the *erhu.* His most celebrated composition, *Er quan ying yue* (Moon Reflection in the Second Spring) has become the pillar of modern *erhu* music and is played very often on the concert stage, either as a solo piece or as an *erhu* concerto with Chinese orchestra.

The *yangqin* is a dulcimer imported to China from the Middle East around the 15th century. Today's *yangqin* is trapezoidal; it is employed as a solo instrument, as a member of an ensemble, and to accompany musical drama.

(ii) Aerophones. Made of bamboo, these have been classified as the "bamboo" category of instruments. Chinese aerophones include transverse and vertical end-blown bamboo flutes, panpipes, mouth organs, ocarinas, and a double-reed flute called *guan.* The transverse flute called the *dizi* has the largest repertory among all the aerophones, and has played an important role as a solo instrument and in instrumental ensembles. The *dizi* is made of bamboo and has six finger holes, a mouth hole, and an extra hole covered by a thin membrane that gives the instrument its characteristic buzzing sound. In the 1950s *dizi* masters of northern and southern China created repertories with regional characteristics. After the 1960s, regional repertories merged to form the modern *dizi* solo repertory of today.

(iii) Idiophones. Chinese idiophones include clappers, suspended bronze bells and stone chimes, cymbals and gongs of varying sizes, and wooden idiophones in varying shapes and sizes. Among these, the *ban,* a clapper consisting of two hard wooden slabs fastened together, is most commonly used.

(iv) Membranophones. *Gu* (drum) is a generic term

for Chinese membranophones. There is a large variety of barrel-shaped drums. The *tanggu* and the *dagu* are medium-size and large single-head drums, respectively, both set on a stand and played with two sticks. The *bangu* is a widely used single-head drum. It is made of a rounded wooden block with its center hollowed out, over which a membrane is stretched and fastened with nails. It is used in many theatrical and narrative ensembles because it is rhythmically versatile.

(v) Instrumental ensembles. The best-known form in the West is the *jiangnan sizhou* (silk and bamboo ensemble of the southern Yangzi region). Popular in the Shanghai area, this ensemble is made up of silk-category instruments such as the *pipa* and *sanxian* plucked lutes and the *yangqin* dulcimer; bamboo-category instruments such as the *dizi, xiao* (end-blown notched flute), and *sheng* (mouth organ); and idiophones such as the clapper, *muyu* (small wooden slit drum), and a pair of cup-size bells; plus a small one-headed flat drum. Its repertory consists of only about two dozen pieces, but because of improvised embellishments, no two performances of a piece are exactly alike. Variations of one basic tune, or of several tunes consecutively, constitute the underlying form. Though divided into sections, a performance has no discernible breaks, the end of one section overlapping with the beginning of the next. Another characteristic feature is the frequent, systematic alternation of silk and bamboo sections, each of which presents a solo instrument supported in heterophony by an ensemble of the same family. A *chuida* (literally, "blow and strike") is a percussion ensemble of drums, gongs, cymbals, and reeds used in processions and festive occasions. Usually in three sections of contrasting timbre, texture, and tempo, a *chuida* piece always has an extensive drum solo. A *logu* (meaning "gong and drum") is an ensemble for gongs, cymbals, and drums used for festive occasions.

4. Traditional musical theater. All forms of Chinese musical theater integrate instrumental and vocal music, speech, dance, and symbolic and stylized gestures into a complex whole. Elaborate costumes and fanciful facial makeup are employed. Actors' role types are divided into *sheng* (male role actor), *dan* (female role actor), *jing* (rough male character-actor who wears a painted face), and *chou* (comic role), plus some subsidiary roles. Two of the better known types of musical theater are *kunqu* and *jingju* (or Peking Opera).

(i) *Kunqu,* a sophisticated and highly polished theater noted for its employment of intricate vocal techniques and word articulation, and expressive and continuous dance and stylized gestures, arose during the mid-15th century in the Kunshan-Suzhou area of Jiangsu province in eastern China. Its creation was a result of collaboration between literary men and professional singers and actors. *Kunqu* rose to a dominant position over other older regional theaters during the 16th century and continued its dominance well into the 18th century. The libretti of *kunqu* were set according to the form of the *chuanqi* drama, which has many scenes divided into a four-part structure. The aria repertory of *kunqu* includes a body of preexistent pentatonic and heptatonic tunes. Arias in each scene are arranged in a prescribed sequential order technically known as *taoshu* (song suite). Professional *kunqu* troupes from the Ming and Qing periods to the present maintain 12 principal types of actors plus a small number of minor actors. The sound ingredients of a *chuanqi* play as realized on the *kunqu* stage consist of alternating arias and spoken passages, either in the mode of everyday speech or in heightened speech and recitation. A *kunqu* actor is expected to have mastery not only of *kunqu* singing but also of the proper delivery of all the modes of speech. In addition, an actor must master complex gestural and dance movements. Arias and movements are accompanied or punctuated by a small instrument ensemble that generally consists of a melodic and a percussive section; the principal melodic instrument that accompanies the singing is the transverse flute *dizi;* subsidiary melodic instruments are the *sheng,* the *sanxian,* the *pipa,* the *ruan* (a four-string, round, plucked lute), and sometimes a *zheng* (a long zither). The principal percussion instruments include a wooden clapper and a small flat drum, a small gong, cymbals, and a barrel drum. For festive or important scenes, a long trumpet called a *changjian* may be used.

(ii) *Jingju* (Peking Opera). A popular theater traditionally catering to a wide spectrum of Chinese audiences, the sources of the plots for *jingju* come mainly from popular legends, historical epics, popular novels, and narratives. The basic musical elements are arias, heightened speech, and instrumental interludes. The instrumental music of *jingju* has many functions: to accompany the singing and the physical movements and dance, to define dramatic situations, and to convey moods and the psychological makeup of characters. The instrumental ensembles have two components: the melodic or *wenchang* (civil instrumentation), and the percussion or *wuchang* (military instrumentation). The percussion ensemble, which provides rhythmical punctuation for movements and singing and communicates to the audience important dramatic information, is made up of the *ban* (clapper), the *bangu* drum, big and small gongs, and cymbals. The melodic ensemble, which accompanies arias and plays overtures and interludes, is made up of a two-string bowed lute called a *jinghu,* which is the chief melodic instrument accompanying singing, the *erhu,* the *yueqin* (a four-string pluck lute with a round sound box), the *dizi,* the *sheng,* and the big and small *suona* (conical double-reed oboes). *Jingju* arias derive from a group of some 30 preexistent tune-and-rhythmic pattern types either in the *xipi* or the *erhuang* category. To appreciate the *jingju* fully, an audience is required to possess "the art of watching and listening."

5. Traditional musical narratives. Storytelling, by highly trained professionals, with or without music, has been one of the most enduring entertainments

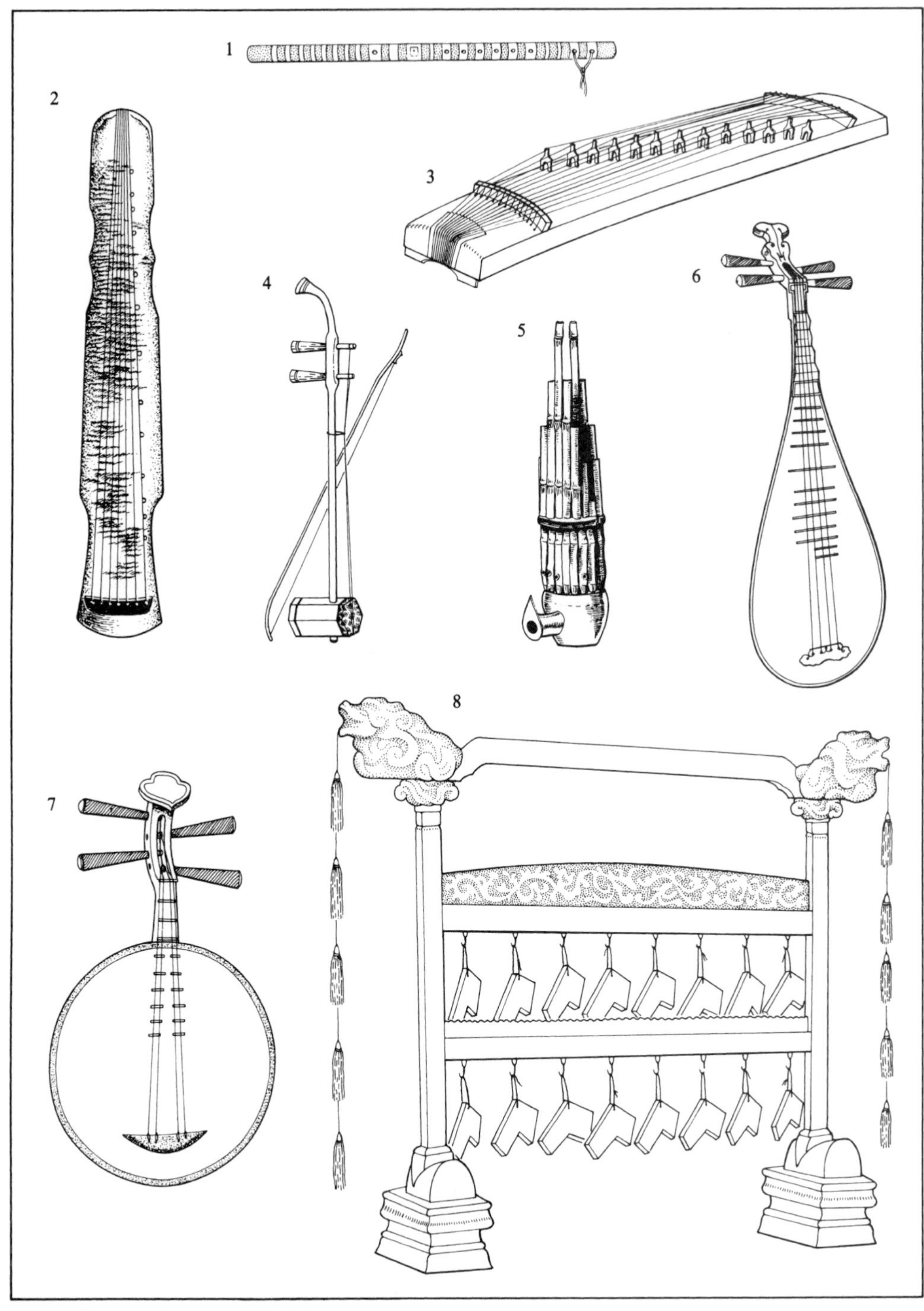

Chinese instruments: 1. Dizi. 2. Qin. 3. Zheng. 4. Erhu. 5. Shend. 6. Pipa. 7. Yueqin. 8. Lithophone or qing.

since the Song dynasty. There are two major forms, *jingyun dagu* and *tanci*. *Jingyun dagu* is commonly known in the West as Peking Drum Song, but the term literally means "musical narrative in Beijing dialect accompanied by drum and clapper." Originating in the countryside of northern China, *jingyun dagu* migrated to Beijing around the late 19th century and underwent changes initiated by a few masters of this narrative form. Very popular in Beijing and its surrounding districts, *jingyun dagu* was and still is usually performed in teahouses by three persons: the singer/narrator, who accompanies him- or herself by striking the surface of a single-headed flat drum, resting on a tripod, with a long thin stick held in the left hand and a pair of clappers held in the right hand (these provide intricate and often syncopated rhythmic patterns); an *erhu* player; and a *sanxian* player. The two string players provide heterophonic, or at times polyphonic, melodic accompaniment to the vocal phrase, which is often heptatonic with wide skips and unpredictable atonal and rhythmic shifts. Spoken passages, either in speech or in half-song, half-speech modes, alternate with vocal phrases. Stories for the narratives derive mostly from historical epics such as the *Sanguo yenyi* (Saga of the Three Kingdoms), which tells of the fight for domination of China by the three kingdoms Wei, Shu, and Wu after the fall of the Han dynasty. The rhythmic and vocal vitality of *jingyun dagu* is particularly suitable for the portrayal of battles.

Tanci, commonly known in the West as southern-style storytelling, literally means "musical narratives accompanied by plucked lutes." *Tanci* became popular in Suzhou and its vicinity in the mid-19th century. In the early 20th century *tanci* also became popular in big cities such as Shanghai, and since then it has commonly been performed by all-female troupes with two or three members. The leading singer/narrator accompanies herself on the *sanxian,* the supporting narrator/singer accompanies herself on the *pipa,* and the third performer plays accompaniment on the *erhu.* The vocal melody, generally lyrical and expressive, is a variation of two basic anhemipentatonic melodies with lyrics in verse, and spoken passages in heightened speech interspersed between vocal phrases. Stories for *tanci* derive from vernacular romantic tales of the Ming and Qing periods. Today a *tanci* performance usually takes place in a small arena specifically for *tanci,* known as a *shuchang.* A performance usually begins with a short independent vocal piece in verse called a *kaipian* (overture), to be followed by longer narratives.

II. *Japan.* 1. History. Japanese musical culture is made up of folk and art traditions. The history of art music can be divided into seven periods corresponding to political and cultural developments.

(i) Antiquity (before the 6th century C.E.). The first evidence of musical life in neolithic Japan is a Chinese reference in the 3rd century C.E. to singing and dancing. Later documents mention instruments such as the *wagon* (six-stringed zither with movable bridges), the *yamato-fue* (flute), and various simple percussion instruments. Music and dance were intimately connected with indigenous shamanistic rituals. By the 5th and 6th centuries, as Japan evolved into an imperial state, early rituals became systematized into the *shinto* religion; the body of court *shinto* music was known as *mikagura.*

(ii) Nara period (553–794). This period saw the establishment of an imperial state and the importation of Buddhism and continental music. In 612 C.E., Chinese *gigaku* (masked dance and music) was imported from Korea, and subsequent importations from Central Asia, China, and Korea made Japanese music international in character. The introduction of *gagaku* court music from China and Korea resulted in the establishment, in 701, of a court music bureau, the *Gagaku-ryō,* which employed several hundred international musicians and dancers. In 749, to celebrate the completion of the Great Buddha of the Tōdaiji Temple, the government sponsored a performance by 400 musicians of various nationalities using some 75 instruments of different types. A collection of some of these instruments is still in the Imperial Treasury in Nara, the *Shōsoin.*

(iii) Heian period (794–1185). The power of the emperor weakened as that of the regent grew. Reflecting a cultural trend, *gagaku* music was modified according to Japanese styles and taste, and its repertory was codified. A Chinese theory for a tonal system was introduced, deriving heptatonic scales from 12 chromatic tones achieved through a series of fifths. The Indian practice of having male voices chant the Buddhist sacred texts *(sutras)* was introduced from China late in this period; the classical theories of this chant, called *shōmyō,* are found in codices of the Tendai and the Shingon sects.

(iv) Kamakura period (1185–1333). Under the military dictatorship of the shōgun, a feudal state evolved. Most traces of the international character of Japanese music disappeared. As court music declined, the popularity of *shōmyō* grew, influencing secular vocal styles. Interest in theatrical and narrative styles also grew. By far the most significant genre of the period was the narrative form called *heikebiwa,* sung by a blind storyteller who also played interludes on the **biwa* (a four-stringed lute played with a plectrum).

(v) Muromachi and Azuchi-Momoyama periods (1333–1615). This war-torn period marked the disintegration of the centralized government of the shogunate and the rise of the merchant class. As the court became impoverished, court music continued to decline. The new song form *kouta* (short song) gained popularity, and new instruments, such as the *hitoyogiri* (a small end-blown bamboo flute) and the *jamisen* (a three-stringed long-necked lute), appeared. The *hitoyogiri* evolved into the present-day **shakuhachi,* and the *jamisen* became the **shamisen.* Theatrical and narrative forms continued to be popular. *Jōruri,* the greatest of Japanese narrative genres, originated at this time from the tales told by itinerant storytellers, and the **noh* theater developed from a host of popular theatricals and ritual dances.

(vi) Edo period (1615–1868). Under the Tokugawa shōgun, Japan was once again unified. In order to maintain stability, the government shut out the outside world. From this isolation developed many distinctly Japanese musical forms. The court was reduced to a ceremonial role in which *gagaku* music played a part. While the aristocracy continued to foster the *noh* theater, the merchant class, by now rich and powerful, supported narrative and theatrical entertainments such as *bunraku* (puppet theater) and *kabuki* (popular drama). Music played by the *zokusō* (or **koto,* a 13-stringed zither), the *shamisen,* and the *shakuhachi* was in vogue.

(vii) Meiji period (1869–1912). Led by the Emperor Meiji, Japan abandoned its isolation and underwent drastic reform and modernization. Western music gained ascendancy over traditional forms. Western band music, Protestant hymns, and American public school songs became part of Japanese life. Late in the 19th century, Western art music was introduced and quickly gained widespread acceptance. Many European virtuosos, composers, and music teachers came to Japan after 1915. The first of a new generation of modern Japanese composers who worked primarily in the Western idiom was Kōsaku Yamada (1886–1966), whose works include symphonic pieces and operas. Yamada and his contemporaries were influenced by German Romanticism, but the generation between the world wars was influenced by French impressionism; some, for example Michio Miyagi (1894–1957), began to combine traditional Japanese and European idioms. The postwar generation followed modern international styles; notable composers include Ikuma Dan (b. 1924), Yashushi Akutagawa (b. 1925), Toshirō Mayuzumi, Kan Ishii (b. 1921), Makoto Moroi (b. 1930), Tōru Takemitsu (b. 1930), Hikara Hayashi (b. 1931), and Akira Miyoshi (b. 1933).

The militant nationalism of the early 20th century helped elevate certain types of traditional music considered representative of the national spirit, such as *gagaku,* and *shamisen* and *koto* music. Lately, traditional Japanese music has shown a steady resurgence, in part because of the continuous presence of a strong system of music guilds.

2. Religious and court music. (i) *Mikagura.* Music performed in court *shinto* ceremonies by male choruses and accompanied by the *wagon* (or the *yamato-goto*), the *kagura-bue* (transverse bamboo flute with six holes), the *hichiriki* (oboe with nine holes), and the *shakubyōshi* (wooden clappers). The present repertory of 15 songs is of two types: *tormino,* songs paying homage to the gods, and *saibara,* songs meant to entertain the gods. Since the Meiji period, *mikagura* songs have been performed by two choruses, each having its own repertory. The leader of each chorus sings the initial phrase accompanying himself on the clappers, followed by unison chorus accompanied by the remaining instruments.

(ii) *Satokagura.* Generic name for the two main types of folk *shinto* rituals: shamanistic rituals paying homage to the gods and rituals connected with festivals. In the former, a priestess sings and dances, accompanied by the *wagon,* transverse flute, and the *suzu* (bell-tree). The latter, called *matsuribayashi* (festival music), is played by a small band or *hayashi* consisting of *o-daiko* (a big two-headed drum), two *taiko* (small one-headed drum), and a transverse flute. The lively syncopated rhythm of the drums accompanies a repetitive melody.

(iii) *Shōmyō.* Buddhist chanting of sacred texts *(sutras)* by male chorus in solo-responsorial style. Chants in Sanskrit are called *bonsan;* in Chinese, *kansan;* in Japanese, *wasan.* The music is a series of stereotyped phrases belonging to either the *ryo* or the *ritsu* scales, each of which has five basic notes and two auxiliary notes. *Shōmyō* chants may be syllabic or melismatic, and more or less regular or free in rhythm. A chant usually begins slowly and gets faster.

(iv) **Gagaku* (elegant music). The traditional court music of Japan. Its repertory includes *mikagura* [see 2 (i) above] and court entertainments. The latter includes two kinds of orchestral music: *komagaku* (music introduced from Korea) and *tōgaku* (courtly entertainment music of T'ang China, 618–907 C.E.), as well as vocal genres such as the *roei* (chanting of Chinese poems), *saibara* (folk song), and *imayō* (court popular song). When *gagaku* music is used to accompany dance, it is called *bugaku.*

3. Theatrical genres. (i) **Noh.* A dance and music theater created by Zeami (1363–1444), who also wrote *Kadensho* (1402), an important treatise on *noh* aesthetics. Popular during the 14th and 15th centuries, the prototypes of *noh* include earlier popular theatricals such as the comic *sarugaku* (monkey music), *sangaku* (Chinese acrobatic show), and *dengaku* (rural dance and music associated with harvest ceremonies). The *sangaku* later lost popularity and was replaced by comic plays called *kyōgin* (mad words). *Noh* plays are performed by two actors (the *shite,* principal actor, and the *waki,* supporting actor), a chorus of eight, and an instrumental ensemble consisting of a *nokan* (a transverse bamboo flute with seven holes) and three drums (*kotsuzumi,* a shoulder-held hourglass drum; *ōtsuzumi,* a side-held hourglass drum; and *taiko,* a shallow barrel drum played with two sticks). Two singing styles are used: the *yowagin* (soft) and the *tsuyogin* (strong).

(ii) *Bunraku.* A 20th-century term for the Japanese puppet theater, which dates to the 12th century. The narrative style used in *bunraku* is called **gidayubushi,* after its developer Gidayu Takemoto (1615–1717) of Osaka. *Bunraku* rose to its artistic and popular heights when Takemoto collaborated with the famous playwright Monzaemon Chikamatsu (1653–1717). *Gi-*

dayu music is performed by a singer/narrator using heightened speech and songs, and an accompanist on *shamisen* who plays preludes, interludes, and postludes made up of stereotyped patterns having symbolic meaning.

(iii) *Kabuki.* A major theatrical form of the Edo period, still popular today. Originally performed by female, now by male, troupes, *kabuki* theater has absorbed elements and repertories from the *noh* and *bunraku* theaters; it also makes use of *shamisen* vocal genres such as the **nagauta, kiyomoto, tokiwazu,* and **gidayubushi,* and offstage ensembles *(geza)* consisting of voices, *shamisen,* flutes, and percussion. The onstage ensembles provide musical commentary or accompany dance; the offstage ensembles provide sound effects and signals, set the mood, reveal the inner thoughts of the characters, and underline dialogue and action.

In general, a *kabuki* play is in four main parts: the *deha* (coming out) contains *okī,* a section that sets the scene or mood, and the *michiyuki,* which introduces the characters. The second part, *chūha,* contains a highly lyrical section, called *kudoki,* and *monogatari,* in which the story develops to a crucial point. The third part, *odoriji,* is the essential major dance. The fourth part, *iriha* (exit section), contains *chirashi,* the musical high point of the play, which resolves in *dangire* (finale).

4. Instrumental and vocal genres. (i) Music for **koto.* The *koto* is a 13-stringed zither made of wood with movable bridges and played with ivory picks. Popular music of the Edo period, known under the generic name of *sōkyoku,* is of two types. The first, *kumiuta,* is a *koto*-accompanied song cycle; the verses of each individual song *(uta)* are derived from preexistent poems whose subjects are unrelated. Typically, an *uta* has duple meter and is in eight phrases divided into four measures. The second type, *danmono,* for *koto* alone, is in several sections *(dan),* each consisting of either 64 or 120 beats; it is usually in a loose rondo-variation form. *Shirabemono,* another type of purely instrumental *koto* music, is a series of variations upon a theme. The *jiuta* is an important hybrid form of *koto* music that combines the techniques of both *kumiuta* and *danmono.* It is sometimes called *tegotomono* after the *tegoto,* the important instrumental interludes between its vocal sections. *Tegotomono* usually contain three parts: a foresong *(maeuta),* an instrumental interlude *(tegoto),* and an aftersong *(atouta).* This basic structure may be extended. In contemporary practice, *jiuta* is played by an ensemble called *sankyoku* consisting of *koto, shamisen,* and *shakuhachi.* The *koto* plays the main melody, while the *shamisen* and *shakuhachi* produce simple heterophony. Important schools of *koto* music perpetuating the tradition include the Ikuta School of Kyoto and the Yamada School of Edo (Tokyo).

(ii) Music of the **shakuhachi.* The *shakuhachi* is an end-blown bamboo flute with five holes. Developed from the *hitoyogiri,* the *shakuhachi* was first played during the 17th century by itinerant Buddhist priests *(komusō)* who used it to solicit alms. The *komusō* tradition was consolidated by the Kinko School of Tokyo and perpetuated by the Tozan School. The *shakuhachi* repertory has two categories: the *honkyoku* (original music), solo pieces in free form and free rhythm created prior to and during the Edo period, and the *gaikyoku* (outside pieces), adapted from *koto* music and having a tighter structure and more metrical rhythm (with frequent changes of tempo) than the *honkyoku. Shakuhachi* music is marked by frequent microtonal effects produced by a combination of half-holing technique and changes in embouchure.

(iii) Music for the **shamisen.* The *shamisen* is a three-stringed long-necked lute played with a plectrum. It is used to accompany various vocal genres, each of which uses different sizes of *shamisen* and plectra. These genres can be grouped under two general headings: the *katarimono* (narrative) and the *utamono* (lyrical). *Utamono* consists of several lyrical song styles, one of which is called *kouta* (short song), a collective name for light and popular songs. *Kouta* were usually combined into song cycles known as *kumiuta.* By far the most important lyrical song cycle style is the **nagauta* (long song); it is performed by an ensemble consisting of voices, *shamisen,* bamboo flute (optional), and drums. Both the *nagauta* and the *kouta* were connected with *shamisen* music used in *kabuki* theater.

The narrative category includes a dozen or more styles, all of them known by the generic name of *jōruri,* sung mostly by solo voices and accompanied by a solo *shamisen.* Individual *jōruri* styles differ in subject matter and in the manner of playing or singing. Among the best known is the *gidayubushi,* which accompanies the puppet theater *bunraku.* Other narrative forms include *naniwabushi, shinnaibushi, kiyomoto,* and *tokiwazubushi,* the latter used in the *kabuki* theater.

5. Folk music. Japanese folk music, either vocal or instrumental, can be classified as children's songs, work songs, dance songs, and festival or ritual songs. Generally, group songs are in duple meter and have a narrow range, while solo songs are characterized by free rhythms and wide range. Instruments used include different types of flutes, drums, cymbals, gongs, *suzu* (a small bell-tree), *binsasara* (a rattle made of strung wooden plaques), and *yotsudake* (bamboo clappers).

Among regional folk traditions, those of the Okinawans in the Ryūkū Islands and the Ainus in the Hokkakō are among the most distinctive. The most vital of the Okinawan folk styles is the *shamisen*-accompanied song genre called *bushi. Bushi* songs are strophic and have *shamisen* ritornelli as prelude, interlude, and postlude. Texts deal with nature, love, dancing, and work. Other instruments used in Okinawa are the *koto,* a small drum *(kudaiko),* and a flute *(fuye).*

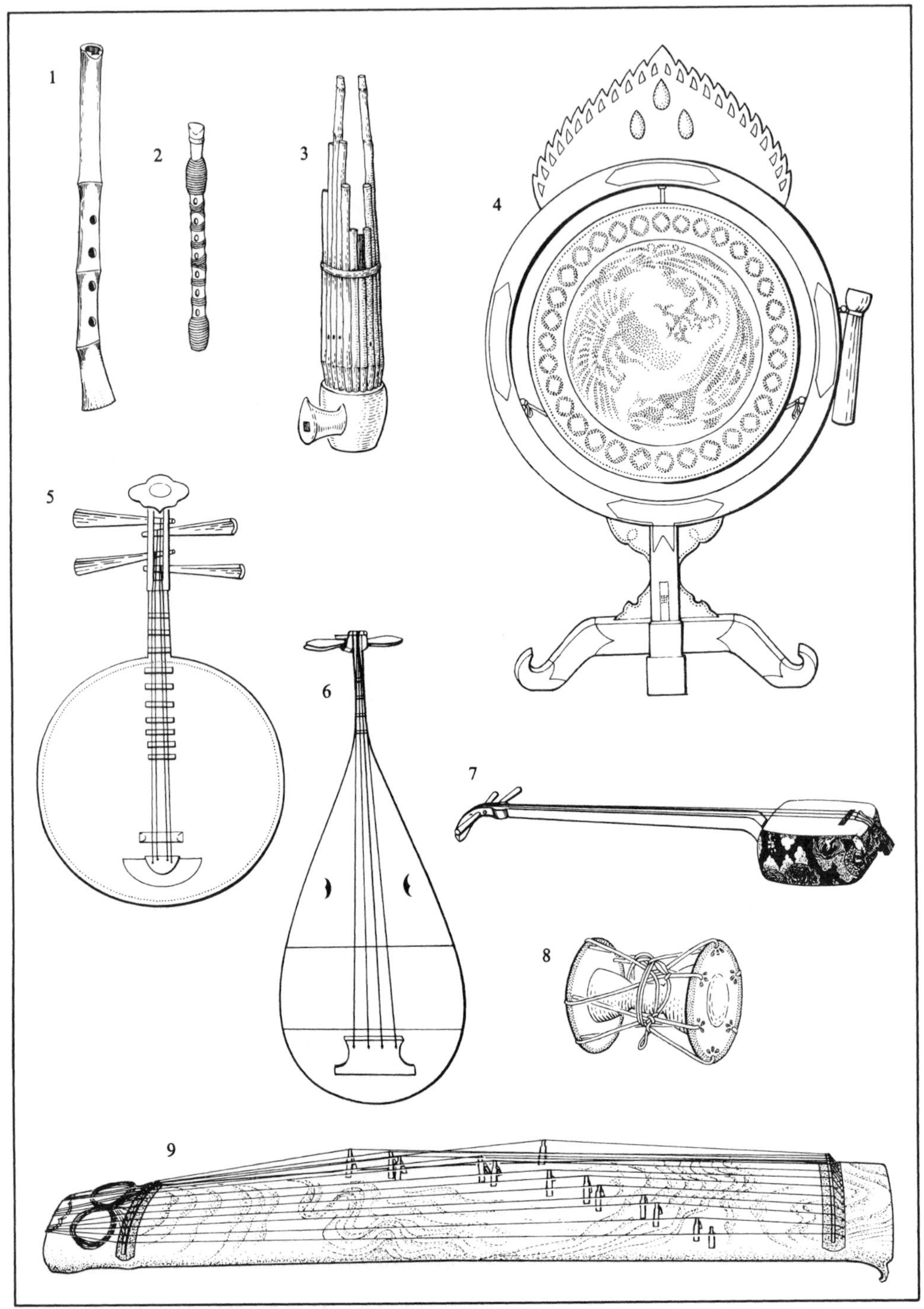

Japanese instruments: 1. Shakuhachi. 2. Hichiriki (shown twice its size in relation to others). 3. Sho. 4. Tsuridaiko. 5. Gekkin. 6. Biwa. 7. Shamisen. 8. Kotsuzumi. 9. Koto.

Predominantly vocal, Ainu music reflects the group's non-Japanese origin. Many songs use onomatopoeic imitations of animal sounds. Among various types of communal songs and dances, one called *upopo* (sitting song) is noted for its polyphonic texture produced by imitative group singing and the beating of chest lids *(hokai)* by the singers. An unusual vocal technique called *rekukkara* is produced by two singers sitting face to face with both of their hands cupping their mouths to form a resonating channel between them; by alternately closing and opening their hands, they change the timbres of their voices. In exorcist rituals, songs for dancing *(chikap-rimse)* are sung in either antiphonal or responsorial manner. Typical instruments include the *tonkori* (a five-stringed zither) and the *mukkuri* (Jew's harp), both played by women.

III. *Korea.* 1. History. Korea was a kingdom until 1910, when it was annexed by Japan. After World War II, it was divided into two political units: the Republic of Korea (South Korea) and the Democratic People's Republic of Korea (North Korea). Korea has distinct art and folk musical traditions. Art music, consisting mainly of court or religious music and music cultivated by the literati, falls into six historical periods.

(i) Antiquity (before 57 B.C.E.). The earliest Korean people probably migrated from present-day Manchuria, northern China, and Mongolia. They apparently practiced shamanism, whose rituals used music. By the 4th century B.C.E., when a league of tribal groups had developed, music was also performed at agricultural rituals and festivals.

(ii) The Three Kingdoms period (57 B.C.E.–668 C.E..). During this period, the kingdoms of Koguryŏ, Paekche, and Silla competed for hegemony. Koguryŏ, which had frequent contacts with China from the late 4th century C.E., adopted the repertory and musical practice of the Sui (581–618 C.E.) and T'ang (618–907) periods of China. One of the most characteristic and prestigious of Koguryŏ instruments was the *kŏmun'go,* a six-stringed zither modeled after the seven-stringed Chinese *ch'in.* Paekche was particularly influenced by music of nearby southern China. The southern Chinese *gigaku* (masked dance and music) was imported and in turn introduced into Japan in 612 C.E. Another Chinese instrument, of central Asian origin, the *k'ung-hou* (an angular harp), was also popular in Paekche. Silla, which did not emerge until the late 4th century, was at first the least developed of the Three Kingdoms, in part because of its isolation from Chinese influences. But it developed rapidly and by the late 7th century had defeated Koguryŏ and Paekche. A typical instrument of Silla was the *kayakum,* a 12-stringed zither with movable bridges related to the 16-stringed Chinese *cheng.*

Buddhism and Confucianism were introduced to Koguryŏ from China in 372 C.E.. and subsequently to Paekche and Silla. By the 5th century, Buddhist chanting of sacred texts *(sutras)* had also been imported.

(iii) Unified Silla period (676–1036). Korea emerged as a unified kingdom under the domination of Silla. The century that followed was a golden age of artistic and cultural achievement during which traveling Korean scholars brought back advanced Chinese culture. The diversified music practice of the Three Kingdoms merged to produce hybrid forms, and two categories of music, *hyangak* (native music) and *tangak* (T'ang music), were systematized. The former is indigenous Korean music as well as pre-T'ang Chinese music already assimilated into the native tradition; the latter is music newly imported from T'ang China. Eventually the word T'ang became synonymous with China, and *tangak* came to denote Chinese music imported after the T'ang period. Buddhism was supported by the government, and Buddhist chanting rose to an art during the Silla period.

(iv) Koryŏ Dynasty (938–1392). Buddhist chanting still flourished, but the most significant musical development of this period was the establishment of Korean court music, *aak* (elegant music), derived from Chinese models. In 1114–16, Korea received from China a set of *aak* instruments divided into two ensembles: *tŭngga* (orchestra on the terrace) and *hŏn'ga* (orchestra on the ground). In addition, Korea received instruction on two types of ritual dance for court ceremonies, the *munmu* (civil dance) and the *mumu* (military dance). By the 12th century, the *aak* repertory included not only *tangak,* but also *hyangak* and a type of court entertainment music for women known as *kyobangak.*

(v) Yi Dynasty (1392–1910). The Yi Dynasty adopted neo-Confucianism as the official state doctrine, leading to a decline in Buddhist chanting. The *hyangak* flourished, and a new type of processional music called *koch'wi* gained great popularity. Many works that combined elements of *hyangak* and *koch'wi* were composed to texts written in the recently developed phonetic vernacular scripts, the *han-gŭl* (Korean letters). With the invention of an abstract mensural notation called *chŏnggan-po* (square notation), music was transcribed for the first time.

During the early Yi period, the court strongly supported *aak.* The noted music theorist Pak Yōn (1378–1458) codified the theoretical system of *aak* and was appointed by Emperor Sejong (1418–50) to establish and head the *Chong'ak-wōn* (Royal Music Department). Subsequently, instrumentation and instrumental tunings used in the *tŭngga* and *hŏn'ga* ensembles were stabilized. A new repertory from China, called *taesŏng akpo* (music of the Confucian Shrine), was absorbed into that of the *aak.* As the native Korean repertory developed and enlarged, the *tangak* became increasingly less important, and *tangak* instruments were modified. Late in the 15th century, two important musical events took place: the invention of a system of tablature for the *kŏmun'go,* modeled after the Chinese *ch'in* tablature, and the publication (1493) of the most important source of Korean music, the *Akhak Kwebŏm (Book of Music)* edited by Sŏng Hyŏn.

Repeated invasions, first by the Japanese during the late 16th century, and then by the Manchu during the mid-17th century, laid waste nearly the whole peninsula. Most of the *aak* instruments were lost, and *aak* was not played. In 1644, the Manchu founded the Ch'ing Dynasty (1644–1912), and the Yi Dynasty became its vassal. In 1645, performance of *aak* resumed at court, by an orchestra of *tangak* and *hyangak* instruments, creating the so-called *hyangdang kyoju* (mixed instruments of *hangak* and *tangak*). By this time, the music of *tangak* had been modified by Korean taste and style, the most notable feature being a predilection for triple meter. Throughout the 18th century, unsuccessful efforts were made to revive the *aak* tradition, for example, by the establishment of the Bureau of Instrument Construction. As the distinction between *tangak* and *hyangak* became blurred, a new term, *habak* (joint music), indicated music played by mixed Korean and Chinese instruments.

From the 18th century on, genres of art music for voice and instrumental accompaniment, such as *kagok, kasa,* and *sijo,* became popular among the literati. Buddhist chanting was barely kept alive by a few monks. In the 19th century, Protestant hymns were brought by missionaries. Later, Western military band music was imported and, around 1900, adopted at court.

(vi) From 1910 to the present. Under the Japanese (1910–45), indigenous traditions were denigrated. *Aak* was discontinued at court, except for the Confucian Ritual music. Under Japanese auspices, the Yi Dynasty Music Department replaced the Royal Music Department. It was the forerunner of the National Classical Music Institute established by the South Korean government in 1951 to train performers of traditional Korean music. By the beginning of the 20th century, Western music had gained widespread acceptance among the educated classes. After World War II, the introduction of Western technology and values and subsequent social changes increased reliance on contemporary Western arts and musical forms and hence strained the sense of cultural continuity. In an effort to revitalize traditional arts and music, to bridge the gap between traditional and modern society, and to consolidate national identity, the government has, since the late 1960s, sponsored numerous art and music festivals. About music in North Korea, little is known.

2. Court and religious music. (i) *Aak.* Originally referring to court music of Chinese origin, the term *aak* came to be used more broadly for repertories of court ritual and entertainment music of both Chinese and Korean origin (*tangak* and *hyangak,* respectively). Only the Confucian Ritual music in the *aak* repertory survives, performed twice a year at the Confucian Shrine. Two orchestras, each with its own repertory, are used in the ritual: *tŭngga* (orchestra on the terrace) and *hŏn'ga* (orchestra on the ground). Both include idiophones (stone chimes, bell chimes, pounded wooden boxes, wooden scrapers, and wooden clappers), aerophones (transverse and end-blown bamboo flutes, ocarina, and panpipes—*tŭngga* only), membranophones (various sizes of barrel drums), and, for *tŭngga,* chordophones (7- and 25-stringed zithers). *Aak* music has a classical symmetry and simplicity reflecting Confucian ideals of balance and universal harmony. The melody, based on a heptatonic scale, is performed in slow tempo with uniform durations, and with minimal ornamentation and dynamic change.

(ii) Buddhist music. Three styles of Buddhist ritual chants are found. *Sutras* (Buddhist invocation) are chanted by unison chorus with texts in Chinese or Chinese transliteration of Sanskrit. They are simple syllabic chants in parlando style accompanied by regular beats of the *mokt'ak* (wooden gong). *Hwach'ŏng* (chants based on folk song) are solo chants accompanied by a small gong (played by the chanter) and a *puk* (suspended barrel drum, played by another priest). *Hwach'ŏng* texts are in Korean, and melodic style is akin to folk song in rhythmic structure and style of delivery. *Hwach'ŏng* is not used in daily monastic services, but at special rites. *Pŏmp'ae* (long solemn chants), the most important type of chant developed from Chinese Buddhist chants, have Chinese texts. In present practice, the *pŏmp'ae* is performed very slowly and in free rhythm. The syllables, set to long sustained tones, are frequently interrupted with vocables. Formulaic motives form the basic melodic material.

3. Vocal art music. (i) *Kagok.* A song cycle sung as a solo or duet, accompanied by *kŏmun'go* (six-stringed zither), *taegŭm* (transverse bamboo flute), *p'iri* (oboe), *haegŭm* (two-stringed bowed lute), and *changgo* (hourglass drum). The present repertory of 27 cycles is categorized by mode: 11 belong to the *ujo* mode (degrees 1, 2, 3, 5, 6 of the diatonic scale), 13 are in the *kyemyŏnjo* mode (degrees 1, ♭3, 4, 5, ♭7 of the diatonic scale), and 2 are in mixed *ujo-kyemyŏnjo* mode. Each song consists of three lines of 12 or 20 syllables. Though all the songs in a cycle are melodically related, their textual contents are not. Each song is divided into five vocal sections framed by an instrumental prelude and postlude *(taeyŏŭm),* and with an instrumental interlude *(chungyŏŭm)* between the third and the fourth. A *kŏmun'go* prelude in free rhythm (known as *tasŭrŭm*) always precedes the first and last song of each cycle; it differs according to the mode of the cycle. The basic rhythmic structure for each song consists of 15 restatements of a 16- or 10-beat cycle, played on the *changgo.* A complex heterophonic texture characterizes *kagok* music.

(ii) *Sijo.* Lyrical songs in a three-line verse form accompanied by the *changgo.* A complex rhythmic structure and subtle dynamic changes are used.

(iii) *Kasa.* A long narrative song in strophic or through-composed form accompanied by *p'iri, taegŭm, haegŭm,* and *changgo* and making extensive use of falsetto.

4. Folk music. (i) *P'ansori.* A solo vocal narrative

accompanied by a *puk* (double-headed barrel drum). It emerged in the 18th century, performed by itinerant entertainers known as *kwangdae* and believed to be related to the shaman. Until the 19th century, when 12 texts were written down, it existed in oral tradition only. Today, *p'ansori* is taught in the National Folk Music Institute. It is performed by a female singer who stands holding a fan and a handkerchief in either hand, while the male drummer sits on the floor. Songs alternate with spoken passages. Sung in a strong and hoarse vocal style, the songs are set in modes characterized by different melodic motives and emotional connotations. The accompanying drum patterns also convey specific dramatic symbolism.

(ii) *Sanjo.* An instrumental duo developed in the 18th century and played by a *kayakum* or, less frequently, by a *komŭn'go* or a *taegŭm,* accompanied by the *changgo.* Originally an improvised form based on stock melodies derived from shamanistic and folk tunes from the Chŏlla province, *sanjo* today has almost completely lost its improvised character and is taught at the National Folk Music Institute.

A *sanjo* piece consists of six continuous movements, each subdivided into several sections whose tempos continuously increase. Each movement uses different tonal centers, rhythmic patterns, and tempos. Generally, melodic phrases in the slow movements have tetratonic structure and frequent ornaments such as portamentos, while those in faster movements have tritonic structure and are played in a virtuosic manner of greater rhythmic complexity.

IV. *Mongolia.* 1. History. The vast central and eastern Asian steppe known as Mongolia has seen several nomadic empires, the most famous being the Mongolian Nation of Genghis Khan in the 13th century. Incorporated into the Chinese Empire in the 17th century, the Eastern Mongols were administratively divided into Inner Mongolia, south of the Gobi desert, and Outer Mongolia, to its north. Western Mongols known as Oriates (or, in Russia and among Turks, as Kalmuks) lived in Xinjian and Qinghai provinces. The northernmost group, the Buriats, lived in forested southern Siberia. Today the Mongols are divided between the nation of Mongolia, which gained independence from the former U.S.S.R. at the end of the 1980s, and the Inner Mongolian Autonomous Region of the People's Republic of China.

Until relatively recently, the inhabitants of the Mongolian steppes were nomadic herders, and much of the rural population remains nomadic. These nomads lived a completely separate existence from the urban and agricultural world of China. As a result, the Mongols have developed a highly individual culture. The indigenous religion is shamanism, but in the 16th century, Tibetan Buddhism was introduced, and monasteries came to control a huge part of Mongolian wealth and productivity.

Music has always been an important element of Mongol life, used to communicate with the spirits and as a means of entertainment and self-expression. Music making is not restricted to specialists. During festivals—particularly the July *Naadam* festivals, a competition of martial arts—or while relaxing around campfires, both men and women expect to be called upon to sing or play; formerly, women sang only in private.

Mongolian music is primarily vocal, with or without instrumental accompaniment. Songs are of two main types: those with free rhythm and those with meter. In both types, the pentatonic scale without semitones predominates.

2. Music and religion. (i) Shamanism. In shamanistic rituals, the shaman sings and accompanies himself on the *khets* (a single-headed round drum with metal jingles, played with a stick) to communicate with the spirits. In the *duudlaga* (invocations), he invokes the spirits, and in the *tamlaga,* he assumes the personae of the spirits and delivers their messages in chant. This chant is syllabic and parlando, using minimal ornamentation, and restricted in range. The *duudlaga* begins slowly and gets gradually faster; it is delivered with frequent sighs, groans, birdcall imitations, and silence. The drum, which serves to induce trance and also acts as the shaman's mount to the spiritual realm, is struck with varying force and rhythm to simulate a horse's gallop.

(ii) Buddhism. The Mongols adopted Tibetan models of monastic rituals and musical practice [see below V, 2 (ii)]. But Buddhism has now very nearly disappeared.

3. Secular music. Two genres of songs survive: the *tuul'* (epic song) and the *duu* (song). Also practiced is the specialized vocal technique known as *köömiy* (pharynx), in which one person sings two tones simultaneously—one being the fundamental, the other a harmonic—by modifying the mouth cavity.

(i) Epic song. Surviving only in reduced form, Mongolian epic song originally consisted of long narratives of historical sagas and mythology, with occasional spoken passages. Sung in a parlando style by a male soloist who may or may not accompany himself with a stringed instrument (either a plucked or a bowed lute), the verses are set syllabically to repetitive melodic motives of limited range and intervals. Improvisation is important to both text and melody. Two shorter song styles, the *domag* (legend) and the *tüühen duu* (historical song), are modern derivatives of the epic song tradition.

(ii) Solo song. By far the most widespread vocal genre is the solo song. Two styles are found, differentiated by length and melodic or rhythmic characteristics: the *urtïn duu* (long song) and the *bogïno duu* (short song). Both can be sung by males or females; accompaniment on a bowed or a plucked lute is optional.

The long song is so called because of its long melodic phrases and very sustained tones. Cast in strophic variation form, the melody consists of formulas set syllabically or melismatically to meaningless syllables. Through skillful improvisatory manipulation of formulaic permutation, a singer can prolong the song at will. When sung by an expert, its range may extend to three octaves through the use of falsetto. The melody is in free rhythm and is highly embellished by mordentlike ornaments, glissandos, terminal glides, and frequent breath-stops. In earlier times, the long song was performed either as entertainment at festivals or as a means of self-expression. This tradition is fast disappearing.

The short song is not only shorter than the long song, but also has regular measures and less-ornamented melodies set syllabically to verses with satirical or romantic themes. Traditional drinking songs sung at wedding banquets also belong to this tradition, which is still very much alive and used by the socialist regimes for patriotic and didactic purposes.

4. Instruments. *Khuur* is a generic name for various indigenous Mongolian bowed lutes, among which the best known is the *morin khuur* (or *khil khuur,* horsehead fiddle). It is a two-stringed, bowed spike lute with a trapezoidal soundbox and a long neck. The head of a horse or a dragon is carved at the end of the neck. Other types of bowed spike lute include the four- or two-stringed *khunchir,* which has a small cylindrical soundbox and is commonly found in East Mongolia.

The Mongols also use various types of plucked lute. The two-stringed *tobshuur* has a trapezoidal sound box and is used by the Oriates to accompany epic songs. The two-stringed *dombra* has a triangular soundbox and a long narrow neck with movable frets and is used by the Volga Kalmuks. The *shandze* is a three-stringed plucked lute of Chinese origin (cf. Chinese *san-hsien*), found especially among the Mongol tribes living close to Chinese culture.

The best-known Mongol flute is the *limbe* (transverse bamboo flute with eight holes) used by shepherds. Other instruments include the *yatag* (a 10- or 14-stringed zither with movable bridges), an ancient court instrument related to the Chinese *cheng* and since the 1930s seldom played. Another instrument of Chinese origin is the *yoochin* (Chinese *yangch'in*), a 14-stringed dulcimer played with two soft-headed sticks.

V. *Tibet.* 1. History. An Autonomous Region of the People's Republic of China since 1965, Tibet has been controlled by China since 1951. The Tibetan spiritual and temporal ruler, the 14th Dalai Lama, has been in exile since 1959. Since the emergence of an organized state around the 6th century C.E., the Tibetan people have continuously dominated the area of the present Autonomous Region. Extensive foreign contact influenced architecture, art, music, and religion. Indian Mahāyāna Buddhism, mixed with an early form of Tantrism, was established at court under King Srong-bstsan-sgam-po (ca. 627–49 C.E.). The indigenous shamanistic faith *bön,* however, remained strong. Since at least the 8th century, the music of Indian Tantric Buddhism has blended with that of *bön,* creating a highly distinctive Tibetan tradition.

In the 10th–14th centuries, Tibet became a feudal theocracy sustained by a vigorous monastic tradition based on a highly syncretic form of Tantric Buddhism that combined late Indian Tantra with the *bön* faith. After Chinese rule during the Yüan Dynasty (1260–1368), Tibet regained its independence, and under strong Indian influence, its arts acquired distinctive forms and styles that have persisted virtually unchanged.

In the 15th century began the rise to power of the dGe-lugs-pa order of Buddhist monks ("yellow hats"), one of whose leaders, the fifth Dalai Lama, became ruler of Tibet in 1642. Chinese control in 1951 brought drastic change. During the Chinese Cultural Revolution (1966–76), Red Guards destroyed nearly all of the holy places and many monasteries. Since 1980, the Chinese government has been more tolerant of religion and traditional culture. Some monasteries have reopened and are accepting novices for training, which includes music. Although many traditional musical forms and styles have changed in Tibet itself, some native music survives in Tibetan refugee communities.

2. Religious music and drama. (i) *Bön.* An essential part of the pre-Buddhist *bön* ritual was the chanting of archetypal myths by the invoking priest. The chants, still essential in *bön* rituals, are strophic with little melodic variation. As the ritual proceeds, the music becomes louder and faster, with special sound effects such as gliding, whistling, and shouting. Instruments include the flute and *rkang-gling* (thigh-bone trumpet), but chiefly the indigenous *phyed-rnga* (single-headed drum) and the *gshang* (flat bell). The drum has particular ritualistic importance, for when the *bön* priest plays his drum, he is mounting the ritual flying steed and communicating with the spirits. There are said to be 300 traditional ways of drumming—a number with symbolic connotations.

(ii) Buddhist music. Tibetan Tantric Buddhism regards music, both vocal and instrumental, as a most important means of preparing the mind for spiritual enlightenment. The standard monastic rituals, which vary among orders, consist of unaccompanied choral chants, instrumental hymns, and antiphony between instrumental ensembles and chorus, sometimes accompanied by cymbals and drums. Choral singing is quiet and in unison, though with occasional oblique organum and vocal drones. There are three main types of chant: parlando recitative in free or measured rhythm; *gdang* (hymn), measured, syllabic, strophic chants of limited range in various tempos, and in dichordal or hexatonic scales; and *dbyangs* (sustained chant), syllabic chants sung in very low register, consisting principally of an inflected monotone interrupted occasionally by short phrases of two or three pitches. Two monastic orders, the rGynd-smad and the rGyud-stod, are famous for their sustained chant in which each chanter simultaneously sings a fundamental plus the fifth or sixth harmonic.

The antiphonal instrumental parts to choral chants are performed by eight or twelve winds and percussion. The wind instruments, always played in pairs, include two *rgya-gling* (shawms), two *dung* (long trumpets of varying size and length), two *rkang-gling,* and, sometimes, two *dung-dkar* (conchs). Supported by a drone or dichordal ostinato on the trumpets and conchs, the principal melody, played on the shawms, consists of short, repeated, monothematic nuclei that are highly ornamented. The result is a complex heterophony. The percussion group consists of *gsill-snyan* (quiet cymbals), *rol-mo* (loud cymbals), *rnga* (double-headed drum struck with a crook-shaped stick), *dril-bu* (handbell), and *damaru* (hourglass rattle drum). The cymbals and the *ruga* play the beats and rhythmic patterns, while the handbell and rattle mark off the sections of the service.

Instrumental hymns are played on shawms with circular breathing. The bithematic melodies are ornate and rhythmically marked.

(iii) *'Cham.* The *'cham* is a solemn ritual mystery drama mimed by masked and costumed monks in the roles of deities. Every movement and gesture follows a pattern of strictly prescribed symbolism, accompanied by chanters, who recite prayers, and an ensemble of shawms, long trumpets, drums, and cymbals, the main purpose of which is to provide dramatic sound effects. Performances take place in the front court of a monastery and are open to the public.

3. Secular music and drama. (i) Secular drama. The *a-che-lha-mo* are music dramas about the piety and miraculous deeds of famous historical figures. Probably of 15th-century origin, the *a-che-lha-mo* are secular entertainments designed to attract religious followers. Until 1959, ten of the most highly trained troupes went to Lhasa each autumn to offer their talents as a sort of corvée to the Dalai Lama, after which they were free to perform for profit. Many lesser companies performed locally.

A *lha-mo* troupe has about ten male members; eight act while two play the *sbub-chal* (cymbals) and the *rnga* (drum). Usually staged in the open air with costumes and masks, the repertory contains about a dozen plays with chanted narration, sung dialogue, and accompanied dance. The narrative texts are in both prose and verse. The prose, which sets the scene, is chanted by an unaccompanied solo singer in rapid parlando style. The verses are chanted by the chorus (with or without instrumental accompaniment) or antiphonally by solo singers. These chants are slow, melismatic, and embellished by frequent glottal stops and microtonal inflections; the scale is pentatonic without semitones. Dialogs are presented either in the slow style of melismatic chant or as measured strophic songs in syllabic style. The instruments accompany the singing and dancing and, by stereotyped patterns, mark scene divisions, indicate character, and evoke moods or situations.

(ii) Epic narratives. The most important of the many epic narratives is the Gesar epic, sung throughout Tibet by traveling bards of nomadic origin *(har-pa).* It is extremely long and extols the heroism of the King of Gling (eastern Tibet), later known as Gesar of Khrom (Caesar of Rome), who was considered the protector of Tibet. Sung unaccompanied and solo, the text alternates sections of prose and verse: the prose sections, always short, are delivered in syllabic parlando style with considerable melodic motion; the verse is in couplets and is sung syllabically to one of about 14 melodic formulas. The melodies use scales of four or five tones without semitones.

(iii) Other secular music. Vocal and instrumental art music is played for entertainment at banquets, festivals, and official occasions by professionals or amateurs. The instrumentation of such pieces, which sometimes accompany dance, is extremely flexible and may combine voices and instruments, the latter including the *sgra-snyan* (unfretted long-necked lute with six, or sometimes three or five, strings played with a plectrum), *pi-wang* (two-stringed, long-necked bowed lute), *rgyud-mang* (25-stringed dulcimer, played with two soft-headed sticks), *ti-gling* (transverse bamboo flute with seven holes), cymbals, and drums.

There are four types of song: songs with auspicious texts, *chang-glu* (humorous and drinking songs), *glu* and *gzás* (dance songs), and popular songs from various regions. Most are strophic with instrumental interludes, some have binary form, and some are linked in a medley. There is no distinction between vocal and instrumental idioms, and instruments may play song tunes without the vocal part. The texture is heterophonic.

Another repertory of instrumental ensemble music for one or more shawms and a pair (or pairs) of *ida-mán* (kettledrums hit with wooden beaters), sometimes with voice, appears to be particularly associated with the southern Himalayan regions of ethnic Tibet, including Ladakh, in present-day Kashmir, and Sikkim. This music is used in many civic contexts such as birthday celebrations, weddings, archery contests, wrestling and polo matches, and festivals. The performers are professional musicians, many of whom belong to an ethnic minority called the *mon,* believed to have come from the valleys of Spiti and Lahul south of the Himalayas. This music is distinct from other Tibetan music. Its rhythm is characterized by lively and varied drum patterns in duple, triple, and compound time; its melodies, played by shawms alone or in antiphony with voices, are very ornate, using pentatonic or even chromatic scales.

4. Folk music. Tibetan folk music is primarily vocal; it may be sung solo, by a group in unison, antiphonally, or responsorially. Though often unaccompanied, the voice may be supported by a drum or a

lute. Four classes of folk songs are found: nomadic pastoral songs, work songs, dance songs, and occasional songs with didactic themes. Except for the nomadic songs, which are improvised and in free form, most are strophic and sung syllabically with measured rhythm, using pentatonic or hexatonic scales without semitones. Since 1950, Tibetan folk songs have been influenced by modern trends, and some new urban occasional songs show increasing westernization.

Bibl.: *China.* Robert H. Van Gulick, *The Lore of the Chinese Lute,* rev. ed. (Rutland, Vt.: Charles E Tuttle, 1969). Mingyue Liang, *The Chinese Ch'in: Its History and Music* (San Francisco: Chinese National Music Association and San Francisco Conservatory of Music, 1972). Colin P. Mackerra, *The Rise of Peking Opera, 1770–1870* (Oxford: Clarendon, 1972). Isabel K. F. Wong, "Geming Gequ: Songs for the Education of the Masses," in *Popular Chinese Literature and Performing Arts in the People's Republic of China, 1949–1979,* ed. Bonnie MacDougall (Berkeley: U of Cal Pr, 1984). Kenneth J. DeWoskin, *A Song for One or Two: Music and the Concept of Art in Early China,* Michigan Papers in Chinese Studies 42 (Ann Arbor: Center for Chinese Studies, Univ. of Mich., 1982). Mingyue Liang, *Music of the Billion: An Introduction to Chinese Musical Culture* (New York: Heinrichshofen, 1985). Bell Yung, *Cantonese Opera: Performance as Creative Process* (Cambridge: Cambridge U Pr, 1989). Fritz Kuttner, *The Archaeology of Music in Ancient China* (New York: Oaragon House, 1990). Isabel K. F. Wong, "From Reaction to Synthesis: Chinese Musicology in the Twentieth Century," in Bruno Nettl and Philip B. Bohlman, eds., *Comparative Musicology and Anthropology of Music* (Chicago: U of Chicago Pr, 1991). Andrew F. Jones, *Like a Knife* (Ithaca: Cornell U Pr, 1992). Stephen Jones, *Folk Music of China: Living Instrumental Tradition* (Oxford: Clarendon, 1992). John E. Myers, *The Way of the Pipa: Structure and Imagery in Chinese Lute Music* (Kent, Ohio: Kent St U Pr, 1992). Lawrence J. Witsleben, *"Silk and Bamboo" Music in Shanghai: The Jiangnon Sizhu Instrumental Ensemble Tradition* (Kent, Ohio: Kent St U Pr, 1995). Jonathan P. J. Stock, *Musical Creativity in Twentieth-Century China: Abing, His Music, and Its Changing Meanings* (Rochester: U of Rochester Pr, 1996). Andrew F. Jones, *Yellow Music: Media Culture and Colonial Modernity in the Chinese Jazz Age* (Durham: Duke U Pr, 2001). Isabel K. F. Wong, "The Incantation of Shanghai: Singing a City into Existence," in Jim Craig and Richard King, ed., *Global Goes Local: Popular Culture in Asia* (Vancouver: U of BC Pr, 2002).

Japan. William P. Malm, *Japanese Music and Musical Instruments* (Rutland, Vt.: Charles E Tuttle, 1959). William P. Malm, *Nagauta: The Heart of Kabuki Music* (Rutland, Vt.: Charles E Tuttle, 1963). Francis Taylor Piggott, *The Music and Musical Instruments of Japan,* 2nd ed. (London: B T Barsford, 1909; R: New York: Da Capo, 1971). Willem Adriaansz, *The Kumiuta and Danmono Traditions of Japanese Koto Music* (Berkeley: U of Cal Pr, 1973). Eta Harich-Schneider, *A History of Japanese Music* (London: Oxford U Pr, 1973). Robert Garfias, *Music of a Thousand Autumns: The Togaku Style of Japanese Court Music* (Berkeley: U of Cal Pr, 1975). Bonnie C. Wade, *Togotomono: Music for the Japanese Koto* (Westport, Conn.: Greenwood, 1975). James R. Brandon, William P. Malm, and Donald H. Shively, *Studies in Kabuki: Its Acting, Music, and Historical Context* (Honolulu: U Pr of Hawaii, 1978). Kunio Komparu, *The Noh Theater: Principles and Perspectives* (New York and Tokyo: Westerhill/Tankosha, 1983). William P. Malm, *Six Views of Japanese Music* (Berkeley: U of Cal Pr, 1986). Shuhei Hosokawa et al., eds., *A Guide to Popular Music in Japan,* trans. Mitsui Toru (Kanazawa: IASPM-Japan, 1st printing, 1991; 2nd printing, 1993). Christine Reiko Yano, *Tears of Longing: Nostalgia and the Nation in Japanese Popular Song* (Cambridge, Mass.: Harvard U Pr, 2002).

Korea. Robert C. Provine, "The Sacrifice to Confucius in Korea and Its Music," *Transactions of the Korean Branch of the Royal Asiatic Society* 1 (1975): 43–69. Patrick Kim, "Sinawi: An Improvisational Style of Korean Folk Music: An Analytical Study" (M.A. thesis, Univ. of Hawaii, 1980). Jonathan Condit, *Music of the Korean Renaissance* (Cambridge: Cambridge U Pr, 1984). Robert C. Provine, "Drumming in Korean Farmers' Music: A Process of Gradual Evolution," in Anne Dhu Shapiro, ed., *Music and Context: Essays for John M. Ward* (Dept. of Music, Harvard Univ., 1985). Ban-song Song, *The Sanjo Tradition of Korean Komungo Music* (Seoul: Jun Eum Sa, 1986). Byongwon Lee, *Buddhist Music of Korea,* Traditional Korean Music Series (Seoul: Jungeumsa, 1987). Keith L. Pratt, *Korean Music: Historical and Other Aspects* (London: Faber Music, 1987). Keith Howard, *Korean Musical Instruments: A Practical Guide* (Seoul: Se-Kwang, 1988). Man-young Hahn, *Kugak: Studies in Korean Traditional Music,* trans. and ed. Ino Paek and Keith Howard (Seoul: Tamgu Dang, 1990). Keith Howard, *Bands, Songs, and Shamanistic Rituals: Folk Music in Korean Society* (Seoul: Royal Asiatic Society, Korean Branch, 1990). Keith Howard, "Samul Nori: A Reinterpretation of a Korean Folk Tradition for Urban and International Audiences," in *Tradition and Its Future in Music* (Tokyo: Mita, 1991), pp. 539–46. Byongwon Lee, "Contemporary Korean Musical Cultures," in Donald C. Clark, ed., *Korea Briefing, 1993: Festival of Korea* (Boulder, Colo.: Westview, 1993), pp. 12–138. Keith Howard, *Korean Musical Instruments* (Oxford: Oxford U Pr, 1995). Byongwon Lee, *Styles and Esthetics in Korean Traditional Music* (Seoul: National Center for Korean Traditional Performing Arts, 1997). Nathan Heselink, "A Tale of Two Drummers: Percussion Band Music in North Cholla Province, Korea" (Ph.D. diss., School of Oriental and African Studies, Univ. of London, 1998). Keith Howard, ed., *Korean Shamanism: Revivals, Survival, and Change* (Seoul: Royal Asiatic Society, Korean Branch, 1998). Bang-song Song, *Korean Music: Historical and Other Aspects* (Somerset, N.J.: Jomoondang International, 2000).

Mongolia. Ernst Emsheimer, *The Music of the Mongols* (Stockholm: Sino-Swedish Expedition, Publication 21, 1943). Petti Aalto, "The Music of the Mongols: An Introduction," in Denis Sinor, ed., *Aspects of Altaic Civilization* (Bloomington: Ind. Univ. Publications, Uralic and Altaic Series 23, 1962). Vargyas Lajos, "Performing Styles in Mongolian Chant," *JIFMC* 20 (1968): 7–72. A. N. Aksenov, "Tuvin Folk Music," *Asian Music* 4, no. 2 (1973): 7–18. Carole A. Pegg, "Tradition, Change, and Symbolism of Mongol Music in Ordos and Xilingol, Inner Mongolia," *Journal of the Anglo-Mongolian Society* 7, no. 1–2 (1989): 64–72. Carole A. Pegg, "The Revival of the Ethnic and Cultural Identity in West Mongolia: The Altai Uriankhai Tsuur, the Turvan Shuur, and the Kazakh Sybyzgy," *Journal of the Anglo-Mongolian Society* 8, no. 1–2 (1991): 1–84. Carole A. Pegg, "Mongolian Conceptualizations of Overtone Singing (Xöömii)," *British Journal of Ethnomusicology* 1 (1992): 31–55. Carole A. Pegg, *Mongolian Music, Dance, and Oral Narrative: Performing Diverse Identities,* with CD (Seattle: U of Wash Pr, 2001).

Tibet. Peter Crossley-Holland, "Forms and Styles in Tibetan Folksong Melody," *JbfmV* 3 (1967): 9–69, 109–26. Id., "The Religious Music of Tibet and Its Cultural Background," in *Centennial Workshop on Ethnomusicology,* ed. Peter Crossley-Holland (Vancouver: Government of Province of Brit. Columbia, 1967; R: 1975), pp. 79–91. Namkhai Norbu Dewang, "Musical Tradition of the Tibetan People: Songs in Dance Measure," *Orientalia Romania: Essays and Lectures* 2 (1967): 205–347. William P. Malm, "East Asia: Tibet," in *Music Cultures of the Pacific, the Near East and Asia* (Englewood Cliffs, N.J.: Prentice-Hall, 1967; 2nd ed., 1977), pp. 138–42. Peter Crossley-Holland, "*rGya-gling* Hymns of the Kama-Kagyu: The Rhythmitonal Architecture of Some Tibetan Instrumental Airs," *Selected Reports* [Institute of Ethnomusicology, U.C.L.A.] 3 (1970): 79–114. Terry Ellingson, "Some Techniques of Choral Chanting in the Tibetan Style," *American Anthropologist* 72 (1970): 826–31. *AsM* 8/2 (1977) [Tibet–East Asia issue], 10/2 (1979) [Tibet issue].

I.K.F.W.

Ecclesiastical mode. See Mode.

Échappée [Fr.]. See Counterpoint II, 6.

Échelette [Fr.]. Xylophone.

Échelle [Fr.]. Scale.

Ēchēma [Gr.]. *Enēchēma.* See *Ēchos.*

Échiquier [Fr.]. *Chekker.

Echo. (1) The acoustical phenomenon in which a sound is heard as having been repeated, usually from some distance, because of the reflection of the sound waves back toward the listener from some, often distant, surface. In the design of concert halls, surfaces must be arranged so as to produce appropriate amounts of sound reflection without leading to the perception of actual repetition or echo of individual sounds. See Acoustics. (2) A musical effect that imitates the acoustical phenomenon (1). Such effects have been created in numerous works since the 16th century. These include 16th-century secular vocal works such as Marenzio's "O tu che fra le selve" and Lassus's "O la, o che bon eccho"; Carissimi's oratorio *Jephthe* (ca. 1645); the last movement of Bach's Partita in B minor from the **Clavier-Übung,* vol. 2; Mozart's *Notturno* K. 286 (269a); Wagner's *Der *fliegende Holländer.* (3) An attachment to a brass instrument that permits the imitation of the acoustical phenomenon (1). On the *cornet it may take the form of a mechanically operated mute. (4) In 17th-century French organs, a division located within the main case, usually with a range from c′ upward. The Echo always contained a *Cornet. (5) In electric-action organs, a division located away from the main organ. (6) A *Swell division of early 18th-century English organs.

Ēchos [Gr.]. In Eastern chant, a system of melodic formulas that characterize the ecclesiastical modes. Hence, the *oktoēchos* is the collection of eight modes that forms the compositional framework of Byzantine, Syrian, and Latin chant. Each mode comprises a restricted set of melody types peculiar to it, and these can be employed in many different combinations and variations. Byzantine theorists refer to the eight sets as Modes I–IV Authentic and I–IV Plagal, a terminology that is borrowed for early Western treatises *(authentus protus, authentus deuteros, . . . plaga protu, plaga deuteri, . . .).*

The origins of the *oktoēchos* are obscure. It appears to have little in common, apart from nomenclature, with the ancient Greek tonal system. Some scholars have speculated that its beginnings lie in Near Eastern musical and philosophical traditions; the authenticity of an 11th-century text of John of Maiuma's *Plerophoriai* (ca. 515), which contains an allusion to "the music of the *oktoēchos,*" is questionable. Also doubtful is the allegation that an anthology of hymns by Patriarch Severus of Antioch (512–19) was an *oktoēchos.* It does seem certain, however, that by the late 7th century, the eight-mode system had become established within the Greek liturgical world; the attribution of its organization to St. John of Damascus (ca. 675–ca. 749), although not totally accurate, may contain some historical fact. In any event, he contributed significantly to the formation of a liturgical book called the *Oktoēchos* (or *Paraklētikē*), which contains the variable hymns of the Office throughout the church year, beginning with the first week after Easter. Since these proper chants recurred every eight weeks in the same order, they were allocated to the eight modes, one for each week.

From the indications in the tonary of St. Riquier, the *Musica enchiriadis,* and *De harmonica institutione* of Hucbald, it is evident that the Byzantine *oktoēchos,* with its corresponding set of intonation formulas *(enēchēmata),* reached the West shortly before the year 800. The *enēchēmata* are short musical inflections sung to meaningless syllables by the precentor *(domestikos)* to introduce the mode of the hymn. Accordingly, there are eight such phrases, one for each of the modes: *ananeanes* (Mode I), *neanes* (Mode II), *nana* (Mode III), *hagia* (Mode IV), *aneanes* (Mode I Plagal), *neeanes* (Mode II Plagal), *aanes* (Mode III Plagal), and *neagie* (Mode IV Plagal).

Bibl.: Henry J. W. Tillyard, "The Modes in Byzantine Music," *Annual of the British School at Athens* 22 (1916–18): 133–56. Id., "Signatures and Cadences of the Byzantine Modes," ibid. 26 (1923–25): 78–87. Oliver Strunk, "The Tonal System of Byzantine Music," *MQ* 28 (1942): 190–204; R: in *Essays on Music in the Byzantine World* (New York: Norton, 1977), pp. 3–18. Id., "Intonations and Signatures of the Byzantine Modes," *MQ* 31 (1945): 339–55; R: in *Essays,* pp. 19–36. Jørgen Raasted, *Intonation Formulas and Modal Signatures in Byzantine Musical Manuscripts, MMB* subsidia 7 (Copenhagen: E Munksgaard, 1966). Dimitri Conomos, "Modal Signatures in Late Byzantine Liturgical Chant," *Actes du XIVe congrès international des études byzantines* 3 (1971): 521–30.

D.E.C.

Éclatant [Fr.]. Brilliant, dazzling.

Eclogue. A poem in which shepherds converse. Such poems were written in classical antiquity by Theocritus and Virgil, and in the 16th century they were sometimes written as plays and staged. Thus, they form part of the pastoral tradition on which early opera drew. Plays of this type, including music, became well established in Spain beginning with the works of Juan del Encina (1468–1529/30). The term has been used as a title for piano pieces with a pastoral character by more recent composers such as Tomášek, Franck, Liszt, and Dvořák.

Eco(s) [Sp.]. A keyboard division of the classic Spanish organ whose pipes are enclosed in a box with a hinged top operated by a pedal.

École d'Arcueil, L'. A group of French musicians (Henri Sauguet, Roger Desormière, Maxime Jacob, Henri Cliquet-Pleyel) formed in 1923 around Erik Satie and taking their name from Arcueil, the working-class suburb of Paris that, after 1898, was Satie's home. See also *Les *six.*

Écossaise [Fr., Scottish]. A type of *contredanse that was very popular in France in the late 18th century. It was related to the *country dance of the British Isles, though its specific origin remains in dispute. The form that was cultivated elsewhere as well in the early 19th century, especially in Vienna, was in a lively 2/4. Examples were composed by Schubert (sets for piano D. 299, 421, 529, 697, etc.), Beethoven (WoO 83, 86), and Weber, among others.

Ecphonetic notation. Notation intended to guide the recitation or *cantillation of liturgical texts, especially those from the Bible; also lectionary notation. Such notation, of which there are various systems, occurs in Latin, Greek, Hebrew, Syriac, Armenian, and Coptic manuscripts, among others. Examples survive from as early as the 5th century and as late as the 15th. Symbols occur most often at the beginnings and endings of phrases, thus reflecting the syntax of the text in the manner of punctuation. Some symbols represent accents or a rising and falling of the voice, and some may be chironomic [see Chironomy]. Their precise musical significance is in every case unknown. In some cases they may simply lack musical significance. The system of *ta'amim* still in use in *Jewish music derives from such notation, however. See also Byzantine chant I, Neume.

Bibl.: Carsten Høeg, *La notation ekphonétique, MMB* subsidia 1/2 (Copenhagen: Levin & Munksgaard, 1935). Gudrun Engberg, "Greek Ekphonetic Notation: The Classical and the Pre-Classical Systems," *Palaeo-Byzantine Notations: A Reconsideration of the Source Material,* ed. J. Raasted and C. Troelsgård (Hernen, 1995): 33–55.

Editio Medicea; Ratisbonensis; Vaticana [Lat.]. See Gregorian Chant VI.

Editions, historical. Works of the past presented in publications carefully prepared from studies of the sources. These publications, usually issued in series, are of three types: (1) the complete works of a composer (Collected works; Fr. *Oeuvres complètes;* Ger. *Gesamtausgabe, Sämtliche Werke, Werke;* It. *Opere complete, Tutte le opere;* Lat. *Opera omnia;* Sp. *Obras completas*); (2) Denkmäler (Eng. and Fr. *Monuments;* Lat. *Monumenta*); and (3) series of performing editions. The German term *Denkmäler,* designating historical collections, has been generally adopted by English-speaking musicians. Historical editions aim to preserve a musical heritage, disseminate a repertory, and make authentic editions available for study and performance. All three types of historical editions are indexed in Anna H. Heyer, *Historical Sets, Collected Editions, and Monuments of Music,* 3rd ed. (1980). This is being superseded by George R. Hill and Norris L. Stephens, *Collected Editions, Historical Series and Sets and Monuments of Music: A Bibliography* (Berkeley: Fallen Leaf, 1997).

I. *History.* Retrospective publications of selected works of individual composers were compiled as early as the 16th century, usually by former pupils or children of the composer. *Choralis constantinus* (Nuremberg, 1550–55) is a collection of Isaac's music compiled by his pupil Senfl. A son of Cabezón issued *Obras de música* (Madrid, 1578) 12 years after the composer's death, and the sons of Lassus collected their father's motets in the publication *Magnum opus musicum* (Munich, 1604). In the 18th century, the music historians Charles Burney and Giovanni Battista Martini issued anthologies as historical musical examples. By this time a curiosity about music of the past was in the air, especially in England, where the Academy of Vocal Music and the Academy of Ancient Music had been active since the 1720s. There was a special interest in resurrecting church music. William Boyce published his *Cathedral Music* (London, 1760–73), a "Collection . . . By the Several English Masters of the Last Two Hundred Years," and in Germany in the first half of the 19th century the Catholic Church's interest in reviving its musical heritage led to multiple-volume collections of vocal music compiled by Franz Commer, Carl Proske, and Friedrich Rochlitz. England was also a leader in collecting the works of individual composers, as Samuel Arnold brought out *The Works of Handel* in 1787–97 in 46 volumes. The rise of public concerts during the 18th century and the increase of music making in the home, spurred on by the development of the piano, led to international fame for some composers and a profitable market for the publication of their music. Breitkopf & Härtel in Leipzig issued 17 volumes of the *Oeuvres complettes de Wolfgang Amadeus Mozart* in 1798–1804 and 12 volumes of the *Oeuvres complettes* of Haydn in 1800–1806. In both cases the volumes consist largely of piano music. Breitkopf & Härtel also issued editions of the "complete" piano music of Muzio Clementi, Jan Ladislav Dussek, Daniel Steibelt, Johann Baptist Cramer, Johann Nepomuk Hummel, and Friedrich Wilhelm Michael Kalkbrenner.

The above examples from the many collections

published before 1850 are not critical editions. They were normally prepared from a single source and without a method for identifying editorial additions. The earliest Denkmäler prepared with a scientific method are Friedrich Chrysander's *Denkmäler der Tonkunst* (Bergedorf, 1869–71) and Robert Eitner's *Publikationen älterer praktischer und theoretischer Musikwerke* (Berlin, 1873–1905), issued in 29 volumes by the Gesellschaft für Musikforschung, a musicological society founded by Eitner. The earliest critical edition of a composer's complete works is Bach's *Werke* (Leipzig, 1851–1926), issued by the Bach Gesellschaft in 46 volumes. This Bach society was formed in 1850 with the main intention of publishing the complete works. The completeness and general accuracy of the edition became a model for subsequent publications, though today it is seen as but a step along the way to more highly developed methods of preparing historical editions.

Breitkopf & Härtel, the publisher of the Bach edition, achieved an astounding production between 1851 and World War I by also undertaking the complete works of Beethoven, Berlioz, Cornelius, Gluck, Grétry, Handel, Haydn, Lassus, Liszt, Loewe, Mendelssohn, Mozart, Obrecht, Palestrina, Schein, Schubert, Schütz, Schumann, Johann Strauss (father), Sweelinck, and Victoria. (Many of these were not completed.) After World War I, musicology spread to countries other than Germany, and works were issued by publishers other than Breitkopf & Härtel, though the market was smaller because of the poor economy. The complete works of Brahms, Buxtehude, Byrd, Josquin, Lully, Monteverdi, Palestrina, Pergolesi, Praetorius, and Scheidt were published between the wars. Since World War II, the publication of collected works has been largely sponsored by composers' societies with the financial assistance of foundations and governments. Advanced editorial methods have led to the re-editing of 19th-century editions, and new editions of the complete works of Bach, Beethoven, Berlioz, Byrd, Gluck, Handel, Haydn, Josquin, Lassus, Liszt, Mendelssohn, Mozart, Schein, Schubert, Schütz, Sweelinck, and Wagner are being published. Bärenreiter has taken over from Breitkopf & Härtel as the chief publisher. The works of many other composers are being collected for the first time. Nevertheless, a list of well-known composers whose works are not available in a collected edition would show that much editing and publishing remain to be done. A remarkable contribution is being made by the American Institute of Musicology, which in its series *Corpus mensurabilis musicae* is publishing the collected works of over 90 medieval and Renaissance composers. This large postwar output reflects the explosion of musicology and also the effects of the invention of photocopying, which has made possible the collection of musical sources at remote locations and consequently the comparison of multiple sources.

Denkmäler soon took on national emphases because they are supported by government funds. Prominent early national Denkmäler and their starting dates are *Denkmäler deutscher Tonkunst* (1892), *Denkmäler der Tonkunst in Österreich* (1894), *L'arte musicale in Italia* (1897), *Denkmäler der Tonkunst in Bayern* (1900), *Tudor Church Music* (1922), *Publications de la Société française de musicologie* (1925), and *Monumentos de la música española* (1941). The U.S. national Denkmäler series, *Music in the United States of America,* began in 1993 and complements a series of facsimiles, *Earlier American Music,* which was begun in 1972.

Scientific methods of editing were not generally adopted in the 19th century for series of performing editions. Editors continued to adapt early music to contemporary styles (e.g., Riemann's *Kantaten-Frühling,* Leipzig: C F W Siegel, 1912) until performers became more concerned with authenticity. Today's minimum standard requires the identification of the editor's source or sources and clear designations of editorial additions. Early widely used series of performing editions and their starting dates are *Collegium musicum* (1903), *The English Madrigal School* (1913), *Organum* (1924), *Nagels Musik-Archiv* (1927), and *Hortus musicus* (1936). Some recent series, e.g., *Le pupitre: Collection de musique ancienne* (1967) and the various *Recent Researches* series published by A-R Editions, can be used equally well by both the scholar and the performer, in keeping with the policy of many of today's publishers.

II. *Editing.* While a general method for editing is widely accepted today, the many speculative aspects of editing can never be resolved to everyone's satisfaction. The editor today collects all of the sources for the work to be edited; collates the sources; in a critical apparatus describes and evaluates the sources and lists their variants; transcribes the sources into modern notation; makes whatever corrections and additions to the sources are necessary to realize the composer's intentions; and carefully designates as editorial whatever is added to the sources. The extent of the critical apparatus and the amount of editorial additions will vary according to whether the edition is intended primarily for scholars or for performers.

The goal of the editor is to present in modern notation a score that will enable the scholar and performer to create the sounds intended by the composer. This poses many problems. The transcription itself distorts the image of the original source, which can provide clues to the composer's intention. The earlier the music, the more changes have to be made in the process of transcription. The original notations vary from the inexplicit indication of melodies and rhythms of the earliest plainchant sources to the detailed instructions of 19th-century composers. The general practice today is to make the modern edition conform to modern notation. Until the 17th century, the sources are in the form of parts, which must be brought together in a score [see Choirbook, Partbook, Score]. *Bar lines are not found in sources until the 17th century, and editors have experimented with various methods of allowing a free flow of the polyphonic voices of the Renaissance, for example, by placing the bar lines between the staves or by using wedges above the staff to indicate the metrical pulse. The variety of *clefs found in sources before 1800 is today reduced to the F- and G-clefs (including the G-clef with subscript 8). The modern practice of key signatures was not solidified until the 18th century; the sharp sign was not adopted in key signatures until the 17th century. The mensuration [see Mensural notation] in music from the 13th to the 17th centuries must be adapted to modern time signatures. Until around 1600, the note-values in use were generally larger than those to which musicians are now accustomed. This poses the special problem of their reduction. Note-values of 13th-century sources are most often reduced in the ratio 8:1 (the longa, the normal pulse, becoming a half note) or even 16:1, while 14th-century sources are reduced 4:1, as the breve became the norm; 15th- and 16th-century sources, in which the semibreve becomes the norm, are reduced usually 2:1, though 4:1 is not uncommon. The editor must also underlay the text, which in sources before 1600 is often not complete and often not precisely placed. While notation may be vague for some aspects of music, it may be of no help at all for others, such as accidentals [see *Musica ficta*], ornamentation, improvisation, and tempo. Until the 17th century, there is often even the question of whether a work should be performed by voices or instruments or some combination of them. Special problems for the editor of 15th- and 16th-century music are *proportions and *ligatures. The editor of Baroque music must deal with the number and type of ornaments to include, the amount of improvisation to suggest, and especially the realization of the basso continuo [see Thoroughbass]. If only a figured-bass line without realization is given, the editor will please the experienced continuo player, but render the edition useless for the performer not capable of original realizations. The normal practice today is to give a simple chordal realization, often in small notes, allowing the experienced player room for improvisation while not neglecting other performers. In music after 1750, the editor has fewer musical judgments to make, for the composers gave instructions in greater detail. Recent advances in the study of *performance practice, however, have made it clear that the notation of works from the late 18th and 19th centuries is also incomplete as a guide to the way in which those works were realized in their own time. Thus, the editor of this music too must wrestle with the problems of ornamentation, articulation, and tempo as well as such matters as realizing cadenzas, the order in which the instruments will appear in the *score, and whether to notate transposing instruments at concert pitch.

To assist the editor in making musical judgments, it is important that the provenance and date of each source and the relationship of sources to one another be determined to the extent possible [see Textual criticism]. Sources may include *autograph scores and parts, editions published during the composer's lifetime (among which one must attempt to identify those authorized by the composer), copies of editions with the composer's manuscript emendations, tablatures, scores and parts made by copyists both during and after the composer's lifetime, and posthumous editions. The most authentic source [see Authenticity] must be identified, for normally the editor bases the edition on that rather than offering a composite of a variety of sources. Variants in the sources, especially variations in pitch and rhythm, should be given in a critical apparatus. Some critical apparatuses today are published as separate volumes and in such detail that they discourage consultation by anyone but the specialist. Since the performer does not require as much detail as the scholar, the critical remarks of the performing edition are usually limited to brief identifications of the sources, their chief variants, and the means of identifying editorial additions. This helps to make possible a lower price for a performing edition (also called a practical or commercial edition) than is normally possible for a scholarly edition.

After an authentic text has been compiled from the sources, including the correction of obvious errors, a major problem for the editor is what, if anything, should be added to assist in the interpretation of the composer's intentions. This is largely determined by the nature of the audience for the edition. The needs of the scholar are normally met with the bare, authentic text presented in score and supplied, as appropriate, with modern note-values, clefs, key signatures, and bar lines, a realized basso continuo, and editorial accidentals. A prefatory staff or page of facsimile is added to give the user a sample of the original notation. The needs of the performer, on the other hand, especially one lacking training in performance practice, might be met by editorial suggestions for tempo, dynamics, phrasing, articulation, ornamentation, and organ registration. In all cases, editorial suggestions must be clearly distinguishable from source material.

The terms scholarly and performing are losing their usefulness in describing editions, for today's demand for accuracy is being met by the editors and publishers of most editions. This has not always been the case, for many abuses have occurred in performing editions over the years. The market for them is considerably larger than that for scholarly editions, and this attracts a greater number of editors and publishers. The market is chiefly for music after 1600, which has fewer notational problems and can thus be edited in some fashion without special training; the publication is often only a few pages, requiring a relatively small outlay of time and money. Thus, performing editions, in series and in single volumes, vary greatly in quality. An edition might be prepared from a secondary source, to which the editor, often a well-known teacher or performer, adds performance marks not distinguishable from those of the source. In reaction to this, some publishers use the term *Urtext,* meaning "original source," to designate critical editions. This term, too, has been abused and is itself misleading, for there is seldom a single source, and when there is, it probably needs correcting by an editor. A true "Urtext" edition would have to be a facsimile of a unique source. Many of the critical performing editions today are edited by performers, which is a tribute to musicological teaching in recent decades. There will nevertheless always be a market for an edition prepared by a well-known performer, giving his or her interpretation in great detail and in notation indistinguishable from that of the composer.

Bibl.: *Editing Early Music: Notes on the Preparation of Printer's Copy* (London: Novello, 1963). Georg von Dadelsen, *Editionsrichtlinien musikalischer Denkmäler und Gesamtausgaben* (Kassel: Bärenreiter, 1967). James Coover, *Gesamtausgaben* (n.p.: Distant Pr, 1970). Alberto Basso, "Repertorio generale dei 'Monumenti musicae,' delle antologie, raccolte e pubblicazioni di musica antica sino a tutto il 1970," *Rivista italiana di musicologia* 6 (1971): 3–135. Thrasybulos G. Georgiades, ed., *Musikalische Edition im Wandel des historischen Bewusstseins* (Kassel: Bärenreiter, 1971). Sydney R. Charles, *A Handbook of Music and Music Literature in Sets and Series* (New York: Free Press, 1972). Robert Donington, *A Performer's Guide to Baroque Music* (London: Faber, 1973). Anna H. Heyer, *Historical Sets, Collected Editions, and Monuments of Music: A Guide to Their Contents,* 3rd ed. (Chicago: Am Lib Assoc, 1980). Howard Mayer Brown, "Editing," *NG* 5 (1980): 839–48. John Caldwell, *Editing Early Music* (Oxford: Clarendon Pr, 1985). James Grier, *The Critical Editing of Music: History, Method, and Practice* (Cambridge: Cambridge U Pr, 1996). George R. Hill and Norris L. Stephens, *Collected Editions, Historical Series and Sets and Monuments of Music: A Bibliography* (Berkeley: Fallen Leaf, 1997). H.E.S., rev. L.C.

Education in the United States. I. *Definition and historical status.* The teaching of music, to individuals or to groups, has been a characteristic of education throughout most of history in both the Western and Eastern worlds. Civic and religious leaders have almost always been trained in musical skills. Public school music, however, is a term that was used at the end of the 19th century in the U.S. in the promotion of a genre of published song books, and it remained in the lexicon for about fifty years. For the past half century the definition of *music education* included the teaching and learning of music, in preschool through adulthood.

The first New England colonists were Protestants whose worship service valued congregational singing. Martin Luther himself composed many of the earliest hymns used in the service of the church. The **Bay Psalm Book* was the first book printed in the English colonies (1639); the earliest editions contained only words, with music notation added in the ninth edition (1698). Incompetent hymn singing in church was an early factor in a continuing call for improved music education. Singing schools flourished in the 18th century and existed for well over 100 years. Instrumental music was important to the Moravians; their brass choirs were well established by the early 1700s, and music was a required subject in Moravian schools. Instrumental music instruction was common in the schools of 18th-century America. It was offered after regular school hours, usually for a fee.

The Massachusetts School Law of 1647 placed the responsibility for education of the young on the community (this education system merged religion and academics); common schools under state supervision were not established until about 1837 in Massachusetts, under the leadership of Horace Mann. By 1850 a similar pattern could be found in most states. Music in grammar schools (grades 4–6) was adopted in the Boston schools in 1848 and quickly spread to schools in most major U.S. cities.

Military, town, and fire department bands flourished in the mid-19th century, and by the end of the century there were more town bands than towns. Playing an instrument in one of these ensembles was seen as a positive experience for boys, and bands were used in boys' reform schools for discipline and morale in the latter part of the 19th century. Many public schools experimented from 1870 on with offering instrumental music as an after-school activity; a fee was usually required.

The large peace festivals arranged by the entrepreneur and band director Patrick Gilmore (1869 and 1872) brought European bands to the U.S. Their tours, the creation of the Sousa band (1892), and the beginning of symphony orchestras in New York (1878) and Boston (1881) each contributed to a strong interest in quality instrumental music by the end of the century. As social and cultural factors (the automobile, radio, and phonograph) brought the demise of professional bands, the music industry switched its support to instrumental music in the public schools, often paying the first year's salary of a school band teacher. Shortly after the beginning of the 20th century, the present schooling configuration was in place, in which public schools assume responsibility for much of the education that had been supported privately by the community and by churches, including music. Normal schools for educating teachers were common.

By 1920, the music contest was established; a system of local, district, state, and national contests for bands, orchestras, and choruses brought wide participation, peaking by 1937, during the Great Depression. Other established characteristics of music education included: academic credit for music classes taught within the school day; music teacher certification requiring a four-year program (programs of six weeks to three years had existed for at least a half century); professional organizations for music education, some serving as accrediting bodies.

At the beginning of the 21st century, most American students can expect, until at least the sixth grade, some regular contact with a music teacher teaching "general" music. (In many schools, students can substitute instrumental music instruction for general music, usually beginning in the fourth or fifth grade.) Instructional time varies from 20–30 minutes every two weeks to daily 30- to 45-minute classes. The regular classroom teacher, who in the first half of the 20th century often followed up on the instruction of the specialist, is today seldom involved.

The content of general music is varied: teachers have the flexibility to use song books published by three or four publishers, to follow methods based on the ideas of Carl Orff or Zoltán Kodály, both introduced to the U.S. in the late 1960s, or to offer an instrument-focused program based on class piano, recorder, or dulcimer. Middle school, which has varying configurations of fifth- through ninth-grade students, offers elective music; where music is required, it is an "exploratory" course of no more than 9 weeks at any one grade level. When there is a middle school requirement for *arts education,* students can substitute another performing art for music instruction.

Widespread criticism of American education, beginning in the 1980s, brought about the adoption of national subject-matter standards for all areas, including music. Forty-nine states have established state standards based on these national standards, moving the U.S. to a more centralized system of education. An active arts advocacy movement in the U.S. has altered some music curricula by bringing professional musicians into the schools and encouraging music teachers to use instructional strategies that might improve test scores in more academic subjects or in general academic ability. Arts advocates also provide financial support for the music curriculum. Innovations in arts education and music education have, during the past half century or so, almost universally been initiated by philanthropic foundations or government agencies, e.g., Ford, Rockefeller, Getty, Annenberg, and the National Endowment for the Arts. Support from the music industry and music publishers continues to be influential. Commercial interests are powerful and growing as evidence accumulates on the economics of the arts. More than 50 percent (a 2002 survey reports 67%) of the financial support for high school bands comes from external sources; interested parents raise funds, or schools turn to corporations to supply instruments to impoverished schools.

Although testing is now nationally mandated in mathematics and language arts, it is unlikely that competence in the arts will be tested as a result of the 1994 arts standards. A few states have developed tests aligned with their state arts curriculum, but these tests are voluntary or there is shared accountability between the state and the local school district.

A majority of the states and many school districts have adopted an arts requirement for high school graduation. To meet this requirement a student may select from visual arts, dance, theater, or music, or other alternatives including foreign language or American literature. This situation makes it impossible to estimate the number of students required to enroll in a music offering at the secondary level. Secondary school offerings in music are usually band, orchestra, and chorus, although the state of New York does require general music for students not enrolled in an ensemble and has developed an elective music competency examination. Solo and small ensemble experiences, including jazz band, continue to be noncredit, meeting before or after the school day. The inclusion of music theory and guitar in the school curriculum is becoming more widespread, and Advanced Placement examinations for college credit are offered in music theory.

Despite the marginalization of music instructional time in grades K–8, participation in instrumental music continues to grow, and bands, string orchestras, and full orchestras are prospering; choral music has suffered a decline in male participants, but female choral organizations have risen accordingly. Ninety percent of all high schools offer band and chorus. These programs have not been affected by the reform movement except through scheduling. Youth orchestras flourish and are excellent, whether due to the influence of the Suzuki string program (introduced into the U.S. in the mid-1960s) or to parents' support of private instruction. The need for public school string teachers is widely recognized; currently they are available in only about 20 percent of the schools. There continues to be interest in drum and bugle corps, which are competitive both in performance and membership and operate primarily in the summer months, attracting hundreds of students. Community (or guild) schools offer music instruction to millions of students of all ages, including ensembles and music for the handicapped. Garage bands, formal and informal instruction on guitar, and the popularity of CDs all contribute to rich experiences and interest in music by American youth.

Music education in the U.S. is more extensive than that found in most countries. For example, British schools require music in grades K–8 taught by the classroom teacher and have an arts requirement in secondary schools, where music is taught by a specialist and focuses on composition; instrumental music and ensembles are after-school activities. Standards in the arts have been accepted in Britain but, on the issue of testing to the standards, little support is evidenced for accountability, as high school music is not a popular subject.

The primary effect of the arts standards and the educational reform movement for music in the U.S. has been to encourage a broadening of the general music curriculum, composition in elementary school being the primary addition, greatly facilitated by the availability of computers.

II. *Higher education.* Music clubs and organizations were present in U.S. colleges almost from the outset, although a full-time faculty appointment in music was not made until Harvard University appointed John

Knowles Paine in 1875. Music is not mandatory in college except through an arts and humanities requirement as part of a liberal arts education. There is, however, a relationship between secondary school music and the music performance curriculum in universities in the U.S. The performing excellence of high school graduates has spurred a recent increase in the applied music enrollment in most colleges, with less growth seen in musicology, music theory (composition), and teacher certification. Musicology and music theory and composition in the U.S. are marked by their excellent graduate programs (the first doctorate in musicology was given shortly after the beginning of the 20th century). The master's degree for teachers has become essential for most continuing teachers and is the primary path for alternative teacher certification. Ethnomusicology is at present a growth industry, one well supported by research funds; beginning with the interest in American folk music stimulated by Charles Seeger, the field has broadened to encompass music of many cultures. Degrees in music therapy and music business appear to be the most specialized recent curricular additions.

Performance on one's major instrument remains the primary basis for admission to tertiary music study, and the quality of the instruction and of the entering students' performance have resulted in many universities having near-professional-quality ensembles. These organizations and student recitals provide, usually at no cost, frequent concerts for the student body and the university and local community.

The teacher education program attracts the largest population of college music majors, although the larger institutions have followed the priorities of the music conservatory and rarely promote music teacher education. The teacher education curriculum is influenced by state teacher certification requirements, and, increasingly, certification examinations are administered by the state. To facilitate transfer of certified teachers among states, a consortium of states has drafted a list of requirements coordinated with those on the National Board of Professional Teaching Standards (Interstate New Teacher Assessment and Support Consortium). Individual states accredit their public schools, but no state has ever found a school system in default because of an inadequate music program. The state, along with professional organizations (primarily the National Council for the Accreditation of Teacher Education and National Association of Schools of Music), accredits college teacher education programs but, again, would not find a university or a school of music in default based on deficiencies in the music teacher program.

Changing priorities in the public schools always affect American music education. In the mid-20th century U.S. rivalry with the Soviet Union placed primary importance on science and mathematics. Later in the century, with the disintegration of the Soviet Union, globalization and the marketplace established the priorities in education (through standards and testing): mathematics and language arts became primary, with science and social studies rounding out the "basic" subjects. Early childhood education is a major current concern and here music is seen as important. Even more recently, the magnet arts school, often established to meet desegregation guidelines, has moved the arts into the center of the curriculum. "National" magnet schools, such as Interlochen, North Carolina School for the Arts, and Walnut Hill are experiencing rapid growth, and local magnet schools are multiplying rapidly when offered as a choice for students and parents. The million or more home-schooled students in the U.S. often attend the local public school to participate in group music experiences and perhaps athletics. In required general music, class singing, originally the staple of the course because of its value to the community, has lost much of its cachet. Students today may graduate from general music programs that have labeled themselves "nonperformance," opening the floodgate to a variety of topics. The definition of music education and now arts education in America is broad indeed.

Bibl.: M. L. Mark and C. L. Gary, *A History of American Music Education* (New York: Schirmer Books, 1992). Consortium of National Arts Associations, *Dance, Music, Theater, Visual Arts: What Every Young American Should Know and Be Able to Do in the Arts* (Reston, Va.: Music Educators National Conference, 1994). John Harland, Kay Kindler, Pippa Lord, *Arts Education in Secondary Schools: Effects and Effectiveness* (National Foundation for Educational Research, 2000). Bennett Reimer, *A Philosophy of Music Education,* 3rd ed. (Upper Saddle River, N.J.: Prentice Hall, 2003). R.J.C.

Egmont. Incidental music by Beethoven, op. 84 (1809–10), composed for Goethe's play. The overture is frequently performed separately.

Eguale [It.]. See *Equale.*

Egypt. The history of Egyptian music stretches from before 3000 B.C.E. to the present. Ancient Egyptian music constituted a continuous tradition from the Old Kingdom (2700–2100 B.C.E.) through the Middle Kingdom (2100–1680 B.C.E.) and the New Kingdom (1580–712 B.C.E.) down to Greek and Roman times. A rich body of documentation about ancient Egyptian musicians, instruments, and musical life has been preserved in pictures, bas-reliefs, statuary, hieroglyphic inscriptions, song texts, musical artifacts, and reports by foreign visitors. Mostly it concerns music in religious contexts: texts of hymns and psalms, statues of music-making gods, and pictures of temple musicians, sacred dancers, and sacred meals to the accompaniment of music. There are also representations of what seems to be secular music making, by professionals and amateurs, men and women. Much of the preserved evidence comes from tombs, where music making, or at least its representation, accompanied important persons to the afterlife.

No ancient Egyptian musical notation has been discovered. From the 3rd millennium B.C.E. on, however, there are many depictions of *chironomy, that is, people giving hand signs to singers and instrumentalists. These signs have been interpreted as representations of pitches and perhaps of rhythms as well. It may even be possible to match the hand signs with depicted fingerings on instruments and thus with pitches or scale degrees. Pictures showing two signs being given simultaneously have been said to indicate the existence of polyphony in ancient Egypt.

Musical instruments typical of the Old and Middle Kingdoms were arched *harps, end-blown *flutes, and *double clarinets. In the New Kingdom, several new instruments were introduced, including the *long-necked lute, the *angle harp, the *lyre, and the *aulos. Other instruments common in ancient Egypt were *clappers, *frame drums, cylindrical drums, the straight trumpet (a soldier's instrument), and the *sistrum (a cult instrument). Specimens of flutes, auloi, trumpets, harps, clarinets, and sistra have all been preserved in tombs. Depictions of ancient Egyptian music making usually show ensembles of musicians playing several types of instruments, along with singers, chironomists, and, often, dancers.

After the conquest of Egypt by Alexander the Great in 332 B.C.E., Egyptian music was exposed to strong influences from Greece and later from Rome. Greek musicians lived and worked in Egypt. Egyptian music had an impact in turn on Greece and Rome, particularly in connection with the cult of Isis. In later Roman times, Egypt was a center of Christian hymnody. After the Arab conquest (640 C.E.), Egyptian music fell into the Islamic sphere of influence.

Modern Egyptian music forms part of international Arabic musical culture [see Near and Middle East]. Cairo is a center for musicians and the music industry. Egyptian singers and composers of the first half of the 20th century—especially Um Kalthum and Muhammad ʿAbd al-Wahhāb—broadened the appeal of classical Arabic music by means of stylistic innovations and through recording and film, and they achieved great popularity throughout the Arab world. The Arabic Music Ensemble, sponsored by the government Ministry of Culture, has successfully revived classical Arabic music from the 19th century and earlier. The Conservatory of Arabic Music in Cairo offers instruction in Arabic music, while the Conservatoire de musique arabe teaches primarily Western music.

The Egyptian government sponsors the Cairo Symphony Orchestra, which from 1990 has been housed in the new Cairo Opera House and Cultural and Educational Center. This facility, inaugurated in 1988, replaced the old Opera House, destroyed in 1971. Many 20th-century Egyptian composers cultivated Western-inspired musical styles, and most received training both in Egypt and Europe. Composers from the older generations include Hasan Rashid (1896–1969), Yusuf Greiss (1899–1961), Abu-bakr Khayrat (1910–63), ʿAziz Al-shawan (1916–93), Gamal ʿAbdal-rahim (1924–88), and Rifʿat Garrana (b. 1924). Composers such as Gamal Salama (b. 1945), Rageh Daoud (b. 1954), and Mauna Ghoneim (b. 1955) combine indigenous *maqāmāt* with Western-derived contrapuntal textures. Several rural musical traditions remain strong in modern Egypt, as does the music of the *Coptic rite. In these, some scholars claim to find surviving remnants of the music of the ancient Egyptians.

Bibl.: Hans Hickmann, *Ägypten,* Musikgeschichte in Bildern, 2/1 (Leipzig: Deutscher Verlag für Musik, 1961). Lise Manniche, *Ancient Egyptian Musical Instruments* (Munich: Deutscher Kunstverlag, 1975). Salwa El-Shawan, "The Socio-Political Context of al-Mūsika al-ʿArabiyyah in Cairo, Egypt: Policies, Patronage, Institutions, and Musical Change (1927–77)," *AsM* 12 (1980): 86–128. Salwa El-Shawan, "Traditional Arab Music Ensembles in Egypt since 1967: 'The Continuity of Tradition within a Contemporary Framework'?" *Ethno* 28 (1984): 271–88. William Stevenson Smith and William Kelly Simpson, *The Art and Architecture of Ancient Egypt* (New York: Penguin, 1981). Salwa El-Shawan (Castelo-Branco), "Western Music and Its Practitioners in Egypt (ca. 1825–1985): The Integration of a New Musical Tradition in a Changing Environment," *AsM* 17, no. 1 (1985): 143–53. Lise Manniche, *Music and Musicians in Ancient Egypt* (London: British Museum, 1991). Samhah Amin Khuli and John Robinson, *Festschrift for Gamal Abdel Rahim* (Cairo: Binational Fulbright Commission in Egypt, 1993). Salwa El-Shawan Castelo-Branco, "Radio and Musical Life in Egypt," *Revista de musicologia* 16, no. 3 (1993): 1229–39. Frédéric Lagrange, *Musiques d'Egypte* (Arles: Cité de la musique: Actes sud, 1996). Virginia Danielson, *"The Voice of Egypt": Umm Kulthum, Arabic Song, and Egyptian Society in the Twentieth Century* (Chicago: U of Chicago Pr, 1997). Sherifa Zuhur, ed., *Images of Enchantment: Visual and Performing Arts in the Middle East* (Cairo: American U in Cairo Pr, 1998). See also Near and Middle East.

Eighteen-Twelve Overture. A festival overture by Tchaikovsky, op. 49 (1880), for orchestra, carillon, and artillery, composed for the commemoration in 1882 of Napoleon's retreat from Moscow in 1812.

Eight-foot. See Foot.

Eights, trade eights. See Trading.

Eilend, mit Eile, eilig [Ger.]. Hurrying.

Einfach [Ger.]. Simple.

Eingang [Ger., entrance]. In a Classical concerto, a short cadenzalike passage for the soloist that precedes and leads into a solo section [see Concerto (2) II].

Eingestrichen [Ger.]. One-line, e.g., c′ [see Pitch].

Einigkeit und Recht und Freiheit. The national anthem of the Federal Republic of Germany, sung to the "Emperor's Hymn" by Haydn [see *Emperor* Quartet]. The text is the third verse of a poem written in 1848 by August Heinrich Hoffmann von Fallersleben, the first line of which is "Deutschland, Deutschland über alles." The poem was adopted in 1922, but because the first line came to be associated with the Nazi party, the third verse was substituted for the first after World War II.

Einklang [Ger.]. *Unison.

Einleitung [Ger.]. Introduction.

Einsatz [Ger.]. (1) Entrance. (2) Attack.

Einstimmig [Ger.]. *Monophonic.

Eintritt [Ger.]. Entrance, as of a fugue subject or the soloist in a concerto.

Eis, eisis [Ger.]. E-sharp, E-double-sharp. See Pitch names.

Eisteddfod [Welsh, session]. A gathering, originally of Welsh *bards, featuring competitions in music and poetry. Although the term was not established until the 18th century, such events are known to have taken place at least as early as the 12th century, and probably before. Through the 16th century, they were occasions for competition as well as for regulating the bards' complicated organization and procedures. They seem not to have been held during the 17th century, but local events were again held in the 18th century, and a movement to revive the ancient traditions began in earnest in the 19th, leading to the establishment of a National Eisteddfod in 1880. These events now feature both solo and choral singing as well as *penillion, instrumental music, and dancing.

Ekphonetic. See Ecphonetic notation.

E la (mi), Elami. See Hexachord.

Élargissant [Fr.]. **Allargando.*

Electric bass. A type of *electric guitar invented by Leo Fender to replace the *double bass. A standard electric bass has a solid body and four strings tuned like those of the double bass and thus an octave below the four lowest strings of the guitar (E A d g). Fretted and fretless models are both popular. It has been widely used in rock since the 1950s and is now used by some jazz players as well. See ill. under Guitar.

Electric guitar. A guitar or guitarlike instrument designed for electronic amplification. It is one component of a system that includes *pickups to translate string vibrations into electrical impulses, an amplifier to modify these impulses, and loudspeakers that turn the electrical impulses back into sound. Most electric guitars have six strings, a fretted neck, two or three pickups mounted under the strings, and knobs on the body for tone and volume control. Additional circuits and controls are often added to the system for special effects.

There are two types of electric guitar: electro-acoustic and solid-body. The electro-acoustic has a sound box like the conventional guitar, and the pickup is driven by both the strings and the sound box. A solid-body guitar has no sound box, only a guitar-shaped slab of wood or fiber glass. The pickup is driven by the vibration of the strings only. Because there is no sound box to disperse the vibrational energy of the strings, the solid-body guitar can sustain a tone much longer than other kinds of guitar. Because there is no feedback from the loudspeakers to the pickup (through a sound box), the solid-body guitar admits of much greater amplification than acoustic or electro-acoustic guitars. These two factors have contributed to the extraordinary success of the solid-body guitar in popular music. See ill. under Guitar.

Pickups were first applied to the guitar in the 1920s, and commercial production of electro-acoustic models began in the 1930s. They were soon widely used in jazz and country music. The solid-body guitar was commercialized in the late 1940s and quickly adopted by black urban blues musicians, who capitalized on its sustaining power to create a style in which the sound of the guitar assumed a quasi-vocal character. This style was adopted in the 1960s by white rock musicians, who formed ensembles consisting principally or even exclusively of electric guitars. Rock guitarists raised amplification to previously undreamed-of levels and exploited sophisticated circuitry to achieve extensive manipulation of the guitar sound. Today the electric guitar is the dominant instrument of popular music in the U.S. and much of Western Europe. It also figures prominently in the urban music of Africa, the Caribbean, and Southeast Asia. See also Electric bass, Electronic instrument, Guitar, Country, Rock.

Bibl.: Tom and Mary Anne Evans, *Guitars: Music, History, Construction and Players from the Renaissance to Rock* (New York: Paddington Pr, 1977). Steve Waksman, *Instruments of Desire: The Electric Guitar and the Shaping of Musical Experience* (Cambridge, Mass.: Harvard U Pr, 1999). Tony Bacon, *Electric Guitars: The Illustrated Encyclopedia* (San Diego: Thunder Bay, 2000).

Electric (electronic) piano. An electronic keyboard instrument designed to emulate to a greater or lesser extent the tone and playing characteristics of the piano. One type, developed in the 1920s, used piano strings and hammers plus *pickups activated by the motion of the strings. More successful designs generate the initial vibrations by other means, usually metal rods or reeds that are struck or plucked. In either case, the electrical impulses generated by the acoustical vibrations are modified by an amplifier and converted back into sound by loudspeakers. The term electronic (as distinct from electric) piano is sometimes reserved for an instrument in which the sounds are generated by wholly electronic means.

Electro-acoustic music. Music that is produced, modified or reproduced by electronic means, including computer hardware and software, and that makes creative use of those technologies. The character of electro-acoustic music depends to some degree on the technology employed, but the term refers to the medium and not a specific style of music. The phonograph has been used since 1948 for the creation of original musical styles ranging from *musique concrète* to *spinning* (live mixing of recorded sound).

I. *Musique concrète.* In the 1950s and 1960s tape recordings of electronically produced and recorded sound were spliced and mixed to produce both *musique concrète* (in France) and tape music (in the United States). Pierre Schaeffer at the Radiodiffusion Française in Paris first described a new way of composing by working directly with sound; he contrasted his *concrète* music with traditional "abstract" music that is conceived in the mind, notated on paper, and realized only by instrumental performance. Composers Pierre Boulez, John Cage, Karlheinz Stockhausen, and Iannis Xenakis were all influenced by the techniques developed in Paris. Composers François Bayle, Luc Ferrari, Beatriz Ferreyra, Pierre Henry, Bernard Parmegiani, Guy Reibel, and others who formed the *Groupe de Recherches Musicales* produced 935 works between 1948 and 1980. Others, such as Luciano Berio, Edgard Varèse, Olivier Messiaen, Michel Redolfi, and Jean-Claude Risset, composed some of their best-known works in the studios now known as the INA/GRM. These studios in Paris, currently under the direction of composer Daniel Teruggi, continue to be the world's leading center for *musique concrète.* Their work is sometimes called acousmatic and performed using a multiple-loudspeaker "orchestra" called the acousmonium. Another notable center for *musique concrète* is Montrèal, Quebec, where composers Francis Dhomont, Robert Normandeau, and others have created a vibrant community for electro-acoustic music.

II. *Electronic music.* Composers Herbert Eimert, Karlheinz Stockhausen, and Gottfried Michael Koenig began working at West German Radio in Cologne in the 1950s. They were attracted by the use of electronic sound as a means of extending techniques of *serial music to the construction of timbre. In the 1970s the term electronic music was used to refer to these various genres but especially to music that used electronic oscillators and other analog equipment to modify and transform the acoustic properties of electronic and acoustic sound sources. Because the equipment was expensive, special studios were constructed at radio stations in Europe and at universities in the United States where students and experienced composers could work in this new medium. The concept of "experimental" music, propelled by the growth of technology, led many composers to electronic music studios. Although "loudspeaker" concerts attracted a specialized public, the phenomenal growth of the record industry and public radio revealed a significant audience for electronic music. Vladmir Ussachevsky, Otto Luening, and Milton Babbitt are often regarded as the first composers in the U.S. to work in this musical medium.

III. *Synthesizers and samplers.* Electronic instruments, today mostly with digital circuitry, are used to produce a variety of timbres, often specified by the user. Leon Theremin invented the Theremin, which is perhaps the first example of a widely used electronic instrument, although it had only one audio oscillator. Between its invention in the 1920s and the early analog synthesizers developed in the 1960s by Donald Buchla and Robert A. Moog in the U.S., there were numerous attempts to create and manufacture electronic performance instruments. The synthesizers of the 1960s used voltages to control parameters such as pitch, amplitude, timbre, and various audio effects. Today, synthesizers are used mostly in rock, pop, and jazz, but they grew out of the work of composers and researchers at various institutions in the U.S., Europe, and Japan. Synthesizers use electronically generated waveforms, often using techniques of Fourier analysis and synthesis. Occasionally musicians will attempt to imitate the sounds of acoustic instruments, but more often a novel timbre is sought. The instruments first attracted popular attention through Wendy Carlos's transcriptions of Bach and by the original compositions of Morton Subotnick. Synthesizers are often confused with samplers. The latter store digitally encoded, and sometimes modified, recordings of natural sounds, including acoustic instruments. Most synthesizers and samplers use keyboards to control pitch and duration; however, an electric guitar or other interface may be employed. In the 1990s a wide variety of controllers (the human interface) were developed, but these have mostly been used experimentally.

IV. *Computers.* The use of computers to produce electro-acoustic music had a parallel development to those production and performance techniques described above. In the 1950s Max V. Mathews at the Bell Telephone Laboratories first used computers for sound synthesis. The early application of computers to make music was perhaps more arduous than any previous sound production method. However, as computers became faster and less expensive, it was possible to use them for nearly every musical application. Composers Herbert Brün, John Chowning, Charles Dodge, Gottfried Michael Koenig, James K. Randall, and Jean-Claude Risset were among the first composers to exploit creatively the use of digital technology. The task of programming early computers to produce complex waveforms, tunings, and so on required special skills that most composers did not possess at the time. Institutes such as the Center for Computer Research in Music and Acoustics (CCRMA) at Stanford University and the Institut de recherche et de coordination acoustique/musique (IRCAM) in France supported research and trained a new generation of composer-programmers who invented hardware and developed software for themselves and others. A minor aspect of the use of computers was their use in the compositional process (sometimes called algorithmic composition). The first commercially produced *digital synthesizer* was called the Synclavier. It produced both synthesized and sampled sounds, allowed for these sounds to be modified, included a digital recording of music performed (sometimes called a sequencer in earlier *analog synthesizers*), and printed the music played. One of its inventors, Jon Appleton, and the rock and pop musicians Michael Jackson, Sting, and Frank Zappa used it in live performance. In the late 1990s most of the functions of the Synclavier and other digital performance instruments were available through less expensive computer software. The software was either in the form of controls for performance instruments or used directly on computers to record, modify, and transmit music. Computer systems incorporating the latter are called digital audio workstations.

V. *Other manifestations of electro-acoustic music.* A period of aesthetic diversity and experimentation in the 1950s until the present brought forth many unusual ways of composing, hearing, and thinking about music. Many of these involved technology and are therefore classified as electro-acoustic music. Concrete poetry gave birth to text-sound composition in which speech sounds became music. The leading composers were Charles Amirkhanian, Lars-Gunnar Bodin, Henri Chopin, Charles Dodge, and Sten Hanson. Electronic circuitry used to construct instruments expressing a single musical idea or technique was created by composers Alvin Lucier, Salvatore Martirano, Gordon Mumma, and Pauline Oliveros. Multimedia experiments involving music "composed" or modified by the movement of dancers or visual installations have been a minor but persistent interest of composers of electro-acoustic music. A category called performance art often involves the manipulation of sound by performers or audience members. Many film scores now also include electro-acoustic music, often combined with instruments.

Bibl.: Pierre Schaeffer, *À la recherché d'une musique concrète* (Paris: Édit Seuil, 1952). Jon H. Appleton and Ronald C. Perera, *The Development and Practice of Electronic Music* (Englewood Cliffs, N.J.: Prentice Hall, 1975). Barry Schrader, *Introduction to Electro-Acoustic Music* (Englewood Cliffs, N.J.: Prentice Hall, 1982). Deta S. Davis, *Computer Applications in Music: A Bibliography* (Madison, Wis.: A-R Eds, 1988; supp. 1, 1992). F. Richard Moore, *Elements of Computer Music* (Englewood Cliffs, N.J.: Prentice Hall, 1990). Curtis Roads, *The Computer Music Tutorial* (Cambridge, Mass.: MIT Pr, 1996). "A Poetry of Reality: Composing with Recorded Sound," *Contemporary Music Review* 15, pts. 1–2 (1996). Joel Chadabe, *Electric Sound: The Past and Promise of Electronic Music* (Saddle River, N.J.: Prentice Hall, 1997). Charles Dodge and Thomas A. Jerse, *Computer Music: Synthesis, Composition and Performance* (New York: Schirmer, 1997). "Aesthetics of Live Electronic Music," *Contemporary Music Review* 18, pt. 3 (1999). Perry Cook, *Real Sound Synthesis for Interactive Applications* (Natick, Mass.: A K Peters, 2002). Trevor Pinch and Frank Trocco, *Analog Days: The Invention and Impact of the Moog Synthesizer* (Cambridge, Mass.: Harvard U Pr, 2002). J.H.A.

Electronic instrument. An instrument in which the tone is produced and/or modified by electronic means. There are two broad classes, in both of which sound is transmitted to the listener by means of loudspeakers.

(1) Instruments in which the sound is generated by mechanical systems, such as vibrating strings or reeds, and modified electronically. These include in the first instance conventional instruments, such as the guitar or saxophone, to which a *pickup or a microphone is attached for the sake of amplifying their sound and, in some cases, modifying their tone color. The use of conventional instruments in this way, however, has often led to specifically electric playing styles and instrument designs, especially in the case of the *electric guitar. Certain types of *electric piano and *electronic organ also employ mechanical systems, but these systems may be quite distinct from those of the conventional instrument that they emulate.

(2) Instruments in which the sound is generated and produced entirely by electronic means. Many such instruments employ one or more oscillators to generate the signals from which a variety of pitches and tone colors is produced by means of frequency dividers, *filters, *ring modulators, and the like. Some *electronic organs are purely electronic in this way. The most versatile of these instruments is the *synthesizer, of which various types are widely used. Some other instruments, however, make use of the techniques of generating sound with the aid of a computer [see Electro-acoustic music].

Among the first electronic instruments was the *Telharmonium (ca. 1900). The first practical types began to appear in the 1920s. Historically important examples include the *Theremin, *Ondes Martenot, and *Trautonium.

Bibl.: Thomas L. Rhea, "The Evolution of Electronic Musical Instruments in the United States" (Ph.D. diss., George Peabody College, 1972). Alan Douglas, *Electronic Music Production* (London: Pitman, 1973). Id., *The Electronic Musical Instrument Manual,* 6th ed. (London: Pitman, 1976). Devarahi [pseud.], *The Complete Guide to Synthesizers* (Englewood Cliffs, N.J.: Prentice-Hall, 1982). Delton T. Horn, *The Beginner's Book of Electronic Music* (Blue Ridge Summit, Pa.: Tab Bks, 1982). Barry Schrader, *Introduction to Electro-Acoustic Music* (Englewood Cliffs, N.J.: Prentice-Hall, 1982).

Electronic music. See Electro-acoustic music.

Electronic organ. An *electronic instrument the first examples of which were designed to approximate the acoustic *organ in sustaining power, tone quality, and playing technique. Like the organ, such an instrument may have two manuals, a pedalboard, *stops or analogous devices for producing a variety of tone colors, and a swell pedal for controlling loudness. Various devices have been used to generate their sound. The first widely successful electronic organ, the Hammond organ developed by Laurens Hammond by 1935, employs rotating tone wheels that electromagnetically produce an oscillating current. The Wurlitzer organ, whose immediate predecessor was also developed in the 1930s, employs vibrating reeds. More recent designs typically employ a number of fixed-pitch oscillators and are thus purely electronic. In all types, the initial vibrations are modified and amplified electronically and then transmitted to the listener by means of loudspeakers.

Because they are much less expensive than comparably equipped acoustic organs, electronic organs have found widespread use in churches. For the same reason, at least initially, they became widely used in the home and for popular music. This led to the development of specific playing styles and to the creation of instruments that do not claim to imitate the acoustic organ. Some instruments, for example, attempt to reproduce the rhythms and tone colors of the rhythm section of a popular-music ensemble.

Electrophone. An *electronic instrument.

Electropneumatic action. In organs, a mechanism connecting the keys and stop controls to the windchest by means of electric contacts and pneumatic pouches or levers. First introduced experimentally in the 1860s, it did not become practical or widely adopted until the beginning of the 20th century.

Elegie für junge Liebende [Ger., Elegy for Young Lovers]. Opera in three acts by Hans Werner Henze (libretto by W. H. Auden and Chester Kallman), produced in Schwetzingen in 1961. Setting: the Austrian Alps in the early 20th century.

Elegy. (1) A sorrowful or melancholy poem, especially one of mourning for someone dead. (2) A musical work of similar character, whether a setting of such a poem or an instrumental work. Other terms for works of mourning include *lament, **planctus,* **tombeau,* **apothéose,* and *dump.

Elektra. Opera in one act by Richard Strauss (libretto by Hugo von Hofmannsthal, after his own play, which is based on the drama by Sophocles), produced in Dresden in 1909. Setting: the royal palace of Mycenae, after the Trojan War.

Elevation [Lat. *elevatio;* It. *elevazione*]. In the Mass, the elevation of the elements of communion following their consecration. Historically, this part of the Mass, or the consecration as a whole, has often been accompanied by a motet or by organ music, e.g., Frescobaldi's works titled *Toccata per l'elevazione.*

Eleventh. See Interval, Chord.

Elijah [Ger. *Elias*]. Oratorio for soloists, chorus, and orchestra by Mendelssohn, op. 70 (completed in 1846, revised in 1847), to texts from the Old Testament. The English version was first performed at the Birmingham Festival in 1846, and the German version in Hamburg in 1847.

Elisir d'amore, L' [It., The Love Potion]. Opera in two acts by Donizetti (libretto by Felice Romani, after Eugène Scribe's libretto for Auber's *Le philtre*), produced in Milan in 1832. Setting: a small Italian village in the early 19th century.

Elmuahim, elmuarifa. Geometrical terms occurring in Arabic translations of Euclid and thence in Latin translations (by Adelard of Bath in the 12th century), used in the 13th century by Coussemaker's Anonymous IV to refer to the rhomboid shape of the semibreve and to the semibreve with tail downward to the left, respectively. The Arabic terms have no specifically musical associations.

Embellishment. See Ornamentation, Counterpoint.

Embolada [Port.]. A traditional song genre of Brazil, especially of the northeastern region of the country, often performed in conjunction with such dances as the **baião* and the *coco.* It demands verbal agility on the part of its singer, with typically comic, alliterative, and onomatopoeic texts, sometimes improvised, that are set syllabically to recitativelike melodies dominated by rapid repeated-note patterns. D.S.

Embouchure. (1) [Eng., Fr.; Ger. *Ansatz*] The placement of the lips, facial muscles, and jaw in the playing of wind instruments. (2) [Fr.] *Mouthpiece. (3) [Eng., Fr.] The mouth hole of a flute.

Emmelēs [Gr., in melos]. (1) According to Plato, a quiet dance associated with tragedy. (2) Tones of definite pitch; also intervals smaller than the fourth that can be expressed as ratios such as 9:8 and 10:9. Tones of indefinite pitch and intervals with complex ratios are *ekmelēs.*

Emperor Concerto. Popular name for Beethoven's Piano Concerto no. 5 in E♭ major op. 73 (1809). The name may have been added by pianist and publisher Johann Baptist Cramer (1771–1858).

Emperor Quartet [Ger. *Kaiserquartett*]. Popular name for Haydn's String Quartet in C major op. 76 no. 3, Hob. III:77 (1797). It is so named because the slow movement consists of variations on "Gott, erhalte [Franz] den Kaiser" (the so-called "Emperor's Hymn"), formerly the Austrian national anthem, which was composed by Haydn (originally as a solo song with keyboard, Hob. XXVIa:43) in 1796–97.

Empfindsamkeit [Ger.]. See *Empfindsam* style.

Empfindsam style [fr. Ger. *empfindsamer Stil*]. The north German "sensitive" or "sentimental" style of the mid-18th century. The noun form of *empfindsam* is *Empfindsamkeit,* sometimes translated as "sensibility" in its earlier meaning of emotional sensitiveness (as in Jane Austen's *Sense and Sensibility*). The goal of *Empfindsamkeit* was the direct, natural, sensitive, and often subjective expression of emotion.

The *empfindsam* style may be considered a dialect of the international **galant* style, characterized by simple homophonic texture and periodic melody. Particular traits of the *empfindsam* style are the liberal use of appoggiatura or sigh figures, exploitation of dynamic nuance, and frequent melodic and harmonic chromaticism. Carl Heinrich Graun's *Der Tod Jesu* (1755) is the principal large-scale work of the *Empfindsamkeit,* while C. P. E. Bach's lieder and his later keyboard pieces (especially the fantasies and sonatas) best express its more intimate side [see also *Klavierlied*]. The *empfindsam* vocal style generally tends toward melodic simplicity, as one would expect given its ideal of pure, heartfelt song. The keyboard idiom, however, is often exceptionally intricate and refined, incorporating extensive ornamentation and complex rhythmic differentiation below the beat level; in part this style reflects the preference of *empfindsam* composers for the clavichord, which allows for greater delicacy of expression and dynamic nuance than the harpsichord.

Bibl.: Gudrun Busch, *C. Ph. E. Bach und seine Lieder* (Regensburg: Bosse, 1957). William S. Newman, *The Sonata in the Classic Era* (Chapel Hill: U of NC Pr, 1963; 3rd ed., New York: Norton, 1983). Eugene Helm, "The 'Hamlet' Fantasy and the Literary Element in C. P. E. Bach's Music," *MQ* 58 (1972): 277–96. Peter Schleuning, *Die Freie Fantasie* (Göppingen: A Kümmerle, 1973). Gerhard Sauder, *Empfindsamkeit,* 2 vols. (Stuttgart: Metzler, 1974–80). Gerhard Kaiser, *Aufklärung, Empfindsamkeit, Sturm und Drang,* 5th ed. (Tübingen: Francke, 1996). E.K.W.

Empfindung, mit [Ger.]. With feeling.

Empressé [Fr.]. Eager, hastening.

Ému [Fr.]. Moved, with emotion.

En [Fr.]. For phrases beginning with this preposition, see the word following.

Enchaînement [Fr.]. Voice leading.

Enchaînez [Fr.]. Continue without pause.

Enchiriadis, enchiridion [Lat., fr. Gr., handbook, manual]. Part of the titles of or references to several medieval treatises, particularly **Musica enchiriadis, Scolica enchiriadis,* and "Enchiridion Oddonis" (a reference in the writings of Guido of Arezzo and Wilhelm of Hirsau to the dialogue until recently attributed to Odo). A number of early publications of Protestant chorales include the word *Enchiridion* in their titles, e.g., the *Erfurt Enchiridien* (1524), a pair of chorale books with titles beginning *Eyn Enchiridion.*

Enclume [Fr.]. *Anvil.

Encore [Fr., again]. When said by members of the audience (usually English-speaking), a request that the performer(s) repeat a composition or perform an additional one not on the program; also the work performed in response to such a request or to enthusiastic applause. The practice of repeating opera arias became established in the 17th century with the rise of the virtuoso singer and continued into the 20th, though it is now generally disapproved. On the Continent, the usual term is *bis* [Lat., twice].

Encyclopedias of music. See Dictionaries and encyclopedias of music.

End-blown flute. A *flute that is played by blowing directly across its open upper end. The blow hole is often beveled or notched to create a sharper edge against which to direct the air stream. End-blown flutes can be documented as far back as the 4th millennium B.C.E. and are distributed worldwide except in Australia. Examples are the **caval,* **nāy,* **quena,* and **shakuhachi.*

Endpin [Fr. *pique;* Ger. *Stachel;* It. *puntale;* Sp. *puntal*]. An adjustable steel or wooden rod fastened in a wooden socket to the bottom block of the cello or double-bass. It is used to support the instrument's weight and control its height above the floor for the convenience and comfort of the player. While fixed supports were sometimes used in the 17th and 18th centuries, the adjustable endpin did not gain popularity until the last half of the 19th century. The Belgian cello virtuoso Adrien François Servais (1807–66) began using an endpin around 1846 to support his very large Stradivari instrument (built in 1708), which is now in the collection of the Division of Musical Instruments, Smithsonian Institution, Washington, D.C. W.L.M.

Enēchēma [Gr.]. See *Ēchos.*

Enfance du Christ, L' [Fr., The Childhood of Christ]. Oratorio for soloists, chorus, and orchestra by Berlioz, op. 25 (1850–54). Berlioz called the work a "trilogie sacrée" and, though the work is not an opera, included stage directions in the score to explain the events portrayed.

Enfant et les sortilèges, L' [Fr., The Child and the Enchantments]. Opera *(fantaisie lyrique)* in two parts by Ravel (libretto by Colette), produced in Monte Carlo in 1925. Setting: a French country house.

Enfant prodigue, L' [Fr., The Prodigal Son]. (1) "Lyric scene" by Debussy (libretto by Ernest Guinand) composed in 1884 (revised 1906–8) for the *Prix de Rome. It was produced as an opera in London in 1910. (2) Ballet by Prokofiev (choreography by George Balanchine), op. 46, produced in Paris in 1929. Most of the ballet music is contained in an orchestral suite arranged by Prokofiev in the same year.

Engführung [Ger.]. *Stretto.

England. I. *Contemporary musical life and related institutions.* Much of English musical life is centered in London, but there is considerable activity outside the capital as well. Decentralization is encouraged by the Arts Council of Great Britain, which may be the single most important factor in the musical life of the country. Since 1946 it has been the agency that distributes government subsidies to the arts. The Arts Council is officially independent of the government and is not intended to be an arbiter of taste through its choice of recipients. It supports a wide range of activities from amateur to professional and is important to the survival of deficit-prone traditional institutions (particularly the Covent Garden opera), as well as more experimental undertakings.

1. Opera. The two principal opera companies in London are the Royal Opera at Covent Garden and the English National Opera (formerly Sadler's Wells), which performs in English, at lower prices, and usually without the great international stars, at the Coliseum. There are also more modest companies, such as the English Music Theatre Company, some of which mostly tour outside London.

Opera is a feature of several English festivals, including Camden, Aldeburgh, and, most notably, Glyndebourne. Occasional productions at English universities have helped awaken interest in works outside the standard repertory. Those at Cambridge in the 1920s and 1930s were of particular historical importance in this respect.

2. Performing groups. (i) Orchestras. London is remarkable for its four major symphony orchestras, the London Symphony (founded in 1904), London Philharmonic (1932), Philharmonia (1945), and Royal Philharmonic (1946). The London Philharmonic and Royal Philharmonic are the result of the activities of Sir Thomas Beecham (1879–1961). The BBC Symphony (1930) is based in London and gives public concerts. There are several excellent symphony orchestras outside London, including the City of Birmingham Symphony (1920), the Bournemouth Symphony (1896), the Royal Liverpool Philharmonic (1840), and the Hallé Orchestra of Manchester (1858), the latter two being much older than the present London orchestras.

Chamber orchestras became an important part of London musical life through such groups as the London Chamber Orchestra (1921) and the Boyd Neel Orchestra (1932). The tradition they began has been carried on by several excellent newer ones, including the Academy of St. Martin-in-the-Fields (1959), the English Chamber Orchestra (1960), the Nash Ensemble (1964), and the Orchestra of St. John's, Smith Square (1973). The London Sinfonietta (1968) and the Birmingham Contemporary Music Group (1987) specialize in contemporary music.

(ii) Choruses. Choral performance has been traditional in England for several centuries and remains popular today, although the tendency to have mammoth choruses singing Handel oratorios, so much favored in the 19th century, was somewhat tempered by the changing taste and greater historical consciousness of the 20th. Amateur choral societies, such as the well-known Huddersfield Choral Society in Yorkshire (1836), are common throughout the country. Among the many in London are the Royal Choral Society (1871), the Bach Choir (1875), and the London Bach Society (1946). London also has several excellent chamber choruses, including the John Alldis Choir (1962) and the Monteverdi Choir (1964). Cathedral choirs and such well-known bodies as the choir of King's College, Cambridge, are also important elements in English choral music.

(iii) Early music. An interest in performing and listening to old music is something of an English tradition, as evidenced by the concerts of the Academy of Ancient Music in 18th-century London, which had hardly a parallel elsewhere in Europe at the time. Arnold Dolmetsch (1858–1940), the central figure in the beginnings of the modern revival of early-music performance, spent most of his career in England and firmly planted the movement there, and the Deller Consort (1950) was later a leader in the field. The work of English musicians, such as David Munrow (1942–76) and his Early Music Consort (1967), was important in arousing audience interest in early music beginning in the 1960s. English activity in this field flourishes at present. One of the best-known groups, the Academy of Ancient Music, founded in 1973, re-creates the mid-18th-century orchestra with authentic instruments. The 1980s and 1990s saw the founding of dozens of early-music groups of varied scope, such as consorts of viols or fretted instruments, cornett and sackbut ensembles, orchestras, choruses, and vocal ensembles focusing on the works of a single composer or specific historical period.

3. Festivals. Music festivals have constituted a flourishing tradition in England since the 18th century, and they are at present almost innumerable. The Three Choirs Festival, begun around 1715 and almost certainly one of the oldest in Europe, represents the traditional type of choral festival, of which several others also survive. Its site alternates among the homes of its choirs, Hereford, Gloucester, and Worcester. Among older English festivals, that at Haslemere was founded by Dolmetsch in 1925 to feature early music, and the Glyndebourne Festival, founded in 1934, early achieved and maintains an international reputation for its productions of operas as integrated dramatic works.

Many British festivals began after World War II. They include the Aldeburgh Festival (1948), long dominated by the personality of its founder, Benjamin Britten; the Bath Festival (1948), similarly associated with Yehudi Menuhin during the 1960s and composer Michael Tippett during the 1970s; the Brighton Festival (1967); the Camden Festival (1954); the Cheltenham Festival (1945), in its early years a potent force in encouraging contemporary English music; the English Bach Festival (1963); and the Tilford Bach Festival (1952).

A festival of sorts and long a central feature of London summers are the Henry Wood Promenade Concerts ("Proms") (1895), mostly given at the Royal Albert Hall.

4. Education. Many aspects of musical activity in England were dominated by foreigners in the 18th and early 19th centuries, and the idea of conservatories and music schools to train native musicians developed slowly. The leading schools are the Royal Academy of Music (1822), the Royal College of Music (1883), both in London, and the Royal Northern College of Music in Manchester, formed in 1972 from the merger of the Royal Manchester College of Music and the

Northern School of Music. Other important schools include Trinity College of Music (1872) of the University of London and the Guildhall School of Music and Drama (1880), London. The Royal College of Organists is mainly an examining body.

The first degrees in music known to have been conferred by a university were awarded at Cambridge in the 15th century, and a professorship of music was created there in the 17th. Oxford awarded music degrees from the early 16th century and in the 17th instituted a lectureship that grew into a professorship, but the establishment of music in anything like a regular, systematic, and modern way as part of the university curriculum at any university in England was almost entirely a 20th-century development. About a dozen English universities now have full music programs.

5. Publishing. London became a major center of European music publishing in the 18th century with the growth of a large and prosperous middle-class market and has remained one, although the industry there as everywhere has declined from its period of greatest prosperity in the 19th and early 20th centuries. In England the field is still dominated by survivors of long-established firms (although several of them have become subsidiaries of conglomerates), including Boosey and Hawkes (two 19th-century firms that merged in 1930), Chappell, J. and W. Chester, J. B. Cramer, J. Curwen, Novello, Oxford University Press (which began publishing music in a regular way in the 1920s), the London branch of Schott, and Stainer and Bell. Faber Music (1966) is one of the few recent additions.

6. Broadcasting. The British Broadcasting Corporation (BBC) included music in its programs almost from its founding as the first regular radio station in Europe in 1922. Growing quickly to a network, the BBC has long been one of the most important forces in the musical life of the country. Serious music (so called) is heard on Radio 3, which in 1970 replaced the famous Third Programme in a general reorganization of the system. Radio 3 broadcasts many public concerts given throughout the country and initiates many of its own, often offering rarely heard large-scale works. The BBC commissions new works, including music for the London Proms, whose sponsorship it took over in 1927. It has also commissioned a series of operatic and orchestral works that have had their premieres on BBC television or radio. Recent works of note by English composers that began as BBC commissions include Britten's *Owen Wingrave* (1970), Peter Maxwell Davies's Symphony no. 3 (1986), and John Tavener's *The Protecting Veil* (1989).

The BBC Symphony (1930) is the principal among several house orchestras. Other performing groups include the BBC Singers, a professional small chorus.

II. *History.* England was an important musical center in the Middle Ages. The Sarum rite, a dialect of the Roman rite originating at Salisbury Cathedral and widely influential throughout the country, gave a local flavor to the chant. The Winchester Tropers show that sacred polyphony was well established by the early 11th century, and by the 13th, English polyphony, as in the *Worcester fragments, had taken on traits distinguishing it from Continental styles. In the early 15th century, John Dunstable (ca. 1390–1453) achieved the widest reputation among several important composers. English music of that time is usually held to have had a decisive influence on the development of Continental musical style and compositional procedures. Thereafter, although works of high quality were written, English music was of mainly local importance, and influences tended to run in the other direction, from Italy and France, producing such English versions of Continental developments as the English *madrigal, the lute *ayre, and the *semi-opera.

The Puritan Commonwealth of the mid-17th century greatly disrupted the English musical tradition; however, the late 17th century produced several distinguished figures, including Henry Purcell (1659–95), one of England's greatest composers. The 18th and 19th centuries were in general a low point in the vitality of native English music, unless Handel is considered to have become an English composer, a not untenable assertion, so completely was his music absorbed into the native tradition. Much of English musical life, particularly that of London, was dominated in this period by foreign musicians attracted by the country's wealth and the large public provided by its sizable middle class. The native tradition survived in church music and in local genres such as the *catch, the *glee, and the *ballad opera, which developed in the late 18th century into the English comic opera and eventually led in the latter part of the 19th century to the operettas of Gilbert and Sullivan, which constitute almost the only part of English 19th-century music surviving in the repertory.

With Edward Elgar (1857–1934), England produced its first native composer of international importance since Purcell, and in the early 20th century an English nationalist school flowered with Ralph Vaughan Williams (1872–1958), Gustav Holst (1874–1934), and others. Herbert Howells (1892–1983), William Walton (1902–83), Michael Tippett (1905–98), the serialist Elizabeth Lutyens (1906–83), and Benjamin Britten (1913–76) dominated their generation. English composers of the next generation include Malcolm Arnold (b. 1921), Harrison Birtwistle (b. 1934), Peter Maxwell Davies (b. 1934), Richard Rodney Bennett (b. 1936), Edwin Roxburgh (b. 1937), Malcolm Williamson (b. 1931 in Australia), Hugh Wood (b. 1932), Anthony Milner (b. 1925), Alun Hoddinott (b. 1929), and Anthony Payne (b. 1936), who completed Elgar's unfinished Symphony no. 3. Younger composers of note include John Tavener (b. 1944), Brian Ferneyhough (b. 1943), Simon Bainbridge (b. 1952), Judith Weir (b. 1954), Robert Saxton (b. 1953), and Michael Finnissy (b. 1946).

III. *Folk music.* Most English folk music is closely related to the song or the dance. Folk songs are generally syllabic and strophic, frequently with a refrain. Notable types include the *ballad, love songs of various sorts, and songs attached to particular occasions or activities, such as *carols, sea *shanties, children's singing games, and *street cries. Two general varieties of folk dance exist: ritual or ceremonial dances, associated with certain seasons of the year and most often performed by costumed groups of men; and *country dances, performed at social occasions by both men and women. Ritual dances include sword, *morris, and processional dances. Country dances most often allow for participation of an unspecified number of couples, positioned in long double lines and reiterating simple figures that focus on one couple after another. Some, however, are round dances or dances for a prescribed number of couples. Dance tunes usually come from folk song and are almost always in duple meter. Instruments used in folk music are the *pipe and tabor, the small-pipes (a sort of *bagpipe), and, especially today, the fiddle, *concertina, or *melodeon. See also Popular music.

Bibl.: Edmund H. Fellowes, *English Cathedral Music* (London: Methuen, 1941; 5th ed., ed. Jack A. Westrup, 1969; R: of 5th ed., Westport, Conn.: Greenwood, 1981). Peter Le Huray, *Music and the Reformation in England, 1549–1660* (Cambridge: Cambridge U Pr, 1967; 2nd ed., 1978). Maud Karpeles, *An Introduction to English Folk Song* (London: Oxford U Pr, 1973). Andrew Wathey, *Music in the Royal and Noble Households in Late Medieval England: Studies of Sources and Patronage* (New York: Garland, 1989). Niall MacKinnon, *The British Folk Scene: Musical Performance and Social Identity* (Buckingham: Open U Pr, 1993). Otto Karolyi, *Modern British Music: The Second British Musical Renaissance, from Elgar to P. Maxwell Davies* (London: Associated U Presses, 1994). Nicky Losseff, *The Best Concords: Polyphonic Music in Thirteenth-Century Britain* (New York: Garland, 1994). Richard Turbet, *Tudor Music: A Research and Information Guide* (New York: Garland, 1994). Ian Woodfield, *English Musicians in the Age of Exploration* (Stuyvesant, N.Y.: Pendragon, 1995). David Atkinson, *English Folk Song: An Introductory Bibliography* (London: English Folk Dance and Song Society, 1996). Andrew Blake, *The Land without Music: Music, Culture and Society in Twentieth-Century Britain* (Manchester: Manchester U Pr, 1997). Tomi Mäkelä, ed., *Music and Nationalism in 20th-Century Great Britain and Finland* (Hamburg: Von Bockel, 1997). John Caldwell, *The Oxford History of English Music,* 2 vols. (Oxford: Clarendon; New York: Oxford U Pr, 1991–99). Bennett Zon, ed., *Nineteenth-Century British Music Studies* (Aldershot: Ashgate, 1999). David Wyn Jones, *Music in Eighteenth-Century Britain* (Aldershot: Ashgate, 2000). Meirion Hughes, *The English Musical Renaissance, 1840–1940: Constructing a National Music* (Manchester: Manchester U Pr, 2001). Victoria Cooper, *The House of Novello: The Practice and Policy of a Victorian Music Publisher, 1829–1866* (Burlington, Vt.: Ashgate, 2002). Gordon S. Cox, *Living Music in Schools, 1923–1999: Studies in the History of Music Education in England* (Aldershot: Ashgate, 2002).

English discant. See Discant.

English flute. In late 18th-century England, the *recorder, as distinguished from the *transverse or *German flute. The term recorder had passed out of use by the end of the Renaissance and was replaced with the simple appellation flute. M.S.

English guitar. A type of *cittern popular in mid-18th-century Britain. It has six courses of metal strings (the top four double), tuned c e g c′ e′ g′, and is plucked with the fingers. Introduced into England from France, it quickly became fashionable with female amateurs. The *keyed guitar* is a later version fitted with a key box, a device with keys and hammers to strike the strings as in the piano. R.L.

English horn [Fr. *cor anglais;* Ger. *Englischhorn;* It. *corno inglese;* Sp. *corno inglés*]. A double-reed woodwind instrument that is a lower-pitched member of the *oboe family. It is a *transposing instrument in F, a fifth below the oboe, with a sounding range of e to a″, a fifth lower than written. Late 18th-century instruments, which seem to be descended from the *oboe da caccia,* are curved and usually covered with leather. The modern instrument is straight, except for a curved *bocal. It has a hollow bulb-shaped bell, which is now known to have only a minimal effect on its tone. There are no satisfactory explanations for the origin of its name. As is usual with subsidiary instruments of a family, the English horn received its modern key system somewhat later than did the treble instrument. See ill. under Reed.

Range.

Bibl.: Philip Bate, *The Oboe,* 3rd ed. (New York: Norton, 1975). M.S.

English Suites. Six suites for harpsichord by Bach, BWV 806–11, usually considered to date from the Cöthen years (1717–23), but perhaps composed in Weimar ca. 1715. Each suite opens with an extended prelude. The title English Suites was not used by Bach himself, so far as is known, and its origins remain obscure.

English violet. A type of *viola d'amore described by Leopold Mozart (1756) as having 14 sympathetic strings, but apparently unknown in England.

Engraving. See Printing of music.

Enharmonic. (1) Of the three genera of tetrachords in the music of ancient *Greece, all of which are bounded by a perfect fourth, the one in which the lower two intervals are quarter tones. (2) In modern theory, pitches that are one and the same even though named or "spelled" differently, e.g., G♯ and A♭ or E and F♭. Pitches related in this way are said to be the enharmonic equivalents of one another. In systems of tuning other than equal *temperament (in which all semitones are the same size), two pitches forming such a pair may not be absolutely the same. Singers and players of fretless stringed instruments may readily preserve such distinctions, and some believe that sharps should be consistently higher and flats consistently lower than their enharmonic equivalents. Much music since at least the 18th century, however, exploits enharmonic equivalence for purposes of *modulation and thus requires that enharmonic equivalents in fact be equivalent. For example, in Schubert's Piano Sonata in B♭ major D. 960, the A♭ in the bass at m. 46 is renamed G♯ as part of a modulation from B♭ major to F♯ minor; similarly, in mm. 52–53 of the third movement of Beethoven's String Quartet in F major op. 59 no. 1, the A♭ in the first violin becomes G♯. In conventional keyboard instruments, where a single string or pipe must produce both members of a pair, the two will always be equivalent, even if the instrument is so tuned that certain intervals are out of tune. This has led on the one hand to systems of temperament and on the other to experiments with enharmonic keyboards with separate keys for at least some pairs that would otherwise be equivalent. The term enharmonic keyboard is also used, however, for instruments intended to produce *microtones for their own sake, e.g., Vicentino's **arcicembalo.*

Enigmatic scale. **Scala enigmatica.*

Enigma Variations. Popular name for *Variations on an Original Theme ("Enigma")* for orchestra by Elgar, op. 36 (1898–99). Each variation depicts a person identified by initials or a nickname.

En Saga. See *Saga, En.*

Ensalada [Sp., salad]. A poem that mixes lines from other poems or in diverse meters, often in several languages and usually with humorous intent; also a musical setting of such a poem, particularly a composition that quotes other compositions or melodies and thus a type of **quodlibet.* The singing of such works was apparently common in 16th-century Spain. The principal surviving examples identified specifically with the term are those by Mateo Flecha the elder (1481–1553) and his nephew of the same name (ca. 1530–1604), published in Prague in 1581 with titles such as "La guerra" (The War), "El fuego" (The Fire), "La bomba" (The Fire Pump). A few of these had been published earlier in the *vihuela* collections of Pisador (1552) and Fuenllana (1554), and one had been published in Lyons by Moderne in a collection with works by Janequin and others. Sebastián Aguilera de Heredia (ca. 1565–1627) employed the term for organ works with an analogous mixture of styles (*CEKM* 14, 1971).

Ensemble. (1) A group of musicians who perform together, whether instrumentalists, singers, or some combination, e.g., a string ensemble, an early-music ensemble. (2) The degree to which a group of performers plays with appropriate balance and well-coordinated articulation; thus, a group may be said to perform with good or poor ensemble. (3) In opera, a set piece for more than two soloists, sometimes also including the chorus, as occurs frequently at the conclusion or finale of an act. (4) Of or pertaining to music intended for performance by more than one player; also music or a performance in which individual parts are performed by more than one performer, as distinct from solo or soloistic music or performance. The distinction between music for one and for more than one performer on each part is often problematical in music of the Middle Ages and Renaissance. It has sometimes also been difficult with respect to music of the 18th century bearing titles such as *divertimento, *serenade, and the like, where the issue concerns orchestral music or performance as against *chamber music in the modern sense. See also Performance practice.

Entendre [Fr.]. To hear; *entendu,* heard.

Entfernt [Ger.]. Distant.

Entführung aus dem Serail, Die [Ger., The Abduction from the Seraglio]. *Singspiel in three acts by Mozart (libretto by Gottlob Stephanie, based on Christoph Friedrich Bretzner's libretto *Belmonte und Constanze*), produced in Vienna in 1782. Setting: Turkey in the 16th century.

Entr'acte [Fr.]. A piece, usually instrumental, performed between the acts of a play (e.g., Beethoven's compositions for Goethe's play *Egmont*) or an opera (Bizet's *entr'actes* in *Carmen*). The terms *entr'acte,* **intermède,* *intermezzo, and *incidental music are, for the most part, coextensive. In Purcell's works, the terms curtain tune and act tune are used.

Entrada [Sp.], **entrata** [It.]. See *Intrada.*

Entrée [Fr.]. (1) In 17th- and 18th-century France, a subdivision of a musico-dramatic work. In **ballet de cour* an *entrée* is a self-contained group of dances, unified by subject, forming part of an act. The later **opéra-ballet* referred to entire acts as *entrées.* (2) The entrance on stage of a character or group of characters, or the music, often marchlike, accompanying such an entrance, or the first piece in a **divertissement.* (3) The first piece of an instrumental suite, having the function of a prelude or introduction. Such an *entrée* may have a marchlike character.

Entremets [Fr.]. **Intermède.*

Entremés [Sp.]. A play, most often comic and sometimes with music, intended for performance between the acts of a larger work. The genre was cultivated by

Cervantes and other 17th-century Spanish authors. See also Intermezzo.

Entry. (1) The point in a composition at which a particular part begins or begins again after a rest; also the musical material with which the part begins at that point. (2) In a fugue, a statement of the subject.

Entschieden [Ger.]. Decided, resolute.

Entschlossen [Ger.]. Resolute, determined.

Envelope. In *acoustics, the characteristics (especially amplitude) of the attack, steady state, and decay of a sound.

Environment. See Mixed media.

Envoi, envoy [Fr.; Prov. *tornada;* It. *commiato*]. In some poetic forms of the Middle Ages such as the *chant royal* and the **ballade,* a concluding half-stanza that usually begins with some form of address such as "Prince," a reference to the prince presiding over a poetic competition. It repeats the refrain line and the rhyme scheme of the immediately preceding lines.

Éoliphone [Fr.]. *Wind machine.

Epic. See Folk music I, 2; *Chanson de geste.*

Epidiapente, epidiatessaron [Gr.]. See *Diapente, Diatessaron.*

Epilogue. *Coda.

Épinette [Fr.]. Spinet, harpsichord.

Epiphonus [Gr.]. See Neume.

Episema [Gr.]. A short horizontal stroke found in association with neumes in some 9th- and 10th-century manuscripts. Editions of *Gregorian chant prepared at Solesmes, which embody a particular theory of the rhythmic interpretation of chant, employ a "vertical episema" to mark the location of the *ictus. This is not found in medieval sources. See Neume.

Episode. A subsidiary passage occurring between passages of primary thematic importance; in a *fugue, a passage, often modulatory, occurring after the exposition of the subject or between subsequent principal statements of the subject [see also Codetta]; in a *rondo, a passage occurring between statements of the principal recurring theme.

Episodic form. *Rondo.

Epistle [Lat. *epistola*]. One of the New Testament Epistles, from which readings are taken for the *Mass of the Roman Catholic Church as well as for the analogous services of other Eastern and Western rites. In the Roman rite, these readings may be sung to a simple recitation formula or tone (*LU,* pp. 104–6) or they may be spoken.

Epistle sonata. An instrumental work intended for performance probably following the *Epistle of the *Mass. The term is especially applied to the 17 sonata-allegro movements by Mozart for various combinations of instruments and for organ. Frescobaldi also composed pieces associated with the Epistle.

Bibl.: Robert S. Tangeman, "Mozart's Seventeen Epistle Sonatas," *MQ* 32 (1946): 588–601. Thomas Harmon, "The Performance of Mozart's Church Sonatas," *ML* 51 (1970): 51–60.

Epithalamium [It. *epitalamio*]. A poem composed for a wedding, especially one to be sung on the wedding night. The genre was cultivated by Sappho and Catullus, among classical Greek and Latin writers, and by numerous poets of the Renaissance. The term has been applied to musical settings of such poems as well as to instrumental works.

Epitritus [Gr.]. A sesquitertian ratio, e.g., 4:3, which characterizes the interval of a perfect fourth.

Epogdous [Gr.]. A sesquioctave ratio, e.g., 9:8. The neuter *epogdoum* (pl. epogdoa) refers to a whole-tone interval, i.e., the difference between a perfect fourth and a perfect fifth.

Equale [Lat., also *aequale;* It. *eguale*]. A piece for voices or instruments all of the same type, especially one for four trombones written for a funeral or other solemn occasion. Beethoven composed three of the latter (WoO 30) in 1812. They were transcribed for four male voices and performed at his funeral.

Equal temperament. See Temperament.

Equal voices. Voices of the same type when employed in a polyphonic work, e.g., all sopranos or all tenors; sometimes also merely all male or all female.

Ergriffen [Ger.]. Moved, stirred.

Erhaben, Erhabenheit [Ger.]. Lofty, noble, sublime; nobility, sublimity.

Erhu [Chin.]. A Chinese *spike fiddle, about 75 cm tall, with two silk strings and a small, hexagonal body covered with snakeskin. It has no fingerboard; the player stops the strings with finger pressure alone. The bow is threaded between the strings, but normally only one string at a time is played. It is used to accompany sung narrative and as an ensemble instrument, particularly in *Peking opera. In the 20th century, it became popular as a solo instrument. See also *Ching-hu;* see ill. under East Asia I.

Erhöhen, Erhöhungszeichen [Ger.]. To sharp, the sharp sign.

Erlöschend [Ger.]. Dying out.

Ermattend [Ger.]. Tiring, weakening.

Ernani. Opera in four acts by Verdi (libretto by Francesco Maria Piave, after Victor Hugo's drama

Hernani), produced in Venice in 1844. Setting: Spain and Aix-la-Chapelle, 1519.

Erniedrigen, Erniedrigungszeichen [Ger.]. To flat, the flat sign.

Ernst, ernsthaft [Ger.]. Earnest, serious.

Eroica. Beethoven's Symphony no. 3 in E♭ major op. 55 (1803). It was composed in homage to Napoleon, but when Napoleon took the title of emperor, Beethoven changed the work's title from *Sinfonia grande: Bonaparte* to *Sinfonia eroica composta per festeggiar il sovvenire d'un gran uomo* (Heroic symphony composed to celebrate the memory of a great man) and dedicated it to Prince Franz Joseph von Lobkowitz. The second movement is headed "Marcia funebre" (Funeral March). The last movement includes a series of variations based on a theme that Beethoven had used in three earlier compositions: *Contretanz* no. 7 in E♭ major WoO 14 (completed in 1802) [see *Contredanse*]; *Die *Geschöpfe des Prometheus; *Eroica Variations.*

Eroica Variations. Variations and fugue in E♭ major op. 35 (1802), by Beethoven, so called because Beethoven later used the work's theme in the last movement of the **Eroica* Symphony. The variations are also called *Prometheus Variations,* after the ballet *Die *Geschöpfe des Prometheus,* in which the theme occurred for the first time.

Ersatz [Ger.]. Substitute; *Ersatzklausel,* substitute *clausula.

Ersterbend [Ger.]. Dying away.

Erwartung [Ger., Expectation]. Opera for soprano and orchestra in one act by Schoenberg (libretto by Marie Pappenheim), composed in 1909 and produced in Prague in 1924. Setting: a forest.

Erweitern [Ger.]. To extend, expand.

Erzähler [Ger.]. (1) Narrator. (2) An organ stop with tapered flue pipes, of soft tone, found in American organs.

Erzlaute [Ger.]. *Archlute.

Es, eses [Ger.]. E-flat, E-double-flat. See Pitch names.

Escapement. See Piano.

Escape note. *Échappée.* See Counterpoint II, 6.

Eschaquier, eschiquier [Fr.]. *Chekker.

Escondido [Sp., hidden]. A traditional couple dance of Argentina. Identified by its choreography, which involves the hiding of dancing partners from one another, it is in many musical features very similar to the Argentine **gato.* Another related dance with a similar choreographic theme is known as *los aires.* D.S.

Esercizio [It.]. Exercise, etude.

Eses [Ger.]. E-double-flat. See Pitch names.

Eskimo music. See American Indian music II.

Espigueta [Sp.]. *Chimney flute.

Espinette [Fr.]. In the 16th century, harpsichord, *spinet.

Espressivo [It., abbr. *espr.*]. Expressive, with expression.

Espringale [OFr.]. A jumping dance, as distinct from the **carole,* a round dance.

Esquinazo [Sp., perhaps fr. *esquina,* street corner]. In Chile, a serenade sung at night or at dawn in honor of a particular person or religious figure and performed on birthdays, saints' days, and during the Christmas season. Its music, traditionally a variety of **tonada,* often concludes with a *cogollo,* the verses making reference to the individual for whom the serenade is intended. D.S.

Estampes [Fr., Prints]. A set of three piano pieces by Debussy, composed in 1903: "Pagodes" (Pagodas), "La soirée dans Grenade" (Evening in Granada), and "Jardins sous la pluie" (Gardens in the Rain).

Estampie [Fr.; Occ. *estampida;* It. *istanpita* or *istanpitta;* Lat. *stantipes*]. A composition of the 13th and 14th centuries, either with text or without. Few text examples survive with music, while 16 textless *estampies* survive, all presumably played instrumentally. The textless *estampie* may be one of the oldest surviving varieties of purely instrumental music composed in Western Europe. The Latin word combines *stati,* standing, with *pes,* feet; the French term (and its cognates in Occitan and Italian) derives from *estamper,* which could mean to stamp, to resound, or to turn around. These etymologies, along with direct associations made by medieval theorists, identify the *estampie* as some kind of dance.

Two Occitan poetic treatises from the late 13th and early 14th centuries describe the poetic type as a love song consisting of several stanzas and a refrain. Music theorist Johannes de Grocheio, around 1300, adds that the text *stantipes* (using the Latin term) has "a diversity of parts" in rhyme and melody, which scholars have taken to mean a heterostrophic versicle structure, often in pairs or double versicles, and akin to the form of the *sequence and the later **lai.* All of the 19 French poems labeled *estampie* in the manuscripts lack a refrain, but most of them are heterostrophic; the few extant Occitan poems called *estampida,* however, are isostrophic like the **canso.*

Grocheio says that the textless *stantipes* has several sections *(puncta),* each consisting of two parts with identical melody and open and closed endings (*aperum* and *clausum*). Two sources preserve musical compositions designated *estampies* or *istanpite.* Eight monostrophic *estampies* were added to the French source *FPn* fr 844 in the late 13th or early 14th century. In the Italian manuscript *GB-Lbm* 29987 (late 14th or early 15th century) is a similar group, headed "Istanpitta," consisting of eight textless monophonic pieces. All of these pieces conform to Grocheio's description, with three to seven *puncta,* each repeated immediately, with first and second endings [Fr. **ouvert* and *clos;* It. *aperto* and *chiuso*]. A single pair of endings (x, y) may serve for any number of *puncta,* as follows: AxAy, BxBy, CxCy, etc. The Italian *istanpite* are considerably longer and more florid than the French pieces. The French pieces are in triple meter, while most of the Italian works are in duple meter, a disparity that poses a problem in determining what the steps of the dance might have been.

Certain other pieces in similar forms but lacking appropriate manuscript labels are sometimes called *estampies* today. Examples include three further textless monophonic pieces in the manuscript *F-Pn* fr. 844; one is untitled, the others called *Dansse real* and *Danse;* all resemble the *estampies* structurally. Seven textless compositions follow the *stanpite* in *GB-Lbm* 29987, each given a title such as *"Saltarello," "La manfredina," "La *rotta della manfredina," "Trotto," and "Lamento di Tristan"; their double-versicle structure, association with dance types, and proximity to the preceding *istanpite* in the manuscript lead some scholars to maintain that these also are *istanpite.* In addition, three keyboard dances, one incomplete, in the Robertsbridge Codex (*GB-Lhm* 28550, ca. 1325) closely parallel this form, as do two in the Faenza Codex (*I-FZc* 117).

The troubadour Raimbaut de Vaqeiras (ca. 1150–1207) was said to have written the text of the song "Kalenda maya" to the tune of an *estampie* he heard played by *jongleurs* from northern France. The song antedates by about a century the first written designations of pieces as *estampies,* and its isostrophic structure and other features have raised doubts recently about whether it conforms to either the poetic or the musical definition provided by theorists.

Bibl.: Pierre Aubry, *Estampies et danses royales* (Paris: Fischbacher, 1907). Jacques Handschin, "Über Estampie und Sequenz," *ZfMw* 12 (1929–30): 1–20; 13 (1930–31): 113–32. Walter Streng-Renkonen, *Les estampies françaises* (Paris: H Champion, 1930). Lloyd Hibberd, "'Estampie' and 'Stantipes,'" *Speculum* 19 (1944): 222–49. Hans J. Moser, "Stantipes und Ductia," *Zeitschrift für Musikwissenschaft* 2 (1944): 194–206. Pierre Bec, *La Lyrique française au moyen-âge,* 2 vols. (Paris: A & J Picard, 1977–78), 1: 241–46, 1: 177–82. Christopher Page, "Johannes de Grocheio on Secular Music: A Corrected Text and a New Translation," *Plainsong and Medieval Music* 2 (1993): 17–41. Timothy J. McGee, *Medieval Instrumental Dances* (Bloomington: Ind U Pr, 1989). Patricia W. Cummins, "Le Problème de la musique et de la poésie dans l'estampie," *Romania* 103 (1982): 259–77. Elizabeth Aubrey, "The Dialectic between Occitania and France in the Thirteenth Century," *EMH* 16 (1997): 1–53.

E.A.

Estey organ. A suction-operated reed organ built in the second half of the 19th century by the firm of Jacob Estey in Brattleboro, Vermont.

Esthetics. See Aesthetics.

Estilo [Sp.]. A genre of lyric song of Argentina and Uruguay, closely related to the **tonada* and the **triste.* Typically for one or two voices with guitar accompaniment, it alternates two distinct sections, a slow *tema* and a faster *alegre,* known in Uruguay as *cielito.* D.S.

Estinguendo [It.]. Dying away.

Estinto [It.]. Barely audible.

Estompé [Fr.]. Toned down.

Estive [Fr.]. A wind instrument mentioned in French medieval sources, possibly a *bagpipe or a *hornpipe.

Estribillo [Sp.]. *Refrain. See also *Villancico.*

Éteindre [Fr., p.p. *éteint*]. To extinguish.

Ethiopic chant. The liturgical chant of the Ethiopian Orthodox Church, performed by musicians *(dabtarā)* trained in improvised hymnody *(qenē),* liturgical dance *(aqqwāqwām),* and the stenographic notation *(melekket),* in which abbreviated words represent melodic formulas. The oldest MSS date from the 14th century, but the notation began in the 17th century. The *Deggwā,* Lenten *Ṣoma Deggwā* (*PO* 32), and the *Mawāse't* contain "antiphons" for the Office; the order of psalmody is in the *Me'rāf* (*PO* 33–34). The *Zemmārē* contains communion hymns for Mass; the *Qeddāsē* is the "missal." There are 3 modes and 13 *qenē* types. A *Malke'* is a chain of *salām* hymns giving a verbal "picture" of a saint. The *Falāshā* sect seems to owe its rite to Christian monks.

Bibl.: Anton Schall, *Zur äthiopischen Verskunst* (Wiesbaden: Steiner, 1961). William F. Macomber and Getatchew Haile, *A Catalogue of Ethiopian Manuscripts* 1– (Collegeville, Minn.: Monastic Manuscript Microfilm Library, St. John's Abbey & Univ, 1975–). Kay Shelemay, *Music, Ritual and Falasha History,* 2nd ed. (East Lansing, Mich.: Mich St U Pr, 1989). Kay Kaufman Shelemay, "The Musician and Transmission of Religious Tradition: The Multiple Roles of the Ethiopian Dabtarā," *Journal of Religion in Africa* 22 (1992): 242–60. Kay Kaufman Shelemay and Peter Jeffery, *Ethiopian Christian Liturgical Chant: An Anthology,* 3 vols., 1 CD, Recent Researches in Oral Traditions of Music 1–3 (Madison, Wisc.: A-R Eds, 1993–97). Kay Kaufman Shelemay, Peter Jeffery, and Ingrid Monson, "Oral and Written Transmission in Ethiopian Christian Chant," *EMH* 12 (1993): 55–117. Peter Jeffery, "The Liturgical Year in the Ethiopian *Deggwā* (Chantbook)," Εὐλόγημα*: Studies in Honor of Robert Taft, S.J.,* Studia Anselmiana 110, Analecta Liturgica 17 (Rome: Pontificio Ateneo Sant' Anselmo, 1993), pp. 199–234. Habtemichael Kidane, *L'Ufficio divino della Chiesa etiopica: Studio storico-critico con particolare riferimento alle ore cattedrali,* Orientalia Christiana Analecta 257 (Rome: Pontificio Istituto Orientale, 1998). P.J.

Ethnomusicology. A subdivision of musicology concerned primarily with the comparative study of musics of the world, music as an aspect of culture, and the music of oral tradition. According to other definitions that have been promulgated, ethnomusicology is the study of non-Western and folk music, or of the music of contemporary cultures, the anthropological study of music, or the study of a music by an outsider to its culture. Although there is disagreement on precise definition, it is clear that most ethnomusicologists do research in non-Western or folk music, take an interest in the role of music in culture, engage in field research, and use concepts developed by anthropology. As their subject is mainly music that lives primarily in oral tradition, they are for the most part limited to materials collected in recent or contemporary times, and as students of music outside their own culture, they are usually obliged to follow a comparative approach. Despite definitional divergence, the field of ethnomusicology offers a reasonably unified perspective.

I. *History.* Although scholarly study of non-Western music in Europe goes back to the Renaissance and flowered briefly in the early 19th century, the formal beginnings of ethnomusicology are placed in the 1880s. Early landmarks are Alexander J. Ellis's "On the Musical Scales of Various Nations" (1885), the first broadly comparative study; Theodore Baker's dissertation on American Indian music (1882); Carl Stumpf's first detailed monograph on the music of one tribal culture, the Bella Coola of British Columbia; and most important, the development of the phonograph. The years following 1900 saw the publication of the first works by scholars who were to dominate the field in its early history. Chief among these was Erich M. von Hornbostel, who was instrumental in founding the "Berlin school," taught many of the prominent scholars of the next generation who were responsible for establishing ethnomusicology as a recognized field, established its earlier name, "comparative musicology," and was to make initial studies of the music of a wide variety of Asian, African, and New World cultures. Béla Bartók, whose research methods became paradigmatic in European folk-music research, and Frances Densmore, who established the importance of research on North American Indian music, were also prominent in the early decades of the century. About 1900, Stumpf and Hornbostel founded in Berlin the first large archive of field recordings of non-Western music and set a pattern for the collection of recordings as a major component of documentation.

The late 1920s and 1930s saw the first attempts to make mechanical transcriptions of music (Milton Metfessel, 1928), publications by George Herzog, Charles Seeger, and Marius Schneider combining anthropological and musicological methods, the first periodicals devoted entirely to this field, and important works by Curt Sachs that were to have a major impact on historical musicology. Another period of great activity began ca. 1950 and includes the development of field research through the study of performance of non-Western music by Western scholars, the coming of Third World scholars into the field, the formalization of ethnomusicology programs in a number of U.S. and European institutions, the establishment of two scholarly organizations, the Society for Ethnomusicology (1955) and the International Folk Music Council (1948; now the International Council for Traditional Musics), and the publication of a series of general books on ethnomusicological theory, method, and approaches. The period after 1970 is characterized by increased influence of anthropology, linguistics, and semiotics on methodology.

II. *Methods.* In its early decades, ethnomusicology was dominated by the desire to preserve the disappearing music of non-Western cultures, by attempts to see exotic musics as representative of historical stages that led ultimately to Western art music, and by the establishment of systems of description and analysis that would make possible a worldview of music based on comparative study. Preservation led to attention to field research, with emphasis on recording, although more comprehensive data collecting was to come later from the anthropological interest in studying music as part of culture and from the development of techniques that made the field worker a participant in the culture under study.

The desire to preserve also led to the development of *transcription as a major technique and activity. Writing music from hearing it on recordings became one of the activities shared by all who worked in the field. Since Western notation had been developed as a prescriptive system for Western music, whereas what was needed was a descriptive system adaptable to all musics, special symbols were developed as early as 1900. Even so, because Western notation is far more satisfactory for the representation of melodic phenomena than for rhythm or aspects of musical sound such as ornamentation, vocal timbre, rasp, nasality, tension, and rubato, and because it is almost impossible to neutralize the transcriber's musical and cultural background, development of mechanical and electronic devices generically called *melographs became necessary. A number of these devices have been perfected, but transcription by ear is still the most widespread method.

Interest in history led to speculation about the origins of music and to attempts to identify in simple tribal repertories the earliest extant music. It also brought ethnomusicology under the influence of anthropological movements that sought to study the prehistory of culture through geographic distribution: the German *Kulturkreis* school in the 1920s and 1930s, to which Hornbostel and Sachs contributed, and the American anthropological school in the 1940s and 1950s, whose major concept was the culture area, a concept used by George Herzog, Bruno Nettl, and Alan P. Merriam. After 1950, the study of recent and current change under conditions of acculturation and influence from Western culture became the chief historical focus.

The analysis of non-Western music has been important from the beginnings of ethnomusicology. Analytical techniques used for Western art music were deemed inadequate, the alternatives being the establishment of a system that would accommodate all musics and the description of each musical system in terms derived from its own culture. The first of these is illustrated by Hornbostel's description of many musics (ca. 1910–35) in essentially the same terms, a method followed and further developed by Herzog; Mieczyslaw Kolinski's publication of classificatory plans for the description of all musics in terms of individual elements such as scale, melodic contour, tempo, and meter (1950s to 1970s); and Alan Lomax's *cantometrics, which concentrates on performance practice and singing style (from ca. 1960 on). Emphasis on culture-specific analysis can be traced to the shift in emphasis, shortly after 1950, from tribal and folk musics to classical musics of Asia. These cultures have theoretical systems articulated in treatises, teaching methods, and terminology used by musicians, but the approach turned out to be possible also for musics without explicitly articulated theory.

An interest in the study of music in culture is found in the earliest writings, but developed greatly after 1950, largely through the work of anthropologists Richard A. Waterman, Alan P. Merriam, John Blacking, and David P. McAllester. Prominent among the many types of studies are the comprehensive description of a musical culture, the study of music as a symbol of cultural values, and the study of cultural change and its effects on music and musical change.

Beginning in the 1970s, the study of music in culture became the principal thrust of ethnomusicology in North America and to a large extent in other regions as well. The typical monographic publication in the 1980s and 1990s was the "ethnography," a work that attempted to relate music to other domains of culture on the basis of field research, with the use of both "insider" and "outsider" voices, and with special interest paid to political, gender, and class relationships. Ethnomusicology was substantially influenced by postmodern cultural studies and critical theory, semiotics, hermeneutics, and developments in literary criticism, and moved away from positivism and toward an emphasis on the interpretive. Ethnomusicologists exhibited increased breadth, influenced by (and influencing) historical musicology, undertaking studies of Western art music, emphasizing various approaches to the study of recent change in the world's musics, and also returning to an interest in older questions they had abandoned, including archeology, musical universals, and the origins of music. Since about 1980, the study of ideas about music and of musical behavior and events has become more prominent than the study of musical styles and sounds. Most noticeable—much in contrast to practices of the 1950s—is the enormous role of the world's popular musics in the ethnomusicological literature of the 1990s. While the profile of ethnomusicology in 2000 might be barely recognizable to the early pioneers of the field, most ethnomusicologists continue to balance an emphasis on the musical diversity of human cultures with an understanding of music as a unified human phenomenon.

Bibl.: Erich M. von Hornbostel, "Die Probleme der vergleichenden Musikwissenschaft," *ZIMG* 7 (1905/6): 85–97. Karl Stumpf, *Die Anfänge der Musik* (Leipzig: Barth, 1911). Robert Lach, *Die vergleichende Musikwissenschaft, ihre Methoden und Probleme* (Vienna: Hölder-Pichler-Tempsky, 1924). Curt Sachs, *Geist und Werden der Musikinstrumente* (Berlin: Reimer, 1929; R: Hilversum: A M Knuf, 1965). Id., *Vergleichende Musikwissenschaft* (Heidelberg: Quelle & Meyer, 1930; 2nd ed., 1959). Fritz Bose, *Musikalische Völkerkunde* (Freiburg i. Br.: Atlantis, 1953). Egon Wellesz, ed., *Ancient and Oriental Music, NOHM* 1 (London: Oxford U Pr, 1957). Jaap Kunst, *Ethnomusicology,* 3rd ed. (The Hague: Nijhoff, 1959). Curt Sachs, *The Wellsprings of Music,* ed. Jaap Kunst (The Hague: Nijhoff, 1962). Mantle Hood, "Music, the Unknown," in Frank Ll. Harrison, Mantle Hood, and Claude Palisca, *Musicology* (Englewood Cliffs, N.J.: Prentice-Hall, 1963), pp. 215–326. Alan P. Merriam, *The Anthropology of Music* (Evanston, Ill.: Northwestern U Pr, 1964). Bruno Nettl, *Theory and Method in Ethnomusicology* (New York: Free Pr of Glencoe, 1964). Alan Lomax, *Folk Song Style and Culture,* ed. Edwin E. Erickson (Washington, D.C.: Amer Assoc for the Advancement of Science, 1968). Mantle Hood, *The Ethnomusicologist* (New York: McGraw-Hill, 1971; new ed., Kent, Ohio: Kent State U Pr, 1982). John Blacking, *How Musical Is Man?* (Seattle: U of Wash Pr, 1973). Walter Wiora, *Ergebnisse und Aufgaben vergleichender Musikforschung* (Darmstadt: Wissenschaftliche Buchgesellschaft, 1975). Alan P. Merriam, "Definitions of 'Comparative Musicology' and 'Ethnomusicology': An Historical-Theoretical Perspective," *Ethno* 21 (1977): 189–204. Charles Seeger, *Studies in Musicology, 1935–1975* (Berkeley and Los Angeles: U of Cal Pr, 1977). Artur Simon, "Probleme, Methoden und Ziele der Ethnomusikologie," *Jahrbuch für musikalische Volks- und Völkerkunde* 9 (1978): 8–52. Marcia Herndon and Norma McLeod, *Music as Culture* (Norwood, Pa.: Norwood Edns, 1979; 2nd ed., 1981). Bruno Nettl, *The Study of Ethnomusicology* (Urbana: U of Ill Pr, 1983). Wolfgang Suppan, *Der musizierende Mensch: Eine Anthropologie der Musik* (Mainz: Schott, 1984). Bruno Nettl and Philip V. Bohlman, eds., *Comparative Musicology and Anthropology of Music: Essays on the History of Ethnomusicology* (Chicago: U of Chicago Pr, 1991). Helen Myers, ed., *Ethnomusicology, an Introduction* (New York: Norton, 1992). Helen Myers, ed., *Ethnomusicology: Historical and Regional Studies* (New York: Norton, 1993). Gregory F. Barz and Timothy J. Cooley, eds., *Shadows in the Field: New Perspectives for Fieldwork in Ethnomusicology* (Oxford: Oxford U Pr, 1997). Nicholas Cook and Mark Everist, eds., *Rethinking Music.* (Oxford: Oxford U Pr, 1999). B.N.

Ethos. In the music of ancient *Greece, the ethical or moral character of music, or, by extension, simply its generalized emotion or mood, especially of the individual modes, each of which was regarded as embodying certain attributes (strength, manliness, passion, lasciviousness, etc.) and as capable of arousing those in the listener. Some writers of the Middle Ages and Renaissance connect the modes of their own day with such qualities, often employing (incorrectly) the Greek names for the modes (Dorian, Phrygian, etc.; see Mode).

Et in terra pax [Lat.]. See Gloria.

Étouffé [Fr.]. Damped, muted; *étouffoir,* *damper.

Etude [Fr. *étude,* study; Ger. *Etüde, Studie;* It. *studio;* Sp. *estudio*]. A composition designed to improve the technique of an instrumental performer by isolating specific difficulties and concentrating his or her efforts on their mastery. A single etude usually focuses on one technical problem; etudes are usually published in groups more or less systematically covering a range of such problems in a range of keys. In present-day usage, the etude falls between the exercise, a short formula not worked out as a formal composition, and the concert etude, which can stand as a self-sufficient piece of music.

The designation etude is seldom found before the early 19th century, although a good deal of earlier keyboard music not now generally thought of as didactic was originally composed at least in part to aid in the mastery of technique. This purpose is explicit in such titles as Bach's **Clavier-Übung* and Alessandro Scarlatti's *Essercizi per gravicembalo* and implicit in a wide range of pieces called only prelude, toccata, and the like. It is clearer when such pieces are included in didactic works, as are the preludes in François Couperin's *L'art de toucher le clavecin* (1716) and Muzio Clementi's *Appendix to the . . . Introduction to the Art of Playing on the Piano Forte, Containing Préludes, Exercises . . .* (1811).

The concept of a series of etudes designed as a course of study combined with sufficient compositional interest and shaping to hold the student's attention is perhaps to be linked to needs arising from the explosion of bourgeois music-making in the late 18th and early 19th centuries. Beginning with Muzio Clementi, Johann Baptist Cramer, Carl Czerny, and others for the keyboard and Rodolphe Kreutzer, Pierre Rode, Charles-Auguste de Bériot, and others for the violin, the 19th century produced a large quantity of such courses. See also Capriccio.

Composers of the 19th century recognized wider musical possibilities in the etude, the development of which led to what is usually called the concert etude. (To some extent this simply continues the earlier tradition of compositions with didactic possibilities.) The etudes of Chopin (op. 10, 1833; op. 25, 1837) are the earliest examples, followed by those of Scriabin (op. 8, 1894; op. 42, 1903; op. 65, 1912), Debussy (twelve in two books, 1915), and many others. In the Lisztian tradition (**Études d'exécution transcendante,* published 1852), the concert etude becomes as much, or perhaps more, a demonstration of triumphant virtuosity to the concert public as a means to its achievement.

Bibl.: Peter Felix Ganz, "The Development of the Etude for Pianoforte" (Ph.D. diss., Northwestern Univ., 1960).

Études d'exécution transcendante [Fr., Transcendental Etudes]. A set of 12 studies by Liszt. The first version was published in 1826 as op. 6 and included 11 pieces related to later versions. The second version was completed and published by 1839. The final version, the first to use the term *transcendante,* was published in 1852. Most of the pieces have descriptive or poetic titles ("Mazeppa," "Vision," "Harmonies du soir," etc.).

Études symphoniques [Fr., Symphonic Etudes]. A set of piano pieces by Schumann, op. 13 (1834–37 with the title *Etüden im Orchestercharakter für Pianoforte von Florestan und Eusebius;* revised in 1852 with the title *Études en formes de variations*), in the form of a theme (by Baron von Fricken, father of Ernestine, the young Schumann's sweetheart) with 12 variations and a finale. Five additional variations not included in either of the earlier versions were published posthumously in 1873.

Etwas [Ger.]. Somewhat.

Eugene Onegin [Russ. *Evgeny Onegin*]. Opera in three acts by Tchaikovsky (libretto by the composer and Konstantin Shilovsky, after Pushkin's poem), produced in Moscow in 1879. Setting: St. Petersburg, about 1820.

Eunuch flute [Fr. *flûte-eunuque*]. A type of *mirliton described and illustrated by Mersenne (1636).

Euouae. The vowels of the words "seculorum Amen," with which the Lesser *Doxology concludes; sometimes also spelled *evovae.* In books and manuscripts containing *Gregorian chant, these letters accompany the pitches of the final cadences or *differentiae* of certain melodic formulas [see Psalm tone]. When the letters and pitches are given together following a melody such as an antiphon, they serve to indicate which formula is to be used for the singing of verses in association with that melody.

Euphonium [Fr. *euphonium, basse à pistons;* Ger. *Euphonium, Baryton;* It. *eufonio;* Sp. *euphonium*]. A valved brass instrument in B♭, an octave lower than the *cornet or *trumpet. It has about 2.75 m (9 ft.) of tube length, usually folded in tuba or upright form with the bell straight up or turned partly forward [see ill. under Brass instruments]. The euphonium has a large bore of bugle or flugelhorn proportions in contrast to the otherwise similar English baritone, which has more modest cornetlike dimensions. Both the euphonium and the baritone have been used extensively in military, community, and school bands since the middle of the 19th century. In bands of the late 19th century, the euphonium became a featured solo instrument with many fine band parts and virtuoso solos written for it.

Valved instruments at 9′ B♭ pitch first appeared in Germany in the 1830s. From almost the beginning there were at least two sizes. The wide-bore instrument was a euphonium in England, a *saxhorn basse* in France, a *Baryton* in Germany, and a *flicorno basso* in Italy. The smaller size was a baritone or Baryton in England, a *saxhorn baritone* in France, a *Baryton B* or *Barytonhorn* in Germany, and a *flicorno tenore* in Italy. In the U.S., several of these terms were used before the English practice of euphonium and baritone was accepted early in the 20th century. The instrument is also known in the U.S. as a tenor tuba.

The range of both euphonium and baritone is that of the cornet one octave lower except when a fourth valve provides additional lower notes down to the fundamental. Parts are written in bass clef at concert pitch or in treble clef sounding a ninth lower.

The double-belled euphonium combines a euphonium or baritone and a valved trombone in the same instrument. Such duplex instruments in several sizes were first made in Europe in the mid-19th century. The double-belled euphonium was made in the U.S. from the 1880s until well into the 20th century. A fourth or fifth valve switches from one instrument to the other. R.E.E.

Eurhythmics. See Dalcroze method.

Euridice. (1) Opera in a prologue and six scenes by Jacopo Peri (libretto on the myth of Orpheus and Eurydice by Ottavio Rinuccini), produced in Florence in 1600. (2) Opera by Giulio Caccini (libretto by Rinuccini), published in 1600 and first produced in Florence in 1602.

Evangeliary [Lat. *evangeliarium*]. See Liturgical books.

Evangelist. In a *Passion, the narrator, whose text is taken from one of the Gospels.

Evangelium [Lat., Ger.]. Gospel.

Evensong. In medieval England, the canonical hour of Vespers. At the Reformation, the name was carried over into the Book of Common Prayer (B.C.P.) formally to designate what subsequently came to be called Evening Prayer: "An ordre for Evensong throughout the yere" (B.C.P., 1549); "An ordre for Evening prayer throughout the yere" (B.C.P., 1552 and later). The informal use of the term Evensong has persisted nevertheless. See also Anglican church music. R.F.F.

Evirato [It.]. **Castrato*.

Evovae. See *Euouae.*

Exaquier [Fr.]. *Chekker.

Exchange of voices. See Voice exchange.

Exequiae [Lat.], **Exequien** [Ger.]. Exequies, i.e., a funeral service.

Exposition. (1) In *sonata form, the first major section, incorporating at least one important modulation to the dominant or other secondary key and presenting the principal thematic material. (2) In a *fugue, the statement of the subject in imitation by the several voices; especially the first such statement, with which the fugue begins.

Expression. (1) With respect to works of music, the representation or conveying of something, usually something beyond the work itself such as a nonmusical idea or emotion, and often something about the composer (thus making it self-expression on the part of the composer). Whether music has the power of such expression and, if so, what the nature and status of musical expression might be, have been central questions of musical *aesthetics. In current use, the term is often employed to distinguish music that is thought to have some direct emotional appeal to listeners from music regarded as more "abstract" or "intellectual." This distinction may be carried to the point of regarding the music of whole periods as largely not expressive. Such a view fails to take account of the extent to which perceptions of expression and emotion in music are culturally and historically determined.

(2) With respect to musical performance, those qualities thought to derive from the activity of the performer as distinct from the pitches and rhythms of the composition itself, hence the term *expression marks for many types of *performance marks. Its domains are thus dynamics, tempo, and articulation. In this sense, the term does not necessarily imply that anything in particular is being expressed, though some connection with emotion, even if undefined, is usually presumed. The expression in question is often thought to be self-expression on the part of the performer. Underlying this sense is a distinction between musical notation and nuance of which notation is regarded as incapable. The musical notation of every period, however, must be interpreted in the light of a historically appropriate set of conventions [see Performance practice]. Thus, the distinction is not entirely tenable. Because notions of expression are so intimately bound up with music of the Romantic period and its performance, it has sometimes been thought that the absence of a particular kind of "expression" or nuance of performance represented a lack of nuance altogether and, conversely, that nuance of a type appropriate to music of the Romantic period constituted the only kind of "expressiveness" in performance.

Expressionism. A movement in German visual art and literature of the early 20th century. The term is sometimes applied to Germanic music of the period, especially that of Schoenberg and his school. The expressionists believed that art should reflect the inner consciousness of its creator: rather than produce a physically accurate depiction of a scene, the painter or writer should "express" his personal feelings toward it. Thus, a major feature of the expressionist style is a restructuring of external reality through exaggeration and distortion. The reliance on external representation increasingly weakened as expressionism developed, and by about 1910, the painter Wassily Kandinsky began producing the first completely nonobjective paintings.

Schoenberg's abandonment of tonality and triadic harmony suggests interesting correspondences with these developments. His tonal works of the early

1900s reveal an analogous tendency to produce extreme expressive effects through distortion of traditional harmonic structures, emphasis upon nontriadic tones, and avoidance of unambiguous tonal regions; and at almost the same time that Kandinsky turned to nonrepresentational painting, Schoenberg composed the first atonal works, breaking completely with the conventions of triadic harmony and the major-minor tonal system. Since Schoenberg knew Kandinsky and actively exchanged ideas with him during this critical period, the expressionist developments in the two arts are in fact explicitly tied to one another. (Schoenberg was, moreover, himself an amateur painter of considerable accomplishment and expressionist leaning.)

Schoenberg's *Erwartung* (1909), with its fragmented text depicting the extremes of psychic disintegration, eerie forest setting, and violently evocative music shorn of virtually all traces of traditional tonal, thematic, and formal conventions, is perhaps the purest embodiment of the expressionist aesthetic in music. Another typical manifestation is the tendency toward intense, highly charged miniatures evident in Schoenberg's own Piano Pieces op. 19 and in a number of works by Webern.

The most important precedents for musical expressionism occur in late Beethoven, Wagner, and Mahler. After World War I, the composers of the Second Viennese School tended to move away from the expressionist aesthetic. Although the movement had no direct historical heirs, expressionist compositions have had an especially important influence on musical developments after World War II, as well as in neo-Romantic tendencies found in much music of the later 20th century. R.P.M.

Expression marks. Symbols and words or phrases and their abbreviations employed along with musical notation to guide the performance of a work in matters other than pitches and rhythms. Such marks in general affect *dynamics, *tempo, and *articulation (including *bowing and *tonguing). The use of the term expression in this context is somewhat misleading, since whatever the nature of musical expression, it does not result exclusively or perhaps even principally from those aspects of music specified by "expression" marks. See Performance marks, Expression.

Expressive organ [Fr. *orgue expressif*]. A pressure-operated *harmonium.

Exsultet [Lat.]. See *Praeconium paschale.*

Extemporization. See Improvisation.

Extravaganza. (1) A musical work characterized by extravagant fancy, often with satirical or parodistic intent. The term was often used in 19th-century Britain and the U.S. for a genre of popular musical stage work descended from the burlesque and itself one of the ancestors of the modern musical comedy. It occurs as a subtitle in Gilbert and Sullivan's *Trial by Jury* and other works. (2) A lavish production.

Eye music [Ger. *Augenmusik*]. Music in which some purely graphic aspect of the notation conveys nonmusical meaning to the eye. Such techniques were used particularly in the 15th and 16th centuries, the most common being the use of blackened notes for texts expressing grief or lament. For example, Josquin's *lament on the death of Ockeghem, "Nymphes des bois," is written in black notes. Black notes were sometimes also used for individual words such as night, dark, and the like, especially in *madrigals of the second half of the 16th century by composers such as Luca Marenzio, though such effects are also encountered in sacred music. In the notation of the period, blackened notes generally represent a shift from duple to triple meter [see Mensural notation]. Hence, in modern transcriptions, such passages often appear as triplets. The term eye music is sometimes also applied to examples of *word painting such as the use of ascending or descending motion in conjunction with words such as up, down, heaven, and hell.

Bibl.: Alfred Einstein, *The Italian Madrigal,* 3 vols. (Princeton: Princeton U Pr, 1949; R: 1971), 1:234–44.

F

F. Abbr. (often in italics, *f*) for **forte.* See also Pitch names, Letter notation, Hexachord, Pitch, Clef, Sound hole.

Fa. See Pitch names, Solmization, Hexachord. *Fa fictum* is f″, i.e., the first pitch above the upper limit of the *gamut of medieval and Renaissance theory; it is therefore part of **musica ficta.* This pitch is sometimes indicated in early manuscripts and prints by what looks like a modern flat sign, which in this context merely instructed the performer to produce *fa,* i.e., F-natural, not F-flat.

Faberdon [Ger.]. (1) One voice of three (four?) named in a 15th-century poem describing Conrad Paumann playing the organ. The reference seems to be to improvisation, perhaps of something related to **fauxbourdon.* (2) A type of instrumental accompaniment to vocal music, as in Heinrich Schütz's *Historia der Aufferstehung Jesu Christi* (1623), probably related to the Baroque **falsobordone.*

Fabordón [Sp.]. (1) **Falsobordone.* (2) **Fauxbourdon.* The first mention of the technique in a Spanish source (Juan de Lucena's *Libro de vida beata,* from the mid-15th century) is disapproving.

Faburden. An English technique of polyphonic vocal improvisation, current from about 1430 until the Reformation in England and until the late 16th century in Scotland. Originally designating the lowest voice of such improvised polyphony, the term faburden was eventually applied to the technique itself and to the entire polyphonic complex [see also Burden (2)]. The original meaning is seen in titles of polyphonic vocal and keyboard pieces that are said to be "on the faburden" (e.g., John Redford's "O Lux on the faburden" and other pieces for organ).

In improvising faburden, singers would begin with a preexisting melody, usually a liturgical chant. This melody would be made the middle of three voices, and the others would be reckoned from it. One would consist of thirds and fifths below, another of parallel fourths above [see Sight]. Ends of phrases were slightly ornamented. The resulting sound, a series of sixth chords with an occasional octave harmonized by a fifth, is similar to that of Continental **fauxbourdon,* which, however, was principally a written technique. In addition, whereas in *fauxbourdon* the preexisting melody was placed in the upper voice, in faburden (at least in England) it was thought of as the middle voice.

Most of what is known of faburden comes from theoretical treatises (such as the anonymous mid-15th-century *The Sight of Faburdon* in *GB-Lbm* Lansdowne 763), indentures of choirmasters, and other literary documents, not from written music. Still, some single-line faburdens (in the original sense) survive in chant books; in rare cases an entire faburden setting was written down in a type of shorthand evidently intended as a performance guide; and some composed pieces show evidence of the style. Literary evidence suggests that the technique was used even by relatively unskilled musicians.

Bibl.: Manfred Bukofzer, *Geschichte des englischen Diskants und des Fauxbourdons nach den theoretischen Quellen* (Strasbourg: Heitz, 1936). Thrasybulos Georgiades, *Englische Diskanttraktate aus der ersten Hälfte des 15. Jahrhunderts* (Munich: Musikwissenschaftliches Seminar der Universität München, 1937). Denis Stevens, "Processional Psalms in Faburden," *MD* 9 (1955): 105–10. Frank Ll. Harrison, *Music in Medieval Britain* (London: Routledge & Kegan Paul, 1958). Id., "Faburden in Practice," *MD* 16 (1962): 11–34. Ernest H. Sanders, "Cantilena and Discant in 14th-Century England," *MD* 16 (1965): 7–52. See also *Fauxbourdon.*

Facile, facilmente [It.]. Simple, simply.

Fackeltanz [Ger., fr. *Fackel,* torch]. A slow torchlight procession forming part of 19th-century Prussian court ceremonies. Spontini, Meyerbeer, and Flotow composed music for such processions.

Fado, fadinho [Port.]. Since the 19th century, the most characteristic genre of urban popular song of Portugal, especially in Lisbon, though it is cultivated in other cities and in the country as well. It is sung in cafés and in the streets to the accompaniment of the guitar and related instruments. Its texts are strophic, and many are in the nature of ballads. Melodies are in duple meter over tonic, dominant, and subdominant harmonies for the most part. Its origins are in dispute.

Bibl.: Rodney Gallop, "The Fado (The Portuguese Song of Fate)," *MQ* 19 (1933): 199–213. Mascarenhas Barreto and George Dykes, *Fado: Lyrical Origins and Poetic Motivation* (Lisbon: Aster, 197?).

Fa fictum [Lat.]. See *Fa.*

Fag. [Ger., It.]. Abbr. for **Fagott, *fagotto.*

Fagott [Ger.]. (1) *Bassoon. (2) An organ reed stop with half-length, flared resonators.

Fagottgeige [Ger.; It. *viola di fagotto*]. In the 17th and 18th centuries, a viola tuned like a cello and played on the arm. Its name derived from its use of overspun strings that produced a buzzing sound similar to that of the bassoon. Leopold Mozart (1756) reports that it was sometimes called a *Handbassel.*

Fagotto [It.]. *Bassoon; *fagottino,* *tenoroon; *fagottone,* contrabassoon.

Fagottzug [Ger.]. A stop on some harpsichords and pianos of the 18th and early 19th centuries, producing a bassoonlike, buzzing sound by bringing a strip of parchment or paper into contact with certain of the strings.

Fairy bells. See Bell harp.

Fairy Queen, The. A *semi-opera in a prologue and five acts by Purcell, the text of which is an anonymous adaptation of Shakespeare's *A Midsummer Night's Dream,* produced in London in 1692.

Fake-book. A collection of popular and jazz melodies with chord symbols (often rudimentary or simply incorrect) [see Fake-book notation] and sometimes words, used especially by musicians in restaurants, nightclubs, and the like as a basis from which to improvise or "fake" their own arrangements. While such books are often produced in violation of copyright laws, a series of legal fake-books were published from the 1970s forward that featured the harmonies indicated on a composer's lead sheet or taken from a canonical recording.

Fake-book notation. The symbols and abbreviations used to indicate the chords of jazz and popular music in *fake-books and elsewhere. Their use is not entirely standardized and may be ambiguous in some cases. Nothing is implied about the inversion or spacing of a chord unless a bass note is specifically indicated (usually by a slash followed by its letter name). The root of a chord is specified by the appropriate letter of the alphabet. A major triad is indicated by a capital letter; a minor triad by a lowercase letter or by the addition of "min," "m," or "−"; an augmented triad by "aug" or "+"; a dominant seventh chord (i.e., a major triad with a minor seventh above the root) by a 7; a minor seventh chord (a minor triad with a minor seventh above the root) by "min 7" or "−7"; a major seventh chord (a major triad with a major seventh above the root) by "maj 7"; a diminished triad by "dim" or "°"; a diminished seventh chord by "dim 7" or "°7"; a half-diminished seventh chord (a diminished triad with a minor seventh above the root) by "ø7." A triad with a sixth added above the root is indicated by a 6, and ninth, eleventh, and thirteenth chords by the numerals 9, 11, and 13, respectively. In each of these cases, the topmost pitch may be specified as raised (by "♯" or "+") or lowered (by "♭" or "−") as compared with the major sixth, ninth, and thirteenth and the perfect eleventh that would ordinarily be formed above the root.

Fa-la, fa-la-la. Nonsense syllables that recur in some types of 16th-century song, especially the **balletto,* and thus pieces of this type, such as Thomas Morley's "Now is the month of Maying."

Falsa [Sp., Port.]. Dissonance. For *tiento de falsas,* see *Tiento* and *Toccata di durezze e ligature.*

Falsa musica [Lat.]. See *Music ficta.*

False. False cadence, deceptive *cadence; false relation, *cross relation; false fifth (triad), diminished fifth (triad). See also Modulation.

Falsetto [It.; Fr. *fausset;* Ger. *Falsett, Fistelstimme;* Sp. *falsete*]. The male voice above its normal range, the latter usually called full or chest voice. It entails a special method of voice production that is frequently used by tenors to extend the upper limits of their range. Male *altos or countertenors use only this method of voice production. The falsetto voice has a distinctly lighter quality and is less powerful than the full voice. The practice of using male falsettists for the upper parts in vocal polyphony, especially the alto, is well documented, along with the term falsetto itself, from the 16th century. Until the widespread introduction of women in church choirs in the 19th century, however, soprano parts were often sung by boys. In opera of the 17th and 18th centuries, male soprano parts were sung by **castrati.* Through at least the 1830s, operatic tenors normally sang falsetto in the upper register. Only in England has the tradition of male altos singing falsetto remained alive. The use of falsetto voice is a prominent feature of some types of black American popular music, from which it and much else were taken up by rock musicians generally.

Falsobordone [It.; Sp. *fabordón*]. In its most characteristic form, a four-part, homophonic, vocal harmonization of a *psalm tone or similar liturgical chant, which may be placed in the tenor or in the uppermost part. It differs from **fauxbourdon,* from which, because of the similarity of the names, it has sometimes been thought to derive, in that all four parts are written out and root-position triads predominate. It is often sung in alternation with chant [see *Alternatim*], principally for Psalm verses, the *Magnificat, and the *Lamentations. The earliest examples come from late 15th-century Italy, Spain, and Portugal. Most popular on the Continent around 1600, *falsobordone* has continued in use to the present day and has influenced the styles of other sorts of music. In England it has survived as *Anglican chant.

In the later Renaissance and the Baroque, *falsibordoni* were composed for more or fewer voices, with or without instrumental accompaniment. The chant might be omitted or treated freely. In addition, the genre gave rise to solo songs and purely instrumental pieces, such as the **glosas* of Antonio de Cabezón (1510–66), often with substantial embellishment. Baroque vocal *falsibordoni,* whether choral or solo, generally include basso continuo.

Bibl.: Murray C. Bradshaw, *The Falsobordone, MSD* 34 (1978).

Falstaff. Opera in three acts by Verdi (libretto by Arrigo Boito based on Shakespeare's *The Merry Wives of Windsor* and *King Henry IV*), produced in Milan in 1893. Setting: Windsor, early 15th century.

Familiar style [It. *stile familiare*]. A style employing four-part vocal, syllabic, *homorhythmic texture such as characterizes simple hymn settings or **falsobordone*. The term was used in the 16th century and was given renewed currency by Giuseppe Baini (1775–1844), the biographer and editor of Palestrina.

Fanciulla del West, La [It., The Girl of the Golden West]. Opera in three acts by Puccini (libretto by Guelfo Civinini and Carlo Zangarini based on a play by David Belasco), produced in New York in 1910. Setting: a California mining camp during the gold rush of the late 1840s.

Fancy. The 16th- and 17th-century English manifestation of the *fantasia [see especially Fantasia II].

Fandango [Sp.]. A dance and dance-song of Spain in a moderately fast triple meter, appearing first in the early 18th century. Examples for keyboard by Soler and Domenico Scarlatti are characterized by regular alternation, in a minor key, of a measure of tonic and a measure of dominant harmony supporting a steadily unfolding upper part of improvisatory character. Sections may conclude on the dominant (also described as the tonic in the E or Phrygian mode of much Spanish folk music; see also *Flamenco*). A melody with elements (including a phrase beginning with the subdominant) shared by Scarlatti's piece was employed by Gluck in the ballet *Don Juan* (1761) and in modified form by Mozart in the finale to act 3 of *Le nozze di Figaro* (1786). More recent examples in art music occur in Rimsky-Korsakov's *Capriccio espagnol* (1887), Granados's *Goyescas* (no. 3, 1912), and Falla's *Sombrero de tres picos* (1919). The folk dance of this name, which is widely disseminated and includes regional variants such as the **malagueña* (from Málaga), *granadina* (Granada), *murciana* (Murcia), and *rondeña* (Ronda), is danced by a couple with castanets and accompanied by guitars, and it includes sung couplets, similar to those of the **jota,* in alternation with instrumental interludes.

Fanfare. (1) Music played by trumpets or other brass instruments, sometimes accompanied by percussion, for ceremonial purposes, especially to call attention to the arrival of a dignitary or to the beginning of a public ceremony; also termed a flourish, as in the "Ruffles and Flourishes" played by military bands in the U.S. to announce the arrival of the President. The term is sometimes extended to include military and hunting signals of similar character [see also Military music]. Since such music was historically performed on *natural instruments, it is often characterized by the use of pitches from a single harmonic series (e.g., c, c′, g′, c″, e″, g″). It has often been imitated in art music (as early as the 14th-century Italian **caccia*), and examples in opera include that for the arrival of the governor in the second act of Beethoven's *Fidelio.* Examples by 20th-century composers include Copland's *Fanfare for the Common Man* for brass and percussion (1942) and Stravinsky's *Fanfare for a New Theatre* for two trumpets (1964).

(2) [Fr.] A brass band.

Bibl.: Johann Ernst Altenburg, *Versuch einer Anleitung zur heroisch-musikalischen Trompeter- und Pauker-Kunst* (Halle, 1795); trans. Edward H. Tarr, *Essay on an Introduction to the Heroic and Musical Trumpeters' and Kettledrummers' Art* (Nashville: Brass Pr, 1974). Georg Schünemann, *Trompetenfanfaren, Sonaten und Feldstücke des 16.–17. Jahrhunderts, EDM,* 1st ser., 7 (1936).

Fantasia [It., fr. Gr. *phantasia,* product of the imagination; Eng. fantasia, fantasy, fancy; Fr. *fantaisie;* Ger. *Fantasie, Phantasie;* Sp. *fantasía*]. An ingenious and imaginative instrumental composition, often characterized by distortion, exaggeration, and elusiveness resulting from its departure from current stylistic and structural norms. Throughout its use, fantasia has often simply meant to improvise [Ger. *fantasieren,* It. *sonar di fantasia,* Sp. *tañer fantasía*]. By extension, it may be applied to a piece that attempts to give the impression of flowing spontaneously from a *player's* imagination and delight in performance. A fantasia may also be an esoteric work that evolves from a *composer's* technical manipulation and mental abstractions. This dichotomy is present in the earliest fantasias and may be observed occasionally in the fantasias of a single composer.

The fantasia has often borrowed antithetical formal procedures and styles, and an inexact use of terminology sometimes compounds the problems in musical definition. In the 16th century, the terms fantasia and *ricercar are often substituted for one another; since then, the fantasia has been equated with the *capriccio, *automaton,* *voluntary, *toccata, *canzona, **fuga,* *rhapsody, and other genres.

I. *The fantasia as quasi-improvisation.* Fantasia has often been used for pieces that attempt to capture the character improvisation as well as for didactic compositions by players wishing to illustrate the art. In their remarks on extemporaneous playing, Diego Ortiz (Rome, 1553), Tomás de Santa María (Valladolid, 1565), C. P. E. Bach (Berlin, 1753), and Carl Czerny (op. 200, Vienna, 1829; op. 300, Leipzig, ca. 1834)—all of whom use fantasia to mean improvisation—attach great importance to a thorough grasp of musical composition. In the Renaissance, this emphasis often resulted in rather sophisticated polyphony and in fantasias that incorporate the **Spagna* or a liturgical melody or the **Bergamasca* harmonies. Other fantasias of the period may use whole passages from vocal polyphony, sometimes in alternation with running passages of sequences [see *Glosa*]; *parody is more prominent in the fantasia than in other genres such as the ricercar and later canzona.

The Italian lutenist Francesco Canova da Milano (1497–1543) is the first master of the fantasia. His fantasias (ed. Ness, 1970) balance compositional methods drawn from vocal polyphony and the requirements of a purely instrumental idiom, employing the techniques of *cantus firmus,* parody, and *paraphrase. These processes may be seen in many later works by Enríquez de Valderrábano (fl. ca. 1550), Bálint Bakfark (1507–76), Giulio Cesare Barbetta (ca. 1540–after 1603), Vincenzo Galilei (ca. 1528–91), and John Dowland (1563–1626), as well as in the 120 or so lute fantasias (each followed by a *fuga*) in Elias Mertel's anthology (Strasbourg, 1615).

Keyboard fantasias, especially those by organists, have always tended toward learnedness, though the element of improvisation is strong in some works of Antonio Valente (Naples, 1576), Charles Guillet (Paris, 1610), the English virginalists (who emphasize *divisions), and Jan Pieterszoon Sweelinck (1562–1621). Their fantasias often range far afield harmonically and may begin with imitation or an ostinato, contrast a dancelike section, and dissolve into a toccatalike close. The Sweelinck tradition was cultivated in the Baroque by central Europeans such as Samuel Scheidt (1587–1654), Johann Jacob Froberger (1616–67), Johann Pachelbel (1653–1706), and Gottlieb Muffat (1690–1770), who brought elements of the concerto, solo and trio sonata, and French overture into their fantasias, sometimes using them as preludes to fugues or sets of dances.

North German composers of the 18th century increased the sense of improvisational freedom in works that owe much to vocal recitative and to the lute and harpsichord *tombeau,* with its plaintive harmonies and rhythmic flexibility. The contrasting moods, sudden deceptive cadences, instrumental recitative, and bold modulations of J. S. Bach's *Chromatic Fantasy and Fugue* BWV 903 illustrate the type. C. P. E. Bach and his father's other students extended it still further by abandoning the bar line and regular meter.

Although the unmeasured fantasia did not survive the post-Bach generation, many features survive in Mozart's Fantasia in C minor K. 457 (1786, intended to preface the Sonata K. 475) and Schubert's Fantasia in C minor D. 2e (1811, with quotations from Mozart's). The *Phantasie* op. 77 by Beethoven (1810), which ends in the key of the raised mediant (moving from G minor to B major), recalls Czerny's prescription for improvising by beginning in one key and proceeding to another with bold and strange modulations. Beethoven's *Choral Fantasy* op. 80, with its opening improvisation—not written down until after the first performance—and its variations on a preexistent lied, both reflects older features of the fantasia and looks forward to the Romantic period.

II. *The fantasia as learned polyphony.* Early ensemble fantasias by Heinrich Isaac (ca. 1450–1517), Ludwig Senfl (ca. 1486–ca. 1543), Giuliano Tiburtino (ca. 1510–69), Adrian Willaert (ca. 1490–1562), and others have subjects from solmization syllables, transformed inventively and elaborated contrapuntally. This tradition ultimately resulted in works of considerable ingenuity by Giaches de Wert (1535–96), Orazio Vecchi (1550–1605), Adriano Banchieri (1568–1634), and Girolamo Frescobaldi (1583–1643) in Italy; Diomedes Cato (before 1570–after 1607) in Poland; Sweelinck in the Low Countries; Eustache Du Caurroy (1549–1609) and Charles Racquet (1597–1664) in France; and William Byrd (1543–1623), John Bull (ca. 1562–1628), John Coprario (ca. 1575–1626), Orlando Gibbons (1583–1625), and John Jenkins (1592–1678) in England. Frescobaldi's fantasias of 1608 illustrate such techniques: twelve fantasias (three each with one, two, three, and four subjects, often sounded simultaneously at the beginning) move progressively through all modes, and the hexachordal and chromatic subjects are augmented, diminished, inverted, and treated to nearly continuous transformation by means of rhythmic distortion, fragmentation, **inganno,* and changes of meter and tempo.

Although the fantasia virtually disappeared in Italy after about 1620, it became central to the chamber music of France and England and the organ music of Germany. The ensemble fancy, which was cultivated in England, especially, and on the Continent, extends from conservative works for consort to works in triosonata texture. Many ensemble fancies strikingly contrast canons and other contrapuntal procedures with "lighter humours" of dance rhythms and harmonic ostinatos, folklike melodies, and chordal "echos." Later English fancies serve as preludes to suites of dances by Coprario, William Lawes (1602–45), Jenkins, and Christopher Gibbons (1615–76). Although Lawes, Louis Couperin (ca. 1626–61), Marin Marais (1656–1728), and especially Henry Purcell (1659–95) each contributed fine specimens, in France and England the fantasia succumbed to arid learnedness. Du Caurroy, Antoine Du Cousu (ca. 1600–58), and Etienne Moulinié (ca. 1600–after 1669) used it to expound upon theoretical controversies, pushing it to an austerity that caused it to be prescribed as the only type of music worthy of performance before the Académie.

In 17th-century Germany, the type of fantasia cultivated by Frescobaldi and Sweelinck survived in the keyboard works of Scheidt, Heinrich Scheidemann (ca. 1595–1663), Froberger, Pachelbel, and others, some of whom also wrote in the improvisatory idiom. J. S. Bach's seven fantasias for organ and eight for harpsichord include both types. The Fantasia in G minor BWV 917, with its thematic fragmentation and three *soggetti* (announced simultaneously in the Frescobaldian manner), the hexachordal Fantasia in G major BWV 572, and the binary Fantasia in C minor BWV 906 are last flourishings of the learned polyphonic fantasia, the substance of which was being taken over in the fugue.

III. *The fantasia after the 18th century.* The 19th and early 20th centuries were inundated with fantasias, capriccios, and rhapsodies that draw upon popular songs, pseudo-folk melodies, and patriotic airs to evoke exotic landscapes, or that quote themes from familiar operas. These range from modest salon pieces to virtuoso vehicles by and for showmen such as violinists Paganini, Bériot, Vieuxtemps, and Sarasate and pianists Thalberg, Gottschalk, Satter, and Tausig, as well as for ubiquitous cornet and piccolo band soloists. The genre also reflected important manifestations of musical Romanticism, as in works for piano by Chopin (Fantaisie op. 49, 1841; Polonaise-Fantaisie op. 61, 1845–46), for violin by Bruch (*Schottische Fantasie* op. 46, 1880), and for orchestra by Tchaikovsky (*Capriccio italien* op. 45, 1880), Rimsky-Korsakov (*Fantasia on Two Russian Themes* op. 33, 1886–87), and Richard Strauss (*Aus Italien* op. 16, 1886). John Field (*Nouvelle fantaisie,* 1833), Smetana (*Fantasie concertante,* 1862), and Busoni (*Indianische Fantasie,* 1913) contributed substantial works for piano. Liszt was the consummate master of the potpourri, particularly in his operatic fantasias, capriccios, and *paraphrases de concert.*

Other 19th-century works fuse the fantasia with the sonata. Such a *sonata quasi fantasia* deviates from the formal norms of the Classical sonata by joining movements together, rearranging their internal sequence, recalling previous ideas, or altering normal tonal and thematic relationships. Early works are by Haydn (Hob. XVII:4, 1789), Beethoven (op. 27, nos. 1 and 2, 1802), Anton Eberl (op. 28, 1805), and Hummel (op. 18, 1805). Following Schubert's influential *Wanderer-fantasie* (D. 760, 1823), many fantasies favored thematic transformation over development, such as Mendelssohn's op. 15 (1827, on an Irish song) and op. 28 (1834, subtitled *Sonate écoissaise* and probably modeled on Beethoven's op. 27, no. 2), Schumann's op. 17 (1836–38, with quotations from a Beethoven lied), and Liszt's *Après une lecture du Dante, fantasia quasi sonata* (ca. 1843).

Orchestral fantasias using the sonata principle include the first version of Schumann's Symphony in D minor and a number on Shakespearean and other dramatic inspirations by Berlioz (*Fantaisie sur la Tempête de Shakespeare,* 1830), Tchaikovsky (*Romeo and Juliet,* 1869–80), and others. Sets of short ternary *Phantasiestücke* with widely varying moods and occasional programmatic titles such as "caprice," "night," and "soaring" represent another extreme in the Romantic fantasia. Examples include Mendelssohn's *Trois fantaisies ou caprices* op. 16 (1829); Chopin's *Fantaisie-Impromptu* op. 66 (1835); Schumann's important *Phantasiestücke* op. 12 (1832–37), his op. 88 for piano trio (1842), and his op. 73 for clarinet and piano (1849); Brahms's op. 116 for piano (1892); and Charles Griffes's *Fantasy Pieces* op. 6 (1912–15). During the late 19th and early 20th centuries, there was a modest vogue for concerto fantasias that are closer in spirit and form to the symphonic fantasia than to the potpourri. Examples include works by Anton Rubinstein (op. 84, ca. 1886), Widor (op. 62, 1889), Debussy (1889–90), and Fauré (op. 111, 1919).

The 20th-century fantasia summarizes many historical features of the fantasia, ranging from the thematic abstraction, *B-A-C-H,* in Busoni's *Fantasia contrappuntistica* (1910–12) to the evocative *Fantasia on "Greensleeves"* (1934) by Vaughan Williams and the *Fantasía baetica* (1922) by Falla; from the potpourri-like Brazilian exoticisms of Milhaud's *Cinema-fantaisie: Le boeuf sur le toit* (1919) to the subsurface distortions in Schoenberg's *Phantasie für Violine* (1949).

Bibl.: Denis Stevens, "Purcell's Art of Fantasia," *ML* 33 (1952): 341–45. John M. Ward, "The Use of Borrowed Material in 16th-Century Instrumental Music," *JAMS* 5 (1952): 88–98. Margarete Reimann, "Zur Deutung des Begriffs Fantasia," *AfMw* 10 (1953): 253–74. Albert Cohen, "The Fantaisie for Instrumental Ensemble in 17th-Century France," *MQ* 48 (1962): 234–47. John M. Ward, "Parody Technique in 16th-Century Instrumental Music," *Sachs,* 1965, pp. 208–28. Dietrich Kämper, *Studien zur instrumentalen Ensemblemusik des 16. Jahrhunderts in Italien, AnMca* 10 (1970). Arthur J. Ness, ed., *The Lute Music of Francesco Canova da Milano,* Harvard Publications in Music 3–4 (Cambridge, Mass.: Harvard U Pr, 1970). Peter Schleuning, *Die Fantasie,* 2 vols., *Mw* 42–43 (Cologne: A Volk, 1971; trans. Eng., 1971). Willi Apel, *The History of Keyboard Music,* trans. and rev. Hans Tischler (Bloomington: Ind U Pr, 1972). Peter Schleuning, *Die Freie Fantasie: Ein Beitrag zur Erforschung der klassischen Klaviermusik* (Göppingen: A Kümmerle, 1973). Gregory G. Butler, "The Fantasia as Musical Image," *MQ* 60 (1974): 602–15. A.J.N.

Fantasiestück [Ger.]. See Fantasia III.

Fantastic Symphony. See *Symphonie fantastique.*

Fantasy. (1) *Fantasia, fancy. (2) The development section of a work in *sonata form.

Farandole [Fr.; Prov. *farandoulo*]. A dance of Provence performed by a chain of alternating men and women who follow the leader in a variety of winding patterns, sometimes passing under the raised arms of couples from the chain. The music is usually in moderate 6/8 and is played on the *pipe and tabor. The dance is thought to have its origins in classical antiquity (Sachs, 1937). It occurs in operas by Bizet (*L'arlésienne,* 1872) and Gounod (*Mireille,* 1864).

Bibl.: Curt Sachs, *World History of the Dance,* trans. Bessie Schönberg (New York: Norton, 1937). Jean Baumel, *Les danses populaires, les farandoles, les rondes, les jeux chorégraphiques et les ballets du Languedoc méditerranéen* (Paris: La grande revue, 1958).

Farce [Fr., Eng., Ger.; It., Sp. *farsa*]. (1) A work of theater characterized by low comedy, often satirical, sometimes obscene, and frequently making use of sudden appearances and other visual humor; also humor of the type found in such works. The first works bearing the term occur in 15th-century France. (2) In 18th-century Italian opera, a comic scene interpolated into a serious work. The term was also used in the 18th century for comic operas performed, like *intermezzi, between the acts of an opera or as an afterpiece. By the 19th century, *farsa* no longer signified an interpolated work, but still indicated an opera normally in one act and often comic. Examples include Rossini's *La cambiale di matrimonio* (Venice, 1810) and *L'inganno felice* (Venice, 1812).

Farewell Symphony. Popular name for Haydn's Symphony no. 45 in F♯ minor Hob. I:45 (1772). The title stems from an episode recounted by Haydn and refers to the design of the closing section of the last movement, which permits players to leave one by one, concluding with only two violins. This jest was intended to dissuade Prince Esterházy, whom Haydn served as conductor and composer, from further prolonging his stay in the palace at Esterháza, allowing the members of the orchestra to return to their families in Eisenstadt instead.

Farse [Lat. *farsa*]. A Latin or vernacular interpolation in a liturgical chant or text, especially in an epistle or other reading; a *trope.

Fasola [contr. of fa-sol-la]. An early English system of *solmization, later called sol-fa or Lancashire sol-fa, in use from the end of the 16th century. Fasola, utilizing only the four syllables *fa–sol–la–mi,* is thus an abridged reconception of the hexachordal system *ut–re–mi–fa–sol–la* commonly attributed to Guido of Arezzo (11th cent.) [see Hexachord].

In fasola, the four syllables, "sufficient for expressing the several sounds, and less burthensome for the memory of Practitioners" (John Playford, *An Introduction to the Skill of Musick,* London, 1654), are employed as shown:

fa	sol	la	fa	sol	la	mi	fa
c	d	e	f	g	a	b	c

Every major scale is composed of the trichord *fa–sol–la* and the tetrachord *fa–sol–la–mi.* In minor, the basic scale becomes *la–mi–fa–sol–la–fa–sol–la.*

Fasola is an early replacement, moving toward what will later be called movable *do,* for the traditional hexachord system as it began to break down in the 16th century. Its attractiveness also lay in its ability easily to effect key changes moving through the circle of fifths; i.e., moving toward the sharp side of the circle, *fa* is raised a semitone and becomes *mi;* moving toward the flat side, *mi* is lowered a semitone and becomes *fa.* See also Shape-note. R.F.F.

Fastoso [It.]. Pompous.

Faust. Opera in five acts by Gounod (libretto by Jules Barbier and Michel Carré, after Goethe's *Faust* part 1), produced in Paris in 1859. It was produced with recitatives instead of spoken dialogue in Strasbourg in 1860 and with the further addition of ballet at the Paris Opéra in 1869. Setting: Germany in the 16th century.

Faust-Symphonie, Eine [Ger., A Faust Symphony]. An orchestral work by Liszt (completed in 1857, though revised at various times thereafter) in three movements described by the composer as "character sketches" of Faust, Gretchen, and Mephistopheles, respectively. The last movement includes a setting for tenor, men's chorus, and orchestra of the final words of Goethe's drama.

Fauvel, Roman de. A long poem by Gervais du Bus that was completed in 1316 and is an allegorical satire of the church (the character Fauvel being a horse). One of the surviving copies (Paris, Bibliothèque nationale, fr. 146), also probably not later than 1316, includes numerous textual and musical interpolations added by Chaillou de Pesstain. The more than 100 musical additions, some bearing directly on the poem, include motets, *lais, ballades, rondeaux,* sequences, *conductus,* refrains, and liturgical chants. Among these are works by Philippe de Vitry and others deriving from the repertory of *Notre Dame.

Fauxbourdon [Fr.]. A 15th-century French technique of composition, employed in short pieces or sections within longer pieces. Two voices are notated, the upper a **cantus prius factus* (usually sacred) an octave higher than ordinary plainchant, the lower forming sixths and octaves below. The words *faux bourdon* or some variant thereof appear at the beginning of the piece or section, usually near the lower part. (This label may be lacking in some copies.)

In the earliest and most widely accepted method of realization, a third voice paralleling the upper part at the fourth below is added in performance. Thus, three voices sound where parts for only two are written out. After about 1450, a method for making four voices from the notated two was sometimes used. The two added voices were both figured from the lower written part, one alternating thirds and fifths below, beginning and ending with a unison or octave, the other alternating thirds and fourths above, beginning and ending with a fifth.

The earliest occurrence of the term *faux bourdon* inscribed on a musical composition is in the older section (finished ca. 1430) of *I-Bc* Q15, on the last item of Dufay's *Missa Sancti Jacobi,* the communion "Vos qui secuti estis me." Only a few compositions from outside the 15th century were originally designated *faux bourdon,* although theorists of the next several centuries mention the term, increasingly confusing it with **falso bordone.*

Although present knowledge of *fauxbourdon* necessarily rests in large part on written compositions, the technique was also used in extemporizing harmonizations of plainchant. This practice was referred to by Guillelmus Monachus and probably implied by a musical example given by Tinctoris in the late 15th century. In such improvisation, the preexisting melody is in the tenor, whereas in written *fauxbourdon* it is in the upper voice.

The relationship of *fauxbourdon* to the English *faburden has been debated extensively, but no thoroughly convincing explanation has yet been advanced. The terms and the practices, although evidently related, probably should be distinguished. As both *fauxbourdon* and faburden arose at roughly the same time, it is not possible to say definitely which was the earlier; evidence advanced to date, however, suggests that *fauxbourdon* developed first.

Bibl.: Heinrich Besseler, "Der Ursprung des Fauxbourdons," *Mf* 1 (1948): 106–12. Id., *Bourdon und Fauxbourdon* (Leipzig: Breitkopf & Härtel, 1950); 2nd ed., ed. Peter Gülke (1974). Manfred F. Bukofzer, "Fauxbourdon Revisited," *MQ* 38 (1952): 22–47. Heinrich Besseler, "Das Ergebnis der Diskussion über 'Fauxbourdon,'" *AM* 29 (1957): 185–88. Suzanne Clercx, "Aux Origines du Faux-Bourdon," *RdM* 40 (1957): 151–65. Ernest Trumble, *Fauxbourdon: An Historical Survey* (Brooklyn: Institute of Mediaeval Music, 1959). Id., "Authentic and Spurious Faburden," *RBM* 14 (1960): 3–29. Ernst Apfel, "Nochmals zum Fauxbourdon (Faburden) bei Guilelmus Monachus," *Mf* 19 (1966): 284–88. Ann B. Scott, "The Beginnings of Fauxbourdon: A New Interpretation," *JAMS* 24 (1971): 345–63. Dagmar Hoffmann-Axthelm, "Faburdon/fauxbourdon/falso bordone," *HMT.*

Favola d'Orfeo, La [It., The Fable of Orpheus; also *L'Orfeo*]. Opera *(favola in musica)* in a prologue and five acts by Monteverdi (libretto by Alessandro Striggio on the myth of Orpheus and Eurydice), produced in Mantua in 1607. See also *Euridice.*

Favorita [It.]. An Italian popular dance of the 16th and 17th centuries in a compound duple meter, based on the harmonic pattern of the **romanesca,* but with a reduction of rhythmic values. In a 6/8 meter, one harmony of the *romanesca* normally covers a complete measure, whereas in the *Favorita,* it covers a half-measure. The earliest settings are in lute tablatures from the middle of the 16th century. Examples also occur in one keyboard collection (Chigi manuscripts, *CEKM* 32, 1968, vol. 3, p. 38) and numerous guitar tablatures of the 17th century.

Bibl.: Lawrence H. Moe, "Dance Music in Printed Italian Lute Tablatures from 1507 to 1611" (Ph.D. diss., Harvard Univ., 1956), pp. 160–62 and 244–47). L.H.M.

Fe fa ut, Fefaut. See Hexachord.

Feierlich [Ger.]. Solemn.

Feldmusik [Ger.]. In the 17th and 18th centuries, music for winds to be played out-of-doors; also a band of musicians who perform out-of-doors. Such music was at first military *fanfares for trumpets. The term was later extended to include all outdoor wind music such as pieces termed *Parthia* or *Feldparthie* [see Partita (3)].

Feldparthie [Ger.]. See Partita (3).

Felix namque [Lat.]. An offertory for certain feasts of the Virgin Mary (*LU,* p. 1271, but see especially the version preserved in the *Sarum rite) that served as the *cantus firmus* for numerous organ and virginal works by English composers of the 15th and 16th centuries, including Redford, Thomas Preston, Blitheman, Shelby, Tallis, and Thomas Tomkins. One source of such pieces is the *Fitzwilliam Virginal Book. Some examples omit the intonation that sets the word "Felix." The earliest example dates from around 1400 (Dart, 1954).

Bibl.: Thurston Dart, "A New Source of Early English Organ Music," *ML* 35 (1954): 201–5.

Feminine cadence. See Masculine, feminine cadence.

Feria [Lat.]. (1) In classical antiquity, a festival day. (2) In the usage of the Roman and other Latin rites, any day of the week except Saturday and Sunday on which no feast falls [see Liturgy], Monday through Friday being numbered two through six, respectively. The adjective ferial (in contradistinction to festal) is used with reference to the liturgy for any day (including Saturday and Sunday) on which no feast falls.

Fermata [It., also *corona;* Fr. *point d'orgue;* Ger. *Fermate;* Sp. *fermata, calderón*]. The symbol 𝄐, placed over a note or rest to indicate that it is to be prolonged beyond its normal duration (usually with a suspension of the regular metrical pulse) or placed over a bar or double-bar line to indicate the end of a phrase or section of a work; also called a pause or hold. In a *concerto, it marks the point at which the soloist is to play a *cadenza.

Ferne [Ger.]. Distance; *wie aus der Ferne,* as if from a distance.

Fernflöte [Ger.]. A soft flute stop sometimes found in *Echo divisions of electric-action organs.

Fernwerk [Ger.]. *Echo (5).

Fes, feses [Ger.]. F-flat, F-double-flat. See Pitch names.

Festal. Pertaining to a day on which a feast occurs [see also *Feria*].

Festa teatrale [It.]. A courtly musico-dramatic entertainment written and performed to commemorate a notable royal or dynastic event such as a birth, baptism, wedding, birthday, or name day. The subject was usually mythological or allegorical. The genre was cultivated in the 17th and 18th centuries at the Hapsburg court in Vienna and at various Italian courts.

Feste romane [It., Roman Festivals]. A symphonic poem by Respighi, composed in 1928, in four movements: "Circenses" (Circus Maximus Games), "Il giubileo" (The Jubilee), "L'ottobrata" (October Festival), "La Befana" (The Epiphany).

Festoso [It.]. Festive.

Festschrift [Ger.]. A collection of articles by colleagues and pupils issued as a tribute to a scholar (in English often with a title such as *Essays in Honor of . . .*, or in French, *Mélanges offerts à . . .*). Normally, the publication is on the occasion of a landmark birthday, e.g., 60th, 65th, or 70th, and contains articles on a variety of topics and often a bibliography of the honored scholar's writings. It is usually a separate publication, though it can be a special issue or volume of a periodical. The earliest Festschrift for a musicologist was published in 1909 for Hugo Riemann on his 60th birthday. Other, less common, types of Festschriften are (a) a collection of a scholar's previously published and unpublished articles; (b) a memorial volume for a composer, issued on an anniversary of his or her birth or death; (c) a volume honoring an organization or institution; and (d) messages of appreciation and sometimes brief compositions, issued as an homage to a well-known composer or performer. The contents of (c) and (d) are often not scholarly in nature. Festschriften are indexed in Walter Gerboth, *An Index to Musical Festschriften and Similar Publications* (New York: Norton, 1969). A later checklist is in *MGG* 16 (1979): 221–69. Analytical indexing of music Festschriften continues in *RILM*. H.E.S.

Festspiel [Ger.]. Festival.

Feuer [Ger.]. Fire, passion; *mit feuer, feurig,* with fire, passionate.

Ff. Abbr. (often in italics, *ff*) for *fortissimo* [see *Forte*].

F fa ut. See Hexachord.

F-hole. See Sound hole.

Fiato [It.]. Breath; *stromenti da fiato* or *fiati,* wind instruments.

Ficta [Lat.]. See *Musica ficta.*

Fiddle. (1) Any bowed stringed instrument. (2) The *violin, especially in colloquial usage. (3) [Lat. *viella, viola;* Fr. *vielle;* Ger. *Fi(e)del;* Sp. *vihuela de arco*] Any of a variety of medieval bowed stringed instruments, especially members of one of the two principal classes of such instruments (the other class being the medieval *viol). Even in the narrow sense that distinguishes the fiddle from the medieval viol, the term fiddle and its cognates are applied to a wide variety of instruments depicted in medieval art beginning in the 11th century. These are bowed instruments with bodies that may be elliptical or with slightly or deeply suppressed waists. They may have a pegdisc with frontal tuning pegs or a pegbox that is turned back and fitted with lateral pegs. The normal playing position was on the shoulder or arm, but instruments of this type are also shown being played upright in the lap, like the viol. See ill. under Violin.

Fiddling. Vernacular violin performance. In North America, Britain, Ireland, and Scandinavia, fiddling constitutes the most vigorous surviving folk music. The fiddle is physically the same as the violin (a notable exception: western Norway's Hardanger fiddle is a viola d'amore relative). However, desirable timbres may be nasal or otherwise piercing to suit the once primary function of fiddling, accompanying dances. Indeed, most fiddlers' repertoires focus on genres of bipartite dance tunes stemming from the 18th through early 20th centuries. However, the contest stage has become the central venue for most fiddle traditions during the last half-century. Fiddlers, while often musically literate, generally learn tunes through oral tradition, and usually play in styles specific to the regions in which they live. For instance, in Norway, a fiddler's ancestral home determines whether he or she will play the normal fiddle or **hardingfele* and which of the dozens of intimately local styles and repertoires the player will explore. In the U.S., style regions are more broadly defined: "old-timey" fiddlers in the Southeast perform rustic "breakdowns" in heterophony with banjos (which are played in a manner evoking 19th-century blackface minstrelsy), while fiddlers in Texas "contest" style vary their breakdowns, waltzes, polkas, and rags systematically and virtuosically.

Fidelio, oder Die eheliche Liebe [Ger., Fidelio, or Conjugal Love]. Opera in three acts by Beethoven, op. 72 (libretto by Josef Sonnleithner after Jean Nicolas Bouilly's *Léonore, ou L'amour conjugal*), first produced in Vienna in 1805 with **Leonore* Overture no. 2; revised in two acts (libretto recast by Stefan von Breuning) and produced in Vienna in 1806 with *Leonore* Overture no. 3; final version (libretto revised by Georg Friedrich Treitschke) produced in Vienna in 1814 with the *Fidelio* Overture. Setting: a state prison near Seville in the 18th century.

Fi(e)del [Ger.]. *Fiddle.

Field holler. Solo singing by blacks in the fields of the southern U.S. Observers in the 19th century describe free rhythmic patterns and falsetto cries. It is often cited among the likely forerunners of country *blues.

Fiero, fieramente [It.]. Proud, high-spirited, fierce.

Fife [Fr. *fifre;* Ger. *Querpfeife;* It. *piffero;* Sp. *pífano*]. A small *transverse flute of narrow cylindrical bore, used almost exclusively in military contexts and traditionally associated with infantry. Since ca. 1700 a small keyless form with six or more fingerholes, usually of wood, has been the most common.

The fife's military associations date from the 15th century, when Swiss infantry techniques, in which the instrument was used for signaling, were copied all over Europe [see Flute]. At this period no systematic distinction was made between the terms flute and fife, and the military instrument was typically about 2½ feet long and played with a drum of a similar diameter and depth. Examples of fife music from the 16th and 17th centuries indicate that players improvised using rapidly repeated scalewise figures in the high register. Reintroduced in a shorter form in the British army in ca. 1745, the fife became an emblem of the American War of Independence (1775–83), its repertoire consisting of marching tunes such as "Yankee Doodle." A vigorous revival of costumed colonial-type fife-and-drum corps took place in late 20th-century North America. A keyed fife known as the Basel piccolo is used in modern festivals in Switzerland, usually playing music in three parts taken from traditional, folk, and jazz styles. See ill. under Flute.

Bibl.: Ardal Powell, *The Flute* (New Haven: Yale U Pr, 2002). A.P.

Fifteenth. An organ stop of *Principal scale at 2′ pitch; so named in English and American organs.

Fifth. See Interval, Scale degrees, Circle of fifths, Parallel fifths.

Figlia del reggimento, La. See *Fille du régiment, La.*

Figura [Lat.]. (1) In *rhetoric, figure. (2) In the Middle Ages, a notational symbol. *Figurae simplices* (simple figures) are single notes such as the long and breve [see Mensural notation]; *figurae compositae* (composite figures) are *ligatures.

Figural, figurate, figured [Lat. *figuratus;* Fr. *figuré;* Ger. *figuriert;* It. *figurato;* Sp. *figurado*]. (1) In the 15th and 16th centuries, mensural music *(musica figurata)* and thus polyphony as distinct from plainsong *(musica plana).* (2) Florid counterpoint such as that codified in fifth-*species counterpoint; especially the florid polyphonic style of late-15th-century composers such as Ockeghem and Obrecht. (3) Music characterized by the use of *figuration. See also Figure, Figured bass, Figured chorale, Rhetoric.

Figuration. Stereotyped *motives or patterns ("figures") that are ornamental in character, at least implying if not actually resulting from the embellishment of simpler, underlying melody or harmony, as in *variations. Figuration may include *diminutions and various types of *ornamentation as well as more mechanical passage work consisting of scales and arpeggios.

Figure. (1) A *motive or pattern that is ornamental in character. See Figuration. (2) See Rhetoric. (3) A number placed below a bass part to indicate the accompanying harmony [see Thoroughbass].

Figured bass [Fr. *basse chiffrée;* Ger. *bezifferter Bass;* It. *basso figurato, cifrato;* Sp. *bajo cifrado*]. A bass part to which Arabic numbers ("figures") have been added to indicate the accompanying harmonies [see Thoroughbass]. The strict realization in four parts of figured basses is a regular feature of instruction in *harmony [see also Harmonic analysis].

Figured chorale. An *organ chorale in which a single motive or figure [see Figuration] is used continuously in the accompaniment to the chorale melody, which may itself remain largely unadorned. There are numerous examples in Bach's *Orgel-Büchlein,* e.g., "Ich ruf' zu dir."

Figures, doctrine of [Ger. *Figurenlehre*]. Any of various attempts made in the 17th and 18th centuries to codify music according to classes of musical figures thought to be analogous to the figures of *rhetoric.

Filar il suono [It.], **filer le son** [Fr.]. (1) In singing, to sustain a tone without interruption for breath and without a change in loudness; similarly in wind playing; in string playing, to sustain a tone without change of bow. (2) In the 18th century, **messa di voce.*

Fill. In jazz, a brief, animated drum solo interpolated between phrases of melody and interrupting a steady, accompanimental drum, usually to highlight phrase endings or other important structural points in a tune.

Fille du régiment, La [Fr., The Daughter of the Regiment]. Opera in two acts by Donizetti (libretto by Jules Henri Vernoy de Saint-Georges and Jean François Alfred Bayard), produced in Paris in 1840; revised in Italian (libretto by C. Bassi) with recitatives by Donizetti instead of spoken dialogue and produced in Milan in 1840. Setting: the Swiss Tyrol about 1815.

Film music. In film, music functioning either as a foreground event to which the visual component draws immediate attention or as a background and secondary event intended to reflect and support the mood or action of a scene. Both uses of music can and often do occur serially in a given film, yet they are clearly enough opposed to constitute a major generic distinction in films: the distinction between movie musicals and films with music. Only rarely have films attempted—as do *Ballet mécanique* (George Antheil, Dudley Murphy, France, 1924), *Windsong* (Harry Partch, Madeline Tourtelot, U.S.A., 1958), and *Hiroshima mon amour* (Alain Resnais, France/Japan, 1959)—to counterpoint the visual and auditory media or to treat narrative and musical discourse as equal partners in the tradition of 19th-century opera.

I. *Background.* Since 1895, when the Lumière brothers hired a pianist to accompany the first commercial projection of a film, the silence of a flickering screen has usually been answered by a solo instrument, by a small ensemble, or by an orchestra. Saint-Saëns (*L'assassinat du duc de Guise,* France, 1908) and Mikhail Ippolitov-Ivanov (*Stenka Razin,* Russia, 1908) were the first to compose scores expressly for film. Other well-known composers who contributed one or more scores to silent films include Mascagni (1915), Milhaud (1916), Charles Wakefield Cadman (1922), Honegger (1924), Sibelius (1926), and Hindemith (1927). But for the most part, silent films were accompanied by small groups, by piano, or by organ, from which emanated (a) medleys of popular tunes whose titles the player(s) associated with the action on the screen, or (b) pastiches either culled from the art-music repertory or written and improvised in styles popularly associated with that repertory. Max Winkler and S. M. Berg formed the most successful of several companies that provided these, along with associated cue sheets, for film palaces.

Early in the history of sound films, the major studios decided that it was cheaper to commission new music than to pay for copyrighted material. Subsequently, there aggregated in the large film centers groups of composers to write for their patrons fluent and occasionally distinguished scores in the established musical idioms of their period. Many composers of earlier film scores were Europeans cast by political events into a new land with economic priorities that did not favor the practice of their craft except in Hollywood. The facility of these professionals is reflected in their prolific outputs: Franz Waxmann (137 scores, 1933–66), Dmitri Tiomkin (104 scores, 1934–68), Miklós Rózsa (79 scores, 1937–73), Daniele Amfitheatrof (66 scores, 1939–65), and Erich Korngold (18 scores, 1935–56). Other important international composers for films include Max Steiner (189 film scores, 1916–65), Alfred Newman (153 scores, 1930–70), Georges Auric (52 scores, 1930–69), Bernard Herrmann (46 scores, 1941–75), Dmitri Shostakovich (23 scores, 1929–64), George Antheil (23 scores, 1935–57), Aaron Copland (10 scores, 1939–61), Sergei Prokofiev (6 scores, 1934–46), and Arthur Bliss (5 scores, 1935–54). In addition, dozens of unheralded composers like William Axt (63 scores, 1925–39) and Paul Sawtell (210 scores, 1941–70) scored the low-budget movies that once served the function now filled by television series.

The aesthetic distance between popular culture and European art music as well as the use of similar late-Romantic musical styles helped determine the nature and function of film background music during the 1930s and 40s. Before Alex North's jazz-inflected score to *A Streetcar Named Desire* (U.S.A., 1951), other idioms were excluded even from dramas set in contemporary urban locales. The first jazzy score to win wide public acceptance was Elmer Bernstein's score to *The Man with the Golden Arm* (U.S.A., 1956). Thereafter, composers like Henry Mancini and André Previn who could write in this idiom were in demand. Scores by mainstream jazz musicians are less common but include such distinguished examples as Duke Ellington's score for *Anatomy of a Murder* (U.S.A., 1959) and Charles Mingus's score for *Shadows* (U.S.A., 1960). Acceptance of jazz emboldened filmmakers to use other popular idioms specific to their film's locale or period: rock and roll in *The Blackboard Jungle* (U.S.A., 1955) and traditional country music in *Deliverance* (U.S.A., 1972). Only rarely, as in composer biographies, do films of the 1930s through the 1950s present classical music as a foreground event. But in films of the 1960s and since, growing musical sophistication has made possible its use as a specific, not generic, style, as in *2001: A Space Odyssey* (Johann Strauss, Richard Strauss, Gyorgi Ligeti), *All That Jazz* and *Kramer vs. Kramer* (Purcell, Vivaldi), *The Hotel New Hampshire* (Offenbach).

II. *Foreground.* Song can intensify narrative or highlight its critical junctures. It can also be used without narrative intent, as in vaudeville or the music revues of the early 20th century. Both narrative and nonnarrative foreground uses of song and dance are important components of film, especially between 1927 and 1942. One year after the invention of the Vitaphone process, *The Singing Fool* (U.S.A., 1928) produced the first soundtrack song to sell over a million records: Al Jolson singing "Sonny Boy." This was the only movie musical of its year, but in 1929 there were 32, and in 1930 there were 72 musical films. The most lavish of these (some in color) imitate vaudeville or Broadway revues. Beginning with *42nd Street* (U.S.A., 1932), movie musicals developed an indigenous style at the hands of director Busby Berkeley and with the assistance of songwriters imported from Broadway (Irving Berlin, Jerome Kern) or developed in Hollywood (Harry Warren, Harold Arlen). Such plots as there are feature aspiring artists who perform the music and dances that are these films' chief attraction. This premise remains popular in similar films of more recent vintage: *A Hard Day's Night* (Britain, 1964), *Saturday Night Fever* (U.S.A., 1978), *Rhinestone* (U.S.A., 1984).

Instrumental music, sometimes with a very singable melody, often has foreground status during the opening credits of a movie. These title tracks were already fully understood in the late 1930s, when Max Steiner wrote "Tara's Theme" for the opening credits of *Gone with the Wind* (U.S.A., 1939). The insertion of a theme song with lyrics into an otherwise instrumental score was spurred by the popular success of Dmitri Tiomkin's "Do Not Forsake Me Oh My Darlin'" (*High Noon,* U.S.A., 1952). In the 1960s and 70s, scores by John Barry [Prendergast] for the James Bond series continued this tradition with consistent success. Instrumental theme songs appear on the pop charts with less frequency than sung theme songs, but with perhaps greater durability (the themes from *A Summer Place,* U.S.A., 1959, and from *Chariots of Fire,* Britain, 1982).

III. *Techniques.* Although the composer is sometimes invited to collaborate with the director and producer of a film from the outset, the composer's involvement with a film most often begins only after it has reached a very nearly final visual form. The composer then views the film and discusses with the director the ways in which music is to be employed. A cue sheet is prepared listing in detail (down to intervals as small as 1/3 or even 1/10 of a second) all scenes that are to include music. Once the music has been composed and orchestrated (the latter sometimes by one or more persons other than the composer), synchronization of music and film are achieved by means of timing with a stop watch or by means of a click track on a copy of the film itself. In either case, the music is recorded as the film is projected in appropriate segments on a screen behind the musicians and facing the conductor (sometimes the composer). If a click track is used, the conductor hears by means of headphones a series of regular clicks, each of which marks off a specific number of frames of the film and in terms of which the score has been composed and marked. The copy that is projected for the conductor may in addition have punches (holes punched in critical frames, producing a flash of light that can be seen without looking at the screen) and streamers (diagonal lines that are produced by scraping off the emulsion from a series of frames and that move across the screen from left to right to warn of an approaching cue) to aid in the synchronization. The final step in the process is dubbing, in which the musical soundtrack is mixed with as many as a dozen or more tracks containing dialogue and sound effects.

Methods like those described continue to be used for both films and television. Other methods employed for both media may avoid the use of musicians in a recording session for a specific project. These include the creation of electronic music, the use of prerecorded music maintained in libraries and classified according to type and mood of scene, and the use of previously recorded music from the concert or other repertories.

Bibl.: Kurt London, *Film Music: A Summary of the Characteristic Features of Its History, Aesthetics, Technique, and Possible Developments,* trans. Eric S. Bensinger (London: Faber, 1936). Jack Burton, *The Blue Book of Hollywood Musicals* (Watkins Glen, N.Y.: Century House, 1953). John Huntley and Roger Manvell, *The Technique of Film Music* (London: Focal Pr, 1957). Earl Hagen, *Scoring for Films* (New York: Wehman, 1972). Tony Thomas, *Music for the Movies* (South Brunswick: A S Barnes, 1973). James L. Limbacher, *Film Music: From Violins to Video* (Metuchen, N.J.: Scarecrow, 1974). Roy M. Prendergast, *Film Music: A Neglected Art* (New York: Norton, 1977). Alain Lacombe, *La musique du film* (Paris: Van de Velde, 1979). James L. Limbacher, *Keeping Score: Film Music 1972–79* (Metuchen, N.J.: Scarecrow Pr, 1981).

Filter. An electronic device that transmits only certain frequencies. A high-pass filter transmits only frequencies above a specified limit; a low-pass filter those below a specified limit; a band-pass filter those between two specified limits. Because the relative strengths of different frequencies within a signal is realized acoustically as *timbre, filters are used in *electronic instruments to create and manipulate timbres. See also Synthesizer, Electro-acoustic music, Acoustics.

Fin [Fr.]. The end.

Final [Lat. *finalis*]. The pitch on which a melody in a given church *mode ends.

Finale [It.]. (1) The final movement of a *sonata or related form such as a symphony, concerto, or string quartet, usually in a fast tempo. (2) In opera, the concluding number of an act, especially an ensemble for the principal characters, perhaps with chorus, in which dramatic tension is created, elaborated, or resolved. A finale is likely to be considerably longer and more elaborate than other numbers such as arias and may consist of several sections of contrasting tempo and key. In operas of the 18th and 19th centuries, they are likely to conclude with a section for all of the principal characters in rapid tempo. Particularly distinguished examples are the finales to the second and fourth acts of Mozart's *Le *nozze di Figaro.* Ensembles of this type emerged in the early 18th century, principally in *opera buffa.* See Opera.

Finalmusik [Ger., final music]. In the Classical period, a type of piece belonging to the family also bearing names such as *cassation, *serenade, and *divertimento and performed at the end of a concert or, especially in the case of the works to which Leopold and W. A. Mozart referred with this term (e.g., K. 185 [167a], 251), at the end of the summer semester of the university in Salzburg.

Fin' al segno [It.]. An instruction to play (usually to repeat) a piece "as far as the sign" (𝄋).

Fine [It.]. The end.

Fingal's Cave. See *Hebriden, Die.*

Fingerboard. In stringed instruments, a strip of hardwood (often ebony) fixed to the neck, over which the strings are stretched and against which they are pressed (stopped) by the fingers to vary their pitch. The fingerboards of some early bowed instruments, such as members of the *viol family, and those of most Western plucked instruments, such as the guitar and lute, are fitted with *frets.

Fingering [Eng., for nonkeyboard instruments, also stopping; Fr. *doigté;* Ger. *Fingersatz, Applikatur;* It. *diteggiatura;* Sp. *digitación*]. (1) A system of symbols (usually Arabic numbers) for the fingers of the hand (or some subset of them) used to associate specific notes with specific fingers. In most 19th- and 20th-century editions of keyboard music, both thumbs are numbered *1,* both index fingers *2,* and so on. This system is already found in Bermudo (1555), Diruta (1593), and Couperin (1708), among others. Most earlier alternatives denote the index fingers with *1,* the middle fingers with *2,* and so on. Much late 18th-, 19th-, and early 20th-century British keyboard music denotes the thumb with an *x.* For the viola da gamba, Ganassi (1543) uses dots to indicate the left hand's index through little fingers (as well as a straight line to indicate the *barré*). In *tablatures for plucked chordophones, the same system of dots is occasionally used to indicate the fingers of the right (plucking) hand. Supplementary numerals have been infrequently used in tablatures to denote left-hand fingerings. In music for the violin and related instruments, the index finger is numbered *1,* the middle finger *2,* and so forth.

(2) Control of finger movement and position to achieve physiological efficiency, acoustical accuracy (or effect), and musical articulation. An aspect of instrumental technique, fingering is directly related to the manner in which vibration is initiated and the means by which its frequency is regulated. Some instruments (e.g., natural horns, slide trombones, pedal timpani) do not use finger articulations for these essential functions; plucked and keyboard instruments usually require them for both; bowed chordophones and most handheld aerophones use them to select pitch but not to initiate vibration.

Valved aerophones such as the trumpet require no lateral shift of hand or fingers. The eight (three-valve) or sixteen (four-valve) possible fingerings combine with variation of *embouchure to produce the full scales of the instruments. Alternate fingerings exist for most pitches above the lowest octave. Cultivation of a quick and vigorous stroke helps the player achieve the illusion of a true legato, as does the precise coordination of tonguing with the movement of the valves [see Valve].

Flute and reed aerophones with side holes require modest lateral shifts of the fingers but none of the hands. On earlier types of side-hole aerophones, such as the recorder, fingering is simplest in the lowest register and in the instrument's tonic scale. In foreign scales, a single pitch can require the simultaneous contrary articulation of two or more fingers [see Cross fingering]. Fingerings for upper registers are modifications of those used for the same pitch classes in the low register. The development of key mechanisms has greatly reduced the need for complicated cross fingerings and minimized the weaknesses of tone and timbre often associated with these [see Boehm system]. Since about 1960, the growing use of *microtones and *multiphonics dramatically increased potentially useful fingerings.

Chordophones with fretted necks admit considerable variations of fingering. Ganassi (1543) offers five methods of fingering a scale on a viol, surpassing the demands of surviving notated music and testifying to a semi-improvisatory, virtuoso tradition. On chordophones with unfretted necks, precise shifts of hand *position are critical for accurate intonation. The division of the fingerboard into standard, diatonically related hand positions became canonical during the 17th century. A competent orchestral player is today expected to be comfortable through at least the seventh position. Most 17th-century scores venture no further than the fourth position; occasional exceptions, such as Marco Uccellini's *Sonate over canzoni da farsi* (Venice, 1649), perhaps reflect more demanding improvisational traditions. In 18th-century pedagogy, fingerings in the even-numbered positions were emphasized; in 19th-century pedagogy, odd-numbered positions dominated. One of the original aims of hand positions was the preservation of a relaxed hand. In the 18th century, however, Locatelli and Geminiani introduced fingerings based on extensions and contractions, and Geminiani introduced a chromatic fingering as well. Leopold Mozart (1756) gives a detailed account of 18th-century fingerings. The late-18th-century Russian violinist Ivan Khandoshkin and, later, Paganini promulgated fingerings that ignore the hand positions altogether. Paganini's imaginative solutions to fingering difficulties seemed to defy the limits of what was possible for the violin and were an inspiration not only to other violinists, but to influential players of other instruments, notably Liszt.

Extant keyboard fingerings from the 16th and 17th centuries tend to isolate finger motion as much as possible and to keep wrist, elbow, and shoulder articulations to a minimum. To this end, the index, middle, and ring fingers are favored, especially in conjunct passage work. But a few sources use the thumb, especially that of the left hand, in scalar passages. For conjunct motion with binary divisions of the beat, paired fingerings are virtually always indicated. Sources of different regions vary only with respect to which fingers constitute the preferred pair. The belief (common through the 18th century except in Spain) that strong fingers (index and ring) should be used on strong beats is given its classic formulation by Diruta (1593).

A toccata by Alessandro Scarlatti has extensive fingerings that indicate a more liberal attitude toward the use of the thumb and little finger in passage work. François Couperin (1716) transmits the old fingerings, but a *leçon* and *menuet en rondeau* by Rameau (1724) are explicitly intended to develop equality of all five fingers (the thumb is not passed under, however).

Clear indication that the relaxed attitude of the hand could be overruled in order to pass the thumb under in a scale occurs in Maichelbeck (1738) and C. P. E. Bach (1753)—the latter widely disseminated in German-speaking regions. A tendency to experimentation and harmonic figurations in Classical keyboard music helped to cause fingering practices to change faster than treatises could keep pace with (see Broder, 1956). Dussek's treatise of 1796 and its better-known offspring, Clementi's of 1802, are the first in which fingerings reflect the new pianoforte styles. Beginning with Johann Baptist Cramer's *Studio per il pianoforte* op. 30 (1804), the best sources for 19th-century fingerings are collections of *etudes. Liszt is said to have practiced every scale with the fingerings of every other scale, thus using the thumb in ways prohibited by the older teaching. The Lisztian demand that the hand be capable of the greatest possible expansion and contraction is exemplified by the fingerings in his *Grandes études de Paganini* (1851) and *Études d'exécution transcendante* (1852) and is formalized in Ferruccio Busoni's *Klavier-Übung* (1918–22). Brahms's approach to the same ideal is documented in his *Studien für das Pianoforte* (1869–79). In the early 20th century, Debussy's *Douze études* (1916) extend the developments of Liszt. More recent music has either refined earlier developments or has explored the timbral potential of the pianoforte in ways that do not depend on consecutive finger articulations at the keyboard.

Bibl.: *Primary.* Sylvestro di Ganassi dal Fontego, *Opera intitulata Fontegara* (Venice, 1535); facs., *BMB* sez. 2, no. 18 (1969; R: 1980); trans. Eng. Dorothy Swainson (Berlin: R Lienau, 1959). Id., *Regola rubertina. Lettione secunda* (Venice, 1543); facs., *BMB* sez. 2, no. 18b (1970); trans. Daphne and Stephen Silvester (Berlin-Lichterfelde: Lienau, 1977). Juan Bermudo, *Declaración de ínstrumentos musicales* (Osuna, 1555); facs., *DM* ser. 1, no. 11 (1957). Girolamo Diruta, *Il transilvano,* 1 (Venice, 1593); facs., *BMB* sez. 2, no. 132 (1969); trans. Murray C. Bradshaw and Edward J. Soehnlen (Henryville, Pa.: Institute of Mediaeval Music, 1984). Jean Denis II, *Traité de l'accord de l'espinette,* 2nd ed. (Paris, 1650); facs. with an introduction by Alan Curtis (New York: Da Capo, 1969); trans. Vincent J. Panetta, Jr. (Cambridge: Cambridge U Pr, 1987). François Couperin, *L'art de toucher le clavecin* (Paris, 1716); facs. of 1717 ed., *MMML* 2nd ser., no. 23 (1969); trans. Margery Halford (New York: Alfred, 1974). Jean Philippe Rameau, *Pièces de clavessin* (Paris, 1724); facs., *MMML* 1st ser., no. 7 (1967). Franz Anton Maichelbeck, *Die auf dem Clavier lehrende Caecilia* (Augsburg, 1738); trans. with commentary of pt. 2, Carole Ruth Terry (D.M.A. diss., Stanford Univ., 1977). Carl Philipp Emanuel Bach, *Versuch über die wahre Art das Clavier zu spielen* (Berlin, 1753); trans. William J. Mitchell, *Essay on the True Art of Playing Keyboard Music* (New York: Norton, 1948). Leopold Mozart, *Versuch einer gründlichen Violinschule* (Augsburg, 1756); trans. Editha Knocker, *A Treatise on the Fundamental Principles of Violin Playing,* 2nd ed. (London: Oxford U Pr, 1951). Jean-Louis Duport, *Essai sur le doigté du violoncelle* (Paris, ca. 1813).

Secondary. Izrail Markovich Yampolsky, *Osnovï skripichnoy applikatur,* 3rd ed. enl. (Moscow: State Music Pubs, 1955); trans. Alan Lumsden, *The Principles of Violin Fingering* (London: Oxford U Pr, 1967). Nathan Broder, "The First Guide to Mozart," *MQ* 42 (1956): 223–29. J. Brian Brocklehurst, "The Studies of J. B. Cramer and His Predecessors," *ML* 39 (1958): 256–61. Sol Babitz, "On Using J. S. Bach's Keyboard Fingering," *ML* 43 (1962): 123–28. David D. Boyden, *The History of Violin Playing from Its Origins to 1761* (London: Oxford U Pr, 1965). Edgar Hunt, *The Recorder and Its Music,* rev. and enl. ed. (London: Eulenburg, 1976), pp. 113–27. Ian Woodfield, "Viol Playing Techniques in the Mid-16th Century: A Survey of Ganassi's Fingering Instructions," *EM* 6 (1978): 544–49. Bruce Haynes, "Oboe Fingering Charts, 1695–1816," *GSJ* 31 (1978): 68–93. Peter Le Huray, "English Keyboard Fingering in the 16th and Early 17th Centuries," in *Source Materials and the Interpretation of Music,* ed. Ian Bent (London: Stainer & Bell, 1981), pp. 227–57. William S. Newman, "Beethoven's Fingerings as Interpretive Clues," *JM* 1 (1982): 171–97. Robert Parkins, "Keyboard Fingerings in Early Spanish Sources," *EM* 11 (1983): 323–31. Albert R. Rice, "Clarinet Fingering Charts, 1732–1816," *GSJ* 37 (1984): 16–41. Peter Walls, "Violin Fingering in the 18th Century," *EM* 12 (1984): 300–15; Sonya Monosoff, "Violin Fingering," *EM* 13 (1985): 76–79. William Drabkin, "Fingering in Haydn's String Quartets," *EM* 16, no. 1 (1988): 50–57. Mark Lindley, "Early English Keyboard Fingerings," *Basler Jahrbuch für historische Musikpraxis* 12 (1988): 9–25. Paul J. White, "Early Bassoon Fingering Charts," *GSJ* 43 (1990): 68–111. Calvert Johnson, "Early Italian Keyboard Fingering," *Early Keyboard Journal* 10 (1992): 7–88. Mark Lindley and Maria Boxall, eds., *Early Keyboard Fingerings: A Comprehensive Guide* (Mainz: Schott, 1992). Mark Lindley, "Handelian Keyboard Fingerings," *Gottinger Handel-Beitrage* 6 (1996): 194–205.

C.C.H.

Finland. Musical life in modern Finland is increasingly rich and varied. Venerable professional ensembles such as the Turku Philharmonic Orchestra (with roots back to 1790), the Helsinki Philharmonic (1882), and the Finnish Radio Symphony Orchestra (1927), have been joined by the Lahti Symphony Orchestra (Sinfonia Lahti, 1949), Ostrobothnian Chamber Orchestra (1972), Avanti! (1983), the Tapiola Sinfonietta (1987), and the Finnish Chamber Orchestra (1990). New concert halls have sprung up around the country, including the Helsinki Opera House, completed in 1993. Finnish operatic activity has increased in prominence since the 1970s and is centered on the Finnish National Opera, founded in 1911 as the Finnish Opera. This institution, now housed at the new opera house, as well as the Savonlinna Opera Festival (revived in 1967) regularly commission new works. Finland has an extensive system of music schools, including eleven conservatories. The principal school for advanced musical training is the Sibelius Academy in Helsinki. Major music festivals include the Helsinki Festival, the Turku Music Festival, Savonlinna for opera, chamber music festivals at Kuhmo, Uusikaupunki, and Naantali, the Korsholma Music Festival, and the Suvisoitto Festival in Porvoo. Three festivals that specialize in contemporary music were founded in the 1980s: Musiikin aika (Time of Music), Musica nova Helsinki (formerly the Helsinki Biennale, now an annual festival), and the Tampere Biennale.

In contrast to Finland's long and rich folk-music heritage, as well as its long-standing participation and interest in European art music (the Finnish Musicological Society was founded 1913), the history of its individual national art music is relatively short. In 1917 the nation finally gained independence from Russia, which had made it a duchy in 1809 after Sweden had ruled it for more than 600 years. A handful of sources survive from before the Reformation, including 14th-century liturgical books from the diocese at Åbo (now Turku). With the rise of Lutheranism during the 16th and 17th centuries, the chorale became central to church music. Secular musical life began to expand during the 18th century; the first music society was established at Åbo in 1790. After 1827, when much of Åbo was destroyed by fire, Helsinki gradually came to be the nation's cultural center.

Early national composers include Erik Tulindberg (1761–1814) and Bernhard Henrik Crusell (1775–

1838). During the 19th century, the native Aksel Gabriel Ingelius (1822–68) was eclipsed somewhat by his foreign-born contemporaries Frederik Pacius (1809–91) and Friedrich Richard Faltin (1835–1919). The single most prominent figure in Finnish music is Jean Sibelius (1865–1957), whose powerful musical personality affected not only contemporaries such as Selim Palmgren (1878–1951), Toivo Kuula (1883–1918), and Leevi Madetoja (1887–1947) but also numerous more recent Finnish composers. His symphonies and tone poems embody the nationalism that was growing in Finland during his lifetime. Significant composers between the world wars include Väinö Raitio (1891–1945), Yryö Kilpinen (1892–1959), Aarre Merikanto (1893–1958), Sulo Salonen (1899–1976), and Uuno Klami (1900–61).

After World War II, Sibelius's influence became somewhat less pervasive. Composers who were particularly prominent in the postwar decades include Erik Bergman (b. 1911), Einar Englund (1916–99), Joonas Kokkonen (1921–96), Einojuhani Rautavaara (b. 1928), Usko Meriläinen (b. 1930), Aulis Sallinen (b. 1935), Paavo Heininen (b. 1938), and Erkki Salmenhaara (1941–2002). Sallinen, Kokkonen, Rautavaara, and Heininen wrote important operas during the 1970s' resurgence of that art form in Finland; Kalevi Aho (b. 1949) and Olli Kortekangas (b. 1955) have continued this operatic tradition. The primary association for contemporary music in Finland, Korvat auki! (Ears Open!), was founded in 1977, and its core group included Kortekangas, Eero Hämeenniemi (b. 1951), Kaija Saariaho (b. 1952), Jouni Kaipainen (b. 1956), Magnus Lindberg (b. 1958), and Esa-Pekka Salonen (b. 1958). Members of this group worked closely with the Avanti! chamber orchestra, as well as with the experimental ensemble Tiomii, founded by Salonen and Lindberg in 1984. Other recent Finnish composers of note are Pehr Henrik Nordgren (b. 1944), Jouni Kaipainen (b. 1956), Kimmo Hakola (b. 1958), and Jukka Tiensuu (b. 1949), who founded the Viitasaari Summer Academy for new music in 1981.

During the 20th century, recordings and transcriptions of nearly 100,000 pieces of folk music have been collected in archives throughout Finland, such as the Finnish-Swedish Folk Music Institute and the Department of Folk Music at the Sibelius Academy in Helsinki. Recent decades have seen a resurgence of popular interest in folk culture, especially in folk dancing and instrumental music. The Ilmajoki Music Festival has staged folk opera productions since the 1970s, and the Kaustinen Folk Music Festival, founded in 1968, has become the biggest event of its kind in the Nordic countries. Among the most important folk dances are the *polska (the oldest group-dance of Finland), the *purpuri* (a set of dances for both groups and couples, used most often at weddings), the *jenkka* (a couple dance), and various dances, usually for couples, known elsewhere in Europe, such as the waltz, polka, and mazurka. Most dances have instrumental accompaniment (sometimes with tunes borrowed from songs), and much independent instrumental music exists. The **kantele,* a kind of trapezoidal zither, has often been called Finland's national instrument, though it is less prominent today than it was in the late 19th century. Other instruments commonly heard in folk ensembles (and occasionally solo) are the violin, the string bass, the accordion, and the clarinet.

A source for much Finnish folk song is the **Kalevala,* an epic including narrative and lyric passages. Folk song influenced by it includes epic recitation and laments (improvised nonmetric poems expressing strong emotion such as grief, incorporating traditional elements and patterns). Other types are functional songs (e.g., sledge songs, herding songs), the *joiku* (a song describing something; related to the Lapp *juoigos*), and the *stiihu* (recitation of a religious legend).

Bibl.: Pekka Gronow, "Popular Music in Finland: A Preliminary Survey," *Ethno* 17 (1973): 52–71. Paavo Helistö, *Finnish Folk Music,* trans. Brad Absetz (Helsinki: Finnish Music Information Centre, 1973). Inkeri Aarnio and Kauko Karjalainen, *Music of Finland* (Helsinki: Finnish Music Information Centre, 1983). Lisa de Gorog, *From Sibelius to Sallinen: Finnish Nationalism and the Music of Finland* (New York: Greenwood, 1989). Helmi Jarviluoma, "Current Research of Folk Music and Popular Music in Finland," in *Finnish-Hungarian Symposium on Music and Folklore Research,* 15.–21.11.1987, ed. Antti Koiranen (Tampere: Tampereen yliopiston, 1991), pp. 17–38. Mikko Heiniö and Erkki Salmenhaara, eds., *Suomalaisia säveltäjiä* [Finnish composers] (Helsinki: Otava, 1994). Kimmo Korhonen, *Finnish Composers since the 1960s* (Helsinki: Finnish Music Information Centre, 1995). Fabian Dahlström, Erkki Salmenhaara, and Mikko Heiniö, *Suomen musiikin historia* [Music History of Finland], 4 vols. (Porvoo: W. Soderström, 1995–1996). Kalevi Aho, *Finnish Music,* trans. Timothy and Philip Binham (Helsinki: Otava, 1996). Erik Tawaststjerna, *Sibelius,* 3 vols., trans. Robert Layton (Berkeley: U of Cal Pr, 1976–97). Hannu-Ilari Lampila, *Suomalainen Ooppera* [Finnish opera] (Porvoo: Werner Söderstrom Osakeyhtïo, 1997). Tomi Mäkelä, ed., *Music and Nationalism in 20th-Century Great Britain and Finland* (Hamburg: Von Bockel, 1997). *Finnish Music Quarterly* (Helsinki: Performing Music Promotion Centre, 1985–).

Finlandia. A symphonic poem by Sibelius, op. 26 (1899; revised 1900), from music for a pageant for press pension celebrations. Although it makes no use of folk music as such, it came to be regarded as the supreme musical embodiment of Finnish nationalism.

Fioritura [It., flowering]. Ornamental passages, improvised or written out. See Diminutions.

Fipple flute. *Duct flute.

Firebird, The. See *Oiseau de feu, L'.*

Fireworks Music. Handel's *Music for the Royal Fireworks,* an instrumental suite composed for performance at a fireworks display in London in 1749 celebrating the Peace of Aix-la-Chapelle.

First-movement form. *Sonata form. See also Sonata.

Fis, fisis [Ger.]. F-sharp, F-double-sharp. See Pitch names.

Fistula [Lat.]. Pipe, flute; *fistula organica,* organ pipe.

Fitzwilliam Virginal Book. A manuscript (Cambridge, Fitzwilliam Museum, 32.g.29, Mu. MS 168) copied by Francis Tregian between 1609 and 1619 containing nearly 300 works for *virginal dating from ca. 1562 to ca. 1612 and including dances, arrangements of songs and madrigals, preludes, and sets of variations by the principal English composers of keyboard works of the period, among them William Byrd, John Bull, and Giles Farnaby. It was edited by J. A. Fuller Maitland and William Barclay Squire (London and Leipzig, 1894–99; R: New York: Dover, 1963).

Five, The. A group of five Russian composers—César A. Cui (1835–1918), Alexander P. Borodin (1833–87), Mily A. Balakirev (1837–1910), Modest P. Mussorgsky (1839–81), and Nikolai A. Rimsky-Korsakov (1844–1908)—who joined in St. Petersburg in about 1875 to create a Russian national music. A slightly larger group including these five were first referred to as The Mighty Handful *(moguchaya kuchka)* by the critic Vladimir Stasov in a newspaper article in 1867.

Five-three chord. A *triad in root position. See Inversion, Thoroughbass.

Fixed-do(h). See Movable do(h), Solmization.

Fl. Abbr. for flute.

Flagellant songs. See *Geisslerlieder.*

Flageolet. (1) A *duct flute similar to the recorder. Two types are distinguished. The French flageolet, originating in the 16th century, has four front finger holes and two thumb holes [see ill. under Flute]. It served both as an instrument for amateurs and as a high orchestral flute. The English flageolet, originating in the early 19th century, has six (sometimes seven) front finger holes and one thumb hole. It was used primarily by amateur musicians. Its music was often written in *tablature, using numbers or note names stamped next to the finger holes. The flageolet was also made in double or triple form.

(2) [Fr.] An organ stop of flute scale at 1′ pitch, especially in 17th-century French organs; also at 2′ pitch in American organs. (1) M.S.

Flageolet tones [Ger. *Flageolett-Töne*]. *Harmonics.

Flam. A common stroke on the snare drum played with the two hands in quick succession: 𝅘𝅥𝅮𝅘𝅥.

Flamenco [Sp.]. A repertory of music and dance of Andalusia in southern Spain. Its origins remain much in dispute and have been variously attributed to Arabic-speaking peoples entering Spain from North Africa and to Gypsies arriving from the east or from the north (including the Low Countries, whence, according to some authorities, the name, which can mean Flemish), among others. On grounds of musical similarities, the strongest arguments point to Arabic and, to a lesser extent, Indian (by way of Gypsies) ties. Its association with Gypsies remains strong. The repertory incorporates characteristic styles of singing (including *cante hondo* or *jondo,* deep song, a term sometimes applied to the repertory as a whole), dancing (featuring erect posture, foot stamping, and finger snapping), and guitar playing (in which both strumming and passage work are prominent). Much of the music embodies the E or Phrygian mode, the descending phrase A, G, F, E being a characteristic concluding melodic gesture, but with significant microtonal inflections. Vocal performances often begin with elaborate melismas on the syllable *ay* and are strongly improvisational in character, being judged by auditors in large measure on the basis of what is perceived to be the extent of the singer's inspiration of the moment. Singers do not normally accompany themselves, and both singing and dancing may be accompanied by the hand clapping of other performers present. Among the numerous individual musical types are the **seguidilla (siguiriya)* and **soleá.* A group of singers, dancers, and guitarists is termed a *cuadro flamenco* or *tablao* (from the platform on which they sit and perform). The continuing evolution of the repertory has resulted in mixed genres and considerable interpenetration of flamenco traditions and other forms of folk and popular music.

Bibl.: Donn E. Pohren, *The Art of Flamenco* (Jerez de la Frontera: Jerez Industrial, 1962; 3rd ed., Morón de la Frontera: Soc of Span Studies, 1972). Id., *Lives and Legends of Flamenco: A Biographical History* (La Mesa, Cal.: Soc of Span Studies, 1964). Ricardo Molina and Antonio Mairena, *Mundo y formas del cante flamenco* (Seville: Libr Al-Andalus, 1971). Manuel Ríos Ruiz, *Introducción al cante flamenco* (Madrid: Ed Istmo, 1972). Arcadio Larrea Palacín, *El flamenco en su raiz* (Madrid: Edit nacional, 1974).

Flat [Fr. *bémol;* Ger. *Be;* It. *bemolle;* Sp. *bemol*]. (1) The symbol ♭, which indicates the lowering of the pitch of a note by a semitone. See Accidental, Pitch names. (2) [adj.] Incorrectly sounded below the correct pitch.

Flatté [Fr., also *flaté*]. According to Montéclair (1736), "a kind of **balancement* that the voice makes with many gentle little breaths *(aspirations)* on a long note . . . without raising or lowering the pitch"; also various kinds of *mordents or an **accent.* See also Ornamentation.

Flattement [Fr.]. (1) On Baroque woodwind instruments, a slow vibrato made by waving the finger over a hole that the written note requires to be open. Thus, according to Hotteterre, it is a pitch vibrato below the written pitch. (2) On Baroque stringed instruments, according to Marais, a two-finger vibrato above the pitch, the fingers being pressed together and rocked. See also Ornamentation.

Flatterzunge [Ger.]. Flutter *tonguing.

Flautado [Sp.]. An organ stop of open flue pipes of *Principal scale.

Flautando, flautato [It., flutelike]. An instruction to bow a stringed instrument over the fingerboard. See Bowing (12).

Flautino [It.]. (1) A small flute, either a small *recorder or *flageolet; not a *piccolo. (2) An organ stop of 2′ pitch and flute scale.

Flauto [It.]. (1) Flute; *f. a becco, diritto, dolce,* *recorder; *f. piccolo,* *piccolo; *f. traverso,* *transverse flute. (2) In the 18th century, *recorder. (3) An organ stop of flute scale.

Flautone [It.]. Alto *flute.

Flaviol [Cat.]. A *duct flute of Catalonia played in a *pipe and tabor combination, particularly in the **cobla* ensemble.

Flebile [It.]. Plaintive, mournful.

Fledermaus, Die [Ger., The Bat]. Operetta in three acts by Johann Strauss, Jr. (libretto by Carl Haffner and Richard Genée, after the French farce *Le reveillon* by Henri Meilhac and Ludovic Halévy, itself after a German comedy by Roderich Benedix), produced in Vienna in 1874. Setting: an Austrian city in the late 19th century.

Flemish school. See Renaissance.

Flex [Lat. *flexa*]. (1) See Psalm tone. (2) *Clivis* [see Neume].

Flexatone. A percussion instrument patented in the 1920s and consisting of a narrow sheet of flexible metal about 25 cm long, on either side of which is mounted a wooden ball on a straight spring, all joined in a handle. When the instrument is shaken, the balls strike the metal sheet, producing a sound similar to that of the *musical saw.

Flexus [Lat.]. See Neume.

Flicorno [It.]. See Flugelhorn, Euphonium.

Fliegende Holländer, Der [Ger., The Flying Dutchman]. Opera in three acts by Wagner (to his own libretto, after Heine's *Aus den Memoiren des Herren von Schnabelewopski*), first produced in Dresden in 1843 and revised in 1846, 1852, and 1860. Wagner originally intended to have the work presented in one continuous act, and present-day productions sometimes follow this practice. Setting: a Norwegian coastal village in the 18th century.

Fliessend, fliessender [Ger.]. Flowing, more flowing.

Florid. Ornamented, characterized by *figuration. In *species counterpoint, the fifth species is termed florid counterpoint. The term florid is also applied to the elaborate polyphony of such composers of the late 15th century as Ockeghem and Obrecht and to the ornamented singing style of the 18th century.

Flos [Lat., pl. *flores*]. In the Middle Ages, ornament. See Ornamentation.

Flöte [Ger.]. Flute.

Flötenuhr [Ger., flute clock]. An *automatic instrument that combines a clockwork with a barrel organ to play music at fixed times of the hour. Haydn, among others, composed works for such instruments.

Flott [Ger.]. Lively, fast.

Flourish. (1) A *fanfare, especially for trumpets. (2) Any florid passage, especially one that calls attention to itself.

Flue chorus. A combination of the *Principal stops of the organ, from 16′ pitch through 8′, 4′, 2 2/3′, 2′, with *mixtures.

Flue pipe. The main class of organ pipework, so called because the wind passes through a flue or opening between the languid and lower lip of the pipe. See diagram under Organ.

Flügel [Ger., wing]. The grand piano, so called because it is shaped like a wing; *Hammerflügel,* the piano as distinct from the *Kielflügel* or harpsichord.

Flugelhorn [also fluegelhorn; Ger. *Flügelhorn;* Fr. *bugle;* It. *flicorno;* Sp. *fiscorno*]. Originally, a half-round, 18th-century, German hunting horn of animal horn or bugle proportions; later, the large-bore German valved *bugle. The flugelhorn or valved bugle was the parent of whole families of similarly proportioned valve instruments that made up the brass bands of the mid-19th century. Soprano flugelhorns in B♭, whose range is the same as that of the cornet, are increasingly used in modern popular music and jazz. See ill. under Brass instruments. R.E.E.

Flüssig [Ger.]. Flowing.

Flüsternd [Ger.]. **Bisbigliando.*

Flute [Fr. *flûte;* Ger. *Flöte;* It. *flauto;* Sp. *flauta*]. Any instrument formed by a hollow chamber of any shape containing a body of air that is set in motion by an airstream striking against the edge of an opening in the chamber.

I. *Classification.* Flutes are classified by the way in which the airstream is shaped and directed over the opening. A player may blow into a slot or duct that directs the air over an internal edge, as on *whistles, *ocarinas, and *recorders; a player's lips may blow over an *embouchure hole or notch, as on *transverse flutes and *shakuhachis; or the air may be wind-driven, as with the *bulu pārinda,* a large (up to 10 m long) aeolian pipe hung in treetops in Southeast Asia. A flute can be further classified by the shape of its air cavity: it may be *globular as in the ocarina, a horizontally held tube like the modern orchestral flute, or a vertically held one like the *pennywhistle. Tubular flutes with an embouchure rather than a duct are classified as *end-blown or transverse. In Europe and the Western world, transverse flutes have been the dominant type for the past three centuries.

II. *The modern orchestral flute.* This transverse flute has developed from a design introduced in 1847 by Theobald Boehm (1794–1881) and modified by French, English, and American makers since that time. Its tube is cylindrical, usually of metal (silver or alloy, or sometimes gold or platinum), and its mechanism is based on the *Boehm system. It has a range of b or c′ to c′′′′. The modern flute comes in several subsidiary sizes, including the *piccolo, an octave higher (its parts written an octave lower than they sound); the alto flute [Fr. *flûte alto;* Ger. *Altflöte;* It. *flautone;* Sp. *flauta baja*], a transposing instrument in G, a fourth below the normal flute (range g to d′′′′); the bass flute in C (c to g′′); and the so-called contrabass, a large-bore C bass flute with an extended lower range down to G. The *flûte d'amour* [Ger. *Liebesflöte*] of the 18th and 19th centuries was pitched in A, a third lower than the normal flute. Renaissance flute consorts generally comprised a bass in G, an alto/tenor in D, and sometimes a discant in A. Military bands before World War II sometimes used flutes in D♭ and E♭, while flute bands of the 19th and 20th centuries employed still other sizes, including the B♭ tenor flute and the G treble.

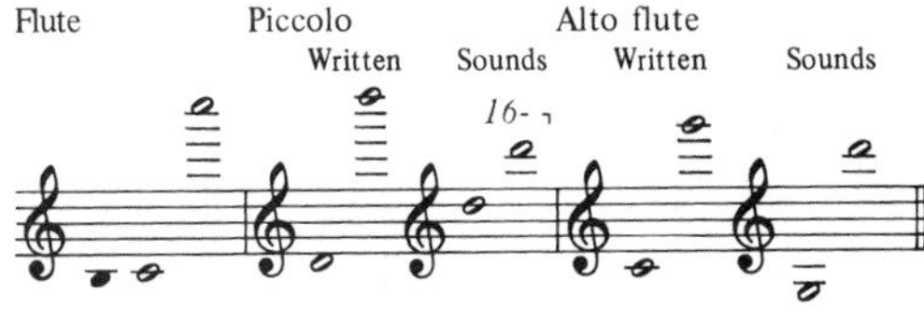

Ranges.

III. *History.* Transverse flutes appear to have reached Europe via Byzantine culture in the 11th century. By ca. 1300 the flute had found a role as a military instrument alongside trumpets, drums, bagpipes, and bells, as well as occasional use in the instrumentarium of minstrels in Germany, Spain, and France.

The flute's employment by Swiss infantry in highly effective new military techniques ca. 1480 spread the instrument all over Europe as German, French, Spanish, Swedish, and English soldiers copied the Swiss maneuvers (see *Fife). The first written instructions for playing the instrument, by Virdung (1511), emphasized this military character, but by 1529 Agricola indicated that sets of flutes in three different sizes (bass, alto/tenor, and discant) were being used to play four-part consort music, in the same way as instruments of most other families. Flute consorts became popular in Lyons and Paris as well as at the courts of England, Spain, Hungary, and Baden-Württemberg, where inventories record their presence in large numbers in the second half of the 16th century. By 1600 transverse flutes more commonly appeared alongside other wind, string, and plucked instruments as well as voices in dramatic and ecclesiastical music composed in Venice, Munich, Leipzig, Florence, and other centers.

French theatrical music of the late 17th century included scores for flutes in a lower part of their range than hitherto, often in scenes of love. These parts signal the presence of a new type of flute, the same size as the Renaissance alto/tenor but with a conical bore, a three-section construction, and a key for E♭ to provide a stronger low range, a more even tone, and a better facility for playing in various tonalities. The new Baroque flute was first depicted on a title page in 1690 and first appeared outside France in a London theater piece of 1701. The first published solo music for flute came in De Labarre's *Pièces* (1703), while the earliest instructions for playing it came in Hotteterre's *Principes* (1707), in which the flute was called "one of the most . . . fashionable instruments," indicating its popularity with cultured and wealthy amateurs.

This popularity grew with northwestern Europe's prosperity in the early 18th century. Production of flutes and printed music for the instrument increased dramatically: sonatas and, later, concertos formed its principal repertoire. A growing number of traveling performers appeared at concerts, while the amateur market expanded as flute playing became one of the marks of a cultivated gentleman.

In the mid-18th century, English makers including Schuchart (ca. 1756) and Cahusac (ca. 1760) began to build flutes with added keys to play B♭, G♯, and F, notes hitherto produced effectively enough by fingerings like those of the recorder and oboe [see *Fingering]. The new keys permitted a harder and more brilliant sound in the low register. During the late 18th and early 19th centuries the number of keys grew as ideals of tone responded to changing tastes, larger concert halls, and new performance practices. During this period Charles Nicholson, Jean-Louis Tulou, Friedrich Ludwig Dülon, and other performers in England, France, and Germany achieved widespread fame as solo performers on keyed flutes.

In 1831 the Bavarian flutist and industrialist Theobald Boehm constructed a flute that used mechanical means to locate tone holes in positions the unaided fingers could not reach. A subsequent Boehm flute of 1832 achieved some success in Paris, London, and New York around 1840, and another new model of 1847, which replaced the conical bore with a cylindrical one, immediately went into production in workshops in Paris and London. French makers soon modified the Boehm flute to make it easier to produce and

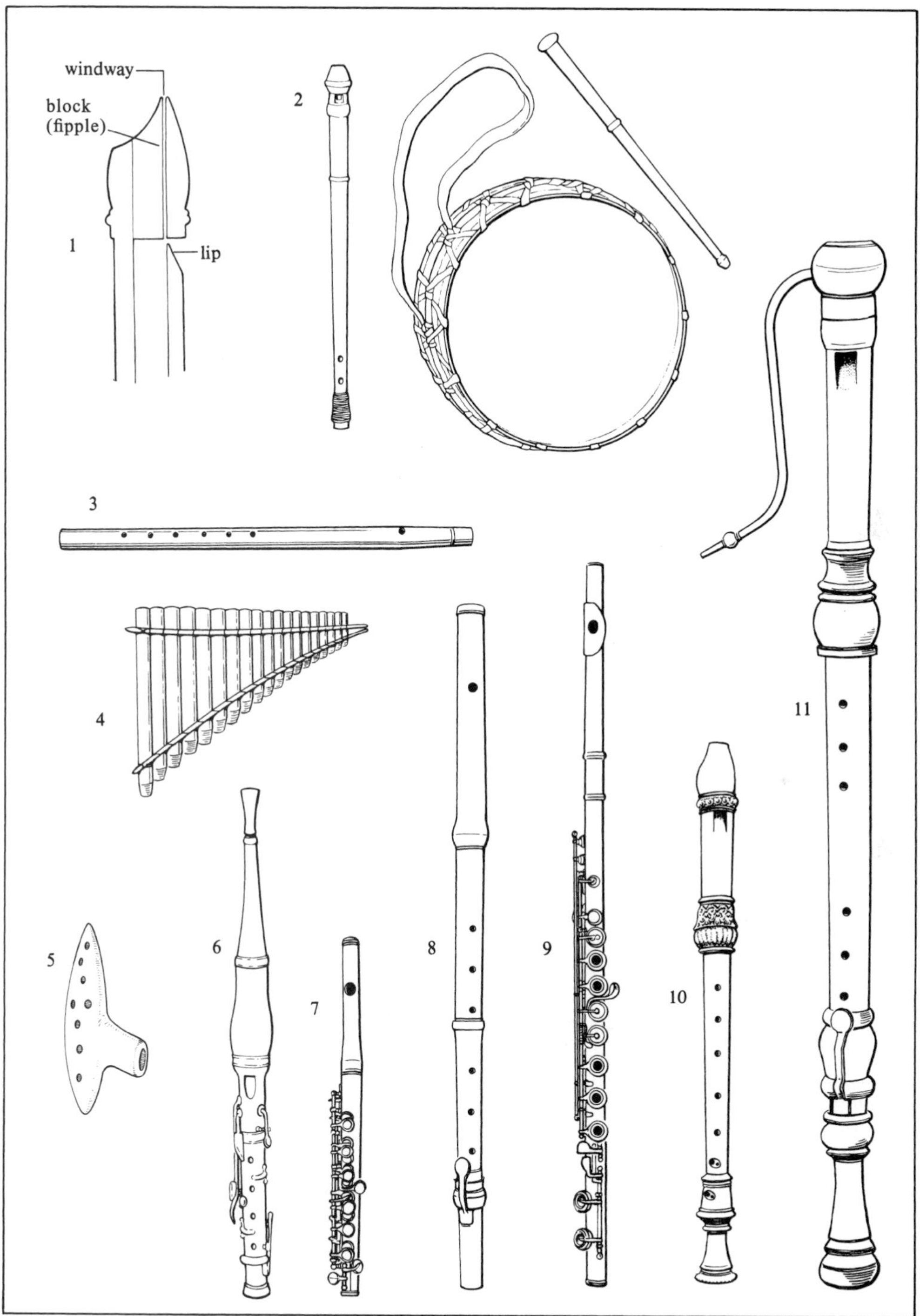

1. Cross section of a duct flute's sounding mechanism (recorder). 2. Pipe and tabor with drum stick. 3. Fife. 4. Panpipes. 5. Ocarina. 6. Flageolet (French). 7. Piccolo. 8. Baroque flute. 9. Flute (Boehm). 10. Alto recorder. 11. Bass recorder.

to market, and by the end of the 19th century French- or English-made Boehm flutes had displaced other models in most of the prominent orchestras of the world. Some German flutists held to the traditional flute with its characteristic sound, however, and Maximilian Schwedler (1853–1940) developed models that increased the old flute's potential to meet the demands of new music. In this period solo flute playing took second place in importance to the instrument's role in the orchestra.

By the end of World War I William S. Haynes (1864–1939) and other American makers dominated the worldwide market for flutes, building copies of French designs by Louis Lot (1807–96), supplier to the influential Paris Conservatoire. Radio and recording increased the hegemony of French and Franco-American instruments and playing styles, which now routinely employed a continuous *vibrato, formerly held in generally low esteem. French soloists, including Marcel Moyse, Louis Fleury, and René le Roy, brought the flute renewed and widespread attention as a solo instrument, influencing prominent players in England and Germany to adopt French instruments and modify their playing styles.

In about 1970 the London flute maker Albert Cooper developed new ways to adapt French flute designs (built at A = 435) to the standard orchestral pitch of A = 440, as well as new styles of cutting the mouth hole to produce a more powerful, though less tonally flexible sound. The Cooper scale and embouchure cuts were quickly adopted by most of the world's leading flute manufacturers, now based in Japan and Korea as well as the U.S., though some manufacturers continued to produce the so-called traditional 19th-century French designs, still highly regarded by many players.

Bibl.: Dayton C. Miller, *Catalogue of Books and Literary Material Relating to the Flute* (Cleveland: Author, 1935). Raymond Meylan, *The Flute* (Portland, Ore.: Amadeus, 1988). Jeremy Montagu, *The Flute* (Buckinghamshire: Shire Publications, 1990). Ardal Powell, *The Flute* (New Haven: Yale U Pr, 2002). A.P.

Flûte [Fr.]. (1) *Flute; *f. à bec, douce,* *recorder; *f. allemande, traversière,* *transverse flute. (2) An organ stop of wide scale, usually stopped, at 8′ or 4′ pitch; *f. à fuseau,* see *Koppelflöte; f. harmonique,* an organ stop of wide-scaled open flue pipes pierced by a small hole at half their length, giving a strong first harmonic, often found in 19th-century French organs; *f. octaviante,* a *flûte harmonique* at 4′ pitch.

Flutter tonguing. See Tonguing.

Flying Dutchman, The. See *Fliegende Holländer, Der.*

Focoso [It.]. Fiery.

Folia [Port., It., insanity; Fr. *Folies d'Espagne*]. A dance and dance song first mentioned in Portuguese documents of the late 15th century and associated in Spain in the early 17th century with wild singing and dancing. From the last quarter of the 17th century, however, compositions on the *folia* have been art music based on a single isometric harmonic pattern, usually accompanied by the same discant tune [Ex.]. *Folia* variations were written by Michel Farinel (1680; publ. John Playford in *The Division Violin,* 1685), D'Anglebert (*Pièces de clavecin,* 1689), Marais (*Pièces de viole,* bk. 2, 1701), Johann Philipp Förtsch (in the opera *Die grossmächtige Thalestris,* 1690), Corelli (*Sonate a violino e violone o cimbalo* op. 5 no. 12, 1700), Alessandro Scarlatti (for harpsichord), Reinhard Keiser (overture to *Der lächerliche Printz Jodelet,* 1726), J. S. Bach (*Bauernkantate,* 1742), C. P. E. Bach (for keyboard, 1778), Grétry (in the opera *L'amant jaloux,* 1778), Cherubini (overture to *L'hôtellerie portugaise,* 1798), Liszt (*Rhapsodie espagnole,* 1867), Nielsen (opera *Maskarade,* 1906), and Rachmaninoff (*Variations on a Theme of Corelli* op. 42, 1931).

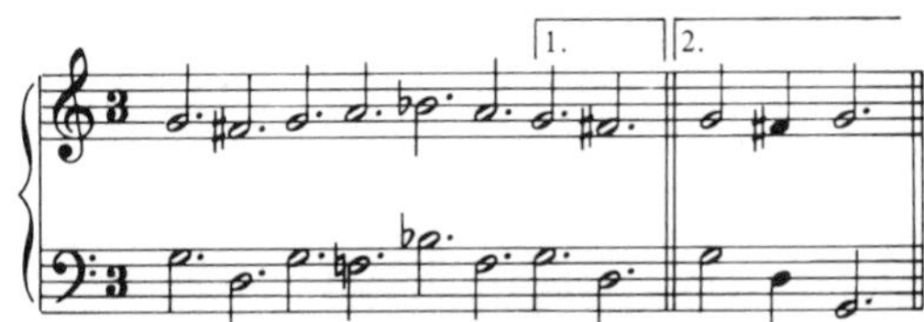

Like other such patterns, the *folia* developed over a long period. Patterns that adumbrate the full-blown *folia* appear in late 15th- and early 16th-century manuscripts in Spain and Italy, the most pronounced differences being a freedom of rhythmic structure. For examples, see *Cancionero Musical de Palacio,* vol. 2, *MME* 10, no. 420, "Adorámoste, Señor" by Francisco de la Torre, and Montecassino MS 871 (ed. Isabel Pope and Masakata Kanazawa, Oxford, 1978), "Dindiri din." In the 16th century, many variants developed without any one taking precedence. The most popular were dances known as "La *cara cosa," "La pavana del duca," and *"Pavaniglia." One of the *folia* discants used most often in the next century is first given by Francisco de Salinas in his *De musica libri septem* (1577, p. 308). An early harmonic pattern that resembles closely the *folia* cited above, in Luis Venegas de Henestrosa's tablature (1557), was written by Antonio (de Cabezón?) and called "Para quien crie yo cabellos" (*MME* 2, no. 119). Johannes Hieronymus Kapsberger was the first to use the title *folia* for a set of variations (*Libro primo d'intavolatura di chitarrone,* 1604, p. 28), but his *folia* is an early adumbration. Countless 17th-century guitarists wrote *folia* variations, some resembling the harmonic patterns of the "Cara cosa" or the "Pavaniglia," and others that of the harmonic sequence of the later *folia.*

Bibl.: Otto Gombosi, "Zur Frühgeschichte der Folia," *AM* 8 (1936): 119–29. Id., "The Cultural and Folkloristic Background of the *Folía,*" *PAMS* 1940: 88–95. John Ward, "The Folia," *Utrecht,* 1952, pp. 415–22. Lawrence H. Moe, "Dance Music in Printed Italian Lute Tablatures from 1507 to 1611"

(Ph.D. diss., Harvard Univ., 1956), pp. 125–28. Richard Hudson, "The *Folia* Dance and the *Folia* Formula in 17th Century Guitar Music," *MD* 25 (1971): 199–221. Id., "The Folia, Fedele, and Falsobordone," *MQ* 58 (1972): 398–411. Id., "The Folia Melodies," *AM* 45 (1973): 98–119. L.H.M.

Folk music. A term denoting a number of different kinds of music, with significant differences in connotation in different parts of the world, in different social classes, and at different points in history. Most typically the term refers to music in the oral tradition, often in a relatively simple style, primarily of rural provenance, normally performed by nonprofessionals, used and understood by broad segments of a population, characteristic of a nation, society, or ethnic group, and claimed by one of these as its own. These criteria apply largely to folk music as it existed in Europe and the Americas in earlier times to the end of the 19th century. In the 20th century the concept of folk music was taken up by urban society, and compositions known as folk songs—some taken over from oral tradition and many especially composed, using stylistic elements of folk music—became major components of political and social movements. These included nationalist initiatives in eastern Europe before World War I, the Nazi movement, the politics of labor unions, peace initiatives in the U.S. in the 1960s and 1970s, and critiques of government environmental policies. In European and North American cultures, 20th-century revivals of folk songs preserved the older traditions but in urbanized and mass-media contexts. The term (and its equivalents in other languages) continues to be used most to identify music associated with a nation, ethnic group, or social class, and while it is most useful for explicating the musical culture of Europe and the Americas before ca. 1920, it has analogues in Asian languages, whose cultures maintain musical taxonomies not unlike those of Europe.

The lines between folk music, popular music, art music, and other classes are difficult to draw; in North American culture, while folk ballads such as "Barbara Allen" and children's songs such as "Oh Where Have You Been, Billy Boy?" are readily accepted as folk songs, it is not always easy to define well-known hymns, Christmas carols, widely known art songs such as Schubert's "Heidenröslein" or Brahms' "Lullaby," college "fight songs" and similar music within this continuum, although they share several of the mentioned characteristics. Some genres of popular music—country, especially, but also folk rock and various European versions of world beat—are also on the boundaries between folk and other classes of music.

Folk music as concept and repertory in Asian societies is discussed in the articles devoted to those cultures; this article focuses on folk music in European and European-derived cultures and concentrates on the tradition outside the scope of special 20th-century developments.

I. *Cultural characteristics.* 1. Transmission. Oral or aural tradition is often considered the central characteristic of folk music. Outside the culture of western Europe, however, the art music of Asia also is learned mainly by hearing. Popular music uses mixed written and oral transmission, as does jazz, which is mainly an art music. Many folk instrumentalists such as fiddlers in the U.S. and Scandinavia can and do read music. Folk singers may use printed versions of song texts, negating the purely oral character of the tradition. Furthermore, the aural components in the transmission of Western art music must not be neglected. A sharp dichotomy along these lines is not properly descriptive.

A piece of folk music, a repertory, or a style may be claimed as the property of a folk community. But composition is normally carried out by individuals and not, as was sometimes asserted in the 19th century, by a group. Many folk songs originate outside the folk community, as hymns or art songs are taken up. In the course of transmission, however, a song may undergo change at the hands of many who learn and in turn teach it, a process called communal re-creation. A song may be shortened or lengthened, its mode, rhythm, or form altered, because of random imperfect learning, but more important, so that it will conform to the musical norms of the culture or to stylistic changes that the repertory may be undergoing as a result of urban influence or contact with neighboring peoples. As a result, folk songs do not have standard authentic forms, but exist, rather, as part of units called *tune families, which may consist of dozens or even hundreds of related tunes within one national repertory. In some cases, two or several national repertories contain related variants of a tune, which has adopted the style of each repertory that it has entered. For example, English, German, Czech, and Hungarian variants of a tune will have absorbed the characteristics of their nations; yet enough of musical identity remains to make recognition possible. Within a nation, the members of one tune family tend to accompany variants of one set of words, such as a ballad story (e.g., "Barbara Allen" or "Lord Randall"), or perhaps of a small number of text families. When a tune crosses national or linguistic boundaries, it seems rarely to be accompanied by a text; and similarly, when a ballad story is sung in several nations, it is normally with unrelated tunes.

2. Uses and functions. Folk music is frequently described as functional, with the implication that it is always used to accompany activities or to help in accomplishing some nonmusical purpose, whereas art music is thought to be exclusively for listening and "art for art's sake." Although this is an oversimplification, it is true that folk music is frequently associated with specific uses, some of which are found in all European and European-derived cultures. A large proportion are calendric songs, which are used to accompany rituals in the life's and year's cycles and include songs for birth, puberty, weddings, and funerals, as well as for solstice, equinox, planting, and harvest. Some of these reflect uses preceding the introduction

of Christianity, and others, such as the begging songs of young people with noisemakers at Easter in Germany, have combined archaic practices with Christian festivals. Such songs often have an archaic musical style.

Another major function shared by all of the West is narration, carried on for entertainment, preservation of history, and maintenance of ethnic identity. The most widespread genre is the *ballad, a strophic song usually dealing with a single incident or a simple plot. Most prominent in the English-speaking world are the Child ballads (identified and classified by Francis James Child), mainly of medieval origin, sung in Britain and North America to pentatonic or modal diatonic tunes monophonically, in a small number of rhythmic settings. Also important are broadside ballads, whose words (and sometimes tunes) were printed on large sheets and sold quickly, passing thereafter into oral tradition. Their texts were often based on incidents in local history or moralistic and sentimental tales, and their music was often more closely related to art music, having longer tunes, mainly in major, often accompanied in performance. Epic singing, comprising songs taking several hours, was once found throughout Europe but remains only in Slavic, Albanian, and Finnish traditions. The Finnish **Kalevala* was performed by pairs of singers. The Yugoslav epics deal with events of national history in the period of Turkish domination (ca. 1300–1600), seen from Christian and Muslim sides, and are sung at lengthy evening entertainments by soloists accompanying themselves on the **gusle,* a one-string fiddle. The singers are professionals who have undergone training at the hand of masters in order to learn complex subject matter and techniques of improvisation.

Other important genres, typically with distinct musical styles, are dance music (usually but not always instrumental), children's songs, work songs, and religious music performed outside the framework of the church. Folk music plays a particularly strong role in the culture of minorities, where it is a special device for underscoring ethnicity, particularly in 20th-century North America. In modern urban life, folk music has absorbed new functions in political, social, and student movements.

II. *Musical style.* 1. Form. Even though each nation has its distinctive style, a few characteristics pervade Western folk music. The typical melodic form is strophic, a stanza consisting of two to eight lines, with four most common. The relationship among the lines varies, progressive form (e.g., ABCD) being very common in older English folk song, and reverting forms (e.g., ABBA, AABA, ABCA, ABAB) more prominent in more recent British material. Similar forms are found in eastern Europe where, however, there is also a tendency to build stanzas from transpositions of a line to various pitch levels. AA^5A^5A or AAA_4A_4 (superscript and subscript numbers indicating intervals of transposition up and down, respectively) are important in Hungarian folk song, and AA^5BA in Czech. Textual and musical lines almost universally coincide in length. In western Europe, a song normally consists of several lines of equal musical length; in eastern Europe, line lengths are more varied.

Children's songs and sung epics include exceptions to the strophic principle. In the latter, the unit may be the line, which is repeated and varied up to dozens of times. Children's ditties may also consist of only one repeated line and tend to be simple in rhythmic and melodic structure as well, using only two, three, or four tones. The style of children's songs is similar throughout Europe and is closely related to the style of the world's simplest tribal music and to that of children's songs in other cultures.

In older repertories, such as that of Romanian Christmas carols, which have hundreds of formal relationships in songs of two to six lines, formal variety is greater than in recently developed genres such as English and German broadside ballads, which, as a result of influence from popular music and Protestant church music, have more standardization, with AABA predominating.

2. Polyphony. Most folk music is monophonic, but harmony and polyphony are found. Instrumental accompaniment probably began with the use of a drone and gradually added chordal materials and, eventually, functional harmony. Vocal folk polyphony is far more common in eastern and southern than in western Europe. Besides the drone principle, rounds and *heterophony are widespread. Parallel singing (not carried through a performance but alternating with other kinds of voice relationships and monophony) is the most common in a variety of intervals. For example, parallel thirds are prominent in Spain, Germany, Austria, and Czechoslovakia; parallel fourths and fifths, in eastern and southern Slavic cultures; seconds and sevenths in Yugoslavia and mountainous areas of Italy. Instrumental folk polyphony is more prominent than vocal folk polyphony. Thus, Scandinavian folk song is largely monophonic, but complex styles of instrumental polyphony were developed on various bowed instruments, particularly the *Hardanger fiddle of Norway.

3. Melody. Generally speaking, the scales of European folk music are compatible with the diatonic system. Intervals outside it—three-quarter tones and "neutral" thirds—are found in the Balkans and may result from Middle Eastern influence. Within the diatonic system, three main scale types are used: (i) Scales of two, three, or four tones separated by minor thirds and major seconds are found mainly in the children's songs and songs of archaic rituals. (ii) Pentatonic scales are of two types, the anhemitonic, composed of major seconds and minor thirds, and five-tone segments of diatonic scales. The former is prominent in northern and western Europe and in Hungary, and the latter in southern Europe. (iii) Diatonic modes

are found throughout the Continent, major being the most common, particularly in styles of recent origin, with substantial use of Dorian and Mixolydian and the occasional appearance of Aeolian, Phrygian, and Lydian. In melodic contour, Western folk music is relatively unified, an arc-shape accounting for a large proportion, but gradual descent also widespread.

4. Rhythm. The aspects of music in which the various repertories differ most are rhythm and singing style or timbre. Regular isometric structure predominates in the West, whereas greater variety and irregularity are found in eastern Europe. This may be related to the tendency to use the metric foot of poetry as the main organizing principle in the West, whereas the total number of syllables per line plays a greater role in the East. Thus, a very common structure of English folk song is the ballad meter, with a four-line stanza alternating lines of four and three iambic feet. In many Hungarian folk songs, all lines may have the same number of syllables, but this number may vary from six to nineteen, with eight, ten, and eleven particularly common. The structure of language may affect folksong rhythm. For example, English and German songs, in their tendency to begin on an anacrusis, reflect the use of unstressed articles and initial unstressed syllables; Czech and Hungarian songs begin on stressed beats, reflecting the tendency to begin spoken utterances with accented syllables. When one can identify the nationality of a tune from its style, it is most commonly on the basis of characteristic rhythms.

5. Singing styles. One of the major differences between folk music and Western art music is in singing style: the way the voice is used and the kinds of sounds that are produced. Neither is the more natural, since each results from aesthetic and cultural values. In folk cultures, even though there is no formal instruction in using the voice, characteristic styles of sound production, ornamentation, nasality, raspiness, tension, vocal blend in group singing, tessitura, etc., are expected of singers. It seems likely that characteristics of a culture such as types of interpersonal relationships, political structure, and degrees of cooperation in labor play a part in determining the singing style of a society.

Although each nation has its one or several distinctive singing styles, it is possible to distinguish three main styles (Lomax, 1968). The "Old European" is relatively relaxed, unornamented, and often used in group singing; it is found in northern Europe, Germany, and parts of eastern Europe. The "Eurasian"—tenser, more nasal and ornamented, often with high tessitura—is common in the Balkans, Italy, Spain, and parts of England; it derives its name from the fact that it has much in common with Middle Eastern singing. A "Modern European" style, found in France, England, Ireland, and northern Italy, is intermediate. Another stylistic distinction partly based on singing style was suggested by Béla Bartók in his classification of the folk music of Hungary and neighboring countries. In the "parlando-rubato" style one finds songs without very precisely demarcated meter sung in somewhat variable tempo with ornamentation. The "tempo giusto" style has steadier tempo and less ornamentation. Although developed for Hungarian songs, these categories are found in many folk musics of Europe, including Spanish and English.

6. Style areas. Although singing-style boundaries cut across Europe in various ways and although each culture has its distinct repertory and style, it is possible to establish some stylistic areas. Some of these follow linguistic relationships, others are separated by natural boundaries, and some result from major historical events. Great Britain, Germany, and Scandinavia share a large repertory in major and pentatonic monophonic song with an emphasis on the ballad. Spain, southern Italy, and part of the Balkans have in common a singing style and scales related to those of the Islamic Middle East, which for centuries dominated the area. Hungarian folk music has relatively little in common with its Slavic neighbors, but shares pentatonic monophony and forms based on transposition of a half stanza with other Finno-Ugric peoples such as Finns and the Cheremis of eastern Russia. East and south Slavic peoples share traditions of choral singing. But linguistically unrelated peoples may also have similar styles, as indicated by the commonality of musical traits in Romania, Bulgaria, and Greece. In general, western European folk music has seen much more influence from art music and the popular music of the cities, and it exhibits, at least in recent times, less scalar, rhythmic, and formal variety than the repertories of eastern Europe, in which a relatively undisturbed folk tradition remained intact longer.

III. *Instruments.* The relationship between folk and art music seems much closer in instruments and instrumental music than in song. Folk cultures received many instruments from cities, courts, the church, and non-Western cultures. It is useful to consider folk instruments by their origin or source. Most widespread is a group that Western folk cultures share with the world's simplest tribal cultures. These include simple percussion instruments such as rattles, the bull-roarer, the musical bow, vertical flutes and wooden trumpets with few or no finger holes, and improvised sound sources such as pots and pans. These are used by children and in remnants of pre-Christian rituals, have a worldwide distribution, and comprise an archaic stratum in cultures as disparate as modern western Germany and eastern Finno-Ugric peoples on the outskirts of European culture. They are surely the oldest instruments of Europe. A second group consists of instruments brought to Europe from non-European cultures since the Middle Ages. Much more complex, they often changed greatly after coming to Europe. Among them are bagpipes, simple fiddles such as the one-string Yugoslav *gusle,* double-reed instruments, especially the twin oboes of the Balkans related to the ancient Greek *aulos, as well as the Yugoslav double recorders, all derived from the Middle East; and, presumably from Africa, banjo and xylophone. Another group comprises instruments developed in the folk cultures themselves from simple materials in imitation of more complex urban or court models. These include a simple fiddle of northwest Germany, the *Dolle,* made from a wooden shoe; the washtub bass, a kind of one-string double bass used in North America; and the more sophisticated bowed lyre once widespread in the British Isles but now known mainly in Finland. Of great importance is a fourth group of instruments taken from urban culture and from classical tradition, but changed. Examples are violins with sympathetic strings, related to the viola d'amore and used in Scandinavia since the 16th century, and the hurdy-gurdy, derived from the medieval organistrum and still played in France under the name *vielle.* Finally, there are instruments from art music that have been taken over into folk cultures, most prominently the violin, double bass, and clarinet. The manner of playing these instruments may, however, differ from that employed in art music. English and American folk fiddling uses less vibrato and few legato passages and makes little use of higher positions.

Although vocal tunes are sometimes performed instrumentally, there is, generally speaking, a separation of repertories and forms. A large proportion of instrumental folk music is intended for dancing. The most widespread form type consists of a series of lines, each repeated, with first and second endings, a form also found in medieval instrumental music. In a related form, a set of stanzalike strains is presented, each likewise repeated with different endings; it is well known in vernacular music such as dances and marches from the 18th century on.

IV. *History.* Because folk music lived for most of its history entirely in oral tradition, there are few documents for historical study, which must thus proceed on the basis of early collections made by musicians and amateurs from outside the folk culture, from the occasional uses of folk songs by art-music composers, and, most important, from extrapolation of processes observed in recent history and conjectures made from comparative study of folk music as it has existed in the last 150 years. The result is more a knowledge of the kinds of things that may normally have occurred than a knowledge of specific events.

1. Folk music and art music. Comparison with other world areas confirms the belief that there was at one time a repertory of extremely simple songs and a stock of equally simple instruments that were held in common with isolated tribal peoples and are still extant but confined to specific functions. The widespread use of pentatonicism in Europe corresponds to a similar development in many non-Western societies. The older, mature folk-music styles in Europe seem to be at least of medieval origin, considering the development of similar polyphonic forms and of scalar and modal types as well as the medieval origin of textual form and content. Development of scales is sometimes attributed to strictly musical determinants such as the filling in of thirds and fourths and the reduplication of tetrachordal structures at intervals of fifths. The latter may be related to the widespread use of forms in which transposition of a line up or down a fifth (e.g., in Hungary, Czechoslovakia, Ukraine, but also England) is the major structural principle.

Since the Middle Ages in western Europe, there seems to have been a constant interchange of materials with art and other urban music. Many folk tunes must have come from art music, and quite likely some melodies by composers had folk origins. Without subscribing to it, it is necessary to mention a once widely held theory to the effect that all folk music and folklore came from city, court, or church, was simplified, and then remained intact while the art of the culture centers changed. This idea, that all folk music is "gesunkenes Kulturgut" (or debased cultural material), cannot be accepted as generally valid, but some folk music surely has this kind of history.

Cultural distance between village and city or court was perhaps not great throughout the Middle Ages, and thus an easily separable body of folk music may not always have existed. The growth of cities in the Renaissance may have isolated rural life, thus separating the strands, but humanistic attitudes tended also to accept folk music as rustic and antique. Renaissance composers made considerable use of folk and popular music in polyphonic settings and *quodlibets, and folk tunes were used as structural and motivic raw material for motets and Masses. Hymns of the Protestant Reformation also used folk material. In the Baroque period, folk music receded somewhat from the consciousness of the literate population, but was itself influenced by the development of printing and the distribution of songs on broadsides. In the late 18th century, folk music and folklore again became important in art music. Their role as raw musical material, as stylistic paradigm, as concept and subject matter in program music and opera rose through the period of 19th- and 20th-century musical nationalism. The late 18th century also saw the beginning of folk-music collecting on a large scale, particularly through the influence of Johann Gottfried Herder, and the growth of urban and industrialized culture subjected folk music increasingly to the influences of art and popular music. In the 19th century, the widespread publication of collections gave it greater acceptance among the educated classes.

With the invention of recording, folk communities (especially in western Europe and the Americas) began to have contact with a way of standardizing tunes and performances easier to comprehend than written music, and recordings by outstanding musicians began to dominate some of the traditions. In the 20th century, folk and popular musics began to merge, oral tradition was replaced or supplemented by written and recorded traditions, and professional singers began to sing versions of folk songs and to compose new songs with elements of folk styles in music, text, and subject matter. Already in the 19th century, folk music had played a role in social and labor movements, and as a concept (more perhaps than in style) it continues to be used in social and political protest, development of ethnic consciousness among minorities, and student movements. A number of developments, such as the performance of folk music by large orchestras of folk instruments in eastern Europe, the popularization of mixed genres such as *bluegrass and *folk rock, and the emergence of urban singers of folk song who achieved mass popularity, such as Bob Dylan, Pete Seeger, and Joan Baez, characterized the history of folk music in the mid-20th century. Many of the best-known folk songs in American culture after 1950 were actually—in the tradition of the broadside ballads—composed by folk singers such as Woody Guthrie, Seeger, and groups such as the Kingston Trio and Peter, Paul, and Mary, and addressed issues of current concern and relevance.

2. Processes. Folk-music styles have changed as a result of cultural change and interaction with art and popular music, but many individual songs have remained in the repertories for centuries, participating in these changes but keeping their identity. The history of the individual song is an important strand of the history of folk music and can best be studied through comparison of versions known since the beginning of widespread collecting. Tune families—groups of tunes that appear to be significantly related—exhibit a number of types of history, some developing in compact form, others in widely divergent strands, some crossing national boundaries, and others remaining geographically restricted. The extant versions of a song may differ greatly in age, some reflecting forms centuries old and others, recent developments. The existence of seemingly related tunes in a variety of countries may indicate that a tune spread through oral tradition over a period of centuries or that, given a limited stylistic vocabulary and repertories of thousands of songs, a group of cultures is bound to create some tunes that are similar.

Among the approaches to conjectural history is the classification of folk songs in large collections, begun ca. 1900, at first for the purpose of placing tunes so they could easily be found by their musical characteristics and then for the purpose of identifying tunes that are genetically related. Ilmari Krohn, Béla Bartók, Bertrand H. Bronson, and Pál Jardyáni were prominent in establishing classification systems. Bartók's work with Hungarian folk music resulted in the identification of an "old" style, partly shared with other Finno-Ugric peoples, a "new," distinctively Hungarian style, and a group of "mixed genera," reflecting influences from urban and neighboring cultures. Classification studies indicate that identifying related tunes requires various criteria. Melodic contour, for example, tends to remain constant in variants of an English folk tune, and rhythmic structure, in Hungarian. Another characteristic of the history of folk music is the tendency of isolated segments of a society, such as European immigrant groups in the Americas and in German enclaves in pre–World War II eastern Europe, to retain old forms of folk music.

V. *Research.* Scholarly study of folk music began in 19th-century England and Germany, with large-scale collecting for the purpose of preservation and providing material for art-music composers. Ludwig Erk and Franz Magnus Boehme made comprehensive collections of German folk music. Early in the 20th century, Cecil Sharp discovered the importance of collecting older European materials in North America. Béla Bartók and Zoltán Kodály provided models for collecting, transcribing, and classifying large eastern European repertories, largely with nationalistic aims. Phillips Barry and, later, Bertrand H. Bronson and Samuel P. Bayard dealt with the nature of folk tradition and tune relationships. By the middle of the 20th century, folk-music research had been absorbed into the methodological framework of *ethnomusicology, and studies similar to those of non-Western cultures were being carried out by scholars such as Charles Seeger, George Herzog, and Alan Lomax.

Bibl.: Ludwig Erk and Franz Magnus Boehme, *Deutscher Liederhort* (Leipzig, 1893–94). Béla Bartók, *Hungarian Folk Music,* trans. M. D. Calvocoressi (London: Oxford U Pr, 1931). Cecil J. Sharp, comp., *English Folk Songs from the Southern Appalachians* (London: Oxford U Pr, 1932). Julian von Pulikowski, *Geschichte des Begriffes Volkslied im musikalischen Schrifttum* (Heidelberg: C Winter, 1933). Kurt Schindler, comp., *Folk Music and Poetry of Spain and Portugal* (New York: Hispanic Institute, 1941). George Herzog, "Song: Folk Song and the Music of Folk Song," in *Funk and Wagnalls Standard Dictionary of Folklore,* vol. 2 (New York: Funk & Wagnalls, 1950). Béla Bartók and Albert B. Lord, eds., *Serbo-Croatian Folk Songs* (New York: Columbia U Pr, 1951). Walter Wiora, comp., *Europäischer Volksgesang, Mw* 4 (Cologne: A Volk, 1952; trans. Eng. Robert Kolben, 1966). Maud Karpeles, ed., *Folk Songs of Europe* (London: Novello, 1956). Walter Wiora, *Europäischer Volksmusik und abendländische Tonkunst* (Kassel: J P Hinnenthal, 1957). Bence Szabolcsi, *Bausteine zu einer Geschichte der Melodie* (Budapest: Corvina, 1959). D. K. Wilgus, *Anglo-American Folksong Scholarship since 1898* (New Brunswick: Rutgers U Pr, 1959). Bertrand H. Bronson, *The Traditional Tunes of the Child Ballads,* 4 vols. (Princeton: Princeton U Pr, 1959–73). Zoltán Kodály, *Folk Music of Hungary,* rev. and trans. Ronald Tempest and Cynthia Jolly (New York: Macmillan, 1960). Alan Lomax, ed., *The Folk Songs of North America* (Garden City, N.Y.: Doubleday, 1960). Albert B. Lord, *The Singer of Tales* (Cambridge, Mass.: Harvard U Pr, 1960). Charles Haywood, *A Bibliography of North American Folklore and Folksong,* 2nd ed. (New York: Dover, 1961). Ernst Emsheimer, *Studia ethnomusicologica eurasiatica* (Stockholm: Musikhistoriska museet, 1964). Karel Vetterl, *A Select Bibli-*

ography of European Folk Music (Prague, 1966). *Annual Bibliography of European Ethnomusicology* (Bratislava: Slowakisches Nationalmuseum, 1967–). Alan Lomax, *Folk Song Style and Culture,* ed. Edwin E. Erickson (Washington, D.C.: Amer Assoc for the Advancement of Science, 1968). Werner Danckert, *Das europäische Volkslied,* 2nd ed. (Bonn: H Bouvier, 1970). Maud Karpeles, *An Introduction to English Folk Song* (New York: Oxford U Pr, 1973). Bruno Nettl, *Folk and Traditional Music of the Western Continents,* 2nd ed. (Englewood Cliffs, N.J.: Prentice-Hall, 1973). Charles Seeger, *Studies in Musicology 1935–1975* (Berkeley and Los Angeles: U of Cal Pr, 1977). James Porter, "The Traditional Music of Europeans in America," *UCLA Selected Reports in Ethnomusicology* 3/1 (1978): 1–23. Bálint Sárosi, *Folk Music: Hungarian Musical Idiom* (Budapest: Corvina, 1986). Philip V. Bohlman, *The Study of Folk Music in the Modern World* (Bloomington: Ind U Pr, 1988). Robbie Lieberman, *"My Song Is My Weapon": People's Songs, American Communism, and the Politics of Culture 1930–50* (Urbana: U of Ill Pr, 1989). James R. Cowdery, *The Melodic Tradition of Ireland* (Kent, Ohio: Kent St U Pr, 1990). Neil V. Rosenberg, *Transforming Tradition: Folk Music Revivals Examined* (Urbana: U of Ill Pr, 1993). Timothy Rice, *May It Fill Your Soul: Experiencing Bulgarian Music* (Chicago: U of Chicago Pr, 1994). Mark Slobin, ed., *Retuning Culture: Musical Changes in Central and Eastern Europe* (Durham: Duke U Pr, 1996). Jan Ling, *A History of European Folk Music* (Rochester: U of Rochester Pr, 1997). Relevant volumes in the *Garland Encyclopedia of World Music* (New York: Routledge): *North America,* ed. Ellen Koskoff (1999), *Europe,* ed. James Porter, Timothy Rice, and Chris Goertzen (2000). See also the various volumes of *Handbuch der europäischen Volksmusikinstrumente* and the "Current Bibliography" in all issues of *Ethno.* B.N.

Folk rock. A fusion of the songwriting styles associated with the urban folk scene of the early 1960s and the amplified instrumentation and vocal harmonies of Beatles-era rock. The Byrds' 1965 recording of Bob Dylan's "Mr. Tambourine Man" is typical of the genre. A.Z.

Follia [It.]. See *Folia.*

Fonds d'orgue [Fr.]. In the classic French organ, a registration consisting normally of the 8′ **Montre,* 4′ **Prestant,* and **Bourdons* at 16′, 8′, and 4′.

Fonola. See Pianola.

Fontane di Roma [It., Fountains of Rome]. A symphonic poem by Respighi, composed in 1916. It is in four movements, each of which depicts a fountain in Rome: Valle Giulia at dawn, Triton in the morning, Trevi at midday, and Villa Medici at sunset.

Fontanelle [Fr.]. See Shawm.

Foot. (1) See Prosody. (2) In organ building, a measure of the pitch at which a pipe sounds. The terminology derives from the fact that an open flue pipe sounding the pitch C (two octaves below middle C) measures about eight feet (2.44 m) in length. This pipe is taken to represent all pipes or ranks of pipes, regardless of length (which will necessarily be different for every pitch), that sound the actual pitch represented by the individual keyboard key or keys to which they are connected. All such pipes are thus said to be at eight-foot (usually written 8-ft. or 8′) pitch. A pipe twice as long sounds an octave lower; one half as long sounds an octave higher, etc. [see Acoustics]. Hence, a pipe or rank that sounds an octave lower than the pitch represented by the key or keys that sound it is said to be at 16′ pitch; an octave higher, at 4′ pitch, etc., regardless of the particular pitch name in question. Thus, if the key corresponding on the keyboard to the pitch d is depressed when coupled to a pipe at 16′ pitch, D will sound; when coupled to a pipe at 4′ pitch, d′ will sound. The system can be extended to include pipes or ranks that sound intervals other than one or more octaves from the standard 8′ pitch, as follows: 8′, actual or untransposed pitch; 16′, one octave below; 32′, two octaves below; 5 1/3′, a fifth above; 4′, one octave above; 3 1/5′, an octave and a third above; 2 2/3′, an octave and a fifth above; 2′, two octaves above; 1 3/5′, two octaves and a third above; 1 1/3′, two octaves and a fifth above; 1′, three octaves above. These terms are also used to describe the relative pitch of the strings or choirs of strings of the *harpsichord; to classify other types of instruments; and to identify octaves within the total range of pitches (the 8′ octave proceeding upward from C, the 4′ from c, the 2′ from c′, etc.).

Forefall. See Backfall, forefall.

Foreground. See Schenker analysis.

Forgeries. See Authenticity.

Fork fingering. On wind instruments with finger holes, a fingering in which the middle finger of either hand is lifted while the two fingers on either side cover their respective holes. See also Cross fingering.

Forlana, furlana [It.; Fr. *forlane*]. A lively dance from the northern Italian province of Friulia. The "Ballo Furlano L'arboscello" in Pierre Phalèse's *Chorearum molliorum collectanea* (1583) and in Jakob Paix's *Ein Schön Nutz und Gebreüchlich Orgel Tablaturbuch* (1583) is in duple meter (2/4), in a style suggesting a folk dance. From the early part of the 17th century until well into the 18th, however, it flourished as an elegant French court dance, one with lascivious connotations. It was a gay dance, in a compound duple meter (6/8 or 6/4), with dotted rhythms. Its popularity is evident by its frequent inclusion in *fêtes* and *ballets* by Campra, Mouret, Lalande, and Rameau. Choreographies exist in Raoul-Auger Feuillet's (*Recüeil de dances,* 1704). Forlanas have been composed from the 18th century to the present as abstract compositions, frequently as a part of a suite.

Bibl.: Paul Nettl, *The Story of Dance Music* (New York: Philosophical Library, 1947), pp. 185ff. L.H.M.

Form. The shape of a musical composition as defined by all of its pitches, rhythms, dynamics, and timbres. In this sense, there can be no distinction between musical form and specifically musical content, since to change even a single pitch or rhythm that might be regarded as part of the content of a composition necessarily also changes the shape of that composition, even if only in detail. The term form is also applied, however, to abstractions or generalizations that can be drawn from groups of compositions for purposes of comparing them with one another. A form in this sense is defined by a loose group of general features shared in varying degrees by a relatively large number of works, no two of which are in fact exactly the same. Only when form is used in this sense can a distinction be made between form and content. Any attempt to define forms of this kind too rigidly will be futile or will at the very least greatly diminish the usefulness of the definition by excluding too many specific compositions.

Both of these senses of the term form apply equally well to notated compositions of the kind that have characterized Western art music and to performances that are partly or entirely improvised, such as characterize much music in all cultures. In many contexts, form in the sense of loose abstraction is in part prescriptive. That is, the composer or performer may consciously work within established forms. In many such contexts, however, originality on the part of the composer or performer is expected and prized in the handling of even the most well-defined forms, and forms may be gradually redefined or cease to be cultivated altogether as a result.

The study of form in Western art music has been shaped in considerable measure by a tension between Western scholarship's urge to classify and the value attached since at least the Romantic period to originality [see also Composition]. And because the tonal system facilitates classification and underlies a central part of the repertory of Western art music, form in tonal music has received the greatest attention. The years from about 1700 to about 1830 provide the bulk of the repertory on which classifications of form have been based, and many 20th-century discussions of form have their roots in writings of the late 18th and early 19th centuries. Compared with attempts to produce taxonomies of form, efforts to explore the underlying principles of musical form and the mechanisms by which the listener perceives form have been rather limited (see Meyer, 1973; see also Analysis, Schenker analysis).

On the largest scale, tonal works may be classified as either single or compound forms. Single (or simple) forms are tonally self-contained and formally complete, and they are not divisible into smaller, self-sufficient works. Compound (or composite) forms are those that include two or more single forms; compound forms thus include forms with more than one *movement, such as the *sonata, *symphony, *string quartet, and *suite. A compound form in which the same or similar music is used in two or more movements is said to be *cyclic. In principle, *opera, *cantata, and *oratorio are also compound forms, though the variety among such works and the considerable length of many examples make difficult the formulation of detailed definitions of them as forms.

Single forms are often classified on the basis of their use of tonality and repetition. A first step in the analysis of form is often the identification of the component sections of a work, and both tonality and repetition are important in the definition of sections. With respect to tonality, a fundamental distinction is made between works in which a major section is incomplete tonally, ending in a key different from the one in which it begins and thus demanding continuation or resolution in a succeeding section, and works in which the principal components are self-contained tonally, beginning and ending in the same key. The former type is said to be open, the latter closed. Most binary forms are open in this sense; most ternary forms are closed [see Binary and ternary form, Sonata form, Aria]. Forms characterized by repetition or recurrence include *rondo, *variation (including *chaconne and *passacaglia), and some types of *concerto movements.

Some types of works often described as forms are characterized more by procedures or techniques than by any well-defined pattern of larger elements. Such types include some cultivated long before the 18th century as well as some cultivated principally in the 18th and 19th centuries. Examples are *fugue, *ricercar, *canzona, *toccata, *fantasia, and the imitative *motet.

Vocal works from all periods may take the larger aspects of their form from their text. The principal types include the **formes fixes* of early French secular music [see also Chanson], the **frottola* and related forms, *bar form, the forms of *Gregorian chant, the *Mass, and *strophic songs and hymns.

The forms of tonal music inherited from the 18th century were considerably modified in the 19th, and with the abandonment of tonality by many composers early in the 20th century, the importance of these forms declined considerably. Analogies were found for some tonal procedures, and the thematic aspects of earlier forms were still readily available. These aspects of form found use in music now sometimes termed *neoclassical. But composers of *twelve-tone and *serial music moved in the direction of forms that avoid repetition altogether and instead unfold continuously. Each new work thus defines its own form without reference to other works. This approach to form and musical time has important precedents in works by Debussy. Composers of *aleatory music, on the other hand, explored radical alternatives to the fixity of the individual *composition and thus to shared concepts of form. Works that can be realized in fundamentally different ways are sometimes termed mobile or open forms. Beginning in the late 1960s, some composers created works in which form results from some process (e.g., *phasing) to which minimal materials are subjected, often over long periods of time [see also Twentieth century, Western art music of the].

Bibl.: George Perle, *Serial Composition and Atonality* (Berkeley and Los Angeles: U of Calif Pr, 1962; 5th ed., 1981). Douglass M. Green, *Form in Tonal Music* (New York: Holt, Rinehart, & Winston, 1965; 2nd ed., 1979). Wallace Berry, *Form in Music* (Englewood Cliffs, N.J.: Prentice-Hall, 1966). Edward T. Cone, *Musical Form and Musical Performance* (New York: Norton, 1968). Leonard B. Meyer, *Explaining Music: Essays and Explorations* (Berkeley and Los Angeles: U of Cal Pr, 1973; R: Chicago: U of Chicago Pr, 1978). Ellis B. Kohs, *Musical Form: Studies in Analysis and Synthesis* (Boston: Houghton Mifflin, 1976). See also Analysis, Theory.

Formant. See Acoustics III.

Format. See Printing of music, Choirbook, Partbook, Score.

Formes fixes [Fr.]. A group of forms that dominated the secular poetry and music of France in the 14th and 15th centuries. The principal *formes fixes* are the **ballade*, the **rondeau*, and the **virelai*. These all probably evolved from late 12th- and 13th-century dance forms with refrain, loosely referred to as *cançon de *carole* or *rondet de carole*. A related form is the **bergerette*, popular especially in the latter half of the 15th century.

Bibl.: Pierre Aubry, "Refrains et rondeaux du XIIIe siècle," *Riemann*, 1909, pp. 213–28. Friedrich Gennrich, ed., *Rondeaux, Virelais und Balladen aus dem Ende des XII., dem XIII. und dem ersten den über Drittel des XIV. Jahrhundert*, 1 (Dresden, 1921); 2 (Göttingen, 1927); 3 (Langen, 1963). Friedrich Gennrich, *Grundriss einer Formenlehre des mittelalterlichen Liedes* (Halle: M Niemeyer, 1932). Gilbert Reaney, "Concerning the Origins of the Rondeau, Virelai and Ballade Forms," *MD* 6 (1952): 155–66. Pierre Le Gentil, *Le Virelai et le villancico* (Paris: Les Belles Lettres, 1954). Willi Apel, "Rondeaux, Virelais, and Ballades in French 13th-Century Song," *JAMS* 7 (1954): 121–30. Marcel Françon, "On the Nature of the Virelai," *Symposium* 11 (1955): 348–52. Gilbert Reaney, "The Ballades, Rondeaux and Virelais of Guillaume de Machaut: Melody, Rhythm and Form," *AM* 27 (1955): 40–58. Gilbert Reaney, "The Poetic Form of Machaut's Musical Works," *MD* 13 (1959): 25–41. Friedrich Gennrich, *Das altfranzösische Rondeau und Virelai*, Summa Musicae Medii Aevi 10 (Langen bei Frankfurt, 1963). Daniel Poirion, *Le poète et le prince* (Paris: Presses universitaires de France, 1965). Nico H. J. van den Boogaard, *Rondeaux et refrains du XIIe siècle au début du XIVe* (Paris: Klincksieck, 1969). Nigel Wilkins, *One Hundred Ballades, Rondeaux and Virelais from the Late Middle Ages* (Cambridge: Cambridge U Pr, 1969). Pierre Bec, *La Lyrique française au Moyen Âge (XIIe–XIIIe siècles)*, 2 vols. (Paris: A & J Picard, 1977–78). Lawrence Earp, "Lyrics for Reading and Lyrics for Singing in Late Medieval France: The Development of the Dance Lyric from Adam de la Halle to Guillaume de Machaut," in *The Union of Words and Music in Medieval Poetry*, ed. Rebecca A. Baltzer, Thomas Cable, and James I. Wimsatt (Austin: U of Tex Pr, 1991), pp. 101–31. Mark Everist, *French Motets in the Thirteenth Century: Music, Poetry and Genre* (Cambridge: Cambridge U Pr, 1994). Mark Everist, "The Polyphonic *Rondeau* c. 1300: Repertory and Context," *EMH* 15 (1996): 59–96.

Fort. (1) [Fr.] **Forte*, strong. (2) [Ger.] Forth, onward; off, as with respect to an organ stop.

Forte [It., abbr. *f*]. Loud; *fortissimo* (abbr. *ff, fff*), very loud; *più forte* (sometimes abbr. *ff*), louder; *mezzoforte (mf)*, moderately loud; *fortepiano (fp)*, loud followed immediately by soft. See Performance marks.

Fortepiano [It.]. (1) See *Forte*. (2) Any of various early forms of the *piano.

Fortissimo [It., abbr. *ff*]. Very loud. See *Forte*.

Fortspinnung [Ger., spinning out]. The process by which melodic material is continuously derived from a brief figure, for example, by means of a sequence [see Sequence (1)], so as to produce a continuous melodic line rather than one characterized by balanced phrases of the type described as *antecedent and consequent. The term has thus been used to characterize textures typical of music of the Baroque period as against those of the Classical period (Kurth). Wilhelm Fischer used the term to describe the modulatory passage occurring in a *sonata-form exposition, which he termed an example of *Fortspinnungtypus* in contrast to a *Liedtypus* (song type) consisting simply of antecedent and consequent phrases or sections.

Bibl.: Wilhelm Fischer, "Zur Entwicklungsgeschichte des Wiener klassischen Stils," *SzMw* 3 (1915): 24–84. Ernst Kurth, *Grundlagen des linearen Kontrapunkts*, 3rd ed. (Berlin: M Hesse, 1927). Friedrich Blume, "Fortspinnung und Entwicklung," *JMP* 36 (1929): 51–70.

Forty-eight, The. Popular name for Bach's **Well-Tempered Clavier*.

Forza [It.]. Strength, force.

Forza del destino, La [It., The Power of Fate]. Opera in four acts by Verdi (libretto by Francesco Maria Piave, after Ángel de Saavedra Duke of Riva's play *Don Álvaro, o La fuerza del sino* and Friedrich Schiller's *Wallensteins Lager*), produced in St. Petersburg in 1862; revised version (libretto revised by Antonio Ghislanzoni) produced in Milan in 1869. Setting: Spain and Italy about the middle of the 18th century.

Forzando, forzato [It., abbr. *fz*]. Forcing, forced, i.e., strongly accented.

Foundation stops. An organ registration including the *flue stops of 16′, 8′, and 4′ pitch. See *Fonds d'orgue*.

Fountains of Rome. See *Fontane di Roma*.

Four-foot. See Foot.

Four-line. See Pitch names.

Fourniture [Fr.]. The main *mixture stop of the classical French organ, usually of four to six ranks, with the lowest pitch at C being 1 1/3′ for an organ based on 8′ pitch, and 2′ for one based on 16′ pitch.

Fours, trade fours. See Trading.

Four Saints in Three Acts. Opera in a prelude and four acts by Virgil Thomson (libretto by Gertrude Stein), produced in Hartford, Connecticut, in 1934. The four saints of the title are Saint Theresa, Saint Settlement, Saint Ignatius Loyola, and Saint Chavez, though 30 or more saints appear in the course of the four (not three) acts. Although the historical subject matter is from 16th-century Spain, the libretto is not intended to reflect a coherent narrative.

Four Seasons, The [It. *Le quattro stagioni*]. The first four concertos of Vivaldi's *Il cimento dell'armonia e dell'inventione* op. 8 (published ca. 1725), a set of twelve concertos for solo violin, strings, and continuo. Each of the four is preceded by a sonnet describing a season, and some lines correspond to specific passages in the music.

Four-shape note. See Shape-note.

Fourth. See Interval; Scale degrees; Consonance, dissonance; Tetrachord.

Fourth chord. A chord consisting entirely or principally of fourths (e.g., c–f–b♭), in contradistinction to the *chords built of thirds that characterize *tonal music. Fourth chords were widely used in music of the 20th century, e.g., by Scriabin [see Mystic chord], Hindemith, and Bartók. See also Quartal harmony.

Foxtrot. The enduring American social dance in 4/4. Introduced in 1913, it became a genre encompassing many patterns of steps. It borrowed freely from extant dance types and engendered new variants (e.g., the *quickstep and slow blues). Dance-band musicians applied the name to thousands of popular tunes in 4/4 in moderate tempo with *two-beat or *walking basslines. B.K.

Fp [It.]. Abbr. for *fortepiano* [see *Forte*].

Fragments [Fr.]. In 18th-century Paris, works for the stage incorporating favorite selections from operas or ballets by one or more composers.

Frame drum. A portable drum with one or sometimes two membranes stretched over a light, narrow, and usually circular frame. Some varieties have jingles attached to the frame, and some have a handle. They are most commonly held in one hand and struck with the other, but some are beaten with a stick. They are distributed almost worldwide and are depicted in Mesopotamian art as early as 2000 B.C.E. See, e.g., *Daff*, Tambourine.

Frame harp. A *harp enclosed on all three sides. One side is a sound box, another a neck, the third a pillar. The strings are stretched between the neck and the sound box. The orchestral harp is of this type. See also Angle harp, Arched harp.

Française [Fr.]. In Germany, the English *country dance and its French derivative the **contredanse*.

France. I. *Current musical life and related institutions.* Paris is the center of French musical life for art music, but much activity also takes place in the provinces. General responsibility is held by the Bureau de musique, which was founded in 1966 as a part of the Ministry of Cultural Affairs.

1. Opera. Paris, for many decades the operatic capital of all Europe as well as of France, gives operatic productions at two main sites—the Palais Garnier (Opéra) and the Salle Favart (Opéra-Studio, successor of the Opéra-Comique). Other French cities that have significant seasons of opera are Avignon, Bordeaux, Dijon, Lille, Lyons, Marseilles, Nancy, Nantes, Nice, Rouen, Toulouse, and Tours.

2. Performing groups. The French government subsidizes more than 30 orchestras, including the Orchestre de Paris and the Orchestre de l'Ile-de-France in Paris and sizable ensembles in many other cities, such as Lyons (Orchestre Philharmonique Rhône-Alpes), Nantes and Angers (Orchestre des Pays de Loire), Amiens, Dijon, and Toulouse. The principal broadcast organization (Office de Radiodiffusion-Télévision Française, or ORTF) supports three full-sized orchestras, a chamber orchestra, and several smaller instrumental groups in Paris, and about six orchestras in the provinces. The country has numerous other chamber ensembles, some of which receive state support.

Organizations cultivating choral music include two choirs, one large and one small, maintained by the ORTF, which also has a choir school for boys. The choir of the Cathedral of Notre Dame of Paris presents public concerts, as do choirs associated with many other religious institutions. Gregorian chant and other early vocal music are widely performed.

3. Festivals. Of the many annual music festivals in France, most take place during the summer and fall. Those in Strasbourg (begun in 1938), Lyons (1945), and Avignon (1946) are among the oldest. The festival at Saintes is devoted to early music, while those in La Rochelle, Royan, and Metz feature contemporary music. The Festival du Marais and Festival Estival are just two of Paris's many annual festivals, and others of importance are located in Prades, Besançon, and Tours.

4. Education. The Paris Conservatory is the foremost national institution of musical education in France. In addition, a number of state-supported music schools or conservatories (often called *Écoles nationales de musique*) are located in cities throughout the country. The curriculum of these institutions is to a large extent standardized, although the latter part of the 20th century saw attempts at decentralization. One

such project was the founding of the Conservatoire National Supérieur in Lyons (1979), meant to become an equal with the Paris Conservatory. There are chairs of musicology at the Sorbonne and the University of Strasbourg. Among the best-known private schools of music are the Schola cantorum (founded in 1894) and the École normale de musique (founded in 1919), both located in Paris.

5. Publishing. In the early 1980s, the music publishing industry in France underwent substantial change, accompanied by mergers of large historic houses (Heugel into Leduc, Eschig into Durand). The most active publishers at present include Durand (founded in 1869 and publisher of many of France's most well-known composers since), A. Leduc (specializing in instructional material, new works by French composers, and music of the 19th century and before), Heugel (20th-century music and practical editions of early music), H. Lemoine (new and instructional works), Salabert (didactic, light, and new music and occasional editions of earlier works), R. Martin (instructional, light, and new music), and G. Billaudot (extremely active; all types of music). R. Martin is in Mâcon; the rest are located in Paris.

6. Broadcasting. The Office de Radiodiffusion-Télévision Française (ORTF) devotes one radio channel, France-Musique, entirely to the discussion and performance of art music. In addition to performing groups [see 2 above], this central broadcast organization supports an electronic music group in Paris [see Electro-acoustic music].

II. *History.* *Gallican chant was the Christian liturgical chant of the region until the 8th century, when it was suppressed in favor of the *Gregorian. From the 9th to the 12th centuries, the country played an important role in the development of additions to the liturgy (especially *trope, *sequence, and *hymn) and of *liturgical drama. The monastery of *St. Martial in Limoges and the Cathedral of *Notre Dame in Paris were centers for the development of early polyphony. Monophonic secular song was cultivated in the 12th and 13th centuries by the *troubadours and *trouvères. Polyphonic secular music (particularly the **rondeau,* **ballade,* **virelai,* **bergerette,* and at times the *motet) began to appear in the 13th century, was brought to a high state of development in the **ars nova* (14th century) by composers such as Philippe de Vitry (1291–1361) and Guillaume de Machaut (ca. 1310–77), and continued to be written in the 15th century [see Chanson]. *Organum (with *discant sections), **conductus,* later *motet, and still later *Mass were the more important polyphonic sacred genres.

Secular music of the 16th century in France included both instrumental music, particularly compositions for the lute and for keyboard, and vocal music, such as the *chanson, **musique mesurée,* and the **air de cour.* Sacred motets and Masses continued to be written. In the 17th century, the patronage of the royal court dominated French musical life, particularly under Louis XIV. The most prominent composers of the time were Jean-Baptiste Lully (1632–87), Michel-Richard de Lalande (1657–1726), Marc-Antoine Charpentier (1645/50–1704), and François Couperin (1668–1733). Important genres included *opera, *ballet, numerous types of relatively brief ecclesiastical music (both vocal pieces, often with rather elaborate instrumental accompaniment, and organ music), and instrumental chamber music, particularly music for harpsichord and for viols [see Suite]. In the 18th century, many of the same genres were cultivated, but taste was dictated less by the royal court. Jean-Philippe Rameau (1683–1764) was the greatest composer of this era and made important contributions to the *theory of music. A recurring theme in French musical life of the 18th century and after was the difference between French and Italian musical styles [see *Bouffons, Querelle des*]. The Centre de Musique Baroque de Versailles, founded in 1988, works to promote French music of the 17th and 18th centuries through education and broadcasting.

Opera (especially *grand opera, but also **opéra comique*) dominated the first half of the 19th century, with works by Giacomo Meyerbeer (1791–1864), Fromental Halévy (1799–1862), Daniel Auber (1782–1871), Adrien Boieldieu (1775–1834), and Ferdinand Hérold (1791–1833), among others. The development of French instrumental music was stimulated in this period by Hector Berlioz (1803–69). In the second half of the century, Jacques Offenbach (1819–80) produced numerous *opéras comiques* and operettas and Georges Bizet (1838–75) various theatrical works. During this period instrumental music again flourished, as did the **mélodie,* with compositions by Bizet, Henri Duparc (1848–1933), Gabriel Fauré (1845–1924), Charles Gounod (1818–93), Edouard Lalo (1823–92), and Camille Saint-Saëns (1835–1921). In the late 19th and early 20th centuries, preeminent composers in France included César Franck (1822–90), Charles-Marie Widor (1844–1937), Vincent d'Indy (1851–1931), Paul Dukas (1865–1935), Erik Satie (1866–1925), Albert Roussel (1869–1937), Maurice Ravel (1875–1937), and Claude Debussy (1862–1918), whose name is often associated with *impressionism.

Between the world wars, composers (especially a group nicknamed *Les *six*) reacted against both German music and impressionism, as embodied in Debussy's works. Among the most revered and respected French composers of the century is Olivier Messiaen (1908–1992), one of a group known as *La *jeune France.* Many of his students also studied with René Leibowitz (1913–72), who encouraged them to use serial techniques. Most prominent among Messiaen's and Leibowitz's pupils is Pierre Boulez (b. 1925), whose activities as a composer, conductor, writer, and organizer of concerts have made an important mark on contemporary music. From 1976 to 1992, he was the director of IRCAM (Institut de recherche et de coordination acoustique/musique), which is concerned with training and research in composition, electronic and computer techniques, acoustics, and instrument building. This organization is only the latest (and most ambitious) in a series of similar research groups that have formed part of the French musical scene from the time of the pioneering work in *musique concrète and other aspects of electronic music done by Pierre Schaeffer (1910–1995), whose Groupe de recherche de musique concrète obtained official recognition in 1951. Other prominent 20th-century composers include Henri Dutilleux (b. 1916), Marius Constant (b. 1925), Betsy Jolas (b. 1926), Pierre Villette (b. 1926), Jean Barraqué (1928–73), Jean-Claude Eloy (b. 1938), Jean-Pierre Guézec (1934–71), Paul Méfano (b. 1937), and Jean-Claude Risset (b. 1938). Prominent among younger French composers are Alexandre Rabinovitch (b. 1945), Graciane Finzi (b. 1945), Renaud Gagneux (b. 1947), Tristan Murail (b. 1947), Anthony Girard (b. 1959), and Nicolas Bacri (b. 1961).

III. *Folk music.* Serious study and publication of French folk music began before the middle of the 19th century. Especially the texts of folk songs were collected in quantity from at least 1860 on, and early in the 20th century, recordings of folk music began to be made. French folk song is most often strophic, monophonic, and solo, and some is used to accompany dancing. Pieces incorporating refrains, responsorial performance, and, in a few areas, vocal polyphony also occur. Rhythm and poetic meter usually correspond, but some songs are recitativelike and in free meter. The repertory includes songs linked with various activities (work; weddings, funerals, and other events having to do with the life cycle; drinking or other leisure-time activities) and religious and magical songs. Instrumental folk music includes noise-making within certain rituals, signaling with bells, whistles, and trumpets, and accompaniment for songs, but the majority is made up of dance tunes. Such tunes may be performed in two-part polyphony, the second part consisting largely or entirely of a melodic or rhythmic drone; in monophony; or in ensemble polyphony. Folk instruments include the fiddle, accordion, cog rattle, bagpipes (including the **biniou*), hurdy-gurdy, shawm, and drum (including the **tambourin*). Folk dances (usually particular to certain regions) include the **farandole,* gavotte, passepied, and **sardana.*

Bibl.: Martin Cooper, *French Music from the Death of Berlioz to the Death of Fauré* (London: Oxford U Pr, 1951). Jean Michel Guilcher, *La tradition populaire de danse en Basse-Bretagne* (Paris: Mouton, 1976). Isabelle Cazeaux, *French Music in the Fifteenth and Sixteenth Centuries* (New York: Praeger, 1975). Christopher Page, *The Owl and the Nightingale: Musical Life and Ideas in France, 1100–1300* (London: Dent, 1989). Adélaïde de Place, *La Vie musicale en France au temps de la Révolution* (Paris: Fayard, 1989). Nigel Wilkins, *The Lyric Art of Medieval France,* 2nd rev. ed. (Fulbourn: New Press, 1989). Marcelle Benoit, ed., *Dictionnaire de la musique en France aux XVIIe et XVIIIe siècles* (Paris: Fayard, 1992). Jérôme de La Gorce, *L'Opéra à Paris au temps de Louis XIV* (Paris: Desjonquères, 1992). Gérard Monnier, *L'Art et ses institutions en France de la Révolution à nos jours* (Paris: Gallimard, 1995). Edith Weber, *Histoire de la musique française: 1500–1650* (Paris: SEDES, 1996). Jean Duron, ed., *Plain-chant et liturgie en France au XVIIe siècle* (Paris: Klincksieck, Fondation Royaumont, 1997). Yves Guilcher, *La Danse traditionnelle en France: D'une ancienne civilisation paysanne à un loisir revivaliste* (Courlay: FAMDT Éditions, 1998). Paul Garapon, "Metamorphoses de la chanson française (1945–1999)," *Esprit* 7 (July 1999): 89–118.

Franco-Flemish school. See Renaissance.

Frauenchor [Ger.]. Women's chorus.

Frauenliebe und Leben [Ger., Woman's Love and Life]. A cycle of eight songs for voice and piano by Schumann, op. 32 (1840), setting poems written by Adalbert von Chamisso and published with the same title.

Frau ohne Schatten, Die [Ger., The Woman without a Shadow]. Opera in three acts by Richard Strauss (libretto by Hugo von Hofmannsthal after his story of the same title), produced in Vienna in 1919. Setting: the imaginary empire of the Southeastern Islands.

Fredon [Fr.]. (1) In 17th-century France, a trill or a short **roulade.* (2) In the 18th century, excessive ornamentation.

Free bop. A style of jazz that emerged in the 1970s and 1980s among musicians like David Murray, Arthur Blythe, and Henry Threadgill, who sought a rapprochement between the performative conventions of *bebop and *free jazz.

Free jazz. A jazz style originating in the late 1950s. Its players, seeking freedom from the stylistic conventions of *bebop, explored new types of collective improvisation, thematic variation, and motivic work, pantonality, drones, nontempered intonation, the melodic possibilities of the bass and of percussion instruments, open-ended forms, new timbres, extreme registers, abrupt rhythmic changes, unmetered pulses, and contrasting dynamics. The style was heralded by pianist Cecil Taylor's recordings of 1956–58 and by saxophonist Ornette Coleman's controversial New York performances in 1959.

Bibl.: Ekkehard Jost, *Free Jazz,* Beiträge zur Jazzforschung 4 (Graz: Universal, 1974). Roger T. Dean, *New Structures in Jazz and Improvised Music since 1960* (Milton Keynes: Open U Pr, 1992). B.K.

Freemasonry and music. From the foundation of freemasonry in London (1717), Paris (1725), and Hamburg (1737), music played an integral part in ceremony and socializing. Ritual music consisted of hymnody with new texts to tunes borrowed largely from the Protestant Church and of processional music for organ (in England) or wind and brass choir (on the Continent) derived from military traditions. Mozart, a lodge brother in Vienna from 1784, composed several vocal works and a *Masonic Funeral Music* K. 477 (as did Sibelius). Social singing after ceremonies resulted in numerous songbooks with new words to popular tunes and operatic airs of the 18th century. In addition, some new tunes were composed by William Boyce, J. A. Scheibe, C. P. E. Bach, and others.

Private concert societies arose under the auspices of freemasonry. London's Societas Appoloni boasted Geminiani as director in 1727, and the Anacreontic Society inspired John Stafford Smith's "Anacreon in Heaven," whose tune became "The Star-Spangled Banner." Haydn, a brother in Vienna from 1785, composed his six *Paris* Symphonies for a similar Parisian organization. Mozart also contributed to Viennese masonic concerts as performer and composer. His Piano Concerto in E♭ K. 482 and his Clarinet Quintet K. 581 and Clarinet Concerto K. 622—both for clarinetist and fellow mason Anton Stadler—may have arisen in that connection.

Masonic themes entered the public musical world as well. Several *pièces de clavecin* by François Couperin suggest masonic mysteries in their titles. Stage works on masonic themes include the ballad opera *The Generous Freemason* (London, 1730), Rameau's *Zoroastre* (Paris, 1749), J. G. Naumann's *Osiride* (Dresden, 1781), and Mozart's *Magic Flute* (Vienna, 1791). The last uses a libretto written by Mozart's lodge brother Emmanuel Schikaneder and dramatizing in allegory the rite and philosophy of masonic initiation; the music embodies masonic symbolism in its principal key of three flats, prominent orchestration for winds, and recurring motif of three repeating chords. In the 19th century, masonic influence waned, though Beethoven and Wagner may have based *Fidelio* and *Parsifal* in part on masonic ideas. Other composer-masons include Spohr, Meyerbeer, Mendelssohn, Liszt, Puccini, John Philip Sousa, and Irving Berlin.

Bibl.: Paul Nettl, *Mozart und die königliche Kunst* (Berlin: F Wunder, 1932); trans. Eng., *Mozart and Masonry* (New York: Philosophical Library, 1957; rev. ed., 1970).

Frei [Ger.]. Free, freely.

Freischütz, Der [Ger., The Freeshooter]. Opera in three acts by Weber (libretto by Friedrich Kind after a folktale), produced in Berlin in 1821. Setting: Bohemia in the 17th century. In its use of folklike subject matter and melody (with spoken dialogue rather than recitative) and its treatment of the supernatural and nature, it is the paradigmatic German Romantic opera.

Freistimmigkeit [Ger.]. Freedom with respect to the number of voices making up a texture. The term is used especially to characterize music for keyboard or plucked strings that gives the impression of stricter counterpoint with a fixed number of voices.

French harp. *Mouth organ.

French horn. *Horn.

French overture. See Overture (1), Suite.

French sixth. See Sixth chord.

French Suites. Six *suites for harpsichord by Bach, BWV 812–17 (the first five of which were originally included in the *Clavierbüchlein* I, composed for Anna Magdalena Bach in the years 1722–25). The name French was not used by Bach himself, and its origins remain obscure, though it appears on some early copies. These works are not more French in character than other keyboard suites by Bach and his German predecessors.

Frequency. In *acoustics, the number of complete vibrations or cycles occurring per unit of time (usually per second; see Hertz) in a vibrating system such as a string or column of air. Frequency is the primary determinant of the listener's perception of *pitch.

Fresco, frescamente [It.]. Fresh, freshly.

Fret [Fr. *touche, ton;* Ger. *Bund;* It. *tasto;* Sp. *traste*]. A strip of material placed across the fingerboard or neck of some bowed or plucked instruments, allowing the strings to be stopped at a predetermined pitch. Frets may be movable or fixed. Movable frets—of gut or cord—are tied around the neck (*sitār, viola da gamba,* lute, early guitar) and can be adjusted to vary the intervals of the pitches. Fixed frets—of metal, ivory, or wood—are inlaid into a groove in the fingerboard (banjo, cittern, modern guitar). The frets of Western instruments are usually placed a semitone apart. See Temperament. R.L.

Frettevole, frettoso, frettoloso [It.]. Hurried.

Fricassée [Fr.]. A type of **quodlibet* occurring among the chansons of the first half of the 16th century and in which quotations are mixed for humorous effect from sources that include polyphonic chansons, folk tunes, and street cries. Examples survive by Henri Fresneau (*La fricassée,* with nearly 100 quotations) and Clément Janequin, among others.

Friction drum. A drum that is sounded by rubbing rather than striking. Most consist of a hollow body covered by a membrane through which passes a stick or string that the player pulls, turns, or rubs. See, e.g., *Cuíca, Zambomba.*

Friss, friszka [Hung.]. See *Csárdás, Verbunkos.*

Frog [Brit. nut; Fr. *hausse, talon;* Ger. *Frosch;* It. *tallone;* Sp. *talón*]. That portion of the *bow of a stringed instrument that is held in the player's hand and by means of which the tension of the hair is adjusted. See also Bowing.

Fröhlich [Ger.]. Joyous.

From My Life [Cz. *Z mého života*]. Smetana's first string quartet, in E minor (1876). Although both

Smetana quartets are meant to be descriptive of his life (the second, composed in 1882–83, is also in E minor), Smetana himself seems to have applied the title only to the earlier quartet.

From the New World. See *New World* Symphony.

Front line. The wind instruments of a *New Orleans or *Dixieland jazz ensemble: clarinet (occasionally saxophone), trumpet (or cornet), and trombone; more generally, non–*rhythm section instruments whose function is primarily melodic.

Frosch [Ger.]. *Frog; *am Frosch,* an instruction to bow near the frog.

Frottola [It.]. A piece from a repertory of secular music written in northern Italy ca. 1480–1520. The word has popular, even rustic connotations, and the poetic forms used for the written repertory of *frottole* were cultivated by improvisers at this time and probably a good deal earlier; but the *frottola* should not be thought of as popular or folklike music. Occasionally printers used *frottola* in a more specific sense as the equivalent of the verse form **barzelletta* (Petrucci, bks. 4 and 6).

The main body of *frottole* survives in manuscripts of northern Italian provenance and in the prints (1504–14) of Ottaviano Petrucci; up to ca. 1525 *frottole* were reprinted, with some new pieces added, in Venice, Siena, Rome, and Naples. Although a few pieces were contributed by *oltremontani* such as Josquin and Compère, most of the music was the work of native Italians, centering in the Veneto, Ferrara, and especially Mantua. These composers, chief among whom were Bartolomeo Tromboncino (ca. 1470–ca. 1535) and Marchetto Cara (ca. 1470–1525), were usually performers and sometimes poets; they were neither *improvvisatori* of note nor celebrated polyphonists, but rather court musicians whose duties included supplying musical settings of fashionable, often local poetry.

Poetic forms favored by the frottolists include the *barzelletta* (most popular of all); other multistanza forms used include the **oda* and **capitolo.* The single-stanza **strambotto,* beloved of improvisers, was set often; but the **canzone* stanza and the sonnet were rare until Petrucci's last books, either because they were too "literary" or because they had been the special province of improvisers. A few pieces, called *modo* or *aere,* provided models for singing any text in the form indicated. Most of the poetry is anonymous; some texts were written by courtiers at Mantua and Ferrara; a few are the work of well-known improvisers; and on occasion the frottolist wrote both words and music.

In musical style, the *frottola* varies from near-homophony among the (usually four) voices to fairly elaborate melodic ornament (mainly in the top voice) and running figuration in the inner voices, serving as, or substituting for, polyphonic activity. Bass lines tend to be strongly harmonic, often approaching the schematic character of the patterned basses of the later 16th century. Many *frottole* use rhythmic formulas suggestive of the dance-song; a favorite pattern (for eight-syllable trochaic verse) is shown in the accompanying example.

Neither printed nor manuscript sources give unequivocal evidence for performance practice; accompanied solo performance may have been the most common, but anything up to four-voice, more or less fully texted singing is possible. The existence of printed books of voice and lute intabulations as well as of *frottole* reduced to keyboard score shows that this music was played and sung in a variety of ways.

Frottole were performed as vocal and/or instrumental chamber music at court; their existence in print made them accessible to a larger though still restricted group of musicians. They were also used in **intermedi* and other theatrical entertainments.

Bibl.: *Editions.* Rudolph Schwartz, ed., *Ottaviano Petrucci: Frottole, Buch I und IV* (Leipzig: Breitkopf & Härtel, 1935; R: Hildesheim: Olms, 1967). Alfred Einstein, ed., *Canzoni, sonetti, strambotti et frottole, libro tertio* [Antico], Smith College Music Archives 4 (Northampton, Mass.: Smith College, 1941). Raffaello Monterosso, ed., *Le frottole nell'edizione principe di Ottaviano Petrucci* [bks. 1–3], Instituta et monumenta, ser. 1, vol. 1 (Cremona: Athenaeum cremonense, 1954). William Prizer, ed., *Libro primo de la Croce* (Madison, Wis.: A-R Edit, 1978).

Literature. Walter Rubsamen, *Literary Sources of Secular Music in Italy (ca. 1500)* (Berkeley and Los Angeles: U of Cal Pr, 1943). Knud Jeppesen, *La frottola,* 3 vols. (Aarhus: Universitetsforlaget, 1968–70). William Prizer, *Courtly Pastimes: The Frottole of Marchetto Cara* (Ann Arbor: UMI Res Pr, 1980). Id., "Isabella d'Este and Lucrezia Borgia as Patrons of Music: The Frottola at Mantua and Ferrara," *JAMS* 38 (1985): 1–33. See also Madrigal. J.H.

Frullato [It.]. Flutter *tonguing.

Fuga [Lat., It., Sp.]. See Fugue.

Fugara. An organ stop of narrow-scaled open pipes that originated in eastern Europe in the early 18th century and is usually found at 4′ pitch.

Fugato [It.]. A fuguelike (and thus contrapuntal and imitative) passage occurring in a larger work or movement that is not itself a fugue, e.g., in the development section of a movement in sonata form; also a fuguelike piece that in one way or another does not incorporate the usual features of a *fugue.

Fughetta [It.]. A short fugue.

Fuging tune, fuge tune. A type of psalm or hymn tune cultivated in Great Britain and the U.S. from the 18th century on, involving contrapuntal writing and the overlapping of text in at least one phrase. It has always been most popular in rural areas.

The fuging tune, unrelated to the fugue, originated

in England in the early 18th century, the first examples appearing in songbooks of itinerant singing masters; the genre reached its peak there around the middle of the century. It then declined in popularity in England, but was taken up enthusiastically in the U.S., receiving substantial attention from both composers and the general public. The peak of growth and popularity of the American fuging tune came in the 1790s.

The American fuging tune is often in the form ABB. Section A is homophonic, often ending with a firm cadence on the tonic. B is imitative, the voices entering in no set order, but all usually having the same text and similar melodic movement (not necessarily strict imitation). This section is then repeated. Most fuging tunes end with homophony, which may extend over only the last few notes.

American composers of early fuging tunes, strongly influenced by the works of the British psalmodist Joseph Stephenson (fl. mid-18th cent.), include William Billings (1746–1800), Supply Belcher (1752–1836), Lewis Edson (1748–1820), Daniel Read (1757–1836), Timothy Swan (1758–1842), and many others.

Early 19th-century reformers of American psalmody objected to the fuging tune because of its supposed crudity and because of the obscuring of the words in the contrapuntal sections. Despite their objections, the American fuging tune continued in vogue into the 20th century. The genre has been kept alive in the southern and western *shape-note tradition long after its disappearance elsewhere.

Bibl.: Irving Lowens, "The Origins of the American Fuging Tune," *JAMS* 6 (1953): 43–52. Nicholas Temperley and Charles G. Manns, *Fuging Tunes in the Eighteenth Century,* Detroit Studies in Music Bibliography 49 (Detroit: Info Coord, 1983).

Fugue [Fr. *fugue;* Ger. *Fuge;* Lat., It., Sp., *fuga*]. (1) The most fully developed procedure of imitative counterpoint, in which the theme is stated successively in all voices of the polyphonic texture, tonally established, continuously expanded, opposed, and reestablished; also the genre designation for a work employing this procedure. (2) In the Renaissance, *imitation. (3) In the Middle Ages, *canon.

I. *Texture, contrapuntal procedure, form.* Fugal texture requires a strict number of voices; two to six are practical, but the usual number is three or four. In a fugal *exposition, the *subject is presented alone in one voice (perhaps accompanied by a *basso continuo), then imitated or answered, usually in the dominant, by a second voice; this answer may be *tonal (modified) or *real (exact), depending on the characteristics of the subject and the composer's intentions with respect to modulation. Typically, the third voice enters with the subject in the tonic, the fourth in the dominant, and so on until all voices have entered. After stating the subject, each voice continues with a *countersubject or free counterpoint, usually moving to a *cadence. An exposition is normally followed by an *episode, the motivic material for which often derives from an aspect of the subject or countersubject. The episodic material is brought into an opposing or contrasting context, an effect often achieved by the use of harmonic sequences; once sufficient contrast has been established, the fugue subject reenters, as a single entry or as a reexposition, in the tonic or in a related key. The alternation of exposition and episode may occur only once or many times. The final section is usually a convincing exposition (complete or incomplete) in the tonic, often concluding with a *pedal point in the bass. See the accompanying example and diagram.

Although many fugues exhibit these features, no single prescription usefully encompasses the variety of form and procedure found in fugues. In general terms, the structure of fugues has been likened to that of formal rhetorical discourse (Butler, 1977): (1) a proposition is formally presented, (2) opposing material is refuted, (3) the initial proposition is strengthened, and (4) a forceful conclusive statement is made. Descriptions of fugue as a conversation, argument, debate, diatribe, or even as a battle among various voices, which occur in sources throughout the 18th century, confirm Forkel's remark that "Bach considered his parts as if they were persons who conversed together like a select company."

A fugue is fundamentally a monothematic work, although the subject itself may be varied by *augmentation, *diminution, *inversion, *retrograde, and other devices or opposed by various countersubjects. Bach's **Art of Fugue* is the comprehensive exemplar of these techniques. In highly unified fugues, all subsequent material derives organically from the theme itself—a process that has been described as continuous expansion (Bukofzer, 1947). Some fugues present two or three subjects, in which case they are called *double or triple fugues. Here, each subject is normally set forth separately, but, later, the multiple subjects are usually combined, though there is considerable variety in these respects as well.

II. *History and theory. Fuga* literally means flight, which suggests the fleeing and chasing characteristic of all fugues. In the Middle Ages, *fuga* was used synonymously with *chace* and *caccia* to denote canon (Jacques de Liège, Oswald von Wolkenstein, the Trent Codices). Occasional use in this sense also occurs until the 18th century, as, for example, in the canonic *Missae ad fugam* of Josquin and Palestrina and in Marpurg's fugue treatise of 1753. Early in the Renaissance, however, the principal meaning came to be *imitation. Ramos de Pareia (1482) described it as "the best manner of part-writing." Vicentino (1555) described the tonal/modal answer, and Zarlino (1558) distinguished fugue from imitation on the basis of intervals: entrances on the fourth, fifth, and octave were fugue, all others were imitation. Tomás de Santa María (1565) discussed fugal technique as a basis for keyboard improvisation, and Thomas Morley (1597) made specific comments on the length and character of fugal themes. Thus, Renaissance composers and

Measure no.:	1	3	5	7	9	11	13	15	17	19	21	23	25	27	29	31
Soprano:		A======	·········	Cs_1 ----	··········	S=======	·········	Cs_1------	········	········	S=======	········	········	Cs_1---	······ S	======
Alto:	S======	Cs_1 -----	·········	Cs_2---	··········	Cs_2-----	·········	A=======	········	········	Cs_1 ------	········	········	·· Cs_2------	········	········
Bass:				S=====	··········	Cs_1 ------	·········	Cs_2-----	········	········	·· Cs_2-----	········	········	S========	······Pedal	——
Section: (Key)	Exposition (c)				Episode	Entry (E♭)	Episode	Entry (g)	Episode		Entry (c)	Episode		Entry (c)	Coda (c)	
Rhetoric:		Propositio/Aetiologia					Confutatio/Refutatio					Confirmatio			Conclusio	

S===== subject; A===== answer (tonal); Cs----- countersubject; ..... continuous expansion of motives from S and Cs.

Bach, Fugue in C minor (in three voices) from *The Well-Tempered Clavier,* bk. 1.

theorists clarified the elements of fugal exposition, but, at most, they thought of fugue as a particular kind of imitation, not as a whole work (which consisted of a series of points of imitation on different themes or motives). Although fugal expositions were common in both vocal and instrumental music of the Renaissance, it was particularly the instrumental forms—*ricercar, *canzona, and *fantasia—that proved important for subsequent development.

Early in the Baroque, the concept of predicating a whole fugue on a single subject generally superseded the polythematic conception of the Renaissance (Cerone, 1613; Zacconi, 1622); the theory of tonal answers appeared (Diruta, 1609); and the idea of "working out" the thematic material was added (Praetorius, 1618). A manuscript treatise by Bertali appears to be the earliest theoretical source in which fugue is described as a series of points of imitation, all based on the same theme but separated from each other in some way. The ricercars and canzonas of Frescobaldi, the motet-type fantasias of Sweelinck, and the "learned" fugues of Scheidt's *Tablatura nova* (1624) are the best examples of such early but self-sufficient fugal compositions. In the toccatas of Froberger and the *praeludia* of Buxtehude, fugue occurs within the context of larger improvisatory forms, either as a procedure for working out thematic material or as an independent section of a larger work. Johann Pachelbel wrote a large number of independent fugues as well as some introduced by a prelude. The "permutation fugue" originated from experiments in the northern German cities of Hamburg and Lübeck within a circle of musicians that included Weckmann, Buxtehude, Reinken, and Christoph Berhard; the first pedagogical example appears to occur in Johann Theile's treatise *Das Musikalisches Kunstbuch,* and the first musically successful example appears to have been composed by Bach. J. C. F. Fischer published a collection of preludes and fugues in many keys (1702). Rameau (1722) recognized that the concept of fugue includes a strong harmonic orientation. Fugues and fugal passages are to be found thoughout the works of Bach and Handel, although Handel's most significant contributions occur in the choruses of his oratorios. Marpurg (1753–54) associated "strict" fugue with Bach, "free" fugue with Handel. Burney (*History,* 1789) called Handel "perhaps the only great Fuguist exempt from pedantry." However, the concise fugues in Bach's **Well-Tempered Clavier* and the majesterial *Art of Fugue* have come to be regarded as the supreme exemplars of fugal composition. Several fugue types have been discerned in the Bach literature: *fuga pathetica,* ricercar-fugue, dance fugue, *Spielfuge,* alla breve fugue, art fugue, simple fugue, double fugue, and counterfugue. Bach's style, with its roughly even balance between the demands of tonal harmony and complex counterpoint, provided the ideal conditions for its full flowering. For both Bach and Handel, fugue provided the best means for the realization of powerful musical ideas; generally, in the works of these composers, fugue represents a climax of musical intensity.

Classic summaries of fugal theory by Fux (1725) and Marpurg (1753) were synthetic works; the accumulated principles—as developed from Palestrina (Fux's model) to Bach (Marpurg's model)—were digested, systematized, and presented in didactic form. These treatises had their influence on virtually every subsequent generation of composers beginning with J. C. Bach and Mozart (via Martini), and Beethoven (via Albrechtsberger). By the end of the 18th century, however, fugue ceased to be a spontaneous, improvisatory procedure, as it had been from the late Renaissance to Bach, and became increasingly associated with academic study and musical antiquarianism. But in works such as the finale of Mozart's *Jupiter* Symphony K. 551, the last movement of Beethoven's *Hammerklavier* Sonata op. 106, and Beethoven's quartets opp. 131 and 133, fugue in a sonata was elevated to a level of artistic accomplishment clearly comparable to that of the Baroque masters. Especially in Beethoven's late works, fugue often became the formal procedure by which the conflicts and tensions of the earlier movements were resolved. The well-established role for fugue as the finale in large-scale sacred vocal works continued in such examples as the Beethoven Masses, Mendelssohn's *Elijah,* and the third movement of the Brahms *Requiem.*

By the middle of the 19th century, fugue became a requirement of much conservatory instruction. Bach's *Well-Tempered Clavier* became an object of widespread attention, and many textbooks on the subject appeared (Prout 1891, Gedalge 1901, etc.). Despite its overwhelming pedagogical and historical—even antiquarian—associations, Schumann, Liszt, and Reger all composed fugues on the notes B-A-C-H; preludes and fugues for organ were composed by Brahms, Liszt, Reger, and Franck; and Chopin was probably the only major 19th-century composer to ignore fugue completely. The finale to Verdi's late opera *Falstaff* is a brilliant jocular fugue.

In the early 20th century, Schoenberg, Berg, and other composers of atonal and *twelve-tone music employed fugal procedures rarely: "Der Mondfleck" in Schoenberg's *Pierrot lunaire* (1912) and the triple fugue in Act II scene ii of Berg's *Wozzeck* (1917–22) are exceptions to the general preference for canon over fugue in serial music. However, in the spirit of 20th-century *neoclassicism, fugue was revived as a compositional procedure within larger forms by many composers after World War I: the second movement of Stravinsky's *Symphony of Psalms* (1930) and the first movement of Bartók's *Music for Strings, Percussion, and Celesta* (1936) are examples. Hindemith's *Ludus tonalis* (1942), and Shostakovich's 24 Preludes and Fugues (1950–51) are notable collections of 20th-century fugue. However, the use of fugue in major compositions appears to have declined precipitously during the second half of the 20th century.

Bibl.: References to theorists and treatises cited above can be located in Alfred Mann, *The Study of Fugue* (New Brunswick, N.J.: Rutgers U Pr, 1958; R: Westport, Conn.: Greenwood, 1981); see also Theory. Ebenezer Prout, *Fugue* (London: Augener, 1891; R: New York: Haskell House, 1969). Heinrich Schenker, "Das Organische der Fuge," *Das Meisterwerk in der Musik* 2 (1926): 55–95. Manfred Bukofzer, *Music in the Baroque Era* (New York: Norton, 1947). John Cockshoot, *Fugue in Beethoven's Piano Music* (London: Routledge & Kegan Paul, 1959). Imogene Horsley, *Fugue: History and Practice* (New York: Free Pr, 1966). S. Kunze, "Gattungen der Fuge in Bachs Wohltemperierten Klavier," in *Bach-Interpretationen,* ed. Martin Geck (Göttingen: Vandenhoeck u. Ruprecht, 1969), pp. 74–93. James Haar, "Zarlino's Definition of Fugue and Imitation," *JAMS* 24 (1971): 226–54. Roger Bullivant, *Fugue* (London: Hutchinson, 1971). Hermann Keller, *The Well-Tempered Clavier by Johann Sebastian Bach,* trans. Leigh Gerdine (New York: Norton, 1976). Gregory Butler, "Fugue and Rhetoric," *JMT* 21 (1977): 49–109. Warren Kirkendale, *Fugue and Fugato in Rococo and Classical Chamber Music,* 2nd ed., trans. Margaret Bent and Warren Kirkendale (Durham: Duke U Pr, 1979). Anthony Newcomb, "The Anonymous Ricerars of the Bourdenay Codex," *Frescobaldi Studies* (Madison, Wis., 1983), pp. 97–123. Paul Walker, "Fugue in German Theory from Dressler to Mattheson" (Ph.D. diss., SUNY Buffalo, 1987). Paul Walker, "Die Entstehung der Permutationsfuge," *Bach-Jahrbuch* (1989): 21–42. George Stauffer, "Fugue Types in Bach's Free Organ Works," in *J. S. Bach as Organist,* ed. George Stauffer and Ernest May (Bloomington: Ind U Pr, 1986), pp. 133–56. L. Dreyfus, "Matters of Kind: Genre and Subgenre in Bach's Well-Tempered Clavier, Book I," in *A Bach Tribute: Essays in Honor of William Scheide,* ed. Paul Brainard and Ray Robinson (Chapel Hill, N.C.: Hinshaw, 1993), pp. 101–19. See also *Art of Fugue, The.*

E.D.M.

Fugue tune, fuguing tune. See Fuging tune, fuge tune.

Full organ. The full sound of the organ, including reed and flue stops.

Functional harmony. A theory of tonal harmony developed by Hugo Riemann according to which all harmonies can be analyzed as having one of three functions: tonic, dominant, and subdominant (designated

T, D, and S, respectively, in analyses of this type). Scale degrees II, III, and VI are often interpreted as the relative minors of IV, V, and I, respectively, and thus as having the functions S, D, and T. III can also function as the "upper relative" of V and thus have the function D, as does VII. The letters T, D, and S are added to in various ways to indicate chromatic alteration and the addition of dissonant tones. The term functional harmony is sometimes loosely applied to tonal harmony in general as it is understood in prevailing methods of *harmonic analysis, which regard each of the seven diatonic scale degrees as having a separate function.

Bibl.: Hugo Riemann, *Vereinfachte Harmonielehre oder die Lehre von der tonalen Funktionen der Akkorde* (London, 1893; trans. Eng., 1896). Hugo Distler, *Funktionelle Harmonielehre* (Kassel: Bärenreiter, 1941).

Fundamental, fundamental tone. In *acoustics, the lowest frequency or tone in a harmonic series and hence the first harmonic, i.e., the frequency of which all remaining frequencies in the series are integral multiples.

Fundamental bass [Fr. *basse fondamentale*]. In the theory of Jean-Philippe Rameau (*Traité de l'harmonie,* 1722), a bass line consisting of the roots of a succession of chords. Rameau's formulation of the principles of chord *inversion and of harmony as governed by a succession of roots underlies much of modern *harmonic analysis.

Fundamentinstrument [Ger.]. According to Michael Praetorius (*Syntagma musicum,* 2, 1618), perhaps borrowing from Agostino Agazzari (*Del sonare sopra il basso,* 1607), chord-playing instruments such as the organ or harpsichord. In the context of the realization of a *thoroughbass, Agazzari distinguishes between such instruments, which provide the foundation, and those that do not play complete harmonies and whose function is therefore ornamental.

Fundamentum [Lat., foundation]. Any of a number of 15th- and 16th-century collections by German keyboard composers that contain works intended for use in the teaching of composition. The pieces consist of one or more florid contrapuntal parts over a *cantus firmus.* The earliest such pieces date from ca. 1440–50 (*CEKM* 1, pp. 13, 23, 25). The most celebrated such collection is Conrad Paumann's *Fundamentum organisandi* (1452) for organ, which is transmitted in several forms (Wolff, 1968; *CEKM* 1, p. 32; facs. in *Locheimer Liederbuch,* ed. Konrad Ameln, *DM* 2nd ser., no. 3, 1972). The **Buxheimer Orgelbuch* contains Paumann's and two anonymous *fundamenta.* Others are by Hans Buchner (1483–1538) and Johannes de Lublin (ca. 1540).

Bibl.: Christoph Wolff, "Conrad Paumanns Fundamentum organisandi und seine verschiedenen Fassungen," *AfMw* 25 (1968): 196–222.

Funebre [It.]. Funereal, gloomy.

Funk(y). Earthy, sexual, danceable, *gospel-influenced. Equated with *soul jazz in 1954, it indicated a desire to unseat the prevailing intellectualized *West Coast style. The term is now applied to many recordings of black popular music, especially those with complex syncopations at the eighth- and sixteenth-note levels. B.K.

Fuoco, con [It.]. With fire.

Furiant [Cz.]. A Bohemian folk dance in a rapid tempo alternating 3/4 and 2/4 meters. Examples in art music are in 3/4 with strong accents forming pairs of beats resulting in occasional hemiola patterns. Composers of such pieces include Smetana (in the **Bartered Bride*) and Dvořák (*Furiant with Dumka* op. 12 for piano; two furiants for piano op. 42; third movement of the Symphony in D op. 60). Daniel Gottlob Türk describes such a piece in his *Clavierschule* of 1789, calling it a *furie.*

Furioso [It.]. Furious.

Furlana [It.]. See *Forlana.*

Furniture. **Fourniture.*

Fusa [Lat., Sp.]. See Note, Mensural notation.

Fusion. A synthesis of *jazz and funk or *rock. The style combines traditional jazz instruments and long, improvised melodies with electronic instruments, experimental tone colors, strong duple (not *swinging) rock, funk, or Latin dance rhythms, and simple *ostinato harmonies. Fashionable since the late 1970s, the term applies to recordings made as early as 1968. See Jazz. B.K.

Futurism [It. *futurismo*]. A movement in literature and the arts founded in 1909 by the Italian writer Filippo Tommaso Marinetti (1876–1942). It emphasized the machine age and the dynamic character of 20th-century life, and it took a radical view of established institutions. Its principles were applied to music in three manifestos (1910–12) by Francesco Pratella (1880–1955) and in his *Musica futurista* (1912), a work for conventional instruments. A more striking manifestation of futurism was in the work of the painter Luigi Russolo (1885–1947), who advocated an "art of noises" that would treat all sounds as musical material and who composed works for various noisemakers *(intonarumori)* of his own invention.

Bibl.: Rodney J. Payton, "The Music of Futurism: Concerts and Polemics," *MQ* 62 (1976): 25–45. Caroline Tisdall and Angelo Bozzolla, *Futurism* (London: Thames & Hudson, 1977). G. Franco Maffina, *Luigi Russolo e l'arte dei rumori* (Turin: Martano, 1978).

Fz [It.]. Abbr. for **forzando, forzato.*

G

G. In French organ music, abbr. for *Grand orgue;* also G.O. See also Pitch names, Letter notation, Hexachord, Clef.

Gadulka [Bulg., also *gusla*]. A Bulgarian fiddle with three or four playing strings and most often seven to eleven sympathetic strings. It resembles the Greek **lira* in form and playing technique. It is used both as a solo and an ensemble instrument to accompany song and especially dancing.

Gagaku [Jap., elegant music]. The traditional court music repertory of Japan codified in the Heian period (794–1185); it includes *mikagura* (court *shinto* music) and court entertainment music [see also East Asia II, 2]. The latter consists of two types of orchestral music—the *komagaku* (music introduced from Korea) and *tōgaku* (court entertainment music of the T'ang period in China, 618–907 C.E.)—and vocal genres such as the *roei* (chanting of Chinese poems), *saibara* (folk song), and *imayō* (court popular songs). When *gagaku* is used to accompany dance, it is termed *bugaku.* A chorus joins the *tōgaku* and *komagaku* orchestras when they are not used to accompany court dances.

Tōgaku music is played by an orchestra consisting of aerophones such as the *hichiriki* (an oboe with nine holes), *ryūteki* (transverse bamboo flute with seven holes), and *sho* (mouth organ with seventeen pipes); chordophones such as the *sō-no-koto* (thirteen-stringed zither with movable bridges), and *biwa* (four-stringed lute played with a plectrum); an idiophone such as the *shōko* (a small suspended gong played with two sticks); and membranophones such as the *kakko* (double-headed barrel drum played with two sticks) and the *tsuridaiko* (a suspended two-headed drum, only one side of which is struck with two sticks). Instrumentation for the *komagaku* orchestra is similar to that of the *tōgaku* except that the *ryūteki* is replaced by the *komabue* (transverse bamboo flute with six holes), and the *kakko* by the *san-no-tsuzumi* (hourglass drum).

The musical style of *gagaku* is characterized by smoothness, serenity, and precise execution without virtuosic display. In *tōgaku* (or *komagaku*) music, the major melody, played on the *hichiriki* and the *ryūteki* (or *komabue*), is supported by chords produced on the *sho.* An abstraction of this major melody is played by the *sō-no-koto* (in octaves) and the *biwa* (in single notes). While smaller sections of a piece are marked off by a *biwa* arpeggio, larger sections are delineated by *tsuridaiko* and *shōko* strokes. Drum patterns played by the *kakko* (or *san-no-tsuzmi*) also serve similar *colotomic functions and regulate the tempo of a piece. When a chorus joins the major melody of the *tōgaku* or the *komagaku,* it sings in a natural voice using very little ornamentation.

Pieces in the repertory of *tōgaku* and *komagaku* are classified according to tempo and meter. *Nobebyōshi* are pieces in slow tempo with eight-beat meters; *hayabyōshi* are in moderate tempo with four-beat meters; and *ozebyōshi* are in fast tempo with two-beat meters. In addition, some pieces with mixed two- and four-beat meters are called *tada byōshi;* others in mixed two- and three-beat meters are called *yatara byōshi.* Influenced by the basic Japanese aesthetic principle of *jo-ha-kyū* (introduction–break away–hurried motion), *gagaku* compositions proceed from slow to fast.

Gagaku pieces are classified according to their length as well as their tempo and meter. Thus, *shōkyoku, chūkyoku,* and *taikyoku* refer, respectively, to small, medium, and large pieces, the latter implying a composition consisting of several pieces. I.K.F.W.

Gagliarda [It.; Fr. *gaillarde;* Sp. *gallarda;* Eng. *galliard*]. A gay, rollicking 16th-century court dance of Italian origin. The music is characterized by a predominantly compound duple (6/8) meter occasionally interspersed with hemiola (3/4) measures. The dance steps of the *gagliarda* are like those of the **saltarello;* both use variations of the same simple steps and the **cinque passi.* The difference is in the execution. The *gagliarda* is danced more vigorously, and the leap on the fifth beat of the *cinque passi* is higher than for the less rambunctious *saltarello.* The music for the two dances is indistinguishable in style. Either is frequently coupled to a **pavana* or a **pass'e mezo.* Early examples are preserved in Pierre Attaingnant's *Six gaillardes et six pavanes* (1530), his *Quatorze gaillardes neuf pavennes* (1531), in Giulio Abondante's *Intabolatura sopra el lauto* (1546), and in Antonio Rotta's *Intabolatura de lauto* (1546). As a dance, the *gagliarda* survived well into the 17th century. The title was also used occasionally for other kinds of music, however. For example, the sets of themes and variations called *gallarda* and written in a simple quadruple (4/4) meter by Juan Cabanilles bear no resemblance to the traditional dance. L.H.M.

Gai, gaiement [Fr., gay, lively]. **Allegro.*

Gaillarde [Fr.]. See *Gagliarda.*

Gaita [Sp., Port.; cf. Ar. **ghayṭah*]. (1) A *bagpipe of

Spain and Portugal. It is usually mouth-blown, with a double-reed *chanter, at least one bass *drone, and often a treble drone. It is still popular in northern Spain and Portugal, especially in Galicia. (2) *Shawm. (3) *Hornpipe (2). (4) In Colombia, a *duct flute.

Galanterie [Fr.]. A short, modish piece for harpsichord or other intimate medium, including chamber ensemble, especially in early 18th-century Germany. It implies French refinement and expressiveness devoid of heavy-handed effects. The term characterized the movements of Bach's harpsichord partitas in their original title: *Clavier-Übung bestehend in Präludien, Allemanden, Couranten, Sarabanden, Giguen, Menuetten, und anderen Galanterien* (1731). Some writers restrict the term to *suite movements other than allemandes, courantes, sarabandes, and gigues, especially those with descriptive rather than dance titles (e.g., badinage). See also *Galant* style. B.G.

Galant style [fr. Fr. *style galant,* fr. *galer,* to amuse oneself, to enjoy; Ger. *galanter Stil*]. In 18th-century writings about music, the free or homophonic style as opposed to the strict, learned, or contrapuntal style. Traits attributed to the *galant* style by various 18th-century theorists include light texture, periodic phrasing with frequent cadences, liberally ornamented melody, simple harmony, and free treatment of dissonance. Historically, the *galant* is the characteristic style of the early *Classical period (as defined here). Some musicologists, however, have also applied the term *galant* style to French *rococo music of the early 18th century such as that of François Couperin (see Bücken, 1923/24; Newman, 1963), an extension in meaning that can lead to unnecessary confusion, as the two styles are substantially distinct.

In general usage, the term *galant* denoted that which was pleasing (especially to ladies), refined, elegant, witty, natural, enjoyable, sophisticated, polite, and in good taste (or, to anti-*galant* writers, frivolous and superficial). A person possessing these and related qualities, for example, was referred to as a *galant homme,* as on the title page of Johann Mattheson's *Das neu-eröffnete Orchestre* (1713). Similar uses of the term may be noted in Watteau's genre paintings known as *fêtes galantes* and in musical works called **galanteries* or, in German, *Galanterien.* In this more general sense, referring to a manner rather than a specific style, the French rococo was, of course, the epitome of the *galant,* standing in opposition to the sober, monumental, and weighty Baroque of Louis XIV.

Bibl.: Ernst Bücken, "Der galante Stil: Eine Skizze seiner Entwicklung," *ZfMw* 6 (1923/24): 418–30. William S. Newman, *The Sonata in the Classic Era* (Chapel Hill: U of NC Pr, 1963; 3rd ed., New York: Norton, 1983). Claude V. Palisca, *Baroque Music* (Englewood Cliffs, N.J.: Prentice Hall, 1968; 3rd ed., 1991). David A. Sheldon, "The Galant Style Revisited and Re-evaluated," *AM* 47 (1975): 240–70. John Walter Hill, "The Anti-Galant Attitude of F. M. Veracini," *Albrecht,* 1980, pp. 158–96. Leonard G. Ratner, *Classic Music: Expression, Form, and Style* (New York: Schirmer Bks, 1980). E.K.W.

Galerón [Sp.]. A dance-song of the *llanos* (plains) region of Colombia and Venezuela. Narrative texts are typically sung by a solo vocalist, with harp, *cuatro* (small four-stringed guitar), and maracas playing a repeated harmonic ground in triple meter. In certain parts of Venezuela, the *galerón* is sung with religious texts in sacred contexts [see *Joropo*]. D.S.

Galin-Paris-Chevé method. See Chevé method.

Gallarda [Sp.]. See *Gagliarda.*

Galliard. See *Gagliarda.*

Gallican chant. The Latin chant of the churches in Gaul before the importation of *Gregorian chant under Pepin and Charlemagne, which began about 750. Because the Gallican chant was forcibly suppressed before the Carolingian invention of neumatic notation, no notated MS survives. Texts of some responsorial psalm refrains for the Mass are given in a 6th-century lectionary (*CLLA* 250) and the "Psalter of St. Germain"; a few others are cited in Gallican sacramentaries or books of Mass prayers (*CLLA* 210, 214). A fragmentary antiphoner (*CLLA* 428) is not definitely Gallican but seems closer to the Roman Office. Some extant psalters and hymnals (*CLLA* 1617, 1670), however, would have been used in the Office, though they tell us little about its specific structure.

A network of diverse local traditions rather than a single uniform repertory, Gallican chant exhibits relationships to traditions in Spain and northern Italy. Church councils, like that of Vaison held in 529, preserve liturgical regulations for particular regions. The decrees of the councils of Tours in particular can be supplemented by the writings of Gregory, bishop of Tours (reigned 573–94; *CPL* 1023–26). The island monastery of Lérins near Cannes produced an important corpus of monastic rules (*CPL* 1840–42, 1859–59b), and its liturgical practices were promoted and developed by its former monks who became bishops of Arles: Caesarius (*CPL* 1009, 1012), Aurelian (*CPL* 1844–46), and John (*CPL* 1848). Caesarius's many sermons also preserve information about the congregational psalmody (*CPL* 1008). A different monastic office was followed at St. Maurice in Agaune near Geneva. The description of the Gallican Mass by Pseudo-Germanus (*CPL* 1925) is especially valuable, despite its dependence on the *De ecclesiasticis officiis* of Isidore of Seville (*CPL* 1207).

Anomalous pieces that survive in French MSS of Gregorian chant appear to be Gallican survivals, such as the litanic *preces,* which were used also in *Mozarabic chant, and the antiphons *post evangelium* and the eucharistic *confractoria,* which had counterparts in *Ambrosian chant. Particularly interesting are the traditions of the continental Irish monasteries Luxeuil and Bobbio; their libraries preserved such MSS as the

Luxeuil lectionary (*CLLA* 255), the Stowe missal and its allies (*CLLA* 101–25), and the Bangor antiphoner and related fragments (*CLLA* 150–63), all important sources of non-Gregorian chant texts. Other Gallican materials, or vestiges of Gallican literary and musical style, may survive in French repertories of tropes and sequences.

Bibl.: Klaus Gamber, *Ordo antiquus gallicanus* (Regensburg: F Pustet, 1965). Kenneth Levy, "Lux de luce: The Origin of an Italian Sequence," *MQ* 57 (1971): 40–61. Bruno Stäblein, "Zwei Melodien der altirischen Liturgie," *Fellerer,* 1973, pp. 590–97. Peter Jeffery, "Litany," *DMA.* Michel Huglo, "Le Répons-graduel de la messe: Évolution de la forme, permanance de la function," *Schweizerisches Jahrbuch für Musikwissenschaft* 2 (1982): 53–77. Charles de Clercq, ed., *Les Canons des conciles mérovingiens (VIe–VIIe siècles),* 2 vols., Sources Chrétiennes 353–54 (Paris: Cerf, 1989). Peter Jeffery, "Eastern and Western Elements in the Irish Monastic Prayer of the Hours," in *The Divine Office in the Latin Middle Ages: Methodology and Source Studies, Regional Developments, Hagiography, Written in Honor of Professor Ruth Steiner,* ed. Margot E. Fassler and Rebecca A. Baltzer (Oxford: Oxford U Pr, 2000), pp. 99–143. P.J.

Galop [Fr.]. A fast dance in 2/4 that was extremely popular in the middle of the 19th century, when it was often used as the concluding number of a ball. It was sometimes made the finale of a **quadrille.* In the dance, embracing couples form a line and move rapidly with a galloping motion. In addition to numerous examples by composers of dance music such as the Johann Strausses, there are examples by Schubert, Liszt, Auber, Bizet, Prokofiev, Khachaturian, Kabalevsky, and Shostakovich. It is parodied in Offenbach's *Orphée aux enfers.*

Galoubet [Fr.]. The pipe of the *pipe and tabor combination of southern France.

Gamak(a) [Hin., Skt., Tel.]. An ornament in Indian music; specifically, a kind of shake that is performed differently in the Carnatic and Hindustani styles. C.C.

Gamba [It.]. (1) See Viol, Viola da gamba. (2) A string-toned organ stop that began appearing in central German organs at the end of the 17th century; sometimes called Viola da Gamba in 19th-century Anglo-American organs.

Gambang [Jav.]. A Javanese *xylophone with 16 to 21 wooden bars of varying length and thickness laid on a trapezoidal wooden frame and struck with two padded mallets. *Gambang* cover three to four pentatonic octaves in **slendro* or **pelog* tuning. See Southeast Asia IX.

Gambe [Ger.]. See Viol, Viola da gamba.

Gambenwerk [Ger.]. A *bowed keyboard instrument. See also *Geigenwerk,* Sostenente piano.

Gamelan [Indonesian, Malay, fr. Jav.]. Musical ensemble. International theoretical usage includes under this term most Indonesian or Malay ensembles that have gongs, gong-chimes, metallophones, and drums. These are found in Indonesia, Malaysia, Surinam, and scattered places around the Western world. This usage is seldom extended to include ensembles with similar components that are found on mainland Southeast Asia (excluding the Malay peninsula) and in the Philippines. The usage closest to that found most often in Java encompasses ensembles that play Javanese music in the **slendro* and **pelog* tunings. These include ensembles with few or no metallophones, gong-chimes, or gongs; for example, *zitran, angklungan,* and *reyog* ensembles, which feature plucked chordophones, shaken bamboo rattles, and quadruple-reed aerophones, respectively. In *gamelan* that have fixed-pitch instruments with a range greater than two octaves, the pitch and interval structures of the *slendro* and *pelog* tunings usually differ from octave to octave, and the pitch and interval structures of these tunings usually differ from one *gamelan* to another. See also Southeast Asia IX. M.H.

Game of Cards, The. See *Jeu de cartes.*

Gamma. The Greek letter Γ, the name of the lowest pitch (G) of the medieval *gamut [see also Hexachord]; by extension, the entire gamut, whence the Italian *gamma* and French *gamme* for scale.

Gamme [Fr.]. *Scale [see also *Gamma*].

Gamut. (1) A contraction of *gamma ut* [see Hexachord, Solmization]. (2) The entire range of diatonic pitches from G to e″ (with the addition of b♭ and b♭′) forming the basis of discussions of pitch in the Middle Ages and Renaissance [see also Guidonian hand]. The pitches of the gamut constitute *musica recta,* the remainder **musica ficta.* (3) Range, compass.

Ganze Note, ganze Pause [Ger.]. Whole note, whole-note rest. See Note.

Ganzton [Ger.]. Whole tone; *Ganztonleiter,* whole-tone scale.

Gapped scale. A scale used in one piece, derived from some tone system, but omitting some of that system's tones. The term is also used (less appropriately) to describe scales that by chance use parts of the diatonic system, e.g., anhemitonic pentatonic scales. B.N.

Garbo, con; garbato [It.]. Graceful, elegant.

Gaspard de la nuit [Fr.]. Three piano pieces composed by Ravel in 1908 and inspired by poems of the same title by Aloysius Bertrand (subtitled *Histoires vermoulues et poudreuses du Moyen Age*), who described them as written by the devil, Gaspard. Ravel's pieces are titled "Ondine" (a water nymph), "Le gibet" (gallows), and "Scarbo" (a goblin appearing in a hallucination).

Gassenhauer [Ger.]. From the 16th century, an urban popular song or street song; from the late 18th century, applied to such songs pejoratively. The term appears in 1535 in the title of Christian Egenolff's *Gassenhawerlin und Reutterliedlin,* which includes polyphonic songs by Isaac, Hofhaimer, and Senfl. Hans Sachs lists it in 1567 among the types of his own poetical works. In the 18th and 19th centuries, German opera and Singspiel were rich sources of street songs, often with new (sometimes obscene) texts.

Gastein or **Gmunden–Gastein Symphony.** A supposedly lost work by Schubert, D. 849 (1825–?), composed in Gastein, the Tyrolian region in which he vacationed in 1825. It is now thought that the symphony that Schubert worked on in Gastein is the Symphony in C major ("Great") D. 944, completed in 1828.

Gat [Hin.]. (1) A Hindustani composition for melodic instruments. The rhythmic pattern for a *gat* in a slow meter of 16 beats *(vilambit tīntāl)* is fixed and begins on the 12th beat. (2) A type of rhythmic composition for **tablā.* C.C.

Gathering note. A note sounded by the organist to give the congregation the pitch for the singing of a hymn.

Gato [Sp.]. The most widely found of several traditional couple dances of Argentina that share many musical features. These include performance by a singer with harp or guitar, or by ensembles of guitar, violin or accordion, and *bombo* (bass drum); and the use of distinctive rhythmic patterns that combine elements of simple triple and compound duple meter in lively tempo. The *gato* and related dances are often distinguished with regard to the details of their formal structures and the choreographic sequences they accompany; with the *gato,* the singing of verses in *seguidilla* form and the predominance of the major mode are also identifying traits.

Bibl.: Isabel Aretz, *El folklore musical argentino* (Buenos Aires: Ricordi americana, 1952). D.S.

Gavotte [Fr., Eng., Ger.; It. *gavotta;* Sp. *gavota*]. A gracious Baroque dance movement in duple meter. Usually it has four-measure phrases that begin and end in the middle of the bar, and its meter is ¢ (or 2). It uses simple rhythmic motives and does not often have syncopations or other complications [Ex.]. It is generally moderate or sprightly in tempo, but slower than a *bourrée or *rigaudon. In the late 16th and early 17th centuries, the dance was a type of **branle.* In the middle of the 17th century, a new dance with similar musical characteristics took the name and became popular at the court of Louis XIV. It was danced in the operas and ballets of Lully and Rameau. It quickly became an important form for independent music for instrumental ensembles and especially harpsichord, written by such composers as Nicolas-Antoine Lebègue (ca. 1631–1702), Purcell, Jean François Dandrieu (1682–1738), and Bach. As such, it kept the

Rameau, Gavotte from *Nais* (1749).

simple rhythms, phrasing, and homophonic texture of music to be danced, but sometimes lost the half-measure upbeat that preceded the choreography. The tempo strained both boundaries of "moderate," with some examples having the qualification "slow" (especially in French harpsichord music, *lentement*), some "fast" *(gai, presto).* The gavotte had pastoral associations from its folk and theater guises, occasionally reflected in drone basses, and it was frequently one of the movements following the sarabande in harpsichord *suites. Although mostly cast in *binary form, it was frequently *en rondeau* [see Rondeau (2)] or was the theme of variations. Later composers (Richard Strauss, Prokofiev, Schoenberg) sometimes used the title as a neoclassical gesture, but the details of their pieces vary considerably. The gavotte is still known as a folk dance in Brittany. B.G.

Gazza ladra, La [It., The Thieving Magpie]. Opera ("melodramma") in two acts by Rossini (libretto by Giovanni Gherardini after the comedy *La pie voleuse* by d'Aubigny and Caignez), produced in Milan in 1817. Setting: a village near Paris.

Gebrauchsmusik [Ger.]. Music for use, functional music. The term was coined in the 1920s for music that was intended to be immediately useful or accessible to a large public, e.g., music for films and the like, but especially music for performance by amateurs in the home, in schools, etc., as distinct from music for its own sake or as strictly a means to the composer's self-expression. It has most often been associated with some of the music of Paul Hindemith (who, however, later objected to the term, preferring *Sing- und Spielmusik,* music to sing and play) and Kurt Weill.

Bibl.: Heinrich Besseler, "Grundfragen des musikalischen Hörens," *JMP* 32 (1925): 35–52. Paul Hindemith, prefaces to scores of *Sing- und Spielmusiken* op. 45 (1928–31), *Lehrstück* (a dramatic work with text by Bertolt Brecht, 1929), *Wir bauen eine Stadt* (a children's opera, 1930), *Plöner Musiktag* (1932).

Gebrochen [Ger.]. Broken, *arpeggiated.

Gebunden [Ger.]. (1) *Legato. (2) With respect to the *clavichord, fretted.

Gedackt, gedeckt [Ger., covered]. Organ registers of flute scale with stopped pipes.

Gedämpft [Ger.]. Muted.

Gedehnt [Ger.]. Prolonged; hence, slow.

Gefällig [Ger.]. Pleasing, pleasant.

Gefühlvoll [Ger.]. With feeling.

Gegen [Ger.]. Toward, against, contrary to; *Gegenbewegung,* contrary *motion, also *inversion, as of a theme or subject; *Gegenfuge,* *counterfugue; *Gegensatz,* contrasting subject or theme; *Gegenstimme,* contrapuntal voice or part; *Gegenthema,* *countersubject in a fugue or second (contrasting) theme in *sonata form.

Gehalten [Ger.]. Sustained.

Gehaucht [Ger.]. Whispered.

Geheimnisvoll [Ger.]. Mysterious.

Gehend [Ger.]. **Andante.*

Geige [Ger.]. Violin [see also Gigue (2)].

Geigenprinzipal [Ger.]. An organ stop with open cylindrical pipes of slightly narrower scale than normal *Principal stops.

Geigenwerk [Ger.]. A *bowed keyboard instrument invented in 1575 by Hans Haiden of Nuremberg. Depressing a key caused a string to be pressed against one of several revolving, parchment-covered wheels that were activated by a treadle. See also Sostenente piano.

Geisslerlieder [Ger., flagellant songs]. Songs sung in the 13th and 14th centuries by flagellants. Penitential flagellation flourished in 13th-century Italy, from which a repertory of associated songs, *laude spirituali* [see *Lauda*], survives. The German repertory dates from the 14th century, when flagellation was prevalent in the context of the Black Plague of 1349. The melodies written down in Germany at the time, some of which are earlier pilgrims' songs and some of which seem to show the influence of the earlier *laude,* set texts most often composed of four-line strophes. They have a relationship to broader repertories of folk song and to the later German *chorale.

Bibl.: Paul Runge, ed., *Die Lieder und Melodien der Geissler des Jahres 1349 nach der Aufzeichnung Hugos von Reutlingen* (Leipzig: Breitkopf & Härtel, 1900). Arthur Hübner, *Die deutschen Geisslerlieder* (Berlin: W de Gruyter, 1931). Walter Wiora, "The Origins of German Spiritual Folk Song," *Ethno* 8 (1964): 1–13.

Geistertrio [Ger., Ghost Trio]. Popular name for Beethoven's Piano Trio in D major op. 70 no. 1 (1808), so called with reference to passages in the second movement in which the pianist plays soft tremolo chords and "mysterious" chromatic scales.

Geistlich [Ger.]. Sacred; *geistliches Konzert,* sacred concerto, i.e., a sacred work for voices and instruments. The latter term is associated particularly with works by Schütz and other German composers of the 17th century that derive in large measure (like the term itself) from the *monody and concerted style of works (termed *concerti ecclesiastici*) by Italian composers such as Giovanni Gabrieli, Adriano Banchieri, and Lodovico Viadana [see Concerto (1); also Chorale concerto]. For *Geistliches Klavierlied,* see *Klavierlied.*

Gekkin [Jap.]. The Japanese "moon-shaped" lute, with flat, round body and short neck; similar to the Chinese **yüeh-ch'in.* See ill. under East Asia.

Gekoppelt [Ger.]. Coupled.

Gelassen [Ger.]. Calm, tranquil.

Geläufigkeit [Ger.]. Technical facility.

Gemächlich [Ger.]. Comfortable, slow.

Gemässigt [Ger.]. Moderate.

Gemeindelied [Ger.]. Congregational hymn, *chorale.

Gemell. See Gymel.

Gemendo [It.]. Moaning, lamenting.

Gemessen [Ger.]. Measured.

Gemischte Stimmen [Ger.]. Mixed voices.

Gemshorn [Ger.]. An organ stop of tapered metal pipes, producing a tone that combines well with flute or Principal-scaled pipes.

Genau [Ger.]. Precise, strict.

Gender [Jav.]. A *metallophone of Java and Bali, with thin bronze bars 4 to 8 cm wide suspended on cords in a wooden frame. Each bar has a tube resonator below it. *Gender* cover one to three octaves in **slendro* or **pelog* tuning. The player strikes the keys with two disk-shaped mallets. *Gender panerus* is a similar instrument pitched an octave higher. See Southeast Asia IX, 4, 5 and ill.

Gender and music. Like musical meaning, the concept of gender is unstable, shifting according to context and historical moment. In music and in the humanities generally, gender was at first understood as a polarity: to study gender meant to devote attention to women's creativity and to specifically female perspectives on works of art. This idea of a feminine outlook that was essentially or innately different from paradigms of male-dominated creation and interpretation was soon supplanted by more flexible views. While sex is usually thought to be based in anatomical difference, most scholars now understand gender as constructed more by mind and social context than by biology, and thus to encompass an infinite number of orientations toward desire, power, and self-expression.

The study of gender in music has evolved in step with this expansion of the definition. Writing about literary studies, Elaine Showalter identified three successive phases of feminist scholarship. An oppositional period directed mainly toward uncovering misogynist values in canonical texts by men (dubbed "feminist critique" by Showalter) was succeeded by one devoted to the recovery and analysis of texts authored by women ("gynocritics"). A third wave of scholarship examined the conceptual basis for the interpretation of texts, revising assumptions about the nature of reading and writing that had been implicitly based on male experience.

Probably because of long-standing resistance to hearing Western art music as linked to social forces, the first two of these phases unfolded in reverse order in musicology. Feminist scholars turned first to excavation of works by women composers and research into women's roles in performance, patronage, and education, endeavors that continue productively to this day. Aspects of feminist critique were explored from the late 1980s on, in studies that sought traces of a distinctly feminine aesthetic in music by women and scrutinized the canonical masterworks for covert patriarchal values. The critical landscape was decisively altered by the publication in 1991 of Susan McClary's *Feminine Endings.* In readings of an ambitious range of repertoire from Monteverdi's *Orfeo* to Madonna's "Live to Tell," McClary decoded tonal processes and manipulations of form and convention as commentaries on relationships of gender and power. A counterpart to Showalter's third phase is going strong today as musicologists and music theorists experiment with models of analysis and musical description less based on mastery of the work and more attuned to the sensory pleasures of listening.

The most controversial aspect of analyses by McClary and others in the early 1990s was the interpretation of the sonata form as a gendered narrative. Following 19th-century terminology that labeled the second key area as feminine, these analysts perceived the encounter between tonic and dominant as symbolic of the confrontation between goal-oriented male and more loosely discursive female models of desire and experience. Subservient nontonic areas might be explored and enjoyed, but they are ultimately subordinated to a normative structure that requires the tonic key to silence all other expressive modalities. Women composers, or those identified with homosocial or other "outsider" identities, might strategically explore alternatives to this traditional tonal binarism. Thus Schubert's well-known reluctance to leave the tonic in his first-movement forms can be heard as a way of exploring alternative models of subjectivity, as can play with the tonic/dominant polarity in works by Fanny Hensel or Cécile Chaminade.

These efforts to find gendered meaning in a musical process usually thought of as purely abstract were crucial to feminism's claim that even "absolute" music has discoverable social meaning. The quest to uncover the gendered content of instrumental music focused on contrasts and oppositions basic to almost all music. Not only the tonic/dominant polarity, but also those of diatonic vs. chromatic, stable vs. unstable, and goal-oriented vs. cyclical form could be read as analogues for the master binary of gender difference. This approach has been criticized for reducing the multiplicity of feminine experience to a narrow set of essential characteristics, as well as for ignoring the ways notions of gender evolve historically. Clearly, musical features such as nondirectional tonality or the distortion of conventional forms do not function as signs of resistance or "otherness" at all historical moments, and it has been the project of a younger generation to propose vocabularies of gender grounded in specific local and historical contexts.

In the early, exploratory phase of work on gender and music, inquiries into texted music seemed exempt from the controversy over social meaning. Poetic texts, and especially operatic plots, offered glaring invitations to gender critique. French philosopher Catherine Clément read plots of famous operas as dramas of violence against women, and a number of musicological studies found her hypothesis confirmed by details of the musical score. One important strand of operatic interpretation moved in a different direction, downplaying the role of the (almost always male) composer to concentrate instead on opera's multivoiced nature. Exemplified by the work of Carolyn Abbate, such interpretations choose to hear specific musical passages or effects as emanating not from the composer but from the fictional characters, or perhaps from an orchestra that temporarily seems to acquire an autonomous and articulate voice. Opera studies has also led the way in shifting attention from the controlling authority of the composer onto the performers for whom a work was written, institutional structures of production and consumption, and the reactions of the often predominantly female audience. The attraction of such multivoiced approaches for feminism is obvious, but these affirmative readings run the risk of seeming to mount apologies for favorite canonical works, using subtle interpretive tools to uncover submerged pro-female messages without seriously confronting the gender politics that lie closer to the surface.

Beginning in the mid-1990s, musicology began to interest itself in populations disenfranchised or objectified by class or ethnicity, with the "otherness" of women's experience claiming less attention. By that point, however, some of the foundational concerns of feminist scholarship had filtered into the musicological mainstream. It is no longer controversial to believe that music bears traces of the society that produced it; feminism did much to push this social dimension to the center of the agenda. Attempts to develop analytical methods that did not reflexively ascribe ultimate authority to the male author helped to spur musicology's move away from composer-centered studies toward the social basis of musical experience, including education, structures of patronage, and reception.

A new sensitivity to the voices of "others" has further provoked a crisis of confidence over the role of analysis and close reading, which is now seen as too likely to reproduce the preferences and prejudices of the analyst in the guise of objective description. A case in point is the perennial question of why there have been "no great women composers." This challenge can be answered with observations about historical restrictions on women's education and public performance, but it should also prompt another question: who decides what greatness is, and based on which criteria? Feminist historiography has revealed the subjective bias of standard evaluative criteria: for example, that large forms such as the symphony have traditionally been valued over intimate genres, and that music that emphasizes harmonic struggle rather than subtle play with timbre or texture has tended to command greater prestige. If close reading is to survive in the new intellectual climate, it may be by ceding some of the analyst's control over the musical text and embracing instead what some see as an essentially feminine relation to the work, acknowledging the overwhelming, untamable, and potentially transgressive nature of the listening experience.

Bibl.: Jane Bowers and Judith Tick, eds., *Women Making Music: The Western Art Tradition, 1150–1950* (Urbana: U of Illinois Pr, 1986). Ellen Koskoff, *Women and Music in Cross-Cultural Perspective* (Westport, Conn.: Greenwood Pr, 1987; Urbana: U of Illinois Pr, 1989). Catherine Clément, *Opera, or the Undoing of Women,* trans. Betsy Wing (Minneapolis: U of Minnesota Pr, 1988; orig. pub. 1979). Susan McClary, *Feminine Endings: Music, Gender, and Sexuality* (Minneapolis: U of Minnesota Pr, 1991). Karin Pendle, ed., *Women and Music: A History* (Bloomington: Indiana U Pr, 1991). Elizabeth Hudson, "Gilda Seduced: A Tale Untold," *Cambridge Opera Journal* 4, no. 3 (November 1992): 229–51. Jeffrey Kallberg, "The Harmony of the Tea Table: Gender and Ideology in the Piano Nocturne," *Representations* 39 (Summer 1992): 102–33. Ruth Solie, "Whose Voice? The Gendered Self in Schumann's *Fraueneliebe* Songs," in *Music and Text: Critical Inquiries,* ed. Steven Paul Scher (Cambridge: Cambridge U Pr, 1992). Ruth Solie, ed., *Musicology and Difference: Gender and Sexuality in Music Scholarship* (Berkeley: U of Cal Pr, 1993). Marcia Citron, *Gender and the Musical Canon* (Cambridge: Cambridge U Pr, 1993). Suzanne Cusick, "Gendering Modern Music: Thoughts on the Monteverdi/Artusi Controversy," *JAMS* 46 (1993): 1–25. Wendy Heller, "The Queen as King: Refashioning *Semiramide* for *Seicento* Venice," *Cambridge Opera Journal* 5, no. 2 (July 1993): 93–114. Fred Everett Maus, "Masculine Discourse in Music Theory," *PNM* 31, no. 2 (1993): 264–93. Suzanne Cusick, "Gender and the Cultural Work of a Classical Music Performance," *Repercussions* 3, no. 1 (1994): 77–110. Susan C. Cook and Judy S. Tsou, eds., *Cecilia Reclaimed: Feminist Perspectives in Gender and Music* (Urbana: U of Illinois Pr, 1994). Suzanne Cusick, "On a Lesbian Relation with Music: A Serious Effort Not to Think Straight," in *Queering the Pitch: The New Gay and Lesbian Musicology,* ed. Philip Brett and Elizabeth Wood (New York: Routledge, 1994), pp. 67–83. Ralph P. Locke and Cyrilla Barr, eds., *Cultivating Music in America: Women Patrons and Activists since 1860* (Berkeley: U of Cal Pr, 1997). Mary Ann Smart, ed., *Siren Songs: Representations of Gender and Sexuality in Opera* (Princeton: Princeton U Pr, 2000). Pirrko Moisala and Beverley Diamond, eds., *Music and Gender* (Urbana: U of Illinois Pr, 2000). Kristina Muxfeldt, "*Frauenliebe und Leben* Now and Then," *19th-Century Music* 25, no. 1 (Summer 2001): 27–48. M.A.S.

Gendhing [Indonesian, fr. Jav.]. (1) Any of the types of pieces that are played on large Javanese **gamelan.* The term usually precedes the proper names of all *gamelan* pieces except those that have the metric-melodic forms *ayak-ayakan, srepegan, kemuda, lancaran, ketawang,* and *ladrang.* This usage was derived in the first half of the 20th century from (2) below. (2) [Jav.] Any piece that is played on large Javanese **gamelan* but that does not use *kempul* (the highest-pitched hanging gongs). Such pieces may also be called *gendhing ageng* (large) to distinguish them from forms known collectively as *gendhing alit* (small). See also Southeast Asia IX. M.H.

Genera [Lat.]. Plural of *genus.

Generalbass [Ger.]. *Thoroughbass.

Generalpause [Ger., abbr. G.P.]. General pause, a rest for the entire orchestra, especially one that occurs unexpectedly.

Género chico [Sp.]. See *Zarzuela.*

Genus [Lat., pl. *genera*]. In ancient Greek music, a tetrachordal tuning. The three categories of tuning were the *diatonic, *chromatic, and *enharmonic genera [see Greece I, 3 (i)]. Some composers and theorists of the Renaissance (e.g., Nicola Vicentino) attempted to revive the use of all three genera. A.B.

Georgian chant. The ecclesiastical music of the Orthodox Church of Georgia, which adopted Byzantine Christianity after the 4th century. Georgian hymnography developed between the 5th and 8th centuries when many translated texts retained the isosyllabic structure and meter of the Greek originals. Thus the Georgian hymns must have been sung to their Greek melodies. Nonmusical sources attest three-voice polyphony from as early as the 12th century, but the evidence is of dubious authenticity. Independent monophonic notations developed in Georgia throughout the Middle Ages; and in the 17th and 19th centuries, new systems of signs, using *neumes and letters, were introduced. D.E.C.

German dance. **Deutscher Tanz.*

German flute. In the 18th century, the transverse flute, as distinct from the English flute or recorder.

German Requiem, A. See *Deutsches Requiem, Ein.*

German sixth. See Sixth chord.

Germany. Germany has been a unified nation only since 1871. Its fragmentation before that date into a multiplicity of independent governments of varying size and character resulted in a highly decentralized and variegated musical life dominated by court musical establishments, such as those of Berlin, Dresden, Munich, Stuttgart, and Mannheim, or the more bourgeois institutions of large commercial centers, such as Hamburg. Traditions thus begun continue strong in German musical life, in spite of the disruptions of more recent political upheavals and wars. Nevertheless, the division of the country in 1945 into communist East and capitalist West had a profound impact on cultural life, for a period of time creating two separate and differently oriented spheres of music activity. In addition to the difference produced by ideology, West Germany was more prosperous and larger, with more major cities and closer links to the rest of Western European culture than East Germany; but three cities traditionally among the most important German musical centers lay in the East: Dresden, Leipzig, and East Berlin (which included the old center of Berlin, with many of the city's leading musical institutions). In part because of this geography and its history, the split had a shorter and less severe impact on German musical institutions, education, and public consumption than might be imagined; the official reunification on October 3, 1990, brought together two Germanys with remarkably similar repertoires, performance standards, and levels of musical education. The rich musical life in many cities, such as Berlin, which has three opera houses and seven orchestras, is a direct result of the importance both countries placed in music institutions during the cold war.

I. *Current musical activity and related institutions.* 1. Opera. The operatic tradition in Germany is very strong and broadly based. The leading houses include the Staatsoper Unter den Linden in Berlin, noted also for its orchestra (the Staatskapelle Berlin) and the musical direction of Daniel Barenboim (1942–); the Komische Oper in Berlin, important for its imaginative stagings by Walter Felsenstein (1901–75) and Harry Kupfer (1935–); the Deutsche Oper Berlin; the Dresden Staatsoper; the Munich Staatsoper at the Nationaltheater, reopened in 1963; the Stuttgart Opera, famous for its often provocative stagings; and the Hamburg Staatsoper, especially prominent during the administration of the composer Rolf Liebermann (1959–73); Hamburg's chamber opera group, Opera Stabile (1973), is one of several permanent ensembles that has been established to present new works.

East Berlin includes the old Staatsoper, reconstructed in 1955; the more modest Komische Oper (established 1947) became better known in the postwar period. The Dresden Staatsoper, long one of Europe's greatest houses, has regained something of its prewar standing and now ranks with Berlin.

Opera is also an important part of the theatrical life of several dozen other cities and towns, thus continuing a long German tradition. This widespread activity has made the smaller German houses an important proving ground for new performers, both German and foreign. In the 1950s and 1960s especially, before there was sufficient opportunity at home, many beginning American singers established their careers in the smaller German houses.

Opera is a specialty of several German music festivals: most famously Bayreuth, devoted to Wagner, and Göttingen, specializing in Handelian opera. Munich offers both a Biennale, founded in 1988 to present the works of composers from the postwar generation, as well as a summer opera festival featuring performances of the standard repertory and recitals by well-known singers. Mannheim, Weisbaden, and Baden-Baden also have summer festivals.

2. Performing groups. The German symphonic tradition is at least equal to the operatic in breadth. The Berlin Philharmonic perhaps stands alone among German orchestras in international reputation. The Leipzig Gewandhaus Orchestra, the Dresden Staatskapelle, and the Staatskapelle Berlin (attached to the Staatsoper Unter den Linden) are of major importance, as are the nearly 150 professional orchestras nationwide. Some of the finest German orchestras are found among those supported by national and regional radio networks. The Akademie für Alte Musik Berlin and the Concerto Köln are two of the most prominent early music ensembles.

There are numerous chamber orchestras in various cities, including Frankfurt, Hamburg, Heidelberg, Mannheim, Munich, and Stuttgart. Amateur choral societies, which became a prominent feature of German musical life in the 19th century, remain popular. Workers' orchestras, choruses, and ensembles, popular throughout the country, are a tradition from the early 20th century that was especially reinforced by the ideological basis of East German society.

Church music remains strong, especially in the great traditions of the Thomaskirche in Leipzig and the Kreuzkirche in Dresden. The ensembles of these institutions now enjoy greater international exposure and freedom to travel and collaborate with institutions worldwide.

3. Festivals. Music festivals of various sorts became relatively frequent in Germany in the 19th century. The most famous was that organized by Richard Wagner to celebrate his music dramas at Bayreuth in 1876, which grew into the present annual festival there. Today there are literally hundreds of annual or biennial festivals of varied focus held throughout Germany. In addition to the opera-oriented festivals, many others are dedicated to a single composer, such as those at Berlin (Mozart), Ansbach and Köthen (Bach), Leipzig (Bach and Mendelssohn), Würzburg (Bach and Mozart), and Bonn (Beethoven). Festivals for new music include those held in Stuttgart, Lüneburg, Heidelberg, Würzburg, Berlin, Hamburg, Hannover, Witten, Düsseldorf, and Donaueschingen, a festival renewed by

Hindemith in 1950 and especially important in furthering avant-garde music in that period. Several festivals are also devoted to early music, jazz, or folk music, and larger all-encompassing festivals exist in cities such as Berlin, Munich, and Passau.

4. Education. In German usage, a Musikhochschule is generally devoted to training professional musicians and ranks higher in the educational hierarchy than a conservatory, which also offers instruction to amateurs; the two types of institution are no longer always kept strictly separate, however. The present system of such schools descends from that developed in the second half of the 19th century, beginning with the establishment in 1843 of the conservatory at Leipzig under Felix Mendelssohn (renamed Mendelssohn Akademie in 1946). This conservatory was followed by many others, including those at Berlin (1869, first headed by Joseph Joachim), Munich (1846, reorganized by Hans von Bülow in 1867), and Cologne (1845, reorganized by Ferdinand von Hiller in 1850), until nearly every sizable German city, as well as many smaller ones, had its own conservatory.

German and Austrian scholars in the 19th century shaped a growing interest in music history into the scholarly discipline of musicology, defining aims and methods that have continued to be influential as musicology has grown into an international undertaking. The first professorship was established at the University of Strasbourg, then part of Germany, in 1897, and more than 20 others have since been created at other German universities. The Nazis drove many German scholars abroad, weakening the German domination of musicology, but ensuring German influence over its foreign development. Since World War II, it has again flourished within Germany.

Among more specialized aspects of the German educational scene, the Internationale Ferienkurse für Neue Musik, founded at Darmstadt in 1946 (held annually until 1970 and biennially since), stands out for its influence on the development of avant-garde music, especially in the late 1940s and 1950s.

5. Publishing. Germany became an important center of music publishing in the earliest days of the industry. In the 16th and 17th centuries, over 1,000 publishers were active at various times in over 200 cities, with Nuremberg the most important. Several firms still in existence had their beginnings in the renewed growth of the industry that began in the second half of the 18th century: Breitkopf, which grew from modest beginnings in Leipzig in the early 18th century and was joined by Härtel in 1795; Schott (Mainz, 1770); and Simrock (Bonn, 1793), the last no longer an independent firm. Leipzig became the principal center of German music publishing in the early 19th century and during the latter part of that century and the beginning of the next was the most important in the world, with dozens of firms having their headquarters there.

The industry was much disrupted by the Nazi regime, which drove several important publishers, such as Eulenburg and Fürstner, out of the country; by World War II, which destroyed or severely damaged the plants and stock of many firms; and by the division of the country into East and West, with Leipzig in the East, where its industry was eventually nationalized. Some of the big Leipzig firms, such as Breitkopf & Härtel, Peters, and Hofmeister, were divided like the country, with independent entities operating in its two parts.

The most important firm established between the wars was Bärenreiter (1923, first at Augsburg, now at Kassel). Postwar firms include Henle (1948) in Munich and the Deutscher Verlag für Musik (1954) in Leipzig.

6. Broadcasting. The first German radio stations were established in 1923–24. The Nazis, highly conscious of radio's importance, organized a centralized network. After the war, radio in West Germany was decentralized into nine semiautonomous regional units: Südwestfunk (SWF, Baden-Baden); Sender Freies Berlin; Radio Bremen; Westdeutscher Rundfunk (WDR, Cologne); Hessischer Rundfunk (Frankfurt am Main); Norddeutscher Rundfunk (NDR, Hamburg); Bayerischer Rundfunk (BR, Munich); Saarländischer Rundfunk (Saarbrücken); and Süddeutscher Rundfunk (SDR, Stuttgart and Heidelberg). A few of these regional networks merged in the late 20th century, while networks in the former East were either added in the style of the West, such as Mitteldeutscher Rundfunk (MDR, Saxony) or became privately owned stations, such as the Berliner Rundfunk, the former center of the East German network, which now belongs to the Europe-wide RTL group. RIAS-Berlin, a descendant of the postwar American-Sector station, was an independent entity until the 1993 Radio Transformation Treaty merged the station with Deutschlandfunk and Deutschlandsender-Kultur to form the nationwide Deutschlandradio network, headquartered in Berlin and Cologne.

German radio stations began to establish orchestras in the 1920s, and those remaining today are among the best in the country.

Another important aspect of German broadcasting has been its encouragement of new music. This began in the 1920s, was interrupted by the Nazi period, and was historically most significant in the 1950s, when Herbert Eimert (1897–1972), using the facilities of Westdeutscher Rundfunk, Cologne, created a pioneer electronic music studio. The SWF at Baden-Baden, first under the leadership of Heinrich Strobel (1898–1970) and now part of the SWR, has also been an important center of the avant-garde. Also, the SWR supports the revived Donaueschingen Musiktage. In addition to supporting two orchestras, a chorus, and a jazz orchestra, the WDR contributed to the growth of the early-music movement by establishing and supporting the Capella Coloniensis (1954).

II. *History.* The broad historical curve of German musical activity traces a rise from relative backwardness and secondary importance to domination of European music from the late 18th to the early 20th century. In ancient times, Germany was located on the edge of European civilization, but whether this has much to do with the slow beginnings of German music in the Middle Ages is debatable. Some German monasteries were important centers of Gregorian chant in that period, but (ironically, in view of its later involvement with the art) Germany seems to have contributed relatively little to the first centuries of the most important musical innovation of the Middle Ages, the rise of polyphony. The creators of the first important surviving body of native German music, the songs of the *Minnesinger (12th–14th centuries) and their successors the *Meistersinger (14th–16th centuries), were much indebted to the *troubadours and *trouvères for the sources of their art. This established a pattern that was long to remain characteristic of much German music, one in which the stimulus for new departures came from foreign influences, which, however, were given a distinctive German character in the process of development.

In one field at least, that of the organ and its music, Germany does seem to have been an early leader, and it has remained one. Germany's preeminence in this field becomes fully apparent in the 15th century with the composer and organist Conrad Paumann (ca. 1410–73) and the sizable body of organ music surviving in sources such as the **Buxheimer Orgelbuch* [see also *Fundamentum*]. The 15th century in general evidences increasing activity in German music, as in the appearance of the polyphonic *lied, in which Oswald von Wolkenstein (ca. 1377–1445) is one of the first distinct figures. This development was also indebted to foreign influence, that of the Burgundian chanson, but it acquired a native character in the *Tenorlied.*

German musical activity further increased in the 16th century, along with the number of important composers, including Heinrich Finck (1444/45–1527), Heinrich Isaac (ca. 1450–1517), Paul Hofhaimer (1459–1537), Thomas Stoltzer (ca. 1480/85–1526), and Ludwig Senfl (ca. 1486–1542/43). This century was dominated by the Reformation, which eventually crystallized in the division of Germany into Protestant north and Catholic south. With music still closely tied to a religious function and with the doctrinal differences between Protestantism and Catholicism strongly affecting the musical practice of each, this division had momentous consequences for the future of German music. For a time, *Lutheran liturgical music remained conservative in style, close to that of the early 16th century, but the development of the *chorale, begun by Luther and his musical associate Johann Walter (Walther) (1496–1570), introduced a factor that was to lead Lutheran music into distinctive paths, while Catholic music remained more directly linked to international styles and practices [see also Church music].

This became evident in the 17th century in the adaptation of new foreign influences—the innovations of the Italian *Baroque, as well as French instrumental and English keyboard styles—to Lutheran needs, particularly in combination with chorales, resulting in such organ genres as the chorale prelude, chorale partita, chorale fantasia, and the like [see Organ chorale], and, in vocal music, the chorale *cantata. Eclecticism, in the form of the absorption and synthesis of elements of various national styles, is a primary trait of most German Baroque composers, from Schütz to Buxtehude to Bach, Handel, and Telemann. The way in which the synthesis was made is usually considered an aspect of their genius and its analysis a principal means of defining and distinguishing their styles.

Regardless of internal growth and retrospective estimates of its achievement, German Baroque music did not acquire much international influence, and in the 18th century the perception of it by foreigners as being characterized by complexity and learnedness, at a time when the general trend was toward simplicity and "naturalness," led to the use of *musica tedesca* as a term of reproach in the eyes of partisans of foreign styles. In the second half of the century, however, with the synthesis of Austro-German and Italian that produced the *Classical style and its associated genres of *symphony, *concerto, *string quartet, and the like, German-speaking composers at last achieved wide international influence and began a lengthy period of domination of most of European music. Yet the center of this influence was not in Germany proper but at Vienna [see Austria], and parallel German beginnings, as at Mannheim [see Mannheim School], were to prove of minor significance beside the Viennese achievements of Haydn and Mozart.

German musical nationalism, stimulated by the Napoleonic wars, was to make "Germanness" a prized element in much 19th-century German music and was to play a significant part in the shaping of German musical *Romanticism, as in the German Romantic *opera, brought to maturity by Weber out of the earlier *Singspiel, and in the newly important genre of lieder [see Lied]. Although Vienna remained the capital of German music, drawing such German-born composers as Beethoven and Brahms, others, such as Mendelssohn, Schumann, and the radical Liszt–Wagner axis, worked mostly within Germany itself.

In the early 20th century, the center of musical progressivism seemed to pass to Paris, as the innovations of Schoenberg and his school, which formed the avant-garde of Austro-German music, were largely ignored in favor of composers who maintained more explicit links to the musical past, such as Richard Strauss (1864–1949) and Max Reger (1873–1916); the *twelve-tone system, introduced in the 1920s and intended by Schoenberg to ensure the continued dominance of German music, began to be widely influential only after World War II, despite the early advocacy of such composers as Heinz Tiessen (1887–1971). The post–World War I period was one of artistic ferment and iconoclasm within Germany, as in the early work of Paul Hindemith (1895–1963), who was to become one of the most imitated composers of the 1930s and 1940s. Among other significant composers of the period were Philipp Jarnach (1892–1982), Ernst Krenek (1900–91), Kurt Weill (1900–50), Hugo Distler (1908–42), Ernst Pepping (1901–81), and Carl Orff (1895–1982). The coming to power of the Nazis in the 1930s stifled progressivism and drove a large proportion of the country's musicians to emigrate and many others to cease overt activity for a time. Much was destroyed in the war, and the postwar period was one of rebuilding in all senses. West Germany won a place in the avant-garde in the early 1950s through electronic music [see Electro-acoustic music] and the union of it with *serialism by Karlheinz Stockhausen (b. 1928). In East Germany, progressivism took the form of broadening music's social basis and exploiting its ability to make ideological statements. The return of the poet and dramatist Bertolt Brecht (1898–1956) and the composer Hanns Eisler (1898–1962) was influential in this regard.

Among composers who rose to prominence in the decades immediately following the war, Stockhausen, Bernd Alois Zimmermann (1918–70), and Hans Werner Henze (b. 1926) are perhaps best known. Also important are Boris Blacher (1903–75), Günter Bialas (1907–95), Wolfgang Fortner (1907–87), Dieter Schnebel (b. 1930), Paul-Heinz Dittrich (b. 1930), Mauricio Kagel (b. 1931 in Buenos Aires), and Siegfried Matthus (b. 1934). The next generation included those who continued to follow the avant-garde trajectories established in the 1950s, such as Tilo Medek (b. 1940), Udo Zimmermann (b. 1943), Johannes G. Fritsch (b. 1941), who founded the electronic music center Feedback Studio Köln in 1970, as well as those who eschewed the extreme experimentation associated with the Darmstadt school, such as Wolfgang Rihm (b. 1952) and Hans-Jürgen von Bose (b. 1953). Other notable composers of this generation include Friedrich Goldmann (b. 1941), Friedrich Schenker (b. 1942), Manfred Trojahn (b. 1949), Wolfgang von Schweinitz (b. 1953), and Detlev Müller-Siemens (1957).

III. *Folk music.* German interest in folk music has been intense since the late 18th century. Although this interest has resulted in much collection and preservation of authentic indigenous music, it has also stimulated the composition and performance of many pieces simply imitating the folk style, largely replacing oral tradition and spontaneous performance. Nevertheless, true folk music is still cultivated in a few areas, and evidence of its characteristics in earlier times survives in various sources. While early German folk song made use of a variety of modes, melismas, and irregular, nonstrophic forms, later music was usually in the diatonic major, syllabic, and strophic. Symmetrical forms and *Sprechgesang* [see *Sprechstimme, Sprechgesang*] have both often been incorporated. Simple part-singing was introduced in the 17th century. The tradition includes love-songs, *Gesellenlieder* (journeymen's songs), *Wanderlieder* (wanderer's songs), class songs, and sacred but nonliturgical songs, among others. German folk dances that are still practiced today in some localities include rounds for masked dancers, leaping processional dances, marches, **Ländler* and waltzes, and the **Zwiefacher.* Instruments used in folk music, both past and present, include noisemakers such as clappers, violin, clarinet, zither, dulcimer, mouth organ, guitar, harp, hurdy-gurdy, concertina, barrel organ, and double bass.

Bibl.: Hans Mersmann, *Eine deutsche Musikgeschichte* (Potsdam-Berlin: Sanssouci Verlag, 1934); 2nd ed. enl., *Musikgeschichte in der abendländischen Kultur* (Frankfurt: H F Menck, 1955; 3rd ed., Kassel: Bärenreiter, 1973). Walter Wiora, *Das deutsche Lied: Zur Geschichte und Ästhetik einer musikalischen Gattung* (Wolfenbüttel: Möseler, 1971). Hermann Strobach, *Deutsches Volkslied im Geschichte und Gegenwart* (Berlin: Akademie Verlag, 1980). Hermann Danuser, *Die Musik des 20. Jahrhunderts* (Laaber: Laaber-Verlag, 1984). Klaus-Michael Hinz, *New Developments in Contemporary German Music* (Reading, J.K.: Harwood Academic Publishers, 1995). Horst Grewer and Michael Thürnau, *Das grosse Lexikon der Volksmusik* (Kiel: M. Jung, 1996). Gianmario Borio and Hermann Danuser, eds., *Im Zenit der Moderne: die Internationalen Ferienkurse für Neue Musik, Darmstadt 1946–1966* (Freiburg: Rombach, 1997). Michael H. Kater, *The Twisted Music: Musicians and Their Music in the Third Reich* (New York: Oxford U Pr, 1997). Pamela M. Potter, *Most German of the Arts: Musicology and Society from the Weimar Republic to the End of Hitler's Reich* (New Haven: Yale U Pr, 1998). Celia Applegate and Pamela Potter, eds., *Music and German National Identity* (Chicago: U of Chicago Pr, 2002).

Ges, geses [Ger.]. G-flat, G-double-flat. See Pitch names.

Gesamtausgabe [Ger.]. Complete edition [see Editions].

Gesamtkunstwerk [Ger., total artwork]. Richard Wagner's term for his mature operas, in which all the arts (including music, poetry, and visual spectacle) were to be perfectly fused [see Opera].

Gesang [Ger.]. Song; *gesangvoll,* songlike, cantabile.

Gesang der Jünglinge [Ger., Song of the Young Boys]. An electronic work by Karlheinz Stockhausen, composed in 1955–56, in which the voice of a boy speaking and singing the *Benedicite* is transformed and combined with purely electronic sounds. It is reproduced through five spatially separated groups of loudspeakers.

Geschöpfe des Prometheus, Die [Ger., The Creatures of Prometheus]. A ballet by Beethoven, op. 43 (choreography by Salvatore Viganò), produced in Vienna in 1801. The overture remains in the concert repertory. Beethoven used a theme from the finale in three other works [see *Eroica, Eroica Variations*].

Geschwind [Ger.]. Quick, fast.

Gesellschaft [Ger.]. See Societies, musical.

Gesellschaftslied [Ger.]. A song for a particular social class, especially the middle class, as distinct from *Volkslied* (folk song) and *Hoflied* (court song). The term has been applied most often to German polyphonic songs of the 16th century, including works of Hofhaimer, Senfl, and others [see Lied].

Geses [Ger.]. See *Ges, geses.*

Ge sol re ut, gesolreut. See Hexachord.

Gesteigert [Ger.]. Increased; hence, **crescendo* or **rinforzando.*

Gestopft [Ger.]. Stopped [see Stopped tones, Horn].

Geteilt [Ger.]. **Divisi.*

Getragen [Ger.]. Sustained, slow, solemn.

Gewandhaus [Ger.]. See Concert, Orchestra, Germany.

Gewandt [Ger.]. Agile.

Gewöhnlich [Ger.]. Usual; an instruction to the player to return to the usual way of playing after a previous instruction to play in a special way, e.g., after an instruction to bow over the fingerboard.

Gezupft [Ger.]. *Pizzicato.

Ghayṭah [Ar.]. (1) A *reedpipe of the Islamic world. (2) In North Africa, a *shawm.

Ghironda [It.]. *Hurdy-gurdy.

Ghost dance. An American Indian religious movement from Nevada that, together with a distinctive musical style, was widely adopted by peoples of the Plains ca. 1890. The songs have small range and paired-phrase form (e.g., AABB, AABBCC).

Bibl.: George Herzog, "Plains Ghost Dance and Great Basin Music," *American Anthropologist* 37 (1935): 403–19.

B.N.

Ghost trio. See *Geistertrio.*

Gianni Schicchi. See *Trittico.*

Gidayubushi [Jap.]. Narrative music of the Japanese puppet theater *(bunraku),* performed by a singer-narrator and a **shamisen* player, both appearing onstage in a kneeling position. The vocal styles of *gidayu* include intonational chants, heightened speech, and lyrical songs. The *shamisen* plays preludes, interludes, and postludes to the singing and uses stereotyped patterns. See also East Asia II, 3 (ii). I.K.F.W.

Giga [It., Sp.]. *Gigue.

Gigelira [It.]. *Xylophone.

Gigue [Fr., fr. Eng. jig; Ger. *Gigue;* It. *giga;* Sp. *giga, jiga*]. (1) A fast Baroque dance movement in binary form, the last movement of the mature *suite. The details of rhythm and texture vary greatly, deriving from Italian and French models. The Italian *giga* features triadic, sequential running figures in even note-values in 12/8 at presto tempo. Its texture is mostly homophonic, and phrases are in four-measure units. French versions are less consistent, often having dotted rhythms in duple meter (usually compound, but also simple), syncopations, hemiolas, and cross rhythms. The most influential type opens each strain with imitation and has irregular phrase lengths. Many composers, especially in Germany, mixed elements of the two schools.

The dance originated in Ireland and England [see Jig]. It was known in France by the 1650s (Chambonnières) and became an important part of the lute and harpsichord repertory (Ennemond and Denis Gaultier, Nicolas-Antoine Lebègue). One type was considered a fast, dotted allemande (the Gaultiers), but the more familiar duple compound variety with upbeats associated with the *canarie, as shown here,

♪♪ | ♩.♪♩ ♩.♪♩

was used in stage music (Lully). In the early 18th century, it often showed more Italian influence (François Couperin, Rameau). Its tempo varied but was usually quick: faster than a *loure, slower than a canarie. In Italy, it was much faster and was particularly common in violin music (Vitali, op. 4, 1668), often as the last movement of solo sonatas (Domenico Zipoli) and trio sonatas (Corelli). In Germany, most composers adopted French imitative texture (Froberger), often making the thematic relationship between the strains closer by using an inversion of the opening motive as the subject of the second strain [see Ex.]. They often favored Italian flowing triplet motion (Handel, Bach). Gigues notated in duple simple meter may call for interpretation in triplets.

Bach, Gigue from French Suite no. 4.

(2) In the Middle Ages, a bowed stringed instrument: a fiddle or *rebec. The term is the root of the modern German word for violin, *Geige.*

Bibl.: Werner Danckert, *Geschichte der Gigue* (Leipzig: Kistner & Siegel, 1924). Michael Collins, "The Performance of Triplets in the 17th and 18th Centuries," *JAMS* 19 (1966): 281–328. Meredith Little and Carol Marsh, *La Danse noble:*

An Inventory of Dances and Sources (Williamstown: Broude Trust, 1992). B.G.

Gimel. See Gymel.

Gioconda, La [It., The Joyful Girl]. Opera in four acts by Amilcare Ponchielli (libretto by Arrigo Boito [pseud. Tobia Gorrio], after Victor Hugo's drama *Angelo, tyran de Padoue*), produced in Milan in 1876. Setting: Venice in the 17th century.

Giocoso [It.]. Jocose, humorous.

Gioioso [It.]. Joyous, merry.

Giorgi flute. A vertically held version of the orchestral *flute, invented by Carlo Tomaso Giorgi and patented in 1896. Eleven finger holes were provided to produce each chromatic tone without *fork fingering. Covering eleven holes with ten fingers proved to be difficult, however, and on later versions some of the holes are covered by open-standing keys. M.S.

Gipsy music. See Gypsy music.

Giraffe piano. A grand *piano of the first half of the 19th century, the wing-shaped portion of which (and thus the plane of the strings) is set upright, perpendicular to the keyboard. Such pianos were often decorated with a scroll formed by the intersection of the curved side with the straight side, the result bearing some resemblance to the shape of a giraffe.

Girl of the Golden West. See *Fanciulla del West, La.*

Gis [Ger.]. G-sharp. See Pitch names.

Giselle (ou Les Wilis). A ballet in two acts by Adolphe Adam (choreography by Jean Coralli and Jules Perrot, book by Vernoy de Saint-Georges, Théophile Gautier, and Jean Coralli, after a story by Heinrich Heine), first produced in Paris in 1841.

Gisis [Ger.]. G-double-sharp. See Pitch names.

Gitana, alla [It.]. See Gypsy music.

Gittern [also gyterne, gitt(e)ron; Fr. *guiterne;* Ger. *Quinterne;* It. *chitarra, ghiterra*]. (1) A small medieval plucked stringed instrument with a pear-shaped body, round back, and sickle-shaped pegbox. Tinctoris (*De inventione et usu musicae,* ca. 1487) says it is strung and played like the *lute. A precursor of the *mandora, the round-backed gittern fell out of favor about 1500. (2) Any of a variety of plucked stringed instruments of the Middle Ages and Renaissance thought to derive from the *guitarra latina* and *guitarra morisca* mentioned in Spanish literature beginning in the 14th century. The term, about which there is considerable confusion, persisted in association with instruments used well into the 17th century.

Giù [It.]. Down; *arcata in giù,* down-bow. See Bowing (1).

Giulio Cesare in Egitto [It., Julius Caesar in Egypt]. Opera in three acts by Handel (libretto by Nicola Francesco Haym, after G. F. Bussani), produced in London in 1724. Setting: Egypt, 48 B.C.E.

Giustamente [It.]. **Giusto.*

Giustiniana [It.]. (1) A setting of poetry by, or in the style of, Lorenzo Giustiniani (d. 1446); four of these, for three voices and in archaic style, are found in Petrucci's *Frottole libro sexto* (1506). (2) A late 16th-century comic subgenre of the **villanella* in which three old men sing, with much written-in stammering, of love. Andrea Gabrieli, Vincenzo Bellavere, and Giuseppe Policreto are among the composers who contributed to the form. J.H.

Giusto [It.]. Just, precise; *tempo giusto,* an appropriate tempo or the usual tempo for the type of work at hand, or a return to regular tempo after a passage in which tempo is flexible.

Glagolitic Mass [Cz. *Glagolská mše*]. A cantata composed in 1926 by Leoš Janáček for soprano, alto, tenor, and bass soloists, chorus, orchestra, and organ, with a text adapted by Miloš Weingart from Old Church Slavonic.

Glanz, glänzend [Ger.]. Brightness, brilliant.

Glass (h)armonica. An instrument invented by Benjamin Franklin in 1761 and called "armonica." It consists of a row of glass bowls of graded sizes fixed concentrically on a horizontal spindle that is made to rotate by a treadle. Sound is produced by gently rubbing the fingers (slightly wetted or dipped in chalk) on the rims of the revolving glasses. Later models are fitted with a trough of water beneath the spindle to keep the glasses constantly wet, and some are fitted with a keyboard that rubs the glasses mechanically. The instrument became very popular in connection with the Romantic movement of the late 18th and early 19th centuries, its delicate, ethereal tones being

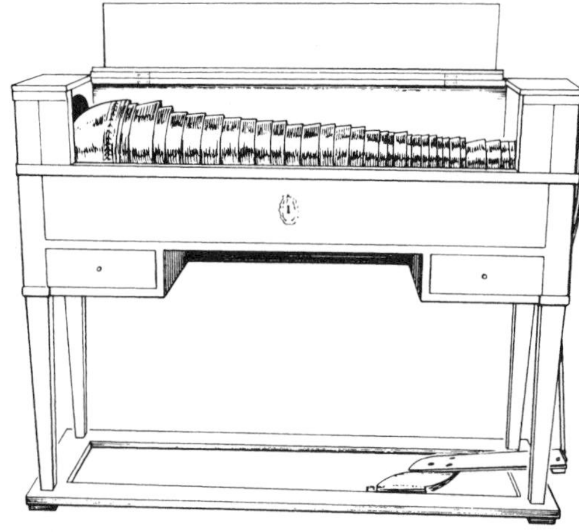

Glass harmonica.

credited with profound psychological and spiritual effects. Mozart, Beethoven, Hasse, Jommelli, and Padre Martini wrote for the glass harmonica. Mozart's Adagio in C major K. 356 (617a) and Adagio and Rondo in C minor (with flute, oboe, viola, and cello) K. 617, both composed in 1791 for the blind virtuoso Marianne Kirchgessner, are the best-known compositions for the instrument. About 1830 it fell into disuse, but Richard Strauss used it in his opera *Die Frau ohne Schatten* (1917). See also Musical glasses.

Bibl.: Alec Hyatt King, "The Musical Glasses and Glass Harmonica," *PRMA* 72 (1945–46): 97–122.

Glass harp [Ger. *Glasharfe*]. A type of *musical glasses invented by the German virtuoso Bruno Hoffmann ca. 1929 and consisting of 46 tuned glasses attached to a resonant table.

Glee. An English composition for three or more voices, usually unaccompanied and male, popular in the 18th and early 19th centuries. The poem (and its music) may be either lighthearted or serious, since this usage of glee does not relate directly to the word's present meaning, but derives from both senses' common Old-English source meaning entertainment, play, sport, and also musical entertainment, the playing of music, and music itself. Used in the sense of melody, it is found in *Beowulf.*

The earliest known designation of a work as a glee is in John Playford's *Select Musicall Ayres and Dialogues* (1652). The glee was at its height in the second half of the 18th century, when it was a favorite for amateur music-making, and clubs devoted to singing glees and similar music and to encouraging their composition were formed in London (and elsewhere), including the Glee Club (1783–1857). The use of *glee club as a name for American school choruses derives from their origin in such groups in the 19th century.

The 18th-century glee tended toward a vigorous style, rather simple in texture, less contrapuntal than most madrigals. It usually consisted of a series of short sections, corresponding to the structure of the poem, each ending with a full cadence, frequently with considerable contrast, even of tempo and meter, from one to the next. In the 19th century, there was a tendency to even more homophonic texture and to sentimental melody, leading to the part song, which eventually replaced the glee. Glees vary considerably in length and form. Some are short, others in two or more movements. The term glee was also applied loosely to music arranged from various sources, including popular songs and the theater.

Originally for male voices exclusively (with the highest part a male alto), glees appeared for mixed voices by the late 18th century, reflecting a change in their social function. Willoughby Bertie's *Twelve Sentimental Catches and Glees* (ca. 1795) were the first published with accompaniment (provided by Haydn). Samuel Webbe (1740–1816) is generally considered the leading glee composer. Other prominent figures include Benjamin Cooke (1734–93), Lord Mornington (1735–81), Stephen Paxton (1735–87), Richard J. S. Stevens (1757–1837), John Danby (ca. 1757–98), John Callcott (1766–1821), Reginald Spofforth (ca. 1768/70–1827), and William Horsley (1774–1858).

Bibl.: William A. Barrett, "English Glees and Part-Songs: An Inquiry into the Glee," *ML* 33 (1952): 346–51. David Johnson, "The 18th-Century Glee," *MT* 120 (1979): 200–202.

Glee club. The term used from the early 1800s in the U.S. for groups devoted to the recreational singing of secular part songs. By the end of the 19th century, glee club signified a student-run collegiate ensemble that, like banjo and mandolin clubs, performed popular and college songs, sometimes in public concerts. College glee clubs since the 1920s—typically either all male or all female—have been more likely to operate under faculty artistic control, often aiming for polished performances and mixing selections by renowned composers of past and present into their repertories. R.C.

Gleemen. See Minstrel.

Gleichmässig [Ger.]. Even, equal.

Gli scherzi [It.]. See *Scherzi, Gli.*

Glissando [It., abbr. *gliss.;* fr. Fr. *glisser,* to slide]. A continuous or sliding movement from one pitch to another. On the piano, the nail of the thumb or of the third finger or the side of the index finger is drawn, usually rapidly, over the white keys or the black keys, thus producing a rapid scale. On the white keys, two such scales can be produced simultaneously at intervals such as an octave or a third by the use of two fingers of one hand. Octave glissandos produced by the thumb and fifth finger are called for in the final movement of Beethoven's *Waldstein* Sonata. A similar effect is much used in harp playing, where the fleshy part of the thumb or finger is drawn across the strings and where the pedal action makes possible the playing of a variety of scales and chords in this fashion [see Harp I, 2].

On stringed instruments such as the violin, on wind instruments (particularly, though not exclusively, the slide trombone), and on the pedal kettledrum, the sliding movement may produce a continuous variation in pitch rather than a rapid succession of discrete pitches. This is often indicated by a straight or wavy line drawn between the starting and ending pitches and is sometimes termed **portamento,* though glissando remains the prevalent term for this effect in musical scores. Some writers have preferred to restrict the meaning of glissando to the motion in which discrete pitches are heard, reserving *portamento* for continuous variation in pitch, but musical practice is not consistent in this respect. Ambiguity in the use of the term glissando is most likely to occur with respect to stringed instruments, which are capable of both effects.

Glissé [Fr.]. In *harp playing, *glissando.

Globular flute. A *flute whose body is not a tube; also called a vessel flute. The player blows either across a blow hole or into a *duct-type mouthpiece. Globular flutes are particularly characteristic of Africa and pre-Columbian South America. A familiar example is the *ocarina.

Glocke [Ger.]. Bell (1).

Glockenspiel [Ger., also *Stahlspiel;* Eng., also bells, but see also Tubular bells; Fr. *carillon, jeu de timbres;* It. *campanelli, carillon;* Sp. *carillón, campanólogo*]. (1) A percussion instrument of definite pitch consisting of metal bars of varying length arranged in two rows, somewhat in the fashion of a piano keyboard, on a frame, usually without resonators. It is mounted horizontally on a stand and played with two or more beaters with hard, small, round heads. Some instruments

Range.

of this general type, which came into use in the mid-18th century, are played from a pianolike keyboard, and some models are equipped with a damper mechanism controlled by a pedal. Its range is notated from g to c″, and it sounds two octaves higher. A similar instrument used in military and marching bands has its bars arranged on a frame shaped like a Greek lyre and is thus often termed a bell lyra or bell lyre. This instrument is supported by a strap around the player and is held upright. See ill. under Percussion instruments. (2) [Ger.] *Carillon.

Gloria (in excelsis Deo) [Lat., Glory to God in the highest]. The second item of the *Ordinary of the Roman Catholic *Mass, except in Advent, Lent, and a few other occasions when it is omitted; also known as the Greater Doxology and the Angelic Hymn. Its text begins with Luke 2:14. The author and date of the remainder of the text are unknown. Greek versions of the text were known at an early date in the East, and a Latin version was known in the West by the 7th century. The text that has remained in use is found first in 9th-century Frankish sources. In performance, the first phrase is intoned by the celebrant, and the choir continues with the phrase "Et in terra pax." Thus it is that most polyphonic settings begin with this phrase. Modern liturgical books contain 19 melodies of varying antiquity. For the complete text with translation, see Mass.

Gloria patri [Lat.]. See Doxology.

Glosa [Sp., ornamentation, gloss]. In 16th-century Spanish music, (1) ornamental figures and passages and (2) a musical gloss.

Diego Ortiz's treatise (1553) provides melodic formulas *(glosas)* that a viol player might use to embellish cadences and fill in intervals when performing from the voice part of a polyphonic composition (ed. *Mw* 12), or when improvising to a harmonic ostinato or *cantus firmus.* Ortiz illustrates the latter with *ricercars *(recercadas)* based on the **folia,* **ruggiero,* and **passamezzo antico* and *moderno* formulas, and on the **Spagna. Glosa* and its adjectival form, *glosado,* thus identify a composition, usually an *intabulation, that has been enlivened with nearly continuous, florid instrumental ornamentations or *divisions. Spanish and Portuguese collections of organ and *vihuela* music are full of such works, many important to the history of *variation (ed. *MME* 22–23, Valderrábano; 27–29, Cabezón; *Portugaliae musica* A/1, Coelho).

In Cabezón's works, published by Luis Venegas de Henestrosa (1557; ed. *MME* 2), *glosa* identifies short figural variations in **fabordón* style on psalm tones (cf. **intonatione*), in contrast to sets of variations called **diferencias.* Alonso Mudarra's tablature (1546; ed. *MME* 7) contains *tiento–fantasia–glosa* sets for *vihuela* in which the *glosas* proper are fairly literal intabulations of Mass movements by Josquin and Févin, except for sections labeled *glosa* that paraphrase (gloss) thematic fragments drawn from the Mass movement.

Bibl.: John M. Ward, "The Editorial Methods of Venegas de Henestrosa," *MD* 5 (1951): 105–13. Id., "The Use of Borrowed Material in 16th-Century Instrumental Music," *JAMS* 5 (1952): 88–98. Id., "Parody Technique in 16th-Century Instrumental Music," *Sachs,* 1965, pp. 208–28. Max Schneider, ed., *Diego Ortiz: Tratado de glosas sobre clausulas y otros generos de puntos en la musica de violones, Roma, 1553,* 3rd ed. (Kassel: Bärenreiter, 1967). A.J.N.

Glückliche Hand, Die [Ger., The Fortunate Hand]. A "drama with music" by Schoenberg (to his own text) with one singing part, for baritone, two mimed parts, and chorus, composed in 1910–13 and produced in Vienna in 1924.

G.O. In French organ music, abbr. for **Grand orgue.*

Goat's trill [Fr. *chèvrotement;* Ger. *Bockstriller, Geisstriller;* It. *trillo caprino;* Sp. *trino de cabra*]. Usually, the rapid reiteration of a single pitch. For this ornament, see Tremolo. According to J. F. Agricola (*Anleitung zur Singkunst,* 1757, a trans. of P. F. Tosi's *Opinioni de' cantori,* 1723), a *Bockstriller* is a trill in which the two pitches are less than a semitone apart or are sung with unequal speed or loudness. According to Leopold Mozart (*Versuch einer gründlichen Violinschule,* 1756), a trill is termed a *Geisstriller* if it is performed too fast and thus sounds like "bleating." Ludwig Spohr (*Violinschule,* 1832) uses *Bockstriller* for a trill at the unison, i.e., a tremolo.

God Save the Queen [King]. The British national anthem. Both words and music are anonymous and seem to have become popular in 1745. In the U.S., the melody is often sung to the words beginning "My country 'tis of thee."

Goldberg Variations. Popular name for Bach's *Aria mit* [30] *verschiedenen Veränderungen* (Aria with [30] Different Variations) BWV 988, named after Bach's pupil Johann Gottlieb Goldberg (1727–56), a harpsichordist in the service of the Russian Count von Keyserlingk. No evidence supports the claim made in 1802 by Bach's biographer Johann Nikolaus Forkel that Keyserlingk commissioned the work, although Bach apparently gave a copy to Keyserlingk for Goldberg's use. The work's plan is a series of threefold units, each consisting of two variations in free style (frequently highly virtuosic) followed by a canonic variation (nos. 3, 6, 9, etc.), the *canon occurring at successively larger intervals; the final variation is a **quodlibet.* The air is played at the beginning and end of the piece. Bach published the work as the fourth part of his **Clavier-Übung* (1741–42). He also composed an additional 14 canons, BWV 1087, on the first eight notes of the air's bass.

Golden Cockerel, The [Russ. *Zolotoy petushok;* Fr. *Le coq d'or*]. Opera in three acts by Rimsky-Korsakov (libretto by V. I. Bel'sky, after Pushkin), composed in 1906–7 and produced in Moscow in 1909. Michel Fokine created a version in French for Diaghilev's Ballets russes (libretto revised by Alexandre Benois) in which the characters were mimed by dancers and the singers were placed in boxes to the side. This version was produced in Paris in 1914. Setting: a mythical kingdom.

Golden Sequence. Popular name for the *sequence "Veni Sancte Spiritus."

Goliards. Wandering scholar-poets who flourished in England, France, and Germany in the 12th and 13th centuries. The origin of the name remains unclear, and it is now generally agreed that they did not constitute an order or guild. The terms goliardic verse and goliardic song have been applied to a large repertory of Latin secular song of the period (including the **Carmina burana*) that is frequently profane, satirical (often directed against the Church and the Pope), amorous (often obscene), and in praise of drink. Only a fraction of the repertory was written by the wandering goliards themselves, however. Other parts of the repertory, even when the voice purports to be that of the vagabond, can be attributed to learned poets of the period, some of them well known (e.g., Hugh Primas, Serlo of Wilton, Walter of Châtillon, Philip the Chancellor). Relatively few poems are provided with musical notation. Goliardic measure is a stanza of four 13-syllable lines with a single rhyme.

Bibl.: Peter Dronke, *The Medieval Lyric,* 2nd ed. (Cambridge: Cambridge U Pr, 1977), with ample bibliography.

Golpe [Sp.]. In Venezuela, a traditional social dance-song genre associated with the nationally popular **joropo.* Also, among Afro-Venezuelan populations in the coastal region, songs known as *golpes* accompany dancing in sacred contexts, performed by solo vocalist and chorus with percussion accompaniment. Examples are the *golpe de tambor grande,* for two single-headed drums (*mina* and *curbata*), and the *golpe de tambor redondo,* for three double-headed drums (*corrío, cruzao,* and *pujao*). D.S.

Gondola song [Ger. *Gondellied;* It. *gondeliera*]. See Barcarole.

Gong. A metal percussion instrument, usually circular, with its circumference turned over to form a lip. In some cases the lip is very deep, making the gong kettle-shaped. The center is often raised into a knob called a boss. A bossed gong has a definite pitch and may be tuned, while a flat gong, such as the *tam-tam, is of indefinite pitch. Gongs are suspended, either horizontally or vertically, and struck with sticks or padded mallets. Tunable gongs may be assembled into sets, called gong chimes. The gong has found its greatest use and development in the Far East and Southeast Asia. In the Javanese *gamelan,* gong denotes the largest gong in the ensemble, the *gong ageng* [see Southeast Asia IX, 5].

Gopak [Russ.], **hopak** [Ukr.]. A Belorussian and Ukrainian dance in rapid duple meter, of which there is an example in Mussorgsky's **Sorochintsy Fair.*

Gorgia [It.]. Improvised *ornamentation, especially that associated with Italian vocal music of ca. 1600 (Lodovico Zacconi, *Prattica di musica,* 1592). The practice is described in detail by Giulio Caccini in the preface to his *Nuove musiche* of 1601 (ed. Wiley Hitchcock, Madison, Wis.: A-R Edit, 1970; excerpts in *SSR*). A modern term for vocal ornamentation of this type, including rapid passage work, is *gorgheggio.*

Gospel. (1) [Lat. *evangelium*]. In all of the Christian liturgies, a reading or lesson from one of the four Gospels of the Bible. In the Roman Catholic *Mass, it may be chanted to a simple tone (*Tonus Evangelii, LU,* pp. 106–9). A *liturgical book in which such lessons are copied in the order of the liturgical year is called an evangeliary. The Gospels have been the source of texts for much music, including *motets and, especially, *Passion music.

(2) Anglo-American Protestant evangelical hymns from the 1870s to the present; also gospel hymn, gospel song. In revival meetings, preacher Dwight Moody (1837–99) and singer Ira Sankey (1840–1908) popularized simple, strophic melodies set homophonically to strong tonal progressions in major keys. The sentimental poetry of Fanny Crosby (1820–1915) exemplified the texts, each assembled around a biblical idea. Texts are often in the first person and concern the Christian life and the anticipated joys of heaven.

Among the best-known examples is George Bernard's "The Old Rugged Cross" (1913).

(3) Black American Protestant sacred singing and an associated 20th-century sacred genre; also gospel music, gospel song. In this style, vocalists radically embellish simple melodies, and in full and falsetto voice, they shout, hum, growl, moan, whisper, scream, cry. By adding florid melismas and tricky syncopations, altering given pitches with *blue notes and glissandos, and interpolating formulaic phrases ("Lord have mercy," "well, well, well"), they freely extend or repeat any fragment of the text. Spontaneous or choreographed dancing, clapping, and stomping may accompany the singing.

Mingled functions, performing media, and repertories confuse stylistic distinctions within the genre "black gospel music." Musicians perform for religious stimulation and for commercial profit, in boisterous services and concerts or in silent recording studios.

Vocalists may be a preacher and congregation (as in the mono- and heterophonic music of numerous Holiness and Sanctified sects), soloists (Mahalia Jackson, Marion Williams), singer-guitarists (Blind Willie Johnson, Rev. Gary Davis, Rosetta Tharpe), quartets and quintets (the Dixie Hummingbirds, the Soul Stirrers, the Clara Ward Singers, the Mighty Clouds of Joy), or choirs (led by James Cleveland, Alex Bradford). Accompanying instruments, if present, are piano, Hammond organ, or guitar, alone or with bass, drums, and tambourine.

Performances may include open-ended ostinatos, in which a soloist's improvised comments alternate with a repeated phrase of text. Many "gospel songs" (exemplified by the compositions of Thomas A. Dorsey) have 16-bar antecedent and consequent tonal schemes. These structures represent only two facets of a repertory that initially drew upon 18th- and 19th-century hymns, Negro spirituals, blues, barbershop singing, ragtime, pop tunes, country, and jazz. Later, after creating (through male quartets) the basis for *rhythm and blues and *soul, black gospel drew upon those secular genres for new material.

Commercial white gospel recordings have sacred texts and occasional imitations of black gospel singing. They are otherwise stylistically indistinguishable from pop, country, or rock.

Bibl.: (2) Sandra S. Sizer, *Gospel Hymns and Social Religion* (Philadelphia: Temple U Pr, 1978).

(3) John Godrich and Robert Dixon, comps., *Blues and Gospel Records 1902–1942* (London: Storyville Pubs, 1969). Tony Heilbut, *The Gospel Sound* (New York: Simon & Schuster, 1971). Cedric J. Hayes, *A Discography of Gospel Records 1937–71* (Copenhagen: Knudsen, 1973). David Evans, "The Roots of Afro-American Gospel Music," *Jazzforschung* 8 (1976): 119–35. (2) (3) B.K.

Gothic music. See Middle Ages, music of the.

Götterdämmerung [Ger.]. See *Ring des Nibelungen.*

Goyescas [Sp.]. (1) Six piano pieces in two sets composed by Enrique Granados in 1911 and inspired by paintings by Francisco Goya (1746–1828). A seventh piece, "El pelele," is usually performed with the original six. (2) Opera in three scenes by Granados (libretto by Fernando Periquet y Zuaznabar), produced in New York in 1916. The opera makes use of the piano pieces of the same name, including especially no. 4, "Quejas, o La maja y el ruiseñor" (Complaints, or The Young Woman and the Nightingale), which was made a song in the second scene.

G.P. (1) Abbr. for **Generalpause.* (2) In French organ music, abbr. for **Grand (orgue)* and **Positif,* indicating that the two divisions should be coupled.

G.R. In French organ music, abbr. for **Grand (orgue)* and **Récit,* indicating that the two keyboards should be coupled.

Grace. In 16th- and 17th-century England, any musical ornament, whether written out in notes, indicated by sign, or improvised by the performer. In lute and viol playing, a distinction was made between smooth graces, produced by sliding the finger along the fingerboard (appoggiaturas, slides, and *Nachschläge*), and shaked graces, for which the finger is shaken, producing several repercussions of the same tone (trills, relishes, and beats). Another distinction is between open graces, which involve a whole fret (i.e., a semitone), and closed graces, which involve a smaller interval (i.e., vibrato). P.A.

Grace note. A note printed in small type to indicate that its time value is not counted in the rhythm of the bar and must be subtracted from that of an adjacent note. Large groups of grace notes sometimes represent an exception to this rule in that together they fill up the time value of a single note that has been omitted from the score (as in works by Chopin and others), in which case the rhythm of the grace notes is flexible and not subject to a strict beat. Most grace notes are used to represent *graces or musical ornaments. See Ornamentation. P.A.

Gracieux [Fr.]. Graceful.

Gracile [It.]. Delicate.

Gradatamente [It.]. Gradually.

Gradevole [It.]. Pleasant, agreeable.

Gradito [It.]. Pleasing.

Gradual [Lat. *graduale*]. (1) In *Gregorian chant, the item of the *Proper of the *Mass that is sung following the reading of the Epistle. An example of responsorial *psalmody, it consists of a respond intoned by soloists and completed by the choir, a verse sung by the soloists, and a repetition by the choir of the last part of the respond. Its texts are most often drawn from the Psalms, and its melodies are highly *melismatic. Most graduals belong to one or another of the authentic *modes. Melodies of the 5th mode constitute a large group and share a number of standard melodic formulas [see Centonization]. A melody assigned to the 2nd mode (often referred to as the type "Justus ut palma") is shared by another less large group and follows the outline of a *psalm tone. St. Augustine (d. 430) and others refer to the responsorial singing of a Psalm after a lesson, and thus the gradual has often been thought to be an ornate abbreviation of an earlier practice that incorporated a whole Psalm. Some of the earliest musical sources employ the term *responsorium graduale.* The surviving ornate melodies, preserved in general with single verses, do not, however, appear to be remnants of that early practice.

(2) The *liturgical book containing the chants for the Mass. The term *antiphonale missarum* was used for some of the earliest surviving examples (ed. Hesbert, 1935; see Gregorian chant).

Gradus ad Parnassum [Lat., Steps to Parnassus (a mountain sacred to Apollo and the Muses)]. (1) A treatise on counterpoint by Johann Joseph Fux (Vienna, 1725; 2nd ed., 1742; for editions, see Theory). See also Species counterpoint. (2) A collection of piano etudes by Clementi, op. 44, in three volumes (1817, 1819, 1826).

Grail [archaic]. *Gradual.

Gramophone. See Recording.

Gran cassa [It.]. Bass drum.

Grandezza, con [It.]. With grandeur.

Grandioso [It.]. Grandiose.

Grand jeu [Fr.]. In the classical French organ, a registration including the *Trompette* 8′, *Clairon* 4′, *Bourdons* 16′ and 8′, and *Cornet,* usually coupled to the *Positiv* with its *Bourdon* 8′, *Cornet,* and *Cromorne.* **Cymbale* and **Fourniture* are never included.

Grand opera. In 19th-century France, a work suitable for performance at the Paris Opéra. This implied a serious work on a historical subject, in four or five acts, including chorus and ballet, with the text fully set musically (that is, without spoken dialogue). An example is Meyerbeer's *Les Huguenots.* More loosely, the term is used to indicate any opera making lavish use of musical and theatrical resources. See Opera.

Grand orgue [Fr.]. The main division of a French organ, based on either an 8′ or a 16′ **Montre* (Principal) stop.

Grand piano. A large, wing-shaped piano, in which the plane of the strings is horizontal.

Gran tamburo [It.]. Bass drum.

Graphic notation. In some works since the early 1950s, visual materials other than conventional musical notation (though sometimes combined with conventional notation) by means of which a composer instructs, guides, or merely hopes to inspire or motivate the activities of performers. The realization of works employing such notation typically allows a great deal of freedom to the performer [see Aleatory music], though the notation may be accompanied by written instructions as well. Composers who have employed such notation include Morton Feldman (b. 1926, perhaps the first to do so), Earle Brown (b. 1926), Karlheinz Stockhausen (b. 1928), Christian Wolff (b. 1934), and Cornelius Cardew (1936–81). Numerous examples were published in the periodical *Source: Music of the Avant Garde* (Davis, Cal.: Composer/Performer Edition, 1967–77), founded and edited by composer Larry Austin. For an example see Notation; see also Twentieth century, Western art music of the.

Grave [It.]. (1) Grave, solemn. (2) Since the 17th century, slow, often equivalent to **adagio* [see Performance marks]. (3) With respect to pitch, low.

Gravicembalo [It.]. In 17th-century Italy, *harpsichord; perhaps a corruption of *clavicembalo.*

Grazioso [It.]. Graceful.

Great antiphons. See O Antiphons.

Greater perfect system. See Greece I, 3 (i), Table 1.

Great Fugue. See *Grosse Fuge.*

Great organ. The main division of an English or American organ. The corresponding French term is **Grand orgue,* the German **Hauptwerk.*

Greece. I. *Antiquity.* The music of ancient Greece was primarily vocal melody, although an instrument often accompanied the voice. Vocal performance was either solo or choral, but in the latter case the chorus sang in unison or in octaves. There did exist, also, a purely instrumental form of *nomos. The rhythm and meter of the vocal music were virtually identical to those of Greek poetry. This may be, in part, a result of the nature of classical Greek, which possessed both long and short vowels and pitch accent.

Music in ancient Greece pervaded most public occasions such as rites of passage and did so among all social classes. Musicians as well as athletes competed at the Pythian and Athenian games. The victors of such musical competitions—both vocal and instrumental—were awarded prizes and honor just as were the victorious athletes. Nearly all forms of Greek poetry and drama were rendered musically or accompanied by music, from the epics of Homer's day to the plays of Aristophanes. In most instances, the poet was probably also the composer. From comments by Plato and Aristotle about music it may be concluded that the study of music formed a part of classical education.

Although much testimony exists about the power and roles of ancient Greek music, and there are some detailed but late descriptions of the music, very few examples have survived. Present knowledge is derived from some 50 fragments, a smattering of mutilated instruments, some paintings on vases, and writings. This last source is the most extensive and can be divided into references to music and musical life in works concerning topics other than music (e.g., Plato's philosophical works), and treatises on music. The degree to which Greek music influenced the development of music in Western Europe is uncertain. The theory of Greek music, however, transmitted to the Latin West primarily by Boethius' *De musica* (ca. 500 C.E.), provided a foundation, albeit shaky, for the description, understanding, and classification of music in the West.

1. History. Work songs, ceremonial songs, and sung epics form the basis of early Greek music. It seems likely that during the 8th through 6th centuries B.C.E., the Greeks were influenced by music from foreign regions, especially the East. During this period, specific musical-poetic forms developed as well as a purely musical form of the nomos. Terpander of Lesbos (7th cent. B.C.E.) is one of the first to receive credit for specific styles or forms of composition, in his case especially the kitharoedic nomos, a solo song based on an epic poetic text and accompanied on the *kithara, probably by the singer himself. Parallel to the kitharoedic nomos, there developed an auloedic nomos and also an *aulos solo. Various figures are credited with the composition of these nomoi, including Polymnestus of Colophon and Sacadas of Argos. The latter won musical competitions at three successive Pythian games during the 6th century B.C.E.

Pindar and the 5th century B.C.E. mark the flowering of classical Greek music and especially of the choral song or hymn. It was during this century and at the turn of the next that Aeschylus, Sophocles, Aristophanes, and Euripides flourished, and music was integral to the production of their plays. Also at this time, Pythagoras and the Pythagoreans took considerable interest in the science of acoustics, if not in music per se.

During the second half of the 5th century B.C.E., the aulos and kithara were improved. With an expanded range, they took on both a more professional and a more ostentatious role in Greek music. Timotheus of Milet (ca. 450–360) is credited with transforming the dithyramb (a choral ode) and the *kitharoedic nomos* into popular music. Subsequent eras seem to have adopted only partially the transformations of Timotheus and others, and contemporary accounts treat the changes effected by Timotheus in at best a neutral tone. In late antiquity, music seems to have lost the prestigious position it held in classical Greece and was produced largely by craftsmen as an ornament to other functions.

2. Instruments. The instruments of ancient Greece can be divided roughly into three categories: strings, winds, and percussion. The *lyra and *kithara were the most important stringed instruments, the former being performed primarily by amateurs and the latter by professionals. Both were strung with gut or sinew and plucked either by the hand or with a plectrum. Neither instrument has a fingerboard, although harmonics and slight variations in pitch may have been obtained by touching the strings. Several varieties of harps were also employed in ancient Greece.

The *aulos was the primary wind instrument, usually played in pairs. In classical times it was probably a double-reed instrument, although there were also single-reed auloi. Before its rapid development during the 5th century, the aulos contained three to five holes; later auloi, however, had as many as fifteen borings. The *syrinx was either a single pipe or an ensemble of pipes bound together, closed at one end, and blown directly. The pipes of the ensemble were stopped at graduated intervals. Various idiophones and membranophones were used as percussion instruments.

3. Theory. (i) Intervals and systems. Musical theory in the West has its roots in the philosophy of the Pythagoreans, and Pythagoras himself is credited with introducing to Greece numerical characterization of consonances, which he discovered in Babylon. The Pythagoreans held number to be reality and thus heard the elementary consonances as material representations of numerical truth. The basic consonances were the octave, fifth, and fourth. These are represented numerically by the ratios 2:1, 3:2, and 4:3, respectively, which represent ratios of string length or frequencies [see also Interval, Pythagorean hammers]. The fifth plus the fourth equals the octave (3:2 + 4:3 = 2:1), and the fifth minus the fourth defines the whole tone (3:2 − 4:3 = 9:8) [see Pythagorean scale]. The numerical quaternary 1, 2, 3, 4 contained great significance for Pythagorean philosophers; the ratios derived from these numbers represented the musical consonances: 2:1, 3:2, 4:3, 3:1 (octave plus fifth), and 4:1 (double octave).

Plato held the rationalist view of music similar to that of the Pythagoreans. Indeed, he is probably in their debt for his own musical philosophy, although the exact relationship between Plato and the Pythagoreans is quite uncertain. Aristotle's primary contribution to music theory was one of method: inductive logic based on empirical evidence. This method is borne out in the work of his student Aristoxenus.

Around the first century B.C.E., Pythagoreanism was revived, and its musical theory was intermingled with Platonic theory. Many writers of late antiquity espoused this Neoplatonic or Neopythagorean musical theory, which culminates in the treatise of Boethius. Another notable late musical treatise is the *De musica* of Aristides Quintilianus (ca. 300 C.E.), which contains much Platonic and Pythagorean philosophy as well as Aristoxenian musical theory.

Aristoxenus (b. ca. 365 B.C.E.) is the most important theorist of ancient Greek music. His incomplete *Elements of Harmony,* a combination of at least two earlier works, is the oldest extant treatise that contains an extensive discussion of music. He also wrote an *Elements of Rhythm,* which survives only in fragmentary form. Aristoxenus relies on Aristotelian method in de-

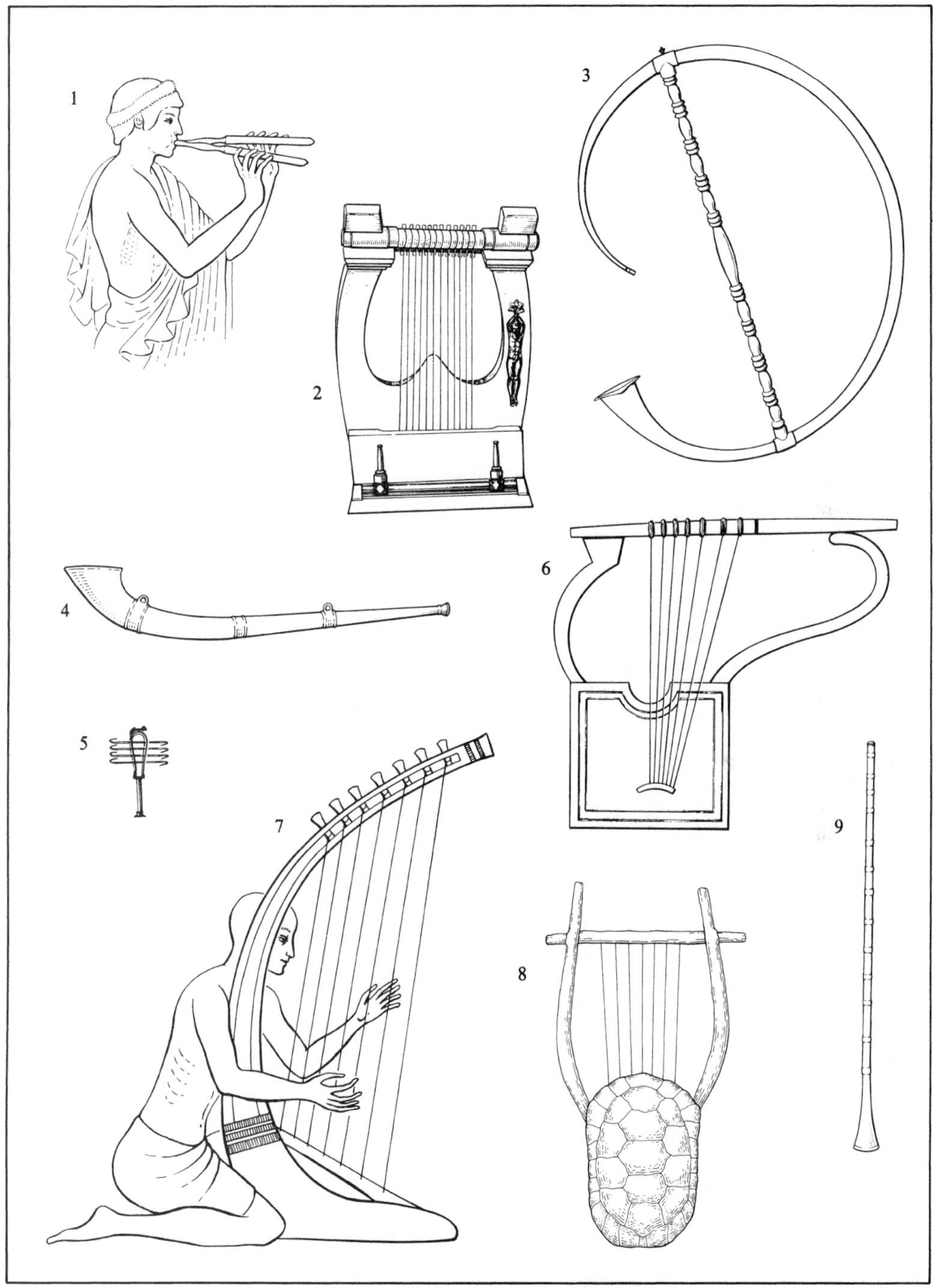

Ancient instruments: 1. Aulos (Greece). 2. Kithara (Greece). 3. Cornu (Rome). 4. Litnus (Rome). 5. Sistrum (Sumeria, Egypt, Rome). 6. Lyre (Egypt). 7. Bow harp (Egypt). 8. Lyra (Greece). 9. Tuba (Rome).

Table 1 The Immutable System

	Greater Perfect System		Lesser Perfect System	
	Nete hyperbolaeon	a′		
Hyperbolaeon tetrachord	Paranete hyperbolaeon	g′		
	Trite hyperbolaeon	f′		
	Nete diezeugmenon	e′		
	Paranete diezeugmenon	d′	Nete synemmenon	
Diezeugmenon tetrachord	Trite diezeugmenon	c′	Paranete synemmenon	Synemmenon tetrachord
	Paramese	b′		
		b♭′	Trite synemmenon	
	Mese	a		
Meson tetrachord	Lichanos meson	g		
	Parhypate meson	f		
	Hypate meson	e		
	Lichanos hypaton	d		
Hypaton tetrachord	Parhypate hypaton	c		
	Hypate hypaton	B		
	Proslambanomenos	A		

vising a theory of music based on his own geometric conception of musical space, in contrast to the arithmetic conception of the Pythagoreans. Aristoxenus viewed the pitch spectrum as a line capable of infinitely many subdivisions. Thus, infinitely many intervals could be produced, although according to Aristoxenus, the smallest musical interval was the enharmonic *diesis or quarter tone. The basic building block of Greek music was the *tetrachord, four notes and three intervals spanning a perfect fourth. Aristoxenus considered the fourth to be exactly 2 1/2 tones.

"Fixed" or "standing" notes bounded a fundamental tetrachord, and the placement of the two inner "movable" notes established the tetrachord's *genus. The enharmonic and chromatic genera were determined by the existence of a **pyknon.* According to Aristoxenus, the enharmonic *pyknon* comprised two quarter tones, leaving an incomposite ditone as the upper interval. Although many chromatic and diatonic genera were possible, Aristoxenus specified only three "shades" or "colors" (**chroai*) of chromatic and two of diatonic. He mentions another arrangement of intervals (tone = unit: 1/3 + 1 1/6 + 1, ascending) that may have been the most common of all tetrachord tunings. This arrangement is virtually identical with the diatonic of Archytas (28:27 + 8:7 + 9:8), and Claudius Ptolemy, five centuries later, confirms this tuning to be the most common. Ptolemy also provides several shades of diatonic and chromatic genera in his *Harmonics* (i.12–16 and ii.14).

According to Aristoxenus, a system was a consecution of intervals. Ptolemy claims that a system is composed of consonances such as the fourth or fifth or octave. Thus larger systems could be composed by combining tetrachords conjunctly or disjunctly. Conjunct tetrachords share a note, and disjunct ones are separated by a whole-tone interval. Eventually a two-octave system, called the Immutable System, became the standard for Greek musical theory. It combined the Greater Perfect and Lesser Perfect Systems (hereafter GPS and LPS). The GPS was a two-octave disjunct system that consisted of four tetrachords plus an added note *(Proslambanomenos)* a whole-tone interval below the lowest tetrachord. The LPS was a conjunct *(*synemmenon)* system comprising the lower octave of the GPS plus a conjunct tetrachord at the top. In the Immutable System, the LPS was used for modulation from one *tonos* to another. The Immutable System is given in Table 1 in a convenient but arbitrary form of the diatonic genus. It seems likely that the names of the notes, with the exception of the *Proslambanomenos,* were derived from the physical position of the strings on the kithara or lyra when held in the hand. Thus the *Hypate hypaton* (highest of the high) was the second-lowest pitch of the system. Conversely, *Nete hyperbolaeon* (very bottom) was the highest pitch of the system. *Meson* indicated the middle or main tetrachord, and *diezeugmenon* the disjunct tetrachord.

(ii) Mode and key. The issues of mode and key have perplexed students of Greek music. Aristoxenus mentions *harmoniai* (tunings) and *tonoi,* providing ethnic names for the latter, e.g., Dorian, Phrygian, Lydian. These are the names that Plato and Aristotle ascribe to the *harmoniai.* The remarks of these writers lead to the conclusion that the *harmoniai* were varied tonally and with respect to *ethos. Both Ptolemy (fl. 150 C.E.) and Cleonides (second cent. C.E.?), an Aristoxenian, list seven species of octave and their names [see Table 2], most of which are the names given by early writers to *harmoniai* and *tonoi.* (Some writers use *tropos* instead of *tonos.*)

Aristides Quintilianus (*De musica* i.9) presents six, apparently very old, *harmoniai,* only one of which—the Lydian—jibes with the species of octave presented by Cleonides and Ptolemy. In addition to the octave species, Cleonides lists thirteen *tonoi* one half-step

Table 2

Species of octave	Boundary notes of GPS
1. Mixolydian	Hypate h. / Paramese
2. Lydian	Parhypate h. / Trite d.
3. Phrygian	Lichanos h. / Paranete d.
4. Dorian	Hypate m. / Nete d.
5. Hypolydian	Parhypate m. / Trite h.
6. Hypophrygian	Lichanos m. / Paranete h.
7. Locrian or Hypodorian	Mese / Nete h.

apart. The *tonoi* apparently take their names from the octave species whose characteristic intervals they bring into the central octave, i.e., within the region of the tetrachords *diezeugmenon* and *meson.* In each *tonos,* the tetrachords bounded by fixed notes could take on any variety of enharmonic, chromatic, or diatonic genus. Cleonides, in his *Introduction to Harmonics,* refers to the Hypodorian as the highest species because its characteristic intervals lie at the top of the GPS. The Hypodorian is at the same time the lowest *tonos* because the system must be tuned downward in order to bring the characteristic intervals (from *Mese* to *Nete hyperbolaeon*) into the central octave. (Thus the GPS, as it stands, has the Dorian octave species as its central octave.) Later Aristoxenians expanded to fifteen the number of *tonoi,* with five central *tonoi* and five of each of the *hyper- and hypovariety [see Table 3].

Scholars are uncertain whether the *tonoi* entailed a sense of tonic or fundamental pitch and whether there existed a variety of ethos corresponding to the various modes. Ptolemy observed that since there are only seven octave species, there need only be seven *tonoi.* He distinguishes between the thetic name of a note, i.e., by position on the GPS, and a note's dynamic or functional name. Thus the fourth note from the bottom of the lower tetrachord of the central octave is the thetic *Mese,* regardless of the octave species that may occupy that position. The dynamic *Mese,* however, occurs at that pitch to which the Dorian *Mese* must be tuned in order to bring the desired octave species into the central octave.

Both the Aristotelian *Problems* and Cleonides assert that the *Mese* is of greater importance than the other notes. It remains unclear, however, whether one should view the *Mese* as a sort of tonic or fundamental pitch, and analyses of musical fragments have proved to be inconclusive in this respect. Plato and Aristotle recognized the ethical qualities of the *harmoniai,* and the testimony of late antiquity argues for the strong character of modes.

Ancient Greek music and theory provided a foundation, albeit shaky, for the development of Western music. Attempting to understand and organize their own music, medieval writers adopted and adapted ancient musical items and categories such as note, interval, system, and mode, as well as a quantified, mathematical disposition. Some Aristoxenian doctrine was passed on to the Middle Ages in Martianus Capella's *On the Marriage of Mercury and Philology* (ca. 425 C.E.), which relies in part on Aristides' *On Music.* But the Pythagorean science of corporeal number, as presented by Boethius, was the most significant Greek musical legacy for the West until the 15th century.

4. Notation. For the notation of pitch, ancient Greek music used two systems, one primarily for vocal and one primarily for instrumental music. Several authors of late antiquity take up the matter of notation, and Alypius gives the most complete account in his *Introduction to Music* (3rd or 4th century C.E.). The Hypodorian *tonos* is conventionally taken to be the natural disposition of this notational system.

The vocal notation is based on the Ionic alphabet and thus dates from no earlier than the 5th century B.C.E., when this alphabet was generally adopted. The instrumental notation, essentially alphabetic also, is believed to be older. Both notations consist of triadic groups. Within each group, a single symbol is rotated through three positions, indicating increasing sharpness of pitch, and thereby the subtlety of tonal inflection associated with the various *chroai. The notation, however, did not distinguish systematically between the chromatic and enharmonic genera.

5. Fragments. There exist some 50 fragments of ancient Greek music, preserved on stone, papyrus, and in manuscripts. Of these, the earliest may be the Leiden Papyrus, a fragment of Euripides' *Iphigenia in Aulis* that dates from ca. 280 B.C.E. Another extant Euripidean fragment, a papyrus dating from ca. 200 B.C.E., preserves a few lines of music and text from *Orestes.* About a century later are the first and second Delphic hymns, and from the 1st century C.E. comes the Epitaph of *Seikilos, all three of which are cut into stone. The latter preserves a complete song.

The corpus of preserved ancient Greek music spans seven centuries. Scholars have attempted to analyze a portion of this material with regard to style, mode, ge-

Table 3 Tonoi with pitch of Mese (assuming Hypolydian Mese = a).

Hypodorian	f
Hypoionian	f♯
Hypophrygian	g
Hypoaeolian	g♯
Hypolydian	a
Dorian	a♯
Ionian	b
Phrygian	c′
Aeolian	c♯′
Lydian	d′
Hyperdorian	d♯′
Hyperionian	e′
Hypermixolydian (or Hyperphrygian)	f′
Hyperaeolian	f♯′
Hyperlydian	g′

nus, form, and the like. These investigations have produced modest results.

II. *Modern Greece.* In modern Greece, a vital tradition of folk and popular music coexists with a burgeoning art music. The latter had its beginnings, under the influence of Italian opera, only after the end of the Ottoman domination in 1830 and reached full fruition in the first half of the 20th century, as the government began to play a more vigorous role in the promotion and dissemination of music. The nation's musical centers are Athens and Salonica (Thessaloniki). Opera is performed primarily by the National Opera (founded 1939), which produces, in the Athens Opera House and at the Athens Festival, standard Italian repertory and national favorites such as Spyridon Samaras's *Flora mirabilis* (1886). The Athens State Orchestra, directed by Dmitri Mitropoulos (1896–1960) before its nationalization in 1942, and since 1976 led by composer Manos Hadjidakis (b. 1925), has shared players with the Radio Symphony Orchestra and the National Opera. Prominent ensembles in Salonica are the Northern Greece Symphony Orchestra and the Small Orchestra of Salonica.

Manolis Kalomiris (1883–1962) attempted to lay the foundation for a national school of composition by advocating the use of elements of modern Hellenic folk music. Of greater impact on composers such as Yannis Papaioannou (b. 1911), Yorgos Sicilianos (b. 1922), Yannis Xenakis (b. 1922), and Jani Christou (1926–1970), however, was the introduction of twelve-tone composition by Schoenberg's pupil Nikolaos Skalkottas (1904–49). Manos Hadjidakis, who has achieved great popularity with his film music and his use of the *rebetiko* (a type of urban folk song), organized a competition in 1962 that brought to Greece the music of many native avant-gardists living abroad, including Xenakis, Anestis Logothetis (b. 1921), and Theodore Antoniou (b. 1935).

The seven or eight distinct regional styles of modern Greek folk music bear similarities to the musics of the nation's Balkan and eastern Mediterranean neighbors. Characteristic song types, all involving a highly developed oral tradition of melodic ornamentation, are the Kleftic song, which describes heroic deeds in the war for independence, the *miroloyi* (lament), usually sung by women, and the *patinada* (wedding procession). Significant dance types are the *kalimatianos*, the slow *tsamikos,* on Crete the *pidichtos* and *sousta,* and on the Aegean and Ionian islands the *ballos,* the *syrtos,* and the *zeibekikos.* The most common folk instruments are the violin, clarinet, **lira* (fiddle), **lauto* (lute), *santouri* (dulcimer) [see also *Santur*], *gaida* (bagpipe), and *daouli* (drum) [see *Davul*]. The music is primarily vocal, usually accompanied heterophonically by various instrumental combinations [see Heterophony]. Meter is often free; patterns of 7/8 (3+2+2) and 8/8 (3+2+3 or 3+3+2) are also typical, as are more regular units of 2/4 and 3/4.

Bibl.: I. *Antiquity.* Diplomatic facsimiles and transcriptions of many musical fragments are given in Egert Pöhlmann, *Denkmäler altgriechischer Musik* (Nuremberg: H. Carl, 1970). A collection of theoretical texts is provided by Karl von Jan, *Musici scriptores graeci* (Leipzig: 1895; R: Hildesheim: G. Olms, 1962). For additional texts see: Ingemar Düring, ed., *Die Harmonielehre des Klaudios Ptolemaios,* Göteborgs Högskolas Årrskrift, 36/1 (Göteborg: Elanders, 1930; R: New York: Garland, 1980). Ingemar Düring, ed., *Porphyrios Kommentar zur Harmonielehre des Ptolemaios,* Göteborgs Högskolas Årrskrift, 38/2 (Göteborg: Elanders, 1932; R: New York: Garland, 1980). Rosetta da Rios, ed. and trans., *Aristoxeni elementa harmonica* (Rome: Typis publicae officinae polygraphicae, 1954). André Barbera, ed. and trans., *The Euclidean Division of the Canon* (Lincoln: U of Nebr Pr, 1991). English translations of several texts are provided in Andrew Barker, *Greek Musical Writings,* 2 vols. (Cambridge: Cambridge U Pr, 1984–89). For additional translations see: Aristides Quintilianus, *On Music: In Three Books,* trans. Thomas J. Mathiesen (New Haven: Yale U Pr, 1981). Ptolemy, *Harmonics,* trans. Jon Solomon (Leiden: Brill, 2000). For historical discussion see: M. L. West, *Ancient Greek Music* (Oxford: Oxford U Pr, 1992). Thomas J. Mathiesen, *Apollo's Lyre: Greek Music and Music Theory in Antiquity and the Middle Ages* (Lincoln: U of Nebraska Pr, 1999). For MSS see: Thomas J. Mathiesen, *Ancient Greek Music Theory: A Catalogue raisonné of Manuscripts, RISM* B11 (Munich: G. Henle, 1988). Additional source studies appear in André Barbera, ed., *Music Theory and Its Sources: Antiquity and the Middle Ages* (Notre Dame: U of Notre Dame Pr, 1990).

II. *Modern Greece.* Samuel Baud-Bovy, *Études sur la chanson cleftique* (Athens, 1958). Sotirios Chianis, *Folk Songs of Mantineia, Greece* (Berkeley and Los Angeles: U of Cal Pr, 1965). Nicolas Slonimsky, "New Music in Greece," *MQ* 51 (1965): 225–35. Brigitte Schiffer, "Neue griechische Musik," *Orbis musicae* 1 (1972): 193–201. Gail Holst, *Road to Rembetika* (Athens: Anglo-Hellenic Publishing, 1975).

I, A.B.

Greghesca [It.]. A Venetian subgenre of the **villanella,* on texts written in a mixture of Venetian dialect and Greek (in imitation of the language of Greek mercenaries) by Antonio Molino (called Manoli Blessi). The music, for four to eight voices, may have been used in the theater; it is often but not always comic (cf. Andrea Gabrieli's lament on the death of Willaert).

Bibl.: Siro Cisilino, ed., *Greghesche, libro I (1564) . . . di Manoli Blessi detto il Burchiella* (Padua: G Zanibon, 1974).

J.H.

Gregorian chant. The *plainsong or liturgical chant of the Roman Catholic Church. It is one of the five principal repertories of Latin liturgical chant of the Middle Ages, the others being *Old Roman, *Ambrosian, *Gallican, and *Mozarabic. As preserved in musical manuscripts beginning in the 10th century, it consists of unaccompanied melodies set to the Latin texts of the *liturgy (of which some understanding is essential to the understanding of the chant itself) including both the *Mass and the *Office. It is named for St. Gregory the Great, pope from 590 until 604, though his role in shaping the surviving repertory is a matter of conjecture and debate.

I. *Texts.* The Book of *Psalms is the principal source of texts for the Gregorian chant. Texts drawn from the Psalms and musical forms associated principally with the singing of the Psalms are termed psalmodic. Some texts are drawn from other parts of the Bible, however, particularly the lyrical passages that make up the *canticles, and a few are drawn from the lives of saints or other early Christian writings. Among the most important nonpsalmodic texts of the Mass are those of the Ordinary; in the Office, the responsories of Matins draw significantly from books of both the Old and New Testaments, often in a way related to the theme of the liturgical season in question. All of these texts, both psalmodic and nonpsalmodic, are treated as prose. Poetic texts make up a much smaller part of the repertory. The most important to continue in use are the *hymns. In the Middle Ages and on through the 16th century, however, *sequences with poetic texts were an important genre, and *rhymed Offices were composed in which forms such as antiphons and responsories that normally employ scriptural texts were set to poetic texts.

II. *Form and performance.* The forms and methods of performance of the chant repertory can be broadly divided into two groups: psalmodic (i.e., forms thought to derive from the various methods of singing the Psalms, even when employed with texts that are not taken from the Psalms) and nonpsalmodic. Three forms of psalmody are usually distinguished, though both medieval and modern practice often obscure the supposed differences among them [see Psalmody for a fuller discussion]: antiphonal psalmody, in which two halves of a choir or schola sing the verses of a Psalm or other text in alternation and in combination with a melody called an antiphon that serves as a refrain; responsorial psalmody, in which one or more soloists or cantors alternate with the schola in singing one or more verses and a refrain often called a respond; and direct psalmody, in which the cantor or cantors sing verses without alternation with the schola and without a refrain.

Nonpsalmodic forms include the strophic form of the hymn, in which a single melody is repeated for all strophes; the double-versicle form of the sequence, in which there is repetition within each couplet, though successive couplets are in general different; the repetitive forms of the *Kyrie and *Agnus Dei, which derive from the repetitive elements in their texts; and the essentially nonrepetitive forms of the *Sanctus and of the longer prose texts of the *Gloria and the *Credo. Thus, in the Mass, the chants of the Ordinary are all nonpsalmodic with respect to both text and form, whereas those of the Proper are (or were at one time) psalmodic in form if not always with respect to text. In modern practice, these nonpsalmodic forms too may employ alternation either between cantors and schola or between the two halves of the schola. The term free form is sometimes applied to any piece that does not employ repetition and is not a formula used for the recitation of a variety of different texts such as the Psalm verses. Thus, it is sometimes applied to the refrainlike components of the psalmodic forms that consist (or are thought to have consisted at one time) of the alternation of a refrain with one or more verses, e.g., antiphons, responsories, and the like.

III. *Melodic style.* Three melodic styles are usually identified: syllabic, in which each syllable of text is borne by only a single note; neumatic (from *neume), in which single syllables are regularly borne by two to a dozen notes; and melismatic, in which single syllables may occasionally be borne by dozens of notes. In general, this range of styles from simple to complex is closely coordinated with the forms and methods of performance outlined above. The antiphonal psalmody of the Office is largely syllabic. The antiphonal psalmody of the Mass, except for the offertory, is neumatic. The responsorial psalmody of the Mass, the offertory, and the great responsories of the Office are most likely to be melismatic. Chants that are primarily choral, such as the Office antiphons and psalm tones, are the simplest and are often syllabic throughout. Chants that are intended for soloists, such as the great responsories of the Office and the gradual, alleluia, and tract of the Mass, are the most elaborate and may be highly melismatic. Among the nonpsalmodic forms, the poetic texts of the hymn and the sequence are set syllabically, as are the long prose texts of the Gloria and the Credo. The Kyrie, which has a relatively short text, is set melismatically. The Sanctus and the Agnus, whose texts are of moderate length, are neumatic.

Many psalmodic chants share stylistic features that cut across their differences in complexity. These are related to the outline of the various recitation formulas for the Psalms [see Psalm tone], in which an introductory or intonation formula rises to a recitation on a single pitch, which is in turn followed by a falling cadential formula. Such elements may be seen to underlie even some of the most complex chants, such as some graduals. An even greater consistency of style is found among the melodies for any one item of the liturgy. This consistency extends beyond the shared outline and general level of complexity to the use of shared melodic elements.

The sharing of melodic elements ranging from a very few notes to longer phrases or melismas is a prominent feature of most types of psalmodic chant [see Centonization]. Specific melodic elements are not generally shared by more than one liturgical type. A single text, however, may be used in a wide variety of liturgical contexts. Within each type, such as the gradual or the tract, shared formulas occur among the melodies of a single *mode or tonal type [see below]; they most often fulfill the same function (intonation, recitation, or cadence) from piece to piece; and they are most likely to occur in prominent positions, namely the beginnings and endings of phrases. In some types, such as the antiphons of the Office and the alleluias of the Mass, whole melodies resemble one another closely as if deriving from a single prototype.

IV. *Modality.* Gregorian melodies are classified tonally according to a system of eight *modes adopted from Byzantine practice in the late 8th century and thus after the early core of the repertory was already formed, but before the earliest sources with musical notation. In the Middle Ages, melodies were listed by mode in *tonaries. Modern liturgical books also indicate the mode for each chant. The modes are not all equally represented within the various types of chant, with some types strongly favoring only a few modes, and the tracts of the Mass being limited to only two.

V. *Rhythm.* The rhythm of Gregorian chant is the subject of considerable controversy. In general, the notations [see Neume] of early sources do not indicate the duration of individual notes. Some early manuscripts employ a short horizontal line, the *episema,* that is thought by some scholars to indicate a lengthening of any neume with which it appears. Some sources, particularly those from St. Gall, employ the so-called *Romanian letters, some of which refer to rhythm and tempo. And some medieval writers discuss rhythm in ways that seem to be relevant to the performance of liturgical chant. But the rhythm of individual melodies and the rhythmic character of the repertory as a whole remain open to a variety of interpretations. Three principal points of view are generally distinguished.

1. The accentualist interpretation was formulated principally by Joseph Pothier (1835–1923), a Benedictine monk from the monastery at *Solesmes, who held that by the time of the formation of the repertory the Latin language had abandoned quantity or length of syllables in favor of stress or accent as its principal rhythmic element and that thus all of the notes in chant are of essentially equal value, with word-accent determining the nature of the generally free and speechlike rhythm except in long melismas, where the first note in each group of neumes is accented.

2. The Solesmes view resulted from the manuscript studies of André Mocquereau (1849–1930), a monk trained at Solesmes under Pothier, whom he succeeded as choirmaster there, and it was upheld and taught by his own student and successor, Joseph Gajard (1885–1972). Mocquereau also regarded the rhythm of chant as essentially free and employing for the most part notes of equal value, but not as deriving primarily from word-accent, even though rhythm and other features of the chant are said to derive from the nature of the Latin language. In this view, rhythm is characterized instead by an alternation of rising (*arsis* or *élan*) and falling (*thesis* or *repos*) and by the free succession of groups of two and three notes. Each of these rhythmic units begins with an *arsis* and concludes with a *thesis,* and units may be combined to produce *arsis* and *thesis* on a larger scale. The beginning of each group is marked by the rhythmic *ictus, which, however, is not an accent and need not coincide with an accented syllable in the text. In modern chant books embodying this interpretation, the horizontal *episema* indicates a slight lengthening of notes, and signs not found in early manuscripts further guide the rhythm: the vertical *episema,* which marks the ictus when its location is not otherwise clear, the dot or *punctum mora,* which indicates a doubling in the length of the final note of some phrases, and the apostrophe, which indicates a pause for breath. Since the 1950s, work carried on or published at Solesmes by Eugène Cardine, based on detailed study (termed *semiology*) of neumes, has put forward a view of a free rhythm deriving from the flexible durations of Latin syllables.

3. The mensuralist interpretation holds that the chant is made up of a variety of different note lengths with a precise relationship to one another, most often two values in the ratio of 2 to 1. Within this framework, however, there is substantial disagreement as to details. Among scholars holding to one or another mensuralist theory have been Antoine Dechevrens, Oskar Fleischer, Alexandre Fleury, Georges Houdard, Hugo Riemann, Peter Wagner, Jules Jeannin, Ewald Jammers, and Jan W. A. Vollaerts.

VI. *History.* Any attempt to trace the early history of Gregorian chant must reckon with the following features of the surviving evidence. The earliest surviving collection of formularies for the Mass of the Roman Church, a collection of prayers known inappropriately as the Leonine Sacramentary, dates from the first quarter of the 7th century, though its contents are attributed to the 5th and 6th centuries, and was copied outside of Rome from Roman models. Despite the many comments on music in the writings of the church fathers, such as St. Augustine (d. 430), the earliest detailed accounts of individual forms of liturgical chant occur in the writings of St. Isidore of Seville (d. 636), and these seem to refer specifically to the Mozarabic rite. The *Ordines romani* (ed. Andrieu, 1931–61), which include practical accounts of specific services, even when they bear witness to Roman practice are known only in Frankish or Germanic collections that do not antedate the 9th century and whose models do not antedate the 8th (Vogel, 1966). The earliest surviving chant books for the Mass (such as those edited by Hesbert, 1935) do not (and were not intended to) contain musical notation and date from the 8th or 9th and early 10th centuries. The earliest surviving books for the Office (ed. Hesbert, 1963–75) are still later. The earliest chant books originally provided with neumes throughout date from the 10th century or perhaps the 9th and were copied in Frankish territory. The Italian sources transmitting the *Old Roman version of the chant date from the 11th, 12th, and 13th centuries. The tradition that associates Pope Gregory the Great (pope from 590 to 604) with the formation of the repertory seems not to antedate the 8th or 9th century. Thus, for much of the first 1,000 years of the Christian era, the specific character of liturgical chant in the West is a matter of speculation.

It seems likely that Christian chant had its roots in the cantillation of Scripture in the Jewish synagogue. Whether specific musical forms and melodies can be traced to Jewish practice (as Abraham Idelsohn and

Eric Werner have attempted to show on the basis of the 19th- and 20th-century oral traditions of isolated Jewish communities in the Middle East) must be seriously questioned, however [see Psalmody]. Recent scholarship has also doubted that the 3rd-century *Oxyrhynchus papyrus, containing a hymn fragment in the letter notation of classical Greece, can be regarded as pointing to origins for Christian chant in classical Greek musical culture. The formation of the Western rites and the musical forms peculiar to them probably began in the 4th century, by which time Latin had superseded Greek as the language of Christian worship in Rome. In this process, however, elements from Eastern Christendom, such as the churches of Antioch and Jerusalem, were probably incorporated. Augustine and Isidore credit the introduction in the West of antiphonal singing, in imitation of Eastern models, to St. Ambrose (d. 397). Isidore attributes the invention of responsories to the Italians, however. The writing of hymns in the West, for which there was ample precedent in the East, also begins in this period with Ambrose and others. *Ordo romanus XIX,* a document composed in France in the third quarter of the 8th century largely with a view to promoting the adoption of Roman practice there, cites a series of popes, beginning with Damasus I (pope from 366 to 384) and including Gregory I (590–604), as having contributed to the formation of a repertory of chant for the liturgical year.

Roman practice began to spread north of the Alps by the 8th century, and during the reigns of Pepin the Short (752–68) and Charlemagne (768–814) its displacement of the native *Gallican rite was imposed. There is abundant testimony to this process of romanization in France and Germany from the 8th, 9th, and 10th centuries—the regions and the periods of the earliest musical documents and notational systems, from which the chant repertory surviving throughout Europe directly derives. The relationship of what is thus a Frankish redaction of the chant (evidently from oral transmission) to the actual practice of Rome at the time and in earlier centuries remains a matter of considerable debate, especially in view of manuscripts from the 11th through 13th centuries that show a somewhat different version of the repertory in use in Rome [see Old Roman chant]. Some scholars (Stäblein, Smits van Waesberghe, Jammers, Van Dijk) have held that in one way or another both the chant of the Frankish sources—what is now known as "Gregorian chant"—and the version of the Roman sources originated in Rome. Others (Hucke, Apel) maintain that the Frankish sources transmit a version of Gregorian chant that is fundamentally Frankish.

Although the development of musical notation facilitated a more uniform dissemination of the repertory, the processes of change have continued into the 20th century. The repertory grew steadily with the composition of new Offices and the cultivation of new forms such as the *trope and the *sequence. Local practices arose, and various monastic orders, particularly the Cistercians in the 12th century, instituted and disseminated their own reformed repertories. The chant was increasingly performed in polyphonic elaborations [see Organum, Mass, Motet]. By the 15th century, the organ was widely used at least for **alternatim* performance in the liturgy, and it has been widely used (if not universally approved) in the accompaniment of chant ever since.

Universal reform of the chant and of sacred music generally was attempted in the wake of the *Council of Trent. Palestrina and Annibale Zoilo were charged with a revision of the chant melodies in 1577 that was not completed, but in 1582 Giovanni Guidetti's *Directorium chori* appeared, in which measured notation was used and melismas were shortened and/or moved from unaccented to accented syllables. This spirit of reform led to the publication under papal auspices by the press of the Medici in 1614 and 1615 of the so-called Medicean edition of the gradual, which incorporated rhythmic interpretations and extensive melodic revisions by Felice Anerio and Francesco Soriano intended to bring the repertory into line with then current views of the correct treatment of Latin and of the relationship of words to music generally. This edition was not universally adopted, however, and France in particular developed its own repertories of measured chant with instrumental accompaniment [see *Plain-chant musical*]. The Medicean edition was largely republished in 1871 by the firm of Pustet in Regensburg (thus the Ratisbon edition) under the editorship of F. X. Haberl and was sanctioned by Pius IX as official.

The first practical result of the study of the earliest manuscripts was the Rheims-Cambrai edition of the gradual published in 1851. Graduals edited by Louis Lambillotte (1857) and Michael Hermesdorff (1863) followed. This activity culminated in the work done at *Solesmes by Pothier, Mocquereau, and others. Pothier's *Liber gradualis* was published in 1883 by the firm of Desclée in Tournai; it employed newly designed typefaces with the predominantly square shapes that remain in widespread use for the representation of neumes. A second edition followed in 1895 along with other books prepared by Pothier and published at Solesmes, including a *Processionale monasticum* (1888), *Variae preces* (1888), a *Liber antiphonarius* (1891), and a *Liber responsorialis* (1895).

A *motu proprio* of 1903 by Pius X established a commission, of which Pothier became the head, to oversee preparations of new Vatican editions of the chant. A bitter controversy ensued in which the participation of Solesmes (which favored the use of only the very oldest sources) came to an end but which left Dom Pothier, who had departed Solesmes in 1893, at the head of the enterprise. The following publications, based in some measure on his earlier editions, resulted: *Kyriale seu ordinarium missae* and *Missa pro defunctis* (1905); *Graduale sacrosanctae romanae ec-*

clesiae, known as the *Graduale romanum* (1908); *Officium pro defunctis* (1909); and *Antiphonale sacrosanctae romanae ecclesiae,* known as the *Antiphonale romanum* (1912). These Vatican editions have remained the officially sanctioned books of the church. Nevertheless, Solesmes editions published by the firm of Desclée and incorporating the rhythmic signs and theories of Mocquereau have been officially permitted and widely used. The *Liber usualis* derives from these. In 1934, Solesmes's *Antiphonale monasticum* was published for the Benedictine order by Desclée, and in 1948, Solesmes embarked on the preparation of a critical edition of the gradual to be published by the Vatican. The Second *Vatican Council (1962–65), however, in revising the shape of the liturgy and the liturgical year and in encouraging the use of the vernacular instead of Latin, fundamentally altered the place of the chant in the worship of the church.

Bibl.: *Scholarly editions and bibliographical tools. Paléographie musicale,* 21 vols. in two series, ed. the Benedictines of Solesmes, including André Mocquereau and Joseph Gajard (Solesmes: Imprimerie St. Pierre, Tournai: Desclée, 1889–; R: Bern: H Lang, 1969–) [facsimiles, often with extended introductions]. Carl Marbach, ed., *Carmina scripturarum* (Strasbourg: F X Le Roux, 1907; R: Hildesheim: Olms, 1963) [Scriptural sources for chant texts]. Michel Andrieu, ed., *Les ordines romani du haut moyen-âge* (Louvain: Spicilegium sacrum lovaniense, 1931–61). René-Jean Hesbert, ed., *Antiphonale missarum sextuplex* (Brussels: Vromant, 1935) [the earliest chant books for the Mass, without notation]. Id., *Corpus antiphonalium officii,* 6 vols. (Rome: Herder, 1963–75) [texts of the earliest chant books for the Office]. *Le graduel romain: Édition critique par les moines de Solesmes* (Solesmes: Abbaye St. Pierre, 1957–). Klaus Gamber, *Codices liturgici latini antiquiores* (Fribourg: Universitätsverlag, 1963; 2nd ed., 1968). Cyrille Vogel, *Introduction aux sources de l'histoire du culte chrétien au moyen âge* (Spoleto: Centro italiano di studi sull'alto medioevo, 1965). *New Catholic Encyclopedia* (New York: McGraw-Hill, 1967). John R. Bryden and David G. Hughes, *An Index of Gregorian Chant,* 2 vols. (Cambridge, Mass.: Harvard U Pr, 1969) [thematic and alphabetical]. Andrew Hughes, *Medieval Music: The Sixth Liberal Art* (Toronto: U of Toronto Pr, 1974; rev. ed., 1980) [critical bibliography]. F. L. Cross and E. A. Livingstone, eds., *The Oxford Dictionary of the Christian Church,* 2nd ed. (Oxford: Oxford U Pr, 1974).

Literature. Peter Wagner, *Einführung in die gregorianischen Melodien,* 3 vols. (I, 3 eds., 2nd ed. trans. Eng., London: Plainsong & Mediaeval Music Soc, 1907; II, 2 eds., Fribourg: Veith, and Leipzig: Breitkopf & Härtel, 1895–1921; R: Hildesheim: Olms, 1962). André Mocquereau, *Le nombre musical grégorien,* 2 vols. (Tournai: Desclée, 1908–27; trans. Eng., Paris: Desclée, 1932–51). Jules Jeannin, *Études sur le rythme grégorien* (Lyons: E Gloppe, 1926). Paolo Ferretti, *Estetica gregoriana,* vol. 1 (Rome: Pontificio istituto di musica sacra, 1934; trans. Fr., Paris: Desclée, 1938); vol. 2, ed. Pellegrino M. Ernetti (Venice: Istituto per la collaborazione culturale, 1964). Ewald Jammers, *Der gregorianische Rhythmus* (Leipzig: Heitz, 1937). Willi Apel, "The Central Problem of Gregorian Chant," *JAMS* 9 (1956): 118–27. Id., *Gregorian Chant* (Bloomington: Ind U Pr, 1958). Jan W. A. Vollaerts, *Rhythmic Proportions in Early Medieval Ecclesiastical Chant* (Leiden: E J Brill, 1958; 2nd ed., 1960). Eric Werner, *The Sacred Bridge* (New York: Columbia U Pr, 1959). Gregory Murray, *Gregorian Chant According to the Manuscripts* (London: L J Cary, 1963). John Rayburn, *Gregorian Chant: A History of the Controversy Concerning Its Rhythm* (New York, 1964). Eugène Cardine, *Is Gregorian Chant Measured Music?* trans. A. Dean (Solesmes: Abbaye St. Pierre, 1964). Karl Gustav Fellerer, ed., *Geschichte der katholischen Kirchenmusik,* 2 vols. (Kassel: Bärenreiter, 1972–76). Leo Treitler, "Homer and Gregory: The Transmission of Epic Poetry and Plainchant," *MQ* 60 (1974): 333–72. James W. McKinnon, "The Exclusion of Musical Instruments from the Ancient Synagogue," *PRMA* 106 (1979–80): 77–87. Helmut Hucke, "Toward a New Historical View of Gregorian Chant," *JAMS* 33 (1980): 437–67. Peter Jeffery, *Re-Envisioning Past Musical Cultures: Ethnomusicology in the Study of Gregorian Chant* (Chicago: U of Chicago Pr, 1992). David Hiley, *Western Plainchant: A Handbook* (Oxford and New York: OUP, 1993). *Hughes,* 1995. Kenneth Levy, *Gregorian Chant and the Carolingians* (Princeton: Princeton U Pr, 1998). For further bibliography see especially Liturgy, Mode, Neume, Old Roman chant, Tonary. D.M.R.

Gr. Fl. [Ger.]. Abbr. for *Grosse Flöte.*

Griffbrett [Ger.]. Fingerboard. See also *Am Griffbrett.*

Groppo [It.]. See *Gruppetto.*

Gross [Ger. masc., sing.; other endings depending on case and gender]. (1) Great, large. (2) With respect to intervals such as the third or sixth, major; with respect to the fourth and fifth, perfect.

Grosse caisse [Fr.]. Bass drum.

Grosse Flöte [Ger.]. The ordinary flute, as distinct from the piccolo.

Grosse Fuge [Ger., Great Fugue]. Beethoven's fugue for string quartet op. 133 (1825–26), originally conceived as the last movement of his String Quartet op. 130. He composed a new finale to the quartet later in 1826 and published the *Grosse Fuge* as a separate composition in 1827.

Grosses Orchester [Ger.]. Full orchestra.

Grosse Trommel [Ger.]. Bass drum.

Ground, ground bass. A pattern of notes, most often a single melodic phrase set in the bass, that is repeated over and over again during the course of a vocal or instrumental composition. Although ground bass is usually used interchangeably with *basso ostinato* to describe this technique in the music of any period [see Ostinato], ground refers most particularly to English music of the late 16th and the 17th century, where it means either a repeating bass line or the entire composition in which that bass appears (e.g., William Byrd, *A Grownde,* ed. in *Mw* 11).

A ground bass may be from one to eight measures long and may or may not contain its own final cadence; it may even modulate in the course of the piece or sustain some light figuration. While the nature of the bass itself does not necessarily differ between instrumental and vocal pieces (grounds in the latter may be more complex), the treatment of the upper parts diverges considerably, and different structures result. In instrumental pieces, the phrases of the upper lines usually coincide with the structure of the ground bass, and the figuration, texture, or melody changes with each repetition of the bass, so that continuous variations result [see Variation]. In these pieces, the ground may not remain in the bass register (Thomas Tomkins, *A Grounde,* in the *Fitzwilliam Virginal Book, hereafter *FVB,* II, 87; Bach, Passacaglia in C minor for organ). In vocal pieces, however, the ground bass tends not to delimit individual variations, but rather acts as the underlying support for a freely and often irregularly phrased setting of the text in the upper line. The vocal melody, expressly designed not to match the phrase structure of the ground, thus creates an affective continuity whose subtle conflict with the bass may build to a moving climax, as in Dido's Lament from Purcell's *Dido and Aeneas.* The term ground was applied to both kinds of pieces, but composers also frequently titled such works *chaconne, *passacaglia, a descriptive name (e.g., William Byrd, *The Bells, FVB* I, 274), or a name referring to the text (e.g., Henry Purcell, *Evening Hymn*). See also Strophic bass, variations.

The 17th century saw a lively tradition of improvisations, especially for viola da gamba, called *divisions on a ground. In Christopher Simpson's *The Division-violist* (1659), the performer was instructed in how to play faster figurations and diminutions over the ground, which was played by harpsichord or organ. While Simpson's treatise stands in a tradition of improvised embellishment and diminution going back to the 16th century (Ganassi, *Fontegara,* 1535; Ortiz, *Trattado de glosas,* 1553), the ground and its divisions (variations) are the English contribution.

Bibl.: Harold Watkins Shaw, "Blow's Use of the Ground Bass," *MQ* 24 (1938): 31–38. Wilfrid Greenhouse Allt, "Treatment of Ground," *PRMA* 72 (1945–46): 73–95. Hugh M. Miller, "Henry Purcell and the Ground Bass," *ML* 29 (1948): 340–47. Ernst Apfel, "Ostinato und Kompositionstechnik bei den englischen Virginalisten der elizabethanischen Zeit," *AfMw* 19–20 (1962–63): 29–39. Rosamond McGuinness, "The Ground-Bass in the English Court Ode," *ML* 51 (1970): 118–40, 265–78. Veronika Gutmann, *Die Improvisation auf der Viola da gamba in England im 17. Jahrhundert und ihre Wurzeln im 16. Jahrhundert* (Tutzing: Schneider, 1979). E.S.

Growl. In jazz, a harsh tone on a wind instrument, imitating the sound of an animal's growl. The sound is especially identified with members of the Duke Ellington band: trumpeter Bubber Miley (in 1926–29) and the brass players who adopted his "jungle" effects. B.K.

Gr. Tr. [Ger.]. Abbr. for **Grosse trommel.*

Grundgestalt [Ger., basic shape]. In the teaching of Arnold Schoenberg, the fundamental, underlying conception of a work in all of its aspects and hence, in *twelve-tone music, not only the row of a work.

Grundstimme [Ger.]. Foundation stop.

Gruppen [Ger., Groups]. A work for three orchestras with three conductors composed by Stockhausen in 1955–57. Its use of spatial deployment of sound sources, a technique first explored in his electronic work **Gesang der Jünglinge,* was widely influential. See also Serial music.

Gruppetto, gruppo, groppo [It.]. In the 16th through 18th centuries, a variety of ornamental note-groups, often written out and often meant to be performed in time or at least not extremely quickly; most commonly, in the earlier part of this period, a trill ending in a *turn; sometimes a turn only. See Ornamentation. D.F.

G sol re ut, Gsolreut, Gesolreut. See Hexachord.

Gsp. Abbr. for *glockenspiel.

Guajira [Sp.]. A traditional song style of rural Cuba (which is generally referred to with the adjective *guajiro*), characterized by the prevalence of 3/4 and 6/8 meters, often in combination, the singing of *décima* texts in a Spanish-derived, high-pitched, and ornamental vocal style, and accompaniment of claves, guitar, and other stringed instruments. It is also a prominent Afro-Cuban urban popular genre, in duple meter and moderate tempo, employing a repeated ground emphasizing tonic, subdominant, and dominant harmonies, and with texts alluding to the Cuban countryside. D.S.

Guaracha [Sp.]. A Cuban song and dance-music genre, prominent in theatrical entertainments in the 19th century, and in the 20th century an important element in the repertories of urban popular dance ensembles. The modern *guaracha* is notable for its picturesque and often satirical texts. It is in moderately rapid duple meter, and like other Cuban popular dance forms, consists of several sections, including ensemble and solo instrumental passages (e.g., for brass and keyboard), verses for solo vocalist, and *call-and-response exchanges between improvising soloist and chorus. Rhythmically complex, multilayered accompaniments in the *guaracha* are similar to those of the **mambo.* D.S.

Guaranía [Sp.]. A popular song form of Paraguay, created by José Asunción Flores (b. 1904) and subsequently adopted by numerous other composers. In slow waltz tempo and usually minor mode, it also draws, as its name would suggest, on the distinctive musical resources of Paraguay and has come to be accepted as a Paraguayan musical tradition. D.S.

Guárdame las vacas [Sp., watch over the cows for me]. The subject of several sets of 16th-century Spanish variations (*diferencias,* e.g., by **vihuela* composers Luis de Narváez, Alonso de Mudarra, and Enríquez de Valderrábano; and by keyboard composer Antonio de Cabezón). It is identical with the *romanesca.

Guerre des bouffons [Fr.], **guerra dei buffoni** [It.]. See *Bouffons, Querelle (guerre) des.*

Guida [It.]. (1) *Direct. (2) The subject of a fugue. (3) An abbreviated orchestral score.

Guidon [Fr.]. *Direct.

Guidonian hand [Lat. *manus Guidonis (Guidonica), palma, manus*]. A diagram of the human hand with the notes and *solmization syllables of the *gamut [see also Hexachord] assigned to joints or fingertips, well known as a teaching aid by the beginning of the 12th century and continuing in widespread use into the 17th or 18th century. Although the hand is mentioned in none of the writings of Guido d'Arezzo (d. after 1033), it is attributed to Guido in the *Chronica* (1105/10) of Sigebertus Gemblacensis (*PL* 160:57–240, mention of Guido in col. 204) and by numerous

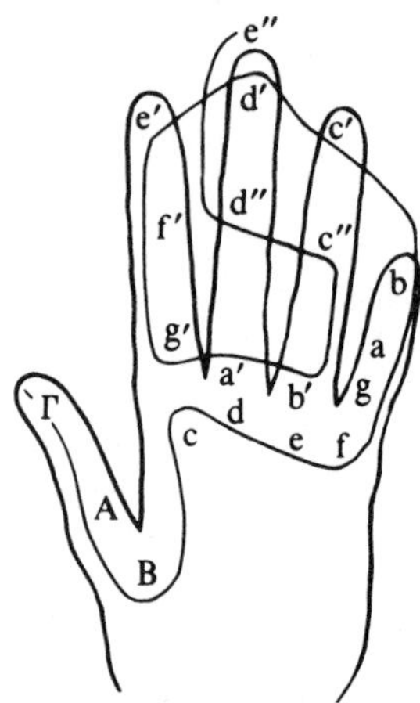

later writers. The accompanying diagram (in which Γ is the lowest note and e″ the highest) shows perhaps the most common of many arrangements of notes on the hand. An early explanation in a music treatise is in *Scientia artis musicae* (1274) by Elias Salomo (*GS* 3:16–64).

Bibl.: Joseph Smits van Waesberghe, *Musikerziehung: Lehre und Theorie der Musik im Mittelalter,* Musikgeschichte in Bildern, vol. 3, pt. 3 (Leipzig: Deutscher Verlag für Musik, 1969). Karol Berger, "The Hand and the Art of Memory," *MD* 35 (1981): 87–120.

Guillaume Tell [Fr., William Tell]. Opera in four acts by Rossini (libretto by Victor Joseph Etienne de Jouy, Hippolyte Louis Florent Bis, and others, after Schiller's play), produced in Paris in 1829. Setting: Switzerland in the 14th century.

Guimbarde [Fr.]. *Jew's harp.

Güiro [Sp.]. A *scraper of Latin America made from a hollow gourd in which notches are cut and across which a stick is rubbed. It is widely used in Latin American popular music. See ill. under Percussion instruments.

Guitar [fr. Gr. *kithara;* Fr. *guitare;* Ger. *Gitarre;* It. *chitarra;* Sp. *guitarra;* Port. *violão*]. A plucked stringed instrument with a hollow resonating chamber, gently waisted sides, a flat or slightly curved back, and a fretted fingerboard. The guitar is used in Western art music; also widely used in folk and popular music, with a variety of modified shapes (e.g., *f*-shaped sound holes, solid bodies), stringings (differences including number, material, and tunings of strings), and performance techniques (e.g., the use of a plectrum) [see also Electric guitar, Guitar family, Steel guitar].

I. *Guitar in art music.* The modern classical guitar has six strings tuned E A d g b e′, geared tuning pegs, an open round sound hole, and normally 19 inlaid metal frets. The table or soundboard is almost always made of spruce or cedar, and the back and sides of a hardwood such as Brazilian rosewood. String length is typically 65 or 66 cm. Since ca. 1946, nylon strings have been employed (the lower three wrapped with fine wire); earlier, strings were made of gut and silk. Until the late 18th century, guitar music was notated in *tablature. Since then it has been written in the treble clef, one octave higher than sounded.

Precursors of the guitar are traceable to early Babylonian and Egyptian instruments, and words similar to guitar (*gitere,* *gittern, *gittarra latina*) appear in medieval literature. The Renaissance four-course guitar appeared in the 15th century, Tinctoris (*De inventione et usu musicae,* ca. 1487) claiming it as an invention of the Catalans. Guitars of the 16th and 17th centuries were much smaller than their modern counterparts (their size being suggested by an instrument by Belchior Dias in the London College of Music that measures only 76.5 cm overall) and featured an inlaid rose and four courses of strings. Juan Bermudo (*Declaración de instrumentos musicales,* 1555) gives the tuning c/c′ f/f a/a d′. The earliest printed music appears in Alonso Mudarra's *Tres libros de música* (1546), a book devoted mainly to the six-course *vihuela. The guitar was especially popular in 16th-century France, where nine books of tablature appeared between 1551 and 1555 (music by Adrian Le Roy, Grégoire Brayssing, Guillaume Morlaye, and others).

The five-course guitar was widely played in the 17th century, particularly in Italy, where it was known as the *chitarra spagnola.* Joan Carlos Amat (1596) and Girolamo Montesardo (1606) invented a notation for stock chord patterns (alfabeto), later refined by Pietro Milioni (1627) and Giovanni Foscarini (ca. 1629) [see Tablature I, 3]. The re-entrant tuning (i.e., involving octave displacement of at least one course) a/a d/d′ g/g b/b e′ was likely the norm for art music and A/a d/d′ g/g b/b e′ for strummed accompaniments, although many others were also used. The most important composers for the five-course guitar were Francesco Corbetta (ca. 1615–81) and Robert de Visée (ca. 1660–ca. 1720), authors of numerous suites, and Gaspar Sanz, eight editions of whose *Instrucción* appeared between 1674 and 1697.

The six-string guitar probably originated in Italy before 1780 and spread throughout Europe by the early 1800s. The leading composer/performers were the Spaniard Dionysio Aguado (1784–1849), whose method-book (first published in 1825 in Madrid) helped to establish modern technique; Fernando Sor (1778–1839), another Spaniard who made his career in London and Paris; the Italian Mauro Giuliani (1781–1829), who established himself in Vienna; and Ferdinando Carulli (1770–1841), a prolific Italian who settled in Paris. The repertory of these virtuosi includes sonatas, sets of variations, and potpourris. Other significant 19th-century guitarists are Matteo Carcassi (1792–1853), Johann Kaspar Mertz (1806–56), Napoléon Coste (1806–83), and Francisco Tárrega (1852–1909). The Spanish luthier Antonio de Torres Jurado (1817–92) is credited with establishing the guitar's present dimensions after 1850.

The modern revival of interest in the guitar is largely attributable to Andrés Segovia (1893–1987), who made the instrument known throughout the world and commissioned much original music for it. His work has been carried on by a number of major artists, including Julian Bream, Christopher Parkening, and John Williams. Important 20th-century composers of guitar music include Manuel de Falla, Heitor Villa-Lobos, Manuel Ponce, Benjamin Britten, Alberto Ginastera, Joaquín Rodrigo, Hans Werner Henze, André Jolivet, William Walton, Elliott Carter, Ned Rorem, and Leo Brouwer. The guitar has also played a role in 20th-century chamber music (e.g., by Schoenberg, Webern, and Boulez).

II. *Guitar in popular and folk music.* The guitar has an extraordinary ability to cross geographical and social boundaries. Throughout the era of European colonialism it carried European musical concepts, such as functional harmony, throughout the world. Its hegemony in world popular music today has also been facilitated by the power of the international music industry. Guitar music has, however, not remained exclusively European in orientation. Musicians throughout the world have indigenized the guitar, treating it as a malleable template, modifying it to make it compatible with local musical ideas. As a result, many countries today boast vibrant syncretic guitar traditions.

Throughout Latin America the guitar has had a strong presence since the early colonial period, Brazil providing an outstanding example. By the early 20th century guitarists were prominent performers in samba and *chôro* ensembles, major exponents being the seven-string guitar pioneer Dino Sete Cordas (b. 1918) and Raphael Rabello (1962–95). In the late 1950s João Gilberto (b. 1931) developed the understated, sophisticated *violão gago* ("stuttering guitar") style that underpinned the new urban popular form *bossa nova. Important contemporary guitarist-composers transcending the popular-classical stylistic continuum include Egberto Gismonti (b. 1947), Toninho Horta (b. 1948), and the Assad family, brothers Sérgio (b. 1952), Odair (b. 1956), and sister Badi (b. 1966).

At the end of the 19th century the steel-string guitar flooded into the rural south of the U.S., the birthplace of blues, jazz, and country music. African American musicians combined the open G "Spanish" and open D tunings used in the earlier parlor guitar tradition with an African technique of playing string instruments with a wood, metal, or glass slide. Singer-guitarists of the new blues genre found the resulting slide guitar a perfect complement to the voice. Pioneers from the Mississippi Delta region included Charlie Patton (1891–1934), Memphis Minnie (1897–1973), Son House (1902–88), and Robert Johnson (1911–38). The next generation of Mississippi-born guitarists took the blues form into the northern urban environment, especially the city of Chicago. The great urban bluesmen Muddy Waters (1915–83), B. B. King (b. 1925), and Buddy Guy (b. 1936) formed electric guitar–based bands that inspired later legions of rock and roll musicians.

In the Piedmont-Appalachian region, a ragtime-oriented finger-picking style was developed by African American and Anglo-American guitarists. Mississippi John Hurt (1892–1966), Elizabeth Cotten (1895–1987), Reverend Gary Davis (1896–1972), and Blind Willie McTell (1901–59) exemplify the Piedmont blues style, while the playing of Merle Travis (1917–83), Doc Watson (b. 1923), and Chet Atkins (1924–2001) became central to both Appalachian folk music and the country music business in Nashville.

The interracial duet of African American guitarist Lonnie Johnson (1899–1970) and Italian American Eddie Lang (1902–33, recording under the pseudonym Blind Willie Dunn) made some of the earliest jazz guitar recordings. Jazz guitar accompaniment style in the big band era was taken to its apogee by Freddie Greene (1911–87), a pillar of Count Basie's All American Rhythm Section for a half century, and the horn-style solo electric guitar style in jazz still preeminent today was pioneered by the great Charlie Christian (1916–42). As jazz grew into an international art form, European guitarists such as Django Reinhardt (1910–53), John McLaughlin (b. 1942), and others have made major contributions.

The gut-string guitar was introduced to Hawaii in the 1830s by Spanish-speaking cowboys from southern California, and steel-string guitars arrived there with sailors from the Portuguese Azores during the 1860s. Despite the fact that the indigenous song tradition had no previous harmonic accompaniment, the guitar was swiftly embraced by Hawaiians, and two important styles developed. Joseph Kekuku (1874–

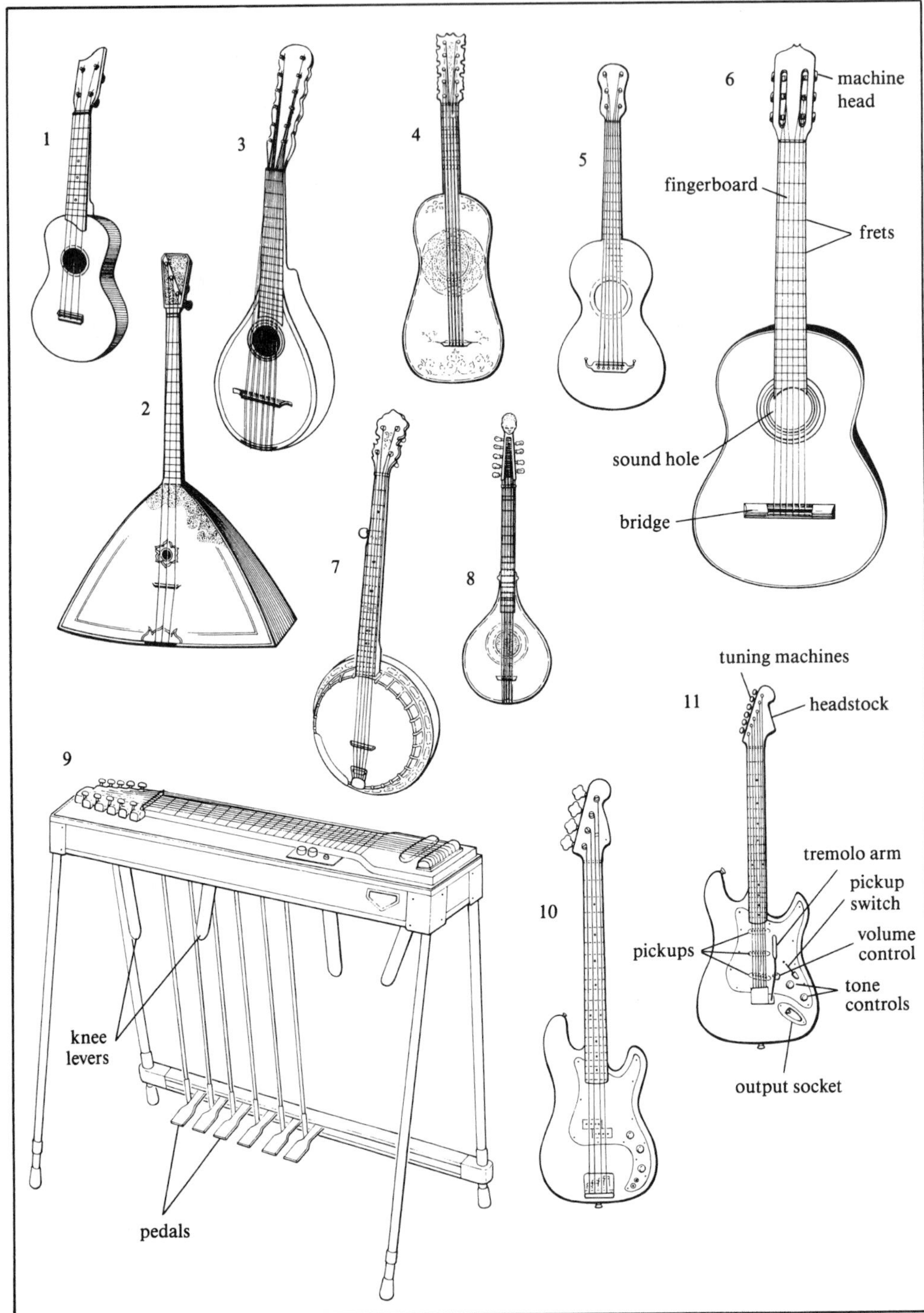

1. Ukulele. 2. Balalaika. 3. Bandurria. 4. 17th-century guitar. 5. Early 19th-century guitar. 6. Modern guitar (not to scale). 7. Banjo. 8. Cittern. 9. Pedal steel guitar. 10. Electric bass guitar. 11. Electric guitar.

1932) was the first to record Hawaiian slide guitar (in 1909), a sound that quickly became a sonic icon for Hawaii worldwide. In *ki ho 'alu,* slack-key guitar, the string tension is "slackened" and a large number of open tunings are used. Auntie Alice Namakelua (1892–1987) was the earliest slack-key guitarist documented on recordings, and Gabby Pahinui (1921–80) was the great 20th-century master of both slide and slack-key styles. His sons Bla and Cyril (b. 1942, 1950), together with Raymond Kane (b. 1925), and Keola Beamer (b. 1951), are major exponents of slack key today.

By the 1920s Hawaiian guitar clubs were thriving in Europe, the U.S., and many Asian countries. In India the slide guitar joined indigenous slide lutes such as the *gottuvadyam,* valued for their ability to replicate vocal nuances and ornaments of the indigenous raga system. Brij Bhushan Kabra (b. 1937) made a seminal recording of Hindustani (North Indian) slide guitar in 1968 that inspired younger players like Vishwa Mohan Bhatt (b. 1952) and Debashish Bhattacharya (b. 1963), active today.

One of the earliest guitar traditions on the African continent was the palmwine guitar style. The Kru sailors of Liberia spread the guitar along the West African coast and across the Atlantic, with the result that the style of palmwine musicians such as Sierra Leone's S. E. Rogie (1919–94) shows kinship with Bahamian guitarist Joseph Spence (1910–84). Ghana's Agya Ko Nimo (b. 1934) is a prominent palmwine and high-life guitarist and researcher. Senegal's Baaba Maal (b. 1954) and Mali's Ali Farka Toure (b. 1949) integrate stylistic aspects and repertoire from the 21-string Mandinka *kora* (lute) into their playing. Central African soukous developed when Congolese musicians syncretized Cuban and indigenous music, creating the irresistible, buoyant dance music that has dominated dance floors across the continent since the 1960s. Major soukous guitarists include the Congolese bandleader Franco (1938–89) and Sam Mangwana (born in Kinshasa in 1945 of Angolan parents).

Returning to Europe, where the colonial travels of the guitar commenced, on the Iberian Peninsula the Rom (gypsy) community is the source of the flamenco guitar tradition, which has evolved over the last century and a half from an exclusively accompanying role (for vocal and dance) to a solo guitar style. Ramón Montoya (1880–1949) was a major transitional figure, an accomplished accompanist who introduced many of the ideas that inspired the next generation of soloists, including Paco Peña (b. 1942) and Paco de Lucia (b. 1947).

Bibl.: *I.* Philip Bone, *The Guitar and Mandolin* (London: Schott, 1914; 2nd ed., 1954; R: 1972). Josef Zuth, *Handbuch der Laute und Gitarre* (Vienna: Verlag der Zeitschrift für die Gitarre, 1926–28; R: Hildesheim: Olms, 1978). Frederic Grunfeld, *The Art and Times of the Guitar* (New York: Macmillan, 1969). Thomas Heck, "The Birth of the Classic Guitar and Its Cultivation in Vienna, Reflected in the Career and Compositions of Mauro Giuliani (d. 1829)" (Ph.D. diss., Yale Univ., 1970). Sylvia Murphy, "The Tuning of the Five-course Guitar," *GSJ* 23 (1970): 49–63. Harvey Turnbull, *The Guitar from the Renaissance to the Present Day* (New York: Scribner, 1974). Tom and Mary Anne Evans, *Guitars . . . from the Renaissance to Rock* (New York: Paddington Pr, 1977). David B. Lyons, *Lute, Vihuela, Guitar to 1800: A Bibliography* (Detroit: Info Coord, 1978). Konrad Ragossnig, *Handbuch der Gitarre und Laute* (Mainz: B Schott, 1978). Giuseppe Radole, *Liuto, Chitarra e Vihuela* (Milan: Suvini Zerboni, 1979). James Tyler, *The Early Guitar* (London: Oxford U Pr, 1980). George Gilmore, *Guitar Music Index,* 2nd ed. (n.p.: George Gilmore, 1981).. Graham Wade, *Traditions of the Classical Guitar* (Riverrun, N.Y.: Riverrun Pr, 1981). Werner Schwarz, *Guitar Bibliography* (New York: Saur, 1984). Periodicals: *Guitar Review* (1946–); *Il "Fronimo"* (1972–); *Guitar* (1972–); *Soundboard* (1974–); *Guitar and Lute* (1974–83); *Gitarre + Laute* (1979–); *Les cahiers de la guitare* (1982–); *Classical Guitar* (1982–).

II. D. George, *The Flamenco Guitar* (Madrid: Society of Spanish Studies, 1969). George Kanahele, *Hawaiian Music and Musicians: An Illustrated History* (Honolulu: U of Hawaii Pr, 1979). Cynthia Schmidt, ed., *The Guitar in Africa,* special issue of *The World of Music* 36, no. 2 (1994). James Sallis, ed., *The Guitar in Jazz: An Anthology* (Lincoln: U of Nebr Pr, 1996). Andy Bennett and Kevin Dawe, eds., *Guitar Cultures* (Oxford: Berg, 2001). Victor Anand Coelho, ed., *The Cambridge Companion to the Guitar* (Cambridge: Cambridge U Pr, 2002).

(I) P.K.D., (II) M.H.A.

Guitar family. A family of instruments that are variants of the guitar but adhere to its general shape [see Guitar; see also Electric guitar, Steel guitar]. The smaller four- and five-course guitars of the 16th through mid-18th centuries are considered the true ancestors of the modern instrument. Other early plucked stringed instruments are harder to classify, but several belong to the *cittern family [see Bandurria, Citole, Gittern, English guitar, Orpharion]. The 16th-century **vihuela* is usually considered a member of the guitar family, as is the later Italian **chitarra battente.*

The 19th-century *Terzgitarre* [It. *chitarrino*] is a small guitar tuned a minor third above the ordinary instrument (G c f b♭ d′ g′). It was used by Mauro Giuliani (1781–1829) in his Third Concerto op. 70 and elsewhere. The lyre guitar, popular in the early 19th century, combined a six-string guitar neck with the stylized shape of the classical Greek *lyra. Many guitars with extra bass strings have been developed, including the *décacorde,* tuned C D E F G A d g b e′, for which Ferdinando Carulli published a method ca. 1827 [see also Harp lute, Mandora (2)]. Guitars with seven or eight strings were common in the later 19th century, and seven-string guitars tuned D G B d g b d′ are still widely played in Russia.

Numerous guitarlike instruments are used to play folk music in many parts of the world, particularly Latin America. These include the Andean *charango* (made of an armadillo shell with five single or paired strings tuned g′ c″ e″ a′ e″) and the *cuatro* of Venezuela (a small guitar with four strings tuned a d′ f♯′ b) [see also Bandola]. The *jarana* (diminutive *jaranita*) is a

Mexican equivalent of the *charango.* The *ukulele (in North America today normally tuned a′ d′ f♯′ b′) is a descendant of the Portuguese *machete* (d′ g′ b′ d″) of the Azores.

Bibl.: Marian G. Harrison, "Small Guitars," *Guitar Review* 34 (1971): 18–24. Stephen Bonner, *The Classic Image: European History and Manufacture of the Lyre Guitar, 850–1840* (Harlow, U.K.: Bois de Boulogne, 1972). Joscelyn Godwin, "Eccentric Forms of the Guitar, 1770–1850," *Journal of the Lute Society of America* 7 (1974): 90–102. Matanya Ophee, "Chamber Music for Terz Guitar," *Guitar Review* 42 (1977): 12–14. P.K.D.

Guitarrón [Sp.]. (1) In Mexico, a very large guitar with six strings, used as the bass in a **mariachi* ensemble. (2) In Chile, a guitar with 21 strings distributed into five courses and an additional four short strings passing over the body but not the fingerboard.

Gurrelieder [Ger., Songs of Gurre]. A cantata by Schoenberg on poems (originally in Danish) by Jens Peter Jacobsen, for five soloists, three male choruses, one mixed chorus, narrator, and large orchestra, begun in 1900–1901 and completed in 1911. Schoenberg began the setting of these texts as a song cycle for voice and piano.

Gusheh [Per., corner]. A constituent part of a Persian **dastgāh,* the basis of an improvised section in nonmetric performance, using a selection (usually a tetrachord) of the *dastgāh*'s scale, and with specific melody or main motif. A *gusheh* may appear in several *dastgāh*s. Designation is by place-name or adjective indicating character or musical position within the *dastgāh.* B.N.

Gusla [Bulg.]. See *Gadulka, Gusle.*

Gusle [Serb.-Cro.; Bulg. *gusla*]. A bowed stringed instrument of Yugoslavia with a pear-shaped body and a single horsehair string. The player, called a *guslar,* holds the instrument between the knees and holds a curved bow in the right hand. The string is stopped with the left hand, using finger pressure only, there being no fingerboard. The *guslar* traditionally sings epic poetry while providing accompaniment on the *gusle.*

Gusli [Russ.]. A *zither used by several nationalities in the former Soviet Union. Its 12 to 36 gut or metal strings are strung across a shallow, usually triangular box. See also Psaltery.

Gusto, con [It.]. With taste, style, relish.

Gutbucket. Rowdy early jazz. Like *barrelhouse, but not restricted to the piano, the term is used informally.

Gymel, gimel, gemel [fr. Lat. *gemellus,* twin]. In English counterpoint of the 15th and 16th centuries, the temporary splitting of one voice part into two of equal range; also the name of each of these two parts. The term first occurs in Continental manuscripts, in connection with anonymous voices added to a piece by John Dunstable and tropes in a Sanctus by Johannes Roullet. The first English references to gymel (also called *semel*) are in the treatise of Pseudo-Chilston (ca. 1450) and in the Eton Choirbook (late 15th century).

In the Eton Choirbook, gymels can be found in pieces by William Cornyshe, John Browne, Walter Lambe, and others. Later composers who made use of gymel include John Taverner, Christopher Tye, and Thomas Tallis. The term was no longer employed after the late 1560s.

The historically inappropriate association of the term gymel with parallel motion in imperfect consonances is due largely to its use ca. 1470 by the Italian theorist Guillelmus Monachus.

Gymnopédies [Fr.]. Three piano pieces by Erik Satie composed in 1888. They take their name from a festival of ancient Sparta. Debussy orchestrated the first and third in 1896, Roland-Manuel the second.

Gypsy music. Gypsies (Roma) are a varied group of people, many of Indic ancestry, living in South Asia, the Middle East, Europe, and the Western Hemisphere. Migrating out of northwest India around the 10th century C.E., they arrived in southeastern Europe starting in the 14th century. They have traditionally had an itinerant, outcast social position, pursuing hereditary trades like metallurgy, soldiery, basketry, and music. Roma are often bilingual in Romani and a mainstream language. During the 20th century many Roma settled, either forcibly or by choice.

In Europe, professional Rom musicians were often settled for centuries, were linguistically assimilated, and developed styles for a multiethnic audience. In southeastern Europe, shawm and drum ensembles played *mehterhane* (military music) at Ottoman garrisons, and they now accompany the sporting events or life-cycle ceremonies of mainstream ethnic groups. Rom ensembles of strings and winds, including the Macedonian *chalgiya,* Greek *koumpania,* and Romanian *taraf,* disseminated from the Ottoman courts to the general public in the 19th century. They perform free-rhythm improvisations and dance music, often in asymmetric meter, and feature virtuoso wind playing like that of the Turkish clarinetist Mustafa Kandirali. In the 18th and 19th centuries, Rom string ensembles in Austria-Hungary helped create the *verbunkos* style, incorporating it into song accompaniments and dances. Rom violinists, including János Bihari, were famous progenitors of this music; the pieces that Bihari played were written down by others and have become standards of the light classical repertoire in Hungary. In Andalusia, the musical cultures of Roma, Muslims, and Jews may have fused to give rise to *flamenco. An intense flamenco style of guitar, dance, hand clapping, and *cante hondo* (deep song) associated with Roma was documented in the 19th century; in the 20th century, Rom performers blended Latin American popular music with flamenco. In Russia during the 18th century, choirs of enserfed Roma began to accompany non-Rom performers of "Gypsy song," a genre that combined popular forms like the *couplet and the romance. The Teatr Romen staged versions of this music in the Romani language during the Soviet period. In the 1930s, Manouche Roma, including the guitarist Django Reinhardt, combined the Parisian *musette with jazz. Sinti (settled Rom musicians) from the German-speaking areas of Europe adopted this style and continue to play it on acoustic instruments. During the 1980s and 1990s in Bulgaria, Roma and members of other ethnic groups developed *svatbarska muzika* (wedding music). Played by clarinet, saxophone, and rock band instruments, it features bebop-inspired improvisation on the melodies and meters of Bulgarian folk dance.

Roma sing for each other, often improvising in the Romani language. Texts dramatize humorous, tragic, or intimate themes arising from a close family life and marginal social position. The melodies and vocal styles reflect transnational tastes by drawing from genres popular across Europe, the Middle East, and South Asia. Travelers, a group similar to the Roma in the British Isles, maintain a ballad-singing tradition. In Yugoslavia, Rom singers like Esma Redžepova performed Romani-language songs for the general public as early as the 1950s. Starting in the 1970s, Roma all over Europe gave song performances, thereby drawing attention to the autonomous aspects of Rom musical culture, the Rom holocaust, and the need for equal rights. At this time the scholarship on Rom music also began to identify the importance of Romani-language song traditions and to recognize syncretic styles.

Non-Roma perform parallel traditions of flamenco, "Gypsy" jazz, and Russian "Gypsy" romances. Composers have long coded the Gypsy for exoticism; many operas feature threatening or sexualized Gypsy figures. Composers such as Franz Liszt and Johannes Brahms incorporated *verbunkos* characteristics, including augmented seconds, in their rhapsodies.

Bibl.: Bálint Sárosi, *Gypsy Music* (Budapest: Corvina, 1978 [1970]). Patrick Williams, *Django* (Montpellier: Éditions du Limon, 1991). Caterina Pasqualino, *Dire le chant: Les Gitans flamencos d'Andalousie* (Paris: CNRS Éditions, 1998). Max Peter Baumann, ed., *Music, Language and Literature of the Roma and Sinti,* Intercultural Music Studies 11 (Bamberg: Verlag für Wissenschaft und Bildung, 2000).

B.R.L.

H

H. (1) Abbr. for horn. (2) [Ger.] B-natural. See Pitch names, Letter notation. (3) Abbr. for **Hauptstimme.*

Habanera [Sp.]. A 19th-century Cuban song and dance form, its name derived from that of the country's capital city of Havana. It is in slow to moderate tempo and in duple meter, with a characteristic accompanimental figure:

The *habanera* is an important antecedent of later Cuban forms such as the **danzón.* It was popular in Spain and Europe (where it was adapted by Bizet in *Carmen* in 1875) as well as elsewhere in Latin America. It is a primary source of the Mexican *danza* of the late 19th and early 20th centuries and a major influence in the early development of the Argentine **tango.* D.S.

Hackbrett [Ger.]. *Dulcimer.

Haffner Serenade. The Serenade in D major for orchestra by Mozart, K. 250 (1776), composed for a festive wedding in the family of Sigismund Haffner, burgomaster in Salzburg. The work consists of nine movements, including an opening march (K. 249) and several movements that feature a solo violin prominently.

Haffner Symphony. Mozart's Symphony no. 35 in D major K. 385 (1782), composed for the ennoblement of Sigismund Haffner in Salzburg. It was originally intended as a serenade with the March K. 408/2 (385a) and another minuet (now lost). The flute and clarinet parts were added later.

Halbe Note, halbe Pause [Ger.]. Half note, half-note rest. See Note.

Halbinstrument [Ger.]. Half-tube instrument [see Wind instruments].

Halbschluss [Ger.]. Half *cadence.

Halbsopran [Ger.]. Mezzo-soprano.

Halbton [Ger.]. Half step, semitone.

Half cadence. A *cadence ending on the dominant.

Half close. Half *cadence.

Half-diminished seventh chord. See Seventh chord.

Half-fall. According to Thomas Mace (1676), an *appoggiatura that rises by a half step.

Half note. See Note.

Half shift. In violin playing, second *position.

Half step. *Semitone.

Half-stop. *Divided stop.

Half-tube. See Wind instruments.

Halil [Heb.]. A *reedpipe of ancient Israel similar to the Greek *aulos and, like the aulos, always played in a pair; usually rendered "flute" in English Bibles.

Hallelujah [Heb., praise ye the Lord]. An expression of praise to God or of general rejoicing. For its occurrence in the Bible and its use in Gregorian chant, see Alleluia. In choral works of the 17th and 18th centuries, its occurrence in a text is often the occasion for an elaborate passage or movement for chorus, often employing imitation. Examples include the "Hallelujah Chorus" from the close of part 2 of Handel's **Messiah* and the first movement of Bach's Cantata no. 4, *Christ lag in Todesbanden.*

Halling [Nor.]. A Norwegian folk dance in a moderately fast duple meter, usually danced by one dancer at a time and accompanied on the **Hardingfele.* Grieg incorporated the *halling* in a number of his works, including the *Lyric Pieces* for piano op. 47 (1888).

Hammer(ed) dulcimer. In the U.S., the *dulcimer, as distinct from the *Appalachian dulcimer.

Hammerklavier [Ger.]. In the early 19th century, a name for the *piano. Beethoven subtitled his Piano Sonatas in A major op. 101 (1816) and B♭ major op. 106 (1817–18) "für das Hammerklavier"; the latter is popularly known as the *Hammerklavier* Sonata.

Hammers, Pythagorean. See Pythagorean hammers.

Hammond organ. See Electronic organ.

Handel Variations. Twenty-five Variations and a Fugue on a Theme by G. F. Handel op. 24 composed by Brahms in 1861. The theme is the Air from Handel's Suite no. 1 in B♭ major for harpsichord, from the second set of suites, published in 1733. The fugue subject is freely derived from the initial notes of Handel's tune.

Handharmonika [Ger.]. *Accordion.

Hand horn. See Horn.

Hand organ. See Barrel organ, Barrel piano.

Handorgel [Ger.]. *Accordion.

Handstück [Ger.]. In the late 18th century (especially among the works of D. G. Türk), a didactic piano piece.

Hänsel und Gretel. Opera in three acts by Engelbert Humperdinck (libretto by his sister, Adelheid Wette, after the fairy tale in the Grimm brothers' collection), produced in Weimar in 1893. Setting: a forest in Germany.

Happening. See Mixed media.

Hardanger fiddle. **Hardingfele*.

Hard bop. A mid-1950s resurgence of *bebop. At times, its practitioners combined the stylistic conventions of the parent style with elements drawn from blues, rhythm and blues, and gospel performance. Its exponents included drummers Art Blakey and Max Roach, pianist Horace Silver, trumpeters Clifford Brown and Lee Morgan, and saxophonists Sonny Rollins and Jackie McLean. T.A.J.

Hardi [Fr.]. Bold, rash.

Hardingfele [Nor.], **hardanger fiddle.** A folk fiddle of western Norway with four melody strings plus four or five metal *sympathetic strings running beneath the fingerboard. In use since the 17th century, it has a special dance-music repertory and a distinctive playing style that makes much use of drone effects.

Harfe [Ger.]. *Harp.

Harmonia. (1) [Gr.] See Greece I, 3 (ii). (2) [Lat.] The relationship between two or more pitches, whether or not sounded simultaneously. Through the 14th century, the term is as likely to refer to melodic relationships as to simultaneities, though as early as the 13th century it may refer to a simultaneity of two pitches. Its use with respect to three pitches sounded simultaneously, and thus in a sense like that of the modern term *harmony, begins with Gaffurius (1496) and is considerably developed by Zarlino (1558) [see also Theory, Harmony of the spheres].

Harmonic. See Acoustics, Harmonics.

Harmonica. (1) *Mouth organ. (2) *Glass harmonica.

Harmonic analysis. Analysis of harmonic functions and their relationship to the larger dimensions of a musical work. Analysis of Western tonal harmony, principally of the 18th and 19th centuries, includes elucidation of chord types and their functional basis (expressed by roman-numeral notation); evaluation of their relative harmonic strength and their patterns within the phrase; the relationship of these to the key and to changes of key; and ultimately the larger and smaller relationships of individual and assembled harmonies to the overall structure of the work [see Harmony].

I. *Types of chords.* The simplest chord is the triad, composed of three pitches: the root (also called the fundamental tone), a third (major or minor), and a fifth, as in Ex. 1, which illustrates a C major triad in its simplest form, without doubling voices. Any other arrangement of C's, E's, and G's would thus constitute some kind of C-major triad. A triad whose root is below the other pitches is said to be in root position. If some other pitch is in the bass, the chord is said to be inverted. See Triad, Inversion II.

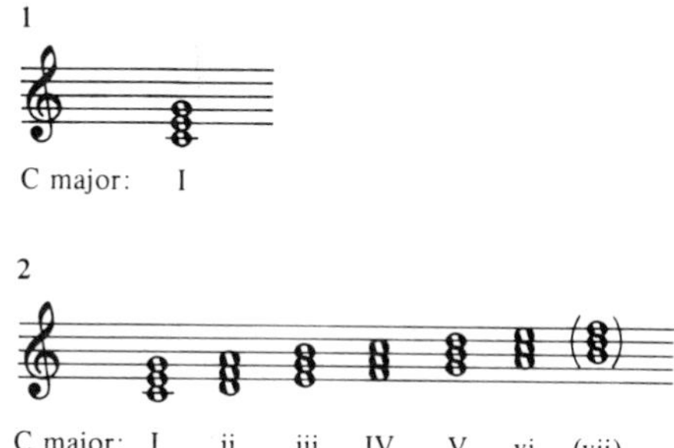

Example 2 shows triads formed on each scale degree in C major, including three major and three minor, which are made up only of consonant intervals and employ no tones from outside the C-major scale; the bracketed chord, formed on the seventh scale degree, is a diminished triad (so called because of the diminished fifth, a dissonant interval) and is the only other type of triad possible in the major mode. It is regarded by some theorists as having a weakened harmonic function and as being an incomplete dominant *seventh chord without the root. Each triad is identified by the roman numeral corresponding to the scale degree that is its root; the roman numeral is capitalized if the triad is major. (If a chord is more complex than a triad [see below] or if it is in some position other than root position, arabic numerals are added to the roman numerals in a variety of ways; for a description of this system of notation, see Thoroughbass.) Because of the variability of scale forms, the *minor mode demonstrates a more complicated set of triads, including augmented (+) and diminished (°) [Ex. 3].

Many different structural types are possible in the family of seventh chords, formed from triads surmounted by a seventh above the root [Ex. 4]. By far the most important of these is the dominant seventh chord (a). Other seventh chords include the major seventh (b), minor seventh (c), major-minor seventh (d), half-diminished seventh (e), and diminished seventh (f); all of these are distinguished from each other by their intervallic content. Next to the dominant seventh, the commonest seventh-chord structure is the diminished seventh; in its commonest usage it is variously described as based on the seventh scale degree or as a dominant ninth chord with the root omitted.

4

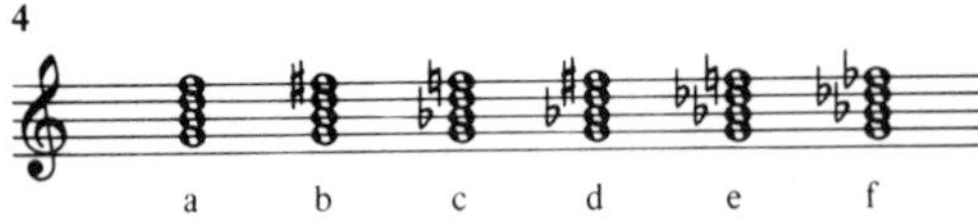

The harmonic weight of most of these seventh chords, as well as of the homologous ninth, eleventh, and thirteenth chords that can be constructed on paper, is attenuated by the nonharmonic values of the dissonant pitches; in most cases, in actual music, such structures arise only as momentary events in the ebb and flow of counterpoint. Late in the period of tonal harmony, however, these complex chords are used independently, for the sake of their particular sonic qualities, e.g., in the music of Debussy, Ravel, and others [see below].

II. *Altered chords.* These are triads or seventh chords with one or more pitches that have been chromatically altered by application of accidental signs so as to include at least one tone not found in the major or minor scales of a particular key. They include the Neapolitan *sixth chord, shown in Ex. 5a, the various types of triads with raised or lowered fifth, particularly the dominant triad (b), the raised supertonic and submediant seventh chords (c), and the augmented sixth chords (d); in Ex. 5 these are shown with their normal resolutions. (Triads of secondary dominant function, discussed below, are considered not as chromatically altered chords, but rather as chords borrowed from other keys.) It is a general rule that resolutions of the altered pitches follow the direction of alteration: raised pitches resolve upward, and lowered pitches resolve downward.

5

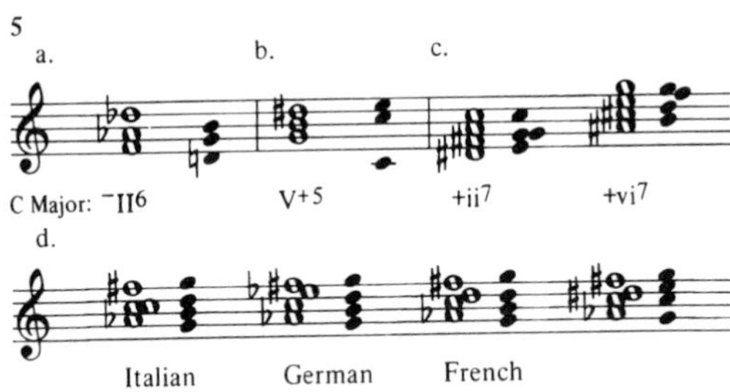

III. *Secondary functions.* In the key of C major, a D-major triad progressing to a G-major triad is usually considered to be not a major triad formed on the supertonic but rather the dominant of the dominant (i.e., the triad formed on the dominant or fifth degree of the scale in which G is tonic, described as V of V and often written V/V). Its tonal strength applies more immediately to G, in which key it is a primary triad, and accordingly with respect to C it is a secondary dominant. Since secondary dominants usually include at least one pitch from outside the scale (e.g., G♯ in V of VI in C major), these pitches are considered as borrowed from the scale of the secondary key and not as alterations of the primary scale. It is apparent that secondary dominants, though not of themselves representing any unique structural types, afford a vast enrichment of harmonic variety by increasing the number of available functions in any one key.

Secondary dominants (sometimes called applied dominants) create a tonal emphasis on the chords to which they apply; V of II, for example, is said to tonicize II (i.e., treat II as if it were tonic). *Tonicization is a temporary state, of short duration, as distinguished from *modulation, which persists long enough to create an actual sense of a new key.

IV. *More complex harmonic types.* The harmonic vocabulary after about 1890 was enlarged and enriched by all kinds of systematic and nonsystematic new chordal types, some of them part of a new common language, others peculiar to certain composers, still others idiosyncrasies of individual works. In Ex. 6 are shown: (a) a stack of thirds (Stravinsky, *Petrushka*); (b) a chord of perfect fourths and one augmented fourth (Satie, *Messe des pauvres*); (c) a chord

6

containing unresolved appoggiaturas (Ravel, "Le gibet" from *Gaspard de la nuit*); (d) a polychord (Ravel, *Daphnis et Chloé*); (e) a C-major chord of unusual spacing (Stravinsky, *Symphony of Psalms*); (f) a tone *cluster (Ives, *Majority*) [see Harmony VII].

For bibl., see Harmony. M.DEV.

Harmonice musices odhecaton [Lat.]. See *Odhecaton.*

Harmonic flute. [Fr. *flûte harmonique*]. A double-length organ stop, pierced with a small hole at the node to produce a strong and pure flute-like overtone.

Harmonic inversion. See Inversion II.

Harmonic mean. See Arithmetic and harmonic mean.

Harmonic minor (scale). See Scale.

Harmonicon. (1) *Glass harmonica or *musical glasses in general. (2) **Vis-à-vis.*

Harmonic rhythm. The rhythm of the changes of harmony in time in a musical work. Strong harmonic rhythm is marked by strong root motions, especially in root position [see Harmony III]; by coincidence of harmonic changes with regular metrical dividing points, especially the downbeat of the measure; by deemphasis of contrapuntal activity of the bass line; and by relatively longer duration of the harmony. Weak harmonic rhythm is marked by weak root progressions, deemphasis of root position, the strength of contrapuntal motions added to the harmony, weak rhythmic placement in the measure, and relatively shorter duration.

Harmonic rhythm does not itself depend on tempo any more than melodic rhythm does; Chopin's Prelude in C minor op. 28 no. 20, for example, shows sixteen changes of root-position harmony in four measures of *Largo,* while the finale of Schubert's Symphony in C major D. 944 *(Allegro vivace)* has extensive stretches where the harmony changes only every eight measures or even longer. But the combination of rapid tempo and rapid harmonic rhythm generally produces an effect of musical compression or intensity, whereas slow harmonic rhythm in slow tempo suggests breadth and freedom from tension.

*Schenker analysis characteristically emphasizes the relatively strong harmonic rhythm, over the larger time-span and considers the relatively weaker harmonic rhythm over the smaller time-span a detail rather than a foundation-post of the overall harmonic structure. See also Harmony.

Bibl.: Jan LaRue, *Guidelines for Style Analysis* (New York: Norton, 1970). Walter Piston, *Harmony,* 5th ed., rev. Mark DeVoto (New York: Norton, 1987). Joseph Swain, *Harmonic Rhythm: Analysis and Interpretation* (New York: Oxford U Pr, 2001). M.DEV.

Harmonics. (1) In acoustics, a series of frequencies, all of which are integral multiples of a single frequency termed the fundamental [see Acoustics I]. The fundamental and its harmonics are numbered in order, the fundamental being the first harmonic and having the frequency 1f, the second harmonic having the frequency 2f, the third harmonic 3f, and so forth. Harmonics above the fundamental are sometimes termed overtones, the second harmonic being the first overtone, etc. The pitches represented by these frequencies, and thus the intervals formed among these pitches, are said to be acoustically pure. In some measure, they correspond to the pitches and intervals employed in much Western music. Most such music, however, requires the use of a tuning system in which relatively few intervals (always the octave and sometimes only the octave) are acoustically pure. Ex. 1 shows the pitches corresponding to the harmonic series for the fundamental C. The pitches shown in whole notes are in general judged to be sufficiently well in tune. Those in black notes are, by the standards of Western tonal music, quite out of tune, and thus their representation on the staff is only approximate. For a detailed comparison of acoustically pure intervals with those employed in various systems of tuning and temperament, see Interval, Temperament.

(2) [Fr. *flageolet, sons harmoniques;* Ger. *Flageolett-Töne;* It. *suoni flautati;* Sp. *sonidos del flautín*] The general class of pitches that are produced by sounding the second or some higher harmonic of a vibrating system such as a string. In the playing of stringed instruments (including the harp and guitar), these are high tones of a flutelike timbre, sometimes called flageolet tones, produced by causing a string to vibrate in segments corresponding to a mode of vibration other than the fundamental and thus suppressing altogether the pitch that is produced when the string vibrates along its entire length [see Acoustics I]. Harmonics are produced by touching the string lightly at a node for the desired mode of vibration at the same time that the string is bowed or plucked. Thus, if a string is bowed or plucked while being touched lightly at a point one-third of the distance from one end, it will produce the harmonic with a frequency three times that of the open string and with a pitch an octave and a fifth higher than that of the open string. This may be notated by placing a small circle above the desired pitch. On the piano, harmonics may be produced by touching a node lightly while the appropriate key is depressed or, more often, by depressing one or more keys in such a way as to release the dampers without allowing the hammers to strike the strings and then inducing vibrations in these strings by striking and releasing other keys.

For instruments of the violin family, natural harmonics are those produced on open strings. Artificial harmonics are those produced on stopped strings and are often notated by a normal note-shape, indicating the pitch for which the string is to be stopped, in combination with a lozenge placed a fourth above, indicating the point at which the string is to be touched lightly so as to produce the harmonic having a frequency four times that of the stopped string and having a pitch two octaves higher than that of the stopped pitch; in Ex. 2, the lower staff shows the notation and the upper staff the sounded pitch.

In violin music, the use of harmonics is thought to

have been introduced by Jean-Joseph Cassanéa de Mondonville (1711–72) in *Les sons harmoniques: Sonates à violon seul avec la basse continue* op. 4 (1738).

Harmonic series. See Acoustics I, Harmonics.

Harmonie [Fr., Ger.]. (1) Harmony. (2) Wind instruments or a band made up of wind instruments. In the late 18th and early 19th centuries, such bands of from two to a dozen instruments were often maintained by the aristocracy, their repertory including works of the type described below under (3) as well as transcriptions of other types of music. (3) [Ger.] Also *Harmoniemusik.* In the late 18th century, a multimovement work for winds (after 1780 often two each of oboes, clarinets, horns, and bassoons) of a type related to the *divertimento and slightly earlier often termed *partita or *Parthie.*

Harmonie der Welt, Die [Ger., The Harmony of the World]. (1) Opera in five acts by Hindemith (to his own libretto), produced in Munich in 1957. Setting: central Europe between 1608 and 1630, the last years of Johannes Kepler's life. (2) A symphony in three movements composed by Hindemith in 1951 and derived from music that was intended ultimately for the opera of the same name.

Harmoniemesse [Ger., Wind-band Mass]. Popular name for Haydn's Mass in B♭ major Hob. XXII:14 (1802) for soloists, chorus, and orchestra, so named because of its generous use of wind instruments.

Harmonika [Ger.]. (1) *Accordion. (2) *Mouth organ. (3) *Musical glasses.

Harmonious Blacksmith. Popular name attached in the 19th century to the air with five variations from Handel's Suite no. 5 in E major for harpsichord, from his first set of suites, published in 1720.

Harmonium. A keyboard instrument with free *reeds sounded by pedal-operated (later electric in some models) bellows; also called a reed organ, though unlike the *organ it has no pipes or resonators. In some instruments of this type (including the first instrument to bear the name harmonium as well as its predecessors the *orgue expressif* and the physharmonica) the bellows generate air pressure; in others (American organ, seraphine, melodeon, cottage organ) the bellows create suction. Stops above the keyboard activate different sets of reeds to provide various timbres. A special feature of many pressure-operated instruments is the "expression" stop, which bypasses the pressure-regulating mechanism and allows the player to control volume by means of foot pressure.

The harmonium was developed in the first half of the 19th century, the name being introduced for a pressure-operated instrument by Alexandre François Debain in 1840. Victor Mustel of Paris introduced several improvements in 1854, including a double expression stop that permitted independent control of the

Harmonium.

volume of two sections of the keyboard. Although the suction principle had been developed in Europe in the 1830s, it was most characteristic of the instruments of American makers of the second half of the 19th century such as the firm of Jacob Estey of Brattleboro, Vermont (purchased by Estey in 1848), and Mason and Hamlin of Boston (founded in 1854). By the turn of the century there were instruments with two keyboards and a pedalboard, and some were equipped to play automatically by means of punched paper rolls.

The harmonium achieved great popularity as a substitute for the pipe organ in churches and theaters and also as a household instrument. Its repertory consisted for the most part of arrangements of organ and orchestral music, though a few composers (including Franck, Dvořák, Mahler, Richard Strauss, and Schoenberg) wrote works for it. By the 1920s the popularity of the harmonium was declining, and electronic organs, introduced in the 1930s, rapidly eclipsed the older instrument. It remains extremely popular, however, on the Indian subcontinent, where small, hand-operated instruments sometimes play along with a vocal melody and sometimes supply a drone. See also Regal.

Bibl.: Auguste Mustel, *L'orgue expressif ou harmonium* (Paris: Mustel, 1903). Ludwig Hartmann, *Das Harmonium* (Leipzig: B F Voigt, 1913). H. F. Milne, *The Reed Organ: Its Design and Construction* (London: Musical Opinion 1930). Robert F. Gellerman, *The American Reed Organ* (Vestal, N.Y.: Vestal Pr, 1973). Robert F. Gellerman, *Gellerman's International Reed Organ Atlas* (Vestal, N.Y.: Vestal Pr, 1985). Arthur W. J. G. Ord-Hume, *Harmonium* (London: David & Charles, 1986).

Harmon mute. Trade name for a type of *wa-wa mute. See also Mute.

Harmony [fr. Gr., Lat. **harmonia;* Fr., Ger. *Harmonie;* It. *armonia;* Sp. *armonía*]. The relationship of tones considered as they sound simultaneously, and the way such relationships are organized in time; also any particular collection of pitches sounded simultaneously, termed a chord. The following concerns the harmony of Western art music, principally that described as tonal [see Tonality]. See also Folk music I, 2.

I. *Chords.* The period of tonal music, from the late 16th century to well into the 20th, is sometimes called the harmonic period, for tonal music is distinguished above all by the importance of its harmonic elements. These comprise a relatively small vocabulary of type-categories called chords. The simplest chordal type in tonal music is the *triad, from which all other types are elaborated [see Harmonic analysis]. Harmonic motion is made up of chords in succession; chord successions in which the motion of successive *roots (i.e., the pitches on which the chords are built) is more or less distinctly perceived are called progressions, which may be regarded as strong or weak. The choice of progression depends on what succession of roots is desired and also on how the various parts of one chord move to the next, which is called voice leading. Voice leading and its motions belong to the domain of *counterpoint [see VI below].

II. *Chord function.* In *tonality, chords relate to each other and to a central harmony, the tonic triad; they are identified by the *root upon which they are built and by the intervallic relationships between the root and the other pitches. The identification of a chord by the scale *degree (indicated with a roman numeral) that is its root is called the function of the chord. In Ex. 1, the C-major triad is labeled with the key designation C and the roman numeral I, indicating that it is formed on the first scale degree in C major and is thus the tonic triad in C; it has tonic function in C. (In the key of F major, this same triad would have dominant function, V; in G major, it would have subdominant function, IV.)

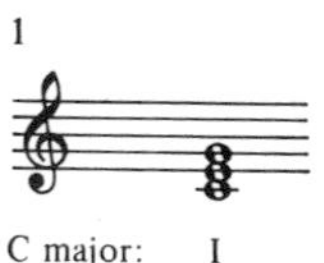

The tonality of a given passage is characteristically defined by the strength of its tonic, dominant, subdominant, and occasionally supertonic functions (on the "tonal degrees" of the scale), and to a lesser extent by its functions on the "modal degrees" (mediant and submediant—scale degrees III and VI, respectively), degrees that establish whether the passage is in major or minor mode. In tonal music, the use of particular functions and progressions is as fundamental as the use of particular words and syntax in language and literature. Tonal works may employ very limited harmonic resources, perhaps only two chords, tonic and dominant, or they may, especially in larger forms, incorporate a rich variety of chords in several different keys.

III. *Harmonic succession, harmonic progression.* In principle, any chord may follow any other, constituting simply a harmonic succession. In practice, however, the vocabulary of tonal music is greatly limited in types of root motion, and these may be regarded variously as strong or weak harmonic progressions. The progression from V to I, dominant to tonic, especially in root position (with the root of each chord in the bass, i.e., as the lowest-sounding pitch), has evolved as not only the strongest progression but also by far the most common in tonal music [see also Cadence]. The subdominant in relation to the tonic, IV–I, is of comparable but lesser force.

Weak progressions are illustrated by triads whose roots are a third apart, such as I–iii or vi–I; such triads have two pitches in common and thus the progression between them involves a change in only one pitch. The weakness is relative, for in root position, the new root obtained by the downward bass motion of a third provides a useful contrast, with a change of harmonic color from major to minor or vice versa. On the other hand, if the bass remains stationary, the progression may be so weak as to be perceived as the result of nonharmonic motion. In Ex. 2a, the bass remains the same, and the A in the uppermost part is analyzed merely as a passing tone between tonic and dominant harmonies; the bass motion of Ex. 2b results in a much stronger progression, in which the A is analyzed as belonging to a new harmony, vi.

Triads with roots a step apart have no common tones; the progression then involves a complete change of pitch collection. Such progressions are regarded as strong, but their usage evolved differently during the period of tonal harmony; IV–V and V–vi are commonly found, for example, while I–ii is found relatively seldom (though often in the 16th century), and ii–iii or IV–iii must be considered rare.

IV. *Harmonic structure of the phrase.* The *phrase is the basic unit in which tonality may be established, projected, or changed by means of harmony. A phrase has harmonic structure as much as melodic or rhythmic structure; harmonic changes in the phrase [see Harmonic rhythm] may serve to enhance the shape of a melody that they support; may stabilize, confirm, or prolong a key; or may bring about a change of key (termed a modulation). Such purposes can be accomplished with many changes of harmony or only a few, with regular or irregular harmonic rhythm, or by means of a sequence [see Sequence (1)]. A *cadence, which can occupy as much as half the phrase or as little as a beat, is always necessary, for rhythmic reasons as much as harmonic. Connections between phrases also have a harmonic significance; phrases in combination add up to formal units [see Form; Antecedent, consequent].

V. *Tonal unity and variety.* A tonal piece is unified harmonically by the strength of its tonic functions, which in turn are established, reestablished, or reinforced by the dominant–tonic (V–I) relationship above all others. Harmonic successions returning to the tonic are called prolongations; they tend to stabilize the key. Variety is afforded by other functions and relationships, which may establish new temporary and subsidiary tonics (*tonicization) in a momentary context, or in larger contexts by *modulation or actual change of key. Such contexts, aided by the faculty of musical memory, serve to project tonality through time. At the most fundamental level, representing the length of an entire movement, the overall tonality is considered a single entity, symbolized by a key designation; the first movement of Beethoven's Symphony no. 1 in C major, for instance, is said to be "in C major" even though a wide variety of keys is plainly established at intermediate levels as its events proceed. The tension between tonal prolongation and tonal progression, between maintaining the established key and disturbing it, is the energy source for all larger aspects of form in tonal music. Establishing and reinforcing tonic function, especially by means of a preceding dominant, is as much a necessity in tonal music as is departing from the established tonic by introducing a different harmony.

A change of key is itself confirmed by a V–I relationship in the new key. Related keys may have one or more shared harmonic functions (pivot chords; see Modulation) as a unifying element, as for instance, V, iii, and vi in C major, which are also, respectively, I, vi, and ii in G major. Distantly related keys may not have this possibility, as for instance C major and F♯ major, which have no triads in common. Nevertheless, the cosmos of functions that can be perceived in any one key is in practice quite large, including triads on the different major and minor scale degrees, secondary functions, and some chromatically altered chords [see Harmonic analysis].

VI. *Harmony and counterpoint.* Harmony is vertical, as melody is horizontal; these popular conceptions arise in the Western notational system, which relates simultaneous events vertically on the staff and successive events along it. Counterpoint designates a generalized relationship of melodies together, or even of melody and harmonic bass. A harmonic bass in turn may be undistinguished melodically or even a mere succession of functional roots, but it symbolizes the harmonic frame within which another melody may move. An exceptional melody may consist entirely of the pitches of one triad—bugle calls are an example—but characteristically a melody moves mostly in stepwise (conjunct) motion, with an occasional skip of a third or larger interval (disjunct motion) as a shaping component. It follows that stepwise motion, so essential to melodic integrity, by its very nature creates dissonances with the harmony sounding simultaneously with it.

In Ex. 3, the passing tones (+) and neighboring tones (N) are the simplest type of what are called nonharmonic tones. By definition, nonharmonic tones are not part of a simultaneous harmony; their function as melodic tones is not only to preserve the continuity of the melodic line to which they belong but also to connect, in a coherent manner, those tones in the melody that are part of the harmony [see Counterpoint II].

In the "modal harmony" of the 15th and 16th centuries, tonal function, with identifiable harmonic progression, is less prominent as a structural element; chords arise more generally as a consequence of contrapuntal relationships, which in turn are guided by melodic progression [see Counterpoint I, III]. This is not to say that harmony is fortuitous in such music, but rather that it is secondary to the continuity of consonance and the resolution of dissonance. By about 1650, however, the actual choice of harmonic function and progression had been elevated at least to an equity with voice-leading considerations, and the century that followed witnessed the great flowering of what some have called harmonic counterpoint. The subsequent history of music shows all manner of balancing of harmonic and contrapuntal elements in many different styles.

VII. *Chromaticism.* This term, deriving from a Greek word meaning color, implies the use of tones from outside the diatonic scale (or, in the 16th century and earlier, the *gamut). In C major, for example, the five sharped tones C♯, D♯, F♯, G♯, and A♯, and their enharmonic equivalents (black keys on the piano), are the chromatic tones that lie between the diatonic major seconds.

In music written from the period of Bach to about the middle of the 19th century, chromatic tones usually appear within a well-regulated diatonicism; modulations occur straightforwardly between closely related keys, and only by exception are they abrupt or remote; relatively few types of chords requiring chromatic signs are used, and though these chords are abundant, they nearly always have a strong diatonic resolution. Beginning in the 19th century with Chopin, and more comprehensively with Liszt and Wagner, the diatonic association of chromatic chords is undermined; the resolution might be guided not by a strong root progression but by common-tone considerations (especially enharmonically) or by contiguity, stepwise connection of one or more voices—in other words, by the contrapuntal relationships between the parts. The same consideration applies in reverse: a primary triad might move to a distantly related dissonant chord by means of smooth, stepwise, chromatic motion in one part or another, with the unexpected root change furnishing part of the element of surprise.

When nonharmonic tones are added to these equations, a virtually limitless set of coloristic possibilities arises, possibilities that were amply explored by composers after the middle of the 19th century. Chopin's Prelude in E minor op. 28 no. 4 is a good illustration of chromatic and diatonic "creeping" in a short nonmodulating piece; the overall motion of the harmonic successions spans less than an octave, and the chromatic elements are mostly passing motions, but the successive root relationships are often distant and difficult to define. Chopin's Prelude is an archetype for the later 19th century, but there are many isolated examples of similar chromatic motions in earlier periods, from the affective madrigalisms of Carlo Gesualdo and others of the late 16th century to Bach's *Chromatic Fantasy* to Mozart's Fantasia K. 475. Wagner's *Tristan und Isolde,* in which the principle of chromatic contiguity is extended to a four-hour opera, is the spiritual ancestor of the "total chromaticism" of the 20th century, discussed in the next section.

VIII. *Harmony after Wagner.* Much more than before, the history of harmony since Wagner can be correlated with the history of styles, even of individuals. The personal liberation of diatonic harmony can be said to have arisen through two means: the elimination of classical functions and voice leading, and the invention of new chord forms "for their own sake." The first of these meant above all the weakening of the dominant function and an increase in modal (third-related) progressions, tendencies first evident in the 19th-century nationalists (especially the Russian *Five) but carried much further by Chabrier, Fauré, and Debussy. The dominant function was weakened by lowering the leading tone in the dominant chord, by adding unresolved nonharmonic tones, and by substituting other chords for the dominant in cadences. Classical voice leading was replaced by a generalized stepwise connection, making possible a freely parallel harmony in fourths, fifths, seconds, complete triads, or even major ninth chords; Debussy's works, and to varying extents contemporaneous works by Ravel, Bartók, Stravinsky, and others, abound in *parallel chord formations of all types, guided in each case only by the melodic lines that they sustain. On the one hand, this symbolizes a reform of contrapuntal practice, and on the other it suggests a growing interest in the chord as a particular entity, having perhaps a root or bass of functional origin or supporting a prominent melody, but otherwise chosen on the basis of vertical considerations, for its own purely sonorous quality.

A whole roster of chord types, commonplace or unique, can be demonstrated during the approximate period 1890–1920, including unresolved major ninths, elevenths, and thirteenths, or any of these with chromatic alterations; chords of stacked thirds, fourths, or fifths, again with possible alterations; stacks of seconds (tone clusters); combinations of these with unresolved or simultaneously resolved appoggiaturas; and many different kinds of *polychords [see the examples in Harmonic analysis IV]. Hardly less important than the structural types might be the special context afforded by the use of a characteristic scale, which serves to relate the chords in a new functional sense. Debussy's modal harmony arises in part from the frequent but constantly changing use of different modal and pentatonic scales; the whole-tone scale, generating augmented triads, also appears frequently, sometimes completely dominating the harmony (Preludes bk. 1 no. 2). Debussy's *Nuages* (*Nocturnes* no. 1) makes extensive use of an artificial scale (B C♯ D E F G A) that defines an idiosyncratic harmonic environment for much of the piece.

The chromaticism of Wagner's Austrian successors (Bruckner, Wolf, Mahler, and Schoenberg) achieved within a diatonic context a certain plateau of functional complexity, but this is dominated by contrapuntal relationships more than by addition of new chordal types to the harmonic vocabulary. In Schoenberg's String Quartet no. 1 in D minor op. 7 and Chamber Symphony no. 1 op. 9, tonality is pushed to the limit, and in the works that followed, Schoenberg's chromaticism goes beyond tonality altogether [see Atonality]. Most of Schoenberg's atonal music is so completely dominated by counterpoint and motivic development that harmonic conceptions, as traditionally conceived, have no real place. The music of Berg, however, though comprehensively influenced by Schoenberg, definitely possesses structural elements of a nostalgic tonality that can nearly always be traced even in the most densely chromatic textures. This paratonality, as it has been called, depends on the emphasis of tone centers and on motivic harmonic progressions, the latter a favorite structural device that can be traced back to Wagner's leitmotifs and even earlier. In Berg's later works, written in *twelve-tone technique, paratonal structures become basic to the overall form (Lyric Suite for string quartet; **Lulu*), and in the Violin Concerto, these structures even include a strongly tonal basis (G minor–B♭ major). Such explorations were not followed up by other composers until relatively recently, when George Perle and a few others achieved a twelve-tone system that is fundamentally harmonic in nature but not serial.

For earlier views of the theory of harmony, see the writers cited under Theory. Pivotal figures are Johannes Lippius (1585–1612) and Jean-Philippe Rameau (1683–1764).

Bibl.: Heinrich Schenker, *Harmony,* ed. Oswald Jonas, trans. Elisabeth Mann Borgese (Chicago: U of Chicago Pr, 1954). William Russo, *Jazz Composition and Orchestration*

(Chicago: U of Chicago Pr, 1968). Arnold Schoenberg, *Structural Functions of Harmony,* rev. ed., ed. Leonard Stein (New York: Norton, 1969). George Perle, *Twelve-Tone Tonality* (Berkeley and Los Angeles: U of Cal Pr, 1977). Walter Piston, *Harmony,* 5th ed., rev. Mark DeVoto (New York: Norton, 1987). Arnold Schoenberg, *Theory of Harmony,* trans. Roy E. Carter (Berkeley and Los Angeles: U of Cal Pr, 1978). See also Theory. M.DEV.

Harmony of the spheres. A Pythagorean belief that the distances between the earth and celestial bodies visible with the naked eye, as well as the speeds at which these bodies rotated around the earth, were related to one another according to the same numerical ratios that characterized the notes of the diatonic scale. The model for this belief occurs in Plato's *Timaeus* (35Aff.), where God composes the World-Soul by inserting *arithmetic and harmonic means in two continuous geometric proportions, one duple and one triple. Writers of late antiquity found this proposition, categorized as *musica mundana* by Boethius (*De musica* i.2), enticing along with the pictorial Myth of Er (*Republic* 616Bff.), though Aristotle (in *De caelo*) had rejected the view that actual sounds were produced. One pairing of notes with celestial bodies is the following [see also Greece I, 3 (i)]: Nete synemmenon, Moon; Paranete synemmenon, Mercury; Trite synemmenon, Venus; Mese, Sun; Lichanos meson, Mars; Parhypate meson, Jupiter; Hypate meson, Saturn. The harmony of the spheres found a late proponent in the astronomer Johannes Kepler (*Harmonices mundi,* 1619). See also *Musica.*

Bibl.: Walter Burkert, *Lore and Science in Ancient Pythagoreanism,* trans. E. L. Minar, Jr. (Cambridge, Mass: Harvard U Pr, 1972). Hans Schavernoch, *Die Harmonie der Sphären: Die Geschichte der Idee des Welteneinklangs und der Seeleneinstimmung* (Freiburg/Munich: K. Alber, 1981). A.B.

Harold en Italie [Fr., Harold in Italy]. A program symphony in four movements (after portions of Byron's *Childe Harold*) by Berlioz, op. 16 (1834), composed at Paganini's request for a work that would feature his newly acquired Stradivarius viola. Paganini never performed the work because the viola part was not sufficiently prominent.

Harp [Fr. *harpe;* Ger. *Harfe;* It., Sp. *arpa*]. A chordophone in which the plane of the strings is perpendicular to the soundboard. Triangular in shape, all harps have three basic structural elements, a resonator, a neck, and strings. Some have a forepillar or column. The resonator is topped with a soundboard and string holder. Strings are attached to the neck directly with special knots, or indirectly through tuning pegs (usually movable). Buzzing mechanisms, attached near either end of the string on the neck or the soundboard, and activated by the plucked string, were used on Renaissance European harps and are found today on most African harps. Harps have from one to 47 strings. Tunings are pentatonic, tetratonic, heptatonic (including diatonic), or chromatic. Chromaticizing mechanisms range from manually operated hooks to complex pedal-activated systems. Strings are usually plucked, but may be strummed, struck by hand or with a plectrum, or slid upon. The resonator may also be used as a percussion instrument and struck by fingers, hand, or hooked rattles. The harp may be played with a single finger, with the thumb of one hand and the thumb and forefinger of the other, and with the thumb and first three fingers of both hands. The little fingers are usually not used.

I. *Double-action harp.* The modern Western concert harp has 47 strings, 7 per octave, from C_1 to g''''. Each string (except C_1 and D_1) can be raised two semitones (double action) using a pedal-activated system. First patented by Sébastien Érard in 1810, the double action made the harp into an equal-tempered chromatic instrument.

1. Construction. The triangular frame consists of a neck at the top (about 1.1 m. long) and a slanting resonator or body (1.7 m. long) connected by an upright column (1.85 m. or about 6 ft. long); it is made of maple, beech, walnut, spruce, or ash. The strings are threaded through the soundboard and wound around tuning pegs on the neck. The lowest 12 strings are usually wound wire; the rest are gut or nylon. The C and F strings are made in different colors from the rest to orient the player.

At the foot or base of the harp are seven pedals, each with three positions. These allow each diatonic pitch to be played flat, natural, or sharp. From left to right, D, C, and B pedals are on the left side, with E, F, G, and A on the right. When a pedal is depressed, all strings of the same note-name are changed in all octaves. With pedals in flat or uppermost position, each string is free to vibrate over its entire sounding length. When the pedals are depressed to the natural or middle position, forks in the upper of two rows rotate to tighten and shorten the strings, raising their pitch a semitone. When the pedals are depressed to the sharp or lowest position, the lower forks act in a similar way, raising the pitch of the strings a second semitone.

2. Performance techniques and notation. Harpists balance the harp on the edge of its base, resting the upper back of the resonator on their right shoulder. They extend their arms around the resonator and play with the thumb and first three fingers of each hand. The right hand usually plays the higher strings, the left hand the lower. As a result, basic harp notation is similar to keyboard notation except that the fingering of the right hand is inverse, and the little fingers are not used. Strings are usually plucked at mid-length or near the soundboard, the latter producing a guitarlike timbre. A glissando (also termed *glissé* and *sdrucciolando*) is produced by strumming across the strings with the fleshy part of the fingers or thumb. Pedals can be set for a particular glissando scale or chord, eliminating all dissonances or extraneous tones with enharmonics. *Harmonics, often played by placing the heel of the hand lightly against the midpoint of the string

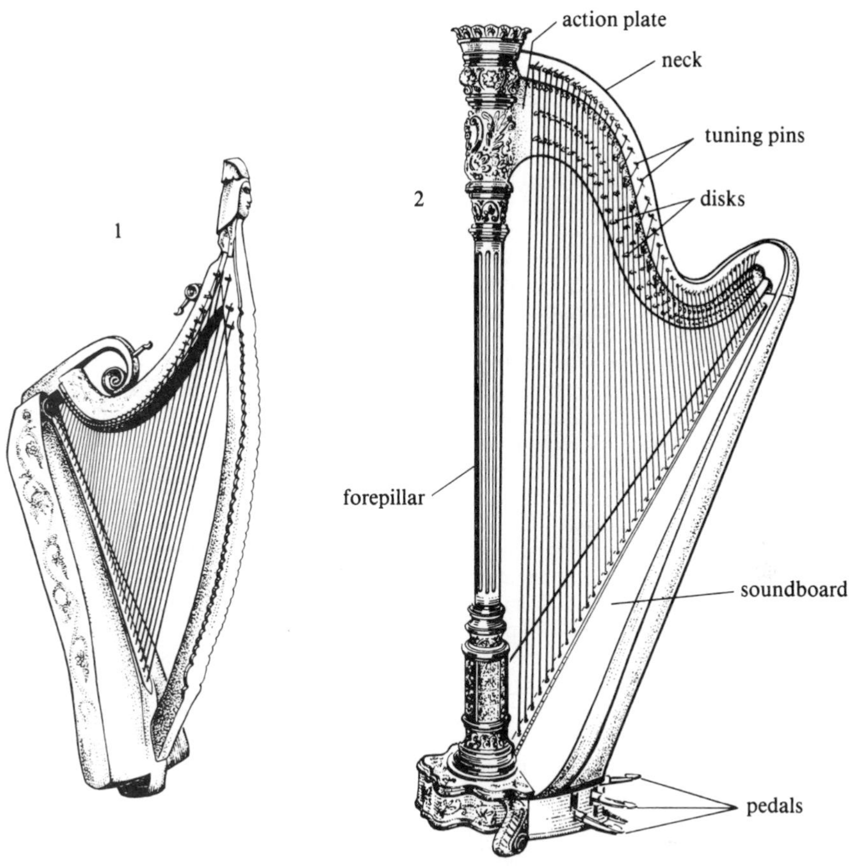

1. Irish harp. 2. Orchestral harp.

while plucking above with the thumb, are a regular feature of harp technique. Numerous modern harp techniques have been developed and a standard notational system devised for them (Inglefield and Neill, 1984).

3. Repertory. There is comparatively little music identified as specifically for harp that predates the double-action harp of 1810. Although the harp was played in the Middle Ages and Renaissance, primarily as a solo instrument but also in ensembles, the earliest extant source is "Tiento IX para harpa u organo" from *Tres libros de musica en cifra para vihuela* (1546) by Alonso Mudarra. Pieces for "keyboard, harp, or lute" were typical of this period in Spain (Luis Venegas de Henestrosa, 1557; Antonio de Cabezón, 1578). There are a few works for harp among the keyboard compositions of the Neapolitan composers Ascanio Mayone (ca. 1565–1627) and Giovanni Maria Trabaci (ca. 1575–1647). The harp appears to have entered the orchestra through opera, notably in Monteverdi's *Orfeo* (1607). Works for solo harp were composed by Jean-Baptiste Krumpholtz (1742–90), Jan Ladislav Dussek (1760–1812), Marie-Martin Marcel Marin (1769–1861), and Louis Spohr (1784–1859). A few works for the instrument were left by Handel (*Esther,* 1720), Gluck (*Orfeo,* 1762), Haydn (*Orfeo,* 1791), Mozart (Concerto for Flute and Harp K. 299/297c), and Beethoven (*Prometheus,* 1801). In the 19th century, the harp's new chromatic capabilities stimulated composition for the instrument in all genres. Most works for solo harp were composed by virtuosos such as Elias Parish Alvars (1808–49), but the harp was also employed as a solo instrument and in ensembles by Berlioz, Liszt, Wagner (*Das Rheingold,* which calls for seven harps), Puccini, Richard Strauss, Saint-Saëns, Debussy, and Ravel among many others. In the 20th century, experimentation with the harp's timbre and with a variety of sound effects resulted in new performance techniques. These are called for in works by Berio, Ginastera, Henze, and Holliger. Harpists, such as Carlos Salzedo, Marcel Grandjany, and Nicanor Zabaleta, have also composed and arranged demanding solo works.

II. *History and distribution.* The harp is an ancient and widely distributed instrument, and its usage ranges from religious ritual to pure entertainment and from solo to ensemble music to accompaniment played by singers of ballads and epic poetry. In the ancient world, solo harpists were usually men, ensemble harpists often women. In the Western world, professional harpists were men until the late 19th century; women took up the harp as a parlor instrument probably in the 17th century. Today, women harpists are still rare in African and Latin American folk traditions.

1. The East. The oldest extant harp, found at Ur in Sumer, dates from ca. 2600 B.C.E. and was already an elegant, sophisticated instrument. Depictions of harps from the same period have been found in the Cyclades and in Egypt, where they existed in a variety of forms and sizes for nearly 2,000 years. The harp appears in Babylonian art beginning in the second millennium B.C.E. and in Assyrian art of the first millennium B.C.E. It figures in Central Asian and Indian iconography from the 2nd century B.C.E. to the Persian and Moghul miniature paintings of the 13th–17th centuries. One type of Indian harp appears in Javanese stone carvings from the 9th century C.E. The harp spread eastward to China during the Han Dynasty (206 B.C.E.–221 C.E.) and on to Korea and to Japan, which possesses the sole extant ancient Chinese harp. The last depiction of a harp in Far Eastern iconography dates from about the 10th century. During this same period it appeared among the Georgians of the Caucasus and the Voguls and Ostyaks of Siberia, continuing in use among them at least into the 1930s. Only three traditions are still practiced in Asia. Two of them, the Burmese Buddhist royal court tradition [see *Saùng-gauk*] and that of the Pardhan epic singer-harpists in central India, share the common ancestry of harps first depicted in Indian iconography in the 2nd century B.C.E. In the third, which is practiced by the Karen of Burma near the Thai border, a different form of harp serves as a young man's courting instrument,

2. The West. Presumed to have moved westward from Egypt in ancient times, and like Egyptian harps in structure, African harps are still used by nearly 50 distinct musical cultures. The harp is represented on vases in Greece and Italy from the 6th to the 4th century B.C.E. It first appears in medieval Europe in illuminated manuscripts and carvings from the 8th to the 10th century. The oldest extant single-rank European harp is from 14th-century Ireland. Related types, also usually tuned to a diatonic scale, are still manufactured and used in Ireland [see Irish harp], Latin America, and the Philippines. They were introduced to the last two regions by Spaniards in the 16th–18th centuries. Many regional styles of harp have emerged in Latin America, and those of Mexico, Venezuela, and Paraguay have attained international renown. In the U.S., the single-rank remains popular because of a folk-harp revival and renewed interest in medieval and Renaissance music.

(i) Harps with two and three ranks of strings. Harps with two parallel rows or ranks of strings *(arpa doppia),* one diatonic, the other with some chromatic tones, were developed in Europe in the 16th century. These harps made possible the first published orchestral use of the harp, in Monteverdi's *Orfeo* (1607). Some attempts at chromatic harps made in the 19th century were not accepted. These had two ranks of strings that crossed at midpoint. One rank corresponded to the white keys of the piano, the other to the black.

Very successful was the chromatic harp called a triple harp, with three parallel rows of strings. The outer two are diatonic; the inner, reachable by either hand, is chromatic. In the early 17th century, a triple harp nearly 2 m. tall quickly became a favorite, starting in Italy. In Wales it is still in limited use. Harps on the Continent were balanced on the right shoulder and had gut strings played with the fleshy part of the fingertips, the left hand playing the bass strings. British harps were balanced on the left shoulder and had wire strings played with the fingernails, the right hand playing the bass strings.

(ii) Hook harps. In late 17th-century Germany, manually operated metal hooks were inserted in the neck below the tuning pegs to raise each string a semitone. In the early 19th century, John Egan added these to Irish harps, some of which are still made in this way, as are the "Troubadour" harps of Lyon and Healy.

(iii) Single-action harps. About 1720, Jakob Hockbrucher, a Bavarian, invented a five-pedal (C, D, F, G, A) and later a seven-pedal mechanism to activate the hooks and raise all the strings a semitone. In 1792, Sébastien Érard of London replaced the hooks with the type of brass fork still in use.

(iv) Double-action harps. In 1782, the Cousineau family of harpmakers in Paris added a second row of pedals to raise the pitches of the strings a second semitone. But the 14 pedals proved cumbersome. Érard's 1810 patent established the basis for the present double-action harp. In the U.S., two firms, both in Chicago, have made harps: Lyon and Healy (1889–) and the Rudolph Wurlitzer Company (1909–36).

See also Angle harp, Arched harp, Frame harp.

Bibl.: Pierre Érard, *The Harp in Its Present Improved State Compared with the Original Pedal Harp* (London, 1821; R: Geneva: Minkoff, 1980). Théodore Labarre, *Méthode complète pour la harpe* (Paris, 1844). *The Lyon and Healy Harp Catalogue* (Chicago: Lyon & Healy, 1897; facs., 1979). Carlos Salzedo, *Modern Study of the Harp* (New York: G Schirmer, 1921). Marcelle Duchesne-Guillemin, "La harpe en Asie occidentale ancienne," *Revue d'assyriologie* 34 (1937): 29–41. Armas Otto Väisänen, "Die obugrische Harfe," *Finnisch-ugrische Forschungen* 24 (1937): 127–53. Claudie Marcel-Dubois, *Les instruments de musique de l'Inde ancienne* (Paris: Presses universitaires de France, 1941). Hans Hickmann, "Les harpes de l'Égypte pharaonique: Essai d'une nouvelle classification," *Bulletin de l'Institut d'Égypte* 35 (1952–53): 309–76a. Roslyn Rensch, *The Harp: Its History, Technique, and Repertoire* (New York: Praeger, 1969). Hans Joachim Zingel, *Lexikon der Harfe* (Laaber: Laaber Verlag H Müller-Buscher, 1977). Sue Carole De Vale, "Prolegomena to a Study of Harp and Voice Sounds in Uganda: A Graphic System for the Notation of Texture," *Selected Reports in Ethnomusicology* 5 (1984): 285–315.

Ruth K. Inglefield and Lou Anne Neill, *Writing for the Pedal Harp* (Berkeley and Los Angeles: U of Cal Pr, 1984). John M. Schechter, "The Diatonic Harp in Ecuador: Historical Background and Modern Traditions," *JAMIS* 10 (1984): 97–118, 11 (1985). Roderic Knight, "The Harp in India Today," *Ethno* 29 (1985): 9–28. S.C.D.V.

Harp lute. Any of a series of instruments invented and produced beginning in 1798 by Edward Light of London. They combine a triangular harp body with a guitar neck, the plane of the strings being parallel to the belly. The harp guitar was first, with 8 strings tuned A♭ B♭ e♭ g b♭ e♭′ g′ b♭′ and notated a major sixth higher. The harp lute guitar followed about two years later. It has a theorbolike pegbox and 11 strings. The harp lute proper (ca. 1810), with neoclassic shiny black lacquer and gold leaf decoration, has 11 or 12 strings supported by a harplike neck and carved pillar. Only a few of its strings pass over a fingerboard. Charles Wheatstone's Regency harp lute (tuned, unlike Light's instruments, as it is notated) is one of several related instruments that followed. Light's British harp lute of 1816 incorporates "ditals," devices operated by the fingers for raising the pitch of the open strings, and this led to the dital harp of 1819, in which the number of strings was increased to as many as 20. R.L.

Harp Quartet. Popular name for Beethoven's String Quartet in E♭ major op. 74 (1809), so called because of several pizzicato arpeggios in the first movement.

Harpsichord [Fr. *clavecin;* Ger. *Cembalo, Kielflügel, Clavicimbel;* It. *clavicembalo;* Sp. *clavicémbalo, clavecín*]. A stringed keyboard instrument in use from the 15th through 18th century and revived since the 1880s.

I. *Construction.* The harpsichord is similar in shape to the modern grand piano, the strings being roughly parallel to the long side of the case. Each string is plucked by a quill plectrum mounted in the pivoted tongue of a fork-shaped jack that stands at the rear end of the key lever. Depressing the key raises the jack until the horizontally projecting plectrum plucks the string. When the key is released, the contact of the descending plectrum with the string causes the tongue to rotate backward on its pivot. As the jack continues to fall, the plectrum is tilted upward and back until its point passes below the string. A spring (of boar bristle, brass wire, or plastic) mounted at the rear of the jack then returns the tongue to its original position, so that the jack is again ready to pluck. A cloth damper is inserted into a slot sawed in one tine of the forked jack, its bottom edge just above the level of the plectrum. When the key is at rest, the damper touches the string, but the slightest depression of the key raises the damper, leaving the string free to vibrate. Thus a harpsichord string, like an organ pipe, can continue sounding only so long as the player holds a key down.

Each rank of jacks is carried in a pair of mortised battens mounted vertically over one another. The lower batten or guide is fixed, but the upper slide or register is movable, usually by means of stop levers located above the keyboard(s) or at the sides of the wrestplank. Some harpsichords, particularly Italian models, have so-called box slides, combining lower guide and slide in one assembly that moves integrally. In many Flemish harpsichords, registers extending through the cheekpiece can be moved in or out directly. Thus each rank of jacks can be moved slightly toward or away from its choir of strings, engaging or disengaging the plectra. In this way, stops or ranks of jacks can be silenced or added to the ensemble.

Harpsichord with two manuals.

The typical 18th-century harpsichord of northern Europe has three choirs of strings, two tuned to 8′ pitch and one an octave higher at 4′ pitch [see Foot]. (Very rarely in late German harpsichords, a fourth choir at 16′ might be added.) Such a harpsichord ordinarily has three ranks of jacks, one for each choir. Frequently there are two keyboards, the upper sounding one 8′ stop and the lower the other 8′ stop and the 4′ stop. The upper manual normally can be coupled to the lower, making all three stops available from the latter.

Three choirs of strings are used singly or in various combinations to provide variations in loudness and timbre. The more nasal sound of a string plucked near one end is noticeable in the upper manual or front 8′ stop of the typical harpsichord. It contrasts with the darker sound of the center-plucked lower manual or back 8′. Sometimes an alternative rank of jacks plucks the upper manual choir of 8′ strings at its extreme end

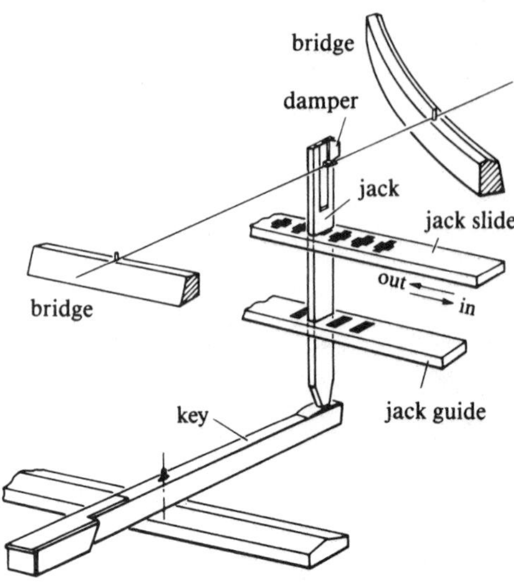

Harpsichord mechanism.

to produce an even more nasal timbre (lute stop). Buff leather pads mounted on a sliding batten can be used to damp one choir of 8′ strings partially to give a harplike effect (buff stop).

The *virginal is a relatively small harpsichord with a case that is rectangular or, if the acoustically inessential rear corners are eliminated, in the form of an irregular polygon. It has a single set of strings running roughly perpendicular to the key levers. Other forms are the *spinet and the clavicytherium, which is upright. See also Arpicordo, Lute harpsichord, and Pedal harpsichord.

During the first years of the harpsichord's modern revival, there was a tendency to employ concepts of design and aesthetic more germane to the piano or organ than to the harpsichord itself. Thus many revival harpsichords did not resemble their antique prototypes in the most essential details. The capacity of the harpsichord to vary timbre was exploited more fully than in earlier centuries, and for many years nearly all harpsichords heard in concert halls were provided with pedals to change the stops. The 16′ stop was for years almost universally fitted to concert instruments, despite the fact that historically it was found only in Germany during the 18th century, and even there only occasionally. Such modernized instruments were of far heavier construction than the early ones, with longer treble strings and shorter bass strings, the latter often overspun like those of the piano. Plectra were of leather instead of the quill almost invariably used in earlier times. All these changes tended to produce a more sustained, but not necessarily stronger tone of less harmonic complexity than is typical of antique instruments.

Since about 1950, makers have increasingly returned to historical principles of construction. Almost all harpsichords now being made closely resemble those for which Renaissance and Baroque keyboard music was composed. Such instruments are almost invariably preferred because they enable the player to solve many of the performance problems that seemed insurmountable to harpsichordists of the first half of the 20th century. Except in some contemporary works composed expressly for it, the modern harpsichord has been effectively replaced by reproductions of antique instruments used in the performance of the historical repertory.

Throughout the Baroque period, the harpsichord was the chief instrument for the realization of *thoroughbass accompaniment, almost always in chamber music and occasionally in church music, where it replaced the organ. Its ability to blend with other instruments while providing a slight rhythmic impulse at the moment of *ictus* makes it unsurpassed for the purpose. Although the harpsichord cannot produce significant dynamic gradations of sound by lighter or heavier touch, this limitation is not felt as such in the context of Baroque style. For contrapuntal music it is definitely superior to the modern piano, since the middle and lower parts of a composition stand out with clarity.

II. *History.* Although the early history of the harpsichord is obscure, the preponderance of evidence about the instrument before 1500 suggests that its early development took place mainly north of the Alps. The first harpsichords were probably made near the end of the 14th century. A document of 1397 refers to Hermann Poll, a Viennese scholar, as the inventor of the *clavicembalum,* but he might have developed just a particular improved form of the instrument. A drawing of the harpsichord in plan view and several suggested mechanisms for jacks with a discussion of their operation are contained in the mid-15th-century manuscript of Henri Arnaut de Zwolle, a member of the retinue of the Duke of Burgundy. Other 15th-century representations are French, German, English, Istrian, Spanish, and Swedish in origin (Bowles, 1977), and another description was written about 1460 by Paulus Paulirinus of Prague. The earliest surviving harpsichord is a south German upright instrument (clavicytherium) datable to the end of the 15th century, in the Royal College of Music in London. The light construction of this instrument anticipates features seen in 16th-century harpsichords throughout Europe.

By the early 16th century there was a distinct school of harpsichord making in Italy. The oldest surviving Italian harpsichord, at the Accademia Chigiana in Siena, was made in Tuscany and signed by its maker, Vincentius, on 18 September 1515. In their style of construction Italian harpsichords from this date until late in the 18th century generally resemble Vincentius's instrument very closely. Their construction was very light, of unfinished cypress or maple ornamented by elegant moldings. The elongated and deeply incurved harpsichords were enclosed in outer boxes ornamented in the prevailing fashion. In the 16th century, large harpsichords usually had a compass of four and a half octaves, C to f‴, with a *short octave in the bass, and two stops, one at 8′ and one at 4′ pitch. Some of these might have been tuned about a fourth below modern pitch. Smaller harpsichords often had a C (short octave) to c‴ compass and a single set of strings at normal 8′ pitch. After about 1600, Italian harpsichords were usually made with two 8′ stops, and most earlier instruments were altered to have this disposition. The lack of development of the Italian type of harpsichord, almost invariably with only a single manual, can perhaps be explained by the Italian emphasis on its role as a continuo instrument. The transparent but rhythmically emphatic tone of the Italian instrument, with its two 8′ stops sounding together, could hardly be improved in this context.

North of the Alps, a harpsichord of 1537 by Hans Müller of Leipzig (now in Rome) and two virginals made in Antwerp by Joes Karest in 1548 and 1550 (now in Brussels and Rome), lightly constructed and decorated with moldings, are similar in style to the 15th-century upright harpsichord in London and to Italian instruments. The Müller harpsichord, however, has three stops, which provide a great variety of tone color, including the nasal sound of strings plucked close to their ends. In Antwerp, which by the 1540s was the major northern European center of harpsichord making, a new style of harpsichord was developed between about 1565 and 1580. Much heavier in construction than earlier instruments, this Flemish type, produced in Antwerp by four generations of the Ruckers family from 1579 to about 1680, subsequently influenced harpsichord making throughout most of northern Europe. Ruckers harpsichords were invariably made with two stops, one 8′ and one 4′; there was also a buff stop to modify the 8′ strings, and this was divided so it could be used separately in the bass or treble. Single-manual instruments usually had a compass of C (short octave) to c‴. Two-manual harpsichords were also made, but the second keyboard, which duplicated the resources of the first, sounded a fourth lower in pitch and was merely a transposition device.

The Flemish school exerted a strong influence on the development of indigenous traditions of harpsichord making in Germany, England, and France. Instruments from Antwerp were enlarged and rebuilt, in France especially, throughout the 18th century.

The true two-manual harpsichord, in which the two keyboards could be used simultaneously or in rapid alternation, was developed in France about 1640. The lower keyboard had the traditional 8′ and 4′ stops, while the upper had a single 8′. There was also a coupler to make the upper 8′ stop playable on the lower keyboard, so that all three stops could sound together. English and Flemish makers of the 18th century commonly provided their upper manuals with a close-plucking nasal register (lute stop). German makers sometimes included a 16′ stop on the lower manual and a nasal on the upper. Late 18th-century expressive devices included the French *peau de buffle,* a very soft 8′ stop resembling the sound of the early piano, and on English harpsichords, machine stops activated by pedals for instant wholesale registration changes and swell mechanisms that opened louvered shutters over the strings or raised a flap of the lid of a half-closed harpsichord. Attempts were even made to combine the piano and harpsichord in one instrument. But all these devices could not prevent the harpsichord's gradual displacement by the piano in the late 18th century. Continued references to *cembalo,* as in the autograph scores of Mozart's piano concertos or on the original editions of Beethoven's piano sonatas, are only evidence of conventional usage rather than of musical practice. In the latter case, publishers' marketing strategies may also have played a part.

Bibl.: Frank Hubbard, *Three Centuries of Harpsichord Making* (Cambridge, Mass.: Harvard U Pr, 1965). Raymond Russell, *The Harpsichord and Clavichord: An Introductory Study,* 2nd ed. rev. Howard Schott (London: Faber, 1973). Donald H. Boalch, *Makers of the Harpsichord and Clavichord, 1440–1840,* 3rd ed., rev. Charles Mould (Oxford: Clarendon Pr, 1995). Howard Schott, "The Harpsichord Revival," *EM* 2 (1974): 85–95. Edmund A. Bowles, "A Checklist of 15th-Century Representations of Stringed Instruments," *Keyboard Instruments: Studies in Keyboard Organology, 1500–1800,* 2nd ed., rev. and enl. Edwin M. Ripin (New York: Dover, 1977): 11–17, plates 1–31a. Howard Schott, *Playing the Harpsichord,* 3rd ed. (New York: St Martin's, 1979). Grant O'Brien, *Ruckers: A Harpsichord and Virginal Building Tradition* (Cambridge: Cambridge U Pr, 1990). John Koster, "Toward a History of the Earliest Harpsichords," *600 Jahr Cembalobau in Österreich,* ed. Alfons Huber (Tutzing: Hans Schneider, 2002).

F.H. REV. H.S., J.Ko.

Harp stop. On the harpsichord, pads of buff leather or other absorbent material mounted on a sliding batten that can be brought into contact with one choir of strings, damping it slightly so as to produce a harplike effect; also buff stop.

Harp way. One of several 17th-century tunings of the lyra *viol.

Hastig [Ger.]. Hurried.

Ḥatzotzerot [Heb., pl.]. Small gold or silver trumpets of ancient Israel, similar to the Greek *salpinx* and the Roman **tuba.* They are mentioned in the Bible and the Dead Sea Scrolls as signaling or ceremonial instruments.

Haupt [Ger.]. Head, principal.

Hauptsatz [Ger.]. The first theme or section in *sonata form. See also *Satz.*

Hauptstimme [Ger.]. (1) The principal or leading part, often the soprano. (2) In *twelve-tone and other nontonal works by Schoenberg, Berg, and others, a voice or part of particular importance, often indicated by brackets formed from the letter H.

Haupttonart [Ger.]. The principal key of a tonal work.

Hauptwerk [Ger.]. The main division of a German organ, based on a Principal stop of 16′ or 8′ pitch.

Hausmusik [Ger.]. Music for informal performance by amateurs in the home. The term dates from the 17th century. In the 20th, it has been associated with **Gebrauchsmusik.*

Hausse [Fr.]. *Frog; *à la hausse,* an instruction to bow near the frog.

Haut, haute [Fr.]. (1) High, e.g., in pitch. (2) [It., Lat., Sp. *alta*]. In the late Middle Ages and Renaissance, instruments or music that was loud rather than soft *(bas, basse).* To the former group belonged the trumpet and especially the *shawm and the *sackbut, which often formed an ensemble [see *Alta* (2), *Basse danse*], and their music; to the latter belonged stringed instruments (both plucked and bowed), the *recorder, and the *crumhorn, and their music.

Hautbois, hautboy [Fr.]. (1) *Oboe. (2) An organ reed stop with half-length resonators, sometimes flared at the top.

Haut-dessus [Fr.]. High treble or soprano, especially the higher of two treble parts, the lower being the *bas-dessus.*

Haute-contre [Fr., fr. Lat. **contratenor altus*]. In France in the late 18th and early 19th centuries, a male *alto or high tenor who sang in full voice rather than *falsetto, except perhaps in the highest register; also an alto part in an instrumental ensemble.

Hawaii. See Oceania and Australia IV.

Hawaiian guitar. See Steel guitar.

Haydn Quartets. Popular name for the six quartets by Mozart K. 387, 421, 428, 458, 464, and 465, composed in the years 1782–85 and dedicated to Haydn.

Haydn Variations. A set of eight variations and a finale by Brahms on a theme entitled "St. Anthony's Chorale," the second movement of a divertimento for winds Hob. II:46*, probably not by Haydn. Brahms's work was composed in 1873 and published in two versions: one for orchestra (op. 56a) and one for two pianos (op. 56b).

Haye, hay, hey, heye [Eng.; perhaps fr. Fr. *haie*]. A dance that Thoinot Arbeau (*Orchésographie,* 1588) calls a type of **branle.* It is a group dance using simple steps and one in which rows of dancers interweave in a serpentine fashion. Its style is characteristic of peasant dances from many countries through the ages. It was well known in Elizabethan England. In the 17th century, it was identified with the **canarie.* John Playford's *Musick's Hand-Maid* of 1678 includes an air entitled "The Canaries or the Hay." L.H.M.

Hb. [Fr.]. Abbr. for *hautbois,* oboe.

Head. In jazz, the melody or theme as distinct from the chord progression, which is known as the *changes.

Head arrangement. A collaboratively created, memorized composition for jazz ensemble. The early *big bands of Duke Ellington, Bennie Moten, and Count Basie, among others, performed such arrangements. B.K.

Head-motive. A motive occurring at the beginning of each of the movements of a work; also *motto. The term is especially applied to the *cyclic Masses of the 15th century and later.

Head voice. The higher register of the voice, as compared with chest voice. See Register, Voice.

Heavy metal. A style of rock featuring a heavy beat, mutated blues inflections, distorted electric guitar, high-decibel volume level, and spectacular theatrics; emerged in England at the end of the 1960s. Preceded by such hard-rocking tracks as the Kinks' "You Really Got Me" (1964) and Jimi Hendrix's "Purple Haze" (1967), the genre came into its own with bands such as Led Zeppelin *(Led Zeppelin II)* and Black Sabbath *(Paranoid),* and eventually spread internationally as it gained worldwide popularity. The emphasis on visual spectacle is apparent with such American bands as Kiss and Alice Cooper, and many of heavy metal's guitarists feature a virtuosic playing style that is equally spectacular (Eddie Van Halen, Yngwie Malmsteen). The open-fifth "power chord" of the distorted electric guitar and an intense, high-pitched vocal style are other signature features. Substyles include glam metal (Poison), death metal (Cannibal Corpse), and thrash (Metallica).

Bibl.: Robert Walser, *Running with the Devil: Power, Gender, and Madness in Heavy Metal Music* (Hanover, N.H.: U Pr of New England, 1993). M.K.

Hebrew music. See Jewish music.

Hebriden, Die, or **Fingals Höhle** [Ger., The Hebrides, or Fingal's Cave]. A concert overture by Mendelssohn, op. 26 (1830, revised in 1832). Originally called *Die einsame Insel* (The Lonely Island), it was inspired by a visit to the famous cave in Scotland during his first tour through the British Isles in 1829.

Heckelclarina [Ger. *Heckelklarina*]. A conical-bore, single-reed wind instrument devised in 1890 by the firm of Wilhelm Heckel of Biebrich to play the part of the shepherd's pipe in Wagner's *Tristan und Isolde* (1857–59). It is not certain if it was actually ever constructed.

Heckelphonclarinet. A wooden, conical-bore, single-reed wind instrument made in 1907 by the firm of Wilhelm Heckel of Biebrich.

Heckelphone [Ger. *Heckelphon*]. A wooden, conical-bore, double-reed woodwind instrument invented in 1904 by the firm of Wilhelm Heckel of Biebrich. It is similar to the bass (or barytone) oboe in range and construction, but it has a larger bore and produces a tone closer to that of the bassoon or saxophone than to the English-horn sound of the low oboes. The instrument has a bulb-shaped bell that is usually fitted with a floor support at the bottom, with the tone opening(s) moved to the side. The heckelphone was originally made in three sizes, but only the bass (pitched in C with range from A to g″) was much used. Works employing it include Richard Strauss's *Salome* (1905). See ill. under Reed. M.S.

Heftig [Ger.]. Violent, impetuous, passionate.

Heirmos [Gr., chain]. The opening model stanza in each *ōdē* of a Byzantine *kanōn* [see Byzantine chant]. All the remaining **troparia* in the *ōdē* are metrical and musical reproductions of the *heirmos*. In content it acts as a linking verse (hence, its name), joining together (1) the theme of the biblical canticle that the *ōdē* of the *kanōn* was originally designed to accompany and (2) the theme of commemoration of the day, which is developed in the *troparia* that follow. The musical book that collects all the *heirmoi* for a given repertory of *kanōns* is called a *Heirmologion* and is one of the principal types of source manuscript for the syllabic tradition of Byzantine chant. D.E.C.

Heiter [Ger.]. Serene, merry, cheerful.

Heldenleben, Ein [Ger., A Hero's Life]. An autobiographical symphonic poem by Richard Strauss, op. 40 (1897–98). It includes quotations of themes from other works by Strauss and depicts the composer's trials (e.g., hostile music critics) and triumphs.

Heldentenor [Ger., heroic tenor]. A tenor voice of considerable brilliance, power, and endurance, suitable for singing the roles of the heros in Wagner's operas, e.g., Tristan and Siegfried.

Helicon [Fr. *hélicon;* Ger. *Helikon;* It. *helicon, elicon;* Sp. *helicón*]. A circular brass instrument possibly first made in Russia about 1845. Ignaz Stowasser of Vienna made F, E♭, and BB♭ sizes in 1849. It was subsequently made in all sizes, sometimes with nonfunctional tubing, and was popular in European and American bands. Also called a cavalry horn, it rested on the left shoulder and under the right arm and could be played comfortably with one hand. A later instrument embodying this idea was John Philip Sousa's *sousaphone. R.E.E.

Hemidemisemiquaver. In British terminology, the sixty-fourth note. See Note.

Hemiola, hemiolia [Gr., Lat. *sesquialtera*]. The ratio 3:2. In terms of pitch, it is the ratio of the lengths of two strings that together sound a perfect fifth [see Interval]. In terms of rhythm, it refers to the use of three notes of equal value in the time normally occupied by two notes of equal value. In *mensural notation of the 14th century and later, it is often expressed with red notes if the prevailing notation is black, or black notes if the prevailing notation is white. Thus, three red semibreves each worth two minims could be substituted for two black semibreves each worth three minims. The resulting rhythm can be expressed in modern terms as a substitution of 3/2 for 6/4 or as two measures of 3/4 in which quarter notes are tied across the bar, as shown in the example.

6/4 𝅗𝅥. 𝅗𝅥. | 𝅗𝅥 𝅗𝅥 𝅗𝅥 | or 3/4 𝅗𝅥. | 𝅗𝅥. | 𝅗𝅥 ♩ | ♩ 𝅗𝅥 |

This rhythmic gesture is common in the music of 15th-century composers such as Dufay, is a characteristic feature of the French Baroque *courante and the Viennese *waltz, and occurs often in the music of Schumann and Brahms (e.g., the opening measures of the third symphonies of both composers). It is also common in some musics of Africa, Latin America, and the Near and Middle East.

Bibl.: Michael B. Collins, "The Performance of Sesquialtera and Hemiolia in the 16th Century," *JAMS* 17 (1964): 5–28.

Hemitonic [fr. Gr., Lat. *hemitonium,* semitone]. Characterized by or including semitones.

Heptachord. A collection of seven pitches, especially the diatonic *scale.

Herabstimmen [Ger.]. To tune down or lower the pitch, e.g., of a string.

Herabstrich [Ger.]. Down-bow. See Bowing (1).

Heraufstimmen [Ger.]. To tune upward or raise the pitch, e.g., of a string.

Heraufstrich [Ger.]. Up-bow. See Bowing (1).

Hermannus letters. Greek and Roman letters used by Hermannus Contractus (1013–54) to designate the interval between one pitch and the next in two didactic songs.

Hermeneutics. The study of musical meaning beyond verifiable facts. The practice of hermeneutics stems initially from biblical exegesis, but musical hermeneutics has come to signify a manner of interpretation that goes beyond grammar and mechanics. Its practice was established in the 19th century with the attempts by E. T. A. Hoffmann and others to hear narratives in instrumental music. Although derided by many as strictly extramusical, hermeneutics often seeks to explain otherwise inexplicable musical events and the way listeners might hear them. In recent years hermeneutic interpretations of music have blended into broader readings emphasizing philosophy, aesthetics, gender, nationalism, and other interdisciplinary approaches to interpretation.

Bibl.: Paul Ricoeur, *The Conflict of Interpretations: Essays in Hermeneutics,* ed. Don Ihde (Evanston: Northwestern U Pr, 1974). Carl Dahlhaus, "A Hermeneutic Model," *The Idea of Absolute Music,* trans. Roger Lustig (Chicago: U of Chicago Pr, 1989), pp. 42–57. Kurt Mueller-Vollmer, ed., *The Hermeneutics Reader: Texts of the German Tradition from the Enlightenment to the Present* (New York: Continuum, 1985). Edward A. Lippman, ed., *Musical Aesthetics: A Historical Reader,* vol. 2: *The Nineteenth Century* (New York: Pendragon, 1988); vol. 3: *The Twentieth Century* (1990). Lawrence Kramer, *Music as Cultural Practice, 1800–1900* (Berkeley: U of Cal Pr, 1990). Umberto Eco et al., *Interpretation and Overinterpretation,* ed. S. Collin (New York: Cambridge U Pr, 1992). Berthold Hoeckner, *Programming the Absolute: Nineteenth-Century German Music and the Hermeneutics of the Moment* (Princeton: Princeton U Pr, 2002).

R.M.

Hero's Life, A. See *Heldenleben, Ein.*

Herstrich [Ger.]. Down-bow. See Bowing (1).

Hertz [abbr. Hz.]. In *acoustics, a measure of frequency equal to one cycle per second and named after the German physicist Heinrich R. Hertz (1857–94).

Hervorgehoben [Ger.]. Prominent, emphasized.

Hervortretend [Ger.]. Brought out, prominent.

Herzlich [Ger.]. Heartfelt, affectionate.

Heses [Ger.]. B-double-flat. See Pitch names.

Hesitation waltz. See Boston dip waltz, Boston waltz.

Heterophony. The simultaneous statement, especially in improvised performance, of two or more different versions of what is essentially the same melody (as distinct from *polyphony). It often takes the form of a melody combined with an ornamented version of itself, the former sung and the latter played on an instrument. The technique is widely found in musics outside the tradition of Western art music, especially in East Asia, South Asia, Southeast Asia, and the Near and Middle East. The term was coined by Plato (*Laws,* vii.812D), but whether his use of it coincides with the modern use of the term described here remains in doubt.

Heure espagnole, L' [Fr., The Spanish Hour]. Opera in one act by Ravel (libretto by Franc-Nohain [pseud. of Maurice Le Grand] after his own comedy), produced in Paris in 1911. Setting: Toledo, Spain, in the 18th century.

Hexachord [fr. Gr., six string]. A collection of six pitches. Hexachords figure prominently in the history of *solmization and in twelve-tone theory. For their use in the latter, see Twelve-tone music.

Solmization by means of a system of hexachords, which prevailed in the 11th–16th centuries, was traditionally attributed to Guido of Arezzo, but none of

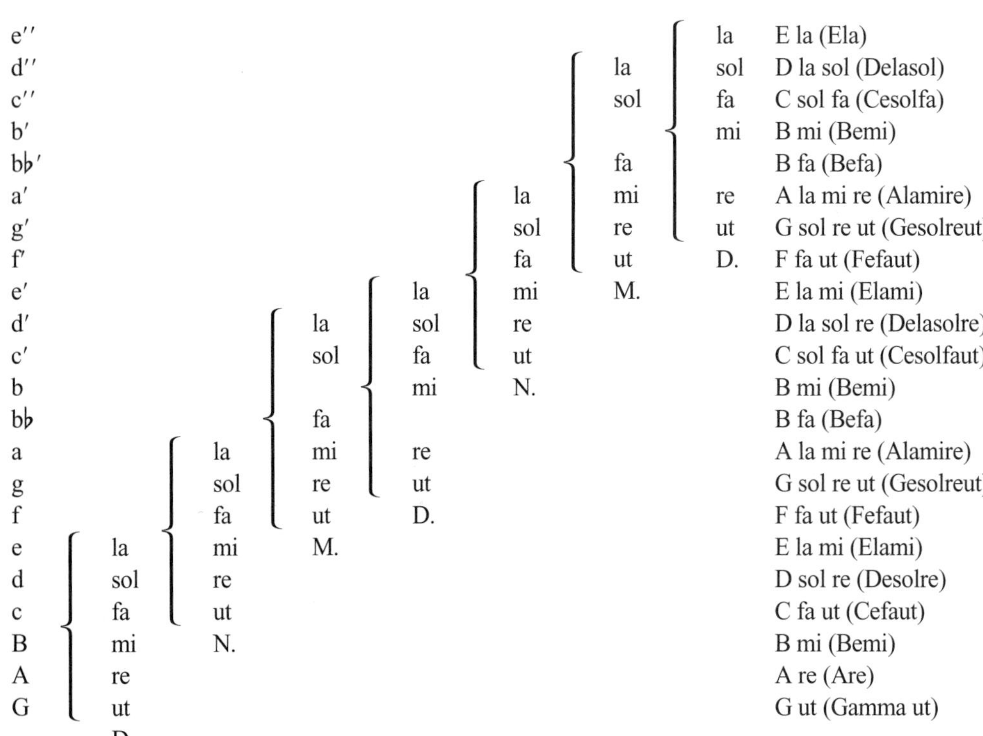

his extant writings gives a full acount of the topic. In the *Epistola de ignoto cantu* (ca. 1028–29), however, Guido did refer to the pitches of the hexachord with the six vocables *ut, re, mi, fa, sol, la,* the initial syllables of the first six lines of the hymn "Ut queant laxis" (*LU,* p. 1504), which begin on the pitches c d e f g a, respectively. The earliest known discussions of the hexachord system are those of the 11th-century anonymous commentary on Guido's *Micrologus,* Elias Salomo (ca. 1274), Jerome of Moravia (ca. 1300), and Engelbert of Admont (ca. 1325).

According to the "Guidonian" system, there were three main types of hexachord: those beginning on C's, F's, and G's. Each hexachord was built from the interval succession tone, tone, semitone, tone, tone, the six syllables being assigned to the six pitches in ascending order. The position of the semitone was critical, always occurring between the syllables *mi* and *fa.* Hexachords formed on C's (e.g., c d e f g a) were called natural hexachords *(hexachordum naturale);* those formed on G's (e.g., g a b♮ c′ d′ e′) were called hard hexachords *(hexachordum durum),* since they contain B♮ (hard b or *b durum,* written with a square-shaped b, the origin of the modern natural sign [see Accidental]); those on F's (e.g., f g a b♭ c′ d′) soft hexachords *(hexachordum molle),* since they contain a B♭ (soft b or *b molle,* written with a rounded b, the origin of the flat sign). Using these three types of hexachord, theorists described the *gamut from G to e″ as a complex of seven overlapping hexachords, as shown in the accompanying table (where D = *durum,* N = *naturale,* and M = *molle*). Pitches lying within the seven hexachords constituted *musica recta;* those lying outside were classed as **musica ficta.*

Each pitch of the gamut is identified by its pitch letter and the syllable or syllables corresponding to its position in one or more hexachords. Thus, middle C may be designated C *sol fa ut,* whereas C one octave below would be C *fa ut,* and C two octaves above that C *sol fa.* Where the same name occurs in two different octaves (e.g., G *sol re ut*), the two pitches are distinguished as high *(acutum)* or low *(grave).* In assigning single syllables to single pitches for purposes of singing, melodies that extend beyond the range of a single hexachord are accommodated by means of mutation, which allows free transfer from one hexachord to another by way of pitches common to both hexachords. Such pitches would have a solmization syllable in each hexachord. During the 15th century, increasing use of chromatic alteration prompted theorists to introduce hexachords starting on pitch classes other than C, F, and G. See Solmization, *Musica ficta.*

Hexameter. See Prosody.

Hey. See Haye.

Hichiriki [Jap.]. A small Japanese oboe with seven finger holes and two thumb holes, used in **gagaku* music. See ill. under East Asia.

Hidden fifths, octaves. See Parallel fifths, octaves.

Highland bagpipe [Gael. *pìob mhór*]. The *bagpipe of the Scottish highlands. It is mouth blown, with a double-reed *chanter and three single-reed *drones. The first secure documentation of the highland bagpipe is from the 16th century. Today it is considered the national instrument of Scotland. The classic musical genre of highland piping is the *pibroch.

Highlife. A type of popular song and dance music prominent especially in West Africa beginning in the 1930s. Associated with and taking its name from urban social life, it incorporates both African and Western instruments and musical idioms. It is most often in duple meter, featuring ostinato rhythmic and melodic figures.

Hi-hat. A pair of cymbals mounted horizontally on a stand and clashed by means of a pedal. It is a regular component of the *drum set used in jazz and popular music, having first appeared in 1927.

Hillbilly music. See Country and western music.

Hinsterbend [Ger.]. Dying away.

Hinstrich [Ger.]. Up-bow. See Bowing (1).

Hintersatz [Ger.]. The large mixture stop behind the facade Principal pipes of the Renaissance German organ; probably the remainder of the earlier **Blockwerk,* which had no sliders for any of its ranks.

Hip hop. While often used to refer to rap music, hip hop more properly denotes the practices of an entire subculture. The term was first coined in the mid-1970s by rapper Afrika Bambaataa as part of a string of vocables or nonsense syllables that he would use while improvising, or "free styling," in rap performances in the South Bronx area of New York City. The phrase quickly caught on with other rappers and became part of a "floating pool" of lyric phrases that were used in rap performances throughout the late 1970s. The term came to national attention in the fall of 1979 when it was featured in the very first line of the very first commercially issued rap recording, "Rapper's Delight" by Sugarhill Gang (Sugarhill Records).

Over time the term hip hop came to refer to the "B-boy" subculture that rap and *DJs were integral parts of. As such, hip hop came to encompass other forms of expressive culture, such as break dancing and "tagging" or "bombing," the style of graffiti art that developed alongside rap. While often simply consisting of highly stylized logos, insignias, or signatures that in one way or another identified the tagger, at its most complex, hip hop graffiti involved large-scale art works most commonly done with spray paint and would cover an entire subway car. Such activity was, of course, illegal and had to be done covertly at night in the subway yards and involved the risk of arrest or physical injury.

Break dancing was a highly athletic dance style involving spinning on the floor, body popping (the dancers isolate various body parts and muscles, moving them precisely, one after another, creating a rippling effect), and jerky, staccato, robotlike moves. Break dancing was commonly done by groups or gangs, known as crews, who would often engage in competitions with other crews. These competitions were similar to rap DJ battles; members of the two crews would perform their most impressive routines individually, the winning crew being decided by the response of the audience.

As is the case with any subculture, hip hop had its own sartorial style and argot. The former initially involved fade hair cuts, untied sneakers, conspicuous gold jewelry (most commonly heavy, overly large medallions on neck chains), and baseball caps worn sideways. The argot of hip hop introduced such words as *dis, def, yo, chill, wack, blunt,* and *fly* into mainstream American English. R.B.

Hirmos [Gr.]. See *Heirmos.*

His, hisis [Ger.]. B-sharp, B-double-sharp. See Pitch names.

Histoire du soldat, L' [Fr., The Soldier's Tale]. A play with music by Stravinsky (libretto by Charles-Ferdinand Ramuz), produced in Lausanne in 1918. The work combines a *ballet d'action* with a story told in dialogue by the characters and a narrator. The music consists of a number of distinct pieces, including "Marche," "Tango," "Valse," "Ragtime," "Petit Choral," and "Grand Choral," composed for an ensemble of clarinet, bassoon, cornet, trombone, violin, double bass, and percussion. Two suites of music from the work were arranged by the composer in 1919 and 1920, the first scored for piano, clarinet, and violin, the second for the original combination of instruments.

Historia [Lat.]. (1) A biblical story or a musical setting of such a story. The Passion story was among the favored texts for musical works among German composers of the 16th–18th centuries [see also Passion music]. Works of this type, by Heinrich Schütz and others, are closely related to the *oratorio. (2) See Rhymed Office.

History of music. The history of Western art music has traditionally been divided into periods adapted from other branches of history. This is in part because the discipline of musicology was established somewhat after related humanistic disciplines and in part because many historians of the 19th and 20th centuries believed that the history of music must necessarily follow the outlines of cultural history generally, each period in history expressing itself equally in all political, social, and cultural spheres. The principal periods so identified are (with approximate and oft-debated dates) the *Middle Ages (500–1430), *Renaissance (1430–1600), *Baroque (1600–1750), *Classical (1750–1820), and *Romantic (1820–1910). No comparable term has yet been widely adopted to describe the *twentieth century. (The music of classical antiquity is discussed in this dictionary under Greece and Rome.) Each of these terms and associated dates has posed considerable problems in the attempt to relate their inherited meanings to specifically musical materials. The dates have usually had to be placed somewhat later than those employed in the fields from which the terms were borrowed. And subperiods, sometimes defined in more specifically musical terms, have been identified to cope with the more unwieldy expanses of time that include radically different kinds of music. The terms nevertheless remain in use at least as conveniences. See also Musicology. D.M.R.

Hitch pin. On a stringed keyboard instrument, any of the pins to which the strings are affixed or around which they pass at the end opposite the tuning pins.

Hob. Abbr. for Anthony van Hoboken's *thematic catalog of the works of Haydn: *Joseph Haydn: Thematisch-bibliographisches Werkverzeichnis* (Mainz: B Schott, 1957–78).

Hoboe [Ger., obs.]. Oboe.

Höchst [Ger.]. In the highest degree.

Hocket [Lat. *hoquetatio, hoquetus, (h)ochetus;* Fr. *hocquet, hoquet;* It. *ochetti*]. In polyphony of the 13th and 14th centuries, a stylistic device or a self-contained composition characterized by the distribution of a melodic line between two voices in such a way that as one sounds the other is silent. As a device, it is first used in *conductus* [see Ex., from *Dic Christi veritas*] and *motets and later in Mass movements and certain of the vernacular forms, above all the **caccia* and the **chace.* As a genre, the hocket is intimately related to the discant **clausula,* its plainchant tenor arranged in modal patterns and ornamented by freely composed voices. What distinguishes it is the overlapping of these voices so that, to quote Johannes de Grocheo, "they continually cut each other off."

Although the genre is often mentioned by the theorists, only eleven examples are known to survive. Seven of these, five of which are based on the popular *In seculum* melisma and one each on *Neuma* and *Virgo,* are preserved in the Bamberg manuscript [see Sources 10]. The Montpellier manuscript [see Sources 9] has two of the *In seculum* pieces and one based on *Portare,* while the manuscript Paris, Bibliothèque nationale, lat. 11411, contains yet another composition on the same tenor, here designated *Sustine[re].*

All of these hockets are for three voices. A fragment of one for four voices has also been identified. Guillaume de Machaut (ca. 1300–77) wrote a single untexted example, the three-voiced *Hoquetus David.*

Several of the hockets in the Bamberg manuscript have identifying tags: *In seculum longum, breve, viellatoris,* and *d'Amiens.* Comparison of the first two shows the second to be a modal transmutation or rhythmic diminution of the first. The term *viellatoris,* thought by some to prove that the hocket was an instrumental genre, may indicate simply that the piece in question was written by a vielle player. More telling in this regard is the text, which is not laid out as for the chant, but copied, here as in other such compositions, at the beginning of the piece.

The hocket and the motet as genres are intertwined. For example, *In seculum longum* and *In seculum breve* reappear in the Montpellier manuscript (as nos. 2 and 3), each with a fourth, texted voice; Montpellier 137 (*RISM* Mo 128) is a French double motet, the tenor and the *motetus* of which correspond to the lower parts of *In seculum longum,* and the *triplum* of which is the same as the fourth voice of Montpellier 2.

In the 14th century, hocket became a prominent device in *isorhythmic motets, audibly signaling in the upper parts the less-noticeable repetition of the tenor rhythmic pattern *(talea).* It is also characteristic of the melismatic "Amen" section of the polyphonic *Glorias in the Mass.

Texture of the hocket type is prominent in the musics of some non-Western cultures and is especially characteristic of some African musics [see Africa].

Bibl.: William E. Dalglish, "The Hocket in Medieval Polyphony," *MQ* 55 (1969): 344–63. Ernest H. Sanders, "The Medieval Hocket in Practice and Theory," *MQ* 60 (1974): 246–56. William Dalglish, "The Origin of the Hocket," *JAMS* 31 (1978): 3–20. Peter Jeffery, "A Four-Part *In seculum* Hocket and a Mensural Sequence in an Unknown Fragment," *JAMS* 37 (1984): 1–48. Wolf Frobenius, "Hoquetus," *HMT* (1988). Juan Carlos Asensio Palacios, "Aproximacion al Hoquetus *In seculum* (quod quidam hispanus fecerat)," *Anuario musical: Revista de musicologia* 53 (1998): 13–28. J.K.

Hofkapelle [Ger.]. See *Kapelle.*

Hoflied [Ger.]. See *Hofweise.*

Hoftanz [Ger.]. A 16th-century German dance, a counterpart of the French **basse danse.* Like its Burgundian model, it was a slow, processional couple dance in a simple triple meter (3/2 or 3/4 depending on the reduction), and like its model it was frequently followed by a **Nachtanz.* The majority of *Hoftänze* are based on traditional melodies, e.g., "Der schwarze Knab," "Bentzenauer," "La *Spagna," "Roti bouilli." *Hoftänze* are found in the lute tablatures of Hans Judenkünig (1515–23; see *DTÖ* 37), Hans Newsidler (1536, 1540, etc.; see *HAM,* no. 105a), and Wolff Heckel (1556). The keyboard tablatures of Hans Kotter (1513–32) contain a number of dances of the genre, but without the title *Hoftanz.* Conversely, the later tablature by Bernard Schmid (1577) includes several dances with this title that are in a duple-quadruple meter more closely resembling a **pass'e mezo.*

Bibl.: Wilhelm Merian, *Der Tanz in den deutschen Tabulaturbüchern* (Leipzig: Breitkopf & Härtel, 1927; R: Hildesheim: Olms, 1968). Otto Gombosi, "Der Hoftanz," *AM* 7 (1935): 50–61. Daniel Heartz, "Hoftanz and Basse Dance," *JAMS* 19 (1966): 13–36. L.H.M.

Hofweise [Ger.]. (1) In the repertory of the *Meistersinger, a courting song. (2) In some modern writings, certain examples of the German polyphonic song of about 1500, associated by implication with courtly life. See also Lied.

Hohlflöte [Ger.]. An organ stop of open, wide-scaled cylindrical pipes, usually of metal.

Ho-hoane [fr. Irish *ochan*]. A *lament. The *Fitzwilliam Virginal Book includes a piece titled "The Irish Hohoane."

Hold. *Fermata.

Holland. See Netherlands.

Holler. See Field holler.

Holpijp [Du.]. A stopped organ register of wide-scaled pipes, usually of metal.

Holz [Ger.]. Wood; *Holzbläser,* woodwind player; *Holzblasinstrument,* woodwind instrument; *Holzblock, Holzblocktrommel,* wood block; *Holzharmonika, Holzstabspiel,* xylophone; *Holzschlegel,* wooden drumstick; *Holztrompete,* alphorn.

Homme armé, L' [Fr.]. A 15th-century melody [Ex.] that was widely used as a **cantus firmus* of polyphonic Masses from the second half of the 15th cen-

L'homme armé. "The armed man, the armed man . . . One should fear the armed man. The warning has been shouted everywhere that everyone should be armed with a suit of mail."

tury through the first part of the 17th and of which there are also several polyphonic chanson settings. Some of the polyphonic settings employ a signature of one flat. Composers of Masses based on this melody include Dufay (*HAM,* no. 66), Busnois, Caron, Ockeghem (*HAM,* no. 73), Obrecht, Tinctoris, Josquin (*HAM,* no. 89), Brumel, La Rue (*HAM,* no. 92), Pipelare, Senfl, de Orto, Morales, Palestrina, and Carissimi. Composers of chanson settings include Morton, Basiron, Japart, and Josquin. A number of the Masses derive from that of Busnois, to whom Pietro Aron attributed the melody (*Thoscanello de la musica,* 1523). The origins of the melody remain in doubt, however.

Bibl.: Lewis H. Lockwood, "Aspects of the *L'homme armé* Tradition," *PRMA* 100 (1973–74): 97–122. Craig Wright, *The Maze and the Warrior: Symbols in Architecture, Theology, and Music* (Cambridge, Mass.: Harvard U Pr, 2001).

Homophony. Music in which melodic interest is concentrated in one voice or part that is provided with a subordinate accompaniment, as distinct from *polyphony, in which melodic interest is distributed among all parts of the musical texture. The term may refer to a variety of melody-plus-accompaniment textures as well as to texture, termed *homorhythmic, in which all parts move with the same or similar rhythm.

Homorhythmic. Characterized by the same or very similar rhythm in all parts making up a musical texture, as in a simple hymn or chorale setting. Texture of this type is also described with the terms chordal style, familiar style, note-against-note style, isometric, and homophonic [see Homophony].

Honky-tonk. See Country.

Hoofdwerk [Du.]. The main keyboard division of a Dutch organ.

Hopak [Ukr.]. See *Gopak.*

Hoquet [Fr.], **hoquetus** [Lat.]. *Hocket.

Horn [also French horn; Fr. **cor;* Ger. *Horn; Ventilhorn,* valve horn; *Waldhorn,* natural horn, hand horn; It. **corno;* Sp. *trompa*]. (1) A circular brass instrument about 35 cm. (14 in.) in diameter with mouthpiece and valve levers at the top and a widely flared end or bell at the bottom. Three or four usually rotary valves, operated with the left hand, and associated extra tubing occupy the center area [see ill. under Brass instruments]. The instrument is usually made of brass and is sometimes nickel or silver plated. Horns made of German silver, copper, and—more rarely—silver also exist. The horn is a prominent solo instrument in European and American symphony orchestras, each of which has a horn section of four or more players. It is also used in bands and in chamber music ensembles such as woodwind and brass quintets.

The most common horn is a double instrument in F/B♭ incorporating a horn in F approximately 3.65 m. (12 ft.) in length with a horn in B♭ alto of about 2.75 m. (9 ft.). The longer or shorter instrument is selected by a left thumb valve. Three double valves for the left hand provide both horns with the usual additional lengths of tubing [see Valve]. Single horns in F are also encountered. Less often found are single instruments in B♭ alto, double horns in F/F alto or B♭/B♭ soprano, and triple horns in F/B♭/F alto.

The F/B♭ horn is the only survivor of a prestigious class of long brasses designed to play normally in the third octave or higher of the *harmonic series. Its tube lengths and fundamentals (lowest tones) are the same as those of the F tuba (F horn) and B♭ trombone (B♭ horn). Yet because of its smaller bore and much smaller mouthpiece it is played in the tenor and alto ranges.

Although small, the horn mouthpiece is long and cone-shaped. The main tube of the instrument is also conical for as much of its length as possible. The sound of the instrument is smooth, lyrical, and mellow in its most characteristic written range of f to f″ (sounding a fifth lower, B♭ to b♭′), more intense but gradually thinner on the increasingly difficult higher notes up to and above (written) c‴, and more and more guttural on the extremely low notes down to c and below.

Range.

The horn is held with the right hand in the bell. Partially closing off the throat of the bell flattens the pitch; fully opening it raises the pitch, giving the player some control of pitches that may be out of tune. Closing the opening tightly with the hand produces a muted or stopped effect [Fr., *sons bouchés;* Ger., *gestopft;* It. *chiuso;* Sp. *tapada*], sometimes specified in musical notation with the sign + and requiring altered fingering. The effect may also be produced with a *mute, which, depending on its type, may or may not require altered fingering.

History. The horn, like the trumpet, grew out of a long tradition of signaling instruments reaching far back beyond even the civilizations of Greece and Rome. Musical use of the instrument, however, did not begin until the late 17th century, after it had become associated with court life and the royal mounted hunt. Horn calls and fanfares became increasingly musical at the lavish hunts of the French courts and were transplanted to the Bohemian (Austrian) courts about 1681 by Count Franz Anton Sporck (1662–1738). There, because of Sporck's wealth and his love of the hunt and of music, the *Waldhorn* or forest horn was used increasingly for indoor musical purposes.

Instrument makers in Vienna, particularly the Leichamschneider brothers, began producing horns in F and *crooks for other keys in the first decade of the 18th century. Before mid-century, Austrian and German horns were often equipped with a master tapered crook and four or more cylindrical crooks or couplers placed between the master crook and the horn, either singly or in combination, to provide the keys commonly needed.

During this period, Bohemian and Austrian horn players—especially in Vienna, Prague, and Dresden—established the range and technical capabilities of the horn to limits approaching what is known today. Hand stopping (partially or fully closing off the bell with the right hand) was developed as a technique for tuning and for providing notes not obtainable in the natural series. Anton Joseph Hampl in Dresden was probably one of the first to bring this technique to public notice about 1760. Hampl is also credited with inventing central crooks, attached by a slide, that allow a permanent mouth pipe and mouthpiece position more convenient for hand stopping. Instruments with this system of crooks were first made for Hampl by Johann Werner of Dresden. The use of this type of instrument, called the *Inventionshorn,* quickly spread throughout the Continent.

Two other types of hand horn with crooks appeared before 1800. In Austria, Germany, and France, horns for orchestral use were developed. These provided separate terminal crooks for the complete range of horn keys (B♭ alto, A, G, F, E, E♭, D, C) and a coupler for B♭ basso. Terminal crooks were tapered from the mouthpiece and avoided the additional amounts of cylindrical tubing necessary when couplers were added between a terminal or master crook and the rest of the horn, or when central *Inventionshorn* crooks were added. A central slide was retained for tuning purposes. In 1780, Joseph Raoux and his son Lucien-Joseph, both of Paris, brought out their *cor-solo* based on the ideas of Carl Thürrschmidt. Less abrupt curves and extra strength were achieved on central *Inventionshorn* crooks by crossing the branches just before the slide. These horns, made for the soloist, were provided with five crooks only—G, F, E, E♭, and D.

The 19th century saw the invention of the *valve and its application to the horn. Although the horn was one of the first instruments fitted with valves by the inventors Stölzel and Blühmel, it was some years before refinements in construction made the valve practical and acceptable to horn players. Contemporary with valve experiments was the attempt to provide the horn with a handy way to change crooks. The first omnitonic horn [Fr. *cor omnitonique*] was made by J. B. Dupont of Paris about 1815; an improved model was patented in 1818. Both used a multiposition slide to direct the windway to eight different loops of tubing. The most successful of the early omnitonic horns operated by such slides was first made in 1824 by Charles-Joseph Sax of Brussels.

By the middle of the 19th century, the valved horn had proven its worth and was being written for by contemporary composers, especially Wagner. As later composers, particularly Richard Strauss, added more and more demanding horn parts to the repertory, the F/B♭ horn, introduced by Fritz Kruspe about 1898, was found to be the best compromise solution to the problems of key, range, tone quality, and chromaticism. Almost the entire repertory of horn music is played today on this instrument, regardless of the crook called for in the original part, the player making the necessary transposition. The increasing use of authentic instruments in the performance of 18th-century music, however, has contributed to a revival of the natural horn [see Performance practice].

(2) In jazz and popular music, any wind instrument.

Bibl.: Reginald Morley-Pegge, *The French Horn* (New York: Philosophical Library, 1960). Robin Gregory, *The Horn: A Comprehensive Guide to the Modern Instrument and Its Music,* 2nd ed, rev. and enl. (New York: Praeger, 1969). Bernhard Brüchle, *Horn Bibliographie* (Wilhelmshaven: Heinrichshofen, 1970). Horace Fitzpatrick, *The Horn and Horn Playing and the Austro-Bohemian Tradition from 1680–1830* (London: Oxford U Pr, 1970). Anthony Baines, *Brass Instruments* (London: Faber, 1976). Bernhard Brüchle and Kurt Janetzky, *A Pictorial History of the Horn* (Tutzing: Schneider, 1976). Wayne Wilkins, *The Index of French Horn Music* (Magnolia, Ark.: Music Register, 1978). Kurt Janetzky and Bernhard Brüchle, *The Horn,* trans. J. Chater (London: Batsford, 1988). Jeremy Montagu, *The French Horn* (Princes Risborough, Buckinghamshire: Shire Publications, 1990).

R.E.E.

Horn fifths. See Parallel Fifths.

Hornpipe. (1) A dance popular in England, Wales, and Scotland from the 16th to 19th centuries, related to the *jig and *country-dance families of dances. The country-dance type is found as a movement in harpsichord and orchestral music and is usually in animated 3/2 time (also 3/4, 2/4, and later 4/4) with simple four-measure phrases. Sixteenth-century examples are continuous variations, often using a two- or four-note ground bass (Hugh Ashton, Byrd). In the late 17th and early 18th century, hornpipes are common in stage music as well as in orchestral and harpsichord suites from England (Handel, **Water Music;* Purcell, keyboard Suites nos. 6 and 7 and *The Married Beau*) and the Continent (Gottlieb Muffat, Telemann), where they are sometimes called **angloises.* Most exploit Scotch-snap syncopations, using repeated short motives and homophonic textures. As a solo dance, the hornpipe has often been associated with sailors. A type in duple meter is a prominent folk dance of *Ireland.

(2) A *reedpipe with a bell made of animal horn. Most are like *shawms, some are *double clarinets, and some are fitted with bags. Some have a horn for the mouthpiece as well as for the bell. They were common in medieval Europe and are still played in Asia and North Africa. Examples include the Scottish stock

and horn and the Welsh *pibgorn, which were still known and played in the 18th century. (1) B.G.

Hornwerk [Ger.]. In Austria in the Middle Ages and Renaissance, a set of flue pipes on their own chest, placed in a tower. At first they sounded only a continuous triad when supplied by wind from a bellows and were used for marking the hours of the day and times of worship. In the Renaissance, they were fitted with barrel and pin mechanisms [see Automatic instruments], enabling them to play tunes. The only complete surviving example is the Salzburg *Stierorgel* of 1502.

Horologium [Lat.]. In the Middle Ages, a wheel to which small bells were attached and that was made to rotate, sometimes mechanically. Eventually such wheels came to be attached to organs. See *Cimbelstern, Cascabeles.*

Hosanna [Lat., fr. Gr. and Heb., save, we beseech Thee]. An acclamation occurring in the phrase "Hosanna in excelsis" (Hosanna in the highest) in the Sanctus of the *Mass. In the Anglican Book of Common Prayer this is rendered "Glory be to Thee, O Lord, most High."

Hours. See Office.

Hptw. [Ger.]. Abbr. for **Hauptwerk.*

Hr. Abbr. for horn.

Huapango [Sp.]. Traditional dance and dance music of the Huasteca region of northern Veracruz and adjacent states in Mexico, also known as *son huasteco.* The *huapango,* with lyric texts most typically sung by two vocalists in alternation and with frequent falsetto, is accompanied by an ensemble of violin, five-string *jarana,* and eight-string *guitarra quinta (huapanguera).* The term *huapango* is also often applied to the related **son jarocho* of the southern Gulf coastal plain of Mexico, and the distinctive *huapango* rhythm, in simplified form, has been widely popularized. D.S.

Huayno, huaiño, wayno. A social dance widely distributed in Andean Peru, also found in Bolivia, northern Chile, and northern Argentina. Of preconquest origin, it is typically in moderate to lively duple meter and is binary in structure, with short, syncopated, anhemitonic-pentatonic melodies. A feature shared with many other Andean genres is a characteristic bimodality, resulting from the alternation of tonal centers a minor third apart. In Ecuador, an important social dance closely related to the *huayno* is the *sanjuanito.* D.S.

Hu-ch'in, huqin [Chin.]. (1) Any *spike fiddle. (2) The **ching-hu.*

Huehuetl [Nahuatl]. A single-headed, cylindrical drum of pre-Columbian Mexico. Aztec examples were made from a section of a tree trunk 75 to 100 cm. long and elaborately carved with hieroglyphs that indicated the history of the instrument, its role in ceremonial functions, and similar information. A smaller, less ornate version is still in use.

Hufnagelschrift [Ger.]. See *Nagelschrift.*

Huguenots, Les [Fr., The Huguenots]. Opera in five acts by Giacomo Meyerbeer (libretto by Eugène Scribe, revised by Émile Deschamps and Meyerbeer), produced in Paris in 1836. Setting: Touraine and Paris in 1572.

Humanism. See Renaissance.

Hummel, hommel, humle [Swed.]. A fretted *zither of Sweden, Denmark, and the Low Countries. Today largely obsolete, it was similar in form and playing technique to the Norwegian **langleik.*

Humoreske [Ger.], **humoresque** [Fr.]. A title used by some composers of the 19th century for pieces of fanciful character. The term derives from humor in the sense of mood rather than wit. Works include Schumann's *Humoreske* in B♭ major for piano op. 20 (1838), which is in five sharply contrasting sections, and Dvořák's set of eight *Humoresques* for piano op. 101 (1894), of which the one in G♭ major is well known.

Hungarian Dances [Ger. *Ungarische Tänze*]. A collection of 21 dances for piano four-hands by Brahms, composed in 1852–69 and published in four volumes (two in 1869 and two in 1880). Brahms arranged nos. 1, 3, and 10 for orchestra in 1873 and nos. 1–10 for piano solo in 1872. Most are freely invented in imitation of the Hungarian **csárdás* and in the style of so-called *Gypsy music, rather than drawing on Hungarian folk music.

Hungarian Rhapsodies [Fr. *Rhapsodies hongroises*]. A group of 19 piano pieces by Liszt, composed in 1846–85 and published in 1851–86. They are based on an earlier set of 21 piano pieces (some of which were called Hungarian Rhapsodies) that draw on Hungarian Gypsy music and that were published by Liszt between 1840 and 1847. Many are freely invented or based on "Gypsy" melodies by various amateur composers and styled in imitation of the Hungarian **csárdás* or so-called *Gypsy music, rather than drawing on Hungarian folk music.

Hungary. I. *Current musical life and related institutions.* Most activity associated with art music in Hungary today is centered in Budapest. Advanced training in all aspects of music, including performance, composition, and scholarship, is available at the Liszt Academy of Music in Budapest. The Hungarian Academy of Science includes an Institute of Musicology, which has supported both musicological and ethnomusicological research since Béla Bartók assembled the first collection of folk music there in the late 1930s. The National Conservatory, renamed the Béla Bartók Musical Training College in 1949, provides intermediate-level training and is affiliated with provincial colleges. Important institutions founded in the second half of the 20th century include the Folk Music Research Group founded by Zoltan Kodály in 1953, the Liszt Memorial Museum and Research Center (1986), and the Kodály Memorial Museum and Archives. Budapest hosts several festivals, including Budapest Music Weeks and those devoted to contemporary and early music; several festivals also occur in Pécs, Sopron, Györ, and Szentendre.

Active performing organizations, many based in Budapest, include the State Opera (1884), the Budapest Philharmonic Orchestra (1853), the Budapest Concert Orchestra MÁV (1945), the Hungarian Radio and Television Symphony Orchestra (known internationally as the Budapest Symphony Orchestra, founded 1943 by Ernst von Dohnányi), and the Hungarian Radio Chorus. There are also a number of chamber groups, such as the Liszt Chamber Orchestra (1963) and the Failoni Chamber Orchestra (1981), various string quartets, and groups for traditional music, such as the State Folk Ensemble (1951) and the Budapest Gypsy Symphony Orchestra (1985).

II. *History of art music.* Art music grew initially from the confluence of a great many outside traditions. The beginnings of Christianity in the nation during the 10th and 11th centuries brought the development of a body of Gregorian chant related to Frankish, north Italian, and St. Gall repertories. From the 12th to the 14th centuries, French-influenced courtly songs flourished among nomadic minstrels. Matthias Corvinus (reigned 1458–90) brought Italian, French, Flemish, and German musicians to his court. The fall of Buda to the Turks in 1541 began a decline in Catholicism and a subsequent spread of Protestant musical culture. Hungarian musicians emigrated in large numbers during the next hundred years, and at the same time Poles and Germans immigrated to Hungarian musical centers such as those of the Báthory and Szapolyai families. Of particular importance during this period are the lute music of Bálint Bakfark (1507–76), the biblical epics in the *Cronica* (1554) of Sebestyén Tinódi (ca. 1505–56), and the dance tunes and folk melodies compiled and intabulated for organ by Ioan Căianu (János Kájoni; 1627–98). After Buda was regained in 1686, it developed into a major European musical center.

During the 18th century, the nation was visited regularly by major international musicians: Albrechtsberger, Dittersdorf, Michael and Joseph Haydn, and the young Mozart, for example. In addition to imported opera such as that presented by Haydn at the Eszterháza Castle, native musical theater such as that begun by Laszló Kelemen's troupe in the 1790s was of growing importance. Protestant vocal polyphony also flourished during this period, as manifested in Calvinist college choirs such as that in Debrecen directed by György Maróthy (1715–44).

The influence of German musicians, many of whom had settled in Hungary, continued to be strong through the 19th century. Significant native composers of the period include Ferenc Erkel (1810–93), Mihály Mosonyi (1815–70), Béni Egressy (1814–51), and especially Franz Liszt (1811–86). During the first half of the 20th century, Jenő Hubay (1858–1937), Ernő von Dohnányi (1877–1960), and Leó Weiner (1885–1960) continued composing in the German romantic tradition. At the same time, the field research of Bartók and Kodály was providing the basis for a reevaluation of the nation's folk song. In his own music, Bartók wrought a new synthesis of artistic tradition and authentic peasant music—not only the music of Hungary but also that of Romania, Bulgaria, and other neighboring regions. Kodály's primary significance as a composer is almost matched by the international importance of the educational system he developed, which uses native folk music as a basis for musical instruction [see Kodály method].

Among the Kodály pupils prominent in the 1920s were György Kósa (1897–1984), Pál Kadosa (1903–83), and Tibor Harsányi (1898–1954). Others influenced by his teachings were Ferenc Farkas (b. 1905) and Rezső Kókai (1906–62). Composers who gained attention in the 1940s and 50s include Ferenc Szabó (1902–69), István Szelényi (1904–72), György Ránki (b. 1907), Béla Tardos (1910–66), István Sárközy (b. 1920), Emil Petrovics (b. 1930), and Sándor Szokolay (b. 1931). The 1950s and 1960s saw a rediscovery of the music of Bartók, by such composers as Endre Szervánszky (1911–77), András Mihály (b. 1917), and Pál Járdányi (1920–66). With the softening of the communist government's stance on the musical avante garde after the 1956 uprising, these composers, along with János Decsényi (b. 1927), Pál Károlyi (b. 1934), Miklós Kocsár (1933), and István Láng (1933), began to explore the hitherto prohibited styles and techniques of the Second Viennese and "Warsaw" schools. Also prominent in this generation are József Soproni (b. 1930), Zsolt Durkó (1934–97), Sándor Balassa (b. 1935), and especially György Ligeti (b. 1923) and György Kurtaág (b. 1926). Many composers of the postwar generation have been associated with the group known as the Új Zenei Stúdió (New Music Studio, founded 1970), including Zoltán Jeney (b. 1943), László Sáry (b. 1940), László Vidovszky (b. 1944), Peter Eotvos (b. 1944), and Barnabás Dukay (b. 1950).

III. *Folk music.* The heritage of folk song in Hungary is especially rich, and in few nations has folk music so thoroughly permeated all levels of musical education and artistic tradition. Among the thousands of songs that Béla Bartók (1881–1945) and Zoltán Kodály (1882–1967) recorded and transcribed beginning in 1905, they distinguished an "old style" of melodies (Kodály called it an "ancient stratum") from a "new style." The older, frequently pentatonic tunes show similarities to Turkish and Central Asian folk music and to Western musical traditions such as Gregorian chant. The new style, which assimilated many elements of the older melodies and lyrics, emerged from the great social changes that followed the withdrawal of the Turks, particularly from the erosion of the feudal system. Bartók described the music of the new independent peasant class as fresher and more vigorous than the old music. It made more frequent use of seven-note modes on D, G, or A and of regularized phrase structures, principally AA^{5}A^{5}A, ABBA, AA^{5}BA, or AABA (the ^{5} indicating the same line of music sung a fifth higher). He also determined that the mobility of soldiers and harvesters during the 18th and 19th centuries had brought about some intermingling of the highly individual styles of isolated regions. A third category included songs imported from other lands and ritualistic songs associated with weddings, harvest, Christmas, May Day, and other special occasions. Some important song types today are the *regös* Christmas songs, the improvised *laments, and the popular *magyarnóta* songs. In the late 1980s an immensely popular outgrowth of the *magyarnóta* tradition known as *lakodalmas,* or wedding rock, quickly established itself throughout Hungary.

Far less research has been devoted to instrumental folk music. The melodies of herdsmen and Gypsy bands are based principally on vocal or vocally inspired tunes. In the 18th and early 19th centuries, the melody-plus-drone instrumental ensemble style gave way to a chordal style better suited to the increasingly popular **verbunkos* and **csárdás* dance music [see also Gypsy music]. Among the folk instruments are the violin, the *kukoricahegedű* (fiddle), the *citera*, the *cimbalom, the *tekerő* (hurdy-gurdy), the *facimbalom* (dulcimer), the *furulya* (fipple flute), the **tárogató,* the *duda* (bagpipes), and the *zőrgősdob* and *nagydob* (drums).

Bibl.: Béla Bartók, *Népzenénk és a szomszéd népek népzenéje* [Our Folk Music and That of Neighboring Peoples] (Budapest: Somlo Béla, 1934; trans. Ger., 1935; Budapest: Zeneműkiadó Vállalat, 1952). Zoltán Kodály, *A magyar népzene* [Hungarian Folk Music] (Budapest: Királyi Magyar Egyetemi Nyomda, 1937); trans. R. Tempest, C. Jolly, and L. Picken, ed. L. Vargas, *Folk Music of Hungary* (New York: Praeger, 1972). Dénes Bartha and Zoltán Kodály, *Die ungarische Musik* (Budapest: Danubia, 1943). Kilián Szigeti, "Denkmäler des Gregorianischen Chorals aus dem ungarischen Mittelalter," *Studia musicologica* 4 (1963): 129–72. Bence Szabolcsi, *A Concise History of Hungarian Music,* trans. Eng. Sára Karig and Fred Macnicol (London: Barrie & Rockliff, 1964); 2nd ed., with an added chapter on modern music by György Kroó (Budapest: Corvina, 1974). Bence Szabolcsi, *Tanzmusik aus Ungarn im 16. und 17. Jahrhundert,* trans. Tilda Alpari (Kassel: Bärenreiter, 1970). Bálint Sárosi, "Instrumentale Volksmusik in Ungarn," *Studia instrumentorum musicae popularis* 4 (1976): 115–41. Benjamin Suchoff, ed., *Béla Bartók: The Hungarian Folksong,* trans. Eng. M. D. Calvocoressi (Albany: State U of NY Pr, 1981). János Breuer, *Negyven év magyar zenekultúrája* [Hungarian Music Culture in the Last Forty Years] (Budapest: Zenemukiadó, 1985). Gyula Czigány, *Contemporary Hungarian Composers,* ed. B. Varga (Budapest: Editio Musica Budapest, 1967; enlarged 5th rev. ed. 1989). Dobszay László, "Plainchant in Medieval Hungary," *Journal of the Plainsong and Medieval Music Society* 8 (1990): 49–78. László Dobszay, Janka Szendrei, and Brian McLean, *Catalogue of Hungarian Folksong Types I* (Budapest: Zoltan Falvy, 1992). Rebecca Gates-Coon, *The Landed Estates of the Esterházy Princes: Hungary during the Reforms of Maria Theresia and Joseph II* (Baltimore: Johns Hopkins U Pr, 1994). Barbara R. Lange, "Lakodalmas Rock and the Rejection of Popular Culture in Post-Socialist Hungary," in *Returning Culture: Musical Changes in Central and Eastern Europe,* ed. Mark Slobin (Durham: Duke U Pr, 1996), pp. 76–91. Judit Frigyesi, *Béla Bartók and Turn-of-the Century Budapest* (Berkeley: U of Cal Pr, 1998).

Hunnenschlacht, Die [Ger., The Battle (Slaughter) of the Huns]. A symphonic poem by Liszt completed in 1857 and inspired by a painting by Wilhelm von Kaulbach.

Hunting horn. See Horn.

Hunt Quartet. Popular name for Mozart's String Quartet in B♭ major K. 458 (1784), no. 3 of the *Haydn Quartets; and for Haydn's String Quartet no. 1 in B♭ major Hob. III:1, composed by 1762. In both quartets, the name refers to the hunting-horn motif in the opening movement.

Hunt Symphony [Fr. *La chasse*]. Haydn's Symphony no. 73 in D major Hob. I:73 (completed by 1782). The title refers to the last movement, which was originally composed as an overture, depicting a hunting scene, to his opera *La fedeltà premiata* Hob. XXVIII:10 (1780).

Hupfauf [Ger.]. See *Nachtanz.*

Hurdy-gurdy [Fr. *vielle à roue, chifonie;* Ger. *Drehleier, Leier, Radleier;* It. *ghironda;* Lat. *symphonia;* Sp. *zanfonía*]. A bowed stringed instrument, most often shaped like a viol, with a crank at the end opposite the pegbox. When the crank is turned, a rosined wooden wheel adjacent to the bridge and touching the strings rotates, causing the strings to sound. Two strings tuned in unison pass over the central bridge and through a long box under what would otherwise be the fingerboard. These strings are stopped by tangents that are connected to keys set into the side of the box. Two pairs of drone strings, tuned in some combination of fifths and octaves, pass over separate bridges, one on either side of the main bridge. The number of strings may vary.

The instrument was introduced into Latin Europe from the East and from Spain in the Middle Ages, when it was at first termed an *organistrum,* as in the treatise *Quomodo organistrum construatur* (How an Organistrum Should Be Constructed, *GS* 1:303, attributed there to the 10th-century writer Odo of Cluny but now thought to date from the 13th century). Its first depictions, in the 12th century, show a large instrument held and played by two players. The smaller size for a single player and the Latin name *symphonia* and its derivatives emerged in the 13th century. By the

17th century, it was regarded as an instrument of the lower classes, including beggars and itinerant musicians. In the 18th century, however, it was taken up along with the *musette by the French aristocracy. Haydn composed five concertos (Hob. VIIh:1–5) and eight **notturni* (Hob. II:25–32) for two instruments of this type (to which organ pipes and bellows were added, the resulting instrument termed a *lira organizzata*) with strings and winds. Mozart included the hurdy-gurdy in mixed ensembles for the four Minuets K. 601 and four German Dances K. 602. It continues in use as a folk instrument in France, Scandinavia, and Hungary. See ill. under Violin. The term is sometimes also applied to the *barrel organ and *barrel piano.

Hurtig [Ger.]. Quick, agile.

H.W. [Ger.]. Abbr. for **Hauptwerk.*

Hydraulis [Gr.; Lat. *hydraulus*]. The organ of ancient Greece and Rome. Its invention is attributed to Ktesibios of Alexandria (ca. 300–250 B.C.E.). As described by ancient sources, it consisted of three components: a set of pipes, a keyboard mechanism, and a wind mechanism that used water to regulate air pressure. The pipes were metal *flue pipes, arranged in ranks, with up to 4 ranks of 4 to 18 pipes per rank. The keyboard was a set of levers connected to sliders. Air pressure was generated by one or two hand-operated pumps that fed air into an underwater chamber *(pigneus)* and thence to a wind-chest. The air in the chamber displaced water, and the weight of the displaced water maintained steady pressure on the wind-chest, thus enabling an even tone. Later instruments, from the 2nd century C.E. on, dispensed with the hydraulic system of pressure regulation, using an inflated leather bag instead to maintain a steady air supply. The range and tuning of the hydraulis cannot be determined, nor is it known whether it was used for polyphony. At first a mechanical curiosity, it became a familiar instrument in ancient Rome. It was often played in the arena together with the **tuba* and **cornu*, and it was found in wealthy households. It is depicted in Roman art and coins, and two scale models have been preserved. In addition, a specimen in a fair state of preservation was excavated from the ruins of Aquincum in what is now Hungary. See also Organ.

Bibl.: Jean Perrot, *L'orgue de ses origines hellénistiques* (Paris: A & J Picard, 1965); trans. Eng. Norma Deane (London: Oxford U Pr, 1971). Werner Walcker-Mayer, *Die römische Orgel von Aquincum* (Stuttgart: Musikwissenschaftliche Vlg, 1970); trans. Eng. Joscelyn Godwin (Ludwigsburg: Musikwissenschaftliche Vlg, 1972).

Hymn [fr. Gr. *hymnos*, a song in praise of gods or heroes]. In Christian churches, a song in praise of God. St. Augustine (353–430) stipulates the essential presence of three elements—song, praise, and God—and thus distinguishes hymns from psalms or spiritual songs (mentioned in the Bible in Ephesians 5:19 and Colossians 3:16). The distinction is often blurred, however. The character and history of the hymn in the West are clearly distinguishable from those of the hymn of classical antiquity or of the closed *Byzantine repertory. From the beginning, the Western hymn has displayed, in varying measure, the influence of vulgar language, didactic (even evangelical) fervor, and congregational participation.

In its use of allegory and symbolism, the Jewish Psalter (first in Greek translation, then in Latin) was the model of the early Christian hymn in the West. But by the fourth century, the hymn had defined itself by language (Latin), form (strophic verse), and manner of performance (some form of alternation) and had begun to relinquish the quantitative accent of classical Latin in favor of the rhythm and rhyme of typically medieval verse. The history of medieval hymnody begins with St. Ambrose (340–97), four of whose hymns ("Aeterne rerum conditor," "Deus creator omnium," "Iam surgit hora tertia," and "Veni redemptor gentium") were certified as genuine by St. Augustine. As early as the 3rd century, the hymn had found a place in the Divine *Office; in the 6th century, the Rule of St. Benedict of Nursia (ca. 480–ca. 547) ordained the singing of hymns at each of the canonical hours. Thus, by the death of St. Gregory the Great (604), the form, language, and use of the medieval hymn were ordered. Its subsequent literary history may be traced through clusters of poets, e.g., Paul the Deacon ("Ut queant laxis") and Hrabanus (Rhabanus) Maurus ("Veni Creator spiritus, Mentes," attribution doubtful) of the Carolingian renaissance, and Bernard of Clairvaux ("Jesu dulcis memoria") and Peter Abelard (a cycle of hymns for the whole year) in the 12th century, and through the numerous works of anonymous poets. The melodies that have been preserved for all of these poems, however, survive only in manuscripts from the 11th or 12th century and later. (The *sequence developed parallel to the hymn and flowered in the 11th and 12th centuries.)

Despite the evidence that the Ambrosian hymn may have been congregational in intent, the subsequent Latin monophonic hymn developed within the Divine Office (principally in Lauds and Vespers), probably utilizing soloists and choir in alternation, in a musical and literary repertory arranged according to the canonical hours and proper to liturgical seasons and saints. The residue of this repertory as given, for example, in the *Antiphonale romanum* (1912), is part of an eclectic mix; Stäblein's collection (1956) catalogs the contents of medieval hymnaries that reveal no consistent association of text and melody. Polyphonic settings, appearing in the 14th century (e.g., in the Apt manuscript), continue the line of general development: in cycles of hymns for the whole year, polyphony, e.g., for the odd-numbered strophes (chant alone being implied for the remaining strophes), is composed around the chant as *cantus firmus.* The cycles of Dufay (even-numbered strophes) in the 15th century and of Costanzo Festa (even-numbered) and Palestrina (odd-numbered, but without incipits) in the 16th are representative, exhibiting the continuing change in polyphonic style observable in all music of their time.

Set against this sophisticated Catholic polyphony, the emergence of the Protestant hymn text is remarkable testimony to the renewed vitality of sacred folk song that marks the transition from the Middle Ages to the Renaissance. Where the Latin hymns of Georg Rhau's *Sacrorum hymnorum liber primus* of 1542, published for the use of the young Lutheran church, are virtually indistinguishable in language and style from their polyphonic contemporaries, the Lutheran German vernacular hymn *(Kirchenlied),* on the other hand, took its place first as congregational replacement for the corresponding sung Latin texts of Ordinary and Proper, then as general confessional and evangelical statement. The printed corpus of texts expanded slowly—during Luther's lifetime, from the eight texts of Jacob Gutknecht's "Achtliederbuch" (*Etlich Cristlich lider,* 1523/24) through the twenty-five texts of the two *Erfurter Enchiridien* (1524) to Valentin Babst's songbook of 1545 containing nearly five times that number. For the Lutheran church, such texts, later known as *chorales, point the way to the future: their combination of vernacular language, folk imagery, strophic form, and hortatory earnestness makes them prototypes of the modern congregational hymn. All subsequent chorale text composition inherited and retained these primary energies.

Though Lutheran texts penetrated into the Anglo-American hymn repertory, particularly through 19th-century translation (e.g., the work of Catherine Winkworth, 1829–78), the rhymed *Psalter translation of the Reformed church had far greater and more basic historical influence. The Elizabethan Injunctions of 1559 provided royal authority for the singing of hymns in the Anglican service; the 1562 Psalter of Thomas Sternhold (d. 1549) and John Hopkins (d. 1570)—the "Old Version"—contained, in addition to the rhymed Psalter translations, nine "original" hymns, the extent of whose use is undocumented but whose very presence posed a classic dilemma: the Sternhold and Hopkins translations, though credited with scriptural fidelity, were poetically awkward; the "original" hymns, though authorized for use, lacked the scriptural stamp. The 17th century sought a resolution by literary style; the inconsequential translation of George Wither (1623) and the *New Version* (1696–98) of Nahum Tate (1652–1715) and Nicholas Brady (1659–1726) virtually superseded Sternhold and Hopkins in urban English parishes and colonial America. The Old Version continued in use, mostly in rural areas, well into the 19th century.

The Psalms of David Imitated in the Language of the New Testament (1719) by the nonconformist Isaac Watts, however, broke decisively with the purely literary solution and indeed with scriptural fidelity itself. Watts's preface explains his remarkable new attitude: no "just translation, but a paraphrase," designed for singing (not reading) and thus stating "our own sense of things" and expressing "our own case," letting the Psalmist "always speak the common sense and language of a Christian." Watts aimed "rather to *imitate* than to translate, and thus to compose a *Psalm-book for Christians* after the manner of the Jewish Psalter." Most of his texts were formed in common, long, or short meter and thus lent themselves conveniently to the rhythmically equivalent melodies.

The whole work of Watts, without forsaking primary scriptural inspiration, marked the modernization of English hymnology. It was quickly followed by the texts of John Wesley (1703–91) and Charles Wesley (1707–88) and of Augustus Toplady (1740–78), among others. On the way to rejoin—indeed, to reform—the mainstream, these texts had to adjust themselves to others born of a heightened sense of liturgical order (e.g., those of Reginald Heber, 1783–1826) and blend with a corpus of new texts translated from Latin (e.g., those of John Mason Neale, 1818–66; John Keble, 1792–1866; and John Henry Cardinal Newman, 1801–90). The full convergence of all these trends produced *Hymns Ancient and Modern* in 1861. But no collection then or now has been authorized for the Anglican Church as an official hymnal. A general openness to distinguished collections was encouraged by the poet Robert Bridges (1844–1930) and tested by Percy Dearmer (1867–1936) in introducing a new hymnal.

The early colonial settlers of North America transplanted their traditional hymns and religious practices into American soil, the diversity of their customs giving rise to the denominational heterogeneity so characteristic of American religious history. Insofar as denominational practices derived from European tradition, the histories of their hymnodies were also derivative, despite adaptations and accretions. Far more interesting are the American attempts to break away from European models. But the first such attempt, the *Bay Psalm Book of 1640, advanced the literary solution with even less success than had its European counterparts.

Despite its poetic clumsiness, the book subsequently went through some 70 editions (not all American). The future of American hymns, however, lay in opportunities hidden beneath three apparent threats to colonial religious prosperity. First, the widespread practice of *lining-out, which ultimately produced a bizarre combination of melodic disagreements, plodding tempos, and textual incoherences. Second, the skill of reading music consequently began to disappear. Third, the transplanted religions could choose either to shut out the unfamiliar environment and sustain an artificial link with the mother churches or to let the practice of religion be influenced by the new environment.

The future lay with education and adaptation. Education produced the New England singing schools (for which John Tufts wrote his *Introduction to the Art of*

Singing Psalm-tunes, 1721) and led subsequently to the compositions of William Billings (1746–1800) [see Fuging tune] and later to the pedagogical work of Lowell Mason (1792–1872). Adaptation is visible in three areas: religious (the Great Awakening, its effect on the Separatist Baptists, their enthusiasm for experiential texts); notational (advent of the four- and seven-shape-notes as devices for teaching singing to the musically unlettered); and musical (the joining of secular folk song to religious text). There resulted white and black *spirituals, America's most distinctive contributions to hymnody, both bound to the 19th-century societies that nurtured them. White spirituals are found in *tune books (e.g., William Walker, *Southern Harmony,* 1835); black spirituals were collected in print after the Civil War. In style, the two are similar, reflecting personal religion, with shared textual sources, use of refrain, repetition, and chorus tag line; in tone, the black spirituals, viewed from the perspective of time, are generally far more eloquent, being born out of the experience of oppression.

The *gospel hymn associated with the urban evangelism of Dwight L. Moody (1837–99) and Ira Sankey (1840–1908), as in Percy P. Bliss and Sankey's *Gospel Hymns and Sacred Songs* (1875), flourished in the last quarter of the 19th century. Its textual and musical practices were not unlike those of the earlier spirituals, but resulted in styles distinctive to white and black congregations (e.g., Holiness and Pentecostal).

In the first half of the 20th century English-language hymnody tended to be conservative—the few new hymns that came into use were usually written, both textually and musically, in older styles. Since the 1960s there has been an extraordinary period of creativity, with many new hymns being written in many different styles. This phenomenon has been called the "hymn explosion" in Britain because of the many new individual hymns that have been written. In America, it has been termed the "hymnal explosion," since during the last quarter of the 20th century an enormous number of denominational and other hymnals were published in North America. This is something of a paradox, for at a time when there are so many new hymns available, congregations and individuals are singing fewer hymns than in earlier generations. See also Church music.

Bibl: *Analecta hymnica medii aevii* (Leipzig: Reisland, 1886–1922; R: New York: Johnson, 1961). John Julian, *Dictionary of Hymnology,* 2nd ed. (London, 1907; R: New York: Dover, 1957). Bruno Stäblein, ed., *Hymnen I: Die mittelalterlichen Hymnenmelodien des Abendlandes* [*MMMA* 1] (Kassel: Bärenreiter, 1956; R: with additional material, 1995). Erik Routley, *The Music of Christian Hymnody* (London: Independent, 1957). Josef Szövérffy, *Die Annelen der lateinischen Hymnendichtung* (Berlin: Schmidt, 1964–65). Erik Routley, *A Panorama of Christian Hymnody* (Collegeville: Liturgical Pr, 1979). Albert Christ-Janer, et al., *American Hymns Old and New* (New York: Columbia U Pr, 1980). Erik Routley, *The Music of Christian Hymns* (Chicago: GIA, 1981). Nicholas Temperley and Charles G. Manns, *Fuging Tunes in the Eighteenth Century* (Detroit: Information Coordinators, 1983). Raymond Glover, ed., *The Hymnal 1982 Companion* (New York: Church Hymnal Corp, 1990–94). Robin A. Leaver, *"Goostly Psalmes & Spirituall Songes": English and Dutch Metrical Psalms from Coverdale to Utenhove 1535–1566* (New York: Oxford U Pr, 1991). Ian Bradley, *Abide with Me: The World of Victorian Hymns* (Chicago: GIA, 1997). J. Richard Watson, *The English Hymn: A Critical and Historical Study* (New York: Oxford U Pr, 1997). Nicholas Temperley, *The Hymn-Tune Index,* 4 vols. (New York: Oxford U Pr, 1998). D. DeWitt Wasson, ed., *Hymntune Index and Related Hymn Materials,* 3 vols. (Lanham: Scarecrow, 1998). J. Richard Watson, ed., *An Annotated Anthology of Hymns* (New York: Oxford U Pr, 2002). R.F.F., rev. R.A.L.

Hypate [Gr.]. See Greece I, 3 (i).

Hypaton [Gr.]. See Greece I, 3 (i).

Hyper-, hypo- [Gr.]. Prefixes meaning literally over or above and under or below, respectively. In ancient Greek music, they were attached to the ethnic names of the *tonoi,* e.g., Hyperdorian, Hypodorian. The Hyperdorian *tonos* was a higher tuning of the Greater Perfect System than the Dorian *tonos;* the Hypodorian was a lower tuning than the Dorian [see Greece I, 3 (ii)]. In the medieval modal system of paired modes (authentic and plagal), hypo- was attached to the low-lying plagal member of each pair [see Mode]. A.B.

Hyperbolaeon [Gr.]. See Greece I, 3 (i).

Hyporchema [Gr.]. In ancient Greek music [see Greece I], a choral song with dancing, usually accompanied by instruments. A.B.

Hz. Abbr. for *Hertz.

I

Iamb, iambic. See Prosody; Modes, rhythmic.

Iastian. Ionian. See Greece I, 3 (ii).

Iberia. (1) A suite of 12 piano pieces by Albéniz, published in four sets of three in 1906–8. Their titles evoke Spanish places or scenes. Although Albéniz orchestrated two pieces himself, the five orchestrations by his friend Enrique Arbós are performed more often. (2) An orchestral work forming part of Debussy's **Images*.

Iconography of music. The study of visual representations of musical subjects. It is important to the understanding of virtually every musical culture, and for some (e.g., those of the ancient Middle East) is the single most important means to such an understanding. It can contribute significantly to the study of musical instruments, performance practice (including performance techniques of individual instruments, the number and combination of instruments and performers in a given repertory or social function, their physical relationship to one another in performance, the physical environment of musical performance, and the staging of theatrical works), the social and cultural roles of music, and biography. Since few of the visual representations were intended primarily to convey information about music, such study requires careful application of the critical tools of both the art historian and the music historian. An assessment must be made of the function of the visual work within the system of signs of which it is a part, since the degree to which a visual work can be interpreted as a reproduction of musical reality varies considerably and does not necessarily depend on a realistic style of representation.

The development of methods of classification and study and the establishment of research centers are being encouraged by the Répertoire international d'iconographie musicale (International Repertory of Musical Iconography, abbr. RIdIM).

Many different categories of pictorial representations of music are being studied today. These include allegorical representations, musical instruments as symbols and in performance, biographical studies, and objects of musical cultures around the world.

Bibl.: Georg Kinsky, ed., *Geschichte der Musik in Bildern* (Leipzig: Breitkopf & Härtel, 1929; trans. Eng., London: Dent, 1930; 2nd ed., New York: Dover, 1951). Heinrich Besseler, Max Schneider, and Werner Bachmann, eds., *Musikgeschichte in Bildern,* 28 vols. (Leipzig: Deutscher Verlag für Musik, 1961–). Emanuel Winternitz, *Musical Instruments and Their Symbolism in Western Art* (New York: Norton, 1967; 2nd ed., New Haven: Yale U Pr, 1979). Tilman Seebass, *Musikdarstellung und Psalterillustration im früheren Mittelalter* (Bern: Francke, 1973). Reinhold Hammerstein, *Diabolus in musica: Studien zur Ikonographie der Musik im Mittelalter* (Bern: Francke, 1974). Albert P. de Mirimonde, *L'iconographie musical sous les rois Bourbons—La musique dans les arts plastiques (XVII–XVIII siècles),* 2 vols. (Paris: A & J Picard, 1975–77). Richard D. Leppert, *The Theme of Music in Flemish Paintings of the Seventeenth Century,* 2 vols. (Munich: Katzbichler, 1977). Id., *Arcadia at Versailles; Noble Amateur Musicians and Their Musettes and Hurdy-Gurdies at the French Court (c. 1660–1789): A Visual Study* (Amsterdam: Swets & Zeitlinger, 1978). James W. McKinnon, "Representations of the Mass in Medieval and Renaissance Art," *JAMS* 31 (1978): 21–52.

Literature. Hugo Leichtentritt, "Was lehren uns die Bildwerke des 14.–17. Jahrhunderts über die Instrumentalmusik ihrer Zeit?," *SIMG* 7 (1905–6): 315–64. Emanuel Winternitz, "The Visual Arts as a Source for the Historian of Music," *New York,* 1961, pp. 109–20. Howard Mayer Brown and Joan Lascelle, *Musical Iconography: A Manual for Cataloguing Musical Subjects in Western Art before 1800* (Cambridge, Mass.: Harvard U Pr, 1972). Barry S. Brook, "RIdIM: A New International Venture in Musical Iconography," *Notes* 28 (1971/72): 652–63. Emanuel Winternitz, "The Iconology of Music: Potentials and Pitfalls," *Perspectives in Musicology,* eds. Barry S. Brook, Edward O. D. Downes, and Sherman van Solkema (New York: Norton, 1972), pp. 80–90. Leopold Vorreiter, "Musikikonographie des Altertums im Schrifttum 1850–1949 und 1950–1974," *AM* 46 (1974): 1–42. *RIdIM/RCMI Newsletter* (New York: Research Center for Musical Iconography, 1975–97). *Imago musicae: Yearbook of RIdIM* (1984–). Tilmann Seebass, "The Illustration of Music Theory in the Late Middle Ages: Some Thoughts on Its Principle and a Few Examples," *Music Theory and Its Sources: Antiquity and the Middle Ages* (South Bend, Ind., 1987), pp. 197–234. Mark Slobin, "Icons of Ethnicity: Pictorial Themes in Commercial Euro-American Music," *Imago musicae* 5 (1988): 129–43. F. Guizzi, "Visual Message and Music in Cultures with Oral Tradition," *Imago musicae* 7 (1990): 7–23. Bonnie C. Wade, *Imagining Sound: An Ethnomusicological Study of Music, Art and Culture in Mughal India* (Chicago, 1998).

Ictus [Lat.]. (1) In prosody, and by analogy in music, a metrical *accent. (2) In the theory developed at Solesmes, the "rhythmic step" or "alighting point" that governs the rhythm of Gregorian chant [see Gregorian chant V, 2]. It marks the beginnings of groups of two or three notes that form the principal rhythmic units of every melody. It need not coincide with the accentuation of the text and in any case "is felt and intimated by tone of voice rather than expressed by any material emphasis" (see *LU,* pp. xxvi–xxxii).

Idée fixe [Fr., obsession]. Berlioz's term for the recurring musical idea linking the several movements of his

Symphonie fantastique and associated in its program with the image of the beloved. See also Cyclic form.

Idiomatic. Of a musical work, exploiting the particular capabilities of the instrument or voice for which it is intended. These capabilities may include timbres, registers, and means of articulation as well as pitch combinations that are more readily produced on one instrument than another (e.g., a *glissando on the slide trombone as opposed to a valved brass instrument or an *Alberti bass on a keyboard instrument as opposed to a slide trombone). Much music from before about 1600 was regarded as suitable for diverse instruments and/or voices, and much music of the Baroque period does not distinguish clearly the melodic styles of certain instruments and voices from one another. The rise of the virtuoso (both singers and instrumentalists) in the 19th century is associated with increasingly idiomatic writing, even in music that is not technically difficult.

Idiomelon [Gr.]. In *Byzantine chant, a **sticheron* whose metrical pattern and melody are original to itself. If borrowed from another *sticheron,* i.e., if it is a **contrafactum,* a *sticheron* is called a *prosomoion.* An *idiomelon* that serves as a model for *prosomoia* receives the special name *automelon.* D.E.C.

Idiophone. Any musical instrument that produces sound by the vibration of its own primary material, i.e., without the vibrations of a string, membrane, or column of air. Idiophones make up a very diverse collection that is broken down further according to construction and playing technique.

1. Concussion idiophone. Two sonorous objects are struck together: *castanets, *claves, *cymbals.

2. Percussion idiophone. A sonorous object is struck with a nonsonorous object: *bell, *celesta, *gong, *metallophone, *slit drum, *xylophone.

3. Rattle. Objects are shaken together or are shaken against a sonorous object: **angklung,* *maraca, *pellet bell.

4. Scraper. A stick is drawn over a notched object: *cog rattle, **güiro,* *washboard, **yü.*

5. Plucked idiophone (*lamellaphone, linguaphone). A flexible tongue, fixed at one end and free at the other, is plucked: *jew's harp, **mbira,* *music box.

6. Friction idiophone. An object is made to vibrate by rubbing: *glass harmonica, *musical saw.

See also Instrument.

Idomeneo, rè di Creta [It., Idomeneo, King of Crete]. Opera in three acts by Mozart (libretto by the Abbé Giovanni Battista Varesco, after a French libretto by Antoine Danchet), produced in Munich in 1781. Setting: Crete after the Trojan wars.

Idyll. (1) A short work in prose or verse depicting rustic life, sometimes synonymous with pastoral or *eclogue. (2) A musical work evoking the quality of pastoral or rural life.

Images [Fr.]. (1) Six piano pieces by Debussy in two sets of three each: I (1905), "Reflets dans l'eau," "Hommage à Rameau," "Mouvement"; II (1907), "Cloches à travers les feuilles," "Et la lune descend sur le temple qui fut," "Poissons d'or." (2) *Images pour orchestre,* three symphonic poems by Debussy (1905–12): *Rondes de printemps, Ibéria, Gigues.* The second, *Ibéria,* consists of three movements: "Par les rues et par les chemins," "Les parfums de la nuit," and "Le matin d'un jour de fête."

Imbroglio [It.]. A scene, usually occurring in a comic opera, in which the illusion of confusion is created by means of polyphonic complexity and rhythmic, metric, and melodic diversity. Originating in 18th-century *opera buffa,* the imbroglio was brought to a high point of artfulness and intricacy in the end of the second act of Wagner's *Die Meistersinger.*

Imitation. The statement of a single motive or melody by two or more parts or voices in succession, each part continuing as the others enter in turn. If successive statements are at the same pitch level, the imitation is said to take place at the unison. Imitation often takes place at different pitch levels, however. Especially common is a regular alternation between statements at the original pitch level and statements at the interval of a fifth above or a fourth below. The distance in time between successive statements may vary, but it often remains constant within any one set of statements. Imitation is generally classified as belonging to one of three types—*canon, *fugue, and free imitation—depending upon the nature of the motive or melody and the preciseness of the restatements. Such techniques are found in all periods of Western art music from the 12th century to the present and in some non-Western musics as well [see, e.g., Africa II, 2].

In canon, each successive voice *(comes)* repeats the complete leading voice *(dux)* literally or in a given transformation (transposition, inversion, retrograde, augmentation, etc.) as prescribed by the "canon" or rule. In fugue, although the entire piece may be based on a single idea or subject (double fugues will have two, etc.), this idea may be developed, possibly reordering motives, and even integrated with new material (e.g., countersubjects, episodes). Furthermore, fugal imitations are often less strict than those in canon; characteristic intervals may be altered so long as the subject keeps its essential contour (e.g., *tonal versus real answers). The terms canonic imitation and fugato refer to sections of canon or fugue that appear within otherwise nonimitative pieces. Free imitation, however, is looser still, and in many cases the only material shared between voices is the opening motive. As in fugue, this motive may be modified in successive statements, so long as it remains recognizable. In all

Imitation. Nicolas Gombert.

types of imitative counterpoint, the imitating voice may be accompanied by independent lines.

Although the term was probably not used until the 15th century, the various imitative techniques emerge as early as the 12th and 13th centuries. Some organa, *conductus,* and motets employ imitation (often in a form termed *voice exchange), and by the 14th century several canonic forms also appear: the *rota, the Italian **caccia,* and the French **chace.* Imitation also occurs in some 14th-century Italian madrigals as well as in some motets of around 1400. During the 15th century, imitation became gradually more important (e.g., in both sacred and secular works by Dufay), but it was not until around 1500 that imitation became established as a paradigm of musical style in works by Josquin and his contemporaries. Josquin himself made frequent use of paired imitation (in which the voices enter in pairs), the time interval between members of a pair being relatively short and that between successive pairs relatively long. About this time, Ramos (1482) became the first to use the term itself to refer to both strict and free repetition. Later theorists, such as Aaron (1516), equated fugue and imitation: "It is called imitation or fugue because the consequent (or antecedent) voice repeats the very notes of the preceding part or else repeats notes identical in name though different in location" (trans. Haar, 1971, p. 232). Later still, however, Aaron observed that imitation was inexact repetition.

Composers of the middle and later 16th century, such as Gombert, Willaert, Clemens non Papa, and Palestrina, made still more extensive use of imitation, sometimes termed pervading imitation [Ger. *Durchimitation,* through imitation]. Here, each line of text was set imitatively with a new melody, each such set of imitative entries termed a point of imitation, with successive points or sections overlapping one another [see Ex.]. Pervading imitation was used in sacred genres (Masses, motets) and secular genres (madrigal, chanson) alike and also became the distinguishing feature of instrumental forms such as the *ricercar, *canzona, *fantasia, and *capriccio. Nevertheless, despite Aaron's recognition of the difference between fugue and imitation, no theorist before Zarlino distinguishes adequately between these two terms and canon. According to Zarlino, successive entries of fugue appear only at perfect intervals (unison, fourth, fifth, octave), whereas imitation can occur at any interval including second, third, sixth, and seventh. Both fugue and imitation may be strict *(legata)* or free *(sciolta)*—*fuga legata* refers to strict canons at perfect intervals whereas *imitatione legata* may denote a free canon.

Most late 16th- and early 17th-century writers adopt Zarlino's definitions of fugue and imitation (e.g., Artusi, Pontio, Cerone). Zacconi (1622), however, used the term in the modern sense for situations where the *dux* is followed only in the most general way. This interpretation became increasingly influential, and by 1700 imitation was generally regarded as a less strict version of fugue (e.g., Rameau, 1722). Imitation remained a basic technique of musical composition through the first half of the 18th century, not only in specifically imitative forms such as fugue and canon, but in a wide variety of vocal and instrumental music as well. The masters of the Classical style—Haydn, Mozart, and Beethoven—all make significant use of imitation also, though that style is usually thought to make distinctly less use of imitation and polyphony than do the styles of preceding centuries.

Throughout the 16th century, the term imitation also had other, wider implications. On the one hand, following rhetorical usage, it referred to the more general use of compositional models and borrowings [see Parody] and even the conscious mimicry of a particular composer's style (e.g., in Tinctoris's introduction to his *Liber de arte contrapuncti*). On the other hand, it referred to the Aristotelian concept of the imitation of nature.

Bibl.: Armen Carapetyan, "The Concept of *Imitazione della natura* in the 16th Century," *MD* 1 (1948): 47–67. James Haar, "Zarlino's Definition of Fugue and Imitation," *JAMS* 24 (1971): 226–54. Howard M. Brown, "Emulation, Competition and Homage: Imitation and Theories of Imitation in the Renaissance," *JAMS* 35 (1982): 1–48.

Imitative. Characterized by *imitation.

Immer [Ger.]. Always, continuously; e.g., *immer stärker,* continuously louder.

Imperfect. See Cadence, Interval, Mensural notation.

Imperfection. See Mensural notation.

Impetuoso [It.]. Impetuous.

Impressionism. A term principally applied to the style cultivated by Claude Debussy during the final decade of the 19th century and the first decade of the 20th. The term was originally introduced in the visual arts to characterize the work of a group of French painters of the late 19th century (e.g., Monet, whose painting *Impression: soleil levant* inspired critic Louis Leroy to coin the term in 1874) who exploited the suffusing effects of light, color, and atmospheric conditions to undermine sharply drawn contours. The subtle gradations produced by haze and smoke were especially favored, giving rise to softly focused, somewhat "blurred" images intended to convey the general "impression" of a scene rather than its precise visual equivalent. By the turn of the century the word was widely current, used to refer not only to French painting but also to other artistic endeavors characterized by rapid change and ephemeral effects (for example, in Germany and Austria, the music of Richard Strauss).

Traditional descriptions of Debussy's style suggest a number of parallels with visual impressionism: finely graded instrumental colors; static, nonclimactic melodies, often circling around a single pitch; harmony conceived as a largely coloristic element; complex textures consisting of elaborate surface figurations, often suffusing whatever melodic material they contain; continuously evolving forms without sharp sectional divisions. Though first used as early as 1887, the term is applicable mainly to music from the *Prélude à "L'après-midi d'un faune"* (1894) to the *Préludes* for piano (1910–13); and, even within this period, it suits certain works (e.g., the opera *Pelléas et Mélisande,* 1893–1902) better than others. Moreover, impressionistic elements are present in works by a number of earlier composers, e.g., in the elaborate pianistic fabrics of Chopin and Liszt and in the soft harmonic colorations of Chabrier and Chausson. At times, similar tendencies are detectable in German composers of the period, notably Wagner, Mahler, and Strauss. Debussy himself disapproved of the term in a letter to Jacques Durand in 1908.

Among Debussy's contemporaries, Ravel is often regarded as an impressionist; but despite corresponding emphasis on color and figuration, the more emphatic rhythm and phrase structure of much of Ravel's music sets it distinctly apart from that of Debussy. The only major composer to exploit impressionistic effects in the period immediately following was Béla Bartók; but such effects have again become common in the music of composers active since World War II, notably Olivier Messiaen, György Ligeti, and George Crumb. R.P.M.

Impromptu [Fr., unpremeditated]. In the 19th century and since, a composition, usually for piano, in an offhand or extemporized style or perhaps intended to suggest the result of sudden inspiration. The term was first used in 1822 by both Jan Václav Voříšek and Heinrich Marschner. The best-known examples are by Schubert (op. 90, D. 899, and op. 142, D. 935, for at least the first set of which the title was supplied not by Schubert but by his publisher), Chopin (opp. 29, 36, 51, 66), and Schumann (op. 5, actually a set of variations, and *Albumblätter* no. 9). Like other types of *character pieces, they are varied in form, though ternary form is common.

Improperia [Lat., reproaches]. In the Roman Catholic Rite, a series of chants sung at the Veneration of the Cross on Good Friday, expressing in alternation God's compassion for Israel and man's ingratitude as seen in the suffering of Christ. As preserved in modern service books (*LU,* pp. 737–41), they consist of three texts based on passages from the Old Testament ("Popule meus, quid feci tibi?" O my people, what have I done to thee; "Quia eduxi te per desertum," Because I led thee out through the desert; and "Quid ultra debui facere tibi," What more ought I to do for thee?), each followed by the *Trisagion, concluding with a series of shorter texts, each followed by "Popule meus." Manuscripts of the 10th and 11th centuries present diverse arrangements of such pieces. Related texts are found in the Byzantine and Mozarabic rites. Palestrina's **falsobordone* settings have been much performed.

Improvisation, extemporization. The creation of music in the course of performance.

I. *The concept.* Even though it is tempting to distinguish simply between composed, or "precomposed," music (determined precisely in advance) and improvisation (created on the spot), the world of music actually comprises repertories and performances in which improvisation of quite different sorts is present in various degrees. Thus, music in oral tradition is normally composed by improvisation of a sort: the audible rendition of pieces (though usually without audience), whose components may then be altered and recombined and finally memorized. The performance of music in oral tradition, however, may or may not involve improvisation. In Western art music, which is heavily dependent on notation for transmission, improvisation includes phenomena such as the addition of extemporized ornaments as well as special improvised genres. Certain cultures with orally transmitted music such as those of South and West Asia also distinguish between improvised and memorized materials. Some improvisational systems are governed by theoretical rules strictly applied by performers. The degree to which a musician departs from a written or memorized work and the extent to which performances differ from each other may also be considered a function of improvisation. Thus, the presence or nature of improvisation is affected by, but does not depend upon, the concept of composition, the use of notation and oral tradition, and the nature of performance practice. But it seems most appropriate to reserve the term improvisation for cultures and repertories in which a distinction from nonimprovised or precomposed forms can be recognized.

With the exception of a small number of experiments in some *aleatory music after 1960, improvised music is not produced without some kind of preconception or point of departure. There is always a model that determines the scope within which a musician acts. In the case of jazz, the model may be a series of harmonies that determine pitches to be selected for a melody; or a melody that is subjected to variation; or a set of motifs from which selection is made. In India, it is partly a set of rules governing melodic and rhythmic movement. In the *mbira* music of the Shona of Zimbabwe, it is a set of stylistically distinct stages through which the variations of a short tune must pass. While improvisation is normally the task of a soloist, group improvisation is found in styles such as Dixieland jazz and the *gamelan* music of Java and Bali.

The world's cultures differ in the value placed on improvisation. In Western culture, it has usually been regarded as a kind of craft, subordinate to the more prestigious "art" of composition. North Indian musicians are evaluated primarily by their ability to improvise and to balance adherence to the prescribed system and individual inventiveness. The most valued and best-paid musicians in a Javanese *gamelan* are those responsible for the maintenance of the regularity principles of group improvisation rather than those whose role is virtuosic departure from the model. In some North American Indian societies, improvisatory change of a composed tune is rejected and even punished; in many African societies, it is encouraged and expected. It seems likely that performers in 18th-century Europe, in their performance practice, departed more from the written notation than did those of the late 19th century, a change paralleling changes in social and aesthetic roles of composer and performer. While improvisatory systems provide more variety in the performance of individual works, they tend to be more compact stylistically than those in which improvisation is absent and in which innovation, inhibited in performance, is reserved for and expected in composition. The elements of risk and of unpredictable achievement are important features in all cultures practicing improvisation.

II. *Western art music.* Improvisation has played its principal role in the supplementation and variation of written compositions. It was probably important in the development of melismatic types of liturgical chant. In the 14th and 15th centuries, the growth of polyphonic practices included improvisatory harmonization. After ca. 1550, melodic improvisation such as the insertion of embellishments or extended ornamental passages (coloraturas) and the improvisation of variations on themes, particularly on keyboard instruments and lutes, developed roles of importance. There was considerable emphasis on the art in the Baroque and Classical periods. A significant development was the practice of extended improvisatory performance of complex polyphonic forms by distinguished composers prized for their intellectual and manual dexterity and their ability to reconcile formal requirements and thematic inventiveness. Virtuosic genres such as the *toccata were sometimes improvised. Sweelinck, Frescobaldi, Buxtehude, Bach, and Handel were famed for their organ improvisations, and on the piano, Mozart and Beethoven. The practice of improvising Baroque forms such as fugues continued in the 19th century, constituting, well into the 20th, an academic requirement in certain European conservatories, and the performance of fugues based on themes given by the audience remained a special genre of modern organ virtuosos. But improvisation of works in contemporary styles continued in the 19th century; Mendelssohn, Liszt, Moscheles, Bruckner, Saint-Saëns, and Franck were famous for improvisations in the style of their own composed works.

An important improvisatory genre of the Classical and Romantic eras was the *cadenza of concertos, in which soloists combined thematic development and technical prowess. With the increased stature of the composer, greater precision of notation, and emphasis on the perfected, finished masterwork in the later 19th century, and with the increased specialization of composer and performer, improvisation was gradually relegated to academic exercise. Yet the concept of an improvisatory style of composition, found, for example, in certain *character pieces for keyboard and in orchestral works with relatively loose formal structure, by composers such as Chopin, Liszt, and Paganini, is an important feature of the Romantic movement.

Revival of improvisation came in the course of the 20th century as a result of several factors. Knowledge of non-Western music with its improvisatory systems stimulated composers, as did the development of jazz, a form principally improvised and in part indirectly derived from the improvised variation technique of West Africa. Techniques of jazz improvisation extend from simple variations of a tune and chaconne-like composition on the basis of a set of chords (*changes), typical of Dixieland, to dissonant genres such as *bop, developed by Charlie (Bird) Parker, all the way to the *free jazz of artists such as Ornette Coleman, and from solo performance and small ensembles in which all musicians improvise to big-band performances in which the ensemble's role is accompaniment and improvisation is limited to the occasional solo. The conceptual association of jazz improvisation with political and social struggles for freedom is significant in the 20th-century history of American and to an extent European music. Complete domination by the musical score led, after 1950, to a reaction by composers such as Lukas Foss who required improvisation in sections of their works. In these, performers are typically directed to improvise for a specific amount of time on the basis of a stated group of tones. Ensembles that devote themselves entirely or partially to improvisation—instrumental as well as vocal, and including the Kronos and Turtle Island string quartets—became an important component of the art music scene in the late 20th century. Composition with the use of aleatoric principles involves improvisation as well. The interest in authentic performance, especially of music from the 18th century and before, has also led to the development of improvisatory performance practice. Robert Levin is among the leaders in the revival of improvisation in the course of performance, including the cadenzas, in the piano concerts of Mozart. In recent decades, improvisation has become an important factor in the music education of children. See also Aleatory music, Jazz, Performance practice.

III. *Non-Western music.* Improvisation is not a major factor in Chinese and Japanese art music. In Korea, the instrumental genre *sanjo,* of recent origin, involves extended melodic improvisation. The *gamelan* music of Java and Bali includes group improvisation of great sophistication, with the many instruments of the ensemble departing in several distinct ways from a composed model, producing simultaneous variations in heterophony. See also Southeast Asia.

The most developed improvisatory systems are those of India and the Middle East. South Indian (Carnatic) music is largely made up of a repertory of composed songs in whose performance improvised passages and variations of lines are inserted. In a full-blown performance, four types of improvisation are used: the nonmetric *ālāpana,* in which the tonal content and relationships of the *rāga* (functioning as model) are explored; *tānam,* roughly similar but with rhythmic pulse; *niraval,* a series of variations on a line from a composed song; and *svarakalpana,* rapid virtuosic passages, each repeated by the accompanying violin, sung with syllables of the Indian solmization system. Improvisation is more prominent in North Indian (Hindustani) music. A full instrumental performance includes nonmetric *ālāp*; *joṛ* and *jhālā,* also nonmetric but with pulse of increasing rapidity; and a *gat,* a rhythmic and melodic line that functions as the model for variation and rapid virtuosic passages. Rhythmic improvisation (including drum solos) involves the juxtaposition of the metric unit, *tāla,* with extemporized units of various lengths, as well as augmentation and diminution of rhythmic lines. See also South Asia.

Middle Eastern improvisation is similar to but less systematized than Indian. The main improvised form in Iran is *āvāz,* nonmetric singing or playing with inserted metric bits, all based on the scalar and motivic material of a *dastgāh.* The *chahār mezrāb,* a virtuosic form with rapid rhythmic ostinato, may be composed or improvised. In Arabic and Turkish music, the main instrumental genre is *taqsīm* (Turkish *taksim*), nonmetric but sometimes with pulse. The improvisor's task is the development of motifs and the modulation from a principal *maqām,* model for tonal content and melodic motifs, to secondary *maqāms*. In much South and West Asian music, improvisation involves the use of a melodic motif that is subjected to repetition, simple variation, extension, contraction, melodic sequence, etc. See also Near and Middle East.

Improvisation is of enormous importance in the music of sub-Saharan Africa, although formal distinction between improvised and composed genres may be absent. Simultaneous performance of variations is found in instrumental ensembles such as the xylophone orchestras of the Chopi of Mozambique. Throughout Africa, the improvisation of variations on a thematic line requiring five to ten seconds is a mainstay of performance. Percussion ensembles similarly perform far-flung improvisations on the basis of simple memorized rhythmic formulas. See also Africa.

Among other cultures, the improvisation of songs in competition among the Inuit (Eskimo), and of song texts requiring melodic and rhythmic changes in North American Plains Indian music, as well as the extemporization of lines and sections, including manipulation of order, in the lengthy epics of Eastern Europe, are examples of this complex art.

Bibl.: Marcel Dupré, *Traité d'improvisation à l'orgue* (Paris: A Leduc, 1926). Ernst Ferand, *Die Improvisation in der Musik* (Zürich: Rhein-Verlag, 1938). Jaap Kunst, *Music in Java,* 2nd ed., trans. Emile van Loo (The Hague: M Nijhoff, 1949; 3rd ed., ed. E. L. Heins, 1973). Ernst Ferand, *Improvisation in Nine Centuries of Western Music,* trans. of *Mw* 12 (Cologne: A Volk, 1961). Gunther Schuller, *The History of Jazz,* vol. 1 (New York: Oxford U Pr, 1968). Ella Zonis, *Classical Persian Music* (Cambridge, Mass.: Harvard U Pr, 1973). Bruno Nettl, "Thoughts on Improvisation: A Comparative Approach," *MQ* 60 (1974): 1–19. Bonnie C. Wade, *Music in India: The Classical Traditions* (Englewood Cliffs, N.J.: Prentice-Hall, 1979). "Improvisation in der Musik des Mittelalters und der Renaissance," *Basler Jahrbuch für historische Musikpraxis* 7 (1983): 11–191. Bernard Lortat-Jacob, ed., *L'Improvisation dans les musiques de tradition orale* (Paris: Selaf, 1987). Leo Treitler, "Medieval Improvisation," *The World of Music* 33, no. 3 (1991). Paul Berliner, *Thinking in Jazz: The Infinite Art of Improvisation* (Chicago: U of Chicago Pr, 1994). Habib Hassan Touma, *The Music of the Arabs, New Expanded Edition* (Portland, Ore.: Amadeus, 1996). Derek Bailey, *Improvisation, Its Nature and Practice in Music* (New York: DaCapo, 1997). Regine Feist, *Der Begriff 'Improvisation' in der neuen Musik* (Berlin: Berliner MusikStudien 14, 1997). Bruno Nettl with Melinda Russell, ed., *In the Course of Performance: Studies in the World of Musical Improvisation* (Chicago: U of Chicago Pr, 1998). B.N.

Im Takt [Ger.]. See *Takt.*

Incalzando [It.]. Pressing on, chasing.

In campo aperto [It., in open field]. Of *neumes, without the aid of lines or other means of fixing pitch precisely.

Incatenatura [It.]. **Quodlibet.*

In Central Asia [Russ. *V sredney Azii*]. A "musical picture" for orchestra by Borodin (1880), evoking the journey of a caravan across the steppes.

Incidental music. Music to be used in connection with a play. It may consist of instrumental music played before an act or between acts (*overture, **entr'acte,* *interlude); it may be vocal or instrumental music accompanying the action of the play (songs and serenades, marches and dances, background music for monologues or dialogues, music for supernatural or transformation scenes); it may underscore the action or be a digression from the action. The use of incidental music extends back to ancient Greek times and continues into the present day. (*Film music may be considered an offshoot of incidental music.) Examples from the 17th century include much of Purcell's dramatic music; from the 18th century, Mozart's incidental music for *Thamos, König in Ägypten.* Many pieces written as incidental music in the 19th century have taken on an independent existence, often in the form of an orchestral suite, e.g., Beethoven's music for Goethe's *Egmont,* Schubert's for von Chézy's *Rosamunde, Fürstin von Zypren,* Mendelssohn's for *A Midsummer Night's Dream,* Bizet's for Daudet's *L'Arlésienne,* Grieg's for Ibsen's *Peer Gynt,* Fauré's and later Sibelius's for Maeterlinck's *Pelléas et Mélisande.*

Incipit [Lat., begins]. The first few words and/or notes with which a work of literature or music begins; in liturgical chant, sometimes also synonymous more specifically with *intonation or *initium* [see Psalm tone]. Works that lack an independent title are often referred to by incipit, and *thematic catalogs and indexes of various kinds are built around lists of incipits. In sources for liturgical chant, a piece that is sung in several services may be copied or printed in full only once, other occurrences being represented by incipits. Sources for polyphonic music often place only the incipit of a text under the beginning of one or more parts. This practice, however, is not a sure indication of which parts should be sung and which played on instruments. In some cases, as in the tenors of early *motets, an incipit may identify the source of the part in question.

Incoronazione di Poppea, L' [It., The Coronation of Poppea]. Opera in three acts by Monteverdi (libretto by G. F. Busenello, after Tacitus), produced in Venice in 1642. Setting: Rome during the reign of Nero, ca. 62 C.E.

Indeterminacy. See Aleatory music.

India. See South Asia.

Indian Queen, The. A *semi-opera in five acts by Purcell (play by John Dryden and Robert Howard, final masque by Daniel Purcell), produced in London in 1695. Setting: Peru and Mexico.

Indians, American. See American Indian music.

Indochina. See Southeast Asia.

Indonesia. See Southeast Asia.

Inégales [Fr.]. See *Notes inégales.*

Inflection, inflexion. (1) See Monotone, Psalm tone. (2) Deliberate deviation from the norm of a pitch. It is prominent in jazz [see Blue note] and popular music and is not unknown in Western art music.

Inganno [It., deception]. A late 16th- and early 17th-century procedure that results in the reshaping of a melody when the names of its *solmization syllables in one hexachord are applied to another. For example, the melodies c B B♭ A c F and F E c A d G may both be expressed *fa, mi, fa, mi, sol, ut,* depending on the hexachords involved.

Bibl.: John Harper, "Frescobaldi's Early *Inganni* and Their Background," *PRMA* 105 (1978–79): 1–12. A.J.N.

Ingressa [Lat.]. The *Ambrosian chant corresponding to the Roman introit.

Initium [Lat.]. The beginning of a liturgical chant, especially a *psalm tone or related form.

Innig [Ger.]. Heartfelt, sincere, fervent.

Inno [It.]. Hymn.

In nomine [Lat.]. Any of over 150 English instrumental compositions of the 16th and 17th centuries, all using the *Sarum antiphon "Gloria tibi Trinitas" as a **cantus firmus* [see Ex.; a related melody is given in *LU,* p. 914].

Glo- ri- a ti- bi Tri- ni-tas ae-qua- lis

These pieces and the associated title *In nomine* arose as follows: The setting of the words "in nomine Domini" in the four-voice Benedictus of John Taverner's six-voice *cantus firmus* Mass *Gloria tibi Trinitas* began to be circulated as a detached piece soon after its composition and was arranged numerous times, most often in four untexted parts. Subsequently, many new compositions incorporating the *cantus firmus* and often other musical features of the Taverner setting were written; most were titled according to the words of the Mass section rather than to those of the antiphon. A tradition of *In nomine* composition had been firmly established by the end of the 1550s.

Although a few examples are for lute and a few more for keyboard, most are for instrumental consort. At first, new works for consort were commonly written for four parts; soon, however, five parts became the norm, and occasionally even more were employed. The antiphon melody is usually in an upper part (most often the alto); it is rarely shared among the voices and rarely appears in the bass even in fragments.

Keyboard pieces based on this antiphon belong more to the tradition of keyboard plainsong setting than to that of the *In nomine* proper; some even bear the title *Gloria tibi Trinitas,* either in addition to or instead of *In nomine.* There are a few compositions that have the title but no other clear connection with the repertory of the *In nomine.*

Important composers of such pieces besides Taverner include Christopher Tye, Robert Parsons, Robert White, Nicholas Strogers, Alfonso Ferrabosco (the elder and the younger), John Blitheman (for keyboard), William Byrd, John Mundy, Orlando Gibbons, and Henry Purcell, who wrote the last 17th-century examples. In the 20th century, Peter Maxwell Davies has made significant use of the *In nomine* tradition.

Bibl.: Ernst H. Meyer, *Die mehrstimmige Spielmusik des 17. Jahrhunderts in Nord- und Mitteleuropa* (Kassel: Bärenreiter, 1934). Robert Donington and Thurston Dart, "The Origin of the In Nomine," *ML* 30 (1949): 101–6. Gustave Reese, "The Origin of the English *In Nomine,*" *JAMS* 2 (1949): 7–22. Warwick Edwards, "In Nomine," *Grove 6* [includes list and cites editions].

Insieme [It.]. Together.

Instrument. (1) [Ger.] In Germany in the 17th and 18th centuries, a stringed keyboard instrument, especially the clavichord; in the early 19th century, the piano. Michael Praetorius (1619) disapprovingly records the generic use of the term, and J. C. F. Fischer, in the preface to his *Musikalisches Blumen-Büschlein* (1698), uses it as a synonym for clavichord.

(2) Any means of producing sounds that are considered to be music by the persons producing them, except the human voice and body areas used for musical purposes. The scientific study of musical instruments is called organology, a Latin-based version of the German word *Instrumentenkunde.* This discipline has two major goals: (a) understanding indigenous terminology and its relation to the culture that generates it and (b) developing study methods and terminology for abstracting and comparing information about all musical instruments. Instruments often fulfill extramusical functions and thus may be studied as well in contexts such as general culture, history, philosophy, technology, and ecology. Specific instruments are discussed separately in this dictionary. Those mentioned here are used to clarify general concepts.

I. *Indigenous terminology.* The terms and classifications of instruments are either "natural" (culture derived) or "artificial" (classifier's method). They tend to fall into three general categories: (1) playing method, (2) structure or material, (3) use or status. These can be either practical or theoretical. Practical examples of the first two categories are the East Asian and Western musicians' terms winds, strings, and percussion. Two of these words refer to what is vibrating and the third deals with how the vibration is generated, but the terms function well as a system in everyday speech about the ensembles of those regions. In contrast, Indonesian musicians speak of slabs, gongs, and drums and place winds and strings with the human voice. These terms properly reflect the use of instruments in *gamelan* music. Mainland Southeast Asians usually separate strings from winds because of their greater variety and use and because of the influence of contiguous East Asian nomenclature and music.

A theoretical division by materials is the ancient Chinese *bayin* system, which classifies instruments as being fundamentally pottery (clay ocarinas), gourd (wind chest of *sheng* mouth organs), silk, skin, metal, stone, wood, or bamboo. This system was created primarily to fit instruments into a design of cosmological numbers rather than practical use. It influenced other written and oral Asian music theories from Japan to Indonesia. Theory and practice both relate to material ecology among the *'Are 'are of the Solomon Islands (Zemp, 1978), who use the word 'au* to mean instruments made of bamboo and from this extrapolate a host of musical terms for ensembles, playing methods, and genres, as well as European instruments and sound equipment. The slit drum *('o'o)* is classified separately, however, because it is an indigenous instrument not made of bamboo. In Java the word *ditabub* (beaten) became a generic term attached to words for playing methods like shaking, blowing, bowing, or plucking and also distinguished between instruments beaten with a padded or a hard hammer. Indonesian and other Southeast Asian instrument classifications include tone system, loud or soft sounds, and male or female. Distinctions by stage location in an ensemble or pay scale are common throughout the world, including Java, India, and the West.

A common functional distinction for instruments is that of sacred and secular. The Jewish *shofar* and New Guinean ancestral flutes are examples of instruments with nontransferable functions, while the Western organ, traditionally a church instrument, serves both functions well. Most European urban instruments may appear in either function, although since medieval times a distinction has been made between loud and soft instruments, as is common elsewhere in the world. The Dutch midwinter horn *(midwinterhoorn)* is an example of a folk instrument that is built and used for only one purpose and season. Musical instruments that may serve as status symbols include the grand (rather than upright) piano in a living room, the pipe (rather than electric) organ in a church, royal drums in East Africa, and the knobbed gong in Kalimantan (as a household possession). This symbolic function indicates the potential value of instruments in nonmusical research.

II. *Organological classifications.* Examples noted above show that diverse classifications exist in both oral and literate cultures. Chinese and Indian are perhaps the oldest written traditions. Western approaches grew out of Greco-Roman and early Christian theories. By the 13th century Islamic influences appeared in Europe. Western writers like Michael Praetorius (*Syntagma musicum,* 1619) and Marin Mersenne (*Harmonie universelle,* 1636) developed taxonomies that emphasized instruments in use more than biblical references. Other new systems flourished in the 18th century. Since the late 19th century, musical instrument research generally has dealt with (a) where and for what purpose an instrument is used, (b) how it is played, or (c) its physical features. The first category is favored by historians and anthropologists. For example, distributions of the *zurna* double reed, the *rebab* spiked fiddle, or the plucked lute are used to study Near Eastern influences in Asia, Europe, and Africa, and similar information about the *mbira/sanza* plucked, keyed instrument and other African instruments aids in the understanding of developments in the Western Hemisphere.

Most organologists find physical features and performance practice more amenable to Western-style classifications. The Mahillon (1880–1922) system was inspired by an ancient Indian set of four classes based upon the nature of the material that vibrates. This was expanded by Hornbostel and Sachs (1914) into a system frequently used today. The electrophone, an instrument in which sound is produced or amplified by electrical means, was added later to the basic four shown below with their first layers of subclasses and a few examples.

1. Idiophone. Vibrations are produced, without stretching the basic material, by striking either one portion of the instrument against another (cymbals) or another object against the instrument (triangle), by scraping, by plucking *(sanza),* by rubbing, or by bowing (nail violin or modern single cymbal).

2. Membranophone. Sound produced by vibrations of a stretched membrane that is struck or rubbed (drum). The mirliton (kazoo) is called a blown membranophone.

3. Chordophone. Sound produced by a vibrating (stretching) string activated by striking, plucking, or bowing (rubbing). Its four basic families are: (i) Lute. Strings are parallel to the soundboard and extend beyond it along a neck or fingerboard (guitar, violin, *sitār*). (ii) Zither. Strings are parallel to the soundboard and functionally its same length (piano, dulcimer, *koto*). (iii) Harp. Strings are at right angles to the soundboard. (iv) Lyre. Strings are parallel to the soundboard and are suspended beyond it on a crossbar of a yoke (Ethiopian *krar* and *beganna*).

4. Aerophone. Sound from a vibrating column of air. It may be activated from a blow hole (flute), a reed (single, double, or quadruple; clarinet, shawm, oboe), or buzzing lips (trumpet, horn).

Using a technique similar to the Dewey decimal system, the Sachs-Hornbostel system moved deeply into details within each class in a manner that predated computerized attempts. Schaeffner (1936) built yet another system with two major divisions: solid materials and columns of air. The first was divided into tensile, nontensile, and flexible materials. Dräger (1948) brought the performer–instrument relation into a graphic system, and Elschek and Stockmann (1967) developed symbols that represent a host of typologies of structure and performance methods. Montagu and Burton (1971) used taxonomies of natural sciences as their base, whereas Hood (1971) entered all physical, performance, social, and tone features into one complex graphic symbol. Heyde (1975) graphed the flow of energies in the performer and the instrument that result in a sound.

A goal of all these systems is consistency, but none

has been fully able to allow for the imagination of instrument makers and performers and the variety exhibited by their work. Thus, in the Sachs-Hornbostel system, the *kora* of Gambia is a harp-lute; the Australian *didjeridoo* is a buzzed-lip aerophone that can be an idiophone if rhythm is struck on its side; a tambourine with jingles in its frame is a hybrid idiomembranophone; and a tube zither, if its "strings" are lifted out of the surface of the bamboo body itself, is an idiochord. The classification of other instruments such as the jew's harp and bullroarer is debatable, as are the more detailed descriptions of nearly every type of instrument whether it be Western, regional, or worldwide. Efforts were made (Malm, 1974) to use less rigorous systems through computers to enhance interdisciplinary exchanges, as instruments reside in a great variety of collections and museums (art, historical, ethnic, regional, private, etc.). Scholars continue their attempts to create better systems and to use the latest electronic and computer tools to learn more about the materials and sounds of individual instruments. The study of these as well as the older and the indigenous approaches will contribute to an understanding, not only of the instruments and their relations to the world at large or to the society that created them, but also to an understanding of the mind-set of the organologists of each period and generation.

Bibl.: Victor C. Mahillon, *Catalogue descriptif et analytique du Musée instrumental du Conservatoire royal de musique de Bruxelles* (Ghent: A Hoste, 1880–1922). Curt Sachs, *Real-Lexikon der Musikinstrumente* (Berlin: J Bard, 1913; R: Hildesheim: Olms, 1962). Erich M. von Hornbostel and Curt Sachs, "Systematik der Musikinstrumente," *Zeitschrift für Ethnologie* 46 (1914): 553–90; trans. Eng. Anthony C. Baines and Klaus P. Wachsmann, *GSJ* 14 (1961): 3–29. André Schaeffner, *Origine des instruments de musique* (Paris: Payot, 1936). Curt Sachs, *The History of Musical Instruments* (New York: Norton, 1940). Hans Heinz Dräger, *Princip einer Systematik der Musikinstrumente* (Kassel: Bärenreiter, 1948). Robert Donington, *The Instruments of Music* (London: Methuen London, 1949; 3rd ed., 1962). Marin Mersenne, *Harmonie universelle* (The Hague: M Nijhoff, 1957). Alexander Buchner, *Musical Instruments through the Ages,* trans. Iris Urwin (London: Batchworth Pr, 1961). Sibyl Marcuse, *Musical Instruments: A Comprehensive Dictionary* (Garden City, N.Y.: Doubleday, 1964; corr. ed., New York: Norton, 1975). Anthony Baines, *European and American Musical Instruments* (London: Batsford, 1966). Michael Praetorius, *Syntagma musicum* (Oxford: Clarendon, 1966). Oskár Elschek and Erich Stockmann, "Zur Typologie der Volksmusikinstrumente," *Brno,* 1967, pp. 11–22. Mantle Hood, *The Ethnomusicologist* (New York: McGraw-Hill, 1971). Jeremy Montagu and John Burton, "A Proposed New Classification System for Musical Instruments," *Ethno* 15 (1971): 49–70. William Malm, "A Computer Aid in Musical Instrument Research," *Emsheimer,* 1974, pp. 119–22. Music Library Association, *A Survey of Musical Instrument Collections in the United States and Canada* (Chapel Hill, N.C., 1974). Herbert Heyde, *Grundlagen des natürlichen Systems der Musikinstrumente* (Leipzig: Deutscher Verlag für Musik, 1975). Diagram Group, *Musical Instruments of the World* (New York: Paddington Pr, 1976). Jean L. Jenkins, ed., *International Directory of Musical Instrument Collections* (Buren, Netherlands: Frits Knuf for International Council of Museums, 1977). Hugo Zemp, "'Are'are Classification of Musical Types and Instruments," *Ethno* 22 (1978): 37–67. Stanley Sadie, ed., *The New Grove Dictionary of Musical Instruments* (London: Macmillan; New York: Grove's Dictionaries of Music, 1984). Margaret J. Kartomi, *On Concepts and Classifications of Musical Instruments* (Chicago: U of Chicago Pr, 1990). For further bibl., see articles on specific instruments. W.P.M.

Instrumentation. (1) The properties and capabilities of individual instruments; also *orchestration. (2) The particular combination of instruments employed in any piece.

Instrument collections. See Music Library Association [William Lichtenwanger, et al.], *A Survey of Musical Instrument Collections in the United States and Canada* (Chapel Hill, N.C., 1974). Jean Jenkins, ed., *International Directory of Musical Instrument Collections* (Buren, Netherlands: Frits Knuf for International Council of Museums, 1977). Laurence Libin, "Instruments, collections of," *Grove 6* [includes list]. James Coover, *Musical Instrument Collections: Catalogues and Cognate Literature,* Detroit Studies in Music Bibliography 47 (Detroit: Info Coord, 1981).

Intabulation [fr. It. *intabolatura, intavolatura;* Fr. *reduicte en tablature;* Ger. *Intabulierung*]. An arrangement of a vocal or instrumental ensemble work for keyboard or plucked string instrument, notated in *tablature. The need to "tabulate" accompaniments in short score from single parts in *choirbook or *partbook formats probably accounts for its inception. The earliest surviving notated keyboard music (ca. 1320) and that for lute, *vihuela,* guitar, etc. (ca. 1470–73), consists overwhelmingly of arrangements of secular polyphony, Mass movements, motets, and (less frequently) ensemble dances and abstract pieces such as ricercars. The model is molded to the playing capabilities of the intended instrument, invariably clothed in ornate coloration [see *Glosa*] with runs, trill-like figures, turns, mordents, etc., that transform the model into an elaborate idiomatic virtuoso display piece. (For early examples, see the Codex Faenza, ca. 1400, ed. Plamenac, 1972, *EDM* 37–39, *CEKM* 1; for later examples before 1600, see works listed in *BrownI.*) Such works can provide much information about performance practices of the time. Lute intabulations in particular (since they provide exact indications of accidentals) can provide important resources for the realization of **musica ficta.* Works by Josquin Desprez enjoyed widespread popularity in both keyboard and plucked-string repertories (for additional exx. for keyboard, see *RRMR* 30). Italian intabulations of chansons by Parisian composers began the history of the *canzona, and intabulations in Elizabethan sources such as the *Fitzwilliam Virginal Book are especially significant in the history of *variation. Although the term intabulation is usually associated only with music before 1600, the procedure did continue into the Baroque. The repertories for plucked stringed instruments, in particular, continued to include similar transcriptions of chorales, opera arias, sonatas for keyboard and other instruments, and ensemble dance music, often in the fashionable *stile brise.*

Bibl.: Jesus Bal y Gay, "Fuenllana and the Transcriptions of Spanish Lute Music," *AM* 11 (1939): 16–27. Ernst T. Ferand, *Die Improvisation, Mw* 12, trans., *Improvisation in Nine Centuries of Western Music* (Cologne: A Volk, 1961). Howard Mayer Brown, "Accidentals and Ornamentation in Sixteenth-Century Intabulations of Josquin's Motets," *Josquin,* 1971, pp. 476–522. Geneviève Thibault, "Instrumental Transcriptions of Josquin's Chansons," *Josquin,* 1971, pp. 455–74. Howard Mayer Brown, "Embellishment in Early Sixteenth-Century Italian Intabulations," *PRMA* 100 (1974–75): 49–84. Marie Louise Göllner, "On the Process of Lute Intabulation in the Sixteenth Century," *Dorfmüller,* 1984, pp. 83–113. A.J.N.

Intavolatura [It.]. *Intabulation. On the title pages of keyboard music of the 16th and 17th centuries, the term often refers to the use of score format with two staves, as distinct from *tablatures of the usual sort. The term and its derivatives can also refer to the use of keyboard *partitura* with one staff for each part in a polyphonic complex, as in Samuel Scheidt's *Tabulatura nova* (1624).

Integer valor [Lat.]. In *mensural notation, the normal value of a note as distinct from an augmented or diminished value such as would be brought about by a *proportion.

Intensity. In *acoustics, the energy of a sound as measured in watts per square meter at some point. It is the principal property responsible for the sensation of loudness of a sound.

Interchange of voices. See Voice exchange.

Interference. In *acoustics, the result of the simultaneous presence in a medium of sound waves from two or more sources.

Interlude. Music played between sections of a composition or of a dramatic work [see also Act tune, *Entr'acte, Intermède, Intermedio, Intermezzo, Zwischenspiel*]. In a dramatic work, it may be purely instrumental music or may include action or narration related to the principal work. In purely instrumental music, it may serve to connect larger movements or sections. In church music, the term is applied to music (often improvised) played between verses (sometimes between lines) of a hymn or Psalm. Pieces of this type were published in 18th-century England by Daniel Purcell, Samuel Wesley, and others. The German Protestant tradition of inserting music between the lines of chorales is reflected in some *organ chorales of Bach (e.g., *In dulci jubilo* BWV 729).

Intermède [Fr.]. A work performed between the acts of a play or opera. Its beginnings in France in the 16th century are closely related to the Italian **intermedio.* The French *intermède,* however, like French opera, soon gave considerably greater play to ballet. In the 17th century, such works were often fully comparable to contemporaneous operas. They were performed between the acts of Latin plays, Italian operas, and the plays of Molière and others. Composers included Marc-Antoine Charpentier, André Campra, and Jean-Baptiste Lully.

Intermedio [It.]. In the Renaissance, a work performed between the acts of a play. Such works were performed beginning in the late 15th century in Ferrara between the acts of plays by Terence and Plautus as well as by playwrights of the time and could consist of instrumental music alone or staged presentations of pastoral or mythological subjects with singers, dancers, and instrumentalists. The **moresca* was an important ingredient of the early *intermedio.* In the course of the 16th century, extremely elaborate *intermedi* were staged for weddings at Italian courts. The subjects of these were more often mythological or allegorical. Although relatively little of their music survives, detailed descriptions together with drawings and engravings make clear the important roles of stage machinery and both vocal and instrumental music, and these documents are important sources of information about instrumentation in the period (Brown, 1973).

Intermedi for plays by Plautus were performed in Ferrara for the wedding of Alfonso d'Este and Lucrezia Borgia in 1502 with Bartolomeo Tromboncino among the singers and instrumentalists. In Florence in the 1520s, **canzoni* by Machiavelli served as *intermedi* to his own plays in settings by Philippe Verdelot; and in 1544, Francesco Corteccia provided madrigals for use between the acts of a play performed at the Florentine *academy. The most elaborate and best-documented *intermedi* of the 16th century were for state occasions in Florence. The wedding of Lorenzo de' Medici and Madeleine de la Tour d'Auvergne was celebrated with a play by Lorenzo Strozzi, who also planned the considerable vocal and instrumental music between acts. The wedding festivities of Cosimo I de' Medici and Eleonora of Toledo in 1539 included Antonio Landi's play *Il commodo* with *intermedi* written by G. B. Strozzi and music composed by Corteccia (published in 1539, ed. in Minor and Mitchell, 1968). The wedding of Francesco de' Medici and Johanna of Austria was celebrated in 1565 with Francesco d'Ambra's comedy *La cofanaria* and *intermedi* planned by G. B. Cini and composed by Alessandro Striggio and Corteccia. The wedding of Ferdinando de' Medici and Christine of Lorraine in 1589 was attended by the most lavish of the *intermedi.* These were performed with Girolamo Bargagli's comedy *La pellegrina* as well as other plays and were written by

Giovanni de' Bardi, Ottavio Rinuccini, and Laura de' Guidiccioni, with music by Cristofano Malvezzi, Luca Marenzio, Jacopo Peri, Giulio Caccini, Emilio de' Cavalieri, and Bardi (published in Venice in 1591, ed. Walker, 1963). This music included solo songs, madrigals, and instrumental pieces for up to 60 singers and 24 instruments.

Early opera made use of the subject matter of the *intermedio* and of some specific works. Operas were themselves provided with *intermedi* through much of the 17th century, however, and the tradition of *intermedi* for spoken plays was continued as well, especially in the literary academies in Italian cities. For the related genre in France, see *Intermède;* for the related 18th-century phenomenon, see *Intermezzo.*

Bibl.: Federico Ghisi, *Feste musicali della Firenze medicea* (Florence: Vallecchi, 1939; R: Bologna: Forni, 1969). *Les fêtes de la Renaissance,* I, *CNRS Abbaye de Royaumont,* 1955; III, *CNRS Tours,* 1972, 2nd ed. 1973–75. D. P. Walker, ed., *Les fêtes du mariage de Ferdinand de Médicis et de Christine de Lorraine, Florence, 1589* (Paris: CNRS, 1963). Andrew C. Minor and Bonner Mitchell, eds., *A Renaissance Entertainment: Festivities for the Marriage of Cosimo I, Duke of Florence, in 1539* (Columbia: U of Mo Pr, 1968). Wolfgang Osthoff, *Theatergesang und darstellende Musik in der italienischen Renaissance* (Tutzing: Schneider, 1969). Nino Pirrotta and Elena Povoledo, *Li due Orfei: Da Poliziano a Monteverdi* (Turin: ERI, 1969; 2nd rev. ed., Turin: Einaudi, 1975; trans. Eng., New York: Cambridge U Pr, 1981). Howard Mayer Brown, *Sixteenth-Century Instrumentation: The Music for the Florentine Intermedii, MSD* 30 (1973).

Intermedium [Lat.]. See *Intermède, Intermedio.*

Intermezzo [It.]. (1) In the 18th century, a comic work performed between the acts of a serious opera. Its origins lie in the **intermedio* (to which the term is also sometimes applied) and in the comic scenes of 17th-century Italian opera. The segregation of the comic scenes *(scene buffe)* into separate and independent works around 1700 and in the years following was an aspect of the reform of *opera seria* [see Opera]. Among the most celebrated works of the type is Pergolesi's *La *serva padrona.*

(2) In the 19th and 20th centuries, a middle movement or section of a larger work, usually lighter in character than its surroundings; or an independent work of small scale, often a lyrical piece for piano of the general type termed *character pieces. Examples can be found among Mendelssohn's Second Piano Quartet, Brahms's Piano Quartet in G minor op. 25 and *Klavierstücke* opp. 116–19, Schumann's *Kreisleriana* and other works, Bartók's *Concerto for Orchestra,* Elgar's *Enigma Variations,* and works for keyboard by Reger. The term has also been used for instrumental music between the scenes of an opera, as in Mascagni's *Cavalleria rusticana.*

Interpretation. Those aspects of the performance of a work that result from the performer's particular realization of the composer's instructions as set down in musical notation. The boundary between notation and performance, however, is not as clear as it has sometimes seemed, for the notation of every period is in some degree incomplete and functions within a set of expectations or conventions that guides (or guided) its realization. Thus, in its narrowest sense, interpretation depends on historically informed taste with respect to the realization of a work as it has been transmitted (most often in notation) to the performer. This is the subject of the study of *performance practice. Beyond this, interpretation is often thought of as the individual performer's unique and personal contribution to the realization of a work. Used in this way, the term is likely to carry with it notions of *expression [see also Aesthetics].

Interrupted cadence. See Cadence.

Interval [Fr. *intervalle;* Ger. *Intervall;* It. *intervallo;* Sp. *intervalo*]. The relationship between two pitches [see Pitch (3)]. A tradition going back at least to Boethius and still current defines interval as the distance between an upper and a lower pitch. This spatial metonymy is convenient for inventories of tempered scales as well as for informal descriptions of intervals. A parallel tradition going back to Greek antiquity defines interval as the ratio between an upper and a lower pitch. This has proved especially useful for untempered tunings such as those prevalent before the 17th century.

I. *Current nomenclature.* For purposes of Western tonal music, intervals are named according to (1) the number of diatonic scale degrees included, as represented in the letter names of the two pitches, and (2) the number of semitones (the smallest interval in the Western system) between the two pitches. The former is expressed as a number, determined by counting the letters of the alphabet beginning with that of the lower pitch and including that of the higher (remembering that only the first seven letters are used and then repeated). Thus, c–c is a prime or unison, c–d a second, c–e a third, c–f a fourth, c–g a fifth, c–a a sixth, c–b a seventh, c–c′ an octave. Intervals larger than an octave can be named similarly (ninth, tenth, eleventh, etc.), though they are also known as compound intervals, since they can be thought of as consisting of an octave plus a smaller interval (e.g., a tenth is the same as an octave plus a third). For most purposes, compound intervals function as do their corresponding simple intervals (e.g., a tenth functions much as does a third, both being consonant [see Consonance, dissonance]). The number of semitones between the two pitches is indicated by a qualifying adjective (perfect, major, minor, diminished, or augmented), as illustrated in Table 1, where the number of semitones in each case is given in parentheses.

This table shows that the fourth, fifth, and octave above the tonic in a major scale (c–f, c–g, c–c′, as illustrated here with the scale of C major) are called perfect. The remaining intervals above the tonic (c–d, c–e, c–a, c–b) are called major. A perfect interval if

Table 1

	Diminished	Minor	Perfect	Major	Augmented
Second	c♯-d♭(0)	c-d♭(1)		c-d(2)	c-d♯(3)
Third	c♯-e♭(2)	c-e♭(3)		c-e(4)	c-e♯(5)
Sixth	c♯-a♭(7)	c-a♭(8)		c-a(9)	c-a♯(10)
Seventh	c♯-b♭(9)	c-b♭(10)		c-b(11)	c-b♯(12)
Fourth	c♯-f(4)		c-f(5)		c-f♯(6)
Fifth	c♯-g(6)		c-g(7)		c-g♯(8)
Octave	c♯-c′(11)		c-c′(12)		c-c♯′(13)

reduced by a semitone becomes diminished. A major interval if reduced by a semitone becomes minor, and a minor interval if reduced by a semitone becomes diminished. Both perfect and major intervals become augmented if increased by a semitone. Augmented and diminished intervals may become doubly augmented or doubly diminished by the addition or subtraction of yet another semitone, respectively. Interval types that contain the same number of semitones but have different names (e.g., the diminished third and the major second) are enharmonically equivalent [see Enharmonic] (though specific examples of each will be enharmonically equivalent only if the specific pitches in question are enharmonically equivalent).

Two intervals that form an octave when added together are the complements of one another, and the *inversion of an interval is its complement. Thus, the inversion of a major sixth (e.g., c–a) is a minor third (a–c′), and these two intervals complement each other in that they form an octave when added together (c–a + a–c′ = c–c′). This feature of inversion, like the function of compound intervals, derives from the phenomenon of octave equivalence, according to which pitches separated by one or more octaves are perceived as in some sense equivalent. Western pitch names reflect this perception in assigning the same letter name to all pitches separated by one or more octaves. All such pitches (e.g., all A's or all C's) are said to belong to the same pitch class (e.g., A or C). Thus, the octave enjoys a unique status among the intervals employed in Western music. Whether this derives from its acoustical properties [see below and Acoustics, Harmonics] is a matter of some debate.

Musical styles have up to now employed only a fraction of the intervals that the human ear can differentiate, and current nomenclature consequently allows a considerable latitude to the range of pitches subsumed by any particular term. Some researchers (e.g., Deutsch, 1975) have suggested that the differentiation of the pitch continuum into discrete intervals is a learned activity analogous to the recognition of phonemes in speech. Perception even of the octave tolerates and sometimes demands departures from the acoustical norm, as is shown by the so-called stretched octaves common on pianos.

II. *Historical terminology.* The Greeks' name for the octave, *diapason* (through all [the tones]), along with their terms *diapente* (through five) and *diatessaron* (through four), survived in the medieval Latin vocabulary. The similar etymologies of these three names reflect the spatial, empirically inflected conception of intervallic collections. The remainder of the medieval Latin intervallic nomenclature reflects the rationalized approach of the parallel speculative tradition. It includes the terms semitone, tone, ditone, and tritone, of which all but the third are used in English today. Even in these rationalized cases, however, a generic name can subsume more than a single specific ratio. For instance, the most authoritative ancient and medieval tuning, the Pythagorean, includes more than one size of semitone.

In counterpoint treatises of the late Middle Ages and Renaissance, there appeared for the first time an informal alternative nomenclature for intervals based on the notion of the scale step and especially useful for practicing musicians. In this system—the basis of current nomenclature—diatonic intervals are called primes or unisons, seconds, thirds, fourths, and so on; chromatic intervals are treated either as inflections or as variants of these.

Intervallum itself is but one of several similar terms found in Latin treatises, and not the most common of these. Related words are the more or less inclusive notions of *modus, spatium,* and *diastema* as well as the somewhat exclusive ones of *symphonia* and *coniunctio.* In his *Terminorum musicae diffinitorium,* Tinctoris preferred the more precise distinction between *concordantia* for simultaneities and *coniunctio* for successions. These terms carry different theoretical burdens. Unlike its companion, *concordantia* asserts not only the existence of simultaneous intervals but a certain hierarchy within the set of these intervals as well. This hierarchy fluctuated over the centuries and survives in today's terminology only as a remnant, a distinction between perfect consonances (the unison, fourth, fifth, and their compounds) and the other intervals. Despite such fluctuations, the numerous musical idioms that have privileged both thirds and fifths inevitably share many further assumptions about intervallic hierarchies.

III. *Calculation of intervals.* The interval between two pitches can be represented as the ratio of the two

Table 2

		Pythagorean			Just intonation			Meantone			Equal temperament		
Interval	Pitch	Ratio	Log	Cents	Ratio	Log	Cents	String length	Log	Cents	String length	Log	Cents
Prime or unison	C	1:1	.00000	0	1:1	.00000	0	200,000	.00000	0	200,000	.00000	0
Minor 2nd	D♭	256:243	.02263	90.2	16:15	.02803	111.7	—	—	—	188,775	.02509	100
Augm. prime	C♯	2187:2048	.02852	113.7	25:24	.01773	70.7	192,120	.01908	76.1	188,775	.02509	100
Major 2nd	D	9:8	.05115	203.9	9:8	.05115	203.9	178,885	.04806	193.2	178,180	.05017	200
Minor 3rd	E♭	32:27	.07379	294.1	6:5	.07918	315.6	167,188	.07783	310.3	168,179	.07526	300
Major 3rd	E	81:64	.10231	407.8	5:4	.09691	386.3	160,000	.09691	386.3	158,740	.10034	400
Perfect 4th	F	4:3	.12494	498.0	4:3	.12494	498.0	149,533	.12629	503.4	149,831	.12543	500
Augm. 4th	F♯	729:512	.15346	611.7	45:32	.14806	590.2	143,108	.14537	579.5	141,421	.15051	600
Perfect 5th	G	3:2	.17609	702.0	3:2	.17609	702.0	133,749	.17474	696.6	133,483	.17560	700
Augm. 5th	G♯	6561:4096	.20461	815.6	25:16	.19382	772.6	128,000	.19382	772.6	125,992	.20069	800
Minor 6th	A♭	128:81	.19873	792.2	8:5	.20412	813.6	—	—	—	125,992	.20069	800
Major 6th	A	27:16	.22724	905.9	5:3	.22185	884.4	119,626	.22320	889.7	118,921	.22577	900
Minor 7th	B♭	16:9	.24988	996.1	9:5	.25527	1017.6	111,801	.25258	1006.9	112,246	.25086	1000
Major 7th	B	243:128	.27840	1109.8	15:8	.27300	1088.3	107,002	.27165	1082.9	105,946	.27594	1100
Octave	C	2:1	.30103	1200.0	2:1	.30103	1200.0	100,000	.30103	1200.0	100,000	.30103	1200

string lengths required to produce those two pitches. Thus, if a string is divided exactly in half, the shorter length will produce a pitch one octave higher than that of the undivided string, with the result that the octave may be represented by the ratio 2:1 [see Table 2]. The ratio of the sum of any two intervals is equal to the product of the ratios of those intervals. Thus, if a fifth (3:2) is added to a fourth (4:3), the result is an octave ($3/2 \times 4/3 = 2/1$). Similarly, the ratio of the difference of any two intervals is equal to the quotient of the larger ratio divided by the smaller, which is the same thing as the product of the larger ratio and the reciprocal of the smaller. (String lengths given in Table 2 are in fact denominators in the ratio 200,000:length.)

In the *Pythagorean scale, all intervals except the octave are multiples of the fifth (3:2). Let A♭–G♯ be a segment of the pitch continuum comprising twelve fifths, as indicated in Table 3. Then if C is arbitrarily assigned the ratio 1:1, the ratios of the remaining intervals can be calculated through multiplication or division of 1/1 by the requisite number of fifths. The vertical lines represent binary multiples of C—i.e., its octaves. To bring the entire series into one octave, ratios to the right of the 1:1 octave must be divided by 2 the appropriate number of times; those to the left of this octave must be multiplied by 2 the appropriate number of times. In this way the standard ratios for the Pythagorean scale (as found in Table 2) are derived.

Intervals in *just intonation may be derived from the Pythagorean scale by keeping the latter's C (1/1, 2/1), F (4/3), G (3/2), and D (9/8); dividing C, G, and F by 16/15 to obtain B, F♯, and E; dividing C and F by 10/9 to obtain B♭ and E♭; multiplying G by 10/9 to obtain A; and, finally, multiplying C and G by 25/24 to obtain C♯ and G♯.

Intervals in *meantone temperament can be approximated by tempering each interval of the Pythagorean series by $37x/10{,}000$, where x equals the number of fifths needed to generate the Pythagorean ratio. Intervals to the left of 1:1 add this temperament; those to the right subtract it. For example, three fifths are needed to generate the Pythagorean E♭ (32/27), so meantone E♭ is approximately $32/27 + 3(37)/10000 = 32000/27000 + 11.1(27)/27000 \approx 32300/27000$ or 323/270.

In equal *temperament, all semitones are of exactly the same size, and the sum of 12 semitones must be an octave with the ratio 2:1. Since the sum of two intervals is the product of their ratios, the ratio for the equally tempered semitone must be a number n that when raised to the 12th power equals 2. That is, given the starting point of 1:1 or simply 1, the semitone above will be $1 \times n$, the next semitone above will be $(1 \times n) \times n$ or n^2, and so forth. Since $n^{12} = 2$, $n = \sqrt[12]{2}$ or 1.05946. To approximate roughly the ratios for equally tempered intervals, let s equal the number of semitones in the desired interval; multiply 106/100 by itself s times; and subtract $7s/10{,}000$ to obtain the final ratio.

For precise calculations of tempered intervals, logarithms are indispensable. By convention musicians use common logarithms to the base 10 when calculating intervals. Recall that $\log MN = \log M + \log N$; $\log M/N = \log M - \log N$; $\log M^k = k\log M$; and $\log M^{1/k} = (1/k)\log M$. Thus, the semitone is represented as log 1.05946 or 0.02509, and an interval of i semitones will be the sum of i semitones or $i \times 0.02509$. The octave is then 12×0.02509 or 0.30108, which is log 2. Since this is a rather cumbersome number for representing the simplest interval, all values in the logarithmic progression from unison to octave can be multiplied by the constant $1200/\log 2 = 3985.7$

Table 3

	Octave												
		−3		−2	−1		+1		+2		+3	+4	
	A♭	E♭	B♭	F	C	G	D	A	E	B	F♯	C♯	G♯
Ratio	$\frac{16}{81}$	$\frac{8}{27}$	$\frac{4}{9}$	$\frac{2}{3}$	$\frac{1}{1}$	$\frac{3}{2}$	$\frac{9}{4}$	$\frac{27}{8}$	$\frac{81}{16}$	$\frac{243}{32}$	$\frac{729}{64}$	$\frac{2187}{128}$	$\frac{6561}{256}$

(rounded off for some purposes to 4000) so as to represent each semitone by the value 100 and the octave by the value 1200 ((1200/log 2) × log 2). The 100 parts into which the semitone is thus divided are termed cents. A similar unit of measure is the *savart, which derives from multiplication by the constant 1000. An octave thus consists of 1000 × log 2 or 301 savarts, one savart being approximately 4 cents. The millioctave divides the octave into 1000 parts by using the constant 1000/log 2 and thus equals 1200/1000 or 6/5 cents. The centitone divides each whole tone into 100 parts and thus each octave into 600 with the constant 600/log 2, making the centitone equal to 2 cents.

Given a reference pitch of frequency *p* Hz, it is possible to determine the value in Hz of any other pitch *q* by first adding to or subtracting from log *p* the log of the interval *pq*, and then taking the antilogarithm of this sum or difference. For example, given a′ = 440 Hz and an equally tempered f′ below it, the value of f′ is the antilog of log 440 − log (major third) = antilog (2.64345 − 0.10034) = antilog (2.54311) = 349.2 Hz.

Bibl.: Alain Daniélou, *Tableau comparatif des intervalles musicaux* (Pondichéry: Institute français d'indologie, 1958). Andrew G. Pikler, "History of Experiments on the Musical Interval Sense," *JMT* 10 (1966): 54–95. Diane Deutsch, "Musical Illusions," *Scientific American* 233 (1975): 92–104. Rosemary N. Killam, Paul V. Lorton, Jr., and Earl D. Schubert, "Interval Recognition: Identification of Harmonic and Melodic Intervals," *JMT* 19 (1975): 212–34. Llewellyn S. Lloyd and Hugh Boyle, *Intervals, Scales, and Temperaments,* 2nd ed. rev. (New York: St Martin's, 1979).

In the Steppes of Central Asia. See *In Central Asia.*

Intonation. (1) The degree to which pitch is accurately produced in performance, especially among the players in an ensemble. (2) A system of tuning, such as *just intonation. (3) The first pitches of a *psalm tone or other form of plainchant, which have the function of establishing the correct pitch for what is to follow and are thus often sung by soloists in preparation for the entrance of the choir. See also *Intonatione.*

Intonatione [It.]. A short liturgical piece for organ intended to establish the pitch and mode of a following vocal composition. The earliest are 22 *intonatione* in all 12 modes by Andrea and Giovanni Gabrieli (Venice, 1593; see *HAM,* no. 135). Perhaps representing a long Venetian tradition of improvising over a "silent" psalm tone harmonized in **falsobordoni* (see Bradshaw, 1972), they resemble the early organ *prelude and homophonic *ricercar; and with their sustained block chords in the left hand against which the right has wide-ranging brilliant scalar passages, they incorporate many features of the longer *toccata. Antonio de Cabezón (1557) called similar short pieces **glosas.* After the Gabrielis, the term was little used, except by a few south German organists such as Johann Erasmus Kindermann (1645), Sebastian Anton Scherer (1664), and Franz Xaver Murschhauser (1696). For bibl., see Toccata. A.J.N.

Intrada [Ger.; It. also *entrata;* Sp., Port. *entrada;* Fr. *entrée*]. A piece that accompanies the entrance of a character on the stage or of an important personage at an event; also music that introduces or marks the beginning of another work or of a dance [see also *Entrée*]. The Spanish term, which occurs in the 16th century in Enríquez de Valderrábano (1547) and Luis Venegas de Henestrosa (1557), has the general meaning entrance or entry, as in polyphony, or introduction, beginning, and is thus probably not directly connected with the repertory of pieces of this title known in Germany at the end of the 16th century and through the 17th. The latter, of which one of the first published collections is the Italian trumpeter Alessandro Orologio's of 1597 for five and six parts, are of four general types (Reimann, 1957): fanfarelike in duple meter; in the style of a solemn pavan; dancelike in faster triple meter; and homophonic and songlike. Such pieces occur in separate publications (e.g., Melchior Franck's *Newe musicalische Intraden* in six parts, 1608; see *DDT* 16) and in orchestral suites (e.g., Johann Hermann Schein, *Banchetto musicale,* 1617; see *GMB,* nos. 153, 154, 157). The term was used for introductory pieces by Gluck (**Alceste,* Italian version of 1767), Mozart (**Bastien und Bastienne*), and Beethoven (**Wellingtons Sieg*).

Bibl.: Margarete Reimann, "Materialen zu einer Definition der Intrada," *Mf* 10 (1957): 337–64.

Introduction [Eng., Fr.; Ger. *Einleitung, Eingang;* It. *introduzione;* Sp. *introducción*]. A passage, usually in a slow tempo, at the beginning of a movement or work and preparatory to the main body of the form. Such passages vary widely in length and complexity. Movements in *sonata form, especially the first movements of symphonies, sonatas, and the like, often have slow introductions (e.g., Haydn, Symphony nos. 101 and 104; Beethoven, Symphony nos. 1 and 7).

Introit [Lat. *introitus*]. In *Gregorian chant, the first item of the *Proper of the *Mass, sung during the procession of the celebrant to the altar. It is an example of antiphonal *psalmody, in *neumatic style, consisting of an antiphon (A), a verse (V, abbr. "Ps." or the like for "Psalmus" in early manuscripts and in liturgical books), and the lesser *Doxology (D) as follows: A V D A. The verse and Doxology are sung to a psalm tone [for an example and further discussion, see Psalm tone], and the antiphon is sometimes also sung between the verse and the Doxology. Texts are most often drawn from the Psalms, and the first word sometimes serves as the name of the feast or Mass as a whole, e.g., Laetare Sunday (the fourth Sunday in Lent) and the *Requiem Mass. The introduction of the introit, consisting of an entire Psalm, is sometimes attributed on questionable authority to Pope Celistinus I (papacy 422–32). *Ordo romanus I* [see Gregorian chant VI], deriving from Roman accounts of the first half of the 8th century, suggests that the singing of verses continued until the celebrant reached the altar and signaled the beginning of the Doxology. This is also permitted in modern practice (*LU,* p. xv). Other treatments of the form are suggested in such documents as well, including the singing of one or more supplementary verses (**versus ad repetendum*) following the Doxology. Some early musical manuscripts preserve such verses with, however, only a single verse preceding the Doxology.

Invention [Eng., Ger.; It. *invenzione;* Lat. *inventio*]. A discovery, an original product of the imagination. The term is associated with musical works beginning in the 16th century, as in Clément Janequin's *Premier livre des inventions musicales* of 1555, which contains "La guerre," and it occurs in the titles of numerous Italian publications of the 17th and 18th centuries. It implies no particular musical characteristics for the works in question. Among German composers and theorists of the 17th and 18th centuries (who often prefer the Latin form), the term is closely tied to its use in *rhetoric, in which *inventio* (according, e.g., to Cicero's *De inventione*) is the first of five stages of creation. Bach's use of the term is in this tradition and probably has little to do with the *Invenzioni* op. 10 (1712), for violin and continuo, by Francesco Bonporti, of some of which Bach made copies. The works by Bach to which the term is generally applied are 15 in two-part counterpoint BWV 772–86 and 15 in three-part counterpoint BWV 787–801, all appearing in the *Clavier-Büchlein* for Wilhelm Friedemann Bach of 1723. Bach originally titled the two-part works *praeambulum* and later substituted *inventio.* The three-part works were first titled *fantasia* and later *sinfonia.* Both *praeambulum* [see Prelude] and **fantasia* have associations with rhetoric similar to those of *inventio* reaching back to the 16th century. The title page of Bach's manuscript of 1723 also evokes the rhetorical tradition in describing the works as showing methods "not only of arriving at good original ideas [*Inventiones*], but also of developing them satisfactorily." No single form characterizes these works, nor do all employ imitation. They make significant use of *invertible counterpoint, and both sets are arranged in the following ascending key scheme (lowercase letters for minor keys): C, c, D, d, E♭, E, e, F, f, G, g, A, a, B♭, b. More recent works employing this term as a title may use it in the most general sense or with reference to the contrapuntal texture of Bach's works.

Inventionshorn [Ger.]. See Horn.

Inventionstrompete [Ger.]. See Trumpet.

Inversion. I. *Intervals.* One interval is the inversion or complement of another if the sum of the two intervals forms a third, fixed interval with respect to which the inversion takes place. Unless something to the contrary is specified, inversion is usually reckoned with respect to the octave. In this case, an interval is inverted by placing the lower pitch class above the upper one, that is by raising the lower pitch class an octave. Thus, the inversion of the interval c–e is e–c′. Since the octave contains 12 semitones, the sum of two intervals related by inversion is 12 (in the preceding example, 4 + 8). With respect to the octave, therefore, the inversion of any interval of n semitones is the complement of n with respect to (with a modulus of) 12, or $12 - n$. In terms of the nomenclature of intervals employed in tonal music, the sum of the numbers associated with the two intervals will always be 9, perfect intervals yielding perfect intervals, major intervals yielding minor, and minor yielding major. Thus, the inversion of a perfect fifth is a perfect fourth; of a major third, a minor sixth; of a minor third, a major sixth; of a major second, a minor seventh; of a minor second, a major seventh.

If, as in some examples of *invertible counterpoint, the inversion takes place at an interval other than the octave, similar principles apply. Thus, in inversion at the twelfth, the lower pitch is raised a twelfth, e.g., c–g becomes g–g′ or a fifth becomes an octave.

Jean-Philippe Rameau incorrectly credited Gioseffo Zarlino with the notion of interval inversion, but the first known use of the concept is by Johannes Lippius (1610, 1612) [see Theory].

II. *Chords.* Two chords are related by inversion if both contain the same pitch classes and have the same root, but have different pitch classes in the bass or lowest-sounding position. In the case of the *triad, a root-position chord has the root in the bass with the third and fifth above. If, however, the third is the lowest-sounding pitch, the chord is in first inversion, and if the fifth is the lowest, the chord is in second inversion. Thus, the root-position triad c–e–g becomes e–g–c′ in first inversion and g–c′–e′ in second inversion. For seventh chords, if the seventh is in the bass, the chord is in third inversion [see Ex. 1]. The nomenclature for chord inversions thus depends solely on the lowest-sounding pitch and is not affected by the particular disposition of the remaining pitches. Because the intervals formed above its lowest-sounding pitch are a sixth and a fourth, the second-inversion triad is termed a six-four chord; similarly, a first inversion triad is termed a six-three chord, or simply a six or sixth chord. See also Harmonic analysis, Thoroughbass.

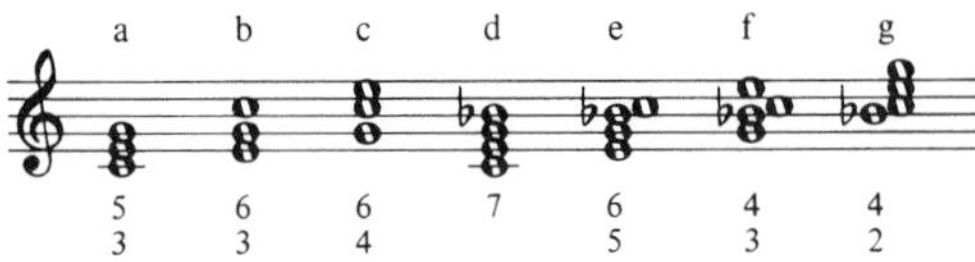

1. Triad in (a) root position, (b) first inversion, and (c) second inversion; seventh chord in (d) root position, (e) first inversion, (f) second inversion, and (g) third inversion.

The origins of chord inversion can be traced to the early 17th century and the writings of Thomas Campion, John Coprario, Joachim Burmeister, Johannes Magirus, and others. The first explicit statements about the relationship between triads and their inversions occurred in the writings of Otto Siegfried Harnisch (1608) and Johannes Lippius (1610, 1612). Even though certain 17th-century writers such as Johannes Crüger and Andreas Werckmeister used the idea, chord inversion did not gain wide currency before Rameau's *Traité* (1722). Rameau considered the major and minor triads (in root position) to be the source of all consonant harmonies, and he regarded the six-four and six-three chords as derived by inversion from them. He did not, however, make any functional distinction between the two inversions—something for which he was severely criticized by figured-bass theorists. Although chord inversion was implied in many figured-bass texts, no priority was necessarily given to root-position triads. Many figured-bass theorists, such as Johann David Heinichen, regarded the second inversion as dissonant at all times, whereas other writers, such as C. P. E. Bach and Johann Philipp Kirnberger, accepted the consonant six-four only in special situations (e.g., passing six-four).

III. *Melodies.* The inversion of a melody is a melody whose contour is the mirror image of the original melody. Thus, where the original melody rises, the inversion falls and vice versa. The intervals between successive pitches may remain exact or, more often in tonal music, they may be the equivalents within the diatonic scale. Hence, c′–d′–e′ may become c′–b–a (where the first descent is by a semitone rather than by a whole tone) instead of c′–b♭–a♭. In either case, the starting pitches need not be the same [see Ex. 2]. Melodic inversion has been common at least since the 15th century, particularly in imitative forms [see Canon, Fugue, Imitation]. Inversion may be indicated by phrases such as "per motu contrario" and "per arsin et thesin."

2. Bach, Fugue in G major from *The Well-Tempered Clavier,* bk. 1.

IV. *Twelve-tone rows.* Inversion is one of the four basic operations used in *twelve-tone composition. Row inversion resembles melodic inversion. But since the crucial property of a row is the order in which pitch classes appear, the particular register in which any pitch class appears being independent of its position in the order, the relations of contour characteristic of melodic inversion need not be preserved between a row and its inversion. Thus, although a row can be inverted by preserving precisely the number of semitones between adjacent pitches while reversing their direction, a more general formulation of the process of inversion in twelve-tone music forms the inversion of a row by taking the complements mod 12 of the pitch numbers of that row. If the pitch classes from C up through B are numbered 0 through 11, respectively, the inversion of the row 0 1 2 3 4 5 6 7 8 9 10 11 (the trivial case of an ascending chromatic scale) can be found by subtracting each pitch number from 12, yielding 12 (= 0) 11 10 9 8 7 6 5 4 3 2 1 (a descending chromatic scale). Both forms may be transposed to begin on any of the 12 pitch classes by adding a constant (mod 12) to their pitch numbers. Thus, in the present example, the inversion transposed up a major third (4 semitones) would be 4 3 2 1 0 11 10 9 8 7 6 5.

Inversional equivalence is an essential element of unordered set theories such as that developed by Forte for free atonal repertories. Forte extends the concept of interval inversion by reducing the 12 intervals to 6 interval classes.

Bibl.: William J. Mitchell, "Chord and Context in 18th-Century Theory," *JAMS* 16 (1963): 221–39. Allen Forte, *The Structure of Atonal Music* (New Haven: Yale U Pr, 1973). Joel Lester, "Root-Position and Inverted Triads in Theory around 1600," *JAMS* 27 (1974): 110–19. John Rahn, *Basic Atonal Theory* (New York: Longman, 1980).

Inverted canon. See Canon.

Inverted fugue. *Counterfugue.

Inverted mordent. See *Schneller.*

Invertible counterpoint. Counterpoint in which the lower voice or voices may also be placed above the higher (or the higher below the lower); thus, counterpoint in which the intervals or chords may be inverted [see Inversion] and remain correct as counterpoint. If for two voices, it is termed double counterpoint; if for three, triple; if for four, quadruple; etc. The inversion

Invertible counterpoint.

may take place at the octave or at some other interval; e.g., the inversion may be achieved by raising the lower voice or lowering the upper voice an octave, a tenth, a twelfth, etc.

Of primary concern in the composition of invertible counterpoint is that the inversion process not introduce parallel perfect intervals [see Parallel fifths] or dissonances that are incorrectly treated [see Counterpoint]. In the simplest case—double counterpoint at the octave—all consonances invert to consonances (thirds become sixths, sixths become thirds) except the perfect fifth, which becomes a perfect fourth; all dissonances invert to dissonances (seconds become sevenths, sevenths become seconds) except the perfect fourth, which becomes a perfect fifth; and all perfect intervals invert to perfect intervals. Thus, only the perfect fifth need be treated with special care, to avoid an incorrect dissonance. Inversion at some other interval is rather more complicated. In inversion at the twelfth, for example, sixths become sevenths, substituting dissonances for frequently used consonances. In inversion at the tenth, thirds become octaves, substituting perfect consonances for imperfect ones and thus posing the risk of creating parallel perfect intervals by the inversion process.

Example 1, from J. S. Bach's Two-part Invention no. 9, shows double counterpoint at the octave; Example 2, from Bach's Three-part Sinfonia no. 9, triple counterpoint at the octave. More complex examples occur in Bach's use of *canon, notably in the *Canonic Variations on Vom Himmel hoch* BWV 769 and in the **Art of Fugue,* and in the Confiteor of the *B-minor Mass.

The earliest examples occur in the melismatic sections of some 13th century **conductus*. By the 16th century, the techniques are well established and are discussed by Nicola Vicentino (*L'antica musica ridotta alla moderna prattica,* 1555) and Gioseffo Zarlino (*L'istitutioni harmoniche,* vol. 3, 1558; trans. Guy A. Marco and Claude V. Palisca as *The Art of Counterpoint,* New Haven: Yale U Pr, 1968).

Bibl.: Ebenezer Prout, *Double Counterpoint and Canon* (London, 1893; R: New York: Greenwood, 1969). Sergei I. Taneev, *Podvizhnoy kontrapunkt strogovo pis'ma* (Leipzig and Moscow, 1909); trans. G. Ackley Brower as *Convertible Counterpoint in the Strict Style* (Boston: B Humphries, 1962). Yvonne Rokseth, "Le contrepoint double vers 1248," *La Laurencie,* 1933, pp. 5–13.

Invitation to the Dance. See *Aufforderung zum Tanz.*

Invitatory [L. *invitatorium*]. Psalm 94 (95), "Venite, exsultemus Domino" (Oh come, let us sing unto the Lord, often referred to as "the *Venite*"), especially as sung with an antiphon at the opening of Matins in the *Office of the Roman Catholic Rite. The Latin text sung in *Gregorian chant derives from a version of the Psalter older than that in the Vulgate and is divided into five sections (corresponding to the Vulgate verses 1–2, 3–4, 5–7, 8–9, and 10–11). Each of these sections is sung to a tripartite *psalm tone in alternation with the antiphon, as follows (where A is the antiphon, A′ the latter part of the antiphon, V one of the five sections of the text, and D the lesser *Doxology): A A V_1 A V_2 A′ V_3 A V_4 A′ V_5 A D A′ A. The first and last statements of the antiphon are begun by the cantors and completed by the choir, all remaining complete or partial statements of the antiphon are sung by the choir, and the verses and Doxology are sung to a psalm tone by the cantors (see *LU,* pp. 368–71 and elsewhere; *Liber responsorialis,* pp. 6ff.). This is the only general category of antiphonal *psalmody in which repetition of the antiphon after verses other than the first and last was preserved. The psalm tones employed are unusual in being tripartite rather than bipartite and in not forming a set of eight, one for each mode. Modes 1 and 8 are lacking altogether, and the number of tones for other modes varies considerably, as does the early manuscript tradition for both tones and antiphons. The Invitatory Psalm was prescribed for the night Office by St. Benedict (d. ca. 547). In the Anglican rite, it is a component of Morning Prayer.

Ionian. See Mode, Greece I, 3 (ii).

Iphigénie en Aulide [Fr., Iphigenia in Aulis]. Opera in three acts by Gluck (libretto by F. L. G. le Bland du Roullet, after Racine's tragedy, based in turn on Euripides), produced in Paris in 1774.

Iphigénie en Tauride [Fr., Iphigenia in Tauris]. Opera in four acts by Gluck (libretto by N. F. Guillard and F. L. G. le Bland du Roullet, after Euripides) produced in Paris in 1779. Gluck revised the work for a German translation by J. B. von Alxinger that was produced in Vienna in 1781.

Īqāʿ [Ar.]. The unit in the classical Arabic system of rhythmic modes. It is a cycle consisting of subdivisions of equal or unequal lengths, marked by sequences of light and heavy beats numbering from 6 to 24 or more, expressed in the percussion accompaniment but not usually audible in the melody. B.N.

Iran. See Near and Middle East.

Iraq. See Near and Middle East.

Ireland. The history of Irish art music is closely interconnected with that of England. The Anglo-Norman invasion of 1172 brought about the replacement of the Celtic rite with the *Sarum rite. English musicians dominated Dublin's musical life during the 16th and 17th centuries, and in the 18th century many musicians active in London visited Dublin frequently; Handel gave the first performance of his *Messiah* there in 1742. A long series of Irish *ballad operas followed the Dublin premiere in 1728 of *The *Beggar's Opera.* The 19th century brought a new awareness of native Irish melodies, though most well-known Irish composers, such as John Field (1782–1837), Michael William Balfe (1808–70), and William Vincent Wallace (1812–65), still lived and worked outside of Ireland. Prominent composers born in the early 20th-century include Frederick May (1911–85), Brian Boydell (1917–2000), Seán Ó Riada (1931–71), and especially Seóirse Bodley (b. 1933). Most recently, Gerald Barry (b. 1952), Raymond Deane (b. 1953), and John Buckley (b. 1951) have gained attention, aided by groups such as the Contemporary Music Centre (Dublin, founded 1986), which has worked in recent years to promote the work of Irish composers.

Concert and festival life in modern Ireland (including the Republic of Ireland and British Northern Ireland) improved considerably during the second half of the 20th century. The postwar expansion of Radio Telefís Éireann (RTÉ) included the founding of the RTÉ National Symphony Orchestra, an ensemble paralleled in the north by the Ulster Orchestra (1966), which is associated with the BBC. The Dublin Grand Opera Society, founded in 1941, provided the city with its first regular seasons of opera, but opera in Ireland remained for several decades the purview of touring companies such as the Irish National Opera (1965), Opera Northern Ireland (now defunct), and the Opera Theatre Company (1986). The Grand Opera Society established Dublin's first permanent opera at the Gaiety Theatre in 1985, a company known from 1996 as Opera Ireland. In Northern Ireland, the Castleward Opera (founded 1985) has grown to fill the void left by Opera Northern Ireland.

A National Concert Hall erected in Dublin in 1981 houses the RTÉ Orchestra and provides venues for diverse groups and festival events, such as Dublin's Living Music Festival of contemporary music. Other festivals include the Cork International Choral Festival (1954), Wexford Opera Festival (1951), Anna Livia International Opera Festival (2000), and Belfast's Sonorities Festival of Contemporary Music and Early Music Festival (1982).

The majority of Irish folk music consists of songs and dances, with a small number of independent instrumental pieces. Although traces of many ancient influences can be found, most of the music now performed dates from no earlier than the late 18th century. The country has two basic folk-song traditions, the Gaelic and the English (which includes both imported and native songs). In both traditions, most songs are lyrical rather than narrative love songs, a large number are diatonic, and more than half employ C modes (sometimes transposed). The Gaelic songs known as slow airs lack the regular pulse usual in European music. The greatest part of the folk repertory today consists of music to accompany dancing. Dances still used include the *jig (in 6/8, 9/8, or 12/8, often in the form AABB, many in 6/8 concluding with a rhythm of three eighth notes followed by a dotted quarter), the *reel (the most prevalent, characterized by groups of eight eighth notes in moderate 2/2 and often in the form AABB), and the *hornpipe (of more recent origin, also with eighth-note motion in moderate duple meter, but often in the form AABA).

Instruments either indigenous to Ireland or developed there to a degree unknown elsewhere include the uilleann or *union pipes, the *Irish harp, and the *bodhrán* (a frame drum); also used extensively are the fiddle, the Scottish *highland bagpipe, flutes of various kinds including the *penny whistle, and the accordion and related instruments [see also *Bouzouki*]. The Irish harp was employed extensively from the late Middle Ages until the 18th century; the last harp composer was the blind itinerant musician Turlough Carolan (1670–1738). During the 18th century, the instrument was suppressed, but in 1792 a harp festival was held in Belfast, and an attempt was made to transcribe the music played. This festival marked the end of traditional harping but the beginning of 19th-century efforts at collection.

The field work done by Edward Bunting (1773–1843), George Petrie (1790–1866), Patrick Weston Joyce (1827–1914), and Francis O'Neill (1849–1938, collecting the music of Irish residents of Chicago), along with voluminous materials on folklore housed at University College, Dublin, have formed the basis of considerable activity in Ireland today. Interest is promoted particularly by the Folk Music Society of Ireland (founded 1971). There are many performing groups, generally influenced by Seán Ó Riada's Ceoltóirí Cualann, and innumerable festivals and competitions focusing on traditional music.

Bibl.: Grace J. Calder, *George Petrie and "The Ancient Music of Ireland"* (Dublin: Dolmen, 1968). Breandán Breathnach, *Folk Music and Dances of Ireland* (Dublin: Talbot Pr, 1971; rev. ed., Dublin: Mercier Pr, 1977). James Porter, *The Traditional Music of Britain and Ireland: A Research and Information Guide* (New York: Garland, 1989). Gerard Gillen and Harry White, *Music and Irish Cultural History* (Blackrock, Ireland: Irish Academic Pr, 1995). Axel Klein, *Die Musik Irlands im 20. Jahrhundert* (Hildesheim: Olms, 1996). Aloys Fleischmann, Mícheál Ó Súilleabháin, and Paul McGettrick, *Sources of Irish Traditional Music c. 1600–1855* (New York: Garland, 1997). Ciaran Carson, *Last Night's Fun: In and Out of Time with Irish Music* (New York: North Point Pr, 1997). Fintan Vallely, *The Companion to Irish Traditional Music* (New York: NYU Pr, 1999). Ann Buckley, "Music in Ancient and Medieval Ireland," in *A New History of Ireland,* vol. 1, ed. T. W. Moody, F. X. Martin, and F. J. Byrne (Oxford: Clarendon, forthcoming).

Irish harp [Gael. *cláirseach*]. A *frame harp with a sound box carved from a single piece of wood, a pillar that curves outward, and 30 to 36 metal strings. An instrument of this type was played in 10th-century Ireland and remained popular until the late 18th century, especially as an accompaniment for songs. Although it became a national symbol, the playing tradition died out at the beginning of the 19th century. A modern version of the instrument employs gut or synthetic strings, each with a tuning hook for raising the pitch one semitone. See also Harp.

Bibl.: Joan Rimmer, *The Irish Harp* (Cork: Mercier Pr, 1969; 2nd ed., 1977).

Islamic music. Music is central to any world religion, and Islam is no exception. Although music and musicians have been viewed with skepticism, the Islamic context has inspired countless musical traditions throughout the world. Core rituals, for example, the call to prayer and the chanting of the Qur'ān, both originating in 7th-century Arabia, still represent archetypal expressions of Near Eastern music today. These rituals, along with the music of Sufi groups, have influenced cultures from Central Asia to Indonesia to southern Africa. At the same time, because the religion has found a home in various communities, its messages have been expressed in diverse musical languages throughout the world.

The influence of Near Eastern music in the Islamic world flows from the call to prayer and the recitation of the Qur'ān, (particularly in the musical *mujawwad* style). In Muslim communities the Islamic call-to-prayer (transliterated as *adhān, athān,* or *azān*) is broadcast from mosques, radio, and television five times a day. The text is:

Allahu Akbar, Allahu Akbar (×2)
Ashhadu Ana La Illaha illa Allah (×2)
Ashhadu Ana Muhammad Rasul Allah (×2)
Hayya ʿala ʿl-Salah (×2)
Hayya ʿala ʿl-Falah (×2)
Al Salat Khayr min al-nawm (×2)
Allahu Akbar, Allahu Akbar (×2)
La Illaha illa Allah

God is great
I testify there is no God but God
I testify Muhammad is the prophet of God
Come to prayer
Come to salvation
Prayer is better than sleep [for the morning call]
God is great
There is no God but God

Although not considered music, the call to prayer is musical, and an excellent muezzin is praised for his vocal ability. While the contemporary muezzin uses a sound system, the minarets of mosques were built so that a muezzin could broadcast his call throughout the community. Even with a sound system, the call is declamatory in nature, never introspective.

Even more illustrative of vocal artistry is the recitation of the Qur'ān. Music and language come together in Quranic recitation, which demands both mastery of a system of rules *(tajwīd)* as well as creative improvisation. No matter what the language of the Islamic community—Spanish, English, Turkish—the Qur'ān is recited in Arabic. *Tajwīd* provides specific guidelines regarding the delivery of the text, however; the creation of melody, although also formulaic, is left to the reciter. While Arabian melodies were the source of original Quranic recitations, and while regional melodies certainly characterize recitation in remote areas of the Islamic world, the Egyptian style of recitation became popular in the Islamic world community in the 20th century. This is due to at least three factors: (1) the education of international students at Cairo's Al-Azhar University, the premier institution of Quranic studies; (2) the dissemination of Egyptian sound recordings of Quranic recitation and traditional music; (3) Egyptian reciters who have traveled and taught their art throughout the world.

Like instrumental improvisation in Near Eastern music *(taqāsīm),* a recitation starts with short and plain phrases in the lowest part of the vocal range and progresses to longer and more fanciful phrases, higher in the reciter's range, that are embroidered with ornamentation and sequence. The peak of a reciter's performance occurs when he or she delivers exceedingly long phrases in one breath, pushing the range to its upper limits while exhibiting impressive control of ornamental filigree. The art of recitation also requires a facility to recite any verses of the 114 chapters of the Qur'ān within a particular musical mode *(maqām)* and then to modulate to other modes, often returning to the initial mode at the end of the recitation.

The recitation of the Qur'ān, due to its divine source and its purpose on earth, is not music. Nevertheless, good recitation informs traditional music, even in nonreligious contexts, in a number of ways. Aspects of recitation heard in other Islamic musics include: (1) the long ornamented melody sung on a single breath; (2) the exposition of *maqām* and the navigation between *maqāmāt;* (3) the characteristic intonation of the Near Eastern modes, particularly the semitones; (4) the freedom of rhythm and the absence of organized, repeated meter; (5) vocal timbre, characterized by the use of nasality and long unvowelled melismas sung on consonants (like *nnn* or *mm*); (6) the use of the chest voice rather than a head or falsetto voice for both men and women; (7) ornamentation; (8) devotional or spiritual intent; (9) the Arabic language. While all of these musical aspects are intrinsic to Quranic recitation, their use in musical performance in both ritual and nonritual contexts can be a sonic symbol of Islam.

Sufi orders or brotherhoods are known for religious rituals (Dhikr, Zikr) that combine group singing, repetitive meter (often played on frame drums), rhythmic breathing, poetry, and movement. Collective performance can lead participants to trance states, resulting in experiences from inner peace to union with God to the ability to perform superhuman acts of strength and endurance. Found throughout the Islamic world, Sufi orders cultivate music that ranges from the very classical and sophisticated instrumental and vocal repertoire of the Turkish Mevlevi order (also Whirling Dervishes), to the folk-like music of the Turkish Bektashi order, the Hamadsha brotherhood of Morocco, or the Baluchi of Iran and Pakistan.

If the philosophies and practices of Sufi orders have

at times been at odds with political powers and mainstream Islam, Sufism has always been allied with the arts, particularly music and poetry. The writing of 13th-century mystic Jalal al Din Rumi, for example, is rich with images and metaphors describing man and his reunion with God, love and companionship, and the evasive presence of nature.

A multitude of genres generated or influenced by the ritual practices of Islam and Sufism permeate Arab, Turkish, and Persian cultural regions as well as areas of Central, South, and Southeast Asia, Africa, and even parts of Europe and the United States. Islamic musics have formed the foundation of traditional and popular musics in these areas, and repertoires have come to be shared by Christian and Jewish musicians who have served as professional entertainers for Muslim patrons. Performed by men and women, professionals and amateurs, the music of Islam has come to the attention of world music audiences through initiatives like the Silk Road Project, the Festival of Sacred Music in Fez, Morocco, the Los Angeles Festival, and the Smithsonian Festival of Folklife, and through organizations like the World Music Institute in New York. The music of Pakistani Qawwali Nusrat Fateh Ali Kahn has been heard on movie sound tracks, Turkish and Syrian Sufi groups conduct international concert tours regularly, and the English-language songs of Yusef Islam, formerly Cat Stevens, are sung by American Sufis. Even popular music, for example Indonesian Dang Dut, Malaysian Qasidah, and Turkish rap music, resonate with the messages and sounds of Islam. See also Quranic chant. A.K.R.

ISMN. International Standard Music Number, ISO Standard 10957.

Isomelic. Characterized by the repetition of melodic material. The term has been applied to the repetition (sometimes varied) of melodic material in the upper parts of polyphonic works of the 15th century that display *isorhythm as well as to the repetition of a *cantus firmus* in differing rhythmic guises in works of this period and later. In the former case, the repetition may coincide with the repetition of either the rhythmic pattern or the melodic pattern of the tenor.

Isometric. *Homorhythmic.

Isorhythm [fr. Ger. *Isorhythmie*]. The repetition of a rhythmic pattern throughout a voice part. The device is found in motets of the 14th and early 15th centuries and on occasion can be found in other genres as well. Most often the tenor of such a piece is isorhythmic, sometimes also the contratenor, and less frequently the upper voices.

An isorhythmic voice normally contains two patterns that are repeated, a rhythmic pattern or *talea* and a melodic pattern or *color.* The two patterns need not be of the same length, however, with the result that successive statements of the rhythmic pattern may occur with different pitches. The repetition of both rhythmic and melodic patterns has precedents in the tenors of 13th-century motets. In the usual motet of that period, the tenor is a preexistent (usually liturgical) melody that is repeated in all but the shortest compositions; such a melody constitutes a *color.* The rhythm of the tenor consists of multiple repetitions of a short pattern based on the rhythmic *modes; a *talea* is simply a longer pattern, most often not connected with the rhythmic modes.

Isorhythm based on the reiteration of a relatively long rhythmic pattern allowed the construction of compositions on a large scale. The earliest such works are early 14th-century motets in the **Roman de Fauvel.* During the decades following the composition of these motets, upper voices became increasingly involved in isorhythmic organization. In the 14th century, the upper parts often reflected the isorhythm of the tenor, perhaps having rests at the same points in each tenor *talea,* for instance, but they were only intermittently isorhythmic themselves. In the late 14th and early 15th centuries, however, many compositions were isorhythmic in all voices; this phenomenon is termed panisorhythm. Most of the motets by Guillaume de Machaut are isorhythmic in the usual manner of the 14th century, e.g., his Motet no. 2, "De souspirant/Tous corps qui de bien amer/Suspiro." Panisorhythm is present in a few of Machaut's motets, such as no. 4, and numerous motets and Mass movements of the later 14th century and the first half of the 15th century, including pieces by Johannes Ciconia, John Dunstable, and Guillaume Dufay. After the middle of the 15th century, isorhythm survived only in modified forms.

Although fully developed isorhythmic construction was first employed in the **Ars nova,* theorists of the time did not discuss the concept. They did use the terms *talea* and *color* together, but most writers report several definitions. The meanings given here are based on some of those reported in the *Libellus cantus mensurabilis,* probably by Jehan des Murs (ca. 1340; *CS* 3:46–58, esp. p. 58). The same terms, defined similarly, occur in *Ars cantus mensurabilis* by Coussemaker's Anonymous V (late 14th cent.; *CS* 3:379–98, esp. pp. 397–98) and in the 15th-century *Tractatus pratice de musica mensurabili* by Prosdocimus de Beldemandis (*CS* 3:200–228, esp. pp. 225–27).

In 1904 Friedrich Ludwig introduced the term isorhythm, a term absent from medieval writings; in 1924 he refined its definition along lines generally accepted today (see Ludwig, 1930).

Bibl.: Friedrich Ludwig, "Die 50 Beispiele Coussemakers aus der Handschrift von Montpellier," *SIMG* 5 (1903/4): 177–224, see p. 223. Id., *Handbuch der Musikgeschichte,* 2nd ed., ed. Guido Adler, vol. 1 (Berlin: Hesse, 1930), p. 273. Rolf Dammann, "Spätformen der isorhythmischen Motette im 16. Jahrhundert," *AfMw* 10 (1953): 16–40. Willi Apel, "Remarks about the Isorhythmic Motet," *Wégimont,* 1955, pp. 139–44. Ursula Günther, "The 14th-Century Motet and Its Development," *MD* 12 (1958): 27–58.

Isosyllabic. Characterized by the repetition of patterns of fixed numbers of syllables without regard for stress or syllable length. It is a feature of some Byzantine and Syrian liturgical poetry.

Israel. I. *Ancient Israel.* The music of ancient Israel was related to the music of other cultures of the ancient Middle East, especially to *Mesopotamian music. These musical cultures assigned a similarly important role in religious observance to choral singing with accompaniment of stringed instruments, and they cultivated some of the same song-types, including hymns, laments, and victory paeans. The music of ancient Israel was not notated. Some song texts have been preserved, and there are descriptions of music making and musical organization in the Bible and in post-biblical sources. However, there is little or no evidence about how the music of ancient Israel actually sounded.

Information about music during the period from the arrival of the Hebrew tribes in Canaan (ca. 1200 B.C.E.) until the Babylonian exile (586 B.C.E.) comes mainly from the Bible. The Bible mentions music in several contexts: singing and dancing to celebrate military victory (Exod. 15:20–21; 1 Sam. 18:6–7), laments for the dead (2 Sam. 1:18–27), singing and dancing at religious festivals (2 Sam. 6:5), solo singing at the royal court (1 Sam. 16:17–23), singing and playing in connection with ecstatic prophecy (1 Sam. 10:5), and trumpet or horn signals in war and in ritual (Num. 10:1–10; Josh. 6:4–20). The organization of music in the Temple during the time of David and Solomon is outlined in detail (1 Chron. 6, 9, 15–16, 23, 25; 2 Chron. 5), though this account was probably written at a later date and may reflect the practices of a subsequent period. Temple music was the responsibility of the Levites, the hereditary priestly caste, whose duties included singing and playing on stringed and percussion instruments to accompany festive and ritual observances.

The music of the second Temple period (516 B.C.E.–70 C.E.) is described not only in the Bible but also by historians like Josephus (ca. 38 C.E.–ca. 100) and in the later reconstructions of the Mishnah (compiled ca. 200 C.E.) and the Babylonian Talmud (5th cent. C.E.). Music in the Temple itself was still the province of the Levites, who acquired considerable wealth and prestige. The most important element of Temple music was choral singing—perhaps in *responsorial and *antiphonal styles as well as in unison—accompanied by stringed instruments, especially the **kinnor* (lyre) and the **nebel* (an angle harp or a lyre). The texts of many of the songs used in this manner are preserved in the biblical Book of Psalms, a collection of 150 religious lyrics, which was codified around 200 B.C.E. and probably represents a selection from a larger repertory created over a period of several centuries. Besides *kinnor* and *nebel,* other instruments mentioned in the Bible are **ḥalil* (a reedpipe), **shofar* (ram's horn), *metziltayim* (cymbals), *tof* (frame drum), and *ḥatzotzerot* (metal trumpets). English Bibles usually render these Hebrew words with anachronistic glosses like flute, timbrel, and psaltery.

In addition to biblical references to Temple music, there are allusions in the Bible to music of a more secular character: work songs (Isa. 16:10; Jer. 48:33), wedding songs (Jer. 25:10), pilgrims' songs (Isa. 30:29), and songs of lamentation (Jer. 9:17–20). Singing and playing instruments at the feasts and private entertainments of the wealthy is depicted in a tone of condemnation by the prophets Isaiah (Isa. 5:11–12) and Amos (Amos 6:4–5).

After the destruction of the Second Temple in 70 C.E., the focus of Jewish religious observance shifted from the Temple to the Synagogue; the Levite musicians lost their position as a caste; and a musical tradition grew up based on sung reading (*cantillation) of the sacred texts. There have been attempts to trace the music of the Synagogue as well as that of the Christian Church back to the Temple, but these remain speculative. See Jewish music.

II. *Modern Israel.* Music in the modern state of Israel may be characterized in terms of two contradictory tendencies: (i) the multiethnic, multicultural character of Israeli society, composed of Palestinians and Jewish immigrants from many parts of the world, all with their own musical traditions; and (ii) the Zionist ideal of a single, distinctly Jewish national culture and music.

1. Institutions. Financial support for music in Israel comes from the state, from international Zionist organizations, and from the Israeli public. The Israel Philharmonic Orchestra, founded in 1936 by German refugees as the Palestine Orchestra, has gained an international reputation. Other Israeli orchestras include the Haifa Symphony Orchestra, the Jerusalem Symphony Orchestra, the Ramat Gan Chamber Orchestra, the Israel Chamber Orchestra, and the Israeli Contemporary Players. Israel's National Opera debuted in 1948, was reorganized in the early 1980s, and reopened in 1985 as the New Israeli Opera. The 1994 dedication of the Tel Aviv Performing Arts Center gave this group a permanent home. A nationwide network of choirs is sponsored by the Histadrut (labor federation). The national radio station is an important force in the dissemination and patronage of several styles of music. The most important music conservatories are two institutions called the Rubin Academy of Music, one in Jerusalem and the other attached to Tel Aviv University. Departments of musicology exist at Hebrew University in Jerusalem, Tel Aviv University, and Bar-Ilan University, and the government Ministry of Education and Culture has a music section, which supports historical and ethnomusicological research on Jewish music. Music festivals in Israel include the Zimriyyah International Choir Festival, the Oriental Song Festival, the Israel Festival, and the Kibbutz Ein Gev Music Festival.

2. History. The music of Palestinian Arabs living in

Israel and adjacent territories belongs to the mainstream of Arabic music [see Near and Middle East], although the traditions of subgroups like the Druse and the Bedouins remain distinct and strong.

Eastern European Jewish immigrants of the late 19th and early 20th centuries wrote Hebrew words for the European tunes they brought with them and also composed Hebrew texts to Arabic melodies they found in their new homeland. As the Zionist presence in Palestine grew, new, self-consciously Israeli songs were created by composers like Joel Engel (1868–1927), Nahum Nardi (1901–77), and Mordechai Zeira (1905–68). Although their composers are known in most cases, these songs have established themselves as Israeli folk song.

Art music in Israel was given impetus by the influx of central European and particularly German immigrants, which accelerated greatly in the 1930s. European-trained composers like Paul Ben Haim (1897–1984), Oedoen Partos (1907–77), and Alexander Uriah Boskovich (1907–64) used elements drawn from Arabic music as well as from the traditions of Sephardic Jewry to create what they called an "Eastern Mediterranean" style, which remained the predominant school of new Israeli music until the 1950s. New music since that time has tended in the direction either of the international *atonal style as represented by Josef Tal (b. 1910) or of a more faithful adherence to Middle Eastern models. Mordecai Seter (1916–1994), after European training, explored the use of Jewish liturgical and folk materials as well as original twelve-tone scales used on the analogy of Middle Eastern modes. The next generation of composers includes Yehezkiel Braun (b. 1922), Ben-Zion Orgad (b. 1926), Tzvi Avni (b. 1927), Yizhak Sadai (b. 1935), Noam Sheriff (b. 1935), Ami Maayani (b. 1936), and Yehuda Yannay (b. 1937).

The immigration of oriental Jews from North Africa, Iraq, Bokhara, and Yemen increased greatly after 1948 and made a strong impression on Israeli music in the late 20th century. Composers from this generation who reflect this increasing integration include Tsippi Fleischer (b. 1946), Yinam Leef (b. 1953), and Betty Olivero (b. 1954). Jerusalem's Rubin Academy has offered study in classical Arab music since 1996, and Jewish musicians who have been raised in the tradition of Arabic music have joined with those from traditional Jewish and European backgrounds, exemplified by the group Bustan.

See also Jewish Music.

Bibl.: *Ancient Israel.* Bathya Bayer, *The Material Relics of Music in Ancient Palestine and Its Environs* (Tel Aviv: Israel Music Institute, 1963). Alfred Sendrey, *Music in Ancient Israel* (New York: Philosophical Library, 1969). Bathya Bayer, "Music—Biblical Period," in *Encyclopedia Judaica,* vol. 12 (1972): 559–66. Periodicals: *Yuval* (1968–), *Musica Judaica* (1976–). Joachim Braun, *Music in Ancient Israel/Palestine: Archaeological, Written, and Comparative Sources* (Grand Rapids, Mich.: Eerdmans, 2002).

Modern Israel. Peter Gradenwitz, *Music and Musicians in Israel,* 3rd ed. (Tel Aviv: Israeli Music Pubns, 1978). Amnon Shiloah and Edith Gerson-Kiwi, "Musicology in Israel, 1960–1980," *AM* 52 (1981): 200–216. Amnon Shiloah and Erik Cohen, "Major Trends of Change in Jewish Oriental Ethnic Music," *Popular Music* 5 (1985): 199–223. Alice Tischler, *A Descriptive Bibliography of Art Music by Israeli Composers* (Warren, Mich.: Harmonie Park Pr, 1989). Philip V. Bohlman, *The World Centre for Jewish Music in Palestine, 1936–1940: Jewish Musical Life on the Eve of World War II* (Oxford: Oxford U Pr, 1992). Jehoash Hirshberg, *Music in the Jewish Community of Palestine 1880–1948: A Social History* (Oxford: Oxford U Pr, 1995). Robert Fleisher, *Twenty Israeli Composers: Voices of a Culture* (Detroit: Wayne St U Pr, 1997).

Israel in Egypt. An oratorio for soloists, chorus, and orchestra by Handel, first performed in London in 1739. The text is from the Bible and the Prayer Book Psalter.

Issue number. See Catalog number.

Istampita, istanpita, istanpitta [It.]. See *Estampie.*

Istar Variations. Seven symphonic variations by Vincent d'Indy, op. 42 (1896). Based on the sixth canto of the Assyrian epic poem of Izdubar, d'Indy's work depicts the voyage of self-discovery and gradual denudation of Istar, daughter of Sin. The most complex variation, presented first, is gradually stripped of its ornamentation to reveal the bare theme, presented last.

Istesso tempo, L' [It.]. The same tempo; hence, an indication that the tempo is to remain the same despite a change in meter and thus in the unit of metrical pulse. In a change from 4/4 to ¢, the half note of the latter will equal the quarter note of the former; in a change from 3/4 to 6/8, the dotted quarter note of the latter will equal the quarter note of the former.

Italiana in Algeri, L' [It., The Italian Woman in Algiers]. Comic opera in two acts by Rossini (libretto by Angelo Anelli, previously set by Luigi Mosca), produced in Venice in 1813. Setting: Algiers in the 19th century.

Italian Concerto. A "Concerto in the Italian Manner" for solo harpsichord with two keyboards by Bach, BWV 971, published in 1735 as the second part of the **Clavier-Übung.* The work is so named because it is in the form and style of the Italian instrumental concerto of the early 18th century, the concerto's characteristic element of contrast being achieved through contrasting *registrations on the harpsichord's two keyboards.

Italian overture. See Overture.

Italian sixth. See Sixth chord.

Italian Symphony. Popular name for Mendelssohn's Symphony no. 4 in A major op. 90 (completed in 1833; many later revisions), begun during a trip to Italy in 1830–31 and containing allusions to Italian folk music, particularly in the last movement, entitled "Saltarello."

Italy. I. *Current musical life and related institutions.* Italy has had a long and continuous tradition of active cultivation of art music in numerous cities and towns. Musical life is entirely decentralized.

1. Opera. Opera remains the most popular form of art music in Italy, although it no longer monopolizes musical life as it did in the 19th century. There are opera houses in more than two dozen cities and towns, some with seasons of a few weeks only and some with seasons lasting most of the year. Preeminent among these are Teatro alla Scala in Milan, Teatro La Fenice in Venice, Teatro dell' Opera in Rome, and Teatro San Carlo in Naples; of major importance also are the opera houses in Bologna, Catania, Florence, Palermo, Trieste, and Turin. In the summer, out-of-door operatic presentations of festival proportions take place at the Baths of Caracalla in Rome and the Arena in Verona.

2. Performing groups. In the 19th century, opera was emphasized in Italy almost to the exclusion of other types of music. Now, however, a number of instrumental groups and semiprofessional choirs are actively supported. Among the most important patrons of music is Radio audizione italiana (RAI), which maintains the RAI National Symphonic Orchestra. Several Italian instrumental groups, such as I musici, I virtuosi di Roma, Vivaldi specialists Il giardino armonico, and the former Quartetto italiano, enjoy international reputations. Concert series of chamber and orchestral music are supported in a number of Italian cities. Amateur groups are not prominent.

3. Festivals. Music festivals take place in nearly every population center in Italy; some are of considerable significance. The Maggio musicale fiorentino, founded in Florence in 1938, is of international scope; it lasts for about two months in the late spring and early summer and encompasses many varieties of music. Also noteworthy is the Festival dei due mondi (Festival of Two Worlds), which takes place in Spoleto. Perugia's Sagra musicale umbra and Palermo's Settimana di Monreale both feature sacred music, whereas Pisa's Primavera musicale is given over to chamber music. Music of the 17th and 18th centuries is the central offering of Siena's Settimana musicale senese, and is a staple of the Settimane musicale in Stresa and Lago Maggiore, summer home of the RAI Orchestra. The Venice Biennale includes a significant international festival of contemporary music, and several festivals founded in the 1970s and 1980s are completely devoted to new music: Musica nel nostro tempo in Milan, Settembre musica and Festival antidogma in Turin, Festival pontino in Latina, Festival nuovi spazi musicali in Rome, Festival G.A.M.O. in Florence, and Festival spaziomusica in Cagliari.

4. Education. Italy has played a leading role in the teaching of music from the Middle Ages through the development of conservatories of music of international repute in the 17th and 18th centuries to the present. Several types of institution offer music education in Italy today. Most prestigious are the national conservatories; there are about 20 such schools, including ones in Bologna, Florence, Milan, Naples, Rome, and Venice. About the same number of less prestigious "equalized institutes" offer diplomas equivalent to those given by the conservatories; locations of schools of this sort, which generally have such titles as *liceo musicale* or *istituto musicale,* include Foggia, Lecce, Messina, and Udine. Music may be studied at the universities in Bologna, Cagliari, Florence, Milan, Naples, Palermo, Rome, and Turin, among others. The country also has a few specialized schools, including the Scuola internazionale di liuteria (for the making of stringed instruments) in Cremona, the Scuola di paleografia e filologia musicale (for the transcription of ancient texts), also in Cremona but affiliated with the University of Parma, and the Pontificio istituto di musica sacra in Rome.

5. Museums, libraries, and archives. Museums dedicated to individual composers, usually located in this person's city of birth, include a Rossini museum in Pesaro, a Donizetti museum in Bergamo, a Bellini museum in Catania, and a Puccini museum in Torre del Lago (near Lucca). The museum connected to the Teatro alla Scala in Milan has a rich collection of documents related to theatrical and particularly operatic history. Important collections of early instruments can be found in the Museo di organologia "A. Stradivari" in the Museo civico in Cremona, in the Conservatory in Florence, and in the Castello sforzesco in Milan. Italy has numerous libraries and archives with significant music holdings. The Ufficio Ricerca fondi musicali in Milan is in the process of compiling catalogs of all manuscript and printed music from before 1900 held in the country. Particularly important collections include the archives of the publishing firm Ricordi in Milan, the libraries of the conservatories "Giuseppe Verdi" in Milan and "S. Cecilia" in Rome, the Biblioteca nazionale centrale (a national copyright depository) in Florence, and the Vatican Library in Vatican City (Rome). The Discoteca di stato in Rome is a national sound archive.

6. Publishing. By far the largest publisher of music in Italy today is Ricordi, founded in 1808 in Milan. In the course of the 19th century, Ricordi published most of the operas of Rossini, Bellini, Donizetti, Verdi, and Puccini. Ricordi increased its attention to contemporary Italian composers during the last decades of the 20th century, although this attention waned somewhat after it became part of international music giant BMG in 1994. De Santis, founded in Rome in 1852, specializes in editions of early Italian music prepared by eminent scholars and in contemporary music. Curci, founded in Naples in 1860, began by publishing operettas by German and Italian composers; in 1936 the central offices of the firm were fixed in Milan. Its cur-

rent publications include performing editions of standard works prepared by eminent interpreters such as Schnabel and Cortot, light music, and contemporary Italian music. Sonzogno, founded in Milan at the end of the 18th century and beginning to specialize in music in 1874, with particular emphasis on opera and operetta, was significant in promoting the careers of Mascagni and Leoncavallo. Suvini Zerboni, founded in Milan in 1907, is an important publisher of contemporary music. Historical and scholarly editions are also undertaken by a number of institutes, while the *Rivista musicale italiana,* founded in 1894, continues to be the main Italian periodical for musicological research.

7. Broadcasting. Radio in Italy was under government control from its beginnings. The present-day network, RAI (Radio audizioni italiana or Radiotelevisione italiana), has grown from a single station in Rome that survived Mussolini's defeat in World War II and the downfall of his broadcast system, EIAR (Ente italiana audizioni radiofoniche). Today RAI has three national networks, of which the first and third broadcast music. From its earliest days, RAI maintained orchestras in Rome, Naples, Milan, and Turin, and an electronic studio (Studio di fonologia musicale) in Milan. In 1994 the four orchestras merged into the RAI National Symphonic Orchestra. All the concerts of the RAI National Symphony Orchestra season are broadcast live on RadioTre, and most of the concerts are televised by various stations.

II. *History.* From the early centuries of the Christian era through the Middle Ages, Rome and Italy are central to the history of Western liturgical chant, including *Gregorian, *Old Roman, and *Ambrosian. The **lauda* of the 13th century is the earliest genre of secular music to have survived. The 14th century saw the composition of much polyphonic secular vocal music, most belonging to the genres **caccia,* **ballata,* and *madrigal, by such composers as Jacopo da Bologna and Francesco Landini. During the 15th and early 16th centuries, the composition of notated art music in Italy was largely in the hands of Netherlandish and Franco-Flemish composers. Native composers seem to have concerned themselves with genres such as the **frottola* (by, e.g., Bartolomeo Trombonicino and Marchetto Cara) and the **canti carnascialeschi.* By the second half of the 16th century, Italian composers had come to the fore once again and were active in sacred genres such as the *Mass and *motet (by, e.g., Palestrina and Andrea Gabrieli), secular vocal music, especially the *madrigal (by, e.g., Luca Marenzio, Carlo Gesualdo, and Claudio Monteverdi), and newer instrumental genres such as the *ricercar, *canzona, and *toccata (by, e.g., Giovanni Gabrieli, Claudio Merulo, and Vincenzo Galilei).

From about 1600, Italy was the source of new styles and techniques, such as *monody or **stile rappresentativo* and basso continuo [see Thoroughbass], as well as new forms and genres such as *opera, *oratorio, *cantata, *sonata, *concerto grosso, *concerto, and *sinfonia. Throughout the 17th and 18th centuries, Italian musicians made significant contributions to both vocal and instrumental music. Important composers, roughly classified according to their field of greatest contribution, include the composers of early opera and vocal music: Giulio Caccini (ca. 1545–1618), Jacopo Peri (1561–1633), and Monteverdi (1567–1643); composers chiefly of instrumental works: Biagio Marini (ca. 1587–1663), Arcangelo Corelli (1653–1713), Antonio Vivaldi (1678–1741), Domenico Scarlatti (1685–1757), and Giovanni Battista Sammartini (1701–55); composers chiefly of vocal works: Emilio de' Cavalieri (ca. 1550–1602), Giacomo Carissimi (1605–74, especially oratorios), Francesco Cavalli (1602–76), Antonio Cesti (1623–69), Giovanni Legrenzi (1626–90), Alessandro Scarlatti (1660–1725), Antonio Caldara (1670–1736), Giovanni Battista Pergolesi (1710–36), Nicolò Jommelli (1714–74), and Nicolò Piccinni (1728–1800).

By the end of this period, however, the country had largely been abandoned by instrumental composers; and in the 19th century, opera dominated compositional activity. Perhaps the greatest contributions were made by Rossini and Verdi, whose works stood in opposition to the German operas of Richard Wagner, but also influential were Vincenzo Bellini (1801–35), Gaetano Donizetti (1797–1848), and Arrigo Boito (1842–1918). Many composers who were born and trained in Italy spent most of their adult lives in other countries, incorporating Italian characteristics into the music of their adopted homelands, as did Luigi Cherubini (1760–1842) and Gaspare Spontini (1774–1851). In the very late 19th century and the early years of the 20th, opera continued to be dominant, with notable works by such composers as Pietro Mascagni (1863–1945), Ruggero Leoncavallo (1857–1919), and Giacomo Puccini (1858–1924), but other influences began to be felt; in particular, studies of earlier music served to remind composers that Italian music had once been more diverse with respect to genre. An important figure in this change of emphasis was the composer Gian Francesco Malipiero (1882–1973), whose edition of the complete works of Monteverdi helped to reveal to Italian composers a part of their instrumental heritage. Some of the most important of Malipiero's contemporaries were Ottorino Respighi (1879–1936), Mario Castelnuovo-Tedesco (1895–1968), and Alfredo Casella (1883–1947).

Under fascism, cultural developments in Italy were held back only mildly, although some musicians, including Castelnuovo-Tedesco, were forced to emigrate. In the years between the wars, numerous institutions for the promotion of new music and the revival of old and at least one excellent periodical (*Il pianoforte,* later renamed *La rassegna musicale*) were founded. Significant composers who began their careers at this time include Luigi Dallapiccola (1904–

75) and Goffredo Petrassi (b. 1904). After World War II, Italian composers began to find stimulation in many sorts of works, including those of the dodecaphonic school, of Stravinsky, and of Cage. The results can be seen in the works of Luciano Berio (b. 1925), Niccolò Castiglioni (1932–96), Aldo Clementi (b. 1925), Bruno Maderna (1920–73), and Luigi Nono (1924–90), among others. Milan's Studio de fonologia musicale (1955) was to be only the first of many centers for electronic music; during the last three decades of the 20th century, similar institutions were created in Florence, Pisa, Padua, Milan, and Naples. Composers who emerged in this period include Francesco Pennisi (1934–2000), Armando Gentilucci (1939–89), and Lorenzo Ferrero (b. 1951), the latter representing a postmodern neo-Romantic reaction against the values of the avant garde.

III. *Folk music.* Various areas of Italy have substantially different indigenous musics. All preserve some archaic traits but have also been affected by art music, as in the virtual replacement of older modes with modern tonality in most regions. Northern Italy has both lyric and narrative song, with florid but not melismatic melody based on triadic harmony; texts are usually strophic and may, in lyric song, incorporate refrains of nonsense syllables. Performance is frequently choral and polyphonic. Southern Italy has mostly lyric song, with modal melismatic melody. Southern narrative song, far less common than the lyric, seldom incorporates melismas. Singers usually perform solo and use a tense vocal style and free rhythms. Polyphony, common in functional songs, is more rudimentary here than elsewhere in Italy. The folk music of central Italy incorporates features from both the northern and southern areas. In Sardinia the principal type of song is a complex lyric form, sung solo with guitar accompaniment. Much music is sung in polyphony, however, involving as many as five parts, which may have either text or nonsense syllables. In addition, Italy incorporates many minority cultures that maintain their own folk music. These include Provençal, German, Tyrolean, Slavonic, Albanian, Ladin, and Waldesian communities. Some traditional Italian dances are the *ballo di Mantova,* **bergamasca,* *gigue, **monferrina,* and **tarantella.* Folk instruments include the tambourine, friction drums, triangles, and castanets; various fipple flutes, accordions, and bagpipes; violin, **launeddas* (triple clarinet), panpipes, and *piffero* (shawm).

Bibl.: Siegmund Levarie, *Musical Italy Revisited* (New York: Macmillan, 1963). Giorgio Colarizi, *L'insegnamento della musica in Italia* (Rome: La boheme italiana, 1967). Roberto Leydi, comp., *I canti popolari italiani* (Verona: Mondadori, 1973). Elaine Brody and Claire Brook, *The Music Guide to Italy* (New York: Dodd, Mead, 1978). Fiamma Nicolodi, ed., *Musica e musicisti nel ventennio fascista* (Florence: Discanto, 1984). Roberto Leydi and Febo Guizzi, *Strumenti musicali e tradizioni popolari in Italia* (Rome: Bulzoni, 1985). Ruth Lakeway and Robert White, *Italian Art Song* (Bloomington: Ind U Pr, 1989). Susanna Forchino, *La Musica contemporanea italiana oggi: Le poetiche delle ultime generazioni* (Turin: U degli Studi di Torino, 1990). David Kimbell, *Italian Opera* (Cambridge: Cambridge U Pr, 1991). Richard Sherr, *Music and Musicians in Renaissance Rome and Other Courts* (Aldershot: Ashgate, 1999).

Ite, missa est [Lat., Go, you are dismissed]. The concluding formula of the *Ordinary of the Roman Catholic *Mass, to which the response "Deo gratias" (Thanks be to God) is made. It dates from at least the 4th century, and the Latin term *missa* for the Mass has its origins here, replacing the earlier *eucharistia.* Up until the reforms following the Second *Vatican Council, this formula was replaced by the **Benedicamus Domino* in Masses lacking the *Gloria (see *LU,* pp. 16–63). It is not normally a part of polyphonic settings of the Mass Ordinary except in the 14th century.

J

Jácara [Sp.]. (1) A **romance* relating the adventures of a lowlife character, often sung, and in the 17th century forming the basis for entertainment between the acts of plays. Becoming more elaborate musically, these entertainments were antecedents of the **tonadilla.* Sacred *jácaras* are also preserved in collections of Spanish polyphony of the 17th and 18th centuries. (2) A dance in triple meter derived from the music for (1) and with rhythms similar to the sarabande, to which it was likened in the 17th century. Examples occur in Spanish keyboard and guitar collections of the 17th and 18th centuries (e.g., for organ by Cabanilles).

Jack. That part of the *harpsichord's action to which the plectrum is fixed and that moves past the string when the key is depressed.

Jagdhorn [Ger.]. Hunting *horn.

Jagdmusik [Ger.]. Music for the hunt.

Jahreszeiten, Die [Ger.]. See *Seasons, The.*

Jale. See Solmization.

Jalousieschweller [Ger.]. An organ *Swell enclosure with Venetian shutters.

Jam. In jazz and rock, to improvise in an informal setting. Jam sessions ordinarily involve changing gatherings of musicians playing for personal pleasure using *standards or other widely known material, but some sessions are institutionalized in concerts or on recordings. B.K.

Janissary music. Music of the elite corps of soldiers known as Janissaries that formed the personal guard of Turkish sultans from the 14th century until 1826, or music of similar character performed on similar instruments; also termed Turkish music or *alla turca.* The typical Turkish ensemble included fifes, shawms, triangle, cymbals, kettledrums, *Turkish crescent, and bass drum and was widely imitated in Europe beginning in the early 18th century. Its influence on European *military music lasted well into the 19th. Among works to draw on this idiom are Mozart's *Die *Entführung aus dem Serail* and Rondo *alla turca* from the Piano Sonata in A major K. 331; Haydn's **Military* Symphony; and Beethoven's *Die *Ruinen von Athen, *Wellingtons Sieg,* and finale to the Ninth Symphony. Around 1800, pianos were sometimes fitted with Janissary stops, which imitated the percussive effects of such music.

Bibl.: Peter Panoff, "Das musikalische Erbe der Janitscharen," *Atlantis* 10 (1938): 634–39. William Lichtenwanger, "The Military Music of the Ottoman Turks," *BAMS* nos. 11–13 (1948): 55–56. H. Powley, "Janissary Music (Turkish Music)," in *Encyclopedia of Percussion,* ed. J. Beck (New York: Garland, 1995), pp. 195–200.

Janko keyboard. See Keyboard.

Japan. See East Asia II.

Jarabe [Sp.]. A traditional Mexican dance and musical form. It is characteristically multisectional with several distinct strains that often contrast in meter and tempo. The "Jarabe Tapatío," well known from **mariachi* performances, is a typical example. D.S.

Jarana [Sp.]. A song and dance genre of the Yucatan peninsula, sharing many features with **son* traditions in other parts of Mexico. The term also designates any of several small Mexican guitars varying in size and shape, string complement, and tuning, according to the regions where they are found. D.S.

Java. See Southeast Asia IX, 5.

Jāvali [Tel.]. A light genre of Carnatic music. Its texts are erotic and are often interpreted in mime toward the end of a **bharata-nāṭyam* recital. C.C.

Jawbone [Sp. *quijada*]. A *rattle made from a horse's, mule's, or donkey's jawbone in which the teeth remain loosely attached. When one side of the open end is struck with the hand, it vibrates in the fashion of a tuning fork, causing the teeth to rattle. It was used in American minstrel shows and is still widely used in Latin American popular music.

Jaw's harp. See Jew's harp.

Jazz. An eclectic, expanding collection of 20th-century styles, principally instrumental and of black American creation. *Swing and improvisation are essential to several styles, but only an emphasis on distinctive individual and group timbres spans all musics called jazz, whether functional or artistic, popular or esoteric, instrumental or vocal, improvised or composed, "hot" or "cool."

Jazz has never been an autonomous genre. It has always been linked to *blues through instrumental adaptations (derived equally from the black church) of improvisatory story telling, *call and response, and vocal inflections (*blue notes, cries, growls, hums, moans, shouts), as well as through performances with blues vocalists and variations on blues progressions. In its early years, jazz absorbed the instrumentation, multithematic structures, strong tonality, and rhythms of American marching band music and *ragtime, the harmonic colors of the piano music of such composers as Debussy and Ravel, the melodies and forms of American popular song, and the rhythms of Latin American dances [see also Latin jazz]. Later it incorporated accompanimental figures and electronic innovations in *rock, *soul, and hip hop, as well as non-Western musics, especially those from Africa, Brazil, and India.

In the years of jazz's emergence, the 1890s through the 1910s, its parent styles developed in many locales, but the majority of its most celebrated players resided in New Orleans. Much of what we know sonically about early jazz comes to us from recordings; those usually recognized as the first were made in 1917 by the Original Dixieland Jazz Band, a group of white New Orleans musicians. Hence, a notion of the first style, New Orleans jazz, must rely in large measure on a comparison of oral histories with later recordings by black and creole innovators, made outside New Orleans after it had lost its geographic centrality. Recordings from 1923 onward featured cornetists Freddie Keppard and King Oliver (with Louis Armstrong playing second cornet and Johnny Dodds clarinet), clarinetist and soprano saxophonist Sidney Bechet, and pianist Ferdinand "Jelly Roll" Morton.

Essential to New Orleans jazz was dense interplay among a front line of wind instruments that varied thematic material borrowed from blues, marches, or rags. Remaining in its middle register, a cornet presented an ornamented melody; a clarinet (generally in a high register) or a saxophone improvised an ornate countermelody; and a trombone lightly embellished tenor harmonies or a bass line derived from the theme. The rhythm section defined pulse and harmony. On each beat, a piano, guitar, or banjo sounded one chord from the theme's strong tonal progressions. A drummer played complex, syncopated march rhythms. On recordings, a tuba, bass saxophone, or piano would play the two-beat bass line (a chord root on beat 1 and the fifth on beat 3 in 4/4). Disrupting these accompanimental roles were frequent breaks (solos one or two bars long) and stop-time choruses (improvised solos against the background of isolated accents in rhythmic unison by the remainder of the ensemble).

The 1920s were a time of greater popularity and stylistic development. James P. Johnson, who first recorded in 1921, was among the first in a school of *stride pianists, including Willy "The Lion" Smith, Fats Waller, William "Count" Basie, and Edward Kennedy "Duke" Ellington. Alternating (i.e., striding) between bass notes and chords with his left hand, Johnson pioneered swinging, virtuosic rhythmic variations on blues and multithematic models. His followers extended his technique to melodic and harmonic improvisations on 32-bar popular songs, which during the decade gradually supplanted marches and rags throughout the jazz repertory.

In carefully composed recordings with his Red Hot Peppers in 1926, Jelly Roll Morton created complex New Orleans ensemble performances. Beyond Morton's work, the only elements consistently retained from the New Orleans tradition in other leading ensembles of the 1920s were breaks and the style of rhythmic accompaniment, with one modification: four-beat bass-lines (one quarter note on each beat) began to replace two-beat lines. Although thickly textured interchanges among winds remained popular in opening choruses and in exciting, climactic final choruses (a device central to the music of cornetist Bix Beiderbecke and other Dixieland and Chicago jazzmen), the focus of attention shifted to individual improvisations and to formal arrangements for large ensembles.

Louis Armstrong became the foremost soloist of the decade. On recordings with his Hot Five and Hot Seven in 1925–28, he established new standards of facility, range, tone, and vibrato for trumpeters; he developed a widely imitated fund of melodic formulas; he popularized scat-singing (improvised vocables imitating instrumental sounds); and above all, he created lengthy, coherent trumpet improvisations with an unparalleled sense of swing. Among fellow bandsmen, he was challenged only by Earl Hines, then (1928) the premier jazz pianist.

Concurrently, distinctive aspects of a new style that would later be called *swing evolved in large ensembles. The widely popular recordings and performances of the Paul Whiteman Orchestra introduced "jazz age" America to this style with the aim of elevating jazz to the level of art. The ensemble's arranger Ferde Grofé, the orchestrator of George Gershwin's *Rhapsody in Blue* (1924), pioneered the division of ensembles into choirs of brass and winds and the writing of different passages for successive choruses. At the same time, beginning in the early 1920s, groups led by Fletcher Henderson, Bennie Moten, and Walter Page gradually expanded, becoming by mid-decade *big bands, in which a rhythm section of piano, banjo or guitar, drums, and double bass or tuba accompanied reeds, trumpets, and trombones. In New York, Henderson's arranger Don Redman adapted Grofé's techniques for big-band orchestration. Redman's arrangements of 1923–27 explored texture through complicated exchanges between sections and provided a showcase for famous soloists, including Armstrong (in 1924–25) and tenor saxophonist Coleman Hawkins, who soon challenged the preeminence of the trumpet in jazz improvisation. Redman's duties were assumed largely by Benny Carter in 1928 and by Henderson in the early 30s.

Steeped in the blues tradition, Moten's band forged the swing style in a series of recordings made in 1932. By this time Moten had acquired bassist Page, William (later Count) Basie, blues singer Jimmy Rushing, trumpeter Oran "Hot Lips" Page (all from Walter Page's Blue Devils), and tenor saxophonist Ben Webster. The group had come to favor memorized *head arrangements featuring solos in alternation with *riffs (brief, tuneful motives repeated over changing harmonies) anchored by Page's walking string-bass line. New in 1932 were the relaxed, precise, swinging orchestral subdivisions of Page's walking string-bass line. The group re-formed under Basie's leadership one year after Moten's death in 1935, the year in which Henderson's arrangements, purchased and polished, earned clarinetist Benny Goodman the popular title "King of Swing." These two dance bands typified the mature swing style: both stressed melodies of antiphonal riffs based on the structures of blues or popular songs; in their rhythm sections, piano, guitar, bass, and bass drum struck each beat, whle the drummer played a swinging cymbal rhythm, as shown in the example. The Goodman orchestra was oriented toward complicated written arrangements, Basie's toward a succession of superior soloists led by Lester Young on tenor saxophone.

Growing up with swing, the unique Duke Ellington Orchestra followed these conventions only in part. During the half century of Ellington's leadership (1923–74), the finest of its distinctive voices were trumpeters Bubber Miley, Rex Stewart, Cootie Williams, Cat Anderson, and Clark Terry; clarinetist Barney Bigard; saxophonists Johnny Hodges, Harry Carney, Ben Webster, and Paul Gonsalves; trombonists Joseph "Tricky Sam" Nanton and Lawrence Brown; and bassist Jimmy Blanton. Ellington utilized their sounds in bluesy "jungle" showpieces, fast dances, romantic mood pieces, new popular songs, program music, miniature concertos, extended concert pieces, film scores, and three Sacred Concerts. He explored novel harmonic subtleties and instrumental combinations, experimented with irregular phrase lengths, and often fixed the details of apparent improvisations. There is still controversy over the extent to which sidemen, most notably Miley from 1926 to 1929 and Billy Strayhorn from 1939 to 1967, contributed to the composition of Ellington's masterpieces.

Goodman's triumph of 1935 marked the merger of big-band jazz with popular music. He opened the door for the commercial success of dance bands led by Tommy Dorsey, Harry James, Glenn Miller, Artie Shaw (with vocalist Billie Holiday), Chick Webb (with Ella Fitzgerald), and others.

As arrangements came to dominate in these large ensembles, remarkable improvisations came most often from solo pianists and small groups. Pianists fell generally into two schools. Incessantly altering popular songs through brief melodic flourishes, unpredictable rhythmic interruptions, or daring harmonic excursions, Art Tatum represented the zenith of an orchestral approach. By contrast, Meade "Lux" Lewis, Albert Ammons, and Pete Johnson played *boogie-woogie, an early blues piano style rediscovered in the late 30s and associated with jazz because of the emphasis on sounds rather than lyrics. Although pianists' repetitive bass-lines and chordal oscillations fell out of favor by the mid-40s, boogie-woogie ostinatos became essential components of blues, rhythm and blues, and rock in, for example, the work of Louis Jordan.

Members or former members of the Henderson, Goodman, and Basie orchestras provided the nuclei of ever-changing combinations of musicians in small groups. Coleman Hawkins excelled in solo interpretations of popular songs. He collaborated with Benny Carter, alto saxophone (from 1928); Henry "Red" Allen, trumpet (in 1933); Django Rheinhart, acoustic guitar; and Roy Eldridge, the foremost trumpeter of the late 30s. Fats Waller and His Rhythm (1934–42) was a forum for the leader's catchy tunes, keyboard virtuosity, and comical singing. Goodman formed a trio in 1934 with his drummer, Gene Krupa, and pianist Teddy Wilson; expanded, the group subsequently included Lionel Hampton, vibraphone, and Charlie Christian, the innovative electric guitarist. Basie's rhythm section supported Lester Young, trumpeter Buck Clayton, and trombonist Dickie Wells. Wilson led sessions featuring Young and Billie Holiday, whose singing delineated a boundary between jazz and pop during these years of merger: her improvisations on popular melodies of the day, delivered with blues inflections, subtle phrasing, and a biting tone, divorced popular lyrics from their cute sentimentality.

The early 1940s began with reactions to the commercialization of swing, which resulted in two additional styles: a resuscitated late New Orleans jazz modified with swing rhythms, and a new style called *bebop. The latter seemed to emerge suddenly in the 1945 quintet recordings of alto saxophonist Charlie "Bird" Parker and trumpeter Dizzy Gillespie, because a recording ban begun in 1942 obscured both its development and its continuity with small-combo swing, particularly a repertory of chord progressions borrowed from blues and popular songs (especially "I Got Rhythm"), concentration on melodic improvisation, a theme-solo-theme format, and swing rhythms. A new virtuosity complemented these conventions in bebop performance: ensembles explored both extremely fast and slow tempos; pianists punctuated irregularly and modified borrowed progressions through chordal extension, alteration, or substitution; rapid, jagged, asymmetrical, improvised melodies and equally difficult, newly composed melodic themes explored these complex harmonies; bassists avoided repeated notes in walking lines; drummers accentuated freely on various drums as they marked subdivisions of measures (with a closed hi-hat cymbal on beats 2 and 4) and of beats (with swinging patterns on a ride cymbal) [see Drum set].

Leading figures in the early years of bebop were saxophonists Parker, Dexter Gordon, and Sonny Stitt; trumpeters Gillespie, Miles Davis, and Fats Navarro;

trombonist J. J. Johnson; pianists Bud Powell and Al Haig; composer-pianists Thelonious Monk and Tadd Dameron; drummers Kenny Clarke and Max Roach. Parker is now regarded as the most talented and influential improviser in the history of jazz. With unsurpassed facility and blues feeling, he invented continuously new melody by flexibly altering the direction, harmonic implications, accentuation, and rhythms of a large body of formulas.

Gillespie initiated in 1947 the first of many modifications of small combo bebop. While he was agile and harmonically imaginative as a bebop soloist, he was also interested in expanding the timbral and rhythmic resources of bebop. His late-1940s big band, at times augmented by the Cuban percussionist Luciano "Chano" Pozo, adapted bebop conventions for larger ensembles and made deft use of Latin dance rhythms.

Teacher-pianist Lennie Tristano (with Lee Konitz, alto saxophone) and Parker's partner of 1947–48, Miles Davis, were influential in the emergence of *cool jazz. Soloists in Tristano's sextet of 1949 played quiet, fast, twisting, chromatic melodies with legato phrasing; his drummer used brushes instead of sticks. The Davis nonet's "Birth of the Cool" recordings of 1949–50 moderated tempo, tone color, dynamics, register, and accentuation, and balanced improvisation with arrangement. At the same time, Stan Kenton's Progressive Jazz Orchestra, much like Whiteman's orchestra in the 1920s, sought to meld big-band jazz with concepts and techniques drawn from concert music.

Through the 1950s, musicians in California were frequently, if incorrectly, associated with the cool substyle under the rubric of *West Coast jazz. Some were innovators: Gerry Mulligan (baritone saxophone) and Chet Baker (trumpet) improvised contrapuntal melodies in a pianoless quartet; pianist Dave Brubeck (with Paul Desmond, alto saxophone) popularized the use of meters other than 4/4. Such experiments declined in popularity when skilled improvisations became subordinate to demanding written arrangements. East Coast–based jazzmen provided alternatives. In 1954–55, drummer Art Blakey and pianist Horace Silver simplified bebop by reasserting jazz's links to blues and gospel music with pentatonic-based melodies, subdominant-oriented progressions, and minor-colored harmonies in the first Jazz Messengers group; their music, sometimes labeled *hard bop and other times funk, acquired the label "soul jazz" after the debut of alto saxophonist Julian "Cannonball" Adderley's second quintet in 1959. Other exemplars of the hard bop style were the quintet led by Clifford Brown (trumpet) and Max Roach (drums) with Sonny Rollins (tenor saxophone) and a number of artists recording for the Blue Note label.

The music of the Modern Jazz Quartet (MJQ) and of Thelonious Monk took bebop in other directions. Starting in 1952, the MJQ, featuring composer-pianist John Lewis and vibraphonist Milt Jackson adapted pre-Classical European forms, concert-hall formalities, and subtlety in dynamics without sacrificing swinging improvisation. A composer of jazz standards (pieces central to the repertory), Monk was a unique soloist at a time when ever-changing formulaic melodies dominated improvisation. He repeated ideas in swing riffs, ornamental variations (after the manner of stride pianists), and motivic work, all modified by a sophisticated sense of rhythmic placement and by a humorously perverse pitch selection that emphasized the most colorful members of bebop chords.

The late 50s brought experimentation and controversy as many jazzmen sought to avoid a single-minded concentration on melodic improvisation based on repeated chord progressions. John Lewis and Gunther Schuller (following paths suggested in the progressive jazz of Stan Kenton's big band of 1947 and in the MJQ) advocated the union of Western art music and jazz in Third Stream music. From 1956, Charles Mingus's sketches for jazz workshop rivaled in significance his dominance of contemporary string bass playing. In ways that obscured distinctions between improvisation and composition, Mingus mixed bebop procedures, Ellingtonian sonorities, downhome gospel music, instrumental conversations (above all with bass clarinetist Eric Dolphy in 1960), nonstandard forms, changing accompanimental styles, and collective invention. Meanwhile, Miles Davis explored new approaches to accompaniment, and ultimately to form, with Bill Evans and Gil Evans. Bill Evans was one of the pianists in Davis's sextet from 1958–59 with Adderley and Coltrane; Gil Evans (a prominent figure in the "Birth of the Cool") created lush arrangements for a big band, expanded to include orchestral instruments, that accompanied Davis's muted trumpet and flugelhorn in recordings from 1957 to 1962. As composer, Davis pursued the flamenco sound of an upper chromatic neighbor in melodic, chordal, and sectional relationships; he substituted slow harmonic rhythm (sometimes changing chords only once every 8 measures), weakly functional chordal oscillations, and bass ostinatos or pedals for the fast-moving chord progressions and walking bass-lines of bebop. As soloists, he and his sidemen responded with long stretches of diatonic improvisation, called modal playing.

Free jazz, the most radical successor of bebop, was neither a style nor free, but rather an amalgamation of individual efforts to refashion bebop conventions. Alto saxophonist Ornette Coleman's collaborations (begun in the late 50s) with trumpeter Don Cherry relied heavily on unfamiliar elements, including non-tempered intonation, "noise" (extreme dynamics, registers, and timbres), themes with changing tempos and intentionally imprecise unisons, and unmetered improvisations based on tonal centers rather than harmonic progressions, all of which disguised the traditional instrumentation, blues inflections, running eighth-note formulas in improvisations, theme-solo-theme formats, and distinctions between soloist and accompanists characteristic of bebop-derived performance practice.

Cecil Taylor, a pianist whose work emphasized pantonality and the percussive nature of his instrument, was similarly tied to tradition in the late 50s. In the 60s, his compositions allowed truly collective improvisation resulting in constantly changing textures (with drummers and bassists freed of accompanimental roles).

John Coltrane, through his career a fine interpreter of ballads, began in the late 1950s to play flurries of pitches at rapid tempos in an attempt to suggest a variety of substitute harmonies over individual chords. Tenor saxophonists Archie Shepp and Albert Ayler subsequently perfected this "sheets of sound" technique in nontraditional contexts, but Coltrane, still a bebop player, shifted in the 60s to an improvisational approach suggested by Miles Davis's ostinato compositions. Playing tenor and soprano saxophone with his quartet of 1961–65 (pianist McCoy Tyner, bassist Jimmy Garrison, drummer Elvin Jones), Coltrane increasingly developed motives in open-ended forms featuring chordal oscillations, bass drones, and swirling drum patterns. By 1965 he had moved to the forefront of free jazz by exploring extreme dissonance, harsh timbres, and intense textures, and adapting elements of African and Indian musics.

Sun Ra's Arkestra and the Art Ensemble of Chicago exemplified the diversity of free jazz from the 1960s forward. In costumed performances, these musicians presented (and sometimes poked fun at) various jazz styles, black American popular music, ethnic musics, poetry, and noise. Other ensembles, such as Horace Tapscott's Pan-Afrikan Peoples Arkestra, various 1970s loft performers in New York City, and European musicians explored similar territory with less emphasis on theatricality.

Miles Davis flirted with an esoteric free jazz approach. His quintet of 1964–68 (saxophonist Wayne Shorter, pianist Herbie Hancock, bassist Ron Carter, drummer Tony Williams) played ostinato tunes and highly chromatic pieces with great flexibility, but strong references to bebop remained. Over time and inspired by James Brown and Sly Stone, the group incorporated elements of funk and rock music—even subdivisions of pulses, unchanging accompaniments, and electronic instruments—popularizing the emergent *fusion style beginning in 1968.

The most celebrated fusion musicians in the 1970s and early 1980s had been Davis's sidemen in 1968–70: Hancock, Chick Corea, Keith Jarrett, and Joe Zawinul (keyboards); Shorter and Bennie Maupin (reeds); George Benson and John McLaughlin (electric guitar); Airto Moreira (percussion); Billy Cobham (drums). (Notable exceptions were Chuck Mangione, flugelhorn, and Pat Metheny, electric guitar.) Hancock, on synthesizer, and Maupin recorded danceable soul tunes. (As an acoustic pianist, Hancock revitalized the mid-60s quintet, with Freddie Hubbard replacing Davis, in the group V.S.O.P.) Shorter and Zawinul founded Weather Report in 1970; although the group improvised collectively in early recordings, rock rhythms and arrangements quickly became central to their repertory. McLaughlin and Cobham played hard rock, modified by jazz harmony, in the Mahavishnu Orchestra. Corea, Moreira, and electric bassist Stanley Clarke emphasized Latin rhythms in their group Return to Forever and in accompaniment to Stan Getz, the tenor saxophonist identified with the **bossa nova*. In the mid-70s, Jarrett became famous for solo interpretations of rock ostinatos on acoustic piano. And in the late 70s, Benson found financial success as a singer. As in swing of the 30s and early 40s, fusion erased the lines separating popular music from jazz.

The period from the mid-70s to the present has been one of stylistic eclecticism in which no single style has dominated and previous styles have been combined in striking ways. Musicians with backgrounds in free jazz, such as saxophonists David Murray, Henry Threadgill, Steve Coleman, and Greg Osby, have increasingly sought to combine the techniques of free jazz with the conventions of bebop as well as those of ragtime, blues, rhythm and blues, hip hop, and African popular musics; some of the resulting amalgams have been called *free bop by critics. Other musicians, such as John Zorn and Bill Frisell, have found inspiration in experimental concert music as well as in country, Eastern European folk musics, and even cartoon and film music. Still others, buoyed by the success of trumpeter Wynton Marsalis, have focused more intently on consolidating the gains of bebop and early free jazz. Important figures in this "neo-traditional" style include saxophonists Kenny Garrett, Joe Lovano, David Sánchez, and Joshua Redman; trumpeters Terence Blanchard, David Douglas, Roy Hargrove, and Nicholas Payton; pianists Geri Allen and Mulgrew Miller; bassist Christian McBride; drummers Jeff "Tain" Watts and Brian Blade; and a host of others. Finally, vocalists such as Betty Carter, Cassandra Wilson, Diana Krall, and Kurt Elling have presented both conventional and boundary-stretching jazz singing to wide audiences, particularly since 1990.

The work of these musicians, as well as those of previous generations, is evidence that as jazz develops, and new fashions emerge, older established techniques remain vital, providing the raw materials that ensure the music's continued growth and importance in the musical landscape.

Bibl.: Nat Shapiro and Nat Hentoff, eds., *Hear Me Talkin' to Ya* (New York: Rinehart, 1955; R: New York: Dover, 1966). André Hodeir, *Jazz: Its Evolution and Essence,* trans. David Noakes (New York: Grove Pr, 1956). Marshall W. Stearns, *The Story of Jazz* (New York: Oxford U Pr, 1956; R: 1970). Nat Hentoff and Albert J. McCarthy, eds., *Jazz* (New York: Rinehart, 1959; R: New York: Da Capo, 1974). Leonard Feather, *The Encyclopedia of Jazz* (New York: Horizon Pr, 1960). Leonard Feather, *The Encyclopedia of Jazz in the Sixties* (New York: Horizon Pr, 1966). Alan P. Merriam and Fradley H. Garner, "Jazz—The Word," *Ethno* 12 (1968): 373–96. Gunther Schuller, *Early Jazz* (New York: Oxford U Pr, 1968). John Chilton, *Who's Who of Jazz: Storyville to Swing Street* (London: Bloomsbury Bk Shop, 1970; 4th ed. rev., London: Macmillan, 1985). Ross Russell, *Jazz Style in Kansas City and the Southwest* (Berkeley and Los Angeles: U of Cal Pr, 1971). Ekkehard Jost, *Free Jazz* (Graz: Universal Ed, 1974). Roger D. Kinkle, *The Complete Encyclopedia of Popular Music and Jazz, 1900–1950* (New Rochelle, N.Y.: Arlington House, 1974). Robert S. Gold, *Jazz Talk* (Indianapolis: Bobbs-Merrill, 1975; R: New York: Da Capo, 1982). Leonard Feather and Ira Gitler, *The Encyclopedia of Jazz in the Seventies* (New York: Horizon Pr, 1976). Albert Murray, *Stomping the Blues* (New York: McGraw-Hill, 1976). James Lincoln Collier, *The Making of Jazz* (Boston: Houghton Mifflin, 1978). Donald Kennington, *The Literature of Jazz* (Chicago: American Library Assoc, 1980). Daniel Allen, *Jazz,* vol. 2 of *Bibliography of Discographies* (New York: Bowker, 1981). Bernhard Hefele, *Jazz Bibliography: International Literature on Jazz* (Munich: Saur, 1981). Joachim E. Berendt, *The Jazz Book: From New Orleans to Jazz Rock and Beyond,* trans. Helmut and Barbara Bredigkeit with Dan Morgenstern (London and New York: Granada, 1983). Carl Gregor Herzog zu Mecklenburg, *International Bibliography of Jazz Books,* vol. I, 1921–1949 (Baden-Baden: Valentin Koerner, 1983). Linda Dahl, *Stormy Weather: The Music and Lives of a Century of Jazzwomen* (New York: Pantheon, 1984). Gunther Schuller, *The Swing Era: The Development of Jazz, 1930–1945* (New York: Oxford U Pr, 1989). Roger T. Dean, *New Structures in Jazz and Improvised Music since 1960* (Milton Keynes: Open U Pr, 1992). Ted Gioia, *West Coast Jazz: Modern Jazz in California, 1945–1960* (Berkeley and Los Angeles: U of Cal Pr, 1992). William Howland Kenney, *Chicago Jazz: A Cultural History, 1904–1930* (New York: Oxford U Pr, 1993). Paul Berliner, *Thinking in Jazz: The Infinite Art of Improvisation* (Chicago: U of Chicago Pr, 1994). Eddie S. Meadows, ed., *Jazz Research and Reference Materials,* 2nd ed. rev. (New York: Garland Publ, 1995). Scott DeVeaux, *The Birth of Bebop: A Social and Musical History* (Berkeley and Los Angeles: U of Cal Pr, 1997). Mark C. Gridley, *Jazz Styles,* 6th ed. (Upper Saddle River, N.J.: Prentice-Hall, 1997). Lewis Porter, ed., *Jazz: A Century of Change* (New York: Schirmer, 1997). Stuart Nicholson, *Jazz-Rock: A History* (New York: Schirmer, 1998).

Periodicals: *Down Beat* (1934–). *Jazz Hot* (1935–39, 1945–). *Jazz Magazine* (1954–). *Jazz Monthly* (1955–71). *Coda* (1958–). *The Jazz Review* (1958–61). *Storyville* (1965–). *Jazzforschung* (1969–). *Journal of Jazz Studies* (1973–79), succeeded by *Annual Review of Jazz Studies* (1982–). *Cadence* (1976–). *JazzTimes* (1980–).

B.K., rev T.A.J.

Jena Symphony. A symphony in C major discovered in Jena, Germany, in 1909. Once thought to be an early work of Beethoven because his name appears on two of the parts found in Jena, it is now believed to be the work of Friedrich Witt (1770–1836) on the basis of two further copies with attributions.

Jenůfa [Cz. originally *Její pastorkyňa,* Her Foster Daughter]. Opera in three acts by Leoš Janáček (libretto by the composer, after Gabriela Preissová's play), produced in Brno in 1904. Setting: the Moravian mountains in the late 19th century.

Jephtha. (1) An oratorio by Handel (English text by Thomas Morell based on the Bible and George Buchanan's *Jepthes sive Votum*), produced in London in 1752. (2) [Lat. *Jephte*] An oratorio by Carissimi (Latin text from the Bible), composed before 1650.

Jeté [Fr.]. See Bowing (5).

Jeu [Fr.]. An organ stop or stop knob; sometimes also a combination of stops, as in **Jeu de tierce,* **Grand jeu,* **Petit jeu,* etc.

Jeu de cartes [Fr., Card Game]. Ballet "in three deals" by Stravinsky (choreography by George Balanchine), composed in 1936 and produced in New York the following year. The dancers represent cards in a poker game.

Jeu de tierce [Fr.]. The pitches of the **Cornet,* drawn separately, in the classical French organ.

Jeu de timbres [Fr.]. *Glockenspiel.

Jeune France, La [Fr.]. A group of French composers formed in 1936 by Olivier Messiaen (b. 1908), Yves Baudrier (b. 1906), André Jolivet (1905–74), and Daniel-Lesur (b. 1908). Their published manifesto proclaimed the wish to "propagate a living music, having the impetus of sincerity, generosity, and artistic conscientiousness" and to "return to the human" in the face of prevailing neoclassicism.

Jeu-parti [Fr.], **joc partit, partimen** [Occ.]. A poetic genre in dialogue form, practiced by the troubadours and especially the trouvères. Like the **tenso,* it consists of a debate on a question of love or some other subject, in alternating stanzas of identical form and melody. According to the strictest definition of the *partimen,* however, the opening speaker, unlike that of the *tenso,* allows his or her opponent to choose which of two positions to defend. In many cases, the two participants call for a judgment in envoys at the end, from the lord or lady of the court or from a designated judge who might also be a poet-composer, sometimes a woman. The **puys* at Arras in particular fostered the genre. About 100 examples in Old French survive with music.

Bibl.: Arthur Långfors, Alfred Jeanroy, and Louis Brandin, eds., *Recueil général des jeux-partis français,* 2 vols. (Paris: H. Champion, 1926). Sebastien Neumeister, *Das Spiel mit der höfischen Liebe: Das altprovenzalische Partimen* (Munich: W Fink, 1969). Michelle F. Stewart, "The Melodic Structure of Thirteenth-Century 'Jeux-Partis,'" *AM* 51 (1979): 86–107. Michel-André Bossy, ed. and trans., *Medieval Debate Poetry: Vernacular Works* (New York: Garland, 1987). See also *Tenso.* E.A.

Jeux [Fr., Games]. Ballet by Debussy (choreography by Vaslav Nijinsky, scenery and costumes by Léon Bakst), produced in Paris in 1913.

Jewish music. Three definitions have traditionally determined the boundaries of Jewish music: (1) music created and performed by Jews; (2) music performed as Jewish liturgy or ritual; (3) music connected to Jewish community and history, whether sacred or not. There has also been a fourth set of definitions that either deny the very possibility that music can convey anything specifically Jewish or limit the musical parameters of Jewishness to an extremely small body of sacred texts. These various definitions may or may not identify related musical practices. Accordingly, there is relatively little agreement about what Jewish music really is, and controversy and debate have surrounded Jewish music and music in Jewish culture. Fundamental issues of ontology accompany all discussions of Jewish music, within and outside Jewish culture. Nonetheless, widespread disagreement about definitions has magnified the deeper importance of music in the construction of Jewish identity and the transmission of Jewish culture throughout centuries of the Diaspora, making music crucial for the maintenance of Jewish tradition.

By including a broad range of musical practice as Jewish and situating them against different cultural contexts, the meanings and definitions of Jewish music emphasize the growing inclusiveness of the modern Jewish experience. If earlier definitions were largely restricted to sacred music, the more general awareness of Jewish communities in the Diaspora and Israel have led to the recognition that Jewish music includes folk music, art music, and popular music, and that the repertories in these categories are diverse and distinctive. Jewish folk musics include repertories and practices in vernacular languages, and they accompany activities that encourage widespread participation within the Jewish community. Jewish popular musics may also utilize vernacular languages, but these may have cosmopolitan functions and lead to exchange with other communities, Jewish and non-Jewish. Jewish classical musics may include languages that are not even Jewish, and participation may be limited to a small number of professionals performing outside Jewish contexts. Despite seeming differences, the sacred, folk, popular, and art musics that constitute Jewish music demonstrate the power of music to define and redefine the Jewish community in its vastly different contexts.

Music provides various means of marking a place as Jewish—as a site given additional meaning through musical performance. The places marked by Jewish music may be textual or contextual, geographic or ritual, restricted to the Jewish community or opened by cultural hybridity. Time, especially history, underscores music's Jewishness by its power to connect contemporary musical practices to specific historical moments. History also juxtaposes concerns for authenticity—whether music is or even can be Jewish—with ongoing processes of change, both preservation and adaptation. The considerations of place and time that follow lead further to sections on musical specialists and Jewish music today.

I. *The place of Jewish music.* Jewish music is fundamentally logogenic, with distinctions between song and instrumental practices critical to the origins of musical sound in worship. The most basic of all texts are biblical and liturgical, and the Hebrew Bible itself provides the basis for different styles, genres, and repertories. The Torah (Five Books of Moses, or Pentateuch) provides a framework for worship through cyclical performance during the year. Whereas the performance of the Torah is technically recitation and not music, reciters recognize musical parameters. A system of notating the direction and syntax of melodic motion, the *te'amim* (masoretic accents), has been employed by most Jewish traditions since the early Middle Ages. *Te'amim* and the tropes that allow for the transmission of recitation permit a common understanding of text while at the same affording different communities and musical specialists the freedom of interpretation at the interstices of oral and written transmission. In several recitation traditions, not least among them the prevalent style of modern Israel, the Jerusalem-Sephardi style, musical parameters are so extensive as to result in the requisite use of specific modes—Arabic *maqamat* (sing., *maqam*) in modern Israel—in the annual cycle. Biblical texts lend themselves to different styles of performance, ranging from the entirely soloistic genres of cantillation to congregational singing, many (e.g., the Psalms) also involving antiphony.

The liturgy of the worship service is the source of many musical practices, some of which are common to most Jewish traditions, while others vary according to historical period and community practice. The liturgy of the service follows an order determined by the service's position in daily, weekly, and annual cycles, as well as specific holidays and celebrations. With extensive emphasis on literacy in Judaism, worshipers follow the order of liturgy in prayerbooks, or *siddurim,* but also rely on the examples set by lay leaders (e.g., the *ba'al tefillah* responsible for leading prayer) and ritual specialists, notably the rabbi and the cantor. In liberal modern traditions musical leadership for the performance of the liturgy is even more extensive, with soloists, chorus, and instruments enriching the texture of worship.

Sacred musical practices outside the synagogue reflect the theological and aesthetic sensibilities of worship to varying degrees. The soloistic practices of recitation often provide a template for melodic style in paraliturgical genres. Similarly, the antiphonal performance practice characteristic of the Psalms and congregational performance of synagogue song may be reflected in community song. Sacred music outside the synagogue may employ paraliturgical texts specific to a holiday or a community's own celebrations, and it is also distinctive because of the ways in which Hebrew texts may be mixed with vernacular texts, be they specifically Jewish—for example, Yiddish, Ladino, or a dialect of Judeo-Arabic—or even nonspecifically Jewish. There are several genres of sacred music practiced in the home (e.g., *zemirot,* or table songs, for Sabbath meals) and many others that have accrued to individual communities (e.g., *piyyutim* and *pizmonim*).

Gender marks virtually every genre and practice of Jewish music, locating it in specific places in Jewish sacred and secular life. In one of the most influential medieval tracts on religious musical practices, Moses ben Maimon, known as Maimonides (1135–1204), called for a separation of male and female practices in the synagogue, asserting that women's voices would distract men from perceiving the word of God in synagogal liturgy. Even though men and women came to worship in separate spaces of the synagogue, the main sanctuary, as a place in which the community gathers as a whole, acquires a feminine character at the beginning of Friday-evening Sabbath services, when the song "Lecha dodi" welcomes *Shechina,* the Sabbath bride, into the sanctuary. The figurative entrance of the Sabbath bride further brings about an orientation of worship toward the altar, or *bima,* which is itself turned toward the East, or *mizrach,* where the ark containing Torah scrolls stands. Outside the synagogue, women's song repertories reconfigure the home for the Sabbath.

Concepts of community shape Jewish musical traditions at various levels. At the most local level, the synagogue distinguishes the place of music in the community, or *kehilla.* More geographically expansive regional, linguistic, religious, or doctrinal boundaries may include the traditions of larger communities, and when these reveal continuity through a long history of tradition they acquire the attributes of *'eda.* Over the course of two millennia of the Diaspora, the most expansive of all concepts of community emerged among the German- and Yiddish-speaking Jews of central and eastern Europe (Ashkenaz), the Ladino-speaking Jews of the Mediterranean, expelled from the Iberian Peninsula at the end of the 15th century (Sepharad), and the culture of Judeo-Arabic–speaking communities in North Africa and the Middle East (Eastern). Larger and smaller Jewish communities, with distinctive music cultures, also developed at a greater distance from the main centers of Diaspora Judaism, such as the Cochin Jews of South Asia and the Fallasha of Ethiopia. The Jewish musical traditions of such communities have historically borne witness to the interaction between Jewish practices and the surrounding cultural environment. Local cultural practices formed patterns of transmission called *minhag,* which left their imprint on musical style, or *nusach,* even in the local synagogue.

When considering the place as a context for defining Jewish music, it is also important to consider the ways in which religious, geographical, and cultural boundaries restrict or encourage musical change. Orthodox views emphasize the need to restrict musical tradition so that various forms of authenticity remain intact. Even the spaces of the synagogue (e.g., between men in the main sanctuary and women in their own worship gallery) are rigidly bounded. By extension, distinguishing practice in the synagogue from that outside the synagogue has functioned, even into 20th-century concepts of Jewish community such as those theorized by A. Z. Idelsohn, as fundamental to what is and is not Jewish music. Liberal views, however, recognize that exchange across cultural and religious boundaries has provided Jewish communities with a means of adapting and surviving as a minority religious culture, and in modern Jewish thought it has become customary to understand music as a measure for acculturation. The sacred music of the reform movement has benefited from musical border-crossing in modern European and North American communities, as have the folk- and popular-music specialists responsible for repertories such as klezmer music in Ashkenazic culture and the art music of many Muslim cultures of the Middle East.

II. *History.* Jewish music reflects deep concerns for time and timelessness, and by extension history and myth. Music is itself a product of the most fundamental myths of Jewish tradition, for example the fashioning of musical instruments by Yuval in the fourth chapter of Genesis. The power to calibrate time through ritual is given to the ram's horn, or shofar, in the story of Abraham's attempted sacrifice of his son Isaac, the "Akeda" (Genesis 22). The biblical origin myths established the conditions for controversies that followed music through Jewish history and that, accordingly, constitute Jewish music history itself. Music produced through artifice (instruments made by human hands) has a more questionable role than music produced within or by the body itself. This distinction, formulated often as a contrast between instrumental and vocal music, has acquired long-term historical dimensions, for example, in the banishment of instruments from synagogue worship after the destruction of the Temple in Jerusalem in 70 C.E.

Jewish music history also reflects reflects the tension between center and periphery. The most powerful symbol of the center has been the Temple, which supported the substantial choruses and instrumental ensembles. Archeological evidence and writings in works of commentary, such as the Mishna, give us some general sense of the earliest forms of music making at the symbolic center, for example, when observers describe performances with considerable volume and a wide array of instruments. With the destruction of the Temple by the Romans, however, the maintenance of musical practices in worship shifted to the synagogue at the periphery. Unlike the canonic traditions of the Temple, those of the synagogue reflected local practice and required flexibility. Whereas historical evidence suggests that professional musicians were responsible for maintaining the musical repertories of the Temple, music making in the synagogue fell to lay worshiper-musicians and, on some occasions, a community's religious leader, the rabbi. The contrast between center and periphery developed as a tension, even a dialectic, between authenticity in an increasingly distant past and the ongoing change confronting Jewish communities in the Diaspora.

In late Antiquity music theoretical systems fixed the rules of biblical recitation and liturgy, on the one hand anchoring them to texts at the center of Jewish tradition and, on the other, allowing sufficient latitude for adaptation to the Diaspora. Recitation and other musically inflected types of performance relied on a mixture of oral and written transmission, which makes it difficult to reconstruct the sound of medieval Jewish music. Among the relatively few examples of notated music that survive are those in the Geniza, a type of archive, of the Ezra-Synagogue in Cairo, which contains, among other manuscripts, 12th-century compositions by Obadiah the Proselyte, a French convert from Christianity, whose Jewish works reflect contemporaneous Norman Christian traditions. Most specific Renaissance and early modern evidence for the sound of music in the synagogue comes from Christian observers, both musicians and theorists (e.g., Johannes Reuchlin and Benedetto Marcello), many of whom sought to emulate what they believed to be the authenticity in Jewish musical practices. At historical moments when anti-Semitism temporarily retreated, there was considerable exchange between Jewish and non-Jewish musicians. The Mantuan composer Salamone Rossi (ca. 1570–ca. 1628), who contributed to the musical life of the Gonzaga court and northern Italian Jewish communities, was one of the most influential composers of early modern Europe, though his position in European music history fell victim to the pogroms against the Italian Jews at the end of his life.

The period of modern Jewish music history began with the Haskala, the Jewish Enlightenment, in the late 18th century. The theological and social reform within European Jewish communities, initiated by Enlightenment thinkers, or *maskilim,* such as Moses Mendelssohn, exposed the musical life of the community to liturgical reform (e.g., the introduction of vernacular languages into the synagogue) and to widespread contact with non-Jewish musical traditions (e.g., the introduction of the organ and music for mixed choruses into the synagogue). The historical tensions between maintaining authenticity and responding to outside cultural pressures led to doctrinal and social conflicts, but they also heightened the awareness of Jewish music itself. By the end of the 19th century, cantors were publishing anthologies of cantorial music, or *chazzanut,* folk-song collectors were publishing volumes of Jewish folk music, and attempts were under way to establish modern traditions of Jewish art music, such as that of the St. Petersburg school from ca. 1910 into the 1920s. The Latvian cantor-musicologist Abraham Zvi Idelsohn (1882–1932) used the recording technologies and nascent methodologies of *Vergleichende Musikwissenschaft* (comparative musicology) to undertake fieldwork in Palestine and to plumb manuscript and archival sources in central and eastern Europe to publish the ten-volume *Hebräisch-orientalischer Melodienschatz* (1914–32).

The historical events of the 20th century profoundly shaped modern and postmodern concepts of Jewish music. The cataclysm of the Holocaust decimated the Jewish communities of central, eastern, and southern Europe and contributed substantially to the reestablishment of Jewish musical traditions in North America and Israel, which achieved statehood in 1948. New movements in music history and attitudes about the relation between the ancient past and the present ensued, among them active attempts to revive presumably destroyed and dying traditions, to instigate new types of fieldwork projects in the increasingly multicultural Jewish communities of Israel and elsewhere, and to open new possibilities for the hybridity of modern Jewish music.

III. *Musical specialists.* Gender serves as one of the most basic distinctions for musical specialization. Boys acquire the necessary knowledge and skills for cantillation in the religious school *(cheder),* and these serve them when they participate in the rituals of the synagogue sanctuary, in orthodox traditions restricted to males. The prayers and songs that girls learn in the home or in community ritual also develop into the specialized practices of family life, rites of passage, or the maintenance of women's practices, such as saint veneration in North Africa or minor pilgrimages in the Middle East.

In the sacred life of a community it is the *chazzan* (cantor) who has been the most distinctive musical specialist since the Middle Ages. Originally responsible for maintaining many different aspects of Jewish tradition at the core of the community, the *chazzan*'s role has increasingly become one of musical specialty; by the late 20th century, many *chazzanim* attended schools of sacred music, sometimes within Jewish seminaries but occasionally even in universities or musical conservatories. From leading prayer and interspersing solos in the liturgy, the *chazzan*'s responsibilities have expanded to include preparing musical ensembles, instruction in Jewish education, and, not uncommonly, the arrangement and composition of new works for the synagogue.

As early as the late Middle Ages, Jewish musical specialists also appear outside the synagogue. Instrumentalists responsible for the accompaniment of dance *(letzim)* or for the various rites of passage accompanying weddings and other celebrations occupy a distinctive presence in the Jewish communities of the late medieval Rhineland (e.g., Speyer and Worms). In early modern Europe, instrumental specialists acquired the designation *klezmer* ("vessel of song"), reflecting the greater acceptance of instrumental genres and secularized repertories as Jewish music. The modernization that swept across the Diaspora communities in the 19th and 20th centuries multiplied opportunities for *klezmorim* and other folk-music specialists, transforming many into popular-music professionals by the mid- and late 20th century.

Jewish musical specialists are frequently active outside the Jewish community. In Muslim societies of North Africa and the Middle East Jewish musicians have often been active as musical "others," for example as instrumentalists in the performance of classical and semiclassical music when Muslim religious practice permits listening to music *(samaᶜ)* but restricts its performance. Elsewhere in the Diaspora, Jewish musicians have become active in non-Jewish classical musics, and this in turn has been a primary motivation for professionalism. Jewish musicians also perform frequently as professionals or semiprofessionals with non-Jewish specialists, such as the Roma, or Gypsies, especially in the border regions of central and east-central Europe.

It may well be that the music that results from the special status of Jewish musicians as cultural "others" is not always or entirely Jewish music, but the musicians who develop these specialties are often responsible for mediating between Jewish and non-Jewish cultural contexts. Jewish popular music, therefore, is highly cosmopolitan, not only in the European and North American communities where Ashkenazic culture dominates, but also in the Sephardic and Eastern communities of the Mediterranean and the Middle East. By the late 19th century, Jewish musicians were beginning to play visible and—in urban centers such as Vienna, Berlin, and Budapest—dominant roles on the musical stage and in the performance of cabaret in Europe and vaudeville in North America. The Yiddish musical stage, for example, was brought to the U.S. by musical specialists, many of whom contributed substantially to the history of the American musical. In the second half of the 20th century, Israeli popular musicians, such as Ofra Haza and Dana International, enjoyed success at international competitions (e.g., the Eurovision Song Contest) and prominence in the world beat scene, where they often played a fusion of global pop and more localized Jewish repertories, notably styles from Yemen, Egypt, and Iraq (e.g., in *musica mizrakhit,* or eastern music).

IV. *Jewish music today.* The capacity to admit and recognize definitions that witness the many different expressive practices gathered together under the single concept of Jewish music is a mark of modernity. The ethno-religious distinction "Jewish" was first applied to different genres and practices of music in the late 19th century. Music, too, was not entirely separable from other religious and cultural practices of sacred and secular life. Once distinctive categories of Jewish music were established in the 19th century, institutions for cultivating Jewish music and supporting Jewish musicians followed at the turn of the 20th century, not least as an accompaniment and response to growing nationalism throughout Europe. The tumultuous events shaping Jewish history in the 20th century had the further impact of moving Jewish musical practices into the public sphere and, in turn, extending modernism to Jewish music. As it spilled beyond the Jewish community in the second half of the 20th century, Jewish music acquired the many attributes of globalization. The time and place of Jewish music today, then, are formed as the different paths of the Diaspora and the different strands of history converge. Diversity may still be extensive, but the possibility for distinctive definitions and patterns of self-identity are intensified rather than disintegrated as Jewish history exerts its palpable presence in world music at the beginning of the 21st century.

Bibl.: Abraham Zvi Idelsohn, ed., *Hebräisch-orientalischer Melodienschatz,* 10 vols. (Leipzig: Breitkopf & Härtel, 1914–32). Alfred Sendrey, *Bibliography of Jewish Music* (New York: Columbia U Pr, 1951). Israel Adler, *La Pratique musicale savante dans quelques communautés juives en Europe aux XVIIe et XVIIIe siècles,* 2 vols. (Paris: Mouton, 1965). Abraham Zvi Idelsohn, *Jewish Music in Its Historical Development* (New York: Schocken, 1975; orig. 1929). Macy Nulman, *Concise Encyclopedia of Jewish Music* (New York: McGraw-Hill, 1975). Joel Walbe, *Der Gesang Israels und seine Quellen* (Hamburg: Christians Verlag, 1975). Max Brod, *Die Musik Israels,* 2nd rev. ed. (Kassel: Bärenreiter, 1976). Eric Werner, *A Voice Still Heard . . . : The Sacred Songs of the Ashkenazic Jews* (University Park: Pa St U Pr, 1976). Robert Lachmann, *Gesänge der Juden auf der Insel Djerba* (Jerusalem: Magnes Pr of Hebrew U, 1978; orig. in English trans., 1940). Hanoch Avenary, *Encounters of East and West in Music* (Tel Aviv: Dept. of Musicology, Tel-Aviv Univ., 1979). Yehiel Adaqi and Uri Sharvit, *A Treasury of Jewish Yemenite Chants* (Jerusalem: Israeli Institute for Sacred Music, 1981). Karl E. Grözinger, *Musik und Gesang in der Theologie der frühen jüdischen Literature: Talmud, Midrasch, Mystik* (Tübingen: J C B Mohr, 1982). Amnon Shiloah, *The Musical Traditions of Iraqi Jews: Selection of Piyyutim and Songs* (Or Yehuda: Iraqi Jews' Traditional Culture Center, 1983). Samuel G. Armistead, Joseph H. Silverman, and Israel J. Katz, *Judeo-Spanish Ballads from Oral Tradition,* 20 vols. (projected) (Berkeley: U of Cal Pr, 1986–). Mark Slobin, ed. and trans., *Old Jewish Folk Music* (Philadelphia: U of Pa Pr, 1982). Irene Heskes, comp., *The Resource Book of Jewish Music: A Bibliographical and Topical Guide to the Book and Journal Literature and Program Materials* (Westport, Conn.: Greenwood, 1985). Kay Kaufman Shelemay, *Music, Ritual, and Falasha History* (East Lansing: African Studies Center, Michigan State Univ., 1986). Mark Slobin, *Chosen Voices: The Story of the American Cantorate* (Urbana: U of Ill Pr, 1989). Alexander L. Ringer, *Arnold Schoenberg: The Composer as Jew* (Oxford: Clarendon, 1990). Walter Salmen, *". . . denn die Fiedel macht das Fest": Jüdische Musikanten und Tänzer vom 13. bis 20. Jahrhundert* (Innsbruck: Helbling, 1991). Philip V. Bohlman, *The World Centre for Jewish Music in Palestine 1936–1940: Jewish Musical Life on the Eve of World War II* (Oxford: Clarendon, 1992). Amnon Shiloah, *Jewish Musical Traditions* (Detroit: Wayne St U Pr, 1992). Jehoash Hirshberg, *Music in the Jewish Community of Palestine, 1880–1948: A Social History* (Oxford: Clarendon, 1995). Edwin Seroussi, *Popular Music in Israel: The First Fifty Years* (Cambridge, Mass.: Harvard College Library, 1996). Kay Kaufman Shelemay, *Let Jasmine Rain Down: Song and Remembrance among Syrian Jews* (Chicago: U of Chicago Pr, 1998). Don Harrán, *Salamone Rossi: Jewish Musician in Late Renaissance Mantua* (New York: Oxford U Pr, 1999). Mark Slobin, *Fiddler on the Move: Exploring the Klezmer World* (New York: Oxford U Pr, 2000). Jeffrey A. Summit, *The Lord's Song in a Strange Land: Music and Identity in Contemporary Jewish Worship* (New York: Oxford U Pr, 2000). Heidy Zimmermann, *Tora und Shira: Untersuchungen zur Musikauffassung des rabbinischen Judentums* (Berne: Peter Lang, 2000). Philip V. Bohlman and Otto Holzapfel, *The Folk Songs of Ashkenaz* (Middleton, Wis.: A-R Eds, 2001). Ellen Koskoff, *Music in Lubavitcher Life* (Urbana: U of Ill Pr, 2001). Edwin Seroussi et al., "Jewish Music," in *Grove 6,* rev. ed. (London: Macmillan, 2001), 13: 24–112. P.V.B.

Jew's harp [also jew's trump, jaw's harp; Fr. *guimbarde;* Ger. *Maultrommel*]. A single tongue of wood or metal fastened at one end to the closed end of a U-shaped or keyhole-shaped frame. The narrow part of the frame is placed lengthwise between the player's lips and the free end of the tongue is then plucked. The player's mouth acts as a resonator; pitch is altered by changing the size of the oral cavity, thus reinforcing different partials. It is distributed through Asia and Southeast Asia, and it has been known in Europe since at least the Middle Ages. From Europe it was exported to America and elsewhere. The name remains unexplained and seems to have no connection with the Jewish people. See ill. under Percussion instruments.

Jhālā [Hin.]. In Hindustani music, a rhythmically animated section of improvisation that often concludes a performance of an **ālāp* or **gat.* Best suited to plucked stringed instruments, the rhythmic animation of *jhālā* is created by repeatedly plucking an instrument's drone-producing strings. C.C.

Jig. A vigorous dance popular in the British Isles from the 16th century onward. The word seems to come from the French *giguer* (to frolic, to leap); the term was repatriated as a musical form and developed specific musical characteristics on the Continent [see Gigue]. In England, it implied no particular rhythmic characteristics except in the hands of composers writing in imitation of Continental (usually Italian rather than French) style. Early examples include settings of or variations on specific jig tunes that sometimes carried the name of stage characters who performed them; thus "Nobody's Jigg" in the **Fitzwilliam Virginal Book* and elsewhere refers to the character played by R. Reynolds in the comedy *Somebody and Nobody.* One type of jig (jigg) developed in the late 16th century into an earthy song-and-dance genre from which sprang the *ballad opera. The jig still current as a folk dance in *Ireland is now thought by some scholars to have been introduced there directly from England rather than indirectly through Italian models. B.G.

Jingling Johnny. *Turkish crescent.

Jitterbug. See Lindy.

Jodel. See Yodel.

Jongleur [Fr.]. See Minstrel.

Jonny spielt auf [Ger., Jonny Strikes Up the Band]. Opera in two acts by Ernst Krenek (libretto by the composer), produced in Leipzig in 1927. Setting: the 1920s.

Joṛ [Hin.]. A markedly pulsed but unmetered section of improvisation following Hindustani **ālāp* and preceding **jhālā.* C.C.

Joropo [Sp.]. A traditional social dance and musical style of the *llanos* (plains) region of eastern Colombia and western Venezuela, now nationally diffused in Venezuela. It is most characteristically performed by solo vocalists, with intricate accompaniments provided by ensembles of, e.g., harp, one or more *cuatros* (small four-string guitars), and maracas. Subtypes of the *joropo* and genres closely associated with it include the **galerón,* **golpe, pasaje,* and *seis por derecho.* D.S.

Jota [Sp.]. A genre of song and dance especially characteristic of Aragón, in northern Spain, but widely disseminated through the Spanish peninsula. In its simplest form, a *copla* consisting of four octosyllabic lines (here numbered 1–4) is set to from two to four phrases of music in a fast triple meter (designated by capital letters) in a seven-member pattern as follows: 2A 1B 2A 3B 4A 4B (or C) 1A (or D). All phrases have two-syllable upbeats, odd-numbered phrases in the pattern beginning on the dominant and cadencing on the tonic, even-numbered ones doing the reverse. It is danced by one or more couples with castanets and is accompanied by guitars and **bandurrias.* Some versions of the choreography require rather high leaps. It began to be widely disseminated in the 18th century, and its existence cannot be firmly documented before the second half of the 17th. As a quintessentially Spanish form of folk music, it has often been taken over into art music: e.g., Liszt, *Rhapsodie espagnole* ("Folies d'Espagne et jota aragonesa"); Glinka, *Capriccio brillante* or First Spanish Overture; Falla **Sombrero de tres picos;* and various works of Albéniz and others.

Bibl.: Arcadio de Larrea Palacín, "Preliminares al estudio de la jota aragonesa," *AnM* 2 (1947): 175–90. Demetrio Galán Bergua, *El libro de la jota aragonesa* (Zaragoza, 1966).

Jouer [Fr.]. To play.

Jouhikantele, jouhikannel, jouhikko [Finn.]. A bowed *lyre of Finland with from two to five horsehair strings, related to the **crwth.*

Jubilus [Lat.]. The melisma sung to the final syllable of the word *alleluia* in the *alleluia of Gregorian chant; also referred to as the neume or **neuma.* It may recur in the verse of the alleluia, especially at the end, and it often incorporates some pattern of repetitions.

Judas Maccabaeus. Oratorio by Handel (libretto by Thomas Morell, based on 1 Maccabees of the Apocrypha and Josephus, Antiquities XII), produced in London in 1747.

Jug band. (1) A small folk ensemble of the U.S. that includes various homemade instruments (e.g., washtub, washboard, and jug), along with a few conventional pitched instruments, particularly guitar and harmonica. (2) An ensemble of a type formed among black musicians in the southern U.S. in the 1920s and 30s, including a jug (played by blowing across its opening) and associated with the blues and some currents of jazz.

Jukebox. An automatic phonograph containing a variety of recordings, principally of current popular music, and operated by inserting a coin and pressing a button to make a selection. Devices of this type date from the late 19th century and were widely disseminated through the middle of the 20th century in modest restaurants and bars.

Julius Caesar. See *Giulio Cesare.*

Jupiter Symphony. Popular name for Mozart's Symphony in C major K. 551 (1788). Mozart's son attributed the name to Haydn's London impresario Johann Peter Salomon. The first edition to use it was Muzio Clementi's arrangement for piano published in London in 1823. The name is usually thought to refer to the majestic character of the opening of the first movement.

Justiniana. See *Giustiniana.*

Just intonation [Fr. *intonation juste;* Ger. *reine Stimmung;* It. *accordatura giusta;* Sp. *entonación justa*]. (1) The beatless tuning of an interval, one that brings it into agreement with some analogous interval in the *harmonic series. Such intervals are considered to be acoustically pure. They are expressed by ratios containing the smallest possible integers corresponding to the lowest analogous partials of the harmonic series. When an interval can be expressed by adjacent partials in the series it has the form (x + 1):x.

(2) Any tuning that incorporates five or more acoustically pure types of interval within the octave; in the case of diatonic or chromatic scales, those based on acoustically pure major thirds and acoustically pure fifths. It is not possible to construct a diatonic scale in which both fifths and thirds are pure. For example, the E produced as the sum of four pure fifths above C will form with C an interval whose ratio is 81:64 rather than the pure third with ratio 5:4. Systems of just intonation typically favor the third at the expense of the fifth. The result is at least one prominent fifth (e.g., D–A) that is distinctly different from the others [see Temperament]. Remedies for this defect proposed as early as the 16th century (Zarlino, *Sopplimenti musicali,* 1588) require the use of two different tunings for one or more pitches (e.g., D). For keyboard and other instruments of fixed pitch, such remedies require a more complex mechanism. The requirements become still more complex if chromatic pitches are to be included in the system to any significant degree so as to permit modulation and transposition of the kind familiar in tonal music, since ultimately an infinite number of pitches within the octave would be required. Instruments with as many as 50 and more pitches per octave have been built, however. Using just intonation with only one tuning per pitch, it is possible to build from the diatonic scale as many as three major and two minor triads with acoustically pure intervals.

The earliest known theorists to assert the superiority of the just third are Theinred of Dover (12th century) and Walter Odington (fl. 1298–1316), both from England, where early polyphony gives considerable prominence to imperfect consonances such as the third. The earliest theorist to publish a complete just tuning is the Spaniard Bartolomeo Ramos de Pareja (ca. 1440–1491?). Apparent ancient antecedents such as Didymus's diatonic and Ptolemy's diatonic syntonic scales have often been cited since the 17th century but are somewhat illusory. The focus of interest in such ancient Greek tunings was on the dimensions of scale steps within tetrachords. Ratios for thirds and sixths are demonstrably incidental. In late medieval accounts of just tunings, on the other hand, the focus is precisely on these two intervals.

In the 18th century, just intonation was sometimes recommended for violin playing (Boyden, 1951). In the 20th century, there has been a modest resurgence of interest in justly intoned multiple divisions of the octave. In the U.S., composers Harry Partch, Ben Johnston, La Monte Young, and Terry Riley have been among the most significant advocates. See also Interval, Temperament.

Bibl.: Adriaan Fokker, *Just Intonation* (The Hague: Nijhoff, 1949). David D. Boyden, "Prelleur, Geminiani, and Just Intonation," *JAMS* 4 (1951): 202–19. James Murray Barbour, *Tuning and Temperament: A Historical Survey,* 2nd ed. (East Lansing: Mich St Coll Pr, 1953). Harry Partch, *Genesis of a Music,* 2nd ed. enl. (New York: Da Capo, 1974).

K

K., KV. Abbr. for *Köchel-Verzeichnis,* the *thematic catalog of the works of Mozart first prepared by Ludwig von Köchel: *Chronologisch-thematisches Verzeichnis sämtlicher Tonwerke Wolfgang Amadé Mozarts* (Leipzig, 1862). A second, revised edition was published in 1905 by Paul von Waldersee; a third in 1937 by Alfred Einstein with a supplement in 1947; and a sixth in 1964 (Wiesbaden: Breitkopf & Härtel) by Franz Giegling, Alexander Weinemann, and Gerd Sievers. Because Köchel numbers are intended to be chronological, advances in the study of the canon and chronology of Mozart's works have led to the reassignment of Köchel numbers for some works. Works for which there have been two numbers are often cited by both (as in this dictionary, where the number from the sixth edition is given in parentheses following the original number if the two are different). The edition being cited is sometimes indicated by a superscript number, e.g., K^6.

Kabuki [Jap.]. A major genre of Japanese music theater. See East Asia II, 3 (iii).

Kadenz [Ger.]. *Cadence, *cadenza.

Kaffeekantate [Ger.]. See *Coffee* Cantata.

Kaiserquartett [Ger.]. See *Emperor* Quartet.

Kalevala. The Finnish national epic. Among the symphonic poems by Finnish composers based on portions of this epic, those by Sibelius include **Lemminkäinen Suite,* **Pohjola's Daughter,* and **Tapiola.*

Kalimba. See *Mbira.*

Kalinda. See Calypso.

Kalkant, Calcant [Ger.]. The operator of a bellows on a nonelectrical organ. In the 18th century, *Kalkanten* were regular members of the musical establishments of churches and large courts; in the latter case, they seem often to have functioned like present-day orchestra managers. E.K.W.

Kalophonic. See Byzantine chant II, *Anenajki.*

Kamānjah, kamancha [Ar., Per.]. (1) A *spike fiddle of the Islamic world, especially Iran. One to four strings pass down a long, unfretted neck and over a small, spherical, wooden body covered with skin. It is held upright and played with a flexible bow. See also *kemençe, rabāb.* See ill. under Near and Middle East. (2) The Western violin or viola. (3) *Kamānjah rūmī,* **lira.*

Kammer [Ger.]. Chamber; *Kammermusik,* chamber music; etc. For *Kammerton* see Pitch.

Kampuchea. See Southeast Asia V.

Kanon [Ger.]. *Canon.

Kanōn [Gr.]. See Byzantine chant II, Monochord (1).

Kantele [Finn.]. A Finnish *zither. The traditional instrument was a narrow trapezoid with 5 strings. The modern version has 12 to 46 metal strings tuned diatonically. It is mentioned in the **Kalevala* and is a national symbol.

Kantionale [Ger.]. See *Cantionale.*

Kantor [Ger.]. The chief musician of a German Protestant (Evangelical) church, whose duties comprised teaching school as well as selecting, composing, rehearsing, and performing music appropriate to liturgical celebrations and public municipal occasions. Bach was Kantor at the church of St. Thomas and its associated school in Leipzig from 1723 until his death. See also Cantor. R.F.F.

Kantorei [Ger.]. In German Protestant cities from the 16th through the 18th century, a voluntary group of townspeople who performed polyphonic music in church under the leadership of the **Kantor;* at Protestant courts in the 16th and 17th centuries, the professional singers and instrumentalists, usually known at Catholic courts as the *Kapelle.*

Kanun [Turk.]. See *Qānūn.*

Kapelle [Ger.]. *Chapel; *Hofkapelle,* court chapel. In the 17th century, this came to mean the entire musical establishment of a court, both sacred and secular, including the opera. Ultimately, the term lost its sacred associations altogether and in the 19th century could refer to any orchestra or ensemble, including a military band (*Militärkapelle*). See also *Kapellmeister.*

Kapellmeister [Ger.]. The leader of a musical *chapel, which might provide both sacred and secular music. Bach held this title at the court at Cöthen from 1717 until 1723. In the 19th century, when the term **Kapelle* could refer to a wholly secular musical establishment, including an opera or any orchestra or ensemble, *Kapellmeister* came to mean simply conductor (even of a military band or dance orchestra), though often the second- or third-ranked conductor under a general music director or chief conductor. Wagner held such a post at Dresden beginning in 1843. The term is now somewhat old-fashioned and often has a pejorative sense suggesting lack of inspiration, as does the term *Kapellmeistermusik* for the compositions of such a person.

Karelia. An orchestral overture, op. 10, and a suite, op. 11, by Sibelius, both drawn from his incidental music to a historical pageant presented in 1893 by students at the university in Vyborg, Karelia (in Russia).

Kát'a Kabanová. Opera in three acts by Leoš Janáček (libretto by the composer, after A. N. Ostrovsky's tragedy *The Storm*), produced in Brno in 1921. Setting: Kalinov, a small town on the Volga, about 1860.

Katerina Izmaylova. See *Lady Macbeth of the Mtsensk District.*

Kathak [Hin.]. (1) A major classical dance of North India. Its style ranges from demonstrations of rhythmically intricate footwork, with little other body movement, to freely mimetic interpretations of traditional mythology. Basic accompaniment includes voice, **tablā,* and **sāraṅgī.* (2) A caste of musicians.
C.C.

Kathakali [Mal.]. A major form of dance-drama in Kerala, South India. Deriving in part from martial exercises, the dramas are performed in vigorous style by men who wear elaborate facial makeup and costumes. Accompaniment is provided by two singers, a pair of drums, cymbals, and gong. C.C.

Katzenmusik [Ger.]. *Charivari.

Kaval. **Caval.*

Kayago, kayagŭm [Kor.]. A Korean *zither with 12 silk strings passing over 12 high, movable bridges, similar to the Japanese **koto* and the Chinese **cheng.* It plays both solo and ensemble music, particularly the *sanjo,* an improvised suite with drum accompaniment [see East Asia III, 4 (ii)].

Kazoo. A voice-operated *mirliton of the U.S. and Europe. A membrane is attached over a hole in the side of a short wooden or metal tube and vibrates with a buzzing effect when the player sings or hums into the tube.

Kehraus [Ger.]. The last dance at a ball.

Kemânğe. See *Kamānjah.*

Kemençe [Turk.]. A three-stringed *fiddle of the Turkish Black Sea region in the shape of an elongated oval or a trapezoid. The player usually stands, holding the instrument vertically with the left hand, often dancing while playing. The *kemençe* of Turkish art music is a somewhat different instrument resembling the Greek **lira.*

Kenner und Liebhaber [Ger.; Fr. *connaisseur* and *amateur*]. In publications of the late 18th century (e.g., by C. P. E. Bach), a phrase often used to suggest that the music in question was suitable both for knowledgeable musicians and the growing number of amateur music-lovers.

Kent bugle, Kent horn. See Keyed bugle.

Kesselpauke, Kesseltrommel [Ger.]. Kettledrum. See Timpani.

Kettledrum. See Timpani.

Key. (1) [Fr. *tonalité, ton;* Ger. *Tonart;* It. *tonalità, tono;* Sp. *tonalidad, tono*]. In tonal music [see Tonality], the pitch relationships that establish a single *pitch class as a tonal center or tonic (or key note), with respect to which the remaining pitches have subordinate functions. There are two types or modes of keys, *major and minor, and any of the twelve pitch classes can serve as a tonic. There are thus in principle 24 different keys. Because a pitch class may have more than one name, however (e.g., C♯ and D♭, which are said to be *enharmonic equivalents), the nomenclature of keys includes more than 24. The key of a composition or passage is described in terms of its tonic and its mode (e.g., C major, D minor), and a work or passage is said to be "in" a certain key.

The key of a work is defined in terms of the particular major or minor *scale from which its principal pitches are drawn. This is indicated in the first instance by a *key signature—an arrangement of sharps or flats (or the absence of both) at the beginning of each staff that specifies the principal pitches. (Other pitches may be used as well, producing *chromaticism.) The notion of scale embodies not only the selection of seven pitch classes from the available twelve, however, but also the organization of the seven in a hierarchy around the one that serves as tonic. When the pitches of a scale are arranged as a scale, the tonic is placed first. Furthermore, each key signature represents one major and one minor key that share the same basic pitch collection, but have different tonics. For example, the pitches of the white keys of the piano (represented by a key signature of no sharps and no flats) can be arranged in a scale with C first and thus as tonic (yielding C major) or with A first as tonic (yielding A minor). These two "modes" of presenting the same pitches differ in the arrangement of tones and semitones on either side of the tonic [for a discussion of these and other modes, see Mode]. Thus, in order to be in a given key, a composition must not only give prominence to the seven pitch classes of the appropriate scale, but it must also treat the tonic as the single pitch class of greatest stability and toward which all tonal movement ultimately tends. A piece in a given key will virtually always conclude with the tonic and will most often include a number of prominent *cadences on the tonic.

Although a tonal piece is usually described as being in a single key, it may incorporate passages in other keys before returning finally to the principal key. The process of moving from one key to another in the course of a piece is called *modulation [see also Key relationship]. Often, though not always, the key signature of a work is left unchanged throughout one or more modulations, the necessary changes of pitch being specified with *accidentals. Pieces consisting of more than one *movement may include one or more movements in a different key altogether [see, e.g., Sonata]. Such movements will have the appropriate key signature.

Like the modes before them [see Mode, Greece I, 3 (ii)], keys have sometimes been associated with ethical or emotional qualities. The most enduring of these associations, with roots in the 16th century, is that of major keys with happiness or brightness and minor keys with sadness or darkness. Keys with sharps in the signature are often said to be bright and keys with flats dark. Keys have sometimes also been associated with colors [see Color and music]. All such associations are learned or rest on convention. The convention regarding major and minor is widely shared or at least recognized, though it should not be thought to operate in every piece in a major or minor key. Other conventions may operate within only a limited period or within the works of a single composer. Often the association of a particular key is not so much with some emotion or abstract quality as with a type of melody, meter, or tempo [for a discussion of emotion and expression in music, see Aesthetics]. Johann Mattheson (*Das neu-eröffnete Orchestre,* 1713), among others, offers extended descriptions of key characteristics, but with a cautionary note (trans. Steblin, 1983): "It is well-known . . . that each key possesses some special characteristic and is very different in its effect from other keys; but what each key actually has for its effect, and how and when this effect is aroused, is greatly disputed."

If equal *temperament is used, the internal relationships of all keys are identical, and keys differ only in their absolute pitch. This has sometimes been used to counter the view that keys have inherent meaning. Even through the Classical period, on the other hand, some tuning systems favored the acoustical purity of certain keys at the expense of others. And some instruments may differ in sound from one key to another depending, e.g., on the disposition of open strings or the harmonic series for the length of tube employed. But this only argues for differences among keys and not for the attachment of any particular meaning to any one of them. Robert Schumann (1835), while dismissing a correlation of specific keys and characteristics, nevertheless argued for differences among keys (trans. Steblin, 1983).

(2) [Fr. *touche;* Ger. *Taste;* It. *tasto;* Sp. *tecla*]. A lever by means of which the movement of a player's hand is transmitted to the action of an instrument, causing it to sound. A set of such levers arranged for ease of playing is a *keyboard, and instruments operated by such a device are keyboard instruments, e.g., the piano, organ, harpsichord, and clavichord.

(3) [Fr. *clef;* Ger. *Klappe;* It. *chiave;* Sp. *llave*]. On a woodwind instrument, a lever used to open or close a hole. The complete mechanism made up of such levers is the keywork.

Bibl.: Robert Schumann, "Charakteristik der Tonleitern und Tonarten," *NZfM* 2 (1835): 43–44. Rudolf Wustmann, "Tonartensymbolik zu Bachs Zeit," *BaJb* 8 (1911): 60–74. Hermann Stephani, *Der Charakter der Tonarten* (Regensburg: G Bosse, 1923). Werner Lüthy, *Mozart und der Tonartencharakteristik* (Strassburg: Heitz, 1931). Hermann Beck, *Die Sprache der Tonart in der Musik von Bach bis Bruckner* (Stuttgart: Urachaus, 1937; 3rd ed., 1977). Ernst Isler, "Vergleichende Charakteristik von c- und d-moll Werken Bachs und Beethovens," *Schweizerische Musikzeitung* 83 (1943): 40–44. Jacques Handschin, *Der Toncharakter* (Zürich: Atlantis, 1948). Paul Mies, *Der Charakter der Tonarten* (Cologne: Staufer, 1948). Hans Keller, "Key Characteristics," in *A Tribute to Benjamin Britten on His Fiftieth Birthday* (London: Faber, 1963), pp. 111–23. Martin Chusid, "The Significance of D Minor in Mozart's Dramatic Music," *MJb* (1965–66): 87–93. Rita Steblin, *A History of Key Characteristics in the Eighteenth and Early Nineteenth Centuries* (Ann Arbor: UMI Res Pr, 1983).

Keyboard [Fr. *clavier;* Ger. *Klaviatur;* It. *tastiera;* Sp. *teclado*]. The whole set of levers in pianos, organs, harpsichords, clavichords, and similar instruments that actuate the tone-producing mechanism. Each octave consists of seven natural and five chromatic keys, arranged as in the accompanying figure. The intervals between the natural keys are whole tones except for the semitone steps E–F and B–C, where no chromatic key intervenes. The interval between any natural key and an adjacent chromatic key is a semitone [see Interval].

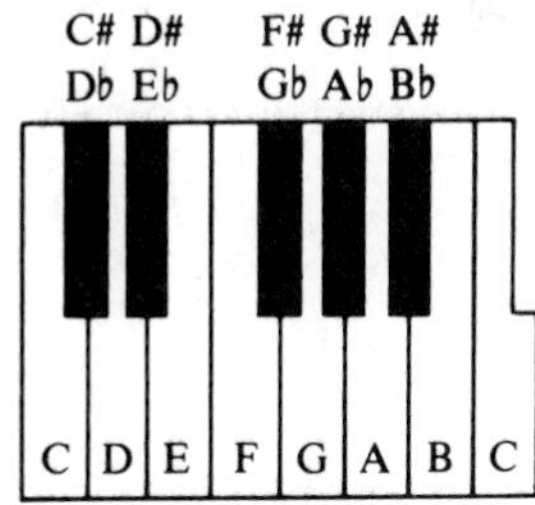

This arrangement of keys dates from the early 15th century and has survived various attempts at reform through adoption of a truly chromatic keyboard on which all scales beginning on either the lower or upper keys would have the same fingering. In Western tonal music, the primacy of the C-major scale, played entirely on the lower keys, must derive in some measure from the traditional keyboard design. The lower keys on the modern piano and organ are invariably made of ivory or white plastic, and the upper keys or sharps of ebony or black plastic. On many types of older keyboard instruments, however, the color scheme was the reverse, with dark-colored naturals and light-colored chromatic keys.

The earliest keyboards were sets of levers played by

the hands rather than the fingers. Until the 13th century, the diatonic keyboard with a compass of two octaves or less usually had only one chromatic note, B♭, often treated as a diatonic lower key. By 1400, the keyboard had become fully chromatic, with five raised keys in each octave, and had an expanded compass. The Robertsbridge Codex (ca. 1360), which contains the earliest surviving keyboard music, calls for a range of two octaves and a third, c to e″, chromatic from f. Typical early 15th-century keyboards are shown in the instrument designs of Henri Arnaut de Zwolle (ca. 1440). They include an organ manual (compass B to f″), a harpsichord and *_dulce melos_ (compass B to a″), and a clavichord (compass B to c‴). Later in the 15th century, a compass of F to a″, often without the low F♯ and G♯ and the top g♯″, became widespread. By the addition of a single key, apparent E but sounding C, at the bass end and by the use of the low F♯ and G♯ keys for D and E, respectively, the C/E *short octave in the bass was created, an arrangement that persisted into the 18th century. The upper limit was soon extended from a″ to c‴ and, in the case of many Italian stringed keyboard instruments, even to f‴. In practice, the actual pitch of these Italian top notes may not have been any higher than those on other instruments extending only to c‴.

In the course of the late 17th century, the harpsichord compass first grew toward the bass, down to G_1 and F_1, and then inched its way from c‴ to f‴. But only the largest clavichords could be extended down to the late 18th-century standard keyboard compass of five octaves (F_1 to f‴). The early piano soon reached the full five-octave compass, expanding it to c⁗ in the 1790s. By 1810 it was six octaves (F_1 to f⁗ in Vienna, C_1 to c⁗ in London), and shortly afterward six and one-half octaves (C_1 to f⁗), the compass of Beethoven's last sonatas and Chopin's works. By mid-century, the seven-octave compass A_2 to a⁗ had become common. The final three keys of today's standard A_2-to-c⁗ 88-note piano keyboard were added after ca. 1870.

Although the range of the organ, with its stops at various pitches, was far greater than that of any stringed keyboard instrument, the European organ manual keyboard kept to a relatively narrow compass, gradually expanding in the 18th century from four octaves with bass short octave (C/E to c‴), first filling in the missing bass notes, then gradually adding treble notes, and finally reaching today's standard manual compass of five octaves, C to c⁗. By the 18th century, Continental organ pedal keyboards had expanded from the original eight-note compass, C to B with B♭ (as on the late 14th-century Norrlanda organ), to their present 27- to 30-note range (C to d′ or C to f′), sometimes even expanded to 32 notes (C to g′) in the 20th century. English organs, however, did not begin to acquire pedal keyboards until the mid-18th century, and they were not widespread until the 19th. In the interim, instruments lacking pedal bass notes often compensated by extending the manual compass below C to G_1.

Experimental keyboards have been designed with six lower keys (C♯, D♯, F, G, A, and B) and six raised keys (C, D, E, F♯, G♯, and A♯) per octave to permit the use of identical fingerings in every tonality. Invented and then improved during the 19th century (most notably by Paul von Janko), they have never succeeded in displacing the standard type. Radiating keyboards in a fanlike shape (Clutsam, 1907, based on a Viennese design of 1824), intended to facilitate playing extreme bass and treble keys, have not gained favor either except on organ pedalboards of the modern type.

Bibl.: G. le Cerf and E.-R. Labande, _Instruments de musique du XVe siècle: Les traités d'Henri-Arnault de Zwolle et de divers anonymes_ (Paris: Éditions Auguste Picard, 1932). Hans Klotz, _The Organ Handbook,_ trans. Gerhard Krapf (St. Louis: Concordia, 1969). Raymond Russell, _The Harpsichord and Clavichord: An Introductory History,_ 2nd ed., rev. Howard Schott (London: Faber, 1973). Peter Williams, _The Organ in Western Culture, 750–1250_ (Cambridge: Cambridge U Pr, 1993). Edwin M. Good, _Giraffes, Black Dragons, and Other Pianos,_ 2nd ed. (Stanford: Stanford U Pr, 2001).

H.S., J.Ko.

Keyboard instruments. Instruments sounded by means of a *keyboard, especially the *piano, *organ, *harpsichord, and *clavichord. The term is often used in the context of music composed before the late 18th century, some of which does not distinguish among the different types then in use.

Keyed bugle, Royal Kent bugle. A trumpet-shaped soprano brass instrument of large, conical bore with five to twelve woodwind-like side holes and keys. Joseph Haliday of Dublin patented the five-key prototype in 1810. By 1815, several inches in length and an additional open key near the bell had been added. The improved instrument was called the Royal Kent bugle in honor of the Duke of Kent, then commander-in-chief of British troops in Ireland. This six-key model in C (with a pigtail crook to B♭) was one of the first fully chromatic soprano brasses. It quickly became the leading voice in newly formed brass bands. By the 1820s, one more key to improve low E♭ brought the basic set of keys to seven—five for the right hand and two for the left. Although valved brasses soon began to replace the keyed bugle in much of Europe, it continued in use, especially in the U.S., until the 1860s. A smaller model in E♭ with up to twelve keys was used by many American band leaders and soloists. Keyed bugles were most often made of copper with brass trim, although examples made of brass, German silver, silver, gold, and even tortoise shell are known.

Bibl.: Ralph T. Dudgeon, _The Keyed Bugle_ (Metuchen, N.J.: Scarecrow, 1993).

R.E.E.

Keyed trumpet. See Trumpet.

Keynote. *Tonic.

Key relationship. The degree to which one *key is related to another is primarily a function of the number of pitches that the two hold in common. The most closely related keys are those adjacent to each other on the *circle of fifths. Their *key signatures differ by a single flat or sharp, and thus they share six of their seven pitches. Conversely, distant keys are those that are distant from each other on the circle of fifths and thus have relatively few pitches in common. Other important relationships are those between parallel keys, i.e., major and minor keys with the same tonic, and between relative keys, i.e., major and minor keys with the same key signature and thus the same basic pitch collection. The relative minor of any major key or scale, while sharing its key signature and pitches, takes as its tonic the sixth scale degree of that major key or scale; e.g., the relative minor of E♭ major is C minor. See also Modulation.

Key signature. In tonal music [see Tonality], an arrangement of sharps or flats (or the absence of both) at the beginning of each staff that defines the principal pitches employed in the composition in question. Each sharp or flat indicates, respectively, a raising or lowering by a semitone of all pitches (in whatever octave) with the letter name of the line or space on which it is placed. This may be countermanded in individual cases by means of a natural sign or other *accidental.

Each key signature defines a diatonic *scale that can be employed in one of two modes, *major or minor, and thus with either of two tonics—one for a major *key and one for a minor key. Since there are twelve pitch classes altogether, there are in principle twelve different key signatures. Since, however, a pitch class can have more than one name (e.g., C♯ and D♭, which are *enharmonic equivalents), the number of key signatures available is greater than twelve. Fifteen are in common use. In the accompanying example, key signatures are presented in order from no sharps or flats through seven sharps and from one flat through seven flats. The whole note in each case indicates the tonic of the corresponding major key; the black note indicates the tonic of the corresponding minor key. Within each key signature, the sharps or flats are always arranged in the order and in the pattern on the staff presented here.

A comparison of this example with the *circle of fifths shows that the addition of sharps corresponds to movement through keys along the circle in a clockwise direction, whereas the addition of flats corresponds to movement through keys along the circle in a counterclockwise direction. The order in which sharps are added (F C G D A E B) can also be seen to be represented by adjacent pitch classes on the circle proceeding clockwise, as can the order in which flats are added (B E A D G C F), proceeding counterclockwise.

The consistent use of this system of key signatures associated with specific keys dates from the later 18th century, even though the tonal system had by then been well established for at least a century. Earlier in the 18th century, minor keys were often written with one less flat than is now usual, as in Bach's *Dorian Toccata and Fugue. This flat corresponds to the sixth scale degree, which is often raised in any case [see Scale]. Less often, keys with sharp signatures were written with one less sharp, as in Handel's Suite no. 5 in E for harpsichord, from the first set.

Before the establishment of the tonal system, the use of signatures was more limited. The use of a single flat on B is found in the earliest staff notation in liturgical chant. In polyphony through the 16th century, the use of one and two flats on B or B and E was common. Often the same signature was not employed in all voice parts of a polyphonic work, though there were certain familiar combinations that have since been termed *conflicting or partial signatures. There is considerable disagreement over the precise theoretical significance of signatures in early music, and the subject is bound up with the use of accidentals in general [see *Musica ficta*]. Although the practical effect of the flat sign in a signature is most often the lowering of the pitch in question by a semitone, this was not always so, since the flat sign was principally an instruction to the performer to sing or play *fa* [see Solmization]. In general, the addition of each flat can be thought of as transposing the tonal system down a perfect fifth, as is in effect the case in modern signatures. The use of sharp signatures did not become common until the 17th century.

Khomonie [Russ.]. See *Anenajki.*

Khovanshchina [Russ., The Khovansky Affair]. Opera in five acts by Musorgsky (libretto by the composer), completed and orchestrated by Rimsky-Korsakov and produced in St. Petersburg in 1886. Setting: Moscow and environs, 1682–89.

Khyāl [Hin.]. The most important genre of Hindustani vocal music. The *khyāl* proper is a texted composition *(bandiś, ciz)* and has two sections (*sthāyī* and

Key signatures.

antarā) differentiated, respectively, by their lower and higher registers. The small portion of the *bandiś* that leads up to the first beat of the measure is called *mukhṛā;* it is frequently used as a cadence to extended passages of improvisation. C.C.

Kielflügel [Ger., obs., fr. *Kiel,* quill]. Harpsichord.

Kinderscenen [Ger., Scenes from Childhood]. A collection of 13 short and simple pieces for piano by Schumann, op. 15 (1838), of which no. 7 is the familiar "Träumerei" (Dreams).

Kindertotenlieder [Ger., Songs on the Death of Children]. A cycle of five songs with orchestra or piano accompaniment by Mahler, composed in 1901–4. The poems, by Friedrich Rückert, are an elegy on the death of two of his children.

King David. See *Roi David, Le.*

Kinnor [Heb.]. A *lyre of ancient Israel, similar to the Greek *kithara. The "harp" of King David was really a *kinnor.* It was both a sacred and a secular instrument, played in the Temple and at social gatherings and festivities.

Kirche [Ger.]. Church; *Kirchengesang,* liturgical chant; *Kirchenjahr,* church or liturgical year; *Kirchenkantate,* church cantata; *Kirchenkonzert,* **concerto da chiesa; Kirchenlied,* a *chorale or other church song in German rather than Latin; *Kirchenmusik,* church music; *Kirchenschluss,* plagal *cadence; *Kirchensonate,* **sonata da chiesa; Kirchenton,* church *mode.

Kit [Fr. *pochette;* Ger. *Tanzmeistergeige, Taschengeige;* It. *sordino*]. A small bowed stringed instrument without frets used primarily from the 16th to the 18th century by dance masters to accompany their students. The instrument's small size made it conveniently portable in a coat pocket; hence the names *pochette* and *Taschengeige.* Kits, with their origin in the medieval *rebec, appear in many varied shapes, usually with four strings tuned like the violin or in higher fifth relationships. There are two primary forms of kit: (1) a rebec-derived, slender, arched, boat-shaped body with short neck and pegbox of hardwood in one piece, with a spruce or pearwood table frequently bearing C-shaped sound holes [see ill. under Violin], and (2) a miniature violin or viol body of traditional maple and spruce with an attached long neck, pegbox, and violin-shaped fingerboard. Kits are often ornamented with ivory, mother-of-pearl, or silver wire and frequently bear delicately carved heads. W.L.M.

Kithara [Gr.; Lat. *cithara, cythara*]. A *lyre of ancient Greece and Rome, the most important stringed instrument of classical antiquity. It had a flat wooden sound box from which two arms rose. The arms, often hollow, were connected by a crosspiece to which were attached gut strings of equal length: 3 to 5 strings in early instruments, 11 or more by the 5th century B.C.E. The player held the instrument vertically, resting it against the left side of the body. The right hand plucked the strings from the front with a plectrum; the left hand remained behind the instrument, plucking or stopping the strings. The kithara was nearly always associated with song. Originally it was played by singers themselves as an accompaniment to epics, hymns, and other song types. By the 6th century B.C.E. there were professional *kitharistēs,* who accompanied singers and played virtuosic instrumental solos as well.

Instruments of this type are depicted in Mesopotamian and Egyptian art and also in the art of Mycenae in the 2nd millennium B.C.E. The instrument is mentioned in the *Iliad* under the name phorminx. The classic seven-stringed kithara is depicted in Greek art from the 6th century B.C.E. It was exported to Rome, where it was popular both as an accompaniment to song and as a solo instrument. In the Middle Ages, the name *cithara* was applied to a variety of stringed instruments: lyre, harp, psaltery, and even the fiddle. See Greece I, 2 and ill.; see also Lyra.

Kl. [Ger.]. Abbr. for *Klarinette,* clarinet. See also Kl. Fl., Kl. Tr.

Klagelied [Ger.]. Lament, elegy.

Klagend, kläglich [Ger.]. Plaintive.

Klagende Lied, Das [Ger., The Plaintive Song]. A cantata by Mahler (setting his own text) for soprano, alto, and tenor soloists, chorus, and orchestra, composed in 1880. Originally in three parts—*Waldmärchen* (Forest Tales), *Der Spielmann* (The Minstrel), and *Hochzeitsstück* (Wedding Piece)—it was revised in 1892–93 and 1898–99 omitting *Waldmärchen.*

Klang [Ger.]. Sound, sonority; *Klangbild,* sound picture; *Klangboden,* soundboard; *Klangfarbe,* tone color, timbre; *Klangfolge,* chord progression; *Klanggeschlecht,* mode, as major or minor; *Klanghöhe,* pitch level; *Klangideal,* the general quality of sound characterizing a period, repertory, or instrument.

Klangfarbenmelodie [Ger., tone-color melody]. A succession of tone colors (even if with only a single pitch) treated as a structure analogous to a melody, which is a succession of pitches. The notion was proposed and the term coined by Arnold Schoenberg in his *Harmonielehre* of 1911. It is reflected in his *Five Orchestral Pieces* op. 16 (1909, rev. 1949), especially the third, which was originally titled "Farben" (Colors). Anton Webern explored the concept extensively, e.g., in the first of his *Five Pieces for Orchestra* op. 10 (1913) and in his orchestral transcription of the six-voice ricercar from Bach's *Musical Offering,* and it has played an important role in the development of *serial music and in some *electro-acoustic music. The texture that results has sometimes been termed pointillism, by analogy with painting.

Klanglich [Ger.]. Sonorous.

Klappe [Ger.]. *Key (3); *Klappenhorn, -trompete,* keyed bugle, keyed trumpet.

Klar [Ger.]. Clear, distinct.

Klarinette [Ger.]. Clarinet.

Klausel [Ger.]. (1) **Clausula.* (2) *Cadence, principally with respect to early music.

Klaviatur [Ger.]. Keyboard.

Klavier [Ger.]. (1) Piano; *Klavierauszug,* piano reduction or arrangement, piano-vocal score; *Klavierkonzert,* piano concerto; *Klavierstück,* piano piece. (2) Keyboard, manual. (3) Keyboard instrument, especially though not necessarily stringed as distinct from the organ. Eighteenth-century titles such as **Clavier-Übung* and *Das *wohltemperirte Clavier* do not specify a particular keyboard instrument. (4) In the later 18th century (spelled *Clavier*), often though not always clavichord. See also Clavier.

Klavierlied [Ger.]. A song with keyboard accompaniment [see Lied III, Berlin school]. The *Geistliches Klavierlied* was a nonliturgical lied on a sacred or devotional strophic text. *Geistliche Klavierlieder* were characteristic products of the north-German *Empfindsamkeit* [see *Empfindsam* style], the best-known examples being C. P. E. Bach's *Geistliche Oden und Lieder* (1758) on texts of Christian Fürchtegott Gellert.

Klein [Ger. masc. sing.; other endings depending on case and gender]. (1) Small. (2) With respect to intervals such as the third or sixth, minor.

Kleine Flöte [Ger.]. Piccolo.

Kleine Nachtmusik, Eine [Ger., A Little Night Music]. Mozart's title for his Notturno or Serenade in G major for string ensemble K. 525 (1787). It was originally in five movements, of which the second, a minuet, is now lost. Although it is often performed with orchestra, it was evidently intended for performance with one player on each part. See Divertimento, Notturno, Serenade.

Kleine Trommel [Ger.]. Snare drum.

Kl. Fl. [Ger.]. Abbr. for *kleine Flöte,* piccolo.

Klezmer music. The primarily instrumental music accompanying Jewish celebrations and rites of passage. Formed from the contraction of the Hebrew words *kli* and *zemer* (lit., vessel of song), klezmer may refer to the dance music itself or to the performers (often collectively in the plural, *klezmorim*). The traditional klezmer ensemble of central and east-central Europe comprised a string band plus a *tsimbl,* or hammered dulcimer, though klezmer ensembles in eastern Europe often contained wind instruments. Klezmer has changed according to three broad periods paralleling the transformation of Ashkenazic Jewry: (1) Klezmer musicians first appeared in the Rhineland during the Middle Ages, spreading to border regions of central Europe and to eastern Europe in the early modern era; (2) modernity, especially following the Jewish Enlightenment, or Haskala, in the late 18th and 19th centuries, stimulated diversification and expanded klezmer's presence outside the Jewish community; (3) in the post-Holocaust decades klezmer underwent a series of revivals, first in North America, and after ca. 1990 in Israel and Europe. Klezmer music enjoys international popularity at the beginning of the 21st century, with repertories ranging from the consciously authentic to the experimentally hybrid to global pop and world beat.

Bibl.: Walter Salmen, *". . . denn die Fiedel macht das Fest": Jüdische Musikanten und Tänzer vom 13. bis 20. Jahrhundert* (Innsbruck: Helbling, 1991). Rita Ottens and Joel Rubin, *Klezmer-Musik* (Kassel: Bärenreiter, 1999). Yaakov Mazor, *The Klezmer Tradition in the Land of Israel* (Jerusalem: Jewish Music Research Center, Hebrew Univ. of Jerusalem, 2000). Mark Slobin, *Fiddler on the Move: Exploring the Klezmer World* (New York: Oxford U Pr, 2000). P.V.B.

Klingen [Ger.]. To sound; *klingen lassen,* allow to sound, do not damp; *klingt wie notiert,* pitch sounds as notated.

Kl. Tr. [Ger.]. Abbr. for *kleine Trommel,* snare drum.

Knaben Wunderhorn, Des [Ger., The Youth's Magic Horn]. A group of German folk-song texts collected and published in three volumes (ca. 1805–8) by Ludwig Achim von Arnim and Clemens Brentano. Mahler composed settings of a number of these texts: nine songs with piano (1887–90), ten songs with piano or orchestra (1892–98), and two songs with piano or orchestra from the so-called "Seven Songs from the Last Years" (1899–1902). An additional three songs were set as parts of his symphonies: "Urlicht" (Primeval Light) in the Second or **Resurrection* Symphony (1888–94, rev. 1903), "Es sungen drei Engel" (Three Angels Were Singing) in the Third Symphony (1893–96, rev. 1906), and "Das himmlische Leben" (The Heavenly Life) in the Fourth Symphony (1892, 1899–1900, rev. 1901–10).

Knarre [Ger.]. *Rattle.

Kniegeige [Ger., obs.]. Viola da gamba.

Knyaz' Igor' [Russ.]. See *Prince Igor.*

Koboz [Hung.; Ger., Russ. *Kobsa*]. A short-necked lute, early and widely distributed from the Middle East, and still in use in Eastern Europe.

Köchel-Verzeichnis [Ger.]. See K.

Kodály method. A system of music education for children developed by the Hungarian composer Zoltan Kodály (1882–1967). The method aims to achieve universal musical literacy by teaching children to sing from notes using a "movable do" *solfège system and a progressive repertory of songs and exercises based on Hungarian folk material. Since 1945, the method has been the basis of music education in the Hungarian school system, and it has been modified for use in other countries. See also Tonic Sol-fa.

Bibl.: Jenő Adam, *Growing in Music with Movable Do* (Budapest, 1944; New York: Pannonius Central Service, 1971). Louise Choksy, *The Kodály Context* (Englewood Cliffs, N.J.: Prentice-Hall, 1981).

Kolęda, kolenda [Pol., pl. *kolędy*], **colindă** [Rom., pl. *colinde*]. A Christmas carol. With roots in pagan winter celebrations, songs of this type were known in Poland from the 12th century and survive in quantity with Polish texts from the 16th century, some in polyphonic settings and instrumental intabulations. The repertory expanded considerably in the 17th and 18th centuries. Both Polish and Romanian repertories continue to flourish, Chopin and Bartók having drawn on them.

Kollektivkoppel [Ger.]. Great coupler.

Kol Nidre [Heb., All the vows]. (1) A prayer from the Jewish service on the eve of Yom Kippur (Day of Atonement). It was set, with some modifications, by Schoenberg for speaker, chorus, and orchestra in 1938. (2) *Kol Nidrei.* An adagio on Hebrew melodies for cello and orchestra by Max Bruch, op. 47 (1881).

Kolorieren [Ger.]. To ornament with *coloraturas, as in 16th-century *intabulations. For *Koloristen,* see Colorists.

Kondakarion [Gr., Russ.]. See Russian and Slavonic chant.

Kontakion [Gr.]. See Byzantine chant II.

Kontakte [Ger., Contacts]. A four-track tape composition by Stockhausen composed in 1959–60 and used in the theater piece *Originale* in 1961. A second version of the work is for piano, percussion, and four-track tape.

Kontertanz [Ger.]. **Contredanse.*

Kontra- [Ger.]. *Kontrabass,* double bass, or as a prefix in the names of instruments, contrabass or double-bass; *-fagott,* contrabassoon; *-faktur, contrafactum; -Oktave,* contra-octave; *-punkt,* counterpoint; *-subjekt,* countersubject.

Konzert [Ger.]. (1) Concert. (2) Concerto.

Konzertmeister [Ger.]. Concertmaster.

Konzertsinfonie [Ger.]. (1) Concert *symphony. (2) Ripieno concerto. See Concerto (2) I, 2.

Konzertstück [Ger., concert piece]. See Concertino (2).

Koororgel [Du.]. *Choir organ (2).

Koppel [Ger.]. (1) A *coupler for organ keyboards. (2) Occasionally, an 8′ stopped flute register in 17th-century German organs.

Koppelflöte [Ger.]. An organ stop of tapered, wide-scaled metal pipes surmounted with inverted cones; in French organs, *Flûte à fuseau;* in English, Spindle flute.

Koranic chanting. See Qur'ānic chanting.

Korea. See East Asia III.

Korean temple block. See Temple block.

Kornett [Ger.]. Cornet.

Kortholt [Ger.]. A *wind-cap, double-reed woodwind instrument described by Michael Praetorius (*Syntagma musicum,* vol. 2, 1619). It has a cylindrical bore and two parallel channels within the same piece of wood. It seems to have been identical to the **sordone* except that the latter has no wind cap. See also *Courtaut.* M.S.

Koto [Jap.]. A Japanese *zither. The term designates several historical zithers with 1 to 17 strings. The prevalent form today has a rectangular body about 80–90 cm long and 24 cm wide. Thirteen silk strings are stretched over movable bridges and tuned in a variety of pentatonic tunings. The player places the instrument on a mat or low table and plucks the strings using plectra on the thumb and the first two fingers of the right hand. With the left hand the player presses on the strings to the left of the bridges, raising pitches and adding ornaments. The *koto* is used in **gagaku* music and in ensembles, especially with the **shamisen,* the **shakuhachi,* and the voice. It is also a popular solo instrument. Traditionally it was played by blind men; recently, many experts have been women. See also *Cheng, Kayago;* see ill. under East Asia.

Kräftig [Ger.]. Strong, energetic.

Krakowiak [Pol.; Fr. *cracovienne;* Ger. *krakauer Tanz*]. A Polish dance from the region of Kraków in rapid duple meter with syncopations. Pieces of this type survive in instrumental tablatures from the 16th century. The dance enjoyed considerable vogue in the 19th century, partly because of performances by the dancer Fanny Elssler, and was employed in art music by Chopin (*Krakowiak* in F op. 14, a rondo for piano and orchestra) and others.

Krar [Amharic]. An Ethiopian *lyre with a bowl-shaped sound box. The player strums six gut strings with the right hand while the left hand damps unwanted strings. It is played by both men and women to accompany secular ballads and love songs. See ill. under Africa.

Krebsgängig [Ger.]. Crabwise, retrograde.

Krebskanon [Ger.]. Crab or retrograde *canon.

Kreisleriana [Ger.]. Schumann's cycle of eight pieces for piano op. 16 (1838). The title refers to Kapellmeister Johannes Kreisler, the protagonist of E. T. A. Hoffmann's autobiographical work of 1810.

Kreutzer Sonata. Popular name for Beethoven's Violin Sonata in A minor op. 47 (1802–3), dedicated to the French composer and violin virtuoso Rodolphe Kreutzer (1766–1831). It was originally composed for the English violinist George Bridgetower (1779?–1860), whom Beethoven accompanied at the first performance in 1803, but with whom he subsequently had a dispute, leading to the change in dedication.

Kreuz [Ger.]. Sharp.

Kriti [Tel.]. A basic Carnatic concert genre. The music and text are divided into three sections (*pallavi, anupallavi,* and *caraṇam*), of which the first, or a portion of it, is used as a refrain. It is often performed with the addition of improvised passages (**niraval, *svarakalpana*). C.C.

Kriuki, krjuki [Russ.]. See Znamenny chant, Russian and Slavonic chant.

Krummhorn [Ger.]. *Crumhorn; **cromorne.*

Kuchipudi [Tel.]. A dance-drama of Andhra Pradesh, South India. It is traditionally performed by males from Brahmin families to whom Kuchipudi village was given by a Muslim king for the maintenance of the tradition. Solo pieces are also occasionally performed by women in recitals of **bharata-nāṭyam.* C.C.

Kuhreigen, Kuhreihen [Ger.]. See *Ranz des vaches.*

Kujawiak [Pol.]. A Polish dance from the region of Kujawy, in 3/4 and similar to the *mazurka, but slower. Examples in art music include Chopin's op. 6 no. 4, op. 30 no. 4, and op. 41 no. 1.

Kunst der Fuge, Die [Ger.]. See *Art of Fugue, The.*

Kunstlied [Ger.]. Art song, as distinct from folk song *(Volkslied).*

Kurz [Ger.] Short; *Kurz-Oktave,* *short octave.

KV. See K.

Kyriale [Lat.]. See Liturgical books.

Kyrie eleison [Gr., Lord, have mercy]. In the Roman Catholic Rite, the first item of the *Ordinary of the *Mass. Its text consists of three petitions, "Kyrie eleison," "Christe eleison," and "Kyrie eleison" (Lord, have mercy; Christ, have mercy; Lord, have mercy), each stated three times. Its *Gregorian melodies often reflect this ninefold structure with forms such as AAA BBB CCC′ or AAA BBB AAA′, though other forms, some distinctly more complex, are also encountered. Successive elements of the form are sung in alternation either between soloists and choir or between the two halves of the choir. The earliest sources, from the 10th and 11th centuries, preserve Kyries both in the melismatic form with Greek text found in modern chant books and in versions with Latin texts set syllabically. These Latin texts usually elaborate upon the Greek text with a series of attributes of the Lord or Christ, e.g., "Kyrie fons bonitatis, Pater ingenite, a quo bona cuncta procedunt, eleison," and the words *Kyrie* and *Christe* themselves may even be replaced by such texts. Although these Latin texts have been suppressed, they serve to identify Kyrie melodies in modern books, e.g., "Kyrie fons bonitatis," which is Kyrie II (in *LU,* p. 19). Scholars have debated whether these texts are later additions or were a feature of Kyries from the beginning. For the terminology for such texts and for additions of both text and melody to the Kyrie, see Trope, Prosula.

Use of the phrase "Kyrie eleison" as a response to a *litany is attested in both East and West from at least the 4th and 5th centuries, and on the basis of one of his letters, St. Gregory the Great (pope from 590 to 604) is often credited with establishing its use along with "Christe eleison" in the Roman Mass. *Ordo romanus I* [see Gregorian chant VI], reporting Roman practice of the first half of the 8th century, describes a variable number of repetitions of these phrases. *Ordo romanus IV,* a derived Frankish document of the late 8th century, describes the ninefold form for the first time. The Kyrie is preserved in translation in a variety of contexts in the Anglican rite and in the Roman rite since the Second *Vatican Council.

Bibl.: Margaretha Landwehr-Melnicki, *Das einstimmige Kyrie des lateinischen Mittelalters* (Regensburg: G Bosse, 1955). See also Gregorian chant.

Kyrieleis [Ger.]. See *Leise.*

L

L. Abbr. for left [Ger. *links*]; L.H., left hand [Ger. *linke Hand*].

La. See Pitch names, Solmization, Hexachord.

Labial pipe [fr. Lat. *labium,* lip]. An organ *flue pipe.

Lacrimoso, lagrimoso [It.]. Tearful, mournful.

Lady Macbeth of the Mtsensk District [Russ., *Ledi Makbet Mtsenskovo uyezda*]. Opera in four acts by Shostakovich (libretto by the composer and A. Preys, after N. S. Leskov's story), produced in Leningrad in 1934 and in the same year in Moscow with the title *Katerina Izmaylova.* The work, and by implication all modern music, was officially condemned in *Pravda* in 1936. It was slightly revised beginning in 1956 with the title *Katerina Izmaylova* and produced in Moscow again in 1962.

Lage [Ger.]. (1) In string playing, *position (*erste,* first; *zweite,* second; etc.). (2) Of a chord, *spacing (*enge,* close; *weite,* wide or open). (3) Of the voice or an instrument, *register (*hohe,* high; *tiefe,* low).

Lai, lay [Fr. and Occ.]. A type of lyric poetry (the *lai lyrique* as distinct from the *lai breton,* a narrative form for which no music survives), sometimes with music, cultivated chiefly in France during the 13th and 14th centuries. Lyric *lais* are usually quite long; with only rare exceptions, the music of *lais* is monophonic. The German *Leich* is similar in history and formal traits. Occitan *lays* generally are on the topic of love, while many French *lais* have a popular or religious theme.

Uncertainty persists regarding an exact definition of *lai.* Medieval writers from as early as the mid-12th century often used the word to mean simply song or, occasionally, a purely instrumental form; a few earlier pieces designated as *lais* have strophic structures like the *chansons* of the *trouvères. By the early 13th century the term refers to lengthy songs of irregular form. Early examples are often made up of long streams of verses of varying lengths and rhymes, which can sometimes be grouped loosely into stanzas. Their simple melodies are made up largely of motives and formulas that may or may not coincide with the poetic features. Gradually the verses and rhymes formed discernible stanzas, or versicles, each with a different poetic form and melody. By the 14th century most *lais* fit into a standard pattern: usually 12 stanzas (double strophes, sometimes called double versicles), each having formally identical halves and in a pattern not used in the preceding stanza, with the first and last stanzas being related or identical in form and music. The music of the last stanza is often the same as that of the first but transposed, usually up a fifth.

The beginnings of the *lai* are difficult to pin down. It probably originated around 1200 and was cultivated throughout the 13th century, first by the troubadours, then by the trouvères and their successors. Several very early 14th-century *lais,* possibly by Philippe de Vitry, are in the *Roman de *Fauvel.* The form reached its peak in the works of Guillaume de Machaut (ca. 1300–1377), of whose numerous *lais* 19 have music. Four of these incorporate polyphony: 2 in canon and 2 by the simultaneous performance of successively notated sections. Most of Machaut's *lais* adhere to the standard pattern outlined above. None of Machaut's successors composed music for *lais,* although poets of the 15th century, in particular, cultivated the form and specified ever-stricter rules for its organization. By the middle of the 16th century, the *lai* was regarded as obsolete. Music for the *Leich* continued to be produced in the 15th century.

While most extant *lais* are French, a few by *troubadours in Occitan survive, several of them called *descort* rather than *lay.* The *descort,* from Latin *discordia,* was defined by poetic theorists as a poem characterized by some kind of discord, as for instance in subject matter or poetic content, including Raimbaut de Vaqueiras's *Ara qun vei verdejar,* with stanzas in Occitan, Italian, French, Gascon, and Galician-Portuguese. This and other *descorts* are isostrophic like the *canso,* but others have the heterostrophic structure characteristic of the *lai;* the music of some of these matches the irregular poetic scheme, although three are through-composed.

The heterostrophic versicle form of the *lai* is similar to that of the *sequence, and some contrafacta between Latin and vernacular songs exist. Although the origins of the sequence are much earlier, the two genres evolved along similar lines and have certain organizational principles in common. The majority of current scholarly opinion sees their histories as largely separate, however.

Bibl.: Alfred Jeanroy, Louis Brandin, and Pierre Aubry, *Lais et descorts français du XIIIe siècle: Texte et musique,* Mélanges de musicologie critique 3 (Paris: Welter, 1901; R: New York: AMS Pr, 1969). Hans Spanke, "Sequenz und Lai," *Studi medievali,* new ser., 11 (1938): 12–68. Gilbert Reaney, "The *Lais* of Guillaume de Machaut and Their Background," *PRMA* 82 (1955/56): 15–32. Id., "Concerning the Origins of the Medieval Lai," *ML* 39 (1958): 343–46. Jean Maillard, *Evolution et esthétique du lai lyrique des origins à la fin du XIVème siècle* (Paris: Centre de documentation universitaire, 1961). Jean Maillard, "Lai, Leich," *Schrade,* 1973, pp. 323–

45. Bruno Stäblein, *Schriftbild der einstimmigen Musik,* Musikgeschichte in Bildern, vol. 3, pt. 4 (Leipzig: Deutsche Verlag für Musik, 1975). David Fallows, "Lai," *Grove 6* [with checklist of music]. Pierre Bec, *La Lyrique française au Moyen-Age (XIIe–XIIIe siècles)* (Paris: A & J Picard, 1977–78), 1: 189–213. Robert Deschauz, "Le Lai et la complainte," *La Littérature française aux XIVe et XVe siècles,* vol. 1, *Grundriss der romanischen Literature des Mittelalters* 8, no. 1 (Winter 1988): 70–85. Ann Buckley, "A Study of Old French Lyric Lais and Descorts and Related Latin Song to c. 1300" (Ph.D. diss., U of Cambridge, 1990). Elizabeth Aubrey, "Issues in the Musical Analysis of the Troubadour Descorts and Lays," in *The Cultural Milieu of the Troubadours and Trouvères,* ed. Nancy Van Deusen (Ottawa: Institute of Medieval Music, 1994), pp. 76–98. Elizabeth Aubrey, *The Music of the Troubadours* (Bloomington: Ind U Pr, 1996), pp. 105–109. E.A.

Laisse [Fr.]. See *Chanson de geste.*

Laisser [Fr.]. To allow; *laissez vibrer,* allow to sound, do not damp.

Lakmé. Opera in three acts by Léo Delibes (libretto in French by Edmond Gondinet and Philippe Gille), produced in Paris in 1883. Setting: India in the middle of the 19th century.

Lamellaphone. An instrument on which sound is produced by plucking one or more flexible tongues, usually of metal; also called a plucked *idiophone. Examples are the **mbira* and the *music box.

Lament. A poem or song of mourning; by extension, an instrumental piece of mournful character. Numerous cultures have, or have had, such songs. Among Western countries, they have been especially important in the music of Ireland and Scotland, both as song and as music for the bagpipe [see also *Caoine, Coronach, Ho-hoane*]. The tradition begins with the medieval Latin *planctus,* from the 9th century, and related vernacular forms [Occ. *Planh,* a lyric form of the 12th and 13th centuries; Fr. *plaint, complainte,* 13th and 14th centuries, often lengthy and nonlyric or irregular in form]; few melodies of these medieval songs survive. They include not only songs on the death of a patron, famous personage, or lover, but also songs on the death of a historical or fictional person (sometimes classical or biblical), songs of exile, laments of the Virgin Mary, and sorrow over a calamity or painful event. The earliest surviving example (in 10th-century neumes that cannot be transcribed) is on the death of Charlemagne (d. 814). Important Latin examples are those by Peter Abelard (1079–1142); the best known troubadour *planh* is by Gaucelm Faidit on the death of Richard the Lion-hearted (d. 1199). Some French and Latin examples from the 13th and 14th centuries, such as the two *lais de plour* by Machaut, share musical features (on occasion whole melodies) with *sequences and **lais,* and some have features of *liturgical drama. Polyphonic works from a later period include **déplorations* on the deaths of Machaut (d. 1377) and Ockeghem (d. 1497). In 17th-century France, composers took over from poetry the term *tombeau,* applying it to instrumental pieces on the deaths of celebrated musicians. Some are in the style of the *pavane. Examples include works by lutenists such as Denis Gaultier as well as *tombeaux* by Louis Couperin and Jean-Henri D'Anglebert on the death of their teacher Jacques Champion de Chambonnières (d. 1672). The term *tombeau* continued to be used in the 18th century along with **apothéose* and was taken up in the 20th century by Ravel (*Le tombeau de Couperin* for piano) and others. Johann Jacob Froberger (1616–67) composed several works in the style of allemandes with titles such as *tombeau, lamentation* (including one each on the deaths of Ferdinand III and IV), *plainte,* and *lamento.* English works in the general tradition of laments include Purcell's elegy for Locke (d. 1677) and Blow's setting of Dryden's ode on the death of Purcell (d. 1695). See also *Lamento.*

Lamentabile, lamentoso [It.]. Sadly, plaintively.

Lamentations. Music for verses from the *Lamentations of Jeremiah* [Lat. *Threni, id est Lamentationes Ieremiae Prophetae*]. The Hebrew letter that precedes each verse in the Bible is retained in musical settings. In the Roman Catholic liturgy, nine groups of these verses are sung, three each at Matins on Maundy Thursday, Good Friday, and Holy Saturday (*LU,* pp. 631–37, 692–97, 754–59) to the *tonus lamentationum,* whose use was prescribed by the Council of Trent (mid-16th cent.), or to a more elaborate Spanish tone (*LU,* pp. 760–61; ninth group only).

The development of polyphonic settings of the Lamentations began in the middle of the 15th century and ended at about the start of the 19th. Most early settings are organumlike, whereas a few are motetlike compositions devoted to single verses, as is Dufay's "O tres piteulx/Omnes amici." Settings from the 16th century vary significantly in the number of verses incorporated. Most earlier ones include the *tonus lamentationum* and are relatively imitative and polyrhythmic in texture, whereas most later ones do not use this tone and are more homorhythmic. Throughout the century, however, Spanish composers made considerable use of the Spanish Lamentation tone. The Hebrew letters are often set in a more elaborate style than is the remainder of the text. In polyphonic Lamentations of this period, expressive devices were used sparingly. Petrucci published two volumes of settings by Tinctoris, Mabrianus de Orto, Tromboncino, and others in 1506. Later composers of notable settings include Carpentras (publ. 1532 and used by the papal chapel until 1587), Crecquillon, Lassus, Palestrina (used by the papal chapel from its publication in 1588), Victoria, and Morales. Settings from England include those of Robert White, Tallis, and Byrd.

Until the middle of the 17th century, most Italian composers of Lamentations used a style rooted in 16th-century polyphony. After that time, monody was commonly employed, and expressive devices were used extensively. Italian composers of Lamentations in the 17th and 18th centuries include Gregorio Allegri (old style), Carissimi, Frescobaldi, Alessandro Scarlatti, and Jommelli. The settings by Palestrina and Allegri have remained in use in the Sistine Chapel. A separate French development led to the composition of *leçons de ténèbres* by Michel Lambert, Marc-Antoine Charpentier, François Couperin, and Michel-Richard de Lalande, among others.

Although the genre largely died out at the end of the 18th century, it has been cultivated in the 20th century by Krenek (*Lamentatio,* 1941–42) and Stravinsky (*Threni,* 1957–58).

Bibl.: Günther Massenkeil, *Mehrstimmige Lamentationen aus der ersten Hälfte des 16. Jahrhunderts* (Mainz: B Schott, 1965). Theodor Käser, *Die Leçon de ténèbres im 17. und 18. Jahrhundert* (Bern: P Haupt, 1966).

Lamento [It., lament]. A song of mourning or great sadness and an important element in Italian opera of the 17th century. Although a few madrigals of the 16th century were given this designation, the *lamento* rose to prominence along with *monody. Monteverdi's *Lamento d'Arianna,* all that survives of his opera *L'Arianna* of 1608, was the first celebrated example and was published separately in its monodic version and in Monteverdi's arrangement of it as a madrigal. The *lamento* was prominent in mid-17th-century Venetian operas, e.g., those of Cavalli, and was often treated as variations on an *ostinato bass of a descending tetrachord. Dido's lament from Purcell's **Dido and Aeneas* belongs to this tradition.

Lancio, con [It.]. Bounding, springing.

Landini cadence, sixth. See Cadence.

Ländler [Ger.]. A dance of Austria and southern Germany in a slow 3/4 time. It originated as a folk dance for couples and in the later 18th century became popular in the ballroom, enjoying a considerable vogue in the early 19th. It was eventually superseded by the *waltz. Mozart (K. 606), Beethoven (WoO 11), and Schubert (D. 378, 734, 790) composed sets of *Ländler,* and movements by Bruckner and Mahler draw on its style.

Langaus [Ger.]. An especially fast and vigorously danced version of the **Deutscher Tanz* of around 1800.

Langleik [Nor.]. A fretted *zither of Norway with a narrow trapezoidal body and four to eight metal strings. One string has frets beneath it and is a melody string; the rest are drones. The player places the instrument horizontally on a table and strums with a plectrum while fingering a melody with the left hand. It was widely popular in the 19th century. See also *Langspil, Hummel.*

Langsam [Ger.]. Slow; *langsamer,* slower; *sehr langsam,* very slow.

Langspil [Icel.]. A bowed *zither of Iceland; similar in form to the **langleik,* but played on the lap with a curved bow.

Laos. See Southeast Asia IV.

Lap organ. A reed organ made in the U.S. in the second quarter of the 19th century in the form of a box held on the player's lap. A keyboard was played with the right hand and the bellows operated with the left. It was also known as an elbow or rocking melodeon.

Larga [Lat.]. In *mensural notation, the *maxima.*

Largamente [It.]. Broadly.

Largando [It.]. **Allargando.*

Large. **Larga.*

Larghetto [It., dim. of *largo*]. Slightly less slow than **largo.* Heinrich Koch (1802) equated it with *andante.*

Largo [It., broad, large]. (1) Very slow; according to some 18th-century theorists, the slowest of the principal divisions of *tempo, though then and later it was often placed between *adagio* and *andante.* (2) A movement whose tempo is *largo.* The piece popularly known as Handel's "Largo" and played in a variety of arrangements is the aria "Ombra mai fù" (Shade never was) from **Serse,* which, however, is actually marked *larghetto.*

Larigot [Fr.]. An organ stop with open flue pipes, usually wide-scale, sounding at 1 1/3′ pitch (the nineteenth).

Lark Quartet. Popular name for Haydn's String Quartet in D major Hob. III:63 (1790), so called because of the high passage played by the first violin at the opening of the first movement. Haydn arranged the fourth movement for **Flötenuhr* (Hob. XIX:30).

Lassú [Hung.]. See *Verbunkos, Csárdás.*

Latin America. South America, Central America, and Mexico and the countries of the Caribbean. This is a region of great ethnic diversity, with indigenous groups, those of Iberian and African descent, and *mestizo* populations resulting from their mixing being most prominent. The following discussion treats, first, indigenous musical culture; second, general characteristics shared by the folk traditions of the Spanish-speaking countries and Brazil, many of which can be related to Iberian antecedents; and third, African-derived traditions.

I. *Indigenous musical culture.* 1. Before the Conquest. Society before the European Conquest exhibited a broad range of complexity and included small bands of nomadic hunters, fishermen, and gatherers, sedentary agricultural and pastoral populations, and in Mesoamerica and Andean South America, several highly developed cultures with stratified populations, large cities with monumental architecture and sculpture, a high level of ceramic and metallurgical achievement, and in some cases, specialized classes of priests, political leaders and warriors, craftsmen and artists. Most is known, thanks largely to 16th-century Spanish chroniclers, about music among the Aztecs of central Mexico and the Inca of Peru.

Music played an integral role in religious and civic life in Aztec and Inca culture. A variety of specific musical contexts are described in contemporary Spanish writings, especially public ceremonials involving the coordinated performance of large groups of instrumentalists, singers, and dancers. Professional musicians included bards in the service of Aztec and Inca rulers and nobles, who created new compositions and maintained extensive traditional repertories. Formal institutions for the rigorous training of musicians existed in both cultures; among the Aztecs, errors in the performance of music or dance in important ceremonies could earn death for the offender. No system of musical notation has been discovered for any pre-Columbian culture, and examination of instruments and other archaeological remains, 16th-century descriptions, and latter-day music of these regions permits only very limited speculation as to the sound and style of these musics.

The **huehuetl*, a footed, single-headed drum, and the **teponaztli*, a slit-drum producing two pitches, were elaborately carved and especially important in Aztec ritual; both were adaptations from older cultures. Other instruments widely diffused in pre-Columbian Mesoamerica include gourd rattles; bone rasps; tortoise-shell drums; jingles of clay, nutshells, and metal; ocarinas; single- and multiple-tube whistle flutes; and long trumpets made from wood and trumpets made from conch shells. Pre-Conquest Andean civilizations used various membranophones and idiophones, conch trumpets and conical trumpets, whistling pots and ocarinas. The region is particularly notable for its development of notched vertical flutes and panpipes, found by the beginning of the Common Era in Paracas and Nazca culture (coastal Peru) and still very important in Andean musical life.

2. Contemporary Amerindian traditions. *Mestizo* populations resulting from the mixing of native Americans, Europeans, and Africans often retain little of pre-Conquest traditions. In remote or marginal regions, however, indigenous society and culture have often survived relatively intact. Many indigenous peoples that have interacted with colonizing populations have still preserved independent ethnic identities and maintain traditions that while acculturated are highly distinctive. In some regions, most obviously in Andean South America, such traditions have had an importance transcending their ethnic base.

A great variety of instruments are found among contemporary indigenous cultures, with idiophones and aerophones, particularly flutes, well developed and widely distributed. Membranophones are important in the Andean region and in Mexico and Central America, but occur only sporadically elsewhere; in many instances, drums based on European models have replaced native types. Stringed instruments are infrequent and may all be adaptations of European and African instruments, although certain of the many musical bows known, for example, among the Huichol and Cora of western Mexico, the Motilón and Guajiro of Colombia and Venezuela, and the Mataco of Patagonia, may be exceptions. The impressive profusion of aerophones includes end- and side-blown trumpets, idioglottal and heteroglottal clarinets, and flutes of all kinds: whistles, simple and notched end-blown flutes, plug and duct flutes, and both mouth- and nose-blown transverse flutes with and without finger holes. Panpipes, most elaborately developed in the Andean region, are also found in Venezuela and Brazil and, farthest north, among the Cuna of Panama.

It is difficult to generalize about indigenous musical styles. Solo song, with and without simple rhythmic instrumental accompaniment, is widespread, but polyphonic styles, both vocal and instrumental, are also cultivated. Examples include the choral singing in parallel harmony of several Brazilian cultures, the heterophonic and imitative choral music of the Shuar (Jívaro) of Ecuador and Peru and the Warao of Venezuela, and the choral music, involving simultaneous and coordinated singing of several individual melodies, of the Brazilian Suya. Apart from those of the Andean region, complex instrumental styles include the interlocking panpipe duets of the Panamanian Cuna, the duets for very large twin-tubed duct flutes among the Camayurá of Brazil, and the music for polyphonic ensembles of as many as 20 instruments, including flutes and large bamboo and bark trumpets, among the Venezuelan Piaroa.

Scales are also varied. Cultures whose music consists largely or entirely of unaccompanied song, with melodies confined to two or three notes at intervals of thirds and major seconds, include Fuegian peoples (Ona, Yahgan, Alacaluf) and the Sirionó of Bolivia. Anhemitonic pentatonic scales are common in and around the Andean region. Scales confined to three pitches corresponding to a major triad are found in northwestern Argentina and Chile (Atacameño, Diaguita-Calchaquí), among the Shuar of Ecuador and Peru, and elsewhere. Chromatic and microtonal intervals occur in the singing styles of several central Brazilian cultures, and the tritone is a conspicuous melodic interval in the complex antiphonal singing of the Brazilian Yaulapiti and Camayurá and in the singing of the Araucanians of Argentina and Chile.

Many contemporary Mayan-speaking societies of Central America and Mexico were contacted early in the Conquest, exploited for their land and labor, and subjected to religious conversion; nonetheless they have retained their ethnic identity and cultivate highly distinctive adaptations of nonindigenous materials. Thus, among the Tzotzil of southern Mexico are ensembles of locally made violins, harps, and guitars that play music only partly explainable by reference to

Western models, in religious ceremonies as much Mayan as Spanish Catholic. The same is true of the quite different Mayan music for ensembles of European-derived drums, flutes, and long brass trumpets reminiscent of pre-Columbian types. Similarly mixed traditions are found elsewhere. The *pascola/venado* dance complex of the Yaqui in northwestern Mexico, which mixes Christian and indigenous symbolism and uses three different ensembles (harp and violins, flute and drum, and wooden rasps with gourd resonators and water drum), is a particularly striking example.

3. The Andean region. Native Andean populations conquered by the Spanish, including those under imperial control of the Inca, also adapted nonindigenous musical and other cultural forms in distinctive ways. The resulting traditions continue to be cultivated among *mestizo* as well as Indian societies throughout the region. Diatonic harps, violins, various guitar types (including the widely found **charango,* fashioned from an armadillo shell), and many other instruments of European derivation are used, but also vertical flutes (**quenas, pincullus*), panpipes (**antaras, sicus*), and other indigenous instruments. The vitality of instrumental and mixed instrumental and vocal ensembles characteristic of the region has a pre-Conquest foundation; for example, the large ensembles of drums, flutes, and panpipes playing in different registers among the Aymara of Bolivia and southern Peru recall 16th-century descriptions. Melodies of descending phrases repeated in pairs, within an anhemitonic framework, are pervasive in these traditions. Where chordal harmony exists, it is highly characteristic and often modal, oscillating between triads built on tonal centers a minor third apart. Polyphony for voices or instruments is often in parallel thirds and reminiscent of Spanish folk styles, but parallel fourths and fifths are also common; Andean polyphonic styles typically display a melodic and rhythmic independence among parts that is likely to be indigenous. The **yaraví,* a song-type, and the **huayno,* a dance and dance-music genre, are but the most important of the secular and sacred musical traditions known before the Conquest that remain important in Andean musical life.

II. *The Iberian heritage in Latin American folk traditions.* Notwithstanding the independent development of the folk traditions of Brazil and the Spanish-speaking countries, their mixing with Amerindian and African elements in several regions, and the impact upon them of changes in popular and elite musical fashion, these traditions exhibit common features, many reflecting a significant degree of continuity with Iberian antecedents.

1. Song and dance forms. Iberian verse forms remain central to traditional folk song of all types. Schemes of general importance include the octosyllabic quatrain (**copla, cuarteta*) characteristic of the Spanish and Portuguese **romance* and other genres; the *seguidilla,* with its alternation of seven- and five-syllable lines; and the *décima,* a ten-line form with various intricate rhyme schemes (e.g., abbaaccdde). Traditions of narrative song are widely established. In some regions, the *romance* itself continues to be cultivated, often preserving Old World texts and, more rarely, melodies, but more important today are traditions such as the **corrido,* which comments on contemporary events as well as preserving tales from the real and legendary past and which takes musically distinct forms in Mexico, Venezuela, Argentina, and elsewhere. Lyric singing is equally important, as in love-song genres such as the *canciones* and **tonadas* in several Spanish-speaking countries and the *toadas* of Brazil, in the many secular dance-song forms with amorous texts, and in the widespread persistence of the romantic serenade. Texts receive special emphasis in Latin American oral traditions. Musicians such as the wandering *corridistas* and *trovadores* of Mexico must command extensive text repertories, and the traditional *payadores* of rural Argentina are esteemed as much for their poetic as for their musical abilities. Traditions involving textual improvisation are found in all countries. These include solo forms and improvisatory contests between two singers, as in the **seis de controversia* of Puerto Rico, varieties of **mejorana* in Panama, the Venezuelan *porfía,* the Argentine *contrapunto,* and the **desafío* of Brazil and elsewhere. The demanding *décima* form is favored for improvisation in many traditions.

Although there are both secular and sacred traditions of unaccompanied singing, accompaniment is more pervasive. As in Spain and Portugal, solo singing self-accompanied on any of several types of guitars, played with a variety of strumming *(rasgueado)* and plucking *(punteado)* techniques, is most common, though diatonic harps, violins, and accordions are also used in several regions. There is also much instrumental ensemble performance, particularly to accompany sung texts. Again, guitars and other fretted stringed instruments along with harps and violins are especially important, with ensembles differing regionally as to instruments, combinations, and performance styles. In Mexico, string ensembles are augmented with trumpets in the **mariachi* and with accordion in the *conjunto norteño* [see *Música norteña*]; in the Andean region, by flutes; and in several regions, by percussion instruments. Nor is the emphasis on strings universal; in Guatemala and southern Mexico, for example, *marimbas, often in pairs of different sizes along with winds and percussion, are more important, though their traditional repertory has much in common with the string-associated styles of Guatemala and Mexico. And throughout Latin America, military bands, typically deriving much of their repertory from the traditional styles of their respective regions, are also important.

Continuity with Iberian traditions is also seen in the many styles of secular dance music. Individual regional traditions themselves are often highly differentiated, as in the many named genres of the *criollo* dance-music tradition of rural Argentina, in the large number of named subtypes of the Puerto Rican *seis,* and in the **son jarocho* tradition of Veracruz (Mexico), where many individual *sones* are distinguished by choreography as well as by text and music. Iberian dances such as the **fandango* and **jota* survive in various regions, but the majority of Latin American dance-music types are of New World origin. Whereas some, such as certain *sones* in Mexico, have been known since colonial times, others, such as the dances of rural Argentina and Chile today, seem to have displaced older styles in the last century. An important factor in the development and diversity of these traditions has been the influence of dance styles fashionable in the cultural centers of Latin America. The incorporation in rural traditions of European salon and ballroom dances such as the *contradanza,* the polka, the schottisch, and above all the waltz—seen in the waltz-derived **pasillo* of Colombia and Ecuador and in the many *valses* and *valses criollos* found in oral tradition in several countries today—is but the most obvious example of such a process. Despite the heterogeneity of the dance traditions of Latin America, however, many forms and styles exhibit common musical characteristics reflecting an Iberian foundation [see 3 below]. Such characteristic elements of Spanish and Portuguese dance as the use of scarfs and handkerchiefs, hand-clapping and finger-snapping, and choreographic patterns with endlessly varied combinations of strolling *(paseo)* and shoe-tapping *(zapateado)* segments are widespread and persistent features of Latin American traditions.

2. Religious traditions. As in Spain and Portugal, a variety of religious musical traditions are associated with the liturgical calendar of the Catholic Church and with *fiestas* of patron saints of individual communities. Although calendric emphases vary regionally and locally, Holy Week, the pre-Lenten festival of Carnival, and the Christmas season are of widespread importance. Particularly well developed are Christmas traditions, including dramatic dances, processions and plays with music (such as the **bailes pastoris* and **reisados* of Brazil and the *posadas* of several Spanish-speaking countries), and many styles and repertories of songs and dance-songs in the Iberian **villancico* tradition (known variously as *villancicos,* **aguinaldos, adoraciones, esquinazos,* etc.). Although religious traditions are occasionally quite different from other styles, as in the polyphonic **tonos de velorio* of central Venezuela, there is often considerable correspondence between a region's religious and secular traditions. The **galerón* of Venezuela has secular or religious texts, as do the *verso* of Chile and the Christmas *aguinaldo* of Puerto Rico. In general, the major feast days and the saints' days of particular communities are extremely important for the maintenance, not only of sacred, but also of secular folk traditions in all Latin American countries.

3. General musical characteristics. Diatonic major and minor (including natural minor) scales are most widely found in Latin American traditional melody, although other modal scales are also common and may in some cases be European survivals. Anhemitonic pentatonic scales and bimodality are distinctive features of Andean traditions; pentatonic scales are also found in certain African-derived styles but are otherwise not characteristic. Although melodic styles vary considerably, the widespread prevalence of conjunct melodies with descending contours, particularly at cadence points, is consistent with Iberian antecedents, as is the wide cultivation of tense and often nasal singing in a high register; but the melismatic and richly ornamented singing of many peninsular traditions, particularly those of southern Spain, is much less common in Latin America.

Vocal styles, with and without accompaniment, include solo and unison singing and polyphonic singing in parallel thirds and sixths; other forms of polyphony are much less common except among certain indigenous cultures. Traditions of antiphonal solo singing, generally with instrumental accompaniment, occur throughout the continent. Responsorial singing, as in the *son jarocho* in Veracruz, is most highly developed in regions of strong African influence.

Song and dance-song genres are most typically strophic in form. In some traditions, for example, the Mexican *corrido* and *canción,* textual strophes may be accompanied by a single musical period of broad and arch-shaped antecedent-consequent phrases; in the dance-song traditions of rural Argentina, on the other hand, strophes have as few as two short, fixed phrases that are repeated in more complex but standardized patterns that vary with specific textual and choreographic schemes. In one widespread practice, for example, in the Argentine *cifra* and **milonga,* the Chilean *verso,* and the Venezuelan *corrido,* strophes have one or two phrases—recitativelike with repeated notes and conjunct motion, descending contours, and often irregular lengths—that are freely varied and repeated.

Harmonic movement often only alternates tonic and dominant triads in both major and minor modes, or restricts progressions to tonic, subdominant, and dominant. Progressions emphasizing major and relative minor triads, alone or with associated primary triads, characterize many Andean accompaniments. Harmonic/rhythmic grounds are also prominent, especially where African settlement has been substantial, and may in some cases be African in origin. In these, alternation between tonic and dominant, with the subdominant as passing chord, is very common, as is the descending minor-key progression, i–♭VII–♭VI–V(7), often associated with descending vocal lines cadencing on the dominant pitch and thus reminiscent of the E-mode so characteristic of Andalusian styles.

Unmeasured rhythm is not uncommon, but regular meter, often used with symmetrical phrasing and regular tempos, is more generally characteristic. Triple meter, both simple and compound, abounds. Simple and compound meters are very often mixed linearly in vocal or instrumental melodies and vertically superimposed in complex, syncopated, instrumental accompaniments whose patterns differ by region.

III. *African-derived traditions.* The importation of slaves from sub-Saharan Africa began in the first years of the Conquest. Today, populations of African descent are most substantial in Brazil, in the Caribbean, along the northern coast of South America, in Panama, and in western Colombia. In all of these regions, distinctive musical traditions of marked African content have flourished.

In Cuba, Haiti, Jamaica, Trinidad, and Brazil, black populations have maintained systems of religious ritual and belief that retain much African (particularly West African) style and content. Musical styles associated with them are among the most African in character in all of Latin America. One index of the vitality of these religious cults (as they are customarily termed) is their diversity, with several distinct forms often found in a single region. But shared among them are the worship of a pantheon of deities of African origin (though often incorporating Christian elements known variously as *orixás, voduns, saints,* or powers), animal sacrifice, spirit possession, and sometimes elaborate systems of cult membership with specialized roles and responsibilities. Music and dance, for general worship but also to effect possession, are of central importance. Repertories of songs, many dedicated to specific deities, with texts in African as well as European languages and often with African mythological content, are sung by soloist and chorus in *call-and-response fashion. Drums are the characteristic and essential accompanying instruments, regarded as the principal agents for communication with the supernatural. In most traditions, three drums of different sizes along with bell or rattle form an ensemble. Rhythms of the lowest-pitched, master drum are varied, through improvisations, against the relatively constant patterns of the bell or rattle; the latter, as in several West African traditions, provides a basic rhythmic orientation for the rest of the ensemble.

Other African-derived religious traditions involve complex drumming, alone and as an accompaniment to call-and-response singing and dancing. Examples are the **baile de palos* of the Dominican Republic and the *baile de tambor* [see *Golpe*], with its many subtypes, in Venezuela; both are associated with Catholic celebrations, and both are generally similar to the music of African-derived cults in other regions. Similar features are also found with the *currulao* in the Pacific coastal lowlands of Colombia and Ecuador. Marimba (an African-derived instrument), drums (including African-derived drums of the *conga type along with the European bass drum), and seed-filled tubular rattles again accompany dancing and call-and-response singing. The *currulao* is performed in secular contexts, but contains ritual and sacred elements of fundamental importance. In many other African-derived traditions as well, the division between secular and sacred is not hard and fast. The Cuban **rumba,* which also involves drum ensemble, call-and-response singing, and dancing, is typically performed in recreational settings in the streets and backyards of black neighborhoods in Havana and other cities, or in folkloric shows.

Many other African-derived secular traditions are found in various regions: some, like the *rumba,* have strong sacred associations; but others, like the Cuban **son,* are a source of entertainment and recreation. A few examples include the **bomba* and **plena* of Puerto Rico, the **merengue* of the Dominican Republic and the *meringue* of Haiti, the *calypso of Trinidad, the **tamborito* of Panama, the **cumbia* of Panama and Colombia's Atlantic coast, and in Brazil, the **batuque* and the **samba,* with its many rural and urban varieties. These traditions vary greatly, in the degrees and ways they have absorbed features of other traditions around them and in the exclusivity with which they are identified with ethnically black groups. But common to all are musical traits that reflect continuity with sub-Saharan African procedures, although it must be stressed that some of these are consistent with features of other Latin American styles possibly untouched by African influence and that others suggest differences in emphasis and degree rather than kind. These traits include (1) measured rhythm with firmly maintained pulse, with predilection for duple and compound duple (and quadruple) meters, and with relatively little use of simple triple meter; (2) rhythmic complexity, seen in the pervasive syncopation of vocal and instrumental melodic lines and in an even greater emphasis than in other Latin American styles on the combination of multiple, rhythmically simple but contrasting ostinatos in accompaniments; (3) emphasis on drums and other percussion instruments, often combined with stringed instruments, and a general tendency to combine instruments (and voices) of contrasting timbres in ensembles; (4) as in Iberian-derived traditions, prevalence of textual improvisation, but with a special bent toward colorful texts, abstract word-play (metaphors, puns, onomatopoeia), and frequently ribald or satirical content; (5) diatonic but also pentatonic and hexatonic scales, and to a greater extent than in other traditions, thirds, fourths, and, not uncommonly, larger melodic intervals, characteristically appearing in freely varied motives; (6) call-and-response patterns; and (7) a characteristic organizational procedure, found in other styles in Latin America but pervasive in African-derived traditions, in which large sections if not entire pieces are formed of repetitions of a short rhythmic or harmonic/rhythmic unit, accompanying improvisation by instrumental or vocal soloists, alone or in alternation with a more fixed choral or instrumental response.

See also Argentina, Brazil, Chile, Mexico.

Bibl.: Raoul and Marguerite d'Harcourt, *La musique des Incas et ses survivances* (Paris: P Geuthner, 1926). Karl Gustav Izikowitz, *Musical and Other Sound Instruments of the South American Indians* (Göteborg: Elanders Boktryckeri Aktiebolag, 1934). Emilio Grenet, *Popular Cuban Music,* trans. Ruby H. Phillips (Havana: Carasa, 1939). Melville J. Herskovits, "Drums and Drummers in Afro-Brazilian Cult Life," *MQ* 30 (1944): 477–92. Carlos Vega, *Panorama de la música popular Argentina* (Buenos Aires: Editorial Losada, 1944). Id., *Los instrumentos musicales aborígines y criollos de la Argentina* (Buenos Aires: Ediciones Centurión, 1946). Erich M. von Hornbostel, "The Music of the Fuegians," *Ethnos* 13 (1948): 61–102. Oneyda Alvarenga, *Música popular brasileira* (Rio de Janeiro: Editôra Globo, 1950). Fernando Ortiz Fernández, *La africanía de la música folklórica de Cuba* (Havana: Dirección de cultura, Ministerio de educación, 1950.) Id., *Los instrumentos de la música afrocubana* (Havana: Dirección de cultura, Ministerio de educación, 1952–55). Isabel Aretz, *El folklore musical argentino* (Buenos Aires: Ricordi americana, 1952). Vicente T. Mendoza, *Panorama de la música tradicional de México* (Mexico City: Imp Universitaria, 1956). Alan P. Merriam, "Songs of the Ketu Cult of Bahia, Brazil," *African Music* 1, no. 3 (1956): 53–67. Raoul and Marguerite d'Harcourt, *La musique des Aymara sur les hauts plateaux boliviens* (Paris: Société des américanistes, 1959). Josafat Roel Piñeda, "El wayno del Cuzco," *Folklore americano* 6–7 (1959): 129–246. Harold Courlander, *The Drum and the Hoe* (Berkeley and Los Angeles: U of Cal Pr, 1960). Vida Chenoweth, *The Marimbas of Guatemala* (Lexington: U Pr of Ky, 1964). George List, "The Folk Music of the Atlantic Littoral of Colombia: An Introduction," *Indiana Univ.,* 1965, pp. 115–22. Charles L. Boilès, "The Pipe and Tabor in Mesoamerica," *Yearbook for Inter-American Musical Research* 2 (1966): 43–74. Isabel Aretz, *Instrumentos musicales de Venezuela* (Cumaná, Venezuela: Universidad de Oriente, 1967). María Ester Grebe, *The Chilean Verso: A Study in Musical Archaism,* trans. Bette Jo Hileman (Los Angeles: Latin American Center, U of Cal, 1967). Francisco López Cruz, *La música folklórica de Puerto Rico* (Sharon, Conn.: Troutman, 1967). Consuelo Pagaza Galdo, comp., *Cancionero andino Sur* (Lima: Casa Mosart, 1967). Frank and Joan Harrison, "Spanish Elements in the Music of Two Maya Groups in Chiapas," *UCLA Selected Reports in Ethnomusicology* 1, no. 2 (1968): 1–44. Samuel Martí, *Instrumentos Musicales Precortesianos,* 2nd ed. (Mexico City: Instituto nacional de anthropología, 1968). Robert M. Stevenson, *Music in Aztec and Inca Territory* (Berkeley and Los Angeles: U of Cal Pr, 1968). Luis F. Ramón y Rivera, *La música folklórica de Venezuela* (Caracas: Monte Ávila, 1969). Norman E. Whitten, Jr., "Personal Networks and Musical Contexts in the Pacific Lowlands of Colombia and Ecuador," *Afro-American Anthropology,* ed. Norman E. Whitten, Jr., and John F. Szwed (New York: Free Press, 1970), pp. 203–17. Martha Ellen Davis, "The Social Organization of a Musical Event: The *Fiesta de Cruz* in San Juan, Puerto Rico," *Ethno* 16 (1972): 38–62. Segundo Luis Moreno Andrade, *Historia de la música en el Ecuador,* vol. 1, *Prehistoria* (Quito: Editorial Casa de la cultura ecuatoriana, 1972). John Storm Roberts, *Black Music of Two Worlds* (New York: Praeger, 1972). E. Thomas Stanford, "The Mexican *Son,*" *YIFMC* 4 (1972): 66–86. Guillermo Abadía Morales, *La música folklórica colombiana* (Bogotá: Universidad nacional de Colombia, 1973). María Ester Grebe, "Presencia del dualismo en la cultura y música mapuche," *Revista musical chilena* 28, nos. 126–27 (1974): 47–79. Id., "La música alacalufe: Aculturación y cambio estilístico," *Revista musical chilena* 28, nos. 126–27 (1974): 80–111. Sandra Smith McCosker, *The Lullabies of the San Blas Cuna Indians of Panama* (Göteborg: Etnografiska museet, 1974). Dale A. Olsen, "The Function of Naming in the Curing Songs of the Warao Indians of Venezuela," *Yearbook for Inter-American Musical Research* 10 (1974): 88–122. Gerard Béhague, "Notes on Regional and National Trends in Afro-Brazilian Cult Music," in *Tradition and Renewal,* ed. Merlin H. Forster (Urbana: U of Ill Pr, 1975), pp. 68–80. Id., *Music in Latin America: An Introduction* (Englewood Cliffs, N.J.: Prentice-Hall, 1977). James Koetting, "The *Son Jalisciense:* Structural Variety in Relation to a Mexican Mestizo *Form Fixe,*" *Wachsmann,* 1977, pp. 162–88. John M. Schechter, "Non-Hispanic Instruments in Mexico and Central America: An Annotated Bibliography," *CM* 24 (1977): 80–104. Id., "The Inca *Cantar Histórico:* A Lexico-Historical Elaboration on Two Cultural Themes," *Ethno* 23 (1979): 191–204. István Halmos, "The Music of the Nambicuara Indians (Mato Grosso, Brazil)," *Acta ethnographica* 28 (1979): 205–350. Carol E. Robertson, "'Pulling the Ancestors': Performance Practice and Praxis in Mapuche Ordering," *Ethno* 23 (1979): 395–416. Anthony Seeger, "What Can We Learn When They Sing?: Vocal Genres of the Suya Indians of Central Brazil," *Ethno* 23 (1979): 373–94. Roberto Rivera, *Los instrumentos musicales de los Mayas* (Mexico: Instituto nacional de antropología e historia, 1980). Max Peter Baumann, "Music of the Indios in Bolivia's Andean Highlands (Survey)," *The World of Music* 25 (1982): 80–98. Julio Estrada, ed., *La música de México,* 5 vols. (Mexico: Universidad nacional autónoma, 1984). Manuel Peña, "From *Ranchero* to *Jaitón:* Ethnicity and Class in Texas-Mexican Music (Two Styles in the Form of a Pair)," *Ethno* 29 (1985): 29–55. See also the articles on Latin American musical topics in the *Latin American Music Review (Revista de música latino americana),* published twice a year beginning in 1980. Important bibliographic sources are the annually published *Handbook of Latin American Studies* and Gilbert Chase, *A Guide to the Music of Latin America,* 2nd ed., rev. and enl. (Washington, D.C.: Pan American Union, 1962). John Mendell Schechter, *Music in Latin American Culture: Regional Traditions* (New York: Schirmer, 1999).

D.S.

Latin jazz. A jazz style that first flourished in the late 1940s when musicians combined elements of bebop with the rhythms and percussion instruments of Afro-Latin popular musics such as the *mambo, especially as arranged for big bands. The Latin American musicians who most inspired and developed the style were trumpeter Mario Bauzá, percussionist Luciano "Chano" Pozo, and bandleader Frank Grillo ("Machito"). Dizzy Gillespie was its most prominent non-Latin exponent. Since the 1970s, figures like Eddie Palmieri and groups like Irakere and Manny Oquendo y Libre have been among the most important musicians working in the style. T.A.J.

Laube Sonata [Ger.]. See *Moonlight* Sonata.

Lauda [It., pl. *laude;* or *laude,* pl. *laudi*]. A nonliturgical religious song, of greatest importance in the 13th and in the 15th–16th centuries, but in continuous use until the mid-19th century, with texts usually in Italian, less often in Latin; also *lauda spirituale.* In diction, subject matter, and musical setting, the *lauda* is familiar, not elite.

Laude of the 13th-century were anonymous, monophonic, and in a relatively simple style suitable for performance by persons without musical training. The genre originated in connection with the Franciscans and lay organizations devoted to religious or devotional activities (such as the guild of *Laudesi della Beata Vergine* in Florence). Surviving sources (most containing texts only) suggest that the *lauda* was vigorously cultivated during the period of penitential fervor of the last half of the 13th century [see also *Geisslerlieder*]. After this time, the rate of production of monophonic *laude* dropped, but songs of this general type continued in use throughout the 14th century and well beyond—even into the 19th century.

In textual and musical form, the medieval *lauda* resembles the Italian **ballata.* A refrain *(ripresa)* alternates with strophes, but the number of strophes and, within formal units, the number of lines and the rhyme scheme vary considerably. Two related musical passages are provided, one for the refrain and one for the strophes. Rhythm is not indicated by the black square notation of the music of the monophonic *laude* in the two principal sources (*I-CT* 91 [Cortona] and *I-Fn* Magl.II.I.122, BR18 [Florence]); hence, this repertory has been subject to many of the same arguments about rhythm as has other nonliturgical medieval monophony [see Troubadour, Trouvère].

The earliest surviving polyphonic *laude* were composed in the 14th century and include an example by Jacopo da Bologna. In the 15th century, polyphonic *laude* may have Italian or Latin texts (increasingly in forms from the **frottola* repertory rather than the *ballata*) and are most often for two or three voices in a simple, homophonic style. The peak of the genre's popularity came in the late 15th and early 16th centuries. Ottaviano Petrucci published two books of *laude* with four-part music, largely homophonic in style, in Venice in 1507–8. The first is devoted entirely to works by Innocentius Dammonis, most with texts in Italian. The second is devoted to Tromboncino, Cara, Fogliano (*HAM,* no. 94), and other frottolists, with more than half of the texts in Latin. Around the same time in Florence, many *lauda* texts were published without music, although in many cases polyphony to which they could be sung was specified. These pieces were performed by trained singers, evidently with instrumentalists, both in and outside of church.

The next printed collections (one by Serafino Razzi and one by Giovanni Animuccia) appeared in 1563, and for a while such prints were issued frequently, many for use by Filippo Neri's Congregazione dell'Oratorio. Polyphonic *laude* of the latter half of the 16th century are stylistically similar to those published by Petrucci. Many of these works employ earlier texts and or melodies or borrow in one way or another from secular monophony or polyphony. After the 16th century, the publication of *laude* was sporadic, lasting, however, into the 19th century.

Bibl.: Knud Jeppesen and Viggo Brøndal, *Die mehrstimmige italienische laude um 1500* (Leipzig: Breitkopf & Härtel, 1935). Fernando Liuzzi, *La lauda e i primordi della melodia italiana,* 2 vols. (Rome: La libreria dello stato, 1935). Giulio Cattin, "Contributi alla storia della lauda spirituale," *Quadrivium* 2 (1958): 45–75. Higinio Anglès, "The Musical Notation and Rhythm of the Italian Laude," *Apel,* 1968, pp. 51–60. A. Ziino, *Strutture strofiche nel laudario di Cortona* (Palermo: Editore Lo Monaco, 1968). Frank D'Accone, "Alcune note sulle compagnie fiorentine dei laudesi durante il Quattrocento," *RIM* 10 (1975): 86–114. Howard E. Smither, *A History of the Oratorio,* vol. 1, *The Oratorio in the Baroque Era: Italy, Vienna, Paris* (Chapel Hill: U of NC Pr, 1977).

Laudes [Lat., praises]. (1) *Lauds. (2) In the *Gallican and *Mozarabic rites, the counterpart of the Gregorian *alleluia. (3) *Laudes regiae,* acclamations addressed to the king or emperor, evidently of Carolingian origin. Beginning with the acclamations "Christus vincit, Christus regnat, Christus imperat," they include invocations similar to those of *litanies. The earliest preserved text is from ca. 800, the earliest melody from the 10th century.

Laudon (Loudon) Symphony. Haydn's name for his Symphony no. 69 in C major Hob. I:69 (completed in 1779), composed in honor of the Austrian field marshal Baron von Laudon (1717–90).

Lauds [Lat. *laudes*]. The second of the services making up the *Office.

Laufwerk [Ger.]. **Flötenuhr.*

Launeddas. A triple clarinet of Sardinia consisting of three cane pipes. Two pipes, one held in each hand, have finger holes; the other is a bass drone. All three single reeds are inserted into the mouth, and circular breathing is used to maintain a continuous sound. The two melody pipes produce a polyphonic texture.

Bibl.: Andreas Weis Bentzon, *The Launeddas* (Copenhagen: Akademisk forlag, 1969).

Laut [Ger.]. (1) [adj.] Loud. (2) [n.] Sound.

Laute [Ger.]. Lute; *Lautenzug,* the buff or *harp stop of the harpsichord; for *Lautenclavicymbel,* see Lute harpsichord.

Lauto, laouto [Gr.]. A fretted *lute of Greece. Four pairs of gut strings are plucked with a quill or a plastic plectrum. It is the traditional accompanying instrument in Greek instrumental ensembles, though lately it has been extensively displaced by the guitar. See also *ʿŪd.*

Lavolta. See *Volta.*

Lay. **Lai.*

Layer. In *Schenker analysis, any of the musical structures underlying a tonal work and understood as related to one another by certain techniques of elaboration.

Leadback. *Retransition [see Sonata form].

Leader. (1) Conductor. (2) [Brit.] Concertmaster.

Leading motive, motif. See *Leitmotiv.*

Leading tone, note [Fr. *(note) sensible;* Ger. *Leitton;* It. *(nota) sensibile;* Sp. *(nota) sensible*]. The seventh degree of the major and harmonic or ascending melodic minor scales, which lies a semitone below the tonic and in tonal music often leads or resolves to the tonic [see Scale, Scale degrees]. Melodic motion from leading tone to tonic, especially when harmonized with the dominant and tonic harmonies (V–I), respectively, is one of the most characteristic gestures of tonal music [see Cadence]. In the major scale, the seventh degree lies naturally a semitone below the tonic. In the pure minor, it lies a whole tone below and is raised by means of an accidental in order to produce the leading-tone effect of the harmonic and melodic minor scales [see Major, minor]. In some of the *modes of early music, too, the seventh degree lies a whole tone below *(subtonium)* the final. Under certain circumstances, however, the seventh degree in such modes could be raised with an accidental to create a semitone below *(subsemitonium)* the final [see *Musica ficta*]. In both tonal and earlier music, leading tones for degrees other than the tonic or final are sometimes introduced with accidentals. In tonal music, this is termed *tonicization and is harmonized with an applied or secondary dominant [see Harmony, Harmonic analysis]. See also Double leading tone.

Lead sheet. In jazz and popular music, a shorthand score or part. It may provide melody and chord symbols [see *Fake-book notation], along with accompanimental figures and/or lyrics. B.K.

Leap. Melodic *motion from one pitch to another that is more than a whole tone away.

Lebendig [Ger.]. Lively.

Lebhaft [Ger.]. Lively, **vivace.*

Lectio [Lat.]. *Lesson.

Lectionary [Lat. *lectionarium, liber comicus*]. A *liturgical book containing Scripture readings or lessons.

Ledger line. A short line parallel to and above or below the staff, representing a continuation of the staff and used to indicate pitches above or below the staff itself [see Notation]. The use of ledger lines can be avoided by the appropriate choice of *clef, as is most often done in music through the 16th century. An early example of their extensive use, however, is Marco Antonio Cavazzoni's *Recerchari motetti canzoni* for organ of 1523.

Leere Saite [Ger.]. Open string.

Legato [It., bound; Fr. *lié;* Ger. *gebunden;* Sp. *ligado*]. Played smoothly with no separation between successive notes; the opposite of *staccato. Although it is sometimes specified by means of a *slur, which on wind and bowed instruments calls for no articulation of successive notes (i.e., no tonguing or change of bow), the term itself does not necessarily imply the absence of articulation, but only a very smooth articulation. On keyboard instruments, the distinction does not exist. Legato *tonguing and *bowing (with changes of bow, now termed *détaché*) are an essential part of playing technique and are now often regarded as the norm. The instruments (including keyboard instruments) and playing styles of the 17th and 18th centuries, however, favored a somewhat lighter sound with clearer articulation, between staccato and legato. See Bowing, Performance practice.

Legende [Ger.], **légende** [Fr.]. Legend; in the 19th century, a title used for shorter instrumental works (Dvořák's op. 59 for piano four hands, also arranged for orchestra) and for symphonic poems intended to depict specific legends (Sibelius's **Lemminkäinen Suite* op. 22). Liszt's *Die Legende von der heiligen Elisabeth* (The Legend of St. Elizabeth) is an oratorio for soloists, chorus, organ, and orchestra composed between 1857 and 1862.

Léger, légèrement [Fr.]. Light, lightly; in the 18th century, also fast.

Leger line. See Ledger line.

Leggiadro, leggiadramente [It.]. Graceful, charming.

Legg(i)ero, leggermente [It.]. Light, nimble, quick; sometimes non- *legato.

Legno [It.]. Wood; *stromenti di legno* or *legni,* woodwinds; *col legno,* in string playing, to strike the strings with the bow stick rather than bow with the hair.

Lehrstück [Ger., teaching piece]. A type of musical theater of the 1920s and 30s written principally by Bertolt Brecht, with music composed by Kurt Weill, Paul Hindemith, Hanns Eisler, and Paul Dessau, and intended for the edification (often political) of its performers, especially members of the working class and children. Examples include *Die Massnahme* (The Precaution; Brecht-Eisler, 1930) and *Der Jasager* (The Yes-sayer; Brecht-Weill, 1930). See also *Gebrauchsmusik.*

Leich [Ger.]. See *Lai.*

Leicht [Ger.]. Light, nimble.

Leidenschaftlich [Ger.]. Passionately.

Leier [Ger.]. (1) Lyre. (2) Hurdy-gurdy; also *Drehleier, Radleier, Bettlerleier.* See also *Leierkasten.*

Leierkasten [Ger.]. *Barrel organ.

Leise [Ger.]. (1) Soft. (2) German sacred songs of the Middle Ages, so called because they included the phrase *Kyrie eleison,* which was contracted to *kirleis* or *leis.* They include pilgrimage and crusading songs as well as songs for congregational use, the latter usually of four-line strophes. The earliest is from the 9th century. Many were based on earlier models, and some survive as *chorales, e.g., "Christ ist erstanden," on the sequence "Victimae paschali laudes," and "Nun bitten wir den heiligen Geist," on the sequence "Veni sancte spiritus."

Leiter [Ger.]. (1) Scale *(Tonleiter).* (2) Leader, director; *Leitung,* direction.

Leitmotif, Leitmotiv [Ger., leading motive]. A musical fragment, related to some aspect of the drama, that recurs in the course of an opera. The term was coined by F. W. Jähns and appears in his study of Carl Maria von Weber (1871); it gained greater currency after Baron Hans Paul von Wolzogen used the concept as a means of elucidating Wagner's *Der *Ring des Nibelungen.*

The term leitmotif is used most often in connection with Wagner's later works, although Wagner himself preferred the terms *Grundthema* and *Hauptmotiv,* among others. Wagner achieved through the leitmotif a synthesis of two important 19th-century compositional techniques—thematic recollection or reminiscence and thematic transformation. Recurring themes are found in French, Italian, and German operas written at least a generation before Wagner. In such cases, the dramatic reference is fairly specific (sometimes words and music recur together), and the musical recollection is fairly exact. For example, in Grétry's *Richard Coeur-de-lion,* the minstrel Blondel sings the same song several times as a means of identifying himself and locating his king; in the mad scenes of Bellini's *I Puritani* and Donizetti's *Lucia di Lammermoor,* the heroine recollects music associated with a happier period in her life. Thematic transformation, on the other hand, is concerned with developmental alterations of a motive. It was used as a means of unifying instrumental works—either with programmatic references, as in Berlioz's **Symphonie fantastique,* or without such references, as in Liszt's Piano Sonata in B minor [see Transformation of themes].

Leitmotifs combine both dramatic and musical functions, often in complex ways. They may simply emphasize aurally what is seen on stage, or suggest to the listener something unseen that is being thought by one of the characters—a recollection, intuition, or prediction. Leitmotifs, thus, can show relationships—between present and past, between action and underlying motivation. Beyond presenting an exegesis of the action, the leitmotifs are the material from which the musical substance is constructed, just as *motifs would be for an instrumental composer; in music drama, however, musical development inevitably suggests dramatic development.

Bibl.: Gerald Abraham, "The Leit-Motif since Wagner," *ML* 6 (1925): 175–90. Karl Wörner, "Beiträge zur Geschichte des Leitmotivs in der Oper," *ZfMw* 14 (1931–32): 151–72. Theodor Adorno, *Versuch über Wagner* (Berlin: Suhrkamp, 1952; 2nd ed., Munich: Droemer/Knaur, 1964). Jack Stein, *Richard Wagner and the Synthesis of the Arts* (Detroit: Wayne St U Pr, 1960). Robert Donington, *Wagner's Ring and Its Symbols* (London: Faber, 1963). Deryck Cooke, *I Saw the World End: A Study of Wagner's Ring* (London: Oxford U Pr, 1979). Robert T. Laudon, *Sources of the Wagnerian Synthesis* (Munich: Katzbichler, 1979). C.G.

Leitton [Ger.]. *Leading tone.

Lemminkäinen Suite [Finn. *Lemminkäis-sarja*]. Four symphonic poems by Sibelius, op. 22, on legends of the warrior Lemminkäinen from the **Kalevala.* Their titles are *Lemminkäinen and the Maidens of the Island* (1895; rev. 1897, 1939), *Lemminkäinen in Tuonela* (1895; rev. 1897, 1939), *The Swan of Tuonela* (1893; rev. 1897, 1900), and *Lemminkäinen's Return* (1895; rev. 1897, 1900).

Lenguetería de la fachada [Sp.]. In Spanish organs, the *trompetas* and other reed stops mounted horizontally in the facade, the first recorded use being in Mondragón in 1677 by José de Echevarría.

Leningrad Symphony. Popular name for Shostakovich's Symphony no. 7 in C major op. 60, begun in Leningrad during the German siege in 1941 and completed in Kuibishev later in the year.

Lent, lentement [Fr.]. Slow [see Performance marks].

Lento, lentamente [It.]. Slow [see Performance marks]; *lentissimo,* extremely slow.

Leonore overtures. The overtures composed by Beethoven for his opera **Fidelio,* originally titled *Leonore,* prior to the composition of the work now known as the *Fidelio* Overture. *Leonore* no. 2 was composed for the first production of the opera in 1805. No. 3 is a revision of no. 2 for a revival of the opera in 1806. No. 1, op. 138 (1806–7), was for a proposed production of the opera in Prague that never materialized. The *Fidelio* overture was composed for the revival of the opera in 1814.

Les adieux [Fr.]. See *Adieux, Les.*

Lesson. (1) [Lat. *lectio*]. In a liturgical service, a reading from Scripture or other source such as the church fathers. In the Roman rite and its *Gregorian chant, these are often associated with responsorial chants: the varying numbers of lessons of Matins [see Office] with *responsories, and the Epistle and Gospel of the *Mass with the *gradual and *alleluia, respectively. The lessons themselves may be sung to simple recitation tones (*LU,* pp. 102–9 for the Mass, pp. 120–23 for the Office). (2) In England from the late 16th century through much of the 18th, a piece for instrumental consort, for lute, or, especially, for keyboard. The term did not imply any particular style or form, and it rarely implied pedagogical aims. By the later 17th century, it often designated a dance movement of the type gathered in suites, a publication consisting of suites often being termed a collection of lessons, as in Matthew Locke's *Melothesia . . . A Choice Collection of Lessons for the Harpsichord and the Organ* of 1673. Later English editions of Domenico Scarlatti's sonatas substituted the term lessons for the *essercizi* of the first English edition of 1738 or 1739.

Letra [Sp.]. The words of a song or other vocal work.

Letter notation. Musical notation that uses the letters of the alphabet to designate pitches. The *pitch names in current use constitute such a notation, especially if combined with a system (e.g., of superscripts and subscripts) to indicate the precise register of each of the pitch classes represented by the first seven letters of the alphabet and associated accidentals. The anonymous 10th-century treatise *Dialogus de musica* (*GS* 1:251–64), formerly attributed to Odo of Cluny, presents an early version of the letter notation that was used for the *gamut and *hexachords of medieval and Renaissance theory. Since the rise of the antecedents of staff notation in the 11th century, this letter notation has been used principally for theory and pedagogy. Other schemes of letter notation are found in the *De institutione musica* of Boethius (ca. 480–ca. 524) and in the 11th-century manuscript Montepellier, Bibliothèque de l'École de médicine, H159 (where the letters a–p serve to make precise the pitches of nondiastematic neumes also used there; ed. in *PM* ser. 1, vols. 7–8). For the letter notation of classical Greece, see Greece I, 4. For the use of letters in notation for instrumental music, see Tablature.

Leuto [It., obs.]. Lute.

Levalto. See *Volta.*

Levare, levate [It.]. Remove, referring to an organ stop or a mute; *si levano i sordini,* the mutes are removed.

Levatio [Lat.], **elevazione, levazione** [It.]. *Elevation.

L.H. Abbr. for left hand [Ger. *linke Hand*].

L'homme armé [Fr.]. See *Homme armé, L'.*

Libero, liberamente [It.]. Freely.

Liber usualis [Lat.]. See Liturgical books.

Libitum [Lat.]. See *Ad libitum.*

Libraries. Considerable progress in making known the contents of libraries has been made in recent decades. The publications of **RISM* have greatly expanded the information given in Robert Eitner's *Biographisch-bibliographisches Quellen-Lexicon* (Leipzig: Breitkopf & Härtel, 1900–1904; 2nd ed., Graz: Akademische Druck- und Verlagsanstalt, 1959–60). The growing number of online catalogs supplementing or superseding the published catalogs of national libraries, which are their nations' depositories for copyright or *depot legal* materials, are especially helpful.

Many of the music libraries of the world are listed in the *Directory of Music Research Libraries* 2nd ed., (Kassel: Bärenreiter, 1983–), which is Series C of **RISM.* This is supplemented by the article "Libraries" in *Grove 6,* rev. ed. (London: Macmillan, 2001). American music libraries are described in Carol June Bradley's *Music Collections in American Libraries: A Chronology* (Detroit: Info Coord, 1981). The journals *Notes* of the Music Library Association (founded in 1931) and *Fontes artis musicae* of the International Association of Music Libraries, Archives, and Documentation Centres (founded in 1951) are sources for current information about music libraries and publishing. *FAM* devotes one issue per year to the libraries of the host country of its annual conference. New technologies have enabled libraries to supply patrons with microfilms and digital images of sources from other collections. Sound and video recordings are widely used for teaching in academic libraries, for listening in public lending collections, and for research in archival collections. The creation of cooperative organizations such as the Online Computer Library Center (OCLC) and the Research Library Group (RLG) and the development of more international standards for descriptive cataloging and handling of electronic information have increased the use of automated, shared cataloging and of resource sharing and conservation efforts. H.E.S., rev. L.C.

Libre, librement [Fr.]. Freely.

Libretto [It.]. The text of an opera or oratorio; sometimes also the text of a *musical comedy, where the term "book" is more often used. Originally, and more specifically, the term refers to the small book containing the text, printed for sale to the audience. As a basic minimum, the libretto gives a list of the cast of characters and the words that are to be performed. In addition, it often gives stage directions and a description of scenes. The libretto may further give a summary of the plot or background information necessary for the comprehension of the plot (called an *argomento* in Italian libretti). Some Italian libretti also contain any parts of the text that the composer did not set; these lines are indicated by quotation marks and are called *versi virgolati.* Libretti from the 17th, 18th, and 19th centuries frequently indicate the time and place of the performance (that is, city, theater, season, and year), the names of the singers, and on occasion the orchestral players. Thus, they are an important source of information regarding the history of the performance of a work.

The relationship between the composer and the librettist varies considerably. In general, the most famous librettists are those who had a fruitful relationship with a great composer. Examples of such successful partnerships are Quinault and Lully, Calzabigi and Gluck, Da Ponte and Mozart, Boito and Verdi, Scribe and Meyerbeer, and Hofmannsthal and Strauss. An exception is Pietro Metastasio (1698–1782), whose texts were set by numerous composers, but whose reputation as a librettist was not established through the settings of any one composer. Starting in the 19th century, composers increasingly acted as their own librettists. The most famous artist to operate as both librettist and composer was Richard Wagner. But composers as diverse as Donizetti, Berlioz, Pfitzner, Menotti, and Schoenberg have provided their own texts, at least on occasion.

There is also much variation in the sources of libretti. A libretto may be wholly original or based on a theatrical work (play or ballet) or literary work (poem, short story, novel). Even when a libretto is based on a play, a certain amount of adaptation is generally necessary to fulfill a musical work's particular needs—for clarity, concision, and, often, for rhymed metrical texts. There are, however, examples of operas using the text of a play almost verbatim, such as Debussy's **Pelléas et Mélisande.* See also Opera.

Bibl.: Oscar Sonneck, *Catalogue of Opera Librettos Printed before 1800,* 2 vols. (Washington, D.C.: Government Printing Office, 1914; R: Johnson Repr, 1968). Edgar Istel, *The Art of Writing Opera Librettos,* trans. Th. Baker (New York: G Schirmer, 1922). Ulderico Rolandi, *Il libretto per musica attraverso i tempi* (Rome: Edizioni dell'Ateneo, 1951). Ralph Müller, *Das Opernlibretto im 19. Jahrhundert* (Winterthur: H Schellenberg, 1966). Leonardo Bragaglia, *Storia del libretto* (Rome: Trevi editore, 1970). Patrick J. Smith, *The Tenth Muse: A Historical Study of the Opera Libretto* (New York: A A Knopf, 1970; R: New York, Schirmer Bks, 1975). Cuthbert Girdlestone, *La tragédie en musique (1673–1750) considerée comme genre littéraire* (Geneva: Droz, 1972). C.G.

Licenza [It., licence]. (1) In the 17th and 18th centuries, a passage or *cadenza added to a composition by a performer. (2) In the 17th and 18th centuries, an epilogue to a stage work, honoring a dignitary on a festive occasion. It might include one or more recitatives, arias, and a closing chorus, sometimes integrated with the main work and sometimes added for the occasion, perhaps by a different composer. Mozart's K. 36 (33i) and K. 70 (61c) are so labeled. (3) *Con alcuna licenza* (pl. *con alcune licenze*), with licence or liberty, either with respect to tempo or (as in the final fugue of Beethoven's Piano Sonata op. 106) the normal requirements of form or composition.

Lichanos [Gr.]. See Greece I, 3 (1).

Lié [Fr.]. (1) Legato. (2) Of the *clavichord, fretted.

Liebes- [Ger.]. As a prefix in the names of instruments, a translation of the Italian *d'amore; Liebesgeige,* *viola d'amore; *Liebesoboe,* oboe d'amore [see Oboe]; *Liebesflöte, flûte d'amour* [see Flute].

Liebeslieder [Ger., Love Songs]. Two groups of 18 and 15 short songs, respectively, by Brahms, op. 52 (1868–69) and op. 65 (*Neue Liebeslieder,* 1874). Each is a waltz scored for vocal quartet and piano four-hands. Brahms arranged nine of the earlier set for voices and small orchestra in 1870 and later arranged all of them for piano four-hands alone, op. 52a (1874) and op. 65a (1877). The texts are taken from Georg Friedrich Daumer's *Polydora,* except for the last song in op. 65, the text of which is by Goethe.

Liebhaber [Ger.]. See *Kenner und Liebhaber.*

Lied [Ger., pl. *Lieder*]. A German poem, usually lyric and strophic; also a song having such a poem for its text; most commonly, a song for solo voice and piano accompaniment in German-speaking countries during the Classical and Romantic periods [see III below]; more broadly, any song setting of a German poetic text for voice(s) alone or for voice(s) with instrument(s).

In German, *Lied* as a musical term means any song (e.g., folk, work, children's, political), whereas in English, lied commonly refers to the German "art song" *(Kunstlied)* of the 19th and late 18th centuries, a poem of literary pretension set to music by a composer. A *Kunstlied* is a consciously artistic creation, distinguished from the functional nature of other songs. The lied *(Kunstlied)* grew out of a minor 18th-century genre—songs composed as a social pastime for amateurs—and became musically significant and part of the concert repertory of the professional singer in the 19th century. The rise of the lied owes much to the historical coincidence of factors such as the burgeoning of Romantic lyric poetry, the popularity of the piano and of music-making in the middle-class home, the commercial success of music publishing, and Franz Schubert (1797–1828), by whose songs the genre was established on a serious artistic level. The general term lied occurs throughout the recorded history of German music, from the earliest notated monophonic songs [see *Minnesinger, Meistersinger*].

I. *The polyphonic lied of the late Middle Ages and Renaissance.* The first polyphonic and rhythmically notated German songs are the two-voice lieder of the Monk of Salzburg (before 1400). The first major composer was Oswald von Wolkenstein (ca. 1377–1445). Of his 120 lieder, some of which are **contrafacta* of French *chansons and Italian **ballate,* about 36 are polyphonic (two to four voices). The text is in one voice only, bottom or top, and *bar form is common. A number of anonymous lied manuscripts (often referred to anachronistically by the modern term **Liederbuch*) date from the latter half of the 15th century. These probably civic collections preserve many monophonic as well as polyphonic lieder, along with French and Italian songs. A distinct German genre is the lied in which parts are composed around a preexistent monophonic melody in the top or a middle voice.

In the 16th century, the preexistent lied was most commonly in the tenor voice (whence the term *Tenorlied* for this genre). Beginning in the early 1500s, lieder were printed in partbooks. Major composers represented in them were Adam von Fulda, Heinrich Isaac, and Paul Hofhaimer. The typical early 16th-century lied was for four voices and increasingly used *imitation. Those of the next generation, including

Isaac's student Ludwig Senfl, exhibited a wide variety of styles and texts, pervasive imitation, and up to six voices; many are *quodlibets. The growing interest of the urban middle class in domestic music making is evidenced by large printed collections, such as Georg Forster's *Frische teutsche Liedlein* (5 vols., 1539–56, 382 songs by 50 composers), with tenors from sources such as *Hofweisen* (court songs) and folk songs. The major lied composer of the later 16th century was Lassus, who dispensed with preexistent melodies and incorporated the styles of the Italian *madrigal and French chanson, of which he also composed numerous examples. The homophonic and dancelike style of the Italian **balletto* is apparent in many of the lieder of Lassus's student Hans Leo Hassler and of other German composers of the period.

II. *The continuo lied of the Baroque period.* German 17th-century vocal music followed trends in Italy and England approximately one generation later. The multivoiced Renaissance lied gave way to the continuo lied, which typically featured one voice with basso continuo accompaniment. This standard disposition was occasionally altered by more singing voices or by a treble instrument or two playing obbligato lines or ritornellos. The texts of these mid-17th-century lieder, conforming with the principles of Martin Opitz's poetic reform, employed regular meter and line length, rhyme, and strophic form. The music was mapped onto this poetic structure, melody syllabically texted, musical phrases coextensive with verse lines, cadences coinciding with rhymes, the often dancelike musical meter coinciding with the poetic meter, and the successive strophes of the poem set to the same (or varied) music.

Seventeenth-century German lieder, both sacred and secular, were aimed at the cultivated urban middle class. Representative composers were Heinrich Albert, Andreas Hammerschmidt, Johann Rist, and Adam Krieger. In the later 17th and 18th centuries, the continuo lied was influenced by Italian cantata and opera. More freely structured nonstrophic texts, sacred and secular, were set to florid melodies, with words, phrases, and lines freely repeated; *da capo form became common. With increasing sophistication and difficulty, popularity decreased. Many published collections contained only cantatas and opera arias (or imitations). Composers of vocal works put their best efforts into cantatas, operas, and oratorios. Handel and Bach composed relatively few continuo lieder; these include Handel's nine German arias (1724–27, containing "Süsse Stille") and Bach's sacred songs in the second *Clavier-Büchlein* for Anna Magdalena Bach (1725, from which the most famous song, "Bist du bei mir," is probably by Gottfried Heinrich Stölzel). An eccentric and popular collection, Johann S. Scholze's (pseudonym Sperontes) *Singende Muse an der Pleisse* (Leipzig, 1736–45, enl. 1747), consisted of popular marches and dances to which Scholze added texts. In later editions, the keyboard accompaniment was fully written out. The popularity of "Sperontic" lieder probably reflects a gradual shift from elaborate Baroque vocal style to a simpler Classical ideal.

III. *The lied of the Classical and Romantic eras.* The so-called *Berlin schools of the later 18th century published songs in a *sangbar* (singable, tuneful) and *volkstümlich* (popular) style, enabling amateurs to learn and enjoy singing and, through it, poetry. Much verse aspired to folk poetry and song to folk song, and it was thought that verse and music belonged together. "The best lied [i.e., lyric poem] without its own melody is a loving heart without its mate," wrote the poet Gellert in the preface to C. P. E. Bach's settings of his odes (1758). Collections of such songs increased dramatically after 1750; e.g., composer-collector Christian Gottfried Krause's *Lieder der Deutschen mit Melodien* (1767–68).

Composers of the first Berlin School were Johann Adam Hiller, Johann Friedrich Agricola, Carl Heinrich Graun, C. P. E. Bach, Friedrich W. Marpurg, and Christian G. Neefe. Their songs tend toward simple melodies, unassuming keyboard accompaniments, plain harmonies, and straightforward strophic or modified strophic forms. The second generation of these composers, e.g., Johann Abraham Peter Schulz, Johann Friedrich Reichardt, and Carl Friedrich Zelter, turned to better poetry, especially that of Goethe, and composed with more varied and extended harmony and greater accompanimental and formal range.

Song composers in southern Germany of the late 18th century included Johann Rudolf Zumsteeg and Christian Friedrich Daniel Schubart. Zumsteeg composed numerous *ballades in long, *through-composed settings that influenced Schubert. In Austria, Haydn and Mozart composed a modest number of lieder in the *volkstümlich* tradition (e.g., Mozart's "Abendempfindung"). But the lied was not a significant compositional category for them or for Beethoven, though he is justifiably noted for his *song cycle *An die ferne Geliebte* (op. 98, 1815–16) and for a few individual songs (e.g., "Maigesang," text by Goethe).

Pre-Schubertian lieder tend (with many fine exceptions) to unremarkable melody, conventional harmony, and stock accompanimental figuration. This is partly the result of the prevailing view (subscribed to by Goethe) that the music should be subsidiary to the poetry.

Schubert composed over 600 lieder. He performed them at private social gatherings with amateur and professional singers. Few were sung in public concerts or published during his lifetime. Schubert set numerous poems by both eminent poets like Goethe and Schiller and minor writers. The superiority of Schubert's lieder lies in the beauty of his melodies, his inventive and pictorial piano writing, his modulations and characteristic use of parallel major and minor keys, and in the variety and genuineness of the lyrical moods expressed in the music. Among Schubert's most famous lieder are "Gretchen am Spinnrade," "Heidenröslein," and "Erlkönig" (Goethe), "Du bist die Ruh" (Rückert), "Die Forelle," "Der Tod und das Mädchen," the two song cycles *Die schöne Müllerin* and *Winterreise* (poetic cycles by Wilhelm Müller), and the late collection of songs, published posthumously as *Schwanengesang,* to texts of Heine, Rellstab, and Seidl (e.g., "Der Doppelgänger"). Ever since the lied became a customary part of the professional singer's concert repertory late in the 19th century, Schubert's songs have been a staple in that repertory.

With the artistic example of Schubert, the appearance of the second generation of German romantic poets (e.g., Rückert, Heine, Eichendorff), with whom Schubert only began to acquaint himself, and the commercial success of both composers and publishers, the lied came into its own as a serious genre. Prolific lied composers of the middle third of the 19th century were Mendelssohn, Schumann, Liszt, Carl Loewe, Robert Franz, and Peter Cornelius.

Loewe was a master of ballades, many still sung (e.g., "Erlkönig," "Edward"). Mendelssohn's lieder are relatively few and generally of modest quality, though some have remained popular (e.g., "Auf Flügeln des Gesanges," Heine).

Schumann, who composed about 250 songs, is noted for his literary taste (superior to Schubert's), the increased expressive role of the piano (often playing alone for long passages, as in postludes), and his portrayal of moods of romantic spontaneity, nostalgia, loneliness, and mystery. Among his most famous lieder are "Widmung" (Rückert) and "Du bist wie eine Blume" (Heine) from the collection *Myrthen* (op. 25), the ballade "Die beiden Grenadiere" (Heine), which quotes the tune of the "Marseillaise," and the song cycles *Dichterliebe* (Heine, op. 48), *Liederkreis* (Eichendorff, op. 39), and *Frauenliebe und Leben* (Chamisso, op. 42). He also set much children's poetry (*Lieder-album für die Jugend* op. 79), contributed significantly to duet, trio, and quartet lieder (e.g., *Spanische Liebeslieder* op. 138), and composed some ballads as recitations with piano accompaniment (*melodrama).

Liszt also composed lieder (including some recitations), but he probably did more for the genre with his piano transcriptions of songs by Beethoven, Schubert, Schumann, and himself (e.g., "Liebestraum"), among others. Wagner's few lieder deserve mention only because of his setting of Heine's "Die Grenadiere" (1840, in French trans.), an interesting foil to Schumann's, and the five *Wesendonck Lieder* (1857–62), several of which were forestudies for *Tristan und Isolde.* Cornelius composed over 100 songs, 50 of them to his own texts; best known are the *Weihnachtslieder* and *Brautlieder.*

Brahms composed about 250 lieder, drawing on major poets (e.g., Goethe, Heine, Tieck, Hölty, Mörike), but also frequently on lesser ones (e.g., Daumer, Groth). Brahms's expansive melodies, rich harmony and modulations, and dark registration and dense piano texture create affective moods. Criticism that the music engulfs the poem and that Brahms was indifferent to detailed coordination of music and text has not deprived his lieder of steady popularity (e.g., "Feldeinsamkeit," "Minnelied," "Die Mainacht," "Vergebliches Ständchen," "Immer leiser wird mein Schlummer"). The *Magelone* songs (op. 33, 1861–69, to poems from Tieck's romance *Die schöne Magelone*) and the *Vier ernste Gesänge* (1896, Biblical texts) are explicit cycles for solo voice. The two sets of *Leibeslieder* waltzes (op. 52, 1869; op. 65, 1875) are cycles for one to four voices and piano four-hands. Brahms also made arrangements of German folk songs (*Deutsche Volkslieder,* 1894).

IV. *The lied of the late 19th and early 20th centuries.* Wolf, Mahler, and Richard Strauss were the outstanding lied composers in the late 19th and early 20th centuries. In their songs, to varying degrees and in different ways, one hears the chromatic tonality of the "new music" of Liszt and Wagner. Their piano writing continues to grow in importance and independence; and seeking more varied instrumental color, they occasionally expanded the lied to an orchestral genre.

Wolf (ca. 250 lieder) was primarily a song composer. Choosing only the best poetry, he spent months reading and setting one poet, and then went to another. His oeuvre consists mainly of the Mörike songs (1889), Eichendorff songs (1889), Goethe songs (1890), *Spanisches Liederbuch* (1891), and *Italienisches Liederbuch* (1, 1892; 2, 1896), the latter two based on German translations of folk poetry. Wolf's meticulous text-setting comes close to dramatic declamation of the poetry; not accidentally he subtitled his lieder "Poems for Voice and Piano." Wolf often adopted the chromatic melody and harmony of Wagner for intense moods, like the Goethe "Mignon" songs, some of which are hyperbolic (e.g., "Kennst du das Land"). He was equally at home in a diatonic style for light, amorous, or comical poetry, as in some Eichendorff songs and in the Spanish and Italian songbooks. Wolf orchestrated a number of his songs.

Mahler, after some early songs with piano, composed *Lieder eines fahrenden Gesellen* (his own texts, 1883–85), a cycle with orchestral accompaniment (published also in the composer's piano version). Mahler's songs exhibit a wide range of feeling, from artful simplicity in the best tradition of romantic naïveté (e.g., songs from *Des Knaben Wunderhorn,* 1892–98) to profound sadness and world-weariness (e.g., *Kindertotenlieder,* Rückert, 1901–4). As in his symphonies, he achieved in his orchestral lieder a delicacy of scoring (with solos and transparent counterpoint) approaching chamber music. Mahler used a number of his songs as movements in his symphonies, and the crowning achievement of his song composition was the symphonic song cycle *Das Lied von der Erde* (Chinese poems in German trans. for tenor and alto/baritone soloists and orchestra, 1908–9).

Richard Strauss composed over 200 songs, many for his singer-wife and himself to perform, the bulk of them preceding his major operas. Drawn to many poets including Goethe, Rückert, and Lenau, he frequently set the poems of Richard Dehmel. He wrote most of his lieder for voice and piano, but orchestrated some (and approved orchestrations by others). Seldom displaying the dense texture of his orchestral tone poems but often reveling in the high soprano tessitura of his operas, Strauss's lieder feature wide-ranging vocal melodies, a relatively conservative chromaticism with frequent modulation, and frankly accompanimental piano writing. Most of his songs can be categorized as excited love songs (e.g., "Zueignung," "Ständchen"), sentimental songs of old age and death ("Allerseelen," "Befreit," "Im Abendrot"), or slow, pensive pieces ("Ruhe mein Seele," "Morgen"). There are no explicit cycles, but many short groups of songs are settings of a single poet. The seldom heard but psychologically telling Ophelia songs (after Shakespeare, op. 67/I, 1918) work as a cycle, and the celebrated *Four Last Songs* (1948, with orch.) are usually performed as a whole. Strauss also composed two melodrama recitations.

The post-Romantic lied has decreased in accessibility for the amateur musician and in popularity. The increasing subjectivity of modern poetry has contributed to the cultivation of correspondingly subjective musical idioms (e.g., atonality), and 20th-century composers have often written with exacting performance demands. Hence, most 20th-century lieder lie outside the aesthetic ideals of the popular and singable *Kunstlied* of the late 18th century.

Lieder in post-Wagnerian tonal styles are prominent among the early compositions of Schoenberg, Webern, and Berg. Schoenberg wrote over 100 lieder (including some cabaret songs), but he is best known for two cycles: *Das Buch der hängenden Gärten* op. 15 (1908–9), in which he broke completely free of tonality for the first time and composed in an athematic, free contrapuntal style to set the symbolist poems of Stefan George; and *Pierrot lunaire* op. 21 (1912), a unique creation for singer and chamber ensemble, in which dense motivic polyphony, kaleidoscopic instrumental colors, and **Sprechstimme* (an outgrowth of melodrama) ideally suit the surrealistic poetry of Albert Giraud. Schoenberg composed few songs after he took up his method of composing with twelve tones in the 1920s.

More than a third of Webern's works are lieder (with piano, chamber ensemble, or small orchestra). Like Schoenberg, he composed most of his songs before he adopted twelve-tone serialism. Already in his opp. 3 and 4 songs (1908–9, Stefan George) he had evolved his characteristic brevity, imperceptible meter, and independence of voice and piano in pitch and meter. By the op. 8 songs (Rilke, 1910), he had begun to develop a fragile lyricism of wide leaps, which requires a singer of great artistry to ensure a musical performance.

Berg's *Seven Early Songs* (1905–8, orchestrated 1928) exhibit a late Romantic style, but in his lieder op. 2 he moved from tonality to atonality. Berg set Theodor Storm's "Schliesse mir die Augen beide" once in a post-Romantic style (1907) and later with his adaptation of the twelve-tone method (1925). His Altenberg songs (op. 4, 1912, with large orchestra) are worthy successors in a modern idiom to Mahler's songs.

Other 20th-century composers of lieder include Kurt Weill, Ernst Krenek, Hanns Eisler, Hugo Distler, Paul Dessau, Wolfgang Fortner, and Hans Werner Henze, but only the lieder of Paul Hindemith have achieved international recognition. These approximately 100 songs, in Hindemith's idiom of nonfunctional tonality and controlled dissonance, include the cycle *Das Marienleben* (1922–23; radically rev. 1936–48; a few orchestrated 1938–59), settings of 15 poems by Rilke on the life of Mary (mother of Christ), using neo-Baroque compositional procedures. *Die Serenaden* (op. 35, 1925), subtitled a "little cantata," is in actuality a cycle of six songs (by as many poets), with three instrumental interludes, for soprano, oboe, viola, and cello.

Bibl.: Max Friedländer, *Das deutsche Lied im 18. Jahrhundert: Quellen und Studien,* 2 vols. (Stuttgart: Cotta, 1902; R: Hildesheim: Olms, 1962). Ernst Bücken, *Das deutsche Lied: Probleme und Gestalten* (Hamburg: Hanseatische Verlagsanstalt, 1939). James Husst Hall, *The Art Song* (Norman: U of Okla Pr, 1953). Helmut Osthoff, *Das deutsche Chorlied, Mw* 10 (Cologne: A Volk, 1955; trans. Eng., 1955). Hans Joachim Moser, *Das deutsche Sololied und die Ballade, Mw* 14 (Cologne: A Volk, 1957; trans. Eng., 1958). Walter Salmen, "European Song (1300–1530)," *NOHM* 3, pp. 349–80. Denis Stevens, ed., *A History of Song* (London: Hutchinson, 1960). Philip Miller, comp. and trans., *The Ring of Words: An Anthology of Song Texts* (Garden City, N.Y.: Doubleday, 1963). Richard H. Thomas, *Poetry and Song in the German Baroque* (Oxford: Clarendon Pr, 1963). Siegbert S. Prawer, ed. and trans., *The Penguin Book of Lieder* (Baltimore: Penguin, 1964). Heinrich Schwab, *Sangbarkeit, Popularität und Kunstlied* (Regensburg: G Bosse, 1965). Dietrich Fischer-Dieskau, *Texte deutscher Lieder: Ein Handbuch* (Munich: Deutscher Taschenbuch-Verlag, 1968); trans Eng., *The Fischer-Dieskau Book of Lieder* (New York: Knopf, 1977; R: New York: Limelight Eds, 1984). Hans Joachim Moser, *Das deutsche Lied seit Mozart,* 2nd ed. (Tutzing: Schneider, 1968). R. A. Barr, *Carl Friedrich Selter: A Study of the Lied in Berlin during the Late Eighteenth and Early Nineteenth Centuries* (Ph.D. diss., Univ. of Wisconsin, 1968). Donald Ivey, *Song: Anatomy, Imagery, and Styles* (New York: Free Press, 1970). Elaine Brody and Robert Fowkes, *The German Lied and Its Poetry* (New York: NYU Pr, 1971). Jack Stein, *Poem and Music in the German Lied from Gluck to Wolf* (Cambridge, Mass.: Harvard U Pr, 1971). Walter Wiora, *Das deutsche Lied: Zur Geschichte und Ästhetik einer musikalischen Gattung* (Wolfenbüttel: Möseler, 1971). Thomas R. Nardone, *Classical Vocal Music in Print* (Philadelphia: Musicdata, 1976). Norbert Böker-Heil, Harald Heckmann, and Ilse Kindermann, eds., *Das Tenorlied: Mehrstimmige Lieder aus deutschen Quellen 1450–1580, Catalogus musicus* 9–11 (Kassel, 1979–86). Lois Phillips, ed., *Lieder Line by Line, and Word for Word* (London: Duckworth, 1979). Anneliese Landau, *The Lied: The Unfolding of Its Style* (Washington, D.C.: U Pr of Am, 1980). Walther Dürr, *Das deutsche Sololied im 19. Jahrhundert: Untersuchungne zu Aprache und Musik* (Wilhelmshaven, 1984). Lawrence Kramer, *Music and*

Poetry: The Nineteenth Century and After (Berkeley, 1984). Kenneth Whitton, *Lieder: An Introduction to German Song* (London, 1984). J. W. Smeed, *German Song and Its Poetry, 1740–1900* (New York, 1987). *Studien zum deutschen weltlichen Kunstlied des 17. Und 18. Jahrhunderts* (Wölfenbüttel, 1990). Lorraine Correll, *The Nineteenth-Century German Lied* (Portland, Ore., 1993). Rufus Hallmark, ed., *German Lieder in the Nineteenth Century* (New York, 1996). Edward F. Kravitt, *The Lied: Mirror of Late Romanticism* (New Haven, 1996). Deborah Stein and Robert Spillman, *Poetry into Song: Performance and Analysis of Lieder* (New York, 1996). R.H.

Liederbuch [Ger.]. Song book. Normally a reference to 15th-century manuscript collections of German monophonic and polyphonic songs [see Lied].

Lieder eines fahrenden Gesellen [Ger., Songs of a Wayfarer]. Four songs for low voice and orchestra or piano by Mahler (composed ca. 1883–85; revised ca. 1891–96; orchestrated in the early 1890s), setting his own poems. The second song was used as the basis of the first movement of his First Symphony, and the last song is quoted in the slow movement of this symphony.

Liederkreis, Liederzyklus [Ger.]. *Song cycle.

Lieder ohne Worte [Ger., Songs without Words]. Forty-eight piano pieces in songlike texture and style by Mendelssohn, published in eight books of six each, opp. 19 (1830, originally published in London as *Melodies for the Pianoforte*), 30 (1835), 38 (1837), 53 (1841), 62 (1844), 67 (1845), 85 (1850), 102 (ca. 1846). A few isolated pieces not published during his lifetime were also titled *Lied ohne Worte.* The titles given to individual pieces in many editions are not Mendelssohn's except for *Venezianisches Gondellied* (Venetian Gondola-Song, nos. 6, 12, 29), *Duetto* (no. 18), and *Volkslied* (Folk Song, no. 23).

Liederspiel [Ger.]. A 19th-century German dramatic entertainment in which songs, newly composed upon preexisting poems, are inserted in the drama. The originator and principal proponent of the genre was Johann Friedrich Reichardt (1752–1814). The *Liederspiel* was meant to appeal to a popular, bourgeois audience. The songs are folklike with simple accompaniments; ensembles, choruses, and more complex musical structures are avoided. By the third decade of the 19th century, the term *Liederspiel* was used more freely, as by Mendelssohn to refer to his comic opera *Die Heimkehr der Fremde* (1829) or by Schumann to refer to his song cycle for quartet and piano, *Spanisches Liederspiel* op. 74 (1849).

Liedertafel [Ger.]. Originally, a group of men gathered around a table [Ger. *Tafel*] for singing and refreshment; later an occasion for such singing and refreshment to which male and female guests might be invited as auditors. The first singing group of this kind was organized in Berlin in 1808 by Carl Friedrich Zelter (1758–1832). Numerous other such groups were founded in the 19th century.

Liedform [Ger.]. *Song form.

Lied von der Erde, Das [Ger., The Song of the Earth]. A cycle of six songs by Mahler (who called it a symphony) for alto (or baritone), tenor, and orchestra, composed in 1908–9 and first performed in 1911, after Mahler's death. The texts are German translations by Hans Bethge of 8th- and 9th-century Chinese poems.

Lieto, lietamente [It.]. Joyful, merry; *lieto fine,* happy ending, as of an opera.

Lieve, lievemente [It.]. Light, easy.

Life for the Tsar, A [Russ. *Zhizn' za tsarya*]. Opera in four acts and an epilogue by Mikhail Ivanovich Glinka (libretto by Georgy Rosen), produced in Moscow in 1836. It is the first historically important Russian opera. In the Russia, Glinka's original title, *Ivan Susanin,* is now often used. Setting: Russia and Poland in the winter of 1612.

Ligatura [It.]. See *Toccata di durezze e ligature.*

Ligature. (1) Any of the notational symbols in use from the late 12th through the 16th centuries that combine two or more notes in a single symbol. They emerged as rectilinear forms (thus, sometimes called square notation) of the neumes with which liturgical chant was notated [for a comparison of the rectilinear shapes with various types of neumes, see Neume]. Around 1200, they were taken up for the notation of the polyphony of the repertory of *Notre Dame. Here they were combined in patterns to indicate the rhythms of the rhythmic modes [see Modes, rhythmic]. The rhythmic meaning of any ligature in this notation is not absolute, but depends instead on the context created by the patterns of ligatures. Since in general a ligature could be sung to only a single syllable, music with text (such as the *motet and *conductus) relied on single notes rather than on ligatures. It was in the late 13th century that theorists systematized the rhythmic meanings of individual symbols, both single notes and ligatures. The formulation of the principles of the notation of this period, which remained the basis of *mensural notation for three centuries or more, is attributed principally to Franco of Cologne, and this notation is thus termed Franconian. The interpretation of ligatures in Franconian and later notation in terms of single note-values is described below. For an account of the meaning of these note-values in terms of modern notation, see Mensural notation, Notation.

Each square represents a note. An oblique stroke represents two notes, one at the line or space at which the stroke begins and another where the stroke ends; nothing unusual is implied by this symbol about the nature of the passage from one note to the other. If two notes are placed directly above and below one another, the lower is read before the upper. Ligatures are loosely classified according to the number of notes they include as binary *(ligatura binaria),* ternary *(ternaria),* quaternary *(quaternaria),* etc.

Rhythmic values are determined with reference to the standard shapes for two-note ascending and descending ligatures, illustrated in the first line of the accompanying table. These standard shapes have the value breve *(B)* followed by long *(L).* They are described by theorists such as Franco as having both propriety (*cum proprietate,* a reference to the shape of the note that begins the ligature) and perfection (*cum perfectione,* a reference to the shape of the note that ends the ligature). If the shape of the beginning note is modified (in descending ligatures by the removal of the tail, in ascending ligatures by the addition of a tail, as in line 2 of the table), the ligature is without propriety, and thus the value of the beginning note becomes *L.* If the shape of the note ending the ligature is altered (in descending ligatures by the use of an oblique shape, in ascending ligatures by placing the ending note to the right of the note preceding instead of directly above it, as in line 3 of the table), the ligature is without perfection, and thus the value of the ending note becomes *B.* (If in an ascending ligature the ending note is both turned to the right *and* supplied with a tail, its value is *L.*) Any ligature (whether ascending or descending) that begins with an upward tail, as in line 5 of the table, is a ligature of opposite propriety *(cum opposita proprietate),* and its first two notes are both semibreves *(S).* If a ligature consists of more than two notes, the values of the beginning and ending notes are determined according to these same principles, the question of ascent or descent being determined with reference to the immediately preceding or following note. Each intervening note has the value *B,* as illustrated in lines 6 and 7 of the table.

	Descending	Ascending	Value
1			*BL*
2			*LL*
3			*BB*
4			*LB*
5	or	or	*SS*
6			*SSBB*
7			*BBBB*

(2) In modern notation, a *slur connecting two or more notes, indicating that all are to be sung to a single syllable.

(3) In instruments of the clarinet family, the adjustable metal band that attaches the reed to the mouthpiece.

Limma [Gr.]. Remnant; in Pythagorean writings, the *diesis or minor semitone [see Pythagorean scale].

Limoges, school of. See St. Martial de Limoges, repertory of.

Lindy. A social dance of the U.S., originating in the late 1920s in New York City and at first associated with the Savoy Ballroom in Harlem. It was danced to music (later, principally *swing) in fast duple meter and was characterized especially by "breakaways," in which the partners in a couple separated and improvised steps individually. It incorporated movements in which partners swung one another around, and it sometimes took on an acrobatic character. Known from the 1930s also as jitterbug, it was widely danced until well into the 1950s and the advent of rock and roll.

Linear analysis. See Schenker analysis.

Linear counterpoint. In the writings of Ernst Kurth (*Grundlagen des linearen Kontrapunkts,* Berne: M Drechsel, 1917) and since, a phrase that stresses the identity and character of individual lines making up the contrapuntal fabric, thus tending to subordinate the harmonic or vertical dimension.

Lingual pipe [fr. Lat. *lingua,* tongue]. An organ reed pipe.

Linguaphone. *Lamellaphone, plucked *idiophone.

Lining (out). In Protestant Psalm and hymn singing in England and America beginning in the 17th century, the practice of leading the congregation by having each line read or sung (sometimes both read and sung) first by the minister or some other person. This practice remains alive in conservative churches in the U.S., though not as the aid for the nonliterate that it was first intended to be.

Linke Hand [Ger.]. Left hand.

Linz Symphony. Popular name for Mozart's Symphony no. 36 in C major K. 425, composed in Linz, Austria, in 1783 and first performed there by the private orchestra of Count Johann Joseph Thun.

Lip. See Embouchure.

Lippenpfeife [Ger.]. *Labial pipe.

Liquescent neume. See Neume.

Lira, lirica, lyra [Gr.]. A bowed stringed instrument of Greece and the Balkans with three strings, a pear-shaped body, and a broad neck without fingerboard, the strings being stopped with the pressure of the fingers or fingernails alone. It is usually held vertically, resting on the player's knee. The *lira* is a favorite instrument for accompanying the dance in Crete and among Pontic Greeks, who play a slender model resembling the Turkish **kemençe.* See also *Gadulka, Rābāb, Lyra.*

Lira da braccio [It.]. A bowed stringed instrument of the late 15th and 16th centuries, shaped like a violin, with a flat, leaf-shaped pegdisk with front pegs, five strings over the fingerboard (tuned g g′ d′ a′ e″), and two drone strings to the left (tuned d d′). It was held on the shoulder with the pegdisk down and was intended to play chords as well as melody. See ill. under Violin.

Lira da gamba [It.]. A bass **lira da braccio* developed in the 16th century, usually fretted, with 9–14 melody strings and 2 drones; also called a *lirone.* It was held between the legs.

Lira organizzata [It.]. See Hurdy-gurdy.

Lirone [It.]. **Lira da gamba.*

Liscio [It.]. Smooth, even.

L'istesso tempo [It.]. See *Istesso tempo, L'.*

Litany [Lat. *litania*]. A prayer consisting of a series of invocations and petitions, each sung or recited by a deacon or other person and responded to by the congregation with a phrase such as *"Kyrie eleison" (Lord, have mercy) or "Ora pro nobis" (Pray for us); also a procession at which such a prayer is sung or recited. When sung, all invocations in the series employ the same syllabic melody. Litanies originated in the East and retain a prominent place in the Byzantine rite. A litany invoking a series of saints (thus, the Litany of the Saints) was instituted in Rome in the 5th century on what later became St. Mark's day (25 April), and this became known in Carolingian times as the *litaniae majores* (Greater or Major Litanies). In modern liturgical books it begins with the Kyrie, continues with invocations of the Trinity, of the Virgin Mary, and of the saints (the list of which varied considerably in the Middle Ages and was fixed only in the 16th century) and a series of supplications, and concludes with *Agnus Dei. Of Gallican origin are the *litaniae minores* (Lesser or Minor Litanies), originally associated with the Rogation Days immediately preceding the feast of the Ascension. Until the reforms following the Second *Vatican Council (1962–65), Greater and Lesser Litanies were sung on the Rogation Days (*LU,* p. 835) and the Greater Litanies on St. Mark's day (*LU,* p. 1431). The Litany of the Saints also forms part of the Paschal Vigil service (*LU,* p. 776v). The Litany of Loreto *(Litania lauretana)* invokes the Virgin Mary and was known by the 12th century (*LU,* p. 1857). The Anglican Litany or General Supplication shares with the Roman litanies the general feature of a series of parallel invocations, each followed by a response.

Litanies were set polyphonically beginning in the 16th century (e.g., by Festa, Lassus, and Palestrina), and the genre continued to be cultivated through the 18th century (e.g., by Michael Haydn, Fux, Caldara, and Mozart).

Lithophone. A stone or set of stones that produces musical sounds on being struck. The stones are either laid on a frame or hung from cords. They are tuned by carving. See, e.g., *Ch'ing.*

Little Hours. See Office, Divine.

Little Russian Symphony. See *Ukrainian* Symphony.

Liturgical books. Books used for the performance of the liturgies or services of the Christian rites. The number and makeup of such books not only vary among rites, but within rites have changed considerably with time.

I. *Roman Catholic rite.* For the structure of the liturgy and the liturgical year, which are naturally reflected in the organization of liturgical books, see Liturgy. The liturgy antedating the Second *Vatican Council (1962–65) was contained in seven fundamental books: the missal *(missale),* containing all of the texts for the Mass, including those of the chants, but without music; the *gradual *(graduale),* containing the chants for the Mass; the breviary *(breviarium),* with the texts for the Office; the *antiphoner *(antiphonale, antiphonarium),* with the chants for the Office (except for Matins, celebrated for the most part only in monastic communities); the martyrology *(martirologium),* with the lives of the saints, read as part of the Office, presented in the order of the liturgical calendar; the pontifical *(pontificale),* containing the ceremonies performed by a bishop, such as confirmation, ordination, and the consecration of a church; and the *rituale,* containing ceremonies performed by a priest in the administration of sacraments such as baptism, marriage, and extreme unction. Other modern books excerpted or derived from one or more of these include the *Kyriale,* with the chants of the Ordinary; the *vesperale,* containing Vespers and sometimes Compline; and the *Liber usualis,* a modern creation combining elements of the missal, gradual, breviary, and antiphoner and thus providing both text and music for both Mass and Office (including Matins in a few cases) for the most important feasts (though with important omissions, such as the weekdays in Lent and the Ember Days). The *Liber responsorialis* includes chants, particularly responsories, for Matins and the *Processionale monasticum* chants for processions before Mass, both for use in monastic communities.

Within the principal books for Mass and Office, and in the *Liber usualis,* where Mass and Office are intermixed, Ordinary and Proper chants are in separate sections, and within the Proper chants, the Proper of the Time or *Temporale* precedes the Proper of the Saints or *Sanctorale,* each series being presented in the order of the liturgical year beginning with Advent. The Common of Saints is in still another section.

In the Middle Ages, there were many more kinds of liturgical books, most arranged according to the liturgical calendar. Among the earliest is the sacramentary *(sacramentarium),* containing the *canon and the proper *collects and *prefaces for the Mass. The earliest surviving book of this general type, known inappropriately as the Leonine sacramentary, dates from the first quarter of the 7th century. Scripture readings or lessons for the Mass were contained in the lectionary (*lectionarium* or *liber comicus*), readings from the Gospels sometimes being in a separate evangeliary *(evangeliarium).* The ordinal (*Liber ordinum* or *ordinarius*) contained sometimes detailed descriptions of individual services in specific localities and is an antecedent of the pontifical of the 10th century and after. The earliest ordinals (included among the *Ordines romani*) are Frankish documents whose direct models date from the 8th century, though they often testify to earlier Roman practice. The rise of the *trope brought with it the *troper *(troparium),* and with the *sequence came the sequentiary *(sequentiarium).* There were also separate hymnals, liturgical psalters, homiliaries (containing homilies or sermons), passionals (containing lives of the saints from which lessons were drawn), and benedictionals (containing blessings said by a bishop at Mass). In the *tonary *(tonale, tonarium, tonarius),* often an adjunct to a gradual or an antiphoner, chants are classified by mode.

The four principal books for Mass and Office themselves changed with time. The earliest graduals, from the 8th or 9th century, evidently antedate the regular use of musical notation and thus contain only texts. The term *antiphonale missarum* (antiphoner of the Mass) is sometimes used as a synonym for these and other early graduals. A related collection was the *cantatorium,* which contained only the chants associated with the readings at Mass—the gradual, the alleluia, and the tract. By the 10th century, there existed plenary missals that contained all of the text and music necessary for the Mass. Similarly, by the 11th century, there were noted breviaries that brought together in one book everything necessary for the Office.

For an outline of the history of the chant, including various editions of chant books, see Gregorian chant.

II. *Anglican rite. The Book of Common Prayer,* first issued under Edward VI in 1549 (revised significantly in 1552 and 1662) is the basic Anglican liturgical text and contains the daily Offices of Morning and Evening Prayer, the order of Communion, other rites (Baptism, Matrimony, Burial), the Psalter, and the ordinal. *The Alternative Service Book 1980,* with a new liturgical psalter, sets forth sevices authorized for use in conjunction with the *Book of Common Prayer;* it is designed to supplement, not to supersede, the 1662 revision. Although the Anglican Church has never had an official hymnal, *Hymns: Ancient and Modern* (1861, rev. 1950), *The English Hymnal* (1906, rev. 1933), *Songs of Praise* (1925, rev. 1931), and *The Anglican Hymn Book* (1965) have been most widely used.

The Protestant Episcopal Church in the U.S. issued its own *Book of Common Prayer* in 1789 (revised 1892, 1928, and 1979, the latter with a new translation of the prose Psalter replacing that of Miles Coverdale, 1539). *The Hymnal 1982* has been authorized for use by the American Episcopal communions.

Other churches of the Anglican communion throughout the world have adapted the English prayer book for their use and produced alternative orders of worship and various hymnals.

Bibl.: Cheslyn Jones et al., *The Study of Liturgy* (New York: Oxford U Pr, 1978). Marion J. Hatchett, *Commentary on the American Prayer Book* (New York: Seabury, 1981; R: San Francisco: Harper, 1995). Geoffrey J. Cuming, *A History of Anglican Liturgy,* 2nd ed. (London: Macmillan, 1982). Marion J. Hatchett, *The Making of the First American Book of Common Prayer, 1776–1789* (New York: Seabury, 1982). Paul Victor Marshall, *Prayer Book Parallels: The Public Services of the Church Arranged for Comparative Study* (New York: Church Hymnal Corp, 1989–90). Raymond Glover, ed., *The Hymnal 1982 Companion* (New York: Church Hymnal Corp, 1990–94). John Harper, *The Forms and Orders of Western Liturgy from the Tenth to the Eighteenth Century: A Historical Instruction and Guide for Students and Musicians* (New York: Oxford U Pr, 1991). Paul Victor Marshall and Lesley A. Northup, *Leaps and Boundaries: The Prayer Book in the 21st Century* (Harrisburg, Pa.: Morehouse Pub, 1997).

(1) D.M.R., (2) R.F.F., rev. R.A.L.

Liturgical drama. Medieval church drama created for or influenced by the liturgy. This vast repertory of works from the 10th to the 15th century is distinguished from spoken dramas such as the mystery plays, in which music was used occasionally, although often in ways vital to the action. Liturgical dramas were sung primarily in Latin, but from the 12th century with ever more frequent forays into the vernacular. The dramas borrow large quantities of their texts and music from the liturgy, and depend upon formal liturgical structures and principles as well, especially those of readings followed by sung responses, antiphons and their tropes as prophetic interpretations of intoned psalm verses or sacramental action, the angelic exegesis of the *sequences, and the processions, with their dramatic action and musical commentary. Most surviving liturgical dramas were written for Easter or Christmas and in the early period are most often contained in tropers or processionals [see Liturgical Books]. The "playbook" of the 12th century forward is a fluid genre, and the far-flung surviving examples suggest that many European cathedral towns and monasteries possessed some form of playbook, but that when religious reform occurred such collections were among the first books to be discarded. The famous 12th century playbook named for the Benedictine monastery of Fleury (Orleans, B.M. MS 201) appears, perhaps deceptively, to be atypical in its size and diversity. Although Cluny's dramatic and luxurious liturgical practices are often cited as the appropriate backdrop to the tropes and liturgical dramas, it does not seem that these forms were featured at Cluny itself or in the majority of its daughter houses. There is a difference between the dramatic in liturgy and liturgical dramas, although the line is blurred.

Almost every medieval church had at least a small-scale dramatic commemoration, whether or not an actual play, centering upon the Easter and Christmas mysteries. The corpus of texts for Easter plays edited by Young has been expanded, most notably by Lipphardt's far more inclusive 6-volume edition. Appropriately enough, the Easter dramas have been studied more than any other, and are commonly categorized (following Young) into three types: Type I consists of a visit to the tomb by the Marys and the encounter with one or more angels (Visitatio Sepulchri or "visit to the sepulcher"); the first known example of this type is found in the *Regularis Concordia* from Winchester (ca. 970), and consists of the famous "Quem quaeritis" dialogue without music, although rubrics say it was sung. Type II consists of the scene at the tomb, with the addition of the Apostles Peter and John racing to the tomb to see if the report is true. Type III also contains a scene including the encounter between Mary Magdalene and the risen Christ. Scholars have rejected the idea of a simple evolutionary line from the simplest stage to the most complex. The greatest controversy has been over the origins of the drama, with most scholars now agreeing that the liturgy was inherently dramatic in several of its aspects, and that actual impersonation developed in many ways; the varied liturgical locations and uses of the early dramas based on the "Quem quaeritis" trope seem to depend upon regional traditions [see also Trope].

Much work has been done recently on the large-scale plays of the 12th and 13th centuries. It is clear that frequently performed works such as the Beauvais Daniel (now believed to have been written for the Feast of Fools, January 1) or the Fleury Herod and Innocents plays were sustained by an enormous repertory of popular music for the Christmas season, the time in which canons came back to the cathedrals they served and were lavishly entertained by the youth who served as choral vicars. The sung morality play *Ordo Virtutum* composed and written by the nun Hildegard of Bingen is one of several masterpieces created in the twelfth century. This particular work is related both musically and thematically to Hildegard's songs and may well have served as a sung commentary upon the Eucharist as celebrated within her community. The brilliant *Ordo representationis Ade* (Play of Adam), which contains spoken scenes punctuated by great responsories from the Lenten liturgy and concludes with a prophets play, offers detailed rubrics suggesting the importance of setting and costume. In the 13th century dramatic traditions were well enough established to make sophisticated parodies possible, as can be seen in the plays found within what is now known as the *Carmina Burana,* the precise origin of which remains a matter of dispute. The disturbing anti-Jewish polemic that often permeated Christian dramatic art in the later Middle Ages (and which was answered back in kind in various Jewish exegetical treatises) poses the most serious problem for modern interpreters, many of whom alter or omit the most offensive texts. Plays in celebration of popular saints, like the mystery plays, often use music borrowed from the liturgy; there is great potential for discovering more of these and other kinds of medieval dramas by better understanding what actually constitutes a play text. Later plays in the vernacular were often a part of civic ceremonies, and have recently been studied by historians for the richly textured pictures they offer of society at the dawn of the Early Modern Period.

Bibl.: Karl Young, *The Drama of the Medieval Church,* 2 vols. (Oxford: Oxford U Pr, 1933). Oscar B. Hardison, *Christian Rite and Christian Drama in the Middle Ages* (Baltimore: Johns Hopkins U Pr, 1965). Carl Stratman, *Bibliography of Medieval Drama,* 2 vols., 2nd ed. (New York: Unger, 1972). C. Clifford Flanigan, "The Liturgical Drama and Its Tradition: A Review of Scholarship 1965–1975," *Research Opportunities in Renaissance Drama* 18 (1975): 81–102, 19 (1976): 109–36. Walther Lipphardt, *Lateinische Osterfeiern und Osterspiele,* 6 vols. (Berlin: de Gruyter, 1975–81). William Smoldon, *The Music of the Medieval Church Dramas* (Oxford: Oxford U Pr, 1980). Susan Rankin, "Liturgical Drama" in *The New Oxford History of Music,* vol. 2: *Early Middle Ages to 1300,* ed. Richard L. Crocker and David Hiley (Oxford: Oxford U Pr, 1990), 310–56. Regula Meyer Evitt, "Anti-Judaism and the Medieval Prophet Plays: Exegetical Contexts for the 'Ordines prophetarum'" (PhD diss., U Virginia, 1992). Margot Fassler, "The Feast of Fools and *Danielis ludus:* Popular Tradition in a Medieval Cathedral Play," in *Plainsong in the Age of Polyphony,* ed. Thomas F. Kelly (Cambridge: Cambridge U Pr, 1992). Peter Dronke, *Nine Medieval Latin Plays* (Cambridge [England]; New York: Cambridge U Pr, 1994). Susan Boynton, "Performative Exegesis in the *Fleury Interfectio Puerorum,*" *Viator: Medieval and Renaissance Studies* 29 (1998): 39–64. Dunbar H. Ogden, *The Staging of Drama in the Medieval Church* (Newark: U of Delaware Pr, 2002). Carol Symes, "The Appearance of Early Vernacular Plays: Forms, Functions, and the Future of Medieval Theater," *Speculum* 77 (2002): 778–831. M.E.F.

Liturgy. The formally constituted services of the various rites of the Christian church; also the particular formal arrangement of any such service. In the West, the term is usually applied to all such services. In the Eastern Orthodox Church, the Divine Liturgy is specifically the analogue of the Mass of the Western rites. The following discussion outlines the liturgy and liturgical calendar of the Roman Catholic Church preceding the reforms of the Second *Vatican Council (1962–65). Some of the fundamental features of this outline are shared among the rites of both East and West, however, and some remained a part of the worship of non-Roman churches after the Reformation. See also Ambrosian chant, Byzantine chant, Gallican chant, Gregorian chant, Mozarabic chant, Anglican church music, Lutheran church music.

The principal services of the Roman Catholic Church are the *Mass or Holy Eucharist, at the heart of which is the reenactment of the Last Supper, and the Divine *Office, which consists of a series of services performed throughout the day. Although the general outline of these services, including the types of readings, prayers, and chants of which they consist, is largely constant, the specific content of services changes in the course of the liturgical year.

Two cycles of observances or feasts make up the calendar of the liturgical year. The first of these, called the Proper of the Time, the *Temporale,* or the feasts of the Lord, commemorates primarily events in the life of Christ and thus includes Christmas (the Nativity, 25 December) and Easter (the Resurrection, celebrated on the Sunday following the first full moon after the vernal equinox and thus between 22 March and 25 April), the seasons that precede each of these (Advent, with which the liturgical year starts on the Sunday closest to St. Andrew, 30 November; Lent, the 40 days preceding Easter, beginning with Ash Wednesday; the three Sundays preceding Lent, known as Septuagesima, Sexagesima, and Quinquagesima, respectively), Ascension (the sixth Thursday or fortieth day after Easter), and Epiphany (6 January, celebrating the adoration of Christ by the Magi); but also Pentecost (or Whitsunday, the seventh Sunday or fiftieth day after Easter, celebrating the descent of the Holy Ghost on the Apostles), the period between Easter and Pentecost (called Paschaltide), the four groups of three Ember Days (Wednesday, Friday, and Saturday after St. Lucy on 13 December, beginning with Ash Wednesday, following Pentecost, and following the feast of the Exaltation of the Holy Cross on 14 September), all Sundays (the long series of 23 or more Sundays following Pentecost and preceding the beginning of the new liturgical year on the first Sunday of Advent being identified by number in the series, up until 1969 when the practice was changed to incorporate these and the Sundays following Epiphany into a single series of Sundays of the Year), and various other days immediately preceding or following major feasts (for example, the vigil or day immediately preceding and days within the octave, i.e., within the week following). Feasts such as Easter that do not occur on the same date every year are said to be "movable" feasts. The structure even of this cycle, which includes the most ancient and solemn occasions, has changed with time, and it includes some feasts of relatively late institution such as Trinity Sunday (the first Sunday after Pentecost, not officially established as a separate feast until the 14th century) and Corpus Christi (Thursday after Trinity Sunday, instituted in the 13th century).

The second cycle of feasts, which overlaps the first, is the Proper of the Saints or the *Sanctorale.* These feasts occur on fixed dates and commemorate individual saints and, in some cases, particular events in their lives, e.g., the Nativity of John the Baptist (24 June) and the Assumption of the Blessed Virgin Mary (15 August). Some of these feasts, too, are of considerable antiquity and importance, though their number grew through the Middle Ages and after and varied somewhat from place to place as did the solemnity with which individual feasts were celebrated. These changes in the liturgical calendar provide an important tool for the study of the chronology and dissemination of the chant repertory. Feasts of both cycles have been ranked so as to make clear which feast is to be observed when feasts from the two cycles occur on the same date. These ranks, which have also changed with time, have included Doubles of the first class, Doubles of the second class, Doubles, Semidoubles, and Simples.

In both Mass and Office, the texts of certain items of the liturgy remain the same for all feasts, though different melodies may be employed for those that are sung. These items make up the *Ordinary. Items that change from feast to feast make up the *Proper. Within the *Sanctorale,* however, some feasts, particularly those of lesser rank, have not been provided with their own complete Propers. For these saints, Propers are drawn from those that have been provided for certain classes of saints (martyrs, confessors, virgins, etc.). These Propers make up the Common of the Saints. *Liturgical books reflect these features of the liturgy.

Bibl.: Anton Baumstark, *Liturgie comparée* (Chevetogne: Monastère d'Amay, 1939); 3rd ed. (Chevetogne: Éditions de Chevetogne, 1953), trans. Eng., *Comparative Liturgy,* ed. F. L. Cross (London: A R Mobray, 1958). Mario Righetti, *Manuale di storia liturgica* (Milan: Ancora, 1946–53; 3rd ed., 1959–66). Josef A. Jungmann, *Missarum sollemnia* (Vienna: Herder, 1948; 5th ed., 1962); 2nd ed. trans. Eng., *The Mass of the Roman Rite* (New York: Benzinger Bros, 1959). John H. Miller, *Fundamentals of the Liturgy* (Notre Dame, Ind.: Fides Publishers Assoc, 1959). Ludwig Eisenhofer and Joseph Lechner, *The Liturgy of the Roman Rite,* trans. A. J. and E. F. Peeler, ed. H. E. Winstone (New York: Herder, 1961), after the 6th ed. of *Liturgik des römischen Ritus* (Freiburg: Herder, 1953). Cyrille Vogel, *Introduction aux sources de l'histoire du culte chrétien au moyen âge* (Spoleto: Centro italiano di studi sull'alto medioevo, 1966). Richard W. Pfaff, *Medieval Latin Liturgy: A Select Bibliography* (Toronto: U of Toronto Pr, 1982). See also Gregorian chant, Liturgical books. D.M.R.

Liturgy of the Hours. See Office, Divine.

Lituus [Lat.]. (1) A trumpet of the ancient Etruscans and Romans, 75–160 cm. long, with its bell bent back in the shape of a J. See ill. under Greece. (2) In the Renaissance, *cornett or *crumhorn. (3) In the 18th century, a brass instrument. The two *litui* requested by Bach in Cantata no. 118 may have been tenor trumpets.

Liuto [It.]. Lute.

Livret [Fr.]. Libretto.

Lleno [Sp.]. (1) The main *mixture of a Spanish or Mexican organ, with the lowest pitch usually 1 1/3′. (2) The complete flue *chorus of a Spanish or Mexican organ.

Lobgesang [Ger.]. (1) Hymn of praise. (2) Mendelssohn's name for his symphony-cantata op. 2 (1840) in B♭ major, the last movement of which adds soloists, chorus, and organ to the orchestra in setting a Biblical text. Although there is no chronological justification, the work is also known as his Second Symphony.

Loco [It., place, abbr. *loc.*]. An instruction to return to the normal register or way of playing after an instruction to play, e.g., an octave higher or lower; also *al loco.*

Locrian. See Mode, Greece I, 3 (ii).

Lohengrin. Opera in three acts by Wagner (to his own libretto, based on Wolfram von Eschenbach and medieval legends), produced in Weimar in 1850. Setting: Antwerp in the early 10th century.

Lombard rhythm. Reversed dotting; a succession of dotted figures whose short notes come on the beat, especially characteristic of Italian music in the style of the 1740s. Without naming it, Johann Adolph Scheibe (*Compendium musices,* 1728–36) described it as a currently fashionable *galanterie* stemming from Tartini and advised composers to use it with caution. Johann Joachim Quantz (*Versuch,* trans. Edward R. Reilly, London: Faber, 1966, p. 323) attributed its popularization to an opera by Vivaldi given in Rome around 1722. It seemed also to exist, he said, in Scottish music [see Strathspey] and had been used by German composers more than 20 years before its vogue in Italy. Burney complained of the overuse of the "Scots catch" in mid-century Italian opera, blaming Gioacchino Cocchi, David Perez, and Nicolò Jommelli. The rhythm had a long and honorable history, however. Tomás de Santa María, Francesco Rognoni Taeggio, and Giulio Caccini advocated it as an embellishment to *diminutions; it was a favorite rhythm in England in the second half of the 17th century (used lavishly by Henry Purcell in his superb realizations of English declamation), and Etienne Loulié mentioned it (as an afterthought, to be sure) in connection with his treatment of *notes inégales;* François Couperin invented a sign for it; and Bach used it as a dominant rhythm in some of his most profound utterances (e.g., *Vater unser im Himmelreich* BWV 682).

Couperin's sign was a slur with a dot over the second note. His term *pointé-coulé* may have meant the same thing; it headed a *courante à l'italienne* (fourth *Concert royal,* 1722), where normal French inequality [see *Notes inégales*] would seem to be excluded, but Lombard rhythm would add sharp characterization. The use of plain slurs over pairs of notes to indicate short-long inequality is much more problematical; such an interpretation can only be valid in a small minority of the vast number of examples. No theorist explicitly states that slurs without dots are a sign for Lombard rhythm. But there are a number of instances of passages that exist in different versions, one with plain notes paired under slurs and one with reversed dotting. These have been found in the music of John Blow (Caldwell, 1973), Henry Purcell (ed. Ferguson, 1965), Matthew Locke (ed. Tilmouth, 1971–72), and Bach (concertos BWV 1042 and 1050, ill. in "Verzierung," *MGG* 13:1547). See also Gerhard Herz's arguments for a Lombard interpretation of *Domine Deus* from the Mass in B minor.

Bibl.: Giulio Caccini, *Le nuove musiche* (Florence, 1601); facs., *MMML* ser. 1, 29 (1973); ed. H. Wiley Hitchcock, *RRMBE* 9 (1970). Francesco Rognoni Taeggio, *Selva di varii passaggi* (Milan, 1620); facs., *BMB* sez. 2, 153 (1970). Etienne Loulié, *Eléments ou principes de musique* (Paris, 1696); trans. Albert Cohen, *MTT* 6 (1965). Johann Adolph Scheibe, *Compendium musices* (MS, 1728–36), ed. in Peter Benary, *Die deutsche Kompositionslehre des 18. Jahrhunderts* (Leipzig: Breitkopf & Härtel, 1961). John Blow, *Six Suites,* ed. Howard Ferguson (London: Stainer & Bell, 1965). Matthew Locke, *Chamber Music,* ed. Michael Tilmouth, *MB* 31–32 (1971–72). John Caldwell, *English Keyboard Music before the Nineteenth Century* (New York: Praeger, 1973). Gerhard Herz, "Der lombardische Rhythmus im 'Domine Deus' der h-Moll-Messe J. S. Bachs," *BaJb* 60 (1974): 90–97. David Johnson, "Scotch Snap," *Grove 6.* See also *Notes inégales.* D.F.

Lombard style. A style mentioned with disfavor by certain 18th-century writers on music. It may include but is not limited to passages incorporating *Lombard rhythm.

In a long passage in his *Versuch* (trans. Reilly, pp. 323ff.) deploring the corruption of Italian string style by two "Lombardic violinists," unnamed but identifiable as Vivaldi and Tartini, Johann Joachim Quantz equates Lombard style and the use of *Lombard rhythm. In Tartini's treatise on violin playing, written around the same time as Quantz's, the writer advised against using long appoggiaturas in a "composizione gaia, vivace, e secondo lo stile corrente (chi si chiama Lombardo)" (gay and lively composition and according to the current style, which is called Lombardo; MS version, p. 6). Since a long appoggiatura would not even be possible in connection with reversed dotting, it seems he had a broader meaning for Lombard style in mind than a purely rhythmic one.

Thus the term may have meant the style of Pietro Antonio Locatelli, Giuseppe Tartini, Pietro Nardini, and others, characterized by much fussy rhythmic detail such as triplets, syncopations, *gruppetti,* ornaments of all kinds, and the Lombard rhythm in the written scores, overlaid by extravagant display in the execution, all this contrasting with the thinnest of accompaniments, usually moving in a moderate, steady pulse of eighth notes articulating a much slower harmonic rhythm. The term **galant* is sometimes applied to this style today.

Bibl.: Giuseppe Tartini, *Traité des agréments de la musique,* ed. Erwin Jacobi, trans. Eng. Cuthbert Girdlestone, with a facs. of the original Italian (Celle: Moeck, 1961). See also Lombard rhythm. D.F.

London Symphony. (1) Popular name for Haydn's Symphony no. 104 in D major Hob. I:104 (1795); also known as the *Salomon* Symphony [see Salomon Symphonies]. (2) Ralph Vaughan Williams's Symphony no. 2, composed in 1912–13 (rev. 1920, 1933). Although the work contains musical evocations of the

Westminster chimes and other London sounds, it has no stated program.

Longa [Lat.], **long.** See Mensural notation.

Long-necked lute. Any of a family of plucked stringed instruments in which the length of the neck is substantially greater than the length of the body. A typical example has a very narrow neck, a wooden body shaped like a halved pear, and two to four strings or courses of strings. Fretted and unfretted models are both common. The pictorial record of long-necked lutes extends back to the 3rd millennium B.C.E. Today they are distributed most heavily in Eastern Europe and Asia. Examples include the **balalaika,* **colascione,* **dömbra,* **saz,* **shamisen,* **sitār,* **tanbur,* and **tār.* See also Lute.

Long playing. Phonograph *recordings that turn at a speed of 33 1/3 revolutions per minute (less often 16) and are for this reason (as well as because of narrower grooves) of longer duration than earlier records turning at a speed of 78 rpm.

Lontano [It.]. Distant.

Loop. See Acoustics II.

Lord's Prayer. See *Pater noster.*

Loudness. The perceived characteristic of a sound that is a function of its intensity, i.e., of the physical energy that the sounding body transmits to the surrounding medium. The term volume is most often used synonymously. The human ear is not equally sensitive to changes in intensity throughout the range of audible frequencies, it being least sensitive at high and low extremes of frequency. This phenomenon is sometimes called the Fletcher-Munson effect, and some phonograph amplifiers are equipped with a "loudness" control (in addition to a "volume" control) that attempts to compensate for it by permitting some control of relative intensities of various ranges of frequencies independent of the intensity (or volume) with which the sound as a whole is reproduced. See also Acoustics, Psychology of music.

Louise. Opera ("musical novel") in four acts by Gustave Charpentier (to his own libretto), produced in Paris in 1900. The work embodies a then novel naturalism. Setting: Paris, ca. 1900.

Lourd [Fr.]. Heavy.

Loure [Fr.]. (1) In the late Baroque period, a slow and majestic French *gigue, with heavy accents (François Couperin marked one *pesament*). It is usually in 6/4 meter, with upbeats, dotted figures, syncopations, and hemiolas, e.g.:

It may have contrapuntal texture and is found in orchestral and harpsichord *suites (Bach, Telemann). (2) In the 16th and 17th centuries, a type of bagpipe with no proven connection to the dance. B.G.

Louré [Fr.]. See Bowing (6).

Lourer [Fr.]. See *Notes inégales.*

Love for Three Oranges, The [Russ. *Lyubov k tryom apelsinam*]. Opera in a prologue and four acts by Prokofiev (libretto by the composer, after Carlo Gozzi's fable), produced in Chicago in French in 1921; produced in Leningrad in 1926. Setting: fairy tale. A suite, a march, and a scherzo from the opera were made into separate works by Prokofiev.

Low Mass. In the Roman Catholic Church, a simplified form of the *Mass, without singing, said by a single celebrant, sometimes in private. Until the reforms of the Second *Vatican Council, it was the usual form of Mass except on Sundays and important feasts.

LP. See Long playing.

Lucernarium [Lat., fr. *lucerna,* lamp]. In the *Ambrosian rite and in some sources for the *Mozarabic rite, the first musical item of Vespers. Its texts most often refer to light because the service coincided with the lighting of lamps at dark.

Lucia di Lammermoor. Opera in three acts by Donizetti (libretto by Salvatore Cammarano, after Sir Walter Scott's novel *The Bride of Lammermoor*), produced in Naples in 1835. Setting: Scotland at the end of the 17th century.

Ludus tonalis [Lat., Play of Tonalities]. A work for piano composed by Hindemith in 1942, consisting of 12 fugues in different keys, linked by 11 modulating interludes, and preceded by a prelude in C that serves, in retrograde inversion, as a postlude. The fugues use many learned contrapuntal devices and are arranged according to Hindemith's principle of decreasing tonal relationship to the tonic of C: C, G, F, A, E, E♭, A♭, D, B♭, D♭, B♮, F♯.

Luftpause [Ger.]. Breathing *pause.

Lugubre [Fr., It.]. Mournful.

Lullaby [Fr. *berceuse;* Ger. *Wiegenlied, Schlummerlied;* It. *ninna nanna;* Sp. *canción de cuna*]. A cradle song, usually with gentle and regular rhythm. A number of instrumental works of the 19th and early 20th centuries evoke such songs. See *Berceuse.*

Lulu. Opera in three acts by Alban Berg (to his own libretto, after Frank Wedekind's plays *Erdgeist* and *Die Büchse der Pandora*). Setting: Germany, France, and England before World War I. At the time of Berg's death in 1935, acts 1 and 2 were entirely complete, and act 3 was complete in short score and partly orchestrated. The first production, in Zürich in 1937, included the first two acts plus two sections from act 3 (orchestrated by Berg for the *Symphonische Stücke aus der Oper "Lulu"*) that were used simply to accompany stage action. The composer's widow subsequently withheld act 3, and only after her death in 1976 did performance of the complete work become possible. The first complete production, based on Berg's materials for the entire work as realized by Friedrich Cerha, was given in Paris in 1979.

Lundu [Port.]. A Brazilian traditional dance of African origin, known since colonial times, but rarely performed today. In the 19th century, the folk *lundu* was adopted and cultivated in the aristocratic salons of Brazil (and Portugal); in the last decades of the century, it also acquired broader popularity as an urban dance-song genre. D.S.

Lungo [It.]. Long; *lunga pausa,* prolonged pause or rest.

Lur [Dan.]. (1) A prehistoric bronze trumpet of Scandinavia, 1.5 to 2.5 m. long and shaped like a loose helix with a flat, ornamented disk for a bell. More than 40 specimens, dated between 1100 and 600 B.C.E., have been excavated, often in pairs, one a left spiral, the other a right spiral. There is no evidence concerning its use. See ill. under Brass instruments. (2) In Scandinavia and the Baltic region, a straight wooden trumpet up to 2 m. long and very similar to the *alphorn.

Bibl.: Hans C. Broholm, William P. Larsen, Gottfred Skjerne, *The Lures of the Bronze Age,* trans. A. Svart (Copenhagen: Gyldendal, 1949).

Lusingando [It.]. Flattering, coaxing.

Lustig [Ger.]. Merry, joyous.

Lustigen Weiber von Windsor, Die [Ger., The Merry Wives of Windsor]. Opera in three acts by Otto Nicolai (libretto by S. H. Mosenthal, after Shakespeare's comedy), produced in Berlin in 1849. Setting: Windsor in the 15th century.

Lustige Witwe, Die [Ger., The Merry Widow]. Operetta in three acts by Franz Lehár (libretto by Viktor Léon and Leo Stein, after Henri Meilhac's comedy *L'attaché d'ambassade*), produced in Vienna in 1905. Setting: Paris, early in the 20th century.

Lute [fr. Ar. *al ʿūd;* Fr. *luth;* Ger. *Laute;* It. *lauto, liuto, leuto;* Sp. *laúd*]. (1) A European plucked-string instrument with an oblong, rounded body, a flat soundboard featuring a rosette, and a short, fretted neck with nearly perpendicular pegbox [see ill.]. (2) In Sachs-Hornbostel terminology [see Instrument], a stringed instrument with a body and neck.

The lute's predecessors are the **pandoura* and **ʿūd.* Moors and Saracens brought the *ʿūd* to Spain and Sicily, where it was later adopted by European musicians and taken north. During the Renaissance, the lute became the dominant musical instrument in Europe and England. It was gradually superseded in popularity by the *theorbo, the violin, and the harpsichord in the 17th century, though it was cultivated in France until the early 18th century, in Italy until ca. 1750, and in Germany and Austria until the time of Mozart. Almost all its music after 1500 was written in *tablature.

The lute had four or five courses (each with one or two strings) in the 15th century; six became standard after 1500. The top string was usually single. The paired strings of the next two to four courses were tuned in unison, the lower ones in octaves, though national practice and string-making technology were responsible for much variation. Around 1580, more bass courses began to be added, and by 1640, 11 courses were the norm in France and Germany, 13 or 14 in Italy [see Archlute]. Thirteen courses became common in Germany by ca. 1720. In the Renaissance, the standard tuning was **vieil ton* (fourths between most courses but a third between the middle two), and the instrument was built in seven sizes, from the small octave lute (highest string or chanterelle at d″) to the contrabass lute (chanterelle at g). Italy retained the old tuning through the Baroque, but experiments during the early 17th century in France [see *Accords nouveaux*] led to the tuning C D E F G A d f a d′ f′, which prevailed in France and Germany through the 18th century.

European lute makers are documented as early as 1380. Increasingly in the 15th century, the town of Füssen (Allgäu) and outlying villages became the center of European lute making. In 1562, a luthiers' guild was established there. Many journeymen left Füssen for Italy or other countries to practice their trade. Hans Frei (erroneously associated with Füssen in Baron, 1727) and Laux Maler, working in Bologna in the early 16th century, are known for slender lutes, half-round in rear profile, with narrow shoulders and 9 or 11 ribs of hardwoods such as maple or ash. In ca. 1580–1630, luthiers such as Magno Tieffenbrucker in Venice and Vendelio Venere and Michael Hartung in Padua, built lutes with an elliptical soundboard outline, a flattened body, and thinner ribs (as many as 41), which were often made of yew wood. The Thirty Years' War destroyed Füssen as a lute-making center, and the increasing popularity of the violin caused later 17th- and 18th-century luthiers to neglect lute building. Many Renaissance lutes were fitted with a wider neck and larger pegbox in the Baroque, so that few Renaissance lutes survive in original condition. Both Joachim Tielke (Hamburg, 1641–1719, known for ornate decoration) and Johann Christian Hoffmann (Leipzig, 1683–1750) revived the slender Bolognese style.

Medieval lutenists played with a quill; performance was thus limited to single-line tunes and strummed chords. In the last quarter of the 15th century, lutenists began to pluck the strings with the thumb and fingers of the right hand. This enabled them to play two or more voices at once in imitation of vocal polyphony. Virtually no attributed lute music written before 1500 survives. Later, Renaissance lutenists cultivated dance music, *fantasias and *ricercars, and vocal *intabu-

1. Chitarrone. 2. Mandolin. 3. Orpharion. 4. Descant lute. 5. Flat-back mandolin. 6. Bandora. 7. Baroque lute. 8. Colascione.

lations, as well as song accompaniments and forms for mixed instrumental ensemble. Dance *suites were the most important genre for Baroque lutenists, who used the archlute and theorbo primarily as continuo instruments. See also Angelica, Colascione, Mandore, Prelude, *Tastar de corde,* Toccata.

Bibl.: Ernst Gottlieb Baron, *Study of the Lute* (Nuremberg, 1727), trans. Douglas Alton Smith (Redondo Beach, Cal.: Instrumenta Antiqua, 1976). Lionel de La Laurencie, *Les luthistes* (Paris: H Laurens, 1928). Stanley Buetens, *Method for the Renaissance Lute* (Menlo Park, Cal.: Instrumenta Antiqua, 1969). Friedemann Hellwig, "Lute Construction in the Renaissance and the Baroque," *GSJ* 27 (1974): 21–30. Robert Lundberg, "Sixteenth and Seventeenth Century Lute-Making," *Journal of the Lute Society of America* [hereafter *JLSA*] 7 (1974): 31–50. Richard Bletschacher, *Die Lauten- und Geigenmacher des Füssener Landes* (Hofheim am Taunus: F Hofmeister, 1978). Adolf Layer, *Die Allgäuer Lauten- und Geigenmacher* (Augsburg: Verlag der Schwäbischen Forschungsgemeinschaft, 1978). David B. Lyons, *Lute, Vihuela, Guitar to 1800: A Bibliography* (Detroit: Info Coord, 1978). Paul Beier, "Right Hand Position in Renaissance Lute Technique," *JLSA* 12 (1979): 4–24. Gerhard Söhne, "On the Geometry of the Lute," *JLSA* 13 (1980): 35–54. Ernst Pohlmann, *Laute, Theorbe, Chitarrone,* 5th ed. (Bremen: Eres, 1982). Douglas Alton Smith, *A History of the Lute: From Antiquity to the Renaissance* (New York: Lute Society of America, 2002). Periodicals: *Lute Society Journal* (1957–; renamed *The Lute,* 1982). *Journal of the Lute Society of America* (1968–). *Il "Fronimo"* (1972–). *Guitar and Lute* (1974–). *Gitarre + Laute* (1979–). D.A.S.

Lute harpsichord [Fr. *clavecin-luth;* Ger. *Lautenclavicymbel, Lautenwerk, Lautenklavier*]. A harpsichord with gut strings (occasionally supplemented by a 4′ choir of metal strings) intended to imitate the sound of the lute rather than the harp, as in the case of the **arpicordo.* Although there are earlier references to such instruments beginning with Sebastian Virdung (1511), the lute harpsichord was primarily cultivated in Germany during the lifetime of J. S. Bach, whose estate included two of them. Bach's pupil Johann Friedrich Agricola, in a note (p. 339) to the sections of Jakob Adlung's *Musica mechanica organoedi* (1768) dealing with the lute harpsichord (pp. 333ff.), recalls having seen and heard one in Leipzig in about 1740 that had been made at Bach's suggestion by Zacharias Hildebrandt. No historical example has survived. H.S.

Lute stop. On the harpsichord, a rank of jacks that plucks one choir of strings at the extreme end, thus producing a more nasal timbre.

Lute tablature. See Tablature.

Luth [Fr.]. Lute.

Lutheran church music. The music of the Lutheran Church, more than that of any other Protestant denomination, derives its character from the views of its founder, Martin Luther (1483–1546). No single document by Luther proclaims a code to which he demanded adherence. Rather, the development of all his views is cumulative and, in the case of music, is most remarkably found not in the major liturgical writings (*Formula missae et communionis pro Ecclesia Wittembergensi,* 1523, and *Deutsche Messe und Ordnung Gottesdienst,* 1526), but in the prefaces to collections of music published for the young Lutheran Church, notably Johann Walter's *Geystliche gesangk Buchleyn* (1524; trans. in *SR,* pp. 341–42) and Georg Rhau's *Symphoniae iucundae* (*Encomion musices,* 1538). In the former, Luther warns against overzealous suppression of the arts, expressing instead the hope that all the arts—and especially music—might be used to serve their creator. In the latter, he defines music as a gift of God that transcends all eloquence and that reaches its full power in the union of text and song in praise of God. Thus, Lutheran church music is characterized by openness to every variety of artistic resource.

The *Formula missae* establishes the evangelical Latin Mass; the *Deutsche Messe* is a vernacular reformation founded on the premise of congregational participation, and to that end, Luther composed and encouraged the liturgical use of vernacular hymns, later known as *chorales. As these two liturgical orders evolved, an elaborate system of substitution became acceptable: German text for Latin (or both in succession), chorale for polyphony (or both), instrumentally performed for texted stanzas (or both). The freedom afforded by these multiple options attracted a distinguished list of composers and manifested itself most conspicuously in organ music (chorale prelude, variation, partita [see Organ chorale]) and in the church *cantatas that developed elaborate but liturgically appropriate musico-textual exegeses. The organ music and church cantatas of J. S. Bach (1685–1750) are paradigms of the genre.

In the later 18th century both the Enlightenment and pietism, for different reasons, diminished the role of Lutheran church music by largely restricting it to congregational hymnody with simple organ accompaniment.

In the early 19th century a liturgical restoration movement was begun, and with it came the concern for the renewal of church music. In Berlin A. W. Bach was one of the pioneers, together with his gifted organ student Felix Mendelssohn. Mendelssohn's revival of Bach's St. Matthew Passion in 1829 fueled not only the Bach movement but also a concern for the renewal of Lutheran church music. Among Mendelssohn's least-known compositions are those written for liturgical use, principally for Berlin Cathedral. In the second half of the 19th century collected editions of the music of Bach, Handel, Schütz, and Schein—much of it written for church use—were published. The movement overflowed into the 20th century, when collected editions of the works of Lübeck, Scheidt, Michael Praetorius, Buxtehude, and Johann Walter appeared. Alongside this recovery of older church music, contemporary composers were writing new music for worship. They include Arnold Mendelssohn, Johann Nepomuk David, Hugo Distler, Karl Marx [*sic*], Siegfried Reda, Günther Raphael, Ernst Pepping, Johannes Petzold, Herman Stern, and Heinz Werner Zimmermann, among others. Hymnals for use by all the *Landeskirchen* were issued in 1930, 1950, and 1993.

Bibl.: K. Ameln et al., *Handbuch der deutschen evangelischen Kirchenmusik* (Göttingen: Vandenhoeck & Ruprecht, 1933–74). Karl Ferdinand Müller and Walter Blankenburg, *Leiturgia: Handbuch des Evangelischen Gottesdienstes* vol. 4: *Die Musik des Evangelischen Gottesdienstes* (Kassel: Stauda, 1961). Friedrich Blume et al., *Protestant Church Music: A History* (New York: Norton, 1974). Robin A. Leaver, "The Lutheran Reformation," in *Music and Society: The Renaissance from the 1470s to the End of the 16th Century,* ed. Ian Fenlon (Englewood Cliffs, N.J.: Prentice Hall, 1989), pp. 263–85. Gustav A. Krieg, *Die gottesdeinstliche Musik als theologische Problem: Darestellt an der kirchenmusikalischen Erneurung nach dem ersten Weltkrieg* (Göttingen: Vandenhoeck & Ruprecht, 1990). Robin A. Leaver, "Lutheran Vespers as a Context for Music," in *Church, Stage, and Studio: Music and Its Contexts in Seventeenth-Century Germany,* ed. Paul Walker (Ann Arbor: UMI Res Pr, 1990), pp. 143–61. Robin A. Leaver, "Theological Consistency, Liturgical Integrity, and Musical Hermeneutic in Luther's Liturgical Reforms," *Lutheran Quarterly,* new ser., 9 (1995): 117–38. Geoffrey Webber, *North German Church Music in the Age of Buxtehude* (New York: Oxford U Pr, 1996). Robin A. Leaver, "Music and Lutheranism," in *The Cambridge Bach Companion,* ed. John Butt (New York: Cambridge U Pr, 1997), pp. 35–45, 253–56. R.F.F., rev. R.A.L.

Lutherie [Fr.]. Lute making; by extension, the making and repair of any stringed instruments, especially those of the violin family.

Luthier [Fr.]. A lute maker; one who makes and repairs stringed instruments, especially those of the violin family.

Luttuoso, luttuosamente [It.]. Mournful.

Lydian. See Mode, Cadence, Greece I, 3 (ii).

Lyra [Gr.; Lat. also *lira*]. (1) A *lyre of ancient Greece with a bowl-shaped, skin-covered resonator (originally a tortoise shell), curved arms, and 5 to 12 gut strings. Compared to the *kithara, another Greek lyre, the *lyra* was smaller and simpler and sounded at a lower pitch. It was considered an instrument of amateurs. See ill. under Greece; see also *Krar.* (2) In the Middle Ages and Renaissance, any of several kinds of stringed instruments, including *fiddles and *hurdy-gurdies. (3) [Ger.] A portable *glockenspiel in the shape of a lyre. See also *Lira.*

Lyra piano. An upright piano of the early 19th century, with case shaped like a Greek lyre.

Lyra viol. See Viol.

Lyra-way. The playing style and associated repertory of the lyra *viol.

Lyre [fr. Gr., Lat. *lyra*]. (1) A stringed instrument whose strings are parallel to the soundboard and attached to a crossbar between two arms extending beyond the soundboard [see Instrument (2) I, 1]. (2) The Greek **lyra.* (3) A musical instrument or other device with curved arms similar to those of the Greek *lyra* or the Greek *kithara [see ill. under Greece], including the clip attached to wind instruments for holding music.

Lyric. (1) Melodious. (2) For lyric soprano and lyric tenor, see Voice. (3) Lyrics [pl.]. The words of a popular song or number from a musical comedy.

Lyric Suite. (1) An orchestral work by Grieg arranged in 1904 from the first four of the six works in his *Lyric Pieces* [Ger. *Lyrische Stücke*], bk. 5, for piano op. 54. (2) A suite in six movements for string quartet by Alban Berg (1925–26), three movements of which were later arranged for string orchestra (1928). The pitch classes B, F, A, B♭ (German *pitch names H, F, A, B) play an important role and are derived from his own initials combined with those of Hanna Fuchs-Robettin.

M

M. Abbr. for *manual, **manualiter,* **main,* **mano,* *metronome, **mezzo* [see Dynamic marks].

Ma [It.]. But; *ma non troppo,* but not too much.

Macbeth. (1) Opera in four acts by Verdi (libretto by Francesco Maria Piave and Andrea Maffei, after Shakespeare's play), produced in Florence in 1847; revised version in French first produced in Paris in 1865. Setting: Scotland in the 11th century. (2) Opera in a prologue and three acts by Ernest Bloch (libretto by Edmond Fleg, after Shakespeare), produced in Paris in 1910.

Macedonia. I. *Current musical life and related institutions.* Skopje, which has had a music school since 1934, is the center of Macedonian musical life. Advanced music education is offered in Skopje at the Faculty of Education (1953) and the Faculty of Music (1966). Opera was occasionally staged after World War I (*Cavalleria rusticana* in 1915); a permanent company was founded in Skopje in 1948 and the ballet was established in the following year. The Makedonska filharmonija was formed in 1950 from the earlier radio symphony orchestra (1944). The conductor Lovro von Matačić (1948–52) played a central role in the early development of both ensembles. Research in traditional music has been done at the Institut za folklor Marko Cepenkov in Skopje (1950). Music scholarship appears in the periodicals *Makedonska muzika* (1977) and *Muzika* (1997). The Sojuz na kompozitorite na Makedonija, which today has about 60 members, was founded in 1947. The Ohridsko ljeto (Ohrid, 1961) and Struška muzička esen (Struga, 1975) are festivals with an international reputation.

II. *History of art music.* Slavic peoples arrived in the region of Vardar Macedonia in the 6th and 7th centuries. Macedonian Orthodox chant, based on melodies of the **oktoēchos (osmoglasnik),* was defined by St. Clement (916) and St. Naum (910)—pupils of St. Cyril and Methodius—who founded in Ohrid and Preslav, respectively, their schools of chant and apparently gave Macedonian church music its autochthonous quality. Ohrid became a significant cultural center during Samoil's empire (969–1018), when the Macedonian Church was raised to the rank of a patriarchate. After Samoil's empire was overtaken by the Byzantines (1018–1187) and the patriarchate was reduced to an archiepiscopate, Greek influences displaced Slavic language and culture. It appears that Joannes Koukouzeles (ca. 1280–1360/75), one of the most significant composers of Byzantine church music, originated from a Slavic family in western Macedonia. After the Ottomans conquered Macedonia in 1371, music literacy and theory deteriorated and musical language became simplified, gradually becoming akin to folk music. The 1814 reform of Byzantine notation was immediately adopted in Macedonia and in 1818 the first manuscript was produced with the reformed Chrysantean notation, indicating renewal of contacts between Ohrid, Constantinople, and Mt. Athos. Western European influences reached Macedonian church music in the 19th century, particularly through works by Atanas Badev (1860–1908), a student of Balakirev and Rimsky-Korsakov, whose polyphonic *Zlatoustova liturgija* (Leipzig, 1898) was published in Western notation. Among other 19th-century composers of church music are Kalistrat Zografski (b. Krstan Sandžak, 1821–1913), Jovan Harmosin Ohridski (Ivan Genadiev, 1829–90), and Dimitar Zlatanov Gradoborski (19th century).

The first collection of folk songs (with 583 Macedonian and 77 Bulgarian songs), *Zbornik so narodni umotvorbi* (A Collection of Folk Creations; Zagreb, 1861), published by the brothers Dimitri and Konstantin Miladin, initiated a cultural and national revival, inspiring Macedonian intellectuals to collect traditional songs. After World War I choral ensembles and military orchestras were established in almost every urban center, determining genres popular among the first generation of Macedonian composers whose style was rooted in Macedonian folklore: Stefan Gajdov (1905–92) Živko Firfov (1906–84; also the leading Macedonian ethnomusicologist of the 1950s and 60s), Todor Skalovski (b. 1909), Trajko Prokopiev (1909–79), and Petre Bogdanov-Kočko (1913–88). The generation that came forward in the 1950s adapted a variety of styles from late Romanticism and neoclassicism to serial and aleatory techniques: Vlastimir Nikolovski (1925–2001), Blagoja Ivanovski (1921–94), Kiril Makedonski (1925–84; the author of the first national opera, *Goce,* 1954), Tomislav Zografski (b. 1934), Dragoslav Ortakov (b. 1928; also a prolific music historian), and Toma Prošev (1931–96), the most prominent among them. In 1968 Prošev founded the ensemble for contemporary music *Sv. Sofija,* which was a vehicle for performances of contemporary Macedonian music. The generation that started composing in the 1960s includes Sotir Golabovski (b. 1937; also author of significant studies on Macedonian church music), Blagoj Canev (b. 1937), Stojan Stojkov (b. 1941), and Risto Avramovski (b. 1943). In the latest generation, Ilija Pejovski (b. 1947), Toma

Mančev (b. 1950), Dimitrije Bužarovski (b. 1952), Goce Kolarovski (b. 1959), and Gorjan Korunoski (b. 1961) have gained attention.

III. *Traditional music.* Macedonia's diversity of traditional music derives from the country's ethnic composition—Macedonians (68%), Albanians (22%), Turks (4%), and Roma (3%)—as well as its two main religions, Eastern Orthodox (67%) and Islam (30%). Traditional music is practiced in two forms: song and dance *(oro).* The diverse and complex rhythms dominating Macedonian music can be divided in two groups: simple and regular meters (2/4, 3/4, 4/4, and 6/4), and compound, usually asymmetric, meters (such as the *čoček* rhythms of the Roma in 3+3+2). Some labor and ritual songs are performed in free rubato guided by the meter of the text. Ritual and everyday songs are often performed by three female singers in the style known as *vikoečki, glasoečki,* and *na glas:* the *kreske* or *viši* singer begins the tune, and the second voice (*slože* or *vleče*) joins in; the third voice doubles the second voice.

Melodies of rural songs usually do not expand over a fourth above the tonic, although extensive ornamentations frequently call for pitches not belonging to the original scale of the melody. Ritual songs are frequently in nontempered scale. More recent urban songs, influenced by *čalgija* instruments, extended tone rows to the full major scale.

Instruments can be classified in four groups. Children's instruments are simple whistles made of clay, leaves, or tree bark. Rural tradition includes end-blown flutes (small *duduk,* also known as *svorče* or *kavalče;* and long *duduk,* also known as *kaval* or *kafal*), a double end-blown flute (*dvojanka,* with melodic and drone pipes), and a bagpipe (*gajdarke* or *surle,* a single-reed clarinet-type instrument with one drone, called *brčalo* or *rog*). The cordophones belonging to the group of mixed rural and urban instruments includes: *gusle* or *čalame,* with three strings, used in eastern and northeastern regions, and various kinds of *tambura* instruments with two (*litarka* or *čitelija*), four (*četvorka* or *karaduzen*), and rarely six *(bozuk)* strings. The membranophones in this tradition are *tapan* (the double-headed drum in different sizes), *daire, def,* and *tarabuka* (goblet drum). Urban music is played by the *čalgija* ensemble usually consisting of a violin, clarinet, lute, *ut, kanun* (zither), and *daire* or *tarabuka.* The fretted lute is used primarily for accompaniment, while the unfretted *ut* is a melodic instrument. To the urban group also belongs the *zurla (surla, zurna),* a double-reed oboe-type instrument played in pairs and accompanied by *tapan* (Albanian *tupan*). Today electrically amplified instruments and synthesizers are also used.

Bibl.: Branko Karakaš, *Muzičkite tvorci vo Makedonija* [Musicians in Macedonia] (Skopje: Makedonska knjiga, 1970). Dragotin Cvetko, *Musikgeschichte der Südslaven* (Kassel: Bärenreiter, 1975). Dragoslav Ortakov, *Muzičkata umetnost vo Makedonija* [Musical Art in Macedonia] (Skopje: Makedonska revija, 1982). Sotir Golabovski, *Tradicionalna i eksperimentalna makedonska muzika* [Traditional and Experimental Macedonian Music] (Skopje: Makedonska revija, 1984). Marko Kolovski, *Sojuz na kompozitorite na Makedonija, 1947–1992: Makedonski kompozitori i muzikolozi* [Sojuz na kompozitorite na Makedonija, 1947–1992: Macedonian Composers and Musicologists] (Skopje: Sojuz na kompozitorite na Makedonija, 1993). Sotir Golabovski, ed., *Macedonian Chant,* 7 vols. (Skopje: Menora, 1993–2002). Sotir Golabovski, *Istorija na makedonska muzika* [History of Macedonian Music] (Skopje: Prosvetno delo, 1999).

Discography. Macedonian Traditional Chant: The Liturgy of Chrysostom; Macedonian octoēchos, prod. by Sotir Golabovski (Delta Records, 2000). Z.B.

Machete [Port.]. See *Cavaquinho.*

Machicotage [Fr.]. The ornamenting of liturgical chant, practiced in France and Italy from the Middle Ages into the 19th century. Ornaments were applied principally to the soloists' portions of chants and were sung by singers called *machicots.*

Machine head. A mechanical device, typically employing worm gears, for controlling the tension of the strings on a stringed instrument, especially the guitar and double bass. Such devices have been in use since the 18th century.

Macumba [Port.]. See *Candomblé.*

Madama Butterfly. Opera in three acts (originally in two acts) by Puccini (libretto by Giuseppe Giacosa and Luigi Illica, based on David Belasco's dramatization of a story by John L. Long). It was first produced in Milan in 1904; the fourth and definitive version was produced in Paris in 1906. Setting: Japan, near Nagasaki, about 1900.

Madrāshā. See Syrian chant.

Madrigal [It.]. (1) A poetic and musical form cultivated in 14th-century Italy. The madrigal as a verse form is mentioned by literary theorists of the early 14th century; neither they nor any subsequent writer has successfully accounted for the etymology of the word. The poems, at first nearly always pastoral in theme but later more varied, usually consist of two or three stanzas of three lines followed by a ritornello of two lines (though the ritornello is sometimes lacking). Typical rhyme schemes are aba bcb dd, abb cdd ee, etc. Seven- and eleven-syllable lines are both used, but the latter predominate.

Musical settings of madrigals for two or (rarely) three voices survive in manuscripts of north Italian and Florentine provenance dating from ca. 1340 to ca. 1440; the sources are on the whole somewhat late in relation to the composition of the music. Composers include the north Italians Giovanni da Cascia and Jacopo da Bologna as well as a group of Florentines of whom the most famous was Francesco Landini (d. 1397). The upper lines of the madrigal show, at first entirely and always chiefly within the confines of Italian Trecento notation, a good deal of melodic fioritura, often slightly varied in the same piece from one source to another, especially at the beginning and end of poetic lines. The supporting tenors, though texted, are less elaborate. Change from one metric pattern to another may occur within the stanza and is all but obligatory from stanza to ritornello. Though basically diatonic, the music has some surprising chromaticisms, and there is no observable principle of modal organization. The intricacy and beauty of the melodic ornamentation suggest a high level of musical culture, probably restricted to small circles of connoisseurs. After ca. 1370, the madrigal lost popularity to the **ballata*, and few madrigals of this type were written after 1400.

(2) A poetic genre popular with 16th-century musicians, distantly if at all related to the 14th-century type. In the writings of 16th-century literary theorists, the madrigal was defined as a one-stanza poem of free rhyme scheme, using a free alternation of seven- and eleven-syllable lines. As such it is similar to a single stanza of a **canzone;* some madrigal texts are closely modeled on *canzoni,* while others resemble the *ballata* or, occasionally, the Trecento madrigal. Petrarchan language is used a great deal, especially in the first half of the 16th century; new currents of epigrammatic, anacreontic, and melic nature find their way into later madrigal texts.

(3) A vocal setting, polyphonic and unaccompanied for most of its history, of any of various kinds of verse from ca. 1520 to the middle of the 17th century. The first printed volume of music to be called *Madrigali* appeared in 1530; but in manuscript sources of the 1520s, the genre is already well represented, and the *Musica di meser Bernardo Pisano sopra le canzone del Petrarcha* of 1520 is an early example of the form in print. The madrigal in its beginning stages was chiefly the work of Florentine composers (Bernardo Pisano, Philippe Verdelot, Jacques Arcadelt) and of men with strong Florentine connections (Costanzo Festa). Sonnets, *ottave rime,* and other poetic forms were used along with the madrigal itself. Petrarch's verse was used, but that of his 16th-century imitators was perhaps more common. In style, this music, normally written for four fully texted voices, is closer to the French *chanson of the early 16th century than to most examples of the **frottola.* The classic form of the early madrigal is found in Arcadelt's *Primo libro* for four voices (published in 1538/39), the most famous and most often reprinted of all madrigal collections.

Madrigals in Arcadelt's style—the poetry set line by line in a basically chordal style animated with graceful points of imitation, expressive in a reticent way but without rhetorical extremes—continued to be written during the middle decades of the 16th century. But beginning about 1540, the madrigal began to take new directions. In the hands of Adrian Willaert, Cipriano de Rore, and their Venetian circle, the madrigal became denser in texture, declamatory in a more individual and less stereotyped manner, and in every way more serious; if the early madrigal resembles a chanson, these works are like motets. Petrarch's sonnets, set in two sections or *partes,* are favorite texts here; five-voice writing is the norm. Some of Rore's madrigals make use of short note-values under the signature C [see *Note nere*], a graphic and musical novelty seen in many of the madrigal anthologies published in the 1540s.

By mid-century, the madrigal for five voices is perhaps the most common, with four-voice texture next; two and three voices are not rare, and madrigals for six, seven, and eight voices appear (the last usually dialogues for two groups of four voices). Problems of register and texture are dealt with in a distinct manner in these various scorings, and it might even be said that compositional conventions and intended use differ somewhat from one to another of them.

By 1550, the madrigal had become in part a vehicle for experiment; thus the chromaticism espoused by the theorist Nicola Vicentino and practiced to some degree by a number of composers, including Rore and the young Lassus, can be seen as an integral part of the history of the genre. In the 1550s, there were further experiments in declamatory rhythm, particularly evident in Roman anthologies called *madrigali ariosi.* Composition of large-scale madrigal cycles became a marked feature after 1550. A new generation of madrigalists, among them Palestrina, Lassus, Philippe de Monte, and Vincenzo Ruffo, came to prominence in the middle 1550s, and a talented group of composers including Giaches de Wert, Alessandro Striggio, Stefano Rossetto, and Andrea Gabrieli rose to prominence early in the 1560s.

A development important for the later history of the madrigal began in the mid-1560s: features of the lighter forms such as the **villanella,* which had intermingled with the madrigal in its earliest stages but thereafter led a separate existence, were absorbed into the serious madrigal. Dancelike rhythms, clear-cut cadence structures, and a bright and simplified harmonic vocabulary reentered the madrigal. These traits are all characteristic of the **canzonetta* of the 1570s. Giovanni Ferretti, Andrea Gabrieli, Marc'Antonio Ingegneri, and others cultivated this new style. During this period, Petrarchan verse was no longer so exclusively cultivated; pastoral poetry was rising in popularity, and much occasional verse for celebrations of various kinds was set.

About 1580, the center of activity changed from Venice to Rome, Mantua, and Ferrara (Wert and Luzzasco Luzzaschi); the court of Alfonso II at Ferrara was particularly important at this time. Professional chamber singers here and elsewhere cultivated a highly ornamented style calling for virtuoso technique, and composers began to write in a style stressing ornament, especially in the upper voices; the polarity of texture evident in music at the end of the century was already manifesting itself. To a certain extent, the greatest madrigal composer of the period, the Roman Luca Marenzio (d. 1599), took part in this development, though his work, which may be regarded as the classic manifestation of the later madrigal, never abandoned contrapuntal texture. In refinement of expressive melodic rhetoric, virtuosic handling of coloristic harmony, and contrapuntal dissonance, Marenzio set a high standard for the genre as the century neared its end.

In the 1580s and 90s, the epic and pastoral poetry of Tasso and especially the pastoral verse of Guarini was in vogue; some of the most impressive madrigals of the period set texts from Guarini's *Pastor fido.* In contrast to this elegant verse was a new repertory of brief, highly charged poems written directly for the use of composers. To a certain extent, musicians now varied their style depending on their choice of text. The experimentalists of the 1590s, chief among them Pomponio Nenna, Carlo Gesualdo, Alfonso Fontanelli, and Luzzaschi, favored short, expressionistic texts that gave them occasion for extremes of melodic and tonal language—what was soon to be called the *seconda prattica* [see *Prima prattica, seconda prattica*]. But madrigals in a more conservative vein continued to be written throughout the 1580s and 90s, some of the music being of great distinction, such as the later work of Monte and Lassus.

About 1600, madrigals with continuo parts began to appear. Solo and few-voice pieces with continuo formed one new genre [see Monody]; concerted madrigals for a variety of vocal and instrumental forces formed another. Giulio Caccini, Sigismondo d'India, and Marco da Gagliano are among the notable figures in this new field. The unaccompanied madrigal continued to be written in the first half of the 17th century, but its vogue had passed and late examples lack conviction and energy.

Monteverdi published his first book of madrigals, for five voices, in 1587; his eight books, the last issued in 1638, are a microcosm of everything important in the final stages of the history of the genre, including the continuo (appearing for the first time in the fifth book of 1605) and concerted madrigal.

Outside Italy, the madrigal flourished in German-speaking lands, where Lassus and Monte spent most of their careers; the Bavarian court was a place of special importance. Italian musicians and their native imitators wrote madrigals in Poland and Denmark; the Netherlands was an important center of madrigal publication as well as composition. In France and Spain, the influence of the genre was indirect. England is a special case. In the last years of Elizabeth's reign, an intense cultivation of the genre—chiefly imitative of Marenzio's earlier style and of the *canzonetta*—took place, led by Thomas Morley and carried to its highest point at the turn of the century by Thomas Weelkes and John Wilbye. Italian madrigal texts were translated and paraphrased to provide words of great charm, and the music serves it well. The English were alone in creating a madrigal style discernibly different from its Italian models.

From the beginning of its 16th-century history, the madrigal served as a diversion for amateur musicians, among them literary dilettantes who wrote texts and commissioned musicians to set them. *Academies for the cultivation of music flourished from the 1540s on, the Accademia filarmonica of Verona (founded 1543) being the first of importance. Only near the end of the century was much of the madrigal literature written for professional performers. Madrigals were used in plays and **intermedi* and on other ceremonial occasions. Although one-to-a-part, unaccompanied vocal performance was the norm, madrigals were intabulated for solo voice and lute, for keyboard, for guitar and cittern; a good deal of freedom in mode of performance doubtless existed.

Bibl.: For (1), see *Ars nova.* (2), (3): Alfred Einstein, *The Italian Madrigal,* trans. Alexander H. Krappe, Roger H. Sessions, and Oliver Strunk (Princeton: Princeton U Pr, 1949). *Isham,* 1961. Joseph Kerman, *The Elizabethan Madrigal* (New York: American Musicological Soc, 1962). Edward J. Dent, "The Sixteenth-Century Madrigal," *NOHM* 4 (1968): 33–95. Don Harrán, "Verse Types in the Early Madrigal," *JAMS* 22 (1969): 27–53. Nino Pirrotta, *Li due Orfei* (Turin: ERI, 1969; rev. ed., Turin: Einaudi, 1975); trans. Karen Eales, *Music and Theatre from Poliziano to Monteverdi* (Cambridge: Cambridge U Pr, 1982). Jerome Roche, *The Madrigal* (London: Hutchinson, 1972). Glenn E. Watkins, *Gesualdo* (Chapel Hill: U of NC Pr, 1974). Anthony Newcomb, *The Madrigal at Ferrara,* 2 vols. (Princeton: Princeton U Pr, 1980). J.H.

Madrigal comedy. A modern term for a group of secular Italian vocal pieces in descriptive or naturalistic style, unified by some kind of plot. Descriptive madrigal cycles may be seen as early as the 1560s (Alessandro Striggio's *Cicalamento,* 1567), but the greatest vogue for these pieces came in the last decade of the 16th century and the first few years of the 17th. Orazio Vecchi's *L'Amfiparnaso* (1597), the most famous madrigal comedy, has a prologue and a succession of scenes and acts, in the manner of the **commedia dell'arte;* it was not, however, meant to be staged. Madrigal comedies were designed for private music making; Vecchi's *Veglie di Siena* (1604) uses as its main theme the games and puzzles that were the diversion of polite company of the time. Adriano Banchieri's madrigal comedies are in part purely descriptive (*Barca di Venetia per Padova,* 1605), in part imitative of Vecchi. The madrigal comedy is a phenomenon of minor importance, really a subgenre of the **villanella;* but its music can, in the hands of Vecchi or Banchieri, have strikingly naturalistic imitative powers and much genuine wit.

Bibl.: Alfred Einstein, *The Italian Madrigal,* trans. Alexander H. Krappe, Roger H. Sessions, and Oliver Strunk (Princeton: Princeton U Pr, 1949). James Haar, "On Musical Games in the 16th Century," *JAMS* 15 (1962): 22–34. J.H.

Madrigale spirituale [It.]. A setting of a vernacular, nonliturgical religious text for general devotional use in Counter-Reformation Italy. Some were *contrafacta* of secular madrigals, but many were new compositions. They differ from the *lauda in not using strophic verse. J.H.

Madrigalism. A musical effect intended to illustrate, usually in a rather literal way, some aspect of the text in a vocal composition, as in many *madrigals of the later 16th century. See also Word painting.

Maestoso [It.]. Majestic.

Maestro [It.]. Master; a form of address used especially for conductors, but often for composers, soloists, or teachers of performance; for *m. de capilla, m. di cappella,* see Chapel master.

Magadis. A stringed instrument of ancient Greece, probably a triangular harp. Greek music theorists use the verb *magadizein* to mean singing or playing in octaves.

Magelone Romances. See *Romanzen aus L. Tieck's Magelone.*

Maggiore [It.]. Major mode.

Magic Flute, The. See *Zauberflöte, Die.*

Magnificat [Lat.]. The *canticle of the Virgin, Luke 1:46–55, the Latin text of which begins "Magnificat anima mea Dominum" (My soul doth magnify the Lord). The Magnificat is used in both Roman Catholic and Anglican services, at Vespers and Evening Prayer, respectively.

The Magnificat has been a part of the Office of Vespers since early times. Like the Psalms, its verses are sung to one of a set of *psalm tones (see *LU,* pp. 207–18) chosen according to the mode of its accompanying antiphon. The verses of the Magnificat proper are followed by the Lesser *Doxology, treated as two additional verses.

The 15th and 16th centuries saw the composition of numerous polyphonic settings of the Magnificat, often but not always incorporating the recitation formulas. Most were vocal, some instrumental (both intabulations of vocal settings and newly composed pieces). Notable examples were contributed by Dufay, Victoria, Lassus, and Palestrina. Such settings were often composed (or transmitted) with **alternatim* performance in mind; that is, polyphony was supplied for only every other verse (usually even-, sometimes odd-numbered), plainchant to be used for the rest.

English Magnificats, never entirely like Continental examples, have been almost completely distinct since the Reformation, when English was substituted for Latin. In general, they are not based on the psalm tones.

In the Baroque and Classical periods, polyphonic settings of the Magnificat came to be divided into self-contained sections not necessarily congruent with verses. Usually, polyphony was supplied for the entire text. In the Baroque, verbal units were differentiated with concertato devices; word painting was commonplace. Prominent among Baroque Magnificats are those by Monteverdi (two, differently scored, from the Vespers of 1610), Schütz, Vivaldi, and Bach (two versions of a single composition, one in E♭ including four Christmas pieces, another in D, BWV 243, not including the Christmas material). Classical settings of the Magnificat often consist of series of comparatively long movements. Examples include those by C. P. E. Bach and Mozart (last movements of the Vespers K. 321 and K. 339).

Romantic composers neglected the Magnificat. In the 20th century, however, the genre was revived. Notable examples are by Alan Hovhaness (1958), Lennox Berkeley (1968), and Krzysztof Penderecki (1974).

Bibl.: Carl-Heinz Illing, *Zur Technik der Magnificat-Kompositionen des 16. Jahrhunderts* (Wolfenbüttel: G Kallmeyer, 1936). Josef Meinholz, "Untersuchungen zur Magnificat-Komposition des 15. Jahrhunderts" (diss., Univ. of Cologne, 1956). Gustave Reese, "The Polyphonic Magnificat of the Renaissance as a Design in Tonal Centers," *JAMS* 13 (1960): 68–78. Edward R. Lerner, "The Polyphonic Magnificat in 15th-Century Italy," *MQ* 50 (1964): 44–58. Robert G. Luoma, "Aspects of Mode in Sixteenth-Century Magnificats," *MQ* 62 (1976): 395–408.

Magnus liber organi [Lat.; lit., a big book of organum]. While modern scholars often treat this designation as a book title, it is more properly the description of a large collection of mainly polyphonic music of the 12th and 13th centuries associated with the Cathedral of Notre Dame in Paris. The description comes from the late-13th-century writer on music known as Anonymous IV, who comments that Leonin made a large book of organum for the gradual (Mass book) and the antiphon (Office book) to enrich the divine service, that it was later revised or edited by Perotin, and that this revision remained in use at Notre Dame even in the later 13th century.

Until recently, most scholars considered Anonymous IV's remarks to refer exclusively to the repertory of two-voice organa, which includes some 100 settings of graduals and alleluias for the Mass, and great responsories and Benedicamus Dominos for vespers, matins, and various processions, though it is accepted that Leonin and Perotin undoubtedly had help from their contemporaries and successors in producing this repertory. Lately Edward Roesner has forcefully argued that the *Magnus liber* comprised works for three and four voice parts as well, in the genres of *organum, *conductus, and *motet, broadening the description that actually accords with those in 13th- and 14th-century library catalogs and inventories. No two surviving copies of the repertory of the *Magnus liber* are exactly alike, and none can be shown to have been copied directly from any other, but they circulated all over Europe. The manuscripts tend to be arranged by genre and by number of voice parts, beginning with *quadrupla* (four-voice organum), *tripla,* and *organa dupla,* then three- and two-voice conductus, then three- and two-voice motets. The youngest extant sources, all fragmentary, show that by the later 13th century the notation of organum was becoming fully mensuralized in accord with contemporary performance practice. The most comprehensive extant manuscript version of the *Magnus liber* is the Florence manuscript (F); more limited sources are the manuscripts W1 and W2, but all postdate the time of Leonin and Perotin.

Overall, the *Magnus liber* represents the largest localized repertory of medieval polyphony, the first appearance of measured rhythm was the notational means to indicate different rhythms (the *rhythmic modes), the first unequivocal examples of three- and four-voice polyphony, and the first polyphonic works attributable to known composers. The *Magnus liber organi,* as a written collection, marks the true beginnings of composed rather than improvised polyphony in European music history; it has been called (by Roesner) "perhaps the greatest single achievement in medieval music." See also *Notre Dame, repertory of.

Bibl.: Friedrich Ludwig, *Repertorium organorum recentioris et motetorum vetustissimi stili,* vol. 1, pt. 1 (Halle: Niemeyer, 1910; R: 1964). Norman E. Smith, "Interrelationships among the Alleluias of the *Magnus liber organi,*" *JAMS* 25 (1972): 175–202. Norman E. Smith, "Interrelationships among the Graduals of the *Magnus Liber Organi,*" *AM* 45 (1973): 73–97. Rebecca A. Baltzer, "Notre Dame Manuscripts and Their Owners: Lost and Found," *JM* 5 (1987): 380–99. Hendrik van der Werf, *Integrated Directory of Organa, Clausulae, and Motets of the Thirteenth Century* (Rochester, N.Y.: Author, 1989). Edward H. Roesner et al., eds., *Le Magnus liber organi de Notre-Dame de Paris,* 7 vols., Musica Gallica (Monaco: Éditions de l'Oiseau-Lyre, 1993–). Edward H. Roesner, "Who 'Made' the *Magnus Liber*?" *EMH* 20 (2001): 227–66. R.A.B.

Magrepha [Heb.]. An organ of the ancient Hebrews containing perhaps 100 pipes and used in the first centuries C.E. as a signaling instrument.

Maid as Mistress, The. See *Serva padrona, La.*

Main [Fr.]. Hand; *m. droite (gauche),* right (left) hand; *à deux (quatre) mains,* for two (four) hands; *m. dans le pavillon,* hand in the bell (of a brass instrument).

Mainstream jazz. A term usually attributed to Stanley Dance in the 1950s to refer to *pre-bebop jazz styles. Since the 1980s, the usage of the term has encompassed all *non-free or *fusion acoustic jazz styles.

Maître de chapelle [Fr.]. *Chapel master [see also *Maîtrise*].

Maîtrise [Fr.]. A choir school attached to a church, under the direction of the chapel master; also a church choir.

Majeur [Fr.]. Major.

Major [Fr. *majeur;* Ger. *Dur;* It. *maggiore;* Sp. *mayor*]. See Interval, Scale, Chord, Triad, Mode, Key, Tonality.

Malagueña [Sp.]. A variety of the **fandango* associated with the region of Málaga in southern Spain, but also known in the New World. Examples in art music include "Málaga" from Albéniz's *Iberia* (1906–8). As a type of *flamenco music, it is in free rhythm with texts composed of five-line octosyllabic strophes.

Malaysia. See Southeast Asia VIII.

Malinconico [It.]. Melancholy.

Mambo [Sp.]. An Afro-Cuban dance-music genre, developed by the early 1940s and quickly popularized internationally. Performed by Cuban *conjunto,* with voices, trumpets, and extensive rhythm section, or by larger, jazz-influenced dance bands, the moderate- to rapid-tempo *mambo* is distinctive in its extensive use

of ostinato or riff passages for brass (and reed) instruments. (Such passages in other Afro-Cuban genres are also known as *mambos.*) The accompanimental pattern [Ex.], while not exclusively found with the *mambo,* is characteristic. The conga-drum figure combines unaccented strokes (♪), sharply accented slap strokes (♪), and open tones (♪). D.S.

Mamelles de Tirésias, Les [Fr., The Breasts of Tiresias]. Comic opera in two acts and a prologue by Poulenc (libretto by Guillaume Apollinaire), produced in Paris in 1947.

Ma mère l'oye [Fr., Mother Goose (Suite)]. A suite by Ravel depicting characters in fairy tales by Charles Perrault (1628–1703) and others. Originally written for piano four-hands (1908–10), it was later orchestrated by Ravel and produced with additional movements and interludes as a children's ballet in 1912.

Man. Abbr. for *manual.

Mancando [It.]. Fading, dying away.

Manche [Fr.]. The neck of a stringed instrument.

Mandolin [Fr. *mandoline;* Ger. *Mandoline;* It. *mandolino;* Sp. *mandolina*]. A small pear-shaped instrument with a round back and short neck developed from the *mandora. The earliest had four to six courses of gut strings and were often finger plucked. After 1730, a version with four double courses intended for plectrum playing only was adapted for metal strings by means of metal frets, a deeply vaulted back, a downward bend in the top below the bridge, and fastenings for strings at the end of the body.

Although mandolins, like lutes, usually had round backs built up of many ribs, some with flat backs were used in France and Portugal in the 1800s. Late in the 19th century, the American Orville Gibson invented a family of mandolins with carved tops and flat backs that were based on the principles of the Cremonese violins.

Other members of the mandolin family are the mandola, either an alto, tuned c g d′ a′, or a tenor, tuned G d a e′; the mandocello, a bass, tuned an octave below the alto, C G d a; the mandolone, a special 18th- and 19th-century bass, tuned F G a d g b e′ a′; the mandobass, a modern contrabass, tuned C_1 G_1 D A.

The earliest music for mandolin (mandola, mandolino) dates from ca. 1650 and is in tablature for a four-course instrument tuned e′ a′ d″ g″. This tuning, with the addition of a fifth and sixth course, remained a standard. Vivaldi (1736) wrote for a six-course mandolin tuned g b e′ a′ d″ g″. Pietro Leone's tutor (Paris, ca. 1750 or ca. 1768) for the Neapolitan mandolin *(mandolino napolitano)* gives a tuning g d′ a′ e″ for four double courses of wire strings. This is used today. One of the most characteristic playing styles on the mandolin produces sustained tones by means of a tremolo with the plectrum. Handel, Mozart, Verdi, Mahler, and Schoenberg have all used the mandolin in major works. In the U.S., flat-backed instruments were popular in mandolin bands around the turn of the 20th century and (including electric versions, some with a cut-out in the body similar to that of the electric guitar) are widely used in country and western music, both as solo instruments and in ensembles. See ills. under Lute.

Bibl.: James Tyler, "The Italian Mandolin and Mandola," *EM* 9 (1981): 438–46. R.L.

Mandora, mandore, mandola [Fr. *mandore;* Ger. *Mandoër, Mandürichen, Mandorlauten;* It. *mandola;* Sp. *vandola*]. (1) A lutelike instrument developed from the medieval *gittern. Mandoras are gut-strung and played with a plectrum. The name was adopted in the mid-16th century with a new tuning and playing method. Early mandoras were carved from solid wood and have three or four courses. By the 17th century, built-up mandoras were also made and the number of courses increased to four or five. As the century progressed, mandoras were built in both smaller and increasingly larger sizes and were given up to eight courses of strings. A very large mandora was sometimes called a colachon. A variety of tunings is documented, among them g d′ g′ d″, c′ g′ c″ g″, c f a d′ g′, and F G c f a d′. The colachon was sometimes tuned a fourth lower than the six-course mandora.

(2) An 18th-century Austrian and German eight-course hybrid combining a lute body and pegbox with a guitar neck. This was played and tuned like the guitar: C D E A d g b e′.

Bibl.: Donald Gill, "Mandores and Colachons," *GSJ* 34 (1981): 130–41. James Tyler, "The Mandore in the 16th and 17th Centuries," *EM* 9 (1981): 22–31. R.L.

Maneria [Lat.]. In the church *modes of the Middle Ages, the pair of authentic and plagal modes associated with any of the four regular finals (D, E, F, G), but without regard for the distinction between authentic and plagal. There are thus four *maneriae,* and these are often identified with the Greek terms [see Byzantine chant] for the four finals, *protus, deuterus, tritus,* and *tetrardus* (first, second, third, fourth).

Maneries [Lat.]. In the 13th century, a rhythmic mode [see Modes, rhythmic].

Manfred. (1) An overture and incidental music by Schumann, op. 115 (1848–49), to Byron's poetic drama of the same name. (2) A symphony in B minor by Tchaikovsky, op. 58 (1885), after Byron's work.

Manfredina. *Monferrina.

Mangulina [Sp.]. A folk dance of the Dominican Republic, performed by vocalists in small ensembles with *tres* (guitar with three double courses) or accordion and such percussion instruments as the *guayo* (metal scraper), *tambora* (double-headed membranophone), and *marimba* (like the Cuban *marimbula,* a metal-keyed lamellaphone with box resonator). The *mangulina* was also a fashionable ballroom dance in the Dominican Republic in the mid-19th century. D.S.

Manica [It.]. In string playing, shift; *mezza manica,* half shift [see Position].

Manico [It.]. (1) The *neck of a stringed instrument. (2) *Mezzo manico,* according to J. J. Quantz (1752), *position or shifting.

Manicorde [Fr.], **manicordio** [Sp.], **manicordo** [It.]. Clavichord.

Maniera [It.]. See Mannerism.

Manieren [Ger.]. In the 18th century, ornaments or *graces [see Ornamentation; see also Mannheim School].

Maṇipuri [Hin.]. A Vaisnava dance-drama of the Meitei people in Manipur, India. Popularized by Rabindranath Tagore in the 1930s through performances by the female students of his university, it helped establish the respectability of the dance arts among the middle class. C.C.

Männerchor [Ger.]. Men's chorus.

Männergesangverein [Ger.]. Male choral society.

Mannerism. An aesthetic principle, recently associated with music from the mid-16th to the early 17th century, according to which individuation of local musical events may seem to take precedence over the exposition of clear and coherent musical structures. Mannerism is thus viewed as a countertendency to classicism. Composers often cited in this connection include Philippe de Monte (1521–1603), Adrian Willaert (ca. 1490–1562), Cipriano de Rore (1515–65), and Carlo Gesualdo (ca. 1560–1613). The Italian *madrigal is the genre most closely associated with the notion.

The modern concept of mannerism emerged in German art criticism of the early 20th century, especially in the work of Max Dvořák. It was introduced to musicology by Trede (1928) and Schrade (1934). The utility of mannerism as a music-historical concept remains controversial. It does not correspond to the 16th-century term *maniera,* from which it etymologically derives, yet it tends to replace this term in discussions of style. *Maniera,* for both its advocates (Giorgio Vasari) and its detractors (Ludovico Dolce), referred to a style that discerns (i.e., abstracts) the most beautiful features of natural objects and then concatenates them into a whole more exquisite than anything naturally beheld. This conception does not transfer easily to musical aesthetics. For whereas an artwork can model itself directly on features of a world seen as imperfect, the stuff of music (tones, intervals, mensurations) already represents a level of abstraction at which beauty has been chosen (or rejected) for its own sake. On the other hand, the modern concept of mannerism is not without its difficulties, for if mannerism is defined by deviations from accepted norms, then the notion of a manneristic style is problematically narrow, and that of a manneristic era a contradiction in terms. Other problems are discussed by Hucke (1961), Finscher (1972), and Lockwood (1974).

The designation of the late 14th-century secular repertory at Avignon as manneristic (first by Willi Apel because he found in this music "deliberate diversification, extravagance, and utmost complexity") has lost favor since Ursula Günther suggested the less biased **ars subtilior.*

Bibl.: Hilmar Trede, "Manierismus und Barock im italienischen Madrigal des 16. Jahrhunderts. Dargestellt an den Frühwerken Claudio Monteverdis" (Ph.D. diss., Erlangen, 1928). Leo Schrade, "Von der 'Maniera' der Komposition in der Musik des 16. Jahrhunderts," *ZfMw* 16 (1934): 3–20, 98–117, 152–70. Helmut Hucke, "Das Problem des Manierismus in der Musik," *Literaturwissenschaftliches Jahrbuch des Görres-Gesellschaft* 2 (1961): 219–38. James Haar, "Classicism and Mannerism in 16th-Century Music," *International Revue of Music Aesthetics and Sociology* 1 (1970): 55–67. Ludwig Finscher, "Gesualdos 'Atonalität' und das Problem des musikalisches Manierismus," *AfMw* 29 (1972): 1–16. Claude V. Palisca, "*Ut oratoria musica:* The Rhetorical Basis of Musical Mannerism," in *The Meaning of Mannerism* (Hanover, N.H.: U Pr of New Eng, 1972), pp. 37–65. Lewis Lockwood, "On 'Mannerism' and 'Renaissance' as Terms and Concepts in Music History," *Studi musicali* 3 (1974): 85–96. Edward E. Lowinsky, "The Problem of Mannerism in Music: An Attempt at a Definition," *Studi musicali* 3 (1974): 131–218. Claude V. Palisca, "Towards an Intrinsically Musical Definition of Mannerism in the 16th Century," *Studi musicali* 3 (1974): 313–46. Maria Rika Maniates, *Mannerism in Italian Music and Culture, 1530–1630* (Chapel Hill: U of NC Pr, 1979). Viktor Ravizza, "Manierismus: Ein musikgeschichtlicher Epochbegriff," *Mf* 34 (1981): 273–84. Carl Dahlhaus, "Musikalischer Humanismus als Manierismus," *Mf* 35 (1982): 122–29.

Mannheim school. A group of performers and composers active at the court of Mannheim in southwestern Germany during the 18th century. The importance of Mannheim as a musical and cultural center began in 1720, when the elector palatine Carl Philipp moved his court there from Heidelberg. Its principal fame, however, was achieved during the reign of Elector Carl Theodor (ruled in Mannheim 1743–78), who assembled some of the finest performers and composers in Europe. Of particular renown was the Mannheim orchestra, widely regarded as the finest in Europe. This brilliant period came to an abrupt end with the removal of the court from Mannheim to Munich in 1778.

The true position of Mannheim in musical history has been the subject of much controversy. Early in the 20th century, Hugo Riemann, basing his studies on the pioneering research of Friedrich Walter, announced his "discovery" of a Mannheim school of symphonists that he proclaimed as the principal creators of the Classical symphonic style (Riemann, 1902, 1906). Riemann's claims were subsequently challenged by musicologists in Austria, Italy, and France, and scholars now generally view Mannheim as "the residence of a talented, up-to-date, though not pre-eminent group of composers" (Newman, 1963).

Recent attention has centered on the debt of the Mannheim symphony to Italy, in particular to the opera overtures of composers such as Niccolò Jommelli and Baldassare Galuppi (Wolf, 1980, 1981; compare Kamieński, 1908/9). For example, the extended crescendo passage or *Walze,* considered by Riemann and others to have been a Mannheim invention, unquestionably originated in Italian opera. The same may be said for the "Mannheim sigh" or melodic appoggiatura, the "Mannheim rocket" (an arpeggio theme rising through several octaves), and numerous other melodic figures or *Manieren* associated by Riemann with Mannheim. On the above points, then, the role of Mannheim may best be described as the adaptation and extension of the dramatic Italian overture style to the concert symphony [see Symphony II, Overture I]. Other important contributions include the earliest consistent use of four movements in the symphony (in the works of Johann Stamitz after ca. 1745) and the idiomatic, frequently virtuosic treatment of the orchestra.

The concept of a unified Mannheim "school" of composers has also been challenged. Eighteenth-century references to the "Mannheim school" refer either to violinists at the electoral court or, more generally, to every aspect of music there, including performance, composition, and taste. The modern concept of a compositional school is clearly inappropriate for the first generation of Mannheim symphonists, including Stamitz, Franz Xaver Richter, and Ignaz Holzbauer; their backgrounds and musical styles are too divergent. By contrast, the music of such second-generation Mannheimers as Anton Fils, Christian Cannabich (Stamitz's successor as concertmaster), and Carl Joseph Toeschi, of whom at least the latter two were students of Stamitz, shows a rather stereotyped approach that conforms to the conventional notion of a "school" of composition.

Bibl.: Friedrich Walter, *Geschichte des Theaters und der Musik am kurpfälzischen Hofe* (Leipzig: Breitkopf & Härtel, 1898). Hugo Riemann, ed., *Sinfonien der pfalzbayerischen Schule, DTB* 3/1 (1902), 7/2 (1906), 8/2 (1907). Lucian Kamieński, "Mannheim und Italien," *SIMG* 10 (1908/9): 307–17. Hugo Riemann, ed., *Mannheimer Kammermusik des 18. Jahrhunderts, DTB* 15–16 (1914–15). Jens Peter Larsen, "Zur Bedeutung der 'Mannheimer Schule,'" *Fellerer,* 1962, pp. 303–9. William S. Newman, *The Sonata in the Classic Era* (Chapel Hill: U of NC Pr, 1963; 3rd ed., New York: Norton, 1983). Eduard Schmitt, ed., *Kirchenmusik der Mannheimer Schule, DTB,* Neue Folge, vols. 2–3 (1980–82). Eugene K. Wolf, "On the Origins of the Mannheim Symphonic Style," *Albrecht,* 1980, pp. 197–239. Id., *The Symphonies of Johann Stamitz* (Utrecht: Bohn, Scheltema & Holkema, 1981). Barry S. Brook et al., eds., *The Symphony, 1720–1840* (New York: Garland, 1979–85), ser. C, vol. 3, *The Symphony at Mannheim: Johann Stamitz, Christian Cannabich,* ed. Eugene K. and Jean K. Wolf (1984). Eugene K. Wolf, "The Mannheim Court," in *Man and Music/Music and Society,* ed. Stanley Sadie, vol. 5: *The Classical Era,* ed. Neal Zaslaw (Englewood Cliffs, N.J.: Prentice Hall, 1989), pp. 213–39. Ludwig Finscher, ed., *Die Mannheimer Hofkapelle im Zeitalter Carl Theodors* (Mannheim: Palatium Verlag im J & J Verlag, 1992). Eugene K. Wolf, "On the Composition of the Mannheim Orchestra, ca. 1740–1778," *Basler Jahrbuch für historische Musikpraxis* 17 (1993): 113–38. *Ballet Music from the Mannheim Court,* ed. Paul Corneilson et al., *RRMCE* 45, 47, 52, 57 (1996–99). Eugene K. Wolf, *Manuscripts from Mannheim, ca. 1730–1778: A Study in the Methodology of Musical Source Research,* Quellen und Studien zur Geschichte der Mannheimer Hofkapelle 9 (Frankfurt am Main: Peter Lang, 2002). E.K.W.

Mano [It.]. Hand; *m. destra (sinistra),* right (left) hand.

Manon. Opera in five acts by Massenet (libretto in French by Henri Meilhac and Philippe Gille, after the novel by the Abbé Antoine François Prévost), produced in Paris in 1884. Setting: Amiens, Paris, and Le Havre about 1721.

Manon Lescaut. Opera in four acts by Puccini, produced in Turin in 1893. The libretto, which appeared without attribution, had been worked on by Ruggero Leoncavallo, Mario Praga, Domenico Oliva, Giacomo Giacosa, and Luigi Illica as well as Giulio Ricordi and Puccini himself and was based on the Abbé Prévost's novel. Setting: France and Louisiana in the early 18th century.

Manual. A keyboard (other than the pedalboard) of an organ or harpsichord.

Manualiter [Lat.]. To be played on the organ keyboards (manuals) only, without use of the pedal keyboard.

Manualkoppel [Ger.]. *Manual coupler.

Manus musicalis [Lat.]. *Guidonian hand.

Manzoni Requiem. The name sometimes given to Verdi's *Messa da Requiem,* which was composed and first performed in 1874 on the first anniversary of the death of the Italian novelist and poet Alessandro Manzoni.

Maqām [Ar., place, pl. *maqāmāt;* Turk. *makam*]. The main modal unit of Arabic music; hence, also Middle Eastern modal practice in general. A *maqām* consists of a diatonic scale (sometimes with 3/4 and 5/4 tones), the lower tetrachord being the most characteristic. Although typical tone sequences, motifs, and cadences as well as nonmusical characterizations are part of the concept, 20th-century practice stresses the scalar aspects. Among the popular *maqāmāt* are *Hijāz, Rāst, Bayātī,* and *Sabā.* The nature, intonation, and organization of *maqāmāt* form the principal subject of the long history of Arabic-Persian theory. See also Near and Middle East. B.N.

Maraca. A Latin American rattle consisting of a round or oval-shaped vessel filled with seeds or similar material and held by a handle. Maracas may be made from gourds, wood, metal, or synthetic materials. An essential element of Latin American popular music, they are almost always played in pairs, one in each hand. See ill. under Percussion instruments.

Marcato [It.]. Marked, stressed, emphasized, often with respect to a melody that is to be made prominent.

Marcellus Mass [Lat. *Missa Papae Marcelli*]. A Mass in six voices by Palestrina composed about 1562–63 and published in his Second Book of Masses in 1567, where it was dedicated to Pope Marcellus II (d. 1555). Because of the clarity with which the text is treated, it was once thought to have been responsible for deterring the *Council of Trent from banishing polyphony from the liturgy. Although the Marcellus Mass reflects directly or indirectly some of the Council's concerns about liturgical music, its specific relationship to the activities of the Council remains a matter of conjecture. See also Mass.

Bibl.: Giovanni Pierluigi da Palestrina, *Pope Marcellus Mass,* ed. Lewis Lockwood [with extensive supplementary material] (New York: Norton, 1975).

March [Fr. *marche;* Ger. *Marsch;* It. *marcia;* Sp. *marcha*]. Music designed to keep the marching of troops or processions of nonmilitary groups uniform, usually through emphatic strong beats embodied in simple, repetitive rhythmic patterns.

By the early 16th century, the marching of European armies was ordered through standard drum patterns, each nation having its own patterns. These were part of the larger system of military signals, including trumpet calls, that were used to direct armies. This is the original meaning of march in a quasi-musical sense. Arbeau's *Orchésographie* (1588) mentions that these drum patterns could be embellished improvisationally by fifes, and this practice can be regarded as the seed from which the more musically developed march began to grow with the beginning of the modern military band around the mid-17th century. The expansion of the band and the improvement of many of its instruments in the 19th century ushered in a golden age of the military march that lasted into the early 20th century, the period of John Philip Sousa (1854–1932), the most notable among a considerable number of march composers popular in that period.

Military marches are categorized by the tempo of the drum beat, corresponding to military function, in ascending order of pace: the slow or parade march [Ger. *Parademarsch;* Fr. *pas ordinaire*]; the quick march [Ger. *Geschwindmarsch;* Fr. *pas redoublé;* Sp. *paso doble*]; and the double-quick or attack march [Ger. *Sturmmarsch;* Fr. *pas de charge*]. The rogue's march accompanies the ceremony when a soldier is drummed out of the army. (In the British Army it is a quick march, traditionally to a tune called "The Tight Little Island.") The normal tempo for a military march in the U.S. is 120 beats per minute; school bands performing at football games are likely to march at a very much faster tempo. Certain marches have become traditional for some nonmilitary functions, such as weddings, funerals, and school graduations.

Various musical types of marches were popular in the late 19th century, such as the patrol, which begins softly, grows gradually louder, and then fades away. (Similar dynamic effects are also found in marches in opera and in such works as Berlioz's Rákóczi March and Debussy's *Fêtes.*) There has been at times a close connection between the march and popular dance music; the march was used for the two-step in the 1890s and was important as a source of *ragtime. The form that the march took in the 19th century was similar to that of contemporary dance music: a series of eight- or, more often, sixteen-measure strains, the principal strain or strains repeated later in the piece, with an introduction and one or more intermediate trios, often in the subdominant.

The stylization of the march in art music, often for programmatic purposes, begins very early with the 16th-century battle piece, such as the "Battell" attributed to William Byrd in *My Ladye Nevell's Booke.* It reaches a height with Beethoven and later 19th-century composers, evocations of the funeral march being especially favored by the Romantics. Many of the marches of Sousa and his contemporaries were composed for concert performances rather than the parade ground.

Bibl.: Jacob Kappey, *Military Music* (London, 1894). Henry G. Farmer, *The Rise and Development of Military Music* (London: W Reeves, 1912; R: Freeport, N.Y.: Books for Libraries Pr, 1970). William C. White, *A History of Military Music in America* (New York: Exposition, 1944; R: Westport, Conn.: Greenwood, 1975).

Marcha [Sp., Port.]. In Iberia and Latin America, the march and associated music; also any of a variety of folk-music genres that accompany processions and marchlike dances. D.S.

Marche [Fr.]. March; *m. harmonique (d'harmonie),* sequence (1).

Marcia [It.]. March; *m. funebre,* funeral march; *alla m.,* in the manner of a march.

Mariachi. A traditional ensemble of western Mexico, and especially the state of Jalisco, now found throughout the country. Today, the typical *mariachi* consists of one or more trumpets and violins, five-string *vihuela,* guitar(s), and *guitarrón* (six-string bass guitar); it performs a varied repertory of **jarabes* and *sones jaliscienses, canciones rancheras* and **corridos, *boleros,* and other genres. D.S.

Marian antiphon. An antiphon for the Virgin Mary [for examples, see Antiphon].

Marienleben, Das [Ger., The Life of Mary]. A song cycle for soprano and piano by Hindemith on 15 texts by Rilke, composed in 1922–23 and revised in 1936–48.

Marimba. (1) A *xylophone with resonators under each bar. Originally an African instrument, it spread to Latin America and remains popular in Mexico and Central America, especially in Guatemala, where it is considered the national instrument. In Africa it may have only 1 or 2 bars, or it may have 20 or more; resonators are generally gourds, sometimes with *mirliton devices added. Marimbas are often assembled into orchestras composed of instruments of different size and pitch accompanied by drums. Sometimes two players play on the same instrument, one player seated on either side.

In Latin America, marimbas are typically mounted on stands. The resonators may be tubular or made from gourds or other material, sometimes with mirliton devices. Marimba orchestras are popular in Mexico and Guatemala. Some Central American marimbas are very large, covering up to seven octaves and played by several players, all standing or sitting on the same side. Tuning is usually chromatic. A marimba constructed of bamboo tubes is played by people of African ancestry along the Pacific coast of Colombia and Ecuador.

Marimbas have been manufactured in the U.S. since the early 20th century for use in popular and concert music, including the symphony orchestra. A typical orchestral instrument covers three to four chromatic octaves ascending from the C below middle C, the bars being arranged on the pattern of piano keys. See ill. under Percussion instruments.

(2) **Mbira.*

Marimbaphone. A variety of *marimba with metal bars, made by J. C. Deagan of Chicago ca. 1920.

Marímbula [Sp.]. An **mbira* of Colombia, Cuba, the Dominican Republic, and Haiti. It consists of several metal tongues mounted over a hole on a wooden box resonator. The player plucks the tongues with his thumbs. The *mbira* was imported to the Caribbean from Africa, and its use is often connected with African-derived cults.

Marinera [Sp.]. A traditional couple dance of Peru, related to the Chilean **cueca* and descended from the *zamacueca (zambacueca)* of the colonial period. In rapid tempo and with rhythmic patterns combining triple and compound duple meters, it often exhibits the distinctive pentatonic melodic framework and bimodal character of the **huayno* and other genres of the Peruvian Andes. D.S.

Marine shell trumpet. A trumpet made from a mollusk shell, most often a conch. The player blows through a hole pierced at or near the small end of the spiral. Today they are most common in Oceania.

Marine trumpet. **Tromba marina.*

Marizápalos [Sp.]. A 17th-century Spanish dance in 3/4 time. Examples survive for guitar and for keyboard.

Markiert [Ger.]. **Marcato.*

Markig [Ger.]. Vigorous.

Marqué [Fr.]. **Marcato.*

Marriage of Figaro, The. See *Nozze di Figaro, Le.*

Marsch [Ger.]. March.

Marseillaise, La. The French national anthem, with words (beginning "Allons enfants de la patrie," Come, children of France) and music composed by Claude-Joseph Rouget de Lisle in 1792. It was adopted in 1795.

Marteau sans maître, Le [Fr., The Hammer without a Master]. A composition in nine movements by Boulez for alto, alto flute, viola, guitar, xylorimba, vibraphone, and percussion, composed in 1952–54 (rev. 1957) on a cycle of poems of the same name by René Char.

Martelé [Fr.]. See Bowing (3).

Martellato [It.]. (1) See Bowing (3). (2) In piano playing, a "hammered" touch.

Martellement [Fr., a hammering]. In the 17th century, a *mordent. In the 18th century, a mordent or a **Schneller;* occasionally a *trill.

Martha. Opera in four acts by Friedrich von Flotow (libretto in German by Wilhelm Friedrich [pseud. for Friedrich W. Riese], after a French ballet scenario by Vernoy de Saint-Georges), produced in Vienna in 1847. Setting: England in the early 18th century.

Mascherata [It.]. A masked Carnival performance in Renaissance Italy. Pieces for such occasions, like **villanelle* in style but for four or more voices, were also called *mascherate* (Giovanni Croce, *Mascarate . . . per il Carnevale,* 1590). J.H.

Masculine, feminine cadence. A cadence is termed masculine if its final pitch or chord occurs on a metrically strong beat [see Meter], feminine if on a metrically weak beat. Feminine cadences occur in both instrumental and vocal music, in the latter often when the final word to be set is accented on the penultimate syllable. In both types of music, the feminine cadence often takes the form of an *appoggiatura to the tonic or other cadential pitch; the underlying harmonic resolution of the cadence may thus take place on the strong beat while the melodic resolution is delayed.

Masked Ball, A. See *Ballo in maschera, Un.*

Masonic music. See Freemasonry and music.

Masque, mask. A form of entertainment, involving costumes, scenery, dances, music, and poetry, that flourished in England in Tudor and Stuart times. The subject matter was usually mythological, allegorical, or heroic. The roots of the masque are more social than theatrical; a group of masked and costumed revelers (sometimes accompanied by torchbearers) would intrude upon a festive gathering, perform a series of dances, recitations, and songs, and then join the party. Models for the masque may be found in similar productions in Italy and France, such as the **ballet de cour.* The English court masque reached a literary and visual high point between 1601 and 1631 when Ben Jonson and Inigo Jones collaborated to produce more than 30 masques. Composers who contributed music to these masques included Alfonso Ferrabosco, John Coprario, Thomas Campion, Nicholas Lanier, and William Lawes. Masques were treated as events for specific occasions, and no complete work, containing all the text and music performed, has survived.

After the Commonwealth, the home for masques was no longer the court but rather the theater, where masquelike entertainments were inserted, generally at the ends of acts of plays or *semi-operas. The greatest examples of such works may be found in Purcell's *Dioclesian, King Arthur,* and *The Fairy Queen.* The masque was revived in the 20th century by Vaughan Williams in *Job: A Masque for Dancing* (1931), and one occurs in Britten's opera *Gloriana* (1953).

Bibl.: Edward J. Dent, *Foundations of English Opera* (Cambridge: Cambridge U Pr, 1928). Otto Gombosi, "Some Musical Aspects of the English Court Masque," *JAMS* 1 (1948): 3–19. Frederick Samuel Boas, ed., *Songs and Lyrics from the English Masques and Light Operas* (London: Harrap, 1949). Eric Walter White, *The Rise of English Opera* (London: J Lehmann, 1951). John P. Cutts, "Jacobean

Masque and Stage Music," *ML* 35 (1954): 185–200. Stephen Orgel, *The Jonsonian Masque* (Cambridge, Mass.: Harvard U Pr, 1965; R: New York: Columbia U Pr, 1981). Murray Lefkowitz, *Trois masques à la cour de Charles Ier d'Angleterre* (Paris: CNRS, 1970). Roger Fiske, *English Theatre Music in the Eighteenth Century* (London: Oxford U Pr, 1973). Stephen Orgel and Roy Strong, *Inigo Jones: The Theatre of the Stuart Court* (Berkeley and Los Angeles: U of Cal Pr, 1973). Andrew J. Sabol, *Four Hundred Songs and Dances for the Stuart Masque* (Providence: Brown U Pr, 1978). C.G.

Mass [Fr. *messe;* Ger. *Messe;* It., Lat. *missa;* Sp. *misa*]. The most important service of the Roman rite, deriving from a ritual commemoration of the Last Supper. The term is taken from the words of dismissal of the congregation at the end of the ceremony ("ite missa est"); an earlier name was *eucharistia.* By the 7th century, the Mass had developed an elaborate liturgy of chants, prayers, and readings placed before and after the central canon [see Canon (3)], and a distinction was made between those parts of the liturgy whose texts (and music) were appropriate only to a particular feast (the Proper) and those whose texts (and music) could be used on any day (the Ordinary) [see also Liturgy, Gregorian chant, *Missa*]. The division of the Mass into musical and nonmusical sections and Proper and Ordinary is shown in the accompanying table. The following is the Latin text of the portion of the Ordinary most often set to music and a translation into English.

Sung		Spoken or recited	
Proper	Ordinary	Proper	Ordinary
1. Introit			
	2. Kyrie		
	3. Gloria		
		4. Collect	
		5. Epistle	
6. Gradual			
7. Alleluia or Tract			
		8. Gospel	
	9. Credo		
10. Offertory			
			11. Offertory Prayers
		12. Secret	
		13. Preface	
	14. Sanctus		
			15. Canon
			16. Pater noster
	17. Agnus Dei		
18. Communion			
		19. Postcommunion	
	20. Ite missa est or Benedicamus Domino		

Kyrie eleison. Kyrie eleison. Kyrie eleison. Christe eleison. Christe eleison. Christe eleison. Kyrie eleison. Kyrie eleison. Kyrie eleison.

Gloria in excelsis Deo. Et in terra pax hominibus bonae voluntatis. Laudamus te. Benedicimus te. Adoramus te. Glorificamus te. Gratias agimus tibi propter magnam gloriam tuam. Domine Deus Rex caelestis, Deus Pater omnipotens. Domine Fili unigenite, Jesu Christe. Domine Deus, Agnus Dei, Filius Patris. Qui tollis peccata mundi, miserere nobis. Qui tollis peccata mundi, suscipe deprecationem nostram. Qui sedes ad dexteram Patris, miserere nobis. Quoniam tu solus sanctus. Tu solus Dominus. Tu solus altissimus, Jesu Christe. Cum Sancto Spiritu, in gloria Dei Patris. Amen.

Credo in unum Deum, Patrem omnipotentem, factorem caeli et terrae, visibilium omnium, et invisibilium. Et in unum Dominum Jesum Christum, Filium Dei unigenitum: et ex Patre natum ante omnia saecula; Deum de Deo, lumen de lumine, Deum verum de Deo vero; genitum, non factum, consubstantialem Patri; per quem omnia facta sunt. Qui propter nos homines, et propter nostram salutem, descendit de caelis. Et incarnatus est de Spiritu Sancto ex Maria Virgine; et homo factus est. Crucifixus etiam pro nobis; sub Pontio Pilato passus, et sepultus est. Et resurrexit tertia die, secundum Scripturas. Et ascendit in caelum, sedet ad dexteram Patris. Et iterum venturus est cum gloria judicare vivos et mortuos: cujus regni non erit finis. Et in Spiritum Sanctum Dominum et vivificantem, qui ex Patre Filioque procedit. Qui cum Patre et Filio simul adoratur et conglorificatur; qui locutus est per Prophetas. Et unam, sanctam, catholicam et apostolicam Ecclesiam. Confiteor unum baptisma in remissionem peccatorum. Et exspecto resurrectionem mortuorum, et vitam venturi saeculi. Amen.

Sanctus, sanctus, sanctus Dominus Deus Sabaoth. Pleni sunt caeli et terra gloria tua: Hosanna in excelsis. Benedictus qui venit in nomine Domini: Hosanna in excelsis.

Agnus Dei, qui tollis peccata mundi, miserere nobis. Agnus Dei, qui tollis peccata mundi, miserere nobis. Agnus Dei, qui tollis peccata mundi, dona nobis pacem.

Lord, have mercy. Lord, have mercy. Lord, have mercy. Christ, have mercy. Christ, have mercy. Christ, have mercy. Lord, have mercy. Lord, have mercy. Lord, have mercy.

Glory to God in the highest, and on earth peace to men of good will. We praise thee. We bless thee. We adore thee. We glorify thee. We give thee thanks for thy great glory, O Lord God, heavenly King. God the Father almighty. O Lord, the only begotten son Jesus Christ. O Lord God, Lamb of God, Son of the Father. Who takest away the sins of the world, have mercy on us. Who takest away the sins of the world, receive our prayers. Who sittest at the right hand of the Father, have mercy on us. For thou only art holy. Thou only art Lord. Thou only, O Jesus Christ, art most high. With the Holy Ghost, in the glory of God the Father. Amen.

I believe in one God, the Father almighty, maker of heaven and earth, and of all things visible and invisible. And in one Lord Jesus Christ, the only begotten Son of God, born of the Father before all ages; God of God, light of light, true God of true God; begotten not made; being of one substance with the Father; by whom all things were made. Who for us men, and for our salvation, came down from heaven; and was incarnate by the Holy Ghost, of the Virgin Mary; and was made man. He was crucified also for us, suffered under Pontius Pilate, and was buried. And the third day he rose again according to the Scriptures; and ascended into heaven. He sitteth at the right hand of the Father; and he shall come again with glory to judge the living and the dead; and his kingdom shall have no end. And [I believe] in the Holy Ghost, the Lord and giver of life, who proceedeth from the Father and the Son, who together with the Father and the Son is adored and glorified; who spoke by the Prophets. And [in] one holy catholic and apostolic Church. I confess one baptism for the remission of sins. And I await the resurrection of the dead, and the life of the world to come. Amen.

Holy, holy, holy, Lord God of hosts. Heaven and earth are full of thy glory. Hosanna in the highest. Blessed is he that cometh in the name of the Lord. Hosanna in the highest.

Lamb of God, who takest away the sins of the world, have mercy on us. Lamb of God, who takest away the sins of the world, have mercy on us. Lamb of God, who takest away the sins of the world, grant us peace.

I. *History to 1400.* The liturgy of the Mass contains 11 musical items: 5 Proper and 6 Ordinary (the latter including the dismissal, Ite missa est). Proper chants are the oldest in the written tradition (beginning around the 9th century, however McKinnon (2000) places the creation of the Proper in the 7th century, before the development of music notation); they are divided among chants employing antiphonal *psalmody (*introit, *offertory, *communion), responsorial psalmody (*gradual, *alleluia), and direct psalmody (the *tract, which occasionally replaces the alleluia). The texts and chants of the Ordinary entered the liturgy at various times, the *Credo not becoming part of the Roman Mass until 1014.

The first five items of the musical Ordinary (i.e., not including the Ite missa est) have so often been set by composers of the polyphonic period that they are sometimes thought of as a unit. Liturgically, however, they are not, as the parts of the Ordinary (with the exception of the *Kyrie and *Gloria) are separated by other chants, readings, and prayers; chant composers made no attempt to make musical links among them in the many melodies created for each text. The chants of the Ordinary and certain chants of the Proper (particularly the introit and alleluia) were also troped [see Trope], and the application of texts to the extended melismas following the alleluia verse gave rise to a new member of the Mass liturgy known as the *sequence. In the 13th century, the Ordinary chants (with the exception of the Credo) were gathered together into plainsong Mass cycles, and they are presented in this way in modern *liturgical books (e.g., *LU*); in modern publications, the cycles are identified by number (Mass IX, etc.), or by title (*Missa de Beata Virgine, Missa de Angelis,* etc.). Apel (1966) has remarked that in many of these cycles the Ite shares the melody of the Kyrie and thus bestows a musical unity upon them.

The responsorial items of the Proper and the sequence were the first Mass chants to inspire polyphonic elaboration, no doubt because they stressed soloistic singing. In the 11th and 12th centuries, the solo sections of the responsorial chants of the Mass and *Office were used by the composers of the *Notre Dame School as the basis of a complex polyphony known as *organum; the **Magnus liber*, ascribed to Leonin, sets the graduals and alleluias of the **Temporale* in two-part polyphony. Perotin, a younger colleague, is credited with composing three- and four-part organa. Eventually, though, the **clausula* and its descendant the *motet became the focus of composition, and by the 13th century, interest in organum (hence, in the Mass) had declined.

The revival of Mass composition in the 14th century concerned the Ordinary rather than the Proper. Manuscripts connected with the papal court at Avignon (1305–78) contain many polyphonic elaborations of the first five elements of the Ordinary (the Ite is rarely set) arranged as groups of Kyries, Glorias, Credos, etc. These were composed in a number of styles—Stäblein-Harder (1962) points to the motet style, discant style, and simultaneous style—and were sometimes, but not always, based on Ordinary chants. When they were, the chant could appear in the tenor or in the uppermost voice and could be rendered exactly or paraphrased [see Paraphrase]. The first presentations of the parts of the Ordinary as a polyphonic cycle (perhaps emulating plainsong cycles) also appear in the 14th century. The earliest such cycles (the Masses of Tournai, Toulouse, Barcelona, and the Sorbonne) cannot be ascribed to any one composer and seem to be miscellanies. The most important early polyphonic cycle, and the first by a known composer, was Machaut's *Messe de Notre Dame,* a setting of all six elements of the Ordinary, including the Ite. The work employs Ordinary chants and isorhythmic procedures in the Kyrie, Sanctus, Agnus, and Ite, though Machaut abandons them in the Gloria and Credo.

II. *1400–1600.* 1. Settings of individual Ordinary texts (with the exception of the Ite, which was by then ignored entirely) abound in the early 15th century; the *Old Hall Manuscript, for instance, contains 40 Glorias, 35 Credos, 27 Sanctus, and 19 Agnus along with other works. (There are no Kyries, perhaps because the manuscript is incomplete or because the Kyrie was omitted from the *Sarum rite.) In these and in other works, paraphrase technique with Ordinary chants in the uppermost voice is quite common, though the chant could also be treated more strictly or could appear in the tenor. The continued concern with the Ordinary also fostered a desire to unite the elements by musical means; Masses so unified are called cyclic Masses (a term introduced in Wagner, 1913). Perhaps the simplest (and, according to Bukofzer, 1950, the first) method of unification consisted of beginning each part of the Ordinary with the same music [see Motto]. More far-reaching was the attempt to unite the five-part Ordinary by basing each polyphonic setting on the same borrowed melody or **cantus firmus* (hence the term *cantus firmus* Mass). The first composers to do this were English, and the idea spread to the Continent no doubt through the great dissemination of English music in Europe at the beginning of the 15th century. In the earliest such Masses, the *cantus firmus* was drawn from non-Ordinary chants (the Marian antiphon "Alma redemptoris mater" for Lionel Power's *Missa Alma redemptoris mater,* for example) and was restricted to the tenor of a three-voice structure (hence, the term tenor Mass). The *cantus firmus* appeared in every movement and could be presented in fairly long note-values and be organized isorythmically (strict *cantus firmus* procedure) as in the *Missa Alma redemptoris*—indeed, in this respect the *cantus firmus* Mass became heir to the dying isorhythmic motet—or it could be paraphrased (free *cantus firmus* procedure) as in John Dunstable's *Missa Rex seculorum* [see Isorhythm].

The first great Continental exponent of the cyclic Mass was Dufay. In what seems to have been his first such Mass, the *Missa Se la face ay pale* of ca. 1450 (the *Missa Caput,* once ascribed to Dufay, is now thought to be an English composition; see Planchart, 1972), he expanded the number of voices from three to four, adding a bass below the tenor, and used the tenor line of one of his own secular works as a *cantus firmus.* The *Missa Se la face ay pale* and the *Missa L'homme armé* (one of the first of many Masses using that melody [see *Homme armé, L'*]) employ strict *cantus firmus* procedure, but the *Missa Ave regina caelorum* of ca. 1472 treats the Gregorian melody freely while still keeping it mainly in the tenor. Dufay also occasionally quoted more than one voice from a polyphonic model, as in the Gloria and Credo of the *Missa Se la face ay pale* and most strikingly in the second Agnus of the *Missa Ave regina,* where a highly personal quotation from his motet of the same name appears. The motto beginning, not utilized by many English composers, was also employed by Dufay in all his cyclic Masses.

The influence of Dufay's Masses can be seen in the works of later composers in at least two distinct ways: (1) the cyclic Mass became an important genre and an outlet for a composer's most serious thoughts; (2) many cyclic Masses were based on the tenors of French chansons (though Gregorian chants were by no means abandoned). Josquin wrote at least 20 cyclic Masses, forming a compendium of all techniques known in his time and introducing several new ones. Strict *cantus firmus* procedure can be found in his *Missa L'homme armé super voces musicales,* and free *cantus firmus* procedure in his *Missa Gaudeamus* (based on an introit), while many Masses are based on secular tenors. The *Missa La sol fa re mi,* however, introduces a new principle in using *solmization syllables as the basis of the Mass. The solmization idea also appears in the *Missa Hercules Dux Ferrariae,* a Mass that flatters a reigning duke by constructing a *cantus firmus* from the syllables of his name [see *Soggetto cavato*]. In the *Missa Pange lingua,* a paraphrased *cantus firmus* moves from voice to voice within an imitative texture—a method of Mass construction that proved extremely attractive to 16th-century composers—while the *Missa Ad fugam* and the *Missa Sine nomine* are strictly canonic and do not seem to use any borrowed melody. Finally, the *Missa Mater patris* stands out within the canon of Josquin's Masses as one based on a three-part motet and consistently quoting more than one voice of its model.

After 1500, the increase in the composition of motets in an imitative-homophonic style had a pronounced effect upon the Mass. In particular, it gave rise to a new type of cyclic Mass, the *parody Mass. Parody Masses were first produced by Josquin's younger French contemporaries (some have claimed the *Missa Mater patris* as an early parody Mass, but this has been disputed; see Lockwood, 1964), and the type became very popular in the 16th century. But at the same time, interest in Mass composition itself seems to have declined, perhaps because there was thought to be no more room for experimentation or individuality in the genre. Instead, from the 1530s through the 1560s, composers such as Adrian Willaert, Nicholas Gombert, and Jacques Arcadelt channeled most of their energies into the production of motets and secular music, relegating the cyclic Mass to a small (and sometimes early and unrepresentative) part of their total oeuvre.

The cyclic Mass returned to prominence in the works of Palestrina and his contemporaries; indeed, Palestrina's 104 Masses are believed by many to be his best compositions. As was fitting for a composer working exclusively in Rome during the late 16th century, Palestrina chose mainly sacred models (Gregorian chants and motets) for his Masses, differing in this respect from his great contemporary Lassus (ca. 60 Masses), who often chose chansons or madrigals (as in the *Missa Je ne mange poinct de porc*). Every type of Mass construction is represented in Palestrina's output, and his personal style became the hallmark of classical polyphony. The *Missa Ecce sacerdotus magnus* (which opens the first book of Masses of 1554) uses the by-then-outmoded strict *cantus firmus* procedure (as do another six Mass settings); some 35 or so other Masses (particularly those based on hymns; see Marshall, 1963) illustrate the imitative paraphrase technique; one, the *Missa Ut re mi fa sol la,* uses solmization syllables; several settings are canonic, and six are freely composed (see *Grove* for a list of all the Masses). But by far the most popular technique for Palestrina, as for his contemporaries, was parody; furthermore, many of his 50 or so parody Masses are based on his own motets. One Mass, the *Missa Papae Marcelli,* was responsible for much of Palestrina's posthumous reputation, since it was believed that the work had saved polyphonic music from banishment by Pope Marcellus II. The story is probably not true—Marcellus II reigned for only a few weeks in 1555 and the Mass was probably written ca. 1562 (see Jeppesen, 1945)—but the *Missa Papae Marcelli* does in fact contain many traits considered by the Council of Trent in its final sessions of 1563: it is not clearly based on a model and thus could not be accused of using profane or secular material, and it furthermore renders the words of the Gloria and Credo particularly intelligible. In this regard, it joins a number of Masses commissioned from composers in Rome and elsewhere (e.g., Vincenzo Ruffo in Milan) by church officials interested in enforcing the Council's dictates (see Lockwood, 1970). But, as these Masses actually illustrate trends already present in late 16th-century music, the true effect of the Council's decrees on Masses and church music in general was probably not as great as has been thought.

2. Settings of the Proper and plainsong Masses. The items of the Proper and plainsong Mass cycles (often in **alternatim* style) were also set polyphonically during the 15th and 16th centuries. Dufay may have been the first to write *alternatim* Kyries (Kovarik, 1975), and he also produced a plainsong cycle of the Ordinary and Propers (the *Missa Sancti Jacobi*) before he turned to the cyclic Mass. The *Trent Codices contain settings of the Proper and plainsong Masses, but it was in German-speaking countries that these genres really took hold. When Heinrich Isaac entered the service of the Emperor Maximilian in 1496, he found it necessary to produce many plainsong *alternatim* Mass cycles and settings of individual Ordinary texts. He also made a great contribution to German tradition with his three-volume set of Proper cycles, the **Choralis constantinus;* no comparable collection of Proper cycles by a single composer appeared thereafter until Byrd published his *Gradualia* in 1605 and 1607. The plainsong Mass, with the exception of the *Missa de Beata Virgine,* did not interest composers outside of Germany. Palestrina did write a set of *alternatim* plainsong Masses, but these were composed on commission to please Guglielmo Gonzaga, Duke of Mantua. Occasional settings of individual Ordinary texts can be found (as in Petrucci's *Fragmenta missarum* of 1505), and items of the Proper were set in the *Lyons Contrapunctus* of 1548 and in Palestrina's cycle of offertories. In general, however, composers from the rest of Europe were immersed in the cyclic Mass.

3. The Protestant Mass. Luther had no objection to the Latin liturgy, and it was perfectly possible for Lutheran churches to perform cyclic Masses and other pieces originally intended for the Roman rite. But it cannot be said that a Protestant tradition of Latin Mass composition developed. Although the Latin liturgy was technically acceptable, there were many attempts to create a liturgy in German, leading eventually to Luther's *Deutsche Messe und Ordnung des Gottesdienstes* of 1526. The German liturgy stressed the *chorale over other elements; indeed, it soon became possible to substitute a chorale for any section of the Mass liturgy. The great emphasis placed on the chorale in Protestant countries tended to discourage composition of the Latin Mass, although isolated settings of Ordinary texts (the Kyrie and Gloria—called *missa*—and the Sanctus) continued to be produced, often only for very special occasions. In England, after the break with Rome and the establishment of a liturgy in English, the elements of the Mass became part of the Communion Service, and the Latin Mass as such ceased to exist. The only important cyclic Masses composed by an Englishman in the late 16th century were those by Byrd, a Catholic, who did not intend them for the Anglican Church.

III. *1600–1900.* In the great musical schism of the early 17th century, Masses were among those works assigned to the **prima prattica,* largely because of the pervasive influence of Palestrina and partly because the Mass text (i.e., the Ordinary) was considered to be impersonal and not apt for expressing the affections. Monteverdi himself made this point when he published with his new-style Vespers of 1610 a six-part Mass based on Gombert's motet *In illo tempore.* This Mass, intended to show its composer as a master of the old style, uses motives from Gombert's motet (ten "fughe" are printed at the head of the partbooks) and is full of imitation (including canon), sequences, and the dense counterpoint so typical of the earlier composer. Furthermore, Monteverdi provided it with a *basso continuo, apparently not thinking that this contradicted the *prima prattica.* This manner of composition, also called *stile antico,* remained the most acceptable for Masses in the 17th century, particularly in bastions of musical conservatism such as Rome, though composers there worked for greater brilliance within the style by composing for many choruses (as in the Masses of Orazio Benevoli and others) [see also Palestrina style, Roman school].

Eventually, however, the new style, or *stile moderno,* was adopted for Mass settings. Monteverdi, for instance, in his *Selva morale e spirituale* of 1641, composed a Gloria entirely in the new concertato style using soloists, choruses, and instruments, and in 1656, his pupil Francesco Cavalli produced an entire *Messa concertata.*

In the 18th century, particularly in Italy, many Masses were written in a mixture of old and new styles, employing soloists and orchestra along with the chorus and borrowing techniques from instrumental music and opera. Masses were no longer based on preexistent models and employed other means of unification; tonality became a favorite means of uniting the five parts of the Ordinary, as did the practice of repeating the music of one of the early sections (the second Kyrie or the "Cum sancto spirito" of the Gloria) as the last section of the Mass (the "Dona nobis pacem"). The Gloria and Credo were divided into many more sections than before—in Pergolesi's Mass in F (1732), the Gloria has seven parts, alternating arialike solos with homophonic and fugal textures for double chorus—and it became possible to compose substantial works merely setting one text (as in Vivaldi's Gloria). But the basic identification of the Mass with the *stile antico* was never lost; it can be seen in the settings of Antonio Caldara and some of those by Johann Joseph Fux. Fux, the most influential composer of sacred music in Vienna and Caldara's colleague, believed that the *stile antico* was best suited to the Mass, but he also allowed for a "stylus mixtus" and used it in many of his 50 Masses. The greatest Mass embodying the early 18th century's mixed style is Bach's *B-minor Mass (believed to have been compiled from a Sanctus written in 1724, a Kyrie and Gloria written in 1733, and other sections added later; see von Dadelsen, 1970), with its *stile antico* choruses, fugues, arias, and duets.

In the later 18th century, what might be called a symphonic Mass tradition developed, especially in Austria. Masses were usually written for orchestra, chorus, and four soloists (who sometimes act as a quartet alternating with the chorus), and new musical forms were introduced (e.g., the Kyrie of Haydn's *Missa in tempore belli,* which is in *sonata form). Conventional ways of setting words and phrases were also adopted: a rising line at the Gloria mirroring the raising of the celebrant's hands, chromatic or dissonant music at the "Crucifixus," a separate setting for the "Dona nobis pacem," etc. These conventions formed part of the Masses of Haydn and Mozart and can also be found in the Masses of Beethoven. Beethoven's *Missa solemnis* in D major of 1823, a supreme example of the symphonic Mass, fits clearly (as Kirkendale, 1970, has shown) into the 18th-century tradition, even though its enormous scope and intensity of expression set it apart as a towering masterpiece of the composer's last period.

Early 19th-century composers continued writing symphonic Masses. Cherubini's *Missa solemnis* in D minor, actually written before Beethoven's, matches it in length if not in quality, and smaller Masses were composed by Schubert, Weber, and others. Nevertheless, the most striking Masses of the 19th century were settings of the *Requiem. This text offered obvious dramatic possibilities, well realized in the settings by Berlioz, Verdi, and Fauré. The perceived theatricality of Masses and other church music spurred a reaction in the later 19th century, evidenced in the *Cecilian movement and in the pronouncements of church officials. In 1893, for instance, Cardinal Giuseppe Sarto, patriarch of Venice, complained about operatic melodies sung in church to sacred words and declared that the only music suitable for the liturgy was Gregorian chant and the polyphony exemplified by Palestrina. When the cardinal became Pope Pius X, his views were incorporated into the *Motu proprio* of 1903, which states that chant and classical polyphony were to be the models for all church composers and bans anything that "is reminiscent of theatrical pieces" (see Hayburn, 1979). These currents of thought are also reflected in a number of Masses composed by Liszt and in the E-minor Mass of Bruckner, works attempting to recapture the feeling of Renaissance polyphony in a 19th-century musical context.

IV. *20th century.* Although the Mass continued to decline in importance as a major musical genre, several composers completed important settings. Stravinsky's Mass (1944–48), the *Missa brevis* of Kodály (1947), and Hindemith's Mass (1963) all strive to be liturgical; they are choral works with subdued instrumental accompaniment, except for Hindemith's, which is *a cappella, and combine contrapuntal and homophonic writing. In contrast, Leonard Bernstein's *Mass* (1970–71) is not a Mass in any strict sense, but uses the Mass liturgy as the framework for a theater piece. The Second *Vatican Council's introduction of vernacular language and music and congregational singing into the Mass liturgy has resulted in rock Masses, folk Masses, even polka Masses. But settings of the original Latin texts have continued to be composed, some clearly referring to older models. Examples include Volker David Kirchner's *Missa Moguntina* (1994), written for the cathedral of Mainz; Paul Chihara's *Missa carminum brevis* (1972), which sets the Kyrie, Benedictus, and Agnus for chorus, integrating Gregorian chant with folk songs used as *cantus firmi;* Ron Nelson's *Mass of Saint La Salle* (1980), which sets the Kyrie, Gloria, Sanctus, and Agnus, each movement composed in "homage" to an earlier composer (Gesualdo, Perotin, Landini, Machaut); Leonard Bernstein's *Missa Brevis* (1988), derived from earlier theatrical music, which sets the Kyrie, part of the Gloria, the Sanctus, and Agnus for a cappella chorus and percussion.

Bibl.: Peter Wagner, *Geschichte der Messe* (Leipzig: Breitkopf & Härtel, 1913). Knud Jeppesen, "Marcellus Probleme," *AM* 17 (1945): 11–38. Manfred Bukofzer, *Studies in Medieval and Renaissance Music* (New York: Norton, 1950). Otto Gombosi, "Machaut's *Messe de Notre Dame,*" *MQ* 36 (1950): 204–24. Joseph A. Jungmann, *Missarum sollemnia,* 2 vols., trans. Francis A. Brunner, *The Mass of the Roman Rite* (New York: Benziger, 1951–55). Leo Schrade, "The Mass of Toulouse," *RBM* 8 (1954): 84–96. Georg Reichert, "Mozarts 'Credo-Messen' und ihre Vorläufer," *MJb* (1955): 117–44. Gustave Reese, *Music in the Renaissance*

(New York: Norton, 1959). Hanna Stäblein-Harder, *Fourteenth-Century Mass Music in France, MSD* 7 (1962). Robert Marshall, "The Paraphrase Technique of Palestrina in his Masses Based on Hymns," *JAMS* 16 (1963): 347–72. Edgar Sparks, *Cantus Firmus in Mass and Motet: 1420–1520* (Berkeley and Los Angeles: U of Cal Pr, 1963). Richard Hoppin, "Reflections on the Origin of the Cyclic Mass," *Van den Borren,* 1964, pp. 85–92. Lewis Lockwood, "A View of the Early Sixteenth-Century Parody Mass," *Queens College,* 1964, pp. 53–77. Anthony Milner, "Music in a Vernacular Catholic Liturgy," *PRMA* 91 (1964–65): 21–32. Egon Wellesz, *Fux* (London: Oxford U Pr, 1965). Willi Apel, *Gregorian Chant* (Bloomington: Ind U Pr, 1966). Edmond H. Fellowes, *English Cathedral Music,* 5th ed., rev. Jack A. Westrup (London: Methuen, 1969). Georg von Dadelsen, "Exkurs über die h-Moll Messe," in *Johann Sebastian Bach,* ed. Walter Blankenberg (Darmstadt: Wissenschaftliche Buchgesellschaft, 1970), pp. 334–52. Warren Kirkendale, "New Roads to Old Ideas in Beethoven's *Missa solemnis,*" *MQ* 56 (1970): 665–701. Lewis Lockwood, *The Counter-Reformation and the Masses of Vincenzo Ruffo* (Venice: Universal, 1970). Max Lütolf, *Die mehrstimmigen Ordinarium Missae-Sätze vom ausgehenden 11. bis zur Wende des 13. zum 14. Jahrhundert* (Bern: P Haupt, 1970). Elizabeth Roche, "Caldara and the Mass: A Tercentenary Note," *MT* 111 (1970): 1101–3. Alejandro Planchart, "Guillaume Dufay's Masses: Notes and Revisions," *MQ* 58 (1972): 1–23. Friedrich Blume, *Protestant Church Music: A History* (New York: Norton, 1974). Edward Kovarik, "The Performance of Dufay's Paraphrase Kyries," *JAMS* 28 (1975): 230–44. Lewis Lockwood, ed., *Palestrina: Pope Marcellus Mass* (New York: Norton, 1975). Martin Staehelin, *Die Messe Heinrich Isaacs,* 3 vols. (Bern: P Haupt, 1977). Robert F. Hayburn, *Papal Legislation on Sacred Music, 95 A.D. to 1977 A.D.* (Collegeville, Minn.: Liturgical Pr, 1979). Joseph Kerman, "Byrd's Settings of the Ordinary of the Mass," *JAMS* 32 (1979): 408–39. Jeffrey G. Kurtzman, *Essays on the Monteverdi Mass and Vespers of 1610,* Rice University Studies, vol. 64, no. 4 (Houston: Rice U Pr, 1979). Graham Dixon, "The Origins of the Roman 'Colossal Baroque,'" *PRMA* 106 (1979–80): 115–28. Joseph Kerman, *The Masses of William Byrd* (Berkeley and Los Angeles: U of Cal Pr, 1981). Elizabeth A. Keitel, "The So-Called Cyclic Mass of Guillaume de Machaut," *MQ* 68 (1982): 307–23. Bruce C. MacIntyre, *The Viennese Concerted Mass of the Early Classic Period* (Ann Arbor, Mich.: UMI Res Pr, 1985). Craig Wright, *Music and Ceremony at Notre Dame of Paris 500–1500* (Cambridge: Cambridge U Pr, 1989). Daniel Leech-Wilkinson, *Machaut's Mass: An Introduction* (Oxford: Oxford U Pr, 1990). Robert Walser, "The Polka Mass: Music of Postmodern Ethnicity," *American Music* 10 (1992): 183–202. Anne Schnoebelen, ed., *Seventeenth-Century Italian Sacred Music* (New York: Garland, 1995). James W. McKinnon, *The Advent Project: The Later-Seventeenth-Century Creation of the Roman Mass Proper* (Berkeley: U of Cal Pr, 2000). Andrew Kirkman, "The Invention of the Cyclic Mass," *JAMS* 54 (2001): 1–48. Peter Ackermann, "Messe," *MGG2.* R.S.

Mässig [Ger.]. Moderate, moderately.

Master number. Often synonymous with *matrix number.

Mastersingers. See Meistersinger.

Mastersingers of Nuremberg, The. See *Meistersinger von Nürnberg, Die.*

Matasin, matassin [Fr.; It. *mattaccino;* Sp. *matachín*]. A dance known in Europe from the 16th through the 18th century and thereafter in Mexico and the southwestern U.S. It has most often been a dance in which combat is enacted, sometimes by buffoons or grotesque characters, sometimes with intricate swordplay. Thoinot Arbeau (*Orchésographie,* 1588) gives a detailed description; other early writers identify it with the *morris or **moresca.* It has also been associated with the dance of death and with church festivals. A melody bearing the name is preserved in August Nörmiger's tablature of 1598 and in a French gittern tablature of 1570.

Mathis der Maler [Ger., Mathis the Painter]. Opera in seven scenes by Hindemith (to his own libretto, after Matthias Grünewald's life), completed in 1934 and produced in Zürich in 1938. A three-movement symphony of the same name was drawn from the opera. Setting: Mainz, Germany, ca. 1525.

Matin, Le [Fr., The Morning]. Haydn's Symphony no. 6 in D major Hob. I:6. Like the Symphony no. 7 in C major Hob. I:7, *Le midi* (Noontime), and no. 8 in G major, *Le soir* (The Evening), it was composed about 1761. Haydn himself gave *Le midi* its name; the other titles are also probably authentic.

Matins [fr. Lat. *matutinus,* early morning]. A service forming part of the Divine *Office.

Matraca [Sp.]. A rattle, often a *cog rattle, of Spain, Portugal, and Latin America.

Matrimonio segreto, Il [It., The Secret Marriage]. Opera in two acts by Domenico Cimarosa (libretto by Giovanni Bertati, after the play *The Clandestine Marriage* by George Colman and David Garrick), produced in Vienna in 1792. Setting: Italy in the 18th century.

Matrix number. A number or combination of numbers and letters designating one side of a phonograph recording, the matrix being the metal plate from which is made the mother, from which in turn is made the stamper that actually stamps or presses one side of a recording. The number often appears in the blank space between a record label and the grooves (though it is sometimes under the paper label) and is often also printed on the label. It provides the best means of uniquely identifying a 78-rpm recording, where it corresponds to a single title, *take (complete or fragmentary), and perhaps manufacturer or series. Since the late 1940s, when master recordings have been made on tape, the matrix number has lost its central significance, representing merely one of many possible specific manufacturing parts made from the same tape master (or combination of tape masters). On many long-playing recordings it identifies only an entire sequence of items; moreover, it may change with the reissuing of such a recording. Compare Catalog number. See also Discography. B.K.

Maultrommel [Ger.]. *Jew's harp.

Má Vlast [Cz., My Fatherland]. A cycle of six symphonic poems composed by Smetana, ca. 1872–79, on subjects from his native Czechoslovakia: (1) *Vyšehrad* (a legendary castle; also, the old citadel of Prague); (2) *Vltava* (the River Moldau); (3) *Šárka* (an Amazon maiden in Czech legend); (4) *Z českých luhů a hájů* (from Bohemian fields and forests); (5) *Tábor* (an ancient city); (6) *Blaník* (a mountain near Prague where, according to legend, heroes slumber awaiting the moment when their country needs their help).

Mavra. Opera in one act by Stravinsky (libretto by Boris Kochno, after Pushkin's "The Little House at Kolomna"), produced in Paris in 1922. Setting: A Russian village long ago.

Mawwāl [Ar.]. An improvised, nonmetric vocal form of Arabic music, used mainly in Egypt, based on a five-line poem with first, second, third, and fifth lines rhyming. B.N.

Maxima [Lat.]. See Mensural notation.

Maxixe [Port.]. An urban dance-music genre of Brazil, originating as an adaptation of the European polka and popular in the late 19th and early 20th centuries. It is in rapid, syncopated, duple meter and is an important antecedent of the urban **samba.* D.S.

Mazeppa. (1) A symphonic poem by Liszt, composed in 1851 and revised in 1854 (orchestrated with Joachim Raff), based on a poem by Victor Hugo describing the insurrection (1708) and death of the Ukrainian Cossack hetman Mazeppa. (2) An etude for piano by Liszt from the **Études d'exécution transcendante* and of which the symphonic poem (1) is an expansion.

Mazurka [Pol.]. A Polish folk dance, in triple time, from the province of Mazovia near Warsaw. Mazurkas in art music, such as those of Chopin, exhibit strong differences in tempo and expressive character. This variability may reflect the subsuming under that name of several different folk dances of Mazovia: the mazurka proper (*mazur* or *mazurek* in Polish), fiery and warlike in character; the *obertas* or *oberek,* livelier in tempo and gayer in expression; and the *kujawiak,* originally from the neighboring province of Kujawy, partly slower in tempo and more sentimental and melancholy. These dances are linked by common rhythmic traits, such as strong accents unsystematically placed on the second or third beat and the tendency to end on the dominant pitch on an unaccented third beat. The music usually contains two or four sections of six or eight measures, each repeated. Traditionally, accompaniment was provided by a bagpipe drone on the tonic or the tonic and dominant pitches. These dances were usually danced by four, eight, or twelve couples, and the movements were highly improvisational.

The mazurka began to spread beyond its original locale and social milieu as early as the 17th century. The Saxon connection with Poland helped carry it to Germany in the 18th. The 1830s and 1840s were the period of its greatest vogue as a drawing-room dance in Western Europe (along with other dances of Slavic origin, such as the *polka and the **redowa*) and thence in the New World.

Chopin's composition of more than 50 mazurkas reflects this contemporary popularity, as well as his nationalistic interest in Polish folk music; its rhythmic and melodic characteristics appear in his stylization of the dance, some frequently, such as pentatonic and modal melodic touches (including the raised fourth degree common in Slavic folk music), others only occasionally, such as the reminiscence of the bagpipe drone in op. 6 no. 3.

The mazurka was not intensively cultivated in art music by Western European composers after Chopin. In Eastern Europe it has continued to have some influence, both in Russia, where the mazurka had taken root, and in Poland, most notably in the works of Karol Szymanowski.

Bibl.: Zofia Stęszewska and Jan Stęszewski, "Zur Genese und Chronologie des Mazurkarhythmus in Polen," *Warsaw,* 1960, pp. 624–27.

Mbira. An African instrument made of 5 to 30 or more thin metal or cane tongues attached to a board or a box resonator. The tongues, which are held in one or two rows by two bars, with one end left free to vibrate, are plucked with the thumbs and or forefingers. The soft sound is sometimes roughened by wrapping the tongues with wire or adding a mirliton device, or the sound may be amplified with a gourd. The instrument is widely distributed in sub-Saharan Africa and has been exported to Latin America. Other names for it are *kalimba, marimba, marimbula, sansa, sanza,* and thumb piano. See also Lamellaphone; Africa IV, 2, and ill.

Bibl.: Paul Berliner, *The Soul of Mbira* (Berkeley and Los Angeles: U of Cal Pr, 1978).

M.d. Abbr. for *main droite* [Fr.] or *mano destra* [It.], right hand.

Meane, mene, mean. (1) In English music of the 14th to 17th centuries, a middle part, usually the middle of three in a polyphonic piece; also, one of the *sights. According to English treatises of the 15th century, the lowest voice discanting above a tenor, beginning at the interval of a fifth, is the mene. Later treatises use the term variously as equivalent to altus or contratenor. Some three-voiced keyboard compositions of the 16th century have a middle voice called meane, which is divided between the hands and may be written in black notes to contrast with the white notes written above and below.

(2) John Playford (17th century) wrote that the sec-

ond and third strings of the viol were called the small and great means. In *A Treatise of Musik* (1721), Alexander Malcolm used the term mean clef to refer to the movable C clef.

Mean-tone temperament. A scale in which justly tuned (i.e., acoustically pure) major thirds (ratio 5:4) above and below the tonic are made up of equal-sized whole tones whose value is thus the geometric mean of 5:4, whence the name.

Mean-tone temperament was widely used on keyboard instruments between ca. 1500 and ca. 1830. It replaced earlier *Pythagorean and *just tunings while preserving some features of both. The Pythagorean scale generates all scale steps from an invariant interval, the pure fifth (ratio 3:2) [see Tuning (2)], and accepts the discrepancies that occur between these intervals and their acoustically pure counterparts, including the syntonic *comma (ratio 81:80) falling between their two major thirds. Although just intonation has acoustically pure intervals, it possesses a crucial disadvantage, namely that between its scale steps are no fewer than four different sizes of semitones. On instruments of fixed pitch this unevenness discourages any but the most rudimentary transposition. Mean-tone temperament, then, adapts the principle of generation used in the Pythagorean scale to preserving the just major third. It does so by contracting slightly each of the four fifths needed to generate a major third. This temperament, which was probably discovered by ear rather than calculation, is a quarter of the syntonic comma. The temperament works well for music that modulates no more than three fifths sharp or two fifths flat of a tuning's tonic. Beyond that tonal domain, the acoustical compromises are particularly severe. They include a G♯–E♭ *wolf fifth some 59 *cents larger than just.

Although the mean-tone temperament had been discussed by Pietro Aaron in his *Toscanello in musica* (Venice, 1523), Gioseffo Zarlino still considered it new in 1571. Abraham Verheijen was the first to provide a close integral approximation of the temperament ca. 1600. Another important early account was provided by Michael Praetorius (*De organographia,* 1618). Many artists now prefer mean-tone temperament to equal temperament when performing 15th-, 16th-, and 17th-century repertories. See also Temperament.

Measure [Fr. *mesure;* Ger. *Takt;* It. *misura;* Sp. *compás*]. A unit of musical time consisting of a fixed number of note-values of a given type, as determined by the prevailing *meter, and delimited in musical notation by two *bar lines; also (especially in British usage) bar. The absolute duration of a measure is a function of tempo, i.e., the rate at which any note-value is performed. Informally, a measure may be said to consist of a given number of *beats, with a given note-value receiving one beat. At very rapid tempos, however, the beating of time may occur at the rate even of one beat per measure, though the meter might be, e.g., 3/4. Thus, the number of beats or pulses perceived as occurring within a measure may also vary with tempo, though the number and type of note-values making up the measure remain fixed. For the arrangement of strong and weak beats or pulses within a measure, see Accent (1), Meter; for the history of the representation of measures with bar lines, see Bar line, Notation; see also Rhythm.

Mechanical instruments. *Automatic instruments.

Mechanik [Ger.]. The action of pianos, etc.

Medesimo [It.]. Same; e.g., *m. tempo.*

Media caña [Sp.]. Along with the closely related *pericón,* a multisectional social dance with elaborate choreography for several couples, fashionable in the salons and theaters of Argentina and neighboring countries in the first half of the 19th century. Possibly of folk origin, these dances were also known in rural Argentina and Uruguay during the period, but have largely fallen into disuse today. D.S.

Medial cadence. See Cadence.

Mediant. See Scale degrees; Psalm tone.

Mediation [Lat. *mediatio*]. See Psalm tone.

Medicean edition. See Gregorian chant.

Medieval music. See Middle Ages, music of the.

Medio registro [Sp.]. A *divided stop. The practice of dividing organ stops into treble and bass halves between c′ and c♯′ became the norm in Castile from the second half of the 16th century.

Medium, The. Opera in two acts by Gian Carlo Menotti (to his own libretto), produced in New York at Columbia University in 1946. Setting: outside a large city in the present.

Medley. A succession of well-known melodies loosely connected to one another; sometimes synonymous with *potpourri. The term was used in the 16th century, especially by the *virginalists. It is now applied principally to popular music, especially to a selection of tunes from a musical or made popular by a particular performer. The overtures of light operas and musicals are often medleys of the most prominent melodies in the associated work.

Meeresstille und glückliche Fahrt [Ger., Calm Sea and Prosperous Voyage]. (1) A cantata for chorus and orchestra by Beethoven, op. 112 (1814–15), setting two contrasting poems by Goethe. (2) An overture by Mendelssohn, op. 27 (1828), evoking the calm and storm of the same two poems by Goethe.

Mehr [Ger.]. More, several; *mehrchörig,* polychoral; *mehrsätzig,* in several movements; *mehrstimmig,* polyphonic; *Mehrstimmigkeit,* polyphony.

Meistersinger. A burgher belonging to one of the guilds of the 14th to 16th centuries formed to perpetuate or emulate the received or presumed artistic traditions of the *Minnesinger. Beginning in western Germany, these guilds spread eastward in the 15th century. By the zenith of the movement (ca. 1500–1550), they were established from Mainz and Strasbourg in the west to Wroclaw and Brzeg in the northeast, with a concentration in southeastern towns such as Augsburg, Steyr, Burghausen, and above all Nuremberg, home of Hans Sachs (1494–1576), the best-known Meistersinger both in his day and since.

The few extant notated sources for *Minnesang* and *Meistergesang* display the conflicts of attribution and the variations and inconsistencies associated with oral transmission. That texts fare better than tunes in this transmission is perhaps evidence of their greater importance to the Meistersinger. This has also been inferred from the melodic notations, which suggest no independent musical meters, but rather free declamation based on speech rhythms. On the other hand, the Meistersinger conceived of melodies as the necessary and specific complements to particular patterns of verse. Both melodies and poetic strophes are typically in *bar form, together constituting a model, or *Ton,* for the production of other songs. For example, in the manuscript *D-Mbs* Cgm4997 (the Colmar manuscript, a central source compiled ca. 1470), the ratio of texts to *Töne* is about 9:1. The use of *Töne* was inherited from the earlier Minnesinger, but there are telling differences between these traditions. The primary organization of *Meistergesang* collections is by formal type, not social hierarchy—a reflection of the fact that Meistersinger were members of amateur fraternities, not individuals dependent on aristocratic patronage. Also, they reduced their forebears' populous hierarchy to a group of 12 founders that begins with the historically strategic Otto the Great (ruled 962–73) and ends with the didactic poet Heinrich von Meissen (called Frauenlob, ca. 1260–1318). Like the related notion of Meistersinger itself, this urge to create a pantheon is already incipient in the works of at least one 13th-century Minnesinger, Rümelant von Swaben.

Meistersinger guilds included several classes of members. A member began as an apprentice *(Schüler),* next became a journeyman (*Geselle* or *Schulfreund*), and (it was hoped) ended as a master *(Meister).* For early members like Fritz Kettner (fl. 1392–1430), a *Meister* was one who had learned some of the 105 or so Minnesinger *Töne* and who could compose new verses on them. Hans Folz (ca. 1450–ca. 1515) is credited with shifting the emphasis from preservation to emulation. In the wake of Folz's 27 additions to the standard corpus, a *Meister,* in addition to fulfilling the previous requirements, had himself to devise at least one new *Ton.* The consequent expansion of the canon (to about 600 *Töne* by 1600) was accompanied by a growing dependency on written tunes and texts as mnemonic aids. But the prestige of oral transmission was reasserted in 1540 in Nuremberg with the prohibition of written aids during public performance.

Meistersinger guilds were governed by town councils. Their high social status enabled them to hold their monthly concerts in town halls and churches and their major singing competitions, or *Singschulen,* during the feasts of Easter, Whitsuntide, and Christmas. *Singschulen* began with a free singing open to nonmembers. The competition proper was limited to guild members and to religious themes. Contestants were graded by three or four *Merker,* chosen for their expertise in ascertaining deviations from the codes of religious discourse and infractions of the 24 rules (as set down in the *Tabulatur*) that govern every *Meistergesang.* These rules were printed by Puschmann (1571).

The Meistersinger saw their art as a means of educating lower- and middle-class audiences in matters both religious and secular. By virtue of their ethics, aesthetics, latent nationalism, and civic prestige, the Meistersinger were superbly situated to help promote Luther's cause. Hans Sachs composed all his 13 *Töne* before 1530; thereafter, his preoccupation was the faithful propagation of Luther's Bible in *Meistergesang* and drama. In areas such as Catholic Augsburg, Meistersinger promoted the Counter-Reformation with similar zeal (Peperkorn, 1982).

Scholars have noted similarities between Meistersinger melody and bar form on the one hand and Lutheran *chorales on the other. But whether they result from a complex interaction or from a common source is not yet established. By the late 17th century (e.g., in Wagenseil, 1697), the focus was on the tradition rather than on the contemporary or didactic aspect of the Meistersinger. By the middle of the 18th century, the guilds had virtually ceased to exist, although isolated groups did not disband until the early 19th century.

Bibl.: *Musical sources.* Georg Münzer, ed., *Das Singebuch des Adam Puschmann. Nebst den Original melodien des Michel Behaim und Hans Sachs* (Leipzig: Breitkopf & Härtel, 1906; R: Hildesheim: Olms, 1970). Günther Kochendörfer and Gisele Kochendörfer, eds., *Mittelhochdeutsche Spruchdichtung. Frühen Meistergesang: Die Codex Palantinus Germanicus 350 der Universitätsbibliothek Heidelberg* (Wiesbaden: L Reichert, 1974). Ulrich Müller, Franz Viktor Spechtler, and Horst Brunner, eds., *Die Kolmarer Liederhandschrift der Bayerischen Staatsbibliothek München (cgm 4997)* (Göppingen: A Kümmerle, 1976).

Literature. Adam Puschman, *Gründlicher Bericht des deutschen Meistergesangs* (Görlitz, 1571). Johann Christoph Wagensiel, *De sacri rom. imperii libera civitate noribergensi commentatio* (Altdorf, 1697), app. *Buch von der Meister-Singer holdseligen Kunst;* facs. of app., ed. Horst Brunner (Göppingen: A Kümmerle, 1975). Clair Hayden Bell, *Georg Hager: A Meistersinger of Nürnberg, 1552–1634* (Berkeley and Los Angeles: U of Cal Pr, 1947). Id., *The Meistersingerschule at Memmingen and its "Kurtze Entwerffung"* (Berkeley and Los Angeles: U of Cal Pr, 1952). Hanns Fischer, "Hans Folz: Altes und Neues zur Geschichte seines Lebens und seinen Schriften," *Zeitshrift für Deutsches Altertum und Deutsche Literatur* 95 (1966): 212–36. Horst

Brunner, *Die alten Meister: Studien zu Überlieferung und Rezeption der mittelhochdeutschen Sangspruchdichter im Spätmittelalter und in der frühen Neuzeit* (Munich: Beck, 1975). Günter Peperkorn, "Meistergesang und Gegenreformation: Zu Fünf Strophen der Kolmarer Liederhandshrift," *Zeitschrift für Deutsches Altertum und Deutsche Literatur* 111 (1982): 60–79. Irene Stahl, *Die Meistersinger von Nürnberg: Archivalische Studien* (Nuremberg: Korn & Berg, 1982).

Meistersinger von Nürnberg, Die [Ger., The Mastersingers of Nuremberg]. Opera in three acts by Wagner (to his own libretto, drawn from several historical and literary sources), produced in Munich in 1868. Setting: Nuremberg in the 16th century. See also Meistersinger.

Mejorana [Sp.]. A song and dance-music genre of Panama. It takes two forms: for instruments alone, it accompanies collective dancing by men and women; performed by singer with accompaniment, it is called *socavón* and traditionally is not danced. Characteristic instruments are the violin or the regional three-string *rabel* and two five-string guitars, the small **mejoranera* and the larger *bocona.* In both *mejorana* and *socavón,* melodies are accompanied by a short, repeated harmonic ground; a two-measure sequence of tonic, subdominant, and dominant chords in compound duple meter and moderate tempo is typical. In the *socavón,* a textual scheme of quatrain *(cuarteta, redondilla)* followed by four ten-line *décimas,* with verbal improvisation by the singer (or in the form called *desafío,* two singers), is also characteristic. D.S.

Mejoranera [Sp.]. A small five-string guitar of Panama with a short neck, frets of string, and, except for the belly, carved from a single piece of wood; also called a *mejorana.* It is tuned d′ a′ a b e′. See also *Mejorana.*

Melanesia. See Oceania and Australia III.

Melisma [Gr., melody]. A group of more than a few notes sung to a single syllable, especially in liturgical chant. In *Gregorian chant, melismas are particularly characteristic of the *alleluia [see also *Jubilus, Sequentia*], the *gradual, the *tract, and the great *responsory. They may consist of as many as several dozen notes. During the Middle Ages, melismas of even greater length were added to some responsories, sometimes having been borrowed from other types of chant such as the *offertory. See also *Neuma* (2), (3).

Bibl.: Ruth Steiner, "Some Melismas for Office Responsories," *JAMS* 26 (1973): 108–31. Thomas Forrest Kelly, "Melodic Elaboration in Responsory Melismas," *JAMS* 27 (1974): 461–74.

Melismatic. Characterized by the presence of *melismas; one of the three principal categories of style in *Gregorian chant.

Mellophone. See Alto horn.

Melodeon. A small, suction-operated reed organ of the first half of the 19th century [see Harmonium].

Melodia. An open wood organ stop, introduced in England in the early 19th century.

Mélodie [Fr.]. (1) Melody. (2) A solo song with accompaniment, usually the French art song of the 19th and 20th centuries, and thus the French counterpart of the German *lied. Forerunners include 17th-century *airs, early 18th-century solo *cantatas, and late 18th-century *romances. The last were simple, tuneful, strophic settings of poems, with square musical phrasing, corresponding to the regular line lengths of the verse, and subordinate keyboard accompaniment. The early 19th-century composers began to pull away from this model on their own artistic initiative and in response to the new French Romantic poetry and to Schubert's lieder, many of which appeared in French editions under the title *Mélodies.* General tendencies of French song through the 1800s are increasingly careful setting of the subtle rhythms and accents of the French language, growing harmonic freedom (e.g., chromaticism, idiosyncratic chord progressions), prominent, mellifluous keyboard accompanimental styles, and a certain elegance and reserve.

Early 19th-century French song composers include Hippolyte Monpou, whose settings of texts by Victor Hugo and Alfred de Musset represent a transition from romances to the newer *mélodies;* Berlioz, whose settings for voice and orchestra of poems by Théophile Gautier are his most famous collection (*Les nuits d'été,* 1840–41); Giacomo Meyerbeer; Henri Reber; and Félicien David. Some German composers, among them Liszt and Wagner, were drawn to the new French poetic and musical style and wrote some genuine *mélodies.*

Gounod wrote approximately 200 songs and, in Ravel's opinion, established the character of the French *mélodie.* With his successful rendering of nuances of the spoken language, occasionally daring harmonies, and arpeggiated piano accompaniments, Gounod was the most influential song composer of the third quarter of the century. Contemporaries who contributed significantly to the genre include Franck, Lalo, Bizet, Délibes, Victor Massé, Ernest Reyer, Saint-Saëns, and Massenet. Among Massenet's approximately 260 songs are found the first true French *song cycles (e.g., *Poème d'avril,* Armand Silvestre, 1866), with musical recurrences as in the cycles of Schumann.

A new chapter in the history of the *mélodie* opens with the few (approximately 15) but exquisite songs of Henri Duparc (1848–1933). His settings of poems by Baudelaire, Gautier, Leconte de Lisle, and others, with their dissonant and unconventional harmonic style, set a new standard of intimate, personal expression. The great master of French song was Fauré. Among his approximately 100 songs are many settings of Paul Verlaine (including the song cycle *La bonne chanson,* 1891–92), a poet to whom many composers were drawn. Fauré's songs exhibit colorful but subdued harmonies, beautiful and balanced melodies, and restraint in his evocation of sensuality, melancholy, and ecstasy. Other song composers of this generation include Ernest Chausson, Emmanuel Chabrier, and Charles-Marie Widor.

Debussy was the great innovator of French song. His early works are comparable in style to those of his predecessors, but from ca. 1887, his songs achieve a unique blend of literary and musical values, with freer declamatory rhythms and forms, combined with his departures from conventional harmonic and melodic language. These tendencies reach their expressive height in Debussy's settings of Verlaine and of Pierre Louÿs's prose lyrics (*Chansons de Bilitis,* 1899). Ravel composed a number of songs, among which the most frequently performed are the cycles (e.g., *Shéhérazade,* 1903; *Chansons madécasses,* 1926). Other turn-of-the-century composers include Jean Rivier, Albert Roussel, Florent Schmitt, Georges Migot, and Lili Boulanger.

All of the 20th-century composers known as *Les *six* (Auric, Honegger, Durey, Milhaud, Poulenc, and Tailleferre) contributed to the repertory of French song with their settings of poets like Guillaume Apollinaire, Stéphane Mallarmé, Jean Cocteau, Gérard de Nerval, and Paul Eluard. Their style, best represented by the prolific Poulenc, is an anti-Romantic, neoclassical one, in which humor, sarcasm, and impudence combine with serious lyricism and detachment. Other modern French song composers include Henri Sauguet, Henry Barraud, Jean Françaix, Olivier Messiaen, and André Jolivet.

Bibl.: Frits Noske, *La mélodie française de Berlioz à Duparc* (Amsterdam: North-Holland Pub Co, 1954); rev. and trans. Rita Benton, *French Song from Berlioz to Duparc* (New York: Dover, 1970). David Cox, "France," in Denis Stevens, ed., *A History of Song* (London: Hutchinson, 1960). Pierre Bernac, *The Interpretation of French Song* (New York: Praeger, 1970). Barbara Meister, *Nineteenth-Century French Song: Fauré, Chausson, Duparc, and Debussy* (Bloomington: Ind U Pr, 1980). D. Tunley, ed., *Romantic French Song 1830–1870* (New York, 1994–95). R.H.

Melodrama. A musico-dramatic technique in which spoken text alternates with instrumental music or, more rarely, is recited against a continuing musical background. There are examples of entire works using this technique (sometimes called monodrama if there is only one character or duodrama if there are two characters), but some of the best-known examples of melodrama appear as parts of a larger work such as an opera.

The first significant example of a work constructed entirely as a melodrama is *Pygmalion,* with text by Jean-Jacques Rousseau and music by Rousseau and Horace Coignet. It was sketched in the 1760s and first performed in 1770 in Lyons. Rousseau called the work a *scène lyrique,* not a melodrama. The text was provided with new music by Franz Asplmayr (Vienna, 1772) and Anton Schweitzer (Weimar, 1772); a German translation was set by Georg Benda (Gotha, 1779). The melodramas composed by Benda were frequently performed and much admired. His first melodrama, *Ariadne auf Naxos* (1775, text by Brandes), was also his most successful, although his *Medea* (1775, text by Gotter) was also well received. Mozart, whose enthusiasm for Benda's melodramas is recorded in several letters to his father, set portions of his incomplete *Singspiel, *Zaide,* as melodrama. Perhaps the most famous examples of melodrama are found in Beethoven's *Fidelio* (act 2, scene 1) and Weber's *Der Freischütz* (act 2, scene 2). Berlioz's *Lélio* applies the technique to a symphonic rather than an operatic work. Another 19th-century development was the recitation of poems to piano accompaniment—a kind of chamber melodrama. Examples are Schubert's "Abschied von der Erde" D. 824 (1826), Schumann's "Schön Hedwig," and Liszt's "Der traurige Mönch." In Italian opera, one situation traditionally calls for melodrama: letters read aloud are usually spoken rather than sung.

A number of 20th-century works make use of melodrama, such as Stravinsky's *Perséphone,* Milhaud's *Christophe Colomb,* Honegger's *Jeanne d'Arc au bûcher,* Walton's *Facade,* and Richard Strauss's *Enoch Arden.* Probably the most striking symbolic use of the technique is in Schoenberg's *Moses und Aron.* In this work, Moses's inability to communicate his revelations to his people is suggested by his inability to sing. Aron, his intermediary, sings, but Moses declaims in **Sprechstimme.*

Bibl.: Heinrich Martens, *Das Melodram* (Berlin: C F Vieweg, 1932). Jan van der Veen, *Le mélodrame musical de Rousseau au romantisme: Ses aspects historiques et stylistiques* (The Hague: M Nijhoff, 1955). Arthur Winsor, "The Melodramas and Singspiels of Georg Benda" (Ph.D. diss., Univ. of Michigan, 1967). Edith Vogl Garrett, "Georg Benda, the Pioneer of the Melodrama," *Geiringer,* 1970, pp. 236–42. James L. Smith, *Melodrama* (London: Methuen, 1973). Edward Kravitt, "The Joining of Words and Music in Late Romantic Melodrama," *MQ* 42 (1976): 571–90. C.G.

Melodramma [It.]. A text to be set as an opera, or the resulting opera; not the same as *melodrama. The term was used in the 17th century; in the 19th century, it was employed in connection with a variety of works, including *Rigoletto* and *Un ballo in maschera,* evidently without implying anything very specific apart from the combination of music and drama.

Melody [fr. Lat. *melodia,* fr. Gr. *melōidia,* fr. *melos*]. In the most general sense, a coherent succession of pitches. Here pitch means a stretch of sound whose frequency is clear and stable enough to be heard as not noise; succession means that several pitches occur; and coherent means that the succession of pitches is accepted as belonging together. The whole of music is often informally divided into three domains: melody, *harmony, and *rhythm. Melody is opposed to harmony in referring to successive rather than simultaneous sounds; it is opposed to rhythm in referring to pitch rather than duration or stress.

In a narrower sense, melody denotes a specific musical entity, and its meaning touches upon those of figure, motive, subject, theme, and, above all, tune; melody is in fact nearly synonymous with tune, though the latter perhaps implies more finitude and closure. Theme or subject denotes a fixed melodic entity that is used as the basis for a larger musical item. The terms motive and figure suggest melodic fragments: a motive is a configuration that forms part of a subject, theme, or melody but that is clearly recognizable in its own right if it recurs in another context; a figure is a protean configuration used for spinning out a melody begun more memorably.

All musical cultures have melody and melodies, and within bounds of larger stylistic consistencies, a culture's melodies resemble and differ from one another in ways easily perceivable, if not always so easily describable; yet the consideration of melodies in relatable groups is the quickest path to grasping their individual modes of coherence. A group of melodies that resemble one another in consistent ways is sometimes called a melody type. In some musics, melody types are named and are describable entities manipulated by musicians; the Indian *rāga* is the outstanding modern instance. The tune types of Anglo-American folk song, on the other hand, are not reified in this way in musical practice, though singers as well as scholars are perfectly conscious of the resemblances they embody.

It is obviously impossible to separate rhythm completely from melody, since every pitch must have a duration, and duration is part of rhythm. Furthermore, a motive, and therefore a theme or melody depending on it, is as likely to be recognizable from its attack pattern—its rhythm—as it is from its pitch contour. Similarly, in Western tonal music, melody is fundamentally inseparable from harmony, since melodies in this system clearly imply simultaneous combinations of sounds such as major and minor triads.

The two primary engines of musical gesture are bodily motion and the voice. Insofar as melody is concerned with coherent successions of pitch, it is ultimately vocal—directly or in indirect instrumental extension. The line between speech and song is sometimes very hard to draw; in some genres the gray area between them is deliberate, as in the *kotoba* vocal style of the Japanese *noh plays or the **Sprechstimme* of Schoenberg's *Pierrot lunaire,* both of which have melodic contour but avoid clear pitches. There are, however, kinds of melody with clear pitches that are just as closely tied to language patterns of one sort or another. Many cultures have more or less fixed tunes for singing standard poetic stanzas, from Javanese *macapat* meters to the *arie da cantar* of 16th-century Italy. Other types of melodic recitation are more flexibly adaptable to prose or to looser verse-forms. The *psalmody of Gregorian chant is a case in point as is the music for *noh* plays.

Example 1, from the *noh* play *Ha-goromo,* is a section from the final *kiri;* it is an instance of a highly constrained melodic recitation named *Age-uta* (high melody) sung within the framework of pitch relationships called *yowagin* (soft style). The three central recitation tones are g, d, and A, and the *Age-uta* melo-

1

2

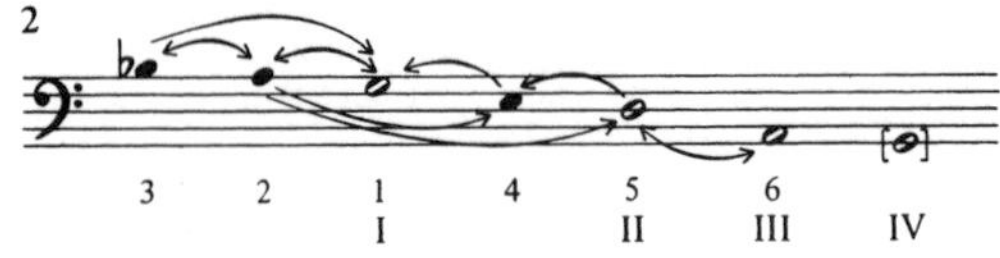

Melody. 1. Excerpt from *Kiri* of Zeami's *noh* play *Ha-goromo (Age-uta, yowagin).* 2. Scale for *Age-uta, yowagin* melodies.

3a WA 340

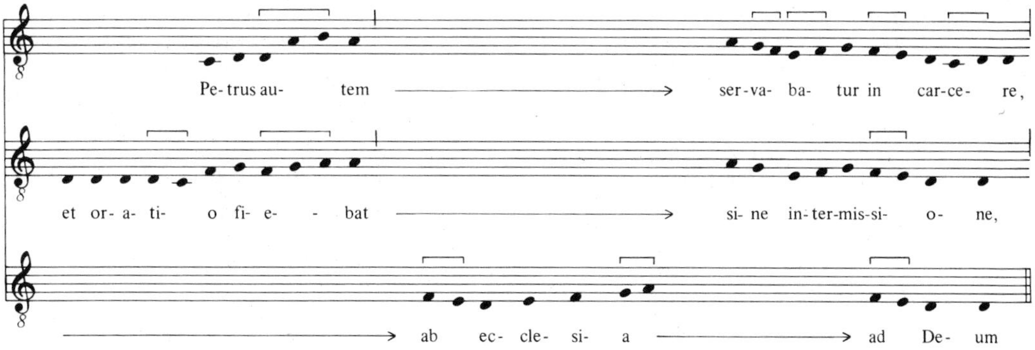

Pe-trus au- tem ——→ ser-va- ba- tur in car-ce- re,

et or- a- ti- o fi- e- - bat ——→ si- ne in-ter-mis-si- o- ne,

——→ ab ec- cle- si- a ——→ ad De- um

3b WA 109

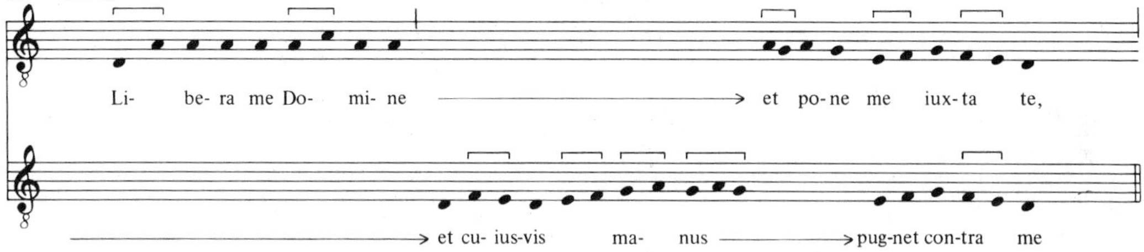

Li- be- ra me Do- mi- ne ——→ et po-ne me iux-ta te,

——→ et cu- ius-vis ma- nus ——→ pug-net con-tra me

3c WA 15

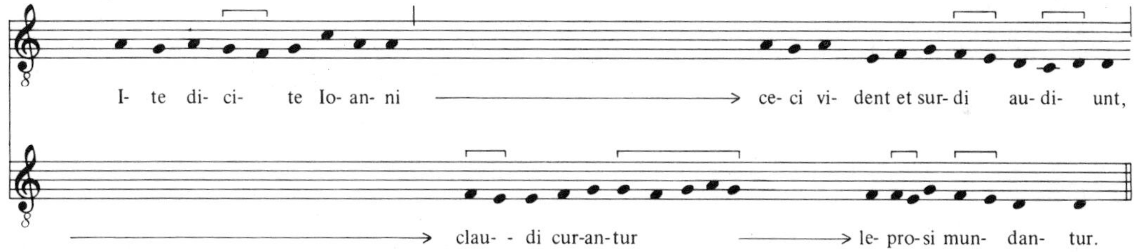

I- te di- ci- te Io- an- ni ——→ ce- ci vi- dent et sur- di au- di- unt,

——→ clau- - di cur-an-tur ——→ le- pro-si mun- dan- tur.

4

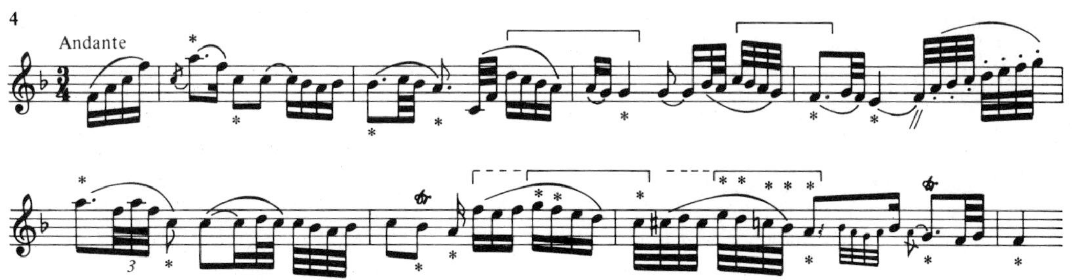

Melody. 3. Three antiphons from the Worcester Antiphoner. 4. Mozart, K. 310, second movement.

dies always begin at the highest level. The two higher central tones in turn have decorative melodic adjuncts: a and b♭ are neighbors to the g, and a is also always used to make the descent to d; e is a passing tone between d and g and is also used as a lower neighbor to g, in preparation for the descent to d. Example 2 shows the "scale"—the pitches in (descending) order—of the *Age-uta* genre; the distinction between main pitches and auxiliary ones is shown by the different note heads, and the order relationships at the structural and ornamental levels are indicated by arrows and roman and arabic numerals.

Two aspects of pitch give *yowagin Age-uta* melodies their easily recognizable generic shape: structural emphasis and consistent contour. Melodic emphasis arises in three ways: from the prolongation, reiteration, or recurrence of certain pitches, to which others are functionally subordinate; from the regular occurrence of certain pitches at temporally significant moments, especially phrase endings; and from the placement of certain pitches in the highest or lowest register of the melody. Consistency of melodic contour arises primarily from a regularly recurring order of pitches, though it is secondarily conditioned by emphases as outlined above.

The three Gregorian antiphons from the 13th-century Worcester antiphoner, shown in Ex. 3, illustrate all of the foregoing. All three end on d and emphasize a, d, and g, in that order. The openings of all three establish a—twice in Ex. 3a—using four quite different motives to do so. The melodies have a common cadential gesture: the conclusions of all phrases but the last start from a, go down to e by step or skip, then stepwise back up to g, and from there stepwise down to d. The last cadence in each antiphon, from f down to d, is preceded by a motive rising only to g decorated by a, rather than by a motive strongly establishing a.

Besides contour and emphasis, the antiphons in Ex. 3 show another important melodic feature: the repetition or cycling of characteristic motives. After the cadential motive in the opening phrase, the tune goes to something else before returning to the cadential phrase. Flexible concatenation of recurring motives is a fundamental device for extending and developing melodies; in musical cultures where melodic types are reified it is essential. Indian **rāga*s and Turco-Arabic **maqām*s are modern instances of such reified melodic types.

In 16th-century vocal polyphony, melodic resemblances are a significant element but are not so controlled as they are in even the Gregorian antiphoner, and they do not form a system of reified melodic types. Nevertheless, in the music of Palestrina, for example, melodies incorporate not only common motives, but often also a larger linear outline overall. Melodies from more familiar Western styles are also often shaped in this way, by the elaboration of an essentially simple line. Example 4, a slow movement theme by Mozart, illustrates this point well. Asterisks under the melody show the basic stepwise motion from c″ to f′; asterisks above show a secondary high-register line from a″ downward that hangs almost until the end, then drops to join the lower line. Main points on both lines are articulated by means of ornamental motives, the most important of which is (like the lower line itself) a stepwise descending fifth, as marked in brackets. In the first half of the melody, this descending-fifth motive elaborates the lower line, and in the second it brings the upper line down from high a″; in both halves, it is used twice in succession, its second occurrence being twice as fast as its first.

Though completely coherent in itself, a melody like that in Ex. 4 actually appears simultaneously with completely different pitch successions sounding in other parts of the texture. It is supported by a bass line whose character is very different from the melody, with other pitches between these outer parts. In Western music, whether the texture is polyphonic or melody with accompaniment, the constraints on what pitches may sound simultaneously and how the independent successions of pitches can proceed are subsumed under the rules of *counterpoint and *harmony.

In other ensemble musics, the restrictions may be more nearly allied to the melody, in that the simultaneously moving lines within the texture are all deemed to have the same melody. In composed Turkish or Arabic genres, for example, all melodic strands have the same pitches, right at the surface level, so that they perform "in unison" (including octave transposition). In other genres, the single melody may be filtered through the possibilities and constraints of various performing media in such a way that what is actually heard may sound like several different pitch successions simultaneously, in a relationship sometimes called *heterophony. The **gagaku* of the Japanese court music ensemble is an extreme case: the melodic identity of what, for example, the *koto* and the *hichiriki* are rendering in a given piece lies very far beneath the surface. Somewhat closer to one another are the multiple strands in Javanese **gamelan* music, though on occasion they too can differ quite strikingly. See also Folk music I, 3.

Bibl.: E. M. von Hornbostel, "Melodie und Skala," *JMP* 1912: 11–25. Robert Lach, *Studien zur Entwicklungsgeschichte der ornamentalen Melopöie* (Leipzig: C F Kahnt, 1913). Arthur C. Edwards, *The Art of Melody* (New York: Philosophical Library, 1956). Bence Szabolcsi, *Bausteine zu einer Geschichte der Melodie* (Budapest: Corvina, 1959); trans. Eng., *A History of Melody* (London: Barrie & Rockliff, 1965). Imogen Holst, *Tune* (London: Faber, 1962). Mieczyslaw Kolinsky, "The General Direction of Melodic Movement," *Ethno* 9 (1965): 240–64. Charles R. Adams, "Melodic Contour Typology," *Ethno* 20 (1976): 179–215. H.S.P.

Melody chorale. An *organ chorale in which the chorale melody is clearly present in the uppermost part.

Melody type. The shared features or underlying pattern of a group of melodies regarded as resembling one another in consistent ways. The concept has been employed principally with respect to repertories transmitted anonymously and often orally and to musics in which the essential creative act lies with the performer rather than with a composer whose activity precedes performance. It may thus embrace, for example, the *tune families of Anglo-American folk song [see also Folk music I, II], the melodic families into which some scholars have classified genres of Gregorian chant such as *antiphons and *graduals, the *$r\bar{a}gas$ of Indian music, and the *$maq\bar{a}ms$ of Turkish and Arabic music. In the latter two cases, among others, the concept is explicitly present in musical practice [see Melody]. It has also played a significant role in discussions of *mode and the processes of *transmission of liturgical chant [see also Centonization]. As a strictly analytical tool, the notion of melody type may prove useful in the study of a wide variety of repertories, though like any attempt at classification, it runs the risk of suppressing significant detail in the individual case. The notion becomes distinctly more problematical if it is given historical status and clothed in biological metaphors suggesting that all members of a melodic family are the descendants of a single historical antecedent.

Melograph. A mechanical device for ethnomusicological *transcription usually producing a kind of graph. Beginning with attempts by Milton Metfessel (1928), various devices have been developed, the most important dating from the 1950s and located at the University of California at Los Angeles (Charles Seeger), the University of Oslo (Olav Gurvin and Karl Dahlback), and Hebrew University (Dalia Cohen and Ruth Katz).

Bibl.: Charles Seeger, "Prescriptive and Descriptive Music Writing," *MQ* 44 (1958): 184–95. Karl Dahlback, *New Methods in Vocal Folk Music Research* (Oslo: Oslo U Pr, 1958). Dalia Cohen and Ruth Katz, "Remarks Concerning the Use of the Melograph," *Yuval* 1 (1968): 55–68. Nazir A. Jairazbhoy, "The Objective and Subjective View in Music Transcription," *Ethno* 21 (1977): 263–74. B.N.

Mélophon [Fr.]. A *reed organ in the shape of a large guitar or hurdy-gurdy, invented in France ca. 1837. Holding the instrument horizontally, the player operated button keys with the left hand while pumping bellows by pushing and pulling a handle with the right hand.

Melopiano. A mechanism, invented in 1873, for converting a piano into a sustaining instrument. The device, which could be installed in a conventional piano, contained metal springs that caused small hammers to bounce repeatedly against the strings, producing a tremolo effect.

Melopoeia [fr. Gr., Lat.]. The art or invention of melody.

Membranophone. An instrument in which sound is produced by the vibration of a membrane, traditionally a stretched animal skin, though now often a synthetic material. Most are *drums, but *mirliton instruments are also included in this category. The membrane may be made to vibrate by striking, rubbing (*friction drum), or, in a mirliton, by the action of sound waves. See also Instrument.

Mene. See Meane.

Ménestrel [Fr.]. *Minstrel; *ménestraudie,* the art of the minstrel, including music; *ménestrandise,* a guild of minstrels or their collective activity.

Meno [It.]. Less; *meno mosso,* slower.

Mensur [Ger.]. (1) Meter, mensuration. (2) In organ building, *scaling.

Mensural (mensurable) music [Lat. *musica (cantus) mensurabilis*]. In the Middle Ages, music in which durations are fixed, as distinct from plainsong *(cantus planus);* thus, music written in *mensural notation.

Mensural notation. A system of notating duration whose principles began to be established around 1260 and that, with various modifications, remained in use until about 1600. Franco of Cologne [see Theory] is usually credited with the first systematic exposition (ca. 1250) of the fundamental principles, and notation of this period embodying these principles is thus termed Franconian. Franco's system made use of three main note-values: long, breve, and semibreve. The long was normally equivalent to three breves and the breve equivalent to three semibreves. A duplex long, equivalent to two longs, was also available. In the first half of the 14th century, Philippe de Vitry and Jehan des Murs increased the number of note-values, extended Franco's principles to govern the relationship among these values, and placed the duple division of note-values on an equal footing with triple division. It is this fuller system that is described in what follows.

Four principal note-values and associated rests are employed: long, breve, semibreve, and minim. When written as single notes, these have the solid black shapes illustrated in the Ex. (a few longer and shorter note-values are also given). As in the Franconian system, longs, breves, and semibreves can be combined to form ligatures, but this does not affect their relationship to one another as note-values [for the identification of the note-values making up a ligature, see Ligature (1)]. The relationship between any two adjacent note-values in the system can be either triple (as with Franco) or duple. The relationship between long and breve is termed *modus* (mood) and is said to be major if there are three breves to the long and minor if there are two; the relationship between breve and semibreve is termed *tempus* (time) and may be perfect (triple) or imperfect (duple); and that between semibreve and minim is termed *prolatio* (prolation) and may be major (triple) or minor (duple). The particular combination of these relationships governing a composition is termed its mensuration and is roughly analogous to

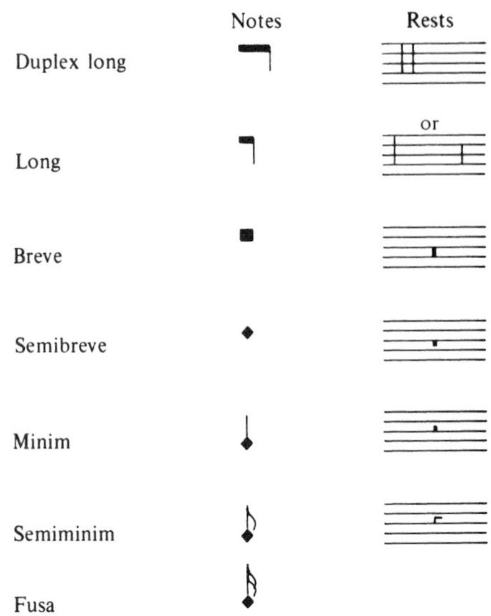

the concept of meter in current musical *notation. In mensural notation, however, the organization of the metrical pulse into recurring patterns of various kinds is not indicated by *bar lines [see also *Tactus*]. The four possible combinations of *tempus* and *prolatio* were termed by Philippe de Vitry the four prolations *(quatre prolacions)* and can be indicated by four signs formed as follows: a complete circle indicates perfect *tempus;* an incomplete circle (C) indicates imperfect *tempus;* a dot in the center of the circle indicates major *prolatio;* and absence of a dot indicates minor *prolatio;* see the accompanying table. These signs, of which the modern use of **C** for 4/4 is a survival, were not much used in sources of the 14th century, with the result that the mensuration of a piece must usually be determined from context.

If the relationship between two adjacent levels of note-values is triple, the particular duration of each note is determined according to the principles applied by Franco to the relationships of long to breve and breve to semibreve (trans. in *SR,* pp. 142–46). The following summary is in terms of longs and breves but applies equally to other levels of the system. A long followed by a single breve is made imperfect (or imperfected) and has the value of two breves (thus creating the succession 2 + 1). If a long is followed by two breves that are in turn followed by a long, the first long remains perfect, the first breve retains its normal value (and is termed a *brevis recta*), and the second breve is altered (termed a *brevis altera*) to have the value of two normal breves (thus creating the succession 3 + 1 + 2). A long followed by three breves remains perfect, and all three breves have the normal value (thus, 3 + 1 + 1 + 1). If a long is followed by four or more breves, the first breve imperfects the long, and the remaining breves are divided into groups of three equal breves. If a single breve remains, it may imperfect a following long; if two breves remain, the second of the two is altered. A note preceding another note of the same type is always perfect. These rules governing imperfection and alteration clearly derive from a wish to notate the patterns of the rhythmic modes [see Modes, rhythmic].

A note can imperfect a following note as well as a preceding one, though not both. A note can also in effect imperfect a note that forms part of a higher value. For example, a long worth three breves, each worth three minims, may be "imperfected" by a minim, thus reducing its value to eight minims; the minim has in effect imperfected one of the three breves of which the long consists. Rests can cause imperfection and alteration, but their own values are fixed and not subject to imperfection and alteration. Notes written in red are imperfect. This is termed coloration and most often serves to introduce three notes of equal value into the time normally occupied by two notes of the same type; e.g., in imperfect *tempus* with major *prolatio,* three red semibreves occupy the same time as two black ones, an effect identical to the shift in 6/8 from two dotted quarters to three undotted quarters, termed *hemiola. The substitution of three red notes for two black ones of the same type may also occur when the

Tempus	Prolatio	Sign	Value	Examples
Imperfect	Imperfect	C		= 2/4
Perfect	Imperfect	O		= 3/4
Imperfect	Perfect	C with dot		= 6/8
Perfect	Perfect	O with dot		= 9/8

Mensural notation.

black ones themselves are normally imperfect, however.

A dot may be placed between adjacent notes in order to prevent imperfection or alteration according to the usual rules. Often, as in the case of a long followed by a dot followed by a breve, the dot has the effect of making the preceding note perfect, i.e., worth three of the next smaller value. For this reason, it was sometimes termed a dot of perfection *(punctum perfectionis).* When it occurs between two breves that occur between two longs, it prevents alteration and forces the preceding breve to imperfect the preceding long, thus causing the long and the breve together to form a perfection, i.e., a group equal to three breves. Because of the way in which it sometimes divides a succession of notes into units of three, Franco termed the dot (or stroke in some sources) a division of the mode *(divisio modi).*

If the relationship between two note-values is duple, as in current notation, imperfection and alteration do not take place. The dot, however, may be used to cause a preceding note to be perfect, i.e., worth three of the next smaller value. Although its function, as most often in triple relationships, is to cause a note to be perfect, it was and is sometimes termed a dot of addition *(punctus additionis),* since it may be thought of as adding to a note a duration equal to half of its own value. By whatever name, this is precisely the way in which the dot has continued to function.

In 14th-century Italy, a somewhat different notation was employed, though derived in part from Franco. The Italian system takes the breve as an unalterable starting point and divides it at three successive levels (termed *divisiones*) either by two or by three, each division resulting in a number of semibreves that are undifferentiated in appearance. Thus, the first division of the breve is perfect into three semibreves *(ternaria)* or imperfect into two semibreves *(binaria).* In the second division in perfect time, the three semibreves may be divided into two each to produce *senaria perfecta* or into three each to produce *nonaria* or *novenaria.* The third division of perfect time divides each of the six semibreves of *senaria perfecta* into two, producing *duodenaria.* The second division of imperfect time is into the four semibreves of *quaternaria* or the six of *senaria imperfecta* or *senaria gallica* (French *senaria*). The third division of imperfect time divides the four semibreves of *quaternaria* into the eight of *octonaria.* The operative grouping is indicated by dots separating them and by letters identifying them. The letters and nomenclature varied over the course of the century. The distribution of unequal values within a series of semibreves not corresponding exactly in number to one of the named divisions is on the basis of established patterns described as *via naturae* (according to nature). Departures from these patterns can be indicated by downward stems *via artis* (according to art). Notes with upward stems (i.e., minims) are used in the French divisions and for the smallest divisions. The end of the century saw the introduction of the *dragma* (a semibreve with both upward and downward stems) and other novel shapes.

By the end of the 14th century, Italian notation was superseded by French. Nevertheless, elements of Italian notation played a role in the creation of quite complex rhythmic relationships by composers of both nationalities. Music by these composers employs new note-shapes such as the *dragma,* additional types of coloration (including hollow red and hollow black notes), and contrasting mensurations simultaneously in different parts, sometimes involving *proportions [see also *Ars subtilior*]. The meaning of some novel note-shapes and types of coloration may vary from piece to piece and must usually be determined from context.

In the course of the 15th century, hollow (or void) black notes were substituted for solid black notes as the norm, the earlier function of red notes being assumed by solid black notes. Except for the use of elaborate *proportions by some composers around 1500, mensural notation thereafter became steadily simpler, the need for the principles of imperfection and alteration being obviated in various ways.

See Notation, *Ars nova,* Editions.

Mensuration. See Mensural notation.

Mensuration canon. See Canon.

Mensurstrich [Ger.]. See Bar line.

Mente, alla [It.]. Improvised.

Menuet [Fr.], **Menuett** [Ger.]. *Minuet.

Mer, La [Fr., The Sea]. An orchestral work by Debussy consisting of three "symphonic sketches," composed in 1903–5: *De l'aube à midi sur la mer* (From Dawn to Noon on the Sea); *Jeux de vagues* (Play of the Waves); and *Dialogue du vent et de la mer* (Dialogue of the Wind and the Sea).

Merengue [Sp.]. A folk and popular dance-music genre of the Dominican Republic. In rapid 2/4 meter, it typically alternates sections of stanza and refrain, with responsorial singing of short phrases common in both sections. Voices, accordion, *guayo* (metal scraper), and *tambora* (double-headed drum played with both bare hand and stick) form a characteristic ensemble. The accompanimental pattern, played by *tambora,* is also characteristic:

The *merengue* is also popular elsewhere in Latin America and is especially well established in Venezuela. In the U.S., there is a strong following among Dominican immigrants and Latino dance music fans. The *méringue* of Haiti is a closely related but distinct dance-music tradition. D.S.

Merry Widow, The. See *Lustige Witwe, Die.*

Merry Wives of Windsor, The. See *Lustigen Weiber von Windsor, Die.*

Merseybeat. A style of popular music that originated ca. 1959 in Liverpool, England. It combined elements of folk music and American *rock and roll. Groups such as Gerry and the Pacemakers and The Searchers defined the style, but its most notable exponents were the Beatles. P.T.W.

Mescolanza [It.]. *Medley.

Mese [Gr.]. See Greece I, 3 (i).

Meson [Gr.]. See Greece I, 3 (i).

Mesopotamia. Mesopotamian music represents a coherent tradition stretching from 3000 B.C.E. to Hellenistic times and encompassing the music of various peoples and empires of the Tigris-Euphrates valley, including Sumeria, Akkadia, Chaldea, Babylonia, and Assyria. Bas-reliefs, cuneiform texts, and archeological remains have transmitted information about Mesopotamian instruments, musicians, and musical organization.

Music played a central role in Mesopotamian religion. Hymns and other liturgical music accompanied sacrifices, ritual purification, and festive occasions. Sacred texts that have been preserved include performance indications suggesting responsorial singing and specifying instrumental accompaniment. Carvings depict musical performances by sizable ensembles of singers and instrumentalists. Sumerian and Babylonian musicians were divided into two castes of professions: *nar* musicians sang the praises of gods and kings, the *gala* sang laments.

The most important musical instruments of Sumeria were arched harps and large lyres, some almost as big as a man. In Babylonian times, both types of instrument became smaller. A few fragmentary remains of both types have been preserved in royal tombs. Other instruments depicted in Mesopotamian art are long-necked lutes, footed drums, frame drums, and instruments resembling the Greek *aulos. Names of instruments are given in Sumerian and Babylonian texts, and Assyriologists have been able to match some names with pictured instruments. The texts also transmit information about the tuning of stringed instruments. One text has been interpreted as notated music for a hymn.

Bibl.: Henrike Hartmann, "Die Musik der sumerischen Kultur" (diss., Frankfurt am Main, 1960). Wilhelm Stauder, "Die Musik der Sumarer, Babylonier und Assyrier," *Orientalische Musik,* Handbuch der Orientalistik, Abt. I, Suppl. IV (1970), pp. 171–243. Anne Draffkorn Kilmer, "The Discovery of an Ancient Mesopotamian Theory of Music," *Proceedings of the American Philosophical Society* 115 (1971): 131–49. David Wulstan, "The Earliest Musical Notation," *ML* 52 (1971): 365–82. Agnes Spycket, "La musique instrumentale mesopotamienne," *Journal des savants* (1972), pp. 153–209. Anne Draffkorn Kilmer, Richard L. Crocker, Robert R. Brown, *Sounds from Silence: Recent Discoveries in Ancient Near Eastern Music* [sound recording, lecture-demonstration] (Bīt Enki Records BTNK 101, 1976). Agnes Spycket, "Louez-le sur la harpe et la lyre," *Anatolian Studies* 33 (1983): 39–49. Anne Draffkorn Kilmer, "A Music Tablet from Sippar (?): BM 65217+ 66616," *Iraq* 46 (1984): 69–80. Subbi Anwar Rashid, *Mesopotamien,* Musikgeschichte in Bildern, vol. 2, pt. 2 (Leipzig: Deutscher Verlag für Musik, 1984).

Mesotonic. *Mean-tone temperament.

Messa di voce [It.]. In singing, a gradual *crescendo* and *decrescendo* on a sustained note. It was first discussed by Giulio Caccini (*Le nuove musiche,* 1601–2) with the phrase "crescere e scemare della voce." It later became one of the primary exercises of **bel canto* and is still often used in teaching. It leads to the mastery of nuance of tone that was one of the most essential elements in *bel canto* singing. Many 18th-century arias begin with a long *messa di voce,* as did the Classical vocal cadenza. It was prescribed as late as 1831 in Bellini's *Norma.*

From vocal style it was adopted into the family of expressive ornaments used for brass (Girolamo Fantini, 1638), woodwind (Johann Joachim Quantz, 1752), string (Christopher Simpson, 1659), and even keyboard (François Couperin, 1717) pedagogy and performance. Michel Pignolet de Montéclair (*Principes de musique,* 1736) claimed to have invented the sign of expanding and tapering solid wedges for it. It should not be confused with **mezza voce.*

Bibl.: John O. Robinson, "The *messa di voce* as an Instrumental Ornament in the Seventeenth and Eighteenth Centuries," *MR* 43 (1982): 1–14.

Messe [Fr., Ger.]. Mass; *Messe des morts* [Fr.], *Requiem Mass.

Messiah. An oratorio in three parts for soloists, chorus, and orchestra by Handel (text compiled by Charles Jennens from various passages in the Bible), first performed in Dublin in 1742. Portions of the work were later revised; the entire oratorio was first published in 1767, after Handel's death.

Messine neumes. Neumes from Metz [see Neume].

Mesto [It.]. Sad, mournful.

Mesure [Fr.]. Meter; measure; *à la m., en m.,* in time or *a tempo.*

Mesuré [Fr.]. Measured.

Metallophone. A *percussion instrument consisting of a row of tuned metal bars, struck in most cases with a mallet. Examples include the *celesta, **gender,* *glockenspiel, **saron,* *tubular bells, *vibraphone. See also Idiophone.

Metamorphosis. See Transformation of themes.

Meter [Fr. *mesure;* Ger. *Takt, Taktart;* It. *tempo, misura;* Sp. *tiempo, compás*]. The pattern in which a steady succession of rhythmic pulses is organized;

also termed time. Most works of Western tonal music are characterized by the regular recurrence of such patterns. One complete pattern or its equivalent in length is termed a measure or bar and in musical notation is enclosed between two *bar lines. The meter of a work or of a passage within a work is indicated by a fraction or by the sign c or ¢. The denominator of the fraction indicates the basic note-value of the pattern, and the numerator indicates the number of such note-values making up the pattern. Thus, a measure of the meter 3/4 consists of three quarter notes or their equivalent. The sign c is the equivalent of 4/4; ¢ is the equivalent of 2/2. Informally, the numerator is sometimes taken as specifying the number of beats per measure, and the denominator as specifying the note-value to receive one beat. The perception of the beat or pulse, however, depends to some extent on tempo. Thus, 3/4 in a very fast tempo may be heard (or conducted) as having only one beat per measure, and 6/8 will be heard as having two beats per measure as often as six.

Meters in Western music are of two principal kinds: duple or triple, depending on whether the basic unit of pulse recurs in groups of two or three. The recurrence of groups of four pulses, as in 4/4, may be termed quadruple meter but is also a special case of duple meter. A meter in which this basic pulse is subdivided into groups of three, however, is said to be a compound meter. Thus, 6/8 is a compound duple meter because it consists of two groups of three eighth notes (three groups of two eighth notes would be written as 3/4 and would be a simple triple meter); 9/8 is a compound triple meter because it consists of three groups of three eighth notes. Before the 20th century, meters other than these are relatively rare, though there are some well-known exceptions such as the second movement of Tchaikovsky's Symphony no. 6, which is in 5/4 or quintuple meter. Composers of the 20th century have employed a variety of other meters as well, sometimes in rapid succession and sometimes simultaneously in different parts. And some music of the 20th century avoids regular meters and even regular pulse altogether.

The perception of meter is a function of the organization of pitch as well as duration. It consists in recognizing every nth pulse or beat as the first in a new recurrence of the metrical pattern. This first beat is thus said to be the strong beat (or downbeat) of the measure. Other beats are described as weak in varying degrees. Thus, in 4/4, the first beat is the strong beat, the third beat is the next strongest, and beats two and four are weak beats. To the extent that the strong beat is thought of as bearing an accent, it is a metrical accent and not one to be necessarily reinforced by increased loudness or sharper attack [see Accent (1)].

The concern for meter in Western music becomes explicit in the 13th century. The present basic scheme of meters, note-values, and their relationships to one another derives from 14th-century practice. See also Mensural notation, Notation, Note, Prosody, Rhythm.

Metrical psalms. See Psalter.

Metronome. A device used to indicate the tempo of a composition by sounding regular beats at adjustable speed. It was invented ca. 1812 by Dietrich Nikolaus Winkler (ca. 1780–1826) of Amsterdam but takes its name from Johann Nepomuk Maelzel (1772–1838), who copied the device, adding a scale of tempo divisions, and patented it as a "metronome." Although the lawsuit that followed acknowledged Winkler as the creator, Maelzel had by then sold many metronomes; the instrument is still sometimes called a Maelzel Metronome. The case of the Maelzel Metronome, still usually pyramid shaped, contains a mechanism based on the principle of the double pendulum, i.e., an oscillating rod with a weight at each end, the upper weight being movable along a scale. Clockwork maintains the motion of the rod and provides the ticking. By adjusting the movable weight away from or toward the axis, the pendulum's swinging, and the ticking, can be made slower or faster, respectively. Some modern electric metronomes do not rely on a pendulum, frequently supplementing or replacing the ticking with a blinking light. An indication in a musical score that some note-value is to be performed at M.M. = 80, for example, means that the pendulum oscillates from one side to the other (and ticks) 80 times per minute and that the note-value specified with the indication should be performed at the rate of 80 per minute.

Prior to the metronome, various efforts were made to use the pendulum as an indicator of exact musical tempos. Lodovico Zacconi, in *Prattica di musica* (Venice, 1592), gauged tempo by using the human pulse as a reference point, as did Johann Joachim Quantz a century and a half later in his *Versuch einer Anweisung die Flöte traversiere zu spielen* (Berlin, 1752); Quantz's measurements are based on a pulse rate of 80 per minute. Following Galileo's determination of the physical laws governing pendulums, a number of writers used his information to measure time. In *Harmonie universelle,* vol. 1, bk. 2 (Paris, 1636), Marin Mersenne published a chart of pendulum lengths for such a purpose. Thomas Mace, in *Musick's Monument* (London, 1676), also speaks of using a pendulum to keep time. Étienne Loulié introduced his *chronomètre* in *Elemens ou principes de musique* (Paris, 1696), and in *A New Musical Grammar* (London, 1746), William Tans'ur treated "the doctrine of pendulums applied to music." Beethoven is thought to have been the first significant composer to use metronome markings; his indications are unreliable, however, because he often changed his mind in the matter of tempo and because his publishers did not always accurately print his markings.

Bibl.: Robert Münster, "Authentische Tempi zu den sechs letzten Sinfonien W. A. Mozarts," *MJb* (1962–63): 185–99. Peter Stadlen, "Beethoven and the Metronome–I," *ML* 48 (1967): 330–49. Hellmuth Christian Wolff, "Das Metronom des Louis-Lëon Pajot 1735," *Larsen,* 1972, pp. 205–17. Standley Howell, "Beethoven's Maelzel Canon: Another

Schindler Forgery?" *MT* 120 (1979): 987–90. Wolfgang Auhagen, "Chronometrische Tempoangaben im 18. und 19. Jahrhundert," *AfMw* 44 (1987): 40–57. William Malloch, "Carl Czerny's Metronome Marks for Haydn and Mozart Symphonies," *EM* 16 (1988): 72–82. David Martin, "An Early Metronome," *EM* 16 (1988): 90–92. Henrike Leonhardt, *Der Taktmesser: Johann Nepomuk Mälzel: Ein lückenhafter Lebenslauf* (Hamburg: Kellner, 1990). Clive Brown, "Historical Performance, Metronome Marks and Tempo in Beethoven's Symphonies," *EM* 19 (1991): 247–58. Rudolf Kolisch, *Tempo und Charakter in Beethovens Musik* (Munich: Text + Kritik, 1992); Eng. trans. in *MQ* 77 (1993): 90–131. Hugh John Macdonald, "Berlioz and the Metronome," in *Berlioz Studies,* ed. Peter A. Bloom (New York: Cambridge U Pr, 1992), pp. 17–36. Rebecca Harris-Warrick, "Interpreting Pendulum Markings for French Baroque Dances," *Historical Performance* 6 (1993): 9–22. Thomas Y. Levin, "Integral Interpretation: Introductory Notes to Beethoven, Kolisch, and the Question of the Metronome," *MQ* 77 (1993): 81–89. Bernard Sherman, "Tempos and Proportions in Brahms: Period Evidence," *EM* 25 (1997): 462–77. Philippe John van Tiggeln, "Über die Priorität der Erfindung des Metronoms," in *Aspekte der Zeit in der Musik: Alois Ickstadt zum 65. Geburtstag,* ed. Herbert Schneider (Hildesheim: Olms, 1997), pp. 98–126. Laszlo Somfai, "Tempo, Metronome, Timing in Bartok's Music: The Case of the Pianist-Composer," in *Der Grad der Bewegung Tempovorstellungen und -konzepte in Komposition un Interpretation 1900–1950,* ed. Jean-Jacques Dunki, Anton Haefeli, and Regula Rapp (Bern: Lang, 1998), pp. 47–71. See also Performance marks.

Mettere [It.], **mettre** [Fr., imperative *mettez*]. To put on, e.g., a mute or an organ stop.

Mexico. I. *Contemporary institutions.* Among Mexico's performing organizations are three major orchestras located in Mexico City, the nation's capital: the Orquesta sinfónica nacional, the Orquesta filarmónica de la Universidad autónoma de México, and the Orquesta sinfónica del Estado de México. There are also professional orchestras in state capitals such as Guanajuato, Morelia, and Guadalajara. The Instituto nacional de bellas artes, a government agency, sponsors the Orquesta sinfónica nacional and also a major opera company.

The two big Mexican music conservatories are the Conservatorio nacional de música, founded in 1877, and the Escuela nacional de música at the Universidad nacional autónoma de México, both located in Mexico City. They are state supported and provide free instruction to their students. The Conservatorio maintains an electronic music studio. In addition there are schools of music in Guadalajara, Guanajuato, Monterrey, Morelia, and Veracruz. The Taller de composición (Composition Workshop), established at the Conservatorio by Carlos Chávez in 1960, offers training to young composers. Despite these resources, many Mexican composers go abroad to study, mainly to the U.S.

Music publishing and the musical press are active in Mexico. Ediciones mexicanas de música is the leading publisher of contemporary music. The magazine *Heterofonía* covers Mexican and Latin American music and musical events. Mexico has no state radio. Although commercial radio has been important in the development of Mexican popular music, it broadcasts little art music.

II. *History.* Before the Spanish Conquest (1519–21), music was a vital part of Indian social life, often integrated with dance. Information about Aztec, Mayan, and Tarascan music has been transmitted in archeological remains and in reports by early Spanish missionaries. The most important native instruments were percussion instruments, like the *teponaztli and the *huehuetl, and flutes. Aboriginal music was rapidly extirpated by the Spaniards. Nevertheless, many remnants of pre-Conquest music have been passed on in Mexican rural culture; new, hybrid forms of Indian music have emerged; and Indian music, past and present, has inspired many 20th-century Mexican composers.

European art music quickly took root and flourished in 16th- and 17th-century Mexico. Spanish missionaries taught the Indians to sing plainchant and sacred polyphony and to play European instruments. Musical institutions and music making centered around the church, especially the cathedrals in Mexico City, Puebla, and Valladolid (now Morelia). New works by Spanish composers quickly made their way to Mexico, and music was composed in Mexico by immigrants like Hernando Franco (1532–85), Pedro Bermúdez (fl. 1600), Juan Gutiérrez de Padilla (ca. 1590–1664), and Francisco Lopez-Capillas (ca. 1615–73). Polyphonic music of the period is preserved in manuscript choirbooks, especially in the archives of the Mexico City and the Puebla cathedrals. There was a substantial demand for monophonic music as well. At least 13 books containing liturgical texts and plainchant were printed in Mexico before 1600.

During the 18th century, secular and instrumental music became more important. The Coliseo nuevo theater, rebuilt in 1753 in Mexico City, presented **zarzuelas, *tonadillas, *sainetes,* and incidental music to dramas. After independence (1810) and especially from the 1830s on, Italian opera dominated the Mexican stage. Even Mexican composers, such as Cenobio Paniagua (1821–82) and Melesio Morales (1838–1908), wrote operas with Italian librettos. In the late 19th century, salon music for piano, much of it by Mexican composers, flourished among the upper classes.

The Mexican Revolution, which began in 1910, wrought fundamental changes in art music. Composers of the revolutionary generation turned to Mexican folk music, Indian music, and even to pre-Conquest Aztec music for inspiration. Manuel M. Ponce (1882–1948), Carlos Chávez (1899–1978), Silvestre Revueltas (1899–1940), and José Pablo Moncayo (1912–58) were outstanding representatives of this movement. Julián Carrillo (1875–1965) is principally known for his use of *microtones. From the 1950s on, musical nationalism abated somewhat, and international contemporary idioms gained influence. This trend may be heard in the later music of Chávez and Blas Galindo (b. 1910) and in works by Rodolfo Halffter (b. 1900), Manuel Enríquez (b. 1926), Mario Kuri-Aldana (b. 1931), Héctor Quintanar (b. 1936), Eduardo Mata (b. 1942), and Mario Lavista (b. 1943).

III. *Folk and popular music.* Some Mexican Indian tribes preserve pre-Conquest musical elements, particularly in their dances. There has been considerable research into Mexican Indian music, and many field recordings are commercially available.

Rural and urban popular music in Mexico derives from many sources. Spanish influence is the oldest and deepest, but black slaves imported in the 16th and 17th centuries brought a strong African component to Mexican music. In the 19th century, European dance music, especially the waltz and the polka, and the Cuban **habanera,* left their mark. The Cuban **bolero,* emerging in the 1880s, had a major impact in the 20th century. Regional styles are strongly differentiated, and songs, dances, and instrumental ensembles are often named after their place of origin. The nationalist movements of the 19th and early 20th centuries, the growth of a national market, and the massive migration to Mexico City in the 20th century, however, have led to the consolidation of a "national" popular style.

The most familiar popular ensemble is the **mariachi.* The *norteño* ensemble—*bajo sexto,* accordion, and acoustic or electric bass—the *marimba ensemble, and the *banda* are also widespread. Characteristic popular song/dance genres are the **son,* the **jarabe,* and the **huapango.* Genres that are sung but not danced include the **corrido* (ballad) and the *canción ranchera.* See also Latin America.

Bibl.: Otto Mayer-Serra, *Panorama de la música mexicana* (Mexico City: El colegio de México, 1941). Jesus Bal y Gay, ed., *El códice del Convento del Carmen* (Mexico City: Instituto nacional de bellas artes, 1952). Robert M. Stevenson, *Music in Mexico* (New York: Crowell, 1952). Samuel Martí, *Instrumentos musicales precortesianos* (Mexico City: Instituto nacional de antropología, 1955; 2nd ed., 1968). Steven Barwick, ed., *The Franco Codex* (Carbondale: S Ill U Pr, 1965). Robert M. Stevenson, *Music in Aztec and Inca Territory* (Berkeley and Los Angeles: U of Cal Pr, 1968). E. Thomas Stanford, "The Mexican *Son,*" *YIFMC* 4 (1972): 66–86. Dan Malmström, *Introduction to 20th-Century Mexican Music* (Uppsala: Akad. avh. Uppsala Univ., 1974). Steven Barwick, ed., *Two Mexico City Choirbooks of 1717* (Carbondale: S Ill U Pr, 1982).

Meyo (meio) registo [Port.]. *Divided stop.

Mezzo, mezza [It.]. Half, medium, middle; *mezzo forte* (abbr. *mf*), moderately loud, less loud than *forte; mezzo piano* (abbr. *mp*), moderately soft, louder than *piano* [see Performance marks]; *mezza voce,* with half voice, restrained (not the same as **messa di voce*); for mezzo-soprano, see Voice.

Mf [It.]. Abbr. for **mezzo forte.*

M.g. [Fr.]. Abbr. for *main gauche,* left hand.

MGG [Ger.]. Abbr. for *Die Musik in Geschichte und Gegenwart* [see Dictionaries and encyclopedias].

Mi. See Pitch names, Solmization, Hexachord, *Mi-fa.*

Mi contra fa [Lat.]. See *Mi-fa.*

Micrologus [Lat.] A treatise by Guido of Arezzo of ca. 1030. See Theory.

Micronesia. See Oceania and Australia V.

Microtone. An interval smaller than a semitone. Microtones have served both melodic and intonational functions in Western music since antiquity. [For discussion of microtones in non-Western music, see the pertinent articles on individual countries and cultures.] In the enharmonic tetrachord of Greek music theory, an interval of a major third is combined with a pair of microtonal intervals that subdivide the tetrachord's remaining semitone. Since the Greek enharmonic scale is a series of such tetrachords, both conjunct and disjunct, its intervallic structure is only periodically microtonal, unlike modern microtonal scales [see Greece I].

The ubiquitous influence of Pythagorean tradition prompted most early theorists to give specific ratios for intervals, including microtonal ones such as the *diesis, various types of comma, the diaschisma, and the schisma [see Comma, schisma]. These, however, are not used in any extant Greek scale. They appeared in tuning theory not by design but by discovery of the fact that pure thirds, fifths, and octaves are incommensurable. Certain other microtonal intervals in ancient sources derive from the Pythagorean emphasis on metaphysics and numerology, e.g., the division of the *limma* (256:243) by Boethius (5th–6th century C.E.) to produce the "intervals" 512:499 and 499:486. More useful for practical music making was a geometrical conception of the whole tone that permitted Aristoxenus and his successors to discuss species of chromatic tetrachords that incorporate quarter-tone, third-tone, and three-eighth-tone intervals.

Pythagorean and Aristoxenian theories were available during the Middle Ages in secondary sources. Yet already in the 2nd century, Aristides Quintilianus reported that the microtonal genera were no longer used by musicians. Some scholars have deduced from the appearance of certain neumes the presence of microtonal melodic ornaments in medieval chant. But this remains speculative, while the century-old belief that the tonary in Montpellier 159 (11th century) contains microtonal notation has been thoroughly refuted by Dom Froger (1978). The only certain context for the medieval discussion of microtones remains the incommensurability of intervals in rational proportions, and it was within this context that interest in microtones chiefly lay between Hellenistic times and the late 19th century. For example, Christiaan Huygens divided the octave into 31 equal tones in the late 17th century in order to permit transposition of diatonic scales in just intonation (see also Herlinger, 1981). The Renaissance, however, saw attempts by some theorists (principally Nicola Vicentino, *L'antica musica ridotta alla moderna prattica,* 1555 [see also *Arciorgano, arcicembalo*]) and composers (e.g., Guillaume Costeley and Anthoine de Bertrand) to reestablish the enharmonic genus of ancient music.

The modern resurgence of interest in microtonal scales coincided with the search for expanded tonal resources in much 19th-century music. Jacques Fromental Halévy was the first modern composer to subdivide the semitone, in his cantata *Prométhée enchaîné* (1847). The first microtonal piece to use Western instrumental forms is a string quartet by John Foulds (1897); and the earliest known published quarter-tone composition, Richard Stein's *Zwei Konzertstücke* op. 26 (1906), is for cello and piano. What most intrigued microtonal composers were the harmonic possibilities of an expanded scale; hence, the development of microtonal keyboard instruments characterized the early decades of experimentation. In 1892, G. A. Behrens-Senegalden published an account of his patented quarter-tone piano; in 1907, Ferrucio Busoni proposed a sixth-tone scale that was realized in a two-manual harmonium built for him ca. 1911; in 1917, Willi von Moellendorff played and discussed his quarter-tone harmonium with the Vienna Tonkünstlerverein. A report of Moellendorff's concert prompted Alois Hába to compose his first quarter-tone piece, a Suite for String Orchestra (1917). In 1920, the Russian émigré composer Ivan Vïshnegradsky began but was unable to complete a quarter-tone piano in France. Hába, who knew Vïshnegradsky's instrument, had greater success building three types of quarter-tone piano in the years 1924–31. In 1924, Hába inaugurated a department of microtonal music at the Prague Conservatory. This forum, in addition to his well-received compositions, soon made him Europe's most effective advocate for the enrichment of the conventional twelve-tone scale by quarter, third, sixth, and finer divisions of the whole tone.

Meanwhile in North America, the Mexican composer Julián Carrillo had begun exploring microtonal intervals on the violin as early as 1895. By 1917, American composers as diverse as Hanson and Ives were experimenting with music for two pianos tuned a quarter tone apart. Quarter tones were used coloristically during the 1920s by such otherwise nonmicrotonal composers as Bloch and Copland. From 1924 on, Carrillo devoted himself almost exclusively to composing microtonal pieces for new or adapted instruments, and in 1930 he formed an ensemble, the Orquesta *Sonido trece, to play them. Carrillo's designs for microtonal pianos, patented in 1940 and built in Germany during the 1950s, are the most successful thus far.

All of these composers adhered to the equal division of the octave and were committed to the extension of the 19th-century heritage. In the 1920s, the American composer Harry Partch followed a similar microtonal path. After 1929, however, he pursued an independent course that combined a concern for acoustic purity (manifested in a 43-tone just division of the octave) with a synthesis of ritual elements borrowed from several ancient and folk traditions. Certain of Partch's younger contemporaries, such as Lou Harrison and Ben Johnston, have been similarly engaged in their own fiercely independent microtonal explorations. John Eaton has been a leading exponent of microtones and has employed them in several operas. Composers of *electro-acoustic music, because of the inherent flexibility and precision of some of the relevant equipment, have made the greatest use of microtones, though not necessarily as the result of a primary wish to employ such intervals for their own sake.

Bibl.: G. A. Behrens-Senegalden, *Die Vierteltöne in der Musik: Begleitschrift zu Erfindung eines achromatischen Klaviers und Entwurf zur Darstellung der Vierteltöne als Notenschrift* (Berlin: Sulzer, 1892). Jörg Mager, *Vierteltonmusik* (Aschaffenburg-Damm: Mager, 1916). Alois Hába, *Neue Harmonielehre des diatonischen, chromatischen, Viertel-, Drittel-, Sechstel- und Zwölftel-Tonsystems* (Leipzig: Kistner & Siegel, 1927). Ivan Vïshnegradsky, "La musique à quarts de ton et sa réalisation pratique," *ReM* 171 (1937): 26–33. Arthur Daniels, "Microtonality and Mean-tone Temperament in the Harmonic System of Francisco Salinas," *JMT* 9 (1965): 2–51, 234–80. Gerald R. Benjamin, "Julián Carrillo and 'sonido trece,'" *Yearbook, Inter-American Institute for Musical Research* 3 (1967): 33–68. Harry Partch, *Genesis of a Music,* 2nd ed., enl. (New York: Da Capo, 1974). Dom Jacques Froger, "Les prétendus quarts de ton dans le chant grégorien et les symboles du ms. H. 159 de Montpellier," *Études grégoriennes* 19 (1978): 145–79. Karol Berger, *Theories of Chromatic and Enharmonic Music in Late Sixteenth-Century Italy* (Ann Arbor: UMI Res Pr, 1979). Jan W. Herlinger, "Fractional Divisions of the Whole," *Music Theory Spectrum* 3 (1981): 74–83. Frank Reinisch, "Französische Vierteltonmusik in der Mitte des 19. Jahrhunderts," *Mf* 37 (1984): 117–22.

Middle Ages, music of the. Music of the period from about 500 until about 1430. Like most ideas traditionally employed in the periodization of the history of music, the idea of the Middle Ages was borrowed from other branches of historical study. Hence, both of the traditional boundaries cited above are problematical and subject to disagreement. The earlier boundary must remain necessarily vague, since musical *notation begins to be used in Western Europe only in the 9th century and is not transcribable until the 11th. The later boundary and the concept Middle Ages itself are most often defined with reference to the period following, namely the Renaissance. Thus, general descriptions of the period often stress explicitly or implicitly the absence of features of later music, such as a particular kind of relationship between words and music and a more familiar type of concern on the part of composers for the harmonic as well as the contrapuntal organization of works. Although the term Middle Ages continues in widespread use, at least as a convenience, some recent scholars have proposed one comprehensive period of musical composition from roughly 1250 to 1600 or smaller units (such as 1380–1500), which blur the traditional dividing lines with the Renaissance. For further discussion of historiographical issues, see Renaissance, History of music, Musicology.

The term Gothic has sometimes been used to describe the period from ca. 1150 to ca. 1430, also by analogy with other branches of history, particularly of art and architecture. It has gained relatively little currency, however. Terms that have gained more acceptance for the designation of subperiods, largely because they are defined more specifically with respect to music, include **Ars antiqua*, **Ars nova*, and **Ars subtilior*. For individual repertories and genres from the Middle Ages, see St. Martial, Notre Dame, Santiago de Compostela, Troubadour, Trouvère, Minnesinger, Meistersinger, Plainsong, Mass, Motet, Liturgical drama, *Lauda, Cantiga,* Chanson.

Bibl.: Heinrich Besseler, *Die Musik des Mittelalters und der Renaissance* (Potsdam: Akademische V-g Athenaion, 1931). Gustave Reese, *Music in the Middle Ages* (New York: Norton, 1940). Jacques Chailley, *Histoire musicale du moyen âge* (Paris: Presses universitaires de France, 1950). *NOHM,* vols. 2–3. John Caldwell, *Medieval Music* (Bloomington: Ind U Pr, 1978). Richard Hoppin, *Medieval Music* (New York: Norton, 1978). Jeremy Yudkin, *Music in Medieval Europe* (Englewood Cliffs, N.J.: Prentice-Hall, 1989). Jessie Ann Owens, "Music Historiography and the Definition of 'Renaissance,'" *Notes* 47 (1990–91): 305–30. Christopher Page, *Discarding Images: Reflections on Music and Culture in Medieval France* (Oxford: Oxford U Pr, 1993). Reinhard Strohm, *The Rise of European Music, 1380–1500* (New York: Cambridge U Pr, 1993). Daniel Leech-Wilkinson, "The Emergence of *ars nova*," JM 13, no. 3 (1995): 285–317. J. A. Owens, "Was There a Renaissance in Music?" in *Language and Images of Renaissance Italy,* ed. A. Brown (Oxford: Clarendon, 1995), pp. 111–25. Graeme M. Boone, ed., *Essays on Medieval Music: In Honor of David G. Hughes* (Cambridge, Mass.: Harvard Univ. Dept. of Music, 1995). James McKinnon, ed., Leo Treitler, gen. ed., *Source Readings in Music History:* vol. 2: *The Early Christian Period and the Latin Middle Ages* (New York: Norton, 1998). Judith A. Peraino, "Re-Placing Medieval Music," *JAMS* 54, no. 2 (2001): 209–64. D.M.R.

Middle C. The C that is closest to the center of the piano keyboard, notated on the first ledger line below the treble staff and the first above the bass staff. See Pitch names, Notation, Clef.

Middle East. See Near and Middle East, Mesopotamia, Egypt, Israel.

Middleground. See Schenker analysis.

Midi, Le [Fr.]. See *Matin, Le.*

Midsummer Night's Dream, A. (1) [Ger. *Ein Sommernachtstraum*] Incidental music by Mendelssohn, op. 61 (completed in 1842), to Shakespeare's play. The overture, op. 21, was composed in 1826. (2) Opera in three acts by Britten (libretto by the composer and Peter Pears, after Shakespeare's play), produced in Aldeburgh, England, in 1960. Setting: a wood near Athens and Theseus' palace in Athens in legendary times.

Mi-fa. In the theory of *hexachords used in the Middle Ages and Renaissance, a combination of *solmization syllables designating any of several dissonant intervals against which singers and composers were warned by theorists. Because each of the syllables could designate several pitches, the combination *mi-fa* could represent *tritones (called the *diabolus in musica* and to which the warning to avoid *mi contra fa* was particularly directed), minor seconds (as well as their inversions and compounds [see Interval]), and *cross relations.

Mignon. Opera in three acts by Ambroise Thomas (libretto in French by Michel Carré and Jules Barbier, after Goethe's *Wilhelm Meisters Lehrjahre*), produced in Paris in 1866. Setting: Germany and Italy in the late 18th century.

Mikrokosmos [Ger., Little World]. A collection of 153 piano pieces (plus supplementary exercises) in six volumes by Bartók, composed in 1926 and 1932–39 and arranged in order from very elementary works to very difficult ones.

Milanese chant. *Ambrosian chant.

Military music. Music used as an adjunct to warfare, and the musical practices and institutions that derive from such usage. Historically, military music consisted mainly of outdoor wind and percussion music played to incite troops and distract the enemy, and it developed the specialized functions of communicating signals (military calls) and regulating the march step. Now, however, military music is employed almost entirely on ceremonial occasions and to inspire patriotism.

Ancient military music was related to religious practices, with which it shared primitive drums and horns as well as forms of song and dance. Technologically more advanced cultures used tubular metal trumpets, such as the Hebrew **ḥatzotzerot* and Greek **salpinx*. The Greeks used fifes, without drums, for the march. The Romans differentiated among military purposes for the **tuba*, **buccina*, and **lituus*, all forms of the trumpet. By extension, such music served for parade, ceremony, and private official functions. Similar practices persisted in Carolingian times and the early Middle Ages, when the military horn acquired legendary status in the *Chanson de Roland.*

The Crusades discovered a wealth of military music employed by Muslim armies as a continuous accompaniment to battle. From the East, the Crusades introduced fife and drum music for the foot soldiers' march, and they appropriated kettledrums to accompany trumpets, already associated with mounted nobility and royal bodyguard. These distinctions were transferred to infantry and cavalry with the rise of organized armies in the 15th and 16th centuries. Shawm and bagpipe choirs were also introduced for elaborately melodic music. At home, military musicians were organized in guilds and served as town *waits and court minstrels.

Under Louis XIV of France and Charles II of England, bands of oboes and bassoons in four parts replaced the shawm choirs; the French "24 oboes du Roi" set the European standard of the late 17th century. In the early 18th century, Frederick the Great of Prussia fixed German regimental music in octets of two oboes, two clarinets, two horns, and two bassoons, called *Harmoniemusik* [see also *Harmonie*]. Military musicians of the day commanded notoriously high salaries. A wave of Turkish enthusiasm brought the importation of black *Janissary musicians to play Oriental percussion, i.e., Turkish crescent, triangle, tambourine, cymbals, and bass drum; from their extravagant costume and gesture derives the showmanship of today's drum major. The integration of complete brass and woodwind family choirs as used today occurred in the late 18th century and the Napoleonic era, during which time the familiar genre of *march with trio took shape.

Since Napoleonic times, military music has largely become dissociated from actual military operations and has assumed primarily ceremonial functions. Civic bands modeled on military ensembles became widespread in the 19th century. They achieved new levels of artistry and size under the influence of bandleaders Wilhelm Wieprecht in Germany, Adolphe Sax in France, and Patrick Gilmore in the U.S., and with the establishment of the Royal Military School of Music in England. About 1850, Sax's introduction of valved brass instruments stimulated the band's development, as did the adoption of the saxophone family as a component choir by bands in France, England, and America. See also Brass band.

In the early 20th century, the present-day symphonic band and the marching band crystallized, reaching their peak of popularity with the eminence of such American bandleaders and composers as John Philip Sousa and Edwin Franko Goldman. Outstanding large bands today include those of various branches of the armed services of France, the United Kingdom, and the United States, as well as those of many American universities, where marching bands perform regularly at outdoor sporting events. The technical sophistication of wind and percussion ensembles has steadily increased, stimulated by a growing repertory of modern compositions, arrangements, and transcriptions of orchestral works. See also Symphonic band.

Bibl.: Georges Kastner, *Manuel général de musique militaire* (Paris: Didot, 1848; R: Geneva: Minkoff, 1973). Henry George Farmer, *The Rise and Development of Military Music* (London: W Reeves, 1912; R: Freeport, N.Y.: Books for Libraries Pr, 1970). Marie Bobillier [pseud. Michel Brenet], *La musique militaire* (Paris: H Laurens, 1917). Hector Ernest Adkins, *Treatise on the Military Band* (London: Boosey, 1931; 2nd ed. rev., 1958). Peter Panoff, *Militärmusik in Geschichte und Gegenwart* (Berlin: K Siegismund, 1938). William Carter White, *A History of Military Music in America* (New York: Exposition Pr, 1944; R: Westport, Conn.: Greenwood, 1975). Henry George Farmer, *Military Music* (London: M Parrish, 1950). David Whitwell, *Band Music of the French Revolution* (Tutzing: Schneider, 1979). Kenneth E. Olson, *Music and Musket: Bands and Bandsmen of the American Civil War* (Westport, Conn.: Greenwood, 1981). Eugen Brixel, *Das ist Österreichs Militärmusik* (Graz: Edit Kaleidoskop, 1982). See also Brass band, Symphonic band.

Military Polonaise. Popular name for Chopin's Polonaise in A major for piano op. 40 no. 1 (1838, published in 1840).

Military Symphony. Popular name for Haydn's Symphony no. 100 in G major Hob. I:100 (1793–94; no. 8 of the *Salomon Symphonies). The second movement, marked *allegretto,* employs triangle, cymbals, and bass drum in imitation of Turkish military music [see Janissary music] and also includes a trumpet fanfare. This movement was originally the second movement of a concerto in G major for two *lire organizzate* [see Hurdy-gurdy] and orchestra Hob. VIIh:3*. After the symphony's success, Haydn made another setting of this movement for military band.

Milonga [Sp.]. A traditional song genre of Argentina. In duple meter, but often with guitar accompaniment in 6/8, it is characteristically sung with wry and playful texts in *romance* or *décima* form; the alternation of passages between two singers in a kind of vocal combat *(payada)* is also a common trait. It became popular in Buenos Aires in the late 19th century and is generally regarded as a principal source of the Argentine **tango.* D.S.

Mimodrame [Fr.]. *Pantomime.

Minaccioso, minacciosamente [It.]. Threatening.

Mineur [Fr.]. Minor.

Minim. In British usage, the half note [see Note; but see also Mensural notation].

Minnesinger [Ger., fr. *Minne,* love]. Any of the contributors to the corpus of Middle High German lyric verse on the topic of love, known as *Minnesang,* as well as to the related corpus of political and didactic verse, all dating from ca. 1150 to ca. 1325.

The Minnesinger probably originated in the Rhineland, but many of the most famous came from Bavaria and Austria. Almost all the first generation were nobles of high degree, most notably Heinrich IV, the Hohenstaufen king. By the late 12th century, some important Minnesinger were *ministeriales,* members of the lesser nobility, including Reinmar (ca. 1160–ca. 1210), Walther von der Vogelweide (ca. 1170–ca. 1230), and Neidhardt von Reuental (ca. 1180–ca.

1250), for whom writing songs had an economic as well as a social function. The *ministerialis* class (e.g., Tannhäuser, ca. 1230–ca. 1280) and the emerging burgher class (e.g., Konrad von Würzburg, ca. 1225–1287) dominated 13th-century *Minnesang,* as knightly *Minnesang* declined with the collapse of Hohenstaufen rule in 1250. Like Heinrich von Meissen (called *Frauenlob,* ca. 1260–1318), influential Minnesinger from the later 13th and the early 14th century were often burghers. Two 14th-century manuscripts, however, order poems according to the real or imagined social status of their authors, each of whom is furnished with (often fanciful) heraldry. Oswald von Wolkenstein (1377–1445) is sometimes considered the last of the Minnesinger, though this gives the term a broader interpretation than many scholars are prepared to accept.

Minnesang (love song) treats various topics of courtly love and was composed to be sung. The *Minnelied* is a man's love song; the *Frauenlied* a woman's. Both derive from the Provençal **canzo* [see also Troubadour]. In the 12th-century *Wechsel* (exchange), a man and woman speak of their common situation in alternating stanzas. In the 13th-century *Tagelied* (dawn song), derived from the Provençal **alba,* lovers part at daybreak. Many similar terms (e.g., *Kreuzlied, Winterlied*) have been coined by modern scholars. All such poetry is typically written in one or more stanzas of equal length and in *bar form. The *Leich* is a song in unequal stanzas influenced by the Provençal **lai* and *descort* and by the Latin *sequence. The *Spruch* (or *Sangspruch*) is formally closer to the *Minnesang* but retains its own identity (see Sayce, 1982, pp. 408–41). Both the *Leich* and the *Spruch* are devoted primarily to political or to religious and secular didactic themes.

The melodies of *Minnesang* were transmitted orally. The three central collections of *Minnesang,* which date from the late 13th and early 14th centuries [see Bibl.], contain no music. The earliest extant notated sources were copied in the later 13th century, when the tradition was already in decline, and, with one exception, are fragmentary. The earliest substantial musical sources are the Jena codex (*D-Ju* E1.f.101), a mid-14th-century manuscript of 133 leaves, probably copied in northwest Germany, and a 14th-century manuscript at Vienna (*A-Wn* 2701) that contains only five *Minnelieder.* The Jena codex comes from the extreme northern periphery of Minnesinger activities. Because of this and its late date, a high proportion of its notated *Minnesang* is attributed to minor figures; most of it is not the *Minnelied* of the early poets, but the *Sangspruch* that dominated the 13th and 14th centuries. This paucity of sources has made the 15th-century Colmar manuscript (*D-Mbs* Cgm4997), compiled by a *Meistersinger, more important than it would otherwise be. Though it ascribes its tunes to earlier Minnesinger, it is impossible to verify the authenticity of these melodies and their ascriptions.

The melodies of the Jena codex are notated in square neumes without mensuration. During the first half of the 20th century, many scholars argued that a meter is intended and can be inferred either directly from the texts themselves (particularly in syllabic settings) or indirectly from the rules for modal rhythm developed for 13th-century Parisian polyphony (see, for example, Spanke, 1929, and Husmann, 1954). These assumptions did not lead to a consensus regarding how specific melodies should be transcribed (see Kippenberg, 1962, pp. 226–27; Müller-Blattau, 1971). Since Kippenberg (1962), there has been less reluctance to confront the sources on their own terms. In *Minnesang,* frequent reference is made to *wort unde wīse,* the uniting of text and melody in a given song into a single system, or *dōn* (later *Ton*), to which future songs may be written at will. The Jena codex transmits 91 of these *Töne.* Since the tune of a *Ton* does not exist independent of a pattern of versification, it is reasonable to suppose that it needs no rhythm apart from the pattern and that performance of *Minnesang* was declamatory. Text settings are not always syllabic: the poems themselves sometimes refer to improvised instrumental accompaniments and melismatic embellishments. Knowledge of how the songs actually sounded must remain inherently limited. Nevertheless, study of the notated sources can expand that knowledge, revealing, for example, that notated melismas tend to occur on accented syllables (Pickerodt-Uthleb, 1975).

Bibl.: *Facsimiles.* Wilhelm Hoffman, ed., *Die Weingartner Liederhandschrift,* 2 vols. (Stuttgart: Müller & Schindler, 1969) [Stuttgart, Landesbibliothek HB XIII poet. germ. I]. Ulrich Müller, ed., *Die grosse Heidelberger "Mannesische" Liederhandschrift* (Göppingen: A Kümmerle, 1971) [Heidelberg, Universitätsbibliothek, Codex pal. germ. 848]. Walter Blank, ed., *Die kleine Heidelberger Liederhandschrift,* Facsimilia heidelbergensia 2 (Wiesbaden: L Reichert, 1972) [Heidelberg, Universitätsbibliothek, Codex pal. germ. 357]. Helmut Tervooren and Ulrich Müller, eds., *Die Jenaer Liederhandschrift in Abbildung* (Göppingen: A Kümmerle, 1975) [Jena, Universitätsbibliothek E1.f.101].

Literature. Hans Spanke, "Romanische und mittellateinische Formen in der Metrik von Minnesangs Frühling," *Zeitschrift für romanische Philologie* 49 (1929): 191–235. Heinrich Husmann, "Das System der modalen Rhythmik," *AfMw* 11 (1954): 1–38. Friedrich Ackermann, "Zum Verhältnis von Wort und Weise im Minnesang," *Wirtschaft und Wettbewerb* 9 (1959): 300–311. Burkhard Kippenberg, *Der Rhythmus im Minnesang: Eine Kritik der literar- und musikhistorischen Forschung mit einer Übersicht über die musikalische Quellen* (Munich: Beck, 1962). Ursula Aarburg, "Probleme um die Melodien des Minnesangs," *Deutschunterricht* 19 (1967): 98–118. Friedrich Maurer, "Sprachliche und musikalische Bauformen des deutschen Minnesangs um 1200," *Poetica* 1 (1967): 462–82. Ronald J. Taylor, *The Art of the Minnesinger,* 2 vols. (Cardiff: U of Wales Pr, 1968). Burkhard Kippenberg, "Die Melodien des Minnesangs," in *Musikalische Edition im Wandel des historischen Bewusstseins,* ed. Thrasybulos Georgiades (Kassel: Bärenreiter, 1971), pp. 62–92. Wendelin Müller-Blattau, "Versuche zur musikalischen Gestaltung des mittelalterlichen Liedes," *Zeitschrift für Deutsche Philologie*

90 (1971) Sonderheft: 153–69. Erdmute Pickerodt-Uthleb, *Die Jenaer Liederhandschrift: Metrische und musikalische Untersuchungen* (Göppingen: A Kümmerle, 1975). Olive Sayce, *The Medieval German Lyric 1150–1300* (Oxford: Clarendon Pr, 1982).

Minor. See Interval, Scale, Chord, Triad, Mode, Key, Tonality.

Minore [It.]. Minor; the term is sometimes used to label a section of a work, e.g., a variation, that is in minor mode.

Minstrel [Fr. *ménétrier, ménestrel;* Ger. *Spielmann;* It. *menestrello;* Sp. *ministril;* Lat. *ministerialis,* an officer of the court]. (1) In English-speaking lands since ca. 1570, a wandering singer of ballads; formerly, one skilled in the performance of music as opposed to its theoretical aspect. In medieval Europe, the term is interchangeable with *ioculator* [Lat., joker; ME. *jogelour;* Fr. *jogleor, jongleur;* It. *gioccolatore;* Sp. *joglar*], rare in classical Latin but frequent in western and southern European sources from the 7th century on. Before ca. 1300, a minstrel might also be any sort of professional entertainer. Several writers (among music theorists, Sowa anonymous [1279]) use *ioculator* synonymously with *mimus* or with *histrio* [Lat., actor].

Minstrels occupied several social stations. In the lowest was the mendicant on the fringe of society, unprotected by feudal or civic law. The moral norms and (frequently pagan) practices of his milieu were regularly condemned by the Church and by educated people. To counter such views, minstrels in the larger cities formed guilds. The earliest known guilds of formerly itinerant musicians are the Nicolai-Bruderschaft (Vienna, 1288) and the Confrérie de St. Julien des Ménestriers (Paris, 1321).

Among the positions open to minstrels in the new bourgeois society of the late Middle Ages was that of town musician or *wait. Beginning with Florence (1291) and Lucca (1308) and spreading rapidly after 1400, many European cities guaranteed a minimum income to one or more minstrels to play for civic and religious functions. In feudal society, the minstrel attached to a noble household occupied a correspondingly elevated social station. Highest of all were trumpeters and drummers who might accompany their lords onto the battlefield. Gatherings or schools of minstrels are documented in Tournai (1330), Geneva (1359), and Cambrai (1366).

At the 13th-century English royal court, and in noble households, servant-minstrels were usually *jestours,* singers of *gestes* who accompanied themselves on the harp. Nonetheless, most minstrels are documented only as instrumentalists. According to Wace (1155), *jongleurs* played *lais, descorts, dansas,* and **chansons de geste* on their *vielles.* In 1180, Raimbaut de Vaqueiras reported "jogleurs, chanteors e troubadours" in Genoa. While such testimony by no means limits minstrels to the role of instrumentalists, it suggests that these and other nonverbal skills were characteristic. Rastall (1970/71) documents the presence of minstrels playing trumpets and shawms in English churches at the enthronement of prelates. In 14th- and 15th-century France and Burgundy, minstrels were especially those who performed on **haut* (loud) instruments.

(2) Since 1843, a member of a troupe of blackface entertainers who mimics, often in a derogatory fashion, the music, dance, language, manners, and appearance of African Americans.

Solo comic blackface entertainers were a fixture on the American stage in the 1830s, most famously Thomas D. Rice (who popularized the song and character "Jim Crow") and George Washington Dixon (known for his "Zip Coon"). In early 1843, four blackface musician-actors in New York City organized themselves along the lines of the then-popular singing families and called themselves the Virginia Minstrels. Over several months, they presented whole evening ("shows") of blackface comedy and music in the American Northeast and in England, planting the seeds for a dynamic and immensely popular new theatrical genre in both countries. The minstrel show quickly established a performance structure that was flexible enough to endure into the mid-20th century. It featured a fluid combination of stock comic characters, singers, instrumentalists, dancers, and actors. Crudely drawn stereotyping of African Americans and their culture provided the show's coherence.

From early in its history, the show featured a "minstrel line" of performers, generally arrayed on stage in a semicircle with the comic characters Mr. Bones and Mr. Tambo at the ends and a pretentiously dignified master of ceremonies ("Mr. Johnson" or the "Interlocutor," usually without blackface makeup) in the middle. Comedy followed from social inversion, since the supposedly dimwitted personifications of blackness—the "trickster" end men—nearly always got the best of the Interlocutor, who represented (and exaggerated) the virtues and values of respectable, white, middle-class life. Interleaved with humorous moments were songs (sometimes comic but often sentimental) and dances. African American musical styles certainly influenced the music of the minstrel shows, but so too did Italian opera, the American fiddle tune tradition, Irish music, the glee, and the parlor song. Important music for the early minstrel show was written by Dan Emmett (one of the original members of the Virginia Minstrels and the author of "Old Dan Tucker" and "Dixie") and Stephen Foster ("Oh! Susanna," "Old Folks at Home," "My Old Kentucky Home," and a host of others). Early on, the minstrel show wedded its musical tradition to its theatrical heritage in the development of the show-closing playlet; these skits often featured slapstick humor, cross-dressed (as well as blackfaced) characters, and a rousing musical finale (the "walkabout"; "Dixie" was a song written for such a closing number).

At its beginning, the blackface minstrel show was a small performance genre for multitalented musicians and actors (generally four to six of them). Audiences tended to be urban, lower-class, white, and male. The shows grew in size and complexity, especially during the last third of the 19th century, and reached a point where dozens of blackface performers might be involved in a production. These extravaganzas tended to draw audiences from a wider social spectrum. Impresarios and managers, such as the famed E. P. Christy, organized far-flung tours of their companies of minstrels, and by century's end the phenomenon had spread throughout the U.S. and the British empire to South Africa, Australia, India, and other points.

Minstrelsy provided the initial means by which blackness was widely represented in the public sphere. It had the effect of stereotyping a place, nature, and character for African Americans, who were generally portrayed as highly musical, good at dancing, lascivious, gluttonous, lazy, unattractive, and altogether ridiculous and worthy of being the butt of any low-order joke. The popular perceptions that issued from minstrelsy have persevered in many forms into the present. It should be surprising, then, that when 19th- and early 20th-century African Americans took to the popular stage, they generally were forced to do so as minstrels in blackface makeup.

The heyday of big-production blackface minstrelsy was past by the turn into the 20th century. It remained very much a part of the early-century entertainment business, though, as an omnipresent element in vaudeville. Movies also featured blackface minstrels, the most popular of whom was Al Jolson. Even early television, especially in Britain ("The Black and White Show"), broadcast blackface entertainment. And hundreds of small professional, semiprofessional, and amateur minstrel troupes performed at local venues well past midcentury.

Bibl.: (1) Walter Salmen, "Zur Geschichte der Ministriles im Dienst geistlicher Herren des Mittelalters," *Anglés,* 1958–61, vol. 2, pp. 811–19. L. M. Wright, "Misconceptions Concerning the Troubadours, Trouvères and Minstrels," *ML* 48 (1967): 35–39. Richard Rastall, "Minstrelsy, Church and Clergy in Medieval England," *PRMA* 97 (1970/71): 83–98.

(2) Hans Nathan, *Dan Emmett and the Rise of Early Negro Minstrelsy* (Norman: U of Okla Pr, 1962). Robert C. Toll, *Blacking Up: The Minstrel Show in 19th-Century America* (New York: Oxford U Pr, 1974). Eric Lott, *Love and Theft: Blackface Minstrelsy and the American Working Class* (New York: Oxford U Pr, 1993). Dale Cockrell, *Demons of Disorder: Early Blackface Minstrels and Their World* (Cambridge: Cambridge U Pr, 1997). William J. Mahar, *Behind the Burnt Cork Mask: Early Blackface Minstrelsy and Antebellum American Popular Culture* (Urbana: U of Ill Pr, 1999).

(2) D.C.

Minué montonero [Sp.]. An urban dance, derived in part from the minuet, in vogue in the first half of the 19th century in Argentina and Uruguay. It was also known as the *minué federal* and, in Uruguay, as "el Nacional." D.S.

Minuet [Fr. *menuet;* Ger. *Menuett;* It. *minuetto;* Sp. *minué, minuete*]. An elegant dance movement in triple meter (usually 3/4) of enormous popularity ca. 1650–1800. It is usually in binary form, with very regular phrases constructed of four-measure units, beginning without upbeat and cadencing on the strong beat [see Ex.]. Its straightforward melodic design did not encourage elaborate ornamentation or contrapuntal texture. The small, quick dance steps have a hemiola relationship to the meter; therefore, accented second beats and hemiola melodic figures are common in minuets. Such pieces were slower when danced, especially in France, and moderately quick as independent instrumental music, above all in Italy where they were often in 3/8 or 6/8.

The minuet is first known in the middle of the 17th century in France, where it was associated with the town of Poitou. It may have derived from the **branle de Poitou,* which had the 3 + 3 phrasing found chiefly in early minuets but occasionally in 18th-century examples (Bach, BWV 820, ca. 1705). It became a rage at the court of Louis XIV, himself an avid minuet dancer. It changed little in character when taken over into harpsichord and orchestral suites (Nicolas-Antoine Lebègue, Telemann), although English composers were sometimes influenced by the quicker Italian version of the dance (Handel). From ca. 1700, pairs of minuets were commonly played **alternativement* (ABA). The second one was often labeled *trio* and was written in a contrasting key and texture.

The minuet with trio was the only Baroque dance form that did not become obsolete as the Classical style emerged in the second third of the 18th century. The minuet often served as the closing movement of an opera overture and thus was one of the original elements of the symphony and related genres. As a last movement, it was often a *tempo di minuetto,* which implied the meter, phrasing, texture, and speed of a minuet divorced from its short binary form and (usually) *alternativement* disposition. Later minuets often include elements of sonata form (Thomas Arne). The *binary (usually rounded binary) minuet with trio ultimately became the standard third movement of the Classical symphony (*Mannheim school, Mozart, Haydn). Haydn especially exploited the form, using canons, retrograde designs, unusual key relationships, or quicker tempos. This loosening of the minuet's definition led to the abandonment of the name in favor of *scherzo, most prominently by Beethoven. Later composers rarely returned to the minuet except as a

Rameau, Minuet from *La Princesse de Navarre* (1745).

neoclassical gesture (Brahms, op. 11; Bizet, Symphony in C; Schoenberg, op. 25).

Bibl.: Helen Meredith Ellis (Little), "The Dances of Jean-Baptiste Lully, 1632–1687" (Ph.D. diss., Stanford Univ., 1967). Wolfram Steinbeck, *Das Menuett in der Instrumentalmusik Joseph Haydns* (Munich: Katzbichler, 1973). Wendy Hilton, *Dance of Court and Theater: The French Noble Style, 1690–1725* (Princeton, N.J.: Princeton Bk Co, 1981). Meredith Little and Carol Marsh, *La Danse noble: An Inventory of Dances and Sources* (Williamstown: Broude Trust, 1992). Christopher Hogwood, "In Defence of the Minuet and Trio," *EM* 30, no. 2 (2002): 237–51. B.G.

Minute Waltz. Popular name for Chopin's Waltz in D♭ major op. 64 no. 1 (1846–47), so called because it lasts approximately one minute when played at an excessively fast tempo (dotted half note = 140).

Miracle play. See Liturgical drama.

Miraculous Mandarin, The [Hung. *A csodálatos mandarin*]. A pantomime in one act by Bartók (scenario by Menyhért Lengyel), composed in 1918–19, orchestrated and revised thereafter, and first produced in Cologne in 1926. Bartók arranged an orchestral suite from the work in 1919 and 1927.

Mirliton. A vibrating membrane that modifies a sound produced in some other way, adding a nasal or buzzing quality. It may be set in motion by the human voice (as in a *kazoo), or by the sound waves of an instrument to which it is attached (e.g., the *marimba, **mbira,* and **ti-tzu*). Mirliton membranes are made of much less elastic materials than drum membranes (e.g., paper, onion skin, spider egg sacs), and they are loose rather than taut.

Miroirs [Fr., Mirrors]. Five piano pieces by Ravel, composed in 1905: *Noctuelles* (Moths); *Oiseaux tristes* (Mournful Birds); *Une barque sur l'océan* (A Boat on the Ocean; orchestrated in 1906, rev. 1926); *Alborada del gracioso* (The Fool's Dawn Song; orchestrated in 1918); and *La vallée des cloches* (The Valley of the Bells).

Mirror composition. A composition that can be performed in *inversion with respect to the intervals of each part as well as the relationship of all of the parts to one another (thus, as if it were being performed from a mirror held below the notation) or one that can be performed in *retrograde (i.e., backward, as if from a mirror held at the end of the notation). Canons and fugues are sometimes composed according to these principles. Examples occur in Bach's *The *Art of Fugue* (*Contrapuncti* 12 and 13; in the latter, the topmost of three voices becomes the bottom voice, and the middle becomes the top). The term is sometimes synonymous simply with *canon by inversion.

Mise [Fr.]. Placing, setting; *m. en musique,* setting to music; *m. en scène,* staging.

Miserere [Lat.]. Psalm 50 [51], "Miserere mei, Deus, secundum magnam misericordiam tuam" (Have mercy upon me, O God, according to thy loving kindness). One of the *Penitential Psalms, it is assigned in the Roman rite to Lauds of Maundy Thursday, Good Friday, Holy Saturday, and the Office of the Dead. It was set polyphonically in the Renaissance by Josquin, Costanzo Festa (in **falsobordone*), and others. A celebrated setting by Gregorio Allegri (1582–1652) has remained in use at the papal chapel.

Missa [Lat.]. *Mass. *Missa solemnis* (solemn or High Mass) is the full form of the Mass with all musical items sung; Beethoven's *Missa solemnis* op. 123 (1818–23), however, like most polyphonic Masses, consists of settings of only the five main parts of the Mass Ordinary, in this case for soloists, chorus, and orchestra. *Missa brevis* (short Mass) in the 16th century refers to a relatively brief setting of all five main parts of the Ordinary; in the 17th century and after, it could also refer to a setting of the Kyrie and Gloria only. *Missa lecta* (read or Low Mass) is the Mass with all texts, including those of musical items, read. *Missa cantata* is sung Mass. *Missa pro defunctis* is Mass for the Dead or *Requiem Mass. For *Missa Papae Marcelli,* see Marcellus Mass. For *Missa L'homme armé,* see *Homme armé, L'.*

Missal [Lat. *missale*]. See Liturgical books.

Mistic(h)anza [It.]. **Quodlibet.*

Misura [It.]. Meter, measure, beat; *alla m.,* in strict meter; *senza m.,* freely, without strict meter.

Mit [Ger.]. With. For phrases beginning with this word, see the second word of the phrase.

Mitte [Ger.]. Middle, e.g., of a drum head (*Fell*).

Mixed cadence. See Cadence.

Mixed media. The merging of elements from different arts into a single, composite expression, usually as in recent works in which live sound (including music) and movement (including dance and dramatic action), film, tape, and setting are combined, often incorporating indeterminate elements [see Aleatory music] and audience participation; also multimedia. Theater necessarily involves a fusion of different arts, so the origins of mixed media with music go back to the origins of opera, which juxtaposes such disparate components as music, text, action, and dance. Wagner gave the concept its first theoretical formulation in his idea of *Gesamtkunstwerk,* the "total work of art" united from separate artistic elements. Early 20th-century developments such as Skryabin's color organ, Stravinsky's innovations in *music theater, and the use of film in stage works (e.g., Berg's *Lulu*) attest to a growing interest in exploring new media combinations.

The main thrust of mixed media in recent music has been away from traditional genres. A major concern has been to develop new modes of theatrical performance. Thus, in the 1950s, John Cage and others began to devise happenings: largely unstructured theatrical events in which indeterminate actions are played out in a specially arranged "enviroment" of heterogeneous sounds and objects. There is no plot or purposeful action, and participants and audience are one.

The development of electronic music has been especially conducive to the creation of new multimedia combinations. Examples include the merging of natural and electronic sounds (Berio's *Omaggio a Joyce,* 1958), the synthesis of tape music with live instrumental or vocal performances (Davidovsky's *Synchronisms* 1–8, 1962–74), and the electronic manipulation of live instrumental or vocal sound sources (Stockhausen's *Mikrophonie I,* 1964). Other examples of mixed media works are Salvatore Martirano's *L's. G. A.* (Lincoln's Gettysburg Address, 1967–68), scored for narrator with gas mask (through which helium is breathed to alter the voice), tape, slides, and film; and John Cage and Lejaren Hiller's *HPSCHD* (1967–69). The latter, probably the most elaborate multimedia event yet staged, included in its original performance (1969) 7 harpsichords, 51 tapes, various films and slides, a light-show, musicians, and several thousand wandering spectators. The emphasis on mixed media throughout the past century mirrors the widespread aesthetic questioning of the advisability or possibility of achieving autonomous "purity" in any of the arts. See also Music theater. R.P.M.

Mixed mode. See Mode.

Mixed voices. A combination of men's and women's voices, as distinct from *equal voices.

Mixolydian. See Mode, Greece I, 3 (ii).

Mixtur [Ger.]. *Mixture; in classic northern European organs, the main mixture stop of the **Hauptwerk,* normally having 1 1/3′ as lowest pitch at C.

Mixture. An organ stop with two or more pipes for each note, always sounding pitches at the octave and twelfth. The lowest pitch at C is related to the basic pitch of the division and also determines the name of the mixture. For an 8′ organ, the following is usual: **Mixtur* or **Fourniture,* 1 1/3′; **Scharff,* **Scherp,* or **Cymbale,* 2/3′.

Mizmār [Ar.]. Any *reedpipe; especially the **zūrnā* and similar instruments.

M.M. Abbr. for Maelzel *Metronome.

Mobile form. See Aleatory music.

Modal. Characterized by the use of a *mode or modes, especially the church modes of the Middle Ages and Renaissance [see also Modality], or by the use of the rhythmic modes [see Modes, rhythmic].

Modality. A musical system based on the use of a *mode or modes, as distinct especially from *tonality; also that quality of a work that is attributable to its use of a specific mode. For the use of the modes in monophonic and polyphonic music of the late Middle Ages and Renaissance, see Mode. The term modality is often applied to the presence within predominantly tonal works of features describable in terms of the modes or to music that is diatonic to a significant degree but not clearly an example of tonality. In such cases the use of the term does not necessarily imply a direct connection with the historical modes, only that any music employing diatonic scales and/or harmonies based on them can be described with the terminology of the modes. Folk music is sometimes described in these terms and in consequence so is art music based on folk music of this type (e.g., some of the music of Chopin and of numerous composers of the later 19th century who used native folk materials). Features that may suggest the term include, for example, a whole tone below the tonic in a scale that is otherwise major (as in the Mixolydian mode); a major sixth above the tonic in a scale that is otherwise minor (Dorian); an augmented fourth above the tonic in a scale that is otherwise major (Lydian); a semitone above the tonic in a scale that is otherwise minor (Phrygian). A celebrated and explicit example is Beethoven's "Dankgesang an die Gottheit in der lydischen Tonart" (Song of Thanksgiving to God in the Lydian Mode) from the String Quartet in A minor op. 132 (1825). The term has also been applied to aspects of the music of Debussy and of 20th-century composers often termed *neoclassical in their avoidance of extreme chromaticism.

Bibl.: Julia d'Almendra, *Les modes grégoriens dans l'oeuvre de Claude Debussy* (Paris: G Énault, 1950). John Vincent, *The Diatonic Modes in Modern Music* (New York: Mills, by arrangement with the U of Cal Pr, Berkeley, 1951).

Modal jazz. See Jazz.

Modal notation. Notation, especially that in the sources for the repertory of *Notre Dame, designed to represent the rhythms of the rhythmic modes [see Modes, rhythmic; Notation].

Modal rhythm. The rhythm of the rhythmic modes [see Modes, rhythmic].

Mode [Lat. *modus*]. (1) In *mensural notation, the relationship between the long and the breve. (2) Any of the rhythmic patterns making up the set of rhythmic modes [see Modes, rhythmic] employed in certain repertories of medieval music. (3) In the writings of some early medieval theorists, e.g., Hucbald (ca. 840–930) and Guido of Arezzo (d. after 1033), interval. (4) In *acoustics, any of the ways in which vibrating systems such as strings and columns of air can be made to vibrate, e.g., in the case of a string, vibration in segments of one-half, one-third, one-fourth, etc., of its total length.

(5) Any of a series of loosely related concepts employed in the study and classification of both scales and melodies. The term is often restricted to scale types defined as collections of pitches arranged from lowest to highest, each including one pitch that is re-

garded as central. At another extreme, some concepts of mode emphasize melody types; any given mode is defined principally by characteristic melodic elements. Other concepts of mode range between these extremes. No single concept usefully embraces all that has been meant by the term throughout the history of Western music as well as all that is meant by the terms associated with non-Western music that have at one time or another been translated as mode. For the related concepts of classical antiquity, see Greece I.

I. *Church modes.* The essentials of the system of modes, termed the church modes, used in the classification of Gregorian chant were formulated by ca. 1000 and may be found in the anonymous *Dialogus de musica* and the *Micrologus* of Guido of Arezzo [see Theory]. Eight modes are defined, each according to final (i.e., the pitch on which melodies in that mode end), the intervallic relationship of other pitches to the final (i.e., the scale type), and ambitus (i.e., the range of pitches available from the scale type). From this period onward, the final is regarded as the most important criterion of mode, though the gamut of diatonic pitches (which, however, could include b♭) is a prior assumption, and thus the intervallic relationship of other pitches to the final is in large measure inseparable from the definition of the final itself.

There are four finals—d, e, f, and g—and for each final there is a high ambitus, termed authentic, and a low one, termed plagal, thus yielding the total of eight modes. Definitions of ambitus vary somewhat. The *Dialogus* describes them as follows. In the authentic modes, the ambitus stretches from the pitch below the final to the octave above the final; in the plagal modes, the ambitus stretches from the fifth below the final to the sixth above the final. Some accounts, however, define each ambitus as an octave, either above the final or from the fourth below to the fifth above, and regard pitches above or below as additional. The pitch below the octave is sometimes termed the *subtonium* or, in the case of an authentic mode, the *subfinalis.* Actual melodies present a more varied picture, however, and this is sometimes reflected in theorists' accounts of individual modes. For example, Gregorian melodies in the authentic mode with final on f almost never employ the pitch below the final.

In the 11th century, theorists began to regard the tenors of *psalm tones as essential characteristics of the modes themselves (and thus sometimes termed dominants of the modes) rather than merely as features of particular types of melodies. The location of these tenors is sometimes described as follows. In authentic modes the tenor lies a fifth above the final and in plagal modes a third above, except that the pitch b is replaced by c′ (in the authentic mode with final on e and the plagal with final on g), and in the plagal mode with final on e, g is replaced by a. Early practice as regards the tenors was a good deal more varied, however, and thus their identity was clearly not essential to the earliest conceptions of the modes.

The first evidence of a system of eight modes in the West is a *tonary from the 8th century. It and others of the period number the four finals in ascending order with terms derived from the Greek ordinal numbers: *protus, deuterus, tritus,* and *tetrardus,* distinguishing authentic and plagal forms for each. They employ the term *tonus.* In the 9th century, Hucbald proposed the numbering 1 through 8 that remains in use, and, like some other theorists, he used the terms *modus* and *tropus* along with *tonus.* The 9th-century treatise *Alia musica* brought together the eight Latin church modes with Boethius's account of octave species and applied the Hellenistic names that have also remained in use in some contexts (though the terms were not used in the way they had been used in Greek theory). These three forms of nomenclature and the characteristics of the modes described above are summarized in the accompanying table.

Apart from the early use of Greek nomenclature, the first testimony on the origin of the Western system of eight modes is found in the 9th-century treatise by Aurelian of Réôme (probably based in part on sources from the early 9th century), where the system is said to be Greek, i.e., from *Byzantine chant. The Greek system or *oktoēchos* [see *Ēchos*] cannot definitely be shown to have existed before the 8th century, however, and it differs from the Western system in some particulars. Although the idea of a system of eight modes was almost certainly imitated from the Greek by Carolingian reformers, scholars (Chailley, Huglo, Claire) now believe that the Western system evolved independently over a period of time. It was in any case applied to a repertory that already existed. This accounts for the early disagreements on the modal classification of some melodies and for the difficulties in classifying some melodies at all. The practical need for classifying melodies and thus the practical need

Mode		Final	Ambitus	Tenor
1. Protus authentic	Dorian	d	d-d′	a
2. Protus plagal	Hypodorian	d	A-a	f
3. Deuterus authentic	Phrygian	e	e-e′	c′
4. Deuterus plagal	Hypophrygian	e	B-b	a
5. Tritus authentic	Lydian	f	f-f′	c′
6. Tritus plagal	Hypolydian	f	c-c′	a
7. Tetrardus authentic	Mixolydian	g	g-g′	d′
8. Tetrardus plagal	Hypomixolydian	g	d-d′	c′
9.	Aeolian	a	a-a′	e′
10.	Hypoaeolian	a	e-e′	c′
11.	Ionian	c	c-c′	g
12.	Hypoionian	c	g-g′	e′

for a system of some kind derived from the need to assign melodies of certain types to an appropriate recitation formula for their verses [see Psalm tone].

Important features of early tonaries and descriptions of the modes are the characteristic melodies or phrases associated with each mode. These include melodic formulas (derived from Byzantine chant) termed **noeane* and the like and model antiphons not taken from liturgical books but with texts from the Bible that incorporate the numbering of the modes (e.g., "Primum quaerite regnum Dei," "Secundum autem simile est huic"). Early writers often assign a melody to a specific mode on the grounds of its similarity to other melodies in that mode [see also Gregorian chant III]. Thus, the early history of the church modes reveals a reliance on concepts of melodic type as well as on the concepts of scale type and final that ultimately became dominant.

In the later 13th century, an explicit connection is made between modal quality and the solmization syllables of the Guidonian hexachord, thus making clear the way in which the modes could be transposed. *Protus, deuterus,* and *tritus* modes had finals on *re, mi,* and *fa,* respectively, and thus on a, b, and c′ as well as on the usual d, e, and f. The *tetrardus* modes could have their final only on g, however. These alternative finals are termed *affinales.* Beginning in the 14th century with the work of Marchetto da Padova (*Lucidarium,* 1318), the outlines of modal theory reaching into the 16th century are established. Among the elements of this theory are the analysis of modes in terms of the species of fifth and fourth that combine to form the modal octave. Authentic and plagal modes with the same final share a fifth rising upward from the final and are distinguished according to whether a fourth is joined to the fifth above or extends downward from the final. The pitch lying a fifth above the final is termed the *confinalis.* Melodies are further classified into five types according to ambitus and constituent species of fifth and fourth: a *tonus perfectus* is one that exactly fills its modal octave; a *tonus imperfectus* is one that does not fill its modal octave; a *tonus plusquam perfectus* is one that exceeds its modal octave, beyond the octave above the final if it is authentic and below the fourth below the final if it is plagal; a *tonus mixtus* is an authentic mode that also descends into the plagal ambitus or a plagal mode that ascends into the authentic ambitus; and a *tonus commixtus* is one that makes use of a species of fourth or fifth that does not belong to it. In the 14th century, too, the possibility of transposition by means of accidentals is also spelled out. The regular use of b♭ makes possible *protus* modes on g and implies the existence of an e♭′ as *fa* in a hexachord on b♭. The use of a B♭ signature is termed *cantus mollis* (from *b mollis*) as distinct from *cantus durus* (from *b durus* or B♮ [see Accidental]); the regular use of E♭ is termed *cantus fictus,* since this was not part of the original gamut at all [see also *Musica ficta*]. Finals other than the regular d, e, f, and g and the *affinales* a, b, and c′ are termed *irregulares.*

II. *Modes in polyphony.* The expansion of the tonal system in some of the ways described brings the concerns of modal theory steadily closer to newly composed music—i.e., polyphony—as distinct from the existing repertory of liturgical chant. This is made explicit first by Johannes Tinctoris, who remarks that his *Liber de natura et proprietate tonorum* of 1476 was undertaken principally with a view to polyphony. Tinctoris and later theorists (including Pietro Aaron and Gioseffo Zarlino) regard the tenor as the crucial voice for determining the mode of a polyphonic work as a whole and in this way maintain the distinction between authentic and plagal modes. The mode of each individual voice may be judged independently, however. Zarlino specifies, for example, that tenor and soprano should be the same as regards authentic or plagal and that alto and bass should be similarly paired in the complementary mode.

It is in this context that the traditional system of eight modes is expanded to twelve, first by Heinrich Glarean (*Dodecachordon,* 1547). He adds authentic and plagal modes with finals on a (numbered 9 and 10 and termed Aeolian and Hypoaeolian, respectively) and c′ (numbered 11 and 12 and termed Ionian and Hypoionian, respectively). In his *Dimostrationi harmoniche* (1571), Zarlino renumbers this system, placing the c modes first and the a modes last, and reassigns the names in order, starting with Dorian on c and ending with Ionian and Hypoionian on g and Aeolian and Hypoaeolian on a. In the 1573 edition of *Le istitutioni harmoniche* (first published in 1558), he dropped the names altogether. Glarean's numbering and nomenclature, which preserved the traditional scheme for the eight-mode system, was preferred everywhere except France, where Zarlino's reassigned numbers and names were taken up, as in collections of music such as Claude Le Jeune's *Octonaires* (1606), Charles Guillet's *Vingt quatre fantasies à quatre parties disposées selon l'ordre des douze modes* (1610), and Denis Gaultier's *La rhétorique des dieux* (ca. 1652).

All modal theorists devoted attention to the set of cadential pitches appropriate to each mode. Accounts of the eight-mode system display considerable variety in specifying these pitches. Zarlino, in contrast, specifies for all twelve modes only the three pitches of the triad formed on the final.

Publications of music from the 1540s and after demonstrate the concern of some composers for the modes. Collections of madrigals (e.g., by Lassus) as well as sacred works (e.g., by Palestrina) are sometimes arranged by order of mode with standard combinations of signatures and clefs [see also *Chiavette*] for each (Powers). More difficult to establish is concern by composers for the supposed ethical or affective qualities of the modes. The attribution of such qualities to the modes has its origins in classical antiquity and persists through the Middle Ages. Writers of the

Renaissance, under the influence of antiquity, take up the matter with renewed vigor. Throughout the Middle Ages and the Renaissance, however, there is steady (though not complete) disagreement on what these qualities are for individual modes. Zarlino's own compositions do not correspond well with his descriptions of the modes, and in modally ordered collections of liturgical music, a correspondence is clearly obviated.

After 1600, a continuing need for the eight modes in liturgical practice is combined with increasing use of transpositions. At about the same time, German theorists such as Lippius formulate the modes in terms of the triad, i.e., in harmonic terms rather than in terms of octave species. Modal theory in the period that follows is still not well studied. But by the early 18th century, Heinichen and Mattheson regard the twelve pitches within each octave as each capable of supporting two scale types distinguished by major and minor thirds. The result is the system of 24 major and minor keys. By the early 19th century, major and minor are seen as the only two survivals of the twelve modes of earlier practice. Although it persists, such a view is at odds with the complex history of the modes, especially in the 17th century. See also Tonality, Modality.

III. *Concepts of mode in folk and non-Western music.* The concepts that have been associated with the term mode in the study of music outside the tradition of Western art music (principally that of the Middle Ages and Renaissance) vary considerably in the relative strength of three elements: scale or pitch collection, usually with some internal hierarchy; melody type; and emotive or other "nonmusical" characteristics. With respect to some repertories, especially of *folk music, these concepts do not form an explicit part of musical practice, but are tools for study and classification by scholars. In some non-Western art musics, on the other hand, such concepts may explicitly underlie a largely improvisatory practice. The latter include the **maqām* and **dastgāh* of musics of the *Near and Middle East and the **rāga* of *South Asia. In *jazz, the term mode has been applied to scales other than the major or minor scale that may serve as the basis for sometimes extended improvisation over a single harmony, as in some music by Miles Davis.

Bibl.: John Vincent, *The Diatonic Modes in Modern Music* (Hollywood: Curlew Music Publications, 1934). Otto Gombosi, "Studien zur Tonartenlehre des frühen Mittelalters," *AM* 10 (1938): 149–74; 11 (1939): 28–39, 128–35; 12 (1940): 21–52. Henri Potiron, *La composition des modes grégoriens* (Paris: Desclée, 1953). Jacques Chailley, *L'imbroglio des modes* (Paris: A Leduc, 1960). Siegfried Hermelinck, *Dispositiones modorum: Die Tonarten in der Musik Palestrinas und seiner Zietgenossen* (Tutzing: Schneider, 1960). Jacques Chailley, "Essai analytique sur la formation de l'octoéchos latin," *Wellesz,* 1966, pp. 84–93. Leeman L. Perkins, "Mode and Structure in the Masses of Josquin," *JAMS* 26 (1973): 189–239. Bernhard Meier, *Die Tonarten der klassischen Vokalpolyphonie* (Utrecht: Oosthoek, Scheltema & Holkema, 1974). Jean Claire, "Les répertoires liturgiques latins avant l'octoéchos: L'office ferial romano-franc," *Études grégoriennes* 15 (1975): 5–192. Joel Lester, "Major-Minor Concepts and Modal Theory in Germany: 1592–1680," *JAMS* 30 (1977): 208–53. Michael Markovits, *Das Tonsystem der abendländischen Musik im frühen Mittelalter* (Bern: P Haupt, 1977). Alberto Turco, "Les répertoires liturgiques latins en marche vers l'octoéchos," *Études grégoriennes* 18 (1979): 177–223. Harold S. Powers, "Tonal Types and Modal Categories," *JAMS* 34 (1981): 428–70. David Hiley, *Western Plainchant: A Handbook* (Oxford: Oxford U Pr, 1993). Ursula Günther et al., eds., *Modality in the Music of the Fourteenth and Fifteenth Century, MSD* 49 (1996). Cristle Collins Judd, ed., *Tonal Structures in Early Music* (New York: Garland, 1998). Harold S. Powers, "Mode," *New Grove 2* 15:775–860. See also Gregorian chant, Psalm tone, Theory, Tonary.
D.M.R.

Moderato [It.]. Moderate with respect to tempo; *allegro m.,* not as fast as *allegro; andante m.,* not as slow as *andante.*

Moderator. A pedal or knee lever found on pianos beginning in the late 18th century that causes a strip of cloth to be inserted between the hammers and the strings, thus softening the tone color.

Modéré [It.]. Moderate with respect to tempo. Rousseau (1768), however, equates it with **adagio.*

Modernism. The avant-garde musical aesthetics from the late 19th century to the mid-20th century. In compositional terms, there are several general traits common to much modernist music: a corrosion, or even refusal, of traditional harmonic and rhythmic organization; the use of unconventional instruments and sounds; and distortions of inherited musical forms.

Starting with the debates about Wagner and his "music of the future," any new music that seemed to introduce fundamentally new styles or procedures came to be called modernist; thus there is no one modernist style of musical composition. The high premium modernism placed on experimentation and innovation meant that compositions and styles once deemed modernist seemed out-dated to subsequent generations—a circumstance reflected in Boulez's famous rallying cry that "Schoenberg is dead." Similarly, many of the aesthetics behind avant-garde music have come into conflict; for instance, the heightened expressivity valued by many early 20th-century modernists was later viewed with disdain by the equally modernist proponents of serialism.

Musical modernism and its innovations cannot be separated from their historical context, for music that was intended to encompass a new modern (and modernist) world necessarily bore the philosophical and societal tensions of that new world. Freudian angst, the suspicion of mass culture and monumental forms, a refusal of decoration, and an embrace of new ideals of beauty have all made their way into modernist musical aesthetics.

In many ways musical modernism simply refers to the most avant-garde music, starting with Wagner. But modernism's fundamental distrust of popular styles and idioms places it apart from most of the neo-Romantic and postmodern music composed in the past decades. As such, the previously close relationship between modernism and new music in general has itself become a historical relic.

Bibl.: Paul Moos, *Moderne Musikästhetik in Deutschland. Historisch-kritische Uebersicht* (Leipzig: H. Seemann, 1902). Ferruccio Busoni, *Sketch of a New Aesthetic of Music,* trans. Theodore Baker (New York: Schirmer, 1911). Igor Stravinsky: *Poétique musicale sous formes de six leçons* (Cambridge, Mass.: Harvard U Pr, 1947; Eng. trans., 1947). Theodor Wiesengrund Adorno, *Philosophy of Modern Music,* trans. Anne G. Mitchell and Wesley V. Blomster (New York: Seabury, 1973). Arnold Schoenberg, *Style and Idea: Selected Writings of Arnold Schoenberg,* ed. Leonard Stein, trans. Leo Black (1950; 2nd ed., New York: St. Martin's, 1975). Milton Babbitt, "Who Cares If You Listen?" *High Fidelity* 8, no. 2 (1958): 38–40. Charles Ives, *Essays before a Sonata and Other Writings,* ed. Howard Boatwright (New York: Norton, 1964). Robert P. Morgan, "Secret Languages: The Roots of Musical Modernism," *Critical Inquiry* 10 (1983–4): 442–61. D. Matore, "Le Modernisme musical français à fin de la Seconde Guerre Mondial," *Revue international de musique française* 18 (1985): 69–78. Jürgen Habermas, *The Philosophical Discourse of Modernity: Twelve Lectures,* trans. Frederick Lawrence (Cambridge, Mass., MIT Pr, 1987). Pierre Boulez and John Cage, *The Boulez-Cage Correspondence,* ed. and trans. Robert Samuels (New York: Cambridge U Pr, 1993). Joseph N. Straus, "The 'Anxiety of Influence' in Twentieth-Century Music," *JM* 9 (1991): 430–47. Marshall Brown, "Origins of Modernism: Musical Structures and Narrative Forms," in *Music and Text: Critical Inquiries,* ed. Steven Paul Scher (New York: Cambridge U Pr, 1992), pp. 75–92. Otto Kolleritsch, ed., *Klischee und Wirklichkeit in der musikalischen Moderne* (Vienna: Universal Ed, 1994). Georgina Born, *Rationalizing Culture: IRCAM, Boulez, and the Institutionalisation of the Avant-Garde* (Berkeley: U of Cal Pr, 1995). Paul Griffiths: *Modern Music and After: Directions since 1945* (New York: Oxford U Pr, 1995). David E. Schneider, "Bartók and Stravinsky: Respect, Competition, Influence, and the Hungarian Reaction to Modernism in the 1920s," in *Bartók and His World,* ed. Peter Laki (Princeton: Princeton U Pr, 1995), pp. 172–99. R.M.

Modern jazz. In the 1950s, *bebop and its derivatives, including *cool jazz. With the advent of *free jazz in the late 1950s, these styles ceased to be regarded as modern, and the term lost currency.

Modern music. See Twentieth century, Western art music of the.

Modes, rhythmic. Patterns of temporal order abstracted by 13th-century theorists from *Notre Dame polyphony above all, the *discant **clausula.* The clearest, most concise description of modal rhythm and its notation is provided by Johannes de Garlandia in *De musica mensurabili* (ca. 1250). There are six modes, each with its own characteristic foot or combination of long (L) and short (B) notes [see Ex. 1].

The value of the normal breve or short note *(brevis recta)* is one temporal unit *(tempus),* and that of the normal long *(longa recta)* is two. The modes that make use of these values only (the first, second, and

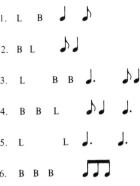

1. L B
2. B L
3. L B B
4. B B L
5. L L
6. B B B

1. The six rhythmic modes.

sixth) are known as *modi recti;* in them each foot contains a total of three *tempora.* The basic values may be altered to accommodate patterns of greater length—the so-called *modi ultra mensuram*—to the ternary rhythm of the shorter ones. Thus, in the third, fourth, and fifth modes the longs have three *tempora,* while in the third and fourth the first breve has one and the second two. Musical phrases *(ordines),* commonly marked off by rests corresponding in duration to the last element of the foot, are created by one or more repetitions of the modal pattern [see Ex. 2].

2

Phrases are described as perfect if they end with the value that initiates the foot, imperfect if they end with another value. Hence, the first-mode phrases illustrated in Ex. 2 are perfect; imperfect phrases in the same mode end with breves. Perfect phrases of the fifth mode have odd numbers of longs; imperfect phrases have even numbers. As in poetic meters, to which the modes are roughly analogous, substitutions for the characteristic members of a given foot are possible: two breves for a long, for example, yielding what the theorists call *fractio modi;* a ternary long for a long and a breve, and so forth.

The melismatic music of the *clausula* is notated chiefly in ligatures, the reading of which is explained by Johannes de Garlandia as follows: the last note is a long, the penultimate is a breve, and everything before that adds up to the value of a long. Hence, the three ligatures most commonly used, *binaria, ternaria,* and *quaternaria* (having two, three, and four notes, respectively), are read with the rhythms shown in Ex. 3.

3

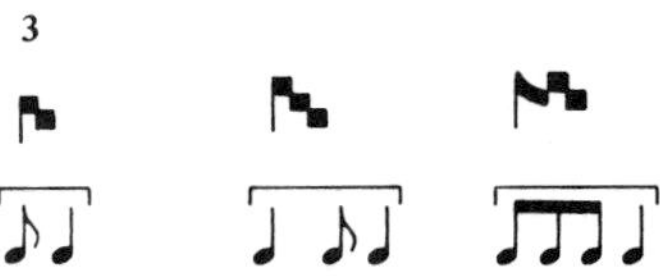

(By convention, the grouping of notes into ligatures is indicated in modern notation by square brackets.)

The mode of a passage is signaled by the sequence of ligatures. For instance, a *ternaria* followed by an indeterminate number of *binariae* indicates the first mode. Certain accidents, however, require the fragmenting of the bound forms: the appearance of repeated notes, which cannot be represented in ligatures but must be construed as if they were; the introduction of a new syllable of text; and an initial ternary long or a series of longs.

The only mode to contain a series of longs is the fifth, and while this often came to be notated, by convention, as a succession of *ternariae* separated by rests, the earliest examples of the mode are written in simple (unbound) notes. The ternary long at the beginning of the third-mode foot is similarly indicated by a simple figure. The original form of this mode, which according to Anonymous IV (ca. 1275) was especially popular in England, proceeded as in Ex. 4. The *ternariae* following the initial long are here read according to rule. When the order of the smaller values was reversed, however, as in Ex. 5 (the rhythm most commonly associated with this mode), the same sequence of forms was maintained, but the ligature was read differently. The last note is a long, and the penultimate is a breve, albeit the longer, second breve *(brevis altera)*, but what comes before is reduced from a long to a breve.

The rule for reading ligatures is distorted even more in the case of the second mode, one of the latest to develop. The opposite of the first mode, it is indicated by an indeterminate number of *binariae* with a final *ternaria.* The smaller ligatures are read breve-long, as the rule would indicate, but the values of the *ternaria* are reversed, to become breve-long-breve. The sixth mode, as such, seems to have evolved slowly. But methods for notating it as a derivative of the first mode had been used from an early period for *fractio modi.* The long at the end of a ligature is subdivided by means of a *plica,* literally a fold, but in appearance a short descending or ascending line drawn from the last member of the ligature [see Ex. 6], indicated in modern notation by a stroke through the stem of the note resulting from this sign. Example 7 gives a sixth-mode rhythm derived from first-mode notation with *fractio modi.*

Johannes de Garlandia's description of the rhythmic modes is followed closely by Anonymous IV and the St. Emmeram (Sowa) Anonymous (1279). Franco of Cologne, writing in the mid-1280s, renumbers the modes, reducing them from six to five by combining the first and the fifth.

Modal rhythm governed not only the *clausula* but also the **conductus* and, in its early stages, the *motet. The latter half of the 13th century saw the gradual dissolution of the modes as the breve was broken down, in the *triplum* of the motet, into ever smaller values—at times up to seven semibreves. If the tenor and the *duplum* still appeared on the page as modal, the ear did not perceive them as such, so extended had both the longs and the breves become.

Bibl: Eric Reimer, ed., *Johannes de Garlandia: De mensurabili musica,* 2 vols. (Wiesbaden: Steiner, 1972). Rebecca A. Baltzer, "Notation, Rhythm, and Style in the Two-Voice Notre Dame Clausula" (Ph.D. diss., Boston Univ., 1974). Jeremy Yudkin, ed., *The Music Treatise of Anonymous IV: A New Translation.* Musicological Studies and Documents 41 (Neuhausen-Stuttgart, 1985). Edward H. Roesner, "The Emergence of *Musica mensurabilis,*" *Studies in Musical Sources and Style: Essays in Honor of Jan LaRue,* ed. Eugene K. Wolf and Edward H. Roesner (Madison, Wis.: A-R Eds, 1990), pp. 41–74. Richard Crocker, "Rhythm in Early Polyphony," *Studies in Medieval Music: Festschrift for Ernest H. Sanders,* ed. Brian Seirup and Peter M. Lefferts (*CM* 45–47 [1991]: 147–77). Norman E. Smith, "The Notation of *Fractio Modi,*" *Studies in Medieval Music: Festschrift for Ernest H. Sanders,* ed. Brian Seirup and Peter M. Lefferts (*CM* 45–47 [1991]: 283–304). Ernest H. Sanders, "The Earliest Phases of Measured Polyphony," *Music Theory and the Exploration of the Past* (Chicago: U of Chicago Pr, 1993), pp. 41–58. Vincent Corrigan, "Modal Transmutation in the 13th Century," *Essays in Honor of Hans Tischler,* ed. David Halperin, *Orbis musicae* 12 (1998): 83–106. Ernest H. Sanders, *"Rithmus," Essays on Medieval Music in Honor of David G. Hughes,* ed. Graeme M. Boone (Cambridge, Mass.: Harvard Univ. Dept. of Music, 1995), pp. 415–40. Roland Eberlein, "Vormodale Notation," *AfMw* 55 (1998): 175–94. For further editions and translations of theoretical treatises, see Theory. See also Notre Dame, repertory of; Notation.

J.K.

Modinha [Port.]. An art song cultivated in Brazil and Portugal beginning in the late 18th century, originally characterized by its simplicity, but from ca. 1800 becoming more elaborate under the influence of Italian opera. In Brazil in the later 19th century, it acquired broader popularity as a kind of sentimental song, and it survives as a lyric folk genre in Brazil today. D.S.

Modo [It.]. Mode; manner.

Modulation. In tonal music, the process of changing

from one *key to another, or the result of such change [see Tonality, Key relationship; for the term as used in electronics, see Modulator]. Modulation is to be found in almost every work of tonal music. It may take the form of a simple modulation to a closely related key and back again (for example, from C major to G major and back to C) in a short piece, or it may occur as part of a whole series of complex modulations involving many keys in larger works. The capacity for modulation, even more than the establishment of key, is the most distinctive and powerful property of the tonal system in Western music, especially since the community of twelve major and twelve minor keys was made intonationally practical by equal *temperament. The possibilities of modulation have been exploited to the fullest by tonal composers since Bach, relying on the ear's remarkable ability to retain, as a function of musical memory, the primacy of an established key to which the music may return even after the most varied and lengthy journeys through distant keys. The first movement of Beethoven's *Eroica* Symphony, for instance, modulates perhaps 17 times between the beginning of the exposition and the beginning of the recapitulation, some 400 measures, without change of key signature.

Modulation characteristically is accomplished by means of a pivot chord, having a particular harmonic function in the initial key but a different function in the second. The harmony following the pivot chord is

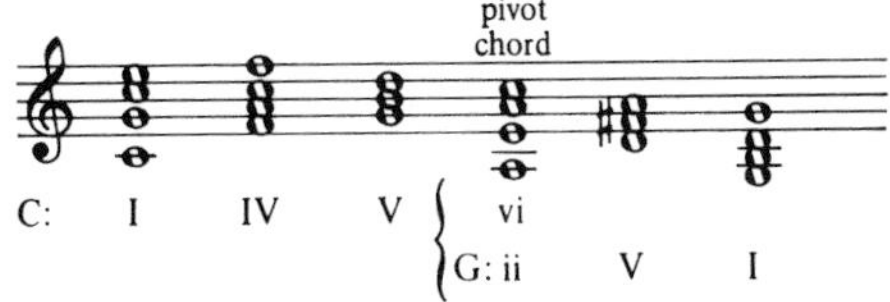

then a distinct harmony of the new key. The process is shown schematically in Ex. 1; in actual music, modulation requires some musical time, at least a phrase, to be carried out. A strong authentic cadence in the new key then helps to confirm the modulation, so that the ear's perception of the old key yields to that of the new. A modulation of no longer than a phrase, allowing for one strong cadence, followed then by a reversion to the old key, still fresh in mind, is called an intermediate modulation (or sometimes false modulation). This state must be distinguished from *tonicization, which is of shorter duration, occurs anywhere within the phrase, and generally affects only primary triads [see Harmonic analysis III]. Gray areas between these three defined states abound, so a distinction between them may be difficult or arbitrary. In the first half of the waltz theme from Beethoven's Diabelli Variations op. 120, for instance, the main key of C is established during eight bars by tonic and dominant harmony alone, followed by successive tonicizations (by means of secondary *dominants) of F major, G

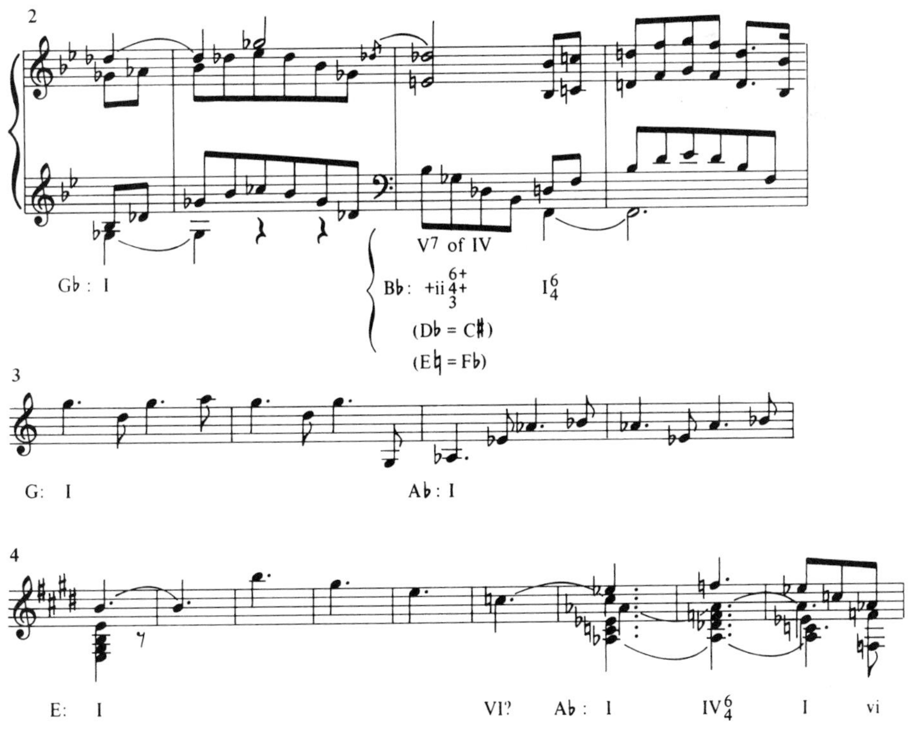

Modulation.

major, and A minor, the last serving as supertonic in an intermediate modulation to G; the second half counterbalances all this harmonic activity by a strong return to C, with proportionate tonicizations of F and G. Such secondary tonal variety, within what is basically a single overall key, is of great advantage in closed forms such as variations, where the allowable space for modulation is intrinsically limited.

The most common modulations are between closely related keys: tonic and dominant, tonic and subdominant, tonic and relative minor or major. The modulation to the key of the dominant (in major mode), or to that of the relative major (in minor mode), is at the heart of the sonata principle, being the most basic tonal aspect of the sonata exposition [see Sonata form]. Nevertheless, modulations between any and all keys are possible, and modulations between distantly related keys, involving complex pivot-chord relationships, can be found everywhere throughout the period in which tonality was the norm for Western art music. In Ex. 2, from Schumann's *Kreisleriana,* the dominant seventh is a pivot chord, enharmonically reinterpreted as an augmented sixth chord. A modulation that is so abrupt as to reveal no apparent pivot chord is called a shift, as in Ex. 3, from Schubert's Symphony in C major D. 944. Or the gap between the two keys may be bridged with a reduced texture, even a single pivot tone symbolizing harmony in the old key, then absorbed into the new, as in Ex. 4, from Schubert's *Unfinished* Symphony D. 759.

A succession of transient modulations (sometimes called passing modulations), traversing several keys before reaching a well-established one, is called a modulation chain. The individual keys are established only briefly, sometimes by as few as two chords, before moving on to the next. Beethoven's Two Preludes for piano or organ, op. 39, show systematic modulations by successive dominants, through all major keys. Modulation chains [see also Sequence (1)] are commonly found in the keyboard fantasies of the late Baroque and in the development sections of the Classical sonata form. In the 19th century, continuous chromatic modulation over a very long musical time, with an apparent main key occurring but seldom, is a distinguishing characteristic of several composers, especially Wagner in his mature operas, and Liszt, Franck, and Bruckner in their orchestral works. The later intensification of this practice, in the late works of Mahler and the early works of Schoenberg, was one of the factors that led to the breakdown of functional tonality altogether [see Atonality].

Bibl.: Hugo Riemann, *Systematische Modulationslehre* (Hamburg, 1887). Thorvald Otterström, *A Theory of Modulation* (Chicago: U of Chicago Pr, 1935; R: New York: Da Capo, 1975). Heinrich Schenker, *Harmony,* ed. Oswald Jonas, trans. Elisabeth Mann Borgese (Chicago: U of Chicago Pr, 1954). Allen Forte, *Tonal Harmony in Concept and Practice* (New York: Holt, Rinehart, & Winston, 1962; 2nd ed., 1974). Arnold Schoenberg, *Structural Functions of Harmony,* rev. ed. Leonard Stein (New York: Norton, 1969). Walter Piston, *Harmony,* 4th ed., rev. Mark DeVoto (New York: Norton, 1978). Arnold Schoenberg, *Theory of Harmony,* trans. Roy E. Carter (Berkeley and Los Angeles: U of Cal Pr, 1978).

M.DEV.

Modulator. (1) An electronic device for varying some characteristic (e.g., frequency, amplitude) of a carrier wave for the purpose of transmitting a signal; the process is termed modulation and is the basis for radio and television transmission, whence the terms amplitude modulation (AM) and frequency modulation (FM). See also Ring modulator. (2) See Tonic sol-fa.

Modus [Lat.]. (1) *Mode. (2) Any of the rhythmic *modes. (3) In *mensural notation, the relationship between the *longa* and the *brevis* (also termed *modus longarum, modus minor*); *modus maximarum* or *modus major* denotes the relationship of the *maxima* to the *longa.* English theorists such as Thomas Morley (1597) sometimes translate these terms as lesser and greater mood, respectively.

Möglich [Ger.]. Possible; *wie m.,* as possible (e.g., as fast, as loud).

Moins [Fr.]. Less.

Mojiganga [Sp.]. In Spanish theater of the 17th and 18th centuries, a short comic work, often with characters wearing animal masks, performed between the acts of a play, sometimes with music. Authors include Pedro Calderón de la Barca.

Moldau, The. See *Má Vlast.*

Moll [Ger.]. Minor.

Molto [It.]. Very.

Momente [Ger., Moments]. A work by Stockhausen for soprano, 4 choral groups, and 13 instrumentalists, composed in 1962–64. It is based on the combination of what he termed moments: brief units of musical time defined by a particular process. In a work in what is termed moment form, such moments may be combined in a variety of ways, perhaps at the discretion of the performers.

Moment form. See *Momente.*

Moments musicaux [Fr., Musical Moments]. The title given by the publisher in 1828 to Schubert's six piano pieces D. 780 (op. 94; 1823–28). The original title page uses the spelling *Momens musicals.*

Monacordio [Sp.]. Clavichord.

Mondscheinsonate [Ger.]. See *Moonlight* Sonata.

Monferrina. A country dance in 6/8 from the Piedmont of northern Italy, popular in England around 1800 and represented in collections such as *Wheatstone's Country Dances for 1810;* also manfredina, monfreda, monfrina. There are examples by Clementi.

Mongolia. See East Asia IV.

Monica, monicha, monaca [It.]. An Italian popular song. The poetic theme of the *monica,* a young girl

whose parents force her to become a nun against her will, can be traced to Italian popular poetry of the 14th century. The text with which the later song is most closely associated was first mentioned in connection with a 15th-century celebration in Siena. The earliest copy of the well-known song with a text on the same theme, "Madre non mi fa monica" (Mother, don't make me be a nun), is in a manuscript of arias compiled by Michele Pazio in 1610 [see Ex.].

Arrangements of the melody exist under various titles in 16th-century lute tablatures. In 17th-century Italy, it was popular as "Aria della monica." Most guitar tablatures contain it, and composers such as Frescobaldi and Biagio Marini based compositions on both the melody and the harmony of the tablatures. Toward the end of the century, it was included in collections of popular religious music (**laude spirituali*).

The earliest extant occurrence of the melody is in Pierre Phalèse's *Luculentum theatrum musicum* (1568), where it is called "Almande nonette." From the early 17th century, the idea of Christmas became firmly attached to the melody, and many 17th- and 18th-century French organists, including Nicolas-Antoine Lebègue, Louis-Claude Daquin, and Jean-François Dandrieu, set it under the titles "Une vierge pucelle," "Noel," and "Noel, Une jeune fillette."

In Germany, the melody entered Lutheran chorale books as "Von Gott will ich nicht lassen" by 1582. Many 17th- and 18th-century German organists, including Bach, wrote chorale preludes on it under this title or as "Wer nur den lieben Gott lässt walten."

Bibl.: Francesco Balilla Pratella, "Anchora dell' *Aria della monicha* e dell' *Aria di Fiorenza,*" *NA* 11 (1934): 214–19. Lawrence H. Moe, "Dance Music in Printed Italian Lute Tablatures from 1507 to 1611" (Ph.D. diss., Harvard Univ., 1956), pp. 184–87. John Wendland, "'Madre non mi fa monaca': The Biography of a Renaissance Folksong," *AM* 48 (1976): 185–204. L.H.M.

Monochord [Gr. *kanōn*]. A *zither with a single string stretched over a rectangular sound box. Calibrations are marked on the sound box to indicate divisions of the string according to mathematical ratios corresponding to various intervals [see Interval]. Usually a movable bridge is provided. The player holds the string firmly against the bridge with one hand and plucks the string with the other. In this way, precisely tuned pitches can be obtained one at a time. The monochord was the principal instrument of ancient Greek music theorists, who used it to investigate the fundamental laws of musical acoustics. Its invention was attributed to Pythagoras. In the Middle Ages, it was used for theoretical demonstrations, for the training of singers, and for tuning instruments. Among Latin writers who discuss it are Boethius, Odo of St. Maur, Guido of Arezzo, Johannes Afflighemensis, Jacques of Liège, and Ramos de Pareja. From the 11th through the 15th century it seems to have found some use as an instrument for practical music-making, though it is not clear in what contexts. Multistringed monochords ("polychords") were introduced as well as keyed models, from which the *clavichord is descended. As late as the 19th century, a metal-stringed monochord was still in common use by organ tuners, and it was used by acousticians and ethnomusicologists into the 20th. See also *Tromba marina.*

Bibl.: Karl-Werner Gümpel, "Das Tastenmonochord Conrads von Zabern," *AfMw* 12 (1955): 143–66. Jacques Chailley, "La monocorde et la théorie musicale," *Smits van Waesberghe,* 1963, pp. 11–20. Cecil Adkins, "The Technique of the Monochord," *AM* 39 (1967): 34–43. Thomas J. Mathiesen, "An Annotated Translation of Euclid's Division of the Monochord," *JMT* 19 (1975): 236–58.

Monocordo [It.]. In string playing, a direction to play a work or passage on a single string. It was first used by Paganini in his Sonata *Napoleone* (1807) for the G string.

Monodrama. See Melodrama.

Monody. (1) Music consisting of a single melodic line [see Monophony]. (2) Any of various types of Italian solo song with instrumental accompaniment that flourished during the first half of the 17th century. Giovanni Battista Doni introduced the term in the 1630s; it was not used by the composers of monody. Although the years around 1600 (which witnessed the performance of the first operas and the publication of Giulio Caccini's important collection of lyric monodies, *Le nuove musiche,* 1602) have usually been considered the starting point of monody, a thriving tradition of accompanied solo song may be traced in Italy at least back to the 15th century. Various "pseudomonodic" styles and genres, then, provide important 16th-century precursors to monody. These include the **frottola,* most often performed by solo voice with accompaniment of lute or viols; the semi-improvised recitation of poetry in fixed forms set to repeating musical units (often bass lines implying harmonic progressions such as the **romanesca* and **ruggiero*); semidramatic solo songs in courtly entertainments such as **intermedi;* light, homophonic, dance-related vocal genres such as the **canzonetta* and **balletto;*

and even a type of polyphonic madrigal, the *madrigale arioso* [see Madrigal (3)], which features a largely homophonic texture and concentration of melodic interest in the uppermost voice.

The transformation of monody into new styles in the mid-17th century is, similarly, difficult to date precisely. In opera, it involves the deemphasis of affective recitative, the central emotional component of early operas, in favor of lyrical *bel canto* *arias and, in solo song, the emergence of the *cantata, a semidramatic alternation of brief recitatives and more elaborate arias. Both of these developments begin in the 1620s and are substantially complete by 1650.

Two more or less distinct sorts of monody may be discerned: lyric and dramatic. Collections of lyric monodies proliferated after Caccini's path-breaking publication. Fortune (1963) counts over 200 surviving collections from the years 1602–35, and many more that are known to have been published are not extant. While Caccini and other composers often referred to their monodies simply as *musiche* (musical works) on their title pages, the contents of the collections usually fall into two distinct genres: the madrigal *(madrigale)* and the air *(aria).* Madrigals for solo voice and continuo extend and develop many of the features of the late polyphonic madrigal. Indeed, some composers of monody, for example Sigismondo d'India, continued throughout their careers to write polyphonic madrigals as well. Such pieces are typically either through-composed settings of freely structured poetry or settings of such poetry with a final section repeated (a common practice in the polyphonic madrigal), and they borrow many devices of text expression—unprepared or extreme dissonance, chromaticism, sequential repetition of important phrases, etc.—from their polyphonic precursors. They differ from the polyphonic madrigal most notably in their increased use of florid embellishments and often in their marked tunefulness. Airs, meanwhile, set strophic poetry, or poetry in fixed forms such as the sonnet. They may consist of repeating musical units adaptable to any example of a particular poetic form (e.g., d'India's *aria da cantar sonetti,* air for singing sonnets); these derive from 16th-century formulas for poetic recitation. More often they employ *strophic variation, in which the strophes of poetry are set to altered versions of the same music, frequently employing the same bass. Perhaps most often they display strict strophic form. This last type of air especially tends toward lively tunes, lilting dance rhythms, and compound or triple meters (or a mixture of both by virtue of frequent hemiola); often it includes instrumental ritornellos between strophes.

Dramatic monody—the **stile rappresentativo* or *recitative—is the fundamental musical novelty of the earliest opera. It attempts, in the words of its first master, Jacopo Peri, "to imitate speech in song" ("imitare col canto chi parla"; see *L'Euridice,* preface, in Solerti, 1903). To this end, its rhythmic pace is freely declamatory, following closely the accentual patterns of the text. Its melodies are less tuneful than those of the monodic madrigal, often declaiming several words on a single pitch. It generally avoids the virtuosic embellishments of lyric monody. But at moments of heightened emotion, it borrows, like the the solo madrigal, the text-expressive devices of the polyphonic madrigal.

In practice, however, the distinction made here between lyric and dramatic monody is blurred in several ways. Even the first operas contain airs that contrast with the prevailing style of recitative. Monteverdi's *Orfeo* (1607) includes light, dancelike songs in strophic form and weightier airs structured as strophic variations; such airs are the precursors of the elaborate arias of later number opera. Occasionally, as in Monteverdi's famous lament from the opera *Arianna* (1608), dramatic monody attains a lyricism that approaches the style of solo madrigals. Finally, many composers of lyric monody, e.g., d'India, Claudio Saracini, and Frescobaldi, included miniature dramatic scenes in recitative style in their collections.

Bibl.: Angelo Solerti, *Le origini del melodramma* (Turin: Fratelli Bocca, 1903). Alfred Einstein, *The Italian Madrigal,* 3 vols. (Princeton: Princeton U Pr, 1949; R: 1971). Nigel Fortune, "Italian Secular Monody from 1600 to 1635: An Introductory Survey," *MQ* 39 (1953): 171–95. Id., "A Handlist of Printed Italian Secular Monody Books, 1602–1635," *RMARC* 3 (1963): 27–50. Jan Racek, *Stilprobleme der Italienische Monodie: Ein Beitrag zur Geschichte des einstimmigen Barocklied* (Prague: Státní Pedagogické Nakladatelství, 1965). Nino Pirrotta, *Li due Orfei* (Turin: ERI, 1969; rev., Turin: Einaudi, 1975); trans. Karen Eales, *Music and Theatre from Poliziano to Monteverdi* (Cambridge: Cambridge U Pr, 1982). Barbara Russano Hanning, *Of Poetry and Music's Power: Humanism and the Creation of Opera* (Ann Arbor: UMI Res Pr, 1980). Claude V. Palisca, *Baroque Music,* 2nd ed. (Englewood Cliffs, N.J.: Prentice-Hall, 1981). Gary Tomlinson, "Madrigal, Monody, and Monteverdi's 'via naturale alla immitatione,'" *JAMS* 34 (1981): 60–108. Id., ed., *Italian Secular Song, 1606–1636,* 7 vols. (New York: Garland, 1986).

G.A.T.

Monophony, monophonic. Music consisting of a single line or melody without an accompaniment that is regarded as part of the work itself, as distinct from *polyphony and homophony. For repertories of Western monophonic music see Plainsong, Trouvère, Troubadour, Minnesinger, Meistersinger, *Cantiga, Lauda.* Most folk song is also monophonic in principle, though it may often be sung with improvised accompaniment.

Monothematic, polythematic. A composition based on one or on several themes, respectively. Most *fugues are monothematic, being based on a single subject. Earlier imitative forms such as the *ricercar, *canzona, and *fantasia may be either monothematic or polythematic, however. Examples of *sonata form are often polythematic, having different themes associated with each of the principal tonal areas of the exposition. Some composers, however (e.g., Haydn), have composed monothematic sonata forms.

Monotone. A single tone on which a liturgical text, most often a prayer or passage of Scripture, is recited. An inflected monotone is a formula for recitation in which a single tone predominates but in which divisions in the text may be marked by brief deviations from the principal tone. See Tone, Psalm tone.

Monter [Fr.]. To raise, e.g., the pitch of an instrument.

Montezuma. Opera in three acts by Sessions (libretto by G. A. Borgese), produced in Berlin in 1964. Setting: Mexico, 1519–20.

Montirandé [Fr.]. A 16th- and 17th-century variety of the **branle,* in 4/4 meter and with dotted rhythms. It is mentioned by Thoinot Arbeau (*Orchésographie,* 1588) as "branle de monstierandel" and by Marin Mersenne (*Harmonie universelle,* 1636) as "branle de montirandé." It is found in Michael Praetorius's *Terpsichore* (1612) and elsewhere.

Montonero [Sp.]. See *Minué montonero.*

Montpellier, Codex. Montpellier, Faculté de médecine, H196 [Mo]. 397 leaves. France, 13th century. The largest medieval motet collection. Modern editions: Yvonne Rokseth, *Polyphonies du XIIIe siècle,* 4 vols. (Paris: L'Oiseau-lyre, 1935–39). Hans Tischler, *The Montpellier Codex,* 6 vols. in 3 (Madison, Wis.: A-R Eds, 1978).

Montre [Fr., to show]. In the classic French organ, the *Principal stop at 8′ or 16′ pitch, whose pipes were mounted in the facade of the organ.

Mood. **Modus* (3) [see also Mensural notation].

Moon guitar (lute). See *Yüeh-ch'in.*

Moonlight Sonata. Popular name for Beethoven's Piano Sonata no. 14 in C♯ minor op. 27 no. 2 (1801), marked *Sonata quasi una fantasia.* The name probably derives from a review written by Heinrich Rellstab (1799–1860) in which the first movement was likened to "a boat visiting, by moonlight, the primitive landscapes of Vierwaldstättersee [Lake Lucerne] in Switzerland." The work has also been called the *Laube-Sonate* [Ger., Bower Sonata].

Moravian music, American. The music of the Moravian Church in America (Brüder-Unität), most highly developed in Bethlehem, Pennsylvania, and Winston-Salem, North Carolina. Other centers include Nazareth and Lititz, Pennsylvania.

The Brüder-Unität was formed by missionaries from the Moravian Church in Herrnhut, Saxony, established in 1722 by the few surviving members of the Unitas Fratrum, a branch of the Bohemian Brethren. The first missionaries to North America arrived in 1735 and founded Bethlehem, Pennsylvania, in 1741, after abandoning a settlement in Georgia.

In Herrnhut, the Moravians had emphasized musical activities, as did the missionaries to North America, even structuring their communities around the musical needs of the church. Provision was made for elaborate choral and orchestral performances, as well as for the playing of chamber music, both secular and sacred. Some music was imported from Europe, but much was composed locally.

The Moravian repertory included hymns, commonly sung to European chorale melodies with organ accompaniment, and a few solo songs with keyboard accompaniment. By far the most prominent type of sacred music, however, was the anthem for mixed chorus and a small instrumental ensemble, usually including organ. Until the middle of the 19th century, the texts of most Moravian anthems were in German.

The first Moravian composers in America were Johann Christoph Pyrlaeus (1713–85) and Christian Friedrich Oerter (1716–93). The first to write concerted anthems was Jeremiah Dencke (1725–95). Perhaps the best and the most important composer was Johann Friedrich Peter (1746–1813). Others included Simon Peter (1743–1819, brother of Johann Friedrich), Georg Gottfried Müller (1762–1821), Johannes Herbst (1735–1812), David Moritz Michael (1751–1827), and Johann Christian Bechler (1784–1857).

After the middle of the 19th century, Moravian music began to decline. Nevertheless, fine composers have occasionally been associated with the church since that time. Archives containing a great many Moravian musical manuscripts are maintained at Bethlehem and Winston-Salem.

Bibl.: Albert G. Rau and Hans T. David, comps., *A Catalogue of Music by American Moravians 1742–1842* (Bethlehem, Pa.: The Moravian Seminary and College for Women, 1938; R: New York: AMS Pr, 1970). Donald M. McCorkle, "Moravian Music in Salem" (Ph.D. diss., Indiana Univ., 1958). Marilyn Gombosi, comp., *Catalog of the Johannes Herbst Collection* (Chapel Hill: U of NC Pr, 1970).

Morceau [Fr.]. Piece, composition.

Mordent [also beat; Ger. *Mordant;* Fr. *martellement, pincement, battement, pincé, agrément;* It. *mordente, tremolo;* Sp. *quiebro*]. An ornament, especially a single or multiple alternation of the principal note with its lower auxiliary [Ex. 1]. The mordent is one of the oldest ornaments for which a description, a sign, and a term exist. In his *Fundamentum* (ca. 1520), Hans Buchner described *mordentes,* which were indicated in the tablature by a descending stem ending with a leftward hook (𝅘𝅥) and played by holding the main (written) note with the third finger of the right hand and rapidly repeating the lower auxiliary with the second finger. His description recalls Jerome of Moravia's late-13th-century recipe for imitating on the organ the vocal *flos harmonicus* (evidently a kind of trill or violent vibrato); there, however, the ornamental note was above rather than below the held principal one (*Tractatus de musica,* ed. Cserba, p. 184). Downward stems with hooks or loops in 15th-century German organ tablatures (e.g., Paumann's **Fundamentum organisandi* and the **Buxheimer Or-*

gan Book) probably indicated similar ornaments. For Martin Agricola (1528), the *Mordant* was any ornament or grace, in contradistinction to diminutions or *Coloratur;* Ammerbach (1571) described *Mordanten* as short trills to the upper or lower auxiliary; the same figures were called *Tremuli* by Praetorius (1619), who said, however, that organists called them *Mordanten.* Capirola, in his lute tablature (ca. 1517), used two dots over the number of the fret for a *tremolo s'un tasto solo,* a lower mordent. Oscillations with the lower auxiliary were included along with other ornaments among Tomás de Santa María's *quiebros* (1555) and Dalla Casa's *groppi* (1584); for most of the 17th and 18th centuries, the French term *martellement* (e.g., in Mersenne, 1636) covered a similar range of ornaments.

The form of the ornament as defined above seems to have crystallized first in England and France. Simpson (1659) and Playford (1660) give a "shaked beat" (a "prepared" and continuous mordent, i.e., one beginning on the auxiliary, Ex. 2a); Nivers (1665) gives a short prepared mordent under the term *agrément* [Ex. 2b]. Later examples generally begin on the main note: Chambonnières's *pincement* (1670), Mace's beat (1676), D'Anglebert's *pincé* (1689), and Purcell's beat (1696; see the correction of this table in Ferguson, 1975, p. 150). Except in connection with the **port de voix,* the mordent was used much more in

instrumental music, especially keyboard music, than in singing. During most of the 18th century, the short and the long mordent were recognized in England, France, and Germany; in Germany, the long "prepared" mordent was called *battement* (Quantz, 1752; Türk, 1789). Normally, all these ornaments took their value from the note they embellished (but see *NeuO,* pp. 415–62, to the contrary). They went out of fashion with the rise of the Classical style. Tartini applied the term *mordente* to a quick *turn designed to lend brilliance to an accented note; Leopold Mozart (1756) applied it to that and to the **Anschlag,* or "double appoggiatura." Heinichen (1728) described a kind of instantaneous, overlapped appoggiatura as one kind of mordent; C. P. E. Bach (1759) admitted an execution in which both notes were struck simultaneously and the auxiliary note immediately released.

Bibl.: Vincenzo Capirola, *Compositione di Messer Vincenzo Capirola,* ed. Otto Gombosi (Neuilly-sur-Seine: Société de musique d'autrefois, 1955). Martin Agricola, *Musica instrumentalis deudsch* (Wittenberg, 1528; facs., Hildesheim: Olms, 1969); trans. William E. Hettrick (Cambridge: Cambridge U Pr, 1994). Hans Buchner, *Sämtliche Orgelwerke,* ed. Jost Harro Schmidt, *EDM* 54–55 (1974). Tomás de Santa Maria, *Libro llamado Arte de tañer fantasia* (Valladolid, 1565; facs., Farnborough: Gregg, 1972); trans. Hans Lampl (Ph.D. diss., Univ. of SC, 1957). Elias Nicolaus Ammerbach, Orgel- oder Instrument-Tabulatur (Leipzig, 1571); trans. Charles Jacobs (Oxford: Clarendon, 1984). Girolamo Dalla Casa, *Il vero modo di diminuir* (Venice, 1584; facs., *BMB* sez. 2, 23, 1970). Christopher Simpson, *The Division-Violist* (London, 1659); 2nd ed., *The Division-Viol* (London, 1665; facs., London: J Curwen, 1955). John Playford, *An Introduction to the Skill of Musick* (London, 1660; facs. of 7th ed., 1674, Ridgewood, N.J.: Gregg, 1966). Guillaume-Gabriel Nivers, *Première livre d'orgue* [*Livre d'orgue contenant cent pièces*] (Paris, 1665); ed. Norbert Dufourcq (Paris: Éditions Bornemann, 1963). Jacques Champion de Chambonnières, *Les pièces de clavessin* (Paris, 1670; facs., *MMML* ser. 1, 3, 1967). Jean Henri D'Anglebert, *Pièces de claveçin* (Paris, 1689; facs., *MMML* ser. 1, 4, 1965). Henry Purcell, *A Choice Collection* (London, 1696; facs., *MMML* ser. 1, 26, 1978). Howard Ferguson, *Keyboard Interpretation* (New York: Oxford U Pr, 1975). See also Ornamentation, Theory. D.F.

Morendo [It.]. Dying, fading away.

Moresca, morisca [It.]. (1) A dance of Renaissance Europe, performed by dancers with blackened faces and with bells attached to their legs, sometimes depicting combat between Moors and Christians. The fool or buffoon was also frequently represented in such dances. No detailed choreography survives, but Thoinot Arbeau (*Orchésographie,* 1588) describes it as being in binary meter and gives a melody. Other melodies appear in the English virginal repertory and elsewhere. It often formed part of the **intermedio* and similar entertainments. Related or at least similar dances are the **matasin* and the English *morris dance. (2) A subgenre of the **villanella* caricaturing Africans or Moors. Published collections include examples by Lassus and others.

Bibl.: Paul Nettl, "Die Moresca," *AfMw* 14 (1957): 165–74.

Mormorando [It.]. Murmuring, whispering.

Morris dance. A type of English folk dance danced by six men, in two groups of three, with bells attached to their legs and each holding a white handkerchief or a stick. At times the tradition has also included dancing with blackened faces. There are numerous morris dances, and the term is sometimes extended to include the sword dance as well. Its historical relationship to the **moresca* and the origins of its name (often said to derive from the representation of Moors) are matters of some dispute.

Moses und Aron [Ger.]. Opera in three acts, of which only the first two were completed (1930–32), by Schoenberg (to his own libretto), performed in concert in Hamburg in 1954 and staged in Zürich in 1957. Setting: Egypt and Mt. Sinai in biblical times.

Mosso [It.]. Moved, agitated.

Motet. A major musical genre from the 13th through the 18th century, of minor importance thereafter. Because no single definition can encompass the characteristics of the motet during the entire course of its development, it is helpful to distinguish three major phases (Dammann, 1959). In the first (ca. 1200–1450), the term motet denoted a particular structure: a tenor derived from chant that serves as the foundation for newly composed upper voices; the resulting composition is heterogeneous both in the musical style of the individual voices and in their texts. In the second phase (ca. 1450–1600), motet denoted a genre: a polyphonic setting of a sacred Latin text. In the third phase (after 1600), the term, while retaining its basic meaning as a type of sacred music, became associated with a particular style *(stilus motecticus):* the serious, imitative style of church polyphony derived from Palestrina.

I. *The medieval motet.* In the 13th century, the term motet had two meanings: first, a brief composition for two or three voices, in which the tenor, drawn from chant, serves as the foundation for one or more upper voices with French or Latin texts; and second, one of the texted upper voices (*motetus,* from the Fr. *mot,* word, and thus, a voice or part to which words have been put) of such a composition. If there is a third voice, it is termed the *triplum.* The principal features of the early compositions of this type are a sharp differentiation in style between the tenor, which consists of a short, repeated rhythmic pattern, and the rhythmically active upper voices and, in works for three voices, the frequent setting of independent texts (sometimes in different languages) in the two upper parts.

The origin of the motet lies in the polyphony of the repertory of *Notre Dame, in which portions of responsorial chants normally sung by a soloist were ornamented by the addition of another voice, creating *organum. Typically, the melismatic portions of the original chant (those containing more than three notes to a syllable) were treated in *discant style, in which the tenor employed a brief, repeated rhythmic pattern. Compositions known as *clausulae* were written to substitute for those portions in discant style. The earliest motets were *clausulae* with text added to the upper voice or voices.

The early development of the motet shows extraordinary richness of invention. A single tenor, for example, "Et gaudebit," often serves as the basis of many different compositions. The upper voices reappear in different guises, combined with other voices or supplied with new texts. Thus, for example, one of the major sources of Notre Dame polyphony (Florence, Bibl. Laurenziana, Plut. 29.1) contains five different settings of the tenor "Et gaudebit" employing the rhythmic pattern shown in the example. The first setting is a discant-style passage within the two-voice organum for the solo passages of the alleluia "Non vos relinquam" (fols. 116–17; *Medieval Music: The Oxford Anthology of Music* [hereafter *MMOA*], no. 43, discant passage on pp. 93–94, tenor and *duplum* or second voice without text). The second is a three-voice substitute *clausula,* with the same *duplum* as the first and an added *triplum* (fols. 45–46). The third is a three-voice motet (sometimes known today as a conductus-motet because both upper voices have the same text), with the same *duplum* as the first (now called a *motetus* because it has a text) and a new *triplum;* the text of the upper voices—an exhortation to good deeds—elaborates the chant text (fols. 386v–87; *MMOA,* no. 43, pp. 93–94, tenor, *motetus,* and *triplum;* also Tischler, 1982 [hereafter *TM*], no. 23). The fourth is a three-voice double motet (i.e., one with two texts), with a new *motetus* and *triplum;* the text of the *triplum* rails against "false prelates, hardened killers of the Church," while the text of the *motetus* praises good priests "whose deeds . . . shine forth like stars in heaven" (fols. 411v–13; *MMOA,* no. 44; *TM,* no. 71). The fifth is a two-voice motet with a new *motetus,* whose text, "Non orphanum," echoes the sense of the chant text (fol. 405r–v; *MMOA,* no. 45, tenor and *motetus; TM,* no. 52).

The motet—begun as a textual decoration of the polyphony that was itself a decoration of the chant, intended to fill a liturgical function and dependent upon the chant in which it was imbedded—soon became an independent composition. The texts, often in French, dealt with love or with political satire. Thus, the tenor "Et gaudebit" appears in several later sources with the same *motetus* as the fifth of the settings listed above, but now with a French text, "El mois de Mai," in which a passing knight asks a pretty young girl for her love, and a new *triplum,* whose text is another French love poem. Motets became "pieces of clerical and aristocratic chamber music" (Sanders, 1973), arranged in anthologies not according to the liturgical function of the tenor, but alphabetically by the text of the *motetus.*

During the second half of the 13th and the beginning of the 14th century, the motet was at the center of the fundamental changes occurring in rhythmic notation. The system of mensural notation, codified by Franco of Cologne (ca. 1250), employed a regular beat (the perfect breve, consisting of three semibreves) and freed the composer from the fixed rhythmic patterns of modal notation [see Modes, rhythmic]. Innovations by Philippe de Vitry (described in the treatise *Ars nova,* early 14th century) allowed duple as well as triple division of the beat at three different levels *(modus, tempus, prolatio)* [see Mensural notation]. These changes permitted rhythmic organization on a larger scale than had been possible before. This style of organization, known today as *isorhythm, employed the repetition of patterns of both pitch *(color)* and rhythm *(talea)*. For example, in *Rex quem metrorum,* Philippe de Vitry arranged the tenor and its accompanying contratenor so that the same series of pitches was repeated three times (the last time twice as fast); each melodic unit was divided into four identical rhythmic units. The upper voices, without using repetition of pitch or rhythmic pattern, consist of phrases of equal length constructed to correspond to the structure of the tenor.

Despite the innovations that led to isorhythm, the 14th century must be seen as a period of decline, particularly in contrast to the 13th century, when the motet was the main form of musical composition (Günther, 1958). The motet lost its place of predominance as composers cultivated instead a new genre of secular music—the French **formes fixes*—that was completely different from the motet in style and conception. This shift in emphasis is evident both in the output of major composers such as Machaut (96 *ballades, rondeaux,* and *virelais,* but only 23 motets) and in major manuscript anthologies (Chantilly [*F-CH* 564]: 99 chansons, 13 motets). By the end of the century, the motet typically had a Latin rather than a French text, employed isorhythm, and consisted of four rather than three voices.

During the first half of the 15th century, the interest in rhythmic organization continued, extending at times to all of the voices (panisorhythm, as in Dunstable's *Veni sancte spiritus*) and often involving proportional relationships among the sections (as in Dufay's *Nuper rosarum flores,* constructed in the ratio 6:4:2:3). During its first three centuries of development, the motet was conceived as a series of lines distinct in character and often employing separate texts and as a structure built upon the foundation supplied by a rhythmically patterned, preexistent tenor.

At the same time, composers were finding different ways of setting short sacred texts in Latin intended for devotional or liturgical use. Some of these settings, now called cantilena-motets or song-motets, employed a style similar to that found in contemporaneous secular music: a two-voice framework between the uppermost voice and the tenor to which a third voice was added; others employed a simple homophony perhaps related to contemporaneous practices of improvisation. Whether or not these settings would have been called motets, they foreshadow the changes that were to take place at the end of the century.

II. *The Renaissance motet.* The period from ca. 1450 to 1600 witnessed a remarkable flowering of the motet. In fact, the repertory is both so vast and so varied that it has not even been catalogued, let alone studied adequately. There can be no doubt, however, that the motet occupied a central position in the work of all the leading composers of the period: Josquin, Willaert, Lassus, Palestrina, and Byrd.

In this phase of its development, the motet was generally understood to be a polyphonic setting of a sacred Latin text; the titles of many of the collections of motets published in the 16th century explain *motectus* (*mottetto,* etc.) as the common translation of *cantio sacra* (sacred song). In his dictionary of musical terminology published in 1495, the theorist Tinctoris offers a somewhat broader definition: a motet is any composition whose text was neither a part of the Ordinary of the Mass nor a *cantilena* (song); it could be on any subject but was frequently sacred. By this definition, which makes no restrictions concerning language, the term motet could include settings of texts in the vernacular such as *Nymphes des bois,* Josquin's lament for Ockeghem, as well as settings of secular Latin texts drawn from Classical poetry or newly composed to honor a person or event. Purely by convention, scholars today exclude from consideration as motets all settings of sacred texts in the vernacular (e.g., anthems, spiritual madrigals) as well as certain categories of liturgical music (e.g., hymns, canticles, lamentations).

The motet of this period is characterized by a dramatic increase in the kinds of texts that were set. In addition to the traditional texts from the liturgy, composers chose passages taken directly from the Bible, for the most part dramatic or emotional in content (for example, Josquin's setting of David's lament *Absalon, fili mi*), and for the first time they set entire Psalms. A large number of the sacred texts are amalgamations of portions of the liturgy or of the Bible. Fewer texts, but still a significant number, come either from classical or humanist Latin poetry; many of the newly composed texts honor a particular person or event.

It seems likely that this variety in the kinds of texts that were set is related to an expansion in the function that the motet was intended to serve. In the past, scholars sought to identify the liturgical assignment of particular motet texts on the assumption that the motet was performed as part of the liturgy. The most recent evidence (Cummings, 1981) suggests, however, that motets served a paraliturgical function as an ornament to the liturgy, not an essential part of it. Furthermore, the motet was part of the musical entertainments at the princely establishments where so many of the composers earned their livings.

In choosing how they would set their motets, composers maintained the close connection that had traditionally existed between Mass and motet. Thus, many motets employ the same techniques as settings of the Mass: canon, ostinato, *cantus firmus,* paraphrase. The technique most characteristic of the motet and indeed of the musical language of this period was imitation. The establishment of the four-voice ensemble, in which all of the voices participate equally in presenting motivic material, as the norm and the abandonment of a preexistent line allowed the composer freedom to fit the music to the individual phrase; in turn, the words influenced his choice of technique. In his setting of *Planxit autem David,* for example, Josquin illustrates the words through his choice of texture (imitation, paired imitation, homophony).

The great variety of texts and of musical structures in Josquin's works (e.g., *Tu pauperum refugium, Miserere mei,* and *Illibata Dei virgo*) characterized the motet during the rest of the century. The style changed (compare Willaert's seamless polyphony to Lassus's evocative imagery), but the overriding concern continued to be the relationship between text and music.

III. *The later motet.* After 1600, the term motet became both more specific and more general in its meaning. In the more specific sense, the word came to be associated with a particular style. "Motet-style" (*stilus moteticus* or *ecclesiasticus*) meant imitative polyphony in the manner of Palestrina, a serious, solemn style considered appropriate for church use [see Palestrina style]. In its general sense, the term motet meant simply a sacred vocal composition intended for liturgical or devotional use; the term no longer had specific connotations concerning language, style, or the nature of the performing forces. In addition to motet, composers also employed a variety of other terms, such as *concerto ecclesiastico* or *symphonia sacra;* the problem of terminology for this period needs further investigation (see Dammann, 1959; Dixon, 1983; Dahlhaus, 1978).

The development of the motet can be seen as a dichotomy between conservative and progressive tendencies. On the one hand, the deliberate retention of a consciously archaic style *(stile antico)* created a conservative musical language, separated from mainstream developments. On the other hand, the constant adaptation of the newest developments in instrumental and dramatic music to motet composition created an unprecedented variety. In addition to this stylistic dualism, two other factors contributed to the complexity of the motet's development. One is the division of Europe into Catholic and Protestant factions. At the most basic level, the differences in practice are evident in language: Latin continued to be employed by Catholics, while Protestants used the vernacular. The other factor is the creation of national styles. Differences in function as well as in musical taste caused the motet to develop separately in France, Germany, Italy, and England.

The developments in Italy illustrate the new variety as composers applied the techniques of the *seconda prattica* (Monteverdi's term for the musical language that evolved ca. 1600). In *Cento concerti ecclesiastici* (1602), Lodovico Viadana drew on the new polarity between melody and bass; the motets, for one, two, three, or four voices with organ accompaniment, employ basso continuo (to be realized according to methods the composer explains in a preface). In *Symphoniae sacrae . . . liber secundus* (1615), a collection of monumental motets designed for Venetian ceremony, Giovanni Gabrieli exploited the principle of contrast in several ways, including harmonic structure (the use of recurring ritornellos) and performing forces. Between these two extremes lies a whole range of compositions for many different performance ensembles by composers such as Alessandro Grandi, Giacomo Carissimi, Maurizio Cazzati, Alessandro Scarlatti, and Vivaldi. The common element is the notion of contrast (usually referred to as the concerto principle or concertato style) in thematic organization, texture (homophony vs. polyphony, recitative vs. aria), and performance forces.

Many elements of the Italian development are also evident elsewhere, perhaps most conspicuously in the work of Schütz. The variety of his motet output ranges from polychoral motets in the Venetian manner (*Psalmen Davids,* 1619) to the sacred vocal concerto (*Symphoniae sacrae,* 1629, 1647, 1650) employing both large and small performing forces. The six motets of Bach (four for double chorus, one for five voices, one for four voices and continuo) represent the peak of the German development. In France, the *grand motet,* cultivated by composers such as Henry Du Mont, Lully, Marc-Antoine Charpentier, Michel-Richard de Lalande, André Campra, François Couperin, and Rameau, was designed primarily for use at the royal court; it had a large-scale episodic structure (many elements of which were drawn from contemporary opera) and employed a large ensemble (soloists, choir, orchestra). The *petit motet,* in contrast, was more modest in its performing forces (one to three voices and continuo) and flexible in form. In England, the development of sacred music—despite the many points of contact with Continental practices—is traditionally considered under the separate category of *anthem.

After 1750, two factors contributed to the decline of the motet. The first was economic: changes in the conditions of patronage meant that major composers no longer derived their income from churches or courts; the composition of church music became incidental to their main output. The second factor was stylistic: the vogue for the "antique," exemplified by the *Cecilian movement, as well as the restrictions imposed by the Catholic Church (e.g., the **Motu proprio* of Pope Pius X, 1903) dictated an artificial style removed from current practice. Motets continued to be written by major composers (including Mozart, Schubert, Brahms, Berlioz, Franck, Liszt, Bruckner, and Verdi), but the absence of unifying elements makes it difficult to characterize the motet after 1750.

Bibl.: Ursula Günther, "The 14th-Century Motet and Its Development," *MD* 12 (1958): 27–58. Rolf Dammann, "Geschichte der Begriffsbestimmung Motette," *AfMw* 16 (1959): 337–77. Edgar Sparks, *Cantus Firmus in Mass and Motet: 1420–1520* (Berkeley and Los Angeles: U of Cal Pr, 1963). Edward Lowinsky, ed., *The Medici Codex of 1518, MRM,* vols. 3–5 (Chicago: U of Chicago Pr, 1968). Albert Dunning, *Die Staatsmotette 1480–1555* (Utrecht: A Oosthoek, 1970). H. Colin Slim, *A Gift of Madrigals and Motets* (Chicago: U of Chicago Pr, 1972). Ernest Sanders, "The Medieval Motet," *Schrade,* 1973, pp. 497–575. James Anthony, *French Baroque Music: From Beaujoyeulx to Rameau* (New York: Norton, 1974; 2nd ed., 1978). Heinrich Hüschen, *Die Motette, Mw* 47 (Cologne: A Volk, 1974; trans. Eng., 1975). W.

Thomas Marrocco and Nicholas Sandon, eds., *Medieval Music: The Oxford Anthology of Music* (London: Oxford U Pr, 1977). Anthony Cummings, "Toward an Interpretation of the Sixteenth-Century Motet," *JAMS* 34 (1981): 43–59. Hans Tischler, *The Earliest Motets (to circa 1270)* (New Haven: Yale U Pr, 1982). Graham Dixon, "Oratorio o mottetto? Alcune riflessioni sulla classificazione della musica sacra del Seicento," *NRMI* 17 (1983): 203–22. Herbert Schneider and Heinz-Jurgen Winkler, *Die Motette: Beitrage zu ihrer Gattungsgeschichte* (Mainz: Schott 1991). Mark Everist, ed., *Music before 1600,* Models of Musical Analysis (Oxford: Blackwell, 1992). Mark Everist, *French Motets in the Thirteenth Century: Music, Poetry and Genre* (Cambridge, 1994). Daniel R. Melamed, *J. S. Bach and the German Motet* (New York: Cambridge U Pr, 1995). Robert L. Kendrick, *Celestial Sirens: Nuns and Their Music in Early Modern Milan* (Oxford: Oxford U Pr, 1996). Dolores Pesce, ed., *Hearing the Motet: Essays on the Motet of the Middle Ages and Renaissance* (New York: Oxford U Pr, 1997). Sylvia Huot, *Allegorical Play in the Old French Motet: The Sacred and the Profane in Thirteenth-Century Polyphony* (Stanford: Stanford U Pr, 1997). Horst Leuchtmann et al., *Messe und Motette,* Handbuch der musikalischen Gattungen *9* (Laaber: Laaber-Verlag, 1998). Julie E. Cumming, *The Motet in the Age of Du Fay* (Cambridge, 1999). J.A.O.

Motet-chanson. A polyphonic work of the Renaissance that combines a Latin sacred text in one voice, usually the tenor or bass, often in relatively longer note-values, with a secular text in the vernacular in another voice or voices. Works of this type were composed by Alexander Agricola, Loyset Compère, Josquin, and others and belong to the tradition of the polytextual motet reaching back to the 13th century [see Motet I].

Motetus [Lat., fr. Fr. *mot,* word]. (1) *Motet. (2) In the 13th century, the second voice of a **clausula,* to which words have been set [see Motet I]; the first (texted) voice above the tenor in a motet.

Mother Goose Suite. See *Ma mère l'oye.*

Motion. Movement from one pitch to another within a single part or simultaneously in two parts. Within a single part, motion is said to be conjunct or by step if it is by an interval not larger than a second; disjunct or by leap if by an interval larger than a second. Motion in two parts simultaneously is parallel if the interval between the two parts remains constant, at least within the general type, e.g., third, sixth, etc. [see also Parallel (consecutive) fifths, octaves]; contrary if one part moves up while the other moves down; similar if both move in the same direction but by different intervals. Motion is oblique if one part remains stationary while the other moves.

Motive, motif. A short rhythmic and or melodic idea that is sufficiently well defined to retain its identity when elaborated or transformed and combined with other material and that thus lends itself to serving as the basic element from which a complex texture or even a whole composition is created. The term is used rather flexibly but is usually taken to refer to something less than a *phrase. A motive may consist of as few as two pitches, or it may be long enough to be seen to consist of smaller elements, themselves termed motives or perhaps cells. The potential for generating more extended material is most often regarded as essential. Much Baroque music consists of a more or less continuous texture spun from one or a few motives, and in the music of this and other periods, passages that modulate are often constructed from a motive, perhaps repeated in a sequence [see Sequence (1)]. Music characterized by the pervasive use of a motive is said to be highly or very motivic, and some works of Beethoven, e.g., the Fifth Symphony, are regarded as paradigms of the technique.

The accompanying example identifies the three motives that make up the opening theme of Beethoven's *Pastoral* Symphony. All three play a prominent role, and the second and third may also be seen to be related to one another through the reversal of rhythmic elements and, to some extent, pitch contour. Development sections of movements in *sonata form are especially likely to be built from motives introduced earlier in the work. Some musical *analysis is carried on principally in terms of motives, often with the aim of demonstrating the organic coherence of the work in question. See also Leitmotif.

Moto [It.]. Movement, motion; often, as in *andante con m.,* to indicate more movement, i.e., a slightly faster tempo, than ordinarily called for by the term being modified.

Moto perpetuo [It.]. See *Perpetuum mobile.*

Motown [fr. Motortown, i.e., Detroit, Michigan]. A fusion of black *gospel, *pop, and *rhythm and blues that began to flourish commercially in the U.S. in the early 1960s. Producer Berry Gordy, Jr., and numerous staff songwriters forged the style, and Gordy's Detroit-based record labels Motown, Tamla, and Gordy and Soul provided the outlet for the numerous black recording artists employed, including Smokey Robinson and the Miracles, Diana Ross and the Supremes, Marvin Gaye, Stevie Wonder, the Temptations, and many others. The Motown recording and publishing company eventually transferred its headquarters to Los Angeles. P.T.W.

Motreb [Ar., Per.]. A principal type of musician in Middle Eastern cultures. In Arabic cultures generally, the term denotes a professional, hired musician, but in rural Iran it refers to one who is both vocalist and instrumentalist and entertains at weddings, circumcisions, and picnic spots. B.N.

Motto. (1) In Masses of the 15th and 16th centuries (e.g., Dufay's *Missa Se la face ay pale*), a musical idea that recurs at the beginning of each major section [see Mass II]; also head-motive. (2) In *arias of the 17th and 18th centuries, the opening gesture of the melody when sung at the outset and followed immediately by an instrumental ritornello, which is then followed by the principal entrance of the voice. Such an aria is termed a motto aria [Ger. *Devisenarie*].

Motu proprio [Lat., by one's own initiative]. A statement issued by the Pope without the official advice of others. Two such statements on the music of the church were issued by Pius X in 1903 and 1904. Among various prohibitions and recommendations, they specified Palestrina's music as the appropriate model for polyphony and disapproved the use of music of a theatrical character, ordered the restoration of *Gregorian chant under the leadership of the monks of Solesmes, restricted the role of the organ, and largely suppressed other forms of instrumental music.

Motus [Lat.]. *Motion; a *canon *per motu contrario* is one by inversion.

Mount of Olives, The. See *Christus am Ölberge.*

Mouth organ [Fr. *harmonica à bouche;* Ger. *Mundharmonika;* It. *armonica a bocca;* Sp. *armónica*]. A wind instrument consisting of several free *reeds that may be sounded individually or in combination by means of blowing and or sucking. Instruments of this type consisting of vertical pipes, each containing a reed, have been known in the Far East since at least 1000 B.C.E. Modern examples there include the Chinese **sheng* and the Japanese **sho.* The Western instrument often called a harmonica (sometimes also mouth harp) was invented in the 19th century. Its reeds are mounted in narrow channels, usually side by side in a rectangular case. In the most common models, each channel contains two brass reeds pitched a *diatonic scale-degree apart, one activated by blowing, one by sucking. Channels can be blown or sucked singly or in combination, producing the diatonic scale as well as some intervals and chords derived from it. More elaborate models, often with a button-operated slider that closes off one set of reeds while making another available, play a chromatic scale. Other types exist as well, including bass instruments with circular cross section that are used principally in ensembles. Blues musicians (especially John Lee "Sonny Boy" Williamson and "Little Walter" Jacobs) developed a strikingly expressive style of playing, and it is widely used also in country and western music. A few virtuosos have inspired a limited concert repertory.

Mouthpiece [Fr. *embouchure* (of brasses), *bec* (of single reeds); Ger. *Mundstück* (of brasses), *Schnabel* (of single reeds); It. *bocchino;* Sp. *boquilla*]. That part of a wind instrument that forms the juncture of the instrument with the player's mouth. Brass instrument mouthpieces are made of brass and are roughly bell-shaped. Three principal components influence tone quality: the cavity for the lips, which is larger or smaller according to the range and tone of the instrument; the throat at the bottom of this cavity; and the back bore leading from the throat to the instrument. A shallow cup-shaped cavity with a sharp-edged throat, as in a trumpet mouthpiece, tends to produce brighter sounds, spicy with *harmonics. A deeper, funnel-shaped cavity with little or no throat or back bore, as in the French horn mouthpiece, encourages a smooth and mellow sound with few harmonics. See ill. under Brass instruments.

Clarinet and saxophone mouthpieces are made of wood, metal, rubber, plastic, or glass and are shaped like a narrow hollow cone sliced off at an angle near the small end to leave a flat surface or table for the reed. A slight curvature of this table away from the reed as well as the dimensions and shape of the cavity within the mouthpiece are important to the instrument's playing qualities and *intonation. See ill. under Reed. R.E.E.

Mouvement [Fr.]. (1) Movement. (2) Tempo. (3) Motion.

Movable do(h). A system of *solmization in which the syllable *do* represents the first scale-degree of the major scale regardless of its transposition and is thus "movable" to any pitch.

Movement [Fr. *mouvement;* Ger. *Satz;* It. *movimento, tempo;* Sp. *movimiento, tiempo*]. Any self-contained and thus at least potentially independent section of a larger work such as a sonata, symphony, concerto, string quartet, suite, cantata, oratorio, or even Mass. In performance, successive movements are usually separated by a brief pause (during which the audience customarily does not applaud). Composers occasionally specify, however, that a movement is to succeed another without pause [see *Attacca*], as in the fourth movement of Beethoven's Fifth Symphony.

Movie music. See Film music.

Movimento [It.]. (1) Movement. (2) Tempo; *doppio m.,* twice as fast. (3) Motion.

Mozarabic chant. The liturgical chant of the Christian church of Spain until its suppression in favor of the Roman rite in 1085. The term Mozarabic refers to Christians living and practicing their own religion under Muslim political rule. It is not, therefore, entirely appropriate, since the writings of St. Isidore of Seville (d. 636) make it clear that the rite existed well before the Muslim invasion of the Iberian peninsula in 711, and an *orationale* (a manuscript containing certain types of prayers) now preserved in Verona suggests that the liturgy, including musical items, as preserved in the musical manuscripts of the 10th and 11th centuries was well established by about 700. Some of the most important musical manuscripts, furthermore, were copied in parts of León and Castile (in the northern half of the peninsula) after their reconquest by Christian rulers. The designation Visigothic chant, sometimes used, is similarly inappropriate, as is the term Hispanic, to a lesser extent.

The surviving manuscripts are notated in nondiastematic *neumes and thus remain untranscribable, except for 20 pieces in a single manuscript, which can be transcribed into modern notation because their original notation was erased and replaced with a diastematic notation from the south of France. This repertory constitutes by far the largest body of evidence for the nature of liturgical chant in the West before the reforms of Charlemagne (d. 814). The practice of *psalmody clearly does not rely on a system of eight *modes. The structures of both Mass and Office and some of the associated terminology show numerous points of contact with other rites, especially the *Ambrosian and *Gallican. Two slightly different liturgical traditions are preserved.

It is not clear to what extent the rite was practiced in the period immediately following its official suppression at the reconquest of Toledo in 1085, though a few parishes in Toledo were granted permission to practice it. Some scholars (especially Mundó) believe the Toledan manuscripts date from the centuries following. In the late 15th century, Cardinal Jiménez de Cisneros sought to restore the rite. The printed books prepared under his auspices are the basis for present-day observances in the Mozarabic chapel of the Cathedral of Toledo. The musical manuscripts prepared at that time contain melodies unrelated to those of the medieval manuscripts.

Bibl.: *Editions. Antifonario visigótico de la Catedral de León,* Monumenta hispaniae sacra, Serie litúrgica V/2, Facsímiles musicales I (Barcelona and Madrid: CSIC, 1953). Louis Brou and José Vives, eds., *Antifonario visigótico de la Catedral de León,* Monumenta hispaniae sacra, Serie litúrgica V/1 (Barcelona and Madrid: CSIC, 1959). José Janini, ed., 4 vols. containing Toledan sources in the series Serie litúrgica, Fuentes I–VIII (Toledo: Instituto de estudios visigótico-mozárabes, 1979–83).

Literature. Juan Francisco Rivera Recio, ed., *Estudios sobre la liturgia mozárabe* [incl. catalogue of sources by J. M. Pinell and extensive bibl.] (Toledo: Diputación provincial, 1965). Anscari M. Mundó, "La datación de los códices litúrgicos toledanos," *Hispania sacra* 18 (1965): 1–25. Don M. Randel, *The Responsorial Psalm Tones for the Mozarabic Office* (Princeton: Princeton U Pr, 1969). Id., "Responsorial Psalmody in the Mozarabic Rite," *Études grégoriennes* 10 (1969): 87–116. Id., *An Index to the Chant of the Mozarabic Rite* (Princeton: Princeton U Pr, 1973). Id., "Antiphonal Psalmody in the Mozarabic Rite," *Berkeley,* 1977, pp. 414–22. Id., "El antiguo rito hispánico y la salmodía primitiva en occidente," *Revista de musicología* 8 (1985): 229–38. Id., "The Old Hispanic Rite as Evidence for the Earliest Forms of the Western Christian Liturgies," *Revista de musicología* 16 (1993): 491–96. D.M.R.

Mp [It.]. Abbr. for **mezzo piano.*

Mṛdaṅgam. A double-headed, barrel-shaped, wooden drum of South India, held horizontally on the player's lap. The right head is damped permanently with a mixture of iron filings, lampblack, and wax to produce a fixed, high pitch. The left head is damped before and during play by a paste of flour and water, producing low and indefinite pitches that vary with the pressure of the heel of the left hand as the fingers strike the head. The *mṛdaṅgam* is an indispensable part of both vocal and instrumental music of South India. A similar North Indian barrel drum *(mṛdang)* is used to accompany **dhrupad.* See ill. under South Asia.

M.s. [It.]. Abbr. for *mano sinistra,* left hand.

Mudanza [Sp.]. See *Villancico.*

Mulliner Book. A manuscript (*GB-Lbm* 30513) compiled by the composer Thomas Mulliner (fl. 1563) and containing 120 works for keyboard, including arrangements of instrumental works and of sacred and secular vocal works, and 11 pieces for cittern and gittern in tablature. Composers, in addition to Mulliner, include John Redford, Thomas Tallis, John Blitheman, John Sheppard, and Richard Alwood.

Bibl.: Denis Stevens, ed., *The Mulliner Book, MB* 1 (London: Stainer & Bell, 1951; 3rd ed., 1962). Id., *The Mulliner Book: A Commentary* (London: Stainer & Bell, 1952).

Multimedia. See Mixed media.

Multimetric. Characterized by frequent changes of meter, as in much music of the 20th century. See also Polymeter.

Multiphonics. Two or more pitches sounded simultaneously on a single wind instrument. They have been increasingly used in art music on a variety of woodwinds since Bartolozzi's (1967) description of them and of the techniques for their production.

Bibl.: Bruno Bartolozzi, *New Sounds for Woodwind,* trans. and ed. Reginald Smith Brindle (London: Oxford U Pr, 1967; 2nd ed., 1982).

Multiple stop. In the playing of bowed stringed instruments, the stopping of two or more strings simultaneously [see Double stop].

Mundharmonika [Ger.]. *Mouth organ.

Mundstück [Ger.]. *Mouthpiece.

Muñeira, muiñeira [Sp.]. A dance in moderately fast 6/8 from Galicia in northwestern Spain, sung and danced to the bagpipe, tambourine, and drum.

Munter [Ger.]. Lively, merry.

Murciana [Sp.]. A variety of **fandango* from the region of Murcia, Spain.

Murky [Ger. also *Murki*]. In keyboard music of the 18th century, a piece employing a left-hand or bass part consisting of broken octaves played on a relatively slowly changing succession of pitches, sometimes notated as a **Brillenbass;* also a bass part of this type, termed a murky bass. It was widespread as a keyboard genre and in song accompaniments (e.g., Sperontes's collection *Die singende Muse an der Pleisse* of 1736–45), principally for the use of amateurs, and is mentioned with condescension by C. P. E. Bach, among others. Its origin is not known, though it has been suggested that it derived from a Polish folk dance.

Muselar [Du.]. A type of *virginal.

Musette [Fr.]. (1) A small French *bagpipe, very popular in aristocratic circles in the 17th and 18th centuries. In its most developed form, it consisted of a bellows-inflated windbag, two double-reed *chanters with keys for semitones, and a set of four to six double-reed *drones cylindrically arranged. Musettes were often lavishly finished: the bags covered with embroidered silks and velvet, the pipes made of ivory. The musette figured prominently in the pastoral ideology and pastoral entertainments of the time, and Boismortier, Hotteterre, and Rameau wrote music for it.

(2) A pseudopastoral dance piece of the 18th century, usually characterized by a drone in the bass imitating the instrument of the same name. Such pieces were danced in French ballets of the early 18th century. Keyboard suites sometimes include a *musette,* e.g., François Couperin's *Pièces de clavecin,* ordre 15, and Bach's English Suite no. 3 (where it is titled "Gavotte ou la musette"). Bartók wrote several pieces in this tradition, including "Bagpipe," from the *Mikrokosmos* (bk. 5, no. 138), and "Dudas," from the *Petite Suite,* and Schoenberg included a musette in his Suite for Piano op. 25.

Musica [Lat., Gr.]. Music. Four important classifications of music are transmitted by ancient and medieval texts. (1) Theoretical and practical. A clear exposition is given by Bellermann's Anonymous 3 (sect. 29), and similar formulations occur in works by Cleonides (early 2nd century) and Aristides Quintilianus (ca. 200). For some medieval readers, the source of this classification was Martianus Capella's *De nuptiis Philologiae et Mercurii,* book 9 (early 5th century). It is central to al-Fārābī's *Classification of the Sciences* (early 10th century), which was translated into Latin and then cited by 13th-century Latin writers including Lambertus, Jerome of Moravia, and Roger Bacon. It appears in Jacques de Liège (writing ca. 1321) and becomes dominant again during the 15th century (Ramos de Pareja, Franchinus Gaffurius).

(2) *Musica mundana, musica humana, musica instrumentalis* (the harmony of the universe, the harmony of the body and of the soul, and music produced by instruments, including the voice). For music history, the direct source of this classification is Boethius (ca. 480–ca. 524). Though this (or any other) classification scheme is ignored by influential early 11th-century pedagogical texts from northern Italy (the *Dialogus* attributed in some sources to an Odo and the writings of Guido of Arezzo), it is emphasized in numerous treatises by Frankish, Lotharingian, and Germanic authors beginning with Aurelian of Réôme (fl. 840–50).

(3) Harmonics, rhythmics, metrics. This classification appears clearly for the first time in the writings of Aristides Quintilianus. Alypius (3rd century?), Martianus Capella, Cassiodorus (ca. 485–ca. 580), and Isidore of Seville (ca. 559–636) pass it on to later ages. Aurelian (*Musica disciplina,* ch. 3) makes this a subclassification of *musica humana.*

(4) Natural and artificial. This dichotomy is made in Aristotle's *Physics* and is applied to music in a 5th-century work by pseudo-Dionysus the Areopagite. This work was translated ca. 860 by John Duns Scotus. Subsequently, natural and artificial music are discussed by Regino of Prüm (ca. 842–915), John of Afflighem (fl. ca. 1100), and other theorists. At the same time, the terms are used by al-Fārābī (d. 950) to distinguish between vocal and instrumental music. This usage was passed by al-Fārābī's translators to 13th-century scholastics in Paris and thence to musical writers like Lambertus and Jerome of Moravia. At the end of the 14th century, the poet Eustache Deschamps appropriated this dichotomy to distinguish spoken from sung lyric verse.

Musica enchiriadis. A treatise probably written ca. 900 and extant today in about 40 manuscript copies. Scholars have disagreed about its authorship. First said to be by Hucbald (in *GS* 1:152–73), it has since been credited to a number of authors, none conclusively, but perhaps most firmly to Otgerus of St. Amand (Smits van Waesberghe, 1969). Related treatises include *Scolica* (not *Scholia*) *enchiriadis* (*GS* 1:173–212), *Commemoratio brevis* [see Psalm tone], and *Alia musica* (ed. Chailley, 1965). *Musica enchiriadis* discusses a musical system based on the tetrachord of the finals of plainchant, d e f g, which is arranged disjunctly [see Ex. under Daseian notation]. It is often cited for its treatment of parallel *organum and for its use of *Daseian notation.

Bibl.: Lincoln Spiess, "The Diatonic 'Chromaticism' of the *Enchiriadis* Treatises," *JAMS* 12 (1959): 1–6. Jacques Chailley, ed., *Alia musica* (Paris: Centre de documentation universitaire, 1965). Joseph Smits van Waesberghe, *Musikerziehung,* Musikgeschichte in Bildern, III/3 (Leipzig: Deutscher Verlag für Musik, 1969). Richard L. Crocker, "Hermann's Major Sixth," *JAMS* 25 (1972): 19–37. Léonie Rosenstiel, trans., *Music Handbook (Musica Enchiriadis), CCT* 7 (1976). Hans Schmid, ed., *Music et scolica enchiriadis: Una cum aliquibus tractatulis adiunctis* (Munich: Verlag der Bayerischen Akademie der Wissenschaften, 1981).

Musica ficta [Lat., feigned music]. In music theory before the end of the 16th century, notes outside of the *gamut or *Guidonian hand. Notes in the gamut or hand constitute *musica recta* or *musica vera* (right or true music). The term *musica falsa* (false music), an earlier equivalent of *musica ficta,* appeared in the 13th century. During the 14th century, *musica ficta* gained the ascendancy, while *musica falsa* became much less common. The synonymous term *conjuncta* first appeared in the 14th century.

Most often, notes classifiable as *musica ficta* are chromatic and thus are specified in modern notation by means of accidentals, but diatonic ones also may qualify. By definition, a note in the hand is not simply a (relative) pitch but both a pitch and a *solmization syllable. For instance, although the gamut includes g, it allows a pitch of that letter name to carry only the syllables *sol, re,* and *ut*—not *mi, fa,* or *la.* Hence, the notes *g sol, g re,* and *g ut* belong to *musica recta,* while *g mi, g fa,* and *g la* belong to *musica ficta.* Conversely, b♭ and b♭′ were included in the gamut and thus belonged to *musica recta* rather than *musica ficta.*

The term *musica ficta* is now often used loosely to describe intended accidentals left unwritten in the original manuscripts or prints of music from before about 1600 but added in performance or editing. In modern editions, added accidentals are often placed above the staff. Sometimes they are placed on the staff but are printed in a different typeface from that of accidentals found in the sources.

Although the theoretical definition of *musica ficta* remained constant in the years before 1600, the degree to which unwritten accidentals were admitted into practice and sanctioned by theorists changed greatly over time. This change is highly significant, because the addition of intended but originally unwritten accidentals is the principal matter of concern to modern scholars investigating *musica ficta.* No single formula for applying accidentals to all types of music has been found, nor is one likely to be.

Certain guidelines for adding accidentals are commonly used. Lowinsky (1964), employing terms used by theorists as early as the 13th century, sums them up under the two headings *causa necessitatis* (by reason of necessity) and *causa pulchritudinis* (by reason of beauty). Under the former heading he classifies guidelines resulting in perfect intervals, under the latter those pertaining to imperfect intervals. Bent (1972) divides them into melodic and harmonic rules. A conflation of the two gives the following set, with which most modern writers and editors seem to agree: (a) Sharp lower neighboring tones or other melodic leading tones. (b) Avoid the melodic tritone between F and B when the melodic line turns down from B. (c) Flat upper returning notes (specifically single notes above *la*) when not doing so would cause a tritone to be outlined melodically; by the 16th century, this principle had been formulated in the Latin rhyme "una nota super *la,* semper est canendum *fa*" (a note above *la* is always to be sung *fa*). (d) Avoid *mi* against *fa* in fourths, fifths, and octaves; that is, make those intervals perfect (some writers exclude fourths). (e) Avoid cross-relations. (f) Approach a perfect consonance from the nearest imperfect consonance; specifically, when the upper voice ascends by step, make a sixth before an octave or a third before a fifth major, and when the upper voice descends by step, make a third before a unison or fifth minor. (g) When a piece ends on a complete minor triad, raise the third of that triad to make it major. More controversial but often applied in practice, if not openly admitted, are the following: (a) Give precedence to the tenor; that is, when possible adjust other parts to it, not it to others. (b) In adding accidentals, observe the principles of context and unity of phrase; that is, do not apply any rule rigidly, for all have exceptions. The first of these two guidelines is stated by Bent, the second by Lowinsky.

Both early theorists and most modern writers agree on the basic meanings of written accidentals, or signs of *musica ficta.* The flat means *fa* and the sharp *mi.* There is no independent natural sign. A few modern writers have suggested that at times written accidentals are warnings that the syllable indicated should *not* be used, although performers might think it should. Such accidentals have been named cautionary signs (Harrán, 1976). On the one hand, rules regarding simultaneities (e.g., *mi contra fa*) may have been directed at composers rather than singers (Urquhart, 1988). On the other hand, properly trained singers could have negotiated the details necessary to achieve appropriate vertical combinations and melodic sonorities at cadences (Bent, 1984). Moreover, false relations appear to have been tolerated (Boorman, 1990).

Scholars differ in their opinions about the evolution of *musica ficta* and the use of accidentals in early music. The principal reason for this lack of unanimity is the variability among sources in the specification of accidentals. Some researchers have concluded that at least at certain times in certain repertories, accidentals were meant to be notated completely; apparent differences between sources are attributable mainly to scribal vagaries (including occasional true error), customs of particular geographical areas or nations (musicians of some regions feeling much freer to alter the written text), and modern misapprehension of the meaning of the transmitted notation. Others think that early musicians never meant written accidentals to be a complete indication of the chromatic alterations to be included in performance.

From earliest times performers added accidentals. As long as notational systems were sufficiently underdeveloped to leave substantial doubt about the pitches or rhythms meant in written music, accidentals tended to be incompletely specified. With the growing sophistication of notational systems came an increase in the number of written accidentals, until in the 14th century all necessary accidentals may have been given (Harden, 1983). Even so, performers never entirely stopped adding accidentals on their own initiative. At least through the 14th century, and fitfully thereafter, many music theorists objected to this practice on the grounds that it was destructive of the mode of the piece being performed or contrary to the meaning of the written music. (A few early theorists stated that certain accidentals did not need to be written, but this was the opinion of only a small minority of those writers whose works survive.)

In the 15th century, however, theorists seem to have decided to stop complaining and instead to try to provide guidance for adding accidentals correctly. By late in the century, many additions were evidently well accepted and widely known. Writing at that time and drawing on common knowledge of a familiar practice, Tinctoris called the written flat on B to avoid the tritone in the fifth and sixth modes asinine. He maintained that the flatting of B in this context was so conventional that indicating it with a written mark was entirely unnecessary.

In the 16th century, the addition of accidentals in performance was a generally accepted practice. This fact, however, did not preclude occasional pleas by theorists that composers write what they mean and that performers adhere to the written text (e.g., Pietro Aaron, supplement to *Toscanello in musica,* 1529; see Lockwood, 1968). The inconsistency of results arrived at by performers adding accidentals was recognized (Lockwood, 1965), and pieces were composed that required strict adherence to written accidentals and their implied *hexachords (Levitan, 1939). Furthermore, musical styles not amenable to notation according to the system of *musica recta* and *musica ficta* developed during the century. Indicating the chromatic alteration of individual notes, without reference to any system of interlocking hexachords, was necessary in pieces such as the chromatic madrigals of Carlo Gesualdo. Experimentation with chromatic and enharmonic tone systems (by Nicola Vicentino and others) further weakened the hold of the gamut on music of the time. By the end of the 16th century, use of the term *musica ficta* had largely died out. Nevertheless, the practice of adding accidentals in performance, particularly in *stile antico,* remained active, though decreasingly, throughout the Baroque.

See also Conflicting signatures, Hexachord, Solmization.

Bibl.: Joseph Levitan, "Adrian Willaert's Famous Duo *Quidnam ebrietas,*" *TVNM* 15 (1939): 166–233. Lloyd Hibberd, "*Musica ficta* and Instrumental Music *c.*1250–*c.*1350," *MQ* 28 (1942): 216–26. Marcus van Crevel, "Secret Chromatic Art in the Netherlands Motet?" *TVNM* 16 (1946): 253–304. Edward E. Lowinsky, *Secret Chromatic Art in the Netherlands Motet,* trans. Carl Buchman (New York: Columbia U Pr, 1946). Suzanne Clercx, "Les accidents sous-entendus et la transcription en notation moderne," *Wégimont,* 1955. Gilbert Reaney, "Musica Ficta in the Works of Guillaume de Machaut," *Wégimont,* 1955. Edward E. Lowinsky, *Tonality and Atonality in Sixteenth-Century Music* (Berkeley and Los Angeles: U of Cal Pr, 1961). Charles Jacobs, "Spanish Renaissance Discussion of Musica Ficta," *Proceedings of the American Philosophical Society* 112 (1968): 277–98. Lewis Lockwood, "A Sample Problem of *Musica ficta:* Willaert's *Pater noster,*" *Strunk,* 1968, pp. 161–82. Karel Ph. Bernet Kempers, "Accidenties," *Lenaerts,* 1969. Gaston G. Allaire, *The Theory of Hexachords, Solmization and the Modal System, MSD* 24 (1972). Margaret Bent, "Musica Recta and Musica Ficta," *MD* 26 (1972): 73–100. Andrew Hughes, *Manuscript Accidentals: Ficta in Focus, 1350–1450, MSD* 27 (1972). Hans Tischler, "'Musica Ficta' in the Thirteenth Century," *ML* 54 (1973): 38–56. Don Harrán, "New Evidence for Musica Ficta: The Cautionary Sign," *JAMS* 29 (1976): 77–98. Bettie Jean Harden, "Sharps, Flats, and Scribes: *Musica ficta* in the Machaut Manuscripts" (Ph.D. diss., Cornell Univ., 1983). Margaret Bent, "Diatonic *ficta,*" *Early Music History* 4 (1984): 1–48. N. Routley, "A Practical Guide to Musica ficta," *EM* 13 (1985): 59–71. Karol Berger, *Musica ficta: Theories of Accidental Inflections in Vocal Polyphony from Marchetto da Padova to Gioseffo Zarlino* (Cambridge: Cambridge U Pr, 1987). Dolores Pesce, *The Affinities and Medieval Transposition* (Bloomington: Ind U Pr, 1987). Robert Toft, "Traditions of Pitch Content in the Sources of Two Sixteenth-Century Motets," *ML* 69 (1988): 334–45. Peter W. Urquhart, "Canon, Partial Signatures, and 'Musica ficta' in Works by Josquin Desprez and His Contemporaries" (Ph.D. diss., Harvard Univ., 1988). Stanley Boorman, "False Relations and the Cadence," *Essays on Italian Music in the Cinquecento,* ed. Richard Charteris (Sydney: Frederick May Foundation for Italian Studies, 1990). David Stern, "The Use of Accidental Inflections and the Musical System in Josquin's Period, ca. 1480–1520" (Ph.D. diss., City Univ. of New York, 1991). Robert Toft, *Aural Images of Lost Traditions: Sharps and Flats in the Sixteenth Century* (Toronto: U of Toronto Pr, 1992). Gaston Allaire, "Debunking the Myth of Musica ficta," *TVNM* 45 (1995): 110–26. Keith Falconer, "Consonance, Mode, and Theories of Musica ficta," in *Modality in the Music of the Fourteenth and Fifteenth Centuries,* ed. Ursula Günther, Ludwig Finscher, and Jeffrey Dean, *MSD* 49 (1996): 11–29. Thomas Brothers, *Chromatic Beauty in the Late Medieval Chanson: An Interpretation of Manuscript Accidentals* (Cambridge: Cambridge U Pr, 1997). Maria Russo and Dale Bonge, "Musica Ficta in Thirteenth-Century Hexachordal Theory," *Studi musicali* 28 (1999): 309–26.

B.J.H., rev. L.D.B.

Musical ability, development of. This field considers what young infants perceive when they hear music, and how this changes with development and experience. A related question concerns what features are common to all (or most) musical systems and what features are specific to particular musical systems and must, therefore, be learned. The first clue perhaps comes from the fact that around the world, caregivers sing to their infants. Furthermore, infant-directed singing is sufficiently different from adult singing that it is recognizable across different musical systems. Why do caregivers sing to infants, and how do infants react to this singing? Given a choice, infants prefer to listen to infant-directed singing over adult-directed singing, the former being higher in pitch, slower in tempo, and rendered in a more loving tone of voice than the latter. Furthermore, infants react differently to different styles of singing, focusing their attention inward during lullabies but outward during play songs. Together, these findings suggest that caregivers sing to infants because the infants react positively to it, and that caregivers use singing for emotional communication and to regulate the infants' attention.

What are infants and children able to perceive about musical structure? Musical structure is often divided into pitch structure and rhythmic structure. Basic pitch perception is similar in infants and adults. However, the essence of music lies in how the pitches are combined sequentially and simultaneously. Some features of musical pitch structure are universal, while others are specific to a particular musical system. One universal feature is the opposition of consonance and dissonance. The frequency ratio between the pitches of consonant intervals can be expressed as small-integer ratios (e.g., octave, 1:2; perfect fifth, 2:3) whereas those of dissonant intervals cannot (e.g., diminished fifth, 32:45). In fact, the most consonant interval, the octave, is universally used as a basic principle of pitch organization. Tones an octave apart sound similar, and scales repeat at the octave. Interestingly, infants are sensitive to consonance, hearing octaves as similar, preferring to listen to consonant intervals over dissonant intervals, and finding two consonant intervals more similar than a consonant and a dissonant interval, even when the pitch frequencies of the latter pair of tones match more closely. This early sensitivity to consonance likely arises from basic features of the auditory system, such as the vibration patterns on the basilar membrane in the inner ear and neural firing patterns in the auditory nerve.

Although it is universal to divide the octave into a small set of discrete intervals, the particular intervals used varies from musical system to musical system. Even musically untrained adults have internalized the scale structure of their culture's music; they find it easier to detect a wrong note in a melody that goes outside the key than one that remains within the key, and this key-membership effect does not apply to unfamiliar scales. Infants are equally good at detecting withkey and out-of-key changes, indicating that they have not yet internalized the scale structure of their culture. By five years, children do have a clear sense of key membership. Rich harmonic structure is rather rare across musical systems. Interestingly, this feature of Western music is acquired rather late in development. It is not until at least six or seven years of age that children have a clear sense of tonality and can perceive implied harmony.

Rhythmic patterning is also a universal feature of musical structures, although different systems vary in the complexity of the rhythms they use. Infants can discriminate rhythmic patterns early in life, and they can recognize rhythmic patterns across changes in tempo. Adults' sense of rhythm is best when the tempo is around 100 beats per minute. Interestingly, the same is true for infants. Metrical structure is hierarchical, with successive layers of the hierarchy typically dividing the beat of the previous layer into groups of two or three. By age seven, children are sensitive to one hierarchical level above and one below the fundamental beat level. However, it is only with musical training that children and adults appear to learn to use more levels of the metrical hierarchy.

Children begin spontaneously singing songs around two years of age. In this initial singing, children generally produce the correct pitch contours (up-down pattern of changes), but the pitch wanders considerably. By age five or six, children are generally able to keep a stable tonality throughout a song. Interestingly, this is also the age at which they become sensitive to key membership.

There are many studies showing that adult musicians are better than nonmusicians at perceiving many aspects of musical structure. Recent research has also shown that there are brain differences between these groups, both at the anatomical level, as shown by PET and fMRI brain-imaging techniques, and at the processing level, as shown by scalp recordings of EEG electrical brain activity over time. Undoubtedly some of these differences result from different musical experiences in childhood, and the brain appears to lose some plasticity for musical learning after about age nine or ten. The question as to the extent to which differences in musical skill arise from innate factors or are due to experiential effects, such as musical training, remains controversial and will likely be a focus of future research.

Bibl.: L. Demany et al., "Rhythm Perception in Early Infancy," *Nature* 266 (1977): 718–19. P. Fraisse, "Rhythm and Tempo," in *The Psychology of Music,* ed. D. Deutsch (San Diego: Academic Pr, 1982). C. L. Krumhansl and F. C. Keil, "Acquisition of the Hierarchy of Tonal Functions in Music," *Memory and Cognition* 10, no. 3 (1982): 243–51. L. Demany and F. Armand, "The Perceptual Reality of Tone Chroma in Early Infancy," *Journal of the Acoustical Society of America* 76, no. 1 (1984): 57–66. J. R. Speer and P. U. Meeks, "School Children's Perception of Pitch in Music," *Psychomusicology* 5, nos. 1–2 (1985): 49–56. L. L. Cuddy and B. Badertscher, "Recovery of the Tonal Hierarchy: Some Comparisons across Age and Levels of Musical Experience," *Perception and Psychophysics* 41, no. 6 (1987): 609–20. S. E. Trehub and L. A. Thorpe, "Infants' Perception of Rhythm: Categorization of Auditory Sequences by Temporal Structure," *Canadian Journal of Psychology* 43, no. 2 (1989): 217–29. M. P. Lynch et al., "Influences of Acculturation and Musical Sophistication on Perception of Musical Interval Patterns," *Journal of Experimental Psychology: Human Perception and Performance* 17, no. 4 (1991): 967–75. M. G. Clarkson, "Infants' Perception of Low Pitch," in L. A. Werner and E. W. Rubel, eds., *Developmental Psychoacoustics* (Washington, D.C.: American Psychological Association, 1992), pp. 159–88. L. J. Trainor and S. E. Trehub, "A Comparison of Infants' and Adults' Sensitivity to Western Musical Structure," *Journal of Experimental Psychology: Human Perception and Performance* 18, no. 2 (1992): 394–402. S. E. Trehub et al., "Adults Identify Infant-Directed Music across Cultures," *Infant Behavior and Development* 16 (1993): 193–211. L. J. Trainor and S. E. Trehub, "Key Membership and Implied Harmony in Western Tonal Music: Developmental Perspectives," *Perception and Psychophysics* 56, no. 2 (1994): 125–32. E. G. Schellenberg and L. J. Trainor, "Sensory Consonance and the Perceptual Similarity of Complex-Tone Harmonic Intervals: Tests of Adult and Infant Listeners," *Journal of the Acoustical Society of America* 100, no. 5 (1996): 3321–28. C. Baruch and C. Drake, "Tempo Discrimination in Infants," *Infant Behavior and Development* 20, no. 4 (1997): 573–77. L. J. Trainor et al., "The Acoustic Basis of Preferences for Infant-Directed Singing," *Infant Behavior and Development* 20, no.

3 (1997): 383–96. C. Drake "Psychological Processes Involved in the Temporal Organization of Complex Auditory Sequences: Universal and Acquired Processes," *Music Perception* 16, no. 1 (1998): 11–26. M. J. A. Howe, J. W. Davidson, and J. A. Sloboda, "Innate Talents: Reality or Myth?" *Behavioral and Brain Sciences* 21, no. 3 (1998): 399–442. C. Pantev et al., "Increased Auditory Cortical Representation in Musicians," *Nature* 392 (1998): 811–14. L. J. Trainor and B. J. Heinmiller, "The Development of Evaluative Responses to Music: Infants Prefer to Listen to Consonance over Dissonance," *Infant Behavior and Development* 21, no. 1 (1998): 77–88. S. E. Trehub and L. J. Trainor, "Singing to Infants: Lullabies and Play Songs," *Advances in Infancy Research* 12 (1998): 43–77. W. J. Dowling, "The Development of Music Perception and Cognition," in D. Deutsch, ed., *The Psychology of Music,* 2nd. ed. (San Diego: Academic Press, 1999). A. M. L. Rock et al., "Distinctive Messages in Infant-Directed Lullabies and Play Songs," *Developmental Psychology* 35, no. 2 (1999): 527–34. L. J. Trainor et al., "A Comparison of Contour and Interval Processing in Musicians and Nonmusicians Using Event-related Potentials," *Australian Journal of Psychology* 51, no. 3 (1999): 147–53. M. J. Tramo et al., "Neurobiological Foundations for the Theory of Harmony in Western Tonal Music," in *The Biological Foundations of Music: Annals of the New York Academy of Science,* ed. R. J. Zatorre (New York: NY Academy of Sciences, 2001). R. J. Zatorre and I. Peretz, eds., *The Biological Foundations of Music* (New York: NY Academy of Sciences, 2001). L.T.

Musical bow. An instrument consisting of a string held taut by a flexible, curved stick. The player plucks or strikes the string to make it vibrate. A resonator is often added to amplify the sound, the simplest resonator being the player's mouth held to one end of the bow. Gourds, coconut shells, and tin cans are also used as resonators. Often a tuning loop is tied between the string and the bow, dividing the vibrating length of the string and giving two pitches. The player can obtain more pitches by stopping the string or by changing the size of the resonator, thereby amplifying different partials. The musical bow is distributed worldwide except Australia. See ill. under Africa; see also *Berimbau.*

Musical clock. See Automatic instruments.

Musical (comedy). A popular form of 20th-century musical theater. Related to *operetta, *comic opera, *revue, and other earlier forms of staged musical entertainment, its main development has taken place in England and the U.S. In structure the musical comedy resembles the European operetta, with spoken dialogue developing dramatic situations that call for song, ensemble numbers, and dance. Musical styles and subjects vary in their connections with the *popular music and social concerns of the day.

In the works of Gilbert and Sullivan, England in the latter half of the 19th century could boast a body of indigenous comic opera to stand beside the operettas of Offenbach in Paris and Johann Strauss in Vienna. It also could claim a corps of well-trained composers, and from their ranks came Sidney Jones, who wrote the music for George Edwardes's production of *A Gaiety Girl* (1893), the first stage work to be labeled musical comedy. Its female glamour, matrimonial plot, fashionable costumes, and lively tunes proved a successful blend, and for years to come these ingredients were remixed and combined with others on the London stage.

New York could also claim by the 1890s a busy musical stage stocked chiefly from overseas. In 1904, however, *Little Johnny Jones* by Rhode Island–born George M. Cohan (1878–1942), with its patriotic entrance song, "The Yankee Doodle Boy," served notice that a vein of American expression less elaborate than the operettas of Victor Herbert and John Philip Sousa was there to be tapped. As author of the show's book, lyrics, and songs, as well as its director and singing and dancing star, Cohan was more a performer-songwriter than a composer. In the next decade Jerome Kern (1885–1945) emerged as a full-fledged American-born theater composer whose works—or shows—made a mark in both London and New York.

By the 1920s, creative leadership in musical comedy had passed to America, where shows generally took one of two forms: the integrated type, in which musical numbers furthered plot and character development, and the song-and-dance type, in which the power and appeal of individual numbers outweighed their dramatic function. The first type, pioneered by Kern and his collaborators at the Princess Theater (1915–18), was continued in *Show Boat* (1927), by Kern and Oscar Hammerstein (1895–1960); *Of Thee I Sing* (1931), by George (1898–1937) and Ira Gershwin (1896–1983); and a series of landmark shows by Richard Rodgers (1902–79) and Hammerstein, from *Oklahoma!* (1943) to *The Sound of Music* (1959). The second type, combining up-to-date romance with down-to-earth (sometimes clever) lyrics and a jazz-tinged musical idiom, flourished in shows like *Lady, Be Good* (Gershwin and Gershwin, 1924); *Good News* (1927), by the team of Henderson, Brown, and DeSylva; and *Anything Goes* (1934), by Cole Porter (1891–1964). Both types transferred well to the screen when, in the late 1920s, Hollywood began to make sound movies [see *film music]. Moreover, both fed into the world of popular song, with numbers circulating on *recordings, *radio, and eventually television and with performances by singers and instrumentalists in a wide range of styles, from jazz-based to symphonic.

After World War II, American dominance continued in such shows as *Guys and Dolls* (1950, Loesser), *My Fair Lady* (1956, Lerner and Loewe), *West Side Story* (1957, Bernstein and Sondheim), *Fiddler on the Roof* (1964, Bock and Harnick), *Company* (1970, music and lyrics both by Stephen Sondheim, b. 1930), *A Chorus Line* (1975, Hamlisch and Kleban), and *La Cage aux Folles* (1983, Herman). Together with a turn toward contemporary problems, the later shows in this group, written after *rock and roll seized dominance in the popular music scene, parted company with reigning popular idioms and no longer supplied songs for that arena. Nevertheless, shows like *Hair* (1967; MacDermott, Ragni, and Rado), dubbed "the American tribal love-rock musical," and *Jesus Christ Superstar* (1971, Andrew Lloyd Webber, b. 1948, and Tim Rice, b. 1944) brought rock idioms to the musical comedy stage with commercial success, opening the way for more such endeavors.

Two recent trends seem noteworthy, and one is the revival. Written for the commercial marketplace of their own day, most of the shows named here have shown a continuing appeal in successful revivals since the early 1980s. The other is the London stage's return to international prominence, especially in the work of Andrew Lloyd Webber, who emphasized dance and experimental staging in *Cats* (1981) and melodramatic spectacle in *Phantom of the Opera* (1986). *Cats* now stands as the longest-running show ever on both the London and the New York stages.

Bibl.: Kurt Gänzl, *The British Musical Theatre,* 2 vols. (Houndmills, Hampshire: Macmillan, 1986). Geoffrey Block, *Enchanted Evenings: The Broadway Musical from* Show Boat *to Sondheim* (New York: Oxford U Pr, 1997). Andrew Lamb, *150 Years of Popular Musical Theatre* (New Haven: Yale U Pr, 2000). Steven Suskin, *Show Tunes: The Songs, Shows, and Careers of Broadway's Major Composers,* 3rd ed. (New York: Oxford U Pr, 2000). Gerald M. Bordman, *The American Musical Theatre,* 3rd ed. (New York: Oxford U Pr, 2001). Richard C. Norton, *A Chronology of American Musical Theater,* 3 vols. (New York: Oxford U Pr, 2002). R.C.

Musical glasses. Drinking glasses tuned by being filled with varying amounts of water and played either by striking with small sticks or rubbing the rims with wetted fingers. They were known in Europe from the 15th century and were fashionable in 18th-century England. See Glass harp, Glass harmonica.

Musical Joke, A. See *Musikalischer Spass, Ein.*

Musical Offering. See *Musikalisches Opfer.*

Musical saw [Fr. *lame musicale;* Ger. *singende Säge*]. A handsaw that is bowed on the smooth edge with a violin or cello bow or struck on the flat side with a soft mallet. The player places one end of the saw between the legs and holds the other with the left hand. Bending the saw raises its pitch, which can be varied continuously.

Música norteña [Sp.]. A distinctive musical tradition of northern Mexico and the U.S.-Mexican border region. It is most typically characterized by ensembles with button-key accordion and *bajo sexto* (12-string bass guitar), a song repertory of *canciones rancheras* and **corridos,* and an instrumental repertory of polkas and other dances of European origin. D.S.

Musica reservata [Lat., also *m. riservata*]. A term occurring (sometimes in vernacular cognates) in about 15 treatises or documents from 1552 until 1625, but for which scholars have been unable to agree on a single and precise meaning. The term is first used by Adrianus Petit Coclico in his treatise *Compendium musices* of 1552, where he praises the music of Josquin for reviving a more text-oriented style of composition, and as the title for a collection of motets, also of 1552, in which chromaticism and other techniques for text illustration are used prominently. A Dr. Seld, writing in 1555 to Duke Albrecht V of Bavaria, describes Philippe de Monte as the best composer "in the new manner and *musica reservata.*" Nicola Vicentino (*L'antica musica,* Rome, 1555) writes that the chromatic and enharmonic genera were reserved *(reservata)* for trained ears in private entertainments. Jean Taisnier (*Astrologiae iudicarie isagogica,* Cologne, 1559) and Eucharius Hoffmann (*Doctrina de tonis,* Greifswald, 1582) use the term to refer to the chromatic genus of music. Samuel Quickelberg, at the court in Munich, uses the term with respect to text expression in the Penitential Psalms and other works of Lassus, without, however, mentioning any specific technique. It seems unlikely that any precise technical meaning will be found to underlie all of the uses of the term. It has variously been thought to refer to the whole range of techniques applicable to text expression, to the sociological phenomenon of music for a limited and privately informed audience, and to cultural currents sometimes described with the term *mannerism.

Bibl.: Willene Clark, "A Contribution to Sources of Musica Reservata," *RBM* 11 (1957): 27–33. Hellmut Federhofer, "Monodie und Musica reservata," *DJbMw* 2 (1957): 30–36. Bernhard Meier, "Reservata-Probleme: Ein Bericht," *AM* 30 (1958): 77–89. Claude V. Palisca, "A Clarification of 'Musica Reservata' in Taisnier's 'Astrologiae,' 1559," *AM* 31 (1959): 133–61.

Música tropical [Sp.]. In Latin America, dance music of "tropical" Caribbean and circum-Caribbean origin, performed today by popular musicians in several countries. Important genres include the **guaracha,* **mambo,* and other Afro-Cuban forms, the **merengue* of the Dominican Republic and Haiti, and the **cumbia* of Panama and Colombia. D.S.

Music box. See Automatic instruments.

Music cognition. Interdisciplinary study of the physical, physiological, and psychological processes engaged in perceiving, remembering, understanding, and performing music. Also the role of cognitive processes in musical development [see Musical ability, development of], preference, and emotion. Music cognition is informed by advances in diverse areas, including acoustics, psychology, music theory, ethnomusicology, cognitive science, linguistics, and neuroscience [see Brain and music].

Traditional fields of inquiry in music cognition are psychoacoustics [see also Acoustics] and psychophysics. These fields are concerned with the sensory encoding of pitch, duration, loudness, and timbre—the basic units of music cognition. Empirical studies use brief, abstract stimulus elements (often single tones or pairs of tones) to measure limits of detection, discrimination, recognition, and identification, and to quantify perceived relations between pairs of elements. The rare ability to identify or produce pitches without reference to a sounded pitch—known as absolute pitch—is thought to be acquired during an early, critical stage of development and may have a genetic basis. Other topics include: masking, the interference of the perception of one element by the presence of another; consonance (dissonance), the degree of smoothness or roughness produced by tone combinations; distortion, audible signals created by nonlinear processes within the auditory system; virtual pitch, the perception of pitch at the fundamental of a harmonic series when the physical fundamental is weak or absent; and perceptual invariance, the perception of constancy despite changes in the physical elements (for example, the recognition of intervals under transposition).

Contemporary developments in music cognition have moved from a concentration on basic elements to a focus on both larger-scale musical patterns and the role of musical knowledge in the perception and interpretation of such patterns. Larger-scale patterns include structured abstract arrays of tones (e.g., rhythmic patterns or melodylike sequences) and are extended to real musical phrases, melodies, and forms. The study of musical knowledge examines levels reaching from informal exposure to the idiom of a musical culture to formal music training (parallels with natural language acquisition are drawn).

Contemporary research may be broadly categorized as taking two complementary directions. The first involves fruitful interactions with both traditional and contemporary music theory, and moves from theory to experiment. It applies the techniques and procedures of cognitive psychology and cognitive science to verify, elaborate, and sometimes modify music-theoretic principles. Experiments testing notions from traditional tonal-harmonic theory have shown that tonal stimuli are better recognized and remembered than nontonal stimuli; that recognition of transposed or modulating melodies is guided by the cycle-of-fifths distance; that tones and chords are organized according to a hierarchy of stability; and that perceived similarities among keys may be described by a multidimensional map of key space. Findings have been extended to tonal hierarchies in non-Western musical idioms. Empirical studies testing more contemporary theoretical proposals have supported the perceptual relevance of the grouping, metric, and hierarchical tree structures of the generative theory of tonal music. Parameters of tonal pitch space predict perceived patterns of musical tension. Empirical studies exploring the implication-realization theory of melodic expectancy have shown the influence both of surface-level and emergent-level expectancy, as defined by the theory, on perceptual judgments of melodic continuation, completion, and cohesion, memory for melodies, and perceived melodic tension.

The second research direction uses musical materials to inform our understanding of how music is perceived and represented in the brain—that is, by studying responses to musical sounds, it aims to discover the mental processes underlying music cognition, using techniques similar to those employed in the study of speech, language, vision, and other psychological domains. Acquisition of the tonal hierarchy reflects the operation of basic cognitive principles—the formation of prototypes, or cognitive reference points, and the sensitivity of the brain to statistical regularities, regularly repeating patterns, in the physical world. The temporal structure of a melody affects judgments of pitch and time. Melodic memory is facilitated when pitch and temporal structures complement one another, as opposed to when they do not. The basic elements of music are initially functionally independent and conjoined at later stages of musical processing. Errors known as illusory conjunctions appear when a pitch is correctly recalled but recalled as having the timbre or duration of another previously heard event. Sequences of musical sounds may form a coherent form (Gestalt) or may fragment into separate "streams" depending on the spectral, temporal, and spatial relations among the sounds; these findings belong to the field of auditory scene analysis. Studies of performance show how a performer develops a conceptual interpretation of a piece and, through skilled motor actions, is able to convey the structural and emotional content to a listener. Units of musical knowledge are revealed through performance errors and systematic deviations from notation in performed timing and dynamics. New research confronts the complex interdependence of cognition and emotion, comparing and contrasting musical emotion with previously established psychological studies of emotion. Studies of musical preference, or taste, track the cognitive and affective components of preference across differences in age, gender, education, and culture, to name but a few influential factors.

Both traditional and contemporary research has further theoretical and practical applications. Theoretical applications include computational and neural models. Practical applications include music pedagogy and musical instrument design. Moreover, within all research directions, individual differences are found that are not necessarily locked to level of music training. Disorders of music cognition may result from developmental delay or acquired brain injury. Other instances of limited ability—such as being "tone deaf"—occur in normally intact populations, and their precise origin is unknown. In general, however, research on music cognition emphasizes the generality of cognitive processes across levels of music training and exposure and the importance of the study of music toward understanding the complexity of the brain.

Bibl.: F. Lerdahl and R. Jackendoff, *A Generative Theory of Tonal Music* (Cambridge, Mass.: MIT Pr, 1983). C. L. Krumhansl, *Cognitive Foundations of Musical Pitch* (Oxford: Oxford U Pr, 1990). A. S. Bregman, *Auditory Scene Analysis* (Cambridge, Mass.: MIT Pr, 1990). E. Narmour, *The Analysis and Cognition of Basic Melodic Structures: The Implication-Realization Model* (Chicago: U of Chicago Pr, 1990). J. Roederer, *The Physics and Psychophysics of Music,* 3rd ed. (New York: Springer-Verlag, 1995). I. Deliège and J. A. Sloboda, eds., *Perception and Cognition of Music* (London: Taylor & Francis, 1997). C. Palmer, "Music Performance," *Annual Review of Psychology* 48 (1997): 115–38. D. Deutsch, ed., *The Psychology of Music,* 2nd ed. (London: Academic, 1999). C. L. Krumhansl, "Rhythm and Pitch in Music Cognition," *Psychological Review* 126 (2000): 159–79. P. N. Juslin and J. A. Sloboda, eds., *Music and Emotion: Theory and Research* (Oxford: Oxford U Pr, 2001). F. Lerdahl, *Tonal Pitch Space* (Oxford: Oxford U Pr, 2001). L.L.C.

Music criticism. See Criticism.

Music drama. See Opera.

Music education. See Education.

Music history. See History of music.

Musicology [Fr. *musicologie;* Ger. *Musikwissenschaft, Musikforschung;* It. *musicologia;* Sp. *musicología*]. The scholarly study of music, wherever it is found historically or geographically. The methods of musicology are any that prove fruitful with respect to the particular subject of study. Because musicology has become steadily more diverse in both subject and method, certain traditional boundaries among its subdisciplines have been blurred. Nevertheless, in practical terms, as reflected in the orientations of professional societies, academic departments, and scholarly publications, several disciplines are usually distinguished.

I. *Disciplines and subjects of study.* 1. *Ethnomusicology. In the broadest terms, ethnomusicology is concerned with music in its human context. In this respect, the disclipline is as broad as musicology itself, and it has been argued that all musicology aims ultimately to be ethnomusicology. In practice, however, ethnomusicology is usually thought of as the study of any music, especially in its cultural context, outside the tradition of Western art music.

2. Musicology, historical musicology. The great majority of scholars who describe themselves as musicologists (as distinct from ethnomusicologists) are students of Western art music. Most would also describe themselves as historians, and most specialize in the music of one or a few historical periods. The subjects of study and the methods brought to bear on these subjects are increasingly diverse, however. The discipline is in general conceived as broadly humanistic; the fields of art history, history, and literature are more closely related to it than anthropology and sociology are, though these play an increasing role in musicology. Much that has characterized musicology derives from the nature of the tradition of Western art music and the view of music deriving from *Romanticism, in which the founders of the discipline were steeped: the importance of writing in Western culture generally and specifically the importance of notation in art music, and the view of the composer as genius and as creator of *compositions of autonomous and enduring value. Major concerns of musicology have thus been to establish the most reliable written texts possible, often under the assumption that there is one and only one best text for each work [see Editions], and to correctly attribute individual works to composers as well as to study and document composers' lives and their processes of composition [see Authenticity, Sketch]. These concerns have made *paleography, *textual criticism, the history of *notation (especially the notation of music before about 1600; see also Mensural notation), and archival research important subjects for many scholars. Musicology in this tradition has often claimed objectivity and quasi-scientific status for its methods and results. These results, in the form of editions and information concerning the techniques, forces, instruments, and circumstances of historical performances [see Performance practice], constitute the principal practical service of musicology to performance. The relationship between musicology and performance has become steadily more intimate and valuable for both.

Musicology has traditionally begun with the attempt to establish accurately the texts and surrounding historical record and then proceeded to the *analysis and classification of works and ultimately to the synthesis of historical narrative. Drawing on the study of music theory [see below], analysis often tries to isolate the similarities and differences among groups of works so as to define a genre, a *form, or the *style of a composer, period, or region. Here, too, the aim has usually been to produce results that can be considered objectively verifiable. Largely absent (though increasingly advocated and practiced with respect to some repertories) has been the kind of *criticism of individual works that has formed a major part of literary studies since the middle decades of the 20th century. The larger historical constructs around which the narrative has been fashioned have been borrowed from the histories of art, literature, and ideas. These constructs include the periods termed *Middle Ages, *Renaissance, *Baroque, *Classical, and *Romantic and such binary frames of reference as sacred and secular, courtly (or classical or high art) and popular, formal (or rational) and expressive (or emotive).

The self-sufficiency of the notated work, and with it the status of the composer, has been undermined in ways that point to changing emphases. This occurred first within traditional methods as the subject of performance practice began to be investigated thoroughly. It was recognized that performance practice is an issue with respect to all music and that all notation requires decoding by an informed reader. From this perspective it is a short step to the recognition that every work has musical meaning only to the extent that a competent listener engages it. This shift of focus onto the listener and away from the composer and the autonomous text opens the way to a listener-oriented criticism along the lines of the reader-oriented criticism of literature, with implications for the nature of the objectivity of musical study and the writing of history. At the same time, some repertories, notably liturgical chant [see Transmission], have been found to be resistant to notions of the unique composer and compositional act. This has implications for such concepts as critical edition and authenticity. In still other repertories, including some secular vocal music of the Middle Ages and Renaissance and much music of the 20th century, the composer works with literary and musical materials that resist easy classification as high art or popular (anonymous) art.

There have been persistent calls for the integration of musicology with the study of the history of ideas, cultural history, or intellectual history. The responses, including the traditional periodization of the *history of music, have been more in the nature of juxtaposition or analogy than integration at the level of musical materials themselves. Study of the historical context of music, including for example its patronage, has yielded great stores of information but has not yet significantly affected the understanding of musical form or style. The *sociology of music aims to understand music in terms of society's most basic social, cultural, and economic structures.

3. *Theory. Two general approaches to the study of music theory may be distinguished: the study of the history of theory, and the study and development of theories of existing repertories. (Allied with composition is the development of speculative theory that explores the bases for future works.) Both approaches are essential to the work of the musicologist even simply as historian, and many musicologists resist regarding the theory of music as the subject of a separate discipline. This separation is more often perceived from the perspective of specialists in theory, and there has been increasing movement in the direction of establishing separate professional organizations, journals, and degree programs dedicated to the study of theory.

4. Other subjects of study. A number of diverse subjects, including theory, have sometimes been grouped under the heading of systematic musicology, a term that has not retained the currency of the parallel historical musicology. These subjects have included *acoustics, *aesthetics, *psychology and physiology of music, *sociology of music, and *education or pedagogy. Other subjects that cut across traditional historical and geographical boundaries include *iconography and organology, or the study and classification of musical *instruments. As in all scholarly disciplines, *bibliography is an essential adjunct, of which *discography is a specialized and close relative. Independent disciplines of increasing relevance to the study of music are linguistics and some aspects of computer science [see Computers, musical applications of].

II. *History.* The first important monuments in the writing of music history were products of the late 17th and 18th centuries. These include Wolfgang Caspar Printz, *Historische Beschreibung der edelen Sing- und Kling-Kunst* (Dresden, 1690; R: Graz: Akadem Druck- & V-a, 1964); Jacques Bonnet, *Histoire de la musique et de ses effets depuis son origine jusqu'a présent,* 4 vols. (Paris, 1715; R: Graz: Akadem Druck- & V-a, 1966); Padre Giovanni Battista Martini, *Storia della musica,* 3 vols. (Bologna, 1757–81; R: Graz: Akadem Druck- & V-a, 1967); Martin Gerbert, *De cantu et musica sacra,* 2 vols. (St. Blasien, 1774; R: Graz: Akadem Druck- & V-a, 1968); Charles Burney, *A General History of Music from the Earliest Ages to the Present Period,* 4 vols. (London, 1776–89; R: New York: Dover, 1957); John Hawkins, *A General History of the Science and Practice of Music,* 5 vols. (London, 1776; new ed. in 3 vols., 1835–75; R: Graz: Akadem Druck- & V-a, 1969); Jean-Benjamin de La Borde, *Essai sur la musique ancienne et moderne,* 4 vols. (Paris, 1780; R: New York: AMS Pr, 1978); Johann Nikolaus Forkel, *Allgemeine Geschichte der Musik,* 2 vols. (Leipzig, 1788–1801; R: Graz: Akadem Druck- & V-a, 1967).

The foundation of musicology as a separate discipline comparable to other humanistic and scientific disciplines was first advocated by Friedrich Chrysander in the preface to his *Jahrbuch für musikalische Wissenschaft* of 1863. Soon thereafter, Guido Adler (1885) outlined its methods and aims, establishing the distinction between historical and systematic musicology that has remained influential (with modifications) ever since. He included what would now be termed ethnomusicology under the heading *Musikologie* (as distinct from *Musikwissenschaft,* the term for the discipline as a whole) within systematic musicology. Among the greatest achievements of late 19th-century scholarship were August Wilhelm Ambros's *Geschichte der Musik,* 5 vols. (Leipzig, 1862–82) and editions of the works of Bach, Handel, and others [see Editions]. Throughout this period and well into the 20th century, Germany and Austria remained the centers of musicology. Professorships in musicology proliferated in German universities in the first half of the 20th century, the first in the U.S. was established at Cornell University in 1930 and held by Otto Kinkeldey. Because of the influx of German scholars at the time of World War II, German scholarship continued to influence the character of musicology as it became established in the U.S., which soon outstripped all other countries in the numbers of scholars being trained and working in this field.

Bibl.: Guido Adler, "Umfang, Methode und Ziel der Musikwissenschaft," *VfMw* 1 (1885): 5–20. Waldo Selden Pratt, "On Behalf of Musicology," *MQ* 1 (1915): 1–16. Guido Adler, *Methode der Musikgeschichte* (Leipzig: Breitkopf &

Härtel, 1919). Glen Haydon, *Introduction to Musicology* (New York: Prentice-Hall, 1941; R: Chapel Hill, U of NC Pr, 1959). Arthur Mendel, Curt Sachs, Carroll C. Pratt, *Some Aspects of Musicology* (New York: Liberal Arts Pr, 1957; R: in Manfred Bukofzer, *The Place of Musicology in American Institutions of Higher Learning* (New York: Da Capo, 1977). Heinrich Husmann, *Einführung in die Musikwissenschaft* (Heidelberg: Quelle & Meyer, 1958). Frank Ll. Harrison, Mantle Hood, Claude V. Palisca, *Musicology* (Englewood Cliffs, N.J.: Prentice-Hall, 1963). Carl Dahlhaus, ed., *Einführung in die systematische Musikwissenschaft* (Cologne: H Gerig, 1971). Barry S. Brook, ed., *Perspectives in Musicology* (New York: Norton, 1972). Walter Wiora, *Historische und systematische Musikwissenschaft* (Tutzing: Schneider, 1972). Denis Stevens, *Musicology: A Practical Guide* (London: Macdonald, 1980). D. Kern Holoman and Claude V. Palisca, eds., *Musicology in the 1980s: Methods, Goals, Opportunities* (New York: Da Capo, 1982). Joseph Kerman, *Contemplating Music: Challenges to Musicology* (Cambridge, Mass.: Harvard U Pr, 1985). Leo Treitler, *Music and the Historical Imagination* (Cambridge, Mass.: Harvard U Pr, 1989). Susan McClary, *Feminine Endings: Music, Gender, and Sexuality* (Minneapolis: U of Minnesota Pr, 1991). Katherine Bergeron and Philip V. Bohlman, eds., *Disciplining Music: Musicology and its Canons* (Chicago: U Chicago Pr, 1992). Ruth Solie, ed., *Musicology and Difference: Gender and Sexuality in Music Scholarship* (Berkeley: U of California Pr, 1993). Philip Brett, Elizabeth Wood, Gary C. Thomas, eds., *Queering the Pitch: The New Gay and Lesbian Musicology* (New York: Routledge, 1994). Nicholas Cook and Mark Everist, eds., *Rethinking Music* (New York: Oxford U Pr, 1999). Regular summaries of musicological activity in various countries are published in *AM.* See also Ethnomusicology.

D.M.R.

Music theater. From the 20th century, the combination of elements from music, drama, and dance in new forms distinct from traditional opera. Although some action is usually specified, music theater is normally nonrealistic and often nonrepresentational. An early example is Schoenberg's *Pierrot lunaire* (1912), scored for *_Sprechstimme_ and small chamber ensemble and originally intended to be presented in cabaret style, with speaker-singer in Harlequin costume. Stravinsky, however, was the most active of the early 20th-century composers in developing alternative musico-theatrical approaches, beginning with *Renard* (1916), a "burlesque in song and dance" combining singing and mimed action to convey something of the atmosphere of a circus performance; this was followed by *Histoire du soldat* (1918), for narrators, actors, dancer, and musicians; *Les noces* (1917, scoring completed in 1923), for voices, instruments, and dancers; and a number of later works. Stravinsky here anticipated the separation of musical and dramatic elements later advocated by the German playwright Bertolt Brecht, who became an important force in creating new modes of music theater in the 1920s and 30s, working in collaboration with such composers as Paul Hindemith and Kurt Weill.

Music theater flourished especially in the latter half of the 20th century, during which time a number of composers came to view much of their work, including purely instrumental music, in essentially dramatic terms. Singers or instrumentalists may be required to wear masks (e.g., George Crumb's *Vox balaenae,* 1971) or full costume (Peter Maxwell Davies's *Eight Songs for a Mad King,* 1969), or the musical performance itself may be treated as a "staged" dramatic event (Luciano Berio's *Recital I,* 1972, and numerous works by John Cage and Mauricio Kagel). See also Mixed media.

Bibl.: W. Anthony Sheppard, *Revealing Masks: Exotic Influences and Ritualized Performance in Modernist Music Theater* (Berkeley: U of Cal Pr, 2001). R.P.M.

Music therapy. The clinical use of music in the treatment especially, though not exclusively, of mental illness or disability. Although healing powers of music are attested from ancient times and in numerous cultures, the scientific understanding of such powers remains limited. The nature of musical perception itself remains imperfectly understood [see Psychology of music]. Nevertheless, music has been found useful in working with patients with a variety of disorders, including autism, cerebral palsy, brain damage, and mental retardation. Therapy, which may include singing, playing musical instruments, dancing, and clapping, can help to establish communication with the emotionally troubled and to enhance motor control and learning ability in some cases. Since the founding of the National Association for Music Therapy in 1950, research and literature on the subject have grown steadily, and a number of universities have established programs leading to degrees in the field.

Bibl.: *Journal of Music Therapy* (1964–). *British Journal of Music Therapy* (1969–). Juliette Alvin, *Music Therapy* (London: Baker, 1966; 2nd ed., New York: Basic Bks, 1975). Mary Priestly, *Music Therapy in Action* (New York: St Martin's, 1975). Paul Nordoff and C. Robbins, *Creative Music Therapy: Individualized Treatment for the Handicapped Child* (New York: John Day, 1977).

Music video. A film or videotape made to be shown to the accompaniment of a recording from any number of popular genres, including rock, rap, country, and pop. It may present a live or staged performance, a direct interpretation of the song's words, or a much more loosely related series of images. Music videos were developed in the mid-1940s. At the time they were shown in movie theaters and in what were in effect video jukeboxes. In the 1960s a handful of videos were made by British rock bands such as the Beatles, the Rolling Stones, and the Kinks. These were sent to various television variety shows in the hope of airplay. With the advent of the cable channel MTV (Music Television) in 1981, music videos became regular promotional vehicles for the music industry. As an alternative promotional format, videos allowed a number of artists to attain substantial sales with little airplay. By 1984 music videos were so central to the promotion of new songs that it became routine for popular artists to have one or more videos made to promote each new CD release. This phenomenon has had an unfortunate effect on A&R decisions, as now record company executives have to take into account how videogenic an artist might be. R.B.

Musikalischer Spass, Ein [Ger., A Musical Joke]. A divertimento by Mozart, K. 522 (1787), for strings and two horns, that caricatures the work of undistinguished composers and performers by the deliberate use of incorrect dissonances, parallel fifths, etc.

Musikalisches Opfer [Ger., Musical Offering]. A work by Bach, BWV 1079 (composed and published in 1747), dedicated to Frederick the Great of Prussia. It consists of 13 compositions—a three-voice ricercar, a six-voice ricercar, ten canons, and a trio sonata—all based on a theme invented by Frederick and on which Bach had improvised during a visit to Potsdam in 1747. The dedication copy bears the inscription "Regis Iussu Cantio Et Reliqua Canonica Arte Resoluta" (Upon the King's Demand, the Theme and Additions Resolved in Canonic Style), which forms the acrostic RICERCAR. Extended controversies have arisen as to the proper order of the pieces and the intended medium of performance. Kirkendale (1980) interprets the parts as corresponding to those of a rhetorical oration.

Bibl.: Christoph Wolff, "New Research on Bach's Musical Offering," *MQ* 57 (1971): 379–408. Ursula Kirkendale, "The Source for Bach's *Musical Offering:* The *Institutio oratoria* of Quintilian," *JAMS* 33 (1980): 88–141.

Musikwissenschaft [Ger.]. *Musicology.

Musique concrète [Fr.]. See Electro-acoustic music I.

Musique mesurée [Fr.]. Music composed in France in the late 16th century in which long and short syllables of text were set by note-values in the ratio 2:1, respectively, without regard for any regular musical meter. Music of this type was at first composed to set poetry, termed *vers mesurés,* written by Jean Antoine de Baïf and his followers in the Académie de poésie et musique (founded in 1570) with the aim of adapting to French the quantitative principles of Latin and Greek poetry (whence the terms *vers mesurés à l'antique* and *musique mesurée à l'antique*). Baïf established French analogues for the classical meters, and these were set syllabically and homophonically with a view to reestablishing the intimate relationship between music and poetry and thus the power of music to move the listener as reported in classical antiquity. The principal composers concerned were Thibault de Courville (d. 1581), Guillaume Costeley (ca. 1530–1606), Nicolas de la Grotte (1530–ca. 1600), Claude Le Jeune (ca. 1530–1600), Eustache Du Caurroy (1549–1609), and Jacques Mauduit (1557–1627). The style of this music was taken up by composers of the *air de cour* for conventional rhymed poetry and persisted into the 17th century.

Bibl.: D. P. Walker and François Lesure, "Claude le Jeune and *musique mesurée,*" *MD* 3 (1949): 151–70. D. P. Walker, "Some Aspects and Problems of *musique mesurée,*" *MD* 4 (1950): 163–86. See also *Air de cour.*

Mustel organ. A *harmonium with an expression stop, invented by Victor Mustel in Paris in 1843.

Muta, mutano [It., imperative and 3rd person plural]. Change, e.g., of instrument and or tuning. Thus, in a timpani part, "muta in G/d" means that the tuning of the timpani should be changed to G and d. In a flute part, "muta in flauto piccolo" means that the player should change to the piccolo.

Mutation. In *solmization, the change from one hexachord to another.

Mutation stop. An organ stop sounding the fifth or its octaves (5 1/3′, 2 2/3′, 1 1/3′, etc.) or the third or its octaves (1 3/5′, etc.) above normal pitch. Thus, a mutation stop 2 2/3′ will sound g′ if the c key is depressed.

Mutazione [It.]. See *Ballata.*

Mute [Fr. *sourdine;* Ger. *Dämpfer;* It. *sordino;* Sp. *sordina*]. A device for reducing the volume and or altering the tone color of an instrument. On the violin and related instruments it produces a veiled, soft tone; on brass instruments a nasal, penetrating tone. In instruments of the violin family, the mute is a comb-shaped clamp that is fastened to the top of the bridge. It damps the vibration of the bridge and thus hinders transmission of vibrational energy from the strings to the sound box. In brass instruments, the mute is a hollow, conical stopper of metal, cardboard, or similar material that fits into the bell. [For the use of the hand to produce stopped tones in the French horn, see Horn.] Such a mute reduces the amount of vibrating air that leaves the bell and at the same time eliminates lower partials and reinforces higher partials. Various types are used for brass instruments, especially in jazz and popular music, including straight, cup, and *wa-wa (or Harmon) mutes [see ill. under Brass instruments]. Jazz trombonists often use a rubber plunger or similar mute that is held in the left hand and moved in front of and away from the bell while playing. Mutes for brass instruments were in use by the 16th century; mutes for strings by the 17th (e.g., in Lully's *Armide,* act 2, scenes 3 and 4, of 1686). Mutes for woodwinds were occasionally used in the 18th and 19th centuries but are rare today.

On the piano, a muted effect is produced by the **una corda* pedal. A related purpose was served by the *moderator on some early pianos. Some confusion has resulted from the fact that the German and Italian words for mute can also mean *damper. Thus, Beethoven's instruction *senza sordini* in the first movement of the Moonlight Sonata means that the passage should be played without dampers, i.e., with the damper pedal depressed. The result on the modern piano is inappropriately different from that on the pianos of Beethoven's day. See Piano.

Muzak. A trade name for music intended solely for use as background in work or public places. Several companies provide music of this type as a commercial service, and it is made available through both radio and closed-circuit broadcast. Such music can be designed for specific environments and schedules so as, it is claimed, to enhance the productivity of workers, increase the receptivity of customers, etc. The name has also come to serve as the generic (and sometimes pejorative) term for any bland background music, often consisting primarily of familiar popular songs or light classics, recorded in instrumental or choral ensemble arrangements.

M.v. [It.]. Abbr. for *mezza voce* [see *Mezzo, mezza*].

My Country (Fatherland). See *Má Vlast.*

Mystery play. See Liturgical drama.

Mystic chord. A chord used by Scriabin consisting of various types of fourths: c–f♯–b♭–e′–a′–d″. It occurs prominently in his tone poem *Prométhée* op. 60 (1908–10) and his Seventh Piano Sonata op. 64 (1911). Other, similar chords are used in his works as well.

N

Nabla [Gr.], **nablium** [Lat.]. **Nebel.*

Nabucodonosor [It., Nebuchadnezzar; usually referred to as *Nabucco*]. Opera in four parts by Verdi (libretto by Temistocle Solera, after a French play of the same name by Auguste Anicet-Bourgeois and Francis Cornue), produced in Milan in 1842. Setting: Jerusalem and Babylon in the 6th century B.C.E.

Nacaire [Fr.]. **Naqqārah.*

Nacchera, naccherone [It.]. (1) **Naqqārah.* (2) [pl. *nacchere*] *Castanets.

Nachdrücklich [Ger.]. Energetic, emphatic.

Nachlassend [Ger.]. Slackening, slowing.

Nachschlag [Ger., after-beat]. (1) In modern German terminology, the suffix of a *trill. (2) The class of ornaments that follow and take their value from the notes they are understood to embellish. The principal ornaments of this class are the *accent* [Ex. 1; see *Accent* (3)], *springer [Ex. 2; see also **Sanglot*], and perhaps *cadent [Ex. 3; see also *Chûte* and Exx. 4 and 5]. Other ornaments may take their value from the note that they follow, but they do not, strictly speaking, embellish it. Such ornaments are connective ones, which decorate the interval itself, especially the **coulé* and *turn, the former of which is always slurred to the following note (sung to its syllable). Both of these may also be executed on the following beat. The term is sometimes also applied in contradictory fashion to the various anticipatory ornaments, such as the **port-de-voix* and the modern *grace note, and, according to Neumann *(NeuO),* to many other ornaments. D.F.

Types of *Nachschlag.* 1. Accent, from Rameau, *Hyppolyte et Aricie* (1733). 2. Springer. 3. Cadent. 4. Montéclair, *Principes de musique* (1736). 5. Armand-Louis Couperin, Sonata for harpsichord and violin op. 2 no. 5, first movement (1765).

Nachspiel [Ger.]. Postlude.

Nachtanz [Ger.]. *After-dance; in German instrumental collections of the 16th and 17th centuries, the second of a pair of dances meant to be played and danced in succession. The *Nachtanz* was in a fast tempo that contrasted with the slow movement of its predecessor, and it used the melodic/harmonic material of the first dance, recomposed into a form of triple meter (3/4 or 6/8). The dance steps consisted of an order of hops, skips, and leaps, probably similar to those of the **saltarello* and the **gagliarda.* The dance appears under a variety of titles and spellings: *Hopp tancz, Hopper dancz, Hopeldantz, Hupfauf, Hupf auff, Proportz, Proportio,* and *Sprung(k).* For examples, see *HAM,* nos. 102b, 105a and b.

Bibl.: Wilhelm Merian, *Der Tanz in den deutschen Tabulaturbüchern* (1927; R: Hildesheim: Olms, 1968). L.H.M.

Nachthorn [Ger.]. An organ stop of wide-scaled open pipes, usually made of metal and most often found at either 4′ or 2′ pitch.

Nachtmusik [Ger.]. *Serenade.

Nachtstück [Ger.]. *Nocturne.

Nāgasvaram [Tamil]. A large *shawm of South India, about 75 cm. long with seven finger holes and a metal bell. Unlike some other shawms, it is played with the lips directly on the double reed and does not require circular breathing. It is traditionally played in

Hindu temples and religious processions, often accompanied by a bass drum and a second shawm. See also *Śahnāi, Zūrnā.*

Nagauta [Jap., long song]. A major lyrical genre connected with the *kabuki* theater [see East Asia II, 3 (iii)], also performed in concert. It is performed by an ensemble of voices, *shamisens* (three-stringed lute), a *nokan* (transverse bamboo flute with seven holes), a *kotsuzumi* (shoulder-held hourglass drum), and an *ōtsuzumi* (side-held hourglass drum). I.K.F.W.

Nagelgeige [Ger.]. *Nail violin.

Nagelschrift, Hufnagelschrift [Ger., fr. *Nagel,* nail; *Huf,* hoof]. A type of neumatic notation employed in Germany in the 14th and 15th centuries, so called because some individual neumes resemble horseshoe nails; also termed Gothic neumes. For examples, see Neume.

Nai [Rom.]. *Panpipes of Romania, consisting of 18 to 30 bamboo pipes arranged from longest to shortest in a single convex row. The common model has 20 pipes tuned to a diatonic scale. The player adds chromatic tones by raising and lowering the pipes.

Nail violin, nail fiddle, nail harmonica [Ger. *Nagelgeige, Nagelharmonica*]. An instrument consisting of a flat, semicircular sound box with nails or U-shaped iron pins of varying lengths driven in around the circumference. It was held in the left hand, and the nails were set into vibration with a violin bow. Invented ca. 1740, it gained popularity in the late 18th and early 19th centuries along with the *aeolian harp and *glass harmonica as part of the vogue, associated with Romanticism, for ethereal sounds. It passed out of use by 1850. A concert model with sympathetic strings was introduced in the late 18th century as the *violino-harmonico.*

Naker. A kettledrum. See *Naqqārah.*

Nänie [Ger., elegy]. A composition for chorus and orchestra by Brahms, op. 82 (1880–81), setting a poem by Friedrich von Schiller.

Napolitana [It.]. See *Villanella.*

Naqqārah [Ar.; Eng. naker; Fr. *nacaire;* It. *nacchera, naccherone;* Sp. *nácara*]. A *kettledrum of the Middle East made of metal, clay, or wood and almost always played in pairs tuned to different pitches. Such drums are played with padded sticks, sometimes while riding a horse or camel. The instrument was brought to Europe by the 13th century. The word *naqqārah* and its cognates denote various sizes of kettledrums from England to Ethiopia *(nagarit)* to India *(nāgarā).* See ill. under Near and Middle East.

National anthems. Patriotic songs adopted by nations through tradition or decree and valued, like a nation's flag, for their ability to arouse feelings of national pride and solidarity. The anthems are played or sung at ceremonial, diplomatic, and sporting events and in concert halls and theaters. The intrinsic value of the music and text might be secondary to an anthem's role in political symbolism. Many countries adopted a national anthem in the 19th century during the rise of nationalism. Developing nations select national anthems as aids in uniting their people, and changes in government can bring about a new or revised anthem. Beethoven's "Ode to Joy" has become a kind of overarching anthem for the European Union and other groups looking for music that speaks to large numbers of people, but it is used without text at EU events.

Bibl.: Paul Nettl, *National Anthems,* trans. Alexander Gode (New York: Storm Pubs, 1952). William Lichtenwanger, "The Music of 'The Star-Spangled Banner': Whence and Whither?" *CMS* 18, no. 2 (1978): 35–81. Ulrich Ragozat, *Die Nationalhymnen der Welt: Ein Kulturgeschichtliches Lexikon* (Freiburg, Basel, and Vienna: Herder, 1982). Caryl Clark, "Forging Identity: Beethoven's Ode as European Anthem," *Critical Inquiry* 23, no. 4 (Summer 1997): 789–807. W. L. Reed and Martin Bristow, eds., *National Anthems of the World,* 9th ed. (London: Cassell, 1997) [gives the original texts, Eng. trans., piano arrangements, names of authors and composers, and dates of adoption for 196 national anthems].

H.E.S., rev. L.C.

Nationalism. Traditionally has denoted the use in art music of materials that suggest a national or regional character. These may include actual folk music, melodies or rhythms that merely recall folk music, or religious music associated with a particular nationality (such as the German chorale).

As a purely musical phenomenon, nationalism has often been associated with the music of the late 19th and early 20th centuries from countries on the periphery of Western Europe, for instance Russia (Glinka, the *Five), Czechoslovakia (Smetana, Dvořák, Janáček), Norway (Grieg), Finland (Sibelius), England (Elgar, Vaughan Williams, Holst), Spain (Pedrell, Albéniz, Granados, Falla), Hungary (Bartók, Kodály), and the U.S. (H. F. Gilbert, Frederick Converse, Ives, Harris, Gershwin, Copland).

But the music of the dominant Western European tradition has also been deemed nationalist, both in terms of musical style and its reception. *Absolute instrumental music, which was thought to be free of any particular connotations, was nonetheless praised as a specifically German music. The memorable melodies of midcentury Italian opera, popular throughout Europe, were in many ways expressions of Risorgimento political aims. Indeed, it would be difficult to find a style, composer, or repertoire of music that at some point has not either aimed to be national or been viewed as such. Even the *twelve-tone system on which much seemingly international 20th-century music was based was viewed by its creator, Arnold Schoenberg, as an advance for German musical superiority.

National interests are also reflected in musical institutions, which are frequently funded by national or regional governments, which in turn benefit from the cultural prestige of the institutions they support.

Bibl.: Jane Fulcher, *The Nation's Image: French Grand Opera as Politics and Politicized Art* (New York: Cambridge U Pr, 1987). Philip Gossett, "Becoming a Citizen: The Chorus in Risorgimento Opera," *COJ* 2 (1990): 41–64. Benedict Anderson, *Imagined Communities: Reflections on the Origin and Spread of Nationalism* (New York: Verso, 1983; rev. and extended ed., 1991). Eric J. Hobsbawm, *Nations and Nationalism since 1780: Programme, Myth, Reality* (New York: Cambridge U Pr, 1990; 2nd ed., 1992). Geoff Eley and Ronald Grigor Suny, eds., *Becoming National: A Reader* (New York: Oxford U Pr, 1996). Richard Taruskin, *Defining Russia Musically: Historical and Hermeneutical Essays* (Princeton: Princeton U Pr, 1997). Celia Applegate, "How German Is It? Nationalism and the Idea of Serious Music in the Early Nineteenth Century," *19th-Century Music* 21 (1997–98): 274–96. Judit Frigyesi, *Béla Bartók and Turn-of-the-Century Budapest* (Berkeley: U of Cal Pr, 1998). Pamela Potter, *Most German of the Arts: Musicology and Society from the Weimar Republic to the End of Hitler's Reich* (New Haven: Yale U Pr, 1998). Michael P. Steinberg, *Austria as Theater and Ideology: The Meaning of the Salzburg Festival* (Ithaca, N.Y.: Cornell U Pr, 2000). Barbara Milewski, "Chopin's Mazurkas and the Myth of the Folk," *19th-Century Music* 22 (1999–2000): 113–35. Celia Applegate and Pamela Potter, eds., *Music and German National Identity* (Chicago: U of Chicago Pr, 2002).
R.M.

Natural. (1) A note that is not affected by either a sharp or a flat, e.g., D-natural as distinct from D-sharp or D-flat. (2) The accidental sign ♮, used to cancel a previous sharp or flat or to warn against the possible use of either [see Accidental].

Natural harmonics. See Harmonics.

Natural horn, trumpet. Brass instruments that lack *valves or keys and thus produce only the tones available in the natural *harmonic series. Crooks—various additional lengths of tubing—are used to obtain the harmonic series of pitches most useful in the composition to be played. By positioning an object (usually the hand) in the instrument's bell or by using lipping techniques, experienced players can inflect certain natural pitches up or down to produce pitches outside the harmonic series. See also Brass instruments. R.E.E.

Natural tones. The pitches of the *harmonic series; especially those produced on a *wind instrument without the aid of *valves or keys.

Naturhorn, Naturtrompete [Ger.]. *Natural horn, natural trumpet.

Nazard [Fr.]. (1) An organ stop of wide-scaled, open cylindrical pipes sounding the twelfth (2 2/3′) or nineteenth (1 1/3′). (2) In French repertory, a registration including (1).

Nāy [Per., Ar.], **ney** [Turk.]. An *end-blown flute of the Middle East. Most are 60 to 70 cm. long, made from cane, and have six finger holes and a thumb hole. The player holds the instrument slightly to one side and blows gently across the open pipe to produce a soft, breathy sound. It is much used in Persian, Arabic, and Turkish art music, in folk music, and in the religious music of the Sufi orders. See ill. under Near and Middle East; see also *Caval, Qaṣabah.*

Neapolitan school. A group of 18th-century composers, known chiefly for their operas, who studied in Naples or were active there for some significant portion of their careers. Nicola Porpora (1686–1768), Leonardo Vinci (ca. 1690–1730), Francesco Feo (1691–1761), Leonardo Leo (1694–1744), Nicola Logroscino (1698–1765), Giovanni Battista Pergolesi (1710–36), Gaetano Latilla (1711–91), Domingo Terradellas (1713–51), Tommaso Traetta (1727–79), Pietro Guglielmi (1728–1804), Niccolò Piccinni (1728–1800), Antonio Sacchini (1730–86), Giacomo Tritto (1733–1824), Giovanni Paisiello (1740–1816), and Domenico Cimarosa (1749–1801) all studied at one or another of the several musical conservatories in Naples. Feo, Leo, Tritto, and Francesco Provenzale (1627–1704, sometimes called the founder of the Neapolitan school) taught in these conservatories. Alessandro Scarlatti (1660–1725) and Niccolò Jommelli (1714–74) are included in the Neapolitan school although they, as well as many of the composers mentioned above, were also active in a number of other cities.

The concept Neapolitan school, or more particularly Neapolitan opera, has been questioned by a number of scholars. That Naples was a significant musical center in the 18th century is beyond doubt. Whether the composers working in Naples at that time developed or partook of a distinct and characteristic musical style is less clear. It must be admitted that only a small proportion of the repertory of 18th-century Italian opera is known, even by specialists. Hence, generalizations about or comparisons between, for example, Neapolitan and Venetian opera, are likely to be imprecise. See Opera, Classical (3).

Bibl.: Francesco Florimo, *La scuola musicale di Napoli,* 4 vols. (Naples, 1880–82; R: Bologna: Forni, 1969). Giampiero Tintori, *L'opera napoletana* (Milan: Ricordi, 1958). Edward Downes, "The Neapolitan Tradition in Opera," *New York,* 1961, pp. 277–84. Helmut Hucke, "Die neapolitanische Tradition in der Oper," *New York,* 1961, pp. 253–77. Daniel Heartz, "Opera and the Periodization of Eighteenth-Century Music," *Ljubljana,* 1967, pp. 160–68. William Stalnaker, "The Beginnings of Opera in Naples" (Ph.D. diss., Princeton Univ., 1968). Gordana Lazarevich, "The Role of the Neapolitan Intermezzo in the Evolution of Eighteenth-Century Musical Style" (Ph.D. diss., Columbia Univ., 1970). Hellmuth Christian Wolff, "The Fairy-tale of Neapolitan Opera," *Geiringer,* 1970, pp. 401–6. Gordana Lazarevich, "The Neapolitan Intermezzo and Its Influence on the Symphonic Idiom," *MQ* 56 (1971): 294–313. Michael Robinson, *Naples and Neapolitan Opera* (Oxford: Clarendon Pr, 1972).
C.G.

Neapolitan sixth. See Sixth chord.

Near and Middle East. An area of West Asia and North Africa whose musical culture is dominated by the Islamic Arabic-, Persian-, and Turkish-speaking peoples and is made up of a single though heterogeneous system including liturgical, classical, folk, and modern popular music. The peoples of Afghanistan, Central Asia, and the Caucasus share in this system peripherally.

I. *Music in culture.* A rich body of folk music and, since the Middle Ages, a body of classical concert music supported until the 20th century by royal and imperial courts, contrasts with a more limited body of Muslim religious music and an ambivalent and even negative attitude toward music that has at various times shaped—and also inhibited—the development of secular and especially instrumental music as well as dance. A subject of controversy in Islamic culture itself, this proscription has had little impact on rural, folk, and vernacular cultures, in which music and dance for entertainment, for producing trancelike states, and as part of folk religion are widely used. It has also brought about a body of secular music with sacred implications such as song texts, and the conception of music as a symbolic seeking of union with God by mystics such as the Sufi movement of Islam. The important historical role of religious minorities such as Jews and Christians in musical life also results from the ambivalent Islamic attitude. Nestorian Christians in particular played a role in the translation of Greek treatises into Arabic. A disproportionate number of Jews have served for centuries as music makers for Muslim society; and in 20th-century Iran, Armenian Christians have been the chief instrument makers. Furthermore, the role of music as intellectual discipline, related to the great flowering of music theory over a period of centuries, mitigated its reputation as an immoral activity. The inhibition of music is also related to the small degree of general participation in performance and the development of specialists who dominate even in the folk cultures, but who are relegated to low social status. Although professional musicians, mainly members of special musical families, have dominated classical music, there is high regard for a class of musical amateurs whose excellence rivals that of those who make their living by music. Performances of classical music have traditionally taken place mainly at small private social gatherings. While it is often referred to as Arabic, the music of this area is as much the creation of Turks and Persians, who contributed greatly to musical life at Arabic courts and to the body of music theory written in the Arabic language.

II. *Religious and ceremonial music.* Despite the religious flavor of much secular music, no body of music actually used in worship has been developed to rival the vast quantity of church music of the West or the temple music of Hindus and Buddhists. Music performed in the mosque is largely limited to reading or chanting the *Qur'ān, which is done by a soloist employing heavy ornamentation. Not technically classified as music, its style is closely related to secular classical song, but it is governed by independent terminology. By contrast, Middle Eastern Jewish cantillation uses the *maqām* system of Arabic classical music. The practice of singing the Qur'ān extends to private social contexts such as small men's clubs in Iran whose members take turns reciting passages. The second major musical function in the mosque is the call to prayer by the *muezzin,* who may be judged by the emotional impact of his voice and musical phraseology.

Outside the mosque ceremonies carried out by Sufis—the Arabic *zikr* and the Turkish *fasil,* for example—consist of music and dance resulting in trances interpreted as union with God. The *ta'azieh* is a kind of morality play performed by Shi'ite Muslims, especially in Iran, recounting the martyrdom of leaders of early Islam, particularly the Imam Hossein at the battle of Kerbala in 680; the characters sing or chant, sometimes with drum accompaniment. Martyrs are also mourned by processions of men antiphonally singing short phrases to the rhythmic accompaniment of beating their chests with fists or chains. A different type of ceremonial music is the accompaniment of traditional gymnastic exercises in establishments called *zurkhāneh* (house of strength) by a *morshed* who, playing drums and bells, sings excerpts from the Iranian national epic, *Shāhnāmeh* by Ferdowsi. No longer extant are fanfares played at city gates by horns, oboes, and drums in Iran and the complex of military *Janissary music performed by large ensembles in the Ottoman Empire.

III. *Folk music.* To a large extent, village and rural music has long been the province of specialists. Singers, many of them women, who were also composers and poets, sang songs of praise, mourning, and satire, and in pre-Islamic times were accorded supernatural power. Group singing, not very common, is carried on responsorially by dervish fraternities. Improvisation of variations on a set tune, and of nonmetric tunes, is prominent. There are work songs to accompany agriculture and camel-driving. Various kinds of specialists are recognized. In northeastern Iran, for example, they include singers of the *Shāhnāmeh,* of the story of Hossein's martyrdom, and of songs for weddings; preachers who include recitation-like singing; minstrels who are also clowns; and beggars who chant musical formulas. A folk music genre is likely to consist of severely limited melodic material, and a singer may make his career from performing variants of one tune type. In Iran, thousands of lyrical quatrains are sung to variants of a single melody called the *chahārbeiti* tune. The figure of the *'asheq,* singer of romantic narratives, is widespread in Turkey, Azerbaijan, Iran, Afghanistan, and Central Asia.

The distance between folk and art music is not great in the central nations of the Middle East. Because of the role of the specialist in folk culture, and since (in contrast to Europe) the singing style of folk music hardly differs from that of art music, the use of art music instruments is widespread in the folk community, and related styles exist in the two repertories. On its outskirts, e.g., Afghanistan and the Caucasus, contrastive folk styles, particularly in their use of polyphony, some of it in fourths, fifths, and seconds, may be found. The folk music of the Balkans and Spain shows the influence of Middle Eastern music in scales, nonmetric improvisation, singing style, and instruments.

IV. *Art music.* 1. General. The history of Middle Eastern art music revolves about a series of political centers that successively dominated large portions of the Islamic heartland: Damascus, Baghdad, Cordoba, Istanbul, Isfahan, etc., each of them drawing on artists and scholars from many regions. It is nevertheless convenient to separate three major traditions—Arabic, Turkish, and Persian—and related systems in Afghanistan, Central Asia, and the Caucasus. Yet all of these have much in common.

The music of all of these traditions is essentially soloistic, with ensembles consisting of a leading vocalist or melodic instrument accompanied by (i) a stringed instrument that plays in unison with the soloist in composed, metric music and follows a note or two behind, also recapitulating phrases, in nonmetric improvisation, and (ii) one or two percussion instruments for metric sections. Distinctions are made between composed and improvised parts of a performance and between metric and nonmetric portions.

Melodic organization follows a system of modes, generally and in Arabic called *maqām,* but also *makam* in Turkish, *dastgāh* and *gusheh* in Persian, *mugam* in Azerbaijan, *shashmaqām* in Uzbekistan. Essence and attributes vary by area and historical period, but in general, a *maqām* has a scale and a hierarchy of pitches whose distribution in the lower tetrachord is the main characteristic. Scalar intervals include those approximating tempered whole and half, three-quarter and five-quarter tones, although there is variation and theoretical controversy regarding their precise tuning. A *maqām* also has characteristic melodic contours, motifs, and interval sequences and is ascribed a specific musical or even nonmusical character. In all of this, and in their complex ornamentation, *maqāmāt* bear important relationships to the Indian *rāga* system.

The rhythm of nonmetric music is closely related to the prosody of Middle Eastern poetry. Though not governed by a cycle of beats, this music has specific rhythmic character, definable by successions of long and short notes and of stresses. Performance of a *maqām* may include characteristic rhythmic formulas. Metric music is governed by systems of rhythmic modes: cycles of beats variously subdivided.

The interrelationship of the various classical systems is such that similar or identical modes or other concepts may have different names, and the same term may have different meanings in Iran, Turkey, Iraq, and Egypt. Although each subdivision of the Middle East emphasizes a particular group of instruments, the entire area has essentially a common stock.

2. Arabic. Although individual pieces may be performed alone or independently in a concert context, the full performances of Arabic music consist of sequences of pieces cast in one *maqām.* Among the important genres is the *beshrev* (also *peshrav, bashraf,* from Persian *pishrāv,* coming before), a stately, metric piece intended for ensemble playing in heterophonic unison, with a form of several sections, each of which is repeated once. Also prominent is the *taqsīm* (division), usually a nonmetric instrumental improvisation in which the performer, after establishing the principal *maqām,* modulates successively to others before returning. In vocal performance, a **mawwāl* or vocal nonmetric improvisation with similar structure may be preceded by an instrumental *taqsīm.* A quick dance-like number may end a performance. A prominent complex form is the *nawbah,* a term once also used for *maqām* and implying a long performance in one mode. Since the 19th century, it has been primarily used in Tunisia and Algeria and has consisted of five contrastive movements. A complex form close to that of Persian music, moving from one *maqām* to others in a group of movements, is found in the so-called Iraqi *maqām* practice, which thus provides a bridge between the principal Arabic and northern-tier traditions. Iraqi practice includes five standardized multi-movement *fusul* (sing. *fasil*). The number of items and their order vary in all of these forms, but the principle of contrast is a constant feature.

More than 30 *maqāmāt* are used in Arabic music. Example 1 gives the lower tetrachord of the eight principal groups (after Touma, 1996), whose constituent *maqāmāt* are differentiated in the upper tetrachord. The example uses notational symbols widely employed in 20th-century Middle Eastern publications, i.e., ♯̸ for a quarter tone sharp, and ♭̸ for a quarter tone flat. The names of *maqāmāt* imply musical character

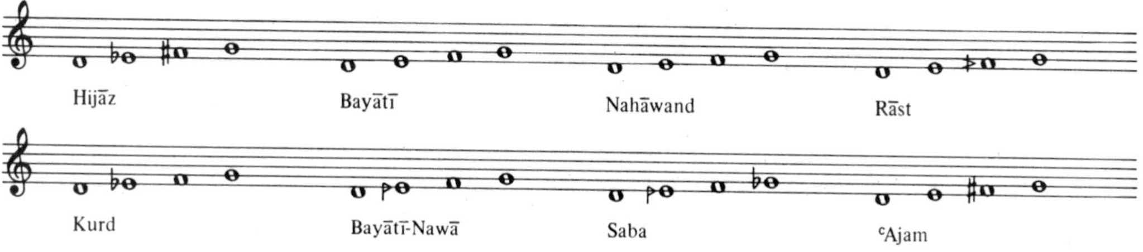

1. Lower tetrachords of a sampling of Arabic *maqām* groups.

derived from a number of sources, some of which (like the names of Greek modes) are place names: *Hijāz* (Arabia), *Nahāwand* (in Iran), and *Kurd* (the Kurds). *Bayātī* is a poetic term, and *Rāst* is Persian for right or straight. *Jahārgāh* (fourth place) and *Sigāh* (third) are also Persian words probably referring to frets or scale degrees. This terminology indicates the diverse origins of *maqāmāt* and suggests that each is the residue of a repertory or style once absorbed into the system.

Īqā', the metric unit of Arabic music, is roughly equivalent to the Western measure but closer to the Indian *tāla*. Each *īqā'* (or *wazn*) has a unique pattern of beats, numbering from 2 to 38. Although over 100 distinct *īqā'āt* are said to exist, in practice a much smaller number is used, and the system has been partially abandoned in favor of simpler Western meters. An *īqā'* has heavy beats (*dum*, representing striking the drum at the center), light beats (*tak*, at the edge), and rests combined into equal or unequal subdivisions of the cycle [Ex. 2]. The rhythmic modes are subject to improvisatory variation and influence the phrasing and accentuation of the melody they accompany.

2. A sampling of *īqā'* (pl. *īqā'āt*) or *wazn* (pl. *awzān*).

3. Turkish. As a result of the concentration of political and cultural power of the Ottoman Empire, Arabic musicians and forms were drawn to Istanbul and established in an organized system that, by the 20th century, emphasized Western notation and the use of composed forms over the improvised. Full performances of Turkish music follow but expand the Arabic principles. The major secular form is the *fasil*, which includes up to seven separate composed pieces beginning with the *beshrev*. Improvised *taksims* (instrumental) and *gazels* (vocal) may be inserted among them. A similar suite accompanies the ceremony of the Mevlevi order of dervishes, largely composed of dancing or whirling to put the worshippers into a trance. An improvised *taksim* (on the flute) and a *peshrev* (by ensemble) precede four long vocal pieces (*Selams*, or greetings) sung in unison by a group of men to texts by the 13th-century Persian poet Rumi, founder of the Mevlevi order. A further *peshrev*, another vocal number, a final *taksim*, and a recited prayer conclude the ceremony, which is cast in one main *makam*.

The Turkish *makam* system is close to the various Arabic ones, but intervals have been standardized by the adoption of a 24-tone scale of unequal intervals generated by the circle of fifths and used as the basis of permanent frets on the chief stringed instrument, the **tanbur*. About 40 or 50 types of rhythmic cycle (*usul*) are used in the contemporary Turkish repertory, which has preserved this aspect of music better than other Eastern cultures.

4. Persian. Although close to Arabic practice before ca. 1880, Persian classical music has for centuries exhibited relationships to India and developed more independently in the 20th century. A full performance includes a stately, metric *pishdarāmad*, a form developed for ensemble performance ca. 1900 but similar to the *beshrev*; *āvāz*, a nonmetric improvisation with some metric or quasi-metric sections inserted, instrumental or vocal, with text from Persian classical poetry; *tasnif*, a composed song with lyrical, satirical, or political text that may also be performed instrumentally; and *reng*, a quick instrumental number derived from the repertory of dance music. A *chahār mezrāb*, an instrumental form, composed or improvised, intended to exhibit instrumental virtuosity, with much use of rhythmic ostinato, may be inserted at various points.

The modal unit of Persian music is the **dastgāh*, with characteristic scale, motifs, and nonmusical character. Example 3 illustrates three of the twelve *dastgāhs*. A *dastgāh*, however, includes a number of subdivisions, **gushehs*, each of which has a typical range, constituent tones that may differ, like accidentals, from those of the basic *dastgāh* scale (and is thus a kind of modulation), as well as typical motifs. The Persian system is taught through the memorization of the *radif*, a body of largely nonmetric music approximately ten hours long, which includes the twelve *dastgāhs* and their constituent *gushehs* in prescribed order, with appropriate melodies and rhythms. Once memorized, the *radif* becomes the basis for composition and improvisation. Musicians determine a *dastgāh* to be performed and then select some of its *gushehs* to be used; these have a function analogous to the modulatory *maqāmāt*, in Arabic *taqāsīm*, but with a standardized role. The principal melodic motif of a *dastgāh* recurs throughout an *āvāz*, often providing a closing formula for the various *gushehs*. The *āvāz*, requiring as much as 45 minutes, is thus intermediate in improvisatory practice between the Arabic and Turkish *taqsīm* and the Indian *ālāpana*. In recent decades, its role in a Persian performance has been reduced in favor of the composed movements.

Although the *iqā'* system has virtually disappeared in Iran, rhythmic sophistication continues in the im-

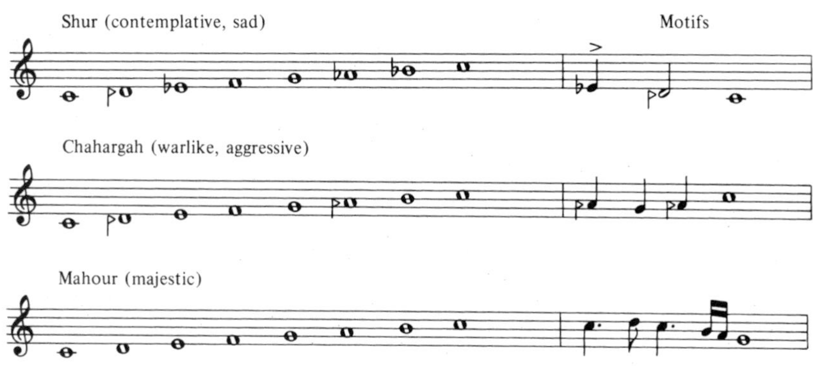

3. Three Persian *dastgāhs:* scale, character, and characteristic motif.

provisations. Rhythmic variety extends from strictly metric with rhythmic ostinato through free rhythm with metric elements to the thoroughly nonmetric. Improvisatory techniques stress development of short motifs through variation, extension, contraction, and melodic sequence. The *mugam* system of Azerbaijan is closely related to the *dastgāh* system of Iran, using almost identical terminology, genres, and improvisatory practices, but with a higher degree of standardization of forms and ensembles, and with historically greater participation of female musicians.

5. Other areas. In Afghanistan, the Caucasus, and Central Asia, versions of the Middle Eastern classical system have been in use, but, in recent centuries with the absence of royal patrons, have occupied a social role more like that of folk music. In Afghanistan, it is the property of the barber caste and of gypsies, along with modern professionals and members of families that have nurtured music as an amateur activity. A number of styles, some influenced by India, have been developed, in part because of the large number of separate ethnic groups.

It is important to mention the practice of Arabic, Turkish, and Persian music in Israel, which, as a result of the immigration of Jewish musicians, functions as a center for both the preservation and the modernization of traditional music.

V. *Instruments.* Most instrument types [see ill.] are distributed throughout the Middle East, but each area has its most characteristic type. String instruments predominate. Most famous is the Arabic *ʿ*ūd,* from which the European lute is physically and terminologically derived. It normally has five courses of two strings tuned mainly in fourths, without frets. Also important are the *bouzouq,* known as **saz* in Turkey, a long-necked lute with frets; and the **qānūn,* a complex, plucked board zither or psaltery. The Western violin has become prominent in classical music throughout the Middle East. The most important Turkish stringed instrument is the **tanbur,* a long-necked lute with round body, a drone string, and 24 frets to the octave. Long-necked lutes predominate in Iran as well: the **tār,* with heavy, waisted body carved from one piece of wood, 6 strings, and 16 frets per octave unequally spaced to make possible performance of all modes; and the smaller, lighter **setār,* with four strings and the same fretting. Also important in Iran is the **santur,* a hammered trapezoid zither with 18 courses of four strings and bridges to provide three octaves, from which the Hungarian **cimbalom* and the Chinese **yang-ch'in* are thought to be derived. Bowed instruments include the *kamancha* (Arabic **kamānjah*), a spike fiddle with three or four strings, held vertically; the *gheichak,* shaped like the Indian **sarinda;* and the **rabāb,* with a variety of shapes and one to three strings.

Idiophones are of modest importance. The most prominent wind instrument is the **nāy* or *ney,* a vertical flute sometimes played with the tongue inserted as a fipple. In folk music, various kinds of oboe *(zūrnā, surnāy)* related to the Indian *śahnāi* are used. Double oboes or single-reed instruments are widely used, with the pipes played in unison or as melody plus drone (Arabic *arghūl,* Persian *qoshmeh,* etc.). Bagpipes are important in North Africa. Among the large number of drum types, the goblet-shaped **darabukkah* is most widespread. Related to it is the goblet-shaped wooden **zarb* or *dombak* of Iran and Turkey, which, like the small kettledrums (**naqqārah*) played in pairs, are used in classical music. Folk and popular instruments include the **davul* (Persian *dohol*), a large cylindrical drum, and tambourines with bells or series of rings. Middle Eastern drums are normally struck with the hands and fingers.

VI. *History.* 1. Early history. The early history of Middle Eastern music, as known from studies of ancient *Greece, *Israel, *Egypt, and *Mesopotamia, gives some evidence of continuity to the Islamic era, mainly by the existence of modal systems and certain instruments. The simplest folk music of today also indicates a prehistory in which the formal and melodic principles now used were found in simpler form centuries ago. From the early Islamic period on, the known history of Middle Eastern music is largely that of theory and conceptualization as found in scholarly treatises, of which some 2,000 from ca. 900 C.E. on exist. The themes dominating these treatises are (1) enumeration and classification of the melodic and rhythmic modes, (2) the scientific rationale of the intervallic structures, and (3) the legitimacy and acceptability of various kinds of music. The relationship of theory to musical practice is often unclear. Thus, in contemporary practice, identities of *maqāms*, *makams*, and *dastgāhs* are much more a matter of school and individual practice and preference than theoretical treatises suggest. Many of the writings about music widely referred to as treatises are in fact historical, entertainment, biographical, and anecdotal literature.

In the history of Middle Eastern theoretical writing, the principal treatises are those of al-Kindī (ca. 790–ca. 874), al-Fārābī (d. 950), the Ikhwān al-Ṣafā' (Brethren of Purity, 10th century), Ibn Sīnā (Avicenna, 980–1037), Ibn Zayla (d. 1048), Ṣafī al-Dīn (d. 1294), and 'Abd al-Qādir (d. 1435) (for an exhaustive catalog, see Shiloah, 1979; for extended translations, see D'Erlanger, 1930–59). The most comprehensive and influential is al-Fārābī's *Kitāb al-mūsīqī al-kabīr* (Great Book on Music). Al-Fārābī discusses in great detail the size of intervals, the combining of intervals into tetrachords (*jins,* pl. *ajnās*), and the combining of tetrachords into "groups" or scales (*jam*ʿ*,* pl. *jumū*ʿ). He draws extensively on classical Greek theory and demonstrates intervallic relationships in terms of the fretting and fingering of the **ʿūd*. Some of his terms remain in use, but the term **maqām,* which is now used in the context of scale and mode, did not come into use in this sense until about the 13th century. Other major topics covered in his treatise include the specific instruments of his day (e.g., two types of **ṭunbūr*) and the intervals and scales played on them; rhythm and its patterns, for which he uses the term still in use, *īqā*ʿ (pl. *īqāʿāt*); and the nature of instrumental and vocal melodies and their composition.

The one Arabic treatise with a direct influence on music theorists of the European Middle Ages is al-Fārābī's *Classification of the Sciences.* The section on music is an outline of his *Great Book on Music,* and it was translated into Latin in Spain in the 12th century. Cited by Jerome of Moravia, Lambert, and others in the 13th century, it contains relatively little technical detail and seems to have interested European writers because of its general system for classifying music [see also *Musica*] rather than because of any need or wish to learn about Arabic music itself (Randel, 1976).

The works of Ṣafī al-Dīn mark the beginning of the Systematist school of theory, which predominated from the 13th century through the 15th (see Wright, 1978). Theorists of this period further developed analyses of the type undertaken by al-Fārābī, and their writings reveal a system shared by Arabs and Persians. From the 16th century to the end of the 19th, however, relatively little theory survives for either Arabic or Persian music. Thus, it has not been possible to study the paths along which Arabic and Persian music diverged.

2. Modern history. Although the precise nature of Middle Eastern influence on medieval Western art music is the subject of controversy, there is little doubt that such influence occurred. Since the 18th century, Middle Eastern influence has taken the form of deliberately exotic effects such as the imitation of *Janissary music. The degree of Western influence on the Middle East is difficult to assess until the 19th century, the era of military conquest and commercial exploitation, when Western military music was introduced (1826 in Turkey, 1856 in Iran), and Western musicians were brought to introduce their music. Late in the 19th century, traditional musicians began modernization of their systems along Western lines. This resulted in the adoption of Western notation with modifications, now widely used, and the creation of large ensembles that performed in heterophonic unison and for which special genres such as the Persian *pishdarāmad* were developed. Early in the 20th century, the record industry produced large quantities of pressings, particularly in Egypt, Turkey, and Iran, adding a new form of transmission and encouraging a system of preeminent musicians who raised the esteem of the profession. In Iran, the traditional system was refurbished along Western lines with the standardization of the *radif* by Mirzā Abdollāh and Darvish Khān, ca. 1900.

The 20th century also saw the introduction of music schools, along the lines of Western conservatories, that teach performance, theory, and aesthetics as separate subjects to large classes. Early in the century, attempts to introduce Western harmony (e.g., by Ali Naqi Vaziri) resulted in composed pieces with tonic-dominant alternation and emphasis on those modes compatible with Western tonalities. After World War I, the desire for cultural Westernization led to the temporary outlawing of traditional music in Turkey and, in Arabic and Persian music, application of Western concepts such as tempered quarter tones. In 1932, a major congress in Cairo, with Middle Eastern and European musicians, led to further modernization and attempts at unification of the various Arabic traditions.

The development of a body of popular music, and of modernized manifestations of classical music, some of it based on classical styles mixed with Western principles of harmony and ensemble, disseminated largely through records, radio, and film, is characteristic of the period after World War I. The popular music caused changes in art music, some of which developed a lighter tone with shorter performances and less improvisation. The Arabic *takht,* an ensemble consisting of two stringed instruments, flute, *darabukkah,* and tambourine, was the standard performance medium through much of the 20th century. Star singers such as Moharam Fuad and Umm Kulthum in Egypt and Delkash in Iran popularized mixed styles with texts of

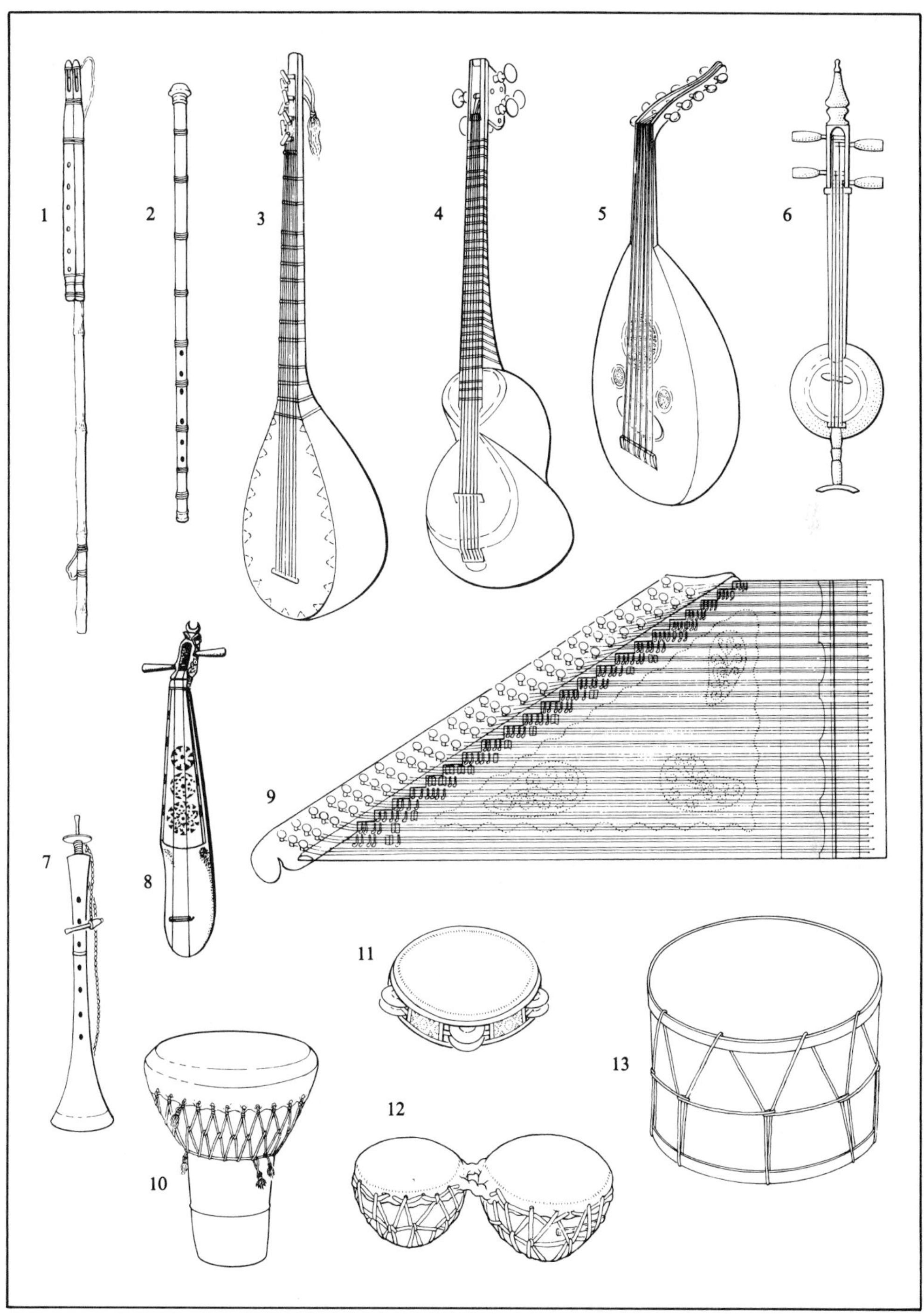

Instruments of the Near and Middle East: 1. Arghūl. 2. Nāy. 3. Saz. 4. Tār. 5. ʿŪd. 6. Kamānjah. 7. Zūrnā. 8. Rabāb. 9. Qānūn. 10. Darabukkah. 11. Daff. 12. Naqqārah. 13. Davul (shown half size in relation to others).

social relevance. Composers of Western art music in contemporary styles but with a vestige of the older Middle Eastern tradition have also been at work since the middle of the 20th century.

The appropriateness of musical activity came into sharp focus again after the 1979 revolution in Iran, when public musical performance was temporarily outlawed; it continues to be controlled in the early 21st century. More radical prohibitions were exercised in Afghanistan in the 1990s, while the development of musical genres such as *Rai* in Algeria, *Arabesk* in Turkey, and *Musika Mizrahi* in Middle East–derived Jewish communities in Israel became significant expressions of nationalism, ethnicity, and protest. At the turn of the 21st century, in the diasporic communities of Persians, Arabs, Turks, and Kurds (mainly in Europe and North America), musical activity is among the most important symbols of ethnic integration as well as a powerful device for communication among different ethnicities. Issues of debate in contemporary Middle Eastern musical cultures include the concept of authenticity, the recovery and preservation of older traditions, the participation of female musicians, and the desirability of modernization.

3. Research. The first landmark in ethnomusicological study is the description of Egyptian music by Villoteau (1809), resulting from Napoleon's invasion of Egypt in 1798. The early 20th century is characterized by studies mainly devoted to the nature of the *maqām* concept and by investigation of medieval theoretical treatises in their relationship to Western theory. After 1950, studies of the Persian classical system were most prominent, along with research in Arabic and Turkish folk music. After 1965, studies of urbanization, modernization, and Western influences are to be noted, along with special interest in Afghanistan. After 1950, Middle Eastern scholars joined the general ethnomusicological effort. Knowledge of Middle Eastern music is quite uneven, the most research having been done in Iran, Afghanistan, and Israel, followed by Egypt and Turkey, with less attention to North Africa and the Arabian peninsula.

Bibl.: Guillaume A. Villoteau, *De l'état actuel de l'art musical en Égypte* (Paris, 1809). Henry George Farmer, *A History of Arabian Music to the XIIIth Century* (London: Luzac, 1929). Rodolphe d'Erlanger, *La musique arabe* (Paris: P Geuthner, 1930–59). *NOHM* 1 (1957). Mehdi Barkechli, *La musique traditionelle de l'Iran* (Tehran: Secrétariat d'état aux beaux-arts, 1963). Nelly Caron and Dariouche Safvate, *Iran: Les traditions musicales* (Paris: Buchet-Chastel, 1966). *Encyclopédie des musiques sacrées* 1 (Paris: Éditions Lagergerie, 1968). Kurt Reinhard and Ursula Reinhard, *Turquie: Les traditions musicales* (Paris: Buchet-Chastel, 1969). Hans Hickmann and Wilhelm Stauder, *Orientalische Musik* (Leiden: E J Brill, 1970). Bruno Nettl with Bela Foltin, Jr., *Daramad of Chahargah* (Detroit: Info Coord, 1972). Artur Simon, *Studien zur ägyptischen Volksmusik* (Hamburg: Verlag der Musikalienhandlung, 1972). Jürgen Elsner, *Der Begriff des Maqām in Ägypten in neuerer Zeit* (Leipzig: Deutscher Verlag für Musik, 1973). Ella Zonis, *Classical Persian Music* (Cambridge, Mass.: Harvard U Pr, 1973). Laurence Picken, *Folk Music Instruments of Turkey* (London: Oxford U Pr, 1975). Béla Bartók, *Turkish Folk Music from Asia Minor* (Princeton, 1976). Ali Jihad Racy, "Record Industry and Egyptian Traditional Music," *Ethno* 20 (1976): 23–48. Don M. Randel, "Al-Fārābī and the Role of Arabic Music Theory in the Latin Middle Ages," *JAMS* 29 (1976): 173–88. Mark Slobin, *Music in the Culture of Northern Afghanistan* (Tucson: U of Ariz Pr, 1976). Karl L. Signell, *Makam: Modal Practice in Turkish Art Music* (Seattle: Asian Music Pubns, 1977). Mohammad T. Massoudieh, *Radif vocal de la musique traditionelle de l'Iran par Mahmud-e Karimi* (Tehran: Ministère de la culture et des arts, 1978). Bruno Nettl, ed., *Eight Urban Musical Cultures* (Urbana: U of Ill Pr, 1978). Owen Wright, *The Modal System of Arab and Persian Music, A.D. 1250–1300* (Oxford: Oxford U Pr, 1978). Harold S. Powers, ed., "Symposium on Art Musics in Muslim Nations," *AsM* 12/1 (1979): 1–169. Amnon Shiloah, *The Theory of Music in Arabic Writings c. 900–1900, RISM* B/X (Munich: Henle, 1979). Lois Ibsen al Faruqi, *An Annotated Glossary of Arabic Musical Terms* (Westport, Conn.: Greenwood, 1981). Hiromi Lorraine Sakata, *Music in the Mind: The Concept of Music and Musicians in Afghanistan* (Kent, Ohio: Kent St U Pr, 1983). Kristina Nelson, *The Art of Reciting the Qur'an* (Austin: U of Tex Pr, 1985). Hans Engel, *Die Stellung des Musikers im arabisch-Islamischen Raum* (Bonn: Verlag für systematische Musikwissenschaft, 1987). John Baily, *Music of Afghanistan: Professional Musicians in the City of Herat* (Cambridge: Cambridge U Pr, 1988). Hormoz Farhat, *The Dastgāh Concept in Persian Music* (Cambridge: Cambridge U Pr, 1990). Jean During et al., *The Art of Persian Music* (Washington, D.C.: Mage, 1991). Bruno Nettl, *The Radif of Persian Music: Studies of Structure and Cultural Context*, rev. ed. (Champaign, Ill.: Elephant & Cat, 1992). Martin Stokes, *The Arabesk Debate* (Oxford: Oxford U Pr, 1992). Amnon Shiloah, *Music in the World of Islam: A Socio-Cultural Study* (Detroit: Wayne St U Pr; Aldershot, U.K.: Scolar Pr, 1995). Habib Hassan Touma, *The Music of the Arabs*, new expanded ed. (Portland, Ore.: Amadeus, 1996). Theodore Levin, *The Hundred Thousand Fools of God: Musical Travels in Central Asia* (Bloomington: Ind U Pr, 1996). Virginia Danielson, *The Voice of Egypt: Umm Kulthum, Arabic Song, and Egyptian Society in the Twentieth Century* (Chicago: U of Chicago Pr, 1997). Ali Jihad Racy, "The Many Faces of Improvisation: The Arab Taqāsīm as a Musical Symbol," *Ethno* 44 (2000): 302–20. Virginia Danielson, Scott Marcus, and Dwight Reynolds, eds., *The Middle East*. Vol. 6 of the Garland Encyclopedia of World Music (New York: Routledge, 2002). B.N.

Nebel, nevel [Heb.; Gr. *nabla;* Lat. *nablium*]. A stringed instrument of ancient Israel, probably a small, triangular harp. English Bibles usually render it *psaltery.

Nebendreiklang [Ger.]. Secondary triad (i.e., not I, IV, or V).

Nebennote [Ger.]. Nonharmonic tone.

Nebensatz, Nebenthema [Ger.]. Secondary or second theme, as in sonata form.

Nebenstimme [Ger.]. Subsidiary voice or part, sometimes indicated in works by Schoenberg and others with brackets formed from the letter N [see also *Hauptstimme*].

Nebentonart [Ger.]. A key other than the tonic in a given composition.

Neck. (1) [Fr. *manche;* Ger. *Hals;* It. *manico;* Sp. *cuello, mango, mástil*] The portion of a stringed instrument that projects from the body, over which the strings pass (usually over a *fingerboard), and by which the instrument is held. (2) The curved, uppermost side of the harp, along which the strings are attached to their tuning pins. (3) The curved, uppermost section of the alto and larger saxophones, to which the mouthpiece is attached.

Negro music. See African American music.

Nehmen [Ger., third person sing. *nimmt*]. To take up, as in an instruction for the flutist to take up or prepare to play the piccolo.

Neighboring tone, neighbor note. See Counterpoint II, 2.

Nelson Mass, Lord Nelson Mass. Popular name for the Mass in D minor by Haydn Hob. XXII:11 (1798). Particularly striking is the use of three trumpets in the Benedictus, sometimes said to have been inspired by news of Lord Nelson's victory in the Battle of the Nile. It is also called the *Imperial* or the *Coronation* Mass.

Neoclassical. A stylistic classification most commonly applied to the works of Stravinsky from *Pulcinella* (1920) to *The Rake's Progress* (1951). Its chief aesthetic characteristics are objectivity and expressive restraint, its principal technical ones, motivic clarity, textural transparency, formal balance, and reliance upon stylistic models. In Stravinsky's music, these models may be specific compositions (e.g., *Pulcinella* and *Le baiser de la fée,* based, respectively, upon actual compositions of the 18th and 19th centuries) or, more commonly, general stylistic traits (e.g., the Piano Concerto and Symphony in C, which contain explicit stylistic references to the Baroque concerto and the Classical symphony, respectively).

As a more general stylistic attribution, neoclassical is also applied to other music of the period between the wars, especially music that—like Stravinsky's—preserves a degree of tonal centricity, as well as characteristics of clarity and expressive detachment. In this broadest sense, it pertains to much music of this period, not only in France (where Stravinsky lived from 1920 until 1939 and had an especially strong influence), but in other countries as well—e.g., Germany (Strauss, Hindemith), Italy (Casella), Russia (Prokofiev), Spain (Falla), and the U.S. (Copland). Moreover, if a still broader stylistic characterization is accepted, the term even applies to the Schoenberg school, whose postwar *twelve-tone music reflects a more rational and systematic compositional approach and a closer affinity to traditional musical forms than did its prewar *expressionistic music.

The term neoclassical was first introduced in art criticism to refer to a stylistic movement of the later 18th century, whose followers favored conscious imitation of antique models. If one accepts only this general idea of conscious imitation, then neoclassical can also apply to a number of pre-20th-century musical developments—e.g., the Baroque-inspired fugues and chorale preludes of 19th-century composers such as Schumann, Mendelssohn, Reger, and Brahms. (Indeed, Brahms's music reveals, in general, strong neoclassical features.) Other earlier manifestations are found in the aesthetic views of Busoni (who first used the term in reference to music), in the later works of Debussy, and in the music of Satie (most notably his *Sonatine bureaucratique* of 1917, which explicitly parodies a sonata by Clementi). See also Classical (3).

R.P.M.

Neo-Gallican chant. Chant composed for any of the reformed liturgies of the Catholic Church in France from the mid-17th century through much of the 19th. It included entirely new melodies as well as substantial reworkings of traditional ones. See also *Plain-chant musical.*

Nete [Gr.]. See Greece I, 3 (i).

Netherlands. I. *Current musical life and related institutions.* 1. Opera. The Netherlands Opera (Nederlandse Operastichting) and Opera Forum (Opera Gezelschap Forum) are the two principal opera companies in the Netherlands. Both companies tour regularly, the Netherlands Opera going to larger cities, primarily Amsterdam, Rotterdam, The Hague, Scheveningen, and Utrecht, and Opera Forum going to towns in the north and east of the country.

2. Performing groups. About 15 orchestras are subsidized by the government. These include the Netherlands Chamber Orchestra and three organizations considered the most important such groups in the country: the Amsterdam Concertgebouw Orchestra (founded in 1888 and having perhaps the greatest international renown), The Hague Residentie Orchestra (1904), and the Rotterdam Philharmonic (1918). The Netherlands Broadcasting Foundation (Nederlandse Omroep Stichting [NOS]) supports the Radio Philharmonic, the Radio Chamber Orchestra, and other instrumental and vocal ensembles. Many smaller instrumental groups are active despite far lower levels of official support (for example, the Netherlands Wind Ensemble [Nederlands Blazers Ensemble, or NBE]). Organizations such as the professional Netherlands Chamber Choir (1937) and some 3,000 amateur choirs attest to the popularity of choral singing. Since World War II, Amsterdam has been a center of the revival of early music.

3. Festivals. Chief among many festivals in the Netherlands is the Holland Festival (founded in 1947), which takes place in the early summer of each year, running concurrently in numerous Dutch cities and towns. It involves concerts, operas, dances, plays, and art exhibits. Performances of contemporary works are encouraged, but standard repertory and revivals of

lesser-known works are by no means excluded. The International Gaudeamus Week (yearly, in September; national and international in alternate years from 1947 to 1959, then fully international) is devoted entirely to the performance of new compositions. Recent additions to Dutch festivals, several devoted to new music, include The Hague's Frans Vester Festival, the Rotterdam Music Festival, New Li(f-v)e on Stage, Utrecht's Festival of Medieval and Renaissance Music, and November Music, an international festival with concerts in 's-Hertogenbosch, the Netherlands; Ghent, Belgium; and Essen, Germany.

4. Education. Most training of professional musicians and teachers of music takes place at conservatories, located in The Hague (Royal Conservatory), Amsterdam, Rotterdam, Utrecht, Enschede, Tilburg, Maastricht, Gronigen, Zwolle, and Arnhem. In addition, there are schools for Catholic church music and Protestant church music in Utrecht and a school for carillon playing in Amersfoort. Musicology is taught at the universities in Amsterdam, Leiden, Utrecht, Gronigen, and Nijmegen. The IJsbreker Music Center, specializing in microtonal music, was established in Amsterdam in 1990, and the electro-acoustic music studio NEAR was founded in 1995.

5. Publishing and recording. The Donemus Foundation, founded in 1947 to promote and support Dutch music, publishes a large proportion of the music written by contemporary Dutch composers. Other companies that publish music and books about music include Frits Knuf, Martinus Nijhoff, and G. Alsbach. Donemus issues many recordings, as does Philips, the only international recording company active in the country. At its Eindhoven headquarters, Philips also maintains an electronic studio for the use of composers.

II. *History.* The current boundaries of the Netherlands were established only in 1830. Before then the area now so named tended to function culturally (and on occasion politically) as part of a larger unit, which also included Belgium, Luxembourg, and at times parts of northern France. This larger unit is commonly referred to as the Low Countries or simply the Netherlands (which includes Flanders). After the Reformation, musical practice differed somewhat in the Protestant north (present-day Netherlands) and the Catholic south (present-day Belgium and Luxembourg).

Music was cultivated in this area at least from the end of the Carolingian era. Medieval contributions include both compositions (plainsong and the Tournai Mass, for instance) and treatises on music theory (such as those of Magister Lambertus, fl. ca. 1270, and Jacques de Liège, ca. 1260–ca. 1330).

Although the musical *Renaissance is usually thought to have flowered in Italy, much of its impetus came from musicians trained in the Netherlands and styles worked out here. As early as the 14th century, large numbers of trained Netherlandish musicians left the area to pursue careers elsewhere in Europe, and their abilities, attributed to the fine training they had received, began to be prized. Emigration of musicians from the Netherlands reached a peak in the years between ca. 1480 and 1520, then declined, especially after 1550. The earliest well-known Netherlandish composer to emigrate (going to Italy) was Johannes Ciconia (ca. 1335–1411). He was followed by such individuals as Guillaume Dufay (ca. 1400–1474), Johannes Ockeghem (ca. 1410–97), Jacob Obrecht (ca. 1450–1505, the only composer in this list born in the territory now called the Netherlands), Adrian Willaert (ca. 1490–1562), Cipriano de Rore (1515 or 1516–65), and Orlande de Lassus (1532–94). The style of Josquin Desprez (ca. 1440–1521), evidently drawing on Ockeghem's, strongly influenced some Netherlandish composers, though Josquin himself was French. Imitation, one characteristic of Josquin's work, was made into a chief structural principle by later Netherlandish composers who did not emigrate. Members of this group wrote in a rather uniform style that is identifiably Netherlandish. Leading individuals include Nicolas Gombert (ca. 1495–ca. 1560), Clemens non Papa (ca. 1515–55 or 56), and Thomas Crecquillon (between ca. 1480 and 1500–1557).

In the latter half of the 16th century, the Netherlands lost its preeminent position in the field of music. Up until the 19th century, the country produced only one more musician whose work gained lasting international attention, Jan Pieterszoon Sweelinck (1562–1621), who was born and spent almost all of his life in the area now called the Netherlands and who was important as a performer, composer, and teacher.

During Sweelinck's life and afterward, cultivation of music for formal worship was discouraged by the precepts of the dominant religion of the area, Calvinism. Musical activity outside church services, however, flourished. Instrument making (especially the manufacture of organs and carillons) and music publishing were pursued with particular vigor. In the 18th century, foreign music (mostly Italian, later also French and German) came to be cultivated in place of indigenous music.

In the 20th century, Alfons Diepenbrock (1862–1921) and Willem Pijper (1894–1947) gave important impetus to the growth of a distinctly Dutch body of compositions. Pijper's students dominated composition in the Netherlands for a time. The most important are Guillaume Landré (1905–68), Henk Badings (1907–87) and Kees van Baaren (1906–70). Ton de Leeuw (1926–96), the most influential composer of his generation, studied with neither Pijper nor any of his students. Kees van Baaren taught many younger composers, such as Peter Schat (b. 1935) and Jan van Vlijmen (b. 1935). Other avant-garde composers who became prominent in postwar decades include Simeon ten Holt (b. 1923), Louis Andriessen (b. 1939), Diderik Wagenaar (b. 1946), electro-acoustic composer Ton Bruynèl (1934–98), and neotonal composer Otto Ketting (b. 1935). The eclectic current generation of Dutch composers includes Peter-Jan Wagemans (b. 1952), Joep Franssens (b. 1955), Theo Verbey (b.

1959), Willem Jeths (b. 1959), Rob Zuidam (b. 1964), Martijn Padding (b. 1956), and Peter van Onna (b. 1966). Compositional activity is fostered by several organizations, such as the Gaudeamus Foundation's Contemporary Music Center, Muziekgroep Nederland (Donemus), and Stichting Nieuwe Muziek Zeeland.

III. *Folk music.* The traditions of modern Netherlands, Belgium, and Luxembourg are largely inseparable and will be discussed together here. The earliest folk melodies preserved in their entirety appear set to religious words in collections dating from the late 15th and first half of the 16th century. The practice of folk music was hampered in the north by Calvinist strictures against singing secular songs and against dancing in the late 16th and early 17th century, but traditions were kept alive in the Catholic south. Most Netherlandish folk songs are largely syllabic and follow the rhythm of the text, but some show German influences in the occasional use of melismas. French influences are prominent in Walloon folk song and borrowings from English and German traditions in Friesian folk song. Polyphony is rare. Folk dances include couple, line, and ritual dances, such as the *zevensprong, crâmignon,* and *maclote,* and types less specific to the area, such as the waltz, polka, reel, and *Schottisch.* Among the many folk instruments of the Netherlands, some of the best known or most frequently used are the *hommel* (zither, extant in many forms with many names), *midwinterhoorn,* accordion, barrel organ, and *pierementen* (large street organ). Instrumental ensembles range in size from duos of melody and bass to sizable bands.

Collection and serious study of Netherlandish folk music began in the early 19th century. Traditional Walloon songs began to be collected only recently, however, and the folk music of Luxembourg has yet to be given close attention. Continuous cultivation of the indigenous repertory largely ceased in the 1920s but has been revived since.

Bibl.: Charles van den Borren, *Geschiedenis van de muziek in de Nederlanden,* 2 vols. (Amsterdam: Wereldbibliotheek, 1949–51). Jos Wouters, "Dutch Music in the 20th Century," *MQ* 51 (1965): 97–110. Leo Samama and Fer Abrahams, *Music in the Netherlands* ([Netherlands]: Dept. of International Relations, Ministry of Cultural Affairs, 1985). Keith Polk, "Instrumental Music in the Low Countries in the Fifteenth Century," in *From Ciconia to Sweelinck: Donum natalicium Willem Elders* (Amsterdam: Rodopi, 1994), pp. 13–29. Keith Polk, "Minstrels and Music in the Low Countries in the Fifteenth Century," in *Musicology and Archival Research,* ed. B. Haggh et al. (Brussels: Regia Belgica, 1994), pp. 392–410. Rudolf Rasch, "The Dutch Republic," in *The Late Baroque Era,* ed. G. J. Buelow (Englewood Cliffs, N.J.: Prentice Hall, 1994), pp. 393–410. Albert Dunning, "Niederlande," in *Europas Musikgeschichte: Grenzen und Offnungen* (Kassel: Bärenreiter, 1997), pp. 52–61. Kenneth Levy, *Gregorian Chant and the Carolingians* (Princeton: Princeton U Pr, 1998). Jolande van der Klis, *The Essential Guide to Dutch Music: 100 Composers and Their Work* (Amsterdam: Amsterdam U Pr, 2000). D. M. R.

Netherlands schools. See Renaissance, music of the.

Neuma [Lat., also *pneuma, neupma*]. (1) *Neume. (2) Any melisma in liturgical chant, but especially those of the *alleluia [see also *Jubilus*], those added to great responsories (including the *neuma triplex* of "Descendit de caelis"; see also Melisma), and the untexted melodies of *sequences. (3) Any of the melismas attached to the Western adaptations of the Byzantine modal intonation formulas in order to form the melodies (**noeane*) used in *tonaries and related treatises of the 9th through the 12th century to characterize the *modes; also termed *stivae, cauda,* and *jubilus.* These same melismas were incorporated in the model antiphons ("Primum querite regnum Dei," etc.) used for the same purpose in tonaries beginning in the 10th century. By the 12th century, they were attached to certain antiphons in the liturgy; and in the 13th and 14th centuries, they were used as motet tenors. Their use in the liturgy, with instrumental accompaniment by the 16th century, persisted into the 19th century in *Neo-Gallican chant.

Bibl.: Michel Huglo, *Les tonaires* (Paris: Société française de musicologie, 1971), pp. 383–90.

Neumatic [fr. *neume]. Characterized by the presence of groups of five or six notes sung to single syllables; one of the three principal categories of style in *Gregorian chant.

Neume [Lat. **neuma,* fr. Gr.]. Any of the signs employed in the notation of plainsong beginning in about the 9th century. The accompanying table gives the names and shows the forms of the principal neumes as they are found in modern liturgical books and in several of the major regional notations of the Middle Ages, together with an approximate equivalent for each (at least in terms of pitch contour) in modern notation. Neumes that represent up to three pitches are termed simple; those that represent more than three, compound. Liquescent neumes form a special category associated with certain features of the sung texts, such as the diphthongs *au, ei,* and *eu,* the semiconsonants *j* and *i,* and the consonants *l, m, n, r, d, t,* and *s* when these are followed by another consonant. In modern liturgical books, the liquescent note itself is made somewhat smaller than the others, and it is to be semivocalized (the Latin term for these being *semivocales*) or sung lightly. Finally, neumes sometimes termed ornamenting neumes seem to imply special types of performance, though their significance is not well understood. Certain supplementary signs may also affect the performance of neumes. These include *Romanian or significative letters found in manuscripts from St. Gall and the **episema.* The latter occurs in two forms in modern liturgical books: horizontal, found also in early manuscripts and interpreted as calling for a slight lengthening of the note over which it appears, and vertical, a sign not found in early sources and used in modern books to mark the placement of the **ictus* according to theories developed at *Solesmes. (For illustrations of the neumes and a guide to their performance according to the methods

		a	b	c	d	e	f	g	h	i
1	Punctum									
	Virga									
	Podatus or Pes									
	Clivis or Flexa									
2	Scandicus									
	Climacus									
	Torculus									
	Porrectus									
	Scandicus flexus									
	Porrectus flexus									
	Torculus resupinus									
	Pes sub-punctis									
3	Epiphonus									
	Cephalicus									
	Ancus									
4	Strophicus									
	Oriscus									
	Quilisma									
	Salicus									
	Pressus									

Types of neumes. 1. Simple. 2. Compound. 3. Liquescent. 4. Ornamenting. a. Modern liturgical books. b. Pitch contour. c. St. Gall (10th century). d. Lorraine or Messine (10th century). e. Beneventan (11th century). f. Aquitanian (11th century). g. English (11th century). h. Northern Hispanic or Mozarabic (11th century). i. Gothic or *Hufnagel* (15th century).

of Solesmes, see *LU,* pp. xix–xxx.) The extent to which neumes represent duration or rhythm has been the subject of considerable controversy [see Gregorian chant V].

Until the 11th century, individual neumes of two or more notes indicated only the general pitch contour of the notes contained, and the relationship of the pitch of one neume to that of the next was most often not implied in their placement on the page. Such neumes are variously described as nondiastematic, staffless, oratorical, and *in campo aperto* (in an open field). The 11th century saw the development of diastematic neumes, the first examples of which are Aquitanian. These specify pitch precisely by their careful arrangement above and below an imaginary line. The earliest type of actual line to be used is termed a dry-point line because it was scratched into the parchment of manuscripts without the use of ink. The use of one or more lines drawn with ink and clefs led in time to the standard practice of using four-line staves with C or F clefs. The square shapes on which those of modern liturgical books are modeled emerged in the 12th century.

The origin of neumes in the West has been the subject of various hypotheses, none universally accepted. Suggested antecedents have included the grave and acute accent signs of Latin or perhaps signs of this type employed in Greek; *ecphonetic notation of various kinds used to guide the recitation of sacred texts; *chironomy, neumes in this view being the graphic representation of gestures used to lead singing; and notations employed for Byzantine and other Eastern rites [for the rather different principles underlying the Byzantine neumes, see Byzantine chant]. The accent signs have attracted the widest support. In this view, the acute accent (representing a rise in pitch) became the *virga,* and the grave (representing a fall) became the *punctum.* The *virga* does typically represent a pitch higher than a *punctum.* More complex neumes would have been formed from combinations of the two.

The earliest surviving manuscripts with notation, which date from the 9th or perhaps 10th century, show that distinct regional families of neumes came into being at about the same time. The use of neumes in the West probably did not antedate these sources by much, since the earliest surviving liturgical manuscripts date from the 8th or 9th and early 10th centuries and were clearly not intended to incorporate musical notation. Much of the later history of the neumes reflects a confluence of traits of the several regional families.

Bibl.: *Paléographie musicale* [see Gregorian chant]. Peter Wagner, *Einführung in die gregorianischen Melodien,* vol. 2, *Neumenkunde* (Freiburg: Universitäts-Buchhandlung, 1905; 2nd ed. rev., Leipzig: Breitkopf & Härtel, 1912; R: Hildesheim: Olms, 1962). H. M. Bannister, ed., *Monumenti vaticani di paleografia musicale latina* (Leipzig: O Harrassowitz, 1913; R: Westmead, U.K.: Gregg, 1969) [numerous facsimiles]. Gregori M. Sunyol [Suñol], *Introducció a la paleografia musical gregoriana* (Montserrat, Spain: Abadía de Montserrat, 1925; rev. and trans. Fr., Paris: Desclée, 1935). Michel Huglo, "Les noms des neumes et leur origine," *Études grégoriennes,* 1 (1954): 53–67. Ewald Jammers, *Tafeln zur Neumenschrift* (Tutzing: Schneider, 1965). Eugène Cardine, *Semiologia gregoriana* (Rome: Pontificio istituto di musica sacra, 1968; trans. Fr. in *Études grégoriennes,* 11 [1970]: 1–158). Constantin Floros, *Universale Neumenkunde* (Kassel: Bärenreiter-Antiquariat, 1970). Solange Corbin, *Die Neumen* (Cologne: A Volk, 1977). See also Notation, Gregorian chant, Ambrosian chant, Byzantine chant, Mozarabic chant, Sarum use.

Nevel [Heb.]. **Nebel.*

New German School [Ger. *Neudeutsche Schule*]. A group of musicians initially gathered around Liszt during his Weimar years (1849–61) and including Hans von Bülow, Peter Cornelius, Joachim Raff, and Carl Taussig. They championed the program music of Berlioz and the music dramas of Wagner. Calling themselves futurists [Ger. *Zukunftsmusiker*], they adopted the name New German School in 1859 and were bitterly opposed in a manifesto issued in 1860 by Brahms and Joseph Joachim. The *Neue Zeitschrift für Musik,* formerly edited by Schumann, became their official journal until 1892.

New Orleans jazz. The first jazz style. The most characteristic features of New Orleans jazz are ensemble passages with dense textures resulting from overlapping rhythms and dissonant clashes among one or two cornets (or trumpets), trombone, clarinet, and perhaps saxophone. Collective improvisations, often guided by informal arrangements and a transparent triadic underpinning, weave around a melody embellished by cornet; the trombone's line is low and deliberate, and the clarinet's is high and florid. On each beat, a piano, banjo, or guitar strikes a chord; drums also keep time; and a string bass, tuba, bass saxophone, or piano plays roots and fifths on beats 1 and 3 of 4/4 measures. Vocallike effects abound: blue notes, glissandi, growls, and wah-wah articulations. *Stop-time passages and *breaks interrupt explicit statements of the pulse. The repertory, based on blues, ragtime, marches, and popular songs, comprises numerous multithematic structures; all employ strong functional harmonic progressions, often in symmetrical antecedent and consequent constructions. See also Chicago jazz, Dixieland, Jazz.

Bibl.: Samuel B. Charters, *Jazz: New Orleans (1885–1963)* (New York: Oak, 1963). Martin Williams, *Jazz Masters of New Orleans* (New York: Macmillan, 1967). Gunther Schuller, *Early Jazz* (New York: Oxford U Pr, 1968). Al Rose and Edmond Souchon, *New Orleans Jazz,* 3rd ed. (Baton Rouge: La U Pr, 1984). B.K.

New wave. A general designation for the *rock music played by numerous English and American bands since the late 1970s. The term is applied to a variety of styles whose direct antecedent was *punk rock but whose forms and rhythms derive directly from the *rock and roll of the 1950s and 60s. New wave began in pubs and small clubs as a rejection of the self-consciousness of *heavy metal and *art rock in favor of a return to simpler forms. Notable exponents include Elvis Costello, Graham Parker, Dave Edmunds, Patti Smith, the Talking Heads, and Brian Eno.

Bibl.: Caroline Coon, *1988: The New Wave Punk Rock Explosion* (New York: Hawthorn, 1978). P.T.W.

New World Symphony [Cz. *Z Nového světa,* From the New World]. Dvořák's Ninth Symphony (formerly no. 5) in E minor op. 95 (1893). It was composed during Dvořák's residence in the U.S. and employs some melodies modeled on traditional African American melodies but does not actually quote any.

New Zealand. Great Britain annexed the country in 1839, and Englishmen and Scots colonized it, partly displacing the native Maoris. The settlers cultivated choral music from the beginning. Bands—first military, then volunteer—gave the earliest concerts and by the 1870s were present in virtually every town. Opera, most often performed by small touring companies, began to dominate musical life in the 1860s. The country's first professional orchestra was the Exhibition Orchestra of the Christchurch Exhibition of 1906–7, conducted by Alfred Hill (1870–1960), a composer born in New Zealand.

The principal patron of music today is the New Zealand Broadcasting Corporation (founded 1925). The National Orchestra (now the New Zealand Symphony Orchestra) was founded in 1946 as part of the company's restructuring, although it had supported several regional orchestras from the 1920s. The New Zealand Symphony has been an independent, Crown-owned entity since 1988. Other professional orchestras now exist in Auckland, Wellington, Dunedin, and Christchurch. Both the New Zealand Chamber Orchestra and the New Zealand String Quarter were founded in 1987, a result of a chamber music federation formed during the 1980s. Operatic institutions in New Zealand had several starts and stutters throughout the 20th century, but several solid companies were formed in the 1980s and 1990s, including the National Opera of Wellington, the Canterbury Opera, and Opera New Zealand. Composers born in the first half of the 20th century include Douglas Lilburn (b. 1915), who established an electronic studio at Victoria University (Wellington) in 1966, Edwin Carr (b. 1926), David Farquhar (b. 1928), Gillian Whitehead (b. 1941), Jack Body (b. 1944), and Lyell Cresswell (b. 1944).

The last three decades of the 20th century saw a dramatic increase in composition and performance, as well as in the institutions that support these activities. The New Zealand International Festival of the Arts has been held biennially in Wellington since 1986, and the Arts Council of New Zealand/Toi Aotearoa regularly commissions works and sponsors concerts. The Composers' Association of New Zealand (1974), the Composers' Foundation (1981), and the New Zealand Music Centre (1991) are also important institutions in this regard. Finally, the national radio network known as Concert FM has consistently championed New Zealand music and performers. The younger generation of composers has been largely trained in New Zealand, benefiting from the increased educational and professional opportunities. Notable figures are Christopher Norton (b. 1953) and Gareth Farr (b. 1968).

For ethnic musics, see Oceania and Australia.

Bibl.: John M. Thomson, *Biographical Dictionary of New Zealand Composers* (Wellington: Victoria U Pr, 1990). John M. Thomson, *The Oxford History of New Zealand Music* (Auckland: Oxford U Pr, 1991). Adrienne Simpson, *Opera's Farthest Frontier: A History of Professional Opera in New Zealand* (Auckland: Reed, 1996).

Ney [Turk.]. See *Nāy.*

Nibelungenring [Ger.]. See *Ring des Nibelungen, Der.*

Nighthorn. **Nachthorn.*

Nightingale, The [Russ. *Solovey;* Fr. *Le rossignol*]. Opera ("musical fairy tale") in three acts by Stravinsky (libretto by the composer and Stepan Mitusov, after Hans Christian Andersen), produced in Paris (in French) in 1914. Setting: China. Stravinsky adapted it for the ballet *Le chant du rossignol* (The Song of the Nightingale; choreography by Leonide Massine, scenery and costumes by Henri Matisse), produced in Paris in 1920.

Night on Bald Mountain [Russ. *Ivanova noch' na Lisoy Jore,* St. John's Night on the Bare Mountain]. A symphonic poem by Musorgsky, inspired by the witches' Sabbath in Nikolai Gogol's story "St. John's Eve." Composed in 1867, it was revised and eventually incorporated into his unfinished opera **Sorochintsy Fair.* It is now usually performed in an orchestral adaptation by Rimsky-Korsakov of Musorgsky's original music.

Nights in the Gardens of Spain. See *Noches en los jardines de España.*

Nimmt [Ger.]. See *Nehmen.*

Ninfale [It.]. *Organetto.

Ninth. See Interval, Chord.

Niraval [Tel.]. A type of improvisation in Carnatic music [see South Asia] in which the pitches in the melodic setting of a text are varied while the original pattern of durations is maintained. C.C.

Noces, Les [Fr., The Wedding; originally Russ. *Svadebka*]. Four choreographic scenes by Stravinsky (choreography by Bronislava Nijinska; text by Stravinsky, after traditional Russian poems), produced in Paris in 1923. Two early orchestrations of the work were abandoned by Stravinsky; the published version is scored for chorus, soloists, 4 pianos, and 17 percussion instruments (including 4 timpani).

Noches in los jardines de España [Sp., Nights in the Gardens of Spain]. Three symphonic impressions for piano and orchestra by Falla, composed in 1911–15: (1) *En el Generalife* (In the Generalife); (2) *Danza lejana* (Distant Dance); (3) *En los jardines de la Sierra de Córdoba* (In the Gardens of the Sierra de Córdoba).

Nocturn. A component of the Office of Matins [see Office, Divine].

Nocturne [Fr., of the night; Ger. *Nachtstück;* It. *notturno*]. The title for certain instrumental works of the 19th and 20th centuries, typically for solo piano; such works do not in general derive from the 18th-century genre of ensemble music termed the **notturno.* The title was first used in 1812 by John Field, whose 18 Nocturnes employed the texture commonly associated with the repertory: a lyrical melody accompanied by broken chords pedaled to collect the harmonies. Chopin's 21 Nocturnes are the best-known examples. Many other pieces whose titles connect them with evocations of night lie outside this tradition of piano writing, e.g., Debussy's **Nocturnes* for orchestra.

Bibl.: Walter Krueger, *Das Nachtstück* (Munich: Katzbichler, 1971). Nicholas Temperley, "John Field and the First Nocturne," *ML* 56 (1975): 335–40.

Nocturnes. Three orchestral pieces by Debussy, composed in 1897–99: *Nuages* (Clouds); *Fêtes* (Festivals); *Sirènes* (Sirens), with women's voices.

Node. With respect to any single mode of vibration of a vibrating string, a point at which the string is stationary [see Acoustics II].

No drama. See *Noh.*

Noeane, noeagis. Combinations of syllables and the melodies set to them found in *tonaries and related treatises of the 9th through the 12th centuries where they serve to characterize each of the eight *modes. Both syllables and melodies are derived from the eight modal intonation formulas or *enechemata* [see *Ēchos*] of *Byzantine chant. Permutations of *noeane* (e.g., *nonenoeane, noannoeane*) serve for the authentic modes, and *noeagis* serves for the plagal modes, whereas in the Greek versions there is a separate combination of syllables for each mode. The Western formulas conclude with an added melisma or **neuma,* though some sources also preserve versions without melismas.

Bibl.: Michel Huglo, *Les tonaires* (Paris: Société française de musicologie, 1971), pp. 383–90.

Noël [Fr., fr. Lat. *natalis,* of birth]. (1) A semireligious Christmas song or *carol of French origin, its text strophic, written in the vernacular, and popular in character. From the 16th century onward, most *noëls* were associated with the Nativity, although their antecedents and relatives include songs used in pre-Christian celebrations and pieces connected with other Christian feasts.

Collections of *noëls*—usually texts only, but sometimes also melodies (rarely polyphony)—were printed in great numbers from the 16th to the 18th centuries. These publications incorporated both newly written and preexisting *noëls.* In collections without music, *timbres* (melodies to which the texts could be sung) were often suggested; these might include plainchant, dances, or song melodies drawn from the music popular at the time—e.g., chansons, *airs de cour,* and *vaudevilles.*

(2) From the latter half of the 17th century, an instrumental piece in the spirit of a vocal *noël,* commonly designed to be played during the Christmas service. Most such *noëls* are for keyboard instruments, particularly the organ; a few are for instrumental ensembles. Many consist chiefly of variations on currently popular *noël* melodies. Composers of keyboard *noëls* include Nicolas-Antoine Lebègue, Jean-François Dandrieu, Louis-Claude Daquin, and Jean-Jacques Beauvarlet-Charpentier. *Noëls* for instrumental ensemble were written by Marc-Antoine Charpentier, Michel-Richard de Lalande, Michel Corrette, and others. With the French Revolution, production of *noëls* stopped, but the genre was revived in the late 19th century. Notable composers of instrumental *noëls* since that time include César Franck, Alexandre Guilmant, and Charles Tournemire.

Bibl.: Jean-Baptiste Weckerlin, *La chanson populaire* (Paris, 1886). Julien Tiersot, *Histoire de la chanson populaire en France* (Paris, 1889). Frédérik Hellouin, *Le noël musical français* (Paris: Joanin, 1906). Adrienne F. Block, *The Early French Parody Noël* (Ann Arbor: UMI Res Pr, 1983).

Noh [Jap., ability]. A Japanese music and dance theater based on philosophical concepts drawn from Zen Buddhism and founded by Zeami Motokiyo (1363–1443) under the patronage of the shogun Ashikago Yoshimitsu.

A *noh* play is performed by *shite* (principal actor), *waki* (supporting actor), several minor actors (*tsure* and *wakizure*), a chorus of about eight who sit on stage left, and an accompanying instrumental ensemble *(hayashi).* The *hayashi,* whose members sit on the stage, play various instruments: a *nōkan* (transverse bamboo flute with seven holes), a *kotsuzumi* (shoulder-held hourglass drum), an *ōtsuzumi* (side-held hourglass drum), and a *taiko* (shallow barrel drum played with two sticks).

Noh plays are divided into five basic categories according to their plots and characters: god plays, warrior plays, woman plays, madwoman plays, and plays on miscellaneous subjects. A *noh* play has one or two acts, and in a two-act play the *shite* assumes a different character in each act. In present-day practice, a complete program of *noh* usually contains five plays with three short humorous plays or *kyōgin* (mad words) inserted between them.

The *shite,* who usually wears a mask, and the *waki,* who does not, both deliver their lines in songs *(fushi)* and in heightened speech *(kotoba),* while the chorus, who also sing or recite in unison, provide commentaries on the drama. There are two main singing styles: the *yowagin* (soft), and the *tsuyogin* (strong). Arias in soft style are built around three principal tones (*jo,* High Tone, *chū,* Middle Tone, and *ge,* Low Tone) a perfect fourth apart. Arias in strong style have two tonal centers (*jo* and *chū* fall on the same tone, and *ge*) a minor third apart.

The instruments play preludes to the drama and accompany the entrance of the actors, the *shite*'s climactic dance, and the final chorus. In addition to playing their instruments, the drummers often exclaim syllables such as "yio" and "hah" that constitute an integral part of the music.

Rhythmic structure is governed by the position of a varying number of textual syllables over an eight-beat framework arranged in the following ways: *ōnori,* one syllable to each beat; *chūnori,* two syllables to each beat; and *hiranori,* 12 syllables, numbers 1, 4, 7, and 12 being one beat each and the remainder each only one-half beat long.

In general, each act of a *noh* play is divided into several distinct sections: instrumental prelude, appearance of the *waki, shidai* (musical representations of the *waki*), *michiyuki* (entrance music for the *shite*), *issei* ("first song" of the *shite*), *sashi* (recitative), *mondō* (dialogue), *kuri* (lyrical song), *kuse* (*shite*'s climactic dance), *rongi* (discussion), and *kiri* (concluding song by the chorus). See also East Asia II.

I.K.F.W.

Noire [Fr.]. Quarter *note.

Nola [Lat.]. A small bell. See also *Cymbalum.*

Nomos [Gr., lit. law or custom]. In ancient Greek music, either an accompanied song or an instrumental piece for aulos or kithara. *Nomoi* were used as tests in musical compositions. The *nomos* had a culmination in the radical and controversial compositions of Timotheus of Milet (ca. 450–360 B.C.E.). A.B.

None. See Office, Divine.

Nonet [Fr. *nonette;* Ger. *Nonett;* It. *nonetto;* Sp. *noneto*]. (1) A composition for nine solo performers. There are relatively few examples. Spohr's op. 31, for string quartet, double bass, and winds, was the 19th-century model. In the 20th century, Webern, Bax, Milhaud, Villa-Lobos, Piston, Eisler, Gerhard, and Copland wrote for various combinations of nine instruments under various titles. (2) An ensemble of nine solo performers.

Nonharmonic tones. In *harmonic analysis, dissonant tones understood as embellishing otherwise consonant harmonies; also embellishing tones. Such tones can almost always be explained in terms of the dissonance treatment embodied in the principles of counterpoint [for examples of specific types, see Counterpoint II] and are components of some of the most conventional harmonies of Western tonal music, e.g., the seventh in dominant seventh chords. The term should be understood as implying, not that such a tone is in any way not a part of the harmony, but that the most fundamental structural level of tonal music is wholly consonant and that dissonance is to be analyzed as occurring at a structural level closer to the musical surface or foreground [see also Schenker analysis].

Nonnengeige [Ger., nun's fiddle]. **Tromba marina.*

Norma. Opera in two acts by Bellini (libretto by Felice Romani, after Alexandre Soumet's play *Norma*), produced in Milan in 1831. Setting: Gaul during the Roman occupation, ca. 50 B.C.E.

Norteño [Sp.]. See *Música norteña.*

Norway. I. *Contemporary institutions.* Musical life flourished in Norway during the 20th century. The annual Bergen International Festival is foremost among the many music festivals in Norway, including those at Harstad, Kristiansand, Trondheim, Elverum, Vestfold, and Risør. In addition to the nation's two major orchestras, the Bergen Philharmonic Orchestra (roots to 1765) and the Oslo Philharmonic Orchestra (1919), the government funds five other orchestras, notably those at Trondheim and Stavanger. The Norwegian Radio Orchestra is based in Oslo, as are the National Opera (founded 1959), the Norwegian State Academy of Music (1973), and an outgrowth of that institution, the Oslo Sinfonietta (1986). Since the 1970s, governmental support of music has increased, resulting in a fine network of lower-level schools and five regional conservatories. The Norwegian Music Information Center (1979) has been an important resource for Norwegian composers, and several smaller groups and chamber orchestras are funded by the Norwegian Cultural Council, including the Norwegian Chamber Orchestra (1975). In 1977 a group of composers founded the association and ensemble for contemporary music Ny Musikk.

II. *History.* The earliest signs of musical activity in Norway are the S-shaped **lur* trumpets that survive from the Bronze Age. The advent of Christianity in the 11th century brought the Gregorian liturgy, including 12th-century chants for St. Olaf, the nation's patron saint. The "Nobilis humilis" hymn for St. Magnus, thought to have originated in the Orkney Islands, is frequently cited as the earliest Norwegian polyphony. Much of this earlier liturgical music was banned and lost after 1537, when the Reformation brought about the use of psalters such as Thomissøn's *Psalmebog* (1569), Jesperssøn's *Graduale* (1573), and later Kingo's *Graduale* (1699). Secular art music waned as Norwegian courts declined in importance after the nation was united with Denmark in 1380, but it received new impetus during the 18th century, with composers such as Johan David Berlin (1714–87) and his son Johan Heinrich Berlin (1741–1807). The separation from Denmark in 1814 and subsequent union with Sweden (1814–1905) coincided with a rise of nationalistic sentiment that found expression in music inspired by folk music and folklore such as that of Waldemar Thrane (1790–1828), Halfdan Kjerulf (1815–68), Thomas Tellefsen (1823–74), and in the more international Romantic idiom of Martin Andreas Udbye (1820–89), Johan Svendsen (1840–1911), Edvard Grieg (1843–1907), Agathe Backer-Grøndahl (1847–1907), and Christian Sinding (1856–1941). Although the Romantic style was carried into the 20th century by Hjalmar Borgström (1864–1925), Johann Halvorsen (1864–1935), and Halfdan Cleve (1879–1951), French impressionism influenced the music of Alf Hurum (1882–1972), Pauline Hall (1890–1969), and David Monrad Johansen (1888–1974). Many composers of the 20th century sought ways to combine folk music and contemporary musical techniques: Johansen, Ludvig Irgens Jensen (1894–1969), Bjarne Brustad (1895–1978), Harald Saeverud (1897–1977), Eivind Groven (1901–92), Sparre Olsen (b. 1903), Klaus Egge (1906–79), and Geirr Tveitt (1908–81). Also significant from this era are Fartein Valen (1887–1952), Finn Mortensen (1922–83), Egil Hovland (b. 1924), Arne Nordheim (b. 1931), Knut Nystedt (b. 1915), and Johan Kvandal (1919–99). Notable postwar composers include Kåre Kolberg (b. 1936), Alfred Janson (b. 1937), Ragnar Søderlind (b. 1945), Olav Anton Thommessen (b. 1946), Lasse Thoresen (b. 1949), Cecilie Ore (b. 1954), Rolf Wallin (b. 1957), Nils Henrik Asheim (b. 1960), and Glenn Erik Haugland (b. 1961).

III. *Folk music.* The predominance of religious songs in Norwegian vocal folk music is a remnant of the nation's powerful religious fervor during the 18th and 19th centuries. Many of these unambiguously diatonic tunes are descended from Kingo's 1699 *Graduál.* The rural *lokk* cattle calls, usually sung by women, comprise speaking, shouting, and long vocal melismas. Other significant song types are the lullabies of the southwest, and the popular, balladlike *stev* poetry. The nation's instrumental music employs such instruments as the *halmpipe,* the *seljefløyte* fipple flute, the modern violin, and, until recently, the **langleik* zither. Of particular significance in western and central Norway is the dance-music repertory of the **hardingfele* (hardanger fiddle), a violinlike instrument with a complement of sympathetic strings. Important folk dances are the duple-meter **halling* and *gangar* and the triple-meter *springar, springleik,* and *pols.* Folk music rose in the national consciousness during the late 20th century, aided by the 1978 federation of amateur folk music organizations into the Council for Music Organizations, an entity that supports folk music concerts and festivals nationwide.

Bibl.: Kristian Lange and Arne Östvedt, *Norwegian Music: A Brief Survey* (London: Dobson, 1958). Olav Gurvin, ed., *Norsk folkemusikk,* 5 vols. (Oslo: Universitet, 1958–67). Nils Grinde, *Norsk musikk historie* (Oslo: Universitet, 1971; 2nd ed., 1975). John H. Yoell, *The Nordic Sound* (Boston: Crescendo Pub Co, 1974). Reidar Sevåg, "Geige und Geigenmusik in Norwegen," *Die Geige in der europäischen Volksmusik,* ed. Walter Deutsch and Gerlinde Haid (Vienna: A Schendl, 1975), pp. 89–101. Nils Grinde, *Contemporary Norwegian Music 1920–80* (London: Universitetsforlaget, 1981). Kjell Habbestad and Kjell Skyllstad, eds., *Norsk samtiddsmusikk gjennom 25 år* (25 Years of Contemporary Norwegian Music) (Oslo: Norsk Komponistforening, 1992). Rolf Wallin, "Wired for Sound: Electro-Acoustic Music in Norway," *Nordic Sounds* 1 (1995): 6–10. Steinar Ofsdal, *Norsk folkemusikk og folkedans: En veiledning for lærere* (Oslo: Grappa Musikkforlag, 2001).

Nose flute. A flute blown through the nose instead of the mouth. The player blows with one nostril only, plugging the other with a finger or some material. *Transverse, *duct, and *globular flutes may be nose-blown. Nose flutes are important in Polynesia and Melanesia, where they have magical and ritual significance.

Nota cambiata [It.]. See Counterpoint II, 7.

Notation. Any means of writing down music.

I. *Current Western notation.* The system of musical notation now most widely in use specifies in varying degrees all four of the components of any musical sound: pitch (or lack of it), duration (and thus rhythm as well as some aspects of *articulation), timbre, and loudness (including changes in loudness over time and some aspects of articulation). The system is principally concerned with pitch and duration, which are represented along a kind of graph. Pitch is notated on the vertical axis, corresponding to its intuitive perception as high or low, and duration along the horizontal axis from left to right. Degrees of pitch are marked on the vertical axis by means of five horizontally parallel lines termed a *staff (pl. staves). Two or more parallel staves increase the range of pitches specifiable (or separate different strands of the composition, termed voices, perhaps played or sung by different performers; see Score). On each staff, a *clef fixes the location of one particular pitch and thus, by extension, determines that of each line or space. *Ledger lines locate pitches lying above or below any staff. The lines and spaces of the staff, in combination with any clef, indicate only the *diatonic scale that underlies Western tonal music. The structure and importance of this scale are reflected in the design of the piano *keyboard, where the scale is embodied in the white keys, and in the nomenclature for pitch, which assigns the first seven letters of the alphabet to the repeating pattern of the white keys alone. Pitches corresponding to the black keys must be indicated with reference to one or another white key by means of an *accidental or a *key signature. Thus, the lines or spaces alone can specify only pitches with the names A through G; e.g., a pitch such as B-flat must be indicated on the staff with the aid of a flat sign (♭).

When any given pitch is to be notated, the rounded head of a symbol termed a *note is placed on the appropriate line or space, preceded by an accidental if necessary. The duration of the pitch is determined by the particular shape and coloring of the note. Silence is specified by means of a rest [see Note]. There are seven basic values of notes and rests, each twice as long as the next smaller value. Other durations are created in a variety of ways. A dot following a note or rest increases its value by one-half. Two or more different values may be joined together by means of curved lines termed ties in order to form a single duration. Notes may be grouped together to form subdivisions other than duple subdivisions of some larger value, e.g., groups of three equal notes are termed triplets and are indicated by placing the number 3 above or below the group. For ease of reading, groups of notes of the same value that ordinarily employ one or more flags may be written with a corresponding number of beams (relatively thick, solid lines) connecting their stems. Partly for ease of reading, but principally because Western tonal music employs both pitch and duration in such a way as to produce recurring patterns of *meter, vertical lines, termed *bar lines, running through the staff or staves mark off a fixed number of some note-value or the equivalent duration. The total duration between adjacent bar lines is termed a *measure or bar.

This system fixes durations only with respect to one another. The absolute duration of any note or rest is a matter of *tempo, i.e., the rate per unit of time at which some particular value (and thus each of the remaining values) is to be performed. This rate is often indicated rather informally by words in Italian or other languages, e.g., *allegro, langsam,* slow. It may, however, be made precise by a *metronome marking, e.g., quarter note = 120 per minute. Tempo, however, may be varied [see Rubato] even over short spans, and tradition and taste will often dictate greater or lesser departures from the precise durations reflected in the available notes and rests. In these respects, duration in Western art music is considerably more susceptible of nuance in performance than pitch, with the result that the notation of duration is, with respect to actual performance, rather crude. The principal respect in which pitch in performance is likely to deviate from its notation is in *ornamentation, generally the addition of notes to those specified as notes. Although there are many supplementary symbols for specifying ornaments rather unambiguously, the practice of unnotated ornamentation has been widespread in some periods. Musical notation, therefore, is like any other sort of text in requiring realization by a reader who brings to bear on it an accumulation of habits and experience. In music, this accumulation is termed *performance practice. No example of musical notation is in this sense transparent and self-sufficient. Because the habits and experience of musicians change with time and place, the music of every period and place requires attention to performance practice.

The specification of timbre is largely a matter of specifying the intended instruments or voices. Some instruments, however, have traditionally been capable of a variety of timbres, and 20th-century composers have demanded greatly expanded timbral variety on instruments in general. The organ and harpsichord achieve considerable variety by means of *registration. Bowed stringed instruments have traditionally employed techniques of *bowing for this purpose, as well as *mutes. Brass instruments regularly make use of mutes, and the French horn in addition employs *stopped tones.

Loudness is least precisely specified, being left in the main, like tempo, to a relatively small number of words and abbreviations. Those employed for loudness, together with some related symbols, are termed *dynamic marks. These and other *performance marks, along with the principal elements of the notation of pitch and duration, are illustrated in Ex. 1.

II. *History.* The notation of classical Greece was a *letter notation [see also Greece I, 4], and notations of this type were again used, principally for theoretical and pedagogical purposes, in the Middle Ages. They are related to systems of *solmization and pitch names [see also Gamut, Guidonian hand, Hexachord]. The earliest surviving notation to employ a staff for fixing pitch occurs in the treatise **Musica enchiriadis* of ca. 900. Here, syllables of the sung text were written in the spaces corresponding to appropriate pitches as indicated on the left by the symbols of *Daseian notation. The history of current musical notation, however, begins in the 11th century with the development of a diastematic notation (i.e., notation that is precise with respect to pitch) that represents pitch on a vertical axis by means of the precise spacing of notational symbols. This development and the related pitch nomenclature are often associated with Guido d'Arezzo. Since about the 9th century, various types of *neume had been employed in the notation of liturgical chant. In general, neumatic notations indicated the approximate contour of a melody and thus served as an aid to the memory. Aquitanian neumes of the 11th century, however, arranged dots carefully around a real or imagined horizontal line. In time more lines were added, and the staff with four lines and a clef became common. By about 1200, square-shaped neumes similar to those still employed in some liturgical books became standard [see ill. under Neume].

Neumatic notations seem not to have indicated durations precisely, though this has been a subject of controversy [see also Gregorian chant V]. By the 13th century, however, square neumes began to be used for polyphony and for secular melodies [see especially Troubadour, Trouvère]. In sacred polyphony, especially that of *Notre Dame, certain of the neumes, termed *ligatures, were employed to indicate dura-

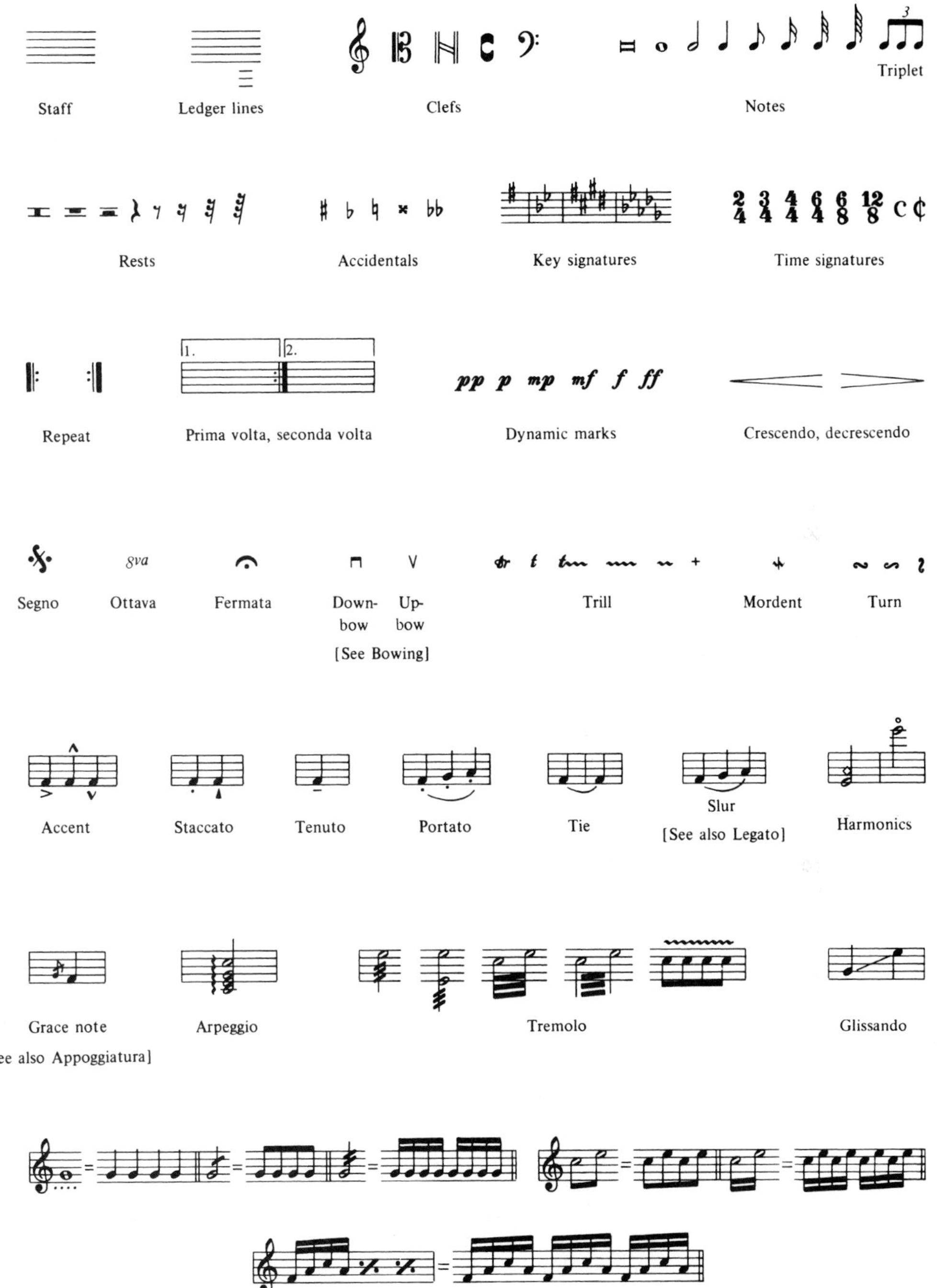

1. Commonly used notational symbols [see separate entry for each].

2. MS F, fol. 167.

3. MS Mo, fol. 292.

4. Machaut MS E, fol. 131.

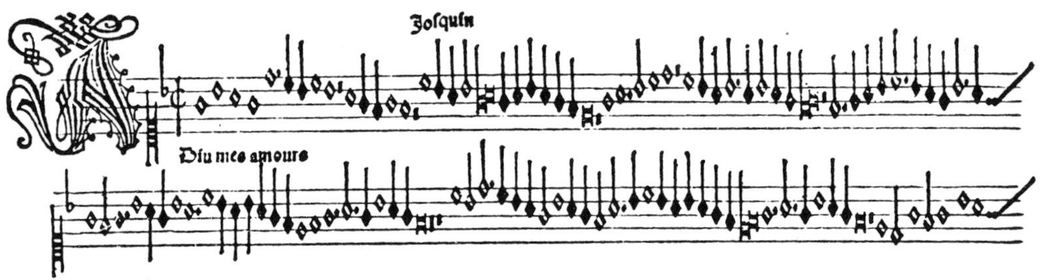

5. *Odhecaton,* fol. 16v.

tions based on the rhythmic modes [see Modes, rhythmic, and Ex. 2]. This is the first Western notation to indicate durations with any precision. Only in the later 13th century, however, did a set of notes with precisely assigned values emerge. This marks the beginning of *mensural (i.e., measurable) notation, a development most often associated with the theorist Franco of Cologne [see Ex. 3; see also Theory].

Franco's notation relied on a triple subdivision of note-values. Early in the 14th century, Philippe de Vitry extended the system to include more note-values and both duple and triple subdivisions [see also *Ars nova*]. This formed the basis of the mensural notation in use through the 16th century and of the system of note-values still in use [Exx. 4 and 5]. In 14th-century Italy, a somewhat different system for notating durations developed [Ex. 6], some features of which were adopted into a predominantly French notation in the late 14th century [see *Ars subtilior*].

In the mid-15th century, mensural notation became somewhat simpler except for occasional *proportions. Longer note-values, instead of being black, began to be written with hollow (void, white) heads, as they are today. By the early 17th century, most of the remaining features of white mensural notation that distinguish it from the notation now in use had largely disappeared. These include the use of triple subdivisions; *partbook and *choirbook formats instead of *score format; the absence of bar lines; the incomplete specification of accidentals [see *Musica ficta*]; the use of angular note-heads instead of rounded ones (though rounded ones can be found as early as the 15th cen-

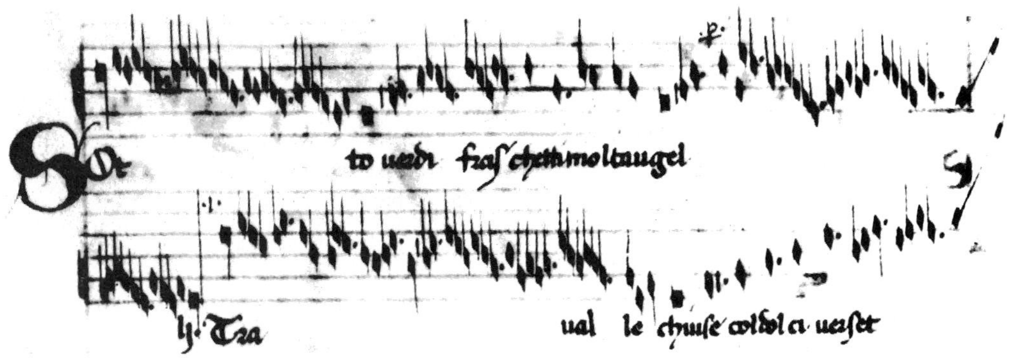

6. MS Pan, fol. 88v.

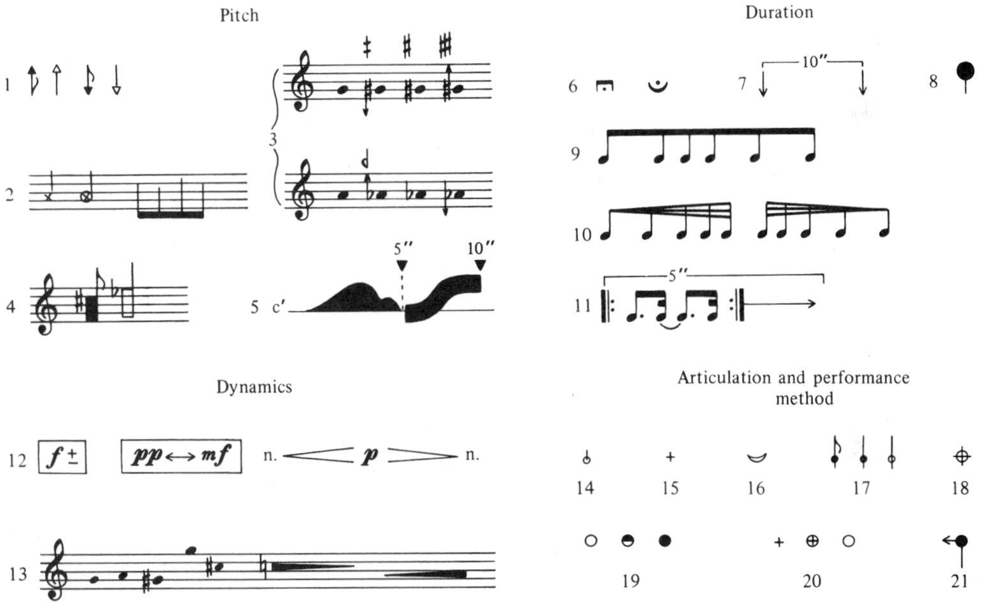

7. Twentieth-century notational symbols.

(1) Highest or lowest possible pitch. (2) Approximate pitch. (3) Quarter tones. (4) Tone clusters with specified range and duration. (5) Tone clusters for ensemble with varying and approximate range and duration. (6) Long and short fermata. (7) Duration between two points. (8) Beginning of unconducted passage. (9) Approximate duration represented by distance. (10) Beamed accelerando and ritardando. (11) Repeat for specified duration. (12) Fluctuating dynamics (n. = It. *niente,* nothing). (13) Loudness, decrescendo, and crescendo represented by note size. (14) Snap pizzicato. (15) Left-hand pizzicato. (16) Pluck with fingernail. (17) Notes for blowing through wind instruments. (18) Damp strings. (19) Open, half-open, and closed valve or key. (20) Stopped, half-stopped, and open tones for horn. (21) Smack or kiss tone for brass and winds.

tury). The 15th and 16th centuries also saw the rise of *tablatures, notations designed for certain instruments.

Although there have been proposals for a general reform of notation, none has gained wide acceptance. Some notations with didactic aims, e.g., *shape-note notation, have been widely adopted. *Braille notation is available for the blind. Some 20th-century music required the creation of numerous new notational symbols, as yet standardized to only a limited degree [Ex. 7; see also Stone, 1980]. The notation of some electronic music has necessarily gone further afield (though it does not usually serve as the basis for performance, as conventional notation does). *Graphic

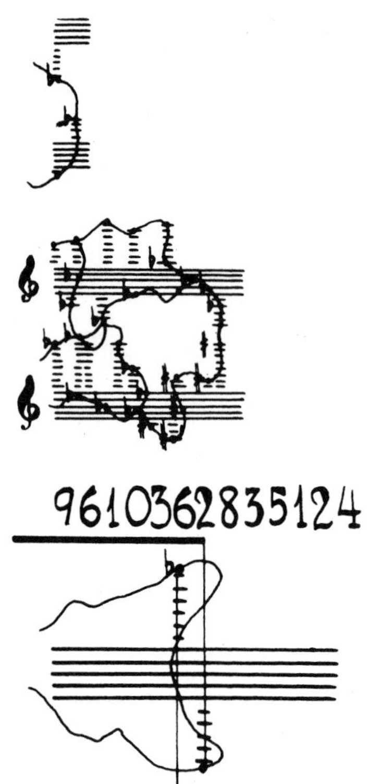

8. John Cage, excerpt from the piano part for *Concert for Piano and Orchestra* (1957–58), © 1960 by Henmar Press, Inc. Used by permission.

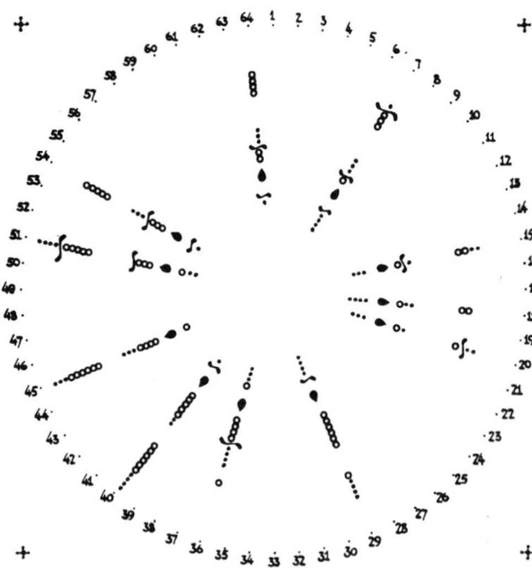

9. Robert Ashley, excerpt from *in memoriam . . . CRAZY HORSE (symphony),* published by Composer/Performer Edition. Used by permission of the composer.

notations may make little or no use of conventional symbols [see Exx. 8 and 9].

III. *Non-Western notations.* Western art music has relied on notation much more than any other music. This is related to the traditional Western view of the musical work of art as the unique historical creation of the composer, set down on paper for all times, and merely reproduced by performers. Such a view is not entirely satisfactory even for Western art music, but it is wholly inapplicable to the musics of many other cultures in which the role of the performer is primary, and the notion of a composer may have little or no importance. Cultures that distinguish between art music and popular music and those that have a body of music theory are most likely to have notation, if only for theoretical or didactic purposes, as in Arabic-speaking cultures. Perhaps the earliest to survive is from *Mesopotamia. The musical cultures of China, Japan, Korea, and India have all made extensive use of notation, often based on solmization syllables of a kind, sometimes with supplementary signs for duration and performance technique, and with instrumental tablatures playing a prominent role. Notation was used in China by the 6th century and underwent considerable development in the 10th [see East Asia]. Perhaps soon thereafter, a neumatic notation was developed in Tibet. A notation based on Sanskrit syllables survives in India from the 13th century, and letter notation is employed in Arabic theory of the same period. By perhaps the 16th century, a notation was in use for *gamelan* music in *Southeast Asia. The 19th century saw the development of more notations for non-Western music, many under the influence of Western notation.

Bibl.: Hugo Riemann, *Studien zur Geschichte der Notenschrift* (Leipzig: Breitkopf & Härtel, 1878; rev. ed. 1970). C. F. Abdy Williams, *The Story of Notation* (New York: C Scribner's Sons, 1903; R: Detroit: Singing Tree, 1968). Johannes Wolf, *Geschichte der Mensural-Notation von 1250–1460,* 3 vols. (Leipzig: Breitkopf & Härtel, 1904; R: Hildesheim: Olms, 1965). Id., *Handbuch der Notationskunde,* 2 vols. (Leipzig: Breitkopf & Härtel, 1913–19; R: Hildesheim: Olms, 1963). Willi Apel, *The Notation of Polyphonic Music, 900–1600* (Cambridge, Mass.: Mediaeval Acad, 1942; 5th ed., 1953). Carl Parrish, *The Notation of Medieval Music* (New York: Norton, 1957). Howard Boatwright, *Handbook on Staff Notation for Indian Music* (Bombay: B V Bhavan, 1960). Charles Hamm, *A Chronology of the Works of Guillaume Dufay Based on a Study of Mensural Practice* (Princeton: Princeton U Pr, 1964). Gardner Read, *Music Notation: A Manual of Modern Practice* (Boston: Allyn & Bacon, 1964; 2nd ed., 1969). Walter Kaufmann, *Musical Notations of the Orient* (Bloomington: Ind U Pr, 1967; R: Gloucester, Mass.: Peter Smith, 1972). Arthur Mendel, "Some Ambiguities of the Mensural System," *Strunk,* 1968, pp. 137–60. J. A. Bank, *Tactus, Tempo and Notation in Mensural Music from the 13th to the 17th Century* (Amsterdam: Bank, 1972). Max Haas, *Byzantinische und Slavische Notationen* (Cologne: A Volk, 1973). Philip Gossett, "The Mensural System and the 'Choralis Constantinus,'" *Mendel,* 1974, pp. 71–107. Richard Rastall, *The Notation of Western Music* (London: Dent,

1982). Leo Treitler, "The Early History of Music Writing in the West," *JAMS* 35 (1982): 237–79. Id., "Reading and Singing: On the Genesis of Occidental Music-Writing," *Early Music History* 4 (1984): 135–208. Anna Maria Busse Berger, *Mensuration and Proportion Signs: Origins and Evolution* (New York: Oxford U Pr, 1993). Kenneth Levy, *Gregorian Chant and the Carolingians* (Princeton: Princeton U Pr, 1998). See also Neume.

New and reformed notation. Jacques Chailley, *Les notations musicales nouvelles* (Paris: Leduc, 1950). Erhard Karkoschka, *Das Schriftbild der neuen Musik* (Celle: Moeck, 1966; trans. Eng., New York: Praeger, 1972). Hugo Cole, *Sounds and Signs: Aspects of Musical Notation* (London: Oxford U Pr, 1974). Benjamin Boretz and Edward T. Cone, eds., *Perspectives on Notation and Performance* (New York: Norton, 1976). David Cope, *New Music Notation* (Dubuque, Iowa: Kendal/Hunt, 1976). Gerald Warfield, *Writings on Contemporary Music Notation: An Annotated Bibliography* (Ann Arbor: Music Library Assoc, 1976). Gardner Read, *Modern Rhythmic Notation* (Bloomington: Ind U Pr, 1978). Kurt Stone, *Music Notation in the Twentieth Century: A Practical Guidebook* (New York: Norton, 1980). D.M.R.

Note. A symbol used in musical notation to represent the duration of a sound and, when placed upon a staff, to indicate its pitch; more generally (especially in British usage), the pitch itself. Types of notes are classed and named according to the relationship of their durations to one another and are sometimes termed note-values. The symbol for indicating silence of a certain duration is termed a rest. The accompanying table gives the notes and rests in current use from largest to smallest, together with their names. Each note or rest is twice as long as the next smaller one. The European names for these notes are as follows. Whole: Brit. semibreve, Fr. *ronde,* Ger. *Ganze (Note),* It. *semibreve,* Sp. *redonda.* Half: Brit. minim, Fr. *blanche,* Ger. *Halbe (Note),* It. *bianca,* Sp. *blanca.* Quarter: Brit. crotchet, Fr. *noire* (quarter rest, *soupir*), Ger. *Viertel,* It. *nera,* Sp. *negra.* Eighth: Brit. quaver, Fr. *croche,* Ger. *Achtel,* It. *croma,* Sp. *corchea.* Sixteenth: Brit. semiquaver, Fr. *double-croche,* Ger. *Sechzehntel,* It. *semicroma,* Sp. *semicorchea.* Thirty-second: Brit. demisemiquaver, Fr. *triple-croche,* Ger. *Zweiunddreissigstel,* It. *biscroma,* Sp. *fusa.* Sixty-fourth: Brit. hemidemisemiquaver, Fr. *quadruple-croche,* Ger. *Vierundsechzigstel,* It. *semi-biscroma,* Sp. *semifusa.*

	Note name	Note	Rest
1.	Whole	𝅝	𝄻
2.	Half	𝅗𝅥	𝄼
3.	Quarter	𝅘𝅥	𝄽
4.	Eighth	𝅘𝅥𝅮	𝄾
5.	Sixteenth	𝅘𝅥𝅯	𝄿
6.	Thirty-second	𝅘𝅥𝅰	𝅀
7.	Sixty-fourth	𝅘𝅥𝅱	𝅁

For ways in which the durations and shapes of notes are sometimes modified and for the history of the notational and metrical systems to which they belong, see Notation, Mensural notation.

Note-against-note style. See Homophony.

Note nere [It., black notes]. A notational development seen in single pieces of the 1530s and advertised in madrigal collections in the 1540s. Under the mensuration sign C (instead of the normal ₵) the tactus is here on the semibreve rather than the breve; there are many semiminims and *fusae,* giving the page a "blackened" appearance. The notation was also called *cromatico* (colored). Conservative theorists disapproved of this novelty, but it became popular among madrigalists and was used even by the austere Cipriano de Rore (1542). The tempo of pieces in this notation is probably somewhat slower than that for music in ₵, but not half the speed; and if all the long values of the old notation are kept, the music has an added rhythmic level. Hence, the phenomenon is more than simple reduction of note-values. Use of blackened notes in the early *villanella* suggests a possible origin for *note nere.* After 1560, use of short values is absorbed into ₵, but the signature C survives for pieces of special character.

Bibl.: James Haar, "The *Note Nere* Madrigal," *JAMS* 18 (1965): 22–41. Don Harrán, ed., *The Anthologies of Black-Note Madrigals, CMM* 73 (1978–81). J.H.

Noter. See Appalachian dulcimer.

Note sensible [Fr.]. *Leading tone.

Notes inégales [Fr., unequal notes]. A performing convention that renders divisions of the beat in alternating long and short values, even if written in equal values, to add grace or liveliness to the music. It is documented in over 85 French treatises from 1550 to ca. 1810, the great majority and the most detailed dating 1690–1780. It is occasionally mentioned in sources from Italy, Spain, England, Holland, and Germany. In the earliest sources, it was usually presented as a way of adding beauty or interest to *diminutions. In our own day, it is so taken for granted in jazz as to be almost never mentioned; a composer or arranger who does not want it must specify "straight eighths" (cf. the 18th-century *croches égales*).

In 18th-century France, the verbs *pointer, piquer, lourer, passer,* and *inégaliser* could all mean "to make unequal," but all except the last had other meanings as well, and their application to inequality was a matter of disagreement. *Pointer* (to dot), the most common, was sometimes held to imply more extreme long and short values than *notes inégales* and sometimes equated with it. Besides *notes* or *croches égales,* terms for equality were *détacher, marteler,* and rarely *couler* (Lacassagne, 1766); all of these had their principal usage as terms of articulation. Italian terms like *andante* or *allegro* implied equality for some writers. No distinction in the application of inequality was made between vocal and instrumental media.

Inequality is usually defined as the alteration in performance of equal written values, but it was very often written out with dots, either as a general practice (Nicolas Gigault, Henry Purcell) or as a cautionary notation (François Couperin and many others). It is the musician's task to decide whether written dotting was meant to be distinguished from inequality—that is, taken literally or even exaggerated—or understood as *notes inégales,* with the expressive liberty of that convention. This was also a problem in the 18th century, recognized by a few theorists. The extent and application of inequality in music preceding the age of recording is disputed; between 1965 and 1970, a major controversy on the subject took place. At present, inequality is still largely ignored in jazz studies, more or less accepted by well-informed players in French Baroque music, treated with great caution and uncertainty in other Baroque music, and avoided in music from before and after that period.

The feature that distinguishes French discussions of inequality from others is the emphasis on the relation between the values to be made unequal and the meter or beat. From the later 17th century to the Revolution, the rule was that in duple meters, values a quarter of that designated by the denominator of the equivalent modern signature were unequal, and in triple and compound meters, values half that of the denominator were unequal [Ex. 1]. Where there were values smaller than those determined by this rule, inequality "descended" to the smaller ones, leaving the larger ones equal; this was relevant especially in courantes in 3/2 time, where the eighths and not the quarters were unequal. The treatment of ¢ depended on whether it was taken in four fast beats or two slow ones (a tempo between those implied by **C** and 2).

1

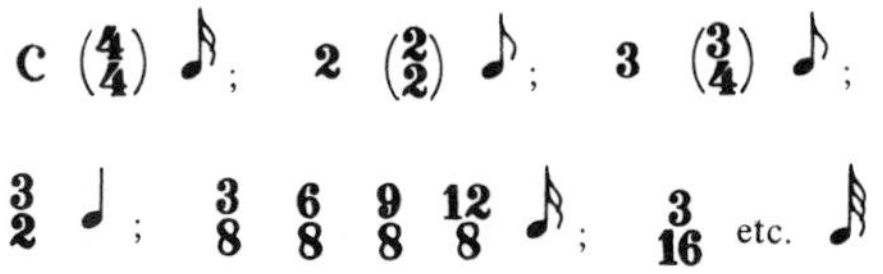

The degree of inequality (the ratio of lengths of the notes of each pair) varied, according to expression and tempo, from sharply dotted to barely perceptible. Occasionally specified (e.g., "les doubles croches un tant-soit-peu pointées" or "pointez fort"), this was usually left to the performer, for whom it was one of the chief problems in taste and expression.

The rules of inequality applied even if the first value of an eligible pair was a rest or a dot instead of a note [Ex. 2]. French inequality was normally long-short, but the short-long variety also existed [see Lombard rhythm]. Theorists do not discuss whether inequality was to be maintained with dogged consistency throughout a piece (as Bach wrote it in *Contrapunctus* 2 of his *Art of Fugue*), but the evidence is that here, too, there was much disagreement and individuality in playing styles. Although there was little disagreement between 1690 and 1780 that inequality was the norm in French music for eligible notes and equality the exception, its character was governed by the style and expressive message of the music and the taste of the moment.

2

The use of inequality was also governed by certain characteristics of the music. The rule with the most theoretical support stated that inequality applied only to predominantly conjunct passages and not to predominantly disjunct ones. Abundant instances of written dotting of disjunct passages, however, suggest that analogous undotted passages were or at least could be played unequally. Though in some cases such written dotting may be evidence that without it the passages would normally be played equally, music in which all the inequality is written out as a matter of consistent policy (e.g., Nicolas Gigault) shows no evidence of the confinement of inequality to conjunct motion. The so-called **style brisé* could also be freely dotted, as is shown by the numerous written examples among François Couperin's harpsichord pieces. Broken-chord accompaniments such as the *Alberti bass, however, were equal.

Some writers said that inequality did not apply to passages in which smaller values were mixed with the theoretically unequal ones. Their examples show that what was especially meant was a rhythmic pattern typical of subsidiary *couplets* of *chaconnes* and *passacailles* [Ex. 3]. In other cases, and perhaps here as well, the rule that inequality descended to the smallest moving values applied.

3

Eugène Borrel's much-copied list of features canceling inequality (1934) also included syncopated notes (from Lacassagne, 1766) and rests of the same value as the notes that would otherwise be unequal (apparently his own idea). Neither of these is generally valid. Borrel's rule (from a treatise of ca. 1810) that inequality is excluded from accompanying parts is also incorrect. Quantz's exclusion of repeated (by which he must have meant reiterated) notes and groupings of more than two notes under a slur has no support in French theory and is sometimes expressly refuted.

There was no body of inequality theory or pedagogy in other countries comparable to the French. A few writers recommended the alteration of equal notes under certain circumstances, e.g., Tomás de Santa María, Pietro Cerone, Giulio Caccini, Girolamo Frescobaldi, Roger North, Johann Joachim Quantz, C. P. E. Bach, Leonard Frischmuth, and Antonio Lorenzoni. Michel Corrette said that the eighths should be unequal in certain English popular songs in 6/4 time; Georg Muffat included the English and Netherlanders among those who followed Lully's performance method (he gave a detailed account of Lully's use of inequality); Hyacinthe Azaïs wrote in 1776 that foreigners (in or out of France?) played unequal eighths in 3/4 time.

It seems clear that although rhythmic alteration was practiced outside of France, it was not practiced systematically, and that if composers particularly desired a dotted effect, they wrote it. Foreign music influenced by French styles shows lavish dotting, furnishing valuable clues to the unwritten French practice. Purcell's music is particularly striking in this regard, but Italian music also has many instances, e.g., some of Corelli's allemandes and courantes. Occasionally Handel and Bach (and French composers as well) dotted only the first few notes of a part meant to be dotted throughout. Alessandro Scarlatti's *Marco Attilio Regolo* (1719) has an aria whose first section, in dotted notation, is marked *allegro alla francese* and whose second, in even notes, is headed simply *allegro.* There was broad though not unanimous agreement among the French, however, that Italian rhythms were to be played as written in the 18th century. This included typical Italianisms like Corelli's walking basses, even when incorporated into French pieces.

The only statement of a code of inequality by a non-Frenchman comparable to those by the French is that in Quantz's *Versuch* (1752), where he makes no mention of French music. Because Quantz was one of the most lucid and comprehensive writers on musical performance of the 18th century, his statement has received an extraordinary amount of attention and has in particular been applied to the music of Bach. Every possible argument for and against this application has been advanced in the controversy mentioned above, but not enough is known about the attitude of Bach and his German contemporaries toward the rhythmic alteration of their own music to permit any conclusions about Quantz's authority in that regard. The precision and completeness of Bach's own notation varied greatly; there can be no one key to the performance of his works. Bach knew French music well, at least on paper; he imitated it and was probably aware of its conventions. But whether, for example, he expected a sarabande in French style to be dotted in performance, as Dolmetsch and Donington would have it, no one can be sure. See also Dotted notes.

Bibl.: Arnold Dolmetsch, *The Interpretation of the Music of the XVIIth and XVIIIth Centuries* (London: Novello, 1915; R: Seattle: U of Wash Pr, 1969). Eugène Borrel, *L'interprétation de la musique française (de Lully à la Révolution)* (Paris: F Alkan, 1934; R: New York: AMS Pr, 1978). Newman Powell, "Rhythmic Freedom in the Performance of French Music from 1650 to 1735" (Ph.D. diss., Stanford Univ., 1958). Frederick Neumann, "The French *Inégales,* Quantz, and Bach," *JAMS* 18 (1965): 313–58. David Fuller, "The 'Dotted Style' in Bach, Handel, and Scarlatti," *Bach, Handel, Scarlatti: Tercentenary Essays,* ed. Peter Williams (Cambridge: Cambridge U Pr, 1985), pp. 99–117. David Fuller, "More on Triplets and Inequality," *EM* 15 (1987): 384–85. David Fuller, "Notes and *Inégales* Unjoined: Defending a Definition," *JM* 7 (1989): 21–28. Stephen E. Hefling, *Rhythmic Alteration in Seventeenth- and Eighteenth-Century Music:* Notes inégales *and Overdotting* (New York: Schirmer, 1993). David Fuller, "Gigault's Dots: Or, *Notes inégales* (wie sie eigentlich gewesen)," in *The Organist as Scholar: Essays in Memory of Russel Saunders,* ed. Kerala J. Snyder (Stuyvesant, N.Y.: Pendragon, 1994), pp. 47–76. Claire Fontijn, "Quantz's *unegal:* Implications for the Performance of 18th-Century Music," *EM* 23 (1995): 54–62. John Byrt, "Some New Interpretations of the *Notes inégales* Evidence," *EM* 28 (2000): 98–112. David Ledbetter, "On the Manner of Playing the Adagio: Neglected Features of a Genre," *EM* 29 (2001): 15–26. For a list of the early sources, see David Fuller, "Notes inégales," in *Grove 6,* 2nd ed. See also Ornamentation, Theory. D.F.

Notre Dame, repertory of. A body of music dedicated above all to the polyphonic categories of *organum, **conductus,* and *motet but including as well a small number of monophonic *conductus* and **rondeaux* [see also *Magnus liber organi*]. The chief sources for this music, which was written between ca. 1150 and ca. 1240, are the manuscripts W1, W2, and F [see Sources 4, 5, 6].

The chant-based organa, of which there are 110 for two voices *(dupla),* 28 for three *(tripla),* and 2 for four *(quadrupla),* are, with few exceptions, appropriate to Parisian cathedral liturgies of the 12th and 13th centuries. In addition to complete organa, W1 and F contain substantial numbers of independent discant sections or **clausulae.* F, the larger of these sources, has 462 such pieces for two voices, 13 for three, and 1 for four. The original or freely composed *conductus,* which by virtue of a preference for the melismatic type constitute a somewhat greater share of the repertory than the liturgical compositions, are similarly for two, three, and four voices (135, 57, and 3 examples, respectively). The youngest of the polyphonic categories, the motet, is most generously represented in W2. Of 200 such pieces, the majority are for two voices, their single texts in Latin or French.

Also to be counted as part of the repertory of Notre Dame are examples of the "late" or "second-epoch" *sequence, which first developed in Paris at both the cathedral and the Augustinian abbey of St. Victor in the 12th century. The most prominent figure in the creation of the late sequence, Adam "of St. Victor," was first the precentor of the cathedral and undoubtedly contributed to the repertory in both institutions.

Bibl.: Friedrich Ludwig, *Repertorium organorum recentioris et motetorum vetustissimi stili,* vol. 1, pt. 1 (Halle: Niemeyer, 1910); vol. 1, pt. 2 and vol. 2, ed. Friedrich Gennrich, Summa musicae medii aevi 7–8 (Langen bei Frankfurt: Gennrich, 1961–62); new ed., ed. Luther Dittmer (New York: Institute of Mediaeval Music, 1964–78). Margot E. Fassler, "The Role of the Parisian Sequence in the Evolution of Notre-Dame Polyphony," *Speculum* 62 (1987): 345–74. Craig Wright, *Music and Ceremony at Notre Dame of Paris, 500–1500* (Cambridge: Cambridge U Pr, 1989). Janet Knapp, "Polyphony at Notre Dame of Paris," *The New Oxford History of Music,* vol. 2: *The Early Middle Ages to 1300,* 2nd ed., ed. Richard Crocker and David Hiley (Oxford: Oxford U Pr, 1990), pp. 557–635. Rebecca A. Baltzer, "How Long Was Notre-Dame Organum Performed?" in *Beyond the Moon: Festschrift Luther Dittmer,* ed. Bryan Gillingham and Paul Merkley (Ottawa: Institute of Mediaeval Music, 1990), pp. 118–43. Andreas Traub, "Das Ereignis Notre Dame," in *Die Musik des Mittelalters* (Laaber: Laaber Verlag, 1991), pp. 239–71. Rebecca A. Baltzer, "The Geography of the Liturgy at Notre-Dame of Paris," in *Plainsong in the Age of Polyphony,* ed. Thomas Forrest Kelly (Cambridge: Cambridge U Pr, 1992), pp. 45–64. J.K.

Notturno [It.]. (1) *Nocturne. (2) An instrumental (occasionally vocal) work intended for performance at night. In the 18th century, most instrumental notturnos were evidently meant to be performed by soloists rather than orchestrally, including Mozart's K. 286/269a (for four sextets, each consisting of two horns and strings) and his *Eine kleine Nachtmusik* (*Nachtmusik* being the German equivalent of *notturno*). Other well-known examples are Haydn's notturnos for two *lire organizzate* (*hurdy-gurdies), two clarinets, two horns, two violas, and bass Hob. II:25–32. Notturnos range in length from two to six or more movements, one or more of which is usually a minuet. They are generally light in character. See also Serenade.

Bibl.: James Webster, "Towards a History of Viennese Chamber Music in the Early Classical Period," *JAMS* 27 (1974): 212–47. Id., "The Scoring of Mozart's Chamber Music for Strings," *Brook,* 1985, pp. 259–96. E.K.W.

Nourri, bien [Fr., well nourished]. With a rich, full sound.

Novelette [Fr.; Ger. *Novellette*]. A title first used by Schumann for his *Novelletten* op. 21 for piano (1838), eight short pieces without further title that he thought of as constituting a story representing Clara Wieck, his future wife. The title implies no particular form, and works bearing it belong in general to the tradition of the *character piece.

Nozze di Figaro, Le [It., The Marriage of Figaro]. Comic opera in four acts by Mozart (libretto by Lorenzo da Ponte, after Beaumarchais's play *La folle journée, ou Le mariage de Figaro*), produced in Vienna in 1786. Setting: a castle near Seville in the 18th century.

Number opera. Opera that makes a pronounced distinction between self-contained pieces—arias, ensembles, or choruses—and recitative or spoken dialogue. These numbers may on occasion be excerpted and published or performed as separate units. The term number opera is applied to 18th-century operas, especially *opera seria,* in which dramatic action is most often carried forward in recitative, arias being more reflective and expressive, as well as to works of the 18th and 19th centuries that include separable numbers without necessarily maintaining the separation between action and reflection. Operas of this type are especially to be distinguished from the music dramas of Wagner and related works that strive for a continuous texture. See Opera.

Nunc dimittis [Lat.]. The *canticle of Simeon (Luke 2:29–32, beginning "Lord, now lettest thou thy servant depart in peace"). In the Roman rite, it is sung at Compline; in the Anglican rite, at Evensong.

Nuove musiche, Le [It., The New Musical Works]. (1) A collection of works by Giulio Caccini published in 1601 (1602 new style), containing strophic songs, madrigals, and dramatic scenes in the then new style of *monody. (2) Music of the period around 1600 employing the new monodic style and including the first operas, cantatas, and oratorios.

Nut. (1) A slightly raised ridge fastened to the upper end of the neck of a stringed instrument, serving to raise the strings over the fingerboard. (2) In British usage, the *frog of a bow.

Nutcracker, The [Russ. *Shchelkunchik;* Fr. *Casse-noisette*]. A ballet by Tchaikovsky (based on a Christmas story by E. T. A. Hoffmann, choreography by Marius Petipa), op. 71, completed in 1892 and produced that year in St. Petersburg. The orchestral suite op. 71a drawn from the ballet was also first performed in 1892.

Nyckelharpa [Swed.; Ger. *Schlüsselfiedel*]. A keyed *fiddle of Sweden. Shaped like a large viola with a broad neck, it has 2 gut melody strings, 1 or 2 bass strings, and 6 to 13 metal sympathetic strings. Protruding from one side of the neck are 9 to 24 wooden keys. When depressed, the keys raise brass tangents to stop the melody strings.

Bibl.: Jan Ling, *Nyckelharpan: Studier i ett folkligt musikinstrument,* with an abbreviated version in English, *The Keyed Fiddle* (Stockholm: P A Norstedt & Söner, 1967).

O

O Antiphons. A set of seven antiphons for the Magnificat, each beginning with the exclamation "O" ("O Sapientia," "O Adonai," "O Radix Jesse," etc.) and sung, one each day, on the seven days preceding Christmas Eve; also Great Antiphons. All share a melody in the second mode. They entered the Roman liturgy by the 9th century, and other antiphons were sometimes added to the series during the Middle Ages.

Obbligato [It., obligatory]. An accompanying part that is nevertheless of considerable importance and thus not to be omitted; the opposite of **ad libitum.* In the Baroque era, the term often referred to keyboard parts that were written out in full rather than realized from a *thoroughbass part. Since that time it has often referred to prominent but largely ornamental accompanying parts such as countermelodies [see also Accompaniment].

Obbligo, obligo [It., obligation]. In the 17th and 18th centuries, a technical requirement or constraint on which a composition is based, e.g., the use of a particular musical subject or of a specified contrapuntal technique. Frescobaldi composed various such works, including a piece in which stepwise motion is avoided ("obligo di non uscire mai di grado") and one based on four pitches ("obligo mi re fa mi"). One of his collections is titled *Ricercari, et canzoni francese fatte sopra diversi oblighi* (1615).

Oberek [Pol.]. A round dance for couples, in quick triple meter, and related to the *mazurka; originally *obertas.* Examples occur in the works of Chopin (Mazurka op. 56 no. 2), Henryk Wieniawski (*Mazurka caractéristique* no. 1), Karol Szymanowski, and others.

Obertas [Pol.]. **Oberek.*

Oberwerk [Ger.]. A secondary division of a German organ, with the wind-chest located in the main case above the **Hauptwerk.*

Obligat [Ger.]. **Obbligato.*

Oblique motion. See Motion.

Oboe [Fr. *hautbois;* Ger. *Oboe;* It., Sp. *oboe*]. Treble double-reed instrument with conical bore used in European art music [for earlier forms, see *Shawm.]

Today the most common form is the Conservatoire oboe, made of African blackwood and equipped with a key system. It is primarily used to play orchestral literature. There are various sizes besides the standard C-oboe (range bb to a'''), including the *hautbois d'amour* in A with a bulb bell (used mostly for performing Bach arias) and various oboes in F (known as the tenor hautboy and *oboe da caccia* in the Baroque period and English horn or *cor anglais* since the 19th century). There are other less-common sizes, both smaller and larger. Another specialized type is the Viennese oboe, which derives from a German tradition that can be traced back to the late 18th century.

Ranges.

The oboe was developed in France during the middle of the 17th century from the shawm, most of whose tasks it took over, such as playing in bands, playing during night watches in cities, and accompanying armies. The new instrument was also used in orchestras, solo obbligatos in operas, solo concertos, church music, and chamber music.

The golden age of the oboe was the period when it appeared in virtually every kind of music, and when its repertoire was most abundant, from roughly 1690 to 1790. The instrument of the time, which has recently begun to be called by its Baroque name, hautboy (pronounced oh-boy) to distinguish it from the keyed Conservatoire oboe, was usually made of boxwood and had two keys (one of which was sometimes doubled). Like the recorder, it used cross-fingerings and half-holing to produce flats and sharps; there was no octave key.

Prior to the mid-19th century the internal and external design of the instrument was in a constant state of change, and it is possible to distinguish some ten distinct designs between about 1670 and 1810. The addition, in the early 19th century, of various keys and key systems with interactive mechanisms changed the basic playing technique but did not arrest the continued evolution in oboe design. Since the appearance of the last Triébert models in 1862 (Barret) and 1872 (Système 6, continued by Lorée and adopted at the Paris Conservatory in 1881), however, changes to the oboe's bore, tone holes, key system, and general dimensions have been minimal.

The 19th and early 20th centuries saw the oboe's role in art music gradually reduced; while composers used the oboe as an important member of symphony and opera orchestras, little solo or chamber music appeared for it, although the oboe is featured in many contemporary movie sound tracks, often associated with evocations of love and romance. Since the 1960s and 1970s the concept of the instrument has been expanded by its participation in experimental forms like the avant garde and the early music movement.

The avant-garde called for effects from the traditional Conservatoire oboe that were never imagined when it was first developed. Sounds that were once considered extraneous, like key noise and breathing, became sonic resources, and to these were added so-called extended techniques, such as multiphonics (or chords), microtones and pitch sliding, double- and triple-tonguing, alternative fingerings, an extended upper range, and combinations with electronic media.

It was also in the 1960s that the early music movement rediscovered the hautboy. The movement's most obvious attribute is its use of historical versions of instruments. But because a so-called early instrument can be played in a later style, and a modern symphonic instrument can be played in an early style, it is not the instruments themselves that are the aesthetic issue but rather the performance style that players bring to the instruments.

Players now have the option to experiment with performing styles beyond the one generally taught on the Conservatoire oboe. These innovative forms and uses of the instrument not only provide new possibilities but also offer a fresh perspective on the basic nature of the Western oboe and its possible uses.

Bibl.: Karl Ventzke, *Boehm-Oboen und die neueren französischen Oboen-System* (Frankfurt am Main: Musikinstrument, 1969). Evelyn Rothwell, *The Oboist's Companion,* 3 vols. (n.p.: Oxford U Pr, 1974–77). Philip Bate, *The Oboe,* 3rd ed. (New York: Norton, 1975). Miroslav Hosek, *Oboen-Bibliographie* (Wilhelmshaven: Heinrichshofen, 1975). Wayne Wilkins, *The Index of Oboe Music* (Magnolia, Ark.: Music Register, 1976). Bruce Haynes, *Catalogue of Chamber Music for the Oboe 1654–c. 1825,* 4th ed. (The Hague: Royal Conservatory, 1980). Virginia Gifford, *Music for the Oboe, Oboe d'amore, and English Horn: A Bibliography of Materials at the Library of Congress* (Westport, Conn.: Greenwood, 1983). Geoffrey Burgess and Bruce Haynes, *The Oboe* (London: Yale U Pr, 2003). B.H.H.

Obra [Sp.]. Work.

Obw. [Ger.]. Abbr. for **Oberwerk.*

Ocarina. A *globular flute invented in the 19th century by Giuseppe Donati; also called a sweet potato or sweet-potato whistle. Made of porcelain, clay, or plastic, and in various sizes, it has a *duct-type mouthpiece, eight finger holes, and two thumb holes. See ill. under Flute.

Oceania and Australia. An area encompassing the islands of the southern Pacific that make up Melanesia, Polynesia, and Micronesia, as well as Australia.

I. *Acculturated music.* Oceanic music has undergone extensive change through contact with outside groups. Christian missionaries, for example, zealously suppressed indigenous singing and dancing, substituting European hymn-singing in its place. In 19th-century Polynesia, the well-known popular "island music" style developed and spread rapidly with the advent of brass bands, accordions, and mouth organs; and in present-day urban Melanesia, traditional music has been largely displaced by new idioms derived from hymn-singing, cowboy songs, and rock music. In more isolated areas, the older traditions have survived almost unchanged. There remain parts of New Guinea where missionaries have not ventured and where European contact has been minimal. Tribal life also continues unabated in the remoter desert regions of Australia. The following discussion is largely concerned with extant nonacculturated styles of music as practiced at the time of first European contact. For Western art music, see Australia, New Zealand.

II. *Australia.* Australian Aborigines have a meager material culture consistent with their life as nomadic hunters and food-gatherers. Musical instruments are mostly confined to a restricted inventory of idiophones, except in the north where the variety is somewhat greater. Hourglass drums are found in Cape York, where they are a recent import from the Torres Strait Islands. A hollow log drum found in Arnhem Land and Northern Queensland may well have entered Australia by the same route. The celebrated Australian instrument known as the *didjeridu* was formerly confined to Arnhem Land and Cape York, but is now spreading southward and westward. It is a hollow tube of wood about 2 m. long that is sometimes fitted with a mouthpiece of wax or clay. It is played with great virtuosity using a rhythmically articulated drone fundamental, in a variety of timbres, alternating with a hooted overtone that may be vocalized to form beats. Australia has neither flutes nor stringed instruments; various kinds of rattles do, however, occur. Rasps are confined largely to Western Australia, while skin bundles beaten by hand seem to appear mostly in the south. By far the most common instruments are paired sticks of hard, resonant wood that are struck together to form a regular accompaniment to singing. Boomerangs may also be beaten together, and percussive effects may be obtained by thumping the ground with billets of wood or by means of handclapping or body-slapping. *Bull-roarers are widespread in Australia but are typically not used as a musical instrument; instead, they are primarily used for love-magic and for simulating the voices of ancestral or totemic beings at initiation ceremonies.

Vocal music is commonly organized into named categories that may be secular or sacred. Secular songs are performed at any time for entertainment. The most popular and numerous are gossip songs. Sacred songs are usually sung in a special setting or in association with ritual. Aboriginal ceremonies are often not only sacred but secret, with separate ceremonies for men and women. In addition to singing, they normally involve dancing, body-painting, the preparation of ceremonial artifacts, and the enactment of myths associated with ancestral beings. Generally there is no concept of song composition. Most songs are said to come from the "dreamtime" or mythological past; others have been acquired by trade together with the associated ceremonies. New songs are learned in dreams and visions from totems or the spirits of the dead.

Aborigine music has developed in geographic isolation and has few affinities with music elsewhere in Oceania. A widespread characteristic is the use of "tumbling strains" or "tile contour" coupled with wide ranges of an octave or more. Group performance is usual and is generally in unison except in Arnhem Land, where canon and three-part polyphony occur in the secular music. This development is attributed to the innovating presence in Arnhem Land of professional "songmen" who own the songs and are allowed latitude to extend and embellish them. Voice quality is distinctive and moderately tense. Scales range from two to seven notes, four to six being apparently most common. In Arnhem Land, the scales are predominantly diatonic. In other areas, the sixth and seventh are often omitted. Songs are organized in song cycles or song series in which as few as a dozen or as many as 300 songs are sung in a prescribed order. Paired sticks or clashing boomerangs provide an isometric accompaniment. Among the Pintupi, Alyawarra, and other people of Central Australia, melodic contours are governed by "word groups" that are subdivided into two, three, or four isorhythmic units, uniform for the song.

III. *Melanesia.* In New Guinea, the instrument used almost everywhere to accompany dancing is the hourglass-shaped hand drum called *kundu* in Pidgin English. Slit gongs or *garamut* are characteristic of the coastal and river-dwelling peoples of New Guinea, particularly along the north coast. Southeastward, they extend throughout the Bismarck Archipelago and along the double chain of Island Melanesia as far as Western and Central Polynesia. South of the Bismarck Archipelago, hourglass drums disappear, and their place is taken by the slit gong. Melanesian slit gongs occur mostly in sets of different sizes and may be up to 3 m. long. They are used for secular and ceremonial signaling and, like the *kundu*, may accompany dance. Most are horizontal to the ground, but in the patrilineal center of Vanuatu (New Hebrides), the dominant form is upright. In Malekula, the standing slit gongs represent ancestors and are thought to speak with their voices. Antiphonal paired flutes or "sacred flutes"—found predominantly in the Sepik and Highland areas of Papua New Guinea—likewise represent "spirit voices" at initiation ceremonies, where they are used to frighten women and uninitiated youths.

Other instruments used to represent the voices of gods, ghosts, or spirits include bull-roarers (especially in the Huon and Papuan Gulf areas), the unique *friction drum or rubbing block *(livika)* of New Ireland, and a variety of other noisemakers including leaf trumpets, whistles, water-drums, and voice disguisers such as megaphones. *Panpipes reach their highest level of development in the Solomon Islands, where they are played in ensemble by groups of men and boys as an accompaniment to dancing. Those of the 'Are'are people of Malaita perform multipart program music based upon the sounds and events of nature and of daily activities. Seven types of ensemble are distinguished in Malaita, each characterized by different numbers of musicians, a different disposition of parts, different organization of the scale, and a distinct repertory. Some of these ensembles use equiheptatonic scales. In addition to the instruments listed above, bamboo *Jew's harps, *musical bows, flutes of many kinds, wooden and shell trumpets, and an immense variety of idiophones including rattles, rasps, *stamping tubes, sticks, and other struck objects are all found in Melanesia.

In Melanesia, social systems are dominated by the so-called big-man, who achieves status either by acquiring and giving away wealth or by buying his way through the ranks of a graded society. The associated ceremonies are occasions for spectacular display and, in common with initiation and other festivities, usually involve dancing and dance music. Possibly because of this, singing styles tend to be metrical and accompanied by handclapping, footstamping with anklet rattles, or percussion instruments that emphasize the beat. Normally the sexes dance separately, and consequently there are distinct songs for men and women. One trait common throughout Melanesia is the use of meaningless song-texts, often the result of trading or purchasing songs from neighboring groups that possess different languages. In some cases, high value is placed on unintelligibility. In the Banks Islands (Vanuatu), there are special song languages that differ from the language of everyday speech.

It is unsafe to generalize about musical styles in New Guinea both because of the large number of peoples and because insufficient studies have been carried out. Recordings have revealed a diversity of styles, and mixtures of style seem often to occur within single cultures. Fanfare melody—once thought to be characteristic only of the interior regions of New Guinea among speakers of non-Austronesian languages—has been documented throughout the Bismarck Archipelago and as far south as the northwest Solomon Islands. Anhemitonic pentatonic styles are widespread among coastal-dwelling Melanesians in New Guinea and predominate in Island Melanesia. In the Solomon Islands, they tend to be associated with singing styles of very wide range and melodic skips extending into the falsetto or yodeling register of the voice. Polyphonic styles have similar distribution. Two-part and occasional three-part styles occur sporadically among Melanesians of coastal New Guinea and extend through the D'Entrecasteaux group and the Bismarck Archipelago, reaching a peak of development in the Solomon Islands, where there are similarities with the arrangements of parts in the panpipe ensembles. A striking feature of Guadalcanal vocal polyphony is a dissonant clash of major seconds and sevenths resulting from the simultaneous sounding of adjacent degrees of the anhemitonic pentatonic scale. Dissonant diaphony takes its most extreme Melanesian form in Manus, Admiralty Islands, where pairs of singers, each of whom may block one ear to aid concentration, perform strings of parallel seconds. Responsorial styles have been reported in parts of the Solomons and in New Caledonia, but center on Vanuatu (New Hebrides), where responsorial verse and refrain forms are typical. Another characteristic of Vanuatu music, contrasting strongly with that of the Solomons, is the absence of polyphony (except in Malekula). Throughout Island Melanesia, forms are commonly strophic with a tendency in some areas toward litany.

IV. *Polynesia.* A musical instrument found nearly everywhere in Polynesia, except New Zealand, is the *nose flute. In Tonga, nose flutes were used to awaken the king. Elsewhere they are often associated with lovemaking and the belief that those who know the art of the instrument could "talk through its tones." As with the rest of Oceania, the shell trumpet or conch is widely distributed. In present-day Tonga, groups of carefully tuned conches—each playing its own note—provide rhythmic music to arouse and sustain excitement during intervillage cricket matches. Elsewhere in Polynesia, they are used primarily for signaling. Throughout Polynesia and the Central Pacific, the conch was the instrument of chiefs and priests and became identified with position, rank, and power.

Most of Western Polynesia's inventory of musical instruments is shared with Island Melanesia. Wooden slit gongs of various sizes are used for signaling and to accompany dancing. Panpipes undoubtedly spread into Western Polynesia from Melanesia, probably by way of Fiji. Stamping tubes are another likely Melanesian import. In Western Polynesia, they occur in graduated sizes and are used to accompany polyphonic singing. Beyond Western Polynesia, they are found only in Hawaii. Rolled mats substituted for drums are unique to Western Polynesia. Membranophones are conspicuously absent except in Tonga, where a double-ended drum has recently been introduced.

Except on Easter Island and in New Zealand, the upright cylindrical drum (*pahu* or *pa'u*) with sharkskin tympanum is typical of Eastern Polynesia. In central Eastern Polynesia, drums are today played with slit gongs and, for added effect, a kerosene tin, to accompany the spectacular "drum dance." Formerly, they were used ceremonially on such occasions as sacrifices or the death or illness of important persons. They range in size from the huge temple drums of the Marquesas, so tall that the players must climb on platforms to reach them, to the little coconut-shell kneedrum *(pūniu),* which is one of many localized percussion instruments in Hawaii. *Musical bows, which are rare in Western Polynesia despite their prevalence in Melanesia, are relatively widespread in Eastern Polynesia. In the Marquesas, the instrument was a women's toy, but in Hawaii, it was used as a communication device by lovers.

Western Polynesian vocal styles have been strongly influenced by those of nearby Melanesia. As in Melanesia, singing is often associated with dance, and there is a corresponding preference for metered styles. Percussion instruments emphasize the beat; handclapping is a frequent accompaniment; and dance songs often finish with sections of increased or accelerating tempo. Drone-based vocal polyphony, generally in two parts, is widespread in Western Polynesia and is undoubtedly pre-European, despite a contemporary overlay of European-derived four-part harmony. In Fiji, which is culturally linked with Western Polynesia, older three-part styles are still extant and feature dissonant note-clusters in which tones a major or minor second apart are sounded together and paralleled a fourth or fifth above and below.

Eastern Polynesian polyphony is confined largely to central areas and probably lacks pre-European antecedents. The two main styles are *himene* or *'imene* (hymns) and *ute* (love songs), both of which developed in Tahiti under the impact of mission hymn-singing. From the Society Islands they have since spread throughout Central Polynesia. Generally there are two main parts, one sung by men and the other by women, upon which four or more additional parts may be superimposed. Notable characteristics include powerful rhythmic unison grunting from the men and a shrill obbligato solo woman's part at the limit of singing range. In marked contrast are the styles of Marginal Polynesia on the outer fringes of Eastern Polynesia. Studies of Easter Island music came too late for the indigenous styles to be distinguished with certainty from Tahitian and other importations. But the cultures of New Zealand, Hawaii, and the Marquesas, especially, have retained common characteristics dating back to the dispersal of these people about 1,000 years ago.

Eastern Polynesia as a whole is differentiated from Western Polynesia by its lack of polyphony (except in the center), fewer dance-regulated styles (with corresponding higher incidence of heterometer), steady tempo, level melodic movement, small melodic range, few notes in the scale, and tonics that are either centric or close to the top of the range. Some traits occur throughout Polynesia; one such is the presence of recited or *parlando* styles side by side with those of more definite pitch. Most islands or island groups have at least one song style performed entirely in this way. Single-note or monotonic styles, with or without added parallel parts, are also widespread, as are responsorial styles in which solo passages performed by a group leader alternate or overlap with choral response. A characteristic device throughout Polynesia—except in Hawaii—is the trailing cadence or terminal glissando. Perhaps the most striking feature of Polynesian music is the large number of styles built upon tonic drones. It is the sole pitch in monotonic styles; it occurs as a durational tonic or intoning note in styles of narrow compass; and it can be heard as a pedal or bordun in polyplane and other polyphonic styles.

V. *Micronesia.* There are few varieties of musical instruments in Micronesia, possibly because of the limited atoll resources with which to make them. Nose flutes were formerly fairly widespread, and on the island of Truk, as in Polynesia, they were used by young men to serenade young women and call them out to rendezvous. Mouth flutes are less often reported. The conch trumpet is found nearly everywhere and, as elsewhere in Oceania, is used solely for signaling. Jew's harps and whizzers seem to be concentrated in Central and Western Micronesia. As a whole, Micronesia is characterized less by the presence of particular instruments than by the absence of instruments that occur in other regions. The Eastern Polynesian cylindrical drum, for example, is not present. Hourglass drums appear only in the eastern areas of Micronesia closest to the Bismarck Archipelago and are probably borrowed from Melanesia. But other Melanesian instruments seem not to have been adopted. Panpipes and slit gongs are reported only for Kosrae, and rattles and the musical bow only for the Marianas. The place of the wooden trumpet is taken entirely by the conch, and stamping tubes likewise do not occur. In the absence of other percussion instruments, dance is accompanied by sticks that are clicked or clashed together, aided by footstamping, handclapping, and other forms of body percussion such as slapping the thigh or clapping the armpit or the crook of the bent arm. A post-European introduction in Kiribati (Gilbert Islands), shared with Tuvalu (Ellice Islands) and Tokelau in Western Polynesia, is the use of upturned boxes as drums.

In Micronesia, vocal music is mainly used to accompany the many varieties of seated and standing dance, but little is as yet known of these styles. Eastern Micronesia in particular still awaits detailed study.

Western Micronesian music was shown long ago by Herzog (1932 and 1936) to share many of its characteristics with Polynesian styles, and a corresponding dissociation is observable with Melanesia. For Tobi, Palau, Yap, Ifaluk, and nearby islands, Herzog distinguished several traits, including scales built on only two notes, dotted rhythms and paired rhythms with few durational values, lack of regular meter, repetition of short motifs, parallel and bordun-type polyphony, and a performing style characterized by uncertain intonation with portamento, transitional notes, grace notes, and terminal glissandos. Handclapping and footstamping may be added to Herzog's list. Most of these traits are either rare or absent in those parts of Melanesia closest to Western Micronesia, thus making influence from this quarter unlikely. This view is further confirmed by the total absence from Western Micronesia of the common Melanesian traits of wide range, anhemitonic pentatonic scales, and fanfare melody. Some of Herzog's traits, such as limited number of notes, irregular meter, and uncertain intonation, are characteristically Eastern Polynesian though by no means absent in the West. Others, such as short motifs and bordun-type polyphony, are convincingly Western Polynesian. The terminal glissando occurs all over Polynesia and is seldom found anywhere else in Oceania except Micronesia. It seems highly probable that Western Micronesia is a last outpost of Polynesian influence, belonging less with the rest of Micronesia than with Polynesian Outliers such as Nukumanu and Ontong Java.

Bibl.: *General.* Hans Fischer, *Schallgeräte in Ozeanien* (Strasbourg: Heitz, 1958); trans., *Sound-Producing Instruments in Oceania* (Boroko: Institute of Papua New Guinea Studies, 1983). Mervyn McLean, "Towards the Differentiation of Music Areas in Oceania," *Anthropos* 74 (1979): 717–36. Mervyn McLean, *An Annotated Bibliography of Oceanic Music and Dance,* rev. and enl. 2nd ed. (Warren, Mich.: Harmonie Park, 1995).

Australia. Adolphus Peter Elkin and Trevor Jones, *Arnhem Land Music* (Sydney: U of Sydney, 1957). Ronald M. Berndt and Catherine H. Berndt, *The World of the First Australians* (London: Angus & Robertson, 1964). Catherine Ellis, *Aboriginal Music Making* (Adelaide: Libraries Board of South Australia, 1964). Trevor Jones, "Australian Aboriginal Music," in *Aboriginal Man in Australia,* ed., Ronald M. Berndt and Catherine H. Berndt (Sydney: Angus & Robertson, 1965). Alice Moyle, *A Handlist of Field Collections* (Canberra: Australian Institute of Aboriginal Studies, 1966). Richard Moyle, *Songs of the Pintupi* (Canberra: Australian Institute of Aboriginal Studies, 1979). Catherine Ellis, *Aboriginal Music, Education for Living: Cross-Cultural Experiences from South Autralia* (St. Lucia, Qld., 1985). Richard Moyle, *Alyawarra Music* (Canberra: Australian Institute of Aboriginal Studies, 1986). Richard Moyle, *Balgo: The Musical Life of a Desert Community* (Nedlands, W.A.: Callaway International Resource Centre for Music Education, School of Music, U of Western Australia, 1997). Adrienne Kaeppler and Jacob Love, *The Garland Encyclopedia of World Music, vol. 9: Australia and the Pacific Islands* (New York, 1998). Clinton Walker, *Buried Country: The Story of Aboriginal Country Music* (Annandale, N.S.W.: Pluto Pr, 2000).

Melanesia. Herbert Hübner, *Die Musik im Bismarck-Archipel* (Berlin: B Hahnefeld, 1938). Dieter Christensen, *Die Musik der Kate und Sialum* (Berlin: Philosophische Fakultät der Freien Universität Berlin, 1957). Karl E. Larsson, "The Conch Shells of Fiji," *Fijian Studies,* pt. 2, *Ethnologiska Studier* 25 (1960): 121–47. Jaap Kunst, *Music in New Guinea,* trans. Jeune Scott-Kemball (The Hague: Nijhoff, 1967). Chris Thompson, "Fijian Music and Dance," *Fiji Society, Transactions and Proceedings* 11 (1971): 14–21. Hugo Zemp, "Instruments de musique de Malaita," *Journal de la Société des océanistes* 27 (1971): 31–53; 28 (1972): 7–48. Kenneth Gourlay, *Sound Producing Instruments in Traditional Society* (Port Moresby: Australian National University,

1975). Gesine Haase, *Studien zur Musik im Santa Cruz-Archipel* (Hamburg: Wagner, 1977). Daniel de Coppet and Hugo Zemp, *'Are'Are: Un peuple mélanésien et sa musique* (Paris: Seuil, 1978). Vida Chenoweth, *The Usarufas and Their Music* (Dallas: SIL Museum of Anthropology, 1979). Steven Feld, *Sound and Sentiment: Birds, Weeping, Poetics, and Song in Kaluli Expression* (Philadelphia: U of Pa Pr, 1982). Mervyn McLean, *Diffusion of Musical Instruments and Their Relation to Language Migrations in New Guinea,* Kuele: Occasional Papers on Pacific Music and Dance 1 (Boroko: Cultural Studies Division, National Research Institute, 1994).

Polynesia. E. S. Craighill Handy, *The Native Culture in the Marquesas* (Honolulu: Bishop Museum, 1923). Id. and Jane L. Winne, *Music in the Marquesas Islands* (Honolulu: Bishop Museum, 1925). Helen Roberts, *Ancient Hawaiian Music* (Honolulu: Bishop Museum, 1926). Edwin G. Burrows, *Native Music of the Tuamotus* (Honolulu: Bishop Museum, 1933; R: New York: Kraus Repr, 1971). Id., "Polynesian Part-Singing," *Zeitschrift für Vergleichende Musikwissenschaft* 2 (1934): 69–76. Peter Buck, "Panpipes in Polynesia," *Journal of the Polynesian Society* 50 (1941): 173–84. Edwin Burrows, *Songs of Uvea and Futuna* (Honolulu: Bishop Museum, 1945; R: New York: Kraus Repr, 1971). Dieter Christensen and Gerd Koch, *Die Musik der Ellice-Inseln* (Berlin: Museum für Völkerkunde, 1964). Ramón Campbell, *La herencia musical de Rapanui* (Santiago: Bello, 1971). Douglas Oliver, "Music and Dance," in *Ancient Tahitian Society,* vol. 1 (Honolulu: U Pr of Hawaii, 1974). Richard Moyle, "Conch Ensembles: Tonga's Unique Contribution to Polynesian Organology," *GSJ* 28 (1975): 98–106. Mervyn McLean and Margaret Orbell, *Traditional Songs of the Maori* (Auckland: Auckland U Pr, revised 2nd ed., 1990). Raymond Firth with Mervyn McLean, *Tikopia Songs* (London: Cambridge U Pr, 1990). Mervyn McLean, *The Structure of Tikopia Music,* Occasional Papers in Pacific Ethnomusicology 1 (Auckland: Archive of Maori and Pacific Music, 1991). Mervyn McLean, *Maori Music* (Auckland: Auckland U Pr, 1996). Mervyn McLean, *Weavers of Song: Polynesian Music and Dance* (Auckland: Auckland U Pr/Honolulu: U of Hawaii Pr, 1999).

Micronesia. George Herzog, "Die Musik auf Truk," in *Ergebnisse der Südsee-Expedition 1908–1910* IIB5 (1932): 384–404. Id., "Die Musik der Karolinen-Inseln," in *Ergebnisse der Südsee-Expedition 1908–1910* IIB9 (1936): 263–350. M.McL.

Ochetus [Lat.]. *Hocket.

Octave. (1) An *interval bounded by two pitches with the same pitch names and the higher of whose frequencies is twice the lower. See also Pitch names. (2) In liturgical contexts, the eighth day or the entire week following a feast.

Octave equivalence. The feature of musical perception according to which all pitches separated by one or more perfect octaves (i.e., all pitches whose frequencies are related by powers of 2) are regarded as belonging to the same class [see Pitch class] or as being in some sense equivalent. This is reflected in the system of Western *pitch names, in which the seven letters employed are repeated for each octave.

Octave species. The particular arrangement of tones and semitones occurring in any given octave of the *diatonic scale. This arrangement is different for the octaves bounded by each of the seven diatonic scale degrees. For example, starting on C and proceeding upward along the white keys of the piano, tones (t) and semitones (s) occur in the order t t s t t t s, whereas proceeding upward from D they occur in the order t s t t t s t. This is an important element in the Western concepts of *mode and *tonality. It also played an important role in the theory of ancient Greek music [see Greece I, 3].

Octet [Fr. *octette, octuor;* Ger. *Oktett;* It. *otteto;* Sp. *octeto*]. (1) A chamber composition for eight solo performers. *Harmoniemusik* [see *Harmonie* (3)] of the Classical period (usually for paired oboes, horns, clarinets, and bassoons) includes several Mozart serenades and Beethoven's op. 103. Stravinsky's Octet (for flute, clarinet, two bassoons, two trumpets, and two trombones) is the best-known later example. There are also octets for strings (Mendelssohn's masterpiece and minor works by a few others) and for mixed winds and strings (Schubert, Spohr, Varèse, Hindemith). (2) An ensemble of eight solo performers.

Octobasse [Fr.]. A large double bass, about 4 m. high, first made by Jean-Baptiste Vuillaume in Paris in 1849. Its three strings, tuned C_1 G_1 C, are stopped by levers.

Octoechos [Gr.]. See *Ēchos.*

Oda [It.]. A verse form used by composers of the **frottola.* It consists of four-line stanzas rhyming aaab, bccc, etc., or abbc cdde, etc. The first three lines of each stanza are of seven syllables; the last varies from four to eleven. When the last is four, composers sometimes treat the last two lines as one. The *oda* has nothing to do with the classical *ode; it may be derived from what poetic theorists called a *moto confetto,* a popular form using a string of proverbs. J.H.

Ode [Gr. *ōdē,* fr. *aeidein,* to sing; Lat. *oda*]. (1) In current usage, a lyric poem of considerable length and complexity, often written for a ceremonial occasion. Poems of this type reflect the tradition of the Greek odes of Pindar (522–442 B.C.E.), which were intended to be performed with song and dance in the theater and on public occasions and whose form is a complex and variable arrangement of irregular lines. The Latin odes of Horace (65–8 B.C.E.), on the other hand, consist of regular stanzas in a few meters and are contemplative rather than ceremonial or public. Horace's odes were set polyphonically by several composers of the Renaissance, including Petrus Tritonius, whose four-voice settings (published in 1507) had been commissioned by the German humanist Conradus Celtes and were in a chordal style that employed a free rhythm based on the classical poetic meters [see *Musique mesurée*]. Tritonius' settings were widely used in schools. Other settings of this type were composed by Ludwig Senfl (1534) and Paul Hofhaimer (1539). Among the Renaissance poets who cultivated the various types of odes from antiquity was Pierre de Ronsard (1524–85), who was widely imitated by French poets in the centuries following.

The Pindaric ode was cultivated in England in the 17th century by Ben Jonson, and this period marks the beginning of the ode in England as a work for an occasion in the life of the monarch or for St. Cecilia's Day, set to music in the fashion of a cantata. Among composers who set such poems were Matthew Locke, Henry Cooke, Pelham Humfrey, John Blow, Purcell, and Handel (settings by Handel including Dryden's "Ode for St. Cecilia's Day").

In north Germany in the mid-18th century, numerous odes were set to music by composers of the first Berlin lieder school and others [see Berlin school, Lied III, *Klavierlied*]. Goethe and Schiller wrote odes, and Schiller's "Ode to Joy" was set by Beethoven in the finale to the Ninth or **Choral* Symphony.

(2) In Byzantine chant, one of the nine sections of the *kanōn* [see Byzantine chant II].

Ode to Napoleon Buonaparte. A composition by Schoenberg, op. 41 (1942), based on Byron's poem on the downfall of dictators, scored for string quartet (later string orchestra), piano, and reciting voice.

Odhecaton. Abbreviated title of the anthology of polyphony published in 1501 by the printer Ottaviano Petrucci as *Harmonice musices odhecaton A* (100 Songs of Harmonic Music, vol. A; collections titled *Canti B* and *Canti C* followed). It is the first publication of polyphonic music printed with movable type and contains 96 (not 100) pieces, mostly French chansons published without texts, by composers such as Agricola, Busnois, Compère, Hayne van Ghizeghem, Isaac, and Josquin. See Notation, Ex. 5.

Bibl.: Helen Hewitt, ed. *Harmonice musices odhecaton A* (Cambridge, Mass.: Mediaeval Acad, 1942; 2nd ed. rev., 1946; R: New York: Da Capo, 1978).

Oḍissi [Hin.]. A solo dance style of Orissa, India. Traditionally performed in temple and court, it is now established as a classical form of concert dance. Because of its regional origin, it is characterized by an amalgam of northern and southern elements of Indian dance and music. C.C.

Oedipus Rex [Lat., Oedipus the King]. An opera-oratorio in two acts by Stravinsky (libretto by Jean Cocteau, translated into Latin by J. Daniélou, after Sophocles' tragedy), performed as an oratorio in Paris in 1927 and staged in Vienna in 1928. Setting: ancient Thebes.

Oeuvre [Fr.]. Work, *opus.

Offerenda [Lat.]. The *Ambrosian chant corresponding to the Gregorian offertory.

Offertory [Lat. *offertorium*]. In *Gregorian chant, the item of the *Proper of the *Mass sung during the presentation of the offering (originally the bread and wine to become the elements of communion). The mention of such a chant by St. Augustine (d. 430) is often interpreted to mean that it originally incorporated a whole Psalm and was thus an example of antiphonal *psalmody. Even though its opening section is consistently identified as an *antiphon, the earliest sources present both antiphons and verses in an extremely ornate or *melismatic style unlike that of other antiphonal pieces. They often employ wide ranges, and some include repetitions of text and melody not found in other types of chant. The two or three verses for each offertory that are included in early sources are unrelated to *psalm tones and do not seem in this context to be remnants of complete Psalms. These verses were gradually discarded beginning in the 12th century and were formally removed in the 16th century by the *Council of Trent, except in the *Requiem Mass, though their use has been permitted in modern practice, as has the singing of a whole Psalm (*LU,* p. xvi).

There are some polyphonic settings of offertories from the 15th and 16th centuries (including the English settings for organ of *"Felix namque"), and in the 16th century the texts were set as free motets by Lassus and Palestrina.

From the 17th century, the offertory was frequently the occasion for the performance of instrumental or vocal music not directly related to the prescribed liturgical item. This tradition has continued in Protestant churches as well, where the term most often refers to any music performed while the collection is taken up.

Bibl.: Karl Ott, ed., *Offertoriale sive versus offertorium* (Paris: Desclée, 1935) [an edition with grave defects]. Ruth Steiner, "Some Questions about the Gregorian Offertories and Their Verses," *JAMS* 19 (1966): 162–81. Harold S. Powers, "Modal Representation in Polyphonic Offertories," *Early Music History* 2 (1982): 43–86. Kenneth Levy, "Toledo, Rome, and the Legacy of Gaul," *Early Music History* 4 (1984): 49–99.

Office, Divine [Lat. *officium*]. The daily series of services of the Western Christian rites, as distinct from the *Mass. The practice of fixed daily hours of prayer derives from Jewish custom and was established early in the Christian communities of both East and West. In the Roman Catholic Church, until the reforms following the Second *Vatican Council of 1962–65 (about which see below), eight services made up this series for each day. The precise arrangement of the services within this series and of the series throughout the liturgical year followed one plan (the Roman cursus) in churches and another (the monastic cursus) in monastic communities. The single most influential document in the establishment of the round of eight services, especially in their observance in monastic communities, was the Rule of St. Benedict, written in about 535. It incorporates an outline according to which the entire Psalter is recited every week. The Psalms are chanted in association with *antiphons. Readings or "lessons" from other parts of the Bible or the lives of the saints, which also form an important part of the Office, are accompanied by *responsories. Other elements of the Office include the *canticles, with their accompanying antiphons, *hymns, *versicles, and prayers. The *liturgical books containing the Office are the antiphoner (see *AntRom,* pp. 1–183, where the *Ordinary of the Office, except for Matins, is given day by day for the week; similarly *LU* beginning p. 112, but especially pp. 221–316; references to the monastic practice of *AntMon* are given below) and the breviary. The eight services or "hours" are as follows:

(1) Matins [Lat. *ad matutinum,* early in the morning], also called the *Night Office* and originally called *Vigils,* a long service held principally in monastic communities at about 3 a.m., though sometimes as early as midnight. It includes versicles, the *Invitatory, a hymn, and from one to three nocturns, each of which, depending on the cursus and other circumstances, includes a variable number of Psalms with antiphons and lessons with responsories (e.g., *LU,* pp. 368–92, for the Nativity; for monastic Matins with a more complete calendar of feasts, see the *Liber responsorialis*). (2) Lauds [Lat. *laudes,* praises], held at daybreak and including versicles and responses, Psalms (among them Psalms 148–50, called *laudes* and from which the service takes its name) and canticles with antiphons, a short lesson or "chapter," a short responsory (in the monastic cursus), and a hymn (*LU,* pp. 221–23; *AntMon,* pp. 25–81). (3) Prime [Lat. *ad primam,* at the first hour of the day, according to the division of the daylight hours into twelve], at 6 a.m., (4) Terce [Lat. *ad tertiam*], at 9 a.m., (5) Sext [Lat. *ad sextam*], at noon, and (6) None [Lat. *ad nonam*], at 3 p.m., all of which together make up the Little Hours and include versicles and responses, hymns, Psalms and canticles with antiphons, short lessons at times with short responsories, and various kinds of prayers (*AntMon,* pp. 1–24, 81–123). (7) Vespers [Lat. *ad vesperas,* in the evening], held at twilight and including, depending on the cursus and other circumstances, versicles and responses, varying numbers of Psalms with antiphons, a lesson, a responsory, the *Magnificat with antiphon, various prayers, and *"Benedicamus Domino" (e.g., *LU,* pp. 250–61 for Sundays, pp. 280–316 for the remaining days of the week, and pp. 364–67, the Proper for the Nativity; *AntMon,* pp. 124–64, for all of the days of the week). Vespers is similar in outline to Lauds. Since the 12th century, parts of Vespers, principally the Psalms, and since the 16th century the Magnificat, have often been set polyphonically. (8) Compline [Lat. *ad completorium,* from *completus,* completed], held before retiring. Its principal elements, depending on cursus, are versicles and responses, several Psalms (not always with antiphons), a hymn, the canticle "Nunc dimittis," a short lesson, a short responsory, prayers, *"Benedicamus Domino," and, in modern practice, one of the four Marian antiphons, *"Alma Redemptoris Mater," *"Ave Regina caelorum," *"Regina caeli laetare," and *"Salve Regina," chosen according to the season of the year (e.g., *LU,* pp. 262[12]–79 for Sundays, and pp. 280–316 for the remaining days of the week; *AntMon,* pp. 167–80).

The Second Vatican Council called for a thorough reform of the Office, and this was promulgated in 1972 as the Liturgy of the Hours *(Liturgia horarum).* Lauds and Vespers, as Morning and Evening Prayer, became the most important hours; Matins became an Office of Readings to be said at any time of the day; Prime was discarded, but Terce, Sext, and None retained; and Compline, as Night Prayer, was kept as the final service before retiring. The content of individual services was also substantially altered.

In the Anglican rite, the corresponding services are Morning Prayer (also called Matins and derived from the Matins of the Middle Ages) and Evening Prayer (also called Evensong and derived from Vespers and Compline of the Middle Ages).

See also Rhymed Office. For bibl. see Gregorian Chant, Liturgy. D.M.R.

Ohne [Ger.]. Without.

Oiseau de feu, L' [Fr., The Firebird]. A ballet by Stravinsky (choreography by Michel Fokine, scenery and costumes by Alexander Golovine and Léon Bakst), produced at the Ballets russes in Paris in 1910. Three versions of a suite taken from the ballet music were made by the composer in 1911, 1919, and 1945, the last two for smaller orchestra.

Oketus [Lat.]. *Hocket.

Oktave [Ger.]. Octave; *Oktavflöte,* piccolo; *Oktavfagott,* contrabassoon.

Oktoēchos [Gr.]. See *Ēchos.*

Old Hall Manuscript. London, British Library, Add. 57950 ("Old Hall Manuscript"). 112 leaves. England (Windsor?), ca. 1410–50. This manuscript contains about 150 Mass movements and motets of English composers (Dunstable, Power, et al.).

Old Hundred(th). A hymn tune used in Bèze's *Genevan Psalter* (1551) for the 134th Psalm, in Knox's *Anglo-Genevan Psalter* (1556) for the 3rd Psalm, and in Sternhold and Hopkins's *Psalter* (1562) for the 100th Psalm (hence its name). In Protestant churches it is often used to sing the *doxology, beginning "Praise God from whom all blessings flow."

Old Roman chant. A repertory of liturgical chant preserved in five Roman manuscripts (three graduals and two antiphoners) dating from the 11th through the 13th century. Nonmusical manuscripts attest to the presence of this tradition in Rome from the 8th century (Huglo, 1954). The liturgy is for the most part that of the *Gregorian chant, and the melodies are in many respects similar as well, though there are significant variants even among the Old Roman manuscripts themselves. The melodies have been said to rely more heavily on melodic formulas and thus to be more archaic than the Gregorian melodies (Connolly, 1972). Variants within the tradition have been attributed to a rather longer period of oral transmission than that of the Gregorian melodies (Cutter, 1967). There has been considerable debate concerning the origins of both traditions and their relationship to each other.

André Mocquereau (1891) regarded this repertory as a late and decadent version of Gregorian chant. Andoyer (1912) held that it is pre-Gregorian in origin. Recent debate began in 1950 with the work of Stäblein, who first held that this repertory is properly called Gregorian and dates from the papacy of Gregory, the Great (590–604). In this view the repertory now known as Gregorian chant dates from the papacy of Vitalian (657–72), when the earlier repertory was recast. Vitalian's role is deduced from his mention in *Ordo romanus XIX* (now generally regarded as an 8th-century Frankish account; see Gregorian chant VI) and a tradition dating from the 12th century according to which Vitalian composed the chant sung in Rome (Hucke, 1980). Jammers (1962) proposed a similar view, attributing the formation of the newer repertory under Vitalian to the supposed introduction of polyphony at the papal court at that time in imitation of Byzantine practice. Van Dijk (1961, 1966) also held that the Gregorian chant was the product of the 7th-century papal court, where it was associated with a specifically papal rite that was ultimately transmitted to Gaul, the Old Roman being the older repertory, which continued in local use in Rome. Smits van Waesberghe (1954, 1966) saw the Gregorian chant as originating in the papal court and the Old Roman as the chant of Roman monasteries, both deriving from a common Roman ancestor. Hucke (1980 and earlier articles cited there) took Gregorian chant to be a specifically Frankish version of a repertory imported from the oral tradition of Rome in the 8th and 9th centuries, the Old Roman version being older though subsequently influenced and then displaced by the Frankish version, which established itself throughout Europe. Apel (1956) also saw the origins of Gregorian chant as Frankish. According to Hucke, Old Roman chant was formed independently from the system of eight *modes, a Frankish system to which the Frankish redaction of Gregorian chant is inextricably bound.

Bibl.: André Mocquereau, ed., *Paléographie musicale,* 2 (Solesmes, 1891). R. Andoyer, "Le chant romain antégrégorien," *Revue de chant grégorien* 20 (1911–12): 69, 107. Bruno Stäblein, "Zur Frühgeschichte des römischen Chorals," *Rome,* 1950, pp. 271–75. Id., "Alt- und neurömischer Choral," *Lüneburg,* 1950, pp. 53–56. Id., "Zur Entstehung der gregorianischen Melodien," *KmJb* 35 (1951): 5–9. Id., "Kann der gregorianische Choral im Frankenreich entstanden sein?" *AfMw* 24 (1967): 153–69. Id., *Die Gesänge des altrömischen Graduale Vat. lat. 5319, MMMA* 2 (Kassel: Bärenreiter, 1970) [edition with commentary]. Michel Huglo, "Le chant 'vieux-romain': Liste des manuscrits et témoins indirects," *Sacris erudiri* 6 (1954): 96–124. Joseph Smits van Waesberghe, "Neues über die Schola cantorum zu Rom," *Vienna,* 1954, pp. 111–19. Id., "'De glorioso officio . . .': Zum Aufbau des Gross-Alleluia in den päpstlichen Ostervespern," *Wellesz,* 1966, pp. 48–73. Willi Apel, "The Central Problem of Gregorian Chant," *JAMS* 9 (1956): 118–27. Robert J. Snow, "Old Roman Chant," in Willi Apel, *Gregorian Chant* (Bloomington: Ind U Pr, 1958), pp. 484–505. S. J. P. van Dijk, "The Urban Papal Rites in Seventh- and Eighth-Century Rome," *Sacris erudiri* 12 (1961): 411–87. Id., "Recent Developments in the Study of the Old-Roman Rite," *Studia patristica* 8 (1966): 299–319. Ewald Jammers, *Musik in Byzanz, im päpstlichen Rom und in Frankreich* (Heidelberg: C Winter, 1962). Paul F. Cutter, "The Question of the 'Old-Roman' Chant: A Reappraisal," *AM* 39 (1967): 2–20 [surveys the literature]. Id., *Musical Sources of the Old-Roman Mass, MSD* 39 (1979) [texts and indexes of the three graduals]. Thomas H. Connolly, "Introits and Archetypes: Some Archaisms of the Old Roman Chant," *JAMS* 25 (1972): 157–74. Helmut Hucke, "Toward a New Historical View of Gregorian Chant," *JAMS* 33 (1980): 437–67. Bonifacio Giacomo Baroffio and Soo Jung Kim, eds., *Biblioteca apostolica vaticana, Archivio S. Pietro B 79* (Rome: Editioni Torre d'Orfeo, 1995). *Hughes,* 1995. Joseph Dyer, "*Tropis semper variantibus:* Compositional Strategies in Offertories of Old Roman Chant," *EMH* 17 (1998): 1–60. D.M.R.

Oliphant [fr. OFr. *cor d'olifant*]. A trumpet made from an elephant's tusk, usually elaborately carved, and regarded in the Middle Ages as a symbol of authority.

Ombra scene. In 17th-century opera, a scene taking place in Hades (as in operas on the Orpheus legend) or one in which ghosts, spirits, or shades are conjured up or appear unsummoned—as when a character is sleeping—to warn, reproach, or deliver a cryptic message. An 18th-century example may be found in Handel's *Alcina,* a 19th-century example in Berlioz's *Les troyens.*

Ondeggiando [It.]. See Bowing (14), Tremolo.

Ondes Martenot. An *electronic instrument introduced by Maurice Martenot in 1928. It generates a single tone whose pitch can be controlled either by a keyboard or by a sliding metallic ribbon that makes the pitch continuously variable. Additional circuits are provided to control volume, timbre, and *envelope. Honegger, Varèse, Milhaud, Messiaen, and Boulez have composed works for it. See also Electro-acoustic music.

Ondulé [Fr.]. See Bowing (14), Tremolo.

One-line. The octave proceeding upward from middle C (c′), or any pitch in that octave [see Pitch names].

One-step. A fast social dance of the decade 1910–20; also a piece for such a dance. It was danced to ragtime and popular songs in 2/4 at about 132 quarter notes per minute.

Ongarese, all' [It.]. In the Hungarian *gypsy style.

Onion flute. *Mirliton.

Op. Abbr. for *opus.

Open fifth, open triad. A perfect fifth or a triad without the third, e.g., c–g–c′.

Open forms. See Aleatory music.

Open harmony. See Spacing.

Open note. (1) On wind instruments, a note played without depressing any key or valve or covering any finger hole. (2) On stringed instruments, a note played on an *open string.

Open pipe. See Wind instruments, Acoustics.

Open position. See Spacing.

Open string. On stringed instruments, a string that is not stopped. Its use may be indicated by a zero where a fingering number might otherwise occur.

Opera. A drama that is primarily sung, accompanied by instruments, and presented theatrically. That opera is primarily sung distinguishes it from dramatic pieces in which music is incidental or clearly subsidiary to the drama. That it is presented theatrically distinguishes it from *oratorio, which has similar musical components.

Opera has had a history of almost 400 years; in that time, it has exhibited many different forms and styles. Thus, overtures, choruses, ballets, and ensembles are present in operas of certain times and places—indeed, they may be the glories of the works in which they appear—but they do not define the genre. Likewise, an opera may be accompanied by an orchestra or by a small group of instruments; it may be sung throughout or it may be interspersed with spoken dialogue. The text of an opera, called a *libretto, may be newly created or may be based on one or more purely literary antecedents; the author of a libretto may be primarily a poet, a dramatist, or simply an adapter. As a staged dramatic work, opera does presuppose an audience (in distinction to, say, madrigals or chamber music, which may very well be performed only for the enjoyment of the performers). Opera, then, is a social art, and its history includes both formal musical and social characteristics.

I. *17th century.* Operatic history, in the sense of a continuous, unbroken tradition of works related to one another, begins in Italy at the end of the 16th century. The theoretical preparations for the new art form (and here theory preceded and encouraged practice rather than following it) were made in the three decades before 1600 by a group of poets, musicians, and classical scholars active in Florence, some of them at first under the sponsorship of Count Bardi in a group later called the *Camerata.

The immediate results were three operas: **Dafne* and two settings of **Euridice.* The librettos for these works were written by Ottavio Rinuccini. *Dafne,* composed by Jacopo Peri in collaboration with Jacopo Corsi, was first performed in Florence in 1598 with the composer singing the role of Apollo. Only some of the music has survived. Peri's *Euridice,* with some additions by Giulio Caccini, was performed and published in Florence in 1600. Caccini's full setting of the text was first published in 1600 but was not performed until 1602.

The subjects of these operas derive from Greek myth, and the Florentines were much concerned with the manner in which ancient Greek drama was performed. But the language and the dramatic presentation of Rinuccini's librettos are largely indebted to contemporary pastoral poetic dramas and to the **intermedio.* The Florentines were also interested in the music of ancient Greece, but their musical ideals in fact had much in common with those of the more progressive madrigalists: a concern for creating text settings that would be emotionally appropriate, expressive, and clearly intelligible.

The first operas, then, began with dramatic pastoral poems written expressly to be set entirely to music. The music itself consisted of songs, madrigallike choruses, dances, instrumental pieces, and most important, a new manner of reciting in music: a type of *monody termed the **stile rappresentativo* or *recitative. The vocal music was written in an abbreviated fashion in which only the outer voices—the melody and the bass line—were written down, while the harmonies supported by the bass line were improvised from numerals representing intervals [see Thoroughbass].

Celebrations at the court of Mantua in 1607 and 1608 brought forth three new operas: *La *favola d'Orfeo* (1607, libretto by Alessandro Striggio) and *Arianna* (1608, libretto by Rinuccini), both by Monteverdi, and *Dafne* (1608, libretto by Rinuccini, an adaptation of the libretto set by Peri in 1598), by Marco da Gagliano. The connections between these operas and their Florentine predecessors are clear (same myth, or libretto, or librettist). But in *Orfeo,* Monteverdi realized more fully than before the expressive and musical power of the *stile rappresentativo. Orfeo* is also more elaborately scored than its operatic predecessors (although the abundance of instruments of different types probably reflects the practice of the older *intermedio*) and shows a much greater richness in the variety and complexity of its musical forms, including instrumental *toccatas and *ritornellos, strophic and ternary *arias, and madrigallike choruses.

Rome became an operatic center in the second quarter of the 17th century. Indeed, in 1600, several months before the production of Peri's *Euridice,* Emilio de' Cavalieri produced a dramatic work making use of the new style, **Rappresentatione di Anima, et di Corpo,* sometimes referred to as the first oratorio because of its allegorical characters, didactic intent, and place of presentation—the oratory of St. Philip Neri. Opera in Rome received encouragement from two important clerical families. The Barberini family (which included Pope Urban VIII) built a theater capable of holding 3,000 spectators. It opened in 1632 with *Il Sant' Alessio,* music by Stefano Landi. Giulio Rospigliosi, who was later to reign as Pope Clement IX, wrote the libretto for *Il Sant' Alessio* and for several other operas (*Chi soffre speri,* 1639; *Dal male il bene,* 1653). Recitative, the great discovery of the Florentines and the expressive heart of the earlier operas, became less important in Roman operas; arias, choruses, and instrumental preludes received a more expansive musical treatment. To the pastoral and mythological subjects preferred in Florence and Mantua were added stories from saints' lives, chivalric epics *(Erminia sul Giordano),* fantasy *(Il palazzo incantato),* and comic subjects. An interest in spectacular scenic effects, which was a part of opera from its earliest days, was taken to even more lavish heights in Rome.

The operas mentioned thus far were produced, in part, by and for an aristocratic avant-garde, or for the enrichment of ducal celebrations, particularly weddings. It was in Venice, an oligarchic republic built on trade, that the first commercial, public opera house was opened in 1637. Several changes accompanied the transformation of a courtly entertainment to a business venture. Spectacular stage effects—flying machines, ships crossing the stage, scenic transformations—were still important but were not always as lavish as in courtly entertainments. Librettos were often constructed to make use of stock scenic devices, and comic scenes were regularly incorporated. Choruses were de-emphasized, and recitative tended to be more formulaic. Arias, on the other hand, of which there might be 30 or more in an opera after mid-century, began to undergo a fuller musical development, tending toward standardized forms such as ABB and, by the final decades of the century, the da capo *aria, which would remain dominant through much of the 18th century. The leading composers of public opera in Venice initially were Monteverdi, his student Pier Francesco Cavalli, and a younger contemporary, Pietro Antonio Cesti. Of the several works Monteverdi wrote for Venice, two have survived, *Il ritorno d'Ulisse* (1640) and *L'*incoronazione di Poppea* (1642). In an operatic career that spanned some 30 years, Cavalli produced 42 operas, 27 of which have been preserved. Cesti's operas were produced not only in Venice, but also in the Hapsburg courts at Innsbruck and Vienna. Prominent through the 1680s was Giovanni Legrenzi.

The sources of French opera can be found in several indigenous French dramatic genres—tragedy, ballet, and *pastorale—reshaped under the impact of Italian opera. The librettos of French opera were taken seriously as literature and judged by standards similar to those of spoken tragedy. **Ballet de cour,* a courtly entertainment involving dance, song, prose recitation, and costume, had enjoyed not only the support but the active participation of French royalty and nobility. *Ballet was an important part of serious French opera from its beginnings through the 19th century. Also important were works in the pastoral tradition, such as Michel de la Guerre's *Le triomphe de l'Amour* (1654) and a work simply called *La pastorale* (or *La pastorale d'Issy*), on the basis of which its librettist, Pierre Perrin, received the permission of Louis XIV to form an Academy of Opera. Italian opera was most enthusiastically supported and encouraged in Paris by Cardinal Mazarin, Richelieu's successor. Between 1645 and 1662, the year of Mazarin's death, Italian operas by Cavalli, Luigi Rossi, Francesco Sacrati, and Carlo Caproli were performed at court.

The most significant figures for the creation and standardization of French opera (called *tragédie en musique* or *tragédie lyrique*) were the composer Jean-Baptiste Lully and the librettist Phillipe Quinault. Lully produced 15 operas between 1672 and 1686, all but three in collaboration with Quinault. These operas are typically in five acts (a form taken over from the theater) with subjects based on classical or chivalric stories. They begin with an *overture in two or more parts, the first stately with dotted rhythms, the second lively and imitative. There follows a prologue in which mythical or allegorical characters, who normally make no further appearance in the opera, make flattering references or allusions to the king, his court, and his policies. Lully was unwilling to allow the text to be undermined by the music. The alternation of word-dominated recitative and music-dominated arias, so serviceable for Lully's Italian contemporaries, was not a pattern he found useful; French recitative and airs did not contrast so strongly with one another. Instead, choruses, ballets, and instrumental pieces, often grouped in **divertissements,* were the pieces in which purely musical expansion was likely to take place.

Lully's operas remained in the repertory of the Académie de musique and continued to be performed well into the 18th century. His principal successors were André Campra, Marc-Antoine Charpentier, and André Destouches. Their works show a lessening of the importance of a central dramatic idea, manifested in an increased use of more or less irrelevant dances and *divertissements.* Still more loosely organized is the *opéra-ballet,* in which each act contains a separate set of characters. Italian influence on French opera after Lully is seen in the appearance of vocally ornate da capo arias called **ariettes.* The culminating master of *tragédie-lyrique* and *opéra-ballet* was Rameau. In his works (from *Hippolyte et Aricie,* 1733, his first *tragédie,* to *Zoroastre,* 1749, his last to be performed), complex harmony and rich orchestration seem to threaten the balance between music and text so much admired in Lully.

Many 17th-century English musicians and writers were aware of operatic developments in Italy and France, and every now and again an attempt would be made at producing an English variety of opera. In 1617, Ben Jonson's *Lovers Made Men* "was sung after the Italian manner, *stylo recitativo,* by Master Nicholas Lanier," but its music is not extant. *The Siege of Rhodes* (1654) is another work in which all of the dialogue was set as recitative; the music, by Henry Lawes, Matthew Locke, and others, is also lost. John Blow's *Venus and Adonis* (ca. 1684) is often cited as a significant influence on Purcell's *Dido and Aeneas* (1689, libretto by Nahum Tate), arguably the greatest English opera until the 20th century. Both works are on a small scale (performance of either would take approximately an hour) but give masterful examples of the use of music to establish character and to underscore intense emotion. These works remained more or less isolated experiments. In general, English audiences preferred either operas that were entirely foreign, that is, set to non-English texts by non-English composers, or dramatic works in which the music was clearly subsidiary or at most separate but equal. Purcell's *Dioclesian* (1690), *King Arthur* (1691), and *The Fairy Queen* (1692), sometimes called *semi-operas, show a close relation to the *masque in that the music is used more for decorative than for dramatic purposes.

Rinuccini's *Dafne,* translated into German by Martin Opitz and set to music by Heinrich Schütz, was performed in Torgau in 1627 for the wedding of the Landgrave of Hesse with the sister of the Elector of Saxony. This, so far as is known, was the first German opera, though its music is lost. German-speaking lands, however, in the midst of the Thirty Years War, were not a likely locale for the development of a new and lavish art form. After the middle of the 17th century, Italian opera was performed at court in Dresden, Munich, Hanover, and Dusseldorf, as well as in Innsbruck and Vienna.

Hamburg, a commercial port-city sometimes called the Venice of the north, attempted commercial opera starting in 1678 with the opening of the Theater am Gänsemarkt. Performances were most often in German, but performances of Italian, French, and polyglot opera (part German, part Italian) were also given. Handel was briefly associated with opera in Hamburg, but the towering figure of Hamburg opera was Reinhard Keiser, who combined the roles of director and manager of the theater with that of its chief composer, writing well over 100 operas in 40 years (1694–1734). His works show a blending of Italian, French, and German stylistic features, French influence emerging most clearly in the overtures and dances.

II. *18th century.* Just as the earliest operas received intellectual impetus from a group of aristocrats and artists, toward the end of the 17th century a similarly composed group of Roman aristocrats and writers, calling themselves the Arcadian Academy, sought to ennoble and purify the exuberantly popular art form opera had become. For ideals they turned to the theories of Aristotle; for models they turned to the French classical theater of Corneille and Racine. The most important authors of the newly reformed librettos, the librettos of **opera seria,* were Apostolo Zeno and his successor as Caesarean poet for the Hapsburg court, Pietro Metastasio. A Metastasian libretto is typically in three acts with each act divided into numerous (from 10 to 20) scenes, a scene being defined by the entrance or exit of a character. There are usually six characters, one or two of whom may be confidants; the remaining characters are connected to one another by links of love, friendship, family ties, or political obligation, any or all of which may be in conflict. The subject matter may be drawn from classical history (the sources cited include Plutarch, Herodotus, Thucydides, and Livy) or from legend. Comic elements are purged from the libretto as being inappropriate to the generally noble tone. The happy resolution of the drama, the *lieto fine,* reaffirmed for the audiences the value of moral and virtuous behavior. *Opera seria* in the 18th century marks the point of greatest importance and influence of the librettist. Each of Metastasio's librettos was set dozens of times; there are 27 *opera seria* librettos by Metastasio and hundreds of Metastasian operas. The words were enduring—they were published and were meant to be read and enjoyed as literature. The musical settings, on the other hand, were transitory.

Opera seria is dominated by the da capo aria. The importance of the aria is a reflection of the significance of the virtuoso singer, particularly the **castrato.* The heroic roles of *opera seria* were written for soprano or alto *castrati,* or for women playing male roles. Ensembles are rare, and the brief homophonic chorus with which an opera may close is often musically negligible. Except for the overture, the instrumental role is largely accompanimental. Most of the text of the libretto is set as simple, continuo-accompanied recitative *(recitativo semplice).* Recitative accompanied by strings or other instrumental groupings (*recitativo stromentato, accompagnato,* or *obbligato*) is reserved for the most dramatic moments and the most important characters in the opera. Although *opera seria* used Italian texts, the musical style was international. That is, the composers, performers, and audiences were drawn from all locations in Europe with the exception of France, which maintained its own national style of opera.

The composers of 18th-century Italian opera were strikingly prolific. Alessandro Scarlatti, who made important contributions to the development and expansion of the aria, composed approximately 115 operas between about 1680 and 1720, of which some 50 are extant. Among the most important composers in the generation following Scarlatti are Leonardo Vinci (40 operas), Leonardo Leo (ca. 60 operas), Francesco Feo (14 operas), Nicola Porpora (44 operas), and Antonio Vivaldi (ca. 46 operas, 21 extant). For many of Italy's most prominent opera composers of the 18th century, Naples was an important center of activity [see Neapolitan school]. Handel, a German composer writing Italian operas for an English audience in

London, exemplifies the international aspects of *opera seria.* That he was active away from the mainstream did not prevent him from producing some of the finest examples of the genre (e.g., **Giulio Cesare in Egitto,* 1724).

The middle of the 18th century saw a trend toward greater musical expansion with the appearance of longer, more richly accompanied arias. Johann Adolf Hasse, active at the court at Dresden and one of Metastasio's preferred composers, was widely admired. At the same time, serious opera underwent certain changes that tended to increase its dramatic component. The major composers in this operatic reform, Niccolò Jommelli, Tommaso Traetta, and Gluck, brought about a certain rapprochement of Viennese, French, and Italian operatic traditions. This led to a reduction in importance of the aria as a static, purely lyrical entity and an increase in importance of accompanied recitative, of choruses, and of instrumental writing—both in the accompaniments of arias and in separate instrumental pieces; there was also greater flexibility in the formal construction of arias. Gluck's prominence as a reformer is due in part to his operas **Orfeo ed Euridice* (Vienna, 1762) and **Alceste* (Vienna, 1767) and in part to his statements on reform, most notably his preface to *Alceste* (trans. in *SR,* pp. 673–75), in which he declares that he has "striven to restrict music to its true office of serving poetry by means of expression" and that he believes that his "greatest labor should be devoted to seeking a beautiful simplicity." Gluck's last operas were written for performance in Paris. They include **Iphigénie en Aulide* (1774), *Armide* (1777), and **Iphigénie en Tauride* (1779), as well as French versions of *Orfeo* and *Alceste.*

The 18th century also saw the vigorous development of comic opera. This development was enhanced and accelerated by the expulsion of comic scenes from serious opera. Comic scenes, such as scenes with comic servants, were found in operas before the middle of the 17th century and were also a feature of entertainment provided between the acts of operas. By the end of the 17th century, such scenes had begun to decline in number and were often placed at the ends of acts. The reforms of this period leading to *opera seria* removed the comic scenes altogether, confining them to independent works termed *intermezzi that were played between the acts of serious operas. Additional sources for comic opera included spoken comedy, which yielded stock situations and characters. Comic opera in dialect was first heard in Naples in the first decade of the 18th century, and this repertoire, featuring larger casts than those used in intermezzi, also contributed to the development of *opera buffa.* In comic operas of the 18th century, distinct musical procedures emerged that point the way from Baroque style to Classical. The weaving of a musical fabric based on short motives that could be easily repeated or interrupted gave music a flexibility more suitable to comedy. Unlike serious opera, comic opera made considerable use of duets, trios, quartets, and larger ensembles, particularly as *finales of acts.

Several national varieties of comic opera arose. Italian *opera buffa,* French **opéra comique,* English *ballad opera, and German *Singspiel have in common that they were in the language of the audience and were popular, commercial works in the sense that they were supported by a largely anonymous audience rather than a specific, known patron. *Opéra comique,* Singspiel, and ballad opera are alike in their alternation of musical numbers with spoken dialogue; *opera buffa* continued to set dialogue as recitative. Comic opera also tended to shed mythological distancing and use contemporary, plebeian characters. An exception to this is Singspiel, which showed a preference for exotic, oriental, or fantastic settings.

Mozart's operatic production includes three genres—*opera seria, opera buffa,* and Singspiel—and brings each to unique heights. **Idomeneo* (1781) and *La *clemenza di Tito* (1791) are both examples of *opera seria,* composed for courtly occasions. *La clemenza di Tito* is a setting of a much-adapted Metastasian libretto. Mozart's three mature *opere buffe, Le *nozze di Figaro* (1786), **Don Giovanni* (1787, a work with more serious overtones), and **Così fan tutte* (1790), are notable for the subtlety and penetration of characterization, the integration of vocal and instrumental factors, and the adaptation of classical symphonic style in their ensemble finales. Mozart's final opera, *Die *Zauberflöte,* is a Singspiel that fuses the most diverse musical and dramatic features.

III. *19th century.* French opera, at the end of the 18th and beginning of the 19th century, responded to the cataclysmic social and political changes taking place in that country. The Opéra (Académie royale de musique, descended from Perrin's academy), previously supported by royal and aristocratic patronage, was largely neglected, while *opéra comique* increased in importance. At the same time *opéra comique* changed significantly in character; lightheartedness and naïve charm were replaced by moral earnestness and explorations of the darker sides of human personality. *Rescue opera came into vogue at this time. Characteristic examples are Jean-François Le Sueur's *La caverne* (1793; heroine rescued from bandits in a cave) and Cherubini's *Les *deux journées* (1800; hero saved from unjust arrest). During Napoleon's reign, the Opéra resumed an important role, producing heroic and grandiose works such as Gaspare Spontini's *La vestale* (1807) and *Fernand Cortez* (1809). At this time Paris could boast three major active opera houses, one producing grand opera (the Opéra), one *opéra comique* (the Opéra-comique), and one Italian opera (the Théâtre italien).

Grand opera, as it developed in the second and third quarters of the 19th century, produced significant works in its own right and influenced the course of Italian and German opera as well. Initiated by Rossini's *Le siège de Corinthe* (1826) and **Guillaume Tell* (1829) and Daniel-François-Esprit Auber's *La muette de Portici* (1828), grand opera reached its apex in the collaborations of Meyerbeer and the librettist Eugène Scribe—**Robert le diable* (1831), *Les *Huguenots* (1836), *Le *prophète* (1849), and *L'*africaine* (1865). These works derive their energy from large-scale conflicts—not just of individuals but of whole national or religious groups—that are frozen at climactic moments into striking, massed tableaux in which all possible aural and visual forces—soloists, chorus, orchestra, ballet, costumes, scenery—contribute to achieve a maximum effect.

Somewhere between the Opéra and Opéra-comique, and a rival to both, was the Théâtre lyrique, which, in the 21 or so years between its founding and its failure in 1870, produced such works as Gounod's **Faust* (1859) and **Roméo et Juliette* (1867), Bizet's *Les *pêcheurs de perles* (1863) and *La jolie fille de Perth* (1867), and a portion of Berlioz's *Les *troyens* (1863). The term lyric opera, though frequently used, does not indicate a distinct genre, though the works given at the Théâtre lyrique (despite the example of *Les troyens*) were generally smaller in scale and more intimate in style than grand opera.

The dominating figure in Italian opera at the beginning of the 19th century was Rossini—the "Napoleon of music." Rossini's best-known works are the comic opera *Il *barbiere di Siviglia* (Rome, 1816) and the grand opera *Guillaume Tell* (Paris, 1829). Although he retired from operatic production early (in 1829, at the age of 36), he remained the model for a succeeding generation of composers, and his works formed the prototype by which theirs were judged. Rossini was influential in matters of orchestration—use of woodwinds, on-stage bands, repetitive orchestral figures—and in the construction of formal designs for solos, duets, and ensembles. The most important composers of Italian opera of the 1830s were Bellini (*La *sonnambula,* 1830; **Norma,* 1831) and Donizetti (*L' *elisir d'amore,* 1832; **Lucia di Lammermoor,* 1836). In the works of Rossini, Donizetti, and Bellini, several significant trends emerge. One is the development of a new set of character stereotypes based on vocal types. The heroic voice became the tenor (rather than the alto or soprano as it had been in 18th-century *opera seria*); the baritone became the rival in love, the villain, or sometimes a father or older adviser. Another trend is the increasing somberness of plots. Tragic endings replaced happy ones in serious operas; comic operas represented the smaller share of Rossini's output and were composed less and less frequently after the first third of the century. Furthermore, the aria, with introductory *scena,* became longer, incorporating more and more action; a leading character was likely to have no more than one aria in an act.

After 1840, Italian opera was dominated by the work of Verdi. From the start of his career, Verdi's operas were associated in the public's mind with hopes for the unification and independence of Italy—an association that Verdi fostered with stirring settings of librettos dealing with the struggle against personal or national oppression. Verdi's early operas are notable for their directness of expression, their rhythmic vitality, and their tendency to favor confrontational duets (rather than arias) at dramatic high points. Vital to this new conception was the emergence of the Verdian baritone, a voice type often set against the hero (tenor) or heroine (soprano). **Rigoletto* (1851), *Il *trovatore* (1853), and *La *traviata* (1853) mark Verdi's full maturity and assured his lasting international reputation. Later works such as **Don Carlos* (1867) and **Aida* (1871) show the important influence of grand opera. The last operas, **Otello* (1887) and **Falstaff* (1893), often singled out for their musico-dramatic continuity, have a chromatically expanded harmonic palette and a new subtlety of scoring, but nevertheless remain essentially true to the Italian tradition.

Among the composers of operas on German texts at the beginning of the 19th century were Beethoven, Spohr, E. T. A. Hoffmann, Weber, and Heinrich August Marschner. On the whole, they preferred a form that alternated spoken dialogue with set numbers, that is, *Singspiel. A solution to the problem of writing convincing recitative to a German text largely evaded composers until Wagner, who, with characteristic boldness, restructured both the texts and the music. The librettos of the operas of this period show Romantic features such as an interest in folk elements, an emphasis on nature as it impinges on man or anthropomorphically reflects his state of mind, and the intrusion of the supernatural upon the everyday world. Examples are Hoffmann's *Undine* (1816), Spohr's *Faust* (1816), Weber's *Der *Freischütz* (1821), and Marschner's *Der Vampyr* (1828).

Although Wagner, especially in his early years, was very much an eclectic, borrowing ideas, themes, and visual impressions wherever he found them, his operas nevertheless represent a new era. The musical changes that Wagner's style underwent in the course of his career were fundamental and radical, leaving no element—rhythm, melody, harmony, counterpoint, tone color, form—unaltered. One category of changes worked in the direction of avoiding small musical units; ends of phrases were obscured by eschewing conventional cadences, and arias and ensembles were merged into the flow of action or replaced by expressive arioso. With *Der *fliegende Holländer* (1843) and *Das Rheingold* (1869), Wagner experimented with merging the acts into one continuous unit, the opera; with *Der *Ring des Nibelungen* (first performed complete in 1876), he suggested that even the single opera was too small a unit, the complete work being no less than a cycle of four operas. As a means of organizing his new structures, Wagner developed the very flexible use of the **Leitmotif.*

Wagner's mature works may be divided into Romantic operas—*Der fliegende Holländer, *Tann-*

häuser (1845, revised 1861 and 1865), **Lohengrin* (1850)—and music dramas—*Das Rheingold, Die Walküre, Siegfried, Götterdämmerung* [see *Ring des Nibelungen, Der*], **Tristan und Isolde* (1865), *Die *Meistersinger* (1868), and **Parsifal* (1882). In these works, Wagner recognized that the apposite subject matter for his operas was legend and myth, subjects that simultaneously emphasized the national (German and Nordic) in their settings and the universal in their issues.

One result of 19th-century *nationalism was the appearance of operas using a broader range of languages and musical idioms, particularly in eastern Europe. Most notable among Polish operas was Stanisław Moniuszko's *Halka* (revised version, 1858); popular Hungarian works were Ferenc Erkel's *Hunyadi László* (1844) and *Bánk bán* (1861). A more significant 19th-century school of opera developed in Czechoslovakia with the works of Smetana (*The *Bartered Bride,* 1866; *Dalibor,* 1868) and Dvořák (*Rusalka,* 1901). Even more important was the development of opera in Russia. The first of the Russian operatic composers to achieve resounding fame in Russia (and international recognition as well) was Mikhail Glinka. He composed only two operas, *A *Life for the Tsar* (1836) and **Ruslan and Lyudmila* (1842), but with these two he explored the wellsprings of Russian nationalist opera: patriotic subjects drawn from earlier Russian history and Russian myth, and legend or fairy tale, particularly as told by the great poet Pushkin. A concern for apt Russian declamation was the overriding musical concern of Glinka's younger contemporary Alexander Dargomïzhsky, and perhaps for that very reason, his last opera, *The Stone Guest* (first performed posthumously in 1872), based on a story by Pushkin, is of more theoretical than musical interest.

In the second half of the 19th century, Russian opera followed two courses. The self-proclaimed nationalistic manner was pursued by Borodin, Musorgsky, and Rimsky-Korsakov. Of this group, only Rimsky-Korsakov was a professional musician, and it was he who completed, revised, and reorchestrated the works of the other two. He composed more than a dozen operas, of which *The *Golden Cockerel* (1909) is perhaps the best known. The Russian opera that has achieved the most enduring international fame is Musorgsky's **Boris Godunov* (1874). The operas of Tchaikovsky were not so overtly nationalistic, although some, such as **Eugen Onegin* (1879) and *The *Queen of Spades* (1890), made use of texts by Pushkin.

IV. *20th century.* Opera in the period since the death of Wagner has exhibited abundant diversity in terms of subject matter, musical styles, philosophical viewpoints, and social aims. Contributing to this diversity was the influence of a number of different artistic and literary movements such as naturalism, impressionism, surrealism, and symbolism. The first operatic masterpiece of the 20th century was Debussy's **Pelléas et Mélisande* (1902), a setting of Maurice Maeterlinck's symbolist play. Notable for its sensitive declamation, emotional reticence, psychological penetration, delicacy of scoring, and evocative atmosphere, it was the only opera Debussy completed.

In Germany, as elsewhere in Europe, Wagner's operas had profound influence but few true successors. Richard Strauss was greeted as Wagner's heir apparent after **Salome* (1905) and **Elektra* (1909), but his later works—*Der *Rosenkavalier* (1911), **Ariadne auf Naxos* (1916), *Die *Frau ohne Schatten* (1919), **Arabella* (1933)—did not pursue the same paths of intense chromaticism and emotionalism. The operas composed in Italy at the turn of the century maintained clear links with the Romantic tradition. The **verismo* movement helped launch the careers of Mascagni (**Cavalleria rusticana,* 1890) and Leoncavallo (**Pagliacci,* 1892) and also had an effect on some of Puccini's operas such as **Tosca* (1900) and *Il tabarro* (1918) [see *Trittico*]. Many of Puccini's works—e.g., *La *bohème* (1896) and **Madama Butterfly* (1904)—have enjoyed enduring success.

Composers from Czechoslovakia, Hungary, and Russia produced works that not only are of interest as examples of nationalistic impulses but that are of absolute value in the international repertory. Among these works are Janáček's **Kát'a Kabanová* (1921), *The *Cunning Little Vixen* (1924), and *The Makropoulos Case* (1926); Prokofiev's *The *Love for Three Oranges* (1921) and *War and Peace* (1945–55); Shostakovich's *The Nose* (1930) and **Lady Macbeth of the Mtsensk District* (1934, revised 1963); Bartók's **Bluebeard's Castle* (1918); and Kodály's *Háry János* (1926). England has experienced a significant operatic renaissance through the works of Britten—**Peter Grimes* (1945), **Billy Budd* (1951), *The *Turn of the Screw* (1954), *A *Midsummer Night's Dream* (1960), and **Death in Venice* (1973)—and Tippett—*The Midsummer Marriage* (1952), *The Knot Garden* (1969), and *The Ice Break* (1976).

Various musical trends that emerged in the 1920s and 1930s affected the operas written then and in successive decades. Jazz was reflected in some operas composed after World War I, notably Krenek's **Jonny spielt auf* (1927) and Weill's *Die *Dreigroschenoper* (1928) and *Aufstieg und Fall der Stadt Mahagonny* (1930), the latter two works written in collaboration with Bertolt Brecht and reflecting his ideas of Epic Theater. Two American operas that make use of jazz are Scott Joplin's *Treemonisha* (1911–15) and Gershwin's **Porgy and Bess* (1935). Operas in which the organizing powers of tonality are either severely challenged or else replaced by the twelve-tone system are Berg's **Wozzeck* (1925) and **Lulu* (1937) and Schoenberg's **Moses und Aron* (first staged performance in 1957). Serial writing is also important in Dallapiccola's *Volo di notte* (1940), *Il prigioniero* (1950), and *Ulisse* (1968), and in Sessions's **Montezuma* (1964). More widely performed, however, have been some operas that follow more traditional lines, including works of Menotti (*The *Medium,* 1945; *The *Consul,* 1949; **Amahl and the Night Visitors,* 1951) and others. The most frequently performed neoclassical opera is Stravinsky's *The *Rake's Progress* (1951). Among more recent innovative works are two operas by minimalist composer Philip Glass, *Einstein on the Beach* (1975) and *Satyagraha* (1980), and *Saint François d'Assise: Scènes franciscaines* (1983), a late work by Olivier Messiaen.

Bibl.: *Reference.* Oscar G. T. Sonneck, *Catalogue of Opera Librettos Printed before 1800* (Washington, D.C.: Government Printing Office, 1914). Ernest Newman, *Stories of the Great Operas and Their Composers* (New York: Garden City Pub Co, 1930). Id., *More Stories of Famous Operas* (New York: A A Knopf, 1943). Gustav Kobbé, *The New Kobbé's Complete Opera Book,* 9th ed., rev. the Earl of Harewood (New York: Putnam, 1976). See also Dictionaries and encyclopedias V, 5.

General. Hermann Kretzschmar, *Geschichte der Oper* (Leipzig: Breitkopf & Härtel, 1919). Oskar Bie, *Die Oper,* 10th ed. (Berlin: S Fischer, 1923). Richard A. Streatfeild, *The Opera,* 5th ed., rev. and enl. (London: G Routledge & Sons, 1925). Paul Bekker, *The Changing Opera,* trans. Arthur Mendel (London: Dent, 1936). Ildebrando Pizzetti, *Musica e dramma* (Rome: Edizioni della Bussola, 1945). Joseph Gregor, *Kulturgeschichte der Oper: Ihre Verbindung mit dem Leben, den Werken, des Geistes und der Politik,* 2nd ed., rev. and enl. (Vienna: Gallus Verlag, 1950). Egon Wellesz, *Essays on Opera,* trans. Patricia Kean (London: Dobson, 1950). Joseph Kerman, *Opera as Drama* (New York: A A Knopf, 1956). Helmut Schmidt-Garre, *Oper: Eine Kulturgeschichte* (Cologne: A Volk, 1963). Ulrich W. Weisstein, ed., *The Essence of Opera* (New York: Free Press of Glencoe, 1964). Edward J. Dent, *Opera,* rev. ed. (Baltimore: Penguin, 1965). Donald J. Grout, *A Short History of Opera,* 2nd ed. (New York: Columbia U Pr, 1965). Charles E. Hamm, *Opera* (Boston: Allyn & Bacon, 1966). Gary Schmidgall, *Literature as Opera* (New York: Oxford U Pr, 1977). Robert Donington, *The Opera* (New York: Harcourt Brace Jovanovich, 1978). John Drummond, *Opera in Perspective* (Minneapolis: U of Minn Pr, 1980). Paul Robinson, *Opera and Ideas: From Mozart to Strauss* (New York: Harper & Row, 1985).

Special topics. Hugo Goldschmidt, *Studien zur Geschichte der italienischen Oper im 17. Jahrhundert* (Leipzig: Breitkopf & Härtel, 1901–4). Jules Ecorcheville, *De Lulli à Rameau, 1690–1730* (Paris: Impressions L.-M. Fortin & Cie, 1906). Edgar Istel, *Die komische Oper: Eine historisch-ästhetische Studie* (Stuttgart: C Grüninger [Klett & Hartmann], 1906). Oscar G. T. Sonneck, *Early Opera in America* (New York: G Schirmer, 1915). Michele Scherillo, *L'opera buffa napoletana durante il settecento,* 2nd ed. (Milan: R Sandron, 1917). Andrea della Corte, *L'opera comica italiana nel '700* (Bari: Laterza & Figli, 1923). Edward J. Dent, *Foundations of English Opera* (Cambridge: Cambridge U Pr, 1928; R: New York: Da Capo, 1965). Lionel de La Laurencie, *Les créateurs de l'opéra français,* new ed. (Paris: F Alkan, 1930). Paul Marie Masson, *L'opéra de Rameau* (Paris: H Laurens, 1930). Nicholas Findeisen, "The Earliest Russian Operas," *MQ* 19 (1933): 331–40. Alfred Einstein, *Gluck,* trans. Eric Blom (London: Dent, 1936). Andrea della Corte, *Tre secoli di opera italiana* (Turin: Edizione Arione, 1938). Donald J. Grout, "The Origin of the Opéra-Comique" (Ph.D. diss., Harvard Univ., 1939). Ludwig Schiedermair, *Die deutsche Oper: Grundzüge ihres Werdens und Wesens,* 3rd ed. (Bonn: F Dümmler, 1943). Edward J. Dent, *Mozart's Operas: A Critical Study,* 2nd ed. (London: Oxford U Pr, 1947). William L. Crosten, *French Grand Opera: An Art and a Business* (New York: King's Crown Pr, 1948). Anna Amalie Abert, ed. *Die Oper von den Anfängen bis zum Beginn des 19. Jahrhunderts, MW* 5 (Cologne: A Volk, 195?). Martin Cooper, *Russian Opera* (London: M Parrish, 1951). Eric W. White, *The Rise of English Opera* (London: J Lehmann, 1951). Simon Towneley Worsthorne, *Venetian Opera in the Seventeenth Century* (Oxford: Clarendon Pr, 1954; R: New York: Da Capo, 1984). Alan Yorke-Long, *Music at Court: Four Eighteenth-Century Studies* (London: Weidenfeld & Nicolson, 1954). Nathaniel Burt, "Opera in Arcadia," *MQ* 41 (1955): 145–70. Hellmuth C. Wolff, *Die Barockoper in Hamburg, 1678–1738* (Wolfenbüttel: Möseler, 1957). Robert L. Weaver, "Florentine Comic Operas of the Seventeenth Century" (Ph.D. diss., Univ. of North Carolina, 1958). Joseph E. Rotondi, "Literary and Musical Aspects of Roman Opera, 1600–1650" (Ph.D. diss., Univ. of Pennsylvania, 1959). Giacomo Meyerbeer, *Briefwechsel und Tagebücher,* 3 vols., ed. Heinz Becker (Berlin: W de Gruyter, 1960–75). Patricia Howard, *Gluck and the Birth of Modern Opera* (London: Barrie & Rockliff, 1963). William Ashbrook, *Donizetti* (London: Cassell, 1965). Robert S. Freeman, *Opera without Drama: Currents of Change in Italian Opera, 1675–1725* (Ph.D. diss., Princeton Univ., 1967; Ann Arbor: UMI Res Pr, 1981). *Grout,* 1968. Herbert Weinstock, *Rossini* (New York: A A Knopf, 1968). Rodolfo Celletti, "Il vocalismo italiano da Rossini a Donizetti," *AnMca* 5 (1968): 267–94; 7 (1969): 214–47. Winton Dean, *Handel and the Opera Seria* (Berkeley and Los Angeles: U of Cal Pr, 1969). Cuthbert M. Girdlestone, *Jean-Philippe Rameau,* rev. and enl. ed. (New York: Dover, 1969). Friedrich Lippmann, *Vincenzo Bellini und die italienische Opera Seria seiner Zeit, AnMca* 6 (1969). Julian G. Rushton, "Music and Drama at the Académie Royale de Musique (Paris) 1774–1789" (Ph.D. diss., Oxford, 1969). Philip Gossett, "Gioachino Rossini and the Conventions of Composition," *AM* 42 (1970): 48–58. Id., "The Operas of Rossini: Problems of Textual Criticism in Nineteenth-Century Opera" (Ph.D. diss., Princeton Univ., 1970). Herbert Weinstock, *Vincenzo Bellini: His Life and His Operas* (New York: A A Knopf, 1971). Michael F. Robinson, *Naples and Neapolitan Opera* (Oxford: Clarendon Pr, 1972). Roger Fiske, *English Theatre Music in the Eighteenth Century* (London: Oxford U Pr, 1973). Robert M. Isherwood, *Music in the Service of the King* (Ithaca, N.Y.: Cornell U Pr, 1973). Mosco Carner, *Puccini: A Critical Biography,* 2nd ed. (London: Duckworth, 1974). Friedrich Lippmann, "Der italienische Vers und der musikalische Rhythmus," *AnMca* 12 (1973): 253–369; 14 (1974): 324–410; 15 (1975): 298–333. Siegfried Goslich, *Die deutsche romantische Oper* (Tutzing: Schneider, 1975). Edward J. Dent, *The Rise of Romantic Opera,* ed. Winton Dean (Cambridge: Cambridge U Pr, 1976). Aubrey S. Garlington, "German Romantic Opera and the Problem of Origins," *MQ* 63 (1977): 247–63. William S. Mann, *The Operas of Mozart* (New York: Oxford U Pr, 1977). Daniel Heartz, "The Creation of the Buffo Finale in Italian Opera," *PRMA* 104 (1977–78): 67–78. John Warrack, "German Operatic Ambitions at the Beginning of the Nineteenth Century," *PRMA* 104 (1977–78): 79–88. James R. Anthony, *French Baroque Music from Beaujoyeulx to Rameau,* rev. ed. (London: Batsford, 1978). Julian Budden, *The Operas of Verdi,* 3 vols. (New York: Oxford U Pr, 1978–81). Barbara R. Hanning, *Of Poetry and Music's Power: Human-*

ism and the Creation of Opera (Ann Arbor: UMI Res Pr, 1980). Robert Donington, *The Rise of Opera* (New York: Scribner, 1981). Carl Dahlhaus, *Vom Musikdrama zur Literaturoper: Aufsätze zur neueren Operngeschichte* (Munich: Katzbichler, 1983). Eric Walter White, *A History of English Opera* (London: Faber, 1983). C.G.

Opéra-ballet [Fr.]. A musico-dramatic form that flourished in France starting in the late 17th century. The principal composers were Campra, Mouret, and Montéclair. The genre makes use of musical types found in ballet (instrumental pieces, dances) and in opera (recitatives, arias, choruses), but the dramatic premise linking the musical numbers is likely to be tenuous. See also Ballet in opera.

Opéra bouffe [Fr.]. A type of French comic opera. The term was used by Offenbach starting in 1858 with **Orphée aux enfers,* a work that had its premiere at the Bouffes Parisiens. See Operetta.

Opera buffa [It.]. Comic opera. See Opera II.

Opéra comique [Fr.]. (1) An opera on a French text with musical numbers separated by spoken dialogue. In the 18th century, the treatment of the subject matter of an *opéra comique* was likely to be lighthearted or sentimental. In the 19th century, *opéra comique* plots incorporated serious or tragic events. In such works, e.g., Bizet's **Carmen,* the adjective *comique* is divorced from the notion of the comic or humorous and refers only to the presence of spoken dialogue. See Opera II. (2) Opéra-comique. The company established by the French government in Paris in 1801 for the purpose of producing *opéra comique.* It was formed from two earlier companies, one with an intermittent history dating to 1715, at times known by this name. It occupied a succession of different theaters, the Salle Favart being the one most closely associated with it and providing the name (since 1976) for its descendant.

Opera houses. The first public opera house was the Teatro San Cassiano in Venice, opened in 1637. In the next hundred years such houses appeared all over Europe. Several 18th-century examples are still in use, although usually more or less altered by remodeling and reconstruction following fires. The small court theater at Drottningholm, Sweden, however, survives almost intact with its machinery and scenery.

Opera houses have often tended toward the grandiose, as demonstrations of dynastic, national, or civic magnificence and pride. The Paris Opéra (1875) came to symbolize its city and its epoch. Wagner's Festspielhaus at Bayreuth (1876) is unique among opera houses for its specialized purpose and as a demonstration of its creator's ideas on opera and drama and their effect on theater design.

The following is a list of the principal opera houses of the present day, in some cases notable more for the company performing there than for the theater itself. *United States:* The oldest American opera house worthy of the name is Philadelphia's Academy of Music (1857), now primarily a concert hall. Others include: New York, Metropolitan Opera House and New York City Opera at the New York State Theater (both at Lincoln Center); Chicago, Lyric Opera at the Civic Opera House; San Francisco, War Memorial Opera House; Houston, Houston Grand Opera at the Wortham Theater Center; Santa Fe, Santa Fe Opera. *Italy:* Naples, San Carlo; Bologna, Comunale; Milan, La Scala; Parma, Regio; Rome, Opera; Venice, La Fenice. *Germany:* Berlin, Staatsoper, Komische Oper, and Deutsche Oper (formerly Städtische Oper); Dresden, Staatsoper; Munich, Nationaltheater; Hamburg, Staatsoper; Stuttgart, Stuttgart Oper at the Staatstheater; Bayreuth, Festspielhaus. *France:* Paris, Opéra National de Paris (at both the Palais Garnier and Opéra Bastille) and Théâtre du Châtelet; Lyons, Opéra National de Lyons. *Austria:* Vienna, Staatsoper and Volksoper. *Great Britain:* London, Royal Opera House (Covent Garden) and English National Opera at the Coliseum; Glyndebourne, Glyndebourne Opera House. *Argentina:* Buenos Aires, Colón. *Russia:* Moscow, Bolshoi; St. Petersburg, Kirov Opera at Mariinsky Theater. *Spain:* Madrid, Teatro Real. *Australia:* Sydney, Sydney Opera House.

In the U.S. in the late 19th and early 20th centuries the term opera house was also used, especially in smaller cities and towns, for any theater or concert hall.

Bibl.: Spike (Patrick Cairnes) Hughes, *Great Opera Houses* (London: Weidenfeld & Nicolson, 1956). Anthony Gishford, ed., *Grand Opera: The Story of the World's Leading Opera Houses and Personalities* (New York: Viking, 1972).

Opera semiseria [It.]. An operatic genre, arising in the second half of the 18th century, in which both comic and serious elements are present. An *opera semiseria* is likely to have ornate arias, such as would not be out of place in *opera seria,* as well as ensemble finales more characteristic of *opera buffa.* The genesis of *opera semiseria* may be seen in part as a conflation of Italian comic and serious opera, but also as a result of the sentimentalizing influence of the *comédie larmoyante* and later of *rescue opera on comic opera. See Opera II.

Opera seria [It.]. A form of opera prevalent through the 18th century. Set to Italian librettos, notably those of Apostolo Zeno and Pietro Metastasio, operas of this type were composed by Italians, Austrians, and Germans and were performed in all the major countries of Europe with the exception of France. The characters of *opera seria* are usually drawn from ancient history. The drama is often one of making the morally right choice rather than a drama of action. An *opera seria* is generally in three acts. Its basic musical components are simple recitative and da capo exit arias—perhaps 25 in the course of an opera. In the second half of the

18th century, orchestrally accompanied recitative, ensembles, and sometimes choruses and ballets were found more frequently in *opera seria* [see Opera II]. The term was also used early in the 19th century for some works by composers such as Rossini, Bellini, and Donizetti.

Operetta. In the 17th and 18th centuries, an operatic work of small scale and pretensions, one that could equally well be classified as *intermezzo, *opera buffa* [see Opera II], **opéra comique,* or *Singspiel. Starting in the middle of the 19th century, operetta developed as a distinct genre, first in France and then in the Austro-Hungarian empire, Germany, England, and the U.S. Operetta is an essentially popular form of entertainment made up of spoken dialogue, song, and dance, whose tone may range from sentimental comedy, through satire and parody, to outright farce.

The originator of the modern operetta is Jacques Offenbach. He composed over 90 works in one, two, three, or four acts; some of these, starting with **Orphée aux enfers* (1858), are designated as *opéras bouffes* and have a pronounced satirical strain. The success of Offenbach's operettas in Vienna provided the impetus for the composition of similar works first by Franz von Suppé and later by Johann Strauss the younger. Strauss composed about 16 operettas, mostly in three acts, the most successful of which is *Die *Fledermaus* (1873). The distinctive flavor of Viennese operettas comes, in part, from their invigorating waltz-rhythm and polka-rhythm numbers. After Strauss, the Viennese tradition was continued in Franz Lehár's *Die *lustige Witwe* (1905). A characteristically English form of operetta was developed by Gilbert and Sullivan. Sullivan's musical style, occasionally parodistic but more often simply eclectic, complemented Gilbert's witty social satire. They produced 14 works together between 1871 and 1896 and also some works with other collaborators.

The operettas performed in the U.S. in the 19th century were mainly importations from Europe or imitations of such works. Victor Herbert, Rudolf Friml, and Sigmund Romberg, all European born and trained, perpetuated the genre in the first two decades of the 20th century. Some of the staged works by Gershwin, such as *Of Thee I Sing* (1931), could be termed operettas.

By the 1920s and 1930s, the terms musical comedy, musical drama, or simply musical came to be preferred to operetta, although it is debatable whether the new terms indicate new genres. See also Musical comedy.

Ophicleide [Fr. *ophicléide;* Ger. *Ophikleide;* It. *oficleide;* Sp. *figle*]. An alto or bass brass instrument, tall and narrow in shape, with nine to twelve woodwindlike side holes and keys. Ophicleides were invented in Paris about 1817 by Jean-Hilaire Asté, known as Halary. They were intended to be the lower members of a brass-instrument family based on the *keyed bugle. In addition to keyed bugles in E♭ and B♭, which Halary called *clavitubes,* this family included *quinticlaves* (alto ophicleides) in six-foot F and E♭ and ophicleides in eight-foot C and B♭. The bass ophicleide was by far the most successful and found use in symphony and opera orchestras as well as in military bands of the 1830s and 1840s and even later. Its parts are now played on the tuba. See ill. under Brass instruments.

Bibl.: Clifford Bevan, *The Tuba Family,* rev. ed. (Winchester: Piccolo, 2000). R.E.E.

Opus [Lat., pl. *opera;* Fr. *oeuvre;* Ger. *Opus;* It. *opera,* pl. *opere;* Sp. *opus*]. Work; often abbreviated op. (pl. opp.). The term is most often used with a number to designate a work in its chronological relationship to a composer's other works. These numbers are often unreliable guides to chronology, however. They may have been assigned by various publishers rather than by the composer. There may be conflicting assignments for individual works. And some genres, notably vocal works and operas, were often not assigned such numbers at all. In the cases of Haydn and Mozart, for example, they are so unreliable that they are rarely used, the numbering of scholarly *thematic catalogs being used instead [see K., Hob.]. The use of the term to designate individual works or collections of works by number begins around 1600 with composers such as Lodovico Viadana, Adriano Banchieri, and Biagio Marini. In the 17th and 18th centuries, an opus often included at first 12 and later 6 separate works, each identified by number, e.g., op. 20 no. 3. The numbering within an opus is not a reliable guide to chronology either.

Orage. In 19th century French organs, a "thunder pedal" that played several bass notes at the same time; popularly used in improvised "storm" pieces.

Oral transmission. See Transmission.

Oratio [Lat.]. Prayer, *collect.

Oratoric(al) neumes. See Neume.

Oratorio. An extended musical setting of a text based on religious or ethical subject matter, consisting of narrative, dramatic, and contemplative elements. The oratorio originated in the 17th century. Throughout most of its history it was intended for performance without scenery, costume, or action. Most oratorios from the 17th century place little emphasis on the chorus, while those from 18th century on tend to use the chorus extensively.

I. *Origins.* Oratorio originally meant prayer hall, a building normally located adjacent to a church and carefully designed as a setting for community experiences that are distinct from the regular liturgy, yet conducive to the goals of religion. Such buildings were brought into existence under the auspices of the Congregation of the Oratory, a religious reform movement in the Catholic Church that had been founded by Saint

Philip Neri (1515–95). Oratorio buildings were rectangular in shape, without transepts, and usually seated between 200 and 400 people. They were acoustically optimal not only for lectures but for music as well. The 16th-century Oratorio di Santa Lucia del Gonfalone in Rome, now regularly used as a concert hall, reveals the exemplary acoustics of such spaces. In these rooms the oratorio as a musical genre was born.

The Baroque oratorio finds its significant roots in certain late 16th-century *motets, which, like some madrigals of the period, contain elements of dramatic narration and dialogue. At the turn of the century, when monody and opera were developed, composers lost no time in imitating these new fashions in the realms of religious music. Emilio de' Cavalieri's *Rappresentatione di Anima, et di Corpo* (Rome, 1600) was a bold attempt to create a religious opera. But because it ill suited the needs and expectations of the oratorio community, it did not lead to further works of its kind.

More indicative of the music that was current in the Roman oratorio in the first decades of the 17th century is Giovanni Francesco Anerio's *Teatro armonico spirituale di madrigali* for five to eight voices (Rome, 1619). All of the texts in this collection are based on biblical passages or the lives of the saints, and many of the texts employ *dialogue. The largest composition in the *Teatro* depicts the conversion of St. Paul, a favorite Counter-Reformation story.

Because the oratorio reflected the Counter-Reformation zeal to attract the broad populace to the Church, most oratorios were written in the Italian language (the *oratorio volgare*). A notable exception was the situation at the important Oratorio associated with the Church of San Marcello in Rome, where the aristocratic membership, the Arciconfraternità del Santissimo Crocifisso, commissioned oratorios with librettos in Latin. This is the language set by the greatest composer of oratorios of the mid-17th century, Giacomo Carissimi. Thirteen of his surviving works are classified as oratorios, and presumably they were all composed for the Santissimo Crocifisso. Most of them involve a narrator *(historicus)* and a story drawn from the Old Testament. The chorus plays an important role in most of Carissimi's oratorios, which is contrary to the norm in Italian oratorios of the 17th century.

In the latter half of the 17th century, oratorios of strongly Roman character were produced in other Italian cities (Venice, Bologna, Modena, Florence, Naples), and trends toward secularization became evident. Oratorios were now regularly performed in locations other than the traditional oratorio buildings (e.g., at the meetings of the *academies in the palaces of the nobility), and they were even performed in public theaters. They acquired a length similar to operas, and poets published the librettos of their oratorios. The stories often involved the lives of the saints and sometimes had a distinctly erotic quality. Female singers were regularly employed, and a strong emphasis was placed on arias, especially the da capo aria. There was little use of a chorus, and the function of the narrator was assumed by the recitatives of the various characters in the story. Principal Italian composers of oratorios in the late 17th century and the first half of the 18th include Bernardo Pasquini, Alessandro Melani, Alessandro Stradella, Alessandro Scarlatti, and Vivaldi. Most of the well-known opera composers of the period also composed oratorios [see, e.g., Neapolitan school], and the two genres remained closely linked. The oratorio was distinguished from opera principally by its subject matter, its division into two parts rather than three acts, and the absence of staged action (though there were occasional exceptions).

II. *The spread of the oratorio.* As the idea of a sacred musical drama spread to other areas of Europe, it was adapted to suit local conditions. In Vienna, under the patronage of Leopold I (1658–1705), himself a composer of oratorios, the genre thrived. In addition to oratorios based on Italian models, there existed in Vienna the *sepolcro,* a shorter work, also with an Italian text, sometimes captioned "rappresentazione sacra." The *sepolcri,* which can be traced back to the 15th century in Vienna, did involve scenery, costume, and action. Performed in the court chapels of the imperial family on Maundy Thursday and Good Friday, they depicted events surrounding the death of Christ. In Vienna, oratorio texts were written by such significant opera librettists as Apostolo Zeno and Pietro Metastasio, whose works were set in Italy and elsewhere as well. The leading oratorio composers in Vienna in the late 17th and early 18th centuries were Antonio Draghi, Johann Joseph Fux, and Antonio Caldara. Cultivation of the Italian oratorio persisted in Vienna into the second half of the century, producing works by Salieri among others. But Italian oratorio also spread wherever Italian opera took root, especially in Roman Catholic centers, e.g., Dresden, where Johann Adolf Hasse set librettos by Metastasio for both operas and oratorios.

In Protestant Germany, the idea of a sacred musical drama was rooted in the Lutheran *historia,* a story of Christ (often associated with Christmas, with Christ's Passion, or with Easter) taken from the Bible, set to music, and performed in the church. The musical format was austere, involving an alternation of unaccompanied liturgical reciting tones sung by soloists with unaccompanied choral polyphony. The greatest master of this repertory was Schütz.

During the 17th century, dramatic music composed for performance in the Lutheran Church increasingly came under the influence of the Italian oratorio, especially with the introduction of basso continuo [see Thoroughbass] and the interpolation of non-biblical texts. The resulting genre has been called the oratorio passion (Smither, 1977). Its earliest example is Thomas Selle's *Passio secundum Johanneum cum intermediis* (1643). The genre culminated in the great examples by Bach, especially his St. John Passion (first version, 1724) and St. Matthew Passion (first version, 1727 or 1729). In such works there is a free alternation of dramatic material that employs text drawn verbatim from Scripture with contemplative material that employs newly created poetry. Soloists and chorus are involved in both of these functions. Extremely important—and unique to music in the Lutheran tradition—is the role of the *chorale. In Bach's passions, the chorales are usually sung in a straightforward and unadorned manner; but occasionally they are woven into choruses and arias with larger forms. See also Passion music.

Oratorio in 17th-century France is represented primarily by the works of Marc-Antoine Charpentier, who studied with Carissimi in Rome. By 1672 he had returned to Paris, and some of his oratorios probably date from the 1670s. He did not call them oratorios, but used such terms as historia, dialogue, and motet. These works all have Latin texts and are similar in many respects to Carissimi's Latin oratorios. In 18th-century France, oratorios were cultivated mainly within the concert series known as the *concerts spirituels.* Among the main composers were J.-J. C. de Mondonville, N.-J. Méreaux, G. M. Cambini, H. J. Rigel, and F.-F. Gossec.

The earliest known Spanish oratorio is the *Historia de Joseph* by Luis Vicente Gargallo, which dates from the 1670s. This is a brief work, more or less comparable to the Italian dialogues of G. F. Anerio. The earliest full-scale Spanish oratorio is the *Oratorio sacro a la Pasiòn de Cristo Nuestro Señor* (1706) by Antonio Teodoro Ortells. Both of these works incorporate Spanish-style music within overall structures borrowed from Italian oratorio. Especially important in the late 18th century are Françesc Queralt's Italianate oratorios composed for the Barcelona Cathedral.

In England during the 17th century, there were sporadic attempts at the production of sacred dialogues, but with no significant later continuity. The flourishing of oratorio in that country in the period 1732–52 was almost exclusively based on the work of one composer, Handel. The Handelian oratorio flourished largely as a result of the vacuum created by the London audience's disaffection with Italian opera. In addition, during the decades following the Peace of Utrecht, English nationalism was finely honed, and the British found righteous parallels between themselves and the God-favored Israelites of the Old Testament, whose tribulations and conquests are repeatedly referred to in Handelian oratorios. This nationalistic spirit is particularly evident in such works as *Israel in Egypt* (1738), *Judas Macabbeus* (1746), *Joshua* (1747), and *Solomon* (1748). Although Handel's *Messiah* (first version, 1741) is obviously the best-known oratorio ever composed, Handel remarked that his own favorite work in this genre was *Theodora* (1749), an oratorio of extraordinary sensitivity.

Many German oratorios of the second half of the 18th century show close parallels with the Italian oratorios of the period. They include works by Telemann and C. P. E. Bach, among others. A more contemplative type also emerged, however, producing works by Telemann, C. P. E. Bach, Graun, and many others. The German oratorio of the Classical period culminates in Haydn's *The *Creation* (1798) and *The *Seasons* (1801).

III. *The 19th century.* The 19th century saw the construction of large concert halls in most cities, as well as the establishment of large orchestras and choral societies. These factors stimulated both the composition of new oratorios and the revival of 18th-century choral works, usually with greatly expanded forces. In the 19th century, the oratorio was influenced by the massive choral ensembles of the contemporaneous grand opera. Oratorios in this era provided an increasingly secular society with a quasi-religious experience, usually outside the setting of the church.

National trends are again apparent. In 19th-century France, Roman Catholic mysticism was reflected in such oratorios as Berlioz's *L'enfance du Christ* (1850–54), Franck's *Redemption* (1871–74), and Théodore Dubois's *Les sept paroles du Christ* (1867). Romantic interest in the legendary, the supernatural, and the apocalyptic was reflected in such 19th-century German oratorios as Carl Loewe's *Die Zerstörung Jerusalems* (1829) and Liszt's *Die Legende von der heiligen Elisabeth* (1857–62). Other German oratorios still drew on biblical stories, as in Schubert's *Lazarus* (1820) and Mendelssohn's *Paulus* (1834–36) and *Elijah* (1844–46). Schumann's *Das Paradis und die Peri* (1841–43) contains the chief elements of oratorio, but is secular. In Brahms's deeply moving *Requiem* (1857–68), the composer selected his own biblical texts and developed a line of thought that dispenses with character and plot.

The cultivation of the oratorio in the 19th and 20th centuries has in no country been so consistent as in England, largely because of the national interest in choral festivals (e.g., those at Leeds and Birmingham). In this setting, not only have works of Continental composers been performed over the generations, but numerous new works have been commissioned, including those by William Crotch, George Macfarren, and C. Hubert H. Parry.

IV. *The 20th century.* Although it occasionally produced works that draw on the basic idea of the oratorio (e.g., Honegger's *Le roi David,* 1923, and Stravinsky's *Oedipus Rex,* 1927), the 20th century in general lacked the institutions and the strong traditions that would stimulate the regular production of large choral works based on religious texts, with or without a plot.

The historical function of the oratorio as a vehicle for propaganda—originally religious, then nationalistic—made it an apt genre for cultivation in socialist countries. A work such as Kabalevsky's *The Mighty Homeland* (1942), produced in the middle of the Second World War, is understandably highly militaristic in character. Prokofiev's *On Guard for Peace* (1950) is only slightly less so. Shostakovich's *Song of the Forest* (1949) was at first withheld by its composer, who sensed it unacceptable in the political climate of the time.

The strong choral tradition of England produced such notable works as Elgar's *The Dream of Gerontius* (1900), Vaughan Williams's *Sancta Civitas* (1925), Walton's *Belshazzar's Feast* (1931), and Tippet's *A Child of Our Time* (1939–41) and *The Mask of Time* (1980–82), which is among the most powerful oratorios of the 20th century. In 1997 Wynton Marsalis's oratorio *Blood on the Fields* won the Pulitzer Prize.

Bibl.: Günther Massenkeil, *Das Oratorium, Mw* 37, trans. A. C. Howie, *The Oratorio* (Cologne: A Folk, 1970). Howard E. Smither, *A History of the Oratorio,* 4 vols. (Chapel Hill; U of NC Pr, 1977–2000). Kurt Pahlen, *The World of the Oratorio,* trans. Judith Schaefer, adds. Thurston Dox, gen. ed. Reinhard G. Pauly (Portland, Ore.: Amadeus, 1990). Günther Massenkeil, *Oratorium und Passion,* 2 vols. (Laaber: Laaber-Verlag, 1998–99). Silke Leopold and Ullrich Scheideler, eds., *Oratorienfüher* (Stuttgart and Weimar: J B Betzler; Kassel: Bärenreiter, 2000). O.J., rev. H.Sm.

Orchestra [fr. Gr. *orchēstra,* dancing area; Fr. *orchestre;* Ger. *Orchester;* It. *orchestra;* Sp. *orquesta*]. A performing body of diverse instruments. The term orchestra may be applied to any such group, such as the *gagaku* orchestra of Japan or the *gamelan* orchestras of Indonesia and Bali [see East Asia, Southeast Asia]. In the context of Western art music, it refers to the symphony orchestra (the subject of the present article), an ensemble consisting of multiple strings plus an assortment of woodwinds, brass, and percussion instruments.

In ancient Greece, the term referred to the area in front of the stage employed by the dramatic chorus for dancing and singing, but by the Middle Ages the term had come to refer to the stage itself. By the mid-18th century, it came to mean the actual performing body, as in current usage. Nevertheless, the term also still denotes the aggregation of seats placed at ground level in front of the stage in theaters and concert halls.

Though the vocal lines of medieval and Renaissance polyphony were often doubled by instruments, these ad hoc instrumental combinations remained unspecified and, in any event, of such small size that they bore little resemblance to modern orchestras. The advent of opera around 1600 helped to provide a greater specificity of scoring and an increasing reliance on multiple strings to provide body and balance with winds and percussion. In his opera *Orfeo* (1607), Monteverdi provided an early example, though at best he only suggested possible scorings for various scenes. Roughly contemporaneous with the establishment of the opera orchestra was the rise of court orchestras in England and France [see *Vingt-quatre violons du roi*], though these at first contained only strings (but without double basses, which were not fully accepted into the orchestra until the advent of the 18th century). These prototypical string orchestras generally contained a core membership of 10 to 25 players that could be augmented when occasions demanded. By 1700, woodwinds were also to be found in certain court orchestras, and by the end of the Baroque era (ca. 1750), composers had come to specify in some detail the composition of the orchestras for which they wrote. The core of such an ensemble consisted of strings (usually in four parts, with each part modestly doubled) and two oboes, with the addition of a continuo part realized by varied combinations of harpsichord (organ for church performances), harp, lute, violoncello solo, or bassoon [see Thoroughbass]. Other instruments (flutes, horns, trumpets, timpani) were often added, and occasionally the oboes were omitted. The ensemble required for Bach's fourth *Ouverture* (D major, ca. 1717–23) is typical of a relatively large late Baroque orchestra: three oboes, bassoon, three trumpets, a pair of timpani, strings, and continuo. While the wind and timpani parts were almost certainly not doubled, each of the string parts (violin 1 and 2, viola) was probably doubled by several players, with cellos and double basses playing the continuo line.

By the middle of the 18th century, numerous changes in instrument design had led to significant improvements in versatility and tone. As the members of the viol family gave way to stringed instruments more closely approximating those in use today, so too was the recorder replaced by the transverse flute and the *oboe da caccia* by the English horn. Trumpets and horns, previously limited in theory to the harmonics of the key in which they were pitched, soon acquired crooks—varied lengths of tubing that could be inserted quickly into the instruments, thereby altering their key and thus their concomitant pitch capacities. Clarinets were accepted as full-fledged members of the woodwind section by 1800, though they had been introduced almost 100 years earlier. Shortly before, the bassoon had divorced itself from the continuo and joined the woodwinds as an equal partner. The composers of the Classical period were vital in creating for the orchestra an increased role as a musically self-sufficient body with its own literature. The advent of the symphonic genre helped to elevate it beyond its previous function as primarily an accompanying ensemble for concertos, operas, and sacred vocal works [see also Mannheim school]. A pair of horns was added to the Baroque core group of two oboes, strings, and continuo, and it was for this combination that Haydn composed a number of his early and middle-period symphonies. He often made use of flutes, either singly or in pairs, as well as two trumpets and a pair of timpani (one rarely occurring without the other). Following Mozart's lead, he also came to employ clarinets in certain of his late symphonies. The symphony orchestra had also dispensed with the continuo by the first decade of the 19th century, although the tradition of a harpsichord accompaniment for recitative continued in *opera buffa* into the early 1800s. The scoring of

Haydn's *London* Symphony no. 104 (1795) well represents the composition of a full high-Classical orchestra: two flutes, two oboes, two clarinets, two bassoons, two horns, two trumpets, a pair of timpani, and strings. Though the number of string players per part varied with the nature of the ensemble (large metropolitan opera orchestras could boast a much richer complement than could most court orchestras), it was not unreasonable to expect at least three players per part. The cello section, however, seems to have been suprisingly small at that time.

More unusual instruments were often found in the Classical opera orchestra. Gluck made telling use of trombones and harps, and his use of various percussion instruments was carried further by Mozart's use of the glockenspiel in *Die Zauberflöte.* Trombones also served important if somewhat limited roles in Mozart's *Requiem* and Haydn's oratorio *The Creation* (which also included a part for the contrabassoon), but it was Beethoven who finally secured a place for them in the early 19th-century orchestra, as he did for the piccolo as well. It was largely through the works of Beethoven and Weber that the standard number of horn parts was increased from two to four. These same composers were among the last to employ percussion instruments such as cymbals, triangle, and bass drum for "Turkish" effects [see Janissary music].

The decline of the aristocracy throughout much of Europe at the end of the 18th century and the concomitant dissolution of numerous court orchestras left the performance of both theatrical and symphonic works to the municipal opera orchestras. With few exceptions, most early 19th-century orchestras were not appreciably larger than those of the previous century. The constitution of the Berlin Opera Orchestra—as recounted by Berlioz after his visit there in 1843—was atypical: four flutes, four oboes, four clarinets, four bassoons, four horns, four trumpets, four trombones, timpani, bass drum, cymbals, two harps, fourteen first violins, fourteen second violins, eight violas, ten cellos, and eight double basses. Although the primary duties of such orchestras were operatic performances, they were hired for symphonic programs as well. But by mid-century, a number of municipal concert orchestras had been established. Notable among them were the orchestras of the Gewandhaus of Leipzig (founded 1781), the Paris Conservatoire (1800), the Philharmonic Society of London (1813), and the Philharmonic Society of New York (1842). The first decades of the 19th century also gave rise to the virtuoso conductor, for the increased musical demands made upon the orchestra by Romantic composers rendered the earlier practice of leading a performance from the keyboard continuo or principal violinist's desk impractical. The first great conductors were also composers (Berlioz, Mendelssohn, Meyerbeer, Wagner), but by the end of the century most conductors specialized only in directing orchestras [see Conducting].

Continued improvements in instrument design during the first decades of the 1800s led to further changes. The development of valved horns and trumpets allowed those instruments to play complete chromatic scales throughout their entire range, and the introduction of the ophicleide (later replaced by the bass tuba) assured the presence of a bass brass instrument in the orchestra. Meyerbeer wrote for the bass clarinet in *Les Huguenots* (1836), and Berlioz made significant demands on the English horn, E♭ clarinet, harp, timpani, and a wide variety of percussion instruments (here no longer employed only for "Turkish" color). While the core group of two flutes, two oboes, two clarinets, two bassoons (sometimes four in France), four horns, two trumpets, three trombones, tuba or ophicleide, three or four timpani, and strings (the last increasing in number throughout the century) remained sufficient for more conservative composers such as Mendelssohn, Schumann, and Brahms, other more radical figures demanded larger forces. Following in Berlioz's footsteps, Wagner substantially enlarged the orchestral apparatus he required: *Die Walküre* (1856) calls for piccolo, three flutes, three oboes, English horn, three clarinets, bass clarinet, three bassoons (with one performer also playing contrabassoon), eight horns (four players also doubling on the Wagner tubas invented for the four operas of the *Ring* cycle), three trumpets, bass trumpet, three trombones, contrabass trombone, bass tuba, four timpani, triangle, cymbals, tenor drum, glockenspiel, six harps, sixteen first violins, sixteen second violins, twelve violas, twelve cellos, and eight double basses. Similarly gargantuan forces are necessary for the late symphonies of Bruckner (nos. 7, 8, and 9), Mahler, and Scriabin as well as for late 19th- and early 20th-century symphonic poems, operas, ballets, and choral works by Richard Strauss, Schoenberg, Stravinsky, and others. In certain of these scores, as in many operas of the late 19th century, an organ is also required.

Such enormous orchestras were reasonably common before 1914, but World War I and its aftermath brought about a slight reduction in the size of standing orchestras for reasons as much economic as aesthetic. The new core ensemble, which remains intact today, included three of each woodwind instrument (with possible use of piccolo, English horn, bass clarinet, saxophone, and contrabassoon), four horns (sometimes five with the first horn doubled), three trumpets, three trombones, tuba, two harps, a keyboard player (for piano, celesta, or possibly organ), timpani, three percussion players, and strings. The number of strings in contemporary orchestras varies considerably, but the best include at least twelve first violins, twelve second violins, ten violas, ten cellos, and eight double basses. As the above numbers suggest, the 20th century brought an enlarged role for percussion instruments, mainly through the influence of composers such as Mahler, Berg, Bartók, Varèse, Orff, and Messiaen. Also in evidence have been occasional uses of electronic instruments or standard instruments amplified electronically. Some composers, particularly those of the *neoclassical movement, have scored works for chamber orchestras roughly equivalent in size to those employed by Haydn and Mozart. The disciples of the Second Viennese School, on the other hand, have given rise to the small orchestra whose core consists of a single performer on each instrument (with string parts undoubled).

Although symphony orchestras in the later 20th and early 21st century continue to play a vital role in musical culture, economic priorities have hindered the preparation and performance of difficult new scores. This has not prevented, however, the creation of a contemporary literature for the orchestra. See also Orchestration.

Bibl.: Hugo Goldschmidt, *Studien zur Geschichte der italienischen Oper im 17. Jahrhundert,* vol. 1 (Leipzig: Breitkopf & Härtel, 1901). Fritz Volbach, *Das moderne Orchester in seiner Entwicklung* (Leipzig: B G Teubner, 1910). Georges Cucuel, *Études sur un orchestre au XVIIIme siècle: L'instrumentation chez les symphonistes de La Pouplinière* (Paris: Fischbacher, 1913). Charles Sanford Terry, *Bach's Orchestra* (London: Oxford U Pr, 1932). Paul Bekker, *The Story of the Orchestra* (New York: Norton, 1936). Ottmar Schreiber, *Orchester und Orchesterpraxis in Deutschland zwischen 1780 und 1850* (Berlin: Junker & Dünnhaupt, 1938). Adam Carse, *The Orchestra in the XVIIIth Century* (Cambridge: W Heffer, 1940). Reginald Nettel, *The Orchestra in England: A Social History* (London: Cape, 1946). Adam Carse, *The Orchestra from Beethoven to Berlioz* (Cambridge: W Heffer, 1948). John H. Mueller, *The American Symphony Orchestra: A Social History of Musical Taste* (Bloomington: Ind U Pr, 1951). Simon Towneley Worsthorne, *Venetian Opera in the Seventeenth Century* (Oxford: Clarendon Pr, 1954). Owen Jander, "Concerto Grosso Instrumentation in Rome in the 1660's and 1670's," *JAMS* 21 (1968): 168–80. Helmut Hell, *Die neapolitanische Opernsinfonie in der ersten Hälfte des 18. Jahrhunderts* (Tutzing: Schneider, 1971). Philip Hart, *Orpheus in the New World: The Symphony Orchestra as an American Cultural Institution* (New York: Norton, 1973). David Charlton, "Orchestra and Image in the Later Eighteenth Century," *PRMA* 102 (1975–76): 1–12. Neal Zaslaw, "Toward the Revival of the Classical Orchestra," *PRMA* 103 (1976–77): 158–87. Joachim Braun, "The Sound of Beethoven's Orchestra," *Orbis musicae* 6 (1978): 59–90. Norman del Mar, *Anatomy of the Orchestra* (Berkeley and Los Angeles: U of Cal Pr, 1981). For a directory of current orchestras, see *Musical America, Annual Directory Issue* (1965–). C.R.

Orchestration. The art of employing instruments in various combinations, most notably the orchestra. Orchestration includes the concept of instrumentation—the study of the properties and capabilities of individual instruments.

During the Middle Ages and Renaissance, parts were assigned to specific instruments on an ad hoc basis for the performance of dance music and for the accompaniment of both sacred and secular vocal music. Since the choice of instrument(s) for a given part rested primarily on what was available in each set of circumstances, orchestration in the usual sense was not employed. The Baroque era brought an increasing specificity of orchestration, one of the earliest instances being Monteverdi's suggestion of certain instrumental combinations for his opera *Orfeo* (1607). Stringed instruments became the bulwark of the orchestra, with wind and percussion parts often scored *ad libitum.* The continuo [see Thoroughbass], made up of a wide assortment of possible instrumental combinations, was also introduced to provide harmonic underpinning. As the period progressed, parts for wind instruments were increasingly specified; among them are the recorder (later the transverse flute), oboe, *oboe d'amore, oboe da caccia,* and trumpet. Parts for horn and bassoon (separate from the continuo) are also encountered, as are solo parts for various stringed instruments. By 1750, a fully orchestrated Baroque concert work might include parts for one or more flutes, oboes (or other members of the oboe family), bassoons, horns, trumpets, timpani, and continuo, plus a body of three- or four-part strings with several players per part. Baroque orchestration frequently featured both contrasts between given orchestral choirs (such as winds versus strings) and simple homophonic doublings (winds plus strings), as in Handel's *Water Music* (1717) and *Music for the Royal Fireworks* (1749). Equally common was a polyphonic approach that achieved homogeneity through the counterpoint of individual, balanced lines. Though doubling sometimes occurred between strings and winds in this context, independent lines requiring equal levels of dexterity were often given to them as well as to trumpets and horns. Only the two timpani (pitched on the tonic and dominant of the work's key) were allotted comparatively simple parts.

The contrapuntal simplification effected during the early Classical period brought about an alteration of orchestrational principles. Since most of this music was based on a melody-and-accompaniment texture, the first violins became the focus of the orchestrator's attention, with lower strings often assigned a rhythmically simple background. Winds—mostly pairs of oboes and horns—found that their new role as sustainers of harmony resulted in parts substantially less complex and demanding than those common in the late Baroque. While Haydn preserved this approach in some of his early works (though often augmenting his forces with flutes and/or trumpets and timpani), he eventually came to be influenced by Mozart, who allotted the woodwinds a much enlarged melodic function. In addition to pioneering the symphonic use of the clarinet, which he had come to appreciate at *Mannheim, Mozart was vital in returning to the woodwinds a role more in balance with that of the strings while also providing them parts requiring greater agility than in the early Classical period. Mozart and the Mannheim composers also gave the bassoon greater independence from the bass line accorded to the low strings and continuo. Beethoven continued this trend toward soloistic writing, increasing the importance not only of woodwinds (including piccolo), but of brass as well. While the earlier Classical composers had stressed the capacity of horns to blend with and buttress the woodwinds, Beethoven also allowed them to be heard as independent brass instruments (e.g., in the third movement of the *Eroica* Symphony). He further promoted a significant symphonic role for trombones (in Symphonies 5, 6, and 9) and scored pitches for timpani other than the tonic and dominant (in Symphonies 7, 8, and 9).

Many of Beethoven's advances in symphonic orchestration had been prefigured in Classical opera orchestration, largely because the obviously dramatic nature of opera necessitated appropriately dramatic orchestration. Gluck's operas had contained numerous elegant passages for instruments not then part of the symphony orchestra (trombones, harp, clarinets, various percussion instruments), and Mozart had also made significant use of trombones and glockenspiel (in *Don Giovanni* and *Die Zauberflöte,* respectively). In the early 1800s, opera orchestration again made important strides. Rossini habitually scored woodwind parts requiring enormous virtuosity, and his lyrical writing for four unaccompanied horns in the overture to *Semiramide* (1823) equaled Weber's challenging horn writing in *Der Freischütz* (1821) in its influence on later Romantics.

In Berlioz, the Romantic era produced perhaps the most important figure in the history of symphonic orchestration. Unlike his predecessors, for whom orchestration was sometimes in effect applied after the fact to completed music, or was largely a matter of convention, Berlioz considered orchestration an integral part of the original compositional process, thus elevating it to the status of other musical elements. To Berlioz and his aesthetic successors, the orchestration of a musical idea was inseparable from the idea itself. He continued to exploit the newly enhanced capabilities of woodwind instruments. At the same time he raised the brass section to equal status with the woodwinds and strings, though generally his brass writing is more chordally conceived than soloistic or melodic. He also was responsible for substantial timbral experimentation, pioneering the symphonic use of string techniques such as *col legno* and *sul ponticello* [see Bowing], string and harp *harmonics, muted and *stopped horn tones, flute glissandos, chordal writing for multiple timpani, and the use of percussion instruments in a role other than the provision of "Turkish" color typical in earlier scores. In addition, Berlioz secured places for the harp, English horn, E♭ clarinet, cornet, and valved trumpet in the symphony orchestra.

The invention of valved horns and trumpets in the first decades of the 19th century was of major importance to composers. These instruments' new-found abilities to play complete chromatic scales throughout their ranges with comparative ease closely followed improvements in the construction of woodwinds. The new instruments understandably sparked a surge of interest among orchestral composers. Schumann made inspired use of valved horns in his symphonies, while Louis Moreau Gottschalk's First Symphony (1858–59) includes a long trumpet solo whose chromaticism would have rendered it virtually unplayable several decades before. Of all the successors to Weber and Berlioz, it was Wagner who contributed the most to orchestration and to the brass section's role within the orchestra. While for Wagner (and virtually all Romantics) the strings remained of paramount importance, the winds—and especially the brass—carried a weight of hitherto unequaled significance. Though some of Wagner's orchestration favored a homogeneous approach involving substantial doubling between orchestral choirs, lengthy solos for various wind instruments (such as the English horn solo in *Tristan und Isolde*), often without string accompaniment, signaled a new importance for those instruments. Horns, trumpets, and trombones, both soloistically and sectionally, became central to the orchestral concept, as did the bass trumpet, contrabass trombone, bass tuba, and the special Wagner tubas invented for the four operas of *Der Ring des Nibelungen.*

Although Wagner's orchestration had a great influence on Mahler, Richard Strauss, Schoenberg, and Berg, other traditions evolved as well. The first, typified by Schubert, Mendelssohn, and Brahms, maintained the fundamental aesthetic of Beethoven: an often heterogeneous blend of orchestral choirs with strings dominant, followed in importance by woodwinds, brass, and percussion. The second, typified by Bruckner and imitated to some extent by Franck and Saint-Saëns (all of whom were organists), favored full orchestral choirs either juxtaposed or contrasted in a fashion reminiscent of the movement to or from various organ manuals. The third, a direct outgrowth of Berlioz's timbral experiments, featured a virtuosic and color-oriented style that encompassed everything from piquantly scored chamber combinations to brilliant tuttis replete with much exotic percussion. This approach reached its zenith during the Romantic era in the middle-period works of Rimsky-Korsakov (e.g., *Capriccio espagnol*) and the later works of Bizet (particularly *Carmen,* 1873–74).

The end of the 19th century brought a significant reaction to Romantic models (especially that of Wagner) in the music of Debussy. His highly subtle orchestration elevates woodwinds, more often scored soloistically than sectionally, to the level of dominance. Imitated by Scriabin (in his later works) and to some extent by Ravel, Debussy preferred the brass section muted and provided equally understated parts for percussion. Most noticeable of all is the greatly reduced role of strings. Such orchestration entrusts them with a largely accompanimental role, making much use of tremolo, coloristic performing techniques such as *sul* ponticello and *sul tasto* [see Bowing], and (again following Berlioz's lead) substantial division of individual sections into two or more parts. Debussy replaced the opulent orchestral overstatement of Wagner and Strauss with equally opulent understatement.

The 20th century brought such a plethora of orchestrational approaches that no one or two can be said to dominate, although a general increase of percussion scoring and an interest in new percussion instruments are clearly observable. Neoimpressionists (Respighi, Messiaen, Schwantner) have built upon the coloristic aesthetic of Debussy, though their scores frequently demand a more extroverted playing style from strings, brass, and percussion. The neoromantics (Nielsen, Prokofiev, Shostakovich, Hartmann, Del Tredici) have similarly conserved many aspects of the Wagner-Mahler-Strauss approach, though economic factors have prevented them from scoring for the gargantuan forces available to their forerunners. Neoclassicists (Stravinsky after *Les noces,* Copland, Piston) have attempted to imitate the clarity and economy of Classical orchestration, though with an elegance of wind writing more reminiscent of Baroque models than of Haydn and Mozart. Pointillists (Webern and many composers of the American and European serial school) have sought to fragment lines through a constantly shifting array of colors in which each instrument or instrumental section plays only a small number of articulations at a given time. The Brucknerian technique of juxtaposing choirs continues in the work of William Schuman (though Schuman's orchestrational brashness contrasts noticeably with Bruckner's sonic monumentality).

One of the most influential and unique styles has evolved from the music of Varèse, whose belief that sound itself could be the principal impetus for composition led him to experiment radically with new scoring concepts. Varèse preferred extreme instrumental ranges, scoring for woodwinds, brass, and especially percussion so strongly that he assured a much decreased role for the strings. Varèse's aesthetic presaged the electronic amplification of instruments (Stockhausen's *Mixtur,* 1964) and the creation of highly unusual ensembles such as the percussion-dominated orchestras of Orff's later scores. Other successors to Varèse have sought to create new textures through extremely thick scoring that effaces individual lines (Lutosławski, Ligeti, Takemitsu, Birtwistle) or to create new timbres through the use of extended instrumental techniques (Crumb), while others (such as Penderecki) have attempted to superimpose both techniques. The "New Romanticism" that flourished in the latter decades of the 20th century effected a return to late 19th- and 20th-century models, as evidenced in the work of such composers as Adams and MacMillan. Simultaneously, the success of international minimalism led to the increased use of synthesizers and other electronic media within the fabric of the traditional orchestra (Andriessen). Common to most of these approaches is a desire to employ the virtuosity of contemporary orchestral performers in the service of new sonic possibilities.

Bibl.: Jean-Georges Kastner, *Traité général d'instrumentation* (Paris: Prilipp, 1837). Id., *Traité général d'instrumentation: Supplément* (Paris: Prilipp, 1844). Louis-Hector Berlioz, *Grande traité d'instrumentation et d'orchestration modernes* (Paris: Schonenberger, 1844). Id., *Grand traité . . . Nouvelle édition revue, corrigée, augmentée . . .* (Paris: Schonenberger, 1855?), trans. M. Cowden Clarke, *A Treatise upon Modern Instrumentation and Orchestration . . . New Edition* (London: Novello, 1856). Ebenezer Prout, *Instrumentation* (Boston: Ditson, 1876). François-Auguste Gevaert, *Nouveau traité d'instrumentation* (Paris: H Lemoine, 1885), trans. Edward Suddard (Paris: H Lemoine, 1906?). Charles-Marie Widor, *Technique de l'orchestre moderne faisant suite au Traité d'instrumentation et d'orchestration de H. Berlioz* (Paris: H Lemoine, 1904), trans. Edward Suddard, *The Technique of the Modern Orchestra* (New York: E Schuberth, 1905). Louis-Hector Berlioz, *Instrumentationslehre, ergänzt und revidiert von Richard Strauss,* 2 vols. (Leipzig: C F Peters, 1905), trans. Theodore Front, *Treatise on Instrumentation, Enlarged and Revised by Richard Strauss* (New York: Kalmus, 1948). Nicolai Rimsky-Korsakov, *Osnovï orkestrovki,* 2 vols., ed. Maximilian Steinberg (St. Petersburg: Rossiiskoe muzykal'noe izdatel'stvo, 1913), trans. Edward Agate, *Principles of Orchestration* (Berlin: Édition russe de musique, 1922; R: New York: Dover, 1964). Adam Carse, *The History of Orchestration* (New York: E P Dutton, 1925). Egon Wellesz, *Die neue Instrumentation,* 2 vols. (Berlin: M Hesse, 1928–29). Bernard Rogers, *The Art of Orchestration: Principles of Tone Color in Modern Scoring* (New York: Appleton-Century-Crofts, 1951). Kent Kennan, *The Technique of Orchestration* (Englewood Cliffs, N.J.: Prentice-Hall, 1952; 3rd ed., with Donald Grantham, 1983). Gardner Read, *Thesaurus of Orchestral Devices* (New York: Pitman, 1953). Charles Koechlin, *Traité de l'orchestration,* 4 vols. (Paris: Max Eschig, 1954–59). Walter Piston, *Orchestration* (New York: Norton, 1955). Alfredo Casella and Virgilio Mortari, *La tecnica dell'orchestra contemporanea* (Milan: Ricordi, 1959). René Leibowitz and Jan Maguire, *Thinking for Orchestra* (New York: Schirmer, 1960). Gardner Read, *Style and Orchestration* (New York: Schirmer Bks, 1979). Alfred Blatter, *Instrumentation-Orchestration* (New York: Longman, 1980). Samuel Adler, *The Study of Orchestration* (New York: Norton, 1982). Stephen Douglas Burton, *Orchestration* (Englewood Cliffs, N.J.: Prentice-Hall, 1982). Andrew Stiller, *Handbook of Instrumentation* (Berkeley and Los Angeles: U of Cal Pr, 1985). C.R.

Orchestrion. An *automatic instrument that imitates the sound of an entire orchestra, employing organ pipes and other devices controlled by a barrel-and-pin, perforated-paper, or similar mechanism. Numerous such instruments were developed beginning in the late 18th century.

Ordinal [Lat. *liber ordinum*]. See Liturgical books.

Ordinario [It., abbr. *ord.*]. Ordinary, normal; an instruction to return to the ordinary way of playing after a passage in which some special technique has been specified, e.g., bowing *col legno.*

Ordinary. Those items of the Mass and Office of the Roman rite whose texts remain the same throughout the liturgical year; as distinct from items making up the *Proper, whose texts vary with the occasion. The melodies of the sung items of the Ordinary may change with the season or the class of feast. In musical contexts, the term most often refers to the *Kyrie, *Gloria, *Credo, *Sanctus, and *Agnus Dei of the Mass, i.e., the sung items of the Mass Ordinary that have most often been set polyphonically. See also Mass, Office, Liturgy, Liturgical books.

Ordo [Lat.]. See Modes, rhythmic.

Ordo romanus [Lat., pl. *Ordines romani*]. Any of the early liturgical books (ordinals) describing the practice of Rome. See Gregorian chant VI, Liturgical books.

Ordre [Fr.]. (1) A series of harpsichord or instrumental ensemble pieces in the same key. François Couperin coined the term in his four harpsichord books (1713, 1717, 1722, 1730) and in *Les nations* (1726). Some of his *ordres* (1, 2, and 4 for harpsichord, and all four in *Les nations*) separate dance movements in traditional sequence from sonata or character pieces. It is not certain whether he conceived these groups of 4 to 24 pieces as performance units [see Suite]. A few French followers (François Dagincour, Philippe François Veras, Coelestin Harst) used the term in place of suite, and some modern editors have supplied it in the works of other composers. (2) *Course. B.G.

Orfeo. See *Favola d'Orfeo, La* (Monteverdi); *Orfeo ed Euridice* (Gluck); *Orphée aux Enfers* (Offenbach).

Orfeo ed Euridice [It., Orpheus and Eurydice]. Opera ("azione teatrale") in three acts by Gluck (libretto by Raniero de Calzabigi), produced in Vienna in 1762. It was revised, with added music and the part of Orpheus, originally a contralto, rewritten for tenor, for a French production (text by Pierre Louis Moline) given in Paris in 1774. Setting: legendary Thrace and Hades.

Orff-Schulwerk. A system of music education developed by the German composer Carl Orff (1895–1982). It is intended for groups of children singing and playing together, and it emphasizes the development of creativity and the ability to improvise. Orff designed a special set of instruments—mainly *xylophones, *metallophones, and other percussion instruments—for which he composed five volumes of "Music for Children" embodying his ideas.

Bibl.: Wilhelm Keller, *Einführung in Musik für Kinder* (Mainz: B Schott, 1954; new ed., 1963); trans. Eng., *Introduction to Music for Children* (London and New York: Schott, 1974).

Organ [Fr. *orgue;* Ger., Du. *Orgel;* It. *organo;* Sp. *órgano*]. A wind instrument consisting of from one to many sets of pipes controlled by one or more keyboards. See also Electronic organ.

The simplest organ has a single keyboard, one pipe for each key, and a wind-chest fed by a bellows. All but the smallest *portative organs have several stops or sets of pipes for each keyboard. Stop actions, moved by knobs, enable the player to combine the sounds of more than one set of pipes as appropriate for the music being played. The English term stop [Fr. *jeu;* Ger. *Register*], although it is of uncertain origin, suggests a means for stopping air from reaching pipes. Disposition refers to the manner in which stops are disposed over several keyboard divisions and pedal, each with its own wind-chest and keyboard. [See alphabetical entries for stop names and organ terms.]

More than any other instrument, the organ depends for success on live acoustics and reverberation and on its placement in the space where it is heard. Optimum placement allows its sound to follow an unobstructed line-of-sight path to listeners, as in its traditional church location in the rear gallery, near a reflective ceiling and walls, speaking directly down the length of the nave. Optimum acoustics are provided by hard reflective surfaces (such as masonry walls and floors) and by a space of large volume created by a room that is high, long, and relatively narrow. Reverberation should approach three seconds (when the room is filled with people), to allow for proper articulation by the player and to ensure development of the organ's complex sound without overpowering loudness.

I. *Components.* An organ may be said to consist of two basic types of components: tonal and mechanical. The tonal portion comprises the pipework and the manner in which it is laid out, scaled, voiced, and tuned. The mechanical portion consists of the wind-chests on which the pipes stand, the key and stop actions connecting the console (or keyboard) to the wind-chests, and the bellows, regulators, and other components of the wind supply.

1. Pipework. Organ pipes are made of various metals or of wood. The commonest pipe material is composed of lead and varying quantities of tin, plus small amounts of stabilizing metals, such as antimony. Metal with 30 percent tin is called common metal; metal with 50 percent tin, spotted metal, due to its characteristic appearance. Nearly pure tin, because of its bright appearance, is sometimes used for facade pipes, and also for interior pipes, particularly those of the principal and string families, although flute-toned pipes are usually of common metal. Other metals used in pipes include copper (for reed resonators and decorative facade pipes) and zinc (for painted facade pipes and large bass pipes). Wooden pipes, rectangular in cross section, may be made of pine, fir, poplar, or hardwoods such as oak. Pipe materials have a subtle effect on sound quality, and thus certain materials are preferred for particular stops.

Organ pipes fall into two general classes, depending on how their sound is generated. Flue pipes sound on the same principle as a penny whistle or recorder. Wind, admitted through the toe hole in the foot of the pipe, passes through the flue (an opening between the languid and lower lip), striking the upper lip and setting in vibration a column of air in the body of the pipe [see Fig. 1]. A pipe that is stopped (closed at the top) sounds an octave lower than an open pipe of the same length, because of the doubling back of the standing wave. Flue pipes (Principals, Flutes, Strings) represent the majority of stops in an organ and contribute a wide range of dynamics and timbres, depending on their scaling, voicing, and material.

Reed pipes sound on the same principle as a clarinet and supply voices of great variety and often brilliance. Their sound is generated by a thin metal tongue, acting as a reed, which vibrates against the open side of a metal or wood shallot (much like a clarinet mouthpiece) when air is forced into the wind-tight housing (boot) surrounding the reed assembly. Reed pipe resonators largely determine tone quality. They may be full length, half length, or fractional length, of flared or cylindrical form, open or partly closed at the top.

The pitch of an organ stop is indicated by the speaking length (in feet) of its longest pipe, not including its foot. Therefore a Principal 8′ (the basic unison stop) has a bottom C pipe eight feet long. Pipe lengths halve at each octave; thus a 4′ stop sounds an octave above an 8′ stop, a 2′ stop two octaves above, and a 16′ stop an octave below. The same system applies to stops sounding intervals other than octaves: 5 1/3′ produces the fifth, 2 2/3′ the twelfth, 1 3/5′ the seventeenth, and so on. These off-unison pitches enrich the harmonic series and are often referred to as mutations. For stopped pipes, the sounding pitch for C is used, although the actual length of the C pipe at 8′ C is only 4′. In reed pipes, pitch is determined by a combination of resonator length and vibrating length of the reed tongue; sounding pitch at C is always designated, even though some reed stops (such as Regals) may have resonators as little as one-fourth of the designated length at bottom C.

Scaling refers to the relation between the diameter and the length of a pipe, and this in turn determines its tone "family." Scales for all stops in a given organ must be carefully planned if good ensemble and blend are to result. Among flue pipes, Principals (which, at various pitches, form the essential chorus of the organ) are of medium scale, Flutes have a wider scale, which suppresses harmonics and gives a more fundamental tone, and Strings have a narrower scale, which suppresses the fundamental and encourages more harmonic development.

Principals are always open pipes, usually of metal but in rare cases of wood. They range from the narrower and more harmonically developed Geigen (or Violin) Principal to the fuller-sounding Open Diapa-

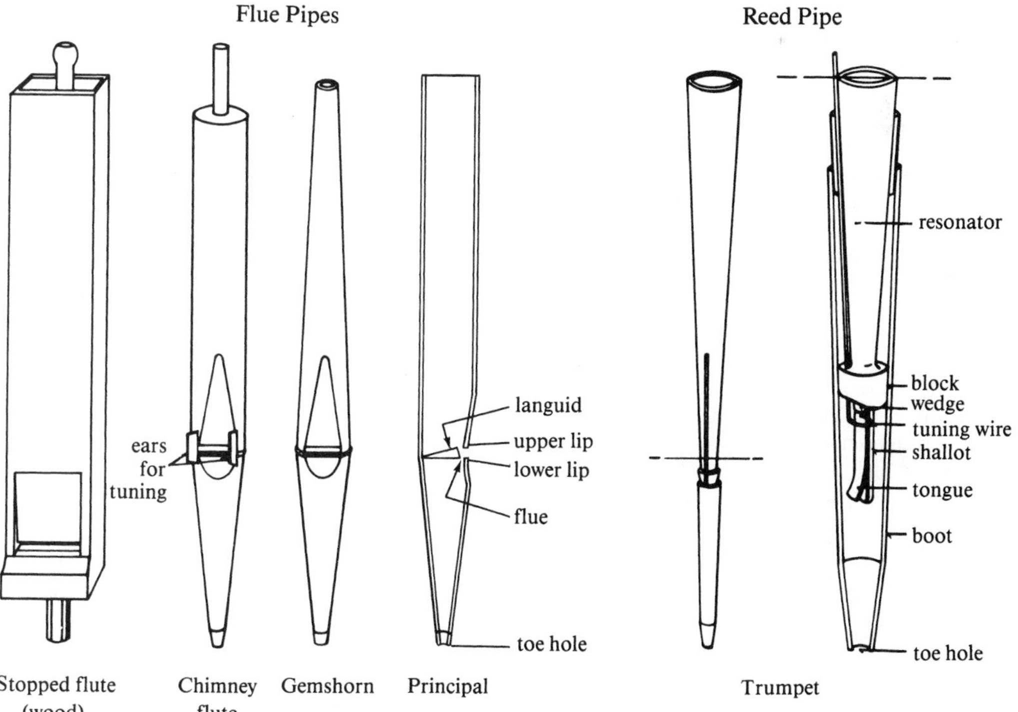

Fig. 1. Organ pipes.

son. Strings (Salicional, Gamba, Aeoline) are always open metal pipes, usually rather softly voiced. The Flute family has the greatest variety of construction and tone color. Stopped Flutes (Stopped Diapason, Gedeckt, Bourdon) can be of either wood or metal and have a fairly foundational tone with a slight fifth harmonic. Half-stopped Flutes (Chimney Fute, Rohrflöte) have a small "chimney" instead of a stopper, can be of wood or metal, and have a brighter harmonic color. Tapered flutes (Spitzflöte, Spillflute) are wide at the mouth and narrower at the top and usually fairly foundational, although a more narrow-scaled stop of this type, the Gemshorn, has more harmonic development and functions as a kind of hybrid color. Open flutes (the metal Night Horn or wood Melodia or Clarabella) are usually of fairly wide scale and foundational tone; a variant is the Harmonic Flute, which is double-length in the treble and produces a very pure flute tone. Scaling in reed pipes relates to the resonators, wider resonators (especially when tapered) producing a fuller and more foundational tone than narrow ones.

Voicing is the regulation of each pipe's tone quality, loudness, and promptness of speech, a demanding and time-consuming operation. Voicing is begun at the workbench and completed (finishing) where the organ is to be heard, to ensure proper balance among all the stops. For flue pipes, critical voicing factors include the sizes of the toe hole and flue opening, the position of upper and lower lips, the precise contour and position of the languid, and the distance (cut-up) between upper and lower lips. For reed pipes, the thickness and degree of curvature of the reed tongue are the voicer's most important concerns.

The tuning of open flue pipes is accomplished by slightly increasing or decreasing the resonating length of the pipe, by adjusting a tuning slide or a slot in the back of the pipe, or by using a metal cone to increase or decrease the opening at the top. Stopped flue pipes are tuned by moving their stoppers or caps, reed pipes by moving a spring wire that bears against the reed tongue or by adjusting a slot near the top of the resonator.

2. Wind supply and wind-chests. Wind pressure affects the loudness and tone quality of an organ. It is held approximately constant by weights or springs on the bellows and is normally determined in accordance with the size and acoustical properties of the space and the tone quality desired. The traditional wind supply consists of a pair or more of wedge-shaped bellows, raised by hand and collapsed in sequence by their weighted tops, the wind reaching the wind-chest through rectangular wooden ducts. Miniature versions of this system may be seen protruding from the side or back of portative organs.

By the late 18th century, single or multifold reservoirs were interposed, located as close as possible to the wind-chests. Other changes made by 19th-century builders included the development of tiered reservoirs capable of supplying different pressure for different stops (especially reed registers) or for treble and bass of the same stop. Because of the influence of historical styles on late 20th- and early 21st-century organ building, any of these types of wind supply may be found in contemporary organs.

Wind-chests of various types were designed during the organ's long history, but by the mid-17th century, the slider chest emerged as the norm. This consists of a rectangular wooden box filled with wind, with the pipes located on its top in rows roughly parallel to the keyboards. A thin wooden strip or slider runs from left to right underneath the pipes of each row or stop. The slider has one hole for each pipe and can be positioned so that the slider holes either are or are not in line with the pipe holes above them. All the pipes for each note stand over a single wind channel or groove (perpendicular to the keyboard), to which air is admitted by a pallet valve connected to the key. By moving the sliders, the player determines which pipes receive wind from their wind channel and thus whether one or more stops will be heard.

3. Key and stop actions. All organs have two distinct actions, one connecting the keys to valves under the pipes, and another to control the stops. Traditional key action employs a direct mechanical connection (by means of a thin wooden tracker, hence tracker action) between each key and the corresponding pallet valve in the wind-chest [see Fig. 2]. The stop action consists of strong wooden connections from the sliders to knobs located near the player, who may place each slider in the on or off position by moving the knob. When the key is depressed, the valve opens, admitting wind to the wind channel for that note and to the pipes with which slider holes are aligned, i.e., to pipes belonging to the stops that have been drawn. Because all the pipes for any note receive their wind from the same note channel, an important blending of combined sounds is achieved.

Various modifications of the traditional actions were tried during the 19th century involving pneumatic means for operating key valves and sliders, most notably the pneumatic lever (Barker machine) first used by Cavaillé-Coll of Paris and soon adopted by builders in other countries for larger organs built during the second half of the 19th century. The introduction of electricity around the turn of the century led to replacement of the traditional actions by either direct electromagnetic valves or a combination of magnets and pneumatic motors. This allowed keyboards to be separated from wind-chests, since no mechanical linkage was required but only an electric cable. For most American builders, the *pitman electropneumatic wind-chest became the standard, along with adjustable combination actions controlled by thumb pistons underneath the keyboards. These systems accounted for practically all the organs built in the U.S. from the early 20th century through the 1960s [see IV below].

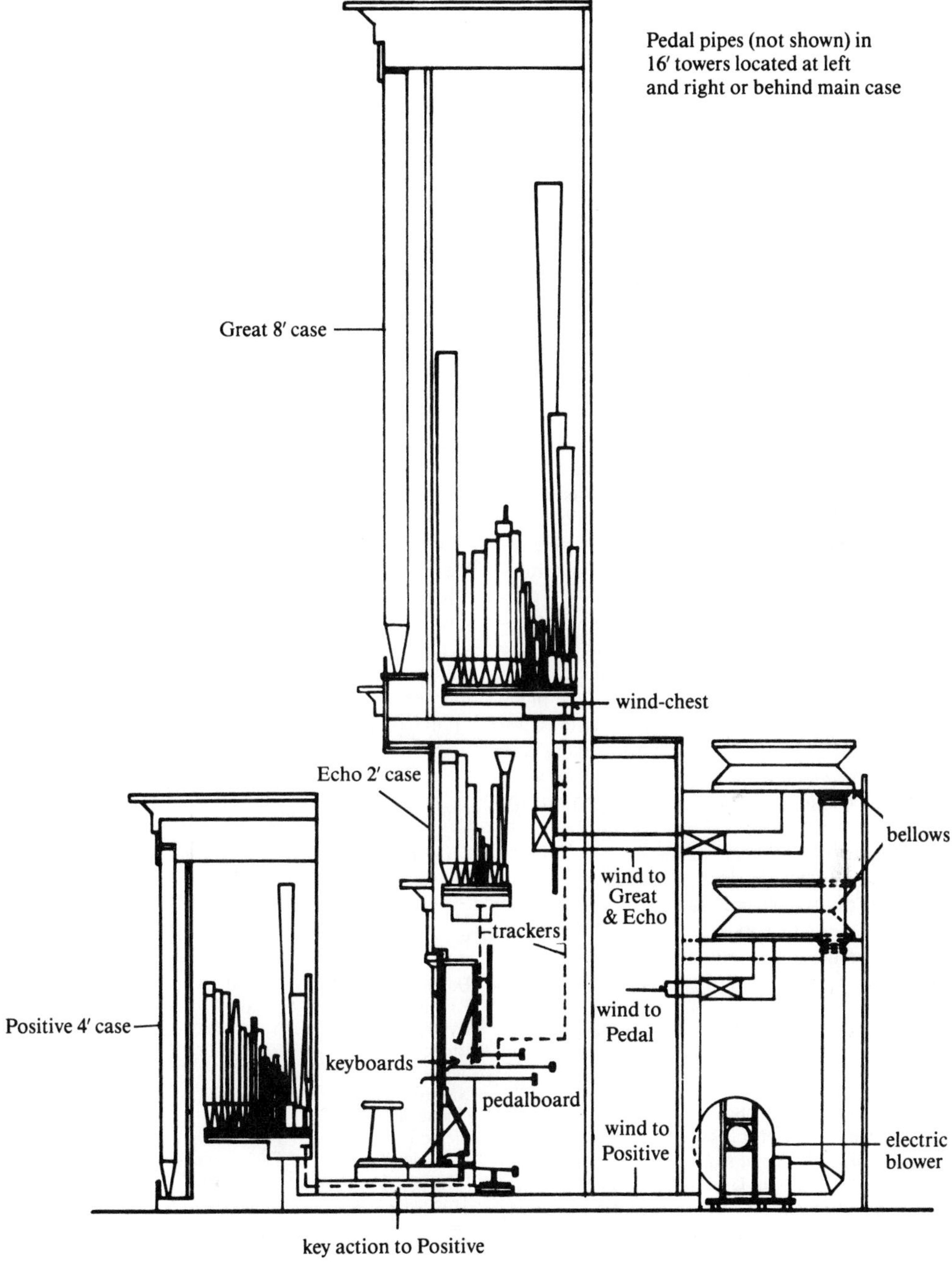

Fig. 2. Section through a three-manual organ.

During the second half of the 20th century there was a renewal of interest among both organists and builders in the traditional all-mechanical type of key action. The study of historic organs and a desire for a more touch-sensitive action were factors in this, and an increasing number of organs have been built with slider chests and tracker key action. In smaller instruments, stop action has also been mechanical, but in larger organs it is not uncommon to find electrically controlled stop and combination actions, and sometimes Barker machine key or coupler actions. An organ built in the early 21st century may thus have either mechanical or electrically controlled action, or a combination of both types.

4. Organ case. The late 20th century also saw a revival of the traditional organ case, which involves placing the pipes for each division in a separate, shallow, wooden enclosure, open at the front, with keyboards located in the center of the main case. Traditional practice places the pipes for the main Principal stop for each division in the facade of its case, suggesting the size and resources of the organ and filtering out the less desirable high-frequency content of organ pipe sound.

Architecturally, the case restores to the organ an identity that had been lost, at least in the U.S., where many instruments were built into recessed spaces whose facades gave no hint of the often extensive instruments behind them. Well-designed and ornamented cases for the Great, Positive, and Pedal divisions, for instance, announce visually the nature of the instrument in relation to the space where it is heard. Acoustically, organ cases project and blend the sound of each division. Free-standing cases, located near reflecting walls and ceiling, provide maximum reinforcement of sound.

Swell boxes, which consist of enclosures with louvered shutters at the front, are usually installed in the main case. Opening and closing the shutters controls the loudness and harmonic development of the pipes contained within the enclosure. Swell divisions became important in 18th-century English organs and from the 19th century in France, although they were not a part of classical designs in France or northern Europe.

II. *Organ stops.* 1. Nomenclature. Stop names ideally are based on the sound, shape, pitch, or location of the pipes. Some nomenclature describes only the general tone family (Principal 8′, Flute 4′), while some suggests the instrument being imitated (Trumpet, Cromorne). Other names arise from the appearance of the pipe: Gedeckt [Ger., covered]; Spitzflöte [fr. Ger. *spitz,* tapering]; Chimney Flute (with its cap pierced by a chimneylike cylinder). Still others imply, by custom, both tone family and pitch: Quint, for Principal 2 2/3′; Nazard, for Flute 2 2/3′. Prestant [fr. Lat. *praestare,* to stand before] is used in northern Europe to mean the main Principal stop, which is displayed in the facade, while Montre [Fr., to show] has the same meaning in France. In reed pipes, resonator length is associated with certain stop names: the Trumpet, Oboe, and Posaune are full length; the Clarinet, Krummhorn, and Fagott are half length; the Regal, Schalmei, and Vox Humana are quarter length or less.

American usage is eclectic and often confusing, mixing several languages without consistent regard for original connotations. Some builders try to be more precise by adhering to English terminology, by making translations, or by using only the appropriate language when designing an instrument in a specific classical style. Nonetheless, it is easier to characterize various European styles than to identify an "American" style, which is likely to be based on some combination of French, German, English, and even Spanish ideas.

2. Mixtures. Mixtures are Principal-scaled stops, having two or more pipes per note, sounding octaves and fifths. Their function is to complete the full flue chorus of the organ [Fr. *Plein jeu*] by reinforcing the harmonic series of 16′, 8′, and 4′ flue registers. A mixture's name traditionally indicates its pitch, which is given for the longest pipe at C. Mixtures for a 16′ *Grand orgue* in the classical French tradition are called *Fourniture* (2′) and *Cymbale* (1′), with the number of ranks (pipes per note) varying with the size of the organ and the acoustics of the building. In

Mixtures for a 16′ *Grand orgue.*

Fourniture V											
C					2′	1⅓′	1′	⅔′	½′		
f			4′	2⅔′	2′	1⅓′	1′				
f′	8′	5⅓′	4′	2⅔′	2′						
Cymbale											
C							1′	⅔′	½′	⅓′	¼′
c						1⅓′	1′	⅔′	½′	⅓′	
f					2′	1⅓′	1′	⅔′	½′		
c′				2⅔′	2′	1⅓′	1′	⅔′			
f′			4′	2⅔′	2′	1⅓′	1′				
c″		5⅓′	4′	2⅔′	2′	1⅓′					
f″	8′	5⅓′	4′	2⅔′	2′						

A 17th-century French organ, Auch Cathedral, 1688. Builder, Jean de Joyeuse.

Grand orgue
Montre 16′
Bourdon 16′
Montre 8′
Bourdon 8′
Prestant 4′
Doublette 2′
Fourniture VI
Cymbale IV
Brode 3⅕′
(Grosse tierce)
Nazard 2⅔′
Quarte de Nazard 2′
Tierce 1⅗′
Flageolet 1′
Dessus de Cornet V
Trompette 8′
Clairon 4′
Voix humaine 8′

Positif
Montre 8′
Bourdon 8′
Prestant 4′
Doublette 2′
Fourniture IV
Cymbale III
Flûte 4′
Nazard 2⅔′
Tierce 1⅗′
Larigot 1⅓′
Cromorne 8′

Echo (from c)
Bourdon 8′
Prestant 4′
Doublette 2′
Fourniture III
Cymbale III
Nazard 2⅔′
Tierce 1⅗′
Voix humaine 8′

Récit (from c′)
Cornet V

Pédale
Flûte (open) 8′
Flûte (open) 4′
Trompette 8′
Clairon 4′

Tremblant doux, Tremblant fort
Rossignol, 6 pipes

northern Europe, the terms are *Mixtur* and *Scharff* [Ger.], and *Mixtuur* and *Scherp* [Du.]; comparable Spanish terms are *Lleno* and *Címbala.* The higher-pitched mixture is intended for use only with the lower one, to avoid a gap in the harmonic series. In smaller instruments, based on an 8′ Principal, there may be only one mixture, pitched at 1 1/3′.

Normal mixtures drop back in pitch as they ascend, one rank at a time, by the intervals of a fourth, fifth, or octave. Hence, the pitch of a 1′ mixture (at C) may become as low as 8′ by the time it reaches c‴. The example given in the table is from Dom Bédos de Celles's *L'art du facteur d'orgues* (Paris, 1766–78), and shows the general procedure for a 16′ *Grand orgue.*

3. Registration. Registration is the selection and combination of stops by the player, according to the style of the music and the design of the organ. The first and oldest principle of all registration practice in any style is the use of the complete flue chorus [Fr. *Plein jeu*], consisting of Principals at 16′, 8′, 4′, 2 2/3′, and 2′ pitches, plus mixtures. In northern European style, the reeds may be added, but couplers are not used, nor are pitches doubled, while in the classical French practice, keyboards are coupled, thereby doubling pitches. Reeds are reserved for the *Grand jeu,* which also includes the *tierces* and flue stops at all pitches, but without the mixtures. Since the music demands appropriate sounds in order to be effective, it is essential for the player to be aware of such fundamental distinctions in different styles.

Registration instructions are often minimal, although French composers usually give clear directions, often including indications in the title of a piece (e.g., François Couperin, "Trio à 2 Dessus de Cromorne et la Basse de Tierce"). Among registrations common to several styles is the Cornet, consisting of 8′, 4′, 2 2/3′, 2′, and 1 3/5′ pitches, drawn either separately or by a single stop knob. The Sesquialtera includes two pitches of the Cornet (2 2/3′ and 1 3/5′), to which the 8′ and other pitches may be added. The five-rank Cornet has great importance as a solo voice and should not be confused with mixtures, since it contains the *tierce* (1 3/5′), and is of Flute scale.

English composers of the 18th century also cite specific registrations in their music, such as Cornet, Trumpet, and Flute (4′) solos; a variety of examples are found in John Stanley's voluntaries. In the 19th century, composers in all countries tended to be quite specific in designating registration, manual changes, and expression in their published music.

III. *Regional styles.* By the late 17th century, French, northern European, Italian, Spanish, and English organs had all achieved their classic identities [see IV]. Each style is clearly related to the repertory created for it, all of which is now available to the modern organist, who usually must perform on instruments whose resources only approximate the sounds needed for large segments of that repertory. Historically, each of the European styles has affected American organ design in varying degrees, beginning with the 18th-century colonial English influence, through the 19th-century influences of English, French, and German fashions, to the 20th-century "organ reform," based

A 17th-century German organ, Steinkirchen, 1687. Builder, Arp Schnitger (using some pipework from a 16th-century organ by D. Hoyer.

Hauptwerk
Quintadena 16′
Principal 8′
Rohrflöte 8′
Oktave 4′
Nasat 2⅔′
Oktave 2′
Gemshorn 2′
Mixtur IV-VI
Cimbel III
Trompete 8′
Rauschpfeife II

Brustwerk
Gedeckt 8′
Rohrflöte 4′
Oktave 2′
Spitzflöte 2′
Quinte 1⅓′
Tertian II
Scharff III-IV
Krummhorn 8′
Tremulant
Cimbelstern

Pedal
Principal 16′
Oktave 8′
Oktave 4′
Nachthorn 2′
Mixtur IV-V
Rauschpfeife II
Posaune 16′
Trompete 8′
Kornett 2′

A mid-19th-century French organ, St. Clothilde, Paris, 1859. Builder, Aristide Cavaillé-Coll.

Grand orgue
Montre 16′
Bourdon 16′
Montre 8′
Viole de gambe 8′
Flûte harmonique 8′
Bourdon 8′
Prestant 4′
Octave 4′
Quinte 2⅔′
Doublette 2′
Fourniture VI
Bombarde 16′
Trompette 8′
Clairon 4′

Positif
Bourdon 16′
Montre 8′
Gambe 8′
Flûte harmonique 8′
Bourdon 8′
Unda maris 8′ (Voix céleste)
Prestant 4′
Flûte octaviante 4′
Quinte 2⅔′
Doublette 2′
Plein jeu
Trompette 8′
Cromorne (Clarinette) 8′
Clairon 4′

Récit
Flûte harmonique 8′
Viole de gambe 8′
Bourdon 8′
Voix céleste 8′
Basson Hautbois 8′
Voix humaine 8′
Flûte octaviante 4′
Octavin 2′
Trompette 8′
Clairon 4′

Pédale
Soubasse 32′
Contrebasse 16′
Basse 8′
Octave 4′
Bombarde 16′
Basson 16′
Trompette 8′
Clairon 4′

Tremolo, 14 *Pédales de combinaison*

A 20th-century American organ, West Church, Boston, 1971. Builder, C. B. Fisk, Inc.

Great	*Swell*
Bourdon 16′	Violin diapsaon 8′
Prestant 8′	Stopped diapason 8′
Spire flute 8′	Flute 4′
Octave 4′	Cornet III
Doublet 2′	Fourniture III
Sesquialter II	Contra Hautboy 16′
Mixture IV-VI	Trumpet 8′
Trumpet 8′	*Pedal*
Clarion 4′	Bourdon 16′
Choir	Octave 8′
Chimney flute 8′	Superoctave 4′ and 2′
Prestant 4′	Mixture III
Night horn 4′	Trombone 16′
Fifteenth 2′	Tremulant
Nasard 2⅔′	
Tierce 1⅗′	
Sharp IV	
Cremona 8′	

largely on (often only partly understood) classical northern European and French models. This embarrassment of riches in both organ design and repertory leaves the modern organ builder and organist far larger areas of artistic discretion than in any other field of musical performance. Indeed, the dividing line between discretion and confusion is difficult to draw, requiring a mature artistic and historical perspective on the part of both player and builder. The accompanying dispositions illustrate some of the similarities and differences among several styles.

IV. *History.* Although the concept of an instrument with several fixed-pitch pipes blown by a single player (such as the *panpipes, or oriental **sheng*) goes back to primitive times, the history of the organ actually begins in the Graeco-Roman period, probably in the 3rd century B.C.E. An early instrument said by Hero (*Pneumatika,* ca. 120 B.C.E.) to have been invented by Ktesibios of Alexandria was the first to possess the basic components of the modern organ—a mechanism to supply air under pressure, a wind-chest to store and distribute it, keys and valves to admit wind to the pipes, and one or more graded sets of fixed-pitch pipes.

In the primitive organ, wind pressure was regulated by water (hence the name *hydraulis) and admitted to the pipes by spring-loaded slides pulled by the player. It was a melodic instrument, secular in usage, sometimes employed for signaling purposes, and frequently used outdoors. Its use spread to Byzantium and Arabian lands; it acquired ceremonial functions and was often a prized possession of rulers and organizations.

In the 6th or 7th century, organs began to be made in which wind was supplied by a bellows similar to a smith's bellows. Organs thus became a symbol of sophisticated technology. Ornamented with ivory and precious metals, they were prized as royal gifts, and it was in this manner that some of the earliest organs reached Europe. In 757 Pepin, King of the Franks, received such a gift from the Emperor Constantine, and Charlemagne was said to have been presented with a similar gift in 812 from the ruler of Constantinople.

It is difficult to ascertain just when the organ began to be used in the ritual of the Christian church. Organs are recorded in western European churches as early as the 8th century, but their usage is open to speculation and may originally have been unconnected to the ritual of the Mass. Pope John VIII is said to have ordered an organ to be built for him in the 9th century, but it may have been needed simply for the purpose of teaching music. By the 10th century, however, definite records appear of the introduction of organs and bells into ritual use, at least on feast days and other special occasions, by the Benedictines. By the end of this century, writers describe large and loud organs in churches of France, England, Spain, Germany, and the Low Countries. By the early 11th century, learned treatises were being written on their construction and the scaling of their pipes by the Benedictine monk Theophilus and many others. In the 12th century, there are indications of a definite liturgical function for the organ, which by this time was technically capable of playing music in at least two parts.

The proliferation of organs was rapid between the 12th and 15th centuries, and their use spread to south central Europe and the Slavic countries. Technical progress was steady during this period, and by the end of the 15th century the organ could be said to possess most of the technical and tonal attributes of its modern successors. Keys became smaller, and the compass expanded to over three octaves. Semitones, beginning with the B♭ required by some *plainsong, made their appearance, and the earliest known organ music manuscript (the Robertsbridge Codex of 1325) requires a full chromatic middle octave. Large church organs had become immense *mixtures (**Blockwerk*) of several ranks of open flue pipes at unison and quint pitches, tuned in *Pythagorean temperament. The continuing expansion of the compass resulted in a partial octave of bass pipes extending downward—the Principal—which by the 14th century was capable of being separated from the other ranks of the *Blockwerk.* These basses were played from an added keyboard, sometimes operated by the player's feet, and were called Trompes or Bordunen. The famous 14th-century organ at Halberstadt, described by Michael Praetorius (*Syntagma musicum,* 1619), possessed all of these features.

Parallel to the development of these large stationary church organs was that of the small portable or semi-portable instruments known as *portatives, *positives, or **organetti.* The smallest were the hand-carried instruments seen in illuminated manuscripts of the Middle Ages and in Renaissance paintings. These had a compass rarely exceeding two octaves and were strictly melodic instruments, used either to guide singers or to take part in instrumental ensembles. One hand was used to play the keys, the other to operate a single bellows at the back. Such instruments could be carried by a shoulder strap. Positives were larger, standing on a table or the floor. They were played with both hands, had a larger compass, and required a second person to operate the bellows, of which there were usually two.

The part played by the positive in the development of the modern organ should not be underestimated. It was in these instruments that the keyboard first reached something resembling its modern proportions, and they were almost certainly the first to have completely separable ranks of pipes controlled by stops. *Reed stops, too, probably made their first appearance in these small organs in the 15th- and 16th-century variant known as the *regal. It is not known who first conceived the idea of placing one of these positives in juxtaposition to a large *Blockwerk* organ to provide the organist with access to a greater variety of sound, but there is little doubt that this was, in the 15th century, the origin of the **Rückpositiv* or *Chair, an important landmark in the tonal and physical development of the organ.

By the end of the 16th century, it was not unusual for large churches, cathedrals, or abbeys to possess as many as four or five organs. English and Netherlandish records in particular make frequent mention of this. One or two of the organs were large, located in elevated places such as the rood loft or "swallow's nest" galleries on the side walls of the nave or choir; west-end organs were also beginning to make an appearance. Smaller organs were likely to be found at floor level in the choir or in chapels, and there were often also a few portatives and/or regals, which could be moved where needed. The custom survives in Spain, where two large organs often face each other across the choir, and in France, where even churches of moderate size usually have both a large west-end *Grand orgue* and a smaller *Orgue de choeur* in the choir.

The most important developments of the 15th and 16th centuries were the division of the tonal resources of the organ into separate stops of varying pitches and colors and the multiplication of sections (divisions) controlled by separate keyboards, particularly in northern Europe. The division of tonal resources began in the Middle Ages with the separation of the unison Principal from the *Blockwerk* and accelerated in the Renaissance when a separate wind-chest bearing colorful and imitative *concertato* stops was added above the *Blockwerk* chest. Later organs had both kinds of stops on a single wind-chest, with separate stop actions for nearly all ranks of pipes. The organ of 1475 in the church of San Petronio, Bologna, is one of the earliest surviving examples of this type. Stops originally put off, or "stopped," individual ranks of pipes, as they still do in the organ of 1521 at Oosthuizen, Holland. In more recent organs, drawing the stop knob puts the rank of pipes on. In northern Europe, the addition of the separately encased **Rückpositiv,* the small but colorful **Brustwerk,* and a Pedal division with its own independent stops laid the foundation for the magnificent Baroque organs of the 17th century. Quite early in the 16th century, the old Pythagorean system of tuning gave way to the more flexible *mean-tone system. All of these developments were paralleled in the rapid advances being made in organ composition.

By the 17th century, organs already possessed virtually all of the varieties of tone and of flue and reed pipe construction found in modern organs, as Praetorius demonstrates in the *Syntagma musicum.* Mechanically the organ was also quite sophisticated. Key action was usually of the "suspended" (direct pull-down) type used by the French and Spanish until well into the 19th century, and the wind-chests either of the slider-and-pallet type still used in tracker-action organs today or of the spring-chest [Ger. *Springlade*] type, in which the stop action was not a perforated slider (register) but an added set of small individual pipe valves. The use of the spring-chest died out in northern Europe in the 17th century, but continued in Italy until early in the 19th century.

Until the 16th century, there had been few regional differences in the style of organ building or composition, partly because all of Europe shared a common religious ritual and partly because both composers and organ builders (the latter frequently in monastic orders) were inclined to travel fairly extensively. After the early 16th century, the Reformation and Counter-Reformation, along with the more rigid national boundaries engendered by the political climate, tended to polarize the liturgical use of the organ along regional lines. This, in turn, had a marked effect on both the tonal and physical development of the instrument in various geographic regions. A brief discussion of each regional style is necessary for the fullest understanding of the remarkable diversity that prevailed during what has been called the Golden Age of the Organ, the 17th and early 18th centuries.

1. Low Countries. Before the Reformation, Flemish builders are recorded as having built organs in France, Spain, Italy, Austria, and England. During the 16th century, the illustrious Niehoff family of 'sHertogenbosch in Brabant built important organs throughout the Netherlands and North Germany, laying the technical and tonal foundations for the North German school of the 17th century. The Calvinist Reformation in 1560 divided the area, the southern part (Belgium) remaining Catholic, the northern (Holland) becoming Protestant, with the result that the Flemish organ continued to develop as a liturgical instrument and as such had a strong influence on the French organ of a century later. From 1560 until the introduction of accompanied congregational singing in the 1630s, the Dutch organ developed as a secular instrument. Although housed in churches, the large Dutch organs of this period were actually owned by the municipalities (which also hired the organists) and were played only for

market-day concerts and for special occasions. The *concertato* (imitative) stops became highly developed, and these large but refined organs were highly versatile. With the reintroduction of the organ to the church service as an aid to congregational singing, the strong Principal chorus was also reintroduced, along with the Cornet stop for the outlining of Psalm-tune melodies. These developments continued into the 18th century with the work of builders such as Müller, Duyschot, and Moreau, which resulted in the monumental organs of the Old and New churches of Amsterdam, Haarlem, Gouda, Rotterdam, and elsewhere. The 18th-century tradition was continued into the 19th century by conservative builders such as Bätz and Freytag, and Holland was only mildly affected by the "symphonic" movement. The 20th century saw a renaissance of Dutch organ building. Drawing upon the example of their many historic instruments, modern Dutch builders such as Flentrop have become internationally known leaders in the revival of classical ideals.

2. North Germany. This area was already rich in organs in the late Middle Ages; small early instruments exist in Krewerd and Rysum, and two fine Gothic cases, containing much early pipework, are found in the Jakobikirche in Lübeck. During the late 16th and early 17th centuries, a school of builders grew up in the Hamburg region that included Stellwagen, Hoyer, Fritzsche (an immigrant from Saxony), and the noted Scherer family. Crowning the work of this school in the 17th and early 18th centuries were Arp Schnitger and his sons. The organs that developed under these builders were unique in all Europe for their size and the scope of their resources. Organs such as Schnitger's instruments in the Nikolaikirche and Jakobikirche in Hamburg would have four manual divisions plus a large independent pedal division and often more than 60 speaking stops ranging from 32′ to 1′ in pitch and including every variety of foundations, mixtures, mutations, flutes, and reeds. These were the instruments that inspired Buxtehude, Scheidemann, Bruhns, Böhm, Tunder, Lübeck, Weckmann, and the young J. S. Bach. The influence of the North German builders was felt in northern Holland, where in Alkmaar, Zwolle, and Groningen some of Schnitger's largest instruments were to be found. In the late 18th and the 19th century, the importance of the area as an organ-building center diminished greatly, and much of the work there consisted simply of rebuilding older organs, often to their detriment. Schnitger's apprentice Cahman built some significant organs in Sweden in the 18th century, and Marcussen built some notable Romantic instruments in Denmark in the 19th century. In the 20th century, a revival occurred in the area, and fine contemporary organs have been built by the Danes Marcussen and Frobenius as well as by a new generation of North Germans such as Von Beckerath, Führer, and Ahrend.

3. South and central Germany, Switzerland, and Austria. Some of the oldest extant organs may be found in Switzerland (Sion, early 15th century) and Austria (Innsbruck, 1555), and Nürnberg was a center of organ-building in the 15th century. Arnolt Schlick of Heidelberg, in his *Spiegel der Orgelmacher und Organisten* (1511), gives valuable information on the well-developed central-German organ of his epoch. Although builders such as Esaias Compenius produced large and influential organs in the 17th century, it was not until the 18th century that the fame of this region's builders exceeded that of builders from the north. Prominent were the French-influenced Riepp and Gabler, builder of the famed Weingarten Abbey organ. Most notable, however, was the Alsatian-trained Saxon, Gottfried Silbermann, whose instruments in Dresden, Freiberg, and elsewhere were known to the mature Bach and whose work was continued by his pupil Hildebrandt. Excellent organs were built in the late 18th century by Stumm, and in the 19th century the large central German firms such as Walcker, Ladegast, and Reubke developed the full-blown German Romantic organ. Massive of tone and often huge in size, these were the instruments for which Reger and Liszt wrote their complex symphonic works. The builders of these organs experimented with many new action designs (such as the ventil chest and pneumatic key-action) to overcome the playing problems generated by the excessive size of these instruments. They also introduced the use of free (as opposed to beating) *reed stops. The 20th century saw a continuation of factory-scale building in this area by firms such as Walcker and Klais, and large factories are also found in Switzerland (Metzler) and Austria (Rieger).

4. France and Alsace. Most of the large 15th-century organs of France were Flemish in origin or design, except in the south, where Italo-Spanish influences prevailed. In the 16th century, a native school began to develop around Paris, and the first references to registrational practices that were to lead to the almost dogmatically fixed rules of the *Jeux* date from the 17th and 18th centuries. Large Gothic and Renaissance cases still exist in places like Amiens and Rouen (St. Maclou), but French organs never exceeded two manuals (*Grand orgue* and *Positif*) until the early 17th century, when a third half-manual *(Récit)* appeared to play a solo Cornet and, later, reeds. A fourth small division was added even later, but until late in the 18th century the Pedal division usually consisted only of 8′ Principal and 8′ Trompette for *cantus firmus* playing. Thierry and Joyeuse were among the noted builders of the 17th century, followed in the 18th century by Isnard, Parizot, LeFèbre, and the celebrated Cliquot family, whose work may be found in such places as Houdan, the cathedral of Poitiers, and St. Gervais in Paris, the church of the Couperins. The highly uniform tonal makeup of the 18th-century Parisian organs provided the retiring Principals, silvery mixtures, colorful mutations, strong Cornets, and fiery reeds for which the Couperins, de Grigny, du Mage, Dandrieu,

Marchand, and Balbastre registrated their organ Masses and **noëls*. A remarkably detailed technical description of these organs is found in Dom Bedos's *L'art du facteur d'orgues* (1766–78).

A parallel school of organ building tempered by German influences, dominated by Andreas Silbermann and his sons, grew up in Alsace in the 18th century, and this led to the conservative work of Callinet and Stier in the 19th century. The French Revolution retarded the progress of organ building for a time, but a new impetus was given in the 19th century by Aristide Cavaillé-Coll, whose instrument for St. Denis in Paris of 1839 broke much new ground tonally and mechanically and introduced the Barker machine (a pneumatic key-action assist invented by the Englishman Charles S. Barker). His tonal innovations included full-bodied Gambas and Harmonic flutes, and harmonic-length trebles for conical reeds to impart greater power. These were the sounds that inspired the late-Romantic Parisian composers such as Franck, Saint-Saëns, Widor, and Guilmant. In the early 20th century, Merklin, Mutin, and others continued to build in this tradition, but in more recent years a neoclassical school taking its inspiration from Silbermann has grown up in the Alsatian region.

5. England. Organs of considerable size, such as that in Winchester Cathedral, are recorded in England as early as the 10th century, and by the early 16th century, organs could be found throughout the realm, many large churches and abbeys containing several. The Reformation, by turns Calvinist and Episcopal in nature, proved a serious setback for English organ building, but organs continued to be built sporadically throughout the 16th and early 17th centuries, not only for churches but also for domestic use. The Commonwealth period (1650–59) caused an almost complete break in the tradition that produced the organs for which Redford, Byrd, Tomkins, Lugge, and Gibbons wrote. Nearly all existing organs were destroyed, but remaining fragments and records reveal the early 17th-century English church organ as an instrument of no more than two manuals (Great and Chaire) and no independent pedal, containing only Flute and Principal stops at various unison and fifth pitches.

The Restoration period in the late 17th century saw considerable organ-building activity, dominated by the contrasting figures of Bernard ("Father") Smith, an immigrant from Holland, and Renatus Harris, the son of an English builder living in Brittany. These two builders brought to England the not uncomplementary traditions of Holland and France, as exemplified in their instruments for St. Paul's, London, and Salisbury Cathedral. Mixtures, Cornets, the *Tierce* mutation, and a variety of reed stops were introduced, as well as a third manual of short compass called *Echo. In lieu of a pedal, the manual compass extended a fifth below that of Continental organs. This was the organ for which Purcell, Locke, and Blow wrote, and it set the pattern for the entire 18th century, the only major change being the growth of the Echo, fitted with Venetian shutters, into the full-compass Swell organ of the 19th century. Notable 18th-century builders included Green, Jordan, the Byfield family, and the Swiss immigrant Snetzler. Green and Snetzler also produced many excellent chamber organs. Stanley, Greene, Boyce, and many others wrote for this 18th-century instrument, exploiting standard registrational formulas in much the same manner as the French.

Beginning with the work of Hill in the 1830s, and continuing with Willis and, later, Lewis and others, larger organs in a developing Romantic tonal style began to be built. Such instruments were found not only in cathedrals but increasingly in town halls (Birmingham, Reading) and concert venues such as Royal Albert Hall in London, where from the second half of the 19th century organists such as W. T. Best gave popular concerts to packed houses. This style of organ carried well into the 20th century, eventually being met by a "neobaroque" backlash in the 1950s and 1960s. By the end of the 20th century, however, builders such as Mander, Walker, and many smaller firms were tending toward eclectic organs that combined historical British practices with Continental influences.

6. Italy. In Italy the process of dividing the *Blockwerk* into individually operated stops is recorded as early as the first half of the 15th century, and springchests came into use toward the end of the century. In the 16th century, the Italian organ became standardized as a large one-manual instrument based on the 8′ *Principale* (sometimes with an added 16′ octave) with a chorus of unison and fifth mutations going as high in pitch (at low C) as 1/2′ and 1/3′, although these broke back in the higher registers. There were also flute stops at unison pitches and the **Voce umana* or *Fiffaro,* a two-rank undulating stop of principal pipes. Among the leading builders of this period was the Antegnati family, and Costanzo Antegnati has left us an important documentation of the work of his era in *L'arte organica* (1608). Second manuals were rare, as were reed stops, although those of the short-length regal type are sometimes found. This was the organ of Frescobaldi, Gabrieli, and Merulo, and it changed little throughout the 17th and 18th centuries. During the late 17th century, there was some influence from Flanders, south Germany, and Austria, but independent pedals did not appear until the 18th century and controlled only a few stops of short compass. Noteworthy builders of this period included Nacchini, Tronci, and Callido. The Serassi family continued the ancient Italian tradition into the 19th century, and while some Romantic concessions in the way of reeds and strings crept into their schemes, the Italian organ did not acquire a third manual or a Pedal division of any scope until nearly the end of the 19th century, when the Romantic practices of other countries began exerting a strong influence on builders of larger organs tonally and mechanically, the Vegezzi-Bossi firm becoming a prominent maker of "symphonic"-style organs. Dur-

ing the second half of the 20th century firms such as Tamburini and Ruffati broke completely with Italian tradition, building organs strongly influenced by German neoclassicism and American eclecticism.

7. Spain and Portugal. The Iberian school developed in a manner similar to the Italian, and, as in Italy, significant early instruments still exist, such as the 16th-century organ in the Escorial. There was also a strong Flemish influence on Iberian organs of the 15th and 16th centuries—an influence that persisted even after a strong regional style had been established. The 17th-century organs of the Echevarria family are typical, being for the most part large, one-manual organs with no independent pedal, containing a principal chorus, mixtures, mutations, flutes, and both short and full-length reeds. Late 17th- and early 18th-century developments were the enclosure of a short-compass manual division (the **Eco*) and the division of all stops (the so-called **medio registro*) so that separate registrations could be played by the right and left hands. "Toy" stops (birdcalls, drums, bells, etc.), though found in other countries, were employed in even greater profusion in Spain and Portugal, as were multiple *tremulants. Horizontal reed stops of all pitches, projecting from the front of the organ case, became a notable feature of large organs from the late 17th century onward and were used on ceremonial occasions and in "battle" pieces. Important composers for these early organs include Cabezón, Cabanilles, Bermudo, Bruno, and Santa María. Churches often had more than one large organ, and in the 18th century, composers such as Soler wrote works for two organs. The traditional Iberian organ was little changed during the 19th century, and even today builders such as Amezúa still base their organs on traditional tonal concepts.

8. America. The earliest organs in the New World were imported from Spain to the South and Central American colonies in the 17th and 18th centuries. Resident builders were soon also producing organs, and many early instruments survive, including the large early 18th-century organs of the Mexico City Cathedral.

To the north, there are records of imported organs being used in the French colonies of Quebec in the late 17th century. Early in the 18th century, German colonists in the Pennsylvania area began to import small organs and by the latter half of the century had established an important if short-lived center of organ building whose dominant figures were Johann Klemm, trained in Saxony, and his illustrious Moravian pupil, David Tannenberg. Also during the 18th century, a significant number of English church and chamber organs were imported to the eastern coastal region, and by the end of the century, organs were being built in the Boston area.

Early in the 19th century, important centers of organ building were established in New York (by Thomas Hall and Henry Erben) and Boston (by William Goodrich and Thomas Appleton). Organs built in these centers were based essentially upon English models with regard to stop lists, compasses, mode of construction, and temperament. By the midpoint of the century, large workshops began to flourish, notably in Boston, where Simmons, Stevens, and the Hook brothers were producing a large volume of organs of all sizes. Erben in New York and Johnson in western Massachusetts were providing some worthy competition, and builders such as Kilgen, Felgemaker, and Pilcher were establishing themselves in the newly settled Midwest. During the latter half of the 19th century, French and German influences began to supplant the English, resulting in a unique expression of the Romantic aesthetic, exemplified in Hook and Hastings's Holy Cross Cathedral organ (Boston) of 1875 and the work of Hutchings (Boston), the Roosevelt brothers (New York), and the Casavant brothers of Quebec.

By the turn of the 20th century, the idea of an orchestrally imitative organ was taking root, and technology was providing a number of pneumatically and electrically operated alternatives to the older tracker and Barker machine actions. Innovators in this field included J. T. Austin of Hartford, Ernest Skinner of Boston, and the English immigrant Robert Hope-Jones. In the early 20th century, self-playing organs for the home became popular, and the Aeolian Co. of New Jersey was a leader in producing them. Hope-Jones's inventions led to the "Mighty Wurlitzer" and similar specialized instruments developed for the accompaniment of silent movies. Skinner's success with imitative voicing won him many important church and concert-hall contracts.

In the 1930s, a reaction to the orchestral concept began to set in, and G. Donald Harrison of Aeolian-Skinner, Richard Whitelegg of Möller, and the Cleveland builder Walter Holtkamp began to produce more balanced tonal schemes doing justice to a wider range of literature. After World War II, the effects of the European "organ reform" began to be felt, resulting in more classically oriented tonal schemes. During the 1960s and 1970s, younger builders such as Fisk, Noack, and Brombaugh, inspired partly by the importation of neoclassical instruments from European builders such as Flentrop and Von Beckerath, led the movement toward more historical mechanical as well as tonal concepts, resulting in a revival of mechanical playing action and free-standing decorative casework. The final quarter of the 20th century saw a broadening of historical influences to include not only 17th- and 18th-century Continental models, but also 19th century influences, primarily French but often with British or American overtones. Toward the end of the century an eclectic type of instrument successfully combining a variety of historical influences, both tonal and mechanical, came into prominence. Firms such as Fisk, Brombaugh, Rosales, and Dobson helped to popularize this trend, having built some notable organs in this style for concert halls and large churches, but its influence is seen even in small organs of this period.

Bibl.: Arnolt Schlick, *Spiegel der Orgelmacher und Organisten* (Speyer, 1511); facs. with parallel transcription and trans. Eng., Elizabeth Berry Barber (Buren: Frits Knuf, 1980); 2nd. ed., Ernst Flade (Mainz: P Smets, 1932; R: 1951). Costanzo Antegnati, *L'arte organica* (Brescia, 1608; facs., *BMB* sez. 4, 44, 1971). Michael Praetorius, *Syntagma musicum,* vol. 2, *De organographia* (Wolfenbüttel, 1619; facs., *DM* ser. 1, 4, 1958); trans. Eng., Harold Blumenfeld (New York: Bärenreiter, 1949; R: New York: Da Capo, 1975). Andreas Werckmeister, *Erweiterte und verbesserte Orgelprobe* (Quedlinburg, 1698; R: Rochester, N.Y.: U of Rochester Pr, 1954); trans. Eng. Gerhard Krapf (Raleigh: Sunbury, 1976). Dom François Bédos de Celles, *L'art du facteur d'orgues,* 4 vols. (Paris, 1766–78; facs., *DM* ser. 1, 24–25, 1963–66); trans. Eng. Charles Ferguson (Raleigh: Sunbury, 1977). Jakob Adlung, *Musica mechanica organoedi* (Berlin, 1768). Johann J. Seidel, *Die Orgel und ihr Bau* (Breslau, 1843; trans. Eng., London, 1852; R: New York: Da Capo, 1982). Edward J. Hopkins and Edward F. Rimbault, *The Organ, Its History and Construction* (London, 1855; 3rd ed., 1877). Arthur G. Hill, *The Organ-Cases and Organs of the Middle Ages and Renaissance,* 2 vols. (London, 1883 and 1891). George A. Audsley, *The Art of Organ Building,* 2 vols. (New York: Dodd, Mead, 1905; R: New York: Dover, 1965). James I. Wedgwood, *A Comprehensive Dictionary of Organ Stops* (London: Vincent Music, 1905). Wallace Goodrich, *The Organ in France* (Boston: Boston Music, 1917). Andrew Freeman, *Father Smith* (London: Office of *Musical Opinion,* 1926); 2nd ed., John Rowntree, with annotations and new material (Oxford: Positif Pr, 1977). Christhard Mahrenholz, *Die Orgelregister, ihre Geschichte und ihr Bau* (Kassel: Bärenreiter, 1930; 2nd ed., 1942). Alexandre Cellier and Henri Bachelin, *L'orgue, ses éléments—son histoire—son esthétique* (Paris: Delagrave, 1933). Norbert Dufourcq, *Esquisse d'une histoire de l'orgue en France* (Paris: Larousse, 1935). Joseph Wörsching, *Die Orgelbauer-Familie Silbermann in Strassburg* (Mainz: Rheingold, 1941). Arie Bouman, *Orgels in Nederland* (Amsterdam: A de Lange, 1943). Noel A. Bonavia-Hunt, *The Organ Reed* (New York: J Fischer, 1951). William L. Sumner, *The Organ: Its Evolution, Principles of Construction, and Use* (London: Macdonald, 1952; 4th ed., New York: St. Martin's, 1973). Ernst Flade, *Gottfried Silbermann,* 2nd ed. (Leipzig: Breitkopf & Härtel, 1953). Joseph Blanton, *The Organ in Church Design* (Albany, Tex.: Venture, 1957). Rudolf Quoika, *Das Positiv in Geschichte und Gegenwart* (Kassel: Bärenreiter, 1957). Maarten A. Vente, *Die Brabanter Orgel* (Amsterdam: H J Paris, 1958; 2nd ed., 1963). Cecil Clutton and Austin Niland, *The British Organ* (London: Batsford, 1963). Wolfgang Metzler, *Romantischer Orgelbau in Deutschland* (Ludwigsburg: E F Walcker, 1965). Jean Perrot, *L'orgue: De ses origines hellénistiques à la fin du XIIIe siècle* (Paris: A & J Picard, 1965); trans. Eng. Norma Deane (London: Oxford U Pr, 1971). Karl Bormann, *Die gotische Orgel zu Halberstadt* (Berlin: Merseburger, 1966). Rudolf Quoika, *Vom Blockwerk zur Registerorgel* (Kassel: Bärenreiter, 1966). Peter F. Williams, *The European Organ, 1450–1850* (London: Batsford, 1966; 2nd ed., Bloomington: Ind U Pr, 1978). Joseph Goebel, *Theorie und Praxis des Orgelpfeifenklanges* (Frankfurt am Main: Musikinstrument, 1967). Michael Wilson, *The English Chamber Organ* (Oxford: Bruno Cassirer, 1968). Poul-Gerhard Andersen, *Organ Building and Design,* trans. Joanne Curnutt (New York: Oxford U Pr, 1969). Fenner Douglass, *The Language of the Classical French Organ* (New Haven: Yale U Pr, 1969). Hans Klotz, *The Organ Handbook,* trans. Gerhard Krapf (St. Louis: Concordia, 1969). Werner Walcker-Mayer, *The Roman Organ of Aquincum,* trans. Joscelyn Godwin (Ludwigsburg: Musikwissenschaftlicher Vlg, 1972). Walther M. Liebenow, *A Bibliography of the History and Construction of Organs* (Minneapolis: Martin Pr, 1973). Rudolf Reuter, *Bibliographie der Orgel: Literatur zur Geschichte der Orgel bis 1968* (Kassel: Bärenreiter, 1973). Jean-Albert Villard, *L'oeuvre de François-Henri Cliquot* (Laval: Imprimerie Barnéoud, 1973). Gustav Fock, *Arp Schnitger und seine Schule* (Kassel: Bärenreiter, 1974). John Fesperman, *Two Essays on Organ Design* (Raleigh: Sunbury, 1975). Orpha Ochse, *The History of the Organ in the United States* (Bloomington: Ind U Pr, 1975). Uwe Pape, ed., *The Tracker Organ Revival in America* (Berlin: Pape, 1977). Barbara Owen, *The Organ in New England* (Raleigh: Sunbury, 1979). Michael I. Wilson, *Organ Cases of Western Europe* (Montclair, N.J.: Abner Schram, 1979). Fenner Douglass, *Cavaillé-Coll and the Musicians* (Raleigh: Sunbury, 1980). John T. Fesperman, *Organs in Mexico* (Raleigh: Sunbury, 1980). Peter F. Williams, *A New History of the Organ* (Bloomington: Ind U Pr, 1980). John Fesperman, *Flentrop in America* (Raleigh: Sunbury, 1982). Peggy K. Reinburg, *Arp Schnitger, Organ Builder* (Bloomington: Ind U Pr, 1982). Walter A. Frankel and Nancy K. Nardone, *Organ Music in Print,* 2nd ed. (Philadelphia: Musicdata, 1984). Homer D. Blanchard, *The Bach Organ Book* (Delaware, Ohio: Praestant Pr, 1985). David C. Wickens, *The Instruments of Samuel Green* (London: Macmillan, 1987). Peter Williams and Barbara Owen, *The Organ* (London: Macmillan, 1988). Raymond J. Brunner, *That Ingenious Business: Pennsylvania German Organ Builders* (Birdsboro, Pa.: Pennsylvania German Society, 1990). Nicholas Thistlethwaite, *The Making of the Victorian Organ* (Cambridge: Cambridge U Pr, 1990). Lynn Edwards, ed., *The Historical Organ in America* (Easthampton, Mass.: Westfield Center, 1992). Peter Williams, *The Organ in Western Culture, 750–1250* (Cambridge: Cambridge U Pr, 1993). Orpha Ochse, *Organists and Organ Playing in Nineteenth-Century France and Belgium* (Bloomington: Ind U Pr, 1994). Lawrence Archbold and William J. Peterson, eds., *French Organ Music from the Revolution to Franck and Widor* (Rochester: U of Rochester Pr, 1995). Stephen Bicknell, *The History of the English Organ* (Cambridge: Cambridge U Pr, 1996). Barbara Owen, *The Registration of Baroque Organ Music* (Bloomington: Ind U Pr, 1997). Carolyn Shuster-Fournier, *Les Orgues de Salon d'Aristide Cavaillé-Coll* (Paris: L'Orgue, Cahiers et Mémoires, 1997). Gustav Fock, *Hamburg's Role in Northern European Organ Building* (Easthampton, Mass.: Westfield Center, 1997). Michael Murray, *French Masters of the Organ* (New Haven: Yale U Pr, 1998). Walter Ladegast, *Friedrich Ladegast, der Orgelbauer von Weissenfels* (Stockach: Weidling Verlag, 1998). Rollin Smith, *The Aeolian Pipe Organ and Its Music* (Richmond: Organ Historical Society, 1998). Nicholas Thistlethwaite and Geoffrey Webber, eds., *The Cambridge Companion to the Organ* (Cambridge: Cambridge U Pr, 1998). Fenner Douglass, *Cavaillé-Coll and the French Romantic Tradition* (New Haven: Yale U Pr, 1999). Jim Berrow, ed., *Towards the Conservation and Restoration of Historic Organs* (London: Church House, 2000). Carol A. Traupman-Carr, ed., *Pleasing for Our Use: David Tannenberg and the Organs of the Moravians* (Bethlehem, Pa.: Lehigh U Pr, 2000). Orpha Ochse, *Austin Organs* (Organ Historical Society, 2001). Rudolf Faber and Philip Hartmann, eds., *Handbuch Orgelmusik: Komponisten—Werke—Interpretation* (Kassel: Bärenreiter, 2002). Kerala J. Snyder, ed., *The Organ as a Mirror of Its Time* (New York: Oxford U Pr, 2002).

I–III J.T.F.; IV, Bibl. B.O.

Organ chorale [Ger. *Orgelchoral*]. A polyphonic prolongation, elaboration, or working out of a Protestant *chorale tune on the organ, for use as a prelude to a congregational chorale, in **alternatim style,* as an interlude between verses, as an independent piece elsewhere in the service, or as a concert piece. Typically, the chorale tune is presented complete in one voice, and/or its motives form the basis of a polyphonic texture. Bach's more than 140 organ chorales (here referred to by *BWV numbers only) represent exemplary achievements in the form.

I. *Types.* Organ chorales are generally classified according to whether the chorale tune is presented in strict form (i.e., in its entirety, even if ornamented) or free form. Strict forms include the chorale motet (sometimes called chorale ricercar), chorale variations, and chorale prelude; free forms include the chorale fantasia and chorale fugue. Both long and short forms of these types are possible.

In the *chorale motet (or chorale ricercar), each line of the chorale serves as the subject of a point of imitation; the overall form is a series of such points analogous to the Renaissance vocal motet (e.g., BWV 686). In a set of *chorale variations, the chorale melody is elaborated several times in contrasting styles (BWV 768, 769). The chorale prelude, frequently intended to serve as the prelude for the singing of a chorale, includes the following types: (1) melody chorale, a short form in which the chorale tune appears as a continuous melody in the soprano accompanied by contrapuntal parts (BWV 644 and many other pieces in the **Orgel-Büchlein*); (2) ornamental chorale, in which the chorale is presented with elaborate ornamentation (BWV 622 and 641, short; 659, long); (3) *cantus firmus* chorale, a long form in which the chorale tune is presented in long notes (often in the pedal) and its successive phrases are separated by interludes (BWV 661); and (4) chorale canon, in which the chorale tune appears in canon supported by accompanying voices (BWV 608 and 634, short; 678 and 682, long). In the chorale fantasia, free treatment of the chorale tune prevails (BWV 615, short; 718, long). Two types of chorale fugue are possible, the short fughettas on the first phrase of the chorale (BWV 677, 679, 681) and the larger free fugues (BWV 680, 733). The accompanying voices in all these forms except the fugue most frequently serve only as modest support for the chorale tune. In the larger examples by Bach, however, the accompaniment is often cast in a clear, self-sufficient structure—invention, fugue, motet, canon, fantasia, duet, aria, trio sonata—to which the chorale tune is added. In BWV 684, for example, the accompaniment constitutes a trio sonata to which the chorale is added in canon.

II. *History.* The first extant organ chorale appears to be an intabulation of *Aus tiefer Not* by the Swiss organist Hans Kotter (1485–1541), while the first publication of organ chorales occurs in Ammerbach's *Orgel oder Instrument Tabulatur* (Leipzig, 1571 and 1583). The Dutch Calvinist organist Jan Pieterszoon Sweelinck (1562–1621) invented the chorale variation by combining the style of the secular keyboard variation, as practiced by the English virginalists, with sacred chorale melodies. Sweelinck normally wrote four variations (for two to four voices) to a set; the chorale tune was usually set in long notes with motivic, patterned, or sequential figuration in other voices. Since organ music was strictly excluded from the Calvinist services, Sweelinck's chorale variations must have been intended only for performance at his frequent organ concerts. Further development stems directly from Sweelinck's leading German pupils Samuel Scheidt (in central Germany), whose monumental *Tabulatura nova* (1624) is a major landmark in the repertory, and Heinrich Scheidemann, who invented the free chorale fantasia by introducing toccata elements into the chorale motet and who influenced many North German composers of organ chorales, including Matthias Weckmann, Franz Tunder, Delphin Strungk, Johann Adam Reincken, Dietrich Buxtehude, Nicolaus Bruhns, Johann Nicolaus Hanff, and Vincent Lübeck.

Buxtehude wrote chorale fantasias and complete sets of chorale variations, but his 30 short chorale preludes constitute his principal historical contribution to the form. Each chorale prelude can be regarded as the reduction of a set of variations to a single variation, which was probably intended to introduce the congregational chorale in the service; the chorale is usually set in the soprano—ornamented with expressive "vocal" embellishments and accompanied by modest lower parts—in such a way as to convey the affect of the chorale text. Clearly, certain pieces by Buxtehude served as models for similar works by Bach.

In central Germany, the chorale motet was compressed into the chorale fughetta by reducing the multiple points of imitation into a single fugue; a set of 44 such pieces was composed by Bach's uncle, Johann Christoph Bach. Johann Pachelbel also developed a distinctive central German chorale prelude style—generally a strict, unadorned *cantus firmus* set against nonmotivic counterpoint, but with each phrase of the chorale anticipated in the accompanying voices. By the early 18th century, the northern and central German styles exerted equal influence, as demonstrated in the works of Georg Böhm, Bach, Telemann, Johann Gottfried Walther, and Georg Friedrich Kauffmann. Bach's great collections—the *Orgel-Büchlein* (BWV 599–644), the *Schübler Chorales (BWV 645–50), the 18 Leipzig chorales (BWV 651–68), the chorales from the **Clavier-Übung* pt. 3 (BWV 669–89), and the Canonic Variations (BWV 769)—clearly represent the artistic apex of the form.

After 1750, Bach's students—Johann Ludwig Krebs, Gottfried August Homilius, Johann Peter Kellner, Johann Philipp Kirnberger, Johann Friedrich Agricola—and others still composed settings, but by 1800, newly composed organ chorales are rare: Mendelssohn's *Sonata VI* (a chorale partita), the 11 chorale preludes op. 122 of Brahms, and Reger's chorale fantasias (1898–1900) are significant exceptions. In the early and middle 20th century, neoclassical impulses in liturgy and music stimulated renewed interest in the form. Heinrich Kaminski, Johann Nepomuk David, Hugo Distler, and Ernst Pepping wrote a large body of organ chorales based on contrapuntal models from the 17th and 18th centuries, but realized in a more dissonant (though often tonal) idiom. At the end of the 20th century, mostly American Lutherans, such as Paul Manz, appeared to be actively composing new works of this type.

Bibl.: Robert Tusler, *The Style of J. S. Bach's Chorale Preludes* (Berkeley and Los Angeles: U of Cal Pr, 1956). Jean Edson, *Organ-Preludes: An Index* (Metuchen, N.J.: Scarecrow, 1970). Willi Apel, *The History of Keyboard Music to 1700,* trans. and rev. Hans Tischler (Bloomington: Ind U Pr, 1972). Friedrich Blume, *Protestant Church Music: A History* (New York: Norton, 1974). Peter Williams, *The Organ Music of Bach* (Cambridge: Cambridge U Pr, 1980). Ernest May, "The Types, Uses, and Historical Position of Bach's Organ Chorales," *J. S. Bach as Organist: His Instruments, Music and Performance Practices,* ed. George Stauffer and Ernest May (Bloomington: Ind U Pr, 1986), pp. 81–101. Russell Stinson, *Bach: The Orgelbuchlein* (New York: Schirmer, 1996). Russel Stinson, *J. S. Bach's Great Eighteen Organ Chorales* (New York: Oxford U Pr, 2001). E.D.M.

Organetto [It.]. (1) A *portative organ, small enough to be carried by a shoulder strap, with a range of less than three octaves, and usually only one set of pipes; small enough also to be pumped by the player's left hand while played with the right. (2) *Barrel organ.

Organ hymn. A set of organ pieces intended to be substituted for the odd-numbered verses of a Latin hymn [see *Alternatim*]. The most famous examples are by Jehan Titelouze (*Hymnes de l'Eglise pour toucher sur l'orgue,* Paris, 1623), but such *versets continued to be improvised and sometimes written down through the 19th century by composers such as Nicolas de Grigny (1672–1703) and Guillaume Lasceux (1740–1831). B.G.

Organillo [Sp.]. *Barrel organ, *barrel piano.

Organista. (1) [Lat., It., Sp.] Organist. (2) [Lat.] In the late 13th-century treatise of Anonymous IV [see Theory], composer of *organum. The composer Leonin is there described as the "optimus organista" (the greatest composer of organum).

Organistrum [Lat.]. *Hurdy-gurdy.

Organ Mass. A set of organ pieces intended to be substituted for portions of plainchant in a *Mass. Organists improvised *versets to alternate [see *Alternatim*] with phrases of sung plainchant in both the Proper and the Ordinary, but usually only Ordinary sections were written down (because they were not limited to a particular liturgical occasion). The possible uses of the organ at Mass were standardized by 1600, and thus most extant organ Masses consist of the same 22 versets, including two movements that are independent of plainchant. They were dispersed in the Ordinary as follows (texts to be sung are given in parentheses):

Kyrie: (1) Kyrie; (Kyrie); (2) Kyrie; (Christe); (3) Christe; (Christe); (4) Kyrie; (Kyrie); (5) Kyrie. *Gloria:* (Gloria in excelsis Deo [priest]); (6) Et in terra pax; (Laudamus te); (7) Benedicamus te; (adoramus te); (8) Glorificamus te; (gratias agimus tibi); (9) Dominus Deus, rex caelestis; (Domine fili); (10) Domine Deus, Agnus Dei; (Qui tollis); (11) Qui tollis; (Qui sedes); (12) Quoniam; (tu solus Dominus); (13) Tu solus altissimus; (Cum Sancto Spiritu); (14) In gloria Dei Patris, Amen [or beginning at Amen]. *Offertory:* (15) [independent movement]. *Credo:* [organ not played *in alternatim*]. *Sanctus:* (16) Sanctus; (sanctus); (17) sanctus; (Pleni sunt). (18) Benedictus [and/or an independent piece for the Elevation]. *Agnus Dei:* (19) Agnus; (Agnus); (20) Agnus. *Communion:* (21) [independent movement]. *Dismissal:* (Ite missa est) (22) Deo gratias.

From ca. 1400 to 1650, organ versets were based closely on the chants they replaced. The *cantus firmus* might be presented unadorned as part of the polyphonic texture, or it might be embellished considerably and used thematically. Composers in the 17th century made little more than slight references to a *cantus firmus,* being careful only to end on the appropriate harmony to give the pitch for the next phrase to be sung. In 1662, the diocese of Paris stipulated that the chants should be recognizable at least in the Kyrie (versets 1 and 5), Gloria (versets 6, 11, and 14), Sanctus (verset 16), and Agnus (verset 20). Composers only partially obeyed. In the 18th century, a type of Christmas organ Mass became popular in which each verset is based on a familiar **noël.* Composers also returned then to writing simple versets based on chants, a style that continued in the 19th century in unpretentious collections of service music. The Church tolerated this decimation of the liturgical texts until 1903, when *alternatim* organ music was discouraged.

The earliest organ Masses consist only of Kyrie and Gloria versets in long-note *cantus firmus* style (Faenza Codex, ca. 1420; see Sources, 27), but the *Buxheimer Orgelbuch (ca. 1470) includes versets for other texts. A variety of versets comes from England in the 16th century (see Stevens, 1969); and in Italy, Girolamo Cavazzoni (1543) inaugurated the use of the *cantus firmus* as the basis for counterpoint, a practice also followed by Andrea Gabrieli and Claudio Merulo. In the 17th century, Masses were published by many composers in Italy (Adriano Banchieri, Giovanni Battista Fasolo), but the most famous examples are the atypical liturgical pieces (mostly not versets) in Frescobaldi's *Fiori musicali* (Venice, 1635). The greatest organ Masses were written in France, where the tradition began with the publisher Pierre Attaingnant's anthology *Tablature pour le jeu d'orgues* (1531) and included works by Nicolas Gigault (ca. 1627–1707), Guillaume Nivers (ca. 1632–1714), André Raison (before 1650–1719), François Couperin (1668–1733), and Nicolas de Grigny (1672–1703). A relatively standard approach to each verset developed there, and the same patterns were used as late as the 19th century (Guillaume Lasceux). The return to chant-based versets began in the 18th century (Michel Corrette) and became the basis of a French improvisatory idiom in the 19th and 20th centuries.

Some writers call the third part of Bach's **Clavier-Übung* an organ Mass, but it has neither the form nor the liturgical function outlined here. In music after 1900, the term is sometimes used for liturgical organ music (Messiaen), but the choice of movements has not been standardized, and *alternatim* performance is not usually assumed.

Bibl.: Almonte Howell, "French Baroque Organ Music and the Eight Church Tones," *JAMS* 11 (1958): 106–18. Denis Stevens, ed., *Early Tudor Organ Music* 2, Early English Church Music 10 (London: Stainer & Bell, 1969). Edward Higginbottom, "French Classical Organ Music and Liturgy," *PRMA* 103 (1976–77): 19–40. Benjamin van Wye, "Ritual Use of the Organ in France," *JAMS* 33 (1980): 287–325. Benjamin van Wye, "Organ Music in the Mass of the Parisian Rite to 1850," in *French Organ Music from the Revolution to Franck and Widor,* ed. Lawrence Archbold and William J. Peterson (Rochester: U of Rochester Pr, 1995). Bruce Gustafson, "France," *Keyboard Music before 1700* (New York: Schirmer 1995), pp. 90–146. B.G.

Organology. The study of musical instruments. See Instrument.

Organo pieno [It.]. Full organ.

Organo pleno [Lat.]. In 17th- and 18th-century music of northern Europe, the complete *flue chorus of the organ, with or without reed stops.

Organ point. *Pedal point [cf. Fermata].

Organum [Lat.]. Medieval polyphony most often based on a **cantus firmus.* Initially improvised, with the added voice (or voices) duplicating the preexistent melody at a given consonant interval, the organum was eventually to be characterized by a sharp distinction, both melodic and temporal, between the original voice and the newly composed material.

The Latin word *organum,* from the Greek *organon,* meaning tool or instrument, was used from the patristic age forward to refer to any musical instrument and, more particularly, to the organ. How it came to be associated with polyphony is not entirely clear, but the most persuasive of several explanations suggested thus far finds the key in the adjectival form *organicus,* a term commonly used to describe the precise measurement of pitches or intervals.

The early history of organum is known not from musical monuments, but from theoretical treatises written before the crystallization of a viable system of notation. The oldest of these are the **Musica enchiriadis* and the closely related *Scolica enchiriadis,* both from the 9th century. The anonymous authors describe three kinds of organum or what they prefer to call diaphony, that is, music composed of distinct but harmonious lines. The first of these is organum at the octave. The second has the added or "organum-making voice" *(vox organalis)* moving parallel with the chant *(vox principalis)* at the fifth below. This simple, two-voiced complex can be expanded to three or four voices by doubling one or both of the lines at the octave. The third kind of organum, which actually involves something other than the simultaneous rehearsal of the chant at more than one pitch, is described as being at the fourth. The difference between this and the first two types arises from the need to avoid the *tritones that almost inevitably occur in the course of an uninterrupted succession of parallel fourths. The illustration provided in the *Musica enchiriadis,* a setting of the first two pairs of versicles from the *sequence "Rex celi domine," shows the chant starting each versicle in unison with the new voice, then ascending stepwise to the fourth. Thereafter in the first pair, the voices proceed in fourths to the penultimate note where again they join. Because of the tessitura of the chant and its overall shape, the setting of the second pair [Ex. 1] is a little more complicated. Because the chant turns down again as soon as the fourth has been reached, another potential tritone must be avoided, and it is not until just past the middle of the phrase that the motion is parallel. The cadence is formed as before.

The *Daseian notation in which the examples are written is an artificially contrived system based on a misunderstanding of Greek practice, and although it is unambigous, it is not appropriate for sight-singing, nor was it intended for that purpose. The ornamentation of the chant was improvisatory, and the authors of the treatises merely wanted to ensure, by means of illustration, an understanding of the rules of improvisation. Mention of parallel organum in theoretical treatises from as late as the 13th and 14th centuries makes it clear that the early practice was by no means abandoned when composers began to cultivate polyphony of greater complexity and sophistication.

The oldest of the practical sources of organum is the Cambridge version of the Winchester Troper. This manuscript, from the middle of the 11th century, contains, under the rubric *Melliflua organorum modulamina,* the organal or newly composed voices for nearly 160 liturgical melodies. Most numerous by far are those for *Proper chants of the Mass and the Office: Alleluias (53), responsories (51), and tracts (19); the remainder are for chants of the *Ordinary, sequences, and tropes.

The nondiastematic notation [see Diastematic] together with the separation of the organal voices from the chants, many of which do not even occur in the manuscript, has made the reconstruction of the organa difficult, but the work of Jammers (1955) and that of Holschneider (1968) have made it possible to form a reasonably clear idea of how they must have sounded. While the organal voice sometimes moves at the fourth below the chant, crossing of the voices is not uncommon. Pitch repetition may occur in the newly composed voice, resulting in the drone effect described in the *Musica enchiriadis.* The unison cadence, whether internal or final, is characteristically approached from the second or, in some cases, the major third. This is precisely the cadence or *occursus* described by the contemporary theorist Guido of Arezzo toward the close of the *Micrologus* (trans. Babb, 1978).

Late 11th- and early 12th-century additions to three Chartres manuscripts (nos. 4, 109, and 130) constitute a repertory of 12 organa. (Although the manuscripts were destroyed in 1944, the relevant folios are preserved in facsimile in *PM* 17.) All of the compositions are settings of soloistic chants from the Mass and the Office. Like the Winchester Troper, MS 4 has only the organal voices, written in staffless neumes. MSS 109 and 130, by contrast, have both parts in score with the *vox organalis* above the chant. MS 109 uses diastematic neumes, MS 130 staff notation. The polyphony has much in common with that of Winchester. Motion is sometimes contrary, sometimes parallel, and there is some crossing of voices; but the drone created by oblique movement does not occur. Perfect consonances, including the octave, appear consistently at phrase beginnings and endings, but elsewhere thirds and seconds are prominent, and there are even occasional sixths. A portion of one of the Eastertide Alleluias from MS 109 is given in Ex. 2.

Interest in polyphonic composition was not limited to the north of Europe, but is also manifested in a group of four Aquitanian manuscripts ranging in date from the end of the 11th century to just past the beginning of the 13th. Altogether there are nearly 100 pieces for two voices, only about half of which are based on *cantus firmi.* A sizable number of the newly composed **versus* are in note-against-note counterpoint, but the preference is now for the melismatic type [Ex. 3]. The use of the term organum to describe this particular kind of polyphony is an anticipation of 13th-century theoretical practice. The several versions of the contemporaneous *Ad organum faciendum* (ed. Eggebrecht and Zaminer, 1970) treat only the older texture.

The same two types of polyphony appear in that part of the late 12th-century Codex Calixtinus devoted to the Offices for St. James. Long housed at *Santiago, the manuscript betrays through its notation and to some extent through the style of its contents a more northerly origin. There are 21 compositions for two voices, 9 of which are based on liturgical chants. Once again the florid style predominates. The melismas tend to be more expansive than those of the Aquitanian pieces, and in the case of the last two compositions, settings of the "Benedicamus domino," they resemble in both contour and duration those of the great Parisian organa of the same period.

The *Notre Dame repertory of organa is dominated by compositions for two voices (110) but includes as well a goodly number (28) for three, and a pair for four. Like those from Chartres, they are based on responsorial chants, of which only the soloistic portions are set polyphonically. The choral portions, though omitted from the manuscripts in the interest of saving time and parchment, were sung monophonically.

The earliest layer of the repertory for two voices, preserved in the manuscript W1 and attributable in part, perhaps, to Master Leonin, shows a marked preference for the florid or *organum purum* style, which is interrupted from time to time by short *discant sections or **clausulae* [Ex. 4]. What distinguished the latter from the surrounding material is not only the faster movement of the *cantus firmus* or *tenor, but the precise rhythmic measurement of the voices. Although some scholars (e.g., Waite, 1954) have interpreted these early Parisian organa as rhythmically ordered throughout, this is not wholly justified by the notation, and it does not accord with the description provided by the theorists. In the final chapter of his *De mensurabili musica* (ca. 1250; ed. Reimer, 1972), Johannes de Garlandia speaks of longer and shorter notes that occur in the organal voice *(organum per se),* depending on consonance, position, etc., but not of any consistent or patterned rhythm. He does mention the device or technique of **copula,* something between organum and discant, in which the second voice *(duplum)* has a brief sequential passage in measured rhythm over a sustained note or notes in the tenor.

Successive layers of organum composition show an ever-increasing preoccupation with the discant *clausula* and with its measurement according to one or more of the rhythmic *modes. The number and the length of the *clausulae,* whether in new compositions or revisions of earlier ones, are greatly increased in the collections of organa transmitted in the manuscripts F and W2.

The three- and four-voiced organa (*tripla* and *quadrupla,* respectively), cultivated in all probability from the last decade of the 12th century, were almost of necessity precisely measured even in the sustained-tenor passages. Johannes de Garlandia explicitly states that *organum cum alio* (one organizing voice with another one) proceeds according to the correct measure *(rectam mensuram)* described in the chapters on discant. Both of the *quadrupla* and several of the *tripla* are attributed by the English Anonymous IV (ca. 1272) [see Theory] to Master Perotin.

It is not known how far into the 13th century organum composition continued. By 1230 or at the very latest 1240, however, it had been superseded by the very genre it had spawned, namely, the *motet.

1
Te hu- mi- les fa- mu- li mo- du- lis ve- ne- ran- do pi- is
Se iu- be- as fla- gi- tant va- ri- is li- be- ra- re ma- lis.
2
Al- le- lu- ia. Al- le ℣ An- ge- lus Do- mi- ni
de- scen- dit de ce- lo
3
Per par- tum vir- gi- nis
4
cap- ti- vi- ta-
All. ℣ Ascendens Christus

Organum.

Bibl.: William Waite, *The Rhythm of Twelfth-Century Polyphony* (New Haven: Yale U Pr, 1954). Ewald Jammers, *Anfänge der abendländischen Musik* (Strassburg: Heitz, 1955). Andreas Holschneider, *Die Organa von Winchester* (Hildesheim: Olms, 1968). Hans Eggebrecht and Frieder Zaminer, *Ad organum faciendum* (Mainz: B Schott, 1970). Erich Reimer, ed., *Johannes de Garlandia: De mensurabili musica,* 2 vols. (Wiesbaden: F Steiner, 1972). Warren Babb, trans., *Hucbald, Guido, and John on Music, MTT* 3 (1978). Ernest H. Sanders, "Consonance and Rhythm in the Organum of the 12th and 13th centuries," *JAMS* 33 (1980): 264–86. Edward H. Roesner, "The Problem of Chronology in the Transmission of Organum Duplum," in *Music in Medieval and Early Modern Europe,* ed. Iain Fenlon (Cambridge: Cambridge U Pr, 1981), pp. 365–99. Sarah Fuller, "Theoretical Foundations of Early Organum Theory," *AM* 53 (1981): 52–84. Edward H. Roesner, "Johannes de Garlandia on *organum in speciale,*" *Early Music History* 2 (1982): 129–60. Jeremy Yudkin, "The Rhythm of Organum Purum," *JM* (1983): 355–76. Irving Godt and Benito Rivera, "The Vatican Organum Treatise—A Colour Reproduction, Transcription, and Translation," in *Gordon Athol Anderson In Memoriam,* 2 vols. (Henryville, Pa.: Institute of Mediaeval Music, 1984), 2: 264–345. Hans Tischler, ed., *The Parisian Two-Part Organa: Complete Comparative Edition,* 2 vols. (New York: Pendragon, 1988). Hendrik van der Werf, *Integrated Directory of Organa, Clausulae, and Motets of the Thirteenth Century* (Rochester, N.Y.: Author, 1989). Charles M. Atkinson, "Franco of Cologne on the Rhythm of Organum Purum," *EMH* 9 (1989 [1990]): 1–26. Sarah Fuller, "Early Polyphony," in *The New Oxford History of Music,* vol. 2: *The Early Middle Ages to 1300,* 2nd ed., ed. Richard Crocker and David Hiley (Oxford: Oxford U Pr, 1990), pp. 485–556. Rebecca A. Baltzer, "How Long Was Notre-Dame Organum Performed?" *Beyond the Moon: Festschrift Luther Dittmer,* ed. Bryan Gillingham and Paul Merkley (Ottawa: Institute of Mediaeval Music, 1991), pp. 118–43. Richard Crocker, "Rhythm in Early Polyphony," in *Studies in Medieval Music: Festschrift for Ernest H. Sanders,* ed. Brian Seirup and Peter M. Lefferts [*CM,* nos. 45–47] (New York: Trustees of Columbia Univ., 1991), pp. 147–77. Theodore Karp, *The Polyphony of Saint Martial and Santiago de Compostela,* 2 vols., (Berkeley: U of Cal Pr, 1992). Hendrik van der Werf, *The Oldest Extant Part Music and the Origin of Western Polyphony,* 2 vols. (Rochester, N.Y.: Author, 1993). Edward H. Roesner et al., eds., *Le Magnus liber organi de Notre-Dame de Paris,* 7 vols., Musica Gallica (Monaco: Éditions de l'Oiseau-Lyre, 1993–). Susan Rankin, "Winchester Polyphony: The Early Theory and Practice of Organum," in *Music in the Medieval English Liturgy: Plainsong and Mediaeval Music Society Centennial Essays,* ed. Susan Rankin and David Hiley (Oxford: Clarendon, 1993), pp. 59–100. David E. Cohen, "Metaphysics, Ideology, Discipline: Consonance, Dissonance, and the Foundations of Western Polyphony," *Theoria: Historical Aspects of Music Theory* 7 (1993): 1–85. Fritz Reckow, "Guido's Theory of Organum after Guido: Transmission—Adaptation—Transformation," in *Essays on Music in Honor of David G. Hughes,* ed. Graeme M. Boone (Cambridge, Mass.: Harvard Univ. Dept. of Music, 1995), pp. 395–413. Alejandro Enrique Planchart, "Organum," in *A Performer's Guide to Medieval Music,* ed. Ross W. Duffin, Early Music America Performer's Guides to Early Music (Bloomington: Ind U Pr, 2000), pp. 23–51. Steven C. Immel, "The Vatican Organum Treatise Re-examined," *EMH* 20 (2001): 121–72.

J.K.

Orgel [Ger., Du.]. *Organ.

Orgel-Büchlein [Ger., Little Organ-Book]. An unfinished collection by Bach containing 46 *organ chorales on 45 *chorale tunes. Numerous pages of the original manuscript are empty except for the title of a chorale tune, indicating that Bach intended to include a total of 164 pieces. All of the compositions are short settings, mostly of the melody-chorale type. The collection, BWV 599–644, was, with few exceptions, probably made toward the end of Bach's stay in Weimar (1708–17). It is described on the title page as a book "in which a beginner at the organ is given instruction in developing a chorale in many diverse ways, and at the same time in acquiring facility in the study of the pedal, since in the chorales contained therein, the pedal is treated as wholly *obbligato.*"

Bibl.: Russel Stinson, *Bach: The Orgelbüchlein* (New York: Schirmer, 1996).

Orgue [Fr.]. *Organ.

Orgue de Barbarie [Fr.]. *Barrel organ; the term derives from a corruption of the name of an 18th-century instrument maker from Modena, Giovanni Barberi.

Orgue expressif [Fr.]. *Harmonium.

Orgue positif [Fr.]. A small, encased organ, usually with one keyboard and no pedals, located in a fixed position. See Positive (2).

Oriscus [Lat.]. See Neume.

Ornamentation. The modification of music, usually but not always through the addition of notes, to make it more beautiful or effective, or to demonstrate the abilities of the interpreter. The resources of ornamentation may be classified as follows:

I. Graces
   1. Additional notes in stereotyped figures.
   2. Alterations or shifts of the written note-values.
   3. Dynamic, color, and pitch ornaments.

II. Diminutions, paraphrase, variation.

III. The elaboration of pauses, cadenzas.

In this dictionary, separate articles are devoted to the principal kinds of ornament as follows: I, 1: *Acciaccatura, Anschlag,* Appoggiatura, Cadent, *Coulé,* Grace note, Mordent, *Nachschlag, Port de voix, Pralltriller,* Relish, *Ribattuta (di gola), Schneller,* Slide, *Tirade,* Trill, Turn. I, 2: Arpeggio, Rubato, Suspension. I, 3: *Balancement, Bebung, Messa di voce, Portamento, Sanglot,* Vibrato. II: Diminutions. III: Cadenza. In addition, articles will be found on the following terms, which apply to more than one kind of ornament: *Accent, Aspiration, Battement, Chûte, Flatté, Gruppetto, Martellement, Plainte, Quiebro, Redoble, Tour de gosier.* For the early Baroque *trillo* (an accelerating repetition of a note, usually the penultimate one in a cadence) see Tremolo, Trill. A few other ornaments are briefly described below along with a historical survey, a discussion of the application of ornaments, and a table of signs. The vast subject of ornamentation in non-Western music is not addressed.

What is and what is not ornamental in a piece of music depends very much upon the style and period or upon the point of view of the observer. For Leopold Mozart (1756), the appoggiaturas in Ex. 1a were ornamental, even though the listener heard them as in 1b. If, however, they had been written down as in 1b, the player might read them as essential and ornament the

1. Leopold Mozart, *Versuch* (trans. Eng.), pp. 167–68.

ornaments (1c); this, Mozart explained, was the reason for the small notes. On the other hand, a Renaissance musician might have regarded the entire passage as the diminution of 1d. In the 17th century, the string vibrato, the shortening of a note, and a *crescendo* and *decrescendo* on a single note were all considered to be ornaments (close shake, Simpson, or *sting, Mace; *détaché,* D'Anglebert; and **messa di voce,* respectively); today they are considered aspects of playing technique, articulation, or expression. (For the distinction between structure and ornament, see *NeuO,* pp. 3–6.)

From the Middle Ages, the notation of Byzantine and Gregorian chant includes signs that show not only what notes or intervals are to be sung but also certain peculiarities of execution that were doubtless thought of as ornamental. Among Gregorian *neumes, the *quilisma, tristropha, oriscus, pressus, trigon,* and others are thought to have indicated some special ways of handling the voice, though precisely what these might have been is a matter of debate. In his late-13th-century *Tractatus de musica,* Jerome of Moravia described three types of *flos harmonicus,* a kind of trill or violent vibrato for the voice, and said that it could be imitated on the organ by holding the main note and reiterating the upper auxiliary (ed. Cserba, 1935, p. 184).

Small circles over certain notes in the Robertsbridge Codex (early 14th century) apparently indicated some kind of keyboard ornament (Apel, 1942, pp. 38–40). In German keyboard tablatures of the 15th and 16th centuries, downward stems with hooks indicated *Mordanten* (a general term for trills and mordents used by German organists from the 15th to the 17th century; see Mordent and Trill). A "t" is probably some kind of trill or mordent in Antonio Valente's *Intavolatura de cimbalo* (1576); trill signs for the lute are found in Vincenzo Capirola's tablature of ca. 1517 [see Trill] and that of Francesco da Milano and Pietro Paolo Borrono (Milan, 1548).

Sixteenth-century treatises on ornamentation are unanimous in asserting that there was no difference between the practices of singers and instrumentalists; the same vocabulary of embellishment served both (Brown, 1976). This vocabulary can be divided roughly into two categories: the graces, more or less stereotyped ornaments applied to single notes, and *diminutions, or *passaggi,* which embellished intervals and melodies. Either type could be written out or improvised; the use of signs to indicate ornaments not written out in notes was limited to a few repertories and was generally vague and rudimentary by comparison with the elaborate codes of the 18th century. The graces of the 16th century fell mainly into the classes of mordents, trills, and *gruppetti.* This unity of ornamental practice was broken in the 17th century with the increasing differentiation of instrumental styles and changing fashions in vocal music.

The first repertory to make lavish use of ornament signs was that of the English virginalists, beginning in the mid-16th century and extending to the mid-17th. Two signs were employed, a double and a single diagonal stroke through the stem of the note to be ornamented (above or occasionally through the note if there was no stem). The meanings of these signs have never been adequately explained, and the inconsistency with which they occur in different sources of the same music suggests that they had no universally recognized meaning. The double stroke, by far the more common, probably meant a simple trill of some kind, since more elaborate trills are so often written out. Various meanings, especially slides and mordents, have been proposed for the single stroke. (For a summary of the problem, see Desmond Hunter, "Ornaments," III, in *Grove 6,* 2nd ed.)

The English signs are also found in early 17th-century Dutch keyboard music. The double strokes, sometimes vertical, found in German keyboard music of the later 17th and early 18th century (Johann Adam Reincken, Johann Kuhnau, Johann David Heinichen, and others) are probably survivals of the English signs. In Purcell's *A Choice Collection* (1696), the double stroke (no longer through the stem) has taken on the explicit meaning of a normal 18th-century trill (i.e., beginning on the beat with the upper auxiliary), and the single stroke through the stem has disappeared.

The use of ornament signs continued in 17th-century lute music, though it is clear from written descriptions of lute ornamentation (such as those in Thomas Robinson's *The Schoole of Musicke,* 1603, and Marin Mersenne's *Harmonie universelle,* 1636–37) that the variety and frequency of ornaments played was very much greater than the signs written in the tablatures would indicate (Poulton, 1975). An important factor in the restraint with which ornament signs were used up to the mid-17th century was the lack of appropriate printer's characters (Mersenne) and the complexity of typesetting they entailed. When engraving became more common, ornament signs proliferated, and scores, particularly of French viol and keyboard music (Marais, D'Anglebert, François Couperin), grew so charged that reading them with attention to every sign is laborious in the extreme.

The *redobles* and *quiebros* with which Spanish keyboard music from the mid-16th century on was richly ornamented were never reduced to a code and were not indicated by signs (Parkins, 1980); Juan Bermudo wrote in 1549 that "the fashion of playing them changes every day." The same is true of Italian keyboard ornaments, according to Girolamo Diruta (*Il transilvano,* 1593); in both repertories, as well as in the German keyboard tablatures and English virginal music of the late Renaissance and early Baroque, a great deal of the ornamentation was written out in notes.

An elaborate code and a terminology for vocal ornaments were developed in connection with Italian monody of the early Baroque period (see Caccini, 1602; Sanford, 1979, pp. 154–213) and elaborated by both Italians and Germans (e.g., Michael Praetorius, Johannes Andreas Herbst) during the 17th century. Caccini described the *trillo* (reiteration of a note), *gruppo* (accelerating trill with turn), **ribattuta di gola* (dotted main-note trill), *cascata* (rapid descending scale), *esclamatione* (*crescendo* or *decrescendo* on a note), **messa di voce* (under the term *crescere e scemare della voce*), *intonazione* (*slide), and various types of rhythmic alteration. Other writers discussed the turn and appoggiatura.

Neither the ornaments nor the terminology remained static, the most complicated case being that of the *trilli, tremuli,* and *gruppi* (or *groppi*). Although the exact nature of Caccini's *trillo* has been a matter of dispute, ornaments ranging from the distinct reiteration of notes (often accelerating) to connected pulsations or a dynamic vibrato can be traced into the 18th century; the *balancement* described by Montéclair (1736), which was notated as repeated notes covered by a wavy line, "que les Italiens appellent, Tremolo," produced the effect of an organ tremulant. At the same time, the term *trillo* was transferred to the trill family of ornaments known earlier as *gruppi* and *tremuli.* Throughout most of the 17th century, and especially in Italy, the introduction of these ornaments in vocal music was left to the singer. As late as 1723, Tosi complained of the growing use of small notes to indicate appoggiaturas as being a crutch for the incompetent.

What is known about French vocal ornamentation in the 17th century applies mainly to the **air de cour.* Two books published within two years of each other (Jean Millet, 1666, and Benigne de Bacilly, 1668) gave detailed accounts of the intricate art of ornamenting such music. The earlier book was retrospective, while the later presented the newer manner of Pierre de Nyert and Michel Lambert. Although the diminution of successive strophes played the largest role, certain codified ornaments such as the trill and *port de voix* were essential to the style. According to Mersenne, the French knew but rejected the more violent Italian ornaments, especially the *esclamazione.*

Toward 1700, signs began to appear along with new ornaments. Loulié (1696) gave nine of them: the *coulé, chûte, port de voix, accent* (an *échappé* or auxiliary taking its value from the preceding note, to which it was slurred), *tremblement* (trill), *martellement* (mordent), *balancement* (a slow fluctuation of loudness but not of pitch), *flatté* (a short trill followed by a *chûte*), and *tour de gosier* (turn). Three others, the *coulade* (a slurred scale connecting two notes and taking its value from the first), *passage* (a kind of turn anticipating a trill), and *diminution* (a rising scale replacing two rising thirds) were indicated by small notes or not at all.

Forty years later, Montéclair (1736) added to this list (probably with his own cantatas in mind) the *trait* (like a *coulade* but with each note articulated), four dynamic ornaments (*son filé, son enflé, son diminué,* and *son enflé et diminué,* that is, steady tone, *crescendo* on a note, *decrescendo* on a note, and *messa di voce*), *son glissé* (a slow glissando over a semitone), and *sanglot* (sob). He also used the term *pincé* instead of *martellement,* redefined *flatté* and *balancement,* subdivided the trill into four types, and considerably changed the code of signs. In introducing the topic of ornamentation, he gave a warning that should be borne in mind by anyone studying the subject: neither the signs nor the terminology of ornaments remained the same from teacher to teacher or medium to medium, even in Montéclair's Paris, so that "a student who has learned from one master does not understand the language and does not know the notation of another."

The first large table of ornament-symbols was included in Christopher Simpson's *The Division-Violist* (1659), where it was credited to Charles Coleman. Several of the ornaments had Continental equivalents, though both terms and signs were unique to England: beat (lower appoggiatura), backfall (upper appoggiatura), elevation (slide), springer *(accent),* cadent *(chûte),* close shake (vibrato), and backfall shaked (trill from upper auxiliary). Others, however, had no such equivalents: the double backfall, shaked beat, double relish of two types, and alternative forms of the

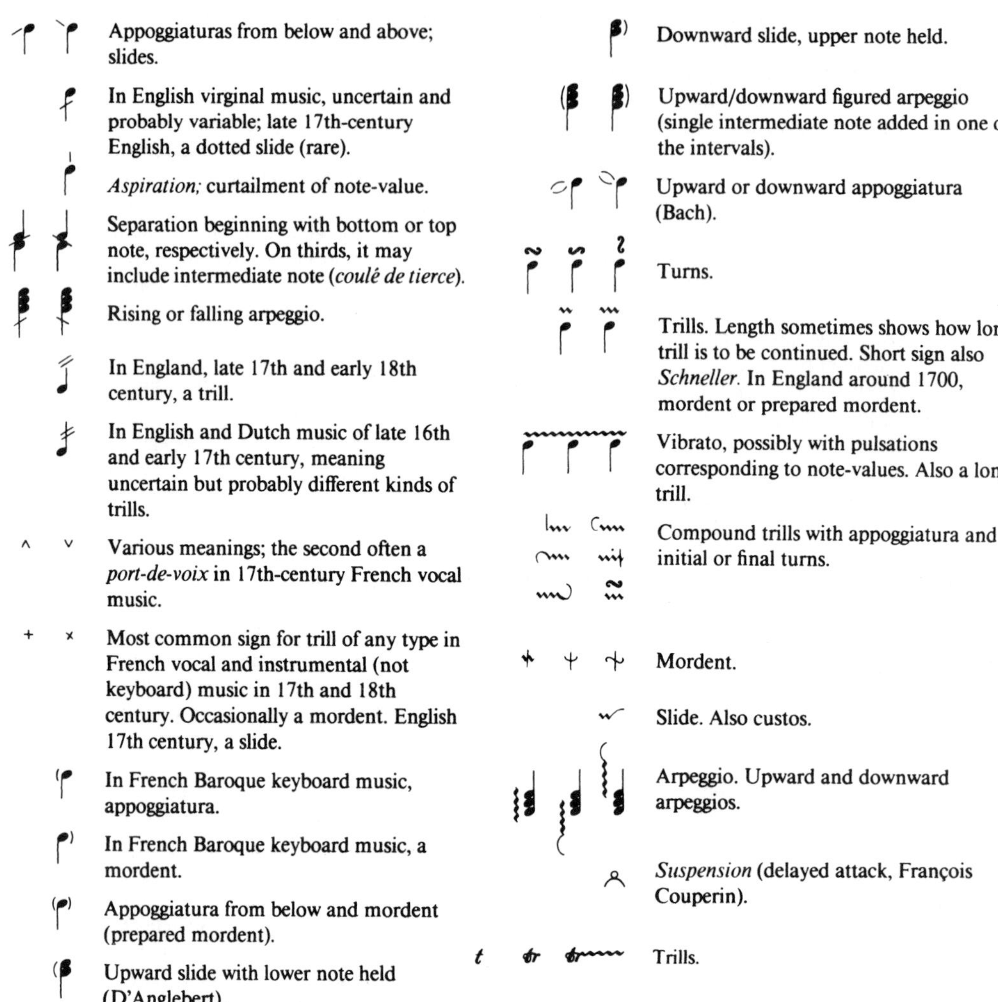

Appoggiaturas from below and above; slides.
In English virginal music, uncertain and probably variable; late 17th-century English, a dotted slide (rare).
Aspiration; curtailment of note-value.
Separation beginning with bottom or top note, respectively. On thirds, it may include intermediate note (coulé de tierce).
Rising or falling arpeggio.
In England, late 17th and early 18th century, a trill.
In English and Dutch music of late 16th and early 17th century, meaning uncertain but probably different kinds of trills.
Various meanings; the second often a port-de-voix in 17th-century French vocal music.
Most common sign for trill of any type in French vocal and instrumental (not keyboard) music in 17th and 18th century. Occasionally a mordent. English 17th century, a slide.
In French Baroque keyboard music, appoggiatura.
In French Baroque keyboard music, a mordent.
Appoggiatura from below and mordent (prepared mordent).
Upward slide with lower note held (D'Anglebert).
Downward slide, upper note held.
Upward/downward figured arpeggio (single intermediate note added in one of the intervals).
Upward or downward appoggiatura (Bach).
Turns.
Trills. Length sometimes shows how long trill is to be continued. Short sign also Schneller. In England around 1700, mordent or prepared mordent.
Vibrato, possibly with pulsations corresponding to note-values. Also a long trill.
Compound trills with appoggiatura and initial or final turns.
Mordent.
Slide. Also custos.
Arpeggio. Upward and downward arpeggios.
Suspension (delayed attack, François Couperin).
t tr
Trills.

Examples of ornamentation.

cadent and elevation. French composers for the solo viol from Du Buisson (1666) to Antoine Forqueray (1747) also had a code of signs and terms, which maintained a certain consistency over the years, though it was considerably less elaborate than Simpson's (a tabular summary is found in Bol, 1973). In his *Florilegium secundum* (1698; trans. 1967), Georg Muffat set forth a dozen ornaments (some with as many as six subtypes) said to represent the performing style of Lully's orchestral dances. Some of the signs and terms (in four languages) are as unusual as Simpson's; they may represent otherwise undocumented Lullian usages.

One of the most elaborate and influential ornament tables was included by D'Anglebert in his harpsichord pieces of 1689. Bach copied this table, and it served as the basis for the ornamental practice of many French harpsichord composers, including Rameau. It contained a total of 29 items using 14 different symbols in a variety of positions and combinations. Howard Ferguson (1966) gives most of them in a comparative table with the corresponding ornaments of Chambonnières, Le Roux, Dieupart, François Couperin, Rameau, and Dandrieu. Another code was established by Chambonnières (1670). It had only seven symbols and also differed in its signs for the mordent, the *coulé sur une tierce,* and arpeggiations; these—especially the first and last—were taken up by François Couperin and others and eventually superseded the D'Anglebert signs. The 13 signs in Bach's *Explication (Clavier-Büchlein vor Wilhelm Friedemann Bach)* are a composite of these two schools. Although the *Explication* made no use of small notes, they are common in Bach's music, as well as in that of Couperin. Small notes increasingly replaced signs during the 18th century. Along with *tr.* for trills, they served for nearly all the formulations of Giuseppe Tartini's 40-page treatment of ornamentation in his *Regole per arrivare a saper ben suonar il violino* (probably written in the 1750s; published in 1771 as *Traité des agrémens de la musique*).

One of the most detailed and certainly the best-known discussion of ornaments occupies most of the second chapter of C. P. E. Bach's *Versuch* (1753), running to 63 pages in the English translation. Although the number of signs and basic types was fewer than ten, these were elaborated into an infinity of variants and subtypes through the lavish use of small notes and the explanation of examples. The 1750s also saw major treatises by Francesco Geminiani, Friedrich W. Marpurg, Johann Joachim Quantz, Jean-Baptiste Bérard, and Leopold Mozart, along with Johann F. Agricola's annotated translation of Pietro Tosi's *Opinioni,* most of which were influential and among which there was sufficient agreement to establish a language of ornamentation that—with dialectal variations—continued to be taught in performance manuals well into the 19th century (e.g., Muzio Clementi's piano method, which was published in 1801 and had gone through 11 editions by 1826). Even Chopin continued to insist upon trills beginning with the auxiliary and appoggiaturas on the beat (sounded with the bass; see Eigeldinger, 1979, pp. 188–92).

Modern doctrine concerning music of the 18th and 19th centuries is based on the mid-18th-century code as modified by Hummel (1828), Spohr (1832), and others. Principal among the modifications are the preference for trills beginning on the main note and the shift of most other ornaments ahead of the beat so as to leave the written note in its notated position. In recent decades, this doctrine has been disrupted by research on early performance (under way since the late 19th century but with little practical effect until the 1960s) and by the countervailing researches of Frederick Neumann (from the 1960s), who sought to find support for traditional performance practices in early documents. None of the vigorous controversy generated by the diverging viewpoints has yet touched the field of *diminutions, where fewer performers and scholars have ventured upon what still strikes modern aesthetic sensibilities as the disfigurement of Renaissance and Baroque melody by streams of mechanical figuration.

One 18th-century ornament, the long appoggiatura, so exploited in the *empfindsamer Stil* of C. P. E. Bach and other German composers of his time, was assimilated into the harmonic language of the 19th century, becoming a salient characteristic of the music of Wagner, Brahms, and especially Mahler. Also, Italian opera continued to be modified and added to by singers, especially at cadences and fermatas (Caswell, 1975). Although musicians are generally taught in school today that the score is sacrosanct and may be neither added to nor subtracted from, a rich and living practice of unwritten ornamentation can be observed in popular music.

The most difficult problem for the modern interpreter of early music is to know where ornamentation is needed and what kind to add in the absence of any sign. In general, ornamentation is richest in solo music, diminishing as the size of the ensemble increases, and the amount to be added decreases as that supplied by the composer increases. Disagreements about the amount and kind of ornamentation to be added to the composer's product are documented from the time of Josquin on, and thus the performer should not imagine that there is only one "right" solution for a given passage.

The most precise models are supplied by *automatic instruments, but their applicability is limited. Next in authority are pieces similar to the one being performed and in which all the ornamentation is written out (see especially Ferand and Erig in the bibliography for Diminutions). Last come the treatises, which vary greatly in the extent to which they tell precisely where ornaments are to be applied. The great danger of treatises is that they are nearly always concerned with a narrow range of styles, which, however, are not specified; consequently, the performer risks applying their prescriptions to the wrong music. The applicability of the treatises of C. P. E. Bach and Quantz to the music of J. S. Bach is, for example, a matter of vigorous dispute.

The following paraphrase (with terminology Americanized) of the anonymous "Rules for Gracing on the Flute" (i.e., recorder) gives an idea of the way musicians around 1700 approached the question of ornamenting music without written indications (see full transcript in Dart, 1959): "Never trill first or last notes. Do not place trills or mordents on two repeated notes. A mordent on all ascending dotted notes, a trill on descending ones; all sharps trilled, either rising or falling. Never trill an eighth or a sixteenth. Of three descending quarters, place a mordent on the first, trill the second, and leave the third plain. Penultimate note of cadence is trilled. Double *relish all long trills if the following note ascends. Of three rising quarters, divide the first in two [substitute two repeated eighths?], double relish the second, and leave the third plain. Trill no ascending flats, trill all descending ones."

Analogous though much more detailed rules are given by Georg Muffat in 1698. In 1791, Francesco Galeazzi summed up the 18th-century consensus when he wrote that "the ornamentation should aid the expression of the principal sentiment, not spoil it; hence the most skillful performer is one who knows how to enter the mind of the composer, be fully conscious of the character of the composition that he is to perform, increasing its energy, uniting his own sentiments with that of its author, so that a perfect whole may result, as if he were part of the same mind" (after Smiles, 1978).

The question of whether repeats should be ornamented has never had comprehensive treatment. The large incidence of varied repeats written out in English virginal music and early 17th-century French lute music suggests that repeats indicated by sign could also be varied. The successive strophes of *airs de cour* were ornamented differently. A few instances of written *doubles* intercalated as varied repeats can be found in French 17th-century lute music, but it is not true, as Margarete Reimann states (*MGG* 3:713), that *doubles* can be treated "without further consideration" as varied repeats. In general, Baroque method books that explain repeat marks say nothing about varying the repeats. Some music, e.g., the harpsichord pieces of François Couperin, would seem to exclude additional ornamentation on repeats; indeed, the composer inveighs against any liberties with his notation. The preface to C. P. E. Bach's *Sonatas with Varied Reprises* implies that such variation was a mid-18th-century fashion, not a long-standing tradition. On the other hand, Tosi (1723) suggests that the reprises of da capo arias had long been varied. Method books of the later 18th century recommend little or no ornamentation on the first appearance of a melody and ornamentation of increasing complexity on further appearances (as in reprises of rondos, sonatas, arias, and other solo music).

The treatises that discuss the accidental inflection of ornaments are agreed that auxiliary notes should conform to the key in force at the moment, and if this is uncertain, then to the immediate context. If the composer wants something different, it must be indicated by an accidental above or below the ornament sign, if any. The sixth and seventh degrees of the minor scale can be a problem, nevertheless, especially when accompanying parts are sounding these degrees in contrary motion to the melody. In such cases, the performer must decide whether the cross-relations produced by chromatic alteration in one part but not in another are consistent with the style and expression of the piece. C. P. E. Bach and Türk recommend raising the auxiliary of certain mordents to give a half step even when the context demands a whole step; this is to enhance its sharpness or brilliance.

The degree to which one should avoid ornamental figures that introduce parallel fifths and octaves is disputed (see *NeuO,* pp. 13–14, for discussion and citations). The question is rarely brought up in early treatises on ornamentation (for one mention, however, see C. P. E. Bach, *Versuch,* trans., p. 95), and varying strictness in counterpoint manuals suggests that opinion on ornaments, too, was not uniform. A safe rule for modern interpreters is to avoid parallels where they would be clearly heard. They are less likely to be offensive when the ornament exists to add color or brilliance (a trill begun rapidly, for example) than if the ornament plays a clear harmonic role, as would a long appoggiatura.

Bibl.: Jerome of Moravia, *Tractatus de musica* [late 13th cent.], ed. Simon Cserba (Regensburg: F Pustet, 1935). Sylvestro Ganassi dal Fontego, *Opera intitulata Fontegara* (Venice, 1535; facs., *BMB* sez. 2, 18, 1980); trans. Eng. Dorothy Swainson (Berlin: R Lienau, 1959). Giulio Caccini, *Le nuove musiche* (Florence, 1601/2); ed. H. Wiley Hitchcock, *RRMBE* 9 (1970). Marin Mersenne, *Harmonie universelle* (Paris, 1636; facs., Paris: CNRS, 1963); Roger E. Chapman, trans., fifth treatise (The Hague: Nijhoff, 1957); Robert F. Williams, trans., fourth treatise (Ph.D. diss., Univ. of Rochester, 1972). Christopher Simpson, *The Division-Violist* (London, 1659; 2nd ed., 1665; facs., New York: G Schirmer, 1955). Jean Millet, *La belle méthode* (Besançon, 1666; facs., New York: Da Capo, 1973). Bénigne de Bacilly, *Remarques curieuses sur l'art de bien chanter* (Paris, 1668; facs., Geneva: Minkoff, 1971); trans. and ed. Austin B. Caswell, *MTT* 7 (1968). Thomas Mace, *Musick's Monument* (London, 1676; facs., *MMML* ser. 2, 17). Étienne Loulié, *Eléments ou principes de musique* (Paris, 1696; facs., Geneva: Minkoff, 1971); trans. and ed. Albert Cohen, *MTT* 6 (1965). Georg Muffat, preface of *Florilegium secundum* (Passau, 1698; trans., *MQ* 53 [1967]: 220–45; trans. David K. Wilson [Bloomington: Ind U Pr, 2001]). Michel de (?) Saint-Lambert, *Les principes du clavecin* (Paris, 1702); trans. Rebecca Harris-Warrick (Cambridge: Cambridge U Pr, 1983). François Couperin, *L'art de toucher le clavecin* (Paris, 1716; facs., *MMML* ser. 2, 23, 1969); trans. Margery Halford (Sherman Oaks, Cal.: Alfred, 1974). Pietro Francesco Tosi, *Opinioni de' cantori* (Bologna, 1723; facs., *MMML* ser. 2, 133, 1968); trans. Eng. Mr. Galliard (London, 1742; 2nd ed., 1743; facs. of 2nd ed., New York: Johnson Repr, 1968); trans. Ger., with annotations, Johann Friedrich Agricola, as *Anleitung zur Singkunst* (Berlin, 1757; facs., Celle: Moeck, 1966); trans. Eng. (Agricola) Julianne Baird (Cambridge: Cambridge U Pr, 1995). Michel Pignolet de Montéclair, *Principes de musique* (Paris, 1736; facs., Geneva: Minkoff, 1972). Francesco Geminiani, *The Art of Playing on the Violin* (London, 1751; facs., London: Oxford U Pr, 1951). Johann Joachim Quantz, *Versuch einer Anweisung die Flöte traversiere zu spielen* (Berlin, 1752; facs., *DM* ser. 1, 2, 1953); trans. Edward R. Reilly, 2nd ed. (New York: Schirmer, 1975). Carl Philipp Emanuel Bach, *Versuch über die wahre Art das Clavier zu spielen* (Berlin, 1753; facs., Leipzig: Breitkopf & Härtel, 1957); trans. William J. Mitchell (New York: Norton, 1948). Jean-Baptiste Antoine Bérard, *L'art du chant* (Paris, 1755; facs., *MMML* ser. 2, 75, 1967; facs., Geneva: Minkoff, 1972); trans. Sidney Murray (Milwaukee: Pro Musica Pr, 1969). Friedrich Wilhelm Marpurg, *Anleitung zum Clavierspielen* (Berlin, 1755; facs., *MMML* ser. 2, 110, 1969; facs., Hildesheim: Olms, 1970). Giuseppe Tartini, "Regole per arrivare a saper ben suonar il violino" (before 1756); publ. as *Traité des agrémens de la musique* (Paris, 1771); facs. of both original and publ. version, plus trans. Eng. Cuthbert Girdlestone (Celle: Moeck, 1961); trans. Sol Babitz (Los Angeles: Early Music Laboratory, 1970). Leopold Mozart, *Versuch einer gründlichen Violinschule* (Augsburg, 1756); facs., Vienna: C Stephenson, 1922; trans. Eng. Editha Knocker (London: Oxford U Pr, 1948; 2nd ed., 1951). Joseph Lacassagne, *Traité général des élémens du chant* (Paris, 1766; facs., *MMML* ser. 2, 27, 1967; facs., Geneva: Minkoff, 1972). Daniel Gottlob Türk, *Klavierschule* (Leipzig and Halle, 1789; facs., *DM* ser. 1, 23, 1962); trans. Raymond H. Haggh (Lincoln: U of Nebr Pr, 1982).

Francesco Galeazzi, *Elementi teorico-pratici di musica* (Rome, 1791–96). Muzio Clementi, *Introduction to the Art of Playing on the Piano Forte* (London, 1801; 11th ed., 1826). Johann Nepomuk Hummel, *Ausführliche theoretisch-practische Anweisung zum Piano-forte-Spiel* (Vienna, 1828; trans., London, 1827). Louis Spohr, *Violin-Schule* (Vienna, 1832; R: Leipzig: C F Peters, 1956); trans. Florence A. Marshall, ed. Henry Holmes (New York, 1832). Manuel García, *Traité complet de l'art du chant* (Paris: 1840 and later eds.); 1847 and 1872 eds. collated, trans., and ed. Donald V. Paschke (Portales, N.M.: Paschke, 1970; R: New York: Da Capo, 1975). Hugo Goldschmidt, *Die Lehre von der vokalen Ornamentik* (Charlottenburg: P Lehsten, 1907; R: Hildesheim: Olms, 1998). Willi Apel, *The Notation of Polyphonic Music, 900–1600* (Cambridge, Mass.: Mediaeval Acad of America, 1942; 5th ed., 1953). Margarete Reimann, "Zur Entwicklungsgeschichte des Double," *Mf* 5 (1952): 317–32; 6 (1953): 97–111. Thurston Dart, "Recorder 'Gracings' in 1700," *GSJ* 12 (1959): 93–94. Howard Ferguson, *Early French Keyboard Music* (Oxford, Oxford U Pr, 1966). Hans Bol, *La basse de viole du temps de Marin Marais et d'Antoine Forqueray* (Bilthoven: Creyghton, 1973). Diana Poulton, "Graces of Play in Renaissance Lute Music," *Early Music* 3 (1975): 107–14. Howard Mayer Brown, *Embellishing Sixteenth-Century Music* (London: Oxford U Pr, 1976). Betty Bang Mather and David Lasocki, *Free Ornamentation in Woodwind Music, 1700–1775* (New York: McGinnis & Marx, 1976). Frederick Neumann, *Ornamentation in Baroque and Post-Baroque Music* (Princeton: Princeton U Pr, 1978) [cited as *NeuO*]. Jean-Jacques Eigeldinger, *Chopin vu par ses élèves,* new ed. (Neuchâtel: La Baconnière, 1979). Robert Parkins, "Cabezón to Cabanilles: Ornamentation in Spanish Keyboard Music," *The Organ Yearbook* 11 (1980): 5–16. Robert A. Green, "Jean Rousseau and Ornamentation in French Viol Music," *Journal of the Viola da Gamba Society of America* 14 (1977): 4–41. John Robison, "The Messa di voce as an Instrumental Ornament in the Seventeenth and Eighteenth Centuries," *MR* 43 (1982): 1–14. Will Crutchfield, "Vocal Ornamentation in Verdi: The Phonographic Evidence," *19th-Century Music* 7 (1983): 2–54. Frederick Neumann, *Ornamentation and Improvisation in Mozart* (Princeton: Princeton U Pr, 1986). John Spitzer and Neal Zaslaw, "Improvised Ornamentation in Eighteenth-Century Orchestras," *JAMS* 39 (1986): 524–77. John Spitzer, "Improvised Ornamentation in a Handel Aria with Obbligato Wind Accompaniment," *EM* 16 (1988): 514–22. Robert Donington, *The Interpretation of Early Music,* new rev. ed. (New York: Norton, 1989). Will Crutchfield, "The Prosodic Appoggiatura in the Music of Mozart and His Contemporaries," *JAMS* 42 (1989): 229–74. Stewart Carter, "On the Shape of the Early Baroque Trill," *Historical Performance* 3 (1990): 9–17. David Fallows, "Embellishment and Urtext in the Fifteenth-Century Song Repertories," *Basler Jahrbuch für historische Musikpraxis* 14 (1990): 59–85. John Butt, "Improvised Vocal Ornamentation and German Baroque Compositional Theory: An Approach to 'Historical' Performance Practice," *Journal of the Royal Musical Association* 116 (1991): 41–62. Charles Jacobs: "Ornamentation in Spanish Renaissance Vocal Music," *Performance Practice Review* 4 (1991): 116–85. Frederick Neumann, "A New Look at Mozart's Prosodic Appoggiatura," in *Perspectives on Mozart Performance,* ed. R. Larry Todd and Peter Williams (Cambridge: Cambridge U Pr, 1991), pp. 92–116. Robert D. Levin, "Improvised Embellishments in Mozart's Keyboard Music," *EM* 20 (1992): 221–33. David Grayson, "Whose Authenticity? Ornaments by Hummel and Cramer for Mozart's Piano Concertos," in *Mozart's Piano Concertos: Text, Context, Interpretation,* ed. Neal Zaslaw (Ann Arbor: U of Mich Pr, 1996), pp. 373–91. H. Diack Johnstone, "Ornamentation in the Keyboard Music of Henry Purcell and His Contemporaries," in *Performing the Music of Henry Purcell,* ed. Michael Burden (Oxford: Oxford U Pr, 1996), pp. 82–104. Neal Zaslaw, "Ornaments for Corelli's Violin Sonatas, Op. 5," *EM* 24 (1996): 95–118. Mary Cyr, "Ornamentation in English Lyra Viol Music, I: Slurs, Juts, Thumps, and Other Graces for the Bow," *Journal of the Viola da Gamba Society of America* 34 (1997): 48–66. Esther Morales-Canadas, *Die Verzierungen der spanischen Musik im 17. und 18. Jahrhundert* (Frankfurt: Lang, 1997). Karin and Eugen Ott, *Handbuch der Verzierungskunst in der Musik,* 5 vols. (Munich: Ricordi, 1997–99). Paul E. Corneilson, "Vogler's Method of Singing," *JM* 16 (1998): 91–109. Mary Cyr, "Ornamentation in English Lyra Viol Music, II: Shakes, Relishes, Falls, and Other Graces for the Left Hand," *Journal of the Viola da Gamba Society of America* 35 (1998): 16–34. Timothy J. McGee, *The Sound of Medieval Song: Ornamentation and Vocal Style According to the Treatises* (New York: Oxford U Pr, 1998). Clive Brown, *Classical and Romantic Performing Practice, 1750–1900* (Oxford: Oxford U Pr, 1999). Charles Gower Price, "Free Ornamentation in the Solo Sonatas of William Babell: Defining a Personal Style of Improvised Embellishment," *EM* 29 (2001): 29–54. See also Diminutions and Performance practice. D.F., rev. S.Z.

Orpharion. A wire-strung plucked instrument with a festooned outline like a *bandora, but smaller, tuned like the *lute (G c f a d′ g′), and possibly derived from the *cittern. Many early 17th-century English lute books call for the orpharion as an alternative instrument, but little printed music specifically for it survives. See ill. under Lute.

Bibl.: Donald Gill, *Wire Strung Plucked Instruments* (Richmond: The Lute Society, 1977). Robin Wells, "The Orpharion," *EM* 10 (1982): 27–40. R.L.

Orphée aux enfers [Fr., Orpheus in the Underworld]. Operetta in two acts by Offenbach (libretto by Hector Crémieux and Ludovic Halévy), produced in Paris in 1858. A revision in four acts was produced in Paris in 1874. Setting: Greek legend.

Orphéon [Fr.]. A male choral society; the first to bear this name was established in Paris about 1830. Such societies multiplied rapidly, principally among the working classes, and by 1900 there were more than 2,000. The movement to found these societies was led by Guillaume Louis Bocquillon Wilhem, and from 1852 until 1860, the Paris society was conducted by Gounod.

Orpheoreon. *Orpharion.

Orpheus in the Underworld. See *Orphée aux enfers.*

Orphica. A small, two- to four-octave piano, invented by Karl Leopold Röllig of Vienna about 1795, that could be carried outdoors and held in the player's lap or suspended from a strap around the player's neck.

Osanna. See *Hosanna.*

Ossia [It.]. Or; used to indicate an alternative (often easier) version of a passage.

Ostinato [It., obstinate]. A short musical pattern that is repeated persistently throughout a performance or composition or a section of one. Repetition of this type is found in the music of cultures throughout the world and is especially characteristic of the music of Africa, whence its presence in much folk and popular music elsewhere (e.g., *rock) and in some 20th-century Western art music [see, e.g., Africa II, American Indian music II]. The following is a survey of its use within Western art music.

Although any musical element may figure as an ostinato, the most memorable patterns result when it is a melody, a chord progression, a rhythm, or some combination of these. The effectiveness of the ostinato derives from the cumulative impact of the repetitions, especially when they occur at the same pitch, although in some pieces, the ostinato statements are widely separated and may begin at different pitch levels. Melodic-harmonic ostinatos were most prevalent in the Baroque period, while melodic-rhythmic ostinatos appear most often in the 20th century.

A repeating melodic phrase set in the bass is called a basso ostinato, or *ground bass, and is usually from one to eight measures in length, as in Purcell's *Evening Hymn,* Biber's Passacaglia in G minor for solo violin, and Bach's Passacaglia in C minor for organ BWV 582. These three pieces exemplify the possible treatments of a Baroque basso ostinato: Purcell's ground bass modulates, Biber's moves to the upper line, where different harmonies accompany it, and Bach's ascends in register, is decorated slightly, and temporarily disappears, replaced by the harmonic progression alone. Although a close relationship often exists between a melodic ostinato and the harmonies associated with it, as in the Bach example, harmonies are by no means fixed in a piece with basso ostinato. Harmonic ostinatos, on the other hand, have no fixed repeating melody, but do permit occasional new chords, as in the variations on dance basses (Giovanni Antonio Terzi, Gagliard Variations over the *passamezzo* bass for lute, *Mw* 11). Melodic and harmonic variations may give rise to a set of continuous variations that develops irresistible momentum when the upper parts are varied with each repetition of the ostinato unit, as in Pachelbel's Canon in D major, Handel's Chaconne in G with 62 Variations, and all of the instrumental examples cited above [see also Variation, Ground, Chaconne, Passacaglia.] In vocal pieces, the sung phrases do not necessarily coincide in structure with the ostinato, so that a variation form does not result (e.g., Monteverdi, *Zefiro torna,* termed *ciacona*). An unusual piece combining melodic-harmonic ostinato with continuous variation is Chopin's *Berceuse,* in which the one-bar ostinato becomes structurally subservient to the four-bar melody and its variations. A short ostinato may thus be grouped into larger repetitive units.

The earliest ostinatos appear in medieval music. Melodic ostinatos, usually very short patterns, are found in a single voice, most often the tenor, of 13th-century motets (e.g., *HAM,* nos. 33b, 35). A well-known early ostinato is the *pes* of *"Sumer is icumen in" (*HAM,* no. 42), which is itself in canon. Rhythmic ostinato became a constructive principle in the isorhythmic motet, although the effect of rhythmic repetition in this context (e.g., Machaut, "S'il estoit nulz," *HAM,* no. 44) is much more diffused than in nearly any melodic ostinato. The ostinato motet with repetitive tenor reemerged in the 15th and 16th centuries, with the phrase recurring on different pitches (e.g., Compère, "Royne du ciel," *HAM,* no. 79, and Morales, *Emendemus in melius, HAM,* no. 128). When this technique is applied to a short phrase, however, the result is sequence rather than ostinato, as in Josquin's *Missa Hercules Dux Ferrariae,* Kyrie II. The 16th century also saw extensive use of harmonic ostinato in the variations (**diferencias, *partitas*) on dance basses (e.g., **romanesca, *ruggiero, *passamezzo*) that arose in Spain and Italy, later moving to England. The basso ostinato, whether or not used as the basis for variations, flourished during the 17th and 18th centuries; in vocal music, its popularity was partially a result of its appropriateness for basso continuo performance in monody. (See, for example, the many "lament" arias on descending tetrachord ostinatos, or such pieces as Monteverdi's *Lamento della ninfa.*) Falling out of favor with the Classical aesthetic of flexible phrase structure, the ostinato returned in 19th-century variations such as Liszt's *Weinen, Klagen, Sorgen, Zagen* and the finales of Brahms's Haydn Variations op. 56 and Fourth Symphony op. 98. In other 19th-century music, ostinatos make more temporary appearances (Bruckner, Symphony no. 4, 4th movt.) or else may be indistinguishable from motivic continuity (Wagner, *Die Walküre,* end of act 3). In the 20th century, the ostinato emerged as a central element in both variation and nonvariation works. Nearly every major composer of the century, and especially of the first half, wrote a passacaglia, in which the ostinato may be treated either with unprecedented freedom (Schoenberg, *Pierrot lunaire* op. 21, "Nacht") or with literal repetition (Shostakovich, Violin Concerto, 3rd movt.). And with Stravinsky, the melodic-rhythmic ostinato finds its most memorable formulations, as in *Le sacre du printemps,* Symphony of Psalms, and Symphony in Three Movements.

Bibl.: Lilli Propper, *Der Basso ostinato als technisches und formbildendes Prinzip* (Hildburghausen: F W Gadow & Sohn, 1926). Richard Litterscheid, *Zur Geschichte des Basso ostinato* (Dortmund: Strauch, 1928). Leopold Nowak, *Grundzüge einer Geschichte des Basso ostinato in der abendländischen Musik* (Vienna: Druckerei Guberner & Hierhammer, 1932). Otto Gombosi, "Italia: Patria del basso ostinato," *La rassegna musicale* 7 (1934): 14–25. Lothar Walther, *Die Ostinato-Technik in den Chaconne- und Arien-Formen des 17. und 18. Jahrhunderts* (Würzburg: K Triltsch, 1940). Robert U. Nelson, *The Technique of Variation* (Berkeley and Los Angeles: U of Cal Pr, 1948). Kurt Westphal, "Der Ostinato in der neuen Musik," *Melos* 20 (1953): 108–10.

E.S.

Otello. Opera in four acts by Verdi (libretto by Arrigo Boito, after Shakespeare's *Othello*), produced in Milan in 1887. Setting: Cyprus in the late 15th century.

Ôter, ôtez [Fr.]. To remove, e.g., a stop or a mute.

Ottava [It.]. The interval of an octave; abbr. *8va. All'ottava, ottava alta, ottava sopra,* or *8va* written above a passage indicates that it should be played an octave higher than written; *ottava bassa, ottava sotto,* or *8va* written below a passage indicates that it should be played an octave lower than written; *coll'ottava* indicates doubling at the octave, either above or below. In arias of the 18th century, *all'ottava* may indicate that the vocal line is to be accompanied only in unison or octaves, without other harmony.

Ottava rima [It.]. See *Strambotto.*

Ottavino [It.]. *Piccolo.

Ottoni, stromenti d'ottoni [It.]. Brass instruments.

Ours, L' [Fr., The Bear]. Popular name for Haydn's Symphony no. 82 in C major Hob. I:82 (1786), the first of the *Paris Symphonies, so called because of the series of "growling" pedal points at the opening of the last movement.

Ouvert, clos [Fr., open, closed; Lat. *apertum, clausum;* It. *aperto, chiuso*]. In secular music of the Middle Ages, especially the **formes fixes,* the first and second endings, respectively, of a section to be repeated; hence, the equivalent of the modern **prima* and *seconda volta.*

Ouverture [Fr.]. Overture.

Overblowing. The process by which a wind instrument is made to sound a harmonic higher than the fundamental (first harmonic) [see Acoustics] and thus the process by which the second and higher registers are produced. An instrument that functions acoustically like an open pipe (e.g., the flute) and thus is capable of sounding the second harmonic (an octave above the fundamental) is said to overblow at the octave. An instrument that functions acoustically like a stopped pipe (e.g., the clarinet) sounds only odd-numbered harmonics and is thus said to overblow at the twelfth (the third harmonic). For some instruments, such as the flute or brass instruments, a change in *embouchure and/or wind pressure produces the change in mode of vibration from the first to the higher harmonics. In other instruments the transition is aided by a *speaker key.

M.S.

Overdotting. See Dotted notes.

Overstrung. An arrangement of the strings of a piano such that those of the bass pass diagonally over those of the middle register.

Overtones, overtone series. See Harmonics, Acoustics.

Overture [fr. Fr. *ouverture*]. (1) A composition for orchestra intended as an introduction to an opera or other dramatic or vocal work. During the 17th and much of the 18th centuries, the most common designations for overtures were *sinfonia* and (less often) *introduzione.* During the same period, overtures to operas and other large dramatic works often served as preludes to acts other than merely the first.

The earliest operas often had no overtures, but rather began with a prologue for one or more singers. The Toccata that precedes the prologue of Monteverdi's *Orfeo* (1607) essentially continued the Renaissance tradition of opening an aristocratic entertainment with a fanfare for trumpets. Later 17th-century overtures, generally called *sinfonie* in the sources, ranged from brief chordal introductions to multisectional *sonata- and *canzona-like pieces (e.g., the sinfonias to Stefano Landi's *Il Sant'Alessio,* 1632; see *HAM,* no. 208). Venetian overtures of the second half of the century were frequently in two movements or sections, the first in duple, the second in triple meter, and often featured trumpets (e.g., Carlo Pallavicino's sinfonia to *Diocletiano,* 1674; see *GMB,* no. 224).

The overture to Alessandro Scarlatti's *Tutto il mal non vien per nuocere* (1681, rev. 1687 as *Dal male il bene*) introduced an important new type consisting of three movements in the pattern fast–slow–fast, the finale generally a dance movement (normally a gigue or fast minuet, but not necessarily so labeled). By 1700 the three-movement overture had become the norm for Italian opera. This type is now sometimes termed an Italian overture.

In France, overtures were of a specific sort consisting of two parts: first a stately slow section in duple meter with pervasive dotted rhythms, then a faster fugal section, usually in triple or compound meter. A return near the end of the second section to the style and often the material of the opening is common, especially in later examples. Double-dotting [see Dotted notes] is expected in the opening section; this section ends on (or in) the dominant or relative major, and both sections are repeated in toto. Hence, the form represents a type of binary or rounded binary form with contrasting parts [see Binary and ternary forms].

Overtures of the type just described, known as French overtures *(ouvertures à la française),* appeared for the first time in Lully's ballet *Alcidiane* (1658). Their basis was evidently the processional entrée of the early **ballet de cour,* which by about 1640 often bore the title *ouverture*. Other possible sources of influence were the allemande–courante pairing and the contemporaneous two-section Italian overture. The French overture remained the standard type in France during the reign of Louis XIV and was quickly adopted by composers in Germany (Johann Sigismund Kusser, Agostino Steffani, Handel), England (John Blow, Purcell, Handel), and elsewhere. In Germany, a French overture often stood at the head of an ensemble or keyboard suite [see Suite III]; in fact, such a suite was usually called an *Ouverture* or *Ouvertüre*. The best-known examples of this practice are Bach's four "suites" for orchestra, which are actually called *ouvertures* in the sources.

The Italian overture of the early Classical period was generally in three movements. First movements from early in the period, for instance those of Pergolesi, often disclose a tri-ritornello structure in which the first section moves to the dominant, the second moves to the submediant or other related key, and the third remains throughout in the tonic [see Ritornello form]. During the 1730s, however, a variant of this scheme began to appear in certain Neapolitan overtures in which the middle section was either omitted entirely or reduced to a short retransition (see Hell, 1971): the result resembles an unrepeated sonata-form exposition followed directly by the recapitulation. The similarity to sonata form without development becomes even closer with the introduction of thematic differentiation (including use of a contrasting secondary theme) beginning in approximately the mid-1730s; this and other stylistic elements of the Italian overture were influential during the early Classical period [see Symphony II].

The movement structure just outlined remained the norm until fairly late in the 18th century, still appearing in Mozart's one-movement overture to *The Marriage of Figaro* (1786). It also formed the basis for the most characteristic type of the so-called da capo or reprise overture, in which the usual dancelike finale is replaced by a restatement of all or part of the opening allegro. Most typically, as in Mozart's overture to *The Abduction from the Seraglio* (1782), a fast-movement exposition leads to the slow movement (in Mozart's case a minor-key version of the opening aria), which is followed in turn by a recapitulation of the opening material. The da capo overture, found in Italy as early as the 1730s, represents a halfway stage in the shift from three- to one-movement overtures.

True one-movement overtures appear sporadically throughout the first half of the 18th century, principally in oratorios and cantatas but occasionally also in operas (e.g., Francesco Conti's *Issicratea* of 1726). Gluck began to utilize the one-movement type in the 1750s (*Il re pastore,* 1756), and by approximately the 1770s it had supplanted the three-movement type as the norm. A related trend was the more intimate connection of the overture with the work it introduced, either by incorporation within the overture of musical material from the opera (as in the above-mentioned overture to Mozart's *The Abduction from the Seraglio*) or by anticipation in it of the action or mood of the first scene. Rameau had already utilized the former procedure, and Gluck was instrumental in establishing the latter. Both are found in late Haydn and Mozart and became standard in Beethoven's time—the *Leonore* Overtures nos. 2 and 3, for example, are like previews of the opera to come. In other respects, late Classical overtures tend to resemble the first movements of contemporaneous symphonies, employing sonata forms (though without repeats) and often slow introductions.

The above trends culminated in the overture of the Romantic era, as in Weber's overture to *Der Freischütz* (1821), which presents the most important thematic material of the opera. An extension of this principle may be seen in the "potpourri" or "medley" overture of comic opera, operetta, and musical comedy from Auber to the present day. An alternative type to the independent overture was the *prelude or introduction in free form, found in Italian opera from Bellini and Donizetti onward and in Wagner beginning with the *Ring*. With numerous exceptions, this type became standard after ca. 1850.

(2) A composition of the 19th and 20th centuries similar to a dramatic overture but intended for independent concert performance. A preliminary stage in the development of the concert overture is represented by the overture to a spoken drama and the overture written for a specific occasion (e.g., Beethoven's *Coriolan* and *Coronation of the House* overtures, respectively). Other composers wrote pieces entitled only "Overture" (e.g., Mendelssohn, op. 101 [1826]). The most characteristic concert overtures, however, were works with generalized programs inspired by literature, history, nature, and the like. The first such composition seems to have been Mendelssohn's overture to *A Midsummer Night's Dream* (1826), inspired by Shakespeare's play but not written originally to precede it. Other early concert overtures of importance include Mendelssohn's *The Hebrides* ("Fingal's Cave") and Berlioz's *Roman Carnival* and *The Corsair*. Though the *symphonic poem absorbed the concert overture to some extent after 1850, numerous composers continued to write overtures, for example Brahms, Saint-Saëns, and such Russian and Czech nationalists as Rimsky-Korsakov and Dvořák.

Bibl.: Henry Prunières, "Notes sur les origines de l'ouverture française," *SIMG* 12 (1910–11): 565–85. Hugo Botstiber, *Geschichte der Ouvertüre und der freien Orchesterformen* (Leipzig: Breitkopf & Härtel, 1913). Gerald Abraham, *A Hundred Years of Music* (New York: Knopf, 1938; 4th ed., London: Duckworth, 1974). Helmut Hell, *Die neapolitanische Opernsinfonie in der ersten Hälfte des 18. Jahrhunderts* (Tutzing: Schneider, 1971). Basil Deane, "The French Operatic Overture from Grétry to Berlioz," *PRMA* 99 (1972–73): 67–80. Susanne Steinbeck, *Die Ouvertüre in der*

Zeit von Beethoven bis Wagner (Munich: Katzbichler, 1973). James R. Anthony, *French Baroque Music from Beaujoyeulx to Rameau,* 2nd ed. (New York: Norton, 1978). Stephen C. Fisher, "Haydn's Overtures and Their Adaptations as Concert Orchestral Works" (Ph.D. diss., Univ. of Pennsylvania, 1985). E.K.W.

Oxford Symphony. Popular name for Haydn's Symphony no. 92 in G major Hob. I:92 (1789). It was performed at Oxford in 1791 when the university awarded Haydn the honorary degree of Doctor of Music.

Oxyrhynchos Hymns. The earliest surviving Christian hymns with music, preserved on fragments of papyrus from the third century found at Oxyrhynchos in Egypt. Two texts are preserved, neither of which has been identified, and are accompanied by Greek letter notation.

Bibl.: Egon Wellesz, *A History of Byzantine Music and Hymnography* (Oxford: Clarendon Pr, 1949; 2nd ed., 1961; R: 1971). *MGG* 4:1052. M. W. Haslam, *Texts with Musical Notation,* The Oxyrhynchus Papyri 44 (London: Egypt Exploration Soc, 1976), pp. 58–72.

P

P. Abbr. for **piano* [see also Performance marks]; in organ and piano music, pedal; [Fr.] **positif.*

Pacato [It.]. Calm.

Padam [Tel.]. A lyrical genre of Carnatic music, in a slow tempo and usually placed following the weightier compositions in a vocal or instrumental recital. Its texts are love songs in which the love of a woman for a man is a metaphor for the love of the soul for a deity. In a recital of **bharata-nāṭyam,* it is performed in mime. C.C.

Padiglione [It.]. The bell of a wind instrument; *p. in alto,* with the bell raised.

Padovana, padoana [It.; Fr. *padouenne*]. Literally, a dance from Padua. As a title, the term was used in various ways, but principally two: (1) In the first half of the 16th century, it is a generic term for the dances of the **pavana–*pass'e mezo* species. The nine dances labeled *pavana* in Joan Ambrosio Dalza's *Intabulatura de lauto Libro quarto* (1508) are described as *padoane diversi* on the title page of the collection, as are the *pass'e mezi* in Giovanni Maria da Crema's *Intabolatura de lauto . . . Libro primo* (1546). Dances of the same type are labeled *padoana* in Vincenzo Capirola's lute book (MS, ca. 1517; see Otto Gombosi, ed., *Compositione di Meser Vincenzo Capirola* [Neuilly-sur-Seine: Société de musique d'autrefois, 1955]) and, anachronistically, in Giulio Cesare Barbetta's *Intavolatura di liuto* (1585) and Giulio Abondante's *Il quinto libro de tabolatura da liuto* (1587). (2) Toward the middle and in the second half of the 16th century, the term *padovana* or *padoana* was usually applied to a quick dance in a quadruple compound meter (12/8) resembling a **piva.* Such dances appear in lute tablatures by Dominico Bianchini (1546), Antonio Rotta (1546), Giacomo de Gorzanis (1561, 1563, 1564, 156?), Giulio Cesare Barbetta (1585), Giulio Abondante (1587), Giovanni Maria Radino (1592), and Giovanni Antonio Terzi (1599).

The inconsistent use of the term in Italian collections is duplicated in many German ones, but in Spanish and French sources, with few exceptions, the word *pavana, pavane,* or *pavenne* (not *padoana*) is a generic term for dances of both the *pavana–pass'e mezo* and the *padoana–piva* types. In German sources of the 17th century, the title reverts to its earlier 16th-century meaning, and introductory dances of the *pavana–pass'e mezo* species in suites by Heinrich Isaac, Isaac Posch, Paul Peuerl, Johann Hermann Schein, and Samuel Scheidt are labeled *paduana.* L.H.M.

Paean. An exuberant song, as of praise or thanksgiving; originally, one addressed to Apollo.

Paganina [It.]. See *Bel fiore.*

Paganini Etudes. (1) Six concert etudes *(Études d'exécution transcendante d'après Paganini)* for piano by Liszt, composed in 1838 and based on Paganini's *Capricci* for solo violin op. 1 (except no. 3, "La campanella," which is after Paganini's "Rondo à la clochette," the last movement of his Concerto in B minor for violin and orchestra op. 7). (2) Two sets of six etudes for piano by Schumann, op. 3 (1832) and op. 10 (1833), on themes from Paganini's *Capricci.*

Paganini Variations. Two sets of variations for piano by Brahms, op. 35 (1862–63), on a theme from Paganini's *Capricci* for solo violin op. 1, the same theme employed by Liszt in no. 6 of his *Paganini Etudes.

Pagliacci [It., The Clowns]. Opera in a prologue and two acts by Leoncavallo (to his own libretto), produced in Milan in 1892. Setting: a village in Calabria on the Feast of the Assumption in the late 1860s.

Paired imitation. *Imitation in which the voices enter in pairs, the members of each pair entering in close succession as compared with the interval of time separating successive pairs. It is especially characteristic of the music of Josquin Desprez (ca. 1440–1521). Most often, a single subject appears in all voices; sometimes, however, imitation does not take place within individual pairs, only between them.

Pajaritos [Sp.]. In Spanish organs, several high-pitched pipes whose open ends are immersed in water to imitate bird sounds when activated.

Paleography [fr. Gr. *palaios,* old, and *graphē,* writing]. The study of the history of writing, dealing in particular with the classification, origin, development, and dissemination of specific types of script, usually within the limits of one alphabet and, at least ideally, on whatever surface they were written. Paleography assumes responsibility for deciphering scripts, i.e., for assigning alphabetical values to their individual graphic signs. This task has in principle been carried out for almost all alphabets, but in practice many reading difficulties remain to be solved, and there is a continuing need to develop the reading facility of new generations of scholars. Because of paleography's role as both an independent and an auxiliary historical discipline, much effort is expended either on establishing rules for dating and localizing types of script or on applying these rules to individual examples. In classifying scripts and tracing their history, paleographers consider both external form and manner of execution. They note the changing shapes of individual letters and ligatures together with certain more general features, such as the slant, the angle of the pen nib (if broad) to the writing line (revealed by the direction of the thickest strokes), the uniformity or lack thereof in the height of the letters (the distinction between majuscule, or capital, and minuscule, or lowercase, scripts), the ratio of the breadth of letters to their height, and the nature of finials or serifs. In terms of manner of execution, special attention is paid to *ductus* or structure (the number, sequence, and direction of strokes for each letter), the degree of deliberateness or currentness, and speed. Paleography also studies abbreviations and punctuation, writing instruments and materials, and the manner of preparing and disposing these materials for writing and preservation. Paleography shares many interests, though not its formal object, with codicology. For musical paleography, see Notation, Neume.

Bibl.: Franz Steffens, *Lateinische Paläographie: 125 Tafeln in Lichtdruck. . .*, 2nd ed. enl. (Trier: Schaar & Dathe, 1909; R: 1929, 1964). Berthold L. Ullman, *Ancient Writing and Its Influence* (New York: Longman, 1932; R: 1980). Léon Gilissen, *L'expertise des écritures médiévales* and *Prolégomènes à la codicologie* (Ghent: Story-Scientia, 1973, 1977). Bernhard Bischoff, *Paläographie des römischen Altertums und des abendländischen Mittelalters,* Grundlagen der Germanistik, 24 (Berlin: E Schmidt, 1979); Eng. trans., *Latin Palaeography: Antiquity and the Middle Ages,* by Dáibhí Ó Cróinín and David Ganz (Cambridge: Cambridge U Pr, 1990). James J. John, "Latin Paleography," in *Medieval Studies: An Introduction,* ed. James M. Powell, 2nd ed. (Syracuse: Syracuse U Pr, 1992), pp. 3–81. J.J.J.

Palestrina. Opera ("musical legend") in three acts by Hans Pfitzner (to his own libretto), produced in Munich in 1917. Setting: Rome and meetings of the *Council of Trent.

Palestrina style. The style of unaccompanied, largely diatonic, polyphonic vocal music embodied in the works of Giovanni Pierluigi da Palestrina (1525 or 1526–1594). Palestrina's music has often been regarded as the model of classical Renaissance polyphony, especially in its controlled treatment of dissonance, though successive generations have varied considerably in their understanding of it. In the 17th century, his music was taken as the model for what was by then termed the *stile antico* (old style), but which was nevertheless still cultivated for some types of sacred music. In the 18th century, Johann Joseph Fux claimed Palestrina as the model for his formulation of the principles of counterpoint in his *Gradus ad Parnassum* (1725). More accurate descriptions of his style were attempted in the 19th century, but the first systematic analysis was carried out in the 20th by Jeppesen, on whose work the teaching of "modal counterpoint" is now often based. Although this style is sometimes taken as representing a *Roman school, it cannot be seen as typifying even just the 16th century, much less the Renaissance more broadly defined. See also *Motu proprio,* Cecilian movement, *Marcellus* Mass.

Bibl.: Knud Jeppesen, *The Style of Palestrina and the Dissonance,* 2nd ed., trans. Margaret W. Hamerick (Copenhagen: E Munksgaard, 1946; R: New York: Dover, 1970; first published in Danish, Cophenhagen, 1923). Karl Gustav Fellerer, *Der Palestrinastil und seine Bedeutung in der vokalen Kirchenmusik des 18. Jahrhunderts* (Augsburg: B Filser, 1929; R: Walluf bei Wiesbaden: M Sändig, 1972). Herbert K. Andrews, *An Introduction to the Technique of Palestrina* (London: Novello, 1959).

Pallavi [Tel.]. (1) The first section of a Carnatic composition, used as a refrain. (2) The most elaborately improvised type of metered Carnatic concert music; it is sometimes based on the *pallavi* of a preexistent composition. C.C.

Pallet. A part of the key action in an organ, consisting of a hinged, narrow, rectangular piece of wood, faced with leather, that can be opened by the movement of the key to admit air to a pipe.

Palo [Sp.]. See *Atabal* (4), *Baile de palos.*

Panconsonant. Manfred Bukofzer's term for the music of John Dunstable and his followers in the mid-15th century, in which consonance (especially the complete triad, often in first inversion) predominates and dissonance is more narrowly restricted, according to certain principles of *counterpoint, than in the music of the 14th century or **ars nova.*

Pandereta, pandero [Sp.]. Tambourine.

Pandiatonicism. Nicolas Slonimsky's term for the predominance in some 20th-century music of the pitches of the diatonic scale, as distinct from the chromaticism of late 19th-century music and of 20th-century *atonal and *twelve-tone music. Such music, including some associated with *neoclassicism, often employs dissonant diatonic harmonies such as added sixth, seventh, and ninth chords. Composers cited include Prokofiev (Third Piano Concerto) and Stravinsky (**Pulcinella*).

Bibl.: Nicolas Slonimsky, *Music since 1900* (New York: Norton, 1937; 4th ed., New York: Scribner, 1971).

Pandora. See Bandora.

Pandoura [Gr.], **pandura** [Lat.]. The long-necked *lute of ancient Greece and Rome.

Pange lingua [Lat.]. (1) The Passiontide hymn "Pange lingua gloriosi proelium certaminis" (Sing, my tongue, the glorious battle) by Venantius Fortunatus (d. ca. 600). (2) The hymn for Corpus Christi "Pange lingua gloriosi corporis mysterium" (Sing, my tongue, the mystery of the glorious body) by Thomas Aquinas (d. 1274).

Panharmonicon. See Automatic instruments.

Panpipes. A wind instrument consisting of a number of small pipes held vertically and blown across the top. Each pipe sounds a single pitch; the longer a pipe, the lower its pitch. Panpipes may be assembled from reeds, hollow bones, or metal tubes, or they may be fashioned from a single piece of wood or clay. The tubes may be arranged in a bundle or in a row. If in a row, they are often arranged from longest at one end to shortest at the other, but they may also be arranged with the longest pipes in the middle or with the shortest pipes in the middle. Amerindian and Melanesian panpipes are often in a double row; each pipe is the same length as the one behind it, but one is stopped and the other open so that they sound an octave. Panpipes are frequently played in pairs, and in Africa in large ensembles. They are an ancient instrument and are found nearly worldwide. Specimens dating from ca. 2000 B.C.E. have been excavated in the Ukraine and from ca. 200 B.C.E. in Peru. They are still much used in the Andean highlands, in East Africa, in Oceania (except Australia), and in Romania. See ill. under Flute; see also *Antara, Fistula, Nai, Rondador,* Syrinx.

Pantaleon, pantalon. (1) A large *dulcimer with up to 275 strings covering five or more octaves, invented ca. 1690 by Pantaleon Hebenstreit. It enjoyed a vogue in the first half of the 18th century, but passed out of use in the 1770s. (2) In the late 18th century, a square piano, especially one with a down-striking action. (3) On a clavichord, a stop that divides the strings from the damping felt, thus permitting them to vibrate sympathetically (as do the strings of Hebenstreit's dulcimer, after which the stop was named) as well as after a key has been released.

Pantomime. The portrayal of emotions and actions or the narration of an event by means of gesture and body movements. The technique of pantomime may be incorporated into opera or ballet. The character Vespone in Pergolesi's *La serva padrona* is a pantomime role, as is the title character of Auber's *La muette de Portici.* Noverre's *ballets d'action* also make significant use of pantomime.

In the 18th century, the term pantomime also referred to a comic entertainment, popular in England, France, and the Hapsburg empire. Populated by stock characters such as the Old Man and his Pretty Daughter, the Wily Servant, the Clown (i.e., Cassandre or Pantaloon, Columbine, Harlequin) drawn from the medieval *sotie* or the Italian **commedia dell' arte,* these entertainments might contain songs, dances, instrumental pieces, and spectacular stage effects as well as scenes in dumbshow. In present-day England, the pantomime, based on a traditional story or a fairy tale, is a popular form of Christmas entertainment.

Pantonal, pantonality. The free use of all twelve pitch classes, as distinct from their restricted use according to the principles of *tonality; hence, synonymous with *atonal, atonality.

Papadikē [Gr.]. See *Akolouthia.*

Papillons [Fr., Butterflies]. Schumann's set of 12 short piano pieces op. 2 (1829–31). It was inspired by a masked ball in a work of Jean-Paul Richter.

Paradiddle. A characteristic series of strokes played on the snare drum with hands alternating as follows: R L R R L R L L; R L R L R R L R L R L L; or R L R L R L R R L R L R L R L L.

Parallel chords. A succession of chords all having the same interval structure and number of parts, the parts thus moving parallel to one another. Because classical *tonal theory prohibits motion in *parallel fifths and octaves, it allows only first-inversion triads [see also Sixth chord, Sixth-chord style] and diminished seventh chords in parallel motion. Composers of the 18th century and earlier, however, sometimes employed otherwise prohibited parallels to evoke a rustic or primitive quality in dance and vocal music, and some composers of the 19th century employed parallel chords in conjunction with folk or folklike melodies.

The repeated or extended use of parallel chords of any type can serve to disrupt the structural hierarchy that is the basis of classical tonality, replacing it with a succession of equally weighted harmonies, none of which may be perceived as the tonic. The music of Debussy (e.g., *Danse sacrée* [Ex. 1]), and thus of *impressionism generally, is frequently associated with this phenomenon, as is that of Satie. It is also encountered in some works of Bartók and of early and middle-period Stravinsky. Some 20th-century music has exploited parallel chords for their percussive effect when used in rapid succession (e.g., Stravinsky, *Petrushka* [Ex. 2] and *Le sacre du printemps*). Jazz and rock music have also used parallel chords [Ex. 3],

often as a result of repeated reliance on characteristic keyboard or fingerboard idioms. They are a widespread feature of polyphony outside the tradition of Western art music, occurring in some European *folk music and in some musics of *Africa and *Oceania.

Parallel (consecutive) fifths, octaves. The simultaneous statement of the same melodic interval in two otherwise independent parts of a polyphonic complex at the distance of a perfect fifth [Ex. 1] or octave [Ex. 2] or equivalent compound interval. *Motion of this type is prohibited in classical tonal harmony and *counterpoint. Although the prohibition has been observed to such an extent that such parallels may sound unusual even to relatively untutored ears, theorists have not always agreed on the grounds for the prohibition. Parallel perfect intervals are often said to destroy the independence of the parts. This is clearly true of parallel octaves, which in effect reduce the number of independent parts. The sound of parallel octaves is not

in and of itself offensive in the context of tonal music, since they are freely used in piano music and orchestral music for the sake of doubling (sometimes for timbral effect) what is in fact a single part. Similar considerations apply to parallel unisons, which are also prohibited.

The prohibition against parallel fifths, however, requires a somewhat different explanation, since their use for any purpose other than to create a deliberately rustic, exotic, or even humorous effect [see also Parallel chords] is quite exceptional. An explanation proposed by Cherubini in the 19th century and taken up by Schenker in the 20th observes that if a melody is harmonized in parallel fifths, its tonality becomes confused, since the harmonization simply states the melody in a different key while employing (with the sole exception of the seventh scale degree) only pitch classes common to the original key. For example, "Mary had a little lamb," if played in the key of C and harmonized diatonically at the fifth above will be stated simultaneously in the keys of C and G. This explanation is more persuasive in the case of a series of parallel fifths than in the case of only two fifths in succession. Nevertheless, it has some historical force in that the observation of the prohibition begins in earnest in the 15th century at a time when tonal coherence around a single tonic emerges as a general concern.

A related phenomenon is variously termed hidden, direct, or covered fifths or octaves. Here a fifth or octave is approached in similar motion in two parts. These are in general avoided when both parts move by leap, especially when the two parts are the outermost voices. Their prohibition has generally been on grounds that they only barely conceal the fifths or octaves that would occur if the movement of both voices were filled in by step. Direct octaves occur frequently between the outermost voices in the chorales of Bach, however, when the soprano moves by step. A familiar type of direct fifth is sometimes termed horn fifths [Ex. 3] because it occurs frequently in parts composed for natural horns.

Some early forms of *organum make extensive use of parallel fifths and octaves. The prohibition against their use first occurs around 1300 in a treatise of Johannes de Garlandia (*Optima introductio in contrapunctum, CS* 3:12). Such progressions continue to occur regularly, however, until the mid-15th century, especially in four-part writing, where they are often found even at cadences. And although most composers of tonal music have taken care to avoid or at least disguise them, they are not altogether absent from great works of this repertory. A number of such passages were collected by Brahms (Schenker, ed., 1933).

Bibl.: August Wilhelm Ambros, *Zur Lehre von Quintenverboten* (Leipzig, 1859). F. E. Gladstone, "Consecutive Fifths," *PMA* 8 (1881–82): 99–113. Maud G. Sewall, "Hucbald, Schoenberg and Others on Parallel Octaves and Fifths," *MQ* 12 (1926): 248–65. Frank T. Arnold, "J. S. Bach and Consecutives in Accompaniment," *ML* 14 (1933): 318–25. Heinrich Schenker, ed., *Johannes Brahms: Oktaven, Quinten u.a.* (Vienna: Universal, 1933). Adolf Ehrenberg, *Das Quinten- und Oktavenparallelen-Verbot in systematischer Darstellung* (Breslau: K Littmann, 1938). Matthew Shirlaw, "Aesthetic—and Consecutive Fifths," *MR* 10 (1949): 89–96. Don M. Randel, "Emerging Triadic Tonality in the Fifteenth Century," *MQ* 57 (1971): 73–86. Heinrich Schenker, ed., *Johannes Brahms: Oktaven, Quinten u.a.* (Vienna: Universal, 1933); Eng. trans. Paul Mast, *Music Forum,* vol. 5 (New York: Columbia U Pr, 1980). See also Counterpoint.

Parallel key. See Key relationship.

Parallel motion. See Motion.

Paralleltonart [Ger.]. Relative (not parallel) key.

Paramese [Gr.]. See Greece I, 3 (i).

Parameter. An independent variable; e.g., in acoustics, amplitude or frequency; in analytical discussions, especially of *serial music, any of the separably specifiable features of a sound, e.g., pitch class, duration, timbre, loudness, register.

Paranete [Gr.]. See Greece I, 3 (i).

Paraphonia [Gr., Lat.]. In late Greek and early medieval writings, the intervals of a fourth and a fifth.

Paraphonista [Lat.]. In some *Ordines romani* of the 7th and 8th centuries [see Gregorian chant VI] and elsewhere, a singer. Peter Wagner interpreted the term as deriving from **paraphonia* and thus as evidence for the early singing of *organum in parallel fourths and fifths. Scholarly opinion has remained divided on this interpretation.

Paraphrase. (1) A metrical rendition in the vernacular of Scripture or the Psalms, set to music (as in Scottish paraphrases or Benedetto Marcello's *Estro poetico-armonico: Parafrasi sopra li primi (secondi) venticinque salmi,* Venice, 1724–26).

(2) In music of the 14th–16th centuries, a melody borrowed from another source (usually chant) and then ornamented. Paraphrase technique has been described as "the process by which a composer quotes a melody faithfully enough, but elaborates freely as he goes along" (Sparks, 1963). It was used in the 14th and 15th centuries in polyphonic settings of the Ordinary of the Mass and also in settings of hymns, sequences, and antiphons. The relevant Gregorian chant would usually appear in the uppermost voice of a three-voice texture in rhythmic guise with a few ornamental notes added—the paraphrase rarely obscured the original melody, however. Paraphrased chants could also serve as the *cantus firmi* of early *cyclic Masses, but here they are restricted to the tenor of a three- or four-part composition, and sometimes they are treated with great freedom [see Mass]. In the 16th century, a highly paraphrased *cantus firmus* might migrate from voice to voice within an imitative structure. This imitative paraphrase technique can be seen in the *Missa Ave maris stella* and *Missa Pange lingua* of Josquin Desprez, and it became a favorite way of using Gregorian chants in Masses, as in Palestrina's paraphrase Masses based on hymns (see Marshall, 1963). It has been suggested that 15th- and 16th-century composers consciously included in their works short citations or paraphrases of sections of well-known chants or even works by other composers, for interpretive or symbolic purposes. Paraphrases of popular tunes are also found in the music of Charles Ives, notably in his Second Symphony (1902).

(3) In the 19th century, a solo work of great virtuosity in which popular melodies, usually from operas, were elaborated (as in Liszt's *Rigoletto: Paraphrase de concert,* 1860); such pieces could also be called Fantasia or Reminiscences and were distinguished from works attempting to be faithful transcriptions. Paraphrases were produced in large numbers by composers of salon music; one catalog of Liszt's works shows 78 such pieces.

Bibl.: Robert Marshall, "The Paraphrase Technique of Palestrina in His Masses Based on Hymns," *JAMS* 16 (1963): 347–72. Edgar Sparks, *Cantus Firmus in Mass and Motet: 1420–1520* (Berkeley and Los Angeles: U of Cal Pr, 1963). Irving Godt, "Renaissance Paraphrase Technique: A Descriptive Tool," *Music Theory Spectrum* 2 (1980); 110–18. J. Peter Burkholder, "'Quotation' and Paraphrase in Ives's Second Symphony," *19th-Century Music* 11 (Summer 1987): 3–25; R in *Music at the Turn of the Century: A 19th-Century Music Reader,* ed. Joseph Kerman (Berkeley: U of Ca Pr, 1990), pp. 33–55. R.S.

Parapter [Gr.]. In the Middle Ages, any of four tones (also termed *medii toni*) used in the classification of melodies regarded as lying outside the system of eight *modes.

Pardessus de viole [Fr.]. A descant *viol of the 17th and 18th centuries [see also *Dessus*], with five strings tuned g c′ e′ a′ d″.

Parhypate [Gr.]. See Greece I, 3 (i).

Paris Symphonies. Haydn's Symphonies nos. 82–87 Hob. I:82–87 (1785–86), composed for the *Concert de la Loge olympique* in Paris. Three of them have popular names: *L'*ours* (no. 82), *La *poule* (no. 83), and *La *reine* (no. 85).

Paris Symphony. Popular name for Mozart's Symphony in D major K. 297 (1778), composed during a stay in Paris and performed there at the **Concert spirituel.*

Parlando [It., speaking]. Speechlike; also *parlante.* The term is used principally with respect to singing, but sometimes also with respect to instrumental music.

Parlante [It.]. (1) **Parlando.* (2) In 19th century Italian opera, music in which continuity is maintained by the orchestra, sometimes employing a recurrent motive, while the voice proceeds in a less melodic and more speechlike fashion. It thus stands between aria and recitative, though it normally occurs within the context of a closed number such as an aria or ensemble.

Parlato [It.]. (1) **Parlando.* (2) Spoken rather than sung, e.g., the dialogue of certain types of comic opera.

Parody. (1) A work that, with humorous or satirical aims, makes distorted or exaggerated use of the features of some other work or type of work. The history of *opera includes numerous examples, beginning with comic interludes in otherwise serious operas of the 17th century and including contemporaneous parodies of the operas of Lully, comic operas intended for performance between acts of serious operas of the early 18th century, some features of *ballad opera, Wagner's portrayal of Beckmesser in *Die *Meistersinger,* and many passages in the works of Gilbert and Sullivan. Among the best-known parodies in instrumental music is Mozart's *Ein *musikalischer Spass.* A 16th-century genre including examples of parody is the **villanella.* See also Burlesque.

(2) A work in which a new text has been substituted for the original, often without humorous intent. A work of this type from the Middle Ages or Renaissance is usually termed a **contrafactum.* Some of the humorous parodies of the works of Lully [see (1)] were of this type.

(3) A composition that seriously reworks the musical material of another composition. Compositions of

this type were common in the 16th and early 17th centuries, the principal genre being the *parody Mass. Numerous instrumental works, too, were based on vocal models in ways that go beyond mere transcription or *intabulation. These include works that bear titles such as *fantasia, **tiento,* and **glosa.* The tradition could also be said to include numerous works of the 19th century (e.g., by Liszt) termed fantasia or rhapsody and works by composers of the 20th century, including Stravinsky, Peter Maxwell Davies, and George Rochberg, that make significant use of earlier music.

Bibl.: Donald J. Grout, "Seventeenth-Century Parodies of French Opera," *MQ* 27 (1941): 211–19, 514–26. John Ward, "The Use of Borrowed Material in 16th-Century Instrumental Music," *JAMS* 5 (1952): 88–98. Howard M. Brown, "The *chanson spirituelle,* Jacques Buus, and Parody Technique," *JAMS* 15 (1962): 145–73. John Ward, "Parody Technique in 16th-Century Instrumental Music," *Sachs,* 1965, pp. 208–28. Paul Brainard, "Bach's Parody Procedure and the St. Matthew Passion," *JAMS* 22 (1969): 241–60.

Parody Mass. A cyclic Mass based on a polyphonic model, making use of the model's motivic construction and quoting more than one of its voices. The term was popularized by August Wilhelm Ambros and Peter Wagner, who mistakenly thought it was common in the 16th century; in fact, what they called a parody Mass was originally designated *Missa super* . . . or *Missa ad imitationem* . . . , and Lewis Lockwood *(Grove 6)* has suggested the use of "imitation Mass" instead of parody Mass. The new term is gradually being adopted by scholars who write in English, but the old term still retains currency. There is some justification for Lockwood's alternative: first, it is closer to 16th-century usage; second, it eliminates confusion with the history of *parody technique. Ludwig Finscher *(MGG),* for example, viewed the imitation Mass as a culmination of an evolutionary process of quoting more than one voice from a model stretching from the 14th century to the 16th. J. Peter Burkholder and others have further pointed to the use of quotations of more than one voice of the model in a number of 15th-century Masses that are based on *cantus firmi,* and have suggested that the parody Mass was not really a new development. But the parody Mass is actually more concerned with motivic construction than with polyphonic quotations. According to Lockwood, the parody Mass is intimately tied to the appearance, ca. 1500, of the four-part, imitative-style motet. In these pieces, individual phrases of the text are set off as points of imitation or as homophonic passages, creating a texture in which no one voice is a linear entity. Composers who wished to base Masses on the new-style motet were forced by its very construction to use its imitative motives rather than any one line; along with this came the quotation of all the voices involved in the motives, either directly or in new contrapuntal combinations. In fact, the idea seems to have been to quote directly as little as possible. Whether this technique is also a reflection of the Renaissance idea of *imitatio* is still a matter of dispute.

The first parody Masses were produced by the younger French contemporaries of Josquin Desprez, whose *Missa Mater patris* is sometimes regarded as a parody Mass. These Masses were all based on new-style motets: Antoine de Févin's *Missa Ave Maria* and *Missa Mente tota* on motets by Josquin, Jean Mouton's *Missa Quem dicunt homines* on the motet by Johannes Richafort, and so on; later it became possible to use madrigals and chansons as models as well. A large percentage of the Masses written in the 16th century were parody Masses [see Mass]. Pietro Cerone, in his *El melopeo y maestro* of 1613 (but following Pietro Pontio's *Raggionamento* of 1588), offered a series of admonitions to composers wishing to write parody Masses: the beginnings of the five major divisions of the Mass should correspond to the beginning of the model; the endings of the major divisions should match the ending of the model; the Christe may be based on a subsidiary motive; the beginnings of the last Kyrie and the second and third Agnus should be freely composed; and the more use made of subsidiary motives in the course of the Mass, the better.

Bibl.: August Wilhelm Ambros, *Geschichte der Musik,* vol. 4 (Leipzig: Breitkopf & Härtel, 1909). Peter Wagner, *Geschichte der Messe* (Leipzig: Breitkopf & Härtel, 1913). Ludwig Finscher, "Parodie und Kontrafaktur," *MGG.* Lewis Lockwood, "Mass" II, 9, *Grove 6.* Lewis Lockwood, "A View of the Early Sixteenth-Century Imitation Mass," (Queens College, 1964), pp. 53–77. "On 'Parody' as Term and Concept in 16th-Century Music," *Reese,* 1966, pp. 560–75. Quentin Quereau, "Sixteenth-Century Parody: An Approach to Analysis," *JAMS* 31 (1978): 407–41. Howard Mayer Brown, "Emulation, Competition, and Homage: Imitation and Theories of Imitation in the Renaissance," *JAMS* 35 (1980): 1–48. J. Peter Burkholder, "Johannes Martini and the Imitation Mass of the Late Fifteenth Century," *JAMS* 38 (1985): 470–523. Honey Meconi, "Does *Imitatio* Exist?" *JM* 12 (1994): 152–78. Murray Steib, "A Composer Looks at His Model: Polyphonic Borrowing in Masses from the Late Fifteenth Century," *TVNM* 46 (1996): 5–41. Veronica Franke, "Borrowing Procedures in the Late 16th-Century Imitation Masses and Their Implications for Our View of 'Parody' or 'Imitation,'" *SzMw* 46 (1998): 7–33. R.S.

Pars [Lat., pl. *partes*]. A self-contained section of a work, especially of a Renaissance motet.

Parsifal. Opera ("stage-dedication festival play" [Ger. *Bühnenweihfestspiel*]) in three acts by Wagner (to his own text, after Wolfram von Eschenbach), produced in Bayreuth in 1882 at the dedication of the festival theater. Setting: Monsalvat, Spain, in the Middle Ages.

Part. (1) [Fr. *voix;* Ger. *Stimme;* It. *voce;* Sp. *voz*] In a polyphonic work for voices or instrument(s), any of the individual lines or melodies making up the texture; sometimes also *voice or voice part, though not usually with respect to works for instrumental ensemble.

In keyboard music, some genres, such as the *fugue, adhere to a fixed number of parts for any work, while others may employ textures in which a fixed number of parts is not readily distinguishable. (2) The music for any single voice or instrument in an ensemble. (3) A section of a larger work or form [see, e.g., Binary and ternary form].

Partbook [Ger. *Stimmbuch*]. A separately bound manuscript or printed book containing the music for only a single voice or instrument in an ensemble. The term is applied chiefly to what was one of the principal formats for the dissemination of ensemble music of the 16th and early 17th centuries [see also Choirbook, Score]. The number of partbooks in a set corresponds to the number of parts making up the texture of individual works, and each partbook is named according to the voice or part contained [see Voice]. The earliest surviving set of partbooks is the manuscript Glogauer Liederbuch of ca. 1480. Printed sets begin with Ottaviano Petrucci's *Motteti C* of 1504.

Parte [It.]. (1) *Part; *colla parte,* an indication that the accompaniment should follow the free rhythmic interpretation of the principal melodic part or that one player is to double the part of another. (2) In the 17th century, a variation [see Partita].

Parthenia [Gr., virgin dances]. A collection of works for *virginal published in 1613 with the title *Parthenia or the Maydenhead of the First Musicke that ever was printed for the Virginalls,* including works by William Byrd, John Bull, and Orlando Gibbons (ed., *EKM* 19). A companion collection of ca. 1614 for virginal and bass viol is titled *Parthenia In-Violata.*

Parthia, Parthie, Partia [Ger.]. *Partita.

Partial. In acoustics, *harmonic.

Partial signature. *Conflicting signature.

Particella [It.; Ger. *Particell*]. A detailed sketch or draft of a composition written on relatively few staves, e.g., with parts for closely related instruments on single staves. Such condensed or short scores have formed part of the compositional procedure of many composers, including Schubert and Wagner.

Partie. (1) [Fr.] *Part. (2) [Fr., Ger.] See Partita.

Partimen [Occ.]. See *Jeu-parti.*

Partimento [It., division]. In the 18th and early 19th centuries, a thoroughbass part with occasional melodic suggestions on the basis of which a complete composition rather than simply an accompaniment was to be improvised. Numerous such pieces, mainly conceived as pedagogical in nature, were composed by Italian, especially Neapolitan, keyboard composers of the 18th century, e.g., *Partimenti, ossia Intero studio di numerati per ben suonare il cembalo* by Francesco Durante. It is not certain that the technique is related to the English *division on a ground.

Bibl.: Karl Gustav Fellerer, ed., *Der Partimento-spieler* (Leipzig: Breitkopf & Härtel, 1940).

Partita [fr. It. *parte,* part], **Parthia** [Ger.; also *Parthie, Partie, Partia*]. (1) In the late 16th and the 17th century, a variation, usually one on a traditional melody such as the **romanesca* or **passamezzo.* This meaning was continued in the chorale partitas of Georg Böhm and Bach.

(2) In the late Baroque period, a *suite. The earliest known use of the term in this sense occurs in Johann Kuhnau's *Neuer Clavier Übung erster Theil, bestehend in sieben Partien* (1689). The best-known examples are Bach's solo violin and keyboard partitas.

(3) In the early Classical period, a type of multimovement instrumental work. According to Heinrich Christoph Koch (*Musikalisches Lexikon,* 1802), partitas are characterized by a mixture of dance and abstract (nondance) movements; many Classical partitas, however, consist entirely of abstract movements. Though the majority of partitas were intended to be performed by solo instruments (either a keyboardist or chamber ensemble), a fair number of examples for orchestra also exist. In Austria during this period, partita was the most common designation for all multimovement chamber works until the 1750s, when it was replaced as the title of choice by *divertimento (Webster, 1974). After about 1760, the term generally designated a work for winds, often entitled *Feldparthie* (partita for outdoor performance). After about 1780, works of this latter type were more often termed *Harmonie.*

Bibl.: Willi Apel, *The History of Keyboard Music to 1700,* trans. and rev. Hans Tischler (Bloomington: Indiana U Pr, 1972). James Webster, "Towards a History of Viennese Chamber Music in the Early Classical Period," *JAMS* 27 (1974): 212–47. Warren Kirkendale, *Fugue and Fugato in Rococo and Classical Chamber Music,* 2nd ed., trans. Margaret Bent and Warren Kirkendale (Durham, N.C.: Duke U Pr, 1979). Eugene K. Wolf, *The Symphonies of Johann Stamitz* (Utrecht: Bohn, Scheltema & Holkema, 1981). Cliff Eisen, ed., *Orchestral Music in Salzburg, 1750–1780, RRMCE* 40 (1994). Jens Peter Larsen, "Zur Vorgeschichte der Symphonik der Wiener Klassik," *SzMw* 43 (1994): 67–143.

E.K.W.

Partition [Fr.], **Partitur** [Ger.], **Partitura** [It., Sp.]. *Score.

Part song. (1) An unaccompanied secular choral work of relatively modest length. Part songs are only sometimes homophonic in texture. The repertory of such works grew strikingly in the 19th century with the spread of amateur choral societies and has continued to grow in the 20th. Composers include Mendelssohn, Schumann, Brahms, Parry, Stanford, Elgar, Vaughan Williams, Holst, Hindemith, Randall Thompson, and many others. See also Choral music. (2) Any unaccompanied secular vocal work, including genres from the Middle Ages and Renaissance such as the chanson and madrigal.

Parture [Fr.]. See *Jeu-parti.*

Part writing. *Voice leading.

Pas [Fr.]. A dance step; *pas de deux,* a dance for two dancers; for *pas de Brabant,* see *Saltarello.*

Pasacalle [Sp.]. (1) Literally, music for walking in the streets. See Passacaglia. (2) In Andean South America, any of various kinds of dance music.

Paseo [Sp.]. **Pasacalle* (1). Juan Cabanilles (1644–1712) employed the term for keyboard variations (*HAM,* no. 239).

Pasillo [Sp.]. A dance originally derived from the European waltz, cultivated in the ballrooms and salons of 19th-century Colombia and Ecuador. Today distinct forms of the *pasillo,* in triple meter but displaying a range of tempos and other musical characteristics, survive in the folk traditions of both countries. Especially typical is the alternation between sections with an accompaniment pattern of three quarter notes and those with the accompaniment pattern ♪♩ ♪♩. The *pasillo* is also known in Venezuela and in Central America as an urban social dance. D.S.

Paso doble [Sp., double step]. One of the most characteristic national social dances of Spain, in moderately fast duple meter with a somewhat marchlike character.

Paspy. **Passepied.*

Passacaglia. A continuous variation form, principally of the Baroque, whose basso ostinato formulas originally derived from *ritornellos to early 17th-century songs. These passacaglias or ritornellos were played on the guitar between stanzas or at the ends of songs, where they were repeated many times, probably with improvised variations; the practice began in Spain [Sp. *pasacalle*] and quickly moved to Italy and France. The passacaglia then developed in a way quite similar to the *chaconne. Its four-bar *ostinato became the basis for long sets of continuous variations as well as vocal pieces (e.g., Frescobaldi, *Partite sopra passacagli* and *Aria di passacaglia*). Early differences between chaconne and passacaglia were the particular chord progressions: the passacaglia tended to be in minor, with a I–IV–V or I–IV–V–I pattern. The bass lines themselves might change in successive phrases, or extra harmonies might be inserted, but these variants fell within a limited set of formulas. One of these formulas is the descending tetrachord used in so many operatic laments but appearing as well in pieces titled passacaglia (e.g., Biber, Passacaglia in G minor for solo violin, *Mw* 11). Bach's Passacaglia in C minor for organ BWV 582 is perhaps the best-known 18th-century passacaglia and was used as a model by many later composers; its eight-bar ostinato appears in the bass for the first eight and last five variations, but in the ninth through fifteenth it is decorated, ascends in register, and even disappears.

Occurring rarely in the later 18th century, the passacaglia then dropped out of sight until the early 20th century, although a case may be made for considering as such Beethoven's *Thirty-Two Variations on an Original Theme* in C minor WoO 80, Liszt's *Weinen, Klagen, Sorgen, Zagen,* and the finale of Brahms's Fourth Symphony op. 98; none is called passacaglia. From Reger on, however, 20th-century composers, including many of the most prominent, have taken an explicit interest in the passacaglia as a constructive framework for a nontonal or serial piece (e.g., Webern, *Passacaglia* op. 1; Schoenberg, *Pierrot lunaire* op. 21, "Nacht"; Berg, *Wozzeck,* act 2, sc. 4; Stravinsky, Septet; see list in Stein, 1959).

Bibl.: Wolfgang Osthoff, "Die frühesten Erscheinungsformen der Passacaglia in der italienischen Musik des 17. Jahrhunderts," *Palermo,* 1954, pp. 275–88. Hans Ludwig Schilling, "Hindemiths Passacagliathema in den beiden Marienleben," *AfMw* 11 (1954): 65–70. Leon Stein, "The Passacaglia in the Twentieth Century," *ML* 40 (1959): 150–53. Manfred Schuler, "Zur Frühgeschichte der Passacaglia," *Mf* 16 (1963): 121–26. Richard Hudson, "The Ripresa, the Ritornello, and the Passacaglia," *JAMS* 24 (1971): 364–94. See also Chaconne. E.S.

Passage. (1) Any section of a work, of indefinite length and not necessarily self-contained. (2) A succession of scales, arpeggios, or similar figures, often of considerable technical difficulty and intended to display virtuosity, but without particular musical substance; also passage work.

Passaggio [It.]. (1) Transition, modulation. (2) *Passage work. (3) An ornamental melodic passage, written or improvised; also the introductory flourishes on manual or pedals in German Baroque toccatas. See Diminutions.

Passamezzo [Eng., also passing measures, passymeasures], **Pass'e mezo** [It., also *pass'e mezzo, passo e mezo, passomezo*]. An Italian dance of the 16th and early 17th centuries similar to a **pavana;* indeed, the musical style of the common *pavana* cannot be distinguished from that of a *pass'e mezo.* The dance steps must also have been similar. Thoinot Arbeau (*Orchésographie,* 2nd ed., 1589, fol. 33) describes the *pass'e mezo* as a "*pavana* played less heavily to a lighter beat." Fabritio Caroso's choreographies for the two dances have the same stylistic characteristics (*Il ballarino,* 1581; *Nobilità di dame,* 1600). Furthermore, Claude Gervaise (*Sixième livre de danseries,* 1555) uses both titles as one: *pavanne-passemaize.* In all probability, the *pass'e mezo* was a type of *pavana.* Like the *pavana,* it was usually coupled to a **saltarello,* a **gagliarda,* or a **padovana.* Dances coupled together were composed on the same melodic and/or harmonic patterns.

The earliest extant example appears in Hans Newsidler's *Ein newgeordent künstlich Lautenbuch* (1536), listed as "Welscher tantz Wascha mesa" (Italian dance Wascha mesa). The curious "Wascha mesa"

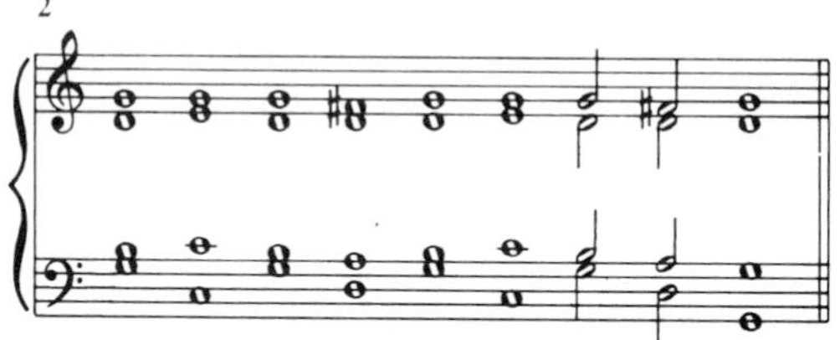

Passamezzo.

is explained in a later collection by Newsidler (*Ein newes Lautenbüchlein,* 1540), in which it is supplanted by the title "Passa mesa: Ein Welscher tantz." The title is not found in Italian books until 1546 (lute tablatures by Giulio Abondante, Domenico Bianchini, Giovanni Maria da Crema, and Antonio Rotta), but it must have existed earlier, since Newsidler cites it as an Italian dance. It did not occur in Spain, but is found in England by the middle of the century. It also appears in the Flemish collections of Pierre Phalèse as early as 1546 and in France in Claude Gervaise's collection printed by the widow of Pierre Attaingnant in 1555.

A large proportion of the *pass'e mezi,* a few *pavane,* and at least one-fifth of all 16th-century dances (including *saltarelli, gagliarde, padovane,* etc.) are composed on two harmonic patterns known as the *pass'e mezo antico* [Ex. 1] and the *pass'e mezo moderno (commune, novo)* [Ex. 2]. No particular discant was associated with the two patterns.

Bibl.: Otto Gombosi, "Italia: Patria del basso ostinato," *La rassegna musicale* 7 (1934): 14–25. Id., "Stephen Foster and 'Gregory Walker,'" *MQ* 30 (1944): 133–46. Georg Reichert, "Der Passamezzo," *Lüneburg,* 1950, pp. 94–97. Imogene Horsley, "The 16th-Century Variation: A New Historical Survey," *JAMS* 12 (1959): 118–32. L.H.M.

Passecaille [Fr.]. *Passacaglia.

Passepied [Fr.]. A lively, simple Baroque dance in triple meter (often 3/8), a fast type of minuet. It has an upbeat, regular two- or four-measure phrases, and homophonic texture. The dance steps encourage the exploitation of a hemiola figure, e.g., a 3/4 measure formed from two measures in the midst of 3/8 motion. It was popular in French stage and harpsichord music of the late 17th and early 18th centuries (Lully, Gaspard LeRoux), as well as in German orchestral and harpsichord suites (J. K. F. Fischer, Bach). Frequently, *passepieds* were in pairs to be performed **alternativement.* Some 19th- and 20th-century composers (Delibes, Debussy) have used the title for simple melodic pieces with broken-chord accompanimental figures. B.G.

Passer [Fr., pass]. In timpani parts, to retune from one specified pitch to another.

Passing chord. A chord occurring within the prolongation of some harmony and introduced over a passing tone [see Counterpoint] in the bass; also any chord whose function is clearly subordinate to those preceding and following and one or more of whose elements is introduced as a passing tone.

Passing tone. See Counterpoint II, 1.

Passion music. A musical setting of Jesus' sufferings and death as related by one of the four Evangelists. In the Roman Catholic liturgy the *Passio Domini nostri Jesu Christi* is enacted or performed on Palm Sunday (Matthew 26:36–75; 27:1–60), Tuesday (Mark 14:32–72; 15:1–46), Wednesday (Luke 22:39–71; 23:1–53), and Good Friday (John 18:1–40; 19:1–42) of Holy Week. The parts of Christ, the narrating Evangelist, and direct speakers other than Christ (Pilate, Judas, etc.) are taken, respectively, by the celebrant, the deacon, and the subdeacon; the part of the crowd *(turba)* is usually taken by the congregation. Since the Second Vatican Council, chanting of the Latin Passion has been replaced in virtually all North American Catholic dioceses by reading of the vernacular Passion.

Plainsong Passions, like other Scriptural readings, are chanted on specific reciting tones, or *tubae.* Major syntactic divisions are punctuated by formulaic melodic inflections. Unlike other readings, Passions are chanted to three distinct reciting tones. In late medieval sources, these typically occur as f′, c′, and f (or e or g). Regional variants of the Passion tones were replaced in 1586 under the authority of Pope Sixtus V by a single set that has remained in use through the 20th century with only minor changes. Between ca. 1450 and ca. 1550, the monophonic Passion tone was either augmented or replaced by polyphony. The manner in which a polyphonic Passion sets its text is closely coordinated with the nature of the text employed.

Responsorial Passions are so named because they preserve both the traditional Passion narratives (according to the Vulgate or Luther's German) and the tripartite division of their recitation. At first, polyphony was restricted to the speeches of the crowds. A primitive stage of augmentation occurs in a treatise from Füssen (ca. 1450), which gives examples of how *turba* speeches may be performed by singing all three recitation tones at once (Schmidt, 1960). A more developed approach is found in two anonymous English Passions (London, British Library, Egerton 3307, ca. 1480). In these, the *turba* speeches are set for six to eight voices. In addition, the *soliloquentiae* (Peter, Pilate, Judas, etc.) are set in a three-voice *faburden style. Richard Davy's St. Matthew Passion (ca. 1490) goes even further by setting all direct speeches with four-voice polyphony.

Davy's Passion anticipates a north Italian repertory that begins with two four-voice Passions (St. Matthew and St. John) written before 1541 by Gasparo Alberti. These works set all direct speech, including Christ's, in polyphonic textures. Antonio Scandello imported this north Italian Passion to German-speaking lands with his setting of St. John (1561). Scandello was the first to integrate the new Lutheran chorale style with the motet style prevalent in the responsorial Passion.

More than 30 years prior to Scandello's Passion, Johann Walter had already set Luther's translation of the Vulgate narratives (St. Matthew and St. John, before ca. 1530) and in so doing had adapted the Latin Passion tones to the requirements of German. Following Walter, Jacob Meiland (1542–77) and Melchior Vulpius (ca. 1570–1615) wrote Passions that heighten the music's dramatic potential by breaking with the earlier practice of using **fauxbourdon* settings of the liturgical Passion tone for the *turba* movements.

Dramatic Passions are 17th-century settings that derive from the work of Scandello. The texts of dramatic Passions follow Luther's Bible, but may be compilations of several Evangelists. The vocal writing is unaccompanied but borrows elements of operatic recitative and aria. These contrast with more conservative melodic elements related to both plainsong and the chorale. The result is a new and vivid kind of unaccompanied Passion that is quite independent of the older Passion tones. The three Passions of Schütz (St. Luke, St. John, and St. Matthew; 1665–66) and the *Historia resurrectionis* of Christian Andreas Schultze (1686) are the outstanding specimens of this genre.

Motet or through-composed Passions conflate the four Gospel narratives into a single condensed text (a *summa passionis* or *Passionsharmonie*) that is then treated like any other motet text. An early (ca. 1500) four-voice *summa passionis* by Antoine de Longueval uses the Passion tone as a migrating *cantus firmus* that stays in the tenor voice for the words of the Evangelists, in the bass voice for the words of Christ, and in the alto voice for the direct speeches. Longueval's example was transmitted to Germany (as a work of Jacob Obrecht) in a publication of 1538 by Georg Rhau. Joachim a Burck took the Longueval Passion as his model in writing a four-voice St. John Passion (1568). The only known German motet Passion to use Longueval's migrating Passion tone, however, is that of Leonhard Lechner, a four-voice work of 1593 that some consider the finest work of its type. The last German motet Passion is a six-voice setting of St. John (1631) by Christoph Demantius. This work eliminates all reference to the Passion tone and points to future oratorio Passions by appending a setting of the related text from Isaiah 53.

Oratorio Passions interpolate non-biblical texts and set the Evangelist's narrative in *recitative style with continuo accompaniment [see also Oratorio]. When an instrumental ensemble is specified, it is used for interpolated sinfonias, arias, and choruses, written in imitation of the latest Italian operatic styles. Another important feature after 1650 is the inclusion of chorale tunes. Thomas Selle composed the first Passions with instrumental interludes (St. Matthew, 1636; St. John, 1641, enl. 1643). Chorales (for both chorus and solo voice) first appear in Johann Sebastiani's St. Matthew Passion (by 1663). Early instances of strophic arias occur in Johann Theile's St. Matthew Passion (1673). Reinhard Keiser's setting of St. Mark (performed by Bach at both Weimar and Leipzig) is noteworthy for its careful attention to tonal construction, its dramatic and coloristic instrumentation, and its setting of the *turba* speeches as terse fughettas.

The apex of the oratorio Passion is reached in the settings of St. John (BWV 245) and St. Matthew (BWV 244) by Bach. The St. John Passion was completed and performed in 1724 and subsequently revised. The St. Matthew Passion was first performed in 1727 or 1729 and revised in 1736. These works show Bach to be keenly aware not only of earlier Passions, but also of unexplored possibilities inherent in Baroque formal procedures of his own day. The St. Matthew Passion is conceived on a grand scale, requiring a large instrumental ensemble and two antiphonal choirs. Its text, more than half of which consists of Picander's verses, places it in the mainstream of 18th-century trends. Bach's St. Mark Passion (BWV 247; 1731) survives only in fragments. These suggest that it was largely a reworking of earlier music. A St. Luke Passion in Bach's hand is an anonymous work performed by him in the early 1730s.

The liturgical oratorio Passion was prominently cultivated also in Hamburg. Telemann wrote one such Passion for each year, 1722–67, alternating between the Gospels of St. Matthew, Mark, Luke, and John (not all have survived). This tradition was continued from 1769 to 1789 by his successor, C. P. E. Bach, who designed his works (all preserved in the Sing-Akademie Collection, Berlin) in pasticcio format by including music by his father, Telemann, Homilius, and others.

Passion oratorios set poetic paraphrases of the biblical accounts that were written under the influence of the early 18th-century Pietist movement. Keiser was the first (1712) of many (including Handel, Telemann, and Mattheson) to set Barthold Heinrich Brockes's *Der für die Sünde der Welt gemarterte und sterbende Heiland Jesus.* The most popular Passion oratorio of the later 18th and the 19th century was *Der Tod Jesu* (1755) by Carl Heinrich Graun. Despite its title, this account completely omits the trial and death of Jesus.

Since the early 20th century, composers have returned to writing responsorial and motet Passions. Hugo Distler's *Choral-Passion* op. 7 (1933) weds Schütz's procedures to a mildly modern vocabulary. Ernst Pepping's St. Matthew Passion (1960) for double choir is a motet Passion written in a dissonant 20th-century idiom. An outstanding American oratorio Passion is Daniel Pinkham's St. Mark Passion (1965). Krzysztof Penderecki's widely performed St. Luke Passion (1963–65) might be loosely termed an oratorio Passion. The 18th-century Passion oratorio found a contemporary counterpart in Andrew Lloyd Webber's rock musical *Jesus Christ Superstar* (1970).

Bibl.: Otto Kade, *Die ältere Passionskomposition bis zum Jahre 1631* (Gütersloh: C Bertelsmann, 1893; R: Hildesheim: Olms, 1971). Konrad Ameln and Karl Gerhardt, "Johann Walter und die ältesten deutschen Passionshistorien," *Monatsschrift für Gottesdienst und kirchliche Kunst* 44 (1939): 105–19; R: (Göttingen: Vandenhoek & Ruprecht, 1939). Hans Heinrich Eggebrecht, "Die Matthäus-Passion von Melchior Vulpius," *Mf* 3 (1950): 143–48. Joachim Birke, "Eine unbekannte anonyme Matthäuspassion aus der zweiten Hälfte des 17. Jahrhunderts," *AfMw* 15 (1958): 162–86. Werner Braun, *Die mitteldeutsche Choralpassion im 18. Jahrhundert* (Berlin: Evangelische Verlagsanstalt, 1960). Günther Schmidt, "Grundsätzliche Bemerkungen zur Geschichte der Passionshistorie," *AfMw* 17 (1960): 100–125. Donald G. Moe, "The St. Mark Passion of Reinhard Keiser" (Ph.D. diss., Univ. of Iowa, 1968). Walter Blankenburg, "Zu den Johannes-Passionen von Ludwig Daser (1578) und Leonhard Lechner (1593)," *Vetter,* 1969, pp. 63–66. Basil Smallmann, *The Background of Passion Music,* 2nd ed. rev. and enl. (New York: Dover, 1970). Id., "A Forgotton Oratorio Passion," *MT* 115 (1974): 118–21. Henning Friedrichs, *Das Verhältnis von Text und Musik in den Brockespassionen Keisers, Händels, Telemanns und Matthesons* (Munich: Katzbichler, 1975). Stanley Malinowski, "The Baroque Oratorio Passion" (Ph.D. diss., Cornell Univ., 1978). Paul Steinitz, *Bach's Passions* (New York: Scribner, 1979). Magda Marx-Weber, "'Musiche per le tre ore di agonia di N.S.G.C.': Eine italienische Karfreitagsandacht im späten 18. und frühen 19. Jahrhundert," *Mf* 33 (1980): 136–60.

Passy-measures. *Passamezzo.

Pasticcio [It., hodgepodge], **pastiche** [Fr.]. (1) Any work assembled from bits of other works and, at least by implication, therefore lacking artistic coherence. (2) A composite vocal work, usually an opera, containing music by several different composers or music originally intended for several different works. In 18th-century public opera, it was rare for a work to be revived without being adjusted to the needs of the singers on hand or else refurbished to increase the number of favorite tunes within the work. Handel and Gluck are particularly notable for their willingness to fashion new operas from their older ones. More commonly, a *pasticcio* was a product of accretion, with several composers and poets making their contributions over an extended period of time.

The popularity of the *pasticcio* illuminates several musical and social features of 18th-century opera. An internationally accepted musical style and the presence of predictable and conventional situations in the librettos made it possible for portions of one opera to be inserted into another without any jarring incongruity. Further, structural unity was not such an issue in the 18th century as it was to become in the 19th century. Moreover, there was little notion of a standard version of a work, in part because relatively few scores of entire operas were printed. The *pasticcio* underlines the lack of concern in the 18th century for individuality of musical style or ownership of musical material.

Although many writers use the term *pasticcio* to describe works written by several composers at the same time, such as *Muzio Scevola* (act 1 by Mattei, act 2 by Bononcini, act 3 by Handel), some restrict the term to works that borrow parts of previously existing works.

Pastorale [Fr., It., pastoral]. A work of literature or music that represents or evokes life in the countryside, especially that of shepherds. The literary genre originated in classical antiquity [see Eclogue] and was widely cultivated through the Renaissance and into the 18th century. Pastoral poetry (especially Torquato Tasso's *Aminta,* 1573, and Giovanni Battista Guarini's *Il pastor fido,* 1590) provided the texts for numerous madrigals of the late 16th century [see Madrigal III], and the tradition of staged pastoral plays was central to the development of *opera [see also *Intermedio*] in both Italy and France. Pastoral themes also provided the subjects for numerous cantatas of the 17th and 18th centuries. In instrumental works of the period, pastoral life was evoked by such features as drone basses [see also *Musette*], dotted rhythms in moderate or slow 6/8 or 12/8 as in the **siciliana,* and the use of double-reed instruments and flutes. Some of these features are still present in the final movement of Beethoven's **Pastoral* Symphony. Perhaps because of the tradition of Italian shepherds [see *Piffero*] playing bagpipes and shawms in the cities at Christmas, such music was often associated with the pastoral element in the Christmas story and thus with Christmas itself. Works in this tradition include Corelli's **Christmas Concerto,* the *Pifa* of Handel's *Messiah,* and the opening sinfonia of Bach's *Christmas Oratorio.*

Pastoral Symphony. Beethoven's Symphony no. 6 in F major op. 68 (1808), published in 1809 with the title *Sinfonie pastorale.* Beethoven's inscriptions for the five movements are (in translation): (1) Awakening of Cheerful Feelings on Arrival in the Country; (2) Scene by the Brook; (3) Merrymaking of the Country Folk; (4) Storm; (5) Song of the Shepherds, Joy and Gratitude after the Storm. His comment on a violin part used at the first performance in 1808 reads, "Mehr Ausdruck der Empfindung als Malerei" (more expression of feeling than painting).

Pastorella [It.]. In the 17th and 18th centuries, a vocal and or instrumental work for Christmas drawing on pastoral elements of the Christmas story and often employing the associated musical conventions [see *Pastorale*]. Such works, of which Haydn wrote three (Hob. XXIIId:1–3), often incorporate folk melodies.

Pastoris [Port.]. **Baile pastoril.*

Pastourelle [Fr.], **pastorela** [Occ.]. A strophic genre of the *troubadours and *trouvères in which the poet narrates his attempt to seduce a shepherdess. In the earliest *pastorelas,* in Occitan, the shepherdess generally fends off the poet's advances, often with great wit and spirit. Such is the case in Marcabru's *L'Autrier jost' una sebissa,* composed in the second quarter of the 12th century and the only Occitan *pastorela* to survive with its melody. The trouvères modeled their *pastourelles* after the Occitan genre from the early 13th century on, and they greatly expanded the genre both in numbers (from the 25 of the troubadours to more than 150 in French) and in poetic treatment (e.g., ranging from light-hearted repartée to rape). Latin, Italian, Galician-Portuguese, and German examples also survive, and many examples in different languages exist today as folksongs.

Bibl.: Michel Zink, *La pastourelle* (Paris/Montréal: Bordas, 1972). Erich Köhler, "La pastourelle dans la poésie des troubadours," in *Etudes de langue et littérature du moyen âge offertes á Félix Lecoy* (Paris: H Champion, 1973), pp. 279–92. Pierre Bec, *La lyrique française au moyen-âge,* 2 vols. (Paris: A & J Picard, 1977–78), 1:119–36, 2:47–58. William D. Paden, ed. and trans., *The Medieval Pastourelle,* 2 vols. (New York: Garland, 1987). Elizabeth Aubrey, *The Music of the Troubadours* (Bloomington: Ind U Pr, 1996), pp. 95–99. Samuel N. Rosenberg, Margaret Switten, and Gérard Le Vot, eds., *Songs of the Troubadours and Trouvères* (New York: Garland, 1998), pp. 43–44, 49–51, 197–205. Elizabeth Aubrey, "Genre as a Determinant of Melody in the Songs of the Troubadours and the Trouvères," in *Medieval Lyric: Genres in Historical Context,* ed. William D. Paden (Urbana: U of Ill Pr, 2000), pp. 273–96. E.A.

Pater noster [Lat., Our Father]. The Lord's Prayer. In the Roman Catholic Church it has formed part of the *Mass and of the hours of Lauds and Vespers. The text was set polyphonically in the Renaissance by Josquin, Willaert, Palestrina, and others, sometimes with the use of an associated liturgical melody (*Missale romanum,* 1920, p. 346).

Patetico [It.]. Pathetic, with great emotion.

Pathet [Jav., fr. constraint, limit]. A system of categories for tonal use in **slendro* and **pelog* **gendhing* and *pathetan* for central Javanese **gamelan;* often rendered *mode. Some Javanese musicians trace use of the term in music theory to descriptions of processes of tuning in *wayang kulit* (shadow-puppet plays), specifically the relationships between parts for fixed-pitch instruments of the *gamelan* and the parts for the nonfixed-pitch *rebab* and the songs of the *dhalang* (puppeteer). The term *pathetan,* used to describe free-meter introductory pieces played by an ensemble consisting of *rebab, gender, gambang,* and *suling* before and after each long *gamelan* piece or suite of pieces, derives from the generic name for one of several types of song sung by the *dhalang,* accompanied by a similar ensemble. For bibl., see Southeast Asia, especially Hood (1954), Becker (1980), and Hatch (1980). M.H.

Pathétique [Fr., pathetic]. (1) Beethoven's Piano Sonata no. 8 in C minor op. 13 (completed ca. 1797–98). The first edition (1799) bears the title *Grande sonate pathétique,* which is possibly Beethoven's title or one sanctioned by him. (2) Tchaikovsky's Symphony no. 6 in B minor op. 74 (1893), titled *Symphonie pathétique* at his brother Modest's suggestion.

Pathetisch [Ger.]. Pathetic, with great emotion.

Patter song. A song whose text, usually humorous, is sung very rapidly. Numerous examples occur in the works of Gilbert and Sullivan.

Pauke [Ger.]. Kettledrum.

Pauroso [It.]. Timid, fearful.

Pausa [It., Sp.]. Rest.

Pause. (1) *Fermata. (2) A breathing pause [Ger. *Atempause, Luftpause*], often indicated by an apostrophe above the staff; it is a slight break in the musical line to allow the singer or player to draw breath or merely to mark the end of a phrase. (3) [Fr., Ger.] Rest. See also *Generalpause.*

Pavan. **Pavana.*

Pavana [It., Sp.; Fr. *pavane, pavenne;* Eng. *pavan, paven, pavin*]. A 16th-century court dance of Italian provenance. The word is derived from Pava, a dialect form of Padua; music and literature as well as dances from Pava or in the Paduan style were described as *alla pavana.* The earliest extant examples of *pavane* are found in Joan Ambrosio Dalza's *Intabulatura de lauto libro quarto* (1508). The dance became popular early in the century and quickly spread throughout Europe. Other early examples are found in Germany in Hans Judenkünig's *Ain schone kunstliche Underweisung* (1523), in France in Pierre Attaingnant's *Dixhuit basses dances* (1530), and in Spain in Luis Milán's *El maestro* (1535 or 1536). The dance remained in vogue for most of the century, though its popularity abated somewhat in the last quarter of the period. It was restored and revitalized in idealized musical form and attained its highest point of artistic perfection under the aegis of the English virginalists, including William Byrd, John Bull, Orlando Gibbons, Thomas Tomkins, Thomas Morley, Giles Farnaby, Peter Philips, and John Dowland. Under the title *paduana,* it flourished briefly in the early 17th century in Germany, where it was used as the introductory movement of the German suite. More recent examples, actually re-creations of the earlier idealized dance form, have been written by Saint-Saëns ("Pavane" in *Étienne Marcel*), Ravel ("Pavane de la belle" in *Ma mère l'oye,* and "Pavane pour une infante défunte"), and Vaughan Williams ("Pavane" in *Job*).

The *pavana* is a slow, processional type of dance, for the most part employing a continuous repetition of basic step patterns: two single and one double step forward followed by two single and one double step backward. There are few choreographic sources. Fabritio Caroso describes a sophisticated *pavana* in his *Il ballarino* (1581). Usually, the *pavana* is followed by one of the faster dances, the **saltarello,* the **gagliarda,* the **padovana,* or the **piva.* Most dances in the genre are in a simple quadruple meter (4/2 or 4/4). Musically they resemble the *pass'e mezo* [see Passamezzo]; indeed it is often difficult to distinguish the music of a *pass'e mezo* from that of a *pavana.*

A few *pavane* are in a simple triple meter (3/2 or 3/4), but this form of the dance is rare. For examples, see Luis Milán's *El maestro,* fol. G5v; Giulio Abondante's *Intabolatura sopra el lauto,* 1546, no. 26; Alonso Mudarra's *Tres libros de música,* no. 18; Pierre Attaingnant's *Six gaillardes et six pavanes,* 1530, no. 2. L.H.M.

Pavaniglia [It.]. An instrumental dance and dance song of uncertain origin, most popular in Italy from the late 16th to the mid-17th century. Non-Italian sources refer to it as the "Spanish pavana," perhaps because it is one of the variant harmonic-melodic patterns that led to the **folia* [see Ex. 1]. The provenance is further confused because the *pavaniglia* itself is a shortened variant of a popular dance song known as the "Pavana del Duca" [Ex. 2] in Italy and by various French titles elsewhere.

The *pavaniglia* is cited in the manuals of Fabritio Caroso, and there are settings by Cabezón, Bull, Sweelinck with Scheidt, and in numerous 17th-century guitar tablatures. The "Pavana del Duca" occurs in Johann Kotter's keyboard tablature and in publications by Attaingnant, sometimes with the title "Jay mis mon coeur," as well as in the tablatures of Hans Newsidler, Alonso Mudarra, Melchiore de Barberiis, and Jacob Paix.

1

2

The abstract pattern of the *pavaniglia* (1) and the "Pavana del Duca" (2).

Bibl.: Lawrence H. Moe, "Dance Music in Printed Italian Lute Tablatures from 1507 to 1611" (Ph.D. diss., Harvard Univ., 1956), pp. 166–67, 249–51. Helga Spohr, "Studien zur italienischen Tanzkomposition um 1600" (diss., Univ. of Freiburg, 1956), pp. 69ff. L.H.M.

Pavillon [Fr.]. (1) The bell of a wind instrument; *p. en l'air,* an instruction to play with the bell raised. (2) *Pavillon chinois,* *Turkish crescent.

Peal. See Change ringing.

Peasant Cantata. See *Bauernkantate.*

Pêcheurs de perles, Les [Fr., The Pearl Fishers]. Opera in three acts by Bizet (libretto by Michel Carré and Eugène Cormon) produced in Paris in 1863. Setting: legendary Ceylon.

Ped. Abbr. for *pedal.

Pedal. (1) On the piano, any of several levers operated by the foot, especially the one that removes all of the dampers from contact with the strings [see Piano]; hence, as a verb, to use the damper pedal [for associated symbols, see Notation]. (2) In organs, the pedal keyboard; also the entire Pedal Division, consisting of wind-chests and pipes [see also Pedalboard]. (3) *Pedal point. (4) *Pedal tone. See also Harp, Harpsichord, Pedal harpsichord, Pedal piano, Timpani.

Pedalboard. The pedal keyboard of the organ, with a modern range of C–f′ or g′. Pedalboards were essential to north European organs. In England before 1850 they were rare, and their range was often limited.

Pedalcembalo [Ger.]. *Pedal harpsichord.

Pedal clarinet. Contrabass *clarinet.

Pedal drum. Pedal kettledrum.

Pedalflügel [Ger.]. *Pedal piano.

Pedal glissando. On the kettledrum, a glissando produced by striking the drum and operating the pedal to vary its pitch. See Timpani.

Pedal harp. Double-action *harp.

Pedal harpsichord [Ger. *Pedalcembalo*]. A *harpsichord equipped with a pedalboard like that of an organ. A number of Italian 16th- and 17th-century harpsichords, even spinets, exist that can be seen formerly to have had pedalboards attached by cords to the corresponding manual keys, the lowest 8 to 15 notes from the low C (*short octave). Separate instruments to be placed under the harpsichord on the floor are known to have existed in 17th- and 18th-century France and Germany. The dispositions of historical pedal harpsichords remain unclear. Probably only in Germany would the most complex 18th-century examples have contained a 16′ stop in addition to those at normal and octave pitch. French pedal harpsichords may indeed have been at 4′ rather than 8′ pitch. No historical pedal harpsichord is extant. In the late 18th century, pedalboards operating a piano action were sometimes placed under French harpsichords, and one such example survives.

Bibl.: Frank Hubbard, *Three Centuries of Harpsichord Making* (Cambridge, Mass.: Harvard U Pr, 1965), pp. 110–21, 270–72. H.S.

Pédalier [Fr.]. Pedal keyboard.

Pedaliter [Lat.]. To be played on the pedalboard of an organ.

Pedalklavier [Ger.]. *Pedal piano.

Pedalkoppel [Ger.]. In organs, the device for coupling a keyboard to the pedalboard.

Pedal organ. The Pedal Division of an organ, including its wind-chest, action, and pipework.

Pedalpauke [Ger.]. Pedal kettledrum.

Pedal piano [Fr. *piano à pédalier;* Ger. *Pedalflügel, Pedalklavier;* It. *pianoforte con pedaliera;* Sp. *piano con pedalero*]. A piano equipped with a pedalboard similar to that of an organ. In some 18th-century instruments, a single set of strings was used for both pedalboard and manual keyboard. The norm in the 19th century was for a wholly independent instrument to be placed on the floor under a grand piano. Schumann (opp. 56, 58), Alkan (opp. 66, 69), and Gounod composed pieces for such instruments.

Pedal point [Fr. *pédale;* Ger. *Orgelpunkt;* It. *pedale;* Sp. *bajo de órgano, nota pedal*]. A sustained tone in the lowest register, occurring under changing harmonies in the upper parts; also pedal, organ point. In tonal music, pedal points may occur on any scale degree (and are often identified by the name of the scale degree), but the most common are those on the dominant, preparing a climactic return to the tonic, and on the tonic, as the final, summarizing statement of the tonic at the conclusion of a work [Ex.]. In organ music, where some of the most characteristic examples occur, such tones are typically played on the pedalboard. A similarly sustained tone in an upper register is sometimes termed an inverted or internal pedal. Sustained tones in the lowest voice are a salient feature of certain types of *organum, and in the form of the *drone, sustained tones used in conjunction with moving parts are widely distributed geographically and historically.

Pedal steel guitar. An electric *zither, much used in *country and western music. Six or more strings are set over an unfretted fingerboard in a rectangular frame mounted on a stand. String tunings can be quickly changed by means of pedals and knee levers. The seated player uses a metal bar to stop the strings, sliding it along to produce a characteristic *portamento. See ill. under Guitar.

Pedal tone. On a brass instrument, the fundamental tone of a harmonic series, of which there will in principle be one for each slide position or combination of valves [see Acoustics]. On some instruments such as the trumpet, however, pedal tones are not easily produced because of the shape and size of the mouthpiece, which is intended to facilitate playing the higher harmonics.

Peer Gynt Suite. Either of two orchestral suites by Grieg, op. 46 (1888) and op. 55 (1891–92), arranged from his incidental music op. 23 (1874–76; rev. 1885) to Ibsen's play *Peer Gynt.*

Pegbox [Fr. *chevillier;* Ger. *Wirbelkasten;* It. *cassetta dei bischeri, cavigliera;* Sp. *clavijero*]. In stringed instruments, a continuation of the neck, into which are inserted the tuning pegs that control the tension of the strings; especially the type found in the violin and related instruments in which the pegs are inserted from the side. When the pegs are inserted from above or below (i.e., perpendicular to the plane of the strings), as on the *ukulele and some *banjos, the terms pegdisc and pegboard are sometimes used. See also Machine head.

Pegdisc. See Pegbox.

Peine entendu, à [Fr.]. Barely audible.

Peking Opera. A type of Chinese musical theater combining speech, stylized gestures, and acrobatics, which has dominated the national stage since the 19th century and is still performed today. The genre uses a repertory of about 30 preexistent tune types divided into two main categories: *hsi-p'i (xipi)* and *erh-huang (erhuang).* Each of the individual tune types is named and may be easily recognized by its melodic structure

Pedal point. Bach, Fugue in C minor from *The Well-Tempered Clavier,* bk. 1.

and other musical features. By setting the same tune to different texts, new arias are produced. Most arias contain a two-phrase unit that sets a rhymed couplet; the constituent lines, which are of equal length, may have either seven or ten syllables. Defined in terms of their rhythm, tempo, and corresponding dramatic functions, five main aria types can be identified: (i) the narrative aria in 4/4 meter and moderate tempo is usually used to provide narration in an unemotional manner; (ii) the lyrical aria in 4/4 meter and slow tempo is used at lyrical moments and is usually melismatic; (iii) the animated aria in measured rhythm and fast tempo is used to reveal a character's excited psychological state; (iv) the dramatic aria in free rhythm, always accompanied by a steady beat from the clappers and the fiddle, is used to propel the dramatic action in a play or to add tension to spoken dialogue; (v) the interjected aria, usually very short (only one phrase) and in free rhythm, is sung at a highly dramatic moment as a signal or call. The orchestra, which sits on stage left, is divided into two ensembles. The melodic ensemble, consisting of an **erh-hu (erhu)* and a **ching-hu* (two-stringed spike fiddles of different sizes), a **yüeh-ch'in* (*yueqin,* a moon-shaped, four-stringed plucked lute), and a *san-hsien* (*sanxian,* a three-stringed plucked lute), accompanies the singing in heterophony. The percussion ensemble, consisting of a *pan-ku* (*bangu,* a one-headed drum resting on a wooden tripod, played with two sticks), a *pan* (*ban,* wooden clappers), a *t'ang-ku* (*tanggu,* a large barrel-drum played with two sticks), and large and small gongs and cymbals, plays conventional rhythmic patterns of varying length and complexity to indicate dramatic situations and changes of mood as well as to provide rhythmic drive for the action. In addition, a *sona* (oboe) is used for special sound effects or in military scenes. See also East Asia I.

Bibl: Rulan Chao Pian, "Text Setting with the Shipi Animated Aria," *Merritt,* 1972, pp. 237–70. Colin P. Mackerras, *The Rise of the Peking Opera, 1770–1870* (Oxford: Oxford U Pr, 1972). Rulan Chao Pian, "Aria Structural Patterns in the Peking Opera," *Chinese and Japanese Music Dramas,* ed. James I. Crump and William P. Malm (Ann Arbor: Center for Chinese Studies, U of Mich, 1975), pp. 65–89. Wu Zhuguang et al., *Peking Opera and Mei Lanfang* (Peking: New World Pr, 1981). I.K.F.W.

Pelléas et Mélisande [Fr., Pelléas and Mélisande]. (1) Opera in five acts by Debussy (to his abridgment of the play by Maurice Maeterlinck), begun in 1893 and produced in Paris in 1902. Setting: the fictional kingdom of Allemonde in legendary times. (2) A symphonic poem by Schoenberg, op. 5 (1902–3), based on Maeterlinck's play. (3) A suite of incidental music to Maeterlinck's play by Fauré, op. 80 (1898).

Pellet bell. A small, rounded, metal vessel with slits or other openings and containing a loose pebble or bit of metal that rattles when the bell is shaken; also called a crotal. Pellet bells are often worn as bracelets or anklets or sewn to the clothing of dancers. They are also frequently attached to animals. *Sleigh bells are of this type. See also Idiophone.

Pelog [Indonesian, fr. Jav.]. One of the two major tunings (the other being **slendro*) that serve as background tunings for the interpretation of melodies performed by **gamelan* instrumentalists and singers in central and east Java [see Southeast Asia IX]. On some instruments in almost every Javanese *pelog gamelan, pelog* is a heptatonic tuning with at least one interval close to a minor second. Most three- to five-note contours that are called *pelog,* however, are heard in relation to a pentatonic background tuning that can be described in descent as a sequence of intervals approximated as follows: major second, minor second, major third, minor second, major third. This definition is based on an interpretation of practices of nonfixed-pitch instrumental and vocal parts. Fixed-pitch instruments with five or seven pitches to an octave are tuned in a compromise of the demands placed on them to accompany the various positions in relation to the heptatonic tuning of the nonfixed-pitch, pentatonic melodies. M.H.

Penillion [Welsh]. An improvised Welsh song sung to the accompaniment of the harp and forming part of the tradition of the *bards. The harpist begins by playing a preexistent tune. This is followed by a series of variations on the tune's harmonic progression, to which the singer improvises text and melody. See also Eisteddfod.

Penitential psalms. Psalms 6, 31 [32], 37 [38], 50 [51], 101 [102], 129 [130], and 142 [143] [for the numbering of the Psalms, see Psalter]. The best-known complete setting of these is Orlande de Lassus's *Psalmi Davidis poenitentiales* (1584). Psalms 50 [51] (the **Miserere*) and 129 [130] (the *De profundis*) have often been set separately.

Penny whistle. A small, metal *duct flute with six finger holes; also called a tin whistle. Among other uses, it was a basic instrument in South African "penny-whistle jive" of the 1950s and 60s, and it remains so in some ensembles of Ireland.

Pentachord. A collection of five pitches; the arrangement of intervals that defines the structure of a collection of five pitches. *Octave species are often defined as consisting of one pentachord plus one *tetrachord, and music of the Middle Ages and Renaissance has sometimes been analyzed in these terms [see also Mode].

Pentatonic. A scale consisting of five pitches or pitch classes; music based on such a scale. Scales of this type, of which there are many, are widely distributed geographically and historically, e.g., in *American Indian music, European and Anglo-American folk music [see Folk music II, 3], the music of Finno-Ugric and Altaic peoples in Eastern Europe and Asia, and in musical cultures of the *Far East and *Southeast Asia [see *Pelog, Slendro*]. Western writers have sometimes given prominence to two types that can be (but, in other cultures, have not necessarily been) derived from the Western diatonic scale: (i) a scale of the form C D E G A or some reordering (or mode, depending on which pitch is taken as central) of this relationship (embodied, e.g., in the black keys of the piano), which, because it lacks semitones, is sometimes termed anhemitonic and which, because it seems to omit members of the seven-tone (heptatonic) diatonic scale, is sometimes inappropriately termed a gapped scale; (ii) scales that do include semitones in the forms C E F G B or C E F A B. Pentatonic scales, especially of this first type, have sometimes been used in 19th- and 20th-century Western art music.

Percussion instruments [Fr. *instruments à percussion* (of the orchestra, *batterie*); Ger. *Schlaginstrument, Schlagzeug;* It. *percussione;* Sp. *percusión, batería*]. Musical instruments that produce sound by being struck or, less often, scraped, shaken, or plucked. In more formal classifications of musical *instruments, they are usually divided between *membranophones and *idiophones, with both categories including instruments of definite as well as indefinite pitch. Percussion instruments, including those illustrated on the following pages, are described in this dictionary in separate entries; see especially Drum.

Bibl.: J. Blades, *Percussion Instruments and Their History* (London: Faber & Faber, 1984). T. Siwe, *Percussion Ensemble and Solo Literature* (Champaign, Ill.: Media Pr, 1993). T. Siwe, *Percussion Solo Literature* (Champaign, Ill.: Media Pr, 1995). *Encyclopedia of Percussion,* ed. John H. Beck (New York: Garland, 1995).

Perdendosi [It.]. Dying away.

Perfect. See Cadence, Interval, Mensural notation, Absolute pitch.

Perfection. See Ligature, Mensural notation.

Performance marks. Words, abbreviations, and symbols employed along with the notation of pitch and duration to indicate aspects of performance. These may be tempo indications, dynamic marks, technical instructions, marks for *phrasing and articulation, and designations for the character of the piece or section.

I. *Tempo.* Tempo marks indicate the speed, and frequently the character, of the music [see also Tempo]. The most commonly used terms are Italian: *grave* (very slow, serious), *largo* (broad), *lento* (slow), *adagio* (slow; literally, at ease), *andante* (literally, walking), *moderato* (moderate), *allegretto, allegro* (fast; literally, cheerful), *vivace* (lively), *presto* (very fast), *prestissimo* (as fast as possible). Gradual and relative changes of tempo are indicated by *ritardando,* abbreviated *rit.* (slowing), *accelerando* (quickening), and *più mosso* (faster).

Prior to the 17th century, tempo designations are rare. A few 10th-century treatises, among them **Musica enchiriadis,* note that pieces are to be performed in different manners, e.g., *morosus* (sadly), *cum celeritate* (with speed). Luis de Milán's vihuela book *El maestro* (Valencia, 1536) contains *apriessa* (quick), *a espacio* (slow), and longer instructions, e.g., "mas respecto a tañer de gala que no a servar compas" (more regard for playing with style than keeping time). Intended for a soloist, this work is a somewhat isolated example for the 16th century. In music of the 14th through 16th centuries, tempo is indicated principally by the mensuration signs and *proportions of *mensural notation in conjunction with the concept of **tactus* or fixed pulse [see Tempo].

In the early 17th century, *tardo* (slow), *presto* (fast), *lento, adagio,* and *allegro* appeared with increasing regularity in Italian and other music. Adriano Banchieri used numerous terms in his *Organo suonarino.* "La battaglia" (ed. of Venice, 1611) contains *allegro, adagio, presto e piano, adagio e vuoto,* and *piano e allegro;* the "Bizaria del primo tuono a Graduale col flauto" (ed. of Venice, 1622) contains *più presto* and *prestissimo. Tardo* and *presto* appear in the sonatas (Venice, 1626) of virtuoso violinist Biagio Marini.

Early tempo marks reflect new expressive musical styles and may have provided contrast to the expected *tempo giusto*—literally "correct tempo"—of earlier practice. The concept of a *tempo giusto* is discussed by Quantz (1752) and Malcolm (1721). Experienced musicianship seems to have been as much a factor as tempo markings; despite the often elaborate tempo directions given in mid-18th-century scores, Leopold Mozart (1756) asserts that "even if a composer endeavors to explain more clearly the speed required . . . one has to deduce it from the piece itself, and this it is by which the true worth of a musician can be recognized without fail." Bemetzrieder (1771, p. 69) succinctly states that "taste is the true metronome." Because of this, definitions of verbal tempo designations given by Purcell (1683), Sebastien de Brossard, Malcolm, Quantz, and Leopold Mozart, among others, are vague and somewhat inconsistent; for example, Brossard (1703) observes that the Italian term *assai,* which modifies markings of *allegro, adagio, presto,* etc., is defined by some as "much" and by others as "enough." Even the adoption of very specific tempo indications and metronome markings in the 19th century did not set authoritative and unchangeable performance speeds; composers often changed their minds and frequently appreciated a considerable range of tempos for a given work [see Metronome]. While this freer attitude is still found today, many composers designate desired speeds in exacting and unchanging detail.

Although Italian markings have predominated, non-Italian composers have always to some degree retained their vernaculars for musical terminology. During the late 17th and early 18th centuries, the French developed a system of terms as comprehensive as the Italian. During the 19th century, German terms were codified into an elaborate system as well.

Tempo marks have frequently designated aspects of a composition other than its speed. An 18th-century *adagio* frequently indicated an appropriate means of

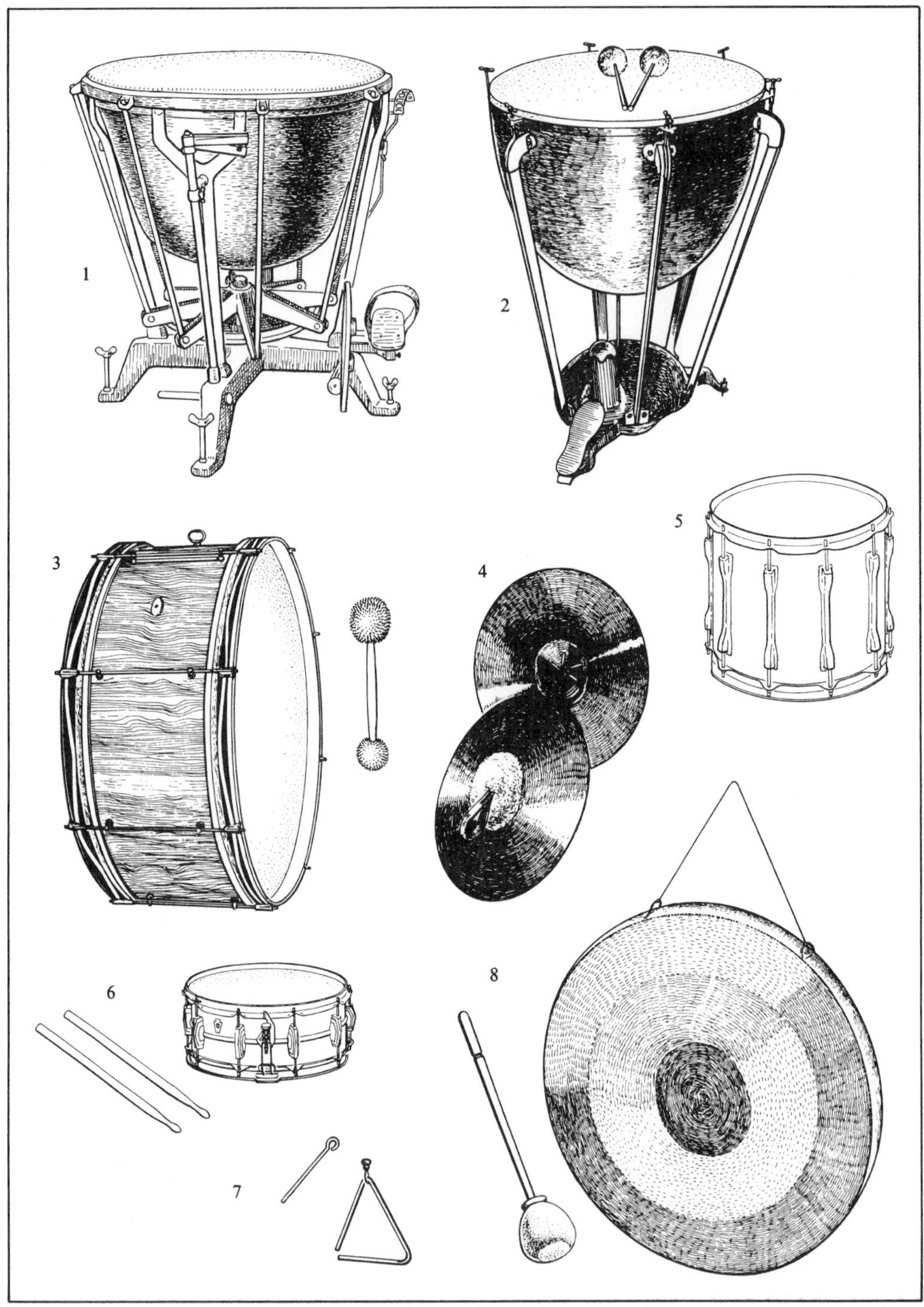

Percussion instruments: 1. Timpani: Ringer type. 2. Timpani: Professional model. 3. Bass drum. 4. Cymbals. 5. Tenor drum. 6. Snare drum. 7. Triangle. 8. Tam-tam.

Percussion instruments: 1. Glockenspiel. 2. Xylophone. 3. Marimba. 4. Crotales. 5. Celesta. 6. Tubular bells.

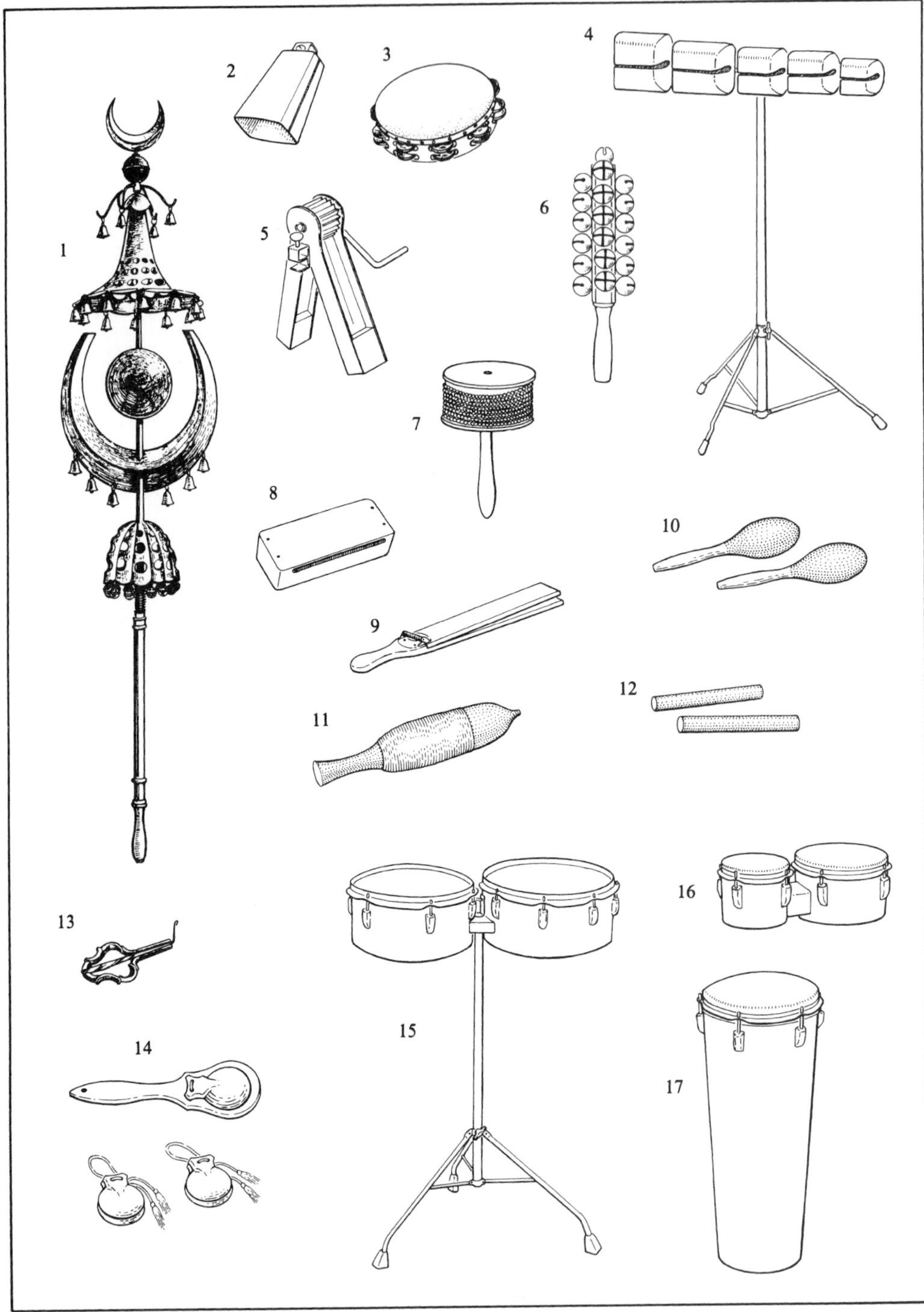

Percussion instruments (not all drawn to same scale): 1. Turkish crescent. 2. Cowbell. 3. Tambourine. 4. Temple blocks. 5. Ratchet. 6. Sleigh bells. 7. Cabaça. 8. Wood block. 9. Slapstick. 10. Maracas. 11. Güiro. 12. Claves. 13. Jew's harp. 14. Castanets. 15. Timbales. 16. Bongos. 17. Conga.

Drum set.

expression and style of improvised ornamentation. Conversely, markings like **gavotte* or **sarabanda,* both dances, implicitly suggested tempos, although, as usual, within broad limits. In music of the mid-18th century, the use of French and Italian terms, often in the same work, implies national stylistic characteristics of composition and performance. With the changed musical climate of the 19th century, most such distinctions were forgotten, and interpretations of tempo markings were considerably altered; an 18th-century *presto,* for example, is likely to have been considerably slower than its 19th-century counterpart.

II. *Dynamics.* Dynamic marks indicate degrees of loudness and are also customarily written in Italian, usually abbreviated: *pianissimo, pp* (very soft); *piano, p* (soft); *mezzo piano, mp* (moderately soft); *mezzo forte, mf* (moderately loud); *forte, f* (loud; literally, strong); *fortissimo, ff* (very loud). Continuous change from one degree of loudness to another may be specified by the terms *crescendo* (getting louder) and *diminuendo* or *decrescendo* (getting softer) or by the symbols < and >, respectively.

Dynamic changes were almost certainly a part of performance earlier, but, like tempos, only came to be notated with any regularity in the 17th century. Until the late 18th century, however, such notations were far from extensive. Isolated 16th-century examples may be found in the solo lute repertory; "Non ti spiqua l'ascoltar" in Vincenzo Capirola's lute manuscript of ca. 1517 contains the direction "tocca pian piano." Giovanni Gabrieli's *Sacrae symphoniae* (Venice, 1597) contains a *Sonata pian e forte.* "Echo" is found, for example, in Monteverdi's 1610 *Vespers.* In his *Polyhymnia caduceatrix* (Wolfenbüttel, 1619), Michael Praetorius observed that the markings *tutti, forte, piano, presto, lento,* and *adagio* "are in full use in Italy." Dynamic gradations were widely used as expressive devices and are discussed at length in Giulio Caccini's *Le nuove musiche* (Florence, 1601/2), where certain of them are termed *esclamazioni.* In the preface to his *Dialoghi e sonetti* (Rome, 1638), Domenico Mazzocchi writes "P., F., E., t, understood for Piano, Forte, Echo, and trill, are certainly common things, known to everyone." Mazzocchi indicates the gradual *crescendo* by the successive use of the terms *pianissimo, piano, forte,* reversing the order for *diminuendo.* His madrigals (Rome, 1638) contain the first examples of symbols for dynamic gradation: *C* for *crescendo,* which he terms **messa di voce,* and *V* for a *crescendo-diminuendo* on a single tone (a more usual form of *messa di voce*). Matthew Locke uses the phrase "lowder by degrees" in the "Curtain Tune" of *The Tempest* (1675); English music for viol consort often contains the indications "loud" and "soft," abbreviated "lo." and "so.," as does Thomas Mace's print, *Musick's Monument* (London, 1676). Giovanni Antonio Piani, in his sonatas for violin and basso continuo (Paris, 1712), was the first to indicate dynamic gradation with blackened wedges, the forerunners of the "hairpin" symbols still in use. The French usage of *fort* and *doux* (loud and soft) became common in mid-17th century.

III. *Other marks.* Further performance marks include verbal technical instructions, e.g., *con sordino* (play with mute), *tutti* (the whole ensemble plays), *arco* (play with the bow); symbols denoting *phrasing and articulation like slurs, dots, lines, accent symbols, wedges, terms like *sforzato, sf,* and strokes over notes—symbols that, like tempo designations, generally have rather different interpretations for different periods and styles; *fingerings for stringed and keyboard instruments, *tonguings for wind instruments, *bowings for stringed instruments, and pedalings for piano, all affecting articulation and phrasing; directions concerning the general character of a piece or section, e.g. *dolce* (sweet), *cantabile* (singing), *con spirito* (spirited), *sostenuto* (sustained), *marcato* (marked, emphasized). For the symbols employed, see Notation; for many of the terms mentioned here, see separate entries. See also Performance practice.

Bibl.: Sebastien de Brossard, *Dictionaire de musique* (Paris, 1703; facs., Amsterdam: Antiqua, 1964); trans. and ed. Albion Gruber, *MTT* 12 (1982). Alexander Malcolm, *A Treatise of Musick, Speculative, Practical, and Historical* (Edinburgh, 1721; facs., New York: Da Capo, 1970). James Grassineau, *A Musical Dictionary* [trans. of Brossard with some new material] (London, 1740; facs., *MMML* ser. 2, 40, 1966). Anton Bemetzrieder, *Leçons de claveçin, et principes d'harmonie* (Paris, 1771; facs., *MMML* ser. 2, 18, 1966). Heinrich Christoph Koch, *Musikalisches Lexicon* (Frankfurt am Main, 1802). Rosamund Evelyn Mary Harding, *Origins of Musical Time and Expression* (London: Oxford U Pr, 1938). Thurston Dart, *The Interpretation of Music* (London: Hutchinson, 1954; 4th ed., 1967). David D. Boyden, *The History of Violin Playing from Its Origins to 1761* (London: Oxford U Pr, 1965). Nicolas Temperley, "Tempo and Repeats in the Early Nineteenth Century," *ML* 47 (1966): 323–36. Robert Donington, *The Interpretation of Early Music, New Version* (London: Faber, 1974; corrected ed., 1977). William S. Newman, "Freedom of Tempo in Schubert's Instrumental Music," *MQ* 56 (1975): 528–45. See also Ornamentation, Theory.

Performance practice [Ger., *Aufführungspraxis*]. The conventions and knowledge that enable a performer to create a performance. In the context of notated music, performance practice is usually thought to encompass everything about performance that is not unambiguously specified in notation. This, however, implies a distinction that is not readily made between what is notated and what is not notated. All notation requires an informed reader for its realization, and thus all notation is fundamentally incomplete. In this respect, performance practice is equally important in written and oral musical traditions. The status of the concept *composition in Western art music has sometimes obscured this similarity among diverse musical cultures and thus among the methods of study appropriate to them [see also Transmission].

The aspects of performance specified in Western *notation have, in general, steadily increased since the beginnings of this system in the Middle Ages. Historically, the study of performance practice has concentrated on periods and repertories in which the gap between what was notated and what was thought necessary for a performance was greatest. The recent history of this study has seen the extent and importance of this gap recognized in repertories ever closer to the present.

Through the 16th century, musical notation omitted information of obvious importance for performance. Pitch began to be specified with precision in the 11th century; the foundations for current methods of notating rhythm were laid in the 13th century; and not until the 17th century were instrumentation and *performance marks regularly provided as a part of notation. In no case, however, did increased precision in notation result in self-sufficiency. Even in the domain of pitch, for example, the precision with which the name of a note is specified does not usually make explicit reference to the *tuning or *temperament in which the note is to be sounded.

Important topics in the study of performance practice for most periods through the 19th century have been *ornamentation and/or *improvisation, the changing character of musical instruments [see, e.g., Piano, Violin, Bow], tuning and temperament, the size and composition of ensembles [see, e.g., Orchestra, Chorus, Chapel (2)], *tempo, *articulation, *dynamics and other performance marks, and the nature of *voice production and *singing styles. Especially important for the music of the Middle Ages and Renaissance has been the investigation of the roles of voices and instruments, separately and together. Except in instrumental *tablatures, the notation of these periods does not usually specify which parts are to be sung and which, if any, played on instruments. Archival and iconographic research have attempted to discover the contexts in which voices and instruments were combined and the numbers of singers and types of instruments employed in specific repertories. Related to the preparation of *editions of early music but also forming a part of performance practice are **musica ficta* and text underlay [see Text and music]. For music of the Baroque period, ornamentation and improvisation [see also Thoroughbass] have been special concerns, and it was with respect to this repertory that the first significant strides were taken in the re-creation of historically appropriate instruments, especially the *harpsichord, *organ, *recorder, and *viol. Only since the 1960s have similar topics in the music of the Classical period been given widespread attention. This has led to the use of restorations or replicas of pianos and of stringed and wind instruments of the period and to the re-creation of orchestras of appropriate size. Related topics have since begun to be investigated for the 19th century as well, a period for which singing styles and vocal ornamentation have also been recognized as important subjects. In music of the 20th century, the domain of performance practice has expanded because of the widely divergent attitudes of composers toward the nature of the musical work and of performance [see Composition, Aleatory]. And even the most carefully notated *serial composition assumes the performer's knowledge of related works and the styles and techniques of performance appropriate to them—knowledge that is in large measure transmitted orally.

Bibl.: Mary Vinquist and Neal Zaslaw, *Performance Practice: A Bibliography* (New York: Norton, 1971). Benjamin Boretz and Edward T. Cone, eds., *Perspectives on Notation and Performance* (New York: Norton, 1976). Jean-Claude Veilhan, *Les règles de l'interprétation musicale à l'époque baroque (XVIIe–XVIIIe s.)* (Paris: Leduc, 1977; trans. Eng., 1979). Josef Mertin, *Alte Musik: Wege zur Aufführungspraxis* (Wien: E Lafite, 1978). Robert Donington, *Baroque Music: Style and Performance* (New York: Norton, 1982). Frederick Neumann, *Essays in Performance Practice* (Ann Arbor: UMI Res Pr, 1982). Jean Saint-Arroman, *L'interprétation de la musique française 1661–1789: I—Dictionnaire d'interprétation (initiation)* (Paris: H Champion, 1983). Gerard Béhague, ed., *Performance Practice: Ethnomusicological Perspectives* (Westport, Conn.: Greenwood, 1984). Stanley Boorman, ed., *Studies in the Performance of Late Medieval Music* (Cambridge: Cambridge U Pr, 1984). Timothy J. McGee, *Medieval and Renaissance Music: A Performer's Guide* (Toronto: U of Toronto Pr, 1985). Robin Stowell, *Violin Technique and Performance Practice in the Late Eighteenth and Early Nineteenth Centuries* (Cambridge: Cambridge U Pr, 1985). Christopher Page, *Voices and Instruments of the Middle Ages: Instrumental Practice and Songs in France, 1100–1300* (Berkeley: U of Cal Pr, 1986). Laurence Dreyfus, *Bach's Continuo Group: Players and Practices in His Vocal Works* (Cambridge, Mass.: Harvard U Pr, 1987). George Houle, *Meter in Music, 1600–1800: Performance, Perception, and Notation* (Bloomington: Ind U Pr, 1987). Roland Jackson, *Performance Practice, Medieval to Contemporary: A Bibliographical Guide* (New York: Garland, 1988). Nicholas Kenyon, ed., *Authenticity and Early Music* (Oxford: Oxford U Pr, 1988). William S. Newman, *Beethoven on Beethoven: Playing His Piano Music His Way* (New York: Norton, 1988). Sandra P. Rosenblum, *Performance Practices in Classic Piano Music: Their Principles and Applications* (Bloomington: Ind U Pr, 1988). Frederick Neumann, *New Essays on Performance Practice* (Ann Arbor: UMI Res Pr, 1989). Neal Zaslaw, *Mozart's Symphonies: Context, Performance Practice, Reception* (Oxford: Clarendon, 1989). Howard Mayer Brown and Stanley Sadie, eds., *Performance Practice: Music before 1600* and *Performance Practice: Music after 1600* (New York: Norton, 1990). John Butt, *Bach Interpretation: Articulation Marks in Primary Sources of J. S. Bach* (Cambridge: Cambridge U Pr, 1990). Peter Le Huray, *Authenticity in Performance: Eighteenth-Century Case Studies* (Cambridge: Cambridge U Pr, 1990). R. Larry Todd and Peter Williams, eds., *Perspectives on Mozart Performance* (Cambridge: Cambridge U Pr, 1991). Mary Cyr, *Performing Baroque Music* (Portland, Ore.: Amadeus, 1992). Barry Millington and Stewart Spencer, eds., *Wagner in Performance* (New Haven: Yale U Pr, 1992). Robert Philip, *Early Recordings and Musical Style: Changing Tastes in Instrumental Performance, 1900–1950* (Cambridge: Cambridge U Pr, 1992). Frederick Neumann, *Performance Practices of the Seventeenth and Eighteenth Centuries* (New York: Schirmer, 1993). Robin Stowell, ed., *Performing Beethoven* (Cambridge: Cambridge U Pr, 1994). Richard Taruskin, *Text and Act: Essays on Music and Performance* (Oxford: Oxford U Pr, 1995). Michael Burden, ed., *Performing the Music of Henry Purcell* (Oxford: Clarendon, 1996). Stewart Carter, ed., *A Performer's Guide to Seventeenth-Century Music* (New York: Schirmer, 1997). Bernard Harrison, *Haydn's Keyboard Music: Studies in Performance Practice* (Oxford: Oxford U Pr, 1997). James R. Briscoe, *Debussy in Performance* (New Haven: Yale U Pr, 1999). Clive Brown, *Classical and Romantic Performing Practice, 1750–1900* (Oxford: Oxford U Pr, 1999). Colin Lawson and Robin Stowell, *The Historical Performance of Music: An Introduction* (Cambridge: Cambridge U Pr, 1999). Ross Duffin, ed., *A Performer's Guide to Medieval Music* (Bloomington: Ind U Pr, 2000).

Performance right. See Copyright and performance right.

Périchole, La. Comic opera in two acts by Offenbach (French libretto by Henri Meilhac and Ludovic Halévy, after a play by Mérimée), produced in Paris in 1868, and in a three-act revision, in 1874. Setting: Peru.

Pericón [Sp.]. See *Media caña.*

Period. (1) A complete musical utterance, defined in tonal music by arrival at a cadence on some harmony that does not immediately require further resolution. In this sense, which is necessarily somewhat flexible, the musical term corresponds to the sentence (or period) in language. In the music of the late 18th and early 19th centuries especially, a period usually consists of two *phrases (an *antecedent and a consequent), each of which may be made up of still shorter subphrases. Periods may be joined to form larger periods (perhaps constituting a section of a movement) and whole movements or forms. The term was used in a much broader way by Wagner, who regarded the musico-poetic period governed by a central tonality as the fundamental component of form in the music drama.

(2) A musical element that is in some way repeated. This sense is derived from the period of periodic motion, e.g., in acoustics. It is sometimes conflated with sense (1) in referring to a well-defined passage or formal element that is repeated in the course of a larger form. Otherwise, and especially in the context of *serial music, it may be applied to the units of any parameter of music that embody repetitions at any level.

Bibl.: Leonard G. Ratner, "Eighteenth-Century Theories of Musical Period Structure," *MQ* 42 (1956): 439–54. Carl Dahlhaus, "Periode," *Riemann Musiklexikon.*

Periodicals. Publications issued at regular or irregular intervals. Music periodicals may include articles giving the results of recent research, news of current events, reviews of books, music, and recordings, lists of recent publications, editorials, letters to the editor, obituaries, and advertisements. Most music periodicals are issued either by societies, which may use them for announcements and reports, or by music publishers, which may use their periodicals to promote their publications.

Few contributors to music periodicals are paid, and the editorial staffs are by and large made up of volunteers. These facts, combined with the relatively small market, often result in delays, cessations, or suspensions of publication; mergers; and changes of title and frequency of publication, all of which may complicate bibliographic citations. An index may exist for a single volume or for an entire periodical, but general indexing is limited to (a) *The Music Index* (Detroit: Information Service, 1949–), which favors more popular and American publications; (b) *RILM Abstracts of Music Literature* (Flushing, N.Y., 1967–), which includes brief abstracts and has international coverage; and (c) *Bibliographie des Musikschrifttums* (Leipzig: Staatliches Institut für deutsche Musikforschung, 1936–39; Frankfurt a/M: Institut für Musikforschung, 1950/51–), which includes books as well as periodicals and favors German literature and is chronically behind.

There are several interesting developments in the world of music periodicals—one is the *International Index to Nineteenth-Century Music Periodicals* known by the acronym for its French title *(RIPM)*. This series of calendars to important 19th-century periodical literature is now available both in paper and via a web subscription. JSTOR, the Mellon Foundation–funded effort to make long runs of important scholarly periodicals available electronically, will soon publish its first segment of music periodicals. At the same time *RILM* will add restrospective indexing of these titles to its online index.

I. *History.* The periodic issuance of music preceded what is commonly accepted as the first music periodical, Johann Mattheson's *Critica musica* (Hamburg, 1722–25). Mattheson's work and the later periodicals of Lorenz Mizler, Johann Adolph Scheibe, and Friedrich Wilhelm Marpurg, all appearing in the first half of the 18th century, are one-man commentaries on a variety of topics. The popularization of art during the Enlightenment led to public concerts, increased amateur music making and music publishing, and consequently to a market for periodicals emphasizing current events. Such a work, directed at the amateur, was Johann Adam Hiller's *Wöchentliche Nachrichten* (Leipzig, 1766–70). By the end of the century, periodicals on current events in music were being issued in most of the European countries. Modern periodicals, calling on an array of contributors and containing articles, reviews, and current events, began with the *Allgemeine musikalische Zeitung* (Leipzig, 1798–1848; 1863–68) in Germany, *Revue musicale* (Paris, 1827–35) and *Le ménestrel* (Paris, 1833–1940) in France, and *The Musical World* (London, 1836–91) and *The Musical Times* (London, 1844–) in England. The first American periodical was *The Euterpeiad* (1820–23), which featured current events in Boston; a more substantial work with wider interests was *Dwight's Journal of Music* (Boston, 1852–81). The establishment of musicology in the second half of the 19th century led to periodicals emphasizing research articles, first in Germany with Friedrich Chrysander's *Jahrbücher für musikalische Wissenschaft* (Leipzig, 1863, 1867) and Robert Eitner's *Monatshefte für Musikgeschichte* (Berlin, 1869–83; Leipzig, 1884–1905), then in other countries as musicological societies were formed. Today current events continue as a feature, but periodicals dealing with particular subjects, genres, or media—already in evidence in the second half of the 19th century—predominate.

Bibl.: Imogen Fellinger, *Verzeichnis der Musikzeitschriften des 19. Jahrhunderts* (Regensburg: Bosse, 1968; "Nachträge" in *FAM* beginning with 17 [1970]: 7–8). Charles E. Lindahl, regular section on periodicals in *Notes* beginning with 32 (1976): 558–66; since 1983, Stephen Fry. Joan M. Meggett, *Music Periodical Literature: An Annotated Bibliography of Indexes and Bibliographies* (Metuchen, N.J.: Scarecrow, 1978). Charles Lindahl, "Music Periodicals in U.S. Research Libraries in 1931: A Retrospective Survey," *Notes* 37 (1981): 864–70. Linda I. Solow, "Index to 'Music Periodicals' Reviewed in *Notes* (1976–1982)," *Notes* 39 (1983): 585–90. Imogen Fellinger, *Periodica musicalia: 1789–1830* (Regensburg: G Bosse, 1986). *International Music Journals,* ed. Linda M. Fidler and Richard S. James (New York: Greenwood, 1990).

H.E.S., rev. L.C.

Permutation fugue. A type of fugue or fugal passage, often found in the choral works of Bach, in which every voice enters with the same succession of a number of musical ideas equal to the number of voices, the second idea in each voice serving to accompany the first in the succeeding voice, etc. The result is that successive entries, especially the last, are marked by a permutation among the voices of material already heard. Often two expositions of this type, the second in a new key, follow one another without interruption (e.g., "Lasset uns den nicht zerteilen" from Bach's *St. John Passion*).

Perpetual canon. See Canon.

Perpetuum mobile [Lat., perpetual motion; It. *moto perpetuo*]. A composition in which rhythmic motion, often in a single note-value at rapid tempo, is continuous from beginning to end. Among composers who have used the term as a title for such a piece are Paganini (op. 11), Weber (Piano Sonata op. 24, last movement), Mendelssohn (op. 119), and Johann Strauss, Jr. (op. 257). The technique is also encountered in some Chopin etudes, and in the finale of Ravel's Violin Sonata (1923–27).

Perséphone. A *melodrama in three scenes for speaker, tenor, choruses, and orchestra by Stravinsky, after a poem by André Gide, first performed in Paris in 1934 and revised in 1949.

Persia. See Near and Middle East.

Pes [Lat.]. (1) *Podatus* [see Neume]. (2) In some medieval English polyphony, the tenor part. In *"Sumer is icumen in," the term is applied to the two lower parts.

Pesante [It.]. Weighty, with emphasis.

Peter and the Wolf [Russ. *Petya i volk*]. A work for small orchestra and narrator by Prokofiev, op. 67 (1936), in which each of the characters of the children's story being narrated is associated with a specific instrument and tune.

Peter Grimes. Opera in a prologue and three acts by Britten (libretto by Montagu Slater, after George Crabbe's poem "The Borough"), produced in London in 1945. Setting: the Borough, a fishing village on the east coast of England, about 1830.

Petit jeu [Fr.]. The full sound of the *Positif* of the classical French organ, including flue ranks at 8′, 4′, and 2′, with **Cymbale* and **Fourniture.*

Petrushka. Ballet by Stravinsky (choreography by Michel Fokine), produced in Paris in 1911 by Diaghilev's Ballets russes. It was revised in 1946.

Peu [Fr.]. Little; *un peu,* a little; *peu à peu,* little by little.

Peyote music. Songs accompanying ceremonies of the Peyote religion, which was widely adopted by North American Indians in the 19th and 20th centuries. Accompanied by water-filled kettledrum and rattle, the melodies have rhythmic intricacy, sequential variation, and texts of special but meaningless syllable groups. They are easily distinguished from other Indian music.

Bibl.: David P. McAllester, *Peyote Music* (New York: Viking, 1949). B.N.

Pezzo [It.]. Piece, composition.

Pf. (1) Abbr. for pianoforte, i.e., the piano. (2) Abbr. for the dynamics *piano* followed immediately by *forte.*

Pfeife [Ger.]. Fife, pipe, organ pipe.

Phagotus, phagotum [Lat.; It. *fagotto*]. A bellows-blown bagpipe of low pitch invented early in the 16th century by Afranio degli Albonesi and illustrated in a book by his nephew Teseo Ambrosiano in 1539.

Phantasie [Ger.]. *Fantasia. Related terms or titles include *Phantasiestücke* (Fantasy Pieces; Schumann, opp. 12, 111) and *Phantasiebilder* (Fantasy Pictures; Schumann, *Faschingsschwank aus Wien* op. 26); *phantasieren,* to improvise.

Phantasy. The title of one-movement works composed for the Cobbet competitions, established in England in 1905. Winners of the competition include Ralph Vaughan Williams, Frank Bridge, John Ireland, and Herbert Howells.

Phasing. A technique developed by Steve Reich in which two subgroups of an ensemble begin by playing the same rhythmic pattern, but with one gradually accelerating until, after a period of being "out of phase," the two are again playing the pattern simultaneously or "in phase." His works incorporating the technique include *Piano Phase* (1967), *Four Organs* (1970), and *Drumming* (1971).

Philharmonic [fr. *phil-,* loving, plus *harmonic,* related to music]. A name taken by various kinds of musical organizations, especially *orchestras. An early example is the Accademia filarmonica of Verona, founded in 1543.

Philippines. See Southeast Asia VII.

Phoebus and Pan. See *Streit zwischen Phöbus und Pan.*

Phonograph. See Recording.

Phonola. See Pianola.

Phorminx [Gr.]. A stringed instrument of ancient Greece, probably a *kithara. It is mentioned often by Homer.

Phrase. By analogy with language, a unit of musical syntax, usually forming part of a larger, more complete unit sometimes termed a *period. A phrase is the product, in varying degrees, of melody, harmony, and rhythm and concludes with a moment of relative tonal and/or rhythmic stability such as is produced by a *cadence. Phrases may also be defined by the repetition of a rhythmic pattern or melodic contour. In tonal music generally, phrases are often composed of multiples of two measures, and in the late 18th and early 19th centuries, the four-measure phrase became especially common. When a phrase is constructed so as to require response or resolution by a following phrase, the two are said to be *antecedent and consequent phrases, respectively. Often pairs of phrases are joined at more than one level to produce a hierarchy: e.g., four pairs of two-measure phrases may form two pairs of four-measure phrases, which in turn form a pair of eight-measure phrases. In such a context, the boundary between what constitutes a phrase as distinct from a larger period is necessarily informal. Elements shorter than the shortest phrase are termed *motives. The analysis of phrase structure in this way has often been a tool of style analysis. The most extended early discussions of the subject occur in Joseph Riepel's *Anfangsgründe zur musicalischen Setzkunst,* vol. 2: *Grundregeln zur Tonordnung insgemein* (1755), and Heinrich Christoph Koch's *Versuch einer Anleitung zur Composition* (Rudolstadt and Leipzig, 1782–93; partial Eng. trans. by Nancy Kovaleff Baker, New Haven: Yale U Pr, 1983). Among the most elaborate of more recent theories of phrase structure are those of Hugo Riemann in his *Musikalische Dynamik und Agogik: Lehrbuch der musikalische Phrasierung* (Hamburg and St. Petersburg, 1884) and *Vademecum der Phrasierung* (Leipzig: M Hesse, 1900; 5th ed., Berlin: M Hesse, 1923, as *Handbuch der Phrasierung*). See also Phrasing.

Phrasing. The realization, in performance, of the *phrase structure of a work; the phrase structure itself. The realization of phrase structure is largely a function of the performer's *articulation. Apart from rests, musical notation employs a variety of symbols as guides to phrasing, principally an arc above the staff, similar to a *slur and termed a phrase mark, an apostrophe or comma placed above the staff to indicate a breathing *pause, and two short parallel lines inclined slightly to the right and crossing the top line of the staff to indicate a *caesura or brief interruption of the musical line. In music for the piano, the use of the damper pedal is crucial to phrasing, and the notation of its use is thus sometimes a guide to phrasing as well.

Although guides to phrasing can be found in notation as early as Emilio de' Cavalieri's *Rappresentatione di Anima, et di Corpo* (Rome, 1600) and François Couperin's *Pièces de claveçin,* bks. 3 and 4 (Paris, 1722, 1730), indications of phrasing, as distinct from the articulation of one or a few notes, are not common in notation until well into the 19th century. Many late 19th- and 20th-century editions (especially those of Hugo Riemann) of music of the Baroque and Classical periods, however, include extensive use of phrase marks that represent almost exclusively the opinions of the editors. This has created a demand for so-called *Urtext* editions in which such supplementary signs have not been added, since interpreters will naturally differ over the precise nature of the phrase structure in many works. See also Notation, Performance practice.

Bibl.: Hermann Keller, *Phrasierung und Artikulation* (Kassel: Bärenreiter, 1955); trans. Eng. Leigh Gerdine (New York: Norton, 1965). Robert Donington, *The Interpretation of Early Music* (London: Faber, 1963; new rev. ed., New York: Norton, 1992). Edward W. Murphy, "Bruckner's Use of Numbers to Indicate Phrase Lengths," *Bruckner-Jahrbuch* 11 (1990): 39–52. Lewis E. Peterman, Jr., "Michel Blavet's Breathing Marks: A Rare Source for Musical Phrasing in Eighteenth-Century France," *Performance Practice Review* 4 (1991): 186–98. Antony Pay, "Phrasing in Contention," *EM* 24 (1996): 291–321.

Phrygian. See Mode, Cadence, Greece I, 3 (ii).

Physharmonica. (1) An antecedent of the *harmonium. (2) In pipe organs, a free reed stop with resonators.

Piacere, a [It.]. At the pleasure of the performer, especially as regards tempo and the use of *rubato.

Piacevole [It.]. Pleasing, agreeable.

Piangendo [It.]. Crying, plaintive.

Pianino [It.]. A small, upright piano.

Pianissimo [It., abbr. *pp*]. Very soft [see Performance marks].

Piano. (1) [It., abbr. *p*] Soft [see Performance marks].

(2) [Fr., It., Sp.; Eng. also pianoforte; Ger. also *Klavier, Hammerklavier,* Rus., Pol. *fortepiano;* fr. It. *pianoforte* or *fortepiano,* soft-loud, loud-soft]. A large stringed keyboard instrument. Its *keyboard is a set of wooden levers attached to the *action, which together operate a system of hammers. The player's fingers press the keys, which move the action levers, driving the hammers to strike tuned strings stretched over one or more wooden bridges glued to a large wooden plate, the *soundboard. The strings vibrate at pretuned pitches. The bridge conveys the vibrations to the soundboard, which amplifies them by the vibration of its entire expanse.

Modern pianos come in two shapes, the grand and the upright. In the wing-shaped grand piano [Fr. *piano à queue,* Ger. *Flügel,* It. *pianoforte a coda,* Sp. *piano de cola*], the strings and soundboard are contained in a horizontal case, and the hammers strike the strings from below [Fig. 2]. The wider keyboard end is about 1.4–1.5 m (4 ft. 7 in. to 4 ft. 11 in.) with the standard musical range of seven and one-third octaves (88 keys), A_2 to c''''' (some have ranges up to 8 octaves, C_1 to c''''', with correspondingly greater widths). The length varies from under 1.5 m (4 ft. 11 in.) for a "baby" grand to about 2.75 m (9 ft.) for a standard concert grand (2.9 m., or 9 ft. 6 in., for eight-octave instruments—one manufacturer makes a grand of 3.1 m, or 10 ft. 2 in.). Upright pianos have the same standard range (a few are smaller), but the action must suit the vertical arrangement of strings, soundboard, and case. The upright action is a more complex mechanical problem than the grand's. Uprights range from spinets, less than 1 m in height (36–38 in.—few are now being made) to larger consoles, studios, and up-

Fig. 1. Grand piano.

rights, about 1 m (3 ft. 5 in.) to 1.3 m (4 ft. 4 in.) in height.

The piano's capacity to vary the volume of its tones depends on the fact that the hammers are not pushed against the strings but are flung in free flight and bounce away. The hammer's speed toward the string determines the volume of sound. In a well-regulated action, the weight of the player's finger on the key is precisely proportional to the loudness of the sound. The action's leverage ratio allows a relatively light touch to produce the sound, usually between 45 and 55 grams (1.45 to 1.77 ounces). The key's movement raises a *damper from the string, which falls back on the key's release.

Piano tone is expected to be rich and mellow but clear, with well-defined attack and adequate sustaining. Tone quality depends on several factors, principally the material and hardness of the hammers and the quality and design of the stringing. Well into the 19th century, wooden hammers were covered in leather, ordinarily deerskin. Other coverings were occasionally tried, but during the 1820s Henri Pape's experiments introduced felt as an adequate alternative to leather. Leather hardens and cracks over time and must be replaced. Repeated blows against strings compact felt and groove it, necessitating reshaping and loosening. The harder the hammer's material, the more strident the tone becomes. If it is too soft, the tone is ill-defined and "fuzzy."

String tone is determined by the combination of *pitch, *duration, and *timbre. Pitch is preestablished by the length of the string, the tension with which it is struck, and its mass. The shorter the string, the higher its tension, and the smaller its diameter, the higher the pitch. None of these qualities can be altered during playing. Duration, or sustain, depends principally on the tension of the wire, and the cast-iron frame on

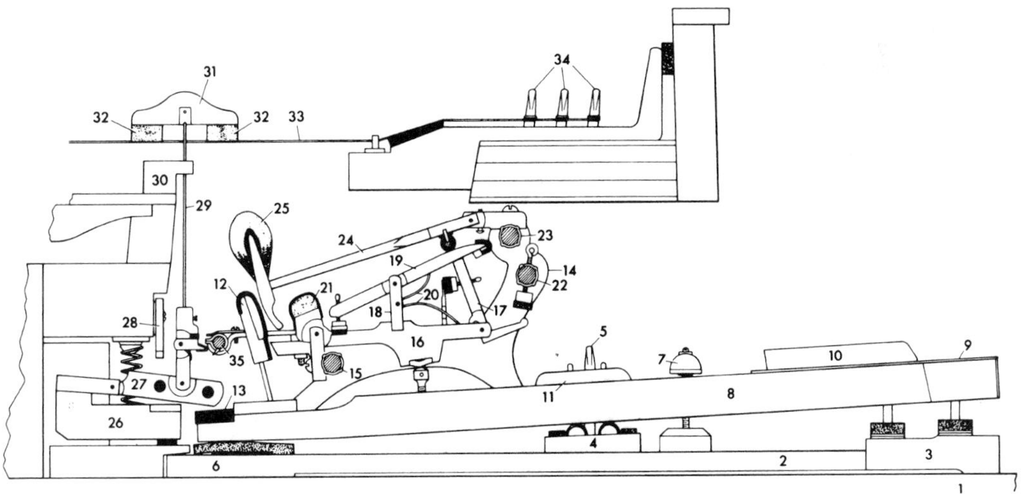

Fig. 2. Cross section of modern grand piano action. 1. Keybed. 2. Keyframe. 3. Front rail. 4. Balance rail. 5. Balance rail stud. 6. Back rail. 7. Key stop rail. 8. White key. 9. Key covering. 10. Black key. 11. Key button. 12. Back Check. 13. Underlever key cushion. 14. Action hanger. 15. Support rail. 16. Support. 17. Fly. 18. Support top flange. 19. Balancer. 20. Repetition spring. 21. Hammer rest. 22. Regulating rail. 23. Hammer rail. 24. Hammer shank. 25. Hammer. 26. Underlever frame. 27. Underlever. 28. Damper stop rail. 29. Damper wire. 30. Damper guide rail. 31. Damper head. 32. Damper felts. 33. String. 34. Tuning pin. 35. Sostenuto rod. (Courtesy of Steinway & Sons)

which the strings are stretched allows high tension. The tone of loosely stretched wire "decays" (fades away) quickly.

Timbre, "tone quality" itself, is a function of the kinds of vibration the string undergoes. A string vibrates in a number of modes simultaneously. It vibrates as a whole at the rate of its fundamental pitch, but it also vibrates in segments: halves, which give a pitch an octave above the fundamental; thirds, sounding a fifth higher than that; quarters, an octave above the half; fifths, a major third above the quarter, and so on [see Harmonics (1) for a partial list of these vibrations]. Acoustical science calls these higher tones overtones or harmonics, but on a piano they are best called partials. The pitches of the partials, theoretically infinite in number, form part of what we hear when a note is played, and the relative strengths among them are the major determinative of tone quality. If the highest partials are relatively too strong, the sound is hard and strident, if relatively too weak, the sound is dull and hollow.

The violinist or flutist can modify pitch with finger or mouth, but keyboard-instrument players cannot alter pitches during playing. In addition, the scales and musical keys used in Western music have some mathematical peculiarities that prevent all the *intervals in pianos from being pure. Tuners work to produce somewhat out-of-tune intervals that are acceptable to the ear. This is *temperament, and it has various types. Early keyboards were tuned mostly in "mean-tone" temperaments, where keys with up to about three sharps or flats were nicely in tune and the others sounded more or less sour. Most familiar today is "equal temperament," in which the 12 notes of the chromatic scale are tuned in a constant ratio to one another. Before equal temperament became the norm, "well temperaments" allowed more pleasing tuning for more keys than mean-tone temperaments, but some keys remained slightly jarring. J. S. Bach's *Well-Tempered Clavier* probably assumed not equal temperament but well temperaments of various kinds. In any case, it is ironically the fact that well-tuned pianos are inevitably out of tune to an extent that only well-trained ears can hear.

The piano began its career in a Medici palace in Florence, where Bartolomeo Cristofori (1655–1732) was harpsichord maker to Ferdinando (1663–1713), prince of Tuscany. In 1700 an inventory of Ferdinando's musical instruments described "An *arpicimbalo* of Bartolomeo Cristofori, of new invention, which produces soft [It. *piano*] and loud [It. *forte*]." The description mentions "hammers, which produce the soft and loud," making it clear that the *arpicimbalo* was a piano. Earlier stringed keyboard instruments with hammers did not succeed. Cristofori can, therefore, be designated—as he designated himself—the piano's inventor. Various names for the instrument boiled down to *pianoforte* or *fortepiano* (now conventionally an instrument from the early 19th century or before), and they were ultimately shortened to piano.

Cristofori made *harpsichords and *clavichords, and we cannot know his motivation to design the hammer-driven piano. He claimed to have done it without help from anyone. His piano looked like a harpsichord, but it embodied the completely new principle of tone production, in which the hammer was propelled in free flight to the string. Scipione Maffei (1675–1755) described and praised the instrument's qualities and gave a somewhat crude action diagram in an Italian journal in 1711. The actions in the three surviving Cristofori pianos (1720, Metropolitan Museum, New York; 1722, National Museum of Musical Instruments, Rome; 1726, Musical Instrument Museum, University of Leipzig, Germany) are wonders of mechanical design. Cristofori modified several parts of the instrument from the usual harpsichord construction: strings were heavier, the harpsichord jacks were altered to become the dampers, and several new aspects of bracing were introduced, because the hammer blows put more strain on the entire mechanism. Cristofori brilliantly solved all the problems of a hammer-action stringed keyboard instrument except

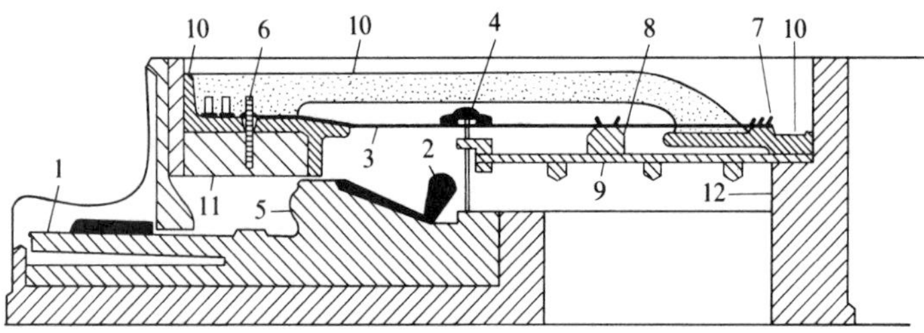

Fig. 3. Cross section of typical modern grand piano. Early instruments are similar but lack the iron frame. (Action details are shown in Fig. 2.) Key (1) propels hammer (2) to string (3) and lifts damper (4) via action mechanism (5). Vibrations of string, stretched from tuning pin (6) to hitch pin (7), pass via bridge (8) into soundboard (9). Iron frame (10) carries tension of strings, positioning pin block (11), and rim of wooden frame and case (12).

Fig. 4. Fortepiano, an early form of the piano.

one: a way to raise all the dampers at once. But the music of the time neither expected nor needed a solution to that problem. In 1732, the year of Cristofori's death, Lodovico Giustini (1685–1743) published the first music specifically for the "harpsichord with soft and loud," 12 sonatas dedicated to the prince of Portugal.

During the 1720s, Cristofori pianos came to the royal court of Portugal, where Domenico Scarlatti (1685–1757) certainly knew them, and, with the removal of Princess Maria Barbara to Spain in about 1730, Madrid came to know them. In 1725, Maffei's article was translated in Germany, and Gottfried Silbermann (1683–1753), a Dresden instrument maker, succeeded by the 1740s in making pianos. He must have studied a Cristofori instrument, as his actions, like those of early pianos from strong Spanish and Portuguese traditions, are exactly like the actions in Cristofori pianos.

Others claimed invention. In 1716, Jean Marius's (d. 1720) designs for "mallet harpsichords" submitted to the French Royal Academy of Sciences were approved, though he made no instruments. Christoph Gottlieb Schröter (1699–1782) submitted action designs to the elector of Saxony in 1721, expecting that an instrument would be built. It never happened, and Schröter later claimed that Silbermann stole his idea.

Both Marius and Schröter heard Pantaleon Hebenstreit (1669–1750), a popular virtuoso on a huge *hammer dulcimer [Ger. *Hackbrett*]. Hebenstreit played expressively, with swells and diminuendos, and achieved an impressive wash of sound with his undamped strings. The instrument came to be named "pantalon." Sometime during the 1720s, people thought of attaching a keyboard to the pantalon, and in 1731, Wahl Friedrich Fickern (or Ficker, fl. 1730s) announced in Leipzig the *Clavir-Cymbal,* which he claimed had the musical attributes of Hebenstreit's instrument. Keyboard pantalons were much easier to play than the *Hackbrett.* They usually had bare wood or horn hammers, sometimes a second set of cloth- or leather-covered hammers, and hand-stops to moderate the bright, hard tone. Many were shaped like clavichords. A number of instruments thought to be square pianos of the middle to late 18th century are actually pantalons. It was a type of piano, with a hammer action and usually metal strings, but its aesthetic was different from that tracing to Cristofori.

The latter 18th century saw many square (actually rectangular) pianos derived partly from the clavichord, typically with a five-octave range, tiny leather hammers, and somewhat rudimentary actions, but, like pantalons, with hand-operated damper stops and other ways of softening or shortening the tone. These instruments were probably invented by 1766 by Johannes Zumpe (1726–90), a German immigrant to London, who became rich making squares, many of which survive. Intended mainly for the drawing rooms of wealthy homes, the piano was still an upper-class artifact.

The growing interest of professional musicians in the piano led to its increasingly displacing the harpsichord as the preferred stringed keyboard instrument for public performance. The earliest known public performance was by Johann Baptist Schmid (dates unknown) in 1763 in Vienna. Two types of wing-shaped pianos (first called grand in an English patent, 1777) came to predominate, one mainly in England and France, the other in Austria and Germany. Their principal difference lay in the actions and in the stringing. The action diagrams [see A, B, C in Fig. 5] demonstrate the designs. The Continental (usually called Viennese) is much the lighter of the two and most unlike the Cristofori action. The English design, perhaps derived from Silbermann's version of Cristofori's action, is heavier, with a deeper dip of the key. The English grands typically had three strings for each note, where the German and Austrian ones had only two. The sound of the English pianos was bigger and often coarser than the small, clear sound of the German instruments. Mozart (1765–91) was the foremost exponent of the German-type grand, which had been designed first by Johann Andreas Stein (1728–92) in Augsburg. Mozart wrote to his father from Augsburg in 1777 praising Stein's pianos. Stein's children, Matthäus Andreas (1776–1842) and Nannette Stein Streicher (1769–1833), became influential piano makers in Vienna, along with Anton Walter (1752–1826), one of whose pianos Mozart owned (still in the Mozarteum in Salzburg). The pianist-composer Muzio Clementi (1752–1832), later a piano maker in Lon-

Fig. 5. Piano actions. In these simplified drawings, moving parts are shown in outline; shaded areas are fixed members; solid black is cloth, felt, or leather.

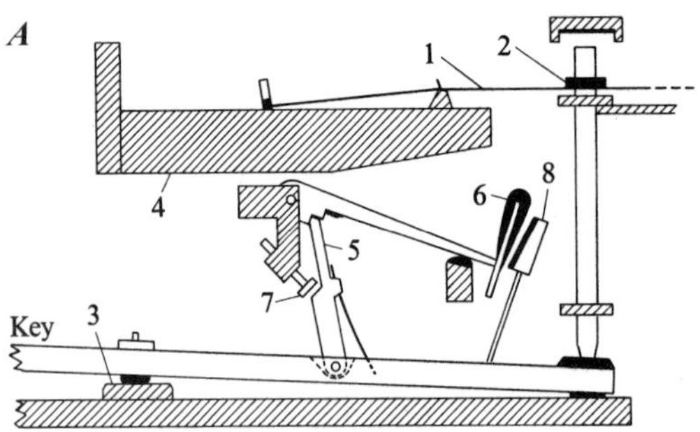

A: English grand action. (1) string; (2) damper; (3) balance rail; (4) pin block. When key is pressed, jack (5) drives hammer (6) until disengaged near end of stroke by set-off button (7). Hammer fall is stopped by back check (8), raised by key motion. When key is released, hammer falls and jack reengages notch.

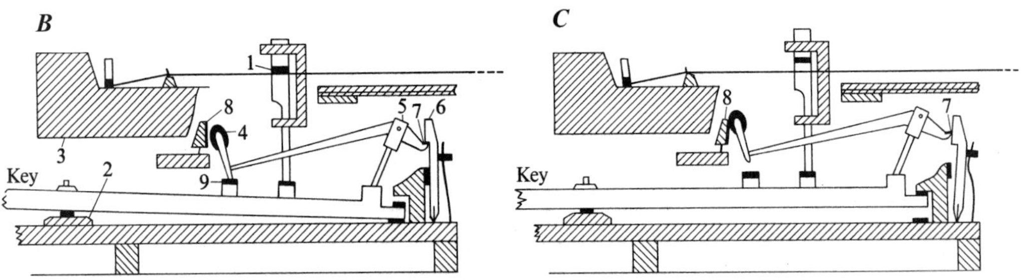

Viennese action: *B:* (1) damper; (2) balance rail; (3) pink block. Key raises hammer (4) via pivot in fork or *Kapsel* (5). Beak (7) slips free of overhang on hopper (6) just before hammer strikes string. *C:* Head of hammer falls, stopping on back check (8), having shifted left while pivoting about balance point at (2). On release, beak reengages hopper (6); hammer head is freed and falls to rest (9).

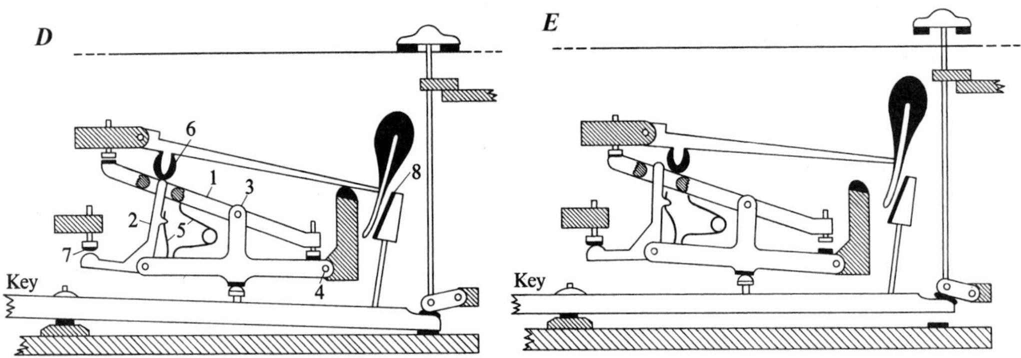

Erard/modern action. *D:* Key at rest. Repetition lever (1) and jack (2) pivot on carrier (3); whole assembly pivots at (4). Jack passes through a rectangular hole in repetition lever (shown cut away). Springs at (5) bear clockwise on (1) and (2). When carrier (3) is slightly raised, repetition lever (1), supported by spring, lifts hammer via roller (6). After partial stroke, left end of repetition lever is stopped; continuing stroke carries jack and carrier upward, compressing spring and lifting right end off position stop at (4). Jack rises until arm is stopped at (7), which snaps other end clear of roller (6) just before note sounds. *E:* When hammer falls as key is held, roller contacts repetition lever. With sufficient momentum on strongly played notes, hammer will force repetition lever down against spring, and hammer head will be caught by back check (8). Slight key release lets jack reengage roller; back check releases hammer. Repetition is now possible from a range of release depths: quicker from partial release, most powerful from full release.

don, was the major influence on players of the English grand, demanding techniques appropriate to its heavier action and larger sound. John Broadwood (1732–1812) founded an enormously successful company and dominated the English and French market.

As the 19th century opened, two other shapes of pianos were emerging, both vertical. "Pyramid" pianos, tall, symmetrical instruments known from the mid-18th century, gave way in England to tall, rectangular instruments, grand pianos standing upright and occupying wall space instead of floor space. In Germany and Austria the favored tall upright was the "giraffe," whose case shape followed that of the grand, with a curved side. About 1800 Matthias Müller (c. 1770–1844) in Germany and John Isaac Hawkins (1772–1855) in the U.S. simultaneously designed small uprights, barely 1.4–1.55 m (4 ft. 6 in. to 5 ft. 1 in.) high, but neither influenced others. Shorter uprights began to appear around 1810–15, especially those of Robert Wornum (1780–1852), whose "cottage pianos" with a newly designed action facilitated the piano's move to more modest homes. As the Industrial Revolution gathered momentum, a middle class acquiring cultural aspirations was a ripe market for the instrument. Though the square continued until about 1860 in Europe and until the turn of the 20th century in America, increasingly the upright displaced it in most homes. The growing piano industry trained most of its energies on instruments for the home, though the 19th century also saw a burgeoning of public concerts, new and larger concert halls, and more and more trained pianists. The result was new developments in the grand.

Prime among them, affecting also squares and verticals, was growth. Cristofori's instruments had four octaves; by Mozart's time the range was five octaves, F_1–f'''. During the 1790s, ranges were widening to c'''', and by 1810 the six octaves from F_1–f'''' (especially in Germany and Austria) and C_1–c'''' (especially in England and France) were coming into use. The next decade saw extensions from C_1–f'''', and in the 1820s, a very few seven-octave pianos, A_2–a'''', though that range was becoming standard only at the middle of the century, and instruments with smaller ranges continued to be made. Five-octave squares were made in America into the 1830s. The main period of the extending range, 1790–1825, coincides with the career of Beethoven (1770–1827) and can be traced through his piano music; the "Hammerklavier" Sonata, op. 106, reaches the C_1–f'''' compass.

As grands grew, problems with existing actions were exacerbated. In 1821 the Parisian maker Sébastien Erard (1752–1831) patented his "repetition" or "double escapement" action, designed so that the player could repeat a note without completely releasing the key [see Fig. 5D, E]. Though other action designs continually appeared, and English and Viennese types continued in use until the early 20th century, Erard's eventually won the day and has come to be used in nearly all contemporary grands.

The piano's growth necessitated an increase in strength. With more and heavier strings, wooden bracing proved inadequate: many fine pianos warped alarmingly, and others collapsed. Wooden braces also exacerbated the fact that humidity changes, making wood shrink or swell, caused pianos to lose their tuning. In the 18th century, English makers had introduced iron braces between the pin block and the belly rail (which supports the front of the soundboard). In 1820, James Thom (fl. 1820s) and William Allen (fl. 1820–40?), working for William Stodart (1762?–ca. 1838) in London, invented a "compensation frame." Tubes of brass and iron, corresponding to brass and iron strings, extended lengthwise in the case and would theoretically expand and contract with temperature changes at the same rate as the strings. Partial frames with metal hitch-pin plates and bars above the strings, bolted into the pin block, were the main solution from the 1820s. In 1825, Alpheus Babcock (1785–1842) in Boston patented a single-piece metal frame for squares. A few American makers adopted it in the 1830s, and Jonas Chickering (1798–1853) of Boston patented it for grands in 1843. This proved the lasting solution both to tuning stability and to the increasing demand for greater volume necessitated by larger concert halls. Its combination in 1859, by Henry Steinway, Jr. (1830–65), with cross-stringing in grands in effect brought the modern piano into being. Cross-stringing (or overstringing) runs the longest bass strings above and across the plane of the tenor strings, allowing for the longest strings possible in the case (an advantage for tone), and had been used sometimes in squares and very small uprights since Henri Pape (1789–1875) invented the design in 1828.

By the middle of the 19th century, the piano industry had largely changed from craft-shop technology to factory technology, with workers performing specialized operations and an increasing use of machines for planing, sawing, and some making of parts. Specialist companies making only actions or cases or keys proliferated in both Europe and America, and some makers became assemblers of parts rather than manufacturers. Production increased rapidly, especially in North America, and export trade began from Europe and America. In America, the opening of the West with railroad transport encouraged an increase in the sale of pianos and the number of manufacturers. The piano had long been an icon of high culture, but as prices fell, it came within the means of even very modest homes, especially as purchase on credit came to be more common.

Since the late 18th century, companies like Broadwood in England and Erard in France had dominated the trade in their countries. Others had come to the fore, notably Chickering in the U.S. A series of world's fairs during the 19th century, beginning with the Crystal Palace exhibition in London in 1851, demonstrated advances in technology and the arts, affording piano makers opportunities to compete and gain reputation. At the fair in Paris in 1867, Steinway & Sons and Chickering gave a boost to the American industry by winning the first prizes. The Germans, with such makers as Bechstein, Blüthner, Schiedmayer, Grotrian, and others, came to dominate the European market. French and English makers, who had led the way in the earlier 19th century, relied on older technologies and fell back from leadership. By the beginning of the 20th century the modern piano had definitively appeared, with cross-stringing and iron frames, steel strings, and the Erard grand action, and the upright had displaced the square in homes everywhere.

The 20th century saw many experiments but little lasting technological change. New materials included resin glues and plastics after World War II. Automation entered piano factories, more in some than in others. Yamaha in Japan led the way, but by no means have all manufacturers followed, nor is Yamaha completely automated. Some important experiments began in the late 1800s. Paul von Jankó (1856–1939) invented a keyboard in which parallel rows of whole-tone keys allow wide stretches and simplified fingering. Emanuel Moór (1863–1931) devised a two-manual piano that allowed simplified playing of octaves, and some concave keyboards were tried. Pianos were designed for quarter tones and for the microtonal scales from 1/3 to 1/16 tones devised by Julián Carillo (1875–1965). That for 1/16 tones required 97 keys to cover one octave.

Most successful were automatic pianos and electric and electronic instruments. Pneumatic player pianos used air or vacuum pressure to run perforated paper rolls on which the music was programmed. E. S. Votey (1856–1931) patented the Pianola, one of the earliest and most successful brands, in 1900. "Piano players" [Ger. *Vorsetzer*] sat in front of an ordinary piano and mechanical fingers touched the keys. "Player pianos" had the mechanism inside the case. Expressive factors such as tempo change and loudness were accomplished by hand-operated levers. More sophisticated "reproducing pianos" recorded actual performers' playing on rolls, with expressive values accomplished automatically. For several years in the 1920s, more automatic pianos were manufactured than ordinary pianos. Electric pianos were relatively short-lived. An early one, the Neo-Bechstein, invented in the 1930s, had no soundboard, but groups of strings converged on electromagnetic pickups connected to an amplifier. Some electric pianos were devised after World War II, most successfully the Fender-Rhodes, invented by Harold Rhodes (1910–2000). Electronic keyboards, now collectively called keyboards, have multiple sounds, including several different piano sounds, programmed on computer chips. Early synthesizers attempted unsuccessfully to imitate piano sound, but keyboards use "sampling," which extends a somewhat simplified recorded piano sound to the entire keyboard. Keyboards, having no strings, are not pianos. The sounds of the best are plausible accounts of the piano, and the keys are weighted to simulate the touch of good pianos. Their flexibility of use recommends them to composers and popular musicians. Whether they will actually displace pianos, as the piano displaced the harpsichord, is not clear.

The center of gravity of the piano industry has moved since about 1970 to Asia, where Japan became the largest producer, Yamaha the largest maker. Korea soon followed suit (Young Chang, Samick), and China's piano industry is expanding (Pearl River, Dongbei). Many old brands are now made in Asia: Knabe and Weber by Young Chang, Kohler & Campbell by Samick, Schiedmayer by Kawai (Japan), and many others. This Asian activity has certainly energized the European and American industries.

Bibl.: *History.* Alfred J. Hipkins, *A Description and History of the Pianoforte,* 3rd ed. (London: Novello, 1929; R: with intr. by Edwin M. Ripin, Detroit: Info Coord, 1975). Rosamond E. M. Harding, *The Piano-Forte: Its History Traced to the Great Exhibition of 1851* (Cambridge: Cambridge U Pr, 1933; 2nd ed., Old Woking, U.K.: Gresham Books, 1978). Arthur Loesser, *Men, Women, and Pianos: A Social History* (New York: Simon & Schuster, 1954). Cyril Ehrlich, *The Piano: A History* (London: Dent, 1976; 2nd ed., Oxford: Oxford U Pr, 1990). Dominic Gill, ed., *The Book of the Piano* (Ithaca, N.Y.: Cornell U Pr, 1981). Cynthia Adams Hoover, "The Steinways and Their Pianos in the Nineteenth Century," *JAMIS* 7 (1981): 47–89. Edwin M. Good, *Giraffes, Black Dragons, and Other Pianos* (Stanford: Stanford U Pr, 2001). Martha Novak Clinkscale, *Makers of the Piano,* vol. 1: *1700–1820;* vol. 2: *1820–1860.* (Oxford: Oxford U Pr, 1993, 1999). David Crombie, *Piano.* (San Francisco: Miller Freeman, 1995). Stewart Pollens, *The Early Pianoforte* (Cambridge: Cambridge U Pr, 1995). Michael Cole, *The Pianoforte in the Classical Era* (Oxford: Clarendon, 1998). James Parakilas et al., *Piano Roles: Three Hundred Years of Life with the Piano* (New Haven: Yale U Pr, 1999). Konstantin Restle, ed., *Faszination Klavier: 300 Jahre Pianofortebau in Deutschland* (Munich: Prestel, 2000). Cynthia Adams Hoover, Patrick Rucker, and Edwin M. Good, *Piano 300: Celebrating Three Centuries of People and Pianos* (Washington, D.C.: National Museum of American History, Behring Center, Smithsonian Institution and NAMM—International Music Products Association, 2001).

Tuning and Maintenance. William Braid White, *Theory and Practice of Piano Construction: With a Detailed, Practical Method for Tuning* (New York: E L Bill, 1906; R: New York: Dover, 1975). Otto Funke, *Das Klavier und seine Pflege: Theorie und Praxis des Klavierstimmens,* 3rd ed. (Frankfurt am Main: Musikinstrument, 1961), trans. W. London and C. H. Wehlau, *The Piano and How to Care for It: Piano Tuning in Theory and Practice* (Frankfurt am Main: Musikinstrument, 1961). Arthur A. Reblitz, *Piano Servicing, Tuning, and Rebuilding* (New York: Vestal Pr, 1976). Owen Jorgensen, *Tuning the Historical Temperaments by Ear* (Marquette: N Mich U Pr, 1977). Ian McCombie, *The Piano Handbook* (New York: Scribner, 1980). Samuel Wolfenden, *A Treatise on the Art of Pianoforte Construction* (London: Unwin Brothers, 1916; R: Old Woking, U.K.: Unwin Brothers, 1977). Anita T. Sullivan, *The Seventh Dragon: The*

Riddle of Equal Temperament (Lake Oswego, Ore.: Metamorphous, 1985). Owen H. Jorgensen, *Tuning: Containing the Perfection of Eighteenth-Century Temperament, the Lost Art of Nineteenth-Century Temperament, and the Science of Equal Temperament Complete with Instructions for Aural and Electronic Tuning* (East Lansing: Mich St U Pr 1991). Larry Fine, *The Piano Book: Buying and Owning a New or Used Piano,* 4th ed. (Boston: Brookside, 2001).

Literature. Luigi Alberto Villanis, *L'arte del pianoforte in Italia (da Clementi a Sgambati)* (Torino: Fratelli Bocca, 1907). Alfred Cortot, *La musique française de piano,* 3 vols. (Paris: Presses universitaires de France, 1944). Walter Georgii, *Klaviermusik,* 2nd ed. (Zürich: Atlantis, 1956). Norman Demuth, *French Piano Music: A Survey with Notes on Its Performance* (London: Museum Pr, 1959). Gerhard Puchelt, *Verlorene Klänge: Studien zur deutschen Klaviermusik 1830–1880* (Berlin: Robert Lienau, 1969). Maurice Hinson, *Guide to the Pianist's Repertoire* (Bloomington: Ind U Pr, 1973). Klaus Wolters, *Handbuch der Klavierliteratur,* 2nd ed. (Zürich: Atlantis, 1977). Joseph Rezits, *The Pianist's Resource Guide: Piano Music in Print,* 2nd ed. (Park Ridge, Ill.: Pallma Music, 1978). Maurice Hinson, *Guide to the Pianist's Repertoire: Supplement* (Bloomington: Ind U Pr, 1979). Linton E. Powell, *A History of Spanish Piano Music* (Bloomington: Ind U Pr, 1980). Katalin Komlós, *Fortepianos and Their Music: Germany, Austria, and England, 1760–1800* (Oxford: Clarendon, 1995).

Technique. Daniel Gottlob Türk, *Klavierschule oder Anweisung zum Klavierspielen für Lehrer und Lernende* (Leipzig & Halle, 1789; facs., *DM* ser. 1, 23, 1962); trans. Raymond H. Haggh, *School of Clavier Playing* (Lincoln: U of Nebr Pr, 1982). Jan Ladislav Dussek, *Instructions on the Art of Playing the Pianoforte or Harpsichord, Being a Compleat Treatise of the First Rudiments of Music* (London: Corri, Dussek and Co., 1796). Johann Nepomuk Hummel, *Ausführliche theoritisch-practische Anweisung zum Pianoforte-Spiel, vom ersten Elementar-Unterricht an bis zur volkommensten Ausbildung* (Vienna: Haslinger, 1828); trans. D. Jelensperger, *Méthode complète théoretique et pratique pour le pianoforte, . . . depuis les premiers élémens jusqu'au plus haut degré de perfection* (Paris: Farrenc, 1827). Adolf Kullak, *Die ästhetik des Klavierspiels,* 3rd ed. rev. Hans Bischoff (Berlin: J Guttentag, 1876); trans. Theodore Baker, *The Aesthetics of Pianoforte-Playing* (New York: G Schirmer, 1893). Malwine Brée, *Die Grundlage der Methode Leschetizky* (Mainz: B Schott, 1902); trans. Theodore Baker, *The Groundwork of the Leschetizky Method* (New York: G Schirmer, 1902; R: New York: Haskell House, 1969). Edith J. Hipkins, *How Chopin Played* (London: Dent, 1937). Harold C. Schonberg, *The Great Pianists* (New York: Simon & Schuster, 1963). József Gát, *A zongorajáték technikája,* 2nd ed. (Budapest: Corvina, 1965); trans. István Kleszky, *The Technique of Piano Playing* (London: Collet's Holdings, 1965). Gerd Kaemper, *Techniques pianistiques: L'évolution de la technologie pianistique* (Paris: Leduc, 1968). Abby Whiteside, *Mastering the Chopin Études and Other Essays,* ed. Joseph Prostakoff and Sophia Rosoff (New York: Scribner, 1969). Walter Gieseking and Karl Leimer, *Piano Technique* (Bryn Mawr, Pa.: Theodore Presser, 1932, 1938; R: New York: Dover, 1972). Konrad Wolff, *Schnabel's Interpretation of Piano Music* [original title: *The Teaching of Artur Schnabel*], 2nd ed. (New York: Norton, 1972). Reginald R. Gerig, *Famous Pianists and Their Technique* (Washington, D.C.: Robert B Luce, 1974). William S. Newman, *The Pianist's Problems,* 3rd ed., enl. (New York: Harper & Row, 1974). Josef Hofmann, *Piano Playing, with Piano Questions Answered* (Bryn Mawr, Pa.: Theodore Presser, 1920; R: New York: Dover, 1976). Malcolm Bilson, "The Viennese Fortepiano of the Late 18th Century: A Performer's Introduction to the Classical Repertoire," *EM* 8 (1980): 158–62. Joan Last, *Freedom in Piano Technique: With an Appendix for Teaching-Diploma Candidates* (London: Oxford U Pr, 1980). James Methuen-Campbell, *Chopin Playing: From the Composer to the Present Day* (New York: Taplinger, 1981). György Sándor, *On Piano Playing: Motion, Sound, and Expression* (New York: Schirmer Bks, 1981). Robert D. Schick, *The Vengerova System of Piano Playing* (University Park: Pa St U Pr, 1982). Kenneth Drake, *The Sonatas of Beethoven as He Played and Taught Them* (Bloomington: Ind U Pr, 1981). Konrad Wolff, *Masters of the Keyboard: Individual Style Elements in the Piano Music of Bach, Haydn, Mozart, Beethoven, and Schubert* (Bloomington: Ind U Pr, 1983). Wilson Lyle, *A Dictionary of Pianists* (New York: Schirmer 1984). Friedrich Wieck, *Clavier und Gesang: Didaktisches und Polemisches* (Leipzig, 1853); trans., ed., and annotated by Henry Pleasants (Stuyvesant, N.Y.: Pendragon, 1986). Sandra P. Rosenblum, *Performance Practices in Classic Piano Music: Their Principles and Applications* (Bloomington: Ind U Pr, 1988). E.M.G.

Piano accordion. An *accordion with pianolike keyboard as distinct from the *concertina and similar instruments with buttons only.

Piano arrangement. An arrangement for piano of a work intended for another medium.

Piano concerto. A *concerto for piano and orchestra.

Piano de cuia [Port.]. **Cabaça.*

Piano duet. A composition for two pianists, playing either one instrument or two. Music to be played on a single instrument is usually described as being for piano four hands.

The earliest known duets for one keyboard are an *In nomine* by Nicholas Carleton (ca. 1570/75–1630) and a fancy by Thomas Tomkins (1572–1656) (both transcribed in Miller, 1943). Only in the late 18th century did the medium begin to be popular. (Earlier the necessary closeness of the players' bodies had been thought indecorous by some, and the fullness of women's skirts had also been an obstacle.) Mozart and his sister played duets in London in 1764–65; the Sonata K. 19d dates from these years. Mozart's later sonatas for four hands are the first important works in the genre. First to be printed were Charles Burney's *Four Sonatas or Duets for Two Performers on One Pianoforte or Harpsichord* (1777). J. C. Bach and Clementi were composing similar pieces at about this time.

Around the turn of the 19th century began the flood of duet arrangements that were the most common means of becoming familiar with large ensemble works before the advent of the radio and phonograph. Composers have continued to produce original four-hand compositions, with Schubert perhaps making the largest contribution among major composers. Keyboard duets have frequently been conceived as teaching pieces, with Haydn's *Il maestro e lo scolare* a notable early example and Stravinsky's *Easy Pieces* (two sets, 1914–15 and 1916–17) a later one.

A smaller amount of music has been written for two pianos, but it includes some very distinguished works. The earliest known piece for two keyboards is an arrangement of a Crecquillon chanson, "Belle sans pere," in Luis Venegas de Henestrosa's *Libro de cifra nueva* (1557; ed. *MME* 2, pp. 158–62). An original piece for two virginals by Giles Farnaby (ed. *MB* 24, p. 71) is in the Fitzwilliam Virginal Book (1609–19). From the late 17th century, activity in this medium, although intermittent, never entirely stops, with examples by Bernardo Pasquini (14 sonatas for two figured basses), François Couperin, Gaspard Le Roux, Bach's sons, Mozart, Clementi, Chopin, Schumann (Andante and Variations op. 46, with cellos and horn), and Brahms (versions of several of his works, including the Haydn Variations), among others. Although duets for one keyboard are seldom played at public concerts, the 20th century produced several notable duo-piano teams, and a considerable number of important works have been produced, including pieces by Debussy, Stravinsky, and Bartók (a sonata with percussion).

Bibl.: Hugh Miller, "The Earliest Keyboard Duets," *MQ* 29 (1943): 438–57. Cameron McGraw, *Piano Duet Repertoire* (Bloomington: Ind U Pr, 1981).

Pianoforte. (1) Piano. (2) As a dynamic mark, *piano* followed immediately by *forte* (abbr. *pf*).

Pianola. (1) The trade name for a *player piano [see also Automatic instruments] manufactured by the Aeolian Piano Company. (2) Any player piano, including such instruments as the Duo-Art, Fonola, Phonola, and Welte-Mignon.

Piano-organ [Fr. *piano organisé, piano-orgue;* Ger. *Orgelklavier*]. An instrument popular in the late 18th century combining a piano, controlled from one manual, with an organ, controlled from another. An example survives from 1772 by Johann Andreas Stein.

Piano quartet. Most often, a *quartet consisting of piano and strings; a work for such a quartet; rarely, a quartet of four pianos.

Piano reduction. An arrangement for piano of a work for orchestra or other ensemble.

Piano score. A score of a work for orchestra or other ensemble arranged on two staves in the fashion of piano music, sometimes with indications of the instruments intended for salient parts.

Piano trio. A *trio consisting of piano, violin, and cello; a work for such a trio.

Piano-vocal score. A score of an opera, oratorio, or other work for voices and orchestra in which the vocal parts are given in full while the orchestral music is reduced or arranged for piano.

Piatti [It.]. *Cymbals.

Pibgorn, pibcorn. A *hornpipe of Wales consisting of a single-reed *chanter with a bell and a mouthpiece of cow's horn. It was used from the Middle Ages into the 18th century, from which century specimens are preserved.

Pibroch [Gael. *pìobaireachd,* piping]. A type of solo Scottish bagpipe music, also termed *ceòl mor* (great music), consisting of highly figured variations on a theme called an *urlar.* Its invention is attributed to a piper of around 1600. A form of solmization used for didactic purposes with this repertory is termed *canntaireachd.*

Bibl.: Roderick S. Ross, *Binneas is Boreraig* (Edinburgh: Macdonald, 1959) [with recordings]. Peter Cooke, "The Pibroch Repertory: Some Research Problems," *PRMA* 102 (1975–76): 93–102.

Picardy third [Fr. *tierce de Picardie*]. The raised or major third of the tonic triad as the final chord in a work otherwise in the minor mode. Its use begins by about 1500 and is very nearly universal in late Renaissance and Baroque music. The term was first used by Jean-Jacques Rousseau (*Dictionnaire de musique,* 1767) and, despite the form given it by him and most writers since, probably derives from the Old French *picart* [fem. *picarde,* sharp, pointed] rather than from Picardie, the name of a region in France.

Picchettato [It.]. In string playing, *spiccato* [see Bowing (4)].

Piccolo [It., small]. (1) [Fr. *petite flûte, flûte piccolo;* Ger. *Pikkoloflöte, kleine Flöte, Pickelflöte, Oktavflöte;* It. *ottavino, flauto piccolo;* Sp. *flautín*] A small *flute pitched an octave higher than the ordinary flute. Its normal range is from d″ to d″″, written one octave lower. It normally lacks a foot joint and may be made of wood or metal. It is sometimes pitched in keys other than C, for bands often in D♭. See ill. under Flute. (2) The smallest or highest-pitched member of a family of instruments, e.g., **violino piccolo,* piccolo *clarinet, piccolo *cornet, piccolo *trumpet.

Pick. (1) *Plectrum. (2) To pluck a stringed instrument, especially a guitar or banjo, rather than strum it; thus, to play melodies as well as chords. The use of one or more plectra is often implied.

Pickelflöte [Ger.]. Piccolo (1).

Pickup. (1) One or more notes preceding the first metrically strong beat (usually the first beat of the first complete measure) of a phrase or section of a composition; anacrusis, upbeat. (2) A device, usually consisting of one or more electromagnetic coils, for converting the movement of a vibrating string (or other object) into electrical impulses. On the *electric guitar and similar instruments, one or more pickups are located on the face of the instrument, directly beneath the strings. The term is also loosely applied to contact microphones, which are sometimes attached to conventional (*acoustic) instruments in order to amplify their sound.

Pictures at an Exhibition [Russ. *Kartinki s vïstavki*]. A suite of descriptive pieces for piano by Musorgsky, composed in 1874. Each piece is inspired by one of the paintings by the Russian artist Victor A. Hartmann (1834–73) shown at a memorial exhibition in 1874. The work is often performed in an orchestral arrangement by Ravel (1922).

Piece [Fr. *pièce, morceau;* Ger. *Stück;* It. *pezzo;* Sp. *pieza*]. A composition, especially but not necessarily an instrumental one. The term, as used informally, implies nothing about length or character. As a title or part of a title, however, it is likely to imply a relatively short composition. In French keyboard music of the 17th and 18th centuries, it frequently occurs in the phrase *pièces de claveçin.* The German term is often part of compounds [see *Stück*].

Piedi [It.]. See *Ballata.*

Pien [Chin. *biann*]. Exchange notes, pitches sometimes substituted for one or more of those making up a scale, the most common examples being pentatonic scales with two such pitches. They occur in the musics of China, Japan, and Java. In Chinese music, the term refers specifically to pitches corresponding to F♯ and B in relation to a scale of the structure C D E G A C and serving as ornamental or passing tones.

Pieno [It.]. Full; *organo pieno,* full organ; *voce piena,* full voice.

Pierrot lunaire [Fr., Moonstruck Pierre]. A work consisting of 21 short pieces by Schoenberg, op. 21 (1912), for a narrator employing **Sprechstimme* and five instrumentalists (three of whom double: flute/piccolo, clarinet/bass clarinet, violin/viola, cello, piano), on poems by Albert Giraud in a German translation by Otto Erich Hartleben.

Pifa [fr. It. **piffero* or **piva*]. The instrumental **pastorale* in Handel's *Messiah.*

Piffero, piffaro [It.]. Shawm; hence, *pifferari* for south Italian shepherds who travel to Rome during Advent to play shawms and bagpipes in the streets in imitation of the shepherds of the Christmas story. See *Pastorale.* In the Middle Ages, the term was used to refer to instrumentalists in general.

Pikkoloflöte [Ger.]. *Piccolo flute.

Pin block. In the *piano and related instruments, the piece of wood into which the tuning pins are inserted.

Pincé [Fr., plucked]. (1) *Pizzicato. (2) In the later 17th and 18th centuries, *mordent. Marais gives the term as a synonym for **flattement* in viol playing.

Pini di Roma [It., Pines of Rome]. A symphonic poem by Respighi composed in 1924, depicting four forested landscapes near Rome: the Villa Borghese, a catacomb, the Janiculum (a hill named after the god Janus), and the Appian Way.

Pìobaireachd [Gael.]. *Pibroch.

P'i-p'a (pipa) [Chin.]. A pear-shaped, fretted, short-necked *lute of China. Its four silk (more recently nylon) strings are usually tuned A d e a. The traditional model has 16 frets extending well up onto the body of the instrument; on more recent models there may be as many as 24. It is held upright, with its lower end resting on the player's lap. The strings are plucked with the fingernails of the right hand using a variety of techniques to produce, e.g., sustained rolls and percussive effects. The prototype of the *p'i-p'a,* a short lute played with a large plectrum, was brought to China from the Middle East in the 6th century and survives in the *biwa* of Japan. Unlike the **ch'in,* the *p'i-p'a* has always been associated with popular entertainment. Today it is played as a solo instrument, in ensembles, and as an accompaniment to song. See ill. under East Asia I.

Pipe. Any wind instrument in the form of a tube. See also Aerophone, Bagpipe, Organ, Pipe and tabor, Reed, Reedpipe, Woodwind.

Pipe and tabor. A *duct flute with three finger holes and a small snare drum, both played by a single player who holds the pipe in the left hand and beats the tabor with a stick held in the right. The tabor, whose depth varies considerably, is hung from the left shoulder or wrist. The pair is distributed widely in western Europe and has served since at least the 13th century as an accompaniment for dancing. In England it disappeared in the 19th century, but the tradition of *galoubet* and *tambourin* survives in southern France and that of **flaviol* and *tamboril* (Catalan), *txistu* and *tamboril* (Basque), and *pito* and *tambor* (Castilian) in Spain. See ill. under Flute.

Pique Dame [Fr.]. See *Queen of Spades, The.*

Pirouette [Fr., Sp. *tudel*]. A wooden disc or cylinder that holds and partly covers the reed of the shawm and similar double-reed instruments.

Pishdarāmad [Per., before the introduction]. A stately, metric piece in Persian classical music, said to have been developed by Darvish Khān for ensemble performance at the first public concert in Tehran (1906), but probably extant earlier. The most traditional pieces consist of a number of repeated lines, each based on one **gusheh* of the **dastgāh* in which it is cast. B.N.

Piston. (1) *Valve. (2) On the organ, a button that controls preset stops.

Pitch [Fr. *hauteur;* Ger. *Tonhöhe;* It. *intonazione;* Sp. *entonación*]. (1) The perceived quality of a sound that is chiefly a function of its fundamental frequency—the number of oscillations per second (called *Hertz, abbr. Hz) of the sounding object or of the particles of air excited by it [see Acoustics]. The perception of pitch may, however, be affected by inharmonicity in the waveform, by the amplitude of the waveform, by the physical relationship between auditor and sound source, by the structure of the ear, and by habitual expectations. In general, pitch is regarded as becoming higher with increasing frequency and lower with decreasing frequency. Pitches may be quantitatively expressed either directly by the value of their frequencies, or indirectly by the ratios their frequencies make with some reference frequency. Unimpaired ears detect frequencies from 16 Hz to ca. 20,000 Hz (as high as 25,000 Hz for young people; as low as 10,000 Hz for those over 40). Musically useful frequencies extend from ca. 20 Hz to ca. 5,000 Hz.

(2) [Fr. *ton;* Ger. *Ton;* It., Sp. *tono*]. Any point on the continuum of musical pitch. This continuum is analogous to the domain of musically useful frequencies, and each point on it corresponds to some definite frequency within that domain. For the nomenclature employed with the pitches used in Western music, see Pitch names.

(3) The position of a point or, in early writings, of a set of points (e.g., a particular range of the scale or staff) on the musical pitch continuum. This position is described as being higher when the corresponding frequency is greater and as being lower when the frequency is smaller. The earliest known instances, found in Thomas Morley's *Plaine and Easie Introduction to Practicall Musicke* (London, 1597), suggest that this was the original musical use of the word.

(4) [Fr. *diapason;* Ger. *Kammerton, Stimmung;* It. *diapason;* Sp. *diapasón*]. The standardized association of some particular frequency and some pitch name (e.g., c′ = 256 Hz). Letter names refer essentially to elements of ordered interval collections (called tunings, scales, etc.) and by extension to the relationships that inhere in such collections. In the 20th century, the standard a′ = 440 Hz became widely used, especially since its endorsement by the British Standards Institution Conference in May 1938 and by the International Organization for Standardization in 1955.

In most times and places, the identification of letter names with specific frequencies has varied. In the 16th–18th centuries, some writers asserted that it does not matter which particular pitch is called (say) a′ so long as players can tune together to it. Thus, when singers and instrumentalists performed in churches they used a standard pitch compatible with the organ's—ideally, its own pitch. In practice, by the early

Mean pitch of	Frequency of a′		Sample pitches, 1495–1812
		506	Halberstadt organ, 1495
		489	Hamburg organ, 1688
15 German organs, 1495–1716	487		
14 Silbermann organs, 1717–50	484		
8 Austrian organs, ca. 1550–1700	466		
48 Venetian *cornettos,* 16th–17th c.	466		
33 German *Zincks,* 16th–17th c.	465		
		464	Störmthal organ, 1723
25 *cornettos* of unknown provenance, 16th–17th c.	461		
		455	Hamburg organ, 1749
		454	Amati violins, high resonance, ca. 1650
		454	London tuning fork, ca. 1720
7 English organs, 1665–1708	450		
32 Italian (non-Venetian) *cornettos,* 16th–17th c.	448		
		440	Paris Conservatoire fork, 1812
		435	Hamburg choir tuning fork, 1761
5 French *cornets,* 16th–17th c.	431		
		427	Sauveur's standard, 1713
		426	Praetorius's *Cammerton,* 1619
		≈ 425	Padua pitch pipe, 1780
		424	Amati violins, low resonance, ca. 1650
		423	"Handel's" tuning fork, 1751
13 English and American organs, 1740–1843	421		
		415	Dresden choir tuning fork, ca. 1754–1824
6 German organs, 1693–1762	412		
92 French oboes, ca. 1670–1750	411		
		408	Hamburg organ, 1762
		405	Deslandes-Sauveur organ, 1704
13 French organs, 1601–1789	399		
		394	De Caus's standard, 1612

17th century, organs (outside of France, at least) tended to be tuned a tone or more higher than either singers or gut strings could tolerate. At the same time, makers of various instruments favored particular—and differing—pitch compasses. It consequently became common during the 17th and 18th centuries to speak of several pitch standards and to identify their interrelations. The terminology was not systematic, and its scope varied in different regions.

The oldest and stablest term is choir pitch [Fr. *ton de choeur, ton de chapelle;* Ger. *Chorton;* It. *tuono chorista*]. This was often contrasted with a chamber pitch [Fr. *ton de chambre;* Ger. *Kammerton*] lying a whole tone lower. Several north German authors described a second chamber pitch a semitone lower still. During Bach's tenure at Leipzig, singers, woodwinds, and strings tuned to *Kammerton;* the organ and trumpets were pitched in *Chorton* a whole tone above. Other terms denoted standard pitch for high winds (*Cornett-Ton, Zinck-Thon, Feldton,* etc.) and for opera *(Operntton).* The accompanying table gives the mean pitches of 13 collections of instruments, whose original pitches can be reliably ascertained. The range of pitches in each collection has been kept fairly narrow so that the mean pitches have more than an arithmetic significance. They should, nonetheless, be compared with the particular historical pitches also included in the table as well as with pitches given by works in the bibliography.

The first proposal of a specific frequency as a standard pitch (equivalent to a′ = 427 Hz) was made by Joseph Sauveur in the early 1700s. In 1711, the tuning fork was invented in England. No concerted effort was made to promulgate a single pitch standard until 1834, however, when the Deutsche Naturforscherversammlung accepted Scheibler's recommendation of a′ = 440 Hz. This had little effect on 19th-century concert halls and opera houses, which used progressively higher pitch standards, until in 1885 an international conference (not including the United Kingdom or United States) at Vienna urged the adoption of the French *Diapason normal,* a′ = 435 Hz, as recommended in 1859 by a French governmental commission as the pitch least taxing to singers. (A selection of 19th-century pitch standards is given in Ellis and Mendel, 1968.) The Viennese conference's a′ = 435 remained the most widely used pitch standard until its replacement by a′ = 440 in the 20th century. Some performers (especially wind players) now adopt a′ = 442 or 443, however, while performers on 18th-century instruments are likely to adopt the lower pitch of that period.

Bibl.: Alexander J. Ellis, "On the History of Musical Pitch," *Journal of the Society of Arts* 28 (1880): 293–336, 400–403; 29 (1881): 109–13. Arthur Mendel, "Pitch in the 16th and Early 17th Centuries," *MQ* 34 (1948): 28–45, 199–221, 336–57, 575–93. Id., "Devices for Transposition in the Organ before 1600," *AM* 21 (1949): 24–40. Id., "On the Pitches in Use in Bach's Time," *MQ* 41 (1955): 332–54, 466–80. David Wulstan, "The Problem of Pitch in 16th-Century English Vocal Polyphony," *PRMA* 93 (1966/67): 97–112. Alexander J. Ellis and Arthur Mendel, *Studies in the History of Musical Pitch* (Amsterdam: Frits Knuf, 1968) [includes Ellis 1880–81 as well as Mendel 1948, 1949, and 1955 with the author's addenda and corrigenda]. Adrian J. M. Houtsma, "What Determines Musical Pitch?" *JMT* 15 (1971): 138–57. William R. Thomas and J. J. K. Rhodes, "Schlick, Praetorius, and the History of Organ Pitch," *Organ Yearbook* 2 (1971): 58–76. Émile Leipp and Michèle Castallengo, "Du diapason et de sa relativité," *ReM* 294 (1977): 1–39. Arthur Mendel, "Pitch in Western Music since 1500: A Re-examination," *AM* 50 (1978): 1–93. Roger Bowers, "The Performing Pitch of English 15th-Century Church Polyphony," *EM* 8 (1980): 21–28. Barbara Owen, "Pitch and Tuning in Eighteenth and Nineteenth Century American Organs," *The Organ Yearbook* 15 (1984).

Pitch aggregate. In discussions of 20th-century music, a collection of pitches, whether or not sounded simultaneously.

Pitch class. A pitch without reference to the octave or register in which it occurs; hence, e.g., the class of all C's as distinct from the pitch c′. Western tonal music uses twelve pitch classes, each of which is represented in each octave of the entire range of pitches. The term is used particularly (though not exclusively) with respect to *twelve-tone and *serial music, having been coined in this context by Milton Babbitt. See also Octave equivalence.

Pitch names. The accompanying table gives the systems for naming pitch classes in English, French, German, Italian, and Spanish. Exceptions to the model for

English	C	D	E	F	G	A	B
German	C	D	E	F	G	A	H
French	ut	ré	mi	fa	sol	la	si
Italian	do	re	mi	fa	sol	la	si
Spanish	do	re	mi	fa	sol	la	si

English	C-sharp	C-flat
German	Cis	Ces
French	ut dièse	ut bémol
Italian	do diesis	do bemolle
Spanish	do sostenido	do bemol
English	C-double-sharp	C-double-flat
German	Cisis	Ceses
French	ut double-dièse	ut double-bémol
Italian	do doppio diesis	do doppio bemolle
Spanish	do doble sostenido	do doble bemol

the addition of suffixes in German include *B* for B-flat (B-natural being represented by *H*), *Es* for E-flat, and *As* for A-flat.

Several competing schemes for the designation of specific octaves are in use. The one employed in this dictionary and widely used elsewhere is the first of the

1.	C_1	C	c	c′	c″	c‴	c⁗
2.	CCC	CC	C	c	c′	c″	c‴
3.	C_2	C_1	C	c	c^1	c^2	c^3

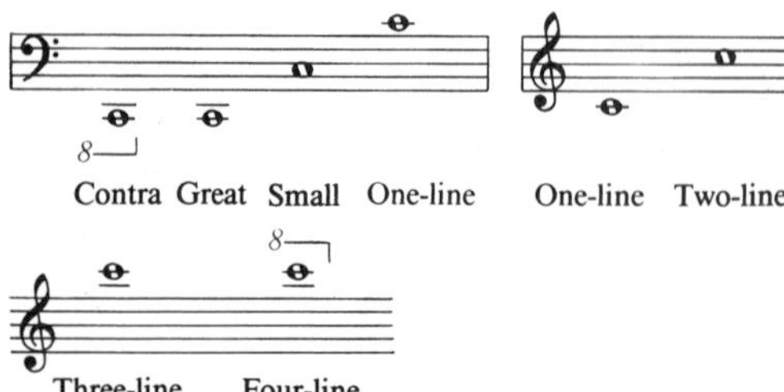

Pitches corresponding to first scheme.

three illustrated here, in which middle C (the C occurring roughly in the middle of the piano keyboard) is designated c′. In all three, the form of the name changes with each C, proceeding upward. Thus, the B above middle C in the first scheme is b′, and the B below middle C is b. For terminology derived from organ building, see Foot (2).

Pitch pipe [Fr. *choriste, flûte d'accord, diapason à bouche;* Ger. *Stimmpfeife;* It. *corista, diapason a fiato;* Sp. *diapasón de boca*]. A small wind instrument used to give an initial pitch to singers or to tune instruments. Pitch pipes from the 18th century were *duct flutes with calibrated movable plungers. In the 19th century, various free-reed pitch pipes were designed. One model has a metal reed of adjustable length. Another is a disc with 11 blown reeds tuned in a chromatic scale. A bundle of 6 pipes, each with a reed, is used to tune guitars.

Pitman wind-chest. A wind-chest used in electropneumatic organ actions, employing a small wooden valve, faced with leather, called a pitman.

Pito [Sp.]. (1) Whistle. (2) A *duct flute of the *pipe and tabor of central Spain.

Più [It.]. More; *più allegro,* faster; *più tosto,* more quickly.

Piuttosto [It.]. Rather; *piuttosto allegro,* rather fast.

Piva [It.]. (1) *Bagpipe. (2) The fastest measure *(misura)* or step unit of the **basse dance (bassadanza).* It consists of a series of rapid steps *(passetti presti)* embellished by leaps and turns. In one dance, Domenico da Piacenza (*De arte saltandi e choreas ducendii,* ca. 1420) suggested that three measures of the *piva* be danced in a herringbone or zigzag pattern. (3) One of the fastest dances of the early 16th century. Seven examples of music survive in Joan Ambrosio Dalza's *Intabulatura de lauto libro quarto* (published by Petrucci in 1508), where they appear as the third dance of a suite that includes a **pavana,* a **saltarello,* and a *piva.* All are in a compound quadruple (12/8) meter. The last dances of the other two suites in the collection are of the same genre as the *piva,* but are called **spingardo.* One isolated *piva* in the *Intabolatura di lauto libro nono* by Melchiore de Barberiis (1549) is in the 6/8 meter of a *saltarello* or a **gagliarda.* L.H.M.

Pivot chord. See Modulation.

Pizzicato [It., abbr. *pizz.*]. In the playing of bowed stringed instruments, an indication that notes are to be plucked rather than bowed. Typically the player uses the right forefinger for pizzicato while continuing to hold the bow. If the passage of pizzicato notes is long enough and an immediate return to bowing (usually indicated by the word *arco*) is not required, the bow may be laid aside. Sometimes all four strings are strummed, and in such a case the thumb may be used. The first notated example occurs in Monteverdi's **Combattimento di Tancredi e Clorinda* (1624).

The technique of plucking with fingers of the left hand while the right hand continues to use the bow was first used extensively by Paganini. Bartók calls for a pizzicato in which the string is plucked so as to cause it to snap back audibly against the fingerboard, notated with the symbol ϕ (e.g., in the Fourth String Quartet). A similar technique, termed a snap pizzicato, is common on the double bass in jazz.

Placido [It.]. Placid, tranquil.

Plagal cadence. See Cadence.

Plagal mode. See Mode.

Plagius [Lat.]. Plagal [see Mode]; *primus plagius,* the first plagal mode, i.e., mode 2.

Plainchant. *Plainsong.

Plain-chant musical [Fr.]. A repertory of liturgical chant composed and performed in France from the 17th through the 19th century. It aimed to correct what were regarded as the deficiencies of the received Gregorian repertory by eliminating melismas, introducing fixed rhythmic values and otherwise revising melodies in such a way as to reflect current norms of Latin declamation, and introducing accidentals, including the sharp. Older melodies were thoroughly revised, and altogether new ones composed. The repertory, which varied from place to place, was accompanied by the organ or the serpent and served as the basis for organ *versets. The first publication of such chants was François Bourgoing's *Directorium chori* (Paris, 1634). An example popular into the 20th century is Henri Du Mont's *Messe royale* from his *Cinq messes en plainchant* (Paris, 1669). Prominent as a composer and theorist of the repertory in the 17th century was Guillaume Gabriel Nivers. A well-known 18th-century method book was *Méthode nouvelle pour apprendre parfaitement les règles du plain-chant et de la psalmodie* (Poitiers, 1784) by François de La Feillée.

Plainsong [fr. Lat. *cantus planus*]. Monophonic Christian liturgical chant in free rhythm, as distinct from measured music [Lat. *musica mensurabilis*]; also plainchant. The principal repertories of Western plainsong are the *Ambrosian, *Gallican, *Gregorian (to which the term is most often applied), *Old Roman, and *Mozarabic. The principal Eastern repertories are the *Armenian, *Byzantine, and *Syrian.

Plainsong Mass. (1) The *Mass in *Gregorian chant. (2) A polyphonic *Mass in which the music for each liturgical item is based on the corresponding liturgical chant.

Plainsong notation. The notation employed for liturgical chant, especially the square-shaped forms that became prominent in the 12th century and were sometimes employed for secular repertories as well. See Neume.

Plainte [Fr.]. (1) *Lament. (2) In Baroque music, a rare term for any of several ornaments: **accent* or **aspiration;* in viol playing, a one-finger vibrato; vocal pulsations; downward *glissando.

Planctus [Lat.]. *Lament.

Planets, The. A suite for orchestra by Holst, op. 32 (1914–16), describing in successive movements the astrological nature of seven planets: Mars, Venus, Mercury, Jupiter, Saturn, Uranus, and Neptune (with women's chorus).

Planh [Occ.]. *Lament.

Plaqué [Fr.]. An instruction to play the notes of a chord simultaneously rather than as an *arpeggio.

Plate numbers. See Publishers' numbers.

Player piano. An *automatic instrument consisting of a piano and a mechanical device that plays it. In some early examples, from the late 19th century, a separate device with fingerlike levers was placed in front of a piano. More characteristic of the player piano's period of greatest popularity in the 1920s were self-contained models. In either case, a perforated roll of paper passes over a bar with holes corresponding to each of the keys of the piano. When a perforation coincides with a hole, the suction created by a pedal mechanism draws air through the hole, activating the pneumatically powered action that causes the instrument to sound. Among the most widely known trade names was *Pianola, and this was often used as a generic term. Rolls could be punched by an actual performance or could be punched directly. Some instruments, termed reproducing player pianos, could replicate the nuances of dynamics and rhythm of an actual performance from which the roll was created. Instruments of this type, usually electrically operated and installed in pianos made by leading manufacturers, included the Ampico, the Duo-Art, and the Welte-Mignon. Stravinsky, Hindemith, and others composed works for such instruments, and rolls were created by Paderewski, Rakhmaninov, Rubinstein, Debussy, Mahler, Richard Strauss, and Gershwin, among others. Conlon Nancarrow (b. 1912) composed numerous works for player piano by punching rolls directly in such a way as to create extremely complex rhythms and textures.

Bibl.: Harvey N. Roehl, *Player Piano Treasury,* 2nd ed. (Vestal, N.Y.: Vestal Pr, 1973). International Piano Archives at Maryland, *Catalog of the Reproducing Piano Roll Collection* (College Park: U of Maryland, 1983).

Plectrum [Fr. *plectre, médiator;* Ger. *Plektrum, Spielblatt, Kiel* (quill); It. *plettro;* Sp. *plectro*]. A piece of some material such as horn, tortoise shell, plastic, quill, or ivory used to pluck a stringed instrument. The *mandolin, **ʿūd,* **biwa,* *zither, and often the *guitar are played with a plectrum. In guitar and *banjo playing, the term pick is more common, and in some styles, picks may be worn on more than one finger. The strings of the *harpsichord are also sounded by plectra incorporated in the jacks.

Plein-jeu [Fr.]. In the classic French organ, the full sound of the **Grand orgue* and **Positif,* employing flue stops at all pitches, with **Fournitures* and **Cymbales,* but without reeds or **Tierces.*

Plena [Sp.]. (1) A Puerto Rican song and dance-music form of both folk and popular traditions, combining European- and African-derived stylistic features. It is in duple meter, with extensive syncopation in vocal and instrumental parts, and sets narrative texts, often with satirical content, in alternating stanzas and refrain for soloist and chorus. A characteristic performance ensemble consists of singers with accompaniment of *sinfonía* or *sinfonía de mano* (concertina), guitar, *güiro,* and *panderetas* (tambourines, without jingles). (2) In the Dominican Republic, a variety of work song, distinct from the *plena* of Puerto Rico.

D.S.

Plenary Mass. A setting of the *Mass that includes both Ordinary and Proper.

Plenum [Lat.]. The full sound of the organ or harpsichord.

Plica [Lat., fold]. A notational symbol derived from the liquescent *neume and employed in both texted and nontexted music until the early 14th century. In its simplest form, its "folded" or U shape was made with a single stroke of the pen, the opening to either the top or the bottom. In either case, the plica represents two pitches. The first is located by the thick, more nearly horizontal part of the stroke. The second lies above when the opening is at the top [Exx. 1, 2] and below when the opening is at the bottom [Exx. 3, 4]. Most often, the pitch following the plica is a third away from the initial note. In such cases, the second of the two notes fills in this interval and is thus a step above or below the initial note. A plica could also be joined to a *ligature (forming a *ligatura plicata*) by the addition of an upward or downward stroke to the final note of the ligature, representing a single note a step above or below [Exx. 5, 6]. It is the convention of modern editions of early music to reproduce this second note in a smaller size or with a slash through the stem (sometimes connecting the note-head to the preceding note with a slur). There is some doubt whether it implies a special or ornamental vocal technique, as the remarks of Lambertus (Pseudo-Aristotle, *CS* 1:273) about closing the epiglottis and subtly vibrating the throat might suggest. Music with text provides some evidence that the plica continued to serve in situations of the sort associated with liquescence.

In the rhythmic *modes of the repertory of Notre Dame, the rhythmic effect of the plica is to subdivide the value of the note to which it is attached. Thus, a two-note ligature that would be transcribed as an eighth note followed by a quarter becomes, with the addition of a plica, three eighth notes. With the systematic distinction between the long [Exx. 1, 3] and the breve [Exx. 2, 4] in the late 13th century, long and breve plicas were also introduced.

Plötzlich [Ger.]. Suddenly.

Plus [Fr.]. More.

Pneuma [Gr., Lat.]. **Neuma.*

Pneumatic action. In organs, a mechanical key or stop action that is assisted by pneumatic pouches.

Poche, pochette [Fr.]. *Kit.

Poco [It.]. Little in amount; *un poco,* a little; *poco a poco,* little by little; *fra poco,* shortly; *pochettino, pochetto,* very little; *pochissimo,* extremely little.

Podatus [Lat.]. See Neume.

Poetic meter. See Prosody.

Pohjola's Daughter [Finn. *Pohjolan Tytär*]. A symphonic fantasia by Sibelius, op. 49 (1906), based on an episode from the **Kalevala.*

Poi [It.]. Then, afterward; *poi la coda,* then (play) the coda, e.g., after the final repetition of the scherzo in a scherzo with trio.

Point. (1) The tip of the violin or similar bow, at the end opposite the one at which it is held. (2) Point of *imitation. In a work making consistent use of imitation, a passage made up of statements of a single subject by each voice in succession. Many polyphonic works of the Renaissance consist of a series of such passages, each on a new subject and often overlapping, a new point of imitation beginning as the last voices to enter in the preceding point conclude. (3) [Lat. *punctus*] The point or dot of perfection [see Mensural notation].

Point d'orgue [Fr.]. (1) *Fermata. (2) *Cadenza, often signaled in notation by a fermata. (3) In the 17th century, rarely, *pedal point (for which the standard term since the 19th century has been *pédale*).

Pointer [Fr.]. To dot [see *Notes inégales*].

Pointillism. By analogy with the technique of this name employed by painters such as Georges Seurat (1859–91), a musical texture in which pitches are presented in varying timbres and largely in linear isolation from one another rather than in successions to be perceived as melodies. See *Klangfarbenmelodie.*

Pointing. See Anglican chant.

Polacca [It.]. *Polonaise; *alla polacca,* in the Polish style.

Poland. I. *Current musical life and related institutions.* Although Poland was devastated in World War II, its musical life revived rapidly afterward; as early as 1947 10 orchestras were active, and today the state's Ministry of Culture and Art supports at least that many (most of which have their own choruses and chamber ensembles), including the National Philharmonic (Warsaw), the Polish Radio and TV Symphony Orchestra, and the Szymanowski, Silesian, Wrocław, and Łódź Philharmonics. Polish Radio has orchestras in Łódź, Bydgoszcz, Wrocław, and Kraków; it has advocated and supported avant-garde music since the 1950s, when it established an electronic studio at Warsaw. Opera and operetta are performed in some 19 state theaters throughout the country, including the National Opera and the Warsaw Chamber Opera. Important choirs include the Polish Radio Choir, the National Philharmonic Choir, and the Poznań Men's and Boys' Choir. The annual "Warsaw Autumn" International Festival of Contemporary Music, founded by the composers Baird and Serocki in 1956, continues to draw musicians from all over the world. Dozens of other festivals are devoted to contemporary music, early music, chamber music, opera,. folk music, choral music, sacred music, music of the organ and other specific instruments. The nation's composers are represented by the Union of Polish Composers (est. 1945), which founded a music library for works by Polish composers in 1950 and established the Polish Music Information Center in 2001. Schools of music are at Warsaw, Gdańsk, Katowice, Kraków, Łódź, Poznań, and Wrocław.

II. *History.* Because of ever-changing borders and frequent influxes of neighboring peoples, Poland's music has drawn upon a rich variety of ethnic and artistic traditions. The recorded history of its art music begins with the adoption of Christianity in 966 and the subsequent dissemination of the Roman liturgy. An expanding musical tradition is attested to by liturgical books, by 14th- and 15th-century Marian songs and *kolędy* [sing. **kolęda,* carol], and by the Burgundy- and Netherlands-influenced polyphony of such native composers as Mikołaj of Radom (fl. first half of

15th century). During the 16th century, which is often called the golden age of Polish music, leading European musicians such as Marenzio and Merula were active in Poland, particularly at the royal chapel at Kraków; music of the first half of the century by native composers such as Sebastian z Felsztyna, Mikołaj z Chrzanów, and Mikołaj z Krakowa shows the influence of these imported styles. Prominent composers and lutenists during the second half of the century include the Hungarian Bálint Bakfark (1507–76), Jakub Polak (1545–1605), and Wojciech Dlugoraj (1558–1619). At the Warsaw court, King Sigismund III (1587–1632) encouraged the development of the polychoral style and imitative instrumental music (canzonas, ricercars), as manifested in the music of Mikołaj Zieleński (fl. ca. 1611), Marcin Mielczewski (d. 1651), and Adam Jarzebski (d. 1648 or 1649). Italian opera flourished in Warsaw throughout the 17th century.

During the 18th century, symphony and public opera flowered in Poland. Prominent symphonists include Jakub Golabek (1739–89), Jan Kleczyński (1756–1828), Feliks Janiewicz (1762–1848), and Jan Wański (1762–1800); among opera composers of the 18th and the early 19th century were Michał Kazimierz Ogiński (1728–1800), Mathias Kamienski (1734–1821), Jan Dawid Holland (1746–1827), Antoni Wejnert (1751–1850), Józef Elsner (1769–1854), Franciszek Lessel (1780–1838), and Karol Kurpiński (1785–1857). In the music of composers such as Ogiński and Józef Kozłowski (1757–1831), nationalistic sentiment manifested itself in the *polonaise, a stylized version of a native folk dance that, with other dances such as the *mazurka, was to form an essential part of the music of Chopin, the first Polish composer whose music had international influence. Other significant composers from around the middle of the 19th century were Stanisław Moniuszko (1819–72), Józef Nowakowski (1800–65), Julian Fontana (1810–65), and composer-violinist Henryk Wieniawski (1835–80). Important composers of the late 19th and early 20th centuries include Władysław Żeleński (1837–1921), Zygmunt Noskowski (1846–1909), Ignacy Jan Paderewski (1860–1941), Henryk Melcer-Szczawiński (1869–1928), Zygmunt Stojowski (1870–1946), and Roman Statkowski (1859–1925). During the first half of the 20th century the more progressive "Young Poland" group included Mieczysław Karłowicz (1876–1909), Ludomir Różycki (1883–1953), and, most important, Karol Szymanowski (1882–1937). Those prominent between the world wars were Witold Maliszewski (1873–1939), Józef Koffler, (1896–1943 or 1944), Witold Friemann (1899–1977), Artur Malawski (1904–57), Grażyna Bacewicz (1909–69), and Michał Spisak (1914–65).

Significant composers of recent years have included Stanisław Wiechowicz (1893–1963), Bolesław Szabelski (1896–1979), Antoni Szałowski (1907–73), Andrzej Panufnik (1914–91), Kazimierz Serocki (1922–81), Stanisław Skrowaczewski (b. 1923), Włodzimierz Kotónski (1925–81), Tadeusz Baird (1928–81), Bogusław Schäffer (b. 1929), Henryk Górecki (b. 1933), and especially Witold Lutosławski (1913–94) and Krzysztof Penderecki (b. 1933). Górecki and Penderecki pursued a "Polish" appropriation of old music and religious genres, a trend that has continued in the music of Zygmunt Krauze (b. 1938), Tomasz Sikorski (1939–88), and Wojciech Kilar (b. 1932), all of whom appropriated folk music in their compositions. The musical styles of current Polish composers, including Marta Ptaszyńska (b. 1943), Krzysztof Baculewski (b. 1950), Pawel Szymański (b. 1954), and Hanna Kulenty (b. 1961), are very diverse.

III. *Folk music.* The Institute of Fine Arts in Warsaw stores more than 70,000 recordings of folk songs accumulated since World War II. Important song types include *przyśpiewki* (ballads), *polne* (field songs), *kolędy* (carols), lullabies, ritual songs for weddings and births, and songs for calendar rituals. Typical dances are the *przytrampywanie* wedding dance, the *zbójnicki* circle dance, the *szewc* and *miotłarz* figure dances, and the **kujawiak, oberek* [see *Obertas*], and *okrąły* round dances. In general, the songs are syllabic, employ a diatonic scale, and are sung monophonically. The syllable divisions of the verse forms are related to the patterns of national dances such as mazurka, polonaise, and *krakowiak. Typical folk instruments are the five types of bagpipe (*koziol, dudy, gajdy, koza,* and *siesieńki*); the *bazuna* or *ligawka* shepherd's trumpets and *fujarki* fipple flute; and stringed instruments such as the *mazanki* and *suka* fiddles, the cellolike *basy,* and the *cymbały* (dulcimer).

Bibl.: Józef M. Chomiński and Zofia Lissa, eds., *Music of the Polish Renaissance,* trans. Claire Grece Dabrowska (Kraków: PWM, 1955). Ludwik Bielawski, ed., *Adolf Chybiński: O polskiej muzyce ludowej: wybór prac etnograficznych* [Adolf Chybiński: On Polish Folk Music: A Selection of His Ethnographical Works] (Kraków: PWM, 1961). Stefan Jarociński, "Polish Music after World War II," *MQ* 51 (1965): 244–58. Id., ed., *Polish Music* (Warsaw: PWM–Polish Scientific Publishers, 1965). Ludwik Bielawski, *Rytmika polskich pieśni ludowych* [The Rhythm of Polish Folksongs] (Kraków: PWM, 1970). Boleslaw Bartkowski, *Polskie spiewy religijne w zywej tradycji* [Polish Religious Songs in Living Tradition] (Kraków: PWM, 1987). Anna Czekanowska, *Polish Folk Music: Slavonic Heritage, Polish Tradition, Contemporary Trends* (Cambridge: Cambridge U Pr, 1990). Teresa Malecka, ed., *Krakowska szkola kompozytorska 1888–1988* [The Kraków Composition School 1888–1988] (Kraków, 1993). Jan Steszewski, "Polish National Character in Music: What Is It?" in *Stereotypes and Nations: Kraków 1991,* ed. T. Walas (Kraków: International Cultural Center, 1995), pp. 225–30. Józef Chominski and Krystyna Wilkowska-Chominska, *Historia muzyki polskiej* [History of Polish Music], 2 vols. (Kraków: PWM, 1995–96). Bernard Jacobson, *A Polish Renaissance* (London: Phaidon, 1996). Jacek Rogala and Ewa Widota-Nyczek, *Polish Music in the Twentieth Century* (Kraków: PWM, 2000).

Polka. A Bohemian dance originating ca. 1830 and becoming extremely popular throughout Europe and in America in the course of the 19th century. It is in a moderately fast 2/4, often incorporating the rhythm shown in the example.

Polkas were composed by the leading composers of ballroom music of the 19th century (including both Johann Strausses), and examples occur in art music by Smetana (**Bartered Bride, *From My Life,* numerous piano pieces), Dvořák, and others. Performed by polka bands, most often with accordion, it has remained popular in American cities among groups of Central and Eastern European origin.

Polo [Sp.]. (1) A song and dance of southern Spain originating in the 18th century and popular into the 19th. Manuel García (1775–1832) composed two examples that became well known outside of Spain, "Polo del Contrabandista" and "Cuerpo bueno," the latter taken up by Bizet in the prelude to act 4 of *Carmen.* (2) A type of *flamenco music belonging to the genre of *cante hondo* and related to the **soleá.* It is probably unrelated to (1). An example in art music is the last of Falla's *Siete canciones populares españolas.*

Polonaise [Fr.]. (1) A festive, processional, couple dance of Polish origin in a moderate tempo. The polonaise, not so named until the 17th century, stems from Polish folk dances accompanied by singing, such as the *chodzony,* the *wolny,* and the *wielki.* Most of the extant music for these dances is in triple meter, lacks upbeats, and has internal short repeated sections.

Before the end of the 16th century, the Polish folk dances that are ancestors of the polonaise were adopted by the lower ranks of the upper classes. At first their sung accompaniment was retained, but as these dances became popular among people of higher status, the music was transferred to the instrumentalists who accompanied court dances. In this form, Polish dances spread throughout Europe.

(2) An instrumental piece, originating in accompaniment to the courtly dance and largely developed outside of Poland. Pieces called Polish dances *(polnischer Tanz, chorea polonica, polacca)* are found in sources of the late 16th century such as the tablatures of Elias Nikolaus Ammerbach (1583) and August Nörmiger (1598) and a manuscript tablature owned by Christoph Loeffelholz (1585). But these lack the features that characterize the later polonaise, which emerged in the 17th century. In the 18th century, the stylized instrumental polonaise acquired the characteristics thereafter considered typical: moderate tempo, triple meter, lack of upbeats, and repetition of rhythmic figures. Certain initial and final rhythmic patterns are less consistently present. A common initial rhythm, often accompanimental rather than melodic, is shown in Ex. 1. Endings of polonaises are usually feminine, the accents occurring after the downbeat. Characteristic final rhythms are shown in Ex. 2.

The first polonaises showing all these features (except the initial rhythm) include those of Bach (French Suite no. 6, Orchestral Suite no. 2). The genre was particularly admired and cultivated in the 18th century by Germanic composers. Telemann, Sperontes (vocal works), Johann Gottlieb Goldberg, Wilhelm Friedemann Bach, Johann Philipp Kirnberger, Johann Schobert, and Mozart made notable contributions. As the polonaise ceased to be essentially a dance with sung accompaniment, becoming chiefly instrumental, it underwent stylistic and formal changes. In particular, melodies became wider in range and more charged with figuration. It was also sometimes given a trio (like the minuet) or set in rondo form.

After 1800, the instrumental polonaise began to be cultivated in Poland by composers including Prince Michael Ogiński, Wojciech Zywny, Józef Elsner, Józef Kozłowski, and Karol Kurpiński. The popularity of polonaises by some of these men contributed greatly to the spread of the genre throughout Europe, in the guise of salon pieces in particular.

The greatest and most prominent composer of polonaises was Chopin, whose works for piano made the dance a symbol of Poland. Notable examples include those in A major op. 40 no. 1 (the so-called *Military* Polonaise, 1838) and A♭ major op. 53 (1842). Other composers of polonaises include Beethoven, Schubert, Schumann, Weber, Liszt, Musorgsky, and Tchaikovsky.

Bibl.: Feliks Starczewski, "Die polnischen Tänze," *SIMG* 2 (1900/1901): 673–718. Tobias Norlind, "Zur Geschichte der polnischen Tänze," *SIMG* 12 (1910/11): 501–25. Wilhelm Merian, ed., *Der Tanz in den deutschen Tabulaturbüchern* (Leipzig: Breitkopf & Härtel, 1927; R: Hildesheim: Olms, 1968). Curt Sachs, *Eine Weltgeschichte des Tanzes* (Berlin: Reimer, 1933); trans. Bessie Schönberg, *World History of the Dance* (New York: Norton, 1937; R: 1963).

Polovtsian Dances. A choral and orchestral interlude in the second act of Borodin's opera **Prince Igor.* The Polovtsy are nomadic invaders of Russia who, in the opera, capture the Russian warrior Prince Igor Svyatoslavich (1151–1202).

Polska. Any of several dances, at first in triple meter, but subsequently also in duple meter, thought to derive from early Polish dances [see Polonaise] and popular elsewhere in Europe, especially in Scandinavia, from the 16th century. The Swedish dance of this name is similar in character to the *mazurka.

Polychoral. Composed with parts for two or more

choirs, most often separately positioned; sometimes also termed antiphonal. In principle, though not always in practice, music of this type exploits an element of contrast or tension between the choirs rather than mere alternation or duplication. It is particularly associated with the *Venetian school of the later 16th century, where the terms *coro battente* and *coro spezzato* (broken choir, pl. *cori spezzati*) were used. The architecture of the Basilica of St. Mark particularly facilitated its performance. The first Venetian composer with whom the technique is closely associated was Adrian Willaert, who published Psalm settings of this type *(salmi spezzati)* in 1550. Venetian exponents from later in the century include especially Andrea and Giovanni Gabrieli. The technique was by no means limited to Venice, however. It is found earlier in the century in music from Bergamo, Padua, and Treviso, and in the later 16th and early 17th centuries it was cultivated widely in Europe, by Palestrina, Victoria, Lassus, Soriano, Benevoli, Hassler, Schütz, and others. Works that deploy choral and/or instrumental forces spatially have been composed regularly since and include Bach's *St. Matthew Passion* and Berlioz's *Requiem.* A resurgence of such techniques in the 20th century can be credited in large part to Henry Brant and Karlheinz Stockhausen.

Bibl.: Denis Arnold, "The Significance of 'Cori spezzati,'" *ML* 40 (1959): 4–14. Paul Winter, *Der mehrchörige Stil* (Frankfurt am Main: C F Peters, 1964). James H. Moore, "The *Vesepro delli Cinque Laudate* and the Role of *Salmi Spezzati* at St. Mark's," *JAMS* 34 (1981): 249–78.

Polychord. (1) See Monochord. (2) In music of the 20th century, a chord made up of two or more simpler, usually familiar types of chord such as a triad, e.g., the so-called **Petrushka* chord, which consists of a C-major triad and an F♯-major triad.

Polychronion [Gr.]. See Acclamation.

Polymeter. The simultaneous use of two or more meters. The term is sometimes applied, however, to the successive use of different meters in one or more parts.

Polyphony [Fr. *polyphonie;* Ger. *Mehrstimmigkeit;* It. *polifonia;* Sp. *polifonia*]. Music that combines several distinct melodic lines simultaneously. In principle, the term is used in contrast to *monophonic music, which consists of a single melodic line, and *homophonic music, which consists of several lines moving at the same time in the same rhythm. In practice, however, such distinctions are often blurred because the categories themselves are hard to define precisely. The distinction between polyphony and monophony is particularly hard to draw. It is unclear, for example, whether melodies sung in octaves or performed against sustained notes or *drones should be treated as monophonic or polyphonic. Moreover, a single melody line can itself project more than one line of counterpoint; such lines are known as polyphonic or compound melodies. To complicate matters further, few pieces belong exclusively to one category; on the contrary, certain music forms often depend on alternating between sections of monophony, homophony, and polyphony.

Within the realm of polyphonic music, it is possible to identify several distinct categories. Two of the most important are so-called equal- and unequal-voice polyphony. In equal-voice polyphony, the individual lines present the same thematic material, though they are staggered in time. The most rigorous works of this type are *canons. Canons are pieces in which each voice, using the same melodic material either exactly or in some transformed state, enters at a fixed time interval. Though less rigorous than canons, most other types of *imitation, including so-called *fugues, also fall under the rubric of equal-voice polyphony. Meanwhile, in unequal-voice polyphony, one or more voices are assumed to have a structural priority over the others. For example, in **cantus firmus* compositions of the 14th and early 15th centuries, the most important polyphonic voice is usually the tenor, for it is the one that projects the preexisting melody, or *cantus firmus.* In contrast, much music of the Common Practice period is controlled by the counterpoint between the soprano and bass; this arrangement is often known as outer-voice polyphony.

When discussing equal- and unequal-voice polyphony of the Renaissance and Common Practice periods, it is important to remember that the individual melodic lines generally conform to certain general principles of music construction. These rules of counterpoint, which vary from one period to another, guarantee that the behavior of one melody is coordinated with that of the others. But such coordination is missing from many kinds of music; one polyphonic line is simply placed above or below another. Such procedures are particularly common in the music of Stravinsky, Ives, and other 20th-century composers. The result is what is usually known as a stratified texture. Another way in which composers have eroded the sense of coordination between polyphonic voices is by employing "pointillist techniques." This usually involves splitting the notes of a melody between different instruments or voices. Such principles appeared in the 13th and 14th centuries in *hockets and resurfaced in the 20th century in Schoenberg's concept of **Klangfarbenmelodie.* M.B.

Polyrhythm. The simultaneous use of two or more rhythms that are not readily perceived as deriving from one another or as simple manifestations of the same meter; sometimes also *cross-rhythm. Familiar examples in tonal music are the simultaneous use of triple and duple subdivisions of the beat, and the simultaneous use of 3/4 and 6/8 or similarly related pairs of meters (whether or not explicitly indicated), termed *hemiola. Much more complex examples are found in some French music of the 14th century [see *Ars subtilior*]. Western art music of the 20th century offers numerous examples, often notated explicitly with conflicting meters. Such techniques are especially prominent in some music of Elliot Carter. Traditional African music abounds in polyrhythm, and it is evident in African-derived musics of the New World.

Polytextuality. The simultaneous use of two texts in a vocal work. It is a prominent feature of the *motet in the 13th and 14th centuries, and it occurs occasionally in genres of secular music of the 14th and 15th centuries as well [see Double *ballade*]. Apart from the simple observation that one text may comment or bear thematically on another, the aesthetics of such works remains little explored, in part because of the Renaissance view that music could and thus should properly "express" only a single set of words at a time. See also Text and music.

Polythematic. See Monothematic, polythematic.

Polytonality. See Bitonality, polytonality.

Pommer, Pomhart [Ger.]. See *Bombard.*

Pomp and Circumstance. Five concert marches for orchestra by Elgar, op. 39 (nos. 1–4 composed in 1901–7, no. 5 completed by 1930). The title is taken from a phrase in Shakespeare's *Othello,* act 3, sc. 3: "Pride, pomp, and circumstance of glorious war!"

Pomposo [It.]. Pompous.

Ponticello [It.]. The *bridge of a stringed instrument [for *sul ponticello,* see Bowing (11)].

Pontifical. See Liturgical books.

Popular music. Most commonly understood to be a musical idiom of recent centuries whose mass-disseminated works appeal to a broad pubic. The 18th and 19th centuries saw the development, chiefly in Europe and America, of a genre distinct from both folk and classical or art music. It differed from the former in being composed and notated and in developing a musical style not distinctive of a certain region or ethnic group. Though many early pieces of popular music shared general features with classical music of the day, they were briefer and simpler, making fewer demands on both performer and listener.

Factors contributing to the development of popular music include the emergence and growth of a middle class, literate and with the means and desire to be involved in newly composed music but without the cultural heritage to be fully involved in classical music; the mass production of chord-playing instruments such as the guitar, concertina, and piano; the development of new, less expensive methods of music printing; and the rise of a popular musical theater, making use of songs that could be widely disseminated in the form of inexpensive items of sheet music for home use.

These factors—all aspects of a growing leisure culture reflecting developing capitalist economies—were at work in England in the second quarter of the 18th century: songs from *ballad operas and *comic operas and from the stages of pleasure gardens were printed as sheet music and bought by accomplished amateurs for home use. Thomas Arne's two song sets *Lyric Harmony* (1745–46)—written for Vauxhall Gardens—are important prototypes, and the remainder of the century brought publication of hundreds of individual songs and collections by Arne, Samuel Arnold, William Shield, William Reeve, Reginald Spofforth, and James Hook. Hook's *A Collection of New English Songs* of 1767 was followed by more than 2,000 songs. The most successful items of this repertory were disseminated and performed throughout the British Isles and also in English-speaking colonies elsewhere in the world.

Increasing musical literacy also brought the composition of choral music that made modest demands on the singer and was intended for amateur or home performance, and a keyboard repertory designed for players of limited technique—variations on familiar tunes, dance and descriptive, or *character, pieces, and simplified transcriptions of items from the classical repertory. There was no sharp differentiation between classical and popular styles on the Continent in the 18th century; C. P. E. Bach and Mozart were among the composers who wrote some pieces that could be performed by talented amateurs. But the first decades of the 19th century brought keyboard-accompanied songs and choral pieces by Franz Abt, Friedrich Wilhelm Kücken, and Weber that were clearly designed for amateur performance.

Arrangements of traditional Irish or Scottish tunes and newly composed songs drawing on stylistic elements of this music were part of the British popular song repertory for most of the 18th century. This trend peaked at the turn of the century and in the first decades of the 19th with the songs of Robert Burns and Thomas Moore. Burns fitted his own lyrics to Scottish folk melodies; publication began in 1787 in *The Scots Musical Museum,* and soon commercial publishers began bringing out individual songs in sheet music form. Some of these, including "Comin' Thro' the Rye" and "John Anderson My Jo," became staples of home and stage music in Britain and North America. Moore's *Irish Melodies,* created in the same way, appeared serially between 1808 and 1834, and several dozen of these became the most widely disseminated songs in the English language of the entire century.

In addition, melodies from the Italian operas of Mozart, Rossini, Bellini, and Donizetti were simplified, fitted with new texts and keyboard accompaniments, and printed as single items of sheet music. By the 1820s and 30s, such hybrid songs were enjoying great popularity as parlor songs in Britain and America and on the Continent.

This same period saw the emergence of the first distinctive songs created in the U.S., melodies from the *minstrel stage. Tunes drawn from the Anglo-American folk tradition were given new texts supposedly reflecting the character of American blacks. The banjo, created by slaves in imitation of instruments they or their ancestors had known in Africa, was the most important accompanying instrument, playing at first nonharmonic ostinato patterns also suggestive of African practice. These minstrel songs spread all over America in the 1830s and were enthusiastically received in Britain and on the Continent as well, being perceived as the first American music of any kind to have taken on an indigenous character.

Europe, particularly the British Isles, continued to produce talented and successful writers of songs for home and stage use in the 19th century—John Braham, Charles Edward Horn, Sir Henry Bishop, Samuel Lover, Claribel (Charlotte Alington Barnard), and Sir Arthur Sullivan—but their songs essentially continued traditions rooted in the 18th century. It was the American Stephen Collins Foster (1826–64) who found new directions for popular music that were both fresh and commercially successful. A well-trained musician with considerable knowledge of classical music, Foster made a deliberate decision to confine his musical vocabulary to the simplest elements of melody, accompaniment, and harmony to ensure that his songs would be accessible to the widest possible range of performers and listeners. Combining elements of Irish, English, German, and minstrel songs into an unmistakable personal style, Foster created masterpieces of the popular repertory ("Old Folks at Home" and "Jeanie with the Light Brown Hair") whose appeal cut across social and economic barriers of 19th-century American life. Though these were composed songs, disseminated as sheet music, they also passed into oral tradition and thus afforded a musical link between distinct cultural groups and musical practices. Sales of Foster's songs made up a significant percentage of the gross income of his several publishers, encouraging the industry to pay more attention to the popular repertory; Foster was able to sustain himself for some years—albeit poorly—with the income from his songwriting.

The years following the American Civil War were dominated by songwriters in the U.S. and Europe who took Foster's music and texts as a point of departure. Typical products were William S. Hays's "We Parted by the River Side" (1866), Thomas Westendorf's "I'll Take You Home Again, Kathleen" (1875), and "Grand-Father's Clock" (1875) by Henry Clay Work, sentimental verse-chorus pieces patterned after Foster's later plantation songs. This period also brought a proliferation of the popular piano literature, made up in large part of European social dances: the *waltz, *polka, *mazurka, *schottisch, *polonaise, and *two-step. The first pieces of this sort having an American character, with rhythms drawn from African American dances (or, in most cases, white perceptions of this music), appeared late in the 19th century as character pieces, with titles referring to blacks: patrols, *cakewalks, and, in the 1890s, the first pieces of *ragtime. Like the music from minstrel shows earlier in the century, such pieces attracted considerable attention in Europe.

A new generation of American songwriters emerged in the 1890s, led by Charles K. Harris, Paul Dresser, and Harry Von Tilzer. These men, their publishers, and the most important *vaudeville theaters in which their songs were first publicized were concentrated in New York City. The texts of their songs were most often concerned with urban life, and both melodies and accompanying harmonies became more sophisticated than they had been in the folk-influenced songs of the previous generation, reflecting the cosmopolitan nature of New York culture and its close ties with European life. A new breed of publishers, concentrating on popular music, succeeded in making sheet music sales of a million or more copies relatively common, beginning with Harris's "After the Ball" of 1892. By the 1910s and 20s, a slightly younger and even more talented group of songwriters, led by Jerome Kern, Irving Berlin, George Gershwin, Cole Porter, and Richard Rodgers, had assumed the leadership of American popular song. By that time, new mechanical means for the dissemination of music had appeared—the *player piano, the nickelodeon and other music machines, the phonograph [see Recording], *radio, and in the late 1920s, the sound film [see Film music]. In addition to expanding the size of the audience for popular music, these new media began contributing to the most profound change in the entire history of the genre, from active consumption of products through performance in the home to a primarily auditory musical experience.

Because of their subject matter and musical style, the new urban popular songs of *Tin Pan Alley had a more limited audience than those of Stephen Foster and his successors, though their popularity was global among the classes for which they were intended. But beginning in the early 1920s, the same new media began disseminating several bodies of music that had previously existed only in oral tradition and, like most folk music, had been the property of specific ethnic, racial, and geographical groups. The phonograph industry and commercial radio began offering several types of African American music (*blues, *jazz, religious music) on a regional basis in the South and in northern cities with substantial black populations. Traditional Anglo-American music and its contemporary dialects, soon labeled hillbilly, were disseminated first in the South and soon in the Midwest, Southwest, and Far West as well [see Country music]. Numerous types of folk music of European, Mexican, Arab, and Asian origin were recorded, sold, and broadcast in urban areas of America boasting enough people of appropriate origin. Thus new technology, disseminating folk music more efficiently and widely than had been possible before, brought to a broad, culturally diverse public sounds confined previously to a specific group. Jazz and blues in particular benefited from this process, gaining exposure among white audiences in

America and Europe who might not have known of their existence otherwise. Indeed, by the 1930s big band jazz, played by blacks and whites, had become the most popular idiom of the day. And in time hillbilly music and its subsequent country and western dialects also spread beyond the cultural environment that had created and nourished it.

The general prosperity in America following the end of World War II in 1945, combined with more new technologies, of which the most important were inexpensive transistor radios and 45-rpm phonograph discs, brought to a new peak the mass dissemination of music in idioms accessible to almost everyone. When the Tin Pan Alley style of songwriting, which had endured for more than half a century, began its inevitable decline, it was succeeded in the mid-1950s by a vibrant new music drawing on elements of African American and Anglo-American styles, soon given the label of *rock and roll. Young people throughout Europe and also in many other parts of the world responded to rock and roll with the same enthusiasm witnessed in America, a process facilitated by the simplicity and directness of both music and lyrics.

During the 1960s and 1970s, popular music moved decisively in the direction of stylistic pluralism. In America, many records of the early 1960s, from both independent and major record companies, worked elements of early rock and roll into professional arrangements of songs by urban songwriters (Neil Sedaka). African American performers produced a succession of related styles, from rhythm and blues (Ray Charles) through vocal doo wop and "girl groups" (Platters, Shirelles) to soul (Otis Redding), Motown (Supremes), funk (James Brown), and disco (Donna Summer). The Kingston Trio; Peter, Paul and Mary; Bob Dylan; and Joan Baez spearheaded a new school of urban folk music, elements of which were subsequently combined with rock elements to form the folk rock genre (Byrds). California pioneered a highly electric style associated with drug usage and social protest (Jefferson Airplane, Grateful Dead). In the early 1970s a specifically southern brand of rock emerged (Allman Brothers); many country performers brought elements of both rock and urban popular styles into their music (Willie Nelson); and in the later 1970s a "new wave" of rock appeared, reinvigorating the idiom with a fresh approach to songwriting, arranging, and record production (Cars). Though all this music is often embraced under the single label of rock or pop, each style has its own primary audience drawn together by perceptions of personal and cultural identity.

With the rise of global music traffic and growing transnational commerce, popular music has taken on an increasingly international complexion. Popular traditions once confined to a specific country or region now claim a voice on the world stage, thanks to sound recording, radio, film, and the tools of mass dissemination and marketing. The worldwide popularity of British rock groups like the Beatles and the Rolling Stones in the 1960s opened a new chapter in postwar popular music as the nearly ubiquitous styles of American popular music were joined by those of other countries. Much of this music bore at least some rock influence, yet indigenous musical elements and cultural sensibilities made for an increasingly syncretic international mainstream, which came to include international hits by artists from Australia (Midnight Oil), Brazil (Sergio Mendes), Canada (Joni Mitchell), Iceland (Björk), Ireland (U2), Jamaica (Bob Marley), Japan (Cibo Matto), Puerto Rico (Ricky Martin), Senegal (Youssou N'Dour), South Africa (Hugh Masekela), and Sweden (Abba), among others. Regional styles such as South African *mbaqanga* (Juluka), Nigerian *juju* (King Sunny Ade), Brazilian bossa nova, Cuban salsa (Celia Cruz), and Jamaican reggae have joined the international tapestry of popular music both as discrete styles and as trace influences. At the same time, the emergence of rap music in the 1980s spread yet another American musical influence throughout the world. The rap style pioneered by African American rappers can now be heard emulated in numerous languages.

In recent decades the wide-ranging musical experience of many popular musicians has led also to hybrid styles that partake of the techniques and aspirations of classical concert music. The ambitious scope of such works is evident in their expanded length, instrumentation, and musical form. Examples are to be found in many different genres, including Argentinean tango (Astor Piazzolla, *Concierto para bandoneón*), jazz (Carla Bley, *Escalator over the Hill*), rock (Who, *Tommy*), and hip hop (DJ Shadow, "What Does Your Soul Look Like?"). Further, the proliferation of affordable computer recording technologies has made for a worldwide culture of desktop music production, with pop composers crafting musical works largely in isolation, much like their concert music counterparts.

Bibl.: Edward Lee, *Music of the People: A Study of Popular Music in Great Britain* (London: Barrie & Jenkins, 1970). Charles Hamm, *Yesterdays: Popular Song in America* (New York: Norton, 1979). Bill C. Malone, *Country Music, U.S.A.* (Austin: U of Tex Pr, 1985). Manuel Peña, *The Texas-Mexican Conjunto: History of a Working Class Music* (Austin: U of Tex Pr, 1985). Peter Manuel, *Popular Musics of the Non-Western World: An Introductory Survey* (New York: Oxford U Pr, 1988). Russell Sanjek, *American Popular Music and Its Business: The First Four Hundred Years* (New York: Oxford U Pr, 1988). Peter van der Merwe, *Origins of the Popular Style: The Antecedents of Twentieth-Century Popular Music* (Oxford: Clarendon, 1989). Richard Middleton, *Studying Popular Music* (Milton Keynes, U.K.: Open U Pr, 1990). Christopher Waterman, *Juju: A Social History and Ethnography of an African Popular Music* (Chicago: U of Chicago Pr, 1990), Eric Lott, *Love and Theft: Blackface Minstrelsy and the American Working Class* (New York: Oxford U Pr, 1993). Charlie Gillett, *The Sound of the City: The Rise of Rock and Roll,* 2nd ed. (New York: Da Capo, 1996). Colin Larkin, ed., *The Encyclopedia of Popular Music* (London: Macmillan,

1998). Paul Oliver et al., *Yonder Come the Blues: The Evolution of a Genre* (Cambridge: Cambridge U Pr, 2001).

C.H., rev. A.Z.

Porgy and Bess. Opera in three acts by George Gershwin (libretto by DuBose Heyward with lyrics by Ira Gershwin, after the play *Porgy* by DuBose and Dorothy Heyward), produced in New York in 1935. Setting: Charleston, South Carolina, in the 1920s.

Porrectus [Lat.]. See Neume.

Portamento [It.]. A continuous movement from one pitch to another through all of the intervening pitches, without, however, sounding these discretely. It is principally an effect in singing and string playing, though for the latter and for other instruments capable of such an effect, the term glissando is often used [for distinctions between the two terms, see Glissando]. In vocal music, the portamento may be indicated by connecting with a slur two pitches that are sung to different syllables. If two pitches are sung to the same syllable, with the slur simply indicating this fact, a portamento is indicated by the term itself.

Portative organ. An organ small enough to be carried or placed on a table, usually with only one set of pipes. Medieval or Renaissance instruments intended to be carried in procession had one or two small bellows reachable by the player and a short range of three octaves or less. Larger portatives might have several stops, with sliders protruding at the sides and a range approaching four octaves. Although the bellows were built into such instruments, large ones required the assistance of a second person to pump them. See also Organetto, Positive organ.

J.T.F.

Portato [It.]. See Bowing (6).

Port de voix [Fr.]. A compound vocal ornament beginning below the principal note (most often, a step lower) and "carrying the voice" up to a resolution that is itself ornamented, the whole being sung to the syllable of the principal note; also an *appoggiatura. It seems to have been developed in the mid-17th century by singer-composers of the *air de cour,* in which it was one of the principal embellishments and whence it spread rapidly to other repertories, both instrumental and vocal. It could be introduced whenever a shorter note was followed by a longer, higher one on a strong part of the measure, except following a cadential trill. Until 1685, there was no sign for the *port de voix,* though it was often partially written out; after that, a *v* over the principal note was sometimes used and, later, other signs, including *petites notes.*

Port de voix. 1. Voice: Mersenne, *Harmonie universelle* (1636), p. 355. 2. Organ: Nivers, *Première livre d'orgue* (1665), preface. 3. Voice: Bacilly, *Remarques curieuses* (1668), trans. Caswell, p. 66. 4. Harpsichord: Chambonnières, *Les pièces de clavessin* (1670), preface. 5. Organ: Gigault, *Livre de musique* (1682), preface. 6. Viol: Jean Rousseau, *Traité de la viole* (1687), p. 87. 7. Harpsichord: D'Anglebert, *Pièces de clavecin* (1689), preface. 8. Voice: Loulié, *Eléments ou principes de musique* (1696), p. 69. 9. Voice: L'Affilard, *Principes très faciles* 2nd ed. (1697), p. 21. 10. Harpsichord: Saint-Lambert, *Les principes du clavecin* (1702), p. 51. 11. General: La Chapelle, *Les vrais principes de la musique* 2 (1737): 14. 12. Flute: Lusse, *L'art de la flûte traversière* (1761), p. 9. 13. Voice: Lacassagne, *Traité général* (1776), p. 69.

To execute the *port de voix* on a given note, the singer divided the preceding note in half and began the ornament on the second half, pronouncing the syllable belonging to the principal note, that is, with an *anticipatione della syllaba.* According to Bacilly (1668), the ornamental note was prolonged into the time of the principal one, delaying it more or less according to the effect desired. The voice then moved (or glided) up to the main note, which it embellished with a *coup de gosier* (a brief mordent, *accent,* or tone repetition) or some kind of vibrato. Whether the delay of the principal note was normal or exceptional in vocal music is disputed (Bacilly, pp. 141–43, as against *NeuO,* p. 55); it is not shown in ornament tables. Some writers recommended that the principal note should be sung more strongly than the ornamental one. Essential in all media was the slurring of the ornamental note to its resolution.

Varieties of *port de voix* were distinguished as *simple, doublé, plein, appuyé, feint, jetté, perdu, demi-port de voix,* or *port de voix par anticipation du son* (this last being Jean Rousseau's term for an appoggiatura). These generally differed in the treatment of the principal note, especially how long it was held and how embellished. Some writers recognized falling *ports de voix,* though the more common terms for these were **coulé* or **chûte.*

Players of melody instruments seem to have imitated the singers' *ports de voix,* interpreting them according to the nature of their instruments. Organists began by doing the same: Nivers (1665) said that in these matters "the organ should imitate the voice," and his examples showed simple, written-out *ports de voix* without any indication of an ornament on the main note (but in the compositions forming the main text, the main note is sometimes ornamented). The extravagant *ports de voix* in Gigault (1682) amounted to a division or paraphrase of the written lines. It is not certain how harpsichordists first interpreted the *port de voix.* The earliest explanation, by Chambonnières (1670), shows the characteristic repetition of the ornamental note, but beginning on the beat. It is possible, however, that this was meant to refer loosely to a variety of rhythmic possibilities. Although D'Anglebert (1689) explained the *port de voix* as an unequivocal appoggiatura, Saint-Lambert (1702) preferred that the ornamental note (or notes, in what he called the *port de voix appuyé*) should take its (or their) value entirely from the preceding note. It seems clear, however, that the old prebeat or straddling *port de voix* largely dropped out of use in all media during the first half of the 18th century in favor of various kinds of appoggiaturas, often with ornamented resolutions (but see *NeuO,* pp. 80–91, and Ex. 10 to the contrary).

Bibl.: Guillaume-Gabriel Nivers, *Première livre d'orgue* [*Liure d'orgue contenant cent pièces*] (Paris, 1665); ed. Norbert Dufourcq (Paris: Éditions Bornemann, 1963). Jacques Champion de Chambonnières, *Les pièces de clavessin* (Paris, 1670; facs., *MMML* ser. 1, 3, 1967). Nicolas Gigault, *Livre de musique dédié à la très Sainte Vierge* (Paris, 1682). Jean Rousseau, *Traité de la viole* (Paris, 1687; facs., Amsterdam: Antiqua, 1965); trans. Robert Green (Ph.D. diss., Indiana Univ., 1979). Jean-Henri D'Anglebert, *Pièces de clavecin* (Paris, 1689; facs., *MMML* ser. 1, 4). See also Ornamentation.

D.F.

Portugal. I. *Current musical life and related institutions.* The state, private organizations, and individuals play significant roles in present-day musical life in Portugal. Since 1934 the country's broadcasting system has maintained performing groups, which today include symphony and chamber orchestras in Lisbon and a symphony orchestra in Porto (Oporto), and has commissioned compositions. Associated with the Teatro São Carlos in Lisbon are a symphony orchestra, an opera company, and a chorus. The Calouste Gulbenkian Foundation, also in Lisbon, supports an orchestra, chorus, and ballet company; provides study grants; commissions compositions; records and publishes Portuguese music; publishes books about music; sponsors festivals; and promotes the cause of music education. Several cities have conservatories or academies of music, providing primary, secondary, and advanced instruction. Festivals are held in Sintra, Figueira Da Foz, Estoril, Faro (two, one dedicated to folklore), Leiria, Lisbon, and Cascais (jazz).

II. *History.* Little is known about early music in Portugal. A Portuguese church musician, Andreas "princeps cantorum," is recorded as early as the 6th century. The *Mozarabic rite was officially replaced on the Iberian peninsula by the Gregorian liturgy in 1085. In the 13th century, Alfonso III (reigned 1248–79) brought Provençal troubadours to his court. Seven Galician-Portuguese love lyrics (*cantigas d'amigo* [see *Cantiga*]), six with music, by Martin Codax survive from the 13th century. The true flowering of the nation's music came in the 16th century, under the influence of Spanish and Italian music, with important polyphonists such as Pedro de Escobar, Fernão Gomes Correia, Vasco Pires, Aires Fernandes, Heliodoro de Paiva, Pedro de Gamboa, and António Carreira. Hierónimo Román's description in 1595 of Portuguese musical culture as "lavish" is borne out by the wealth of music printed in Lisbon beginning at about that time, including works by Duarte Lobo (ca. 1565–1646), Manuel Cardoso (1571–1650), João Lourenço Rebello (1609–61), King John IV (1604–56), Manuel Cardoso (1566–1650), Filipe De Magalhães (ca. 1570–1652), and Manuel Rodrigues Coelho (ca. 1555–ca. 1635).

Italian influence was strong in the music composed at the court of John V (reigned 1706–50), such as the cantatas of André da Costa (fl. early 18th century) and Francisco José Coutinho (1680–1724). Domenico Scarlatti's Italianate church music written for the royal chapel (where he served from 1721 to 1729) contains none of the "Spanish" elements found in his keyboard music. Portuguese composers of opera in the 18th century also looked to Italy, as evident in the works of

João De Sousa Carvalho (1745–98), Marcos Antonio da Fonseca Portugal (1762–1830), and Antonio Leal Moreira (1758–1819). Other significant composers during the second half of the 18th century include Luciano Xavier dos Santos (1734–1808), José Maurício (1752–1815), António da Silva Leite (1759–1833), and João José Baldi (1770–1816). The symphonies of João Domingos Bomtempo (1775–1842) are in the style of the late Classical period in Austria. Other notable composers during the 19th and early 20th centuries were Joaquim Casimiro Júnior (1802–62), Alfredo Keil (1850–1907), and José Vianna da Motta (1868–1948). Recent composers include Fernando Lopes-Graça (b. 1906), Joly Braga Santos (b. 1924), Luis Filipe Pires (b. 1934), Alvaro Leon Cassuto (b. 1938), Jorge Peixinho (b. 1940), and Cláudio Carneyro (1895–1963). During the 1960s many composers were supported by the Gulbenkian Foundation.

III. *Folk music.* Most surviving Portuguese folk songs are thought to have originated during the 16th and 17th centuries. Vocal music is most prominent today and includes heroic and epic ballads, lyric songs dealing with aspects of everyday life (the two most typical types are *despedidas,* songs of farewell, and *saudades,* songs of desire and longing), and the widespread urban music called **fado.* The last named is heard in cafés and taverns and is frequently accompanied by the *viola* (four- or five-stringed guitar) or the *guitarra portuguesa* (a long-necked lute). Characteristic dances are the *vira* waltz, the *corridinho* (fast polka), and the *charamba* (circle-dance for couples). The *romaria* festivals bring together traditional dances and songs corresponding to specific calendar rituals.

Bibl.: Santiago Kastner, *Contribución al estudio de la música española y portuguesa* (Lisbon: Editorial Atica, 1941). Albert T. Luper, "The Music of Portugal," in Gilbert Chase, *The Music of Spain* (New York: Norton, 1941; 2nd ed. rev., New York: Dover, 1959). Kurt Schindler, ed., *Folk Music and Poetry of Spain and Portugal* (New York: Hispanic Institute in the U.S., 1941). Albert T. Luper, "Portuguese Polyphony in the 16th and early 17th Centuries," *JAMS* 3 (1950): 93–112. Solange Corbin, *Essai sur la musique religieuse portugaise au moyen âge (1100–1385)* (Paris: Les belles lettres, 1952). Fernando Lopes Graça, *A canção popular portuguesa* (Lisbon: Publicações Europa-America, 1953). João de Freitas Branco, *História de música portuguesa* (Lisbon: Publicações Europa-America, 1959). Robert Stevenson, *Portuguese Music and Musicians Abroad (to 1650)* (Lima, 1966). Ernesto Veiga de Oliveira, *Instrumentos musicais populares portugueses* (Lisbon: Gulbenkian, 1966; 2nd ed., 1982). José Sasportes, *História da dança em Portugal* (Lisbon: Gulbenkian, 1970). *Music in Portugal in the 20th Century* (Lisbon: Office of the Secretary of State for Information and Tourism, 1971).

Portuguese hymn. See *Adeste fideles.*

Pos. Abbr. for **Posaune, *positif,* *position.

Posaune [Ger.]. Trombone.

Positif (à dos) [Fr.]. The *Positive division of an organ, located at the player's back.

Position. (1) In harmony, the proximity in register of the several parts to one another, e.g., close position, open position [see Spacing]. (2) In string playing, the location of the hand on the fingerboard. In first or natural position on the violin, the first or index finger stops the pitch a whole tone above the open string, the fourth or little finger reaching a perfect fifth above the open string. Successively higher positions are numbered in order as the first finger is used to stop successively higher pitches of the diatonic scale. A movement from one position to another is termed a shift. The second position (first finger a minor third above the open string) is sometimes termed the half shift, the third position (first finger a perfect fourth above the open string) the whole or full shift, and the seventh position (first finger an octave above the open string) the last shift. By the late 17th century, music for virtuosos called for the seventh position. In the 18th century, Leopold Mozart and Francesco Geminiani regarded positions as high as the seventh as normal for good players, but still higher positions were sometimes required. Because of their larger size, the cello and double bass employ somewhat different systems. See also Fingering. (3) On the *trombone, any of the seven locations at which the slide is normally held. In first position, the slide is fully retracted, providing the shortest possible length of tubing and the fundamental tone by which the instrument is named (typically B♭). Successive positions lower the fundamental by a semitone.

Positive organ [Fr. *positif (à dos);* Ger. *Positiv, Rückpositiv;* It., Sp. *positivo*]. (1) The secondary division of an organ, with its pipes located behind the player, the key and stop actions running under the floor; also called Chair, because it is located behind the organist's chair or bench. Its disposition includes a full flue chorus, based on a 4′ Principal in modest instruments and on an 8′ Principal in large ones. One or more reed stops are usually included. The Positive is intended as a foil or even an equal to the Great organ and not merely as an echo division, although it has many antiphonal uses in the traditional repertory. A minimal disposition might include (in classic French style) **Bourdon* 8′, **Prestant* 4′, **Doublette* 2′, **Cymbale* III ranks, **Cromorne* 8′, and **Cornet* V ranks.

(2) A small, one-manual organ, usually without independent Pedal stops, rarely with a pedalboard (which, if present, is permanently coupled to the bass of the manual). Such organs are too large to be easily moved and contain a full flue chorus, normally based on a 4′ Principal, with one or more reed stops often included. J.T.F.

Post horn [Fr. *cornet de poste;* Ger. *Posthorn;* It. *cornetta da postiglione;* Sp. *corneta de postillón*]. A small horn sometimes straight or curved but usually coiled in a circle only a few inches across with mouthpiece and bell ends protruding at approximately a right angle to each other. From the beginning of postal service in the 16th century, small horns were used to signal the approach of the mail wagon. At first very short and sounding only an octave, they gradually acquired more length and the ability to play fanfarelike calls on pitches two to eight of the *harmonic series. Although usually of narrow proportions, they were occasionally as wide-bored as a *bugle. The post horn is one of the ancestors of the valved *cornet. R.E.E.

Postlude. A work forming the conclusion of a larger work or one performed at the end of a ceremony; especially a piece played (sometimes improvised) on the organ at the conclusion of a church service.

Postmodernism. See Twentieth century, Western art music of the.

Potpourri [Fr., "rotten pot," a stew of various meats and vegetables]. A composition based on selections from other works; sometimes also a *medley. The term was used early in the 18th century for miscellaneous collections of songs (e.g., the **brunettes* published by Ballard in 1703) and by the end of the century for medleys of opera melodies. Works titled *Potpourri* by Czerny and others sometimes elaborated considerably on their materials rather than merely weaving them loosely together.

Poule, La [Fr., The Hen]. Popular name for Haydn's Symphony no. 83 in G minor Hob. I:83 (1785; no. 2 of the **Paris* Symphonies), so called because the repeated woodwind figures accompanying the second theme of the first movement suggest the cackling of a hen.

Poussé [Fr.]. Up-bow [see Bowing (1)].

Pp. Abbr. for *pianissimo,* very soft [see *Piano*]. Sometimes three or more *p*s are used to specify even softer playing.

P.R. [Fr.]. In French organ music, abbr. for coupling the **Positif* to the **Récit.*

Praeambulum [Lat.]. *Prelude.

Praeconium paschale [Lat.]. A prayer of *Gallican origin forming part of the Easter Vigil and the blessing of the Paschal candle (*LU,* p. 776M), also termed the *Exultet* (from the opening phrase, "Exultet jam turba angelica") or *Benedictio cerei.* It has been sung to simple reciting tones as well as to more ornate melodies.

Praefatio [Lat.]. *Preface.

Praelegenda [Lat.]. In the *Gallican and *Mozarabic rites, the chant corresponding to the Gregorian *introit.

Praeludium [Lat.]. *Prelude.

Praestant. See Prestant.

Prague Symphony. Popular name for Mozart's Symphony no. 38 in D major K. 504, composed in Vienna in 1786 and first performed in Prague in 1787. Its three movements do not include a minuet.

Pralltriller [Ger.]. See *Schneller.*

Préambule [Fr.], **preambulum** [Lat.]. *Prelude.

Precentor. In an Anglican cathedral, the cleric who directs the singing; in some Protestant churches, the person who leads the congregational singing by *lining out.

Preces [Lat., prayers]. In the Roman rite, prayers consisting of a series of supplications in alternating *versicles and responses and sung or recited at Prime on ordinary Sundays [*LU,* p. 231]. In the *Gallican and *Mozarabic chant such prayers play a more prominent role and often have rhythmic texts and elaborate melodies (see examples published in *Variae preces,* Solesmes, 1888, and subsequent eds.). In form and origin they are closely related to the *litany. In the Anglican services of Morning and Evening Prayer, the term is sometimes applied to the versicles and responses beginning "O Lord, open thou our lips."

Precipitato [It.]. Rushed.

Preface [Lat. *praefatio*]. The introduction, together with the immediately following Sanctus, to the Canon [see Canon (3)] of the *Mass (*LU,* pp. 3–4). In the Middle Ages, there were a great many Proper prefaces, but this number was reduced to only a few by the 16th century (*LU,* pp. 8–10, all beginning with the words "Vere dignum").

Preghiera [It.]. An aria or chorus in which the character or characters plead for divine assistance. *Preghiere* are principally associated with 19th-century Italian opera (e.g., "Del tuo stellato soglio" in Rossini's *Mosè in Egitto* and the "Ave Maria" sung by Desdemona in Verdi's *Otello*); analagous numbers are found in French and German operas.

Prelude [fr. Lat. *praeludere,* to play beforehand; Fr. *prélude;* Ger. *Präludium, Preambel, Vorspiel;* It., Sp. *preludio;* also Lat. *preambulum*].

(1) A composition establishing the pitch or key of a following piece. In France and northern Europe, prelude has been a preferred title for pieces that have been equated with, and are virtually identical in style and function to, the **tiento,* *toccata, *ricercar, *fantasia, *arpeggiata, tastata, entrada,* etc. All feature an idiomatic virtuosity, rhythmic freedom, and loose thematic construction, reflecting frequent contemporaneous observations that they were usually improvised, particularly when serving a preludial function [Fr. *préluder,* Ger. *preludieren,* It. *sonar di fantasia,* etc., to play impromptu]. The improvisatory element is particularly evident in the unmeasured preludes *(préludes*

non mesurés) of 17th-century French lutenists and *clavecinistes* Denis Gaultier, Louis Couperin, and their contemporaries. In these works, undifferentiated notes are grouped into irregular and unbarred patterns whose rhythmic interpretation is left to the performer. More fully written-out preludes (e.g., those in Bach's *Das Orgel-Büchlein;* see Chorale prelude, Organ chorale) may serve the dual purposes of instructing the novice in the art of a famed composer-improviser and providing music for the composer's own performance.

The essential function of the prelude is to attract the listener's attention and define the pitch, mode, or tonality of a following Mass movement, motet, hymn, secular song, ricercar, fugue, set of dances, etc. Most are thematically unrelated to the piece or pieces they preface. Accordingly, collections of preludial pieces will often provide a selection with one in each of the 8 (or 12) modes, or 24 major and minor tonalities. This practical consideration has produced a long tradition of cycles of preludial pieces in all current keys: Adam Ileborgh (preludes, 1448), Alonso Mudarra (*tientos,* 1546), Andrea and Giovanni Gabrieli (*intonazione,* 1593), Girolamo Frescobaldi (toccatas, 1615), Johann Erasmus Kindermann (preludes, 1645), J. C. F. Fischer (preludes and fugues, 1702), Gottlieb Muffat (toccatas, 1726), and preludes by Clementi (op. 19, 1787), Hummel (*24 Präludien* op. 67, 1814), Moscheles (*50 Präludien* op. 73, 1827), Heller (including *24 Präludien* op. 81, 1853; *32 Präludien* op. 119, 1867), and Busoni (*24 preludi* op. 37, 1879–80). The crowning work is Bach's *Das wohltemperirte Clavier* (The *Well-Tempered Clavier), with its 48 preludes and fugues in all major and minor tonalities.

German organ preludes of the 17th century frequently begin in free style and end with a short fugal section, anticipating the later dichotomy of prelude and fugue as distinct pairs in the works of Buxtehude and Bach. The form was revived particularly by Mendelssohn (op. 35, 1832–37), Brahms (Two Preludes and Fugues, 1856–57), Franck (*Prélude, choral et fugue,* 1884), Reger (op. 117, 1909–12; op. 131, 1914–15), and Honegger (*Prélude, arioso et fughetta sur le nom de BACH,* 1932). Other single-movement preludes may modulate continuously through available keys ("de tutti li toni," "sur chacun ton") allowing the player to "prelude" until an appropriate tone is reached: Francisco Spinacino (ricercar, 1507), a work published by Pierre Attaingnant (prelude, 1531), Marguerite Bocquet (prelude, ca. 1630), Johann David Heinichen (1728), Adam Falckenhagen (ca. 1742), and Beethoven (op. 39, 1789?). These and similar works represent the legacy that Carl Czerny cites when he states that one method of improvising is to pass boldly though a number of keys.

Chopin's *Préludes* op. 28 (1836–39) are best considered as improvisations rather than as the apparent paradox of preludes prefacing preludes: they move through a logical tonal sequence of major and minor keys (C major, A minor, G major, E minor, . . . F major, D minor). Emanating from this tradition as well as from Bach's is Hindemith's *Ludus tonalis* (1942), with continuously joined modulating interludes and tonally stable fugues, framed by a prelude and its retrograde, a postlude.

(2) A short work for piano. Since Chopin's op. 28, prelude has connoted for many composers a tightly constructed, unattached, evocative miniature for piano that grows (as do many of the preludes of Bach and Chopin) from small, pervasive melodic or rhythmic fragments. Some of these essay programmatic moods, as in the two books of preludes by Debussy (1910, 1913, each piece being followed by a descriptive phrase) and the one by Messaien (1929). Other unattached preludes, many of which acknowledge Chopin's model, include those of Scriabin (op. 11, 1888–96; op. 74, 1914; many others), Cui (op. 64, 1903), Rakhmaninov (op. 23, 1901–03; op. 32, 1910), Gershwin (Three Preludes, 1926), and Ginastera (*Twelve American Preludes* op. 12, 1944).

(3) An introductory orchestral piece that elides with the opening scene of a drama, such as an opera. Pieces termed *overture most often come to a rousing close before the curtain rises and are often unrelated thematically to the work following. A prelude is integrated into the whole and draws upon thematic ideas and motives from the opera to evoke an essence of the drama's mood and conflicts. Most music dramas and operas after about 1850 use preludes. Representative examples include the preludes to Wagner's *Das Rheingold* and *Tristan und Isolde* and to Verdi's *Aida.*

Bibl.: Lloyd Hibberd, "The Early Keyboard Prelude: A Study in Musical Style" (Ph.D. diss., Harvard Univ., 1941). Frank E. Kirby, *A Short History of Keyboard Music* (New York: Free Press, 1966). Davitt Moroney, "The Performance of Unmeasured Harpsichord Preludes," *EM* 4 (1976): 143–51. Siegfried Hermelink, "Das Präludium in Bachs Klaviermusik," *Jahrbuch des Staatlichen Instituts für Musikforschung 1976* (1977): 7–80. A.J.N.

Préludes, Les [Fr.]. A symphonic poem by Liszt, composed in 1848 (revised in 1852–54). It was orchestrated by Joachim Raff and originally served as an introduction to Liszt's unpublished choral work *Les quatre élémens* (The Four Elements). When Liszt decided to use the introduction as a separate work, he attached Alphonse de Lamartine's poem *Les préludes* as a "programme."

Prelude to "The Afternoon of a Faun" [Fr. *Prélude à "L'après-midi d'un faune"*]. A symphonic work by Debussy inspired by Stéphane Mallarmé's poem *L'après-midi d'un faune,* completed and performed in 1894. In 1912, it was choreographed and danced by Vaslav Nijinsky for Sergei Diaghilev's Ballets russes in Paris.

Prendere [It.], **prendre** [Fr.]. Take up, prepare to play; e.g., *prendere il flauto,* take up the flute (after a passage for piccolo).

Preparation. The introduction of some pitch as a consonance immediately preceding its statement as a dissonance, especially as part of a suspension [see Counterpoint II, 3].

Prepare [Fr. *préparer;* Ger. *vorbereiten;* It. *preparare;* Sp. *preparar*]. In harp playing, to set the pedals in the appropriate positions for a passage to follow, e.g., prepare F-sharp minor; in organ playing, to ready a combination of stops.

Prepared piano. A piano whose sound has been altered by inserting material such as bolts, rubber, cloth, and paper between the strings, thus altering pitch, loudness, and especially timbre. The preparation is usually carried out according to the instructions of a composer, who for each composition specifies the materials and their exact placement in relation to individual strings. The prepared piano was introduced by John Cage, who has composed numerous works for it, including *Bacchanale* (1938), *A Book of Music* (for two pianos, 1944), and *Sonatas and Interludes* (1946–48). Other composers to write for prepared pianos include Lou Harrison, Christian Wolff, and George Crumb.

Bibl.: Richard Bunger, *The Well-Prepared Piano* (Colorado Springs: Colo Coll Music, 1973).

Près [Fr.]. Near; *près de la touche,* an instruction in string playing to bow near or over the fingerboard; *près de la table,* an instruction in harp playing to pluck the strings at a point near the soundboard.

Presa [It.]. In a *canon, the sign, often shaped somewhat like an S, that indicates the point reached by one voice when the succeeding voice begins.

Pressante [It.], **en pressant** [Fr.]. Hurrying.

Pressus [Lat.]. See Neume.

Prestant [fr. Lat. *praestare,* to stand before]. (1) [Fr. *montre;* Ger. *Praestant*] In north European organs, the main Principal stop of each division, displayed in the facade of the case. (2) In the classic French organ, the 4′ Principal register of the **Grand orgue* or **Positif.*

Presto [It.]. Very fast, i.e., faster than *allegro; prestissimo,* as fast as possible. Before the late 18th century, however, *presto* could be the equivalent of *allegro* or could indicate simply the normal, moderately fast tempo [see Tempo, Performance marks].

Priamel [Ger.]. A 16th-century spelling of *Praeambel* (*prelude).

Prick song. In England from the late 15th through the early 17th centuries, music notated in mensural notation and thus polyphony as distinct from plainsong.

Prima donna [It.]. The singer of the principal female role in opera, or the leading female singer in an opera company. The corresponding male designation, less frequently used, is *primo uomo.* The term was in use by the middle of the 17th century, spurred on, it has been conjectured, by the development of public opera houses. It connotes a performer of overbearing temperament and arrogance. Terminology for the hierarchy of singers has at times been subject to an inflation resulting in the use of terms such as *prima donna assoluta* (absolute first lady) or *diva* (goddess).

Prima prattica, seconda prattica [It., first practice, second practice]. In the early 17th century, the musical practice of 16th-century polyphony as codified by Zarlino, and the new styles of *monody and dissonance treatment, respectively. The terms were employed in polemical exchanges between the conservative theorist Giovanni Maria Artusi and the brothers Claudio and Giulio Cesare Monteverdi (excerpts trans. in *SR,* pp. 393–412). According to Giulio Cesare, the guiding principle of the *seconda prattica* was that the words should govern the music, thus justifying previously unacceptable dissonance treatment and the like. He credited the rediscovery of this practice (its principles having been lost since classical antiquity) to Cipriano de Rore, who was followed by Marenzio and others and ultimately by Peri, Caccini, and Claudio Monteverdi. See also Baroque.

Primary triads (chords). The tonic, subdominant, and dominant triads in any key; in the view of Schenker theory, the tonic and dominant triads only.

Prima vista [It.]. At first sight, i.e., *sight-reading.

Prima volta, seconda volta [It., first time, second time]. The first and second endings of a passage that is repeated. These are usually numbered 1 and 2, respectively, and marked off by horizontal brackets above the staff [see Notation]. In music of the Middle Ages, the terms **ouvert* and *clos* were sometimes used.

Prime. (1) The *interval of a unison. (2) The third hour of the *Office. (3) In *twelve-tone music, the original form of a row.

Primgeiger [Ger.]. First violinist; sometimes also concertmaster.

Primo, secondo [It., first, second]. In a duet (e.g., for piano four-hands), the two parts, the *primo* usually being the leading part; in an orchestra, the two parts into which a section has been divided (e.g., first and second violins); *primo tempo,* the tempo with which a work began; *primo uomo,* the leading male singer in an opera.

Prince Igor [Russ. *Knyaz' Igor'*]. Opera in a prologue and four acts by Borodin (libretto by the composer on a scenario by Vladimir Stasov, after the Russian chronicle *The Story of Igor's Army*), composed in 1869–70 and 1874–87. It was completed by Rimsky-Korsakov and Glazunov and first produced in St. Petersburg in 1890. Setting: semilegendary Russia in the 12th century. See also *Polovtsian Dances.*

Principal. (1) The characteristic tone of the organ, produced by open *flue pipes of medium scale. (2) In 18th-century English organs, the 4′ stop of the Principal chorus. (3) In an orchestra or large wind ensemble, the leader of any section (e.g., trumpets, violas, but not the first violins, whose leader is called the *concertmaster); also called the first chair.

Principal chorus. See *Plein-jeu.*

Principale [Ger., also *Prinzipal(e)*]. The principal or lower register of the natural trumpet, as distinct from the **clarino.*

Printing of music. Prior to Gutenberg's development of printing by movable type in the 1450s, the production and sale of manuscripts flourished throughout Europe. While printed music gradually competed with, and then overtook, the sale of manuscripts, the market for manuscripts continued into the 19th century. The printing of music, which is complicated by the large number of symbols needed, developed considerably more slowly than the printing of literary texts, which need only the letters of an alphabet. During the 15th century, music was added in manuscript to a printed text, or the staff lines were preprinted and the notes added in manuscript, or vice versa, or a double impression was made: first the lines were printed, then the notes. The earliest known book of printed music is a German gradual done in double impression, probably in 1473. Only chant and one-line musical examples in texts were printed by movable type during the 15th century. Another early system, widely used into the first half of the 16th century and still found in isolated examples up to the 19th century, was printing from blocks of wood or metal. This was the system used for the earliest existing music printed in North America, the ninth edition of the *Bay Psalm Book* (Boston: B Green and J Allen, 1698; the first eight editions have no music).

Remarkable progress was made by Ottaviano Petrucci, whose **Odhecaton* (Venice, 1501) is the first printed mensural music. In *choirbook format, the printing was done in three impressions: first the staves, then the text, then the notes. Printing from one impression, first used by John Rastell in London, was developed by Pierre Attaingnant beginning in 1527–28. A single type-unit combined a note head, stem, and lines, and this was the system used for partbooks for the next 200 years by such well-known printers as Jacques Moderne and Robert Ballard in France, Antonio Gardane and the Scotto family in Italy, Hieronymus Formschneider and Georg Rhau in Germany, and Pierre Phalèse, Christopher Plantin, and Tylman Susato in Belgium, to name only 16th-century printers. Music was first printed from movable type in America in 1752. The last development in this process was by J. G. I. Breitkopf in the 1750s; the music was a mosaic formed from a font of type consisting of note heads, stems, and flags, each attached to lines.

By this time, music had become more complex, and movable type was not well suited for the printing of florid melodies, the chords of keyboard music, or scores for operas. That was best done by engraving, in which music is drawn with a steel point on a copper plate (or, in a later technique, punches are used on a pewter plate). Engraving was first used for music in the 16th century and spread slowly over Europe during the 17th century. By 1700, it was more common than typography, and printers such as Estienne Roger in Amsterdam and John Walsh in London were meeting the middle class's new demand for chamber and keyboard music. Amsterdam, London, and Paris were the chief music printing centers then, as Venice had been in the 16th century and as Vienna became later in the 18th century. A greatly increased market for printed music during the 19th century led to the establishment of music stores and of publishers [see Publishing], who became middlemen between the printers and consumers.

A fourth printing system, lithography, was invented by Alois Senefelder in 1796 and was fully developed by 1850. This chemical process, based simply on the principle that grease repels water, eventually allowed music to be written on paper as the preparation for plates. Weber prepared lithographic plates in 1800 for a set of his piano variations, as did Wagner in 1845 for the full score of *Tannhäuser.* Engraving was not superseded by lithography, however, and is still widely used for the preparation of camera-ready copy. Practically all music is printed today by the offset process, which uses photographic plates prepared from copy from engravings, music typewriters, transfers, or composers' or autographers' manuscripts. As in the beginning of printing, the complexities of music delayed somewhat the development of music typesetting by computer even after the computer had begun to be widely used for the typesetting of books and newspapers in the 1970s.

Although printing of music using computers has come a long way, it is still a work in progress. There are a number of different methods for inputting the data, of which the two most essential elements are the pitch and the duration, but in addition there are the myriad pieces of ancillary information (e.g., slurs, stems, ornaments, fingerings) that also must be present to form a complete representation of the work. The rapid rate of change of computer operating software has left developers of music writing software scurrying to finish their work before the next iteration of the operating software makes their programs obsolete.

There are several ways of encoding music in the computer; most now result in a musical image on the computer screen that can be edited. These methods include encoded data entry, graphical programs, and playing from a MIDI (musical instrument digital interface) keyboard or other electronic device. Scanning, using optical character recognition software, is still in its infancy for music.

Bibl.: *History.* Cecil Hopkinson, *A Dictionary of Parisian Music Publishers, 1700–1950* (London: C Hopkinson, 1954). Cari Johansson, *French Music Publishers' Catalogues of the Second Half of the Eighteenth Century,* 2 vols. (Stockholm: Library of the Royal Swedish Academy of Music, 1955). Alexander Weinmann, *Wiener Musikverleger und Musikalienhändler von Mozarts Zeit bis gegen 1860* (Vienna: Commissioned by R M Rohrer, 1956). Claudio Sartori, *Dizionario degli editori musicali italiani* (Florence: Olschki, 1958). Mariangela Donà, *La stampa musicale a Milano fino all'anno 1700* (Florence: Olschki, 1961). A. Hyatt King, *Four Hundred Years of Music Printing,* 2nd ed. (London: British Museum, 1968). Hans-M. Plesske, "Bibliographie des Schrifttums zur Geschichte deutscher und österreichischer Musikverlage," *Beiträge zur Geschichte des Buchwesens* 3 (1968): 135–222. Charles Humphries and William C. Smith, *Music Publishing in the British Isles,* 2nd ed. with supp. (New York: Barnes & Noble, 1970). Ted Ross, *The Art of Music Engraving and Processing* (Miami: Hansen Bks, 1970). Donald W. Krummel, *Guide for Dating Early Published Music* (Hackensack, N.J.: Boonin, 1974); supp. in *FAM* 14 (1977): 175–84. Donald W. Krummel, *English Music Printing, 1553–1700* (London: Bibliographical Soc, 1975). Anik Devriès, *Édition et commerce de la musique gravée à Paris dans la première moitié du XVIIIe siècle* (Geneva: Minkoff, 1976). Richard J. Wolfe, *Early American Music Engraving and Printing . . . 1787 to 1825* (Urbana: U of Ill Pr, 1980). A. Peter Brown, "Notes on Some Eighteenth-Century Viennese Copyists," *JAMS* 34 (1981): 325–38. Oscar Mischiati, *Indici, cataloghi e avvisi degli editori e librai musicali italiani dal 1591 al 1798* (Florence: Olschki, 1984). Stanley Boorman, "Early Music Printing: Working for a Specialized Market," in *Print and Culture in the Renaissance: Essays on the Advent of Printing in the Renaissance,* ed. G. P. Tyson and S. S. Wagonheim (Newark, Del.: Associated U Pr, 1986), pp. 222–45. Donald W. Krummel and Stanley Sadie, eds., *Music Printing and Publishing* (London: Macmillan, 1990). Donald W. Krummel, *The Literature of Music Bibliography* (Berkeley: Fallen Leaf, 1993). Jane A. Bernstein, *Print Culture and Music in Sixteenth-Century Venice* (New York: Oxford U Pr, 2001). H.E.S., rev. L.C.

Prinzipal [Ger.]. In German organs, the 8′ stop of *Principal tone. See also *Principale.*

Prix de Rome. A prize awarded on the basis of a competition held by the Académie des Beaux-Arts in Paris from 1803 until 1968. The competition entailed the composition of a cantata on a prescribed libretto, and the first prize or Grand Prix de Rome was a four-year stay at the Villa Medici in Rome. The winners include Halévy (1819), Berlioz (1830), Bizet (1857), Debussy (1884), Gustave Charpentier (1887), Florent Schmitt (1900), Lili Boulanger (1913), and Henri Dutilleux (1938). There is also a Belgian Prix de Rome, and the American Academy in Rome awards fellowships to composers as well.

Processional. (1) A work performed during a procession at the beginning of some ceremony. (2) [Lat. *processionale*] See Liturgical books.

Prodaná Nevěsta [Cz.]. See *Bartered Bride, The.*

Prodigal Son, The. See *Enfant prodigue, L'.*

Program music [fr. Fr. *musique à programme;* Ger. *Programmusik*]. Music that, most often explicitly, attempts to express or depict one or more nonmusical ideas, images, or events. The composer usually indicates the "program" (the subject or subjects being evoked) by a suggestive title or preface, which may be quite vague or may be specific and detailed. A seemingly simple title—e.g., *Romeo and Juliet* (Tchaikovsky)—may suggest a rather precise sequence of characters and events (e.g., Friar Laurence, street fights between the Montagues and Capulets, balcony scene, tomb scene). Other titles do little more than label a piece's mood, style, or dance characteristics (e.g., Liszt's *Consolations,* Schumann's *3 Romanzen* op. 28, or Chopin's *Tarantelle*) or suggest an image that is not essential to an understanding of the music's spirit (e.g., Schumann's "Vogel als Prophet" [The Prophet Bird] op. 82 no. 7, MacDowell's "To a Wild Rose," and many of the Debussy Preludes).

Programmatic music has flourished at different times [see III below], but especially in the 19th century. The Romantics were fond of associating music with literature, landscape, or the visual arts. Furthermore, the program became a weapon in the battle to gain respect for instrumental music [see I]. And untutored listeners could "understand" a piece of music by reading the program and letting their imaginations roam. Indeed, many pieces not supplied with programs by their composers were given inauthentic but enduring nicknames (e.g., Beethoven's **Moonlight* Sonata op. 27 no. 2; Mendelssohn's "May Breeze" op. 62 no. 1 from the **Lieder ohne Worte;* and Chopin's etudes "Butterfly" op. 25 no. 9, "Winter Wind" op. 25 no. 11, and "Revolutionary" op. 10 no. 12).

The predominant genres of Romantic program music were the *program symphony and the *symphonic poem, followed by *concert overtures, *character pieces for piano or small ensemble, and, later, even an occasional string quartet such as Smetana's **From My Life* (1876). The symphony orchestra was a particularly fertile medium for program music, because its rich variety of instrumental colors and color combinations aided in characterizing and differentiating states of mind, events, or even individual characters. (Richard Strauss represents the title figure in *Don Quixote* by a solo cello, Sancho Panza by a viola, and a flock of sheep by muted brass.)

I. *Program vs. absolute music.* The term program was first applied to the program symphonies (or "characteristic" symphonies) composed in the late 18th century by Dittersdorf and others and was rather neutral in connotation. During the early 19th century, it became entangled in the passionate controversies over whether (or to what extent) music is a means of *expression. E. T. A. Hoffmann, Berlioz, and others argued that instrumental music is more than diverting sounds, that it can be as lofty and as expressive of human experience as more obviously representational art forms, such as painting or literature (or music that carries a sung text). Some claimed that of all art forms, instrumental music can best express the deepest levels of experience, because it is not trammeled by words or visual images. Nonetheless, many 19th-century composers felt compelled to announce their subjects in words in order (as Liszt put it) to "guard against erroneous poetical interpretations" (1855). The critic Eduard Hanslick and others noted this contradiction and argued that the highest form of music is *"absolute" music—music free of explicit external reference. (Even Hanslick, though, allowed that great instrumental music could give the listener access to realms of divine truth, analogous to those touched on in philosophy, religious writings, and great literature.) The debate raged for a century, with Stravinsky, for example, insisting—simplistically, as he later admitted—that "music is, by its very nature, powerless to express anything at all."

Recent scholars (e.g., Wiora, Dahlhaus) argue that the dichotomy between absolute and program music is false, that the best program music can be appreciated without knowledge of the program. (Berlioz said as much of his own *Symphonie fantastique,* as did Liszt of Wagner's Overture to *Tannhäuser.*) Furthermore, some of the finest absolute works (e.g., the symphonies of Haydn) are rich in references to dance rhythms and other stylistic conventions that a listener must recognize in order to follow the composer's thought fully (Ratner, 1980). And the recent surge of interest in theories of musical narrative/narrativity—rooted in part in Adorno's 1960 study of Mahler—has further eroded the understood boundary between "abstract" or absolute musical works and the possibility of extramusical readings. In any case, many works, e.g., *character pieces, or certain symphonies of Mendelssohn, Schumann, and Bruckner, have long been understood as evincing characteristics of both categories. Composers themselves often reveal a mixed attitude toward the programmaticism in their works. Beethoven's warning about looking for detailed "painting" in the *Pastoral* [see Program symphony] suggests that he would not have denied that various "feelings" were portrayed or "expressed" (his words) in his other works as well. Gustav Mahler in 1907 declared to Sibelius: "The symphony must be like the world. It must embrace everything." But he rarely explained, and then mostly in private letters and conversations, how a listener might establish more precise parallels between symphony and world. Even George Crumb, in the midst of admitting the frankly programmatic intent in much of his music, qualifies it: *Black Angels* is "*a kind of* parable on our troubled contemporary world," filled with "numerous *quasi*-programmatic allusions" (emphasis added).

In the end, the distinction between program music and whatever its opposite might be is not fixed and open to consensus. Rather, it is negotiated anew by each listener in contact with a given musical work. And such negotiations are shaped and colored by the information (or misinformation) that the listener has received about the work, the particular performance that he or she hears, and his or her more general beliefs about the relationship between music and the rest of life (nature, feelings, other human thoughts and activities).

II. *Methods.* The three main compositional approaches to program music may be called the *expressive,* the *depictive,* and the *narrative.* A composer may attempt to express a mood or character trait, depict a more concrete subject, or narrate a sequence of events or emotional states.

The expressive approach can take the modest form of a short piece that maintains its announced mood—e.g., *La gaieté*—more or less unchanged. Such a piece may not be substantially more "gay" than works lacking a program (e.g., a sonata movement marked *allegro giocoso* or even simply *allegro*). The expressive approach can also shade off into the depictive. The many character portraits in music, from those of Dowland to Elgar's *Enigma* Variations and the dozens of portraits for piano by Virgil Thomson, rarely give more than the name of the subject being portrayed; thus, whether a given piece is "expressing" the emotional essence of its subject (e.g., "Chiarina" [Clara] in Schumann's *Carnaval*) or "depicting" him or her in more concrete detail (e.g., George R. Sinclair and his gamboling dog in the *Enigma* Variations, no. 11, entitled simply "G. R. S.") may be apparent to the composer and his circle but not to posterity.

The depictive approach exists in several shades; all are based on the principle of depicting an aspect of nonmusical reality by imitating its sounds, motions, or processes. Among the more common subjects of imitation are nature (singing birds, flowing water, wind, thunder), human activities (spinning, travel by horse or train, walking, running, laughing, weeping), or sounds or musical styles with strong associations (bells for church worship, marches for battle, gentle tunes in 6/8 meter for pastoral scenes and lullabies, horn calls for the hunt). Since some of these subjects can be less directly and unambiguously "described" in music than others, and since many things in life, especially feelings, suggest no clear tonal equivalent, musicians have created systems of symbolism that set up a (perhaps artificial) correspondence between the desired subject and one that is more easily portrayed musically. Thus, sorrow or grief is often represented by descending melodic motion (by association with sighing or by analogy to physical staggering or collapse), e.g., chromatic *ostinato basses in Monteverdi and Purcell, "sighing" two-note figures in Bach. Similarly, Haydn portrays primeval chaos (in *The Creation*) by unpredictable modulations. The depictive approach, like the expressive, is most often used in a modest way: it helps generate the main melodic or accompanimental motive or figure, but purely internal considerations of continuity, contrast, development, etc., guide the work otherwise.

In contrast, the narrative approach allows the program to determine to some extent the way a piece proceeds from beginning to end. The resulting succession of programmatic moments or movements—of the expressive or depictive types or a mixture thereof—gives the listener the impression of a continuous story, argument, or emotional progression. It is this sort of program music that diverges most strikingly from other instrumental music and that has been most controversial. A piece written to follow a verbal program may be aptly illustrative but musically choppy and unsatisfactory. Nonetheless, several pieces in the standard repertory do follow a narrative program closely yet manage to be musically coherent (e.g., Vivaldi's *Four Seasons,* Smetana's *Moldau,* and Strauss's *Don Quixote*).

III. *History.* Instrumental music during the Middle Ages and Renaissance rarely attempted to portray or represent nonmusical subjects. Vocal music, on the other hand, was rich in such practices, both depictive and expressive. The 14th-century Italian **caccia* made use of canonic imitation to depict the chase of the hunt and the cries of the marketplace. Composers of sacred vocal music during the 14th through 16th centuries sought a convincing expressive relationship between *text and music, e.g., by suiting the music to the mood (reflective, funereal, glorifying, etc.) of the words. The depictive and expressive approaches were used extensively—separately and in combination—in 16th-century chansons and madrigals; indeed, text-motivated changes in texture, rhythmic activity, melodic direction, mode, etc., may occur so rapidly, at times in response to a single word or phrase, that the technique is often described as *word painting. Similar techniques are found in Baroque opera, cantata, and oratorio [see also Affections, Doctrine of; Rhetoric].

In the early Baroque, when instrumental music began to establish itself as an art in its own right, it adopted expressive and depictive vocal techniques. Certain English pieces for *virginals or lute are character pieces whose titles are "expressed" in the mood of the music (e.g., Giles Farnaby's "His Humour"). Others are depictive, e.g., John Mundy's meteorological Fantasia ("Faire Wether," "Lightning," etc.) and *Mr [William] Bird's Battle,* whose 13 titled sections ("The battels be ioyned," "The retreat," etc.) use procedures differing little from those of Janequin, for example, in his chanson *La bataille.*

By around 1700, programmatic writing was well established in instrumental music. Lutheran church chorale preludes for organ may reflect the central image or emotion *(Affekt)* of the (silent) chorale text, and Johann Kuhnau and Heinrich Biber composed "sonatas" illustrating stories from the Bible. Kuhnau not only provided a lengthy preface to each of his six "Biblical Sonatas" (1700), but added explanatory rubrics to make clear that, for example, the sudden rising scale in the first sonata represents David slinging the stone at Goliath.

French harpsichord composers of the same period generally avoided detailed narrative of this sort. Some of their pieces bear the names of individuals (e.g., François Couperin's "La Forqueray," meaning "the piece for [or describing] Forqueray"); Couperin himself stated (introduction to his first book, 1713) that these are "portraits of a sort." Other pieces by Couperin have titles indicating an emotional quality ("La séduisante" [The Charming One]) or depicting a natural object or a human activity ("Les ondes" [Waves], "Les tricoteuses" [Knitters]). But in these and similar pieces such as Rameau's "La poule" (The Hen), the imitation of natural sounds serves mainly to suggest a musical figure that remains constant from first note to last. Only rarely, as in Couperin's chamber suites *L'apothéose de Lully* and *L'apothéose de Corelli,* did French instrumental composers of the period string movements together to illustrate a narrative program.

In the theater, however, the use of instrumental music for vivid depictive and narrative purposes was the rule. Ballet suites by Rameau and Jean-Féry Rebel and scenes of shepherds, dreams, and storms in operas by Lully and Handel became testing grounds for new programmatic techniques. Similar techniques were employed in oratorios (e.g., the pastoral orchestral interludes in Handel's *Messiah* and Bach's Christmas Oratorio), concerti grossi (e.g., the "Christmas" concertos of Torelli, Corelli, and others, or, again, in Vivaldi's *Four Seasons*), suites (*Neuer und sehr curios-Musicalischer Instrumental-Calender* [*New and Very Curious Musical Instrument Calendar*], 1748, of Gregor Joseph Werner, 12 pieces representing the months, complete with December snores), and the early program symphonies of Dittersdorf and others.

With some exceptions (e.g., František Kočzwara's enormously popular *The Battle of Prague* and Beethoven's *Wellington's Victory;* see *Battaglia*), Classical instrumental music (including most of Haydn's and Mozart's music) was not programmatic. Beethoven's *Pastoral* Symphony (1808) is thus remarkable as a serious attempt by a major composer to fuse many of the programmatic traditions of the previous century with recent achievements in large-scale form. Beethoven called the work "more an expression of feeling than painting," but a number of instances of true depiction are evident: flowing water, birdcalls, peasant dances, a thunderstorm, and an Alpine horn call. A few other Beethoven pieces are programmatic in a less detailed way, e.g., the *Coriolan* Overture and the Piano Sonata in E♭ op. 81a, with movements marked "Lebewohl," "Abwesenheit," and "Wiedersehen" (Farewell, Absence, Return).

Beethoven's example no doubt helped encourage prominent composers of the next generation to produce a flood of programmatic works. Schumann's **Noveletten* and **Davidsbündlertänze* and Chopin's Preludes and Impromptus are character pieces of the vaguest sort, but other works—Schumann's **Carnaval,* Weber's **Aufforderung zum Tanz* (Invitation to the Dance), and Berlioz's **Symphonie fantastique* and

Harold en Italie—have passages that may be puzzling unless the composer's program is taken into account.

This wide range continued in the symphonic poems of Liszt and his followers. Some have only vague titles (Liszt's *Hungaria* and *Festklänge* [Festive Sounds]), whereas others carry either a detailed program or a poetic epigraph (Saint-Saëns's **Danse macabre*) that clarifies the meaning of the musical imagery. Occasionally, a composer changed, withheld, or withdrew the descriptive titles or program for a work (e.g., respectively, Liszt, *Les *préludes;* Weber, *Konzertstück,* and Tchaikovsky, Symphony no. 4; Mahler, Symphony no. 1), confirming that the musical impulse was the crucial one.

For much of the 20th century, program music became ever less fashionable among composers who considered themselves modern and thus anti-Romantic. Nonetheless, some composers continued to evoke images openly in their piano music (Debussy and Ravel), symphonic poems (Strauss, Sibelius, Respighi), program symphonies (Shostakovich), and suites from dance scores, opera, and film (e.g., Copland's *Appalachian Spring;* Britten's "Four Sea Interludes" from *Peter Grimes;* "The Battle on the Ice" from Prokofiev's *Alexander Nevsky*).

In socialist countries, late into the 20th century, program music remained respectable (e.g., Penderecki's *Tren ofiarom Hiroszimy* [*Threnody for the Victims of Hiroshima*], the collectively composed Chinese violin concerto *The Butterfly Lovers,* and the epic symphonies and folk-derived national rhapsodies of many Soviet composers).

Even in the West during the mid-20th century, when modernism dominated academia and certain other aspects of musical life, the programmatic impulse still found occasional proponents, such as Leonard Bernstein, David Del Tredici, and, as mentioned, Crumb. Olivier Messiaen's organ, piano, and orchestral works are filled with highly personal religio-philosophical symbolism and with birds songs that are rigorously transcribed and often identified in the score. Even the seemingly abstract works of Elliott Carter are sometimes based on a kind of program: in his Second String Quartet (1959), each of the four instruments has a distinctive personality, resulting in conversations, arguments, even some eventual persuasion and consensus. Recent years have seen a resurgence of the programmatic. John Tavener's *The Protecting Veil,* for cello and string orchestra (1987), contains movements representing the birth of Mary, the Annunciation, and her lament at the cross. The various movements of Tan Dun's *2000 Today: A World Symphony for the Millennium* (1999) incorporate sounds of nature (running water), distinctive regional instruments and performance styles (didgeridoo, klezmer clarinet), and a chorus singing brief texts from Lao-Tzu, the Bible, Dante, and Tennyson. Other recent composers incorporating literary or programmatic elements into their instrumental works include John Adams, Sally Beamish, Philip Glass, Michael Gordon, Osvaldo Golijov, Steve Reich, and Joan Tower.

See also Aesthetics.

Bibl.: Hector Berlioz, "On Imitation in Music" (1837), trans. Jacques Barzun and Edward Cone, in Cone, ed., *Hector Berlioz: Fantastic Symphony* (New York: Norton, 1971), pp. 36–46. Franz Liszt, "Berlioz and His 'Harold' Symphony" (1855), excerpts in *SR.* Ernest Newman, "Programme Music," *Musical Studies* (London: J Lane, 1905; R: New York: Haskell House, 1969), pp. 101–86. Theodor W. Adorno, *Mahler: A Musical Physiognomy,* trans. Edmund Jephcott (1960; Chicago: U of Chicago Pr, 1992), chaps. 4 and 8. Donald Francis Tovey, *Essays in Musical Analysis,* 6 vols. (London: Oxford U Pr, 1935–39; R: 1972; new ed. in 2 vols., 1981), vol. 4, *Illustrative Music* (1936). Leonard B. Meyer, *Emotion and Meaning in Music* (Chicago: U of Chicago Pr, 1956), pp. 256–72. Deryck Cooke, *The Language of Music* (London: Oxford U Pr, 1959; R: 1962). Wolfgang Stockmeier, ed., *Die Programmusik, Mw* 36 (Cologne: A Volk, 1970; trans. Eng., 1970). Edward Lockspeiser, *Music and Painting* (New York: Harper & Row, 1973). Donald Mitchell, *Gustav Mahler,* vol. 2: *The Wunderhorn Year: Chronicles and Commentaries* (1975; 2nd rev. ed., Berkeley: U of Cal Pr, 1995). Leslie Orrey, *Programme Music* (London: Davis-Poynter, 1975). Edward A. Lippman, *A Humanistic Philosophy of Music* (New York: NYU Pr, 1977). Leonard G. Ratner, *Classic Music: Expression, Form, and Style* (New York: Schirmer Bks, 1980). Peter LeHuray and James Day, *Music and Aesthetics in the Eighteenth and Early Nineteenth Centuries* (Cambridge: Cambridge U Pr, 1981). Jacques Barzun, *Critical Questions,* ed. Bea Friedland (Chicago: U of Chicago Pr, 1982). Carl Dahlhaus, *Esthetics of Music,* trans. William Austin (Cambridge: Cambridge U Pr, 1982), pp. 24–31, 57–63. Peter Kivy, *Sound and Semblance: Reflections on Musical Representation* (Princeton: Princeton U Pr, 1984). Anthony Newcomb, "Once More 'Between Absolute and Program Music': Schumann's Second Symphony," *19th-Century Music* 7 (1984): 233–50. Bojan Bujic, ed., *Music in European Thought: 1851–1912* (Cambridge: Cambridge U Pr, 1988). Scott Burnham, "Criticism, Faith, and the *Idee:* A. B. Marx's Early Reception of Beethoven," *19th-Century Music* 13 (1989–90): 183–92. Carolyn Abbate, *Unsung Voices: Opera and Musical Narrative in the Nineteenth Century* (Princeton: Princeton U Pr, 1991), pp. 119–54. Lawrence Kramer, *Classical Music and Postmodern Knowledge* (Berkeley: U of Cal Pr, 1995), pp. 98–121. Thomas S. Grey, *Wagner's Musical Prose: Texts and Contexts* (Cambridge: Cambridge U Pr, 1995), pp. 1–129. Mark Evan Bonds, "Idealism and the Aesthetics of Instrumental Music at the Turn of the Nineteenth Century," *JAMS* 50 (1997): 387–420. David Fuller, "Of Portraits, 'Sapho' and Couperin: Titles and Characters in French Instrumental Music of the High Baroque," *ML* 78 (1997): 149–74. Lawrence Casler, *Symphonic Program Music and Its Literary Sources,* 2 vols. (Lewiston, N.Y.: Edwin Mellen, 2001).

R.P.L.

Program symphony. An orchestral work in the form of a *symphony and bearing a descriptive title or program, like that of a *symphonic poem; also called descriptive or characteristic symphony [see Character piece]. A few 18th-century symphonies were programmatic, in large or small degree (Dittersdorf, 12 symphonies after the *Metamorphoses* of Ovid; Justin Heinrich Knecht, *Le portrait musical de la nature;* Haydn, Symphonies no. 6–8, 26, 60; Clementi, *Great*

National Symphony), but the Sixth Symphony of Beethoven (**Pastoral*, 1808) became the principal model [see Program music]. Program symphonies of Spohr (nos. 4, 6, 7, 9), Mendelssohn (nos. 3–5), Berlioz (**Symphonie fantastique*, 1830), and Liszt (**Faust-Symphonie*, 1857; **Dante*, 1855–56) gave further impetus to such composers as Joachim Raff, Karl Goldmark, Tchaikovsky (**Manfred*, 1885), Anton Rubinstein, Richard Strauss, Roussel, Glière, and—more recently—Honegger, Shostakovich, Vaughan Williams, Messiaen, Tippett, Corigliano, Glass, and Tan Dun. Each movement of a program symphony generally bears its own title, indicating one aspect or episode of the general program. Still, Beethoven cautiously described his *Pastoral* as "more expression of feeling than [tone-]painting." Nearly two hundred years later, John Harbison echoes the warning: though his Symphony no. 2 consists of movements entitled Dawn, Daylight, Dusk, and Darkness, he claims to be interested "in the symphony as a tone poem *without a plot*" (emphasis added).

When composers include singing voices or solo instruments, the result may incorporate features of another genre, such as concerto (Berlioz, *Harold in Italy*, 1834; Bernstein, *Age of Anxiety*, 1949), song cycle (Mahler, *Das Lied von der Erde*, 1909), cantata or oratorio (Mendelssohn, Symphony no. 2, *Lobgesang*, 1840; Mahler, Symphony no. 2, *Resurrection*, 1888–94; Britten, *Spring* Symphony, 1949), and opera (Berlioz, *Roméo et Juliette*, 1839). When composers ask for the sections to be played without pause or even provide transitional passages and other musical links between the sections (as in Strauss's *Ein Heldenleben*, 1897–98), the effect is more that of a single symphonic poem.

Bibl.: Nicholas Temperley, "The *Symphonie fantastique* and Its Program," *MQ* 57 (1971): 593–608. James Webster, *Haydn's "Farewell" Symphony and the Idea of Classical Style* (Cambridge: Cambridge U Pr, 1991). Owen Jander, "The Prophetic Conversation in Beethoven's 'Scene by the Brook,'" *MQ* 77 (1993): 508–59. David Wyn Jones, *Beethoven: "Pastoral Symphony"* (Cambridge: Cambridge U Pr, 1995). Michael Steinberg, *The Symphony* (New York: Oxford U Pr, 1995). Thomas Sipe, *Beethoven: "Eroica" Symphony* (Cambridge: Cambridge U Pr, 1998). John Rice, "New Light on Dittersdorf's Ovid Symphonies," *Studi musicali* 29 (2000): 453–98. James Hepokoski, "Beethoven Reception: The Symphonic Tradition," in *The Cambridge History of Nineteenth-Century Music*, ed. Jim Samson (Cambridge: Cambridge U Pr, 2001), pp. 424–59. Richard Will, *The Characteristic Symphony in the Age of Haydn and Beethoven* (Cambridge: Cambridge U Pr, 2002). See also Program music. R.P.L.

Progression. A succession of two or more chords; also chord progression, harmonic progression; in jazz and popular music also termed changes.

Progressive jazz. A jazz style heralded by Stan Kenton's "Progressive Jazz Orchestra" of 1947–48 (and its arrangers, including Bob Graettinger, Bill Holman, and William Russo). Its complex, often loud, brassy, densely voiced *big-band arrangements were usually intended for concert performance. Titles such as "Elegy" and "Fugue" and those beginning "Artistry in . . ." evoked concert music. B.K.

Prolation [Lat. *prolatio*]. See Mensural notation.

Prologue. The preface or introduction to a dramatic work, often serving to give the audience either background or a frame of reference. The prologue may be delivered by one allegorical figure (Musica in Monteverdi's *Orfeo*) or several (Fortuna, Virtù, and Amor in Monteverdi's *L'incoronazione di Poppea*). The characters in the prologue may stand apart from the drama or interact with it (as in Lully's *Amadis*). Precedents for prologues in operatic works are found in the earlier dramatic works of the same culture. Thus, the prologues of the Florentine operas have models in the pastoral plays of Tasso and Guarini; the prologues of Lully's operas have models in works of Molière and Racine. The ultimate source is Greek and Roman drama. Prologues are found in many Italian operas of the first half of the 17th century. They are a necessary feature of Lully's operas, in which they often make direct and flattering allusions to Louis XIV. The use of prologues waned in the 18th century. They reappeared in the 19th and 20th centuries under special circumstances, as in Leoncavallo's *Pagliacci*, Boïto's *Mefistofele*, and Berg's *Lulu*.

Prolongation. See Schenker analysis.

Prolongement [Fr.]. The sostenuto pedal of the piano.

Prometheus. (1) See *Geschöpfe des Prometheus*. (2) A symphonic poem by Scriabin, *Prométhée, le poème du feu* (Prometheus: The Poem of Fire) op. 60 (1908–10), for large orchestra, piano, organ, choruses, and *color organ. The music is based on the so-called *mystic (Promethean) chord.

Pronto, prontamente [It.]. Quick(ly).

Prooemium [Lat.]. *Prelude.

Proper. Those items of the Mass and Office of the Roman rite whose texts and melodies vary with the occasion, as distinct from those whose texts remain the same throughout the liturgical year and thus make up the *Ordinary. In *liturgical books, the Proper is presented in such a way as to reflect the two major cycles of feasts in the liturgical year: the Proper of the Time, including especially feasts commemorating events in the life of Christ, and the Proper of the Saints, including feasts commemorating the saints [see Liturgy]. Items of the Proper that are shared among the feasts of certain categories of saints (Virgins, Confessors, etc.), rather than being assigned to the feasts of specifically named saints, make up the Common of the Saints. See also Mass.

Prophecies. Readings from the Old Testament books

of the Prophets. In the Roman Catholic rite, these are read (or sung to a special tone, *LU,* pp. 102–4) in place of the Epistle at Mass on certain occasions such as Ember Days, the Epiphany, and Monday, Tuesday, and Wednesday of Holy Week. A series of nine (formerly as many as twelve) prophecies are read in the course of Holy Saturday.

Prophète, Le [Fr., The Prophet]. Opera in five acts by Meyerbeer (libretto by Eugène Scribe), produced in Paris in 1849. Setting: the Anabaptist uprising in 16th-century Münster.

Proportion [Lat. *proportio*]. In *mensural notation, a ratio expressing the relationship between the note-values following the ratio and those preceding it or between the note-values of a work or passage and an assumed normal relationship of note-values to metrical pulse or **tactus.* When the proportion is written as a fraction, the numerator (the first term when written as a ratio) expresses the number of notes of a certain value that are to occupy the same time as was previously occupied by the number of notes of the same value expressed in the denominator. In the accompanying example, four semibreves following the proportion are to take the time occupied by three semibreves

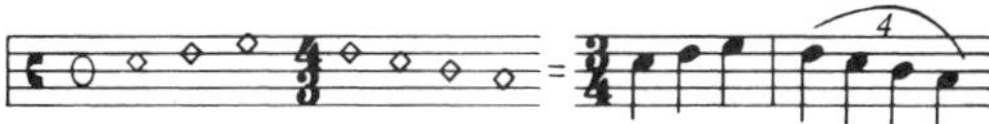

preceding it. A proportion thus specifies diminution or augmentation. Among the most common proportions are 2:1 (or simply 2, also expressed by a line, usually vertical, through the mensuration sign C or O, thus ¢ or Φ, or by turning the mensuration sign C backward, thus Ɔ; termed *proportio dupla* or simply *dupla* or *diminutio*), 3:1 (or simply 3; *proportio tripla* or *tripla*), and 3:2 (*sesquialtera,* which is equivalent to the use of coloration [see Mensural notation]).

If a proportion occurs in only one or a few voices of a polyphonic work, the context will normally make clear the precise relationship of tempos that is intended. If the proportion occurs in all voices simultaneously or at the beginning of a work, however, there may be ambiguity (as theorists of the 15th and 16th centuries and modern scholars agree). This results from the need to establish which note-value is the one in terms of which the ratio is stated. By the 16th century, it was generally agreed that the semibreve was this note-value and represented the normal pulse or *tactus.* Notes not governed by a proportion were said to have *integer valor* (whole, normal value). Thus, normal notation or *integer valor* was termed *alla semibreve. Proportio dupla* or diminution by half was said to be *alla breve.* The latter term is still used in the same way, together with the sign ¢, to imply movement twice as fast as that of **C** or 4/4.

Proportio dupla is encountered in theory (Jehan des Murs) and practice early in the 14th century. Proportions increased in variety and complexity through the 15th century, reaching a peak around 1500 in works by composers such as Johannes Ockeghem and Heinrich Isaac (notably the **Choralis constantinus*). Theorists who provide extended discussions, sometimes exceeding in complexity anything represented in compositions, include Prosdocimus de Beldemandis (*Tractatus practice cantus mensurabilis,* 1408), Guillelmus Monachus (*De preceptis artis musice libellus,* ca. 1460), Johannes Tinctoris (*Proportionale musices,* ca. 1473–74), Franchinus Gaffurius (*Practica musicae,* 1496), and Martin Agricola (*Musica figuralis deudsch,* 1532). For bibl., see Mensural notation, Theory.

Proportz, proportio [Ger.]. See *Nachtanz.*

Proposta [It.]. The subject of a fugue, as distinct from the answer or *riposta.*

Propriety [Lat. *proprietas*]. See Ligature.

Proprium Missae [Lat.]. *Proper of the *Mass.

Proprium Sanctorum, Proprium de Tempore [Lat.]. *Proper of the Saints, Proper of the Time.

Prosa [Lat.], **prose** [Fr.]. A term used in many medieval sources, especially those of French or English origin, for the text added to the extended melisma, or *sequentia,* that followed the verse of the Alleluia in the Mass [see Sequence]. Although the resulting combined form of words and music is usually referred to today as a sequence by writers in English, the word *prose* is still frequently found in French literature on the subject. The term *prosa* seems originally to have been applied specifically to the added words themselves, which were at the outset in prose rather than a poetic meter, thus making the term particularly suitable. It frequently occurs in the manuscripts in some such phrase as *sequentia cum prosa* (i.e., "sequence melody with added prose text").

Bibl.: Heinrich Husmann, "Sequenz und Prosa," *AnnM* 2 (1954): 61–91. P.E.

Proslambanomenos [Gr.]. See Greece I, 3 (i).

Prosody. Originally versification alone, but currently extended to refer to all features of a language involving stress, pitch, and length of syllables. [See also Text and music.] Variations in prosodic features occur in the sound-structure (phonology) of every known language. In any given language, variation in one or more aspects of prosody may, although phonetically present, be nonsignificant in determining structural contrasts, whereas in another language the same variation may have structural (phonemic) significance.

Stress is the amount of force involved in expelling air from the lungs in speaking, and it may vary from quite weak to quite strong. In Hungarian, this phonetic contrast is present in extreme form, but since stress falls automatically on the first syllable of each word, it is not phonemically significant. In French, there is very little phonetic contrast in stress between syllables, but since the last syllable of each breath-group automatically has slightly stronger stress than those preceding, stress is likewise not phonemic. In languages in which stress is structurally significant (e.g., the Germanic languages and the Romance languages except for French), levels of significant stress may vary from four (as in English) to three (Italian) or two (Spanish). Languages having phonemically significant stress are often termed accentual.

In some languages (e.g., Germanic), in ordinary speech as well as in poetry, heavy stresses come at regular intervals, with one, two, or more weak stresses sandwiched in between. Such languages are stress-timed, in contradistinction to syllable-timed languages. In the latter, the syllables of a sequence, whether stressed or unstressed, are uttered (as in the Romance languages), at a regular, even rate.

Pitch, in linguistic structure, is not absolute but relative. (A sentence spoken with a given pitch-contour is regarded as having the same intonation whether spoken by a man in low register or a woman in a high register.) Variations in sequences of pitch distinguish various types of sentences (e.g., declarative, interrogative, imperative) in all known languages. Such variation is, in linguistics, termed intonation. In some languages, called tone-languages (e.g., Chinese, Swedish, Norwegian), a difference in pitch on individual syllables marks a difference in the meaning of a word.

Length is the actual duration in milliseconds of a syllable in pronunciation. Syllable length is often correlated with the duration of the vowel sound that forms the center of the syllable and with the presence or absence of a consonant sound following the vowel. In some languages (e.g., French), almost all syllables are of equal duration, and hence length is not phonemic. In others (e.g., English), differences in syllable length are present but automatic and hence nonphonemic. In still others (e.g., Latin, ancient Greek, modern Hungarian, and Finnish), vowel length (and hence syllable length) is structurally significant. In such languages, the contrast in length is normally a binary opposition between long and short, although a third degree, extra-long, has been reported for Estonian.

Versification in each language is a function of the phonological prosodic resources available to its speakers. Poetry depends upon the recurrence of certain prosodic features in a predetermined and hence predictable pattern or meter, e.g., a specific alternation of long and short syllables, or the presence of a certain number of stresses or syllables, in each verse. (In normal conversational prose, on the other hand, the speaker is not bound in advance to any specific prosodic pattern.) In longer verses of any type, there is normally a break in the prosodic structure, corresponding to a break in the sense, termed caesura, in the middle of the line.

Classical Latin and Greek verse prosody was quantitative, i.e., dependent on the relation of long (–) and short (⌣) syllables in each line of a poem. A unit of two or three syllables was a foot. A verse consisted of anywhere from two to six feet (dimeter, trimeter, tetrameter, pentameter, hexameter). The main types of foot were the iamb (⌣ –), the trochee (– ⌣), the anapaest (⌣⌣ –), the dactyl (– ⌣ ⌣), the spondee (– –), and the tribrach (⌣ ⌣ ⌣). Verse types were named according to the type of foot and the number of feet in each line. The most common classical verse types were iambic pentameter and dactylic hexameter. In classical Greek and Latin, word stress was not correlated with the type of syllable contained in a foot. Skillful poets used this absence of correlation to create a tension between word stress and the structure of the metrical feet in the middle of each line, resolving the tension by bringing the two into harmony again at the end.

In the Germanic languages, stress is the major factor in versification, involving a sequence of stressed syllables in regular rhythm (in accordance with the stress-timed nature of the language), with unstressed syllables (usually one or two at a time) falling in between. Common to all Germanic languages is a four-stressed line, with a caesura after the second stress (exemplified in some Old Norse sagas and in the Old English poem *Beowulf*). In earlier Germanic verse and later imitations of it (as in Wagner's *Ring*), stress was supplemented by alliteration [Ger. *Stabreim*], i.e., sequences of the same initial consonant or consonant-group in successive words in each line.

In contrast to Germanic versification, that of the Romance languages is primarily syllable-timed, i.e., based on the number of syllables (often miscalled feet, in imitation of classical terminology) in each line. Verses are found with any number of syllables from two (exceptionally) to twelve. The most frequent types in lyric poetry involve six, seven, or eight syllables; longer verses usually contain ten, eleven, or twelve. The more conservative Romance languages (including Old French and Old Provençal) have phonemic stress. In these, the favorite longer verse is of ten syllables, with a caesura after a stressed fourth or sixth syllable and with a stress on the tenth. The tenth syllable may be followed by another, weakly stressed syllable, forming a "feminine" ending. In modern French, which has no phonemic stress, the favorite longer verse is the twelve-syllable or Alexandrine, with the possibility of a caesura after the fourth, sixth, or eighth syllable and of subdivisions within a six-syllable sequence, thus forming a very flexible type of line.

In setting poetic texts in their own languages, composers have naturally tended to follow their native prosodic patterns. Some composers are more sensitive than others in their perception of subtle variations in versification, e.g., Parry or Holst as compared with Elgar in setting English lyrics. A composer can often depart from the minor details of prosody (e.g., stress or pitch contours) with resultant beneficial tension between habitual speech patterns and a special emphasis attained by their violation, but the basic prosodic patterns of the language cannot be abandoned. The same is true of performance: a singer or chorus cannot introduce into a rendition features that are not characteristic of the language being sung (e.g., heavy stress on the first beat of each measure in a French art song).

A special problem is posed by settings of languages no longer spoken and for which no native-speaker models are available, such as Latin, Old French, and Old Provençal. Composers have tended to treat Latin texts in accordance with the prosodic patterns of their own native language: for instance, French composers have usually paid little or no attention to Latin word stress in settings of liturgical texts; in contrast, greater care has been shown by native speakers of languages in which word stress is significant. For Old Provençal and Old French, evidence for their speech rhythm is lacking, so opinions inevitably diverge concerning the manner of singing *troubadour and *trouvère songs: in triple rhythm, in duple, or in free declamatory style with varying rhythm.

Bibl.: Rudolf Baehr, *Manual de versificación española,* trans. and adapted by K. Wagner and Francisco López Estrada (Madrid: Gredos, 1969). Pierre Guiraud, *La versification* (Paris: Presses universitaires de France, 1970). Fritz Schlawe, *Neudeutsche Metrik* (Stuttgart: Metzler, 1972). W. K. Wimsatt, ed., *Versification: Major Language Types* (New York: Mod Lang Assoc, 1972). Mario Pazzaglia, *Teoria e analisi metrica* (Bologna: Pàtron, 1974). John Hollander, *Rhyme's Reason: A Guide to English Verse* (New Haven: Yale U Pr, 1981). R.A.H.

Prosomoion [Gr.]. See *Idiomelon.*

Prosula [Lat.]. The medieval term for the texts added to the internal melismas of certain liturgical chants of the Mass and less frequently of the Office. The creative process involved—that is, the addition of words to a preexistent melody—is related to that of the *sequence or **prosa,* the word itself being a diminutive form of *prosa.* But unlike the sequence, which could eventually become a form independent of the Alleluia, since it was sung after the official chant and since its melody was itself an addition, the prosula was integrally linked to the chant it embellished and therefore could only rarely take on a life of its own. Prosulae occur most frequently in connection with the melismas of Alleluias, Alleluia verses, and Offertory verses in the Proper of the Mass and the Osanna and Kyrie in the Ordinary. The titles of certain Kyrie prosulae are still used in modern chant books to identify the Kyries to which they were originally attached. One special category of prosulae consists of additions to an addition—namely, the so-called *Regnum* prosulae, which were textual additions to an internal melisma of a Gloria trope.

Bibl.: Ruth Steiner, "The Prosulae of the MS Paris, Bibliothèque Nationale, f. lat. 1118," *JAMS* 22 (1969): 367–93. Olof Marcusson, *Prosules de la messe,* Corpus troporum 2 (Stockholm: Almqvist & Wiksell International, 1976) [critical edition of the texts of Alleluia prosulae]. Richard Hoppin, *Medieval Music* (New York: Norton, 1978), pp. 149–51. David A. Bjork, "The Kyrie Trope," *JAMS* 33 (1980): 1–41.

P.E.

Protestant church music. See Church music.

Protus [Gr.]. See Mode.

Prussian Quartets. (1) A set of three string quartets by Mozart, K. 575 in D major, K. 589 in B♭ major, and K. 590 in F major, composed in 1789–90, possibly at the suggestion of Friedrich Wilhelm II of Prussia, who in 1789 had invited Mozart to Berlin. The monarch played the cello, and the cello parts are unusually elaborate. (2) Haydn's six string quartets op. 50, Hob. III:44–49 (1787). The title page of the Artaria first edition of 1787 bears a dedication to Friedrich Wilhelm II.

Ps. (1) Abbr. for *Psalm. (2) [Ger.] Abbr. for *Posaune* (trombone).

Psalm [Gr. *psalmos;* Lat. *psalmus;* Fr. *psaume;* Ger. *Psalm;* It., Sp. *salmo*]. A sacred poem or song; specifically, one of the 150 such poems making up the Book of Psalms of the Bible, also termed the Psalter. For the numbering system employed in different versions of the Psalter and for the history of its use in liturgical contexts and its translation in metrical versions, see Psalter. For the methods of Psalm singing employed in the Gregorian and other repertories of plainsong, see Psalmody, Latin. See also Psalmody, British and North American; Penitential Psalms; Anglican chant; *Falsobordone.*

Psalmellus [Lat.]. The *Ambrosian chant corresponding to the Roman gradual.

Psalmo [Lat.]. The *Mozarabic chant corresponding to the Roman gradual.

Psalmodikon. A bowed *zither of Scandinavia with one to four melody strings over a fret board and several drone strings. It was used in the 19th century to accompany choral singing in the absence of an organ or piano, but passed out of use with the advent of the harmonium. See also *Langleik.*

Psalmody, British and North American. In the English-speaking Protestant and Reformed churches of the 17th, 18th, and 19th centuries, the singing of Psalms according to published metrical *psalters; by extension, the performance of any concerted sacred vocal music either for worship or for recreation. In the Anglican- and Calvinist-rooted denominations, psalmody provided an approximate equivalent to the slightly older use of *chorales in the German Lutheran Church. It gradually gave way after about 1790 to the increased use of hymns and choral singing in the Anglican cathedral style (anthems, responses, etc.), features that persist today in these churches. A few metrical Psalms still survive as hymns, e.g., "Old Hundredth" ("All people that on earth do dwell").

The earliest English metrical psalms (Sternhold 1547–49) were written in meters of popular ballads and were probably sung to ballad tunes, though their identities are difficult to establish. Clament Marot was said to have sung his Psalm versions to French *chanson melodies, and the earlier Dutch **Souterliedekens* (1540) set its 150 Psalms to various European folk songs. Thus there was Continental precedent for singing metrical Psalms to popular melodies. The parallel connections between balladry and psalmody in later generations of English speakers is an underresearched area, but some ballads were set to Psalm tunes, and others alluded to psalmody.

In English town churches, statutory choirs of "charity children" led the psalmody with the parish clerk *lining out the text; after the Restoration, organs were added. In the poorer country churches, psalmody was led by the clerk alone or, after about 1680, by amateur men's choirs and instrumental groups. Although psalmody originated as spirited syllabic singing, by the late 17th century it had generally slowed to a drawl and admitted spontaneous congregational ornamentation, resulting in discordant heterophony. During the 18th century, its debased state prompted frequent clerical criticism and attempts at reform (e.g., Symmes, 1720). Increasingly, psalmody also subsumed new music composed in imitation of cathedral or theater music but suitable for the limited forces available to churches, by such composers as William Tans'ur, William Knapp, and John Arnold. The conservative Scottish Presbyterian Church preserved relatively simple Psalm singing, a practice continued to the present.

The Pilgrims and Puritans came to North America with a thorough grounding in psalmody, which provided their sole musical form of recreation as well as devotion (see Cotton, 1647). Succeeding generations of Americans possessed sharply less musical skill, and by the 1720s, the New England clergy saw fit to promote musical literacy by instituting singing schools and by publishing tune books on an extensive scale. The success of the effort resulted in the growing importation of new British psalmody in the mid-18th century. In the wake of this influx, America produced a nationalistic strain of self-taught native composers of psalmody, with William Billings (1746–1800) in the forefront. While their work had a following, it provoked 19th-century criticism on stylistic and qualitative grounds, and the newly composed psalmody of the early national period converged more and more with then current English-European style.

In much of the 20th century, 18th-century psalmody was not always taken seriously. In recent decades both the music of English parochial psalmody and that of Billings and his successors in America have received increasing study and performance. They are now understood within their own terms.

Bibl.: John Cotton, *Singing of Psalmes, a Gospel-Ordinance, Or, a Treatise, wherein are handled these Foure Particulars. 1. Touching the Duty It Selfe. 2. Touching the Matter to be Sung. 3. Touching the Singers. 4. Touching the Manner of Singing* (London: M.S. for Allen, 1647). Thomas Symmes, *The Reasonableness of Regular Singing, or Singing by Note; in an Essay, to Revive the True and Ancient Mode of Singing Psalm-tunes, According to the Pattern of our New England Psalm-books*. . . (Boston: Green for Gerrish, 1720). Hyder E. Rollins, *An Analytical Index to the Ballad-Entries in the Registers (1557–1709) of the Company of Stationers of London* (Chapel Hill: U of NC Pr, 1924; R. New York: Johnson, 1967). Henry Wilder Foote, *Three Centuries of American Hymnody* (Cambridge: Harvard U Pr, 1940; R: [Hamden]: Archon, 1968). H. C. Macdougall, *Early New England Psalmody: An Historical Appreciation, 1620–1820* (Brattleboro: Daye, 1940). Millar Patrick, *Four Centuries of Scottish Psalmody* (New York: Oxford U Pr, 1949). Claude M. Simpson, *The British Broadside Ballad and Its Music* (New Brunswick, N.J.: Rutgers U Pr, 1966). Richard Crawford, *Andrew Law, American Psalmodist* (Evanston: Northwestern U Pr, 1968; R: New York: Da Capo, 1981). Nicholas Temperley, *The Music of the English Parish Church* (New York: Cambridge U Pr, 1979). Bernarr Rainbow, *English Psalmody Prefaces: Popular Methods of Teaching, 1562–1835* (Kilkenny, Ireland: Boethius, 1982). Robin A. Leaver, *"Goostly psalmes and spirituall songes": English and Dutch Metrical Psalms from Coverdale to Utenhove 1535–1566* (Oxford: Clarendon, 1991). Tessa Watt, *Cheap Print and Popular Piety, 1550–1640* (New York: Cambridge U Pr, 1991). Christopher Turner, ed., *Georgian Psalmody 1 and 2* (Corby Glen, U.K.: SG Publishing, 1998–99). Thomas A. M. Barnett and Richard G. Leggett, *Psalmody in the Canadian Churches* (Vancouver: Chalmers Institute, 2001). rev. R.A.L.

Psalmody, Latin. The singing of the Psalms in the Western Christian rites; also the several musical forms associated principally, though not exclusively, with the singing of Psalms. The psalmodic forms have often been thought to derive from the earliest practices of Psalm singing in biblical times. The form of individual Psalm verses, which consist of two parallel elements, and the form of some whole Psalms, such as Psalm 135 (136), in which all verses conclude with the same words, suggest possible models for the surviving forms of psalmody. Attempts to find their specific origins in Jewish practice, however, have been seriously questioned. Formally constituted psalmody as a part of the Christian liturgy perhaps dates from as late as the 4th century, and regular psalmody in the synagogue is perhaps later still (McKinnon, 1979–80; see Gregorian chant VI). In any case, all of these forms evidently underwent considerable change between the time of the earliest accounts of Psalm singing even in the West and the earliest surviving musical records of these forms from the 9th and 10th centuries. All of the Western Christian chant repertories share these forms. The following descriptions refer principally to the Gregorian chant [see also Ambrosian chant, Gallican chant, Mozarabic chant; for Eastern practice see Byzantine chant]. Three forms of psalmody are usually distinguished, though both medieval and modern practice often obscure the supposed differences among them.

In antiphonal psalmody, the verses of a Psalm are

sung alternately by the two halves of a choir or schola seated facing one another in front of and on opposite sides of the altar. The singing of the Psalm itself, to a relatively simple melodic formula called a *psalm tone that is adapted and repeated for each verse, is preceded and followed by the singing of a separate melody with a brief text usually drawn from the Psalm and called an *antiphon. St. Augustine (d. 430) credits St. Ambrose (d. 397) with having introduced antiphonal singing into the West in imitation of Eastern Christian models. The refrainlike antiphon seems not to have been a feature of antiphonal singing at first, but may have been added by the 4th century in imitation of the earliest forms of responsorial singing. The resulting scheme would have been as follows (where A is the antiphon, V a verse, and D the lesser *Doxology): A V_1 A V_2 . . . A D A. As late as the 9th century, Amalarius of Metz suggests that this repetition of the antiphon after each verse was the norm. The principal examples of antiphonal psalmody in the Office are the Psalms, canticles, and the *Invitatory. Of these, only the Invitatory preserves a scheme in which the antiphon is sung following verses other than the last. In modern practice for the Psalms and canticles, the antiphon is sung only at beginning and end, the lesser Doxology being divided and treated as two verses sung to the same psalm tone as the verses themselves: A V_1 V_2 . . . D_1 D_2 A. The antiphon is begun by a soloist and continued by the choir. The first half of each verse is also often sung by the soloist and the second half by the choir. Thus, alternation between soloist and choir is substituted for the original practice of alternation between the two halves of the choir. In the Mass, the *introit is the clearest example of this type of psalmody. Even the earliest sources provide only one or two verses for the introit, however. Here too, modern practice often employs alternation between soloists and choir rather than between the two halves of the choir. The *offertory and the *communion of the Mass are also usually regarded as antiphonal chants, though the style of surviving offertories and their verses is quite different from that of other antiphonal pieces, and both offertory and communion were ultimately stripped of all verses, as early as the 12th century in some sources. According to this classification, all of the antiphonal chants of the Mass are associated with actions: the entrance at the beginning of the Mass, the offering, and the communion.

In responsorial psalmody, one or more soloists or cantors sing one or more verses, and a choir sings a refrain or respond at the beginning and end and perhaps following each of the verses. Although the earliest forms of responsorial psalmody may have incorporated whole Psalms, surviving examples include only one or a very few verses. It is unlikely that the surviving examples (even the few with more than one verse) are the remnants of pieces that at one time included many more verses or whole Psalms. The writings of Isidore of Seville (d. 636) suggest that a single verse was the norm for responsories as early as the 7th century and that both this and performance practice distinguished responsories from antiphons. He attributes the invention of responsories to the Italians, though the general scheme of responsorial singing is widely attested in both East and West; thus the general practice, as opposed to any specific embodiment of it, may not have spread through the West from any single center. Indeed, it is possible that an early and widespread general practice of responsorial singing is the antecedent of both the antiphonal and the responsorial psalmody that were incorporated into the Latin rites. Amalarius reports that among the Franks only the last part of the respond of responsories was repeated following the verse, whereas in Rome the whole of the respond was repeated. In the *gradual it became the norm for the choir to join the soloist in singing the end of the verse rather than repeat any of the respond. The principal examples of responsorial psalmody in the Office are the great *responsories, the verses of which are sung to relatively elaborate psalm tones, and the brief responsories. The responsorial chants of the Mass are the gradual and the *alleluia. In both Mass and Office, responsorial chants are associated with readings.

In direct psalmody, a Psalm is sung without alternation among singers and without the refrainlike additions found in antiphonal and responsorial psalmody. In the Mass this is usually said to be represented by the elaborate melodies of the *tract. Amalarius remarks in the 9th century that although the choir responds in responsories, no one responds in tracts. In modern practice, successive verses of the tract are usually sung in alternation either between the soloists and the choir or between the two halves of the choir rather than by soloists alone. For the Office, the singing of a Psalm without an antiphon (*psalmus in directum* or *directaneus*) is mentioned along with the other two types of psalmody in the Rule of St. Benedict (ca. 535), and a simple psalm tone is used for this purpose (*LU,* p. 118; *AntMon,* p. 1219).

Bibl.: Jacques Hourlier, "Notes sur l'antiphonie," *Schrade,* 1973, 1:116–43. Helmut Hucke, "Das Responsorium," *Schrade,* 1973, 1:144–91. James W. McKinnon, "The Exclusion of Musical Instruments from the Ancient Synagogue," *PRMA* 106 (1979–80): 77–87. See also Gregorian chant.

D.M.R.

Psalm tone. A melodic formula to which the verses of the Psalms and certain other texts are sung [see Psalmody, Latin]. The use of such tones in the Western Christian rites is linked to Byzantine practice [see Byzantine chant] as is the system of eight *modes with which the Gregorian tones described here are inextricably linked. Although the existence of these tones along with the modes in Gregorian chant is implied in a *tonary of the late 8th century, the earliest preserved source for the tones themselves is a treatise of the 10th century, the *Commemoratio brevis de tonis et psalmis modulandis* (ed. and trans. Bailey, 1978). The use of psalm tones in other Western rites such as the *Ambrosian, *Mozarabic, and *Old Roman seems not to have been linked to a system of modes.

The following items of the Gregorian liturgy employ psalm tones for their verses, each item having its own set of eight tones, one for each mode: the Psalms, canticles, and great responsories of the Office, and the introit of the Mass. The Invitatory at Matins also employs psalm tones for its verses, though modes 1 and 8 are not represented, and the number of tones for other modes varies. The communion of the Mass, as long as it retained verses, shared the tones of the introit. Within the appropriate set, the psalm tone is chosen according to the mode of the accompanying antiphon (for the Psalms, canticles, and Invitatory), responsory, or introit.

The underlying scheme for the tones, which may be seen to underlie other types of chants as well, is generally bipartite. In the first half, an intonation formula (*initium* or *inchoatio*) leads to a reciting tone (tenor or *tuba*), and this is followed by a cadence (mediant or *mediatio*). The second half may begin with another intonation, returns to a reciting tone, and ends with a final cadence (termination or *terminatio*). Because in the simpler tones much of the text is sung to the reciting tone, psalm tones are often said to be inflected monotones or recitatives. In some of the more elaborate tones, however, the reciting tone is not particularly prominent. The pitch of the reciting tone is sometimes said to be a fundamental feature of the mode in question. These pitches have nevertheless varied somewhat with time and liturgical type. The separate sets of tones modify the general scheme in other ways as well.

The tones for the Psalms of the Office begin with a simple intonation that does not take account of the accentuation of the text (see *LU,* pp. 112–17, 128–220, *AntMon,* pp. 1210–22, *AntRom,* pp. 3*–24*; also *LU,* pp. 917–39, Matins for the feast of Corpus Christi, which includes a series of antiphons in the order of the eight modes and with the psalm tones and verses written out). In modern practice, the intonation is sung by the cantor and for the first verse only, all remaining verses beginning directly with the tenor. If the first half of the verse is sufficiently long, the tenor is inflected (flex or *flexa*) before proceeding to the mediant. Early sources sometimes provide a second intonation for the second half of the tone, though this is not found in modern chant books. The tone concludes with the termination, which, like the flex and the mediant, is adjusted for the accentuation of the text. The number of text accents incorporated into the mediant and termination varies from tone to tone, the seventh tone, shown in the example, having both mediant and termination of two accents. In the accompanying examples, the black notes with accent marks are applied to the last two accented syllables of the appropriate section of the text, and the hollow notes are applied to intervening syllables, if any. The flex is similarly applied to a single accented syllable. Cadences that are adjusted to the tonic accent of the text in this way are tonic cadences [see Cursive and tonic]. (Like their Byzantine models, however, the earliest terminations used in the West seem to have been four-element formulas applied to the last four syllables of text without regard for accent. See Strunk, 1945, 1957, 1960; Randel, 1977.) The terminations are further modified melodically in order to smooth the transition from the end of the tone to the beginning of the accompanying antiphon. These alternative terminations are known as differences *(differentiae)* and have been a feature of the psalm tones since the earliest surviving records, though their number and relationship to particular antiphons varied from source to source [see Tonary]. In modern chant books they are identified by the number of the mode followed by the pitch on which they end and, if there is more than one for any single pitch, a second number. Antiphons are usually preceded by this designation for the difference and followed by the musical notation for the difference placed over the final syllables of the lesser *Doxology (E u o u a e, from *seculorum Amen*), with which the singing of a Psalm concludes.

The *tonus peregrinus* (wandering or foreign tone) lies outside the system of eight tones but is found in the earliest sources (though the name is slightly later) and is similar to the other tones in design except for its use of different pitches for the reciting tones of the two halves. It is used principally for the singing of Psalm 113 (114–15), *In exitu Israel,* and is thought by some scholars to be of Jewish origin.

On some occasions, as in the Office for the Dead, a Psalm is sung without an antiphon, and for this purpose one or another *tonus in directum* is prescribed (*LU,* p. 118, *AntMon,* p. 1219, *AntRom,* pp. 25*–27*). These tones are similar in design to the psalm tones used with antiphons, though they constitute examples of direct psalmody.

Medieval sources provide a slightly more elaborate set of tones for the canticles. In modern practice, the tones for the canticles are virtually the same as those for the Psalms except on important feasts when more elaborate "solemn tones," which derive from medieval practice, may be used for the first half of each verse. Here both intonation and mediant are usually very slightly embellished versions of the corresponding tones for the Psalms, and the intonation is repeated for each verse. For the second half of each verse the regular tones for the Psalms are used (*LU,* pp. 213–18, *AntMon,* pp. 1220–22, *AntRom,* pp. 3*–25*).

The tones for the introit are also somewhat more elaborate than those for the Psalms, though their general plan is the same. A second intonation is provided for the second half of the verse. They differ principally in their use (except in the fifth mode) of a termination of five elements applied to the last five syllables of text without regard for accent. Such a cadence is said to be *cursive. The tone for the sixth mode is exceptional in employing different reciting pitches for the two halves. When sung with the introit, the Doxology departs from the general plan and is treated in three

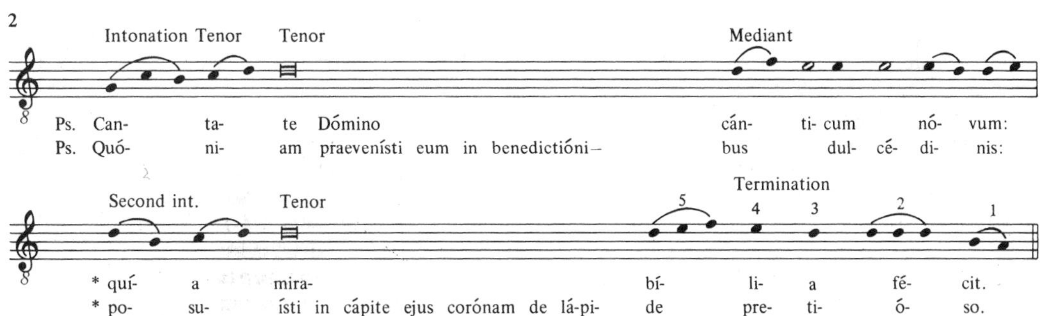

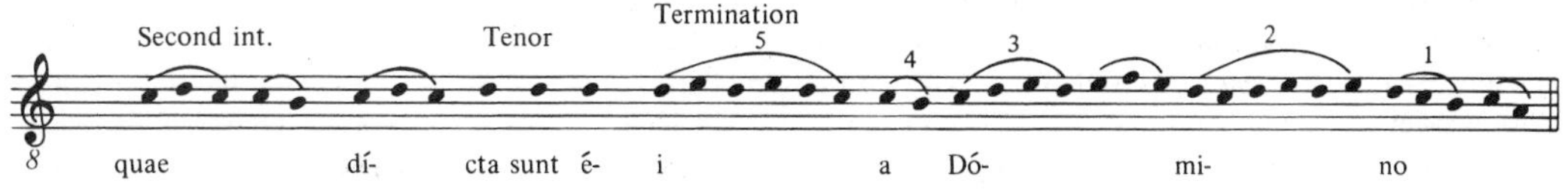

Psalm tone. 1. Psalm 111, Tone 7.c (*LU,* pp. 146–47). 2. Introit, Tone 7 (*LU,* pp. 408, 1136). 3. Great responsory, Tone 7 (*LU,* p. 383).

parts. The first and second parts employ the same mediant, and the second and third parts generally employ the same intonation (*LU,* pp. 14–16).

Still more elaborate are the tones for the Invitatory. These do not embody the eightfold system of other psalm tones, since the first and eighth modes are lacking. Medieval sources differ strikingly from one another in their presentation of these tones. The tones consist of three parts, each with intonation, reciting tone, and cadence. Within each tone, intonations and reciting pitches may or may not be shared among the parts. The final cadences or terminations are cursive.

The eight tones for the great responsories follow the outline of the tones for the Psalms but are in every respect distinctly more elaborate. Intonations, unlike those for the Psalms, are adjusted for text accent. Except in the fifth mode, the reciting pitch is different in the two halves, though the elaborate character of the intonations and cadences greatly reduces the prominence of the reciting tones, especially for shorter texts. The terminations are cursive cadences of five elements.

Bibl.: Oliver Strunk, "Intonations and Signatures of the Byzantine Modes," *MQ* 31 (1945): 339–55; R: in *Essays on*

Music in the Byzantine World (New York: Norton, 1977), pp. 19–39. Id., "The Influence of the Liturgical Chant of the East on that of the Western Church," first publ. in It. trans. in 1957; R: in *Essays,* pp. 151–56. Id., "The Antiphons of the Oktoechos," *JAMS* 13 (1960): 50–67; R: in *Essays,* pp. 165–90. Hugo Berger, *Untersuchungen zu den Psalmdifferenzen* (Regensburg: G Bosse, 1966). Clyde W. Brockett, Jr., "*Saeculorum amen* and *Differentia:* Practical versus Theoretical Tradition," *MD* 30 (1976): 13–36. Don M. Randel, "Antiphonal Psalmody in the Mozarabic Rite," *Berkeley,* 1977, pp. 414–22. Terence Bailey, ed. and trans., *Commemoratio brevis de tonis et psalmis modulandis* (Ottawa: U of Ottawa Pr, 1978). See also Gregorian chant, Psalmody, Antiphon, Responsory. D.M.R.

Psalmus [Lat.]. *Psalm.

Psalter. The collected Book of Psalms of the Old Testament, as an independent entity or as a section of a liturgical book (with or without separate pagination). The authorship of David (King of Israel ca. 1012–ca. 972 B.C.E.) is no longer assumed. No other book of the Bible is so musically conceived or has left such a strong imprint on the music associated with prayer, praise, and thanksgiving.

The numeration of the Psalter in the Latin (Vulgate) and the King James Version (1611, which corresponds to the Hebrew and Lutheran numeration), is as follows:

Latin (Vulgate)	King James Version
1–8	1–8
9	9, 10
10–112	11–113
113	114, 115
114, 115	116
116–145	117–146
146, 147	147
148–150	148–150

Thus, of a total of 150 Psalms, only the first eight and the last three have the same number in both numerations. In all versions, the ordering of the Psalms is identical: five books, each of the first four concluding with a brief doxology, and the final Psalm 150 constituting the doxology to the entire Psalter. In the numeration of the King James Version, the doxologies conclude Psalms 41, 72, 89, and 106. The Latin numbering is employed in this dictionary, followed by the King James numbering in parentheses if it is different.

The musical importance of the Psalter is directly related to the structure of the Psalms and their content. Structurally, the verses of the Psalms are composed of parallel halves that may be related as idea and restatement of idea (synonymously), or as idea followed by contrasting idea (antithetically), or as antecedent and consequent, the former completed by the latter (synthetically). This structure is itself indicative of the variety and depth of the Psalter's spiritual content, evidenced also by the incorporation of the entire Psalter into the Roman Breviary and the Book of Common Prayer. The rubrics of the former direct its recitation once a week (a practice embodied in the Rule of St. Benedict, ca. 535), and those of the latter once a month. For the methods of Psalm singing employed in Gregorian chant and related repertories, see Psalmody, Latin.

The Psalter has always been privileged in liturgy and worship, but during the Reformation of the 16th century, it acquired special and renewed importance, particularly in the liturgies of the Reformed (Calvinist) and related churches. Calvin held that only singing of unaccompanied Psalm texts in the vernacular (thus being immediately intelligible) was proper to his Reformed liturgy. The 1562 editions of the so-called Geneva (Huguenot) Psalter *(Les Psaumes mis en rime francois . . .),* comprising 152 texts set to 125 different melodies, were the first containing rhymed paraphrases in French of the complete Psalter (plus the Decalogue and Canticle of Simeon). The texts are by Clément Marot (1496?–1544) and Théodore de Bèze (1519–1605), and the melodies are of varied provenance, though many are attributed to Loys Bourgeois (ca. 1510–60).

The Genevan experiment, in which a series of smaller collections culminated in the complete 1562 Psalter, became the prototype for a plethora of similar complete rhymed paraphrases, termed metrical Psalters, in other languages—notably, in English, the so-called 1562 Old Version of Thomas Sternhold (d. 1549), John Hopkins (d. 1570), and others; the 1612 Psalter of Henry Ainsworth (1571–1622?) brought to North America by the Pilgrims in 1620; and the New England Version or so-called *Bay Psalm Book of 1640, the first indigenous Psalter to be published in the colonies. The first Dutch metrical Psalter, the **Souterliedekens,* was published in Antwerp in 1540 by Symon Cock and employed Dutch and French folk songs. Between 1551 and 1566 Jan Utinhove produced Dutch metrical Psalms, published in London and Emden. These were replaced by those of Petrus Daltheen (Heidelberg, 1566), which follow the French models more closely. These were the metrical Psalms early Dutch immigrants brought to North America, and in some parts of the Netherlands they are still sung today. The tunes of the Geneva Psalter are particularly remarkable, many of them combining melodic and rhythmic stencils into patterns that convey a quite modern eloquence and that achieved such instant and widespread popularity that they spread quickly abroad.

Through rhymed translations into German by the Lutheran Ambrosius Lobwasser (1515–85), which were designed to fit Genevan tunes, the Genevan melodies also penetrated deeply into German-speaking lands, both Reformed and Lutheran (provoking, in turn, the opposing Lutheran translation of Cornelius Becker in 1602, later set by Schütz). There are over 2,000 polyphonic settings of the Genevan Psalms from the 16th century by composers such as Pierre Certon, Clément Janequin, Jacques Arcadelt, Claude

Goudimel (three complete settings), and Claude Le Jeune (two complete settings). These are in a variety of styles, from simple homophony to elaborate motets, many making use of the Genevan melodies. Such settings were not intended for use in church. Harmonized Psalters in England included Thomas East's *The Whole Booke of Psalmes* of 1592, with settings of the whole of Sternhold and Hopkins, and Thomas Ravenscroft's *The Whole Booke of Psalmes* of 1621, which introduced a great many new tunes.

All the Reformed translators strove for literal fidelity to the Hebrew texts, expressed in vernacular idioms of the time; thus, the subsequent history of the rhymed or metrical Psalter must be recounted within each idiom, recognizing that the art of translation was universally experimental, aiming now at "literal" translation, slipping into paraphrase, incorporating evangelical expansion, inflating portions of themes at the expense of the remainder, and always having to compromise theological accuracy with literary intransigence. The history of the rhymed English Psalter exhibits all of these tendencies, but its course is set toward the goal of poetic felicity, marked by the "New Version" (1696) of Nahum Tate (1652–1715) and Nicholas Brady (1659–1706), and beyond that to the paraphrases, literary and evangelical distortions, and expansions of the 1719 collection of Isaac Watts (1674–1748), *The Psalms of David Imitated in the Language of the New Testament.* Watts's highly influential work openly broke with literalism and comprehensiveness and attempted to modernize the language, even abbreviating the message of the Psalter when necessary, recognizing prophecies of the Old Testament as fulfilled in the New, and generally letting the Psalms speak "the common sense and language of a Christian." Thus, Watts composed, as he says, a Psalmbook for Christians after the manner of the Psalter.

The unrhymed translation of the Psalter by Miles Coverdale (1488–1568), taken from the Great Bible of 1539, was incorporated into the Book of Common Prayer in 1549 and persists beneath all subsequent English and American revisions until 1979/80. It has thus retained its liturgical primacy and authority for over four centuries, parallel to the rhymed translations and paraphrases.

Bibl.: Maurice Frost, *English and Scottish Psalm and Hymn Tunes* (London: Oxford U Pr, 1953). J. A. Lamb, *The Psalms in Christian Worship* (London: Faith Pr, 1962). Pierre Pidoux, *Le Psautier Huguenot* (Basel: Bärenreiter, 1962). Friedrich Blume, et al., *Protestant Church Music: A History* (New York: Norton, 1974). Richard G. Appel, ed., *The Music of the Bay Psalm Book, 9th Edition (1698)* (Brooklyn: ISAM, 1975). Nicholas Temperley, *The Music of the English Parish Church* (New York: Cambridge U Pr, 1979). Lorraine Inserra and H. Wiley Hitchcock, eds., *The Music of Henry Ainsworth's Psalter (Amsterdam, 1612)* (Brooklyn: ISAM, 1981). J. A. Smith, "The Ancient Synagogue, the Early Church, and Singing," *ML* 65 (1984): 1–16. James W. McKinnon, "On the Question of Psalmody in the Ancient Synagogue," *EMH* 6 (1986): 159–91. Victor H. Matthews and Ivor H. Jones, "Music and Musical Instruments," in *The Anchor Bible Dictionary,* ed. David Noel Freedman et al. (New York: Doubleday, 1992), 4: 930–39. Robin A. Leaver, *"Goostly psalmes and spirituall songes": English and Dutch Metrical Psalms from Coverdale to Utenhove 1535–1566* (Oxford: Clarendon, 1991). William L. Holladay, *The Psalms through Three Thousand Years: Prayerbook of a Cloud of Witnesses* (Minneapolis: Fortress, 1993). J. A. Smith, "Which Psalms Were Sung in the Temple?" *ML* 71 (1990): 167–86. J. A. Smith, "First-Century Christian Singing and Its Relationship to Contemporary Jewish Song," *ML* 75 (1994): 1–15.

R.F.F., rev. R.A.L.

Psalterium [Lat.; Gr. *psaltērion*]. In ancient Greece, any stringed instrument, but especially the harp; in the Middle Ages, any of a variety of stringed instruments, including the *harp, *crwth, and *psaltery; in the Renaissance, almost always the *psaltery. In the Vulgate, the term is a translation of the Hebrew **nebel.*

Psaltery [Lat. *psalterium;* Fr. *psaltérion;* Gr. *Psalterium;* It., Sp. *salterio*]. A plucked *zither of medieval Europe with a flat, wooden sound box and a variable number of strings. Medieval illustrators and commentators identified the biblical *psalterium* with frame harps and triangular zithers. Sometime in the 11th or 12th century, the Arabic **qānūn* reached Europe (whence the Latin term *canon* and its cognates such as the Spanish *caño*) and thereafter the vernacular term psaltery referred primarily to this instrument and its variants. No medieval psalteries have been preserved or excavated, but many are depicted in illustrations and carvings of the period. They were made in several shapes: trapezoidal like the *qānūn,* square, triangular, and "pig's snout" (a trapezoid with inward-curving sides). Instruments with the shape of a half trapezoid (i.e., with only one oblique side) were given various names deriving from the Latin *canon,* e.g., *medius canon, medicinale, micanon, Metzkanon, mezzocanone, medio caño.* Several playing positions and techniques are shown: horizontal in the lap or vertical against the chest, plucked with the fingers or with a plectrum. A few sources show a triangular psaltery held upright like a harp and with a second, harplike sound box. Some scholars have dubbed this a harp-psaltery and have speculated that it may have had strings on both sides of the vertical sound box. The psaltery seems to have been extremely widespread from the 12th through the 15th century, but its popularity declined thereafter. Its principal features survive in many folk zithers and *dulcimers. See also *Arpanetta, Gusli, Psalterium, Rote.* See ill. under Zither.

Publishers' numbers. Numbers assigned to publications by their publishers. Because these numbers are ordinarily assigned in chronological sequence, they are often useful in establishing the date when a work was issued. The most common type of publisher's number is the plate number, which usually appears centered at the bottom of each page of an engraved publication, the same number for each page. These numbers probably designated where in a publisher's warehouse the engraved plates were stored. They doubtless also assisted in keeping track of the various sheets after they were printed.

Tentative dates can often be determined for a series of publishers' numbers by correlating them with other types of evidence. To give a hypothetical example, it might be possible to establish a date of 1750 for plate numbers 1 and 3 of a given publisher because the prints they designate were first advertised in that year. In that case, one could tentatively assign a date of 1750 to a print by the same publisher with the plate number 2, even though no advertisement for that print has been found. Lists of dated numbers useful in applying such a procedure have been published by several scholars.

There are a number of pitfalls to this method, however, most notably the fairly common reuse of a given number by a publisher after the original work has gone out of print. Also, some publishers seem to have applied plate numbers in wholly random fashion. Hence, the appropriate use of publishers' numbers as chronological evidence requires a comprehensive knowledge of the firm in question.

Bibl.: Otto Erich Deutsch, *Musikverlags-Nummern,* 2nd ed. (Berlin: Merseburger, 1961). O. W. Neighbour and Alan Tyson, *English Music Publishers' Plate Numbers in the First Half of the Nineteenth Century* (London: Faber & Faber, 1965). Donald W. Krummel, comp., *A Guide for Dating Early Published Music* (Hackensack, N.J.: Boonin, 1974). Anik Devriès and François Lesure, *Dictionnaire des éditeurs de musique français* (Geneva: Minkoff, 1978–88), 2 vols. in 3. Phillip Gossett, "The Ricordi Numerical Catalogue: A Background," *Notes* (Sept. 1985): 22–28.
E.K.W.

Publishing of music. The branch of the book trade that entails the selection, production, and marketing of music. Publishers of concert or art music make up only a small fraction of today's industry. Some publishers feel a responsibility to issue a selection of recently composed music, which they solicit or which is submitted to them. A publisher must have a broad base of items that sell well, such as standard works and educational materials, in order to support editions of recently composed music, whose sales may not cover the printing costs. Most publishers have long-standing agreements with certain composers, whose works they invest in and promote. Recently composed music may derive income from performance rights and rental of parts, while older music has income only from the sale of printed editions. The publication of historical editions such as Denkmäler and collected works is often subsidized by foundation or government grants. Most American publishers also derive income as American agents for European publishers. Publishers generally prefer to deal with music stores, which today are found primarily in large cities or in educational centers, rather than deal directly with the consumer.

Publishers of *popular music dominate today's market, and their income is derived not primarily from the sale of printed music, but from recording royalties and performance fees, as collected by ASCAP, BMI, and SESAC [see Copyright and performance right]. This arrangement is dependent on the copyright law, which allows composers to contract with publishers for the use of works for a limited time. Many of these publishers are affiliated with a record or motion-picture company, which in turn may be part of a larger conglomerate.

The history of music publishing from the invention of printing to the 18th century is largely a history of printers, for they were also the publishers and usually, too, the dealers. Some, such as John Playford (1623–86) and John Walsh (1665 or 1666–1736), both active in London, were successful businessmen in the promotion of their publications. Several composers have been publishers, notably Claudio Merulo, Muzio Clementi, Pleyel, Dussek, Cramer, the Andrés, Telemann, Diabelli, Litolff, and Novello. In the first half of the 20th century, American composers, frustrated by their lack of opportunities for publication, established their own enterprises, e.g., the Wa-Wan Press, the New Music Society, the Arrow Press (Cos-Cob Press), and the Society for the Publication of American Music.

During the Enlightenment, the market for music increased greatly, and publishers became the middlemen between composers and consumers. As composers left the employment of the church and the court, the chief new employers were publishers and impresarios. Two major periods in the popularization of music led to large increases in publishing; in both cases social change coincided with technological innovations. Early in the 19th century, *character pieces and favorite opera arias (and arrangements of them) for amateur music making were in demand at the same time as the modern piano was being developed. A second period of popularization was brought on early in the 20th century with the advent of radio, recordings, and sound movies, at the same time as a demand for entertainment arose from a new leisured class, especially in the U.S. Mass communications made everyone a potential customer for music, and publishing popular music became big business. A worldwide market was created for American popular music by dissemination during World War II. Two professional organizations serve music publishers in the U.S.: the Music Publishers' Association for publishers of educational, church, and concert music, and the National Music Publishers' Association for publishers of popular music. The Music Publishers Association website, *http://www.mpa.org/agency/pal.html,* contains a directory of American music publishers and a list of publishers from other countries whom they represent in the American market.

Bibl.: "Music Publishing Today—A Symposium," *Notes* 32 (1975–76): 223–58. Leonard Feist, *An Introduction to Popular Music Publishing in America* (New York: National Music Publishers' Assoc, 1980). Harvey Rachlin, *The Encyclopedia of the Music Business* (New York: Harper & Row, 1981). Agostina Z. Laterza, *Il catalogo numerico Ricordi 1857 con date e indici* (Rome: Nuovo istituto editoriale italiano, 1984). D. W. Krummel and Stanley Sadie, eds., *Music Printing and Publishing* (New York: Norton, 1990). Rita Benton, *Pleyel as Music Publisher: A Documentary Sourcebook of Early 19th-Century Music* (Stuyvestant, N.Y.: Pendragon, 1990). David Baskerville, *Music Business Handbook and Career Guide,* 6th ed. (Thousand Oaks, Calif.: Sage, 1995). Kate van Orden, ed., *Music and the Cultures of Print* (New York: Garland, 2000). See also Printing of music.

H.E.S., rev. L.C.

Pui [OFr.]. See *Puy.*

Pulcinella. A ballet with song by Stravinsky for soloists and chamber orchestra, commissioned by Sergei Diaghilev (choreography by Leonide Massine, decor and costumes by Pablo Picasso) and produced in Paris, 1920. The music makes free use of numerous passages from works by Pergolesi and works formerly attributed to him.

Pumhart [Ger.]. See *Bombard.*

Punctum [Lat.]. See Neume, Punctus.

Punctus [Lat.]. (1) The dot employed in mensural notation. For its meaning in various contexts and the associated nomenclature, see Mensural notation. (2) [pl. *puncta*] A section of an **estampie.*

Punk Rock. A subgenre of *rock music that evolved as a form of social protest among English and working-class youths in the mid-1970s. Punk groups rejected rock's emphasis on technique and professionalism and relied instead upon sheer volume and rhythmic energy applied to rhythms and forms derived from *rock and roll of the early 1960s. Their dress and behavior were often intended to shock. The Sex Pistols, an English quartet, are credited with initiating the genre; by the time of their breakup in 1977, punk had already fallen prey to the same commercial aesthetic it was meant to criticize [see New Wave]. P.T.W.

Punta [It.]. Point; *p. d'arco,* the point or tip of the violin or similar bow.

Punteado [Sp.]. The style of guitar playing in which individual strings are plucked, as distinct from that in which all are strummed [see also *Rasgado, rasgueado*].

Punto [Sp.]. A traditional song genre of rural Cuba, with several subtypes. It is most typically in major mode and combines 6/8 and 3/4 meters; solo vocalists sing *décima* texts in a high register and with ornamentation reminiscent of southern Spain, accompanied by guitar, *tres* (guitar with three double courses), and, in the *punto fijo,* claves. The *punto* is also found in various forms in other countries of the Spanish-speaking Caribbean and circum-Caribbean region. D.S.

Purajhei [Guaraní; Sp. *canción*]. Any of several varieties of traditional song in bilingual Paraguay. D.S.

Purfling [Fr. *filet;* Ger. *Einlage;* It. *filetto;* Sp. *filete*]. The inlaid borders of the belly and back of the violin and some related instruments. It often consists of three strips of wood of varying color (especially black and white), but is sometimes much more elaborate, including mother-of-pearl. It serves as ornament and as reinforcement for the edges of the instrument [see ill. under Violin].

Puritani di Scozia, I [It., The Puritans of Scotland]. Opera in three acts by Bellini (libretto by Carlo Pepoli after the play *Têtes rondes et cavaliers* by François Ancelot and Xavier Boniface Saintine, in turn loosely related to Sir Walter Scott's *Old Mortality*), produced in Paris in 1835. Since the story has nothing to do with Scotland, the title is sometimes given simply as *I Puritani.* Setting: near Plymouth, England, early in the 1650s.

Puy, pui [OFr.]. A French literary or musical society of the period from the 12th century through the early 17th. Such societies, which existed in a number of French cities and in London, were presided over by an elected *prince du puy* (sometimes addressed as such in poems; see *Envoi*) and held regular competitions at which the winning poet was crowned. The winning poem was sometimes referred to as a *chanson couronée.* The musical *puy* founded in Évreux in about 1570 by Guillaume Costeley and others was dedicated to St. Cecilia. Among its prize winners were Orlande de Lassus, Eustache Du Caurroy, and Jehan Titelouze.

Pyknon [Gr.]. In ancient Greek music, a composite interval extending from the lowest standing note of a *tetrachord to the higher of the two movable notes. It is smaller than the remaining incomposite interval at the top of the tetrachord. The upper interval of a *pyknon* usually equals or approximately doubles the lower interval. The presence of a *pyknon* characterizes a *genus as enharmonic or chromatic [see Greece I, 3 (i)]. A.B.

Pyramid piano. An upright grand piano in the shape of a truncated pyramid. Such pianos, which at first had curved sides, were made beginning in the first half of the 18th century and were popular until about 1825.

Pythagorean comma. See Comma, schisma.

Pythagorean hammers. Elements of a myth, first appearing in the 2nd century, that ascribes to Pythagoras the discovery of the numerical characterization of basic musical intervals. He was said to have discovered that four blacksmith's hammers, weighing 12, 9, 8, and 6 pounds, produced musical intervals when struck in pairs: octave (12:6), fifth (12:8 and 9:6), fourth

(12:9 and 8:6), and whole tone (9:8). Although these numbers correctly represent the ratios of frequencies of the intervals, the myth is unsound acoustically.

A.B.

Pythagorean scale. A diatonic scale characterized by pure fifths (3:2), pure fourths (4:3), and whole tones defined as the difference between a fifth and a fourth (3:2 – 4:3 = 9:8). The scale can be deduced from Philolaus' remarks on intervals (frag. 6, 5th century B.C.E.), but the earliest complete presentation occurs in Plato's *Timaeus* (35Aff.). There, each fourth is subdivided into two whole tones and a remainder, called **diesis* (difference) and later, **limma* (remnant). Thus, 4:3 – $(9:8)^2$ = 256:243. Thus, the diatonic scale from c to c′ would consist of five whole tones, each with the ratio 9:8, and two semitones (e–f and b–c′), each with the ratio 256:243. The same scale can be derived by assuming a series of perfect fifths, beginning with F. If this series, F c g d′ a′ e″ b″, is collapsed into a single octave, the Pythagorean scale is produced.

Since the whole tone is easily obtained from the perfect tunings of a fifth and a fourth, this scale formed the basis of ancient and medieval divisions of the monochord. An early such division occurs in the Euclidean *Division of the Canon (Sectio canonis),* and Boethius' division (*De musica* iv.5–11) served as a model throughout the Middle Ages.

It seems likely that the ancient Greek process of continuous subtraction *(antanairesis)* played a role in establishing several intervals based on the Pythagorean scale. An octave minus a fifth leaves a fourth (2:1 – 3:2 = 4:3); a fifth minus a fourth leaves a tone (3:2 – 4:3 = 9:8); a fourth minus a tone leaves an impure minor third (4:3 – 9:8 = 32:27); this minor third minus a tone leaves the *diesis* or *limma* (32:27 – 9:8 = 256:243); a tone minus the *diesis,* also called a minor semitone, leaves the *apotome* (cut off), also called a major semitone (9:8 – 256:243 = 2187:2048); finally, the *apotome* minus the *diesis* leaves the Pythagorean *comma (2187:2048 – 256:243 = 531441:524288).

Bibl.: André Barbera, ed. and trans., *The Euclidean Division of the Canon* (Lincoln: U of Neb Pr, 1991). Boethius, *Fundamentals of Music,* trans. Calvin M. Bower (New Haven: Yale U Pr, 1989).

A.B.

Q

Qānūn [Ar.; fr. Gr. *kanōn;* Turk. *kanun*]. A plucked *zither of the Middle East. Its 50 to 100 strings of metal, gut, or nylon are strung in courses of three over a shallow trapezoidal or half-trapezoidal box. The player holds it horizontally in the lap and plucks or strums the strings with plectra on the fingers of both hands. It is distributed from India to the Maghrib and is particularly favored in the art music of Turkey and the Arab countries. See ill. under Near and Middle East; see also Psaltery.

Qaṣabah [Ar.]. An end-blown flute similar to the **nāy.* The term was at first associated with this instrument throughout the Arabic-speaking world. By the 9th century it was replaced in the easternmost countries by the Persian term *nāy,* but it continues in use in the westernmost countries.

Quadran pavan, quadro paven. In late 16th- and early 17th-century England, the *pass'e mezo moderno* [see Passamezzo]. These terms were used by John Bull, William Byrd, Thomas Morley, and other Elizabethans. They refer to the term B *quadro* (B♮), which often appears with the Italian title *pass'e mezo moderno* to indicate a major mode, in contrast to the *pass'e mezo antico,* which uses B♭ and is in a minor mode. L.H.M.

Quadrat [Ger.]. The natural sign (♮).

Quadreble. See Sight.

Quadrille [Fr., from Sp. *cuadrilla,* a group of horsemen]. (1) A dance for four or more couples, popular in the 19th century and consisting of five sections in either 2/4 or 6/8: *Le pantalon, L'été, La poule, La pastourelle,* and *Finale.* Although the names are those of the specific **contredanses* that originally made up a quadrille, they were retained for the large repertory of music that was composed or adapted from a variety of popular tunes, operatic music, and even sacred works. (2) In the 18th century, an even-numbered group of dancers that performed an **entrée* in a ballet such as those of Lully and Campra.

Quadrivium [Lat.]. In the Middle Ages, the subjects making up the mathematical or upper group of the seven liberal arts: arithmetic, music, geometry, and astronomy. The rhetorical or lower group, known collectively as the *trivium,* were grammar, logic, and rhetoric.

Quadruple counterpoint. See Invertible counterpoint.

Quadruple-croche [Fr.]. Sixty-fourth *note.

Quadruple fugue. See Double fugue.

Quadruple meter, time. *Meter consisting of recurring groups of four pulses.

Quadruplet. A group of four notes of equal value occurring in the time normally occupied by three notes of the same value and identified by the figure 4.

Quadruplum [Lat.]. In music of the *Notre Dame repertory, the fourth or uppermost part of an *organum in four parts; *organum quadruplum,* an organum in four parts.

Quarrel of the Buffoons. See *Bouffons, Querelle des.*

Quartal harmony. Harmony based on combinations of the interval of a fourth, as distinct from tertian harmony (e.g., Western tonal harmony), which is based on combinations of the third.

Quarte [Ger.]. The interval of a fourth. As a prefix (*Quart-*) to the name of an instrument, it indicates that the instrument is pitched a fourth above or below the standard instrument.

Quarte de nazard [Fr.]. An organ stop of 2′ pitch and flute scale, so named because it is a fourth higher than the **Nazard* 2 2/3′.

Quarter note. See Note.

Quarter tone. An interval equal to half of a semitone [see Microtone].

Quartet [Fr. *quatuor;* Ger. *Quartett;* It. *quartetto;* Sp. *cuarteto*]. (1) A composition for four solo performers, with or without accompaniment. (2) An ensemble of four solo performers.

Four parts replaced three as the normal texture of vocal composition in the 15th century, with soprano, alto, tenor, and bass established as the standard distribution in the 16th century. Considerable Renaissance secular vocal and instrumental music is in four parts, usually performed by soloists.

Four-part texture is again prominent in Classical chamber music, especially in the *string quartet. Quartets combining strings and winds were also fairly common, but all-wind quartets less so than quintets. After ca. 1750, the quartet for keyboard and strings also began to be cultivated, first for harpsichord, two violins, and cello (Haydn, 11 extant quartets), then for the standard later ensembles of piano, violin, viola, and cello (Mozart, K. 478, 493). Later examples are relatively few but include notable works by Schumann, Brahms, and Fauré. Among the few quartets for piano and winds, Messiaen's *Quatuor pour le fin du temps* is especially notable.

Use of the quartet as an operatic ensemble with orchestral accompaniment began in the early 18th century; many celebrated examples were written later. The unaccompanied vocal quartet (male, female, or mixed) was very popular, especially as social music, in the 19th century, and remained so in popular music, especially black, in the 20th century [see also Barbershop singing].

Quartet for the End of Time. See *Quatuor pour la fin du temps.*

Quartfagott [Ger.]. A *bassoon pitched a fourth below the normal bassoon; sometimes, however, a bassoon pitched a fourth above the normal bassoon.

Quartflöte [Ger.]. In the 17th and 18th centuries, a recorder with the lowest pitch c″, a fourth above the normal alto on g′.

Quartgeige [Ger.]. **Violino piccolo.*

Quartole [Ger.], **quartolet** [Fr.]. *Quadruplet.

Quartposaune [Ger.]. In the 17th and 18th centuries, a bass trombone in F, a fourth below the normal tenor trombone.

Quasi [It.]. Almost, as if.

Quaternaria. (1) [Lat.] A *ligature of four notes. (2) [It., also *quadernaria*] A faster measure *(misura)* or step unit of the **basse danse (bassadanza),* also known as the *saltarello todescho.*

Quatreble. See Sight.

Quattro [It.]. Four; *quattro mani,* four hands; *quattro voci,* four voices.

Quatuor [Fr.]. *Quartet.

Quatuor pour la fin du temps [Fr., Quartet for the End of Time]. Premiered in 1941 by the composer Olivier Messiaen and his fellow prisoners in a German prison camp, the work's eight movements incorporate religious mysticism and symbolism, using the Book of Revelation as a point of departure.

Quaver. In British terminology, the eighth *note.

Queen, The. See *Reine, La.*

Queen of Spades, The [Russ. *Pikovaya dama;* Fr. *Pique dame*]. Opera in three acts by Tchaikovsky (libretto by Modest Tchaikovsky and the composer, after Pushkin), produced in St. Petersburg in 1890. Setting: St. Petersburg at the end of the 18th century.

Quempas [fr. Lat. *Quem pastores laudavere,* He whom the shepherds praised]. A German Christmas song popular in the 16th century; also in the 16th century, any Christmas song. The singing of such songs from house to house by Latin-school students in hopes of alms was termed *Quempas singen.* A collection of songs copied for the purpose by the student was termed a *Quempasheft.*

Quena [Quechua *kena*]. An end-blown flute of the Andes. The common modern version is made of cane, is 25 to 50 cm. long, and has five or six finger holes and a thumb hole. A notch is cut in the upper rim, and the player blows across the sharp edge. It is popular in Bolivia and Peru and is played both as a solo instrument and in ensembles. Specimens of bone and clay have been excavated from pre-Columbian sites in Peru and dated as early as 900 B.C.E.

Querelle des bouffons [Fr.]. See *Bouffons, Querelle des.*

Querflöte [Ger.]. Transverse flute.

Querpfeife [Ger.]. Fife.

Queue [Fr.]. Tail or stem, e.g., of a note; *piano à queue,* grand piano.

Quickstep. (1) Since the 18th century, a fast military march. (2) A fast version of the *foxtrot, introduced in London in 1923.

Quiebro [Sp.]. Tomás de Santa María's term in the 16th century for a *trill *(quiebro reyterado)* or *mordent, normal or inverted *(quiebro senzillo).* See Ornamentation, *Redoble.*

Quijada [Sp.]. *Jawbone.

Quijongo [Sp.]. **Caramba.*

Quilisma [Lat.]. See Neume.

Quilt canzona. A *canzona made up of short sections in contrasting styles.

Quint. (1) [Fr. *quinte*] An organ stop of Principal scale sounding the interval of the fifth or its octaves (5 1/3′, 2 2/3′, 1 1/3′, etc.). (2) [Ger.] A prefix in the names of some instruments, indicating that they sound a fifth above or below the standard instrument. See also *Quinte, Quintsaite.*

Quinta, quinta vox [Lat.]. In Renaissance polyphony, a fifth voice or part in addition to the normal complement of *superius, altus, tenor,* and *bassus.*

Quintadena [Lat.]. An organ stop with stopped pipes of modest scale and mild tone quality, characterized by the prominence of the third harmonic, i.e., the interval of a twelfth.

Quinte [Fr., Ger.]. (1) The interval of a fifth. (2) *Quint. (3) [Fr.] *Quinte (de violon),* viola.

Quintenquartett [Ger., Fifths Quartet]. Popular name for Haydn's String Quartet in D minor op. 76 no. 2

Hob. III:76 (1797), so called because of the descending fifths in the first theme of the opening movement.

Quintern [Ger. *Quinterne*]. *Gittern.

Quintet [Fr. *quintette,* formerly *quintuor;* Ger. *Quintett;* It. *quintetto;* Sp. *quinteto*]. (1) A composition for five solo performers, with or without accompaniment. (2) An ensemble of five solo performers.

Five-part writing was highly favored in the 16th century and appears in much vocal and instrumental music of the period. In the 17th century, it continued to be common in music for orchestra and certain types of solo ensemble (e.g., the viol consort), but otherwise it was not much used again until the Classical period. The string quintet is less common than the string quartet, but there are notable examples by Mozart, Beethoven, Dvořák, Bruckner, and Brahms. These employ the usual ensemble of string quartet with extra viola. An extra cello appears in most of the quintets of Boccherini, as well as in Schubert's great String Quintet in C major D. 956.

Quintets for string quartet and a woodwind instrument were popular in the Classical period, as seen in Mozart's Clarinet Quintet (1789). Brahms's Clarinet Quintet (1891) is the best-known later example. The usual wind quintet includes flute, oboe, clarinet, bassoon, and horn. Brass quintets (usually two trumpets, horn, trombone, and tuba) have become popular in North America in recent decades.

The piano quintet (usually for piano and string quartet) seems to have arisen out of the many Classical concertos whose accompaniments could be played by a string quartet. Some piano quintets of this period do achieve a genuine chamber-music texture. Romantic composers (Schumann, Brahms, Dvořák, Franck, Fauré) produced several important examples, later ones fewer (Bloch, Shostakovich). Mozart's Quintet in E♭ major K. 452 for piano and winds was the model for Beethoven's op. 16 but had few later followers.

The operatic quintet is found in 18th-century comic opera and later in serious opera, the most famous probably being that in Wagner's *Die Meistersinger.*

Quintfagott [Ger.]. In the 17th century, a bassoon pitched a fifth below the ordinary bassoon; in the 18th and 19th centuries, also a bassoon pitched a fifth above the normal instrument.

Quintole [Ger.], **quintolet** [Fr.]. *Quintuplet.

Quinton [Fr.]. (1) In the 17th century, the **pardessus de viole.* (2) In the late 18th century, a hybrid of the viol and violin with a body similar, except for its sloping shoulders, to that of the violin and with its neck fretted like that of the viol. Its five strings were tuned g d′ a′ d″ g″.

Quintsaite [Ger.]. (1) The highest string of the lute, even if the instrument is of six courses. (2) The E-string of the violin.

Quintuor [Fr.]. *Quintet.

Quintuple meter. *Meter consisting of recurring groups of five pulses. In Western art music, it has been relatively rare, though by no means unknown, until the 20th century. Often the five pulses are in effect subdivided into two plus three, as in the third movement of Tchaikovsky's Symphony no. 6, or three plus two. Quintuple meter has occasionally been employed in jazz, as in Dave Brubeck's *Take Five.*

Quintuplet. A group of five notes of equal value to be played in the time normally occupied by four notes of the same value and indicated by the figure 5.

Quintus [Lat.]. **Quinta pars, quinta vox.*

Quire [obs.]. Choir.

Qui tollis [Lat.]. A section of the *Agnus Dei of the Mass.

Quodlibet [Lat., what you please]. A composition in which well-known melodies or texts are presented simultaneously or successively, the result being humorous or displaying technical virtuosity. Examples date from the late Middle Ages to the present.

As early as the 15th century, pieces that could be called quodlibets were used as illustrations in theoretical treatises. The term was first applied to music in a print edited by Wolfgang Schmeltzl (1544). But it was first defined in the third book (1618) of Michael Praetorius's *Syntagma musicum.* Quodlibets can be categorized as catalog, successive, or simultaneous.

The texts of catalog quodlibets are lists or series of items classifiable under a single heading (e.g., noses, proverbs about drinking, or chanson refrains); their music is most often newly composed. The first such pieces were written in the late Middle Ages, and their production reached a peak in the early 18th century.

The principal voice of a successive quodlibet is a string of textual and musical quotations. The other voices form a homophonic accompaniment and may be textless or may carry the same text as the principal voice. Successive quodlibets were written beginning in the late 15th century but were never very common. Particularly fine examples appear in *Musicalischer Grillenvertreiber* by Melchior Franck (1622). The type was popular as entertainment music throughout the 16th, 17th, and 18th centuries, as was its descendant, the **potpourri,* in 19th-century Vienna.

In a simultaneous quodlibet, two or more voices make use of preexisting musical material (and perhaps its text) at the same time, each consisting of either a patchwork of quotes or a single preexisting melody. This sort of quodlibet is musically the most challenging. Among numerous Renaissance examples are pieces by Caspar Othmayr, Matthias Greiter, and Ludwig Senfl. A famous simultaneous quodlibet is the last variation of Bach's *Goldberg Variations, in which two German songs are set against each other as well as against the theme's harmonic framework.

Terms designating compositions similar to the quodlibet (but commonly not exact equivalents) include *farrago* [Lat.], **fricassée* [Fr.], **ensalada* [Sp.], and *messanza, misticanza, centone,* and *incatenatura* [It.].

Bibl: Kurt Gudewill, "Ursprünge und nationale Aspekte des Quodlibets," *New York,* 1961, 1:30–43. Wolfgang Rogge, *Das Quodlibet in Deutschland bis Melchior Franck* (Wolfenbüttel: Möseler, 1965). Maria Rika Maniates, "Quodlibet Revisum," *AM* 38 (1966): 169–78.

Quranic chant. Melodic cantilation of the holy text of the Islamic religion according to a system of rules governing pronunciation, phrasing, and duration of the Arabic text collectively known as *tajwīd.*

Two styles of recitation *(qirā'āt)* are practiced: *murattl,* which is chantlike, employing alternation between two to five tones and a quick and clear delivery of the text, and *mujawwad* (also *tartil*), a more public, performative style demanding a florid, melodic delivery of the text with generous ornamentation and vocal artistry.

The recited Qur'ān is practiced, performed, and experienced as ritual, musical oratory. Both sound and the text are believed to emanate from God in its revelation and in contemporary recitation. The sound of the recited Qur'ān permeates life in Islamic communities and is a summarizing symbol of the power and presence of the divine.

Recitation is taught by master to apprentice in the circular process of oral tradition—demonstration, imitation, correction—the way it was revealed to and rehearsed with the prophet Muhammad over a period of 20 years in 7th-century Arabia. Pedagogy is extended today with an array of published manuals, CD-ROM, and video programs, speedy intensive workshops, and audio recordings of fine reciters.

The Egyptian style of recitation is imitated throughout the Islamic world, although regional variations, often reflecting local musico-linguistic variation, are common. Egyptian recitation is studied by international students of the Qur'ān at Al-Azhar University in Cairo; Egypt's reciters have been recorded and broadcast internationally, and its reciters have traveled widely to recite and teach their style. Muslim women also study and recite; however, their role as professional reciters, teachers, and judges is much more prominent in Southeast Asia than elsewhere.

The melodies of *mujawwad* recitation are improvised by the reciter, who draws from a vast repository of practical phrases, ornaments, and cadence formulae *(qaflah/qaflāt)* essential to the system of Egyptian melodic modes *(maqām/maqāmāt).* Due to its divine quality the Qur'ān is in a category separate from music, which can be associated with less honorable contexts. However, the relationship between traditional Arab music and recitation is acknowledged, and great reciters are admired for their musical virtuosity and artistry. The sound, style, and technique of Quranic recitation are the apex of vocal music in much of the Islamic and Arab world.

Bibl.: Kristina Nelson, *The Art of Reciting the Qur'an* (Austin: U of Tex Pr, 1985). Michael A. Sells, *Approaching the Qur'an: The Early Revelations* (Ashland, Ore.: White Cloud, 1999), includes CD with recordings of several examples of call to prayer and Quranic recitation. Anne K. Rasmussen, "The Qur'ān in Indonesian Daily Life: The Public Project of Musical Oratory," *Ethno* 45, no. 1, ed. Bruno Nettl (2001): 30–57. A.K.R.

R

R. Abbr. for **ripieno, *récit,* *responsory (℟), **ritardando.*

Rabāb [Ar.; variant spellings and cognates include *rabōb, rbāb, rebab, ribab*]. Any of several distinct stringed instruments of the Islamic world, most of them held upright and bowed. (1) In the writings of al-Fārābī in the 10th century, a bowed instrument with from one to four strings, evidently similar to instruments known in Greece [see *Lira*] and Persia. The European *rebec descends from this group. (2) In North Africa, especially Morocco, a bowed instrument with a narrow, boat-shaped body and no neck. Two strings pass down a hollow fingerboard and over a bridge resting on a piece of skin. (3) In Afghanistan, a plucked instrument similar in form and playing technique to the North Indian **sarod.* (4) In eastern Arabic-speaking countries, a *spike fiddle with one or two strings, no fingerboard, and a sound box that is usually square and covered on both sides with skin. If square, the sound box may be pierced diagonally from one corner to the opposite corner. It accompanies singing and recitation. (5) The *rebab* of Southeast Asia is a *spike fiddle with a heart-shaped, skin-covered sound box and two metal strings. In Java, it plays a leading role in some *gamelan* ensembles. See ills. under Near and Middle East, Southeast Asia.

Bibl.: Joseph Kuckertz, "The Origin and Development of the Rabāb," *Sangeet Natak* 15 (1970): 16–30.

Rabbia, con [It.]. With rage, fury.

Rabel [Sp.]. (1) *Rebec. (2) A fiddle of Spain and Latin America with one to four strings.

Race record. A recording intended for black Americans, who emerged as a new commercial market in 1920 with Mamie Smith's "Crazy Blues." From the 1920s through the 1940s, companies assigned specific series of *catalog numbers to "race records," which included blues (the most profitable discs), gospel songs, sermons, spirituals, jazz, comic dialogues, and jug bands. In the late 1940s, the industry replaced this now-offensive reference to "the race" with the newly fashionable term *rhythm and blues, which, however, did not include the earlier diversity of genres. B.K.

Racket [Fr. *cervelas, cervelat;* Ger. *Rankett, Rackett*]. A small, cylindrical, double-reed woodwind instrument of the 16th and 17th centuries. The bore of the instrument is constructed of a number of parallel channels arranged in a circle within a cylinder of solid ivory or wood. The channels are connected at alternating ends to effect a long bore within a very small space. Rackets were produced in a number of sizes, the smallest being ca. 12 cm long [see ill. under Reed]. In the 18th century, the racket was redesigned and renamed the racket bassoon [Fr. *cervelat à musique, basson à serpentine;* Ger. *Rackettenfagott, Stockfagott, Wurstfagott* (Eng. sausage bassoon)]. M.S.

Rada drum. A Haitian cult drum; in Cuba, *arará.* Carved from a tree trunk, it is cylindrical or conical, has a single head laced to pegs, and is played with the hands or sticks. Rada ensembles contain three drums of graduated size and accompany rituals.

Raddolcendo [It.]. Becoming softer, sweeter.

Raddoppiare [It.]. To *double, often at the octave.

Radel [Ger.]. From the 14th century, a round or canon; synonymous with **rota.*

Radical bass. *Fundamental bass.

Radio and television broadcasting. The dissemination of information and entertainment by means of radio and television transmission intended for public reception.

I. *Radio.* Although Marconi had developed the techniques necessary for wireless broadcasting by 1896, the first continuous public radio transmission did not begin until 1920, when KDKA in Pittsburgh broadcast the election returns of that year. The establishment of the Radio Corporation of America (RCA) in 1919 and the subsequent pooling of technical patents among RCA, General Electric, and other companies opened the way for the manufacture of inexpensive receivers and their sale to the general public.

The consolidation of national broadcast systems began with the state-supported British Broadcasting Company (BBC), which commenced operations in 1922. Despite several experiments with government control during World War I, U.S. broadcasting remained in private hands, and local radio stations were supplemented by the development of large, corporate-owned networks: the National Broadcasting Company (NBC, an RCA affiliate, 1926), the Columbia Broadcasting Company (CBS, 1927), and others. The Federal Radio Commission (FRC) and the Federal Communications Commission (FCC), created in 1927 and 1933, respectively, provided government regulation for all privately owned stations. All early stations broadcast on AM (amplitude modulation) frequencies; the development of FM (frequency modulation) in 1935 led to improved signal quality and, in the 1960s, to public availability of stereo broadcasts.

Music has always occupied a large percentage of broadcast time, both in Europe and in the U.S. Until the 1950s, live performances provided the bulk of U.S. musical programming, as a result in part of the technical limitations of 78-rpm recordings [see Recording] and in part of a ruling in 1922 by the Secretary of Commerce prohibiting the use of phonograph records by larger stations. The BBC set the standards for live-music programming in the 1920s with broadcasts of operas from Covent Garden and of numerous symphony and chamber concerts from other locations. In the early 1930s, the New York Philharmonic and the Metropolitan Opera began a series of broadcasts that have continued each season since then. In 1930, the BBC assembled an orchestra intended solely for on-air performance, and the next 25 years saw a proliferation of such ensembles, including the NBC orchestra under Arturo Toscanini, the Orchestre nationale in Paris, and more than 20 regional orchestras in Germany. *Popular music, particularly that by the American *swing bands of the 1930s, was aired almost exclusively live from studios, ballrooms, and nightclubs.

The broadcast of art or classical music included a number of educational programs, such as NBC's "Music Appreciation Hour," directed by Walter Damrosch. North German Radio presented numerous programs on music, including talks by Schoenberg (on Brahms, 1933) and an influential series of lectures by Theodor W. Adorno on the *sociology of music. Arthur Bliss, during his association with the BBC, produced programs such as "Music Magazine" and "Music in Our Time," which were broad in scope and of lasting influence.

Contemporary and avant-garde music received relatively little support from U.S. broadcasting companies, although CBS offered commissions to Copland, Piston, Harris, and others during the 1930s. The commercial considerations of private ownership kept U.S. programming conservative in this regard, leaving new music to a small group of public stations, or to those few commercial stations that had begun to specialize in art music. National Public Radio (NPR), the largest public network in the U.S. (founded 1971), was for some time the only consistent outlet for new music available to the American public. European broadcasting, on the other hand, has always been receptive to new music, and in England, France, and postwar Germany, state-sponsored radio has continued a close, supportive association with current musical and cultural developments.

The rise of television [see below] in the 1940s nearly destroyed network radio broadcasting in the U.S., as NBC, CBS, and the newly formed American Broadcasting Company (ABC) pursued the financial opportunities of the new medium. Local radio stations began to program more recorded music, as the general prohibition was eased, and competition forced many to narrow the content of their programming. This specialization led, in the mid-1950s, to the creation of *"rhythm and blues," "good music," and other types of stations that competed for smaller, more specific audiences than were sought by the networks. In order to better accommodate audience tastes, program directors began to monitor popular record sales and to program accordingly, an action resulting in the creation of *"Top 40" and "Rock Radio" in the late 1950s. Since the mid-1960s, radio programming has been dominated by popular music (which has in turn become more and more oriented toward radio as an outlet), and the programmers of art music have become increasingly conscious of the current record market as well.

By the end of the 20th century, there were fewer commercial classical-music radio stations in the U.S., and some limited themselves to the most accessible kind of classical music in an attempt to retain as large an audience as possible. Some of their tactics included broadcasting only single movements from symphonic works, concentrating on "easy to listen to" Baroque music, and minimizing or eliminating modern music and vocal works. In many cities the slack was taken up by public radio, which grew significantly in the 1970s and 1980s. But the degree of musical programming depended on the views of the executives of each local station, and many preferred to concentrate on public affairs or other spoken programming. In the last quarter of the 20th century, many markets lost full-time classical music stations, and serious programming of the full range of concert music was available in fewer cities than had been the case 40 years earlier. Still, replacement stations seemed to pop up, often from the public radio sector, and by the year 2000 it seemed possible to remain optimistic about finding concert music on the radio in many communities in the U.S. At the same time, it was more difficult to retain that optimism when considering jazz, folk music, or Broadway musicals—American musics that found only sporadic programming on selected public radio stations. Commercial radio seemed to aim more and more at the youth market, or for specialist nonmusical interest groups (all-sports talk stations, for instance, became extremely widespread at the end of the century).

II. *Television.* The development of the technical innovations necessary for the broadcast of transient images and sound began as early as 1873. Both British and U.S. scientists were responsible for the refinement and consolidation of the techniques that eventually led to the development of electronic television receivers and the beginning of commercial television in 1941.

The quality of television transmission and reproduction of sound has never been high enough to sustain the commercial networks' long-term interest in music broadcasts, although there were a few notable exceptions such as Leonard Bernstein's series of Young People's Concerts. On television as on radio, art music has found its most sympathetic outlet in the listener-supported or Public Broadcasting Stations (PBS, founded 1969). These stations have offered numerous concert series by nationally known orchestras. Televised opera has become quite popular as well, sometimes in filmed productions and sometimes in live broadcasts. Compositions intended solely or originally for television productions, such as Menotti's opera *Amahl and the Night Visitors* (telecast December 25, 1952) and Stravinsky's musical play *The Flood* (June 14, 1962), have been rare, however. In the late 1970s, the New York City Opera and other companies began to combine television and FM radio broadcasts of the same production (simulcasting) to achieve better audio reproduction. The early 1980s saw the first efforts to improve the quality of both the audio and video components of television to levels comparable with those of high-fidelity sound recordings.

Popular music, however, remains the predominant form of music broadcast on television. From the beginning of the medium through the 1960s and 70s, popular music was presented on various dance and concert programs, such as "American Bandstand" and Don Kirshner's "Rock Concert," and on a number of variety programs, such as "The Ed Sullivan Show," which featured musical performers. In 1980, Warner Communications Corporation developed a cable television network known as Music Television (MTV) that broadcast exclusively *music videos, music news, and interviews with current pop music stars. It quickly became profoundly influential on popular music taste, styles, and sales.

By the end of the 20th century, art music was limited exclusively to public television (PBS). While simulcasting with their partner NPR stations offered excellent sound quality, PBS officials found that decreasing governmental funding forced them toward a more populist programming approach. Their emphasis began to focus on crossover rather than purely classical artists (Andrea Bocelli, the Three Irish Tenors, Charlotte Church, Sarah Brightman), or on opera, which offered the visual element of staging. Orchestral concerts became a TV rarity because producers couldn't find a way to make them visually interesting, and their limited appeal hurt the stations' chances of attracting underwriters. The increasing number of cable outlets in the U.S. did not meaningfully change the amount of art music available. At the beginning of the 21st century, new possibilities were being explored through the Internet, digital broadcasting, and home theater systems.

Bibl.: Asa Briggs, *The History of Broadcasting in the United Kingdom,* 2 vols. (London: Oxford U Pr, 1961). Eric Barnouw, *A History of Broadcasting in the United States,* 3 vols. (New York: Oxford U Pr, 1966–70). Walter B. Emery, *National and International Systems of Broadcasting: Their History, Operation, and Control* (East Lansing: Mich St U Pr, 1969). Jack Bornoff, *Music and the Twentieth-Century Media* (Florence: Olschki, 1972). Hans-Christian Schmidt, ed., *Musik in den Massenmedien Rundfunk und Fernsehen* (Mainz: B Schott, 1976). Tom Burns, *The BBC: Public Institution and Private World* (London: Macmillan, 1977). John Kittross and Christopher Sterling, *Stay Tuned: A Concise History of American Broadcasting* (Belmont, Cal.: Wadsworth Pub Co, 1978). P.T.W., rev. H.F.

Radleier [Ger.]. *Hurdy-gurdy.

Raffrenando [It.]. Slowing down.

Rāg(a) (-am) [Hin., Skt., Tel.]. (1) *Mode in Indian music. Besides the designation of a particular scale, a *rāga* includes other modal prescriptions such as pitch ranking, characteristic ascent and descent patterns, motives, use of ornaments, performance time, and emotional character. (2) In the Carnatic usage, *rāgam* may also mean **ālāpana.* C.C.

Ragtime. A composed instrumental genre, primarily for piano and principally created by black Americans, that combines syncopated melodies with the forms of the march; the syncopated style of this genre. Piano rolls played an important part in the dissemination and popularization of ragtime. Existing also in various ensemble arrangements, classic rags of Scott Joplin (1868–1917), James Scott (1886–1938), and Joseph Lamb (1887–1960) present three or four distinct 16-bar themes (strains) in duple meter. Tempos are most often moderate, suitable for dances such as the *cakewalk, *two-step, *one-step (in a fast tempo), or *polka. Portions of the melody stress syncopated motives in rhythmic contrast to the "oom-pah" (bass note and chord) motions and series of repeated chords that define simple, strong, functional harmonic progressions. Strains consist of eight-bar antecedents and consequents, which are subdivided into four-bar phrases; the material of the first phrase returns in the second (leading to a half cadence) or in the third, but the fourth (mm. 13–16) may introduce a new texture in the drive to a full cadence. Strains recur literally in schemes such as I:AABBA—IV:CCDD(C) or I:AABB—IV:CC—I:AA (where I and IV represent the tonic and subdominant keys, respectively). Common are four-bar introductions to the opening and transitions to the section on IV, where the climax and ending generally occur.

Bibl.: Rudi Blesh and Harriett Janis, *They All Played Ragtime,* 4th ed. (New York: Oak Pubns, 1971). William Schafer and Johannes Riedel, *The Art of Ragtime* (Baton Rouge: La St U Pr, 1973). Edward A. Berlin, *Ragtime* (Berkeley and Los Angeles: U of Cal Pr, 1980). B.K.

Raindrop Prelude. Popular name for Chopin's Prelude in D♭ major op. 28 no. 15 (the 24 preludes of op. 28 dating from 1836–39), so called because the continuously repeated A♭ (G♯ in the middle section) suggests the sound of raindrops.

Rake's Progress, The. Opera in three acts by Stravinsky (libretto by W. H. Auden and Chester Kallman, inspired by William Hogarth's series of prints of the same name), produced in Venice in 1951. Setting: England in the 18th century.

Rákóczi March. A Hungarian national air set down ca. 1810 by János Bihari in homage to Prince Ferenc Rákóczi II (1676–1735), leader of the Hungarian revolt against Austria. The melody was used by Berlioz in *La *damnation de Faust* and by Liszt in the **Hungarian Rhapsody* no. 15.

Ralentir [Fr.]. To slow down.

Rallentando [It., abbr. *rall.*]. Slowing down.

Range. The span of pitches between highest and lowest of an instrument, voice, or part; also compass. See also Tessitura.

Rank. A row of pipes, one for each note of the organ keyboard, making up a stop. *Mixture stops have two or more pipes for each note, designated by a Roman numeral, e.g., Mixture IV.

Rankett [Ger.]. *Racket.

Rant. A spirited dance movement similar to a *jig, in simple or compound duple meter. It appears occasionally in English suites beginning ca. 1650 (e.g., by Matthew Locke), and it is still known as a polka-like folk dance. B.G.

Ranz des vaches [Fr.; Ger. *Kuhreigen, Kuhreihen*]. A type of Swiss melody, sometimes sung, but most characteristically played on the *alphorn by herdsmen to call their cows; also *Lobetanz,* after the opening words of some examples "Lobet, o lobet" (fr. *loba,* cow). A repertory of about 50 such melodies survives. One example is preserved in Rhau's *Bicinia gallica* of 1546; others are quoted in Theodor Zwinger's *Fasciculus dissertationum medicarum* of 1710 (reproduced in the Breitkopf & Härtel edition of Liszt's *Pianofortewerke,* vol. iv, p. iv) and in Jean-Jacques Rousseau's *Dictionnaire de musique* of 1768. Such melodies have been used in operas on Swiss subjects, e.g., the versions of *Guillaume Tell* by Grétry (1791) and Rossini (1829), and the style is evoked in works such as the last movement of Beethoven's *Pastoral* Symphony, the "Scène aux champs" in Berlioz's *Symphonie fantastique,* Liszt's *Album d'un voyageur,* and the beginning of the third act of Wagner's *Tristan und Isolde.*

Bibl.: Alec Hyatt King, "Mountains, Music, and Musicians," *MQ* 31 (1945): 395–419. Carl-Allan Moberg, "Kühreihen, Lobetanz und Galder," *Handschin,* 1962, pp. 27–38.

Rap. A style of music that arose in the South Bronx in New York in the early and mid-1970s with antecedents in black oral forms such as the "dozens" and "toasting" that can be traced back to the expressive culture of sub-Saharan African. More immediate antecedents include late sixties and early seventies Jamaican toasting and dub recordings; the fusion of poetry and African drumming of late-1960s ensembles such as the Last Poets and the Watts Prophets; and the highly developed verbal delivery of late forties and fifties African American personality DJs on the radio.

Rap ensembles consist of a DJ who manipulates preexistent sounds via the cutting and mixing of vinyl records and, since 1983 and the development of the sampler, the triggering of digitized samples, and one or more MCs (masters of ceremonies) who rhythmically declaim spoken rhymes. Although existing in embryonic form within the South Bronx community as early as 1973, the first rap recordings were issued in 1979 by the Fatback Band ("King Tim III (Personality Jock)") and the Sugarhill Gang ("Rapper's Delight").

Using such techniques as cutting rapidly between different records, rhythmically scratching the needle of a turntable on records at various speeds, looping samples, and building dense collages by overlapping several samples, the earliest rap DJs turned a technology of consumption (the turntable) into a technology of production. Their innovative and increasingly virtuosic ability to manipulate found sound via repetition, juxtaposition, alteration of pitch, alteration of rate of articulation, and placement in time eventually created the subgenre of *turntablism as embodied in the 1990s by artists such as the Scratch Pickles.

Cutting and mixing and digital sampling brought into open question the whole notion of ownership of sound. By the early 1990s a series of legal and informal precedents had brought about a system in which most artists asked permission and negotiated a form of compensation for the use of samples. Some commonly sampled musicians, such as George Clinton, actually released CDs containing several dozen sound bites specifically for sampling. A residual effect of sampling was a newfound sense of musical history among black youth. Such earlier artists as James Brown and Parliament/Funkadelic were lionized as cultural heroes, their recordings reissued and bought by the thousands. By the late 1990s the cost of licensing samples had become so prohibitive that many rap artists opted to create completely original tracks using drum machines and synthesizers.

In its earliest stages rap was produced and consumed exclusively within the black and Latino communities in New York City. While much of the lyrical content of early rap focused on the time-honored theme of love and relationships, many rap lyrics were rife with braggadocio and, in the tradition of the black folk expressive form of the "dozens," often included put-downs or "disses" between competing rap artists.

In the late 1980s a large segment of rap became highly politicized, manifesting the most overt social agenda of any form of popular music since the 1960s urban folk movement. Coming to prominence with their second album, 1988's *It Takes a Nation of Millions to Hold Us Back,* Public Enemy embodied this aesthetic more than any other group. In an apt and often quoted phrase, lead singer Chuck D. referred to rap as "CNN for black people." Against the backdrop of conservative political programs that were systematically decimating the inner city, rap functioned as a voice for a community without access to the mainstream media. As such, it served to promote pride and self-help, communicating a sense of black history as positive and fulfilling that was largely absent from any other American institution.

Parallel to the rise of politicized rap was the appearance of *gangsta rap* with NWA's (Niggas with Attitude) 1989 album *Straight Outta Compton.* Songs such as "——— tha Police" generated an extraordinary amount of controversy and brought pressure from a wide range of sources, including the FBI, local PTA committees, and Parents' Music Resource Center. As is always the case, such attempts at censorship only served to publicize the music and made it more attractive to both black and white youths.

With the emergence of gangsta rap, a substantial white audience developed for the music. Over the course of the 1990s, this audience broadened further as rap became an integral element in the music of both mainstream R 'n' B artists, such as Janet Jackson and Mary J. Blige, and mainstream hard rock groups, such as Korn and Lincoln Park.

Bibl.: David Toop, *The Rap Attack: African Jive to New York Hip Hop* (Boston: South End, 1984, 1991). Brian Cross, *It's Not About a Salary: Rap, Race and Resistance in Los Angeles* (London: Verso, 1993). Tricia Rose, *Black Noise: Rap Music and Black Culture in Contemporary America* (Hanover, N.H.: Wesleyan U Pr, 1994). Rob Walser, "Rhythm, Rhyme and Rhetoric in the Music of Public Enemy," *Ethno* 39 (1995): 193–217. William Eric Perkins, ed., *Droppin' Science: Critical Essays on Rap Music and Hip Hop Culture* (Philadelphia: Temple U Pr, 1996). R.B.

Rape of Lucretia, The. Opera in two acts by Britten (libretto by Ronald Duncan after André Obey's play *Le viol de Lucrèce,* in turn after Shakespeare and Livy), produced in Glyndebourne in 1946. Setting: in or near Rome, ca. 510 B.C.E.

Rappresentatione di Anima, et di Corpo [It., Representation of the Soul and the Body]. A work for the stage by Emilio de' Cavalieri (text in part from a dialogue by Agostino Manni), first performed in Rome in 1600 and published there in the same year (the first publication to include a *basso continuo*). Because of its religious themes, it is sometimes regarded as the first *oratorio. It was, however, staged with scenery, costumes, and dancing, the music consisting of recitatives, strophic airs, madrigals, and short homophonic choruses intended for dancing.

Rappresentativo [It.]. See *Stile rappresentativo.*

Rappresentazione sacra, sacra rappresentazione [It.]. In the 16th century, a religious play with music and thus an antecedent of *oratorio, especially of Cavalieri's **Rappresentatione di Anima, et di Corpo.*

Rapsodie espagnole [Fr., Spanish Rhapsody]. A suite for orchestra by Ravel, composed in 1907–8 and evoking Spanish themes. Its four movements are titled "Prélude à la nuit," "Malagueña," "Habanera," and "Feria." The "Habanera" was originally part of Ravel's *Sites auriculaires* (1895–97) for two pianos.

Rasch [Ger.]. Quick, lively.

Rasgado, rasgueado [Sp.]. A style of guitar playing in which the strings are strummed, as distinct from *punteado,* in which individual strings are plucked.

Rastrology. The study of musical staving. Before the advent of printed staff paper in the 19th century, the lines of the staff were normally drawn simultaneously using a single- or multistave *rastrum. Careful comparative study of such characteristics as the spacing between the lines and staves, the thickness of the lines, and irregularities in the staving can, under appropriate circumstances, lead to identification of a specific rastrum and to useful conclusions regarding the date and provenance of a manuscript.

Bibl.: Jean K. and Eugene K. Wolf, "Rastrology and Its Use in Eighteenth-Century Manuscript Studies," in *Studies in Musical Sources and Style: Essays in Honor of Jan LaRue,* ed. Eugene K. Wolf and Edward H. Roesner (Madison, Wis.: A-R Eds, 1990). E.K.W.

Rastrum [Lat., rake, pl. *rastra;* Ger. *Rastral, Raster*]. In its simplest form, a five-pointed pen used in drawing a musical staff. Compound (multinib) rastra combining two or more simple rastra were also common, especially during the 18th and first half of the 19th centuries. See also Rastrology. E.K.W.

Rasumovsky Quartets. Beethoven's three string quartets op. 59 (1805–6), dedicated to the Russian Count Andreas Rasumovsky; also termed the Russian Quartets. In nos. 1 (fourth movement) and 2 (third movement), Beethoven used Russian folk songs (labeled in each case "Thème russe") taken from a collection first published by Johann Gottfried Pratsch (Ivan Prach) in 1790.

Ratchet. *Cog rattle.

Ratisbon Edition. See Gregorian chant VI.

Ratsche [Ger.]. *Cog rattle.

Rattenando, rattenuto [It.]. Holding back.

Rattle. An instrument that is shaken to produce sound. One familiar type consists of a vessel (made of gourd, clay, metal, wood, or basketwork) filled with seeds, pebbles, or pellets and often provided with a handle. Such rattles are very ancient and distributed worldwide. In rattles of the stick and frame type, rattling or jingling objects are fastened or strung together, attached to a rigid object, and shaken against one another. Similarly, dancers may string objects together, tie them around their arms and legs, and rattle them as they dance. In many cultures, rattles are important in religious rites, magic, and healing. See also *Angklung, Cabaça,* Cog rattle, Idiophone, Maraca, Sistrum, Turkish Crescent.

Rauscher [Ger.]. **Batterie* (4).

Rauschpfeife [Ger.]. (1) A 16th-century German *shawm made in various sizes, with and without a *wind cap. (2) [Du. *Ruispijp*] A low-pitched *mixture stop in the organ, usually of two or three *ranks, beginning at 2 2/3′ pitch in an 8′ division and at 5 1/3′ in a 16′ division.

Ravvivando [It.]. Quickening.

Razor Quartet. Popular name for Haydn's String Quartet in F minor op. 55 no. 2 Hob. III:61 (1788), so called because the English publisher John Bland claimed that Haydn jokingly gave him the autograph manuscript in exchange for an English razor. The work was not published by Bland, however.

Re. See Pitch names, Solmization, Hexachord.

Reading Rota. *"Sumer is icumen in."

Real. See Tonal and real.

Rebab [Jav.]. See *Rabāb* (5).

Rebec [Fr. *rebec, rebecq, rebecquet;* Ger. *Rubebe, Rebec;* It. *rebeca, ribeca;* Sp. *rabel*]. A bowed instrument, commonly with three strings, derived from the ancient Arab **rabāb* and perhaps introduced into Europe during the 10th century, though it cannot be documented before the 13th century. The *rubeba* described by Jerome of Moravia in the late 13th century may have been a transitional instrument between the *rabāb* and the rebec proper. The rebec was primarily used during the Middle Ages and the Renaissance. Later, in the 16th century, it inspired the development of the dance master's fiddle or *kit. The rebec generally bears an arched back with a pear-shaped body of hardwood extending in one piece to form a short, narrow neck and an open pegbox. A flat hardwood fingerboard covers the neck, extending slightly over a flat softwood table with inverted-*c* sound holes, hardwood bridge, and tailpiece. The three strings, tuned in fifths, pass over a flat bridge and are often played in pairs with the middle string acting as a drone. A typical tuning would be g d′ a′, with all three strings of plain gut. Iconographic sources show the rebec played either vertically on the lap or on the shoulder, with an outcurved bow held in the overhand position. Today the rebec can be found in use among folk cultures of southeastern Europe. See ill. under Violin.

Bibl.: Margaret Downie, "The Rebec: An Orthographic and Iconographic Study" (Ph.D. diss., Univ. of West Virginia, 1981). Ian Woodfield, *The Early History of the Viol* (Cambridge: Cambridge U Pr, 1984). W.L.M.

Rebube [Fr., obs.]. *Jew's harp.

Recapitulation. See Sonata form.

Reception [Ger. *Rezeption*]. The impact of artworks as reflected in the responses of audience, critic, and artist. Studies in reception regard the history of response to an artwork [Ger. *Rezeptionsgeschichte*] as part of the work's modern meaning. Knowledge of the aesthetic and social conditions surrounding the production of a work allows a sharper definition of the work's meaning in its historical context, as it was "received" by its original audience.

The most highly developed theories of aesthetic response [Ger. *Rezeptionsästhetik, Rezeptionstheorie*] have appeared in literary studies, where the areas of research are broadly bounded by reader-response criticism (the phenomenology of reading), genre theory, and reception theory. Case studies such as Schrade (1942) and Austin (1975) stand as somewhat isolated examples of work in English in the historical reception of music; Kropfinger (1975) represents a surge of interest among German scholars in the 1970s. A lack of data for many historical periods limits much of the work on musical reception to the development of theoretical categories.

Bibl.: Leo Schrade, *Beethoven in France* (New Haven: Yale U Pr, 1942). Hans Heinrich Eggebrecht, *Zur Geschichte der Beethoven Rezeption* (Mainz: Verlag der Akademie der Wissenschaften und der Literatur, 1972). Peter Faltin and Hans-Peter Reinecke, *Musik und Verstehen: Aufsätze zur semiotischen Theorie, Ästhetik und Soziologie der musikalischen Rezeption* (Cologne: A Volk, 1973). William W. Austin, *"Susanna," "Jeannie," and "The Old Folks at Home": The Songs of Stephen Foster from His Time to Ours* (New York: Macmillan, 1975). Klaus Kropfinger, *Wagner und Beethoven: Untersuchungen zur Beethoven-Rezeption Richard Wagners* (Regensburg: G Bosse, 1975). Carl Dahlhaus, "Probleme der Rezeptionsgeschichte," in *Grundlagen der Musikgeschichte* (Cologne: Gerig, 1977), pp. 237–59. Hans Robert Jauss, *Towards an Aesthetic of Reception,* trans. Timothy Bahti (Minneapolis: U of Minn Pr, 1982). P.T.W.

Recercada [Sp.], **recercar** [It.]. See Ricercar.

Rechant [Fr.]. In some types of polyphonic chanson of the 16th century, a refrain.

Récit [Fr.]. (1) In French music of the 17th and 18th centuries, a passage or a complete composition (e.g., an aria) for solo voice or, in the later part of this period and beyond, for a solo instrument; not the same as *recitative, though a *récit* may be in recitative style. (2) A division of the classical French organ with its wind-chest mounted in the main case and with a range from c′ in the treble, often containing only a **Cornet.* (3) In the 19th-century French organ, a large, full-compass division, with a full *Principal chorus, reeds, and a **Celeste.*

Recital. A concert given by a small number of performers, most often a soloist, perhaps with an accompanist. The term was first used in this way in an advertisement for a performance on the piano by Liszt in London in 1840.

Recitative [Fr. *récitative;* Ger. *Rezitativ;* It., Sp. *recitativo*]. A style of text setting that imitates and emphasizes the natural inflections, rhythms, and syntax of speech. Such a setting avoids extremes of pitch and intensity and repetition of words, allowing the music to be primarily a vehicle for the words. The term recitative is used most often in connection with dramatic music—opera, oratorio, and cantata—but this type of text setting is far more widespread historically and geographically than are these genres.

Recitative became a particular concern of composers from the beginning of the 17th century onward [see also Monody, Baroque]. Peri, Caccini, Cavalieri, Gagliano, and Monteverdi all proclaimed a new style of declamation that is variously referred to as *stile rappresentativo* and *stile recitativo.* In the first half of the 17th century, recitative was valued for its expressivity in the sense that the music supported and emphasized the text rather than obscuring it. For example, the most affective moments of Monteverdi's *Orfeo*—Silvia's announcement of Euridice's death, Orfeo's response to this announcement, Euridice's farewell to Orfeo after he has violated the command not to look at her—are set in recitative; madrigal, song, and dance are used for emotionally simpler moments.

As the recitative style spread from Italy to Germany, France, and England, it was valued not only for its expressive capacity but also for its sheer novelty. Schütz states in a preface to his *Psalmen Davids* (1619) that the *stile recitativo* in his work is "almost unknown in Germany at present." In England, masques were advertised as being "sung after the Italian manner, *stylo recitativo,*" as early as 1617 (Ben Jonson's *Lovers Made Men,* music by Nicolas Lanier). The acknowledged master of English recitative, who found musical accents uniquely suited to the English language, was Henry Purcell. French recitative, as developed first by Lully, maintained a distinct style. Perhaps influenced by **vers mesuré,* French recitative emphasized correct and accurate rhythmic declamation. A notational indication of this concern is the presence of changing meters and a relatively large number of rhythmic values.

By the end of the 17th century in Italy, perhaps in response to longer libretti with more involved and complicated plots, a simpler and more perfunctory style of setting text evolved, *recitativo semplice.* The sparse texture and slow harmonic rhythm of the accompaniment, played by continuo instruments only, allowed for the clear and rapid presentation of a large amount of text. Two functions of recitative at this time may be distinguished: dramatic and musical. The dramatic function was expository or narrative, advancing the action. The musical function was one of modulation, creating a transition between one aria or ensemble and the next [see Aria]. The term *recitativo secco,* now used interchangeably with *recitativo semplice,* came into use in the 19th century, after that style of recitative was no longer being composed.

Recitative may be classified in terms of the instruments that accompany the voice. *Recitativo semplice* is accompanied by continuo instruments. Orchestrally accompanied recitative is called *recitativo accompagnato* or *recitativo stromentato.* When the accompanying instruments not only provide harmonic support but also present prominent motivic or melodic material, the term *recitativo obbligato* may be used. Fully accompanied recitative was reserved, in 18th-century opera, for the most important characters at climactic moments in the drama.

An urge for greater continuity of music and action—a desire to lessen the musical disparity between recitative and aria—was one of the principal concerns of Gluck in his reform operas. In *Orfeo ed Euridice* (1762) and *Alceste* (1767), the recitatives are all accompanied by the orchestra. By the third decade of the 19th century, recitative accompanied by continuo alone had largely disappeared except in Italian comic opera, where it continued in use until mid-century. Although in some cases the change from continuo to orchestral accompaniment was primarily a change in tone color, the trend in 19th-century opera was toward an increasingly important musical role for the orchestra. A motivically constructed orchestral part could provide the musical continuity of a whole scene, while the voice parts were declamatory and of lesser musical interest. The opening scenes of Verdi's *Rigoletto* or *La traviata,* in which the orchestra plays dance tunes through which the voices float conversationally, are examples of this method, termed **parlante.* The works of Wagner achieve the goal of blending recitative and aria into an endless melody supported by a motivically rich orchestral part.

A 20th-century addition to techniques of recitative is the practice of **Sprechstimme* or *Sprechgesang.* This technique is precise with regard to rhythm and deliberately indefinite with regard to pitch. Thus, it stands somewhere between speaking and singing. In a sense, *Sprechstimme,* particularly as it is exploited by Schoenberg and Berg, approaches the ideals of the earliest composers of *stile recitativo* by using heightened speech to express extreme affective states.

Starting in the 17th century, recitative style was occasionally transferred to instrumental music, sometimes producing an effect of inarticulate instruments striving to speak. An early example is found in Johann Kuhnau's *Biblische Historien* (1700). Recitativelike passages are found with some frequency in the keyboard works of C. P. E. Bach. They also occur in works of Haydn (Symphony no. 7) and Beethoven (Piano Sonatas op. 31 no. 2 and op. 110, finale of Symphony no. 9)—both frank admirers of C. P. E. Bach. Later examples of instrumental recitative are to be found in works by Schumann (*Kinderscenen,* "The Poet Speaks"), Berlioz *(Roméo et Juliette),* and Schoenberg (*Variations on a Recitative* for organ).

Bibl.: Jack Westrup, "The Nature of Recitative," *Proceedings of the British Academy* 42 (1956): 27–43. Edward Downes, "Secco Recitative in Early Classical Opera Seria," *JAMS* 14 (1961): 50–69. Jack Westrup, "The Cadence in Baroque Recitative," *Jeppesen,* 1962, pp. 243–52. Mary Phillips, "Recitative-Arioso: A Survey with Emphasis on Contemporary Opera" (Ph.D. diss., U.C.L.A., 1965). Sven Hansell, "The Cadence in 18th-century Recitative," *MQ* 54 (1968): 228–48. Paul Mies, *Das instrumentale Rezitativ* (Bonn: Bouvier, 1968). Claude V. Palisca, *Baroque Music* (Englewood Cliffs, N.J.: Prentice-Hall, 1968; 2nd ed., 1981). Herbert Seifert, "Das Instrumentalrezitativ von Barock bis zür Wiener Klassik," *Schenk,* 1975, pp. 103–16. Winton Dean, "The Performance of Recitative in Late Baroque Opera," *ML* 58 (1977): 389–402. Margaret Murata, "The Recitative Soliloquy," *JAMS* (1979): 45–73. C.G.

Reciting tone, note. See Psalm tone.

Recorder [Fr. *flûte à bec, f. douce;* Ger. *Blockflöte, Schnabelflöte;* It. *flauto diritto, f. dolce;* Sp. *flauta de pico*]. A *duct flute—end-blown with a block (also called fipple) mouthpiece—used from the Middle Ages through the Baroque era. In England, this instrument was called a recorder in the Renaissance and a flute in the Baroque era. On the Continent, it was known throughout both periods as the *Blockflöte, flûte,* or *flauto.* The *transverse or cross flute was specifically identified as such (with terms such as German flute, *flauto traverso*) to distinguish it from the recorder or English flute. The English name perhaps derives from the Italian *ricordo* (a keepsake). See ill. under Flute.

Two principal types are distinguished: Renaissance and Baroque. The Renaissance recorder is constructed in one section, except for the larger sizes. It is usually provided with a total of nine holes: a thumb hole on the back and seven finger holes on the front, the lowest of which (played by the little finger) is doubled to allow either hand to play uppermost. The unused hole is stopped with wax. The bore is usually slightly conical, being larger at the top. The exterior is a smooth shape, wider at the top and bottom than in the center, somewhat like the tibia bone of the leg (from which very early instruments were made). Michael Praetorius (*Syntagma musicum,* vol. 2, 1619) lists eight sizes of recorders (including discants at both c″ and d″). The Baroque instrument has a much more ornate profile and is usually made in three sections. Because the bottom section can be turned to accommodate either hand uppermost, the ninth hole is not provided.

The modern recorder family is regarded as including only instruments in C, no matter what the individual ranges or basic scales of its members. It includes the sopranino (lowest pitch f″), the soprano (in Britain, descant, c″), the alto (in Britain, treble, f′), the tenor (c′), the bass (f), the great bass (c), and the contrabass (f). All normally have a range of two octaves and a whole step, though this may be extended upward by accomplished players. Music for the two highest members of this family is often notated an octave lower than it sounds. Because of their length, the two lowest instruments are provided with a curved mouth pipe similar to that of the bassoon. Basses, and sometimes the tenor, are also provided with a single key for the lowest pitch. The single lowest hole may also be replaced, especially on modern instruments, by two small holes placed beside one another to facilitate the playing of the lowest semitone.

In the Baroque era, the alto instrument was the major instrument of the family, and others were denoted by their pitch relationship to it; hence, fifth flute (soprano in c″), sixth flute (soprano in d″), etc. The voice flute, also popular in the 18th century, was an alto recorder in d′, treated as a transposing instrument.

Two forms of fingering have developed: German, based on a misunderstanding of Baroque practice and requiring its own arrangement of the finger holes; and English, a minor modification of the fingerings given in Baroque manuals.

Recorders have been made of boxwood, maple, and other woods as well as of ivory and, today, plastic. The block or fipple [see Duct flute] of Baroque instruments is generally made of softwood, usually of cedar. Renaissance instruments invariably had blocks of maple or another hardwood.

Arnold Dolmetsch (1858–1940) can properly be credited with the revival of the instrument in this century. As a result of this revival, recorders are again popular as a means of re-creating music of the past, for teaching beginning music lessons, and as serious instruments for contemporary music.

Bibl.: Edgar Hunt, *The Recorder and Its Music,* rev. ed. (London: Eulenberg, 1977). M.S.

Recording. I. *Technical history.* The modern phonograph has its origins in techniques developed in 1857 by the French physicist Léon Scott, whose phonautograph was the first machine capable of etching (though not reproducing) patterns of sound waves in solid material. In April 1877 a French poet and amateur scientist, Charles Cros, proposed (but did not construct) a workable disc-playing machine. Independent of Cros, in December 1877 American Thomas Edison produced and patented the first machine that could both record and reproduce sound. Edison inaugurated the device, which he called the phonograph, with a recording of "Mary Had a Little Lamb." This purely acoustic (i.e., mechanical rather than electronic) apparatus channeled sound waves through a speaking horn and a diaphragm to a metal point capable of engraving consecutive grooves on a tin or wax-covered cylinder. The recording could then be played back by reversing the process on the hand-driven machine. Though a remarkable achievement, this early technology could not capture the full frequency and dynamic range of concert music; moreover, early cylinders could not be copied and generally held only two minutes of music. At the turn of the century the recorded repertory was therefore rather small, consisting mainly of short works performed by small ensembles of voices or instruments that could project a focused and powerful sound to the phonograph's acoustic horn.

In 1887, Emile Berliner secured a patent for and in 1895 commercially produced a machine called the gramophone, replacing the Edison cylinder with a flat disc. (At the time gramophone and phonograph referred to disc- and cylinder-playing machines, respectively, and were not interchangeable. It was not until the 1920s, when cylinder recording all but disappeared, that both terms referred to disc players, with phonograph used in the U.S. and gramophone preferred in Great Britain.) The disc presented an immediate commercial advantage over the cylinder in that it could be reproduced quickly and in great quantity, and generally allowed longer playing times. Most early discs were designed to rotate at a speed of between 70 and 82 rpm (the arbitrary standard became 78), allowing playing times of about 3 and 4½ minutes per side on 10- and 12-inch discs (the latter were first widely introduced in 1903); the capacity doubled with the introduction of two-sided discs in 1902. Berliner later collaborated with E. R. Johnson on the motorized "improved gramophone," which, along with techniques for improving the sound quality of discs, provided the commercial basis for the Victor Talking Machine Company (formed in 1898, an RCA affiliate by 1929).

Until about 1925, both recording and playback techniques were acoustic. In the mid-1920s, the introduction of electrical recording greatly increased the accuracy of sound reproduction. The new process, which borrowed the microphone and amplifier from radio *broadcasting, widened the range of frequency response, making it possible to record works in their original full scoring and to capture the resonance of the performance space.

With a few experimental (and ultimately unsuccessful) exceptions, it was not until the advent of the long-playing (LP) record that the 4½-minute limit of the 78-rpm disc was surpassed. In 1948, Columbia Records introduced the 12-inch, 33⅓-rpm microgroove disc, which averaged 20 minutes of playing time per side and was pressed on vinyl rather than shellac, providing a much quieter surface for reproduction. The development of the LP revolutionized the approach to the issuing of music on disc. Several movements and often entire works could fit on a single side, and there was a rush to record and rerecord as many works as possible. RCA entered the microgroove market in 1949 with a 7-inch, 45-rpm disc, but it could not compete with the practicality of the larger disc and eventually became limited to the distribution of popular music.

Almost concurrent with the appearance of the microgroove disc was the development of magnetic tape, which completely altered sound recording and reproduction. In this process, sound waves are converted to electronic signals, imprinted on magnetic tape, and then transferred to disc. Tape recording provided a greater signal-to-noise ratio and a longer uninterrupted playing time than disc recording. Furthermore, the easy manipulability of tape allowed performers to edit their recordings, most notably by splicing together several different performances of the same work. With such advantages, tape emerged as the essential medium for recording.

Nearly all recordings issued on disc until the late 1950s were monaural and thus reproduced all recorded information as though it emanated from a single point in space. The development of stereophonic (binaural) recording in the mid-1950s lent a new realism to recorded music, imitating the spatial distribution of sound that a listener might experience at a live performance. A boom in recording not seen since the introduction of the LP followed the development of the stereo disc. Further experiments in the 1970s led to quadrophonic, or four-channel, recording and reproduction, which effectively created a three-dimensional sound image through the use of four speaker outputs. This technique was short-lived, however, because of the expense of home equipment and the relative incompatibility of quadrophonic discs with stereo systems.

The most significant advance in recording technology since the introduction of the electrical process has been the development of digital recording. The digital recorder uses a computer to encode the sound signal from the microphone and is capable of storing a more precise representation of the sound than the approximation offered by analog techniques. Fully digital playback capabilities became commercially available in 1983 with the mass production of the compact disc (CD) system by Sony and Philips. CD players use laser light to "read" the musical information encoded on a plastic disc with reflective aluminum coating on one side. The 4¾-inch playback-only disc is the current standard format (recordable and/or smaller discs are also in use), and with an 80-minute capacity it can hold all but the longest works. Digital audio tape (DAT), introduced in 1986, is a cassette-based storage medium that is typically used in professional recording studios. Developed in the early 1990s, MP3 (short for Motion Picture Experts Group 1, Layer 3) is a digital compression format that allows CD-quality sound to be stored and distributed over the Internet as data files. MP3 (and related formats) has had an enormous impact on both the listening public and the music industry because of the ease with which recordings are copied and disseminated (often at no cost to the user).

II. *Position in musical life.* In its impact on modern musical life, recording is both a documentary tool and a catalytic agent. The former aspect of the technology is clear, if not fully appreciated. Since the turn of the 20th century, nearly every notable composer has conducted or performed on record: Bartók, Elgar, Hindemith, Ives, Prokofiev, Rachmaninoff, Stravinsky, and many others have provided posterity with a new type of primary musical document of immense value. The documentary role of the technology is particularly important for popular music and jazz, where there is seldom a written score and the record remains the only tangible embodiment of the work. Similarly, recordings made in the field have been central to the study of non-Western musics. The systematic preservation of recordings began in 1899 with the establishment of the first sound archives in Vienna; significant collections were later established throughout Europe. In the U.S., important archives have been established at Yale, Stanford, and Syracuse Universities, the New York Public Library, and the Library of Congress. Every area of music is represented on disc; thus, far more music is immediately available to scholars and amateurs than ever would be possible through live performance alone.

Though the purpose of recording is to preserve sound, the technology has also indelibly shaped the activities of composers, performers, and listeners. The manipulability of recorded sound has given rise to wholly new genres (e.g., *musique concrète*) and compositional practices (e.g., digital sampling). The sensitivity of the microphone has made new performance practices possible, such as the soft, restrained crooning of Bing Crosby and others. [See Croon.] With the ubiquity of recorded sound, musical listening, once almost solely a communal activity, is now perhaps predominantly a solitary pursuit. In these and countless other ways, a technology designed to reproduce sound has played a profound role in the development of modern musical life.

III. *Industry trends.* A remarkable breakthrough in art music in the last two or three decades of the 20th century is the availability of previously obscure repertoire. As late as the 1950s and early 1960s, some Mahler and Bruckner symphonies remained unrecorded, and others were available only in inadequate performances by specialist conductors. The symphonies of Carl Nielsen were available only on hard-to-find Danish recordings, and not one of the 32 symphonies of Havergal Brian could be purchased. By 2000, there were hundreds of recordings of Mahler and Bruckner, there were duplicate cycles of Nielsen's six symphonies, and many of Brian's were on disc as well. Virtually all corners of the repertoire were explored in a way that had never before been the case in the record industry. Composers unheard in the concert hall became available on disc to an unprecedented degree, and many obscure operas that one had no chance of encountering in the opera house could be listened to at home.

The glut of repertoire, duplicate performances, and previously recorded material being made available in dressed-up sound as "historic reissues" had an inevitable effect on the marketplace. No new disc could duplicate the sales figures that were normal in the 1970s and 1980s. Whereas a new recording of a Tchaikovsky symphony by a major artist in 1975 might sell 25,000 to 50,000 copies in the first two years after its release and particularly successful classical releases passed the 200,000 mark in that span of time, by the late 1990s those numbers had dropped by half or more. As a result, by 2000 the classical recording industry was in retreat, making far fewer new recordings and existing more on reissues of their old catalogs.

Another development, led by a company called Naxos, was the budget label devoted to recording a wide range of repertoire, familiar and obscure, using largely unknown artists and smaller European orchestras (often radio orchestras) that charged only nominal fees for recordings. At first ignored by the recording establishment, Naxos gained a serious foothold in the marketplace and became an important force. By the late 1990s it also entered the "historical reissue" arena, with high-quality transfers of recordings from the beginning of the 20th century, and its market share continued to grow at the expense of the major labels.

As the 21st century arrived, yet another trend was making an impact: the DVD (digital video disc). One major conglomerate announced in early 2002 that it would no longer make audio-only recordings of operas, but only complete video performances. Since this company owned labels with a long and important history of operatic recordings, its decision represented a potential sea change in the industry.

Bibl.: Oliver Read and Walter L. Welch, *From Tin Foil to Stereo: Evolution of the Phonograph,* 2nd ed. (Indianapolis: Howard W Sams, 1976). Roland Gelatt, *The Fabulous Phonograph,* 2nd rev. ed. (New York: Macmillan, 1977). Evan Eisenberg, *The Recording Angel: Explorations in Phonography* (New York: McGraw-Hill, 1987). John Harvith and Susan Edwards Harvith, eds., *Edison, Musicians, and the Phonograph: A Century in Retrospect* (Westport, Conn.: Greenwood, 1987). Robert Philip, *Early Recordings and Musical Style: Changing Tastes in Instrumental Performance, 1900–1950* (Cambridge: Cambridge U Pr, 1992). Guy A. Marco, ed., *Encyclopedia of Recorded Sound in the United States* (New York: Garland, 1993). John Borwick, ed., *Sound Recording Practice,* 4th ed. (London: Oxford U Pr, 1996). Erika Brady, *A Spiral Way: How the Phonograph Changed Ethnography* (Jackson: U Pr of Miss, 1999). Mark Katz, "The Phonograph Effect: The Influence of Recording on Listener, Performer, Composer, 1900–1940" (Ph.D. diss., Univ. of Michigan, 1999). Timothy Day, *A Century of Recorded Music: Listening to Musical History* (New Haven: Yale U Pr, 2000).

I–II, M.K.; III, H.F.

Reco-reco, reso-reso [Port.]. A *scraper of Brazil made of notched bamboo and scraped with a stick. See also *Güiro.*

Recoupe [Fr.]. The first *after-dance of the **basse dance commune* in Pierre Attaingnant's collections. Usually, an after-dance would be composed on the same melodic-harmonic materials as its preceding dance, but in Attaingnant's *Dixhuit basses dances* (1530), all of the *recoupes* are independently conceived.

Bibl.: Daniel Heartz, *Preludes, Chansons, and Dances for Lute Published by Pierre Attaingnant, Paris (1529–1530)* (Neuilly-sur-Seine: Société de musique d'autrefois, 1964).
L.H.M.

Recte et retro [Lat.]. Forward and in *retrograde.

Recueilli [Fr.]. Contemplative.

Redoble [Sp.]. In Spanish keyboard music of the Renaissance, a trill-like ornament of several repercussions that may be begun or ended with turns or other figures. The term appears not to have applied to very short ornaments; otherwise its use was not very different from that of **quiebro* [see also Ornamentation]. For a comparative table of *quiebros* and *redobles* in the various treatises, see Robert Parkins, "Cabezón to Cabanilles: Ornamentation in Spanish Keyboard Music," *The Organ Yearbook* 11 (1980): 6. D.F.

Redoute [Fr.]. See **Ridotto.*

Redowa [fr. Cz. *rejdovák*]. A social dance that became popular in Paris and elsewhere ca. 1840. Its Czech antecedents were the *rejdovák,* in 3/4 and similar to the *mazurka, and its following *rejdovačka,* in 2/4.

Reduction [Fr. *réduction*]. An arrangement, especially for piano (piano reduction, *réduction pour le piano*), of a work originally for orchestra or other ensemble.

Reed [Fr. *anche;* Ger. *Rohrblatt;* It. *ancia;* Sp. *lengüeta, caña*]. A thin, elastic strip, fixed at one end and free at the other, set into vibration by moving air. Reeds are the sound generators in *woodwind instruments (except flutes) and many other *aerophones [see ill.]. Woodwinds generally use reeds made from cane, particularly from the *arundo donax* grown in southern France. Plastic reeds have recently found limited acceptance, however. Organs and accordions have steel or brass reeds.

Cane reeds are constructed as either double reeds or single reeds. A double reed, used in the oboe, the bassoon, and *shawms, consists of two pieces of cane carved and bound into a hollow, round shape at one end and flattened out and shaved thin at the other. The single reed of the clarinet or saxophone is a flat strip of cane shaved at one end and fastened at the other to a mouthpiece. Bagpipes and folk clarinets use idioglot single reeds, which are formed by a narrow, U-shaped slit in a tube of cane.

In woodwinds, a reed and a pipe constitute a coupled system with a soft reed. The vibrating reed sets the air column in motion, but, because the reed is capable of vibrating over a wide range of frequencies, the length of the pipe determines the frequency of the system. Metal reeds, on the other hand, are hard: they vibrate at one pitch only. Thus metal-reed instruments characteristically have many reeds and, except in the organ, no pipes (e.g., the *mouth organ and *harmonium). Metal reeds, except in the organ, are usually free reeds: they do not strike the frame that holds them and do not interrupt the flow of air. Cane reeds usually act as beating reeds: they beat against the frame that holds them (or, in the case of double reeds, the two halves beat against one another), periodically cutting off the airstream and producing a sharper sound, rich in upper partials. The reeds of organ pipes behave in this way as well, though they are made of metal.

Woodwind instruments such as the oboe, bassoon, clarinet, and saxophone are played by setting the lips directly onto the reed, thus damping it slightly and enabling fine tuning. In many *reedpipes, however, the reed is removed from the player's control and enclosed in a *wind cap, producing a harsher, "reedier" sound.

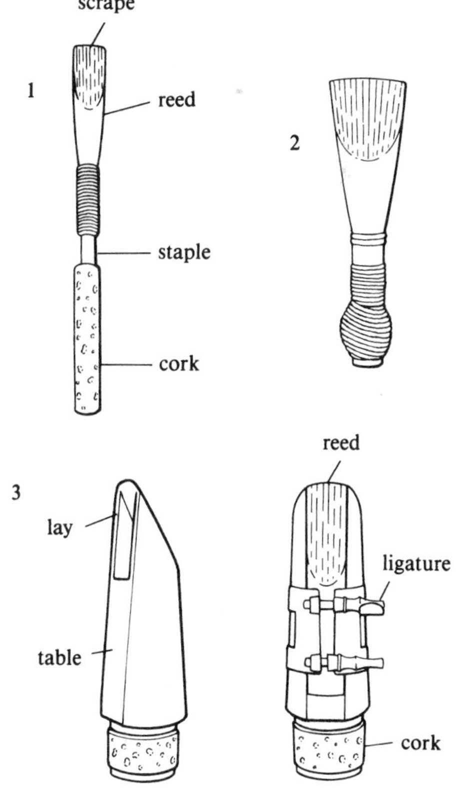

1. Oboe reed. 2. Bassoon reed. 3. Clarinet reed.

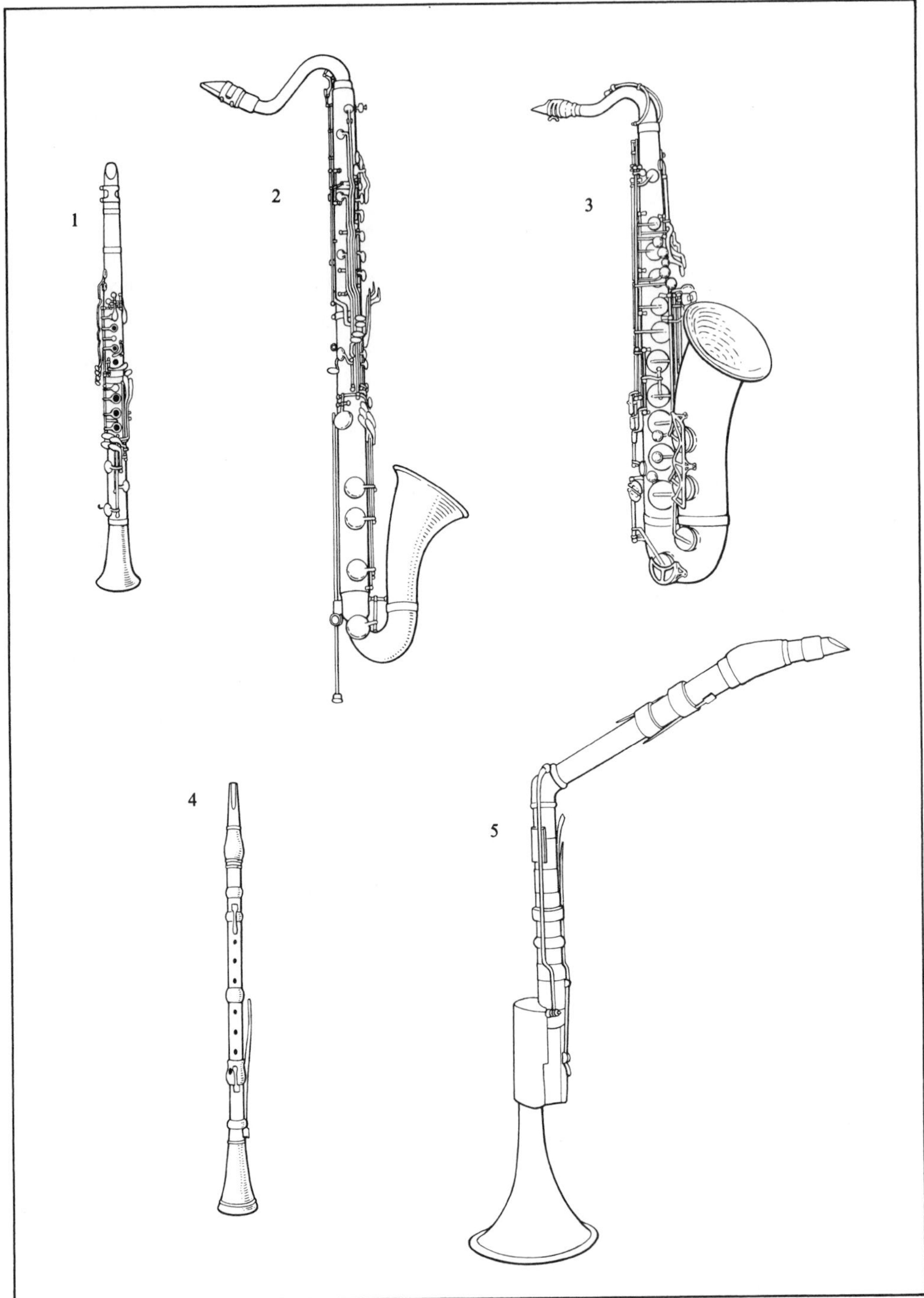

Reed instruments: 1. B♭ clarinet. 2. Bass clarinet. 3. Tenor saxophone. 4. Late 18th-century clarinet. 5. Basset horn.

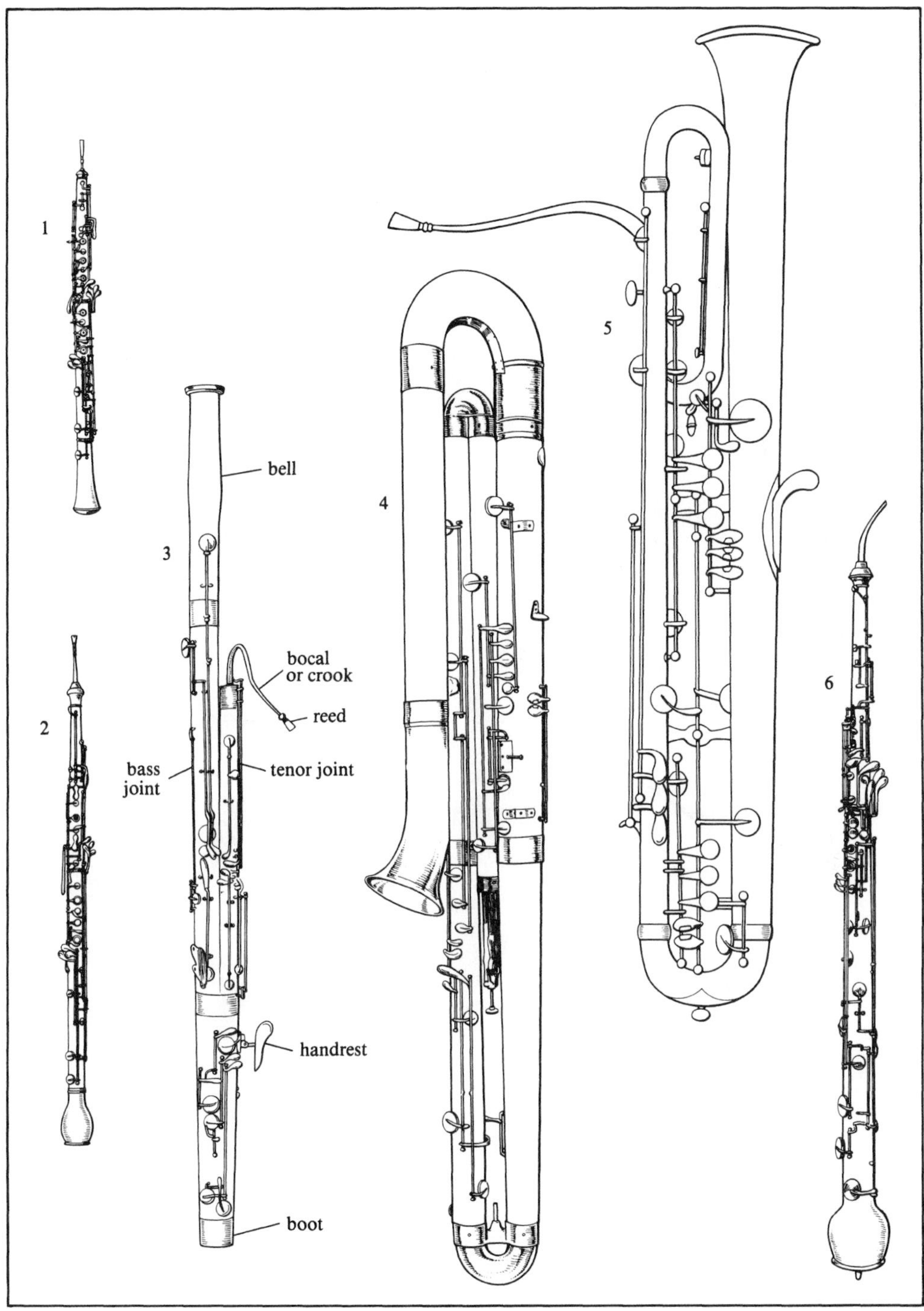

Reed instruments: 1. Oboe. 2. English horn. 3. Bassoon. 4. Contrabassoon. 5. Sarrusophone. 6. Heckelphone.

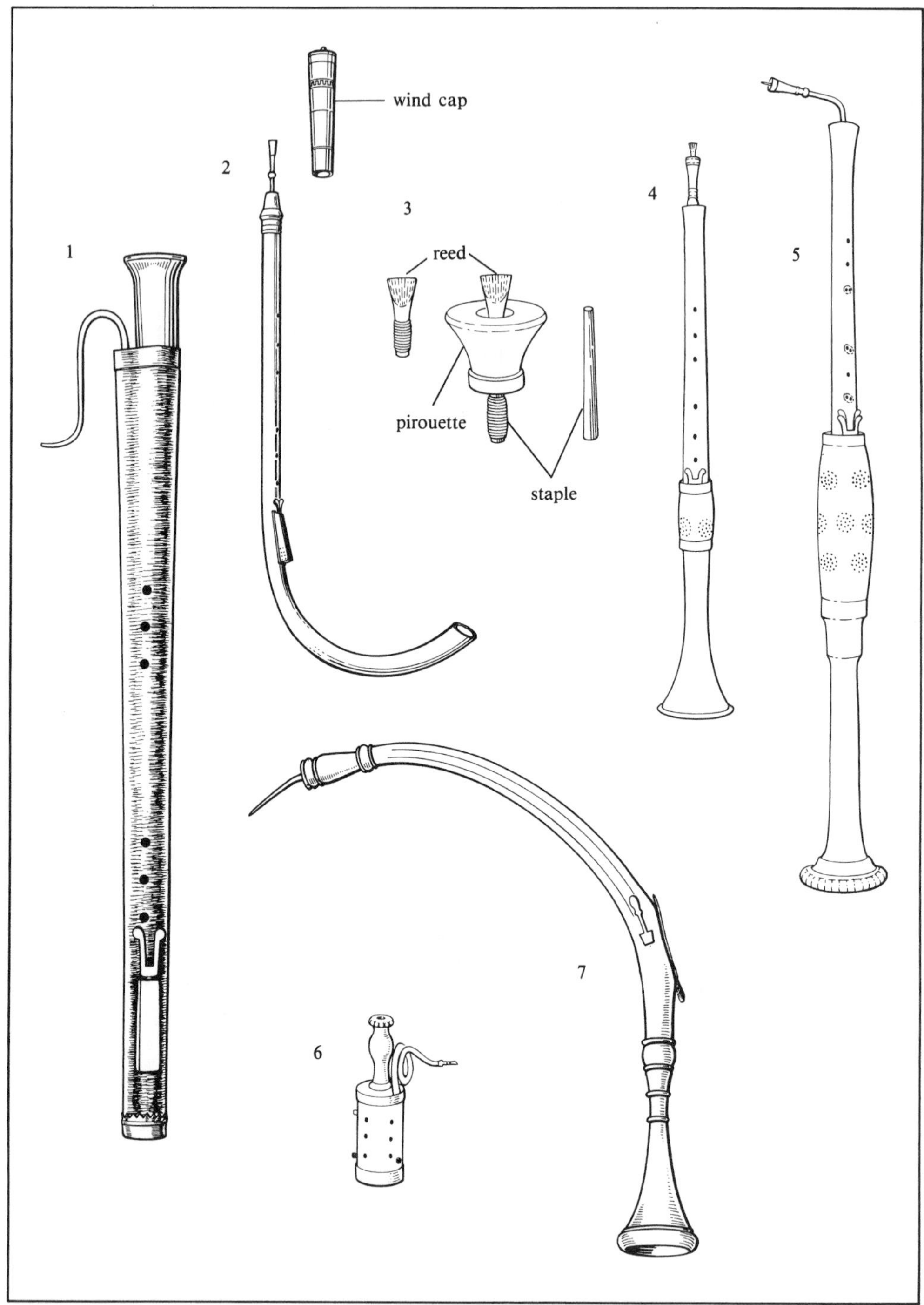

Reed instruments: 1. Curtal. 2. Crumhorn (with wind cap removed). 3. Shawm reed and pirouette (not to scale). 4. Alto shawm. 5. Tenor shawm. 6. Racket. 7. Oboe da caccia.

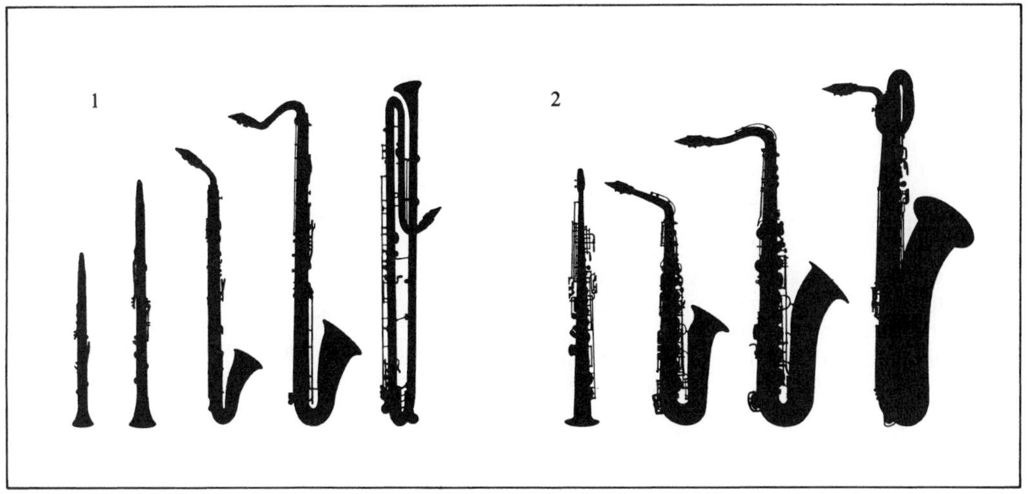

Reed instruments: 1. Clarinets: E♭ soprano, B♭, E♭ alto, B♭ bass, BB♭ contrabass. 2. Saxophones: soprano, alto, tenor, baritone.

Reed cap. *Wind cap.

Reed organ. An *organ in which all notes sound by means of blown reeds rather than flue pipes. See also Harmonium, Regal.

Reed pipe, stop. In organs, a pipe whose sound is generated by a metal tongue vibrating against a wooden or metal *shallot, as distinct from a *flue pipe; a stop made up of such pipes. See ill. under Organ.

Reedpipe. A wind instrument consisting of a tube and a vibrating *reed. The reed may be double or single and may be held in the player's mouth or vibrate freely. See also Aerophone.

Reel. A dance for couples, usually four to eight, documented in Scotland as early as the 16th century and disseminated in Scandinavia, Ireland, and the U.S., where the Virginia reel is familiar in square dancing. Its music is in a moderately fast duple meter, and it includes steps done in place as well as steps entailing movement from one place to another. A related dance in a slower tempo is the *strathspey.

Reformation Symphony. Mendelssohn's Symphony no. 5 in D minor op. 107 (1829–30), composed for a proposed celebration in 1830 of the 300th anniversary of the adoption of the Augsburg Confession as the articles of faith of the Lutheran Church; not performed until 1832, however. The work makes recurring use of the Dresden Amen (composed in the late 18th century by J. G. Naumann), and the last movement is based on Luther's chorale "Ein' feste Burg."

Refrain [Fr. *refrain;* Ger. *Kehrreim;* It. *ritornello, ripresa;* Sp. *estribillo*]. Text or music that is repeated at regular intervals in the course of a larger form; also burden. In music with text, the refrain (both text and music) typically recurs following each of a series of strophes of identical structure also sung to recurring music. The alternation between strophes and refrain is sometimes associated with an alternation between soloist(s) and chorus. The device characterizes a wide variety of both folk and art music and poetry, including some of the principal forms of liturgical chant [see Psalmody, Latin] and musico-poetic genres such as the **ballade,* **ballata,* *carol, 14th-century *madrigal, **rondeau,* **villancico,* and **virelai.* See also Ritornello.

Regal(s). (1) A small portable reed organ used in the 16th and 17th centuries. A row of metal reeds (sometimes two or three rows) was set directly behind the keyboard, and air was driven past the reeds by a pair

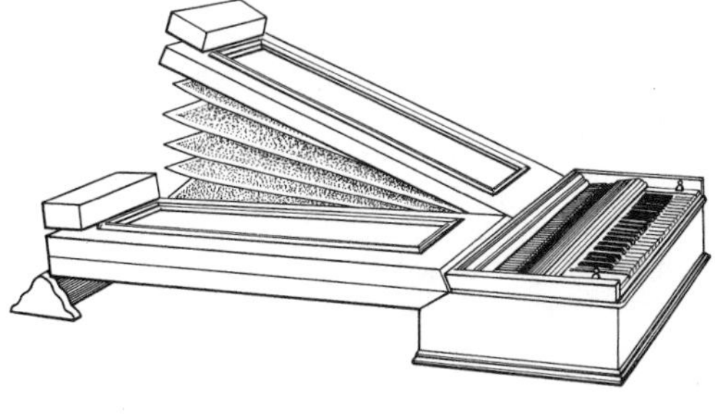

Regal.

of bellows worked by a second person facing the player. Short pipes were sometimes provided above the reeds to reinforce the sound. A small regal that could be folded like a book for storage was called a bible regal. (2) An organ reed stop with short resonators, which occur in various shapes.

Reggae. A style of Jamaican popular music that evolved out of "rock steady" in 1968. Prominent musical characteristics include a pronounced accent on beat three in 4/4 time on the bass drum (referred to by reggae musicians as the "one drop"), rhythm guitar and keyboard playing on the upbeats, and gapped, patterned bass lines. The latter are typically prominent in the mix, as the bass commonly serves the function of the lead instrument. Reggae became an international phenomenon in the 1970s when Bob Marley and the Wailers were marketed to the mainstream rock audience by the British label Island Records. Marley was heavily influenced by the Rastafarian religion, and his international fame helped spread Rastafarianism, alongside reggae, around the world. Marley died of cancer in 1980 and subsequently has been embraced as an iconic figure by indigenous and oppressed peoples in the Caribbean, Africa, the U.S., and New Zealand. Subgenres of reggae have included dub, toast, and, in the 1990s, dancehall. The latter, which substituted highly sexualized lyrics for the political consciousness of earlier Rasta-influenced reggae, has proven to be extremely popular. R.B.

Regina caeli laetare [Lat., Rejoice, Queen of Heaven]. One of the four *antiphons for the Blessed Virgin Mary, sung in modern practice at Compline from Easter Sunday through Friday after Pentecost (*LU,* p. 275). In the Renaissance, it was often set polyphonically and was the basis of many polyphonic *Masses.

Regisseur [Fr.]. The stage manager of a theatrical production.

Register. (1) A specific segment of the total range of pitches available to a voice, instrument, or composition. It may often be described loosely simply as high, low, etc. For the nomenclature of registers of the voice, see Voice. (2) In *serial music, the specific location of a pitch, as opposed simply to its designation as a member of a *pitch class. (3) Organ *stop.

Registration. In organ and harpsichord playing, the selection and combination of *stops (registers) employed in the performance of a work. In the absence of instructions by the composer, which, except in French and English organ music, are rare as late as the 18th century, the player's choice of registration must rely on historically informed taste that takes account of the history of instrument building and the style of the music in question.

Bibl.: E. Harold Geer, *Organ Registration in Theory and Practice* (Glen Rock, N.J.: J Fischer, 1957). Stevens Irwin, *Dictionary of Pipe Organ Stops* (New York: G Schirmer, 1962; 2nd ed., 1983). Jack C. Goode, *Pipe Organ Registration* (New York: Abingdon, 1964). Fenner Douglass, *The Language of the Classical French Organ* (New Haven: Yale U Pr, 1969). Thomas Fredric Harmon, *The Registration of J. S. Bach's Organ Works* (Buren: Frits Knuf, 1978). Ferdinand Klinda, *Orgelregistrierung* (Leipzig: Breitkopf & Härtel, 1987). Barbara Owen, *The Registration of Baroque Organ Music* (Bloomington: Ind U Pr, 1997). Joachim Walter, *"This Heaving Ocean of Tones": Nineteenth-Century Organ Registration Practice at St. Marien, Lübeck* (Göteborg Univ., 2000). See also Harpsichord, Organ.

Regola dell' ottava [It.]. *Rule of the octave.

Regulation. The adjustment of the action of a *piano or *harpsichord so as to produce a consistent tonal quality and response to the fingers throughout its range.

Reigen [Ger.]. Round dance.

Rein [Ger.]. (1) With respect to the tuning of intervals, acoustically pure; *reine Stimmung,* *just intonation. (2) With respect to types of intervals, perfect.

Reine, La [Fr., The Queen]. Popular name for Haydn's Symphony no. 85 in B♭ major Hob. I:85 (1785?; no. 4 of the *Paris Symphonies), so called because Queen Marie Antoinette was said to have been particularly fond of it. The title first appears in the Imbault edition of 1788.

Reisado [Port.]. A kind of dramatic dance or *bailado* of Brazil, primarily found in the northeast of the country and associated with the Christmas season. Of the several *reisados* formerly popular, the *bumba-meu-boi,* itself often performed to conclude other *reisados,* enjoys greatest vitality today. A dramatization of the death and resurrection of an ox *(boi),* the *bumba-meu-boi* includes songs performed by the characters and also, unusual among Brazilian *bailados,* by a female chorus; accompaniment is provided by an ensemble of various strings, winds, and percussion instruments. D.S.

Rejdovák [Cz.]. See *Redowa.*

Réjouissance [Fr., celebration]. A descriptive title for a festive movement in some orchestral suites (e.g., by Bach, Telemann, Handel).

Related key, relative key. See Key relationship.

Relative pitch. The ability to identify specific intervals or to notate music by ear alone, without the ability to identify individual pitches independent of context (termed *absolute pitch). This ability exists in widely varying degrees, and its development is a central aim of *ear training.

Release. In jazz and popular music, *bridge.

Relish. An ornament used in performing early English music for lute, viol, and keyboard. The term single relish was used for any ornament formed by the alternation of two adjacent notes. The double relish consists essentially of a trill upon each of two successive notes [see Ex.]. P.A.

Remettre, remettez [Fr.]. In French organ music, an instruction to take off a stop.

Renaissance, music of the. Music of the period from about 1430 until about 1600. Like others of the principal concepts employed in the periodization of the *history of Western art music, the concept Renaissance [Fr., rebirth] was borrowed from other branches of the study of history. The term was first applied to an entire epoch by the French historian Jules Michelet in 1855, and the concept received its most widespread and influential formulation in Jacob Burckhardt's *The Civilization of the Renaissance in Italy,* first published in German in 1860. The birth of individualism was the crucial element for Burckhardt, and this he saw as the unique product in the 14th century of Italian social and political life and of the revival by Italians of classical learning. Other historians explored the implications of this view in other aspects of Italian culture and sought to trace the subsequent spread of similar phenomena elsewhere in Europe. The result was a view of a period stretching from around 1300 to beyond 1600 characterized by individualism, discovery, and freedom from a childish faith and illusion that had kept mankind's spirit in check during the Middle Ages. The Renaissance was seen as the beginning of the modern age. This view became the subject of vigorous debate among historians but remained widely influential nevertheless.

The attempt to incorporate this view into the history of music met with several difficulties from the outset. Although an important repertory of secular polyphony is preserved from 14th-century Italy [see *Ars nova*], relatively little music by Italian composers survives from major parts of the 15th century, a period in which significant changes in musical style appear in the work of composers from northern Europe active in Italy. And because, unlike literature and the visual arts, music afforded no actual examples of works from classical antiquity, the influence of antiquity on musical style was largely theoretical and did not make itself felt even in writing about music until near the end of the 15th century in the works of Johannes Tinctoris.

It was also Tinctoris (a northerner, though active in Italy) who, in his *Liber de arte contrapuncti* of 1477 (see *SR,* pp. 197–99), proclaimed for the first time a rebirth in the art of music. Citing Dufay, Binchois, and Dunstable as the founders of the new art, he asserted that no work over 40 years old was worth hearing. Succeeding generations of writers on music echoed the claim of rebirth, though citing successively later composers as responsible, and appeals to the authority of classical antiquity on the nature and effects of music increased steadily. These writers, beginning with Tinctoris, provide the principal intellectual links between music and other aspects of culture in this period, though the notion of rebirth had emerged in other spheres well over a century earlier. This current of Renaissance humanism led in the course of the 16th century not only to theoretical explorations of the chromatic and enharmonic genera of ancient music, such as Nicola Vicentino's *L'antica musica ridotta alla moderna prattica* (Rome, 1555), but also to the use of *chromaticism and *microtones by some composers seeking to imitate ancient music, to settings of the *odes of Horace and other classical texts, to attempts to recover the rhythm and meter of ancient music as in **musique mesurée,* and to various practical expressions of the wish to allow words (at the level of accentuation and syntax as well as meaning and affective character) to dominate aspects of vocal music [see Text and music]. But the quite radical changes in musical style occurring around 1600 [see Baroque] were also carried out largely in the name of rediscovering the art of music as it had been practiced in classical antiquity.

On purely musical grounds, Tinctoris's boundary of about 1430, represented by the music of Dufay, Binchois, and Dunstable, is undeniably important, largely because of an increasing reliance in this music on imperfect consonances and a more narrowly restricted use of dissonance [see Counterpoint]. But many of the genres in which they worked and the formal techniques that they employed (e.g., secular works in the **formes fixes* and sacred works based on a **cantus firmus*) belong to unbroken traditions stretching from the 14th century to the very end of the 15th century. And the late 15th century saw changes in musical style and structure (e.g., the adoption of four-voice texture as a norm, the increased use of *imitation, and abandonment of the *formes fixes*) that made themselves felt through the end of the 16th century. Jessie Ann Owens has suggested one single period from roughly 1250 to 1600, which could accommodate the continuities of musical style and its historical and cultural context.

The beginning of the musical Renaissance has thus been placed as early as 1300 (by Hugo Riemann and Heinrich Besseler), as late as 1600 (by Edward J. Dent), and at various dates in between (see Blume, 1967). The consensus that has emerged with respect to the year 1430 owes much to Tinctoris and to a wish to maintain the use of the term Renaissance in some relation (even if uncomfortable) to its use in the study of history generally. The principal danger in its use derives from the extent to which, as framed in the 19th century and still widely used, it describes the Middle Ages in the essentially negative terms of shackles needing to be thrown off by modern heroes (as in Lowinsky, 1954). Such large-scale conceptions of the Middle Ages and the Renaissance as broad cultural phenomena run the risk of falsifying the individual works of both periods that they purport to explain and may inhibit an appropriate critical response to them.

The 15th century saw the emergence of a musical language that ultimately spread throughout all of Western Europe. This language and its dissemination was due in large measure to the work and travels of musicians from the Low Countries, including what is now part of northern France. These musicians, whose culture was principally French, were especially prominent in Italy in the 15th century. They have sometimes been described as constituting one or more schools spanning the 15th and 16th centuries. Raphael Georg Kiesewetter, in 1826, defined three "Netherlands schools," the first headed by Guillaume Dufay (ca. 1400–74), the second by Johannes Ockeghem (ca. 1410–97) and Jacob Obrecht (ca. 1450–1505), and the third by Josquin Desprez (ca. 1440–1521). In part because the term Netherlands is misleading with respect to the geographic and cultural origins of these composers, some more recent writers (including Willibald Gurlitt, Heinrich Besseler, and Paul Henry Lang) have preferred to term the first of these *Burgundian and the second and third variously as Flemish and Franco-Flemish, respectively, or simply (combining the second and third) Flemish, Netherlandish, or Franco-Netherlandish (Gustave Reese). Each such label, however, entails its own compromises.

For the principal genres of the period, see Mass, Motet, Chanson, Madrigal, *Frottola, Lauda, Villancico,* Canzona, Ricercar, Intabulation; see also Mode, Theory, Council of Trent, Roman School, Venetian School, Mannerism.

Bibl.: Heinrich Besseler, *Die Musik des Mittelalters und der Renaissance* (Potsdam: Akademische Verlag Athenaion, 1931). André Pirro, *Histoire de la musique de la fin du XIVe siècle à la fin du XVIe* (Paris: H Laurens, 1940). Gustave Reese, *Music in the Renaissance* (New York: Norton, 1954; rev ed., 1959). Nino Pirrotta, "Music and Cultural Tendencies in 15th-Century Italy," *JAMS* 19 (1966): 127–61. Friedrich Blume, *Renaissance and Baroque Music: A Comprehensive Survey,* trans. M. D. Herter Norton (New York: Norton, 1967). Iain Fenlon, ed., *The Renaissance: From the 1470s to the End of the 16th Century* (Englewood Cliffs, N.J.: Prentice Hall, 1989). Edward E. Lowinsky, *Music in the Culture of the Renaissance and Other Essays,* ed. Bonnie J. Blackburn (Chicago: U of Chicago Pr, 1989). Jessie Ann Owens, "Music Historiography and the Definition of 'Renaissance,'" *Notes* 47 (1990–91): 305–30. Mark Everist, ed., *Music before 1600* (Oxford: Blackwell Reference, 1992). Tess Knighton and David Fallows, eds., *Companion to Medieval and Renaissance Music* (New York: Schirmer, 1992). Gary Tomlinson, *Music in Renaissance Magic: Toward a Historiography of Others* (Chicago: U of Chicago Pr, 1993). Reinhard Strohm, *The Rise of European Music, 1380–1500* (New York: Cambridge U Pr, 1993). Honey Meconi, "Does *Imitatio* Exist?" *JM* 12, no. 2 (1994): 152–78. Jessie Ann Owens, *Composers at Work: The Craft of Musical Composition 1450–1600* (New York: Oxford U Pr, 1997). Allan W. Atlas, *Renaissance Music: Music in Western Europe, 1400–1600* (New York: Norton, 1998). Gary Tomlinson, ed., Leo Treitler, gen. ed., *Source Readings in Music History,* vol. 3: *The Renaissance* (New York: Norton, 1998). Howard Mayer Brown and Louise K. Stein, *Music in the Renaissance,* 2nd ed. (Englewood Cliffs, N.J.: Prentice Hall, 1999). Leeman L. Perkins, *Music in the Age of the Renaissance* (New York: Norton, 1999). D.M.R.

Renard [Fr., The Fox; Russ. *Bayka*]. Burlesque in one act for dancers, singers, and small orchestra by Stravinsky (libretto by Stravinsky, after Russian folktales; original choreography by Bronislava Nijinska; later versions by Serge Lifar and George Balanchine), produced by Diaghilev's Ballets russes in Paris in 1922.

Renforcer [Fr.]. To reinforce, make louder.

Repeat [Fr. *reprise;* Ger. *Wiederholung;* It. *replica;* Sp. *repetición*]. To play a passage again; repeat sign, either of the symbols (‖: and :‖) used to mark the beginning and end, respectively, of a passage that is to be repeated. In the absence of a sign like the first, the repetition is from the beginning of the work or movement. Unless otherwise indicated, these symbols call for a single repetition. If the first and second statements of the passage have different endings, these are identified by number and termed **prima volta* and *seconda volta,* or first and second endings, respectively [see ill. under Notation].

Repercussa [Lat. *vox r.,* repeated tone]. In a church *mode, the pitch second in importance to the final, also termed (especially in the context of a *psalm tone) the tenor, *tuba,* or reciting note.

Repercussio [Lat.]. (1) The repetition of a pitch occurring within a *neume such as the *bistropha* or *tristropha.* (2) In a church *mode, the interval between the final and the tenor; also the tenor itself (hence, synonymous with *repercussa*).

Répertoire international . . . See *RILM, RISM, RIdIM.*

Repetendum [Lat.]. In Latin liturgical chant, especially *responsories, the concluding section of the respond or refrain, which is repeated following the verse. Where there is more than one verse or where the lesser *Doxology is sung in addition to a verse, two or more different *repetenda* may be indicated. See also *Versus ad repetendum.*

Répétiteur [Fr.]. Coach; one who rehearses singers or soloists apart from general rehearsals.

Repetition. (1) The restatement of a musical idea or section of a work. The perception of repetition is one of the principal elements in the perception of musical *form. Repetition may be literal or varied in some way; it may involve extended passages or only a few notes. Techniques that rely on repetition of one kind or another include *ostinato, *sequence, *imitation, and **Stimmtausch.* (2) The characteristics of the action of a piano that permit the rapid repetition of notes [see Piano].

Répétition [Fr.]. Rehearsal; *répétition générale,* dress rehearsal.

Repiano [fr. **ripieno*]. In some bands, a cornet or clarinet player other than the principal player [see Brass band].

Replica [It.]. *Repeat; *senza r.,* without repeat, as when a minuet or similar piece is played **da capo.*

Répons [Fr.]. *Responsory.

Réponse [Fr.]. An answer in a fugue.

Reports. In the 17th century, imitation (so defined in Henry Purcell's revision of the treatise in John Playford's *Introduction to the Skill of Musick,* 12th ed., London, 1694); also contrapuntal texture generally (as in the "Psalmes in Reports" of the Scottish Psalter of 1635).

Reprise [Fr.; also Eng., Ger.]. *Repeat, repetition. The term may refer to either literal or varied repetitions: in C. P. E. Bach's *Sechs Sonaten für Clavier mit veränderten Reprisen* (1760), the "varied" repetitions, here written out, of the expositions of sonata forms; in 17th- and 18th-century French keyboard music, the second section of a *binary form, the refrain of a **rondeau,* or a short phrase repeated at the end of a movement; in some accounts of *sonata form, the recapitulation; in musicals or operettas, an abbreviated repetition of a prominent number, usually after some intervening dialogue.

Reproaches. **Improperia.*

Requiem [Lat.]. The Mass for the Dead *(Missa pro defunctis),* called Requiem after the first word of its introit ("Requiem aeternam dona eis Domine," Grant to them eternal rest, O Lord). The term has also been used in the 20th century in works not strictly liturgical but written in honor of the dead, as in Britten's *War Requiem* (1962) and Stravinsky's *Requiem Canticles* (1965–66). German Requiems, such as the *Musikalische Exequien* (1636) of Schütz or Brahms's *Ein Deutsches Requiem* op. 45 (1868), employ German texts drawn from the Bible or from chorales.

The Latin Requiem Mass, though part of the liturgy from the earliest times, was not actually standardized until after the Council of Trent (1545–63) in the Missal of Pius V (1570), which prescribed the following *Proper and *Ordinary items: introit ("Requiem aeternam"), Kyrie, gradual ("Requiem aeternam"), tract ("Absolve Domine"), sequence ("Dies irae"), offertory ("Domine Jesu Christe"), Sanctus and Benedictus, Agnus (with "Dona eis requiem" and "Dona eis requiem sempiternam" in place of "Miserere nobis" and "Dona nobis pacem"), and communion ("Lux aeterna"). The absolution (the responsory "Libera me Domine"), set by a few composers of Requiems, belongs not to the Mass itself but to the burial service. Polyphonic settings of the Requiem Mass begin in the 15th century; a lost Requiem has been attributed to Dufay, but the first extant setting is the one by Ockeghem. The polyphonic Requiem always includes some of the Proper (particularly, the introit) but does not always set all of the Ordinary. Before 1570, Requiems reflected local traditions in the choice of certain Proper items and tended not to contain a polyphonic setting of the "Dies irae," although one can be found in the version by Antoine Brumel. Renaissance Requiems also generally employ Gregorian intonations at the beginnings of movements or sections, and Gregorian chant invariably forms the basis of the polyphony.

After the Requiem Mass was liturgically fixed, the number of settings increased dramatically. During the 17th century, they were often written in **stile antico*—as were Masses generally—but new styles were eventually incorporated. Many important Requiems were composed in the 18th and 19th centuries (by Mozart, Berlioz, and Verdi, to name but a few); in these works, the formerly neglected "Dies irae" became the central musical event, greatly expanded and divided into many sections with full advantage taken of the dramatic implications of its description of the Last Judgment. The "Dies irae" of Cherubini's Requiem in C minor (1816) begins with the arresting sound of trumpets and a Chinese gong, but this pales beside the theatrical fury of the "Tuba mirum" of Berlioz's *Grande Messe des morts* (1837) with its 4 brass bands, 16 timpani, and 10 cymbals. Just as dramatic is Verdi's *Manzoni Requiem* (1874), with its offstage trumpets at the "Tuba mirum" and agitated soprano recitative in the "Libera me"; significantly, this Requiem, though first performed in a liturgical context, was later taken by Verdi on a tour of the opera houses and concert halls of Europe. Other 19th-century composers were more restrained, particularly Liszt, whose *Requiem* (1867–68) is written in *a cappella* style, and Fauré, who even chose not to set the "Dies irae" (1887). There have been a number of Requiems written in the 20th century; of these, that by Maurice Duruflé (1947, rev. 1961) is perhaps the best known.

Bibl.: Charles Warren Fox, "The Polyphonic Requiem before about 1615," *BAMS* 7 (1943): 6–7. Alec Robertson, *Requiem: Music of Mourning and Consolation* (London: Praeger, 1967). David B. Rosen, "The Genesis of Verdi's *Requiem*" (Ph.D. diss., Univ. of Cal., Berkeley, 1976). Edward T. Cone, "Berlioz's Divine Comedy: The *Grande Messe des morts,*" *19th Century Music* 4 (1980): 3–16. William Prizer, "Music and Ceremonial in the Low Countries: Philip the Fair and the Order of the Golden Fleece," *EMH* 5 (1985): 113–53.

R.S.

Rescue opera. A category of *opéra comique* in which the hero or heroine, threatened by a natural catastrophe (e.g., avalanche or volcano), a villainous outlaw, or an unjust ruler, is rescued at the last moment by a person showing great personal courage and heroism. The genre was popular in France in the decade between the fall of the monarchy and the rise of Napoleon. Afterward it was taken up in Italy and Germany. The best-known example of a rescue opera is Beethoven's **Fidelio.*

Reservata [Lat.]. See *Musica reservata.*

Res facta [Lat.; Fr. *chose faite*]. A composition, usually but not necessarily written, in which each voice is constructed with regard for all others [cf. *Cantare super librum*]. Since the first occurrence of the term (in the works of Tinctoris, ca. 1435–1511), writers have exhibited considerable confusion over its meaning. It has most commonly been used to designate written, as opposed to improvised, counterpoint.

Bibl.: Ernest T. Ferand, "What Is *Res Facta?*" *JAMS* 10 (1957): 141–50. Margaret Bent, "*Resfacta* and *Cantare Super Librum*," *JAMS* 36 (1983): 371–91.

Resolution. A progression from a dissonant tone or harmony to one that is consonant; the consonant tone or harmony itself. In classical tonal counterpoint, every dissonant tone must be resolved, normally by stepwise motion [see Counterpoint].

Resonance. See Acoustics VI, Sympathetic string.

Resonator. A device that amplifies or reinforces a musical sound by vibrating at the same frequency. A resonator may be a column of air such as that contained in an organ pipe, or it may be an elastic surface such as the piano soundboard. Often it is both, for example, the sound box of a guitar. A resonator like the *marimba tube is specific—i.e., its natural frequency matches exactly the frequency of the driving sound. Other resonators (e.g., the sound box of the violin or the gourd resonator of the **sitār*) are general—they vibrate in response to many different pitches. See also Acoustics VI, Reed, Sympathetic string.

Reso-reso [Port.]. **Reco-reco.*

Respond. *Responsory; also the refrain of a responsory as distinct from its verse.

Response. A short text (often preceded by the abbreviation ℟), spoken or sung by congregation or choir, in reply to a versicle (another short text spoken or sung by the officiant, identified by the abbreviation ℣), occurring as a single pair (℣ Benedicamus domino, ℟ Deo gratias) or in more elaborate sets (℣ Lord have mercy upon us, ℟ Lord have mercy upon us, ℣ Christ have mercy upon us, ℟ Christ have mercy upon us, etc.). As an element of liturgical dialogue, the response, representing the congregation, picks up and develops the versicle text by rhetorical devices such as repetition, amendment, accretion, and expansion, all aimed at effecting an intensified congregational participation. The most elaborate form of versicle and response is the *litany. R.F.F.

Responsorial singing. Singing, especially in liturgical chant, in which a soloist or group of soloists alternates with a choir [see Psalmody]; in nonliturgical contexts, synonymous with *call and response.

Responsory. A type of liturgical chant common to the *Gregorian and other Western chant repertories and an example of responsorial *psalmody. As a general category within the repertory of Gregorian chant, it may be said to include the great and short responsories described here as well as the *gradual (to which the term *responsorium graduale* is applied in some early sources).

The great responsories or *responsoria prolixa* are a prominent feature of Matins in the Office (included in the *Liber responsorialis;* for a few important feasts also in *LU*), where they are associated with lessons or readings from Scripture. They are also sung at Vespers on solemn feasts (*AntMon,* pp. 1183–1204) and in processions (in the *Processionale monasticum*). In general, each consists of two parts: a respond (R, with R′ representing its last part, called the *repetendum*) intoned by the soloists and continued by the choir, and a verse (V) sung by the soloists. To this the first half of the lesser *Doxology (D) may be added, as follows: R V R′ D R′. Other schemes including the use of the full rather than the abbreviated refrain are encountered, and a few responsories have more than one verse, sometimes with a different *repetendum* for each. The responds are moderately elaborate melodies with occasional long *melismas. Beginning in the 9th century, a melisma *(neuma)* was sometimes added to an existing responsory. Some of these melismas were borrowed from other chants, especially offertories, and some were shared among a number of responsories. Such melismas were sometimes texted to produce **prosulae.* The verses and the lesser Doxology are most often sung to one or another of a set of eight *psalm tones, according to the mode of the respond. The texts are drawn from a variety of books of the Bible, including the Psalms, and from some nonbiblical sources. These texts were often set in the 16th century as elaborate *motets in two sections, the first section setting the respond and the second section setting the verse and the repeated section of the respond.

The short responsories or *responsoria brevia* are sung following the short readings or chapters of the lesser hours and Compline in the secular Office and at Lauds and Vespers as well in the monastic Office. Although the medieval repertory is quite varied, the repertory in modern use consists of simple melodies, three of which serve for many texts and change with the liturgical season. Both verse and respond sometimes have the character of a psalm tone, though there is no fixed set of eight such tones. Their form is often as follows: R R V R′ D R, in which the verse and lesser Doxology are sung by the soloists and the respond is sung by the choir except in its first and last statements, where it is intoned by the soloists and continued by the choir.

Bibl.: Walter Howard Frere, ed., *Antiphonale sarisburiense* (London: Plainsong and Mediaeval Music Society, 1901–25; R: Farnborough: Gregg, 1966). Helmut Hucke, "Das Responsorium," *Schrade,* 1973, pp. 144–91. Ruth Steiner, "Some Melismas for Office Responsories," *JAMS* 26 (1973): 108–31. See also Gregorian chant. D.M.R.

Rest. A span of time in which there is silence; a notational symbol specifying a silence of some duration. For examples and nomenclature, see Note.

Restatement. A recurrence, often after intervening

contrast, of an element of a musical form; also the recapitulation in *sonata form.

Restringendo [It.]. Becoming faster.

Resultant bass. In organs, a stop sounding a unison (16′ or 8′) and its fifth (10 2/3′ or 5 1/3′) simultaneously, to produce the pitch an octave below the unison. For the acoustical phenomenon entailed, see Combination tone.

Resultant tone. See Combination tone.

Resurrection Symphony. Popular name for Mahler's Symphony no. 2 in C minor, composed in 1888–94 (rev. 1903). The fourth movement is a setting for alto and orchestra of "Urlicht" (Primeval Light, a song from *Des *Knaben Wunderhorn*); the fifth and last movement is a setting of Friedrich Gottlieb Klopstock's poem "Auferstehung" (Resurrection) for soprano, chorus, and orchestra.

Retard. To slow down; a slowing down; **ritardando*.

Retardation [obs.]. Suspension [see Counterpoint II, 3].

Retenu [Fr.]. Held back.

Retirada [It., retreat]. A closing movement in some Baroque suites, the counterpart of the opening **intrada*. The title is found occasionally in Italy (Biagio Marini) and Eastern Europe. B.G.

Retirez [Fr.]. In organ music, an instruction to withdraw a specified stop.

Retransition. A passage that leads to a restatement of some element of a musical form; specifically, in *sonata form, a passage that concludes the development and prepares the return to the tonic and the original thematic material in the recapitulation.

Retrograde [Lat. *cancrizans,* crab motion, *recte et retro;* Ger. *Krebsgang;* It. *al rovescio*]. Backward, i.e., beginning with the last note and ending with the first. The device is found in *canons (some as early as the 14th and 15th centuries) and is central to *twelve-tone music.

Retrograde inversion. The *inversion of a series of notes presented from last to first. The device is central to *twelve-tone music.

Revolutionary Etude. Popular name for Chopin's Etude in C minor op. 10 no. 12 for piano (1831?), so called because Chopin supposedly composed it on hearing that Warsaw had been captured by the Russians, crushing the Polish Revolution of 1830–31. There is no evidence for the anecdote, and the etude may in fact have been composed in the previous year.

Revue. Beginning in the 19th century, a theatrical production featuring a series of songs, dances, and other entertainments, often humorous, often organized around a theme but usually without plot. Prominent use is usually made of a group of young women ("chorus girls") who dance and sing in costume, sometimes intended to be sexually provocative. Such productions were common in the U.S. musical theater through the 1920s and include the several *Ziegfeld's Follies.*

Rf., Rfz. Abbr. for **rinforzando.*

R.H. In keyboard music, abbr. for right hand.

Rhapsodie (Fragment aus Goethe's Harzreise im Winter) [Ger.]. Brahms's op. 53 (1869) for alto, men's chorus, and orchestra, setting a fragment of Goethe's *Harzreise im Winter* (Winter Journey through the Hartz Mountains); also known as the *Alto Rhapsody.*

Rhapsodies hongroises [Fr.]. See *Hungarian Rhapsodies.*

Rhapsody. (1) [fr. Gr. *rhapsōidos,* a singer or reciter of epic poetry] A section of an epic poem that is separately recited. (2) In the 19th and 20th centuries, a title chiefly for instrumental pieces. Borrowed from 18th-century literature, it implied no particular form, content, or compositional method. Václav Jan Tomášek's 15 rhapsodies (1810ff.) were the first individual piano pieces to bear the title, and the piano remained the principal medium for the repertory until the last quarter of the 19th century. Liszt's 19 **Hungarian Rhapsodies* (1846–86), with their loose, episodic forms (like epic poetry), their exaggerated, contrasting moods, and their supposed folk themes, initiated a long tradition of nationalistic rhapsodies, many of which use folk or folklike materials (e.g., Dvořák's *Slavonic Rhapsodies* and Vaughan Williams's *Norfolk Rhapsodies*). On the other hand, Brahms's well-known Rhapsodies op. 79 for piano depart from this tradition, the second in G minor being a clear example of sonata form. See also Character (characteristic) piece.

Bibl.: Walter Salmen, *Geschichte der Rhapsodie* (Zürich: Atlantis, 1966).

Rhapsody in Blue. Rhapsody for piano and dance band by Gershwin, composed in 1924. Both the original version and the later version for piano and symphony orchestra were orchestrated by Ferde Grofé.

Rheingold, Das [Ger.]. See *Ring des Nibelungen, Der.*

Rhenish Symphony. Popular name for Schumann's Symphony no. 3 in E♭ major op. 97 (1850, and thus the fourth in order of composition), composed after his arrival in Düsseldorf and in some measure inspired by the region along the Rhine. The fourth movement, originally inscribed "In the Style of an Accompaniment to a Solemn Ceremony," evokes a service for the elevation of a cardinal attended by Schumann in the cathedral in Cologne.

Rhetoric. The principles governing the invention, arrangement, and elaboration of ideas in a piece of music. Drawing on classical models of oration, music theorists cultivated the concept of musical rhetoric in earnest during the 16th, 17th, and 18th centuries, especially for works with texts. Such activity blossomed into the so-called doctrine of *figures and doctrine of *affections. Although rhetorical models for music were supplanted in the 19th century, they continue to influence the various modes of musical analysis, whether or not the music in question is based on an explicit text or program.

Traditionally, discussions of musical rhetoric have borrowed extensively from ancient Greek and Roman treatises on public oratory. These texts show how successful speeches are produced and presented according to rational principles. Some, such as Aristotle's *De Rhetorica,* are philosophical in nature and treat rhetoric as a social science, akin to logic and psychology. But others, including Cicero's *De Inventione* and Quintilian's *Institutio oratorio,* are more practical in tone and describe how the aspiring orator can move, delight, or instruct the listener. Broadly speaking, these treatises address five main issues: (1) how to invent a suitable topic *(inventio),* (2) how to arrange the argument systematically *(dispositio),* (3) how to elaborate particular ideas appropriately (*elaboratio, elocutio,* or *decoratio*), (4) how to memorize a text accurately and efficiently *(memoria),* and (5) how to deliver a speech effectively *(pronuntiatio).* In particular, they suggest that successful arguments are normally arranged into six sections: *exordium, narratio, divisio* (or *propositio*), *confirmatio, confutatio,* and *peroratio* (or *conclusio*). To show how particular ideas are elaborated, rhetoricians not only discussed the concept of style but also classified numerous figures of speech, such as metaphor, metonymy, and hyperbole. They also advocated the use of mnemonic aids to memorize texts.

Given the intimate connections that often exist between music and language and the central role rhetoric played in medieval education (it was one of the seven liberal arts) [see Quadrivium], music theorists started to borrow the rhetorical concept of figures, topoi, clausula, copula, and so on. Since most of the discussion focused on vocal music, theorists insisted that the music should follow the punctuation of the text; some even introduced musical analogues to the various points of punctuation (e.g., colon, comma, and period). Guido and his successors also used mnemonic and visual aids to help singers memorize tunes, perhaps the most famous being the *Guidonian hand. Interest in musical rhetoric expanded in the early 16th century, thanks to the rediscovery of the treatises by Cicero and Quintilian. A particular treatise in this regard was Listenius's *Musica Poetica* (1537); by widening the scope of theoretical discourse from the traditional distinction between *musica theorica* and *musica practica* [see Theory], this text became a model for many later theorists. Meanwhile, other theorists, such as Heyden (1540) and Glarean (1547), invoked the notion of musical figures to explain successful text setting, whereas Coclio (1552) and Finck (1556) focused on the appropriate manner of delivery for vocal compositions. In his *Praecepta musicae poetica* (1563), Dressler even suggested that musical compositions should follow the simple rhetorical plan: *exordium, medium, finis.*

It was during the 17th and 18th centuries that rhetorical models came to dominate discourse about music theory. Among the most important treatises of the period were Burmeister's *Musica autoschediastike* (1601) and *musica poetica* (1606). Building on earlier writers, Burmeister transformed the various figures of speech invoked by rhetoricians to elaborate ideas (i.e., *elaboratio*), and he created a complex system of stereotypical musical figures that connected particular words or phrases in a text to their musical setting. Some of these figures were simply borrowed from traditional rhetorical terminology, but others were newly minted. Later writers followed Burmeister's lead, adding new figures of their own; the list includes Lippius, Nucius, Thuringus, Herbst, Kircher, Bernhard, Printz, Ahle, Janovka, Walther, Vogt, Scheibe, Spiess, and Forkel. Although there is no single doctrine of figures for Baroque music, they had a direct bearing on the emotional impact of works, and this influenced the doctrine of affections. Besides discussing musical figures, Burmeister also connected the large-scale structure of musical compositions to the sixfold scheme mentioned earlier. Since Lassus was widely regarded as the greatest musical orator, he even analyzed Lassus's motet *In me transierunt* according to its rhetorical structure and musical figures.

Just as some theorists used the rhetorical concept of figures to explain details of text setting, so they also incorporated them into various classifications of musical style. Debates about musical style date at least back to Monteverdi's celebrated exchanges with Artusi. The result of this polemic was to distinguish between two distinct modes of composition—the **prima prattica,* which followed the principles of dissonance treatment and musical structure exemplified by composers such as Willaert and Palestrina, and **seconda prattica,* which followed the practices of more radical composers, such as Rore and Monteverdi [see Baroque]. This distinction soon became ubiquitous in music theory treatises. But as compositional practices diversified, theorists began to differentiate styles more carefully. For example, Scacchi (1649) claimed that, whereas Renaissance music conformed to one practice and one style, modern music conformed to two practices and three styles, namely those for church, chamber, and theater. Within these three styles, Scacchi identified various other types. In his *Tractatus compositions augmentatus* (ca. 1657) Bernhard tried to connect differences in style with musical figures; these figures were often closely connected with patterns of dissonance.

Theorists did not, however, simply adapt the rhetorical concept of elaboration *(elaboratio),* they also borrowed the concepts of invention *(inventio)* and arrangement *(dispositio).* Heinichen (1728), for example, drew on the rhetorical idea of *loci topici* to help the composer find an appropriate topic from which to create suitable material for invention. Although Heinichen apparently confined his discussion of *loci topici* to one particular type of topic, the *loci circumstantiarum,* Mattheson subsequently widened the discussion to include others, such as the *locus descriptionis, locus notationis,* and *locus causae materialis.* Also in his celebrated treatise *Der vollkommene Capellmeister* (1739), Mattheson classified musical rhetoric according to the five main issues mentioned above and even mentioned the sixfold disposition of works. As Buelow and others have stressed, Mattheson did not suppose that all works follow this rigid plan; however, he implied that they provide helpful models by which composers could approach the problems of musical composition.

By the late 18th century, however, interest in musical rhetoric began to wane, as music theorists turned their attention to new modes of analytical discourse based on phrase models and tonal structure. However, several authors continued to propose rational models to explain the process and products of musical composition. Sulzer (1771–74), for example, suggested that composers start with a plan *(Anlage)* that they execute in broad terms *(Ausführung)* before working out in detail *(Ausarbeitung).* Meanwhile, Kollmann (1799) suggested that pieces should follow a threefold tonal plan: "setting out," "elaboration," and "return." This plan overlapped with a fourfold thematic scheme in which the basic material is initially proposed and then elaborated in three sections. Koch developed similar ideas in his *Versuch einer Anleitung zur Composition* (1782–93), though his analysis of phrase structure owes much to Riepel.

Although the idea of musical rhetoric lived on the idea of formal stereotypes and the various principles of thematic analysis, such as Schoenberg's concepts of liquidation, developing variation, and **Grundgestalt,* many 19th-century writers turned away from the idea that musical compositions could ever be explained rationally by generalized principles. Spurred on by idolization of the genius, the masterpiece, and the virtuoso, Romantic theorists often focused their attention on describing the unique properties of individual compositions, rather than properties shared among large repertories of music. Even when they discussed works with extra musical associations or programs, they generally explored the ways in which the composer responded to the specifics of the source, rather than offering catalogs of stereotypical musical figures. Similarly, music theorists frequently explained musical form in more organic terms: A. B. Marx, for example, suggested that "there are as many forms as works of art." By the same token, they regarded the processes of composition as mysterious and ineffable. These Romantic notions still live on in contemporary analytical writing. See also Theory. M.B.

Rhumba. See Rumba.

Rhyme, musical. The recurrence of the same musical material at the conclusion of two or more lines or sections of a work, especially when the recurrence occurs on a level comparable to that of the analogous phenomenon in poetry rather than between major sections of a large-scale work. It is a feature of some examples of liturgical chant, some medieval **ballades,* and the **estampie.*

Rhymed Office. A set of the services making up the *Office for some feast, most often that of a local saint, in which the antiphons and responsories have rhymed, metrical texts; also termed *historia.* The melodies for such Offices frequently follow one another in the order of the eight modes. The tradition of writing rhymed Offices lasted from the 9th through the 16th century and reached its peak in the 12th and 13th centuries. The Office for Trinity Sunday, attributed to Hucbald of St. Amand (d. 930), is an early example that has remained in use.

Bibl.: Karlheinz Schlager, "Reimoffizien," in Karl Gustav Fellerer, ed., *Geschichte der katholischen Kirchenmusik* (Kassel: Bärenreiter, 1972), 1:293–97.

Rhythm [fr. Gr. *rhythmos;* Lat. *rhythmus;* Ger. *Rhythmus;* Fr. *rhythme;* Sp., It. *ritmo*]. The pattern of movement in time. The traditional derivation from Greek and Indo-European roots meaning flow has been questioned; one suggested alternative derivation would refer the Greek word to roots meaning uphold/maintain. As with the closely associated term meter, contexts for the word rhythm throughout Western history have been poetic as well as musical.

In modern English musical usage, the word rhythm appears on two semantic levels. In the widest sense, it is set beside the terms melody and harmony, and in that very general sense, rhythm covers all aspects of musical movement as ordered in time, as opposed to aspects of musical sound conceived as pitch (whether singly or in simultaneous combination) and timbre (tone color). In the narrower and more specific sense, rhythm shares a lexical field with meter and tempo. Rhythm in that specific sense—where it can be preceded by an indefinite article ("a rhythm")—denotes a patterned configuration of attacks that may or may not be constrained overall by a meter or associated with a particular tempo. The acoustic medium may be of any kind, from unclouded pitches or harmonies to percussive noises of jumbled or indeterminate frequency; it is necessary only that there be more than one attack, that the attacks not be too far apart, and that the musical convention in play accept the succession of attacks as mutually connected and not independent of each other. A succession of attacks can be articulated in many ways: by striking or blowing an instrument; by articulation of a consonant in singing; by change of density in a multilayered texture; by change of harmony or timbre; even by mere change of pitch in an otherwise unarticulated melodic line. A perceivable pattern of temporal space between attacks constitutes a rhythm.

The particular relationship between the two levels of usage for the term rhythm—specifically (as opposed to meter and tempo) and generally (as opposed to melody and harmony)—is peculiar to Western musical terminology. The double usage, however, is not. In modern Hindustani musical theory, for instance, music *(saṅgīta)* is divided overall into *svara* (scale degree) and *laya* (tempo); in Javanese *gamelan* music *(karawitan),* the corresponding overall bifurcation is *lagu* (melody) and *irama* (a kind of temporal density). In all three cases—Western, Indian, Javanese—the general term used to refer to temporal flux in music is also a term designating some particular aspect of temporal flux, presumably the most significant one for each culture: a change of rhythm in Western music is a change in the patterning of temporal flow; a change of *laya* in Indian music is a change in the rate of temporal flow; a change of *irama* in Javanese music is a doubling or halving of the number of secondary attack points between primary attack points—a change in the density of temporal flow—that is accompanied by a modest adjustment downward or upward, respectively, in the overall tempo.

On the face of it, the specific Javanese concept *irama* (temporal density) seems more complex than Hindustani *laya* (tempo) or European rhythm (patterned succession of attacks), not only because tempo is always coordinated with *irama,* but also because two layers of attack pattern are explicit, a primary sequence moving faster perceived against a secondary sequence moving slower. But in fact, both tempo *(laya)* and rhythm (in the sense of "a rhythm") also imply at least two layers of motion even where only one is explicit. "Fast," "medium," and "slow" in musical time exist on a continuum, and they are relative proximately not only to one another but also ultimately to some sort of biological sense of a normal pace against which they are perceived; the heartbeat at rest, the breath rate at ease, or a comfortable walking pace have all been considered manifestations of that norm. Similarly, rhythmic patterns are necessarily separated one from another in some way and usually are also differentiated internally. The means of separation and differentiation are various—by shorter and longer durations between attacks, by softer and louder dynamic stress, by thinner and thicker textural density, by simple and complex (or "consonant" and "dissonant") simultaneous sonorities, by lower and higher pitch, by duller and sharper percussive sound, or by any combination thereof—but there is always at least a bipolar contrast, at least two structural layers.

As may be seen from several of the foregoing continua, rhythm is necessarily a part of the pitch and textural aspects of music as well, and one can speak of durational rhythm, accentual rhythm, textural rhythm, harmonic rhythm, melodic rhythm, or timbral rhythm, depending on which aspect is to the fore in any particular context. But a closer look shows that a separable sense of durational or accentual contrast is entailed in the pitch and texture continua in any case. Alternations in any of the last five of the six continua above (e.g., louder versus softer) will serve as a rough measure of time elapsed between successions on each level (e.g., between successive louds); thus, temporal duration is often a part of accentual and other rhythmic parameters. Similarly, certain extremes on any of the textural and pitch continua will sound out more prominently—being strikingly more or less complex in frequency structure or nearer to one end or the other of the pitch continuum—so that even in contexts without overt durational or dynamic contrast, accentual highlighting is often present.

Though both durational and accentual rhythmic distinctions play some role in most musical practices in any particular musical idiom, one or the other normally has clear primacy. A summary outline of the degrees of progressive temporal constraint in the modern Hindustani instrumental art-music tradition will illustrate the significance of durational rhythm as distinct from accentual rhythm and will at the same time introduce the important subrhythmic and superrhythmic concepts pulse and meter.

The first phase of improvisatory presentation of an Indian melodic type—the *ālāpa* of a *rāga*—uses longer and shorter note values contrasted in the purest possible way: they are irrationally related, indeed unrelated save in the contrast itself, occasionally garnished with rapid flourishes in extrashort values or broken up by extralong prolongations or pauses. The next phase of temporal constraint in Hindustani music (*nom-tom* in vocal music, *joḍ* in instrumental) introduces a link between longs and shorts in the form of pulse: though still in more or less random sequence determined entirely by melodic needs, longs and shorts are now proportionally related—usually as 2:1, occasionally as 3:1 or even 4:1—so that running through the whole is an underlying implied stratum of shorts, a unit value in terms of which all note values are counted out; the Greek theorist Aristoxenus called it *chronos protos.* In the third phase of temporal constraint (*jhālā* in Hindustani instrumental music), the sequences of pulsed longs and shorts are no longer rhythmically random, subordinate to melody: they are presented in various short repeating groups, rather like bits of Morse code, and have become rhythmic patterns, or simply rhythms. In the final stage of temporal constraint, meter is introduced: melodic-rhythmic patterns of whatever kind are brought under the control of a larger temporal span of constant duration—called a *tāla* in Indian music—that repeats cyclically and is moreover articulated within each cycle in its own way, independently of the melodic-rhythmic successions under its control. In many musical practices (including Indian), the sectional articulations within a single metric cycle are marked in performance, either instrumentally (with timbral or pitch contrast patterns on membranophones or idiophones) or with hands (in clapping or beating patterns).

As may be inferred from the orderly introduction of duration, pulse, rhythm, and meter one after the other, each of these four rhythmic dimensions must be deemed independent of the others, and they could theoretically be present in any combination. In the slow *khayāl* genre of Hindustani vocal music, for instance, the improvisatory *ālāpa* is accompanied by a *tablā* drummer. The drummer plays what Judith Becker has called (in quite another context) a "configurative drum pattern": a succession of timbrally and durationally articulated simple rhythmic patterns, in this case with an underlying regular pulse, is repeated over and over again to mark out the metric cycle of the *tāla* and articulate its internal segments. Such a configurative drum pattern in Hindustani music is called a *ṭheka,* and each *tāla* has its own. The drummer rigidly, almost mechanically, maintains a regular pulse and marks out the metric cycle; the singer's durationally irrational *ālāpa* phrases float and drift over the surface of pulse and meter. At the very end of each metrical cycle, at the approach to count number 1 of whichever long slow *tāla* is being used (a single cycle lasting as long as 30 to 45 seconds), the vocalist pulses his melody for a few seconds. The pulsed fragment is timed so as to reach the main note of a little fixed motive (around which the free-floating *ālāpa* is draped) precisely at count number 1, together with the drummer. In short, the vocal line is controlled metrically in the large, but is mostly without pulse or rhythmic pattern; often the succession of notes is so slow as to seem wholly arrhythmic; even when the attacks are close enough together to give a sense of rhythmic shape, it is still a purely durational contrast that is heard, without fixed proportion or rhythmic pattern. In other musical idioms, other combinations of independent rhythmic variables may be heard.

In Western European and some other musical idioms whose primary rhythmic manner is accentual, meter (in its sense of general measure) is conceptually prior to rhythm (in the sense of individual rhythmic pattern). Raw rhythmic matter is conceived as an endless stream of evenly spaced and unaccented pulses. Pulses are then grouped by regularly recurrent stresses; it is often said that even unaccented pulses will begin to seem regularly grouped if listened to for more than a few seconds. Groups of evenly spaced pulses (call them counts) are set off one from another by equally evenly spaced accented counts (often called beats), and these are the constituents of meters.

In Western practice, the recurring accented count in a meter (always reckoned as number 1) can receive its accent in a number of ways; one usually thinks of a louder sound followed by a given number of softer sounds, but a low sound followed by a given number of higher sounds, or a thick sound followed by a given number of thins, will do as well. A particularly significant convention through which metric accent is defined by texture and pitch relationships alone is the cadential form of a standard sequence of intervallic harmonies in Renaissance polyphony. It proceeds from a consonant preparation to a dissonant suspension and then on to a consonant resolution; cadential closure is possible when the consonant resolution is a harmonic interval that can expand or contract to a perfect consonance. This four-place harmonic and melodic succession—preparation-suspension-resolution-cadence—is always construed as weak-strong-weak-strong accentually and always defines those metric accents in the idiom to which it pertains. It is also the prototype, model, and underlying skeleton of what is called harmonic rhythm in Western tonal-harmonic practice of the 18th and 19th centuries. The unaccented pulse of harmonic rhythm is provided by regular changes of harmony, and the accentuation is provided by the particular harmonies involved. The four-place chord succession that corresponds to consonant preparation–dissonant suspension–consonant resolution–cadence, which may cycle back onto itself, is as follows. A harmony of any sort (but often a tonic or tonic-equivalent harmony) leads to an accentually strong harmony of the predominant class (often dissonant and often containing the tonic scale degree), which then moves on into an accentually weak dominant harmony (containing the leading tone and/or a dissonant fourth scale degree); the succession concludes with an accentually strong tonic or tonic substitute resolving the leading tone.

The distinction of durational rhythms and meters from accentual meters and rhythms has often been described with other pairs of terms: quantitative (durations) versus qualitative (accents), borrowed from poetic metrics, is one such pair. Particularly suggestive is the designation additive for quantitative meters and rhythms of the Indian type versus divisive for accentual meters like those of Western music; this distinction may be illustrated in the way nine-count meters are treated additively as opposed to divisively. As in Hindustani music, metric cycles and their internal articulations in Turco-Arabic music are marked off by configurative drum patterns called *uṣūl;* each meter is characterized by its own particular *uṣūl,* with strokes of contrasted timbres separated by pauses of a determined number of evenly spaced pulses or counts. The fast nine-count *uṣūl* sometimes called *aqṣaq ifranjī* has two units, comprising on the first level a four-count segment *added* to a five-count segment, marked as in Ex. 1. The deeper "dum" strokes mark off two

"beats" of unequal duration in pulses, in the proportion 4:5. The nine-count 9/8 meter of Western music, conversely, has three beats of equal duration, each in turn *divided* into three pulses, as in Ex. 2. Where

the grouping of pulses into beats in *aqṣaq ifranjī* is 9 = 4 + 5, in 9/8 it is 9 = 3 × 3.

In both Turco-Arabic music and Western polyphonic and tonal-harmonic music, all meters and rhythms are ultimately construed in terms of durational values of two and three. But where the larger rhythmic-metric numbers in the Near East are consequences of the addition of twos and threes and their sums, in Western traditional art music they arise as products of twos and threes and their multiples. In the Middle Ages and the Renaissance, in fact, the principle of systematically dividing or multiplying by two or by three was built right into the system of *mensural notation: every graphic symbol represented a relative value that could be either multiplied or divided by either two or three, except for the largest and the smallest. Little enough is left of mensural notation in modern Western notation (which is now all in duple proportion), but the underlying divisive rhythmic bias continues in force. Additive rhythms, however, became more familiar in the 20th century, largely under exotic influences.

Example 3 illustrates the principal rhythmic patterns of a quartet movement "alla bulgarese" by Bartók. It is indeed a Bulgarian dance rhythm, and like a number of Eastern European and Eastern Mediterranean musical types, it is almost certainly of Turkish origin—it has exactly the same (2 + 2) + (2 + 3) rhythm as the *aqṣaq ifranjī* quoted above. The upper line—representing a quiet and ubiquitous arpeggio motive and more vigorous stepwise diatonic melody—shows the pulse. The lower line is the underlying pattern of three unequal beats into which the pulses are grouped; it is played as an accompaniment figure, by the cello at the beginning of the movement, and is heard frequently throughout.

Patterning one or more movements of a cyclic instrumental work, such as a sonata, quartet, or symphony, on a traditional dance-music form—albeit often highly stylized and remote from actual courtly or popular dance—was a tradition in European art music for several centuries. More than that, it is symptomatic of the more abstract descent of many *topoi* and techniques of European art music from musical gestures associated with dance and other bodily movements. This points to another useful terminological polarity: speech rhythm versus body rhythm, or more narrowly, poetic rhythms versus dance rhythms.

Example 4 shows the rhythmic patterns of two moderately slow movements in triple meter from Bach's Partita in D minor for violin alone. Both are instances of common 17th- and 18th-century instrumental movements having titles of dances; these two dances, the sarabande and the chaconne, are said to have come from Latin America to Spain in the 16th century and from Spain to Italy and the rest of Europe in the 17th century. By Bach's time, both were completely stylized into instrumental types and were no longer danced. Their origin as dance is still reflected nonetheless, not only in the continuing succession of eight-measure segments, but even more in the characteristic "hesitation" rhythm, with its durational emphasis at the second count of almost every three-count measure. The sarabande rhythmic *topos,* like many other motives originating in dance rhythms, can still be recognized in movements not directly modeled on the stylized instrumental dance, such as the last movement of Brahms's Symphony no. 4 (a variation movement like the Bach chaconne) and the principal theme of the slow movement of Mozart's *Jupiter* Symphony K. 551.

Of course, not all body rhythms are dances. Physical labor of many kinds involves repetitive effort cycles, often in simple alternations, and accentual rhythmic music has always and everywhere been found helpful. A particularly fatiguing effort that has been traditionally enlivened by music with accentual rhythms is the day's march of infantry troops—and the military march accompanied by drums and trumpets has given rise to some of the fundamental rhythmic *topoi* of Western music. In the Viennese Classical style, the beat or roll of drums and the fanfare of trum-

= 46

4 + 2 + 3 / 8 ... etc.

4x 2x 3x

3. Bartók, String Quartet no. 5, third movement, "Scherzo alla bulgarese" (da capo mm. 2b–3b; cf. also mm. 1 ff).

4. Bach, Sarabande and Chaconne from Partita for unaccompanied violin no. 2 in D minor.

pets is the rhythmic source for many opening movements of instrumental pieces, e.g., Mozart's Piano Concerto in C major K. 503. The form of the *topos* here comprises the twofold statement of a motive that uses three unaccented shorts on the same pitch as upbeat to an accented long (which is often inflected or protracted, as in the first-movement themes of Beethoven's Symphony no. 5 and the trumpet fanfare that begins Mahler's Symphony no. 5). The slow-tempo, muffled-drum patterns used for processions at the funerals of important personages have given rise to a funeral-march variety of the military-upbeat *topos,* as in the "Marcia funèbre" movement of Beethoven's *Eroica* Symphony and the accompaniment rhythm of repeated chords that leads off the final ensemble of Verdi's *La traviata* (Violetta's death scene).

Repetitive rhythms rooted in bodily movements, whether of work or of play, lie behind much of the world's instrumental music. Repetitive need not mean monotonous, however. Repeating cyclic patterns may be very complex internally, for one thing; but in combination, even simple patterns may result in great complexity. Example 5 shows combined rhythmic cycles from a West African dance piece; it is played by an ensemble comprising three drums and a bell, to which is added the clapping of otherwise unoccupied dancers. There is a steady underlying pulse, and each pattern occupies a span of pulses numbering twelve or some factor of twelve. The high-drum pattern fills six pulses, the lead-drum and respond-drum patterns fill four pulses each; the lead drum, however, has three different four-pulse patterns, and a set of three makes up the full twelve-pulse metric cycle. The bell pattern, on which the other players rely for orientation to each other and for tempo control, also cycles only every twelve pulses; each of the successive clapping patterns fills six pulses, the first with three even claps, the second with four.

The individual rhythms are by no means without interest, but the greater effect arises from the polyrhythmic combination. Not only are the patterns at cross-rhythmic odds with one another's internal structuring, their metric cycles are also askew. Each metric cycle comprises twelve pulses, but they do not coincide; each has its own beginning–returning point. The only cycles that run simultaneously are those of the respond drum and the lead drum. The high-drum pattern has the same number of pulses as the patterns of the clapping cycle—six—but it begins and returns one pulse later than they do. The cycle of the guiding bell runs with neither the clapping nor any of the drum parts.

Rhythms rooted in bodily movements are always fundamentally accentual; rhythms oriented toward speech have more varied orientations. Some languages feature contrasts in syllabic stress, which (requiring effort) is closely allied to bodily movement. Some other languages rely on contrasts in syllabic length, especially as regards vowel quantity; the momentary continuation of breath requires little effort, so that contrast of longer and shorter temporal spans between consonant articulations constitutes the fundamental rhythmic feature of the language. When poetic language comes into the picture, a third possibility for speech rhythms—the mere number of syllabic attacks per line—comes into play. Musical rhythms based on duration or on a fixed number of attacks need not be tied directly to language, but in fact purely durational rhythms are most often found in musical cultures whose language rhythms are based predominantly on syllabic quantity rather than on stress. A setting of a Sanskrit text is likely to show long and short syllables clearly correlated with long and short durations, whereas in 19th-century Italian opera, musical rhythms will grow out of poetic rhythms based on both syllabic stress and on the number of syllabic attacks per group.

Musical rhythms whose fundamental property is the number of attacks in the pattern need not be connected with either speech or accentual rhythm. The most important cadential formula in South Indian drumming in unelaborated form comprises merely three groups

5. Polyrhythm in Eve dance music *Agbadza* after David Locke, "Principles . . . in . . . Eve Dance Drumming," *Ethno* 26 (1982): 235, Ex. 17.

of five strokes each; the individual strokes are contrasted timbrally, as represented by the onomatopoeic drum syllables *ta-diṅ-giṇ-ṇa-tom.* This five-stroke formula can be realized durationally in many different ways, depending on the pauses between attacks, and—especially in the versions with more pauses—on the manner of filling in with rapid flourishes between the main strokes.

A contrast with the fundamentally durational rhythms, even though beaten on a drum, of South Indian music is provided by George Gershwin's "Fascinating Rhythm," whose rhythms are accentual, precisely (as it turns out) because they are sung [Ex. 6]. Its three opening phrases make up 7 + 7 + 7 = 21 pulses, with 11 left over to fill out the 32 pulses of the four-bar phrase; in this it is similar to one of the South Indian *ta-diṅ-giṇ-ṇa-tom* patterns mentioned above. The song differs from Indian patterns, however, in one fundamental rhythmic particular that is clarified by the lyrics, which Ira Gershwin wrote afterward to fit the tune that his brother had already composed. Any version of any Indian rhythmic formula is an independent pattern; it is adjusted into the metric frame of a particular *tāla* merely by starting it in the right place. Whatever timbral or other accents there may be will be the same each time. In the George Gershwin song, conversely, normal English stress forces onto the second group of five shorts plus a long a dynamic shape that is completely at variance with the dynamic shape of the first group; the groups have been made to match qualitative musical accents already built into the 4/4 meter and the four-bar phrase, as may be seen in the stress patterns of their words, so that they have become completely dependent upon them. The third phrase is saved from rhythmic incoherence, cutting across the fixed metric accents as it does, by the secondary stress in "fascinating." In short, in this instance, George Gershwin's musical rhythms were originally metrically free of all but the four-bar period—they were in effect durational—but as soon as they got Ira Gershwin's English lyrics, they became accentual. See also Folk music II, 4.

Bibl.: Mathis Lussy, *Le rythme musical* (Paris, 1883; 4th ed., 1911); trans. Eng., *A Short Treatise on Musical Rhythm* (London: Vincent, 1908). Hugo Riemann, *System der musikalischen Rhythmik und Metrik* (Leipzig: Breitkopf & Härtel, 1903; R: Wiesbaden: M Sändig, 1971). Jaap Kunst, *Metre, Rhythm, Multi-Part Music* (Leiden: E J Brill, 1950). Curt Sachs, *Rhythm and Tempo: A Study in Music History* (New York: Norton, 1953). Bruno Nettl, *Music in Primitive Culture* (Cambridge, Mass.: Harvard U Pr, 1956). Grosvenor W. Cooper and Leonard B. Meyer, *The Rhythmic Structure of Music* (Chicago: U of Chicago Pr, 1960). Judith Becker, "Percussive Patterns in the Music of Mainland Southeast Asia," *Ethno* 12 (1968): 173–91. Steven Winick, *Rhythm: An Annotated Bibliography* (Metuchen, N.J.: Scarecrow, 1974). Wilhelm Seidel, *Rhythmus: Eine Begriffsbestimmung* (Darm-

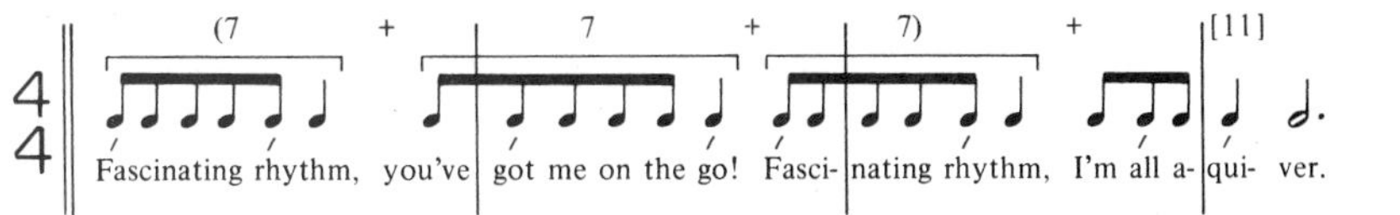

6. Music by George Gershwin, lyrics by Ira Gershwin.

stadt: Wissenschaftliche Buchgesellschaft, 1976). John Miller Chernoff, *African Rhythm and African Sensibility* (Chicago: U of Chicago Pr, 1979). Judith Becker, "A Southeast Asian Musical Process: Thai *Thăw* and Javanese *Irama,*" *Ethno* 24 (1980): 453–64. H.S.P.

Rhythm and blues [also rhythm 'n' blues, R 'n' B]. Black American popular music from the late 1940s through the early 1960s. It was predominantly a vocal genre, often used for dancing, that featured lead singers (e.g., Clyde McPhatter, Sam Cooke) who worked independently or as members of a (usually male) vocal quartet or quintet (e.g., the Ravens, the Orioles, the Drifters, the Coasters). Other group members harmonized using nonsense syllables ("ooo," "doo-wop") and catchy phrases ("shake, rattle, and roll"). A bass voice sometimes provided an independent lower line. Lyrics, increasingly oriented toward teenagers through the 1950s, concerned romance. Singers were often accompanied by piano, electric guitar, bass, and drums, with a prominent, honking tenor saxophone. Harmonic and metric structures were clearly derived from 32-bar popular song forms and 12-bar *blues, even when peculiarities of lyrics demanded adjustments in phrase lengths or sectional divisions.

These generalizations do not describe the whole phenomenon. "Rhythm and Blues" was as much an economic, sociological, and chronological designation as a musical one; *Billboard* magazine's R 'n' B Top 40 listed records by black artists that were hits in black communities from 1949 through 1964. Hence, urban bluesmen (Joe Turner, B. B. King) became R 'n' B artists by virtue of increased sales; they still shouted AAB blues lyrics to the accompaniment of 12-bar *boogie-woogie blues patterns played by a small combo. Conversely, some R 'n' B hit singles with a female lead singer (Dinah Washington, Ruth Brown), a backup group, or a prominent tenor saxophone were otherwise identical to urban blues.

In the mid-1950s, one branch of R 'n' B became *rock and roll, as white musicians usurped black creations and as black innovators (Chuck Berry, Fats Domino, Little Richard) reached white audiences. In the late 1950s, another branch merged with *pop music, as producers introduced plush arrangements with strings. In the early 1960s, a third branch became *soul music, as impassioned, screaming singing (Ray Charles, James Brown) gained widespread popularity.

Bibl.: Irwin Stambler, *Encyclopedia of Pop, Rock, and Soul* (New York: St Martin's, 1974). Don Heckman, "Straighten Up and Fly Right," *New World Records* 261, liner notes. Arnold Shaw, *Honkers and Shouters* (New York: Collier Bks, 1978). B.K.

Rhythmic modes. See Modes, rhythmic.

Rhythmicon. An electronic instrument designed to produce complex polyrhythms. It was built by Leon Theremin in 1931 at the request of Henry Cowell, who composed for it.

Rhythm section. The chord-playing, bass, and percussion instruments in a jazz or rock/popular music group; the players of those instruments. A standard rhythm section comprises keyboard and/or guitar, double bass (played pizzicato) or electric bass, and drums. In an organ trio (organ, guitar, and drums), the organist fulfills both keyboard and bass functions.

Rib. Any of the parts of the body of a stringed instrument connecting the back and the table or belly.

Ribattuta [It.]. In Italian and German music of the 17th and 18th centuries, a trill in dotted rhythm (long-short) beginning on the main note. It usually accelerates to end either on a **tremolo* (in early Italian vocal music, *ribattuta di gola*) or in an ordinary trill.

Ribibe, ribible. See *Rabāb,* Rebec.

Ricercar, ricercare [fr. It. *ricercare,* to seek; also It. *ricercata;* Fr. *recherché;* Ger. *Ricercar;* Sp. *recercario, recercada*]. An instrumental composition of the 16th and 17th centuries, of which two varieties existed concurrently: a rhapsodic type in homophonic texture and a polyphonic type that exploits learned contrapuntal artifices and is a precursor of the *fugue. In the 16th century, both types frequently appear in German, English, Spanish, and French sources titled, respectively, *prelude, *fancy, **tiento,* and *fantasia. They have sometimes served as *etudes or studies.

The ricercar often had a preludial function, "seeking out" the key or mode of a following song, *intabulation, dance, motet, psalm, or portion of the Mass (see W. Kirkendale, 1979). Frescobaldi specified toccatas before the Mass and ricercars (some preceded by a toccata) before the Eucharist. Although ricercars do not always stand directly before the piece they are intended to introduce, they are often arranged and identified by mode or key, simplifying selection of one to match the following piece. Ricercars may follow an intabulation of vocal music or other work. In many such cases the term seems to refer to "searching out" (using *paraphrase and *parody procedures) permutations and combinations of thematic materials drawn from the model, as in the *ricercari ariosi* of Andrea Gabrieli (Venice, 1571, 1605) and the *canzoni francese-recercata* for theorbo published by Filippo Thomassini (Rome, 1645). In the 17th century, ricercars could appear in sets with a preceding *toccata and following *canzona, or with just a toccata, anticipating the later prelude and fugue.

I. *The homophonic ricercar.* The earliest ricercars of the homophonic rhapsodic type appear in lute manuscripts of the late 15th century and Petrucci prints (1507–11; *GMB,* no. 63b). These were followed by organ works of Marco Antonio Cavazzoni (Venice, 1523) and of Claudio Maria Veggio (ca. 1510–after 1544) in the Castell'Arquato manuscript (see Slim, 1962; ed. *CEKM* 37). These thin-textured pieces lack formal organization and thematic unity and freely mingle chords with running passagework as in an improvisation. They are usually attached to a following intabulation or dance, though a few may have been played between verses of a **frottola* or dances in a suite, particularly those that modulate (e.g., dances on the **romanesca* and *cara cosa* formulas). Some are clearly intended as codas. Others, such as those by Joan Ambrosio Dalza (fl. 1508; *HAM,* no. 99a), are preceded by a **tastar de corde.*

After mid-century, the terms *tasteggiata, tastata,* and *toccata* ousted *ricercar* as a designation for preludial improvisationlike pieces. The term appears very frequently through the 18th century, however, being equated with testing the tuning of an instrument, cadential flourishes and difficult passages, or toccatalike compositions.

Instruction manuals such as those of Sylvestro di Ganassi dal Fontego (Venice, 1535), Diego Ortiz (Rome, 1553), and Giovanni Bassano (Venice, 1585; see Horsley, 1961) use *recercata* to identify either ornate pieces, for a single-line instrument, that explore a technical device, such as trill-like figures, running sequences, or double stops, or pieces that illustrate procedures for embellishing a line in a vocal ensemble work or for improvising over a *cantus firmus* or bass pattern [see *Glosa*]. As late as 1685, Domenico Gabrieli and Giovanni Battista Degli Antoni wrote ricercars for solo cello (*GMB,* no. 228) that are, in essence, etudes.

II. *The polyphonic ricercar.* Polyphonic ricercars, usually **bicinia,* by composers such as Lassus (Venice, 1585) and Giovanni Gentile (Rome, 1642) served as solfeggio exercises; and in his *Seconda parte del Transilvano* (Venice, 1609), Girolamo Diruta included 12 for keyboard that illustrate contrapuntal methods and may be used as exercises in transposition.

The polyphonic ricercar is sometimes (perhaps incorrectly) described as an instrumental counterpart to the motet. Many Renaissance instrumental genres were influenced by parallel vocal ones, but they were generally separate in development. Early works by lutenists Marco Dall'Aquila (Milan, 1536; *GMB,* no. 94) and Francesco Canova da Milano (1536ff.) and by organists Giacomo Fogliano (composed ca. 1530) and Girolamo Cavazzoni (Venice, 1543) and ensemble ricercars by Adrian Willaert and his circle printed in *Musica nova* (Venice, 1540) and by the publisher Antonio Gardane (Venice, 1551ff.) are all remarkable for their reconciliation of compositional procedures of the Josquin generation with the needs of idiomatic instrumental styles. Compared with the motet, thematic materials are generally more animated rhythmically and more angular melodically, the individual lines more sweeping. Even the earliest ricercars tend to divide into sections developing short points of imitation in a considerable number of entries, separated by episodes of running passagework and harmonic sequences that anticipate the fugue.

Mid-century lute ricercars approach the part-writing complexities of the ensemble and keyboard ones, especially those by Bálint Bakfark (Lyons, 1553) and Melchior Neusidler (Venice, 1566; Strasbourg, 1574) and the 24 in all modes by Vincenzo Galilei (Rome, 1563). The ensemble ricercars of Giuliano Tiburtino (Venice, 1549) and Annibale Padovano (Venice, 1556) and those of Jacques Buus (Venice, 1547, 1549) for organ and for ensemble sometimes derive subsequent subjects from the opening one, heralding the monothematic ricercar. The keyboard ricercars of the Neapolitan composers Rocco Rodio (Naples, 1575) and Antonio Valente (Naples, 1576) are notable for their sectional structure and passagework. Sebastián Raval's ensemble ricercars (Palermo, 1596) contain canonic procedures and are scored for an ensemble of bowed, plucked, and keyboard instruments. The ricercars of Andrea Gabrieli (ca. 1560–70; publ. Venice, 1589, 1595, 1596, 1605) are generally built from a few subjects; five of them are monothematic and treat the subject in augmentation, in contrary motion, and with regular countersubjects. These devices—as well as syncopation, diminution, and subjects that are chromatic, move only by leap, or are founded in solmization syllables—permeate the ricercars of Frescobaldi (Rome, 1615; Venice, 1635), turning the genre into a font of learned counterpoint, which it was to remain.

By 1632, ensemble ricercars disappeared, and by mid-century keyboard ones had taken on increasing severity and archaic connotations, the term being reserved for fugal compositions in long notes and *alla breve* meter—"in stile antico e grave," as Fabrizio Fontana (Rome, 1677) called his. Such works were composed by, among others, Frescobaldi's student Johann Jacob Froberger (1616–67), whose ricercars are all monothematic. Bach's *Musical Offering* (1747) contains two ricercars that are thought to serve as preludes to the first and second parts, although an acrostic identifies the entire work as a ricercar, its contents "seeking out" the many canonic and other guises in which the royal theme might be presented (see U. Kirkendale, 1980).

The connotation of a learned fugal piece *(Kunst-*

fuge) continued into the 19th century, and in this sense Beethoven described his *Grosse Fuge* op. 133 as "tantôt recherchée." Twentieth-century neoclassicism produced ricercars that evoke a similar meaning. The two in Igor Stravinsky's *Cantata* (1952) incorporate canons at various time and pitch intervals using inversion, mirror, retrograde, and retrograde inversion.

Bibl.: Otto Kinkeldey, *Orgel und Klavier in der Musik des 16. Jahrhunderts: Ein Beitrag zur Geschichte der Instrumentalmusik* (Leipzig: Breitkopf & Härtel, 1910). Gordon Sutherland, "The Ricercari of Jacques Buus," *MQ* 31 (1945): 448–63. Willi Apel, "The Early Development of the Organ Ricercar," *MD* 3 (1949): 139–50. Imogene Horsley, "The Solo Ricercar in Diminution Manuals: New Light on Early Wind and String Techniques," *AM* 33 (1961): 29–40. H. Colin Slim, "The Keyboard Ricercar and Fantasia in Italy, ca. 1500–1550, with Reference to Parallel Forms in European Lute Music of the Same Period" (Ph.D. diss., Harvard Univ., 1961). Id., "Keyboard Music at Castell'Arquato by an Early Madrigalist," *JAMS* 15 (1962): 35–47. Dietrich Kämper, *Studien zur instrumentalen Ensemblemusik des 16. Jahrhunderts in Italien, AnMca* 10 (1970). Arthur J. Ness, ed., *The Lute Works of Francesco Canova da Milano,* Harvard Publications in Music, 3–4 (Cambridge, Mass.: Harvard U Pr, 1970). Willi Apel, *The History of Keyboard Music to 1700,* trans. and rev. Hans Tischler (Bloomington: Ind U Pr, 1972). Eleanor Selfridge-Field, *Venetian Instrumental Music from Gabrieli to Vivaldi* (New York: Praeger, 1975). James Leslie Ladewig, "Frescobaldi's *Ricercari, et canzoni franzese* (1615): A Study of the Keyboard Idiom in Ferrara, Naples, and Rome, 1580–1620" (Ph.D. diss., Univ. of California at Berkeley, 1978). Warren Kirkendale, "Ciceronians versus Aristotelians on the Ricercar as Exordium from Bembo to Bach," *JAMS* 32 (1979): 1–44. Ursula Kirkendale, "The Source for Bach's *Musical Offering:* The *Institutio oratoria* of Quintilian," *JAMS* 33 (1980): 99–141. A.J.N.

Ricochet [Fr.]. See Bowing (5).

Riddle canon. See Canon.

RIdIM. Acronym for Répertoire international d'iconographie musicale [see Iconography of music].

Ridotto [It.]. (1) Reduced, arranged, e.g., for piano, from a work for ensemble. (2) [Fr. *redoute*] An 18th-century entertainment consisting of music and dancing.

Riduzione [It.]. *Reduction.

Rienzi [Ger. *Cola Rienzi, der letzte der Tribunen,* Cola Rienzi, the Last of the Tribunes.]. Opera in five acts by Wagner (to his own libretto, based on a drama by Mary Russell Mitford and a novel by Edward Bulwer-Lytton), produced in Dresden in 1842. Setting: Rome, about 1350.

Riff. In jazz, a short motive repeated over changing harmonies. It may serve as accompaniment or as melody and may be presented in call-and-response fashion with other riffs. Many hits of the *swing era feature riffs. The accompanying example, from Count

Basie's "Jumpin' at the Woodside," features two overlapping riffs repeated over the A sections of a 32-bar AABA song form. B.K., rev. T.A.J.

Rigaudon, rigodon [Fr.; Eng. rigadoon]. A cheerful Baroque dance movement in duple meter. It typically has a quarter-note upbeat, four-measure phrases in ¢ (or 2), and binary form. Often phrases begin with half-note motion, increasing to no more than eighths [see Ex.]. Like a *bourrée (from which it is sometimes indistinguishable), it is moderately quick, faster than a gavotte. It may have been based on one of the southern

Rameau, Rigaudon from *Les Fêtes d'Hébé* (1730).

French folk dances of the same name; it gained popularity at the French court after Lully's death (1687) and was quickly adopted in Germany and especially England. It was danced frequently in Rameau's operas. As independent music for instrumental ensemble or harpsichord (François Couperin, Telemann, Muffat), it retains the simple rhythms, phrasing, and homophonic texture of music to be danced. B.G.

Rigoletto. Opera in three acts by Verdi (libretto by Francesco Maria Piave, after Victor Hugo's drama *Le roi s'amuse*), produced in Venice in 1851. Setting: Mantua and environs in the 16th century.

Rigoroso [It.]. Rigorous, in strict time.

Rilasciando [It.]. Slowing down.

RILM. Acronym for Répertoire international de littérature musicale [see Periodicals].

Rim. The hoop affixing the head of a drum to the shell. Percussion parts may direct that the drum be struck at or on the rim. A rim shot is a loud stroke produced by striking the rim and the head simultaneously.

Rinforzando [It., abbr. *r., rf., rfz., rinf.*]. Becoming stronger, i.e., louder, usually over a shorter span of time than is called for by *crescendo;* also (sometimes *sforzato*) a sudden accent on a single note, similar to **sforzando.*

Ring des Nibelungen, Der [Ger., The Ring of the Nibelung]. A cycle of four operas by Wagner (to his own "poems," after Scandinavian, Icelandic, and Germanic sagas, including the *Nibelungenlied*), intended for performance on a preliminary evening and the following three days, respectively: (1) *Das Rheingold* (The Rhine Gold) in four scenes (composed in 1853–54), which serves as the prelude (*Vorspiel;* also termed the *Vorabend,* preparatory evening) to the entire cycle. (2) *Die Walküre* (The Valkyrie) in three acts (1854–56). (3) *Siegfried* in three acts (1856–71). (4) *Götterdämmerung* (The Twilight of the Gods) in a prologue and three acts (1869–74). The entire cycle was first performed in Bayreuth in 1876. The first poem to be completed, in 1848, was titled *Siegfrieds Tod* (Siegfried's Death). This was followed by *Der junge Siegfried* (The Young Siegfried), *Die Walküre,* and *Das Rheingold,* in that order. *Siegfrieds Tod* and *Der junge Siegfried* were then revised as *Götterdämmerung* and *Siegfried,* respectively, the entire poem in its present order being completed in 1852. Sketches of the music for *Siegfrieds Tod* were undertaken in 1850.

Ring modulator. An electronic device named for the characteristic arrangement in its circuitry of four diodes in a ring. It accepts two signals as input and produces as output frequencies that are the sum and difference of the two input frequencies [see also Electroacoustic music, Electronic instrument].

Ring shout. An ecstatic, religious dance of black American slaves. Prohibitions against dancing (crossed feet) and drumming engendered its circular shuffle step to the music of energetic spirituals accompanied by claps and stamps.

Ripetizione [It.]. Repetition; rehearsal.

Ripieno [It.]. (1) Played with doubled parts; *tutti. (2) In a Baroque concerto grosso, the larger ensemble, as distinct from the soloists [see Concerto (2) I, 1; see also Repiano]. (3) In Italian organs, the full organ with upperwork.

Ripieno concerto. See Concerto (2) I, 2.

RIPM. Acronym for Répertoire international de la presse musicale, an international index to 19th-century music periodicals.

Riposato [It.]. With repose.

Riprendere [It.]. To resume (the original tempo).

Ripresa [It.]. (1) Repeat, repetition. (2) Refrain [see *Ballata, Barzeletta*]. (3) In some 16th- and 17th-century dances and songs, a short instrumental passage occurring in conjunction with the repetitions of the principal sections; also termed ritornello [for bibl., see Passacaglia].

Riservata [It.]. See *Musica reservata.*

RISM. Acronym for Répertoire international des sources musicales; International Inventory of Musical Sources; Internationales Quellenlexikon der Musik, a project sponsored jointly by the International Association of Music Libraries, Archives, and Documentation Centres and the International Musicological Society. Activated in 1952, the project calls on each nation to submit to a central office its holdings of manuscript and printed music by composers active before 1800 and books about music published before 1801. That original plan, which was conceived as an updating of Robert Eitner's *Biographisch-Bibliographisches Quellen-Lexikon* (Leipzig, 1900–1904) and *Bibliographie der Musik-Sammelwerke* (Berlin, 1877), was expanded to include 18th-century anthologies, a separately published list of books, bibliographies on several special topics, and a directory of music libraries. The volumes are in three series, of which A and C are published by Bärenreiter (Kassel) and B by Henle (Munich):

A/I: *Einzeldrucke vor 1800,* 9 vols. (1971–81).

A/II: *Handschriften vor 1800.* National lists are being collected at the international RISM office in Kassel; the composite list is being published on the web by NISC (2001–).

B/I/1: François Lesure, *Recueils imprimés XVIe–XVIIe siècles* (1960).

B/I/2: François Lesure, *Recueils imprimés XVIIIe siècle* (1964).

B/III: *The Theory of Music from the Carolingian Era up to 1400,* vol. 1, *Austria-Netherlands,* ed. Joseph Smits van Waesberghe (1961); vol. 2, *Italy,* ed. Pieter Fischer (1968); vol. 3, *Manuscripts from the Carolingian Era up to c. 1500 in the Federal Republic of Germany* (D-brd), ed. Michel Huglo and Christian Meyer (1986); vol. 4, *Manuscripts from the Carolingian Era up to c. 1500 in Great Britain and the United States of America: Descriptive Catalogue,* ed. Michel Huglo and Nancy C. Phillips (1992); vol. 5, *The Theory of Music: Manuscripts from the Carolingian Era up to c. 1500 in the Czech Republik, Poland, Portugal and Spain: Descriptive Catalogue,* ed. Christian Meyer, Elzbieta Witkowska-Zaremba, and Karl Werner Güpel (1997); vol. 6, *The Theory of Music from the Carolingian Era up to c. 1500: Descriptive Catalogue of Manuscripts: Nachträge zu Italien und Frankreich,* ed. Cesarino Ruino, Michel Huglo, and Claire Maître (forthcoming).

B/IV/1–2: Gilbert Reaney, *Manuscripts of Polyphonic Music,* vol. 1, *11th–Early 14th Century* (1966); vol. 2, ca. 1320–1400 (1969); suppl., 1100–1400, ed. Andrew Walthey (1993).

B/IV/3–4: Kurt von Fischer and Max Lütolf, *Handschriften mit mehrstimmiger Musik des 14., 15. und*

16. Jahrhunderts, vol. 3, *Austria bis France* (1972); vol. 4, *Great Britain bis Yugoslavia* (1972).

B/IV/5: Nanie Bridgman, *Manuscrits de musique polyphonique, XVe et XVIe siècles: Italie* (1991).

B/V/1: Heinrich Husmann, *Tropen- und Sequenzenhandschriften* (1964).

B/V/2: Nancy van Deusen, *Katalog der mittelalterlichen Sequenzen* (in preparation).

B/VI: François Lesure, *Écrits imprimés concernant la musique,* 2 vols. (1971).

B/VII/1: Wolfgang Boetticher, *Handschriftlich überlieferte Lauten- und Gitarrentabulaturen des 15. bis 18. Jahrhunderts* (1978).

B/VIII/1: Konrad Ameln, Marcus Jenny, and Walther Lipphardt, *Das deutsche Kirchenlied. Kritische Gesamtausgabe der Melodien,* vol. 1, *Verzeichnis* (1975); vol. 2, *Verzeichnis/Register* (1980).

B/IX/1/1–2: Israel Adler, *Hebrew Notated Manuscript Sources up to circa 1840: A Descriptive Catalogue with a Checklist of Printed Sources* (1989).

B/IX/2: Israel Adler, *Hebrew Writings Concerning Music* (1975).

B/X: Amnon Shiloah, *The Theory of Music in Arabic Writings (ca. 900–1900)* (1979).

B/XI: Thomas J. Mathiesen, *Ancient Greek Music Theory: A Catalogue Raisonné of Manuscripts* (1988).

B/XII: Mohammad Taghi Massoudieh, *Manuscrits persans concernant la musique* (1996).

B/XIII/1: Jan Kouba and Maria Skalicka, *Hymnologica Bohemica et Slovaca* (forthcoming).

B/XIII/2: Leon Witowski, *Hymnologica Polonica* (forthcoming).

B/XIII: Gerhard Schuhmacher, *Hymnologica Sorbica* (forthcoming).

B/XIV/1: Michel Huglo, *Les Manuscrits du processionnal, I: Autriche à Espagne* (1999).

B/XIV/1: Michel Huglo, *Les Manuscrits du processionnal, II* (forthcoming).

C: *Directory of Music Research Libraries,* ed. Rita Benton, vol. 1, *Canada and the United States* (1967; 2nd ed., 1983); vol. 2, *Thirteen European Countries* (1970); *Austria, Belgium, Switzerland, Germany, Denmark, Spain* (2nd rev. ed., 2001); vol. 3, *Spain, France, Italy, Portugal* (1972); vol. 3/1: *France, Finland, United Kingdom, Ireland, Luxembourg, Norway, Netherlands, Portugal, Sweden* (2nd rev. ed., 2001); vol. 4, *Australia, Israel, Japan, New Zealand* (1979); vol. 5, *Czechoslovakia, Hungary, Poland, Yugoslavia* (1985); supp., *RISM-Bibliothekssigel, Gesamtverseichnis* (1999). H.E.S., rev. L.C.

Risoluto [It.] Resolute, energetic.

Rispetto [It.]. A stanza of poetry consisting of eight 11-syllable lines with the rhyme scheme abababcc or ababccdd. Poems in this form were set polyphonically in the 14th century and in the **frottola* repertory of the 15th and 16th centuries [see also *Strambotto*].

Risposta [It.]. In a fugue, an answer.

Risqolo [Syrian]. In *Syrian chant, an original monostrophic melody used as a model for other strophes of similar rhythmic pattern. It is the precursor of the Byzantine *automelon* [see *Idiomelon*]. D.E.C.

Ritardando [It., abbr. *rit., ritard.*]. Slowing down gradually; also indicated by *rallentando* [see also *Ritenuto*].

Ritenuto [It.]. Held back, slowed down; usually a more sudden reduction in tempo than called for by *ritardando* and *rallentando.*

Rite of Spring, The. See *Sacre du printemps, Le.*

Ritmico [It.]. Rhythmic.

Ritmo [It.]. Rhythm; for *ritmo di tre (quattro) battute,* see *Battuta.*

Ritornello [It., little return]. (1) In the 14th-century *madrigal and *caccia, the final couplet of the 8- or 11-line poem. The ritornello is set to different music and is often in a meter different from that of the preceding strophes of three lines. Despite the name ritornello, this final couplet is not a refrain, because it is stated only once. (2) In the 17th century, an instrumental section of an opera, cantata, strophic aria, or other vocal work. Ritornellos may be either recurrent, functioning as refrains, or nonrecurrent; in the latter case, the term probably refers to the "return" of the instrumental ensemble, not the thematic material. Ritornellos generally differ from sinfonias in being more dependent structurally on the vocal sections they punctuate, though considerable overlap in terminology occurs. (3) In the late 17th and 18th centuries, the recurring tutti section of a concerto movement or an aria [see Concerto (2) I, 2–3, II; Aria]. See also *Ritournelle.* E.K.W.

Ritornello form. The characteristic form of the first and often the last movement of a late-Baroque or Classical concerto, based on an alternation of tutti (ritornello) and solo sections [see Concerto (2) I, 2–3, II]. Ritornello form also occurs in concerto-based movements such as the choruses of many Bach cantatas, in which the choir functions as the "soloist." By extension, the term may be applied to movements without tutti/solo contrast (e.g., sonatas and ripieno concertos of the late Baroque, fugues) in which the principal formal event is the recurrence of the main theme in various keys. E.K.W.

Ritorno d'Ulisse in patria, Il [It., The Return of Ulysses to His Country]. Opera in a prologue and five acts by Monteverdi (libretto by Giacomo Badoaro, after Homer's *Odyssey*), produced in Venice in 1640.

Ritournelle [Fr.]. (1) *Ritornello. (2) In French stage music from the late 17th to the early 19th century, an instrumental prelude to an air or vocal ensemble, or a similar passage that serves as an interlude or conclusion [see also Ritornello]. Because French Baroque operas use triple meter and dances so extensively, the term has sometimes been mistakenly thought to denote a triple-meter dance form. B.G.

Rituale [Lat.]. See Liturgical books.

Riverso [It.]. Reversed; either *inversion or *retrograde.

Rivolto [It.]. *Inversion.

Robert le diable [Fr., Robert the Devil]. Opera in five acts by Meyerbeer (libretto by Eugène Scribe), produced in Paris in 1831. Setting: Palermo in the 13th century.

Rock. A popular music idiom related to, but in some ways distinct from *rock and roll. Beginning in the early 1970s, some writers began making the distinction to highlight the differences between the teen-oriented rock and roll artists of the 1950s and early 1960s and later groups such as the Doors, the Velvet Underground, and the Jimi Hendrix Experience. The differences include song topics, song length and form, stylistic range, and recording techniques. The Velvet Underground's "Heroin" (1967), for example, is a 7-minute, 10-second evocation of narcotic transcendence; the Doors' "The End" (1967) is more than 11 minutes of rambling stream-of-consciousness imagery laced with Oedipal references; and in Hendrix's "1983 . . . (A Merman I Should Turn to Be)/Moon, Turn the Tides . . . Gently Gently Away" (1968) we hear pop song, psychedelic soundscape, blues, and free improvisation woven together through the course of an ode to utopia beneath the sea lasting almost 15 minutes. Styles of rock songwriting and performance came to include elements of urban folk (Bob Dylan, "Like a Rolling Stone"), blues (Big Brother and the Holding Company, "Ball and Chain"), avant-garde concert music (the Velvet Underground, "Sister Ray"), English music hall (Kinks, "Village Green Preservation Society"), Indian raga (Beatles, "Within You Without You"), and virtually anything else that artists were willing to adopt, adapt, or experiment with. The music of the multiracial and mixed-gender band Sly and the Family Stone, under the direction of songwriter-musician-producer Sylvester Stewart, exemplifies rock's pluralistic spirit and eclectic range.

Together with a growing stylistic reach came an expanded menu of instrumental sounds and sound-processing effects. Recording practices, too, grew increasingly sophisticated and time consuming as multitrack recording increased to 4 tracks, then to 8, 12, 16, and beyond. Along with extensive use of overdubbing and a deepening interest in electronic sound manipulation, the increased complexity of the recording process extended to mixing. The mixing stage of recording projects, where multiple tracks are assembled to form a composite sound image, came to include its own set of compositional techniques and criteria.

While the musical differences between rock and rock and roll are significant, rock represents a further development of rock and roll fundamentals—including an emphasis on songs and singing, the backbeat, small amplified ensembles, recording, mass media exposure, and artists' public personae—subsuming both into a larger continuous tradition. Thus, many writers and artists make no distinction between the two, referring to the entire tradition as either rock and roll or rock. The continuity from rock and roll to rock is apparent in the work of groups like the Beatles and the Band. Both began as rock and roll bands and developed into rock bands. In the 1970s both the Band and John Lennon released albums of rock and roll covers *(Moondog Matinee, Rock 'n' Roll)* partly in tribute to the music that had shaped them. Further, in the decades following the 1960s there have been repeated efforts—the various manifestations of punk music, for example—to strip the music of what some have seen as mannered artifice and return, at least in spirit, to its rock and roll roots.

One of rock's key distinguishing traits is the presence and powerful influence of British musicians and songwriters. In 1963 the Beatles spearheaded the so-called British invasion, which the following year would populate the American sales charts with an unprecedented array of records by British bands. For the first time, an imported reworking of an American popular music idiom became better known than the original one. Many young American musicians learned their rock and roll not from Chuck Berry or Elvis Presley but from bands like the Beatles, the Rolling Stones, the Who, and the Kinks. Other significant factors in the music's development include a growing emphasis on record albums rather than singles, the rise of FM radio, and the growth of a concert culture with dedicated performing venues such as the Fillmore Auditorium in San Francisco, the Fillmore East in New York, and large-scale festivals such as Monterey (1967) and Woodstock (1969).

To a certain extent, rock represents the next phase in the experience of the rock and roll generation. As the young Americans for whom rock and roll was a source of both cultural and personal identity matured, the music reflected their changing concerns and interests. While such perennial pop song topics as romantic relationships remained central, new ones, like civil rights struggles, the Vietnam war, drugs, sexual freedom, and political protest, found expression in songs of the mid- to late 1960s. The influence of urban folk music, and in particular the songs of Bob Dylan, brought to the world of rock the idea that pop could encompass the entire spectrum of this generation's experience. Similarly, the wider embrace of stylistic elements from other musical idioms reflected the growing experience and increased awareness of artists and audiences.

The term rock eventually came to refer in at least a loose way to most popular music in the West after about 1965, and indeed the basic features of rock have remained, even as the music has continued to expand its scope of musical style and cultural expression. Emerging in the 1980s, *hip hop was seen by many as a new and distinct musical idiom, rather than a rock subgenre. Yet many of its artists refer to their own work as rock. With its particular emphasis on recording as both a means of production and a connection to the past (through sampling, allusive reference, and parody), hip hop would seem a fitting product of the rock tradition. Other subgenres include: glam (David Bowie, *The Rise and Fall of Ziggy Stardust and the Spiders from Mars*), *heavy metal (Black Sabbath, *Paranoid*), *soul (Aretha Franklin, *Lady Soul*), *punk (Sex Pistols, *Never Mind the Bollocks Here's the Sex Pistols*), *folk rock (Byrds, *Mr. Tambourine Man*), *new wave (Talking Heads, *Fear of Music*), *funk (James Brown, *The Payback*), disco (Donna Summer, *Love to Love You Baby*), bubblegum (Tommy James and the Shondells, *Crimson and Clover*), psychedelic (Jimi Hendrix, *Axis Bold as Love*), progressive (King Crimson, *In the Court of the Crimson King*), and techno (Moby, *Everything Is Wrong*), each of which claims subgenres of its own.

Rock music has proven extremely flexible in serving the needs of artists and audiences for a wide range of social activities and aesthetic expression. It has been, for example, the locus for gatherings of dancers from the sock hop of the 1950s to the techno raves of today; its songs have been adopted by an international public as anthems reflecting collective attitudes ranging from idealism (Lennon, "Imagine") to sports competition (Queen, "We Will Rock You"); and its records, played on the radio, have provided a musical soundtrack for the daily activities of millions. At the same time, it has provided a language for individuals with fertile poetic visions and sophisticated verbal and musical skills (Joni Mitchell, Paul Simon). It is, in some measure, rock's flexibility and inclusiveness that have made for its enduring appeal.

Bibl.: Steve Chapple and Reebee Garofalo, *Rock 'n' Roll Is Here to Pay: The History and Politics of the Music Industry* (Chicago: Nelson-Hall, 1977). Anthony DeCurtis et al., eds., *The Rolling Stone Illustrated History of Rock and Roll: The Definitive History of the Most Important Artists and Their Music,* 3rd ed. (New York: Random House, 1992). Gillian Garr, *She's a Rebel: The History of Women in Rock and Roll* (Seattle: Seal, 1992). Gerald Early, *One Nation under a Groove: Motown and American Culture* (Hopewell, N.J.: Ecco, 1995). Robert Palmer, *Rock and Roll: An Unruly History* (New York: Harmony, 1995). Paul Friedlander, *Rock and Roll: A Social History* (Boulder, Colo.: Westview, 1996). Charlie Gillett, *The Sound of the City: The Rise of Rock and Roll,* 2nd ed. (New York: Da Capo, 1996). Theodore Gracyk, *Rhythm and Noise: An Aesthetics of Rock* (Durham: Duke U Pr, 1996). Rob Bowman, *Soulsville, U.S.A.: The Story of Stax Records* (New York: Schirmer, 1997). Greil Marcus, *Mystery Train: Images of America in Rock 'n' Roll Music,* 4th rev. ed. (New York: Plume, 1997). Martin Strong, *The Great Rock Discography* (New York: Random House, 1998). Michael Hicks, *Sixties Rock: Garage, Psychedelic, and Other Satisfactions* (Urbana: U of Ill Pr, 1999). Eric Olsen, Paul Verna, and Carlo Wolff, *The Encyclopedia of Record Producers* (New York: Billboard Books, 1999). William McKeen, *Rock and Roll Is Here to Stay: An Anthology* (New York: Norton, 2000). Albin J. Zak III, *The Poetics of Rock: Cutting Tracks, Making Records* (Berkeley: U of Cal Pr, 2001). A.Z.

Rockabilly. One of the earliest styles of *rock and roll, emerging in the mid-1950s and combining elements and repertory from the blues, rhythm and blues, and *country music. Rockabilly style is infused with a driving, moderate to up-tempo rhythmic feel that permeates the musical texture, extending to the percussive "slapped" bass and to the so-called slapback echo effect. The latter adds a second layer of electronically generated attacks (echoes), which increase the density of the rhythmic fabric. Ensembles are usually small—perhaps only two guitars (at least one electric) and a bass—and singing is usually unharmonized and highly energetic. Many of the most prominent rockabilly records were produced by Sam Phillips for his own Sun Records in Memphis, Tennessee (Elvis Presley, "Blue Moon of Kentucky"; Carl Perkins, "Blue Suede Shoes"; Jerry Lee Lewis, "Whole Lotta Shakin' Goin' On"), and Phillips's sonic and musical sensibilities were important factors in the style's development.

Bibl.: Craig Morrison, *Go Cat Go! Rockabilly Music and Its Makers* (Urbana: U of Ill Pr, 1996). A.Z.

Rocket. See Mannheim school.

Rocking melodeon. *Lap organ.

Rock and roll. A popular musical idiom that emerged in the U.S. in the 1950s and quickly enjoyed worldwide dissemination and popularity, aided largely by radio, television, and film exposure. Adopted from song lyrics and referring at first to the *rhythm and blues repertory, the term rock and roll came to be applied to music covering a broad stylistic range and appealing primarily to young people, regardless of race or class. Many rock and roll records appeared simultaneously on pop, country, and rhythm and blues sales charts. Such early star performers as Bill Haley, Little Richard, Elvis Presley, and Chuck Berry show the influence of rhythm and blues in their many recordings of songs in 12-bar *blues form and in their high-energy performances with a rhythmic excitement based on an emphatic *backbeat. What eventually set the music apart from other idioms, however, was (1) the stylistic range of its songs, arrangements, and performances; (2) the youth-oriented tone of its lyrics ("Teen Angel," "School Days," "Summertime Blues"); and (3) its creative approach to sound recording. Records identified as rock and roll might bear the mark of country music (Everly Brothers, "Bye Bye Love"), Western swing (Haley, "Crazy, Man, Crazy"), gospel (Sam Cooke, "Bring It on Home to Me"), blues (Presley, "Mystery Train"), pop ballad (Johnny Ace,

"Pledging My Love"), or novelty song (Coasters, "Yakety Yak")—indeed, elements of discrete styles were often combined within a single track. The song topics, together with the images of young performers, helped make the music a significant component of teenage identity, setting the young apart from their elders as symbolized by the prominence of Bill Haley's "(We're Gonna) Rock around the Clock" in the soundtrack of the 1955 film *The Blackboard Jungle.* Sonically, the records—primarily 45-rpm singles—made little attempt at transparency. Instead, sonic manipulation in the form of electronic balancing, added echo and reverb, compression, and various kinds of timbral manipulation became an integral aspect of the music's overall effect.

Among the factors that made for the rise of rock and roll, the part played by independent record companies was crucial. In cities across the U.S., small operations such as Sun (Memphis), Atlantic (New York), Specialty (Los Angeles), King (Cincinnati), and Chess (Chicago) brought to the public musicians and songs in which the major record and publishing companies at first showed no interest. As independent releases won widespread success with young record buyers, however, a sweeping change took place in the popular music landscape. Many records by established African American performers crossed over from the rhythm and blues charts, long the province of independent labels, to the pop mainstream as white audiences increasingly tuned in to radio stations featuring a combination of high-energy music and such lively disc jockeys as Dewey Phillips and Alan Freed. The records themselves often had a sound as raw and electric as their performances, further distancing them from the more polished products released by the major labels. Further, the independents were quick to take a chance on young and inexperienced performers, both black and white, whose energy and image were thought to pack youthful appeal. Many of the songs recorded by the newcomers were covers of rhythm and blues hits, but increasingly rock and roll developed its own repertory of songs, written by such songwriters as Jerry Leiber and Mike Stoller as well as writer-performers such as Chuck Berry, Buddy Holly, and Carl Perkins.

The patchwork of musical styles identified as rock and roll in the 1950s and early 1960s resulted in part from record producers' uncertainty about the nature of the new youth market and its nascent aesthetic sensibilities. Experimentation was in the air as dozens of record companies across the country cast about for the combination of song, arrangement, and sound that would produce a hit. Among the rock and roll subgenres that resulted were rockabilly (Carl Perkins, "Blue Suede Shoes"), doo wop (Frankie Lymon and the Teenagers, "Why Do Fools Fall in Love"), surf (Dick Dale, "Let's Go Trippin'"), girl groups (Shangri-Las, "Leader of the Pack"), and uptown soul (Drifters, "There Goes My Baby"). Instrumentation usually included bass, drums, guitar, piano, and saxophones, but it is not uncommon also to hear strings and various sound effects. The fundamental role of records in developing and disseminating the music gave recording engineers, producers, and their studios key importance. Distinctive and influential contributions came from Sam Phillips at Sun Studio in Memphis; Cosimo Mattasa at J&M Studio in New Orleans; Norman Petty in Clovis, New Mexico; Jerry Wexler and Tom Dowd at Atlantic in New York; Stan Ross, Larry Levine, and Phil Spector at Gold Star Studio in Los Angeles; and the various Motown producers at Hitsville, U.S.A., in Detroit.

Bibl.: John Broven, *Rhythm and Blues in New Orleans* (Gretna, La.: Pelican, 1978). Colin Escott and Martin Hawkins, *Good Rockin' Tonight: The Sun Records Story* (New York: St. Martin's, 1991). Craig Morrison, *Go Cat Go! Rockabilly Music and Its Makers* (Urbana: U of Ill Pr, 1996). Nick Tosches, *Country: The Twisted Roots of Rock 'n' Roll,* 3rd ed. (New York: Da Capo, 1996). James M. Salem, *The Late Great Johnny Ace and the Transition from R&B to Rock 'n' Roll* (Urbana: U of Ill Pr, 1999). Anthony J. Gribin and Andrew M. Schiff, *The Complete Book of Doo-Wop* (Iola, Wis.: Krause, 2000). See also Rock. A.Z.

Rococo [fr. Fr. *rocaille,* rockwork, possibly combined with *coquille,* shellwork]. In the visual arts, a style originating in France in the last decade of the 17th century and extending to approximately the 1760s. It is characterized by ornamental delicacy, graceful elegance, and (often) sophisticated wit; it shows a general lightening in color and tone and a reduction in scale by comparison with the more serious, monumental Baroque. Recent scholars, however, have stressed the formal kinship of the Baroque and rococo styles, a kinship especially obvious in south German and Austrian architecture and in large-scale allegorical and religious painting such as that of Tiepolo.

In the study of music, the term rococo has been used in various ways, not always judiciously. Its most appropriate application is to French music of the same period as the rococo in the visual arts, particularly small-scale lute and harpsichord works (e.g., descriptive pieces of François Couperin), works for chamber ensemble (especially with flute), and *opéra-ballets,* as well as to comparable music by French-influenced composers such as Telemann. Such works provide direct equivalents for rococo art, not only in style—including retention of Baroque traits such as motivic play and relatively linear bass lines—but also in content (often amorous or witty) and patronage (aristocratic and upper-class).

Periodic attempts by musicologists to extend the term rococo to all European music of the time and, in particular, to the subperiod designated in this dictionary as early *Classical, have met with a number of difficulties. In the first place, the new **galant* or early Classical style had its origins in Italy—specifically, in Italian opera—and not in France, where it did not take root until decades later. Second, the patronage enjoyed by Italian opera of the period was mixed and partly public, whereas the patronage of the French rococo was aristocratic and mostly private; this difference appears most obviously in *opera buffa,* with its many popular elements. Finally, the new Italian style represents a significant break with the past, whereas (as noted above) true rococo maintains strong links with the Baroque. There are, of course, certain rococo aspects within the visual arts of Italy during this period, but few direct parallels with Italian music exist—certainly not enough to warrant application of the term to the entire subperiod.

Bibl.: Ernst Bücken, *Handbuch der Musikwissenschaft,* vol. 4, *Die Musik des Rokokos und der Klassik* (Potsdam: Akademische V-g Athenaion, 1927). Sidney Fiske Kimball, *The Creation of the Rococo* (Philadelphia: Philadelphia Museum of Art, 1943). Nikolaus Pevsner, *An Outline of European Architecture,* 6th ed. (Baltimore: Penguin, 1960). Michael Levey, *Rococo to Revolution: Major Trends in Eighteenth-Century Painting* (New York: Praeger, 1966). James R. Anthony, *French Baroque Music from Beaujoyeulx to Rameau* (New York: Norton, 1974; rev. ed., 1978). E.K.W.

Rodeo. A ballet in two scenes by Copland (book and choreography by Agnes de Mille) produced in New York in 1942. Copland excerpted and arranged four dance episodes from the work for orchestra.

Rohrblatt [Ger.]. *Reed; *Rohrblattinstrumente,* reed instruments.

Röhrenglocken [Ger.]. *Tubular bells.

Rohrflöte [Ger.]. *Chimney flute.

Rohrstimmen, Rohrwerk [Ger.]. The *reed stops of the organ.

Roi David, Le [Fr., King David]. Opera ("Dramatic Psalm") in two parts by Honegger (libretto by René Morax), produced in Mézières, Switzerland, in 1921. It was revised and performed as an oratorio in New York in 1925. Setting: the lifetime of the biblical King David.

Roll. On a drum, a rapid and continuous succession of indistinguishable strokes produced by the alternation of two sticks, on the snare drum usually L L R R, etc. It may be notated with the diagonal strokes of a **tremolo* or with the abbreviation *tr* (for trill).

Rolle [Ger.]. A *turn beginning on the main note, also called a *Walze* (F. W. Marpurg) or *geschnellter Doppelschlag* (C. P. E. Bach).

Rollschweller [Ger.]. On an organ, a roller pedal for obtaining a *crescendo.* See Crescendo pedal.

Rolltrommel [Ger.]. Tenor *drum.

Roman Carnival, The. See *Carnaval romain, Le.*

Romance. (1) [Sp.] *Ballad. The most characteristic type is in stanzas of four eight-syllable lines, with assonance in the even-numbered lines. Examples from the later 16th century and since sometimes include a refrain. *Romances* have been transmitted in large numbers both orally and in writing from the Middle Ages to the present. The publication of collections of such poems began in the 16th century. The repertory includes anonymous popular poetry, poems on epic and historical subjects (sometimes thought to be the earliest types), and learned poetry by known poets. They were sung from the earliest times, though relatively few melodies survive in early sources. The early 16th-century **Cancionero musical de palacio* contains about 50 polyphonic settings of such texts, presumably based on their preexistent melodies; the **vihuela* composers of the 16th century included a number of settings for voice and *vihuela* in their publications; and Francisco Salinas published some traditional melodies in his *De musica libri septem* (1577). The 17th century saw a flowering of polyphonic secular and sacred *romances,* similar in character to the polyphonic **villancico* of the period.

(2) [Fr.] Beginning in the 18th century, a lyrical, strophic poem on an amorous or epic subject; also a musical setting of such a poem. Composers of the 18th century, including Jean-Jacques Rousseau, cultivated a simple style in such works, some incorporated in *opéra comique* and others intended for private performance. The character of the genre changed considerably in the early 19th century, and it ultimately merged with the **mélodie,* though the term continued in use. See also *Romanza, Romanze.*

Roman chant. See Gregorian chant, Old Roman chant.

Roman de Fauvel [Fr.]. See *Fauvel, Roman de.*

Romanesca. A harmonic bass, widely used for the composition of *arie per cantar* and dance variations from the middle of the 16th through the 17th centuries [see Ex. 1]. Its provenance is uncertain; extant sources indicate that musicians in both Italy and Spain played a significant role in its early history. Because in *arie per cantar* singers improvised discant tunes to the bass pattern, many different discant melodies are found in extant versions of the *romanesca.*

1

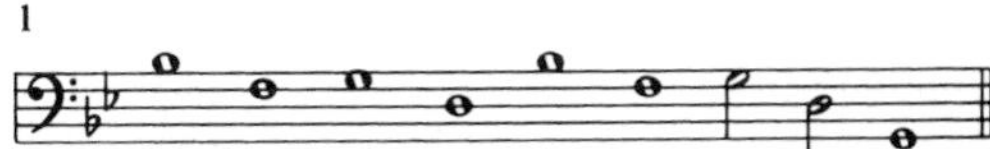

The isometric pattern cited in Ex. 1 developed over a long period. Many late 15th- and early 16th-century sources in both Italy and Spain include adumbrated examples that are more complicated rhythmically than the isometric pattern. Indeed, numerous variants existed side by side with the isometric pattern, under titles such as **Favorita, El poverin, La desperata, La comadrina, L'herba fresca* [Ex. 2], *La pigna, La meza notte, La canella, Todeschin.*

2

Among the earliest examples of pieces written on the isometric pattern are a "Gaillarde" in Pierre Attaingnant's *Dixhuit basses dances* (1530, fol. 24), a set of variations on "Guárdame las vacas" in Luis de Narváez's *Los seys libros del Delphin* (1538, no. 32; *MME* 3), "Ein gütter Venecianer tantz" in Hans Newsidler's lute tablature (1540, fol. E4), and a "Pass'e mezo a la villana" in Antonio Rotta's lute tablature (1546, fol. 18v). The earliest extant appearances of the title *Romanesca* with the bass pattern are in Alonso Mudarra's *Tres libros de música* (1546, nos. 14 and 23, "Romanesca, o Guárdame las vacas"; *MME* 7) and in Pierre Phalèse's *Carminum pro testudine liber III* (1546, no. 49, "Romanescha"). Settings also appear in 16th-century collections by Enríquez de Valderrábano (1547; *MME* 22; *HAM,* no. 124), Francesco Bianchini (1540s), Diego Pisador (1552), Diego Ortiz (1553), Bernardino Balletti (1554), Antonio di Becchi (1568), Adrian Le Roy (1568), Pierre Phalèse (1568, 1574), Antonio Valente (1576), Antonio de Cabezón (1578), Fabritio Caroso (1581), and many others.

In the 17th century, keyboard variations were written by Giovanni Maria Trabaci (1603), Ascanio Mayone (1609), and Frescobaldi (*HAM,* no. 192); strophic bass arias [see Aria] by Caccini (*Le nuove musiche,* 1601), Monteverdi (*Madrigali,* bk. 7), Stefano Landi (*RiHM,* vol. 2, pt. 2, pp. 91–92), and Kaspar Kittel (ibid., pp. 353–54); and violin variations by Biagio Marini (*HAM,* no. 199) and Salomone Rossi (*RiHM,* vol. 2, pt. 2, pp. 88–89). The pattern was also used for countless compositions for the guitar.

Bibl.: Otto Gombosi, "Italia: Patria del basso ostinato," *La rassegna musicale* 7 (1934): 14–25. L.H.M.

Romania. Before Romania freed itself from Turkish rule in 1878, its art music was cultivated primarily in church. Byzantine and Gregorian chant developed simultaneously, hymns were composed at the Cozia monastery during the 14th and 15th centuries, and Psalm settings employing the Romanian language became prevalent in the 18th century. Secular music was cultivated from the 17th century in courts such as those at Bucharest and Jassy (Iaşi). The establishment of conservatories at Bucharest and Iaşi during the 1860s and the founding of the Romanian Opera in 1877 encouraged the development of a nationalist movement, represented by the music of Alexandru Flechtenmacher (1823–98) and Isidor Vorobchievici (1836–1903). A renewed interest in folk music during the first half of the 20th century was manifested in the music of Mihail Jora (1891–1971, the founder of the Romanian Composers' Society), Sabin Drăgoi (1894–1968), Filip Lazăr (1894–1936), and most significantly in the "parlando rubato" style of George Enescu (1881–1955). Other significant composers of the mid-20th century are Ion Nonna Otescu (1888–1940), Martian Negrea (1893–1975), Theodore Rogalski (1901–54), Mihail Andricu (1894–1974), and Paul Constantinescu (1909–63). The next generation included Ion Dumitrescu (b. 1913), Gheorghe Dumitrescu (1914–96), Anatol Vieru (1926–98), Pascal Bentoiu (b. 1927), and Aurel Stroe (b. 1932). Romanian radio was begun in 1926, the Radio Symphony Orchestra in 1933, and a studio orchestra in 1955. The advent of socialism after World War II brought a reorganization of the system of musical education and formation of the Union of Composers and Musicologists (1949), the Institute of Ethnography and Folklore (1949), and a large number of state-controlled orchestras and opera houses.

The 1989 revolution had a minimal impact on Romania's musical life, but increased involvement in the international scene is evident in Bucharest's New Music Week, an international contest of contemporary music founded in 1991. The most recent generation of Romanian composers includes Costin Miereanu (b. 1943), Liviu Danceanu (b. 1954), and Adrian Pop (b. 1958).

Central to the language of Romanian folk music is the *doina,* a style of improvisatory melody constructed of established formulas; melodies employing this style emphasize D modes, the interval of a fourth, and a highly flexible *portamento style. Widespread are the *colinde* (carols [see Kolęda]) and fertility dances such as the *căluşul* or the *drăgaica.* An essential aspect of the dance style is the *aksak* rhythm, consisting of metrical combinations expressing the ratios 2:3 or 3:2. Other musical types are *bocete* laments, narrative ballads, shepherds' pastorals, *al miresei* wedding songs, and the more recent *hora* and *sîrbă.* Bartók found in the songs proper, which constitute the richest part of the repertory, a great variety of regional musical dialects, each with a distinct set of scales, cadences, and melodic formulas. A significant number of the folk instruments are aerophones: the *bucium* (*alphorn), the *cimpoi* (*bagpipes), and the *fluier* (flute); also important are the *cobza* (lute), **nai* (panpipes), and *tambal* (*cimbalom).

Bibl.: Nicolas Slonimsky, "Modern Composition in Rumania," *MQ* 51 (1965): 236–43. Benjamin Suchoff, ed., *Béla Bartók: Rumanian Folk Music,* 5 vols. (The Hague: Nijhoff, 1967–75). Viorel Cosma, ed., *Muzicieni români: compozitori şi muzicologi; Lexicon,* new ed. (Bucharest: Editura muzicală, 1970). Viorel Cosma, *Duoă milenii de muzică pe pămîntul României* (Bucharest: Ion Creangă, 1977). Vasile Tomescu, *Musica Daco-Romana* [Music of Romano-Dacia] (Bucharest: Editura Muzicala, 1978–82). Tiberiu Alexandru, *Romanian Folk Music* (Bucharest: Musical Pub, 1980). Corneliu D. Georgescu, *Jocul popular românesc: Tipologie muzicala* [The Romanian Folk Dance Melody: A Musical

Typology] (Bucharest: Editura Muzicala, 1984). Corneliu D. Georgescu, *Improvisation in der traditionellen rumänischen Tanzmusik* (Eisenach: K D Wagner, 1995). Paula Boire, *A Comprehensive Study of Romanian Art Song* (Lewiston, N.Y.: E Mellen, 2002).

Romanian (Romanus) letters [Lat. *litterae significativae,* significative letters]. Letters employed in conjunction with certain neumatic notations, notably that of St. Gall (but to some extent also those of Metz and Chartres; see Neume), to indicate aspects of pitch, rhythm, and performance presumably not indicated by the neumes themselves. They include *t* (for *trahere,* to drag, or *tenere,* to hold), *x* (*expectare,* to retard), *m* (*mediocriter,* moderately), and *c* (*celeriter,* quickly). They were attributed to a Roman singer named Romanus, said to have brought Gregorian chant to St. Gall in the late 8th century, and were described in a letter by Notker (*GS* 1:96; facs. in *PM* 4).

Bibl.: Jacques Froger, "L'épitre de Notker sur les 'lettres significatives,'" *Études grégoriennes* 5 (1962): 23–71.

Roman school. Composers of sacred polyphonic music active in Rome in the late 16th and early 17th centuries; principal among them is Giovanni Pierluigi da Palestrina (1525 or 1526–94), whence the term *Palestrina style to describe their music. Their unaccompanied or *a cappella* vocal music, with its controlled treatment of dissonance, is often regarded as representing a fundamental and conservative contrast with the instrumentally accompanied *polychoral works of the so-called *Venetian school of the period. Neither style, however, was limited to the city for which it is named. Composers sometimes identified as members of a Roman school include Annibale Stabile (ca. 1535–95), Giovanni Andrea Dragoni (ca. 1540–98), Giovanni Maria Nanino (1543 or 1544–1607), Francesco Soriano (1548 or 1549–1621), Ruggiero Giovanelli (ca. 1560–1625), Felice Anerio (ca. 1560–1614), Gregorio Allegri (1582–1652), Virgilio Mazzocchi (1597–1646), and Francesco Foggia (1604–88).

Romantic. A period in European music history usually considered to have lasted from the early 19th century until the modernist innovations of the early 20th and sometimes subdivided, with an early phase before about 1850 and a late one from about 1890. Terms such as pre-Romantic and neo-Romantic have been used for historical prefigurations and survivals of Romantic traits.

The word romantic derives from the romance [Fr. *roman*], a long narrative in prose or verse that arose in the Middle Ages and was the principal antecedent of the novel. Having no counterpart in Classical literature, the romance remained free of the limits and rules imposed on most literary genres with the revival of the Classical literary tradition in the Renaissance. Romantic thus came to signify freedom from the Classical tradition and, in its place, the uncontrolled play of the individual creative imagination, with resulting connotations of the highly idiosyncratic and even the fantastic.

German Romanticism arose in the late 18th century in opposition to the declining *Classical tradition. It was based on an almost mystical conception of the work of art and the creative artist. Art gave entry into a transcendent spiritual world, indefinable and infinite; this raised its creators out of the ordinary human sphere. Because the artist's primary obligation was to be true to his inner creative urges, Romanticism encouraged the breaking down of traditions of subject matter, artistic conventions, limits set to genres, canons of taste and beauty—all fundamental to Classical aesthetics. Romantic form often embodied the Romantic emphasis on the indefinable and the infinite, weakening Aristotelian concepts of beginning, middle, and end. Works were often intentionally given the character of a fragment or an improvisation. Music reached new extremes of lengthiness and brevity (the latter often found in the newly prominent genres of short piano piece and art song). The exploration of distant harmonic and tonal relations (previously used with great caution) and new kinds of texture and instrumental sonority contributed to the creation of new Romantic effects. Performers were no longer encouraged to add creatively to a composition through ornamentation; rather they became conveyors of the composer's "intentions."

Music was placed much higher in the Romantic hierarchy of the arts than in the Classical tradition, because the indefinable nature of its meaning made it quintessentially Romantic. Music was thus freed from the notion prevalent earlier that it had no intrinsic meaning; on the other hand, Romantic music became tied even more closely than before to literature and other extramusical elements through the belief that it could express their indefinable essence. This belief led to such typically Romantic musical genres as the *symphonic poem of Liszt and the *program symphony of Berlioz as well as to aspects of Wagner's music dramas and the subtle relations between poem and music in many *lieder. It also led many writers and critics to interpret works of *absolute music as if they were programmatic by adding extramusical narratives.

Early Romantic writers, such as E. T. A. Hoffmann, found Romantic traits in the works of 18th-century composers such as Haydn and Mozart. Beethoven's music was even more fertile ground. In the later 19th century, however, a school of Romantic composers directly and consciously influenced by Romantic thought and literature was usually said to begin with Weber (1786–1826), regarded as the founder of German Romantic opera, followed by Schubert (1797–1828), Berlioz (1803–69), Mendelssohn (1809–47), Chopin (1810–49), Schumann (1810–56), and Liszt (1811–86), although whether these men were all true Romantics was debated. The idea that the earlier Viennese masters embodied a Classicism fundamentally different from this Romanticism is connected with the growth in the 19th century of the misconception of *sonata form as a formula, which was seen to contrast with the (supposed) freedom of Romantic form, and a diminished estimate of Haydn and to a lesser extent Mozart as simply composers of charm and perfection, lacking in passion and daring. Beethoven escaped this distortion and continued to be regarded as a seminal influence by figures as diverse as Berlioz and Wagner (1813–83).

There are several problems with the use of Romanticism as a general period designation in music: (1) Romanticism is difficult to define both comprehensively and coherently in terms of musical style and technique because its emphasis on creative individualism and originality led to stylistic and technical procedures that often varied considerably. (2) The comprehensive use of the term obscures the varying degrees to which music of the period can be called Romantic. This usage does reflect the newly achieved dominance of German music. Yet there continued to be independent French and Italian traditions, increasingly influenced by German music and its Romanticism, but in selective, adaptive ways. And although a folk-oriented nationalism is an important strain in German Romanticism itself, the spread of musical nationalism in the later 19th century often involved, as with Mussorgsky (1839–81), the use of folk materials as a means of escaping German influence. (3) Some have argued that the term should be restricted to the first group of Romantic composers, mostly working before about 1850, and that to extend it as far as Mahler (1860–1911), Strauss (1864–1949), and beyond requires diluting its meaning so much that it ceases to be useful. (4) Longer historical perspective has led some to reject or qualify the older view of a Classical-Romantic polarity in music and to stress the elements of continuity over those of change, with Classicism and Romanticism seen as phases within the continuum of development. For these and other reasons, the more neutral term 19th century is now often used in place of Romantic to designate the period as a whole.

Bibl.: Jacques Barzun, *Berlioz and His Century: An Introduction to the Age of Romanticism* (New York, 1950; 3rd ed., 1969; rev. ed., Chicago: U of Chicago Pr, 1982). Rey Longyear, *Nineteenth-Century Romanticism in Music* (Englewood Cliffs, N.J.: Prentice-Hall, 1969; 2nd ed., 1973). Friedrich Blume, *Classic and Romantic Music: A Comprehensive Survey* (New York: Norton, 1970). Leon Plantinga, *Romantic Music* (New York: Norton, 1984). Gary Tomlinson, "Italian Romanticism and Italian Opera: An Essay in Their Affinities," *19th-Century Music* 10 (1986): 43–60. Carl Dahlhaus, *Nineteenth-Century Music,* trans. J. Bradford Robinson (Berkeley: U of Cal Pr, 1989). Carl Dahlhaus, *The Idea of Absolute Music* (Chicago: U of Chicago Pr, 1989). Peter Rummenhöller, *Romantik in der Musik: Analysen, Portraits, Reflexionen* (New York: Bärenreiter, 1989). John Daverio, *Nineteenth-Century Music and the German Romantic Ideology* (New York: Schirmer, 1993). Martin Geck, *Von Beethoven bis Mahler. Die Musik des deutschen Idealismus* (Stuttgart: Metzler, 1993). Hans Lenneberg, "Classic and Romantic: The First Usage of the Terms," *MQ* 78 (1994): 610–25. Charles Rosen, *The Romantic Generation* (Cambridge, Mass.: Harvard U Pr, 1995). Berthold Hoeckner, "Schumann and Romantic Distance," *JAMS* 50 (1997): 55–132. Mark Evan Bonds, "Idealism and the Aesthetics of Instrumental Music at the Turn of the Nineteenth Century," *JAMS* 50/2–3 (1997): 387–420. Celia Applegate, "How German Is It? Nationalism and the Idea of Serious Music in the Early Nineteenth Century," *19th-Century Music* 21, no. 3 (1998): 274–96. Ruth Solie, ed., Leo Treitler, gen. ed., *Source Readings in Music History,* vol. 6: *The Nineteenth Century* (New York: Norton, 1998). Jim Samson, ed., *The Cambridge History of Nineteenth-Century Music* (New York: Cambridge U Pr, 2002).

Romantic Symphony. (1) Bruckner's Symphony no. 4 in E♭ major, the original version of which was composed in 1874 and the revised version, in 1878–80. (2) Howard Hanson's Symphony no. 2, completed in 1930.

Romanus letters. See Romanian letters.

Romanza [It.]. *Ballad. The term was used by Rossini, Donizetti, and Verdi, though not always consistently, for a somewhat more intimate and less elaborate piece than an aria [see also *Romance, Romanze*].

Romanze [Ger.]. (1) *Ballad. The term was often used interchangeably with **Ballade.* Examples from the 18th century were similar in character to the French **romance* and include two collections by Johann Adam Hiller (1762 and 1767). The *Romanze* was often folklike and was frequently found in *Singspiel (e.g., Mozart's *Die Entführung aus dem Serail*) and opera (e.g., Weber's *Der Freischütz*). (2) In the 18th and 19th centuries, an instrumental work of lyrical character in a slow tempo, often in ABA, rondo, or variation form and sometimes part of a symphony or other multimovement work (e.g., Haydn's *La *reine,* Mozart's Piano Concerto in D minor K. 466). In the 19th century, the term was often taken as a title for *character pieces in a variety of forms (e.g., Schumann's *Drei Romanzen* op. 28 and *Albumblätter* no. 11).

Romanzen aus L. Tieck's Magelone [Ger.]. A cycle of 15 songs for voice and piano by Brahms, op. 33 (1861–ca. 1868), setting poems from Ludwig Tieck's *Liebesgeschichte der schönen Magelone und des Grafen Peter von Provence* (The Love Affair of the Beautiful Magelone and Count Peter of Provence).

Rome. The richness and diversity of musical life in Roman antiquity is amply attested in literary and historical references and in iconographical and archeological remains. Detailed accounts of music theory, however, largely continue the tradition of ancient *Greece and form the basis for the transmission of Greek theory to the Middle Ages. Musical instruments of the period include the *buccina, cithara* [see *Kithara*], **cornu,* **crotalum,* cymbals, drum, *harp, *hydraulis, **tibia,* and **tuba.* See ill. under Greece.

Bibl.: J. E. Scott, "Roman Music," *NOHM* 1:404–20. Günter Fleischhauer, *Etrurien und Rom,* Musikgeschichte in Bildern, II/5 (Leipzig: Deutscher Verlag für Musik, 1964). Günther Wille, *Musica romana* (Amsterdam: P Schippers, 1967). Id., *Einführung in das römische Musikleben* (Darmstadt: Wissenschaftliche Buchgesellschaft, 1977).

Romeo and Juliet. Works inspired by or based on Shakespeare's play include (1) A dramatic symphony for soloists, chorus, and orchestra by Berlioz, op. 17 (1839). (2) An opera in five acts by Gounod (1867). (3) A fantasy overture by Tchaikovsky (1869; rev. 1870, 1880). (4) A ballet by Prokofiev, op. 64 (1935–36).

Rom music. See Gypsy music.

Rondador [Sp.]. *Panpipes of Guatemala, Ecuador, and Colombia.

Ronde [Fr.]. (1) Whole *note. (2) Round dance.

Rondeau [Fr., pl. *rondeaux*]. (1) One of the three **formes fixes,* prominent in the poetry and music of France in the 14th and 15th centuries. During the second quarter of the 13th century, dance songs with refrains were emerging, many of them called simply *cançon de *carole,* or occasionally *rodet de carole,* referring to its choreography as a round dance. By the late 13th century the *rondeau* had begun to emerge as a form distinct from other *formes fixes,* notably the **ballade* and **virelai.* In its most common form it has eight lines in the pattern ABaAabAB (capital letters indicating a refrain), notable for its internal half-refrain. Music is provided for A and B and is repeated according to this pattern. In the 14th and, especially, later centuries, A or B might have two or three poetic lines, the latter never having more than the former.

The earliest surviving *rondeaux* in French are monophonic insertions in the *Roman de la rose ou de Guillaume de Dole* by Jean Renart (from before 1230). Despite frequent irregularities, all can be seen as having, in essence, six lines in the same poetic and musical pattern as the later eight-line *rondeau,* minus the initial refrain. In early examples, the words of the half-refrain A may differ slightly from those of A in the full refrain. In later poems, complete identity of the two is usual. Before the end of the 13th century, the initial full refrain is found in many examples.

Adam de la Halle (1245/50–85/88 or after 1306) wrote the first polyphonic settings of *rondeaux,* 14 of them, in a note-against-note style in three voices. Guillaume de Machaut (ca. 1300–77) composed 22 polyphonic settings, with one texted part and, most often, two untexted parts. His immediate successors, although preferring the *ballade,* wrote some *rondeaux* on the same plan. In the 15th century, the *rondeau* (its text now at times having 21 lines) was by far the most popular of lyric forms, numerous examples being composed by Dufay, Binchois, and many others. Instrumental introductions, the texting of all parts, and imitation were employed increasingly.

In religious drama at least as early as the 14th century, *rondeaux* were used to indicate the passage of time and to accompany scene changes. On occasion they were employed without any such implication or function. Secular *rondeaux* occurred in other sorts of dramas in the 15th century.

See also Chanson, Trouvère, Troubadour.

(2) In the Baroque era, a simple refrain form, usually employed in dance movements. The term is sometimes used alone as a title but does not have implications of tempo, meter, or texture. The first strain closes in the tonic (rather than in the dominant or the relative minor) and serves as a refrain or *grand couplet* to be repeated following the succeeding strains or *couplets,* which are often in related tonalities (Rameau) [see Rondo]. The number of *couplets* was never standardized. When a dance usually in binary form was so treated, it was said to be *en rondeau.* This was the norm for *chaconnes* and *passacailles* in France (Jean-Baptiste Lully, Louis Couperin) but was not unusual for gavottes, sarabandes, and minuets. In the early 18th century, character pieces were often treated in the same manner (François Couperin, Jacques Duphly).

Bibl.: (1) Pierre Aubry, "Refrains et rondeaux du XIIIe siècle," *Riemann,* 1909, pp. 213–28. See also *Formes fixes.*

(2) B.G.

Rondellus [Lat.]. (1) In Continental medieval treatises, the Latin equivalent of **rondeau.* (2) In 13th-century England, a technique of composition for three voices based on *voice exchange; a piece exhibiting this technique. The lowest voice (the tenor or *pes*) of an English *rondellus* may be an independent part made up of a repeated phrase, or it may participate equally with the upper voices in voice exchange. The parts begin together [see Canon (5) II]. Excluding any independent part, the voices of a *rondellus* all have the same melodic material (in phrases that remain intact throughout) but present it in different orders. Writing ca. 1300, the English theorist Walter Odington described the *rondellus* as a piece in which "what is sung by one may be sung by everybody in turn."

Rondeña [Sp.]. See *Fandango.*

Rondo [It.]. (1) A multisectional form, movement, or composition based on the principle of multiple recurrence of a theme or section in the tonic key.

I. *The rondo.* In a standard rondo, the principal theme or section (usually symbolized A), known also as the refrain or rondo, alternates with subsidiary sections called couplets or episodes (symbolized B, C, etc.); it then returns at or near the end to complete the movement. All statements of the refrain are normally in the tonic key, whereas the couplets or episodes favor contrasting tonalities. Thus, rondo form differs fundamentally from *ritornello form, in which the refrain recurs in various keys. The refrain itself is frequently in binary or rounded binary form and may be shortened or otherwise varied in appearances after the first; the systematic application of variation may produce a hybrid form known as a variation rondo [see Variation III, 2 (ii)]. Transitions and (especially) retransitions between sections are common, as are codas in all but the earliest examples.

Typical rondo designs include the two-couplet ABACA (common throughout the history of the rondo and its predecessor, the French Baroque **rondeau*), the multicouplet or serial ABACADA type (also characteristic of the *rondeau* as well as of early Classical rondos), the symmetrical or arched ABACABA scheme, and truncated forms such as ABACBA (a favorite of Mozart). Some writers also consider ABA (ternary) forms to be rondos (the "first rondo form" of 19th-century theory; see also Binary and ternary form).

The rondo originated in the French *rondeau* of the Baroque period, of which the rondo basically represents a Classical version. The principal agent in the shift from *rondeau* to rondo seems to have been Italian *opera buffa,* in which vocal rondos and rondo finales are common. In fact, most faster rondos retain elements of *buffo* style in the character of their melodies, the simplicity of their texture, and the clear sectionalization of their form. Rondo form also appears in serious opera, as in the well-known aria "Che farò senza Euridice" from act 3 of Gluck's *Orfeo* (ABACA).

Independent rondos, sometimes with slow introductions, were fairly common during the Classical period; notable examples are the rondos of C. P. E. Bach, Mozart, and Beethoven. During the Romantic era, the independent rondo was popular as a virtuoso display piece, as illustrated by works of Chopin, Mendelssohn, and Liszt. The greatest importance of the rondo, however, lies in its use as one movement of a larger work, in which function it provided the principal alternative to sonata and related forms. After ca. 1770, the rondo became the standard finale of the concerto and **symphonie concertante,* and it occurs in the same capacity in many sonatas, chamber works, and symphonies. Less complex rondo designs, especially ABACA, are also frequent in slow movements of both the Classical and Romantic periods.

II. *Sonata-rondo form.* As the name indicates, sonata-rondo is a mixed form incorporating the sonata and rondo principles in varying degrees. Typical sonata-rondos follow an ABACAB′A plan in which the first A and B are treated as the primary and secondary themes of an exposition (i.e., B is generally in the dominant or relative major), the C section becomes a development, and the second A and B (AB′) are treated as a recapitulation (i.e., both A and B are in the tonic [see Sonata form]). Nevertheless, sonata-rondos cover a broad range of structural types, from near-sonatas to near-rondos, and no single scheme can account for the many variants. Haydn, for example, often omitted the final B′ and A or merely the final A of the above scheme; the result inclines more toward an ABACA rondo in the first case, toward sonata form in the second (see, e.g., the finales of his Symphonies no. 88 and 103, respectively). By contrast, Mozart often omitted the third statement of A in his late sonata-rondos, avoiding a strong sense of recapitulation (as in the finale of his Piano Quartet K. 493).

Sonata-rondos appeared as early as 1768 in London, which was an important center of rondo composition (Pietro Alessandro Guglielmi, Cembalo Quartets op. 1 nos. 4 and 6; see Stern, 1979). Mozart first utilized the form in his String Quartet K. 157 of 1772/73 and his Symphony K. 181 (162b) of 1773, and it rapidly became a favorite type for Viennese Classical finales, doubtless owing to its fusion of the lightness of the rondo and the serious musical treatment of the sonata. Sonata-rondos continued to appear throughout the 19th century in instrumental finales by conservative Romantic composers (e.g., the finales of Brahms's Second and Third Symphonies).

(2) A two-section aria of the latter half of the 18th century, the first section slow, the second fast; both sections are usually repeated. In this meaning, the term is generally spelled *rondò.*

Bibl.: Witold Chrzanowski, *Das instrumentale Rondeau und die Rondoformen im XVIII. Jahrhundert* (Leipzig: A Hoffmann, 1911). Rudolf von Tobel, *Die Formenwelt der klassischen Instrumentalmusik* (Bern: P Haupt, 1935). Malcolm S. Cole, "The Development of the Instrumental Rondo Finale from 1750 to 1800" (Ph.D. diss., Princeton Univ., 1964). Id., "Sonata-Rondo, the Formulation of a Theoretical Concept in the 18th and 19th Centuries," *MQ* 55 (1969): 180–92. Id., "The Vogue of the Instrumental Rondo in the Late Eighteenth Century," *JAMS* 22 (1969): 425–55. Stephen C. Fisher, "Sonata Procedures in Haydn's Symphonic Rondo Finales of the 1770s," *Haydn,* 1975, pp. 481–87. Marion G. Stern, "Keyboard Quartets and Quintets Published in London, 1756–75" (Ph.D. diss., Univ. of Pennsylvania, 1979). Malcolm S. Cole, "Haydn's Symphonic Rondo Finales: Their Structural and Stylistic Evolution," *Haydn Yearbook* 13 (1982): 113–42. William E. Caplin, *Classical Form: A Theory of Formal Functions for the Instrumental Music of Haydn, Mozart, and Beethoven* (New York: Oxford U Pr, 1998).

E.K.W.

Root. In tonal harmony, the fundamental or generating pitch of a triad or *chord. If the pitches of a chord are arranged as a series of superimposed thirds, the lowest pitch is the root. A chord sounded with the root as the lowest pitch (even if the remaining pitches are not sounded as superimposed thirds) is said to be in root position. Otherwise, the chord is in *inversion. In *harmonic analysis, the root of a chord is represented by a Roman numeral that designates it as a particular *scale degree in the prevailing key.

Rorantists [Lat. *Collegium Rorantistarum*]. A chapel choir of nine singers established by Sigismund I in Kraków in 1543 to sing polyphony daily. It remained in existence until 1872. The name derives from a repertory of music and its associated votive Masses, which in turn take their name from the introit for the fourth Sunday in Advent, "Rorate caeli." Rorate chants, as the repertory is known, were sung first in Latin and then also in Czech from the 14th century until well into the 20th.

Rosalia [It., fr. the song "Rosalia mia cara"; Ger. *Schusterfleck*]. A pejorative term for a sequence [see Sequence (1)] that embodies exact transposition up a step.

Rosamunde. Incidental music by Schubert, D. 797 (1823), for the play *Rosamunde, Fürstin von Zypern* (Rosamunde, Princess of Cyprus) by Helmina von Chézy, produced in Vienna in 1823. Schubert composed no overture specifically for this work, using at various times instead the overtures to *Die Zauberharfe* (now called the *Rosamunde* overture) and *Alfonso und Estrella.*

Rose. In lutes and related instruments and in harpsichords, a round *sound hole in which a decorative, openwork carving has been inserted.

Rosenkavalier, Der [Ger., The Knight of the Rose]. Opera ("comedy for music") in three acts by Richard Strauss (libretto by Hugo von Hofmannsthal), produced in Dresden in 1911. Setting: Vienna, about 1745.

Rosin, resin. A hard, brittle substance derived from oil of turpentine. Rubbed on the hair of the bow of a stringed instrument, it leaves a white, powdery deposit that helps to create the friction required to set the strings in motion when the bow is drawn across them.

Rossignol [Fr., nightingale]. In the classical French organ, several pipes set in a metal container of water to produce bird sounds. J.T.F.

Rossignol, Le [Fr.]. See *Nightingale, The.*

Rota [Lat.]. A *round. The term is found only in the manuscript copy of *"Sumer is icumen in." See also Rote.

Rote. In the Middle Ages, any of several stringed instruments, including plucked and bowed *lyres and the *psaltery.

The word *rote* and a whole family of cognates occurs from the 8th through the 16th century in literary texts: *cruit* and *crot* in Gaelic, **crwth* in Welsh, crowd and rote in English, *chrotta, rota,* and *rotta* in Latin, *Rotte* in German, *rote* and *rota* in French. In most of these texts, it is clear that the word refers to a stringed instrument, but it is seldom clear just which instrument is meant. Some scholars believe that these words were generic terms that might be applied to any stringed instrument; others hold that each word denoted a specific instrument. Steger (1971) has proposed that these words are not true cognates but fall into two groups: one group (Gaelic, Welsh, English) denoting lyres and another (German, French, Latin) denoting psalteries.

In paintings, illuminations, and sculpture of the same period, three broad classes of plucked stringed instruments are depicted: *lyres, *harps, and *zithers. Because the pictures are seldom labeled and the literary references rarely descriptive, it is extremely difficult to match the names with the instruments. A carved figure at the Moissac cloister dating from ca. 1100, however, shows a man holding a triangular psaltery and is inscribed "eman cum rotta." A few medieval references give the number of strings or indicate whether the instrument was bowed or plucked. Occasionally these words are glossed by the names of other instruments: cithara, psalterium, lira, figella (fiddle). All of this evidence must be interpreted cautiously.

Bibl.: Hortense Panum, *The Stringed Instruments of the Middle Ages,* rev. ed. Jeffrey Pulver (London: W Reeves, 1939). Hugo Steger, *Philologia musica* (Munich: W Fink, 1971). Tilman Seebass, *Musikdarstellung und Psalterillustration im früheren Mittelalter* (Bern: Francke, 1973).

Rotrouenge, rotruenge [OFr.], **retroncha** [Occ.]. Any of a small number of poems (some with music) so identified (sometimes in the texts themselves) in the *troubadour and *trouvère repertories; only four survive with melodies. Occitan poetic treatises describe the *retroncha* as a love song with four stanzas and a refrain. Most of the extant self-identified *rotrouenges* and *retronchas* have text refrains. But refrains are not uncommon in the troubadour and trouvère repertories, and it is impossible to discern what makes these songs different from others that are not given this special designation. E.A.

Rotta. (1) [Lat.] A medieval stringed instrument [see Rote]. (2) [It.] In 14th-century Italian dances, an *after-dance, a metrical variant of the main dance (see *HAM,* no. 59a; *GMB,* no. 28). (3) In the 16th century, a rare term used to designate dances. The *Libro primo d'intabulatura da leuto* by Antonio di Becchi (1568) includes one *rotta* without choreography, which, following the older tradition, is in a simple quadruple (4/4) meter that contrasts with its preceding dance (p. 38, "Favorita e la sua rotta"). The *rotte* in Fabritio Caroso's manuals (*Il ballarino,* 1581, and *Nobiltà di dame,* 1600) are all listed as **sciolte* (after-dances) in his choreographic descriptions. The *rotta* incorporates a common group of steps that can be adapted to various *tempi* and can assimilate the style of other dances such as the **saltarello* and the **gagliarda* and on occasion the **piva.* L.H.M.

Roulade [Fr.]. An ornamental passage of melody, especially a vocal melisma in music of the 18th century. See Diminutions.

Round. A perpetual canon at the unison [see Canon (5) I, 4]. One singer or group begins an appropriately composed melody (e.g., "Three blind mice") and, on reaching a certain point, is joined by a second group that begins the melody. When the second reaches the same point, a third begins, and so on until all voices or parts have entered, which will have occurred before the first singer or group reaches the end and is itself ready to begin the melody again. On reaching the end, each part may return to the beginning immediately, and the piece may continue indefinitely or until one part has made an agreed-upon number of repetitions. See also Catch.

Rounded. A composition consisting of two sections, the second ending with a return to the material of the first, as in rounded binary form [see Binary and ternary form II]; also a composition in which the two principal sections conclude with the same material, as in many French **ballades,* the latter termed rounded chansons [see also *Rundkanzone*].

Roundelay [fr. Fr. *rondelet*]. In the 14th century, **rondeau.*

Round O. An anglicization of **rondeau* (2), found mostly in harpsichord and chamber ensemble music around 1700 (Jeremiah Clarke, Matthew Locke, Henry Purcell).

Rovescio [It.]. Either *retrograde (i.e., from the end to the beginning, as in the minuet of Haydn's Piano Sonata in A major Hob. XVI:26) or *inversion (as in the trio to the minuet of Mozart's Serenade in C minor K. 388 [384a]).

Row. An ordered set of the twelve pitch classes, as employed in the composition of *twelve-tone music.

Roxelane, La [Fr.]. Haydn's Symphony no. 63 in C major Hob. I:63 (completed by 1781). Haydn so named the work because the second movement is a set of variations on the French tune of that name.

Rubāb. A *long-necked lute of several Central Asian peoples, including Uzbeks, Kazakhs, and Tadjiks. See also *Rabāb.*

Rubato [It. *tempo rubato,* stolen time]. In performance, the practice of altering the relationship among written note-values and making the established pulse flexible by accelerating and slowing down the tempo; such flexibility has long been an expressive device.

Two varieties of rubato are usually discussed. In the first, the underlying pulse remains constant while the rhythmic values are minutely inflected. This was extensively done as an expressive nuance in the 18th century, especially in the solo part or melody of slow movements (the instrumental *adagio* and vocal *cantabile*) while the accompaniment held the beat steady. This technique is referred to by many contemporaneous writers, including Tosi, Quantz, C. P. E. Bach, Leopold Mozart, and Türk [for citations of their works, see Ornamentation, Theory]. Traces of it still occur in the 19th century, most notably in connection with Chopin (quoted in Edward Dannreuther, *Musical Ornamentation,* London, ca. 1895, 2:161).

The second type is the more common, present-day understanding of rubato. Changes in tempo and rhythmic figuration (**accelerando* and **ritardando*) are made in all parts at the same time without any compensation; the original tempo is simply resumed at the performer's discretion. Even though this expressive rhythmic freedom is frequently associated with the playing styles of 19th-century virtuosos such as Liszt, it is discussed by 17th- and 18th-century writers such as Frescobaldi (in the preface to his *Toccate e partite d'intavolatura di cimbalo . . . Libro primo;* Rome, 1615), Thomas Mace (in *Musick's Monument;* London, 1676), and C. P. E. Bach and Türk. Freedom of pulse for flexibility of declamation has always been an integral part of vocal *recitative, as it was of early *monody, being recommended in the preface to Caccini's *Le nuove musiche* (Florence, 1601/2) and in the works of many later writers.

A less common meaning for rubato may be found in Türk and in the *Musikalisches Lexicon* (Frankfurt am Main, 1802) of Heinrich Christoph Koch. They describe rubato as the displacement of normal metric accents within the measure, e.g., strengthening the second and fourth beats in a 4/4 meter.

Bibl.: Sol Babitz, "'Concerning the Length of Time that Every Note Must Be Held,'" *MR* 28 (1967): 21–37. Edward F. Kravitt, "Tempo as an Expressive Element in the Late Romantic Lied," *MQ* 59 (1973): 497–518. Sandra P. Rosenblum, *Performance Practices in Classic Piano Music: Their Principles and Applications* (Bloomington: Ind U Pr, 1988). Hao Huang and Rachel V. Huang, "Billie Holiday and Tempo Rubato: Understanding Rhythmic Expressivity," *Annual Review of Jazz Studies* 7 (1994): 181–99. Richard Hudson, *Stolen Time: The History of Tempo Rubato* (Oxford: Oxford U Pr, 1994). Sandra P. Rosenblum, "The Uses of *Rubato* in Music, Eighteenth to Twentieth Centuries," *Performance Practice Review* 7 (1994): 33–53. David E. Rowland, "Chopin's Tempo Rubato in Context," in *Chopin Studies,* vol. 2, ed. Jim Samson (Cambridge: Cambridge U Pr, 1994), pp. 199–213. See Performance marks, Tempo.

Rubeba [Lat.], **Rubebe** [Ger.]. See Rebec.

Rückpositiv [Ger.]. The *Positive division of an organ, whose pipes and wind-chest are in a wooden case located behind the player.

Rueda [Sp., wheel]. A round dance from Old Castile, Spain, in rapid quintuple meter and related to the Basque **zortziko.*

Ruf [Ger., call]. A congregational acclamation of one or two lines with origins in the Middle Ages, some examples of which, as with the related **Leise,* survive in *chorales.

Ruff. A common stroke on the snare drum, executed by the two hands in rapid alternation: ♬♪♩

Ruggiero [It.]. A harmonic bass of Italian provenance, popular from the mid-16th through the 17th century [see Ex.]. Alfred Einstein (1911–12) suggested that the title comes from the first word in Ludovico Ariosto's *Orlando furioso:* "Ruggier, qual sempre fui, tal' esser voglio." The word *Fedele* is sometimes substituted for *Ruggiero* and the piece labeled *Aria sopra Fedele.* The practice of chanting epic poetry to a skeletal bass is an old one; examples of its most developed form are found in Italian collections under the title "Aria per cantar ottave" [see also Aria]. A singer usually improvised a discant tune to the harmonic pattern represented by the bass, a fact that accounts for the many different discant melodies found in extant versions.

Many settings of the *ruggiero* have survived. An early example is the final *recercada* for viola da gamba and harpsichord in Diego Ortiz's *Tratado de glosas* of 1553. Others include keyboard variations by Giovanni de Macque (ca. 1580), Giovanni Maria Trabaci (1603), Ascanio Mayone (1603), Ercole Pasquini (ca. 1600), and Frescobaldi ("Partite 12 sopra l'aria di ruggiero," 1616; "Capriccio sopra l'aria di ruggiero," 1624; and "Capriccio Fra Jacopino sopra l'aria di ruggiero—Partite 6," 1637) and seven pieces in the Chigi manuscripts (ed. in *CEKM* 32). Lute settings are found in tablatures by Vincenzo Galilei and in English collections from ca. 1600 (see Gustave Reese, *Music in the Renaissance,* rev. ed., New York: Norton, 1959, p. 848, n. 130). A violin sonata was written by Salomone Rossi (1613; *RiHM,* vol. 2, pt. 2, p. 94), a two-voice aria by Antonio Cifra (*Li diversi scherzi,* 1613), a "Canzon Ruggiero" by Tarquinio Merula (1637), and a virtuoso solo aria by Kaspar Kittel (*RiHM,* vol. 2, pt. 2, pp. 349–51). Other musical formulas for singing verses of the *Orlando,* some of them titled *Ruggiero,* are found in 16th-century sources, but the pattern shown above was the most popular.

Bibl.: Alfred Einstein, "Die Aria di Ruggiero," *SIMG* 13 (1911–12): 444–54. Id., "Ancora sull' 'aria di Ruggiero,'" *RMI* 41 (1937): 163–69. Dragan Plamenac, "An Unknown Violin Tablature of the Early 17th Century," *PAMS* 1941: 144–57. L.H.M.

Rugwerk [Du.]. The *Positive division of a Dutch organ.

Ruhig [Ger.]. Calm, peaceful.

Rührtrommel [Ger.]. Tenor *drum.

Ruinen von Athen, Die [Ger., The Ruins of Athens]. Incidental music by Beethoven, op. 113 (1811), for a play by August von Kotzebue, produced in Budapest in 1812. It contains an overture, choruses, an aria, and a Turkish March (this last adapted from Beethoven's variations for piano op. 76, composed in 1809).

Ruispijp [Du.]. **Rauschpfeife.*

Rule of the octave [It. *regola dell' ottava*]. In 18th-century *thoroughbass practice, a scheme for harmonizing a bass line consisting of a scale that ascends and descends through an octave. Various such schemes were discussed by the theorists of the period.

Rumania. See Romania.

Rumba [Sp.]. An Afro-Cuban recreational event, dance, and accompanying music. The rumba, of which there are several named subtypes (e.g., *guaguancó, yambú, columbia*), is secular but contains elements from African-derived sacred traditions. It is performed by a vocal soloist and chorus with an accompaniment of two or three drums of the conga type (low-pitched *tumba,* often a *segundo,* and a higher-pitched *quinto*), a pair of wooden sticks *(palitos, cáscara)* beaten on a wooden surface, and sometimes *claves.* The rumba begins with a short introduction (*diana* or *llorao*) followed by improvised verses, both sections for solo singer with choral refrain passages; a third and concluding section is one of *call-and-response exchanges between soloist and chorus.

Adopted and transformed by Cuban urban popular ensembles, the rumba became known internationally in the 1930s. Although the term has been loosely applied, the popular rumba is most typically dance music in rapid duple meter, with the energetic character, emphasis on call-and-response patterns, and intricate percussion playing of its traditional counterpart. D.S.

Rundkanzone [Ger., rounded chanson]. A *bar form in which the *Abgesang* concludes with most or all of the material of the *Stollen.* The whole piece is in the form AABA.

Ruslan and Lyudmila [Russ. *Russlan i Lyudmila*]. Opera in five acts by Glinka (libretto by Valeryan Fedorovich Shirkov and others, after Pushkin's poem), produced in St. Petersburg in 1842. Setting: Russia in legendary times.

Russia. I. *Western art music and related institutions.* In land area, Russia is the world's largest country. Its population of 146 million people includes divergent ethnic groups, most of whom speak their own languages and maintain distinctive folkways, including music. While Russia was one of the 15 constituent republics of the former Soviet Union (1917–1991), the entire nation was rigorously unified by a cultural bureaucracy that covered all aspects of music making, from accreditation of performers through authorization for publication and the funding of musical collectives. Having absorbed prerevolutionary traditions and institutions, the communist Soviet government developed its own monopolistic structures for support and control of the country's musical creativity. Although this was accomplished at the expense of artistic freedom and self-determination, the state placed a high premium on music and music making as exportable commodities and a valuable source of international prestige. The end of communist rule, and the accompanying demise of a musical life lavishly subsidized by the state, found musicians ill-equipped to deal with the harsh economic realities and political instability of the postcommunist nation, as well as with the sudden marginalization of "serious" music. Many musicians emigrated. Musical life became more diversified and less centralized in the last decade of the 20th century, with new initiatives joining existing ones, but as Russia entered the 21st century it was still in a period of transition and few of its musical institutions could boast a sound infrastructure and stable financing.

1. Professional organizations. Following the collapse of the Soviet empire, the Union of Composers of the U.S.S.R., which had functioned as the most important musical organization in the Soviet Union, soon dissolved, ceding its assets to the existing affiliates on the republic and local levels. The Union of Composers of Russia became the national organization, an umbrella to large, autonomous branches in Moscow and St. Petersburg [formerly Leningrad], as well as regional branches around the country. Stripped of its political authority and influence, and most of its funding, in the post-Soviet period the union has continued to serve a useful function as an artistic guild. While composers and musicologists still aspire to membership, which remains selective, it is no longer obligatory for professional security and advancement, nor can it furnish the access to performance, copying, publication, and subsidized creative retreats that it guaranteed during the Soviet period.

2. Opera and ballet. The Bolshoi Theater (founded in 1776) in Moscow, the most prestigious opera and ballet company during the Soviet era, has been surpassed in stature by the Mariinsky Theater (1783) in St. Petersburg, which records and tours abroad under the name it acquired during the Soviet period, the Kirov Opera and Ballet. Moscow also boasts the Nemirovich-Danchenko and Stanislavsky Theater (1941) and St. Petersburg the Mussorgsky Theater (formerly the Maly; 1918), smaller companies that initially focused on more experimental ventures. Moscow's Chamber Opera Theater (1971) gained a reputation for its productions of both contemporary and 18th-century Russian operas. The Helicon Opera in Moscow and the St. Petersburg Opera are among the more successful of the new chamber companies started up in the 1990s. Additionally, some regional companies, like the Perm Opera, have gained recognition for the production of new or rarely performed repertory. Although in the Soviet period it was customary to perform Western operas in the vernacular, in recent years it has become more common to hear them performed in their original language.

3. Performing groups. Philharmonic societies established in major cities during the Soviet period remain the most prominent concert-producing organizations, offering subscription series of chamber and symphonic concerts. The Russian State Symphony Orchestra (formerly the State Symphony of the U.S.S.R.; 1936), the Moscow State Symphony Orchestra (1943), and the Moscow Philharmonic Orchestra (1953), all based in the nation's capital, were joined in 1990 by a new orchestra, the Russian National Symphony, the first to be created since 1917 independent of the government and supported entirely by private funding. Together with the Moscow Chamber Orchestra (1955), the Moscow Virtuosi (1979), the Moscow Soloists (1992), and many other chamber ensembles, they are now maintained through corporate sponsorship, cultural foundations, and extensive foreign touring. The Shostakovich Philharmonia in St. Petersburg hosts the oldest orchestra in the country, the St. Petersburg Philharmonic Orchestra (formerly the Leningrad Philharmonic Orchestra; 1882), which actually comprises two separate ensembles.

Choral activities, both professional and amateur, have traditionally been popular. Among the finest professional ensembles are the Sveshnikov State Academic Russian Choir (formerly State Academic Russian Choir of the U.S.S.R.; 1943), the Russian State Symphonic Capella (1971), the Moscow State Chamber Choir (1972), and the Choir of the State Academic Capella of St. Petersburg (formerly the Leningrad Glinka Academic Capella; 1763), the oldest Russian choral collective. The lifting of Soviet-era constraints on religious observance, together with the reconsecration of hundreds of Russian Orthodox churches, helped pave the way for a broad revival of the rich legacy of Russian liturgical music and the emergence of many new choral ensembles devoted to singing it.

4. Festivals, competitions, and prizes. The Moscow's annual Russian Winter Festival (since 1964) and December Evenings Festival (1981) have achieved international stature as showcases of Russian musical accomplishments in all spheres, as has the Stars of the White Nights Festival (1993; successor to the White Nights Festival established in 1965) in St. Petersburg. The Golden Mask Performing Arts Festival (1994) in Moscow features performances of, and awards to, the theatrical productions selected by a panel of experts as the best in the nation of the previous season. The Moscow Autumn Festival (1979) and St. Petersburg Spring Festival (1965) were established to highlight the work of contemporary composers from those cities, but both have expanded their reach to include music by other Russian and Western composers. With increased opportunities in the post-Soviet period, festivals of early and contemporary music became more widespread.

Soviet performers were encouraged to participate in regional, national, and international competitions, and the competitive urge has not diminished in the post-Soviet period. The Tchaikovsky Competition, established in 1958 and held every four years in Moscow, remains among the most important in the world, regularly attracting outstanding violinists, cellists, pianists, and vocalists. Distinguished contributions to musical life are honored by means of a number of prizes and titles. Among the most prestigious of these are the President's Prize of Russia and the title People's Artist of Russia.

5. Education. A complex network of specialized primary and secondary education in music set up during the Soviet period continues to provide early recognition, encouragement, and training both for potential professionals and for amateurs. Despite a broader range of educational options made available in the post-Soviet period, higher musical education still takes place primarily in conservatories, of which the oldest, the St. Petersburg Rimsky-Korsakov State Conservatory (1862), the Moscow Tchaikovsky State Conservatory (1866), and the Gnesin Russian Academy of Music (1944) in Moscow, are the most illustrious. Musicologists and theorists pursue advanced studies either in conservatories or in specialized research institutes such as the Russian Institute for the History of the Arts in St. Petersburg (1921) and the National Institute for the Study of the Arts in Moscow (1943). The doctoral degree is awarded after significant scholarly contribution to the discipline. The Glinka State Central Museum of Musical Culture (1943) in Moscow is a major archival repository.

6. Publishing, recording, and broadcasting. The successor firms to the publishers of music and books on music of the Soviet era are Muzyka and Kompozitor (previously Sovetskii kompozitor), the former based in Moscow and the latter, since 1993, the name employed by separate imprints in Moscow and St. Petersburg. In the post-Soviet era, the focus of music publishing shifted to pedagogical literature and the classics; the music of contemporary composers became a rarity. Musicological literature, often issued under the imprint of a conservatory or research institute, is typically subsidized by private donations or grants from foundations, Russian and Western. Popular titles can be found under a wide variety of nonspecialized imprints. Among the many new ventures, the Moscow-based DSCH Publishers (1993) has been active in publishing and promoting the music of Dmitri Shostakovich.

During the Soviet period, all Russian authors were obliged to affiliate with the All-Union Agency for Authors' Rights (VAAP). In the post-Soviet era, many exercised their right to choose whether to affiliate with Western agencies or with the Russian Authors' Society (RAO; 1993). The Soviet Union only ratified the Universal Copyright Convention in 1973. U.S. legislation implementing the General Agreement on Tariffs and Trade (GATT) in 1994 allowed for the restoration of copyright protection for many Russian works that had previously been in the public domain in the U.S., including the music of Prokofiev, Shostakovich, Khachaturian, Kabalevsky, and others.

Melodiia, the state monopoly for the production and distribution of all sound recordings during the Soviet era, continues its existence chiefly as an archival treasury of recorded sound. It has not been replaced by any major national producer; the recordings that are still frequently made in Russia are almost invariably produced by foreign labels. Similarly, the prominent position once occupied by broadcasts of academic music on radio and television in the Soviet Union has greatly diminished in the postcommunist era.

7. History. Although traditions of folk and liturgical music [see Russian and Slavonic chant] flourished in Russia from early times, the cultivation of an art-music tradition is a relatively recent development. The 18th century saw the rise in popularity of Italian and French opera at the imperial court, the genre that would dominate secular art music until well into the 19th century. Foreign composers, including Francesco Araja (1709–ca. 1770), Giovanni Paisiello (1740–1816), Guiseppe Sarti (1729–1802), and Catterino Cavos (1775–1840), dominated Russian musical life, and native-born composers, including Maxim Berezovsky (1745–77) and Dmitri Bortniansky (1751–1825), studied extensively in Italy. The beginnings of a distinctive national art music in Russia are usually traced to the performance of Mikhail Glinka's opera *A Life for the Tsar* (1836). Glinka (1804–57) is credited with creating a consummate fusion of the melodies, harmonies, and rhythms associated with the Russian national idiom with the forms and techniques of Italian opera, a fusion shown in this and other works. The characteristic Russian interest in brilliant orchestral tone color is also traced to his example.

Through Alexander Dargomyzhsky (1813–69), Glinka's legacy was passed to Mily Balakirev (1837–1910) and to the members of the circle of composers that grouped around him in St. Petersburg in the 1860s, the Mighty *Five (or Mighty Little Heap): Balakirev, Alexander Borodin (1833–87), César Cui (1835–1918), Modest Mussorgsky (1839–81), and Nikolai Rimsky-Korsakov (1844–1908). The group's members, none of whom had formal musical training, were united more by their opposition to Anton Rubinstein (1829–94), to the continuing dominance of Western musical influences, and to the formation of the country's first conservatories in St. Petersburg (1862) and Moscow (1866), than by common stylistic tendencies or progressive ideals, though all found folk music a major source of inspiration. Mussorgsky, the most original composer of the Five, combined a flair for the nuances of Russian musical "realism," with unusual harmonic juxtapositions and flexible, textually motivated rhythmic techniques in his songs and his operatic masterpiece, *Boris Godunov* (1869–72). After joining the faculty of the St. Petersburg Conservatory, Rimsky-Korsakov eventually became the elder statesman of Russian music and the chief link to its future generations.

Piotr Tchaikovsky (1840–93), educated at the St. Petersburg Conservatory and subsequently a professor at the Moscow Conservatory, developed a more catholic approach in his compositions without rejecting his national heritage. He was the first Russian composer to make lasting contributions to a wide variety of genres, including symphonies, concerti, program music, opera, ballet, chamber music, choral music, and songs. Later in the century, a new generation of nationalists trained by Rimsky-Korsakov at the St. Petersburg Conservatory, including Alexander Glazunov (1865–1936) and Anatoly Liadov (1855–1914), gained recognition, as did their Moscow colleague Sergei Taneev (1856–1915). A distinguished legacy of virtuoso performers, especially pianists and violinists, was also appearing. Sergei Rachmaninoff (1873–1953) and Alexander Scriabin (1872–1915), contemporaries as students at the Moscow Conservatory, pursued successful international careers as pianist-composers and interpreters of their own works. Scriabin's music incarnated the fascination with the symbolist aesthetic.

The startling originality and exoticism of 19th-century Russian music was fully exposed to the West through the lavish productions of Sergei Diaghilev in Paris beginning in 1907. His Ballets russes launched the career of the young Igor Stravinsky (1882–1971), most notably with the premiere of *The Rite of Spring* (1913).

The revolutions of 1917 were a watershed in Russian musical life, not simply because of the political and social upheaval. Many of the older generation of musicians had recently died, and others, including Stravinsky and Rachmaninoff, elected to pursue their careers in the West. Sergei Prokofiev (1891–1953), who received his musical education at the St. Petersburg Conservatory during czarist times, spent more than 15 years composing and concertizing in the West; he repatriated to the Soviet Union only in the mid-1930s. Among the many émigré performers who enhanced the legend of the Russian performance school were the bass Feodor Chaliapin (1873–1938), the conductor Serge Koussevitzky (1874–1951), the pianist Vladimir Horowitz (1903–89), the cellist Gregor Piatigorsky (1903–76), and the violinists Jascha Heifetz (1899–1987) and Nathan Milstein (1904–92).

Despite the upheavals, the period of the 1920s was marked in Soviet Russia by a spirit of artistic innovation that gave rise to many experiments, including a demonstration in 1920 of the prototype of the first electronic instrument by Leon Theremin (1896–1993) and a composition performed on the factory whistles of Moscow (1923). Soviet musicians kept abreast of the latest developments in Western music, and jazz was influential. By the late 1920s, a new generation of "Soviet" composers had emerged, headed by Dmitri Shostakovich (1906–75). Strong opposition to the avant-garde tendencies of many young composers, the formation of the government-sponsored Union of Soviet Composers (1932), and the rise of the doctrine of socialist realism ("founded on the truthful, historically concrete representation of reality in its revolutionary development") brought an end to the permissive period in Soviet culture, a move consolidated by the official condemnation in 1936 of Shostakovich's highly popular opera **Lady Macbeth of the Mtsensk District*. Over the next 20 to 30 years, Soviet music developed in relative isolation from Western musical influences.

Shostakovich reestablished his leading reputation with his Fifth Symphony (1937), which became a model for successful Soviet symphonic writing. Aram Khachaturian (1903–78) and Dmitri Kabalevsky (1904–87) also emerged as important Soviet composers, and all three gained international prestige. After his return to the Soviet Union, Prokofiev composed many of his most popular works, including *Peter and the Wolf* (1936), *Romeo and Juliet* (1935), and *Alexander Nevsky* (1938). The high visibility enjoyed by Soviet music was enhanced by the world-class performers who championed it, including the violinist David Oistrakh (1908–74), the pianist Sviatoslav Richter (1915–97), the cellist Mstislav Rostropovich (b. 1927), and the conductor Evgeny Mravinsky (1903–88). The war years saw energetic activity by Soviet composers, and Shostakovich's Seventh Symphony (*Leningrad*, 1941) became an international symbol for heroic resistance against fascism. In 1948, many of the most prominent composers—including Prokofiev, Shostakovich, and Khachaturian—were subjected to officially inspired attacks, and the rehabilitation of their stature, as well as that of many of their suppressed works, was accomplished only after the death of Stalin in 1953.

The latter half of the 20th century witnessed a gradual rapprochement with the modern compositional developments of the West, both in the works of the older generation and, more particularly, in the works of "nonconformist" composers who came to maturity in the post-Stalin period, including Edison Denisov (1929–96), Sofia Gubaidulina (b. 1931), and Alfred Schnittke (1934–98). These composers and others used serial, aleatoric, and other contemporary techniques, fusing them into distinctively individual styles. At the same time, strong ties to tradition were maintained in the music of composers like Rodion Shchedrin (b. 1932) and Georgy Sviridov (1915–98). The advent of the glasnost period sparked the discovery of many Russian composers—including Galina Ustvolskaya (b. 1919) and Alexander Knaifel (b. 1943)—previously unknown by audiences in the West. The widespread emigration by composers and other musicians following the disintegration of the Soviet Union left the musical life of Russia in disarray. At the beginning of the 21st century, the long-term consequences for Russian music remain unclear. What affords hope for yet another renaissance is the nation's undiminished and deeply ingrained love of music.

II. *Folk and popular music*. The Russian Federation sustains an ethnically diverse population that includes

70 distinct nationalities. The Russians, who make up about 86 percent of this population, descend from eastern Slavs who had dispersed into Russia, Ukraine, and Belarus by the 8th century. Orthodox Christianity, embraced in 988, remains the principal religion.

1. Folk music. (i) Ritual song. Until the early 1900s most Russians were peasants who engaged in agriculture and animal husbandry. Ritual life corresponded closely with nature's cycles; pre-Christian Slavs revered the sun and earth, and vestiges of this belief system became incorporated into Christian celebrations after conversion. Some ritual songs *(obriadovye pesni)* accompanied calendrical rites that marked the solstices and equinoxes, the changing seasons, and crop cultivation. Others pertained to life-cycle rites, of which women's wedding and funeral laments are particularly evocative. In general, songs reveal that the human life cycle and natural calendar were envisioned as metaphorically linked; thus plants and animals often symbolized human beings in song lyrics.

(ii) Secular song and dance. The secular domain featured narrative, lyric, and dance songs. *Byliny* (epic songs) related fantastical episodes of medieval Rus and its knightly, often supernatural heroes. Such epics, which date largely from the 10th to the mid-13th centuries, were likely composed and performed by *skomorokhi* and *gusliari,* professional court minstrels active from the 11th to the mid-17th centuries. In the late 1500s a briefer, more factual narrative genre, the historical song *(istoricheskaia pesnia),* emerged to chronicle significant events of Muscovite Russia and its rulers. "Songs of everyday life" *(bitovye pesni),* such as love, work, and family songs, provided entertainment and accompanied daily activities. On autumn evenings young women gathered for *posidelki* (work bees), singing such songs while they engaged in handicrafts. In late spring and early summer, women (and some mixed groups) performed outdoor ring and figure dances (sing. *khorovod*), whose open or closed circular form symbolized the sun, while singing moderately paced songs *(khorovodnye pesni).* By contrast, rapid dance songs *(pliasovye pesni)* using simple meters, symmetrical phrase structures, and short, repeated, rhythmic melodies accompanied solo *pliaski* (fast dances; sing. *pliaska*). In winter similar dancing took place indoors or on frozen rivers or lakes; it was also integral to weddings. The most widespread genre of *bitovye pesni* was the poetic, highly embellished protracted song *(protiazhnaia pesnia),* whose name derives from its slow tempo, considerable length, metric elasticity, and use of melismas, repetition, and other devices to draw out the text. In the 1860s the *chastushka,* whose brief, improvised, humorous, sometimes socially critical texts commented on current events and personages, became widely popular, and they remain so today. Sung for all occasions, they may be accompanied by balalaika or accordion and dancing.

(iii) Texture and timbre. Songs were rendered by both men and women, monophonically or polyphonically in regionally specific a cappella part-singing styles related to those of Belarus and Ukraine. Throughout Russia the latter were initiated by a leader and then joined by a chorus that improvised parts derived from an underlying melody, resulting in a largely heterophonic texture. Vocal production emanated from the chest and open throat except in Arkhangelsk, where women tended to sing in a high-pitched, "thin," head voice. In the north, monophony, wide unison, minimal heterophony, and homophony prevailed, while in southern regions a dense, compact, heterophonic texture featuring numerous variant parts and, often, a descant voice, was most common.

2. Instrumental music. Instrumental music making was predominantly a male activity. Indigenous instruments include two strummed or plucked, fretted, three-string wooden chordophones, the triangular balalaika and circular *domra;* the *gudok,* a vertical, wooden, three-string bowed lute with a tear-drop shape base and unfretted short neck; the *gusli,* a plucked zither; the *zhaleika,* a single-reed aerophone with horn-shaped bell; the *sopel,* a duct flute; the *kuvikly* (panpipes); the *ruzhok* (wooden trumpet), the chromatic *bayan* and diatonic *garmonika,* both button accordions; *loshki* (spoons); and *bubni* (tambourines). The *gusli* and *gudok* are ancient instruments once probably associated with the *skomorokhi* and *gusliari,* who likely used them to accompany their *byliny* and historical songs. The balalaika and *domra,* which date from at least the 1600s, were peasant instruments that accompanied song and dance. In the 1880s they were reconstructed by Vasily V. Andreyev (1868–1918) to facilitate the creation of large balalaika orchestras. Andreyev developed symphonic-like families of chromatic instruments—six customary sizes of balalaika and four of *domra*—and standardized their tuning. He combined these new chordophones with other traditional instruments, such as (modified) *gusli,* and symphonic instruments, like classical flute.

Andreyev's innovations permitted the performance of works written in western European four-part polyphony using major-minor tonality and chordal harmonies. His Great Russian Orchestra of Folk Instruments played arrangements of traditional folk dances and songs, new compositions written in a traditional vein, solo vocal and instrumental pieces with orchestral accompaniment, newly composed symphonic works (overtures, fantasias), brief tone poems or musical pictures, and transcriptions of well-known classical works, especially those by native composers. Similar mixed folk choirs, which first emerged in the 1860s on the basis of late 18th-century serf choruses, performed Russian and other Slavic songs locally and abroad, in arrangements and traditional form.

3. Folklife after 1917. Following the socialist revolution, folk choirs, orchestras, and dance troupes, singly and in combination, became the principal vehicles for folklore performance, which entailed stylized,

choreographed, and costumed theatrical productions of music and dance. Early groups, such as Andreyev's orchestra and the Agrenev-Slaviansky Cappella, became state enterprises and prototypes for the hundreds of other amateur and professional ensembles associated with workplaces, schools, unions, the military, and Houses of Culture throughout all Soviet republics. Such organizations reflected governmental concern with modernization, the development of Soviet culture, and aesthetic education through amateur involvement in the arts *(samodeitel'nost')*. Since the 1970s a few ensembles, such as that of Dimitri Pokrovsky (1944–96), have revived older traditions by learning performance techniques from villagers with whom they conduct ethnomusicological fieldwork.

4. Minority groups. Russia's 70 nationalities include at least 5 significant minority populations with distinct musical cultures: the Jews and Roma of western Russia; the Finnish-speaking peoples bordering Finland and the Baltic countries; the Finno-Ugric groups settled between the Volga and Urals; and the Turkic peoples of the Volga-Ural region and Siberia. Historically, many of these were indigenous peoples, some nomadic, whose music exhibited profound connections to nature and, often, shamanism. Pentatonicism and zithers figure prominently among Volga-Ural populations. The music of south Siberian groups, such as the Tuvans and Bashkirs, renowned for their biphonic ("throat") singing, is closely related to Central Asian and Mongolian traditions.

5. Popular music. Since the 1920s various jazz, pop, rock, and variety trends have flourished, with and without governmental sanction, especially in major metropolises. The Soviet administration promoted mass song (anthems, marches, patriotic songs, and contemporary lyric songs with socialist themes) and *estradnaia muzyka,* a category incorporating cabaret and show tunes, folk-chanson, and pseudo-operatic light pop songs with sentimental or optimistic texts performed by soloists and bands in state employ. By contrast, in the 1950s and 1960s solo male poet-singers, such as Vladimir Vysotsky, Bulat Okudzhava, and Aleksandr Galich, created "guitar poetry," an initially underground genre whose lyrics, set to simple, acoustic guitar accompaniments, offered comparatively honest commentaries on Soviet life. Such songs, like jazz and rock created outside official venues, were disseminated through an informal cassette culture *(magnitizdat)*. Ragtime, big band, and swing, once ideologically problematic, gained increased state support in the mid-1960s, as young people turned steadily to pop and rock, including numerous underground or semi-official heavy metal bands. Free jazz, rock operas, and avant-garde musical theater were important experimental genres in the 1970s and 1980s; some post-Soviet artists have combined rock and ethnic idioms to create new pop genres with a distinctively Russian sound.

Bibl.: *Western art music.* Gerald Seaman, *History of Russian Music,* vol. 1 (New York: Praeger, 1967). Boris Schwarz, *Music and Musical Life in Soviet Russia,* enl. ed. (Bloomington: Ind U Pr, 1983). Richard Taruskin, *Defining Russia Musically: Historical and Hermeneutical Essays* (Princeton: Princeton U Pr, 1997). Levon Hakobian, *Music of the Soviet Age, 1917–1987* (Stockholm: melos music lit, 1998). Francis Maes, *A History of Russian Music: From* Kamarinskaya *to* Babi Yar (Berkeley: U of Cal Pr, 2002).

Folk and popular music. Russell Zguta, *Russian Minstrels: A History of the Skomorokhi* (U of Pennsylvania Pr, 1978). S. Frederick Starr, *Red and Hot: The Fate of Jazz in the Soviet Union* (Oxford: Oxford U Pr, 1983). Gerald S. Smith, *Songs to Seven Strings: Russian Guitar Poetry and Soviet "Mass Song"* (Bloomington: Ind U Pr, 1984). Artemy Troitsky, *Back in the USSR: The True Story of Rock in Russia* (London: Omnibus, 1987). Elizabeth A. Warner and Evgenii S. Kustovskii, *Russian Traditional Folksong* (Hull: Hull U Pr, 1990). Thomas Cushman, *Notes from Underground: Rock Music Counterculture in Russia* (Albany: SUNY Pr, 1995). Susannah L. Smith, *Soviet Arts Policy, Folk Music, and National Identity: The Piatnitskii State Russian Folk Choir, 1927–45* (Ph.D. diss., Univ. of Minnesota, 1997). Izaly Zemtovsky, "Russia," in *The Garland Encyclopedia of World Music,* vol. 8: *Europe,* ed. Timothy Rice, James Porter, and Chris Goertzen (New York: Garland), 754–89. Laura Olson, *Making Memory: Russian Folk Music Revival and the Fashioning of Cultural Identity* (in press). I, L.E.F.; II, D.A.B.

Russian and Slavonic chant. The medieval, sacred plainsong of Russia and of the South Slavic lands. Both were entirely indebted to Byzantine forms that were brought over by Greek missionaries in the 9th century.

I. *Russia.* The monumental work of Saints Cyril and Methodios, who translated the Greek service books into Slavonic, also involved the transmission of *Byzantine chant, its notation, and its *oktoēch* [see *Ēchos*] organization. By comparative analyses with Greek sources, the earliest Russian musical manuscripts, which date from the late 11th century, reveal the coexistence of both archaic and contemporary notational features. The contemporary notational features (many also of Byzantine origin) identify *neumes that behave in ways quite dissimilar to those of Byzantium, and at least one, the *stopitsa,* is an original invention. Otherwise, the system in the Greek books that is most like the Russian system is an early version of the obscure Coislin notation as exemplified in the *Heirmologia* [see *Heirmos*] of the late 10th and early 11th centuries. In common with other chant dialects, Russian and Slavonic chant is entirely vocal, monodic, and unaccompanied.

Byzantine notation developed and evolved into less ambiguous forms, but the Russian neumes for a long time remained unchanged and unaffected by modernizations that took place elsewhere. Research has demonstrated that the earliest stratum of Slavonic chant was essentially a syllabic tradition. Among its monuments are the celebrated *Triodion* MS Chilandar 307 and *Heirmologion* MS Chilandar 308. The melismatic chants may be just as early as the syllabic chants, but there is no positive proof of this. The oldest florid melodies survive in five Russian **Kondakaria* that date from the 11th to the 13th centuries. These volumes correspond to the Constantinopolitan and Greco-Italian *Asmatika* of the 12th and 13th centuries, except that the neumatic notation of the former, known as *Kondakarion* notation, remains undecipherable, belonging as it does to an archaic stage of the paleobyzantine tradition. Using Greek books in round notation as controls, it is possible to make tentative transcriptions of the *Kondakarion* chants, basing conclusions on a comparison of centonate-formulaic designs. It has become obvious that for many Eastern liturgical chants, the Slavonic musical recensions are older and more authoritative than the Greek.

By the late 15th century, there emerged a new school of notation different in character from the Byzantine tradition. Neumatic nomenclature was arranged in alphabetic lists called *azbuki,* among which appear the terms **krjuk* (hook) and *znamya* (sign). Eventually the new chant received the name **Znamenny raspev* (chanting by signs), and it followed an independent development in Russia [see *Anenajki*].

II. *Serbia and Romania.* The year 1219 marks the independence granted to the Serbian Church under its first archbishop, St. Sava, by the Patriarch of Nicaea. Although there is a lack of musical documents from the earliest period, evidence from written sources suggests an active use of sung Offices in the new Serbian Church. The bulk of surviving documents of or connected with Serbian chant comes from the 15th to the 18th centuries. Recently, the names of a few significant composers have come to light: Stefan the Serb, Isaiah the Serb, and Nicolas the Serb. All three followed faithfully the Byzantine musical traditions, writing in the late kalophonic style of the 14th and 15th centuries. The existence of bilingual Greek and Slavonic settings identifies a mixture of linguistic usage in Serbian services.

With the advance of the Ottoman invasion, bearers of Byzantine culture tended to migrate north and west. The 15th century in Wallachia and the 16th century in Moldavia saw an extraordinary flowering of Christian art, architecture, literature, and music. In addition to chants written by Serbian and Greek composers, Romanians, still worshipping in Greek and Slavonic, produced their own scribes and musicians, including the monk Evstatie of Putna, Antonie, Theodosie Zotika, and Dometian the Vlach.

Bibl.: Erwin Koschmieder, *Die ältesten Novgoroder Hirmologion-Fragmente* (Munich: Verlag der Bayerischen Akademie der Wissenschaften, 1952–58). Carsten Høeg, "The Oldest Slavonic Tradition of Byzantine Music," *Proceedings of the British Academy* 39 (1953): 37–66. Raina Palikarova-Verdeil, *La musique byzantine chez les bulgares et les russes, MMB,* subsidia 3 (1953). Miloš Velimirović, *Byzantine Elements in Early Slavic Chant,* 2 vols., *MMB,* subsidia 4 (1960). Constantin Floros, "Die Entzifferung der Kondakarien-Notation," *Musik des Ostens* 3 (1965): 7–71; 4 (1967): 12–44. Dimitrije I. Stefanović, *Stara srpska muzika* [Old Serbian Music], 2 vols. (Belgrade: Muzikoloshki Institut Srpske Akademije Navka i Umetnosti, 1974–75). Ann E. Pennington, "Music in Sixteenth-Century Moldavia: New Evidence," *Oxford Slavonic Papers* 11 (1978): 64–83. Dimitri Conomos, "The Monastery of Putna and the Musical Tradition of Moldavia in the Sixteenth Century," *Dumbarton Oaks Papers* 36 (1982): 15–28. J. Roccasalvo, "The Znamenny Chant," *MQ* 74 (1990): 217–41. D.E.C.

Russian bassoon. A tall narrow variety of the *serpent with two parallel tubes in sections joined at the bottom in a wooden, bassoon-like butt joint. A mouthpiece and gracefully curved or looped mouth pipe or *bocal of brass leads into the top of the narrow tube. The upper part of the larger tube ends in either a wooden or metal bell or a fanciful dragonhead. Several varieties were made by at least 1788. They were more convenient to hold than the serpent, but they shared the serpent's playing technique and compass. R.E.E.

Russian horn. A straight or slightly curved metal hunting horn from about 30 cm to 2 m in length. A band of 37 such instruments, each playing only its second harmonic, was organized in 1751 by Jan Antonín Mareš (Maresch), horn player to the Empress Elizabeth of Russia. Such bands, which played marches, songs, dances, and the like, performed successfully until well into the 19th century.

Russian Quartets. See *Rasumovsky* Quartets; *Scherzi, Gli.*

Rute [Ger.]. A birch brush used in playing drums of various kinds. Introduced to Europe in the 18th century along with *Janissary music, it was largely replaced in the 20th century by the wire *brush.

S

S. (1) In current musical notation, abbr. for *segno, *sinistra, *soprano, *subito. (2) In liturgical books, abbr. for *schola. (3) In music of the 16th century, abbr. for *superius. (4) In the analysis of *functional harmony, abbr. for subdominant. (5) Abbr. for Wolfgang Schmieder's catalog of the works of Bach. See BWV.

Sacabuche [Sp.]. Sackbut [see Trombone].

Saccadé [Fr.]. Jerked, abrupt, especially with respect to a bow stroke.

Sackbut. The early *trombone.

Sackgeige [Ger.]. *Kit.

Sackpfeife [Ger.]. *Bagpipe.

Sacramentary [Lat. *sacramentarium*]. See Liturgical books.

Sacra rappresentazione [It.]. See *Rappresentazione sacra.*

Sacre du printemps, Le [Fr., The Rite of Spring; Russ. *Vesna svyashchennaya,* Sacred Spring]. Ballet ("Scenes of Pagan Russia") by Stravinsky (choreography by Vaslav Nijinsky, book by the composer and Nicholas Roerich, décor and costumes by Roerich), produced in Paris in 1913 by Sergei Diaghilev's Ballets russes. It is in two parts, titled *L'adoration de la terre* (The Adoration of the Earth) and *Le sacrifice* (The Sacrifice), each divided into several scenes.

Sacrificium [Lat.]. In the *Mozarabic rite, the chant corresponding to the Gregorian *offertory.

Saeta [Sp., arrow]. In Andalusia, Spain, a song sung to a passing religious statue or float (usually the Virgin Mary or Jesus) during the processions of Holy Week. The term implies a spontaneous eruption of sentiment such as characterizes the singing style of *flamenco music generally, to which the *saeta* belongs.

Bibl.: Diego de Valencina, *Historia documentada de la saeta* (Seville: Editorial católica española, 1947). Arcadio de Larrea, "La saeta," *AnM* 4 (1949): 105–35.

Saga, En [Finn., A Saga]. A symphonic poem by Sibelius, op. 9 (1892; revised in 1902). Despite its title, the work has no known program.

Sagbut. Sackbut [see Trombone].

Śahnāi [Hind.]. A *shawm of North India, smaller than the South Indian *nāgasvaram,* but similar in construction, playing technique, and social role. See also *Zūrnā;* see ill. under South Asia.

Sainete [Sp.; Fr. *saynète*]. A type of Spanish comedy originating in the late 18th century, portraying scenes from everyday life and sometimes set to music or including a few musical numbers. It was traditionally in one act and performed at the end of a larger work. Blas de Laserna (1751–1816) composed numerous *sainetes.* The term was borrowed for a similar genre in France. See also *Tonadilla, Zarzuela.*

St. Anne's Fugue. Popular name for Bach's organ fugue in E♭ BWV 552 from the *Clavier-Übung* III (published in 1739), so called because its theme is similar to the beginning of the English hymn tune "St. Anne" (sung to the text "O God, our help in ages past").

St. John Passion [Lat. *Passio secundum Joannem*]. Bach's setting BWV 245 of the Passion story according to St. John (with free poetic texts by Barthold Heinrich Brockes and others for arias and large choruses) for soloists, chorus, and orchestra, first performed in Leipzig in 1724 and revised at various times thereafter. See also Passion music.

St. Martial, repertory of. A body of music of the 9th through 12th centuries transmitted in manuscripts that by historical accident all came to be held in the library of the monastery of St. Martial of Limoges (southwest France). Of these manuscripts, only a few (none containing polyphony) originated there. The repertory might more accurately be called Aquitanian.

The monophony of St. Martial is notable for its *tropes and *sequences. The well-known repertory of polyphony associated with St. Martial dates from the 11th and 12th centuries and includes both *discant (note-against-note or neume-against-neume) and *organum (with long tenor notes set against a florid upper part). Although the notation of these pieces gives no hint of rhythm, there has been considerable debate over the applicability of rhythmic modes (and the relation between this music and the repertory of *Notre Dame).

A prominent form in St. Martial manuscripts, cultivated as both monophony and polyphony, is the *versus,* a setting of rhymed, strophic Latin poetry, sometimes said to be a precursor of the *conductus.*

Bibl: Jacques Chailley, *L'école musicale de Saint-Martial de Limoges jusqu'à la fin du XI siècle* (Paris: Les livres essentiels, 1960). Bruno Stäblein, "Modale Rhythmen im Saint-Martial-Repertoire?" *Blume,* 1963, pp. 340–62. Leo Treitler, "The Polyphony of St. Martial," *JAMS* 17 (1964): 29–42. Id., "The Aquitanian Repertory of Sacred Monody in the Eleventh and Twelfth Centuries" (Ph.D. diss., Princeton Univ.,

1967). Paul Evans, *The Early Trope Repertory of Saint Martial de Limoges* (Princeton: Princeton U Pr, 1970). Sarah Fuller, "The Myth of 'Saint Martial' Polyphony: A Study of the Sources," *MD* 33 (1979): 5–26.

St. Matthew Passion [Lat. *Passio secundum Matthaeum*]. Bach's setting BWV 244 of the Passion story according to St. Matthew (with free poetic texts by Picander [pseudonym of Christian Friedrich Henrici] for arias and large choruses) for soloists, two choruses, and orchestra, first performed in Leipzig in 1727 and revised for a performance in 1736. See also Passion music.

St. Paul (Paulus). An oratorio for soloists, chorus, and orchestra by Mendelssohn, op. 36, completed in 1836 and first performed in Düsseldorf in that year. The text is from the Bible's Acts of the Apostles.

Saite [Ger.]. String; *Saitenchor,* *course of strings; *Saiteninstrument,* stringed instrument; *leere Saite,* open string.

Salicional [Ger., *Salizional*]. An organ stop of open metal flue pipes of narrow scale, first appearing in the 17th century.

Salicus [Lat.]. See Neume.

Salmo [It., Sp.]. *Psalm.

Salome. Opera in one act by Richard Strauss (libretto translated into German by Hedwig Lachmann from Oscar Wilde's play of the same name), produced in Dresden in 1905. Setting: the terrace of Herod's palace in Galilee, about 30 C.E.

Salomon Symphonies. Haydn's Symphonies nos. 93–104 Hob. I:93–104 (1791–95), named for the impresario Johann Peter Salomon, who brought Haydn to London in 1791/92 and 1794/95. Only the first nine symphonies (93–101) were actually composed for Salomon's concerts; the last three (102–4) received their first performances in 1795 at a new series, the Opera Concerts. The twelve are also termed the *London* Symphonies, though the name **London* Symphony specifically applies to no. 104 (sometimes also called the *Salomon* Symphony). Others are the **Surprise* (no. 94), **Military* (no. 100), **Clock* (no. 101), and **Drum-Roll* (no. 103).

Salón México, El. A descriptive piece for orchestra by Copland composed in 1933–36 and named for a dance hall in Mexico City that he had visited in 1932. In evoking this atmosphere, he made use of folk songs gathered in collections by Francis Toor and Rubén M. Campos (especially "El mosco," no. 84 in Campos's collection).

Salpinx [Gr.]. A straight trumpet of ancient Greece, similar to the Roman **tuba.*

Salsa [Sp., sauce, connoting spiciness or soul]. A collective label for contemporary Latin American dance music, based principally on the styles and forms of Afro-Cuban urban popular tradition. The designation first began to be employed consistently in the late 1960s in Puerto Rico and among Latin musicians in New York and other cities in the U.S. A second term widely used in Latin America for varieties of urban popular dance music, including those of Afro-Cuban origin, is **música tropical.* D.S.

Saltarello [It.]. A gay, sprightly dance of Italian provenance.

(1) 14th century. The music of four *saltarelli* without choreographies is preserved in *GB–Lbm* Add. 29987. In varying meters (3/8, 3/4, 6/8, 4/4), all are monophonic pieces cast in the four-repeated-phrase form of the **estampie.*

(2) 15th century [Fr. *pas de Brabant;* Sp. **altadanza*]. One of the faster measures *(misura)* or step units of the **basse danse (bassadanza).* The term was sometimes applied to the **quaternaria,* another step unit of the *basse danse* family that, because of its popularity in Germany, was known to the Italians as the *saltarello todesco.*

(3) 16th century [Fr. *sauterelle, tordion, *tourdion;* Ger. *Hopp tancz, Hupfauf, Proportz, *Nachtanz, Sprung*]. In the 16th century, the music of the *saltarello* was indistinguishable from that of the **gagliarda.* The difference is in the style of the dancing as suggested by the respective titles: *saltarello,* a small leap; *gagliarda,* vigorous. The *gagliarda* is simply a more vigorous version of the *saltarello.* A *saltarello* or a *gagliarda* is usually coupled to either a **pavana* or a **pass'e mezo,* and the coupled dances are composed on the same musical material (harmonic patterns, melodies, etc.).

The *saltarello* continued in vogue until late in the 19th century. Indeed, its steps are still used in present-day folk dances. By the 17th century, however, any function it had as an elegant court dance waned. As a folk dance, its movements were executed more rapidly and with greater violence. The *saltarelli* in the last movement of Mendelssohn's **Italian* Symphony are stylized apotheoses of the dance, but they do suggest its hopping and jumping movements. L.H.M.

Saltato, saltando [It.]. *Sautillé* [see Bowing (4)].

Saltbox. A wooden box with a lid, used as a makeshift percussion instrument in 17th- and 18th-century England and sometimes struck with a rolling pin.

Salterio [It., Sp.]. *Psaltery, *dulcimer.

Salve Regina [Lat., Hail, Queen]. One of the four *antiphons for the Blessed Virgin Mary, sung in modern practice at Compline from the Feast of the Trinity through Saturday before the first Sunday in Advent (*LU,* p. 276). It was formerly attributed to Hermannus Contractus (d. 1054). From the 15th through the 17th century, both text and melody (separately and together) were made the basis for numerous compositions for voices (Dunstable, Ockeghem, Obrecht, Josquin) and for organ (**Buxheimer Orgelbuch,* Paul Hofhaimer, Hans Kotter, Arnolt Schlick, John Bull, Sebastián Aguilera de Heredia, José Ximénez, Pablo Bruna).

Sam(a) [Hin., Skt., Tel.]. The first beat of a **tāla.* The approach to *sam* is often signaled by increased rhythmic activity or the use of a thrice-repeated rhythmic phrase [Hin. *tihāi,* Tel. *mōrā*] and or by tonal direction toward a modally significant degree. C.C.

Samba [Port.]. An Afro-Brazilian dance and dance-music form. Varieties of samba include the rural *sambas de roda,* round dances formerly widespread and still important in northeastern Brazil; the *sambas de morro* of the hillside slums *(favelas)* of Rio de Janeiro, prominent in the city's annual Carnival celebrations; and the internationally known urban popular samba, established in Rio by the 1920s. Characteristics shared among samba types include duple meter, verses for solo singer alternating with choral refrain, syncopated and often disjunct melodic lines, and accompaniments that combine layers of patterns such as the following:

over marchlike bass figures such as:

D.S.

Sambuca [Lat.; Gr. *sambykē*]. (1) A stringed instrument of ancient Greece and Rome, probably an *angle harp. It was an instrument of low status, associated with banquets and prostitutes. (2) In the Middle Ages, any of a number of stringed instruments, including the harp, the *crwth, and the *hurdy-gurdy *(sambuca rotata);* occasionally a wind instrument, probably a *reedpipe. (3) The *sambuca lincea* of the early 17th century was an enharmonic harpsichord with 17 notes to the octave. See also *Trigōnon.*

Samisen [Jap.]. **Shamisen.*

Samplers. See Electro-acoustic music.

Sampogna [It.]. **Zampogna.*

Samson et Dalila [Fr., Samson and Delilah]. Opera in three acts by Saint-Saëns (libretto by Ferdinand Lemaire, after the biblical story), first produced in Weimar in 1877 in German. Setting: Gaza, Palestine, ca. 1150 B.C.E.

Sanctorale [Lat.]. In the liturgical year, the feasts of the saints [see Liturgy].

Sanctus [Lat., holy]. The fourth item of the *Ordinary of the Roman *Mass, beginning with the threefold acclamation "Sanctus, sanctus, sanctus" and sung by the choir following the *Preface. The first part of its text is from Isaiah 6:3, and it is one of the oldest parts of the Mass. The Greek East and the Latin West may originally have shared a single melody for it, sung by the congregation [for a related Greek text, see Trisagion]. Numerous melodies to the Latin text were composed during the Middle Ages. Up to the word "Benedictus," the text is retained in English in the Anglican service of Holy Communion. For the complete text with translation, see Mass.

Bibl.: Peter Joseph Thannabaur, *Das einstimmige Sanctus der römischen Messe in der handschriftlichen Überlieferung des 11. bis 16. Jahrhunderts* (Munich: W Ricke, 1962).

Sanft [Ger.] Soft.

Sanglot [Fr., sob]. According to Montéclair (1736), a note attacked with a kind of sob from the bottom of the chest ("une aspiration violente") and ended with an **accent* or **chûte;* also termed *hélan* (*élan,* outburst). It was used on interjections and outcries in all sorts of situations. See *Nachschlag.* D.F.

Sangsaite [Ger.]. **Cantino.*

Sanjuanito [Sp.]. See *Huayno.*

Santiago de Compostela, repertory of. A repertory of 20 polyphonic pieces and various monophonic pieces contained in the so-called *Codex Calixtinus* in Santiago de Compostela, Spain. The nonmusical parts of the manuscript are largely associated with pilgrimage to the shrine of St. James in Santiago and include a letter falsely attributed to Pope Calixtus II (1119–24). The manuscript and its music originated in central France, however, reaching Santiago by 1173.

Santur [Per., Turk.]. A *dulcimer of the Middle East with a shallow, trapezoidal sound box, 12 to 18 courses of metal strings, and two rows of movable bridges. The player strikes the strings on either side of the bridges with light wooden hammers. It originated in Persia in about the 10th century C.E. and seems to be the prototype of dulcimers from Europe to Korea.

Sanza, sansa. See *Mbira.*

Saqueboute [Fr.]. Sackbut [see Trombone].

Sarabande [Fr.; also Ger.; It. *sarabanda;* Sp. *zarabanda*]. A Baroque dance movement in triple meter. In France and Germany, it was usually slow and majestic, characterized by an accented dotted note on the second beat, beginning without upbeat, and cadencing on the third beat. It was normally in binary form, with fairly regular four- or eight-bar phrases and simple melodies that invited profuse ornamentation, sometimes written out or following as a **double* [see Ex.]. It became a regular member of the solo and chamber *suite, following the courante.

The *zarabanda* is first known as a fast and wildly erotic dance in Mexico and Spain in the 16th century, accompanied by castanets and guitar. It was banned in Spain in 1583, but it nevertheless survived both there and in Italy as a fast dance until the end of the Baroque

Bach, Sarabande from Partita for unaccompanied violin no. 2 in D minor.

era. The earliest extant examples are in Italian guitar sources from the early 17th century. The sarabande was conceived primarily as a harmonic scheme (Luis de Briçeño, Antonio Carbonchi) until the middle of the century, when metric features (e.g., straightforward triple meter, not necessarily including an accented second beat) became the distinguishing characteristics. In solo and chamber sonatas of the mature Baroque, tempo markings are often given, usually *allegro* or *presto* (Torelli, Corelli), but sometimes *largo* or *adagio* (Vitali, Corelli).

It was in France that the sarabande was transformed into an essentially slow dance. It came to be considered a slow minuet by the beginning of the 18th century and was highly expressive, either tender or majestic. Even here, however, the intended tempo is not always clear, perhaps because the dance's early history was too colorful to be forgotten. The sarabande appeared in lute music throughout the 17th century (Ennemond and Denis Gaultier, Germain Pinel, René Mesangeau) and in harpsichord music until the demise of the suite as a collection of dance movements in the 1730s (Chambonnières, Louis and François Couperin, Rameau). It was also popular in stage music from Lully to Rameau. A *petit reprise* (an extra repetition of the last four measures) is often indicated in French sarabandes, and they are sometimes written *en rondeau* [see *Rondeau* (2)].

German composers generally followed French rather than Italian models, adopting their slow tempo and accented second beat in music for harpsichord, lute, and chamber ensembles (Froberger, Alessandro Poglietti, J. C. F. Fischer, Bach). Here the sarabande was almost always part of the core of a dance suite (allemande, courante, sarabande, gigue). England borrowed from both the Italian and French traditions, tending toward a fast "toyish" concept of the dance (Thomas Mace, 1676) in 17th-century music for harpsichord and chamber ensembles (William Lawes, Matthew Locke, Purcell).

Bibl.: Daniel Devoto, "De la zarabanda à la sarabande," *RMFC* 6 (1966): 27–72. Richard Hudson, "The *Zarabanda* and *Zarabanda Francese* in Italian Guitar Music of the Early 17th Century," *MD* 24 (1970): 125–49. Meredith Little and Carol Marsh, *La Danse noble: An Inventory of Dances and Sources* (Williamstown: Broude Trust, 1992). Rainer Gstrein, *Die Sarabande, Tanzgattung und musikalisher Topos* (Innsbruck: Studien Verlag, 1997). B.G.

Sarambo [Sp.]. A traditional dance-music genre of the Dominican Republic. Danced by couples with characteristic *zapateo* (foot-stamping) patterns, it is in rapid 6/8 meter with frequent hemiola and is typically performed by singers with accordion, *guayo* (metal scraper), and *tambora* (double-headed membranophone). The *callao, guarapo,* and *yuca* are closely related forms. D.S.

Sāraṅgī [Hind.]. A bowed stringed instrument of northern India and Pakistan. Three gut strings pass down a broad, unfretted neck and over a waisted, skin-covered belly. Ten to forty metal sympathetic strings run beneath the melodic strings. It is held upright and the strings are stopped with the fingernails of the left hand. It is a favorite instrument for accompanying the voice. See also *Sarinda;* see ill. under South Asia.

Sardana [Sp.]. The national dance of Catalonia, in rapid 6/8 meter and danced in a circle to music performed by a **cobla.*

Sarinda [Hind.]. A three-stringed *fiddle of Pakistan, India, and Bangladesh. It is smaller and simpler than the **sāraṅgī* and is considered an instrument of folk rather than art music.

Sarod [Hind.]. A plucked, stringed instrument of northern India. Four or five melody strings plus three to five drone strings and 11 to 16 sympathetic strings, all of metal, pass down a broad, unfretted, metal-covered neck and over a bowl-shaped, skin-covered sound box. A round, metal-covered resonator is attached to the underside of the pegbox. Plucked with a plectrum, it is most often a solo instrument, accompanied by **tablā* and **tamburā.* It is a relatively recent descendant of a lutelike instrument termed a *rabāb.* See Rabāb (3); South Asia VI and ill.

Saron [Jav.]. An Indonesian *metallophone. Thick bronze or iron bars are set on top of a wooden frame and struck with wooden mallets. Most contain six or seven bars and encompass one octave. They are important in many *gamelan* ensembles. *Saron demung* is the lowest-pitched of the family, *saron barung* is an octave higher, and *saron peking* an octave higher still. See ill. under Southeast Asia.

Sarrusophone [Eng., Fr.; Ger. *Sarrusophon;* It. *sarrusofono;* Sp. *sarrusofón*]. A family of brass, conical-bore, double-reed woodwind instruments invented by the French bandmaster W. Sarrus and constructed for him by P. L. Gautrot, Sr., of Paris. The sarrusophone was patented by Gautrot in 1856. The instruments exist in eight sizes, ranging from sopranino to subcontrabass. The smaller instruments resemble the straight soprano *saxophone, while the lower members of the family are constructed with vertical loops and an upward-facing bell. The fingering is based on that of the saxophone, and all have the same written range as the saxophone: b♭ to f‴. The member of the family to gain the widest use is the contrabass in B♭ or C (lowest sounding pitch $A♭_2$ or $B♭_2$), which often substitutes for the *contrabassoon in French orchestral scores written around 1900. See ill. under Reed. M.S.

Sarum Use. The modification of the Roman Catholic rite developed and used at the Cathedral of Salisbury between the 13th and the 16th century, adopted throughout much of the British Isles and influential elsewhere. The Sarum Use had substantial effects on the makeup of the Anglican Book of Common Prayer. In 1559, it was officially abolished in England. Sarum modifications of Roman practice include certain variations in plainchant melodies, adaptations of the calendar to reflect local interests, the inclusion of some prayers and a number of chants (particularly troped Kyries and one troped Gloria) peculiar to this rite, and provision for elaborate processions.

The Sarum Use has provided the plainchant melodies that form the basis of many polyphonic compositions, including much English sacred music and some pieces by French composers of the 15th and early 16th centuries.

Bibl.: Francis Proctor and Christopher Wordsworth, eds., *Breviarum ad usum Sarum,* 3 vols. (Cambridge, 1879–86; R: Farnborough: Gregg, 1970). Walter H. Frere, ed., *Graduale sarisburiense* (London, 1894; R: Farnborough: Gregg, 1966) [facs.]. Id., ed., *Antiphonale sarisburiense* (London: Plainsong and Mediaeval Music Society, 1901–25; R: Farnborough: Gregg, 1966) [facs.]. J. Wickham Legg, ed., *The Sarum Missal* (Oxford: Clarendon Pr, 1916; R: London: Oxford U Pr, 1969). Frank Ll. Harrison, *Music in Medieval Britain* (London: Routledge & Kegan Paul, 1958; 2nd ed., 1963). Id., "Music for the Sarum Rite," *AnnM* 6 (1958–63): 99–144. Terence Bailey, *The Processions of Sarum and the Western Church* (Toronto: Pontifical Institute of Mediaeval Studies, 1971). Leslie Hewitt, ed., *Richard Pynson: Processionale ad Usum Sarum 1502* (Clarabricken, Ireland: Boethius Pr, 1980) [facs.].

Sassofono [It.]. Saxophone.

Sattel [Ger.]. *Nut (1).

Satz [Ger.]. (1) Movement, e.g., of a sonata. (2) *Phrase, *period. (3) Theme; *Hauptsatz* and *Seitensatz* or *Nebensatz,* the first and second themes, respectively, in *sonata form. (4) The structure, fundamental style, or texture of a work; e.g., *strenger (freier) Satz,* strict (free) style.

Saul. An oratorio for soloists, chorus, and orchestra by Handel, first performed in London in 1739. The text, compiled by Charles Jennens, is from the Bible (I Samuel 17–II Samuel 1) and Abraham Cowley's *Davideis.*

Saùng-gauk [Burmese]. An *arched harp of Burma with a boat-shaped sound box covered with skin and 14 silk or nylon strings. It has been used since the 7th century C.E. to accompany court songs. See ill. under Southeast Asia.

Sausage bassoon. See Racket (bassoon).

Sauterelle [Fr.]. **Saltarello.*

Sautillé [Fr.]. See Bowing (4).

Savart. A logarithmic measure of intervals introduced by Félix Savart (1791–1841) of France. An octave is represented by $2 \times \log 2 = 301$ savarts. A semitone is approximately 25 savarts, and one savart is approximately 4 cents. See Interval.

Saw, musical. See Musical saw.

Saxhorn. A valved brass instrument, usually in upright tuba form, made in uniformly proportioned sizes from sopranino to contrabass. Saxhorns were an early attempt to create a uniform and complete family of brass instruments, an attempt made possible by the invention of the *valve. They were first produced about 1845 by (Antoine-Joseph) Adolphe Sax (1814–94) in Paris and were widely used by military and community bands in France, Belgium, England, and the U.S. during the last half of the 19th century. Some sizes of present-day band instruments—notably *alto horns, *euphoniums, and baritones—are direct descendants of the corresponding saxhorns. Sets of brasses made by many other manufacturers in the second half of the 19th century copied the bugle-flugelhorn bore proportions and alternating E♭ and B♭ sizes made standard by the success of the saxhorns.

Bibl.: Clifford Bevan, *The Tuba Family,* rev. ed. (Winchester: Piccolo, 2000). R.E.E.

Saxophone [Eng., Fr.; Ger. *Saxophon;* It. *sassofono;* Sp. *saxofón*]. A family of metal, conical-bore, single-reed woodwind instruments invented by Adolphe Sax (1814–94) of Brussels in 1841 and patented by him in 1846 after he settled in Paris. From the beginning, the instruments have been made in two shapes. Smaller saxophones are made in straight form, while larger ones have the bell bent up and toward the front and the neck bent back toward the player. Because Sax intended the instruments for both orchestral and band use, the family actually comprises two parallel groups. The orchestral group has seven sizes, pitched alternately in C and F. The band (or military) group also has seven sizes, pitched alternately in B♭ and E♭. In 1904, the firm of C. G. Conn in Elkhart, Indiana, added a subcontrabass. From the orchestral group only the C tenor (called the melody saxophone) is in use today.

All saxophones are notated in the treble clef and have a written range of b♭ to f‴, though some instruments may have additional keys for extending the range downward to written a or below, and skilled players may extend the range upward considerably. Saxophones used today include the sopranino in E♭ (sounding a minor third higher than written), soprano in B♭ (a major second lower), alto in E♭ (a major sixth lower), tenor in B♭ (or, less often, C, sounding a major ninth or an octave lower than written), baritone in E♭ (an octave and a major sixth lower), bass in B♭ (two octaves and a major second lower), contrabass in E♭ (two octaves and a major sixth lower), and subcontrabass in B♭ (three octaves and a major second lower). The principal instruments of the family are the alto in E♭, the tenor in B♭, and the baritone in E♭ [see ill. under Reed]. The saxophone has a fingering system similar to that of the Boehm flute in the right hand [see Boehm system]; the left hand retains some characteristics of the earlier *simple system.

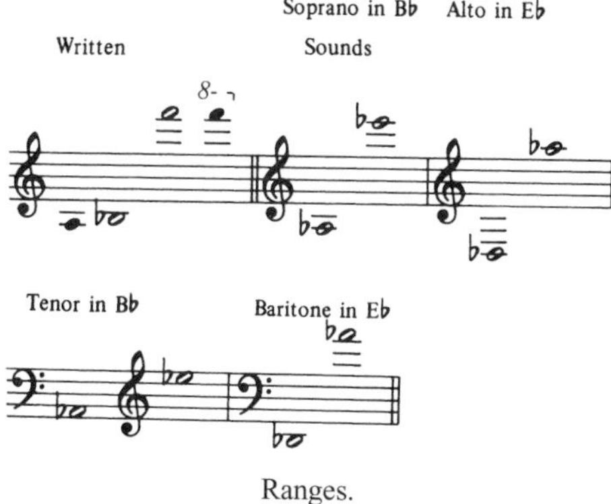

Ranges.

The instrument has been used extensively in jazz and popular music and in military bands and other large wind ensembles. It has been used to some extent in orchestral and chamber music as well.

The term saxophone has also been used occasionally by organologists as a generic term for a conical-bore, single-reed woodwind that produces a second register by *overblowing the octave. This is in distinction to the clarinet type. The **tárogató*, for example, could be said to be of the saxophone type.

Bibl.: Jaap Kool, *Das Saxophon* (Leipzig: J J Weber, 1931). Marcel Perrin, *Le saxophone* (Paris: Fischbacher, 1955). Karl Ventzke and Claus Raumberger, *Die Saxophone: Beiträge zur Baucharakteristik und Geschichte einer Musikinstrumentenfamilie* (Frankfurt am Main: Musikinstrument, 1979). Malou Haine, *Adolphe Sax, 1814–1894: Sa vie, son oeuvre et ses instruments de musique* (Brussels: Éditions de l'Université de Bruxelles, 1980). William McBride, "The Early Saxophone in Patents 1838–1850 Compared," *GSJ* 35 (1982): 112–21. M.S.

Saxotromba. A valved brass instrument in upright tuba form for mounted military use. Saxotrombas, which were patented in 1845 by Adolphe Sax, have narrower bore proportions than the instruments of his *saxhorn family. They were not successful. R.E.E.

Sax tuba. A valved brass instrument in circular form. Adolphe Sax made 15 of them in various sizes for Halévy's opera *Le juif errant* in 1852. R.E.E.

Saynète [Fr.]. See *Sainete.*

Saz [Turk.]. A *long-necked lute of Turkey with three courses of metal strings (tuned E D A or G D A, the middle string thus sounding lowest), a fretted neck, and a bulging, pear-shaped body. Of the instruments of varying size that make up the family of this name, the most common is the *bağlama.* The performer uses a flexible plectrum to play a melody on the highest string, adding accompaniment on the others. The *saz* is considered the Turkish national instrument and is used to accompany many kinds of songs and dances. See ill. under Near and Middle East.

Scala [It.]. *Scale.

Scala enigmatica [It.]. The scale c d♭ e f♯ g♯ a♯ b c′, employed by Verdi in his *Ave Maria* ("Scala enigmatica armonizzata a quattro voci miste") for mixed chorus (original version, 1889; revised version, 1898).

Scale. (1) [Fr. *gamme, échelle;* Ger. *Tonleiter, Skala;* It. *scala, gamma;* Sp. *escala, gama*] A collection of pitches arranged in order from lowest to highest or from highest to lowest. The pitches of any music in which pitch is definable can be reduced to a scale. The concept and its pedagogical use have been especially prominent in the history of Western art music. The importance of the concept in non-Western systems varies considerably and is often associated with concepts of melody construction and internal pitch relationships that go well beyond any simple ordering of pitches from lowest to highest [see also Mode, Melody type]. Even in Western tonal music, however, scales are only a reflection of compositional practice that includes notions of appropriate melodic progression and the functions of individual pitches in relation to one another. With respect to nontonal Western music, a scale is likely to be simply an arbitrary representation of pitch content that contributes little to an understanding of a given work.

The total pitch world of Western tonal music [see Tonality] is defined by the chromatic scale—a scale in which each pitch is separated from its neighbors by a semitone, the smallest *interval in use in the system. This scale thus includes twelve different pitch classes or pitch names, and by convention, as with other scales, the starting pitch name is repeated at the top of the scale [see the accompanying table]. A scale of this structure may be formed beginning on any of the twelve possible pitch classes and may be repeated through any number of octaves. It is embodied in all of the white and black keys of the piano keyboard taken together.

Central to the structure of Western tonal music is the *diatonic scale—a scale that includes two semitones (s) and five whole tones (t) arranged in the pattern embodied in the white keys of the piano: taking C

Chromatic	c	c♯	d	d♯	e	f	f♯	g	g♯	a	a♯	b	c′
Major	c		d		e	f		g		a		b	c′
Minor, natural	c		d	e♭		f		g	a♭		b♭		c′
Minor, melodic													
ascending	c		d	e♭		f		g		a		b	c′
descending	c		d	e♭		f		g	a♭		b♭		c′
Minor, harmonic	c		d	e♭		f		g	a♭			b	c′
Whole tone	c		d		e		f♯		g♯		a♯		c′
Gypsy	c		d	e♭			f♯	g	a♭			b	c′
Pentatonic	c		d			f		g		a			c′
Octatonic	c	c♯		d♯	e		f♯	g		a	a♯		c′
Blues	c		d	e♭	e	f	g♭	g		a	b♭	b	c′

as the starting point, t t s t t t s. In principle, any of the seven pitches of such a scale can be taken as the starting point, thus rearranging the order in which the tones and semitones occur, though not the underlying pattern from which the order derives. There are thus seven different versions of the diatonic scale, termed octave species, since, by convention in Western tonal music, every scale is understood as being bounded by an octave. In historical practice, however, only some of these octave species have been important. By the end of the Renaissance, six (all but the one produced by starting upward from B) were recognized in both theory and practice, forming a central part of the system of modes. For a discussion of this system, see Mode.

In tonal music, from the late 17th century on, only two octave species or modes are at work: major and minor. The major mode or major scale takes the pattern produced by starting upward through the diatonic scale from C. The natural or pure minor mode or scale takes the pattern starting upward from A: t s t t s t t. The distinction among starting points and the resulting orders of tones and semitones reflect a feature of compositional practice, namely, that pitches are treated in a hierarchical relationship and that each pitch in a tonal composition has a particular function with respect to the others. Each step or degree of a particular scale is thus numbered and named [see Scale degrees]. The starting pitch is of the greatest importance in the hierarchy, and since major and minor scales can be formed on any of the twelve available pitch classes, any given example is named for its starting pitch or tonic, e.g., C major, G minor, etc. A composition based primarily on a given scale is said to be in the *key of that scale, e.g., C major, G minor, etc. An important property of these scales is that the twelve different starting points or tonics produce twelve different scales, no two of which contain precisely the same pitch classes and each of which is uniquely and precisely related to all of the others. For the nature of this relationship, see Key relationship, Circle of fifths.

Compositions in the minor mode often approach the tonic from below by semitone, thus raising the seventh scale degree of the natural minor scale by a semitone to produce what is termed the harmonic minor scale [see table, where all scales are illustrated starting on c]. This produces an interval of three semitones between the sixth and seventh scale degrees—an interval called an augmented second that is regarded as melodically awkward. Hence, in approaching the tonic from below, compositions in the minor mode often raise both the sixth and seventh scale degrees by a semitone. This results in what is termed the melodic minor scale, which, however, when descending from the tonic is identical with the natural minor scale. Here again, scales are simply abstractions from musical practice rather than musical objects with prior or independent standing.

Some kinds of Western music can be understood to employ scales that are largely modifications of major or minor scales (or perhaps one of the other octave species or modes), the music in question being essentially tonal, e.g., *gypsy music, the *blues, and most 19th- and 20th-century examples of *modality. Among the most familiar nontonal scales is the whole-tone scale, which includes no semitones. This scale includes only six pitch classes, and there are only two different pitch collections reducible to a scale of this structure. *Pentatonic scales, found in both Western and non-Western music, include five pitches in differing patterns of intervals. The octatonic scale includes eight pitches per octave arranged in a pattern of alternating whole tones and semitones. There are only three different pitch collections reducible to a scale of this structure. This scale figures prominently in music by Stravinsky and others.

(2) For the scale of organ pipes, see Scaling.

Scale degrees. The numbered positions of individual pitches within a major or minor *scale. Because in Western *tonality each pitch of a scale functions in a particular way with respect to the others, scale degrees are both numbered (traditionally with roman numerals) and named, as follows: I tonic, II supertonic, III mediant, IV subdominant, V *dominant, VI submediant, VII *leading tone or *subtonic. The numbering and nomenclature are extensively used in *harmonic analysis.

Scaling [Fr. *diapason;* Ger. *Mensur;* It. *misura;* Sp. *mensura*]. (1) The diameter of organ pipes in relation to their length. Scales for organ pipes are determined with regard for the size of the instrument and the acoustics of the space in which it is to be heard. Wide scaling of *flue pipes produces varieties of flute tone (characterized by few audible harmonics), and narrow scaling produces *Principal tone. Extremely narrow scaling produces a variant known as string tone. (2) [Fr. *taille, mesure*] The length of the strings of a stringed keyboard instrument in relation to their pitch. Since, in addition to length, mass and tension are variables in the determination of the pitch of a string [see Acoustics], the length of lower-sounding strings on such instruments is usually made somewhat shorter than it would have to be if length were the only variable.

Scandicus [Lat.]. See Neume.

Scandinavia. See entries for individual countries.

Scat singing. *Jazz singing primarily composed of vocables. Although earlier recordings exist, Louis Armstrong's 1926 "Heebie Jeebies" is the most celebrated early example of the practice. After 1944, the style came to be represented by virtuosic interpretations (e.g., by Ella Fitzgerald, Eddie Jefferson, and Jon Hendricks) of rapid *bebop instrumental improvisation. Since the 1970s, yodels (by Leon Thomas) and percussive or non-Western sounds (by Al Jarreau and Bobby McFerrin) expanded the vocal palette.

B.K., rev. T.A.J.

Scena [It.]. (1) Stage, or the scene represented on the stage. (2) A subdivision of an act of an opera. In the librettos of *opera seria,* each entrance or exit of a character is designated as a new scene. (3) In formulations such as *scena ed aria* or *scena e duetto,* which appear frequently in the scores of 19th-century operas, the recitative portion of the number. A setting of a portion of a libretto for concert performance by a solo singer plus orchestra, e.g., Beethoven's "Ah! perfido" or Mozart's "Misera, dove son," may also be called *scena ed aria.*

Scenario. An outline for a libretto, usually indicating characters, scenes, and actions. The German term *Scenarium,* however, means a libretto with complete dialogue, stage directions, and indications of setting and scenery.

Schachtbrett [Ger.]. *Chekker.

Schalkhaft [Ger.]. Roguish.

Schall [Ger.]. Sound.

Schallbecher [Ger.]. *Bell (2).

Schallbecken [Ger.]. Cymbals.

Schalloch [Ger.]. *Sound hole.

Schallplatte [Ger.]. Phonograph record.

Schallstück [Ger.]. *Bell (2).

Schalltrichter [Ger.]. *Bell (2); *S. auf,* an instruction to brass players to play with the bell raised.

Schalmei [Ger.]. *Shawm.

Scharff [Ger.]. The main *mixture of the **Positiv* division of German organs, usually at 2/3′ pitch at C.

Schauspieldirektor, Der [Ger., The Impresario]. *Singspiel in one act by Mozart (libretto by Gottlieb Stephanie), performed at the Orangery of the Schönbrunn Palace in Vienna in 1786. Setting: Salzburg, 1786. The music consists only of an overture, two arias for sopranos, a terzett, and a finale.

Scheherazade. See *Sheherazade.*

Scheitholt, Scheitholz [Ger.]. A rectangular *zither, now obsolete, similar in playing technique to the Norwegian **langleik,* Swedish *hummel,* and *Appalachian dulcimer.

Schelle [Ger., pl. *Schellen*]. *Pellet bell, *sleigh bells.

Schellenbaum [Ger.]. *Turkish crescent.

Schell(en)trommel [Ger.]. *Tambourine.

Schelomo [Heb., Solomon]. A rhapsody for cello and orchestra by Ernest Bloch composed in 1915–16, inspired by the Book of Ecclesiastes, which is attributed to Solomon.

Schenker analysis. A method of analysis for tonal music, developed over some 30 years by the Austrian theorist Heinrich Schenker (1868–1935); sometimes also called linear analysis or layer analysis. Applied to a given work, Schenker's analytical technique aims to discover and reveal tonal relationships by their intrinsic linear connections in a hierarchy of structural levels *(Schichten)* or layers. The most immediate level of a composition, called the foreground *(Vordergrund),* includes all of the composition's most prominent note-to-note motions (Schenker sometimes employed the term to refer to the work itself). The second general level of a work is the middleground (*Mittelgrund,* of which there may be several specific levels), in which the linear relationships between the pitches of structurally important harmonies within and between phrases become apparent and in which structurally important melodic elements may be retained from the foreground. At the highest, or first level of the middleground, only the most fundamental harmonies of the piece are shown in their linear relationship; at this level even an entire modulation, lasting for a whole formal section, might be symbolized by a single triad. Beyond the middleground is the background-level elaboration of the tonal projection through time of a tonic triad, which is arpeggiated in the bass by a leap from tonic to dominant and back *(Bassbrechung)* so as to support in the upper part a linear, stepwise motion from the third, fifth, or eighth degree of the scale down through the intermediate degrees to the first degree or tonic. This fundamental structure is called the *Ursatz;* the upper part, the *Urlinie* (fundamental line).

In Schenker's own view, the musical foreground emanates from the *Ursatz* by means of the composing-out *(Auskomponierung)* of its elements. The techniques of composing-out are termed diminution and are based on the principles of strict counterpoint, which underlie events on all levels. Schenker regarded the *Ursatz* (and its relationship to the foreground), however, as a feature only of the greatest works, the organic unity of which it guarantees. He did not treat his theory as a theory of all tonal music, nor did he explain his analytical technique as one of reduction,

Schenker's analysis of Bach's chorale "Ich bin's, ich sollte büssen" from the St. Matthew Passion.

stripping away features of the foreground to reach the background.

In practice, however, many of Schenker's followers have employed an analytical method involving a number of systematic reductional techniques based on his concepts, and displayed in a special graphic style developed by Schenker and using ordinary musical notation supplemented by some new symbols and explanatory remarks. In a typical Schenker graph, the foreground is shown at the bottom, the *Ursatz* at the top, and the other levels in between, the corresponding structural elements between the levels being aligned vertically on the page. The accompanying example, from Schenker's *Fünf Urlinie-Tafeln,* shows his analysis of Bach's chorale "Ich bin's, ich sollte büssen" from the St. Matthew Passion. Numbers with circumflexes or carets indicate scale degrees. Fundamental linear motions *(Züge),* involving stepwise motion over an interval, are indicated by notes connected by slurs. White and black notes denote greater and lesser structural weight, respectively; their stepwise connection in time is shown with a solid horizontal beam. Linear connection of nonsuccessive notes of the same melodic part is fundamental to this understanding. Slurs may also be used to indicate arpeggiation *(Brechung),* which is melodic (but not linear) motion over the pitches of a triad. A diagonal beam is used to show the unfolding of an interval, connecting a tone in one voice to one understood to be in another voice.

A connection between a particular pitch and its duplicate later in time, identified by a dotted slur or dashed beam, is called a prolongation *(Prolongation);* prolongation may also apply to triads, to the point where, for instance, the entire coda section of a sonata movement may be considered as the prolongation of the final tonic triad of the recapitulation, at the background level. Such characteristic relationships, which are fundamental to Schenker's analytical conceptions, are often of profound significance in understanding the deeper tonal structure of both larger and smaller works.

Notwithstanding the power and penetration of Schenker's method, it is open to widely different interpretations when applied by different analysts; nor were Schenker's own principles always consistent over his lifetime. He intended his method to be comprehensive, but he limited its application to music he himself considered valid, namely that of Austrian and German composers from Bach through Brahms, including Chopin but excluding Wagner. He was hostile to the music of his own time and claimed that his analytical method proved it to be inferior to the masterworks of the past.

Bibl.: Adele Katz, *Challenge to Musical Tradition* (London: Putnam, 1947). Felix Salzer, *Structural Hearing* (New York: C Boni, 1952; new ed., New York: Dover, 1962). Felix Salzer and Carl Schachter, *Counterpoint in Composition* (New York: McGraw-Hill, 1969). Maury Yeston, *Readings in Schenker Analysis and Other Approaches* (New Haven: Yale U Pr, 1977) [contains a comprehensive bibliography of Schenker's writings]. Allen Forte and Steven Gilbert, *Introduction to Schenkerian Analysis* (New York: Norton, 1982). Oswald Jonas, *Introduction to the Theory of Heinrich Schenker: The Nature of the Musical Work of Art,* trans. and ed. John Rothgeb (New York: Longman, 1982). David Beach, ed., *Aspects of Schenkerian Theory* (New Haven: Yale U Pr, 1983). *Schenker Studies,* ed. Hedi Siegel (Cambridge: Cambridge U Pr, 1990). *Schenker Studies 2,* ed. Carl Schachter and Hedi Siegel (Cambridge: Cambridge U Pr, 1999). Allen Cadwallader and David Gagné, *Analysis of Tonal Music: A Schenkerian Approach* (New York: Oxford U Pr, 1998).

Works by Heinrich Schenker: *Der freie Satz* (Vienna: Universal, 1935); in Eng., *Free Composition,* trans. and ed. by Ernst Oster (New York: Longman, 1979). *Fünf Urlinie-Tafeln* (New York: private publication, 1933); in Eng. *Five Graphic Music Analyses,* ed. Felix Salzer (New York: Dover, 1969). *Kontrapunkt,* in Eng. as *Counterpoint,* trans. and ed. John Rothgeb and Jürgen Thym (New York: Schirmer, 1987). *Das Meisterwerk in der Musik,* 3 vols. (Munich: Drei Masken Verlag, 1925–26, 1930); Eng. trans. Ian Bent (Cambridge: Cambridge U Pr, 1994–97). *Die Kunst des Vortrages,* in Eng. as *The Art of Performance* (New York: Oxford U Pr, 2000).
See also Harmonic rhythm. M.DEV.

Scherp [Du.]. The main *mixture of the **Rugwerk* (*Positive) division of the classical Dutch organ.

Scherzando [It.], **Scherzhaft** [Ger.]. Playful.

Scherzi, Gli [It.]. Popular name for Haydn's six String Quartets op. 33, Hob. III:37–42 (1781), so called because the minuets are headed "Scherzo." The quartets are also known as the *Russian* Quartets because later editions bear a dedication to the Grand Duke Pavel Petrovich, who visited Haydn while in Vienna in 1781; and as the *Maiden* Quartets [Ger. *Jungfern Quartette*] because the title page of the Hummel edition of 1782 shows a female figure.

Scherzo [It., joke]. (1) In the Baroque period, a vocal or instrumental work of lighter character. Most uses of the term before about 1650 refer to vocal pieces of the **balletto* type (e.g., Monteverdi's *Scherzi musicali* of 1607), while after 1650, the term usually signifies an instrumental work.

(2) In the 18th century, one movement of a suite or other multimovement work, quick in tempo and light in style. Scherzos of this sort are most often in 2/4 time (see, e.g., the penultimate movement of Bach's A-minor Partita and the finale of Haydn's Sonata Hob. XVI:9, both for solo keyboard).

(3) From the late 18th century to the present, a standard movement-type introduced as a replacement for the minuet in multimovement cycles. Scherzos are normally in rapid 3/4 time; they range in character from the light and playful to the sinister and macabre. Most scherzos are in rounded binary form [see Binary and ternary form II]. As in the minuet, there is usually a contrasting trio, after which the scherzo is restated.

Haydn employed the term scherzo for the dance movements of his String Quartets op. 33 of 1781;

most of these movements do not, however, differ substantially from the usual minuet and trio. Beethoven began to write true scherzos early in his career (see the Wind Octet of 1792–93, published posthumously as op. 103, and the Piano Trios op. 1 of 1794–95). His introduction of the scherzo within the symphony was especially influential; scherzos are found in every Beethoven symphony but the First and Eighth, though in the former case the movement is a scherzo in all but name. In the Seventh Symphony, Beethoven extends the movement by including an additional statement of the trio and scherzo, creating a Scherzo–Trio–Scherzo–Trio–Scherzo plan, while in the Ninth the scherzo is the second rather than the third movement, its usual position.

The scherzo was a standard component of the Romantic and post-Romantic symphony and related genres. The Romantic affinity for the scherzo may also be seen in the many independent or semi-independent scherzos of the period, for example, Chopin's four for piano, Mendelssohn's first entr'acte from the incidental music to *A Midsummer Night's Dream* (probably influenced by the "Queen Mab" scherzo of Berlioz's *Romeo and Juliet*), and Dukas's programmatic *The Sorcerer's Apprentice.*

Bibl.: Gustav Becking, *Studien zu Beethovens Personalstil: Das Scherzothema* (Leipzig: Breitkopf & Härtel, 1921). Josef Gmeiner, *Menuett und Scherzo: Ein Beitrag zur Entwicklungsgeschichte und Soziologie des Tanzsatzes in der Wiener Klassik* (Tutzing: Schneider, 1979). E.K.W.

Schicksalslied [Ger., Song of Destiny]. A setting for chorus and orchestra by Brahms, op. 54 (1868–71), of a poem from Johann Hölderlin's *Hyperion.*

Schietto, schiettamente [It.]. Open(ly), sincere(ly).

Schillinger system. A theory that proposes a mathematical basis for music (and other arts), introduced by Joseph Schillinger (1895–1943) and published posthumously in 1946 as *The Schillinger System of Musical Composition.* Schillinger's system in music reduces all possible horizontal (scales), vertical (dyads, triads, etc.), and rhythmic combinations to arithmetic formulas and seeks to offer theorems for composing aesthetically pleasing results. His methods were most influential in the 1930s and 40s, especially in popular music, where his ideas on orchestration and thematic and rhythmic variation were widely used. Schillinger's pupils included Benny Goodman, George Gershwin, and Glenn Miller.

Bibl.: Arnold Shaw and Lyle Dowling, eds., *The Schillinger System of Musical Composition* (New York: C Fischer, 1946). Vernon Duke, "Gershwin, Schillinger, and Dukelsky—Some Reminiscences," *MQ* 33 (1947): 102–15. Frances Schillinger, *Joseph Schillinger: A Memoir* (New York: Greenberg, 1949).

Schisma. See Comma, schisma.

Schlag [Ger.]. (1) Beat, blow; *Schlaginstrumente, Schlagzeug,* percussion instruments. (2) A popular song hit.

Schlägel [Ger.]. See *Schlegel.*

Schlagmanieren [Ger., manners of beating]. A repertory of rhythmic patterns, elaborations, and embellishments employed by 17th- and 18th-century timpanists, running the gamut from eighth-, sixteenth-, and thirty-second-note figures to rolls and cross-beating. Altenburg (1795) distinguishes between strictly written music and impromptu playing, listing 14 formulas that the apprentice drummer had to perfect and commit to memory. The *Schlagmanieren* were played with varying dynamics and tempos, along with posturing, body movements, and turns of the wrist. Final cadences, especially, provided opportunities for players to exhibit improvisatory skill.

Bibl.: Daniel Speer, *Grund-richtiger . . . Unterricht der musicalischen Kunst* (Ulm, 1687; facs., Leipzig: Peters, 1974), p. 104f. Johann Ernst Altenburg, *Versuch einer Anleitung zur heroisch-musikalischen Trompeter- und Pauker-Kunst* (Halle, 1795), pp. 128–30; trans. Edward H. Tarr, *Essay on an Introduction to the Heroic and Musical Trumpeters' and Kettledrummers' Art* (Nashville: Brass Pr, 1974), pp. 124–25. Georges Kastner, *Méthode complète et raisonée de timbales* (Paris: Schlesinger, 1845?), pp. 28–32. Georg Fechner, *Die Pauken und Trommeln in ihren neueren und vorzüglicheren Konstruktionen* (Weimar, 1862), pp. 20–28. Gerassimos Avgerinos, *Lexikon der Pauke* (Frankfurt am Main: Musikinstrument, 1964), pp. 76–77. Edmund A. Bowles, "The Double, Double, Double Beat of the Thundering Drum: The Timpani in Early Music," *EM* 19 (1991): 419–35. Peter Downey, "On Sounding the Trumpet and Beating the Drum in 17th-Century England," *EM* 24 (1996): 263–77. John Michael Cooper, "Percussion and Timpani," in *A Performer's Guide to Seventeenth-Century Music,* ed. Stewart Carter (New York: Schirmer, 1997), pp. 133–52. E. A. Bowles, *The Timpani: A History in Pictures and Documents* (Hillsdale, N.Y.: Pendragon, 2002). E.A.B.

Schlegel [Ger.]. Drumstick.

Schleifer [Ger.]. *Slide (3).

Schleppen [Ger.]. To drag; *nicht schleppen(d),* do not drag.

Schlummerlied [Ger.]. Lullaby.

Schluss [Ger.]. Conclusion, *cadence; *Schlusssatz,* concluding movement.

Schlüssel [Ger.]. *Clef.

Schlüsselfiedel [Ger.]. See *Nyckelharpa.*

Schmachtend [Ger.]. Languishing, pining.

Schmeichelnd [Ger.]. Flattering, coaxing.

Schmerzlich [Ger.]. Sad, painful.

Schmetternd [Ger.]. Blaring, brassy, especially in horn playing.

Schnabel [Ger., beak]. The mouthpiece of the recorder or clarinet.

Schnabelflöte [Ger.]. *Recorder.

Schnarre [Ger.]. *Rattle.

Schnarrsaite [Ger.]. Snare.

Schnarrwerk [Ger., obs.]. The reed stops of the organ.

Schnell [Ger.]. Fast.

Schneller [Ger.]. An 18th-century ornament involving alternation of the written note with the note immediately above it, to be performed as a short, rapid trill beginning on the beat; sometimes also termed an inverted mordent. The *Schneller* was not one of the French *agréments,* having been introduced after 1750 by C. P. E. Bach, who always indicated it by two small grace notes [Ex. 1]. Later composers often designated the *Schneller* with a short wavy line [Ex. 2], which originally indicated a somewhat different ornament called a *Pralltriller.* This is a rapid trill of four notes, beginning with the upper auxiliary, as was customary with trills in that period. This trill was used only on the lower note of a descending second and tied to the preceding note, sometimes giving the erroneous impression that the *Pralltriller* begins with the main note. The *Schneller,* on the other hand, can occur only on a detached note, that is, the upper note of a descending second, so that the position of the sign [Ex. 2] usually indicates whether a *Schneller* [Ex. 3] or a *Pralltriller* [Ex. 4] is meant.

After 1800, the *Pralltriller* dropped out of use; hence, the sign [Ex. 2] always indicates the *Schneller.* Simultaneously, however, the name *Schneller* dropped out of use and the ornament illustrated in Ex. 3 became known as a *Pralltriller,* the current German term for the *Schneller.* The former restriction regarding its position on the first note of a descending second has, of course, been long abandoned, and the *Schneller* is frequently found in connection with skips, to which it adds crispness and a determined attack (e.g., in the last movement of Beethoven's *Hammerklavier* Sonata op. 106). About 1830 (Hummel, Moscheles), the *Schneller* began to be performed before the main note, and today this is generally considered the proper manner of execution. As late as in Chopin, however, examples abound in which the old method appears to be preferable, owing to its greater expressiveness [Ex. 5, Waltz in A♭].

Bibl.: Putnam Aldrich, "On the Interpretation of Bach's Trills," *MQ* 49 (1963): 289–310. P.A.

Schola (cantorum) [Lat., school of singers]. (1) The body of singers of the papal court in Rome, founded perhaps as early as the papacy of St. Gregory (590–604). Their number and organization are described in *Ordines romani* [see *Ordo romanus*] from the 8th century. It was dissolved in the late 14th century and its functions taken over by the papal chapel. (2) A choir that performs Gregorian chant. (3) An institution founded in Paris in 1894 by Vincent d'Indy, Alexandre Guilmant, and Charles Bordes, at first dedicated to instruction in church music, especially Gregorian chant, but subsequently concerned with early music generally and with thorough training in counterpoint.

Schöne Müllerin, Die [Ger., The Fair Maid of the Mill]. A cycle of 20 songs by Schubert, op. 25, D. 795 (1823), setting poems by Wilhelm Müller.

Schools of music. See Education, Conservatory.

Schöpfung, Die [Ger.]. See *Creation, The.*

Schöpfungsmesse [Ger.]. See *Creation* Mass.

Schottisch [Ger.]. A round dance of the 19th century in the nature of a slow polka and not the same as the **écossaise.* In England it was termed the German polka.

Schrammelmusik [Ger.]. From the late 19th century, music of the Viennese wine houses, named for the brothers Johann and Josef Schrammel, both violinists, who in 1878 founded a trio with a guitarist. A clarinetist was added in 1886 (whence the term *Schrammelquartett*); after 1893 an accordion replaced the clarinet. The repertory of these and similar ensembles consists of waltzes, marches, songs, and the like.

Schrittmässig [Ger.]. Measured; **andante.*

Schübler Chorales. Popular name for a collection of six chorale preludes for organ by Bach, BWV 645–50, published ca. 1748–49 by Johann Georg Schübler. Five of the chorale preludes are arrangements of arias from Bach's cantatas.

Schusterfleck [Ger., cobbler's patch]. **Rosalia.*

Schütteln [Ger.]. To shake.

Schwach [Ger.]. Weak, soft; *schwächer,* weaker, softer.

Schwanda the Bagpiper. See *Švanda Dudák.*

Schwanengesang [Ger., Swan Song]. A collection (not properly a cycle) of Schubert's last songs, D. 957 (1828), setting seven poems by Ludwig Rellstab, six by Heinrich Heine, and one by Johann Gabriel Seidl, published in Vienna by Tobias Haslinger, who chose the title.

Schwärmer [Ger.]. **Bombo* (3) [see also Tremolo].

Schwebung [Ger.]. (1) [pl. *Schwebungen*] *Beats. (2) In German organs, a **Céleste* stop; sometimes also *Tremulant.

Schwegel [Ger.]. (1) [also *Schwegelpfeife*] A cylindrical-bore woodwind instrument of the *flute family. *Schwegel* has referred to both a three-holed, whistle-mouthpiece *pipe and an embouchure-hole *transverse flute. Both types were built in several sizes. The first documentation of the embouchure-hole transverse flute is a 12th-century depiction of a *Schwegel.* The transverse instrument is still played in the Austrian Alps.

(2) [also *Schwiegel*] On the organ, a flute stop of mild tone, usually found at 2′ or 1′ pitch. (1) M.S.

Schweigen [Ger.]. To be silent.

Schweller, Schwellkasten [Ger.]. The organ *swell box.

Schwellwerk [Ger.]. The *Swell division of an organ.

Schwer [Ger.]. Heavy, ponderous; difficult; grave.

Schwindend [Ger.]. Dying away, becoming softer.

Schwungvoll [Ger.]. Spirited, energetic.

Sciolta [It.]. In the dancing master Fabritio Caroso's *Il ballarino* (1581) and *Nobilità di dame* (1600), any of a variety of *after-dances following a **balletto,* including the **saltarello,* **gagliarda,* and **rotta.* L.H.M.

Sciolto [It.]. Free, unconstrained.

Scolica enchiriadis. See *Musica enchiriadis.*

Scordatura [It., from *scordare,* to mistune]. Unconventional tuning of stringed instruments, particularly lutes and violins, used to facilitate or make available otherwise difficult or impossible pitch combinations, alter the characteristic timbre of the instrument to increase brilliance, reinforce certain sonorities or tonalities by making them available on open strings, imitate other instruments, etc. Scordatura appeared early in the 16th century and became common in the 17th, but much less so after about 1750. Lute music of the 16th century provides the earliest examples. Italian lutenists appear to have originated the idea of extending the range of their instruments by tuning the lowest or two lowest strings down a tone; the practice was termed *bordone descordato* [Fr. *à corde avalée*, Ger. *Abzug*]. Examples occur in Joan Ambrosio Dalza, *Intabulatura de lauto libro quarto* (Venice, 1508), and in Alberto da Ripa, *Second livre de tabulature de leut* (Paris, 1554). More elaborate ones by Italian, French, and German lutenists followed.

Violin scordatura occurs often in 17th-century violin music. Biagio Marini, in the second sonata of his opus 8 (Venice, 1629), requires the retuning of the violin's top string from e″ down to c″, to facilitate consecutive thirds between the upper two strings. Such violinist-composers as Marco Uccellini and Giovanni Maria Bononcini also used scordatura. The German violin repertory of the 17th century, particularly the works of Heinrich Ignaz Franz von Biber, contains its most thorough exploration. Fourteen of Biber's fifteen Mystery (or Rosary) Sonatas [and Passacaglia] (ca. 1676; ed. *DTÖ* 25, 1905) call for different tunings, from the simple lowering of the top string to d″ in the tenth sonata to the extraordinary g g′ d′ d″ tuning of the eleventh. Five trio sonatas in Biber's *Harmonia artificiosa-ariosa* (Nuremberg, 1712; ed. *DTÖ* 92, 1956) call for various scordaturas. Other 17th-century German composers using the technique include Johann Erasmus Kindermann (perhaps the first German to employ it), Johann Heinrich Schmelzer, Johann Pachelbel, and Johann Paul von Westhoff.

Scordatura is far less prevalent in 18th-century German music; two famous examples are Bach's Fifth Suite for unaccompanied cello in C minor BWV 1011, in which the highest string is lowered from a to g, and Mozart's *Sinfonia concertante* K. 364 (320d), in which all the strings of the solo viola are tuned a semitone sharp. It is more common in 18th-century French and Italian music. By tuning the violin's lowest string from g down to d, Antonio Lolli enabled players to accompany themselves in a lower register; pieces using this tuning were termed "in the style of Lolli." The first French use of violin scordatura appears, with the heading "Pièces à cordes ravallées," in Michel Corrette's treatise *L'école d'Orphée* (Paris, 1738). It is also called for by Vivaldi, Tartini, and Pietro Nardini.

Examples from the 19th and 20th centuries include Paganini's Violin Concerto no. 1 in D op. 6, in which the solo violin is tuned a semitone above the orchestra; the Andante cantabile in Schumann's Piano Quartet in E♭ major op. 47, in which the cello must tune the C-string to B♭; and part of the final movement in Bartók's *Contrasts* (Sz. 111), in which the violin is tuned g♯ d′ a′ e♭″, so that tritones can be played with pairs of open strings.

With rare exceptions, violin scordatura is written as a tablature: opening with the given tuning or *accordo,* the notes on the page refer to usual positions on the violin's fingerboard, rather than the resulting pitch within the nonstandard tuning. The notation assumes that the violinist will use the first position and open strings wherever possible.

Folk musicians in the southern Appalachian and

Ozark Mountains of the U.S. often employ scordatura for traditional dance tunes and ballads. The most common tuning is a e′ a′ e″.

Bibl.: Max Schneider, "Zu Bibers Violinsonaten," *ZIMG* 8 (1906–7): 471–74. Guido Adler, "Zu Bibers Violinsonaten," *ZIMG* 9 (1907–8): 29–30. Gustav Beckmann, *Das Violinspiel in Deutschland vor 1700* (Leipzig: Simrock, 1918). Andreas Moser, "Die Violin-Skordatur," *AfMw* 1 (1918–19): 573–89. Lionel de La Laurencie, *L'école française de violon de Lully à Viotti,* 3 vols. (Paris: Delagrave, 1922–24). Elizabeth Lesser, "Zur Scordatura der Streichinstrumente," *AM* 4 (1932): 123–27, 148–60. Theodore Russell, "The Violin 'Scordatura,'" *MQ* 24 (1938): 84–96. Willi Apel, *The Notation of Polyphonic Music, 900–1600* (Cambridge, Mass.: Mediaeval Acad, 1942; 5th ed., 1953). Michael Morrow, "Ayre on the F♯ String," *Lute Society Journal* 2 (1960): 9–16. David D. Boyden, *The History of Violin Playing from Its Origins to 1761* (London: Oxford U Pr, 1965). Frank Traficante, "Lyra Viol Tunings: 'All Ways have been Tryed to do It,'" *AM* 42 (1970): 183–205. Robin Stowell, *Violin Technique and Performance Practice in the Late Eighteenth and Early Nineteenth Centuries* (Cambridge: Cambridge U Pr, 1985). Jason Paras, *The Music for Viola Bastarda* (Bloomington: Ind U Pr, 1986). Ekkehard Schulze-Kurz, *Die Laute und ihre Stimmungen in der ersten Hälfte des 17. Jahrhunderts* (Wilsingen: Tre Fontane, 1990).

Score. (1) [Fr. *partition;* Ger. *Partitur;* It., Sp. *partitura*] The notation of a work, especially one for ensemble, presented in such a way that simultaneous moments in all voices or parts are aligned vertically. In a full score, each voice or part is notated on its own staff (though two parts for instruments of the same kind, e.g., two flutes or two oboes, may be placed on a single staff). In a short or condensed score, related parts (e.g., woodwinds, brass) may be combined on a single staff. A piano-vocal score (usually of an opera, oratorio, or similar work) presents vocal parts on individual staves, with orchestral parts reduced to two staves and arranged so as to be performable on the piano. A single set of all of the necessary staves running across a page is termed a system and is linked at the left and right margins by a continuous bar line. Otherwise, bar lines, while drawn through each individual staff, may run between the staves only of related instruments. There may be several systems on a page if space permits; for ease of reading, they may be separated at the left margin by a pair of bold diagonal strokes.

Although practice has varied somewhat even since the mid-19th century, the normal arrangement of parts from top to bottom in an orchestral full score places choirs of related instruments together and, within these groups, arranges individual instruments from highest down to lowest in register, as follows: piccolo and flutes, oboes, clarinets, bassoons, horns (though the order of bassoons and horns has sometimes been inverted), trumpets, trombones, tuba, timpani, other percussion (for instruments of indefinite pitch, often on a single line each rather than a five-line staff), celesta, piano, harp, the solo part in a concerto or the part for a vocal soloist, first violins, second violins, violas, vocal soloists and choral parts (in two groups, both from top to bottom in range; sometimes placed above the first violins), organ, cellos, and double basses. The first page of a score may show staves, each one identified, for all of the required instruments and voices. Thereafter, only those necessary at any time are shown, the order from top to bottom being preserved, however. Sometimes the complete list of required performers is given on a page preceding the score itself, and even the first page of the score presents only the needed staves.

Each of the larger groups, such as winds, brass, strings, etc., may be linked at the beginning of each system by a bracket. Within these groups, specific instruments whose parts are notated on more than one staff (e.g., horns if there are four, or harp and keyboard, which normally require two staves each) may have their staves linked by curved braces.

Notation in score format was employed in the sources for the polyphonic repertories of *Notre Dame and *St. Martial, especially for the **conductus*. By the middle of the 13th century and the rise to prominence of the *motet, however, it was abandoned for vocal music except in England, where it survived into the 15th century. Because the upper parts of motets included many more notes than the tenors, each part was written separately on its own set of staves, usually arranged on a single page or on facing pages, with page-turns, if any, coordinated in all parts. This format, often termed *choirbook format in the case of larger manuscripts, remained common for polyphonic music through the 16th century, even though individual parts soon ceased to be of such disparate length. *Partbooks were the other principal format for ensemble music of the 16th century. Score format was employed for keyboard music as early as the 14th century and was widespread in printed sources for keyboard music of the early 16th century [see also *Intavolatura,* Tablature]. In the later 16th and the 17th century, the term *partitura* could refer to keyboard scores in which each part of a polyphonic complex was notated on a separate staff. Manuscript scores of vocal music do not reappear until the second half of the 16th century, but steadily increase in number in this period. The first example of vocal music in a printed score is from Auctor Lampadius's treatise *Compendium musices* of 1537, and it has been argued on the basis of this treatise and the complexity of vocal music well before this time that composers had already by this date adopted the practice of using scores on erasable materials in the process of composition (Lowinsky, 1960). The first independent publications of vocal music in score date from 1577 and include madrigals by Cipriano de Rore, but these seem to have been intended for study and keyboard performance rather than for the use of singers. By the 17th century, score format was the norm for both vocal and instrumental music. The *thoroughbass part was normally placed at the bottom, with vocal parts, if any, immediately above. Otherwise the layout for scores remained flexible well into the 19th century.

(2) [v.] To create a score, often from a more abbreviated form of notation; to orchestrate [see Orchestration]; to arrange [see Arrangement].

(3) A work such as would normally be notated in score.

Bibl.: Edward E. Lowinsky, "Early Scores in Manuscript," *JAMS* 13 (1960): 126–73. Klaus Haller, *Partituranordnung und musikalischer Satz* (Tutzing: Schneider, 1970). See also Notation, Orchestration, Tablature.

Score reading. The internal realization of the sound of a work by means of simply reading the score; also the performance at the piano of a work for ensemble notated in score format.

Scoring. *Orchestration; the combination of instruments employed in a work or the character of their use.

Scorrendo, scorrevole [It.]. Flowing.

Scotch snap. *Lombard rhythm.

Scotch (Scottish) Symphony. Popular name for Mendelssohn's Symphony no. 3 in A minor op. 56 (begun in 1830, completed in 1841–42), inspired by a visit to Scotland in 1829.

Scotland. I. *Current musical life and related institutions.* Scottish musical life today is centered in Glasgow, although significant activity also takes place in both Aberdeen and Edinburgh (the capital city and until the late 19th century the cultural capital of the country). Distribution of resources is overseen by the Scottish Arts Council, which has its headquarters in Edinburgh. Glasgow is home to the Scottish Opera and its chorus, the Royal Scottish National Orchestra, the BBC Scottish orchestras, and the Scottish Early Music Consort. Edinburgh is the site of the national copyright library and a number of comparatively small ensembles, including the Scottish Chamber Orchestra, as well as several choruses and specialized instrumental groups. Major festivals include the long-established Edinburgh International Festival, the St. Magnus Festival in Orkney, Glasgow's Mayfest, and the Perth Festival of the Arts. Aberdeen has an independent broadcasting company and sponsors numerous concerts by touring groups and many festivals. Universities in all three of these cities offer advanced training in music, but the only conservatory is located in Glasgow. The BBC, the Arts Council, the Saltire Society, the McEwen Bequest, and the Edinburgh Contemporary Arts Trust are all significant patrons of contemporary music and support interest in older Scottish music as well. The Scottish Music Information Centre (founded in 1968 as the Scottish Music Archive) at the University of Glasgow is intended eventually to cover all of the country's music.

II. *History.* The music of Scotland past and present is an amalgam of native and derived traditions. One of Scotland's earliest surviving musical sources, the manuscript Wolfenbüttel 677 (W1), thought to have originated at St. Andrews Priory, is a chief source both of *Notre Dame polyphony and of music that appears to be of local origin. Native music represented in the 16th-century manuscripts known as the Scone Antiphoner and the St. Andrews Psalter shows the influence of English and Italian polyphony. Edinburgh became an important musical center during the 18th century, beginning in 1725 with the establishment of the Edinburgh Musical Society, which sponsored concerts of German, Italian, and English music, and of Scottish *ballad operas.

Scotland's first music professor was the composer John Thomson (1805–41), appointed to Edinburgh's Reid Chair of Music in 1839. At the beginning of the 20th century the German-influenced music of Alexander MacKenzie (1847–1935), resident in England after 1885, helped reestablish British composition in Europe; also in England during this period were the Scottish composers William Wallace (1860–1940) and John B. McEwen (1868–1948). The works of composers such as Francis George Scott (1880–1958) began to show less influence of German and English models and more reliance on Scotland's rich folk materials. More recent composers include Ian Whyte (1901–60), Erik Chisholm (1904–65), William Wordsworth (1908–88), Robin Orr (b. 1909), Cedric Thorpe Davie (1913–83), Iain Hamilton (1922–2000), Thomas Wilson (b. 1927), and, perhaps most important, Thea Musgrave (b. 1928). Significant among the younger generation are David Dorward (b. 1933), Sebastian Forbes (b. 1941), and Martin Dalby (b. 1942).

III. *Folk music.* Each of Scotland's two language cultures, lowland Scots and highland Gaelic, has a more or less distinct body of folk music. The lowlands are known for vocal songs and ballads and for instrumental dance styles such as the *strathspey, the *reel, and the bagpipe *lament. Of highland origin is the **pibroch* (great music) for bagpipe, consisting of ornate variations on a theme called an *urlar.* Other characteristic highland styles are the Heroic Ballad, the *ôran môr* (great song), the Gaelic psalm, the "waulking" song, and the *puirt-a-beul.* The music of the Shetland and Orkney Islands is more closely related to Scandinavian folk repertory than to that of the British Isles.

Bibl.: Francis Collinson, *The Traditional and National Music of Scotland* (Nashville: Vanderbilt U Pr, 1966). Helena Mennie Shire, *Song, Dance and Poetry of the Court of Scotland under King James VI* (Cambridge: Cambridge U Pr, 1969). George S. Emmerson, *Rantin' Pipe and Tremblin' String: A History of Scottish Dance Music* (London: Dent, 1971). David Johnson, *Music and Society in Lowland Scot-*

land in the 18th Century (London: Oxford U Pr, 1972). Roger Fiske, *Scotland in Music* (Cambridge: Cambridge U Pr, 1983). John Purser, *Scotland's Music: A History of the Traditional and Classical Music of Scotland from Earliest Times to the Present Day* (Edinburgh: Mainstream, 1992). Bridget Mackenzie, *Piping Traditions of the North of Scotland* (Edinburgh: J. Donald, 1997). Ailie Munro and Morag MacLeod, *The Democratic Muse: Folk Music Revival in Scotland* (Aberdeen: Scottish Cultural Pr, 1997). G. W. Lockhart, *Fiddles and Folk: A Celebration of the Re-Emergence of Scotland's Musical Heritage* (Edinburgh: Luath, 1998).

Scraper. An instrument made by cutting notches in a stick, bone, gourd, piece of bamboo, etc., and scraping with a stick or metal rod. See also Cog rattle, *Güiro, Reco-reco, Yü.*

Scrittura [It.]. A contract, usually one drawn up between a composer and an impresario or opera company for the composition of a new opera.

Scroll. The coiled ornamental carving above the pegbox of the violin and related instruments.

Scucito [It.]. Detached, *non legato.*

Sdrucciolando [It.]. In harp playing, *glissando.

Seasons, The. An oratorio for soloists, chorus, and orchestra by Haydn, Hob. XXI:3 (1799–1801), with a German libretto *(Die Jahreszeiten)* by Gottfried van Swieten, based on an English poem by James Thomson translated by Barthold Heinrich Brockes. Its four parts portray spring, summer, fall, and winter. See also *Four Seasons, The.*

Sea Symphony, A. Vaughan Williams's Symphony no. 1, composed in 1903–9 (final revisions, 1923), for soloists, chorus, and orchestra, based on texts from Walt Whitman's *Leaves of Grass.*

Sec [Fr.]. Dry, staccato.

Secco recitative. See Recitative.

Sechszehntel, Sechszehntelnote, Sechszehntelpause [Ger.]. See Note.

Second. See Interval, Scale degrees.

Seconda prattica [It.]. See *Prima prattica, seconda prattica.*

Secondary dominant. See Dominant, Tonicization.

Seconda volta [It.]. See *Prima volta, seconda volta.*

Seelenamt [Ger.]. *Requiem Mass.

Seelenvoll [Ger.]. Soulful.

Segno [It.]. A sign (𝄋) used to mark the beginning or end of a repeated section of a work. If the former, the end of the section bears the instruction *dal segno* (from the sign, often abbreviated *D.S.*); if the latter, the beginning of the section bears the instruction *al segno* (to the sign), *sin' al segno* (until the sign), or *fin' al segno* (end at the sign). See also *Da capo.*

Segue [It., follows]. (1) An indication that the next section of a work is to follow immediately without interruption, e.g., *segue l'aria, segue la coda.* (2) An instruction to continue a manner of execution that is at first written out in full, but thereafter abbreviated, e.g., a pattern of broken chords [for abbreviations of this type, see Notation].

Seguidilla [Sp.]. (1) A Spanish verse form consisting of one or more strophes of four or seven lines each, as follows: 7.5.7.5 or 7.5.7.5.5.7.5, with assonance within the pair(s) of five-syllable lines. Originally a form of popular poetry, it was taken up increasingly by poets in the later 16th century. Musical settings occur from around 1600 through the **zarzuelas* of the 19th and 20th centuries. (2) [pl. *seguidillas*] A couple dance, widely distributed in Spain, done to the singing of a text of the type described under (1), accompanied by guitar, and in a moderately fast triple meter. The dance is first mentioned by Cervantes and other writers around 1600. (3) [*siguiriya, seguidilla gitana*] One of the principal types of *flamenco music, also termed *playera,* with a text (perhaps derived from (1) above) often of four lines, 7.5.11.5, with assonance between lines 2 and 4. The guitar accompaniment freely alternates measures of 6/8 and 3/4 under the flexible rhythm of the vocal part.

Sehnsucht [Ger.]. Longing; *Sehnsuchtvoll,* filled with longing.

Sehr [Ger.]. Very.

Seikilos epitaph. An epitaph of the 2nd century B.C.E. or later inscribed on stone for the wife of one Seikilos and discovered in Asia Minor. It includes one of the few surviving examples of the music of ancient *Greece (see *HAM,* no. 7c).

Seis [Sp.]. A traditional song and dance-music genre of Puerto Rico, with numerous named subtypes corresponding to distinctions in choreography, region or locale, particular musicians with whom they are associated, and stylistic features. It is in 2/4 meter and moderate to rapid tempo, complicated by syncopation and characteristic triplet figuration in both melody and accompaniment, and it most typically sets *décima* texts that are often improvised. The *seis de controversia* involves a contest of textual improvisation between two singers. A common performance ensemble consists of one singer (or two, singing in alternation), *cuatro* (guitar with five double courses of strings), six-string guitar, and *güiro.* D.S.

Seises [Sp.]. From the 16th through the 19th century in the cathedrals of Seville and a few other cities of Spain and the New World, a group of six *(seis)* choirboys who sang polyphony and who, in Seville, danced in elaborate costumes, sometimes to specially composed music, on the feasts of Corpus Christi and the Immaculate Conception.

Bibl.: Simón de la Rosa y López, *Los seises de la Catedral de Sevilla* (Seville: F de P Díaz, 1904).

Seite [Ger.]. Side, as of an instrument.

Seitensatz, Seitenthema [Ger.]. The second subject in sonata form.

Semele. A dramatic oratorio by Handel (libretto based on a play by William Congreve), first performed in London in 1744. Setting: classical mythology.

Semi- [Lat.]. Half; for *semibiscroma, semibreve (semibrevis), semicroma, semifusa, semiminima, semiquaver,* see Note, Mensural notation; *semidiapente,* diminished fifth; *semiditonus,* minor third; *semiditas, proportio dupla* [see Proportions].

Semi-opera. In England in the late 17th century and the first years of the 18th, a dramatic work in which the principal characters employed only speech but in which there were elaborate musical scenes for lesser characters. The first such work was Thomas Betterton's version of Shakespeare's *The Tempest,* produced in 1674 with music by Pelham Humfrey, Matthew Locke, and others. The best-known examples are Purcell's *Dioclesian* (1690), *King Arthur* (1691), *The *Fairy Queen* (1692), and *The *Indian Queen* (1695).

Semiramide. Opera in two acts by Rossini (libretto by Gaetano Rossi, based on Voltaire's tragedy), produced in Venice in 1823. Setting: ancient Babylon.

Semitone. The smallest interval in use in the Western musical tradition. There are twelve such intervals to the octave, i.e., between two pitches with the same pitch name. The semitone is represented on the piano keyboard by the distance between any two immediately adjacent keys, whether white or black. See Interval.

Semplice [It.]. Simple, without ornament. For *recitativo semplice,* see Recitative.

Sempre [It.]. Always, continuously.

Senario [It.]. In the writings of the 16th-century theorist Gioseffo Zarlino, the first six numbers and the ratios between them, 1:2:3:4:5:6, from which he derived the ratios for all consonant *intervals.

Sennet [perhaps fr. It. *sonata;* also senet, sennate, signate, synnet, cynet]. In the stage directions of Elizabethan plays, music played by trumpets or cornetts to signal the entrance or exit of a group of actors. See also Tuck, tucket.

Sensible [Fr.]. Leading tone.

Sentito [It.]. Felt, expressive.

Senza [It.]. Without; *s. tempo, s. misura,* without strict measure; for *s. sordini,* see Mute.

Sepolcro [It., sepulchre]. In 17th-century Vienna, an oratorio in one part on the Passion story, set at the holy sepulchre and staged in the court chapel with scenery and costumes.

Septet [Fr. *septour;* Ger. *Septett;* It. *septetto;* Sp. *septeto*]. (1) A chamber composition for seven solo performers. (2) An ensemble of seven solo performers. Most compositions of this type employ mixed winds and strings, as does Beethoven's Septet op. 20, one of his works most popular with his contemporaries. Hummel's once-celebrated Septet uses a piano, as do those of Spohr and Saint-Saëns. Later septets include Ravel's *Introduction and Allegro,* Schoenberg's Suite op. 29, Hindemith's Wind Septet, and Stravinsky's Septet. There are a few operatic septets.

Septuor [Fr.]. *Septet.

Septuplet. A group of seven notes of equal value to be played in the time normally occupied by four or six notes of the same value.

Sepulchrum play. A *liturgical drama set at the holy sepulchre.

Sequela. A textless melody to which a text was fitted in order to produce a sequence [see Sequence (2)]. The term was coined by Dom Anselm Hughes ca. 1930.

Sequence. (1) The repetition of a phrase of melody (melodic sequence) and or a harmonic progression (harmonic sequence) at different pitch levels, the succession of pitch levels rising or falling by the same or similar intervals. In a melodic sequence (as distinct from *imitation), the repetition occurs within a single voice. A melody may be transposed exactly, retaining its precise interval content and thus probably effecting a change of key, or the sequence may proceed diatonically, the melody retaining only its general contour and remaining in the same key. Many sequences mix the two procedures, and sequences are often employed to bring about modulations. In the case of a melodic sequence, the harmony may or may not remain the same in relationship to the melody. Sequences occur frequently in the music of Baroque composers such as Handel [Ex.] and in the development sections of works in sonata form and similar modulatory passages of the Classical period. The sequential treatment of *leitmotifs is a prominent feature of the musico-dramatic technique of Wagner. See also *Rosalia.*

(2) [Lat. *sequentia;* Fr. *prose*] In medieval music, and continuing into later periods in some regions, one of the most important genres of proper *Mass chants in the Roman rite. Terminology has proved problematic because medieval manuscripts themselves are inconsistent, and because the sequence existed in two forms in the Carolingian period, texted and untexted. In modern English scholarship the term *sequentia* is commonly employed for the untexted form of the genre and *sequence* for the texted form; *prose* appears occasionally for the texted form and predominates in modern French scholarship. From the 9th century, sequences were sung in the Mass after the Alleluia and

Sequence.

before the intoning of the Gospel on major feast days, although they were sometimes adopted for use in the Divine Office, especially at Vespers, and sometimes as processional pieces or in liturgical dramas. Because Alleluias were not sung in penitential times, the sequences too were usually not sung in Lent. In centers east of the Rhine, they tended not to be sung at Advent, whereas west of the Rhine they usually were. Although many famous early melodies are well known in both East and West Frankish repertories, the families of texts vary, and the strong regionality of sequence repertories is of major importance, making the works evidence of the highest order for the study of religious and musical cultures in the Middle Ages.

Individual works are often related either musically, textually, or both, to the Alleluia of the day, and the nature of the relationship between Alleluias and sequences, especially in the earliest layers of the repertory, is complex. It is clear from the writings of medieval liturgical commentators that the Alleluia of the Mass liturgy had a rich tradition of theological interpretation, and that sequence poets and composers were influenced by this tradition and the early history of the genre as established in the famous preface to the *Liber hymnorum* by the learned and prolific monk of St. Gall, Notker Balbulus (c. 840–912). In this work he claimed that *longissimae melodiae,* the long melismas that often closed Alleluias, were very difficult for young singers to remember. When a monk from Jumièges came to St. Gall, he brought examples of syllables designed to be sung to the melodies, thereby making the music easier to retain. Notker's teachers were able to critique his own efforts at writing similar pieces, and persuaded him to compose more works in the genre and create the famous compilation, which is a collection of texts only. In spite of the many ambiguities of Notker's account, it is one of the few contemporary references to the sequence and suggests a northern French origin for the form and a date from before the mid-9th century. It also implies that sequences were, to begin with at least, texted jubili of Alleluias, and that they—like the Alleluias at Mass—were commonly sung by children and youth, an assumption borne out by study of early medieval monastic customaries. Repetition of melodic phrases is characteristic of Alleluia melodies and of the sequence. Short, sharply marked, often triadic melodic units prevail, making the early sequence a matrix for the development of melodic style in the late Carolingian period. The regional bodies of texts have differing exegetical strategies: those written in the Notkerian vein emphasize biblical typologies; early sequences from West Francia often embody liturgical commentary, exploring what it means for humans to sing with the angels and employing deliberately strange turns of phrase.

Throughout the various stages of its history, the sequence had certain formal characteristics that were more or less constant and inherited from the earliest repertories, especially (1) a through-composed form, with different music for each successive pair of lines or each successive strophe; (2) repetition within each section so that each unit of melody, whether a single phrase or a whole hymnlike stanza, was repeated with new text before the introduction of the next melodic unit; and (3) a largely syllabic setting of the text. Thus sequences, no matter when they were written, commonly consist of a series of melodically paired versicles with the form aa bb cc dd ee ff, etc., with repetition sometimes wanting in the opening or closing melodic units. Earlier repertories of sequences tend to be found in manuscripts called *tropers or prosers, which also included tropes; in the 12th century sequences are found in missals or graduals, sometimes in separate sections, sometimes mixed with other proper chants, feast by feast. In the Middle Ages, sequences are found in separate sections in missals, or gathered as collections of texts for devotional reading. It seems clear that the performance practice of the sequence varied from place to place and time to time, with the genre being predominantly for soloists in the first centuries and sung antiphonally by the choir in the later Middle Ages, sometimes with various uses of the organ or with improvised polyphony.

The later history of the sequence demonstrates much experimentation, as well as dependence on the authority of early examples that remained popular for centuries. In the *Analecta hymnica* and other compendia, sequences have been organized into three groups: (1) the early (or first epoch) style, with its heightened but free art-prose; (2) the "transitional" style of the 11th century, which increasingly used rhyme and accentual patterns; and (3) the late (or second epoch) style of Adam of St. Victor (d. 1146) and others from the 12th century, which used hymn-like stanzas marked by strong accentual patterns and rhyme, especially at the ends of half-lines and lines. Recent scholarship suggests that this traditional scheme is an over-simplification, and that there really was no "transitional" style in the 11th century but rather a number of competing styles, with the rhyming, accentual poetry championed by the Victorines and other Augustinians eventually becoming predominant, and this at a time when poetry in the rhythmic style was gaining in other liturgical genres as well.

Although once studied primarily for the imagistic richness and poetic innovations of their texts, Victorine sequences have recently been recognized as of major importance in the history of western music as well. The poet Adam of St. Victor is now identified with Adam, precentor of the Cathedral of Notre Dame, a musician who lived in the first half of the 12th century, dying in 1146, and a contemporary of Abelard and of Hildegard of Bingen, both of whom also wrote distinguished sequences. The texts by Adam and the Parisian school are recognized as commentaries on religious life by reforming Augustinians, commentaries in which music plays a major role. By the end of the 12th century, over 100 new sequences had been adapted for liturgical use in Paris, and well over half of these were composed in Paris itself. This extraordinary musical activity first marked Paris as a musical center and initiated the activities of the repertory of *Notre Dame. Sophisticated techniques of contrafacta were used in this repertory to capitalize upon the symbolic power of music and to link texts in a variety of ways. The sequence *Laudes crucis,* for example, which may have been written by Adam of St. Victor, was reset many times, joining a large group of texts into a magnificent commentary upon the meanings of the Cross and of the ideals of Augustinian canons regular. In addition, the Victorine sequences, whose texts fell into sharply marked trochaic accentual patterns, offered composers rhythmic grids against which they experimented with various techniques of melodic variation and rhythmic shapes, both of which were essential background for the newer polyphonic styles developed at this place and time. The late sequences of Paris formally resemble through-composed hymns, and are the forerunners of the popular styles of strophic song that came to predominate later in many religious movements. Of the new religious orders founded in the 13th century, only the Dominicans wrote substantial numbers of sequences, the majority of which were in honor of the Virgin Mary. The most famous of the Dominican sequences is *Laude Sion salvatorem,* whose text is set to the melody *Laudes crucis;* this piece, composed for the feast of Corpus Christi, is often attributed to Thomas Aquinas. Sequence texts were of major importance both as devotional texts and as the subjects of numerous commentaries in the 14th through the 16th centuries.

In the 15th century composers continued both to write new monophonic sequences and to set older examples polyphonically, making a new day for the genre at the dawn of the Early Modern period. However, the 16th-century reforms of the Council of Trent were unkind to the medieval sequence, as they were to any genre that did not advance the humanists' taste for classical Latin forms and meters. In the same age when Roman Catholics were losing their sequence repertories to the reforms of the Counter-Reformation, Protestant reformers were seizing upon the popular melodies and forms of the genre, often setting tunes with new words that advanced particular theological agendas. Modern chant books reflect the Tridentine cutting away of medieval sequences, and retain only five examples of the genre, none of which is from the early repertory: *Victimae paschali,* a late 11th-century Easter sequence; and four works from the 12th through the 14th centuries, *Lauda Sion Salvatorem* (Corpus Christi); *Veni sancte spiritus* (Pentecost); *Stabat Mater Dolorosa* (Sorrows of the Virgin); and *Dies irae* (Mass of the Dead).

Bibl.: Eugene Misset and Pierre Aubry, *Les proses d'Adam de Saint-Victor* (Paris: H. Welter, 1900). Wolfram Von den Steinen, *Notker der Dichter,* 2 vols. (Bern: Francke, 1948). Richard Crocker, *The Early Medieval Sequence* (Berkeley: U of Cal Pr., 1977). Margot E. Fassler, "Who Was Adam of St. Victor," JAMS 37 (1984): 233–69. Chrysogonus Waddell, "'Epithalamica': An Easter Sequence by Peter Abelard," *Musical Quarterly* 72 (1986): 239–71. Id., "Accent, Meter, and Rhythm in Medieval Treatises *De rithmis,*" JM 5 (1987): 345–374; Id., "The Role of the Parisian Sequence in the Evolution of Notre-Dame Polyphony." *Speculum* 62 (1987): 345–74. Franz Karl Prassl, *Psallat Ecclesia Mater: Studien zu Repertoire und Verwendung von Sequenzen in der Liturgie österreichischer Augustinerchorherren* (Klagenfurt, 1987); Joseph Szövérffy, *Latin Hymns,* Typologie des sources du moyen âge occidental, 55 (Turnhout: Brepols, 1989). Craig Wright, "Dufay's *Nuper rosarum flores,*" JAMS 47 (1994): 395–441. Susan Boynton, "Rewriting the Early Sequence: *Aureo flore* and *Aurea virga,*" *Comitatus* 25 (1994): 19–42. David Hiley, "The Repertory of Sequences at Winchester," in *Essays on Medieval Music in Honor of David Hughes,* ed. Graeme M. Boone (Cambridge: Harvard U Pr., 1995), 153–93. Susan Rankin and Wulf Arlt, eds., *Stiftsbibliothek Sankt Gallen Codices 484 & 381* (Winterthur, 1996). Michael McGrade, "Gottschalk of Aachen," JAMS 49 (1996): 351–408. Lori Kruckenberg-Goldenstein, "The Sequence from 1050–1150" (Ph.D. diss., U of Iowa, 1997). Lance Brunner, ed., *Early Medieval Chants from Nonantola,* part IV: *Sequences* (Madison, A-R Editions, 1999). Alejandro Planchart, "Proses in the Manuscripts of Roman Chant and Their Alleluias," in *The Study of Medieval Chant,* ed. Peter Jeffery (London: Boydell and Brewer, 2001). Margot E. Fassler, *Gothic Song: Victorine Sequences and Augustinian Reform,* 2nd ed. (South Bend: U Notre Dame Pr, 2003). (2) M.E.F.

Sequentia [Lat.]. In the Middle Ages, the textless melody to which a text (termed a *prosa*) was fitted in order to create what is now usually called a sequence [see Sequence (2)].

Seraphine. A small reed organ invented in England ca. 1830. See also Harmonium.

Serbia and Montenegro (Srbija i Crna Gora). I. *Current musical life and related institutions.* The federation consists of Serbia, with cultural centers in Belgrade and Novi Sad, and Montenegro, with the center in Podgorica. The first music school in Belgrade was founded in 1899, while university-level education began in 1937 at the Academy of Music (today Fakultet muzičke umetnosti). Music academies also exist in Novi Sad (1973), Priština (1975), Cetinje (1980), and Niš (1987). Research in Serbian music history, Orthodox chant, and traditional music is mainly carried out at the Muzikološki institut (1948), affiliated with the Srpska akademija nauka i umetnosti (Serbian Academy of Sciences and Arts), the publisher of the journal *Muzikogija* (2001). Other scholarly periodicals are *Zbornik Matice srpske za scenske umetnosti i muziku* (Novi Sad, 1987), and the English-language *New Sound* (Belgrade, 1993) published by the Savez organizacija kompozitora Jugoslavije (1950). The Belgrade Opera (1920), well known for its Slavic repertoire, was at the forefront of European opera productions during the tenure of Oskar Danon (b. 1913) as its artistic director (1945–60). The ballet ensemble of the opera was founded in 1923. The leading orchestras in Belgrade are the Beogradska filharmonija (1923), the Simfonijski orkestar RTV (1937), chamber ensembles Dušan Skovran (1965) and Gudači svetog Djordja (1992); in Novi Sad, the Vojvođanska filharmonija (1978); and in Podgorica, the Simfonijski orkestrar RTV (1959). Choral singing has had a strong tradition since the early 19th century, the leading ensembles presently being the choir of Belgrade RTV (1939), Obilić/Krsmanović (1884), and the women's choir Collegium musicum (1963). The Studijski hor Muzikološkog instituta in Belgrade (1969), directed by Dimitrije Stefanović, is dedicated to interpretation of Serbian Orthodox chant. The festival Beogradske Muzičke Svečanosti (BEMUS, 1969) has gained an international reputation.

II. *History of art music.* Medieval a cappella singing, which developed within the Serbian Orthodox church (autocephalous since 1219), was influenced by the Byzantines and based on the *octoechos *(osmoglasnik).* The largest repository of Serbian medieval manuscripts, the earliest being from the 15th century, is at the Hilandar and Great Lavra monasteries on Mt. Athos. They include the earliest Serbian-attributed compositions by Nikola Srbin (fl. late 14th century), Stefan Srbin (fl. ca. 1450), and Isaija Srbin (fl. late 15th century), notated with middle-Byzantine neumes. Indirect evidence about musical life in medieval Serbia is found in frescoes in churches throughout southern Serbia and Kosovo. With the 1690 migration of the Serbs from Kosovo to Vojvodina and the establishment of the religious center in Sremski Karlovci, contacts with European rationalism became frequent and church music was prodded into new life. Earlier orally transmitted chants were first transcribed in Western staff notation in Sremski Karlovci in the mid-1850s by the composer Kornelije Stanković (1831–65).

Secular music was reborn after the withdrawal of the Ottomans in the early 19th century, almost directly adopting Romanticism. Its main forms were theater plays with musical numbers *(komad s pevanjem)* and choral music, which provided the repertoire for numerous choral societies formed throughout the 19th century. The first orchestra, Knjaževsko-srbska banda, conducted by Josif Šlezinger (1794–1870) was formed in Kragujevac in 1830. The leading music personalities toward the end of the century were Davorin Jenko (1835–1914), Josif Marinković (1851–1931), Robert Tolinger (1859–1911), and particularly Stevan St. Mokranjac (1856–1914), who formulated in his 15 *rukoveti* (1883–1909) the form of choral rhapsody consisting of arranged folk songs. After the turn of the 20th century, musical life in Serbia matched its European models. The first performance of a national opera, *Na uranku* (At Dawn) by Stevan Binički (1872–1942), was staged in Belgrade in 1904. The period between the two world wars was defined by Petar Konjović (1883–1970), who introduced several genres into Serbian music and was instrumental in founding the Muzikološki institut and the Belgrade Music Academy; the composer, journalist, and musicologist Miloje Milojević (1884–1946); Stevan Hristić (1884–1958); and the Croatian composer Josip Štolcer Slavenski (1896–1955), who lived in Belgrade after 1924. The generation of composers who studied in Prague during the 1930s opened up to a variety of styles: Mihajlo Vukdragović (1900–86), Mihovil Logar (1902–98), Dragutin Čolić (1907–87), Milan Ristić (1908–82), Ljubica Marić (b. 1909), and Stanojlo Rajičić (1910–2000). Stylistic pluralism became even greater with the following generation: Ludmila Frajt (1919–99), Vasilije Mokranjac (1923–84), Konstantin Babić (b. 1927), Aleksandar Obradović (b. 1927), Dejan Despić (b. 1930), Peter Ozgijan (1932–79), Rajko Maksimović (b. 1935), and Mirjana Živković (b. 1935). The generation born in the 1940s and 1950s, marked by the postmodern sensibility, includes Srđan Hofman (b. 1944), Milan Mihajlović (b. 1945), Vuk Kulenović (b. 1946), Vlastimir Trajković (b. 1947), and Zoran Erić (b. 1950). Among the youngest composers to have achieved distinction are Miloš Petrović (b. 1952), Žarko Mirković (b. 1952), Nebojša Jovan Živković (b. 1962), and Goran Kapetanović (b. 1969).

Electronic music received impetus with the founding of the Elektronski studio Radio Beograda in 1971, directed by Vladan Radovanović (b. 1932).

III. *Traditional music.* Vocal tradition is conveyed in diaphonic and monophonic singing. Diaphonic singing has two distinct styles. The older style (singing *na glas,* or at full voice) is characterized by a narrow melodic range and the second as the main chord interval. The newer style (singing *na bas*), featuring a soloist with accompaniment, has the third as the main interval, with the perfect fifth at the end of melopoetic units. Monophonic songs are performed during *sedeljka* (leisurely gatherings) or rituals, such as the *koleda* during Christmastime; the *lazarica* on Lazarus's Saturday, before Easter; Pentacostal ritual, or *kraljičke pesme,* and the *dodole* ritual performed to invoke rain. The Montenegrin songs are one-part and polyphonic, with the melody and singing style similar to those in western Serbia. A significant vocal-instrumental tradition in both Serbia and Montenegro is the singing of epic songs accompanied by the **gusle.*

Instrumental music is associated with leisure time, rituals, or as an accompaniment of the *kolo* (round dance). The main aerophones are the *frula* (short flute), *duduk, cevara* (long flutes), and *dvojnice* (double flute), and *gajde* (bagpipes). The *zurle* (shawm) is used by ethnic Albanians in Kosovo, usually accompanied by the *tupan* (big drum). String instruments include *tambura* (mostly in Vojvodina) and the violin (in urban ensembles). The accordion has been popular since World War I. The popularity of brass bands was greatly advanced by the festival Dragačevski sabor trubača, held yearly in Guča since 1961. Brass-band music is homophonic, with penetrating sound and intense rhythm produced by the *tupan* with cymbals.

Adjacent to Serbia proper are two culturally and ethnically distinct areas: Vojvodina to the north, with Hungarian, Slovak, and Romanian ethnic minorities, and Kosovo to the south with an Albanian majority.

Bibl.: Vlastimir Peričić, *Muzički stvaraoci u Srbiji* [Composers in Serbia] (Beograd: Prosveta, 1969). Stana Djurić-Klajn, *A Survey of Serbian Music through the Ages* (Beograd: SANU, 1972). Dragotin Cvetko, *Musikgeschichte der Südslaven* (Kassel: Bärenreiter, 1975). Danica Petrović, *Osmoglasnik u muzičkoj tradiciji Južnih Slavena* [Oktōēchos in the music tradition of South Slavs] (Beograd: SANU, 1982). Mirjana Veselinović, *Stvaralačka prisustnost evropske avangarde u nas* [The Creative Presence of the European Avant-Garde in Serbia] (Beograd: Univerzitet umetnosti, 1983). Roksanda Pejović, *Predstave muzičkih instrumenata u srednjovekovnoj Srbiji* [Musical Instruments in Medieval Serbia] (Beograd: SANU, 1984). Nadežda Mosusova, ed., *Srpska muzička scena* [Serbian Music Theater] (Beograd: SANU, 1995). Roksanda Pejović et al., *Srpska muzika od naseljavanja slovenskih plemena na Balkansko poluostrvo do kraja XVIII veka* [Serbian Music from the First Settlements of Slav Tribes on the Balkan Peninsula until the End of the 18th Century] (Beograd: Univerzitet umetnosti, 1998).

Discography: *Srpsko pojanje* [Serbian Chant], prod. by Dimitrije Stefanović (SOKOJ, 1997). *Serbia: An Anthology of Serbian Folk Music,* prod. by Dimitrije O. Golemović and Katarina Knezović (VDE-GALLO, 1999). *Kosovo Roma,* prod. by Svanibor Pettan (Nika/Arhefon, Ljubljana 2001).

Z.B.

Serenade. A vocal or instrumental work intended for performance in the evening and usually addressed to a lover, friend, or person of rank. More loosely, music performed to seek the favor of someone.

The custom of serenading was already frequent in the Renaissance. In its most traditional form, an admirer sings beneath a lady's window (as in the aria "Deh vieni alla finestra" from Mozart's *Don Giovanni*), though part songs are also common.

The most important type of serenade during the 18th century was that for instruments. Such works were often commissioned for a specific occasion. Mozart's six Salzburg serenades are festive, large-scale pieces for orchestra, while his three Viennese serenades are for six to thirteen winds. Serenades for a small chamber ensemble were also common, however, especially in Vienna; scoring of this type is still found in Beethoven's Serenades op. 8 (for string trio) and op. 25 (for flute, violin, and viola).

The overall form of the 18th-century serenade is usually based on the standard three-movement (fast–slow–fast) succession of Classical instrumental music, to which are added marches (often as a processional or recessional), minuets (usually two or three), and often movements featuring one or more soloists. It should be noted that the terms *notturno and *cassation were used interchangeably with serenade by many composers of the 18th century.

The serenade continued to be cultivated during the 19th century, examples including two by Brahms and the Dvořák and Tchaikovsky serenades for strings. A late example of the wind serenade is Richard Strauss's op. 7; an example of the chamber serenade is Hugo Wolf's *Italian Serenade* (in its original version for string quartet).

See also Serenata.

Bibl.: Günter Hausswald, *Mozarts Serenaden* (Leipzig: Breitkopf & Härtel, 1951). Carl Bär, "Zum Begriff des 'Basso' in Mozarts Serenaden," *MJb* (1960–61): 133–55. Reimund Hess, "Serenade, Cassation, Notturno und Divertimento bei Michael Haydn" (diss., Univ. of Mainz, 1963). James Webster, "Towards a History of Viennese Chamber Music in the Early Classical Period," *JAMS* 27 (1974): 212–47. Id., "The Scoring of Mozart's Chamber Music for Strings," *Brook,* 1985, pp. 259–96.

E.K.W.

Serenata [It.]. (1) *Serenade. (2) In the Baroque period, a cantata composed to celebrate a special occasion such as the name-day of a prince or the arrival of an important visitor. Serenatas were often performed in the evening and outdoors, hence the name. They were usually longer and more elaborate than solo cantatas, with several characters and a plot or theme of pastoral, mythological, or allegorical content. Serenatas commonly featured impressive costumes and scenery but little or no stage action. Important composers of serenatas include Alessandro Stradella and Alessandro Scarlatti in Italy and Johann Joseph Fux and Antonio Caldara in Vienna. E.K.W.

Serial music. Music constructed according to permutations of a group of elements placed in a certain order or series. These elements may include pitches, durations, or virtually any other musical values. Strictly speaking, serial music encompasses *twelve-tone music as well as music employing other types of pitch series, i.e., those containing fewer than twelve pitches (e.g., certain "pre–twelve-tone" movements from Schoenberg's *Five Piano Pieces* op. 23 and Serenade op. 24; Stravinsky's *In Memoriam Dylan Thomas*) and those containing more than twelve pitches (e.g., Messiaen's *Quatuor pour la fin du temps*). Normally, however, the term is reserved for music that extends classical Schoenbergian twelve-tone pitch techniques and, especially, applies serial control to other musical elements, such as duration. Such music, mainly developed after World War II (although there were also earlier tendencies in this direction, notably in the music of Berg and Cowell), is often distinguished from twelve-tone serialism as "integral" or "total" serialism. It is usually characterized by a high degree of precompositional planning and thus also of compositional determinacy.

The leading figures in the early development of integral serialism were Stockhausen and Boulez in Europe and Babbitt in the U.S. Boulez, influenced by Messiaen's piano piece *Mode de valeurs et d'intensités* of 1949 (which, although not strictly serial, exhibits considerable precompositional determination of pitch, registral, durational, and attack characteristics), developed a method for controlling different musical parameters through permutations of a single series of twelve numbers. This approach is employed most systematically in his *Structures 1a* for two pianos (1952), for which the pitches, durational values, dynamics, and attack types are all precompositionally ordered into "scales" of twelve elements. In the case of durations, for example, the first element in the scale is a thirty-second note, while each successive element adds a thirty-second note to the previous value. Thus, the second value is a sixteenth note, the third a dotted sixteenth, the fourth an eighth, etc. Then each member of each scale of elements (i.e., those for pitch, duration, dynamics, and attack) is assigned a number from 1 to 12, so that the numbers of the numerical series can be assigned various musical values. Since most compositional choices are thus determined by the numerical series (and there is also a higher-order series selecting the choice of serial permutations), the compositional process takes on an almost automatic quality. Moreover, the constant permutation of all the musical elements tends to cancel out any significant distinctions in the musical details. In his subsequent music, Boulez has developed a much freer and more flexible approach to serial technique.

Whereas Boulez's early serialism is oriented toward the permutation of individual musical units, widely separated from one another in pointillistic textures [see Pointillism], Stockhausen in the 1950s favored the use of serial structures to control the more generalized characteristics of large-scale organization. In his **Gruppen* for three orchestras (1957), for example, the basic series consists of a succession of numerical proportions that governs the length of formal sections, the tempos of these sections, and even such general textural features as the overall pitch range of each segment, the number of events within the segment, the speed of these events, etc. Stockhausen called this approach group composition, the musical character of a group being defined primarily by its overall statistical qualities rather than the combination, or summation, of its individual pointillistic elements.

The earliest composition to control both pitch and nonpitch components through serial means was Babbitt's *Three Compositions for Piano,* written in 1947. The opening movement of this work, for instance, has an essentially traditional twelve-tone pitch structure, but it also integrates dynamics into this structure by associating specific loudness levels with specific row forms. In addition, there is a rhythmic series based upon the proportion 5:1:4:2, which is musically interpreted in several different ways. For example, it may determine the durations of a succession of four notes, the numbers being interpreted as multiples of sixteenth notes:

Or it may determine the placement of slurs and accents in a series of twelve sixteenth notes:

As with other series, this one may be retrograded or inverted. Since interval inversion can be mathematically represented as complementation to 12, Babbitt interprets inversion of the series as complementation to 6: thus 5:1:4:2 becomes 1:5:2:4.

In the *Three Compositions for Piano,* as well as in other Babbitt works of this period, the rhythmic and pitch series are essentially independent structures. Subsequently, however, Babbitt developed a "time-point" rhythmic system enabling him to translate pitch relationships into durational ones. This translation assumes an equivalence between pitch interval and time interval, the former being defined as the number of half steps upward from the first pitch class of a series to each successive pitch class, while the latter is defined as the number of basic rhythmic units between the downbeat of any given measure and the point of attack of each note in a rhythmic series. Thus, for the following twelve-tone series (that of Babbitt's Third String Quartet), the interval series can be expressed as a series of numbers measuring the half steps upward from the first pitch class to each of the following pitch classes:

Interval series	0	11	6	7	5	1	10	2	9	3	4	8
Pitch series	F	E	B	C	B♭	F♯	E♭	G	D	G♯	A	C♯

Translated into "time points," this produces the following rhythmic series (for which the sixteenth note is taken as the basic unit and the sixteenth on each downbeat is counted as zero):

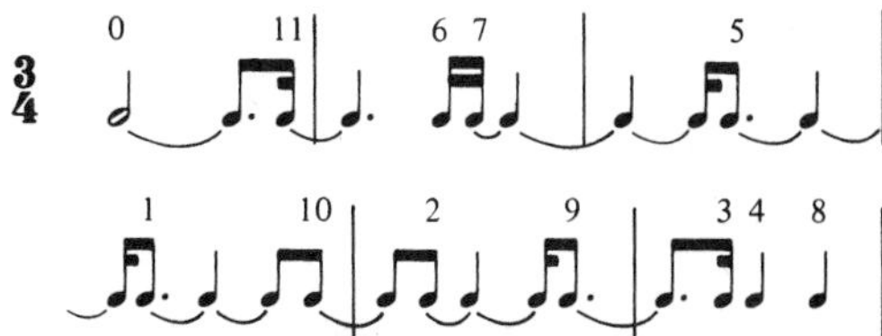

The numerical values of the time-point series thus do not measure the total distance between attacks, but the distance between each attack and the downbeat of the measure within which the attack falls. Moreover, the actual durations of the notes are not determined, but only their attack points (so that, for example, each note in the preceding example could also be represented by a sixteenth note followed by a rest filling in the time interval before the next attack). Through such translation (this example being relatively simple), Babbitt was able to develop serial rhythmic structures analogous in form and complexity to the pitch structures of his compositions.

Babbitt's approach to integral serialism has proved to be more fruitful, at least in the sense of being open to further extension, than the approaches of his European contemporaries. Thus, unlike his European colleagues, Babbitt, along with a number of American followers (e.g., Donald Martino and Charles Wuorinen), has continued to develop an essentially serial idiom, introducing various innovative techniques such as multiplicative operations, compositional arrays, and systematic derivations of secondary sets. It should be noted, however, that in the U.S. as well as in Europe, the general trend in recent years has been away from serialism, especially as represented by its more systematic forms [see Twentieth century, Western art music of the].

Other prominent composers who have at some point in their careers written serial music include Luciano Berio, Luigi Nono, Ernst Krenek, George Rochberg, and Henri Pousseur. See also Twelve-tone music.

Bibl.: Karlheinz Stockhausen, ". . . wie die Zeit vergeht . . . ," *Die Reihe* 3 (1957): 13–42, trans. Eng., *Die Reihe* 3 (1959): 10–40. György Ligeti, "Pierre Boulez: Entscheidung und Automatik in der Structure 1a," *Die Reihe* 4 (1958): 38–63, trans. Eng., *Die Reihe* 4 (1960): 36–62. Milton Babbitt, "Twelve-tone Rhythmic Structure and the Electronic Medium," *PNM* 1 (1962): 49–79. Karlheinz Stockhausen, *Texte zur elektronischen und instrumentale Musik* (Cologne: DuMont Schauberg, 1963). Pierre Boulez, *Penser la musique aujourd'hui* (Paris: Gonthier, 1964); trans. Susan Bradshaw and Richard Rodney Bennett, *Boulez on Music Today* (Cambridge, Mass.: Harvard U Pr, 1971). Herbert Eimert, *Grundlagen der musikalischen Reihentechnik* (Vienna: Universal, 1964). Richard Toop, "Messiaen/Goeyvaerts, Fano/Stockhausen, Boulez," *PNM* 13 (1974): 141–69. *Sounds and Words: A Celebration of Milton Babbitt at 60, PNM* 14, no. 2, through 15, no. 1 (1976) [in one issue]. Andrew Mead, *An Introduction to the Music of Milton Babbitt* (Princeton: Princeton U Pr, 1994). R.P.M.

Series. See Twelve-tone music, Serial music.

Serinette [Fr., fr. *serin,* canary]. A *barrel organ used to teach birds to sing.

Serioso [It., serious]. Beethoven's String Quartet in F minor op. 95 (1810), described by Beethoven on the title page of the autograph manuscript as a "Quartett[o] serioso."

Serpent [Fr. *serpent;* Ger. *Serpent, Schlangenrohr, Schlangenbass;* It. *serpentone;* Sp. *serpentón*]. A wide-bore, lip-vibrated wind instrument made in an undulating serpentine shape of wood covered with leather; a relative of the *cornett. It has six finger holes, a short brass mouth pipe, and an ivory or wood mouthpiece. It is usually about 2.45 m. (8 ft.) long, pitched in C or D, and plays from a note or two below this fundamental upward about three octaves. The serpent first appeared in France in the late 16th century. By the early 17th century it was being used to support Gregorian chant in many French churches. Late in the 18th century it began to be used in orchestras and military bands as well. An English model with tighter curves, more bracing, and a right-hand position opposing the left hand was designed for military use. Three or four keys were added in the early 19th century. In 1840, near the end of the instrument's career, a whole set of 14 keys was tried with little success. The tone of the serpent is gentle and mellow, but will become harsh if *overblown. See ill. under Brass instruments. R.E.E.

Serrant [Fr.]. Becoming faster.

Serse [It., Xerxes]. Opera in three acts by Handel (libretto adapted from one by Niccolò Minato for Cavalli in 1654 and revised for Bononcini in 1694), produced in London in 1738. Setting: Persia in the 5th century B.C.E.

Serva padrona, La [It., The Maid as Mistress]. Comic opera in two acts by Pergolesi (libretto by Gennaro Antonio Federico), composed as an **intermezzo* to be played between the three acts of his serious opera *Il prigioner superbo* (The Haughty Prisoner), produced in Naples in 1733. Setting: 18th-century Naples.

Service. In religious use, the serving of God by obedience, piety, and good works. The word has also come to denote (1) worship, especially public worship according to form and order; (2) a celebration of public worship; (3) a ritual or series of words and ceremonies prescribed for public worship or for some particular occasion (a service of communion, of thanksgiving); or (4) a musical setting of those portions of public worship that are sung; more particularly, in the Anglican church, settings of certain texts used for Morning and Evening Prayer and Holy Communion. It is in this last sense that the term service has acquired particular musical significance.

The musical settings of such texts, though often published together, are not intended to be performed without interruption, since such treatment obliterates liturgical meaning; all such performances are mere aggregates of musical settings extracted from context.

The musical service of the Anglican Church (as applied to music, the term service is not current until the 17th century) generally implies settings of three groups of texts taken from three principal services of the Anglican liturgy as found in the Book of Common Prayer (from 1552): Morning Prayer, Holy Communion, and Evening Prayer. The incipits and sources of the texts are as follows: *Morning Prayer:* O come let us sing unto the Lord ("Venite exultemus," Psalm 95, Vulgate 94); We praise thee, O God ("Te Deum laudamus," 5th century hymn in rhythmical prose); All ye works of the Lord, bless ye the Lord ("Benedicite opera omnia Domini Domino," Apocrypha, Song of the Three Children; Vulgate, Daniel 3); Blessed be the Lord God of Israel ("Benedictus Dominus Deus Israel," Luke 1: 68–79); Be joyful in the Lord, all ye lands ("Jubilate Deo omnis terra," Psalm 100, Vulgate 99). *Holy Communion:* Lord, have mercy upon us and incline our hearts to keep thy law (Kyrie); I believe in one God (Creed); Holy, holy, holy, Lord God of hosts (Sanctus); Glory be to God on high ("Gloria in excelsis"). *Evening Prayer:* My soul doth magnify the Lord ("Magnificat anima mea Dominum," Luke 1:46–55); O sing unto the Lord a new song ("Cantate Domino canticum novum," Psalm 98, Vulgate 97); Lord, now lettest thou thy servant depart in peace ("Nunc dimittis servum tuum, Domine, secundum verbum tuum in pace," Luke 2:29–32); God be merciful unto us ("Deus miseratur nostri," Psalm 67, Vulgate 66).

The musical importance of these texts attaches to the long list of polyphonic settings of some or all of them, commencing with John Day's publication *Certaine notes set forth in foure and three parts to be song at the morning Communion and evening praier* (1560/65), in which musical settings by Thomas Caustun (d. 1569) are identified. The next and far more important printed collection is that of John Barnard in 1641: *The First Book of Selected Church Musick, consisting of services and anthems, such as are now used in the cathedrall, and collegiat churches of this Kingdome,* which preserves all or parts of 15 services by 11 deceased composers, including three by William Byrd and two each by Orlando Gibbons and Thomas Morley.

The three services by Byrd, along with a fourth (the Great Service) rediscovered in the 20th century (all employing organ), may be taken as typical. Two of them, the so-called Short Service and the Great Service, set the same seven texts (Venite, Te Deum, Benedictus, Kyrie, Creed, Magnificat, Nunc dimittis), and thus neither brevity nor grandeur can be attributed to choice of text alone but rather to its treatment. In the Short Service, Byrd strives for maximal verbal clarity by setting the text syllabically and simultaneously in all lines, a practice consonant with Reformation views on textual intelligibility. The more elaborate Great Service (for up to ten voices) is generally regarded as the masterpiece of its type. Despite its polyphonic complexity and the rhythmic intricacies of its syllabic treatment, Byrd still succeeds in giving the individual word a musical distinctiveness that is, in its own style, the musical counterpart of the considerably more severe treatment in the shorter piece. Both works utilize to great effect the possibilities of antiphonal dialogue between the two parts of the choir facing each other from opposite sides—designated **decani* and *cantoris.* Byrd's so-called Second Service (called in *The First Book of Selected Church Musick* "service with verses to the organ") is the earliest surviving example of the use of solo voices and instrumental accompaniment in an Anglican liturgical context and is thus the prototype of the "verse" style that spread through later services and anthems. In a given service, all the text settings tended to use a single tonal center, often designated as a key or mode (e.g., Service in B♭, Dorian Service).

Despite liturgical constraints, the musical possibilities inherent in the various combinations of choir, organ, and solo voices (the number of written parts often masking the performing forces required) have led to a distinguished series of liturgical settings, among them those of John Blow, Pelham Humphrey, Henry Purcell, Maurice Green, Samuel S. Wesley, John Stainer, Ralph Vaughan Williams, Herbert Howells, Michael Tippett, and Benjamin Britten. In each of these, fully contemporary musical materials are adapted to liturgical use. See Anglican church music; Canticle; Liturgical books II, Anglican rite.

Bibl.: Christopher Dearnley, *English Church Music, 1650–1750: In Royal Chapel, Cathedral, and Parish Church* (New York: Oxford U Pr, 1970). Kenneth R. Long, *The Music of the English Church* (New York: St. Martin's, 1972). Friedrich Blume et al., *Protestant Church Music: A History* (New York: Norton, 1974). Peter Le Huray, *Music and the Reformation in England, 1549–1660,* corrected ed. (New York: Cambridge U Pr, 1978). Ian Spink, *Restoration Cathedral Music, 1660–1714* (New York: Oxford U Pr, 1995).

R.F.F., rev. R.A.L.

Sesqui- [Lat.]. A prefix denoting a fraction whose numerator is larger by one than its denominator, e.g., *sesquialtera* (3/2, in some contexts equivalent to *hemiola), *sesquitertia* (4/3), *sesquiquarta* (5/4), *sesquioctava* (9/8). The terms were used especially by writers of the Middle Ages and Renaissance in discussions of *proportions and *intervals. See also *Sesquialtera.*

Sesquialtera [fr. Latin]. (1) An organ stop of two *ranks sounding the twelfth (2 2/3′) and seventeenth (1 3/5′) with narrow-scaled open flue pipes. (2) In 18th- and 19th-century Anglo-American organs, a chorus mixture of three or four ranks on the Great division, containing a tierce. See also *Sesqui-.*

Sestetto [It.]. *Sextet.

Set. In the context of *twelve-tone music, *row.

Setār [Per.]. A *long-necked lute of Iran with four strings, one of which functions as a drone. It is similar in form to the Turkish **saz.* See also *Sitār.*

Set-piece. (1) In Anglo-American sacred music of the 18th and 19th centuries, a through-composed setting of a metrical text. (2) In a musico-dramatic work, a composition such as an aria that is musically self-contained; also termed a number.

Set theory. In mathematics, a set refers to an unordered collection of objects; mathematicians study the properties of sets and define operations on and relations in them. In principle, such sets can be musical; set theory allows music theorists to study musical structure in terms of unordered collections of musical objects and to investigate ways in which these sets can be transformed and related mathematically. Today the term usually refers more specifically to the study of sets of pitches and pitch structures; in this form it has become the main theoretical and analytical tool for dealing with post-tonal music.

Originating in the writings of Milton Babbitt and others, set theory received its primary formulation in the hands of Allan Forte (1973), who used it to tackle the hitherto elusive language of "free" (i.e., pre-serial) atonality. Other theorists, like David Lewin, Robert Morris, and John Rahn, subsequently developed the theory into a versatile analytical and compositional tool. Its versatility is due to the fact that the theory can address atonal pitch structures in an abstract manner, generalizing and unifying a number of music theoretic concepts, such as *chords, chord *inversion, *scales, *motives, twelve-tone rows, and twelve-tone procedures [see Twelve-tone music]. More recently, set theory has been extended to other domains, including the study of rhythm in minimalist or *African music. In the guise of diatonic set theory, it has even been used to study properties of tonal pitch structures that occur in the diatonic system of Western or ethnic music.

Fundamental to set theory is the notion of a pitch class. A pitch class is a collection of all pitches related to each other by octave, enharmonic equivalence, or both: thus C♯4, C♯5, and D♭4 all belong to the same pitch class. The integer representation of pitch class assigns an integer between 0 and 11 to each of the 12 possible pitch classes, usually taking C to be 0; thus C♯/D♭ is represented by 1, D by 2, and so on. While octave equivalence also underlies many aspects of tonal theory, enharmonic equivalence is peculiar to post-tonal theory. The development of a theory of pitch-class sets, or pc-sets for short, was motivated by the desire to study post-tonal sonorities in their own terms, free of tonal associations and references to triad-derived structures, especially in contexts where the latter are not analytically pertinent. For instance, the chord in the example can be represented as the set {3, 5, 8, 11} irrespective of its possible tonal interpretations [see Ex.]. In this light, a pitch-class set can be viewed as a generalized chord, and its different registral realizations correspond to chord inversions. But when realized horizontally, it can also be seen as a scale, or scale segment. Even though a set is unordered, set theory can define and manipulate ordered collections as well. Ordered collections of pitch classes are used to identify melodic ideas or motives, and twelve-tone rows become particular instances of ordered collections [see Serial music].

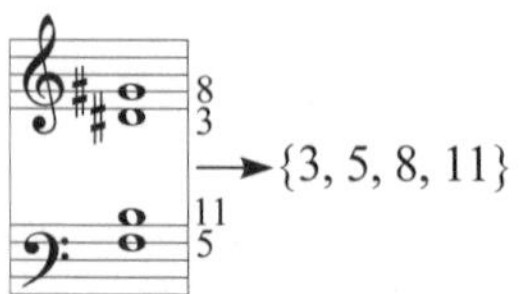

Identifying pc-sets allows music theorists to add standard mathematical operations and relations to their toolbox. Thus, union, intersection, and complementation can be applied to pc-sets to obtain other such sets; and subset/superset (inclusion) relations can be identified among sets. The analyst can thus demonstrate the coherence of a musical passage by relating to each other in set-theoretic terms the pc-sets that occur in the passage. But there are additional advantages that extend beyond the borrowing of mathematical tools. One advantage is that new types of operations and relations can be defined on pc-sets beyond those of abstract set theory, to capture specifically musical relations. For instance, we can apply to pc-sets the familiar musical concepts of transposition and inversion. Musical operations on sets formalize and generalize various processes of motivic transformation, relating pc-sets that may look superficially different in their specific context. Another specifically musical property defined on pc-sets is interval content; interval content is captured by the interval vector, a tally of all possible intervals contained in the pc-set, and presented as an array of numbers. The interval vector can account for the sound qualities of the chord, thereby bringing out its similarities with other chords.

Sets can be related in two main ways: by equivalence and by similarity. One type of equivalence relation links pc-sets that are related by transformations, such as transposition or inversion; sets related to each other by one of these two operations are said to belong to the same set class. When pc-sets are viewed as chords, set class generalizes the idea of chord quality. Another type of equivalence relates sets, or set classes, that share some common property, like the interval vector. Set classes with identical interval vectors that cannot be related to each other by transposition or inversion are known as Z-related.

Similarity relations among sets are particularly important in musical contexts, because many aurally and analytically pertinent relations among pc-sets are based on approximate, not exact, identity or equivalence; the latter is often too rigid and limiting a criterion for musical purposes. Various similarity relations have been defined on pc-sets and set classes, based on the sets' common properties, most notably on their interval vector and on subset/superset relations. Similarity relations can divide the set world into broad similarity types that represent intuitive characteristics of the sets, and that are hard to define in exact terms. As similarity plays a central role in cognitive psychology, pc-set similarity also offers music theory the possibility to interface with cognitive studies.

Set theory has given music theorists the opportunity

to study structural properties of the sets that had not been addressed in older frameworks. Sets with special symmetries, often known as cyclic sets, have figured prominently in some theories of atonal structure; sets with special symmetries are also believed to play an important role in organizing the similarity types.

Central to the analytical application of set theory is the idea of segmentation, or the parsing out of a musical surface into pitch sets and pc-sets, based on the notes' sharing certain salient characteristics, like simultaneity, proximity, register, or timbre. Although there have been several attempts at systematization, it is generally acknowledged that mechanical application of segmentation criteria does not guarantee that the results will be audible or analytically pertinent.

Bibl.: A. Forte, *The Structure of Atonal Music* (New Haven: Yale U Pr, 1973). J. Rahn, *Basic Atonal Theory* (London: Collier Macmillan, 1987). J. Straus, *Introduction to Post-Tonal Theory,* 2nd ed. (Upper Saddle River, N.J.: Prentice Hall, 2000). R. D. Morris, *Class Notes for Advanced Atonal Music Theory* (Lebanon, N.H.: Frog Peak Music, 2001). P.M.

Seul [Fr.]. Solo.

Seven (Last) Words, The. The seven last words (actually phrases) of Christ, compiled from the four Gospels, which have been used as a text for *Passion music, e.g., by Schütz (*Die sieben Wörte* SWV 478, composed ca. 1645), Haydn, and Gounod (*Les sept paroles de N. S. Jésus-Christ sur la croix,* 1858). Haydn's composition, commissioned by the Bishop of Cádiz, was originally a series of seven instrumental "sonatas," one to be played after the recitation of each of the seven "words," plus a musical depiction of an earthquake. As such, its title was *Musica instrumentale sopra le sette ultime parole del nostro redentore in croce o sieno sette sonate con un introduzione ed al fine un teremoto* (Instrumental Music on the Seven Last Words of Our Savior on the Cross, or Seven Sonatas with an Introduction and at the End an Earthquake). It appeared in four versions: (1) for orchestra, Hob. XX/1 A (1785); (2) for string quartet, Hob. XX/1 B (also Hob. III:50–56; 1787); (3) for harpsichord or piano, Hob. XX/1 C (1787; a version not actually by Haydn but approved by him); and (4) an oratorio version for soloists, chorus, and orchestra, Hob. XX/2 (appearing by 1796), choral parts having first been added by Joseph Friebert to his own text, which was later revised by Haydn and Baron Gottfried van Swieten.

Seventh. See Interval, Scale degrees.

Seventh chord. A chord formed by the addition of pitches a third, a fifth, and a seventh above the lowest pitch or root. Such a chord can be formed on any of the seven *scale degrees of the major or minor scale, the intervals above the root varying by type (i.e., major, minor, etc.) accordingly. For the various types of seventh chords that can result, see Harmonic analysis I; for inversions of seventh chords, see Inversion II; for the types and nomenclature of seventh chords used in jazz and popular music, see Fake-book notation. Since the seventh is dissonant with the root (forming a seventh or, in inversion, a second), all seventh chords are dissonant. In tonal harmony and counterpoint, therefore, the seventh chord requires resolution through the resolution of the dissonant pitch, usually downward by step, as in Ex. 1. This dissonant pitch is most often introduced as a passing tone [Ex. 2], neighboring tone [Ex. 3], or suspension [Ex. 4], according to the principles of voice leading or counterpoint. It is from these principles that the seventh chord derives its force [see Counterpoint].

When formed on the fifth scale degree or dominant, the chord is termed a dominant seventh. Because of the presence in this chord of both the fourth and the seventh scale degrees, any given dominant seventh chord can exist in only one key. It therefore strongly implies a single tonic and is often resolved by the tonic triad. The progression from dominant seventh to tonic is termed a dominant-seventh *cadence and is one of the most familiar and powerful progressions in tonal music.

A diminished seventh chord consists of a diminished triad with a diminished seventh added above the root. It is thus made up of only minor thirds placed above one another. In tonal music, it occurs most often formed on the seventh scale degree. In the minor mode, this occurs when the seventh scale degree is raised; in the major mode, the sixth scale degree must be lowered. Because this chord is symmetrical with respect to the octave, all inversions have the same structure. There are, furthermore, only three different diminished seventh chords as far as actual pitches are concerned (though the pitch names may vary according to context). In consequence, each diminished seventh chord can be made to function for four different tonics in both major and minor, resolving in each case

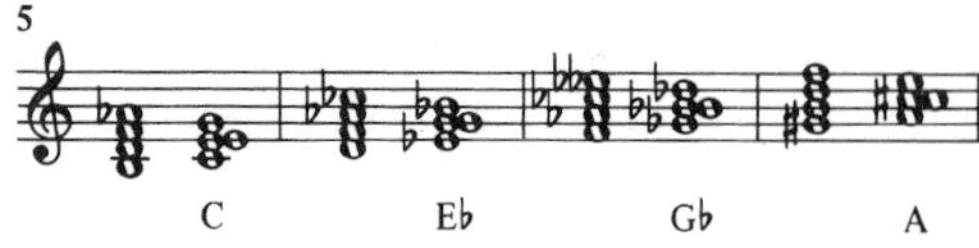

to the tonic triad [Ex. 5]. The diminished seventh chord is sometimes interpreted to be a dominant ninth chord with the root omitted. Because diminished seventh chords can be resolved in a variety of directions, they are especially useful as pivot chords in *modulations. A diminished triad with a minor seventh added above the root is termed a half-diminished seventh.

Sevillanas [Sp.]. A slightly faster variant from Andalusia of the *seguidillas* [see *Seguidilla* (2)]; also a type of **flamenco* music derived from this variant.

Sext. See Office, divine.

Sexta, sexta vox [Lat.]. In Renaissance polyphony, a sixth voice or part.

Sextet [Fr. *sextette, sextuor;* Ger. *Sextett;* It. *sestetto;* Sp. *sexteto*]. (1) A composition for six solo performers, with or without accompaniment. (2) An ensemble of six solo performers. Compositions of this type for winds or mixed winds and strings occur primarily among Classical divertimentos. The string sextet (usually paired violins, violas, and cellos) was used by Brahms, Dvořák, Schoenberg, and others. There are sextets with piano by Mendelssohn, Poulenc, and Copland. The sextet as an operatic ensemble is first found in 18th-century *opera buffa,* but later also in serious opera.

Sextolet, sextuplet [Fr. *sextolet;* Ger. *Sextole;* It. *sestina;* Sp. *seisillo*]. A group of six notes of equal value to be played in the time normally occupied by four notes of the same value and identified by the figure *6.* The effect may be the same as two triplets of appropriate value or as three groups of two notes each. Beams may be drawn so as to distinguish between these effects.

Sextuor [Fr.]. *Sextet.

Sf. Abbr. for **sforzando, sforzato.*

Sfogato [It.]. With respect to expression, vented, unburdened, unrestrained.

Sforzando, sforzato [It., abbr. *sf., sfz.*]. Forcing, forced; accented (usually a single pitch or chord) at least with respect to the prevailing dynamic, but often simply loud.

Sfp. [It.]. Abbr. for **sforzando* followed immediately by *piano,* i.e., a sudden (often loud) accent followed immediately by a soft continuation.

Sfz. Abbr. for **Sforzando, sforzato.*

Shake. Formerly, *trill. For closed and open shake, see Grace. A shaked beat is a repeated lower *appoggiatura; a shaked cadent is a repeated **Nachschlag.*

Shakuhachi [Jap.]. An *end-blown bamboo flute of Japan with four finger holes and one thumb hole. A notch is cut in the lip to facilitate sound production. Originally an instrument of Buddhist monks, it is now also played in ensembles with the **shamisen* and the **koto.* See ill. under East Asia.

Shallot. In organ *reed stops, the half-cylindrical backing, made of wood or metal, against which the reed tongue vibrates. See ill. under Organ.

Shamisen [Jap.]. A *long-necked lute of Japan. Three strings of silk or nylon pass down an unfretted neck and over a small, square sound box covered front and back with cat or dog skin. The strings are plucked with a large, triangular plectrum. Introduced to Japan in the 16th century, the *shamisen* has become a favorite instrument for accompanying the voice. It is used in the **kabuki* and *bunraku* (puppet) theater, in **nagauta,* and in popular singing. See ill. under East Asia.

Shank. A relatively short, straight piece of tubing that can be inserted in a brass instrument to receive the mouthpiece and alter the instrument's fundamental pitch. See also Crook.

Shanty, chanty, chantey [perhaps fr. Fr. *chanter,* to sing]. A work song sung by sailors, especially one that rhythmically coordinates strenuous effort. Such songs typically feature alternation between a leader or shantyman and the chorus of sailors, and they are classed according to the type of work to be performed.

Bibl.: Joanna C. Colcord, comp., *Songs of American Sailormen,* rev. and enl. ed. (New York: Oak Pubns, 1964). Stan Hugill, *Shanties and Sailors' Songs* (New York: Praeger, 1969).

Shape-note. A type of notation employed in tune books and hymnals in the U.S. (especially in the South and Midwest) from the 19th century until the present in which the shape of the note head indicates the solmization syllable to be sung; also called character notation, or patent notes (because copyright was sought for competing systems), or buckwheat or dunce notes (stigmatizing singers who required such assistance). The first such system, introduced in *The Easy Instructor* (Philadelphia, 1801) by William Little and William Smith, was based on sol-fa solmization and assigned a different shape to each of the four syllables employed (hence, four-shape notation): *fa, sol, la,* and *mi* [Ex.]. A few earlier books had simply placed on a staff the letters F, S, L, M for the same purpose. By the mid-19th century, the use of seven shapes corresponding to seven syllables began in some regions to supersede the four-shape system.

Rhythmic values were indicated with stems and flags in the conventional way. Shape-note tune books fostered singing schools and encouraged local styles of composition. See also Hymn, Tune book, Gospel.

Bibl.: Allen P. Britton, Irving Lowens, and Richard Crawford, *American Sacred Music Imprints 1698–1810: A Bibliography* (Worcester: American Antiquarian Society, 1990), p. 438. George Pullen Jackson, *White Spirituals in the Southern Uplands* (Chapel Hill: U of North Carolina Pr, 1933; R: 1965). R.C.

Sharp [Fr. *dièse;* Ger. *Kreuz;* It. *diesis;* Sp. *sostenido*]. (1) The sign ♯, which indicates the raising of the pitch of a note by a semitone. See Accidental, Pitch names. (2) [adj.] Incorrectly tuned above the correct pitch.

Shawm [fr. Lat. *calamus,* reed; Fr. *chalemie;* Ger. *Schalmei;* It. *cennamella;* Sp. *chirimía*]. A conical-bore, double-reed woodwind instrument used in Europe from the 13th through the 17th century with many close relatives still in use elsewhere [see *Hichiriki, Nāgasvaram, Śahnāi, Zūrnā*]. It survives as a folk instrument in some parts of Europe as well [see *Chirimía, Ciaramella, Dulzaina*]. See ill. under Reed.

The older European instrument exists in at least seven sizes, as described by Michael Praetorius (*Syntagma musicum,* vol. 2, 1619). The higher instruments are generally made in one piece and the lower instruments in several. A usual feature of the instrument is that its length is considerably longer than necessary for the pitch, the additional length being a widely flaring bell. Vents or tuning holes raise the lowest pitch to the proper level. Keys covered by a pierced wooden cover or fontanelle are applied to the larger sizes. A disk called a pirouette is usually provided below the reed to support the player's lips. Shawms were used in early European music with other "loud" instruments [see *Haut*], often in outdoor settings. The *deutsche Schalmei* is a transitional form of treble shawm made in two pieces with a key and fontanelle. It was rapidly replaced by the *oboe. See also *Bombard.* M.S.

Sheherazade. (1) A symphonic suite by Rimsky-Korsakov, op. 35 (1888), based on tales from the *Thousand and One Nights* and named for the woman who tells the stories. In 1910, it was presented in Paris as a ballet by the Ballets russes (choreography by Michel Fokine). (2) [Fr. *Shéhérazade*] A cycle of three songs for voice and piano or orchestra by Ravel, composed in 1903, on poems by Tristan Klingsor inspired by the *Thousand and One Nights.*

Shenai [Hind.]. See *Śahnāi.*

Sheng [Chin.]. A Chinese *mouth organ consisting of a bowl-shaped wind-chest around the perimeter of which 12 to 19 bamboo pipes are inserted vertically. Each sounding pipe has a brass reed at its lower end and a hole that must be covered to produce a sound. The player holds the *sheng* cupped in both hands and inhales and exhales through a mouthpiece, covering several holes at a time to produce chords. It is used in Confucian temple rites and in various secular celebrations. See ill. under East Asia; see also *Sho.*

Shift. In the playing of stringed instruments, the movement from one *position to another.

Shimmy. A dance popular in the U.S. in the 1910s and 1920s whose characteristic motion is the rapid movement of the two shoulders in opposite directions, forward and backward. It was danced to music in a relatively fast tempo.

Shivaree. See *Charivari.*

Sho [Jap.]. A Japanese *mouth organ, very similar to the Chinese **sheng.* It is used in **gagaku* music. See ill. under East Asia.

Shofar [Heb.]. A ram's-horn trumpet of ancient Israel and modern Jewish worship. It produces primarily two pitches, corresponding to the second and third harmonics and thus a fifth apart, though other pitches may be produced by lipping. Today it is sounded on Rosh Hashanah (New Year) and Yom Kippur (Day of Atonement).

Bibl.: David Wulstan, "The Sounding of the Shofar," *GSJ* 26 (1973): 29–46.

Short octave. In keyboard instruments, the omission of one or more pitches from the lowest octave, the keys corresponding to the omitted pitches causing other, usually lower pitches to sound instead. The practice began with the earliest keyboards and lasted well into the 18th century in Europe and even later in Mexico and Spanish America. It was justified by the lack of need for certain low pitches (especially accidentals); in organs, there was a substantial saving when large bass pipes could be omitted. The resulting reassignment of lower pitches to higher keys also made larger intervals reachable under the player's hand.

Examples of various treatments of the short octave, taken from instruments at the Smithsonian Institution, follow: a Flemish virginal of 1620 by Andreas Ruckers with a range beginning at C on apparent E, omitting C♯ and D♯, with apparent F♯ and G♯ sounding D and E, F sounding its normal pitch, becoming chromatic at A; an English chamber organ of 1761 by John Snetzler with a range beginning at G_1 on apparent B_1, sounding A_1 on apparent C♯, omitting $G♯_1$, $A♯_1$, and B_1, becoming chromatic at D. In an Italian virginal of 1617 by Iohannes Battista Boni, bass accidental keys are split, the front half sounding one pitch, the back half another: apparent E sounds C, while the back half of F♯ and G♯ sound D and E, respectively, with the front half of these keys sounding their normal pitch; C♯ and D♯ are omitted. Such a scheme is known as a broken octave. In this instrument, d♯, g♯, d♯′, and g♯′ are also split to provide proper thirds for the d♯/e♭ and g♯/a♭ in mean-tone tuning. J.T.F.

Short score. A *score in which parts are consolidated on relatively few staves. See also Particella.

Shout. (1) *Ring shout. (2) In jazz, a vigorous tune played by a *stride pianist (e.g., James P. Johnson's "Carolina Shout"); the performer of such a piece may be termed a shout pianist. (3) In blues, jazz, and rhythm and blues, a shout singer (e.g., Jimmy Rushing) is one who shouts more than sings the lyrics.

Si. See Pitch names, Solmization.

Siam. See Southeast Asia III.

Siciliana, siciliano [It., Eng., Ger.; Fr. *sicilienne;* Sp. *siciliana*]. (1) A late Baroque instrumental movement or an aria that evokes a gentle pastoral mood [see also *Pastorale*], usually through slow 6/8 or 12/8 time and simple phrases with repeated dotted figures (♪.♬♪), often beginning with an upbeat. It frequently appears as a slow movement in sonatas and dance suites (Bach, Telemann) and was considered to be a sort of slow *gigue, though little is known of it as an actual dance. Arias with the same characteristics, as well as the use of the Neapolitan sixth chord at cadences, are very common (Alessandro Scarlatti, Handel), but they are rarely labeled *siciliano* by the composers.

(2) In the early 17th century, a musical setting of the Sicilian version of a **strambotto.* B.G.

Side drum. Snare *drum.

Sideman. Any member of a jazz or popular-music ensemble other than the leader.

Siege of Rhodes, The. The first English opera, with a libretto in five entries by William Davenant and music (now lost) by Henry Lawes, Henry Cooke, Matthew Locke, George Hudson, and Charles Coleman; produced in London in 1656.

Siegfried. See *Ring des Nibelungen, Der.*

Siegfried Idyll. A composition for small orchestra by Wagner, composed in 1870 and first performed on his wife Cosima's birthday at their home Tribschen (hence, also the *Tribschen Idyll*), near Lucerne. It is named for their son Siegfried, then a year old, and includes themes from the opera *Siegfried* as well as the lullaby "Schlaf, Kindlein, schlaf" (Sleep, baby, sleep).

Sight, sighting [Lat. *discantus visibilis, fictus visus, perfectio ocularis*]. In English discant treatises of the 15th century, a system of improvising counterpoint while visualizing it on the same staff as a given liturgical melody sung by the tenor. Each improvised part or sight (or "degree of discant") is allowed to sound consonances within a certain range reckoned from the tenor, the parts from highest to lowest being quadreble, treble, mene (meane), countertenor (moving both above and below the tenor), and counter (countir, lying always below the tenor).

A note of such an improvised part is identified in two ways: "in sight" (what the singer would visualize) and "in voice" (the pitch actually sung). A singer discanting in roughly the same range as the given melody could visualize his part at pitch, but most sights involve transposition. That is, the note in sight and the note in voice differ by a certain interval. For example, if the quadreble is to sound the pitch an octave above the tenor, its note would be visualized on the staff a fifth below the tenor and sung a twelfth higher. The counter involves transposition of the sighted note to the fifth below (for extremely low notes a twelfth), the mene and countertenor do not transpose, the treble transposes to the octave above, and the quadreble to the twelfth above.

Acceptable intervals (in voice) for sights include all consonances within specified ranges except fourths or elevenths. Sources disagree on these ranges. In general, each sight above the tenor has a range of approximately one octave; the counter extends in voice to two octaves below the tenor. The lowest sounding notes of the quadreble, treble, and mene are the octave, fifth, and unison with the tenor, respectively; the highest sounding note of the counter is the unison with the tenor.

Faburden is a special application of sights. The top voice is sighted in unison with the given melody but is a fourth above in voice. The part called faburden may sight only the unison and the third above the tenor, transposing down a fifth (like the counter) to sound the fifth and the third below. See also Faburden, *Fauxbourdon.*

Sight-reading, sight-singing [Fr. *lecture à vue;* Ger. *Blattspiel;* It. *suonare a prima vista;* Sp. *lectura a primera vista*]. The performing of a piece of music on seeing it for the first time. The ability to sing at sight requires the ability to imagine the sound of pitches or intervals without the aid of an instrument, and training in this skill forms an important part of instruction in basic musicianship or *ear training. *Solfège and other systems of *solmization are among the principal means for carrying out this training. Performing at sight on an instrument requires the ability to grasp the meaning of musical notation quickly and call upon the relevant technical skills for execution; this should be accompanied by the skills of the ear as well. The ability to perform efficiently at sight and the ability to give finished performances of distinction do not necessarily go together, and both should be among the goals of musical instruction.

Bibl.: Paul Hindemith, *Elementary Training for Musicians* (New York: Assoc Music Pubs, 1946; 2nd ed., 1949). Samuel Adler, *Sight Singing: Pitch, Interval, Rhythm* (New York: Norton, 1979). Allen Trubitt and Robert S. Hines, *Ear Training and Sight-Singing,* 2 vols. (New York: Schirmer Bks, 1979–80). Leland D. Bland, *Sight Singing through Melodic Analysis* (Chicago: Nelson-Hall, 1984). Earl Henry and James Mobberley, *Musicianship: Ear Training, Rhythmic Reading, and Sight Singing* (Englewood Cliffs, N.J.: Prentice Hall, 1986–87). John R. Stevenson and Marjorie S. Porterfield, *Rhythm and Pitch: An Integrated Approach to Sight-singing* (Englewood Cliffs, N.J.: Prentice Hall, 1986). Robert D. Levin and Louis Martin, *Sight Singing and Ear Training through Literature* (Englewood Cliffs, N.J.: Prentice Hall, 1988). Daniel Kazez, *Rhythm Reading: Elementary through Advanced Training,* 2nd ed. (New York: Norton, 1997). Gary S. Karpinski, *Aural Skills Acquisition: The Development of Listening, Reading, and Performing Skills in College-Level Musicians* (Oxford: Oxford U Pr, 2000).

Signature. See Key signature, Time signature, Conflicting signatures.

Significative letters. *Romanian letters.

Signum congruentiae [Lat., sign of congruence]. A sign, often in the form of a fermata or a **segno* (𝄋), used especially in music of the Middle Ages and Renaissance for a variety of purposes, including the indication of the boundaries of repeated sections and the point of entry for succeeding voices in canons.

Silbenstrich [Ger., syllable stroke]. In the sources for the repertory of *Notre Dame, a short vertical stroke through some part of the staff to indicate a change of syllable in the text of a melismatic piece.

Silence [Fr.]. Rest.

Sillet [Fr.]. *Nut.

Similar motion. See Motion.

Simile, simili [It.]. An instruction to continue in the same manner of execution as has just been indicated explicitly.

Simon Boccanegra. Opera in a prologue and three acts by Verdi (libretto by Francesco Maria Piave and Giuseppe Montanelli, based on a play by Antonio García Gutiérrez), produced in Venice in 1857; revised version (libretto revised by Arrigo Boito) produced in Milan in 1881. Setting: Genoa and environs in the mid-14th century.

Simple system. Any of the most common types of woodwind fingering used prior to the innovations of Theobald Boehm (1794–1881); also called old system. The term is applied most often to the flute, but is applicable to other woodwinds as well. The simple system can be distinguished by the large number of *cross fingerings and *fork fingerings and by the production of a major scale when the six principal finger holes are opened sequentially. M.S.

Simultaneity. Any two or more pitches sounded simultaneously.

Sin' al fine (segno) [It.]. Until the end (or the **segno*); usually in conjunction with the instruction to repeat **da capo* or **dal segno.*

Sinfonia [It., pl. *sinfonie*]. (1) Symphony. (2) In the Baroque period, an alternate designation for *sonata or *canzona, especially a trio or other ensemble sonata [see also *Sonata da chiesa*]. This meaning reflects the derivation of sinfonia from the Greek word for "sounding together" [see Symphony] and probably explains Bach's use of the term for his three-part inventions. Sinfonias for keyboard or instrumental ensemble also served during this period as preludes to Mass and motet sections and to sets of dances. (3) In operas and other extended vocal works of the 17th and 18th centuries, an instrumental piece serving as a prelude or *overture, interlude, or postlude. As interludes, sinfonias were usually in one section or movement and often recurred several times, as in act 3 of Monteverdi's *Orfeo* [cf. Ritornello (2)].

Bibl.: William S. Newman, *The Sonata in the Baroque Era* (Chapel Hill: U of NC Pr, 1959; 4th ed., New York: Norton, 1983). Ernst Apfel, *Zur Vor- und Frühgeschichte der Symphonie* (Baden-Baden: Koerner, 1972). E.K.W.

Sinfonia concertante [It.]. See *Symphonie concertante.*

Sinfonie pastorale [Fr.]. See *Pastoral* Symphony.

Sinfonietta [It.]. An orchestral work similar to a symphony but on a smaller scale; sometimes also a small orchestra.

Sinfonische Dichtung [Ger.]. *Symphonic poem.

Singakademie [Ger.]. A society founded in Berlin in 1791 by Carl Friedrich Christian Fasch for the purpose of giving concerts of sacred vocal music; the building occupied by this society from 1829 until after World War II.

Singend [Ger.]. In a singing style.

Singhiozzando [It.]. Sobbing.

Singing. The use of the voice as a musical instrument with the mouth open (as distinct from humming).

As the most common and instinctual form of music making, singing has had the widest possible links to other human activities, the singer having been at times also priest, healer, actor, poet, and much else. In European art music, the singer's function has been progressively circumscribed. The poet-composer-singer of classical antiquity and the Middle Ages survives today only in popular and folk music. The role of singing as determiner of musical style, nearly all-encompassing through the Renaissance, diminished with the growth of idiomatic instrumental styles thereafter (a change reflected also in the giving way of the combination of composer-singer so frequent in the Renaissance and earlier to that of composer-instrumentalist in the Baroque and after). From at least the 17th century to the early 19th, solo singers, especially in the Italian tradition, were encouraged to develop the individual qualities of their voices and musical temperaments, and music was composed to display them, the composer also making the singer a creative collaborator in the final result by leaving much of the surface detail to be more or less spontaneously added or adjusted in performance. With the elevation of the composer's function in the Romantic period, singers (and performers in general) were reduced to interpreters of the composer's intentions. As music came increasingly to consist of a standard repertory, singers tended to shape their voices to its requirements, although the practice of composing for specific singers has never entirely disappeared. It is only in other genres, popular music and jazz especially, that voices have remained free to develop more individually.

The most complex of all musical instruments, the voice is highly adaptable to different methods of singing, and preferences in timbre, register, tessitura, and tone quality, among other aspects, vary greatly among cultures and even among genres within a culture. The strong cross-cultural currents of the 20th and early 21st century, as well as other factors such as the use or avoidance of electronic sound amplification, have widened the divergence of operatic and concert singing and the various kinds of popular singing in Western music.

It is also likely that even within the European classical tradition, ideals of vocal sound have changed over time and that before the 19th century a lighter registration and a sweeter and less rich quality of tone may have been favored. This is difficult to prove (and some authorities strongly dispute it), since ignorance of the functioning of the vocal mechanism long prevented the sort of technical analysis or the formation of precise terminology necessary for detailed historical investigations. Much indirect evidence supports it, however, such as the long popularity of voice types such as falsettist and *castrato.*

Gregorian chant, the earliest surviving body of western European vocal music, already reflects a highly developed singing style. The solo sections of responsorial chants suggest vocal virtuosity of a high order, the exact nature of which is no longer entirely clear because of the loss of authentic performance traditions.

Early vocal composition was oriented almost entirely toward the natural male voice. An interest in female voices and in the *castrato* becomes evident in the 16th century. Improvised florid singing reached a first peak of development in this period and is described in several treatises. Giulio Caccini's *Le nuove musiche* (Florence, 1601/2) reacted against such ornamentation by diminution, rethinking the relation between words and vocal style in terms of the derivation of melodic line and ornamentation from an affective declamation of the text. This was to remain an important element in Baroque singing, when new genres such as opera, cantata, and oratorio provided the ground for the extraordinary development of solo singing during the following centuries. The basis of the art was vocal flexibility, not so much in the sense of acrobatic agility, as is often assumed, but more essentially in a mastery of gradation of tone to impart to the vocal line a sensitive nuance that was the main source of expressiveness. By the 18th century, the Italian singing style had developed clear-cut genres, principally the *cantabile, grazioso, parlante,* and *bravura.* High voices were favored and the upper limits of the range much extended. Pier Francesco Tosi and Giambattista Mancini, two of the period's many celebrated teachers, produced the principal treatises.

During this time the French maintained their own manner of singing, as described by Bénigne de Bacilly in the 17th century and Jean-Antoine Bérard in the 18th. Quite distinct in their approaches to many of the basic elements of singing and in their ideals of sound, the French and Italian styles each had their partisans who decried the other.

The first half of the 19th century marks the transition to the present period of the classical singing tradition. The change is embodied in new types of singers, such as the dramatic soprano and *tenore robusto,* characterized by a heavier registration and more forceful manner of singing reflective of new ideals of dramatic expression and larger accompanying orchestras. In some ways, the new style can be seen as a synthesis of elements from the French and Italian styles. As a meeting ground for these, the French grand opera appears to have been one of the main arenas in which this synthesis was accomplished. Adumbrated in the music of Bellini and Donizetti, the new style appears fully in the works of Verdi, and it was then that the term *bel canto* began to be applied in retrospect to the previous Italian style. Wagnerian singing, while reflecting Wagner's theories on the proper relation of words and music, had much in common with the general trend in singing. At the same time the intense development of the art song opened a new field for a more intimate and nuanced manner of singing. See also Singing style, Voice.

Bibl.: Albert Lavignac and Lionel de la Laurencie, eds., *Physiologie vocal et auditive; technique vocale et instrumental,* Encyclopédie de la musique et Dictionnaire du Conservatoire, pt. 2, vol. 2 (Paris: Delagrave, 1926). Frederick C. Field-Hyde, *The Art and Science of Voice Training* (London: Oxford U Pr, 1950). Cornelius Reid, *Bel Canto, Principle and Practice* (New York: Coleman-Ross, 1950; R: New York: J Patelson, 1972). Philip A. Duey, *Bel Canto in Its Golden Age* (New York: King's Crown Pr, 1951). Fritz Müller-Heuser, *Vox humana: Ein Beitrag zur Untersuchung der Stimmästhetik des Mittelalters* (Regensburg: G Bosse, 1963). Rodolfo Celletti, *Le grandi voci: Dizionario critico-biografico dei cantanti* (Rome: Instituto per la collaborazione culturale, 1964). Frederick Husler and Yvonne Rodd-Marling, *Singing: The Physical Nature of the Vocal Organ* (New York: October House, 1965). Henry Pleasants, *The Great Singers: From the Dawn of Opera to Our Own Time* (New York: Simon & Schuster, 1966). William Vennard, *Singing, the Mechanism and the Technique,* rev. ed. (New York: C Fischer, 1967). Franz Thomas, *Die Lehre des Kunstgesanges nach der altitalienischen Schule* (Berlin: Achterberg, 1968).

Singing school. See United States; Psalmody, British and North American.

Singing style. In ethnomusicology, those aspects of

singing not normally indicated in Western notation, including timbre, tessitura, nasality, and tension. Recognized by scholars before 1900 as a principal distinguishing feature of musical cultures, but difficult to describe, it has been the subject of various analytical and transcription systems, including verbal (by Erich M. von Hornbostel, George Herzog), *cantometric, and *melographic. See also Folk music I, 5.

Bibl.: Charles Seeger, "Singing Style," *Western Folklore* 17 (1958): 3–11. *Selected Reports in Ethnomusicology,* vol. 2, no. 1 (1974): 1–175. B.N.

Singspiel [Ger.]. A musico-dramatic work with a German text, especially a work written in the 18th or early 19th century in which spoken dialogue alternates with songs and sometimes with ensembles, choruses, or more extended musical pieces. The setting of such works is frequently rural, sometimes fantastic or exotic; the characters are often artisans or from the lower middle class and exhibit simpler or humbler virtues than characters from serious opera. There were two principal schools of Singspiel composition in the 18th century, the Viennese and the north German. The Leopoldstadt Theater in Vienna was the home of German plays interspersed with music from early in the 18th century. In 1778, Joseph II sought to encourage the growth of native German-language operas by the foundation of a national theater. The experiment lasted only a decade, but among its most successful products was Mozart's *Die *Entführung aus dem Serail* (1782, text by Stephanie). Other significant composers of Viennese Singspiel were Ignaz Umlauf, Karl Ditters von Dittersdorf, Wenzel Müller, Johann Schenck, and Joseph Weigl. Mozart's *Die *Zauberflöte* (1791, text by Schikaneder) represents a culmination of the genre.

North German Singspiel may be said to have begun in 1752 with the performance in Leipzig of a German adaptation of Charles Coffey's *ballad opera *The Devil to Pay* (*Der Teufel ist los,* text by Christian Friedrich Weisse, music by Johann C. Standfuss). For much of its history, north German Singspiel was susceptible to influences from English and French comic opera. The most notable composer of north German Singspiel was Johann Adam Hiller, who composed about 14 Singspiele between 1766 and 1779, most to librettos adapted by Weisse and almost all produced in Leipzig. Georg Benda was also a significant contributor to the genre.

In the 19th century, Singspiel was replaced on the one hand by German Romantic opera, Beethoven's **Fidelio* and Weber's *Der *Freischütz* being significant works of transition, and on the other hand by *operetta.

Bibl.: Georgy Calmus, *Die ersten deutschen Singspiele von Standfuss und Hiller* (Leipzig: Breitkopf & Härtel, 1908; R: Walluf: Sändig, 1973). Kurt Lüthge, *Die deutsche Spieloper* (Braunschweig: W Piepenschneider, 1924). Ludwig Schiedermair, *Die deutsche Oper: Grundzüge ihres Werdens und Wesens* (Leipzig: Quelle & Meyer, 1930; 3rd ed., Bonn: F Dümmler, 1943). Arthur Winsor, "The Melodramas and Singspiels of Georg Benda" (Ph.D. diss., Univ. of Michigan, 1967). Peter Branscombe, "The Singspiel in the Late 18th Century," *MT* 112 (1971): 226–28. Id., "Music in the Viennese Popular Theatre of the Eighteenth and Nineteenth Centuries," *PRMA* 98 (1971–72): 101–12. Hans-Albrecht Koch, *Das deutsche Singspiel* (Stuttgart: Metzler, 1974). C.G.

Sinistra [It.]. Left (hand).

Sink-a-pace. **Cinque passi.*

Sirventes [Occ.]. A type of *troubadour poetry concerned with topics such as politics, literary satire, current events, and moralizing, but not with love. Such poems, which are strophic, were sometimes based on the poetic structure of a preexisting *canso* or other song, and thus could use its melody. E.A.

Sistine Chapel. The principal chapel in the Vatican palace, employed by the pope and named for Pope Sixtus IV (1471–84), for whom it was built. Under Pope Leo X (1513–21), its choir came to include 32 musicians, among them some of the most celebrated composers of the period, and it continues today the tradition of performing Renaissance polyphony of the *Palestrina style.

Sistre [Fr.]. *Cittern.

Sistrum [Lat.]. A *rattle of ancient Sumeria, Egypt, and Rome. Heavy wires are set loosely into a U-shaped frame with a handle, and jingles are sometimes threaded onto the wires. It was sacred to the goddess Isis and traveled from Egypt to Rome with her cult. It is still used in the Coptic church. See ill. under Greece.

Sitār [Hind.]. A *long-necked lute of northern India. It has a wide fingerboard with movable frets, a pear-shaped gourd body, and a gourd resonator at the top of the neck. There are 7 principal strings—4 melody strings and 3 drones—all made of metal, plus 12 to 20 sympathetic strings. The player plucks the strings with a wire plectrum. The *sitār* is a solo instrument, usually accompanied by the **tablā* and the **tamburā.* See ill. under South Asia.

Sitole. *Citole.

Six, Les [Fr., The Six]. A name given by Henri Collet in 1920 to a group of six French composers—Louis Durey, Arthur Honegger, Darius Milhaud, Germaine Tailleferre, Georges Auric, and Francis Poulenc—who shared the aesthetic ideals of Erik Satie and for whom Jean Cocteau subsequently became an advocate.

Six-four chord. A *triad in second *inversion (i.e., with the fifth as the lowest-sounding pitch, e.g., g–c′–e′), so called because the third of the triad then forms a sixth with the lowest-sounding pitch while the root forms a fourth; it is notated in *thoroughbass notation and in *harmonic analysis with the figures $^6_4$. Because the interval of a fourth sounds above the lowest pitch, such a chord is normally treated in tonal music as a dissonance and must be resolved. It is often introduced as a suspension [see Counterpoint II, 3]. An especially familiar cadence resolves the tonic six-four chord to the dominant, which in turn moves to the tonic in root position (I$^6_4$–V–I). The *cadenza in concertos is often an elaboration of the progression from tonic six-four to dominant.

Bibl.: Glen Haydon, *The Evolution of the Six-Four Chord* (Berkeley and Los Angeles: U of Cal Pr, 1933; R: New York: Da Capo, 1970).

Sixteen-foot. See Foot.

Sixth. See Interval; Scale degrees; Consonance, dissonance; Added sixth.

Sixth chord. A *triad in first *inversion (i.e., with the third as the lowest-sounding pitch, e.g., e–g–c′), so called because the root then forms a sixth with the lowest-sounding pitch while the fifth of the triad forms a third; hence, also termed a six-three chord. It is notated in *thoroughbass notation and in *harmonic analysis with the figures $^6_3$. Because the sixth chord is wholly consonant when formed from a major or minor triad, it is freely used in tonal music [see Sixth-chord style].

Five chromatically altered sixth chords are also often found in tonal music. These are shown with their most common resolutions in Exx. 1–5. The names given are widely used, but have no historical or geographic significance. The first is the first inversion of a triad formed on the lowered second scale degree in either major or minor and most often resolves to the dominant; the root position of this triad is sometimes employed as well. The remaining four are termed augmented sixth chords because they are characterized by the interval of an augmented sixth above the lowest-sounding pitch. This interval is typically formed between the lowered sixth scale degree and the raised fourth scale degree, resolving in each case to an octave on the fifth scale degree or dominant. In consequence, these chords most often function as dominants to the dominant. Because of their interval content and the corresponding figures, these four chords are sometimes termed, respectively, augmented sixth, augmented six-five-three, augmented six-four-three, and doubly augmented fourth. See also Added sixth.

Sixth-chord style. A manner of composition characterized by the use of successions of *sixth chords, i.e., first-inversion triads. Passages made up of sixth chords have occurred occasionally in tonal music since the 18th century. The persistent use of sixth chords (though they are not described as such in contemporaneous theory) is more striking, however, in some music of the Middle Ages and Renaissance. In the 15th century, **fauxbourdon* and *faburden rely almost exclusively on such harmonies, and the music of composers such as Dunstable, Dufay, and Binchois gives them a prominent place. A familiar *cadence of this period, first encountered in 14th-century Italian music, is characterized by descending sixth chords approaching the cadential goal. Like the significant use of imperfect consonances generally, sixth chords first appear in quantity in English music of the late 13th century and after [see Worcester, repertory of].

Sixth tone. An interval equal to one-sixth of a whole tone [see Microtone].

Sizzle cymbal. See Drum set.

Ska. A popular urban dance music that flourished in Jamaica between 1960 and 1965. The form originated from the imitation by black Jamaican musicians of the *rhythm and blues styles (notably that of Fats Domino) broadcast from New Orleans in the 1950s. The style was characterized by the mechanical use of fast, offbeat rhythms and was best represented by artists such as the Skatalites and Minnie Small. A slower version of ska known as rock steady became popular ca. 1965; it was this latter style that developed into the internationally popular *reggae. Ska groups have remained active in England. P.T.W.

Skala [Ger.]. Scale.

Sketch. A composer's autograph notation of a work in progress. Sometimes a sketch can be identified as an early stage of a known composition, or sometimes it represents a projected but unfinished work. A sketch may be no more than a brief fragment, or it may be a draft of extensive segments of a piece.

Sketches by well-known composers survive in quantity beginning in the 18th century. Some composers (e.g., Beethoven, Webern, and Richard Strauss) systematically kept sketchbooks in which such material has been preserved. For others (e.g., Mozart, Chopin, and Berlioz), only scattered fragments survive. Beethoven's sketchbooks were the first musical sketches to receive scholarly attention (Nottebohm,

1872, 1887), and study of this copious body of material (over 5,000 manuscript pages) has remained intense.

Sketches have been used as an aid to biography and to establish chronology. They have also been used to gain insight into the creative process. Some commentators have used sketches as an aid to analysis, claiming to find in them evidence that makes some interpretations of the work more plausible than others, though this has occasioned some controversy (Johnson, 1978). Finally, sketches of unfinished compositions have occasionally been used as the basis for posthumous completion: Süssmayr's completion of the Mozart Requiem is an early example and Deryck Cooke's version of Mahler's Tenth Symphony a relatively recent one.

Sketches by many well-known composers, among them Beethoven, Debussy, Schubert, Stravinsky, Verdi, and Webern, have been published in facsimile and or in transcription.

Bibl.: Gustav Nottebohm, *Beethoveniana* (Leipzig, 1872; R: New York: Johnson Repr, 1970). Id., *Zweite Beethoveniana* (Leipzig, 1887; R: New York, Johnson Repr, 1970). Paul Mies, *Beethoven's Sketches,* trans. Doris L. Mackinnon (London: Oxford U Pr, 1929; R: New York: Johnson Repr, 1969). Allen Forte, *The Compositional Matrix* (Baldwin, N.Y.: Music Teachers National Assoc, 1961). Lewis Lockwood, "On Beethoven's Sketches and Autographs: Some Problems of Definition and Interpretation," *AM* 42 (1970): 32–47. Alan Tyson, "Sketches and Autographs," in *The Beethoven Reader,* ed. Denis Arnold and Nigel Fortune (New York: Norton, 1971), pp. 443–58. Curt von Westernhagen, *Die Entstehung des "Ring," dargestellt an den Kompositionsskizzen Richard Wagners* (Zürich: Atlantis, 1973); trans. Eng. Arnold and Mary Whittall, *The Forging of the Ring* (Cambridge: Cambridge U Pr, 1976). Philip Gossett, "Beethoven's Sixth Symphony: Sketches for the First Movement," *JAMS* 27 (1974): 248–84. Deryck Cooke, "Mahler's Tenth Symphony," *MT* 117 (1976): 563–65, 645–49. Douglas Johnson, "Beethoven Scholars and Beethoven's Sketches," *19th-Century Music* 2 (1978): 3–17. Douglas Johnson, Alan Tyson, and Robert Winter, *The Beethoven Sketchbooks: History, Reconstruction, Inventory* (Berkeley and Los Angeles: U of Cal Pr, 1985).

Skiffle. A folklike English popular music of the 1950s in which guitars, bass, and drums were used to accompany simple songs. Skiffle groups provided training grounds for many future rock stars.

Skip. *Leap.

Skolie [Ger., fr. Gr. *skolion*]. A drinking song.

Slancio [It.]. Dash, impulse, impetus.

Slapstick. Two narrow, flat pieces of wood about 30 cm. long, hinged so that they can be slapped together, producing a sound like the cracking of a whip; also termed a whip. See ill. under Percussion instruments.

Slargando [It.]. Broadening, slowing down.

Slavic music. See entries for individual countries; Russian and Slavonic chant.

Sleeping Beauty, The [Russ. *Spyashchaya krasavitsa*]. A ballet by Tchaikovsky, op. 66 (1888–89; choreography by Marius Petipa), produced in St. Petersburg in 1890.

Sleigh bells. In musical performance, small *pellet bells mounted in rows on a piece of wood with a protruding handle. See ill. under Percussion instruments.

Slendro [Indonesian, fr. Jav.]. One of the two major tunings (the other being **pelog*) that serve as background systems for the interpretation of melodies performed by **gamelan* instrumentalists and singers in central and east Java [see Southeast Asia IX, 5]. In all of its instrumental and vocal realizations, *slendro* is a pentatonic tuning that mixes thirds that are closer to minor thirds than major seconds (abbr. m) with seconds that are closer to major seconds than minor thirds (abbr. s+). This mix is organized so that contours consist of pitch and interval structures that can be generalized into the following single-octave interval set: s+ s+ m s+ m. Seldom are two m intervals found next to each other in fixed-pitch realizations, but the varying uses of the *slendro* interval structure in nonfixed-pitch parts places different demands on the interval structure of accompanying fixed-pitch instruments. These demands are compromised in the fixed-pitch tunings, none of which closely matches the nonfixed-pitch intervals.

M.H.

Slentando [It.]. Becoming slower.

Slide. (1) On the *trombone and slide *trumpet, a U-shaped segment of cylindrical tubing fitted over two straight segments of tubing in such a way as to be able to slide easily in and out, thus changing the instrument's effective total length, and with it, its fundamental pitch. On brass instruments generally, a tuning slide is a much shorter device of similar design intended for minor adjustments of the instrument's pitch. Instruments with *valves may permit in this way the adjustment of the instrument as a whole as well as of each of the segments of tubing controlled by a valve.

(2) In the playing of bowed stringed instruments, movement from one pitch to another by sliding the finger that has stopped the first pitch toward the second pitch, which is then stopped by an adjacent finger at the rhythmically appropriate moment, an effect sometimes also termed a *portamento; also, any movement from one pitch to another or through a series of discrete pitches by sliding the finger (or fingers, in the case of double stops) from one to the next. The technique was developed early in the 19th century.

(3) [Ger. *Schleifer*] An ornament consisting most commonly of two notes ascending stepwise to the principal note and slurred to it. It is very often written out in full notes, but when it is indicated by small notes, a sign, or not at all, its rhythmic interpretation can be a problem. The dotted slide, called *intonazione, clamatione,* or *accento,* was a favorite Italian orna-

1a. Caccini, "Non più guerra," *Le nuove musiche* (1601/2). 1b. Caccini, "Fortunato augellino."
2a. Montéclair, *Principes* (1736), p. 87.
2b. D'Anglebert, *Pièces de clavecin* (1689).
3b. C. P. E. Bach, *Versuch* (1753).

ment of the late Renaissance and early Baroque periods. Recommended by Bovicelli, it was decried as commonplace by Caccini, who nevertheless wrote it out frequently in his songs [Ex. 1]. In France, the slide sometimes formed part of a *port-de-voix doublé* (a **port-de-voix* from a third below), but more often it was shown as one kind of *coulade* (a group of notes moving scalewise from one pitch to another and taking their value from the first note) or, in keyboard music, a rising *coulé de tierce* [Ex. 2]. Only in the last case did the ornament fall on the beat. C. P. E. Bach illustrated three types of slides. The first [Ex. 3a] is the most familiar; it was used to fill up intervals and was played on the beat (though *NeuO* argues at length for a prebeat performance of this ornament in the music of J. S. Bach). The second was an inverted *turn. The third, the dotted slide, for which C. P. E. Bach gave a dozen examples, some with more than one realization, often resulted in odd distortions of the written rhythms [Ex. 3b]. For bibl. see Ornamentation. (3) D.F.

Slide guitar. *Bottleneck.

Slider. A wooden strip running the length of an organ wind-chest, with a series of holes corresponding to the pipe holes for a particular stop. By means of a stop knob or other device, the slider can be positioned either with its holes aligned with the pipe holes, in which case wind reaches the pipes when keys are depressed, or with the pipe holes cut off from the wind supply. J.T.F.

Slide trumpet. See Trumpet.

Slit drum. A length of wood or bamboo hollowed out through a slit on one side and beaten with a stick. In the Americas, the slit is often cut in the form of an H to make two tongues of different pitch. African instruments sometimes have several tongues. Slit drums are often carved to resemble animals or humans. See also *Teponaztli.*

Slovakia. In 1993, the Slovak and Czech republics became autonomous states, no longer joined as Czechoslovakia, the independent country established in 1918 following centuries of Hapsburg rule. The earliest music known in Slovakia dates from around the 9th century, when Christianity reached the region; liturgical music was at first Byzantine, then Gregorian, as several extant missals and antiphoners testify. Secular music, practiced by minstrel groups, *igrici,* is recorded from the 12th to the 18th century.

Vocal polyphony developed mainly in larger centers such as Bratislava, Bardejov, Levoča, Košice, and Prešov in the 16th and 17th centuries; the major composers were Johannes Ján Šimbracký (d. 1657), Zachariáš Zarewutius (ca. 1605–67), S. F. Capricornus (1628–65), Samuel Marckfelner (1621–74), and Johann Kusser (1626–96). Instrumental music in the 17th century and vocal music in the Baroque period were greatly influenced by folk music, as in the works of Paulinus Bajan (1721–92) and Georgius Zrunek (1734–89), with Italian characteristics only gradually being assimilated by such composers as F. X. Budinský (1676–1727, Pantaleon Roškovsky (1734–89), and Gaudentius Dettelbach (1739–1818).

From the mid-18th century on, Bratislava became an important musical center, attracting some notable composers, such as Anton Zimmermann (ca. 1741–81) and Georg Druschetzky (1745–1819). Elsewhere, in western and central regions of Slovakia, towns and religious establishments cultivated local music making, aided by patronage and cross-fertilized by a variety of different nationalities. In eastern Slovakia, sacred music remained dominant.

The rise of nationalism in the 19th century brought about the study and collection of folk music, culminating in *Slovenské spevy* [Slovak Songs] (1880–1926), and influencing composition and musical life. Significant composers include Ján Levoslav Bella (1843–1936), Mikuláš Schneider-Trnavský (1881–

1958), Mikuláš Moyzes (1872–1944), and Viliam Figuš-Bystrý (1875–1937). At the same time, musical institutions and societies flourished and music teaching became more formalized, trends that intensified after the establishment of Czechoslovakia in 1918. This period also saw more progressive trends in composition from such composers as Eugen Suchoň (1908–93), Ján Cikker (1911–89), and Jozef Kresánek (1913–86), subsequently muted somewhat in the 1950s by the demands of socialist realism. By the 1960s, reflecting developments elsewhere in Europe, a more avant-garde group of composers emerged, including Roman Berger (b. 1930) and Ilja Zelenka (b. 1932). The end of the socialist state in 1989 consolidated new trends toward postmodernism in composition.

The musical institutions developed during the socialist era have similarly blossomed since 1989, despite economic difficulties, with flourishing orchestras in Bratislava, Košice, and Žilina, and opera companies in Košice and Prešov. Music education in local primary music schools, in conservatoires in Žilina, Košice, and Banská Bystrica, and in universities, has ensured the development of high standards in musicology and performance. A new generation of performers, now more free to travel, is gaining a more international audience, and regular festivals in Bratislava, Žilina, and other towns bring artists from abroad to Slovakia.

Slovakia's distinctive folk music continues to exert its influence on mainstream composition, while still a central theme of Slovak musical research and regularly performed by ensembles and at festivals. Most Slovak folk songs belong to one of three broad stylistic categories: "magico-ritual" songs, peasant songs, and shepherd songs. From the 13th to the 19th century, influences from the folk traditions of many neighboring or occupying peoples were assimilated, producing songs dealing with love, politics, and military recruiting; such influences also resulted in a freer use of polyphony, syncopation, and large intervals. Slovak instrumental music, which derives from song, employs more than 200 different instruments, including the *gajdy* (bagpipes), the single-reed *drček,* the 1.8-m *fujara* flute, the *oktáva* and *shlopcoky* violins, the *kôróva basa* (bark bass), and the *cymbal* (dulcimer).

Bibl.: Vladimír Štěpánek and Bohumil Karásek, *An Outline of Czech and Slovak Music* (Prague: Orbis, 1964). Čeněk Gardavský, ed., *Contemporary Czechoslovak Composers* (Prague: Panton, 1965). Peter Faltin, "New Music in Slovakia," *Slovenská hudba* 11 (1967): 341–47. Ladislav Leng, *Slovenské l'udové nástroje* [Slovak Folk Instruments] (Bratislava: vydavatel'stvo Slovenskej akadémie vied, 1967). Duššn Holý and Ladislav Mokrý, "Slovenská hudba" [Slovak Music], *Československá vlastivěda,* no. 3 (1971): 315–86. Ladislav Leng, "L'udová hudba Zubajovcov" [The Folk Music Ensemble of the Zubaj], *Musicologica slovaca* 3 (1971): 25–140. Ladislav Leng and A. Mó i, *Nauka o slovenskom folklóre* [Theory of Slovak Folklore] (Bratislava, 1973). Ladislav Burlas, *Slovenská hudobná moderna* [Modern Slovak Music] (Bratislava, 1983). Ladislav Burlas, *Pohlady na súčasnú slovenskú hudobnú kultúru* [An Overview of Contemporary Slovak Musical Culture] (Bratislava, 1988). Boris Banáry, *Slovenské národné obrodenie v hudbe* [The Slovak National Revival and Music] (Martin: Matica slovenská, 1990). Igor Wasserberger, "Vývoj slovenskej populárnej hudby v rokoch 1920–1944" [Development of Slovak Popular Music 1920–1944], *Slovenská hudba* 20 (1994): 203–16. Peter Faltin, "Slovenská hudobná tvorba v rokoch 1956–1965" [Slovak Composition 1956–65], *Slovenská hudba* 23 (1997): 175–210. Zuzana Martináková, "Súčasná slovenská hudba z konca tisícročia" [Contemporary Slovak Music from the End of the Millennium], *Slovenská hudba* 23 (1997): 234–52.

P.T.

Slovenia (Slovenija). I. *Current musical life and related institutions.* Advanced music education is offered in Ljubljana at the Music Academy (1939; with roots in the music school of the Glasbena matica, 1919), and the Faculty of Education in Maribor (1964). In 1962, on the initiative of Dragotin Cvetko (1911–93), the musicology department was transferred from the Music Academy to the Faculty of Philosophy. Organized musicological research is conducted at the Muzikološki inštitut (1980) and research on traditional music and dance at the Glasbenonarodopisni inštitut (1934), both affiliated with the Slovenska akademija znanosti in umetnosti (Slovenian Academy of Sciences and Arts). The leading musicology journal is *Muzikološki zbornik* (1965). The Society of Slovene Composers was founded in 1945 and the Slovene Musicological Society in 1992.

Permanent opera companies exist in Ljubljana (1892) and Maribor (1922). The main professional orchestras are the Slovenska filharmonija (1908) and the Simfoniki RTV Slovenije (1955). A collection of approximately 270 historical instruments is housed at the Pokrajinski muzej in Ptuj. The Festival Ljubljana (1952), with concert and opera performances, has achieved an international reputation.

II. *History of art music.* Records of the beginnings of sacred music in Slovenian territory are found in 17 medieval codices with music and more than 600 folios, remnants of destroyed music books produced between the 11th and 15th centuries, preserved in Slovenian libraries. The older fragments are in German adiastemic neumatic notation, while more recent fragments are mainly in Gothic (Messine) notation. Secular music was disseminated mainly by minstrels and German *Minnesinger,* among whom were Ulrich von Liechtenstein (13th century) and Oswald von Wolkenstein (15th century).

In the second half of the 16th century the country was briefly overwhelmed with Protestantism, the leading exponent of which was Primus Trubar (1508–86), who published more than 50 books, among them a translation of the Bible (1584), *Catechismus* (1550) with six hymns, and the Slovenian hymnal *Eni Psalmi* (five editions, 1567–95). The country was from the 13th century ruled by the Hapsburgs, and the exchange of musicians between Slovenia and other parts of the monarchy was extensive. The German-born Wolfgang Striccius (b. ca. 1555/60) and Austrian-born Isaac Posch (1591–1622/23) worked for the Ljubljana Estates, while Slovene composers went to work abroad: Jacobus Handl (Gallus, 1550–91), one of the leading European late-Renaissance composers, lived in Vienna, Olomouc, and Prague; Georg Prenner (d. 1590) and Janez Krstnik Dolar (1620–73) in Vienna; Daniel Lagkhner (after ca. 1550–after 1607) in lower Austria; and Gabriel Plavec (Plautzius; ca. 1590–1641) in Mainz. The restoration of the Catholicism at the end of the 16th century temporarily curtailed musical life, but through efforts of Tomaž Hren (1560–1630), the prince-bishop of Ljubljana, musical life became vigorous again. As a 1620 inventory of music of the Ljubljana Cathedral testifies, contemporary Italian music and German music were performed equally, juxtaposing Italian (primarily Venetian) influences against the southern German currents.

The Society of Jesus established its residence in Ljubljana in 1597 and soon started training seminarians in singing and playing instruments, in order that they could participate in performances of religious plays (scholastic comedies) with music interludes. Although the first opera (*Euridice* by Caccini) was performed in Ljubljana before 1620, visiting opera companies performed intermittently after 1660 and regularly after 1740. Central to 18th-century musical life in Ljubljana was the Academia Philharmonicorum (1701–ca. 1869), a music society founded after the model of similar Italian societies that regularly organized concerts and participated in municipal celebrations. With the rise of the middle class in the second half of the 18th century, music amateur societies were founded in Ljubljana (*Filharmonična Družba/ Philharmonische Gesellschaft,* 1794), Klagenfurt (*Philharmonische Gesellschaft,* 1811), Maribor (*Musikverein,* 1828), Trieste (*Società filarmonico-drammatica,* 1829), and Celje (*Lavanter Musikverein,* 1836). The first Slovenian opera, *Belin* by Jakob Zupan (1734–1810), composed in 1780/82 (now lost), was followed by music for the comedy *Ta veseli dan ali Matiček se ženi* (ca. 1790) by Janez Krstnik Novak (1756–1833). Other notable composers from the early 19th century were Ferdinand Schwerdt (ca. 1770–1854), František Benedikt Dussek (1765–after 1817), and Gašpar Mašek (1794–1873).

The March Revolution of 1848 brought nationalism to the fore, and musical life became split between Slovene and German societies. Central to Slovene cultural life were *čitalnice* (reading rooms), which provided an environment for performances of choral and instrumental salon compositions by Benjamin Ipavec (1829–1908), Anton Foerster (1837–1926), and Fran Gerbič (1840–1917). Later the Glasbena matica (Music Society, 1872) came to the scene, a choral society that performed throughout the country (including Vienna in 1896, conducted by Dvořák) and supported a music school (founded 1882). The Slovene opera was housed from 1892 at the Deželno gledališče (State Theater). The German repertoire remained present at the Filharmonična družba (Filharmonische Gesellschaft, 1794), and the Stanovsko gledališče (in 1762 renamed Deželno gledališče, where Mahler conducted in 1881/82), which retained Italian and German opera. With its 388 graduates, the Orglarska šola in Ljubljana (1877–1945) created a solid basis of church musicians throughout the country.

At the turn of the century a generation of well-educated and capable composers came on the scene, able to deal with the large forms of late Romanticism: Viktor Parma (1858–1924), Emil Adamič (1877–1936), and Risto Savin (1859–1948). The 1920s were dominated by the expressionist Marij Kogoj (1895–1956), and the 1930s by Slavko Osterc (1895–1941) whose works reflect the avant-garde and neoclassicism. The generation that marked the central part of the century includes Janko Ravnik (1891–1982), Matija Bravničar (1897–1977), Lucijan Marija Škerjanc (1900–73), Danilo Švara (1902–81), Vilko Ukmar (1905–91), Pavel Šivic (1908–95), and Marijan Lipovšek (1910–95). After a brief disalignment with the European trends in the 1950s, connections with Darmstadt and the new Polish school were established in the 1960s by Primoš Ramovš (1921–99), Zvonimir Ciglič (b. 1921), and the group of composers Pro Musica Viva, who used twelve-tone techniques, serialism, and later electronic music and aleatory: Alojz Srebotnjak (b. 1931), Milan Stibilj (b. 1929), Dorijan Božič (b. 1933), Ivo Petrić (b. 1931), Jakob Jež (b. 1928), Igor Štuhec (b. 1932), and Lojze Lebič (b. 1934).

III. *Traditional music.* Most often in major key, performed by two voices in parallel thirds or sixths, where the accompanying voice can be above or under the leading voice. In three-part homophonic singing the leading voice is usually in the middle voice *(naprej),* accompanied by tenor *(čez)* a third above, with bass *(bas)* providing harmonic foundation. The older four- or five-voice polyphony is still practiced in Koruška, Gorenjsko, and occasionally in Štajersko. Pentatonic scale appears in Prekomurje and Val Resia. Meter of traditional songs is only trochaic and dactylic, with isorhythmic scheme most often consisting of six, seven (3 + 4, particularly frequent in ballads), and eight (4 + 4 or 3 + 2 + 3) syllables.

Besides a large repertoire of simple children's instruments (mostly idiophones), musicians generally use instruments from art music: the *oprekelj* (also known as *šenterija, cimbale, trklje*), a dulcimer played with sticks that can be traced back to the 14th century; although it is no longer in use, it was the most frequently played instrument until the appearance of the accordion in the late 19th century. In the 17th century plucked zithers were introduced with 7 to 12 strings, mostly played in the western and Alpine regions. In the 18th and 19th centuries the most common ensemble was a trio of violin, dulcimer, and double bass. In eastern regions the common ensemble consists of *cimbale* (large dulcimer), violin, viola, and clarinet. In Val Resia (now in Italy), the only instruments used are the *citira* (fiddle) and *bunkula* (cello with three strings tuned a third higher than Western equivalent).

Bibl.: Dragotin Cvetko, *Zgodovina glasbene umetnosti na Slovenskem* [History of Musical Art in Slovenia] (Ljubljana: Državna Založba Slovenije, 1958–60). Dragotin Cvetko, *Histoire de la musique slovene* (Maribor: Obzorja, 1967). Zmaga Kumer et al., eds., *Slovenske ljudske pesmi* [Slovene Traditional Songs] (Ljubljana: Slovenska Matica, 1972–98), 4 vols. Andrej Rijavec, *Slovenska glasbena dela* [Slovene music works] (Ljubljana: Državna založba Slovenije, 1979). Milko Bizjak and Edo Škulj, *Organs in Slovenia* (Ljubljana: Državna založba Slovenije, 1985). Zmaga Kumer, *Die Volksmusikinstrumenten in Slowenian,* Handbuch der europaische Volksmusikinsturmente 1/5 (Leipzig: Deutscher Verlag für Musik, 1986). Jurij Snoj, *Medieval Music Codices: A Selection of Representative Samples from Slovene Libraries* (Ljubljana: Znanstvenoraziskovalni center SAZU, 1997). Mirko Ramovš, *Polka je ukazana: Plesno izročilo na Slovenskem* [Polka Is Ordered: Dance Expression in Slovene Lands] (Ljubljana: Kres; 1995–2000), 6 vols.

Discography. Slovenske ljudske pesmi [Slovene traditional songs], prod. by Zmaga Kumer, *Iz arhiva Glasbenonarodopisnega Instituta,* 4 vols. (Ljubljana: SAZU, 1998). Z.B.

Slur. A curved line placed above two or more notes of different pitch to indicate that they are to be performed *legato. In the case of bowed instruments, this generally means in a single bow; in the case of wind instruments, without *tonguing or taking breath [see also Articulation]. In vocal music, notes sung to a single syllable or in a single breath may be notated in this way. For uses of the slur in conjunction with staccato dots and some other marks, see Bowing; see also Tie. Slurs may also be used to indicate phrasing on a larger scale, as distinct from detailed articulation of notes within a *phrase.

Sly Vixen, The. See *Cunning Little Vixen, The.*

Sminuendo [It.]. **Diminuendo.*

Smorzando [It.]. Dying away.

Snare [Fr. *timbre;* Ger. *Schnarrsaite, Trommelsaite;* It. *corda, bordoniera;* Sp. *bordón*]. Heavy strings or wires, now often overspun with metal, stretched across the center of one head of the snare or side *drum (and sometimes of larger drums) so as to vibrate against it when the other head is struck.

Snare drum. See Drum I, 1.

Snello [It.]. Nimble, graceful.

Soave [It.]. Sweet, gentle.

Sobrecímbala [Sp.]. In Spanish and Mexican organs, the *mixture a fourth or fifth higher than the **Címbala.*

Societies, musical [Ger. *Gesellschaft, Verein*]. Organizations of people with common artistic or scholarly goals, whose activities are regulated by a constitution and bylaws. The activities can include congresses for the exchange of ideas and for business meetings [see Congress report]; the publication of journals, monographs, and editions of music; sponsorship of concerts; encouraging and rewarding outstanding research and performance; and serving as a watchdog over the national and international interests of the organization's areas of knowledge. Prominent today are musicological societies and societies devoted to the music of particular composers. Both began development during the second half of the 19th century. The earliest composer's society was the Bach Gesellschaft, formed in 1850 to publish the collected works of J. S. Bach. The earliest musicological society, founded in 1868 by Robert Eitner, was the Gesellschaft für Musikforschung, which published *Monatshefte für Musikgeschichte* and a series of editions of early music [see below]. In recent years, many societies devoted to the teaching, performance, and literature of a particular instrument or the voice have been formed.

The idea of joining forces for professional interests can be traced back to medieval guilds and, for the performance of music, to **collegia musica.* *Academies of artists and scholars, e.g., the Florentine Camerata, were active throughout Europe from the 15th to the 18th century. Bach was a member of such an academy, the Societät der musicalischen Wissenschaften, in Leipzig. In the late 18th and 19th centuries, concert and singing societies were formed to promote public concerts. Well known among them, some of which are still in existence, are the Academy of Ancient Music in London (1710 or 1726–92), the Gewandhaus-Konzertgesellschaft in Leipzig (1781–), the Gesellschaft der Musikfreunde in Vienna (1812–), the Allgemeine Musik-Gesellschaft in Zürich (1812–), the Royal Philharmonic Society in London (1813–), the Handel and Haydn Society in Boston (1815–), the Sacred Harmonic Society in London (1832–82), the Philharmonic Symphony Society in New York (1842–), and the Association des concerts Lamoureux in Paris (1881–).

The following list emphasizes current professional societies, arranged as follows: I. *Musicological;* II. *Composers;* III. *Modern Music;* IV. *Instruments;* V. *Educational;* VI. *Other.* For each society, the founding date (and ending date, if appropriate) and the titles and dates of some publications (CE = Collected Editions, D = Denkmäler, MS = Monographic Series, P = Periodical) are given. Current addresses are in the societies' journals.

I. *Musicological.* Am. Musicological Soc., 1934 (*Doctoral Dissertations in Musicology,* 1952–96, continued by Doctoral Dissertations Online, 1996–; MS: *Studies and Documents,* 1962–; P: *JAMS,* 1948–). Associazione dei musicologi italiani, 1908 (P: *Bollettino,* 1919–). Dansk Selskab for Musikforskning,

1954 (P: *Dansk årbog for musikforskning,* 1961–). Deutsche Musik-Gesellschaft, 1918–35 (P: *ZfMw,* 1918–35). Gesellschaft für Musikforschung, 1868–1906 (P: *MfMg,* 1869–1905). Gesellschaft für Musikforschung, 1946 (P: *Mf,* 1948–). Instituto español de musicología, 1943 (D: *Monumentos de la música española,* 1941–; P: *AnM,* 1946–). Int. Musical Soc., 1899–1914 (P: *SIMG,* 1899–1914, *ZIMG,* 1899–1914). Int. Musicological Soc., 1927 (*RIdIM, RILM, RISM, RIPM;* P: *AM,* 1928–). Plainsong and Mediaeval Music Soc., 1888 (P: *Journal of the Plainsong and Medieval Music Society,* 1978–90, *Plainsong and Medieval Music,* 1992–). Royal Musical Assoc., 1874 (D: *MB,* 1951–; P: *PRMA,* 1874–1984/5, *RMARC,* 1961–85). Schweizerische musikforschende Gesellschaft, 1919 (CE: Ludwig Senfl, 1937–; D: *Schweizerische Musikdenkmäler,* 1955–; MS: *Publicationen,* Serie II, 1952–, *Schweizer Beiträge zur Musikwissenschaft,* 1972–; P: *Mitteilungen,* 1934–36, *Mitteilungsblatt,* 1937–, *Schweizerisches Jahrbuch für Musikwissenschaft,* 1924–38). Sociedad española de musicología (P: *Revista de musicología,* 1978–). Società italiana di musicologia, 1964 (P: *Rivista italiana di musicologia,* 1966–). Société belge de musicologie, 1946 (P: *RBM,* 1946–). Société de musique d'autrefois, 1927 (P: *AnnM,* 1953–). Société française de musicologie, 1917 (P: *RdM,* 1917–). Société "Union musicologique," 1921–27 (P: *Bulletin,* 1921–26). Svenska Samfundet för Musikforskning, 1919 (P: *Musik i Sverige,* 1969–, *STMf,* 1919–). Verband der Komponisten und Musikwissenschaftler der DDR (P: *BzMw,* 1959–, *Musik und Gesellschaft,* 1951–). Vereniging voor Nederlandse Muziekgeschiedenis, 1868 (D: *Monumenta musica neerlandica,* 1959–; P: *Bouwsteenen,* 1869–81, *TVNM,* 1882–). Vereeniging voor Muziekgeschiedenis, 1930 (P: *Vlaamsch Jaarboek voor Muziekgeschiedenis,* 1939–59).

II. *Composers.* Bach-Gesellschaft, 1850–1900 (CE: 1850–1900). Bruckner Soc. of Am., 1931 (P: *Chord and Discord,* 1932–69). Deutsche Mozart-Gesellschaft, 1951 (P: *Acta Mozartiana,* 1954–). Gilbert and Sullivan Soc., 1924 (P: *Gilbert and Sullivan Journal,* 1925–). Georg-Friedrich-Händel Gesellschaft, 1955 (CE: *Hallische Händel-Ausgabe,* 1955–, P: *Händel Jahrbuch,* 1955–). Int. Bruckner Soc., 1929–39, 1950? (CE: ed. Haas, 1930–44, ed. Nowak, 1951–; P: *Bruckner Blätter,* ?–1940, *Mitteilungsblatt,* 1971–). Internationale Gustav Mahler Gesellschaft, 1955 (CE: ca. 1966–). Internationale Bach-Gesellschaft, 1946. Internationale Schönberg-Gesellschaft. Internationale Schubert-Gesellschaft (CE: 1964–). Internationale Hugo Wolf-Gesellschaft (CE: 1960–). Internationale Felix-Mendelssohn-Gesellschaft (CE: 1960–). Internationale Heinrich-Schütz-Gesellschaft (CE: 1955–; P: *Jahrbuch,* 1979–, *Sagittarius,* 1966–). Internationale Richard Strauss Gesellschaft, 1951 (P: *Mitteilungen,* 1952–70, *Richard Strauss Blätter,* 1971–78, Neue Folge, 1979–). Internationale Stiftung Mozarteum, 1880 (CE: *Neue Mozart Ausgabe,* 1955–; MS: *Schriftenreihe,* 1966–; P: *Mitteilungen,* 1952–, *MJb,* 1950–). Neue Bach-Gesellschaft, 1900 (P: *BaJb,* 1904–). Purcell Soc., 1876 (CE: 1878–).

III. *Modern Music.* Am. Soc. of University Composers, 1966 (P: *Proceedings,* 1966–76/77, *ASUC Journal of Music Scores,* 1973–). Composers' Guild of Great Britain, 1944 (P: *Composer,* 1958–88). Int. Soc. for Contemporary Music, 1922. League of Composers, 1923–54 (P: *Modern Music,* 1924–47). Schweizerische Tonkünstlerverein, 1900 (P: *Schweizerische Musik Zeitung,* 1861–1984, *Dissonanz/Dissonance,* 1984–). Soc. for the Publication of Am. Music, 1919–69. Society of Composers (P: 1989–). Soiuza Sovetskikh Kompozitorov SSSR (P: *Sovetskaia musyka,* 1933–91). Soiuz kompozitorov Rossiiskoi Federatsii Russia (P: Muzykal'naia akademiia, 1992–).

IV. *Instruments.* Am. Choral Foundation, 1957 (P: *Am. Choral Review,* 1958). Am. Guild of Organists, 1896 (P: *The Am. Organist,* 1918–70, 1979–, *Music,* 1967–78, *Quarterly,* 1956–67). Am. Musical Instrument Soc., 1971 (P: *Journal,* 1974–, *Newsletter,* 1971–). Am. Recorder Soc., 1939 (P: *The Am. Recorder,* 1960–). European Piano Teacher's Assoc. (P: *Piano Journal,* 1980–). The Galpin Soc., 1946 (P: *Galpin Soc. Journal,* 1948–). The Guitar Foundation of Am., 1973 (P: *Soundboard,* 1974–). Int. Assoc. for Experimental Research in Singing, 1975 (P: *Journal of Research in Singing,* 1977–). Int. Clarinet Soc., 1973 (P: *The Clarinet,* 1973–). Int. Double Reed Soc., 1969 (P: *The Double Reed,* 1978–, *Journal,* 1973–). Int. Horn Soc., 1971 (P: *The Horn Call,* 1971–). Int. Soc. of Bassists, 1967 (P: *Bass World,* 1975–, *Bass Sound Post,* 1967–71, *Newsletter,* 1974–, *Probas,* 1972–). Int. Trombone Assoc. (P: *Journal,* 1971–, *Newsletter,* 1973–81). Int. Trumpet Guild, 1974 (P: *Journal,* 1976–, *Newsletter,* 1974–). Int. Viola Research Soc. (P: *Die Viola,* 1979–). Lute Soc. [England], 1956 (MS: *The Lute Soc. Booklets,* 1975–, P: *Journal,* 1959). Lute Soc. of Am., 1965 (P: *Journal,* 1968–, *Newsletter,* 1965?–). National Assoc. of Harpists, 1919 (P: *Eolus,* 1921–32?). National Assoc. of Teachers of Singing, 1944 (P: *The NATS Bulletin,* 1944–). The North Am. Saxophone Alliance, 1975 (P: *The Saxophone Symposium,* 1976–). Organ Historical Soc., 1956 (P: *The Tracker,* 1956–). Percussive Arts Soc., 1963 (P: *Percussive Notes,* 1963–, *Percussionist,* 1963–). Soc. of the Classic Guitar, 1936 (P: *Guitar Review,* 1946–). Tubists Universal Brotherhood Assoc., 1973 (P: *T.U.B.A. Journal,* 1974–). Viola da Gamba Soc. [London], 1948 (P: *Chelys,* 1969–). Viola da Gamba Soc. of Am., 1963 (P: *Journal,* 1974–, *VdGSA News,* 1963–). Violoncello Soc., 1956 (P: *Newsletter,* 1968–).

V. *Educational.* College Music Soc., 1957 (*Directory of Music Faculties,* 1967–, MS: *Bibliographies in*

Am. Music, 1974–, P: *Symposium,* 1961–). Int. Soc. for Music Education, 1953 (P: *Int. Music Educator,* 1960–73; continued as *Int. Music Education: ISME Yearbook,* 1973–; *Int. Journal of Music Education,* 1983–). Music Educators National Conference, 1907 (P: *Journal of Research in Music Education,* 1953–, *Music Educators' Journal,* 1914–, *Yearbook,* 1907–). Music Teachers' National Assoc., 1876 (P: *The Am. Music Teacher,* 1951–, *Papers and Proceedings,* 1906–50).

VI. *Other.* Am. Assoc. for Music Therapy, 1971 (P: *Music Therapy,* 1981–). Am. Bandmasters Assoc., 1928 (P: *Journal of Band Research,* 1964–). Am. Soc. for Jewish Music, 1974 (P: *Musica Judaica,* 1975–). Chinese Music Soc. of North Am., 1976 (P: *Chinese Music,* 1978–). Church Music Assoc. of Am., 1964 (P: *Sacred Music,* 1965–). English Folk Dance and Song Soc., a continuation of the Folk-Song Soc., 1898 (P: *English Dance and Song,* 1936–, *Folk Music Journal,* 1965–, *Journal,* 1899–1931). Hymn Soc. of Am., 1922 (P: *The Hymn,* 1949–). Int. Assoc. for the Study of Popular Music, 1981 (P: *Review of Popular Music,* 1982–). Int. Assoc. of Music Libraries, Archives and Documentation Centres, 1951 (*RIdIM, RILM, RISM, RIPM;* P: *Brio* [by United Kingdom Branch], 1964–, *FAM,* 1954–). Int. Folk Music Council, 1947 (P: *Journal,* 1949–68, *Yearbook,* 1969–). Int. Jazz Federation, 1969 (P: *Jazz Forum,* 1967–). Int. Soc. for Jazz Research, 1969 (P: *Beiträge zur Jazzforschung,* 1969–, *Jazzforschung,* 1969–). Music Library Assoc., 1931 (P: *Music Cataloguing Bulletin,* 1970–, *Notes,* 1934–42, 1943–). Musical Antiquarian Soc., 1840–47. National Assoc. for Music Therapy, ca. 1949 (P: *The Journal of Music Therapy,* 1964–). Soc. for Asian Music, 1959 (P: *Asian Music,* 1968–). Soc. for Ethnomusicology, 1955 (P: *Ethno-Musicology,* 1953–57, *Ethnomusicology,* 1957–). Soc. for Music Theory, 1978 (P: *Music Theory Spectrum,* 1979–). Soc. for Research in Psychology of Music and Music Education, 1966 (P: *Psychology of Music,* 1973–). The Soc. for American Music, formerly known as the Sonneck Soc., 1975 (P: *Newsletter,* 1975–, *American Music,* 1983–).

Bibl.: John R. Douglas, "Musician and Composer Societies: A World Directory," *Notes* 34 (1977): 39–51.

H.E.S., rev. L.C.

Sociology of music. The systematic study of the relationship between music and society. This is a general field of inquiry that is not unified by a single specific methodology, but depends instead upon the traditions of sociology, *musicology, and philosophy for its analytic techniques.

By examining the interdependence of music and its social milieu, the sociology of music attempts to determine not only the function of that music in society, but also the ways in which society influences and affects particular musical structures. Thus, for example, this field is interested both in the evolution of concert activity from private to public life in the later 18th century and equally well in the possible effects of that change on the emergence of sonata form.

The sociological examination of musical life concerns all periods of cultural history. The breadth of the field and the irregular nature of available data make it impossible to describe a continuous orientation and methodology, since numerous topics demand individual analytic methods. Contemporary sociological tools, such as the interviews utilized by Charles Keil in *Urban Blues* (Chicago: U of Chicago Pr, 1966) and by Simon Frith in *Sound Effects* (New York: Pantheon, 1981), are unavailable for most historical studies. In general, however, the analyst begins by establishing the social climate of a particular society in the attempt to define the variables of musical production, form, and *reception.

Questions that arise in this type of inquiry are as varied as the cultures under investigation. General concerns include the determination of why a society during one historical period will produce a certain type of music; how the historical nature and progress of a society are affected by the production and reproduction of music; and how musical, social, and cultural structures might be related to one another. The sociology of music is not primarily an aesthetic discipline; musical styles are considered for their social significance. Thus, as material categories, *popular and *folk music are as important as art music.

Although Plato and Aristotle explored the political implications of music in society, contemporary theory has its origins in the work of the sociologists Dilthey and Simmels (Etzkorn, 1973). The sociology of music is primarily a product of German scholarship. Max Weber's *Die rationalen und soziologischen Grundlagen der Musik* (1911; publ. 1921), the first attempt, projects interrelations between the fundamental technical foundations of Western music and the historically parallel social structures. The development of the tempered scale, for instance, is perceived as both indication and result of the increasing rationalization of socioeconomic structures. Although the value of this approach for 20th-century music has been disputed, Weber's work remains important for its influence on later thinkers and for its initiation of a link between sociology and musicology.

New directions, all currently vital, developed in the 1930s. There are two major schools of thought, one primarily empirical, the other essentially historical. The empiricist school is represented by Blaukopf, Engel, Karbusický, and Silbermann. Generally, their approach presupposes the existence of the musical work and concentrates on its context and function within the society. Consequently, the social genesis and its possible meaning or content are often bypassed in favor of the analysis of the use of a particular type of music and the profile of its users. The area most receptive to this approach is the contemporary dissemination and reception of both serious and popular music. Through demographic and related methods, the consumption of various musics is linked to particular social groups.

The theories of Hegel and Marx provide the basis for the two main factions of the historical school. Theodor Adorno (1903–1969) developed an approach whose terminology borrows heavily from Marxism but whose critical principles remain rooted in Hegelian idealism. Although Adorno saw some value in empirical studies, he generally viewed them as superficial indicators, preferring to rely on technical and aesthetic analysis of the music itself. Adorno considered the inner structural coherence of the music, and the progressive character of the musical "material," to be the most reliable social indicators, a theory that places particular emphasis on the production of the avant-garde (1962). Popular music, with its "standardized" structures and nonfunctional use of detail, becomes a false ideology and a symptom of domination in late capitalist societies. For Adorno, the most advanced music produced in a culture is at once social criticism and an aesthetic depiction of the society that produced it. Thus, his sociology of music is in many ways intended as "social criticism through the artistic realm" (Blomster, 1976). Although Adorno's work has been criticized as abstract and elitist, it remains the central influence in the field.

The Marxist sociology of music, which is generally opposed to Adorno's theories, proceeds from the tenet that all change in the social and cultural superstructure is the result of change in economic or material foundations. Thus, changing musical styles and values result from historical fluctuations in the economic and social function of music in society rather than of an autonomous chronological development of musical aesthetics. This approach favors the politically oriented and class-conscious works of Brecht and Weill, Blitzstein, and Eisler over the isolated avant-garde promoted by Adorno. Hanns Eisler (1898–1962), who produced most of his sociological writings in the 1920s and 30s, commands a central position in the sociology of music based on historical materialism.

Although a large percentage of work done in the sociology of music has been epistemological, there has been a tendency in recent decades toward objective empirical work (Karbusický, 1975). It has been hoped for some time that sociology would become an aid to musicological investigation rather than remain an independent science; this goal may only be completely realized through a consolidation of interest and methodology between the two fields.

Bibl.: *Bibliographies.* Martin Elste, *Verzeichnis deutschsprachiger Musiksoziologie 1848–1973,* 2 vols. (Hamburg: K D Wagner, 1975). Ivo Supičić et al., "The Sociology of Music—A Selected Bibliography," *IRASM* (1976–).

Literature. Max Weber, *Die rationalen und soziologischen Grundlagen der Musik* (Munich: Drei Masken Verlag, 1921); trans. and ed. Don Martindale, Johannes Riedel, and Gertrude Neuwirth, *The Rational and Social Foundations of Music* (Carbondale: Southern Ill U Pr, 1958). Wilhelm Dilthey, *Der Aufbau der geschichtlichen Welt in den Geisteswissenschaften* (Leipzig: Teubner, 1927). Theodor W. Adorno, "Zur gesellschaftlichen Lage der Musik," *Zeitschrift für Sozialforschung* 1 (1932): 103–24, 356–78. Paul Lazarsfeld, *Radio Research* (New York: Essential Bks, 1940–41). Kurt Blaukopf, *Musiksoziologie* (St. Gall: Zollikofer, 1950). François Lesure, "Musicologie et sociologie," *ReM* (1953): 4–11. Alphons Silbermann, *Wovon lebt die Musik? Die Prinzipien der Musiksoziologie* (Regensburg: G Bosse, 1957), trans. Corbet Stewart, *The Sociology of Music* (London: Routledge & Kegan Paul, 1963). Theodor W. Adorno, *Einleitung in die Musiksoziologie* (Frankfurt: Suhrkamp, 1962; rev., Reinbek: Rohwohlt, 1968), trans. E. B. Ashton, *Introduction to the Sociology of Music* (New York: Seabury Pr, 1976). Konrad Boehmer, *Zwischen Reihe und Pop: Musik und Klassengesellschaft* (Vienna and Munich: Jugend & Volk, 1970). Ivo Supičić, *Musique et societé—Perspectives pour une sociologie de la musique* (Zagreb: Institut de musicologie, Académie de musique, 1971). Gilbert Chase, "American Musicology and the Social Sciences," in Barry S. Brook, Edward Downes, and Sherman Solkema, eds., *Perspectives in Musicology* (New York: Norton, 1972). Hanns Eisler, *Musik und Politik—Schriften 1924–48,* ed. Günter Mayer (Munich: Rogner & Bernhard, 1973). Peter Etzkorn, ed., *Music and Society: The Later Writings of Paul Honigsheim* (New York: J Wiley, 1973). Bernd Buchhofer, Jürgen Friedrichs, and Hartmut Lüdtke, *Musik und Sozialstruktur: Theoretische Rahmenstudie und Forschungspläne* (Cologne: A Volk, 1974). Daniel Mendoza de Arce, "Contemporary Sociological Theories and the Sociology of Music," *IRASM* 5 (1974): 231–50. Vladimír Karbusický, *Empirische Musiksoziologie—Erscheinungsformen, Theorie, und Philosophie des Bezugs "Musikgesellschaft"* (Wiesbaden: Breitkopf & Härtel, 1975). Tibor Kneif, ed., *Texte zur Musiksoziologie* (Cologne: A Volk, 1975; 2nd ed., n.p.: Laaber, 1983). Wesley Blomster, "Sociology of Music: Adorno and Beyond," *Telos* 28 (1976): 80–112. Peter Rummenhöller, *Einführung in die Musiksoziologie* (Wilhelmshaven: Heinrichshofen, 1978). Elizabeth Haselauer, *Handbuch der Musiksoziologie* (Vienna: Böhlau, 1980). Kurt Blaukopf, *Musik im Wandel der Gesellschaft: Grundzüge der Musiksoziologie* (Munich: R Piper, 1982). P.T.W.

Sofort [Ger.]. Immediately, **attacca.*

Soft pedal. See *Una corda,* Piano.

Soggetto [It.]. Subject, theme. In the 16th century, the term referred to the entirety of a melody forming the basis of a canon. By the 18th century, it referred to a fugue subject of the type found in the early *ricercar, consisting of relatively few notes of relatively long duration (e.g., the subject of the Fugue in C♯ minor from the first book of Bach's **Well-Tempered Clavier*). In this sense, it is distinguished from an *andamento,* a longer fugue subject, perhaps in two phrases (e.g., from the Fugue in G major, *Well-Tempered Clavier,* bk. 1), and from an *attacco,* a short motive such as might be used for imitative treatment in a motet.

Soggetto cavato (dalle parole) [It., subject carved from the words]. A musical subject or **cantus firmus* derived from a text by employing *solmization syllables whose vowels correspond to the vowels in the text. Thus, Josquin's Mass dedicated to *Hercules dux Ferrarie* (Hercules, Duke of Ferrara, d. 1505) derives its subject from this dedication by employing the six solmization syllables of the time *(ut, re, mi, fa, sol, la)* as follows: *re ut re ut re fa mi re,* corresponding to the vowels *e u e u e a i e,* yielding the pitches d c d c d f e d. The term was coined by Gioseffo Zarlino (*Le istitutione harmoniche,* 1559, 3:66).

Soir, Le [Fr.]. See *Matin, Le.*

Sol. See Pitch names, Solmization, Hexachord.

Soldier's Tale, The. See *Histoire du soldat, L'.*

Soleá [Sp., pl. *soleares*]. One of the principal general categories of *flamenco music, incorporating many subtypes. The most prominent types of text or *copla* are the *grande* (great), consisting of four octosyllabic lines, with lines 2 and 4 rhyming, and the *corta* (short), consisting of three octosyllabic lines, with lines 1 and 3 rhyming. The guitar accompaniment employs a variety of patterns in 6/8 and 3/4.

Solemn Mass. See Mass, Missa.

Solenne [It.]. Solemn.

Solennel [Fr.]. Solemn.

Solesmes. A Benedictine monastery in Solesmes, France, a village on the Sarthe River, southwest of Le Mans. Since its reestablishment in 1833 by Dom Prosper Guéranger, this community has carried on scholarly study of Gregorian chant aimed in part at its restoration. This work has resulted in a series of scholarly publications (e.g., *Paléographie musicale* and *Études grégoriennes*) as well as liturgical books, some of which have been declared the official books of the Roman Catholic Church. Another central activity has been the interpretation of chant in performance, especially as regards rhythm, accentuation, and the relationship of melodies to texts. Among the monks who have played an important role in the work of Solesmes are Joseph Pothier, André Mocquereau, Joseph Gajard, Eugène Cardine, and Jean Claire. See also Gregorian chant V, VI.

Sol-fa. See Tonic sol-fa.

Solfège [Fr.], **solfeggio** [It.]. (1) In the 17th century and subsequently, a textless vocal exercise (first Italian, later also French). At first rarely published, *solfeggi* were frequently printed after this type of exercise was adopted in France. The related vocal *ricercar (a polyphonic genre) was commonly published as early as the 16th century.

(2) Particularly from the late 18th century to the present, the singing of scales, intervals, and melodic exercises to *solmization syllables. The term has also been used to encompass all aspects of the teaching of basic musical skills; in France particularly, extensive courses of solfège (in this sense) were developed. The 20th century saw a considerable increase of interest in solfège, in the sense of solmization. For instance, Zoltán Kodály developed a highly successful choral method intended for the teaching of children [see Kodály method; see also Tonic sol-fa].

Currently, the (revised Guidonian) syllables *do, re, mi, fa, sol, la, si (ti)* are applied to notes in two different ways, called fixed *do* and movable *do.* In fixed *do,* the syllables are equivalent in meaning to letter names: *do* = C, *re* = D, *mi* = E, and so forth; they are assigned without regard to accidentals. In movable *do,* the syllables indicate the scale degrees of a major scale (e.g., in D major, *do* = D, *re* = E, *mi* = F♯, and so forth). Chromatic notes are assigned syllables in various ways. For instance, in many systems, *ti* is used for the seventh syllable, so that the seven basic solmization syllables begin with seven different consonants; when chromatically altered, a note takes the initial consonant of the syllable it would carry if unaltered and a different vowel, which indicates the alteration. The ascending chromatic scale (with sharps) is thus *do, di, re, ri, mi, fa, fi, sol, si, la, li, ti, do;* the descending chromatic scale (with flats) *do, ti, te, la, le, sol, se, fa, mi, me, re, ra, do.* German *Tonwort* systems combine characteristics of both types of solmization: fixed correspondence between letter names and syllables, but variation of syllables according to chromatic alteration.

Bibl.: Lévesque and Bêche, comps., *Solfèges d'Italie* (Paris, 1768; 4th ed., 1788). Henri Lemoine, *Solfège des solfèges* (Paris: H Lemoine, 1910–13). Sol Berkowitz, Gabriel Fontrier, Leo Kraft, *A New Approach to Sight Singing* (New York: Norton, 1960). Marta Árkossy Ghezzo, *Solfège, Ear Training, Rhythm, Dictation, and Music Theory: A Comprehensive Course* (University, Ala.: U of Ala Pr, 1980).

Solfegietto [It. also *solfeggieto*]. A short piece similar in character to an etude or study. A well-known example (originally titled "Solfeggio") is a piece in C minor by C. P. E. Bach.

Solmization. The designation of pitches for aural recognition by means of conventional syllables rather than letter names. Many of the principal musical cultures of the world have systems of solmization, which may be employed in oral transmission or in the teaching or reading of music. The syllables most commonly used in Western cultures today are *do (doh), re, mi, fa, sol, la,* and *si* (or *ti*). These are derived from the Guidonian system [see below].

Early solmization systems include Chinese, Indian, Greek, and Byzantine methods of assigning syllables to pitches. Some of these are still in use. The system that has survived into modern Western use, first recorded in the early 11th century, is traditionally associated with Guido of Arezzo. [For a system of assigning syllables to pitches with a somewhat different purpose, see *Noeane.*]

Guidonian solmization is based on a set of interlocking *hexachords. The system is based on the text and tune of the hymn *Ut queant laxis,* in which each of the first six lines begins one step higher than the previous line; the six initial tones of these lines constitute a hexachord. The syllables sung to the notes of the hexachord in the hymn tune, and associated with them in Guidonian solmization, are *ut, re, mi, fa, sol,* and *la.* Between *mi* and *fa* is a semitone; a whole tone separates other adjacent syllables. Other texts are sometimes linked with the tune. One gives the syllables *tu, rex, mi, fons, sol, laus* and another *tri, pro, de, nos, te, ad.* Solmization was conceived as a method for *sight-reading. To solmize a melody, one gives a syllable to each written note and sings the pitch associated with that syllable.

In the Guidonian system, regular hexachords begin on C, F, and G, within the range G to g′; the notes of these hexachords constitute the gamut, which reaches from G to e″. Hexachords other than the basic ones are not members of the gamut; before the end of the Middle Ages, however, theorists had recognized the usefulness of irregular (or *ficta*) hexachords in justifying the existence of chromatically altered notes. For example, to explain the note F♯, a hexachord beginning on D, in which F♯ would be *mi,* was constructed. Early in the 15th century, hexachords beginning on every note, altered or unaltered, were described by theorists.

When a melody to be solmized moves beyond the limits of a single hexachord (regular or *ficta*), the device of mutation is used to change from one hexachord to another. Mutation takes place on a note belonging to both the hexachord currently in use and the one to which it is necessary to change. To make the mutation, one simply changes the solmization syllable of the note in question from that which it carries in the first hexachord to that belonging to it in the second hexachord.

With the proliferation of *ficta* hexachords and with the development of musical styles dependent on extensive chromaticism and transposition (as in the mid- to late 16th century), Guidonian solmization began to lose its usefulness. Music theorists responded with two types of suggestions: rejection of the system in favor of alternative methods, and retention of elements of the system but elimination of its more troublesome features (especially mutation).

The first alternative to the Guidonian system was suggested in 1482: Ramos de Pareia proposed a set of eight syllables, *psal–li–tur per vo–ces is–tas,* for an ascending series of notes (without chromatic alteration) from C to c; the seventh syllable could be used for either b♭ *(b is)* or b♮ *(is* ♮). Other alternatives include Hubert Waelrant's (ca. 1517–98) Bocedization (beginning on C or F and ascending diatonically, *bo, ce, di, ga, lo, ma, ni;* in 1600 expanded by Sethus Calvisius to include the syllable *pa* for the lowered seventh scale degree); Daniel Hitzler's (1576–1635) Bebization (ascending diatonically from C, *ce, de, mi, fe, ge, la, bi,* plus syllables for two flatted tones and most sharped tones; expanded and revised in 1659 by Otto Gibelius); and Carl Heinrich Graun's (1704–59) Damenization (from C, *da, me, ni, po, tu, la, be,* with provision for all chromatic tones). None of these systems had a lasting influence. More recent alternatives include the "Jale" method of Richard Münnich (1887–1970), a simplification of the "Tonwort" system of Carl A. Eitz (1848–1924), and the Jamization of Karel Ph. Bernet Kempers.

Most theorists of the 16th century advanced no substantial changes in Guidonian solmization but simply tried to make it easier to use. Around the year 1600 the syllable *si* was added to the original six, so that the series could encompass an octave. As part of his revision of Bebization, Otto Gibelius both adopted Guido's syllables for the diatonic notes and, following Italian writers of the 16th century, used *do* in place of *ut.* Since then, many methods of using Guidonian solmization and of expanding it to include extra syllables, particularly for chromatically altered notes, have been advanced [see Solfège (2)]. None has become universal. In the 18th century, a simplified method called *fasola was widely used in the U.S. Recently, several systems, including *Tonic sol-fa (especially in England) and Zoltán Kodály's method (developed in Hungary, now used elsewhere as well), have achieved considerable currency.

Bibl.: Georg Lange, "Zur Geschichte der Solmisation," *SIMG* 1 (1899/1900): 535–622. Carl Parrish, "A Renaissance Music Manual for Choirboys," *Reese,* 1966, pp. 649–64. Robert Vladimir Henderson, "Solmization Syllables in Musical Theory" (Ph.D. diss., Columbia Univ., 1969). Gaston G. Allaire, *The Theory of Hexachords, Solmization and the Modal System: A Practical Application* (American Institute of Musicology, 1972). Gene H. Anderson, "*La Gamme du si:* A Chapter in the History of Solmization," *Indiana Theory Review* 3 (1979): 40–47. Carol Berger, "The Hand and the Arts of Memory," *MD* 35 (1981): 87–120. Daniel Zager, "From the Singer's Point of View: A Case Study in Hexachordal Solmization as a Guide to *Musica recta* and *Musica ficta* in Fifteenth-Century Vocal Music," *CM* 43 (1987): 7–21. Leeman L. Perkins, "Ockeghem's *Prenez sur moi:* Reflections on Canons, Catholica, and Solmization," *MD* 44 (1990): 119–83. Timothy A. Smith, "A Comparison of Pedagogical Resources in Solmization Systems," *Journal of Music Theory Pedagogy* 5 (1991): 1–23. Timothy A. Smith, "Liberation of Solmization: Searching for a Common Ground," *Journal of Music Theory Pedagogy* 6 (1992): 153–168; responses in *Journal of Music Theory Pedagogy* 6 (1992): 137–51; 8 (1994): 221–25, 227–30. Daniel Taddie, "Solmization, Scale and Key in Nineteenth-Century Four-Shape Tunebooks: Theory and Practice," *American Music* 14 (1996): 42–64. Lionel Pike, *Hexachords in Late-Renaissance Music* (Aldershot: Ashgate, 1998). Allen Scott, "Bobization and Bebization: Two Alternative Solmization Systems of the Early Seventeenth Century," *Theoria* 9 (2001): 25–47. See also *Musica ficta.*

B.J.H., rev. L.D.B.

Solo [It., alone]. (1) A work for a single instrument without accompaniment or one in which a single instrument is prominently featured throughout, even if with accompaniment. (2) In a work for ensemble, a passage to be played by a single player instead of an entire section or one in which a single player has an especially prominent part. (3) In a concerto, a passage featuring the soloist, as distinct from a *tutti, in which the orchestra predominates.

Solo organ. A division, usually found in electric-action organs, containing *stops suitable for solo use.

Sombrero de tres picos, El [Sp., The Three-Cornered Hat]. A ballet by Manuel de Falla (choreography by Leonide Massine; décor by Pablo Picasso; based on a novel by Pedro Antonio de Alarcón), produced in London in 1919. It is an expanded version of Falla's unpublished "farsa mímica" *El corregidor y la molinera* (The Magistrate and the Miller's Daughter), composed in 1916–17.

Son. (1) [Fr.] Sound; *s. bouché, étouffé,* in horn playing, *stopped tone; *s. ouvert,* an open or natural tone on a wind instrument; *s. harmonique,* harmonic. (2) [Sp.] In Cuba, a rural song and dance-music style combining Hispanic and African-derived elements. *Sones* are performed by singers with accompaniment of *tres* (three-course guitar) and maracas, and by larger ensembles with, e.g., *tres,* guitar, *marimbula* (wooden-box lamellaphone) and *botija* (earthenware-jug aerophone), bongos, maracas, claves, and other hand-held percussion instruments. In moderate to rapid tempo, syncopated, and in duple meter, *sones* are varied in structure; a typical form alternates two sections, one with verses sung to a short repeated phrase, the other with a repeated *call-and-response refrain. In the early 20th century, the *son* became an important urban popular form, performed by ensembles that gradually modified its traditional instrumentation and musical style. (3) [Sp.] Any of a number of types of pieces of traditional dance music in several regions of Mexico. Mexican *son* traditions share certain traits such as emphasis on combinations of simple triple and compound duple meter and *zapateado* (foot-tapping) in the dances they accompany, but they are also regionally distinct in terms of performance ensemble, repertory, and many stylistic features. See also *Son chapín, Son jarocho.* (2) (3) D.S.

Sonata [It.]. A work for one or more solo instruments, usually in several movements, and prevalent from the 17th century on. This definition must be refined for each historical period and must allow for exceptions, since the term sonata has at times been used for instrumental works that include a part for voice (Monteverdi, *Sonata sopra "Sancta Maria,"* 1610) or, in the 17th and 18th centuries, for works that could also be performed by orchestra [see Trio sonata]. It should also be noted that *sonata form refers not to the disposition of several movements collected under the rubric sonata, but rather to a formal convention widely used by composers since the Classical period for individual movements in a sonata, as well as in chamber and symphonic music.

The term has a long history before 1600, but has always denoted instrumental music. The variant *sonade* is found in a 13th-century literary source. Another variant, *sennet, was used in the Elizabethan theater. Luis de Milán used the form *sonada* for pavanes and fantasias in his *vihuela* book, *El maestro* (Valencia, 1536). During the latter half of the 16th century the term sonata was used at times for dances in the Italian lute repertory (Giacomo Gorzanis, 1561). At the end of the century, a new kind of sonata emerged as an important genre.

I. *Baroque.* In the Baroque period, the term sonata was applied in Italy not only to dance collections but also to a new type of instrumental work in an abstract style. Outside Italy, betraying both Italian origins and influence, only this new type was normally called sonata, dance collections being entitled **ordre,* *partita, or *suite. Sonatas in an abstract style were composed for a variety of instruments, both keyboard and ensemble, and in a variety of settings, from unaccompanied solo to polychoral works for as many as 22 parts grouped in five instrumental choirs. Giovanni Gabrieli's two sonatas in his *Sacrae symphoniae* (Venice, 1597), one of which is the famous *Sonata pian e forte,* are the earliest examples in this abstract style. They are also the earliest *polychoral settings, a type current through the 1660s and particularly popular with German composers. All but one of Gabrieli's seven sonatas were of this kind and differed from his *canzonas mainly in their graver character. In a late Italian example, Giovanni Legrenzi's six-voice *La buscha* (in op. 8; Venice, 1663), each choir has the instrumentation of the trio sonata.

Keyboard sonatas in the new abstract style, though one of the oldest types, were rare until the 1740s. Adriano Banchieri's one-movement organ sonatas (*L'organo suonarino,* 1st version; Venice, 1605), intended for use in church, were followed by similar works by Tarquinio Merula (1594?–1665) and Giovanni Marco Martini (ca. 1650–1730). The earliest sonatas for harpsichord, by Gioanpietro Del Buono (Palermo, 1641), were based on the plainchant hymn "Ave maris stella." Later sonatas for this instrument normally had several movements; such pieces were composed by Bernardo Pasquini (1637–1710), Benedetto Marcello (1686–1739), and Johann Kuhnau (1660–1722), among others.

Far more common than any of the aforementioned types were ensemble sonatas for one to four melody instruments and basso continuo. Their appearance heralds the rise to prominence of the violin family, and they were the main vehicle for the development of a style appropriate to these instruments. The names applied to these works may be misleading as to the number of performers involved. A solo sonata, for example, often (but not always) requires three: the solo instrument, usually a violin; a chord-producing instrument, usually either organ or harpsichord, to realize the harmonies of the continuo [see Thoroughbass];

and a bass instrument, usually stringed, to reinforce the bass line. Thus, Giovanni Gabrieli's *Sonata per tre violini* (Venice, 1615), among the earliest examples of the ensemble sonata, requires five performers. Giovanni Paolo Cima's sonatas (Milan, 1610) have scorings common through the 1640s: violin and violone; and violin, cornett, violone, and trombone. The most common scoring, however, was to be that of the trio sonata.

Through the 1650s, it is often difficult to distinguish between the canzona and the sonata stylistically. Both have a number of sections contrasting in tempo, meter, and character, though the sonata tends to be more virtuosic and exploits such special effects for the violin as *double stops and *scordatura. Prominent composers include Carlo Farina (ca. 1600–ca. 1640), Biagio Marini (ca. 1587–1663), Johann Heinrich Schmelzer (ca. 1620–80), and Heinrich Biber (1644–1704). A popular type in Italy through the 1640s was the variation sonata, written by Marini and Francesco Turini (ca. 1589–1656), among others, and based on popular tunes such as "Tanto tempo ormai" and "Quest e quel luoco." Corelli's *La follia* (in his op. 5; Rome, 1700), is a late example of this type.

The title of a publication by Merula, *Canzoni overo sonate concertate per chiesa e camera* (op. 12; Venice, 1637), indicates two significant trends before 1650: the gradual fusion of the canzona and sonata, and the emergence of a concern with the uses of the sonata. Both trends crystallized in the 1650s in the sonatas of Giovanni Legrenzi (1626–90) and others, which are of two types, **sonata da chiesa* and **sonata da camera,* differentiated in both style and function. The former, suitable for use in the church, employs an abstract style; the latter, intended for use in the chamber, is most often a collection of dances. By the 1650s, the number of contrasting sections in the two precursors of the *sonata da chiesa* had decreased, and those that remained took on the character of independent movements, normally three to five. Further standardization in format for both types is evident in the works of Corelli at the end of the 17th century. Significant composers from 1650 through 1700 include Maurizio Cazzati (ca. 1620–77), Giovanni Battista Vitali (1632–92), Giuseppe Colombi (1635–94), and Giovanni Maria Bononcini (1642–78).

Toward the end of the 17th century, the sonata gained a foothold in England with Henry Purcell's two published sets (1683 and 1697, the former described by the composer as a "just imitation of the most fam'd Italian Masters"), and through works by Nicola Matteis (fl. ca. 1670–ca. 1690) and other immigrant composers. In France, native composers such as François Couperin and Élisabeth-Claude Jacquet de La Guerre (ca. 1666/67–1729) began to write sonatas during the 1690s, followed in the early decades of the 18th century by Jean-Féry Rebel (1666–1747), Michel Blavet (1700–68), Jean-Marie Leclair the Elder and many others. Sonatas written after 1700, including those of Bach, Handel, and Telemann, tend to employ the four-movement format (slow-fast-slow-fast) found in about half of Corelli's *sonate da chiesa,* though the church-chamber dichotomy was no longer in effect. These works include solo sonatas, trio sonatas, and (especially in Germany) quartet sonatas, of which the *Quadri* (Hamburg, 1730) and *Nouveaux quatuors* (Paris, 1738) of Telemann are the best known examples. Paralleling the spreading popularity of the redesigned Baroque woodwinds, many sonatas of the early 18th century specify the recorder, flute, and oboe, often in combination with string instruments. Italian composers during these same years often favored either fewer or more movements. Francesco Veracini (1690–1768) wrote sonatas having from five to eight movements, whereas both Giuseppe Tartini (1692–1770) and Pietro Locatelli (1695–1764) preferred a three-movement format, also common in German sonatas around midcentury.

Three other types of Baroque sonatas should be mentioned: the unaccompanied sonata, of which those by Bach for violin and for cello are the most famous; the duo sonata for obbligato keyboard and violin or flute, examples of which were composed in Germany by Bach and Telemann, and in France by Jean-Philippe Rameau and Jean-Joseph Cassanéa de Mondonville (1711–72); and the 17th-century German **Turmsonate.*

II. *Classical.* The rise to prominence of solo sonatas for stringed keyboard instruments in the 1740s is one sign of the beginnings of Classical style, especially in the works of such eminent composers as Domenico Scarlatti and Carl Philipp Emanuel Bach. The former probably composed primarily for the harpsichord, the preferred instrument through the 1760s. The latter early in his career favored the clavichord because of its suitability to the expressive **empfindsam* style of which he was the most gifted practitioner; in the 1760s, Emanuel Bach turned to the more powerful fortepiano.

Scarlatti's sonatas are one-movement *binary forms. Many that share the same tonic but differ in tempo may have been intended to be played in pairs or occasionally in threes. Emanuel Bach, on the other hand, composed sonatas in a three-movement format, fast–slow–fast, that was to become standard for the Classical sonata, regardless of instrumentation, though other plans are found as well. Most sonatas by both these composers, in the custom of the period, were intended for amateur music-making. Solo sonatas of this type were extremely popular with the three late Classical Viennese composers: Haydn, Mozart, and Beethoven. Haydn is credited with 62 and Mozart with 21. It is generally acknowledged, however, that the 37 sonatas composed by Beethoven are unsurpassed in their seriousness of purpose and control of large-scale forms, a judgment that is supported by their continuing popularity from his day to ours.

More popular initially than the solo keyboard sonata, and first appearing at about the same time, was the *accompanied keyboard sonata, which was of two types: the first included the violin, the second both violin and cello. In both types, the stringed instruments either reinforce the melody (or melody and bass) of the keyboard part or supply sustained notes against it. The first type, composed by the young Mozart among others, was to evolve into the violin sonata that balanced the roles of the instruments, a type that Mozart himself wrote in his maturity and that Beethoven was later to write for violin, for cello, and for horn. The second, composed in great numbers by Emanuel Bach and Haydn, was by a similar balancing of instrumental roles to evolve into the piano trio, a genre popular with Mozart, Beethoven, and composers in the Romantic era [see Trio (3)].

The formal conventions employed for individual movements of the Classical sonata, regardless of instrumentation, were shared with other contemporary kinds of chamber music and with the symphony. Most evolved in some fashion from the *binary form associated with the dance. Most often, the first movements of such works are in *sonata form. The slow middle movements, normally in a different key, often also employ sonata form, occasionally with a short retransition replacing the development. Emanuel Bach preferred the free fantasia. Other conventions used for this movement include the simple binary form (common in Haydn), a ternary design (favored by Mozart and Beethoven), the variation set, and—rarely—the *rondo. If a fourth movement is present (and it was seldom included before Beethoven), it most often relates to the dance and is normally placed between the slow movement and the finale. In early Classical sonatas it is commonly a *minuet and trio; in Beethoven's works it is usually a *scherzo. For final movements, the two most common conventions are the dance (again a minuet and trio) and the rondo. The former was more popular with early Classical composers, the latter with the three Viennese masters, who often furnished their rondos with a development, creating what is commonly called a sonata-rondo [see Rondo (1) II]. Other possibilities for the final movement include sonata form and the variation.

Beethoven's practices with the sonata, which he composed throughout his lifetime, set him somewhat apart from his predecessors and served as guides to later composers. His sonatas can have from two to four movements. In two sonatas, each labeled *quasi una fantasia* (op. 27 no. 1, 1800–1801; op. 27 no. 2, 1801), he used conventions other than sonata form for the opening movements and called for no pause between movements. In several late sonatas, fugal writing plays a prominent role. And there is no grander, more symphonic work than his *Hammerklavier* Sonata op. 106 (1817–18).

III. *Romantic.* During Beethoven's last years, such early Romantic composers as Schubert, Weber, and Mendelssohn wrote numerous sonatas, mainly for piano solo or for piano and violin. Though infused with a new spirit, these works still employ Classical conventions for the number of movements and their formal schemes. Following Beethoven's death in 1827, however, there was a marked decline in interest in the genre, even by such major composers as Schumann, Chopin, Liszt, and Brahms. The reasons for this decline are many and appear to be interdependent. (1) The change in intended performer—already evident in Beethoven's works—from the competent amateur to the skilled professional reflected the growing importance of the sonata in public concerts. (2) As both Schumann and Wagner reported, a shift in public taste made publishers increasingly reluctant to publish sonatas. (3) A shift in aesthetic purpose—doubtless hastened by the continued performance of Beethoven's piano sonatas, with their skillfully wrought large-scale structures—increasingly favored small-scale character pieces for piano. (4) Among many younger composers, there was a perception—probably reinforced by such prescriptive accounts on the makeup of the sonata as Czerny's in his op. 600 (ca. 1840), which was based on Beethoven's practices—that the genre held little promise for further exploitation.

Yet the fact that Schumann, Chopin, Liszt, and Brahms all chose, early in their careers, to compose examples of the sonata testifies to the continuing high regard for the genre. Schumann's early ambivalence toward the sonata is evident in his *Phantasie* (op. 17, 1836–38), which he originally called a *grosse Sonate.* Chopin composed three piano sonatas (1828, 1839, 1844) and a sonata for cello and piano (1845–46). After 1850 the sonata reflected current trends in symphonic writing. Liszt's virtuosic piano sonata (1852–53) is in one movement that comprises sections in different tempos and employs the technique of thematic *transformation already evident in his symphonic poems. Franck's violin sonata (1886), in four movements, employs a cyclic principle whereby thematic material from one movement recurs in others. Brahms, the most prolific sonata composer of the period, also favored a four-movement sonata that was strongly Classical in form and syntax. Other sonata composers of the time include Dvořák, Fauré, Grieg, MacDowell, Reger, Rubinstein, Saint-Saëns, Richard Strauss, Tchaikovsky, and Wagner.

IV. *20th century.* Interest in the sonata continued in a limited fashion, though the genre was often transformed in both style and general form. Among significant examples before 1920 are those by Debussy, Scriabin, Ives, and Berg. Sonatas by the first three in particular opened new paths in musical expression, substituting for thematic process syntaxes based on intervals, sonorities, and textures. Between 1920 and 1940, many composers wrote sonatas that have been somewhat misleadingly labeled *neoclassical, since they reintroduce not only Baroque formal conventions but often rhythms and counterpoint of that period as well. Noteworthy examples are piano sonatas by Stravinsky (1924) and Bartók (1926), and Bartók's *Sonata for Two Pianos and Percussion* (1937). Others writing in the same vein include Martinů, Hindemith, and Poulenc. After 1940, composers increasingly turned to other names for chamber works that earlier might have been called sonata, suggesting either an uneasiness with the implications of the term or a decreasing interest in abstract musical forms. Many composers who had earlier in their careers written examples had abandoned the term by 1960: Boris Blacher, Pierre Boulez, John Cage, Elliott Carter, George Crumb, Peter Maxwell Davies, Wolfgang Fortner, Karel Husa, Ernst Krenek, George Rochberg, and Karlheinz Stockhausen.

Bibl.: Eleanor Selfridge-Field, *Venetian Instrumental Music from Gabrieli to Vivaldi* (1975; 3rd rev. ed., New York: Dover, 1994). Terence Best, "Handel's Solo Sonatas," *ML* 58 (1977): 430–38. William S. Newman, *The Sonata in the Baroque Era,* 4th ed., rev. (New York: Norton, 1983). Christopher Hogwood, *The Trio Sonata* (London: BBC, 1979). Willi Apel, *Die Italienische Violinmusik im 17. Jahrhundert* (Wiesbaden: Steiner, 1983; Eng. trans., enlarged 1990 by Thomas Binkley). John Daverio, "In Search of the Sonata da Camera before Corelli," *AM* 57 (1985): 195–214. Sandra Mangsen, "Instrumental Duos and Trios in Printed Italian Sources, 1600–1675" (Ph.D. diss., Cornell Univ., 1989). Gary Zink, "The Large-Ensemble Sonatas of Antonio Bertali and Their Relationship to the Ensemble Sonata Traditions of the Seventeenth Century" (Ph.D. diss., Washington Univ., 1989). Sandra Mangsen, "The Trio Sonata in Pre-Corellian Prints: When Does 3 = 4?" *Performance Practice Review* 3 (1990): 138–64. Andrew Dell'Antonio, "Syntax, Form and Genre in Sonatas and Canzonas, 1621–1635" (Ph.D. diss., Univ. of California, Berkeley, 1991). Peter Allsop, *The Italian "Trio" Sonata* (Oxford: Clarendon, 1992). Jeanne R. Swack, "On the Origins of the *Sonate auf Concertenart,*" *JAMS* 46 (1993): 369–414. Sandra Mangsen, "The Sonata da Camera before Corelli: A Renewed Search," *ML* 76 (1995): 19–31. Peter Allsop, "Sonata da Chiesa: A Case of Mistaken Identity?" *The Consort* 53 (1997): 4–15. Gregory Richard Barnett, "Musical Issues of the Late-Seicento: Style, Social Function, and Theory in Emilian Instrumental Music" (Ph.D. diss., Princeton Univ., 1997). Steven Zohn, "When Is a Quartet not a Quartet?: Relationships between Scoring and Genre in the German Quadro, ca. 1715–40," in *Johann Friedrich Fasch und sein Wirken für Zerbst,* ed. Konstanze Musketa and Barbara Reul (Dessau: Anhaltische Verlagsgesellschaft, 1997), pp. 263–90. Peter Allsop, *Arcangelo Corelli: New Orpheus of Our Times* (Oxford: Oxford U Pr, 1999).

II. Roger Kamien, "Style Change in the Mid-18th-Century Keyboard Sonata," *JAMS* 19 (1966): 37–58. Ronald Kidd, "The Emergence of Chamber Music with Obbligato Keyboard in England," *AM* 44 (1972): 122–44. Charles Rosen, *The Classical Style: Haydn, Mozart, Beethoven,* (1972; expanded ed., New York: Norton, 1997). David Fuller, "Accompanied Keyboard Music," *MQ* 60 (1974): 222–45. Hans Hering, "Das spielerische Element in der klassichromantischen Klaviersonate," *NZfM* 135 (1974): 227–32. James Webster, "Towards a History of Viennese Chamber Music in the Early Classical Period," *JAMS* 27 (1974): 212–47. Leonard Ratner, *Classic Music: Expression, Form, and Style* (New York: Schirmer Bks, 1980). Charles Rosen, *Sonata Forms* (New York: Norton, 1980; rev. ed., 1988). William S. Newman, *The Sonata in the Classic Era,* 3rd ed., rev. (New York: Norton, 1983). A. Peter Brown, *Joseph Haydn's Keyboard Music: Sources and Style* (Bloomington: Ind U Pr, 1986). Katalin Komlos, "The Viennese Keyboard Trio in the 1780s: Sociological Background and Contemporary Reception," *ML* 68 (1987): 222–34. Basil Smallman, *The Piano Trio: Its History, Technique, and Repertoire* (New York: Oxford U Pr, 1990). Basil Smallman, *The Piano Quartet and Quintet: Style, Structure, and Scoring* (New York: Oxford U Pr, 1994). Katalin Komlos, *Viennese Fortepianos and Their Music: Germany, Austria and England, 1760–1800* (New York: Oxford U Pr, 1995). László Somfai, *The Keyboard Sonatas of Joseph Haydn: Instruments and Performance Practice, Genres and Styles* (Chicago: U of Chicago Pr, 1995). John A. Irving, *Mozart's Piano Sonatas: Contexts, Sources, Style* (Cambridge: Cambridge U Pr, 1997). Huei-Ming Wang, *Beethovens Violoncell- und Violinsonaten* (Kassel: Bosse, 1997). Glenn Stanley, "Genre Aesthetics and Function: Beethoven's Piano Sonatas in Their Cultural Context," *Beethoven Forum* 6 (1998): 1–29.

III. William S. Newman, "Wagner's Sonatas," *Studies in Romanticism* 7 (1968): 129–39. Martin Weyer, *Die deutsche Orgelsonate von Mendelssohn bis Reger* (Regensburg: Bosse, 1969). William S. Newman, *The Sonata since Beethoven,* 3rd ed., rev. (New York: Norton, 1983). Anatoly Leikin, "The Dissolution of Sonata Structure in Romantic Piano Music, 1820–1850" (Ph.D. diss., U.C.L.A., 1986). Klaus Korner, *Die Violinsonaten von Johannes Brahms: Studien* (Augsburg: Wissner, 1997).

IV. Robert Moevs, "Intervallic Procedures in Debussy: Serenade from the Sonata for Cello and Piano, 1915," *PNM* 8 (1969): 82–101. Sondra Clark, "The Element of Chance in Ives's Concord Sonata," *MQ* 60 (1974): 167–86. Iwenka Stoianowa, "La Troisième Sonate de Boulez et le projet mallarméen du Livre," *Musique en jeu* 16 (1974): 9–28. Siegfried Borris, "Die Krise der Sonata im 20. Jahrhundert," in *Musa—Mens—Musici: Im Gedenken an Walther Vetter,* ed. Heinz Wegener (Leipzig: VEB Deutscher Verlag fur Musik, 1969), pp. 361–78. Johann Peter Vogel, "Die Wiederbelebung der Klaviersonate: Deutscher Klassizismus im 20. Jahrhundert," *Musica* 39 (1985): 353–59. Lisa Hardy, *The British Piano Sonata, 1870–1945* (Woodbridge: Boydell, 2001). S.B., rev. S.L.

Sonata da camera [It., chamber sonata or court sonata]. A work for instrumental ensemble, prevalent from the 1650s through the 1740s. Written for one or more melody instruments, normally of the violin family, and basso continuo [see Thoroughbass], it was associated with the dance throughout the 17th century. The earliest examples, by Giovanni Legrenzi (op. 4, 1656), consist of a single binary form. Later examples by Giovanni Maria Bononcini (op. 2, 1667) and Pandolfi Mealli (1669) consist solely of dances [see also Suite IV]. Beginning with Giovanni Buonaventura Viviani (op. 4, 1678), the *sonata da camera* increasingly embodied the format associated later with Corelli: an introductory free movement followed by two to four dances. Late in the 17th century, several other terms were occasionally used for the genre: *trattenimenti da camera* (Giovanni Bononcini, 1686), *concerti da camera* (Giuseppi Torelli, 1686), and *allettamenti per camera* (Giorgio Buoni, 1693). Following the numerous printings of Corelli's two famous sets (op. 2, op. 4), the genre was less favored, though new examples were being published at least through 1744 (Francesco Veracini, op. 2). Other uses of the term appear occasionally: works with the characteristics of the **sonata da chiesa* (Antonio Veracini, op. 2), pieces made up of numbers from popular theatrical works (Agostino Steffani, ca. 1705). Late examples using the term appear in a posthumous publication of Johann Stamitz (op. 6, ca. 1759) and in numerous works by Johann Janitsch (op. 1, 1760).

S.B.

Sonata da chiesa [It., church sonata]. A work for instrumental ensemble, prevalent from the 1650s through the 1770s. It has one to seven or more sections or movements, contrasting in meter, tempo, and texture, and is written for one or more melody instruments, normally of the violin family, and basso continuo [see Thoroughbass]. Though called simply sonata in most 17th-century publications, suggesting use outside the church as well, it is identifiable by a serious style, manifest in much fugal writing, by the relative scarcity of the dance movements characteristic of the **sonata da camera,* and by the common specification of organ as the continuo instrument. Late in the century the term was on occasion equated with sinfonia (Giovanni Battista Bassani, op. 5, 1683). With Corelli the form of the church sonata became standardized. Most have four movements: slow–fast–slow–fast. Composers employing this format in the 18th century—still under the name *sonata*—include Vivaldi, Handel, Bach, Telemann, and Jean-Marie Leclair *l'aîné.* Several three-movement sonatas can also be identified with the term (Giuseppe Tartini, 1734; Leopold Mozart, 1740). The 17 so-called Epistle sonatas of Mozart (written in Salzburg, 1772–80), all in one movement, are late examples of the genre. Available evidence suggests that the church sonata, in part or as a whole, was used in Italy, and doubtless elsewhere, in the Mass of the Roman rite as a substitute for the gradual and communion, and at Vespers for Psalm *antiphons. On occasion, church performances entailed doubling of parts, making them in fact orchestral performances.

S.B.

Sonata form. The most characteristic movement form in instrumental music from the Classical period to the 20th century. The term is misleading in two respects. First, it refers to the structure of an individual movement, not to the overall form of a multimovement work. Second, sonata form occurs not merely (or even most typically) in sonatas, but also in a wide variety of other orchestral and chamber genres—symphonies, overtures, string quartets, and so forth. Because this form is common in slow movements and finales as well as opening fast movements, the more general term sonata form is preferable to such designations as sonata-allegro form and first-movement form.

I. *Structure.* Sonata form is best viewed not as a rigid, prescriptive mold, but rather as a flexible and imaginative intersection of modulation, the thematic process, and numerous other elements. The basis for sonata form is the open modulatory plan of binary form, in which an initial modulation from the tonic to a new key (normally the dominant in a movement in major) is answered by a complementary modulation from the new key back to the tonic [see Binary and ternary form]. This scheme results in two large divisions or parts.

The first part, which modulates to the new key, is known traditionally as the exposition. It is repeated in most Classical and many 19th-century examples. The second part, which leads eventually back to the tonic, was also generally repeated until the late 18th century, when composers began to omit this repetition, especially in large-scale works. The second part is usually more extended than the first; it consists of two large sections, each of which may rival the exposition in size and importance: the development and the recapitulation. The development section ordinarily modulates still farther afield and provides varied and often dramatic treatment of material already heard in the exposition. This combination of tonal instability and intensive thematic development can create a high degree of tension at the midpoint of the movement. The recapitulation, the second section of part 2, is based thematically upon the exposition but now ends as well as begins in the tonic. (In minor-key movements, however, a shift to the tonic major may occur at any point in the recapitulation.) Once again tonality and thematic process coordinate, for the reentry of the tonic coincides with the return to original material in its approximately original form and order. Moreover, the material formerly heard in the new key now recurs in the tonic, providing a long-range resolution of the tonal tension created by the modulation in the exposition.

Exposition. Expositions vary widely in structure, revealing a highly flexible interaction of tonality, thematic material, and large-scale rhythmic motion. In one standard pattern, the tonic is established by means of a harmonically clear-cut primary theme or themes. After this section comes a more vigorous or brilliant transition that accomplishes the modulation to the new key. At this point, in order to confirm or stabilize the new key, the composer may introduce one or more contrasting secondary themes, often *piano.* The exposition then closes with cadential material, which may range from conventional chordal passages to full-fledged themes. Other common procedures in expositions include (1) omission of a separate transition section; (2) use of a nonmodulatory transition, the new key being established only with the entrance of the secondary theme; (3) omission of secondary themes entirely in favor of a more direct connection between the transitional and closing areas; (4) reuse of the primary theme later in the exposition in a new function, for example as the secondary theme (the so-called monothematic exposition frequent in Haydn) or as a

(*Intro.*)	Part 1 *Exposition*	Part 2 *Development*	*Recapitulation*	(*Coda*)
	‖: Pr. Tr. Sec. Cl. :‖(:)	(Pr.) Retr.	Pr. Tr. Sec. Cl.	(:‖) ‖
(I)	I ——→ N ———	N or other ∿∿→ (V)	I ———	(IV) ——

Sonata form.

closing theme; (5) return to *forte* transitional material after the secondary theme, leading either to another secondary theme or to the closing area (a passage of this type may be labeled a secondary transition); and (6) combination of secondary and closing functions in one theme or section.

Development. Construction of the development section follows no stereotyped plan. Most early development sections, and many later ones, begin with a restatement of the primary theme in the new key—an obvious vestige of their binary origin. Others introduce new or related material at this point, frequently transitional in character (see Beethoven's Symphony no. 3, first movt.; unless otherwise noted, all subsequent citations refer to the first movement of the work in question). Most textbook descriptions of development sections emphasize the intensive, concentrated character of their thematic treatment. A majority of the development sections in Haydn, late Mozart, Beethoven, and Brahms do indeed fit this description, applying such techniques as melodic variation, fragmentation, expansion or compression, contrapuntal combination, textural and contextual change, reharmonization, and reorchestration to one or many themes of the exposition [see Development]. Others, however, from all chronological periods, merely restate material from the exposition with little change other than the key, or are basically episodic in nature. Yet even these sections often represent the dramatic culmination or high point of the movement, if only because of their more extensive modulatory excursions.

A majority of development sections conclude with a passage known as a retransition, which sets the stage for the dramatic and dual return of the tonic key and original thematic material at the beginning of the recapitulation, usually by suspensefully stressing the dominant.

Recapitulation. Recapitulations run the gamut from nearly exact restatement of the material of the exposition, the only alteration being transposition to the tonic of the new-key material, to thoroughgoing recomposition involving extensive compression or expansion. Two variant types of recapitulation deserve mention. In the first, the primary theme recurs in the subdominant rather than the tonic key. The normal progression of the exposition, up a fifth from tonic to dominant, therefore leads from subdominant to tonic for the return of the secondary and closing sections. Though the best-known subdominant recapitulations occur in works by Mozart (Piano Sonata K. 545) and Schubert (Symphony no. 5, numerous sonatas), examples may be found throughout the Classical period.

A second type of recapitulation, common in the early Classical period but also present in some Romantic works (e.g., Chopin's Piano Sonatas opp. 35 and 58), is the partial recapitulation. In this type, reestablishment of the tonic after the development section is entrusted to the secondary and closing themes alone; the primary theme does not reappear. Opinion is divided as to whether movements with partial recapitulations of this sort are best designated as more elaborate types of binary form (e.g., "polythematic binary form") or as types of sonata form (e.g., "binary sonata form"). Related to this type are those "mirror" forms in which the return of the primary theme is delayed until after the secondary theme has recurred.

In addition to the three obligatory sections, exposition, development, and recapitulation, a movement in sonata form may begin with an introduction and end with a coda, the latter returning once again to the primary theme and often generally emphasizing the subdominant at some point. An entire movement in full sonata form might therefore proceed as in the accompanying figure (N = new key, arrows = modulations; Pr. = primary material, Tr. = transitional material, Sec. = secondary material, Cl. = closing material; Retr. = retransition).

II. *History.* 1. 18th century. The early history of sonata form is exceedingly complex, for in effect it represents a history of how the many structural principles and processes enumerated above—open tonal organization, thematic development and recapitulation, thematic contrast and function, and so on—became associated with one another to produce the structure that we call sonata form. The basic framework was provided by late Baroque binary form, especially of the rounded binary type [see Binary and ternary form I–II]. With few exceptions, the modulatory goal of the exposition throughout the 18th century remained the dominant in a major key (frequently the dominant minor in overtures and symphonies about mid-century), the relative major or (less often) dominant minor in a minor key, just as in binary form. Also important, especially for the symphony, was a roughly contemporary tri-ritornello structure, the three sections of which paralleled the three main divisions of rounded binary and sonata form, though without repeat signs [see Concerto (2) I, 2; Overture (1)].

In both the binary and ritornello types, however, the motivic and textural continuity, fast harmonic rhythm, and rapid change of key characteristic of late Baroque style tended to forestall the dramatic treatment of modulation on which Classical sonata form is based; the original modulation to the new key, and even the start of the recapitulation, may seem almost incidental. Hence, the development of sonata form depended upon the development of Classical style, with its hierarchical phrase and *period structure, homophonic texture, slower harmonic rhythm, and broader, more plateaulike key areas. By the same token, an isolated early movement in Baroque style that happens to prefigure later sonata form holds little importance for the history of that form. It should be noted in this connection that many later examples of "sonata form," for instance most of the keyboard sonatas of C. P. E. Bach, are more closely related to the older tradition of the rounded binary form than to later Classical sonata form.

Composers of sonatas and chamber music in the modern **galant* idiom made use of an increasingly variegated thematic apparatus in the first half of the 18th century. However, the principal thrust toward thematic differentiation within the exposition seems to have come in orchestral music, particularly the Italian opera overture. From about 1740 on, the first movements of Italian (especially Neapolitan) opera overtures rarely failed to include relatively clear primary, transitional, secondary, and closing sections of the types described above, all within a generally Classical stylistic framework. The combination of a stereotyped, easily copied pattern and the extremely wide distribution of these works made them highly influential, and in one form or another their innovations quickly found their way into symphonies and other works from Italy, Mannheim, Austro-Bohemia, and elsewhere [see Symphony II, Overture (1)].

Where thematic differentiation of this kind was incorporated within a rounded-binary tradition, as in northern Italy and Vienna, the result was an early sonata form with full recapitulation. By contrast, where the tradition was predominantly a binary one, as in the sonatas of Domenico Scarlatti and at Mannheim, the result was a "polythematic binary" or "binary sonata form" of the type outlined earlier, in which the recapitulation begins with the secondary theme. The Italian overture mentioned above presents a third large-scale configuration [see also Overture (1)]. In most first movements of these works from the late 1730s on, a full recapitulation enters in the tonic either immediately after the close of the exposition or after a brief retransitional passage. No development section is present, and repeat signs are nearly always omitted (an option in the other types, as well). Historically, this "exposition-recapitulation" form (Jan LaRue) was derived from tri-ritornello form by reduction or elimination of the middle section (see Hell, 1971). It is found in overtures until late in the century (e.g., Mozart's overture to *The Marriage of Figaro,* 1786) as well as in many sonatinas, slow movements, and arias.

All these and many other designs existed side by side at approximately mid-century. By about 1765, however, full sonata form—though never the rigid textbook variety—was rapidly becoming the norm in fast movements and many slow movements of symphonies and related genres, works for chamber ensemble, and solo and accompanied sonatas in all but a few major centers. Slow introductions began to appear in symphonies ca. 1760. The works of Haydn and Mozart extended the dramatic and expressive possibilities of early sonata form by introducing various kinds of strict and free counterpoint, by intensifying the development of themes—not just within the development section but also, especially in Haydn, in the exposition and recapitulation—and by treating the different thematic areas of the exposition with great variety and subtlety. Furthermore, the clarity of function and relative regularity of mature Classical sonata form provided the opportunity for imaginative exploitation of the listener's expectations, as in Haydn's frequent use of false transitions and false recapitulations.

The Classical period saw the introduction of sonata-form principles within both secular and sacred vocal music, as well; arias, ensembles, and choruses are often patterned to a greater or lesser extent on sonata form. Such hybrid forms as ritornello-sonata and sonata-rondo also arose at this time through the combination of sonata principles and the ritornello and rondo principles, respectively [see Concerto (2) II, Rondo (1) II].

Theorists of the 18th century were not as blind to the above developments as is sometimes stated. All regarded sonata form as essentially binary rather than ternary, for they considered the harmony to be central. As early as 1755, Joseph Riepel's *Grundregeln zur Tonordnung insegemein* prints and discusses numerous sonata-form movements of various types, including one with a clear secondary ("piano") theme. Heinrich Christoph Koch's account (*Versuch einer Anleitung zur Composition* 3, 1793) is exceptionally detailed and precise, even describing the thematic process of development. Neither theorist presents sonata form as an abstract norm or prescription; the form goes unnamed, and no functional labels are supplied for the various sections and themes. Such labels begin to appear only with Francesco Galeazzi (1796; see Churgin, 1968), whose approach presages that of the 19th century to some extent.

2. 19th century. Beethoven's highly dramatic conception of sonata form resulted in several influential innovations. On the large scale, use of an extended coda, already fairly common in Mozart, becomes frequent in Beethoven as one means of resolving the extraordinary tension and excitement of his development sections. In a related change, many Beethoven movements deemphasize the beginning of the recapitulation as a significant point of resolution, as in the highly unstable return of the primary theme over a dominant pedal in the *Appassionata* Sonata op. 57. In addition, Beethoven occasionally employs a formal variant for first movements in which a brief return of the primary theme in the tonic precedes the development section; the exposition is not repeated (see his String Quartet op. 59 no. 1). This design, obviously related to sonata-rondo form [see Rondo (1) II], reappears in works by

several later composers (e.g., the Fourth Symphonies of Brahms and Mahler). Within the exposition, Beethoven's evident dislike of conventional melodic material led him to treat the transition and closing areas with great flexibility. Particularly noteworthy is his expansion of the modulatory goals of the exposition to include third-related keys, for example the major mediant (*Waldstein* Sonata op. 53; *Leonore* Overtures no. 2 and 3) and submediant major (Symphony no. 8, soon moving to the dominant; *Archduke* Trio op. 97; *Hammerklavier* Sonata op. 106).

Beethoven's use of sonata form provided the model for most Romantic composers of *absolute music, though major differences in emphasis are evident. Romantic sonata form often gives the impression of being fundamentally a vehicle for the presentation of striking thematic material, as seen especially in the tendency to focus on the secondary theme as a self-contained, highly expressive cantabile melody. This view of sonata form is clearly reflected in writings of the theorists of the time, who formulated the academic concept of sonata form familiar today. Sonata form is presented as an abstract compositional framework or norm, understood to a significant extent in terms of its thematic material. These theorists included Antoine Reicha (*Traité de haute composition musicale,* 1824–26), Heinrich Birnbach (articles in *BamZ,* 1827–28, the first theorist to treat sonata form as ternary), Adolf Bernhard Marx (*Die Lehre von der musikalischen Komposition,* 1837–47), and Carl Czerny (*School of Practical Composition,* 1840). Marx was evidently the first writer to use the term sonata form ("Sonatenform"), which appears in an essay of his in *BamZ* for 1824.

The expanded tonal system of the 19th century, typified by chromaticism at all structural levels, naturally manifested itself in Romantic sonata form. One noteworthy effect of this expansion was the use of increasingly remote keys for many secondary themes; these were commonly followed, however, by progression to the dominant by the end of the exposition (see Webster, 1978/79). The choice of novel keys often seems dictated by coloristic considerations rather than the tensional/structural concerns characteristic of Beethoven. Other attributes of Romantic sonata form include (1) more frequent omission of repeat signs; (2) in the development section, a tendency toward variation—sequential restatement, reharmonization, reorchestration—or episodic treatment rather than structural development (Mendelssohn and Brahms being notable exceptions); and (3) in many composers, a tendency to deemphasize and shorten the recapitulation in various ways in favor of the coda, which now generally contains the climax or apotheosis of the movement. It should be noted that the large one-movement composite forms found in symphonic poems and other works of the period (e.g., Liszt's Piano Sonata in B minor) usually incorporate the principles of sonata form in some degree.

3. 20th century. Numerous 20th-century composers adapted sonata form to their own styles, though often with significant modifications in the traditional design. Tonal examples range from the free, highly personal interpretations of Sibelius to quite conventional usages like those of Prokofiev. At the opposite extreme, sonata form appears in many atonal and especially serial works (e.g., Schoenberg's String Quartets no. 3 and 4, Webern's String Trio op. 20, 2nd movt.), even though the basic organizing force of tonality is lacking. For this last reason, the frequent use of sonata form by Bartók, Hindemith, and Stravinsky is often considered more successful, since these composers introduce various individual substitutes for traditional functional tonality in order to assure an integrated overall structure (see, e.g., Bartók's String Quartet no. 4 and *Music for Strings, Percussion, and Celesta,* 2nd movt.; Hindemith's symphony *Mathis der Maler;* Stravinsky's Symphony in C).

Bibl.: Donald Francis Tovey, "Sonata Forms," *Encyclopaedia Britannica,* 11th ed. (1911), R: in *The Forms of Music* (New York: Meridian Bks, 1956), pp. 208–32. Rudolf von Tobel, *Die Formenwelt der klassischen Instrumentalmusik* (Bern: P Haupt, 1935). Kurt Westphal, *Der Begriff der musikalischen Form in der Wiener Klassik* (Leipzig: Kistner & Siegel, 1935). Leonard Ratner, "Harmonic Aspects of Classic Form," *JAMS* 2 (1949): 159–68. Jens Peter Larsen, "Sonatenform-Probleme," *Blume,* 1963, pp. 221–30. William S. Newman, *The Sonata in the Classic Era* (Chapel Hill: U of NC Pr, 1963; 3rd ed., New York: Norton, 1983). Ian Spink, *An Historical Approach to Musical Form* (London: Bell, 1967). Edward T. Cone, *Musical Form and Musical Performance* (New York: Norton, 1968). Bathia Churgin, "Francesco Galeazzi's Description (1796) of Sonata Form," *JAMS* 21 (1968): 181–99. William S. Newman, *The Sonata since Beethoven* (Chapel Hill: U of NC Pr, 1969; 3rd ed., New York: Norton, 1983). Fred Ritzel, *Die Entwicklung der "Sonatenform" im musiktheoretischen Schrifttum des 18. und 19. Jahrhunderts,* 2nd ed. (Wiesbaden: Breitkopf & Härtel, 1969; with extensive bibliography). Jan LaRue, *Guidelines for Style Analysis* (New York: Norton, 1970; 2nd ed., Warren, Mich.: Harmonie Park, 1992). Helmut Hell, *Die neapolitanische Opernsinfonie in der ersten Hälfte des 18. Jahrhunderts* (Tutzing: Schneider, 1971). James Webster, "Schubert's Sonata Form and Brahms's First Maturity," *19th Century Music* 2 (1978/79): 18–35, 3 (1979/80): 52–71. Leonard G. Ratner, *Classic Music: Expression, Form, and Style* (New York: Schirmer Bks, 1980; rev. ed., 1988). Charles Rosen, *Sonata Forms* (New York: Norton, 1980). Eugene K. Wolf, *The Symphonies of Johann Stamitz: A Study in the Formation of the Classic Style* (Utrecht: Bohn, Scheltema & Holkema, 1981). Mark Evan Bonds, *Wordless Rhetoric: Musical Form and the Metaphor of the Oration* (Cambridge, Mass.: Harvard U Pr, 1991). William E. Caplin, *Classical Form: A Theory of Formal Functions for the Instrumental Music of Haydn, Mozart, and Beethoven* (New York: Oxford U Pr, 1998). James Hepokoski, "Beyond the Sonata Principle," *JAMS* 55 (2002): 91–154. James Hepokoski and Warren Darcy, *Elements of Sonata Theory: Norms, Types, and Deformations in the Late-Eighteenth-Century Sonata* (New York: Oxford U Pr, forthcoming). E.K.W.

Sonata-rondo. See Rondo (1) II.

Sonatina [It., dim. of sonata]. A work with the formal characteristics of a *sonata (usually of the type cultivated in the Classical period), but on a smaller scale and often less technically demanding for the performer. Composers who cultivated the genre, which is especially though not exclusively associated with the piano, include Muzio Clementi (1752–1823), Jan Ladislav Dussek (1760–1812), and Friedrich Kuhlau (1786–1832). The term was revived in the 20th century by composers such as Busoni, Ravel, Bartók, Prokofiev, Milhaud, Chávez, and Boulez.

Son chapín [Sp.]. A traditional dance-music genre of Guatemala, also known as the *son guatemalteco.* In moderate to rapid tempo and combining elements of compound duple and simple triple meters, it accompanies couples dancing with characteristic *zapateado* (foot-stamping) patterns. It is performed in instrumental versions by the marimba, the national instrument of Guatemala, and also by small ensembles of vocalists with guitars and other instruments. D.S.

Song. A form of musical expression in which the human voice has the principal role and is the carrier of a text; as a generic term, any music that is sung; more specifically, a short, simple vocal composition consisting of melody and verse text. In this latter, narrower sense, song would exclude, for example, the ornate Baroque solo *cantata or the extended opera *aria. (In German, the generic and specific meanings are distinguished as, respectively, *Gesang* and **Lied.*) This article is limited primarily to Western secular art song. See also Folk music, Ballad, Shanty, Popular music.

I. *General considerations.* 1. Text. Song verse most commonly is strophic poetry with short, regular line lengths, simple rhyme schemes, and often some kind of refrain. Subjects of song verse vary greatly, with love (courtly, metaphysical, erotic, bawdy, sacred, or sentimental) probably the most common. Judged as poetry, song verse may be inferior or of the highest literary achievement.

2. Music. A song is most commonly for a solo voice, and its music may be considered to be primarily its melody or tune, whether accompanied or unaccompanied. In some periods, *polyphonic song, with no single voice predominating, is prevalent. A musical setting may be composed to an existing text, a text may be written to fit a melody, or the two may be created together. The authors of the text and music may be the same or different persons.

3. Relation of music and text. The music of a song may be related to its text in terms of form (or structure), sound, and meaning. Gross form is a matter of how the overall structure of the poem is manifested in the music: e.g., whether a setting of a strophic poem is musically *strophic (or modified strophic) or *through-composed. Particular form concerns the relation between the line structure of the text and the phrase structure of the music.

Form and sound overlap, since sound elements such as meter and rhyme in poetry and rhythm and *cadences in music articulate structure. On a level of finer detail, the sound qualities of the text may be related to musical elements in a variety of ways. The relatively flexible declamation of speech must be translated into fixed musical rhythms; accented syllables may be placed on strong beats and receive longer temporal values. Text inflection may be reflected in melodic contour. The text may be set in a basically syllabic fashion, or important syllables and long vowels may be set melismatically. Literary end rhyme may be matched by musical rhyme at phrase endings, but exact parallelism is rare because of the requirements of tonal cadences.

Song may also reflect, enhance, or construe the meaning of the text through mode, tempo, dynamics, word-painting, sets of conventionalized or personal musical symbols, and musical analogs to emotional effects (e.g., an unexpected harmonic progression to depict surprise). Changes in texture or in the pace of declamation may correspond to structural, phonetic, or semantic features of the text.

An abiding question in all text-music relations is whether song allows the poetry to be appreciated or overwhelms it. Even if the latter is true, a secondary question is whether this makes or should make any difference in our enjoyment of the song itself [see also Text and music].

4. Function, performer, and audience. In its generic sense, song can be avocational or invocational. It may be a diversion or pastime (for example, work songs or audience entertainment), or it may direct human or divine attention (for example, in religious chant or ceremonial motets). The singer may sing privately or for an audience. Song may be conceived for trained musicians or for amateurs, for an educated and sophisticated class or for the general populace. For most of Western music history, song means that of the literate aristocracy and merchant class and the composers that served them. Until the beginning of folk-song collecting in the 18th century, there is almost no written record—and hence little knowledge—of the song of the general population.

II. *Historical outline.* 1. Ancient song. Early literate societies have left evidence in their narrative and religious poetry of the importance of song (e.g., the Hebrew Psalms). Almost no songs from ancient Greece and Rome have survived with their melodies intact or transcribable (an exception being the *Seikilos epitaph), but surviving epic and lyric poetry abundantly attests to the prominence of song in classical cultures.

2. Medieval monophonic song. The largest body of medieval song is Christian liturgical *plainsong, within which the Latin *hymns are closest to the narrow definition of song. The secular monophonic song of the early Middle Ages may have constituted just as vast a repertory. The little that survives includes *Goliard songs from the 12th century, the most famous of which are the **Carmina burana.* At the same

time, the paraliturgical *conductus* existed also as a secular strophic Latin song.

The high Middle Ages developed a significant repertory of vernacular song: the epic **chansons de geste,* *troubadour and *trouvère songs in France, the *Minnesang (and later *Meistergesang) in German-speaking areas, **laude* and **cantigas* in Italy and Spain, respectively, *minstrel songs (and later *carols) in England. The songs manifest a great variety of textual and musical forms. Rhythmic notation is usually less precise than pitch notation in the manuscripts, and the manner of performance is unclear (for example, whether instrumental accompaniment was intended). In some medieval song, dance appears to be a strong influence.

3. Polyphonic song of the Middle Ages and Renaissance. In the 13th century, the polyphonic *motet, which had originated as a sacred genre, began to be given secular Latin and vernacular texts (sometimes two simultaneously), while retaining a *tenor from the chant repertory. In the 14th and 15th centuries, the motet became a vehicle for texts of courtly love and of secular ceremony.

In the 14th century, France and Italy saw a great burgeoning of secular polyphonic song. In the French **ars nova,* the huge variety of trouvère genres was largely narrowed to the **formes fixes:* **rondeau,* **virelai,* and **ballade* (as in the works of Guillaume de Machaut). Three-part texture was most common, one part sung and two probably instrumental. In trecento Italy, the *madrigal and **ballata* predominated (composed by, e.g., Jacopo da Bologna and Francesco Landini); two sung parts, often joined by an instrumental one, were the norm. Elaborate *canonic songs were also composed (the **chace* in France, the **caccia* in Italy), and some genres remained partly or wholly monophonic (e.g., the **lai*).

English song tradition remained relatively separate from that of the Continent, and the sources transmit a smaller repertory, including the first *round (*"Sumer is icumen in," 13th century, anon.) and the *carol, which was often purely secular and was not originally associated only with Christmas.

In the 15th century, the standard number of parts in polyphonic song gradually increased from three to four, *imitation among the parts began to be common, and the *formes fixes* gave way to freer verse (though vestiges remained, as in the **bergerette,* a one-strophe virelai). The Franco-Flemish or Burgundian *chanson flourished in the mid-15th century (by, e.g., Binchois, Dufay). For a while, composers from the *Netherlands (broadly defined) led in the composition of chansons and established what became the international style of polyphonic imitation.

Though polyphony predominated in the 15th and 16th centuries, composers also produced significant amounts of solo song with accompaniment, notably in the **villancicos* and **romances* of 16th-century Spain for voice and **vihuela.* The extent and nature of popular songs of the time can only be guessed at from the occasional appearance of their tunes in polyphonic compositions (e.g., "L'*homme armé").

In the early 16th century, pervasive imitation became the norm, as did the texting and singing of all parts (e.g., in the works of Josquin Desprez). The Parisian chanson (Claudin de Sermisy, Clément Janequin) and Italian **frottola* (Marchetto Cara, Bartolomeo Tromboncino) and *madrigal (Jacques Arcadelt, Philippe Verdelot, Cipriano de Rore) were the most common genres. A growing body of German-texted polyphonic songs, especially the **Tenorlied* (Heinrich Isaac, Ludwig Senfl), set a preexisting monophonic popular or folk song in the tenor part, surrounded by other composed parts.

Later, the texture of polyphonic songs (e.g., by Adrian Willaert) was enriched to five and sometimes six voices. The Italian madrigal of the late 16th and early 17th centuries (Luca Marenzio, Claudio Monteverdi, Carlo Gesualdo) was the leading song genre of its time. English composers (Thomas Weelkes, John Wilbye, Thomas Morley) subsequently produced English madrigals that, though modeled on the Italian, maintained a distinct identity.

4. Accompanied song of the Baroque. In the early 17th century, there was a widespread revival of interest in setting texts for solo voice, often in a speechlike manner over a simple, chordal accompaniment [see Monody, Thoroughbass], as cultivated in the new *opera (Jacopo Peri, Giulio Caccini), but also in the solo madrigal (Caccini, Sigismondo d'India). At the same time there continued to be regularly metrical songs growing out of the 16th-century *ground bass and dance traditions. In Elizabethan England, lute songs or *ayres flourished, written by madrigal composers such as Morley and lutenists such as John Dowland. In France, analogous songs were **airs de cour* and **vaudevilles.* In both English and French repertories, many songs were based on popular dance rhythms and patterns (e.g., *pavane and *galliard).

Purcell integrated Italian and English vocal styles in a significant body of solo songs in the late 17th century. In a lighter vein, Purcell and his contemporaries produced humorous and bawdy *part songs called *catches and *glees.

During the 17th century, the solo songs or *arias in opera, largely following Italian models, became more complex in range and rhythm, more gymnastic vocally, and increasingly oriented toward projection of the emotion or *affect of the text as much as toward clear and straightforward setting of the words. This trend reached its height in arias of Alessandro Scarlatti (opera), Handel (opera and oratorio), and Bach (cantata) in the 18th century. Vocal repertory of this sort tended to eclipse simpler solo song in the late Baroque period, except in such pointedly reactive genres as the English *ballad opera (e.g., John Gay's *The *Beggar's Opera*), which employed well-known popular tunes (*broadside ballads), and French **opera comique.*

5. Art song in the 18th–20th centuries. In the 18th century, the middle class came to be highly influential as audience for and consumer of music. Song composers often attempted to create vocal music accessible to this public. Also, the harpsichord was gradually replaced by the hardier and dynamically more expressive piano, which was eventually produced and sold in large quantities. These factors helped produce the modern keyboard-accompanied solo song.

At approximately the same time, the collection and printing of folk songs provided a body of accessible song as well as a style to be assimilated into the artistic tradition. Folk melodies were given keyboard accompaniments by Beethoven and Haydn, among others, and left their mark on original compositions such as Papageno's arias in Mozart's opera *The Magic Flute.*

In the late 18th and early 19th centuries, national traditions were important in the development of solo song. Foremost was the German, giving rise to the *lied, of which the chief exponents were Schubert and Schumann (followed later by Brahms, Wolf, Mahler, and Richard Strauss). The best German lieder tend toward the selection of first-rank poetry and an expressive rather than primarily accompanimental role for the piano. The French art song, the **mélodie,* shares these features, but embodies the unmistakably French style of its composers (e.g., Berlioz, Fauré, Henri Duparc). Also significant in 19th-century art song was the Russian national tradition, evident especially in the songs of Musorgsky, which combine an often naturalistic style of declamation with an idiomatic harmonic and pianistic sense.

America and England made no notable contribution to the 19th-century art-song repertory (though they did produce a substantial body of Protestant hymnody). Their importance to the history of song lies primarily in popular song (e.g., American minstrel songs and British music hall songs), which provided the basis for the achievements of Stephen Foster and Sir Arthur Sullivan.

In quantity, popular song completely overshadowed art song in the 20th century, and the best music in its many branches (e.g., folk, jazz, show tunes, rock and roll) possesses undeniable beauty, genius, and expressiveness. [See Song, American popular.] The art song, if numerically sparse, continued strong in the music of such composers as Debussy, Ravel, Poulenc, and Messiaen in France; Vaughan Williams, Britten, and Tippett in England; Schoenberg, Berg, Webern, and Hindemith in Germany and Austria; and Ives, Copland, Barber, and Rorem in the U.S.

Bibl.: Denis Stevens, ed., *A History of Song* (London: Hutchinson, 1960; R: Westport, Conn.: Greenwood, 1982). Philip Miller, comp. and trans., *The Ring of Words: An Anthology of Song Texts* (Garden City, N.Y.: Doubleday, 1963; R: New York; Norton, 1973). British Broadcasting Corporation, *Song Catalogue,* 4 vols. (London: BBC, 1966). Donald Ivey, *Song: Anatomy, Imagery, and Styles* (New York: Free Press, 1970). Judith E. Carman, *Art-Song in the United States 1801–1976: An Annotated Bibliography* (n.p.: National Assoc of Teachers of Singing, 1976; suppl., 1978). Thomas R. Nardone, *Classical Vocal Music in Print* (Philadelphia: Musicdata, 1976; annual suppl.). Barbara Meister, *An Introduction to the Art Song* (New York, 1980). Mark Booth, *The Experience of Songs* (New Haven: Yale U Pr, 1981). James Winn, *Unexpected Eloquence: A History of the Relations between Poetry and Music* (New Haven: Yale U Pr, 1981). *Music and Language,* Studies in the History of Music, vol. 1 (New York: Broude Bros, 1983). Stephen Banfield, *Sense and Sensibility in English Song: Critical Studies in the Early 20th Century* (Cambridge, 1985). J. E. Carmen, *Art Song in the United States 1881–1987: An Annotated Bibliography* (Jacksonville, Pa., 1987). Kenneth Whitton, *Lieder: An Introduction to German Song* (London, 1984). J. W. Smeed, *German Song and Its Poetry, 1740–1900* (New York, 1987). Lorraine Correll, *The Nineteenth Century German Lied* (Portland, Ore., 1993). Rufus Hallmark, ed., *German Lieder in the Nineteenth Century* (New York, 1996). R.H.

Song, American popular. The history of popular song in America since the late 1800s has been marked by significant changes both in authorship and in what constitutes the text of the song itself. These changes occurred largely because new media for circulating music emerged, and because popular music now includes music previously considered folk or traditional. A continuum exists between the idea of a song as a work existing in notation and as a work existing in performance or recording. Songs recorded many times (in what have come to be called cover versions) may be said to enjoy a stronger identity independent of a particular recording than songs with few or no cover versions—i.e., those whose identity is tied to one recording, presumably the first. Similarly, a composer (or composers) may exercise a great deal of control over a recording, or that control may be shared among composers (who still receive the credit), singers, instrumentalists, arrangers, and studio personnel.

I. *1890–1920.* Popular song publishing was built around a sheet-music trade aimed at home performers. During the 1890s, theatrical producers and organizers of the variety entertainment known as vaudeville consolidated their offices increasingly in New York City, which had already become the center of the music publishing business. Located first on West 28th Street in Manhattan, then moving uptown (eventually to the neighborhood between West 42nd and West 56th Streets), the area where the publishers set up shop became known as Tin Pan Alley, a name that would later stand for the kind of songs created there. There was a close connection between the stage and the publishing trade, and both the vaudeville circuit and the Broadway show relied on Tin Pan Alley songwriters for their music; in turn, the stage, with its national circuits and touring attractions, popularized and circulated the music among customers who enjoyed listening to, singing, and playing it.

The decade of the 1890s dawned on a popular music scene dominated by Victorian-style ballads and waltz songs. Composed by such songwriters as

Charles K. Harris, Paul Dresser, and Harry von Tilzer, songs for solo voice featured diatonic melody and harmony with occasional strings of applied dominant chords (resulting in "barbershop harmony"). Before the decade was over, however, a vigorous new style called ragtime was introduced—syncopated in rhythm and down-to-earth in spirit. Both types of song (as well as others) persisted through the years 1900–20, each developing in its own way. The well-schooled Broadway composer Jerome Kern brought a cosmopolitan harmonic and melodic richness to the first type. As for the second, in the hands of the self-taught Russian-immigrant songwriter Irving Berlin, ragtime rhythm and exuberance (closely associated with African American musicians) came to stand less for ethnic difference than for social liberation, especially as expressed in such new dances as the grizzly bear and the turkey trot. Songs from Tin Pan Alley (and from Broadway, its higher-toned relative) were heard live on stage and in other entertainment venues across the country and overseas, and on phonograph records and player-piano rolls, as well as being performed at home. Most songs followed a verse-chorus form that, as time passed, gave greater weight to the chorus.

II. *1920–1955.* The maturing of phonograph recording and radio as components of the music industry during the 1920s contributed to far-reaching changes in popular song. While sheet music remained important for distribution, performance, and economics, listeners could now "consume" a song by listening to a recording or a broadcast. Repeated listening to a record, especially after the advent of the electric microphone in 1925, meant that the nuances of a specific recorded performance—the timbre of particular vocalists and instrumentalists, their accompaniments and improvised embellishments, the particular balance between voices and instruments—could now become part of what listeners identified as the "song," previously defined by the sheet music's harmonic-melodic template.

For the most part, the effect of these technological changes was not felt directly by the songwriters of Tin Pan Alley, whose top luminaries were composing for dramatic venues: the Broadway stage and, after the advent in 1927 of the sound film, the Hollywood movie. In the history of American song, this era—especially the interwar years—has sometimes been called the Golden Age because many of its songs, written with ephemeral entertainment in mind, have endured. Composers such as Berlin, Kern, George Gershwin, Cole Porter, and Richard Rodgers, in collaboration with lyricists such as Ira Gershwin, Dorothy Fields, Lorenz Hart, E. Y. Harburg, and Oscar Hammerstein II, developed an urbane style of song that merged witty lyrics with a sophisticated harmonic-melodic sense in a blend that could evoke the emotional gamut of male-female romance, from euphoria and tenderness to risk and heartache. Harmony and melody were adapted from late-19th-century European light classical music, with chromatic, functional harmony enriched with upper chordal extensions (ninths, elevenths, thirteenths), and altered tones redolent of late Romanticism and Impressionism. Kern, in particular, was known for his advanced chromatic harmony and modulations and the graceful arc of his melodies, while Gershwin was attuned to jazz harmony, melody, and syncopation.

Songs continued to be written in verse-chorus structure. In onstage performances, approaching the effect of the recitative-aria pattern of opera, the verse often served as a set-up for the chorus or refrain, the heart of the song. Choruses were typically in 32 bars, with 8-bar sections in the pattern AABA the most common, and a "two-halves" pattern (ABAC or ABAB) also widely used. In professional offstage performances the verse was increasingly viewed as optional.

1. "Race" music / rhythm and blues. Some African American professionals made music for popular consumption in sheet-music form, performed chiefly in vaudeville or by urban dance bands. But much black music had no way of reaching a mass audience before the advent of recording and broadcasting. Recordings made possible the distribution of a whole new range of music from oral tradition, including country blues and various sacred forms, beyond the context in which it originated. Many such songs share melodic phrases and lines of lyrics, making it hard to draw a line between performer and composer. A musician such as Blind Lemon Jefferson, the most successful country blues artist of the 1920s, may be considered the author of the music he recorded not because his lyrics or melodic-harmonic templates were unique and original, but because his way of performing them was distinctive.

By the 1940s and early 1950s, recordings of black popular music were likely to feature instrumental and vocal ensembles, some using written arrangements (as in the case of composer-arranger Jesse Stone's songs recorded by artists such as Ruth Brown) but others developed entirely by year (such as the recordings of Muddy Waters). As early as the "classic blues" of the 1920s, the blues form had been stabilized in its now familiar 12-bar pattern, perhaps out of the need to coordinate ensembles. Other songs employed forms adapted from gospel music or the AABA chorus structure. Compared with Tin Pan Alley, lyrics in blues-oriented songs tended toward the unsentimental and earthy, featuring double entendres and tales of personal success and misfortune presented in a relatively realistic way.

2. Hillbilly music and country. The advent of recording also allowed the music of white rural southerners to be heard beyond its home turf. Dubbed hillbilly by the music industry, this music quickly grew popular throughout North America. Songs varied from fiddle-led dance numbers for string bands, built around a two-part structure, to strophic ballads with narrative lyrics to blues such as those sung by Jimmie

Rodgers, hillbilly music's first big star. Lyrics followed a predominantly narrative impulse, though uptempo tunes might be sung to ribald or nonsense words. Recording sparked the composition of new tunes that fit within the general style of traditional music, such as "The Prisoner's Song," recorded by Vernon Dalhart in 1924. Credited to Guy Massey, this song is made up of melodic and lyric fragments that had long been in circulation.

In the 1940s and early 1950s, country songs adapted elements from Tin Pan Alley, especially the AABA form, while still reaching the public chiefly in recordings full of improvised elements. Songwriter-vocalist Hank Williams produced a particularly compelling blend of the traditional and the new, setting the stage for contemporary country music.

III. *1955 to the present.* The importance of the recording studio as a compositional force increased greatly during this period, with figures such as the producer and the engineer assuming creative roles in the shaping of a recording. Sheet music for popular songs remained, but only as a document—often an inaccurate one—of music that consumers experienced in recorded form. Recordings, and thus songs, could be constructed in the studio through overdubbing, a process in which different elements of the songs were recorded at different times. Such recordings therefore correspond to no actual performance, nor to a preexisting template for performance such as a musical score.

With the onset of rock and roll in the mid-1950s, many of the traits separating the three main types of popular music—mainstream, rhythm and blues, and country—merged. Among the key songwriters of the early rock and roll era, Chuck Berry relied largely on variants of the blues form with a narrative impulse adapted from country music, while Otis Blackwell (who wrote many of Elvis Presley's hits) and Jerry Leiber and Mike Stoller eclectically combined blues forms with those derived from Tin Pan Alley. Rock and roll lyrics tended to focus on teenage concerns.

During the 1960s, songwriters affiliated with rhythm and blues (known as soul by mid-decade), such as Smokey Robinson, Otis Redding, and the teams of Isaac Hayes and David Porter, and Eddie Holland, Lamont Dozier, and Brian Holland, fused contemporary gospel music with early rock and roll and with jazz. Their songs feature a mixture of precomposed elements with instrumental parts and vocal inflections created during the act of recording.

Bob Dylan, after winning fame as part of the urban folk revival of the early 1960s, expanded the subject matter and poetic range of popular music, largely by incorporating influences from Beat poetry. His songs were mostly strophic, occasionally with a refrain or chorus, but with complex internal arrangements of lines, striking imagery, and flavored by a hard-edged absurdist humor. Dylan's music drew from a range of blues and country music, delving back into the ballad forms that had constituted a good part of hillbilly music in the 1920s.

John Lennon and Paul McCartney, the primary songwriters for the Beatles, synthesized many earlier styles of popular music—rockabilly, Motown, early rock and roll, and even Tin Pan Alley pop—while also making innovative use of the recording studio. Their early songs relied largely on AABA forms, sometimes with phrases of irregular length. Many of their melodies were pentatonic, with harmony combining functional and modal approaches. Their lyrics focused at first on teenage romance but, partly through Dylan's influence, grew increasingly surreal, especially those later attributed to Lennon. The Beatles also made experimental use of overdubbing and other recording techniques, so that their recordings might be as memorable for their timbres—the use of electronically modified sounds and tape effects as well as instruments unusual for rock music—as for their melodies and harmonic progressions.

Other trends in the late 1960s include the development of the riff-based song. In genres such as blues-rock, heavy metal, and psychedelic rock, long sections were based on short *ostinati* or riffs derived from blues tonality. The so-called funk genre also developed during this period, inspired mainly by the recordings of James Brown, in which long open-ended sections were built on interlocking, polyrhythmic riffs.

The singer-songwriter movement of the early 1970s looked back to Dylan in rejecting the riff-based approach and using song forms derived from traditional music and Tin Pan Alley. Songwriters such as Joni Mitchell, James Taylor, and Carole King extended the autobiographical implications of their lyrics beyond Dylan's model. The singer-songwriter genre has remained important in popular music to the present.

Since the mid-1970s, dance music genres, such as disco, house, and techno, almost entirely products of the recording studio, have depended heavily on ostinato-based sections. "Samples" of previous recordings are often used as an important textural element in these genres. The remix, in which elements of a recording are taken apart and put back together again in the studio, symbolizes both this mode of composition and the growing textual instability of the popular song.

Hip hop, in which lyrics are often spoken (rapped) rather than sung, places more emphasis on lyrical complexity than the other electronically based genres noted here. Favorite topics include quasi-cinematic representations of male-female relationships, the harshness of inner-city life, and, conversely, the opulence of a recording artist's successful career. Creative duties may be entirely split in hip hop, with producers constructing backing tracks from samples or electronically generated rhythmic patterns, which are then matched with lyrics written by a rapper.

Songs in other genres such as punk and alternative follow from heavy metal, often being based on rhythmic patterns developed from guitar riffs. Except for the singer-songwriters' work, all these post-1970 popular genres tend to steer clear of functional harmony and melody (though exceptions do exist), to develop songs collectively (although one person may receive most of the credit), and to present the recording as the definitive version of the song.

Bibl.: Alec Wilder, *American Popular Song: The Great Innovators, 1900–1950,* ed. James T. Maher (New York: Oxford U Pr, 1972). Charles Hamm, *Yesterdays: Popular Song in America* (New York: Norton, 1979). Bill C. Malone, *Country Music U.S.A.,* rev. ed. (Austin: U of Tex Pr, 1985). David Toop, *Rap Attack 2: African Rap to Global Hip Hop* (London: Serpent's Tail, 1991). Theodore Gracyk, *Rhythm and Noise: An Aesthetics of Rock* (Durham: Duke U Pr, 1996). Richard Crawford, *America's Music Life: A History* (New York: Norton, 2001). Albin J. Zak III, *The Poetics of Rock: Cutting Tracks, Making Records* (Berkeley: U of Cal Pr, 2001).

D.B.

Song cycle [Ger. *Liederkreis, Liederzyklus*]. A group of songs, usually for solo voice and piano, constituting a literary and musical unit. The song cycle is associated primarily with the 19th-century German *lied.

The poems of a song cycle are usually by a single poet and often exist as a poetic cycle, taken over in whole or in part by the composer. The poems may be related in general theme (e.g., love, nature, travel) and sometimes suggest a narrative outline. Many of the most familiar song cycles are examples: Beethoven's *An die ferne Geliebte* (Alois Jeitteles), Schubert's *Die schöne Müllerin* and *Winterreise* (Wilhelm Müller), Schumann's *Frauenliebe und -Leben* (Adalbert von Chamisso). In other cases, the song texts are the composer's selection and arrangement of poems by a single poet (e.g., Schumann's *Liederkreis* op. 39, from Joseph Eichendorff), from a single source (e.g., Brahms's *Vier ernste Gësange,* from the Bible; Mahler's *Das Lied von der Erde,* from Hans Bethge's *Die chinesische Flöte*), or, less commonly, from different poets (e.g., Schumann's *Myrthen,* from Goethe, Rückert, Heine, Burns, et al.).

The songs in a cycle are sometimes drawn together by musical means. Beethoven's use of connective piano interludes between the songs of *An die ferne Geliebte* is unique, but his reprise of music from the beginning of the cycle at the end had imitators (e.g., Schumann in *Frauenliebe und -Leben*), as did his writing the songs in closely related keys and ending the cycle in the key in which it had begun. Songs may also be related by common musical motives. However, Schubert's cycles, for example, manifest none of these traits.

The 19th-century German song cycle bears some resemblance to 16th-century madrigal cycles and to the 18th-century German lied cantata, but the nearest antecedents appear to be the English and German song collections of the late 18th century by James Hook and Christian Gottlob Neefe, respectively, in which the individual songs touch upon a common theme or were composed for a particular occasion or dedicatee. Beethoven's *An die ferne Geliebte* does not stand alone in the early 19th century; there were other song cycles by Friedrich Heinrich Himmel, Carl Maria von Weber, Sigismund Neukomm, Ludwig Berger, Ferdinand Ries, and Conradin Kreutzer, those by Kreutzer being among the most popular and critically acclaimed of the day. Schubert's cycles appeared in the 1820s and gave the genre a more serious tone. In the next decade, Mendelssohn, Heinrich August Marschner, and especially Carl Loewe contributed cycles. Schumann's numerous song cycles, which appeared in the 1840s, are among the most highly unified musically; in addition to those mentioned above, these include *Liederkreis* op. 24 and *Dichterliebe* (both Heine). Schumann probably invented the cycle for mixed voices (*Minnespiel,* from Friedrich Rückert, and *Spanische Liebeslieder,* from Emanuel Geibel). In addition to his solo cycles, Brahms composed works for mixed voices (*Liebeslieder* and *Neue Liebeslieder*). Hugo Wolf's large collections of songs on poems by single poets (Mörike-, Eichendorff-, and Goethe-Lieder) or from single sources (*Spanisches* and *Italienisches Liederbuch*) do not constitute song cycles in the ordinary sense. Mahler enriched the song cycle with orchestral accompaniment (e.g., *Kindertotenlieder,* Friedrich Rückert) and enlarged it to symphonic proportions *(Das Lied von der Erde).* Notable 20th-century song cycles are Schoenberg's *Pierrot lunaire* (Albert Giraud, trans. Otto Erich Hartleben, for **Sprechstimme* and chamber ensemble) and *Das Buch der hängenden Gärten* (Stefan George), Berg's *Altenberg Lieder* (with orchestra), Hindemith's *Das Marienleben* (Rainer Maria Rilke), and Richard Strauss's *Ophelia-Lieder* and *Vier letzte Gesänge.*

Among French examples are Berlioz's *Les nuits d'été* (Théophile Gautier), Fauré's *La bonne chanson* (Paul Verlaine), Debussy's *Les chansons de Bilitis* (Pierre Louÿs), and Ravel's *Chansons madécasses* (Évariste de Parny, with instrumental ensemble), *Shéhérazade* (Tristan Klingsor, with orch.), and *Histoires naturelles* (Jules Renard). Mussorgsky composed three cycles, *The Nursery, Sunless,* and *Songs and Dances of Death.* English and American composers made distinguished contributions to the genre in the 20th century: e.g., Vaughan Williams's *On Wenlock Edge* (A. E. Housman, with piano and string quartet) and *Songs of Travel* (Robert Louis Stevenson); Britten's *Serenade* (various poets, for tenor, horn, and strings), *The Poet's Echo* (Pushkin), and *Winter Words* (Thomas Hardy); Copland's *Twelve Poems of Emily Dickinson;* Barber's *Hermit Songs.* The song cycle has been given new life in such compositions as Lukas Foss's *Time Cycle* (Auden, Kafka, Housman, Nietzsche), Luciano Berio's *Circles* (e. e. cummings), and George Crumb's *Ancient Voices of Children* (Federico García Lorca), each in a strikingly expressive modern musical and vocal idiom and with unique instrumentation.

Cycles, like lieder generally, were originally composed as private entertainments and pastimes. Individual songs from cycles began to appear in concert programs in the 1830s. Complete performances were uncommon before the late 19th century, but have since become the norm.

Bibl.: Lotte Lehmann, *Eighteen Song Cycles* (London: Praeger, 1945). Helen Mustard, *The Lyric Song Cycle in German Literature* (New York: King's Crown Pr, 1946). Don Lee Earl, "The Solo Song Cycle in Germany: 1800–1850" (Ph.D. diss., Indiana Univ., 1952). Edward Kravitt, "The Lied in 19th-Century Concert Life," *JAMS* 18 (1965): 207–18. Luise Eitel Peake, "The Song Cycle: A Preliminary Inquiry into the Beginnings of the Romantic Song Cycle and the Nature of the Art Form" (Ph.D. diss., Columbia Univ., 1968). Barbara Turchin, "Robert Schumann's Song Cycles in the Context of the Early Nineteenth-Century 'Liederkreis'" (Ph.D. diss., Columbia Univ., 1981). Barbara Turchin, "Schumann's Song Cycles: the Cycle within the Song," *19th-Century Music* 8 (1984–85): 231–44. Barbara Turchin, "The Nineteenth-Century *Wanderlieder* Cycle," *JM* 5 (1987): 498–525. Arnold Feil, *Franz Schubert. Die Schöne Müllerin, Winterreise,* trans. Ann Sherwin (Portland, Ore., 1988). R. O. Bingham, *The Song Cycle in German-Speaking Countries, 1790–1840: Approaches to a Changing Genre* (Ph.D. diss., Cornell Univ., 1993). Susan Youens, *Retracing a Winter's Journey: Schubert's* Winterreise (Ithaca, N.Y., 1991). Richard Kramer, *Distant Cycles: Schubert and the Conceiving of Song* (Chicago, 1994). Susan Youens, *Schubert, Müller, and Die Schöne Müllerin* (Cambridge, 1997). See also Lied, Song. R.H.

Song form [Ger. *Liedform*]. Ternary form, ABA [see Binary and ternary form].

Song-motet. See Motet I.

Song of Destiny. See *Schicksalslied.*

Song of the Earth, The. See *Lied von der Erde, Das.*

Songs of a Wayfarer. See *Lieder eines fahrenden Gesellen.*

Songs without Words. See *Lieder ohne Worte.*

Sonido trece [Sp., sound thirteen]. Mexican composer Julián Carrillo's term for his use of *microtones, including intervals equal to 1/3, 1/4, 1/8, and 1/16 of a whole tone.

Son jarocho [Sp.]. The traditional **son* of the Jarocho region of Mexico, the Gulf coastal plain south of the city of Veracruz. Such pieces are rhythmically and contrapuntally complex, with lyric, often elaborately improvised texts accompanied by ensembles with harp and, most typically, *requintos* and *jaranas* (small four- and eight-string guitars). D.S.

Sonnambula, La [It., The Sleepwalker]. Opera in two acts by Bellini (libretto by Felice Romani, based on Eugène Scribe's scenario for a ballet), produced in Milan in 1831. Setting: a Swiss village early in the 19th century.

Sonnenquartette [Ger.]. See *Sun* Quartets.

Sonnerie [Fr.]. A signal sounded by trumpets or bells.

Sono [Lat.]. In the *Mozarabic rite, a melismatic chant sung at Matins and Vespers; in the *Gallican rite, the chant corresponding to the Gregorian *offertory.

Sonore [Fr.], **sonoro, sonoramente** [It.]. Sonorous(ly).

Sonority. (1) In discussions of 20th-century music, a sound defined by some combination of timbres or registers, especially one that plays a significant role in a work. (2) The tonal quality produced by a performer on an instrument. (3) Simultaneity.

Sopra [It.]. Above; *come sopra,* as above; *M. s.* (or *M. d.*) *sopra,* left (or right) hand above the other in piano playing.

Sopranino [It., dim. of and thus higher in pitch than soprano]. In the modern *recorder family, the highest pitched instrument; in the *clarinet family, an instrument pitched between the highest-pitched member, in A♭, and the clarinet in C.

Soprano. (1) The highest-pitched general type of human voice, normally possessed only by women and boys [for subtypes and ranges, see Voice; see also *Castrato,* Falsetto]. (2) In music for the conventional combination of four vocal parts, the highest part. (3) In some families of wind instruments, notably the *saxophone and *recorder, the highest-pitched conventional member [but see also Sopranino].

Soprano clef. See Clef.

Sorcerer's Apprentice, The. See *Apprenti sorcier, L'.*

Sordino [It.]. (1) *Mute. (2) *Damper. (3) *Kit. (3) *Clavichord.

Sordone [It.; Fr. *sourdine;* Ger. *Sordun*]. A double-reed woodwind instrument described early in the 17th century by Michael Praetorius. It has a cylindrical bore and two parallel channels within the same piece of wood. It seems to have been identical to the **Kortholt,* except that the latter is played with a *wind cap. See also *Courtaut.* M.S.

Sorochintsy Fair [Russ. Sorochinskaya Yarmarka]. Unfinished comic opera by Musorgsky (libretto by the composer, after Gogol), composed in 1874–80 and edited and completed by various composers after Musorgsky's death. One version was produced in Moscow and St. Petersburg in 1913. A version by Nicolas Tcherepnin was produced in Monte Carlo in 1923. Setting: Ukraine in the mid-19th century.

Sortisatio [Lat.]. In the 16th and 17th centuries, improvised counterpoint, as distinct from *compositio,* composed counterpoint.

Sospirando [It.]. Sighing.

Sostenente (sostinente, sustaining) piano. Any keyboard-operated stringed instrument that, unlike a piano or harpsichord, can sustain a pitch indefinitely. Many such instruments, all more or less ephemeral, have been invented, following three basic designs. In the **anémocorde*, the strings are set into vibration by currents of air. In the *melopiano, they are struck repeatedly by spring-operated hammers. The most successful approach to the problem is found in the family of *bowed keyboard instruments. In many of these, the strings are "bowed" by revolving cylinders, a design similar to that of the *hurdy-gurdy. Leonardo da Vinci sketched such an instrument in his notebooks of 1488–89, but the first working instrument was Hans Haiden's **Geigenwerk* of 1575. Here, one or more parchment-covered cylinders were kept constantly rotating by a treadle; each key caused a string to be pressed against a wheel. It produced a sound resembling a string ensemble and was widely imitated in the 17th and 18th centuries. Related designs used separate wheels for each string, a long loop of horsehair to bow all strings (e.g., the *Bogenflügel* invented by Johann Hohlfield in 1752, for which C. P. E. Bach wrote a work), or even a hand-drawn bow similar to the violin's. In some instruments, the sounding strings were not bowed directly, the vibrations being transmitted to the strings by an intermediate device. The harmonichord (ca. 1810) of Gottfried and Friedrich Kaufmann, for which Weber composed an Adagio and Rondo, employed a rod for this purpose. In Isaac Henry Robert Mott's sostinente piano forte of 1817, revolving wheels acted on silk threads that transmitted their vibration in turn to the strings. See also Clavicylinder.

Sostenido [Sp.]. (1) The sharp sign [see Accidental, Pitch names]. (2) Sustained.

Sostenuto, sostenendo [It., abbr. *sost.*]. Sustained, sustaining in duration; sometimes with the implication of a slowing in tempo.

Sostenuto pedal. On a modern piano with three pedals, the center pedal, which causes to remain undamped only those strings whose keys are depressed at the moment that the pedal itself is depressed.

Sotto [It.]. Under, below; *sotto voce,* in an undertone, subdued; *M. s.* (or *M. d.*) *sotto,* with left (or right) hand below the other in keyboard playing.

Soubrette. In opera, particularly comic opera of the 18th century, a clever female servant or lady's maid, often given to flirtation or intrigue. Her ancestress is the *damigella* of the *commedia dell'arte,* by way of the plays of Marivaux. Examples from the 18th century are Serpina in Pergolesi's *La serva padrona,* Blonde in Mozart's *Die Entführung aus dem Serail,* and Despina in Mozart's *Così fan tutte;* a 19th-century example is Adele in Johann Strauss's *Die Fledermaus.* The term is also used to describe the type of voice generally called for in such roles, that is, a light and agile soprano. A related French term is *dugazon,* from the name of a well-known singer at the Opéra-comique, Louise-Rosalie Dugazon (1755–1821).

Soul. A type of black American *popular music that emerged in the mid-1960s. Typically, a single prominent element of musical spontaneity is combined with pervasive musical and extramusical control. Spontaneity (or a well-rehearsed impression of spontaneity) comes from featured vocalists (e.g., Ray Charles, James Brown, Aretha Franklin, Stevie Wonder, Otis Redding, Wilson Pickett, Gladys Knight, Sam and Dave, the O'Jays) or saxophonists who function by analogy as vocalists (Junior Walker, King Curtis, Grover Washington, Jr.). They bring to secular singing the impassioned improvisatory vocal devices of black *gospel music (sudden shouts, falsetto cries, moans, etc.) and a collection of church-derived, idiomatic formulas ("feel all right," "have mercy baby"). All other performers have fixed roles. Final segments of pieces exemplify this contrast: as a singer improvises to a climax, electric bass and drums establish a loud, one-, two-, or four-bar ostinato; electric guitars, keyboards, and a "horn" section of saxophones, trumpets, and trombones overlay crisp, syncopated patterns; strings may add still another line; backup vocalists, if present, repeat a catchy phrase, perhaps the song's title. Often, control extends to matters of technology on record (synthesized sounds, complex overdubbing) and of ritual in live performance (uniforms, detailed choreography).

Songs are built on brief tonal progressions corresponding to alternating verses and refrains, on open-ended, hypnotic, interlocking one- or two-chord ostinatos (as described above), or, less often, on traditional 32-bar popular song forms and 12-bar blues. Since the late 1960s, some performers have addressed social issues (James Brown, the Impressions, the Temptations, Stevie Wonder); but the principal topic of lyrics remains love life, ranging from raw adult sexuality (Brown) to teen love (the Supremes, the Jackson 5). A few performers (Smokey Robinson, Stevie Wonder) have become known for the quality of their lyrics.

Bibl.: Irwin Stambler, *Encyclopedia of Pop, Rock, and Soul* (New York: St Martin's, 1974). Ian Hoare, ed., *The Soul Book* (London, 1975). Gerri Hirshey, *Nowhere to Run: The Story of Soul Music* (New York: Times Bks, 1984). B.K.

Soul jazz. A *gospel-influenced adaptation in the mid-1950s to early 60s of *bebop. This *funky style emphasized subdominant-oriented progressions evoking church hymns; "soulful," minor harmonies; moderate tempos; and catchy, symmetrical melodies, in combination with bebop structure (e.g., 12-bar blues or 32-bar popular song forms), format (theme-solo(s)-

theme), and instrumentation (small combos led by saxophone or trumpet, or organ trios). See Hard bop. B.K.

Soundboard [Fr. *table d'harmonie;* Ger. *Resonanzboden;* It. *piano armonico, tavola armonica;* Sp. *caja armónica*]. On the *piano and related stringed instruments, a thin sheet of wood over which the strings pass and that is largely responsible for transmitting the vibrations of the strings to the surrounding air. On the *harp, the strings are attached to the soundboard and are stretched in a plane perpendicular to it. The analogous part of the *violin and related instruments is termed the belly or table.

Sound box. In stringed instruments, the hollow body, which is responsible for enhancing and transmitting the vibrations of the strings to the surrounding air.

Sound hole [Fr. *ouïe;* Ger. *Schalloch;* It. *occhio;* Sp. *abertura acústica*]. In stringed instruments, an opening or openings, both ornamental and functional, cut into the table to amplify sound and help focus musical quality. Instruments of the violin family traditionally have two sound holes, in the shape of an *f* and thus known as F holes, one on either side of the bridge. Viols similarly have such holes, usually in the shape of a *c* or an elaborate *f.* Other early bowed strings like the viola d'amore bear sword-shaped openings called flame holes. Regardless of shape, these sound holes afford increased plate flexibility and lie just outside the location of the bridge feet to increase lateral table rocking. The guitar, lute, and other plucked instruments usually have one or more round sound holes beneath the strings between the fixed bridge and fingerboard. In early plucked strings, these sound holes are often carved with elaborate geometric patterns or are inlaid with decorative parchment to form rose holes. These openings, too, while often visually beautiful, have the primary function of increasing sound volume. Sound holes or roses in early keyboard instruments, however, are usually placed to punctuate and enhance decorative ornamentation and have little bearing on musical quality. W.L.M.

Sound post [Fr. *âme;* Ger. *Stimmstock;* It. *anima;* Sp. *alma*]. In the *violin and other bowed strings, a slender movable dowel placed inside the instrument body behind the treble bridge foot connecting the table with the back. It functions to support string and bridge pressure on the table while transmitting and balancing string vibrations between the table and back. The sound post is fitted just snugly enough to be held in place without string tension, and its location and adjustment play an important role in sound production. For this reason, it is known in French and other romance languages as the soul. The normal diameter of a violin sound post is .65 cm. W.L.M.

Soupir [Fr.]. A quarter rest [see Note].

Soupirant [Fr.]. Sighing.

Sources (pre-1500). All of the surviving sources for polyphonic music that predate Petrucci's **Odhecaton* (Venice, 1501) are manuscripts, the majority of which contain sacred music. None has been identified as a composer's autograph.

The chief finding tools are **RISM* for manuscripts before 1600 and printed sources before 1800, the *Census-Catalogue of Manuscript Sources of Polyphonic Music, 1400–1550* (1979–), and Ludwig and Gennrich (1910–62). The advent of photoduplication and the publication of facsimile editions have made possible the study of sources at distant locations and especially the comparison of multiple sources, which can vary considerably. In the U.S., sizable microfilm collections of early sources have been established at Harvard's Isham Library, the Musicological Archive for Renaissance Manuscript Studies at the University of Illinois (*FAM* 16 [1969]: 148–49), St. John's Abbey and University in Collegeville, Minnesota (*Notes* 36 [1979/80]: 849–63), and St. Louis University (Vatican Film Library; *Notes* 14 [1956/57]: 317–24).

Bibl.: Friedrich Ludwig and Friedrich Gennrich, *Repertorium organorum recentioris et motetorum vetustissimi stili,* vol. 1, pt. 1 (Halle: M Niemeyer, 1910); vol. 1, pt. 2 & vol. 2, ed. Friedrich Gennrich, Summa musicae medii aevi 7–8 (Langen bei Frankfurt: Gennrich, 1961–62); new ed., ed. Luther Dittmer (New York: Institute of Mediaeval Music, 1964–78). Solange Corbin, ed., *Répertoire de manuscrits médiévaux contenant des notations musicales,* 3 vols. (Paris: CNRS, 1965–74). Masakata Kanazawa, "Polyphonic Music for Vespers during the Fifteenth Century," 2 vols. (Ph.D. diss., Harvard Univ., 1966). Gilbert Reaney, ed., *Manuscripts of Polyphonic Music, 11th–Early 14th Century, RISM* B/IV/1 (Munich-Duisburg: Henle, 1966). Id., ed., *Manuscripts of Polyphonic Music (c. 1320–1400), RISM* B/IV/2 (Munich-Duisburg: Henle, 1969). Kurt von Fischer and Max Lütolf, eds., *Handschriften mit mehrstimmiger Musik des 14., 15. und 16. Jahrhunderts, RISM* B/IV/3–4 (Munich-Duisburg: Henle, 1972). Viola L. Hagopian, *Italian Ars Nova Music: A Bibliographic Guide,* 2nd ed. (Berkeley and Los Angeles: U of Cal Pr, 1973). Joshua Rifkin, "Scribal Concordances for Some Renaissance Manuscripts in Florentine Libraries," *JAMS* 26 (1973): 305–26. *Census-Catalogue of Manuscript Sources of Polyphonic Music 1400–1550,* 5 vols. (Neuhausen-Stuttgart: Hänssler, 1979–1988). Thomas R. Ward, *The Polyphonic Office Hymn, 1400–1520: A Descriptive Catalogue* (Neuhausen-Stuttgart: Hänssler, 1980). María del Carmen Gómez, "Más códices con polifonía del siglo XIV en España," *AM* 53 (1981): 85–90. *Les sources en musicologie* (Paris: CNRS, 1981). Peter M. Lefferts and Margaret Bent, "New Sources of English Thirteenth- and Fourteenth-Century Polyphony," *Early Music History* 2 (1982); 273–362. Hans Tischler, *The Earliest Motets (to circa 1270): A Complete Comparative Edition,* 3 vols. (New Haven: Yale U Pr, 1982). William J. Summers, ed., *English Fourteenth-Century Polyphony: Facsimile Edition of Sources* (Tutzing: Schneider, 1983). Roger Bowers and Andrew Walthey, "New Sources of English Fourteenth- and Fifteenth-Century Polyphony," *Early Music History* 3 (1983): 123–73. Id., "New Sources of English Fifteenth- and Sixteenth-Century Polyphony," *Early*

Music History 4 (1984): 297–346. Frank A. D'Accone, "Una nuova fonte dell'ars nova italiana: Il codice di San Lorenzo, 2211," *Studi musicali* 13 (1984): 3–31. Mark E. Everist in *Anderson,* 1984, pp. 97–118. Gilbert Reaney in *Anderson,* 1984, pp. 495–504. Hans Tischler, *The Style and Evolution of the Earliest Motets (to circa 1270),* 3 vols. in 4 (Henryville, Pa.: Institute of Mediaeval Music, 1985). H.E.S.

Sourd [Fr.]. Muffled, muted.

Sourdine [Fr.]. (1) *Mute. (2) **Sordone.*

Sousaphone. A circular tuba in BB♭ or E♭ with a large bell pointing forward above the player's head and coils of tubing balanced on the left shoulder and against the right hip for ease of carrying while marching. John Philip Sousa (1854–1932) suggested its design to J. W. Pepper of Philadelphia. Either Pepper or one of his suppliers made the first model in 1892. The bell, which originally pointed straight up, was turned forward by the C. G. Conn Company of Elkhart, Indiana, in 1908. Like other tubas, sousaphones have traditionally been made of brass, usually lacquered to prevent tarnish, but occasionally plated with nickel. Fiberglass is now sometimes substituted for brass. A related instrument is the *helicon. See ill. under Brass instruments. R.E.E.

Soutenu [Fr.]. Sustained.

Souterliedekens [Du., little Psalter-songs]. The first Dutch metrical *Psalter, published in Antwerp in 1540 by Symon Cock. The author of the translation has not been established with certainty. Preexisting melodies were employed (and printed), including chiefly Dutch folk songs, but also some French and German folk songs. Texts and melodies were set polyphonically by Clemens non Papa (1556–57), Gherardus Mes (1561), and Cornelis Buscop (1568).

South America. See Latin America, Argentina, Brazil, Chile.

South Asia. The region called South Asia is centered on India and includes the countries on its periphery with which India has close cultural and historical ties. While the term South Asia implies a unit with more than mere geographic contiguity among its constituents, it does not signify ethnic, cultural, linguistic, or musical uniformity any more than does the term Europe. Within this region, therefore, there is a musical diversity based on class, ethnicity, religion, and education, as well as a contrasting unity that is aided by modern media and marketing.

The medium that has done the most to create a broad public for certain kinds of music is the Indian film industry, the world's most productive. Sound films began in 1931, and a few years later the practice began of having professional singers overdub the half dozen or so songs commonly included in any film. The phenomenal productivity of the film studios and their reliance on songs to help sell a film rapidly made film songs *(filmigāt)* a quasi-genre with an exceptionally broad audience that crossed many ethnic, linguistic, social, and geographic boundaries, so that for several decades after World War II it was unrivaled in popularity. Western influence was evident in these songs, which often used large orchestras—with heavy emphasis on strings and instrumental introductions and interludes—as well as harmonic accompaniment, but equally important were elements taken from classical *rāgas,* regional folk styles, and religious genres like Muslim *qavvāli* and Hindu *bhajan.* Music directors such as Naushad Ali (b. 1919) and Sachin Dev Burman (1906–75) could often make a film a success by their contributions, but the most extraordinary power of this sort is held by playback singers—especially Lata Mangeshkar (b. 1929), who is said to have recorded more than 30,000 songs in nearly two dozen languages. In many dozens of film hits, no matter what starlet appeared on the screen, it was Lata's voice that emanated from the actor's mouth when she opened it to sing. High, sweet, and girlish even into middle age, Lata's voice changed the aesthetic criterion for female voices in *filmigāt,* just as the crooningly mellow voice of the actor-singer K. L. Saigal (1905–47) had done for male voices in the early days of sound film.

In the 1970s and 1980s, while *filmigāt* retained its exceptional popularity, a modernized version of *ghazal,* a light classical genre of Indo-Islamic musical culture, gave it some competition, particularly among a middle-class urban population that found its nostalgic quality appealing because of its associations with a romanticized past of aristocratic elegance and sophistication. Starting with the Pakistani singers Ghulam Ali and Mehdi Hasan, the vogue was soon taken up in India, where it was aided by the rapidly developing music cassette industry. Less sophisticated in its poetry and Urdu language than the older styles, which were the specialty of courtesan singers, its music also relied less on improvisation and was more easily accessible.

While Indian art music, especially that of the north, had a sporadic presence in Europe and America throughout the 20th century, it became fashionable when pop stars like the Beatles brought it to the attention of youth in the 1960s and 1970s and started using some of its instruments and characteristic sounds in their own music. In India, Western pop influences became increasingly evident in *filmigāt* of the 1970s and 1980s, but the spread of television among the middle class during that time prepared the way for a more direct and current connection with international pop styles through media outlets like MTV and Star TV in the 1990s. Fusion styles now work in both directions. The Pakistani *qavvāli* singer Nusrat Fateh Ali Khan (1949–97) made an international mix of traditional Sufi devotional styles and contemporary pop sounds, and remix artists have used his samples in any number of techno-trance-jungle combinations. Nusrat epitomizes the quandary of the traditional artist in the new global world of sound: while appealing to an enormous international youth public with his trendy sounds, he has been criticized by some fans for selling out his heritage after being brought to the Western limelight by Peter Gabriel and the World of Music and Dance Festival (WOMAD).

While Nusrat's music was consciously aimed at an international audience, newer styles of dance music have originated within the Indian diaspora. Starting with the Punjabi folk dance *bhangra,* Indian youth in Britain in the 1970s and 1980s developed a fusion with styles current among Caribbean blacks, as a means of distinguishing themselves from dominant white British culture and of expressing discontent with its racial attitudes. Styles range from the modernized folk songs of Punjabi singers like Hans Raj Hans to the studio-savvy remixes of Hindi film song by artists like the British Bally Sagoo, whose music, with the help of Sony, has passed out of the diaspora community.

In discussing the realm of art music, one concept that is helpful in making possible generalizations about the area is that of the Great and Little Traditions. Developed in the 1950s and 60s at the University of Chicago, its chief proponent for South Asia is the anthropologist Milton Singer. In music, the Great and Little Traditions are distinguished primarily by the extensive geographic spread of the former and the localization of the latter. The lateral spread of the Great Tradition has been achieved through the codification and standardization of theory and performing practice by the literati and by a professional class of musicians, both of which have been supported by the patronage of privileged classes. The local circumscription of the Little Tradition depends on such things as sectarian, linguistic, ethnic, political, or caste constraints. To a certain extent, the distinction between the two traditions is that between art and folk, but some types of art music are bound to their locales and lack the lateral spread necessary for being recognized as part of the Great Tradition, and some aspects of folk music may be adapted to performance in the styles of the Great Tradition. Because of the enormous diversity and complexity of musics of the Little Tradition, the following discussion deals only with the Great Tradition.

I. *The written canon (śāstra).* Although tangential mention of music is to be found in the ancient primers of Vedic grammar *(prātiśākhya)* and phonetics *(śikṣā),* the earliest extant and extensive discussion of the art is found in a treatise on dramaturgy, the *Nāṭya Śāstra* (ca. 5th cent.) by Bharata. The allied arts of vocal and instrumental music and dance, collectively called *saṅgīta,* were included in the *Nāṭya Śāstra* as constituents of the Sanskrit theater. Among the aspects of musical theory described in the treatise is a tuning system of 22 intervals *(śruti)* in the octave from which two heptatonic species of octave *(grāma)* are derived. Serially permuted, these octave species give rise to 14 different scales *(mūrcchana)* from which 18 modes *(jāti)* evolve. Scholars are divided, however, in their opinions about the niceties of this theory.

The discussion of instruments in the *Nāṭya Śāstra* is divided into four sections, one for each class: chordophones (*tata,* stretched); membranophones (*avanaddha,* covered); idiophones (*ghana,* solid); and aerophones (*suṣira,* hollow, tubular). This classification scheme, transmitted to Victor Mahillon by Sourindro Mohun Tagore in the 1880s, became the basis for the Sachs-Hornbostel system of instrument classification.

Considerable attention is paid in the *Nāṭya Śāstra* to the affective quality of music, and prescriptions are given concerning the choice of modes and musical forms for the expression of particular sentiments *(bhāva)* whose end is to create in the connoisseur *(rasika)* a particular aesthetic sensation *(rasa).*

The *Nāṭya Śāstra* continued to be a basic source for other treatises written in the succeeding centuries. In addition to building upon the *Nāṭya Śāstra,* Matanga's *Bṛhad-deśī* (9th cent.) includes the first discussion of *rāga* and the names of some *rāga*s that are still extant. Also new in the *Bṛhad-deśī* is a metaphysical/physiological interpretation of the nature of sound based upon the precepts of Tantra yoga. This interpretation is particularly evident, too, in the last and most comprehensive treatise of the ancient period, the *Saṅgīta-ratnākara* (13th cent.) by Śārṅgadeva. While retaining an unequaled prestige today, the *Saṅgīta-ratnākara* contains many enigmas. Even so, it can be shown that some of its information—e.g., on improvisation—can be related to contemporary practice.

After the 16th century, theoretical treatises reflect a split of the Great Tradition into two styles, now called the Hindustani and Carnatic systems *(paddhati).* The former is prevalent in northern, Indo-Aryan-speaking areas of the subcontinent, including Pakistan, Bangladesh, and less significantly, Afghanistan and Nepal. The latter is common in the southern, Dravidian-speaking areas such as the Tamil-speaking areas of Sri Lanka. Among the Sinhalese inhabitants of Sri Lanka, the Hindustani *paddhati* is more established.

An illustration of the way in which the two systems grew apart is provided by the different approaches to *rāga* classification that each developed. The Carnatic approach emphasized a method of scale *(mela)* construction that would allow classification of the *rāga*s according to their pitch content. All 72 scales possible in the 12-tone division of the octave within the Carnatic system were described in the *Caturdaṇḍi prakāśika,* written in 1660 for the court of Tanjore by Veṅkaṭamakhī; at that time only 19 of the scales were in use, but since then *rāga*s have been devised for all the scales. Although a number of treatises written in the north starting in the 16th century contain discussions of scale structure as the basis for *rāga* classification, they also discuss a distinctive system that designates several chief *rāgas* (usually six) and subordinates to each of these another group of *rāgas* (usually five). Eventually these groups came to be described as families, with the subordinates called wives and sons of the chief *rāgas*. Contemporaneous with this new system of *rāga* classification there arose the practice of accompanying each description of a *rāga* with an iconographical epitome in verse. A separate painters' tradition of *rāga* iconography *(rāga-mālā)* emerged at the same time.

In Carnatic music, the system of 72 *melas* remains the basis for classifying *rāgas*; in Hindustani music, however, the early 20th-century Marathi theoretician Vishnu Narayan Bhatkhande devised a different scheme based on a group of 10 scales derived from fretting arrangements for the *sitār (thāṭ)*. His contributions to theory have been widely adopted in music curricula but often meet with criticism from musicians and connoisseurs for being too simple.

II. *Traditions of performance (sampradāya).* The theory and philosophy of music in South Asia have been transmitted through literature, but the transmission of repertory and of performing practice is achieved almost entirely through oral instruction. Notation is used mainly as an aid to memory, not for the production of authoritative texts. The tradition is accepted as valid because of its having been handed down in a succession *(paramparā)* of masters *(guru)* and disciples *(śiṣya)*. In both Hindustani and Carnatic styles, one man, in particular, is viewed as the most authoritative source for the *sampradāya.*

In the Hindustani style, this man is Tansen (ca. 1500–1589), who in his maturity was associated with the court of the Mughal Emperor Akbar. He is commemorated in an annual festival at Gwalior, where he had been trained in his youth and where he is buried. The *bīn* player Dabir Khan (1902–74?) was a direct descendant in both of the important lineages stemming from Tansen: on his mother's side, the *bīn*-playing lineage in the line from Tansen's daughter Sarasvatī, and, on his father's side, the *rabāb*-playing lineage descending from Tansen's son Bilas Khan. The most revered of all modern Hindustani musicians, Alauddin Khan (1881–1972), though not a direct descendant of Tansen, was in the discipular *paramparā,* having studied with Tansen's collateral descendant Wazir Khan (1861–1926), a court musician of Rampur.

Because Islam was the religion of the Mughal court, many Hindu musicians, Tansen's descendants among them, found it convenient to convert, and since the 17th century, Hindustani musicians have been predominantly Muslims. Persian, the language of religion, government, and culture in the Mughal Empire, contributed new musical terms and provided some equivalents for Sanskrit ones. The Sanskrit terms *guru–śiṣya,* for example, were replaced by the Persian *ustād–śāgird;* this particular change was accompanied by a change in meaning as well, since lineages of professional musicians came to look upon their traditions as private property that only disciples from the family were entitled to inherit in their complete form. In this way, the *paramparā* was viewed as a family lineage *(gharāna)* to which outsiders could be only partially admitted.

Upon the dissolution of the Mughal Empire from the late 18th century on, and particularly after Victoria was declared Empress, musicians who had been attracted to the court at Delhi began to disperse to other centers of patronage, and the place names of these centers were sometimes associated with the *gharānas* arising in them. The *gharānadār* musicians, mostly singers of *khyāl* and *dhrupad,* were the elite of the Hindustani musical world not only because they controlled specialized knowledge but also because they were socially superior to the Mirasi and Kathak families of professional musicians who specialized in accompaniment, particularly of dancing girls.

The social distinction between musicians who are basically vocal soloists and those who are connected with accompaniment for dance is evident in Carnatic musical life as well. The Brahmin singer-saint Tyāgarāja (1767–1847) is revered by all Carnatic musicians, many of whom are his discipular descendants and are also Brahmins. Tyāgarāja was not from a family of professional musicians, and his musical career was a by-product of his life as a devotee of the god Rama; many of his disciples were devotees, too, rather than musicians, but Tyāgarāja's compositions, along with those of two of his contemporaries, Śyāma Śāstri (1762–1827) and Muttusvāmi Dīkṣitar (1775–1835), eventually became the foundation of the modern Carnatic concert repertory.

The increasing number of professional musicians and dancers from the Brahmin caste and the middle classes in the last few generations has created occasional tension with traditional professionals from lower castes, particularly during periods of anti-Brahmin agitation. There has, however, always been mutual recognition and exchange between the caste groups, as is illustrated, for example, by the career of Veena Dhanam (1867–1938). Born in a family that provided dancers to the Tanjore court, she became a disciple of Śyāma Śāstri's son, learning an instrument and a repertory outside the dance tradition. Her artistry and recognition were such that the name of her chosen instrument, *vīṇā,* became an epithet to precede her given name. When her daughter Jayammal determined to revive the dance tradition in the family by having her own daughter Balasaraswati (1920–84) trained by a traditional dancing master, Jayammal was criticized. By this time, however, interest in the performing arts was arising among the urban intelligentsia, who were to create a new class of patrons and a new respectability for all the performing arts.

The course followed by Veena Dhanam's family

from the Tanjore court to the Madras concert stage is that of Carnatic music itself, since the basis for the contemporary repertory and style took shape in Tanjore from the 17th to the 19th century, and the music now finds its main source of patronage among the urban elite, particularly of Madras. The Tanjore court, though some 200 miles south of Madras in Tamilnadu, was originally ruled by viceroys of the Telugu Vijayanagar Empire (1336–1565); even when it was later taken over by Marathi adventurers in the 17th century and many aspects of Marathi culture were maintained among nobles, Telugu remained the important language for music. This fact explains why even today, when Madras is the center of Carnatic musical life, Telugu retains its significance for Carnatic music.

III. *Rāga.* 1. Scalar bases. In contemporary practice, the tonal material from which heptatonic scales *(saptak)* and their associated modes *(rāga)* are derived is a 12-tone octave species. Considerable ingenuity is exercised by theorists of Hindustani music who attempt to accommodate the 22 *śruti*s of Bharata's tuning system to the 12 tones, and many Hindustani musicians demonstrate 22-interval octaves on their instruments. Both feats are meant to validate the claim that *rāga*s are diagnostically characterized by microtonally different placement of scale degrees, but this claim has been empirically demonstrated to be questionable in Hindustani music (Jairazbhoy and Stone, 1963).

Since the Carnatic system of scales *(mela)* makes considerable use of enharmonics, the question of modally diagnostic microtones is less apt to arise in connection with it. In both systems a complete scale consists of seven degrees *(svara)* having the following names in ascending order: *ṣaḍja, ṛṣabha, gāndhāra, madhyama, pañcama, dhaivata, niṣāda.* When solfège *(sargam)* is sung, these names are abbreviated to *sa, ri* [Car.] or *re* [Hin.], *ga, ma, pa, dha, ni.* Of these pitches, the first and fifth are unalterable, while the remainder may be changed in particular ways [see Table 1].

To be noted in Table 1 are the possibilities in the Carnatic scale for enharmonic overlaps between the second and third, and the sixth and seventh degrees; in the Hindustani scale there are no such possibilities, and two versions only are allowed of any alterable degree. Since only two versions of a degree are available, the term *śuddha* (pure) is often dispensed with, and degrees are called either *komal* (soft) or *tīvra* (acute). Confusion arises, however, when English terms for accidentals are equated with Hindustani, i.e., when *komal, śuddha,* and *tīvra* are translated as flat, natural, and sharp. Thus, when it is said of *rāga kalyāṇ* that all the notes are sharped (translation of *tīvra*), what is meant is that all degrees are in their higher positions, i.e., the second, third, sixth, and seventh are *natural,* while the fourth is sharped. Conversely, when *rāga bhairavī* is said to have all notes flatted (translation of *komal*), the fourth is, in fact, natural.

Table 1. Carnatic and Hindustani *svaras*

	Carnatic	
kākalī ni, B♮		
kaiśikī ni, B♭		A♯, ṣaṭśruti dha
śuddha ni, B♭♭		A♮, catuśśruti dha
		A♭, śuddha dha
		G, pañcama
		F♯, prati ma
		F♮, śuddha ma
		E♮, antarā ga
ṣaṭśruti ri, D♯		E♭, sādhāraṇa ga
catuśśruti ri, D♮		E♭♭, śuddha ga
śuddha ri, D♭		
ṣaḍja, C		
	Hindustani	
B, śuddha ni		F, śuddha ma
B♭, komal ni		E, śuddha ga
A, śuddha dha		E♭, komal ga
A♭, komal dha		D, śuddha re
G, pañcama		D♭, komal re
F♯, tīvra ma		C, ṣaḍja

2. Carnatic *mela.* The 72 *mela*s first outlined in *Caturḍaṇḍi prakāśika* are divided into antecedent and consequent groups (*pūrvāṅga* and *uttarāṅga*) according to whether the lower tetrachord has the natural fourth degree or the sharped. Each *aṅga* has six cycles *(cakra)* in each of which the lower tetrachord (also called *pūrvāṅga*) remains unaltered while the upper *(uttarāṅga)* is put through the six possible permutations [Table 2]. When each of the six permutations of the lower tetrachord has been combined with the six of the upper tetrachord, the 36 *mela*s of the *pūrvāṅga* are complete, and the process is repeated with the sharped fourth degree substituted for the natural in order to complete the *uttarāṅga* of 36 *mela*s.

Table 2. First *cakra*

				G	A♭	B♭♭	C
				G	A♭	B♭	C
C	D♭	E♭♭	F	G	A♭	B♮	C
				G	A♮	B♭	C
				G	A♮	B♮	C
				G	A♯	B♮	C

Since the time of this system's devising, when *rāga*s were found in only 19 *mela*s, additional *rāga*s have been created for all the *mela*s.

3. Hindustani *thāṭ.* The ten *thāṭ*s selected by Bhatkhande to accommodate the scales of Hindustani *rāga*s include six that are like the Western diatonic modes and four others [Table 3].

4. *Rāga.* All *thāṭ*s and some *mela*s are assigned more than one *rāga. Rāga*s using the complete scale *(sampūrṇa)* are designated parent *rāga*s [Car. *mela-rāga;* Hin. *āśray-rāg;* both, *janaka-rāga*]; those using a pentatonic *(auḍava)* or hexatonic *(ṣāḍava)* selection

Table 3. Hindustani *thāṭs*

kalyān	C	D	E	F♯	G	A	B
bilāvāl	C	D	E	F	G	A	B
khamāj	C	D	E	F	G	A	B♭
kāfī	C	D	E♭	F	G	A	B♭
āsāvarī	C	D	E♭	F	G	A♭	B♭
bhairavī	C	D♭	E♭	F	G	A♭	B♭
bhairav	C	D♭	E	F	G	A♭	B
pūrvī	C	D♭	E	F♯	G	A♭	B
mārvā	C	D♭	E	F♯	G	A	B
toḍī	C	D♭	E♭	F♯	G	A♭	B

from a scale and those requiring accidentals are designated as derivative *(janya).*

Characteristic manners of using the scales distinguish the various *rāga*s from one another. A description of a *rāga* may mention such things as the number and order of pitches and whether or not the manner of ascent *(ārohaṇa)* and descent *(avarohaṇa)* is crooked *(vakra);* the predominant pitch [Car. *jīvasvara;* Hin. *vādi, amśa*]; diagnostic motives and phrases [Car. *piṭṭipu, sañcāra;* Hin. *pakaṛ, calan*]; characteristic tessitura; affective class *(rasa);* and suitable season or time of day for performance.

A certain number of *rāga*s are common to both Hindustani and Carnatic music; *kalyāṇ* (C D E F♯ G A B) is one such case that is recognizably the same performed in either style. Other *rāga*s that sound similar occur under different names; Hindustani *mālkoś* (C E♭ F A♭ B♭), for example, is equivalent to Carnatic *hindolam.* And finally, some names are shared, but they indicate different *rāga*s; as an illustration, the scalar material of Carnatic *toḍī* (C D♭ E♭ F G A♭ B♭) may be contrasted with that of the Hindustani *toḍī* (C D♭ E♭ F♯ G A♭ B). Despite this difference in scales, however, some modal features are common to both *toḍī*s. On the other hand, although Hindustani *bhairavī* shares its scale with Carnatic *toḍī,* there is a great difference in the modal characteristics of these two *rāga*s, and it is emphasized by different performance traditions. A characteristic element of Carnatic *toḍī,* for example, is the ornament *(gamaka)* with which the third degree is invariably performed. The most common rendering of this pitch is with *kampita,* a kind of tremolo or wide vibrato [Ex.]. The apparent ambiguity of the intended degree when performed with *kampita*

is never encountered in Hindustani performance, where even the broadest ornament stays within the outer limits of the degree. In *rāg darbāri,* for example, *andolan,* a slow, wide vibrato, is required for the proper rendition of the third degree, but, unlike the *ga* of Carnatic *toḍī,* it does not trespass upon the fourth or second degree. The peculiar microtonal inflections occurring in the performance of this type of ornament have given rise to the generalized use of the term *śruti* (microtonal interval) to mean ornament in Hindustani theory while *gamaka,* strictly speaking a particular kind of ornament, has been similarly generalized in Carnatic terminology.

IV. *Tāla.* The word *tāla* signifies beating or striking together and suggests the handclapping or striking together of small cymbals with which musical time is often measured in South Asia. No regularly recurring pattern of accents is implied by the beating of a *tāla.* Instead, the beats are arranged in an abstract hierarchy according to whether they are indicated with a clap, a wave, or a finger count.

1. Carnatic system. The basis of *tāla* in modern Carnatic music is the group of seven *sūlādī tāla*s. These consist of cyclic measures *(āvartana)* made up of three types of units *(aṅga),* which are written with the symbols | *(laghu),* O *(drutam),* and U *(anudrutam).* The last two are fixed units of two beats *(akṣara)* and one beat, respectively. *Drutam* is indicated with a clap *(taṭṭu, ghāṭa)* and a wave *(vīccu, visarjitam); anudrutam* is shown with a clap only. *Laghu,* indicated with a clap and successive finger counts, is a unit whose varieties *(jāti)* are based upon the number of *akṣara*s it contains; this number is chosen from a standard progression: 3 *(tiśra),* 4 *(caturaśra),* 5 *(khaṇḍa),* 7 *(miśra),* and 9 *(sankīrṇa).* The arrangements of aṅgas for the seven *tāla*s are given in Table 4. All *laghu*s in a *tāla* are of the same *jāti;* the subscripts in Table 4 indicate the number of *akṣara*s in the *laghu*s of what are considered the basic forms of the particular *tāla*s. *Caturaśra jāti tripuṭa tāla* ($|_4$ O O) is commonly called *ādī* (primary) *tāla* and is the most widely used.

Table 4. *Sūlādī tāla*s

dhruva	$\vert_4$	O	$\vert_4$	$\vert_4$	jhampā	$\vert_7$	U	O	
mathya	$\vert_4$	O	$\vert_4$		tripuṭa	$\vert_3$	O	O	
rūpaka	O	$\vert_4$			āṭa	$\vert_5$	$\vert_5$	O	O
				eka $\vert_4$					

Each beat of a *tāla* is divided in two ways: the first division *(kala)* is unitary, duple, or quadruple; the second *(gati)* is based on the pulse, of which 3, 4, 5, 7, or 9 make up each *kala* of a beat.

Supplementing the *sūlādī tāla*s is a group of four *cāpu tāla*s, which are generally performed in quick tempo. Each is divided into two parts, the second being a beat longer than the first [Table 5]. The name *cāpu* used alone means the *miśra* version; it and *khaṇḍa cāpu* are the commonest varieties.

2. Hindustani system. The cyclic measures *(āvard)*

Table 5. *Cāpu tāla*s

tiśra cāpu	1 + 2	miśra cāpu	3 + 4
khaṇḍa cāpu	2 + 3	sankīrṇa cāpu	4 + 5

of Hindustani *tāla* consist of divisions *(vibhāg)* having a number of beats *(mātrā)*. The *vibhāg*s are classed as struck *(tālī)* or void *(khālī),* depending on whether they commence with a clap or a wave, and the *mātrā*s are counted on finger joints beginning at the base of the little finger.

There is no conventional system of *tāla*s in Hindustani music like the *sūlādī tāla*s. There is, however, a conventional rhythmic pattern *(ṭhekā)* associated with each *tāla.* The *ṭhekā* may be spoken using meaningless syllables *(bol)* as well as played on drums; similar syllables *(śolkaṭṭu)* are used for speaking rhythmic patterns in Carnatic music, but not for constructing fixed *ṭhekā*s. Table 6 lists some of the *ṭhekā*s for common *tāla*s, with each *mātrā* written as a single word. Most of these *tāla*s are associated primarily with a certain genre: *tīntāl* is the main *tāla* for instrumental *gat*s; *ektāl* for *khyāl; cautāl* for *dhrupad; dhamār* for *hori-dhamār; dādrā, kaharvā,* and *dīpcandī* for *ṭhumrī* and other light classical forms.

There is no direct correlation between the spoken syllables and the drum strokes in *ṭhekā,* but a significant correlation can be observed between syllables beginning with unaspirated dentals or retroflexes (*din, tā, ṭa, tin, nā,* etc.) or unvoiced gutturals *(ka, ki, kat)* and damping the bass resonance; and in some *tāla*s, this correlation extends to a connection with *khālī vibhāg*s.

V. *Performing practice and forms.* The basic South Asian ensemble consists of a melodic soloist supported by a drone and accompanied by a drummer. In Carnatic ensembles, secondary percussion is often included, and except in the case of Hindustani instrumental soloists, melodic accompaniment is normally provided.

Table 6. *Ṭheka*s

tīntāl:	$^{+}$dhā dhin dhin dhā / ^{2}dhā dhin dhin dhā
	^{0}dhạ tin tin tā / ^{3}tā dhin dhin dhā
ektāl:	$^{+}$dhīn dhīn / ^{0}dhāge tirakiṭa / ^{2}tū nā
	^{0}kat tā / ^{3}dhāge tirakiṭa / ^{4}dhī nā
cautāl:	$^{+}$dhā dhā / ^{0}dhīn tā / ^{2}kiṭa dhā / ^{0}dhīn tā
	^{3}tiṭa kata / ^{4}gadi gina
dhamār:	$^{+}$ka dhi ṭa dhi ṭa / ^{2}dhā-
	^{0}ga ti ṭa / ^{3}ti ṭa tā-
jhūmrā:	$^{+}$dhin dhā tirakiṭa / ^{2}dhin dhin dhāge tirkiṭa
	^{0}tin tā tirakiṭa / ^{3}dhin dhin dhāge tirakiṭa
rūpak:	^{0}tin - traka / ^{2}dhin - / ^{2}dhā ge
jhaptāl:	$^{+}$dhī nā / ^{2}dhī dhī nā / ^{0}tī nā / ^{3}dhī dhī nā
dādrā:	$^{+}$dhā dhī nā / ^{0}dhā tū nā
kaharvā:	$^{+}$dhā ge nā tī / ^{0}nā ka dhin -
dīpcandi:	$^{+}$dhā dhīn - / ^{2}dhā dhā dhīn -
	^{0}tā tīn - / ^{3}dhā dhā dhīn -

\+ indicates *sam,* the first *mātrā,* except in *rūpak,* which begins with a *khālī vibhāg.*
0 indicates a *khālī vibhāg.* Arabic numbers indicate *tāli vibhāg*s other than *sam.*

Both improvisation and the rendition of precomposed pieces play important roles in South Asian musical performances, but there is greater emphasis on the latter in the Carnatic style than in the Hindustani. Further, in the Carnatic style there is no distinction between vocal and instrumental concert repertories, and composed vocal *kriti*s form the mainstay of any Carnatic recital, whether sung or played on an instrument. Many of the *kriti*s are rendered with no improvisation.

In the Hindustani style, where there is some independence of the instrumental practice from the vocal, both practices nevertheless follow similar principles. These require considerable improvisation in every performance, since composed material is used only incidentally.

1. Carnatic improvisation. *Rāga ālāpana,* improvisation that may precede performance of a composition, is a free exploration of the *rāga* without meter. Performance of *ālāpana* generally follows a structural pattern based upon a gradual increase of ambitus. The overall tempo is moderately slow, although ornamentation is dense; occasional fast passages of virtuosic fioriture *(bṛikka)* interrupt the otherwise sedate flow of *ālāpana. Tānam* may follow *ālāpana,* which it more or less repeats in structural terms with the addition of pulsed rhythm. In *tānam,* groups of pulsed phrases are separated from one another by momentary returns to the free rhythmic style of *ālāpana.*

In the course of metered compositions, two types of improvisation may be introduced: *niraval,* in which the text of a chosen line and its rhythmic articulation are maintained while the pitch content is altered, and *svarakalpana,* the singing of solfège over increasingly greater spans of time and with proportionally graduated increase in rhythmic density. Both types of improvisation are sectioned by periodic returns to a portion of the composed line into which the improvisation has been inserted. The beginning *(graha, eṭuppu)* of such a line must be artfully caught with extreme precision as regards its placement within the *tāla.* To increase the sense of expectation for the catching of the *eṭuppu,* some improvisations are ended with a thrice-repeated pattern *(mōrā)* calculated to end precisely before the *eṭuppu.* At the end of extended passages of *svarakalpana,* longer, formulaically conceived rhythmic patterns *(kōrvāi, kōrappu)* are used. These are usually worked out beforehand or are familiar enough to allow all accompanists to join with the soloist. When artfully conceived and skillfully executed, they create tension that the return of *eṭuppu* releases—to the appreciative exclamations of the connoisseurs.

2. The Carnatic recital *(kacceri).* The typical Carnatic recital may be considered to have four parts, classed according to the types of pieces performed in each or by the style of rendition. (1) To begin with, an

etudelike *tāna vārṇam* is performed, a piece selected from a relatively small number and therefore familiar. It is usually performed in a straightforward manner as a kind of warming up, but it may be elaborated with augmentation and diminution of some of its sections. (2) Next, simple *kriti*s are performed with little or no improvisation. (3) At this stage, more complex *kriti*s are introduced, and these are preceded by *rāgam (ālāpana)* and *tānam* and elaborated with *niraval* and *svarakalpana;* alternatively, *rāgam-tānam-pallavi,* a largely improvised form, may be sung or played with augmentation and diminution of the *pallavi* theme as well as *niraval* and *svarakalpana.* (4) To conclude a recital, the soloist normally chooses a number of short lyrical pieces from the repertory of dance music *(padam, jāvali),* a fast-tempo *tillanam* emphasizing rhythmic excitement, and or *maṅgalam* or *ślokam,* Sanskrit devotional verses contemplatively rendered in free melody often employing a series of *rāga*s *(rāgamālika).* The effect of this arrangement is to build toward the difficult pieces requiring much improvisation and then to relax after their accomplishment.

3. Carnatic forms. Most types of Carnatic compositions are divided into three sections, *pallavi, anupallavi,* and *caraṇam,* most of whose lines, including variations *(saṅgati),* are repeated. The very opening of the *pallavi* is repeated after the completion of the *pallavi* section, and this rounding is maintained when the *pallavi* or one of its *saṅgati*s is repeated after the *anupallavi* and the *caraṇam.* In many compositions, the latter part of the *caraṇam* has the same music as the *anupallavi.* Exceptions to these general comments are *vārṇam*s, both concert type *(tāna)* and dance type *(pada, cauka),* in which the *pallavi* is not repeated at the end of the *caraṇam,* since the *caraṇam* itself is repeated after each in a series of solfège passages *(ettugaḍa svara).*

4. Hindustani improvisation. Types of Hindustani improvisation, like Carnatic ones, may be classed as with or without meter. The structure of *ālāp,* without meter, is similar to that of *ālāpana,* but the tempo, starting very broadly, increases in a series of plateaus until articulatory density precipitates the introduction of pulse for the *joṛ* (instrumental) or *nom-tom* (vocal), during which tempo and rhythmic density continue to increase. Once pulse has been introduced, it is more consistently maintained than in *tānam,* and throughout both *ālāp* and *joṛ/nom-tom,* a pulsed cadential formula *(moharā)* is used to conclude sections *(sam dikhānā).* In instrumental music, another type of pulsed improvisation may follow *joṛ,* namely *jhālā.* The articulatory density achieved at the end of *joṛ* is usually maintained at the beginning of *jhālā* while the tempo is halved, and there is a sudden increase in the use of drone strings *(cikāri),* or of repeated tonguing, for rhythmic patterning. This section concludes in a virtuosic frenzy. After a pause, the metered composition is begun in slow or moderate tempo (*vilambit* or *madhya lay*), and this again gradually increases to a fast tempo *(drut lay).*

Preceding the performance of *khyāl,* the most important genre of contemporary Hindustani vocal music, *ālāp* without meter is very abbreviated *(āocār ālāp)* in the styles of most *gharāna*s. A fuller *ālāp* is often sung within the *khyāl* composition *(bandiś, ciz)* using the words of the text *(bol ālāp)* or an open vowel *(akār ālāp).* As these types of *ālāp* are accompanied by *ṭheka* performed on *tablā,* there is a tantalizing disparity between their extreme rubato and the mechanical orderliness of the *ṭhekā.* Although the melody goes on seemingly unrelated to the meter, occasionally there is a momentary coincidence of drum pulse and vocal articulation. This coincidence is particularly marked at *sam* and is signaled by the singer's catching a small phrase of the composition *(mukhṛā)* that effectively cadences on that beat. The use of *mukhṛā* in this way is similar to that of *moharā* in unmetered *ālāp,* and it continues to be so used when the singer eventually switches to other types of improvisation. These are, principally, wide-ranging, melismatic phrases *(tān)* that may be rendered with or without text and with rubato or with a clearer relation to the pulse; syllabically articulated rhythmic phrases *(bol bāṇṭ);* and solfège *(sargam).* An alternative method to the use of *mukhṛā* for the conclusion of such passages of improvisation is the use of a thrice-repeated rhythmic pattern *(tihāi)* ending on *sam* or just before *mukhṛā.*

In metered instrumental performance, improvisation follows the same pattern as *ālāp-joṛ-jhālā* except that it is bound by meter. Some performers use extreme rubato, similar to that of vocal style *(gāyakī aṅg)* in the *ālāp* section, generally called *vistār* (unfolding) in instrumental style. The *mukhṛā* section of the instrumental composition *(gat)* and *tihāi* are used for concluding sections of improvisation *(toṛā),* which may end at *sam,* or when *tihāi* is used, just before the *mukhṛā.* When the soloist stops improvising for a time and continues repeating the *gat,* it assumes the timekeeping function of the *ṭhekā.* During this time, the *tablā* player is free to play intricate rhythmic compositions and to improvise.

Toward the end of *jhālā,* there may be quick alternation of improvised rhythmic passages between soloist and drummer (*savāl-javāb,* question-answer, alternation); this technique is derived from the Carnatic *korappu* and has been popularized in Hindustani music by Ravi Shankar. When the drummer tries to anticipate the soloist's rhythmic patterns (*tār paran,* instrumental; *bol bāṇṭ,* vocal) in order to play them simultaneously, the practice is called *sāth saṅgat;* it is now considered somewhat learned and archaic.

Bol bāṇṭ and *sāth saṅgat* are basic in the performance of *dhrupad,* the oldest South Asian repertory and performance style; the fact that the drum accompaniment (on *pakhāvaj*) is less bound to keeping a *ṭhekā* may account for the emphasis on metrically bound improvisation in the performance of *dhrupad* compositions. The elaboration of *dhrupad*s often involves augmentation and diminution in a manner similar to that used in *pallavi;* this fact and the relative insignificance of *ṭhekā* make *dhrupad* the Hindustani genre closest in style to Carnatic music.

5. The Hindustani recital *(jalsā).* Unlike Carnatic *kacceri,* which follow a similar plan whether vocal or instrumental, the Hindustani *jalsā* is devoted primarily to the single genre specialized in by the soloist: *dhrupad, khyāl,* or *gat-toṛā.* Each of these is normally followed by lighter genres: respectively, *hori-dhamār, ṭhumrī* or *bhajan,* and *ṭhumrī* or *dhun.* Commonly, several artists perform in succession in order to create greater variety in a recital.

6. Hindustani forms. Most Hindustani compositions *(bandiś)* are divided into two sections, *sthāyī* and *antarā,* which are differentiated, respectively, by their lower and higher tessituras. In addition to these, most *dhrupad*s have two other sections, *sañcārī* and *ābhog,* which are rarely performed. In performances of *khyāl* and *gat-toṛā,* the usual procedure is to begin with a composition in slow tempo *(vilambit lay)* and later to change to another, normally in the same *rāga,* in fast tempo *(drut lay);* occasionally, a third composition in medium tempo *(madhya lay)* is interposed between them.

Slow and fast vocal compositions are called *baṛā* (large) and *choṭā* (small) *khyāl;* instrumental ones are called, respectively, *masītkhānī* (in the style of Masit Khan) and *razākhānī* (in the style of Raza Khan) *gat. Masītkhānī gat*s in *tīntāl* follow a fixed rhythmic pattern that evenly divides in two; the first part *(mukhṛā)* begins on beat 12 and cadences on *sam* with a two-beat extension, and the second part repeats the pattern, with different pitch content, from beat 4 through beat 11. *Gat*s in other *tāla*s and *razākhānī gat*s do not have such fixed patterns.

Often, in the performance of slow compositions, the *antarā* is omitted, and in slow *khyāl,* when the *antarā* is sung, its entrance may be delayed until the *ālāp* has been brought to the appropriate tessitura. *Tarānā,* a type of briskly rhythmic composition employing frequently repeated nonsense syllables, is sometimes substituted for *choṭā khyāl.*

VI. *Instruments.* 1. Drones. The foundation of South Asian ensembles is normally an instrumental drone, the *tamburā,* a long-necked lute with a broad bridge that slants toward the neck *(javarī).* Between the bridge and the strings, threads are placed that create the peculiar timbre and long life of the instrument's sound. There are four to six strings tuned to tonic and fifth degrees; in the Hindustani version, besides this tuning, a number of others are used to accommodate the scales of various *rāga*s. Drones are also produced on *śruti-peṭṭi,* a kind of keyboardless harmonium, and on double-reed instruments through the use of circular breathing.

2. Melody-producing instruments. Plucked, fretted, long-necked lutes—the Hindustani *sitār* and Carnatic *vīṇā*—hold pride of place among South Asian concert instruments. Both these instruments have necks that are broad as well as long, allowing for the deflection of strings to produce the portamento effects and legato ornaments characteristic of Indian melody. The *vīṇā* has four strings for melody tuned in the relationship c′ g c G, of which the chanterelle *(sāraṇī)* is most used; there are also three strings for a drone, tuned c″ g′ c′, and these are struck to indicate the clapped beats of the *tāla* and to aid in creating the rhythmic patterns of *tānam.*

While the stringing and tuning of the *sitār* are, to a degree, a matter of individual taste, all tunings have the chanterelle *(bāj tār),* by far the most played, at the natural fourth degree (about f♯). Most often the other one to three strings for melody are tuned to tonic and fifth in the lower octaves. Three strings for a drone *(cikāri)* are tuned to the second octave and the twelfth above the tonic in the strings for melody *(joṛi).* In addition to these strings, there are about a dozen sympathetic strings *(taṛap)* whose tuning depends on the scale of the *rāga* being played. The bridge of the *sitār* is similar to that of the *tamburā* and produces a similar timbre but without the use of threads. Both *vīṇā* and *sitār* are played with wire plectrums called, respectively, *nakhi* and *mizrāb.* The frets of the *vīṇā* are fixed and panchromatic, while those of the *sitār* are movable.

The Hindustani *bīn,* used for instrumental performance of *dhrupad,* is a stick zither having traditionally fixed, panchromatic frets; some now have movable frets like those of the *sitār.* Its four strings for melody are tuned in the relationship f c G C; there are three strings for a drone tuned to octaves of the tonic.

The most important fretless stringed instrument of South Asia is the Hindustani *sarod.* A rival to the *sitār* in the performance of *gat-toṛā,* though somewhat less popular, the *sarod* has an extremely deep and broad neck that is carved from the same block of wood as the sound box; it is covered with sheet metal, and the steel and bronze strings are stopped against it with the tips of the fingernails. The four (sometimes five) strings for melody are tuned in the relationship f′ c′ g c (G), and there are three drone strings (c″ c″ c′) and more than a dozen sympathetic strings. The sound box is covered with a membrane that is often struck with a plectrum (*javā,* a thick, triangular piece of coconut shell) during performance of emphatic rhythmic patterns. This technique is inherited from that of the Seniya *rabāb,* an instrument now virtually extinct through which, with the *bīn,* the instrumental tradition of Tansen's lineage has descended. The *sarod* itself, however, is descended from the Afghani *rabāb.* Established about 200 years ago in the Hindustani Great Tradition by the forebears of Amjad Ali Khan, a prominent contemporary *sarodīyā,* the Afghani *rabāb* continues in use in the Little Traditions of Kashmir and Afghanistan.

Bowed stringed instruments are primarily accompa-

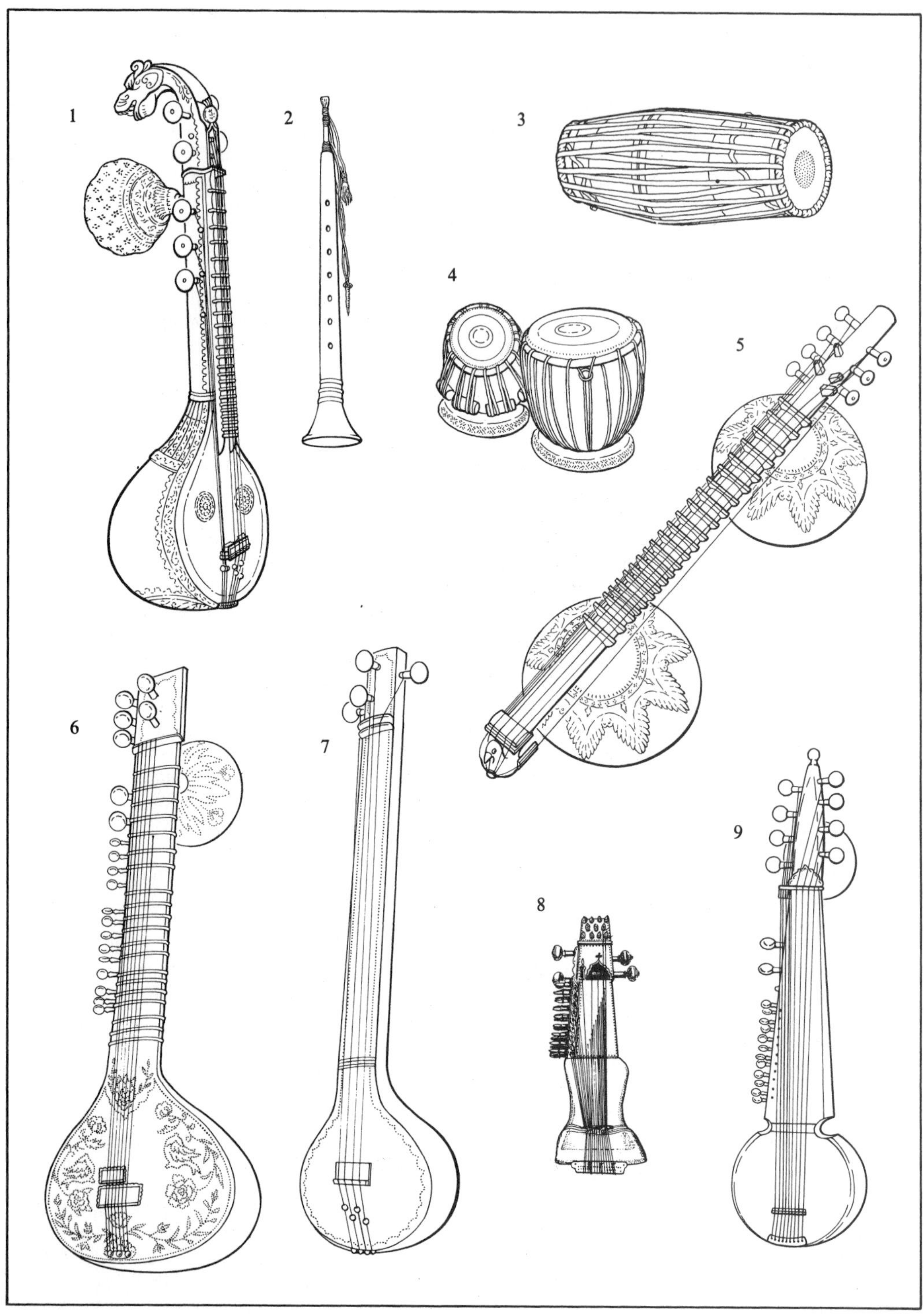

Instruments of South Asia: 1. Vīṇā. 2. Śahnāi (shown one and a half times size in relation to others). 3. Mṛdaṅgam. 4. Tablā. 5. Bīn. 6. Sitār. 7. Tamburā. 8. Sāraṅgī. 9. Sarod.

nying instruments in both Carnatic and Hindustani styles. The Western violin has become a fixture in the Carnatic ensemble in the accompanying role since it was first introduced about 1800. Its metal strings are tuned alternately to *sa* and *pa,* and it is played while braced between the foot and the chest of the performer, who is seated on the floor. The player's fingering hand is thus free to perform the necessary sliding movements for the portamento and ornamentation of the melody. The instrument is also used for solo performance in Carnatic music, and it is as a solo instrument that it has become established in the Hindustani style.

The indigenous bowed lute of Hindustan, the fretless *sāraṅgī,* has recently become accepted as an instrument for solo recitals, though in the past it was used mainly to accompany vocalists, particularly singers of *ṭhumrī,* and dancing girls. The inferior social status of traditional accompanists such as *sāraṅgī* players prevented them from being accepted as true carriers of *sampradāya,* a stigma that has been partly removed by the great success of the contemporary *sāraṅgī* soloist Ram Narayan. The instrument has a membrane-covered sound box, three gut strings, which are lightly stopped with the base of the fingernails, and very numerous sympathetic strings.

Double-reed instruments and transverse flutes, both keyless, have only recently come to be used for concert recitals. The double reeds have been associated with ceremonial ensembles including loud drums ever since they were introduced by the Muslim military and court establishments. The Carnatic *nāgasvaram* is part of the "great ensemble" *(periya melam)* of temples. Paradoxically, some *nāgasvaram* players are Muslims or members of castes that would ordinarily be denied admittance to the temple. In concert recitals, *nāgasvaram* players perform the standard concert repertory but are still accompanied by the same drum, *tāvil,* that is used in the *periya melam.*

The *naubat* ensemble of Hindustan is the traditional milieu for the double-reed instrument *śahnāi* and its accompanying pair of kettle drums, *naqqārā.* This ensemble played—in some places, still plays—on the masonry portals to courts, at Hindu temples, and at the tombs of Sufi saints, and a similar ensemble provides the necessary music for wedding celebrations. In concert recitals, the *śahnāi* is used to perform *gat-toṛā.*

Transverse, keyless flutes of bamboo are now used in both Carnatic and Hindustani concert recitals. The short, high-pitched Carnatic *kuzhal* is a standard instrument in the "little ensemble" *(cinna melam)* used in the accompaniment of the classical temple and court dance *sadir nāc,* now called *bharata-nāṭyam.*

The Hindustani *bāṣurī* is considerably larger and deeper in pitch than the *kuzhal.* Its establishment as a concert instrument is largely credited to the late Pannalal Ghosh. *Bāṣurī* players usually perform *khyāl* rather than *gat-toṛā.*

3. Instruments for rhythmic accompaniment. The basic drum of the Carnatic ensemble is the *mṛdaṅgam,* a wooden barrel drum with two heads struck with the hands. The higher-pitched head is tuned to the soloist's tonic (various sizes of drum are available) and has permanently affixed to it a spot of dried paste made from rice, powdered metal, and other ingredients. During performance, the drummer fixes a temporary spot of coarse wheat-flour paste to the lower-pitched head. These spots aid in producing the desired timbres.

Secondary percussion in the Carnatic ensemble is most often provided by *kañjira* (a kind of tambourine), *ghaṭam* (a large clay jug with a wide mouth), or more rarely by *morsing* (jew's harp). The latter, of course, is not a percussion instrument, but it is used for rhythmic accompaniment.

Tablā and *bāyā,* also called *dāhinā* and *ḍuggi,* are the pair of drums used in the standard Hindustani ensemble. Although these drums have a more resonant and sweeter sound than that of the *mṛdaṅgam,* the heads are somewhat similarly constructed. Both the higher-pitched *tablā* and the lower-pitched *bāyā,* however, have permanent spots of paste.

While *tablā* and *bāyā* are used to accompany *khyāl* and *gat-toṛā, pakhāvaj* is used to accompany *dhrupad* and *kathak* dance. This drum closely resembles the *mṛdaṅgam,* by which name it is also known, but its sound, unlike that of the Carnatic *mṛdaṅgam,* is booming and stately rather than crisp and dry. The impressive sound of the *pakhāvaj* is emphasized by the playing technique, which uses many open strokes.

Bibl.: Charles Russell Day, *The Music and Musical Instruments of Southern India and the Deccan* (London: Novello, 1891; R: Delhi: B R Publishing Corp, 1974). Arthur Henry Fox-Strangways, *The Music of Hindostan* (Oxford: Oxford U Pr, 1914; R: Oxford: Clarendon Pr, 1965). Bharata Muni, *Nāṭya-śāstra,* trans. Manomohan Ghosh, 2 vols. (Calcutta: Asiatic Society, 1951–61). P. Sambamoorthy, *A Dictionary of South Indian Music and Musicians* (Madras: Indian Music Publishing House, 1952–71). Nazir A. Jairazbhoy and A. W. Stone, "Intonation in Present-day North Indian Classical Music," *Bulletin of the School of Oriental and African Studies* 26 (1963): 119–32. Robert E. Brown, "The Mṛdanga: A Study in Drumming in South Indian Music" (Ph.D. diss., U.C.L.A., 1965). P. Sambamoorthy, *South Indian Music* (Madras: Indian Music Publishing House), 1 (1966), 2 (1960), 3 (1964), 4 (1963), 5 (1963), 6 (1969). Walter Kaufmann, *The Ragas of North India* (Bloomington: Indiana U Pr, 1968). Harold S. Powers, "An Historical and Comparative Approach to the Classification of Ragas (with an Appendix on Ancient Indian Tunings)," *Selected Reports* [Institute of Ethnomusicology, U.C.L.A] 1/3 (1970): 1–78. Nazir A. Jairazbhoy, *The Rāgs of North Indian Music: Their Structure and Evolution* (Middletown, Conn.: Wesleyan U Pr, 1971). Milton Singer, *When a Great Tradition Modernizes* (New York: Praeger, 1972). Bonnie Wade, "Chīz in Khyāl: The Traditional Composition in the Improvised Performance," *Ethno* 17/3 (1973): 443–59. Rebecca Stewart, "The Tablā in Perspective" (Ph.D. diss., U.C.L.A., 1974). T. Viswanathan, "The Analysis of Raga Alapana in South Indian Music," *AsM* 9 (1977): 13–71. Kathleen and Adrian L'Armand, "Music in Madras: The Urbanization of a Cultural Tradition," in *Eight Urban Musical*

Cultures: Tradition and Change, ed. Bruno Nettl (Urbana: U of Ill Pr, 1978), pp. 115–45. Daniel M. Neuman, *The Life of Music in North India: The Organization of an Artistic Tradition* (Detroit: Wayne St U Pr, 1979). Harold S. Powers, "India," I–II, *Grove 6,* 9:69–141. Bonnie C. Wade, *Khyal: Creativity within North India's Classical Music* (Cambridge: Cambridge U Pr, 1984). James Kippen, *The Tabla of Lucknow: A Cultural Analysis of a Musical Tradition,* Cambridge Studies in Ethnomusicology (Cambridge: Cambridge U Pr, 1988). Lewis Eugene Rowell, *Music and Musical Thought in Early India,* Chicago Studies in Ethnomusicology (Chicago: U of Chicago Pr, 1992). Peter Manuel, *Cassette Culture: Popular Music and Technology in North India,* Chicago Studies in Ethnomusicology (Chicago: U of Chicago Pr, 1993). Allyn Miner, *Sitar and Sarod in the 18th and 19th Centuries* (Wilhelmshaven: F Noetzel, 1993). Gerry Farrell, *Indian Music and the West* (New York: Oxford U Pr, 1997). Bonnie C. Wade, *Imaging Sound: An Ethnomusicological Study of Music, Art, and Culture in Mughal India,* Chicago Studies in Ethnomusicology (Chicago: U of Chicago Pr, 1998). Alison Arnold, ed., *South Asia: The Indian Subcontinent,* vol. 5 of *The Garland Encyclopedia of World Music* (New York: Garland, 2000). Martin Clayton, *Time in Indian Music: Rhythm, Metre, and Form in North Indian Rāg Performance,* Oxford Monographs on Music (Oxford: Oxford U Pr, 2000). C.C.

Southeast Asia. A geographic region south of *East Asia and east of *South Asia, situated between 30° north and 10° south latitude, consisting of 1.7 million square miles of land and more than twice that amount of seas. This area encompasses present-day Burma, Thailand, Laos, Cambodia (Kampuchea), Vietnam, Singapore, Malaysia, Brunei, Indonesia, and the Philippines.

I. *Historical and cultural background.* Until the mid-20th century, Southeast Asians lived in diverse societies, in rural, village, or urban-court environments. Most societies were closely related in some aspects of musical culture to their immediate neighbors; some were linked to more distant Southeast Asian societies or to other Asian, African, Middle Eastern, or European peoples, resulting in a complex dynamic of intra- and interregional social relationships. The diversity of many urban-court and some village environments meant that, even as early as the 10th century C.E., in several regions of Southeast Asia, groups of people with different cultures, but speaking the same language, lived in what can be called the same society. Cross-fertilization of musical traditions has been one result of these diverse social forces. Some understanding of the history of the complex interactions of these many different cultures is necessary in order to appreciate the many types of music that have developed in Southeast Asia and to avoid making premature judgments about the relative value of any one type.

The land and people can be studied in various groupings, the most useful for musicological purposes being ethnolinguistic. This division is perhaps most profitable when musical practices are tied to language—as in song and dramatic presentations. It is also useful in a discussion of instrumental ensembles, some of which, such as the *beepat (piphat)* of mainland Southeast Asia, have spread among the elite-court class of the Siamese Tai society, in part as an index of social standing. The same is true of particular *gamelan* ensembles (Munggang or Sekaten) in Javanese elite-court classes. There, ethnolinguistic similarities reflect historical developments—times when certain ethnic groups (Siamese Tai or Javanese) and their languages were dominant in a region and influenced the survival of musical practices associated with their activities.

Until the development of large 20th-century urban centers, density of settlement in Southeast Asia usually depended on soil fertility, the possibility of irrigation, and easy access to the sea and trade winds. Court centers arose with relatively dense population. In the past, the population of Southeast Asia was fairly small—an estimated 80 million as late as the beginning of the 19th century—but concentrations of population occurred in many of the same areas as today. The peoples of the economic and political centers of some of these areas were in documented contact with one another and with other parts of the world by at least the 5th century C.E. and probably long before.

The mountains, plateaus, and hills of the mainland and the islands were often places of refuge and retreat for groups out of favor in lowland societies, or for vanquished lowland groups. Sometimes these areas were also alternative centers of authority to those of the lowland societies. For many of the ethnic groups of Indonesia, Vietnam, Cambodia, and Thailand, the mountains and hills were sacred centers. Mining for copper, tin, and iron, and metal work in iron or bronze, pursuits that had religious power in many Southeast Asian societies, often took place in the mountains and hills, and these areas often provided many of the valuable goods that lowland societies traded in international markets. Thus, even though relatively few and small, the upland groups had disproportionate strength and prestige up to the last century.

The major urban centers are now ethnically and linguistically heterogeneous. These populations include each of the major national ethnic groups, as well as communities of nationals who still actively trace their ancestry to other national areas of Southeast Asia or elsewhere in the world and groups of people with citizenship or ancestry outside the nation. Up to the 19th century, court centers had small populations of advisers and commercial brokers from all over the realm and sometimes small communities of foreign brokers, while coastal trading centers usually had larger foreign populations. Throughout the 19th century, European communities grew larger in most urban centers. Court cultures, including music, thrived as expressions of the richness of the realm. Sometimes a particular musical ensemble with its repertory was an offshoot of the regional rural culture, with variants unique to the court (*ma'yong* in Kelantan); sometimes it was a mixture of styles and instruments from throughout the realm (*gamelan ageng* in central Java); sometimes it was a mixture of regional practices and others foreign to the realm (*mahori* in Siamese, Lao, and Khmer courts); and sometimes it was adopted with little change from a court culture outside the region (*nobat* of Malay courts).

Developments in court cultures were usually influenced by trade, political alliances made by marriages, and tribute or gifts, including musicians and instruments. Thus, Southeast Asian music traveled in instruments and in theory and practice in the minds of traveling and donated musicians. Other carriers of traditions of music, mostly song, were Buddhist monks, devotees of Siva, Brahmanic chanters of the Veddhas, Islamic muezzins and ketibs, and Christian priests. Traveling merchants were sources of change, through the sale or barter of musical instruments from afar. In coastal trading centers, musical genres such as *gambang kromong,* and *kroncong* on the north coast of Java or *gambus* on the Malay peninsula developed. These genres show, even more clearly than the music discussed above, the influence of one or more foreign sources. Initially, music of this type was tied to aspects of culture that were tangential or marginal in the region where it was found. Often, as time passed, features of these types of music became integrated into the music of the entire region. These processes of establishment and rooting in the local cultures were accelerated by 20th-century communication technologies and by the decline of the forms and functions of earlier music in court centers and rural communities.

Early evidence of musical activities and instruments is found in the bas-reliefs on the Buddhist temple Borobudur (late 8th, early 9th century C.E.) in central Java, and on temples and "state" buildings at Angkor (11th–14th centuries C.E.) in central Cambodia. This information can be compared with references in indigenous literary sources attributable to particular periods in the Southeast Asian past and in exogenous sources: travelers' accounts, records of tribute and trade missions, and dynastic histories, from China, beginning in the first millennium C.E., and from India, the Near East, and Europe in the second millennium C.E. The resulting outline can be filled out a bit by comparative analysis with present-day cultures, mostly rural, that have maintained some of the musical instruments, forms, and practices prevalent in past eras.

Most of the musical reliefs on the Borobudur show ensembles that accompany dances in processions and on prosceniums, that accompany meditation, or that provide entertainment for presumed members of court society or an elite class. Only a few show musical activities in contexts other than religious or courtly ceremonies or diversions. The musical reliefs of Angkor have yet to be systematically investigated, but most that have been show ensembles played for processions—usually battle processions—and for gatherings of an apparently elite class or court society.

Instruments shown on the levels of the Borobudur associated with stories of the life of the Buddha are temple bells, hanging bells, goblet drums, flanged cymbals, strapped barrel drums, cylindrical drums, truncated conical drums, earthenware drums, a ten-key vertical xylophone, a single pot-gong, two- and three-string plucked lutes, bar zithers, arched harps, a single-tone trumpet, and transverse flutes. The lowest level of the Borobudur, which illustrates "life bound up in earthly desires," depicts some of the same instruments, as well as free-reed mouth organs, scraping sticks, and a slit drum. Angkor reliefs show tuned gong-chime sets on semicircular frames, large and small hanging bossed gongs, goblet cymbals, flanged cymbals, bells, strapped drums of various shapes, shawms, arched harps, bar zithers, two- and three-string plucked lutes, and two-string bowed lutes.

Gongs and gong-chimes do not appear on island temple reliefs until the 13th century (at Panataran temple), after their appearance on mainland reliefs. Yet it is on the islands that metal gong and bar/slab ensembles have achieved their most elaborate development. Drums are prominent on early island temple reliefs, and drum choirs are the most common ensembles pictured there. Although the bowed spike-fiddle plays an important role in many present-day island ensembles, bowed instruments are pictured only on mainland reliefs.

Until about the 16th century, island and coastal-mainland centers of economic and political power were linked to each other and to the rest of the world by Southeast Asian seafaring societies. The cultures that developed in them and in the supporting agrarian areas around them were dynamic and syncretistic. The economic and political powers of these societies were increasingly eclipsed and their cultural riches increasingly called into question from the 16th century on.

Since the mid-20th century, pressures of expanding population, increasing interactions of cultures and societies, cultural and social dislocation and change caused by wars and migrations, and radical changes in communication, agriculture, and manufacturing have resulted in processes known throughout the region by the foreign terms development or modernization. Of the large variety of forms of such processes, many have several aspects in common: the growth of proportionately larger urban centers than ever before existed; the development of a large gap between economic classes; the growth of centralization of economic and political power in urban centers; state ownership of communications media; the tight control of the resources of the countryside by urban elites. Yet, even now, many past patterns of diversity in settlement, social organization, and cultivation persist in each of the Southeast Asian nations. Even Singapore (238 square miles), which is mostly urban and Chinese, and Brunei, which consists of two small sections of the north coast of Borneo, still reflect older patterns of social diversity. The former has some rural agrarian population and sizable Malay and Indian minorities, while the latter has a coastal urban center with a mix of Chinese and Malay residents and a moderately large rural population of Malay and other ethnic groups who speak Austronesian languages.

Over ten million ethnic Chinese live in Southeast

Asia. They make up 75% of the population of Singapore, and there are also significant numbers in Thailand, Indonesia, the Philippines, and Malaysia. In Thailand, Indonesia, and the Philippines, as in Singapore, most Chinese live in cities and towns and are engaged in commerce. In Malaysia, a million are farmers in rural areas. The music of the ethnic Chinese of Southeast Asia has yet to be systematically investigated. Though closely related to music of East Asian peoples, it also shows assimilation from other ethnic groups in its area of origin.

This survey will concentrate on the types of music that were most widespread in earlier times, before the extensive changes of the past 50 years. The following discussion will present some of the principal older ensembles and instruments used by most of the largest ethnic groups in each nation. The focus is on material culture—musical instruments and ensembles—rather than on the functions and meanings of music.

II. *Burma* (9% of the population of Southeast Asia). Burmans, most of whom live in the broad Irrawaddy valley and down the coast to the south, constitute about 70% of the population of Burma. The central government has set aside autonomous, mostly highland, districts for several of the largest ethnic minorities. Kachin, Chin, Lisu, Lahu, and Akha (about 6% of the population) are related to Burmans in language and culture, and cultivate a highly developed vocal music, centering around community rituals and the playing of various kinds of free-reed mouth organs—*naw* (Lahu), *fu-ru* (Lisu)—and bamboo or forged-iron jaw harps—*ya-eah* (Akha). They usually accompany dance with singing or with narrow-rim, bossed gongs and a flute.

The largest ethnic minority in Burma, the Karen (11%), have been Christian for more than a century, and their music includes Christian hymns, songs in pre-Christian styles, and recent mixes between them. Many Karen households own bronze drums *(hpa-si),* regarded as signs of wealth and high status, but which can be played as musical instruments. The Karen often consider a drum's sound an important measure of its value. Other Karen musical instruments include the *t'na* (similar to the Burmese harp), the *mo* (a medium-sized gong), and the *pa:ku* (a bamboo xylophone).

Groups that speak languages in the Tai family, mainly Shan, represent 4% of the population. Shan are primarily Theravada Buddhist. They have lived in centralized, permanent communities in these areas and in northern Thailand for centuries. They have small musical ensembles similar to those of their neighbors, consisting of mouth organ *(hnyin),* flute, and bossed gong, and larger ensembles that use many Burman instruments, performance techniques, and melodies.

Mon (4%) were a strong influence on the cultural and social development of mainland peoples up to the 12th century C.E. They were assimilated or subjugated from the 10th century on by Khmer (in the east), Tai (who expanded south from the northern reaches of the Mekong river along the Mekong and Chao Phraya rivers), and Burmans (who moved closer to the sea over the centuries). Mon were responsible for the spread of Theravada Buddhism in the first millennium C.E. They were probably in close and productive alliances with Malay sea-faring peoples. Musical instruments attributed to Mon include the crocodile zither (known in different areas as *mi gyaun, jake* [*chakei*], *krapeu,* and *kacapi* or its variants), the boat-shaped xylophone *(pat-tala),* gong-chimes in a U-shaped frame *(kawng mawn),* the large strapped-barrel drum *(daphon mawn/taphon mon),* and the arched harp. Sea-faring Malay peoples probably occupied the coastal areas of the Malay peninsula and the river deltas of Burma from early times. Malay (1%) remain the main occupants of the islands off the Burmese coast. Little has been written about their music.

The most significant Burman ensemble is the *hsaing-waing,* named after one of its instruments, a circle of 21 tuned drums (*hsaing* or *pat-waing*). Its smallest version consists of *hsaing,* a circle of 21 gong-chimes *(kyi-waing),* barrel drum *(pat-ma),* cymbals *(yagwin),* goblet cymbals *(si),* and wooden clappers *(wa).* Larger versions may include additional rhythmic punctuators and melodic percussion and the double-reed shawm *(hne). Hsaing-waing* ensembles perform as adjuncts to many activities in Burman life, including Buddhist or spirit ceremonies and dramatic and dance performances throughout central and southern Burma. Other Burman ensembles have been associated with royal ceremonies or village festivals and commemorate important events or accompany processions. The *hsaing* and several other ensembles frequently accompany songs, in both dramatic and chamber-music settings. In chamber music, the Burman flute *(palwei)* and the arched harp (**saùng-gauk*) may also be employed in the ensemble or as solo instruments. Seldom played now, the arched harp has a rich history and repertory.

III. *Thailand* (10.5% of the population of Southeast Asia). Thailand can be divided into four culture regions: central, south, north, and northeast. Most people in each of the large ethnic minorities, except Lao, Mon, and Malays, live in the northern region. The musical heritage of these groups, including the Karen, Shan, and Mountain Tibeto-Burmans, is similar to that of their counterparts in Burma, with the important exception that the central government in Thailand has stimulated more exposure to 20th-century technologies, more extensive mobility of ethnic groups, and greater development of urbanized centers. Thus, mixed forms of music are more pronounced among these ethnic groups than they are in Burma.

The Siamese Tai, 55% of the population, live mostly in the central culture region. They are close in language and some aspects of culture to the Lao Tai (20%), who live primarily in the northeast and to some extent in the north. Although the lives of Siamese Tai are tied to urban centers, most still farm and live in rural areas. The Lao are basically rural village and farming people. Elaborate court musical ensembles (principally the *beepat, mahori,* and *kruang sai*) and pieces that show assimilation of court and rural music of several other Southeast Asian groups developed in Siamese courts over the past six centuries. Under the constitutional monarchy, court and elite patronage for the court arts has declined, but the central government has established schools for their study and promotion. This appears to have resulted in the development of local clubs and performance groups for these ensembles in smaller cities and towns throughout Thailand.

The principal instruments in the *kruang sai* are strings: *saw duang, saw oo,* and *jake (chakay).* Other instruments in the smallest typical ensemble are flute *(klui paing aw),* drums *(ton* and *rummanah),* and goblet cymbals *(ching). Kruang sai,* generally considered to be the oldest of the Siamese ensembles, is seldom heard now. Its past repertory included melodies said to be of Mon and Khmer origin. It performed for receptions of guests in court and high administrative households and halls and sometimes in wedding receptions.

Even at their smallest, *mahori* ensembles have many of the same instruments as *kruang sai.* Elementary ensembles include all the items listed above, plus the stringed *saw sam sai* and the melodic idiophones *ranat ek* and *kawng wong.* The styles of performance and instrumentation of this ensemble, generally recognized to be a mix of Tai and Chinese ingredients, give its repertory a decidedly East Asian cast. *Mahori* ensembles formerly performed in court households to accompany dramas with contemporary themes.

Of the three principal central Thai ensembles, *beepat (piphat)* have spread the farthest. In the past, uses of *beepat* included the accompaniment of popular Ramayana stories, *kon* masked dramas, and *like* dramas in towns and villages of central Thailand and larger towns in the north and south. The name derives from the quadruple reed shawm, *bee nai (pinai),* an indispensable part of the ensemble. Other instruments in the smallest form of this ensemble are melodic idiophones (*ranat ek* and *kawng wong yai;* larger than the corresponding members of the *mahori* ensemble), drums (*daphon* [*taphon*] and *glawng tut* [*klong that*]), and *ching.* Larger ensembles are common, with the largest employing all the same aerophones and idiophones, complemented by their lower or higher versions, a set of bronze metallophones (*ranat ek lek* and *ranat toom lek*), cymbals *(chap lek),* gong *(kawng mong),* and wood clappers *(grup sepah).* Solo instrumental traditions in central Thailand exist for the *saw duang, saw oo, saw sam sai, ranat ek, kong wong yai,* and *jake.* Central Thai shadow puppetry *(nang)* was formerly accompanied by the smallest form of *beepat,* but with *kawng wong* instead of *kawng wong yai.*

The southern culture area is the home of the *manora* stories, staged dramas accompanied by an ensemble consisting of a double-reed oboe *(bee jawa),* a pair of pegged drums *(glawng daloong),* two tuned gongs *(kawng koo),* and *ching.* The ensemble accompanying *nung daloong (nang talung),* Siamese shadow-puppet play of the south, is similar, having *bee jawa, glawng daloong,* and usually *kawng koo,* but substituting *grup sepah* for *ching.* In comparison with the central Thai, southern Thai shadow puppetry has much smaller puppets, and they are worked by one puppeteer, in the manner of Malay and Javanese *wayang kulit/wayang jawa/wayang siam.* Both the Tai and the Malay shadow plays concentrate on the Ramayana stories. Tai shadow-boxing *(klang kaek)* is accompanied by *bee jawa,* gong *(kong),* and a set of drums *(glawng kaek).* In this and in musical content, it is close to Malay and Khmer shadow-boxing.

Most ethnic Malays (4%) live in the southern culture area, near the Malaysian border. Their music shows some assimilation of Tai musical instruments and pieces, notably in the accompaniment for *wayang siam,* and possibly also in the musical ingredients of *ma'yong,* dance drama interspersed with solo song and choral heterophonic singing.

Northern Thailand displays a large variety of types of music, a result of the rich mix of ethnic groups and the cross-fertilization of musical traditions. Many sorts of song exist, most falling into the broad categories of solo or repartee song, accompanied by free-reed mouth organ *(kaen)* or small ensembles of various instruments. Songs called *mawlum* fall into several general types: dramatic or story-telling performances, spirit ceremonies, and male-female repartee. Each type has subtypes with specific musical or poetic characteristics and social contexts.

The music of the Shan (5% of Thailand's population) and Karen (less than 3%) is similar to that of the Shan and Karen of Burma. Lao (20%) of the north engage in types of *mawlum* singing and *kaen (khene, khaen)* performance similar to those of the Lao in the northeast and in Laos. The music of the northeast is mostly Lao, with *kaen* performance and *mawlum* singing as the predominant musical activities. Usually these two occur together, song accompanied by *kaen,* alternating with short *kaen* solos at breath points in lines of text. Other instruments join *kaen* in accompanying some types of *mawlum;* possibilities include *pin (sung),* a two-to-four string lute; *hoon (hun),* a bamboo jaw harp; *saw bip,* two-string fiddle; and *kaw law (bong long),* a twelve-key vertical xylophone. Khmer equivalents to one form of *mawlum* story-telling, accompanied by *kaen,* have the name *jarieng khmer.* Buddhist chant and song accompanying festivals are common throughout Thailand.

IV. *Laos* (1% of the population of Southeast Asia). The Lao Tai are the major ethnic group (64%). Little information exists on the musical culture of postwar Laos, Cambodia, and Vietnam, but probably Laos has the greatest number of remaining varieties of practices among the unassimilated ethnic minorities, the largest of which are the Miao-Yao (9%) and the Mon-Khmer

(13%). Their vocal music is well developed, and their instrumental music employs jaw harp, free-reed mouth organ *(gaeng),* and reed flutes.

The Miao-Yao are in the Sino-Tibetan ethnolinguistic family and are related to several peoples of Southern China. Most of the mountain Mon-Khmer live in the southern quarter, near to the borders with Vietnam and Cambodia, and are closely related in culture to the Mon-Khmer of those nations. The history of all major Mon-Khmer groups is closely tied to that of lowland Khmer. These groups cultivate vocal music connected with village ceremonies and several types of instrumental ensembles, notably groups of flat, rimmed gongs performing interlocking, varied melodic lines in binary rhythmic structures.

The music of the rural Lao of Laos is similar to that of the Lao of Thailand; increased communication through mass media and a higher standard of living among the Lao of Thailand has produced slightly more elaborate traditions of *mawlum* there. But in both countries, various performance styles persist in the same genres. Over the past 100 years, the Lao courts at Luang Prabang developed *beepat* and *mahori* ensembles under the direction of court musicians from Thailand. Though the performers were Lao and some of the compositions were based on Lao melodies, the ensembles never took root in Laos, and it is presumed that they are no longer played there.

V. *Cambodia (Kampuchea)* (1.5% of the population of Southeast Asia). The musical culture of the 19th- and 20th-century Khmer courts was a focus for 20th-century documentation and definition of Cambodian music, but this culture was largely derived from that of the Siamese courts, taught to Khmer court musicians in the 18th century. This represented, however, a return to the Khmer of musical practices and types of instruments that the Siamese had assimilated from the Khmer over three previous centuries.

The Khmer *pinpeat* and *mohori* ensembles closely paralleled Siamese *beepat* and *mahori* in instruments and repertory, except that the vocal sections in pieces for the *mohori* ensembles had smoother melodic flow and were more often accompanied by instruments, perhaps because the Tai are tonal languages while Khmer is not. Thus, multioctave pentatonic and hexatonic melodies can accompany poetic texts in Khmer without the constraint of locating pitches in relation to the tones of the spoken text syllables. The number of instruments in *pinpeat* and *mohori,* as in Siamese ensembles, was not fixed. Most of the Khmer instruments in these ensembles have variants of Siamese names, with the following exceptions: the Khmer equivalent of the *bee nai* is usually known as *sralay,* of *daphon* as *sampho,* and of *glawng tut* as *skor thom. Pei shenai,* a less common Khmer name for the *sralay,* reveals a connection between this double-reed shawm and the Malay and Javanese double-reed shawms called *serunai.* A similarity of names also connects the entire set of instruments to the family of Persian oboes known as *surnāy* [see *Zūrnā*] and South Asian shawms known by the name **śahnāi. Pinpeat* ensembles primarily accompanied court dances and ceremonies, shadow plays, and Ramayana dance dramas. A small version of *pinpeat,* consisting only of *sralay, roneat ek, kong thom, kong,* and *skor thom,* can accompany funerals. Since 1980, several Khmer *pinpeat* and *mohori* ensembles have been revived in the U.S. by immigrants, and in Cambodia to accompany dance in schools teaching traditional Khmer arts.

The large Mon-Khmer minority in Cambodia, significantly different from lowland Khmer of towns and urban-oriented rural agriculture, has much smaller musical ensembles and music that is closely related to rural life and religious or agricultural rituals. More common than the *pinpeat* and *mohori* in Cambodian villages are *arak (phleng Khmer)* ensembles. Basic instruments for *arak* are frame drums *(skor arak),* flute *(khloy),* long-neck lute *(chapei),* and three-string spike fiddle *(tro Khmer).* An ensemble of these instruments might play for spirit ceremonies. *Arak* ensembles that add lap fiddles (*tro u* and *tro i*) and substitute quadruple-reed shawm *(pey)* for flute accompany weddings. Another sort of ensemble, the *chhayam,* consists of a set of drums *(skor klawng kaek),* hanging bossed gongs *(kong chhayam),* and *sralay;* it formerly played at Buddhist ceremonies and today accompanies Cambodian martial arts.

While the mountain Mon-Khmer probably retain many characteristics of early Cambodian peoples, another minority, the Cham (an Austronesian ethnic group), has a musical culture similar to some Malay and other Austronesian ones. Both the Cham and Mon-Khmer minorities are closely linked in culture to ethnic minorities in the central and southern highlands of Vietnam. Mon-Khmer groups in rural areas in both nations have traditions of play on iron jaw harp (*angkouch* in central Cambodia), free-reed horn *(sneng),* and leaf *(slek).* They also employ flat-rimmed gongs in interlocking patterns for village rituals, as do Mon-Khmer of Laos. Cham use bossed gongs *(kong)* in ensembles with oboe *(shanai)* and drums *(ganang)* for spirit ceremonies and buffalo sacrifice rituals. Solo instrumental traditions among the Khmer and Mon-Khmer of Cambodia exist for *chapei, tro khmer,* and the bar zither *(khse diev).*

VI. *Vietnam* (14.5% of the population of Southeast Asia). The ethnic majority in Vietnam is Vietnamese (83%). From at least the 10th century C.E. to the 18th, contact with the Austronesian Cham, the Austroasiatic Mon-Khmer, and the Tai allowed their music to influence Vietnamese music through the introduction of the barrel drum *(trong com),* the hourglass drum *(phong yeu co),* and several pentatonic modes. The instrumentation and formal characteristics of repertory in musical ensembles from all of the four basic categories of Vietnamese ensembles, theater, court, chamber, and ceremonial, closely parallel Chinese ensembles used for similar purposes. Most of this music is no longer played, although some is being revived in government schools and institutes in order to maintain Vietnamese traditions.

Vietnamese musical genres developed in the last century have assimilated Western instruments and formal ingredients, including equal-tempered tuning. Orchestras combining Western and Vietnamese instruments have performed settings of Vietnamese and ethnic minority melodies and newly composed pieces of international style. This type of music remains of interest primarily to Vietnamese in urban areas.

The music of the upland Tai (4% of Vietnam's population) and Miao-Yao (2%), mostly in northern Vietnam, and the Cham (2%) and Mon-Khmer (3%), mostly in southern and central Vietnam, is similar to the music of these groups elsewhere in Southeast Asia. The Mon-Khmer of Vietnam play on vertical xylophones (*to rung* among one Mon-Khmer group), and flat, rimmed gongs, the latter in ensembles of up to 13 gongs, carried in processions and struck with the hand or with mallets. Some Cham and upland Cham have bossed gong ensembles as well as the ensembles of the Cham of Cambodia.

VII. *The Philippines* (13.4% of the population of Southeast Asia). Over the past 400 years, almost all Philippine ethnic groups have come into close syncretistic contact with Western and syncretized Philippine cultures. Thus, about 90% of the population participate in a pan–Philippine-Island musical culture that is best described in relation to Western musical cultures. The other 10% participate in diverse societies in the Austronesian ethnolinguistic family.

There are three basic types of syncretized music: music connected with Philippinized Catholic rituals, "folk songs" connected with village celebrations, and popular, mass-mediated music of urban origin but broadcast nationwide. All three types display indigenous characteristics, notably the use of Austronesian languages (usually Tagalog). The mass-mediated "popular" genres are by far the most widespread and the greatest in quantity and variety.

The Muslim ethnic minorities (2%) in the southern islands of Magindanaon and the Sulu archipelago play music closely related to several types of Indonesian music. Ensembles similar to the southern Philippine *kulintang,* which consists of a gong-chime row *(kulintang),* hanging bossed gongs (*gandingan, babendil,* and *agung*), and drums *(debakan),* are found throughout the northern Indonesian islands (except Sulawesi) and in Malaysian Borneo. Some of the music played by these ensembles is similar to some *talempong* music of Minangkabau peoples of Sumatra. Both *talempong* and *kulintang* are usually played by women. Among the Maranao of southern Philippines, *kulintang* are played as a part of courtship activities. A *kulintang*-like gong row called *trompong* is the central melodic instrument in Balinese ensembles called Semar Pegulingan. Other instrumental musics of these Philippine Muslim groups center around pentatonic xylophones *(gabbang),* violin *(biola),* single-reed oboe *(saunay),* and ring-flute *(suling).* These instruments are played alone, in combination, or as accompaniment to secular song. A type of wide-rim bossed gong called *agung* is played both by southern Philippine Muslims in *kulintang* ensembles and by non-Muslim Filipinos of that area in ensembles of several *agung* gongs. These gong ensembles are similar in instrumentation and some aspects of organization to the gong ensembles of some Dayak peoples in northern and central Borneo. Other instruments shared by these southern Philippine groups are lip-valley flute *(palendag),* percussion beams *(kagul),* bamboo jaw harp *(kubing),* two-string plucked lute *(kudyapi),* and bamboo *tube zither (*saluray* and *takumbu*), the last three being instruments common to peoples throughout Southeast Asia, and in the case of the tube zither, also to Austronesian peoples of Madagascar.

Instruments of the ethnic minorities of the northern and central Philippines are tied in similarly diverse ways to musical cultures of other Southeast Asian peoples. Tube zithers *(kolitong/patanggu)* are common among minorities of Luzon and Mindoro. Other instruments of these peoples are the nose flute *(kalaleng),* lip-valley flute *(paldong),* bamboo xylophone *(patatag),* musical bow *(gitaha),* jaw harp *(bikkung),* and three-string bowed lute *(gitgit).* Ensembles of rimmed flat gongs *(gangsa)* of bronze or brass are prominent among minorities of Luzon. These gongs are played with sticks or with the hand in community ceremonies or celebrations, often accompanying dance. The patterns are interlocking, usually in binary form, and are close in some aspects of style to the mainland ensembles of the Mon-Khmer.

All of these minorities have well-developed traditions of song—ballads, allegorical verse, love songs—reflecting a vigorous interplay between oral and written transmission, the writing of song texts perhaps having begun more than 1,000 years ago.

VIII. *Malaysia* (3.8% of the population of Southeast Asia). Malays are the largest ethnic group in Malaysia (50%). The music of the Malays of the peninsula (West Malaysia) is rich and varied.

Two types of ensemble have been prominent at Malay courts. The *nobat,* performed at most court ceremonies, was a sign of the ruler's sovereignty. Instrumentation varies by region, but usually consists of a metal kettle drum (*negara* in the state of Kedah), several strapped barrel drums *(gendang),* trumpet *(nafiri),* and quadruple-reed shawm *(serunai).* A type of *gamelan,* brought from Java, was formerly maintained in one court to accompany *joget* dances and later found favor in another. This ensemble, still occasionally played, consists of a pair of six-key bronze metallophones *(sarun),* xylophone *(gambang),* a double-row gong-chime *(keromong)* with five small kettle-gongs in each row, a row of larger kettle-gongs *(kenong),* and a pair of gongs.

Ma'yong dance-drama is accompanied by ensembles consisting of three-string spike fiddle *(rebab),* two *gendang,* and a pair of gongs, known as *tawak-tawak.* Various types of shadow-puppet theater *(wayang kulit)* are found in the north. In one of the Malay types, *wayang siam,* the *dalang* (puppeteer) tells mostly stories based on the Ramayana. His chanted, sung, and spoken narration alternates with instrumental music played by an ensemble usually consisting of *serunai,* a pair of goblet cymbals *(kesi),* a pair of kettle-gongs *(canang/celempung), tawak-tawak,* and pairs of *gendang,* goblet drums *(gedumbak),* and pegged drums *(geduk).* Another type, *wayang jawa,* uses Mahabharata and Panji stories and an ensemble consisting of two-string *rebab,* six-gong *canang,* various hanging gongs, and *gendang.*

In spirit ceremonies and curing rituals called *main puteri,* the officiant sings, sometimes accompanied by *rebab, gendang, canang, kesi,* and *tawak-tawak.* Martial arts are accompanied by gong, *gendang,* and *serunai,* as is poetic repartee, chanted by competing teams of men *(dikirbarat).* Islamic religious chanting and dancing accompanied by ensembles that feature *rebana* (frame drums) are found in a wide variety of regional styles, with each name for this complex of activities *(dikir, rodat, hadrah)* reflecting the relative weight placed on dance, song, or instrumental music. *Dondang sayang,* the music of Malaysians of the state of Malacca, combines song with an instrumental ensemble including gong, *rebana,* and violin or accordion as accompaniment for social dances. Recently, this genre has enjoyed a resurgence of popularity in nearby Johore and Singapore. In the cities of west Malaysia, a variety of danced dramatic performances involving musical ensembles, which bring together aspects of Malay music and that of other Malaysian ethnic groups, developed in the later part of the 20th century.

Orang asli (original people) is an administrative name for the aboriginal peoples of west Malaysia. These Mon Khmer–speaking groups have been subdivided into Negritos, Senoi, and Aboriginal Malays. Among the Senoi, songs about the spirit world of the forest are important in social life. Bamboo instruments, such as the tube zither *(karanting/kereb),* several flutes, and *stamping tubes, figure prominently. Jaw harps *(genggong)* are fashioned from the stalks of palm leaves. Ensembles of more than two or three instruments are few and are associated with dancing. An ensemble of one Senoi group can consist of several sets of bamboo stamping tubes, two drums, a bossed gong, male solo, and female chorus.

East Malaysia consists of the regions of northern Borneo known as Sabah and Sarawak. Apart from Chinese and a few ethnic Malays on the coast, both regions are populated mainly by Austronesian ethnic groups in the Bedayuh, Iban, Kenyah/Kayan, Murut, and Dusun ethnolinguistic subfamilies. The four largest of these groups have ensembles in which gongs are played, and gongs are generally valued as heirlooms that display both the wealth and the power of the owners. In one type of Bedayuh ensemble, three sizes of bossed gongs (*ketawak, bandai,* and *sanang*) are played together with flat gongs *(puum)* to welcome visitors and to accompany dance at agricultural or religious festivals or ceremonies. Iban, Kenyah/Kayan, and Dusun ensembles used for similar purposes have fewer gongs but often include gong-chime instruments with eight to twelve pot gongs in a row *(engkerumong/kulintangan).* Drums *(kandang/dumbak)* are usual parts of these ensembles. The Dusun and Kenyah/Kayan play xylophones *(gambang),* usually as accompaniment to the chanting of long stories. Bamboo jaw harps *(junggotan/seruding/bungkau),* ring flutes *(suling/kesuling),* and nose flutes *(sangui/selengut/turali)* are played by all groups, usually as solo instruments. The Iban, Kenyah/Kayan, and Murut have tube zithers *(satong/lotong/tongkungon)* and lutes with two to six strings *(belikan sampeh/sundatang).* These groups, as well as the Dusun, have free-reed mouth organs *(engkerurai/lkedi/keluri/kediri/sumpotan).* These instruments formerly accompanied dances in community ceremonies. Now they are also played alone and in groups for community or personal entertainment. Spike fiddles of one *(merebab)* and two *(engkerabab)* strings are played by the Iban.

IX. *Indonesia* (42.5% of the population of Southeast Asia). The fifth most populous nation in the world, Indonesia is a mix of diverse peoples. This section will survey the music of only a few of the largest ethnic groups on the largest islands. Most of the peoples of Irian Jaya (Indonesian New Guinea) are in the Papuan ethnolinguistic family. The music of these groups is best presented in relation to that of the peoples of Papua New Guinea. The other large islands—Sumatra, Sulawesi, Kalimantan (Indonesian Borneo), and Java—have great ethnic diversity. Even on several of the smaller islands, such as Lombok, Bali, and Nias, several cultural complexes exist for people who speak essentially the same language. Early attempts to categorize ethnic groups in Indonesia are now being revised, as are descriptions of musical activities and instruments. Even within the area of a single ethnic group, musical practices—the composition of ensembles, styles of performance, names of pieces, or melodies of pieces that have the same name—differ from village to village.

1. Ethnic groups of Indonesian Borneo (Kalimantan) can be divided into Malays, unassimilated recent migrants, Dayak, and Punan. Little has been written about the music of the Punan, who live in the foothills and mountains of central Borneo. Most Malays live in coastal cities and towns and in towns along Kalimantan's many rivers. Their ancestors were migrants from elsewhere in Indonesia and Malaysia. Some of the more recent migrants, principally Bugis,

Javanese, and Madurese, retain their native languages. Among both assimilated and unassimilated migrants, some musical practices persist from their places of origin. Among Javanese of coastal Kalimantan, some of the smaller *gamelan* ensembles of Java are maintained.

The main ethnolinguistic groups of the Kalimantan Dayak are Kenyah and Kayan in the east, the Maanyan and Ngaju in the center and south, and the Malayic Dayak in the west. Some musical instruments of east Kalimantan are similar to those of Malaysian Borneo. Kenyah and Kayan of east Kalimantan have traditions of performance on several flat gongs *(mehbiang/mebang)* or bossed gongs *(agong/tawak),* usually together with long conical drums *(tuwung/ jatung),* to accompany dance. Rhythmic patterns are associated with particular dances and patterns of gestures within a dance. As among east-Malaysian peoples, some Dayak groups have well-developed solo and small ensemble repertories for *kediri, sampeh,* and jaw harps *(tong buweh/uding).* Tube zithers *(lutong/kedutong)* are also found here, but with a less highly developed repertory than in Malaysian Borneo. Performance on ring or nose flute *(lukunwut/kedinget)* and vertical hanging xylophones *(jatung utang)* frequently occurs in combinations of several of the same instrument and with *sampeh.* Rhythmic pounding of large rice mortars is an essential part of harvest festivals.

Ngaju musical ensembles in central Kalimantan perform in funerary, curing, and harvest ceremonies. Among one Ngaju group, these ensembles consist of large bossed gongs *(gendring)* and cylindrical strapped drums. Another ensemble that accompanies a kind of courtship dance during *selamatan* festivals consists of a four-kettle gong-chime *(kenganong)* and three cylindrical drums *(duung).* This is one of the few examples of *kulintang*-like gong-chimes in the Dayak areas.

Closer to the southern coast of Kalimantan, metallophones are included in ensembles that accompany regional variants of these Ngaju ceremonies. These metallophones are thought to be substitutions for the *kenganong* through assimilation from *gamelan* of the ethnic Javanese, who have lived on the south coast for centuries.

2. There has been little written about the music of the peoples of northern Sulawesi (Celebes). The culture of the Minahasans, the largest ethnic group in the area, was strongly influenced by the Portuguese and Dutch. Minahasans are almost all Christian, and many early practitioners of Europeanized music—hymns and topical songs in homophonic style or with homophonic guitar accompaniment—were from this area. Southern Sulawesi is the home of the Toraja, Macassar, and Bugis. All three groups are related in culture and language, but the Macassar and Bugis have been influenced by Javanese and Malay peoples. Music of Toraja is connected with funerary rites of noble families, rituals of curing, spirit exorcism, courtship, and village harvest celebrations, and is usually accompanied by dance. Cylindrical strap-drums *(gandang),* bossed gongs *(padaling),* short ring flutes *(suling passailok),* and songs mark various stages of funerary rites. Each instrument or set of instruments plays alone, and songs are monophonic, sung as solos or in unison chorus. *Gandang,* pellet drums *(kamaru),* bamboo jaw harps *(karombi),* long flutes *(suling deata),* and songs are essential to rituals of curing and spirit exorcism. Religious feasts are often occasions for repartee songs by young men and women. The rice-stalk horn *(pakbarrung)* is played to announce harvest time, as well as in spirit possession and house-consecration ceremonies.

Even though the Bugis and Macassar adopted Islam several centuries ago, Islamic-influenced music has not entirely displaced earlier music. The *gambus* lute and *orkes melayu* ensembles are popular, especially in urban areas, and Qur'ānic chant is heard in mosques. Yet several pre-Islamic rituals, mainly those connected with the nobility, are still practiced. Ritual pounding of rice mortars, in interlocking patterns, is still found in Bugis and Macassar villages. Rice-stalk horn *(panoni),* bamboo jaw harp *(genggong),* leg xylophone *(gandong-gandong),* and tube zither *(genrang bulo)* are solo instruments, played for personal entertainment in rural areas. Transverse flutes *(suling),* violin *(biola),* lute *(kacapi/hasapi),* and drum *(gandang)* are also played solo or together in ensembles. Both the Bugis and Macassar have vigorous and long-standing traditions of singing poetry—epics, love ballads, or chronicles—memorized or written. These songs are frequently accompanied by *hasapi, biola,* or *biola* and *suling;* they can last up to two hours.

3. Music of the Achenese of the northern tip of Sumatra is the closest in style to Arabic music of any Indonesian music. Although Qur'ānic chant is found throughout Indonesia, it is a larger part of the musical training of Achenese than of other ethnic groups. *Dabus,* religious songs accompanied by Arabic lute *(gambus),* and secular songs accompanied by *orkes melayu* ensembles or *gambus,* in Arabic and Indonesian, are also important in Achenese music.

Batak is a name given to five ethnic groups of northern Sumatra. These groups have many cultural characteristics in common, including aspects of musical culture. But there is also much cultural variation among the five, and some regional variation within each group. Most Batak are Christian, and many are Muslim. Both religions arrived within the past two centuries and, especially in the mountainous interior of north Sumatra, have not entirely replaced earlier religious practices and the music associated with them, such as the chanting of long stories, formerly a part of many Batak ceremonies. Muslim and Christian Batak have large repertories of religious songs, and many of their secular songs have been influenced by Middle Eastern Islamic and European Christian music.

The main musical ensembles of most Batak groups are called *gondang/gordang*. Usually accompanying dance, they are played at village ceremonies, including weddings and funerals and as a part of kinship rites for noble or wealthy families. Among two Batak groups, Mandailing and Angkola, a *gondang* ensemble consists of two large, hanging, bossed gongs *(ogung),* a set of goblet cymbals *(talisasayap),* two to four small hand-held gongs *(momongan),* a small hanging gong *(doal),* a shawm *(sarune),* a solo male singer, and two strapped barrel-drums *(gondang)*. *Gordang* ensembles of these groups are the same, except that *gondang* drums are replaced by a set of five or nine large tuned drums *(gardang)*. In other Batak groups, this set is called *taganing,* and the entire ensemble is called *gondang.*

In some Mandailing regions, the drums of *gondang* are replaced by large bamboo tube-zithers *(gondang buluh),* the strings of which are struck with sticks to produce pitches of interlocking melodies, or other melodies with limited pitch content. These ensembles play to accompany martial-arts exercises or for entertainment. Other Batak instruments played alone, in small ensembles, or in accompaniment to song include rice-stalk horns *(ole-ole/saleot),* ring flutes *(suling),* end-blown flutes *(sordam),* transverse flutes *(salahot),* xylophones *(gambang),* and lutes *(hasapi)*. Among some Batak groups, five or more of these instruments are combined, often with Western instruments, into ensembles that play Westernized Batak melodies as entertainment.

The Minangkabau are an Islamic people in west and central Sumatra. Their music can be divided into coastal and interior. The former reflects long contact with other Islamic peoples, including the Achenese to the north. *Orkes melayu* ensembles probably originated among Minangkabau people of central Sumatra and the west coast of the Malay peninsula. They accompany many different kinds of secular song, usually in the Indonesian/Malay language, and often consist of harmonium, tambourine, electric or acoustic guitars, Indian flute, violin, bass, piano, electric organ, and accordion, with Indian, Indonesian, and Western drums.

The principal ensemble of the Minangkabau in the interior is *talempong,* named after its central instrument, a gong-chime of five to nine small kettle gongs. It also usually includes small bossed gongs *(canang),* large bossed gongs *(aguang),* and a pair of large and small strapped barrel-drums *(gandang),* and sometimes double-reed shawms *(sarunai),* rice-stalk horns *(puput),* or tube zithers *(kacapi bambu)*. These ensembles play interlocking melodies to accompany ceremonial dance or drama or in harvest festivals. Minangkabau of the interior also chant religious poetry in Arabic or Minangkabau accompanied by frame drums *(rabana/indang)*. Many types of secular poetry, distinguished by textual content, melodic character, and sociocultural function, are also chanted, sometimes accompanied by long bamboo ring-flutes *(saluang)*.

4. Even though Bali is one of the smaller Southeast Asian islands, has not been a central participant in large kingships, and has only about 1% of Indonesia's present population, it is home to an especially rich variety of musical genres. Almost all Balinese practice a form of Hinduism in which religious rituals are integral to daily life. Music, both as accompaniment to other performing arts and as an independent form, e.g., in the songs and chants of Hindu priests and teachers, is a part of most rituals. According to modern classification, almost all musical ensembles are varieties of *gamelan,* tuned to scales that have either *slendro* or *pelog* characteristics. The largest recent *gamelan,* known by the generic name *gong gede,* were five-tone *pelog* sets used to accompany religious rituals and festivals. These great ensembles almost certainly developed in the royal courts of Bali, where sufficient resources existed for their construction and maintenance, but by the 1920s they had spread to most of the large villages of the island. The largest *gong gede* employed almost 40 musicians and consisted of metallophones with and without suspended keys; rows of gong-chimes for melody-playing and paired gong-chimes for melodic punctuation and ornamentation; hanging gongs; cymbals; and drums. Other prominent *pelog* ensembles of the past were *gamelan gambuh, semar pegulingan,* and *pelegongan,* each having particular functions in accompaniment to dance dramas, classical court and temple dances, and royal celebrations. Important *slendro* ensembles are the *gender wayang,* a duo or quartet of suspended-key bronze metallophones used to accompany shadow-puppet plays, and *gamelan angklung,* village ensembles that provide music for many religious and civic occasions. In the early 20th century, by the melting down and reforming of some instruments and the addition or subtraction of others, many *gong gede* ensembles were transformed into *gamelan kebyar,* ensembles that were different in many aspects of timbre, repertory, and function. New forms of dance developed around the *kebyar* ensembles. Performance techniques were similar to earlier ones, though *kebyar* pieces and performance styles were often faster and flashier than before, involving the precise execution of intricate, presto, interlocking parts, in systematic, patterned elaborations of melodic ideas.

5. The largest ethnolinguistic groups on the island of Java are the Sundanese (8 million), mostly in the western third of the island, and the Javanese (70 million), concentrated in the central third. Most Sundanese and Javanese profess Islam, and Islamic chant and Middle Eastern song play clear roles in the musical life of Java. The Sundanese also have rich traditions of instrumental music—both *gamelan*-like en-

sembles and others—and song in both *slendro* and *pelog* tunings. *Gamelan*-like ensembles, those which have a significant number of metallophones or gongs, differ in size and instrumentation from one large town (former court center) to another or one large village (regional center) to another. Bamboo idiophones *(angklung)* and flutes *(suling)* are featured in some Sundanese *gamelan.* Several types of chamber ensembles found in large towns both accompany sung poetry (*pantun* and *tembang*) and play wholly instrumental repertories. These ensembles center on one or more *kacapi* (zither), *rebab* (two-stringed fiddle), or *suling.*

Musical ensembles composed predominantly of hanging gongs, gong-chimes, or drums are found in many areas of Southeast Asia. *Gamelan ageng* (big gamelan), which developed over the past 200 years in the courts of central Java, represent high points in the coalescence and refinement of such ensembles. Schools for the study of *gamelan* and associated performing arts are now found in several large towns of that region. A center for research in Javanese performing arts and a *gamelan* conservatory are maintained by the Indonesian government in the city of Surakarta (Solo). Future teacher-musicians of central Java are trained in the theories and practices of the more intricate styles of the arts that once flourished in the royal courts. Creation of new functions for *gamelan* and variation of old forms of performing arts are also encouraged.

Though *gamelan* are probably best known for their metal percussion instruments, the strong vocal tradition of central Java has been important in the development of most *gamelan* music. In soft-playing pieces of the large court *gamelan,* the vocal and vocal-oriented instrumental parts are more evident than in the strong-playing pieces, which once served to honor arriving guests, accompany processions, or signal the occurrence of court events, inside and outside the palaces.

The instruments of a large *gamelan* divide into several functional groups: metallophones play a one-octave condensation of the skeletal melody *(balungan);* gongs of various sizes punctuate that melody at important structural points; other instruments, such as a two-stringed spike fiddle *(rebab)* and a pentatonic xylophone *(gambang),* play elaborating melodies of various complexities that wind around the skeletal melody; and drums set and maintain the rhythm and tempo.

The pulse *(keteg)* structure of most *gamelan* pieces is in units of four *(gatra),* and most *gamelan* pieces have as a part of their name a designation of a multiple of this four-pulse unit. For example, *ladrang* is the name of a type of meter in **gendhing* that usually precedes the proper name of a piece of that metric type. It means that there are 32 basic pulses in each section of the piece marked by the sound of the large gong. This unit is called one *gongan.* The *kenong,* a set of large horizontally placed kettle-gongs, subdivides one *gongan* into units of 8 basic pulses (each unit, one *kenongan*). Other instruments punctuate at other important places. Elaborating metallophones *(gender),* zither *(clempung),* ring flute *(suling),* male chorus *(gerong),* female singer *(psindhen), gambang,* and *rebab* play various styles of patterns *(cengkok)* with variations *(wiletan)* that are appropriate to one- and two-*gatra* sections of the melody. Elaborating gong-chimes *(bonang)* play in one of three techniques (*mipil, gembyangan,* and *imbal-sekaran*), depending on the tempo level and function of the *gendhing.*

In a large central Javanese *gamelan,* there are usually two tunings *(laras)* available, **slendro* and **pelog.* The intervals between the pitches of the fixed-pitch metal keys are not best measured according to principles of equal temperament. In fact, although general parameters for intervallic relationships exist, the theory of pitch organization in *gamelan* pieces leaves room for variation in horizontal pitch relationships. Thus, although the instruments in one *gamelan* are usually in tune with one another, that tuning is usually slightly different from the tuning of every other *gamelan.* Each set of instruments is said to have its own character and is named accordingly.

In the course of the 1990s, Smithsonian-Folkways issued a monumental compilation of 20 compact discs from a wide range of geographic and cultural areas and contexts in the Indonesian archipelago. Selected from hundreds of hours of recordings made under the close direction of Philip Yampolski in the late 1980s and 1990s (and edited, produced, and with extensive notes by Yampolski), the set intentionally has only a few examples of music that are called *gamelan,* giving clear, incontrovertible evidence of the rich and variegated musical cultures in Indonesia today.

X. *New music.* The most common and conspicuous types of music in almost all areas of Southeast Asia today can be called new music because of the close association between their growth and the recent development of electronic media and concert-stage performance. These types differ from nation to nation or, within one nation, from region to region, but all are recognizably different from the types of music discussed above, and all have several common ingredients: they include some influence of Western popular genres, either directly through recordings or actual study with Western performers, or indirectly through an Asian type of new music—usually Indian, Chinese (primarily from Taiwan and Hong Kong), Middle Eastern, or Japanese. Thus, for example, many of the types of new music in Thailand, and among the Cambodians on the border between Thailand and Cambodia, show the influence of popular music of Hong Kong, which is a mixture of Western harmonic changes and scales, sometimes even Western melodies, and vaguely Chinese scale and modal practices. Radio, television, films, cassette tape, and live stage shows are the most common media through which these genres of Southeast Asian new music are communicated. The incidence of performance and the

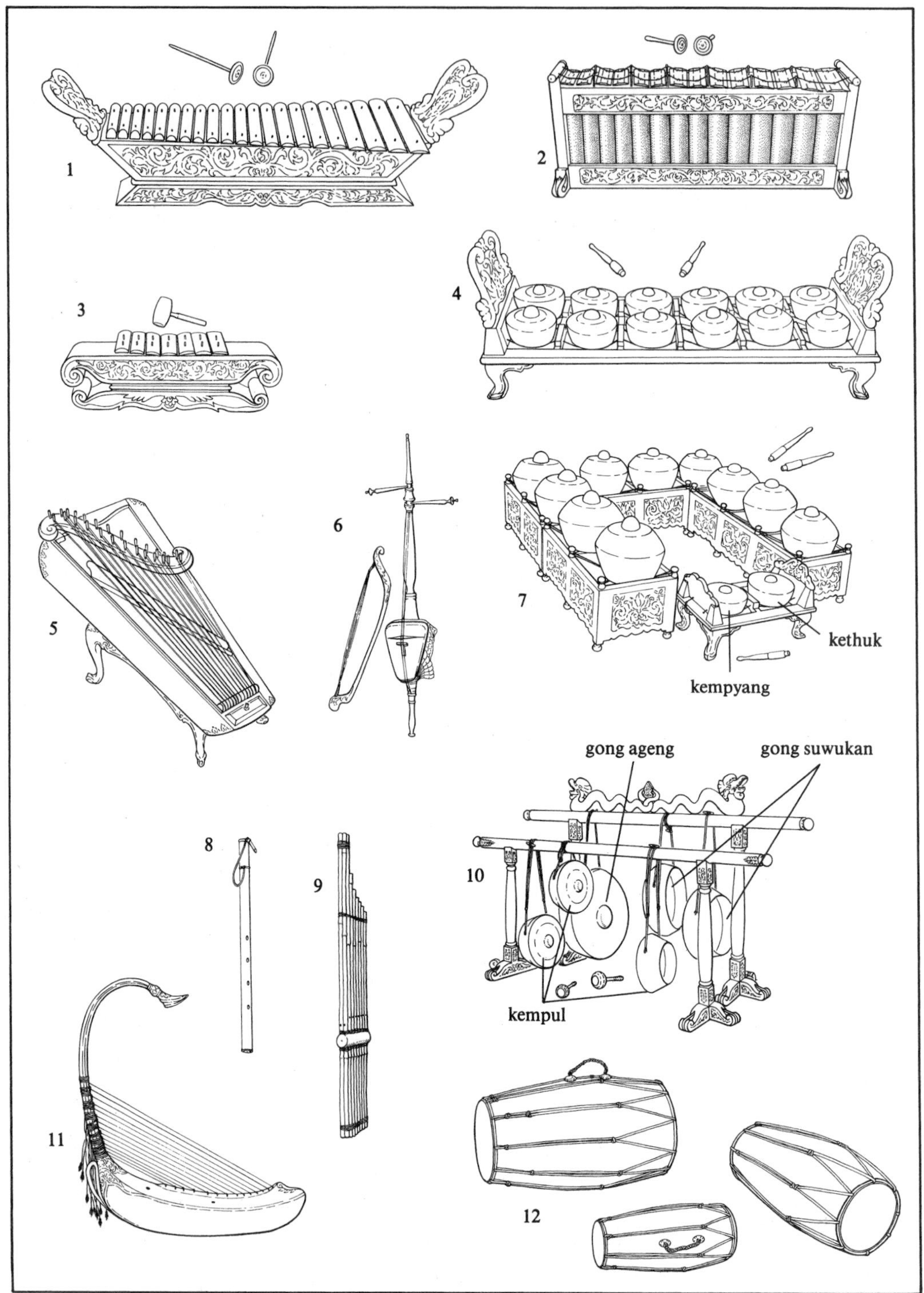

Instruments of Southeast Asia: 1. Gambang. 2. Gender. 3. Saron. 4. Bonang. 5. Clempung. 6. Rebab. 7. Kenong with kethuk and kempyang (shown half size in relation to others). 8. Suling (shown one and a half times size). 9. Khene. 10. Gong ageng, gong suwakan, and kempul (shown three-quarter size). 11. Saùng-gauk. 12. Kendang.

availability of electronic media are increasing in all Southeast Asian nations, but unevenly, affected by national policies such as the Burmese government's prohibition of television and foreign films. After changing several times, recent Indonesian policy is relatively liberal, and inexpensive cassette recordings of all types of contemporary music from around the world can now be found there. Because it has the greatest variety of peoples, the largest population, the largest land area, and the greatest isolation of individual ethnic groups, Indonesia has the most genres of new music.

New music in Indonesia falls into three general types, each known by at least two different names, the most common being *kroncong, dang dut,* and *pop.* All have pre-electronic roots. Those of *kroncong* extend to the 17th-century songs and string ensembles of communities of Portuguese sailors and merchants on the northwest coast of Java. The roots of *dang dut* can be found in *kroncong* as well as in Malay-Arabic singing accompanied by *orkes melayu* or by frame drums and flutes, which were present in northern Sumatra and the west coast of the Malay Peninsula as early as the 18th century. The roots of *pop* are in the hymnody and secular song of the Christianized peoples of northern Sumatra, Ambon, and northern Sulawesi. Early forms of *kroncong* and *pop* were restaurant and street music that appealed to a small number of city-dwelling Indonesians and Europeans. Early forms of *dang dut* were relatively isolated in the back streets of Jakarta and several towns of northern Sumatra and the Malay Peninsula. *Kroncong* was the first to grow into a pan-Indonesian phenomenon, when it was carried to urban centers throughout Indonesia on radio and phonograph records earlier in the 20th century. Several varieties of *pop* had become known in Java by the mid-20th century, but in the 1960s, many of them were banned from broadcast and performance to stop "westernization" of Indonesian cultures and values. By the late 1960s, *dang dut* had a strong following throughout Indonesia. This popularity grew during the 1970s, aided by the growth of the new Indonesian cassette industry. Old genres of *pop* began to reappear, and new ones had developed by the beginning of the 1970s. By the end of that decade, several of them were thriving among segments of urban society throughout Indonesia, though none was as widespread and well received as *dang dut. Kroncong* retained its following throughout these decades. There was some evidence in the early 1980s of a decline in popularity of *dang dut* and an increase for some forms of *kroncong* and *kroncong*-related forms.

Some of the subgenres of new music in Indonesia differ from others only in the language of song texts. For example, some songs in the repertory called *kroncong asli* are close in character to some songs in the category *langgam jawi.* Both are subgenres of *kroncong;* the former have texts in Indonesian, the latter in Javanese. There are subgenres of *langgam jawi* that mix instruments or tunings of Javanese *gamelan* with the typical *kroncong* ingredients, while some other subgenres are more clearly *kroncong,* rendered in the Javanese language. In some cases, the *gamelan*-mixed songs have influenced other *kroncong* subtypes in text content, melodic style, and accompaniment, thus yielding Indonesian *kroncong* that are imitations of *langgam jawi.*

Recent developments in the new music of Southeast Asia are the inclusion of instruments, aspects of melody, schemes of metric organization, rhythmic motifs, and sometimes fragments of text or language of songs from older local music. In Indonesia, these syncretizations occur primarily with the older music of Java and Bali. Cross-mixing has been occurring among all three types of new music in Indonesia, and additions from other Asian and from Euro-American music continue.

In the 1960s, several European and American record companies began to produce or increased their production of recordings of Southeast Asian music (for current discographies of Asian Music see *Ethno;* for reviews, see *Ethno* and *AsM*). Record companies in Thailand, Singapore, Indonesia, and the Philippines are well developed, and a large proportion of their production is of music that is indigenous to Southeast Asia.

Bibl.: *General, on history, ethnology, and the arts of Southeast Asia.* Frits Wagner, *Indonesia: The Art of an Island Group,* trans. Ann E. Keep (New York: McGraw-Hill, 1959). Bernard Groslier, *The Art of Indochina,* trans. George Lawrence (New York: Crown, 1962). Frank LeBar, Gerald Hickey, and John Musgrave, *Ethnic Groups of Mainland Southeast Asia* (New Haven, Conn.: Human Relations Area Files, 1964). James R. Brandon, *Theatre in Southeast Asia* (Cambridge, Mass.: Harvard U Pr, 1967). Claire Holt, *Art in Indonesia* (Ithaca, N.Y.: Cornell U Pr, 1967). Frank LeBar, ed. and comp., *Ethnic Groups of Insular Southeast Asia* (New Haven, Conn.: Human Relations Area Files, 1972–75). Mubin Sheppard, *Taman Indera* (Kuala Lumpur: Oxford U Pr, 1972). Amin Sweeney, *The Ramayana and the Malay Shadow-Play* (Kuala Lumpur: Penerbit Universiti Rebangsaan Malaysia, 1972). Mohamed Taib Osman, ed., *Traditional Drama and Music of Southeast Asia* (Kuala Lumpur: Dewan Bahasa dan Pustaka, Kementerian Pelajaran Malaysia, 1974). Charles Keyes, *The Golden Peninsula* (New York: Macmillan, 1977). Ralph B. Smith and William Watson, eds., *Early South East Asia* (New York: Oxford U Pr, 1979). Daniel G. E. Hall, *A History of South-East Asia,* 4th ed. (New York: St Martin's, 1981). Oliver W. Wolters, *History, Culture, and Region in Southeast Asian Perspectives* (Singapore: Institute of Southeast Asian Studies, 1982).

Specific, on music of Southeast Asia. See articles in *Grove 6* under the following headings: bronze drum, Burma, gong, gong-chime, Indonesia, Kampuchea, Laos, Malaysia, Philippines, Southeast Asia, Thailand, and Vietnam. Walter Kaudern, *Ethnographic Studies in Celebes,* vol. 3, *Musical Instruments in Celebes* (The Hague: Nijhoff, 1927). Jaap Kunst, *The Music of Java* (The Hague: Nijhoff, 1934; 3rd ed., enl., ed. Ernst L. Heins, 1973). Mantle Hood, *The Nuclear Theme as a Determinant of Patet in Javanese Music* (Groningen: J B Wolters, 1954; R: New York: Da Capo, 1977).

Dhanit Yupho, *Thai Musical Instruments,* trans. David Morton (Bangkok: Siva Phorn, 1960). Colin McPhee, *Music in Bali* (New Haven: Yale U Pr, 1966). Tran-van-Khe, *Vietnam* (Paris: Buchet-Chastel, 1967). Judith Becker, "Percussive Patterns in the Music of Mainland Southeast Asia," *Ethno* 12 (1968): 173–91. Jaap Kunst, *Hindu-Javanese Musical Instruments,* 2nd ed., enl. (The Hague: Nijhoff, 1968). La commission de musique, Cambodia, *Musique Khm'ere* (Phnom Penh, Cambodia: URBA, 1969). Van Giang, *The Vietnamese Traditional Music in Brief* (Saigon: Ministry of State in Charge of Cultural Affairs, 1971). Usopay Cadar, "The Role of Kulintang Music in Maranao Society," *Ethno* 17 (1973): 234–49. Margaret Kartomi, "Music and Trance in Central Java," *Ethno* 17 (1973): 163–208. William Malm and Amin Sweeney, *Studies in Malaysian Oral and Musical Traditions* (Ann Arbor: Center for South and Southeast Asian Studies, Univ. of Michigan, 1974). *AsM* 7/1 (1975, Southeast Asia Issue). Martopangrawit, *Catatan pengetahuan karawitan* (Surakarta: ASKI Surakarta, 1975–). David Morton, ed., *Selected Reports* [Institute of Ethnomusicology, U.C.L.A.] 2/2 (1975, Southeast Asia Issue). Martin Hatch, "The Song is Ended: Changes in the Use of Macapat in Central Java," *AsM* 7/2 (1976): 59–71. Margaret Kartomi, "Performance, Music, and Meaning of Réyog Ponorogo," *Indonesia* 22 (1976): 85–130. David Morton, *The Traditional Music of Thailand* (Berkeley and Los Angeles: U of Cal Pr, 1976). William R. Pfeiffer, *Filipino Music: Indigenious [sic], Folk, Modern* (Dumaguete City, Philippines: Silliman Music Foundation, 1976). Tilman Seebass, I Gusti Bagus Nyoman Panji, I Nyoman Rembang, and I Poedijono, *The Music of Lombok: A First Survey* (Bern: Francke, 1976). Margaret Kartomi, ed., *Studies in Indonesian Music* (Clayton, Australia: Centre of Southeast Asian Studies, Monash Univ., 1978). R. Anderson Sutton, "Notes toward a Grammar of Variation in Javanese Gender Playing," *Ethno* 22 (1978): 275–96. José Maceda, "A Search for an Old and a New Music in Southeast Asia," *AM* 51 (1979): 160–68. Harold Powers, "Classical Music, Cultural Roots, and Colonial Rule: An Indic Musicologist Looks at the Muslim World," *AsM* 12/1 (1979): 5–39. Judith Becker, "A Southeast Asian Musical Process: Thai *Thaw* and Javanese *Irama,*" *Ethno* 24 (1980): 453–64. Id., *Traditional Music in Modern Java* (Honolulu: U of Hawaii Pr, 1980). Wayne Forrest, "Concepts of Melodic Pattern in Contemporary Solonese Gamelan Music," *AsM* 11/2 (1980): 53–127. Martin Hatch, "Lagu, Laras, Layang: Rethinking Melody in Javanese Music" (Ph.D. diss., Cornell Univ., 1980). Mantle Hood, *The Evolution of Javanese Gamelan,* bk. 1 (New York: C F Peters, 1980). Rüdiger Schumacher, *Die Suluk-Gesänge des Dalang im Schattenspiel Zentraljavas* (Munich: Katzbichler, 1980). Andrew Toth, comp. and annot., *Recordings of the Traditional Music of Bali and Lombok* (n.p.: Society for Ethnomusicology, 1980). Richard Wallis, "Voice as a Mode of Cultural Expression in Bali" (Ph.D. diss., Univ. of Michigan, 1980). Monni Adams, "Instruments and Songs of Sumba, Indonesia: A Preliminary Survey," *AsM* 13/1 (1981): 73–83. Margaret Kartomi, "Dualism in Unity: The Ceremonial Music of the Mandailing Raja Tradition," *AsM* 12/2 (1981): 74–108. Terry Miller, "Free-Reed Instruments in Asia: A Preliminary Classification," *Kaufmann,* 1981, pp. 63–99. Terry Miller and Jarernchai Chonpairot, "The Ranat and Bong-Lang: The Question of Origin of Thai Xylophones," *Journal of the Siam Society* 69 (1981): 145–63. Endo Suanda, "The Social Context of Cirebonese Performing Artists," *AsM* 13/1 (1981): 27–42. Sumarsam, "The Musical Practice of the Gamelan Sekaten," *AsM* 12/2 (1981): 54–73. Sooi-Beng Tan, "The Glove Puppet Theater (Po Te Hi) in Malaysia," *AsM* 13/1 (1981): 53–72. Roger Vetter, "Flexibility in the Performance Practice of Central Javanese Music," *Ethno* 25 (1981): 199–214. William Frederick, "Rhoma Irama and the Dangdut Style," *Indonesia* 34 (1982): 103–30. Patricia Matusky, "Musical Instruments and Musicians of the Malay Shadow Theater," *JAMIS* 8 (1982): 38–68. Ghulam-Sarwar Yousof, "Mak Yong: The Ancient Malay Dance-Theater," *Asian Studies* 20 (1982): 108–21. Id., "Nora Chatri in Kedah," *JMBRAS* 60/1 (1982): 53–61. Marc Perlman, Judith Becker, and Alton Becker, "Reflections on 'Srepegan,'" *AsM* 14/1 (1983): 9–73. Terry Miller, *Traditional Music of the Lao* (Westport, Conn.: Greenwood, 1985). R. Anderson Sutton, "Musical Pluralism in Java: Three Local Traditions," *Ethno* 29/1 (1985): 56–85. Terry Miller and Sean Williams, eds., *Southeast Asia,* vol. 4 of *Garland Encyclopedia of World Music* (New York: Garland, 1998). M.H.

Sp. [Ger.]. Abbr. for **Spitze.*

Spacing. The registral placement of the elements of a chord. In traditional four-part harmony, assuming all three elements of a triad to be present, a chord is said to be in close position if the three uppermost parts lie as close to one another as possible; otherwise it is in open position.

Spagna [It.]. The most famous of the 15th-century Italian *bassedanze* [see *Basse danse*] tenors. It is preserved as a monophonic tune in one manuscript, Antonio Cornazano's *Libro dell'arte del danzare* (1455), where it is called "Re di Spagna," and in one print, Michel de Toulouse's *L'art et instruction de bien danser* (ca. 1496), titled "Casulle [Castille?] la novele." The earliest surviving polyphonic setting is a two-part one from the second half of the 15th century attributed to Guglielmo Ebreo. A three-part setting, "Alta," by Francisco de la Torre was written around 1500 (*HAM,* no. 102a). In the 16th century and early 17th, it was widely used as a *cantus firmus* for instrumental music and even for a few vocal compositions. Gombosi lists 240 extant pieces on the melody. Costanzo Festa's 120 *contrapunti* on it are now lost.

Bibl.: Otto Gombosi, ed., *Compositione di Meser Vincenzo Capirola* (Neuilly-sur-Seine: Société de musique d'autrefois, 1955), pp. xxxvi–lxiii. Frederick Crane, *Materials for the Study of the Fifteenth Century Basse Danse* (Brooklyn: Institute of Mediaeval Music, 1968). L.H.M.

Spagnoletta [It.; Sp. *españoleta*]. An Italian dance and dance song of the late 16th century that remained popular through the 17th [see Ex., where the pattern is transposed]. It is sometimes set in a compound duple (6/8) meter and sometimes in a simple quadruple (4/4). The melody most commonly associated with the dance is found in a *ballo* in a 15th-century manual by Giovanni Ambrosio (perhaps identical with Guglielmo Ebreo da Pesaro) under the title "Voltate in ça Rosina." It first appears under the title *Spagnoletta* in Fabritio Caroso's dance manuals (1581, fols. 163v–164; 1600, p. 153). In lute tablatures by Giulio Cesare Barbetta (1585, p. 19) and Giovanni Antonio Terzi (*Il*

secondo libro . . . , 1599, p. 21) it is titled "Balletto francese." The term *Spagnoletta* is used with the same music in Cesare Negri's dance manual (1602, p. 117) and in numerous guitar tablatures of the 17th century. Keyboard variations were written by Giles Farnaby (*Fitzwilliam Virginal Book,* no. 289), Girolamo Frescobaldi (1624), and Bernardo Storace (1664).

Bibl.: Lawrence H. Moe, "Dance Music in Printed Italian Lute Tablatures from 1507 to 1611" (Ph.D. diss., Harvard Univ., 1956), pp. 136–38, 276–77. L.H.M.

Spain. I. *Current musical life and related institutions.* The leading cities for art music in Spain are Barcelona and Madrid. Spain's only international opera house is the Gran teatro del liceo in Barcelona (1847), which also presents a brief season in Madrid each year. The Teatro de la zarzuela in Madrid now offers only a few **zarzuela* performances each year along with a variety of concerts and works for theater by Spanish and foreign artists. Leading orchestras are the Orquesta nacional de España and the Orquesta de la Radiotelevisión española in Madrid and the Orquesta Ciudad de Barcelona in Barcelona. The numerous other cities with orchestras include Bilbao, León, Valencia, and Seville. Apart from religious musical establishments, the best-known choral organization is the Orfeó català (1891) of Barcelona. In recent decades, festivals devoted to a wide variety of music have been held throughout Spain, some under national and some under regional sponsorship. Among annual events, the Festival internacional de música y danza held in Granada in the spring is the most prominent. Others include Madrid's Festival de otoño (which includes all of the arts), the Semana de música religiosa in Cuenca, and festivals devoted to the classical guitar in Santiago de Compostela and to Baroque performance practice in Daroca (near Zaragoza). Broadcasting is dominated by state-supported, national networks with headquarters in Madrid: Radio nacional de España and Televisión española. The leading publisher of art music in Spain in the last century has been La unión musical española in Madrid.

The principal conservatories are located in Madrid (1830), Barcelona (1838), Seville (1882), Granada, Valencia, and Pamplona. Professorships in musicology began to be established in Spanish universities in the 1980s, including positions at Oviedo, Barcelona, Seville, Salamanca, and Madrid. The leading centers for the scholarly study and publication of music in the last century have been the music department of the Biblioteca central de Cataluña and the Instituto español de musicología, both of Barcelona. The base of musicological activity was considerably expanded with the founding of the Sociedad española de musicología in Madrid in 1978.

The Roman Catholic Church has played a central role in the history of music in Spain, though the musical fortunes of individual cathedrals and churches have fluctuated considerably. The seat of the Spanish Church is the cathedral in Toledo. Important in the study and performance of Gregorian chant have been the Benedictine monasteries at Santo Domingo de Silos and Montserrat.

After considerable pressure for centralization during the Franco years after the Civil War of 1936, the return of democracy brought movement toward regionalization that accelerated in the 1980s. This marked the beginning of a period of change in the character and relative importance of many institutions affecting the musical life of the nation.

II. *History.* *Mozarabic chant was the liturgical chant of the Christian church in Spain until 1085, when it was suppressed in favor of Gregorian chant. Medieval repertories of Latin monophony and polyphony include those associated with *Santiago de Compostela and Las Huelgas, and there was some contact with the repertory of *Notre Dame as well. The court of Alfonso X (The Wise, 1221–84) was rich in learning and the arts and produced a large repertory of vernacular **cantigas* to the Virgin Mary. In the 14th and 15th centuries, the royal house of Catalonia and Aragon supported considerable musical activity, some of it in close contact with musicians in southern France [see *Ars subtilior*] and Italy.

The late 15th century produced the first large collections of polyphonic **villancicos* [see also *Cancionero*], including works by Juan del Encina (1468–1529 or 1530) and others. The *villancico* remained the principal genre of secular polyphony into the 17th century, though there were also settings of **romances* and **ensaladas,* and a few composers wrote works similar to the contemporaneous Italian *madrigal. The greatest international prominence was achieved by 16th-century composers of Latin sacred music, including Cristóbal de Morales (ca. 1500–1553), Francisco Guerrero (1528–99), and Tomás Luis de Victoria (1548–1611). The 16th century also saw publications devoted to works for **vihuela* and for voice accompanied by *vihuela* by Luis de Milán (ca. 1500–ca. 1561), Alonso Mudarra (ca. 1510–80), Luys de Narváez (fl. 1530–50), Enríquez de Valderrábano (fl. 1550), Diego Pisador (d. after 1557), Miguel de Fuenllana (d. after 1568), and Estéban Daza (fl. 1575). Genres cultivated by these composers and by Antonio de Cabezón (1510–1566) and later keyboard composers include the **diferencia, *tiento, *glosa,* and *fantasia. Theorists of the period include Diego Ortiz (*Tratado de glosas,* 1553), Juan Bermudo (*Declaración de instrumentos musicales,* 1555), Tomás de Santa María (*Arte de tañer fantasía,* 1565), and Francisco Salinas (*De musica libri septem,* 1577).

Sacred choral music of the 17th century included works in the *Palestrina style as well as elaborate polychoral works with instrumental accompaniment (e.g., by Juan Bautista Comes, 1582–1643) and **villancicos* of a type that were composed for major feasts in both Spain and Spanish America. The publication of Joan Carlos Amat's *Guitarra española de cinco órdenes* in 1596 marked the beginning of a long history of guitar methods and anthologies, an important example of which is Gaspar Sanz's *Instrucción de música sobre la guitarra española* of 1674.

Spain's indigenous form of musical theater, the **zarzuela,* had its beginnings in the 17th century and, undergoing many transformations, became central to the musical life of Spain into the 20th century. For much of the 18th and 19th centuries, however, Italian opera dominated all other musico-dramatic forms [see also *Tonadilla, Sainete*]. A strong native tradition of organ music was continued in the 17th and 18th centuries by Sebastián Aguilera de Heredia (ca. 1565–1627), Francisco Correa de Arauxo (ca. 1576–1654), Pablo Bruna (1611–79), Juan Cabanilles (1644–1712), and José Elías (fl. 1715–51). Domenico Scarlatti held an appointment at the court in Madrid from 1729 until his death in 1757 and was joined in the creation of a large repertory of harpsichord music by native composers such as Antonio Soler (1729–83).

Italian opera by the leading Italian composers of the day overshadowed all other forms of art music in the early 19th century, a period in which even the *zarzuela* was eclipsed (though in part by the lighter *tonadilla escénica*). Spanish composers who wrote operas in Italian included Ramón Carnicer (1789–1855), Baltasar Saldoni (1807–89), and Hilarión Eslava (1807–78). Francisco Asenjo Barbieri (1823–94) was among the composers who reestablished the *zarzuela,* and in the second half of the century, he and Felipe Pedrell (1841–1922), both of whom were influential scholars and writers on music, led efforts to rediscover Spain's musical past and establish a genuinely national art music, including opera. Tomás Bretón (1850–1923) composed nine operas between 1875 and 1914 but is nevertheless best remembered for his *zarzuelas.* Paris-trained Juan Crisóstomo Arriaga (1806–26) later became the object of considerable attention for his instrumental music, but in general, Spanish instrumental music of the 19th century remains little studied.

The most widely known composers from the turn of the 20th century, remembered principally for their piano music, were Isaac Albéniz (1860–1909) and Enrique Granados (1867–1916); perhaps the single most important figure of the first half of the 20th century was Manuel de Falla (1876–1946). All three used elements of Spanish folk music that have made their works seem quintessentially Spanish. Later composers exploring similar paths have included Oscar Esplá (1886–1976), Joaquín Turina (1882–1949), Rodolfo Halffter (b. 1900), Ernesto Halffter (b. 1905), and Joaquín Rodrigo (b. 1901). Less well-known outside of Spain are Conrado del Campo (1878–1953, a prolific and influential composer within Spain), Jesús Guridi (1886–1961), Federico Mompou (b. 1893), and Xavier Montsalvatge (b. 1912). By the 1960s, works representing all of the major currents in Western art music, from serialism to aleatory music, were being widely performed. Leaders of the new generation that came to prominence in this period are Cristóbal Halffter (b. 1930), Luis de Pablo (b. 1930), Ramón Barce (b. 1928), and Juan Hidalgo (b. 1927). Other prominent composers then and since include Carmelo Bernaola (b. 1929), Josep María Mestre-Quadreny (b. 1929), Antón García Abril (b. 1933), Gerardo Gombau (b. 1937), Tomás Marco (b. 1942), Francisco Guerrero (b. 1951), and José Ramón Encinar (b. 1954).

III. *Folk music.* The folk music of Spain is unusually rich and diverse, in part because of the linguistic and cultural diversity of the country itself. Large, regionally distinct repertories of traditional poetry and song continue to be transmitted orally and include **romances* with origins in the Middle Ages. *Flamenco music and dance are products of Andalusia in southern Spain, though some melodic elements of this tradition have been assimilated elsewhere to such an extent that they are often (especially in art music) taken to represent Spanish traditional music generally. Also broadly representative, though with specific links to Aragon, is the **jota.* Basque music is perhaps the most isolated and distinct [see also *Aurresku, Zortziko*]. Characteristic of Catalonia is the **sardana* and the **cobla* ensemble. Bagpipes are prominent in northern Spain, especially in Galicia [see *Gaita*]. The *pipe and tabor and various types of shawm [see *Chirimía, Dulzaina*] are also distributed through northern and central Spain. The guitar and castanets are widely distributed over the entire Iberian peninsula; the tambourine *(pandereta)* somewhat less so.

Bibl.: Adolfo Salazar, *La música en España* (Buenos Aires: Espasa-Calpe, 1953). José Subirá, *Historia de la música española e hispanoamericana* (Barcelona: Salvat, 1953). Gilbert Chase, *The Music of Spain,* 2nd rev. ed. (New York: Dover, 1959). Robert M. Stevenson, *Spanish Music in the Age of Columbus* (The Hague: Nijhoff, 1960). Id., *Spanish Cathedral Music in the Golden Age* (Berkeley and Los Angeles: U of Cal Pr, 1961). Israel J. Katz, "The Traditional Folk Music of Spain: Explorations and Perspectives," *YIFMC* 6 (1974): 64–85. María del Carmen Gómez Muntané, *La música en la casa real catalano-aragonesa durante los años 1336–1432* (Barcelona: Antoni Bosch, 1977). Jacqueline Andrea Shadko, "The Spanish Symphony in Madrid from 1790 to 1840: A Study of the Music in Its Cultural Context" (Ph.D. diss., Yale Univ., 1981). Pablo López de Osaba, ed., *Historia de la música española* (Madrid: Alianza, 1983–); vol. 1, Ismael Fernández de la Cuesta, *Desde los orígenes hasta el "ars nova"* (1983); vol. 2, Samuel Rubio, *Desde el "ars nova" hasta 1600* (1983); vol. 3, José López-Calo, *Siglo XVII* (1983); vol. 5, Carlos Gómez Amat, *Siglo XIX* (1984); vol. 6, Tomás Marco, *Siglo XX* (1983), trans. *Spanish Music in the Twentieth Century* (Cambridge, Mass.: Harvard U Pr, 1993); vol. 7, Josep Crivillé i Bargalló, *El folklore musical* (1983).

Spanisches Liederbuch [Ger., Spanish Song Book]. A collection of 44 songs by Hugo Wolf, composed in 1889–90 to German translations (by Emanuel Geibel and Paul Heyse) of 16th- and 17th-century Spanish poetry. Wolf later arranged five of the songs for voice and orchestra.

Spanish Rhapsody. See *Rapsodie espagnole.*

Spanish Song Book. See *Spanisches Liederbuch.*

Spasshaft [Ger.]. Jocose.

Speaker key. On a woodwind instrument, a key that facilitates *overblowing. The hole for a speaker key is usually small and so placed that when uncovered it prevents the formation of one or more of the lower harmonics. The key was first applied to the clarinet in the 18th century and to the oboe in the early 19th century. Most modern woodwind instruments use some form of the key. Some, like the modern conservatory-system oboe, often have as many as four keys providing such a function. M.S.

Speaking stop. In organs, a *stop whose pipes are used only for one register and not unified at higher or lower pitches. See Unit organ.

Species counterpoint. A method of instruction in 16th-century counterpoint, based on a categorization of contrapuntal relationships into five species, first promulgated by Johann Joseph Fux in his *Gradus ad Parnassum* of 1725. The progressive arrangement of the method, in dialogue form, with the rules for each species dependent more or less on the restrictions of the preceding, was widely admired for its pedagogical value. Haydn, Mozart, Beethoven, and several 19th-century composers studied from Fux's *Gradus* or taught from it; the method was reinvigorated in the 20th century, with some modifications adapting it to the major and minor scale systems [see also Counterpoint].

Fux's method of instruction is based on exercises consisting of a given *cantus firmus,* represented in whole notes, for which a counterpoint is to be constructed. This begins with a single melody above or below the cantus firmus; at a later stage, exercises in three or more parts are introduced.

In the first species, also called note-against-note [Lat. *punctus contra punctum*], one note of the counterpoint is matched to one of the *cantus firmus.* This is the most restrictive species. All intervals must be consonant; parallel motion of perfect intervals is forbidden, nor may any perfect interval be approached by similar (direct) motion; disjunct motion (i.e., by skip) is used sparingly; certain formulas are required at the end of the phrase; and various other rules and guidelines pertain. In the second species, two notes are matched to one of the *cantus firmus.* All the first-species rules apply to the first note of each pair; the second note may be a passing tone, the only dissonance allowed in this species. The third species, or four against one, introduces further flexibilities, including the cambiata, the dissonant neighbor note, and the double neighbor note (changing tone, disallowed by Fux but allowed by others; see Counterpoint). The fourth species consists of two notes against one, like the second species, but the second note of each pair is tied to the first of the next, thus introducing the possibility of suspensions. The fifth species, called florid, allows the most melodic freedom and includes all the conditions of the first four species, but only with their appropriate note-values.

Bibl.: A. Tillman Merritt, *Sixteenth-Century Polyphony* (Cambridge, Mass.: Harvard U Pr, 1939). Johann Joseph Fux, *Steps to Parnassus: The Study of Counterpoint,* trans. Alfred Mann (New York: Norton, 1943; rev. ed., London: Dent, 1965). Arnold Schoenberg, *Preliminary Exercises in Counterpoint,* ed. Leonard Stein (London: Faber, 1963). Erich Hertzmann and Cecil B. Oldman, eds., *Thomas Attwoods Theorie- und Kompositionsstudien bei Mozart,* in Wolfgang Amadeus Mozart, *Neue Ausgabe sämtlicher Werke* (Kassel: Bärenreiter, 1965). Felix Salzer and Carl Schachter, *Counterpoint in Composition* (New York: McGraw, 1969). M.DEV.

Specification. In organs, the formal description of the stops, divisions, and other parts of the instrument. See Disposition.

Speech song. **Sprechstimme.*

Sperdendosi [It.]. Fading away.

Spezzato [It.]. Divided, broken; for *coro spezzato,* see Polychoral; *registro spezzato,* *divided stop.

Spianato [It.]. Smooth, even.

Spiccato [It.]. See Bowing (4).

Spiegando [It.]. Spreading out, becoming louder.

Spieldose [Ger.]. Music box.

Spieloper [Ger.]. In the 19th century, a comic opera with spoken dialogue.

Spike fiddle. A bowed stringed instrument with a neck that pierces the body and emerges from the lower end. Spike fiddles commonly have two or three strings, no frets, and are held vertically. They are distributed through North Africa, the Middle East, Central Asia, and East and Southeast Asia. Examples include the **ching-hu,* **kamānjah,* and **rabāb.*

Spindle flute. **Koppelflöte.*

Spinet [Fr. *épinette;* Ger. *Spinett, Querflügel;* It. *spinetta, cembalo traverso;* Sp. *espineta*]. (1) A small *harpsichord, almost always with a single keyboard and set of jacks, strung diagonally from left to right with the bass strings at the rear. The jacks are arranged in pairs in the register, back to back, with plectra pointing in opposite directions. As in a harpsichord, one bridge rests on the wrest plank, the other on the soundboard, rather than having both on the latter, as is usual in a *virginal. The design imposes an irregular trapezoidal shape on the instrument, as seen in early 17th-century spinets at octave pitch. This was modified to the wing shape, with a bent side, typical of the larger spinets at normal pitch made from the middle of the 17th century to the end of the 18th in England, France, Germany, and occasionally Italy. Spinets were essentially domestic instruments. The compass paralleled that of contemporary harpsichords, being 4 octaves (C to c‴, bass *short octave) in earlier 17th-century instruments and extending in the latter years of the century down to G_1 (probably as a G_1/B_1 short or broken octave) and up to d‴. By about 1730, the spinet finally attained a full five-octave range, F_1 to f‴ or, in many English instruments, G_1 to g‴. Octave spinets at 4′ pitch were built during the 16th to 18th centuries to save both space and cost. In Italy, the term *spinetta* was most often used for virginals, as was the French *épinette* before the late 17th century. (2) A small upright piano. H.S., rev. J.Ko.

Spingardo [It.]. An Italian dance of the early 16th century, known only from two examples in Joan Ambrosio Dalza's *Intabulatura de lauto libro quarto* (1508), where it occurs in two suites. Each is arranged in the order **passamezzo*–**saltarello*–*spingardo* instead of the usual *passamezzo*–*saltarello*–**piva.* The music is in the same meter as the *piva.* L.H.M.

Spinto, lirico spinto [It.]. A lyric soprano or tenor voice, but one capable of being "pushed," i.e., of some dramatic power.

Spire flute. **Spitzflöte.*

Spirito, spiritoso [It.]. Spirit, spirited, usually in association with a fast tempo; in the 18th century, however, the terms were sometimes closer in meaning to spiritual and called for a relatively slow tempo.

Spiritual. A Christian religious folk song of the U.S., the term perhaps deriving from the biblical injunction to sing hymns and spiritual songs (Ephesians 5:19, Colossians 3:16). Related types were cultivated by both whites and blacks throughout the 19th century and into the 20th, and scholars have differed on the relationship between the two repertories. Among whites, the term referred especially to songs used in revival meetings as early as the late 18th century, as distinct from *metrical psalms and traditional hymns. These white spirituals were gathered in *shape-note publications. The term now most often refers to the religious songs of blacks beginning in the 19th century, a repertory genuinely *African American in character and largely transmitted orally. Such songs, hundreds of which were collected in the later 19th century, often have words of a melancholy character with regularly recurring refrain lines. Their original contexts included work as well as religious meetings, and contemporaneous accounts describe singing in unison, sometimes with heterophonic or polyphonic and rhythmic accompaniment, in *call-and-response patterns. Their introduction to large, white audiences in the U.S. and Europe by the Fisk [University] Jubilee Singers beginning in 1871 led to the production of numerous choral arrangements in the 20th century that are widely sung by whites and blacks alike. Spirituals have also been performed widely as solo art songs since early in the 20th century.

Bibl.: William Francis Allen, Charles Pickard Ware, and Lucy McKim Garrison, *Slave Songs of the United States* (New York, 1867). George Pullen Jackson, *White and Negro Spirituals* (New York: J J Augustin, 1943). Id., "Spirituals," *Grove 5.* John Lovell, Jr., *Black Song: The Forge and the Flame* (New York: Macmillan, 1972). See also African American music.

Spitze [Ger., point]. (1) In violin playing, the tip of the bow. (2) In organ playing, the toe of the foot.

Spitzflöte [Ger.]. Spire flute, an organ flue stop whose pipes are tapered inward at the top, producing a rather broad flute tone.

Spitzharfe [Ger.]. **Arpanetta.*

Spondee, spondaic. See Prosody.

Sprechstimme, Sprechgesang [Ger., speaking voice, speech-song]. A use of the voice midway between speech and song. In general, it calls for only the approximate reproduction of pitches and in any case avoids the sustaining of any pitch. It is often notated with *x*'s as note heads (sometimes with *x*'s through the stems), their placement on a staff indicating at least a pitch contour, and stems and flags being used in the conventional way to indicate rhythm. It was first employed by Engelbert Humperdinck in *Königskinder* (1897). Schoenberg made the greatest use of it, however, in works such as **Pierrot lunaire* (1912), *Die *glückliche Hand* (1910–13), and **Moses und Aron* (1930–32).

Sprezzatura [It.]. The lack of regular rhythm in the performance of *monody around 1600. The term is used by Giulio Caccini in the prefaces to *Euridice* (1600) and *Le *nuove musiche* (1601/2).

Springbogen [Ger.]. See Bowing (4).

Springer. An unaccented *échappé* or auxiliary note coming at the very end of the note-value on which it is placed; hence, the same as the French **accent* [see also *Nachschlag* (2)].

Spring Sonata. Popular name for Beethoven's Sonata for Violin and Piano in F major op. 24 (1800–1801).

Spring Symphony. Schumann's Symphony no. 1 in B♭ major op. 38 (1841).

Spruch [Ger.]. A type of poem cultivated by the **Minnesinger.*

Sprung(k) [Ger.]. See *Nachtanz.*

Spurious compositions. See Authenticity.

Squarcialupi Codex. Florence, Biblioteca medicea laurenziana, Med. Pal. 87 ("Codex Squarcialupi") [Sq, Fl]. 216 leaves. This beautiful Florentine manuscript of the first half of the 15th century contains 354 secular works of Italian composers (Landini et al.): *ballate, cacce,* madrigals. Facsimile edition: *Il codice Squarcialupi: Ms. mediceo palatino 87, Biblioteca medicea laurenziana de Firenze,* ed. F. Alberto Gallo (Firenze: Giunti Barbera; Libreria Musicale Italiana, 1992).

Square. In 15th- and 16th-century England, a part taken from one polyphonic work and made the basis of another.

Square dance. A folk dance of the U.S. danced by groups of four couples forming a square; also, an occasion on which such dances are danced. The dance itself was derived from the French **quadrille* in the 19th century. It employs music in moderately fast duple meter performed by a fiddle and or various other instruments while the steps are called out to the dancers by a caller.

Square neumes. Square-shaped *neumes of the type that became current in the 12th century and that form the basis for the notation of some polyphony and secular monophony [see Square notation] and for the neumes employed in some modern liturgical books.

Square notation [Ger. *Quadratnotation*]. *Notation employing predominantly square shapes, such as that for the repertory of *Notre Dame; sometimes also termed modal notation because of its use in association with the rhythmic *modes.

Square piano. A *piano whose case is a horizontal rectangle. Pianos of this type were common from the late 18th through the 19th century and varied in size from quite small instruments similar to clavichords to quite large and elaborately decorated instruments of the 19th century.

St. Abbr. for (and alphabetized as) Saint.

Stabat Mater dolorosa [Lat. The pained Mother stood]. A sequence often attributed to the Franciscan Jacopone da Todi (d. 1306) and adopted in the Roman Catholic rite in 1727, assigned to the Feast of the Seven Dolours (September 15; *LU,* pp. 1634v–37). There are numerous polyphonic settings of the text dating from the 16th century to the 20th.

Stabreim [Ger.]. *Alliteration.

Stabspiel [Ger.]. *Xylophone.

Staccato [It., abbr. *stacc.*]. Detached. Notes to be played in this fashion, marked by a dot (now most common), a solid black wedge, or a vertical stroke above or below, are decisively shortened in duration and thus clearly separated from the note following. A light accent is also implied. The term is thus the opposite of **legato.* For various related techniques of execution on the violin, see Bowing. *Staccatissimo* indicates an extreme form of such shortening.

Stadtpfeifer [Ger.]. Town piper, *wait; a musician, usually one of a group, employed by a municipality to perform music on public occasions of various kinds. Such musicians, especially wind players, were used in Germany from the 14th century.

Staff, stave [Fr. *portée;* Ger. *Liniensystem, System;* It. *sistema, rigo;* Sp. *pentagrama, pauta*]. A group of equidistant horizontal lines, now always five, on which notes are placed in such a way as to indicate pitch. Successive lines and spaces from lowest to highest represent rising steps of the diatonic *scale (embodied in the white keys of the piano) and bear the corresponding letter names, the first seven letters of the alphabet. Notes are sharped or flatted (to produce the pitches of the black keys of the piano) by means of *accidentals. The assignment of specific lines and spaces to specific letter names is made by means of a *clef placed at the beginning of each staff. Pitches lying above and below the lines of the staff proper are notated with the aid of *leger lines. Two or more staves connected by a brace are termed a system. Piano music is notated on two staves connected by a brace, the upper with a treble clef, the lower with a bass clef; this arrangement is sometimes termed the great or grand staff. See also Notation, Score, *Rastrum.*

The staff rests on the principle of precise measurement of pitch along a vertical axis. This principle was established in Aquitanian *neumes of the 11th century, which employ a single horizontal line for the purpose scratched into parchment (hence, dry-point line). Guido of Arezzo (d. after 1033) recommended the use of several lines of different color, one with a clef, with pitches being notated on both lines and spaces. By the 13th century, the use of five lines was common, though six were sometimes used in polyphonic music of the 14th and 15th centuries, and four lines were (and still are) used for liturgical chant. The number of lines per staff in early keyboard music is somewhat more variable. For types of notation using parallel lines in a different way, see Tablature.

Staff liner. **Rastrum.*

Stage band. *Big band.

Stahlspiel [Ger.]. *Glockenspiel.

Stamping tube. A tube, usually of bamboo and usually closed at one end, that is beaten on the ground in order to produce sound. Stamping tubes are played in South America, Africa, Southeast Asia, and in Oceania, especially Melanesia.

Standard. A popular song that has retained its popularity over a period of years; especially one that has become part of the jazz repertory. Jazz standards, based on similar forms, include songs composed by jazz musicians (e.g. Duke Ellington, Thelonious Monk, Wayne Shorter) that have similarly entered into the jazz repertory.

Bibl.: Richard Crawford and Jeffrey Magee, *Jazz Standards on Record, 1900–1942* (Chicago: Center for Black Music Research, 1992).

Ständchen [Ger.]. *Serenade.

Stantipes [Lat.]. See *Estampie.*

Stark [Ger.]. Strong, loud; *stärker werdend,* becoming louder.

Star-Spangled Banner, The. The national anthem of the United States of America, officially adopted in 1931. The words were written by Francis Scott Key (1779–1843) in September 1814 as he watched the British bombardment of Fort McHenry, near Baltimore. The melody, for which Key intended his words, is by the English composer John Stafford Smith (1750–1836) and was sung in Anacreontic Societies in England and America to the words "To Anacreon in Heaven."

Bibl.: William Lichtenwanger, "The Music of 'The Star-Spangled Banner': Whence and Whither?" *CMS* 18, no. 2 (1978): 35–81.

Steel drum. A percussion instrument made from an oil drum. The drum is cut to a relatively shallow depth, and the end is made concave, subdivided by grooves, and hammered into shape so as to create up to 30 segments, each of which produces a tuned pitch when struck with a rubber-headed stick. Steel drums are made in a variety of sizes and played in ensembles called steel bands. The instrument was developed in Trinidad in the 1940s and has since spread through the Caribbean and to other areas where there are West Indian populations.

Steel guitar. A guitar with metal strings that is held horizontally with the belly up and played by sliding a metal bar along the strings with the left hand, plucking with the right, rather than by pressing the strings against the frets; also called a Hawaiian guitar. It is now typically an electric instrument lacking a sound box, rectangular rather than guitar-shaped, and mounted on a stand. See also Pedal steel guitar.

Steg [Ger.]. The *bridge of a stringed instrument; *am Steg,* an instruction to bow at the bridge.

Stegreifausführung [Ger.]. Improvisation.

Stegreifkomödie [Ger.]. A type of comic opera on a German text with improvised dialogue, popular in Vienna in the second half of the 18th century.

Steigern [Ger.]. To intensify, increase; *Steigerung, crescendo.*

Stem. The vertical line attached to a note head [see Note].

Stemma, stemmatics. See Textual criticism.

Stendendo [It.]. Stretching out, slowing.

Stentando, stentato [It.]. Labored, halting.

Step. (1) A *scale degree. (2) The interval between one scale degree and the next, whether a semitone or a whole tone [see also Motion].

Stepwise. *Motion from one scale degree to an adjacent one.

Sterbend [Ger.]. Dying away.

Steso [It.]. Stretched, slow.

Stesso [It.]. Same [see *Istesso tempo*].

Sticheron [Gr.]. A short monostrophic Byzantine hymn. Such a hymn originally functioned as an appendage to a verse *(stichos)* of a Psalm or as an intercalation between verses. Later, *stichera* assumed a variety of functions in the Office, and entire sets in syllabic or near-syllabic style were arranged in a type of manuscript called a *Sticherarion* [see Byzantine chant, *Idiomelon*]. D.E.C.

Stick zither. A *zither whose strings are stretched along a solid stick as distinct from a resonating body. A resonator of some type is often attached.

Stierhorn [Ger.]. *Cow horn.

Stil [Ger.], **stile** [It.]. *Style.

Stile antico [It.]. See Palestrina style.

Stile concertante [It.]. See *Concertant, concertante;* Concerto.

Stile concertato [It.]. See *Concertato.*

Stile concitato [It.]. See *Concitato.*

Stile familiare [It.]. *Familiar style.

Stile rappresentativo [It.]. The dramatic or theatrical style of *recitative used in the earliest operas and semidramatic works of the first decades of the 17th century. It is characterized by freedom of rhythm and irregularity of phrasing; the vocal line readily forms dissonances with an accompaniment improvised by one or several chordal instruments reading from a figured bass. The term *stile rappresentativo* first appeared in print on the title page of Giulio Caccini's *Euridice* (1600). It was used more or less interchangeably with the term *stile recitativo* for the first third of the 17th century; but by 1635, Giovanni Battista Doni suggested that the *stile recitativo* was more songlike in style.

Stimmbogen [Ger.]. *Crook; tuning *slide.

Stimme [Ger.]. (1) Voice. (2) *Part. (3) Organ *stop.

Stimmen [Ger.]. (1) Plural of **Stimme.* (2) To tune.

Stimmgabel [Ger.]. Tuning fork.

Stimmstock [Ger.]. (1) *Sound post. (2) *Pin block.

Stimmtausch [Ger.]. *Voice exchange.

Stimmung [Ger.]. (1) Mood; *Stimmungsbild* (mood picture), a piece intended to express some particular mood. (2) Tuning, intonation; *reine Stimmung,* *just intonation.

Stimmzug [Ger.]. (1) Tuning slide. (2) The slide of the trombone.

Sting. In Thomas Mace's *Musick's Monument* (1676), a single-finger *vibrato on the lute.

Stinguendo [It.]. Fading away.

Stiracchiando, stiracchiato, stirando, stirato [It.]. Stretching out, slowing down.

Stock and horn. See Hornpipe (2).

Stockfagott [Ger.]. See Racket.

Stockflöte [Ger.]. **Czakan.* See also Walking-stick instrument.

Stollen [Ger.]. See Bar form.

Stomp. A term found in jazz titles of the 1920s and 1930s connoting fast dance music with a strong beat. "Jelly Roll" Morton claimed to have been the first to use it in his "King Porter Stomp," copyrighted in 1924 but composed more than a decade earlier. Morton's publisher, the Chicago-based Melrose Brothers Music Co., thereafter used it as a marketing category, with its "famous series of Blues and Stomps."

Stop. (1) In *organs, a row of pipes, one for each key, that can be made to sound when the stop knob is drawn by the player. Each keyboard and pedal division of the organ has its own wind-chest, on which one to many such rows of pipes are placed. *Mixture stops have two or more pipes for each key, sounding octaves and fifths to reinforce the natural harmonic series. See also Divided stop. (2) In *harpsichords, a set of jacks that can be brought into play or retired by the player in order to sound one or another choir of strings. The choirs of strings may be at different pitch (usually 8′ and 4′), and the timbre produced by each stop varies according to the point along the length of the strings at which they are plucked by the jacks. A buff stop, however, is simply a set of buff leather pads or a similar device that partially damps one choir of strings while it is being played.

(1) J.T.F.

Stopped pipe. (1) A pipe that is closed at one end. Such a pipe (including those on organs; see below) sounds a pitch an octave lower than an open pipe of the same length. See Acoustics, Wind instruments. (2) In organs, a *flue pipe whose top is closed by a metal cap or wooden stopper.

Stopped tones. Tones produced on the French horn by closing the opening in the bell with the hand or with a mute [see Horn]. In addition to producing a change in tone color, the technique may produce a change in pitch, requiring altered fingerings.

Stopping. (1) On a stringed instrument, altering the vibrating length of a string by pressing it against the fingerboard. This is the principal means of executing the variety of pitches available on such instruments. See also Double stop. (2) On the French *horn, the production of *stopped tones.

Stop-time. In tap dancing, jazz, and blues, accompaniment consisting of a regular pattern of attacks (e.g., on the first beat of each measure) separated by silences. Interrupting normal accompanimental rhythms (the "time"), such single, accented attacks alternate, often every two bars, with a solo.

Storm and stress. **Sturm und Drang.*

Storto [It., crooked]. *Crumhorn.

Straff [Ger.]. Tense, rigid, strict.

Straight organ. An organ in which all *stops are used only on one division and at one pitch, without being "borrowed" between keyboards. See also *Unit organ.

Strambotto [It.]. A verse form popular among Italian improvisers in the 15th century and taken over into the repertory of the **frottola.* It consists of a single stanza of eight hendecasyllabic lines, normally rhyming abababcc *(strambotto toscano),* less often abababab. In structure, it is identical with the *ottava rima* stanza. Musical settings of the *strambotto* often have only two phrases, each to be repeated four times in alternation; a separate phrase for the final couplet may be included. The *strambotto* is sometimes through-composed, however.

J.H.

Strascicando, strascinando [It.]. Dragging.

Strathspey. A type of Scottish *reel, slower in tempo, in duple meter, and characterized by dotted rhythms, including the inverted dotting termed the Scotch snap [see Lombard rhythm].

Stratification. A term borrowed from geology, stratification refers to polyphonic textures in which the individual strands of counterpoint are placed above or below one another without any attempt to coordinate their activity. Such procedures are particularly common in 20th-century music, especially works by Ives, Stravinsky, and their successors. Stratified textures stand in direct contrast to the textures found in most polyphonic music of the Renaissance and Common Practice periods. In music of these repertories, the motion of one line is coordinated with that of the others. But in stratified textures the lines are simply superimposed in an unrelated fashion. A good case in point is the orchestral piece *Central Park in the Dark* (ca. 1909) by Charles Ives. While the strings play a slow ostinato that represents "the night sounds and silent darkness," the wind, brass, percussion, and piano parts superimpose more active melodies that recreate various city noises. Just as in real life, the superimposed sounds are layered haphazardly; Ives even notated them in completely different meters from the ostinato.

M.B.

Stravaganza [It.]. A piece that is in some way extravagant or unconventional in style, in demands on the performer, or in conception. The term appears in the late 16th century in the title of a work for organ by Giovanni Macque (*HAM,* no. 174) and was later used by Vivaldi (op. 4) and others.

Straw fiddle [Ger. *Strohfiedel*]. See Xylophone.

Straziante [It.]. Agonizing, heart-rending.

Street cries. Cries, often with a definable musical shape, used by street vendors to advertise their wares. Such cries, a type of folk music, are found throughout the world and have been preserved in Western art music from as early as a late 13th-century motet with the tenor "Frèse nouvele, muere france" (Fresh strawberries, wild blackberries; *HAM,* no. 33b). Steadily increasing numbers of examples are preserved in this way in French and Italian music of the 14th through 16th centuries, especially in various types of **quodlibet* [see also *Caccia*]. English composers of around 1600, including Thomas Weelkes, Orlando Gibbons, and Richard Dering, composed pieces based almost entirely on street cries, and Thomas Ravenscroft's *Pammelia* (1609) and *Melismata* (1611) include rounds made from such cries. In all such cases, independent musical documentation of the cries is lacking. As late as Handel's *Serse* (1738) and even in the case of Gershwin's *Porgy and Bess* (1935), the use of authentic cries can only be suspected.

Street organ. See Barrel organ, Barrel piano.

Streich [Ger.]. Bow; *Streichinstrumente,* bowed stringed instruments; *Streichorchester,* string orchestra; *Streichquartett,* string quartet; *Streichklavier,* *bowed keyboard instrument.

Streit zwischen Phöbus und Pan, Der [Ger., The Contest between Phoebus and Pan]. A secular cantata ("dramma per musica") by Bach, BWV 201 (1729?). The text by Picander is based on Ovid's account of the musical contest between Phoebus Apollo and Pan. The character Midas may satirize one of Bach's critics, Johann Scheibe (1708–76).

Streng [Ger.]. Strict.

Strepitoso [It.]. Noisy, boisterous.

Stretta [It.]. **Stretto* (2).

Stretto [It., narrow, close]. (1) [Ger. *Engführung*] In a *fugue, the imitative treatment of the subject at a shorter interval of time than is employed in the initial exposition [see Ex., from the Fugue in D major in the *Well-Tempered Clavier,* bk. 2]. The technique is often

reserved for a climactic moment near the end. It is also employed in the *ricercar, beginning in the 16th century. (2) In nonimitative works, a climactic, concluding section in a faster tempo; often *stretta.* Examples occur in the finales of Italian opera (e.g., Rossini's *Il *barbiere di Siviglia,* act 1). The term is also often applied to passages such as the conclusion of the fourth movement of Beethoven's Fifth Symphony.

Strich [Ger.]. Bow stroke. See also Bowing, *Mensurstrich, Silbenstrich.*

Strict composition. Composition in a predetermined, usually historical, form. For strict counterpoint, see Species counterpoint.

Stride. An accompanimental technique perfected by Harlem jazz pianists of the 1920s, including James P. Johnson, Fats Waller, and Willie "the Lion" Smith. Modifying the two-beat ("oom-pah") style of *ragtime, the left hand flows between bass note and chord in *swing rhythms, often sounding a tenth with the bass note on strong beats.

String [Fr. *corde;* Ger. *Saite;* It. *corda;* Sp. *cuerda*]. A stretched cord fastened under tension to the resonant chamber of an instrument. Such a cord can be bowed, plucked, or struck to produce a musical sound. Strings can be made from many materials but are commonly fashioned of lamb gut, silk, wire, horsehair, and nylon or other synthetics. The development of bowed stringed instruments can be linked to the technology of strings and their musical characteristics.

Before the 18th century, strings for bowed instruments were generally made from slit strands of lamb gut, tightly twisted and polished for even thickness. The degree of tightness of twisting influenced brightness and clarity of sound, while the number of strands fashioned together allowed strings to achieve appropriate tension at different pitches. Lower-register strings, like the violin g, viola g and c, and cello G and C, were constructed of two or more twisted strings refashioned and wound together to form the roped string or Catline. The Catline twist allowed considerably larger string diameters to "speak" or vibrate easily under the bow but required generally longer vibrating length to function with musical volume. For this reason, early cellos were larger of body than is common today, with an extended vibrating string length.

In the last decades of the 17th century, Catline strings and twisted gut strings were wound with brass, copper, or silver wire to increase mass and tension with shorter vibrating length. The new strings allowed the lower registers to be stronger and focused on instruments of smaller body, helping to create the proportions of the bowed stringed instrument family that we know today. Until the 20th century, the lower two strings of the violin, viola, and cello were usually of silver- or copper-wound gut, with plain gut upper registers. Over the course of the first half of the 20th century, aluminum-covered middle strings and a plain steel violin E became the standard to create clarity and brilliance in sound. More recently strings with braided steel or nylon-like synthetic rather than traditional gut cores have become popular with musicians for their pitch stability and durability. W.L.M.

String band. See Bluegrass music.

String bass. *Double bass.

String drum. A *friction drum in which a string that passes through a membrane is rubbed to produce sound.

Stringed instrument. An instrument in which one or more strings constitute the principal vibrating system; also chordophone. The string or strings may be set in motion by bowing, plucking, or striking. For the various types, see Instrument II, 1. The term is often used informally to refer to instruments of the violin family.

Stringendo [It.]. Pressing, becoming faster.

String quartet. A composition for an ensemble consisting of four solo string instruments, normally two violins, viola, and cello; the ensemble itself [see also Quartet]. Since the second half of the 18th century, the string quartet has been the most widely cultivated and influential chamber-music genre.

I. *Classical.* The string quartet was a creation of the Classical era. Early in that period the textural ideal of four relatively independent solo performers began to supplant the polarized continuo texture of the Baroque trio sonata and related genres. Four-part writing for string orchestra had long been utilized in such Baroque genres as the overture and concerto, and in a more modern idiom in the early Classical symphony *a 4.* The same four-part texture, but now for solo strings with continuo, may be found in the late Baroque period in the four-part concertino sections of concerti grossi by Geminiani, Locatelli, Giuseppe Sammartini, and others who added a viola to the usual concertino of two violins and cello/continuo. Complete compositions utilizing this scoring include the north German *sonata a 4* or *Quadro* with continuo—too isolated to have a direct connection with the later string quartet—and occasional Italian sonatas *a 4.* Finally, certain Italian works called *concertini* in Parisian sources from ca. 1740 may have been intended for solo performance (as claimed in Finscher, 1974); if so, they may be considered progenitors of such early quartets as Luigi Boccherini's op. 2 of 1761 (printed in Paris as op. 1), the first of 90 works he contributed to this genre.

The most important precursors of the string quartet were, however, Austro-Bohemian—namely the various informal chamber genres of the early Classical period such as the string *trio and quintet and the sextet for string quartet and two horns. Austrian chamber music of this type was not only soloistic, but it seems generally to have been performed without a keyboard continuo (see Webster, 1974), the latter circumstance owing in part to the custom of playing these works outdoors [see Serenade].

It is within this context that Joseph Haydn created his first string quartets, which eventually numbered 68. Haydn's early biographer Georg August Griesinger tells us that the composer was invited from time to time to Weinzierl, the country estate of his patron Carl Joseph von Fürnberg, to play in a quartet consisting of Fürnberg's pastor, his steward, Haydn, and "Albrechtsberger" (either Johann Georg Albrechtsberger or his brother, Anton Johann) on cello. According to Griesinger, Haydn's earliest quartets were written for these occasions. These works may be dated from the second half of the 1750s, with 1757–59 the most plausible period (see Webster, 1975); they are thus the most likely candidates for the title of the first "true" string quartets.

Haydn's early quartets were subsequently published as part of opp. 1–2 ("op. 3" is spurious). Like most of his other early chamber works, they are in five movements with a minuet and trio in both second and fourth place, an indication of their generally light, informal character. Haydn's next sets, opp. 9, 17, and 20 (ca. 1769–72), brought a change to four longer movements with the minuet in second place. This is also the form of four of the six quartets of op. 33 (1781) and three from Mozart's principal set, the quartets dedicated to Haydn (1782–85). Thereafter the standard symphonic cycle, with the minuet in third place, became the norm.

In both style and expression, Haydn's opp. 9–20 grow increasingly serious in nature. They evince a particular concern on Haydn's part for the creation of a balanced, varied, and idiomatic texture, a tendency that culminates in the quartets of op. 33; Haydn may have been referring to the equal distribution of thematic material among all the parts when he described op. 33 as written in "an entirely new and special way." His 39 quartets after op. 33 combine the textural principles, wit, and accessible style of that set with the large scale, formal and stylistic inventiveness, and wide range of expression characteristic of his late works in every genre.

While Austria, in particular Vienna, was preeminent in the composition of string quartets, Paris and London were the leading centers for their publication and dissemination. After ca. 1770 the title *quatuor concertant* was used in French prints to designate quartets in which all the parts were necessary to the texture, not merely accompanimental; many such works are virtuoso display pieces, illustrating a tendency that continued in the 19th century.

II. *19th century.* Beethoven's great series of 16 quartets falls neatly into the three traditional periods of his compositional activity. The early quartets op. 18 (1798–1800) show the strong influence of Haydn, especially in the economy of their motivic development. The five "middle" quartets (the *Razumovsky* Quartets op. 59, the *Harp* op. 74, and the *Serioso* op. 95, 1805–10) echo the extraordinary increase in dramatic intensity and time span heralded by Beethoven's *Eroica* Symphony (1803). At the same time, the expanded pitch range and technical difficulty of these works reflect the fact that they were written for performance by a professional quartet, the Schuppanzigh; the appropriate milieu for these quartets was no longer the intimate princely soirée or amateur gathering but, like the symphony, the large-scale concert (whether private or public).

Beethoven's late quartets (opp. 127, 130–32, and 135, 1823–26) are highly individual in conception. Perhaps most obvious about them is the variety of their large-scale forms, which range from the four movements (with scherzo) of opp. 127 and 135 to the seven connected movements of op. 131. The basic approach of the late quartets might be described as abstractly linear, a characteristic evident in their frequent melodic terseness or neutrality and their pervasive interest in contrapuntal procedures (seen especially in the *Grosse Fuge* op. 133, originally intended as the finale to op. 130). A still more fundamental trait is their enormous range of contrasts (see Kerman, 1967); introspective, highly complex movements exist side by side with movements in which the appeal is direct and even childlike, as in the "Hymn of Gratitude to God from a Convalescent, in the Lydian Mode" (op. 132, 3rd movt.).

The efflorescence of the string quartet in the late 18th and early 19th centuries was followed by a gradual decline in interest. The more radical Romantic composers such as Berlioz, Liszt, and Wagner turned almost entirely from chamber music, and those composers who did write quartets often treated them as miniature orchestral works or virtuoso showcases (e.g., the *quatuors brillants* of composer-violinists like Louis Spohr). Schubert's early quartets are written in a somewhat orchestral style, mostly for performance by his family's string quartet. After a four-year hiatus, he returned to the genre with the important *Quartettsatz* (1820) and his three masterpieces of 1824–26, including *Death and the Maiden.* The lyricism, interest in sonority, extended tonal goals (especially third relationships), and expressive content of these works mark them as both Schubertian and Romantic. Many of the same qualities are apparent in Mendelssohn's six numbered quartets (1827–47), recently the subject of renewed interest, and Schumann's three (all from 1842, his "chamber music year").

The string quartet experienced a minor renascence in the latter part of the century in the works of Dvořák (14 quartets, 1862–95), Brahms (3 quartets, 1873–76), and Smetana (2 quartets, 1876–96). Dvořák's and Smetana's quartets, the latter autobiographical in content, are notable for their inclusion of Czech folk material, particularly dances. In France, César Franck's single quartet of 1889, one of the few string quartets until that time to make use of *cyclic form, spurred the composition of similar works by his student Vincent d'Indy (3 completed quartets, 1890–1929) and others. In Russia, the first noteworthy quartets were by Anton Rubinstein, followed somewhat later by Tchaikovsky (3 quartets, 1871–77) and the more nationalistic Alexander Borodin (2 quartets, 1874–81).

III. *20th century.* The repertory of string quartets from the modern era incorporates most of the stylistic innovations found in other works of the period. The Debussy and Ravel quartets (1893, 1902–3) combine impressionist harmony and scoring with formal procedures deriving from the Franck quartet. Shortly thereafter, Vienna saw the production of Schoenberg's first two quartets, no. 1 (1904–5) in a single large movement and no. 2 (1907–8) with soprano, as well as Berg's op. 3 of 1910. These works were followed much later by Schoenberg's last two quartets (1927–36) and Webern's op. 28 (1936–38), all three dodecaphonic. By contrast, a neoclassical approach characterizes many of Darius Milhaud's 18 string quartets (1912–50), as it does the very different quartets of Ernst Toch (13, 1902–54) and Paul Hindemith (6, 1919–45).

Among the most important quartets of the century are Bartók's set of six (1908–39), notable for their assured handling of form and their expansion of the timbral possibilities of the quartet, including the use of harmonics, various percussive effects, and even quarter-tones (in the Burletta of no. 6). Somewhat similar in style, but programmatic in content, are Leoš Janáček's two fine quartets (1923–28). In Russia, the leading composers of string quartets have been Nikolay Myaskovsky, Prokofiev (2 quartets, 1930–41), and Shostakovich (15 quartets, 1935–74), in Poland Karol Szymanowski and more recently Krzysztof Penderecki (2 quartets, 1960–68).

Of numerous British string quartets, those of Michael Tippett (4 quartets, 1934–79), Alan Rawsthorne (3, 1939–64), and Benjamin Britten (3, 1941–75) are worthy of mention. Except for a few negligible examples from the 19th century, American composition in this genre may be said to begin with Charles Ives's two quartets, the first (1896) entitled *From the Salvation Army,* the second (1907–13) with programmatic titles for each movement. More recent quartets include Ruth Crawford's String Quartet *1931,* which includes serial techniques; 5 quartets (1933–62) by Walter Piston, in a neoclassical idiom; 2 (1936–51) by Roger Sessions; 1 (1936) by Samuel Barber, best known as the origin of his Adagio for Strings; 5 (1950–95) by Elliott Carter, featuring his technique of musical characterization or personification of each part; *Black Angels* (1970) by George Crumb; and 7 quartets (1952–1979) by George Rochberg, the second and seventh with voice. The formation of the Kronos Quartet in 1973 and the Arditti Quartet in 1974 has contributed to a revival of interest in the string quartet on the part of contemporary composers, including the minimalists Philip Glass (5 quartets, 1966–91) and Steve Reich (Triple Quartet for quartet and tape, 1999).

Bibl.: Eugene Goossens, "The String Quartet since Brahms," *ML* 3 (1922): 335–48. Mary D. Herter Norton, *String Quartet Playing* (New York: C Fischer, 1925). Wilhelm Altmann, *Handbuch für Streichquartettspieler,* 4 vols. (Berlin: M Hesse, 1928–31). Homer Ulrich, *Chamber Music* (New York: Columbia U Pr, 1948). Athol Page, *Playing String Quartets* (London: Longman, 1964). Joseph Kerman, *The Beethoven Quartets* (New York: A A Knopf, 1967). Ludwig Finscher, *Studien zur Geschichte des Streichquartetts,* vol. 1, *Die Entstehung des klassischen Streichquartetts* (Kassel: Bärenreiter, 1974). James Webster, "Towards a History of Viennese Chamber Music in the Early Classical Period," *JAMS* 27 (1974): 212–47. Id., "The Chronology of Haydn's String Quartets," *MQ* 61 (1975): 17–46. Warren Kirkendale, *Fugue and Fugato in Rococo and Classical Chamber Music,* 2nd ed., trans. Margaret Bent and Warren Kirkendale (Durham, N.C.: Duke U Pr, 1979). Roger Hickman, "The Nascent Viennese String Quartet," *MQ* 67 (1981): 193–212. Wolfgang Oberkogler, *Das Streichquartettschaffen in Wien von 1910 bis 1925* (Tutzing: Schneider, 1982). Paul Griffiths, *The String Quartet* (New York: Thames and Hudson, 1983). James Webster, "The Scoring of Mozart's Chamber Music for Strings," *Brook,* 1985, pp. 259–96. E.K.W.

String quintet. See Quintet.

Strings. The stringed instruments (string section) of an orchestra.

String trio. See Trio.

Strisciando [It.]. *Glissando.

Strohfiedel [Ger.]. See Xylophone.

Stromentato [It.]. Accompanied by instruments. In *recitativo stromentato,* the standard continuo instruments are reinforced by others, usually strings. See Recitative.

Stromento [It.]. See *Strumento.*

Strong beat. See Meter.

Strophic. (1) With respect to a poem, made up of units (strophes), all with the same number of lines, rhyme scheme, and meter. (2) With respect to a musical setting of a strophic text, characterized by the repetition of the same music for all strophes, as distinct from *through-composed.

Strophicus [Lat.]. See Neume.

Strophic variations. (1) In 17th-century vocal music, an aria or song whose bass line remains the same (or very nearly the same) for every stanza of text, while different melodies are set to it at each repetition; also called strophic bass. (2) In instrumental music of the 17th, 18th, and 19th centuries, a sectional theme-and-variations form in which the variations retain the structure of the theme; the melodies of the variations may or may not resemble or ornament that of the theme, though the harmonic structure, at least at cadences, is quite similar. The structural principle in both (1) and (2) is repetition. Strophic variations, both vocal and instrumental, are sectional and thus differ from variations on a *ground or an *ostinato. In addition, the strophic bass or theme is usually quite a bit longer than a typical ground.

Theorists of the 17th and 18th centuries did not use the term strophic to describe these structures, but one good precedent may be found in Walther's *Musicalisches Lexicon* of 1732, s.v., "Double": "the second *verse* of an air, varied."

Examples of (1) include Monteverdi's duet on the **romanesca* bass, "Ohimè, dov'è il mio ben" (Seventh Book of Madrigals, 1619), and Frescobaldi's "Aria di Romanesca" (*Arie musicali,* 1630). The practice died out soon after this. Examples of (2) include most independent sets of variations as well as variation movements of the 17th through mid-19th centuries, such as Bach's *Goldberg* Variations, Beethoven's *Eroica* Variations for piano op. 35, and the finale of Brahms's String Quartet op. 67.

Bibl.: Nigel Fortune, "Solo Song and Cantata," *NOHM* 4 (1968): 125–217. Elaine R. Sisman, "Haydn's Variations" (Ph.D. diss., Princeton Univ., 1978). E.S.

Strumento [It., sometimes also *instrumento, stromento*]. A musical instrument; *s. d'arco,* bowed instrument; *s. a corde,* stringed instrument; *s. a fiato,* wind instrument; *s. di legno,* woodwind instrument; *s.*

d'ottone, brass instrument; *s. a percussione,* percussion instrument; *s. da tasto,* keyboard instrument.

The *strumento d'acciaio* (steel instrument) specified in Mozart's *The Magic Flute* has been variously thought to be the *glockenspiel or a keyboard instrument like the *celesta.

Stück [Ger.]. Piece, composition.

Study. *Etude.

Stürmend, stürmisch [Ger.]. Stormy, impetuous.

Sturm und Drang [Ger., storm and stress]. A movement in German literature of the second half of the 18th century that had as its goal the powerful, shocking, even violent expression of emotion. Its principal influence occurred in the period from 1773, the publication date of Goethe's *Götz von Berlichingen,* until 1781, the date of Schiller's *Die Räuber.* However, earlier manifestations of a *Sturm und Drang* spirit have been noted in Rousseau and in Herder's *Fragmente* (1767) and Gerstenberg's *Ugolino* (1768). A play from 1776 by Maximilian Klinger was titled *Sturm und Drang.*

The most appropriate parallels between music and the literary *Sturm und Drang* can be drawn with German opera and other stage music of the 1770s, notably the melodrama (Heartz, 1970). Certain earlier works such as Gluck's ballets and operas of the 1760s, with their scenes of terror, have also been cited as examples of the *Sturm und Drang.* Yet such works antedate the *Sturm und Drang* proper, and the forcefulness and intensity of their expression can be related equally well to standard 18th-century aesthetic concepts, in particular the "sublime."

The same may be said for a series of minor-key instrumental pieces of the period ca. 1765–75, including symphonies, overtures, string quartets, and sonatas by Haydn, Mozart, Johann Vanhal, Carl Ditters von Dittersdorf, Johann Christian Bach, and others. Though commonly designated as *Sturm und Drang* compositions, the early dates and predominantly Austrian origins of these works, as well as what we know of their composers, make it highly unlikely that any direct influence of the literary *Sturm und Drang* was involved.

Bibl.: Roy Pascal, *The German Sturm und Drang* (New York: Philosophical Library, 1953). Hans Heinrich Eggebrecht, "Das Ausdrucksprinzip im musikalischen Sturm und Drang," *Deutsche Vierteljahrsschrift für Literatur- und Geistesgeschichte* 29 (1955): 323–49. Daniel Heartz, "Sturm und Drang im Musikdrama," *Bonn,* 1970, pp. 432–35. Barry S. Brook, "Sturm und Drang and the Romantic Period in Music," *Studies in Romanticism* 9 (1970): 269–84. Max Rudolf, "Storm and Stress in Music," *Bach: The Quarterly Journal of the Riemenschneider Bach Institute* 3, no. 2 (April 1972): 3–13; no. 3 (July 1972): 3–11; no. 4 (October 1972): 8–16. R. Larry Todd, "Joseph Haydn and the *Sturm und Drang:* A Revaluation," *MR* 41 (1980): 172–96. Gerhard Kaiser, *Aufklärung, Empfindsamkeit, Sturm und Drang,* 5th ed. (Tübingen: Francke, 1996). E.K.W.

Stürze [Ger.]. The bell of a wind instrument; *S. hoch,* an instruction to play with the bell raised.

Style [Fr. *style;* Ger. *Stil;* It. *stile;* Sp. *estilo*]. The choices that a work or performance makes from among the possibilities available. Style thus comprehends all aspects of a work or performance. As often used with respect to music, the concept style is borrowed from a rhetorical tradition (reaching back at least to Aristotle) that distinguishes style from content—the manner in which something is said as distinct from what is being said. Such a distinction is difficult to sustain even with respect to language. Its application to music is still more problematic, because music is essentially nonrepresentational. The pitches and durations that define the style of a composition also constitute its content. In this sense, music has only style.

The concept style is employed principally for the sake of comparing works or performances with one another and identifying the significant characteristics that distinguish one or more works or performances from others. Style may thus refer to features that characterize the works or performances of a period, region, genre, or individual composer or performer. An individual work may also be described as having a style that distinguishes it from other works by the same composer. In all of these cases, the attempt to define a style requires consideration of all aspects of the music being studied. Thus, the analysis of style makes use of all of the techniques of *analysis (including, e.g., the analysis of form) and *criticism. Its emphases may differ, however. It is more likely to concentrate on the establishment of normative categories against which to test the individual work than it is to concentrate on the uniqueness of the individual work. Here it runs the risk of circularity. The norms of a particular style can only be discovered through careful study of individual works. But the criteria for significance employed in the study of the individual work are likely to rest in some measure on a prior definition of the style to which the individual work is thought to belong. The danger is greatest where the aims are broadest, as in the attempt to define the style of a historical period that has itself been defined at least in part on the basis of nonmusical criteria [see History of music].

Historically, classifications of musical styles derive from the tradition of classifications of style in rhetoric [see Rhetoric I], and they begin to flourish in the late 16th and early 17th century when writers on music were most heavily influenced by theories of rhetoric. To this period belong distinctions between the *stile antico* (old style; see Palestrina style) and various new styles (termed *nuovo, moderno, luxurians,* etc.), especially the **stile rappresentativo* or *recitativo* [see also Monody; *Prima prattica, seconda prattica*]. Other terms associated with music of this period are *stile *concitato* and *stile *concertato.* A widely shared classification of the second half of the 17th century and the first half of the 18th distinguished styles appropriate to church, chamber, and theater. The 18th century also saw discussion of national styles. In France, this took the form of a dispute over the relative merits of French and Italian music [see *Bouffons, Querelle des*], a dispute with echoes into the 19th century.

Bibl.: Jan LaRue, *Guidelines for Style Analysis* (New York: Norton, 1970). Leonard B. Meyer, *Explaining Music* (Berkeley and Los Angeles: U of Cal Pr, 1973). Oswald Ducrot and Tzvetan Todorov, *Encyclopedic Dictionary of the Sciences of Language,* trans. Catherine Porter (Baltimore: Johns Hopkins U Pr, 1979). See also Analysis, History of music.

Style brisé [Fr., broken style]. A texture in which melodic lines are subservient to the broken chords and composite rhythms they create. Voices merge and change roles frequently, and even melody notes are delayed to create continuous rhythmic presentation of the harmony [see the canon in the accompanying example]. *Style brisé* was an essential feature of 17th-century French lute music (whence the term *style luthé*) and was imitated by French harpsichordists (Chambonnières, d'Anglebert), as well as by Germans in harpsichord suites (Froberger, Bach). The term itself is modern. B.G.

Style galant [Fr.]. See *Galant* style.

Style luthé [Fr.]. **Style brisé.*

Subdiapente, subdiatessaron. See *Diapente, Diatessaron.*

Subdominant. The fourth *scale degree of a major or minor scale, so called because it lies the same distance below the tonic as the *dominant lies above the tonic, namely a perfect fifth. In *harmonic analysis it is identified by the roman numeral IV or by the letter S [see also Functional analysis]. It often precedes the dominant at cadences (IV–V–I). The progression IV–I is termed a plagal (or amen) *cadence.

Subfinalis [Lat.]. In an authentic *mode, the tone below the final.

Subito [It.]. Suddenly, quickly.

Subject. A melody or melodic fragment on which a composition or a major portion of one is based. The term, which has been in use since the 16th century, implies that the material in question is developed or treated in some special way. It is now used principally with respect to the *fugue and other imitative forms such as the *ricercar and with respect to *sonata form (where it may be synonymous with theme). It may also denote the material on which any use of *imitation is based. See also *Soggetto, Soggetto cavato.*

Subjugalis [Lat.]. A plagal *mode.

Submediant. The sixth *scale degree.

Subsemitonium modi [Lat.]. The pitch lying a semitone below the final of a *mode. This occurs naturally if the final is C or F. For other finals, however, an accidental is required to produce such a semitone. For a discussion of the use of accidentals in this context, see *Musica ficta.*

Substitution chord. A chord that can be substituted for another while retaining its harmonic function [see Functional analysis]. Jazz makes use of a variety of such chords (often chromatically altered), especially in the performance of popular songs or *standards that are adapted for the jazz repertory. The tritone substitution, for example, replaces a dominant or dominant-seventh chord with a seventh or ninth chord on the lowered supertonic.

Subtonic. The *scale degree immediately below the tonic, especially when it lies a whole tone below the tonic; otherwise the term *leading tone is preferred.

Subtonium modi [Lat.]. Originally, the pitch lying immediately below the lowest pitch of the normal ambitus of a *mode; in the case of the authentic modes, this is the pitch below the final. In the 16th century, the term was applied to the pitch below the final in both authentic and plagal modes when this occurred naturally at the interval of a whole tone, thus, in all modes except those with finals on C and F. See also *Subsemitonium modi.*

Succentor. In some Anglican cathedrals, the deputy of the *precentor.

Successive composition. A process of composition in which voices or parts are largely composed one after

Style brisé. Gaultier, *Courante le canon* for lute, transcribed by Perrine (1680).

another rather than more or less simultaneously and with a view to the harmonies created from moment to moment by all parts at once. Some music of the Middle Ages seems to have been composed in this way, and the *Renaissance has sometimes been characterized as the result in part of a shift to simultaneous composition. This view is made plausible by the remarks of some theorists and the absence of *scores from before about 1500. The music of these periods suggests, however, that the distinction has often been too rigidly applied and that the control of simultaneities is as careful in much music from well before 1500 as it is in music composed thereafter. The term is also used in reference to New England psalmody and shape-note hymnody.

Suffrages. Intercessory prayers; commonly a series of liturgical intercessory petitions pronounced by the officiant and answered by the people or its surrogate. Formally, such series are often indistinguishable from sets of versicles and responses. The Book of Common Prayer of 1549 for Evensong instructs the repetition of "the suffrages before assigned at Mattyns" preceding the final collects. John Barnard (1641) calls musical settings of such suffrages "Responce" and designates as "Preces" suffrages occurring earlier, e.g., at Matins before the *Venite.* Many passages of the Litany have the character of suffrages, though the term (as in the phrase Litany and suffrages) is sometimes reserved for the concluding versicles and reponses. R.F.F.

Sughithā [Syrian]. See Syrian chant.

Suite [Fr., succession, following]. A series of disparate instrumental movements with some element of unity, most often to be performed as a single work. The number of movements in a suite may be just large enough to constitute a series (three) or may be so great as to suggest that the work was intended to be treated as an anthology from which to make selections (e.g., 24 pieces in François Couperin's second **ordre*). Individual movements are almost always short and contrasting. A suite's unity may result from nothing more than a common key or from its origins in a larger work, such as an opera or ballet, from which it is excerpted; unity may occasionally involve thematic connections and some sense of overall form. In some suites, the relationship among movements is defined by an extramusical program. The Baroque solo suite came close to having a specific pattern of dance movements at its core (*allemande–*courante–*sarabande–*gigue), but even then looseness of definition and variability of design were implicit in the term.

I. *Before ca. 1630.* The origins of the suite are found in dance music pairing two contrasting dances. Among the earliest such pairs are two in a manuscript of the 14th century (*GB-Lbl.* Add. 29987). By the 16th century, pairs of this type were commonplace, usually consisting of a slower gliding dance in duple meter followed by a faster leaping dance in triple meter (e.g., *Tanz* and **Nachtanz,* *pavan and *galliard; see also After-dance). Groups of three dances appeared during the 16th century as well, such as Joan Ambrosio Dalza's lute arrangements published by Petrucci in 1508, in which he calls attention to the *pavana–salterello–piva* groupings. There are similar groupings in lute tablatures of 1546 by Antonio Rotta and Domenico Bianchini. In such groups, the dances are often thematically related, placing them as much in the history of variations as in that of the suite. The term suite was first used by Estienne du Tertre (1557) for sequences of **branles* following established choreographic traditions of progressing from the sedate to the lively.

In the last quarter of the 16th century and the beginning of the 17th, dances for instrumental ensemble and for lute were published with varying contents, generally grouped by key, sometimes without overt thematic connections (Mathäus Waissel, 1573; Robert Ballard, 1611 and 1614). The first composer to adopt a consistent pattern and thus demonstrate a concept of the suite as a coherent musical whole was Paul Peuerl (1611), using the order *paduana–intrada–Dantz–galiarda* ten times. Other composers in Germany wrote thematically related dances in a single key with a specific order, each composer creating his own choice of dances (Johann Hermann Schein, 1617; Isaac Posch, 1618). But such "variation suites" did not dominate instrumental publications, which more often contained pairs of unrelated dances.

II. *Baroque solo suite.* Bach wrote nearly 40 suites (some called *partitas) for solo instruments (harpsichord, lute, violin, cello, and flute), a little over half of which have the following pattern: prelude–allemande–courante–sarabande–optional–gigue (henceforth P–A–C–S–O–G). This has given rise to the notion that the Baroque suite was by definition the sequence A–C–S–G, which might be prefaced by a nondance movement and which could allow optional dances to intervene before the gigue. Although the core of A–C–S–G did evolve to be the most frequent pattern in solo suites, the suite was less an architecturally conceived whole than a series of separate units. The opening of solo suites tended to follow the pattern (P)–A–C–S, but the number, choice, and character of closing dances remained variable even with Bach, not always including a gigue. Furthermore, suites for other media [see III–IV] developed different traditions, and these patterns were sometimes taken over into suites for solo instruments.

A–C–S groupings seem first to have appeared in French lute music ca. 1630. The pattern was adopted by German harpsichordists who, after the addition of the gigue, ca. 1665, used it more than any other scheme. In England, the A–C–S sequence was a commonplace but not a rule in harpsichord music. In Italy, the solo suite was not a significant genre for any medium [see *Sonata da camera*].

Datable suite literature for the Baroque lute and

its relatives begins with A–C–S groupings in a 1629 mandora volume by François de Chancy. It was primarily through music of other French lutenists (anthologized by the publisher Pierre Ballard, 1631) that the notion was disseminated. Gigues were included after mid-century (Denis Gaultier, ca. 1655, 1669), but most such suites were very large groupings of pieces in a single key not centering around an A–C–S–G core (Jacques Gallot, 1673–75; Perrine, 1680; Charles Mouton, 1698–99). German lutenists, however, wrote A–C–S–G suites until the very end of the Baroque period, by then in the shadow of the more popular harpsichord (Silvius Weiss, Adam Falckenhagen). In Italy, some exceptional guitar collections include A–C–S suites (Angelo Michele Bartolotti, 1640; Giovanni Battista Granata, 1651).

The solo suite is principally a harpsichord genre. German harpsichordists in the second third of the 17th century imitated several aspects of French lute style, including A–C–S sequences. Johann Jakob Froberger created a norm (ca. 1650) of A–G–C–S, but virtually all succeeding composers in Germanic areas placed the gigue at the end, and Froberger's publishers (17th and 19th century) felt compelled to "correct" his ordering. The large body of German harpsichord suites includes music by Johann Erasmus Kindermann, Dietrich Buxtehude, and Georg Böhm. The last composer in this tradition was Bach, whose partitas as well as "French" and "English" suites (the nicknames are not from Bach and carry no stylistic implications) tower over their antecedents and have no successors. The English Suites are the most regular, using the pattern P–A–C–S–O–G, with the optional dances being a pair of *bourrées, *gavottes, *minuets, or *passepieds. One suite includes two courantes, and two include **doubles*. The French Suites have no preludes, and the optional dances vary both in number (one to four) and kind. The partitas show the greatest diversity within the same basic scheme, using five types of opening movement and occasionally placing a dance between the courante and sarabande; one ends with a *capriccio rather than a gigue. Even within the German harpsichord tradition, many suites ignore the A–C–S–G concept altogether, such as those that imitate the orchestral suite (J. C. F. Fischer).

In French harpsichord music, the suite was more an ordering of pieces for publication or performance than a compositional form. Preexisting movements were compiled by composers or performers to create groupings in a single key. Often suites were put together from the music of more than one composer. The published harpsichord music from 1670 until ca. 1710 shows the greatest consistency. The serious dances (A–C–S) preceded lighter ones, which might include a gigue. Often there was more than one courante; *doubles* [see Double (5)] were included for a few movements; there was a tendency to end with a minuet (Nicolas-Antoine Lebègue, Elisabeth Jacquet de la Guerre); and the opening of a suite was often an unmeasured prelude [see Prelude (1)]. Jean-Henri d'Anglebert (1689) followed such groups with, in effect, a second suite modeled after orchestral suites, consisting of transcriptions from Lully's operas. Beginning with François Couperin (1713), harpsichord suites (his term was **ordre*) increasingly contained character pieces rather than dances, and no consistent organizational pattern emerged except for a tendency to include programmatic sets of pieces as subgroups (Jean-François Dandrieu, 1724). Even unity of key was occasionally challenged (Simon Simon, 1761).

English harpsichord composers did write (P)–A–C–S–G suites in the late 17th century (Purcell), but here also the gigue was not to be counted on. Suites did not always have an A–C–S opening before the usually short series of dances and transcriptions from stage music that are characteristic. Handel's suites combine the German proclivity for the A–C–S–G pattern with English and French elements, including the assembling of miscellaneous pieces in the same key. In his composed (rather than compiled) suites, he sometimes made obvious thematic connections among the movements.

In Italy, pieces were usually grouped together by type, not as multimovement forms. Harpsichord dances were occasionally placed in suitelike sequences, though the patterns were more closely related to the **sonata da camera* (Bernardo Pasquini).

Suites for other solo instruments are less numerous, but the patterns follow those of the lute and harpsichord. Viol and cello suites usually had the A–C–S–G pattern in Germany (Peter Zachau, Konrad Höffler, Bach). In France, dances other than the gigue tended to be the conclusion of suites that vary from 5 to 40 movements (de Machy, Marin Marais).

III. *Baroque orchestral suite.* In the second half of the 17th century, the popularity of French ballet and especially of the music of Lully surged. With this came the practice of excerpting dances and airs from stage works, presenting the aggregate as an independent work. Such a suite might restrict itself to tunes from a single work or might mix extracts in the same key from various works. By the 1680s, such extract-suites inspired composers to write original suites in a similar style. In Germany, the vogue was spurred by the set of suites of 1682 by Lully's former intimate friend Johann Sigismund Kusser. Telemann is said to have written about a thousand such suites, 135 of which survive. Bach wrote four masterly examples (BWV 1066–69), but the most famous are Handel's *Water Music* (ca. 1717) and *Music for the Royal Fireworks* (1749). Most orchestral suites begin with a French *overture, and thus *ouverture* may stand as the title of a complete suite (Bach). Dances follow in no particular order, but in the same key (except for pairs of dances to be played alternatively in which the second might be in a closely related key). The choice of dances emphasizes those popular in stage works and in the ballroom (e.g., minuet, bourrée, gavotte, passepied) and does not usually include the older forms of allemande and courante. Pieces with descriptive titles such as *réjouissance* are also common.

IV. *Baroque chamber suite.* A sharp distinction between chamber and orchestral music is a modern concept, but suites especially for trios did develop differently from the solo or orchestral varieties. At about the same time that the solo suite in Germany crystallized in the A–C–S–G pattern, the *sonata da camera* became the principal genre for dance music for small ensembles. In English consort music, A–C–S groups may date from as early as the 1620s (William Lawes), but the pattern remained exceptional for chamber music. For example, although the harpsichord suites of Johann Erasmus Kindermann use the A–C–S pattern, his collection of dances for ensemble (1640–43) shows no organization into suites. In Germany, the A–C–S succession (with the addition of the gigue from ca. 1665) did gain a foothold until the 1680s (Johann Rosenmüller, Clamor Heinrich Abel). In France, chamber suites paralleled the orchestral suite with the exception that the overture might be replaced by a prelude for bass. François Couperin wrote some suites that are tied together programmatically. Suite, sonata, and even opera converged in *La gamme en forme de petit opera* by Marin Marais (1723). In Italy, the *sonata da camera* reigned supreme and did not admit suites of other sorts.

V. *After ca. 1750.* As dances gave way to sonata designs in the middle of the 18th century, the dance suite all but disappeared for a time. Genres such as the *divertimento had the same looseness of definition as the Baroque suite without the strong attachment to dance forms [see also Partita]. The dance suite then assumed a retrospective gesture for composers, even as early as Mozart (K. 399/385i). Neoclassicists of the 19th and 20th centuries (Saint-Saëns, Hindemith) created a large corpus of such suites, and others contributed to a major revival of the orchestral suite (Debussy, Sibelius). Sometimes the title suite is used for collections of movements that could be considered multimovement tone poems (Massenet, Holst), often with a nationalistic flavor.

Beginning in the middle of the 19th century, the extract-suite regained nearly the popularity it had enjoyed in the 17th century. Composers sometimes merely assemble coherent excerpts from larger works such as ballets, or may weave them together into a continuous whole, making key and orchestration changes as necessary. Famous examples include the *Nutcracker Suite* by Tchaikovsky and the *Firebird Suite* of Stravinsky.

Bibl.: Jules Armand Joseph Écorcheville, *Vingt Suites d'orchestre du XVIIe siècle français* (Paris: L M Fortin, 1906). Karl Nef, *Geschichte der Sinfonie und Suite* (Leipzig: Breitkopf & Härtel, 1921). Margerete Reimann, *Untersuchungen zur Formgeschichte der französischen Klaviersuite* (Regensburg: G Bosse, 1940). Mildred Pearl, "The Suite in Relation to Baroque Style" (Ph.D. diss., New York Univ., 1957). Hermann Beck, *Die Suite, Mw* 26 (1964), trans. Robert Kolben, *The Suite* (1966). Willi Apel, *The History of Keyboard Music to 1700,* trans. and rev. Hans Tischler (Bloomington: Ind U Pr, 1972). Barry A. R. Cooper, "The Keyboard Suite in England before the Restoration," *ML* 53 (1972): 309–19. Bruce Gustafson, *French Harpsichord Music of the 17th Century: A Thematic Catalog of the Sources,* 3 vols. (Ann Arbor: UMI Res Pr, 1979). B.G.

Suite bergamasque [Fr.]. A suite for piano by Debussy in four movements: Prélude, Menuet, Clair de lune, and Passepied, composed in 1890 (revised in 1905). Its title is probably derived from a phrase in Paul Verlaine's poem "Clair de lune": "masques et bergamasques."

Suivez [Fr., imp., follow]. (1) **Attacca.* (2) An instruction for the accompaniment to follow the lead of the soloist.

Sul, sulla [It.]. At, on, on the; *sul G,* an instruction in music for stringed instruments to play on the G string (or, similarly, another string identified by letter or by roman numeral); *sul ponticello,* to bow at the bridge; *sul tasto, sulla tastiera,* to bow over the fingerboard [see Bowing].

Suling [Jav.]. A *duct flute of Java made of bamboo, with four to six finger holes, depending on the scale to be played. A bamboo ring guides the air stream across a notch, making the *suling* an external rather than an internal duct flute. It is played as a solo instrument and in **gamelan* ensembles. See ill. under Southeast Asia.

Sumeria. See Mesopotamia.

Sumer is icumen in. A mid-13th-century infinite *canon or round at the unison for four voices over a texted two-voice **pes* involving *voice exchange (*HAM,* no. 42); also known as the Summer Canon and the Reading Rota (from Reading, England, the probable place of composition). A Latin text for the canonic part ("Perspice christicola"), written beneath the English text in the single surviving manuscript copy of the piece (*GB–Lbm* Harl.978, fol. 11v), may not have been part of the work originally. The text of the *pes* is related to the English text of the canonic part. The manuscript includes instructions for performance.

Summation(al) tone. See Combination tone.

Sumponyah [Heb., Aramaic, fr. Gr.?]. In the Book of Daniel (3:5, 7, 10, 15), a term that has been variously translated or thought to mean dulcimer, bagpipe, or ensemble.

Sun Quartets [Ger. *Sonnenquartette*]. Popular name for Haydn's six string quartets op. 20, Hob. III:31–36 (1772). The Hummel edition of 1779 had an engraving of the rising sun as part of its frontispiece.

Suor Angelica [It.]. See *Trittico.*

Superdominant. The *scale degree above the dominant, normally termed the submediant.

Superius [Lat.]. In polyphonic vocal music of the 16th century, the highest part. The term is often applied to the highest part in earlier polyphony as well, though such parts are not normally given a name in sources before the advent of printed *partbooks.

Superoctave. An organ flue stop of *Principal tone, pitched an octave higher than the main Principal stop of the division in which it appears.

Supertonic. The second *scale degree.

Supplying. See Verset.

Sur [Fr.]. On, over; *sur le chevalet,* an instruction in music for stringed instruments to bow at the bridge; *sur la touche,* to bow over the fingerboard [see Bowing].

Surnāy [Pers.]. See *Zūrnā.*

Surprise Symphony. Popular name for Haydn's Symphony no. 94 in G major Hob. I:94 (1791, no. 2 of the *Salomon Symphonies), so called because of a loud chord in the middle of the quiet first theme of the second movement. Haydn later incorporated this celebrated second movement into his oratorio *The *Seasons,* in the aria "Schon eilet."

Susannah. Opera in two acts by Carlisle Floyd (to his own libretto), produced in Tallahassee, Florida, in 1955. Setting: the mountains of Tennessee.

Suspension. (1) See Counterpoint II, 3. (2) An ornament described in the 18th century by François Couperin and others as the delaying of a note by a short rest of flexible duration [see Ex.].

Suspirum [Lat.]. A rest equal in value to a *minima* [see Mensural notation].

Sussurando [It.]. Whispering.

Sustaining pedal. The *sostenuto pedal of the piano; sometimes also the *damper pedal.

Suzuki method. A system of musical instruction for children developed by Shinichi Suzuki (b. 1898). The child begins at an early age (preferably 3–4 years) with lessons on an instrument, usually the violin, learning a fixed repertory of pieces (most, except the most elementary ones, by composers of the 18th and 19th centuries), arranged in order of increasing difficulty. Instruction is by ear and by rote, often aided by listening to recordings of the assigned pieces; emphasis is on correct technique and musicality from the beginning; practice entails substantial repetition and active participation of a parent until the student is quite advanced; note reading is not introduced until the child has acquired a basic technique. The method is also used to teach piano, cello, and flute.

Bibl.: Shinichi Suzuki, *Nurtured by Love: A New Approach to Education,* trans. Waltraud Suzuki (Smithtown, N.Y.: Exposition, 1969). Id., *Ability Development from Age Zero,* trans. Mary Louise Nagata (Athens, Ohio: Ability Development Associates, 1981; first Japanese ed., 1969). John D. Kendall, *The Suzuki Violin Method in American Music Education* (Washington: MENC, 1973).

Švanda Dudák [Cz., Schwanda the Bagpiper]. Opera in two acts by Jaromír Weinberger (libretto by Miloš Kareš and Max Brod, after the tale by Tyl), produced in Prague in 1927. Setting: fairy tale.

Svarakalpana [Tel.]. The improvisation of solfège in Carnatic music; ordinarily preceded by **niraval.*

C.C.

Svelto [It.]. Quick, nimble.

Sw. Abbr. for the *Swell division of an organ.

Swan Lake [Russ. *Lebedinoye ozero*]. A ballet in four acts by Tchaikovsky, op. 20 (1875–76), produced in Moscow in 1877 with choreography by Wenzel Reisinger. The choreography by Marius Petipa (acts 1 and 3) and Lev Ivanov (acts 2 and 4) that has remained in the repertory was for a new production in St. Petersburg in 1895.

Swan of Tuonela. See *Lemminkäinen Suite.*

Swan Song. See *Schwanengesang.*

Sweden. I. *Contemporary institutions.* Important to Sweden's concert life are active opera companies at the Royal Opera House and the Rotundan, both in Stockholm, at the 18th-century court theater in Drottningholm, and at Göteborg and Malmö. Annual festivals in Stockholm, Umeå, and elsewhere feature chamber music, opera, concerts, film, and jazz. Music by contemporary Swedish composers has been promoted by a number of institutions and organizations, such as Fylkingen (the Society for Contemporary Music), the Samtida Musik concert society, the "Nutida Musik" (contemporary music) radio series, and STIM (Svenska Tonsättares Internationella Musikbyrå), the Swedish performing-rights organization.

II. *History.* The S-shaped **lur* trumpets from the Nordic Bronze age (ca. 1100–ca. 500 B.C.E.) attest to early musical activity in Scandinavia. The earliest extant music from Sweden is liturgical chant, brought to the region by Christian missionaries during the 11th century. Parisian *organum was apparently performed at Uppsala during the 13th century, and several organs survive from after 1400. Secular court music became established only after the nation was separated from Denmark in the early 16th century. The Thirty Years War (1618–48) brought a large influx of German musicians, including Sweelinck's pupil Andreas Düben (ca. 1597–1662), who served the Stockholm court. Important early native composers include the Handel-influenced Johan Helmich Roman (1694–1758) and the organist Johan Wikmanson (1753–1800). The court of Gustav III (reigned 1771–92) attracted prominent foreign-born composers, including Francesco Uttini (1723–95), Johann Gottlieb Naumann (1741–1801), Georg Joseph Vogler (1749–1814), and Joseph Martin Kraus (1756–92). Romanticism in Sweden was manifested in the songs and choral music of Erik Gustav Geijer (1783–1847), Carl Jonas Love Almqvist (1793–1866), Adolf Fredrik Lindblad (1801–78), Otto Lindblad (1809–64), Jacob Axel Josephson (1818–80), Gunnar Wennerberg (1817–1901), and Prince Gustaf (1827–52).

Many consider Franz Berwald (1798–1868) to be Sweden's greatest composer, though this composer of exceptional symphonies and string quartets was strongly criticized during his lifetime. Significant composers in the second half of the 19th century were Ludvig Norman (1831–85), Johan August Söderman (1832–76), and Emil Sjögren (1853–1918), and in opera Ivar Hallström (1826–1901) and Andreas Hallén (1846–1925). The last part of the 19th century and the first part of the 20th saw the emergence of Wilhelm Peterson-Berger (1867–1942), Wilhelm Stenhammar (1871–1927), Hugo Alfvén (1872–1960), Edvin Kallstenius (1881–1967), Ture Rangström (1884–1947), Kurt Atterberg (1887–1974), and Oskar Lindberg (1887–1955). During the 1920s the music of Gösta Nystroem (1890–1966), Hilding Rosenberg (b. 1892), and Finnish-born Moses Pergament (1893–1977) showed a strong influence of European trends. Other significant composers have included, among an older generation, Dag Wirén (1905–86), Lars-Erik Larsson (1908–86), Erland von Koch (b. 1910), Allan Pettersson (1911–80), Karl-Birger Blomdahl (1916–68), Sven-Erik Bäck (1919–94), Sven-Eric Johanson (1919–97), Torsten Nilsson (1920–99), and Ingvar Lidholm (b. 1921), and among the next generations, Jan Carlstedt (b. 1926), Lars Johan Werle (1926–2001), Hans Eklund (1927–99), Maurice Karkoff (b. 1927), Knut Wiggen (b. 1927), Bengt Hambraeus (1928–2000), Karl-Erik Welin (1934–92), Bo Nilsson (b. 1937), and Jan Morthenson (b. 1940).

III. *Folk music.* Traditionally, a large portion of Swedish folk music has been associated with herding, specifically with the nomadic *fäbod* lifestyle, though the industrialization of the 19th century has destabilized the rural economy that nurtured such musical styles as the *lockrop* (a high-pitched vocal cattle call). Also of significance are the *visor,* or strophic "sung poems," the true folk songs, such as those for singing-games, lullabies, and work in the fields, and the ballads, some of whose tunes still bear resemblances to the medieval French songs from which they appear to have been derived. Remnants survive of a previously strong fiddle tradition, including such dance tunes as the *polska, the *waltz, the *schottische, the polkett, and the *stenbockslåtar.* Important instruments are the *nyckelharpa* (keyed fiddle), the modern violin (often in ensembles), the *psalmodikon* (bowed zither), and the birchbark *lur* (not related to the ancient bronze trumpet).

Bibl.: Åke Davidsson, *Bibliografi över Svensk Musiklitteratur 1800–1945* (Uppsala, 1948; 2nd ed. 1980). John Horton, *Scandinavian Music* (London: Faber, 1963). Carl-Allan Moberg, *Studien zur schwedischen Volksmusik* (Uppsala: Universitet, 1971). Axel Helmer, *Svensk solosång 1850–1890,* 2 vols. (Stockholm: Almquist & Wiksell, 1972). Bengt Emil Johnson and Knut Wiggen, *Electronic Music in Sweden* (Stockholm: STIM, 1972). Arne Aulin and Herbert Connor, *Svensk musik,* 2 vols. (Stockholm: Bonnier, 1974–77). John H. Yoell, *The Nordic Sound* (Boston: Crescendo Pub Co, 1974). Fred K. Prieberg, *Musik und Musikpolitik in Schweden* (Herrenburg: Döring, 1976). Lena Roth, ed., *Musical Life in Sweden,* trans. Michael Johns (Stockholm: Swedish Institute, 1987). Inger Mattsson, ed. *Gustavian Opera* (Stockholm: Royal Swedish Academy, 1991).

Sweet potato. *Ocarina.

Swell. In organs, a keyboard division whose pipes are placed within a large wooden box with Venetian louvers at its front. When the louvers are opened by the Swell pedal, the sound is louder. Closing the louvers both softens the sound and reduces its harmonic development. The Swell is important in 19th-century French organs and in England starting in the 18th century.

Swing. (1) The popular, dance-oriented, *big band jazz style that first flourished in the 1930s [see also Jazz]. Featured are combinations such as five saxophones, four trumpets, and four trombones, and often a vocalist. A *rhythm section smoothly accentuates each beat in 4/4; a "swinging" rhythmic pattern [Ex.] is played on the ride cymbal [see Drum set]. Based on

popular songs (especially 32-bar AABA forms) and 12-bar *blues, the repertory ranges from complex, entirely written arrangements to impromptu *head arrangements in which simple *riffs provide thematic material and accompaniment to improvisations.

(2) Term for characteristic rhythmic momentum in jazz. Specifically manifested in a variety of uneven (2:1 or 3:2) durational relationships between eighth notes within a single beat and/or differing relationships between a song's pulse and the attacks of instruments or vocal sounds (e.g., slightly before or after the beat), swing is sometimes difficult to quantify. But it is meaningful as a general stylistic concept: in, e.g., swing [see (1) above] and *bebop, "swinging" uneven subdivisions of quarter notes (or of eighths at slow tempos, halves at fast tempos) contrast with even subdivisions of pulses in, e.g., *ragtime, Latin American dances, *rock, and *soul. B.K., rev. T.A.J.

Switzerland. Musical activity in Switzerland is entirely decentralized, partly as a result of linguistic diversity. German, French, Italian, and Romansch are each used by some segments of the population and are recognized as official. For this reason, education (including music education) is overseen by local governments. The national government acts as a patron of music through the Fondation Pro Helvetia, the Swiss Office for Culture (which established the Swiss Center for Computer Music in 1985), and the Swiss Music Information Center.

I. *Present-day musical life.* 1. Performing activity. Opera is cultivated in Basel, Bern, Biel, Geneva, Lucerne, St. Gall, and Zürich. About ten cities have resident orchestras, some more than one, of which the best known is the Orchestre de la Suisse Romande of Geneva. Swiss orchestras include full-sized, chamber, and specialized ensembles, a few supported by broadcasting companies, which also maintain small professional choirs.

Numerous festivals are held in towns and villages across the country. Prominent among these are the Menuhin Festival in Gstaad, the Lucerne International Festival, the Montreux Jazz Festival, and international festivals that include exhibitions and theatrical events as well as music in Bern and Zürich. Choral music, religious music, and folk music are emphasized in various other festivals.

2. Education, libraries, and museums. Advanced musical training is available in conservatories in about ten cities. The universities in Zürich, Basel, Geneva, and Fribourg have departments of musicology. Significant music libraries include the Private Library of Dr. Anthony van Hoboken in Ascona, the Musikbibliothek of the Benedikterkloster in Einsiedeln, the Stiftsbibliothek St. Gallen in St. Gall, and the Paul Sacher Foundation. In Lucerne is the Richard Wagner Museum, located at Triebschen, which was Wagner's home from 1866 to 1872.

3. Broadcasting. Switzerland has several broadcasting companies, each dedicated to one language or group of languages. Separate companies exist for German, Italian, French, and English, and one for German and Romansch. Through the commissioning and broadcasting of new works, these organizations are important forces in musical life.

II. *History.* In the Middle Ages, Switzerland was important in the development of religious music. Contributions of the monks of the Benedictine monastery at St. Gall (including Notker Balbulus) include many early *sequences, *tropes, and **versus,* as well as a body of 9th- and 10th-century manuscripts of Gregorian chant in a notation unusually well-supplied with rhythmic indications. In the 13th and 14th centuries, Passion plays were cultivated in several Swiss towns, including Basel and Einsiedeln. Secular music of the late Middle Ages and early Renaissance included songs of Swiss Minnesinger and instrumental music used in main cities on public holidays and in official ceremonies.

In the 16th century, under the influence of Swiss leaders of the Reformation (Zwingli and Calvin), musical development came almost completely to a halt. The Reformers' strictures against the use in church services of any music but the unaccompanied, monophonic singing of Psalms had the effect of suppressing the development of even secular music.

From the 17th century on, both sacred and secular music were freed from the limitations placed on them during the Reformation, but no specifically Swiss music culture developed; rather each linguistic group adopted the culture belonging to other Europeans speaking the same language. This was especially true of French- and German-speaking Swiss in the 19th century. Only in the late 19th century did a native tradition begin to emerge, based in part on the synthesis of various national characteristics. Perhaps the best known Swiss composer whose works exhibit such a synthesis of German and French styles is Arthur Honegger (1892–1955). Others of international renown and active chiefly in the first half of the 20th century are Othmar Schoeck (1886–1957), Ernest Bloch (1880–1959), and Frank Martin (1890–1974). More recently active and generally of more radical orientation are Klaus Huber (b. 1924), Wladimir Vogel (1896–1984), Rudolf Kelterborn (b. 1931), Jacques Guyonnet (b. 1933), Jürg Wyttenbach (b. 1935), Pierre Mariétan (b. 1935), Jean Balissat (b. 1936), Hans Ulrich Lehmann (b. 1937), Heinz Holliger (b. 1939), Urs Peter Schneider (b. 1939), and Roland Moser (b. 1943).

III. *Folk music.* Switzerland has both true folk music (associated with traditional culture and transmitted orally) and folklike music (composed in imitation of true folk styles but fixed in and transmitted by way of notation). Systematic study and collection were pursued from the 18th century.

There is virtually no folk music that is common to all of Switzerland; rather the folk styles of various linguistic groups tend to be strongly affiliated with the styles of neighboring peoples speaking the same language. Most folk songs are for solo voice, in some areas with choral refrain; a few regions have traditional part-singing. Various sorts of *yodels, the **ranz des vaches* or *Kühreihen,* and the *Betruf* (a prayer call using *Sprechgesang;* see *Sprechstimme, Sprechgesang*) are traditional vocal genres. Some traditional couple dances survive. Instruments used in indigenous music include fife and drum; noisemakers such as *Scharren, Chlefeli,* and *Klapperbretter; Hackbrett* (dulcimer), zither, alphorn, and church bells and carillons.

Composed folklike music was first written early in the 19th century, starting with arrangements of genuine folk tunes. From its beginnings, such music was used for commercial purposes, especially to entertain tourists. These compositions were performed chiefly by urban musical societies, many founded for this purpose; yet their texts for some time continued to reflect rural concerns. Eventually societies concerned with folk dancing and traditional costumes arose, and supposedly traditional dances began to be presented as theatrical events, accompanied by small ensembles composed usually of melody instruments (such as fiddle, trumpet, clarinet, or fipple flute), accordion, and string bass.

Bibl.: Willi Reich, "On Swiss Musical Composition of the Present," *MQ* 51 (1965): 78–91. Hans Steinbeck and Walter Labhart, comps. and eds., *Schweizer Komponisten unserer Zeit* (Zürich: Atlantis, 1975). Elaine Brody and Claire Brook, *The Music Guide to Belgium, Luxembourg, Holland, and Switzerland* (New York: Dodd, Mead, 1977). Brigitte Bachmann-Geiser, *Die Volksinstrumente der Schweiz* (Zürich: Atlantis, 1981). Brigitte Bachmann-Geiser et al., *Volksmusik in der Schweiz* (Zofingen: Ringier, 1985). Dominique Rosset, *Music in Switzerland,* trans. J. Gartmann (Zurich: Pro Helvetia, 1992). Mathes Seidl and Hans Steinbeck, eds., *Schweizer Komponisten unserer Zeit: Biographien, Werkverzeichnisse mit Diskographie und Bibliographie,* new ed. (Winterthur: Amadeus, 1993).

Syllabic. Characterized by the singing of only one note for each syllable; applicable to any type of vocal music and one of the three principal categories of style in *Gregorian chant.

Sylphide, La [Fr., The Sylph]. A ballet in two acts by Jean Schneitzhoeffer (choreography by Filippo Taglioni), first produced in Paris in 1832. A Danish production of 1836 employed music by Herman Løvenskjold and choreography by Auguste Bournonville.

Sylphides, Les [Fr., The Sylphs]. A ballet in one act with choreography by Michel Fokine, employing music by Chopin (orchestrated by Glazunov), first produced in Paris in 1909.

Sylvia, ou La nymphe de Diane. A ballet in three acts by Delibes (choreography by Louis Mérante), first produced in Paris in 1876.

Symbolum [Lat.]. *Creed; *Symbolum Nicenum,* Nicene Creed.

Sympathetic string. A string that is not normally played upon directly but that is set in motion by the acoustical phenomenon of resonance [see Acoustics VI]. Such a string thus vibrates "in sympathy" with the strings played upon directly, contributing to the tone color of the instrument. Instruments incorporating sympathetic strings include the *viola d'amore, *baryton, and **sitar.* Some pianos include such strings, termed *aliquot strings.

Symphonia [Gr.]. (1) In Greek theory, the unison. (2) In late Greek and medieval theory, consonance, as distinct from *diaphonia,* dissonance. (3) In the Middle Ages, any of several instruments, including the drum (St. Isidore of Seville), *hurdy-gurdy or *chifonie* (Jehan des Murs), and *bagpipe (whence perhaps **zampogna*). Praetorius (1619) used the term for all stringed keyboard instruments. (4) From the 17th century, **sinfonia.*

Symphonia domestica. A "domestic symphony" for orchestra by Richard Strauss, op. 53 (1902–3), depicting a typical day spent at home by the composer, his wife, and young son.

Symphonic band, concert band. The name concert band is applied to a group of wind and percussion players performing band music (transcriptions of orchestral music, arrangements of light and popular music, and originally composed music) in which the parts are duplicated (e.g., four or more first clarinets). Within this definition, there may be any number of performers. Most American high school and community/adult bands are concert bands; there are presently thousands of these organizations. Symphonic band is a term reserved for wind organizations with full, balanced instrumentation, often consisting of 90–120 performers and truly analogous to a symphony orchestra. A concert band can also have balanced instrumentation—i.e., the instrumentation that was established by leading professional and college band directors (members of the American Band Association) in the early part of the 20th century and quickly became standard. Standard instrumentation made it economically feasible for Boosey and Company, and Chappell, the two leading publishers at that time (both British), to publish music for bands, providing the impetus for the enormous growth of school bands in the U.S. Prescribed parts were: 2 flute (3 or 4 players), 2 oboe, 2 bassoon, 3 clarinet (12 players), 1 bass clarinet, 4 saxophone, 4 horn, 3 trumpet or cornet (6 players), 3 trombone, 1 baritone horn (substitute for the euphonium), 1 tuba (three players), and 3 or 4 percussion, resulting in an ideal concert band of 40–45 performers. The symphonic band has larger sections on each part and in addition possibly a string bass, harp, bass trombone, piccolo, English horn, and occasionally a contrabassoon and a bass and/or soprano saxophone. See also Wind ensemble.

Bibl.: Fred Fennell, *Time and the Winds* (Kenosha, Wis.: Leblanc, 1954). Richard F. Goldman, *The Wind Band: Its Literature and Technique* (Boston: Allyn & Bacon, 1961). David Whitwell, *The History and Literature of the Wind Ensemble,* 9 vols. (Northridge, Calif.: Winds, 1982–84). Frank Battisti, *The Winds of Change: The Evolution of the Contemporary American Wind Band/Ensemble and Its Conductor* (Galesville, Md.: Meredith Music, 2002). R.J.C.

Symphonic etudes. See *Études symphoniques.*

Symphonic poem [Fr. *poème symphonique;* Ger. *symphonische Dichtung*]. An orchestral piece whose music is accompanied by a program, i.e., a text, generally poetic or narrative in nature, which is meant to be read by the audience before listening to the work. As is true for other types of *program music, the program may be rather brief and vague (and may even consist merely of a suggestive title), or it may be long and detailed. Similarly, the music may be related to the program only very generally or in a myriad of specific ways. Usually the term is reserved for a composition in one movement, as opposed to the multimovement *program symphony; though many symphonic poems do contain several contrasting sections, these sections tend to flow into one another (through transitional passages) and are usually unified by tonal or motivic interrelationships. The term tone poem was preferred by Richard Strauss, and it has sometimes been used to refer to all works in the genre. Certain works for smaller performing groups are in other respects analogous to symphonic poems (e.g., Balakirev, *Islamey,* 1869, for piano; and Schoenberg, *Verklärte Nacht,* 1899, for string sextet). The symphonic poem, by its very freedom of form, has also lent itself to hybridization with other genres, e.g., the solo concerto (Strauss, *Don Quixote,* 1896–97; Bloch, *Schelomo,* 1915–16), cantata (Franck, *Psyché,* 1887–88), or concert aria (Barber, *Knoxville: Summer of 1915,* 1947).

The term symphonic poem was coined by Liszt for a performance of his *Tasso* in 1854, and he subsequently applied it to all of his other works in the genre, including earlier ones, originally described as overtures. The descriptive concert overtures of Beethoven (e.g., *Coriolan,* 1807), Berlioz (*Le Roi Lear,* 1831), Mendelssohn (*Hebrides,* 1829–32), and Wagner (*Eine Faust-Ouvertüre,* 1840, rev. 1855) are generally considered the clearest predecessors of Liszt's symphonic poems, but Liszt himself had also helped pave the way with his descriptive pieces for piano solo (*Album d'un voyageur,* 1835–38, rev. as *Années de pélerinage,* bk. 1, "Suisse"). The first of Liszt's symphonic poems, *Ce qu'on entend sur la montagne* (1848–49), is based on a poem by Victor Hugo; other works of art or literature, including ancient legends, are invoked by most of the others—*Hunnenschlacht* (1857, after a painting by Klaubach), *Tasso* (1849, after Byron), *Orpheus* (1853–54), *Prometheus* (1850), *Hamlet* (1858), etc. Many of these provide as programs only brief, evocative extracts from the literary works in question. *Les préludes* (rev. 1854, "after Lamartine") probably derives from a (lost) overture to an oratorio based on a text by Autran; nonetheless, the phases of the Lamartine poem can be seen as parallel to the character of the music's successive episodes. This work also illustrates Liszt's fondness for capping his symphonic poems with an extended, grandiloquent coda in which one or more of the earlier themes are subjected to thematic *transformation.

Many composers after Liszt eagerly seized upon this new, archetypally Romantic genre. Like him, they tended to avoid highly detailed musical depictions, but their programs were sometimes quite lengthy, especially if the work dealt with events or characters unlikely to be familiar to an audience (e.g., the six symphonic poems of Smetana, **Má Vlast,* 1872–79). The symphonic poems of Dvořák, Franck, Saint-Säens, Tchaikovsky, Balakirev, Musorgsky, Rimsky-Korsakov, Borodin, and Scriabin contain some of these composers' finest music. Wagner's *Siegfried Idyll* (1870) is likewise closely related to the Lisztian symphonic poem.

With Richard Strauss, the genre reached its culmination, in such works (termed tone poems) as *Till Eulenspiegels lustige Streiche* (1894–95) and *Also sprach Zarathustra* (1895–96). Skill in motivic manipulation, orchestral invention, and tonal coherence enabled Strauss to create the longest examples of the genre still in the standard repertory and the ones that are perhaps the most detailed in their programmaticism. The "realism" sometimes protrudes in his later tone poems, e.g., *Eine Alpensinfonie* (1915), after which he abandoned the genre until near the end of his life (*Metamorphosen,* 1944–45, for 23 solo strings).

Contemporary with Strauss, many other composers—Debussy, Ravel, Loeffler, Sibelius, Elgar, Nielsen, Delius, Rachmaninoff, Ives, and others—composed important one-movement orchestral works that may be regarded as symphonic poems. The level of descriptive detail ranges from vague evocation (Griffes, *The White Peacock,* 1915, orchestrated 1919?) to explicit, almost measure-by-measure narration (Dukas, *L'apprenti sorcier,* 1897). Occasionally a composer would, as Smetana had done, group into a single suitelike work several short or medium-length symphonic poems that were either related in subject matter and style (Debussy, *La mer,* 1903–5; Sibelius, *Lemminkäinen Suite,* 1893–95) or intentionally contrasted (Debussy, *Images,* 1905–12; Holst, *The Planets,* 1914–17). In some cases, the larger work is both varied and unified enough to be performed in its entirety (e.g., Respighi, *Pini di Roma,* 1924), but in others the individual movements make a stronger impression when performed separately (Ives, *Holidays,* 1904, 1909–13).

Around 1920, the anti-Romantic prejudices of the modernist movement led many composers away from the symphonic poem. Its influence, though, could occasionally still be seen in certain stylistically advanced works (Schoenberg, *Begleitungsmusik zu einer Lichtspielszene,* 1929–30), and it flourished for a time in the hands of more traditional composers, such as Honegger, Milhaud, Villa-Lobos, Gershwin, and Copland. In recent years, perhaps attracted by the unprecedented virtuosity of contemporary symphony orchestras and the continuing appeal of descriptive musical procedures, composers of varied stylistic persuasions—Jacob Druckman, Hans Werner Henze, David Del Tredici, John Tavener, Philip Glass *(The Light)*—have written works that are effectively symphonic poems, though not always so named.

Bibl.: Richard Wagner, "On Franz Liszt's Symphonic Poems" (1857), in William Ashton Ellis, trans., *Richard Wagner's Prose Works* (London, 1891) 3:235–54. Donald Francis Tovey, *Essays in Musical Analysis,* vol. 4 (London: Oxford U Pr, 1937; R: 1972). Gerald Abraham, *A Hundred Years of Music,* 4th ed. (London: Duckworth, 1974). Edward Downes, *The New York Philharmonic Guide to the Symphony* (New York: Walker, 1976). Carl Dahlhaus, *Die Musik des 19. Jahrhunderts* (Wiesbaden: Akademische V-g Athenaion, 1980). Carl Dahlhaus, *Nineteenth-Century Music,* trans. J. Bradford Robinson (Berkeley: U of Cal Pr, 1989). James Hepokoski, "Fiery-Pulsed Libertine or Domestic Hero? Strauss's *Don*

Juan Reinvestigated," in *Richard Strauss: New Perspectives on the Composer and His Work,* ed. Bryan Gilliam (Durham: Duke U Pr, 1992), pp. 135–75. Bryan Gilliam, "Richard Strauss," In *The Nineteenth-Century Symphony,* ed. D. Kern Holoman (New York: Schirmer, 1997), pp. 345–68. Keith T. Johns, *The Symphonic Poems of Franz Liszt,* rev. and ed. Michael Saffle (Stuyvesant, N.Y.: Pendragon, 1997). Vera Micznik, "The Absolute Limitations of Programme Music: The Case of Liszt's 'Die Ideale,'" *ML* 80 (1999): 207–40. R.P.L.

Symphonic variations. See *Variations symphoniques.*

Symphonie concertante [Fr.; It. *sinfonia concertante*]. In the 18th and early 19th centuries, a type of concerto for two or more solo instruments (normally strings or winds) and orchestra. Though called *symphonies,* these works belong, with few exceptions, to the history of the concerto. They are in two or three movements, the first in Classical ritornello or ritornello-sonata form [see Concerto (2) II], the last typically in rondo form. The style tends generally toward the light and popular rather than the heroic or grand.

The earliest *symphonies concertantes* date from the late 1760s; despite frequent statements to the contrary, the genre has little or no connection with the Baroque concerto grosso. From 1770 through the first decades of the 19th century the *symphonie concertante* experienced an exceptional vogue, centered primarily on Paris. The masterwork of the genre, however, is Mozart's *Sinfonia concertante* for violin and viola K. 364 (320d), written in Salzburg in 1779; the work for oboe, clarinet, bassoon, and horn attributed to him as K. 297b (C14.01) is now considered of doubtful authenticity, at least in its present form. Also worthy of note are Johann Christian Bach's 15 works in this genre and Haydn's *Sinfonia concertante* in B♭ for violin, cello, oboe, and bassoon (London, 1792). In the 19th century the term *symphonie concertante* fell into disuse, comparable works being designated by such titles as Triple Concerto (Beethoven), *Konzertstück* (Schumann), and Double Concerto (Brahms).

Bibl.: Franz Waldkirch, *Die konzertanten Sinfonien der Mannheimer im 18. Jahrhundert* (Ludwigshafen: J Waldkirch, 1931). Barry S. Brook, "The *Symphonie Concertante:* An Interim Report," *MQ* 47 (1961): 493–516, 48 (1962): 148. Id., "The Symphonie Concertante: Its Musical and Sociological Basis," *IRASM* 6 (1975): 9–28. Barry S. Brook et al., eds., *The Symphony, 1720–1840,* ser. F, vol. 5: *The Symphonie Concertante,* ed. Jean Philippe Vasseur and Barry S. Brook (New York: Garland, 1983). E.K.W.

Symphonie fantastique [Fr., Fantastic Symphony]. A symphony by Berlioz, op. 14 (1830; revised 1831–45), an important example of *program music. The work (subtitled *Épisode de la vie d'un artiste*) consists of five movements—"Rêveries-Passions"; "Un bal" (A Ball); "Scène aux champs" (Scene in the Country); "Marche au supplice" (March to the Gallows); "Songe d'une nuit du sabbat" (Dream of a Witches' Sabbath) —which are united by a recurring theme, called an *idée fixe.* The final movement includes the *"Dies irae" from the Requiem Mass.

Symphonie pathétique [Fr.]. See *Pathétique* (2).

Symphony [fr. Gr. *symphōnía,* Lat. *symphonia,* sounding together, concord]. A work for orchestra in multiple movements (or occasionally one movement with multiple sections). Though symphonies are normally abstract or absolute in content, many from the 19th and 20th centuries, and some from the 18th, have more or less explicit programs [see Program music, Program symphony]. Likewise, although most symphonies are for orchestra alone, many later examples include parts for voice, chorus, or solo instrument.

I. *Origins.* Numerous earlier genres contributed to the formation of the concert symphony. The most important precursor seems to have been the late Baroque ripieno concerto (*concerto ripieno, concerto a 4* or *a 5;* see Concerto (2) I, 2). These works, though called concertos, did not generally contain solo parts and were scored for the same ensemble as early symphonies—string orchestra plus continuo. In addition, beginning with Giuseppe Torelli's *Concerti musicali* op. 6 (1698), ripieno concertos frequently utilized the standard formal cycle of the early symphony, three movements in a fast–slow–fast pattern, the last a binary dance or dance-related movement. Finally, ripieno concertos were intended for the same audiences, venues, and occasions as early symphonies. Indeed, the only significant difference between the more modern type of ripieno concerto and the early concert symphony is the prevalence in the ripieno concerto of first movements in *ritornello form; early symphonies made more extensive use of *binary and rounded binary formal types, though ritornello structure was also common. Likewise, binary form occurs in the first movements of some ripieno concertos. However, the principal sources for bipartite structure within the symphony were probably the late Baroque solo and trio sonata (the latter often performed orchestrally), the longer movements of various kinds of *suites (especially those for orchestra), and the binary first movements of some early overtures.

The three-movement Italian opera *sinfonia or *overture, established by Alessandro Scarlatti as early as the 1680s, furnished another important avenue for development. In addition to being the main source for the name "symphony," these pieces were frequently detached from their operas for independent performance. However, their expanded instrumentation (with winds) and more facile style set them apart to some extent from the earliest concert symphonies, as does the difference in performance circumstances and function. For these reasons, the influence of the opera overture as a source or model for the earliest symphonies now seems less important than the influence it exerted somewhat later, during the 1740s and 50s [see below].

II. *Classical.* Symphonies were performed at a wide

variety of events in the 18th century. These included "academies" (private concerts) and less formal gatherings in palaces, monasteries, and private residences; various civic and institutional functions; and, of ever-increasing importance throughout the century, public concerts, ranging from ale-house and coffee-house performances and the many amateur series to the formal subscription and benefit concerts characteristic of the second half of the century. Symphonies were also ubiquitous in church (see Zaslaw, 1982), the usual practice being to distribute the movements of a work throughout the Mass as substitutes or accompaniments for items of the *Proper.

The earliest symphonists of importance were from Lombardy in northern Italy, most notably the Milanese composer Giovanni Battista Sammartini (1700/1701–75), whose twenty-odd early symphonies from the 1720s to ca. 1740 provided a firm foundation for the nascent genre. These works continue the tradition of the ripieno concerto in their scoring (string orchestra) and use of a three-movement cycle, but depart from it both in their increasingly Classical style and their adoption of a rounded binary or early sonata form for most of their fast movements.

At about the time Sammartini was composing his early symphonies, Italian opera composers, particularly such Neapolitans as Leonardo Vinci, Giovanni Battista Pergolesi, Leonardo Leo, and later Niccolò Jommelli and the Venetian Baldassare Galuppi, were developing a fundamentally new style for their overtures that by the 1740s manifested the following Classical characteristics: use of a larger, more powerful orchestra (strings, pairs of oboes or flutes and horns, often trumpets and timpani); homophonic texture with blocklike rather than linear treatment of the winds; slow harmonic rhythm and extensive use of pedal point; reliance upon dynamic effects, especially the *crescendo* passage; and increasing use of thematic contrast in first-movement expositions [see Sonata form II, 1]. Some conservative centers simply disregarded these innovations for the most part. For example, north German symphonists such as Johann Gottlieb Graun (1703–71) and C. P. E. Bach (1714–88) continued throughout their lives to write in a style influenced by the Baroque concerto, while other northern symphonists reflected the influence of the suite. But most composers, including Sammartini himself, proceeded during the 1740s and 50s to adapt the new overture style to the quite different aesthetic requirements of the concert symphony.

Perhaps the most striking example of such assimilation occurred at the important German court of Mannheim [see Mannheim school]. Indeed, the list of style traits of the overture given above corresponds closely with the list of innovations often credited by earlier scholars to the Mannheim symphony. There is no question, however, that the Italian overture provided the principal model for these and other characteristics of the Mannheim style. To give only one example, the famous "Mannheim crescendo" appeared years earlier in the Italian opera overture. At the same time, the Mannheim symphonists generally extended and enhanced each of the elements they borrowed from the overture. Orchestration, for instance, is much more varied and challenging to the performer in a Mannheim symphony than in an Italian overture, as would be expected in works written for performance by the famous Mannheim orchestra. Clarinets appear beginning in the 1750s, and exposed passages for winds are frequent.

Mannheim also deserves credit for expansion of the symphonic cycle from three movements to four by insertion of a minuet and trio before the finale. Four-movement symphonies appeared from approximately the mid-1740s on in the works of Johann Stamitz (1717–57), concertmaster at the court and the most important Mannheim symphonist. However, later Mannheim composers returned eventually to the three-movement type, for example Stamitz's successor Christian Cannabich (1731–98). As for the individual movements, sonata form with partial rather than full recapitulation (i.e., polythematic binary form or binary sonata form) predominated at Mannheim until the mid-1770s [see Sonata form I–II, 1].

The earliest Viennese symphonists such as Mathias Georg Monn (1717–50) and Georg Christoph Wagenseil (1715–77) were on the whole more conservative, as one might expect given the strong Baroque tradition of the imperial capital. Like Sammartini in Milan, however, these composers favored the use of binary formal types with full recapitulation. The symphonies of the next generation, including Leopold Hofmann (1738–93), the prolific Carl Ditters von Dittersdorf (1739–99), and Johann Vanhal (1739–1813), are characterized by clarity of structure in their sonata forms and by considerable lyricism, even in primary themes. A majority of the symphonies of this generation are in four movements, some with slow introductions to the first movement, and rondo finales occur beginning in the 1760s. Similar traits are found in the symphonies of such later Viennese contemporaries of Mozart as Franz Anton Hoffmeister (1754–1812) and Paul Wranitzky (1756–1808).

The symphonies of Haydn, now considered to number 106, range from the modest works of the late 1750s to the 12 great *"London" symphonies of 1791–95—like the *"Paris" symphonies of 1785–86, written for public concerts. The majority of Haydn's symphonies were composed for the Esterházy court, with which Haydn became associated in 1761. Because of the length and conditions of his employment, Haydn was, in his words, "forced to be original," and indeed the inventiveness and variety of his symphonies are extraordinary. This diversity encompasses form at every level, choice and use of instruments, texture (often contrapuntal), rhythm and phrase structure, and theme (often folklike). A consistent element in Haydn's symphonies is his interest in thematic development or manipulation, which pervades not only the development sections but also the expositions and recapitulations of his sonata and sonata-rondo movements (the latter found in many of his late finales). Finally, the dramatic intensity and frequent wit of Haydn's symphonies, together with the pathos of his many minor-key (*"Sturm und Drang") works, represent a significant expansion of the expressive range of the symphony.

Mozart's approximately 50 symphonies (some no longer extant) appeared rather sporadically, reflecting his travels and changing circumstances. Most of the early works show an Italianate orientation in their smooth and uncomplicated flow, clear thematic contrasts, choice of formal types, and use of three movements. In these and other respects one can discern the influence of the important overtures and symphonies of Johann Christian Bach (1735–82), the "Milan" and later "London" Bach. The small number of symphonies from Mozart's Viennese period, especially the *Prague* of 1786 (K. 504) and the great trilogy of 1788 (K. 543, K. 550 in G minor, and K. 551, the *Jupiter*), are remarkable for their synthesis of strict and free counterpoint within the symphonic idiom—the finale of the *Jupiter* is only the best-known example—as well as for their adoption of the intensive developmental techniques of Haydn, the exquisite quality of their melodic material, and the richness of their harmony and orchestration. Other symphonists of the Haydn-Mozart period who should at least be mentioned are Antonio Rosetti in southern Germany, Michael Haydn in Salzburg, François-Joseph Gossec in Paris, Carl Friedrich Abel in London, and Luigi Boccherini and Gaetano Brunetti in Spain.

III. *19th century.* The nine symphonies of Beethoven represent a culmination of the Classical symphony as embodied in the later works of Mozart and particularly Haydn. Though Beethoven extended and expanded virtually every element of the symphony, his ideal remained the dramatic sonata principle of the late 18th century, based upon a coordination of tonal and thematic process in all its ramifications. His brilliant use of fugato, for instance, exemplifies his abiding interest in intensive thematic development. A similar motivation may be seen in his use of theme-and-variation forms in Symphonies no. 3, 7, and 9.

Beethoven's orchestra is somewhat larger than that of earlier symphonists. Most notably, he adds trombones in the Fifth, Sixth, and Ninth Symphonies. More important are the changes he wrought in the overall form of the symphony, such as the replacement of the minuet with the *scherzo. In a highly influential development, the finales of the Fifth and Ninth Symphonies (and to some extent the Third) function as a climax or apotheosis of all that has gone before, far removed from the lighter finales of most 18th-century symphonies. This shift in the center of gravity from the beginning to the end of the symphony—already foreshadowed in Haydn's *Farewell* and Mozart's *Jupiter* Symphony—is designated by the term finale-symphony. Related to this change is Beethoven's return to material from the scherzo in the finale of the Fifth and, in the choral finale of the Ninth, his quotation of themes from the first three movements—both examples of a *cyclic approach to the symphony. Also influential was the direct connection of the last two movements of the Fifth Symphony, a trait found in many symphonies of the 18th century as well (e.g., by C. P. E. Bach).

These innovations are bound up with the more concrete and specific conceptual content of many of Beethoven's symphonies—the heroic character of the Third *(Eroica),* the struggle and ultimate triumph of the Fifth and Ninth, and the depiction of nature in the Sixth (*Pastorale;* see also Program symphony). In all but the Fifth, the poetic content is made explicit by the use of titles or, in the Ninth, text (Beethoven's setting of Schiller's "Ode to Joy" for vocal quartet and chorus). Yet even in the Ninth, the "program" is a general one, paralleling but not taking precedence over the symphonic ideal. (The Ninth was not the first symphony to add voices, an earlier instance being Peter Winter's *Battle Symphony* of 1814.)

For many 19th-century composers, the symphony seems to have functioned as a convenient (though not always comfortable) framework for Romantic lyricism, harmonic and orchestral color, and individual expression. The two late symphonies of Schubert (nos. 8 and 9, 1822–28) provide an illustration of this trend. They are memorable above all for the beauty and expressivity of their lyrical themes; the *forte* passages tend to be conventionally dramatic, and the development sections consist mainly of large harmonic sequences. Similarly, the structural use of tonality that provided the foundation for Beethoven's vast forms often yields to Schubert's striking sense of harmonic color; this appears clearly in his preference for third-related keys and chords, for example the famous G-major secondary theme—recapitulated in D—of the B-minor Symphony (no. 8, the "Unfinished").

The principal German Romanticists were for the most part rather conservative in their approach to the symphony. Of Mendelssohn's five numbered symphonies, the first is a youthful work related to his twelve early string sinfonias. The four mature symphonies (1832–42) comprise two on religious themes and two inspired by the composer's travels, the *Italian* (no. 4) and the *Scottish* (no. 3). These works combine Mendelssohn's characteristic lyricism and superlative orchestration with the use of classicistic forms reflecting the influence of Mozart. Schumann's four symphonies (1841–51) are more adventuresome formally. On the largest scale, he utilizes cyclic form in all but the First Symphony, a device he adopted from Beethoven and especially Berlioz. His sonata forms are also rather free and rhapsodic; recapitulations are often abbreviated, codas extended and climactic. Like Mendelssohn, Schumann supplied evocative titles for two of his symphonies, the *Spring* and *Rhenish* (nos. 1 and 3).

Brahms's four symphonies, the first completed only at the age of 43 (1876), consciously return to the symphonic technique of Beethoven. Romantic and individual elements are by no means lacking, as may be seen in the cyclic form of the Third Symphony, the preference for tender *Allegretto grazioso* third movements, and the expressive lyricism that pervades these works. But Brahms rejected such overtly Romantic traits as the use of programmatic titles and a larger and more varied orchestra, and his only true finale-symphony, the First, is obviously modeled on the Beethoven Fifth and Ninth Symphonies, not on later examples. Moreover, in the sonata-form movements a high degree of discipline is evident in the logic of the tonal organization, the clarity of thematic function and articulation, and especially the rigor and intensity of the thematic development. Equally disciplined, and still more retrospective, is Brahms's last symphonic movement, the Baroque *chaconne or *passacaglia that closes the Fourth Symphony (1884–85).

The foregoing composers represent a generally conservative trend within the symphony, one that was carried on by composers in other countries. In Russia, the symphonies of Tchaikovsky (6 symphonies, 1866–93) exemplify some of the problems in the Romantic approach to the symphonic form. For many listeners, the most cherished moments are the lyrical outpourings—secondary themes, slow movements—and the dance and dance-derived movements. The ostensibly more dramatic intervening sections often seem merely bombastic, inserted because the abstract form required them. An original stroke on the large scale is Tchaikovsky's conclusion of the Sixth Symphony *(Pathétique)* with an *Adagio lamentoso*—a portrayal of death, according to the composer's private program for the work.

Though Tchaikovsky occasionally quoted Russian folk material in his symphonies, his style is for the most part cosmopolitan or personal rather than specifically national. In fact, the growth of *nationalism in 19th-century orchestral music took place primarily in genres other than the symphony, notably the *symphonic poem. Among nationalist composers of symphonies, the most important were the Russian Alexander Borodin (2 symphonies, 1867–76) and the Czech Antonín Dvořák (9 symphonies, 1865–93). Dvořák's symphonies stand firmly within the conservative tradition, the early ones being modeled on those of Schubert and Mendelssohn, the later ones on those of his friend and champion Brahms. A Czech national idiom, observable not only in the thematic material but also in the rhythm and harmony, appears primarily in the last symphonies, nos. 3–9—the latter, paradoxically, entitled *From the New World* and written in America.

In opposition to the basically conservative continuum just outlined, Romantic composers such as Berlioz, Liszt, and Wagner advocated the creation of new forms and a more radical union of music and poetic content. Although this approach led some composers away from the symphony (notably Wagner), others could not resist the challenge it presented. Berlioz's three most important symphonies are all programmatic in one sense or another. The **Symphonie fantastique* (1830) depicts sensational and lurid scenes deriving from the composer's personal experience. The more restrained *Harold in Italy* (1834), based on Byron's *Childe Harold,* personifies the hero in a solo viola part. Most innovative of all is *Roméo et Juliette* (1839), which presents the story (taken from Shakespeare) through the use of vocal soloists and chorus. Berlioz's most important technical innovations are his cyclic use of an *idée fixe* (a symbolic theme recurring in each movement) and his brilliant instrumentation and orchestration. The most obvious successors to the symphonies of Berlioz were Liszt's *Faust* and *Dante* symphonies (1854–57, the former with tenor soloist and male chorus in the finale), though in both, the "program" consists primarily of the movement titles. In turn, Liszt's technique of thematic *transformation affected numerous symphonies within the French orbit, notably Vincent d'Indy's *Symphony on a French Mountain Air* (1886, with piano) and César Franck's Symphony in D minor (1889). More traditional are Camille Saint-Saëns's three symphonies (1853–86), the last with organ.

Anton Bruckner's nine numbered symphonies (1865–96; no. 9 incomplete, plus the early "no. 0") are a highly individual blend of Wagnerian proportions and dynamic range, clear and generally traditional formal types, the style of the organ and of Catholic church music, and religious inspiration and expressive content. Though Bruckner somewhat naively linked himself with Wagner, his symphonies in fact eschew both explicit programs and the use of voices.

The symphonies of Bruckner's fellow Austrian Gustav Mahler are very different, though they doubtless owe something of the vastness of their conception to the older composer's works. Of Mahler's nine symphonies (ca. 1884–1909; no. 10 incomplete), four utilize voices, ranging from the single soloist of the finale of the Fourth to the huge ensemble of the Eighth (**Symphony of a Thousand*). In addition, numerous quotations and derivations from Mahler's songs appear within the symphonies. Also in contrast to Bruckner, most of Mahler's symphonies have narrative content of a general nature, though in many cases he eventually suppressed the actual programs and movement titles. Other points of importance are Mahler's use of "progressive tonality," with the work ending in a different key from the one in which it began (e.g., c–E♭ in no. 2, b/G–E in no. 4); the size of Mahler's orchestra, which is nonetheless employed quite sparingly, even delicately; the use of extended slow movements to conclude the Third and Ninth Symphonies; and the fascinating amalgam of folk, military, sacred, and popular styles in many of the works.

Though Jean Sibelius (7 symphonies, 1899–1924) and Carl Nielsen (6 symphonies, 1894–1925) are often classified as Post-Romanticists, the later works of Sibelius in particular show a more compact and objective approach than do such symphonies as those of Mahler, Rachmaninoff (3, 1895–1936), and Elgar (2, 1910–12)—not to mention Richard Strauss's magniloquent *Symphonia domestica* (1902–3) and *Alpensinfonie* (1911–15). Sibelius's Symphony no. 7, for example, is rather spare in both style and form; its one-movement plan incorporates elements of sonata and rondo form as well as the standard symphonic cycle.

IV. *Modern.* World War I marked the beginning of an overt reaction to both the form and content of the Romantic symphony. A *neoclassical view of the symphony may be seen in Prokofiev's parody of Mozart and Haydn in the Symphony no. 1 (*Classical,* 1916–17) and in symphonies by two members of **Les Six,* Darius Milhaud (6 chamber symphonies of 1917–23; 12 others, 1939–62) and Arthur Honegger (Symphony no. 1, 1930; 4 later symphonies, 1941–50). Albert Roussel's eclectic Symphonies nos. 3–4 and *Sinfonietta* (1929–34) also reveal a neoclassical concision and clarity, especially when compared with his programmatic Symphony no. 1 (1904–6) and his modernist Symphony no. 2 (1919–21). At the opposite end of the stylistic spectrum is Messiaen's expansive *Turangalîla* Symphony, scored for piano, *ondes martenot, and large orchestra (1946–48, rev. 1990).

Stravinsky's symphonies likewise fall in varying degrees within the neoclassical orbit, at least if one disregards his early Symphony in E♭ (1905–7) and understands neoclassical to include neo-Baroque: the *Symphonies of Wind Instruments* (1920, the title used in the older sense of "sounding together" or "soundpiece"), the choral **Symphony of Psalms* (1930), and the Symphony in C (1939–40) and Symphony in Three Movements (1945). These works integrate the composer's individual conception of tonality, based on assertion, static polarity, and ultimate convergence, with his flexible adaptation of inherited forms and procedures. The same may be said for the symphonies of Hindemith, though the tonal system differs and the forms are generally more traditional. Hindemith's six symphonies include *Mathis der Maler* (1934, from the opera of that title), the Symphony in E♭ (1940), and the symphony *Die Harmonie der Welt* (1951). The German tradition of the symphony has been continued more recently in the nine symphonies of Hans Werner Henze (1947–97).

Unlike such neo-tonal composers as Stravinsky and Hindemith, the Viennese serialists showed little interest in the symphony. In fact, Webern's Symphony op. 21 (1928) is the only twelve-tone symphony by this group. Neither of Schoenberg's two Chamber Symphonies is serial, the first (op. 9, in one movement) dating from 1906, the second (op. 38, 1939) being based on sketches and drafts from the same year as the first, 1906.

Numerous national centers have been prolific in their cultivation of the symphony in the 20th century, in part because of a continuing interest in the development of national idioms within the context of traditional genres. In Poland one can cite Karol Szymanowski's four symphonies (1909–32, the last with piano) as well as symphonies by the later composers Witold Lutosławski (2, 1947–67), Krzysztof Penderecki (2, 1973–78), and Henryk Górecki (3 symphonies, 1959–76, the latter two with voice). By contrast, the most notable Czech symphonies, at least if one excludes Leoš Janáček's popular *Sinfonietta* (1926), are the six by Bohuslav Martinů—all, ironically, written in the U.S. (1941–53). In Hungary, Bartók left no works in this genre, Kodály only one (1961). The most important Finnish symphonist after Sibelius is Einojuhani Rautavaara (8 symphonies, 1956–99).

The Russian proclivity for the symphony, evident already in the 19th century, continued in the 20th in works by Scriabin (3 symphonies, 1900–1904), Glière (3 symphonies, 1900–11), Nikolay Myaskovsky (27 symphonies, 1908–50, many on political themes), Prokofiev (7 symphonies, 1916–52), and Shostakovich (15 symphonies, 1924–71). Only Prokofiev's last three symphonies were written after his final return to the U.S.S.R. from Paris in 1936, a move that brought a shift to a more lyrical, accessible style. Like Prokofiev, but perhaps more surprisingly, Shostakovich generally disregarded folk-derived traits and even a specifically Russian idiom in his symphonies; the influence of socialist realism appears most obviously in his program symphonies with chorus.

The symphony in both Britain and the U.S. shows a history of early domination by the German academic-Romantic tradition followed by assertion of a more national approach. In Britain the former trend is exemplified by the symphonies of Charles Villiers Stanford (7, 1875–1911), the latter by the symphonies of Ralph Vaughan Williams (9, 1903–58). Vaughan Williams rarely quoted directly from the folk songs he had collected and studied so assiduously, but rather assimilated them within his personal melodic and harmonic idiom. Other English symphonists of the Vaughan Williams generation are Havergal Brian (32 symphonies, ca. 1907–68) and Arnold Bax (7 symphonies, 1922–39), while later composers include William Walton (2 symphonies, 1932–60), Benjamin Britten (3 symphonies, 1933–63), Michael Tippett (4 symphonies, 1944–77), Oliver Knussen (3 symphonies, 1966–79), and Peter Maxwell Davies (7 symphonies, 1975–2000).

The late 19th-century German Romantic school is represented in the U.S. by John Knowles Paine (2 symphonies, 1875–80) and the more individual George Chadwick (3 symphonies, 1882–94). Against this background the symphonies of Charles Ives (4, 1895–1916, plus a fifth, the *Universe Symphony,* left incomplete) seem all the more startling, especially the extraordinary Fourth, with its synthesis of transcendental program, collage technique, and vast range of styles. Yet Ives's music was generally unknown at the time, and the establishment of a distinctively American school of symphonists had to await a second generation: Aaron Copland (4 symphonies, 1925–46), Roy Harris (13 symphonies, 1933–76), and Walter Piston (8 symphonies, 1937–65), all of whom had studied in Paris with Nadia Boulanger in the 1920s. Their symphonies range in style from the neoclassicism of Piston and early Copland to the evocations of the American West characteristic of Harris. To this generation of symphonists may be added Howard Hanson (7 symphonies, 1922–77); Roger Sessions (8 symphonies, 1927–68), who espoused a more cosmopolitan approach; and Henry Cowell (20 symphonies, 1938–65). More recent American composers notable for their symphonies include Samuel Barber (2 symphonies, 1935–44), William Schuman (10 symphonies, 1935–76), Alan Hovhaness (67 symphonies, 1937–92), Paul Creston (5 symphonies, 1940–55), David Diamond (8 symphonies, 1940–60), Peter Mennin (8 symphonies, 1941–73), Vincent Persichetti (8 symphonies, 1942–70), Elliott Carter (3 symphonies, 1942–97), George Rochberg (6 symphonies, 1949–87), and William Balcom (6 symphonies, 1957–97). Many contemporary composers, however, prefer to give descriptive or evocative titles to works that might earlier have been called symphonies.

The most noteworthy Latin American symphonists have been the Brazilian Heitor Villa-Lobos, whose 12 symphonies (1916–57) incorporate many popular elements, and the Mexican Carlos Chávez (7 numbered symphonies, 1933–61).

Bibl.: Karl Nef, *Geschichte der Sinfonie und Suite* (Leipzig: Breitkopf & Härtel, 1921). Robert Sondheimer, *Die Theorie der Sinfonie* (Leipzig: Breitkopf & Härtel, 1925); index in *AM* 37 (1965): 79–86. Donald Francis Tovey, *Essays in Musical Analysis,* vols. 1–2, 6 (London: Oxford U Pr, 1935–39; new ed. in 2 vols., 1981). Gerald Abraham, *A Hundred Years of Music* (New York: Knopf, 1938; 4th ed., London: Duckworth, 1974). Homer Ulrich, *Symphonic Music* (New York: Columbia U Pr, 1952). Barry S. Brook, *La symphonie française dans la seconde moitié du XVIIIe siècle,* (Paris: L'institut de musicologie de l'Université de Paris, 1962). William W. Austin, *Music in the Twentieth Century* (New York: Norton, 1966). Robert Simpson, ed., *The Symphony* (Baltimore: Penguin, 1966). Bathia Churgin, ed., *The Symphonies of G. B. Sammartini,* vol. 1, *The Early Symphonies* (Cambridge, Mass.: Harvard U Pr, 1968). George R. Hill, *A Preliminary Checklist of Research on the Classic Symphony and Concerto to the Time of Beethoven (Excluding Haydn and Mozart)* (Hackensack, N.J.: J Boonin, 1970). Helmut Hell, *Die neapolitanische Opernsinfonie in der ersten Hälfte des 18. Jahrhunderts* (Tutzing: Schneider, 1971). Charles Rosen, *The Classical Style* (New York: Viking Pr, 1971; 2nd ed., New York: Norton, 1997). Louise Cuyler, *The Symphony* (New York: Harcourt Brace Jovanovich, 1973; 2nd ed., Warren, Mich.: Harmonie Park, 1980). Preston Stedman, *The Symphony* (Englewood Cliffs, N.J.: Prentice-Hall, 1979). Barry S. Brook et al., eds., *The Symphony, 1720–1840,* 61 vols. (New York: Garland, 1979–86). Bellamy Hosler, *Changing Aesthetic Views of Instrumental Music in 18th-Century Germany* (Ann Arbor: UMI Res Pr, 1981). Eugene K. Wolf, *The Symphonies of Johann Stamitz* (Utrecht: Bohn, Scheltema & Holkema, 1981). Neal Zaslaw, "Mozart, Haydn, and the *Sinfonia da chiesa,*" *JM* 1 (1982): 95–124. Christopher Ballantine, *Twentieth-Century Symphony* (London: Dennis Dobson, 1983). Jan LaRue, *A Catalogue of 18th-Century Symphonies,* vol. 1: *Thematic Identifier* (Bloomington: Ind U Pr, 1988). Stefan Kunze, *Die Sinfonie im 18. Jahrhundert: von der Opernsinfonie zur Konzertsinfonie,* vol. 1 of *Handbuch der musikalischen Gattungen,* ed. Siegfried Mauser (Laaber: Laaber-Verlag, 1993). Robert Layton, ed., *A Companion to the Symphony* (New York: Simon & Schuster, 1993). Jens Peter Larsen, "Zur Vorgeschichte der Symphonik der Wiener Klassik," *SzMw* 43 (1994): 67–143. Eugene K. Wolf, "I *Concerti grossi* dell'Opera I (1721) di Pietro Antonio Locatelli e le Origini della Sinfonia," in *Intorno a Locatelli: Studi in occasione del tricentenario della nascita di Pietro Antonio Locatelli,* ed. Albert Dunning (Lucca: Libreria Musicale Italiana, 1995), pp. 1169–93. Mark Evan Bonds, *After Beethoven: Imperatives of Originality in the Symphony* (Cambridge, Mass.: Harvard U Pr, 1996). D. Kern Holoman, ed., *The Nineteenth-Century Symphony* (New York: Schirmer, 1997). Richard Will, *The Characteristic Symphony in the Age of Haydn and Mozart* (Cambridge: Cambridge U Pr, 2002). E.K.W.

Symphony of a Thousand. Popular name for Mahler's Symphony no. 8 in E♭ major, composed in 1906. The impresario Emil Guttmann, who organized the Munich premiere of the work, so named it in a publicity slogan because of the extremely large orchestral and choral forces required. The first part is a setting of the hymn "Veni, creator spiritus"; the second part a setting of the closing scene of Goethe's *Faust.*

Symphony of Psalms. A work for chorus and orchestra (without violins or violas) by Stravinsky, composed in 1930 (rev. 1948). Its three movements are based on Latin Psalms.

Symponia. See *Sumponyah.*

Syncopation. A momentary contradiction of the prevailing *meter or pulse. This may take the form of a temporary transformation of the fundamental character of the meter, e.g., from duple to triple or from 3/4 to 3/2 [see Hemiola], or it may be simply the contradiction of the regular succession of strong and weak beats within a measure or a group of measures whose metrical context nevertheless remains clearly defined by some part of the musical texture that does not itself participate in the syncopation. The former type may have the effect of "shifting the bar line," e.g., of causing one of the weak beats to function as a strong beat. It is frequently encountered in the music of Beethoven, among many others. The latter type may entail attacks between beats rather than on them and is particularly common in ragtime, blues, and some styles of jazz. Elaborate examples are found in French secular

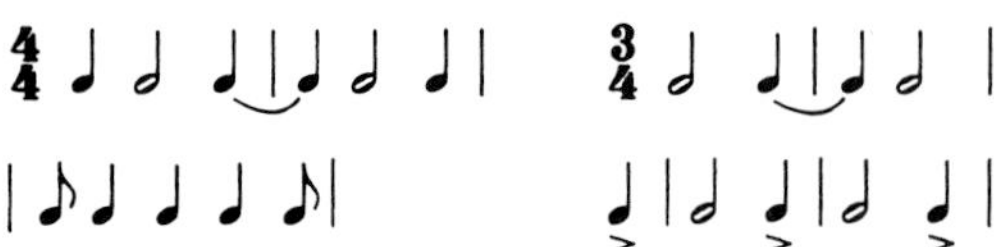

music of the late 14th century [see *Ars subtilior*]. The accompanying example includes some common types of syncopation. Syncopation may be created by the types of note-values themselves or by accentuation, articulation, melodic contour, or harmonic change in the context of an otherwise unsyncopated succession of note-values.

Synemmenon [Gr.]. The conjunct *tetrachord connected at the Mese to the lower octave of the Greater Perfect System [see Greece I, 3 (i)], thus producing the Lesser Perfect or Synemmenon System, which may have existed prior to the Greater Perfect System. In medieval theory, the diatonic synemmenon tetrachord (semitone–tone–tone, ascending) was used to introduce a b♭ to the scale (Mese = a). A.B.

Synthesizer. An instrument that produces sounds, modifies them, and in some circumstances orders them in time by purely electronic means. In principle, such an instrument can create, or synthesize, any sound whose characteristics can be precisely specified in acoustical terms. That is, it generates electronically and permits independent control of the frequency, waveform, intensity, and envelope that together make up a musical sound [see Acoustics]. It consists of a collection of modular components that can be connected in a great variety of ways, the electronic output of one component serving as the input of the next, until the signal reaches a loudspeaker and is turned into sound. Modern synthesizers are distinguished by two features: (1) initial signals are generated electronically, usually by means of oscillators; (2) these signals are modified by means of voltage control. A given voltage applied to a voltage-controlled oscillator produces a certain frequency (heard ultimately as a pitch); a higher voltage produces a higher frequency (or higher pitch). Similarly, as higher voltages are applied to a voltage-controlled amplifier, the amplitude (heard ultimately as loudness) of the amplified signal is increased. Control voltages regulate many other parameters besides pitch and loudness, and they are manipulated in a variety of ways, especially by means of control knobs, keyboards, and secondary signals.

Machines for synthesizing sounds electronically were introduced as early as 1929. The first synthesizer of consequence was the RCA Music Synthesizer developed early in the 1950s and installed at the Columbia–Princeton Electronic Music Center in New York. But not until the introduction of the principle of voltage control by Robert Moog around 1964 did synthesizers become commercially viable. At first they were used primarily in the studio in conjunction with tape recorders to create recorded electronic compositions. Transistors soon made it possible to build small, flexible, and relatively inexpensive synthesizers suitable for live performance. Computer technology has led to automated control of many synthesizer functions and to direct digital synthesis of sound. See Electro-acoustic music.

Bibl.: Trevor Pinch and Frank Trocco, *Analog Days: The Invention and Impact of the Moog Synthesizer* (Cambridge, Mass.: Harvard U Pr, 2002).

Syrian chant. The ecclesiastical plainsong of a number of ancient Christian churches following the Eastern rite and originating ultimately from the Patriarchate of Antioch. These include the Syrian Orthodox, Assyrian, Syro-Antiochene, Chaldean, Maronite, Malabar, Malankar, and Melkite churches. Medieval historians attribute the genesis of Syrian chant to a countermove by St. Ephrem, who wrote orthodox hymns (words and music) directed against the hymnodic propaganda of heretics, chief among whom were Bardesanes and his son Harmonius. In its later development, Syrian chant assumed the Byzantine system of the eight modes, which certain groups (Assyrians, Chaldeans, and Maronites) called *maqāmāt.*

According to the Byzantine historian Sokrates (ca. 380–450), St. Ignatius, bishop of Antioch in the first century, introduced antiphonal psalmody into his diocese. This is generally considered too early an appearance; current opinion holds that the early churches in Syria used a primitive responsorial form that was superseded in the 4th century by antiphonal singing. The former required two performers: a soloist and a choir (in early times, the whole congregation) that responded with a pendant refrain to the Psalm verses chanted by the soloists. The later antiphonal form needed two groups of performers: two soloists and two choirs, each choir responding to its soloist with a hemistich or *'enyānā* (analogous to the Byzantine **troparion*), and each soloist alternating with the other in singing the successive verses of the Psalm.

Chief among the hymnodic forms of Syrian chant are the *qālā,* the *madrāshā,* and the *mimra.* The first, found in manuscripts as early as the 9th century, is a poem consisting of several stanzas that are interpolated between the verses of Psalms and canticles. Most of them are attributed to Simeon the Potter (ca. 500) and are arranged in a developed AABBCC . . . structure that includes an alleluia. Occasionally, the opening melody of the stanza of a *qālā* is used for the preceding Psalm verse. The *madrāshā* is a category of independent strophic hymn that reached its supreme development in the hands of St. Ephrem. It consists of four to six lines sung by a soloist and a constant refrain sung by a choir. Most of the existing chants are *contrafacta* dealing with such subjects as the Incarnation, death, and paradise; a large number of these *contrafacta* gained liturgical acceptance. By emphasizing apologetics, Ephrem laid the foundation of later Christian hymnody and also influenced its development in the West.

A variant form of the *madrāshā* is the *sughithā,* which features a developing dramatic dialogue in direct speech and often includes alphabetical acrostics in its text. Finally, the *mimra,* also popularized by Ephrem, is a poetic homily or exposition of Scripture in uniform meter and without strophic division. Surviving musical fragments of *mimre* show that only short sections remain in the same mode, for there is constant modulation. In this genre, a melody that could be rhythmically adapted to serve not only the different stanzas of one poem, but any number of different poems (provided the verse pattern was the same), was called a **risqolo.*

Musical notation is lacking in all but the Melkite liturgical books. One example is a 13th-century *Sticherarion* in St. Katherine's Monastery, Mt. Sinai (MS syr. 261), a palimpsest containing both paleobyzantine and round symbols [see Byzantine chant]. Other primitive and still undecipherable systems have been discovered, including a sophisticated network of dots found in *ecphonetic lectionary sources.

Bibl.: Dahlia Cohen, "An Investigation into the Tonal Structure of the *Maqamat,*" *JIFMC* 16 (1964): 102–6. Louis Hage, "Les mélodies-types dans le chant maronite," *Melto* 3 (1967): 325–409. Heinrich Husmann, "Ein syrisches Sticherarion mit paläobyzantinischer Notation (Sinai syr. 261)," *Hamburger Jahrbuch für Musikwissenschaft* 1 (1975): 9–57. J. Raasted, "Musical Notation and Quasi Notation in Syro-Melkite Liturgical Manuscripts," *Cahiers de l'institut du Moyen Age grec et latin* 31 (1979): 11–37, 53–77. A. Cody, "The Early History of the Octoechus in Syria," in *East of Byzantium: Syria and Armenia in the Formative Period,* ed. N. Garsoïan, T. F. Mathews, and R. W. Thomson (Washington, D.C., 1982), pp. 89–113.

D.E.C.

Syrinx [Gr.]. The *panpipes of ancient Greece and Rome. The syrinx was associated with the god Pan and by extension with pastoral life.

System. Two or more staves connected by means of braces or bar lines for the purpose of allowing notation of music not readily accommodated on a single staff [see also Score].

T

T. Abbr. for *tenor, *tonic, *trill, toe (in pedal parts for organ), *tutti.

Ta'amim [Heb.]. See Ecphonetic notation, Jewish music.

Tabarro, Il [It.]. See *Trittico.*

Tabatière de musique [Fr.]. Music box.

Ṭabl [Ar.]. (1) Drum. (2) A cylindrical drum with two heads, widely distributed in various sizes in the Islamic world. (3) In the Maghrib, a kettledrum, usually played in pairs [pl. *aṭbāl,* whence Sp. **atabal*].

Tablā [Hind., fr. Ar.]. A pair of drums of North India. The conical right-hand drum (*tablā* or *dāhinā*) is made of wood and is tuned to a definite pitch. The kettle-shaped left-hand drum *(bāyā)* is made of metal or clay and is tuned to a lower but indefinite pitch. The player sits cross-legged on the floor and strikes both drums with the fingers, occasionally raising the pitch of the left-hand drum by pressing with the heel of the hand. *Tablā* are the principal percussion instrument of North Indian art music, accompanying both vocal and instrumental performance. See ill. under South Asia.

Tablature [fr. Lat. *tabula,* table, score; Fr. *tablature;* Ger. *Tabulatur;* It. *intavolatura;* Sp. *tablatura, cifra*]. Musical notation using letters, numerals, or diagrams to specify pitch in terms of the playing technique of a given instrument (e.g., which strings to stop at which frets, which keys to depress, which finger holes to cover) rather than abstractly, as in conventional Western staff notation. Systems of tablature are as old as notated music itself and are widely distributed. They include the principal notations of *East Asia and are familiar to a large audience in the form of the guitar and ukulele chord symbols published with Western popular music since the 1920s. The following is a survey of the principal tablatures in use for stringed and keyboard instruments in Western art music of the 15th through the 18th century.

I. *Stringed instruments.* From the late 15th century through the 18th, music for lute was notated in several systems of tablature that were also applied to other plucked and bowed stringed instruments such as the *vihuela,* guitar, orpharion, theorbo, cittern, bandora, mandora, viola da gamba, lyra viol, baryton, and violin. All systems entail some method of specifying the string on which a pitch is to be played and the fret (if any) at which that string is to be stopped, assuming some particular tuning of the instrument. Tunings for individual instruments varied considerably.

1. Italian, French, and Neapolitan (or "Spanish") lute tablatures. Six horizontal lines (sometimes five in French tablature) represent the courses of the instrument arranged from the highest-pitched down to the lowest, except in Italian tablature, where the order is reversed, the bottom line denoting the highest-pitched string. Ciphers (letters in French and numerals in the other tablatures) indicate open and stopped courses that are plucked individually: *0* (sometimes *1* in Neapolitan) or *a* = open course, *1* or *b* = first fret, *2* or *c* = second fret, *3* or *d* = third fret, etc. [see Ex. 1 and Ex. 2, the opening of a ricercar for lute by Francesco Canova da Milano that was printed during the 16th century in four types of lute tablature]. Since frets were placed chromatically (though some cittern tablatures have frets placed diatonically), the ciphers represent notes a semitone, tone, minor third, major third, etc., above an open course. Notes or note stems above the lines show durations separating successive attacks, sometimes recurring only when the note-value changes. The tablature thus gives only the beginning of each pitch, not how long it is to be sustained. Hence, the performer or transcriber must assign note-values to individual pitches. This may entail reconstructing a polyphonic texture consisting of several individual lines. (Some tablatures show held notes with an asterisk or other sign placed next to the affected cipher, or with a diagonal line, but these indications of "covered play" are rare and inconsistently used.) Dots under some individual ciphers tell the player to pluck the string upward with the index finger.

During the 16th century, Italian tablature was also used in Spain, southern France, and Bavaria; Neapolitan in southern Italy and in one Spanish print; and French in England, the Low Countries, and in an Italian manuscript of the late 15th century. After ca. 1600,

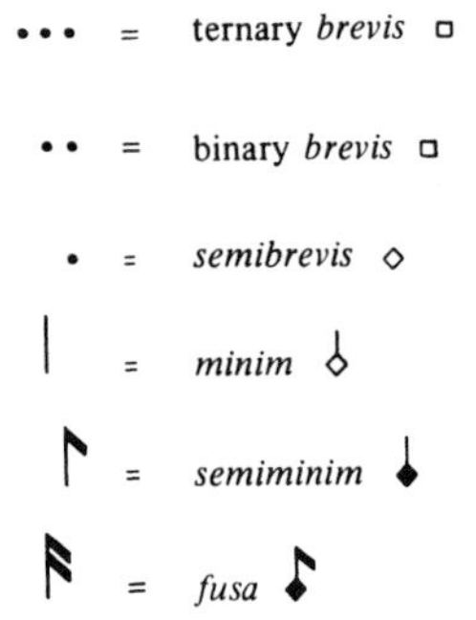

ternary *brevis*
binary *brevis*
semibrevis
minim
semiminim
fusa

1. Note-values.

2. Four types of lute tablature with transcription.

French tablature gained international ascendancy except in Italy and Spain. At that time, the lute and related instruments also acquired as many as eight unfingered courses (or diapasons), which were tuned, according to the key of the piece, in a descending scale, indicated /a, //a, ///a, /4, /5, etc.

2. German lute tablature. Devised for the five-course lute of the 15th century, German lute tablature notates the open strings with numbers, 1–5 starting with the lowest, and the frets with letters in like succession [see Ex. 3]. Various systems for notating the sixth course appear in the sources. Notes plucked upward with the index finger are indicated with hooks on the rhythmic signs. Although it is the oldest (the earliest source dates from ca. 1470–73) and was also used in eastern Europe, Austria, and Scandinavia, German tablature did not survive beyond 1620.

3. *Alfabeto* and mixed guitar tablatures. Hundreds of 17th- and 18th-century guitar books assign letters and other symbols (the so-called Castilian and Catalan systems use numerals) to represent specific **rasgueado* chords, strummed upward or downward according to placement of the letter above or below a horizontal line. Other books indicate the direction of strumming by vertical dashes that extend upward or downward from the line. In Italian or French tablature, the letters do not directly represent the actual harmonies (e.g., G for a G-major triad), but refer to a diagram or an illustration showing the frets to be stopped.

The most common guitar *alfabeto* is shown with its transcription in Ex. 4 (Giovanni Paolo Foscarini, ca. 1632). Small dots (replaced with superscript numerals in Ex. 4) indicate the finger used to press the fret. Further refinements include chords shifted to higher positions, indicated by superscript numerals (Ex. 4b), or chords altered with dissonance, indicated by crosses (Ex. 4c). Rhythm may be indicated with notes or note stems, though long and short notes are frequently

	OPEN	1st FRET	2nd FRET	3rd FRET	4th FRET	5th FRET	6th FRET	7th FRET	
I.	5 = g′	e = a♭′/g♯′	k = a′	p = b♭′	v = b′	9 = c″	$\overline{\text{e}}$ = c♯″	$\overline{\text{k}}$ = d″	
II.	4 = d′	d = e♭′	j = e′	o = f′	t = f♯′	& = g′	$\overline{\text{d}}$ = a♭′	$\overline{\text{j}}$ = a′	
III.	3 = a	c = b♭	h = b	n = c′	s = c♯′	z = d′	$\overline{\text{c}}$ = e♭′	$\overline{\text{h}}$ = d′	
IV.	2 = f	b = f♯	g = g	m = a♭	r = a	y = b♭	$\overline{\text{b}}$ = b	$\overline{\text{g}}$ = c′	
V.	1 = c	a = c♯	f = d	l = e♭	q = e	x = f	$\overline{\text{a}}$ = f♯	$\overline{\text{f}}$ = g	
VI.	+ = G	A = A♭/G♯	F = A	L = B♭	Q = B	X = c	Ā = c♯	F = d	(1512)
	A	B	C	D	E	F	G	H	(1523)
	+	A	B	C	D	E	F	G	(1536)
	$\overline{1}$	$\overline{2}$	$\overline{3}$	$\overline{4}$	$\overline{5}$	$\overline{6}$	$\overline{7}$	$\overline{8}$	(1552)
	+	$\overline{\text{a}}$	$\overline{\text{f}}$	$\overline{\text{l}}$	$\overline{\text{q}}$	$\overline{\text{x}}$	$\overline{\text{aa}}$	$\overline{\text{ff}}$	(1552)

3. German lute tablature.

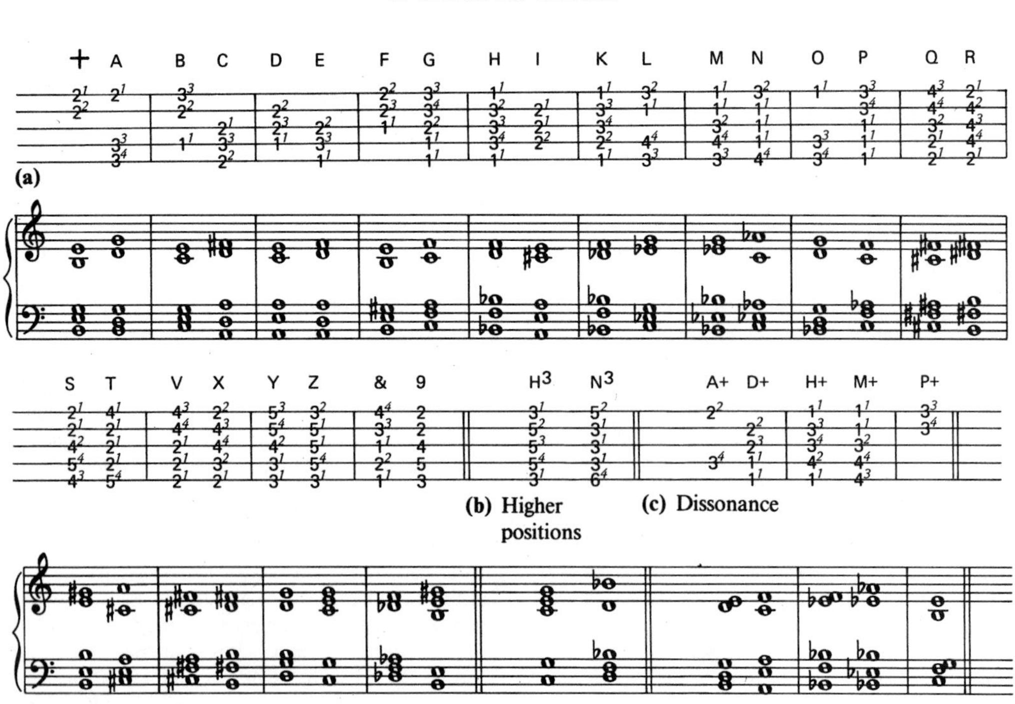

4. Guitar *alfabeto* with transcription.

shown simply with uppercase and lowercase letters. The player must determine the rhythm by examining the position of strong (downward) and weak (upward) strokes. Suggestions for resolving these notational ambiguities are given in Tyler (1980), p. 70, and Wolf (1919), pp. 179f.

Mixed tablature combines *alfabeto* with French or Italian lute tablature. Chords and direction of *rasgueado* strokes are indicated at the bottom of a five-line "staff" on which the individually sounded *(punteado)* notes are given in ciphers. Stems of the rhythmic signs show up and down strokes, and a rhythmic sign without ciphers indicates that the previous chord should be strummed again. When a stroke mark appears with a cipher, the previous *alfabeto* chord is altered as indicated by the cipher. Although pure *alfabeto* tablatures persisted sporadically until ca. 1800, French (and to a lesser extent Italian) tablature—modified to reflect the newer composite *rasgueado/punteado* playing style inherent in mixed tablature—gradually displaced earlier systems [Ex. 5]. Individual *punteado* notes are specified in the usual way, and finger placements for *rasgueado* chords are given, though only stopped frets are indicated. Open courses must be sounded with fingered courses in a continuous stroke unless specifically canceled with a dot.

II. *Keyboard instruments.* From the earliest document, the Robertsbridge Codex (ca. 1320), through the time of Bach, much keyboard music was notated in systems employing numerals, letters of the alphabet, and combinations of letters and the staff. In letter tablature, keys of the organ or harpsichord are designated by the conventional a to g with some modifications. B♭ and B, both part of the hexachord system, are differentiated as *b rotundum* and *b quadratum* (written h, ♯, ♮, or ♭), respectively. Accidentals are indicated by attaching to the letter a small loop, representing the Latin abbreviation of *-is,* "of the" (i.e., the black key "of the" white key below); thus a C with loop = *Cis* (C♯), D with loop = *Dis* (E♭, rarely D♯), etc., the exact modern spelling being determined by context. The central octave is usually B to b♭, with octaves above and below it distinguished with one or two lines over the letter and uppercase or underscoring [see Ex. 6d].

In other systems, the keys are numbered. In the first [Ex. 6a], each white key and black key is assigned a number between 1 and 42. In the second [Ex. 6b], only the white keys are numbered (from 1 to 23), and a black key is indicated with an *x* or ♯, thus $\overset{x}{3}$ = D in the *short octave, and $\overset{x}{9}$ = f♯. The third, more practical method [Ex. 6c] assigns the numbers 1 through 7 to a diatonic scale from f to e′, with higher and lower octaves designated with dots and commas or one and two dashes. The numeral 4 may stand for b♭ or b, according to a key signature (B or ♮) placed at the head of the piece. In tablatures using numbers and letters, rhythmic values are indicated with diamond-shaped notes, or more frequently with the flagged note stems used in lute tablature [see Ex. 2].

Staff notation, when incorporated into tablature, draws from contemporaneous black and white *mensural notation, but differs in using only imperfect *tempus* and *prolatio,* ties, and bar lines. Accidentals are frequently indicated with a dot above or below the altered note, or with a second stem or loop extending below the note head. Depending on context, B, E, and A are usually lowered, and F, C, and G raised. Confusion sometimes results because a double-stemmed note may indicate that the rhythmic value is twice as long, and the loop may also mark an ornament (usually a mordent).

1. German keyboard tablature. Two systems are generally recognized. One, called Old German, was in use in many parts of Europe from the 14th century until replaced in the late 16th century by the New German system, which remained common, particularly in northern lands, until well into the 18th century. Old German tablature notates the upper part(s) on a staff and the lower with letters. Sometimes the bass is directly below the staff, and the alto and tenor below

5. Mixed tablature with transcription.

Black keys			D		E		B♭			c♯		e♭			f♯		a♭/g♯		b♭					
White keys	C	F		G		A		B	c		d		e	f		g		a		b	c′	b′	c″	a″
a. Bermudo	1	2	3	4	5	6	7	8	9	10	11	12	13	14	15	16	17	18	19	20	21. . .	32	33	42
b. Valente	1	2	X 2	3	X 3	4	X 4	5	6	X 6	7	X 7	8	9	X 9	10	X 10	11	X 11	12	13. . .	19	20	
c. Henestrosa	5	+	6	2	7	3	4	4	5		6		7	1		2		3	4	4	5	4′	5′	3′
d. German	C	F	D	G	E	A	B	h	c	cis	d	dis	e	f	fis	g	gis	a	b	$\bar{h}$	$\bar{c}$	$\bar{\bar{h}}$	$\bar{\bar{c}}$	$\bar{\bar{a}}$
	$\underline{c}$	$\underline{f}$	$\underline{d}$	$\underline{g}$	$\underline{e}$	$\underline{a}$	$\underline{b}$															hh	cc	aa

6. Tablature for keyboard instruments.

that. New German tablature uses only letters [see Ex. 7].

2. Spanish keyboard tablatures. Three systems occur in Spanish and southern Italian prints and manuscripts. The one in Ex. 6c appears in keyboard, harp, guitar, and *vihuela* sources from Luis Venegas de Henestrosa (Alcalá de Henares, 1557) to Lucas Ruiz de Ribayaz (Madrid, 1677); the one in Ex. 6a is known only from Juan Bermudo's treatise (Osuna, 1555). In both, the numerals are placed on two to six horizontal lines, each of which represents one part in the polyphonic complex. The third type [Ex. 6b], appearing first in works by Antonio Valente (Naples, 1576), distributes the numerals above and below a line that divides notes for the right hand from those for the left. A difficulty in many tablatures is in showing the durations of the inner parts. Valente used subsidiary signs following the numerals: ; = dotted minim, : = semibreve, ⁝ = dotted semibreve, and ? = breve. In all number tablatures, rhythmic signs are placed above the tablature proper.

3. Italian (French, English) keyboard tablature. Although not true tablatures (since they employ notation either on two staves with from five to eight lines each or on a single staff with as many as 13 lines), many 16th- and early 17th-century prints of keyboard music carry designations such as *intabolatura* and *reduicte en tablature,* referring to the reduction of part-music to short score. A preferable modern term for these is keyboard score, though this may be confused with keyboard *partitura,* a format in which each part is given a separate staff.

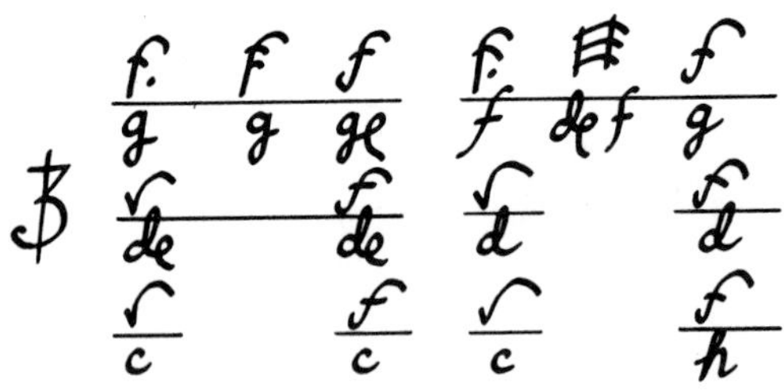

7. New German tablature with transcription.

Bibl.: Johannes Wolf, *Handbuch der Notationskunde,* vol. 2 (Leipzig: Breitkopf & Härtel, 1919; R: Hildesheim: Olms, 1963). Willi Apel, *The Notation of Polyphonic Music, 900–1600,* 5th ed. rev. (Cambridge, Mass.: Mediaeval Acad, 1953). Sylvia Murphy, "Seventeenth-Century Guitar Music: Notes on *Rasgueado* Performance," *GSJ* 21 (1968): 24–32. Hans Radke, "Zum Problem der Lautentabulatur-Übertragung," *AM* 43 (1971): 94–103. Jürgen Eppelsheim, "Buchstaben-Notation, Tablatur und Klaviatur," *AfMw* 31 (1974): 57–72. Thomas Heck, "Lute Music: Tablatures, Textures, and Transcription," *JLSA* 7 (1974): 19–30. James Tyler, *The Early Guitar: A History and Handbook,* Early Music Series 4 (London: Oxford U Pr, 1980). A.J.N.

Table. (1) The belly or upper plate of the sound box of stringed instruments such as the violin and guitar. (2) [Fr.] The *soundboard of the harp [see also *Près*].

Tabor, taborel, tabour, tabourin, tabret [Eng., Fr.]. A small, shallow drum of Europe, often with a snare. See Pipe and tabor, Tambourin, Tambourine.

Tabulatur [Ger.]. *Tablature.

Tace [It.], **tacet** [Lat.]. Be (is) silent. The terms are used in parts and scores for ensemble music to indicate extended passages or movements in which a part remains silent.

Tactus [Lat.]. In the 15th and 16th centuries, beat. This was marked by a falling and rising motion of the hand, and in the 16th century, one *tactus* was equal to the value of a normal semibreve (or the corresponding value in cases of augmentation and diminution; see Mensural notation, Proportions). According to Franchinus Gaffurius (1496), the rate of such beats was equal to the pulse of a man breathing normally, thus, perhaps 60–70 per minute. That this remained fixed throughout the 16th century, as was once thought, seems unlikely because of the effects of certain proportions and some evidence that tempo could be varied [see Tempo].

Bibl.: Carl Dahlhaus, "Zur Theorie des Tactus im 16. Jahrhundert," *AfMw* 17 (1960): 22–39. Antoine Auda, *Théorie et pratique du tactus* (Brussels: Oeuvres de Don Bosco, 1965). J. A. Bank, *Tactus, Tempo, and Notation in Mensural Music from the 13th to the 17th Century* (Amsterdam: Annie Bank, 1972).

Tafelklavier [Ger.]. *Square piano.

Tafelmusik [Ger., table music; Fr. *musique de table*]. Music to be performed at a banquet or at dinner. This and related terms were widely used in publications of the 17th and 18th centuries (e.g., Johann Hermann Schein, *Banchetto musicale,* 1617; Telemann, *Musique de table,* 1733).

Tagelied [Ger.]. A song of the *Minnesinger related to the **alba.*

Taille [Fr.]. From the 16th century through the 18th, tenor, with respect to both voices and families of instruments (e.g., *taille des hautbois, taille de violon,* etc.).

Tailpiece [Fr. *cordier;* Ger. *Saitenhalter;* It. *cordiera;* Sp. *cordal*]. On the *violin and related instruments, a piece of wood (often ebony) to which the strings are attached below the bridge.

Take. A single, distinct, continuous *recording. In a recording session, there are usually several takes of each piece or movement; the recording issued to the public is a selection from or, in some cases, a composite of these. Some jazz discographies give a take number following the matrix number to identify the different versions of a single title.

Takt [Ger.]. (1) Beat; *Taktmesser,* metronome. (2) Measure; *Taktstrich,* bar line. (3) Meter (also *Taktart*); *im Takt, taktmässig,* in strict meter or tempo; *Taktvorzeichnung, Taktzeichen,* time signature.

Tāl(a)(am) [Hin., Skt., Tel.]. Meter in Indian music [see South Asia]. An abstract pattern of beats serving as a time frame for musical composition and improvisation, the *tāla,* particularly in Carnatic music, may not be evident in the musical sound and is consequently demonstrated with hand gestures. C.C.

Talea [Lat.]. See Isorhythm.

Tales of Hoffmann, The. See *Contes d'Hoffmann, Les.*

Talharpa [Swed.]. A bowed *lyre of Sweden with three or four gut or metal (formerly horsehair) strings, related to the **crwth.*

Tallone [It.]. *Frog.

Talon [Fr.]. *Frog.

Tambor [Sp.]. Drum.

Tambora [Sp.]. A two-headed drum of Latin America. In the Dominican Republic, where it is particularly prominent, it is made from a hollowed tree trunk and played with the bare left hand and a stick held in the right hand.

Tamborito [Sp.]. A Panamanian dance and its music, combining Hispanic and African-derived elements. The *tamborito* is traditionally danced by one couple at a time, with responsorial singing by female vocalists, hand-clapping, and drum ensemble; the two-headed *tambora* and the single-headed *pujador* and *repicador* are typical instruments. The *tamborito* is in moderate duple meter, with complex instrumental accompaniments combining contrasting figures; in a characteristic vocal procedure, a varying four-measure phrase for improvising soloist alternates with a fixed refrain of equal length for unison chorus. D.S.

Tambour [Fr.]. Drum, drummer; *t. de Basque,* *tambourine; *t. militaire,* snare drum.

Tambourin [Fr.]. (1) A long, two-headed drum of Provence (sometimes called a *tambourin provençal*) played with the **galoubet* as a *pipe and tabor. (2) *Tambourine. (3) An 18th-century French dance found in the theatrical works of Rameau and others, perhaps based on a Provençal folk dance, and often employing a texture imitating the *galoubet* and *tambourin* [see (1) above] with a regular, static bass and a lively melody, usually in duple meter. Examples also occur in keyboard and other purely instrumental works.

Tambourine [Fr. *tambour de basque;* Ger. *Schellentrommel, Tamburin;* It. *tamburello, tamburino;* Sp. *pandereta*]. A shallow, single-headed frame drum with a wooden frame in which metal disks or jingles are set; also sometimes timbrel. It is most often held in one hand and struck with the other; sometimes the head is rubbed along the perimeter with the thumb, producing a continuous sound from both head and jingles; it may also be simply shaken or played upon with sticks. It is of Middle Eastern origin and in the West is particularly associated with Spain. See also *Tambourin;* see ill. under Percussion instruments.

Tamburā, tānpura [Hin.]. A *long-necked lute of India used exclusively as a drone. It has a hollow neck, a pear-shaped body, and four metal strings. The player holds it vertically and strums the open strings with the right hand throughout vocal and instrumental performances. See also *Tanbur;* see ill. under South Asia.

Tamburello [It.]. *Tambourine.

Tamburin [Ger.]. *Tambourine.

Tamburino [It.]. Tenor *drum; *tambourine.

Tamburo [It.]. Drum; *t. grande, grosso,* bass drum; *t. rullante,* tenor drum; *t. militare,* snare drum.

Tampon. A drumstick with a soft head on each end, used with the bass drum and permitting the execution of a roll by means of rapid, rotary oscillations of the hand.

Tam-tam. A percussion instrument of indefinite pitch consisting of a broad circular disk of metal, slightly convex, with the rim turned down, giving the appearance of a shallow plate with low vertical sides. It is hung vertically and struck in the center with a soft-headed beater. See also Gong; see ill. under Percussion instruments.

Tānam [Tel.]. A pulsed form of melodic improvisation in Carnatic music. Its varied rhythmic patterns are achieved by frequent articulation of syllables like *ta* and *nā,* or by frequent strokes of the plectrum, tonguing, or bowing changes. C.C.

Tanbur [Turk.; Per. *ṭanbūr;* also *danbura, tambur, tambura, tamburica, ṭunbūr*]. A *long-necked lute distributed from the Balkans through the Middle East to Central Asia. A typical member of this family has a small pear-shaped body, a long fretted neck, and two or three metal strings. The *tanbur* of Turkish art music has a hemispheric body and six strings in courses of two. The Afghan *tanbur* has added sympathetic strings. In Yugoslavia, the *tambura* is made in varying sizes that are played together in ensembles to accompany dance. See also *Saz, Dutār, Tamburā, Ṭunbūr.*

Tañer [Sp.]. To play a musical instrument.

Tangent. In a *clavichord, the metal blade attached to each key that both strikes the string and determines its vibrating length when the key is depressed.

Tango [Sp.]. An Argentine genre of urban song and dance music. It is generally regarded as originating in the poor neighborhoods of Buenos Aires in the late 19th century, with important antecedents in the traditional Argentine **milonga* and in Cuban dances such as the **habanera,* then in vogue. The tango is a dramatic form in several respects. The dance, for couples in tight embrace, is characterized by almost violent movement. The often lengthy texts of the sung tango are emotional, sentimental, and sometimes intensely negative in tone, and the music of the tango, frequently in minor mode, is one of abrupt rhythmic and dynamic contrasts. In a typical tango accompaniment, a prevailing pattern in which all beats are sharply accented will be occasionally interrupted by sudden pauses and by emphatically syncopated passages [see Ex.]. Traditional performance media include solo

voice with guitar accompaniment; trios with violin, flute, and guitar or **bandoneón* (accordion); and ensembles of various sizes with *bandoneones,* strings, and piano. D.S.

Tannhäuser und der Sängerkrieg auf Wartburg [Ger., Tannhäuser and the Song Contest at the Wartburg]. Opera in three acts by Wagner (to his own libretto, based on a conflation of several medieval legends). First produced in Dresden in 1845, it was revised for a production in Paris in 1861. Setting: Venusberg and the Wartburg (near Eisenach) in the early 13th century.

Tānpura [Hin.]. See *Tamburā.*

Tanto [It.]. So much; *non tanto,* not so (too) much, e.g., *allegro non tanto.*

Tanz [Ger.]. Dance.

Tap dance. A type of popular theatrical dance in which rhythmic patterns are sounded on the floor with the heels and toes of shoes fitted with metal taps for the purpose. It is danced by a single dancer, two or a few working together, or an entire chorus line. The accompanying music often makes use of *stop time to permit the most intricate or demanding tap patterns to be heard clearly. It originated in the 19th century from clog dancing and was much influenced by black entertainers. In the first half of the 20th century, tap dancing was a regular feature of revues and similar musical entertainments, and it was prominent in many musical films. It regained some of its popularity in the 1970s and 80s with musicals such as *42nd Street.*

Tape music. See Electro-acoustic music.

Tape recording. See Recording.

Tapiola. A symphonic poem by Sibelius, op. 112 (1926), named for Tapio, the forest god of Finnish legend [see *Kalevala*].

Taqsīm [Ar., division; Turk. *taksim*]. A major improvised instrumental form in Arabic and Turkish music, usually nonmetric, one to ten minutes in length and often used to open a performance. Most frequently performed on lutes or *qānūn* in rapid tempo, it may be slow when played by bowed instruments or flutes. A *taqsīm* consists of a series of short sections of increasingly high pitch, some of them modulating from the principal *maqām* to others. Some *taqāsīm* have metric introductions *(dūlāb)* or inserts, and a few are completely metric. B.N.

Tār. (1) [Per.] A fretted, *long-necked lute of Iran and the Caucasus. The Persian *tār* has six strings in courses of two and a double-pear-shaped body covered with skin. See ill. under Near and Middle East. (2) [Ar. *ṭār*] A circular *frame drum of the Middle East and North Africa with one head and jingles.

Tarantella [It.]. A folk dance of southern Italy that takes its name from the town of Taranto (not, as is often said, from the tarantula or from a dance to cure its bite). It is in a rapid, accelerating 6/8 with shifts between major and minor. The tarantella was taken up by various composers of the 19th century (Chopin, Liszt, Heller, Weber), often as a piece with continuous eighth notes (or eighth-note triplets in simple meters) and of some technical difficulty.

Tardo, tardamente [It.]. Slow, slowly; *tardando,* slowing.

Tárogató [Hung.]. (1) A Hungarian woodwind instrument similar to the soprano saxophone, with a single reed and a conical bore, but made of wood. It is often pitched in B♭, with a range from b♭ to d'''. It was invented in the 1890s by Joseph Schunda and is played mainly as an unaccompanied solo instrument. (2) A double-reed instrument, similar to the **zūrnā,* in use in Hungary from the 13th century through the 18th. The modern *tárogató* developed by Schunda was inspired by this instrument, which in the 19th century became a symbol of freedom.

Tartini's tone. See Combination tone.

Tartöld [Ger.]. A *racket, brightly painted and in the shape of a dragon. Five survive from the 16th century.

Taschengeige [Ger.]. *Kit.

Tasnif [Per.]. The most important genre of composed, metric vocal music in 20th-century Iran, with lyrical, satirical, and sometimes political texts. In popular music, the term refers to songs in general. A classical *tasnif* may be performed alone or, in a full performance, follow the *āvāz* [see Near and Middle East IV, 4] and may use the tonal and structural principles of a **dastgāh.* Its most prominent composers were 'Ali Akbar Sheydā and 'Aref. B.N.

Tasso. A symphonic poem by Liszt, after a poem by Byron, first performed in 1849 (orchestrated by August Conradi) as an overture to Goethe's drama *Torquato Tasso.* It was revised in 1850–51 (reorchestrated by Joachim Raff) and 1854.

Tastar de corde [It., to test the strings]. In the 16th century, a short piece intended to probe the tuning of a lute or similar instrument. The five pieces so titled in Joan Ambrosio Dalza's collection (Venice, 1508; *HAM,* no. 99) are virtually indistinguishable from the homophonic *ricercar and *prelude of the same time, although the *tastar de corde* is generally shorter and more chordal. In four instances, Dalza's are attached to a following ricercar and may be precursors of the preludial *tastata* and *tasteggiata* in the lute, theorbo, and keyboard repertories of Italy and Austria in the 17th century. Spanish *vihuela* prints and manuscripts include **tientos* that are specified as appropriate for testing the tuning of the instrument. A.J.N.

Taste [Ger.]. A key of a keyboard; *Tasteninstrument,* keyboard instrument; *Tastenmusik,* keyboard music; *Obertaste,* upper or accidental key; *Untertaste,* lower or natural key.

Tastiera [It.]. (1) Keyboard; *t. per luce,* *color organ. (2) Fingerboard; *sulla t.,* an instruction to bow over the fingerboard [see Bowing (12)].

Tasto [It.]. (1) A key of a keyboard; *t. solo,* in *thoroughbass parts, an instruction to play the bass note only, without chords. (2) Fingerboard; *sul t.,* an instruction to bow over the fingerboard [see Bowing (12)].

Tattoo. A call sounded on bugles, drums, or fifes to summon soldiers to their quarters at night.

Tāvil. See *Davul.*

Tavola [It.]. The table or belly of a stringed instrument; *t. armonica,* soundboard; *presso la t., sulla t.,* an instruction in harp music to pluck near the soundboard.

Tecla [Sp.]. Key, keyboard, keyboard instrument.

Tedesca [It.]. (1) In the 17th century, *allemande. (2) Around 1800, **Deutscher Tanz.* (3) In the German style *(alla tedesca).*

Te Deum [Lat.]. A song of praise to God ("Te Deum laudamus," We praise thee, O God) sung in the Roman rite at the end of Matins on Sundays and feast days, in the Middle Ages following the last responsory, in modern practice replacing it. As a "Hymn of Thanksgiving" (as it is termed in modern liturgical books), it has also long been sung at both religious and secular ceremonies such as coronations and celebrations of victory in battle. In the Anglican rite, it is a canticle at Morning Prayer. Although attributed in the Middle Ages to St. Ambrose (whence sometimes termed Ambrosian Hymn), its authorship remains in doubt. Nicetus of Remesiana (d. 568) has been proposed, but Kähler (1958) argues for origins in the early 4th century. The text employs a variety of styles and quotes the Sanctus of the Mass and several Psalms. Preserved versions of the complete melody (*LU,* pp. 1,832–37) have not been shown to occur in manuscripts from before the 12th century.

The earliest of numerous polyphonic settings is a setting of the verse "Tu Patris sempiternus es Filius" as an example of organum in the treatise **Musica enchiriadis* (ca. 900). Polyphonic settings from the late Middle Ages and Renaissance include works by Binchois, Taverner, Hugh Aston, Festa, Palestrina, Lassus, Anerio, and Kerle, and settings for organ published by Attaingnant and in the *Mulliner Book. The 17th century saw the beginning of a tradition of elaborate choral and orchestral settings, often for particular festive occasions. Composers of such works include Benevoli, Lully, Graun (1757, for the Battle of Prague), Michael Haydn, Joseph Haydn (two examples), Berlioz (for the Paris Exhibition of 1855), Bruckner, Dvořák, Verdi, Kodály, and Pepping. Luther's German translation, "Herr Gott dich loben wir," led to settings by Michael Praetorius and organ works by Scheidt, Buxtehude, and Bach (BWV 725). English settings include those by Purcell, Handel (for the Peace of Utrecht, 1713; for the victory at Dettingen, 1743), Sullivan, Parry, Stanford, and Walton (for the coronation of Elizabeth II in 1953).

Bibl.: Ernst Kähler, *Studien zum Te Deum* (Göttingen: Vandenhoeck & Ruprecht, 1958).

Telephone, The. Comic opera in one act by Gian Carlo Menotti (to his own libretto), written to precede performances of *The *Medium* and produced in New York in 1947. Setting: a city apartment in the present.

Telharmonium. An early electromechanical keyboard instrument, invented by Thaddeus Cahill, who built the first model in 1900. It contained many design features of later electronic instruments, but it lacked an amplifier and in consequence was very large, weighing over 200 tons. Its music was to be distributed over telephone lines.

Telyn [Welsh]. A gut-strung *frame harp of Wales. Known as early as the 11th century, it was displaced in the 18th century by the triple harp. See also Harp.

Tema [It.]. Theme, subject.

Temperament [Fr. *tempérament;* Ger. *Temperatur;* It. *temperamento, sistema participato;* Sp. *temperamento*]. (1) The slight modification of an acoustically pure or just interval [see Just intonation, Interval]. (2) Any scale or system of tuning employing intervals that have been so modified. Tempered intervals sometimes deviate from just intervals by more than 3 percent. For more than two millennia, most theorists have taken the desirability of acoustical purity to be self-evident. Temperaments have thus been practical compromises made necessary by the fact that the desire for acoustical purity and for musical transposition or modulation are not compatible in any closed system, be it a tuning theory or an instrument that lacks a convenient means of varying intervallic size with changing melodic or harmonic contexts.

The chromatic scale can be expressed as a linear series of 12 fifths bounded by the pitch class A♭ and its enharmonic equivalent, G♯: A♭–E♭–B♭–F–C–G–D–A–E–B–F♯–C♯–G♯. If these fifths are kept acoustically pure (as happens in the Pythagorean tuning), then enharmonic pitch classes such as A♭ and G♯ will differ by an amount known as the Pythagorean or ditonic comma, equivalent to 23.5 *cents. This enharmonic discrepancy is a practical disadvantage when, for example, an organist, transposing in order to match (say) the range of some singers, must use the out-of-tune G♯–E♭ as a proxy for the true fifth A♭–E♭. The remedy for this is temperament, which dilutes the acoustic discrepancy by distributing it among several intervals. The distribution may be in 12 or fewer parts and may be equal or unequal.

I. *Equal distributions.* In the 20th century, a temperament with 12-part equal distribution predominated. In this, each of the Pythagorean scale's fifths (3:2, worth 702 cents) is diminished by about 2 cents so as to eliminate over the sum of 12 fifths the accumulation of the nearly 24 cents of the Pythagorean comma. If the 12 pitch classes are arranged in a chromatic scale within a single octave, the result is a succession of 12 semitones of equal size. Since the frequency of the higher of two pitches an octave apart must be two times the frequency of the lower pitch, the frequency of the higher of two pitches separated by such a semitone must be $\sqrt[12]{2}$ or about 1.05946 times the frequency of the lower one.

The first evidences of temperament come from northern Italy. In 1496, Franchinus Gaffurius testified that organists were subjecting fifths to a small diminution known as *participata.* Pietro Aaron used this same term in 1523 in describing *meantone temperament. The earliest source for a temperament that attempts to distribute the comma equally is Giovanni Lanfranco's *Scintille di musica* (Brescia, 1533). Equal temperament did not become the norm for another 300 years, for three reasons. First, in a tradition still permeated by Pythagorean numerology, savants were reluctant to give irrational intervals the same ontological status as that possessed by Pythagorean or just intervals. A second obstacle was the difficulty of extracting $\sqrt[12]{2}$. Lanfranco's own general guidelines for tuning instruments (unspecified, but with a keyboard) eschew the quantitative altogether, although elsewhere he instructs the reader in the extraction of square roots. The only early numerical method to win practical acceptance was Vincenzo Galilei's fortuitous discovery (before 1581) that $(18{:}17)^{12}$ very nearly equals 2:1 (in fact, about 199:100). A prominent mathematician, Simon Stevin, was the first Westerner to show (ca. 1596) how to tune a monochord in equal temperament using numerical methods. But his solution remained in manuscript, unknown to musicians. Marin Mersenne's numerical method (1636), on the other hand, was widely disseminated.

The tuning and construction of fretted instruments gave a strong practical impetus to the creation of equal temperament. Because the frets of such instruments intersect all strings and must produce, for example, an A at the seventh fret of a string tuned to D that is in tune with the A produced at the second fret of a string tuned to g′ (and, of course, many other such combinations), the frets must be positioned so as to produce semitones as nearly equal as possible, and the open strings must be tuned to reflect the size of the semitones.

Most methods for obtaining an equal and proportional division of the octave were geometrical. A few theorists advocated the use of an ancient mechanical instrument, the mesolabium, but the majority preferred the less cumbersome medium of Euclidean geometry. Mersenne's geometrical method was especially successful, obtaining by simple means a rather recondite value for the semitone equivalent to 100.433 cents. This comes closer to the ideal value of the equally tempered semitone than do most actual semitones on tuned nonelectronic instruments.

Another class of temperaments begins with just intonation instead of the Pythagorean scale and equally distributes the syntonic comma. Indeed, the most widely used of all keyboard temperaments before the 19th century narrows each of the scale's 12 fifths by 1/4 of a syntonic comma [see Meantone temperament]. Francisco Salinas described (1577) an influential temperament that narrows each fifth by 1/3 of a syntonic comma.

II. *Irregular and unequal distributions.* The third factor that retarded the full acceptance of equal temperament was the relative circumscription of modulation schemes before ca. 1765. Little-used keys can be tempered more. This works best if they lie a semitone or tritone away from the key of the tuning. Irregular temperaments make up for any lack of formal elegance by their ease of application. The earliest instructions for a complete chromatic tuning, given by Arnolt Schlick in 1511, appear to be for an irregular temperament. The practical and effective temperament described in 1518 by Heinrich Schreiber (Henricus Grammateus) distributes the Pythagorean comma to ten semitones. As late as 1779, Johann Kirnberger suggested that a single division of the comma be applied to fifths on D and A.

Historically, the most important unequal distributions are those that eliminate the *wolf fifth. A number of these "circulating" temperaments were propagated during the 17th and 18th centuries, and it is to them rather than to equal temperament that the term well-tempered (as in Bach's *Das Wohltemperirte Clavier*) rightly refers. The most famous of these was given by Andreas Werckmeister in his *Musikalische Temperatur* (Frankfurt and Leipzig, 1691; facs., Utrecht: Diapason Pr, 1983). In this, the Pythagorean comma is distributed equally to fifths on C, G, D, and B. Probably the most prolific propagandist for temperaments was Johann Georg Neidhardt. His Model Temperament #3 (1732) distributes the Pythagorean comma unequally: fifths on E♭ and G♭ are 1/12th of a comma (two cents) flat; on C and G, 1/6th of a comma (four cents) flat; and on D and A, 1/4th of a comma (six cents) flat. Neidhardt's own favorite temperament (1724) distributes the comma unequally to nine fifths in the scale. Those on B♭, A, B, F♯, C♯, and G♯ are 1/12th of a comma flat; those on C, G, and D are 1/6th of a comma flat. As late as 1776, Friedrich Marpurg considered this temperament to be worthy of citation. See also Tuning.

Bibl.: Robert H. M. Bosanquet, "On Temperament, or The Division of the Octave," *PRMA* 1 (1874/75): 4–17. Id., "On the Beats of Mistuned Harmonic Consonances," *PRMA* 8 (1881/82): 13–27. A. R. McClure, "Studies in Keyboard Temperaments," *GSJ* 1 (1948): 28–40. James Murray Barbour, *Tuning and Temperament: A Historical Survey* (East Lansing: Mich St Coll Pr, 1951; 2nd ed., 1953). Heinrich Husmann, "Zur Charakteristik der Schlickschen Temperatur," *AfMw* 24 (1967): 253–65. Clare G. Raynor, "Historically Justified Keyboard Variations on Equal-Tempered Tuning," *GSJ* 28 (1975): 121–29. John Barnes, "Bach's Keyboard Temperament," *EM* 7 (1979): 236–49. William Blood, "'Well-Tempering' the Clavier," *EM* 7 (1979): 491–95. Dale Carr, "A Practical Introduction to Unequal Temperament," *The Diapason* 65 (Feb. 1979): 6–8. Dirk de Klerk, "Equal Temperament," *AM* 51 (1979): 140–50. Mark Lindley, "Mersenne on Keyboard Tuning," *JMT* 24 (1980): 167–203. Id., *Lutes, Viols, and Temperaments* (Cambridge: Cambridge U Pr, 1984).

Temperatur [Ger.]. *Temperament; *gleichschwebende, ungleichschwebende T.,* equal, unequal temperament.

Tempest, The. Popular name for Beethoven's Piano Sonata in D minor op. 31 no. 2 (1802). When Anton Schindler asked Beethoven to explain the "meaning" of this sonata and the sonata op. 57 (**Appassionata*), Beethoven cryptically suggested that Schindler read Shakespeare's *Tempest.* The title has been associated only with the earlier sonata, however.

Tempestoso [It.]. Tempestuous, stormy.

Temple block. A percussion instrument carved from hardwood into a round or oval shape and made hollow, with a slit spanning most of the lower half; also called a Chinese or Korean temple block (and sometimes confused with the rectangular *Chinese block). It is usually played in a set of five of differing pitches (approximating a pentatonic scale) with soft-headed mallets or drum sticks. See ill. under Percussion instruments.

Tempo [It., time]. (1) The speed at which music is performed, i.e., the rate per unit of time of metrical pulses in performance; *a tempo,* an instruction to return to the original tempo after a temporary departure specified by **ritardando* or a similar term. Speeds of performance may range from quite slow to quite fast and, in Western art music beginning in the 17th century, are usually indicated on a score in words, or sometimes *metronome markings. Most pieces have a range of acceptable tempos. Even seemingly absolute metronome markings are seldom unchangeable. A tempo is chosen for a variety of reasons: it may be better suited to the interpretive and expressive requirements of the performer, or it may be better adapted to ensemble size, instrumentation, or the dimensions and acoustical makeup of a performance space. While performance speeds are, therefore, often a matter of taste, tempos should be selected with a view to the date and style of the music.

Until the introduction of words or phrases to specify tempo in the 17th century, tempo was expressed in notation by the combination of mensuration or meter [see Mensural notation], the prevailing note-values in a given work, and the concept of **tempus* or **tactus*—a pulse of fixed rate assigned to some particular note-value. Although writers as late as the 18th century continued to discuss tempo in these terms (e.g., Michel de Saint-Lambert, 1702), the system was not wholly unambiguous even in the 16th, especially as regards the fixity of the *tactus.* Notational devices such as **note nere* and some *proportions imply a flexibility of *tactus,* and theorists as early as Zarlino (1558) complain of the system's inadequacy. Nevertheless, every period has had its conventions of tempo expressed in combinations of meter and note-value. In the music of Mozart, for example, 3/4 with motion in quarters and eighths is generally associated with slower tempos than is 3/8 with motion in eighths and sixteenths (see Zaslaw, 1972).

By the 18th century, Italian terms for tempo were widespread, and theorists such as Quantz (1752) attempted to relate them to conventions based on meter and note-value. There was general agreement about the relative position of some basic tempos, e.g., from slowest to fastest, *adagio, andante, allegretto, allegro,* and *presto.* But disagreements about the precise meanings of these terms and, especially, those for intervening tempos were widespread (for comparative lists, see Zaslaw, 1972). Conventions with respect to their use have changed steadily since. For a survey of the terms used to designate tempo and their history, see Performance marks; see also Rubato.

In some studies of non-Western music (e.g., Lomax's *cantometrics), whole repertories or musical cultures may be characterized by a typical tempo.

(2) [It.] *Movement.

Bibl.: Rudolf Kolisch, "Tempo and Character in Beethoven's Music," *MQ* 29 (1943): 169–87, 291–312. Curt Sachs, *Rhythm and Tempo: A Study in Music History* (New York: Norton, 1953). Mieczyslaw Kolinski, "The Evaluation of Tempo," *Ethno* 3 (1959): 45–57. Dieter Christensen, "Inner Tempo and Melodic Tempo," *Ethno* 4 (1960): 9–14. Robert Münster, "Authentische Tempi zu den sechs letzten Sinfonien W. A. Mozarts," *MJb* (1962–63): 185–99. Neal Zaslaw, "Mozart's Tempo Conventions," *Copenhagen,* 1972, pp. 720–33. Robert Donington, *The Interpretation of Early Music, New Version* (London: Faber, 1974; corrected ed., 1977). William S. Newman, "Das Tempo in Beethovens Instrumentalmusik—Tempowahl und Tempoflexibilität," *Mf* 33 (1980): 161–83.

Tempo giusto [It.]. See *Giusto.*

Tempo marks. See Performance marks.

Tempo ordinario [It.]. (1) Common time, 4/4. (2) A tempo neither particularly fast nor slow.

Tempo primo [It.]. An instruction to return to the original tempo after some temporary departure.

Temporale [Lat.]. In the liturgical year, the feasts of the Time, i.e., principally those commemorating (or organized around the commemoration of) events in the life of Jesus [see Liturgy].

Tempo rubato [It.]. See *Rubato.*

Temps [Fr.]. Beat.

Tempus [Lat.]. In *mensural notation, the relationship (whether duple or triple) between the *brevis* and the *semibrevis.* As an index of tempo, a *tempus* was described in the 13th century by Franco of Cologne as "that which is a minimum in fullness of voice" ("minimum in plenitudine vocis") and was represented by the *brevis.* By the 14th century, however, smaller note-values had been introduced, and the *brevis* had become a relatively long note-value. An analogous concept in the 16th century regarding tempo is **tactus.*

Ten. [It.]. Abbr. for **tenuto.*

Tender Land, The. Opera in two acts by Copland (libretto by Horace Everett), produced in New York in 1954 (revised in three acts in 1955; orchestral suite arranged in 1956). Setting: a Midwestern farm in the early 1930s.

Tendre, tendrement [Fr.]. Tender(ly).

Tenebrae [Lat., darkness]. In the Roman rite, the service made up of Matins and Lauds on Thursday, Friday, and Saturday of Holy Week, so called because a candle is extinguished after each Psalm, the final portion being conducted "in tenebris" (in darkness). The *Lamentations and **Miserere* form prominent parts of the service.

Teneramente [It.]. Tenderly.

Tenor [fr. Lat. *tenere,* to hold]. (1) In medieval polyphony up to the 15th century, the part that "holds" or is based on a preexistent melody or **cantus firmus,* most often a liturgical chant [see Organum, Clausula, Motet]. This was in general the lowest sounding part. (2) In three-voice secular polyphony of the 14th and 15th centuries, the lowest part structurally (though often crossed by the *contratenor), forming at times a structural pair with the uppermost part. (3) In vocal textures for four parts, the part immediately above the lowest part or bass. This usage was established in the late 15th century, at which time the tenor still sometimes retained the function of presenting the *cantus firmus* in long note-values. By the 16th century, however, it was most often not distinguished from the other voices in the character of its music. Since the 18th century, it has formed part of the most characteristic texture for polyphonic vocal music, namely (from highest to lowest) soprano, alto, tenor, and bass. (4) The highest naturally occurring voice type in adult males. See Voice. (5) In some families of instruments, by analogy with the voice, one of the lower members (e.g., in the *trombone, the one immediately above the bass; in the *saxophone, the one immediately above the baritone). (6) In a *psalm tone, the reciting note. See also Clef.

Tenor cor [Fr. *cor alto*]. A brass instrument with piston valves operated by the right hand, round in shape like the French horn, and pitched in F an octave above the French horn. It was introduced by the firm of Besson in Paris ca. 1860.

Tenor drum. See Drum I, 2.

Tenorgeige [Ger.]. *Tenor violin.

Tenor horn. See Alto horn.

Tenorlied [Ger.]. A German polyphonic song of the 16th century in which a preexistent song is placed in the tenor [see Lied].

Tenor Mass. A polyphonic *Mass of the Renaissance based on a **cantus firmus* placed in the tenor.

Tenoroon. A 19th-century tenor member of the *bassoon family. It is a transposing instrument, sounding a fourth or a fifth higher than the normal bassoon. It is played with the usual type of double reed and has the same form as its larger relative. M.S.

Tenor violin. The tenor-voiced instrument of the violin family, largely unknown today. The violin (treble), viola (alto), and cello (bass) with the double bass complete the modern bowed string ensemble. In the 16th and 17th centuries, however, the viola existed in two sizes, known as the tenor and the contralto. In its larger compass, the tenor violin was tuned in fifths upward from F or G, an octave below the violin, and was sometimes large enough to be placed vertically like a small cello.

By the 17th century, the tenor was simply a very large viola with a short neck, in contrast to the smaller viola alto; both were tuned in fifths from c, an octave above the cello. But the larger tenor usually played in a lower tessitura, because plain gut and Catline strings could not easily concentrate the sound of the c string on the contralto. An instrument grouping would have included two violins, a contralto, tenor, and cello. The tenor was so large that it was taxing to hold the instrument when playing in first position.

As late as 1690 in Cremona, Antonio Stradivari was constructing instruments in both sizes. Plans for a tenor viola, marked *TV,* were used in making several instruments, including the famous Tuscan or "Medicea" tenor, now in the City Museum of Florence, with a body length of 47.9 cm. In contrast is his plan for the smaller *TA* or contralto viola with a body length of 41.1 cm. It is clear that these two forms of the viola were in common usage as labeled by Stradivari in these plans from the Della Valle Collection, now in the Civic Museum of Cremona.

With the development of covered strings by the 18th century, the sound of the lower register in the viola contralto could be concentrated and focused to a greater extent with shortened string length. For the cello, improved string technology and players' technique in upper registers allowed extension of its practical range into and through that of the tenor.

An experimental search for an enlarged viola sound continued into the 18th century. The tenor violin was revived by Johann Ritter in his viola-alto with versions having four or five strings, but again the extremely long body length made the instrument impractical. The idea of a balanced grouping of instrument sizes and proportions has been revived by the work of Carleen M. Hutchins of Montclair, New Jersey, who has introduced a violin family of eight instruments, including a tenor violin, held vertically and tuned as was its 16th-century counterpart, in G with ascending fifths, an octave below the violin. W.L.M.

Tenso [Occ.], **tenson, debat** [Fr.]. A form of troubadour and trouvère poetry that consists of a discussion between two or more poets maintaining opposing views on a given question. Love is the most frequent topic of debate, but religion, politics, literature, and other subjects are also treated. Usually, the dialogue alternates between the participants stanza by stanza, each strophe employing an identical poetic structure and melody. In some cases, however, two separate poems using the same metric scheme are recited in succession by the contenders. See also *Jeu-parti.*

Bibl.: Arthur Långfors, Alfred Jeanroy, and Louis Brandin, eds., *Recueil général des jeux-partis français,* 2 vols. (Paris: H Champion, 1926). David J. Jones, *La tenson provençale: Étude d'un genre poétique suivie d'une édition critique de quatre tensons et d'une liste complète des tensons provençales* (Paris: Droz, 1934). Erich Köhler, "Zur Entstehung des altprovenzalischen Streitgedichts," in *Trobadorlyrik und höfischer Roman* (Berlin: Rütten & Loening, 1962). Michel-André Bossy, ed. and trans., *Medieval Debate Poetry: Vernacular Works* (New York: Garland, 1987).

P.E., V.P., rev. E.A.

Tenth. See Interval.

Tento [Port.]. **Tiento.*

Tenuto [It., abbr. *ten.*]. Held, sustained. In the 18th century, notes so marked were to be held to their full value rather than detached somewhat, as was the norm. In music of the 19th century and since, the term may call for a delay of the beat following. It may be indicated by a short horizontal stroke over or under the note.

Teponaztli [Nahuatl]. A *slit drum of the Aztecs and other Mesoamerican tribes. An H-shaped slit was cut into a hollowed-out section of log, forming two tongues that were struck with mallets. Such instruments were often elaborately carved into animal and human shapes. In Aztec society they were used, along with the **huehuetl,* in dancing and in religious ritual, often in connection with human sacrifice. They were also used by the Mayans (who called them *tunkul*) and the Tarascans, and small drums of this type are still used in Mexico.

Terce. See Office, divine.

Teretismata. See *Anenajki.*

Ternary form. See Binary and ternary form.

Ter Sanctus [Lat.]. The threefold Sanctus occurring in the *Sanctus of the Mass, in the **Trisagion,* and in the **Te Deum.*

Tertian. See *Terzian.*

Tertian harmony. Harmony based on combinations

of the interval of a third, such as characterizes Western tonal harmony.

Terz [Ger.]. (1) The interval of a third. (2) *Terzflöte, Terzfagott,* a flute and a bassoon, respectively, pitched a minor third above the standard instrument. (3) The organ stop **Tierce.*

Terzett [Ger.], **terzetto** [It.]. A vocal work for three voices with or without accompaniment (a work for three instruments being a *trio). Three-part writing was the norm from the late 12th to the 15th century, when it was generally displaced by four-part texture [see Quartet]. Compositions in three parts remained popular throughout the Renaissance, however, especially in lighter forms such as the **villanella* [see also *Tricinium*]. Opera, oratorio, cantata, and related genres of the 17th century made fairly frequent use of three-part vocal ensembles accompanied by continuo. The terzett with orchestral accompaniment became a standard ensemble type in opera of the Classical and Romantic periods, Mozart's numerous examples being among the most famous.

Terzian [Ger.]. An organ stop of two ranks of open *flue pipes, normally pitched a nineteenth and a tenth above unison (1 1/3′ and 1 3/5′).

Terzina [It.]. Triplet.

Terzo suono [It.]. See Combination tone.

Tessitura [It.]. The particular range of a part (especially a vocal part) that is most consistently exploited, as opposed to the total range or compass of such a part. Thus, a soprano part may have a high or a low tessitura.

Testo [It.]. In an *oratorio, *Passion, or similar work, the narrator, whose part is often set in recitative.

Testudo [Lat., tortoise]. (1) In ancient Rome, the Greek **lyra.* (2) In the Middle Ages and Renaissance, the *lute. See also *Chelys.*

Tetrachord. Four pitches. In ancient Greek music, the tetrachord spanned the interval of a perfect fourth and was the smallest system commonly used. Larger systems were constructed by combining tetrachords, culminating in the Greater Perfect System, which comprised four tetrachords: *Hypaton, Meson, Diezeugmenon,* and *Hyperbolaeon* [see Greece I, 3 (i)]. Theorists of the 10th and 11th centuries adopted the double-octave Greater Perfect System in its diatonic form, dividing it into four tetrachords, but differently from the Greek system. These theorists analyzed the two-octave system into two pairs of conjunct tetrachords, A–d–g (*graves* and *finales*) and a–d′–g′ (*superiores* and *excellentes*), with an added note, a′, at the top. The basis for this revision was the tetrachord of the four modal *finales,* d–e–f–g. See also Genus, Diatonic, Chromatic, Enharmonic.

Octave species are often defined as consisting of one pentachord (five pitches) plus one conjunct tetrachord, e.g., c–g and g–c′, or, in the case of a plagal *mode, A–d and d–a. Both monophonic and polyphonic music of the Middle Ages and Renaissance has sometimes been analyzed in these terms. Similarly, the major scale is sometimes described as consisting of two disjunct tetrachords separated by a whole tone, e.g., c–f and g–c′. A.B.

Tetrardus [Gr.]. See Mode.

Text and music. The relationship between a text and the music that sets it may bear on the text's phonetic, syntactic, and semantic features. Repertories of vocal music vary widely, however, with respect to the nature of this relationship.

In Western art music, ideas formulated in the 16th century under the influence of Renaissance humanism have been influential into the 20th century. At the heart of these ideas is the view that text must guide music. This has meant that music should respect the *prosody of its text through proper *declamation, that musical phrase structure should not contradict or obscure the syntax of its text, and that music should in some way express or reinforce the meaning of its text. These same principles have been repeatedly invoked in the course of the centuries in the name of reform. The relationship of music to the semantic features of texts has been a special concern and is closely bound up with views of the expressive and representational powers of music generally [see Aesthetics]. This concern was expressed by Zarlino (see, e.g., *SR,* pp. 255–59) and other 16th-century writers, who often cited classical authorities, and it was reflected in the devices of *word painting found in some music of that period and the centuries following. But similar concerns were later expressed to justify very different kinds of music, including *monody and the **stile rappresentativo* around 1600 (see *SR,* pp. 363–92, 405–15), **opera seria* around 1700, the reform of *opera seria* by Gluck and others in the late 18th century (see *SR,* pp. 657–83), and Wagner's music drama in the mid-19th century (see *SR,* pp. 874–903). In the 17th and 18th centuries, these concerns were closely associated with views of the relationship between *rhetoric and music.

The study of the relationship between text and music has often been guided by the same preoccupation with semantic connections, and this has been reinforced by the considerable attention given in literary studies to the analysis of themes. Structuralist and poststructuralist literary analyses of the second half of the 20th century, however, have suggested alternative approaches to the study of this relationship by attaching greater importance to the sound and structure of texts as inseparable from what texts may be thought to mean and by reformulating the roles of author, text, and reader in the creation of meaning. These approaches are particularly relevant to the study of music from before the 16th century, because scholarship has often understood the absence of concerns proclaimed in the 16th century to mean the absence of any significant relationship between text and music at all.

A major concern in the editing and study of music with text composed before the late 16th century is text underlay—the alignment of individual syllables with individual notes. Both manuscript and printed sources often fail to make this alignment clear, and it is often not possible to resolve ambiguities of this type editorially, even in the light of principles enumerated by theorists such as Zarlino (see *SR,* pp. 259–61). That 16th-century principles of text underlay do not apply to earlier music, however, does not imply that the relationship of individual syllables to individual notes in this music is arbitrary.

Composers of the 20th century have greatly expanded the range of relationships between text and music. Berio, Nono, Stockhausen, and others have sometimes employed texts principally as sound sources to be fragmented and recombined. Dodge and others have employed electronic means to this end [see Electro-acoustic music V]. Babbitt and other composers of serial music have fully integrated the phonemic makeup of texts with the pitch structures of some works. In works by Cage and other composers of aleatory music, the relationship between music and text is the chance result of their simultaneous performance. And in the prose music or word scores of La Monte Young, Christian Wolff, Yoko Ono, and others, the text itself is the music.

See also Folk music, Lied, Opera, Song.

Bibl.: Edward E. Lowinsky, "A Treatise on Text Underlay by a German Disciple of Franciso de Salinas," *Besseler,* 1961, pp. 231–51. Don Harrán, "New Light on the Question of Text Underlay Prior to Zarlino," *AM* 45 (1973): 24–56. Leeman L. Perkins, "Towards a Rational Approach to Text Placement in the Secular Music of Dufay's Time," *Dufay,* 1974, pp. 102–14. *Music and Language,* Studies in the History of Music 1 (New York: Broude Bros, 1983). James Anderson Winn, *Unsuspected Eloquence: A History of the Relations between Poetry and Music* (New Haven: Yale U Pr, 1981). John Neubauer, *The Emancipation of Music from Language: Departure from Mimesis in Eighteenth-Century Aesthetics* (New Haven: Yale U Pr, 1986).

Textual criticism. A method for restoring corrupted texts as closely as possible to their original state. It seeks to identify and account for the new errors almost inevitably introduced every time a text is copied by hand, but successive printed editions can generate the same problem. Hellenistic, medieval, and humanistic scholars were often aware of defects in their texts and sometimes made very perspicacious emendations, but not until the 19th century was a systematic method developed for dealing with varying readings in different copies of the same text.

The method has two stages: *recensio* and *examinatio. Recensio* tries to establish the text of the archetype, i.e., the closest common ancestor of all the extant manuscripts. It takes the varying readings that are significant enough to enable one to affirm or deny dependence of one manuscript on another and uses this information to construct a *stemma,* a family tree that shows the interrelationship of the various manuscripts. In establishing the text of the archetype, one counts not the absolute number of manuscripts favoring a given reading but rather the number of independent family branches. If these numbers are evenly divided between readings, *recensio* leaves the archetype with alternatives to be dealt with in the second stage of textual criticism. The archetype may turn out to be the author's autograph, but for early works, it is usually a later copy likely to include some errors. *Examinatio* tries to detect these errors and proposes emendations, using knowledge of the common causes of error and a sense of the author's argument and style.

Recensio assumes that each copy was made from one exemplar without conscious effort to correct it. If, as may have happened more often than not, scribes "corrected" their exemplar or introduced readings from other exemplars *(contaminatio),* a *stemma* may be difficult or even impossible to construct. In this case, or if an author issued several revisions of his work or if a text suffered extensive interpolations, a critical edition may not be appropriate.

Bibl.: Paul Maas, *Textual Criticism,* trans. Barbara Flower (Oxford: Clarendon Pr, 1958). Martin L. West, *Textual Criticism and Editorial Technique Applicable to Greek and Latin Texts* (Stuttgart: Teubner, 1973). Vinton A. Dearing, *Principles and Practice of Textual Analysis* (Berkeley: U of Cal Pr, 1974). Jacqueline Hamesse, ed., *Les Problèmes posés par l'édition critique des textes anciens et médiévaux* (Louvain-la-Neuve: Institut d'Études Médiévales, 1992). See also bibliography of Editions, historical. J.J.J.

Texture. The general pattern of sound created by the disposition in time of the elements of a work or passage. For example, the texture of a work that is perceived as consisting of the combination of several melodic lines is said to be contrapuntal or polyphonic [see Counterpoint, Polyphony]. A work consisting primarily of a succession of chords sounded as such is said to have a chordal or homophonic texture [see Homophony]. Between these two extremes, there are numerous gradations for which there is no very precise terminology. *Freistimmig* [see *Freistimmigkeit*] and pseudocontrapuntal are sometimes used to describe a texture with some of the attributes of counterpoint but in which the number of voices is not fixed. A familiar texture in much non-Western music is *heterophony. Other aspects of texture include *spacing, *tone color [see also Orchestration], loudness, and *rhythm. The terms used with respect to these aspects of texture are most often rather imprecise adjectives such as sparse, thin, dense, and thick.

Although the control of texture and the creation of textural contrast within works have been significant parts of compositional technique in Western art music since the Middle Ages, a concern with texture comparable to that with other, more traditional concerns such as melody and harmony came to the fore only in the 20th century, partly in consequence of the breakdown of the tonal system [see Twentieth century, Western art music of the]. Among the most striking departures from traditional textures occurred first in the works of *twelve-tone (and later *serial) composers, especially Webern, in which elements such as melody and harmony in the usual sense are greatly deemphasized in favor of a kind of discontinuity that is sometimes termed *pointillism [see also *Klangfarbenmelodie*]. Composers of quite different persuasions such as Ives and Varèse, on the other hand, created equally striking textures of very disparate elements, sometimes treated in the fashion of a collage. In some *aleatory music, texture may be a more important factor than the specific pitches executed to create it. This is true of some fully composed music as well. The work of Crumb, Ligeti, and many others is characterized as much by its distinctive textures as by its other features.

Thailand. See Southeast Asia III.

Theater music. See Incidental music, Music theater.

Ṭhekā [Hin.]. In Hindustani music, a standard pattern of drum strokes or rhythmic syllables representing a particular **tāla*. C.C.

Thematic catalog (index). A list of compositions in a collection or of an individual composer, using the opening notes as a positive means of identification. Because the opening notes may not embrace the opening theme, the designation "incipit catalog" is more descriptive. A thematic catalog may cover a collection in a library (e.g., Duckles and Elmer, 1963, or the series of Bavarian music library catalogs), works of a publisher (Breitkopf, 1762–87), or a repertory (Dodd, 1980–, or Barlow and Morgenstern, 1975), but the great majority are catalogs of the works of individual composers. Here the works are arranged chronologically (Deutsch's Schubert catalog), by opus number (Kinsky and Halm's Beethoven), or by medium (Schmieder's Bach, Hoboken's Haydn), whichever best accommodates a composer's work. After putting the works in order, the compiler assigns each one a sequential number, which becomes the standard identification for that work, e.g., D. 795 for Schubert's *Die schöne Müllerin.*

The use of incipits to identify works was not uncommon in the 18th century. Mozart compiled a thematic catalog of his works beginning in 1784 (incomplete), giving title, instrumentation, date, and incipit. Three catalogs of Haydn's works were compiled during the composer's lifetime, one in Haydn's hand (Larsen, 1939). Thematic catalogs have grown from simple indexes to extensive bibliographic descriptions of individual works. They blossomed in the second half of the 19th century, at the same time as the publication of collected works. Köchel's catalog of Mozart's works, first published in 1862, is the first to give expanded information. Today, a thematic catalog may include title, an identifying letter and number (K. = Köchel), the opening measures of a work or of each movement (usually on two staves), the date and place of composition, location of the autograph manuscript, information about the first edition and other editions and arrangements published during the composer's lifetime, a reference to an edition of the composer's collected works, date and place of first performance, instrumentation, performance time, and a bibliography of references to the work. The amount of information varies according to what is available, and the result is a history of each work. The catalog may also include indexes of publishers, copyists, names, titles, watermarks, paper mills, text incipits, and thematic locators. Such a publication is often affordable only by institutions, though it is immensely valuable for research and reference. The use of data processing for thematic catalogs has enormous potential. Thematic catalogs, both of collections and composers, are listed in Brook, 1972. Adequate catalogs have been compiled for perhaps only a third of the well-known composers. Some well-known composers lack adequate catalogs. See also BWV, D., Hob., K., S.

Bibl.: Jens Peter Larsen, *Die Haydn-Überlieferung* (Copenhagen: E Munksgaard, 1939). Harold Barlow and Sam Morgenstern, *A Dictionary of Vocal Themes* (New York: Crown Pubs, 1950); rev. ed., *A Dictionary of Opera and Song Themes: Including Cantatas, Oratorios, Lieder, and Art Songs* (1976). Barry S. Brook, ed., *The Breitkopf Thematic Catalogue . . . 1762–1787* (New York: Dover, 1966). *Kataloge Bayerischer Musiksammlungen* (Munich: Henle, 1975–). Barry S. Brook, *Thematic Catalogues in Music* (Hillsdale, N.Y.: Pendragon, 1972; 2nd ed., with Richard Viano, 1997). Harold Barlow and Sam Morgenstern, *A Dictionary of Musical Themes,* rev. ed. (New York: Crown Pubs, 1975). Thematic Catalogue Series (Hillsdale, N.Y.: Pendragon, 1977–). Hermann Wettstein, *Bibliographie musikalischer thematischer Werkverzeichnisse* (n.p.: Laaber-Verlag, 1978). Barry S. Brook, "The Past, Present, and Future of the Music Library Thematic Catalogue," *King,* 1980, pp. 215–42. Hermann Wettstein, *Thematische Sammelverzeichnisse der Musik* (n.p.: Laaber-Verlag, 1982). H.E.S.

Thematic transformation. See Transformation of themes.

Thematische Arbeit [Ger.]. The working out or *development of a theme by transformation or by separation of its component *motives and elaboration of these.

Theme [Fr. *thème;* Ger. *Thema;* It., Sp. *tema*]. A musical idea, usually a melody, that forms the basis or starting point for a composition or a major section of one. Although the terms theme and *subject are sometimes used interchangeably, as in the context of *sonata form, theme often (though only since the 19th century) implies something slightly longer and more self-contained than subject. In the context of theme and *variations, it usually refers to an entirely self-contained melody or short piece. See also Thematic catalog, Transformation of themes.

Themenaufstellung [Ger.]. *Exposition.

Theorbo [Fr. *théorbe;* Ger. *Theorbe;* It., Sp. *tiorba*]. A large six-course bass lute to which have been added seven or usually eight diatonically tuned contrabass courses held in a second pegbox glued to an extension of the first. Developed late in 16th-century Italy to provide accompaniment for a new style of singing, *musica recitativa,* the theorbo was quickly adopted throughout Europe as an important *thoroughbass instrument. Its great length—six to seven feet—accommodates unstopped contrabasses twice as long as its fretted courses; and its top two courses are an octave low, giving a usual tuning of G_1 A_1 B_1 C D E F G A/A d/d g/g b/b e/e a/a. See also *Chitarrone.*

Bibl.: Robert Spencer, "Chitarrone, Theorbo, and Archlute," *EM* 4 (1976): 407–23. Douglas Alton Smith, "On the Origin of the Chitarrone," *JAMS* 32 (1979): 440–62. R.L.

Theory. A branch of music scholarship that studies the materials and structure of music. Music theory deals with the properties of single sounds—*pitch, *duration, *timbre, *dynamics, *tuning, and *temperament—as well as those of collections of sounds, *intervals, *consonance and dissonance, *scales, *modes, *melody, *counterpoint, *harmony, *rhythm, *themes, *meter, *form, texture, *analysis. Today, the term also refers specifically to the rudiments of music—*ear training, *solfège, general musicianship, and so on. Many ancient and non-Western cultures also have rich traditions of music theory; see Greece, East Asia, and South Asia.

I. *The scope of music theory.* The oldest branch of music scholarship, music theory has a history that dates back to ancient Mesopotamia, Egypt, China, and Greece. Although the discipline has changed considerably over the centuries, it has traditionally been concerned with understanding pieces of music in terms of their materials and structure rather than their historical background or social significance. Perhaps the most immediate task facing music theorists is that of providing ways to conceptualize music; at least since the Middle Ages they have focused much of their energy on finding ways to categorize and classify the pitch and rhythm of musical sounds. Drawing on translations and paraphrases of ancient Greek sources, such as Boethius's *De institutione musica* (ca. 500 C.E.), medieval theorists not only devised ways to classify and represent individual notes within the *gamut, but they also developed more complex concepts such as intervals, consonance and dissonance, and mode. This conceptualization of pitch space was reinforced by the investigations in tuning systems and by the proliferation of staff notation by Guido of Arezzo and others in the 11th century [see Notation]. With the rise of polyphony, music theorists turned their attention to rhythm. By the end of the 13th century, Franco of Cologne and others developed a way to conceptualize and notate rhythm by means of a proportional mensural system. Having said this, it was not until the 20th century that music theorists tried to conceptualize sound quality in any systematic way; they are now actively involved in developing comprehensive theories of musical timbre.

When finding ways to conceptualize music, music theorists have tried to ground their concepts in those of other disciplines. Prior to 1600, they frequently associated the properties of intervals with arithmetic ratios; this view reflected the fact that music was widely regarded as a branch of the *quadrivium. In fact, the term *musica theorica* was synonymous with that of *musica arithmetica* and was used in contrast with the terms *musica practica,* which dealt with topics such as *plainsong, *solmization, mode, *mensural notation, and counterpoint, and *musica poetica,* which considered music from a rhetorical and affective perspective. But starting in the 18th century, theorists drew on more recent developments in acoustics; for example, theorists such as Rameau, Schenker, Schoenberg, and Hindemith tried to derive the properties of major triads from the first five members of the overtone series. Instead of grounding their work in the physical properties of sounds, some theorists have turned to music psychology and cognitive science. The rationale is simple: since music is a product not of nature, but of the human mind, it seems reasonable to relate the concepts of music theory to the ways people actually listen to and think about music. This cognitive perspective can be found in the writings of theorists ranging from Aristoxenus to Meyer, Narmour, and Lerdahl and Jackendoff.

Besides categorizing the basic materials of music, music theorists have also been concerned with understanding how these materials are structured in broad repertories, such as modal polyphony or functional tonality. In particular, they have tried to find general patterns among each type of music. They have often expressed the patterns in conditional form: if X occurs in context Y, then Z happens. Perhaps the most famous examples are the so-called laws of strict counterpoint formulated in the 15th and 16th centuries by Prosdocimus, Tinctoris, Gaffurius, Zarlino, and others, and codified in the early 18th century by Fux. With the shift to triadic tonality, theorists tried to formulate analogous laws to explain the behavior of tonal harmony; these laws generalize not only about what sorts of harmonies typically occur in tonal music but also about how these harmonies are arranged to create functional progressions. Some of the most important contributions in this area were made by Rameau, Kirnberger, Marpurg, Vogler, Weber, Fetis, Riemann, Schoenberg, and Schenker. More recently, Schoenberg, Forte, Babbitt, Perle, Lewin, and others have developed theories to explain the behavior of free atonal and serial music of the 20th century. These models often call for powerful mathematical techniques, such as *set theory and group theory.

But not all music theorists have been involved with explaining the materials of music or with finding covering laws to explain the behavior of large repertories; on the contrary, many have focused their attention on analyzing the structure of specific pieces. This trend can be traced at least back to the 16th and early 17th centuries in works such as Nicholas Listenius's *Musica poetica* (1537), Burmeister's *Musica poetica* (1606), and Berhard's *Tractatus compositionis augmentatus* (ca. 1657). The field of music analysis subsequently blossomed in the late 18th and early 19th centuries in the writings of Riepel, Koch, Kollmann, Momigny, Reicha, and Marx. These theorists provided the field with powerful techniques for analyzing the small- and large-scale structure of individual pieces. Analytically driven music theory continues to thrive to this day, thanks to the contributions of writers such as Schenker, Tovey, Cone, Schachter, Lewin, and others.

II. *The functions of music theory.* Just as music theory encompasses a broad range of subjects, so it also caters to a wide array of audiences. Some treatises are clearly intended for other music theorists. They are often highly speculative in nature and take the form of technical books or specialized papers for academic institutions, such as universities or national societies. For the most part, these writings draw on observations taken from existing musical practice, though the connections to this practice may be difficult to determine; Aristoxenus's *Harmonics* and Rameau's *Traite de l'harmonie* are works of this type. Meanwhile, some treatises are concerned less with explaining the structure of past practices and more with devising new methods for creating music in the future. Such texts are often written by composers for composers; Schoenberg's *Harmonielehre* (1911), Busoni's *Entwurf einer neuen Aesthetik der Tonkunst* (1907), and Xenakis's *Musiques formelles* (1963). Still other texts are aimed at teaching performers how to learn and respond to specific types of music. Perhaps the most obvious examples are the many diminution treatises from the 15th, 16th, 17th, and 18th centuries. These treatises show how to ornament pieces by adding melodic diminutions. Along the same lines are the many figured bass treatises of the 17th and 18th centuries; the list of such treatises includes works by Agazzari, Penna, Heinichen, Mattheson, and C. P. E. Bach. We can even find important theoretical insights in editions of music; for example, Schenker's editions of Beethoven's late piano sonatas contain some of his first graphic analyses, and Tovey provided analytical commentaries to editions of Bach's *Well Tempered Clavier* and Beethoven's piano sonatas. Similarly, many music theory texts are directed toward beginners or nonmusicians. For example, Tovey contributed celebrated articles for the *Encyclopaedia Britannica* (1944). Other important dictionaries include Tinctoris's *Terminorum musicae diffinitorium* (1495) and Heinrich Koch's *Musikalisches Lexicon* (1802) [see Dictionaries and Encyclopedias]. Alongside these general texts, many theorists have produced tutors for basic musical instruction. Some of the most famous pedagogical texts include Guido's *Micrologus* (ca. 1025–26 or 1028–32), which teaches singing through the use of solmizing syllables; Fux's *Gradus ad Parnassum* (1725), which teaches species counterpoint and imitation, among other things; and Schoenberg's *Structural Functions of Harmony,* which was written for music students at the University of California, Los Angeles (1948).

III. *The methods of music theory.* Given its extraordinary scope and diverse functions, the discipline of music theory also embraces a wide range of different methods. Broadly speaking, these methods seem to pull in two quite different directions: some treatises aim toward mathematics and the sciences, and others tend toward aesthetics and criticism. For those committed to a scientific image of music theory, the goal is to explain what is known about pieces of a particular type and to predict the behavior of unanalyzed pieces of the same type. Successful theories should therefore explain all and only all music of that particular type and should be capable of being tested intersubjectively by other theorists. Rival theories are evaluated according to various epistemic values, such as their accuracy, explanatory scope, fruitfulness, consistency, simplicity, and coherence. Following scientific models, music theories are built and tested in the following manner. Theorists usually begin by observing a particular phenomenon in a well-defined test sample. These observations are described and categorized by means of concepts. Next, theorists guess some laws that explain their observations. They then predict the unobserved consequences of those laws. Finally, they see if their predictions are confirmed by further observation. If they are, then the theory is confirmed, but if they aren't, then the theory/laws must be modified or replaced entirely. But simple as it may seem, the task of building and testing theories is often fraught with difficulties. Not only is it hard to establish the precise nature of specific covering laws, but it is also unlikely that covering laws are necessary and sufficient for all successful explanations. Even if theorists can devise plausible covering laws, the task of confirming them is equally problematic. Problems arise because it is hard to propose theory-neutral tests for theoretical claims, because it is hard to definitively confirm or falsify a given theory, and because a given set of data can always give rise to a variety of theoretical explanations. Likewise, when comparing rival theories, it is not always easy to measure accuracy, explanatory scope, fruitfulness, consistency, simplicity, coherence, and so on.

Although the scientific image of music theory has been extremely influential, many music theorists have preferred to endorse methods drawn from aesthetics and criticism. Instead of focusing their attention on exploring the general nature of musical systems or the behavior of specific repertories of music, some theorists see as their goal uncovering the unique properties of particular works. Using models drawn from literary theory and art criticism, they are more concerned with understanding the meaning and significance of musical compositions than with explicating a work's structure in some putatively objective manner. They often insist that the success of an analysis can be measured not in terms of its truth or its predictive power, but in terms of its capacity to heighten the listener's aesthetic response. They claim that music can be analyzed only within some cultural, intertextual, or subjective context and insist that music theory should not embrace the empirical methods of the sciences. Although advocates of criticism are right to discuss the limitations of scientific methods, their criticisms often exaggerate the problems and underestimate the extent to which their own views are shaped by conventional theoretical ideas. Ideally the one image should inform and be informed by the other.

Bibl.: *Bibliographies.* James B. Coover, "Music Theory in Translation: A Bibliography," *JMT* 3 (1959): 70–96; supp., *JMT* 13 (1969): 230–48. Joseph Smits van Waesberghe, Pieter Fischer, and Christian Maas, eds., *The Theory of Music from the Carolingian Era up to 1400, RISM,* B/III/1–2 (Munich-Duisberg: Henle, 1961–68). François Lesure, ed., *Écrits imprimés concernant la musique, RISM,* B/VI/1–2 (Munich-Duisberg: Henle, 1971). David Russell Williams, *A Bibliography of the History of Music Theory,* 2nd ed. (Fairport, N.Y.: Rochester Music Pubs, 1971).

Periodicals. Die Reihe, 8 vols. (Austrian ed., 1955–62; trans. Eng., 1958–68). *Journal of Music Theory* (1957–). *Perspectives of New Music* (1962–). *The Music Forum* (1967–). *Zeitschrift für Musiktheorie* (1970–78). *In Theory Only* (1975–). *Music Theory Spectrum* (1979–). *Music Analysis* (1982–). *Musiktheorie* (1986–).

General. Hugo Riemann, *Geschichte der Musiktheorie im IX.–XIX. Jahrhundert* (Leipzig, 1898; 2nd ed., Berlin: M Hesse, 1921, R: Hildesheim: Olms, 1961); trans. Eng., bks. 1–2 by Raymond H. Haggh (Lincoln: U of Nebr Pr, 1962) and bk. 3 by William Mickelsen (Lincoln: U of Nebr Pr, 1977). Oliver Strunk, *Source Readings in Music History* (New York: Norton, 1950). Gustave Reese, *Fourscore Classics of Music Literature* (New York: Liberal Arts Pr, 1957). David Kraehenbuehl, Norman Phelps, Howard Murphy, Gordon Binkerd, and Robert Melcher, "The Professional Music Theorist—His Habits and Training: A Forum," *JMT* 4 (1960): 62–84. Francisco José León Tello, *Estudios de historia de la teoría musical* (Madrid: CSIC, 1962). Michael Kassler, "A Sketch of the Use of Formalized Languages for the Assertion of Music," *PNM* 1/2 (1963): 83–94. Milton Babbitt, "The Structure and Function of Music Theory," *CMS* 5 (1965): 49–60. David Lewin, "Behind the Beyond," *PNM* 7/2 (1969): 59–69. Benjamin Boretz, "Meta-Variations: Studies in the Foundations of Musical Thought," *PNM* 8/1 (1969): 1–74; 8/2 (1970): 49–111; 9/1 (1970): 23–42; 9/2 and 10/1 (1971): 232–70; 11/1 (1972): 146–223; 11/2 (1973): 156–203. Thomas Clifton, "Some Comparisons between Intuitive and Scientific Descriptions of Music," *JMT* 19 (1975): 66–110. Richmond Browne, Vernon L. Kliewer, Peter Westergaard, Carl E. Schachter, Carlton Gamer, and Allen Forte, "Music Theory: The Art, the Profession, and the Future," *CMS* 17 (1977): 135–62. John Rahn, "Aspects of Musical Explanation," *PNM* 17/2 (1979): 204–24. Harold S. Powers, "Language Models and Musical Analysis," *Ethno* 24 (1980): 1–60. Richmond Browne, ed., *Music Theory: Special Topics* (New York: Acad Pr, 1981).

II. *Representative theorists 350–1200.*

Augustine (354–430). *De musica* (On Music), 387–91. *PL* 32:1081–1194; Giuseppe Vecchi, ed., *Praecepta artis musicae; collecta ex libris sex Aurelii Augustini "De Musica,"* Reale accademia delle scienze dell'Istituto di Bologna, Classe di scienze morali, Memorie, ser. 5, vol. 1 (Bologna, 1950), pp. 93–153; R. Catesby Taliaferro, trans., *On Music,* in *Writings of Saint Augustine,* pt. 2, *The Fathers of the Church: A New Translation,* vol. 4 (New York: Fathers of the Church, 1947). Defines music as the "art of measuring well." Books 1–5 consider musical rhythm and quantitative poetic meter and may have been impetus behind modal rhythm.

Boethius (ca. 480–ca. 524). *De institutione musica* (The Principles of Music). *PL* 63:1167–1300; Gottfried Friedlein, ed., *A. M. T. S. Boetii. De institutione arithmetica libri duo. De institutione musica libri quinque* (Leipzig, 1867; R: Frankfurt: Minerva, 1966); Calvin M. Bower, trans., "Boethius, *The Principles of Music*" (Ph.D. diss., George Peabody College, 1967); *SR,* pp. 79–86; *RFsC,* pp. 12–13. See Calvin Bower, "The Modes of Boethius," *JM* 3 (1984): 252–63. Principal text for the transmission of Greek theory to the Middle Ages. Bks. 1–4 probably translated from Nicomachus (with material from Euclid [?], *Sectio canonis* in bk. 4) and bk. 5 from Ptolemy. Covers harmonics, arithmetic proportions, tones and semitones, comma, notation, tuning, and modes. Divides music into *musica mundana, musica humana,* and *musica instrumentalis* (bk. 1).

Isidore of Seville (ca. 559–636). *Etymologiarum sive originum libri xx,* bk. 3, chaps. 15–23, bk. 6, chap. 19. *PL* 82:163–69, 251–60; *GS* 1:20–25; Wallace M. Lindsay, ed. (Oxford: Clarendon Pr, 1911); *SR,* pp. 93–100 (chaps. 15–23 complete); *CCT* 12 (1980): 11–20. Book 3 treats music as a branch of mathematics (with arithmetic, geometry, astronomy) and outlines three parts of music—harmonics, rhythmics, metrics (chap. 18), then divides sounds into harmonic (vocal), organic (wind instruments), and rhythmic (string and percussion instruments) (chaps. 19–22). Book 6 discusses singing in the Office.

Aurelian of Réôme (fl. 840–50). *Musica disciplina* (The Discipline of Music). *GS* 1:28–63; Lawrence Gushee, ed., *CSM* 21 (1975); Joseph Ponte, trans., *CCT* 3 (1968). Chapters 1–7 discuss general topics (drawn from Boethius, Cassiodorus, and Isidore), chaps. 8–18 examine the eight modes, chap. 19 explains recitation formulas, and chap. 20 lists classes of plainsong.

Hucbald (ca. 840–930). *De harmonica institutione* (The Principles of Harmony). *GS* 1:104–25; Yves Chartier, ed., trans. Fr., "La *Musica* d'Hucbald de Saint-Amand" (Ph.D. diss., Paris IV, 1973); Warren Babb, trans., *YTS* 3 (1978): 3–46. Synthesizes Greater Perfect System and tetrachords with eight modes and

Byzantine **noeane* syllables. Considers intervals, consonances and dissonances, tones and semitones three times—without musical notation, with neumatic notation and tetrachords, and with the Greater Perfect System plus Greek letter names.

Anonymous (ca. 900). **Musica enchiriadis* (Music Handbook). *GS* 1:152–73; *CS* 2:74–78; Hans Schmid, ed. (Munich: Verlag der Bayerischen Akademie der Wissenschaften, 1981); Ernst Waeltner, ed., trans. Ger., chaps. 13–18, *Die Lehre von Organum bis zur Mitte des 11. Jahrhunderts* (Tutzing: Schneider, 1975), pp. 2–19; Léonie Rosenstiel, trans., *CCT* 7 (1976); *RFsC,* pp. 13–15. Also related texts: *Scolica enchiriadis, GS* 1:173–212; *SR,* pp. 126–38. *Commemoratio brevis, GS* 1:213–29; Terence Bailey, ed. (Ottawa: U of Ottawa Pr, 1979). *Alia musica, GS* 1:125–52; Jacques Chailley, ed. (Paris: Centre de documentation universitaire, 1965); Edmund B. Heard, ed. and trans. (Ph.D. diss., Univ. of Wis., 1966). Examines intervals, hexachords, modes, parallel and free organum. Gives gamut built only from disjunct tetrachords in Daseian notation.

Anonymous (ca. 1000). *Dialogus de musica* (Dialogue Concerning Music). *GS* 1:252–64; P. Bohn, trans. Ger., *MfMg* 12 (1880): 23–34, 39–48; *SR,* pp. 103–16; Michel Huglo, "L'auteur du 'Dialogue sur la Musique' attribué à Odon," *RdM* 55 (1969): 119–71. Starts with division of monochord (chaps. 1–2) and consonances (chaps. 4–5), then gives lengthy account of eight modes as defined by final (chaps. 6–18). Uses 16-note gamut (G–a′). Formerly attributed to Odo of Cluny.

Guido of Arezzo (ca. 991–after 1033). *Micrologus* (Little Discourse), 1025–26 or 1028–32. *GS* 2:2–24; Joseph Smits van Waesberghe, ed., *CSM* 4 (1955); Warren Babb, trans., *YTS* 3 (1978): 49–83; *RFsC,* pp. 15–16. Also *Alia regulae, GS* 2:34–42; *Regulae rhythmicae, GS* 2:25–34; *Epistola de ignoto cantu, GS* 2:43–50; *SR,* pp. 121–25. Guido expands the gamut of the *Dialogus* to 21 steps (chap. 2), considers the monochord (chaps. 7–13), modes by ambitus and final (chap. 14), melodic design (chaps. 15–17), and free organum (especially the *occursus*) (chaps. 18–20). The *Epistola* gives six solmization syllables—*ut, re, mi, fa, sol, la*—while *Alia regulae* and *Regulae rhythmicae* introduce staff notation. Neither the Guidonian hand nor the system of natural, hard, and soft hexachords appears in Guido's extant works.

Johannes Afflighemensis (fl. ca. 1100). *De musica* (On Music). *GS* 2:230–65; Joseph Smits van Waesberghe, ed., *CSM* 1 (1950); Warren Babb, trans., *YTS* 3 (1978): 87–190; *RFsC,* pp. 17–18. Modeled on the *Micrologus.* Covers general definitions (chaps. 1–4), the monochord (chaps. 5–7), intervals (chaps. 8–9), modes (chap. 10), chant (chaps. 14–19), solmization syllables (chap. 20), notation (chap. 21), and free organum (chap. 22). Prefers contrary to parallel motion in organum. Chapters 23–27 are reserved for a tonary.

Bibl.: *GS,* vols. 1–2. Edmond de Coussemaker, *Histoire de l'harmonie au moyen âge* (Paris, 1852; R: Hildesheim: Olms, 1966). Adrien de La Fage, *Essais de diphtérographie musicale* (Paris, 1864). *CS,* vols. 1–2. Hans Peter Gysin, *Studien zum Vokabular der Musiktheorie im Mittelalter* (Zurich: A Köhler, 1959). *RISM,* B/III. Gilbert Reaney, "The Question of Authorship in the Medieval Treatises on Music," *MD* 18 (1964): 7–17. Joseph Smits van Waesberghe, *Musikerziehung: Lehre und Theorie,* Musikgeschichte in Bildern 3, pt. 3 (Leipzig: Deutscher Verlag für Musik, 1969). Michel Huglo, *Les tonaires: Inventaire, analyse, comparaison* (Paris: Société française de musicologie, 1971). F. Alberto Gallo, "Philological Works on Musical Treatises of the Middle Ages," *AM* 44 (1972): 78–101. Lawrence Gushee, "Questions of Genre in Medieval Treatises on Music," *Schrade,* 1973, pp. 365–433. Ernst Waeltner, *Die Lehre von Organum bis zur Mitte des 11. Jahrhunderts* (Tutzing: Schneider, 1975). Mathias Bielitz, *Musik und Grammatik: Studien zur mittelalterichen Musiktheorie* (Munich: Katzbichler, 1977). Michael Markovits, *Das Tonsystem der abendländischen Musik im frühen Mittelalter* (Bern: P Haupt, 1977). Andrew Hughes, *Medieval Music,* rev. ed. (Toronto: U of Toronto Pr, 1980). Sarah Fuller, "Theoretical Foundations of Early Organum Theory," *AM* 53 (1981): 52–84. Charles M. Atkinson, "The *Parapteres: Nothi* or Not?" *MQ* 68 (1982): 32–59. Calvin M. Bower, review of *YTS* 3 in *JAMS* 35 (1982): 157–67. Hans Heinrich Eggebrecht, "Die Mehrstimmigkeitslehre von ihren Anfängen bis zum 12. Jahrhundert," in *Geschichte der Musiktheorie,* vol. 5, ed. Frieder Zaminer (Darmstadt: Wissenschaftliche Buchgesellschaft, 1984), pp. 9–87.

III. *Representative theorists 1200–1400.*

Anonymous (fl. early 13th century). *Discantu positio vulgaris* (General Types of Discant). *CS* 1:94–97; Simon M. Cserba, ed., *Hieronymous de Moravia* (Regensburg: F Pustet, 1935), pp. 189–94; Janet Knapp, trans., *JMT* 6 (1962): 200–207; *RFsC,* p. 19. Short treatise on discant rules and six rhythmic modes. Also defines sound, ligatures, consonance, etc., and lists various polyphonic forms—e.g., organum, motet, conductus, hocket. Transmitted by Jerome of Moravia.

Anonymous IV (fl. ca. 1270–80). *De mensuris et discantu* (Concerning Mensuration and Discant). *CS* 1:327–65; Frits Reckow, ed., with commentary, *AfMw,* Beihefte 4–5 (1967); Luther Dittmer, trans., *MTT* 1 (1957); *RFsC,* pp. 20–21; Jeremy Yudkin, ed. and trans. (Ph.D. diss., Stanford Univ., 1982). Lengthy synopsis of rhythmic modes, consonance and dissonance, discant and organum, plus references to specific two-, three-, and four-part compositions. Preserves essential historical data about Notre Dame School.

Johannes de Garlandia (fl. ca. 1240). *De mensurabili musica* (Concerning Measured Music). *CS* 1:175–82; Erich Reimer, ed., with commentary, *AfMw,* Beihefte 10–11 (1972); Stanley H. Birnbaum, trans., *CCT* 9 (1978); Rudolf Rasch, ed., *Johannes de Garlandia,* IMM Musicological Studies 20 (New York: Institute of Mediaeval Music, 1969); *RFsC,* p. 20. Describes three types of organum—discant, copula, organum—and focuses on the notation of rhythmic modes both in pure form and in combination in different voices.

Franco of Cologne (fl. ca. 1250). *Ars cantus mensurabilis* (The Art of Measured Singing). *GS* 3:1–16; *CS* 1:117–36; Friedrich Gennrich, ed., *Magistri Franconis Ars cantus mensurabilis* (Darmstadt: Gennrich, 1957); Gilbert Reaney and André Gilles, eds., *CSM* 18 (1974); *SR,* pp. 139–59 (complete). Detailed treatise on mensural notation, discant, consonance and dissonance, copula, organum, and hocket. Provided basis for many later theorists—e.g., Marchetto da Padova, Jehan des Murs, Jacques de Liège.

Jerome of Moravia (fl. 1272–1304). *Tractatus de musica* (Treatise on Music). *CS* 1:1–94; Simon M. Cserba, ed., *Hieronymous de Moravia* (Regensburg: F Pustet, 1935); *RFsC,* pp. 21–22. Encyclopedic survey of definitions, gamut, solmization, intervals, modes, plainsong, etc. Quotes identified extracts from other writers and transmits four complete discant treatises—*Discantus positio vulgaris,* Johannes de Garlandia, Franco of Cologne, and Petrus de Picardia (*CS* 1:94–154).

Johannes de Grocheo (fl. 1300). *Ars musice* (The Art of Music). Facs., ed., trans. Ger. with commentary, Ernst Rohloff, *Die Quellenhandschriften zum Musiktraktat des Johannes de Grocheio* (Leipzig: Deutscher Verlag für Musik, 1972); trans. Eng. Albert Seay, *CCT* 1 (1967); *RFsC,* pp. 23–24. Discusses music in use in Paris, dividing it into *musica vulgaris, musica mensurabilis,* and *musica ecclesiastica,* and describes specific forms of sacred and secular music at length.

Walter Odington (fl. 1298–1316). *Summa de speculatione musicae* (Highest Speculations about Music). *CS* 1:182–250; Frederick F. Hammond, ed., *CSM* 14 (1970); Jay A. Huff, trans., pt. 6, *MSD* 31 (1973); *RFsC,* pp. 22–23. Comprehensive treatise in six parts: pts. 1–4 deal with speculative topics, including arithmetic proportions, intervals, and divisions of the monochord; pt. 5 provides a tonary; pt. 6 surveys mensural notation and discusses *rondellus, conductus, copula,* motet, and hocket.

Marchetto da Padova (fl. 1305–26). *Lucidarium in arte musicae planae* (Explanation of the Art of Plainsong), 1309–18. *GS* 3:65–121; Jan W. Herlinger, *The* Lucidarium *of Marchetto of Padua: A Critical Edition, Translation, and Commentary* (Chicago: U of Chicago Pr, 1985); id., "Marchetto's Division of the Whole Tone," *JAMS* 34 (1981): 193–216. *Pomerium arte musicae mensuratae* (Orchard of the Art of Measured Music), 1318–26; *GS* 3:121–87; Giuseppe Vecchi, ed., *CSM* 6 (1961); *SR,* pp. 160–71; *RFsC,* pp. 24–25. *Lucidarium* outlines the arithmetic aspects of interval ratios, modes, and chant construction, while the *Pomerium* codifies Trecento Italian mensural notation. *Pomerium* precedes and is probably independent of the *Ars nova* tradition.

Jehan des Murs (ca. 1300–ca. 1350). *Notitia artis musice* (Knowledge of the Art of Music) or *Ars nove musice* (The Art of New Music), 1321. Bk. 1, "musica theorica," *GS* 3:312, 256–57, 313–15; bk. 2, "musica practica," *GS* 3:292–301 (the whole condensed as *Compendium musice practice,* ca. 1322, *GS* 3:301–6); Ulrich Michels, ed., *CSM* 17 (1972); *SR,* pp. 172–79. Also *Musica speculativa, GS* 3:249–83; *Libellus cantus mensurabilis, CS* 3:46–58; beginning of *Ars contrapuncti, CS* 3:59–68. See Ulrich Michels, *Die Musiktraktate des Johannes de Muris, AfMw,* Beihefte 8 (1970). "Musica theorica" treats tuning, proportions, etc., and "musica practica" conforms with Vitry's ideas on duple and triple notation.

Philippe de Vitry (1291–1361). *Ars nova* (The New Art), ca. 1322–23. *CS* 3:13–22; Gilbert Reaney, André Gilles, Jean Maillard, eds., trans. Fr., *CSM* 8 (1964); Leon Plantinga, trans., *JMT* 5 (1961): 204–23; *RFsC,* pp. 25–26. Following a description of intervals, gamut, hexachords, *musica ficta,* etc., Vitry explains duple and triple notation at four levels—maximodus, modus, tempus, prolatio—and introduces four time signatures.

Jacques de Liège (ca. 1260–after 1330). *Speculum musice* (The Mirror of Music), not before 1330. *CS* 2:193–433 (bks. 6, 7); Roger Bragard, ed., complete in 7 vols., *CSM* 3 (1955–73); *SR,* pp. 180–90; *RFsC,* pp. 27–28; F. Joseph Smith, *Iacobi Leodiensis Speculum musicae,* IMM Musicological Studies 13, 22, 42 (Brooklyn: Institute of Mediaeval Music, 1966–). Largest extant treatise on music from the Middle Ages (7 bks., 518 chaps.). Books 1–5 mostly devoted to intervals, consonances and dissonances, proportions, etc.; bks. 6–7 survey modes, 13th- to 14th-century polyphony, and mensural notation.

Bibl.: *GS,* vol. 3. Edmond de Coussemaker, *Traités inédits sur la musique du moyen âge* (Lille, 1865–69). *CS,* vol. 3. Richard Crocker, "Discant, Counterpoint, and Harmony," *JAMS* 15 (1962): 1–21. Id., "Hermann's Major Sixth," *JAMS* 25 (1972): 19–37. See also bibl. for II above.

IV. *Representative theorists 1400–1600.*

Prosdocimus de Beldemandis (ca. 1380–1428). *Tractatus musicae speculative* (Treatise on Speculative Music), 1425. D. Raffaello Baralli and Luigi Torri, eds., *RIM* 20 (1913): 707–62. Also *Tractatus practice cantus mensurabilis, CS* 3:200–228. *Contrapunctus, CS* 3:193–99; Jan Herlinger, ed. and trans. (Lincoln: U of Nebr Pr, 1984). *Tractatus practice cantus mensurabilis ad modum ytalicorum, CS* 3:228–48; Jay A. Huff, ed. and trans., *MSD* 29 (1972); *RFsC,* p. 30. Includes a polemic against Marchetto's *Lucidarium;* rejects Marchetto's division of the tone into five dieses and restores Pythagorean ratios. Stresses advantages of Italian trecento notation over French *ars nova.*

Ugolino of Orvieto (ca. 1380–1457). *Declaratio musice discipline* (Declaration of the Discipline of Music), 1430–35. Albert Seay, ed., 3 vols., *CSM* 7 (1959–62); id., "Ugolino of Orvieto, Theorist and Composer," *MD* 9 (1955): 111–66, 11 (1957): 126–

33; Andrew Hughes, trans., chap. 34, *MSD* 27 (1972), pp. 21–39; *RFsC,* p. 31. Treatise in two sections: bks. 1–3 consider practical problems of mode, intervals, chant, counterpoint, and mensural notation; bks. 4–5 are more speculative and deal with the arithmetic foundations of music.

Johannes Tinctoris (ca. 1435–1511?). *Liber de arte contrapuncti* (The Art of Counterpoint), 1477. *CS* 4:76–153; Albert Seay, ed. and trans., *MSD* 5 (1961); *SR,* pp. 197–99; *RFsC,* pp. 33–34. Also *Liber de natura et proprietate tonorum, CS* 4:16–41; *CCT* 2 (1967; 2nd ed., 1976). *Proportionale musices, CS* 4:153–77; *CCT* 10 (1979); *SR,* pp. 193–96. *Expositio manus, CS* 4:1–16; Albert Seay, trans., *JMT* 9 (1965): 194–232. See *CSM* 22 (1975). Taken together, Tinctoris's 12 treatises cover the spectrum of 15th-century music theory. *Liber de arte contrapuncti* has prologue and three books. Book 1 defines counterpoint and gives the 22 consonances of note-against-note style; bk. 2 describes 27 dissonances and false concords; and bk. 3 lists 8 general rules for counterpoint.

Bartolomeo Ramos de Pareia (ca. 1440–91 or thereafter). *Musica practica* (Practical Music), Bologna, 1482. Facs., *BMB* sez. 2, 3 (1969); Johannes Wolf, ed. (Leipzig: Breitkopf & Härtel, 1901); *SR,* pp. 200–204; *RFsC,* pp. 36–37. Text in three parts with prologue and epilogue. One of the most original of all music theorists, Ramos challenges the work of Boethius and Guido by proposing an eight-syllable *solmization based on the octave *(psal-li-tur per vo-ces is-tas),* an alternative gamut, and a revised tuning system. Also covers *musica ficta,* modes, mensural notation, and counterpoint.

Franchinus Gaffurius (1451–1522). *Practica musicae* (Practical Music), Milan, 1496. Facs. (Farnborough: Gregg, 1967), *BMB* sez. 2, 26 (1972), *MMML* ser. 2, 99 (1979); Clement A. Miller, trans., *MSD* 20 (1968); Irwin Young, trans. (Madison: U of Wis Pr, 1969); *RFsC,* pp. 37–38. Also *Theorica musicae* (Milan, 1492); facs. (Rome: Reale Accademia d'Italia, 1934); *BMB* sez. 2, 5 (1969). *De harmonia musicorum instrumentorum opus* (Milan, 1518); facs. *BMB* sez. 2, 7 (1972), *MMML* ser. 2, 97 (1979); Clement A. Miller, trans., *MSD* 33 (1977). Parts of *Practica musicae* date back to early 1480s. Book 1 covers the gamut, solmization, modes; bk. 2, mensural notation; bk. 3, counterpoint, including list of eight rules; bk. 4, proportions. Gaffurius also commissioned Latin translations of Greek texts.

Pietro Aaron (ca. 1480–ca. 1550). *Thoscanello de la musica* (Thoscanello of Music), Venice, 1523. Facs., *MMML* ser. 2, 69 (1969). Revised with supp. as *Toscanello in musica,* Venice, 1529–62; facs., *DM* ser. 1, 29 (1970); Peter Bergquist, trans. (1523–62 eds.), 3 vols., *CCT* 4 (1970); *RFsC,* pp. 40–41. Also *Trattato della natura et cognitione di tutti gli tuoni di canto figurato* (Venice, 1525); facs., *MMML* ser. 2, 129 (1979); *SR,* pp. 205–18. A general manual with lengthy discussion of mensural notation, intervals, genera, counterpoint, chords, etc. Gives modal ascriptions to polyphonic works of famous composers.

Heinrich Glarean (1488–1563). *Dodecachordon* (Twelve Strings), Basel, 1547. Facs., *MMML* ser. 2, 65 (1967) and (Hildesheim: Olms, 1969); Clement A. Miller, trans., *MSD* 6 (1965); *SR,* pp. 219–27; *RFsC,* pp. 44–45. Also *Isagoge in musicen* (Basel, 1516); ed. and trans., *JMT* 3 (1959): 97–139. In bk. 2 (39 chaps.), Glarean derives 12-mode system (mode 1 on D) from 14 possible authentic and plagal octave species, giving examples from plainchant. He dismisses two hypothetical modes on B. Book 3 considers mode in polyphony. Also discusses Greek theory, Guidonian solmization, intervals (bk. 1, 21 chaps.), contemporary practice, and notation (bk. 3, 26 chaps.).

Nicola Vicentino (1511–ca. 1576). *L'antica musica ridotta alla moderna prattica* (Ancient Music Reduced to Modern Practice), Rome, 1555. Facs., *DM* ser. 1, 17 (1959); *RFsC,* p. 47. See Henry W. Kaufmann, *The Life and Works of Nicola Vicentino (1511–c. 1576), MSD* 11 (1966). A central figure in the revival of Greek ideas and especially of the three genera (diatonic, chromatic, and enharmonic). Vicentino divides his treatise in two parts: bk. 1, "della theorica musica," gives Pythagorean harmonics derived from Boethius; bks. 2–5, "della practica musicale," treat solmization, modes, and counterpoint in all three genera. Book 5 introduces the *archicembalo,* Vicentino's keyboard instrument for playing chromatic and enharmonic genera.

Gioseffo Zarlino (1517–90). *Le istitutioni harmoniche* (The Principles of Harmony), Venice, 1558–89. Facs., *MMML* ser. 2, 1 (1965) and (Ridgewood, N.J.: Gregg, 1966); Guy A. Marco and Claude V. Palisca, trans., pt. 3, *YTS* 2 (1968; R: 1976); Vered Cohen, trans., pt. 4, *YTS* 7 (1983); *SR,* pp. 228–61; *RFsC,* pp. 48–49. Also *Dimostrationi harmoniche* (Venice, 1571); facs. (Ridgewood, N.J.: Gregg, 1966), *MMML* ser. 2, 2 (1965). *Sopplimenti musicali* (Venice, 1588); facs. (Ridgewood, N.J.: Gregg, 1966). *De tutte l'opere* (Venice, 1588–89). *Le istitutioni* is a seminal work in four parts: pt. 1 classifies music and shows its arithmetic basis; pt. 2 describes Greater Perfect System and intervals; pt. 3 is an extensive study of counterpoint, composition, and mensural notation; pt. 4 treats mode (after 1572 renumbers Glarean—mode 1 on C), and chap. 33 gives ten rules for text underlay in polyphony.

Vincenzo Galilei (late 1520s–1591). *Dialogo della musica antica et della moderna* (Dialogue on Old and New Music), Florence, 1581. Facs. (Rome: Reale Accademia d'Italia, 1934), *MMML* ser. 2, 20 (1967); Robert Herman, trans., "*Dialogo* . . . of Vincenzo Galilei" (Ph.D. diss., North Texas State Univ., 1973); *SR,* pp. 302–22; *RFsC,* pp. 51–52. Also *Fronimo* (Venice, 1568, and, with subtitle revised, 1584); facs., *BMB* sez. 2, 22 (1969). *Discorso intorno all'opere di Messer Gioseffo Zarlino* (Florence, 1589); facs. *BBM* (1933). Following a long discussion of tuning systems, Galilei compares Greek and modern theory, focusing on modes; argues against polyphony in favor of monody; and concludes with a history of instruments and notation. The dialogue is between Giovanni Bardi and Pietro Strozzi.

Thomas Morley (1557/58–1602). *A Plaine and Easie Introduction to Practicall Musicke,* London, 1597, 1608, 1771. Facs. (London: Oxford U Pr, 1937); R. Alec Harman, ed. (New York: Norton, 1952); *SR,* pp. 274–78. See Otto Erich Deutsch, "The Editions of Morley's *Introduction,*" *Library* ser. 4, vol. 23 (1942–43): 127–29. Written as a dialogue between teacher and student, Morley's treatise considers melodic construction and notation (pt. 1), discant (pt. 2), and the rules for composing polyphony in three, four, five, or more parts. Also describes numerous musical forms such as motet and madrigal.

Bibl.: *CS,* vols. 3–4. Dénes von Bartha, "Studien zur musikalischen Schrifttum des 15. Jahrhunderts," *AfMf* 1 (1936): 59–82, 176–99. Claude V. Palisca, "The Beginnings of Baroque Music: Its Roots in Sixteenth-Century Theory and Polemics" (Ph.D. diss., Harvard Univ., 1954). Åke Davidsson, *Bibliographie der musiktheoretischen Drucke des 16. Jahrhunderts* (Baden-Baden: Heitz, 1962). Edward Lowinsky, "Renaissance Writings on Music Theory," *Renaissance News* 18 (1965): 358–70. *RISM,* B/IV. Peter Bergquist, "Mode and Polyphony around 1500: Theory and Practice," *The Music Forum* 1 (1967): 99–161. Don M. Randel, "Emerging Triadic Tonality in the Fifteenth Century," *MQ* 57 (1971): 73–86. Joel Lester, "Root-Position and Inverted Triads in Theory around 1600," *JAMS* 27 (1974): 110–19. Bernhard Meier, *Die Tonarten der klassischen Vokalpolyphonie* (Utrecht: Oosthock, Scheltema & Holkema, 1974). Benito V. Rivera, "Harmonic Theory in Musical Treatises of the Late Fifteenth and Early Sixteenth Centuries," *Music Theory Spectrum* 1 (1979): 80–95. Karol Berger, *Theories of Chromatic and Enharmonic Music in Late Sixteenth Century Italy* (Ann Arbor: UMI Res Pr, 1980). Harold S. Powers, "Tonal Types and Modal Categories in Renaissance Polyphony," *JAMS* 34 (1981): 428–70.

V. *Representative theorists 1600–1800.*

Giovanni Maria Artusi (ca. 1540–1613). *L'arte del contraponto* (The Art of Counterpoint), Venice, 1598. Facs. (Hildesheim: Olms, 1969). Also *L'Artusi, overo Delle imperfettioni della moderna musica* (Venice, 1600). See Claude V. Palisca, "The Artusi-Monteverdi Controversy," *The Monteverdi Companion,* ed. Denis Arnold and Nigel Fortune (London: Faber, 1968), pp. 133–66. Arranged as a set of 76 annotated tables (chaps.) that cover many topics, including classification of music theory, intervals, consonances and dissonances, and contrapuntal technique. Expands theories of Zarlino. Artusi is also famous for his debate with Monteverdi over **prima* and *seconda prattica.*

Joachim Burmeister (1564–1629). *Musica poetica* (The Poetics of Music), Rostock, 1606. Facs., *DM* ser. 1, 10 (1965). Also *Hypomnematum musicae poeticae* (Rostock, 1599); *Musica autoschediastikē* (Rostock, 1601). See Martin Ruhnke, *Joachim Burmeister* (Kassel: Bärenreiter, 1955). Outlines a comprehensive system of musical rhetoric. Divides compositions into four types according to complexity: *genus humile* (stepwise, consonant motion), *genus grande* (larger intervals, consonant and dissonant), *genus mediocre* (between *humile* and *grande*), *genus mixtum* (all three genera mixed). Distinguishes between major and minor modes.

Johannes Lippius (1585–1612). *Synopsis musicae novae* (Synopsis of New Music), Strasbourg, 1612. Benito V. Rivera, trans., *CCT* 8 (1977). See Rivera, *German Music Theory in the Early 17th Century: The Treatises of Johannes Lippius* (Ann Arbor: UMI Res Pr, 1980). First part explains intervals, notation, consonance and dissonance, counterpoint, triads, modes from triads, etc. Second part lists biblical and Lutheran references to music. Uses principle of octave inversion to form intervals. Coined the term triad and distinguishes between inversions, then classifies modes as major or minor according to the quality of the final triad.

Michael Praetorius (ca. 1571–1621). *Syntagma musicum* (Treatise on Music), 3 vols., Wolfenbüttel, 1614–19. Facs., *DM* ser. 1, nos. 14, 15, 21 (1958–59); Harold Blumenfeld, trans., vol. 2, pts. 1–2 (New Haven: Yale University, The Chinese Printing Office, 1949); Hans Lampl, trans., vol. 3 (D.M.A. diss., Univ. of Southern California, 1957); *RFsC,* pp. 59–60. Volume 1, in Lat., outlines vocal and instrumental church music; vol. 2, in Ger., considers instruments (pt. 1), instrumental range and tone (pt. 2), ancient organs (pt. 3), modern organs (pt. 4), individual instruments (pt. 5, with 42 woodcuts of different instruments); vol. 3, also in Ger., treats musical form (pt. 1), notation and rhythm (pt. 2), and concludes with a dictionary of musical terms and figured bass.

Marin Mersenne (1588–1648). *Harmonie universelle,* Paris, 1636–37. Facs. (Paris: CNRS, 1963); Roger E. Chapman, trans., fifth treatise (The Hague: Nijhoff, 1957); Robert F. Williams, trans., fourth treatise (Ph.D. diss., Univ. of Rochester, 1972); *RFsC,* p. 61. See Albion Gruber, "Mersenne and Evolving Tonal Theory," *JMT* 14 (1970): 36–67. Extensive text in five treatises: the first concerns nature of sound (bk. 1) and movements (bks. 2–3); the second deals with mechanics; the third considers voice (bk. 1) and singing (bk. 2); the fourth explains consonances (bk. 1), dissonances (bk. 2), genres and modes (bk. 3), composition (bks. 4–5), and singing (bk. 6); the fifth is on instruments—introduction (bk. 1), lutes, etc. (bk. 2), keyboard (bk. 3), violins, etc. (bk. 4), wind (bk. 5), organs (bk. 6), and percussion (bk. 7).

Christoph Bernhard (1628–92). *Tractatus compositionis augmentatus* (An Augmented Treatise on Composition), MS., ca. 1657. Josef Maria Müller-Blattau, ed., *Die Kompositionslehre Heinrich Schützens in der Fassung seines Schülers Christoph Bernhard* (Leipzig: Breitkopf & Härtel, 1926; 2nd ed., Kassel: Bärenreiter, 1963); Walter Hilse, trans., "The Treatises of Christoph Bernhard," *The Music Forum* 3 (1973): 30–196; *RFsC,* p. 62. Distinguishes between old *(gravis)* and new *(luxurians)* styles of free counterpoint according to dissonance treatment and figures and then outlines three functions for music—church *(gravis),* chamber, and theater *(luxurians).* The treatise, in 70 chaps., also deals with various aspects of counterpoint, culminating in sections on fugue and multipart polyphony.

Christopher Simpson (ca. 1605–69). *A Compendium of Practical Musick,* London, 1667. Philip J. Lord, ed. (Oxford: Blackwell, 1970). Pedagogical tract in five parts: pt. 1, rudiments of song; pt. 2, principles of composition; pt. 3, use of discords; pt. 4, figuration in discant; pt. 5, canon. A revised and enlarged ed. of *The Principles of Practical Musick* (London, 1665).

Lorenzo Penna (1613–93). *Li primi albori musicali per li principianti della musica figurata* (First Light for Beginners in Figured Music), Bologna, 1672–96. Facs., *BMB* sez. 2, 38 (1969). Popular treatise in three vols. that treats rudiments of music, counterpoint, and continuo playing.

Johann Gottfried Walther (1684–1748). *Praecepta der musikalischen Composition* (Precepts of Musical Composition), MS, 1708. Peter Benary, ed. (Leipzig: Breitkopf & Härtel, 1955). Also *Musikalisches Lexicon* (Leipzig, 1732); facs., *DM* ser. 1, 3 (1953); *RFsC,* pp. 70–71. See Hermann Gehrmann, "Johann Gottfried Walther als Theoretiker," *VfMw* 7 (1891): 468–578. Compiled from various 17th-century treatises: pt. 1 discusses rudiments (notation, scales, etc.), giving a brief index of terms; pt. 2 ("Musicae poëticae") considers compositional technique (intervals, consonance and dissonance, counterpoint, figures, affections, etc.).

Jean-Philippe Rameau (1683–1764). *Traité de l'harmonie* (Treatise on Harmony), Paris, 1722. Facs., *MMML* ser. 2, 3 (1965); Erwin R. Jacobi, ed., *Complete Theoretical Writings* [hereafter *CTW*], vol. 1 (Rome: AIM, 1967); Philip Gossett, trans. (New York: Dover, 1971); *SR,* pp. 564–74; *RFsC,* pp. 66–67. Also *Nouveau Système* (Paris, 1726); facs., *MMML* ser. 2, 7 (1965); *CTW,* vol. 2 (1967); B. Glen Chandler, trans. (Ph.D. diss., Indiana Univ., 1974). *Dissertation sur les différents méthodes d'accompagnement* (Paris, 1732). *Génération harmonique* (Paris, 1737); facs., *MMML* ser. 2, 6 (1966); *CTW,* vol. 3 (1968); Deborah Hayes, trans. (Ph.D. diss., Stanford Univ., 1968). *Démonstration du principe de l'harmonie* (Paris, 1750); facs., *MMML* ser. 2, 4 (1965); *CTW,* vol. 3 (1968); Roger Lee Briscoe, trans. (Ph.D. diss., Indiana Univ., 1975). See Joan Ferris, "The Evolution of Rameau's Harmonic Theories," *JMT* 3 (1959): 231–56. Building on the acoustical theories of Descartes and Sauveur, Rameau codifies the principles of harmonic generation (triad source for all consonance, dominant seventh source for all dissonance), harmonic inversion (all inversions consonant), and fundamental bass (progressions governed by tonic, subdominant, and dominant roots). *Traité* is in four books: bk. 1 describes ratios and proportion in harmony; bk. 2 explores the nature and properties of chords; bk. 3 outlines principles of counterpoint; bk. 4 explains principles of accompaniment.

Johann Joseph Fux (1660–1741). *Gradus ad Parnassum* (Steps to Parnassus), Vienna, 1725 (Lat.); Leipzig, 1742 (Ger.); Carpi, 1761 (It.); Paris, 1773–75 (Fr.); London, 1791 (Eng., free paraphrase and condensation). Facs., *MMML* ser. 2, 24 (1966); Alfred Mann, trans. (New York: Norton, 1943; rev. ed., *The Study of Counterpoint,* London: Dent, 1965), and *The Study of Fugue* (New Brunswick: Rutgers U Pr, 1958), pp. 78–138; *SR,* pp. 535–63. Text in two parts: pt. 1, "pars speculativa," gives mathematical explanations of intervals, scales, etc.; pt. 2, "pars activa," contains studies of counterpoint and fugue. Concludes with a few short chaps. on church modes and current stylistic trends. Codifies five *species of counterpoint, and became the basic counterpoint text for major composers of the Classical period.

Johann David Heinichen (1683–1729). *Der General-Bass in der Composition* (Thoroughbass in Composition), Dresden, 1728. Facs. (Hildesheim: Olms, 1969); George J. Buelow, trans. (Ph.D. diss., New York Univ., 1961); *RFsC,* pp. 67–68. See Buelow, "Heinichen's Treatment of Dissonance," *JMT* 6 (1962): 216–75; id., *Thorough-Bass Accompaniment according to Johann David Heinichen* (Berkeley and Los Angeles: U of Cal Pr, 1966). Long two-part treatise on thoroughbass. Part 1 has two chaps. on chords and then four chaps. dealing with realization of figured basses. Part 2 considers topics such as the resolution of dissonances in theatrical style (chap. 1), realization of unfigured basses (chap. 2), accompaniment of recitatives (chap. 3), application of these rules to a complete cantata (chap. 4), and the circle of keys (chap. 5). The final chap. gives additional exercises. Classifies six-four chord as dissonant. Also *Neu erfundene und gründliche Anweisung . . . zu vollkommener Erlernung des General-Basses* (Hamburg, 1711).

Johann Mattheson (1681–1764). *Grosse General-Bass-Schule* (The Great Thoroughbass School), Hamburg, 1731. Ed. (Mainz: Schott, 1956); facs. (Hildesheim: Olms, 1968); *RFsC,* pp. 68–69. Also *Der vollkommene Capellmeister* (Hamburg, 1739); facs., *DM* ser. 1, 5 (1954; 3rd ed., 1980); Ernest C. Harriss, trans. (Ann Arbor: UMI Res Pr, 1981). See Hans Lenneberg, "Johann Mattheson on Affect and Rhetoric in Music," *JMT* 2 (1958): 47–84, 193–236. Comprehensive account of thoroughbass practice in three parts: pt. 1, general matters divided into 291 subsections; pt. 2, 24 easy examples; pt. 3, 24 examples of greater difficulty. *Der vollkommene Capellmeister* gives an important codification of rhetorical models.

Joseph Riepel (1709–82). *Anfangsgründe zur musicalischen Setzkunst* (Rudiments of Musical Composition), 5 vols., Regensburg and Vienna, Frankfurt and Leipzig, Augsburg, 1752–68. See Wilhelm Twittenhoff, *Die musiktheoretischen Schriften Joseph Riepels (1709–1782)* (Halle: Buchhandlung des Waisenhouses, 1935); Leonard Ratner, "*Ars Combinatoria:* Chance and Choice in Eighteenth-Century Music," *Geiringer,* 1970, pp. 343–63. Long and unsystematic five-part treatise written in dialogue form. Covers rhythmic/metrical classification, tonal classification, and counterpoint. Gives important description of phrase and period analysis. Assumed that the same principles governed both small- and large-scale works. Established the basis of chord hierarchy.

Friedrich Wilhelm Marpurg (1718–95). *Abhandlung von der Fuge* (Essay on Fugue), 2 vols., Berlin, 1753–54. Facs. (Hildesheim: Olms, 1970); Alfred Mann, trans., *The Study of Fugue* (New Brunswick, N.J.: Rutgers U Pr, 1958), pp. 142–212. Also *Handbuch bey dem Generalbasse und der Composition* (Berlin, 1755–60; facs., Hildesheim: Olms, 1974). *Anfangsgründe der theoretischen Musik* (Leipzig, 1757). See Joyce Mekeel, "The Harmonic Theories of Kirnberger and Marpurg," *JMT* 4 (1960): 169–93; Howard Serwer, "Marpurg versus Kirnberger: Theories of Fugal Composition," *JMT* 14 (1970): 209–36. Prolific writer who expands the ideas of Rameau while criticizing those of Kirnberger. Emphasizes practical rather than mathematical basis for theory. Develops triad classification and hierarchic scheme of keys. Author of seminal treatise on fugue.

Giuseppe Tartini (1692–1770). *Trattado di musica* (Treatise on Music), Padua, 1754. Facs., *MMML* ser. 2, 8 (1966); Alfred Rubeli, trans. Ger. (Düsseldorf: Gesellschaft zur Förderung der systematischen Musikwissenschaft, 1966); *RFsC,* pp. 73–74. See Alejandro Planchart, "A Study of the Theories of Giuseppe Tartini," *JMT* 4 (1960): 32–61; D. P. Walker, "The Musical Theories of Giuseppe Tartini," *Modern Musical Scholarship,* ed. Edward Olleson (New York: Oriel Pr, 1980), pp. 93–111. Tries to relate major, minor, and dissonant harmony to *a priori* geometric principles. Bulk of calculation and proof in chaps. 2–3. Other chaps. deal with harmony in general (chap. 1), diatonic scale (chap. 4), old and new modes (chap. 5), intervals and new music (chap. 6).

Johann Philipp Kirnberger (1721–83). *Die Kunst des Reinen Satzes* (The Art of Strict Musical Composition), 2 vols., Berlin and Königsberg, 1771–79; supp. by Johann A. P. Schulz, *Die wahren Grundsätze zum Gebrauch der Harmonie,* Berlin and Königsberg, 1773. Facs. (Hildesheim: Olms, 1968; supp., 1970); David Beach and Jurgen Thym, trans., *YTS* 4 (1982) and (supp.) *JMT* 23 (1979): 163–225. Also *Grundsätze des General-Basses* (Berlin and Königsberg, 1781); facs. (Hildesheim: Olms, 1974). See sources listed under Marpurg and Cecil Powell Grant, "The Real Relationship between Kirnberger's and Rameau's Concept of the Fundamental Bass," *JMT* 21 (1977): 324–38. Critical of Rameau's theories, Kirnberger develops his own system of fundamental bass in which dissonances are explained through part-writing. Distinguishes between essential and nonessential dissonances. First part of *Die Kunst* includes discussions of temperaments (chap. 1), intervals (chap. 2), dissonances (chap. 5), modulation (chaps. 7–8), counterpoint (chaps. 10–11). Second part considers harmonization of melodies (chap. 1), tuning and keys (chap. 2), melody and song (chap. 3), rhythm and meter (chap. 4).

Georg Joseph (Abbé) Vogler (1749–1814). *Tonwissenschaft und Tonsetzkunst* (The Science of Sound and the Art of Composition), Mannheim, 1776. Facs. (Hildesheim: Olms, 1970). Also *Betrachtungen der Mannheimer Tonschule* (monthly, 1778–81; facs., Hildesheim: Olms, 1974). *Handbuch zur Harmonielehre* (Prague, 1802). See Floyd K. Grave, "Abbé Vogler and the Study of Fugue," *Music Theory Spectrum* 1 (1979): 43–66; id., "Abbé Vogler's Theory of Reduction," *CM* 29 (1980): 41–69. Short treatise in two parts arranged as succession of numbered paragraphs. *Tonwissenschaft* (54 pars.) concerns the derivation of triad, scale, consonant and dissonant intervals, etc. *Tonsetzkunst* (100 pars.) explains use of these resources—e.g., preparation and resolution of dissonances, cadences, chord progressions, part writing, keys, and modulation. Also proposes system of harmonic reduction.

Heinrich Christoph Koch (1749–1816). *Versuch einer Anleitung zur Composition* (Introductory Essay on Composition), 3 vols., Leipzig, 1782–93. Facs. (Hildesheim: Olms, 1969); secs. 3 and 4 trans. Nancy K. Baker, *YTS* 6 (1983). See Nancy K. Baker, "Heinrich Koch and the Theory of Melody," *JMT* 20 (1976): 1–48. Extensive discussion of composition, from the foundations of harmony to the construction of symphony movements. Volume 1 starts with description of keys and chords and leads to treatment of counterpoint; vol. 2 examines nature of composition (three stages: "Anlage" or plan, "Ausführung" or completion of design, and "Ausarbeitung" or refining and polishing), aesthetics, and phrase and period structure (with analyses of specific works). Volume 3 studies large forms in various genres (recitative, aria, rondo, sonata, concerto, overture, symphony) and provides guides for writing exposition and development for the first movement of a symphony, sonata, etc.

Bibl.: Matthew Shirlaw, *The Theory of Harmony* (London: Novello, 1917). Frank T. Arnold, *The Art of Accompaniment from a Thorough-Bass* (London: Oxford U Pr, 1931). Leonard Ratner, "Harmonic Aspects of Classic Form," *JAMS* 2 (1949): 159–68. Id., "Eighteenth-Century Theories of Musical Period Structure," *MQ* 42 (1956): 439–54. Erwin R. Jacobi, *Die Entwicklung der Musiktheorie in England nach der Zeit von Jean-Philippe Rameau* (Strasbourg: Heitz, 1957–60). Alfred Mann, *The Study of Fugue* (New Brunswick, N.J.: Rutgers U Pr, 1958). Peter Benary, *Die deutsche Kompositionslehre des 18. Jahrhunderts* (Leipzig: Breitkopf & Härtel, 1961). Ernst Apfel, "Satztechnische Grundlagen der neuen Musik des 17. Jahrhunderts," *AM* 34 (1962): 67–78. William J. Mitchell, "Chord and Context in 18th-Century Theory," *JAMS* 16 (1963): 221–39. James W. Krehbiel, "Harmonic Principles of Jean-Philippe Rameau and His Contemporaries" (Ph.D. diss., Indiana Univ., 1964). Albert Cohen, "Survivals of Renaissance Thought in French Theory 1610–1670: A Bibliographical Study," *Reese,* 1966, pp. 82–95. Fred Ritzel, *Die Entwicklung der "Sonatenform" im musiktheoretischen Schrifttum des 18. und 19. Jahrhunderts,* 2nd ed. (Wiesbaden: Breitkopf & Härtel, 1969). Albert Cohen, "*La Supposition* and the Changing Concept of Dissonance in Baroque Theory," *JAMS* 24 (1971): 63–84. Walter Atcherson, Albert Cohen, George Buelow, Imogene Horsley, and Almonte Howell, "National Predilections in Seventeenth-Century Music Theory: A Symposium," *JMT* 16 (1972): 2–71. Walter Atcherson, "Key and Mode in Seventeenth-Century Music Theory Books," *JMT* 17 (1973): 204–32. Lyn Tolkoff, "French Modal Theory Before Rameau," *JMT* 17 (1973): 150–63. David W. Beach, "The Origins of Harmonic Analysis," *JMT* 18 (1974): 274–306. Gregory G. Butler, "Fugue and Rhetoric," *JMT* 21 (1977): 49–109. Joel Lester, "Major-Minor Concepts and Modal Theory in Germany, 1592–1680," *JAMS* 30 (1977): 208–53. Id., "The Recognition of Major and Minor Keys in German Theory: 1680–1730," *JMT* 22 (1978): 65–103. Jamie Croy Kassler, *The Science of Music in Britain, 1714–1830* (New York: Garland, 1979). Albert Cohen, *Music in the French Royal Academy of Sciences* (Princeton: Princeton U Pr, 1981). Benito V. Rivera, "The Seventeenth-Century Theory of Triadic Generation and Invertibility and Its Application in Contemporaneous Rules of Composition," *Music Theory Spectrum* 6 (1984): 63–78. Joel Lester, *Compositional Theory in the Eighteenth Century* (Cambridge, Mass.: Harvard U Pr, 1992).

VI. *Representative theorists 1800–1950.*

Gottfried Weber (1779–1839). *Versuch einer geordneten Theorie der Tonsetzkunst* (Attempt at a Systematically Arranged Theory of Musical Composition), Mainz, 1817–21. James F. Warner, trans. (Boston, 1846), later ed. with additions, John Bishop (London, 1851). Also *Generalbasslehre zum Selbstunterricht* (Mainz, 1833). Part 1 of this two-part treatise examines music in general (chap. 1), tone systems, notation, intervals (chap. 2), and rhythmics (chap. 3). Part 2 considers specific theoretical points in detail—voices (chap. 1), harmony (chap. 2), keys (chap. 3), modulation (chap. 4), harmonic progressions (chap. 5), large-scale modulation (chap. 6), etc. Popularized Roman numerals for harmonic analysis.

Antoine Reicha (1770–1836). *Traité de haute composition* (Treatise on Composition), 2 vols., Paris, 1824–26. Also *Cours de composition musicale* (Paris, 1816?–18); Arnold Merrick, trans., and John Bishop, ed. (London, 1854). *Traité de mélodie* (Paris, 1814). See Ernst Bücken, "Anton Reicha als Theoretiker," *ZfMw* 2 (1919–20): 156–69. Treatise devoted to counterpoint, harmony, canon, and fugue. Book 6 is a manual of form and includes 26-page analysis of sections, cadences, phrasing, and motives in Mozart's overture to *Le nozze de Figaro.* Borrows rhetorical terms exposition, bridge, and development for sections of musical works.

Adolf Bernhard Marx (1795?–1866). *Die Lehre von der musikalischen Komposition* (The Theory of Musical Composition), 4 vols., Leipzig, 1837–47. Herrman S. Saroni, ed. and trans., vols. 1–2 (New York, 1854). See Birgitte Moyer, "Concepts of Musical Form in the Nineteenth Century with Special Reference to A. B. Marx and Sonata Form" (Ph.D. diss., Stanford Univ., 1969). Volume 1 considers the elements of musical composition for one, two, and three parts (including harmony, chord inversions, and modulation); vol. 2 treats the accompaniment of melodies (particularly chorales); vols. 3 and 4 cover higher forms and include a famous discussion of three-part form in sonatas (exposition, development, recapitulation) and fugues.

François-Joseph Fétis (1784–1871). *Traité complet de la théorie et de la pratique de l'harmonie* (Complete Treatise on the Theory and Practice of Harmony), Paris and Brussels, 1844. Also *Esquisse de l'histoire de l'harmonie* (Paris, 1840); Mary Irene Arlin, trans. (Ph.D. diss., Indiana Univ., 1971). See Robert Nichols, "François-Joseph Fétis and the Theory of *Tonalité*" (Ph.D. diss., Univ. of Michigan, 1971); Bryan Simms, "Choron, Fétis and the Theory of Tonality," *JMT* 19 (1975): 112–38. Among the first theorists to adopt the term tonality, Fétis divided his *Traité* into four books: bk. 1, intervals, consonance and dissonance; bk. 2, chords, consonant (pt. 1), dissonant (pt. 2), modified (pt. 3); bk. 3, tonality and modulation in harmony, with description of chord hierarchy; bk. 4, critical examination of principal systems of generation and classification of chords.

Moritz Hauptmann (1792–1868). *Die Natur der Harmonik und Metrik* (The Nature of Harmony and Meter), Leipzig, 1853. William E. Heathcote, trans. (London, 1888). See Peter Rummenhöller, *Moritz Hauptmann als Theoretiker* (Wiesbaden: Breitkopf & Härtel, 1963). Attempts to give a Hegelian explanation of the laws of music based on universals. In particular, uses Hegel's thesis, antithesis, and synthesis, and advocates harmonic dualism (major and minor keys mirroring each other, both equally valid). The text is in three parts: pt. 1, harmony (sound, triads, keys, scales, dissonance, modulations, etc.); pt. 2, meter, accent, rhythm; pt. 3, metrical harmony, harmonic meter (especially metric position of dissonances and syncopation).

Simon Sechter (1788–1867). *Die Grundsätze der musikalischen Komposition* (The Principles of Musical Composition), 3 vols., Leipzig, 1853–54. Carl C. Müller, ed. and trans., vol. 1, *The Correct Order of Fundamental Harmonies* (New York, 1871). See William Earl Caplin, "Harmony and Meter in the Theories of Simon Sechter," *Music Theory Spectrum* 2 (1980): 74–89; Walter Zeleny, *Die historischen Grundlagen des Theoriesystems von Simon Sechter* (Tutzing: Schneider, 1979). Famous Viennese pedagogue who taught Schubert and Bruckner. Volume 1 outlines intervals, harmonic progressions, and modulation and introduces *Stufentheorie.* Volume 2 offers theory of pitch and rhythm.

Hugo Riemann (1849–1919). *Grosse Kompositionslehre* (Complete Theory of Composition), 3 vols.,

Berlin and Stuttgart, 1902–13; vol. 1, *Der homophone Satz;* vol. 2, *Der polyphone Satz;* vol. 3, *Der Orchestersatz und der dramatische Gesangstil.* Also *Musikalische Syntaxis* (Leipzig, 1877), *Musikalische Dynamik und Agogik* (Hamburg, 1884), *Präludien und Studien* (Frankfurt am Main and Leipzig, 1895–1901), *System der musikalischen Rhythmik und Metrik* (Leipzig, 1903). See William Mickelsen, *Hugo Riemann's Theory of Harmony: A Study* (Lincoln: U of Nebr Pr, 1977), pp. 3–103; Elmar Seidel, "Die Harmonielehre Hugo Riemanns," *Beiträge zur Musiktheorie des 19. Jahrhunderts,* ed. Martin Vogel (Regensburg: G Bosse, 1966), pp. 39–92; Gerhard Wuensch, "Hugo Riemann's Musical Theory," *Studies in Music from the University of Western Ontario* 2 (1977): 108–24. Writings fall into three periods: speculative (1872–77); practical (1877–1909); speculative/aesthetic (1909–19). Basing his work on theories of Hauptmann, Helmholz, and Oettingen, Riemann outlines three tonal functions (I, IV, V) and, assuming harmonic dualism, uses subharmonic series to derive minor chords. He developed an analytic theory of rhythm and form based on an underlying, normative eight-measure phrase. His *Geschichte der Musiktheorie* remains the standard history of music theory.

Heinrich Schenker (1868–1935). *Neue musikalischen Theorien und Phantasien* (New Musical Theories and Fantasies), 3 vols., Stuttgart and Vienna, 1906–35. Vol. 1, *Harmonielehre* (R: Vienna: Universal, 1978), Oswald Jonas., ed., and Elizabeth Borgese, trans. (Chicago: U of Chicago Pr, 1954); vol. 2, pts. 1–2, *Kontrapunkt;* vol. 3, *Der freie Satz* (Free Composition), Ernst Oster, ed. and trans. (New York: Longman, 1979); *RFsC,* pp. 83–84. Also *Der Tonwille,* 10 issues (Vienna, 1921–24). *Das Meisterwerk in der Musik,* 3 vols. (Vienna, 1925–30). *Fünf Urlinie-Tafeln* (Vienna, 1932); Felix Salzer, trans. (New York: Dover, 1971). See David Beach, "A Schenker Bibliography," *JMT* 13 (1969): 2–37, 23 (1979): 275–86. Proposes revolutionary method, vocabulary, and graphic notation for showing the structure of tonal works. Schenker conceived of tonal structure as a series of hierarchic levels or *Schichten,* which extend from the *Ursatz* (an unfolding of the tonic triad) to the surface or foreground of the piece. Emphasizes contrapuntal aspect of composition. See Schenker analysis.

Arnold Schoenberg (1874–1951). *Harmonielehre* (Theory of Harmony), Vienna, 1911, 3rd ed. enl., 1922. Robert D. W. Adams, trans. (New York: Philosophical Library, 1948); Roy Carter, trans. (Berkeley and Los Angeles: U of Cal Pr, 1978); *RFsC,* pp. 84–85. Also *Structural Functions of Harmony* (1948), Leonard Stein, ed. (New York: Norton, 1969). *Style and Idea* (1950), Leonard Stein, ed., and Leo Black, trans. (London: Faber, 1975). See Alexander Goehr, "The Theoretical Writings of Arnold Schoenberg," *PNM* 13, no. 2 (1975): 3–16. Influenced by theories of Sechter, Schoenberg develops a theory of monotonality in which all modulations within a movement are digressions within the main key. Argues that since all dissonances occur in overtone series, there is no qualitative distinction between them and consonances; proposes the "emancipation of dissonance" as theoretical justification of free atonal and twelve-tone music.

Milton Babbitt (1916–). "The Function of Set Structure in the Twelve-Tone System," unpub., 1946; "Twelve-Tone Invariants as Compositional Determinants," *MQ* 46 (1960): 246–59; "Set Structure as a Compositional Determinant," *JMT* 5 (1961): 72–94. See Robert Pazur, "A Babbitt Bibliography," *PNM* 14, no. 2, and 15, no. 1 (1976): 26–28. Using mathematical concepts such as group and set theory, Babbitt codifies twelve-tone system. Introduces terms such as pitch-class and interval-class into theoretical vocabulary. Focuses on invariant properties of ordered sets, especially combinatoriality.

Allen Forte (1926–). *The Structure of Atonal Music* (New Haven: Yale U Pr, 1973). Employing some of Babbitt's concepts, Forte develops unordered set theory for free atonal music, makes detailed catalog of set types (3–9 members), and proposes theory of set-complexes for comparing sets of different elements.

Bibl.: Matthew Shirlaw, *The Theory of Harmony* (London: Novello, 1917). Donald Packard, "Seven French Theorists of the Nineteenth Century" (Ph.D. diss., Univ. of Rochester, 1952). Mark Hoffman, "A Study of German Theoretical Treatises of the Nineteenth Century" (Ph.D. diss., Univ. of Rochester, 1953). Charles Finney, "British Theorists of the Nineteenth Century" (Ph.D. diss., Univ. of Rochester, 1957). Ann Basart, *Serial Music: A Classified Bibliography* (Berkeley and Los Angeles: U of Cal Pr, 1961). Martin Vogel, ed., *Beiträge zur Musiktheorie des 19. Jahrhunderts* (Regensburg: G Bosse, 1966). Peter Rummenhöller, *Musiktheoretisches Denken in 19. Jahrhundert* (Regensburg: G Bosse, 1967). Fred Ritzel, *Die Entwicklung der "Sonatenform" im musiktheoretischen Schrifttum des 18. und 19. Jahrhunderts,* 2nd ed. (Wiesbaden: Breitkopf & Härtel, 1969). Benjamin Boretz and Edward T. Cone, eds., *Perspectives on Contemporary Music Theory* (New York: Norton, 1972). Manfred Wagner, *Die Harmonielehren der ersten Hälfte des 19. Jahrhunderts* (Regensburg: G Bosse, 1974). Richmond Browne, ed., "Index of Music Theory in the United States: 1955–1970," *ITO* 3, nos. 7–11 (1977–78). John D. Vander Weg, "An Annotated Bibliography of Articles on Serialism: 1955–1980," *ITO* 5, no. 1 (1979). Ian Bent, "Analytical Thinking in the First Half of the Nineteenth Century," in Edward Olleson, ed., *Modern Musical Scholarship* (New York: Oriel Pr, 1980), pp. 151–66. David M. Thompson, *A History of Harmonic Theory in the United States* (Kent, Ohio: Kent State U Pr, 1980). Carl Dahlhaus, *Die Musiktheorie im 18. und 19. Jahrhundert. Erster Teil: Grundzüge einer Systematik,* Geschichte der Musiktheorie, vol. 10 (Darmstadt: Wissenschaftliche Buchgesellschaft, 1984). Robert W. Wason, *Viennese Harmonic Theory from Albrechtsberger to Schenker and Schoenberg* (Ann Arbor: UMI Res Pr, 1985). M.B.

Therapy. See Music therapy.

Theremin. An *electronic instrument invented in the 1920s by Leon Theremin. It generates a single tone whose pitch and loudness are controlled by the proximity of the player's hands to a straight antenna and a loop, respectively, that protrude from it. It was produced commercially in the U.S. and achieved some popularity on the concert stage as well as in film scores.

Theresienmesse [Ger., Theresa's Mass]. Popular name for Haydn's Mass in B♭ major Hob. XXII:12 (1799), often supposed (without conclusive evidence) to have been written for Empress Maria Theresa.

Thesis. See Arsis and thesis.

Third. See Interval; Scale degree; Consonance, dissonance; Tertian harmony; Picardy third; Just intonation.

Third-stream. Music that combines elements of jazz and of 20th-century art music. In the late 1950s, Gunther Schuller, who coined the term, and John Lewis led an effort to compose complex forms without destroying the vitality of jazz improvisation.

Thirteenth. See Interval, Chord.

Thirty-two foot. See Foot.

Thoroughbass, figured bass [Fr. *basse continue, chiffrée, figurée;* Ger. *Generalbass, bezifferter Bass;* It. *basso continuo;* Sp. *bajo cifrado*]. An independent bass line continuing throughout a piece (whence the Italian *continuo*), on the basis of which harmonies are extemporized on keyboard or other chord-playing instruments. Individual chords may be specified by figures written above, below, or beside the bass notes (whence, figured bass and related terms). The thoroughbass method was essential to ensemble music in Europe from about 1600 to about 1750, the period sometimes being called the thoroughbass period [Ger. *Generalbass-Zeitalter,* as Hugo Riemann termed it; see also Baroque]. The technique reflects a conception of music as embodying a polarity between a foundation, consisting of a bass line with its implied harmonies, and one or more supported melodic parts above. The creation of a complete texture from a figured-bass part is termed its realization. The realization of figured basses in four parts (sometimes at sight at the keyboard) is still often part of instruction in harmony.

I. *Figures.* In historical practice, the conventions governing the use of figures and the completeness of figures in specifying the intended harmonies has varied considerably. Generally, Arabic numbers are used to specify intervals formed above the bass note, much as they are used with Roman numerals in *harmonic analysis. Unless modified, the figures specify the intervals occurring naturally above the bass note in the prevailing key signature. If chromatic alteration is required, an accidental is placed immediately before the figure. The sharp may also be indicated by a small stroke drawn through some part of the figure. The pitches specified can be played in any register and doubled at will, though in general the principles of correct voice leading should be observed. Hence, figures for intervals larger than a ninth are not normally used. If no figure is given, the chord is assumed to be in root position. If only an accidental is given, it is assumed to modify the pitch a third above the bass and thus the third in a triad in *root position. The figure 0 indicates that only the bass note is to be played (termed *tasto solo*).

Example 1 shows the root position and first and second *inversions of a triad with the appropriate figures. The figures in brackets are most often omitted by way of abbreviation. Example 2 illustrates the figures for a seventh chord and its inversions in similar fashion. (In harmonic analysis, in the absence of a notated bass part, these harmonies would be notated with the same Arabic numbers placed following a Roman numeral designating the *scale degree of the root. In Ex. 1, in C major, this would be I; in Ex. 2, also in C major, V.) Figures may also be used to specify details of voice leading, including dissonances. For example, suspensions or appoggiaturas [see Counterpoint] in which a fourth above the bass resolves to a third are often indicated by the horizontal placement of the figures 4 and 3 connected by a dash; similar successions may be notated in similar fashion [Ex. 3]. A horizontal line following a figure and over changing bass notes indicates that the pitch or pitches originally specified are to be sustained. Diagonal slashes with changing bass notes indicate that the last figure given is to be applied to each succeeding bass note.

The realization of a thoroughbass part in performance normally requires at least two instruments: a harpsichord, organ, or other chord-playing instrument to realize the harmonies, and a melody instrument such as the cello or viola da gamba to play the bass line itself. Although the bass line is not to be modified, the player realizing the harmonies has considerable freedom and is not bound by the rhythm of the bass line or the simplest form of the harmonies specified. Within the bounds of historically informed taste, a realization may entail elaborate improvisation that interacts prominently with the written-out melody parts [see III below].

II. *Origins and history.* Traditions of accompanying vocal or instrumental music from some sort of harmonic shorthand can be traced back to the 16th century. Church organists frequently accompanied polyphonic part-music from various types of score, usually playing the lowest-sounding part together with the appropriate chords (organ bass, *basso per l'organo*). In polychoral works, such bass parts were distilled from different lines by playing the lowest-sounding pitch at any moment and were termed *basso seguente.* Examples are found in Alessandro Striggio's 40-part motet *Ecce beatam lucem* (1587) and in Adriano Banchieri's collection *Concerti ecclesiastici* (1595). Early organ basses give sporadic accidentals, but figures occur rarely before 1610. The term *basso continuo* became popular following the publication of Lodovico Viadana's *Cento concerti ecclesiastici . . . con il basso continuo* (1602). The continuo part of these pieces was not extracted from other bass parts like the *basso seguente,* but was composed independently to run throughout each piece. Viadana's musical style, however, preserves the character of imitative polyphony, and several early thoroughbass writers recommend imitation by the continuo.

Continuo accompaniments may well be older in secular than in sacred music, but no examples survive from before 1600. For the early monodists, continuo accompaniment allowed the accompanist sufficient flexibility and metric freedom to match the expressive qualities of the text, as befitted the new *stile recitativo* [see Recitative, Monody]. Monodic continuo parts were invariably written on a single staff and were more systematically figured than organ basses in sacred music. The first publications to employ figures were Cavalieri's **Rappresentatione di Anima, et di Corpo,* Peri's **Euridice* (1600), and Caccini's **Euridice* (1600) and **Nuove musiche* (1601/2), all of which sometimes employ figures higher than 9 to specify the precise register above the bass. At about the same time, theorists, notably Banchieri (1605), Agazzari (1607), and Bianciardi (1607), offered the first descriptions of thoroughbass method. The technique also spread rapidly outside of Italy and led to the addition of continuo parts to existing works (e.g., Palestrina Masses) as well as the composition of original figured-bass compositions.

In the 18th century, thoroughbass emerged as the major tool for teaching composition; more manuals were published on this subject than on any other musical topic. Many of these texts focused on standard situations that the pupil learned by rote (e.g., the *rule of the octave). Others cataloged chord types (Heinichen, 1711, 1728) and provided the basis for harmonic theory. From 1725, however, this approach was seriously challenged by the theories of Rameau. Writers such as C. P. E. Bach (1753) and Kirnberger (1774, 1781) responded vigorously, attacking the inconsistencies of Rameau's system. But by the late 18th century, thoroughbass practice was no longer the dominant compositional technique.

III. *Instrumentation and performance.* The practice of thoroughbass varied widely with time, place, and genre, and because of its improvisatory character, few precise details of actual practice survive. Church performance was invariably on the organ, perhaps doubled by other instruments in larger concerted pieces. Chamber organs were also widely used in secular contexts, where a wide variety of continuo instruments was possible. Among the most elaborate continuo groups were those assembled for lavish court spectacles and early operas around 1600. The continuo for the Medici wedding celebrations of 1589 included harps, psalteries, lutes, chitarroni, citterns, mandolas, guitars, harpsichords with bells, regals, and chamber organs. Monteverdi's *Orfeo* (1607) called for two harpsichords, three chitarroni, harp, regals, and two *organi di legno,* enabling the composer to mix timbres and colors to suit a given context. It is unlikely that large numbers of players were used at any one time.

According to Agazzari, there were two types of continuo instrument: foundation instruments, which sustain the harmonies (e.g., organ, gravicembalo, lute, theorbo), and ornamenting instruments, which highlight the harmonies with counterpoints (e.g., lute, theorbo, harp, lirone, cittern, chitarrone, spinet, violin, pandora). Praetorius (1619) adds a list of instruments suitable for reinforcing the bass line itself—e.g., trombone, bassoon, violone. Other theorists insist that small groups were more typical and specify organ or harpsichord with bass viol, violone, or cello support. In general, the larger the ensemble the larger the continuo group. In a *concerto grosso, separate continuo groups might be used for the concertino and the ripieno. In opera, particularly Italian opera, the choice of continuo instruments was also governed by the action, text, and symbols of the plot. From studies of harpsichord playing, it seems that French players used a florid, arpeggiated style, often doubling the bass line. Italian players, on the other hand, seem to have distinguished between two styles—one ornate, the other simple.

Bibl.: *Sources.* Adriano Banchieri, *L'organo suonarino* (Venice, 1605; 4th ed. enl., 1638). Agostino Agazzari, *Del sonare sopra il basso* (Siena, 1607; facs., *BBM,* 1933); partial trans. Eng., *SR,* pp. 424–31. Francesco Bianciardi, *Breve regola per imparar' sonare sopra il basso* (Siena, 1607); ed. in *Wolf,* 1929, pp. 48–56. Matthew Locke, *Melothesia or Certain General Rules for Playing upon a Continued-Bass* (London, 1673; facs., *MMML* ser. 2, 30, 1975). Andreas Werckmeister, *Die nothwendigsten Anmerckungen und Regeln, wie der Bassus continuus oder General-Bass wol könne tractiret werden* (Aschersleben, 1698; 2nd ed., 1715). Friedrich Erhardt Niedt, *Musicalische Handleitung, Erster Teil* (Hamburg, 1700; 2nd ed., 1710). Michel de Saint-Lambert, *Nouveau traité de l'accompagnement du clavecin* (Paris, 1707; facs., Geneva: Minkoff, n.d.). Gottfried Keller, *Rules or a Compleat Method for Attaining to Play a Thorough-Bass* (London, 1705; 6th ed., 1717). Francesco Gasparini, *L'armonico prattico al cimbalo* (Venice, 1708; 6th ed., 1802; facs., *MMML* ser. 2, 14, 1967); trans. Frank S. Stillings, ed. David L. Burrows (New Haven: Yale U Pr, 1963; R: New York: Da Capo, 1980). David Kellner, *Treulicher Unterricht im General-Bass* (Hamburg, 1732; 8th ed., 1796). Georg Philipp Telemann, *Singe-, Spiel-, und Generalbass-Übungen* (Hamburg, 1733–34; new eds., Berlin: Liepmannssohn, 1914; Kassel: Bärenreiter, 1935). Carl Philipp Emanuel Bach, *Versuch über die wahre Art das Clavier zu spielen* (Berlin, 1753–62; 2nd ed., 1787–97; facs., Leipzig: Breitkopf

& Härtel, 1957); trans. William J. Mitchell (New York: Norton, 1949; 2nd ed., 1951). Francesco Geminiani, *The Art of Accompaniment* (London, 1754). Daniel Gottlob Türk, *Kurze Anweisung zum Generalbass-spielen* (Leipzig, 1791; 5th ed., 1841; facs., Amsterdam: Frits Knuf, 1971). See also references to works on thoroughbass under Theory V: Michael Praetorius, Lorenzo Penna, Jean-Philippe Rameau, Johann David Heinichen, Johann Mattheson, Friedrich Wilhelm Marpurg, Johann Philipp Kirnberger.

Literature. Hugo Riemann, *Anleitung zum Generalbass-Spielen* (Berlin, 1889; 2nd ed., Leipzig: M Hesse, 1903). Max Schneider, *Die Anfänge des Basso continuo und seiner Bezifferung* (Leipzig: Breitkopf & Härtel, 1918; R: 1971). Frank Thomas Arnold, *The Art of Accompaniment from a Thorough-Bass as Practised in the XVIIth and XVIIIth Centuries* (London: Oxford U Pr, 1931; R: New York: Dover, 1965). Peter Williams, *Figured Bass Accompaniment* (Edinburgh: Edinburgh U Pr, 1970). Walter Kolneder, *Schule des Generalbassspiels, Teil I: Die Instrumentalmusik* (Wilhelmshaven: Heinrichshofen, 1983).

Three-Cornered Hat, The. See *Sombrero de tres picos, El.*

Three-line. The octave proceeding upward from c‴, or any pitch in that octave [see Pitch names].

Three-part form. Ternary form, sometimes also termed song form [see Binary and ternary form].

Threepenny Opera, The. See *Dreigroschenoper, Die;* Ballad opera.

Threni [Lat.]. *Lamentations.

Threnody [Gr. *thrēnos;* Lat. pl. **threni*]. *Lament.

Throat singing. See Tuva.

Through-composed [Ger. *Durchkomponiert*]. Without internal repetitions, especially with respect to the setting of a *strophic or other text that might imply the repetition of music for different words; thus, e.g., a song in which new music is composed for each stanza of text.

Ṭhumrī [Hin.]. A light, romantic genre of Hindustani vocal music. Traditionally associated with the courtesan entertainers of Lucknow and Benares, it is now often used to conclude recitals by singers of **khyāl* and by instrumentalists. C.C.

Thunder machine. A drum containing hard balls that strike the heads when it is rotated, thus producing a sound reminiscent of thunder. A sound like that of thunder is also sometimes produced by a long metallic sheet (termed a thunder sheet) that is shaken.

Thunder stick. *Bull-roarer.

Thus Spake Zarathustra. See *Also sprach Zarathustra.*

Tibet. See East Asia V.

Tibia [Lat.]. (1) A *reedpipe of ancient Rome, identical to the Greek *aulos. It was important in Roman official worship, especially as an accompaniment to sacrifices. It was also played in the theater, at weddings, at banquets, and at funerals. (2) An organ stop of wide-scale, open flue pipes, on high wind pressure, found in theater organs.

Tie, bind. A curved line connecting two successive notes of the same pitch, indicating that the second note is not to be attacked, but that its duration is to be added to that of the first. It is identical in appearance to a *slur. In modern notation, it is most often used to notate a duration that extends from one measure into another, thus permitting both measures to be notationally complete. It is also used to create durations that cannot be created in any other way (e.g., the value of seven eighth notes, created by tying a half note to a dotted quarter). The advent of the tie coincides with the advent of the *bar line.

Tiento [Sp., fr. *tentar,* to feel, try out; Port. *tento*]. A Spanish or Portuguese composition for harp, *vihuela,* or keyboard from the 16th through the early 18th century. In style and function, the *tiento* has at times resembled pieces called *ricercar, *fantasia, *toccata, or *prelude, and varies from short flourishes of chords mixed with running scales to long and complex contrapuntal works. Important *vihuela* collections include those of Luis de Milán (Valencia, 1536), Alonso Mudarra (Seville, 1546), and Miguel de Fuenllana (Seville, 1554). Mudarra's short *tientos* are preludes to longer pairs of fantasias and *intabulations. Juan Bermudo's treatise (Osuna, 1555) illustrates the contrapuntal foundations of 16th-century solo instrumental music with keyboard *tientos* notated in parts. The tablature edited by Luis Venegas de Henestrosa (Alcalá de Henares, 1557) for keyboard, harp, or *vihuela* includes as *tientos* Italian ensemble ricercars by Julio Segni (da Modena) and fantasias by Mudarra, as well as original *tientos* by the Spanish organists Pere Alberch Vila, Francisco Soto de Langa, and Francisco Fernández Palero.

A high point in the early *tiento* is reached with Antonio de Cabezón's works, edited in Venegas de Henestrosa's book and by his own son (Madrid, 1578). Some use themes from sacred and secular part-music and liturgical chant. With their sectional structure, thematic transformation, and polarities of restrained counterpoint and florid coloratura, many anticipate the more Baroque works of Bernardo Clavijo del Castillo (1549–1626), Sebastián Aguilera de Heredia (ca. 1565–1627), José Ximénez (1601–72), and the theorist Francisco Correa de Arauxo (Alcalá de Henares, 1626) in Spain; Manuel Rodrigues Coelho (Lisbon, 1620) in Portugal; and even Jan Pieterszoon Sweelinck (1562–1621) in the Low Countries. Their *tientos* use features common to the Italian toccata and fantasia, such as elaborate figuration, sudden changes of mood, episodic sections, and punctuating passages in brilliant improvisatory style. Some *tientos* are monothematic in the manner of the ricercar or are styled after the canzona. The 200 manuscript *tientos* of Juan Bautista José Cabanilles (1644–1712) are the final flowering of the genre. They are large works of great stylistic diversity, some with programmatic content. Correa de Arauxo, Cabanilles, Clavijo del Castillo, Aguilera de Heredia, and Pablo Bruna (1611–79) also wrote a special type called *tiento de falsas* [see *Toccata di durezze e ligature*]. In the **flamenco* repertory, the name *tiento* is still applied to the guitarist's preludial improvisations, suggesting a tradition related to the early *tientos* of Mudarra.

Sources of the *tiento* often preface them with explicit written descriptions and instructions. Modal designation, number of parts, harmonic peculiarities, and tempo are often specified; sections of paraphrase may be labeled *glosa,* and fugal sections, *discurs.* When borrowed material is present, it is usually cited in the title or in the course of the piece. Some *vihuela* tablatures have subsidiary signs that show voice leading or a part for voice, and 17th-century organ *tientos* may specify registration. Many *tientos* address technical problems such as loosening and equalizing the hands, applying ornamentation, playing in an elegant manner or with rubato, and testing the instrument's tuning. They are frequently graded according to difficulty, further reflecting a didactic intent.

Bibl.: Willi Apel, "Early Spanish Music for Lute and Keyboard Instruments," *MQ* 20 (1934): 289–301. John M. Ward, "The Editorial Methods of Venegas de Henestrosa," *MD* 5 (1951): 105–13. Id., "The *Vihuela de Mano* and Its Music" (Ph.D. diss., New York Univ., 1953). Willi Apel, "Spanish Organ Music of the Early 17th Century," *JAMS* 15 (1962): 174–81. Id., ed., *Spanish Organ Masters after Antonio de Cabezón, CEKM* 14 (1971). Murray C. Bradshaw, "Juan Cabanilles: The Toccatas and Tientos," *MQ* 59 (1973): 285–301. Louis Jambou, *Les origines du tiento* (Paris: CNRS, 1982).

A.J.N.

Tierce [Gr.]. (1) The interval of a third. For *tierce picarde (de Picardie),* see Picardy third; for *tierce coulé,* see *Coulé.* (2) An organ stop of open flue pipes pitched a tenth above unison (1 3/5′). The *Tierce* is an essential pitch for the **Cornet* in the classical French organ, along with pitches of 8′, 4′, 2 2/3′, and 2′.

Till Eulenspiegels lustige Streiche [Ger., Till Eulenspiegel's Merry Pranks]. A symphonic tone poem by Richard Strauss, op. 28 (1894–95), in the words of the title, "based on the old rogue's tale [the 16th-century folktale of Till Eulenspiegel], set for large orchestra, in rondo form."

Timbal [Sp.]. Kettledrum, *timpani. See also *Timbales.*

Timbale [Fr.]. Kettledrum, *timpani.

Timbales [Sp., pl.]. (1) Kettledrums. (2) A pair of single-headed, shallow cylindrical drums of Cuban origin that are tuned to different pitches, clamped side by side to a waist-high stand, and played with two sticks. One or two *cowbells are often attached to the same stand. *Timbales* are an essential element in Latin American urban popular music and have found some use in concert music as well. See ill. under Percussion instruments.

Timballo [It.]. Kettledrum, *timpani.

Timbre [Fr.]. (1) *Tone color. (2) A melody, especially an anonymous or popular one, that is used for different texts. The term, which came into use in the late 18th century, has been employed in connection with the *sequences of Adam of St. Victor and some other liturgical chant, the **noël* of the 16th century and after, **vaudeville,* and **opera comique.* Such a melody is usually identified by the first phrase of its presumed original words, and was specified in early publications with a phrase such as "to the tune of . . ." (3) In the Middle Ages, either a small bell or a small frame drum (sometimes the *tambourine).

Timbrel. (1) *Tambourine. (2) A *frame drum. (3) The English translation of the biblical Hebrew *toph.*

Time. See Meter, *Tempus,* Tempo, Duration.

Time signature. The sign placed at the beginning of a composition to indicate its meter. This most often takes the form of a fraction, but a few other signs with origins in the system of *mensural notation and *proportions are also employed [see Meter].

Timpan. (1) In the Middle Ages, kettledrum. (2) **Tiómpán.*

Timpani [Eng. sing. and pl.; It., sing. *timpano;* Fr. *timbale;* Ger. *Pauke;* Sp. *timbal, atabal.*]. Kettledrum; *t. coperti, t. sordi,* muted or muffled timpani. The most important orchestral percussion instrument, and the only member of the drum family of Western art music capable of producing notes of definite pitch. It consists of a large hemispherical shell of metal or fiberglass across which is stretched a head, ordinarily of calfskin or plastic, mounted (lapped) on a hoop that is held in place by a metal ring (counterhoop) through which pass threaded screws or rods that allow the skin's tension to be varied. Timpani come in standard sizes, from 50 to 82 cm (20 to 32 in.) in diameter, with a range from high b♭ to low D. Typical sets of four drums will include drums that are 58, 64, 71, and 76 cm (23, 25, 28, and 30 in.) or now often 58, 66, 74, and 81 cm (23, 26, 29, and 32 in.) in diameter, each with a range of approximately a perfect fifth, upward from d, B♭, F, and D or E♭, respectively. If only two drums are used, they are usually the middle two. They are played with two wooden sticks with heads of felt or other material, varying in shape, size, weight, and texture. See ill. under Percussion instruments.

Timpani arrived in western Europe during the 15th century as a cavalry instrument played on horseback by the Muslims, Ottoman Turks, and Mongols [see *Naqqārah*]. Following eastern custom, they were paired with the trumpet and were soon appropriated as

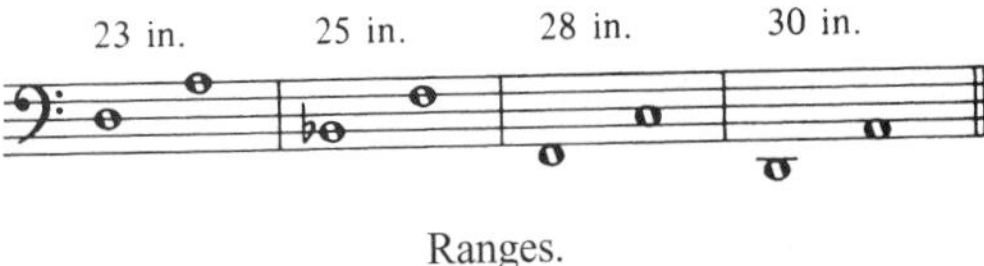

Ranges.

exclusive insignia of rank. For several centuries, construction remained constant, and tuning was by means of threaded bolts around the rim, tightened or loosened by a key. Around 1790, the screw with a T handle was introduced for faster changes of pitch. During the 19th century, numerous inventors developed devices for rapid tuning. The most successful of these so-called machine drums were tuned either by turning a single master screw or lever (Gerhard Cramer, 1812; Johann Einbigler, 1836), rotating the bowl itself (Johann Stumpff, 1821), or manipulating a foot pedal (Carl Pittrich, 1881). Other approaches included cable tuning with a turnbuckle (Cornelius Ward, 1837), concentric rings pressing up against the skin (Darche, ca. 1849), and gears rotated by the foot (August Knocke, ca. 1841).

By the 16th century, timpani were found in military regiments as well as at court. The music was at first improvised, but later both outdoor carrousel music and indoor polychoral liturgical music were written for one or two pairs of instruments; for example, Schmelzer's music for a *Pferdeballet* (1667) and the *Salzburger Festmesse* by Biber or Hofer (1682). Stage directions to early English masques, such as Jonson's *The Golden Age Restored* (1615), included references to timpani. Their introduction into the orchestra took place around 1670: by Lully in *Thésée* (1675) and by Purcell in his *Ode for St. Cecilia's Day* ("Hail, bright Cecilia," 1692) and *The Fairy Queen* (1692). The timpani solo in Bach's Cantata no. 214, *Tönet, ihr Pauken* (1733) was used again in his *Christmas Oratorio.* Occasional pieces for four to as many as eight timpani were written by Graupner (1749), Molter (ca. 1750), and J. C. C. Fischer (ca. 1780s). Haydn, a drummer himself, wrote significant parts for the instrument, particularly in his *Drum-Roll* Symphony no. 103 (1795) and *Missa in tempore belli* or *Paukenmesse* (1796). Beethoven liberated the timpani from merely rhythmic functions wedded to the trumpets and from the usual tonic and dominant tunings.

Vogler, in his opera *Samori* (1803), and his student Weber, in the revised overture to *Peter Schmoll* (1807), were the first symphonic composers to call for three drums. Four were required in Reicha's *Die Harmonie der Sphären* (before 1826) and Meyerbeer's *Robert le diable* (1831), where they were given a melodic solo. Berlioz asked for ten players on sixteen drums in his *Requiem* (1837). Wagner used two players, each with a pair of instruments, throughout the *Ring.* Russian composers made particularly full use of timpani, often writing very high pitches. Mahler's symphonies often require two players with four to six drums covering all possible pitches. Verdi's *Otello* (1887), Strauss's tone poems, and D'Indy's Symphony no. 2 (1903) require the use of machine drums in order to effect instantaneous pitch changes. Bartók wrote sequences of glissandos for timpani in his *Music for Strings, Percussion, and Celeste* (1936) and Sonata for two pianos and percussion (1937), and Britten wrote ascending and descending passages in his *Nocturne* (1958). Carter's *Concerto for Orchestra* (1969), among many other pieces (some for solo timpani), makes the ultimate demands on the performer.

See also Drum; *Schlagmanieren.*

Bibl.: Ernst G. B. Pfundt, *Die Pauken: Ein Anleitung dieses Instrument zu erlernen* (Leipzig: Breitkopf & Härtel, 1849). Georg Fechner, *Die Pauken und Trommeln in ihren neueren und vorzuglichen Konstruktionen* (Weimar: B F Voigt, 1862). Georges Kastner, *Méthode complète et raisonnée de timbales* (Paris: Schlesinger, 1845?). P. A. Browne, "The Orchestral Treatment of the Timpani," *ML* 4 (1923): 334–39. Percival R. Kirby, *The Kettle-Drums* (London: Oxford U Pr, H Milford, 1930). Henry George Farmer, *Handel's Kettledrums, and Other Papers on Military Music* (London: Hinrichsen, 1950). Caldwell Titcomb, "Baroque Court and Military Trumpets and Kettledrums: Technique and Music," *GSJ* 9 (1956): 56–81. Gerassimos Avgerinos, *Lexikon der Pauke* (Frankfurt am Main: Musikinstrument, 1964). Henry Walter Taylor, *The Art and Science of the Timpani* (London: J Baker, 1964). G. Facchini, *Il timpano: Sua evoluzione storica e tecnologica dalle origini ad oggi* (Padua, 1977). Herbert Tobischek, *Die Pauke: Ihre spiel- und bautechnische Entwicklung in der Neuzeit* (Tutzing: Schneider, 1977). Nancy Benvenga, *Timpani and the Timpanist's Art: Musical and Technical Development in the 19th and 20th Centuries* (Göteborg: Göteborg U, Dept of Musicology, 1979). Edmund A. Bowles, "Nineteenth-Century Innovations in the Use and Construction of the Timpani," *JAMIS* 5–6 (1979–80): 74–143. Edmund A. Bowles, "Mendelssohn, Schumann, and Ernst Pfundt: A Pivotal Relationship between Two Composers and a Timpanist," *JAMIS* 24 (1988): 5–26. Edmund A. Bowles, "The Double, Double, Double Beat of the Thundering Drum: The Timpani in Early Music," *EM* 19 (1991): 419–38. Harald Buchta, *Pauken und Paukenspiel im Europa des 17.–19. Jahrhunderts* (Heidelberg, 1996). Edmund A. Bowles, *The Timpani: A History in Pictures and Documents* (Hillsdale, N.Y.: Pendragon, 2002). Jeremy Montagu, *Timpani and Percussion* (London/New York, 2002).
E.A.B., rev. H.P.

Tin Pan Alley. The *popular music business in the U.S. from the late 19th century through the 1950s; its geographical center, beginning in the 1920s, around West 28th Street in New York City; also the style of U.S. popular song of the period. Often sentimental in character, such songs were at first usually in verse-and-chorus form. By the 1920s, the verse was often less prominent and the chorus in 32-bar AABA form [see Ballad (3)].

Tintinnabulum [Lat.]. A small *bell; in the Middle Ages, often synonymous with **cymbalum.*

Tin whistle. *Penny whistle.

Tiómpán, timpán [Gael.]. A stringed instrument of

medieval Ireland, most likely a *lyre like the Welsh *crwth.*

Tiorba [It.]. *Theorbo.

Tiple [Sp.]. (1) Treble, soprano. (2) A small guitar of Spain and Latin America with varying stringings and tunings. A typical Colombian *tiple* has four courses (three of which are triple) tuned like the highest four strings of the guitar. (3) A treble *shawm of the Catalan **cobla* ensemble. See also *Chirimía.*

Tirade [Fr.], **tirata** [It.]. A Baroque ornament consisting of a scale passage of more than three notes serving as a transition between two principal melody notes. It was written out or indicated by the sign illustrated in Ex. 1, but was often improvised to fill in large intervals. *Tirades* are typical of the French overture style

[Ex. 2, from Bach's Goldberg Variations]. A late example appears in the fourth measure of Beethoven's Piano Concerto no. 4 in G major op. 58. P.A.

Tirana [Sp.]. An Andalusian dance song, usually in 6/8 and common in **tonadillas* of the late 18th century. The "Tirana del trípili" by Blas de Laserna (1751–1816) became well known in Europe after being used by Mercadante in the overture to his opera *I due Figaro* (1835).

Tirando [It.]. Dragging.

Tirare [It., to draw]. (1) Down-bow. See Bowing (1). (2) To draw an organ stop; *tiratutti,* a *coupler.

Tirasse [Fr.]. In organs, a *coupler for connecting a keyboard to the pedalboard.

Tiratutti, tirapieno. In 18th-century Italian organs, a knob for drawing the full organ.

Tirer, tirez, tiré [Fr., to draw, draw, drawn]. (1) Down-bow. See Bowing (1). (2) To draw an organ stop.

Titan. Mahler's Symphony no. 1 in D major (1885–88, rev. 1893–96), originally termed a symphonic poem and including five movements with programmatic titles, which, like *Titan* itself, are after a novel by Jean Paul Richter. The Andante "Blumine" was subsequently removed, as were the titles of the other movements.

Ti-tzu (dizi) [Chin.]. A transverse bamboo flute of China with six finger holes. Near the mouth hole is another hole that is covered with a skin or paper *mirliton, giving a penetrating, reedy sound.

Toada [Port.]. See *Tonada.*

Toc [Cat.]. In Catalan folk music, a festival piece played on *grallas* (shawms) during the building of a human pyramid.

Toccata [fr. It. *toccare,* to touch; to hit or tap, e.g., a drum or bell; Ger. *Tokkata*]. (1) A virtuoso composition for keyboard or plucked string instrument featuring sections of brilliant passage work, with or without imitative or fugal interludes. Early descriptions include "a prelude that an organist, starting to play, . . . fantasizes out of his head before commencing a motet or fugue" (Michael Praetorius, 1619), and a piece "intended to make the impression of being played impromptu," in which "nothing is more inappropriate than order and constraint" (Johann Mattheson, 1757, 1759). The principal elements of toccata style are quasi-improvisatory disjunct harmonies, sweeping scales, broken-chord figuration, and roulades that often range over the entire instrument. In some periods, this style is also found in pieces called *prelude, **tiento,* *ricercar, and *fantasia.

Toccatas (labeled *tochata*) first appeared in a 1536 Milanese anthology as codas to sets of lute dances (*Nachleuffl,* "after-run," is used in some German sources). These short pieces by Francesco Canova da Milano and Pietro Paolo Borrono are virtually indistinguishable from the earlier homophonic preludial ricercars and **tastar de corde* published by Petrucci (Venice, 1507–11) and from *tientos* by Alonso Mudarra (Seville, 1546). Only toward the century's end did Venetian organists firmly establish the toccata and its style, which spread quickly throughout Europe, becoming one of the most influential keyboard genres. In works by Annibale Padovano (Venice, 1604), Sperindio Bertoldo (Venice, 1591), Giovanni Gabrieli (Venice, 1597, 1615), and especially Claudio Merulo (Rome, 1594–1604; *HAM,* no. 153; *GMB,* no. 149), sustained pedal tones and chords animated by passage work alternate with brief protofugal episodes, resulting in a homophonic/polyphonic duality that characterizes the toccata throughout most of its history.

Toccata style is prefigured in preludes, *intabulations, and **cantus firmus* settings in 15th- and early 16th-century French, German, Spanish, and Italian keyboard sources. A direct model for the early toccata was most likely the embellished **falsobordone* illustrated by Giovanni Battista Bovicelli (Venice, 1594) and contained in the **glosas en fabordón* of Alonso Mudarra (Seville, 1546), Miguel de Fuenllana (Seville, 1554), and Luis Venegas de Henestrosa and Antonio de Cabezón (Alcalá de Henares, 1557, and Madrid, 1578). Similarly underlying the tonal construction of many toccatas and **intonazione* may be a psalm tone, which, beyond providing material for imitation, is never sounded outright (Bradshaw, 1972). Thus, toccatas by Venetian organists and their south German successors—Hans Leo Hassler (Strasbourg, 1607, and Basel, 1617), Christian Erbach (ca. 1570–

1635), Johann Ulrich Steigleder (Stuttgart, 1624), and even Johann Jacob Froberger (1616–67)—belong more to the tradition of improvisation *supra librum* than to one of free rhapsodic composition. In the first volume of his *Transilvano* (Venice, 1593), Girolamo Diruta uses toccatas by his contemporaries to illustrate ornamentation in improvisation.

The toccatas of Giovanni Maria Trabaci (Naples, 1603) and other Neapolitans link the Renaissance toccata, with its evenly flowing figuration, and the more articulated sectional toccata of the early Baroque. The genre's first high point was reached with Frescobaldi (*HAM,* no. 193). His longer toccatas frequently juxtapose many segments that contrast greatly in figuration, meter, tempo, and texture, yet balance fugal elements with dramatic harmonic clashes and agitated virtuosity. Shorter ones are sometimes paired with a following ricercar, anticipating the prelude and fugue. Runs in contrary motion, or in parallel sixths or tenths, are reminiscent of the toccatas and *toutches* of Elizabethan virginalists and the 12 toccatas of Sweelinck. Frescobaldi's disciples Froberger (e.g., Mainz, 1693, composed ca. 1640–60), Michelangelo Rossi (Rome, 1657, composed ca. 1645), and Johann Kaspar Kerll (Munich, 1686) often emphasize the fugal sections by unifying them with thematic transformation and other contrapuntal devices drawn from the variation ricercar and canzona, a procedure favored by north German organists through the time of Bach. Later Catholic organists shunned fugal writing and elaborate pedal parts, preferring to enrich the figural elements. Although some toccatas are long chains of loosely connected segments of contrasting figuration, many are short pieces (sometimes called toccatinas) that may spin a single idea through a series of modulating sequences, as in examples by Franz Xaver Murschhauser (Augsburg, 1696, and Nuremberg, 1707), Johann Pachelbel (1653–1706), Gottlieb Muffat (Vienna, 1726), and Johann Ernst Eberlin (Augsburg, 1747). They are often joined to a following ricercar, fantasia, or canzona, or to miniature fugal versets. Many of these composers also cultivated the **toccata di durezze e ligature.*

In Protestant north Germany, the toccatas of composers such as Matthias Weckmann (ca. 1619–74), Dietrich Buxtehude (ca. 1637–1707), Johann Adam Reincken (1623–1722), Georg Böhm (1661–1733), and Bach often attain great heights of virtuosity and fugal maturity. Many include several lively and thematically related fugues and contrasting recitative-like adagios *(con discrezione),* framed and interspersed with brilliant passage work. Others approach the sonata by having distinct movements, as do Bach's for harpsichord (BWV 912–16) and his organ toccata in C major (BWV 564, sometimes incorrectly called Toccata, Adagio, and Fugue). Terminology being inexact, numerous preludes (or fantasias) and fugues are cast in the usual toccata structure of toccata–fugue–toccata, e.g., Franz Tunder (1614–67; *HAM,* no. 234) and early Bach (BWV 550–51, 561).

In the Italian harpsichord and lute/theorbo repertories, toccatas (sometimes called *tastatas,* e.g., pieces to test the instrument's tuning) are often preludes to sets of dances. Lutenists Joachim van den Hove (ca. 1620), Alessandro Piccinini (Bologna, 1623), Bernardo Gianoncelli (Venice, 1650), and Wenzel Ludwig von Radolt (Vienna, 1701) wrote many that are not far removed from those of 1536. Because of the influence of the Gaultier school of Parisian lutenists, the term prelude was favored by most non-Italian lutenists, e.g., German Bohemians such as Wolff Jacob Lauffensteiner (1676–1754), Johann Georg Weichenberger (1676–1740), and Silvius Leopold Weiss (1686–1750), for toccatalike introductions to dance suites. Driving figurations often approach perpetual motion in the harpsichord toccatas by Bernardo Pasquini (1637–1710), Giovanni Battista Ferrini (fl. ca. 1661), Alessandro Scarlatti (1660–1725), Azzolino Della Ciaia (Bologna, 1727), and a notable Viennese circle that includes Alessandro Poglietti (composed ca. 1670–80) and the elder Georg Reutter (1656–1738).

After 1750, the term toccata fell into disuse. The continuous drive of the late Italian harpsichord toccata was transferred to virtuoso etudes, some subtitled toccata, e.g., Czerny's *Toccata ou exercice pour le piano forte* op. 92 (1826?), a few of Johann Baptist Cramer's studies (1804–10), and Francesco Pollini's *32 esercizi in forma di toccata* (1820). This perpetual-motion idiom was incorporated into more substantial works such as Beethoven's finales to his Sonatas opp. 26 and 54, String Quartet op. 59, no. 3, and Seventh Symphony op. 92. Clementi's Toccata in B♭ op. 11 (1784), Czerny's *Toccatine brilliante et facile* op. 63 (1824), Schumann's Toccata in C op. 7 (composed 1829–32), Liszt's Toccata R. 60 (composed 1865–81), and Widor's familiar finale to the Fifth Organ Symphony op. 42 (composed ca. 1880) are among the relatively few pieces that carry the title.

The Bach revival inspired multimovement toccatas modeled on the C-major toccata, such as the organ sonatas of Mendelssohn (op. 65, 1844–45), the 20 cyclical ones by Joseph Rheinberger (1839–1901), the fantasias and fugues by Max Reger, Ferrucio Busoni's *Toccata: Preludio-Fuga-Ciaccona* (1921), and Joaquín Turina's *Ciclo pianistico: Tocata y fuga* op. 50 (1930).

The 20th century produced single-movement toccatas by Debussy (*Pour le piano,* 1901), Balakirev (1902), Prokofiev (op. 11, 1912), Ravel (*Le tombeau de Couperin,* 1917), Krenek (*Toccata und Chaconne,* 1923), Holst (*Toccata for Piano, Founded on a Northumbrian Tune,* 1924), Poulenc (*Trois pièces pour piano,* 1928), and Goffredo Petrassi (1933), among others.

(2) A processional fanfare for trumpets and timpani

for entrances and departures at coronations, royal weddings, state banquets, and the like. From as early as 1393 through the late 18th century, literary sources refer to the *toccata de trompettes, tocade de guerra,* etc. Seldom notated, most were improvised by members of courtly trumpeters' guilds, who closely guarded their art. The term probably refers to the striking of the drums [see Tuck, Toccato]. Many sustain a single harmony (like the beginnings of many organ toccatas), enlivened with fanfarelike tattoos and rapid figuration for the *clarino* instrument. The treatises (both translated by Tarr, 1976) of Cesare Bendinelli (MS, 1614) and Girolamo Fantini (Frankfurt, 1638) and the handbook by Danish court trumpeters Hendrich Lübeck and Magnus Thomsen (ca. 1598) contain numerous toccatas in one part, the other parts apparently being improvised. The best-known toccata opens Monteverdi's *La favola d'Orfeo* (Mantua, 1607); others include Francesco Rognoni Taeggio's *Toccata per sonar con il piffaro* (Milan, 1608) and an **Aufzug* by Daniel Speer (Ulm, 1697; compare *Tusch*). An ensemble toccata by Giovanni de Macque (ca. 1607), which also survives in a keyboard version, suggests a relationship with the fanfarelike openings of organ *tientos,* toccatas, and toccatinas by Juan Bautista José Cabanilles, Johann Caspar Ferdinand Fischer, and Murschhauser. In the same tradition are the first movements of *canzoni da farsi* by Marco Uccellini (Venice, 1649) and Vivaldi (op. 2 no. 2, Venice, 1709), opera sinfonias of the 17th and 18th centuries, and even the *Concerto à 7 clarini e tympani* attributed to Johann Ernst Altenberg (Halle, 1795). A modern contribution is Vaughan Williams's *Toccata marziale* (1924) for military band.

(3) In *clarino trumpet playing, the fifth partial of the harmonic series.

Bibl.: Erich Valentin, *Die Entwicklung der Tokkata im 17. und 18. Jahrhunderts (bis J. S. Bach)* (Münster: Helios-Verlag, 1930). Ernst Kaller and Erich Valentin, eds., *Tokkaten des XVII und XVIII Jahrhunderts,* Liber organi 5 (Mainz: B Schott, 1933). Otto Gombosi, "Zur Vorgeschichte der Tokkata," *AM* 6 (1934): 49–53. Susanne Clercx, "La toccata: Principe du style symphonique," in *La musique instrumentale de la Renaissance,* ed. Jean Jacquot (Paris: CNRS, 1955), pp. 313–25. Erich Valentin, *Die Tokkata, Mw* 17 (Cologne: A Volk, 1958; trans. Eng., 1958). Murray C. Bradshaw, *The Origin of the Toccata, MSD* 28 (1972). Id., "Tonal Design in the Venetian Intonation and Toccata," *MR* 25 (1974): 101–19. Eleanor Selfridge-Field, *Venetian Instrumental Music from Gabrieli to Vivaldi* (New York: Praeger, 1975). A.J.N.

Toccata di durezze e ligature [It., toccata with dissonances and suspensions]. A quiet, slow-moving organ piece of the late 16th and 17th centuries. Luzzasco Luzzaschi (1545?–1607), Giovanni de Macque (ca. 1550–1614), Frescobaldi, Bernardo Pasquini (1637–1710), Georg Muffat (1653–1704), and many others cultivated a special toccata to accompany solemn liturgical moments such as the Elevation. It features *alla breve* meter, imitation, chromaticism, many suspensions and unorthodox ("harsh") nonharmonic tones, and is generally played in the lower registers of the organ. A Spanish counterpart, **tiento de falsas,* uses simultaneous cross relations to intensify the chromaticism. A.J.N.

Toccatina [It.]. A short toccata, often introducing further movements. See Toccata.

Toccato [It., struck, hit]. In 17th- through 19th-century music for trumpets, the tenor (usually fourth) trumpet part, which may be doubled or replaced with timpani in the performance of processional fanfares and other pieces; also *touquet.* See Toccata (2). A.J.N.

Tocotín. A **villancico* of the 17th century partly or wholly in the Aztec Nahuatl language. The name derives from syllables *(to, ti, ko, ki)* used to describe the pitches sounded on accompanying drums. A.J.N.

Tod und das Mädchen, Der [Ger., Death and the Maiden]. Popular name for Schubert's String Quartet in D minor D. 810 (1824), the second movement of which consists of variations on his song of the same name, D. 531 (1817).

Tod und Verklärung [Ger., Death and Transfiguration]. A symphonic poem in four sections by Richard Strauss, op. 24 (1888–89). The work depicts a dying artist, his visions, his painful death, and the transfiguration of his soul. The poem by Alexander Ritter printed at the head of the score was written after the work was completed.

Tombak [Per.]. **Zarb.* See also *Darabukkah, Dumbalak.*

Tombeau [Fr., tombstone]. See Lament.

Tom-tom. (1) A cylindrical drum without snares, usually double headed, used in *drum sets, often in more than one size. Typical examples are 20 to 50 cm high, 15 to 25 cm in diameter, and are played with sticks, mallets, and brushes. (2) In colloquial usage, any African or American Indian drum, or the steady beating of such a drum.

Ton [Fr.]. (1) Pitch, tone. (2) Mode, key. (3) Whole tone. (4) Crook of a horn *(ton du cor, ton de rechange).* (5) Pitch pipe.

[Ger.] (6) Pitch, tone. (7) See Meistersinger.

Tonabstand [Ger.]. Interval.

Tonada [Sp.], **toada** [Port.]. Melody, tune. The term is widely applied in Spanish-speaking Latin America and in Brazil to a variety of lyrical song types. Especially important is the traditional *tonada* of Chile and Argentina, a song with guitar or accordion accompaniment, generally in major mode and slow to moderate compound duple meter, and frequently with a refrain in faster tempo.

Bibl.: Raquel Barros and Manuel Dannemann, "Introducción al estudio de la tonada," *Revista musical chilena* no. 89 (1964): 105–14. D.S.

Tonadilla escénica [Sp.]. A short, one-act popular or comic Spanish opera, usually performed between the acts of a larger work. The word *tonadilla* is the diminutive form of *tonada* (from *tono*), meaning song. The *tonada* became important in the latter half of the 17th century as a long, strophic set piece that generally dominated an entire scene within a musical court play.

In the 18th century, the *tonadilla* began as a self-contained solo song (literally, "little song") appended as the epilogue to a minor theatrical piece such as a **sainete*. When more than one character was introduced into the *tonadilla,* an independent short theatrical form, the so-called *tonadilla escénica,* was born. Antonio Guerrero (ca. 1700–1776) and Luis Misón (d. 1766) were the first composers to cultivate the new genre enthusiastically around 1750. It reached its apogee in the compositions of Pablo Esteve y Grimau (ca. 1730–94) and Blas de Laserna (ca. 1751–1816). The generally satirical or burlesque *tonadilla escénica* dealt with colorful situations and stock characters from everyday urban life. Its immense popularity lasted through the first decade of the 19th century.

Bibl.: José Subirá, *La tonadilla escénica,* 3 vols. (Madrid: Tipografía de Archivos, 1928–30). Id., *La tonadilla escénica: Sus obras y sus autores* (Barcelona: Labor, 1933). Id., *Historia de la música teatral en España* (Barcelona: Labor, 1945). Gilbert Chase, *The Music of Spain,* 2nd ed. (New York: Dover, 1959). José Subirá, *Temas musicales madrileños* (Madrid: Instituto de Estudios Madrileños, 1971). L.K.S.

Tonal. Exhibiting the principles of tonic-dominant *tonality, as distinct from *modality and other systems of organizing pitch. See also Atonality.

Tonal and real. Two types of answer that may be employed in a *fugue or related imitative work. An answer is termed tonal if it modifies the intervallic content of the subject in certain ways while preserving its essential contours. The most characteristic modification is the answering of a leap of a perfect fifth from tonic to dominant in the subject by a leap of a perfect fourth from dominant to tonic in the answer, as in the accompanying example from Bach's *The *Art of Fugue.* This causes the subject and its answer together

to outline prominently the octave over the tonic and thus to emphasize the original tonic, even though the answer may proceed in such a way as to modulate to the dominant. A tonal answer does not necessarily cause the piece to remain in the tonic. An answer is termed real if the subject is simply transposed to another scale degree, usually the dominant, thus preserving its intervallic content precisely.

Tonale [Lat.]. *Tonary.

Tonality. In Western music, the organized relationships of tones with reference to a definite center, the *tonic, and generally to a community of *pitch classes, called a *scale, of which the tonic is the principal tone; sometimes also synonymous with *key. The system of tonality (sometimes termed the tonal system) in use in Western music since about the end of the 17th century embraces twelve major and twelve minor keys, the scales that these keys define, and the subsystem of triads and harmonic functions delimited in turn by those scales [see Harmonic analysis], together with the possibility of interchange of keys (*modulation). A piece embodying this system is said to be tonal.

A particular tonality or key is defined and reinforced by the presence of a tonal center, embodied harmonically in the tonic triad; by harmonic progressions pointing to the tonic, especially by strong *cadences; by *pedal points and *ostinato basses; and by essential diatonicism as opposed to chromaticism. Avoidance of the tonic, whether by direct deemphasis of the tonic triad itself, by suppression of the dominant harmony that points to it, or by *deceptive cadence, may weaken the sense of key or divert it toward another center. So may emphasis on chromatic chords, on chords with many dissonant pitches, or on contrapuntal writing. Continuous modulation involving many chromatic chords may suspend the sense of key entirely for a time [see Harmony VII].

Tonality in a very limited sense can be said to exist in the tone-centering properties of monophonic Christian chant; the same kind of centricity can be traced, in varying degrees, in surviving instances of much older Semitic and Asian monophony, even in nondiatonic music. Some pentatonic music suggests two simultaneous tonalities, related as relative major and minor; this obvious aspect of some folk song has not been without influence on Western diatonic music. The organization of pitch relationships in 15th- and 16th-century music, characteristically in contrapuntal textures where harmonic functions are a by-product, generates a quasi-tonality that is only partially comparable to the tonality of the 18th century and since; nothing like the regular relationship of sharp and flat keys in equal temperament was practical (though a tendency toward exaggerated chromaticism, briefly appearing at the end of the period in the works of Carlo Gesualdo and others, does point to the freedoms of the 19th century). Functional harmony [see Harmony], with strong root progressions not subjugated to contrapuntal motions of the bass, appears increasingly in the 16th century, particularly in secular music, but the appearance of secondary dominant functions [see Dominant] around 1600 even more strongly suggests the beginning of a major-minor system.

The tonal family of keys could be proclaimed as fully established by the 18th century (e.g., in Bach's

The Well-Tempered Clavier, two books, each of 24 preludes and fugues in all the major and minor keys, 1722 and 1742); however, composers continued to prefer the simpler keys and the simpler relationships between them, notwithstanding some remarkable chromatic exceptions, until the 19th century. At the end of the 19th century, both tonal harmony and tonal form had been carried nearly to their limits. The crisis was resolved in the second decade of the 20th century by the "total chromaticism" of *atonality on the one hand and by a reevaluated diatonic tonality on the other; these two main tendencies have continued to prevail in art music, with a spectrum of different harmonic conditions in between. In much Western popular music and jazz, however, the system of tonality practiced through the 19th century has remained in effect with relatively minor, though characteristic, changes in harmonic vocabulary.

Bibl.: Joseph Yasser, *A Theory of Evolving Tonality* (New York: American Library of Musicology, 1932). Armand Machabey, *Genèse de la tonalité musicale classique des origines au XVe siècle* (Paris: Richard-Masse, 1955). Rudolph Richard Réti, *Tonality, Atonality, Pantonality: A Study of Some Trends in Twentieth-Century Music* (New York: Macmillan, 1958). Edward Lowinsky, *Tonality and Atonality in Sixteenth-Century Music* (Berkeley and Los Angeles: U of Cal Pr, 1961). Ernst Apfel, "Die klangliche Struktur der spätmittelalterlichen Musik als Grundlage der Dur-Moll-Tonalität," *Mf* 15 (1962): 212–27. Allen Forte, *Tonal Harmony in Concept and Practice* (New York: Holt, Rinehart and Winston, 1962; 2nd ed., 1974). Carl Dahlhaus, *Untersuchungen über die Entstehung der harmonischen Tonalität* (Kassel: Bärenreiter, 1968). Richard Norton, *Tonality in Western Culture: A Critical and Historical Perspective* (University Park: Pa St U Pr, 1984). Walter Piston, *Harmony,* 5th ed., rev. Mark DeVoto (New York: Norton, 1987). See also Counterpoint, Harmony, Theory. M.DEV.

Tonart [Ger.]. *Key (1).

Tonary [Lat. *tonarium, tonarius, tonale*]. A medieval *liturgical book (often incorporated into other books such as the antiphoner or gradual or into theoretical treatises) in which chants of the *Gregorian repertory are classified and listed by *mode. Such classification was of particular practical value (especially in the period before the development in the 11th century of musical notation that is precise with respect to pitch) in the case of antiphonal chants whose verses are sung to one of a set of *psalm tones chosen according to the mode of the accompanying antiphon. For these chants, tonaries make clear which psalm tone is to be chosen and, within any psalm tone, which termination or difference is to be sung. Other types of chant, however, including responsories and graduals, are included even in early tonaries. Tonaries differ significantly from one another in the number of differences available for any single psalm tone and in the assignment of certain chants to a particular tone and difference. Thus, they provide important evidence of the ways in which the chant repertory was accommodated to evolving notions of the system of eight modes that was adapted (along with some Greek terminology found in tonaries [see Noeane]) from Byzantine practice.

The earliest surviving example is the tonary of St. Riquier (ed. Huglo, 1971), which dates from the end of the 8th century. Other early examples are the tonaries of Metz (or Carolingian tonary, ca. 830, ed. Lipphardt, 1965), Aurelian of Réôme (ca. 850, ed. Gushee, 1975, trans. Joseph Ponte, 1968), Regino of Prüm (ca. 900, ed. *CS* 2), and Odo of Arezzo (late 10th century, ed. *CS* 2). Some examples are from as late as the 16th century.

Bibl.: Walther Lipphardt, ed., *Der karolingische Tonar von Metz* (Münster: Aschendorff, 1965). Michel Huglo, *Les tonaires: Inventaire, analyse, comparaison* (Paris: Société française de musicologie, 1971). Lawrence Gushee, ed., *Aureliani reomensis: Musica disciplina, CSM* 21 (1975).

Tondichtung [Ger.]. Tone poem [see Symphonic poem, Program music].

Tone [Fr. *ton;* Ger. *Ton;* It., Sp. *tono*]. (1) A sound of definite pitch; a pitch. (2) The interval of a whole tone. (3) The character of the sound achieved in performance on an instrument. (4) [Lat. *tonus*] A *psalm tone or other formula for the chanting of a liturgical text.

Tone cluster. A highly dissonant, closely spaced collection of pitches sounded simultaneously, at the piano usually by striking a large number of keys with the hand or arm. The term was coined by Henry Cowell, who made considerable use of tone clusters in his own music from at least 1912.

Bibl.: Henry Cowell, *New Musical Resources* (New York: Knopf, 1930; R: New York: Something Else Pr, 1969).

Tone color [Fr. *timbre,* also Eng.; Ger. *Klangfarbe;* It. *timbro, colore;* Sp. *timbre, color*]. The character of a sound, as distinct from its pitch; hence, the quality of sound that distinguishes one instrument from another. It is largely, though not exclusively, a function of the relative strengths of the harmonics (and sometimes nonharmonic frequencies) present in the sound. See Acoustics I.

Tone language. A language in which the relative pitch of syllables contributes to the lexical meaning of a word. Examples include most languages of sub-Saharan Africa (with two to four tones), Navajo (two), and Chinese (up to nine flat and sliding tones). In Jabo (Liberia), the word *ba* at different pitch levels means namesake, to be broad, and tail, and denotes command. Although not themselves music, linguistic tone systems affect composition and in Africa are the bases for instrumental signaling.

Bibl.: George Herzog, "Speech-melody and Primitive Music," *MQ* 20 (1934): 452–66. B.N.

Tone poem [Ger. *Tondichtung*]. *Symphonic poem.

Tone row. See Twelve-tone music.

Tonfarbe [Ger.]. *Tone color.

Tongeschlecht [Ger.]. Mode, type, as between major and minor.

Tonguing. The use of the tongue for articulation in the playing of wind instruments. The tongue releases the wind stream for an initial attack and interrupts it for successive notes that are separately articulated. Single tonguing, the simplest type, consists in using the tongue as if to pronounce the letter *t* one or more times. On a reed instrument, this will consist in removing the tongue from contact with the tip of the reed. On brass instruments, a sharp attack is produced if the tongue touches the opening between the lips, and a softer attack is produced by touching the roof of the mouth farther back or by producing a *th.* On brass instruments and the flute, rapid notes in duple divisions may be played with double tonguing *(t–k, t–k . . .).* Similarly, rapid notes in triple divisions may be played with triple tonguing (*t–t–k, t–t–k* . . . or *t–k–t, t–k–t* . . .). In flutter tonguing [Ger. *Flatterzunge;* It. *frullato*], the tongue is fluttered or trilled against the roof of the mouth, just behind the front teeth.

Tonhöhe [Ger.]. *Pitch (1).

Tonic. See Scale, Scale degrees, Tonality.

Tonic accent. An accent produced by a rise in pitch. See also Accent, Cursive and tonic.

Tonicization [Ger. *Tonikalisierung*]. The momentary treatment of a pitch other than the tonic as if it were the tonic, most often by the introduction of its own leading tone or fourth scale degree or both. The resulting harmony is most likely to be the dominant of the tonicized pitch and is in such a case often termed a secondary or applied *dominant. The triad formed on the leading tone of the tonicized pitch may also function in this way. Tonicization, which may be prolonged beyond a single chord or two, is nevertheless a local phenomenon, as distinct from *modulation, which implies an actual change in tonic. The boundary between the two, however, is not always easily fixed in practice.

Tonic Sol-fa. A type of musical notation and its associated method of sight-singing, developed in England in the 19th century. Similar systems have been adopted in many countries (e.g., *Tonika-Do* in Germany and the *Kodály method in Hungary and elsewhere).

The system was developed by the Rev. John Curwen (1816–80), beginning in 1841, with the aim of teaching beginners to sing accurately. Adopting many aspects of the method advocated and used by Sarah Glover of Norwich, Curwen employed the *solmization syllables *doh, ray, me, fah, soh, lah,* and *te* for the ascending pitches of the major scale. *Doh* is movable to any pitch, depending on the key of the piece in question [see also Solfège]. For purposes of notation, each syllable is represented by its initial consonant, and the precise pitch is specified in the form "Key C" or "Doh is C." In a minor scale, the tonic is represented by *lah.* If a modulation occurs within a piece, the location of *doh* is shifted. Octaves above and below the central octave are represented, respectively, by superscript and subscript vertical strokes following the consonants; sharped notes add the vowel *e* (pronounced *ee*) to the initial consonant; and flatted notes add the vowel *a* (pronounced *aw*). Curwen indicated rhythm with the aid of conventional bar lines, colons, commas, periods, and dashes, but this aspect of the notation has been dropped. For drill with students, the teacher may point to a chart, termed a Modulator, that arranges the notation for the scale pattern vertically. Hand signs corresponding to the syllables are also used.

Curwen published much music in Tonic Sol-fa notation and eventually established the Tonic Sol-fa College in London. Large numbers of people became proficient in reading Curwen's notation while remaining almost entirely ignorant of staff notation, contrary to Curwen's original intentions. Modifications of the system have been aimed in part at reincorporating standard notation.

Bibl.: John Curwen, *Tonic Sol-fa* (London: Novello, 1878). William G. Whittaker, "The Claims of Tonic Solfa," *ML* 5 (1924): 313–21; 6 (1925): 46–53, 161–73. Bernarr Rainbow, *The Land without Music* (London: Novello, 1967).

Tonika [Ger.]. Tonic; for *Tonika-Do,* see Tonic Sol-fa.

Tonkunst [Ger.]. Music; *Tonkünstler,* composer.

Tonleiter [Ger.]. Scale.

Tono [It., Sp.]. (1) Tone, pitch. (2) Key. (3) Mode. (4) Whole tone. (5) [Sp.] Tune, melody (especially in the period around 1600).

Tono de velorio [Sp.]. Among several folk-music genres referred to as *tono* in Latin America, a distinctive song tradition associated with **velorios* (wakes and other religious observances) in Venezuela. It is most characteristically sung by three male vocalists, often without accompaniment, in parallel harmony or in simple improvised counterpoint around a principal melody. D.S.

Tonos [Gr., pl. *tonoi*]. See Greece I, 3 (ii).

Tonsatz, Tonstück [Ger.]. Composition, piece.

Tonschrift [Ger.]. Notation.

Tonus [Lat., fr. Gr. *tonos*]. (1) Whole tone. (2) Any of the formulas to which liturgical texts are chanted, especially the *psalm tones (including the *tonus peregrinus*) [see also Psalmody]. (3) *Mode. (4) Tone, pitch.

Top 40. A format for commercial radio broadcasting that organizes pop songs for play on the air according to their sales and relative popularity, i.e., according to a ranked list of the 40 songs presumed to be most popular. Network AM stations developed the system in the 1950s in an attempt to make their programming more uniform and to take advantage of the growing youth market. In the 1980s, the term became synonymous with any mainstream popular music. P.T.W.

Torbellino [Sp., whirlwind]. A social dance of the Andean region of Colombia. It is typically in moderate, strongly accented triple meter; syncopated melodies with hemiola patterns, and complex rhythmic relationships between melody and accompaniment are also characteristic. Perhaps related to the Andean *torbellino* is a genre of the same name found among black populations in the Pacific lowlands of Colombia and Ecuador. D.S.

Torculus [Lat.]. See Neume.

Tordion [Fr.]. See *Tourdion.*

Tornada [Prov.]. See *Envoi.*

Tosca. Opera in three acts by Puccini (libretto by Giuseppe Giacosa and Luigi Illica, based on Victorien Sardou's drama of the same name), produced in Rome in 1900. Setting: Rome in June of 1800.

Tosto [It.]. Quickly, at once; *più tosto, *piuttosto,* rather, somewhat.

Tost Quartets. Popular name for the 12 string quartets by Haydn dedicated to the Viennese merchant and violinist Johann Tost: op. 54, Hob. III:57–59 (completed in 1788); op. 55, Hob. III:60–62 (completed in 1788); and op. 64, Hob. III:63–68 (1790).

Totenmesse [Ger.]. *Requiem Mass.

Touch. In piano playing, the way in which the keys are depressed so as to produce the desired qualities of sound; also the particular characteristics of any keyboard action according to which greater or lesser force is required in order to depress the keys.

Touche [Fr.]. (1) A key of a keyboard. (2) Fingerboard; *sur la touche,* an instruction to bow over the fingerboard. (3) In the 16th century, fret. (4) Toccata (2).

Touquet [Fr.]. See *Toccato.*

Tour de gosier [Fr.]. According to Montéclair (1736), a five-note *turn beginning and ending on the same note. After resting on the first, the singer sings the middle three notes lightly and quickly, but with a slight trill on the second. D.F.

Tourdion, tordion [Fr.; It. *tordiglione*]. A 16th-century dance most commonly found as an *after-dance to the **basse danse commune.* In Pierre Attaingnant's *Dixhuit basses danses* (1530), it follows the **recoupe* as the third element of a three-dance suite. Both Antonius de Arena (*Ad suos compagnones,* 1529) and Thoinot Arbeau (*Orchésographie,* 1588) describe it as a kind of *gaillarde (*gagliarda),* but lighter, faster, and without its vigorous movements. Although frequently described as the same as the French *tourdion,* the *tordiglione* in the dance manuals by Fabritio Caroso (1581, 1600) and Cesare Negri (1602) is a freely conceived dance that bears no relation to the one described by Arena and Arbeau. L.H.M.

Tourte bow. A *bow of the type developed and made beginning in the 1780s by François Tourte (1747–35).

Toy(e). A light piece for lute or virginals from the end of the 16th century or the first half of the 17th.

Toy Symphony. A composition often attributed to Haydn (Hob. II:47*) and scored for violins, violas, horns (in some versions), and continuo, and for such instruments as toy drum, rattle, wind machine, whistle, cuckoo, quail (in some versions a screech owl), toy trumpet, and *cimbelstern* (an organ stop with a continuous tinkling sound). The piece, completed by 1786, is now variously attributed to Leopold Mozart (whose attributed version contains additional movements), Michael Haydn, and P. Edmund Angerer.

Tpt. Abbr. for trumpet.

Tr. Abbr. for trill, treble, transpose.

Tracker action. The traditional key action of the organ, in which the key is directly connected by a thin wooden strip, called a tracker, to the valve beneath the pipe. See Organ I, 3.

Tract [Lat. *tractus*]. In *Gregorian chant, an item of the *Proper of the *Mass that is sung before the Gospel, in the place of the *alleluia, on certain days during the season from Septuagesima Sunday through Lent to Holy Saturday, on certain of the Ember Days, and in the *Requiem Mass. Its texts consist of from two to ten or more verses, usually from the Psalms. Its melodies are *melismatic elaborations of the outline of a *psalm tone and are restricted to the second and eighth modes, within each of which certain melodic formulas are shared [see Centonization]. Since it is sung without any refrain or response, as Amalarius of Metz points out in the 9th century in distinguishing it from responsories, it is an example of direct *psalmody. In modern practice, however, it is sung in alternation by the two halves of the choir or by the soloists and the choir (*LU,* p. xv) rather than by the soloists alone. There is no evidence for its history before the first liturgical documents to preserve examples from the 8th or 9th century; thereafter the repertory of tracts continued to grow. A few of the earliest tracts are identified as *gradual responsories in early sources and were presumably performed in this fashion. Tract melodies are also employed for the Old Testament canticles of the Easter Vigil.

Trading. In jazz, improvised solos—usually in units of four or eight bars—by successive members of an ensemble, most often two in alternation, such as a trumpeter and saxophonist. One or more choruses may be played in this way following the whole choruses taken by individual soloists and just before the return of the original tune. In some cases, an ensemble heightens the effect by trading successively smaller units—eights, fours, twos, ones, etc.

Tragédie lyrique [Fr.]. French serious opera of the 17th and 18th centuries. The term was first used in connection with *Cadmus* (1673), Lully's musical setting of Quinault's dramatic text. A *tragédie lyrique* normally contains a prologue plus five acts and draws its subject from Greek mythology or chivalric romance. The term was used interchangeably with *tragédie en musique.*

Tragic Overture. See *Tragische Ouvertüre.*

Tragic Symphony. Schubert's title for his Symphony no. 4 in C minor D. 417 (completed in 1816); also the popular name for Mahler's Symphony no. 6 in A minor (1903–4, rev. 1906 and after) and Bruckner's Symphony no. 5 in B♭ major (1875–76).

Tragische Ouvertüre [Ger., Tragic Overture]. An orchestral composition by Brahms, op. 81 (1880, rev. 1881). It may have arisen from a request for incidental music to a new production of Goethe's *Faust* at the Vienna Burgtheater, a production that failed to materialize.

Traîner [Fr.]. To drag; *sans traîner,* without dragging.

Tranquillo [It.]. Tranquil, calm.

Transcendental Etudes. See *Études d'exécution transcendante.*

Transcription. (1) The adaptation of a composition for a medium other than its original one, e.g., of vocal music for instruments or of a piano work for orchestra, a practice that began in Western music by the 14th century; also the resulting work [see also Arrangement, Intabulation]. (2) The translation of music from one notational system into another, a major technique of historical musicology. Mainly used in the study and publication of medieval and Renaissance music, its principal difficulty has been the correct interpretation of rhythm. (3) The reduction of music from live or recorded sound to written notation. Important in ethnomusicology, it differs, by being "descriptive," from the "prescriptive" use of notation by composers as directions to performers. Western notation is most used, but as it does not adequately render the sounds or the musical conceptions of other cultures, other approaches have been attempted, including graph notation, staves of more or less than five lines, various supplementary symbols, the *melograph, and principles derived from non-Western notational systems. Recording and videotaping are recent substitutes for transcription.

Bibl.: Nazir A. Jairazbhoy, "The Objective and Subjective View in Music Transcription," *Ethno* 21 (1977): 263–74. Bruno Nettl, *The Study of Ethnomusicology* (Urbana: U of Ill Pr, 1983). B.N.

Transfigured Night. See *Verklärte Nacht.*

Transformational theory. A range of theoretical and analytical activities that adopt a dynamic view of musical structure, placing emphasis upon, or granting structural priority to, the intervals or relationships between musical objects (e.g., pitches, chords, durations), rather than upon those objects themselves. The theory is limited neither to a particular repertoire nor to a particular domain of musical structure.

The term transformation has both a colloquial and a technical meaning. Colloquially, it refers to the process by which one musical object (a pitch, a pitch class, a pitch-class set, a tone row, a rhythmic duration) becomes transformed into another. Transformation of a pitch-class set might be a particular transposition (T) or inversion (I), or some contextually defined operation. A rhythmic-durational transformation might be augmentation or diminution by a specific factor or ratio. In its technical meaning, a transformation is a type of reversible mathematical operation or function that maps elements of a set onto itself in a one-to-one fashion. Transpositions acting on the set of 12 pitch classes fulfills this technical definition: the operation "transpose by 4 semitones" (T_4) uniquely maps each pitch class in the set to a pitch class in the set (C maps to E, C♯ to F, D to F♯, and so on) and the operation is reversed by T_8.

The dynamic nature of the transformational perspective is most apparent when contrasted with the static, "thing-oriented" perspective common in early formulations of classical *twelve-tone and *set theories. Having selected some prime form of a set or row (P_0), these early theories identified and labeled other manifestations of those sets or rows always with reference to that prime form (e.g., $T_7 \cdot P_0$ or $T_5I \cdot P_0$). Such a labeling system, which subsumes relations within the things it labels (T_7 is here less a way of getting from any set or row to another than a label for one particular set or row form), can obscure direct structural relationships. For example, given the two pitch collections A = [G, G♯, B] and B = [D♯, E, G], the labels $T_7 \cdot P$ and $T_3 \cdot P$ indicate the relationships between those two sets and an arbitrary "prime form" collection P = [C, C♯, E], a referential form which may or may not have musical significance in a particular context. But such nomenclature only indirectly reflects the direct and possibly more significant relationship, T_8, that exists between collections A and B. A transformational perspective, by contrast, brings the direct relation between those sets to the fore, reflecting its significance in language such as "T_8 maps A to B" or "A progresses to B via T_8."

Transformational relationships are often expressed graphically. If we add a third collection, C = [E, F, G♯], to collections A and B above, the relations between the three collections could be expressed as a *transformational network,* a graph consisting of nodes that represent musical objects and arrows that represent transformations between those objects. Figure 1 illustrates a transformational network describing certain relations between collections A, B, and C. Collection A placed in the leftmost node of Figure 1 maps to B in the middle node via T_8 and B maps to C in the rightmost node via T_1. The sequence of transformations T_8-then-T_1 is called a *transformational pathway.* The nodes of Figure 1 are left empty to illustrate how the same network can describe relations among other objects, such as pitches of collections A, B, or C themselves: the pathway T_8-then-T_1, for instance, describes the intervals from B to G to G♯ in collection A. Figure 1 demonstrates how internal relations, the intervals within a collection, can be projected externally, defining progression between collections. The figure also reveals the potential of transformational theories to express commonalities of structure among different kinds of musical objects or across structural domains: the abstract network of Figure 1 may be realized by single pitches, by ordered or unordered pitch collections, by key areas, and so on.

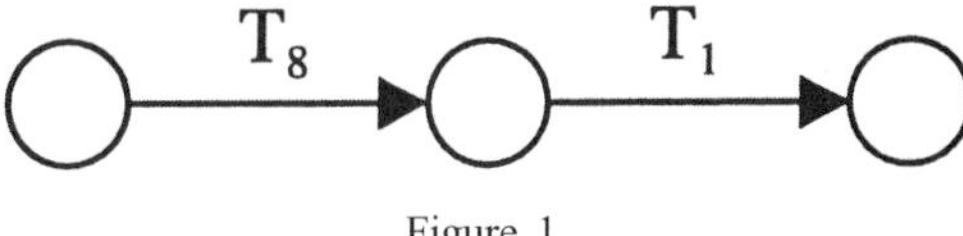

Figure 1.

Transformational perspectives have been largely assimilated into recent set-theoretical and twelve-tone analytical writings. More recently, transformational reinterpretations of certain 19th-century ideas about triadic relations have inspired a subdiscipline or transformational theory known as neo-Riemannian theory.

Bibl.: David Lewin, "Transformational Techniques in Atonal and Other Music Theories," *PNM* 21 (1982–83): 312–71. David Lewin, *Generalized Musical Intervals and Transformations.* (New Haven: Yale U Pr, 1987). David Lewin, *Musical Form and Transformation.* (New Haven: Yale U Pr, 1993). Richard Cohn, "Introduction to Neo-Riemannian Theory: A Survey and Historical Perspective," *JMT* 42:2 (1998): 167–80. E.G.

Transformation of themes. The alteration of themes for the sake of changing their character while retaining their essential identity. It differs from *development in that the resulting theme is likely to be treated with as much independence as the original. The term normally excludes such abstract devices as *augmentation and *diminution. Although the technique is found early in the history of the *suite of dance movements, the term is most often applied to music of the 19th century. The first characteristic use of the technique occurs in Berlioz's treatment of the *idée fixe* in his **Symphonie fantastique* [see Ex.]. Liszt used it extensively in his symphonic poems. Wagner's use of the **Leitmotif* is at the least very closely related.

Transient. See Acoustics III.

Transition. *Bridge (2).

Transitorium [Lat.]. In the *Ambrosian rite, the chant corresponding to the Gregorian *communion.

Transmission. Any of the means by which music (or literature) is preserved over time. A distinction has traditionally been made between oral and written transmission. In many cultures and repertories, transmission is almost exclusively oral, i.e., without the aid of musical notation. Western art music has usually been thought to rely almost entirely on written transmission [for some of the methods used in the study of written transmission generally, see Textual criticism]. The distinction is not easily maintained, however, because traditional Western notation requires for its realization a significant body of information and habit external to its written form [see Performance practice]. The distinction is still more problematical with respect to some repertories of early music such as liturgical chant, which was evidently transmitted orally for an extended period before being committed to notation. Recent scholarship has attempted to identify features of these repertories that result from oral transmission and to suggest ways in which the preserved written versions must be interpreted in consequence. Traditional notions of authorship and of procedures such as

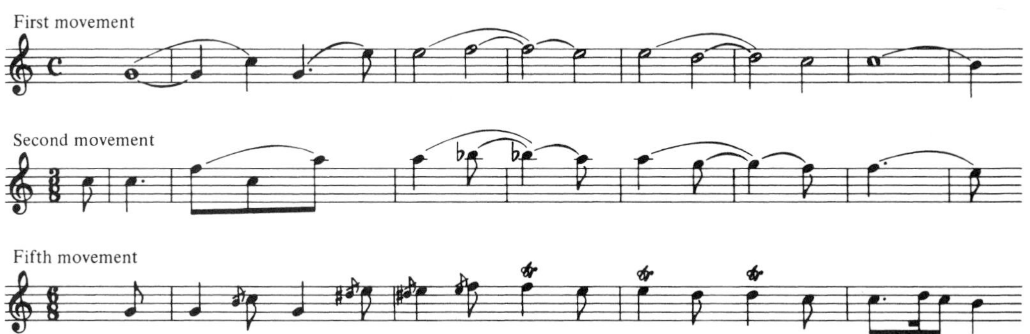

Transformation of themes. Berlioz, *Symphonie fantastique.*

*centonization have as a result been seriously called into question.

Bibl.: Leo Treitler, "Homer and Gregory: The Transmission of Epic Poetry and Plainchant," *MQ* 60 (1974): 333–72.

Transposing instruments. Instruments whose notated pitch is different from their sounded pitch. Except for those whose notated and sounded pitches differ by one or more octaves (usually for the sake of avoiding the use of multiple ledger lines), most such instruments are identified by the letter name of the pitch class of their fundamental, e.g., trumpet in B♭. The letter name identifies the pitch class that is sounded when a notated C is played. Thus, when the alto saxophone in E♭ plays a notated C, an E♭ a sixth below sounds. A few nontransposing instruments are also identified in this way, however: e.g., the tenor trombone in B♭ and the tuba in BB♭, which sound as notated. The direction of transposition may be up or down and may exceed an octave. For precise intervals of transposition, see the entries on individual instruments; see also orchestration books cited under Orchestration.

The use of transposing brass instruments derives from the need, before the advent of *valves, to have a separate natural instrument for each of the principal keys to be played in. The use of transposition for differently pitched valved instruments of the same family permits the player to employ the same relationship of fingerings to notation for all instruments of the family. This is also true of reed families such as the saxophone. The different instruments within a family make available a variety of tone colors and registers. Orchestral scores have traditionally presented the parts for transposing instruments in their transposed pitches. Beginning in the 20th century, however, some scores notate all parts at (sounding) pitch.

Transposition. The rewriting or performance of music at a pitch other than the original one. This entails raising or lowering each pitch of the original music by precisely the same interval. In tonal music, it results in changing the key of the original. Works are often transposed to accommodate the ranges of singers. The player of an instrument at one pitch will be required to transpose in order to perform a part written at another pitch; e.g., the player of a trumpet in B♭ will be required to transpose in order to perform from a part for trumpet in C or D, in the first case by raising every pitch a whole tone, in the second by raising every pitch a major third. See also Transposing instruments.

Transverse flute. A *flute in which the airstream is directed across the axis of its length rather than along it; thus, e.g., the modern flute as distinct from the *recorder.

Traps. *Drum set; also the nondrum items used in such a set by theater drummers.

Traquenard [Fr., ambling gait]. A *gavotte-like dance movement in some late 17th-century German orchestral suites (Georg Muffat, J. C. F. Fischer). The solo dance was said to involve special movements of the body, apparently related to the literal 17th-century meaning of the word. B.G.

Trascinare, trascinando [It.]. To drag, dragging; *senza trascinare,* without dragging.

Traste [Sp.]. Fret.

Trattenuto [It.]. Held back, **ritardando.*

Tratto [It.]. Drawn out.

Trauermarsch [Ger.]. Funeral march.

Trauermusik [Ger.]. Funeral music.

Trauernd [Ger.]. Mourning, lamenting.

Trauer-Ode [Ger., Funeral Ode]. A secular cantata by Bach, BWV 198 (1727), composed on the death of the Electress Christiane of Saxony. The text, beginning "Lass, Fürstin, lass noch einen Strahl," is an ode by Johann Christoph Gottsched.

Trauer-Symphonie [Ger., Mourning Symphony]. Popular name for Haydn's Symphony no. 44 in E minor Hob. I:44 (completed by 1772), apparently so called because the third movement (Adagio) was performed at a memorial concert in Berlin in September 1809.

Träumerisch [Ger.]. Dreamy.

Traurig [Ger.]. Sad, mournful.

Trautonium. An *electronic instrument exhibited in 1930 by Friedrich Trautwein. It produced, by entirely electronic means, only one pitch at a time, though its timbre could be varied widely. The performer controlled pitch by varying the point at which a wire was pressed against a metal bar. It was popular in the 1930s, and Richard Strauss, Hindemith, and Paul Dessau composed works for it.

Traverso [It.], **traversière** [Fr.], **Traversflöte** [Ger.]. *Transverse flute.

Traviata, La [It., The Strayed One]. Opera in three acts by Verdi (libretto by Francesco Maria Piave, after the play *La dame aux camélias* by Alexandre Dumas), first produced in Venice in 1853. Setting: Paris and environs, about 1700 (now more often set about 1850).

Tre [It.]. Three; *a tre voci,* for three voices; for *tre corde,* see *Una corda.*

Treble [fr. Lat. **triplum*]. The highest part; the highest range of voices; the highest-pitched members of some families of instruments, e.g., treble *viol or *recorder (in this case not the single highest). With respect to voices, the term is now generic for high voices, having been displaced as the specific term by soprano. See also Clef, Descant, Sight, Voice.

Trecanum [Lat.]. In the *Gallican rite, the chant corresponding to the Gregorian *communion.

Trecento [It.]. The 14th century [see *Ars nova*].

Treibend [Ger.]. Driving, hurrying.

Tremblant doux, fort [Fr.]. The light and heavy *tremulants, respectively, of the classical French organ. *Tremblant doux* consists of a weighted valve inside the windtrunk; *tremblant fort* consists of two valves, one inside the windtrunk, the other outside and weighted.

Tremblement [Fr.]. In the 17th and 18th centuries, the *trill, the most important French ornament of the period.

Tremolando [It.]. With *tremolo.

Tremolo [It.]. Usually, the quick and continuous reiteration of a single pitch. On stringed instruments, it is produced by a rapid up-and-down movement of the bow, indicated as in Ex. 1. This effect is called for in violin music of the early 17th century, and is a feature of Monteverdi's *stile *concitato.* It has remained in continuous use. Eighteenth-century names for the string tremolo are [It.] *bombo* and [Ger.] *Schwärmer.* The term tremolo also refers, however, to a succession of repeated notes slightly articulated without a change in direction of the bow, as in Ex. 2, this being termed a slurred tremolo and sometimes indicated by a wavy line, and to a rapid alternation between two pitches of a chord, as in Ex. 3, this being termed a fingered tremolo because it is produced by rapid movement of a finger on the fingerboard rather than by rapid movement of the bow.

In violin music of the 18th century, a tremolo known as the undulating tremolo [It. *ondeggiando;* Fr. *ondulé*] occurs frequently. It is produced by an undulating motion of the bow arm, resulting in alternate bowing on two strings (or more when the technique is applied to the playing of arpeggios). This bowing can be used to produce either a reiteration of a single pitch alternately on a stopped string and an open string (in which case it is called *bariolage,* Ex. 4) or an alternation between two (or more) pitches. It is indicated by a wavy line, as in Ex. 5. The addition of a slur indicates that several notes are to be taken in a single bow stroke, i.e., without a change in the direction of the bow. The term tremolo was also used in the 18th century for *vibrato produced by the left hand, and this too could be indicated by a wavy line. Finally, the term could also mean *trill.

In piano music the rapid repetition of a single pitch is a device used mainly in highly virtuosic compositions such as Liszt's *La campanella,* where it also occurs in the form of quickly repeated octaves. The tremolo of strings is sometimes imitated on the piano by the rapid alternation of a pitch and its octave, or of the several pitches of a chord. In organ music, the term tremolo is applied to the effect produced by the *tremulant stop. This effect, however, more nearly approximates the string player's *vibrato.

In singing, the term now usually refers to excessive vibrato that leads to deviations in pitch. The rapid repetition of a single pitch, however, is called for in liturgical chant by *neumes such as the *bistropha* and *tristropha* and is described by Aurelian of Réôme (ca. 850). Thirteenth-century terms for this effect include *repercussio gutturis* and *reverberatio.* Termed a *trillo,* the effect was widely used in the 17th century and was usually written out in small note-values. During this period, tremolo referred to various kinds of *trill or *mordent. In the 18th century, the rapid repetition of a single pitch in vocal music fell into disuse and began to be known by such pejorative terms as [Fr.] *chevrotement* and [Ger.] *Bockstriller* (goat's trill). See also Ornamentation, Bowing.

Tremulant. A mechanical device applied to the wind supply of organs to cause regular fluctuations of pressure to the wind-chests, thus producing a *vibrato. See *Tremblant doux, fort.*

Trenchmore. An English country dance of the 16th and 17th centuries in fast triple meter with dotted rhythms. It was very popular in the late 17th century at the court of Charles II.

Trent, Council of. See Council of Trent.

Trent Codices. Six manuscript volumes (Codice 87–92) of 15th-century polyphonic music in the National Museum in the Castello del Buonconsiglio at Trent. A seventh volume (Codice 93) is almost identical to the fourth, differing only in the last three gatherings (of a total of 33). The six volumes contain 1,585 compositions from the first 74 years of the 15th century by English, Flemish, French, German, and Italian composers (incipit catalog in *DTÖ* 14). The source is the largest and most important for 15th-century music and a major source for the music of Dufay.

Bibl.: Facsimile edition, 7 vols. (Rome: Vivarelli & Gullà, 1970). Modern editions: *DTÖ* 14–15, 22, 38, 53, 61, 76, and 120 (1900–1970); Margaret Bent, *Four Anonymous Masses,* Early English Church Music 22 (London: Stainer & Bell, 1979); Richard Loyan in *CMM* 38 (1967). Lorenzo Feininger, *Il Codice 87 del Castello del Buonconsiglio di Trento* (Bologna: Forni, 1971). Peter Wright, "The Compilation of Trent 87 and 92," *Early Music History* 2 (1982): 237–71. H.E.S.

Trepak [Russ.]. A Cossack dance in fast duple meter. An example occurs in Tchaikovsky's **Nutcracker.*

Tres [Sp.]. A small guitar of Latin America with three courses, which are sometimes double or triple.

Tresca, tresche, tresce [Occ., It., Fr.]. A dance mentioned in literary sources from the 11th through the 15th century, evidently danced with jumping movements by a circle of couples or in a straight line, and sometimes sung. See *Carole.*

Trezza. In some German suites of the late 17th century, a dance similar to the *courante or *galliarde.

Triad [Fr. *triade, accord parfait;* Ger. *Dreiklang;* It. *triade, accordo perfetto;* Sp. *tríada, acorde perfecto*]. A chord consisting of three pitches, the adjacent pitches being separated by a third, and thus the whole capable of notation on three adjacent lines or three adjacent spaces of the staff; also termed the common chord. There are four types [Ex.]: (1) the major triad,

in which the interval between the lower two pitches is a major third and that between the upper two a minor third, the interval between the lowest and highest pitches thus being a perfect fifth; (2) the minor triad, in which the lower interval is a minor third and the upper a major third, the outer interval being a perfect fifth; (3) the diminished triad, in which both internal intervals are minor thirds and the outer interval is a diminished fifth; and (4) the augmented triad, in which both internal intervals are major thirds and the outer interval is an augmented fifth. The major and minor triads include only consonant intervals and are thus consonant chords. The diminished and augmented triads both include a dissonant interval and are thus dissonant chords [see Consonance, Dissonance]. For the various positions in which triads can be stated, see Inversion II; see also Harmony, Harmonic analysis.

Triads can be formed on any *scale degree of the major or minor scale (i.e., with any degree as the lowest pitch), those on degrees I, IV, and V being termed the primary triads. Together these three include all of the pitches of the scale in question. In a major scale, the triad on the tonic is major; in a minor scale it is minor. The concepts triad and triad inversion have been central to discussions of tonality since the 18th century, the first explicit theoretical accounts of them dating from around 1600 [see especially the citations of Lippius and Rameau under Theory]. The major and minor triads themselves occur regularly in English music beginning in the 13th century. They are prominent in Continental music from the 15th century on, in part because of an increasing preference for four-voice texture, combined with the fact that the major and minor triads are the only consonant simultaneities of more than two pitches that can be produced from the intervals regarded as consonant at the time [see also Counterpoint].

Trial of Lucullus, The. Opera in one act by Sessions (libretto by Bertolt Brecht), produced in Berkeley, California, in 1947.

Triangle [Fr. *triangle;* Ger. *Triangel;* It. *triangolo;* Sp. *triángulo*]. A percussion instrument made from a steel rod bent into the shape of a triangle but with the ends of the rod not joined at the corner. It is struck with a metal beater, producing a sound of high but indefinite pitch. Known in Europe since the Middle Ages (then usually with rings on the lowest side), it became especially prominent in the 18th century under the influence of *Janissary music. See ill. under Percussion instruments.

Tribrach, tribrachic. See Prosody.

Tricesimoprimal temperament. A division of the octave into 31 equal intervals advocated in the 17th century by Christian Huygens [see Microtone].

Trichord. A collection of three pitches, especially any one of the four making up a *twelve-tone row.

Tricinium [Lat.]. A three-voice vocal or instrumental composition of the 16th and 17th centuries, especially one related in some measure to the didactic repertory of the **bicinium.* Hieronymus Formschneider (Nuremberg, 1538) was among the first publishers to issue such works. Collections employing the term include Georg Rhau's *Tricinia . . . latina, germanica, brabantica et gallica* (1542), Caspar Othmayr's *Tricinia in pias aliquot* (1549), Wolfgang Figulus's *Tricinia sacra ad voces pueriles* (1559), Georg Aichinger's *Tricinia Mariana* (1598), Sethus Calvisius's *Tricinia* (1603), and Melchior Franck's *Tricinia nova* (1611). The term is now often applied, however, to a broad range of works in three voices, including madrigals and motets by composers such as Costanzo Festa, Jhan Gero, and Lassus.

Tricotet [Fr., also *tricotée, triquotée*]. Any of several dance tunes of the 16th and 17th centuries, quoted or preserved in chansons (e.g., Josquin's "Je me complains de mon amy") and instrumental settings dating in some cases from as late as the 18th century.

Trigon [Lat.]. See Neume.

Trigōnon [Gr., triangle]. A harp of Greece and Rome, apparently either an *angle harp or one with a post. It is depicted held in the player's lap.

Trihori(s) [Fr.]. See *Triori.*

Trill [also shake; Fr. *tremblement, cadence;* Ger. *Triller;* It. *trillo, tremolo, groppo;* Sp. *trino, quiebro reyterado, redoble*]. An ornament consisting of the more or less rapid alternation of a note with the one next above in the prevailing key or harmony. In current musical notation, it is often indicated by the abbreviation *tr,* but the signs used have varied in the course of its history, as have such conventions of its execution as whether it begins on the main note or the ornamenting note, whether it is preceded by an auxiliary ornamenting note, and whether any preceding note is to be played on the beat or before it.

Trill-like ornaments for both voice and organ were described by Jerome of Moravia toward the end of the 13th century, those for voice perhaps being more like a violent vibrato and those for organ requiring that the main note be held while the upper one was reiterated [see Ornamentation, Mordent]. Ornament signs in 14th- and 15th-century keyboard tablatures may have indicated trills as well as mordents. Vincenzo Capirola (ca. 1517) indicated a lute trill in his tablature by placing after the main fret number the fret number of the auxiliary note written in red dotted lines. Written models for trills and trill-like ornaments appeared in treatises beginning with Ganassi (1535). These were generally known by some variant of the name *tremolo* or, when followed by a suffix (turn), *groppo; tremolo* was also applied to mordents and *groppo* to ornamental passages containing trill elements, but winding around two or more notes [Exx. 1–3]. *Trillo* was used by Caccini (in *Le nuove musiche,* Florence, 1601/2) and others for the rapid or accelerating reiteration of a

1. Giovanni Luca Conforti, *Breve et facile maniera* (1593?). 2, 3. Girolamo Diruta, *Il transilvano* (1593).

single pitch, but the meanings of *trillo* and *tremolo* were sometimes reversed, and there was no consistency in the use of any of these terms. The Spanish *quiebro* and *redoble* were roughly analogous in range of meaning to the Italian (and later, German) *tremolo* and *groppo,* respectively. *Groppi* were often written out by 16th- and 17th-century composers, but performers were expected to supply others, especially at cadences. Simpler trills were ordinarily left to the performer. Signs for the trill were rare until the mid-17th century, except (probably) in English virginal music (ca. 1560–ca. 1650); the precise meaning of the oblique strokes, ubiquitous in that repertory, remains unknown. Not until the second half of the 17th century are trills indicated by signs whose meaning is spelled out in tables, prefaces, or treatises, and this growing precision of usage narrowed options and engendered the elaborate codes of the 18th century. Much was still left to the performer, however; samples of directions for supplying unindicated trills may be seen under Ornamentation.

Trills on intervals narrower than a minor second or wider than a major second are occasionally mentioned, the former resembling a wide vibrato and the latter necessary for some wind-instrument fingerings; Ganassi (1535) admitted *tremoli* on the third. Tartini (1771) allowed, but did not recommend, trills on the augmented second to avoid a clash between the chord and the trill auxiliary [Ex. 4]; Quantz (1752) called

4. Tartini, *Traité des agréments* (1771; Italian original, 1750s).

such trills "formerly customary." Otherwise, the auxiliary of a trill obeys the same rules with regard to accidentals as other ornamental notes [see Ornamentation].

In the 16th century, simple *tremoli* rarely exceeded half the written value of the note (Brown, 1976, p. 5), while cadential trills *(groppi)* took most or all of the value. In the Baroque period, except for certain short trills (accent trills, like the *Schneller and *martellement,* and trills resolving appoggiaturas, the **Pralltriller,* etc.), which never exceeded two or three repercussions, the longer the trill the better, whatever the symbol.

The speed of a trill is important to its effect and was often mentioned. Jerome of Moravia's vocal trills were slow or accelerating; his keyboard equivalent was slow or accelerating if on a semitone, moderate if on a whole tone. The *groppi* in 16th-century music were apparently very fast; written-out examples sometimes have more notes than seem playable and may not have been intended to be taken literally. In the Baroque period, keyboard trills were normally rapid and even, though some writers allowed a slight broadening in slow, expressive pieces. Vocal trills evidently varied considerably, some writers specifying slower speeds for pieces in slower tempos, some saying that the speed should be governed by the expressive content. French Baroque singers had a reputation for slow trills, Italians for fast. A few writers seem to imply an uneven execution, with the main notes receiving more emphasis than the auxiliaries. Unevenness was an essential characteristic of the *ribattuta* [see Ex. 5]. Accelerating trills other than the *ribattuta* were common in the Baroque period, but may have become unfash-

5. Mattheson, *Der vollkommene Capellmeister* (1739).

ionable later, at least in some circles; Lacassagne's singing method of 1766 recommended that trills should be as fast and even as possible, acknowledging that some readers might regret the abandonment of the old *cadence à progression,* a kind of *ribattuta.* Yet in 1781, Dellain, describing the trills "now" used at the Opéra and required by the new (Classical) style of composition, specified acceleration from slow to extremely fast. Instruction books for melody instruments generally fall between voice and keyboard. Leopold Mozart's violin treatise (1756) divided trills into slow, medium, fast, and accelerating, and warned against too much speed. Trills in 19th- and 20th-century music are usually fast.

The issue that has most engaged modern scholarship, often passionately, is whether the starting note should be the main note or the auxiliary. In the 16th century, *tremoli* (which included trills and mordents) began on the main note, while cadential *groppi* (trills on the leading note with suffixes and sometimes additional figures) generally began on the auxiliary, sometimes after dwelling on the main note [Ex. 1]. Usage in the 17th century appears to have varied greatly according to time, place, and medium, and sources are inadequate to establish common practices within this diversity. As noted above, the riddle of English virginal ornamentation, which must have profoundly influenced north German keyboard practice, has never been solved. It appears, nevertheless, that a preference for upper-note starts developed in French and English instrumental music during the second half of the century, and that by 1700 it had spread to Germany and perhaps to Italy. Whether the initiative lay in lute music, in French keyboard music, or in the Lullian orchestra is impossible to say; the tables of Nivers (1665), Chambonnières (1670), and D'Anglebert (1689), and those in orchestral collections by Lully's pupil Georg Muffat and by J. C. F. Fischer, both of whom were imitating the French style, have only upper-note starts, while, as Neumann *(NeuO)* has shown, the *air de cour* preserved a type of trill analogous to the **port de voix,* in which the auxiliary is sounded as a measured note preceding the trilled main note. A similar trill was taught in Jean Rousseau's viol method of 1687 [Ex. 6].

6. Jean Rousseau, *Traité de la viole* (1687).

By 1696, Loulié's general treatise defined the trill as a succession of **coulés* beginning on the beat; Montéclair's text on singing (1736) did the same, and Marpurg's treatise on keyboard playing (1765) called it a series of appoggiaturas. This theoretical postulate was borne out by the overwhelming majority of ornament tables and other 18th-century descriptions. The upper-note, on-beat start was clearly normal for trills from the late 17th to the early 19th century, in all countries and all media [Ex. 7]. Within this common practice, however, there was the greatest possible diversity of subspecies, conflicting terminology, and contradictory descriptions. Certainly, many trills were begun on the main note. Most fell into one of two types: trills following a written note a step above a trilled one, which was felt to do duty as the initial upper auxiliary (but even here, many writers preferred a repetition of the auxiliary, where time allowed, or a delay of the main note to give the effect of a tie to a downbeat auxiliary) [Ex. 8], and short, main-note trills that served as accents *(martellement, *Schneller).*

7. Bach, *Clavier-Büchlein vor Wilhelm Friedemann Bach* (begun 1720). 8. Rameau, "De la méchanique des doigts," in *Pièces de clavecin* (1724).

The terms preparation, *Vorbereitung,* and *appuy,* all of which refer to the initial auxiliary of a trill, were used with the greatest inconsistency to mean either the simple presence of this first note or its prolongation, which might vary from a slight dwelling to half the value of the written note to nearly all its value. In the absence of a clear description or table, there is no way to be sure which was meant. The same is true of a small note indicating the auxiliary; this may or may not mean a prolongation. Marpurg (1765, p. 57) complained of composers who add such *Vorschläge* without meaning anything by them. Thus, a trill *sans appuy* (without preparation) or without the auxiliary shown by a small note does not necessarily start on the main note. Trills may also begin with turns in either direction; these, however, are usually indicated unambiguously by small notes or a sign. Parallels (octaves, fifths, sevenths, etc.) were apparently not a consideration in the execution of trills though Neumann often adduces them in favor of main-note or prebeat trills. Dissonance was sometimes held to be desirable, and recently, Robert Winter (1977, 1979) has elevated it to a principle for the performance of trills in Beethoven's music: trills should begin on whichever note is more dissonant (a view disputed by Newman, 1978).

The upper-note start was gradually abandoned during the first half of the 19th century, though Chopin preferred it, and it evidently persisted in Italian opera (García, 1847 and 1872). Hummel (1828) and Czerny (1842) may have established the norm of the main-note start, which still persists and is applied by many pianists and orchestral players to 18th-century repertory. When the upper auxiliary is written as a small note, it is now normally played before the beat so that the trill may begin with the main note (Neumann's "grace-note trill").

It is often more difficult to decide how to end a trill than how to begin it. One may stop, usually with a slight acceleration or "snap" (C. P. E. Bach) on the main note, early if the trill is short, or just for an instant at the end if it is long (François Couperin's *point d'arrêt*). One may stop, then very lightly anticipate the following note (Bacilly's *liaison*). One may trill smoothly into the following note (unavoidable if the trilled note is very short). Finally, one may add a "suffix" *(Nachschlag),* a dip to the lower auxiliary before the final main note [Exx. 1 and 9]. (The resemblance to an appended mordent or turn is reflected in

9. Johann Gottfried Walther, "Praecepta der musicalischen Composition" (1708).

two of the signs for a trill with suffix; Ex. 10.) Normally one trills smoothly into the suffix, which connects without a break to the following note, but occasionally the suffix is separated from the trill by a pause or rest. The suffix is also used to end a trill that

10

is not immediately followed by another note, e.g., a trilled fermata. Suffixes are indicated by signs or (more commonly) written out. They may also be added by the performer when not indicated. The chief problems occur on dotted notes. Here the performer must decide whether the complementary short note or notes are intended as a suffix to the trill or must be articulated separately from it. A similar problem occurs with changing-note figures. The lower auxiliary may be intended to be sounded on time in full value or to be incorporated into the trill as the lower tone of a suffix. In rapid tempos, a trill with suffix can sometimes be compressed into a turn.

Bibl.: For treatises cited, see Ornamentation. Putnam Aldrich, "On the Interpretation of Bach's Trills," *MQ* 49 (1963): 289–310. Frederick Neumann, "Misconceptions about the French Trill in the 17th and 18th Centuries," *MQ* 50 (1964): 188–206. Jean-Jacques Eigeldinger, *Chopin vu par ses élèves* (Neuchâtel: La Baconnière, 1970). Michael Collins, "In Defense of the French Trill," *JAMS* 26 (1973): 405–39. Howard Mayer Brown, *Embellishing 16th-Century Music* (London: Oxford U Pr, 1976). William Newman, "The Performance of Beethoven's Trills," *JAMS* 29 (1976): 439–62. Robert Winter, "Second Thoughts on the Performance of Beethoven's Trills," *MQ* 63 (1977): 483–504. Elfrieda F. Hiebert, "Letter," *JAMS* 31 (1978): 173–75. William Newman, "Second and One-Half Thoughts on the Performance of Beethoven's Trills," *MQ* 64 (1978): 98–103. Robert Winter, "And Even More Thoughts on the Beethoven Trill . . . ," *MQ* 65 (1979): 111–16. Julianne Baird, "An 18th-Century Controversy about the Trill: Mancini v. Manfredini," *EM* 15 (1987): 36–45. Stewart Carter, "On the Shape of the Early Baroque Trill," *Historical Performance* 3 (1990): 9–17. Paul Badura-Skoda, "Mozart's Trills," in *Perspectives on Mozart Performance,* ed. R. Larry Todd and Peter Williams (Cambridge: Cambridge U Pr, 1991), pp. 1–26. See also Mordent.

D.F.

Triller [Ger.]. *Trill; *Trillerkette,* chain or series of trills.

Trillo [It.]. In 17th-century Italy, a vocal *tremolo (rapid repetition of the same pitch); later, a *trill [see also Ornamentation].

Trinklied [Ger.]. Drinking song.

Trio [It.]. (1) An ensemble of three solo instruments or voices.

(2) In dance movements from the 17th century onward, a contrasting second or middle section appearing between the principal dance and its repetition (e.g., minuet–trio–minuet da capo). Trios are also found in *scherzos and *marches. The term derives from the 17th-century practice of scoring the second of two alternating dances for three instruments, frequently two oboes and bassoon. See also *Alternativo.*

(3) In the Baroque period, a strict contrapuntal composition in three parts without continuo.

(4) From the Classical period to the present, a composition for three solo instruments. The most important types of trio are the piano trio, for piano, violin, and cello, and the string trio, for violin, viola, and cello or two violins and cello. The piano trio derives from the *accompanied sonata for keyboard and violin [see also Sonata II], the cello being added initially as simplified doubling for the bass line of the keyboard part. In the earliest examples, the violin is also subsidiary. In Haydn's many piano trios, the violin achieves considerable independence; the cello, however, continues its doubling function for the most part. Mozart's six late piano trios give the cello somewhat greater freedom, and in Beethoven's opp. 70 and 97 (the *Archduke* Trio) and Schubert's opp. 99–100, both string instruments attain true obbligato status.

The piano trio remained popular throughout the 19th century, with notable contributions by Mendelssohn (2), Franck (4), Schumann (3), Brahms (3), Smetana (1), and Dvořák (3). Examples from the 20th century include single works by Roussel, Ives, Ravel, and Fauré.

The string trio is a descendant of the *trio sonata of the Baroque; indeed, for many early Classical "trios," a keyboard continuo was doubtless intended. However, Haydn's many early string trios—some evidently dating from before 1760—are probably analogous to his early string quartets in dispensing with continuo [see String quartet I]. All but one of these works are scored for two violins and bass; the exception, Hob. V:8 (before 1765), ranks among the earliest known trios for the favorite later ensemble of violin, viola, and cello. Haydn also composed 126 trios for *baryton, viola, and cello for use by his patron Prince Nikolaus Esterházy.

A special mid-18th-century type of trio was the so-called orchestral trio for two violins and bass, which could be performed either with doubled parts or with a single player on each part. The best-known example of this genre is Johann Stamitz's op. 1, published in 1755.

The small repertory of later Viennese string trios, nearly all for violin, viola, and cello, includes Mozart's K. 563, Beethoven's four trios opp. 3 and 9, and two trios by Schubert (one incomplete). The later 19th century generally neglected the string trio, but the 20th century produced works by Hindemith, Webern (op. 20, 1927), Roussel, Schoenberg, and Milhaud, among others.

(5) A composition for three solo voices with or without accompaniment (more properly termed a *terzett; see also *Tricinium*).

(6) In jazz, an ensemble consisting of piano, bass, and drums.

Bibl.: Wilhelm Altmann, *Handbuch für Klaviertriospieler* (Wolfenbüttel: Verlag für musikalische Kultur und Wissenschaft, 1934). Ruth Blume, "Studien zur Entwicklungsgeschichte des Klaviertrios im 18. Jahrhundert" (diss., Univ. of Kiel, 1962). Hubert Unverricht, *Geschichte des Streichtrios* (Tutzing: Schneider, 1969). Charles Rosen, *The Classical Style* (New York: Viking Pr, 1971; new ed., New York: Norton, 1972). James Webster, "Towards a History of Viennese Chamber Music in the Early Classical Period," *JAMS* 27 (1974): 212–47. Michelle Fillion, "The Accompanied Keyboard Divertimenti of Haydn and His Viennese Contemporaries (c. 1750–1780)" (Ph.D. diss., Cornell Univ., 1982). Eugene K. Wolf, "The Orchestral Trios, Opus 1, of Johann Stamitz," *Brook,* 1985, pp. 297–322. Katalin Komlós, "The Viennese Keyboard Trio in the 1780s: Sociological Background and Contemporary Reception," *ML* 68 (1987): 222–34. Basil Smallman, *The Piano Trio: Its History, Technique, and Repertoire* (New York: Oxford U Pr, 1990). E.K.W.

Triole [Ger.], **triolet** [Fr.]. Triplet.

Trionfo di Dori, Il [It.]. See *Triumphes of Oriana, The.*

Triori [Fr., also *trihoris*]. A Breton dance of the 16th century, described in Arbeau's *Orchésographie* (1589) as a kind of **branle* in duple meter.

Trio sonata. The commonest type of Baroque instrumental chamber music. Written in three parts—two upper lines, normally in the same register, and basso continuo [see Thoroughbass]—it often includes a **concertante* bass as well. It usually requires four performers: two melody instruments for the top lines, normally violins; a melody bass instrument (bass viol, violone, cello) that either reinforces the bass line of the continuo part or, as a *concertante* part, participates in imitations with the upper parts; and a chord-playing instrument such as organ, harpsichord, or theorbo to realize the harmonies of the continuo. In some repertories, such as Corelli's opp. 2 and 4, the two melody instruments are supported by a single bass part (in this case, violone or harpsichord). Until the 1660s, occasional options in instruments were offered, such as *cornetto* for the violin, and trombone or bassoon for the stringed bass instrument. In the 18th century, recorders, flutes, and oboes were often alternatives to the violin.

The origins of the genre lie in the adaptation to instruments of the three-part scoring common in Italian vocal music at the end of the 16th century. The earliest published trio sonatas are by Salomone Rossi (titled sinfonia, 1607) and Giovanni Paolo Cima (1610). At mid-century, two different types appeared: the **sonata da camera* and the **sonata da chiesa.* Corelli's examples of both, first published between 1681 and 1694, are justly famous. From the 1750s, the term was often equated with *trio, *partita, *divertimento, and, as it had been since the 17th century, *sinfonia. A frequent option in performance can be seen in Stamitz's *Sonates à trois parties concertantes qui sont faites pour exécuter ou à trois ou avec toutes l'orchestre* op. 1 (1755). During the 1760s, the continuo was increasingly abandoned, and by 1775 the trio sonata had largely disappeared.

The term has also been applied to Bach's organ sonatas for two manuals and pedal BWV 525–30 and to sonatas for violin and harpsichord by Bach and Jean-Joseph Cassanéa de Mondonville (1711–72) in which the keyboard supplies two obligatory parts—the second upper part and the bass. See also Sonata.

S.B., rev. S.Z.

Tripla [Lat.]. (1) Plural of **triplum.* (2) With respect to *proportions, triple. (3) *Proportz* [see *Nachtanz*].

Triple concerto. A concerto for three solo instruments and orchestra, e.g., Beethoven's op. 56 for violin, cello, and piano with orchestra.

Triple counterpoint. See Invertible counterpoint.

Triple-croche [Fr.]. Thirty-second *note.

Triple fugue. See Double fugue.

Triple meter, time. See Meter.

Triplet [Fr. *triolet;* Ger. *Triole;* It. *terzina;* Sp. *tresillo*]. Three notes of equal value to be played in the time normally occupied by two notes of the same value, indicated by the figure 3, often with a slur, above or below the group. See also Dotted notes.

Triple tonguing. See Tonguing.

Triplum [Lat., pl. *tripla*]. In music from the *Notre Dame repertory until the 15th century, the third part above the tenor; *organum triplum,* *organum in three parts.

Trisagion [Gr., thrice holy]. A chant of the Office and the Mass (where it is sung before the lections) of the

Eastern Christian rites. Its text, beginning "Hagios o Theos, Hagios Ischyros, Hagios Athanatos" (Holy God, Holy and Mighty, Holy and Immortal), is not to be confused with the threefold *Sanctus associated with the Eucharistic prayers in both Latin and Greek rites. It was adopted into the Gallican and Mozarabic liturgies, and it is sung in both Greek and Latin with the **Improperia* or Reproaches of the Roman Adoration of the Holy Cross on Good Friday (*LU,* p. 737).

Tristan chord. The first chord sounded in Wagner's **Tristan und Isolde* and prominent elsewhere in the work: f–b–d♯′–g♯′. Although it can be described as a half-diminished *seventh chord, its function in terms of *harmonic analysis has been a matter of dispute.

Tristan Schalmei [Ger.]. A shawm pitched in F built by the firm of Wilhelm Heckel to play the part of the shepherd's pipe at the opening of act 3 of Wagner's *Tristan und Isolde.* See also Heckelclarina.

Tristan und Isolde. Opera ("music drama") in three acts by Wagner (to his own "poem," based on Gottfried von Strassburg), composed between 1856 and 1859 and produced in Munich in 1865. Setting: aboard a ship, Cornwall, and Brittany, in legendary times.

Triste. (1) [Fr., Sp.] Sad. (2) [Sp.] A love song of sad character found in Peru and Argentina, closely related to the Andean **yaraví.* The *triste* is slow, varied in meter, and often with an alternating or concluding section in faster tempo. D.S.

Tristropha [Lat.]. See Neume.

Trite [Gr.]. See Greece I, 3 (i).

Tritone [Lat. *tritonus*]. An interval consisting of three whole tones; hence, the augmented fourth (e.g., f–b) or, because in equal temperament the inversion of this interval yields an interval of the same size, the diminished fifth (e.g., b–f′). It has been regarded as a dissonance since the Middle Ages, when it was nicknamed the *diabolus in musica* (the devil in music) and was the object of prohibitions by theorists [see also *Mi-fa, Musica ficta,* Hexachord]. Its presence as an interval formed with the final (f) of the fifth or Lydian *mode led in the course of the Middle Ages to the regular addition of B♭'s to that mode. Its role as a dissonance in tonal music has been principally as part of the dominant *seventh chord, in which it represents the fourth and seventh scale degrees, both of which are separated from members of the tonic triad by only a semitone and thus account for a considerable measure of the force of the progression from dominant seventh to tonic. Because it divides the octave precisely in half and is thus its own inversion, the sound itself may function in two different ways that depend on context. For example, F and B may be part of a dominant seventh chord on G and resolve to E and C, respectively, as part of C major. Spelled E♯ and B, however, these same pitch classes may be part of a dominant seventh on C♯ and resolve to F♯ and A♯, respectively, as part of F♯ major. It is because the diminished seventh chord consists of two tritones equidistant from one another that such a chord is able to serve a cadential function equally well in four different keys. The tritone is also a prominent element in the whole-tone scale, and its symmetry with respect to the octave gives it a special role in *twelve-tone music as well.

Trittico, Il [It., The Triptych]. A cycle of three independent one-act operas by Puccini, first produced in New York in 1918. (1) *Il tabarro* (The Cloak), libretto by Giuseppe Adami, after Didier Gold's play *La Houppelande.* Setting: a barge on the Seine, early in the 20th century. (2) *Suor Angelica* (Sister Angelica), libretto by Giovacchino Forzano. Setting: a convent in Italy at the end of the 17th century. (3) *Gianni Schicchi,* libretto by Giovacchino Forzano, developed from a few lines in Dante's *Inferno,* canto 30. Setting: a bedroom in a house in Florence in 1299.

Tritus [Lat.]. See Mode.

Triumphes of Oriana, The. A collection of 25 English madrigals in five and six voices by Morley, Weelkes, and 21 others, in praise of Elizabeth I and published by Thomas Morley in 1601 (ed. in *EMS* 32). Each piece concludes with the line "Long live fair Oriana," a feature modeled on the Italian collection *Il trionfo di Dori* of 1592.

Trobairitz. A woman who composed lyric songs in Old Occitan (sometimes called Old Provençal) in the Midi, including Languedoc and Provence, between about 1180 and 1260; female counterpart to a *troubadour. The feminine word *trobairitz,* derived like the masculine noun *trobador* from the verb *trobar,* meaning to find or to compose, is found in only one medieval source, the 13th-century romance *Flamenca.* There are at least 20 *trobairitz* named as authors in 13th-century manuscripts of Occitan song, and some 32 songs are attributed to them.

The tone of the poetry of the *trobairitz* is generally more personal and direct than that of the male troubadours. *Trobairitz* tend to express emotions—both good and bad—more intensely; they provide a glimpse of the personalities of real women that belies some of the stereotyped images of the cold or frivolous lady found in male-voiced poems.

The best-known *trobairitz* is referred to in the sources only as the Comtessa de Dia. Her identity is uncertain, but most scholars accept the hypothesis that she was Beatriz, daughter of Count Isoard II of Dia, which would date her work to the late 12th and early 13th century. Four **cansos,* or love songs, are attributed in the manuscripts to the Comtessa, and one of them—the only one by a *trobairitz*—"A chanter m'er de so qu'eu no volria," survives with music. Other named *trobairitz* include Castelloza (who also left behind four poems), Gormonda de Monpeslier, Clara d'Anduza, Bietris de Roman, Azalais de Porcairagues, Maria de Ventadorn, Lombarda, and Alamanda. Very little is known for certain about these authors, for most of whom only one song survives.

There were women among the *trouvères as well, and although fewer names survive, more of the songs of these *troveresses* survive with music. Blanche de Castille, wife of Louis VII and mother of Louis IX (Saint Louis), who was credited with a devotional chanson and was a participant in a **jeu-parti* with Thibaut de Champagne; Maroie de Diergnau, who exchanged a *jeu-parti* with a Dame Margot; Dame de Gosnai, who was listed as a member of the **puy* (trouvère confraternity) of Arras in the 13th century; and the Duchesse de Lorraine—possibly identified as Marguerite de Champagne, the daughter of the famed trouvère Thibaut IV—who composed a **plainte* mourning the loss of her lover, and a *chanson de malmariée.*

In both the Occitan and the French repertoires there are many anonymous songs whose subjects are in the feminine voice, and it is likely that at least some of them were composed by women who either did not take, or were not given, credit for their work.

Bibl.: *Editions.* Angelica Rieger, ed., *Trobairitz: Der Beitrag der Frau in der altokzitanischen höfischen Lyrik: Edition des Gesamtkorpus* (Tübingen: Niemeyer, 1991). Matilda Tomaryn Bruckner, Laurie Shepard, and Sarah White, eds., *Songs of the Women Troubadours: An Edition and Translation* (New York: Garland, 1995). Eglal Doss-Quinby et al., eds., *Songs of the Women Trouvères,* with Eng. translations and music (New Haven: Yale U Pr, 2001).

Literature. Meg Bogin, *The Women Troubadours* (New York: Paddington, 1976). William D. Paden, ed., *The Voice of the Trobairitz: Perspectives on the Women Troubadours* (Philadelphia: U of Pa Pr, 1989). Elizabeth Aubrey, *The Music of the Troubadours* (Bloomington: Ind U Pr, 1996). E.A.

Trochee, trochaic. See Prosody.

Trojans, The. See *Troyens, Les.*

Tromba [It.]. Trumpet; *t. a macchina (ventile),* valved trumpet; *t. bassa,* bass trumpet; *t. da tirarsi, t. spezzata,* slide trumpet.

Tromba marina [It., marine trumpet or trumpet marine; Fr. *trompette marine;* Ger. *Nonnengeige, Trumscheit*]. A one-stringed, bowed instrument, common in Europe from the 15th through the 18th century. In its most developed form it was about two meters long with a narrow, slightly tapered sound box; the bridge had one leg shorter than the other so that it vibrated against the instrument's belly. The *tromba marina* was held at an angle away from the player and bowed near the upper end. The string was not stopped but touched lightly below the bow to produce *harmonics. The vibration of the bridge amplified the clear tone of the harmonics to produce a trumpetlike sound. Some late examples were fitted with sympathetic strings inside the sound box and with a *guidon,* a device for increasing and decreasing the vibration of the bridge, thus changing the timbre. It enjoyed a vogue in the late 17th century, when sonatas, suites, and many arrangements were written for it. The origin of its name is not known. See ill. under Violin.

Bibl.: Cecil Adkins, "New Discoveries in the Development of the Trumpet Marine," *Copenhagen,* 1972, pp. 221–27. Id. and Alis Dickinson, "A Trumpet by Any Other Name: Towards an Etymology of the Trumpet Marine," *JAMS* 8 (1982): 5–15.

Trombone [Fr., It.; Ger. *Posaune;* Sp. *trombón*]. A long, narrow brass instrument with tube ends folded to overlap in the center. One resulting U-shaped section is a cylindrical telescoping slide that begins with a mouthpiece. The other section is more conical and ends with an expanded opening or bell. About one-third of the tube length is conical, the rest cylindrical. Trombones are used in European and U.S. symphony orchestras and bands as well as in many types of jazz and popular music. They are most often made of brass (sometimes plated with nickel or silver), but have also been made of German silver and, more rarely, of copper. Special chromium alloys are now used in the slide to lessen friction. See ill. under Brass instruments.

The most common trombone is a tenor instrument in B♭ (fundamental note B♭$_1$) folded to about 1.2 m in length with approximately 2.75 m (9 ft.) of tubing. The slide when extended provides enough additional length to lower the pitch of the instrument by up to six half-steps. The seven harmonic series of pitches [see Harmonics (1)] made possible by these seven positions (including the first or fully retracted position) together provide every chromatic note from low E to b♭′ and, depending on the player's ability, above as high as f″. Other sizes of trombone, although not often used today, include the soprano or treble in B♭, alto in F or E♭, bass in G$_1$, bass in F$_1$ or E♭$_1$ (*Quart-* or *Quintposaune*), and contrabass in B♭$_2$. The longer slides of old bass trombones in G$_1$, F$_1$, and E♭$_1$ usually have a hinged handle so that the lower positions can be reached. The extra-long tubing necessary for the contrabass is usually arranged in a double slide and in extra loops before the bell. Bass trombones are now made with the same tube length as the tenor but with a larger bore and one or two valves, which add enough tubing to lower the pitch a fourth to a sixth. Since the invention of the valve, trombones having valves and no slide have also been made. Valve trombones are more agile than the slide instruments but cannot match them in intonation or tone quality.

The mouthpiece of the trombone is a moderately

Range.

deep cup with pronounced but rounded shoulders joining the bore. The sound of the tenor instrument in its most characteristic range (E to b♭′) is bright with overtones and penetrating. The upper register to d″ and above is more mellow and increasingly difficult, while the low fundamentals or pedal tones from $B♭_1$ lower can tend to rattle. The addition of one or two valves allows production of the pitches from E♭ down to the fundamentals. On larger-bore bass trombones these can be full round tones.

Music for tenor or bass trombone is written at concert pitch in the bass clef, switching freely to the tenor clef (c′ fourth line) for higher passages. Alto trombone parts are most often written in the alto clef (c′ center line).

The earliest evidence suggests that trombones first appeared in southern France or northern Italy sometime in the 15th century. Their ancestry, though vague, probably lies with the longer medieval trumpet, the *buisine* or *tromba.* A larger *tromba* in Italian was a *trombone,* while *buisine* gradually through varied spellings probably became *Posaune* in German. Spanish *(sacabuche)* and French *(saqueboute)* origins are suggested for the English term sackbut, thought to mean literally draw pipe, draw out, or push-pull. By the 16th century, the trombone was well established in England and on the Continent, and Nuremberg, Germany, had become a center of trombone making. The earliest surviving trombones are by Erasmus Schnitzer (Nuremberg, 1551) and Jörg Neuschel (Nuremberg, 1557). The first half of the 17th century is represented by many more surviving specimens as well as by good written descriptions by Michael Praetorius, Marin Mersenne, and Daniel Speer.

Trombones of the 16th and 17th centuries are surprisingly similar to modern instruments. Not only are the basic proportions the same, but they were made in the same sizes, with the tenor in B♭, then as now, being the most common member of the family. The bell was not flared as widely, loose stays with hinged clasps held the instrument together, and the slide may not have worked as freely. But a modern performer would have little difficulty understanding the instrument and negotiating parts written for it. During this period, trombones were regular members of town and court bands. With cornetts they were the principal instruments used to support singing in many churches and were most effectively used in works of Giovanni Gabrieli and Schütz.

During the 18th century, the trombone received a more widely flared bell, and loose stays were replaced by firmly soldered braces. The earlier part of that century also saw a general decline in the use of the instrument. But this trend was reversed later in the century when military bands found the trombone useful and when its ecclesiastical and supernatural associations drew it into the opera orchestras of Gluck and Mozart.

In the late 18th and early 19th centuries, some communities of Moravian immigrants in the U.S. used the trombone choir extensively for community and religious activities. Until the invention of the valve, trombones and some slide trumpets were the only brass instruments capable of performing the parts of a chorale. The trombone also found specialized use in Belgian and French military bands, where grotesque dragon heads—sometimes with rattling tongues—replaced the usual bell. This type of instrument was called a *buccin,* possibly after the early Roman instrument of that name.

By the 1830s, valve instruments flourished in most military bands. The valve trombone without slide was made as early as the late 1820s, and F valve attachments for the tenor slide instrument were invented by 1839. In the U.S., slide trombones with bells pointing to the rear over the player's shoulder were in use by the late 1830s.

Slide trombones in alto, tenor, and bass sizes were regular members of the symphony orchestra by the mid-1800s, though even then the alto part was sometimes played on a tenor. The use of a larger-bore B♭ trombone with valve attachment to F or E♭ bass instead of the regular bass trombone began in Germany in the early 20th century. This, together with the neglect of the alto, led to the present practice of using two B♭ tenor instruments and a B♭/F or E♭ bass trombone for the usual three orchestral parts. The second and often the first player may also have a valve attachment to F because of its technical advantage as an alternate to the lower slide positions. The soprano trombone was revived briefly in the early 20th century for dance-band and novelty use, but was not very successful. The B♭ tenor trombone, however, has been a staple of jazz throughout its history.

Bibl.: Robin Gregory, *The Trombone: The Instrument and Its Music* (London: Faber, 1973). Anthony Baines, *Brass Instruments* (London: Faber, 1976). Harry J. Arling, *Trombone Chamber Music: An Annotated Bibliography* (Nashville: Brass Pr, 1978). Philip Bate, *The Trumpet and Trombone: An Outline of Their History, Development, and Construction,* 2nd ed. rev. (New York: Norton, 1978). Thomas G. Everett, *Annotated Guide to Bass Trombone Literature* (Nashville: Brass Pr, 1978). David M. Guion, *The Trombone: Its History and Music, 1697–1811* (New York: Gordon & Breach, 1988). G. B. Lane, *The Trombone: An Annotated Bibliography* (Lanham, Md.: Scarecrow, 1999). R.E.E.

Trommel [Ger.]. *Drum; *Trommelschlegel,* drumstick.

Trommelbass [Ger., drum bass]. A bass part, common in music of the mid-18th century, in which single pitches are persistently repeated.

Trompete [Ger.], **trompette** [Fr.]. Trumpet; *trompette à coulisse,* slide trumpet; for *t. en chamade,* see *Chamade.*

Trompetengeige [Ger.]. **Tromba marina.*

Tronca [It.]. Cut off, accented.

Trop [Fr.]. Too much.

Troparion [Gr.]. See Byzantine chant.

Troparium [Lat.]. *Troper.

Trope [Lat. *tropus*]. In the Middle Ages, a generic term for a variety of musical interpolations and sung commentaries upon the *proper and *ordinary chants of the Mass, and, although with far less frequency, upon the great responsories of the Divine *Office. Tropes for the proper of the Mass include both textual and musical introductions and/or intercalations to the introit, offertory, and communion chants and, in the case of the introit, to psalm verses and doxologies as well. Proper tropes relate to themes of particular feasts as well as to the liturgical purposes of the particular genre of chant they decorate and explain. These may be contrasted with the tropes for the ordinary of the Mass, that is, for the Kyrie, Gloria, Sanctus, Agnus Dei, and Ite missa est. These tropes serve primarily to explicate liturgical sense and relate secondarily to particular feasts and seasons; some early examples within the ordinary trope repertories are thought to have been composed in conjunction with the chants themselves. Tropes are categorized in two ways: (1) more specifically by the kinds of chants with which they function (e.g., introit tropes or Sanctus tropes), and in these categories the tropes are seen as controlled by the style of the "parent" chant; and (2) more generally by the ways in which they introduce, ornament, or explain the proper or ordinary chants with which they are associated. This second way of categorizing tropes employs the following categories:

1. Addition of melody alone. Wordless melismas were on occasion added to the ends of phrases of various Mass chants, such as the Introit or Gloria. The most important of these was the very long melisma added to the repetition of the Alleluia after its verse [see Sequence].

2. Addition of words to a preexisting melody. Texts were often added to the melismatic sections of both ordinary and proper chant melodies, and these additions are commonly called *prosulae.* Because such texts are generated by the structure of the melodies to which they are set, they are termed *melogenous.*

3. Addition of both words and music, commonly called *logogenous.* This category contains by far the largest number of tropes, and some scholars apply the term trope to this situation exclusively. Tropes of this sort are powerfully exegetical and serve to explain and comment upon both the chants they ornament and the liturgical meanings of any given chant genre.

It is assumed that the first tropes were born in the late 8th or early 9th century, when the fusion of liturgical and musical materials that produced the Gregorian repertory began to supplant local practices in many European regions. Just as the Carolingian reforms inspired liturgical commentators—the greatest of whom was Amalarius of Metz—they also inspired the tropes, which served to explain and promote the Gregorian texts and their music. It appears that the art of troping occasionally allowed for the preservation of liturgical styles and even specific texts and melodies that were otherwise dying. The debates surrounding its origins have produced something of a consensus: the first centers of trope composition were in northern Europe and diffusion through oral traditions and the production of *libelli* (booklets) spread a core repertory outward from the centers to other regions, where many local elements were added and the repertories were eventually anthologized. The nature of the repertories is further complicated because each genre of trope relates to the chant it ornaments in a unique way and each of these genres has its own history, depending upon region. Thus, the manuscript tradition allows for no overriding system of affiliation, and the relationships between pieces and families of pieces cannot be forced into stemmata. Rather it seems that the tropes existed in each region in an oral tradition long enough to become independent of points of origin, and that copying tropes from libelli into compendia organized according to the church year happened only gradually and took more than a century. The earliest of the surviving large trope collections found in Paris, B.N.lat. 1240, has been dated by internal evidence to the fourth decade of the 10th century and associated with the Basilica of the Holy Savior in Limoges. This source, like the first tropers from St. Gall (St. Gall 484 and 381), reflects the use of small collections in its preparation.

Repertorial problems were long exacerbated by the way tropes were collected and studied in the late 19th and early 20th centuries. The *Analecta Hymnica,* the standard repository of medieval hymn, sequence, trope, and other non-Gregorian liturgical texts, contains only tropes written purely in verse, and ignores various important layers of the repertory, such as the southern Italian proper tropes. The standard reference work on the trope manuscripts compiled by Heinrich Husmann includes only books that are "troper/prosers"; a second volume that was to include other sources, including tropes and sequences, was never completed. If the texts of the tropes were poorly served, the situation was even worse for trope music. There were no editions or even transcriptions of trope repertories until the work of Günther Weiss and Paul Evans in the second half of the 20th century. In recent decades all this has changed: the *Corpus Troporum,* a team of scholars from Sweden, has produced critical editions of both proper and ordinary trope texts. These editions include evaluations of sources as well as discussions of various genres of tropes. In addition the *Corpus Troporum* has sponsored several symposia whose published papers provide interdisciplinary analyses of the tropes and the analytical work of several music historians. As the necessary supplement for these studies, music historians have worked tirelessly to catalog, transcribe, and edit various genres of tropes and regional repertories, and have pushed the study of tropes into the especially neglected areas of southern

Europe. Scholars have also turned their attention to the performance practice of tropes, with attention to the differences between regions, establishing that the tropes were, for the most part, the property of soloists. The massive introit tropes and other proper tropes did not survive the liturgical reforms of the 12th century in most regions, whereas proper tropes were generally more long lived. The "Quem Quaeritis," used in northern Europe as a trope for the introit "Resurrexi" of Easter Sunday, is the most discussed of all tropes [see also Liturgical drama]. The literature on this work is a microcosm for the study of tropes, revealing that the liturgical use of the trope depended upon regionality and that this trope, like all others, is best studied through attention to both texts and music, and to liturgical and regional contexts as well. The tropes, like the sequences, are the counterparts of the liturgical exegesis and other liturgical arts of the late 9th through the later 12th centuries. The work of the future is to explore the ways in which these liturgical arts are interrelated.

Bibl.: Richard Crocker, "The Troping Hypothesis," *MQ* 52 (1966): 183–203. Günther Weiss, ed., *Introitus-Tropen 1: Das Repertoire der südfranzösischen Tropare des 10. und 11. Jahrhunderts* (Kassel, 1970); Paul Evans, *The Early Trope Repertory of Saint Martial de Limoges* (Princeton: Princeton U Pr, 1970). Alejandro Planchart, *The Repertory of Tropes at Winchester* (Princeton: Princeton U Pr, 1977). Ritva Jacobsson, Gunilla Björkvall, Gunilla Iversen, et al., eds., *Corpus Troporum* (Stockholm: Almquist & Wiksell, 1975–). Michel Huglo, *Les Livres de Chant Liturgique,* Typologie des Sources du Moyen Age Occidental 52 (Turnhout: Brepols, 1988). Wulf Arlt and Gunilla Björkvall, eds., *Recherches nouvelles sur les tropes liturgiques: Recueil d'études* (Stockholm: Almquist & Wiksell, 1993). Margot Fassler, "Liturgy and Sacred History in the Twelfth-Century Tympana at Chartres," *Art Bulletin* 75 (1993): 499–520. Alejandro Planchart and John Boe, eds., *Beneventanum troporum corpus,* in 28 vols. (Madison: A-R Editions, 1994–). Eva Louise Lillie and Nils Holger Petersen, eds., *Liturgy and the Arts in the Middle Ages: Studies in Honor of C. Clifford Flanigan* (Copenhagen: Museum Tusculanum, 1996). M.E.F.

Troper [Lat. *troparium*]. A medieval Latin *liturgical book containing *tropes and *sequences as well as various other types of chants and additions to the official liturgy of the Western Church. A very few tropers date from as early as the 10th century—one of the earliest being the *St. Martial troper *F-Pn* lat. 1240—but the number of manuscripts increases significantly after the year 1000. The monasteries of St. Martial de Limoges in southwestern France and of St. Gall in Switzerland preserved particularly large collections of tropers. For the Winchester troper, see Sources 1.

Bibl.: Heinrich Husmann, *Tropen- und Sequenzenhandschriften, RISM,* B/V/1 (1964). P.E.

Tropical [Sp.]. See *Música tropical.*

Tropos [Gr.]. See Greece I, 3 (ii).

Troppo [It.]. Too much; *(ma) non troppo,* (but) not too much.

Tropus [Lat.]. (1) *Mode, octave species. (2) *Trope.

Troubadour. Any of the poet-musicians of Occitania, the area from Aquitaine and Limousin south through Languedoc, Catalonia, and Provence (southern France and northeastern Spain), who composed and performed songs between about 1100 and 1300. Their language was Old Occitan (*langue d'oc,* sometimes called Old Provençal), a Romance language closely related to Catalan and sister to Old French, the language of the *trouvères. The Occitan word *trobador* derives from the verb *trobar,* meaning to find or to compose.

Among the antecedents of these vernacular songs, and possibly influential in their development, were the *kharjas* of Mozarabic poets in the Iberian Peninsula. But the songs of the troubadours are so diverse, expressive, and numerous that they are viewed as the earliest significant repertoire of vernacular lyric song in Europe. They were imitated by the trouvères, the *Minnesinger,* and the composers of the Old Portuguese *cantigas de Santa Maria* and the Italian *laude spirituale.*

The troubadours developed the poetic aesthetic of *fin' amors* [Occ., refined or true love]—in simple terms, erotic longing or desire. Sometimes misleadingly called courtly love, this desire was not restricted to aristocratic settings but embraced all classes and myriad social situations, and it was expressed by both men and women. It was sometimes satisfied in the poetry, sometimes not. It is the theme of the most important genre, the **canso,* and also underlies the more narrative and light-hearted **pastorela,* the *planh* or lament, the dawn-song *(*alba),* the extended **lais* and *descorts,* dialogue forms *(*tenso, *partimen),* and sometimes even the poems of political or social satire *(*sirventes).*

The first troubadours were concentrated in the western regions of Poitou, Limousin, and Auvergne, an area that also saw the rise of polyphony and the development of Latin lyric song, the *versus* associated with the monastery of St. Martial in Limoges. Although its exact nature has not been fully explained, there was no doubt some connection between the troubadours' songs and this Latin repertoire. The first known troubadour was Guilhem de Peitieus (1071–1126), seventh count of Poitiers and ninth duke of Aquitaine, only a fragment of whose music survives. Early troubadours for whom some music has been preserved include Jaufre Rudel (fl. 1125–48), Marcabru (fl. 1129–49), Rigaut de Berbezilh (fl. 1140–1162), and Bernart de Ventadorn (fl. 1147–80). Between about 1160 and 1210 the art of the troubadours expanded into Provence and Catalonia, and a golden age began that included works by Giraut de Bornelh (fl. 1160–1200), Berenguier de Palol (fl. 1160–1209), Gaucelm Faidit (fl. 1170–1202), Folquet de Marseille (fl. 1179–95), who became bishop of Toulouse and ceased composing songs in 1195 (d. 1231), and Peire Vidal (fl. 1183–1205).

Women *(*trobairitz)* also composed songs, and poetry by at least 20 of them survives, including several by the Comtessa de Dia (fl. end of the 12th century), who was possibly Beatriz, daughter of Count Isoard II of Dia. One of her melodies survives.

The Albigensian Crusade of 1209–29, called to eliminate the Catharist heresy widespread in the Midi, brought much economic and social devastation to the entire region. To escape its effects many troubadours migrated to France, Italy, and Spain. The turmoil eventually led to a decline in the art of the troubadours. Languedoc and Provence were finally subsumed under the French monarchy in 1271. Troubadours who continued composing during and after the Crusade include Peirol (fl. 1185–1221), Raimon de Miraval (fl. 1185–1229), and Guiraut Riquier (fl. 1250–92).

More than 2,500 troubadour poems are extant, but only 246 of these, by 42 composers, survive with music. Of these, 51 are preserved with two or more musical readings. Most of the songs have monophonic melodies that are repeated for each strophe of the poem; they range in texture from syllabic to quite melismatic. They are largely through-composed, often with irregularly repeated phrases; many of them have the structure ABAB*x*, with the first two musical phrases repeated before concluding with unrepeated phrases—a scheme much more common among the melodies of the northern trouvères.

There are more than 30 major sources of troubadour poetry, but only four manuscripts preserve melodies. Two of these are important French sources of trouvère songs: Paris, Bibliothèque nationale de France, fonds français 844 (MS *W,* also known as trouvère MS *M*) and 20050 (MS *X,* also known as trouvère MS *U*); the largest source of troubadour melodies was copied in Languedoc at the end of the 13th century: Paris, Bibliothèque nationale de France, fonds français 22543 (MS *R*); another late source was produced in Italy: Milan, Bibl. Ambr. R 71 *sup.* (MS *G*).

All four manuscripts employ chant notation that gives scant indication of rhythm. This paucity of evidence has generated much controversy since the early 20th century. The earliest theory involved the application of rhythmic modes, but in recent years other theories have been advanced, including one postulating a declamatory delivery dependent on the flow of the words and the poetry; the isosyllabic theory, according to which each syllable receives roughly the same time value; and more flexible views that depend on analysis of each individual reading.

There has also been considerable debate over whether instrumental accompaniment was used and, if so, what its nature was. The manuscripts and other medieval sources offer little concrete evidence on this subject, but because the poetry was central to the songs, any use of instruments was probably simple and unobtrusive.

Bibl.: *Facsimiles.* Jean Beck and Louise Beck, eds., *Le Manuscrit du Roi, fonds français no. 844 de la bibliothèque nationale* (Philadelphia: U of Pa Pr, 1938). Paul Meyer and Gaston Raynaud, eds., *Le Chansonnier français de Saint-Germain-des-Prés (Bibl. Nat. fr. 20050)* (Paris: Société des Anciens Textes Français, 1892; R: New York: Johnson Reprints, 1968).

Editions. Friedrich Gennrich, *Der musikalische Nachlass der Troubadours,* 3 vols. (Darmstadt, 1958–65). Ismael Fernández de la Cuesta and Robert Lafont (text editor), *Las cançons dels trobadors* (Tolosa: Institut d'estudis occitans, 1979). Hendrik van der Werf and Gerald A. Bond (text editor), *The Extant Troubadour Melodies* (Rochester, N.Y., 1984). Matilda Tomaryn Bruckner, Laurie Shepard, and Sarah White, eds., *Songs of the Women Troubadours* (New York: Garland, 1995). Samuel Rosenberg, Margaret Switten, and Gérard Le Vot, *Songs of the Troubadours and Trouvères* (New York: Garland, 1998).

Literature. Jean-Baptiste Beck, *Die Melodien der Troubadours* (Strassburg: K J Trübner, 1908). Pierre Aubry, *Trouvères et troubadours* (Paris: F Alcan, 1909; 2nd ed., 1910). Alfred Pillet and Henry Carstens, *Bibliographie der troubadours* (Halle: M Niemeyer, 1933). Alfred Jeanroy, *La Poésie lyrique des troubadours,* 2 vols. (Toulouse: Privat, 1934). Ugo Sesini, "Le melodie trobadoriche nel canzoniere della Biblioteca Ambrosiana R 71 *sup,*" *Studi medievali* 12 (1939): 1–101; 13 (1940): 1–107; 14 (1941): 31–105. Alois R. Nykl, *Hispano-Arabic Poetry and Its Relations with the Old Provençal Troubadours* (Baltimore: J H Furst, 1946). István Frank, *Répertoire métrique de la poésie des troubadours,* 2 vols. (Paris: Champion, 1953, 1957). Raffaello Monterosso, *Musica e ritmica dei trovatori* (Milan: Giuffrè, 1956). Robert H. Perrin, "Some Notes on Troubadour Melodic Types," *JAMS* 9 (1956): 12–18. Bruno Stäblein, "Zur Stilistik der Troubadour-Melodien," *AM* 38 (1966): 27–46. Peter Dronke, *Medieval Latin and the Rise of European Love-Lyric,* 2 vols., 2nd ed. (Oxford: Clarendon Pr, 1968). Alan R. Press, ed. and trans., *Anthology of Troubadour Lyric Poetry* (Austin: U of Tex Pr, 1971). Hendrik van der Werf, *The Chansons of the Troubadours and Trouvères: A Study of the Melodies and Their Relation to the Poems* (Utrecht: A Oosthoek, 1972). Frederick Goldin, *Lyrics of the Troubadours and Trouvères* (Garden City, N.Y.: Anchor Bks, 1973). Ewald Jammers, *Aufzeichnungsweisen der einstimmigen ausserliturgischen Musik des Mittelalters* (Cologne: A Volk, 1975). Martín de Riquer, *Los trovadores: Historia literaria y textos,* 3 vols. (Barcelona: Planeta, 1975) [includes discography]. Ian Parker, "The Performance of Troubadour and Trouvère Songs: Some Facts and Conjectures," *EM* 5 (1977): 184–207. Robert A. Taylor, *La littérature occitane du moyen âge: Bibliographie sélective et critique* (Toronto: U of Toronto Pr, 1977). Christopher Page, *Voices and Instruments of the Middle Ages: Instrumental Practice and Songs in France, 1100–1300* (Berkeley: U of Cal Pr, 1986). John Stevens, *Words and Music in the Middle Ages: Song, Narrative, Dance and Drama, 1050–1350* (Cambridge: Cambridge U Pr, 1986). Elizabeth Aubrey, "References to Music in Old Occitan Literature," *AM* 61 (1989): 110–49. F. R. P. Akehurst and Judith M. David, eds., *A Handbook of the Troubadours* (Berkeley: U of Cal Pr, 1995). Margaret Switten, *Music and Poetry in the Middle Ages: A Guide to Research on French and Occitan*

Song, 1100–1400 (New York: Garland, 1995). Elizabeth Aubrey, *The Music of the Troubadours* (Bloomington: Ind U Pr, 1996). Geneviève Brunel-Lobrichon and Claudie Duhamel-Amado, *Au temps des troubadours, XIIe–XIIIe siècles* (Paris: Hachette, 1997). Elizabeth Aubrey, "The Dialectic between Occitania and France in the Thirteenth Century," *EMH* 16 (1997): 1–53. Simon Gaunt and Sarah Kay, eds., *The Troubadours: An Introduction* (Cambridge: Cambridge U Pr, 1999). Elizabeth Aubrey, "Genre as a Determinant of Melody in the Songs of the Troubadours and the Trouvères," in *Medieval Lyric: Genres in Historical Context,* ed. William D. Paden (Urbana: U of Ill Pr, 2000), pp. 273–96. Elizabeth Aubrey, "Non-liturgical Monophony: Introduction" and "Non-liturgical Monophony: Occitan," in *A Performer's Guide to Medieval Music,* ed. Ross W. Duffin (Bloomington: Ind U Pr, 2000), pp. 105–14, 122–33. E.A.

Trough zither. A *zither in which a single string is laced a variable number of times across the opening of a wooden trough or bowl and plucked. It is found in Central and East Africa.

Trout Quintet. Popular name for Schubert's Quintet in A major op. 114, D. 667 (1819), for violin, viola, cello, double bass, and piano, in five movements, the fourth being a set of variations on his song "The Trout" [Ger. "Die Forelle"] D. 550a–e (several versions, ca. 1817–21).

Trouvère. Any of the poet-musicians of France—mainly north of the Loire—who composed songs in the Old French language from the late 12th through the late 13th century. The trouvères modeled their songs initially on those of the *troubadours of Languedoc and Provence in the south, whose songs in Old Occitan (sometimes called Old Provençal) established a new style of vernacular lyric poetry. The word *trouvère,* analogous to Occitan *trobador,* derives from the verb *trouver,* to find or to compose.

Although the languages differed, cross-fertilization between north and south was an inevitable result of several circumstances: (1) the development of Latin lyric poetry in Limousin that paralleled the rise of troubadour song in Occitan, which probably also spawned the development of lyric poetic forms in the northern vernacular; (2) the influence of patrons like Aliénor d'Aquitaine (1122–1204)—granddaughter of the first troubadour, Guilhem IX de Peitieus (Poitou), wife first of Louis VII of France and then of Henry II of England, and mother of Richard Coeur-de-Lion (d. 1199, a poet-composer himself)—who evidently encouraged the careers of several troubadours and trouvères; (3) the migration of troubadours to the north after the opening of the Albigensian Crusade in the early 13th century (see *troubadour).

The earliest trouvères—including Blondel de Nesle (fl. 1175–1210), Gautier de Dargies (fl. 1190–1236), Gontier de Soignies (fl. 1180–1220), and the Chastelain de Couci (fl. 1170–1203)—practiced their art in the aristocratic courts of Champagne, Picardy, Burgundy, and Paris. Aliénor's daughter Marie, countess of Champagne (1145–98), was a patron of Canon de Béthune (fl. 1180–1219/20) and Gace Brulé (fl. 1179–1212). Several trouvères went on Crusades to the Holy Land during the late 12th and the 13th centuries. This courtly art reached its high point in the first half of the 13th century with the works of Marie's grandson Thibaut IV, count of Champagne and king of Navarre (1201–53).

During the 13th century, cities in Artois and Picardy established poetic fraternities. The most notable of these was the Confrérie des jongleurs et des bourgeois d'Arras. Known as **puys,* some of them were lay societies dedicated to honor the Virgin Mary, who was credited with their miraculous foundation. Other *puys* were professional trade guilds, and some of these organized annual festivals to which trouvères of all classes and from all regions were invited to enter their songs in a competition for prizes. Trouvères who worked within this bourgeois environment, and some of whom were listed on the rolls of the confraternities, included the canon Richard de Fournival (1201–59/60), Guillaume le Vinier (a cleric, fl. 1220–45), Moniot d'Arras (also a cleric, fl. 1213–39), Colin Muset (a **jongleur,* second third of the 13th century), Jehan Bretel (a long-time *prince,* or presiding judge, of the *puy* at Arras, fl. 1245–72), Perrin d'Angicourt (fl. 1245–70), and Gillebert de Berneville (fl. 1246–70). Adam de la Halle (ca. 1240/50–88), the best known of the Artesian trouvères—some sources give him the title *maistre*—composed not only monophonic and polyphonic songs but also Latin motets and theatrical works.

Women also composed songs, although most of them did not take, or were not given, credit for them. One notable *troveresse* was Blanche de Castille (1188–1252), wife of Louis VIII and mother of Louis IX. Two extant songs attributed to her survive, both with music. Another aristocratic *troveresse* was called the Duchesse de Lorraine and was possibly Marguerite de Champagne, daughter of Thibaut IV; she left behind two chansons. Women also participated in the bourgeois environment of Arras; several are listed among members of the confraternity there, and others served as judges during the *puy* competitions.

Although the trouvères drew their inspiration from the troubadours, especially in appropriating the theme of *fin' amors* [Occ., refined or pure love; see *troubadour], their works encompass a much wider variety of genres, from the serious chansons [Occ. **canso*], *sirventois,* laments, crusade songs, and debate songs—especially the **jeu-parti*—adapted from the troubadour repertoire, to more popular indigenous types such as **rotrouenges,* dances, *ballettes,* **estampies,* and simple refrains. Some types, like **pastourelles* and **lais,* borrowed language and style from both aristocratic and popular registers. One often finds short songs and single-line musical "refrains" inserted in the manuscripts of long narrative works. Many of these short phrases are found also in longer songs and motets, and their interpolation into narrative and polyphonic works has been understood as evidence of their currency as popular "ditties."

The music of the trouvères is closely bound up with the development of the *motet, which also was fostered in Arras. Many motets share one or more melodies, texts, or short quotations with extant trouvère songs, and even though the motets remain unattributed in the manuscripts, it seems likely that other trouvères besides Adam de la Halle composed them.

About two-thirds of the roughly 2,130 extant Old French lyric poems have been preserved with melodies; most survive with more than one melodic reading. Stylistically the monophonic songs are similar in many respects to those of the troubadours. In contrast to the somewhat freer forms of the troubadours' melodies, by far the most common form of the melodies of the trouvères is ABAB*x,* wherein the music of the first two phrases is repeated for the next two. Some of the late 13th-century songs, notably by Adam de la Halle, have strict repetition schemes that eventually evolved into the 14th-century *formes fixes,* especially the *virelai* and *rondeau.* A unique collection of monophonic songs in fixed forms, by Jehannot Lescurel, is bound in with the manuscript of the *Roman de Fauvel* of 1316–17 (Paris, Bibliothèque nationale de France, f. fr. 146).

The songs of the trouvères survive in about 22 large manuscripts and dozens of fragmentary sources, the majority of which were produced in Artois, Picardy, Burgundy, or Lorraine during the second half of the 13th century. Several of them (Paris, Bibliothèque nationale de France, f. fr. 844 [MS *M,* also known as troubadour MS *W*], 12615 [MS *T*], 25566 [MS *W*]; Rome, Biblioteca apostolica Vaticana, Reg. lat. 1490 [MS *a*]) include motets, and two (Paris, Bibliothèque nationale de France, f. fr. 844 [MS *M*] and 20050 [MS *U,* also known as troubadour MS *X*]) have significant collections of troubadour songs.

As with the troubadours, there is disagreement about the rhythm of the trouvères' songs and whether they were accompanied by instruments. About 200 of the surviving melodic readings, most of them in Paris, Bibliothèque nationale de France, f. fr. 846 [MS *O*], are in mensural notation. Since the early 20th century some scholars have argued that this circumstance, along with the close connection of the monophonic repertoire with motets, must mean that all trouvère songs were performed with modal rhythms. Others have argued recently that the songs were performed with a free rhythm dependent on the declamation of the text, or that each syllable was given roughly equal duration (isosyllabism). Some scholars argue that songs in a courtly register were performed without instruments, while the popular genres were more likely to be accompanied by instruments and also to have measured rhythms. Others have pointed out the ubiquity of musical instruments in northern French culture and the fluidity of distinctions among genres that makes generalizations about performance practices untenable.

Bibl.: *Facsimiles.* Pierre Aubry, ed., *Le chansonnier de l'Arsenal* (Paris: P Geuthner, 1909–12). Alfred Jeanroy, ed., *Le chansonnier d'Arras* (Paris, 1925). Jean Beck and Louise Beck, eds., *Le chansonnier Cangé: Manuscrit français no. 846 de la Bibliothèque nationale de Paris* (Philadelphia: U of Pa Pr, 1927; R: New York: Broude Bros, 1964) [with transcriptions]. Id., ed., *Le manuscrit du roi: Fonds français no. 844 de la Bibliothèque nationale* (Philadelphia: U of Pa Pr, 1938; R: New York: Broude Bros, 1970). Paul Meyer and Gaston Raynaud, eds., *Le Chansonnier français de Saint-Germain-des-Prés (Bibl. Nat. fr. 20050)* (Paris: Société des Anciens Textes Français, 1892; R: New York: Johnson Reprints, 1968).

Editions. Hendrik Van der Werf, *Trouvères-Melodien,* 2 vols., *MMMA* 11–12 (Kassel: Bärenreiter, 1977–79). Samuel N. Rosenberg and Hans Tischler, eds., *Chanter m'estuet: Songs of the Trouvères* (Bloomington: Ind U Pr, 1981). Hans Tischler, ed., *Trouvère Lyrics with Melodies: Complete Comparative Edition,* 15 vols., Corpus Mensurabilis Musicae 107 (American Institute of Musicology, 1997). Samuel Rosenberg, Margaret Switten, and Gérard Le Vot, eds., *Songs of the Troubadours and Trouvères* (New York: Garland, 1998). Eglal Doss-Quinby et al., eds., *Songs of the Women Trouvères* (New Haven: Yale U Pr, 2001).

Literature. Friedrich Gennrich, *Rondeaux, Virelais und Balladen,* 3 vols. (Dresden, 1921; Göttingen, 1927; Langen, 1963). Hans Spanke, *G. Raynauds Bibliographie des altfranzösischen Liedes neu bearbeitet und ergänzt* (Leiden: E J Brill, 1955). Roger Dragonetti, *La technique poétique des trouvères dans la chanson courtoise* (Brugge: De Tempel, 1960; R: Geneva: Slatkine, 1979). Irénée Marcel Cluzel and Léon Pressouyre, eds., *La poésie lyrique d'oïl: Les origines et les premiers trouvères,* 2nd ed. (Paris: Nizet, 1969). Ulrich Mölk and Friedrich Wolfzettel, *Répertoire métrique de la poésie lyrique française des origines à 1350* (Munich: Fink, 1972). Paul Zumthor, *Essai de poétique médiévale* (Paris: Édit Seuil, 1972). Pierre Bec, *La lyrique française au moyen-âge,* 2 vols. (Paris: A & J Picard, 1977, 1978). Robert White Linker, *A Bibliography of Old French Lyrics* (University, Miss.: Romance Monographs, 1979). Christopher Page, *Voices and Instruments of the Middle Ages: Instrumental Practice and Songs in France, 1100–1300* (Berkeley: U of Cal Pr, 1986). John Stevens, *Words and Music in the Middle Ages: Song, Narrative, Dance and Drama, 1050–1350* (Cambridge: Cambridge U Pr, 1986). Sylvia Huot, *From Song to Book: The Poetics of Writing in Old French Lyric and Lyrical Narrative Poetry* (Ithaca: Cornell U Pr, 1987). Sylvia Huot, "Voices and Instruments in Medieval French Secular Music: On the Use of Literary Texts as Evidence for Performance Practice," *MD* 43 (1989): 63–113. Mark Everist, *French Motets in the Thirteenth Century: Music, Poetry and Genre* (Cambridge: Cambridge U Pr, 1994). Margaret Switten, *Music and Poetry in the Middle Ages: A Guide to Research on French and Occitan Song, 1100–1400* (New York: Garland, 1995). Elizabeth Aubrey, "The Dialectic Between Occitania and France in the Thirteenth Century," *EMH* 16 (1997): 1–53. Elizabeth Aubrey, "Genre as a Determinant of Melody in the Songs of the Troubadours and the Trouvères," in *Medieval Lyric: Genres in Historical Context,* ed. William D. Paden (Urbana: U of Ill Pr, 2000), pp. 273–96. Elizabeth Aubrey, "Non-liturgical Monophony: Introduction" and "Non-liturgical Monophony: French," in *A Performer's Guide to Medi-*

eval Music, ed. Ross W. Duffin (Bloomington: Ind U Pr, 2000), pp. 105–14 and 134–43. See also Troubadour. E.A.

Trovatore, Il [It., The Troubadour]. Opera in four parts by Verdi (libretto by Salvatore Cammarano completed by Leone Emanuele Bardare, based on a play by Antonio García Gutiérrez), produced in Rome in 1853. Setting: Spain, 1409.

Troyens, Les [Fr., The Trojans]. Opera in five acts by Berlioz (libretto by Berlioz, after Virgil's *Aeneid* and a passage in Shakespeare's *The Merchant of Venice,* act 5), composed in 1856–58, revised and enlarged in 1859–60, and divided into two parts in 1863: *La prise de Troie* and *Les troyens à Carthage.* Part 2 was produced in Paris in 1863; the first complete production took place in Karlsruhe, Germany (in German), in 1890. Setting: Troy and Carthage.

Trumpet [Fr. *trompette;* Ger. *Trompete;* It. *tromba;* Sp. *trompeta*]. A soprano brass instrument commonly about 1.4 m (4½ ft.) in tube length, folded twice to a narrow rectangular shape about 35 cm (14 in.) long. A mouth pipe with mouthpiece protrudes from one end of the rectangle, and an expanded opening or bell extends from the other. The center of the rectangle is occupied by three valves and associated extra tubing. The bore of the trumpet is mostly cylindrical, though like the *cornet it expands just before the bell. Most trumpets are now made of brass, either lacquered or plated with silver, nickel, or more rarely gold. Other materials occasionally used besides brass include German silver, copper, silver, and very rarely gold. See ill. under Brass instruments.

Trumpets are commonly available in several sizes named according to the pitch class of their fundamental. Instruments in B♭, C, D, E♭, F, and piccolo B♭ or A have actual fundamentals B♭, c, d, e♭, f, and b♭ or a. The B♭ instrument is used mostly in school bands and popular music. The C trumpet is the favorite among professional orchestra players. The higher trumpets are becoming more common and find use in certain segments of the repertory written for instruments in those keys or demanding an extremely high register. For the latter use, piccolo trumpets are made in a variety of shapes, some (occasionally called Bach trumpets) straight except for the valves and their associated tubing, and some with four rather than three valves. American trumpets are now almost invariably equipped with Périnet piston valves for the right hand, though orchestra players sometimes use instruments with rotary valves. Better-quality instruments also have levers or rings for adjusting the length of the first and third valve tubes [see also Valve].

The trumpet mouthpiece is generally a shallow cupped shape with formerly rather pronounced but recently more rounded corners surrounding the bore or throat. The sound of the instrument is brilliant and commanding in its most characteristic range from written c′ to c‴, gradually less brilliant on the increasingly difficult notes above this range, and more and more dark and grainy on the lower tones to f♯. Special timbres and effects can be produced by using various kinds of *mutes in the trumpet bell [see ill. under Brass instruments].

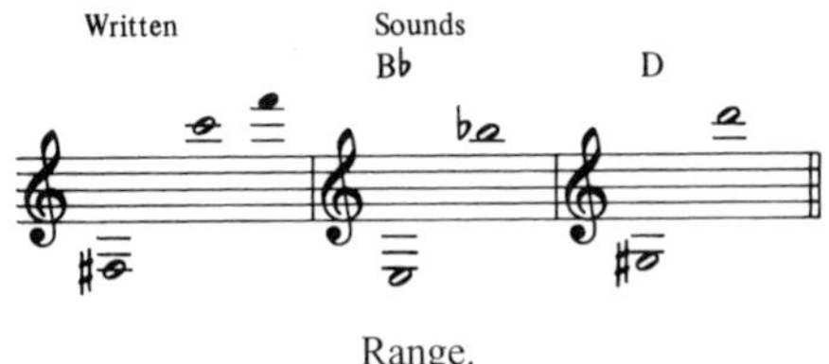

Range.

Most trumpet parts since about 1900 are written either for B♭ trumpet, sounding one tone lower, or for C trumpet at concert pitch. Orchestral parts from earlier periods were written for trumpets that could be put in the appropriate key for the composition to be played by means of crooks (small loops of extra tubing). These parts were commonly in B♭, C, D, E♭, and F, sounding from a tone lower to a fourth higher than written. Some late 19th-century parts were written for trumpets with an extra valve or slide to put them in A, sounding a minor third lower. Orchestra players today usually play all of these parts on B♭ or C instruments, making the necessary transposition as they play.

The trumpet has a very long history, having been used in ancient Egypt, the Near East, and Greece. During much of that time, however, it was a signaling device sounding only one or two tones. Even in the Roman era, trumpetlike instruments, though prominent in art and literature, are not known to have been used in music. They remained instruments of only a few tones for signaling, announcing, commanding, and ceremonial purposes.

It was not until the 14th and 15th centuries that the more musical possibilities of the long trumpet began to be recognized and used, and the instrument acquired its characteristic folded form. The instruments of this period were natural trumpets, on which only the tones of the *harmonic series were available. Evidence exists that toward the end of this period, however, some instruments may have been fitted with a single slide at the mouth pipe, theoretically providing a chromatic scale, except for one pitch, from the fourth harmonic upward. Such an instrument was called a *tromba da tirarsi.*

The 16th century saw increasing use of the trumpet in a variety of more musical situations in addition to court ceremony and military communication. Craftsmen in Nuremberg, Germany, began to excel in trumpet making during this period and supplied instruments to most of Europe. At the end of this century and the beginning of the next, the first written accounts of trumpet playing occur. In these works are found trumpet calls, fanfares, toccatas, and sonatas using mostly the low register of the instrument. Among the later of these writings are the first illustrations of melodic playing on the higher pitches of the harmonic series.

During the 17th and 18th centuries, the natural trumpet reached its peak of development and was used with brilliant effect by Bach, Handel, and many other composers. The instruments were from about 1.8 to 2.5 m (6 to 8 ft.) in total length, folded to traditional form, and pitched usually in D and C for court use and in E♭ and F for the military. Players specialized in different registers, allowing the *clarino* or high-range players to concentrate on the top dozen or so tones where melodic playing is possible. This type of playing reached its zenith in the mid-1700s and gradually declined toward the end of the century. The lower range was called the *principale.*

The orchestral trumpet of the late 18th and the early 19th century was in F, with crooks for lower keys down to C or B♭ to match the key of the composition played. Its sound was not as loud as the modern trumpet's, and it balanced well with other instruments in smaller ensembles. The limitations of an instrument that could play only the tones of the natural harmonic series, however, became gradually more perplexing toward the end of the 18th century and led to a number of attempts to improve the instrument mechanically.

Hand stopping, used on horns since about 1750, was tried on specially constructed trumpets [Ger. *Inventionstrompete*] beginning in the 1770s. The keyed trumpet was tried with limited success by several makers and players in the last 30 years of the century. Four or five keys like those on clarinets of the time provided pitches missing in the natural harmonic series. Concertos by Haydn and Hummel exploited the capabilities of these instruments. The slide trumpet, never completely forgotten since the 15th and 16th centuries, was revived again in England in the late 1700s. The improved slide mechanism was fairly successful in that country throughout the 19th century, and such instruments continued to be made into the 20th century in the U.S. as well.

The most important mechanical improvement, however, was the invention of the *valve for brass instruments about 1814. Valves were very quickly applied to the trumpet, and, although crude at first, were gradually refined until they provided the trumpet with a fairly even chromatic scale. By the mid-19th century, the orchestral trumpet in F had two or three valves instead of the crooks used earlier in the century.

Late in the 19th century, as larger orchestras played for larger audiences, the long F trumpet was finally given up in favor of shorter valved trumpets in B♭ and C. The new instruments were louder, more brilliant, and somewhat easier to play accurately. After the mid-1920s, the trumpet also replaced the cornet in dance bands.

Bibl.: James Murray Barbour, *Trumpets, Horns, and Music* (East Lansing: Mich St U Pr, 1964). Don L. Smithers, *The Music and History of the Baroque Trumpet before 1721* (Syracuse: Syracuse U Pr, 1973). Norbert Carnovale, *Twentieth-Century Music for Trumpet and Orchestra* (Nashville: Brass Pr, 1975). Anthony Baines, *Brass Instruments* (London: Faber, 1976). Linda Farr, *A Trumpeter's Guide to Orchestral Excerpts* (Nashville: Brass Pr, 1977). Philip Bate, *The Trumpet and Trombone: An Outline of Their History, Development, and Construction,* 2nd ed. rev. (New York: Norton, 1978). Edward Tarr, *The Trumpet,* trans. from the German by S. E. Plank and Edward Tarr (London: Batsford, 1988). Don L. Smithers, *The Music and History of the Baroque Trumpet before 1721,* 2nd ed. (Buren: Fritz Knuf, 1988; Carbondale: Southern Ill U Pr, 1988). Edward H. Tarr, "The Romantic Trumpet," *Historic Brass Society Journal* 5 (1993): 213. John Webb, "The English Slide Trumpet," *Historic Brass Society Journal* 5 (1993): 262. Art Brownlow, *The Last Trumpet: A History of the English Slide Trumpet* (Stuyvesant, N.Y.: Pendragon, 1996). Trevor Herbert and John Wallace, eds., *The Cambridge Companion to Brass Instruments* (Cambridge: Cambridge U Pr, 1997). R.E.E.

Trumpet marine. **Tromba marina.*

Trumpet Voluntary. A work often played in an arrangement for trumpet, organ, and drums and misattributed to Purcell. The original is by Jeremiah Clarke (ca. 1674–1707) and survives in a version for harpsichord titled *The Prince of Denmark's March* as well as in a suite for winds. See also Voluntary.

Trumscheit [Ger.]. **Tromba marina.*

Trutruka. A straight trumpet of the Araucanian Indians of southern Chile and Argentina. It is made from a piece of bamboo about 3 m long. A diagonal cut at one end serves as a mouthpiece, and a horn is attached at the other end to form a bell. It is used in rituals, either as a solo instrument or with a drum.

T. s. Abbr. for **tasto solo.*

Tuba. (1) [Lat.] A *trumpet of ancient Rome. A straight tube of bronze or iron, 1.25–1.6 m long, with a slightly flaring bell, it was first and foremost a military instrument, sounding the attack and retreat in battle. In civilian life it was heard in funeral processions, at games and gladiatorial contests, and in religious rituals, particularly sacrifices.

(2) [Lat.] The reciting tone of a *psalm tone.

(3) [Eng., Fr., Ger., It., Sp.] The largest and lowest of the brass instruments, with a widely expanding tube as long as 5.5 m (18 ft.). Tubas are usually wrapped in a rectangular shape about 45 cm wide by 75 cm tall. The narrow end with *mouthpiece points back from high on one side of the rectangular body, while the expanded end or bell rises above the body of the instrument either straight up or, less often, turned forward. Three or four *valves for the right hand are provided. The instrument is commonly used in European and American symphony orchestras as well as in school, community, and military bands. Tubas are usually made of brass or, less often, of German silver. Brass is usually lacquered but is sometimes plated with silver or nickel. In marching bands, circular tubas called

*sousaphones are also common. See ill. under Brass instruments.

Tubas are now made mostly in four sizes, BB♭ (pronounced "double B-flat"), CC, E♭, and F (*fundamental tones B♭$_2$, C$_1$, E♭$_1$, and F$_1$). The first two sizes are the most common, with E♭ a distant third, and F a rather remote last. There are also smaller tubas at baritone or *euphonium pitch. They are commonly used in brass bands as well as in some French orchestras and usually have additional valves for lower notes. A few larger tubas have been made a fifth or even an octave below the BB♭ instrument (11 m in tube length, fundamental tone B♭$_3$), but they have been more curiosities than useful musical instruments.

Tubas are nontransposing bass-clef instruments except in brass bands where occasionally parts are written in treble clef, the B♭ instrument sounding two octaves and a tone lower, the E♭ sounding one octave and a major sixth lower. The most characteristic and dependable range of the BB♭ and CC tubas is from E$_1$ or F♯$_1$ to b♭ or c′. Lower pitches produced by additional valves or as pedal tones are slow to respond, but useful at least down to C$_1$. Upper pitches are increasingly difficult, but useful to f′ or g′ with a good player and careful approach. The smaller tubas in E♭ and F have correspondingly higher ranges, but can often play just as low as the larger ones if provided with additional valves. The tone of these pitches is less full. The smaller tubas are more secure in the upper register, but reach b♭′ or c″ only with great difficulty and thin tone.

The mouthpiece most often used on the tuba is quite deep and is shaped somewhere between a cup and a cone, like a small wine glass. There are usually no pronounced shoulders where the throat begins. The resulting tone is smooth and mellow but with enough edge to give it definition, body, and carrying power.

Tubas belong to the bugle or cornet families [see Brass instruments], instruments having widely expanding bores and round, mellow tone qualities. The earliest examples were bass tubas and **bombardons* in F and E♭ designed and made in Berlin by Wilhelm Wieprecht (1802–72) and Johann Gottfried Moritz (1777–1840, founder of the firm later operated and known by the name of his son C[arl] W[ilhelm] Moritz, 1811–55); the first was patented in 1835. These instruments were the logical result of attempts to complete a choir of valved brasses for use in military bands.

Predecessors of the tuba include a number of bass instruments using side holes to alter their sounding length. The earliest of these is the *serpent, dating from the late 16th century. Late in the 18th century and on into the 19th, a number of improved serpents were built, including the *bass horn, several so-called *Russian bassoons, the keyed serpent, and the *ophicleide. Made of either metal or wood, they were designed for more durability, easier holding, and better intonation.

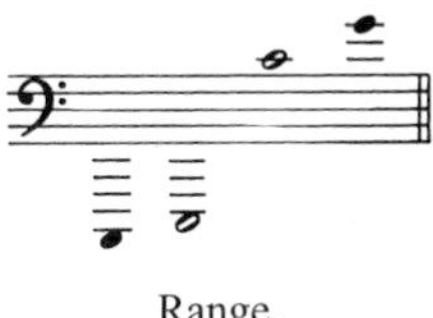

Range.

From Berlin, tuba making spread quickly to Prague, Vienna, and Paris. By the end of the 1840s, the larger sizes in BB♭ and CC had been introduced by Václav František Červený (1819–96) of Königgrätz (now Hradec Králové) near Prague; circular tubas called *helicons or cavalry horns had been designed by Ignaz Stowasser (active ca. 1838–78) of Vienna; and Adolphe Sax (1814–94) of Paris was making his bass *saxhorns in the upright form still most common today. During the 1840s and 1850s many other shapes and styles of tuba were tried. The most successful of these were the over-shoulder models used in the U.S. through Civil War times.

Bibl.: Winston R. Morris, *Tuba Music Guide* (Evanston, Ill.: Instrumentalist, 1973). Anthony Baines, *Brass Instruments* (London: Faber, 1976). Clifford Bevan, *The Tuba Family* (New York: Scribner, 1978). R. Winston Morris and Edward R. Goldstein, eds., *The Tuba Source Book* (Bloomington: Ind U Pr, 1996). Clifford Bevan, *The Tuba Family,* rev. ed. (Winchester: Piccolo, 2000). (3) R.E.E.

Tuba mirabilis [Lat.]. A loud reed stop with full-length, flared resonators, found in English organs.

Tubaphone. An instrument similar to the *glockenspiel, but with a softer sound, being made with metal tubes rather than solid bars.

Tube zither. A wooden or bamboo tube with one or more strings running its length above its surface. It is widely distributed in Africa and Asia. Several strings may be distributed around the circumference of the tube, which acts as a resonator. A common method of construction is to make two slits in a section of bamboo and to insert small wedges under the bamboo "string" thus formed. Other types add strings of silk, fiber, or metal. Tube zithers may be plucked, struck, bowed, or used as *aeolian harps. See also *Bīn, Valiha,* Zither.

Tubular bells [Fr. *cloches tubulaires;* Ger. *Röhrenglocken, Glocken;* It. *campane tubolari;* Sp. *campanólogo*]. A set of metal tubes of varying length, hung vertically in a frame in an arrangement similar to that of the piano keyboard, and struck at the top with one or two rawhide mallets; also called chimes. They are tuned chromatically, usually from c′ to f″, notated at pitch. Their pitch is better defined than that of cup-

Range.

shaped bells. Tubular bells were introduced in the 1880s and have become a standard part of the orchestral percussion section, often being called upon to imitate the sound of church bells. See ill. under Percussion instruments.

Tuck, tucket [possibly fr. Ar. *tuqā,* alarm, or It., Sp., Fr., and Eng. *tocco, toc-toc, toque, tick-tack,* imitation of the sounds of bells or percussion instruments when hit]. A flourish on trumpets and timpani, often used as a fanfare or military signal from the 14th through the 18th century [see also *Tusch,* Toccata (2)]. The earliest usage of the term refers only to drums, e.g., "The dandring drums aloud did tuik" (*Battle of Harlow,* ca. 1513), though it is later encountered frequently as a stage direction upon the entrance of a noble ("Then let the trumpets sound the tucket sonnance," *Henry V,* act 4, scene 2; compare *sennet, used when a group of ordinary people enters or exits). In 17th-century military music, a *tucquet* is a march for trumpets, fifes, and drums. A.J.N.

Tumba [Sp.]. (1) A large, single-headed, Afro-Cuban barrel drum. (2) A dance of Santo Domingo that originated in the 19th century and spread by way of Haiti to eastern Cuba, where it was called the *tumba francesa.*

Tuna [Sp.]. In Spain and several countries of Latin America, a student ensemble of singers and instrumentalists dedicated to the performance of folk and popular song, typically in serenades. Such ensembles are also known as *estudiantinas* or *rondallas.* D.S.

Ṭunbūr [Ar.]. A fretted, long-necked lute with a variable number of strings. In the 10th century, al Fārābī described two types, both with two strings: the *ṭunbūr al baghdādī* (of Baghdad) and the larger *ṭunbūr al khurāsānī* (of Khurāsān). Among instruments still in use, the **buzuq* perhaps derives from the former; the larger *ṭunbūr al turkī* (Turkish), with four strings or double courses, derives from the latter. See also *Tanbur, Bouzouki, Saz.*

Tune. (1) *Melody. (2) To adjust the pitch of an instrument.

Tune book. Psalm and hymn tunes, circulated in printed collections since the early Protestant Reformation. Aimed at a variety of users (e.g., congregations, singing schools, musical societies), these collections were widespread in Great Britain and later in America, where they came to be called tune books. The story of the sacred tune book is properly an Anglo-American one. Yet in early America the singing school and its tune books, providing economic support for musicians and an outlet for composition where no others existed, proved so important to musical life that the American part of the story is told here.

Intended for singing schools, a typical 18th- or 19th-century American tune book is oblong in shape, starts with a didactic introduction, and presents a selection of unaccompanied choral pieces. The first such book, Thomas Walter's *The Grounds and Rules of Musick Explained* (Boston, 1721), followed its introduction with 16 pages of psalm tunes, all of them composed overseas. Although the format changed little thereafter, native-born composers began to emerge after midcentury, and compilers gradually transformed the repertory from a British one to an Anglo-American blend. *Urania* (Philadelphia, 1761), compiled by James Lyon, was the first tune book to declare its inclusion of new (i.e., American) music; William Billings's all-original *The New-England Psalm-Singer* (Boston, 1770) was a creative landmark. By 1790, it was common for American and foreign tunes to appear side by side in tune books. Shortly after 1800, however, a number of compilers criticized such mixtures, touting the refinement and solemnity of European tunes and launching a stylistic reform. (A favorite reform target was the *fuging tune, scorned for the vociferous singing it encouraged.)

In the 19th century, repertory was linked in some regions to a new musical notation. William Little and William Smith's *The Easy Instructor* (Philadelphia, 1801) introduced *shape-notes, which simplified the reading of music by assigning a differently shaped note head to each of the four sol-fa syllables then in use. Ignored in New England and the Northeast, shape-notes caught on in the rural West and South. A pair of tune books issued by Pennsylvania printer John Wyeth suggest the trend. His *Repository of Sacred Music* (Harrisburg, 1810) maintains the blend—including many of the same American pieces—found in earlier New England books. His *Repository of Sacred Music, Part Second* (Harrisburg, 1813) broke new ground by printing folk hymns: melodies from oral tradition, both sacred and secular, harmonized and supplied with new texts. In popular books compiled by many Wyeth successors, these two strains, plus new pieces by local composers, were combined: Ananias Davisson, *Kentucky Harmony* (Harrisonburg, Va., 1816); Allen D. Carden, *Missouri Harmony* (Cincinnati, 1820); William Walker, *Southern Harmony* (compiled in South Carolina, printed in New Haven, 1835); Benjamin Franklin White and E. J. King, *The Sacred Harp* (Philadelphia, 1844, compiled by two Georgians). Meanwhile, in the Northeast, the tune books of composer-compiler Lowell Mason and others dominated the market with a blend of foreign and American music, the latter in a simple idiom with orthodox European harmonies.

As midcentury approached, the didactic part of northeastern tune books was subsumed into public school music programs, while congregational hymnals took over the musical component. In the South and West, the shape-note tune book—sometimes in a variant of the seven-shape system introduced in Jesse Aikin's *Christian Minstrel* (Philadelphia, 1846)—persisted well into the 20th century, maintaining ties with the singing school and with local composers. See also Psalmody, British and North American.

Bibl.: George Pullen Jackson, *White Spirituals in the Southern Uplands* (Chapel Hill: U of NC Pr, 1933; R: 1965). Irving Lowens, *Music and Musicians in Early America* (New York: Norton, 1964). Buell E. Cobb, Jr., *The Sacred Harp* (Athens: U of Ga Pr, 1978). Nicholas Temperley, *The Music of the English Parish Church,* vol. 1 (Cambridge: Cambridge U Pr, 1979). Allen P. Britton, Irving Lowens, and Richard Crawford, *American Sacred Music Imprints, 1698–1810: A Bibliography* (Worcester, Mass.: American Antiquarian Society, 1990). Richard Crawford, "'Ancient Music' and the Europeanizing of American Psalmody, 1800–1810," in *A Celebration of American Music,* ed. Richard Crawford, R. Allen Lott, and Carol J. Oja (Ann Arbor: U of Mich Pr, 1990), pp. 225–55. Nicholas Temperley, *The Hymn Tune Index: A Census of English-Language Hymn Tunes in Printed Sources from 1535 to 1820,* vol. 1 (Oxford: Clarendon, 1998).
R.C.

Tune family. In folk music, a group of tunes presumably derived, through oral tradition, from a single parent tune. Since it is not known whether the original is extant, relationship must be extrapolated from comparative study of similar tunes. All similarity cannot be ascribed automatically to genetic relationship, since it may also result from imitative composition and creation within strict stylistic limits.

Bibl.: Samuel P. Bayard, "Prolegomena to a Study of the Principal Melodic Families . . . ," *Journal of American Folklore* 63 (1950): 1–44. Bertrand H. Bronson, *The Traditional Tunes of the Child Ballads,* vol. 1 (Princeton: Princeton U Pr, 1959).
B.N.

Tuning [Fr. *accord;* Ger. *Stimmung;* It. *accordatura;* Sp. *afinación*]. (1) The act of adjusting the fundamental sounding frequency or frequencies of an instrument, usually in order to bring it or them into agreement with some predetermined pitch. Whether or not two sound sources are in tune depends both on the acoustical identity of their fundamentals and on that of their significant shared upper partials. (Just which and how many partials are significant varies with the sound source.) Thus, a sounding c is potentially in or out of tune with every pitch whose fundamental or upper partials it shares, including C, e♭, f, a, c′, g′, e″, and so on. When two pitches are slightly out of tune, the ear experiences fluctuations in intensity, or *beats. Tuners listen closely to the beats between upper partials, especially those in the range of 100–1600 Hz. Guitarists and some other string players frequently tune by harmonics and thus avoid fundamentals altogether.

Piano tuners begin by inserting felt dampers and rubber wedges so that no more than one string can sound for every pitch on the keyboard. Next they set a *temperament or tuning in some central octave (e.g., f–f′) of the instrument. This central octave is then expanded outward by tuning the octaves of its pitches. Octaves toward the further extremities of the keyboard may be made slightly larger than an acoustically perfect octave. Such octaves are referred to as stretched. Finally, the damping material is removed, and the unison strings are put in tune.

Early accounts of tuning parallel the rise of keyboard instruments and the corresponding interest in temperaments. The writings of Arnolt Schlick, Giovanni Lanfranco, Pietro Aaron, and others in the 16th century are rudimentary and suggest an aural pedagogy that lacked adequate vocabulary. Marin Mersenne's *Harmonie universelle* (Paris, 1636–37) inaugurated the modern era with its very full accounts and its cognizance of the usefulness of upper partials in tuning temperaments. More sophisticated accounts of the relationship between beats and tuning were published by Joseph Sauveur (*Mémoires de l'académie royale des sciences,* 1701 and 1711) and by Rameau in his *Génération harmonique* (Paris, 1737). Stretched octaves were first suggested by Michel Corrette in his *Le maître de claveçin pour l'accompagnement* (Paris, 1753).

(2) Any ordered interval collection all of whose members can be expressed precisely by rational numbers. Interval collections not displaying this property are *temperaments.

The quantification of practical or speculative tuning systems has always been a major preoccupation of music theorists. Of surviving Greek, Hellenistic, and Roman tunings (see Barbour, 1951), the most authoritative for later times was the *Pythagorean, well established in Plato's time and dominant in Europe until ca. 1550. This tuning permits beatless octaves and fifths in a diatonic scale. Many musicians of the 15th century and after preferred one of the several forms of *just intonation. Just tunings mix beatless thirds with beatless fifths and are apt for styles that treat both intervals as harmonic concords. Of the so-called irregular tunings also surviving in Renaissance sources, some favor keyboard idioms of the time. A second group promotes the easy division of a string, thereby aiding demonstrations of the monochord and fretting the neck of an instrument. A third group displays scholastic elegance or ingenuity for its own sake. Other irregular tunings include as many as 53 tones to the octave and permit considerable freedom to keyboard transposition. Appropriate keyboards were built but did not prevail. By ca. 1650, it had been found simpler to retain the now-familiar chromatic arrangement and adopt a temperament instead of a tuning. Although temperaments have flourished ever since, some performers use tunings for early repertory, and among 20th-century composers there was some interest in *just intonation.

Bibl.: (1) William Braid White, *Piano Tuning and Allied Arts,* 4th ed. (Boston: Tuners Supply, 1943) [see esp. table, p. 68]. W. Dean Howell, *Professional Piano Tuning* (Deep River, Conn.: New Era Printing, 1966). Owen Jorgensen, *Tuning the Historical Temperaments by Ear* (Marquette: N Mich U Pr, 1977). Mark Lindley, "Instructions for the Clavier Diversely Tempered," *EM* 5 (1977): 18–23. Herbert A. Kellner, *The Tuning of My Harpsichord* (Frankfurt am Main: Musikinstrument, 1980).

(2) James Murray Barbour, *Tuning and Temperament: A Historical Survey* (East Lansing: Mich St Coll Pr, 1951; 2nd

ed., 1953; R: New York: Da Capo, 1972). Charles Shackford, "Some Aspects of Perception," *JMT* 5 (1961): 162–202; 6 (1962): 66–90, 295–303. Jan Herlinger, "Fractional Divisions of the Whole Tone," *Music Theory Spectrum* 3 (1981): 73–83.

Tuning cone. A tool made of brass, ivory, or other hard material, with one concave and one convex end, used for tuning metal organ pipes.

Tuning fork [Fr. *diapason;* Ger. *Stimmgabel;* It. *corista;* Sp. *diapasón*]. A two-pronged metal fork that sounds a given pitch when struck. Such forks are used to provide reliable pitches (especially a′ = 440 *Hz. [see Pitch, Acoustics]) for tuning instruments and for acoustical experiments. A tuning fork produces a pure, clear sound with few *harmonics, and it retains its pitch over wide ranges of temperature and long periods of time. Its small sound can be amplified by means of a *resonator or simply by pressing the stem against a wooden surface. It is usually said to have been invented in the first half of the 18th century by the English trumpeter John Shore; the date most often cited is 1711, but it has been disputed.

Tuning pin. On the *piano and related instruments, including the harp, a short piece of metal of round cross section at one end, which is fitted into a hole in the pin block, and square or rectangular in cross section at the other, so as to fit into a wrench or "hammer" by means of which it is turned; also termed a wrest pin. Each of the instrument's strings is wrapped around such a pin at one end, and its pitch is adjusted by turning the pin so as to increase or decrease its tension.

Tuning slide. (1) On a brass instrument, a length of tubing, usually U-shaped, that can be made to slide in such a way as to alter the instrument's effective length, thus making it possible to adjust its pitch slightly. (2) An adjustable metal collar fitted to the top of an organ *flue pipe, by means of which the pipe is tuned.

Tuning wire. In an organ *reed pipe, a stiff wire bearing against the reed tongue and projecting above the top of the reed assembly. The wire is moved up or down to lower or raise the pitch. See ill. under Organ.

Tuono [It.]. **Tono.*

Tupan, topan. A large, double-headed cylindrical drum of the Balkans, similar to the Turkish **davul* and likewise played in ensemble with a shawm [see *Zūrnā*].

Turandot. Opera in three acts by Puccini, left unfinished at his death and completed by Franco Alfano (libretto by Giuseppe Adami and Renato Simoni, based on Carlo Gozzi's play of the same name), produced in Milan in 1926. Setting: Peking in legendary times.

Turangalîla Symphony. Symphony in ten movements by Olivier Messiaen. It was commissioned by Serge Koussevitsky for the Boston Symphony and premiered in 1949 with Leonard Bernstein conducting. Its title is made up of two Sanskrit words: *Turanga,* which denotes time, and surging ever onward; and *Lîla,* meaning play. Significantly, its instrumentation includes a large percussion section and an *ondes Martenot.* As its title suggests, Messiaen's symphony incorporates Eastern religious mysticism and music, including chromatic modes based on Hindu ragas and Balinese gamelan.

Turba [Lat., crowd]. In *Passion music, the words spoken by crowds, often set in the works of Bach and others as short, imitative choral movements in a fast tempo; also, such a movement.

Turca, alla [It.]. In the Turkish style, i.e., in the style of *Janissary music.

Turkey. See Near and Middle East.

Turkish crescent [also Jingling Johnny, Chinese pavilion or hat; Fr. *pavillon (chapeau) chinois;* Ger. *Schellenbaum;* It. *mezzaluna, cappello cinese;* Sp. *chinesco, sombrero chino*]. The crescent that was hung with small bells atop a pole seems to be a European adaptation of several Turkish elements (e.g., military standard with horsetail [*tug*] that often preceded the *mehter* [Turkish military band]). Few if any examples of Turkish crescents made before the early 19th century exist, and all extant instruments are of European origin. See ill. under Percussion instruments.

Bibl.: H. Powley, "Janissary Music," in *The Encyclopedia of Percussion,* ed. John H. Beck (New York: Garland, 1995), pp. 195–200.

Turmmusik, Turmsonate [Ger., tower music (sonata)]. In Germany in the 16th through the 18th century, music for brasses, often in four or five parts, played from a tower by town musicians (**Stadtpfeifer*). It included signals of various kinds to mark the hours, harmonized chorales, and more elaborate "sonatas." Published collections include Johann Christoph Pezel's *Hora decima* (Leipzig, 1669) and *Fünff-stimmigte blasende Music* (Frankfurt, 1685; selections from both ed. in *DDT* 63).

Turn [Fr. *double cadence, doublé, tour de gosier;* Ger. *Doppelschlag;* It. *groppo, circolo mezzo, gruppetto;* Sp. *grupeto*]. An ornament that "turns around" the main note. It consists most often of a stepwise descent of three notes beginning with the upper auxiliary, followed by a return to the principal note [Ex. 1]. But there are also "rising turns" and turns that begin with the main note and descend to the third below [Exx. 3a and 2]. The principal note may be prefixed as part of the ornament, and the return may be included as well [Ex. 3b]. If the turn connects a note to one a third higher, the passing note can be added to the ornament. A turn may be added to the beginning, middle, or end of a trill, producing various compound ornaments better considered under *trill.

Turns may come at the beginning, middle, or end of

a note, or they may occupy its whole value; in some cases they may also anticipate the note they are meant to embellish. In each case, they have a different effect. A rapid turn placed at the beginning of a note and starting on the auxiliary gives brilliance and accent, like a *mordent, and was indeed so named by Giuseppe Tartini (1771) and Leopold Mozart (1756). In the middle, it prepares for melodic activity to come; at the end, it connects the note with the one that follows. Turns, usually slower, that occupy the whole value of a note connect the preceding and following notes. Turns seem to have been generally performed in notes of equal value, but C. P. E. Bach (1753) recommended playing the first two notes of a turn beginning on the upper auxiliary faster than the third in slow tempos [Ex. 4].

Various kinds of turns are found written out in 16th-century *diminutions, most often in association with trills. Tomás de Santa María (1565) included several examples under the more general terms *redobles* and *quiebros.* They can be found also among the "figures" in 17th-century German treatises. The first appearance of the turn in a table of signs and terms seems to be in Chambonnières's *Pièces de clavessin* (1670), where it is indicated by the reverse curve that has remained the normal sign ever since [Ex. 2]. The melodic figure itself differs from the norm, however, as shown in the example; the same melodic figure is given by Saint-Lambert (1702) for cases in which the turn is followed by a trill on the same note, while the usual melodic figure is used in other circumstances. The sign for a turn is often placed between the note it embellishes and the following note, showing that the turn is to be delayed until the principal note has sounded for a while; this execution may be desirable even when the sign is over the note [Ex. 5]. In the 18th and increasingly in the 19th century, turns are indicated by small notes or notes of full value. Wagner, who employed this melodic figure often, used the sign in *Rienzi,* but used small or large notes in the late operas. See bibl. under Ornamentation. D.F.

Turns. 2. Chambonnières, *Les pièces de clavessin* (1670). 3. Wagner, *Götterdämmerung.* 4. C. P. E. Bach, *Versuch* (1753). 5. Loulié, *Eléments ou principes de musique* (1696).

Turnaround, turnback. In jazz, generally a one- or two-bar passage occurring at the end of one section of a form leading harmonically or melodically to the next, especially to the repetition of the section or of the entire form, e.g., the repetition of the A section in AABA song forms or the repetition of the 12-bar *blues pattern (in which bar 12 may turn to the dominant). See also Break (1).

Turn of the Screw, The. Opera in two acts and a prologue by Britten (libretto by Myfanwy Piper, adapted from the story by Henry James), produced in Venice in 1954. Setting: Bly, an English country house, in the mid-19th century.

Turntablism. A musical practice with origins in hip hop, in which prerecorded discs are manipulated in live performance. Typically using two phonographs and an electronic mixer, turntablists (also known as DJs or scratch DJs) generate compositions (routines) through scratching (the rhythmic movement of a record underneath the stylus) and beat juggling (the combination of discrete recorded passages in counterpoint). Turntablism arose in the New York hip-hop scene in the 1970s but is now heard globally and in many musical genres. See also DJ.

Tusch [Ger., fanfare; fr. Fr. *touche,* stroke]. A noisy, improvised flourish of arpeggios, runs, and high, sustained notes, performed on trumpets and timpani, usually over a single harmony. According to Johann Ernst Altenberg (1795), a *Tusch* is played when a toast is proposed at a state banquet and is similar in style to a processional fanfare *(*Aufzug),* which often preceded it. A.J.N.

Tutte le corde [It.]. See *Una corda.*

Tutti [It., all]. In a *concerto, the ensemble as distinct from the soloist(s); a passage for the ensemble.

Tuva. An autonomous republic within the Russian Federation situated in the Altai region of south Siberia and bordering on western Mongolia, with which Tuva shares many aspects of musical life. Best known among these is *khöömei,* usually translated as throat singing. In *khöömei* a single vocalist simultaneously produces two distinct tones: a low sustained fundamental pitch and a series of reinforced harmonics high above the fundamental. Using the throat as a precise type of band-pass filter that reinforces certain frequencies while attenuating others, singers are able to isolate and reinforce a single harmonic to such an extent that it sounds louder than the fundamental. By sequencing different reinforced harmonics in quick succession, vocalists produce the effect of "singing" a melody composed solely of harmonics. Tuvan musicians typically classify throat singing into some half-dozen styles distinguished by timbre, tessitura, and rhythmic pulse. A rich instrumentarium includes metal and wooden Jew's harps, two-string upright fiddles, plucked lutes, zithers, and a range of natural horns and idiophones designed to imitate the sounds of animals.

Bibl.: Theodore Levin and Michael Edgerton, "The Throat Singers of Tuva," *Scientific American* 281, no. 3 (Sept. 1999): 70–77. *Tuva: Among the Spirits,* Smithsonian Folkways CD 40452. T.L.

Tuyau [Fr.]. Organ pipe; *t. à anche,* *reed pipe; *t. à bouche,* *flue pipe.

Twelfth. (1) See Interval. (2) An organ stop of *Principal scale sounding a twelfth above the unison.

Twelve-tone music. Music based on a serial ordering of all twelve chromatic pitches. The series of twelve pitches (also known as the row), whose form is uniquely determined for each composition, serves as the referential basis for all pitch events in that composition (in distinction to the seven-note diatonic basis used in tonal music). The term is most commonly applied to music by Arnold Schoenberg and his followers, though Josef Matthias Hauer actually developed a somewhat different type of twelve-tone composition shortly before Schoenberg.

I. *Evolution.* Schoenberg's twelve-tone music, which came into being during the early 1920s, was a direct result of the crisis brought on by the dissolution of the traditional tonal system in the early years of the 20th century. The composer's own early compositions, though still tonal, clearly reflect the impact of this crisis: the music's triadic harmonic basis, as well as the distinction between diatonic and chromatic elements, is increasingly obscured by the richness and freedom of the contrapuntal writing. By 1907, Schoenberg abandoned the old tonal system entirely, producing his first atonal works. In these compositions, key centers are completely avoided, the triad disappears as the basis for harmonic reference, and all elements of the total chromatic are treated as essentially equal in importance. Schoenberg's so-called free atonal period, encompassing his post-tonal works composed without reference to a conscious, integrated system of pitch control, extended until 1916, the year in which the Four Orchestral Songs op. 22 appeared. It was followed by a hiatus of some seven years in which no new compositions were published, the result in part of World War I and in part of a crisis in the composer's own creative development. Schoenberg had come to believe that a new compositional system, based on the full chromatic, was necessary if composers were to be able to continue to write large-scale instrumental works exhibiting a degree of complexity and coherence comparable to that of tonal music. (His own atonal compositions, for example, were without exception either brief or relied upon texts to aid continuity.)

Schoenberg thus gradually evolved a new system of composition based on an ordering of the full chromatic scale. Although music written in this system is also atonal, since there is no key center (at least in the traditional sense), it is referred to as twelve-tone to distinguish it from "free" atonal music. As early as 1917, in the unfinished oratorio *Die Jakobsleiter,* Schoenberg experimented with twelve-tone structures; and in a number of movements from the first three compositions published after his period of silence—the Five Piano Pieces op. 23, the Serenade op. 24, and the Piano Suite op. 25, all published in 1923–24 but individually dating back as far as 1920—he gradually developed a systematic approach to twelve-tone composition. Each of these three works contains portions that are twelve-tone, and op. 25 is composed exclusively in the new system.

II. *The twelve-tone system.* In Schoenberg's twelve-tone music, the twelve pitches of the chromatic scale are ordered into a row, or series, that provides the basic pitch structure (or **Grundgestalt*) for a given composition and is thus an essential element in the work's fundamental conception. Any order may be chosen, with different orderings normally used for different pieces; ordinarily, the ordering chosen has certain intervallic properties that the composer wishes to exploit. The entire pitch structure of the composition is then derived from the row, including its melodic, contrapuntal, and harmonic features. The row thus represents an abstract structure that is fleshed out in the actual music: it supplies the sequences of pitch classes, for example, but not their registers or durations; nor does it determine (though it may influence) the formal or textural aspects of the music.

In addition to the principal or prime form of the row (designated P), new forms may be derived through three basic operations: the row can be reversed (the retrograde, designated R), inverted (the inversion, I), and both reversed and inverted (the retrograde-inversion, RI). Moreover, each of these four basic versions may be transposed to begin on a different pitch. In analysis, transpositions are designated by an Arabic numeral following the row designation, indicating the number of half-steps upward from the prime form in the transposition: thus, P-0 indicates the untransposed principal form, and P-6 indicates the principal form transposed up six half-steps, or a tritone (though some analysts now prefer to number pitch classes from C

1. Schoenberg, Piano Suite op. 25.

upward starting with 0 and identify transpositions by the number of the pitch class on which they begin). The four basic forms, multiplied by the twelve possible transpositions of each, produce a total of 48 possible versions in all. Rarely, however, are all forms used in a single work; more commonly, a small collection is chosen for particular compositional reasons.

Example 1 gives the four basic forms of the row used in Schoenberg's Piano Suite op. 25 and presents the opening measures of the Trio of the fifth movement. This particular row begins on E and ends on B♭, a tritone away, a fact exploited by Schoenberg throughout the Suite by using only transpositions beginning on E and B♭ (and thus ending, respectively, on B♭ and E). Hence, besides the four basic forms, the only other forms that occur are P-6 (P beginning on B♭), R-6 (R on E), I-6 (I on B♭), and RI-6 (RI on E). Four of these eight are used in the opening measures of the Trio: P-0, I-6, I-0, and P-6 (shown in the example). These are disposed as a canon in contrary motion between the two hands.

Schoenberg also developed a technique, known as combinatoriality, for controlling the relationship between two different forms of a row used simultaneously. A row is combinatorial if half of one of its forms (i.e., one of this form's two hexachords) can be combined with half of one of its other forms without producing any pitch duplications between the two halves. Thus, the two hexachords, one from each row form, combine to create a new twelve-tone aggregate (as, of course, do the remaining two hexachords from the same two row forms). Not all twelve-tone rows are combinatorial (except for the limited case that the first half of every row can be combined with the first half of its own retrograde to produce a twelve-tone aggregate). Many rows do have this property, however, and Schoenberg came to favor them almost exclusively, since they enabled him to combine rows without pitch duplication. A typical case in point is given in Ex. 2, a passage from Schoenberg's Piano Piece op. 33a. The two row forms are shown above the music. The upper parts have P-0, while the lowest part has I-5, the first hexachords of the two rows combining to form a twelve-tone aggregate in the first two and one-half measures, the second hexachords doing so in the next two and one-half measures. Thus, the "harmonic" relationship of the two row forms is also controlled by twelve-tone considerations. This passage also indicates the freedom with which Schoenberg often employs note repetitions in his twelve-tone music, both of individual pitches and of groups of pitches. Indeed, in certain compositions, such as the Three Songs op.

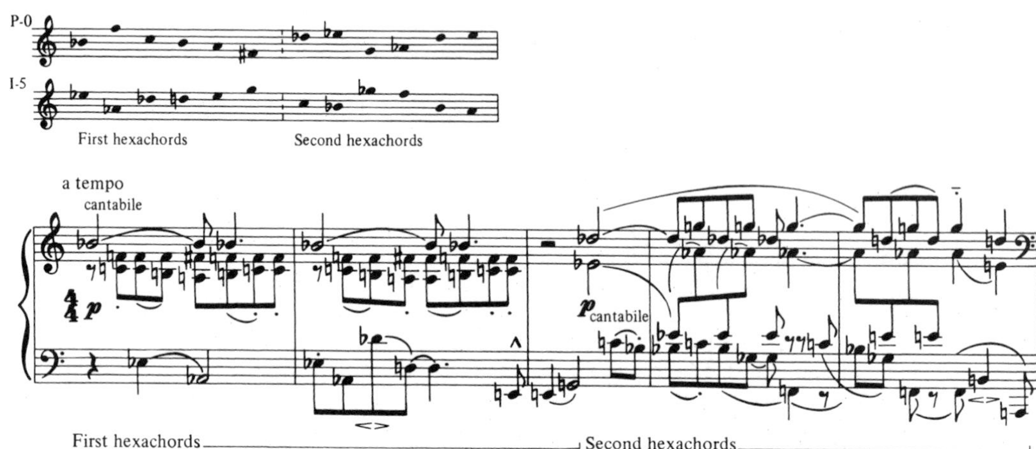

2. Schoenberg, Piano Piece op. 33a.

48 (1933) and the Violin Phantasy op. 47 (1949), he may ignore the original ordering entirely within a given row segment (such as a hexachord). In such cases, his approach to twelve-tone composition nears that of Hauer, who consistently conceived of the twelve-tone aggregate as a combination of two *unordered* hexachords, called tropes.

The twelve-tone system lends itself to markedly different compositional realizations, even within Schoenberg's own output. During his early twelve-tone period, for example, he felt that octave doublings and triadic harmonies should be rigorously avoided as too suggestive of tonal practice, whereas in later works he made frequent use of such doublings and triads. Moreover, his pupils Berg and Webern, both of whom adopted the twelve-tone technique, brought radically different conceptions of the method. Even in his earliest twelve-tone works, Berg, for example, favors rows that allow for strong triadic and tonal suggestions; and rather than adhering to transformations of a single basic row, he employs elaborate techniques to generate new, "derived" rows from the original one. Webern, on the other hand, largely avoids associations with traditional music and develops as much as possible the structural characteristics of each composition out of the properties of its own row. Indeed, Webern's rows are themselves often generated from an opening segment through operations derived from the twelve-tone system. Example 3, the series of his Concerto op. 24, begins with a three-note unit (P) followed by three transposed permutations of it: RI, R, and I.

III. *Subsequent developments.* Among the many

3. Series from Webern, Concerto op. 24.

composers of the generation following Schoenberg and his school who eventually adopted the twelve-tone system (and adapted it for their own personal use) were Krenek, Dallapiccola, and Sessions. After World War II, twelve-tone music continued to flourish both independently and as a component of integral *serial music. It has played a significant role in the music of such important postwar figures as Babbitt, Boulez, and Nono; and even Stravinsky adopted the system in his final years. Babbitt has also been a leading theorist of twelve-tone music. More recently, George Perle has developed a more generalized theory of total chromaticism, which he calls twelve-tone tonality, that is applicable not only to twelve-tone music as such but to other types of post-tonal chromatic music as well (e.g., Bartók). See also Serial music.

Bibl.: Josef Matthias Hauer, *Zwölftontechnik: Die Lehre von den Tropen* (Vienna: Universal, 1926). Arnold Schoenberg, "Composition with Twelve Tones," I (1941), add. (1946), II (ca. 1948), in *Style and Idea,* ed. Leonard Stein, trans. Leo Black, 2nd ed. (New York: Faber, 1975), pp. 214–49. Milton Babbitt, "Some Aspects of Twelve-tone Composition," *The Score* 12 (1955): 53–61. Id., "Twelve-tone Invariants as Compositional Determinants," *MQ* 46 (1960): 246–59. Ann P. Basart, *Serial Music: A Classified Bibliography of Writings on Twelve-tone and Electronic Music* (Berkeley and Los Angeles: U of Cal Pr, 1961; R: 1976). George Perle, *Serial Composition and Atonality* (Berkeley and Los Angeles: U of Cal Pr, 1962; 4th ed. rev., 1977). Id., *Twelve-tone Tonality* (Berkeley and Los Angeles: U of Cal Pr, 1978). Ethan Haimo, *Schoenberg's Serial Odyssey: The Evolution of His Twelve-tone Method, 1914–1928* (Oxford: Oxford U Pr, 1990). R.P.M.

Twentieth century, Western art music of the. Perhaps the single most dominant characteristic of 20th-century Western art music is its variety and eclecticism and thus its resistance to easy categorization and generalized stylistic descriptions. This stems in significant (if essentially negative) measure from one

1. Schoenberg, Piano Suite op. 25.

upward starting with 0 and identify transpositions by the number of the pitch class on which they begin). The four basic forms, multiplied by the twelve possible transpositions of each, produce a total of 48 possible versions in all. Rarely, however, are all forms used in a single work; more commonly, a small collection is chosen for particular compositional reasons.

Example 1 gives the four basic forms of the row used in Schoenberg's Piano Suite op. 25 and presents the opening measures of the Trio of the fifth movement. This particular row begins on E and ends on B♭, a tritone away, a fact exploited by Schoenberg throughout the Suite by using only transpositions beginning on E and B♭ (and thus ending, respectively, on B♭ and E). Hence, besides the four basic forms, the only other forms that occur are P-6 (P beginning on B♭), R-6 (R on E), I-6 (I on B♭), and RI-6 (RI on E). Four of these eight are used in the opening measures of the Trio: P-0, I-6, I-0, and P-6 (shown in the example). These are disposed as a canon in contrary motion between the two hands.

Schoenberg also developed a technique, known as combinatoriality, for controlling the relationship between two different forms of a row used simultaneously. A row is combinatorial if half of one of its forms (i.e., one of this form's two hexachords) can be combined with half of one of its other forms without producing any pitch duplications between the two halves. Thus, the two hexachords, one from each row form, combine to create a new twelve-tone aggregate (as, of course, do the remaining two hexachords from the same two row forms). Not all twelve-tone rows are combinatorial (except for the limited case that the first half of every row can be combined with the first half of its own retrograde to produce a twelve-tone aggregate). Many rows do have this property, however, and Schoenberg came to favor them almost exclusively, since they enabled him to combine rows without pitch duplication. A typical case in point is given in Ex. 2, a passage from Schoenberg's Piano Piece op. 33a. The two row forms are shown above the music. The upper parts have P-0, while the lowest part has I-5, the first hexachords of the two rows combining to form a twelve-tone aggregate in the first two and one-half measures, the second hexachords doing so in the next two and one-half measures. Thus, the "harmonic" relationship of the two row forms is also controlled by twelve-tone considerations. This passage also indicates the freedom with which Schoenberg often employs note repetitions in his twelve-tone music, both of individual pitches and of groups of pitches. Indeed, in certain compositions, such as the Three Songs op.

2. Schoenberg, Piano Piece op. 33a.

48 (1933) and the Violin Phantasy op. 47 (1949), he may ignore the original ordering entirely within a given row segment (such as a hexachord). In such cases, his approach to twelve-tone composition nears that of Hauer, who consistently conceived of the twelve-tone aggregate as a combination of two *unordered* hexachords, called tropes.

The twelve-tone system lends itself to markedly different compositional realizations, even within Schoenberg's own output. During his early twelve-tone period, for example, he felt that octave doublings and triadic harmonies should be rigorously avoided as too suggestive of tonal practice, whereas in later works he made frequent use of such doublings and triads. Moreover, his pupils Berg and Webern, both of whom adopted the twelve-tone technique, brought radically different conceptions of the method. Even in his earliest twelve-tone works, Berg, for example, favors rows that allow for strong triadic and tonal suggestions; and rather than adhering to transformations of a single basic row, he employs elaborate techniques to generate new, "derived" rows from the original one. Webern, on the other hand, largely avoids associations with traditional music and develops as much as possible the structural characteristics of each composition out of the properties of its own row. Indeed, Webern's rows are themselves often generated from an opening segment through operations derived from the twelve-tone system. Example 3, the series of his Concerto op. 24, begins with a three-note unit (P) followed by three transposed permutations of it: RI, R, and I.

III. *Subsequent developments.* Among the many composers of the generation following Schoenberg and his school who eventually adopted the twelve-tone system (and adapted it for their own personal use) were Krenek, Dallapiccola, and Sessions. After World War II, twelve-tone music continued to flourish both independently and as a component of integral *serial music. It has played a significant role in the music of such important postwar figures as Babbitt, Boulez, and Nono; and even Stravinsky adopted the system in his final years. Babbitt has also been a leading theorist of twelve-tone music. More recently, George Perle has developed a more generalized theory of total chromaticism, which he calls twelve-tone tonality, that is applicable not only to twelve-tone music as such but to other types of post-tonal chromatic music as well (e.g., Bartók). See also Serial music.

3. Series from Webern, Concerto op. 24.

Bibl.: Josef Matthias Hauer, *Zwölftontechnik: Die Lehre von den Tropen* (Vienna: Universal, 1926). Arnold Schoenberg, "Composition with Twelve Tones," I (1941), add. (1946), II (ca. 1948), in *Style and Idea,* ed. Leonard Stein, trans. Leo Black, 2nd ed. (New York: Faber, 1975), pp. 214–49. Milton Babbitt, "Some Aspects of Twelve-tone Composition," *The Score* 12 (1955): 53–61. Id., "Twelve-tone Invariants as Compositional Determinants," *MQ* 46 (1960): 246–59. Ann P. Basart, *Serial Music: A Classified Bibliography of Writings on Twelve-tone and Electronic Music* (Berkeley and Los Angeles: U of Cal Pr, 1961; R: 1976). George Perle, *Serial Composition and Atonality* (Berkeley and Los Angeles: U of Cal Pr, 1962; 4th ed. rev., 1977). Id., *Twelve-tone Tonality* (Berkeley and Los Angeles: U of Cal Pr, 1978). Ethan Haimo, *Schoenberg's Serial Odyssey: The Evolution of His Twelve-tone Method, 1914–1928* (Oxford: Oxford U Pr, 1990). R.P.M.

Twentieth century, Western art music of the. Perhaps the single most dominant characteristic of 20th-century Western art music is its variety and eclecticism and thus its resistance to easy categorization and generalized stylistic descriptions. This stems in significant (if essentially negative) measure from one overriding historical factor: the final collapse during the early years of the 20th century of the tonal system used in 18th- and 19th-century music. Although this system had betrayed signs of serious erosion as far back as the mid-19th century, and although it had in fact never represented a completely stable, immutable set of conventions, it nevertheless provided composers of the "common-practice" period of 1700–1900 with a fundamental musical constant. It served as a general set of limitations on what was considered compositionally possible, yet also formed a highly flexible framework allowing for controlled expansion of the previously available musical resources. The loss of this system suddenly made available unimagined new compositional possibilities. But it also represented something like the loss of a mother tongue; and the course of subsequent 20th-century music can be understood to a significant extent as a series of strategies developed to compensate for this loss. The one conspicuous feature of all these developments, however, has been the failure of a new mother tongue—that is, a new set of generally accepted conventions—to emerge. This technical fact, together with the more general social and political realities of the period (of which this fact represents an unmistakable symptom) goes far in explaining the fragmented character of the music of this age.

The profound effects of the dissolution of tonality on subsequent music were immediately evident. The first atonal works of Schoenberg, Berg, and Webern, in which not only key centers but other conventions of the tonal system, such as triadic harmony, were assiduously avoided, appeared before 1910. Other composers such as Stravinsky and Bartók developed new approaches to tonality that, though they preserved the idea of pitch centricity, were based upon assumptions of harmonic structure and the relationship of consonance and dissonance entirely different from those of earlier music. Still more extreme indications of the entirely new compositional situation were evident in the music of Ives, who mixed together radically contrasting musical styles, materials, and techniques in unprecedented combinations; Satie, whose conception of composition often seemed to transform music into a sort of private joke; and the composers of the *Futurist movement, who believed that all possible sounds, including industrial noises and other mechanistic strains of modern life, had become the rightful province of music.

Following World War I, however, there was a widespread tendency to reemphasize connections with older Western musical tradition. Although few composers returned to traditional tonality, many favored formal structures based on Baroque or Classical models, as well as more diatonic pitch structures than had been common in the prewar years. The leading figure in this movement, usually known as *neoclassicism, was Stravinsky; but many other prominent composers of the time, including Bartók, Prokofiev, Hindemith, Copland, and the composers known as *Les *six,* displayed similar inclinations. Moreover, the twelve-tone music of Schoenberg and his school, composed during the same years, also revealed certain formal and stylistic features suggesting a related aesthetic orientation.

Yet even during the period between the two world wars, dominated by neoclassicism, the more experimental attitude toward composition fostered by the absence of tonality persevered. It remained particularly strong in the U.S., where the heritage of Ives was carried on by such figures as Henry Cowell, Lou Harrison, and Harry Partch. Also Edgard Varèse, who took up permanent residence in the U.S. in 1916, evolved an innovative style with relatively few traditional ties.

The period following World War II witnessed the emergence of two widespread tendencies that seemed diametrically opposed: *serial music, which reflected a highly conscious and rational approach to composition, and *aleatory music, which reflected an essentially intuitive one. The principal composers of serial music included Babbitt, Stockhausen, and Boulez; the leaders of the aleatory movement were John Cage, Morton Feldman, and Earle Brown. By the later 1950s, however, many composers came to see these two approaches as simply the extremes of a single continuum of virtually unlimited compositional possibilities. This attitude fostered a number of new developments: music conceived primarily in terms of texture and color (Kryzsztof Penderecki, György Ligeti), music that reinterpreted earlier music through quotation and distortion (Luciano Berio, Lukas Foss), *microtonal music (John Eaton, Ben Johnston), new approaches to *music theater (Cage, Mauricio Kagel), improvised music with audience participation (Frederic Rzewski, Cornelius Cardew), etc.

Viewed from one perspective, the highly eclectic quality of music during the final quarter of the century, a period now commonly designated as postmodern, can be seen as the logical culmination of these varied post-serial and post-indeterminate developments. Postmodernism, however, rejects their experimental, risk-taking aesthetic in favor of a pervasive laissez-faire pluralism. One especially notable feature associated with recent tendencies is a renewed interest in the social role of music—not so much in a political sense (as a means of achieving cultural transformation) as simply part of a commitment to finding a larger public for contemporary composition.

*Electro-acoustic music has played an especially important role during the latter half of the 20th century. Although the sources of this music go back to the turn of the century, it flourished only after the tape recorder became generally available following World War II. Many recent compositional concerns, such as the widespread interest in timbral and acoustical effects and in *mixed media, are directly attributable to this medium. Indeed, the general explosion of technology in the 20th century, resulting in such critical inventions as the radio, phonograph, and *computer, had a profound impact on 20th-century music and musical attitudes.

Throughout the 20th century and beyond, there has been a constant cross-fertilization between Western art music and *popular music. Indeed, the borderlines between contemporary idioms of *jazz and *rock and certain types of recent concert music, such as that of the minimalist school (Steve Reich, Philip Glass), often seem quite unclear. The music of other, often remote, cultures is also becoming increasingly influential on Western music. Another significant development has been the return in recent years to more traditional conceptions of tonality, melody, harmony, and form (George Rochberg, David Del Tredici). Such references to earlier musical conventions have an unavoidable "quotational" quality when heard within today's musical context (especially since most composers tend to juxtapose them with post-tonal techniques). Nevertheless, at the present time the pervasive trend in composition appears to be away from more experimental and innovative approaches toward more traditional ones. But whether this represents the beginning of a long-term development and thus indicates a wish, or need, to formulate a new "common practice" remains at best a problematic question.

Bibl.: William W. Austin, *Music in the Twentieth Century* (New York: Norton, 1966). John Vinton, ed., *Dictionary of Contemporary Music* (New York: Dutton, 1971). Jim Samson, *Music in Transition* (London: Dent, 1977). Paul Griffiths, *Modern Music and After: Directions since 1945* (Oxford: Oxford U Pr, 1995). Hermann Danuser, *Die Musik des 20. Jahrhunderts* (Laaber: Laaber-Verlag, 1984). Robert P. Morgan, *Twentieth-Century Music: A History of Musical Style in Modern Europe and America* (New York: Norton, 1991). Elliott Schwartz and Daniel Godfrey, *Music since 1945: Issues, Materials, and Literature* (New York: Schirmer, 1993). Arnold Whittal, *Musical Composition in the Twentieth Century* (Oxford: Oxford U Pr, 1999). R.P.M.

Twilight of the Gods, The. See *Ring des Nibelungen, Der.*

Two-beat. In jazz, emphasis on beats 1 and 3 (as when the bass plays only on these beats) in 4/4; music characterized by such rhythm.

Two-foot. See Foot.

Two-line. The octave proceeding upward from c″, or any pitch in that octave [see Pitch names].

Two-part form. See Binary and ternary form.

Two-step. The most popular pattern in social dancing ca. 1893–1913. Initially in 6/8 and associated with John Philip Sousa's march of 1889 "The Washington Post" (the title of which became a name for the dance in Europe), the simple steps came to be danced to music in duple meters at ca. 60 bars per minute. See also One-step.

Txistu [Basque]. See Pipe and tabor.

Tympani. *Timpani.

Tympanon [Gr.], **tympanum** [Lat.]. (1) A *frame drum of ancient Greece and Rome, usually round with two heads. (2) In the Middle Ages, any of several instruments including the *dulcimer, the *psaltery, and the Irish *tiómpán.* (3) [Fr. *tympanon*] *Dulcimer.

Tyrolienne [Fr.]. A Tyrolean folk song and dance similar to the **Ländler* and sung with a *yodel. Tyrolean folk music became popular in the U.S. and Europe in the 19th century and was often evoked in piano pieces and ballets (e.g., in Rossini's **Guillaume Tell,* act 3) titled *tyrolienne.*

Tzigane [Fr.]. *Gypsy.

U

Über [Ger.]. Over, above; *überblasen,* to overblow; *Übergang, Überleitung,* transition, bridge passage; *übergreifen,* to cross the hands in piano playing; *übermässig,* augmented (interval); *übersetzen,* to pass one finger over another; *übertragen,* to transcribe; *Übertragung,* transcription.

Übung [Ger.]. *Etude.

U.c. Abbr. for **una corda.*

ʿŪd [Ar., also *oud*]. A Middle Eastern, short-necked, fretless *lute with a pegbox set back at an angle, a bulging, pear-shaped body, and strings in double courses. The most common model has five double courses of gut or nylon strings tuned g a d′ g′ c″. A sixth course is sometimes added and tuned to f″. A North African type usually has only four courses. The ʿūd has a shorter neck than the European lute, is played with a plectrum rather than with the fingers, and is played in monophonic rather than polyphonic style. In the view of some scholars, it was originally provided with frets and retained these until perhaps the 15th century. Known to the Arabs since the 7th century, it had become by the 9th century the premier instrument of Arabic music theory and practice. From Muslim Spain it spread through Europe, where it became the lute. Today it is very popular throughout the Arabic-speaking world and is well known in Iran, Turkey, Greece, and the Balkans. See ill. under Near and Middle East.

ʾUgab [Heb.]. One or more woodwind instruments mentioned in the Bible; usually rendered in English as pipe.

Uguale [It.]. Equal, uniform.

Uilleann pipe. *Union pipe.

Ukelin. A zither with a sound box approximately 70 cm long, 19 cm wide, and 6 cm deep, one end of which is curved in the shape of a guitar. There is a sound hole at each end and two sets of 16 strings, one tuned to triads on C, D, F, and G, the other to the C-major scale. Such instruments were made and sold (often door-to-door) in the U.S. from the 1920s through the 1960s.

Ukrainian Symphony. Popular name for Tchaikovsky's Symphony no. 2 in C minor op. 17 (1872, rev. 1879–80), so called because it incorporates Ukrainian folk songs; also termed *Little Russian* (Little Russia being another name for the Ukraine).

Ukulele, ukelele. A small *guitar of Hawaii with four gut or nylon strings tuned g′ c′ e′ a′ (or some transposition thereof). A larger, baritone model is tuned like the highest four strings of the guitar, d g b e′. The ukulele was developed in the late 19th century from the **cavaquinho* brought to Hawaii by Portuguese sailors, and it became very popular in the U.S. during and after World War I and again in the 1940s and 50s. It is sometimes a part of *string bands. See ill. under Guitar.

Umfang [Ger.]. Compass, range.

Umkehrung [Ger.]. Inversion.

Umstimmen [Ger.]. To retune to another pitch.

Una corda [It., one string, abbr. *u.c.*]. In piano playing, an instruction to depress the leftmost or soft pedal [Ger. *Verschiebung*], which, on a grand piano, reduces loudness by shifting the keyboard and action in such a way that the hammers strike only one string (usually two on modern instruments) for each pitch instead of the usual two or three provided for all but the extreme bass. The instruction may be canceled with the phrases *tre corde* (three strings) and *tutte le corde* (all strings, abbr. *t.c.*). On early pianos in which one string is struck with the pedal fully depressed, two *(due corde)* are struck with the pedal partially depressed, an intermediate effect called for by Beethoven in the slow movement of the Fourth Piano Concerto op. 58. See also Piano.

Un ballo in maschera [It.]. See *Ballo in maschera, Un.*

Unbetont [Ger.]. Unaccented.

Under-third cadence. See Cadence.

Unequal temperament. Any *temperament in which all semitones are not of the same size, especially one in which acoustically pure or *just intonation is favored for some keys at the expense of others.

Unequal voices. Mixed voices, i.e., men's and women's.

Unfinished Symphony. Popular name for Schubert's Symphony no. 8 in B minor D. 759 (1822), so called because only the first two movements are complete. Schubert sketched a considerable part of the third movement, a Scherzo. In 1823, he sent the two completed movements to his friend Josef Hüttenbrenner as a gift to Josef's brother Anselm. The work was first performed in 1865 and published in 1867. Why Schubert failed to complete the work remains a matter of controversy.

Ungaresca [It.]. In lute and keyboard music of the 16th century, a dance tune of Hungarian origin, usually consisting of repeated phrases over a drone.

Ungarische Tänze [Ger.]. See Hungarian Dances.

Ungebunden [Ger.]. Free, unrestrained.

Ungeduldig [Ger.]. Impatient.

Ungerader Takt [Ger.]. Triple *meter.

Ungestüm [Ger.]. Turbulent, violent.

Ungezwungen [Ger.]. Free, unbridled.

Unheimlich [Ger.]. Sinister, uneasy.

Union (uilleann) pipe. A bellows-blown bagpipe of Ireland, developed in the 18th century and still popular. It includes three kinds of pipes: a double-reed, keyed *chanter, tuned chromatically with a range of two octaves, three single-reed *drones, and three or four regulators, which produce chords when opened by means of keys. It is an indoor instrument with a sweet tone and great technical capabilities. See ill. under Bagpipe.

Unis [Fr.]. (1) In orchestral music, together (after a passage in which a section has been divided). (2) In organ music, 8′ stops only; without octave couplers.

Unison [It. *unisono*]. (1) [Ger. *Prim*]. The *interval formed by two statements of the same pitch and hence consisting of zero semitones; also termed prime. (2) Simultaneous performance at the same pitch, or sometimes at one or more octaves. This may be specified by the phrase *all'unisono.* An *all'unisono* aria is one in which the accompaniment consists exclusively of instruments playing in unison.

Unisono, all' [It.]. See Unison.

United States. America's musical life has been shaped by an interaction of peoples from three continents: North America, Europe, and Africa.

When Europeans began colonizing America in the 1500s, they encountered settlements of Amerindians with their own musical practices. Foreign and strange to Western ears, this music was preserved orally in tribal traditions and legends, surviving into the 19th and 20th centuries despite the predations and disruptions the Indians' way of life suffered. Traditional *American Indian music—monophonic, functional, often tied to ritual that includes dance—seems inextricably woven into a worldview blending human beings with animals, trees, weather, and topography into a sacralized web of interconnection. Yet since the 1880s, and with the help of *transcription and sound *recording, more observers outside this web have shown an interest in it—a prospect hardly foreseeable in earlier days.

Europeans journeyed to the New World seeking economic gain. But having found there an unchurched population, the Roman Catholic Church set about converting the natives to Christianity. Establishing a capital in Mexico City, the Spanish carried their missionary effort across the Rio Grande before the mid-1500s. By 1680, the Southwest could boast some 25 missions, including "schools for reading and writing, singing and playing all instruments," as an early missionary reported. In the next century this network reached California, and by 1800, native musicians there were performing polyphonic sacred music that could have been heard in Europe.

Meanwhile, in the 1620s, Protestants from the British Isles launched their own colonial enterprise. In the name of religious freedom, they set up in Massachusetts a plain style of worship that renounced musical elaboration (organs, choirs, expert performers) in favor of congregational psalm singing from *psalters brought from overseas. As time passed, however, oral transmission introduced so much variation into *psalmody that, in the early 1700s, the clergy took up the cause of reform. Singing schools were instituted and books published for their use, the first in Boston in 1721. Psalm singing as a written practice caught on in New England. By the mid-1760s, singing schools and the meeting-house choirs they fostered were performing from sacred *tune books with four-part settings of psalms, *hymns, and *anthems.

English-speaking settlers also carried to the New World secular traditions that included *ballads, lyric and topical songs, and dance music played on fiddles and pipes. Moreover, the colonies became a Western extension of the London stage and of British concert life as professional musicians in search of work traveled to North America. The first known public *concert was given in Boston in 1729. By the 1760s concerts were regularly staged in Boston, New York, Philadelphia, Baltimore, and Charleston, and by the 1790s each of these cities boasted a theater company whose offerings included *ballad and *comic operas by English composers. Growing affluence after the War of Independence (1776–81) drew to American shores such musicians as Alexander Reinagle, Victor Pelissier, Benjamin Carr, and Gottlieb Graupner. Trained overseas, these men settled in cities on the Eastern seaboard, composed, gave concerts, taught, and worked in the theater, the music trades, and in Episcopal and Catholic churches.

With a supply from overseas assured, demand for homegrown compositions was felt most keenly in psalmody: psalm and hymn tunes, *fuging tunes, and anthems for unaccompanied singers. Self-taught New England singing masters filled that demand: most notably William Billings (1746–1800) but also Daniel Read, Timothy Swan, and Oliver Holden, among others. In Philadelphia, the gentleman amateur Francis Hopkinson (1737–91) began in the 1750s to write songs in the style of English comic opera, publishing a small collection of them in 1788. Local composers also cropped up in German-speaking settlements: Ephrata Cloister (Pennsylvania) and Moravian settlements in Pennsylvania and North Carolina. There is no denying the historical importance of these first American composers. Yet their impact on the nation's musical life was limited, as would be the role of American composers in the years to come, for musical life is shaped more by performance than by composition. During the 19th century, musicians marketing their services in America helped to create an infrastructure that included teaching, *publishing, distributing, and instrument making, with performances the chief commodity they had to sell.

One key branch of performance was instructional, and the desire to learn musical skills boomed as edification—an impulse toward intellectual, moral, and spiritual improvement—became big business. In Boston, Lowell Mason extended the singing school's mission into secular terrain. In 1837 he and several associates began to teach singing in the city's public schools. While compiling and composing for sacred tune books, Mason added to them books for youngsters and manuals for their teachers. Perceiving a social need and offering a way to meet it, he promoted music instruction with great effectiveness. Mason was also the first American to get rich through music.

The 19th century saw theatrical and concert venues multiply. Residents of New Orleans were hearing French *opera before 1800, and in 1825 a traveling troupe introduced Italian opera to New York City. Like other branches of pre–Civil War concert life, opera performances offered a blend of entertainment and edification. Rather than music dramas controlled by composers' scores, operas in this era were freely adapted and arranged, often in English translations, for maximum impact on audiences drawn to the theater by the promise of spectacle, drama, and full-blooded singing. Proof of the opera star's charisma may be seen in the half-million-dollar profit reaped by American promoter P. T. Barnum when, in 1850–51, he presented Swedish soprano Jenny Lind in an American concert tour.

While opera was imported from Europe, the blackface *minstrel show, a more popular entertainment, reflected America's interaction with Africa. Contradicting principles of equality in British law (and the later U.S. Constitution), African slavery had been introduced in Virginia as early as 1619 to make farming more profitable. Slavery wrenched Africans from their native environment and transported them to North America as a species apart. Yet some aspects of their culture survived, including powerfully distinctive traditions of dance and *African American music. Indeed, from the bottom echelon of the social order, Africans in the U.S. made their mark on a society that scorned them. In minstrel shows, for example, white entertainers imitating black ways of speaking, moving, and syncopating, darkened their faces and sang, danced, and joked onstage as "Ethiopian" characters. From the 1840s on, blackface troupes toured in the U.S. and overseas. Using a variety format, these performers were always on the lookout for new music, and songwriters like Daniel D. Emmett from Ohio, himself a stage minstrel, and Stephen C. Foster (1826–64), born near Pittsburgh, supplied it.

By midcentury, the teaching boom, the proliferation of concerts and theaters, and the growth of the music trades had made the American home a major marketplace for sheet music. Songs and keyboard pieces—new and old, European and American—were widely purchased, sung, and played on *pianos that mass production was making affordable. Sheet music aimed to satisfy the talents and tastes of its buyers. But written music comes in two forms. In one, the composer's invention is subject to the whim of performers and arrangers. In the other, the composer's score rules. The authority of the notation—is it treated prescriptively or nonprescriptively?—determines whether the performer or the composer is in charge of a composition's performance.

In that difference lay the primary distinction between *popular music and what came to be called classical music. Writers on the subject in the 19th century generally agreed that the popular sphere, devoted to accessibility (acceptance by its target audience), was ephemeral, hence historically insignificant. Music history was thought to be made in the composer-centered classical sphere, devoted to the ideal of "transcendence" (making music that outlives the time and place of its origin). Fundamental, too, though ephemeral in a different way, was music that circulated orally, in the traditional (or *folk) sphere, which tended toward continuity (the wish to maintain the music's original spirit).

As oral tradition and 19th-century enterprise supplied Americans with music they wanted to sing, play, and listen to, venues were also being established where works by past and present composers could be heard. Led by European immigrants, most notably the conductor Theodore Thomas, this endeavor revolved around choral *societies and *orchestras devoted to European classics. A few pre–Civil War Americans offered compositions of their own, including the Bohemian-born Anthony Philip Heinrich (1781–1861), who kept writing large orchestra works despite a lack of performances, and William Henry Fry (1813–64) of Philadelphia, who in 1845 witnessed the premiere of his *Leonora,* the first American grand opera in English. More successful was Louis Moreau Gottschalk (1829–69) of New Orleans, a piano soloist who launched his career in Europe and later spent time in the Caribbean. In some of his compositions, Gottschalk brought together elements from all three spheres: the virtuosity and form of the classical, the accessibility of the popular, and the artless charm of traditional melodies remembered from his Louisiana boyhood.

After the Civil War, wealthy patrons stepped forward to support a concert life dedicated to artistic edification, a development encouraging to the efforts of such native-born composers as John Knowles Paine (1839–1906), George Whitefield Chadwick (1854–1931), Edward MacDowell (1860–1908), and Amy Beach (1867–1943), who, except for Beach, earned their living as teachers. As the end of the century approached, however, and a Wagnerian cult emerged in the classical sphere, the homegrown American music most in demand lay in the popular sphere. Wind band *marches by John Philip Sousa (1854–1932); *ragtime by Scott Joplin (1868–1917) for piano, *player piano, and dance orchestra; *spiritual song arrangements for black choirs; variety shows, soon to be called *vaudeville and fostering a dynamic New York–based songwriting industry (*Tin Pan Alley); *musical comedy, which brought to Broadway shows by such skilled composers as Will Marion Cook (1869–1944) and Victor Herbert (1859–1924)—these were among the genres and works that most delighted audience members and home performers.

In the name of *nationalism, borrowings from popular and traditional sources had put a stamp on music by composers in Russia, Bohemia, Scandinavia, and elsewhere. The U.S. seemed ripe for a similar effort, according to the Czech composer Dvořák, who concluded after a stay in New York (1892–95) that "the germs for the best" American classical works lay "hidden among all the races that are commingled in this great country." In 1915 Arthur Farwell, who had based some of his own compositions on American Indian melodies, revisited this provocative issue when he wondered in an article what might result in the future from contact between "the tractable and still unformed art of music" and "our unprecedented democracy."

In fact, Farwell's question had already been addressed thoroughly by a major American composer. But because Charles Ives (1874–1954) earned his living as a businessman and did little to circulate his works until late in life, his answer went almost unheard. The son of a town musician in Connecticut, Ives was raised thinking of sound exploration as part of musical composition. In the cowboy song "Charlie Rutlage," for example, he gradually undermines a simple, homey beginning by having the singer, in telling how the hero is killed in a cattle drive, move to speech and then to shouting over a piano accompaniment that—evoking heat, dust, and chaos—erupts into a cacophonous roar. An admirer of the New England transcendentalists Emerson and Thoreau, Ives discovered musical substance in country fiddling, hymn singing, and other vernacular performance practices, and he looked for ways to bring this spirit into his works.

As a classical composer who valued informal performance modes and the repertories they came from, Ives claimed territory for the classical sphere broader than that of his predecessors. The democratic aura of his blending of classical, popular, and traditional elements has been widely recognized. Less obvious, however, has been that aura's link to a transforming contribution of technology: the impact of sound recordings, which by the 1920s were raising the prestige of popular and traditional music while also making their presence concrete. While Ives sought to catch in notation the spirit of vernacular singing and playing, recording reified that spirit in sound, in effect turning performances into works that could be repeated, learned from, and even written about, as well as sold. Music once considered ephemeral now enjoyed permanence. And its cultural stock began to rise.

Artistically and economically, the years after World War I were banner ones in the popular and traditional spheres. Prewar ragtime was superseded by another product of African influence, *jazz, which in the 1920s wore several faces (including that of youth, modernity, and social liberation) and from the 1930s on, as *swing, dominated the urban popular scene. In the rural South, efforts to collect traditional African American music alerted record companies to its commercial potential; by the mid-1920s, the genre of hillbilly (later *country) music was flourishing commercially. Elsewhere in the South, African Americans were singing *blues songs, a folk form that, written, published, and recorded, remained a force through the rest of the century. Meanwhile, on Broadway's musical comedy stage, a talented corps of songwriters, including Irving Berlin, Jerome Kern, Cole Porter, George Gershwin, and Richard Rodgers, blended European and African American influences in a sophisticated style that enriched the repertory of popular song while delighting theater audiences with shows that, from 1927 on, included movie musicals. [See Film music.] These and other genres won a place in a burgeoning entertainment business that complemented live performances with records, movies, and *radio, the latter having the advantage of being free to listeners.

The classical sphere also carried high hopes into the 1920s. Some composers followed European leads, especially those of Schoenberg (*atonality, later *serialism) and Stravinsky (*neoclassicism), pioneers of modernism who sought to invigorate composition with anti-Romantic approaches. Others worked in a more nationalist vein. Yet most performers, still dedicated to European classics (which more Americans were coming to know through the mass media), were slow to embrace modern music, except for an occasional work like *Rhapsody in Blue* by George Gershwin (1898–1937). Only after the Depression hit in the 1930s did American composers find a nationalistic approach that won favor with both performers and audiences, in such works as the ballets *Billy the Kid, Rodeo,* and *Appalachian Spring* by Aaron Copland (1900–90); Gershwin's opera *Porgy and Bess;* and Virgil Thomson's (1896–1992) film score for *The River* and his opera *Four Saints in Three Acts.*

If a musical democracy is one respectful of individual choice, then developments in the U.S. since World War II have answered Arthur Farwell's 1915 question emphatically. In a prosperous market with a vast array of choices, technology has made musical sound more and more accessible, first through phonographs and radios, then cassette and compact disc players, and then, in more personalized form, the Internet. Thanks to computers, sound synthesizers, and digital technology, the composition of music and its commercial packaging now lie within the capacity of individuals, as dramatized in the 1970s by *hip hop, an urban African American style. This trend has roots in the 1950s, in *rock and roll and the family of *rock styles it inspired. Before that time, music outside oral tradition had existed in the form of composers' scores, and in performances, live or on record. But rock and roll was defined by recordings, made to be played on the radio and marketed increasingly as symbols of personal identity. Originating among record producers and white country performers with a taste for *rhythm and blues, *gospel, or both, and scorned at first as unrefined teenage expression, the music had such broad appeal and staying power that, at the century's end, references to "the King" would cause most Americans to think of rock and roll star Elvis Presley. With recordings seen as the equivalent of works, rock music, like jazz before it, became the subject of written *criticism, and the classical sphere's monopoly on musical transcendence melted away.

Nevertheless, composition in the classical sphere flourished in many forms and styles in the U.S., while concert performance and *conservatories maintained their dedication to older classics. Systems as different as the *serial approach of Milton Babbitt (b. 1916), in which much was predetermined, and the *aleatoric approach of John Cage (1912–92), in which unintended sounds were valued no less than intended ones, held in common their absorbing sound worlds and their lack of appeal to most concertgoers. In the 1950s and 1960s, academia's support of composition as a branch of research widened the gap between composers and nonspecialist audiences. But by the 1970s, minimalism—also systematic, but more accessibly so—proved that composers such as Steve Reich (b. 1936), Philip Glass (b. 1937), and John Adams (b. 1947) were interested in narrowing that gap.

Finally, just as America's music has been shaped through interaction with peoples from elsewhere in the world, so interactions among the three spheres of musical endeavor have grown more and more common—not only in *crossover borrowings but also in the movement of genres from one sphere to another. Jazz, for example, originated as an oral (improvised) approach to playing popular dance music. Yet in the hands of such musicians as trumpeter Louis Armstrong (1901–70), pianist-composer-bandleader Duke Ellington (1899–1974), and saxophonist Charlie Parker (1920–54), working as entertainers in the clubs, dance halls, and theaters of the popular sphere, the music took on a power that seemed worth preserving not just on record but on paper, through transcription, as well. Today their music and that of other jazz musicians, prescriptively notated and with the original sounds in mind, is formally taught in schools and performed on concert stages: an ephemeral music now classicized and outliving the time and place of its origin.

Bibl.: Gilbert Chase, *America's Music: From the Pilgrims to the Present* (New York: McGraw-Hill, 1955; 3rd ed., rev., Urbana: U of Ill Pr, 1987). D. K. Wilgus, *Anglo-American Folksong Scholarship since 1898* (New Brunswick, N.J.: Rutgers U Pr, 1959). Wilfrid Mellers, *Music in a New Found Land* (London: Barrie & Rockliff, 1964; New York: Knopf, 1966). Bill C. Malone, *Country Music USA: A Fifty-Year History* (Austin: U of Tex Pr, 1968). Gunther Schuller, *Early Jazz: Its Roots and Musical Development* (New York: Oxford U Pr, 1968). H. Wiley Hitchcock, *Music in the United States: An Introduction* (Englewood Cliffs, N.J.: Prentice Hall, 1969; 4th ed., with Kyle Gann, Upper Saddle River, N.J.: Prentice Hall, 2000). Charlie Gillett, *The Sound of the City: The Rise of Rock and Roll* (New York: Outerbridge & Dienstfrey, 1970; 2nd ed., New York: Dell, 1972). Martin Williams, *The Jazz Tradition* (New York: Oxford U Pr, 1970; 2nd rev. ed., 1993). Tony Heilbut, *The Gospel Sound: Good News and Bad Times* (New York: Simon & Schuster, 1971; updated and rev., New York: Limelight, 1985). Eileen Southern, *The Music of Black Americans* (New York: Norton, 1971; 3rd ed., 1997). Philip Hart, *Orpheus in the New World: The Symphony Orchestra as an American Institution* (New York: Norton, 1973). Robert C. Toll, *Blacking Up: The Minstrel Show in Nineteenth-Century America* (New York: Oxford U Pr, 1974). William W. Austin, *"Susanna," "Jeanie," and "The Old Folks at Home": The Songs of Stephen C. Foster from His Time to Ours* (New York: Macmillan, 1975). Dena J. Epstein, *Sinful Tunes and Spirituals: Black Folk Music to the Civil War* (Urbana: U of Ill Pr, 1977). Charles Hamm, *Yesterdays: Popular Song in America* (New York: Norton, 1979). Edward A. Berlin, *Ragtime: A Musical and Cultural History* (Berkeley: U of Cal Pr, 1980). Charles Hamm, *Music in the New World* (New York: Norton, 1983). William Lichtenwanger, ed., *Oscar Sonneck and American Music* (Urbana: U of Ill Pr, 1983). *The New Grove Dictionary of American Music,* 4 vols., ed. H. Wiley Hitchcock and Stanley Sadie (London: Macmillan, 1986). Russell Sanjek, *American Popular Music and Its Business: The First Four Hundred Years,* 3 vols. (New York: Oxford U Pr, 1988). Gunther Schuller, *The Swing Era: The Development of Jazz, 1930–1945* (New York: Oxford U Pr, 1989). Richard Crawford, *The American Musical Landscape* (Berkeley: U of Cal Pr, 1993; updated and with new preface, 2000). John Dizikes, *Opera in America: A Cultural History* (New Haven: Yale U Pr, 1993). Helen Myers, ed., *Ethnomusicology: Historical and Regional Studies* (New York: Norton, 1993). Katherine K. Preston, *Opera on the Road: Traveling Opera Troupes in the United States, 1925–60* (Urbana: U of Ill Pr, 1993). Joseph Horowitz, *Wagner Nights: An American History* (Berkeley: U of Cal Pr, 1994). Tricia Rose, *Black Noise: Rap Music and Black Cul-*

ture in Contemporary America (Hanover, N.H.: Wesleyan U Pr and U Pr of New England, 1994). Samuel A. Floyd, Jr., *The Power of Black Music: Interpreting Its History from Africa to the United States* (New York: Oxford U Pr, 1995). Theodore Gracyk, *Rhythm and Noise: An Aesthetics of Rock* (Durham: Duke U Pr, 1996). Scott DeVeaux, *The Birth of Bebop: A Social and Musical History* (Berkeley: U of Cal Pr, 1997). Kyle Gann, *American Music in the Twentieth Century* (New York: Schirmer, 1997). Timothy D. Taylor, *Global Pop: World Music, World Markets* (New York: Routledge, 1997). Richard Crawford, *America's Musical Life: A History* (New York: Norton, 2001). Ellen Koskoff, ed., *The Garland Encyclopedia of World Music,* vol. 3: *The United States and Canada* (New York: Garland, 2001). R.C.

Uniti [It.]. United, together.

Unit organ. An electric-action organ so designed that some or all of its *stops are made to sound at more than one pitch (i.e., 8′ and 4′) by a system of wiring between the keys and stop switches.

Unmerklich [Ger.]. Imperceptible.

Un peu [Fr.], **un poco** [It.]. See *Peu, Poco.*

Unruhig [Ger.]. Restless.

Unter [Ger.]. Under, below; *Unterdominante,* subdominant; *Unterklavier,* lower manual; *Untermediante,* submediant; *untersetzen,* to pass the thumb under in piano playing; *Unterstimme,* lower or lowest voice; *Untertaste,* white key; *Unterwerk,* *choir organ.

Upbeat [Fr. *anacrouse;* Ger. *Auftakt;* It. *anacrusi;* Sp. *anacrusa*]. One or several notes that occur before the first bar line and thus before the first metrically accented beat (downbeat) of a work or phrase; anacrusis, pickup.

Up-bow. See Bowing (1).

Upright (piano). See Piano.

Urlar [Gael.]. See *Pibroch.*

Urlinie, Ursatz [Ger.]. See Schenker analysis.

Urtext [Ger.]. A text in its presumed original state, without subsequent alterations or additions by an editor; an edition purporting to present a work in such a state [see Editions, historical, II].

Usul [Turk.]. The unit in the Turkish system of rhythmic modes, similar to the Arabic **īqā*ʿ, performed on a pair of drums (*kudüm* or *nakkare*). The simplest type, *semaī,* has 3 beats, and the longest (now obsolete) 88. For memorization, a set of syllables denoting strokes and their sequences are used: *düm* (low), *tek* (high), and combinations. B.N.

Ut. See Hexachord, Pitch names, Solmization.

Ut supra [Lat.]. As above, as before.

V

V. Abbr. for *verse (℣), *verso, *vide,* violin (also V°, VV), **voce* (pl. *voci*), **vox.*

Va. Abbr. for viola.

Vagans [Lat., vagrant]. In 15th- and 16th-century polyphony, a fifth voice (also *quinta vox*) added to the normal complement of four *(superius, altus, tenor, bassus)* but not restricted with respect to range and thus "wandering," depending on the piece, from one range or singer to another.

Vaghezza, con [It.]. With longing, with charm.

Valiha. A *tube zither of Madagascar with 7 to 20 strings, each passing over two bridges, distributed around the circumference of the tube. It is held vertically and plucked and is considered the national instrument of the Malagasy Republic. See ill. under Africa.

Valkyrie, The. See *Ring des Nibelungen, Der.*

Valor [Lat.]. In *mensural notation, the value of a note [see also *Integer valor,* Proportion].

Valse [Fr.], **vals** [Sp.]. Waltz; *valse à deux temps* [Fr.], a form of waltz popular in the 19th century in which two steps (the first occupying two beats) are taken per measure. Its tempo is faster than the usual waltz.

Valse, La. "Poème chorégraphique" (dance poem) for orchestra by Ravel, composed in 1919–20 (arranged for two pianos in 1921) and evoking the Viennese waltz. It has been choreographed by Bronislava Nijinska, Michel Fokine, Harald Lander, Frederick Ashton, and George Balanchine.

Valses nobles et sentimentales [Fr., Noble and Sentimental Waltzes]. A set of waltzes for piano by Ravel, composed in 1911 and later orchestrated by the composer to serve as music for his ballet *Adelaïde, ou Le langage des fleurs* (Adelaide, or The Language of Flowers), produced in Paris in 1912. The title of the waltzes alludes to Schubert's *Valses nobles* op. 77, D. 969 (composed by 1826), and *Valses sentimentales* op. 50, D. 779 (ca. 1823), both for piano.

Valse triste [Fr., Sad Waltz]. A waltz for orchestra by Sibelius, originally composed in 1903 as part of his incidental music op. 44 to the play *Kuolema* and revised in 1904.

Valve [Fr. *piston, cylindre;* Ger. *Ventil;* It. *pistone, cilindro;* Sp. *pistón*]. A mechanical device used on brass instruments to change rapidly their sounding length. The two most common types are the piston valve, used on most American trumpets, and the rotary valve, more often seen on horns. In the modern piston valve, a piston moves up and down within a cylindrical casing. In a modern rotary valve, a rotor rotates on its own axis within a cylindrical casing. Both have exactly the same function. When the valve is at rest or in "open" position, where it is held by a spring mechanism, the air column passes through one passage; but when the finger button or key controlling the valve is pressed, holes or depressions in the piston or rotor are aligned so as to bring another longer or sometimes shorter passage into play. A basic set of three valves is arranged so that the first adds enough tubing to lower the pitch of the instrument two semitones, the second a single semitone, and the third three semitones. Combinations of these can be used to lower the pitch an additional three semitones.

Without some means of changing its length, a brass instrument can sound only a series of pitches corresponding approximately to the *harmonic series. The three-valve system provides every chromatic pitch from the second pitch of this series upward. For example, the trumpet in C, whose tube is 48 inches long, sounds c′ as the second pitch of its series and g′ as the third. Between these pitches there are six intermediate ones; hence, six different pipe lengths are required, each obtained by lengthening the tube with the appropriate valve or valve combination. These six additional pipe lengths also make available the six semitones below c′. Altogether, valves provide such an instrument with a chromatic scale from f♯ to c‴ and above.

There are two flaws in this system. First, as more valves are brought into play, the air column is interrupted with more cylindrical tubing and more corners and bends, with the result that pitches requiring two or three valves may be stuffier and less stable. Fortunately, these combinations are needed for only a few pitches.

The second flaw concerns intonation when two or more valves are used together. In the case of the hypothetical C trumpet, the first valve must increase the tube length by about 1/8, or 6 inches, to lower the pitch by two semitones and thus sound b♭ or f′ [see Interval, Acoustics]. In order to lower the pitch another semitone to a or e′, the first and second valves together or the third valve alone must increase the 48-inch tube by about 3/16, or 9 inches, to a total of 57 inches. In order to descend still another whole tone to g or d′, the tube that is now 57 inches long must itself be lengthened by 1/8 of its own length, or more than 7 inches. In producing a total of five semitones with the combination of the first and third valves, the first valve adds only about 6 inches to the 9 or so of the third. This combination is therefore more than an inch too short, and the pitches g and d′ will be noticeably sharp. This will be true to an even greater extent for f♯ and c♯′.

This problem is dealt with in several ways. The third valve passage is often made a bit longer because it is most often used in combinations and because valves one and two together are available as a substitute for valve three. Trumpets often have levers or rings that enable the player to lengthen the third and sometimes also the first valve slides. On lower-pitched instruments, a fourth valve is often provided that has the correct length of tube for the first and third valve combination and that can be lengthened to correct the combination of second and fourth valves as an alternative to the extremely sharp combination of valves one, two, and three. Another common solution, especially on baritones and tubas, is a compensating valve system, the most successful of which, invented by David James Blaikley in 1874, has double valves that automatically add compensating lengths of tubing when used in combination.

Valves for brass instruments were first conceived in 1814–15 by two German musicians, Heinrich Stölzel of Breslau and Friedrich Blühmel of Silesia. A conical rotary valve, square piston valves, and tubular piston valves were tried. In 1818, Stölzel bought Blühmel's rights and patented his tubular piston valve, which then was widely produced throughout the 19th century. This valve has narrow pistons and tubes exiting from the bottom of each valve.

In 1821, Christian Friedrich Sattler of Leipzig published a description of his double-tube valve. The Sattler valve was also used in many 19th-century instruments, first in its original form (becoming the first type of valve commercially produced in the U.S.) and then in an improved version by Leopold Uhlmann of Vienna and known as the Vienna valve.

The modern rotary valve was a result of work by Blühmel in 1828. It was improved by a Prague hornist, Joseph Keil, in 1829 and was patented by Joseph Riedl of Vienna in 1832. The Berlin valve *(Berliner-Pumpe)* was developed in 1833 by Wilhelm Wieprecht of Berlin with ideas from an improved Stölzel design and from Blühmel's conical rotary valve. The Berlin valve was a short, fat piston valve copied by Adolphe Sax [see Saxhorn] and many other 19th-century makers. The modern piston valve was invented by Etienne François Périnet of Paris in 1839.

Other valve mechanisms were developed in several countries, but few were very successful. In the U.S., about 1825–30, Nathan Adams of Lowell, Massachusetts, made conical rotary valves and valves using vanes in the windways. Thomas D. Paine of Woonsocket, Rhode Island, patented his three-tube rotary valves in 1848 and, also about 1848, created the string action for rotary valves, the most important American contribution to valve development.

A new type of rotary valve has been successfully applied to trombones. Called the axial-flow valve or Thayer valve, after its inventor, Ed Thayer of Waldport, Oregon, it provides perfectly clear windways and only a gentle 30-degree curve through the valve rotor. First conceived in 1947, a cylindrical version was patented in 1978, and the current cone-shape model was patented in 1984.

Bibl.: Robert E. Eliason, "Early American Valves for Brass Instruments," *GSJ* 23 (1970): 86–96. Anthony Baines, *Brass Instruments* (London: Faber, 1976). Herbert Heyde, "On the Early History of Valves and Valve Instruments in Germany (1814–1833)," *Brass Bulletin* 24 (1978): 9–33; 25 (1979): 41–50; 26 (1979): 69–82; 27 (1979): 51–61. Reine Dahlqvist, "Some Notes on the Early Valve," *GSJ* 33 (1980): 111–24. Edward H. Tarr, "The Romantic Trumpet," *Historic Brass Society Journal* 5 (1993): 213. Trevor Herbert and John Wallace, eds., *The Cambridge Companion to Brass Instruments* (Cambridge: Cambridge U Pr, 1997). Ron Babcock, "The Story of Ed Thayer and His Axial-Flow Valve," *International Trombone Association Journal,* Winter 1998: 38.

R.E.E.

Valve instruments. Brass instruments provided with *valves, as distinct from natural instruments [see Natural horn, trumpet]; instruments fitted with slides, such as the slide trombone and slide trumpet; and instruments with keys for covering side holes.

Vamp. A simple introductory or accompanimental phrase or chord progression that can be repeated indefinitely until a soloist enters; hence, the expression "vamp till ready."

Vanessa. Opera in four acts by Samuel Barber (libretto by Gian Carlo Menotti), produced in New York in 1958. Setting: Vanessa's castle, in a northern country about 1905.

Variant. A distinct performance of a folk song, the minimal constituent member of a *tune family. In the terminology of folk music research, a group of closely related variants constitutes a version, several versions make up a form, and a number of forms may constitute a tune family. See also Textual criticism. B.N.

Variation. A technique of modifying a given musical idea, usually after its first appearance; a form based on a series of such modifications. Variation is one of the most basic and essential of musical techniques and is widely distributed, playing an important role in, for example, the musics of *South Asia, *Southeast Asia, and *Africa. It is the underlying technique in much *jazz.

In the context of Western art music, the term commonly means elaboration of melody or accompaniment; other kinds of modifications, such as *development or *transformation, are often considered to be outside the scope of variation. Variation form, in its simplest sense the "theme and variations," embodies a principle of strophic repetition: a theme with a particular structure is followed by a series of discrete pieces with the same or very similar structure. In each variation, some elements of the theme remain constant while others change, and this form-defining relationship between constant and changing elements depends on historical and stylistic context, on genre, and on whether the set is an independent piece or a movement in a larger work.

Variation forms are not necessarily always sectional and strophic. If the theme is a short *ostinato or *ground bass, its repetitions will generate a continuously unfolding piece over which figuration and textures change with each statement of the theme; this is known as continuous variation. If variations recur after intervening material, the form will not be strophic because recurrence rather than repetition becomes the structural principle. The resulting hybrid variation forms include rondo-variations and alternating variations, in which the theme and its variations alternate with rondo couplets or with another theme and its own variations, respectively. Types of variation forms are thus located within sets of oppositions: sectional/continuous, strophic/hybrid, independent set/variation movement. In addition, there is an essential stylistic opposition between stricter variation sets, in which variations are relatively faithful to the structure and some elements of the theme, and freer variations, which may diverge considerably from the theme.

I. *Theme.* The material to be varied may be a bass line, chord progression, melody, or thematic complex that includes these and other elements. In the continuous variation types, the theme is a melodic pattern set in the bass (that is, a ground bass or ostinato) and is rarely more than eight bars long. The harmonies suggested by or accompanying the theme may stand in for it if the ostinato disappears but are not considered part of the theme except in certain dance types. Continuity is assured by the brevity of the theme and its typical conclusion on the dominant rather than on the tonic; a strong cadence is delayed until the end of the piece. In sectional variations, at least until the later 19th century, the theme is most often a two-reprise structure, about 16 to 32 bars in length, with a relatively clear phrase structure, a simple or affecting melody, and a cadence in the tonic at the close. But within this sectional structure, the actual theme may in essence be the bass line or chord progression, as in Bach's Goldberg Variations. In such pieces, the melody of the theme is the feature least likely to be retained or embellished in the variations that follow.

As a complex of elements, the theme presents the primary constructive features—bass, chords, phrase structure, melody—and their attendant characterizing elements—rhythm, meter, tempo, mode, texture, instrumentation, and dynamics. Character or affect, the intangible sum of all of these, acts as a kind of "extrathematic" quality that may change dramatically when thematic elements are varied or replaced. In individual variations, one or more of the constructive elements are usually retained, together with one or more of the characterizing elements. Sets of alternating themes have two themes of markedly different character, as in Haydn's Variations for Piano in F minor, so that characterizing elements need change but little in the course of the piece. In strophic variations on a single theme, however, every characterizing element of the theme is subject to variation.

II. *Relationship of variations to the theme.* Because every variation retains elements of the theme while artfully altering or replacing others, the degree of relationship may be expressed in what is constant, modified, or new. Most important in these respects are the constructive elements (bass, harmony, structure, melody); because they offer the clearest lines of resemblance, most composers of variations retain at least one. But even "retention" allows considerable freedom. For example, between the extremes of literally restating the theme's melody and replacing it with a new melody, options include keeping its main notes and adding some ornaments or figurations, partially obscuring the original melody with figuration while returning to it at cadence points, or treating it motivically. Between keeping and discarding the theme's harmony are the possibilities of substituting some chords and cadences, changing the mode, and expanding it chromatically. And the characterizing elements of the theme may also be modified or replaced to provide articulations in the set that help to organize the whole.

The following list of variation types is based primarily on the constant constructive elements within each set, because these chart the history of the form and point up the most consistent distinctions. Only type 1 is normally continuous; only type 6 regularly dispenses with the theme's structure.

1. Basso ostinato or ground bass variation. The theme, a short bass line, repeats essentially unchanged in each variation, resulting in a continuous variation form (e.g., Bach, Passacaglia in C minor for organ).

2. Constant-melody variation. The theme's melody remains the same and, although usually retained in the highest voice, may move from voice to voice and be reharmonized as well (e.g., Haydn, String Quartet in C major op. 76 no. 3, second movt.). This type is sometimes referred to as *cantus firmus* variation, but its appearance as late as the 19th century discourages the use of the older term.

3. Constant-harmony variation. The harmonic structure is fixed, although changes in mode and some substitutions in chords are possible (e.g., Bach, Goldberg Variations). A subcategory is the constant-bass variation, in which the bass line of the theme remains the same (e.g., Haydn, String Quartet in B♭ major Hob. III:12, "op. 2 no. 6," first movt.).

4. Melodic-outline variation. The theme's melody is recognizable despite figuration, simplification, or rhythmic recasting. In a figured melodic-outline varia-

tion, the principal melodic notes of the theme appear within a highly elaborated melodic line. Simplified or rhythmically changed melodic-outline variation is usually unfigured, with a melodic outline similar to that of the theme. In the late 18th century, melodic-outline variation is often found in conjunction with retention of the theme's harmony (e.g., Mozart, variations on "Ah! vous dirai-je, Maman" K. 300e [265]).

5. Formal-outline variation. Aspects of the theme's form and phrase structure remain constant in this predominantly 19th-century type of variation. Nonetheless, phrase lengths may expand or contract within the general outline. Harmonies usually refer to the theme at the beginning and end of a variation (e.g., Beethoven, Diabelli Variations op. 120; Brahms, Handel Variations op. 24).

6. Fantasy variation. In this product of the 19th century, the variations only allude to the constructive elements, especially the structure and melody; the format may be sectional or "developmental." Sometimes the relationship is purely incidental, whereas at other times constructive elements of the theme come to the fore. Examples include most late 19th-century variations except those of Brahms, but sometimes this type is difficult to distinguish from formal-outline variation (e.g., Strauss, *Don Quixote;* Elgar, *Enigma* Variations).

7. Serial variation. Modifications of a serial theme (a twelve-tone row or some slightly longer or shorter configuration) in which figuration and accompaniment are derived from the row. The structure of the theme usually remains the same. Serial variation thus differs from serial pieces in which variation technique means manipulation of the row, not the theme (e.g., Schoenberg, Serenade op. 24, third movt.; Webern, Symphony op. 21, second movt.).

Each of these constructive variation types may govern an entire set, or the set may mix two or even more of them (except for ostinato variation, which applies to the whole piece). Baroque, Classical, and Romantic composers commonly included types 2 through 4 within a single work, whereas 5 and 6 are characteristic of the 19th century, and 6 and 7 of the 20th. Within each type, any constructive elements that are not fixed may change, and the characterizing elements are all allowed to change: individual variations may then be typed as contrapuntal or coloristic, dance-type or character-piece. Of course, characterizing elements may be altered without a single, easily identifiable type emerging; for example, the texture may be thickened without being made contrapuntal, or the meter and tempo may change without creating a dance-type. And the character-variation is an elusive creature because the term may be so broadly applied.

III. *Formation of the cycle.* Composers have sought to organize the additive, open-ended variation form into a musically coherent and convincing whole. To this end, they employ either technical manipulations of the theme's elements, as listed above, or large-scale formal procedures that may change the basic nature of the form. The following list sets out the main structural categories.

1. *Strophic variation. Corresponding to the "theme and variations" itself, with its principle of strophic repetition (AA′A″. . .), this type has a variety of technical means at its disposal to inflect or articulate the series of variations [see II above]. Strophic sets may also include an introduction, coda, and even transitions between the variations.

2. Hybrid variation. Variation sets that use recurrence rather than repetition as their structural principle are different from variations per se. The main types are in evidence from the late 18th to the early 20th century, although considering types (ii) and (iii) below as variation is somewhat controversial.

(i) Alternating variations, in which two themes are set forth and then varied in turn, ending either with a variation on the first theme (ABA′B′A″) or on the second theme (ABA′B′A″B″); the former is more like a rondo, the latter more like a strophic variation set with a higher-level repetition of A and B. Alternating variations of both types are sometimes called double variations because of the double theme, but the term is better avoided here because it is also used for variations in which each reprise is varied further instead of being repeated (as in Mozart's Divertimento K. 563).

(ii) Rondo-variation or variation rondo. This form (ABA′CA″) may be perceived in two ways: as a theme and variations separated by couplets and as a rondo with varied refrains. The extent of the variation determines the precise designation, but there are no agreed-upon limits in this hybrid.

(iii) Ternary variation (ABA′), a *da capo* format with considerable embellishment of the return. This hybrid poses a problem similar to that of rondo-variation: where repetition is not the main principle, variation technique rather than variation form is perhaps at issue.

3. Genre variation, such as the variation motet, variation ricercar, variation canzona, and variation suite. These genres use systematic variation technique, though only the last has some structural relationship between its sections. Indeed, theorists show how to construct a suite from a single bass line (e.g., Friedrich Erhard Niedt, *Handleitung zur Variation,* 1706), and the resulting variation suite could be regarded as constant-bass variations of the dance type. Genre variations are not usually considered variation forms, however.

IV. *History.* The history of the variation proper begins in Italy and Spain in the early 16th century and develops from the practice of repeating several times a strain of dance music, retaining the bass and varying or changing the upper line(s). Originating in such dances as the *passamezzo and **romanesca,* the variations are either the constant-harmony type, when the theme is a bass line, or the melodic-outline type, when the dance bass is used in conjunction with a popular melody (e.g., the *romanesca* bass plus the "Guárdame las vacas" melody, *HAM,* no. 124). Difficulties thus arise in maintaining a distinction between these dance-bass variations and so-called song variations. See also *Diferencias.*

Later in the 16th century, English keyboard composers brought both variation types to a high point (see the many examples in the *Fitzwilliam Virginal Book, e.g., Byrd's "Jhon come kisse me now," I:47). In addition to constant-harmony and melodic-outline types, constant-melody variation also appears. A striking degree of harmonic freedom is evident, in that phrases and cadences may substitute new chords for the originals. These variation sets also sustain interest through contrapuntal motivic treatment.

Sweelinck and his pupils wrote many sets of song variations, using either constant-melody or melodic-outline techniques. His most famous set, "Mein junges Leben hat ein End," varies each half of the theme twice, so that the opportunities for textural and figural varying increase. Sweelinck also wrote variations on sacred themes, usually chorales, the melodies of which are accorded constant-melody treatment in a contrapuntal setting. Such chorale variations are usually not quite strophic, however, because contrapuntal or figural episodes extend and join individual variations or even phrases of the chorale melody.

The rest of the 17th century follows the paths already made plain during Sweelinck's time. Song variations and chorale variations continued through Pachelbel and Buxtehude, Muffat and Biber. The dance-bass variation developed into *ostinato types on the one hand and sectional constant-bass types on the other as the century wore on. In Italy, dance basses and songs predominate as sources of variations, and both Italian and French composers began to write varied versions of suite movements *(doubles),* a purely ornamental melodic-outline type.

J. S. Bach's variations sum up the possibilities of the late Baroque in the constant-harmony type (Goldberg Variations), melodic-outline type *(Aria variata alla maniera italiana),* ornamental and figurative melodic-outline (B minor Partita for solo violin), ostinato variations (Passacaglia in C minor for organ, Chaconne in D minor for solo violin), and chorale variations ("Vom Himmel hoch"). All but the suites erect elaborate contrapuntal scaffolding; later writers of the 18th and 19th centuries upheld the contrapuntal and canonic organization of the Goldberg and "Vom Himmel hoch" sets as the first rank of variation writing, relegating *doubles* to a much lower position. These writers do not mention Handel, who was known more for his figurative melodic-outline style than Bach (e.g., the "Harmonious Blacksmith" variations in the Harpsichord Suite in E major).

Haydn's variations in their turn span the range of possibilities of the Classical variation. At first writing only constant-bass and constant-harmony sets, he gradually added greater numbers of melodic-outline variations until this type began to predominate around 1770 (e.g., Symphony no. 47, second movt.). At the same time, he turned to writing hybrid variations and is especially known for his sets of alternating variations on themes in the parallel major and minor (e.g., Symphony no. 103, *Drumroll,* second movt.). He also developed the rondo-variation and ternary variation and included variation technique extensively in all of his instrumental forms. In this he was preceded and probably influenced by C. P. E. Bach, whose "Sonatas with Varied Reprises" (1760; W. 50, H. 126, 136–40) reveal the importance of variation technique to his compositional thinking. C. P. E. Bach's own theme and variation works, like those of his north German contemporaries, change mode, character, and harmony more often than their Viennese counterparts.

Mozart's variations reflect his virtuoso career in 14 independent sets mostly on popular themes (as opposed to Haydn's four or five on original themes), with their melodic-outline figurations and cadenzas. He stereotyped the *adagio–allegro* pair to round off a set that has the proportions of a sonata cycle. Yet his variation movements equal the seriousness and complexity of Haydn's, with greater contrast and diversity of techniques afforded by the larger number of variations within a movement (e.g., finale of the C minor Piano Concerto K. 491). His careful organization of strophic sets—he wrote very few hybrids—is attested by the variation movement of the string trio Divertimento K. 563.

Beethoven's variations occupy a central role in his oeuvre and in the history of the form as well. His early piano variations are, like Mozart's, the fruit of a career as a virtuoso, whereas his later variation movements continue in Haydn's path. Notable in his strophic sets after the 1790s is the return of the constant-harmony variation (*Eroica* Variations for piano op. 35) and a marked increase in the number of characterizing elements that are altered in individual variations. Because the melodic-outline variation was at this time degenerating into empty figurative display in the hands of salon composers, Beethoven was credited with revitalizing the form by casting off the hegemony of the theme melody. Even when he returned to melodic-outline variation in his late piano sonatas, he imbued the decorative aspect with a contemplative, even ethereal, character. He also took on and transformed the alternating variation, first by welding together the themes and creating a progressive structure in the *Eroica* Symphony finale and Fifth Symphony slow movement, and later by contrasting the themes in tempo, key, and, especially, character, in the Ninth Symphony slow movement and "Heiliger Dankgesang" of the A minor String Quartet op. 132. And his Diabelli Variations op. 120 are usually considered the successor to the Goldberg Variations as the summit of the variation form to that time. In this formal-outline set, Beethoven freely changed harmony, structure, and character without ever losing the thread connecting the segments.

Schubert's variations reflect his preoccupation with beautiful melody, especially in the prominent place accorded constant-melody technique in conjunction with melodic-outline technique (*Trout* Piano Quintet D. 667). Occasionally writing hybrid variations (C minor Piano Sonata D. 958, slow movt.) and introducing quite remote keys into a set *(Trout),* Schubert contributed the first example of fantasy variation in the slow movement of the *Wanderer* Fantasy D. 760, with its melody richly arrayed in different keys and figurations without a strict structural frame. Precedents lie outside the variation entirely, in C. P. E. Bach's rondos and Haydn's fantasias.

Other 19th-century composers tried their hand at variations, notably Mendelssohn *(Variations sérieuses)* and Schumann, but the true inheritor of Beethoven's variation mantle is Brahms, who not only wrote more variations than anyone else after Beethoven but also conveniently explained his thoughts on the form in letters to his friends (to Joachim in 1856, Schubring in 1869, and Herzogenberg in 1876). Brahms identified the bass as the essence of the theme, thus claiming descent from an older tradition, and used the bass to control the structure and character of individual variations and the entire set. He interpreted the concept of the bass rather broadly, however; and together with variations clearly inspired by earlier models (String Sextet op. 18; Handel Variations op. 24; Haydn Variations op. 56), he also indulged in more formal-outline and even fantasylike constructions (Schumann Variations op. 9; String Quintet op. 111).

The trend toward greater freedom in the later 19th-century variation meant fewer constant elements. Fantasy variations, a type mentioned by Brahms as not even belonging to the form, came to the fore in such works as Elgar's *Enigma* Variations and Franck's Symphonic Variations, although in the latter piece, the variations themselves are rather strict but are embedded in a larger developmental fantasy. This freedom extended toward variation movements as well, such as the alternating variations in Mahler's Fourth Symphony. Long continuous programmatic pieces, such as Strauss's *Don Quixote* (subtitled "Fantastic Variations") stretch the limits of the form.

A stricter approach to thematic elements, especially structure and melody, reemerged in the 20th century, together with a striking resurgence of interest in the *passacaglia. The older forms work as effective organizational frameworks for nontonal or serial musical languages, but the relationship between theme and variations is often difficult to discern. Schoenberg usually keeps to the structure of his theme, which may be based on a row (e.g., Serenade op. 24, third movt.), and his variations increase in complexity and density as the pieces proceed, a historically sanctioned protocol. His Variations for Orchestra op. 31 conjure up the image of the character change associated with Beethoven and Brahms. Webern's serial variations in his Symphony op. 21 retain the palindromic structure of the theme while exploring rhythmic and timbral relationships in a tightly organized sequence. Coloristic variation procedures and the *concertante* treatment of instruments is important to Schoenberg and Webern. Stravinsky claimed that the melody of the theme was the only important element and then, like Brahms, interpreted it broadly and freely; the relationship is clearest in such pieces as the Octet, in which the first variation returns several times as a ritornello, and the Sonata for Two Pianos. After the middle of the century, works titled variation seem to bear no resemblance to any historical sense of the form (e.g., Benjamin Boretz, Group Variations), but challenging "true" variations, such as Elliott Carter's Variations for Orchestra, show a serious attempt to redefine the meaning of constant and changing elements by introducing nonthematic materials fully as important as the theme itself. With minimalist repetition of melodic or melodic-harmonic patterns (Terry Riley, Philip Glass, Steve Reich), the cycling of ostinato and strophic repetition leads to processes quite different from variation form.

Bibl.: Herbert Viecenz, "Über die allgemeinen Grundlagen der Variationskunst, mit besonderer Berücksichtigung Mozarts," *MJb* 2 (1924): 185–232. Victor Luithlen, "Studie zu Brahms' Werken in Variationenform," *SzMw* 14 (1927): 286–320. Werner Schwarz, *Robert Schumann und die Variation* (Kassel: Bärenreiter, 1932). Paul Mies, "W. A. Mozarts Variationenwerke und ihre Formungen," *AfMf* 2 (1937): 466–95. Robert U. Nelson, *The Technique of Variation* (Berkeley and Los Angeles: U of Cal Pr, 1948). Joseph Müller-Blattau, *Gestaltung-Umgestaltung: Studien zur Geschichte der musicalische Variation* (Stuttgart: J B Metzler, 1950). Kurt von Fischer, "C. Ph. E. Bachs Variationenwerke," *RBM* 6 (1952): 190–218. Margarete Reimann, "Zur Entwicklungsgeschichte des Double," *Mf* 5 (1952): 317–32; 6 (1953): 97–111. Kurt von Fischer, *Die Variation, Mw* 11 (Cologne: A Volk, 1955; trans. Eng., 1962). Id., "Zur Theorie der Variation im 18. und beginnenden 19. Jahrhundert," *Schmidt-Görg,* 1957, pp. 117–30. Elsie Payne, "The Theme and Variation in Modern Music," *MR* 19 (1958): 112–24. Imogene Horsley, "The 16th-Century Variation: A New Historical Survey," *JAMS* 12 (1959): 118–32. Arnold Schoenberg, "The Orchestral Variations, Op. 31," *The Score* 27 (1960): 27–40. Adolf Albrecht, *Die Klaviervariation im 20. Jahrhundert* (diss., Cologne, 1961). Robert U. Nelson, "Stravinsky's Concept of Variations," *MQ* 48 (1962): 327–39. Id., "Schönberg's Variation Seminar," *MQ* 50 (1964): 141–64. Id., "Webern's Path to the Serial Variation," *PNM* 7 (1968–69): 73–93. Kurt von Fischer, "Arietta Variata," *Geiringer,* 1970, pp. 224–35. Rudolf Flotzinger, "Die barocke Doppelgerüst-Technik im Variationsschaffen Beethovens," *Beethoven,* 1970, pp. 159–94. Willi Apel, *The History of Keyboard Music to 1700,* trans. and rev. Hans Tischler (Bloomington: Ind U Pr, 1972). Stefan Kunze, "Die 'wirklich gantz neue Manier' in Beethovens Eroica-Variationen Op. 35," *AfMw* 29 (1972): 124–49. Gerhard Puchelt, *Variationen für Klavier im 19. Jahrhundert*

(Hildesheim: Olms, 1973). András Batta and Sándor Kovács, "Typbildung und Grossform in Beethovens frühen Klaviervariation," *Studia musicologica* 20 (1978): 125–56. Elaine R. Sisman, "Haydn's Hybrid Variations," *Haydn,* 1975, pp. 509–15. David R. B. Kimbell, "Variation Form in the Piano Concertos of Mozart," *MR* 44 (1984): 95–103. Elaine R. Sisman, *Haydn and the Classical Variation* (Cambridge, Mass.: Harvard U Pr, 1993). E.S.

Variations on a Theme by Diabelli (Handel, etc.). See Diabelli Variations, Handel Variations, etc.

Variations symphoniques [Fr., Symphonic Variations]. A work for piano and orchestra by Franck, composed in 1885, in which theme-and-variation structure is combined with elements of development such as those that occur in the first movement of a symphony.

Varṇam [Tel.]. Either of two types of composition in Carnatic music. One type *(tāna varṇam)* is a preliminary piece in vocal or instrumental recitals; the other (*pada* or *cauka varṇam*) is the most demanding piece in a recital of **bharata nāṭyam.* C.C.

Varsovienne [Fr.]. A dance popular in Paris in the period 1850–70, named for the city of Warsaw and similar to a slow mazurka, with an accented note on the first beat of the second and fourth measures.

Vater unser [Ger., Our Father]. The German version of the Lord's Prayer, sung to a 16th-century *chorale melody (perhaps by Luther) and made the basis of numerous vocal and instrumental works (e.g., *organ chorales and variations by Bach and others).

Vatican Council II. An Ecumenical Council that was summoned by Pope John XXIII and met in several sessions from 1962 through 1965 (under Paul VI beginning in 1963). It set in motion the work carried out by postconciliar commissions that led to the introduction of the vernacular and to extensive revisions of the liturgy, changes culminating in the publication of a new missal in 1970 and a new breviary in 1971. These books superseded the *Liber usualis (LU)* and other books that are cited in this dictionary for historical reasons. See also Gregorian chant VI; Liturgy; Liturgical books; Office, Divine.

Vatican edition. See Gregorian chant VI.

Vaudeville [Fr.]. In the 16th century, a lyrical or amatory strophic poem sung to a simple melody, often with chordal accompaniment. In this period, the form *voix de ville* was preferred, as in the first preserved collection devoted to such pieces, Adrien Le Roy's *Le second livre de guiterre, contenant plusieurs chansons en forme de voix de ville* (1555). Some melodies also served as dance tunes, and some were employed in polyphonic chansons, in either the tenor or the uppermost voice. Related works occur among the chansons of Arcadelt and others in the first half of the century. In a publication of 1571, Le Roy equates the *vaudeville* with the **air de cour.* In the 17th century, *vaudeville* increasingly referred to light or satirical texts sung most often to preexistent melodies [see *Timbre* (2)]. In the first half of the 18th century, such songs were the principal type of music in the genre of comedy *(comédie en vaudevilles)* that led to both *ballad opera and **opera comique.* Large collections of *vaudevilles* include J. B. C. Ballard's *La clef des chansonniers, ou Recueil des vaudevilles* (1717), A. R. Le Sage's *Le théâtre de la foire, ou L'opéra comique* (1721–37), and P. Capelle's *La clé de caveau* (1810). By the 19th century, the term referred to light comedies interspersed with music; in the later 19th century, throughout Europe and the U.S., it came to designate variety shows or revues featuring singers of popular song, dancers, comedians, and acrobats. In the U.S., vaudeville coexisted with film in some movie theaters into the second half of the 20th century, when it gradually succumbed to television, some of the most popular early programs of which were patterned on vaudeville.

Bibl.: Kenneth Levy, "Vaudeville, vers mesurés, et airs de cour," in *Musique et poésie au XVIe siècle* (Paris: CNRS, 1953), pp. 185–201. Clifford Barnes, "Vocal Music at the 'Théâtres de la Foire' 1697–1762," *RMFC* 8 (1968): 141–60. Daniel Heartz, "Voix de ville: Between Humanist Ideals and Musical Realities," *Merritt,* 1972, pp. 115–35. Bill Smith, *The Vaudevillians* (New York: Macmillan, 1976).

Vau de Vire [Fr., valley of the Vire]. A type of popular song, often topical or concerned with drinking, first associated with the city of Vire in Normandy in the 15th century and attributed to one Olivier Basselin. Collections of such songs persisted into the 16th century, when the term became confused with *voix de ville* and **vaudeville.*

Vc., Vcl. Abbr. for violoncello.

V-Disc. A noncommercial record label for 78-rpm, 12-inch records produced by the U.S. War Department in the period 1943–49 for the use of military personnel. Such records included classical, jazz, and popular music.

Bibl.: Richard S. Sears, *V-Discs* (Westport, Conn.: Greenwood, 1980).

Vela [Sp.]. See *Velorio.*

Velato [It.]. Veiled.

Veloce, velocemente [It.]. Fast.

Velorio, vela [Sp.]. In Latin America, a wake for a deceased adult or child (often, in the latter case, *velorio de angelito*); also, any of a number of other rituals, such as ceremonies dedicated to the saints or the Cross. In several countries, distinctive musical traditions are associated with the *velorio,* e.g., the Venezuelan **tonos de velorio.* D.S.

Venetian school. A group of northern and Italian composers active in Venice in the late 16th and early

17th centuries, many associated with the Basilica of St. Mark. The first of the group was Adrian Willaert (ca. 1490–1562), who became chapel master at St. Mark's in 1527. Others include Cipriano de Rore (1515 or 1516–65), Andrea Gabrieli (ca. 1510–86)—both pupils of Willaert—Girolamo Dalla Casa (d. 1601), Baldassare Donato (ca. 1525–1603), Gioseffo Guami (ca. 1540–1611), Giovanni Gabrieli (ca. 1555–1612), Giovanni Croce (ca. 1557–1609), the organ composers Jacques Buus (ca. 1500–1565), Annibale Padovano (1527–75), Vincenzo Bellavere (d. 1587), and Claudio Merulo (1533–1604), and the theorists Nicola Vicentino (1511–ca. 1576) and Gioseffo Zarlino (1517–90) [see Theory]. Their music has often been contrasted with that of a so-called *Roman school of the period in its use of instruments (especially by Giovanni Gabrieli; see Canzona) and *polychoral style and was influential in the work of German composers such as Jacob Handl (1550–91), Hieronymus Praetorius (1560–1629), Hans Leo Hassler (1562–1612), Michael Praetorius (ca. 1571–1621), and Heinrich Schütz (1585–1672), the last of whom studied in Venice with Giovanni Gabrieli.

Venetian swell. The louvered wooden shades at the front of a *Swell division of an organ. They may be opened or closed by the player to increase or decrease loudness. A Venetian swell for the harpsichord was patented in England in 1769 by Burkat Shudi.

Veni Sancte Spiritus [Lat., Come, Holy Spirit]. The *sequence for Pentecost; also called the Golden Sequence.

Venite exultemus [Lat.]. The *Invitatory.

Vent [Fr.]. Wind; *instruments à vent,* wind instruments.

Ventil [Ger.], **ventile** [It.]. *Valve; *Ventilhorn* [Ger.], valve horn.

Veränderungen [Ger.]. Variations.

Verbunkos [Hung., fr. Ger. *Werbung,* recruiting]. A Hungarian dance originating in the second half of the 18th century and used in the recruitment of soldiers until the advent of conscription in 1849; the dance and its associated music have nevertheless survived, principally in the closely related **csárdás*. Music was provided by Gypsy bands, who added their characteristic performing style to a repertory of folk tunes. The result was a central part of what is usually termed *Gypsy music. At first largely improvised, music in this style reached a peak in the first part of the 19th century in the works of the violin virtuosos János Bihari (himself of Gypsy origin), Antal György Csermák, and János Lavotta. The *verbunkos* itself typically includes an alternation between a slow introductory section *(lassú)* and a section in a fast tempo *(friss).* Composers of art music drawing on this tradition include Liszt *(*Hungarian Rhapsodies),* Brahms, Bartók, and Kodály.

Verdoppeln [Ger.]. To *double.

Vergleichende Musikwissenschaft [Ger.]. Comparative musicology, now usually termed *ethnomusicology.

Vergrösserung [Ger.]. Augmentation.

Verhallend [Ger.]. Fading away.

Verismo [It.]. A style of operatic composition, prevalent in Italy in the 1890s, with repercussions extending to other European countries and later decades. *Verismo* in Italy began as a literary movement, exemplified by the novels and plays of Giovanni Verga, showing analogies with the naturalism of Zola and de Maupassant. The landmark veristic opera, Mascagni's **Cavalleria rusticana* (1890), is based on a story by Verga. The veristic operas that followed, such as Leoncavallo's **Pagliacci* (1892), Giordano's *Mala vita* (1892), and Puccini's *Il tabarro* (1918) [see *Trittico*], have certain traits in common. The settings are contemporary; the characters are often rural and generally impoverished; the passions run high and lead to violence. There is a tendency in these works to wed the sordid with the sensational.

Verismo is also used, more loosely, to describe any of the operas by Mascagni, Leoncavallo, Puccini, Giordano, and Cilea, who were also collectively referred to as the young school *(nuove giovane).* The term then expands to include Puccini's **Tosca,* Cilea's **Adriana Lecouvreur,* and Giordano's **Andrea Chénier,* although they have historical settings; Puccini's **Madama Butterfly* and Mascagni's *Iris,* which have exotic settings; and Puccini's *La *bohème,* which sentimentalizes its characters in a way alien to ideals of realism or naturalism. C.G.

Verkaufte Braut, Die [Ger.]. See *Bartered Bride, The.*

Verklärte Nacht [Ger., Transfigured Night]. A work in one movement for two violins, two violas, and two cellos by Schoenberg, op. 4 (1899), inspired by a poem of Richard Dehmel. It was later arranged for string orchestra (1917, rev. 1943), and it has served as the basis for many ballets, including *Pillar of Fire* (1942, choreography by Antony Tudor).

Verkleinerung [Ger.]. Diminution.

Verkürzung [Ger.]. Shortening of a note-value; diminution.

Verlöschend [Ger.]. Dying away.

Vermindert [Ger.]. Diminished.

Vers [Occ., Fr., Ger.]. Poetry; a line of poetry; a verse, as of a Psalm; [Occ.] general term for song in the 12th century, eventually replaced by **canso* and other words referring to specific thematic content; [Ger.] stanza, strophe.

Verschiebung [Ger.]. See *Una corda.*

Verschwindend [Ger.]. Disappearing, fading away.

Verse. (1) Poetry; a line of poetry. (2) A group of lines making up a unit of a poem, usually one of several based on the same meter and rhyme scheme; strophe, stanza. Several such units may be separated by a recurring *refrain. (3) In one of the most typical forms of American popular song of the mid-20th century, words and music preceding the chorus or refrain, which constitutes the body of the song itself. The form and nomenclature derive from verse-and-refrain form [see (2)], but in practice there may be only one set of words for the verse, and it is often not performed at all [see Ballad (3)]. (4) The small units into which chapters and books of the Bible (including the Psalms) are divided, often identified in liturgical books with the symbol ℣. For the singing of Psalm verses and related texts, see Psalmody, Latin; Psalm tone. (5) *Versicle.

Verset [Fr.; Ger. *Versett, Versetl;* It. *verso, versetto;* Sp. *versillo*]. A brief organ piece intended to replace a verse of plainchant in the liturgy. Organists customarily played it in place of the odd-numbered verses of a liturgical item, the even-numbered verses being sung by the choir. Such pieces were improvised in virtually all Roman Catholic countries from ca. 1400 to 1903 [see Organ Mass]. Composers wrote out versets for liturgical items that were most frequently used, such as the Mass Ordinary, Magnificat, Te Deum, and certain Latin hymns. The practice of substituting organ music for plainsong is sometimes termed supplying.

Early versets (Buxheim Organ Book, ca. 1400; Girolamo Cavazzoni, 1553) were based on the chants they replaced, but by the mid-17th century they were often completely independent compositions. Large collections were written in southern Germany (Johann Pachelbel, Magnificat fugues), but the greatest flowering was in France during the next hundred years. Prominent contributors include Nicolas-Antoine Lebègue (ca. 1631–1702), Guillaume Nivers (ca. 1632–1714), François Couperin (1668–1733), Louis Marchand (1669–1732), Nicolas de Grigny (1672–1703), and Michel Corrette (1704–95). Written versets were often grouped by tone into "suites" because the same verset could serve in any number of places in the liturgy as long as it ended with the appropriate harmony for the ensuing verse of plainchant. In France, they fell into highly standardized categories of registration, texture, mood, and tempo. Three liturgical items remained separate and provided occasions for much more extended pieces: the offertory and elevation of the Mass (the former usually a spirited *dialogue sur les grands jeux* and the latter a somber *récit de tierce* in either the soprano or the tenor range); and the "judex crederis" of the Te Deum (in the late 18th century and onward, the occasion of unabashed storm pieces). Versets continued to be written in the 19th century as functional liturgical music, once again bound to chants. After 1900, composers including Messiaen and Jean Langlais have also used the term for organ pieces intended for liturgical use, but not for *alternatim* performance, which subsisted primarily as a French improvisatory art after the papal reforms of 1903. B.G.

Versetto [It.]. *Verset.

Versetzung [Ger.]. Transposition; *Versetzungszeichen,* accidental.

Versicle [abbr. ℣.]. (1) In the Western Christian rites, a phrase or sentence, often from Scripture, said or sung by the officiant and to which the choir or congregation answers with a phrase called a response (abbr. ℟.). In the Roman rite, the hours of the Office begin with the following versicle and response: ℣. Deus in adjutorium meum intende. ℟. Domine ad adjuvandum me festina. (℣. O God, come to my assistance. ℟. O Lord, make haste to help me; from Psalm 69 [70]; e.g., in *LU,* p. 250, and *AntMon,* p. 1.) Versicles and responses sometimes occur in longer series in the manner of a *litany. In the Anglican rite such series are variously termed **preces,* *suffrages, and responses. (2) In the *sequence, either of the two parallel lines that make up a couplet or "double versicle."

Versification. See Prosody.

Versillo [Sp.]. *Verset.

Vers mesuré [Fr.]. See *Musique mesurée.*

Verso [It., Sp.]. (1) *Verse. (2) *Verset. (3) [Lat.] In a manuscript or book, the reverse or second side of a leaf, the first side being termed *recto.*

Verstärken [Ger.]. To reinforce, amplify.

Versus [Lat.]. (1) Verse, as of a Psalm or some forms of liturgical chant [see Psalmody, Psalm tone, *Versus ad repetendum*]. (2) A line of poetry. (3) Rhymed, rhythmic, strophic Latin poetry set to music (both monophonic and polyphonic) beginning in the late 10th century and especially prominent in the repertory of *St. Martial. It had a strong influence on the development of *troubadour music. See also *Conductus.*

Versus ad repetendum [Lat.]. In *introits and *communions, one or more verses to be sung following the *Doxology. Such verses are preserved in some of the earliest sources and are described still earlier, though not entirely consistently, in the *Ordines romani* [see Gregorian chant VI].

Verticalization. In *twelve-tone music, the statement as a simultaneity of two or more adjacent elements of a row.

Vertical piano. Upright *piano.

Verzierung [Ger.]. Ornament, *ornamentation.

Vesperal [Lat. *vesperale*]. See Liturgical books I.

Vespers [fr. Lat. *vesper,* evening]. A service forming part of the Divine *Office.

Vessel flute. *Globular flute.

Via [It.]. Away; *via sordini,* remove mutes.

Vibraharp, vibraphone. A percussion instrument of definite pitch consisting of graduated metal bars arranged horizontally in a fashion similar to that of the piano keyboard. Beneath each bar is a vertical resonating tube, in the upper part of which is a flat disk. The disks for each of the two rows of resonators (one for diatonic pitches, the other for chromatic) are connected by a rod that can be rotated by a motor, causing the disks to open and close the resonators, thus producing a *vibrato. The instrument may be played either with the motor on or off and is struck with beaters of various hardnesses. It is also fitted with dampers controlled by a pedal. Its normal compass is f–f‴. The instrument was developed in the U.S. in the 1920s and became widespread in popular music and jazz. Since the 1930s, it has been increasingly used in art music as well.

Vibrare [It.]. To vibrate; *lasciar vibrare,* allow to vibrate, do not damp.

Vibrations. See Acoustics.

Vibrato [It., from Lat. *vibrare,* to shake]. A slight fluctuation of pitch used by performers to enrich or intensify the sound. In modern string playing, vibrato is produced by rocking the left hand, usually from the wrist, as a note is played; in modern wind playing, it is effected by regulating the air flow into the instrument or by varying the tension of the lips or the pressure of the mouth on the reed or mouthpiece. Since the early decades of the 20th century, vibrato, particularly on bowed stringed instruments, has become essentially an organic feature of tone production, a means of adding continuous intensity to the sound; vibrato has become a standard feature of the unchanging legato sound most often taught at present.

Until the 20th century, vibrato, or **tremolo,* as it was generally termed, was produced in a number of ways and was considered to be an ornament, an expressive device that, like many others available to the performer, was used sparingly. Mersenne (1636), calling it *verre cassé,* and Mace (1676), using the term sting, described lute vibrato; both say that it was little used, Mersenne reporting that its lack of popularity was a reaction against its overuse in former times. Vibrato on the viola da gamba is discussed by authors like Ganassi (1543), who found it appropriate for "sad and aggrieved" music, Simpson (1659), who also recommends a bow tremolo, De Machy (1685), Marais (1686), Danoville (1687), and Jean Rousseau (1687). These writers distinguish between two-finger vibrato—a kind of microtonal trill—and the more familiar one-finger variety. Two-finger vibrato is termed close shake by Simpson, *tremblement sans appuyer* by De Machy, *battement* by Danoville and Rousseau, and *flattement* by Marais. One-finger vibrato, termed *langeur* by Rousseau and *plainte* by Marais, is recommended for notes played with the fourth finger, when two-finger vibrato was impossible. Flute treatises by Hotteterre (1707) and Corrette (1735) describe *flattement* that, like the gambist's two-finger vibrato, requires the sounded note to be alternated with one a microtone higher, produced by partially closing the flute's next hole with an adjacent finger. Quantz (1752) mentions vibrato, calling it **Bebung,* only to say that it is appropriate when swelling and diminishing a long-note *messa di voce.*

Bow vibrato on the violin, an undulating movement of the bow, seems to have been preferred by such diverse writers as Ganassi (1535), Brossard (1703), Walther (1732), and Mattheson (1739). Left-hand, one-finger vibrato is mentioned in 1545 by Martin Agricola as "sweetening" the sound of "Polish violins." Eighteenth-century treatises by Tartini (MS, ca. 1752; pub. 1771) and Leopold Mozart (1756), who repeats much of Tartini's material, recommend specific and limited use of violin vibrato. Only Geminiani, who calls vibrato close shake, wrote that "it should be made use of as often as possible." But Leopold Mozart speaks disapprovingly of players who "tremble upon every note as though they had palsy," and subsequent editions of Geminiani's treatise delete the advice to use it as often as possible. Spohr (1832) and other 19th-century violinists continue to recommend limited, deliberate use of vibrato; in the autograph of Mendelssohn's violin concerto, the composer has specified moments at which vibrato should be used. In general, vibrato is said to be useful on long notes and to highlight expressive moments; the modern use of vibrato to add intensity is never mentioned.

Vocal vibrato is more difficult to define. What is often termed vibrato and widely cultivated is at least as much a fluctuation in intensity as in pitch; some authorities maintain that it is entirely a fluctuation in intensity. An excessive fluctuation in pitch (sometimes termed in this context tremolo) is, of course, agreed by all to be undesirable. In general, vocal vibrato is the norm in Western art music today, its momentary restraint or absence serving an expressive purpose. Singers attempting to re-create the performing styles of some early music may employ vibrato sparingly or not at all, however. For vocal ornaments consisting of the rapid repetition of a pitch, see Tremolo; see also Singing, Voice, Performance practice.

Bibl.: David D. Boyden, *The History of Violin Playing from Its Origins to 1761* (London: Oxford U Pr, 1965). Robert Donington, *The Interpretation of Early Music, New Version* (London: Faber, 1974). *NeuO.* Bruce Dickey, "Untersuchungen zur historischen Auffassung des Vibratos auf

Blasinstrumenten," *Basler Jahrbuch für historische Musikpraxis* 2 (1978): 77–142. Clive Brown, "Bowing Styles, Vibrato and Portamento in Nineteenth-Century Violin Playing," *Journal of the Royal Musical Association* 113 (1988): 97–128. Greta Moens-Haenen, *Das Vibrato in der Musik des Barock: Ein Handbuch zur Aufführungspraxis für Vokalisten und Instrumentalisten* (Graz: Akademische Druck- und Verlagsanstalt, 1988). Frederick Neumann, "The Vibrato Controversy," *Performance Practice Review* 4 (1991): 14–27. Neal Zaslaw, "Vibrato in Eighteenth-Century Orchestras," *Performance Practice Review* 4 (1991): 28–33. Frederick K. Gable, "Some Observations concerning Baroque and Modern Vibrato," *Performance Practice Review* 5 (1992): 90–120. See also Bowing, Mordent, Ornamentation, Performance marks, Performance practice, Singing.

Vibrer [Fr.]. To vibrate; *laissez vibrer,* allow to vibrate, do not damp.

Victimae paschali laudes [Lat., Praises to the Paschal victim]. The *sequence for Easter.

Vida breve, La [Sp., The Brief Life]. Opera in two acts by Falla (libretto by Carlos Fernández Shaw), produced (in French) in Nice in 1913. Setting: the Gypsy quarter of Granada.

Vidala [Sp.]. A traditional song genre of northern and central Argentina associated, like the tritonic **baguala,* with the celebration of carnival. The *vidala* and the closely related *vidalita* are sung collectively and individually, with drum (*caja* or *tambor*), or guitar and drum accompaniment. Melodies, often in parallel thirds, are set to verses typically in *copla* form, with distinctive interpolated refrains. D.S.

Vide. (1) [Fr.] Empty; *corde à vide,* open string. (2) [Lat.] See. The instruction to proceed directly from one point in a score to some other may be indicated by placing the syllable *Vi-* at the first and *-de* at the second.

Vieil ton [Fr., old tuning]. The Renaissance tuning in fourths for lute, *vihuela,* viola da gamba, and related instruments. The G tuning (G c f a d′ g′) is most frequently encountered in the sources, though the tuning on A was favored by some German lutenists. Renaissance lute tunings are "nominal," however, since the actual pitch would be determined by the instrument's size. Players conceived the fingerboard as representing a number of movable hexachords. Disparate tunings that today would be called D, E, B♭, or even F♯ do not represent pitch levels but rather were selected for ease in the *intabulation of vocal music and, in collections of music for voice and lute, to assure that the vocal tessitura remained the same throughout. The *vieil ton* was gradually displaced after 1600 by the many **accords nouveaux,* though its use was continued by the Dowland school, in the **air de cour* repertory, and in tablatures for chitarrone and theorbo (in which the top two courses were frequently tuned an octave lower). Today the G tuning has become standard in transcriptions of Renaissance music.

Bibl.: John M. Ward, "Changing the Instrument for the Music," *Journal of the Lute Society of America* 15 (1982): 27–39. A.J.N.

Vielle [Fr.]. Any of a variety of bowed stringed instruments of the Middle Ages, including both the medieval *viol and *fiddle; *v. à roue,* *hurdy-gurdy.

Vielstimmig [Ger.]. Polyphonic.

Viennese classical school. The principal composers of the *Classical period, Haydn, Mozart, and Beethoven, the major part of whose activity was in Vienna. The term is sometimes broadened to include their contemporaries and predecessors.

Viennese school, second. Arnold Schoenberg (1874–1951) and his two pupils Anton Webern (1883–1945) and Alban Berg (1885–1935), the first major exponents of *twelve-tone music.

Vierhändig [Ger.]. For four hands, i.e., for two players at a single piano.

Vierhebigkeit [Ger.]. The divisibility of music into units of four, whether of beats, accents, measures, phrases, etc. Hugo Riemann (1849–1919) was largely responsible for elevating this to a universal principle of Western music. Even in the Classical period, however, where such divisions (especially in the form of the four-measure *phrase; see also Antecedent, consequent) are most readily observable, this view is not consistently applicable. Riemann's analyses and transcriptions of some medieval repertories on the basis of such principles have largely been discredited.

Viertel [Ger.]. Quarter; *Viertelnote,* quarter *note; *Viertelton,* quarter tone.

Vietnam. See Southeast Asia VI.

Vif [Fr.]. Lively, fast.

Vigil [Lat. *vigilia,* wakefulness, watchfulness]. A liturgical service held in anticipation of a given feast, especially on the night preceding. Vigils have been assigned to only the most important feasts of the year, the most prominent being the Easter or Paschal Vigil, which begins after sundown on Holy Saturday and concludes with a Mass at about midnight (*LU,* pp. 776H–776MM).

Vihuela [Sp.]. A waisted, stringed instrument of medieval and Renaissance Spain. Three varieties are most often encountered: *vihuela de arco,* a bowed *vihuela; vihuela de peñola,* played with a quill; *vihuela de mano,* plucked with the fingers. By the 16th century, the unqualified term meant the *vihuela de mano.* In 16th-century Italy, the *vihuela* was called the *viola* or *viola de mano.*

The *vihuela (de mano),* often seen in Renaissance

sources, is a large instrument, quite like a modern guitar in size and appearance. It has a flat top and back, rather shallow sides, a narrow neck (with ten gut frets) and peghead, an elaborate rosette, and sometimes decoration. The peghead is bent slightly back with pegs inserted from the rear. Only one example from the period is known to survive, and it is thought to be abnormally large.

Six unison courses of double gut strings are typical, though printed music for five- and seven-course instruments is preserved. The *vihuela*'s tuning uses intervals identical to the lute's: fourth, fourth, major third, fourth, fourth. The exact pitch of the instruments varied because of the variety in *vihuela* sizes. In his tutor *El maestro* (1536), Luis de Milán recommends tuning the **chanterelle* as high as it will go without breaking, then tuning the other strings to it. Luys de Narváez (1538) gives the nominal tuning for the *chanterelle* of six sizes of *vihuela* as c″, b♭′, a′, g♯′, g′, and f′.

The *vihuela* repertory includes accompaniment to songs of the **romance* and **villancico* types, some beautiful and difficult solos (*fantasias, **diferencias,* and **tientos*), and *intabulations of vocal works and a few dances [see also Spain II]. It is printed in a variety of *tablature forms. Playing techniques are very similar to those of the 16th-century lute. By the beginning of the 17th century, the *vihuela* had been largely replaced by the four-course guitar.

Bibl.: John Ward, "The Vihuela de Mano and Its Music (1536–1576)" (Ph.D. diss., New York Univ., 1953). David B. Lyons, *Lute, Vihuela, Guitar to 1800: A Bibliography* (Detroit: Info Coord, 1978). James Tyler, *The Early Guitar: A History and Handbook* (London: Oxford U Pr, 1980). Donald Gill, "Vihuelas, Violas, and the Spanish Guitar," *EM* 9 (1981): 455–67. R.L.

Villancico [Sp.]. In the 15th and 16th centuries, a form of Spanish poetry consisting of a refrain *(estribillo)* that alternates with one or more strophes (*coplas* or *pies*), each of which is made up of a *mudanza* (change, i.e., of rhyme) and a *vuelta* (return, i.e., to the rhyme of the refrain). The number of lines and the rhyme scheme of these components is variable; the most common line length is of eight syllables. The accompanying diagram gives two common schemes. In the first, the rhyme scheme of the *vuelta* agrees with that of the refrain. In the second, a rhyme from the *mudanza* is carried over into the *vuelta,* with the result that the return to the music of the refrain begins before the return to its rhymes. In some examples, the *vuelta* repeats literally the last line or two of the refrain, thus contracting the two. The form is employed, though not so termed, in the 13th century **cantigas;* and it is closely related to the 12th-century Hispano-Arabic **zajal,* the French **virelai,* and the Italian **ballata* (the terminology for which is similar to that for the *villancico*). The repertory includes courtly, popular, and sacred elements and many poems in the feminine voice.

	Estribillo (refrain)	Copla (strophe)	
		Mudanza	Vuelta
Music	A	BB	A
Text	ABB	cdcd	abb
	ABB	cdcd	dBB

The first large collections are **cancioneros* from around 1500, especially the *Cancionero musical de Palacio* (ed. *MME* 5, 10, 14). These contain polyphonic settings in three and four voices by Juan del Encina (1468–1529 or 1530; the principal exponent of the genre in this period), Francisco Millán, Francisco de Peñalosa, Francisco de la Torre, Juan de Anchieta, and others. Some works employ polyphonic textures reminiscent of the 15th-century French chanson (sometimes with text supplied in only the uppermost of three voices), whereas others are largely homophonic (sometimes with text in all voices). Composers cultivating the genre later in the 16th century include Juan Vázquez (*MME* 4) and Francisco Guerrero (*MME* 16, 19). In this period, the number of voices is often reduced (sometimes to one) for the *mudanza,* and there is a growing repertory of sacred works, including *contrafacta.* Composers for the **vihuela* such as Luís de Milán, Luis de Narváez, Miguel de Fuenllana, and Alonso Mudarra also contributed settings.

The vast repertory of *villancicos* from the 17th century remains largely unpublished and unexplored. It includes secular works that continue the traditions of the 16th century, but by mid-century some *villancicos* had instrumental accompaniment. At the same time, the addition of refrains *(estribillos)* to the form of the **romance* leads to a merging of the musical forms of the *villancico* and *romance,* and the sources of the period often label as *villancicos* works more properly described as *romances* with added *estribillos.* Such works may also be termed *tonada* or *tono humano.* Composers represented in the period's *cancioneros* (described and selections published in *MME* 32) include Mateo Romero ("Maestro Capitán"), Juan Pujol, Juan Arañés, Francisco Gutiérrez, and Bartolomé Murillo. This period also saw the rapid expansion of a repertory of increasingly elaborate sacred works. Many of these works, which are accompanied by instruments, begin with an *introducción* for solo voices, followed by a *responsión* or *estribillo* for soloists and one or more choirs in as many as a dozen parts and by *coplas* for one or a few soloists. Such works were composed by chapel masters all over Spain for the principal religious feasts, especially Christmas. Composers include Juan Bautista Comes (1582–1643), Joan Cererols (1618–76), and Sebastián Durón (1660–1716). In the first half of the 18th century, the *villancico* increasingly took on the character of the Italian cantata in its use of arias, recitatives, and instrumental movements, as in works by Durón that were sharply criticized in some quarters at the time on this account. In 1765, the performance in church of works of this type with vernacular texts was suppressed.

The *villancico* followed a similar course in Latin America in the 17th and 18th centuries, in part through the spread of works by peninsular composers such as Durón and in part through the activity of composers working there, e.g., Juan Gutiérrez de Padilla (ca. 1590–1664), whose cycles of *villancicos* were composed for and are preserved at the Cathedral of Puebla, Mexico. The foremost poet of the repertory was Mexico's Sor Juana Inés de la Cruz (1651–95), whose texts were set by Miguel Matheo de Dallo y Lana, José de Loaysa y Agurto, and others. Works intended for use in church, a major fraction of which were for Christmas, were often arranged in cycles to be sung in place of the responsories at Matins. Regional types within the repertory include the *gallego, portorrico, tocotín, canario, negrilla, jácara,* and *irlandés.* Several types of Latin American folk songs also derive from the *villancico,* including the *adoración, *alabado, *aguinaldo,* and **esquinazo.*

The term is now sometimes simply synonymous with Christmas carol.

Bibl.: For sources and editions (in the case of *MME,* often with extended introductory studies), see *Cancionero.* Isabel Pope, "Musical and Metrical Form of the Villancico," *AnnM* 2 (1954): 189–214. Miguel Querol [Gavaldá], "El romance polifónico en el siglo XVII," *AnM* 10 (1955): 111–20. José Romeu Figueras, "Mateo Flecha el Viejo, la corte literario-musical del duque de Calabria y el Cancionero llamado de Upsala," *AnM* 13 (1958): 25–101. Robert M. Stevenson, *Spanish Music in the Age of Columbus* (The Hague: Nijhoff, 1960). Gertraut Haberkamp, *Die weltliche Vokalmusik in Spanien um 1500* (Tutzing: Schneider, 1968). Miguel Querol [Gavaldá], "La producción musical de Juan del Encina (1469–1529)," *AnM* 24 (1969): 121–31. Antonio Sánchez Romeralo, *El villancico (estudios sobre la lírica popular en los siglos XV y XVI)* (Madrid: Gredos, 1969). Ramón Adolfo Pelinski, *Die weltliche Vokalmusik Spaniens am Anfang des 17. Jahrhunderts: Der Cancionero Claudio de la Sablonara* (Tutzing: Schneider, 1971).

Villanella [It.]. A form of vocal music popular in Italy from ca. 1530 to the end of the 16th century. The earliest examples, called *canzone villanesche alla napolitana,* are stanzas similar in poetic form and content to a chain of **strambotti* but have a refrain placed between adjacent couplets (abR abR abR ccR). The material is often but not invariably rustic; parodies of high-flown poetic language are common, and many proverbial expressions are used. The music, for three voices in homophonic style and with the chief tune in the top voice, is simple and rhythmically lively (usually written in **note nere*), with dancelike syncopations and well-marked cadences. The celebrated parallel fifths in the texture may be a deliberate rusticity and may also imitate the effect of a strumming instrument. Neapolitan composers such as Giovanni Domenico da Nola (1541 and after) and Giovan Tomaso di Maio (1546) wrote quantities of these pieces, the popularity of which soon spread throughout Italy.

The *villanella* was taken up by Adrian Willaert (1544) and other Venetian composers; they paraphrased the originals, adding a fourth voice, moving the tune to the tenor, and smoothing out the counterpoint. *Villanelle,* like other popular forms such as the **villotta,* were used in plays; in Naples, leading roles in comedies were given to well-known singers.

In the 1550s, the term *villanella* began to replace the older *villanesca.* Orlande de Lassus included four-voice *villanelle* in his "op. 1" of 1555; these pieces and Lassus's later work in the genre are among the best of their kind. Subgenres such as the *moresca* (Moorish song), *mascherata,* and *todesca* (German soldier's song) in the music of Lassus and others are *villanelle* in form and style.

The three-voice, simple-textured *villanella* continued to flourish in the later 16th century, with Venetian subgenres such as the *giustiniana* and *greghesca* adding to its variety of subject matter. Three-voice *villanelle* of a more polished nature were also being written (Giovanni Ferretti, *Napolitane,* 1568; Ruggiero Giovannelli, 1588; Luca Marenzio, 1584 and after); Ferretti and others wrote multivoice *villanelle* that are really identical to the **canzonetta.* In the early 17th century, Adriano Banchieri used *villanelle* of parodistic content in his madrigal comedies.

Bibl.: *Editions.* Filippo Azzaiolo, *Il secondo libro de villote . . . con alcune napolitane,* Maestri bolognesi 2 (Bologna: Antiquaria Palmaverdi, 1953). Donna G. Cardamone, ed., *A. Willaert and His Circle: Canzone Villanesche alla Napolitana and Villote, RRMR,* vol. 30 (Madison, Wis.: A-R Edit, 1978).

Literature. Alfred Einstein, *The Italian Madrigal,* 3 vols. (Princeton: Princeton U Pr, 1949). Wolfgang Osthoff, *Theatergesang und darstellende Musik in der italienischen Renaissance* (Tutzing: Schneider, 1969). Donna G. Cardamone, "The Debut of the Canzone Villanesca alla napolitana," *Studi musicali* 4 (1975): 65–130. Id., "Forme metriche e musicali della canzone villanesca e della villanella alla napolitana," *RIM* 12 (1977): 25–72. J.H.

Villanesca [It., fr. *canzone villanesca alla napolitana*]. The term used for the early repertory of the **villanella. Villanesca* is an adjective meaning countrified; *villanella* is a noun meaning, originally, a country girl. J.H.

Villano [Sp., peasant; It. *vallan di Spagna*]. A sung dance of Spain, also popular in Italy in the 16th and 17th centuries. Music based on the harmonic progression I–IV–I–V–I was provided in numerous Spanish and Italian guitar tablatures.

Villotta [It.]. A type of vocal music popular in Venice and Padua during the early 16th century. The poems, of one or more stanzas varying in length and form, are of a rustic, unsentimental character and often include portions of popular song texts. At some point in the poem comes a group of nonsense syllables called *lilolela;* before or after it is a refrain called *nio.* The music of the *villotta* is for four voices, often with a popular tune in the tenor. The texture is basically chordal, although there are points of imitation. The *nio* is often in triple meter. Some *villotte* are *quodlibets or *incatenature* of popular song texts and tunes; an example is Giacomo Fogliano's "Fortuna d'un gran tempo" (published by Petrucci in *Frottole,* bk. 9, of 1509). The chief sources for the *villotta* are a group of prints and manuscripts of the late 1520s, collections that also include *frottolas and early examples of the madrigal. There is no reason to think, as does Torrefranca, that the music in these sources is of 15th-century origin.

Bibl.: Knud Jeppesen, "Venetian Folksongs of the Renaissance," *PAMS* (1939): 62–75. Fausto Torrefranca, *Il segreto del Quattrocento* (Milan: U Hoepli, 1939; R: Bologna: Forni, 1972). J.H.

Vīṇā. A South Indian *long-necked lute. Four playing strings and three drone strings are stretched over a broad neck that extends from its pear-shaped body. The neck has 24 frets, and a gourd resonator and backward-curving pegbox are attached to its upper end. The body and pegbox make it a long-necked lute in contrast to the North Indian **bīn,* which is a stick zither. The player sits cross-legged and holds the instrument more or less horizontally, plucking the playing strings with plectra on the fingers of the right hand. It is much used in South Indian art music, mainly as a solo instrument but also to accompany song. See ill. under South Asia.

Vingt-quatre violons du roi. A string ensemble of 24 players in five parts (6, 4, 4, 4, 6) at the French court under Louis XIII, Louis XIV, and Louis XV (1626–1761); this ensemble was famous throughout Europe under the directorship of Lully. It was also termed *La grande bande,* in contradistinction to the *petite bande,* an ensemble of 16 (later 21) players that Lully had begun to conduct by 1656, and it inspired the formation of similar groups elsewhere, e.g., at the court of Charles II of England [see also Band (1)]. On some occasions, such as opera performances, it was joined by winds.

Viol [fr. It. *viola da gamba;* Fr. *viole;* Ger. *Gambe;* Sp. *viola de gamba*]. Any of a family of fretted, bowed stringed instruments in use from the 16th through much of the 18th century; also viola da gamba, gamba. The Italian term *viola da gamba* (leg viol) distinguishes the instruments of this family, which are played upright, resting on or between the legs, from instruments termed **viola da braccio,* which are played on the arm. In addition to its seven gut frets, the usual distinguishing features of the viol are sloping shoulders, a flat back with a section that slopes toward the neck, deep ribs, *sound holes in the shape of a *c* rather than an *f,* six (or, in the case of the French *basse de viole,* seven) strings tuned in fourths except for a major third between the two middle strings, and relatively wide and flat bridge and fingerboard [see ill.]. The shape of the viol varied considerably, however. Like other instruments of its period, including the violin, its strings are lighter and under less tension than those of the modern violin family. The bow is held with the palm upward, and its stick curves slightly away from the hair [see also Bow, Bowing].

Terminology and tunings were often inconsistent for the viol, especially in the 16th century. In the 17th and 18th centuries, however, there were in general three standard sizes: the treble [Fr. *dessus de viole*], tuned d g c′ e′ a′ d″ and supported on the knees; the tenor [Fr. *taille de viole*], tuned G c f a d′ g′ and held between the legs; and the bass [Fr. *basse de viole*], tuned D G c e a d′ or A_1 D G c e a d′ and also held between the legs. A *chest of viols ordinarily included two of each type. The terms viola da gamba and gamba now usually refer to the bass. Other sizes and types included a smaller, higher-pitched instrument, often with five strings tuned g c′ e′ a′ d″, termed a descant or *pardessus de viole;* the double-bass viol [Fr. *contre-basse de viole;* It. **violone*], tuned an octave below the bass; the division viol [It. *viola bastarda*], a bass viol slightly smaller than the normal consort viol and used for playing *divisions; and the lyra viol, a still smaller bass viol with a somewhat flatter bridge, played in a variety of tunings, and for which a considerable literature in a polyphonic style was composed in 17th-century England. More distant relatives include the *viola d'amore and the *baryton.

The viol originated in late 15th-century Spain under the influence of the playing technique of the Arabic **rabāb,* which was held upright on the knee. Medieval *fiddles played in this way and sometimes termed medieval viols died out in the 14th century and are thus not the ancestors of the Renaissance instrument. Although the viol therefore predates the violin by about half a century, the two instrumental families coexisted for nearly 250 years. The oft-asserted claim that the cello "evolved" from the bass viol is simply erroneous.

The first treatise on viol playing was Silvestro Ganassi's *Regola rubertina* (Venice, 1542; facs., *BMB* sez. 2, 18, 1970; trans. Bodig, 1981–82), which also includes the first published music for solo viol. Diego Ortiz's *Trattado de glosas* of 1553 is devoted to improvising divisions or ornaments, often on polyphonic vocal models, which constituted the principal repertory of 16th-century viol consorts. The end of the 16th century saw the viol lose ground to the violin, especially in Italy. But the viol was well established in England by this time and gave rise to a large and varied repertory there [see Consort, Division, Fantasia, In nomine]. In the late 17th century and most of the 18th, French performers and composers of viol music were the most celebrated in Europe. These included Marin

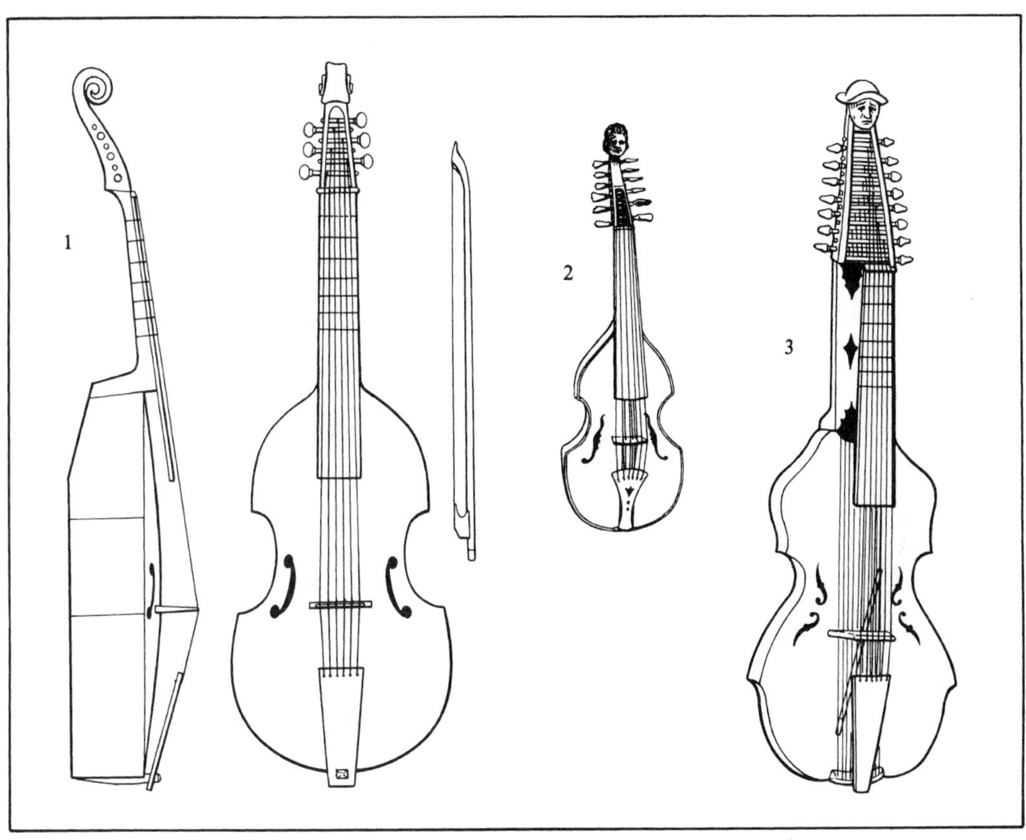

1. Viola da gamba (bass viol). 2. Viola d'amore. 3. Baryton.

Marais (1656–1728), Antoine Forqueray (1671 or 1672–1745), Louis de Caix d'Hervelois (d. ca. 1760), and Jean-Baptiste Forqueray (1699–1782). Perhaps the last great performer and composer of viol music, however, was the German Carl Friedrich Abel (1723–87), active from 1758 in London (where he produced concerts jointly with J. C. Bach). Other German composer-performers included August Kühnel (1645–ca. 1700), Johannes Schenck (1660–ca. 1712), and Ernst Christian Hesse (1676–1762). J. S. Bach employed the viol as an obbligato instrument in a number of vocal works (including arias in the St. Matthew and St. John Passions) and composed three sonatas for viol and harpsichord (BWV 1027–29, ca. 1720).

By the mid-18th century, the bass viol gave way to the cello in ensembles, and it soon ceased to be cultivated widely as a solo instrument. The extensive modern revival of the viol dates from the end of the 19th century and the work of Arnold Dolmetsch.

Bibl.: Gerald R. Hayes, *Musical Instruments and Their Music 1500–1750,* 2 vols. (London: Oxford U Pr, H Milford, 1930), vol. 2, *The Viols and Other Bowed Instruments* (R: New York: Broude Bros, 1969). Nathalie Dolmetsch, *The Viola da Gamba: Its Origin and History, Its Technique and Musical Resources* (New York: Hinrichsen, 1962). Hans Bol, *La basse de viole du temps de Marin Marais et d'Antoine Forqueray* (Bilthoven: A B Creyghton, 1973). Veronika Gutmann, *Die Improvisation auf der Viola da gamba in England im 17. Jahrhundert und ihre Wurzeln im 16. Jahrhundert* (Tutzing: Schneider, 1979). Gordon Dodd, comp., *Thematic Index of Music for Viols* (London: Viola da Gamba Society, 1980). Julie Ann Sadie, *The Bass Viol in French Baroque Chamber Music* (Ann Arbor: UMI Res Pr, 1980). Richard D. Bodig, trans., "Ganassi's Regola Rubertina," *Journal of the Viola da Gamba Society of America,* 18 (1981): 13–66, 19 (1982): 99–163. John Hsu, *A Handbook of French Baroque Viol Technique* (New York: Broude Bros, 1981). Ian Woodfield, *The Early History of the Viol* (Cambridge: Cambridge U Pr, 1984). Annette Otterstedt, *Die Gambe. Kulturgeschichte und praktischer Ratgeber* (Kassel: Bärenreiter, 1994); rev., enlarged ed. trans. Hans Reiners, *The Viol: History of an Instrument* (Kassel: Bärenreiter, 2002).

Viola. (1) [It., Sp.; Fr. *alto;* Ger. *Viola, Viole, Bratsche*]. The second-highest member of the violin family. Its four strings are tuned c g d′ a′, a fifth below those of the violin, and its music is normally notated in the alto clef. The viola varies in size, with a body length of from 38 to 44 cm (15 to 17¼ in.). It is thus larger than the violin (which has a normal body length of 35.5 cm), but not as much larger as would be necessary if the violin's ratio of size to pitch were to be maintained. This facilitates its being played on the shoulder but results in tonal characteristics different from the violin's, notably a less rich and powerful sound in the extreme low register. The viola is otherwise similar in construction to the violin. For the early history of the viola and relatively recent designs of larger size, see Violin II, Tenor violin; see ill. under Violin.

In the orchestra, it is the second highest of the four bowed stringed instruments, and its part lies below the two violin parts and above the parts for the violoncello and double bass. In the string quartet, it has the second lowest part, lying below those of the two violins and above that of the violoncello. In the string trio, it has the middle part, between those for violin and violoncello. Although it has played an important role in orchestral and chamber music since the 18th century, its solo repertory remains limited. Orchestral works with solo viola include Mozart's *Sinfonia concertante* K. 364 (320d), Berlioz's **Harold en Italie,* and Richard Strauss's **Don Quixote* and concertos by Walton, Bartók (posthumous), Hindemith (himself a violist), and Piston.

(2) [It.] In the 16th and 17th centuries, any bowed stringed instrument. If played on the arm, such an instrument was a **viola da braccio* (whence the German *Bratsche*); if played on or between the legs, it was a **viola da gamba.*

Bibl.: Henry Barrett, *The Viola: Complete Guide for Teachers and Students* (University, Ala.: U of Ala Pr, 1972). Maurice W. Riley, *The History of the Viola* (Ann Arbor, 1980). See also Violin, Bibliography II.

Viola alta [It.; Ger. *Altgeige*]. A large viola (body length about 48 cm with the exact proportions of the violin) built by Karl Adam Hörlein according to the specifications of the violist Hermann Ritter and exhibited in 1876. It was used in the orchestra at Bayreuth. In 1898, Ritter had a fifth string added, tuned e″.

Viola bastarda [It.]. *Division viol.

Viola da braccio [It. *braccio,* arm]. In the 16th and 17th centuries, a bowed stringed instrument played on the arm, as distinct from one played on or between the legs *(*viola da gamba);* thus, any of several instruments of the violin family, as distinct from viols. See also Viola.

Viola da gamba [It. *gamba,* leg]. In the 16th and 17th centuries, a bowed stringed instrument played on or between the legs, as distinct from one played on the arm *(*viola da braccio);* thus, any of the members of the *viol family. Since the 17th century, the term (now often abbreviated *gamba*) has most often designated the bass viol; see ill. under Viol.

Viola d'amore [It.; Fr. *viole d'amour;* Ger. *Liebesgeige*]. A bowed stringed instrument prominent in the late 17th and 18th centuries, approximately the size of the viola and played on the shoulder, but with the body of a viol and most often provided with *sympathetic strings. The pegbox terminates in the figure of a head, the fingerboard is fretless, and the sound holes are in the shape of flaming swords [see ill. under Viol]. Typical 18th-century examples have six or seven gut playing strings and a corresponding number of metal sympathetic strings that pass through the bridge and under the fingerboard to the pegbox. Early in the century, tunings varied considerably. By the end of the century, a widely used tuning was A d a d′ f♯′ a′ d″, the sympathetic strings being tuned in unison or at the octave with the playing strings. Music for the instrument was often notated in *scordatura, as if the highest four strings were tuned like the four strings of the violin. A 17th-century type is slightly smaller and has metal playing strings and no sympathetic strings.

Composers who wrote for the instrument in the 18th century include Attilio Ariosti (a leading player of the first half of the century), Alessandro Scarlatti, Telemann, Bach (Cantatas 152 and 205 and the St. John Passion), Graupner (including nine concertos), Vivaldi (eight concertos), Carl Stamitz (a virtuoso of the second half of the century), Quantz, and Haydn. A much sparser repertory from the 19th and 20th centuries includes works by Meyerbeer *(Les Huguenots),* Puccini *(Madama Butterfly),* Charpentier *(Louise),* Richard Strauss *(Sinfonia domestica),* and Hindemith (a sonata op. 25 no. 2 and a concerto op. 46 no. 1).

Bibl.: Karl Stumpf, *Neue Schule für Viola d'amore* (Vienna: Österreichischer Bundesverlag, 1957; 2nd ed., 1965). Harry Danks, *The Viola d'Amore* (Halesowen, England: Bois de Boulogne, 1976; 2nd ed., 1979). Myron Rosenblum, "Contributions to the History and Literature of the Viola d'Amore" (Ph.D. diss., New York Univ., 1976).

Viola da spalla [It., *spalla,* shoulder]. In the early 18th century, a small cello with four to six strings held against the chest by a shoulder strap. By mid-century, the term was synonymous with cello, in contradistinction to viola da gamba.

Viola di bordone, viola paradon [It.]. *Baryton.

Viola di fagotto [It.]. **Fagottgeige.*

Viola pomposa [It.]. A viola of the mid-18th century, with five strings tuned either c g d′ a′ e″ or perhaps d g d′ g′ c″. The only surviving works for the instrument are two duets with flute by Telemann, a concerto by Graun, and a sonata by Cristiano Lidarti. Graun and Heinrich Koch also use the term *violino pomposo.* In the late 18th century, its invention was incorrectly attributed to Bach, perhaps because of confusion with the **violoncello piccolo.*

Bibl.: Francis W. Galpin, "Viola pomposa and Violoncello piccolo," *ML* 12 (1931): 354–64.

Viola tenore [It.]. See Tenor violin.

Viole [Fr.]. *Viol; *viole d'amour,* *viola d'amore.

Violet [dim. of viol]. In the 16th century, the violin. See also English violet.

Viole-ténor [Fr.]. A large viola, held like a cello, constructed by R. Parramon of Barcelona in 1930; also termed *alto moderne.*

Violetta [It.]. Any of a variety of bowed stringed instruments. At the time of the emergence of the violin, Lanfranco in 1533 uses the term *violetta* to describe what is probably an early form of the violin, i.e., a three-string instrument without frets. Such an instrument is depicted in a painting by Gaudenzio Ferrari, ca. 1530, documenting the basic form of the instrument with corners and stylized F holes and with shallow ribs unlike those of instruments of the viol family. In the 17th and 18th centuries, *violetta* refers to the viola, particularly in Germany; *violetta marina* to the viola d'amore. The term *English violet probably also derives from *violetta.* W.L.M.

Violin [Fr. *violon;* Ger. *violine, Geige;* It. *violino;* Sp. *violín*]. A bowed stringed instrument consisting of a hollow resonating wooden body with an attached neck and pegbox. Its four strings are tuned in fifths, g d′ a′ e″. The body is distinguished by rounded shoulders where it joins the neck and by indented center bouts, which allow free bow clearance when playing on the outer strings. An extended, fretless fingerboard over the neck is used for stopping the strings with the fingers of the left hand. A *bow, with its ribbon of rosined horsehair, sets the strings in motion, and this string vibration is transmitted through the bridge to the table (top, belly) and resonating body, thereby creating the instrument's characteristic sound [see Fig. 1].

I. *Construction.* The violin table is traditionally fashioned from European spruce, a soft wood similar to pine and grown in cool mountain elevations that

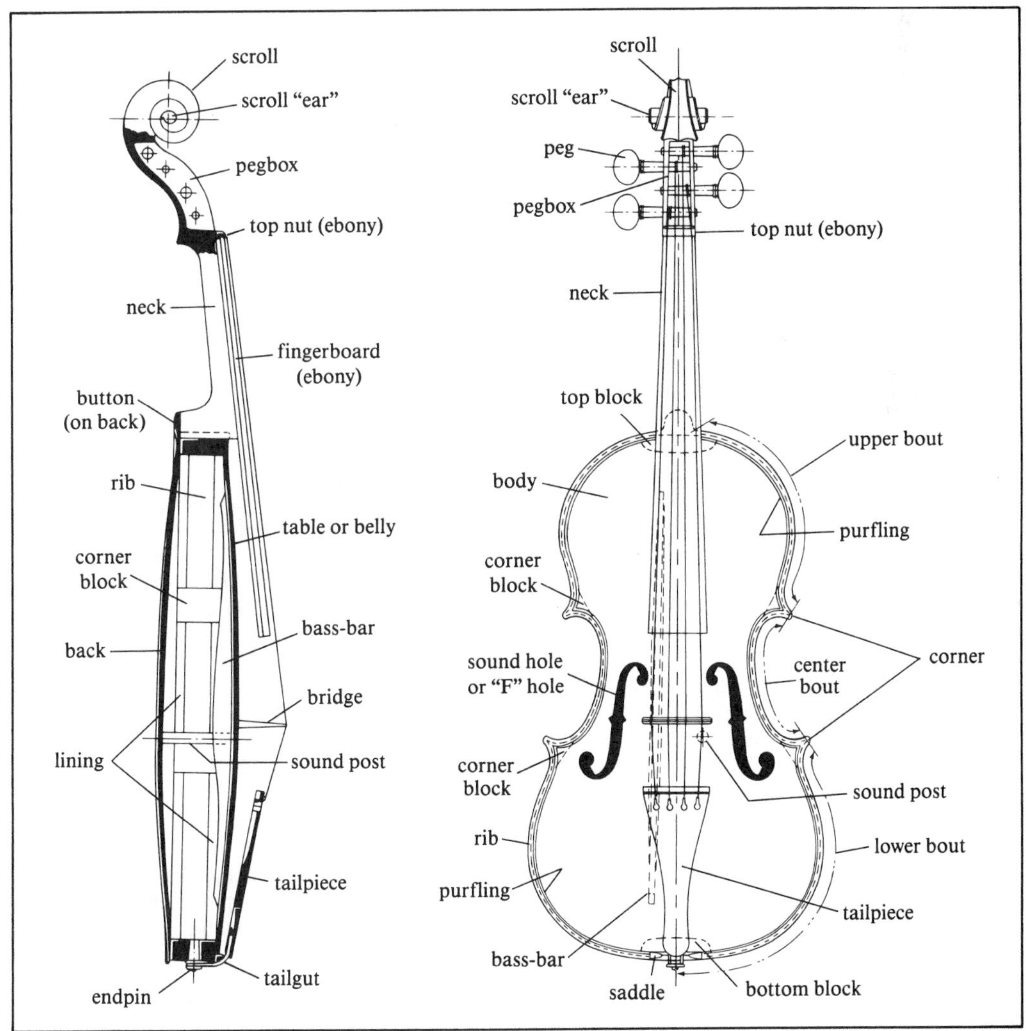

Fig. 1. Violin: cross-section and front view.

produce trees with compact, fine, even grain. The violin back, ribs, and neck are usually of maple, less often of poplar or willow, and very rarely of ash, chestnut, or beech. One special element of beauty in the violin is the choice of figured (flame) wood for the back. The grain of the back, like the table, runs longitudinally, but the figure is more or less at right angles. Although similar figured maple is used for the ribs, maple of milder figure is often used for the neck, pegbox, and scroll, where string tension could cause warping in weaker, highly figured wood. Recognition of specifically figured maple or even-grained spruce can be helpful in instrument identification and dating.

The interior blocks and linings are usually of spruce or willow, chosen for lightness and resistance to splitting. Blocks strengthen the instrument at the rib corners and at areas of string tension in the bottom where the strings are fastened by the tailpiece and at the top with the joining of the neck. Linings (six) allow an increased gluing surface between the thin ribs (usually 1 mm in thickness), table, and back.

The table and back are carved and shaped to form archings and then hollowed inside to maximize vibrations, while retaining sufficient strength to sustain string tension. The edges extend slightly beyond the ribs to allow a delicate rounding of the form and to accentuate the shape of the body. *Sound holes, called F holes, are cut in the spruce top both for beauty and for sound production. The body is ornamented with an inlay of *purfling to emphasize the outline of the table and back and to aid in preventing cracks on the edges from continuing into the body of the instrument. Purfling also affects sound by increasing edge flexibility.

The spruce *bass-bar is fitted longitudinally beneath the left or g-string side under the bridge foot and glued in place under mild tension. It influences sound while strengthening the table against string pressure exerted by the bridge. The *sound post, also of spruce, is fitted between the table and back, near the right or treble bridge foot, and is held in place by string pressure. The sound post is readily movable, and its adjustment has a significant influence on musical quality and bow response, transmitting vibration of the strings to the maple back.

The *bridge is fitted to the arching of the table between the inner notches of the F holes and is held in place by string tension. From the button (endpin), which is set into the bottom block for strength, a tailgut of gut, nylon, or wire passes over a protective saddle and is secured to the tailpiece. The strings, fastened to the tailpiece, pass over the bridge, above the fingerboard, along fixed notches in the top-nut, and on to the four tuning pegs. Modern strings are usually of lamb gut wound with silver wire on the g and aluminum wire on the d′ and a′, and plain steel of considerable tension for brilliance of sound on the e″. Pegs, button, and tailpiece are usually of ebony, rosewood, or boxwood. The fingerboard, top-nut, and saddle are of ebony.

Varnish preserves the wood and protects it from wear and dirt while providing a flexible penetrating "blanket" that has a profound influence on sound. Excessively hard and brittle varnishes tend to emphasize brightness of tone, whereas overly soft varnish inadequately resists wear and abrasion. During the 17th century in northern Italy, especially in Cremona, varnish was developed with a nearly perfect combination of flexibility, texture, and lustrous depth of color. The basic formula was common knowledge in the 17th and early 18th centuries, but by 1750 it was lost. Research and experimentation by makers and scientists since then have failed to rediscover the process and ingredients for making the classical varnish and to explain the exact means by which it influences sound.

II. *History.* It is unlikely that the violin was developed by a single craftsman. Its antecedents include the medieval *fiddle, *rebec, and **lira da braccio.* By at least 1520, the violin with only three strings was in existence, judging from iconography of the period. One is depicted in a painting of 1529 by Gaudenzio Ferrari. By 1550, the fourth string, the top e″, had been added. Between 1520 and 1550, the viola and cello also emerged, completing the family of bowed stringed instruments still in use. There is no concrete evidence to support the popular theory that the viola was developed prior to the violin and cello.

The violin probably emerged in Cremona and Brescia. Andrea Amati (before 1511–before 1580), who founded violin making in Cremona and established its preeminence there, developed the basic proportions of the violin, viola, and cello. His sons Antonio (ca. 1540–?) and Girolamo (Hieronymous) (1561–1630) continued his work, refining the style of the body outline, F holes, purfling, and scroll. Antonio and Girolamo evidently worked together and often labeled their instruments jointly; they are believed to have developed the contralto viola, a small form of the tenor viola and still the standard of viola dimension.

In 1562, Gasparo da Salò (1540–1609) moved from Salò to Brescia, where there already existed a tradition of lute, viol, and keyboard instrument making. Here Gasparo produced many fine tenor violas, violins, and double basses. His violas frequently bear double inlays of purfling and elaborate purfled geometric ornaments copied and modified by makers throughout Europe. Gasparo's student Giovanni Paolo Maggini (ca. 1580–ca. 1632) became the most famous Brescian maker of violins and cellos, and his work strongly influenced makers in the 17th century.

Before 1600, instruments with body lengths both larger and smaller than the eventual standard of 14 inches (35.5 cm) were being produced. Bridge placement and vibrating string length also varied as makers sought to improve the quality of sound produced by strings of plain gut. Although twisted plain gut worked reasonably well for the top two strings, e″ and a′, it was much too slack for the lower d′ and g strings. Roped strings from multiple strands of twisted gut,

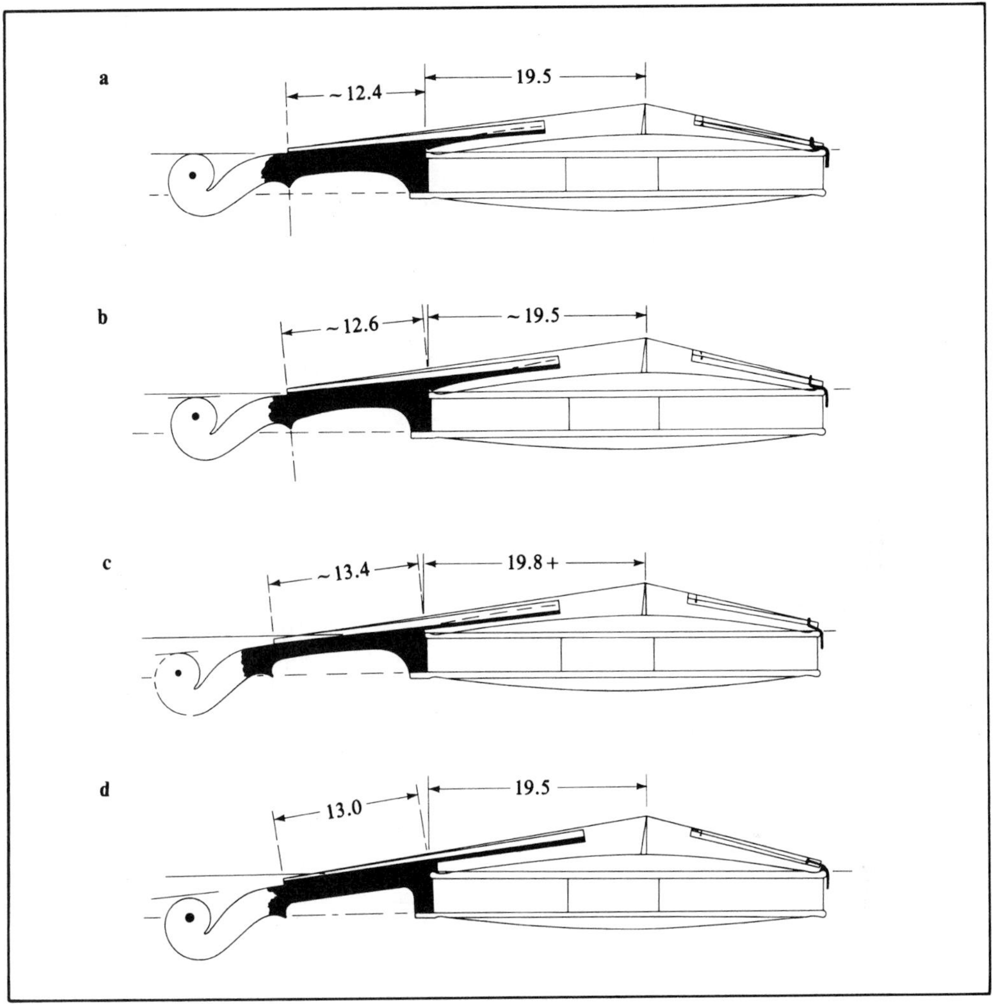

Fig. 2. Changing geometry of the violin.

called Catlines, were more successful than plain gut, but spoke slowly under the bow and lacked focus and concentration of sound [see also String]. The violin neck was short and simply extended in a straight projection from the upper edge of the table. The fingerboard was also short and wedge-shaped to allow string elevation for a low bridge that exerted only gentle downward string pressure onto the table of the instrument [Fig. 2a]. Bass-bars were frequently small and short, and the sound post is believed to have been quite thin, probably less than 5 mm in diameter. Plain gut strings did not make heavier structuring necessary, and instruments tended to be warm and resonant in musical quality, though somewhat lacking in power and projection.

The early cello was unusually large, with a body length that exceeded 31 inches (79 cm) and was required to concentrate sound volume on the highly flexible C and G strings of roped Catline gut. With an overly long vibrating string length, fingering was difficult and a very heavy bow was required to achieve articulation. The viola also emerged as a large instrument, the tenor. With a body length of more than 18 inches (46 cm), the tenor viola had a short neck, a feature allowing the instrument to be held on the shoulder with the left arm almost completely extended. The instrument was tuned c g d′ a′, an octave above the cello [see also Tenor violin].

Violin proportion became largely standardized as we know it today in the 17th century, with a body length of roughly 14 inches (35.5 cm). The viola and cello were, however, still in development. It was probably the brothers Amati who reduced the size of the tenor viola to the contralto, still with tenor tuning (c g

1. Violoncello. 2. Violin. 3. Viola. 4. Double bass (reduced in size).

d′ a′) but with a body length under 17 inches. Such an instrument from their hand emerged as early as 1616 and had a body 16¼ inches long. The small cello, destined to become a guide for the great Venetian makers in the late 17th and 18th centuries, was possibly created in the first quarter of the 17th century by Maggini in Brescia. The short body length (less than 30 inches) of the small cello was compensated with a broadening of the outline and higher ribs to retain interior volume. Maggini's violins were a strong influence on makers throughout Europe, but his death in 1632 marked the end of violin making in Brescia.

After Girolamo Amati's death in 1630, his son Nicolo (1596–1684) became the most prominent maker in Italy. Demand for Nicolo's violins forced the creation of a full shop with apprentices after 1640. His development of channeling and other arching details led to an improvement in musical quality, and his influence as a teacher created a new generation of gifted makers, including Andrea Guarneri, Francesco Rugeri, and Antonio Stradivari. Jacob Stainer may also have received his training in part from Nicolo Amati.

New richness of sound resulted in part from highly built archings of the table and back. Instruments of great reputation with such archings were made by Jacob Stainer (ca. 1617–83), of Absam in the Austrian Tyrol. His instruments of German model rivaled and in many ways surpassed the instruments of the brothers Amati in Cremona. Until the 19th century, Stainer violins were considered among the very best and were widely imitated throughout Europe.

It was Antonio Stradivari (1644–1737), however, who refined and finalized the form, symmetry, and beauty of the violin. He is universally recognized as the greatest violin maker in history. After 1690, he departed from the popular Amati models, creating the "long-pattern" (14⁵⁄₁₆ inches) violin. About the same time, string technology leapt forward as plain gut and Catline strings were covered with metal wire. Covered strings created quicker response and concentration of sound with increased mass and tension, allowing the lower register to become greatly focused with shorter vibrating length. With covered strings, the cello and tenor could be reduced in size without sacrifice of

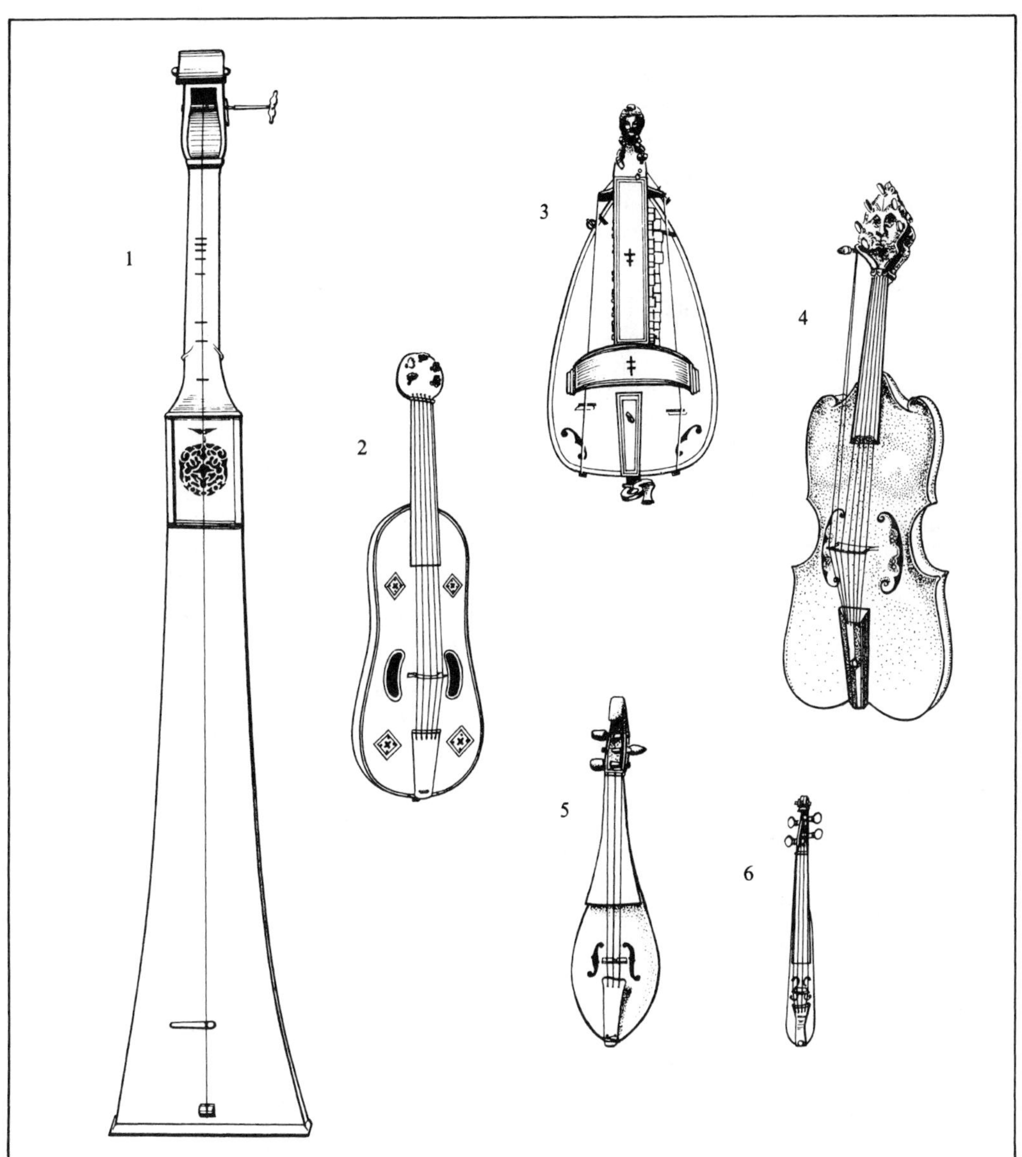

1. Tromba marina. 2. Medieval fiddle. 3. Hurdy-gurdy. 4. Lira da braccio. 5. Rebec. 6. Kit.

musical quality. The tenor violin disappeared in favor of the smaller contralto viola; large cellos were also replaced with instruments of less than 30-inch body length.

Aware of the implications of concentrating sound with the new covered strings at higher tension, Stradivari abandoned the "long-pattern" after 1700, creating a new model of exactly 14 inches (35.5 cm), with strong, flatter archings. He also applied these proportions to a smaller cello of 29⅞ inches. Both models in this new form have remained the standard of excellence to the present. What has become known as Stradivari's golden period extended from 1700 until after 1724.

By 1675, makers were experimenting with instrument tension, finding that setting the neck back at an angle from the body and correspondingly increasing the bridge height were helpful in concentrating the sound of plain gut strings [Fig. 2b]. The neck also became longer to increase overall vibrating string length. The advent of covered strings by 1700 spurred further experimentation with neck angles and length of vibrating string. In Prague and Mittenwald, in the course of work on models influenced by Stainer, the neck length increased slowly to 12.8 cm, and the neck tilt continued to increase. The new string tensions created the need for longer and higher bass-bars and thicker sound posts. Makers experimented widely with bass-bar location and grain direction, seeking to amplify violin sound.

Paris in the 18th century exerted a strong influence on the development of violin sound. Claude Pierray, Jacques Boquay, and Jean Baptiste Salomon continued experiments with violin tension and neck placement and with others evolved a French neck that was by 1740 even longer (13.4 cm) than the established standard today [Fig. 2c], with an extended string length and thin body graduations producing unusual clarity, response, and brilliance. Louis Lagetto even attempted full-size tables with short backs (like a ¾-size violin) in hopes of increasing sound clarity and projection.

Despite change and innovation, the violins of Nicolo Amati and Jacob Stainer remained the most sought-after instruments until the end of the 18th century. Although golden-period Stradivari were acclaimed for their perfection of form, the increased projection of flatter archings on these and the violins of Giuseppe Guarneri ("del Gesù," 1698–1744) was not truly appreciated until the 19th century, when bigger sound and projection were required for larger concert halls and the new, demanding concerto literature.

The 19th century firmly established the basic violin in use today. The modern *bow had been invented by François Tourte (1747–1835) with a weight, length, and balance capable of achieving increased power on the higher tensions of the violin. Instruments from the 17th and 18th centuries were already being "modernized" with respect to neck and bass-bar by the great maker and connoisseur J. B. Vuillaume (1798–1875). Stradivari's reputation gained momentum through the musicianship of Viotti, and the playing of Paganini brought acclaim to the work of Guarneri.

The combined thickness of neck and fingerboard, difficult for the player to negotiate in the 17th century because it increased toward the body, had become virtually uniform on the modern instrument, and this, together with Spohr's invention of the chin rest around 1820, made holding the instrument and shifting positions with the left hand easier and cleared the way for modern playing technique. Beginning in the 20th century, the plain gut d′ and a′ have been wound with aluminum, and the e″ has been fabricated of steel wire to provide clarity, power, and projection. The geometry of the neck [Fig. 2d] in relation to the height of the bridge, however, has remained largely unchanged. Although instruments by Stainer are no longer widely popular, their delicacy of sound is being sought after again by specialists in the re-creation of Baroque music, who use original instrumentation and Baroque performance practice.

Experimental improvements of violin acoustics by François Chanot and Felix Savart in the 19th century have proved to be unsuccessful. The Ritter viola in tenor size also has attracted little attention. Lionel Tertis developed a viola with improvements in playing ease in the 1950s; and in the 1960s and 70s, Carleen Hutchins developed a new group of eight bowed stringed instruments designed to provide acoustic improvement over the entire musical range [see also Tenor violin]. Instruments by the Cremonese, and Stradivari in particular, remain the unchallenged masterpieces, however.

Bibl.: Wilhelm Joseph von Wasielewski, *Die Violine und ihre Meister,* 4th and later eds., ed. and enl. by Waldemar von Wasielewski (Leipzig: Breitkopf & Härtel, 1868; 8th ed., 1927; R: Wiesbaden: M Sändig, 1968). George Hart, *The Violin: Its Famous Makers and Their Imitators* (London: Dulau, 1875; new ed., 1909). Edward Heron-Allen, *Violin-Making, as It Was and Is* (London: Ward, Lock, 1884; 2nd ed., 1885; R: 1984). Willibald Leo von Lütgendorff, *Die Geigen- und Lautenmacher vom Mittelalter bis zur Gegenwart* (Frankfurt: H Keller, 1904; 2nd ed., 1913). Lionel de La Laurencie, *L'école française de violon de Lully à Viotti,* 3 vols. (Paris: Delagrave, 1922–24). Andreas Moser, *Geschichte des Violinspiels,* with an introduction, *Das Streichinstrumentenspiel im Mittelalter,* by Hans Joachim Moser (Berlin: M Hesse, 1923; 2nd ed., Tutzing: Schneider, 1966–67). William Henry Hill, Arthur F. Hill, and Alfred E. Hill, *The Violin-Makers of the Guarneri Family (1626–1762)* (London: W E Hill, 1931; R: London: Holland Press, 1965). René Vannes, *Essai d'un dictionnaire universel des luthiers* (Paris: Fischbacher, 1932; 2nd ed., with supplement, Brussels: Les amis de la musique, 1951–59; 3rd ed., 1959–72; 4th ed., 1979). Edmond van der Straeten, *The History of the Violin* (London, Cassell, 1933). David D. Boyden, *The History of Violin Playing from Its Origins to 1761* (London: Oxford U Pr, 1965). Herbert K. Goodkind, *Violin Iconography of Antonio Stradivari (1644–1737)* (Larchmont, N.Y., 1972). Walter Kolneder, *Das Buch der Violine* (Zurich: Atlantis, 1972). Sheila M. Nelson, *The Violin and Viola* (New York: Norton, 1972). Simone F. Sacconi, *The Secrets of Stradivari,* trans. Andrew Dipper and Cristina Rivaroli (Cremona: Libreria del Convegno, 1979). Dominic Gill, ed., *The Book of the Violin* (New York: Rizzoli, 1984). Robin Stowell, *Violin Technique and Performance Practice in the Late Eighteenth and Early Nineteenth Centuries* (Cambridge: Cambridge U Pr, 1985). Robin Stowell, ed., *The Cambridge Companion to the Violin* (Cambridge: Cambridge U Pr, 1992). See also Bibliography II; Periodicals II, 8.

W.L.M.

Violin concerto. A *concerto for violin and orchestra.

Violino piccolo [It.; Ger. *Quartgeige, Terzgeige*]. A small violin with a body length of roughly 33 cm (13 in.), similar to a ¾-size child's instrument. It is known to have been used in the 16th and 17th centuries and was tuned a third or fourth higher than the normal violin. Such instruments have a clear, bright sound at higher tunings and allow comfortable playing in a higher register with lower left-hand positions and limited position-shifting technique. Bach wrote for one in the first *Brandenburg* Concerto, with the instrument tuned up a third. As techniques for playing in higher positions were developed, the *violino piccolo* fell out of use. The instrument is frequently difficult to identify because of its similarity to small violins intended for use by children. W.L.M.

Violon [Fr.]. Violin.

Violón [Sp.]. (1) Bass viol, double bass viol. (2) An organ stop of flute scale with stopped pipes. See also *Gedackt.*

Violoncello, cello [It., diminutive of **violone;* Ger.; Fr. *violoncelle;* Sp. *violoncelo, violonchelo*]. The bass instrument of the violin family. Its four strings are tuned C G d a, an octave below those of the viola. The cello has a body length of 74–76 cm (29–30 in.) and an overall length of ca. 120 cm (47 in.). It is played between the legs, its weight being supported on the floor by the *endpin, and it is bowed with the palm downward. Except for its deeper ribs, it is similar in proportions and contruction to the violin [see ill. under Violin].

The cello emerged in the early 16th century along with the violin and viola and was first distinguished as the bass member of this family by terms such as *basso di viola da braccio, Bass-Klein-Geig,* and *basse de violon.* The terms *violoncino* and *violoncello* date from the mid- to late 17th century. In the 18th century in Austria and southern Germany, it was often termed *Bassetl* or *Bassett.* The modern tuning is described by 16th-century writers, as is a tuning a whole step lower that survived into the 18th century in England and France. Throughout the 17th century and into the early 18th, the cello sometimes had five strings tuned F_1 C G d a or C G d a e′ [see also *Violoncello piccolo;* for the early history of the cello, see Violin II]. In the late 18th and the 19th century, it underwent modifications similar to those of the violin to produce a larger, more powerful tone. The last step in the development of the modern instrument was the widespread adoption of the adjustable endpin in the second half of the 19th century.

In the symphony orchestra, the cello is the second-lowest of the bowed stringed instruments, its part lying just above that of the double bass. In music earlier than the symphonies of Beethoven, however, the cello often plays the same part as the double bass, sounding an octave higher. The cello is the lowest-sounding member of the string quartet, string trio, and string quintet (in which there may be two cellos), and it forms part of the piano trio along with the piano and violin.

Until the late 17th century, the cello was an ensemble instrument, often playing the bass line in *thoroughbass parts. The earliest known works for solo cello are *ricercars by Domenico Gabrielli published ca. 1675. Since the beginning of the 18th century, however, there has been an extensive literature for the cello as a solo instrument with orchestra and in smaller ensembles. Cello concertos of the 18th century include works by Giuseppe Maria Jacchini (1701), Evaristo Felice Dall'Abaco (1712), Leonardo Leo (1737–38), Vivaldi, Tartini, C. P. E. Bach, Wagenseil, Monn, composers of the *Mannheim school, and Haydn (especially the Concerto in D major Hob. VIIb:2 of 1783, one of five that he is thought to have composed). Sonatas for cello in this period include works by Jacchini (some from before 1700), Gaetano Boni (1717), Giacobbe Basevi Cervetto (published 1741–61 in London, where he was active), Giovanni Bononcini, and Vivaldi. Among the most prolific of all composers for the cello was Luigi Boccherini (1743–1805), whose works include numerous sonatas and concertos and more than 100 string quintets with two cellos. Among the best-known works of any period are Bach's six suites for unaccompanied cello BWV 1007–12 (ca. 1720).

An important early method for the cello is Michel Corrette's *Méthode théorique et pratique pour apprendre en peu de temps le violoncelle dans sa perfection* (Paris, 1741; facs., *MMML* ser. 2, 85, 1972). The foundations of modern cello playing are laid down in the *Essai sur le doigté du violoncelle et sur la conduite de l'archet* (Paris, ca. 1813) by Jean-Louis Duport (1749–1819), a virtuoso performer and a composer of concertos, sonatas, and much chamber music for cello.

The best-known 19th- and 20th-century works for orchestra with solo cello include concertos or other compositions by Beethoven (concerto for piano, violin, and cello op. 56, 1808), Schumann (op. 129, 1850), Saint-Saëns (op. 33, 1872, and 119, 1902), Tchaikovsky (*Variations on a Rococo Theme* op. 33, 1876), Lalo (1877), Bruch (*Kol nidrei* op. 47, 1881), Brahms (concerto for violin and cello op. 102, 1887), Dvořák (op. 104, 1895), Strauss (**Don Quixote* op. 35, 1897), Bloch (**Schelomo,* 1916), Elgar (op. 85, 1919), Prokofiev (op. 58, 1938, and Symphony-Concerto op. 125, 1951), Walton (1956), and Shostakovich (op. 107, 1959, and op. 126, 1966). Sonatas and similar works include compositions by Beethoven (5), Brahms (2), Saint-Saëns (2), Fauré (2), Reger (4), Webern, Debussy, Hindemith (2), and Britten.

Bibl.: Klaus Marx, *Die Entwicklung des Violoncells und seine Spieltechnik bis J. L. Duport, 1520–1820* (Regensburg: Gustav Bosse Verlag, 1963). Edmund Sebastian Joseph van der Straeten, *History of the Violoncello, the Viola da Gamba, Their Precursors, and Collateral Instruments,* 2 vols. (London: W Reeves, 1914; R: 1971). Elizabeth Cowling, *The Cello* (London: Batsford, 1975). Stephen Bonta, "From Violone to Violoncello: A Question of Strings?," *JAMS* 3 (1977): 64–69. William Pleeth, *Cello,* comp. and ed. Nona Pyron (New York: Schirmer Bks, 1983). Winifred Pape and Wolfgang Boettcher, *Das Violoncello: Geschichte, Bau, Technik, Repertoire* (Mainz: Schott, 1996). Valerie Walden, *One Hundred Years of Violoncello: A History of Technique and Performance Practice, 1740–1840* (Cambridge: Cambridge U Pr, 1998). Robin Stowell, ed., *The Cambridge Companion to the Cello* (Cambridge: Cambridge U Pr, 1999). See also Violin.

Violoncello piccolo [It.]. A small cello, with either four or five strings, tuned C G d a, G d a e′, or C G d a e′. Bach calls for an obbligato violoncello piccolo in a number of cantatas, and his Sixth Suite for unaccompanied cello was written for an instrument with five strings, but since five-string celli of normal size also existed (particularly in the 17th century), it is not known if the cantata solos and the Sixth Suite were intended for the same instrument. The four-string violoncello piccolo is frequently difficult to identify because of its similarity to small celli intended for use by children. In the case of Bach, confusion with the *viola pomposa has also arisen surrounding a five-string instrument with an overall length of 76 cm built, supposedly to Bach's specifications, by J. C. Hoffmann of Leipzig in 1732. K.S.

Violoncino [It.]. In the 17th century, violoncello.

Violone [It.]. (1) Now usually the double-bass *viol and thus the immediate ancestor of the *double bass. The term has designated a variety of instruments, however. In the 16th century, it referred to any viol as distinct from a violin. From about 1600 onward, it was applied to bass or contrabass viols. In the first half of the 18th century, it could refer to an instrument tuned G_1 C F (or E) A d g, to one tuned a fourth lower, or to a larger four-stringed instrument *(violone grosso)* tuned C_1 G_1 D A, among others. In Italian publications of the first half of the 18th century, it sometimes designated the violoncello. By the mid-18th century, it was falling out of use and referred increasingly to the double bass.

(2) An organ stop of open flue pipes of narrow scale, usually found in the Pedal; also violoncello.

Violon-ténor [Fr.]. See Tenor violin.

Violotta [It.]. A *tenor violin built by Alfred Stelzner beginning in 1891, measuring about 71 cm (28 in.) and tuned G d a e′.

Virelai [Fr.; OFr. *vireli,* virely]. One of the three **formes fixes,* prominent in the poetry and music of France in the 14th and 15th centuries. It was called *chanson balladée* in the 14th century. In outline, the poetic structure of a virelai stanza is AbbaA (capital letters indicating a poetic and musical refrain). Each letter stands for several lines; the exact number is quite variable. The section b often has different endings on its two occurrences (**ouvert* and *clos*). Ordinarily there are three stanzas. Some scholars maintain that the entire form, including both statements of the refrain, should be repeated for each; others say that the refrain should be presented only once between stanzas (as well as once at the beginning and again at the end of the complete piece).

The word *virelai* comes from the Old French *virer* (to turn or to twist). This etymology, along with the term *chanson balladée,* suggests that the form was originally associated with dance. Two general accounts of the ancestry of the *virelai* have been offered. One theory suggests a connection with Arabic song forms of the 11th century in North Africa and Spain [see *Zajal*], which may have influenced *troubadour songs and later also some trouvère songs. Another account holds that the *virelai,* like the **rondeau* and **ballade,* evolved from the refrain type of round dance loosely called **carole* in the 12th and 13th centuries. The distinctive AbbA structure, as with the forms of other refrain types, was not well delineated until the late 13th century, when it appears in several genres—the French *vireli,* the Occitan *dansa* and *balada,* the Italian **ballata* and **lauda,* and the Galician-Portuguese **cantigas,* which contributed to the rise of the Spanish **villancico* in the 15th century.

In the 13th century, motets sometimes contained one or more voices in forms similar to that of the *virelai.* The first polyphonic song in the form of a *virelai* was composed in the late 13th century by Adam de la Halle. The poetico-musical form as it came to be practiced in the 14th century took definitive form in some monophonic works of Jehannot de l'Escurel (d. 1304).

Guillaume de Machaut (ca. 1300–1377) wrote numerous *virelais,* setting 33 of them to music; most are monophonic and largely syllabic, the few polyphonic settings being comparatively simple. The late 14th century saw the composition of pieces today sometimes termed realistic *virelais,* in which the hunt, battle, a fire, and birdcalls are depicted. In comparison to the other *formes fixes,* however, the *virelai* was not frequently used.

In the 15th century, the *virelai* was rare, even as poetry without music. The late 15th-century **bergerette,* however, has the form of a *virelai* with only one stanza.

See also Chanson, Troubadour, Trouvère; for bibl. see *Formes fixes.* E.A.

Virga [Lat.]. See Neume.

Virgil practice clavier. A silent practice keyboard patented in the U.S. by Almon K. Virgil in 1892. The touch can be regulated, and if desired, clicks are produced when the keys are either depressed or released.

Virginal [Fr. *virginale, épinette;* Ger. *Virginal, Instrument;* It. *virginale, spinetta, spinettina;* Sp. *virginal*]. A small *harpsichord, almost always with one set of strings and jacks and a single keyboard. The strings run at right angles to the keys rather than obliquely as in the *spinet. In 16th- and 17th-century England, virginal or pair of virginals referred to any quilled keyboard instrument. In other European languages, an inconsistent nomenclature often fails to distinguish between virginals and spinets. The origin of the term virginal is not known, despite various hypotheses.

Unlike the spinet, the virginal has its long bass strings at the front, so that instruments could be built in various shapes, rectangular and polygonal, with inset or projecting keyboards. Typically the jacks are arranged in pairs in the register, back to back, plucking in opposite directions, and run in a line from the left

Virginal.

front to the right rear of the virginal. Thus, the key levers in the bass are much shorter than in the treble, giving the instrument a characteristic but uneven touch. The earliest references to the virginal (Paulus Paulirinus, ca. 1460, and Sebastian Virdung, 1511) are to rectangular instruments. But by the early 16th century, polygonal virginals of thin-cased construction are depicted in Italian intarsias and paintings. To judge from 16th- and 17th-century works of graphic art, virginals seem to have been far more numerous than harpsichords during this period.

As can be seen in the sole surviving examples (by Joes Karest, 1548 and 1550) and in mid-16th-century Flemish pictures, the older type of north European virginal is of thin-cased polygonal construction, protected by an outer case, but has a recessed keyboard rather than the projecting one found on Italian models. By the 1560s, the thick-cased rectangular virginal, the typical instrument in later Flemish paintings, was displacing the earlier thin-cased type. Three models of Flemish virginal were made, with their keyboards to the left (confusingly termed *spinett*), in the center (obsolete by ca. 1585), and to the right *(muselar)*, respectively. Keyboard placement, with its effect on the point at which the strings are plucked, determines the timbre. *Muselar*s, whose strings are plucked near the center, have a fairly uniformly flutelike sound from bass to treble, whereas *spinetten,* like harpsichords, change gradually from flutelike at the top to reedy at the bottom of the compass. *Muselar*s were made only in the Low Countries. Elsewhere, only models with keyboards placed to the left (or, in Germany, occasionally of the central-keyboard type) were made.

Flemish makers also constructed combination instruments, consisting of a normal-pitch virginal (the mother, as it was termed) with a compartment next to its off-center keyboard in which an octave virginal (the child) was housed. The child could be removed and placed on top of the mother, creating a two-manual instrument with 8′ and 4′ on the lower and 4′ alone on the upper keyboard. Similar combination instruments are known to have been made in Germany and Austria, some even of three components, but none has survived. One English child virginal, dated 1638, has survived, but without its mother.

Except in Italy, the virginal seems by the close of the 17th century to have been replaced by the more graceful spinet of wing shape, despite a certain tonal loss, especially in the bass. The compass of virginals paralleled that of contemporary harpsichords and spinets of the 16th and 17th centuries.

Bibl.: Miloš Velimirović, "The Pre-English Use of the Term 'Virginal,'" *Plamenac,* 1969, pp. 341–52. John Koster, "The Mother and Child Virginal and Its Place in the Keyboard Instrument Culture of the 16th and 17th Centuries," *The Brussels Museum of Musical Instruments Bulletin* 7 (1977): 78–96. Grant O'Brien, *Ruckers: A Harpsichord and Virginal Building Tradition* (Cambridge: Cambridge U Pr, 1990). See also Harpsichord. H.S., rev. J.Ko.

Virginalist. Any of the English composers of music for *virginal and related keyboard instruments of the late 16th and early 17th centuries, including William Byrd (1543–1623), Thomas Morley (1557 or 1558–1602), Peter Philips (1560 or 1561–1628), Giles Farnaby (ca. 1563–1640), John Bull (ca. 1562–1628), Thomas Weelkes (1576–1623), Thomas Tomkins (1572–1656), and Orlando Gibbons (1583–1625). Their repertory includes dances, *variations, *preludes, *fantasias, arrangements of songs and madrigals, and liturgical pieces. Sources for this music include the *Fitzwilliam Virginal Book, the *Mulliner Book, *My Lady Nevells Booke* (privately owned, completed 1591), and other manuscripts now in Europe and the U.S. and the print titled **Parthenia.*

Bibl.: John Caldwell, *English Keyboard Music before the Nineteenth Century* (New York: Praeger, 1973).

Virtuoso [It.]. A performer of great technical ability. The term is now most often associated with the tradition of celebrated soloists that began in the 19th century with performers such as Paganini and Liszt and is applied to conductors and singers as well as to instrumentalists. It sometimes pejoratively implies technical skill in the absence of musical sensitivity. Earlier uses of the term reaching back to the 16th century imply training in theory or composition as much as skill in performance.

Vis-à-vis [Fr., facing]. An instrument combining a piano and a harpsichord that could be played from separate keyboards by two players seated facing one another. It was designed by Johann Andreas Stein, and an example by him, also termed a harmonicon, survives from 1777.

Visigothic chant. *Mozarabic chant.

Visitation, The. Opera in three acts by Gunther Schuller (libretto by the composer, after Franz Kafka), produced in Hamburg in 1966. Setting: the American South in the 20th century.

Vista [It.]. Sight; *a prima vista,* at sight, *sight-reading.

Viste [Fr., obs.]. **Vite.*

Vite, vitement [Fr.]. Fast; in the 18th century, the fastest of the principal divisions of *tempo.

Vivace [It.]. Lively, brisk. In isolation, the term may indicate a *tempo equivalent to *allegro* or faster. It has also been used to modify various terms (e.g., *allegro vivace*), usually, but not always, implying a faster tempo than the term modified. The intensifiers *vivacissimo* and *vivacissimamente* are also used.

Vivement [Fr.]. Lively.

Vivo, vivamente [It.]. Lively, brisk.

Vl. Abbr. for violin.

Vla. Abbr. for viola.

Vlc. Abbr. for violoncello.

Vocalise [Fr.]. A composition for voice without text. Numerous such pieces, often with piano accompaniment, were published beginning in the 19th century as exercises in vocal technique or in *solfège. Textless didactic vocal works occur as early as some *ricercars of the 16th and 17th centuries, however. Concert pieces for voice without text, sometimes titled *vocalise,* date largely from the 20th century and include Fauré's *Vocalise-étude* (1907), Ravel's *Vocalise en forme d'habanera* (1907), Rachmaninoff's *Vocalise* op. 34 no. 14 (1912), Metner's *Sonata-Vocalise* op. 41 no. 1 and *Suite-Vocalise* op. 41 no. 2 (1922–26?), Respighi's *3 vocalizzi* (1933), and Vaughan Williams's *Three Vocalises* for soprano and clarinet (1958). The term has sometimes also been used to refer to any melismatic passage in a vocal work with text.

Vocalization, to vocalize. To sing without text, often for didactic purposes or to warm up before performance, thus often arpeggios or other exercises. The terms are also applied to singing by one or more voices without text, called for in works such as Debussy's *Sirènes* (from his **Nocturnes*), Ravel's **Daphnis et Chloé,* Vaughan Williams's *Pastoral* Symphony (1921), and Holst's *The *Planets.*

Voce [It., pl. *voci*]. Voice, part; *voce di petto,* chest voice; *voce di testa,* head voice; *a due* (*tre,* etc.) *voci,* for two (three, etc.) voices; *voci pari* or *eguali,* *equal voices. See also *Colla, Mezza, Sotto.*

Voces [Lat.]. Plural of **vox.*

Voce umana. A characteristic stop of Principale pipes in Italian organs from the late 17th to the early 19th century, usually of short compass and tuned slightly sharp to the Principale; when drawn with it, a gentle undulating effect is produced, often called for in the toccatas of Frescobaldi and others.

Vodun. See Latin America III.

Voice. (1) The human mechanism for producing sound from the mouth. Every musical culture has its own distinct *singing style, with characteristic ranges and timbres. Thus, even the most basic terms and categories for describing vocal sound in one culture may not be relevant to others. What follows concerns the voice as employed in Western art music.

Since the 19th century, voices have usually been classified in six basic types, three male and three female, according to their range, roughly as shown in the accompanying example. Most voices, especially untrained ones, fall into the intermediate ranges, baritone and mezzo soprano, the extremes being more rare (as is reflected in the difficulty of filling the tenor and alto sections of choruses). The limits of range vary among individuals, although trained singers often much exceed those given in the example. Voices of similar range may be unlike in tessitura—that part of the range that is most comfortable for the singer and sounds best. The voice categories also differ in timbre, with the result that singers of different categories can be distinguished even on the same pitch. In practice, however, singers of one type often have an admixture of the timbre of another, such as a tenor with some baritonal quality.

Kinds of voices and ranges now unusual have been cultivated at other times, for example, Russian basses of very low range; the male alto, countertenor, or falsettist [see Falsetto], who, after long employment in European music, went out of favor in the 19th century, regaining some of it in the 20th; or the **castrato,* a dominant figure in Italian singing from the 16th to the early 19th century.

The voice is a much more complicated musical instrument than any man-made one and by its nature resistant to scientific investigation. Many, perhaps most, aspects of its mechanical functioning are still only imperfectly understood, and almost any assertion by one authority is still liable to contradiction by another, especially if among authorities one includes not only scientific researchers but singers and singing teachers as well. The latter group, dedicated less to abstract understanding than to singing itself, draws at times on the conclusions of the former, but also frequently employs terminology and concepts of dubious scientific

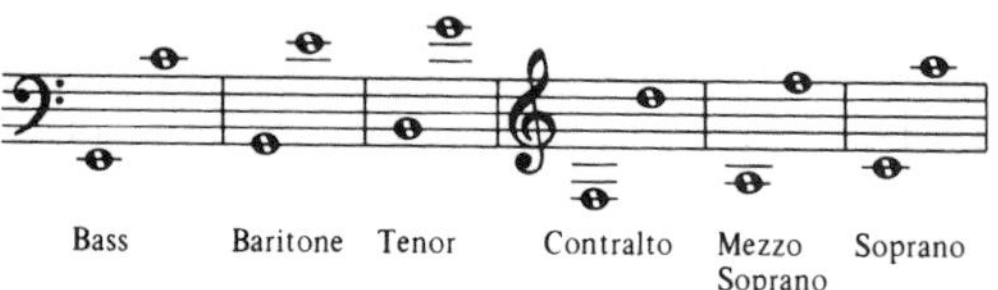

Ranges.

validity, held to be of value in achieving practical ends. Because important components of the vocal mechanism are not subject to direct conscious control, training the voice and keeping it in good order cannot be a straightforward scientific undertaking and often depend on methods of an indirect, intuitive sort, utilizing psychological suggestion. Because the voice is usually seen as a highly integrated mechanism, singers and teachers often fix on one of its elements as the key to the whole, whose proper management will cause the rest to fall into place. For these reasons singing methods vary greatly, and the successful combination of singer and teacher is often difficult to achieve.

The voice is usually considered a kind of wind instrument (but even this has been strongly contested), its mechanism consisting of three main parts: air supply, vibrator, and resonator. Air is drawn into the lungs by the inspiratory muscles, of which the diaphragm is the chief, and expelled by the expiratory. At the top of the trachea (or windpipe) within the larynx (or voicebox) is a set of muscles (popularly but misleadingly called the vocal cords; more accurately, vocal folds) that act as a kind of valve, opening and closing to regulate the flow of air. During expiration their resistance to air escaping between them through the opening called the glottis causes them to vibrate, thereby producing sound. (This sums up a mechanism and its workings that are both rather complex if followed in detail.) Before leaving the body, the sound produced in the larynx proceeds to the resonance cavities, which act as secondary vibrators, altering tonal quality by reinforcing some partials and muffling others. The principal resonators are the pharynx and the mouth (the importance of nasal resonance is much disputed). The resonating properties of these cavities are highly complex because of their irregular shape and the varying nature of their surfaces and materials. The shaping of these resonators for the control of tone quality, difficult in itself, is further complicated by the articulation of words in the mouth. Other parts of the body, such as the chest and sinuses, have in the past been considered important resonators. This is now discredited, but the idea of "placing" the tone by directing it to various locations in the head, neck, or chest is still maintained as a useful fiction among singers.

The voice can produce sounds of very different tonal character. In singing, register refers to series of pitches that are of like tonal character because of a consistent vocal production. The question of registers has been subject to profound disputes, and the terminology to considerable confusion. Falsetto, for example, has been used in rather different ways over time. At present, sometimes two, sometimes three principal registers are recognized in the classically trained voice. Often, but not invariably, these are called chest, head, and falsetto in men, and chest, middle, and head in women. (Some hold the falsetto to be nonexistent in women; others disagree.) The terms chest and head reflect the tonal quality of those registers and, sometimes, sensations felt in singing them. But it is now generally held that registral differences do not depend on the resonating cavities, but result from different functions within the laryngeal mechanism itself. For this reason some now prefer the terms heavy and light register to chest and head, though the latter remain in common use.

The sudden shift from one register to another is called a register break. Much of classical singing technique is directed toward eradicating register breaks by extending the pitches common to two registers and blending the registers together on those pitches. The principal registral break, at the top of the chest voice, occurs at close to the same absolute pitch area in both male and female voices and so at different points in their ranges. As a result the chest register is more extensive in voices of low range.

Difference of registral emphasis is one of the principal factors distinguishing types of singers. The coloratura soprano is characterized by very light registration, high tessitura, and agility. Most young tenors and sopranos use a predominantly light registration; this makes them, in standard terminology, lyric voices. Some remain in this category, but others adopt heavier registration and more powerful sound with age and experience. A *lirico spinto* is a voice of basically lyric quality that can "push" (the meaning of *spinto*) the voice more powerfully in climaxes; a tenor of this sort is called a *tenore di forza.* The dramatic soprano sings more powerfully and with heavier registration more of the time and throughout her range. *Tenore robusto* is the tenor equivalent, *Heldentenor* that for Wagnerian singing. Basses and contraltos sing mainly in chest voice, the bass using falsetto only for comic effect. The *basso profondo* [Fr. *basse profonde*] emphasizes a rich, low tessitura, the *basso cantante* [Fr. *basse chantante*] a higher one, of lighter register and more flexibility.

The voice can sing with varying degrees of *vibrato or without it (straight tone). A wide but controlled vibrato is encouraged in classical singing to add richness to the tone. How long this has been the case is disputed. Less vibrato is used in much popular and folk singing, in singing early music, and in some choruses. For bibl., see Singing.

(2) In American usage, the study of singing (e.g., "voice teacher").

(3) A single melodic line or part in polyphonic music, as in a four-voice fugue. Used in this way, voice implies no specific manner of performance, vocal or instrumental, solo or doubled. Part and voice part are also used in this sense. *Voice leading is derived from this usage.

(4) In the interpretation of music, the presumed personage behind a particular passage. Many writers and listeners have traditionally invoked a "composer's voice" evident throughout much music to highlight those musical characteristics that seem indicative of

Voice exchange.

the composer's self. Recent interpreters have broadened the idea to explain musical passages that seem to emanate from a particular subjective standpoint not necessarily identical with that of the composer.

Voice exchange [Ger. *Stimmtausch*]. The exchange between two voices (sometimes also among three voices) of phrases that are sounded simultaneously; thus, the first voice takes the phrase just sung by the second, while the second takes the phrase just sung by the first; also termed part exchange. The technique occurs frequently in the 12th-century repertory of *Notre Dame between the upper voices of three- and four-part organa and in the melismatic sections of polyphonic **conductus* [see Ex.]. It is also widely used in English polyphony of the 13th century [see *Rondellus*] and is a feature of the two-part *pes* of *"Sumer is icumen in."

Voice flute. See Recorder.

Voice leading. The conduct of the several voices or parts in a polyphonic or contrapuntal texture [see Counterpoint].

Voice part. See Voice (3).

Voicing. (1) The adjustment of the general tonal quality of a stringed keyboard instrument or of individual pitches to produce consistency throughout. On the piano, this entails principally the use of needlelike tools to prick the felt of the hammers and reduce their hardness. On the harpsichord, it entails modifying the shape and flexibility of the plectra. (2) The adjustment of organ pipes for proper speech, loudness, and tone quality. This is done on a flue pipe principally by modifying the characteristics of the mouth; on a reed pipe principally by altering the characteristics of the reed.

Voilé [Fr.]. Veiled, subdued.

Voix [Fr.]. Voice.

Voix céleste [Fr.]. See *Céleste.*

Voix de ville [Fr.]. See *Vaudeville.*

Voix humaine [Fr.]. An organ reed stop of thin, bright quality, sometimes associated with the sound of the singing voice. It was an important solo register in the classical French organ and appears in altered forms in later organs.

Vokal [Ger.]. (1) Vowel. (2) Vocal; *vokalisieren,* to vocalize; *Vokalise,* *vocalization, **vocalise.*

Volante [It.]. Flying, rushing. See also Bowing (7).

Volkslied [Ger.]. Folk song.

Volkstümliches Lied [Ger.]. The folklike lied cultivated by composers such as Schulz, Reichardt, and Zelter beginning in the later 18th century [see Lied III]. Such songs were often marked *im Volkston.*

Volles Werk [Ger.]. The full sound of the organ, employing the main *Principal stops of a keyboard division.

Volonté, à [Fr.]. **Ad libitum.*

Volta [It.]. (1) [Fr., Ger. *Volte*] A dance from Provence popular in much of Europe around 1600. Arbeau (*Orchésographie,* 1588) described it as similar to the **gagliarda.* Examples are notated in compound duple meter. It was danced in an embrace and included a step in which the man helped the woman to execute a high jump. Shakespeare and others used the terms lavolta or levalto. (2) A component of the **ballata.* (3) Time, occasion [see *Prima volta, seconda volta; Ouvert* and *clos*].

Volteggiando [It.]. Crossing the hands in keyboard playing.

Volti [It.]. Turn (the page); *volti subito* (abbr. *v.s.*), turn quickly.

Volume. *Loudness [see also Acoustics].

Voluntary. An English organ piece performed or improvised before, during (in earlier practice), or after an Anglican church service. The musical term is derived from one of the word's general definitions: "growing wild or naturally; of spontaneous growth." It was applied in this sense to musical improvisations. One of the definitions of *preludio* in Florio's Italian-English dictionary of 1598 is "a voluntary before the song," and this usage continued into the 19th century ("Sitting down to the piano, she rattled away a triumphant voluntary on the keys," Thackeray, *Vanity Fair,* chap. 48). The term came to be most firmly attached to the organ music, whether improvised or not, played before (sometimes called In-Voluntary) and after (Out-Voluntary) the Anglican service. (The old practice of playing a voluntary during the service, still followed in the 19th century, is no longer found.)

The earliest known organ composition designated as a voluntary, by Richard Alwood in the Mulliner Book (ca. 1560; ed. *MB* 1, no. 17), is in an imitative, ricercarlike style. Fugal writing remained the most common texture in the organ voluntary, often prefaced by a preludelike movement or section, but the voluntary is not limited to any style or form, being ultimately defined by its function more than by its materials. Voluntaries of the period of Byrd and Tomkins are often similar to pieces called fantasia, verse, or the like by the same or other early 17th-century composers. Later examples can resemble the suite, concerto, or sonata, or consist of arrangements or variations of hymn tunes. Exploitation of organ stops led to standard types such as the diapason voluntary and the cornet or trumpet voluntary [see also *Trumpet Voluntary*].

The voluntary had its last great flowering in the 18th and early 19th centuries, prominent composers including William Croft (1678–1727), Thomas Roseingrave (1688–1766), Maurice Greene (1696–1755), William Boyce (1711–79), John Stanley (1712–86), John Bennett (ca. 1725/30–84), Samuel Wesley (1766–1837), and Thomas Adams (1785–1858). The 19th-century voluntary is usually dismissed as a degeneration into Victorian sentimentality.

Bibl.: John Caldwell, *English Keyboard Music before the Nineteenth Century* (Oxford: Basil Blackwell, 1973). Francis Routh, *Early English Organ Music from the Middle Ages to 1837* (London: Barrie & Jenkins, 1973).

Voodoo. Vodun [see Latin America III].

Vorbereiten [Ger.]. *Prepare.

Vorimitation [Ger.]. In a work such as an organ chorale in which a melody or *cantus firmus* is stated in long note-values, the imitation of that melody in shorter note-values in other parts before its entrance. The first and succeeding phrases of the principal melody may be treated in this way.

Vorschlag [Ger.]. *Appoggiatura; *grace note.

Vorspiel [Ger.]. (1) Prelude, overture. (2) Audition, performance; *vorspielen,* to perform before an audience.

Vortrag [Ger.]. Interpretation, performance; *mit freiem Vortrag,* in a free style; *Vortragszeichen, Vortragsbezeichnung,* *performance mark.

Vorwärts [Ger.]. Forward, continue; *vorwärtsdrängend,* **accelerando.*

Vorzeichen [Ger.]. (1) Accidental. (2) [also *Vorzeichnung*] Key signature *(Tonartvorzeichen),* time signature *(Taktvorzeichen).*

Votive antiphon. Any of the four *antiphons for the Blessed Virgin Mary sung at Compline or a polyphonic setting of one of these [see also Votive Mass].

Votive Mass [Lat. *missa votiva*]. A Mass for some special circumstance (e.g., in time of war, the consecration of a bishop, a wedding) or devotion (e.g., to the Blessed Virgin Mary, the Trinity, certain saints). Such Masses have varied greatly in number through the centuries. Some have at times been assigned to be celebrated on particular days of the week, normally only when no major feast falls on that day (e.g., the Mass for the Virgin or Lady Mass on Saturday).

Vox [Lat., pl. *voces*]. (1) Pitch, note, solmization syllable. (2) In polyphonic music, voice part. (3) Voice, either the human voice or the "voice" of an instrument.

Vox angelica [Lat.]. An organ stop of thin-toned flue pipes; in reed organs, a soft 8′ stop.

Vox coelestis [Lat.]. **Céleste.*

Vox humana [Lat.]. **Voix humaine.*

V.s. Abbr. for **Volti subito.*

Vuoto [It.]. Empty, void; *corda vuota,* open string.

VV. Abbr. for violins, voices.

Wachsend [Ger.]. Growing, increasing.

Wagner tuba. A type of tuba developed for use in Wagner's *Der *Ring des Nibelungen;* also tuben. It uses a French horn mouthpiece and was intended to be played by horn players. The tubing, which has a wide conical bore, is coiled in an upright ellipse. Four rotary valves are arranged at the center in such a way as to be operated with the left hand. A tenor size is pitched in B♭ (sounds E♭ to f″) and a bass size is pitched in F (sounds $B\flat_1$ to a′). The Wagner tuba is also used in works by Bruckner, Richard Strauss, and Stravinsky.

Wait. (1) Beginning in the 13th century, a town or castle watchman, who signaled with a horn. By the late 13th century, those in noble households were sometimes *minstrels and played the shawm, whence the beginning of the association of this instrument with the term wait or wayte. By the 14th century, the term was applied to household musicians who were not also watchmen. (2) In the 15th through the 18th century, a town musician, analogous to the German **Stadtpfeifer.* Such musicians, at first in ensembles of several shawms and slide trumpet or sackbut, played for civic functions. From the 16th century onward, they also included singers and players of other instruments, and they performed in the streets as well as on ceremonial occasions. The term is also applied to the melodies (preserved in collections such as John Playford's *The English Dancing Master,* 1651) that served as trademarks of individual groups and, probably because these groups performed Christmas music in the appropriate season, to any group of wandering performers of Christmas music.

Bibl.: Walter L. Woodfill, *Musicians in English Society . . . from Elizabeth to Charles I* (Princeton: Princeton U Pr, 1953; R: New York: Da Capo, 1969).

Waldflöte [Ger.]. An organ stop of flue pipes, open or tapering inward at the top, of wide scale; often at 2′ pitch.

Waldhorn [Ger.]. *Horn, especially the natural horn, but also the modern French horn with valves.

Waldstein Sonata. Popular name for Beethoven's Piano Sonata in C major op. 53 (1803–4), dedicated to his patron Count Ferdinand von Waldstein.

Wales. In its abundant body of folk songs and its popular choral *eisteddfod festivals, this bilingual region of the United Kingdom (a separate country until the English annexation in 1284) still manifests the rich song traditions of its Celtic and English musical ancestry. An important part of this ancestry is the heritage of the *bards, pre-Christian and medieval Celtic minstrels who performed and competed at courts in Ireland and Wales, accompanying their poetry on the **crwth* (lyre) or **telyn* (harp). In the 18th century, Wesley-inspired Methodists began a tradition of hymns that is still strong. The medieval eisteddfods were reinstated during this period, primarily as choral contests, and the tradition has continued to grow. Today numerous local festivals complement the larger ones, most notably the National Eisteddfod, the Welsh League of Youth *(Urdd)* Eisteddfod, and the International Eisteddfod at Llangollen. Other significant festivals, including folk music, opera, and a variety of concerts, are at Cardiff, Swansea, and Fishguard.

The years following World War II saw the establishment of the Welsh National Opera, the BBC Welsh Orchestra (now the BBC National Orchestra of Wales), the Welsh College of Music and Drama, the Welsh Folk Dance Society, and groups to support native composers, such as the Welsh Arts Council and the Guild for the Promotion of Welsh Music. Folk music, whose dissemination has been encouraged by the Welsh Folk Song Society (founded 1906), exerted a strong force on prominent 20th-century composers such as David Wynne (1900–1983), Daniel Jones (1912–93), and William Mathias (1934–92), while the music of recent composers such as John Metcalf (b. 1946) is more international in scope. Several operatic singers from Wales, including Stuart Burrows (b. 1933), Gwyneth Jones (b. 1937), Margaret Price (b. 1941), and Bryn Terfel (b. 1965), have gained widespread acclaim, and the Wales Millennium Centre in Cardiff, scheduled to open in 2004, will house the National Opera as well as a number of other leading arts organizations.

Native folk songs, ballads, carols, and *penillion have continually been supplemented with English contributions from the south and east. Most Welsh folk songs are sung by solo voice and stay within a fairly narrow pitch range. Ballads and carols employ a wider range and freer rhyme and meter. Dance tunes, usually played on harp or fiddle, are generally associated with calendar rituals such as May Day. Other significant folk instruments are the *tabwrdd* (tabor), the corn or catgorn (types of trumpets), and various types of bells.

Bibl.: William Sidney Gwynn Williams, *Welsh National Music and Dance* (London: J Curwen, 1933; 5th ed., Llangollen: Gwynn Pub Co, 1975). Peter Crossley-Holland, ed.,

Music in Wales (London: Hinrichsen, 1948). William Sidney Gwynn Williams, ed., *Caneuon traddodiadol y Cymry* [Traditional Songs of the Welsh], 2 vols. (Llangollen: Gwynn Pub Co, 1961–63). Emrys Cleaver, *Gwŷr y gân* (Llandybie: Llyfrau'r Dryw, 1964); trans. as *Musicians of Wales* (Ruthin: John Jones, 1968). Ian Parrott, *The Spiritual Pilgrims* (Llandybie: C Davies, 1969). Hywel Teifi Edwards, *The Eisteddfod* (Cardiff: U of Wales Pr, 1990). Wyn Thomas, *Cerddoriaeth draddodiadol yng Nghymru: llyfryddiaeth* [Traditional Music in Wales: A Bibliography], 2nd ed. (Denbigh: Gwasg Gee, 1996).

Walking bass. A type of bass line in which rhythmic motion is predominantly in one note-value, often quarters or eighths when the pulse is equal to the quarter note. Stepwise melodic motion is characteristic and pitch repetition is generally avoided. The term is applied to Baroque music as well as to jazz in which the bass sounds a pitch on each beat in 4/4 (as distinct from *two-beat), often with a sustained or legato sound.

Walking-stick instrument. An instrument in the form of a functional walking stick. A 19th-century vogue for such instruments produced, among others, walking-stick flutes, recorders, oboes, clarinets, trumpets, bassoons, and violins, and in England the umbrella flute. See also *Czakan.*

Walküre, Die [Ger.]. See *Ring des Nibelungen, Der.*

Waltz [Ger. *Walzer,* fr. *walzen,* to turn about; Fr. *valse;* It. *valzer;* Sp. *vals*]. A couple dance in triple time, popular in various versions since the late 18th century. The waltz is the most long-lived and continuously favored among modern ballroom dances, in part because of its ability to adapt to new styles of dancing and music and to changing social conditions. Beginning as a daring, even risqué, intrusion from the lower classes into the polite world, it evolved into a symbol of grace, sophistication, and elegance.

The waltz grew out of southern German and Austrian country dances known generally as **Deutsche* or German Dances (and having no connection with the *allemande of the Baroque suite). Often of similar character, these dances appear under a multiplicity of names, including some referring to local versions or different developmental stages. The best known of them, the **Ländler* and the waltz, were originally closely related, but the **Ländler* retained a slower tempo and more rustic character, whereas the waltz in the late 18th century took on a faster tempo and greater refinement, keeping the turning movements that had given it its name. By the 1780s, the waltz had achieved considerable popularity across Europe, and this increased in the early years of the next century, though it was still considered daring and, by some, morally objectionable because of the close embrace in which the couple danced.

The popularity of the waltz across Europe was given a new impetus in the middle decades of the 19th century by the vogue of the Viennese waltz. This vogue was stimulated by waltz-composing Viennese dance-orchestra leaders, beginning with Joseph Lanner (1801–43) and climaxing with the Strauss family. Around 1910 the slower English waltz (derived from the Boston, which was imported from America in the 1870s) replaced the Viennese as the favorite ballroom waltz.

Early waltzes usually consisted of two repeated eight-measure periods. Gradually the dances became longer, and a form evolved comprising a series of such periods framed by an introduction and coda, as in many 19th-century waltzes. The evocative possibilities of the waltz began to be recognized by Romantic composers at least as early as Weber's *Aufforderung zum Tanz* (1819), and the stylization of the dance was pursued in various directions by Schubert, Chopin, Liszt, Brahms, Tchaikovsky, and many others in most of the genres of instrumental, vocal, and dramatic music. The Viennese waltz was even used anachronistically by Richard Strauss to characterize 18th-century Vienna in *Der Rosenkavalier* (1911). After the destruction in World War I of the society that the dance had come to symbolize, it took on even greater evocative potency, as in Ravel's *La valse* (1919–20).

Walze [Ger.]. (1) The **crescendo* pedal of an electric-action organ. (2) In the 18th century, a stereotyped accompaniment figure such as the *Alberti bass. (3) A roll for a player piano. (4) For *Mannheimer Walze,* see Mannheim school.

Wandererfantasie [Ger., Wanderer Fantasy]. Popular name for Schubert's Fantasy in C major op. 15, D. 760 (1822), for piano, actually a sonata in four movements played without pauses, so called because the second movement is a set of variations on a theme from his song "Der Wanderer" D. 489a–c (1816). Portions of this theme are also used in the other three movements.

Wärme, mit [Ger.]. With warmth, passionately.

War of the Buffoons. See **Bouffons, Querelle des.*

War Requiem. Britten's setting of the Requiem Mass with interpolated poems by Wilfred Owen, for soprano, tenor, baritone, boys' choir, chorus, organ, orchestra, and chamber orchestra, completed in 1961 and first performed in Coventry Cathedral in 1962.

Washboard. A *scraper consisting of the domestic laundry implement (a piece of corrugated metal set in a wooden frame) scraped with a metal rod or with thimbles worn on the fingers. It has been used as a rhythm instrument to accompany blues singing and in *jug, *string, and jazz bands.

Washtub bass. A folk string bass of the U.S. made from a metal washtub. A single string is affixed at one end to the center of the tub (which is turned upside down) and at the other end to a stick approximately four feet long. Bracing the free end of the stick against the rim of the tub, the player pulls on the stick in such a way as to vary the tension of the string and thus the pitch produced when the string is plucked.

Watermark. A design in paper visible when the sheet is held up to the light. Watermarks result from slight variations in the thickness of the paper. In handmade paper, they are produced by wires affixed to the sieve-like mold, in machine-made paper by raised portions of the processing roller.

Watermarks usually consist of devices or characters relating to the maker of the paper (e.g., name or monogram), its place of manufacture (often a coat of arms), or its size and quality. Two different marks frequently appear in the same sheet of paper, one on the left side, the other, called a countermark, on the right. In addition, most batches of handmade paper contain two different forms or "twins" of the same basic watermark, a result of the papermaker's use of two different molds in alternation.

Watermarks can provide useful evidence of the provenance and date of a source, the latter owing to the fact that paper molds were subject to deterioration, damage, and eventual replacement. Such evidence must, of course, be used with appropriate caution, as paper could obviously be both transported and kept for a period of time before being used.

Bibl.: Jan LaRue, "Watermarks and Musicology," *AM* 33 (1961): 120–46 [with further bibliography]. Alan Tyson, *Mozart: Studies of the Autograph Scores* (Cambridge, Mass.: Harvard U Pr, 1987). E.K.W.

Water Music. Popular name for three orchestral suites by Handel in F, D, and G major, the original order of movements of which is, however, uncertain. Some or all movements were presumably performed during a royal procession on the River Thames on 17 July 1717.

Water organ. *Hydraulis.

Wa-wa [also wah-wah, wow-wow]. An undulating musical sound obtained by mechanical or electronic means. Jazz and dance-band trumpeters and trombonists produce the effect with a Harmon or wa-wa *mute by covering and uncovering the bell-like opening in the end of the mute with the fingers of the left hand. A related effect is produced by covering and uncovering the bell of the instrument itself with a plunger (sometimes the domestic plumbing implement). On electric pianos and guitars, the effect is produced electronically and activated by a pedal.

Wayte. See Wait.

Wechsel [Ger.]. Change; *Wechselgesang,* antiphonal singing; *Wechselnote,* any of several contrapuntal devices such as the neighbor note, changing note, and cambiata; *Wechseldominante,* the dominant of the dominant; *wechseln,* in harp playing, to change the key of the instrument by adjusting the pedals (e.g., *wechseln in D-dur,* change to D major).

Wedge fugue. Popular name for Bach's organ fugue in E minor BWV 548 (composed between 1727 and 1731), so called because the subject consists of increasingly wider intervals around a central axis.

Wehmütig [Ger.]. Sad, melancholy.

Weich [Ger.]. Soft, delicate.

Weihe des Hauses, Die [Ger., The Consecration of the House]. An overture by Beethoven, op. 124 (1822), composed for the opening of the Josephstadt Theater in Vienna.

Weihnachts Oratorium [Ger.]. See *Christmas Oratorio.*

Wellingtons Sieg [Ger., Wellington's Victory]. A "battle symphony" [see *Battaglia*] by Beethoven (full title, *Wellingtons Sieg, oder Die Schlacht bei Vittoria*), op. 91 (1813), written in celebration of Wellington's victory over Napoleon. It depicts battle scenes and quotes English and French fanfares, "Rule Britannia," "Marlborough s'en va-t-en guerre," and "God Save the King." The second part was originally composed for Maelzel's panharmonicon [see Automatic instruments], but the entire work was later orchestrated by Beethoven for strings, "opposing" wind bands, and miscellaneous artillery.

Well-Tempered Clavier, The [Ger., Das wohltemperirte Clavier]. Bach's collection of 48 preludes and fugues, grouped in two parts, BWV 846–69 and 870–93 (assembled in 1722 and 1738–42), each of which contains 24 paired preludes and fugues, one prelude and fugue for each major and minor key beginning with C major and ascending chromatically. The pieces making up the collections date from various periods in Bach's life and employ a variety of styles. The title refers to the use of a *temperament in which all keys are satisfactorily in tune, but not necessarily an absolutely equal temperament. These collections are the first to exploit such a possibility fully. A related precedent, however, is J. C. F. Fischer's *Ariadne musica* for organ (1702), 20 preludes and fugues in 19 different keys (ex. in *HAM,* no. 248). It cannot be said with certainty that either the harpsichord or the clavichord was the sole intended medium of performance for Bach's pieces.

Welsh harp. See *Telyn.*

Wenig [Ger.]. Little, slightly; *ein wenig,* a little; *weniger,* less.

Werk principle. A system of traditional organ design according to which each division of the instrument, including Pedal, is conceived as an entity, with its own *flue chorus and is housed in its own separate wooden case.

Werther. Opera in four acts by Massenet (libretto in French by Édouard Blau, Paul Milliet, and Georges Hartmann, after Goethe's novel), first produced in

German in Vienna in 1892 and in French in Paris in 1893. Setting: Wetzlar, Germany, in 1772.

West Coast jazz. Small-combo jazz in California in the 1950s. Although many performances were indistinguishable from their East Coast, *bebop-derived counterparts, the most celebrated sounds emphasized complex arrangements in the restrained *cool jazz style or in clear, contrapuntal improvisations by the pianoless Gerry Mulligan–Chet Baker Quartet and in the Dave Brubeck Quartet's experiments with meters other than 4/4. B.K.

Whip. *Slapstick.

Whistle. A small, end-blown pipe, usually a *duct flute, made of wood, cane, metal, or plastic. Whistles may produce only a single pitch or they may produce several with the aid of finger holes or a plunger that varies the effective length of the pipe. The pipe may be open or stopped. See also Penny whistle.

Whistle flute. *Duct flute.

White noise. A sound, somewhat like a hiss, made up of a random distribution of audible frequencies at equal intensities.

Whizzer. *Bull-roarer.

Whole note. See Note.

Whole tone. An *interval consisting of two semitones (e.g., C–D or E–F♯).

Whole-tone scale. A *scale consisting only of whole tones. Such a scale includes six pitches in each octave, and only two different examples can be constructed from the twelve pitch classes of Western music: C D E F♯ G♯ A♯ and C♯ D♯ F G A B (or their enharmonic equivalents). It lacks all intervals consisting of an odd number of semitones, such as the minor third and perfect fifth. Since such a scale is perfectly symmetrical about any of its pitches, it greatly restricts the possibility of scale-degree functions (such as tonic) that characterize the diatonic major and minor scales. This feature of the whole-tone scale has often been exploited to represent the sensation of floating or drifting. It is often associated with works of Debussy (e.g., "Voiles," from the *Préludes* for piano bk. 1 of 1910) and others termed impressionist, but the association is easily overemphasized. Precedents in the 19th century, in the context of traditional tonality, include works by Russian composers such as Glinka *(*Ruslan and Lyudmila)* and Dargomizhsky (*The Stone Guest,* 1860s).

Whole-tube instrument. See Wind instruments.

Wie [Ger.]. As, as if, like [see *Ferne*].

William Tell. See *Guillaume Tell.*

Winchester Troper. 11th century. Cambridge, Corpus Christi College, Ms. 473 [Cb 473]. 199 leaves. Winchester, England. The content and notational style of this important liturgical source link it to French repertories of the period, but no collection of organa or tropers from related institutions survives. Modern editions: Walter Howard Frere, *The Winchester Troper* (London, 1894; R: New York: AMS Pr, 1973). Andreas Holschneider, *Die Organa von Winchester* (Hildesheim: Olms, 1968).

Bibl.: Jaques Handschin, "The Two Winchester Tropers," *Journal of Theological Studies* 37 (1936): 34–49, 156–72. Armand Machabey in *Besseler,* 1961, pp. 67–90. Alejandro Panchart, *The Repertory of Tropes at Winchester* (Princeton: Princeton U Pr, 1977).

Wind band. See Band.

Wind-band Mass. See *Harmoniemesse.*

Wind cap [Ger. *Windkapsel*]. A wooden cover enclosing and concealing the double reed of certain woodwind instruments of the 14th through the 17th century. A blowing hole was provided at the top or rear edge of the cap. The lack of direct lip contact with the reed prevented such instruments from being *overblown, and thus limited their range to pitches of the first *harmonic. The principal example of such instruments is the *crumhorn. See ill. under Reed. M.S.

Wind-chest. A rectangular, airtight wooden construction containing the *pallet valves and *stop action for the pipes of a division of the organ and to which wind is supplied by the bellows. Each division has its own wind-chest. See ill. under Organ.

Wind ensemble. The modern wind ensemble was born when Frederick Fennell created the Eastman Wind Ensemble in 1952. Fennell used the instruments generally found in symphonic or concert bands, but reduced the size of sections to feature one player on each part. This allowed players to rise to the challenge of playing as soloists in an ensemble context and to receive professional-level training in the wind ensemble as well as in the orchestra. Wind ensemble members could perform repertoire from all eras of written wind music, and Fennell began programming works that followed the one-on-a-part guideline, such as the Mozart Serenades for wind octets and works for brass choirs by Gabrieli. Early wind ensemble programs also included the relatively few but excellent works for military and symphonic bands by composers such as Holst and Vaughan Williams, with part assignments adjusted for balance. Major works not found on traditional band programs, such as Hindemith's Symphony in B-flat, Schoenberg's Theme and Variations, op. 43a, Stravinsky's Symphonies of Wind Instruments, and Husa's *Music for Prague 1968* became staples in the wind ensemble literature and models for new wind and percussion compositions. Fennell's philosophy also encouraged contemporary composers to write for this new instrumentation, referring to it as an expanded orchestral winds and percussion section that could include (but did not require) characteristic color instruments generally associated with the concert band, such as saxophones and euphonium.

The wind ensemble does not relate historically to the traditional band. Instead, the wind ensemble is a 20th-century idea, but for its historical identity it draws on various important historical genres in wind chamber music and orchestral chamber music. The period closing the 18th century and the first third of the 19th century saw the single most influential thrust of serious wind music, known as Harmonie-Musik, (wind octets) flourishing until the 1830s in and around Vienna. The period from 1830 to the end of the 19th century witnessed little wind band writing, although the increasing wind section in the ever expanding orchestras of Wagner and the late Romantics certainly laid a foundation for large woodwind and brass sonorities to have a singular identity. It was the wind music of Richard Strauss and Igor Stravinsky that brought a focus to the myriad timbral possibilities in the wind band and established, once again, an important place in the music world for this medium.

The wind ensemble is now standard in most colleges and universities and has found a home in many community organizations throughout the world. Despite the youth of the wind ensemble in comparison to other musical media, in the past 50 years more contemporary composers have written music for this collection of 40 individual wind and percussion artists than for any other type of large ensemble. See also Symphonic band. M.D.S.

Wind gauge [also water gauge, water manometer, anemometer]. A device for measuring wind pressure in organs. It is an S-shaped glass tube, placed on its side in such a way that one curve can be filled with water. One end is connected to the source of pressure, which is then measured in inches or centimeters as the difference in height between the resulting two columns of water.

Wind instruments. A class of instruments having an enclosed mass of air, especially those sounded by means of the breath. The technical term for such instruments is *aerophone, which, however, properly refers to all instruments in which air or wind is the primary agent of sound production, whether or not the vibrations produced are those of an enclosed column of air and whether or not the player's breath is the wind supply. As the term wind instruments is often used, this group usually excludes keyboard instruments such as the *organ, *accordion, and related instruments but occasionally includes a few instruments in which a bellows has replaced the lungs (Irish *union pipes, *musette).

Wind instruments are generally divided into two classes, called *woodwinds and *brass winds. The terms woodwind and brass originated at a time when *flutes, *oboes, *clarinets, and *bassoons were all commonly made of wood, and when *trumpets, *horns, *trombones, *ophicleides, and *tubas were made of brass. The names of both classes persist, though in current practice several instruments of the woodwind class are usually made of metal (flute, *saxophone), and some revived early instruments related to the present-day brass group are usually made of wood (*cornett, *serpent).

With respect to sounding method, the brass winds are a homogeneous group. All are sounded by the vibration of the player's lips, which are supported by a cup- or funnel-shaped *mouthpiece. But with respect to bore (i.e., the diameter of the tube and whether the tube is more nearly cylindrical or conical) and pitch-modification method, they are more diverse. A number of methods have been devised to allow the player to produce more than one pitch. The first is the use of a more relaxed or tightened *embouchure to excite lower or higher *harmonics in a tube of fixed length [see also Acoustics]. This allows a player of the *natural trumpet or horn of the 18th century, for example, to play any of the first 13 or so pitches of the harmonic series. As one ascends through the series, more pitches become available within the space of an octave, and scale passages become possible. The second method combines playing the natural pitches with the process of altering them by means of hand positions within the bell [see Horn]. The third method uses a slide to vary the length of the tube (as on the *trombone). The fourth uses *valves for the same purpose. A fifth uses side holes that can be covered or left open so as to vary the effective length of the tube. Although this last method has been used on lip-vibrated instruments such as the cornett, ophicleide, serpent, and *keyed bugle, no present-day brass instrument uses it.

Woodwind instruments are homogeneous in terms of pitch-changing apparatus. All have side holes that can be covered or left open so as to vary the sounding length of the tube. But they are diverse in sounding method and are thus often classed according to the method by which the air column is set into motion, whether by single reed, double reed, or no reed. These classes can be further divided [see Reed, Flute, Woodwind].

Another basic distinction within the family of wind instruments is between whole-tube and half-tube instruments. In the former, the lowest obtainable pitch corresponds to the vibration of the column of air in its fundamental mode, i.e., the mode in which frequency is directly related to the whole length of the tube [see Acoustics]. These include brass instruments with wide bore, such as the tuba, and all woodwinds. In half-tube instruments, the fundamental is produced only with difficulty or not at all, the lowest readily obtainable pitch being the second harmonic, i.e., the one resulting from the vibration of the column of air in two halves. These include brass instruments of narrow bore, such as the trumpet, trombone, and horn.

It is obvious that much of the usual classification system for winds is arbitrary, reflecting more accurately those European types that have become commonplace than all of the combinations that are possible. For a discussion of classification schemes, see Instrument.

Bibl.: Curt Sachs, *Real-Lexikon der Musikinstrumente* (Berlin: J Bard, 1913); 2nd ed., rev. and enl. (New York: Dover, 1964). Adam Carse, *Musical Wind Instruments* (London: Macmillan, 1939). Anthony Baines, *Woodwind Instruments and Their History,* 3rd ed. (London: Faber, 1967). Sibyl Marcuse, *Musical Instruments: A Comprehensive Dictionary,* corr. ed. (New York: Norton, 1975). Anthony Baines, *Brass Instruments* (London: Faber, 1976). William Waterhouse, *The New Langwill Index of Musical Wind-Instrument Makers* (London: T Bingham, 1992). Phillip T. Young, *4900 Historical Woodwind Instruments* (London: T Bingham, 1992). M.S.

Wind machine [Fr. *Éoliphone;* Ger. *Windmaschine*]. A device for imitating the sound of wind, usually a horizontally mounted large wooden cylinder with spaced slats that rub against canvas or other material when it is rotated. Among works that call for it are Strauss's **Don Quixote* and Ravel's **Daphnis et Chloé.*

Winterreise, Die [Ger., Winter Journey]. A cycle of 24 songs by Schubert, D. 911 (1827), in two parts, setting poems by Wilhelm Müller.

Wirbel [Ger.]. A tuning peg of a stringed instrument; *Wirbelkasten,* *pegbox. (2) A drum roll; *Wirbeltrommel,* tenor *drum.

Wohltemperirte Clavier, Das [Ger.]. See *Well-Tempered Clavier, The.*

Wolf. (1) On any bowed stringed instrument, a pitch whose quality or loudness differs in an undesirable way from others. Such pitches are created by an imbalance between the enclosed air volume and plate resonances [see Acoustics] at specific frequencies, resulting in an amplification or muting of those frequencies. Unstable intonation or sympathetic beating between a pitch being played and closely adjacent resonances may create a wavering that is also termed a wolf note. For example, a wolf is frequently found on the cello near the f♯ on the G string, and to a lesser degree in the octave above and below. It can be partially controlled by gently squeezing the lower bout ribs with the legs (altering plate vibration) or by fitting a small metal weight or "wolf eliminator" to the G string between the bridge and tailpiece. The wolf may be prominent even when an instrument is in excellent resonant adjustment.

(2) A perfect fifth that is noticeably out of tune with respect to others in a given *tuning system or *temperament, especially the fifth that results from a succession of 11 acoustically pure fifths; also the Pythagorean *comma. W.L.M.

WoO. In the *thematic catalog of Beethoven's works compiled by Georg Kinsky and Hans Halm, abbr. for *Werk ohne Opuszahl* (work without opus number).

Wood block. *Chinese block.

Woodwinds. *Wind instruments that have an enclosed, vibrating air column set into motion by a *reed or by blowing across or through an aperture [see Flute]; as distinct from *brass instruments, in which the air column is set into motion by the vibration of the player's lips. Keyboard instruments sounded by the same means as woodwinds (e.g., the *organ) are excluded. Despite the name woodwind, this group of instruments is no longer composed only of wooden-bodied instruments. *Flutes, *piccolos, and *saxophones are now usually made of metal. Conversely, some early instruments made of wood, such as the *cornett and the *serpent, are not regarded as woodwinds because they are lip vibrated.

Woodwinds may be classified according to the means by which the air column is set into motion as well as by the extent to which the tube of which they consist more nearly approximates a cylinder or a cone. All, however, vary their pitch by the same method: all have side holes that can be covered or left open so as to vary the effective length of the tube [see Acoustics]. The principal families of European woodwinds encountered today and their principal characteristics are listed in the accompanying table.

Instrument	Reed	Body	Bore
Flute	None	Metal (wood)	Cylindrical
Recorder	None	Wood	Conical
Clarinet	Single	Wood (metal)	Cylindrical
Saxophone	Single	Metal	Conical
Oboe	Double	Wood	Conical
Bassoon	Double	Wood	Conical
Sarrusophone	Double	Metal	Conical

Entries for each of these instruments will be found elsewhere in this dictionary. Early European woodwinds include the *crumhorn and the *shawm. See also Aerophone, Instrument, Wind instruments. M.S.

Worcester, repertory of. A repertory of over 100 polyphonic works (mostly in three parts) preserved on leaves and fragments thought to have originated and most still preserved at Worcester, England (whence the term Worcester fragments), and dating from the 13th and early 14th centuries. They include **rondelli, *conductus,* *motets, and settings of various types of liturgical items; many employ *voice exchange and make extensive use of imperfect consonances, complete triads, and first-inversion triads or six-three chords.

Bibl.: Luther A. Dittmer, *The Worcester Fragments, MSD* 2 (1957). Id., *Worcester Add. 68, Westminster Abbey 33327, Madrid, Bibl. Nac. 192,* Publications of Mediaeval Musical Manuscripts 5 (Brooklyn: Institute of Mediaeval Music, 1959). Id., *Oxford, Latin Liturgical D20; London, Add. MS 25031; Chicago, MS 654 App.,* ibid. 6 (Brooklyn: Institute of

Mediaeval Music, 1960). Ernest H. Sanders, ed., *English Music of the 13th and Early 14th Centuries,* Polyphonic Music of the Fourteenth Century 14 (Monaco: L'oiseau-lyre, 1979).

Word painting. The musical illustration of the meaning of words in vocal music, especially the literal meaning of individual words or phrases. It is a prominent feature of some music of the late Renaissance (especially some *madrigals, whence the synonym madrigalism) and of the Baroque, but examples occur throughout the history of music. The devices used rely principally on the relationship between qualities of the thing illustrated and certain characteristics of music. In the simplest cases, natural sounds, such as those of birds, thunder, sighing, and sobbing, are imitated. Otherwise, music that is high, low, ascending, descending, loud, soft, fast, or slow may be associated, respectively, with these same concepts in the abstract or with concepts or things that share these qualities. Thus, for example, the word heaven may be associated with music that is high or ascending in pitch. The shape of a melodic line may illustrate words such as crooked and straight. More abstractly, dissonance may be associated with pain, imitation with following, the minor mode with sorrow, and so forth. The rise to prominence of such techniques in the 16th century and after coincides with increasing expressions of the view that music should serve words by expressing their meaning and with the application to music of the Aristotelian view that art should imitate nature. Joachim Thuringus (*Opusculum bipartitum,* 1625) classifies words that can be "expressed and painted" into three types: (1) *verba affectuum* (words of affection), such as rejoicing, weeping, laughing, as well as words that suggest sound, such as bird; (2) *verba motus et locorum* (words of motion and place), such as to stand, to run, to jump, heaven, hell, mountain; and (3) *adverbia temporis, numeri* (adverbs of time and number), such as quick, slow, twice, often, rarely. Such techniques are sometimes also prominent in nonvocal *program music. See also Text and music, Eye music.

Words and music. See Text and music, Word painting.

Work song. A song synchronizing the rhythm of group tasks. Such songs are distributed throughout the world and include many types (e.g., the sea *shanty). West African work songs contributed, under slavery, the following elements of what later became American blues, jazz, black gospel, etc.: the leader's improvised, formulaic lyrics and melodies, alternating with the group's recurrent rhythmic punctuation (*call and response); the timbres of black dialects; a flexible conception of pitch (blue notes, glissandos); and brief, cyclic, open-ended forms. B.K.

Wozzeck. Opera in three acts by Berg (libretto in German by Berg, adapted from Georg Büchner's play of the same name), produced in Berlin in 1925. Setting: Germany in the early 19th century.

Wrest pin. *Tuning pin.

Wrest plank. *Pin block.

W.T.C. Abbr. for **Well-Tempered Clavier, The.*

Wuchtig [Ger.]. Weighty, vigorous.

Würdig [Ger.]. Dignified, stately.

Wurstfagott [Ger.]. *Sausage bassoon.

Wütend [Ger.]. Raging, furious.

X

Xácara [Sp., obs.]. See *Jácara.*

Xerxes. See *Serse.*

Xirimía [Cat.]. **Chirimía.*

Xota [Sp., obs.]. See *Jota.*

Xylophone [fr. Gr. *xylon,* wood; Fr. *xylophone,* also obs. *claquebois;* Ger. *Xylophon;* It. *xilofono;* Sp. *xilófono*]. A percussion instrument of definite pitch consisting of suspended wooden bars struck with a beater. The modern orchestral instrument has bars made of hardwood or a synthetic material suspended horizontally on a frame and arranged in the fashion of a keyboard. Beneath each bar is a vertical tubular resonator whose length corresponds to the pitch of the bar. The instrument is mounted on a stand and struck with two (or more) beaters of various hardnesses. The back of each bar is longitudinally concave, a feature that contributes to definition of pitch. The pitch of a bar is determined by both its length and thickness; a decrease in length raises pitch, a decrease in thickness lowers it.

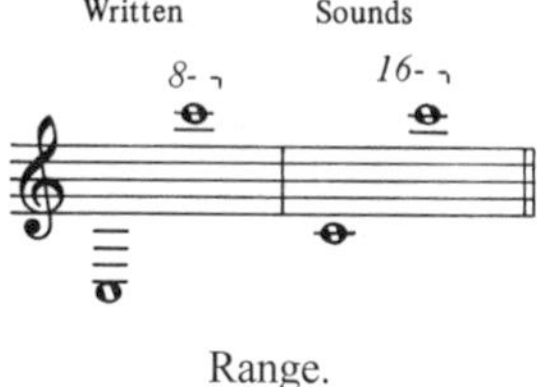

Range.

The range of the modern instrument varies, the largest being four octaves upward from c′ to c′′′′′, another standard size being from f′ or g′ to c′′′′′. It is normally notated on a single treble staff an octave below sounding pitch. See ill. under Percussion instruments.

Instruments of this general type are documented in Southeast Asia and Africa from the 14th century and are still widely disseminated in a variety of types in these regions as they are in the Americas, to which they were brought from Africa [see also Marimba]. In Southeast Asian instruments, a wooden trough often serves as a resonator. In African instruments, gourds may be used, though bars may also be suspended between the legs or between two logs. In Europe, Arnolt Schlick (*Spiegel der Orgelmacher und Organisten,* 1511) described such an instrument as *hültze glechter* (wooden percussion), and soon after the term *Strohfiedel* (straw fiddle) came into use owing to the fact that the bars were sometimes simply laid on ropes of straw. The latter type of instrument was played by the Pole Michał Józef Guzikow, who aroused the interest of Mendelssohn, Chopin, and Liszt. It persisted into the 20th century, when the modern form was developed. Marin Mersenne (*Harmonie universelle,* 1636–37) depicted a keyed instrument and one with the bars suspended vertically like a ladder and termed *échelette.* Other terms have included [Ger.] *Holzharmonika,* [It.] *gigelira,* and [Lat.] *ligneum psalterium.* The term xylophone came into use early in the 19th century. The instrument's earliest well-known use in the orchestra was to represent the rattling of skeletons in Saint-Saëns's **Danse macabre* (1874). It has been widely used in art music since then.

Bibl.: J. A. Strain, "Published Literature for Xylophone (ca. 1880–ca. 1930)," *Percussive Notes* 31, no. 2 (1992): 65–98.

Y

Yang-ch'in (yangqin) [Chin.]. A Chinese *dulcimer, popular as a solo instrument, in some theater ensembles, and as accompaniment for sung narrative. Like European dulcimers, it has a trapezoidal body and two bridges.

Yankee Doodle. A tune of unknown origin first published, with this title but without words, in James Aird's *A Selection of Scotch, English, Irish, and Foreign Airs* (Glasgow, ca. 1778). It has been associated with various words and was sung during the Revolutionary period by both British and American troops. In the U.S., it has come to represent the American revolutionaries.

Bibl.: Oscar G. T. Sonneck, *Report on the "Star-Spangled Banner," "Hail Columbia!" "America," and "Yankee Doodle"* (Washington, D.C.: Music Division of the Library of Congress, 1909; R: New York: Dover, 1972), pp. 79–156.

Yaraví [Sp.]. A song genre of the Andean regions of

Peru, Bolivia, Ecuador, and northern Argentina, probably derived from the Quechua *harawi* or *harahuí* of pre-Conquest times. The *yaraví* is typically slow in tempo, often in triple meter, with Quechua as well as Spanish texts lamenting amorous loss. The pentatonicism and bimodality found in many other Andean songs and dances also characterize the *yaraví*. D.S.

Yodel [Ger. *Jodel*]. A style of folk singing, to a succession of vowels, characterized by rapid shifts between full voice and *falsetto combined with rapid alternation between two pitches or the arpeggiation of several. A passage in this style [Ger. *Jodler*] is sometimes appended to a song with text. The technique may be employed polyphonically and is typical of Switzerland and Austria, the music of African pygmies, and some singers of American *country music.

Bibl.: Joseph Pommer, ed., *Jodler und Juchezer* (Vienna, 1890), and several later collections. Erich M. von Hornbostel, "Die Entstehung des Jodels," *Basel,* 1924, pp. 203–10. Max Peter Baumann, *Musikfolklore und Musikfolklorismus: Eine ethnomusikologische Untersuchung zum Funktionswandel des Jodels* (Winterthur: Amadeus-Verlag, Bernhard Päuler, 1976). Gustl Thoma, *Die Kunst des Jodelns: Alpenländnische Jodelschule* (Munich: Heimeran, 1977). Heinrich J. Leuthold, *Der Naturjodel in der Schweiz: Entstehung, Charakteristik, Verbreitung* (Altdorf: R Fellmann, 1981). Claudia Luchner-Löscher, *Der Jodler: Wesen, Entstehung, Verbreitung und Gestalt* (Munich: Katzbichler, 1982). Susanne Fürniss, *Die Jodeltechnik der Aka-Pygmaen in Zentralafrika: Eine akustisch-phonetische Untersuchung* (Berlin: Reimer, 1992). Franz Födermayr, "Zur Jodeltechnik von Jimmie Rodgers: The Blue Yodel," in *For Gerhard Kubik: Festschrift on the Occasion of His 60th Birthday,* ed. August Schmidhofer and Dietrich Schuller (Frankfurt: Lang, 1994), pp. 381–404. Graeme Smith, "Australian Country Music and the Hillbilly Yodel," *Popular Music* 13 (1994): 297–311. Bart Plantenga, "Will There Be Yodeling in Heaven?" *American Music Research Center Journal* 8–9 (1998): 106–38.

Youth's Magic Horn, The. See *Knaben Wunderhorn, Des.*

Yü (yu) [Chin.]. A Chinese *scraper made of wood carved in the shape of a tiger and scraped with a split bamboo stick. It is used in Confucian temple worship.

Yüeh-ch'in (yueqin) [Chin.]. A *short-necked lute of China; also called a moon guitar. Its round sound box is flat in back and front, and it has four strings tuned in pairs a perfect fifth apart and stretched over ten frets that are distributed along the neck and well onto the body. It is mainly an ensemble instrument. See ill. under East Asia.

Z

Zählzeit [Ger.]. Beat.

Zajal [Ar.; Sp. *zéjel*]. A form of poetry appearing in early 12th-century Arabic Spain (al-Andalus), similar in form to the *muwashshaha* (a form developed in al-Andalus in the 9th or 10th century), but written in colloquial rather than classical Arabic, sometimes incorporating Romance vocabulary and treating themes of more popular character. Both forms employ rhyme and versification according to the methods typical of Romance poetry rather than classical Arabic poetry. This, combined with the presence of Romance vocabulary in both (confined in the *muwashshaha* to the concluding *kharja,* an element of form that disappears from the *zajal*) suggests Romance influence on Arabic poetry rather than the reverse. The *zajal* is in form very closely related to the **villancico* (in many cases identical) and thus to the **virelai* and **ballata.*

Bibl.: Emilio García Gómez, *Poesía arábigoandaluza: Breve síntesis histórica* (Madrid: Instituto Faruk I de estudios islámicos, 1952). Samuel M. Stern, *Les chansons mozarabes* (Palermo: U Manfredi, 1953). James T. Monroe, ed., *Hispano-Arabic Poetry* (Berkeley and Los Angeles: U of Cal Pr, 1974) [with introduction]. Id., in *Berkeley,* 1977, pp. 22–23. See also *Villancico, Virelai.*

Zamba [Sp.]. An Argentine couple dance, probably derived from the *zamacueca (zambacueca)* of colonial Peru. It shares features with other widely known Argentine dances, such as the **chacarera* and the **gato,* but is distinctive with regard to its musical and choreographic structure, its moderate tempo, and its principally instrumental performance.

Zambra [Sp.]. A lively party with **flamenco* music and dancing.

Zambomba [Sp.]. A *friction drum of Spain and Latin America, now often made from a tin can rather than the traditional earthenware and particularly associated with the Christmas season.

Zambumbia [Sp.]. **Caramba.*

Zampogna, cornamusa [It.]. A *bagpipe of southern Italy and Sicily, the only such instrument that uses double reeds in all pipes. It has two separate *chanters, one fingered with each hand. It is played by shepherds and itinerant musicians, particularly during the Christmas season and usually in ensemble with the **piffero.*

Zampoña [Sp.]. (1) A *bagpipe of Spain, particularly the Balearic Islands. (2) In Andean Latin America, a panpipe.

Zamr [Ar.]. (1) Any wind instrument [see also *Miz-*

mār]. (2) A double clarinet of North Africa [see also *Zummārah*]. (3) **Zūrnā*.

Zanfonía [Sp.]. *Hurdy-gurdy.

Zapateado [Sp. fr. *zapato,* shoe]. Any of various, sometimes quite intricate, patterns of stamping of the feet that characterize certain dances of Spain and Latin America.

Zarabanda [Sp.]. *Sarabande.

Zarb, dombak, tombak [Per.]. A clay, goblet-shaped drum of Iran. See also *Darabukkah.*

Zart [Ger.]. Delicate, soft.

Zarzuela [Sp. from *zarza,* bramble bush]. A Spanish theatrical genre characterized by a mixture of singing and spoken dialogue. Throughout its history, the *zarzuela* has included elements from the Spanish popular tradition.

The term *zarzuela,* probably chosen initially to distinguish shorter court plays with music and dancing from the strictly defined *comedia* in three acts, originated in the 17th century with the musical court plays intended for performance at the royal hunting lodge or Palace of the Zarzuela outside of Madrid. Both the two-act pastoral *zarzuelas* and the three-act mythological spectacle plays by Pedro Calderón de la Barca (1600–1681) and contemporary dramatists were hybrids, consisting of a mixture of sung and spoken dialogue and incorporating elements from the native tradition and forms from opera. Although the earliest works called *zarzuelas* date from 1657 (Calderón's *El golfo de las sirenas,* a "piscatory eclogue" in one act, and *El laurel de Apolo,* a pastoral in two acts), recitative was introduced for the speech of the gods as early as 1652 in Calderón's *La fiera, el rayo, y la piedra.* The hybrid design is exemplified in the extant score of Calderón's *Fortunas de Andrómeda y Perseo* (1653).

The classical theatrical genre and the musical style developed by Juan Hidalgo (1614–85) remained essentially stable to the last decade of the 17th century, when the *zarzuela* adapted to a change in literary fashion and a new interest in contemporary foreign musical styles. Antonio Zamora (1664–1728) and José de Cañizares (1676–1750) were the leading dramatists of the new epoch, and they provided texts for *zarzuelas* by Sebastián Durón (1660–1716) and Antonio Literes (1673–1747). *Zarzuelas* by Durón and especially Literes include longer and more elaborate set pieces, a clearer distinction between recitative and air, and some da capo arias. Although early 18th-century *zarzuelas* still retain the characteristic Spanish theatrical style inherited from the era of Calderón and Hidalgo, they also reveal a self-conscious cultivation of the Italian or pan-European operatic style. From ca. 1710 to 1750, the *zarzuela* increasingly approximated the musical styles and conventions of contemporary *opera seria,* which quickly replaced *zarzuela* as the favorite court entertainment. The ultimate absorption of the late Baroque operatic style is seen in José de Nebra's (1702–68) highly successful *Viento es la dicha de Amor* (1743, text by Zamora).

After ca. 1710, *zarzuelas* were largely commissioned for the public theaters, and the demands of the theater-going public became more important than royal taste. The decline in commercial success of the traditional *zarzuela heróica* after ca. 1730 may have been a reaction against the increasingly "foreign" musical style and the conventions of *opera seria* as applied to *zarzuela.*

Around 1760, Spanish composers regained public support by self-consciously cultivating a popular native style and returning to Spanish theatrical conventions. In this nationalistic movement, the importance of the dramatist Ramón de la Cruz (1731–94) and the influence from the smaller comic forms (the **sainete* and the **tonadilla*) cannot be overestimated. The first important work of this type *(zarzuela burlesca)* performed in Madrid was *El tío y la tía* (1767) by the composer Antonio Rosales (ca. 1740–1801) to a one-act *sainete*-like text by Ramón de la Cruz. This was followed in 1769 by the production of a two-act work with music by Antonio Rodríguez de Hita (ca. 1724–87) on a text by Ramón de la Cruz, *Las labradoras de Murcia.* The latter work can be defined as the first extant *zarzuela de costumbres,* because the plot is not only injected with popular humor but devoted to local customs—a hallmark of the later and better-known examples of the genre. In both works, there are obvious traces of contemporary *opera buffa.* But *Las labradoras de Murcia* also includes elements from Murcian folk music.

The *zarzuela* disappeared for roughly 50 years, primarily because Ramón de la Cruz did not write *zarzuela* texts after ca. 1776, but also because the genre was eclipsed by the tremendous success of the smaller ephemeral **tonadilla escénica.* During the Rossini epoch, the *zarzuela* was banished from Madrid stages by Italian opera.

The first 19th-century *zarzuela* production in Madrid took place in 1839 with the one-act *El novio y el concierto* (termed *zarzuela-comedia*) by the Italian Basilio Basili (1803–95) and the poet Manuel Bretón de los Herreros (1796–1873), a declared enemy of Italian opera. The popular native musical forms returned to the stage as novelties, ensuring instant success. By the middle of the century, the resurgence of *zarzuela* was fired by a nucleus of young Spanish composers, the "grupo de los cinco" (group of five), who, in essence, founded the modern *zarzuela* genre: Francisco Asenjo Barbieri (1823–94), Rafael Hernando (1822–88), Joaquín Gaztambide (1822–70), Cristóbal Oudrid y Segura (1825–77), and José Inzenga (1828–91). The two-act *Colegiales y soldados* (1848) by Hernando was the first product of this group, followed by Barbieri's *Gloria y peluca* (1850) and his *zarzuela grande* (in three acts) *Jugar con fuego* (1851).

Barbieri was behind the founding of Madrid's Teatro de la Zarzuela in 1856, and his efforts in support of the genre were crucial to the future of Spanish musical theater. In a letter published in 1885, Barbieri listed 475 writers and 240 composers of *zarzuela* active between 1832 and 1885 and hailed the *zarzuela* as the "national lyric-dramatic genre." Yet the 19th-century *zarzuela* was inextricably linked to Madrid, which provided its typical subjects and characters and whose working middle class was its principal audience.

The *zarzuela* was an ephemeral entertainment, and the continual demand for new works made the one-act *zarzuelas* referred to as *género chico* (small genre) more practical. Federico Chueca (1846–1908) was a leading exponent of this genre, and his *La Gran Vía* (1886) is still one of the most frequently performed works of the period. Several works by Ruperto Chapí (1851–1909), including *La tempestad* (1882) and *La revoltosa* (1897), have remained favorites in the standard repertory as well. The high point of the *género chico,* however, was reached by Tomás Bretón (1850–1923) with *La verbena de la paloma* (1894), which has enjoyed unflagging popularity.

In the opening decades of the 20th century, the *zarzuela* continued as popular theater and attracted many talented composers, most notably Amadeo Vives (1871–1932), whose reputation was established with *Bohemios* (1904) and whose *Doña Francisquita* (1923) is the archetype of the sentimental *zarzuela.* Among the most respected and revered works of the entire genre is Federico Moreno Torroba's (1891–1982) *Luisa Fernanda* (1932). Although performances of established works continue to appeal to a wide audience in Spain (and to have some appeal in the Western Hemisphere), the production of new works has virtually ceased.

Bibl.: Felipe Pedrell, *Teatro lírico español anterior al siglo XIX* (La Coruña, 1897–98). Emilio Cotarelo y Mori, *Historia de la zarzuela* (Madrid: Tipografía de Archivos, 1934–). Id., *Orígenes y establecimiento de la ópera en España hasta 1800* (Madrid: Tipografía de la "Revista de archivos," 1917). José Subirá, *Historia de la música teatral en España* (Barcelona: Editorial Labor, 1945). José Deleito y Piñuela, *Origen y apogeo del "género chico"* (Madrid: Revista de Occidente, 1949). Antonio Peña y Goñi, *España desde la ópera a la zarzuela,* ed. Eduardo Rincón (Madrid: Alianza, 1967). Jack Sage, "La música de Juan Hidalgo para *Los celos hacen estrellas,*" in Juan Vélez de Guevara, *Los celos hacen estrellas,* ed. J. E. Varey and N. D. Shergold (London: Tamesis, 1970). William M. Bussey, *French and Italian Influence on the Zarzuela 1700–1770* (Ann Arbor: UMI Res Pr, 1982). Louise Kathrin Stein, "Un manuscrito de música teatral reaparecido: *Veneno es de amor la envidia,*" *Revista de musicología* 5 (1982): 225–33. See also Spain. L.K.S.

Zauberflöte, Die [Ger., The Magic Flute]. Opera (*Singspiel) in two acts by Mozart (libretto by Emanuel Schikaneder, after various sources, including Liebeskind's fairy tale "Lulu, oder Die Zauberflöte," published by Wieland in 1786–89), produced in Vienna in 1791. Setting: ancient Egypt.

Zeitmass [Ger.]. (1) Tempo; *im ersten Z., *tempo primo; im früheren Z., a *tempo; im freien Z.,* in free tempo. (2) *Zeitmasse* [pl.], Stockhausen's work no. 5 for flute, oboe, English horn, clarinet, and bassoon, which simultaneously combines independent tempos.

Zeitmesser [Ger.]. Metronome.

Zéjel [Sp.]. See *Zajal.*

Zhizn' za tsarya [Russ.]. See *Life for the Tsar, A.*

Zibaldone [It.]. *Medley.

Ziehharmonika [Ger.]. Accordion.

Ziemlich [Ger.]. Rather.

Zigeunerbaron, Die [Ger., The Gypsy Baron]. Operetta in three acts by Johann Strauss, Jr. (libretto by Ignaz Schnitzer, after a story by Mor Jókai), produced in Vienna in 1885. Setting: the Austro-Hungarian Empire in mid-18th century.

Zigeunermusik [Ger.]. *Gypsy music.

Zimbalon. **Cimbalom.*

Zimbel [Ger.]. (1) **Cimbel.* (2) *Antike Zimbeln,* *crotales.

Zimbelstern [Ger.]. **Cimbelstern.*

Zingarese, alla [It.]. In the *gypsy style.

Zink [Ger.]. *Cornett.

Zither. (1) Any of a class of stringed instruments in which the string or strings run the length of the body [see ill.]. The body is usually the principal *resonator, and the strings are stretched above it over bridges. Zithers may be plucked, struck, bowed, or set into vibration by the wind (as in *aeolian harps). They are widely distributed, especially in Europe, Asia, and Africa, and take a great variety of forms, ranging from the simple *trough zither to the refined **koto* to the technically intricate *piano. Zithers may be divided into broad classes on the basis of shape, construction, and playing technique:

(i) *Trough zither.
(ii) *Stick zither: **bīn.*
(iii) *Tube zither: **valiha.*
(iv) Long zither: **cheng,* **ch'in,* **koto.*
(v) Board or box zither (the latter incorporating a *sound box): *Appalachian dulcimer, *autoharp, **gusli,* **hummel,* **kantele,* **langleik,* *monochord, *psaltery, **qānūn,* **Scheitholt,* zither (2). Zithers with a sound box also include instruments whose strings are struck by the player, e.g., the *dulcimer, **cimbalom,* **santur,* and **yang-ch'in,* and instruments whose strings are struck or plucked by means of a keyboard, e.g., the *clavichord, *harpsichord, and *piano.

For more detailed classification schemes, see bibl. for Instrument. See also Chordophone.

(2) A box zither native to Austria and southern Germany. It has four or five metal melody strings pass-

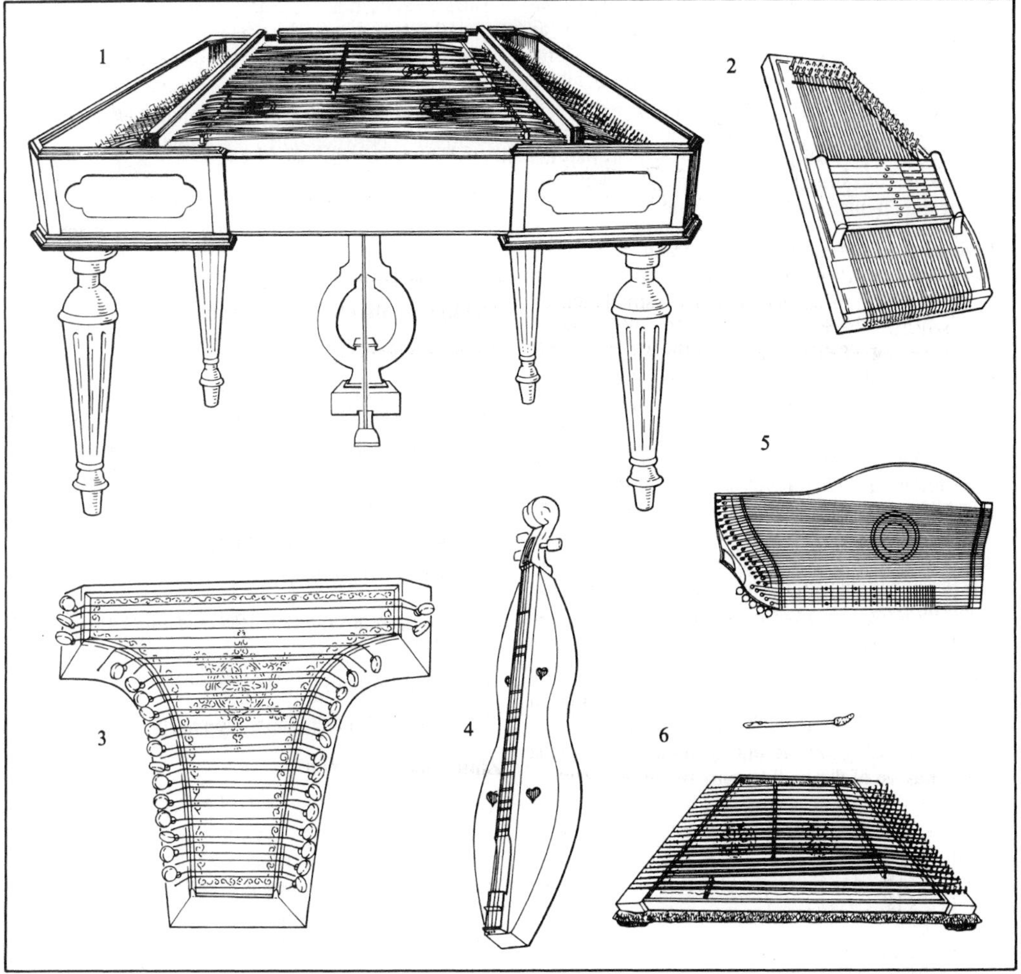

1. Cimbalom. 2. Autoharp. 3. Psaltery. 4. Appalachian dulcimer. 5. Zither. 6. Dulcimer.

ing over a chromatically fretted fingerboard that runs along the straight side closest to the player. Parallel to these are 30 to 40 gut or nylon accompaniment strings stretched over a flat sound box with sound hole and an outward curve opposite the player. The player stops the melody strings with the left hand and plucks them with a plectrum worn on the right thumb. The remaining fingers of the right hand add accompaniment on the open strings. This type of zither was developed in the 19th century and has been used as both a solo and an ensemble instrument.

Zitternd [Ger.]. **Tremolando.*

Znamenny chant. A type of Russian chant originating in the 15th century and characterized by the nondiastematic *krjuki* or hook notation that superseded the Byzantine neumes. The 17th-century reforms of Ivan Shaydurov, based on Western theoretical principles, reduced the number of signs and provided cinnabar letters to fix the height of the pitches. See also Russian and Slavonic chant. D.E.C.

Zögern [Ger.]. To hesitate, to retard.

Zopfstil [Ger., fr. *Zopf,* pigtail]. A pejorative term used in the 19th century to refer to music, by then out of date, from the period of pigtails and powdered wigs of the 18th century.

Zoppa, alla [It., lame, limping]. A typical rhythm of the 18th-century **galant* style consisting of a syncopated quarter note between two eighths in 2/4 time, usually preceded by an anacrusis.

Zortziko [Basque]; also *zortzico.* A Basque dance in rapid quintuple meter with dotted rhythms, related to the Castilian *rueda,* which lacks dotted rhythms.

Zu [Ger.]. To, too, toward, for; *zu 2, a *due.*

Zufolo [It.]. *Whistle, *duct flute.

Zug [Ger.]. (1) Slide; *Zugposaune,* slide trombone; *Zugtrompete,* slide trumpet. (2) Organ stop. (3) See Schenker analysis.

Zummārah [Ar.]. A *double clarinet of the Middle East. Both pipes are of cane and of the same length, and the finger holes (usually six) are cut in parallel. The two reeds are taken all the way into the mouth and blown using circular breathing. See also *Zamr.*

Zunge [Ger.]. Tongue, as of an organ *reed pipe; *Zungenpfeife,* an organ reed pipe.

Zūrnā [Ar., also **ghayṭah, *mizmār, *zamr;* Turk. *zurna;* Per. *surnāy*]. A *shawm of the Middle East and regions influenced by Islam. A typical example is a wooden tube 30 to 35 cm in length with a conical bore, a flared bell, and seven finger holes plus a thumb hole. It has a small reed, often with a metal lip-disk below it. The whole reed is usually taken into the mouth and circular breathing is used so as to produce a continuous sound. Related instruments are distributed from Spain to Bulgaria to Java to China. They are characteristically played in ensemble with a bass drum *(*davul, *tupan)* and are used in a variety of social contexts. See also *Chirimía, Hichiriki, Nāgasvaram, Śahnāi;* see ill. under Near and Middle East.

Zurückhalten [Ger.]. To hold back, *rallentando.*

Zusammen [Ger.]. Together, as after a passage in which a section of the orchestra has been divided.

Zusammenschlag [Ger.]. *Acciaccatura.

Zwerchpfeife [Ger., obs.]. Transverse flute.

Zwiefacher [Ger.]. A German folk dance with regular alternation between duple and triple meter.

Zwischen [Ger.]. Between; *Zwischensatz,* the middle section in ternary form or the development section in sonata form; *Zwischenspiel,* interlude, intermezzo, an episode in a fugue or rondo, *ritornello,* a *tutti* section in a concerto, music played between the stanzas of a song or hymn.

Zydeco [fr. Fr. *les haricots,* French beans]. A type of music originating among blacks in Cajun Louisiana and combining elements of French Cajun traditions with blues, rhythm and blues, rock and roll, Caribbean music, and country music. The closely related music as performed by white musicians is usually termed Cajun. Traditional instruments are the accordion and washboard, to which have been added electric guitar, bass, and drums. Its first exponent to achieve widespread recognition was Clifton Chenier (b. 1925).

Bibl.: Jon Albris and Anders Laurson, "Zydeco & Cajun," *FAM* 31 (1984): 108–12.

Zyklus [Ger.]. Cycle.

Zymbel [Ger.]. **Zimbel.*

DON MICHAEL RANDEL was for many years Professor of Music at Cornell University. He is now Professor of Music and President of the University of Chicago.